Goldmine

Country & Western

RECORD PRICE GUIDE

Second Edition

Tim Neely

Published by

700 E. State Street • Iola, WI 54990-0001
Telephone: 715/445-2214

Please call or write for our free catalog of music publications.
Our toll-free number to place an order or obtain a free catalog is 800-258-0929
or please use our regular business telephone 715-445-2214
for editorial comment and further information.

Library of Congress Catalog Number: 96-76683
ISBN: 0-87341-949-9
Printed in the United States of America

Contents

Introduction to the 2nd Edition

This is the *Goldmine Country & Western Record Price Guide, 2nd Edition*. But if you were at all familiar with the first edition, the only real resemblance between this and its predecessor is in the title.

Fred Heggeness, who did the first edition, passed away not too long after it was released. After his death, Krause Publications bought the rights to the two books he had done for the company – the C&W guide and the *Goldmine Promo Record & CD Price Guide*. As Heggeness had done little revising to his first C&W guide before he died, we decided for the second edition to completely overhaul it.

A cursory glance will show that it looks nothing like the first edition. Instead, we have made it more like most other *Goldmine* price guides. In the process, we feel we have created the most comprehensive country & western price guide ever published.

In so doing, we eliminated some material from the first edition that took away from the book's intended focus on country & western records.

Gone is the "& CD" from the title of the book, as we've removed all compact discs. There weren't very many to begin with; all of them we found in the first edition were syndicated radio shows. So this isn't a significant deletion.

Gone are the "general" listings for record labels. All records are now listed individually with no grouping by label. If we couldn't confirm any releases on a particular label that Heggeness listed, we didn't list any.

Gone are the numerous double listings for stock copies and promo copies. We kept those that are significantly different, such as the large numbers of 1980s RCA and MCA promotional 45s on colored vinyl. But the others we deleted to make room for other unique listings. We'll talk more about promos later in this introduction.

Gone are the listings for syndicated radio shows, even on vinyl. Most country & western collectors are far more interested in the "meat and potatoes" – the original discs.

And finally, gone are many of the one-record rockabilly artists who were listed in the first edition. We found that they took away from the focus of the book, which is "country and western" and not rockabilly. That said, you'll still find plenty of rockabilly in this book. Many of the more prolific rockers, either at the time or later on, also made country music. Those performers are still here.

What's new?

We told you what we've eliminated between the first and second editions. The additions, we feel, more than make up for them.

- For most artists, we include complete pre-CD era discographies (or at least as complete as we know about) without regard to the value of the record.
- We have added hundreds of artists who were not listed in the first edition. Some of them have never been listed in any price guide before.
- We've beefed up the singles listings considerably. After all, country & western music, throughout its entire recorded history, has been a song-driven, rather than an album-oriented, genre. (To some degree, this remains true even today.) So probably 75 percent of this book consists of singles.
- We don't ignore older country music. For the first time in a book that comes from the *Goldmine* records database, we've added listings of selected 78s, which help give a truer picture of the prolific output of some of the C&W pioneers.
- We don't ignore newer country music, even though this book consists entirely of records. Until the late 1990s, almost every country hit was pressed on a domestic, legitimately produced 7-inch 45 rpm single. And even today, more than half of all country hits still appear on the small record with the big hole. (You'll find well over 100 singles in this book with a release date of "2000"!) Almost every country 45 produced in the 1990s by a major label is included in this book. If it's from the '90s and

it's not listed, it probably didn't come out on vinyl.

Market insights

In general, country & western records are undervalued compared to their rarity. There are several reasons for this. One of them is that country is not collected that heavily in the major collecting centers of the Northeast and the West Coast. Another is that country music, much like another great American music called jazz, doesn't get as much respect here in the U.S. as it does overseas. It's sad that most of the major American record labels ignore the vast amount of classic country and western music in their archives. Most career retrospectives are spotty at best and shoddy at worst. (A major exception is the first-class treatment that Hank Williams' recorded legacy has received in America.) Instead, it's a German label, Bear Family, that does by far the best job of rescuing old country from obscurity. But until the Internet came along, Bear Family collections were tough to get Stateside.

There's always the possibility of changing attitudes, though. Until the 1990s, blues records did not hold the same collecting cachet as vocal group or early rock 'n' roll records.

That said, there are some upward trends in the C&W record market, among which are:

Country-only or country-predominant labels. A couple of dealers have reported that when they get original LPs from the 1960s on the Starday label, they can't keep them in stock. And when they put them up for auction, they get much more than they expected.

An important thing to remember about Starday, though, is that not all of their LPs are sought-after. In the 1970s, after the label became part of the Gusto family, the albums are almost universally scorned. But the original editions from the 1960s are well regarded in collector's circles.

The giants. Members of the Country Music Hall of Fame, or those who are likely to be inducted some day, are generally more sought-after than those who are not. Not including Country Music Hall of Famer Elvis Presley, who is in a class by himself among collectible artists, the most collected country artists include (not necessarily in this order) Hank Williams, George Jones, Buck Owens, Jim Reeves, Ernest Tubb, Loretta Lynn, Dolly Parton, and the biggest of the "singing cowboys," Gene Autry. All of these artists have early discs that can fetch in the hundreds of dollars, and in some cases more.

Independent labels of the 1980s. From about the late 1970s until 1990, the lower portions of the Billboard country singles charts were a haven for dozens of tiny, mostly Nashville-based, labels. One of these labels, Door Knob, had 100 different songs make the national charts, yet few of them got even as high as the top 50! Many of these labels, which generally released only 45s (those that did LPs didn't do very many), had no distribution outside Music City. In fact, some of these charted records may not even exist at all except as promos, and in some cases, even the existence of promos has been questioned! As chart collectors find some of these lower-rung "hits" impossible to find, the prices they are willing to pay for them increases as well.

Big hits. Conversely, many of the biggest hits in country music history are tough to find in near-mint condition, or even in VG+. That's because, since the earliest days of country music, many of the hits have ended up in jukeboxes. And today, most of the market that remains for 45s is in the jukebox trade. Today, you can, without much trouble, find stashes of country singles that formerly spent time in jukeboxes, and most of the extremely popular titles are in sad shape. They got *played!* And I can speak from experience.

When I first really got into country music, I figured that a good history lesson would be to collect all the 45s that had hit number 1 on the *Billboard* charts since 1968. (That's the year that the word "western" was dropped from the chart.) It didn't take long to find 90 percent of the records that had done so. Finding copies that were in acceptable playing condition was another story entirely. To this day, almost a decade after I started that collection, there are *still* some chart-topping hits of the past 30-plus years that I haven't found in better than VG condition.

In addition, there are two areas that we see as having potential for growth:

Record club exclusive LPs. From 1989 through 1992, both Columbia House and the BMG Music Service (labeled as "BMG Direct Marketing") pressed dozens, if not hundreds, of country LPs that were not available on vinyl at regular retail stores. These editions were rather limited and are difficult to find in the secondary market. Artists as diverse as Dolly Parton, Shenandoah, Reba McEntire, George Strait, Randy Travis, Trisha Yearwood, Wynonna Judd and Billy Ray Cyrus (and this is far from a complete list) had at least one album pressed on vinyl by the record clubs but not otherwise. The most sought-after today are the record club pressings of Garth Brooks' *No Fences* (both clubs did vinyl on that one) and *Ropin' The Wind* (only Columbia House pressed this one).

45s of the 1990s. We've mentioned it before: The 7-inch vinyl single did not die in the 1990s. Almost every hit country song of the decade was pressed on 45. Today, many of these can still be commonly found for $3-$4 each, if you know where to look. But just try to find Shania Twain's ultra-popular "Any Man of Mine" or the original stock pressing of Garth Brooks' "Friends in Low Places," or, for that matter, Tracy Byrd's popular wedding favorite "The Keeper of the Stars." These, and others, have been known to bring much more than their original $2-$3 retail price for the 45.

What's in here, and what isn't

First, let me reiterate that this book consists entirely of *records*. No tapes or compact discs are listed. This may come as a surprise to readers who thought that records stopped being made in the early 1990s. We list literally thousands of 45s from the 1990s, all of which have been confirmed to exist! The observant reader will also note that very few albums after 1990 are listed – and that's because they don't exist as records.

Our starting point for deciding which artists to include was the *Billboard* magazine charts from 1944 to the present. By definition, if a song or album made the country charts, it's country, and it ought to be listed in a country & western book. But we didn't stop there. Once we decided to list someone, we tried to list *all* their records, not only the ones that made the charts.

There are some exceptions, however. Not every artist has all their records listed. These fall into two categories:

- Some performers with long non-country careers had records big enough or "country" enough to cross over to the country charts. Examples include Nat King Cole, Paul McCartney, Bobby Darin, Bob Seger, Vaughn Monroe, and Louis Jordan. Their appearance on the country charts was so anomalous that we could not in good conscience list any records other than their country chart hits, which we do for the sake of completeness.
- Other artists either were country early in their career and radically different afterwards (Pia Zadora, for example), or came to country late in their careers after not having done country-style material before (Pat Boone and Dean Martin, for example). In those cases, we only listed those records that seemed most relevant to country & western.

That said, there are some artists who began making the country charts late in their career, not because their music changed significantly, but because radio's definition of "country" had. (Guy Mitchell and Bobby Vinton come to mind, as does Creedence Clearwater Revival.) In those cases, we cover the artist's entire career. Other artists went through "non-country" periods, yet had significant country success otherwise. (The most obvious case is Elvis Presley, who was still a relevant country artist at the time of his death, but it also fits Olivia Newton-John.) Again in those cases, we list the entire discography, even the "non-country" material.

Fortunately, most of the important country artists of the past 50 years also made the charts at least once. But some didn't. So we've made a few judgment calls on other artists that we felt belonged. The most obvious place was in the 1950s, when the country charts still were in their infancy and rarely listed more than 20 songs in any given week. We also chose to include some of the "country rock" music of the late 1960s and early 1970s. Most of the country establishment considered it blasphemous at the time. Today much of this is hailed as an influence on more recent country music and cannot be ignored. In fact, depending on what your definition of "country" is, much of this formerly shunned music is more "country" than some of today's "country"!

Grading your records

When it comes to records, and how much you'll get for them, remember this above all:

Condition is (almost) everything!

Yes, it's possible to get a high price for a beat-up record, if it's exceptionally rare. But for common material, if it's not in at least Very Good condition – and preferably closer to Near Mint – you won't get many buyers. Or at least you won't the second time around. So accurately grading your discs is important, whether you're selling your records to a dealer or selling them to another collector.

Visual or play grading? In an ideal world, every record would be played before it is graded. But the time involved makes it impractical for most dealers, and anyway, it's rare that you get a chance to hear a record before you buy through the mail. Some advertisers play-grade everything and say so. But unless otherwise noted, records are visually graded.

How to grade. Look at everything about a record – its playing surface, its label, its edges – under a strong light. Then, based on your overall impression, give it a grade based on the following criteria:

Mint (M): Absolutely perfect in every way – certainly never played, possibly even still sealed. (More on still sealed under "Other considerations.") Should be used sparingly as a grade, if at all.

Near Mint (NM or M-): A nearly perfect record. Many dealers won't give a grade higher than this, implying (perhaps correctly) that no record is ever truly perfect.

The record should show no obvious signs of wear. A 45 RPM or EP sleeve should have no more than the most minor defects, such as almost invisible ring wear or other signs of slight handling.

An LP jacket should have no creases, folds, seam splits or any other noticeable similar defect. No cut-out holes, either. And of course, the same should be true of any other inserts, such as posters, lyric sleeves and the like.

Basically, an LP in Near Mint condition looks as if you just got it home from a new record store and removed the shrink wrap.

Near Mint is the highest price listed in all *Goldmine* price guides. Anything that exceeds this grade, in the opinion of both buyer and seller, is worth significantly more than the highest *Goldmine* book value.

Very Good Plus (VG+): Generally worth 50 percent of the Near Mint value.

A Very Good Plus record will show some signs that it was played and otherwise handled by a previous owner who took good care of it.

Record surfaces may show some slight signs of wear and may have slight scuffs or very light scratches that don't affect one's listening experience. Slight warps that do not affect the sound are OK.

The label may have some ring wear or discoloration, but it should be barely noticeable. The center hole will not have been misshapen by repeated play.

Picture sleeves and LP inner sleeves will have some slight ring wear, lightly turned-up corners, or a slight seam split. An LP jacket may have slight signs of wear also and may be marred by a cut-out hole, indentation or corner indicating it was taken out of print and sold at a discount.

In general, if not for a couple minor things wrong with it, this would be Near Mint. All but the most mint-crazy collectors will find a Very Good Plus record highly acceptable.

A synonym used by some collectors and dealers for "Very Good Plus" is "Excellent."

Very Good (VG): Generally worth 25 percent of the Near Mint value.

Many of the defects found in a VG+ record will be more pronounced in a VG disc.

Surface noise will be evident upon playing, especially in soft passages and during a song's intro and fade, but will not overpower the music otherwise. Groove wear will start to be noticeable, as will light scratches (deep enough to feel with a fingernail) that will affect the sound.

Labels may be marred by writing, or have tape or stickers (or their residue) attached. The same will be true of picture sleeves or LP covers. However, it will not have all of these problems at the same time, only two or three of them.

This *Goldmine* price guide lists Very Good as the lowest price. This, not the Near Mint price, should be your guide when determining how much a record is worth, as that is the price a dealer will normally pay you for a Near Mint record.

Good (G), Good Plus (G+): Generally worth 10-15 percent of the Near Mint value.

Good does not mean Bad! A record in Good or Good Plus condition can be put onto a turntable and will play through without skipping. But it will have significant surface noise and scratches and visible groove wear (on a styrene record, the groove will be starting to turn white).

A jacket or sleeve will have seam splits, especially at the bottom or on the spine. Tape, writing, ring wear or other defects will start to overwhelm the object.

If it's a common item, you'll probably find another copy in better shape eventually. Pass it up. But if it's something you have been seeking for years, and the price is right, get it... but keep looking to upgrade.

Poor (P), Fair (F): Generally worth 0-5 percent of the Near Mint price.

The record is cracked, badly warped, and won't play through without skipping or repeating. The picture sleeve is water damaged, split on all three seams and heavily marred by wear and writing. The LP jacket barely keeps the LP inside it. Inner sleeves are fully seam split, crinkled, and written upon.

Except for impossibly rare records otherwise unattainable, records in this condition should be bought or sold for no more than a few cents each.

Other grading considerations. Most dealers give a separate grade to the record and its sleeve or cover. In an ad, a record's grade is listed first, followed by that of the sleeve or jacket.

With **Still Sealed (SS)** records, let the buyer beware, unless it's a U.S. pressing from the last 10-15 years or so. It's too easy to re-seal one. Yes, some legitimately never-opened LPs from the 1960s still exist. But if you're looking for a specific pressing, the only way you can know for sure is to open the record. Also, European imports are not factory-sealed, so if you see them advertised as sealed, someone other than the manufacturer sealed them.

Grading scale for 78s

Most dealers in 78s have a slightly different grading system than the *Goldmine* system. The system uses only single-letter abbreviations and a series of pluses and minuses as follows:

N – New. Exactly that. This is a 78 that obviously has never been played and is in its original company paper sleeve. This grade is almost never used except for unplayed store stock. In this book, the "NM" value would be the "N" value for a 78, and should only be used for truly new 78s.

E – Excellent. The highest grade used by most 78 rpm dealers, with the occasional "+" to designate a really strong record. It's equivalent to "VG+" in this book. (If this book were all 78s, this is the highest price we'd list.)

V – Very Good. Most 78 rpm collectors are happy with a V record. It's roughly equivalent to a VG record for LPs and 45s. It's been played a bit and shows some obvious wear, but it is far from being abused.

G – Good. Here's where things start to get dicey. A record may have been played enough to cause some enlargement of the center hole, or the groove may be turning white, or some chips that don't affect the play have flaked off the edges.

F – Fair. See Good, except that the record has probably got an audible crack in it, too.

P – Poor. A truly unpleasant listening experience. Only acceptable for extremely rare, one-of-a-kind discs.

Common collecting abbreviations

In addition to the letters used to designate a record's grade, it's not uncommon to see other abbreviations used in dealer advertisements. Knowing the more common ones helps to prevent confusion. Here are some:

boot: bootleg (illegal pressing)
cc: cut corner
co: cutout
coh: cut-out hole
cov, cv, cvr: cover
demo: demonstration record (synonym for promo, this is the more common term overseas)
dh: drill hole
dj: disc jockey (promotional) record
ep: extended play (can be used for both 45s and LPs)
gf: gatefold (cover)
imp: import
ins: insert
lbl: label
m, mo: monaural (mono)
m/s: mono/stereo (usually used to describe a promo single that has the same song on both sides, with the only difference in the type of sound)
nap: (does) not affect play
noc: number on cover
nol: number on label
obi: not actually an abbreviation, "obi" is the Japanese word for "sash" and is used to describe the strip of paper usually wrapped around Japanese (and occasional US) pressings of LPs
orig: original
pr, pro, promo: promotional record
ps: picture sleeve (the cover that appears with some 45s and most 7-inch extended play singles)
q: quadraphonic
re: reissue
rec: record
repro: reproduction

ri: reissue
rw: ring wear
s: stereo
sl: slight
sm: saw mark
soc: sticker on cover
sol: sticker on label
ss: still sealed
s/t: self-titled
st: stereo
sw: shrink wrap
toc: tape on cover
tol: tape on label
ts: taped seam
w/: with
wlp: white label promo
wobc: writing on back cover
woc: writing on cover
wofc: writing on front cover
wol: writing on label
wr: wear
wrp: warp
xol: "x" on label

Some notes on the pricing

The prices listed in this book were determined from many sources.

The more common items reflect a consensus of used record shops and collectors, plus prices in ads over the past few months. In some ways, these items are more difficult to get a handle on; they sell without much publicity because of their low value, thus they aren't reported as often.

The rarer items are often the matter of conjecture because they so rarely come up for public sale. A high auction price for a truly rare piece can be the only way such an item's "worth" can be gauged, no matter what someone says about the value being inflated. Records, as with all collectibles, are only worth what someone will pay for them.

Because of the inexact nature of this undertaking, that's why we always urge you to use a book such as this as a guide and not as the final word on pricing.

We, too, can always use more input on the subject. See the **How you can help** section for more information.

And by the way, the publisher of the book does not engage in the buying and selling of records. So the prices listed in here should not be construed as "offers to buy" or "offers to sell" from Krause Publications.

Some notes on promotional records

To list every promotional version of every record in this book would be a consumption of space better used for unique listings. It would come close to doubling the length of the book. Some selected promos are listed, either because they are unique – in other words, the only version of the record is promotional or because it was pressed on a different color of wax than the stock copies – or because there is a significant, verifiable price difference between the promo and stock copies.

Obviously, not all promos are created equal.

It's probably easier to say which promotional copies are *not* going to fetch a premium. Those are copies that are otherwise identical to stock copies – the same label, the same number, the same everything – but are merely stamped on the front or back cover with (usually) a gold "For Promotion Only" indicator. There's nothing special about these records for the most part; any time the record company wants to create a promo, it can take a stock copy and gold-stamp it!

These are known as "designate promos" and rarely get more than 10 percent above the price of a regular stock copy, if that. For some sought-after rare items, such as Tori Amos' early album *Y Kant Tori Read*, designate promos go for much, much less than copies not so designated.

Some albums that appear to be "designate promos" do have collector value. These are copies pressed on special "audiophile vinyl," the most notable of which are the "Quiex II" pressings from the Warner-Reprise-Geffen family. Some of these fetch as much as 4-5 times the regular editions! These will *always* be marked on the cover with a sticker advertising the "Quiex II" record within.

Other promos of little collector value are those with a hole punch in the corner. This was Capitol's preferred method of creating promos during much of the 1970s. These are never worth more than the stock copy, and usually go for less.

Also, Columbia for a time merely used a "timing strip" on the front or back cover to designate a promo; these, too, also have little extra value above the stock copy. There is a major exception, though: The earliest promos for Bruce Springsteen's *Greetings From Asbury Park, N.J.* included both an attached timing strip and a glossy

8 1/2 x 11 "Bruce Springsteen Fact Sheet" glued to the back cover along the top. By the way, no white-label promos were ever pressed of this title.

Promos that *do* attract interest are those with custom promotional labels. Most of the time, these are white versions of the regular label, thus the term "white label promo." Of course, the label isn't always white; sometimes it's yellow or blue or pink or some other color. But it will always have as part of the label typesetting, "Promotional Copy" or "Audition Copy" or "Demonstration" or some other such term. Sometimes, the label will be almost identical to the stock versions, but some sort of words alluding to the promotional nature of the record will have been added to the typeset copy.

What makes these promos special? They are far more likely to have been mastered from the actual master mixdown tape, rather than a several-generations-removed copy, thus making them of higher sonic quality than later editions. They are among the first to come off the presses – after all, promos get sent out before stock copies Sometimes they are specially mastered to sound better over the air or through a store's loudspeakers. Regardless, they are sought after, and their value ranges from the same as a stock copy to as much as twice that of a stock copy.

Another rule of thumb when it comes to promos: In most cases, the more valuable a stock copy is, the *less* valuable the promo is. That's because in these instances, there are fewer stock copies known to exist than the promos.

Some more notes on 78s

In addition to a slightly different grading standard for 78s, we have a different standard for listing them in the book.

We use the heading "Selected 78s" for a reason. First, we only list 78s where there is either no 45 rpm equivalent or none was issued until some time later. So most of the 78s are from the late 1920s to the late 1940s (in some cases the early 1950s). When a 78 and 45 were issued simultaneously, we only list the 45. The 78 usually is valued at a small fraction of the 45's value, at least until about 1956. This is because once there is a choice, the collector tends to want the easier-to-handle 45. After 1956, 78s become rare enough that they overtake the 45 in value, even with less competition for them.

Also, we figure that most people who pick up this book are interested in the country artists from the 45 and LP era (roughly the past 50 years). Those artists whose recording career did not last into the "vinyl era" are not listed, unless they were around long enough to make the *Billboard* country charts. We made two obvious exceptions: First, no self-respecting country book could omit the original Jimmie Rodgers. And second, we listed the first major country-oriented hit record, which is purported to have sold a million copies – "The Prisoner's Song" by Vernon Dalhart.

You'll also see that, even in those time periods where there were only 78s, we're missing quite a few. In some cases we only know one side; in others, we only know the number but not what songs were on that disc. Any help you can give us on filling in these holes will be appreciated (see "How you can help" for more information).

Making sense of the listings

The artists' names are in bold capital letters. They are alphabetized, for the most part, the way our computer did, so blame anything that seems way out of line on that. We've programmed in some "fudge factors" – artists who have numbers in their names are listed as if they spelled out the name; artists with "Mr." are listed as if their name was "Mister," and the same with "St." and "Saint."

On the next line under some artists are cross-references or other information we feel is helpful. In some cases, you'll see a number after an artist in parentheses. That means we have more than one different artist by that name in our database. If you have records by, say, Sylvia or Shorty Long and they are not listed in here, then they are most likely not by the country singer we list.

One of the few, if not the only, cases in this book where we list different artists with the same name is with Jimmie Rodgers. As most collectors know, there were two distinct, unrelated artists who used this name, and both had country music success. Their records are listed separately.

Records are listed in five formats, in this order: "12-Inch Singles"; "45s"; "Selected 78s"; "7-Inch Extended Plays"; "Albums."

These are defined for the purposes of this book as follows:

A **12-inch single** is meant to promote or make available one particular song. These rarely have a name other than that of the song being promoted. Album-sized records with three or four songs on them that are not meant to specifically "sell" one song are 12-inch extended plays, and are listed under "Albums." Sometimes we had to make a judgment call as to where to put some of these.

A **45** is a seven-inch record, usually with one song on each side. It need not have a big hole. It need not even play at 45 rpm – for simplicity's sake, we've included Columbia Microgroove 33 1/3 rpm singles of the late 1940s and early 1950s in this category. They always have a note attached to them explaining what they are. Sometimes we list a 45 with more than one song on a side; either that's because the record was sold as a 45 or it was part of a record company's regular numbering system for 45s.

A **78** is usually a 10-inch record (larger than a 45, smaller than most LPs), usually with one song on each side. They are heavy, thick and brittle compared to newer records, which is one reason why they are not as avidly collected as 45s and LPs.

A **7-Inch Extended Play**, a product of the 1950s and early 1960s, is a hybrid. Most of the time they contain two songs on each side and had big holes, like 45s. But they almost always came with cardboard sleeves, like albums. Again, until only a few years ago, price guides always treated these items as inseparable. Consumers, however, often treated EPs like 45s – they threw out the covers. Reflecting that, all EP listings here have separate lines, and values, for the cover and the record.

An **album** is defined here as a 10- or 12-inch record (never 7 inches) that has a small hole and isn't a 12-inch single. Defining it any more than that is problematical. Some albums have only one song on a side, others have over a dozen; some play for 15 minutes, others for over an hour; some albums even play at 45 rpm rather than the standard 33 1/3 rpm. Unless noted, however, all albums are assumed to be 33 1/3s. No 78s are listed under albums.

Under each format listing, the records are sorted alphabetically by label, which are printed in all capital letters, then numerically within each label, ignoring prefixes. The one exception is with RCA Victor 45s, which are arranged with APBO issues first, then PB issues, then 447- series reissues, then other issues in order of prefix.

After many of the numbers is a number or letter in brackets. These designate something special about the listing as follows:

DJ: some sort of promotional copy, usually for radio stations and not meant for public sale

EP: extended play album (only used with album listings for 12-inch releases with 4 to 6 tracks and not as long as a regular album)

M: mono record

P: partially stereo record (rarely are records advertised as such; the determination has been made by careful listening)

PD: picture disc (the artwork is actually part of the record; these proliferated in the late 1970s and early 1980s and tend to have inferior sound quality)

PS: picture sleeve (this is the value for the sleeve *alone*; combine the record and sleeve value to get an estimated worth for the two together)

Q: quadraphonic record

R: rechanneled stereo record (these will usually be labeled with such terms as "Electronically Re-Channeled for Stereo"; "Enhanced for Stereo"; "Simulated Stereo"; or "Duophonic," but sometimes they aren't labeled as rechanneled)

S: stereo record

10: a 10-inch LP

(x) where x is a number: the number of records in a set (this is in parentheses inside the brackets so that in those rare instances where they exist, 10-record sets won't be confused with 10-inch LPs)

Most albums after 1968 do not have a stereo content designation. After 1968, if no designation is listed, it's probably stereo, though not necessarily. More importantly, it means that there was only one purchasing option available (except for the quadraphonic years of 1972-1977).

In the next, widest, column, we list the titles.

In the 12-inch single listings, we mention whether the version is extended, or how long it is, or something to identify it. We also mention, when known, whether a record has the same version on both sides.

For 45s, we list both the A- and B-side.

Each EP has two listings, one with its contents in order, one with the title of the EP as listed on the cover. In many cases, the title of the EP is found nowhere on the actual label – another reason to list the record and its sleeve separately.

If the contents of the EP are preceded by an asterisk (*), we know that these are the songs on this record, but we're not sure this is the correct order. Readers with this information are welcome to supply confirmation.

As most albums are almost worthless without a cover, they have one listing with the title as shown on the cover (assuming a title is shown on the cover). Most album listings have a prefix, usually from one to five letters. These prefixes often tell you whether your album is a first pressing and can have a considerable effect on an album's value.

The next column lists the year of release. Please note that the year of release and the year of recording are not necessarily the same! For example, if an album had several singles taken from it, the later singles may not have come out until another year, even though all of the singles have the same year on them. Also note that many archival recordings are reissued many times. Just because an album claims to be "recorded in 1941" doesn't mean that it actually came out in 1941. It's far more likely to be a more modern release.

That said, some of these dates may be off by a year; sometimes a record is released in December of the year before or January of the year after. Other years we can only guess the decade, and the year will have a question mark in it.

The next three columns are the values in Very Good (VG), Very Good Plus (VG+), and Near Mint (NM) condition. For all but the rarest pieces, the Very Good Plus value is twice the Very Good value, and the Near Mint value is twice the VG+ listing or four times the VG listing.

In some cases, dashes appear in the pricing column. That means that the VG or VG+ value is under $2 (bargain bin, yard sale, thrift shop material). If all three columns have dashes, there is some other reason, and we mention that in the explanatory notes below the listing. Every item with no value listed in any column is explained. If not, it's our error.

Finally, many items have a descriptive line in italics under the entry. This often purveys important information that plays a role in the above record's value, such as label design, cover design or colored vinyl. Sometimes, relatively insignificant differences can make a huge difference in value. Just look at the Elvis Presley listings for proof.

Making sense of the listings in back

Because of the nature of these items, we've used a slightly different format for the four sections that appear after the letter Z. These four sections are "Original Cast Recordings"; "Soundtracks"; "Television Albums"; and "Various Artists Collections."

Within each category, these are arranged alphabetically by the *title* of the release, again as our computer did them, and ignoring the words "A," "An" or "The." The exception is if the title begins with a number. Computers have this nasty tendency to put these first, before things beginning with "A."

Underneath each title are the applicable releases, arranged alphabetically and numerically by label. Those lines start with a check box, then are followed by the label and number listed together; any applicable abbreviations in brackets (which are the same as in the rest of the book – M for mono, S for stereo, etc.); the year of release; and the prices in three grades of condition.

Finding duets

Country & western music has a long tradition of otherwise solo artists teaming up for duets. Jimmie Rodgers and the Carter Family did a couple songs together in the early days; later we have Elton Britt and Rosalie Allen, Conway Twitty and Loretta Lynn, George Jones and Tammy Wynette, and dozens of others, not to mention all the artists with whom Willie Nelson did a duet. More recently, we have Tim McGraw and Faith Hill, Clint Black and Martina McBride, Garth Brooks and Trisha Yearwood, and Dwight Yoakam and Patty Loveless, among others.

If the duet was a one-shot deal, it's generally listed in the discography of the artist on whose record label the song appeared. For example, the Brooks/Yearwood duets were issued on MCA, Yearwood's label, so they are in her listings. If both artists were on the same label, we tried to find out which solo artist was on the B-side of the record; we then listed it under that artist.

Artists who did a lot of songs together get their own listings, usually in the order they appear most often on the label. For example, we have all the Loretta Lynn/Conway Twitty duets listed under "Conway Twitty and Loretta Lynn," even though not all of them are credited that way. The vast majority of duos are cross-referenced so you can find them.

As much effort as we made to try to make a confusing area less confusing, we've probably made some unintentional errors of consistency in the listings. Feel free to bring them to our attention, but don't make a federal case of them, OK?

Selling your records

At some point, perhaps after looking through this book, you may decide that you want to sell your collection. Good for you! And you want to take them to your local used record store with the idea that you'll get the prices you see in this book. Bad for you!

What the values in here reflect are *retail* prices – what a collector might pay for the item from a dealer, and *not* what a dealer will pay a collector for resale. Too many non-collectors (and even some collectors) don't understand that.

I know one dealer who has told me that he won't buy records from someone who tells him they consulted a price guide first. While that is extreme, it shows the distrust some dealers have for books like this and how the public uses (and abuses) them.

Just as importantly, the highest values are for records in the best condition (re-read the section on "Grading your records"). And there is a reason for that: Truly pristine records are very difficult to find! Many collectors are willing to pay handsomely for them – but for many of the records in this book, Near Mint examples aren't even known to exist!

One reason we've expanded the price listing to three grades of condition is to reflect that. There's a tendency to look at the highest price listed for something and assume that's what your record is worth. More realistically, though, such a small percentage of records are truly Near Mint – especially from the 1950s and 1960s and earlier – that your own records, if you were a typical accumulator and not a collector, are considerably less than Near Mint.

Even if you do end up trying to sell to a dealer, choose him or her carefully. Many dealers want nothing to do with country music because they have no clientele for it. It's always best to find someone who has a customer base for your kind of records.

There is only one way you'll be able to get anything close to the prices listed for most items, and that's to sell them direct to the collector.

The "old-fashioned" way is through record collecting magazines. The oldest and most widely read remains *Goldmine*, which was founded in 1974. Published every two weeks, the magazine is loaded with ads from people selling records of all kinds and from all eras. *Goldmine* has advertising salespeople who will help you put your ad together for maximum impact. To see what *Goldmine* is about, pick up a copy. It is available at all Tower Records stores in the U.S., most Barnes and Noble and Borders bookstores and hundreds of independent record dealers. If you still can't find a copy, call 1-800-258-0929.

Admittedly, *Goldmine's* country content is somewhat limited. But there are country collectors who read the paper, so if you do have country records for sale, you will have much less competition than you might in some other places. Also, in every other issue there is a section called "Country Junction," which has a short interview with a country artist and many CD reviews.

The "new" way to sell records and other memorabilia is over the Internet. The most popular method is through the online auction, and the most popular of these sites is eBay (www.ebay.com).

Online selling seems to draw two widely different audiences. One is very much the same audience as a stand-alone record store, except on a global scale rather than a regional one. Browsers who know next to nothing about record collecting and the relative scarcity of the listed pieces are common. These are people who can sometimes be fooled into paying too much for a common piece, especially certain million-selling compact discs, because of three magic letters: "OOP," short for "out of print." Just because something's out of print doesn't mean it has vanished off the face of the earth!

The other audience drawn to online sales are the hyper-specialists, and this is often where items can justifiably go for much larger sums than in a retail store. Thanks to search engines on most of the better sites, a fan of, say, Jim Reeves can type in the words "Jim Reeves" and find nothing but the Jim Reeves-related material. People who specialize in one artist will usually pay more – sometimes a *lot* more – than someone who collects a more broad range of artists. But because they are specialists, they also know which items are common, so they don't get taken on the easy stuff.

I have bought records over the web, and have yet to have significant problems. It's faster than "snail mail" and less expensive than a long-distance telephone call. But it's not perfect. Just as in real life, it pays to be wary.

As a seller, you are reaching a larger audience than you would in a record collecting magazine, but also a much less targeted one. The Internet seems to be a good place to sell lower-priced items that might take up valuable space in an expensive print ad. But many more valuable pieces sit or fetch less than they might through more traditional means.

Also, many sellers have found that eBay overreacts if you say you are selling a promo.

Promos are an accepted part of record collecting; there's even an entire book on collecting promotional records and CDs, and it's from the same publisher as this book. Despite that, eBay can, and does, remove these items, almost at random, for no good reason. (It's one thing if you're selling an advance copy of a CD that hasn't been issued to the general public yet. It's another to try to sell a 25-year-old vinyl promo.) So if you're selling promos, be aware of this.

As a buyer, you have to watch out for overgraded, under-described items. Photos of the items help. Also, buying from someone who deals in records as a primary area rather than as an obvious sideline to his/her Beanie Baby business is recommended. Look for dealers with strong feedback ratings; that is a sign of satisfied customers. Also, check for use of something resembling the *Goldmine* grading system. People who say their albums are in "good condition" don't know record collecting, because "good" is a low grade in the world of records (as it is in some other collecting areas, such as coins).

Also as a buyer, don't be afraid to e-mail the seller if you have any questions about the item. If you don't get a satisfactory answer, or get no answer at all, don't bid.

We feel the online world will continue to grow in importance over time. At some point it may become *the* biggest market for collectible records. So we'll continue to keep an eye on it. But even with its growth, it's still far from eclipsed other proven selling methods.

How you can help

Within this book, we have well over 50,000 listings of country & western records – 45s, 78s, LPs and picture sleeves. All the information is located in a growing database of records, which will make both our future price guides and *Goldmine* magazine better products in the long run.

But as you look through this book, you may see holes large enough to drive a convoy of 18-wheelers through. Certain parts of the book aren't as good as they could be. Readers have helped tremendously with other *Goldmine* projects; we know you can lend a hand with this one.

While any information is helpful, here are some areas where the most help is needed:

78s. This is the first book that we've compiled with information on 78 rpm records. In some cases we have detailed and accurate data, and in others, we don't. I'm sure we're missing many of these discs from the pre-1949 era.

You'll also see that we're missing a lot of B-sides, and in some cases we only know the number, but neither of the songs that appeared on the disc.

We also know that many discs that originally appeared on the Vocalion label in the late 1930s were reissued on the Okeh label in the 1940s. We know some of these, but not all of these.

We also know that several labels in the 1930s released the same records simultaneously. Some of these labels are Perfect, Romeo, Conqueror and Banner. Others include Bluebird, Montgomery Ward, Sunrise and Velvet Tone. Not every record that came out on one came out on the others; some had different pairings on them as well. We've only listed those records we have confirmed. Again, any good information will be appreciated.

Missing B-sides; repeated A-sides. Some records are listed as "(B-side unknown)." In some cases, it's because the record never was issued with a different B-side. Some of the Nashville independent labels issued the same version of the same song on both sides, even on stock copies! We figure that many of these unknown B-sides actually are the A-side repeated, but we could not confirm this with certainty. If you have any of these discs, we'd like to know for sure about B-sides.

Picture sleeves. Country music generally has had fewer 45 rpm picture sleeves than pop or rock music. Several major artists are only known to have one sleeve! Certainly there must be more country picture sleeves than we have listed.

Extended plays. Hundreds of extended play 7-inch singles are listed in this book. Most of them are certainly collectible, and many fetch healthy sums. But some of them we don't yet know about.

Anywhere you see the words "(contents unknown)," we'd like to know exactly what's on the record. What we need is side 1 and side 2, plus sleeve variations. As the titles of extended plays are often not listed on the records, we feel that actually listing the songs will be of greater help to the collector.

For the best results, follow these guidelines:

- Use the *record*, not the jacket, to determine the exact order of songs. Often, the titles on the sleeve are arranged to look better and don't necessarily correspond to the playing order.

- Not all EPs list Side 1 and Side 2 explicitly. So how do you tell? Look for the master numbers, which are usually found below the main number. On most EPs, the master number for Side 1 is one smaller than the master number for Side 2. For example, one of the Conway Twitty EPs listed in these pages has a Side 1 master number of "59-EP-33" and a Side 2 number of "59-EP-34." Another example: One of the Elvis Presley EPs has a Side 1 master number of "G2WH-7209" and a Side 2 number of "G2WH-7210." You get the idea.

Also, on those EP listings with an asterisk before the contents, we need confirmation of the exact order of tracks.

So if you're an EP collector, you can play a big role in helping us.

Albums. We're sure there are many missing albums from the listings. Most of these probably fall into two categories:

- Reissues of older material on different labels.
- Albums from small independent labels.

If you have albums that don't appear in the book, let us know. Please note, though, that we're only interested in albums on American labels. We don't intentionally list imports in here, nor do we plan to in the future.

The back section. We've barely scratched the surface with the various artists section, I'm reasonably sure. We're interested in any U.S. various artists LP with all, or mostly, country music on it. This includes additional soundtracks, original cast records and TV albums as well. Remember, though, that just because a film or TV has a western or rural setting doesn't mean that the music is country & western.

Early 45s. With two labels in particular – King and 4 Star – we're quite hazy as to when country 45s began to be produced. We tended to err on the side of caution. With both labels we continued to list only 78s well into 1951. But it's indeed possible that 45s exist of some of the titles we list as 78s only. If you have original 45s (maroon King labels, for example) of anything we list as 78 only, we want to know about it. And not only on King or 4 Star, but any American label.

Any incorrect information. In a book such as this, typographical errors are bound to happen, regardless of how hard we try to prevent them. If your record number or prefix doesn't match what's listed in here, let us know.

Missing artists. We think we have as broad a listing of country & western artists as you'll find in one book. That said, I'm sure someone of importance is not listed.

Some artists aren't in here because, as of press time, none of their music has come out on vinyl – SheDaisy, Phil Vassar, Rascal Flatts and Yankee Grey come to mind immediately. Others aren't in here because they stopped recording in the 1930s and were basically forgotten by the time LPs and 45s were invented.

Make your case for an artist who belongs in the book, preferably one who had releases on either 45 or LP, and who knows, we may include them in the third edition!

Basically, any information you have on a country artist's U.S. record releases that isn't in the book is welcome. We receive many contributions and suggestions, so not everyone can be acknowledged. But rest assured that even your one little correction helps in the long run.

You can contact me by mail:

Tim Neely
Goldmine Country & Western Price Guide
700 E. State St.
Iola, WI 54990

or by telephone:
445-2214 or 4612, ext. 782

or by e-mail:
neelyt@krause.com

If you write or e-mail, please include a *daytime* telephone number where I can contact you in case I have any questions.

Acknowledgments

First off, I'd like to thank Fred Heggeness for his first edition of this book. He gave us a good starting point, and even though this book looks vastly different than if he were still doing it, a fair amount of the information, especially on EPs and LPs, was retained.

Some artists in this book had appeared in prior *Goldmine* books, including the *Standard Catalog of American Records 1950-1975*, so a fair amount of information was already gathered and corrections made from those listings. Thanks to all the people who supplied me with information in response to appeals from that book and others.

Several photos of rare country & western items in this book came from Good Rockin' Tonight, an auction house in California. Its primary specialties are rock 'n' roll, rhythm & blues, and blues, but it does sell some classic country occasionally, both in its four-times-a-year auctions and in its more regular set sales. For more information on GRT, see the web site www.goodrockintonight.com or call (949) 833-1899.

Some people who deserve special mention for their contributions to this edition include Michael Sharritt, Bruce Krohmer, Maggie Thompson (who, while rummaging several years ago, found a "Victor and Bluebird Numerical Catalog" from 1942 – I never knew it would actually come in handy some day!), Mike Devich (I still use those catalogs he sent me several years back), Steve Kauffman, and all the country music lovers on the Internet who have done web sites in tribute to their favorite artists and genres. You all have been most helpful in giving me a greater perspective, and I hope you can get some use out of this book as well.

I want to thank the Krause book department for its patience, as it seemed this project would never end. Well, it finally has! I also want to thank my family members for their patience as well.

And finally, thank *you*, the reader and buyer of this book. I sure hope the wait was worth it!

Tim Neely
January 2001

A

ABBOTT, JERRY

45s

CHURCHILL

Number	Title (A Side/B Side)	Yr	VG	VG+	NM
❑ 7712	I Want a Little Cowboy/When It Comes to Cowgirls (I Just Can't Say No)	1978	—	2.50	5.00
❑ 7715	I Owe It All to You/Jack of All Trades	1978	—	2.50	5.00

DALLAS STAR

Number	Title (A Side/B Side)	Yr	VG	VG+	NM
❑ 102581	One Night Stanley/(Love Is Still) The Main Attraction	1981	—	3.00	6.00

ELLIOTT

Number	Title (A Side/B Side)	Yr	VG	VG+	NM
❑ 100/101	Christmas Is a Whispering Time of the Year/Jing-A-Ling	197?	2.00	4.00	8.00

ABERNATHY, MACK

45s

CMI

Number	Title (A Side/B Side)	Yr	VG	VG+	NM
❑ 1988-8	Slippin' Around/Pocket Rocket Ranger	1988	—	3.00	6.00
❑ 1988-9	Different Situations/Dos Hermanos Cantina	1988	—	3.00	6.00

ACE IN THE HOLE BAND

Also see GEORGE STRAIT.

45s

D

Number	Title (A Side/B Side)	Yr	VG	VG+	NM
❑ 1309	I Just Can't Go On Dying Like This/Honky Tonk Downstairs	1978	12.50	25.00	50.00
❑ 1313	The Way I Feel About You/Lonesome Rodeo Cowboy	1978	10.00	20.00	40.00
❑ 1316	I Don't Want to Talk It Over Anymore/Loneliest Singer in Town	1979	7.50	15.00	30.00

ACUFF, ROY

45s

CAPITOL

Number	Title (A Side/B Side)	Yr	VG	VG+	NM
❑ F2385	What Will I Do/Tied Down	1953	6.25	12.50	25.00
❑ F2460	Lonesome Joe/Is It Love or Is It Lies?	1953	6.25	12.50	25.00
❑ F2548	Don't Say Goodbye/Sixteen Chickens and a Tambourine	1953	6.25	12.50	25.00
❑ F2642	Swamp Lily/Sweep Around Your Own Back Door	1953	6.25	12.50	25.00
❑ F2738	Rushing Around/Whoa Mule	1954	6.25	12.50	25.00
❑ F2820	Sunshine Special/I Closed My Heart's Door	1954	6.25	12.50	25.00
❑ F2901	I'm Planting a Rose/Streamlined Heartbreaker	1954	6.25	12.50	25.00
❑ F3064	Don't Judge Your Neighbors/Thief Upon the Tree	1955	6.25	12.50	25.00
❑ F3115	That's What Makes the Juke Box Play/Night Spots	1955	6.25	12.50	25.00
❑ F3209	Little Moses/Oh Those Tombs	1955	6.25	12.50	25.00

COLUMBIA

Number	Title (A Side/B Side)	Yr	VG	VG+	NM
❑ 1-355 (?)	Lonesome Old River Blues/It's Just About Time	1949	10.00	20.00	40.00
—Microgroove 33 1/3 rpm 7-inch single					
❑ 1-483	The Day They Laid Mary Away/It's All Right Now	1950	10.00	20.00	40.00
—Microgroove 33 1/3 rpm 7-inch single					
❑ 4-20792	Plastic Heart/Your Address Unknown	1951	7.50	15.00	30.00
❑ 4-20804	Pliney Jane/Baldknob, Arkansas	1951	7.50	15.00	30.00
❑ 4-20828	Doug MacArthur/In the Shadow of the Smokies	1951	7.50	15.00	30.00
❑ 4-20858	Advice to Joe/When My Money Ran Out	1951	7.50	15.00	30.00
❑ 4-20877	Just Friends/Thy Burden's Greater	1952	6.25	12.50	25.00
❑ 4-20912	Ten Little Numbers/My Tears Don't Show	1952	6.25	12.50	25.00
❑ 4-20951	Cheating/Don't Hang Your Dirty Linen on the Line	1952	6.25	12.50	25.00
❑ 4- 21018	Wonder Is All I Do/She Isn't Guaranteed	1952	6.25	12.50	25.00

DECCA

Number	Title (A Side/B Side)	Yr	VG	VG+	NM
❑ 9-29748	Crazy Worried Mind/Along the China Coast	1955	5.00	10.00	20.00
❑ 9-29935	Goodbye Mr. Brown/Mother Hold Me Tight	1956	5.00	10.00	20.00
—With Kitty Wells					
❑ 9-30141	I Like Mountain Music/It's Hard to Love	1956	5.00	10.00	20.00

ELEKTRA

Number	Title (A Side/B Side)	Yr	VG	VG+	NM
❑ 45515	That's the Man I'm Looking For/(B-side unknown)	1978	—	2.50	5.00
❑ 46515	Freight Train Blues/Don't Worry 'Bout the Walk	1979	—	2.50	5.00
❑ 47040	I Can't Help It (If I'm Still in Love with You)/Cold, Cold Heart	1980	—	2.50	5.00
❑ 47480	Smokey Mountain Memories/What Have They Done to the Trains	1982	—	2.50	5.00
❑ 69937	Fireball Mail/The Stage	1982	—	2.50	5.00
—B-side by Boxcar Willie					

HICKORY

Number	Title (A Side/B Side)	Yr	VG	VG+	NM
❑ 1073	Once More/I Don't Care (If You Don't Love Me)	1958	3.75	7.50	15.00
❑ 1081	The One I Love (Is Gone)/Searchin' for Happiness	1958	3.75	7.50	15.00
❑ 1090	So Many Times/They'll Never Take Her Love from Me	1958	3.75	7.50	15.00
❑ 1097	Come and Knock (On the Door of My Heart)/My Love Came Back to Me	1959	3.75	7.50	15.00
❑ 1106	Nero Played His Fiddle/Write Me Sweetheart	1959	3.75	7.50	15.00
❑ 1113	Don't Know Why/Thanks for Not Telling Me	1960	3.00	6.00	12.00
❑ 1134	Mountain Guitar/Till No Longer You Care (For Me)	1960	3.00	6.00	12.00
❑ 1142	Streamlined Cannon Ball/Time Will Make You Pay	1961	3.00	6.00	12.00
❑ 1149	Little Mary/Lost John, He's Gone	1961	3.00	6.00	12.00
❑ 1160	Six More Days/Willie Boy, The Crippled Boy	1962	3.00	6.00	12.00
❑ 1178	Wabash Cannonball/Old Age Pension Check	1962	3.00	6.00	12.00
❑ 1191	Fireball Mail/The Great Speckled Bird	1962	3.00	6.00	12.00
❑ 1206	Don't Make Me Go to Bed and I'll Be Good/Pins and Needles (In My Heart)	1963	3.00	6.00	12.00
❑ 1223	The Great Titanic/The Birmingham Jail	1963	3.00	6.00	12.00
❑ 1244	Low and Lonely/Wabash Cannonball	1964	2.50	5.00	10.00
❑ 1271	Do You Wonder Why/Things That Might Have Been	1964	2.50	5.00	10.00
❑ 1291	Freight Train Blues/All the World Is Lonely Now	1965	2.50	5.00	10.00
❑ 1316	Life to Go/Rising Sun	1965	2.50	5.00	10.00
❑ 1331	I'm Planning a Rose/Tennessee Central	1965	2.50	5.00	10.00
❑ 1365	Pan American/Don't Tell Mama	1966	2.50	5.00	10.00
❑ 1394	Golden Treasure/Lost Highway	1966	2.50	5.00	10.00
❑ 1424	Kaw-Liga/Couldn't Believe It Was True	1966	2.50	5.00	10.00
❑ 1479	I Love You Because/I'm Movin' On	1967	2.50	5.00	10.00
❑ 1497	I'll Go On Alone/Uncle Pen	1967	2.50	5.00	10.00
❑ 1519	Don't Be Angry/The Nearest Thing to Heaven Is You	1968	2.50	5.00	10.00
❑ 1581	Life to Go/Each Season Changes You	1970	2.00	4.00	8.00
❑ 1627	Somebody Touched Me/Carry Me Back to the Mountains	1972	2.00	4.00	8.00
❑ 1636	A Pale Horse and His Ride/Sing a Country Song	1972	2.00	4.00	8.00
❑ 1644	Satisfied Mind/Just a Friend	1973	2.00	4.00	8.00

HICKORY/MGM

Number	Title (A Side/B Side)	Yr	VG	VG+	NM
❑ 314	Back in the Country/Jole Blon	1974	—	3.00	6.00
❑ 319	Old Time Sunshine Song/This World Can't Stand Long	1974	—	3.00	6.00
❑ 336	Back Down to Atlanta/A Most Reasonable Guy	1974	—	3.00	6.00
❑ 341	Fireball Mail/Roof Top Lullaby	1975	—	3.00	6.00
❑ 348	A Whole Month of Sundays/I Can't Find a Train	1975	—	3.00	6.00
❑ 355	That's Country/Take Me Home, Country Roads	1975	—	3.00	6.00
❑ 362	Walk a Mile in Your Neighbor's Shoes/Waltz in the Wind	1975	—	3.00	6.00

Selected 78s

COLUMBIA

Number	Title (A Side/B Side)	Yr	VG	VG+	NM
❑ 20003	Pins and Needles/We Live in Two Different Worlds	1948	3.00	6.00	12.00
—Reissue of 36856					
❑ 20009	I Think I'll Go Home and Cry/No One Will Ever Know	1948	3.00	6.00	12.00
—Reissue of 36891					
❑ 20021	All the World Is Lonely Now/That Glory Bound Train	1948	3.00	6.00	12.00
—Reissue of 36974					
❑ 20031	Great Speckled Bird/My Mountain Home Sweet Home	1948	3.00	6.00	12.00
—Reissue of 37005					
❑ 20032	Great Speckled Bird No. 2/Tell Mother I'll Be There	1948	3.00	6.00	12.00
—Reissue of 37006					
❑ 20033	Steel Guitar Chimes/Steel Guitar Blues	1948	3.00	6.00	12.00
—Reissue of 37007					
❑ 20034	Wabash Cannon Ball/Freight Train Blues	1948	3.00	6.00	12.00
—Reissue of 37008					
❑ 20038	Mule Skinner Blues/The Streamlined Cannonball	1948	3.00	6.00	12.00
—Reissue of 37012					
❑ 20041	Blue Eyed Darling/Beneath That Lonely Mound of Clay	1948	3.00	6.00	12.00
—Reissue of 37015					
❑ 20043	Come Back Little Pal/The Precious Jewel	1948	3.00	6.00	12.00
—Reissue of 37017					
❑ 20046	Be Honest with Me/Worried Mind	1948	3.00	6.00	12.00
—Reissue of 37020					
❑ 20056	I'll Reap My Harvest in Heaven/Don't Make Me Go to Bed and I'll Be Good	1948	3.00	6.00	12.00
—Reissue of 37031					
❑ 20057	The Prodigal Son/Not a Word from Home	1948	3.00	6.00	12.00
—Reissue of 37032					
❑ 20060	I'll Forgive You But I Can't Forget/Write Me Sweetheart	1948	3.00	6.00	12.00
—Reissue of 37035					
❑ 20064	Blues in My Mind/I Hear a Silver Trumpet	1948	3.00	6.00	12.00
—Reissue of 37039					
❑ 20068	Wait for the Light to Shine/It's Too Late Now to Worry Anymore	1948	3.00	6.00	12.00
—Reissue of 37045					
❑ 20079	Tell Me Now or Tell Me Never/Waiting for My Call to Glory	1948	3.00	6.00	12.00
—Reissue of 37099					
❑ 20090	Gone, Gone, Gone/Let Me Be the First to Say I'm Sorry	1948	3.00	6.00	12.00
—Reissue of 37202					
❑ 20106	(Our Own) Jole Blon/Tennessee Central (No. 9)	1948	3.00	6.00	12.00
—Reissue of 37287					
❑ 20120	Po' Folks (All the Time)/There's a Big Rock in the Road	1948	3.00	6.00	12.00
—Reissue of 37345					
❑ 20140	Just Inside the Pearly Gates/It Won't Be Long	1948	3.00	6.00	12.00
—Reissue of 37???					
❑ 20148	Things That Might Have Been/No Letter in the Mail	1948	3.00	6.00	12.00
—Reissue of 37421					
❑ 20151	I Know We're Saying Goodbye/You Are My Love	1948	3.00	6.00	12.00
—Reissue of 37???					
❑ 20156	Brother Take Warning/The Great Judgment Morn	1948	3.00	6.00	12.00
—Reissue of 37429					
❑ 20163	You're My Darling/Branded Wherever I Go	1948	3.00	6.00	12.00
—Reissue of 37436					

Number	Title (A Side/B Side)	Yr	VG	VG+	NM
❑ 20169	Are You Thinking of Me Darling?/I Called and Nobody Answered	1948	3.00	6.00	12.00
—Reissue of 37442					
❑ 20182	I Talked to Myself About You/Short Changed in Love	1948	3.00	6.00	12.00
—Reissue of 37505					
❑ 20195	Wreck on the Highway/Fire Ball Mail	1948	2.50	5.00	10.00
—Reissue of 37596					
❑ 20196	Pins and Needles/The Precious Jewel	1948	2.50	5.00	10.00
—Reissue of 37597					
❑ 20197	Wabash Cannon Ball/Freight Train Blues	1948	2.50	5.00	10.00
—Reissue of 37598					
❑ 20198	Wait for the Light to Shine/Low and Lonely	1948	2.50	5.00	10.00
—Reissue of 37???					
❑ 20213	New Greenback Dollar/Steamboat Whistle Blues	1948	3.00	6.00	12.00
—Reissue of 37614					
❑ 20320	Smoky Mountain Rag/Smoky Mountain Moon	1948	3.00	6.00	12.00
—Reissue of 37743					
❑ 20357	Blue Eyes Crying in the Rain/The Devil's Train	1948	3.00	6.00	12.00
—Reissue of 37822					
❑ 20378	They Can Only Fill One Grave/Do You Wonder Why	1948	3.00	6.00	12.00
—Reissue of 37943					
❑ 20385	Easy Rockin' Chair/Golden Treasure	1948	3.00	6.00	12.00
—Reissue of 37961					
❑ 20396	The Waltz of the Wind/The Songbirds Are Singing in Heaven	1948	3.00	6.00	12.00
—Reissue of 38042					
❑ 20409	I Saw the Light/Thank God	1948	3.00	6.00	12.00
—Reissue of 38109					
❑ 20425	Unloved and Unclaimed/I Had a Dream	1948	3.75	7.50	15.00
—Reissue of 38189					
❑ 20454	This World Can't Stand Long/It's So Hard to Smile	1948	5.00	10.00	20.00
—First "new" Acuff issue in Columbia 20000 series					
❑ 20475	A Sinner's Death/Midnight Train	1948	5.00	10.00	20.00
❑ 20478	Great Shining Light/That Beautiful Picture	1948	5.00	10.00	20.00
❑ 20479	Just to Ease My Worried Mind/Blue Ridge Sweetheart	1948	5.00	10.00	20.00
❑ 20480	Farther Along/What Would You Do with Gabriel's Trumpet	1948	5.00	10.00	20.00
❑ 20505	Heartaches and Flowers/When They Take That Last Look at Me	1948	5.00	10.00	20.00
❑ 20528	I'll Always Care/You'll Reap Those Tears	1948	5.00	10.00	20.00
❑ 20550	They Crucified My Lord/Pale Horse and His Rider	1948	5.00	10.00	20.00
❑ 20551	Tennessee Waltz/Sweeter Than the Flowers	1948	5.00	10.00	20.00
❑ 20558	Black Mountain Rag/Dance Around Molly	1949	3.00	6.00	12.00
❑ 20559	Smoky Mountain Rag/Pretty Little Widow	1949	3.00	6.00	12.00
❑ 20560	Grey Eagle/Lonesome Indian	1949	3.00	6.00	12.00
❑ 20561	Bully of the Town/Polk County Breakdown	1949	3.00	6.00	12.00
❑ 20626	Lonesome Old River Blues/It's Just About Time	1949	3.75	7.50	15.00
❑ 20664	The Day They Laid Mary Away/It's All Right Now	1950	3.75	7.50	15.00
❑ 20684	Jesus Died for Me/If I Could Hear My Mother Pray Again	1950	3.00	6.00	12.00
❑ 36856	Pins and Needles/We Live in Two Different Worlds	1946	5.00	10.00	20.00
❑ 36891	I Think I'll Go Home and Cry/No One Will Ever Know	1946	5.00	10.00	20.00
❑ 36974	All the World Is Lonely Now/That Glory Bound Train	1946	5.00	10.00	20.00
❑ 37005	Great Speckle Bird/My Mountain Home Sweet Home	1946	3.75	7.50	15.00
❑ 37006	Great Speckle Bird No. 2/Tell Mother I'll Be There	1946	3.75	7.50	15.00
❑ 37007	Steel Guitar Chimes/Steel Guitar Blues	1946	3.75	7.50	15.00
❑ 37008	Wabash Cannon Ball/Freight Train Blues	1946	3.75	7.50	15.00
❑ 37012	Mule Skinner Blues/The Streamlined Cannonball	1946	3.75	7.50	15.00
❑ 37015	Blue Eyed Darling/Beneath That Lonely Mound of Clay	1946	3.75	7.50	15.00
❑ 37017	Come Back Little Pal/The Precious Jewel	1946	3.75	7.50	15.00
❑ 37020	Be Honest with Me/Worried Mind	1946	3.75	7.50	15.00
❑ 37028	Wreck on the Highway/Fire Ball Mail	1946	3.75	7.50	15.00
❑ 37029	Night Train to Memphis/Low and Lonely	1946	3.75	7.50	15.00
❑ 37031	I'll Reap My Harvest in Heaven/Don't Make Me Go to Bed and I'll Be Good	1946	3.75	7.50	15.00
❑ 37032	The Prodigal Son/Not a Word from Home	1946	3.75	7.50	15.00
❑ 37035	I'll Forgive You But I Can't Forget/Write Me Sweetheart	1946	3.75	7.50	15.00
❑ 37039	Blues in My Mind/I Hear a Silver Trumpet	1946	3.75	7.50	15.00
❑ 37045	Wait for the Light to Shine/It's Too Late Now to Worry Anymore	1946	3.75	7.50	15.00
—All of the above from 37005 to 37045 are reissues of material that originally appeared on Vocalion or Okeh					
❑ 37099	Tell Me Now or Tell Me Never/Waiting for My Call to Glory	1946	5.00	10.00	20.00
❑ 37202	Gone, Gone, Gone/Let Me Be the First to Say I'm Sorry	1947	5.00	10.00	20.00
❑ 37287	(Our Own) Jole Blon/Tennessee Central (No. 9)	1947	5.00	10.00	20.00
❑ 37345	Po' Folks (All the Time)/There's a Big Rock in the Road	1947	5.00	10.00	20.00
❑ 37421	Things That Might Have Been/No Letter in the Mail	1947	3.75	7.50	15.00
❑ 37429	Brother Take Warning/The Great Judgment Morn	1947	3.75	7.50	15.00
❑ 37436	You're My Darling/Branded Wherever I Go	1947	3.75	7.50	15.00
❑ 37442	Are You Thinking of Me Darling?/I Called and Nobody Answered	1947	3.75	7.50	15.00
❑ 37505	I Talked to Myself About You/Short Changed in Love	1947	5.00	10.00	20.00
❑ 37596	Wreck on the Highway/Fire Ball Mail	1947	3.00	6.00	12.00
❑ 37597	Pins and Needles/The Precious Jewel	1947	3.00	6.00	12.00
❑ 37598	Wabash Cannon Ball/Freight Train Blues	1947	3.00	6.00	12.00
—The above three were issued in an album					
❑ 37614	New Greenback Dollar/Steamboat Whistle Blues	1947	5.00	10.00	20.00
❑ 37743	Smoky Mountain Rag/Smoky Mountain Moon	1947	5.00	10.00	20.00
❑ 37822	Blue Eyes Crying in the Rain/The Devil's Train	1947	5.00	10.00	20.00
❑ 37943	They Can Only Fill One Grave/Do You Wonder Why	1947	5.00	10.00	20.00
❑ 37961	Easy Rockin' Chair/Golden Treasure	1947	5.00	10.00	20.00
❑ 38042	The Waltz of the Wind/The Songbirds Are Singing in Heaven	1948	5.00	10.00	20.00
❑ 38109	I Saw the Light/Thank God	1948	5.00	10.00	20.00
❑ 38189	Unloved and Unclaimed/I Had a Dream	1948	6.25	12.50	25.00
CONQUEROR					
❑ 9434	The Streamlined Cannon Ball/Weary River	193?	6.25	12.50	25.00
❑ 9741	The Precious Jewel/The Broken Heart	193?	6.25	12.50	25.00
OKEH					
❑ 04374	Great Speckle Bird No. 2/Tell Mother I'll Be There	193?	7.50	15.00	30.00
❑ 04466	Wabash Cannon Ball/Freight Train Blues	194?	7.50	15.00	30.00
❑ 04505	She No Longer Belongs to Me/You're the Only Star (In My Blue Heaven)	1939	10.00	20.00	40.00
❑ 05163	Beautiful Brown Eyes/Living on the Mountain	1940	6.25	12.50	25.00
❑ 05587	When I Lay My Burden Down/Will the Circle Be Unbroken	194?	6.25	12.50	25.00
❑ 5695	Blue Eyed Darling/Beneath That Lonely Mound of Clay	194?	6.25	12.50	25.00
❑ 5956	Come Back Little Pal/The Precious Jewel	193?	6.25	12.50	25.00
❑ 06229	Worried Man/Be Honest with Me	194?	6.25	12.50	25.00
❑ 6550	I Know We're Saying Goodbye/You Are My Love	194?	6.25	12.50	25.00
❑ 6685	Wreck on the Highway/Fire Ball Mail	1943	6.25	12.50	25.00
❑ 6693	Night Train to Memphis/Low and Lonely	1943	6.25	12.50	25.00
❑ 6704	I'll Reap My Harvest in Heaven/(B-side unknown)	1943	6.25	12.50	25.00
❑ 6716	The Prodigal Son/Not a Word from Home	1943	6.25	12.50	25.00
❑ 6723	I'll Forgive You But I Can't Forget/Write Me Sweetheart	1944	6.25	12.50	25.00
❑ 6745	Wait for the Light to Shine/It's Too Late Now to Worry Anymore	1945	6.25	12.50	25.00
VOCALION					
❑ 04252	Great Speckle Bird/(B-side unknown)	1938	12.50	25.00	50.00
❑ 04466	Wabash Cannon Ball/Freight Train Blues	1938	10.00	20.00	40.00

Albums

CAPITOL

Number	Title	Yr	VG	VG+	NM
❑ T 617 [M]	Songs of the Smoky Mountains	1955	15.00	30.00	60.00
❑ DT 1870 [R]	The Best of Roy Acuff	1963	5.00	10.00	20.00
❑ T 1870 [M]	The Best of Roy Acuff	1963	7.50	15.00	30.00
❑ DT 2103 [R]	The Great Roy Acuff	1964	3.75	7.50	15.00
❑ T 2103 [M]	The Great Roy Acuff	1964	6.25	12.50	25.00
❑ ST 2276 [S]	The Voice of Country Music	1965	10.00	20.00	40.00
❑ T 2276 [M]	The Voice of Country Music	1965	7.50	15.00	30.00
COLUMBIA					
❑ CL 9004 [10]	Songs of the Smoky Mountains	1949	50.00	100.00	200.00
❑ CL 9010 [10]	Old Time Barn Dance	1949	37.50	75.00	150.00
❑ CL 9013 [10]	Songs of the Saddle	1950	37.50	75.00	150.00
❑ FC 39998 []	Columbia Historic Edition	1985	2.50	5.00	10.00
ELEKTRA					
❑ E-C 10-1-78 [DJ]	An Interview with Roy Acuff	1978	6.25	12.50	25.00
HARMONY					
❑ HL 7082 [M]	Great Speckled Bird	1958	6.25	12.50	25.00
❑ HL 7294 [M]	That Glory Bound Train	1961	5.00	10.00	20.00
❑ HL 7342 [M]	The Great Roy Acuff	196?	3.75	7.50	15.00
❑ HL 7376 [M]	Waiting for My Call to Glory	196?	3.75	7.50	15.00
HICKORY					
❑ LPM-H-101 [M]	Once More It's Roy Acuff	1961	7.50	15.00	30.00
❑ LPM-109 [M]	King of Country Music — All-Time Greatest Hits	1962	6.25	12.50	25.00
❑ LPM-113 [M]	Roy Acuff — Star of the Grand Ole Opry	1963	6.25	12.50	25.00
❑ LPM-114 [M]	The World Is His Stage	1963	6.25	12.50	25.00
❑ LPM-115 [M]	Roy Acuff Sings American Folk Songs	1963	6.25	12.50	25.00
❑ LPM-117 [M]	Hand-Clapping Gospel Songs	1963	6.25	12.50	25.00
❑ LPM-119 [M]	Country Music Hall of Fame	1964	5.00	10.00	20.00
❑ LPM-125 [M]	Great Train Songs	1965	5.00	10.00	20.00
❑ LPM-134 [M]	Roy Acuff Sings Hank Williams	1966	10.00	20.00	40.00
❑ LPS-134 [S]	Roy Acuff Sings Hank Williams	1966	10.00	20.00	40.00
❑ LPS-139	Famous Opry Favorites	1967	5.00	10.00	20.00
❑ LPS-145	Living Legend	1968	5.00	10.00	20.00
❑ LPS-147	Treasury of Country Hits	1969	5.00	10.00	20.00
❑ LPS-156	Roy Acuff Time	1970	5.00	10.00	20.00
❑ DT-90698 [R]	Great Train Songs	1965	6.25	12.50	25.00
—Capitol Record Club edition					
METRO					
❑ M 508 [M]	Roy Acuff	1965	3.75	7.50	15.00
❑ MS 508 [R]	Roy Acuff	1965	2.50	5.00	10.00
MGM					
❑ E-3707 [M]	Favorite Hymns	1958	12.50	25.00	50.00
❑ E-4044 [M]	Hymn Time	1962	6.25	12.50	25.00
❑ SE-4044 [R]	Hymn Time	196?	5.00	10.00	20.00
ROUNDER					
❑ SS-23	1936-1939: Steamboat Whistle Blues	1985	2.50	5.00	10.00
❑ SS-24	1939-1941: Fly Birdie Fly	1985	2.50	5.00	10.00

ACUFF, ROY, JR.

45s

HICKORY

Number	Title	Yr	VG	VG+	NM
❑ 1349	Baby Just Said Goodbye/Wabash Cannonball	1965	2.50	5.00	10.00

Number	Title (A Side/B Side)	Yr	VG	VG+	NM
❑ 1371	Stand Tall/You Won't Ever See Me Here Again	1966	2.50	5.00	10.00
❑ 1398	I Wish It Were Me/Turn That Frown Upside Down	1966	2.50	5.00	10.00
❑ 1425	Looks Like the Sun Ain't Gonna Shine/Victim of Circumstances	1966	3.00	6.00	12.00
—As "Roy Junior"					
❑ 1456	The Lament of the Cherokee Reservation/Luckiest Guy in the World	1967	3.00	6.00	12.00
❑ 1476	As Long As I Live/You, You, You, You	1967	2.50	5.00	10.00
❑ 1505	My World Has Stopped/Follow Your Drum	1968	2.50	5.00	10.00
❑ 1515	Blue Train (Of the Heartbreak Line)/Thru the Windows of Your House	1968	2.50	5.00	10.00
❑ 1535	Luckiest Guy in the World/The Guy Who Played Bass (So Well in Harlin Mason's Band)	1969	2.50	5.00	10.00
❑ 1551	Looks Like Baby's Gone/Through the Windows of Your Mind	1969	2.50	5.00	10.00
❑ 1583	Back Down to Atlanta/Outlaw	1970	2.00	4.00	8.00
❑ 1597	Running/Street Singer	1971	2.00	4.00	8.00

HICKORY/MGM

Number	Title (A Side/B Side)	Yr	VG	VG+	NM
❑ 321	California Lady/Take Me Back	1974	—	3.00	6.00
❑ 331	Don't Worry 'Bout the Mule/Precious Memories	1974	—	3.00	6.00
❑ 344	Good Morning Country Rain/Sittin' Around the Campfire	1975	—	3.00	6.00
❑ 351	Good Time and T-Bird Wine/Turpentine Blues	1975	—	3.00	6.00
❑ 358	Baby, Maybe, Some Day/When She's Thirty	1975	—	3.00	6.00

ACUFF, ROY, JR., AND SUE THOMPSON

45s

HICKORY

Number	Title (A Side/B Side)	Yr	VG	VG+	NM
❑ 1542	Thoughts/Are You Teasing Me	1969	2.50	5.00	10.00
❑ 1558	Talk Back Trembling Lips/Till I Can't Take It Anymore	1970	2.00	4.00	8.00
❑ 1573	Don't Let the Stars Get In Your Eyes/Why You Been Gone	1970	2.00	4.00	8.00

ADAMS, CHARLIE

45s

COLUMBIA

Number	Title (A Side/B Side)	Yr	VG	VG+	NM
❑ 4-21195	Hey Liberace/Will You Love Me When I'm Old	1954	6.25	12.50	25.00
❑ 4-21230	I'll Tickle Your Toeses/You've Wounded the Heart	1954	5.00	10.00	20.00
❑ 4-21239	Jolie Fille/I'm a Railroad Daddy	1954	5.00	10.00	20.00
❑ 4-21300	Gee, But It's Dry in Texas/Waltzing with Sin	1954	5.00	10.00	20.00
❑ 4-21355	Cat'n Around/Man Was the Cause of It All	1955	6.25	12.50	25.00
❑ 4-21401	Flower of My Heart/Hidin' Out	1955	5.00	10.00	20.00
❑ 4-21443	Pistol Packin' Mama/They Can't Make a Devil	1955	5.00	10.00	20.00
❑ 4-21524	Sugar Diet/Black Land Blues	1956	5.00	10.00	20.00

DECCA

Number	Title (A Side/B Side)	Yr	VG	VG+	NM
❑ 9-46335	If a Beer Bottle Had a Nipple On It/You're Getting Too Old	1951	6.25	12.50	25.00
❑ 9-46358	I'm Gonna Love You Pretty Baby/I'm Gonna Put My Foot Down	1951	7.50	15.00	30.00
❑ 9-46373	Stop Your Bawlin' Baby/Give Me Back My Kisses	1951	6.25	12.50	25.00
❑ 9-46391	I Lost an Angel/Without You I'm Lost	1952	6.25	12.50	25.00

ADAMS, DON

45s

ATLANTIC

Number	Title (A Side/B Side)	Yr	VG	VG+	NM
❑ 4002	I'll Be Satisfied/All for the Love of a Girl	1973	—	2.50	5.00
❑ 4009	I've Already Stayed Too Long/Oh What a Future She Had	1973	—	2.50	5.00
❑ 4017	Baby Let Your Long Hair Down/Little Girl Blue	1974	—	2.50	5.00
❑ 4027	That's Love/I Just Lost My Favorite Girl	1974	—	2.50	5.00

D

Number	Title (A Side/B Side)	Yr	VG	VG+	NM
❑ 1268	You Introduced Me to the Blues/I Just Lost My Favorite Girl	196?	3.75	7.50	15.00

JACK O' DIAMONDS

Number	Title (A Side/B Side)	Yr	VG	VG+	NM
❑ 1002	Two of the Usual/Wake Me 100 Years from Now	1967	2.50	5.00	10.00
❑ 1003	Plant a Little Heartache/Why I Still Love You	1967	2.50	5.00	10.00
❑ 1004	Brand New Bed of Roses/Tear Talk	1967	2.50	5.00	10.00
❑ 1015	I Miss You/Just Say You Love Me	1968	2.50	5.00	10.00

MUSICOR

Number	Title (A Side/B Side)	Yr	VG	VG+	NM
❑ 1078	Heartaches Deep in Sorrow/Kill Me with Kindness	1965	2.50	5.00	10.00
❑ 1136	Big Town Baby/There Are Some Things	1965	2.50	5.00	10.00
❑ 1172	Heartaches Morning, Noon and Night/Painting Pictures	1966	2.00	4.00	8.00

ADAMS, KAY

45s

CAPITOL

Number	Title (A Side/B Side)	Yr	VG	VG+	NM
❑ 3551	Step Aside Girl/Second Hand Sugar Spoon	1973	2.00	4.00	8.00
❑ 3624	Hearts of Stone/I Can, I Can	1973	2.00	4.00	8.00
❑ 3692	Reason to Feel/Ain't It Funny	1973	2.00	4.00	8.00

GRANITE

Number	Title (A Side/B Side)	Yr	VG	VG+	NM
❑ 521	I Never Got to Nashville/Eli Whitney	1975	—	3.50	7.00
❑ 525	Country Dreamer/Henry in the Centerfold	1975	—	3.50	7.00

OVATION

Number	Title (A Side/B Side)	Yr	VG	VG+	NM
❑ 1015	Let George Do It/You Better Not Do That	197?	2.00	4.00	8.00

TOWER

Number	Title (A Side/B Side)	Yr	VG	VG+	NM
❑ 177	Don't Talk About Trouble to Me/Honky Tonk Heartaches	1965	3.75	7.50	15.00
❑ 201	Roll Out the Red Carpet/She Didn't Color Daddy	1966	3.00	6.00	12.00
❑ 235	Anymore/Old Heart Get Ready	1966	3.00	6.00	12.00
❑ 269	Little Pink Mack/That'll Be the Day	1966	3.00	6.00	12.00
❑ 294	Where Did the Good Times Go/You Taught Me Everything I Know	1966	2.50	5.00	10.00
❑ 305	Trapped/Rocks in My Head	1967	2.50	5.00	10.00
❑ 329	Six Days a-Waiting/Be Nice to Everybody	1967	2.50	5.00	10.00
❑ 360	Husband Stealer/I Let a Stranger (Buy the Wine)	1967	2.50	5.00	10.00
❑ 395	Big Mac/Get Out of My Heart	1968	2.50	5.00	10.00
❑ 470	Good Morning Love/Too Used to Being with You	1969	2.50	5.00	10.00

Albums

TOWER

Number	Title (A Side/B Side)	Yr	VG	VG+	NM
❑ ST 5033 [S]	Wheels & Tears	1966	7.50	15.00	30.00
❑ T 5033 [M]	Wheels & Tears	1966	6.25	12.50	25.00
❑ ST 5069	Make Mine Country	1967	5.00	10.00	20.00
❑ T 5069 [M]	Make Mine Country	1967	6.25	12.50	25.00
❑ ST 5087	Alcohol & Tears	1968	5.00	10.00	20.00

ADAMS, KAYLEE

45s

WARNER BROS.

Number	Title (A Side/B Side)	Yr	VG	VG+	NM
❑ 28567	I Can't Help the Way I Don't Feel/Love You 'Til It Hurts	1986	—	—	3.00

ADEN, TERRY

45s

AMI

Number	Title (A Side/B Side)	Yr	VG	VG+	NM
❑ 1303	She Doesn't Belong to You/What's So Good About Goodbye	1982	—	2.50	5.00

B&B

Number	Title (A Side/B Side)	Yr	VG	VG+	NM
❑ 21	What's So Good About Goodbye/I'm Here	1981	—	3.00	6.00

ADKINS, TRACE

45s

CAPITOL NASHVILLE

Number	Title (A Side/B Side)	Yr	VG	VG+	NM
❑ S7-19117	There's a Girl in Texas/A Bad Way of Saying Goodbye	1996	—	2.00	4.00
❑ S7-19224	Every Light in the House/If I Fall (You're Goin' with Me)	1997	—	2.00	4.00
❑ S7-19524	(This Ain't) No Thinkin' Thing/634-5789	1997	—	2.50	5.00
❑ S7-19579	I Left Something Turned On at Home/I Can Only Love You Like a Man	1997	—	2.00	4.00
❑ S7-19698	The Rest of Mine/Wayfaring Stranger	1997	—	2.00	4.00
❑ S7-19897	Lonely Won't Leave Me Alone/Nothin' But Taillights	1998	—	2.00	4.00
❑ S7-19976	Big Time/Snowball in El Paso	1998	—	2.00	4.00
❑ 38701	More/The Night He Can't Remember	2000	—	—	3.00
❑ 58744	The Christmas Song/Wayfaring Stranger	1998	—	—	3.00
❑ 58812	Don't Lie/All Hat, No Cattle	1999	—	—	3.00
❑ 58817	The Christmas Song/Santa Claus Is Coming to Town	1999	—	—	3.00
—B-side by Chris LeDoux					
❑ 58880	I'm Gonna Love You Anyway/I Can Dig It	2000	—	2.00	4.00

ADKINS, WENDEL

45s

HITSVILLE

Number	Title (A Side/B Side)	Yr	VG	VG+	NM
❑ 6050	I Will/Show Me the Way	1977	—	2.50	5.00
❑ 6055	Laid Back Country Picker/Texas Moon	1977	—	2.50	5.00

MC

Number	Title (A Side/B Side)	Yr	VG	VG+	NM
❑ 5002	Julieanne (Where Are You Tonight)/She Gives Me Love	1977	—	2.50	5.00
❑ 5008	You've Lost That Loving Feeling/Show Me the Way	1978	—	2.50	5.00

Albums

HITSVILLE

Number	Title (A Side/B Side)	Yr	VG	VG+	NM
❑ H6-406S1	The Sundowners	1977	3.75	7.50	15.00

MC

Number	Title (A Side/B Side)	Yr	VG	VG+	NM
❑ MC6-503S1	The Sundowners	1977	3.00	6.00	12.00
—Reissue of Hitsville LP					

AKINS, RHETT

45s

DECCA

Number	Title (A Side/B Side)	Yr	VG	VG+	NM
❑ 54910	What They're Talking About/(B-side unknown)	1994	—	—	3.00
❑ 54974	I Brake for Brunettes/I Brake for Brunettes (Dance Mix)	1994	—	2.00	4.00
❑ 55034	That Ain't My Truck/Same Ol' Story	1995	—	2.00	4.00
❑ 55085	She Said Yes/Old Dirt Road	1995	—	—	3.00
❑ 55166	Don't Get Me Started/I Was Wrong	1996	—	2.00	4.00
❑ 55223	Love You Back/No Match for That Old Flame	1996	—	—	3.00
❑ 55291	Every Cowboy's Dream/Carolina Line	1997	—	—	3.00
❑ 72022	More Than Everything/Better Than It Used to Be	1997	—	—	3.00
❑ 72036	Better Than It Used to Be/I'm Finding Out	1998	—	—	3.00
❑ 72049	Drivin' My Life Away/A Man with 18 Wheels	1998	—	—	3.00
—B-side by Lee Ann Womack					

ALABAMA

45s

BNA

Number	Title (A Side/B Side)	Yr	VG	VG+	NM
❑ 65312	Angels Among Us/Make a Miracle	1997	—	—	3.00
—B-side credited to "Various Artists"					

GRT

Number	Title (A Side/B Side)	Yr	VG	VG+	NM
❑ 129	I Wanna Be with You Tonight/Lovin' You Is Killin' Me	1977	3.75	7.50	15.00
❑ 129 [PS]	I Wanna Be with You Tonight/Lovin' You Is Killin' Me	1977	5.00	10.00	20.00

Number	Title (A Side/B Side)	Yr	VG	VG+	NM
MDJ					
❑ 1002-JB	My Home's in Alabama/Some Other Time, Some Other Place	1980	2.50	5.00	10.00
—Jukebox pressing with one B-side					
❑ 1002-R	My Home's in Alabama//Some Other Time, Some Other Place/Why Lady Why	1980	3.00	6.00	12.00
—Regular pressing with two B-sides					
❑ 7906	I Wanna' Come Over/Get It While It's Hot	1979	3.00	6.00	12.00
RCA					
❑ 2519-7-R	Pass It On Down/The Borderline	1990	—	—	3.00
❑ 2519-7-R [PS]	Pass It On Down/The Borderline	1990	—	2.00	4.00
❑ 2643-7-R	Jukebox in My Mind/Fire on Fire	1990	—	—	3.00
❑ 2706-7-R	Forever's As Far As I'll Go/Starting Tonight	1990	—	2.50	5.00
❑ 2778-7-R	Down Home/Goodbye (Kelly's Song)	1991	—	—	3.00
❑ 2828-7-R	Here We Are/Gulf of Mexico	1991	—	—	3.00
❑ 5003-7-R	Touch Me When We're Dancing/Hanging Up My Travelin' Shoes	1986	—	—	3.00
❑ 5051-7-R	Christmas in Dixie/Tennessee Christmas	1986	—	2.00	4.00
❑ 5081-7-R	"You've Got" The Touch/True, True Housewife	1987	—	—	3.00
❑ 5222-7-R	Tar Top/If I Could Just See You Now	1987	—	—	3.00
❑ 5222-7-R [PS]	Tar Top/If I Could Just See You Now	1987	2.00	4.00	8.00
—Promo-only sleeve					
❑ 5328-7-R	Face to Face/Vacation	1987	—	—	3.00
❑ 6902-7-R	Fallin' Again/I Saw the Time	1988	—	—	3.00
❑ 8744-7-R	Song of the South/(I Wish It Could Always Be) '55	1988	—	—	3.00
❑ 8817-7-R	If I Had You/I Showed Her	1988	—	—	3.00
❑ 8937-7-R	Fallin' Again/Song of the South	1989	—	—	3.00
—Gold Standard Series reissue					
❑ 8948-7-R	High Cotton/"Ole" Baugh Road	1989	—	—	3.00
❑ 9083-7-R	Southern Star/Barefootin'	1989	—	—	3.00
❑ PB-12008	My Home's in Alabama/I Wanna Come Over	1980	—	2.00	4.00
❑ PB-12008 [PS]	My Home's in Alabama/I Wanna Come Over	1980	—	3.00	6.00
❑ PB-12018	Tennessee River/Can't Forget About You	1980	—	2.00	4.00
❑ PB-12091	Why Lady Why/I Wanna Come Over	1980	—	2.00	4.00
❑ PB-12091 [PS]	Why Lady Why/I Wanna Come Over	1980	—	2.50	5.00
❑ PB-12169	Old Flame/I'm Stoned	1981	—	2.00	4.00
❑ PB-12236	Feels So Right/See the Embers, Feel the Flame	1981	—	2.00	4.00
❑ PB-12288	Love in the First Degree/Ride the Train	1981	—	2.00	4.00
❑ GB-12310	Why Baby Why/My Home's in Alabama	1981	—	—	3.00
—Gold Standard Series reissue					
❑ GB-12369	Tennessee River/Old Flame	1981	—	—	3.00
—Gold Standard Series reissue					
❑ PB-13019	Mountain Music/Never Be One	1981	—	2.00	4.00
❑ PB-13019 [PS]	Mountain Music/Never Be One	1981	—	2.50	5.00
❑ PB-13210	Take Me Down/Lovin' You Is Killin' Me	1982	—	2.00	4.00
❑ PB-13294	Close Enough to Perfect/Fantasy	1982	—	2.00	4.00
❑ PB-13358	Christmas in Dixie/Christmas Is Just a Song for Us This Year	1982	—	2.50	5.00
—B-side by Louise Mandrell and R.C. Bannon					
❑ PB-13446	Dixieland Delight/A Very Special Love	1983	—	2.00	4.00
❑ GB-13489	Feels So Right/Mountain Music	1983	—	—	3.00
—Gold Standard Series reissue					
❑ GB-13492	Take Me Down/Close Enough to Perfect	1983	—	—	3.00
—Gold Standard Series reissue					
❑ PB-13524	The Closer You Get/You Turn Me On	1983	—	2.00	4.00
❑ PB-13590	Lady Down on Love/Lovin' Man	1983	—	2.00	4.00
❑ PB-13664	Christmas in Dixie/Never Be One	1983	—	2.00	4.00
❑ PB-13716	Roll On (Eighteen Wheeler)/Food on the Table	1984	—	2.00	4.00
❑ PB-13763	When We Make Love/Oklahoma Mountain Dew	1984	—	2.00	4.00
❑ GB-13786	Dixieland Delight/Lady Down on Love	1984	—	—	3.00
—Gold Standard Series reissue					
❑ PB-13840	If You're Gonna Play in Texas (You Gotta Have a Fiddle in the Band)/I'm Not That Way Anymore	1984	—	2.00	4.00
❑ PB-13926	(There's A) Fire in the Night/Rock on the Bayou	1984	—	2.00	4.00
❑ PB-13992	There's No Way/The Boy	1985	—	2.00	4.00
❑ GB-14067	Roll On (Eighteen Wheeler)/When We Make Love	1985	—	—	3.00
—Gold Standard Series reissue					
❑ PB-14085	Forty Hour Week (For a Livin')/As Right Now	1985	—	2.00	4.00
❑ PB-14085 [PS]	Forty Hour Week (For a Livin')/As Right Now	1985	—	2.50	5.00
❑ PB-14165	Can't Keep a Good Man Down/If It Ain't Dixie (It Won't Do)	1985	—	2.00	4.00
❑ GB-14174	Love in the First Degree/The Closer You Get	1985	—	—	3.00
—Gold Standard Series reissue					
❑ GB-14176	(There's a) Fire in the Night/If You're Gonna Play in Texas (You Gotta Have a Fiddle in the Band)	1985	—	—	3.00
—Gold Standard Series reissue					
❑ PB-14213	Thistlehair the Christmas Bear/Santa Claus (I Still Believe in You)	1985	—	—	—
—Unreleased					
❑ PB-14219	Joseph and Mary's Boy/Santa Claus (I Still Believe in You)	1985	—	2.00	4.00
❑ PB-14281	She and I/The Fans	1986	—	2.00	4.00
❑ PB-14281 [PS]	She and I/The Fans	1986	—	2.50	5.00
❑ GB-14347	There's No Way/(There's a) Fire in the Night	1986	—	—	3.00
—Gold Standard Series reissue					
❑ GB-14350	Forty Hour Week (For a Livin')/Can't Keep a Good Man Down	1986	—	—	3.00
—Gold Standard Series reissue					
❑ 60211	We Made Love/Small Stuff	2000	—	—	3.00
❑ 62059	Then Again/Hats Off	1991	—	—	3.00
❑ 62168	Born Country/Until It Happens to You	1991	—	—	3.00
❑ 62253	Take a Little Trip/Pictures and Memories	1992	—	—	3.00
❑ 62336	I'm In a Hurry (And Don't Know Why)/Sometimes Out of Touch	1992	—	—	3.00
❑ 62428	Once Upon a Lifetime/American Pride	1992	—	—	3.00
❑ 62495	Hometown Honeymoon/Homesick Fever	1993	—	—	3.00
❑ 62623	The Cheap Seats/This Love's on Me	1994	—	—	3.00
❑ 62636	Reckless/Clean Water Blues	1993	—	—	3.00
❑ 62643	Angels Among Us/Santa Claus (I Still Believe in You)	1993	—	2.00	4.00
❑ 62712	T.L.C.A.S.A.P./That Feeling	1993	—	—	3.00
❑ 62894	We Can't Love Like This Anymore/Still Goin' Strong	1994	—	—	3.00
❑ 64273	Give Me One More Shot/Jukebox in My Mind	1995	—	—	3.00
❑ 64346	She Ain't Your Ordinary Girl/Heartbreak Express	1995	—	—	3.00
❑ 64419	In Pictures/Between the Two of Them	1995	—	—	3.00
❑ 64436	Christmas in Dixie/Thistlehair the Christmas Bear	1995	—	—	3.00
—Reissue with edit of A-side					
❑ 64473	It Works/Katy Brought My Guitar Back Today	1996	—	—	3.00
❑ 64543	Say I/My Love Belongs to You	1996	—	—	3.00
❑ 64588	The Maker Said Take Her/Nothing Comes Close	1996	—	—	3.00
❑ 64775	Sad Lookin' Moon/Give Me One More Shot	1997	—	—	3.00
❑ 64849	Dancin', Shaggin' on the Boulevard/Very Special Love	1997	—	—	3.00
❑ 64965	Of Course I'm Alright/(I Wish It Could Always Be) '55	1997	—	—	3.00
❑ 65409	She's Got That Look in Her Eyes/That Feeling	1998	—	—	3.00
❑ 65561	How Do You Fall in Love/Keepin' Up	1998	—	—	3.00
❑ 65759	God Must Have Spent a Little More Time on You/Sad Lookin' Moon	1999	—	2.00	4.00
❑ 65935	Small Stuff/God Must Have Spent a Little More Time on You	1999	—	—	3.00
❑ 69019	When It All Goes South/Feels So Right	2000	—	—	3.00
SUN					
❑ 1173 [DJ]	I Wanna Be with You Tonight (Standard Version/Edited Version)	1982	7.50	15.00	30.00
—Promo only on yellow vinyl; stock copies were not released					
Albums					
ALABAMA					
❑ ALA-78-9-01	The Alabama Band	1978	100.00	200.00	400.00
HEARTLAND					
❑ HL 1186/7 [(2)]	The Very Best of Alabama	1992	3.75	7.50	15.00
LSI					
❑ 0177	Deuces Wild	1977	300.00	600.00	1200.
—As "Wild Country"					
❑ 0275	Wild Country	1975	750.00	1125.	1500.
—As "Wild Country"					
PLANTATION					
❑ 44	Wild Country	1981	15.00	30.00	60.00
RCA					
❑ 5649-1-R	The Touch	1986	2.00	4.00	8.00
❑ 6495-1-R	Just Us	1987	2.00	4.00	8.00
❑ 6825-1-R	Alabama Live	1988	2.00	4.00	8.00
❑ 8587-1-R	Southern Star	1989	2.00	4.00	8.00
❑ 9574-1-RDJ [DJ]	Open-Ended Interview	1988	7.50	15.00	30.00
RCA VICTOR					
❑ AHL1-3644	My Home's in Alabama	1980	3.75	7.50	15.00
❑ AYL1-3644	My Home's in Alabama	1986	2.00	4.00	8.00
—"Best Buy Series" reissue					
❑ AHL1-3930	Feels So Right	1981	2.00	4.00	8.00
❑ AHL1-4229	Mountain Music	1982	2.00	4.00	8.00
❑ AHL1-4663	The Closer You Get	1983	2.00	4.00	8.00
❑ AHL1-4939	Roll On	1984	2.00	4.00	8.00
❑ AHL1-5339	40 Hour Week	1985	2.00	4.00	8.00
❑ ASL1-7014	Christmas	1985	3.00	6.00	12.00
—Original copies have gold embossed letters on cover					
❑ ASL1-7014	Christmas	1986	2.50	5.00	10.00
—Later copies have white non-embossed letters on cover					
❑ AHL1-7170	Greatest Hits	1986	2.00	4.00	8.00

ALAN, BUDDY

Also see BUCK OWENS.

Number	Title (A Side/B Side)	Yr	VG	VG+	NM
45s					
CAPITOL					
❑ 2305	When I Turn Twenty-One/Adios, Farewell, Goodbye, Good Luck, So Long	1968	2.00	4.00	8.00
❑ 2305 [PS]	When I Turn Twenty-One/Adios, Farewell, Goodbye, Good Luck, So Long	1968	3.75	7.50	15.00
❑ 2580	Alabama, Louisiana or Maybe Tennessee/You Can't Make Nothing Out of That But Love	1969	2.00	4.00	8.00
❑ 2653	Lodi/I Wanna Be Wild and Free	1969	2.00	4.00	8.00
❑ 2715	Big Mama's Medicine Show/When a Man Can't Call His Home a Home	1969	2.00	4.00	8.00
❑ 2784	Down in New Orleans/I've Never Had a Dream Come True Before	1970	2.00	4.00	8.00
❑ 2852	Santo Domingo/That's Quite a Ride	1970	2.00	4.00	8.00
❑ 3010	Lookin' Out My Back Door/Corn Liquor	1970	2.00	4.00	8.00
❑ 3110	Fishin' on the Mississippi/If I Could Love You More	1971	2.00	4.00	8.00
❑ 3146	I Will Drink Your Wine/Doin' the Best I Can	1971	2.00	4.00	8.00
❑ 3266	White Line Fever/Another By Your Side	1972	2.00	4.00	8.00
❑ 3346	I'm in Love/The Happiness Song	1972	2.00	4.00	8.00
❑ 3427	Things/One Good Woman	1972	—	3.50	7.00
❑ 3485	Move It On Over/Magic Man	1972	—	3.50	7.00
❑ 3555	Why, Because I Love You/She's Been On My Mind for So Long	1973	—	3.50	7.00
❑ 3598	Caribbean/Please, Friend, Take Me Home	1973	—	3.50	7.00
❑ 3680	Summer Afternoons/Maybe Things Would Be Better	1973	—	3.50	7.00

Until Alabama came along in the early 1980s, it was thought that a self-contained group – one that not only sang, but played its own instruments – could not succeed in Nashville. (Top left) "My Home's in Alabama," originally released on the small MDJ label, managed to make the top 20 of the charts even without the distribution power of a major label. After this song's success, Alabama was signed to RCA. (Top right) "Why Lady Why," which had been one of the B-sides on some copies of the MDJ version of "My Home's in Alabama," became Alabama's second No. 1 single after RCA re-released it as an A-side. (Bottom left) "She and I" was the "new" track on Alabama's first greatest-hits collection. And like every non-holiday single on RCA before it, it hit the top. (Bottom right) In 1999, Alabama raised some eyebrows by not only covering the pop hit "God Must Have Spent a Little More Time on You," but also inviting the song's pop artists, 'N Sync, to join in on background vocals.

Number	Title (A Side/B Side)	Yr	VG	VG+	NM
❑ 3749	All Around Cowboy of 1964/You Are My Everything	1973	—	3.50	7.00
❑ 3861	I Never Had It So Good/She Always Wears a Yellow Rose	1974	—	3.00	6.00
❑ 3944	Call My Number, Call My Name/If I Hurt Her I Know She'll Cry	1974	—	3.00	6.00
❑ 4019	Chains/A Whole Lot of Somethin'	1974	—	3.00	6.00
❑ 4075	Another Saturday Night/Nickels, Dimes and Quarters	1975	—	3.00	6.00
❑ 4144	Something She's Got/1,000 Miles	1975	—	3.00	6.00
SUN DEVIL					
❑ 1001	Ride 'Em Cowboy/(B-side unknown)	1978	2.50	5.00	10.00
Albums					
CAPITOL					
❑ ST-592	Whole Lot of Somethin'	1970	5.00	10.00	20.00
❑ ST-11019	Best of Buddy Alan	1972	3.75	7.50	15.00

ALAN, BUDDY, AND DON RICH

Number	Title (A Side/B Side)	Yr	VG	VG+	NM
45s					
CAPITOL					
❑ 2928	Cowboy Convention/We're All Gonna Get Together	1970	2.00	4.00	8.00
❑ 3040	I'm On the Road to Memphis/I'll Be Swingin' You	1971	2.00	4.00	8.00
Albums					
CAPITOL					
❑ ST-769	We're Real Good Friends	1971	5.00	10.00	20.00

ALBERT, UREL

Number	Title (A Side/B Side)	Yr	VG	VG+	NM
45s					
CINNAMON					
❑ 786	One Man's Woman at a Time/Just Wait	1974	2.50	5.00	10.00
TOAST					
❑ 311	Country and Pop Music/Just Wait	1973	3.75	7.50	15.00

ALEXANDER, DANIELE

Number	Title (A Side/B Side)	Yr	VG	VG+	NM
45s					
MERCURY					
❑ 874330-7	She's There/Goodbye Me	1989	—	—	3.00
❑ 876228-7	Where Did the Moon Go Wrong/First Move	1989	—	—	3.00
❑ 878256-7	It Wasn't You, It Wasn't Me/Fairytale Fool	1990	—	—	3.00
—A-side with Butch Baker					
❑ 878970-7	I Know What I Do Know/It Wasn't You, It Wasn't Me	1991	—	—	3.00
Albums					
MERCURY					
❑ 838352-1	First Move	1989	3.00	6.00	12.00

ALEXANDER, WYVON

Number	Title (A Side/B Side)	Yr	VG	VG+	NM
45s					
GERVASI					
❑ 633	Frustration/Old Familiar Feeling	1981	—	2.50	5.00
❑ 644	Old Familiar Feeling/(B-side unknown)	1981	—	2.50	5.00
❑ 659	Women/Don't Lead Me On	1981	—	2.50	5.00
❑ 660	Alice in Dallas (Sweet Texas)/Hungry Man's Dream	1982	—	2.50	5.00
❑ 661	Midnight Cabaret/Same Old Song	1982	—	2.50	5.00
❑ 662	Good Lovin' Bad/(B-side unknown)	1983	—	2.50	5.00
❑ 663	The Look of a Lovin' Lady/High Time	1983	—	2.50	5.00

ALIBI

Number	Title (A Side/B Side)	Yr	VG	VG+	NM
45s					
COMSTOCK					
❑ 1833	It Only Hurts When I Cry/(B-side unknown)	1987	—	3.00	6.00
❑ 1856	Roller Coaster/(B-side unknown)	1987	—	3.00	6.00
❑ 1884	Do You Have Any Doubts/(B-side unknown)	1988	—	3.00	6.00

ALLAN, GARY

Number	Title (A Side/B Side)	Yr	VG	VG+	NM
45s					
DECCA					
❑ 55227	Her Man/Wake Up Screaming	1996	—	2.00	4.00
❑ 55289	Forever and a Day/Living in a House Full of Love	1996	—	—	3.00
❑ 72003	From Where I'm Sittin'/Wine Me Up	1997	—	—	3.00
❑ 72018	Living in a House Full of Love/Of All the Hearts	1997	—	—	3.00
❑ 72039	It Would Be You/Send Back My Heart	1998	—	—	3.00
❑ 72059	No Man in His Wrong Heart/Baby I Will	1998	—	—	3.00
❑ 72079	I'll Take Today/I've Got a Quarter in My Pocket	1998	—	—	3.00
MCA NASHVILLE					
❑ 72109	Smoke Rings in the Dark/Right Where I Need to Be	1999	—	—	3.00
❑ 088 172140 7	Lovin' You Against My Will/I'm the One	2000	—	—	3.00

ALLANSON, SUSIE

Number	Title (A Side/B Side)	Yr	VG	VG+	NM
45s					
ABC					
❑ 12219	Love Is a Satisfied Woman/Me and Charlie Brown	1976	—	3.00	6.00
ELEKTRA					
❑ 46009	Words/We Can Make It Up to Each Other	1979	—	2.50	5.00
❑ 46036	Two Steps Forward and Three Steps Back/I Will Never Leave You	1979	—	2.50	5.00
❑ 46503	Without You/Heart to Heart	1979	—	2.50	5.00
❑ 46565	I Must Be Crazy/I Can't See Me Without You	1979	—	2.50	5.00
ENIGMA					
❑ 75001	Where's the Fire/I Can't Say It on the Radio	1986	—	2.50	5.00
❑ 75005	She Don't Love You/(B-side unknown)	1987	—	2.50	5.00
LIBERTY					
❑ 1383	Dance the Two Step/You Never Told Me About Goodbye	1980	—	2.00	4.00
❑ 1408	Run to Her/Send Me Somebody to Love	1981	—	2.00	4.00
❑ 1422	Hearts (Our Hearts)/Strength of a Woman	1981	—	2.00	4.00
❑ 1425	Lay a Little Lovin' on Me/Love Is Knockin' at My Door	1982	—	2.00	4.00
❑ B-1460	Wasn't That Love/Falling in Love for the Last Time	1982	—	2.00	4.00
OAK					
❑ 1001	Baby, Don't Keep Me Hangin' On/It's Gone	1977	2.00	4.00	8.00
TNP					
❑ 75001	Where's the Fire/(B-side unknown)	1986	—	3.00	6.00
❑ 75005	She Don't Love You/(B-side unknown)	1987	—	3.00	6.00
UNITED ARTISTS					
❑ 1365	While I Was Makin' Love to You/Michael	1980	—	2.00	4.00
WARNER BROS.					
❑ 8429	Baby, Don't Keep Me Hangin' On/It's Gone	1977	—	2.50	5.00
❑ 8473	Baby, Last Night Made My Day/Will There Really Be a Morning	1977	—	2.50	5.00
❑ 8534	Maybe Baby/Hide Me in Your Love	1978	—	2.50	5.00
❑ 8597	We Belong Together/I Don't Want to Cry Anymore	1978	—	2.50	5.00
❑ 8686	Back to the Love/I Want This Feeling to Last	1978	—	2.50	5.00
Albums					
ELEKTRA					
❑ 6E-177	Heart to Heart	1979	2.50	5.00	10.00
WARNER BROS.					
❑ BSK 3217	We Belong Together	1978	2.50	5.00	10.00

ALLEN, CLAY

Number	Title (A Side/B Side)	Yr	VG	VG+	NM
45s					
DECCA					
❑ 9-46324	Can't Keep Smiling/Evalina	1951	6.25	12.50	25.00
❑ 9-46360	A Little Bit of Heaven/If I Live a Thousand Years	1951	6.25	12.50	25.00
LONGHORN					
❑ 506	You've Got the Cleanest Mind/I Can't Stop the Blues from Moving In	196?	3.00	6.00	12.00
❑ 510	Long Long Trailer/What Are We Gonna Name Our Baby	196?	3.00	6.00	12.00
❑ 512	Crazy Crazy World/Just a Stone's Throw Away	196?	3.00	6.00	12.00
❑ 515	Takkiti Takki Tu/Doubtfulness	196?	3.00	6.00	12.00
❑ 516	Broken Home/This Time It's Really Goodbye	196?	3.00	6.00	12.00
❑ 522	The Password to Your Heart/It Doesn't Surprise Me	196?	3.00	6.00	12.00
❑ 528	B.M. Loves B.J./Old Love and New Tears	196?	3.00	6.00	12.00
❑ 533	Classified/I'm Gonna Lock the Door	196?	3.00	6.00	12.00
❑ 541	Lies/How Long Will You Win	196?	2.50	5.00	10.00
❑ 547	I'm Changing the Numbers on My Telephone/One Too Many	196?	2.50	5.00	10.00
❑ 557	The Only Thing I Can Count On (Is My Fingers)/2:45	196?	2.50	5.00	10.00
❑ 587	Promise Her Anything (But Give Her Money)/The Way You Are	196?	2.50	5.00	10.00

ALLEN, DEBORAH

Also see JIM REEVES.

Number	Title (A Side/B Side)	Yr	VG	VG+	NM
45s					
CAPITOL					
❑ 4903	If I Had Known Then/You Never Cross My Mind	1980	—	2.00	4.00
❑ 4945	Nobody's Fool/Let Me Down	1980	—	2.00	4.00
❑ 5014	You (Make Me Wonder Why)/Next to You	1981	—	2.00	4.00
❑ 5080	You Look Like the One I Love/It's Cold Outside	1981	—	2.00	4.00
❑ B-5110	After Tonight/Don't Worry 'Bout Me Baby	1982	—	2.00	4.00
❑ B-5186	Don't Stop Lovin' Me/Let's Stop Talkin' About It	1982	—	2.00	4.00
GIANT					
❑ 18199	Break These Chains/Talkin' to My Heart	1994	—	2.00	4.00
❑ 18426	All the Loving and the Hurting Too/Long Time Lovin' You	1993	—	2.00	4.00
❑ 18530	If You're Not Gonna Love Me/Long Time Lovin' You	1993	—	2.00	4.00
❑ 18566	Rock Me (In the Cradle of Love)/Natural Tears	1992	—	2.50	5.00
RCA					
❑ 5136-7-R	Telepathy/You Better Come Back to Me	1987	—	2.00	4.00
❑ 5214-7-R	You're the Kind of Trouble/Don't You Think I Don't Love You	1987	—	2.00	4.00
❑ PB-13600	Baby I Lied/Time Is Taking You Away from Me	1983	—	2.00	4.00
❑ PB-13600 [PS]	Baby I Lied/Time Is Taking You Away from Me	1983	—	2.50	5.00
❑ PB-13694	I've Been Wrong Before/Fool's Paradise	1983	—	2.00	4.00
❑ PB-13776	I Hurt for You/Cheat the Night	1984	—	2.00	4.00
❑ JK-13904 [DJ]	Rockin' Little Christmas (same on both sides)	1984	—	2.50	5.00
❑ PB-13904	Rockin' Little Christmas/It's a Good Thing	1984	—	2.00	4.00
❑ JK-13921 [DJ]	Heartache and a Half (same on both sides)	1984	3.00	6.00	12.00
—Promo only on red vinyl					
❑ PB-13921	Heartache and a Half/It Makes Me Cry	1984	—	2.00	4.00
❑ PB-13921 [PS]	Heartache and a Half/It Makes Me Cry	1984	—	2.50	5.00
❑ GB-14356	Baby I Lied/Time Is Taking You Away from Me	1983	—	—	3.00
—"Gold Standard Series" reissue					
WARNER BROS.					
❑ 8271	Take Me Back/Do You Copy	1976	—	3.00	6.00
Albums					
CAPITOL					
❑ ST-12104	Trouble in Paradise	1980	3.00	6.00	12.00

RCA VICTOR

Number	Title (A Side/B Side)	Yr	VG	VG+	NM
❑ AHL1-5318	Let Me Be the First	1985	2.00	4.00	8.00
❑ AHL1-5806	You Can't Say No	1986	2.00	4.00	8.00
❑ MHL1-8514 [EP]	Cheat the Night	1983	—	3.00	6.00

ALLEN, JOE

45s

WARNER BROS.

Number	Title (A Side/B Side)	Yr	VG	VG+	NM
❑ 7791	Big Band Days/The Girl I Used to Run Around On	1974	—	2.50	5.00
❑ 8052	Should I Come Home (Or Should I Go Crazy)/ What Kind of a Fool	1975	—	2.50	5.00
❑ 8098	Carolyn at the Broken Wheel Inn/Again	1975	—	2.50	5.00
❑ 8149	Bedroom Ballad/Busted	1975	—	2.50	5.00

ALLEN, JUDY

45s

POLYDOR

Number	Title (A Side/B Side)	Yr	VG	VG+	NM
❑ 14440	Sweet Little Devil/He Was Fine	1977	—	2.50	5.00
❑ 14480	Fear of a Feeling/Going Down for the Third Time	1978	—	2.50	5.00

STOP

Number	Title (A Side/B Side)	Yr	VG	VG+	NM
❑ 1583	Losing You Is What I Get/Yankee Man	197?	—	3.00	6.00

ALLEN, MELODY

45s

MERCURY

Number	Title (A Side/B Side)	Yr	VG	VG+	NM
❑ 73424	Goodbye for the Last Time/Virginia, You've Taken My Man	1973	—	3.00	6.00
❑ 73456	All the Love You Can Stand/Well, For Goodness Sake	1974	—	3.00	6.00
❑ 73638	Once Again I Go to Sleep with Lovin' on My Mind/ You've Got a Way with Love	1975	—	2.50	5.00
❑ 73674	May You Rest in Peace/When Someone Wants to Leave	1975	—	2.50	5.00
❑ 73701	Virginia, You've Taken My Man/Two Little Faces	1975	—	2.50	5.00
❑ 73773	I'm Sorry/Our Piggy Bank	1976	—	2.50	5.00

ALLEN, REX

45s

DECCA

Number	Title (A Side/B Side)	Yr	VG	VG+	NM
❑ 9-27952	The Waltz of the Roses/As Long As the River Flows On	1952	5.00	10.00	20.00
❑ 9-28146	Till the Well Goes Dry/Rack Up the Balls	1952	5.00	10.00	20.00
❑ 9-28341	Jambalaya (On the Bayou)/The Two-Faced Clock	1952	5.00	10.00	20.00
❑ 9-28446	No One Will Ever Know/Hootin' and Howlin'	1952	5.00	10.00	20.00
❑ 9-28556	Knocking on the Door/Why My Darlin' Why	1953	3.75	7.50	15.00
❑ 9-28758	Crying in the Chapel/I Thank the Lord	1953	5.00	10.00	20.00
❑ 9-28897	To Be Alone/If God Can Forgive You, So Can I	1953	5.00	10.00	20.00
❑ 9-28933	Where Did My Snowman Go?/Why Daddy?	1953	5.00	10.00	20.00
❑ 9-28998	He Played the Steel Guitar/Somewhere	1954	5.00	10.00	20.00
❑ 9-29111	Bringing Home the Bacon/I Could Cry My Heart Out	1954	3.75	7.50	15.00
❑ 9-29168	In the Chapel in the Moonlight/Chapel of Memories	1954	3.75	7.50	15.00
❑ 9-29297	You Took My Name/I'm Learning to Live	1954	5.00	10.00	20.00
❑ 9-29397	Tomorrow's Another Day to Cry/L-O-N-E-S-O-M-E Letter Blues	1955	3.75	7.50	15.00
❑ 9-29586	That's What Makes the Juke Box Play/Pedro Gonzales, Tennessee Lopez	1955	5.00	10.00	20.00
❑ 9-29610	Daddy, You Know What/The Albino Stallion	1955	3.75	7.50	15.00
❑ 9-29729	The Last Round-Up/I'm a Young Cowboy	1955	3.75	7.50	15.00
❑ 9-29851	The Last Frontier/Sky Boss	1956	3.00	6.00	12.00
❑ 9-30066	Trail of the Lonesome Pine/Nothin; to Do	1956	3.00	6.00	12.00
❑ 9-30204	Drango/Little White Horse	1957	3.00	6.00	12.00
❑ 9-30205	Westward Ho the Wagons/Wringle Wrangle	1957	3.00	6.00	12.00
❑ 9-30364	Money, Marbles and Chalk/Flowers of San Antone	1957	3.00	6.00	12.00
❑ 9-30511	Blue Dream/Blue Light Waltz	1957	3.00	6.00	12.00
❑ 9-30651	Knock, Knock, Rattle/Invitation to the Blues	1958	6.25	12.50	25.00
❑ 9-30833	I Know the Reason Why/The Mystery of His Way	1959	3.00	6.00	12.00
❑ 9-31039	Take Me Lord/Sheltered in the Arms of the Old Rugged Cross	1959	3.00	6.00	12.00
❑ 32072	A Waltz That Never Ends/A Woman (Can Change a Man)	1967	2.00	4.00	8.00
❑ 32322	Tiny Bubbles/Jose Villa Lobo Alfredo Thomaso Vincente Lopez	1968	—	3.00	6.00
❑ 32401	Bummin' Around/When I Leave This World Behind	1968	—	3.00	6.00
❑ 32467	It Happens Over and Over Again/Sai Finis	1969	—	3.00	6.00
❑ 32612	Ain't That Beautiful Singing/A Voice	1970	—	3.00	6.00
❑ 9-46390	I've Got So Many Million Years (I Can't Count 'Em)/Is He Satisfied	1952	5.00	10.00	20.00
❑ 9-88161	Where Did My Snowman Go?/Why Daddy?	1953	3.75	7.50	15.00
—Yellow label "Children's Series" release					
❑ 9-88161 [PS]	Where Did My Snowman Go?/Why Daddy?	1953	7.50	15.00	30.00

MCA

Number	Title (A Side/B Side)	Yr	VG	VG+	NM
❑ 41071	So Long Duke/At the Rainbow's End	1979	—	3.00	6.00

MERCURY

Number	Title (A Side/B Side)	Yr	VG	VG+	NM
❑ 5573-X45	The Roving Kind/John B.	1950	6.25	12.50	25.00
❑ 5597-X45	Sparrow in the Tree Top/Always You	1951	6.25	12.50	25.00
❑ 5619-X45	I'm a Sentimental Fool/Ten More Miles to Go	1951	6.25	12.50	25.00
❑ 5647-X45	Mister and Mississippi/Lonely Little Robin	1951	6.25	12.50	25.00
❑ 5713-X45	Angel to Joe/Cowpoke	1951	6.25	12.50	25.00
❑ 6297-X45	I Ain't Gonna Cry No More/You Drifted	1951	6.25	12.50	25.00
❑ 6349-X45	Naggin'/Albuquerque Polka	1951	6.25	12.50	25.00
❑ 70373	True Blue Lou-Lou-Lou/Save a Little Corner in Your Heart for Me	1954	5.00	10.00	20.00
❑ 71844	Marines, Let's Go/Heartaches of a Fool	1961	2.50	5.00	10.00
❑ 71997	Don't Go Near the Indians/Touched So Deeply	1962	2.50	5.00	10.00
❑ 72095	Roll Up Your Sleeve/Oohin' and Aahin'	1963	2.00	4.00	8.00
❑ 72137	Silver Spoon Lonely Me/To-Ra	1963	2.00	4.00	8.00
❑ 72205	Tear After Tear/I'm Just Killing Time	1964	2.00	4.00	8.00
❑ 72205 [PS]	Tear After Tear/I'm Just Killing Time	1964	3.75	7.50	15.00

MUSICOR

Number	Title (A Side/B Side)	Yr	VG	VG+	NM
❑ 1132	Take It Back and Change It for a Boy/Rodeo Twist	1965	2.00	4.00	8.00

Selected 78s

MERCURY

Number	Title (A Side/B Side)	Yr	VG	VG+	NM
❑ 6171	Song of the Hills/Tennessee Tears	1949	3.75	7.50	15.00
❑ 6192	Afraid/Cottage in the Clouds	1949	3.75	7.50	15.00
❑ 6203	Arizona Waltz/Tell Me Little Darlin'	1949	3.75	7.50	15.00
❑ 6214	I'm So Alone with the Crowd/Over Three Hills	1949	3.75	7.50	15.00

Albums

BUENA VISTA

Number	Title (A Side/B Side)	Yr	VG	VG+	NM
❑ BV-3307 [M]	Rex Allen Sings 16 Golden Hits	1961	10.00	20.00	40.00

DECCA

Number	Title (A Side/B Side)	Yr	VG	VG+	NM
❑ DL 8402 [M]	Under Western Skies	1956	12.50	25.00	50.00
❑ DL 8776 [M]	Mister Cowboy	1959	10.00	20.00	40.00
❑ DL 75011 [S]	The Smooth Country Sound of Rex Allen	1968	5.00	10.00	20.00
❑ DL 75205	The Touch of God's Hand	1970	5.00	10.00	20.00
❑ DL 78776 [S]	Mister Cowboy	1959	15.00	30.00	60.00

HACIENDA

Number	Title (A Side/B Side)	Yr	VG	VG+	NM
❑ WWLP-101 [M]	Rex Allen Sings	1960	50.00	100.00	200.00

MERCURY

Number	Title (A Side/B Side)	Yr	VG	VG+	NM
❑ MG-20719 [M]	Faith of a Man	1962	6.25	12.50	25.00
❑ MG-20752 [M]	Rex Allen Sings and Tells Tales	1963	6.25	12.50	25.00
❑ SR-60719 [S]	Faith of a Man	1962	7.50	15.00	30.00
❑ SR-60752 [S]	Rex Allen Sings and Tells Tales	1963	7.50	15.00	30.00

ALLEN, REX, AND TEX WILLIAMS

Also see each artist's individual listings.

45s

DECCA

Number	Title (A Side/B Side)	Yr	VG	VG+	NM
❑ 9-29254	This Ole House/Two Texas Boys	1954	5.00	10.00	20.00

ALLEN, REX, JR.

45s

IMPERIAL

Number	Title (A Side/B Side)	Yr	VG	VG+	NM
❑ 66288	Before I Change My Mind (I'm Going Home)/The World I Live In	1968	3.00	6.00	12.00

JMI

Number	Title (A Side/B Side)	Yr	VG	VG+	NM
❑ 16	Reflex Reaction/Today I Started Loving You Again	1973	—	3.50	7.00
❑ 19	Everglades/(B-side unknown)	1973	—	3.50	7.00

MOON SHINE

Number	Title (A Side/B Side)	Yr	VG	VG+	NM
❑ 3017	The Air That I Breathe/You Should Care	1983	—	2.50	5.00
❑ 3022	Sweet Rosanna/You Sure Could Have Fooled Me	1984	—	2.50	5.00
❑ 3030	Dream On Texas Ladies/(B-side unknown)	1984	—	2.50	5.00
❑ 3034	Running Down Memory Lane/Shameless Love	1984	—	2.50	5.00
❑ 3036	When You Held Me in Your Arms/(B-side unknown)	1985	—	2.50	5.00

PLANTATION

Number	Title (A Side/B Side)	Yr	VG	VG+	NM
❑ 77	Uncle Boogar Red and Byrdie Nelle/Other Husbands and Wives	1971	—	3.50	7.00
❑ 89	I Honky Tonked All the Way Back Home/Corner of My Life	1972	—	3.50	7.00

SSS INTERNATIONAL

Number	Title (A Side/B Side)	Yr	VG	VG+	NM
❑ 813	Wake Up Morning/You Weren't There	1970	2.00	4.00	8.00
❑ 837	Country Comfort/The Father Needs a Man	1971	2.00	4.00	8.00

TNP

Number	Title (A Side/B Side)	Yr	VG	VG+	NM
❑ 75010	We're Staying Together/Diamond in the Rough	1987	—	3.00	6.00

WARNER BROS.

Number	Title (A Side/B Side)	Yr	VG	VG+	NM
❑ 7753	The Great Mail Robbery/Start Again	1973	—	3.00	6.00
❑ 7788	Goodbye/The Same Old Way	1974	—	3.00	6.00
❑ 8000	Another Goodbye Song/Yes We Have Love	1974	—	3.00	6.00
❑ 8046	Never Coming Back Again/I Can See Clearly Now	1974	—	3.00	6.00
❑ 8095	Lying in My Arms/She Just Said Goodbye	1975	—	2.50	5.00
❑ 8133	Then I'll Be Over You/Paying the Price for Staying Free	1975	—	3.00	6.00
❑ 8171	Play Me No Sad Songs/She Just Said Goodbye	1976	—	2.50	5.00
❑ 8204	Can You Hear Those Pioneers/Streets of Laredo	1976	—	2.50	5.00
❑ 8236	Teardrops in My Heart/Home Made Love	1976	—	2.50	5.00
❑ 8297	Two Less Lonely People/I Gotta Remember to Forget You	1976	—	2.50	5.00
❑ 8354	I'm Getting Good at Missing You (Solitaire)/Don't Say Goodbye	1977	—	2.50	5.00
❑ 8418	Don't Say Goodbye/There's No Use Hanging On	1977	—	2.50	5.00
❑ 8482	Lonely Street/Don't It Make You Want to Go Home	1977	—	2.50	5.00
❑ 8541	No, No, No (I'd Rather Be Free)/I Got a Name	1978	—	2.50	5.00
❑ 8608	With Love/You Turned It On Again Last Night	1978	—	2.50	5.00
❑ 8697	It's Time We Talk Things Over/Watch Me Cry	1978	—	2.50	5.00
❑ 8786	Me and My Broken Heart/Lovin' You Is Everything to Me	1979	—	2.50	5.00
❑ 29890	Ride Cowboy Ride/Three Friends Have I	1982	—	2.00	4.00
❑ 29968	Cowboy in a Three Piece Business Suit/Round Up Time	1982	—	2.00	4.00
❑ 49020	If I Fell in Love with You/Pick Up the Pieces	1979	—	2.00	4.00
❑ 49128	It's Over/Why Did You Stop Lovin' Me	1980	—	2.00	4.00
❑ 49168	Yippi Cry Yi/She Has My Heart	1980	—	2.00	4.00

Number	Title (A Side/B Side)	Yr	VG	VG+	NM
❑ 49562	Drink It Down, Lady/What Was Your Name?	1980	—	2.00	4.00
❑ 49682	Just a Country Boy/Cat's in the Cradle	1981	—	2.00	4.00
❑ 49844	Arizona/The One I Sing My Love Songs To	1981	—	2.00	4.00
❑ 50035	Last of the Silver Screen Cowboys/Round Up Time	1982	—	2.00	4.00
—A-side with Roy Rogers and Rex Allen Sr.					
❑ 50035 [PS]	Last of the Silver Screen Cowboys/Round Up Time	1982	2.50	5.00	10.00
—A-side with Roy Rogers and Rex Allen Sr.					

Albums

WARNER BROS.

Number	Title (A Side/B Side)	Yr	VG	VG+	NM
❑ BS 2821	Another Goodbye Song	1974	2.50	5.00	10.00
❑ BS 2958	Ridin' High	1976	2.50	5.00	10.00
❑ BS 3054	Rex	1977	2.50	5.00	10.00
❑ BSK 3122	The Best of Rex	1977	2.50	5.00	10.00
❑ BSK 3190	Brand New	1978	2.50	5.00	10.00
❑ BSK 3300	Me and My Broken Heart	1979	2.50	5.00	10.00
❑ BSK 3403	Oklahoma Rose	1980	2.50	5.00	10.00

ALLEN, REX, JR., AND MARGO SMITH

45s

WARNER BROS.

Number	Title (A Side/B Side)	Yr	VG	VG+	NM
❑ 49626	Cup of Tea/Goodbye	1980	—	2.00	4.00
❑ 49738	While the Feeling's Good/Watered Down Love	1981	—	2.00	4.00

ALLEN, ROSALIE

Also see CHET ATKINS; ELTON BRITT.

45s

RCA VICTOR

Number	Title (A Side/B Side)	Yr	VG	VG+	NM
❑ 47-4425	Shoot Him High Paw/I've Paid	1951	6.25	12.50	25.00
❑ 47-4683	Tomboy/Hills of Pride	1952	6.25	12.50	25.00
❑ 47-4853	It Wasn't God Who Made Honky Tonk Angels/It'd Surprise You	1952	6.25	12.50	25.00
❑ 47-4987	I Laughed at Love/I Gotta Have You	1952	6.25	12.50	25.00
❑ 47-5121	Let Me Share Your Name/Hard Hearted Woman	1953	5.00	10.00	20.00
❑ 47-5308	Bring Your Sweet Self Back to Me/Just Wait Till I Get You Alone	1953	5.00	10.00	20.00
❑ 47-5379	Castaway/My Old Familiar Heartache	1953	5.00	10.00	20.00
❑ 48-0068	The Yodeling Bird/Square Dance Polka	1949	10.00	20.00	40.00
—Original on green vinyl					
❑ 48-0121	Yodelin' Boogie/Mama, What'll I Do	1950	10.00	20.00	40.00
—Original on green vinyl					
❑ 48-0305	My Dolly Has a Broken Heart/Chocolate Ice Cream Cone	1950	7.50	15.00	30.00
—Original on green vinyl					
❑ 48-0343	Green As Grass/I Wanna Sit	1950	7.50	15.00	30.00
—Original on green vinyl					
❑ 48-0403	I've Got the Craziest Feeling/One and One Is Two	1951	6.25	12.50	25.00
❑ 48-0434	Station L-O-V-E Signing Off/Cranberry Kisses	1951	6.25	12.50	25.00
❑ 48-0470	Just a Sailor's Sweetheart/Somebody	1951	6.25	12.50	25.00

STOP

Number	Title (A Side/B Side)	Yr	VG	VG+	NM
❑ 256	Fire on the Mountain/There Goes My World Again	1969	2.00	4.00	8.00

Selected 78s

RCA VICTOR

Number	Title (A Side/B Side)	Yr	VG	VG+	NM
❑ 20-1924	Guitar Polka (Old Monterey)/I Want to Be a Cowboy's Sweetheart	1946	5.00	10.00	20.00

Albums

GRAND AWARD GA-33-262

Number	Title (A Side/B Side)	Yr	VG	VG+	NM
❑ GA-33-330 [M]	Songs of the Golden West	1957	10.00	20.00	40.00

RCA VICTOR

Number	Title (A Side/B Side)	Yr	VG	VG+	NM
❑ LPM-2313 [M]	Rosalie Allen	1961	5.00	10.00	20.00
❑ LSP-2313 [S]	Rosalie Allen	1961	6.25	12.50	25.00

WALDORF

Number	Title (A Side/B Side)	Yr	VG	VG+	NM
❑ 150 [10]	Rosalie Allen Sings Country and Western	1955	20.00	40.00	80.00

ALLEY, JIM

45s

AVCO

Number	Title (A Side/B Side)	Yr	VG	VG+	NM
❑ 606	Her Memory's Gonna Kill Me/If I Didn't Have a Dime	1975	2.00	4.00	8.00
❑ 615	Her Memory Is Here Tonight/(B-side unknown)	1975	2.00	4.00	8.00

DOT

Number	Title (A Side/B Side)	Yr	VG	VG+	NM
❑ 17051	Only Daddy That'll Walk the Line/When You Were Here	1967	3.75	7.50	15.00

ALLSUP, TOMMY

Albums

GRT

Number	Title (A Side/B Side)	Yr	VG	VG+	NM
❑ 20004	Tommy Allsup and the Tennessee Saxes Play the Hits of Tammy Wynette	1970	5.00	10.00	20.00

METROMEDIA

Number	Title (A Side/B Side)	Yr	VG	VG+	NM
❑ MM 1004	Tommy Allsup and the Nashville Survey Play the Hits of Charley Pride	1969	6.25	12.50	25.00

REPRISE

Number	Title (A Side/B Side)	Yr	VG	VG+	NM
❑ R 6182 [M]	Tommy Allsup Plays the Buddy Holly Songbook	1965	10.00	20.00	40.00
❑ RS 6182 [S]	Tommy Allsup Plays the Buddy Holly Songbook	1965	12.50	25.00	50.00

ALMOST BROTHERS, THE

45s

MTM

Number	Title (A Side/B Side)	Yr	VG	VG+	NM
❑ B-72053	Don't Tell Me Love Is Kind/Nighttime Fantasy	1985	—	2.00	4.00
❑ B-72062	Birds of a Feather/I Wanna Kiss the Bride	1986	—	2.00	4.00
❑ B-72072	What's Your Name/Adventures in Love	1986	—	2.00	4.00
❑ B-72079	I Don't Love Her Anymore/Nighttime Fantasy	1986	—	2.00	4.00

ALVIN, DAVE

45s

EPIC

Number	Title (A Side/B Side)	Yr	VG	VG+	NM
❑ 34-07394	Every Night About This Time/Brother on the Line	1987	—	2.00	4.00

Albums

EPIC

Number	Title (A Side/B Side)	Yr	VG	VG+	NM
❑ FE 40921	Romeo's Escape	1987	2.50	5.00	10.00

ALVIN AND THE CHIPMUNKS

See THE CHIPMUNKS.

AMARILLO

See BARRY GRANT.

AMAZING RHYTHM ACES

Also see RUSSELL SMITH.

45s

ABC

Number	Title (A Side/B Side)	Yr	VG	VG+	NM
❑ 12078	Third Rate Romance/Mystery Train	1975	—	2.50	5.00
❑ 12142	Amazing Grace (Used to Be Her Favorite Song)/Beautiful Lie	1975	—	2.00	4.00
❑ 12202	Same Ol' Me/The End Is Not in Sight	1976	—	2.00	4.00
❑ 12242	Dancin' the Night Away/If I Just Knew What to Say	1976	—	2.00	4.00
❑ 12272	Two Can Do It Too/Living in a World Unknown	1977	—	2.00	4.00
❑ 12287	Just Between You and Me and the Wall/Never Been to the Islands	1977	—	2.00	4.00
❑ 12359	Burning the Ballroom Down/All That I Had Left (With You)	1978	—	2.00	4.00
❑ 12369	Ashes of Love/All That I Had Left (With You)	1978	—	2.00	4.00
❑ 12454	Lipstick Traces (On a Cigarette)/Whispering in the Night	1979	—	2.00	4.00

COLUMBIA

Number	Title (A Side/B Side)	Yr	VG	VG+	NM
❑ 10983	Love and Happiness/Homestead in My Heart	1979	—	2.00	4.00

WARNER BROS.

Number	Title (A Side/B Side)	Yr	VG	VG+	NM
❑ 49543	Living on Borrowed Time/What Kind of Love Is This	1980	—	2.00	4.00
❑ 49600	I Musta Died and Gone to Texas/Give Me Flowers While I'm Living	1980	—	2.00	4.00

Albums

ABC

Number	Title (A Side/B Side)	Yr	VG	VG+	NM
❑ D-913	Stacked Deck	1975	5.00	10.00	20.00
❑ D-940	Too Stuffed to Jump	1976	3.75	7.50	15.00
❑ AB-1005	Toucan Do It Too	1977	3.75	7.50	15.00
❑ AA-1063	Burning the Ballroom Down	1978	3.75	7.50	15.00
❑ AA-1123	The Amazing Rhythm Aces	1979	5.00	10.00	20.00

COLUMBIA

Number	Title (A Side/B Side)	Yr	VG	VG+	NM
❑ JC 36083	The Amazing Rhythm Aces	1979	3.00	6.00	12.00
—Reissue of ABC 1123					

WARNER BROS.

Number	Title (A Side/B Side)	Yr	VG	VG+	NM
❑ BSK 3476	How the Hell Do You Spell Rythum?	1980	3.00	6.00	12.00

AMES, DE DE

45s

ADVANTAGE

Number	Title (A Side/B Side)	Yr	VG	VG+	NM
❑ 175	Dancin' in the Moonlight/(B-side unknown)	1987	—	3.00	6.00
—As "Durelle Ames"					
❑ 185	Break Down the Walls/(B-side unknown)	1987	—	3.00	6.00

AMES, DURELLE

See DE DE AMES.

AMY

45s

SCORPION

Number	Title (A Side/B Side)	Yr	VG	VG+	NM
❑ 0570	Please Be Gentle/Jump Into My Love	1979	—	3.00	6.00

ANDERSON, BILL

45s

CURB

Number	Title (A Side/B Side)	Yr	VG	VG+	NM
❑ 76855	Deck of Cards/Thank You Darling	1991	—	2.50	5.00

DECCA

Number	Title (A Side/B Side)	Yr	VG	VG+	NM
❑ 9-30773	That's What It's Like to Be Lonesome/Thrill of My Life	1958	3.75	7.50	15.00
❑ 9-30914	Ninety-Nine/Back Where I Started From	1959	3.75	7.50	15.00
❑ 9-30993	Dead or Alive/It's Not the End of Everything	1959	3.75	7.50	15.00
❑ 31092	The Tip of My Fingers/No Man's Land	1960	3.00	6.00	12.00
❑ 31168	Walk Out Backwards/The Best of Strangers	1960	3.00	6.00	12.00
❑ 31262	Po' Folks/Goodbye Cruel World	1961	3.00	6.00	12.00
❑ 31358	Get a Little Dirt on Your Hands/Down Came the Rain	1962	3.00	6.00	12.00
❑ 31404	Mama Sang a Song/On and On and On	1962	2.50	5.00	10.00
❑ 31458	Still/You Make It Easy	1963	2.50	5.00	10.00
❑ 31521	8 x 10/One Mile Over — Two Miles Back	1963	2.50	5.00	10.00
❑ 31521 [PS]	8 x 10/One Mile Over — Two Miles Back	1963	5.00	10.00	20.00
❑ 31577	Five Little Fingers/Easy Come — Easy Go	1964	2.50	5.00	10.00
❑ 31630	Me/Cincinnati, Ohio	1964	2.50	5.00	10.00
❑ 31681	In Case You Ever Change Your Mind/Three A.M.	1964	2.50	5.00	10.00
❑ 31743	Certain/You Can Have Her	1965	2.50	5.00	10.00
❑ 31825	Bright Lights and Country Music/Born	1965	2.50	5.00	10.00
❑ 31890	Bright Guitar/I Love You Drops	1966	2.50	5.00	10.00
❑ 31999	I Get the Fever/The First Mrs. Jones	1966	2.00	4.00	8.00
❑ 32077	Get While the Gettin's Good/Something to Believe In	1967	2.00	4.00	8.00
❑ 32146	No One's Gonna Hurt You Anymore/Papa	1967	2.00	4.00	8.00

Number	Title (A Side/B Side)	Yr	VG	VG+	NM
❑ 32215	Stranger on the Run/Happiness	1967	2.00	4.00	8.00
❑ 32276	Wild Week-End/Fun While It Lasted	1968	2.00	4.00	8.00
❑ 32360	Happy State of Mind/Time's Been Good to Me	1968	2.00	4.00	8.00
❑ 32417	Po' Folks' Christmas/Christmas Time's a-Coming	1968	2.00	4.00	8.00
❑ 32417 [PS]	Po' Folks' Christmas/Christmas Time's a-Coming	1968	3.75	7.50	15.00
❑ 32445	My Life (Throw It Away If I Want To)/To Be Alone	1969	—	3.50	7.00
❑ 32514	But You Know I Love You/A Picture from Life's Other Side	1969	—	3.50	7.00
❑ 32643	Love Is a Sometimes Thing/And I'm Still Missing You	1970	—	3.50	7.00
❑ 32744	Where Have All Our Heroes Gone/Loving a Memory	1970	—	3.50	7.00
❑ 32793	Always Remember/You Can Change the World	1971	—	3.50	7.00
❑ 32850	Quits/I'll Live for You	1971	—	3.50	7.00
❑ 32930	All the Lonely Women in the World/It Was Time for Me to Move Anyway	1972	—	3.50	7.00
❑ 33002	Don't She Look Good/I'm Just Gone	1972	—	3.50	7.00
MCA					
❑ 40004	If You Can Live With It (I Can Live Without It)/Let's Fall Apart	1973	—	2.00	4.00
❑ 40070	The Corner of My Life/Home and Things	1973	—	2.00	4.00
❑ 40164	World of Make Believe/Gonna Shine on It Again	1973	—	2.00	4.00
❑ 40243	Can I Come Home to You/I'm Happily Married	1974	—	2.00	4.00
❑ 40304	Every Time I Turn the Radio On/You Are My Story	1974	—	2.00	4.00
❑ 40351	I Still Feel the Same About You/Talk to Me Ohio	1975	—	2.00	4.00
❑ 40404	Country D.J./We Made Love	1975	—	2.00	4.00
❑ 40443	Thanks/Why's the Last Time Have to Be the Best	1975	—	2.00	4.00
❑ 40595	Peanuts and Diamonds/Your Love Blows Me Away	1976	—	2.00	4.00
❑ 40661	Liars One, Believers Zero/Let Me Whisper Darling One More Time	1976	—	2.00	4.00
❑ 40713	Head to Toe/Love Song for Jackie	1977	—	2.00	4.00
❑ 40794	Still the One/This Ole Suitcase	1977	—	2.00	4.00
❑ 40893	I Can't Wait Any Longer/Joanna	1978	—	2.00	4.00
❑ 40964	Double S/Married Lady	1978	—	2.00	4.00
❑ 40992	This Is a Love Song/Remembering the Good	1979	—	2.00	4.00
❑ 41060	The Dream Never Dies/One More Sexy Lady	1979	—	2.00	4.00
❑ 41150	More Than a Bedroom Thing/Love Me and I'll Be Your Best Friend	1979	—	2.00	4.00
❑ 41212	Mike Mine Night Time/Old Me and You	1980	—	2.00	4.00
❑ 41297	Rock 'N' Roll to Rock of Ages/I'm Used to the Rain	1980	—	2.00	4.00
❑ 51017	I Want That Feelin' Again/She Made Me Remember	1980	—	2.00	4.00
❑ 51052	Mister Peepers/How Married Are You, Mary Ann	1981	—	2.00	4.00
❑ 51150	Homebody/One Man Band	1981	—	2.00	4.00
❑ 51204	Whiskey Made Me Stumble (The Devil Made Me Fall)/All That Keeps Me Goin'	1981	—	2.00	4.00
SOUTHERN TRACKS					
❑ 1007	Southern Fried/You Turn the Light On	1982	—	2.50	5.00
❑ 1011	Laid Off/Lovin' Tonight	1982	—	2.50	5.00
❑ 1014	Thank You Darling/Lovin' Tonight	1983	—	2.50	5.00
❑ 1021	Son of the South/20th Century Fox	1983	—	2.50	5.00
❑ 1026	Your Eyes/I Never Get Enough of You	1984	—	2.50	5.00
❑ 1030	Speculation/We May Never Pass This Way Again	1984	—	2.50	5.00
❑ 1067	Sheet Music/Maybe Go Down	1986	—	2.50	5.00
❑ 1077	No Ordinary Memory/Sheet Music	1987	—	2.50	5.00
SWANEE					
❑ 4013	Wino the Clown/Wild Weekend	1985	—	2.50	5.00
❑ 5015	Pity Party/Don't She Look Good	1985	—	2.50	5.00
❑ 5018	When You Leave That Way, You Can Never Go Back/Quits	1985	—	2.50	5.00
TNT					
❑ 146	Empty Room/Take Me	1957	17.50	35.00	70.00
❑ 165	Empty Room/Take Me	1958	15.00	30.00	60.00
❑ 9015	City Lights/No Song to Sing	1958	20.00	40.00	80.00
Albums					
DECCA					
❑ DL 4192 [M]	Bill Anderson Sings Country Songs	1962	5.00	10.00	20.00
❑ DL 4427 [M]	Still	1963	5.00	10.00	20.00
❑ DL 4499 [M]	Bill Anderson Sings	1964	3.75	7.50	15.00
❑ DL 4600 [M]	Bill Anderson Showcase	1964	3.75	7.50	15.00
❑ DL 4646 [M]	From This Pen	1965	3.75	7.50	15.00
❑ DL 4686 [M]	Bright Lights and Country Music	1965	3.75	7.50	15.00
❑ DL 4771 [M]	I Love You Drops	1966	3.75	7.50	15.00
❑ DL 4855 [M]	Get While the Gettin's Good	1967	3.75	7.50	15.00
❑ DL 4859 [M]	Bill Anderson's Greatest Hits	1967	5.00	10.00	20.00
❑ DL 4886 [M]	I Can Do Nothing Alone	1967	6.25	12.50	25.00
❑ DXSA 7198 [(2)]	The Bill Anderson Story	1969	3.75	7.50	15.00
❑ DL 74192 [S]	Bill Anderson Sings Country Songs	1962	6.25	12.50	25.00
❑ DL 74427 [S]	Still	1963	6.25	12.50	25.00
❑ DL 74499 [S]	Bill Anderson Sings	1964	5.00	10.00	20.00
❑ DL 74600 [S]	Bill Anderson Showcase	1964	5.00	10.00	20.00
❑ DL 74646 [S]	From This Pen	1965	5.00	10.00	20.00
❑ DL 74686 [S]	Bright Lights and Country Music	1965	5.00	10.00	20.00
❑ DL 74771 [S]	I Love You Drops	1966	5.00	10.00	20.00
❑ DL 74855 [S]	Get While the Gettin's Good	1967	5.00	10.00	20.00
❑ DL 74859 [S]	Bill Anderson's Greatest Hits	1967	5.00	10.00	20.00
❑ DL 74886 [S]	I Can Do Nothing Alone	1967	5.00	10.00	20.00
❑ DL 74998	Wild Weekend	1968	3.75	7.50	15.00
❑ DL 75056	Happy State of Mind	1968	3.75	7.50	15.00
❑ DL 75142	My Life/But You Know I Love You	1969	3.75	7.50	15.00
❑ DL 75161	Bill Anderson's Christmas	1969	3.75	7.50	15.00
❑ DL 75206	Love Is a Sometimes Thing	1970	3.00	6.00	12.00
❑ DL 75254	Where Have All Our Heroes Gone?	1971	3.00	6.00	12.00
❑ DL 75275	Always Remember	1971	3.00	6.00	12.00
❑ DL 75315	Bill Anderson's Greatest Hits, Vol. 2	1971	3.00	6.00	12.00
❑ DL 75339	Singing His Praise	1972	3.00	6.00	12.00
❑ DL 75344	Bill Anderson Sings For "All the Lonely Women in the World"	1972	3.00	6.00	12.00
❑ DL 75383	Don't She Look Good	1972	3.00	6.00	12.00
MCA					
❑ 13	Bill Anderson's Greatest Hits	1973	2.50	5.00	10.00
—Reissue of Decca 74859					
❑ 320	Bill	1973	3.00	6.00	12.00
❑ 416	"Whispering" Bill Anderson	1974	3.00	6.00	12.00
❑ 454	Every Time I Turn the Radio On/Talk to Me Ohio	1974	2.50	5.00	10.00
❑ 693	Love and Other Sad Stories	198?	2.00	4.00	8.00
—Reissue					
❑ 694	Ladies' Choice	198?	2.00	4.00	8.00
—Reissue					
❑ 766	Nashville Mirrors	198?	2.00	4.00	8.00
—Reissue					
❑ 2222	Peanuts & Diamonds & Other Jewels	1975	2.50	5.00	10.00
❑ 2264	Scorpio	1976	2.50	5.00	10.00
❑ 2371	Love and Other Sad Stories	1977	2.50	5.00	10.00
❑ 3075	Ladies' Choice	1979	2.50	5.00	10.00
❑ 3214	Nashville Mirrors	1980	2.50	5.00	10.00
❑ 4001 [(2)]	The Bill Anderson Story	1973	3.00	6.00	12.00
—Reissue of Decca 7198					
❑ 35032	Whispering	197?	2.50	5.00	10.00
MCA CORAL					
❑ 20002	I Can Do Nothing	1973	2.50	5.00	10.00
VOCALION					
❑ VL 3835 [M]	Bill Anderson's Country Style	196?	3.00	6.00	12.00
❑ VL 73835 [S]	Bill Anderson's Country Style	196?	3.75	7.50	15.00
❑ VL 73927	Just Plain Bill	197?	2.50	5.00	10.00

ANDERSON, BILL, AND ROY ACUFF

Also see each artist's individual listings.

45s

Number	Title (A Side/B Side)	Yr	VG	VG+	NM
MCA					
❑ 52290	I Wonder If God Likes Country Music/Ride Off Into the Sunset	1983	—	2.00	4.00

ANDERSON, BILL, AND JAN HOWARD

Also see each artist's individual listings.

45s

Number	Title (A Side/B Side)	Yr	VG	VG+	NM
DECCA					
❑ 31884	I Know You're Married (But I Love You Still)/Time Out	1966	2.50	5.00	10.00
❑ 32197	For Loving You/The Untouchables	1967	2.00	4.00	8.00
❑ 32511	If It's All the Same to You/I Thank God for You	1969	2.00	4.00	8.00
❑ 32689	Someday We'll Be Together/Who's the Biggest Fool	1970	2.00	4.00	8.00
❑ 32877	Dis-Satisfied/Knowing You're Mine	1971	2.00	4.00	8.00
Albums					
DECCA					
❑ DL 4959 [M]	For Loving You	1967	6.25	12.50	25.00
❑ DL 74959 [S]	For Loving You	1967	5.00	10.00	20.00
❑ DL 75184	If It's All the Same to You	1970	5.00	10.00	20.00
❑ DL 75293	Bill & Jan (Or Jan & Bill)	1972	5.00	10.00	20.00

ANDERSON, BILL, AND MARY LOU TURNER

Also see each artist's individual listings.

45s

Number	Title (A Side/B Side)	Yr	VG	VG+	NM
MCA					
❑ 40488	Sometimes/Circle in a Triangle	1975	—	2.00	4.00
❑ 40533	That's What Made Me Love You/Can We Still Be Friends	1976	—	2.00	4.00
❑ 40753	Where Are You Going, Billy Boy/Sad Ole Shade of Gray	1977	—	2.00	4.00
❑ 40852	I'm Way Ahead of You/Just Enough to Make Me Want It All	1978	—	2.00	4.00
Albums					
MCA					
❑ 2182	Sometimes	1976	3.00	6.00	12.00
❑ 2298	Billy Boy & Mary Lou	1977	3.00	6.00	12.00

ANDERSON, IVIE

Selected 78s

Number	Title (A Side/B Side)	Yr	VG	VG+	NM
EXCLUSIVE					
❑ 3113	Mexico Joe/When the Ships Come Sailing Home Again	1944	12.50	25.00	50.00

ANDERSON, JOHN

45s

Number	Title (A Side/B Side)	Yr	VG	VG+	NM
ACE OF HEARTS					
❑ 0500	Swoop Down, Sweet Jesus/(B-side unknown)	1975	2.00	4.00	8.00
BNA					
❑ 62062	Who Got Our Love/Steamy Windows	1991	—	2.00	4.00
❑ 62140	Straight Tequila Night/Seminole Wind	1991	—	2.00	4.00
❑ 62235	When It Comes to You/Cold Day in Hell	1992	—	2.00	4.00
❑ 62312	Seminole Wind/Steamy Windows	1992	—	2.00	4.00
❑ 62410	Let Go of the Stone/Look Away	1992	—	2.00	4.00
❑ 62443	Money in the Bank/Nashville Tears	1993	—	2.00	4.00
❑ 62621	I Fell in the Water/All Things to All Things	1993	—	—	3.00
❑ 62709	I've Got It Made/Can't Get Away from You	1993	—	2.00	4.00
❑ 62795	I Wish I Could Have Been There/Solid Ground	1994	—	2.00	4.00
❑ 62935	Country 'Til I Die/Swingin'	1994	—	2.00	4.00

Number	Title (A Side/B Side)	Yr	VG	VG+	NM
❑ 64260	Bend It Until It Breaks/Keep Your Hands to Yourself	1994	—	2.00	4.00
❑ 64274	Mississippi Moon/It Ain't Pneumonia, It's the Blues	1995	—	2.00	4.00
❑ 64465	Paradise/Bad Weather	1995	—	—	3.00
❑ 64498	Long Hard Lesson Learned/Paradise	1996	—	—	3.00
❑ 64573	My Kind of Crazy/Long Hard Lesson Learned	1996	—	—	3.00
MCA					
❑ 53155	When Your Yellow Brick Road Turns Blue/Lying in Her Arms	1987	—	—	3.00
❑ 53155 [DJ]	When Your Yellow Brick Road Turns Blue (same on both sides)	1987	2.50	5.00	10.00
—Promo only on red vinyl					
❑ 53226	Somewhere Between Ragged and Right/Just for You	1987	—	—	3.00
❑ 53307	It's Hard to Keep This Ship Together/There's Nothing Left for Me to Take for Granted	1988	—	—	3.00
❑ 53366	If It Ain't Broke Don't Fix It/Just to Hold a Little Hand	1988	—	—	3.00
❑ 53441	Down in the Orange Grove/The Will of God	1988	—	—	3.00
❑ 53485	Lower on the Hog/The Ballad of Zero and the Tramp	1989	—	—	3.00
MERCURY					
❑ 568496-7	Takin' the Country Back/Brown Eyed Girl	1998	—	—	3.00
❑ 574640-7	Somebody Slap Me/We've Got a Good Thing Goin'	1997	—	—	3.00
❑ 574948-7	Small Town/The Fall	1997	—	—	3.00
UNIVERSAL					
❑ UVL-66020	Who's Lovin' My Baby/There Was a Time When I Was Alone	1989	—	2.00	4.00
WARNER BROS.					
❑ 8480	I've Got a Feelin' (Somebody Stealin')/It's All the Way Together	1977	—	2.50	5.00
❑ 8585	Whine, Whistle, Whine/If There Were No Memories	1978	—	2.50	5.00
❑ 8705	The Girl at the End of the Bar/You're Pleasin' Me	1978	—	2.50	5.00
❑ 8770	My Pledge of Love/Why Baby Why	1979	—	2.50	5.00
❑ 8863	Low Dog Blues/Girl, for You	1979	—	2.50	5.00
❑ 28433	What's So Different About You/Life's Little Pleasures	1987	—	2.00	4.00
❑ 28502	Countrified/Yellow Creek	1986	—	2.00	4.00
❑ 28639	Honky Tonk Crowd/If I Could Have My Way	1986	—	2.00	4.00
❑ 28748	You Can't Keep a Good Memory Down/What's So Different About You	1986	—	2.00	4.00
❑ 28855	Down in Tennessee/I've Got Me a Woman	1985	—	2.00	4.00
❑ 28916	Tokyo, Oklahoma/Willie's Gone	1985	—	2.00	4.00
❑ 29002	It's All Over Now/Only Your Love	1985	—	2.00	4.00
❑ 29127	Eye of a Hurricane/Chicken Truck	1984	—	2.00	4.00
❑ 29207	She Sure Got Away with My Heart/Lonely Is Another State	1984	—	2.00	4.00
❑ 29276	I Wish I Could Write You a Song/The Sun's Gonna Shine (On Our Back Door)	1984	—	2.00	4.00
❑ 29385	Let Somebody Else Drive/Mexico	1984	—	2.00	4.00
❑ 29497	Black Sheep/Call on Me	1983	—	2.00	4.00
❑ 29585	Goin' Down Hill/If a Broken Heart Could Kill	1983	—	2.00	4.00
❑ 29788	Swingin'/Honky Tonk Saturday Night	1982	—	2.50	5.00
❑ 29917	Wild and Blue/Honky Tonk Heart	1982	—	2.00	4.00
❑ 49089	Your Lying Blue Eyes/Mountain High, Valley Low	1979	—	2.00	4.00
❑ 49120	Girl, For You/Your Lying Blue Eyes	1979	—	2.00	4.00
❑ 49191	She Just Started Liking Cheatin' Songs/I Wish I Could Write You a Song	1980	—	2.00	4.00
❑ 49275	If There Were No Memories/Shoot Low Sheriff	1980	—	2.00	4.00
❑ 49582	1959/It Looks Like the Party Is Over	1980	—	2.00	4.00
❑ 49699	I'm Just an Old Chunk of Coal (But I'm Gonna Be a Diamond Someday)/Havin' Hard Times	1981	—	2.00	4.00
❑ 49772	Chicken Truck/I Love You a Thousand Ways	1981	—	2.00	4.00
❑ 49860	I Just Came Home to Count the Memories/Girl, For You	1981	—	2.00	4.00
❑ 50043	Would You Catch a Falling Star/I Danced with San Antonio Rose	1982	—	2.00	4.00

Albums

Number	Title	Yr	VG	VG+	NM
MCA					
❑ 42037	Blue Skies Again	1988	2.00	4.00	8.00
❑ 42218	10	1988	2.00	4.00	8.00
WARNER BROS.					
❑ BSK 3459	John Anderson	1980	3.00	6.00	12.00
❑ BSK 3547	John Anderson 2	1981	2.50	5.00	10.00
❑ BSK 3599	I Just Came Home to Count the Memories	1981	2.50	5.00	10.00
❑ 23721	Wild & Blue	1982	2.00	4.00	8.00
❑ 23912	All the People Are Talkin'	1983	2.00	4.00	8.00
❑ 25099	Eye of a Hurricane	1984	2.00	4.00	8.00
❑ 25169	Greatest Hits	1984	2.00	4.00	8.00
❑ 25211	Tokyo, Oklahoma	1985	2.00	4.00	8.00
❑ 25373	Countrified	1986	2.00	4.00	8.00

ANDERSON, LES

45s

Number	Title (A Side/B Side)	Yr	VG	VG+	NM
DECCA					
❑ 9-46303	I Was Sorta Wondering/Just Like Two Drops of Water	1951	6.25	12.50	25.00
❑ 9-46326	T-T-Tucky Ty/Las Vegas, Nevada	1951	6.25	12.50	25.00
❑ 9-46352	My Baby Buckaroo/Dimples Dumplins	1951	6.25	12.50	25.00
❑ 9-46370	Tennessee Moon/She's Dynamite in Blue Dungarees	1951	6.25	12.50	25.00

ANDERSON, LIZ

45s

Number	Title (A Side/B Side)	Yr	VG	VG+	NM
EPIC					
❑ 5-10782	It Don't Do No Good to Be a Good Girl/That's What Loving You Has Meant to Me	1971	—	3.00	6.00
❑ 5-10840	I'll Never Fall in Love Again/You Buy the Wine	1972	—	3.00	6.00
❑ 5-10896	Astrology/Living One Day at a Time	1972	—	3.00	6.00
❑ 5-10952	Time to Love Again/Wearing a Smile	1973	—	3.00	6.00
HOBBY HOUSE					
❑ CSA-1 [DJ]	Christopher the Christmas Seal (same on both sides)	196?	2.00	4.00	8.00
❑ CSA-1 [PS]	Christopher the Christmas Seal	196?	2.00	4.00	8.00
RCA VICTOR					
❑ 47-8778	Go Now Pay Later/The Bottle Turned Into a Blonde	1966	2.50	5.00	10.00
❑ 47-8861	So Much for Me, So Much for You/Release Me	1966	2.50	5.00	10.00
❑ 47-8999	The Wife of the Party/Fairytale	1966	2.50	5.00	10.00
❑ 47-9163	Mama Spank/To the Landlord	1967	2.00	4.00	8.00
❑ 47-9271	Tiny Tears/Grandma's House	1967	2.00	4.00	8.00
❑ 47-9378	Thanks a Lot for Tryin' Anyway/Come Walk in My Shoes	1967	2.00	4.00	8.00
❑ 47-9508	Like a Merry-Go-Round/Thanks, But No Thanks	1968	2.00	4.00	8.00
❑ 47-9586	Cry, Cry Again/Me, Me, Me, Me, Me	1968	2.00	4.00	8.00
❑ 47-9650	Love Is Ending/Blue Are the Violets	1968	2.00	4.00	8.00
❑ 47-9796	Husband Hunting/All You Add Is Love	1970	2.00	4.00	8.00
❑ 47-9876	All Day Sucker/Wonder If I'll Feel This Bad Tomorrow	1970	2.00	4.00	8.00
❑ 47-9924	When I'm Not Lookin'/Only for Me	1970	2.00	4.00	8.00
❑ 74-0112	Free/Nothing Between Us	1969	2.50	5.00	10.00
❑ 74-0166	Excedrin Headache #99/The Rainy Season's Over	1969	2.50	5.00	10.00
❑ 74-0220	If the Creek Don't Rise/Only for Me	1969	2.50	5.00	10.00
SCORPION					
❑ 0565	After You/The World Has Music	1978	—	2.50	5.00

Albums

Number	Title	Yr	VG	VG+	NM
RCA VICTOR					
❑ LPM-3769 [M]	Liz Anderson Sings	1967	7.50	15.00	30.00
❑ LSP-3769 [S]	Liz Anderson Sings	1967	5.00	10.00	20.00
❑ LPM-3852 [M]	Cookin' Up Hits	1967	7.50	15.00	30.00
❑ LSP-3852 [S]	Cookin' Up Hits	1967	5.00	10.00	20.00
❑ LPM-3908 [M]	Liz Anderson Sings Her Favorites	1968	10.00	20.00	40.00
❑ LSP-3908 [S]	Liz Anderson Sings Her Favorites	1968	5.00	10.00	20.00
❑ LSP-4014	Like a Merry-Go-Round	1968	5.00	10.00	20.00
❑ LSP-4222	If the Creek Don't Rise	1969	5.00	10.00	20.00
❑ LSP-4346	Husband Hunting	1970	5.00	10.00	20.00

ANDERSON, LIZ, AND LYNN ANDERSON

Also see each artist's individual listings.

45s

Number	Title (A Side/B Side)	Yr	VG	VG+	NM
RCA VICTOR					
❑ 47-9445	Mother, May I/Better Than Life Without You	1968	2.00	4.00	8.00

ANDERSON, LYNN

45s

Number	Title (A Side/B Side)	Yr	VG	VG+	NM
CHART					
❑ 1001	Too Much of You/If This Is Love	1967	2.00	4.00	8.00
—Reissue of 1475					
❑ 1010	Promises, Promises/It Makes You Happy	1967	2.00	4.00	8.00
❑ 1026	No Another Time/The Worst Is Yet to Come	1968	2.00	4.00	8.00
❑ 1042	Big Girls Don't Cry/I Keep Forgettin'	1968	2.00	4.00	8.00
❑ 1059	Flattery Will Get You Everywhere/A Million Shades of Blue	1968	2.00	4.00	8.00
❑ 1330	My Heart Keeps Walking the Floor/In Person	1966	2.50	5.00	10.00
❑ 1375	Ride, Ride, Ride/Tear By Tear	1966	2.00	4.00	8.00
❑ 1430	If I Kiss You (Will You Go Away)/Then Go	1967	2.00	4.00	8.00
❑ 1475	Too Much of You/If This Is Love	1967	2.50	5.00	10.00
❑ 5001	Our House Is Not a Home (If It's Never Been Loved In)/Wave Bye-Bye to the Man	1969	2.00	4.00	8.00
❑ 5013	Where's the Playground Bobby/There Oughta Be a Law	1969	2.00	4.00	8.00
❑ 5021	That's a No No/If Silence Is Golden	1969	2.00	4.00	8.00
❑ 5040	He'd Still Love Me/All You Add Is Love	1969	2.00	4.00	8.00
❑ 5053	I've Been Everywhere/Penny for Your Thoughts	1970	2.00	4.00	8.00
❑ 5068	Rocky Top/Take Me Home	1970	—	3.50	7.00
❑ 5098	I'm Alright/Pick of the Week	1970	—	3.50	7.00
❑ 5113	It Wasn't God Who Made Honky Tonk Angels/Be Quiet Mind	1971	—	3.50	7.00
❑ 5125	Jim Dandy/Strangers	1971	—	3.50	7.00
❑ 5136	He Even Woke Me Up to Say Goodbye/A Pillow That Whispers	1971	—	3.50	7.00
❑ 5146	Love of the Common People/Simple Words	1971	—	3.50	7.00
❑ 5151	There Oughta Be a Law/Too Much of You	1972	—	3.50	7.00
COLUMBIA					
❑ AE7 1056 [DJ]	Frosty the Snowman/Don't Wish Me Merry Christmas	1972	2.00	4.00	8.00
❑ 10041	What a Man, My Man Is/Everything's Falling in Place	1974	—	2.00	4.00
❑ 10100	He Turns It Into Love Again/Someone to Finish What You Started	1975	—	2.00	4.00
❑ 10160	I've Never Loved Anyone More/He Worshipped Me	1975	—	2.00	4.00
❑ 10240	Paradise/You've Got It All Together Now	1975	—	2.00	4.00
❑ 10280	All the King's Horses/If All I Have to Do Is Just Love You	1975	—	2.00	4.00

Number	Title (A Side/B Side)	Yr	VG	VG+	NM
❑ 10337	Rodeo Cowboy/Dixieland, You Will Never Die	1976	—	2.00	4.00
❑ 10401	Sweet Talkin' Man/A Good Old Country Song	1976	—	2.00	4.00
❑ 10467	Wrap Your Love All Around Your Man/I Couldn't Be Lonely (Even If I Wanted To)	1976	—	2.00	4.00
❑ 10545	I Love What Love Is Doing to Me/Will I Ever Hear Those Church Bells Ring	1977	—	2.00	4.00
❑ 10597	He Ain't You/It's Your Love What Keeps Me Going	1977	—	2.00	4.00
❑ 10650	We Got Love/Sunshine Man	1977	—	2.00	4.00
❑ 10721	Rising Above It All/My World Begins and Ends with You	1978	—	2.00	4.00
❑ 10809	Last Love of My Life/When You Marry for Money	1978	—	2.00	4.00
❑ 10909	Isn't It Always Love/A Child with You Tonight	1979	—	2.00	4.00
❑ 11006	I Love How You Love Me/Come As You Are	1979	—	2.00	4.00
❑ 11104	Sea of Heartbreak/Say You Will	1979	—	2.00	4.00
❑ 11296	Even Cowgirls Get the Blues/See Through Me	1980	—	2.00	4.00
❑ 11374	Blue Baby Blue/The Lonely Hearts Café	1980	—	2.00	4.00
❑ 45101	Stay There 'Til I Get There/I'd Run a Mile to You	1970	—	2.50	5.00
❑ 45190	No Love at All/I Found You Just in Time	1970	—	2.50	5.00
❑ 45251	Don't Wish Me Merry Christmas/Ding-a-Ling the Christmas Bell	1970	—	3.00	6.00
❑ 45251 [PS]	Don't Wish Me Merry Christmas/Ding-a-Ling the Christmas Bell	1970	2.00	4.00	8.00
❑ 45252	Rose Garden/Nothing Between Us	1970	—	2.50	5.00
❑ 45356	You're My Man/I'm Gonna Write a Song	1971	—	2.00	4.00
❑ 45429	How Can I Unlove You/Don't Say Things You Don't Mean	1971	—	2.00	4.00
❑ 45527	Don't Wish Me Merry Christmas/Ding-a-Ling the Christmas Bell	1971	—	2.50	5.00
❑ 45529	Cry/Simple Words	1972	—	2.00	4.00
❑ 45615	Listen to a Country Song/That's What Loving You Has Meant to Me	1972	—	2.00	4.00
❑ 45692	Fool Me/What's Made Milwaukee Famous	1972	—	2.00	4.00
❑ 45768	Keep Me in Mind/Rodeo	1973	—	2.00	4.00
❑ 45843	Sing About Love/Home Is Where I Hang My Head	1973	—	—	—
—Canceled?					
❑ 45857	Top of the World/I Wish I Was a Little Girl Again	1973	—	2.00	4.00
❑ 45918	Sing About Love/Fickle Fortune	1973	—	2.00	4.00
❑ 46009	Smile for Me/A Man Like Your Daddy	1974	—	2.00	4.00
❑ 46056	Talkin' to the Wall/I Want to Be a Part of You	1974	—	2.00	4.00

MCA

Number	Title (A Side/B Side)	Yr	VG	VG+	NM
❑ 52408	Running from the Real Thing/The Heart of the Matter	1984	—	—	3.00

MERCURY

Number	Title (A Side/B Side)	Yr	VG	VG+	NM
❑ 870528-7	Under the Boardwalk/Turn the Page	1988	—	—	3.00
❑ 872154-7	The Angel Song (Glory to God in the Highest)/When a Child Is Born	1988	—	—	3.00
—With Butch Baker					
❑ 872220-7	What He Does Best/It Goes Without Saying	1988	—	—	3.00
❑ 872602-7	How Many Hearts/How Many Hearts (Long Version)	1989	—	—	3.00
❑ 888209-7	Didn't We Shine/We Must Be Doing It Right	1986	—	—	3.00
❑ 888597-7	It Goes Without Saying/So Little Love in the World	1987	—	—	3.00
❑ 888839-7	Read Between the Lines/If This Ain't Love	1987	—	—	3.00

PERMIAN

Number	Title (A Side/B Side)	Yr	VG	VG+	NM
❑ 82000	You Can't Lose What You Never Had/This Time the Heartbreak Wins	1983	—	2.00	4.00
❑ 82001	What I Learned from Loving You/Mr. Sundown	1983	—	2.00	4.00
❑ 82003	You're Welcome To Tonight/Your Kisses Lied	1983	—	2.00	4.00
—A-side with Gary Morris					

Albums

CHART

Number	Title	Yr	VG	VG+	NM
❑ CHM-1001 [M]	Ride, Ride, Ride	1967	5.00	10.00	20.00
❑ CHS-1001 [S]	Ride, Ride, Ride	1967	3.75	7.50	15.00
❑ CHM-1004 [M]	Promises, Promises	1968	5.00	10.00	20.00
❑ CHS-1004 [S]	Promises, Promises	1968	3.75	7.50	15.00
❑ CHS-1008	Big Girls Don't Cry	1969	3.75	7.50	15.00
❑ CHS-1009	The Best of Lynn Anderson	1969	3.75	7.50	15.00
❑ CHS-1013	With Love, From Lynn	1969	3.75	7.50	15.00
❑ CHS-1017	At Home with Lynn	1969	3.75	7.50	15.00
❑ CHS-1022	Songs That Made Country Girls Famous	1970	3.00	6.00	12.00
❑ CHS-1028	Uptown Country Girl	1970	3.00	6.00	12.00
❑ CHS-1032	Songs My Mother Wrote	1970	3.00	6.00	12.00
❑ CHS-1037	I'm Alright	1970	3.00	6.00	12.00
❑ CHS-1040	Lynn Anderson's Greatest Hits	1971	3.00	6.00	12.00
❑ CHS-1043	Lynn Anderson with Strings	1971	3.00	6.00	12.00
❑ CHS-1050 [(2)]	Lynn Anderson	1972	3.75	7.50	15.00

COLUMBIA

Number	Title	Yr	VG	VG+	NM
❑ CS 1025	Stay There 'Til I Get There	1970	3.00	6.00	12.00
❑ C 30099	No Love at All	1970	3.00	6.00	12.00
❑ C 30411	Rose Garden	1970	2.50	5.00	10.00
❑ PC 30411	Rose Garden	197?	2.00	4.00	8.00
—Reissue					
❑ KC 30793	You're My Man	1971	2.50	5.00	10.00
❑ CG 30902 [(2)]	The World of Lynn Anderson	1971	3.00	6.00	12.00
❑ KC 30925	How Can I Unlove You	1971	2.50	5.00	10.00
❑ 3C 30957	Christmas Album	198?	2.00	4.00	8.00
—Reissue of KC 30957					
❑ KC 30957	Christmas Album	1971	3.00	6.00	12.00
❑ KC 31316	Cry	1972	2.50	5.00	10.00
❑ KC 31641	Lynn Anderson's Greatest Hits	1972	2.50	5.00	10.00
❑ PC 31641	Lynn Anderson's Greatest Hits	197?	2.00	4.00	8.00
—Reissue					
❑ KC 31647	Listen to a Country Song	1972	2.50	5.00	10.00
❑ KC 32078	Keep Me in Mind	1973	2.50	5.00	10.00
❑ KC 32429	Top of the World	1973	2.50	5.00	10.00
❑ KC 32719	Queens of Country	1974	2.50	5.00	10.00
❑ KC 32941	Smile for Me	1974	2.50	5.00	10.00
❑ KC 33293	What a Man, My Man Is	1974	2.50	5.00	10.00
❑ KC 33691	I've Never Loved Anyone More	1975	2.50	5.00	10.00
❑ PC 34089	All the King's Horses	1976	2.50	5.00	10.00
❑ PC 34308	Lynn Anderson's Greatest Hits Volume II	1976	2.50	5.00	10.00
❑ PC 34439	Wrap Your Love All Around Your Man	1977	2.50	5.00	10.00
❑ JC 34871	I Love What Love Is Doing to Me/He Ain't You	1977	2.50	5.00	10.00
❑ JC 35776	Outlaw Is Just a State of Mind	1979	2.50	5.00	10.00
❑ JC 36568	Even Cowgirls Get the Blues	1980	2.50	5.00	10.00
❑ FC 37354	Encore	1981	2.50	5.00	10.00
❑ PC 37354	Encore	1983	2.00	4.00	8.00
—Budget-line reissue					

HARMONY

Number	Title	Yr	VG	VG+	NM
❑ KH 32433	Singing My Song	1973	2.00	4.00	8.00

MERCURY

Number	Title	Yr	VG	VG+	NM
❑ 834625-1	What She Does Best	1988	2.00	4.00	8.00

MOUNTAIN DEW

Number	Title	Yr	VG	VG+	NM
❑ 7047	Lynn Anderson	197?	2.50	5.00	10.00

PERMIAN

Number	Title	Yr	VG	VG+	NM
❑ 8205	Back	1983	2.50	5.00	10.00

PICKWICK

Number	Title	Yr	VG	VG+	NM
❑ PTP-2049 [(2)]	Lynn Anderson	1973	3.00	6.00	12.00
❑ SPC-3267	Flower of Love	197?	2.00	4.00	8.00
❑ SPC-3296	It Makes You Happy	197?	2.00	4.00	8.00

ANDERSON, LYNN, AND JERRY LANE

45s

CHART

Number	Title (A Side/B Side)	Yr	VG	VG+	NM
❑ 1003	Keeping Up Appearances/You've Gotta Be the Greatest	1967	2.00	4.00	8.00
—Reissue of 1425					
❑ 1300	For Better or For Worse/We're Different	1965	2.50	5.00	10.00
❑ 1425	Keeping Up Appearances/You've Gotta Be the Greatest	1967	2.50	5.00	10.00

ANDERSON, RANDY

45s

COMSTOCK

Number	Title (A Side/B Side)	Yr	VG	VG+	NM
❑ 1959	It's Christmas (I Wish You Were Here)/(B-side unknown)	1988	—	3.00	6.00

ANDI AND THE BROWN SISTERS

45s

DOOR KNOB

Number	Title (A Side/B Side)	Yr	VG	VG+	NM
❑ 323	Labor of Love/(B-side unknown)	1989	—	2.50	5.00
❑ 329	Gently Hold Me/(B-side unknown)	1989	—	2.50	5.00
❑ 331	Lighter Shade of Blue/(B-side unknown)	1989	—	2.50	5.00
❑ 337	Shows You What I Know/Lighter Shade of Blue	1989	—	2.50	5.00
❑ 354	Dreamin' That Dream Again/(B-side unknown)	1990	—	3.00	6.00

KILLER

Number	Title (A Side/B Side)	Yr	VG	VG+	NM
❑ 115	This Old Feeling/(B-side unknown)	1988	—	3.00	6.00
❑ 1013	I'd Do Anything for You, Baby/(B-side unknown)	1988	—	3.00	6.00

ANDREWS, JESSICA

45s

DREAMWORKS

Number	Title (A Side/B Side)	Yr	VG	VG+	NM
❑ 59021	I Will Be There for You (same on both sides)	1999	—	—	3.00
❑ 459042-7	Unbreakable Heart/Unbreakable Heart (Acapella Version)	2000	—	—	3.00

ANDREWS, SHEILA

45s

OVATION

Number	Title (A Side/B Side)	Yr	VG	VG+	NM
❑ 1116	Too Fast for Rapid City/Bigger Fool Than I Am	1978	—	2.50	5.00
❑ 1121	Love Me Like a Woman/It'll Be Love	1979	—	2.50	5.00
❑ 1128	I Gotta Get Back the Feeling/Diggin' and a Grindin' For His Love	1979	—	2.50	5.00
❑ 1138	What I Had with You/I Gotta Get Back the Feeling	1980	—	2.50	5.00
—A-side with Joe Sun					
❑ 1146	It Don't Get Better Than This/The Softer You Touch Me The Harder I Fall	1980	—	2.50	5.00
❑ 1160	Where Could You Take Me/Pretty Lies	1980	—	2.50	5.00
❑ 1165	Maybe I Should Have Been Listening/(B-side unknown)	1981	—	3.00	6.00

ANDREWS SISTERS, THE

This popular group appeared on several country hits, but had none on their own. See BING CROSBY; ERNEST TUBB.

ANGELLE, LISA

45s

CAPITOL

Number	Title (A Side/B Side)	Yr	VG	VG+	NM
❑ B-44292	The First Time I Loved Forever/(B-side unknown)	1989	—	2.50	5.00

DREAMWORKS

Number	Title (A Side/B Side)	Yr	VG	VG+	NM
❑ 59032	I Wear Your Love/Midnight Rodeo	1999	—	2.00	4.00

EMI AMERICA

Number	Title (A Side/B Side)	Yr	VG	VG+	NM
❑ B-8258	Love, It's the Pits/Biloxi Blue	1985	—	3.00	6.00
❑ B-8258 [PS]	Love, It's the Pits/Biloxi Blue	1985	—	3.00	6.00
❑ B-8294	Bring Back Love/Poor Baby	1985	—	3.00	6.00

ANNE CHRISTINE

45s

Number	Title (A Side/B Side)	Yr	VG	VG+	NM
CME					
❑ 4633	Fool, Fool, Fool/Mountain of Lies	1971	2.50	5.00	10.00
❑ 4634	Summer Man/How Important Can It Be	1971	2.50	5.00	10.00
❑ 4635	It's Gonna Take a Little Bit Longer/Silver Threads and Golden Needles	1971	2.50	5.00	10.00

ANTHONY, RAYBURN

45s

Number	Title (A Side/B Side)	Yr	VG	VG+	NM
AUDIOGRAPH					
❑ 444	Tennessee Whiskey, Texas Women/(B-side unknown)	1983	—	3.00	6.00
❑ 459	Dance for a Crystal Ball/(B-side unknown)	1983	—	3.00	6.00
MEGA					
❑ 0048	Binoculars/Wild Flowers	1971	—	3.50	7.00
MERCURY					
❑ 55042	I Thought You Were Easy/This One's for You	1978	—	2.00	4.00
❑ 55053	Shadows of Love/Fire in the Night	1979	—	2.00	4.00
❑ 55063	It Won't Go Away/Baby Take It from Me	1979	—	2.00	4.00
❑ 57006	The Wild Side of Life/I Don't Believe I'll Fall in Love Today	1979	—	2.00	4.00
—A-side with Kitty Wells					
❑ 57024	Married Women/Cheatin' Fire	1980	—	2.00	4.00
❑ 57040	What Do You Need with Another Man/(B-side unknown)	1980	—	2.00	4.00
MILLION					
❑ 19	Memphis Morning/(B-side unknown)	1972	2.00	4.00	8.00
MONUMENT					
❑ 1004	I've Worn Out My Welcome Home/Walkin' on My Heart in High Heel Sneakers	1967	2.50	5.00	10.00
❑ 1023	There'll Be Many Tomorrows (Before I Forget Yesterday)/A Woman Whose Love Is Hard to Keep	1967	2.50	5.00	10.00
MUSICOR					
❑ 1073	You're Driving You Out of My Mind/Big Foot Again	1965	2.50	5.00	10.00
POLYDOR					
❑ 14346	Crazy Again/Mother Country Music	1976	—	2.50	5.00
❑ 14367	If You Don't Like Hank Williams/This Time Marie	1976	—	3.00	6.00
❑ 14380	Lonely Eyes/Walkin'	1977	—	2.50	5.00
❑ 14398	Hold Me/Don't Fall in Love	1977	—	2.50	5.00
❑ 14423	She Keeps Hangin' On/Talk About a Feeling	1977	—	2.50	5.00
❑ 14457	Maybe I Should've Been Listenin'/This Time Marie	1978	—	2.50	5.00
❑ 14482	Ain't No California/Talk About a Feeling	1978	—	2.50	5.00
STOP					
❑ 240	You Still Turn Me On/Bag Is You	1969	2.00	4.00	8.00
SUN					
❑ 333	Alice Blue Gown/St. Louis Blues	1959	5.00	10.00	20.00
❑ 339	There's No Tomorrow/Who's Gonna Shoe Your Pretty Foot	1960	5.00	10.00	20.00
❑ 373	Big Dream/How Well I Know	1962	5.00	10.00	20.00

ANTHONY, VINCE

45s

Number	Title (A Side/B Side)	Yr	VG	VG+	NM
MIDNIGHT GOLD					
❑ 160	Call Me Friend/Leave Me Tonight	1982	2.00	4.00	8.00

ARATA, TONY

45s

Number	Title (A Side/B Side)	Yr	VG	VG+	NM
MCA					
❑ 52782	Same Old Story/Rollin'	1986	—	2.00	4.00
NOBLE VISION					
❑ 106	Come On Home/Maybe I'm Over You	1984	—	2.50	5.00
❑ 108	Sure Thing/Enjoy the Ride	1985	—	2.50	5.00

ARCHER PARK

45s

Number	Title (A Side/B Side)	Yr	VG	VG+	NM
ATLANTIC					
❑ 87181	We Got a Lot in Common/I Still Wanna Jump Your Bones	1994	—	2.00	4.00
❑ 87211	Where There's Smoke/'Til Something Better Comes Along	1994	—	2.00	4.00

ARGO, JUDY

45s

Number	Title (A Side/B Side)	Yr	VG	VG+	NM
ASI					
❑ 1019	Night Time Music Man/Country Hall of Shame	1979	—	3.00	6.00
MDJ					
❑ 4633	Hide Me (In the Shadow of Your Love)/Millionaire Lover	1979	—	2.50	5.00
❑ 51379	He's a Good Man/Why Me	1979	—	2.50	5.00
❑ 51379 [PS]	He's a Good Man/Why Me	1979	2.00	4.00	8.00

ARMSTRONG, BILLY, AND THE GENERAL STORE

45s

Number	Title (A Side/B Side)	Yr	VG	VG+	NM
HILLSIDE					
❑ 8107	Christmas Is Bigger in Texas/Tater Pie	1981	—	3.00	6.00

ARMSTRONG, WAYNE

45s

Number	Title (A Side/B Side)	Yr	VG	VG+	NM
NSD					
❑ 57	Hot Sunday Morning/I Don't Want to Be Alone	1980	—	2.50	5.00

ARNOLD, EDDY

45s

Number	Title (A Side/B Side)	Yr	VG	VG+	NM
CURB					
❑ 73088	Cattle Call (with LeAnn Rimes)/I Walk Alone	1999	—	—	3.00
MGM					
❑ 14478	So Many Ways/Once in a While	1972	—	2.50	5.00
❑ 14535	If the Whole World Stopped Lovin'/My Son, I Wish You Everything	1973	—	2.00	4.00
❑ 14600	Oh, Oh, I'm Falling in Love Again/Anyway You Want Me	1973	—	2.00	4.00
❑ 14672	She's Got Everything I Need/I'm Glad You Happened to Me	1973	—	2.00	4.00
❑ 14711	Just for Old Times Sake/I Got This Thing About You	1974	—	2.00	4.00
❑ 14734	I Wish That I Had Loved You Better/Let It Be Love	1974	—	2.00	4.00
❑ 14769	Butterfly/If You Could Only Love Me Now	1974	—	2.00	4.00
❑ 14780	Red Roses for a Blue Lady/I Will	1975	—	2.00	4.00
❑ 14827	Middle of a MemoryI Just Had You on My Mind	1975	—	2.00	4.00
RCA					
❑ 2750-7-R	You Don't Miss a Thing/Just One Time	1990	—	2.00	4.00
❑ PB-10794	Put Me Back Into Your World/Goodnight Irene	1976	—	2.00	4.00
❑ PB-10899	(I Need You) All the Time/I've Never Loved Anyone More	1977	—	2.00	4.00
❑ PB-11031	Freedom Ain't the Same as Being Free/Till You Can Make It On Your Own	1977	—	2.00	4.00
❑ PB-11133	Where Lonely People Go/Penny Arcade	1977	—	2.00	4.00
❑ PB-11257	Country Lovin'/I've So Much to Be Thankful For	1978	—	2.00	4.00
❑ PB-11319	I'm the South/You Are My Sunshine	1978	—	2.00	4.00
❑ PB-11422	If Everyone Had Someone Like You/You're a Beautiful Place to Be	1978	—	2.00	4.00
❑ PB-11537	What In Her World Did I Do/Love of My Life	1979	—	2.00	4.00
❑ PB-11668	Goodbye/You're So Good At Lovin' Me	1979	—	2.00	4.00
❑ PB-11752	If I Ever Had to Say Goodbye to You/Love of My Life	1979	—	2.00	4.00
❑ PB-11918	Let's Get It While the Gettin's Good/You Cared Enough (To Give Your Very Best)	1980	—	2.00	4.00
❑ PB-12039	That's What I Get for Loving You/Undivided Love	1980	—	2.00	4.00
❑ PB-12136	Don't Look Now (But We Just Fell in Love)/There's Women (Then There's My Woman)	1980	—	2.00	4.00
❑ PB-12226	Bally-Hoo Days/Two Hearts Beat Better Than One	1981	—	2.00	4.00
❑ PB-13000	All I'm Missing Is You/Don't It Break Your Heart	1981	—	2.00	4.00
❑ PB-13094	Don't Give Up on Me/In Love with Loving You	1982	—	2.00	4.00
❑ PB-13339	The Valley Below/Make the World Go Away	1982	—	2.00	4.00
❑ PB-13452	The Blues Don't Care Who's Got 'Em/Wooden Heart	1983	—	2.00	4.00
❑ 62598	Out of the Blue/On a Night Like This	1993	—	2.00	4.00
RCA VICTOR					
❑ PB-10701	Cowboy/Don't Let the Good Times Roll Away	1976	—	2.00	4.00
❑ 47-2729	Anytime/What a Fool I Was	1949	7.50	15.00	30.00
❑ 47-2730	Bouquet of Roses/Texarkana Baby	1949	7.50	15.00	30.00
❑ 47-2776	I'm Thinking Tonight of My Blue Eyes/Rockin' Alone	1949	7.50	15.00	30.00
❑ 47-2777	It Makes No Difference Now/Molly Darling	1949	7.50	15.00	30.00
❑ 47-2778	The Prisoner's Song/Seven Years with the Wrong Woman	1949	7.50	15.00	30.00
❑ 47-3310	That's How Much I Love You/Chained to a Memory	1949	6.25	12.50	25.00
❑ 47-3311	Will the Circle Be Unbroken/Who, At My Door, Is Standing	1949	6.25	12.50	25.00
❑ 47-4243	When My Blue Moon Turns to Gold Again/White Azaleas	1951	5.00	10.00	20.00
❑ 47-4244	When You and I Were Young, Maggie/Roll Along Kentucky Moon	1951	5.00	10.00	20.00
❑ 47-4245	That Little Boy of Mine/Sinner's Prayer	1951	5.00	10.00	20.00
❑ 47-4273	Somebody's Been Beating My Time/Heart Strings	1951	5.00	10.00	20.00
❑ 47-4413	Bundle of Southern Sunshine/Call Her Your Sweetheart	1951	5.00	10.00	20.00
❑ 47-4490	Take My Hand, Precious Lord/Open Thy Merciful Arms	1952	5.00	10.00	20.00
❑ 47-4569	Easy on the Eyes/Anything That's Part of You	1952	5.00	10.00	20.00
❑ 47-4597	Bouquet of Roses/Texarkana Baby	1952	5.00	10.00	20.00
❑ 47-4598	It's a Sin/Anytime	1952	5.00	10.00	20.00
❑ 47-4599	That's How Much I Love You/A Heart Full of Love	1952	5.00	10.00	20.00
❑ 47-4600	I'll Hold You in My Heart (Till I Can Hold You in My Arms)/Don't Rob Another Man's Castle	1952	5.00	10.00	20.00
❑ 47-4787	A Full Time Job/Shephard of My Heart	1952	5.00	10.00	20.00
❑ 47-4954	Older and Bolder/I'd Trade All My Tomorrows (For Just One Yesterday)	1952	5.00	10.00	20.00
❑ 47-5020	My Desire/I Want to Thank You Lord	1952	5.00	10.00	20.00
❑ 47-5108	Eddy's Song/Condemned Without a Trial	1952	5.00	10.00	20.00
❑ 47-5189	When Your Hair Has Turned to Silver/Angry	1953	5.00	10.00	20.00
❑ 47-5192	Moonlight and Roses/Missouri Waltz	1953	5.00	10.00	20.00
❑ 47-5193	You Always Hurt the One You Love/I'm Gonna Lock My Heart	1953	5.00	10.00	20.00
❑ 47-5196	The Old Rugged Cross/Have Thine Own Way, Lord	1953	5.00	10.00	20.00
❑ 47-5197	Someday Somewhere/When I've Done My Best	1953	5.00	10.00	20.00
❑ 47-5305	Free Home Demonstration/How's the World Treating You	1953	5.00	10.00	20.00
❑ 47-5415	Mama, Come Get Your Baby Boy/If I Never Get to Heaven	1953	5.00	10.00	20.00
❑ 47-5525	I Really Don't Want to Know/I'll Never Get Over You	1953	5.00	10.00	20.00

Number	Title (A Side/B Side)	Yr	VG	VG+	NM
❑ 47-5601	Rose of Calvary/Prayer	1954	5.00	10.00	20.00
❑ 47-5634	My Everything/Second Fling	1954	5.00	10.00	20.00
❑ 47-5753	Chapel on the Hill/A Touch of God's Hand	1954	5.00	10.00	20.00
❑ 47-5805	This Is the Thanks I Get (For Loving You)/Hep Cat Baby	1954	5.00	10.00	20.00
❑ 47-5905	Christmas Can't Be Far Away/I'm Your Private Santa Claus	1954	5.00	10.00	20.00
❑ 47-6000	I've Been Thinking/Don't Forget	1955	3.75	7.50	15.00
❑ 47-6001	It Took a Miracle/I Always Have Someone to Turn To	1955	3.75	7.50	15.00
❑ 47-6069	Two Kinds of Love/In Time	1955	3.75	7.50	15.00
❑ 47-6139	The Cattle Call/The Kentuckian Song	1955	5.00	10.00	20.00
❑ 47-6198	Just Call Me Lonesome/That Do Make It Nice	1955	3.75	7.50	15.00
❑ 47-6290	The Richest Man/I Walked Alone Last Night	1955	3.75	7.50	15.00
❑ 47-6365	Trouble in Mind/When You Say Goodbye	1955	3.75	7.50	15.00
❑ 47-6407	Bayou Baby/Do You Know Where God Lives	1956	3.75	7.50	15.00
❑ 47-6502	You Don't Know Me/The Rockin' Mockin' Bird	1956	3.75	7.50	15.00
❑ 47-6601	Casey Jones (The Brave Engineer)/You Were Mine for Awhile	1956	3.75	7.50	15.00
❑ 47-6699	The Ballad of Wes Tancred/I Wouldn't Know Where to Begin	1956	3.75	7.50	15.00
❑ 47-6708	Mutual Admiration Society/If'n	1956	3.75	7.50	15.00
—With Jaye P. Morgan					
❑ 47-6773	A Dozen Hearts/A Good Lookin' Blonde	1956	3.75	7.50	15.00
❑ 47-6842	One/Do You Love Me	1957	3.00	6.00	12.00
—With Jaye P. Morgan					
❑ 47-6905	Gonna Find Me a Bluebird/Little Bit	1957	3.00	6.00	12.00
❑ 47-6975	Crazy Dream/Open Your Heart	1957	3.00	6.00	12.00
❑ 47-7040	Little Miss Sunbeam/When He Was Young	1957	3.00	6.00	12.00
❑ 47-7089	Wagon Wheels/You're Made Up for Everything	1957	3.00	6.00	12.00
❑ 47-7143	Too Soon to Know/I Need Somebody	1958	3.00	6.00	12.00
❑ 47-7221	Peck a Cheek/Before You Know It	1958	3.00	6.00	12.00
❑ 47-7292	The Day You Left Me/Real Love	1958	3.00	6.00	12.00
❑ 47-7340	Till You Come Back Again/I'm a Good Boy	1958	3.00	6.00	12.00
❑ 47-7435	Chip Off the Old Block/I'll Hold You in My Heart (Till I Can Hold You in My Arms)	1959	2.50	5.00	10.00
❑ 47-7542	Tennessee Stud/What's the Good (Of All This Love)	1959	2.50	5.00	10.00
❑ 47-7619	Did It Rain/Sittin' By Sittin' Bull	1959	2.50	5.00	10.00
❑ 47-7661	Boot Hill/Johnny Reb, That's Me	1959	2.50	5.00	10.00
❑ 47-7727	Little Sparrow/My Arms Are a House	1960	2.50	5.00	10.00
❑ 47-7794	Before This Day Ends/Just Out of Reach	1960	2.50	5.00	10.00
❑ 47-7861	(Jim) I Wore a Tie Today/Just Call Me Lonesome	1961	2.50	5.00	10.00
❑ 47-7926	One Grain of Sand/The Worst Night of My Life	1961	2.50	5.00	10.00
❑ 47-7984	Tears Broke Out on Me/I'll Do As Much for You Someday	1962	2.00	4.00	8.00
❑ 47-8048	A Little Heartache/After Loving You	1962	2.00	4.00	8.00
❑ 47-8102	Does He Mean That Much to You/Tender Touch	1962	2.00	4.00	8.00
❑ 47-8160	Yesterday's Memories/Lonely Balladeer	1963	2.00	4.00	8.00
❑ 47-8160 [PS]	Yesterday's Memories/Lonely Balladeer	1963	3.75	7.50	15.00
❑ 47-8207	A Million Years or So/Just a Ribbon	1963	2.00	4.00	8.00
❑ 47-8253	Jealous Hearted Me/I Met Her Today	1963	2.00	4.00	8.00
❑ 47-8296	Molly/The Song of the Coo Coo	1963	2.00	4.00	8.00
❑ 47-8363	Sweet Adorable You/Why	1964	—	3.00	6.00
❑ 47-8445	I Thank My Lucky Stars/I Don't Cry No More	1964	—	3.00	6.00
❑ 47-8516	What's He Doing in My World/Laura Lee	1965	—	3.00	6.00
❑ 47-8632	I'm Letting You Go/The Days Gone By	1965	—	3.00	6.00
❑ 47-8679	Make the World Go Away/The Easy Way	1965	2.00	4.00	8.00
❑ 47-8679 [PS]	Make the World Go Away/The Easy Way	1965	3.75	7.50	15.00
❑ 47-8749	I Want to Go With You/Better Stop Tellin' Lies (About Me)	1965	2.00	4.00	8.00
❑ 47-8749 [PS]	I Want to Go With You/Better Stop Tellin' Lies (About Me)	1965	3.75	7.50	15.00
❑ 47-8818	The Last Word in Lonesome Is Me/Mary Claire Melvina Rebecca Jane	1966	—	3.00	6.00
❑ 47-8818 [PS]	The Last Word in Lonesome Is Me/Mary Claire Melvina Rebecca Jane	1966	3.00	6.00	12.00
❑ 47-8869	The Tip of My Fingers/Long, Long Friendship	1966	—	3.00	6.00
❑ 47-8869 [PS]	The Tip of My Fingers/Long, Long Friendship	1966	3.00	6.00	12.00
❑ 47-8965	Somebody Like Me/Taking Chances	1966	—	3.00	6.00
❑ 47-8965 [PS]	Somebody Like Me/Taking Chances	1966	3.00	6.00	12.00
❑ 47-9027	The Angel and the Stranger/The First Word	1966	—	3.00	6.00
❑ 47-9080	Lonely Again/Love on My Mind	1967	—	3.00	6.00
❑ 47-9182	Misty Blue/Calling Mary Names	1967	—	3.00	6.00
❑ 47-9265	Turn the World Around/The Long Ride Home	1967	—	3.00	6.00
❑ 47-9368	Here Comes Heaven/Baby That's Loving	1967	—	3.00	6.00
❑ 47-9387	Jolly Old St. Nicholas/This World of Ours	1967	2.00	4.00	8.00
❑ 47-9437	Here Comes the Rain, Baby/The World I Used to Know	1968	—	3.00	6.00
❑ 47-9525	It's Over/No Matter Whose Baby You Are	1968	—	3.00	6.00
❑ 47-9606	Then You Can Tell Me Goodbye/Apples, Raisins and Roses	1968	—	3.00	6.00
❑ 47-9667	They Don't Make Love Like They Used To/What a Wonderful World	1968	—	3.00	6.00
❑ 47-9801	Soul Deep/(Today) I Started Loving You Again	1969	—	3.00	6.00
❑ 47-9848	A Man's Kind of Woman/Living Under Pressure	1970	—	2.50	5.00
❑ 47-9889	From Heaven to Heartache/Ten Times Forever More	1970	—	2.50	5.00
❑ 47-9935	Portrait of My Woman/I Really Don't Want to Know	1970	—	2.50	5.00
❑ 47-9968	A Part of America Died/Call Me	1971	—	2.50	5.00
❑ 47-9993	Welcome to My World/It Ain't No Big Thing	1971	—	2.50	5.00
❑ 48-0001	Bouquet of Roses/Texarkana Baby	1949	12.50	25.00	50.00
—Originals on green vinyl					
❑ 48-0001	Bouquet of Roses/Texarkana Baby	1949	6.25	12.50	25.00
—Second pressings: Green label, black vinyl					

Number	Title (A Side/B Side)	Yr	VG	VG+	NM
❑ 48-0001 [PS]	Bouquet of Roses/Texarkana Baby	1949	20.00	40.00	80.00
—Brown and dark brown title sleeve					
❑ 48-0002	Anytime/What a Fool I Was	1949	12.50	25.00	50.00
—Originals on green vinyl					
❑ 48-0002	Anytime/What a Fool I Was	1949	6.25	12.50	25.00
—Second pressings: Green label, black vinyl					
❑ 48-0016	I'm Thinking Tonight of My Blue Eyes/Rockin' Alone	1949	12.50	25.00	50.00
—Originals on green vinyl					
❑ 48-0016	I'm Thinking Tonight of My Blue Eyes/Rockin' Alone	1949	6.25	12.50	25.00
—Second pressings: Green label, black vinyl					
❑ 48-0017	It Makes No Difference Now/Molly Darling	1949	12.50	25.00	50.00
—Originals on green vinyl					
❑ 48-0017	It Makes No Difference Now/Molly Darling	1949	6.25	12.50	25.00
—Second pressings: Green label, black vinyl					
❑ 48-0018	The Prisoner's Song/Seven Years with the Wrong Woman	1949	12.50	25.00	50.00
—Originals on green vinyl					
❑ 48-0018	The Prisoner's Song/Seven Years with the Wrong Woman	1949	6.25	12.50	25.00
—Second pressings: Green label, black vinyl					
❑ 48-0019	Will the Circle Be Unbroken/Who at My Door Is Standing	1949	12.50	25.00	50.00
—Originals on green vinyl					
❑ 48-0019	Will the Circle Be Unbroken/Who at My Door Is Standing	1949	6.25	12.50	25.00
—Second pressings: Green label, black vinyl					
❑ 48-0025	A Heart Full of Love (For a Handful of Kisses)/ Then I Turned and Walked Slowly Away	1949	12.50	25.00	50.00
—Originals on green vinyl					
❑ 48-0025	A Heart Full of Love (For a Handful of Kisses)/ Then I Turned and Walked Slowly Away	1949	6.25	12.50	25.00
—Second pressings: Green label, black vinyl					
❑ 48-0026	Just a Little Lovin' (Will Go a Long, Long Way)/ My Daddy Is Only a Picture	1949	12.50	25.00	50.00
—Originals on green vinyl					
❑ 48-0026	Just a Little Lovin' (Will Go a Long, Long Way)/ My Daddy Is Only a Picture	1949	6.25	12.50	25.00
—Second pressings: Green label, black vinyl					
❑ 48-0030	I'll Hold You in My Heart (Till I Can Hold You in My Arms)/Don't Bother to Cry	1949	12.50	25.00	50.00
—Originals on green vinyl					
❑ 48-0030	I'll Hold You in My Heart (Till I Can Hold You in My Arms)/Don't Bother to Cry	1949	6.25	12.50	25.00
—Second pressings: Green label, black vinyl					
❑ 48-0042	There's Not a Thing (I Wouldn't Do for You)/Don't Rob Another Man's Castle	1949	12.50	25.00	50.00
—Originals on green vinyl					
❑ 48-0042	There's Not a Thing (I Wouldn't Do for You)/Don't Rob Another Man's Castle	1949	6.25	12.50	25.00
—Second pressings: Green label, black vinyl					
❑ 48-0080	I'm Throwing Rice (At the Girl That I Love)/Show Me the Way Back to Your Heart	1949	12.50	25.00	50.00
—Originals on green vinyl					
❑ 48-0080	I'm Throwing Rice (At the Girl That I Love)/Show Me the Way Back to Your Heart	1949	6.25	12.50	25.00
—Second pressings: Green label, black vinyl					
❑ 48-0083	One Kiss Too Many/The Echo of Your Footsteps	1949	12.50	25.00	50.00
—Originals on green vinyl					
❑ 48-0083	One Kiss Too Many/The Echo of Your Footsteps	1950	6.25	12.50	25.00
—Second pressings: Green label, black vinyl					
❑ 48-0127	C-H-R-I-S-T-M-A-S/Will Santa Come to Shanty Town	1949	12.50	25.00	50.00
—Originals on green vinyl					
❑ 48-0127	C-H-R-I-S-T-M-A-S/Will Santa Come to Shanty Town	1949	6.25	12.50	25.00
—Second pressings: Green label, black vinyl					
❑ 48-0136	The Nearest Thing to Heaven/The Cattle Call	1949	12.50	25.00	50.00
—Originals on green vinyl					
❑ 48-0136	The Nearest Thing to Heaven/The Cattle Call	1949	6.25	12.50	25.00
—Second pressings: Green label, black vinyl					
❑ 48-0137	There's No Wings on My Angel/You Know How Talk Gets Around	1949	12.50	25.00	50.00
—Originals on green vinyl					
❑ 48-0137	There's No Wings on My Angel/You Know How Talk Gets Around	1949	6.25	12.50	25.00
—Second pressings: Green label, black vinyl					
❑ 48-0138	Just a Little Lovin' (Will Go a Long, Long Way)/ I'm Throwing Rice (At the Girl That I Love)	1949	12.50	25.00	50.00
—Originals on green vinyl					
❑ 48-0138	Just a Little Lovin' (Will Go a Long, Long Way)/ I'm Throwing Rice (At the Girl That I Love)	1949	6.25	12.50	25.00
—Second pressings: Green label, black vinyl					
❑ 48-0150	Take Me in Your Arms and Hold Me/Mama and Daddy Broke My Heart	1949	12.50	25.00	50.00
—Originals on green vinyl					
❑ 48-0150	Take Me in Your Arms and Hold Me/Mama and Daddy Broke My Heart	1949	6.25	12.50	25.00
—Second pressings: Green label, black vinyl					
❑ 48-0165	The Lily of the Valley/Evil, Tempt Me Not	1950	12.50	25.00	50.00
—Originals on green vinyl					
❑ 48-0165	The Lily of the Valley/Evil, Tempt Me Not	1950	6.25	12.50	25.00
—Second pressings: Green label, black vinyl					
❑ 48-0166	When Jesus Beckons Me Home/Beautiful Isle	1950	12.50	25.00	50.00
—Originals on green vinyl					

Number	Title (A Side/B Side)	Yr	VG	VG+	NM
❑ 48-0166	When Jesus Beckons Me Home/Beautiful Isle	1950	6.25	12.50	25.00
—Second pressings: Green label, black vinyl					
❑ 48-0167	Hills of Tomorrow/Softly and Tenderly	1950	12.50	25.00	50.00
—Originals on green vinyl					
❑ 48-0167	Hills of Tomorrow/Softly and Tenderly	1950	6.25	12.50	25.00
—Second pressings: Green label, black vinyl					
❑ 48-0174	That Wonderful Mother of Mine/Mother	1950	12.50	25.00	50.00
—Originals on green vinyl					
❑ 48-0174	That Wonderful Mother of Mine/Mother	1950	6.25	12.50	25.00
—Second pressings: Green label, black vinyl					
❑ 48-0175	Bring Roses to Her Now/I Wish I Had a Girl	1950	12.50	25.00	50.00
—Originals on green vinyl					
❑ 48-0175	Bring Roses to Her Now/I Wish I Had a Girl	1950	6.25	12.50	25.00
—Second pressings: Green label, black vinyl					
❑ 48-0176	My Mother's Sweet Voice/I Wouldn't Trade the Silver	1950	12.50	25.00	50.00
—Originals on green vinyl					
❑ 48-0176	My Mother's Sweet Voice/I Wouldn't Trade the Silver	1950	6.25	12.50	25.00
—Second pressings: Green label, black vinyl					
❑ 48-0197	To My Sorrow/Easy Rockin' Chair	1950	12.50	25.00	50.00
—Originals on green vinyl					
❑ 48-0197	To My Sorrow/Easy Rockin' Chair	1950	6.25	12.50	25.00
—Second pressings: Green label, black vinyl					
❑ 48-0198	It's a Sin/I Couldn't Believe It Was True	1950	12.50	25.00	50.00
—Originals on green vinyl					
❑ 48-0198	It's a Sin/I Couldn't Believe It Was True	1950	6.25	12.50	25.00
—Second pressings: Green label, black vinyl					
❑ 48-0199	What Is Life Without Love/Be Sure There's No Mistake	1950	12.50	25.00	50.00
—Originals on green vinyl					
❑ 48-0199	What Is Life Without Love/Be Sure There's No Mistake	1950	6.25	12.50	25.00
—Second pressings: Green label, black vinyl					
❑ 48-0300	Little Angel with the Dirty Face/Why Should I Cry?	1950	12.50	25.00	50.00
—Originals on green vinyl					
❑ 48-0300	Little Angel with the Dirty Face/Why Should I Cry?	1950	6.25	12.50	25.00
—Second pressings: Green label, black vinyl					
❑ 48-0342	Cuddle Buggin' Baby/Enclosed, One Broken Heart	1950	12.50	25.00	50.00
—Originals on green vinyl					
❑ 48-0342	Cuddle Buggin' Baby/Enclosed, One Broken Heart	1950	6.25	12.50	25.00
—Second pressings: Green label, black vinyl					
❑ 48-0382	The Lovebug Itch/A Prison Without Walls	1950	12.50	25.00	50.00
—Originals on green vinyl					
❑ 48-0382	The Lovebug Itch/A Prison Without Walls	1950	6.25	12.50	25.00
—Second pressings: Green label, black vinyl					
❑ 48-0390	White Christmas/Santa Claus Is Comin' to Town	1950	12.50	25.00	50.00
—Originals on green vinyl					
❑ 48-0390	White Christmas/Santa Claus Is Comin' to Town	1950	6.25	12.50	25.00
—Second pressings: Green label, black vinyl					
❑ 48-0412	There's Been a Change in Me/Tie Me to Your Apron Strings Again	1950	12.50	25.00	50.00
—Originals on green vinyl					
❑ 48-0412	There's Been a Change in Me/Tie Me to Your Apron Strings Again	1950	6.25	12.50	25.00
—Second pressings: Green label, black vinyl					
❑ 48-0425	May the Good Lord Bless and Keep You/I'm Writing a Letter to the Lord	1951	12.50	25.00	50.00
—Originals on green vinyl					
❑ 48-0425	May the Good Lord Bless and Keep You/I'm Writing a Letter to the Lord	1951	5.00	10.00	20.00
—Second pressings: Green label, black vinyl					
❑ 48-0444	Kentucky Waltz/A Million Miles from Your Heart	1951	12.50	25.00	50.00
—Originals on green vinyl					
❑ 48-0444	Kentucky Waltz/A Million Miles from Your Heart	1951	5.00	10.00	20.00
—Second pressings: Green label, black vinyl					
❑ 48-0476	I Wanna Play House with You/Something Old, Something New	1951	6.25	12.50	25.00
❑ 48-0495	Jesus and the Atheist/He Knows	1951	6.25	12.50	25.00
❑ 74-0120	Please Don't Go/Heaven Below	1969	—	2.50	5.00
❑ 74-0175	But For Love/My Lady of Love	1969	—	2.50	5.00
❑ 74-0226	You Fool/You Don't Need Me Anymore	1969	—	2.50	5.00
❑ 74-0282	Since December/Morning of Our Mind	1969	—	2.50	5.00
❑ 74-0559	I Love You Dear/Long Life, Lots of Happiness	1971	—	2.50	5.00
❑ 74-0641	Lonely People/If It's Alright with You	1972	—	2.50	5.00
❑ 74-0705	Poison Red Berries/Just Out of Reach	1972	—	2.50	5.00
❑ 74-0747	Lucy/The Last Letter	1972	—	2.50	5.00
❑ 74-0842	An Angel Sleeps Beside Me/Sweet Bunch of Daisies	1972	—	—	—
—Unreleased					

Selected 78s

BLUEBIRD

Number	Title (A Side/B Side)	Yr	VG	VG+	NM
❑ 33-0520	Mother's Prayer/Mommie Please Stay Home with Me	1945	20.00	40.00	80.00
❑ 33-0527	Each Minute Seems Like a Million Years/The Cattle Call	1945	15.00	30.00	60.00
❑ 33-0535	Did You See My Daddy Over There?/I Walk Alone	1945	12.50	25.00	50.00
❑ 33-0540	Many Tears Ago/You Must Walk the Line	1946	12.50	25.00	50.00

RCA VICTOR

Number	Title (A Side/B Side)	Yr	VG	VG+	NM
❑ 20-1801	I Talk to Myself About You/(I'll Have to) Live and Learn	1946	10.00	20.00	40.00
❑ 20-1855	All Alone in This World Without You/Can't Win, Can't Place, Can't Show	1946	7.50	15.00	30.00
❑ 20-1871	Many Tears Ago/Mommie Please Stay Home with Me	1946	7.50	15.00	30.00
—Reissue of Bluebird sides					
❑ 20-1948	That's How Much I Love You/Chained to a Memory	1946	7.50	15.00	30.00
❑ 20-2058	What Is Life Without Love/Be Sure There's No Mistake	1947	5.00	10.00	20.00
❑ 20-2067	Each Minute Seems a Million Years/You Must Walk the Line	1947	5.00	10.00	20.00
—Reissue of Bluebird sides					
❑ 20-2128	Cattle Call/I Walk Alone	1947	5.00	10.00	20.00
—Reissue of Bluebird sides					
❑ 20-2241	It's a Sin/I Couldn't Believe It Was True	1947	3.75	7.50	15.00
❑ 20-2332	I'll Hold You in My Heart (Till I Can Hold You in My Arms)/Don't Bother to Cry	1947	3.75	7.50	15.00
❑ 20-2481	To My Sorrow/Easy Rocking Chair	1947	3.75	7.50	15.00
❑ 20-2488	Rockin' Alone (In an Old Rocking Chair)/I'm Thinking Tonight of My Blue Eyes	1947	3.00	6.00	12.00
❑ 20-2489	Molly Darling/It Makes No Difference Now	1947	3.00	6.00	12.00
❑ 20-2490	The Prisoner's Song/Seven Years with the Wrong Woman	1947	3.00	6.00	12.00
❑ 20-2491	Will the Circle Be Unbroken/Who at My Door Is Standing	1947	3.00	6.00	12.00
—The above four comprise album P-195, "All Time Hits from the Hills"					
❑ 20-2700	Anytime/What a Fool I Was	1948	3.00	6.00	12.00
❑ 20-2806	Bouquet of Roses/Texarkana Baby	1948	3.00	6.00	12.00
❑ 20-3013	Just a Little Lovin' (Will Go a Long, Long Way)/ My Daddy Is Only a Picture	1948	3.00	6.00	12.00
❑ 20-3174	A Heart Full of Love (For a Handful of Kisses)/ Then I Turned and Walked Slowly Away	1948	3.00	6.00	12.00
—All later 78s were released simultaneously (or nearly so) with the 45, though not always with the same number.					

7-Inch Extended Plays

RCA VICTOR

Number	Title (A Side/B Side)	Yr	VG	VG+	NM
❑ 547-0100	I'll Hold You in My Heart (Till I Can Hold You in My Arms)/A Heart Full of Love (For a Handful of Kisses)//Anytime/Texarkana Baby	1952	5.00	10.00	20.00
—Part of 2-EP set EPB-3027					
❑ EPA 260	The Cattle Call/The Nearest Thing to Heaven// I'm Throwing Rice (At the Girl That I Love)/Just a Little Lovin' (Will Go a Long, Long Way)	195?	5.00	10.00	20.00
❑ EPA 260 [PS]	Eddy Arnold Sings	195?	5.00	10.00	20.00
❑ EPB 3027 [PS]	Anytime (Country Classics)	1952	5.00	10.00	20.00
—Two-pocket jacket for two-EP set					

Albums

MGM

Number	Title	Yr	VG	VG+	NM
❑ SE-4878	If the World Stopped Loving	1973	3.00	6.00	12.00
❑ SE-4912	She's Got Everything I Need	1974	3.00	6.00	12.00
❑ SE-4916	I Wish I Had Loved You Better	1974	3.00	6.00	12.00
❑ MG-1-4992	The Wonderful World of Eddy Arnold	1975	3.00	6.00	12.00
❑ MJB-5107 [(2)]	World of Hits	1976	3.00	6.00	12.00

PAIR

Number	Title	Yr	VG	VG+	NM
❑ PDL2-1000 [(2)]	The Mellow Side of Eddy Arnold	1986	3.00	6.00	12.00

RCA

Number	Title	Yr	VG	VG+	NM
❑ 9963-1-R	Hand-Holdin' Songs	1990	3.75	7.50	15.00

RCA CAMDEN

Number	Title	Yr	VG	VG+	NM
❑ CAL-471 [M]	Eddy Arnold (That's How Much I Love You)	1959	5.00	10.00	20.00
❑ CAS-471(e) [R]	Eddy Arnold (That's How Much I Love You)	1966	2.50	5.00	10.00
❑ CAL-563 [M]	More Eddy Arnold	1960	5.00	10.00	20.00
❑ CAS-563(e) [R]	More Eddy Arnold	1966	2.50	5.00	10.00
❑ CAL-741 [M]	Country Songs I Love to Sing	1963	3.75	7.50	15.00
❑ CAS-741(e) [R]	Country Songs I Love to Sing	1966	2.50	5.00	10.00
❑ CAL-799 [M]	Eddy's Songs	1964	3.75	7.50	15.00
❑ CAS-799(e) [R]	Eddy's Songs	1966	2.50	5.00	10.00
❑ CAL-897 [M]	I'm Throwing Rice (At the Girl That I Love) And Other Favorites	1966	3.75	7.50	15.00
❑ CAS-897(e) [R]	I'm Throwing Rice (At the Girl That I Love) And Other Favorites	1966	2.50	5.00	10.00

RCA VICTOR

Number	Title	Yr	VG	VG+	NM
❑ APL1-0239	The World of Eddy Arnold	1973	3.00	6.00	12.00
❑ PRS-346	Christmas with Eddy Arnold	1971	3.75	7.50	15.00
—Special-products issue					
❑ ANL1-1078	Pure Gold	1975	2.50	5.00	10.00
❑ LPM-1111 [M]	Wanderin' with Eddy Arnold	1955	12.50	25.00	50.00
❑ LPM-1223 [M]	All-Time Favorites	1955	12.50	25.00	50.00
—New version of LPM 3117					
❑ LPM-1224 [M]	Anytime	1955	12.50	25.00	50.00
—New version of LPM 3027					
❑ LPM-1225 [M]	The Chapel on the Hill	1955	12.50	25.00	50.00
—New version of LPM 3031					
❑ LPM-1293 [M]	A Dozen Hits	1956	12.50	25.00	50.00
❑ LPM-1377 [M]	A Little on the Lonely Side	1956	12.50	25.00	50.00
❑ LPM-1484 [M]	When They Were Young	1956	12.50	25.00	50.00
❑ LPM-1575 [M]	My Darling, My Darling	1957	10.00	20.00	40.00
❑ LPM-1733 [M]	Praise Him, Praise Him	1958	10.00	20.00	40.00
❑ APL1-1817	Eddy	1976	3.00	6.00	12.00
❑ LPM-1928 [M]	Have Guitar, Will Travel	1959	6.25	12.50	25.00
❑ LSP-1928 [S]	Have Guitar, Will Travel	1959	7.50	15.00	30.00
❑ LPM-2036 [M]	Threrby Hangs a Tale	1959	6.25	12.50	25.00
❑ LSP-2036 [S]	Threrby Hangs a Tale	1959	7.50	15.00	30.00
❑ LPM-2185 [M]	Eddy Arnold Sings Them Again	1960	6.25	12.50	25.00
❑ LSP-2185 [S]	Eddy Arnold Sings Them Again	1960	7.50	15.00	30.00
❑ LPM-2268 [M]	You Gotta Have Love	1960	6.25	12.50	25.00
❑ LSP-2268 [S]	You Gotta Have Love	1960	7.50	15.00	30.00
❑ APL1-2277	I Need You All the Time	1977	3.00	6.00	12.00

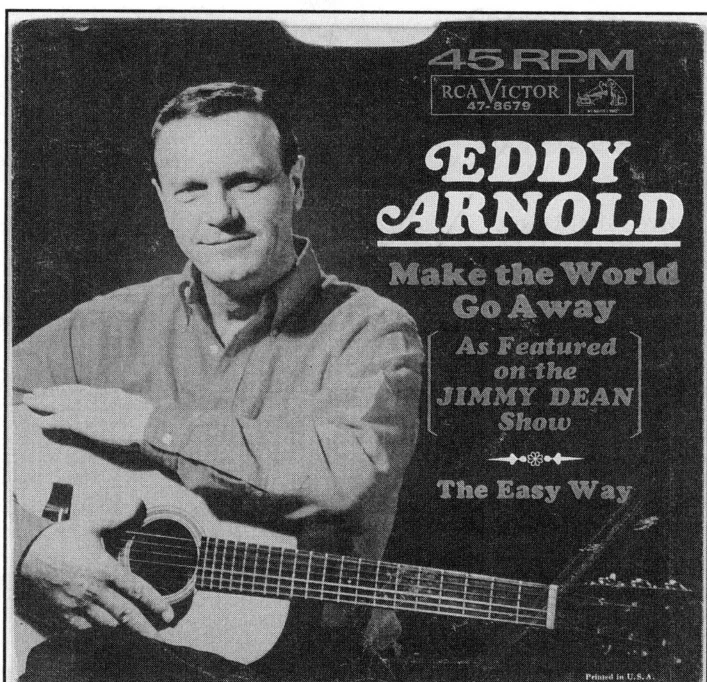

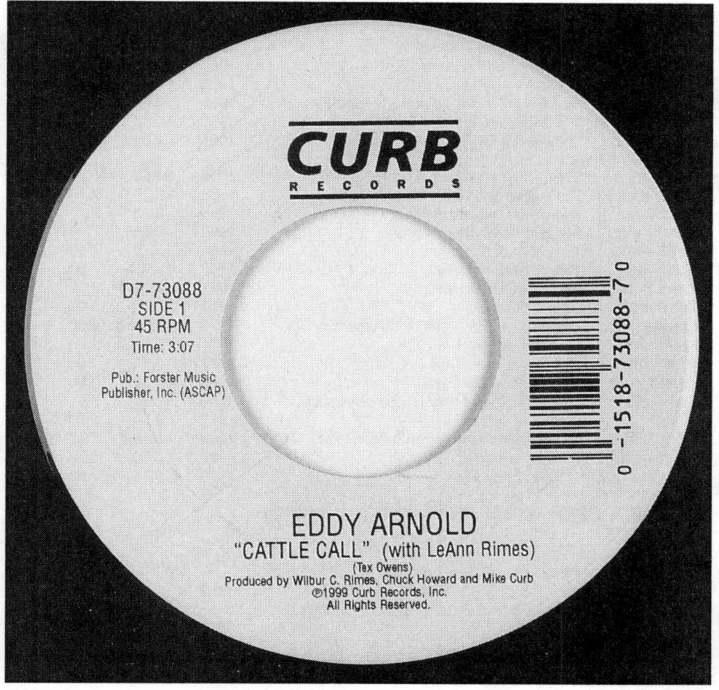

Eddy Arnold remains, even today, the most successful singles artist in the history of the *Billboard* charts. His music has made the charts in seven different decades! (Top left) "Bouquet of Roses" spent 19 weeks at the top in 1948, spent over a year on the charts, is generally believed to have sold a million singles, and was honored as the first country release (48-0001) when RCA introduced 45 rpm records on March 31, 1949. (Top right) An even bigger hit, based on weeks on top, was the often-remade "I'll Hold You in My Heart (Till I Can Hold You in My Arms)." In 1947, it spent 21 weeks – almost half a year! – at No. 1. It was the first of an amazing string in which an Arnold song was on top for almost a full year without interruption! (Bottom left) When "Make the World Go Away" made the top 10 on the pop charts in 1965, as it was topping the country charts, it was Arnold's first Top 20 pop hit since 1949. (Bottom right) During the first week of 2000, Arnold's new recording of his classic "Cattle Call" with LeAnn Rimes made the country sales charts, thus giving him a 55-year span of hits.

Number	Title (A Side/B Side)	Yr	VG	VG+	NM
❑ LPM-2337 [M]	Let's Make Memories Tonight	1961	5.00	10.00	20.00
❑ LSP-2337 [S]	Let's Make Memories Tonight	1961	6.25	12.50	25.00
❑ LPM-2471 [M]	One More Time	1961	5.00	10.00	20.00
❑ LSP-2471 [S]	One More Time	1961	6.25	12.50	25.00
❑ LPM-2554 [M]	Christmas with Eddy Arnold	1962	5.00	10.00	20.00
❑ LSP-2554 [S]	Christmas with Eddy Arnold	1962	6.25	12.50	25.00
❑ LPM-2578 [M]	Cattle Call	1962	6.25	12.50	25.00
❑ LSP-2578 [S]	Cattle Call	1962	7.50	15.00	30.00
❑ LPM-2596 [M]	Our Man Down South	1962	6.25	12.50	25.00
❑ LSP-2596 [S]	Our Man Down South	1962	7.50	15.00	30.00
❑ LPM-2629 [M]	Faithfully Yours	1963	6.25	12.50	25.00
❑ LSP-2629 [S]	Faithfully Yours	1963	7.50	15.00	30.00
❑ LPM-2811 [M]	Folk Song Book	1964	5.00	10.00	20.00
❑ LSP-2811 [S]	Folk Song Book	1964	6.25	12.50	25.00
❑ LPM-2909 [M]	Sometimes I'm Happy, Sometimes I'm Blue	1964	5.00	10.00	20.00
❑ LSP-2909 [S]	Sometimes I'm Happy, Sometimes I'm Blue	1964	6.25	12.50	25.00
❑ LPM-2951 [M]	Pop Hits from the Country Side	1964	5.00	10.00	20.00
❑ LSP-2951 [S]	Pop Hits from the Country Side	1964	6.25	12.50	25.00
❑ LPM-3027 [10]	Anytime	1952	30.00	60.00	120.00
—Label calls this "Country Classics"					
❑ LPM-3031 [10]	All-Time Hits from the Hills	1952	25.00	50.00	100.00
❑ LPM-3117 [10]	All-Time Favorites	1953	25.00	50.00	100.00
❑ LPM-3219 [10]	The Chapel on the Hill	1954	25.00	50.00	100.00
❑ LPM-3230	An American Institution Booklet	1954	12.50	25.00	50.00
❑ LPM-3230 [10]	An American Institution	1954	25.00	50.00	100.00
❑ AHL1-3358	Somebody	1979	2.50	5.00	10.00
❑ LPM-3361 [M]	The Easy Way	1965	3.75	7.50	15.00
❑ LSP-3361 [S]	The Easy Way	1965	5.00	10.00	20.00
❑ LPM-3466 [M]	My World	1965	3.00	6.00	12.00
❑ LSP-3466 [S]	My World	1965	3.75	7.50	15.00
❑ LPM-3507 [M]	I Want to Go with You	1966	3.00	6.00	12.00
❑ LSP-3507 [S]	I Want to Go with You	1966	3.75	7.50	15.00
❑ LPM-3565 [M]	The Best of Eddy Arnold	1967	5.00	10.00	20.00
❑ LSP-3565 [S]	The Best of Eddy Arnold	1967	3.75	7.50	15.00
❑ AHL1-3606	A Legend and His Lady	1980	2.50	5.00	10.00
❑ LPM-3622 [M]	The Last Word in Lonesome	1966	3.00	6.00	12.00
❑ LSP-3622 [S]	The Last Word in Lonesome	1966	3.75	7.50	15.00
❑ AYL1-3675	The Best of Eddy Arnold	1980	2.00	4.00	8.00
—"Best Buy Series" reissue					
❑ LPM-3715 [M]	Somebody Like Me	1966	3.00	6.00	12.00
❑ LSP-3715 [S]	Somebody Like Me	1966	3.75	7.50	15.00
❑ LPM-3753 [M]	Lonely Again	1967	5.00	10.00	20.00
❑ LSP-3753 [S]	Lonely Again	1967	3.75	7.50	15.00
❑ LPM-3869 [M]	Turn the World Around	1967	5.00	10.00	20.00
❑ LSP-3869 [S]	Turn the World Around	1967	3.75	7.50	15.00
❑ AHL1-3914	A Man for All Seasons	1980	2.50	5.00	10.00
❑ LPM-3931 [M]	The Everlovin' World of Eddy Arnold	1968	10.00	20.00	40.00
❑ LSP-3931 [S]	The Everlovin' World of Eddy Arnold	1968	3.75	7.50	15.00
❑ AYL1-3937	The Best of Eddy Arnold, Volume II	1981	2.00	4.00	8.00
—"Best Buy Series" reissue					
❑ LPM-4009 [M]	The Romantic World of Eddy Arnold	1968	37.50	75.00	150.00
❑ LSP-4009 [S]	The Romantic World of Eddy Arnold	1968	3.75	7.50	15.00
❑ LSP-4089	Walkin' in Love Land	1968	3.75	7.50	15.00
❑ LSP-4110	Songs of the Young World	1969	3.75	7.50	15.00
❑ LSP-4179	The Glory of Love	1969	3.75	7.50	15.00
❑ LSP-4231	The Warmth of Eddy	1969	3.75	7.50	15.00
❑ AHL1-4263	Don't Give Up on Me	1981	2.50	5.00	10.00
❑ LSP-4304	Love & Guitars	1970	3.00	6.00	12.00
❑ LSP-4320	The Best of Eddy Arnold, Volume II	1970	3.00	6.00	12.00
❑ LSP-4471	Portrait of My Woman	1971	3.00	6.00	12.00
❑ LSP-4625	Loving Her Was Easier	1971	3.00	6.00	12.00
❑ AHL1-4661	Close Enough to Love	1983	2.50	5.00	10.00
❑ LSP-4738	Eddy Arnold Sings for Housewives and Other Ladies	1972	3.00	6.00	12.00
❑ CPL2-4885 [(2)]	The Legendary Performances (1945-1971)	1983	3.00	6.00	12.00
❑ AHL1-5467	Collector's Series	1985	2.50	5.00	10.00
❑ VPS-6032 [(2)]	This Is Eddy Arnold	1972	3.75	7.50	15.00

ARNOLD, EDDY & JO ANN

45s

RCA VICTOR

Number	Title (A Side/B Side)	Yr	VG	VG+	NM
❑ 490	A Present For Santa Claus/Sittin' On Santa Claus' Lap	195?	—	2.50	5.00
❑ 490 [PS]	A Present For Santa Claus/Sittin' On Santa Claus' Lap	195?	—	2.50	5.00

ARNOLD, RICK

45s

LYNN

Number	Title (A Side/B Side)	Yr	VG	VG+	NM
❑ 51088	I Must Be Dreaming/(B-side unknown)	1989	—	3.00	6.00

ASHLEY, LEON

45s

ASHLEY

Number	Title (A Side/B Side)	Yr	VG	VG+	NM
❑ 22	Ain't Gonna Worry/Illusions of Life	1969	2.50	5.00	10.00
❑ 100	Our Old Love Song/She Picked Me Up	197?	2.00	4.00	8.00
❑ 350	If Love Had Died/How Can We Divide These Little Hearts	197?	2.00	4.00	8.00
❑ 764	The Weakness of a Man/Most Men	197?	2.00	4.00	8.00
❑ 768	Before You Were Mine/Su-Sow	197?	2.00	4.00	8.00
❑ 2003	Laura (What's He Got That I Ain't Got)/With the Help of the Wine	1967	2.50	5.00	10.00
❑ 2025	Anna, I'm Taking You Home/Curtain of Sadness	1967	2.50	5.00	10.00
❑ 2075	Mental Journey/All I Can Stand	1968	2.50	5.00	10.00
❑ 4000	Flower of Love/Prayers Can't Reach Me	1968	2.50	5.00	10.00
❑ 7000	While Your Lover Sleeps/That's Alright	1968	2.50	5.00	10.00
❑ 7600	I'll Be There/If I See Over the Mountain	197?	2.00	4.00	8.00
❑ 7876	Losing Man/There Ain't No Easy Way	197?	2.00	4.00	8.00
❑ 7996	There's Not a Single Thing/Before the Next Teardrop Falls	197?	2.00	4.00	8.00
❑ 9000	Walkin' Back to Birmingham/It's All Over But the Crying	1969	2.50	5.00	10.00
❑ 35001	A Life for a Wife/The Bees Are Making Honey	197?	—	3.00	6.00
❑ 35003	Tell Him Daddy Said Hello/Brace Up and Face It	197?	—	3.00	6.00
❑ 35005	Mama's Ten/Keeping Her Memory Alive	197?	—	3.00	6.00
❑ 35008	There Ain't No Easy Way/Losing Man	197?	—	3.00	6.00
❑ 35010	Ease Up/Until Dawn	197?	—	3.00	6.00
❑ 35011	Not a Single Thing About Her (That I'd Change)/Before the Next Teardrop Falls	197?	—	3.00	6.00
❑ 35013	Love Fits Me Better/Off and Running	197?	—	3.00	6.00

DOT

Number	Title (A Side/B Side)	Yr	VG	VG+	NM
❑ 16649	You Gave Me a Reason to Live/You've Got a Heartbreak	1964	3.75	7.50	15.00

GOLDBAND

Number	Title (A Side/B Side)	Yr	VG	VG+	NM
❑ 1104	He'll Never Go/If I Were King of the Universe	1960	6.25	12.50	25.00

IMPERIAL

Number	Title (A Side/B Side)	Yr	VG	VG+	NM
❑ 5795	It's Alright Baby/Court of Two Sisters	1961	5.00	10.00	20.00

Albums

RCA VICTOR

Number	Title (A Side/B Side)	Yr	VG	VG+	NM
❑ LPM-3900 [M]	Laura (What's He Got That I Ain't Got)	1967	7.50	15.00	30.00
❑ LSP-3900 [S]	Laura (What's He Got That I Ain't Got)	1967	5.00	10.00	20.00

ASHLEY, LEON, AND MARGIE SINGLETON

Also see each artist's individual listings.

45s

ASHLEY

Number	Title (A Side/B Side)	Yr	VG	VG+	NM
❑ 600	Dear Willie (Letter from Leach)/Laura	197?	2.00	4.00	8.00
❑ 700	Love Me or Leave Me (For Love to Find)/Here We Go Again	197?	2.00	4.00	8.00
❑ 702	Can You Live with the Way/Watching Your Memory Grow	197?	2.00	4.00	8.00
❑ 2015	Hangin' On/Four O'Clock	1967	2.50	5.00	10.00
❑ 3000	You'll Never Be Lonely Again/Parting of the Ways	1968	2.50	5.00	10.00
❑ 8000	Love Me or Leave Me (For Love to Find)/Here We Go Again	1969	2.50	5.00	10.00

MONUMENT

Number	Title (A Side/B Side)	Yr	VG	VG+	NM
❑ 990	If Love Has Died/How Can We Divide These Little Hearts	1966	3.00	6.00	12.00

ASHTON, SUSAN

45s

CAPITOL NASHVILLE

Number	Title (A Side/B Side)	Yr	VG	VG+	NM
❑ 58757	Faith of the Heart/Spinning Like a Wheel	1999	—	—	3.00
❑ 58787	You're Lucky I Love You/Think of Me	1999	—	—	3.00

ASHWORTH, ERNEST

Also includes records as "Ernie Ashworth."

45s

DECCA

Number	Title (A Side/B Side)	Yr	VG	VG+	NM
❑ 31085	Each Moment (Spent with You)/Night Time Is Cry Time	1960	3.00	6.00	12.00
❑ 31156	You Can't Pick a Rose in December/You'll Hear My Heart Break	1960	3.00	6.00	12.00
❑ 31237	Forever Gone/Life of the Party	1961	3.00	6.00	12.00
❑ 31292	Be Mine Again/No Room Left for Me	1961	3.00	6.00	12.00

HICKORY

Number	Title (A Side/B Side)	Yr	VG	VG+	NM
❑ 1170	Everybody But Me/(I Just Spent) Another Sleepless Night	1962	2.50	5.00	10.00
❑ 1189	I Take the Chance/King of the Blues	1962	2.50	5.00	10.00
❑ 1214	Talk Back Trembling Lips/That's How Much I Care	1963	3.00	6.00	12.00
❑ 1237	A Week in the Country/Heartbreak Avenue	1964	2.50	5.00	10.00
❑ 1265	I Love to Dance with Annie/My Heart Would Know	1964	2.50	5.00	10.00
❑ 1281	Pushed in a Corner/Gooder Than Good	1964	2.50	5.00	10.00
❑ 1304	Because I Cared/Love Has Come My Way	1965	2.50	5.00	10.00
❑ 1325	The D.J. Cried/Scene of Destruction	1965	2.50	5.00	10.00
❑ 1358	I Wish/Crazy Me, Foolish You	1966	2.50	5.00	10.00
❑ 1400	At Ease Heart/The Nearest Thing to Heaven	1966	2.50	5.00	10.00
❑ 1428	Sad Face/I'm from Missouri	1966	2.50	5.00	10.00
❑ 1445	Just an Empty Place/Just One Time	1967	2.50	5.00	10.00
❑ 1466	My Love for You (Is Like a Mountain Range)/You're Tearing My Heart Out	1967	2.50	5.00	10.00
❑ 1484	Tender and True/Back on My Mind Again	1967	2.50	5.00	10.00
❑ 1503	A New Heart/The Next Ones (You Love)	1968	2.50	5.00	10.00
❑ 1513	I Feel Better (Than I Meant To)/You Don't Have to Be an Angel Anymore	1968	2.50	5.00	10.00
❑ 1528	Where Do You Go (When You Don't Go with Me)/Hocus-Pocus	1969	2.50	5.00	10.00
❑ 1538	Love, I Finally Found It/King of the Blues	1969	2.50	5.00	10.00
❑ 1549	The Joker's Gonna Cry/Talk Back Trembling Lips	1969	2.50	5.00	10.00
❑ 1570	That Look of Good-Bye/A Woman's Touch	1970	2.50	5.00	10.00
❑ 1580	Let's Start Talking Before Her Feet Start Walking/My Heart Would Know	1970	2.50	5.00	10.00
❑ 1599	She's Love/Jesus Is a Soul Man	1971	2.00	4.00	8.00
❑ 1609	Another Sleepless Night/Bottle of Blues	1971	2.00	4.00	8.00
❑ 1620	Wanted Man/I Love to Dance with Annie	1972	2.00	4.00	8.00
❑ 1647	Dreaming Again/I Wish	1972	2.00	4.00	8.00

Number	Title (A Side/B Side)	Yr	VG	VG+	NM
O'BRIEN					
❑ 320	Little Rosa/Each Moment Spent with You.	197?	2.00	4.00	8.00
❑ 322	This Ole Boy Ain't Gonna Walk Your Line/Each Moment Spent with You	197?	2.00	4.00	8.00
❑ 325	Catfish and Bones/Memphis Memory	197?	2.00	4.00	8.00
❑ 327	Irene/The Beginning of the End	197?	2.00	4.00	8.00
Albums					
HICKORY					
❑ LPM-118 [M]	Hits of Today and Tomorrow	1964	6.25	12.50	25.00

ASLEEP AT THE WHEEL

Also see RAY BENSON.

Number	Title (A Side/B Side)	Yr	VG	VG+	NM
45s					
ARISTA					
❑ 2045	Keepin' Me Up Nights/Pedernales Stroll	1990	—	—	3.00
❑ 2122	That's the Way Love Is/Beat Me, Daddy (Eight to the Bar)	1990	—	—	3.00
❑ 2178	Dance With Who Brung You/Quittin' Time	1991	—	—	3.00
CAPITOL					
❑ 4115	The Letter That Johnny Walker Read/(B-side unknown)	1975	—	2.50	5.00
❑ 4187	Bump Bounce Boogie/Fat Boy Rag	1975	—	2.50	5.00
❑ 4238	Nothin' Takes the Place of You/Tonight the Bartender Is on the Wrong Side of the Bar	1976	—	2.50	5.00
❑ 4319	Route 66/Shout Wa Hey	1976	—	2.50	5.00
❑ 4357	Miles and Miles of Texas/Blues for Dixie	1976	—	2.50	5.00
❑ 4393	The Trouble with Lovin' Today/Ragtime Annie	1977	—	2.50	5.00
❑ 4438	Somebody Stole His Body/Let's Face Up	1977	—	2.50	5.00
❑ 4601	Ghost Dancer/Louisiana	1978	—	2.50	5.00
❑ 4659	Texas Me & You/One O'Clock Jump	1978	—	2.50	5.00
❑ 4725	Choo Choo Ch'Boogie/Too Many Bad Habits	1979	—	2.50	5.00
CAPITOL NASHVILLE					
❑ S7-18844	Lay Down Sally/Hightower	1995	—	2.00	4.00
EPIC					
❑ 06671	Way Down Texas Way/String of Pars	1987	—	—	3.00
❑ 06671 [PS]	Way Down Texas Way/String of Pars	1987	—	2.00	4.00
❑ 07125	House of Blue Lights/Big Foot Stomp	1987	—	—	3.00
❑ 07610	Boogie Back to Texas/(B-side unknown)	1987	—	—	3.00
❑ 07659	Blowin' Like a Bandit/String of Pars	1987	—	—	3.00
❑ 07966	Walk On By/Sugarfoot Rag	1988	—	—	3.00
❑ 08087	Hot Rod Lincoln/String of Pars	1988	—	—	3.00
❑ 08461	House of Blue Lights/Blowin' Like a Bandit	1988	—	—	3.00
—Reissue					
❑ 50045	Choo Choo Ch'Boogie/Our Names Aren't Mentioned	1974	—	2.50	5.00
❑ 68620	Chattanooga Choo Choo/Sugarfoot Rag	1989	—	—	3.00
LIBERTY					
❑ S7-17715	Red Wing/Bring It On Down to My House	1993	—	2.00	4.00
❑ S7-17970	Blues for Dixie/Got a Letter from My Kid Today	1993	—	2.00	4.00
MCA					
❑ 51020	Cool as a Breeze/Don't Get Caught Out in the Rain	1980	—	2.00	4.00
UNITED ARTISTS					
❑ XW-245	Take Me Back to Tulsa/Before You Stop Loving Me	1973	—	3.00	6.00
❑ XW-344	Daddy's Advice/Drivin' Nails in My Coffin	1973	—	3.00	6.00
Albums					
ARISTA					
❑ AL-8550	Keepin' Me Up Nights	1990	3.00	6.00	12.00
CAPITOL					
❑ ST-11441	Texas Gold	1975	3.00	6.00	12.00
❑ ST-11548	Wheelin' and Dealin'	1976	3.00	6.00	12.00
❑ ST-11620	The Wheel	1977	3.00	6.00	12.00
❑ SW-11726	Collision Course	1978	3.00	6.00	12.00
❑ ST-11945	Served Live	1979	3.00	6.00	12.00
❑ SN-16306	Served Live	1984	2.00	4.00	8.00
—Budget-line reissue					
CAPITOL SPECIAL MARKETS					
❑ SL-8138	Drivin'	1980	3.00	6.00	12.00
DOT/MCA					
❑ 39036	Asleep at the Wheel	1985	2.50	5.00	10.00
EPIC					
❑ KE 33097	Asleep at the Wheel	1974	3.75	7.50	15.00
❑ PE 33097	Asleep at the Wheel	197?	2.00	4.00	8.00
—Reissue					
❑ BG 33782 [(2)]	Fathers and Sons	1974	6.25	12.50	25.00
—With Bob Wills					
❑ EG 33782 [(2)]	Fathers and Sons	197?	3.00	6.00	12.00
—Reissue					
❑ BFE 40681	10	1987	2.00	4.00	8.00
❑ FE 44213	Western Standard Time	1988	2.00	4.00	8.00
LIBERTY					
❑ LN-10296	Comin' Right At Ya!	1986	2.00	4.00	8.00
—Budget-line reissue					
MCA					
❑ 742	Framed	1982	2.00	4.00	8.00
—Reissue of 5131					
❑ 5131	Framed	1980	2.50	5.00	10.00
UNITED ARTISTS					
❑ UA-LA038-F	Comin' Right At Ya!	1973	5.00	10.00	20.00

ATCHER, BOB

Number	Title (A Side/B Side)	Yr	VG	VG+	NM
45s					
CAPITOL					
❑ F975	Smoke Comes Out My Chimney/Ain't You Ashamed	1950	6.25	12.50	25.00
❑ F1007	My Pillow Knows/One Kind Word	1950	6.25	12.50	25.00
❑ F1147	Guilty Conscience/Walk Chicken Walk	1950	6.25	12.50	25.00
❑ F1258	Blue Christmas/Christmas Island	1950	6.25	12.50	25.00
❑ F1364	Chain Around My Heart/Peek-a-Boo	1951	5.00	10.00	20.00
COLUMBIA					
❑ 2-310 (?)	Nightingale/I'll Remember You in My Prayers	1949	10.00	20.00	40.00
—Microgroove 7-inch 33 1/3 rpm single					
❑ 2-320 (?)	Why Don't You Haul Off and Love Me/Warm Red Wine	1949	10.00	20.00	40.00
—Microgroove 7-inch 33 1/3 rpm single					
❑ 2-460 (?)	I Can't Think of Love Without You/To Make You Mine	1949	10.00	20.00	40.00
—Microgroove 7-inch 33 1/3 rpm single					
❑ 4-43193	I'm Thinking Tonight of My Blue Eyes/Old Fiddler Joe	1964	2.50	5.00	10.00
❑ 4-43365	Flash Flood/Indoor Plumbing	1965	2.50	5.00	10.00
❑ 4-43524	Buck Private's Lament/Foreclose on a Mortgage	1966	2.50	5.00	10.00
Selected 78s					
COLUMBIA					
❑ 20024	I Must Have Been Wrong/I Want to Be Wanted	1948	3.00	6.00	12.00
—Reissue of 36983					
❑ 20083	Long Gone Baby/One Little Teardrop Too Late	1948	3.00	6.00	12.00
—Reissue of 37173					
❑ 20115	Long Road Ahead/I Traded In My Heart for a Tear	1948	3.00	6.00	12.00
—Reissue of 37326					
❑ 20134	Pins and Needles/Time Alone	1948	3.00	6.00	12.00
—Reissue of 37???					
❑ 20136	Sorrow on My Mind/Why Should I Cry Over You	1948	3.00	6.00	12.00
—Reissue of 37???					
❑ 20138	Don't Let Your Sweet Love Die/Honest I Do	1948	3.00	6.00	12.00
—Reissue of 37???					
❑ 20145	In the Echo of My Heart/Let's Tell Our Dream to the Moon	1948	3.00	6.00	12.00
—Reissue of 37418					
❑ 20159	Walking the Floor Over You/Sweethearts or Strangers	1948	3.00	6.00	12.00
—Reissue of 37???					
❑ 20170	Crying Song/You Love Me Or You Don't	1948	3.00	6.00	12.00
—Reissue of 37443					
❑ 20248	She's Not My Curly Headed Baby/I Dream of Your Bonnie Blue Eyes	1948	3.00	6.00	12.00
—Reissue of 37649					
❑ 20328	Now I Know Somebody Doesn't Care/I Won't Care	1948	3.00	6.00	12.00
—Reissue of 37751					
❑ 20330	A Face I See at Evening/You Waited Too Long	1948	3.00	6.00	12.00
—Reissue of 37753					
❑ 20332	No One to Kiss Me Goodnight/We Never Dream the Same Dream Twice	1948	3.00	6.00	12.00
—Reissue of 37???					
❑ 20354	Cool Water/Pennsylvania Pal	1948	3.00	6.00	12.00
—Reissue of 37815					
❑ 20363	On Account of You/Wasted Tears	1948	3.00	6.00	12.00
—Reissue of 37878					
❑ 20379	I Don't Want Nobody/I'll Never Grow Too Old to Love You	1948	3.00	6.00	12.00
—Reissue of 37944					
❑ 20382	Don't Give Your Heart/Never Trust a Woman	1948	3.00	6.00	12.00
—Reissue of 37958					
❑ 20393	Signed, Sealed and Delivered/Mountain Maw	1948	3.00	6.00	12.00
—Reissue of 37991					
❑ 20410	Down with the Feminine Gender/Your Broken Vow	1948	3.00	6.00	12.00
—Reissue of 38132					
❑ 20468	In My Heart/Time Will Tell	1948	3.75	7.50	15.00
❑ 20527	Nobody Knows But Me and You/Now That You're Gone	1948	3.75	7.50	15.00
❑ 20538	Blue Tail Fly/Foggy Foggy Dew	1948	3.75	7.50	15.00
❑ 20556	Money, Marbles and Chalk/Smiling with a Broken Heart	1949	3.75	7.50	15.00
❑ 20557	Tennessee Border/Don't Rob Another Man's Castle	1949	3.75	7.50	15.00
❑ 36983	I Must Have Been Wrong/I Want to Be Wanted	1946	3.75	7.50	15.00
❑ 37173	Long Gone Baby/One Little Teardrop Too Late	1946	3.75	7.50	15.00
❑ 37326	Long Road Ahead/I Traded In My Heart for a Tear	1947	3.75	7.50	15.00
❑ 37418	In the Echo of My Heart/Let's Tell Our Dream to the Moon	1947	3.75	7.50	15.00
❑ 37443	Crying Song/You Love Me Or You Don't	1947	3.75	7.50	15.00
❑ 37649	She's Not My Curly Headed Baby/I Dream of Your Bonnie Blue Eyes	1947	3.75	7.50	15.00
❑ 37751	Now I Know Somebody Doesn't Care/I Won't Care	1947	3.75	7.50	15.00
❑ 37753	A Face I See at Evening/You Waited Too Long	1947	3.75	7.50	15.00
❑ 37815	Cool Water/Pennsylvania Pal	1947	3.75	7.50	15.00
❑ 37878	On Account of You/Wasted Tears	1947	3.75	7.50	15.00
❑ 37944	I Don't Want Nobody/I'll Never Grow Too Old to Love You	1947	3.75	7.50	15.00
❑ 37958	Don't Give Your Heart/Never Trust a Woman	1947	3.75	7.50	15.00
❑ 37991	Signed, Sealed and Delivered/Mountain Maw	1947	3.75	7.50	15.00
❑ 38132	Down with the Feminine Gender/Your Broken Vow	1948	4.50	9.00	18.00

Number	Title (A Side/B Side)	Yr	VG	VG+	NM
OKEH					
❑ 6689	Pins and Needles/Time Alone	1943	5.00	10.00	20.00

ATKINS, BIG BEN

45s

Number	Title (A Side/B Side)	Yr	VG	VG+	NM
GRT					
❑ 161	We Don't Live Here, We Just Love Here/Baby Blue Eyes	1978	—	2.50	5.00

ATKINS, CHET

Also see SUZY BOGGUSS.

45s

Number	Title (A Side/B Side)	Yr	VG	VG+	NM
COLUMBIA					
❑ AE7 1776 [DJ]	East Tennessee Christmas/Winter Wonderland	1983	—	2.00	4.00
❑ 03984	Run Don't Walk/Walk Me Home	1983	—	—	3.00
❑ 04859	The Boot and the Stone/Sunrise	1985	—	—	3.00
❑ 05662	Please Stay Tuned/Some Leather and Lace	1985	—	—	3.00
❑ 06165	The Official Beach Music/Alicia	1986	—	—	3.00
❑ 07929	I Still Can't Say Goodbye/The Mockingbird	1988	—	—	3.00
RCA					
❑ PB-10902	La Chicana/Four in the Morning	1977	—	2.00	4.00
—With Danny Davis and Floyd Cramer					
❑ PB-11071	Me and My Guitar/Cascade	1977	—	2.00	4.00
❑ PB-11892	Blind Willie/Dance with Me	1980	—	2.00	4.00
❑ PB-12064	I Can Hear Kentucky Calling Me/Strawberry Man	1980	—	2.00	4.00
❑ PB-12263	Orange Blossom Special/Ready for the Times to Get Better	1981	—	2.00	4.00
RCA VICTOR					
❑ APBO-0146	Fiddlin' Around/Paramaribo	1973	—	2.00	4.00
❑ PB-10046	The Entertainer/Dizzy Fingers	1974	—	2.00	4.00
❑ PB-10346	The Night Atlanta Burned/Old Folks of Okracoke	1975	—	2.00	4.00
—As "The Atkins String Co."					
❑ PB-10448	Sonora/Mostly Mozart	1975	—	2.00	4.00
—As "The Atkins String Co."					
❑ PB-10614	Frog Kissin'/Bill Cheatham	1976	—	2.00	4.00
❑ 47-4377	In the Mood/Sweet Bunch of Daisies	1951	6.25	12.50	25.00
❑ 47-4491	Goodbye Blues/Rainbow	1952	6.25	12.50	25.00
❑ 47-4684	Spanish Fandango/Your Mean Little Heart	1952	6.25	12.50	25.00
❑ 47-4896	Meet Mr. Callaghan/Chinatown, My Chinatown	1952	6.25	12.50	25.00
❑ 47-4922	Gallopin' on the Guitar/(B-side unknown)	1952	6.25	12.50	25.00
❑ 47-4931	Tennessee Rag/My Little Girl	1952	6.25	12.50	25.00
❑ 47-5010	Midnight/Rustic Dance	1952	6.25	12.50	25.00
❑ 47-5100	Guitar Polka/Dream Train	1952	5.00	10.00	20.00
—With Rosalie Allen					
❑ 47-5181	Fig Leaf Rag/High Rockin' Swing	1953	5.00	10.00	20.00
❑ 47-5300	Country Gentlemen/The Bells of St. Mary's	1953	5.00	10.00	20.00
❑ 47-5484	Three O'Clock in the Morning/City Slicker	1953	5.00	10.00	20.00
❑ 47-5565	Barber Shop Rag/Centipede Boogie	1953	5.00	10.00	20.00
❑ 47-5638	Wildwood Flower/Simple Simon	1954	5.00	10.00	20.00
❑ 47-5650	Georgia Camp Meeting/Jealous Hearted Me	1954	5.00	10.00	20.00
—With Minnie Pearl					
❑ 47-5704	Downhill Drag/Kentucky Derby	1954	5.00	10.00	20.00
❑ 47-5813	San Antonio Rose/Mister Misery	1954	5.00	10.00	20.00
—With Red Kirk					
❑ 47-5956	Mr. Sandman/Set a Spell	1954	5.00	10.00	20.00
❑ 47-6108	Hey Mr. Guitar/Unchained Melody	1955	3.75	7.50	15.00
❑ 47-6199	Somebody Stole My Gal/Shine On Harvest Moon	1955	3.75	7.50	15.00
❑ 47-6314	Christmas Carols/Jingle Bells	1955	3.75	7.50	15.00
❑ 47-6366	Jean's Song/Honey	1955	3.75	7.50	15.00
❑ 47-6550	Cecilia/The Lady Loves	1956	3.75	7.50	15.00
❑ 47-6796	Trambone/Blue Echo	1957	3.75	7.50	15.00
❑ 47-6808	Tricky/Peanut Vendor	1957	3.75	7.50	15.00
—With the Rhythm Rockers					
❑ 47-6919	Martinique/Dig These Blues	1957	3.75	7.50	15.00
—With the Rhythm Rockers					
❑ 47-7048	Hidden Charms/Colonial Ballroom	1957	3.75	7.50	15.00
❑ 47-7589	Boo Boo Stick Beat/Django's Castle	1959	3.00	6.00	12.00
❑ 47-7684	One Mint Julep/Teensville	1960	3.00	6.00	12.00
❑ 47-7747	Slinkey/Rainbow's End	1960	3.00	6.00	12.00
❑ 47-7796	Hocus Pocus/Theme from The Dark at the End of the Stairs	1960	3.00	6.00	12.00
❑ 47-7847	The Slop/Hot Mocking Bird	1961	3.00	6.00	12.00
❑ 47-7891	Man of Mystery/Windy and Warm	1961	3.00	6.00	12.00
❑ 47-7971	Jingle Bells/Jingle Bell Rock	1961	3.00	6.00	12.00
❑ 47-8029	Down Home/Melissa	1962	3.00	6.00	12.00
❑ 47-8246	Guitar Country/Waitin' for the Evening Train	1963	3.00	6.00	12.00
—With the Anita Kerr Quartet					
❑ 47-8342	Freight Train/Dobro	1964	3.00	6.00	12.00
❑ 47-8492	Travelin'/Cloudy and Cool	1965	2.50	5.00	10.00
❑ 47-8590	Yakety Axe/Letter Edged in Black	1965	2.50	5.00	10.00
❑ 47-8781	From Nashville with Love/Rhythm Guitar	1966	2.50	5.00	10.00
❑ 47-8829	Tennessee Waltz/Country Gentleman	1966	2.50	5.00	10.00
❑ 47-8927	Prissy/La Fiesta	1966	2.50	5.00	10.00
❑ 47-9116	Charlie Brown/What'd I Say	1967	2.50	5.00	10.00
❑ 47-9578	Huntin' Boots/Blue Angel	1968	2.00	4.00	8.00
❑ 47-9672	Light My Fire/Mrs. Robinson	1968	2.00	4.00	8.00
❑ 47-9725	Theme from Zorba the Greek/Those Were the Days	1969	—	3.00	6.00
❑ 47-9824	Love Beads/Passion Flower	1969	—	3.00	6.00
❑ 47-9827	Steeplechase Lane/Love Beads	1970	—	2.50	5.00
❑ 47-9890	Tennessee Stud/Cannonball Rag	1970	—	2.50	5.00
—With Jerry Reed					
❑ 47-9956	Snowbird/Chaplain in New Shoes	1971	—	2.50	5.00
❑ 48-0062	Guitar Waltz/Barber Shop Rag	1949	12.50	25.00	50.00
—Originals on green vinyl					
❑ 48-0062	Guitar Waltz/Barber Shop Rag	1949	6.25	12.50	25.00
—Second pressings: Green label, black vinyl					
❑ 48-0089	Dance of the Goldenrod/Telling My Troubles to My Old Guitar	1949	12.50	25.00	50.00
—Originals on green vinyl					
❑ 48-0089	Dance of the Goldenrod/Telling My Troubles to My Old Guitar	1949	6.25	12.50	25.00
—Second pressings: Green label, black vinyl					
❑ 48-0142	Centipede Boogie/Wednesday Night Waltz	1949	12.50	25.00	50.00
—Originals on green vinyl					
❑ 48-0142	Centipede Boogie/Wednesday Night Waltz	1949	6.25	12.50	25.00
—Second pressings: Green label, black vinyl					
❑ 48-0173	One More Chance/Old Buck Dance	1950	6.25	12.50	25.00
—Originals on green vinyl					
❑ 48-0173	One More Chance/Old Buck Dance	1950	6.25	12.50	25.00
—Second pressings: Green label, black vinyl					
❑ 48-0329	Main Street Breakdown/Under the Hickory Nut Tree	1950	12.50	25.00	50.00
—Originals on green vinyl					
❑ 48-0329	Main Street Breakdown/Under the Hickory Nut Tree	1950	6.25	12.50	25.00
—Second pressings: Green label, black vinyl					
❑ 48-0367	Boogie Man Boogie/Was Bitten By the Same Bug Twice	1950	12.50	25.00	50.00
—Originals on green vinyl					
❑ 48-0367	Boogie Man Boogie/Was Bitten By the Same Bug Twice	1950	6.25	12.50	25.00
—Second pressings: Green label, black vinyl					
❑ 48-0402	The Birth of the Blues/Confusin'	1950	12.50	25.00	50.00
—Originals on green vinyl					
❑ 48-0402	The Birth of the Blues/Confusin'	1950	6.25	12.50	25.00
—Second pressings: Green label, black vinyl					
❑ 48-0428	Indian Love Call/Music in My Heart	1951	12.50	25.00	50.00
—Originals on green vinyl					
❑ 48-0428	Indian Love Call/Music in My Heart	1951	6.25	12.50	25.00
—Second pressings: Green label, black vinyl					
❑ 48-0439	My Life with You/A Trinket of Shiny Gold	1951	6.25	12.50	25.00
—With the Carter Sisters					
❑ 48-0440	You're Always Brand New/Mountain Melody	1951	6.25	12.50	25.00
❑ 48-0471	Jitterbug Waltz/My Crazy Heart	1951	6.25	12.50	25.00
❑ 48-0500	Crazy Rhythm/Hybrid Corn	1951	6.25	12.50	25.00
❑ 74-0236	Delilah/Ode to Billie Joe	1969	—	2.50	5.00
—With Arthur Fiedler and the Boston Pops					
❑ 74-0536	Black Magic Woman/Wabash Blues	1971	—	2.50	5.00
❑ 74-0696	Red, White and Blue Medley/Kentucky	1972	—	2.50	5.00
❑ 74-0775	Nashtownville/Jerry's Breakdown	1972	—	2.50	5.00
—With Jerry Reed					
❑ 74-0914	Ruby, Are You Mad at Your Man/Somewhere, My Love	1973	—	2.00	4.00

Selected 78s

Number	Title (A Side/B Side)	Yr	VG	VG+	NM
BULLET					
❑ 617	Guitar Blues/Blue Eyes Crying in the Rain	1947	30.00	60.00	120.00

7-Inch Extended Plays

Number	Title (A Side/B Side)	Yr	VG	VG+	NM
RCA VICTOR					
❑ EPA-685	Arkansaw Traveler/Londonderry Air//Ouch Chornya/La Golondrina	195?	5.00	10.00	20.00
❑ EPA-685 [PS]	Chet Atkins in 3 Dimensions Vol. 1: Folk	1955	5.00	10.00	20.00
❑ EPA-687	Minuet and Prelude No. 2/Intermezzo//Schon Rosmarin/Minute Waltz	195?	5.00	10.00	20.00
❑ EPA-687 [PS]	Chet Atkins in 3 Dimensions Vol. 3: Classical	195?	5.00	10.00	20.00
❑ EPA-796	(title unknown)	195?	5.00	10.00	20.00
❑ EPA-796 [PS]	Indian Love Call/Memphis Blues//St. Louis Blues/Black Mountain Rag	195?	5.00	10.00	20.00
❑ 547-0919	Oh By Jingo/Indian Love Call//Alice Blue Gown/The 3rd Man Theme	1956	5.00	10.00	20.00
—One record of 2-EP set EPB 1236					
❑ 547-0920	Memphis Blues/12th Street Rag//Gallopin' Guitar/St. Louis Blues	1956	5.00	10.00	20.00
—One record of 2-EP set EPB 1236					
❑ EPB 1236 [PS]	Stringin' Along with Chet Atkins	1956	5.00	10.00	20.00
❑ EPA-4194	Say "Si Si"/Villa//Yankee Doodle Dandy/You're Just in Love	1958	3.75	7.50	15.00
❑ EPA-4194 [PS]	Chet Atkins at Home	1958	3.75	7.50	15.00
❑ EPA-5052	The Poor People of Paris/Chinatown, My Chinatown//San Antonio Rose/Country Gentlemen	195?	3.75	7.50	15.00
❑ EPA-5052 [PS]	(title unknown)	195?	3.75	7.50	15.00

Albums

Number	Title (A Side/B Side)	Yr	VG	VG+	NM
COLUMBIA					
❑ FC 38536	Work It Out with Chet Atkins C.G.P.	1983	2.50	5.00	10.00
❑ PC 38536	Work It Out with Chet Atkins C.G.P.	1985	2.00	4.00	8.00
—Budget-line reissue					
❑ PC 39003	East Tennessee Christmas	1983	2.50	5.00	10.00
❑ FC 39591	Stay Tuned	1985	2.50	5.00	10.00
❑ FC 40256	Street Dreams	1986	2.00	4.00	8.00
❑ FC 40593	Sails	1987	2.00	4.00	8.00
❑ FC 44323	Chet Atkins, C.G.P.	1989	2.00	4.00	8.00
DOLTON					
❑ BLP-16506 [M]	Play Guitar with Chet Atkins	1967	6.25	12.50	25.00
❑ BST-17506 [S]	Play Guitar with Chet Atkins	1967	7.50	15.00	30.00
PAIR					
❑ PDL2-1047 [(2)]	Tennessee Guitar Man	1985	3.00	6.00	12.00
❑ PDL2-1115 [(2)]	Guitar for All Seasons	1986	3.00	6.00	12.00
RCA CAMDEN					
❑ CAL-659 [M]	Chet Atkins and His Guitar	196?	3.75	7.50	15.00

Number	Title (A Side/B Side)	Yr	VG	VG+	NM
❑ CAS-659(e) [R]	Chet Atkins and His Guitar	1964	3.00	6.00	12.00
❑ CAL-753 [M]	Guitar Genius	196?	3.75	7.50	15.00
❑ CAS-753(e) [R]	Guitar Genius	196?	3.00	6.00	12.00
❑ CAL-981 [M]	Music from Nashville, My Home Town	196?	3.00	6.00	12.00
❑ CAS-981 [S]	Music from Nashville, My Home Town	196?	3.75	7.50	15.00
❑ CAL-2182 [M]	Chet	196?	3.00	6.00	12.00
❑ CAS-2182 [S]	Chet	196?	3.75	7.50	15.00
❑ CAS-2296	Relaxin' with Chet	1969	3.00	6.00	12.00
❑ CAS-2523	Chet 'n Boots	1972	3.00	6.00	12.00
❑ CAS-2555	Nashville Gold	1972	3.00	6.00	12.00
❑ CAS-2600	Finger Pickin' Good	1973	2.50	5.00	10.00
❑ ACL1-7042	Love Letters	197?	2.50	5.00	10.00
RCA RED SEAL					
❑ LM-2870 [M]	The "Pops" Goes Country	1966	3.75	7.50	15.00
❑ LSC-2870 [S]	The "Pops" Goes Country	1966	5.00	10.00	20.00
—Above two with the Boston Pops Orchestra, Arthur Fiedler, conductor					
❑ LSC-3104	Chet Picks On the Pops	1969	3.75	7.50	15.00
—With the Boston Pops Orchestra, Arthur Fiedler, conductor					
RCA VICTOR					
❑ APL1-0159	Alone	1973	3.00	6.00	12.00
❑ APL1-0329	Superpickers	1974	3.00	6.00	12.00
❑ APL1-0545	Chet Atkins Picks On Jerry Reed	1974	3.00	6.00	12.00
❑ APL1-0645	Chat Atkins Goes to the Movies	1973	3.00	6.00	12.00
❑ ANL1-0981	Chet Atkins Picks the Best	1975	2.50	5.00	10.00
❑ LPM-1090 [M]	A Session with Chet Atkins	1954	15.00	30.00	60.00
—Red cover					
❑ LPM-1090 [M]	A Session with Chet Atkins	1961	5.00	10.00	20.00
—Woman and guitars cover					
❑ LSP-1090(e) [R]	A Session with Chet Atkins	1967	2.50	5.00	10.00
❑ LPM-1197 [M]	Chet Atkins in Three Dimensions	1956	12.50	52.00	50.00
—Black-and-white guitar cover					
❑ LPM-1197 [M]	Chet Atkins in Three Dimensions	1961	5.00	10.00	20.00
—Red guitar cover					
❑ LSP-1197(e) [R]	Chet Atkins in Three Dimensions	1967	2.50	5.00	10.00
❑ APL1-1233	The Night Atlanta Burned	1975	3.00	6.00	12.00
❑ LPM-1236 [M]	Stringin' Along with Chet Atkins	1956	12.50	25.00	50.00
—Orange cover					
❑ LPM-1236 [M]	Stringin' Along with Chet Atkins	1961	5.00	10.00	20.00
—Full-color cover					
❑ LSP-1236(e) [R]	Stringin' Along with Chet Atkins	1967	2.50	5.00	10.00
❑ LPM-1383 [M]	Finger Style Guitar	1956	12.50	25.00	50.00
—Chet's face not visible on cover					
❑ LPM-1383 [M]	Finger Style Guitar	1961	5.00	10.00	20.00
—Chet's face visible on cover					
❑ LSP-1383(e) [R]	Finger Style Guitar	1962	3.00	6.00	12.00
❑ LPM-1544 [M]	Chet Atkins at Home	1957	12.50	25.00	50.00
—Title in block letters on cover					
❑ LPM-1544 [M]	Chet Atkins at Home	1961	5.00	10.00	20.00
—Title in script on cover					
❑ LSP-1544(e) [R]	Chet Atkins at Home	1967	2.50	5.00	10.00
❑ LPM-1577 [M]	Hi-Fi in Focus	1957	12.50	25.00	50.00
—No guitars on cover					
❑ LPM-1577 [M]	Hi-Fi in Focus	1957	5.00	10.00	20.00
—Guitar on cover					
❑ LSP-1577(e) [R]	Hi-Fi in Focus	196?	2.50	5.00	10.00
❑ ANL1-1935	Christmas with Chet Atkins	1976	2.00	4.00	8.00
—Reissue of LSP-2423					
❑ APL1-1985	The Best of Chet Atkins	1975	3.00	6.00	12.00
❑ LPM-1993 [M]	Chet Atkins in Hollywood	1959	7.50	15.00	30.00
—Night-time cover					
❑ LPM-1993 [M]	Chet Atkins in Hollywood	1961	5.00	10.00	20.00
—Daylight "blonde" cover					
❑ LSP-1993 [S]	Chet Atkins in Hollywood	1959	12.50	25.00	50.00
—Night-time cover					
❑ LSP-1993 [S]	Chet Atkins in Hollywood	1961	7.50	15.00	30.00
—Daylight "blonde" cover					
❑ LPM-2025 [M]	Hum & Strum Along	1959	6.25	12.50	25.00
—Add $10 NM if instruction book is included					
❑ LSP-2025 [S]	Hum & Strum Along	1959	10.00	20.00	40.00
—Add $10 NM if instruction book is included					
❑ LPM-2103 [M]	Mister Guitar	1959	7.50	15.00	30.00
—Lone guitar on cover					
❑ LPM-2103 [M]	Mister Guitar	1961	5.00	10.00	20.00
—Guitar and woman on cover					
❑ LSP-2103 [S]	Mister Guitar	1959	12.50	25.00	50.00
—Lone guitar on cover					
❑ LSP-2103 [S]	Mister Guitar	1961	7.50	15.00	30.00
—Guitar and woman on cover					
❑ LPM-2161 [M]	Teensville	1960	7.50	15.00	30.00
—Title overlaps cover photo					
❑ LPM-2161 [M]	Teensville	1961	5.00	10.00	20.00
—Title in black strip at top of cover photo					
❑ LSP-2161 [S]	Teensville	1960	12.50	25.00	50.00
—Title overlaps cover photo					
❑ LSP-2161 [S]	Teensville	1961	7.50	15.00	30.00
—Title in black strip at top of cover photo					
❑ LPM-2175 [M]	The Other Chet Atkins	1960	5.00	10.00	20.00
❑ LSP-2175 [S]	The Other Chet Atkins	1960	7.50	15.00	30.00
❑ LPM-2232 [M]	Chet Atkins' Workshop	1961	5.00	10.00	20.00
❑ LSP-2232 [S]	Chet Atkins' Workshop	1961	7.50	15.00	30.00
❑ LPM-2346 [M]	The Most Popular Guitar	1961	5.00	10.00	20.00
❑ LSP-2346 [S]	The Most Popular Guitar	1961	7.50	15.00	30.00
❑ AHL1-2405	My Guitar	1977	3.00	6.00	12.00
❑ LPM-2423 [M]	Christmas with Chet Atkins	1961	5.00	10.00	20.00
❑ LSP-2423 [S]	Christmas with Chet Atkins	1961	7.50	15.00	30.00
❑ LPM-2450 [M]	Down Home	1962	5.00	10.00	20.00
❑ LSP-2450 [S]	Down Home	1962	6.25	12.50	25.00
❑ CPL1-2503	A Legendary Performer	1977	3.00	6.00	12.00
❑ LPM-2549 [M]	Caribbean Guitar	1962	5.00	10.00	20.00
❑ LSP-2549 [S]	Caribbean Guitar	1962	6.25	12.50	25.00
❑ LPM-2601 [M]	Back Home Hymns	1962	5.00	10.00	20.00
❑ LSP-2601 [S]	Back Home Hymns	1962	6.25	12.50	25.00
❑ LPM-2616 [M]	Our Man in Nashville	1963	5.00	10.00	20.00
❑ LSP-2616 [S]	Our Man in Nashville	1963	6.25	12.50	25.00
❑ LPM-2678 [M]	Travelin'	1963	5.00	10.00	20.00
❑ LSP-2678 [S]	Travelin'	1963	6.25	12.50	25.00
❑ LPM-2719 [M]	Teen Scene	1963	5.00	10.00	20.00
❑ LSP-2719 [S]	Teen Scene	1963	6.25	12.50	25.00
❑ LPM-2783 [M]	Guitar Country	1964	3.75	7.50	15.00
❑ LSP-2783 [S]	Guitar Country	1964	5.00	10.00	20.00
❑ LPM-2887 [M]	The Best of Chet Atkins	1964	3.75	7.50	15.00
❑ LSP-2887 [S]	The Best of Chet Atkins	1964	5.00	10.00	20.00
❑ LPM-2908 [M]	Progressive Pickin'	1964	3.75	7.50	15.00
❑ LSP-2908 [S]	Progressive Pickin'	1964	5.00	10.00	20.00
❑ LPM-3079 [10]	Chet Atkins' Gallopin' Guitar	1952	37.50	75.00	150.00
❑ LPM-3169 [10]	Stringin' Along with Chet Atkins	1953	25.00	50.00	100.00
❑ AHL1-3302	The First Nashville Guitar Quartet	1979	3.00	6.00	12.00
❑ LPM-3316 [M]	My Favorite Guitars	1965	3.75	7.50	15.00
❑ LSP-3316 [S]	My Favorite Guitars	1965	5.00	10.00	20.00
❑ LPM-3429 [M]	More of That "Guitar Country"	1965	3.75	7.50	15.00
❑ LSP-3429 [S]	More of That "Guitar Country"	1965	5.00	10.00	20.00
❑ AHL1-3505	The Best of Chet On The Road...Live	1980	3.00	6.00	12.00
❑ LPM-3531 [M]	Chet Atkins Picks On the Beatles	1966	6.25	12.50	25.00
❑ LSP-3531 [S]	Chet Atkins Picks On the Beatles	1966	7.50	15.00	30.00
❑ LPM-3558 [M]	The Best of Chet Atkins, Volume 2	1966	3.00	6.00	12.00
❑ LSP-3558 [S]	The Best of Chet Atkins, Volume 2	1966	3.75	7.50	15.00
❑ LPM-3647 [M]	From Nashville with Love	1966	3.00	6.00	12.00
❑ LSP-3647 [S]	From Nashville with Love	1966	3.75	7.50	15.00
❑ LPM-3728 [M]	It's a Guitar World	1967	7.50	15.00	30.00
❑ LSP-3728 [S]	It's a Guitar World	1967	3.00	6.00	12.00
❑ AYL1-3741	The First Nashville Guitar Quartet	1981	2.00	4.00	8.00
—"Best Buy Series" reissue					
❑ LPM-3818 [M]	Chet Atkins Picks the Best	1967	7.50	15.00	30.00
❑ LSP-3818 [S]	Chet Atkins Picks the Best	1967	3.00	6.00	12.00
❑ LPM-3885 [M]	Class Guitar	1967	7.50	15.00	30.00
❑ LSP-3885 [S]	Class Guitar	1967	3.00	6.00	12.00
❑ LPM-3992 [M]	Solo Flights	1968	12.50	25.00	50.00
❑ LSP-3992 [S]	Solo Flights	1968	3.00	6.00	12.00
❑ LSP-4017	Hometown Guitar	1968	3.75	7.50	15.00
❑ AHL1-4044	Still Country — After All These Years	1981	2.50	5.00	10.00
❑ LSP-4061	Solid Gold '68	1968	3.75	7.50	15.00
❑ LSP-4135	Lover's Guitar	1968	3.75	7.50	15.00
❑ LSP-4244	Solid Gold '69	1969	3.00	6.00	12.00
❑ LSP-4331	Yestergroovin'	1970	3.00	6.00	12.00
❑ LSP-4396	Me & Jerry	1971	3.75	7.50	15.00
—With Jerry Reed					
❑ LSP-4464	For the Good Times	1971	3.75	7.50	15.00
❑ AHL1-4724	Great Hits of the Past	1983	2.50	5.00	10.00
❑ LSP-4754	Chet Atkins Picks the Hits	1973	3.75	7.50	15.00
❑ AHL1-5495	Collector's Series	1985	2.50	5.00	10.00
❑ VPS-6030 [(2)]	This Is Chet Atkins	1972	3.75	7.50	15.00
❑ VPXS-6079 [(2)]	Now & Then	1972	3.75	7.50	15.00
TIME-LIFE					
❑ 117	Country Music	1981	3.00	6.00	12.00

ATKINS, CHET, AND LES PAUL

45s

RCA

Number	Title (A Side/B Side)	Yr	VG	VG+	NM
❑ PB-11330	I'm Your Greatest Fan/Hot Toddy	1978	—	2.00	4.00
RCA VICTOR					
❑ PB-10642	Moonglow/Avalon	1976	—	2.50	5.00

Albums

RCA VICTOR

Number	Title (A Side/B Side)	Yr	VG	VG+	NM
❑ APL1-1167	Chester and Lester	1976	3.00	6.00	12.00
❑ APL1-2786	Guitar Monsters	1978	3.00	6.00	12.00
❑ AYL1-3682	Chester and Lester	1980	2.00	4.00	8.00
—"Best Buy Series" reissue					

ATKINS, CHET, AND HANK SNOW

Also see each artist's individual listings.

45s

RCA VICTOR

Number	Title (A Side/B Side)	Yr	VG	VG+	NM
❑ 47-5995	Silver Bell/Old Spinning Wheel	1954	5.00	10.00	20.00
❑ 47-6558	Reminiscing/New Spanish Two-Step	1956	3.75	7.50	15.00
❑ 47-9803	Wheels/Difficult	1969	2.00	4.00	8.00

ATKINS, CHET, AND DOC WATSON

45s

RCA

Number	Title (A Side/B Side)	Yr	VG	VG+	NM
❑ PB-12138	Medley-Tennessee Rag & Beaumont Rag/On My Way to Canaan's Land	1981	—	2.00	4.00

Albums

RCA VICTOR

Number	Title (A Side/B Side)	Yr	VG	VG+	NM
❑ AHL1-3701	Reflections	1980	2.50	5.00	10.00

ATKINS, RODNEY

45s

CURB

Number	Title (A Side/B Side)	Yr	VG	VG+	NM
❑ D7-73026	In a Heartbeat/God Only Knows	1997	—	—	3.00

ATLANTA

45s

MCA

Number	Title (A Side/B Side)	Yr	VG	VG+	NM
❑ 52336	Sweet Country Music/Seven Bridges Road	1984	—	2.00	4.00
❑ 52391	Pictures/Long Cool Woman (in a Black Dress)	1984	—	2.00	4.00
❑ 52452	Wishful Drinkin'/Blue Side of Grey	1984	—	2.00	4.00
❑ 52552	My Sweet-Eyed Georgia Girl/Dancin' on the Bayou	1985	—	2.00	4.00
❑ 52603	Why Not Tonight/Dancin' on the Bayou	1985	—	2.00	4.00
❑ 52671	Can't You Hear the Whistle Blow/Long Ago Shoes	1985	—	2.00	4.00

MDJ

Number	Title (A Side/B Side)	Yr	VG	VG+	NM
❑ 4831	Atlanta Burned Again Last Night/Tumblin' Tumbleweeds	1983	—	2.50	5.00
❑ 4832	Dixie Dreaming/Orange Blossom Special-Rocky Top	1983	—	2.50	5.00
❑ 4832 [PS]	Dixie Dreaming/Orange Blossom Special-Rocky Top	1983	2.50	5.00	10.00

SOUTHERN TRACKS

Number	Title (A Side/B Side)	Yr	VG	VG+	NM
❑ 1074	We Always Agree on Love/Close Enough for Country	1987	—	2.50	5.00
❑ 1079	Good Vibrations/We Always Agree on Love	1987	—	2.50	5.00
❑ 1087	A Thing Called Love/(B-side unknown)	1987	—	2.50	5.00
❑ 1091	Sad Cliches/We Always Agree on Love	1988	—	2.50	5.00
❑ 1097	Look at Us Now/(B-side unknown)	1988	—	2.50	5.00

Albums

MCA

Number	Title	Yr	VG	VG+	NM
❑ 5463	Pictures	1984	2.00	4.00	8.00
❑ 5576	Atlanta	1985	2.00	4.00	8.00

ATLANTA RHYTHM SECTION

Not known as a country group, but some of its records did make the country charts.

45s

COLUMBIA

Number	Title (A Side/B Side)	Yr	VG	VG+	NM
❑ 18-02471	Alien/Southern Exposure	1981	—	2.00	4.00

DECCA

Number	Title (A Side/B Side)	Yr	VG	VG+	NM
❑ 32928	All in Your Mind/Can't Stand It No More	1972	2.00	4.00	8.00
❑ 32948	Earnestine/Another Man's Woman	1972	2.00	4.00	8.00
❑ 33051	Back Up Against the Wall/It Must Be Done	1973	2.00	4.00	8.00

MCA

Number	Title (A Side/B Side)	Yr	VG	VG+	NM
❑ 40059	Cold Turkey, Tennessee/Conversation	1973	—	3.00	6.00
❑ 40719	All in Your Mind/Earnestine	1977	—	2.50	5.00

POLYDOR

Number	Title (A Side/B Side)	Yr	VG	VG+	NM
❑ 2001	Spooky/It's Only Music	1979	—	2.50	5.00
❑ 2039	Back Up Against the Wall/Large Time	1980	—	2.50	5.00
❑ 2079	Conversation/Indigo Passion	1980	—	2.50	5.00
❑ 2125	Putting My Faith in Love/I Ain't Much	1980	—	2.50	5.00
❑ 2142	Silver Eagle/Strictly R & R	1981	—	2.50	5.00
❑ 14248	Doraville/Who Are You Going to Run To	1974	—	2.50	5.00
❑ 14262	Angel (What in the World's Come Over Us)/Help Yourself	1975	—	2.50	5.00
❑ 14273	Get Your Head Out of Your Heart/Jesus Hearted People	1975	—	2.50	5.00
❑ 14289	Bless My Soul/Crazy	1975	—	2.50	5.00
❑ 14323	Jukin'/Beautiful Dreamer	1976	—	2.50	5.00
❑ 14339	Free Spirit/Police Police	1976	—	2.50	5.00
❑ 14373	So In to You/Everybody Gotta Go	1977	—	2.50	5.00
❑ 14397	Neon Nites/Don't Miss the Message	1977	—	2.50	5.00
❑ 14411	Dog Days/Cuban Crisis	1977	—	2.50	5.00
❑ 14459	Imaginary Lover/Silent Treatment	1978	—	2.50	5.00
❑ 14484	I'm Not Gonna Let It Bother Me Tonight/Ballad of Lois Malone	1978	—	2.50	5.00
❑ 14504	Champagne Jam/Great Escape	1978	—	2.50	5.00
❑ 14568	Do It or Die/My Song	1979	—	2.50	5.00
❑ 14582	Spooky/It's Only Music	1979	—	—	—

—Unreleased?

Albums

COLUMBIA

Number	Title	Yr	VG	VG+	NM
❑ FC 37550	Quinella	1981	2.50	5.00	10.00
❑ PC 37550	Quinella	1982	2.00	4.00	8.00

—Budget-line reissue

DECCA

Number	Title	Yr	VG	VG+	NM
❑ DL 75265	Atlanta Rhythm Section	1972	6.25	12.50	25.00
❑ DL 75390	Back Up Against the Wall	1973	6.25	12.50	25.00

MCA

Number	Title	Yr	VG	VG+	NM
❑ 2-4114 [(2)]	Atlanta Rhythm Section	1977	3.00	6.00	12.00

—Combines the two Decca LPs into one package

MOBILE FIDELITY

Number	Title	Yr	VG	VG+	NM
❑ 1-038	Champagne Jam	1981	10.00	20.00	40.00

—Audiophile vinyl

POLYDOR

Number	Title	Yr	VG	VG+	NM
❑ PD 6027	Third Annual Pipe Dream	1974	2.50	5.00	10.00
❑ PD 6041	Dog Days	1975	2.50	5.00	10.00
❑ PD-1-6060	Red Tape	1976	2.50	5.00	10.00
❑ PD-1-6080	A Rock and Roll Alternative	1977	2.50	5.00	10.00
❑ PD-1-6134	Champagne Jam	1978	2.50	5.00	10.00
❑ PD-1-6200	Underdog	1979	2.50	5.00	10.00
❑ PD-2-6236 [(2)]	Are You Ready!	1979	3.00	6.00	12.00
❑ PD-1-6285	The Boys from Doraville	1980	2.50	5.00	10.00

AUSTIN, BOBBY

45s

ATLANTIC

Number	Title (A Side/B Side)	Yr	VG	VG+	NM
❑ 2913	Knoxville Station/Bitter Chill of Lonely	1972	—	3.00	6.00
❑ 2942	Forgotten Footprints/Time for One More Dream	1973	—	3.00	6.00

CAPITOL

Number	Title (A Side/B Side)	Yr	VG	VG+	NM
❑ 2039	This Song Is Just for You/Do-Die	1967	2.00	4.00	8.00
❑ 2152	Is This the Beginning of the End/Sweet Evelina	1968	2.00	4.00	8.00
❑ 2306	The Robin/Ten Years Ago	1968	2.00	4.00	8.00
❑ 2552	Goodbye Again/Play Me a Good Old Country Song	1969	2.00	4.00	8.00
❑ 2681	For Your Love/(Leaning On) Your Everlasting Love	1969	2.00	4.00	8.00
❑ 2757	The Great Pretender/Tommy Jekyll and Linda Hyde	1970	2.00	4.00	8.00
❑ 2851	Little Boy Don't Live Here Anymore/Scatter Your Seeds to the Wind	1970	2.00	4.00	8.00
❑ 2971	Garden of My Mind/When Your Sweet Love Carried On	1970	2.00	4.00	8.00
❑ 5867	Cupid's Last Arrow/Mary's Merry Go Round	1967	2.00	4.00	8.00
❑ 5923	Some of Us Never Learn/Feet Keep Walkin'	1967	2.00	4.00	8.00

TALLY

Number	Title (A Side/B Side)	Yr	VG	VG+	NM
❑ 500	Apartment #9/Going Home to Momma	1966	3.75	7.50	15.00

TRIUNE

Number	Title (A Side/B Side)	Yr	VG	VG+	NM
❑ 7201	Knoxville Station/Bitter Chill of Lonely	1973	—	3.00	6.00
❑ 7208	I'll Run Get You/Carol	1973	—	3.00	6.00
❑ 7213	Your Love Made a Man Out of Me/I'll Run and Get You	1973	—	3.00	6.00

Albums

CAPITOL

Number	Title	Yr	VG	VG+	NM
❑ ST 2773 [S]	Apartment No. 9	1967	5.00	10.00	20.00
❑ T 2773 [M]	Apartment No. 9	1967	6.25	12.50	25.00
❑ ST 2915	Old Love Never Dies	1968	5.00	10.00	20.00

AUSTIN, BRYAN

45s

PATRIOT

Number	Title (A Side/B Side)	Yr	VG	VG+	NM
❑ 17932	Radio Active/Limo Driver	1994	—	2.50	5.00

AUSTIN, CHRIS

45s

WARNER BROS.

Number	Title (A Side/B Side)	Yr	VG	VG+	NM
❑ 27531	Blues Stay Away from Me/We Will Take a Lot of Memories When We Go	1989	—	2.00	4.00
❑ 27661	I Know There's a Heart In There Somewhere/Somehow Tonight	1988	—	2.00	4.00
❑ 27815	Lonesome for You/The Reason	1988	—	2.00	4.00
❑ 27815 [PS]	Lonesome for You/The Reason	1988	—	2.00	4.00

AUSTIN, DARLENE

45s

CBT

Number	Title (A Side/B Side)	Yr	VG	VG+	NM
❑ 4146	Guilty Eyes/When Do We Stop Starting Over	1986	—	3.00	6.00
❑ 4146 [PS]	Guilty Eyes/When Do We Stop Starting Over	1986	2.00	4.00	8.00

MAGI

Number	Title (A Side/B Side)	Yr	VG	VG+	NM
❑ 4444	I Had a Heart/(B-side unknown)	1987	—	3.00	6.00

MYRTLE

Number	Title (A Side/B Side)	Yr	VG	VG+	NM
❑ 1002	Sunday Go to Cheatin' Clothes/Why Baby Why	1982	—	3.00	6.00
❑ 1003	Take Me Tonight/Then You Can Tell Me Goodbye	1982	—	3.00	6.00
❑ 1004	I'm on the Outside Looking In/Heartaches by the Number	1983	—	3.00	6.00

AUSTIN, KAY

45s

E.I.O.

Number	Title (A Side/B Side)	Yr	VG	VG+	NM
❑ 1122	The Rest of Your Life/(B-side unknown)	1980	—	2.50	5.00
❑ 1127	Two Hearts Beat (Better Than One)/Like the Seasons	1980	—	2.50	5.00

MC

Number	Title (A Side/B Side)	Yr	VG	VG+	NM
❑ 5014	Big Red Roses (And Little White Lies)/Try Me	1978	—	2.50	5.00

AUSTIN, SHERRIE

45s

ARISTA NASHVILLE

Number	Title (A Side/B Side)	Yr	VG	VG+	NM
❑ 13083	Lucky in Love/Put Your Heart Into It	1997	—	2.50	5.00
❑ 13099	One Solitary Tear/I Want to Fall in Love (So Hard It Hurts)	1997	—	2.50	5.00
❑ 13122	Put Your Heart Into It/That's No Way to Break a Heart	1998	—	2.50	5.00
❑ 13140	Never Been Kissed/Words	1999	—	2.00	4.00
❑ 13184	Little Bird/Never Been Kissed	1999	—	2.00	4.00

AUTRY, GENE

45s

CHALLENGE

Number	Title (A Side/B Side)	Yr	VG	VG+	NM
❑ 1009	No Back Door to Heaven/You're the Only Good Thing	1957	3.00	6.00	12.00
❑ 1010	Rudolph the Red-Nosed Reindeer/Here Come Santa Claus	1957	3.00	6.00	12.00

—Re-recordings of originals on Columbia

Number	Title (A Side/B Side)	Yr	VG	VG+	NM
❑ 59030	Rudolph, the Red-Nosed Reindeer/Here Come Santa Claus	1958	3.00	6.00	12.00
❑ 59030 [PS]	Rudolph, the Red-Nosed Reindeer/Here Come Santa Claus	1958	5.00	10.00	20.00

COLUMBIA

Number	Title (A Side/B Side)	Yr	VG	VG+	NM
❑ 4-56	Rudolph, the Red-Nosed Reindeer/If It Doesn't Snow on Christmas	1951	5.00	10.00	20.00

—Yellow label, red print; second number on label is 90049

Number	Title (A Side/B Side)	Yr	VG	VG+	NM
❑ 4-56 [PS]	Rudolph, the Red-Nosed Reindeer/If It Doesn't Snow on Christmas	1951	6.25	12.50	25.00
—Sleeve was manufactured with a hole in the middle					
❑ 4-68	Peter Cottontail/Funny Little Bunny	1950	5.00	10.00	20.00
—Yellow label, red print; second number on label is unknown					
❑ 4-68 [PS]	Peter Cottontail/Funny Little Bunny	1950	6.25	12.50	25.00
—Sleeve was manufactured with a hole in the middle					
❑ 4-75	Frosty the Snow Man/When Santa Claus Gets Your Letter	1951	5.00	10.00	20.00
—Yellow label, red print; second number on label is 90072					
❑ 4-75 [PS]	Frosty the Snow Man/When Santa Claus Gets Your Letter	1951	6.25	12.50	25.00
—Sleeve was manufactured with a hole in the middle					
❑ 4-84	Here Comes Santa Claus/He's a Chubby Little Fellow	1951	5.00	10.00	20.00
—Yellow label, red print; second number on label is 90088					
❑ 4-84 [PS]	Here Comes Santa Claus/He's a Chubby Little Fellow	1951	6.25	12.50	25.00
—Sleeve was manufactured with a hole in the middle					
❑ 4-121	Thirty-Two Feet — Eight Little Tails/(Hedrock, Coco and Joe) The Three Little Dwarfs	1952	5.00	10.00	20.00
—Yellow label, red print; second number on label is 90135					
❑ 4-121 [PS]	Thirty-Two Feet — Eight Little Tails/(Hedrock, Coco and Joe) The Three Little Dwarfs	1952	6.25	12.50	25.00
—Sleeve was manufactured with a hole in the middle					
❑ 4-122	Poppy the Puppy/He'll Be Coming Down the Chimney (Like He Always Did Before)	1952	5.00	10.00	20.00
—Yellow label, red print; second number on label is 90136					
❑ 4-122 [PS]	Poppy the Puppy/He'll Be Coming Down the Chimney (Like He Always Did Before)	1952	6.25	12.50	25.00
—Sleeve was manufactured with a hole in the middle					
❑ 4-150	Merry Texas Christmas, You All!/The Night Before Christmas (In Texas, That Is)	1953	3.75	7.50	15.00
—Yellow label, red print; second number on label is 90172					
❑ 4-150 [PS]	Merry Texas Christmas, You All!/The Night Before Christmas (In Texas, That Is)	1953	5.00	10.00	20.00
—Sleeve was manufactured with a hole in the middle					
❑ 4-176	Santa Claus Is Comin' to Town/Up on the Housetop (Ho! Ho! Ho!)	1954	3.75	7.50	15.00
—Yellow label, red print					
❑ 4-176 [PS]	Santa Claus Is Comin' to Town/Up on the Housetop (Ho! Ho! Ho!)	1954	5.00	10.00	20.00
❑ 2-210 (?)	Ellie Mae/Sun Flower	1949	10.00	20.00	40.00
—Microgroove 33 1/3 rpm single					
❑ 2-270 (?)	My Empty Heart/I Wish I Had Stayed Over Yonder	1949	10.00	20.00	40.00
—Microgroove 33 1/3 rpm single					
❑ 2-320 (?)	Santa, Santa, Santa/He's a Chubby Little Fellow	1949	10.00	20.00	40.00
—Microgroove 33 1/3 rpm single					
❑ 2-340 (?)	When the Silver Colorado Turns to Gold/Whirlwinds	1949	10.00	20.00	40.00
—Microgroove 33 1/3 rpm single					
❑ 2-370 (?)	Riders in the Sky/Cowboy Trademarks	1949	10.00	20.00	40.00
—Microgroove 33 1/3 rpm single					
❑ 1-375	Rudolph, the Red-Nosed Reindeer/If It Doesn't Snow on Christmas	1949	10.00	20.00	40.00
—Microgroove 33 1/3 rpm single					
❑ 6-375	Rudolph, the Red-Nosed Reindeer/If It Doesn't Snow on Christmas	1950	6.25	12.50	25.00
—Reissue on 45 of a single originally on 33 1/3 Microgroove single					
❑ 2-430 (?)	Mule Train/Cowboy Serenade	1950	10.00	20.00	40.00
—Microgroove 33 1/3 rpm single					
❑ 2-480 (?)	Poison Ivy/A New Star Is Shining	1950	10.00	20.00	40.00
—Microgroove 33 1/3 rpm single					
❑ 2-550 (?)	Take Me Back to My Boots and Saddle/Dust	1950	10.00	20.00	40.00
—Microgroove 33 1/3 rpm single					
❑ 1-575	Peter Cottontail/Funny Little Bunny	1950	10.00	20.00	40.00
—Microgroove 33 1/3 rpm single					
❑ 1-630 (?)	Roses/The Roses I Picked for Our Wedding	1950	10.00	20.00	40.00
—Microgroove 33 1/3 rpm single					
❑ 1-741 (?)	Blue Canadian Rockies/Onteora	1950	10.00	20.00	40.00
—Microgroove 33 1/3 rpm single					
❑ 6-741 (?)	Blue Canadian Rockies/Onteora	1950	6.25	12.50	25.00
❑ 1-742	Frosty the Snow Man/When Santa Claus Gets Your Letter	1950	10.00	20.00	40.00
—Microgroove 33 1/3 rpm single					
❑ 6-742	Frosty the Snow Man/When Santa Claus Gets Your Letter	1950	5.00	10.00	20.00
❑ 1-765 (?)	Goodnight Irene/Texans Never Cry	1950	10.00	20.00	40.00
—Microgroove 33 1/3 rpm single					
❑ 6-765 (?)	Goodnight Irene/Texans Never Cry	1950	6.25	12.50	25.00
❑ 1-810 (?)	Little Johnny Pilgrim/Guffy the Goofy Gobbler	1950	10.00	20.00	40.00
—Microgroove 33 1/3 rpm single					
❑ 6-810 (?)	Little Johnny Pilgrim/Guffy the Goofy Gobbler	1950	6.25	12.50	25.00
❑ 38-06189	The Statue in the Bay/God Bless America	1986	—	2.00	4.00
❑ 4-20377	Here Comes Santa Claus (Down Santa Claus Lane)/An Old-Fashioned Tree	1950	5.00	10.00	20.00
—Reissue on 45 of a single originally on 78					
❑ 20709	I Love You Because/The Last Straw	1950	6.25	12.50	25.00
❑ 20727	Silver Haired Daddy/Mississippi Valley Blues	1950	6.25	12.50	25.00
❑ 20763	Rose Colored Memories/Let Me Cry on Your Shoulder	1950	6.25	12.50	25.00
❑ 20775	The Statue in the Bay/The Place Where I Worship	1951	5.00	10.00	20.00
❑ 20814	At Mail Call Today/I'll Be Back	1951	5.00	10.00	20.00
❑ 20865	When It's Springtime in the Rockies/I Don't Want to Set the World on Fire	1951	5.00	10.00	20.00
❑ 20899	Heartsick Soldier/I'm Learning to Live	1952	3.75	7.50	15.00
❑ 20904	Am I a Pastime/I Was Just Walkin'	1952	3.75	7.50	15.00
❑ 20929	Diesel Smoke/Stop Your Gambling	1952	3.75	7.50	15.00
❑ 21035	I've Lived a Lifetime for You/Story Book of Love	1952	3.75	7.50	15.00
❑ 21144	Love Is So Misleadin'/Don't Send Your Love	1953	3.75	7.50	15.00
❑ 21207	Bimbo/Roly Poly	1954	3.75	7.50	15.00
❑ 21229	Angels in the Sky/A Voice in the Choir	1954	3.75	7.50	15.00
❑ 21252	Closing the Book/My Lazy Day	1954	3.75	7.50	15.00
❑ 21269	20-20 Vision/You're the Only Good Thing	1954	3.75	7.50	15.00
❑ 21280	I'm a Fool to Care/A Broken Promise Means a Broken Heart	1954	3.75	7.50	15.00
❑ 21304	When He Grows Tired of You/It Just Don't Seem Like Home	1954	3.75	7.50	15.00
❑ 21329	Barney the Bashful Bullfrog/Little Peter Pumpkin Eater	1954	3.75	7.50	15.00
❑ 21358	I'm Innocent/You're an Angel	1955	3.75	7.50	15.00
❑ 21481	You've Got to Take the Bitter with the Sweet/Two Cheaters in Love	1956	3.75	7.50	15.00
❑ 21527	God's in the Saddle/If Today Were the End of the World	1956	3.75	7.50	15.00
❑ 33023	Back in the Saddle Again/Tumbling Tumbleweeds	196?	2.00	4.00	8.00
—"Hall of Fame" reissue; red and black label					
❑ 33165	Rudolph, the Red-Nosed Reindeer/Here Comes Santa Claus (Down Santa Claus Lane)	1970	—	2.50	5.00
—"Hall of Fame" reissue; red and black label					
❑ 33165	Rudolph, the Red-Nosed Reindeer/Here Comes Santa Claus (Down Santa Claus Lane)	198?	—	—	3.00
—"Hall of Fame" reissue; gray label					
❑ 38610	Rudolph, the Red-Nosed Reindeer/If It Doesn't Snow On Christmas	1951	3.75	7.50	15.00
—Second 45 issue of this song					
❑ 38907	Frosty The Snowman/When Santa Claus Gets Your Letter	1951	3.75	7.50	15.00
—Second 45 issue of this song					
❑ 3-39086	My Heart Cries for You/Teardrops from My Eyes	1950	7.50	15.00	30.00
—Microgroove 33 1/3 rpm single					
❑ 4-39086	My Heart Cries for You/Teardrops from My Eyes	1950	5.00	10.00	20.00
❑ 39217	Sonny the Bunny/Bunny Roundup Time	1951	5.00	10.00	20.00
❑ 39347	Crime Will Never Pay/Gold Can Buy Anything	1951	3.75	7.50	15.00
❑ 39371	Mr. and Mississippi/How Long Is Forever	1951	3.75	7.50	15.00
❑ 39405	Old Soldiers Never Die/God Bless America	1951	3.75	7.50	15.00
❑ 39461	Frosty the Snow Man/An Old-Fashioned Tree	1951	3.00	6.00	12.00
❑ 39462	When Santa Claus Gets Your Letter/He's a Chubby Little Fellow	1951	3.00	6.00	12.00
❑ 39463	Rudolph, the Red-Nosed Reindeer/Here Comes Santa Claus (Down Santa Claus Lane)	1951	3.00	6.00	12.00
❑ 39464	Santa, Santa, Santa/If It Doesn't Snow on Christmas	1951	3.00	6.00	12.00
❑ 39542	Poppy the Puppy/He'll Be Coming Down the Chimney (Like He Always Did Before)	1951	3.75	7.50	15.00
❑ 39543	Thirty-Two Feet — Eight Little Tails/(Hedrock, Coco and Joe) The Three Little Dwarfs	1951	3.75	7.50	15.00
❑ 39808	Don't Believe a Word They Say/God's Little Candles	1952	3.75	7.50	15.00
❑ 39876	The Night Before Christmas Song/Look Out the Window	1952	3.75	7.50	15.00
—With Rosemary Clooney					
❑ 40092	Where Did My Snowman Go?/Freddie the Little Fir Tree	1953	3.75	7.50	15.00
❑ 40135	I Wish My Mom Would Marry Santa Claus/Sleigh Bells	1953	3.75	7.50	15.00
❑ 40167	Easter Morning/The Horse with the Easter Bonnet	1954	3.75	7.50	15.00
❑ 40589	Round, Round the Christmas Tree/Merry Christmas Tree	1955	3.75	7.50	15.00
❑ 40790	Everyone's a Child at Christmas/You Can See Old Santa Claus	1956	3.75	7.50	15.00
❑ 40931	Johnny Reb and Billy Yank/Happy Little Island	1957	3.00	6.00	12.00
❑ 40960	Half Your Heart/Darlin' What More Can I Do	1957	3.00	6.00	12.00
❑ 44632	Back in the Saddle Again/Home on the Range	1968	2.00	4.00	8.00

CRICKET

Number	Title (A Side/B Side)	Yr	VG	VG+	NM
❑ CX-6	Rudolph, the Red-Nosed Reindeer/Tinker Town Santa Claus	196?	3.00	6.00	12.00
—B-side by the Cricketones					

MISTLETOE

Number	Title (A Side/B Side)	Yr	VG	VG+	NM
❑ 801	Rudolph, The Red-Nosed Reindeer/Up On The House Top	196?	2.00	4.00	8.00

REPUBLIC

Number	Title (A Side/B Side)	Yr	VG	VG+	NM
❑ 001	Back in the Saddle Again/The Last Round-Up	1977	—	2.50	5.00
❑ 326	Rudolph the Red-Nosed Reindeer/Here Comes Santa Claus	1976	—	2.00	4.00
❑ 1405	Rudolph the Red-Nosed Reindeer/Here Comes Santa Claus	1969	2.00	4.00	8.00
❑ 2001	Nine Little Reindeer/Buon Natale (Means Merry Christmas)	1959	3.00	6.00	12.00
❑ 2001 [PS]	Nine Little Reindeer/Buon Natale (Means Merry Christmas)	1959	3.00	6.00	12.00
❑ 2002	Santa's Comin' in a Whirlybird/Jingle Bells	1959	3.00	6.00	12.00

Selected 78s

BANNER

Number	Title (A Side/B Side)	Yr	VG	VG+	NM
❑ 32349	That Silver Haired Daddy of Mine/Mississippi Valley Blues	193?	17.50	35.00	70.00
❑ 32843	There's an Empty Cot in the Bunkhouse Tonight/Louisiana Moon	193?	17.50	35.00	70.00
❑ 33055	After Twenty-One Years/Little Farm Home	193?	17.50	35.00	70.00

Number	Title (A Side/B Side)	Yr	VG	VG+	NM
❑ 33102	The Stump of the Old Pine Tree/Seven More Days	193?	17.50	35.00	70.00
❑ 33348	Tumbling Tumbleweeds/Old Missouri Moon	1934	17.50	35.00	70.00
CHAMPION					
❑ 16030	I'll Be Thinking of You Pretty Girl/(B-side unknown)	193?	25.00	50.00	100.00
❑ 16050	In the Shadow of the Pine/(B-side unknown)	193?	25.00	50.00	100.00
❑ 16073	Hobo Bill's Last Ride/(B-side unknown)	193?	25.00	50.00	100.00
❑ 16096	Hobo Yodel/Cowboy Yodel	193?	25.00	50.00	100.00
❑ 16119	Texas Blues/Dust Pan Blues	193?	25.00	50.00	100.00
❑ 16141	In the Jailhouse Now No. 2/(B-side unknown)	193?	25.00	50.00	100.00
❑ 16166	High Powered Mama/(B-side unknown)	193?	25.00	50.00	100.00
❑ 16210	Mean Mama Blues/(B-side unknown)	193?	25.00	50.00	100.00
❑ 16228	Pistol Packin' Papa/(B-side unknown)	193?	25.00	50.00	100.00
❑ 16230	Any Old Time/(B-side unknown)	193?	25.00	50.00	100.00
❑ 16245	Blue Days/(B-side unknown)	193?	25.00	50.00	100.00
❑ 16275	T.B. Blues/(B-side unknown)	193?	30.00	60.00	120.00
❑ 16328	True Blue Bill/(B-side unknown)	193?	37.50	75.00	150.00
❑ 16372	Dad in the Hills/(B-side unknown)	193?	37.50	75.00	150.00
❑ 16485	That's How I Got My Start/(B-side unknown)	193?	37.50	75.00	150.00
CLARION					
❑ 5025	Hobo Yodel/(B-side unknown)	193?	20.00	40.00	80.00
❑ 5026	No One to Call Me Darling/(B-side unknown)	193?	20.00	40.00	80.00
❑ 5058	I'll Be Thinking of You Little Girl/(B-side unknown)	193?	20.00	40.00	80.00
❑ 5075	Cowboy Yodel/(B-side unknown)	193?	20.00	40.00	80.00
❑ 5154	Dust Pan Blues/(B-side unknown)	193?	20.00	40.00	80.00
❑ 5155	Waiting for a Train/(B-side unknown)	193?	20.00	40.00	80.00
❑ 5239	Left My Gal in the Mountains/(B-side unknown)	193?	20.00	40.00	80.00
❑ 5240	Daddy and Home/(B-side unknown)	193?	20.00	40.00	80.00
❑ 5243	Lullaby Yodel/(B-side unknown)	193?	20.00	40.00	80.00
❑ 5272	True Blue Bill/(B-side unknown)	193?	20.00	40.00	80.00
❑ 5308	A Gangster's Warning/(B-side unknown)	193?	20.00	40.00	80.00
COLUMBIA					
❑ 20001	Don't Hang Around Me Anymore/Address Unknown	1948	3.75	7.50	15.00
—Reissue of 36840					
❑ 20007	Don't Live a Lie/I Want to Be Sure	1948	3.75	7.50	15.00
—Reissue of 36880					
❑ 20012	Silver Spurs (On the Golden Stairs)/Good Old Fashioned Hoedown	1948	3.75	7.50	15.00
—Reissue of 36904					
❑ 20020	I Wish I Had Never Met Sunshine/You Only Want Me When You're Lonely	1948	3.75	7.50	15.00
—Reissue of 36970					
❑ 20025	Wave to Me, My Lady/Over and Over Again	1948	3.75	7.50	15.00
—Reissue of 36984					
❑ 20027	Tumbling Tumbleweeds/Old Missouri Moon	1948	3.75	7.50	15.00
—Reissue of 37000					
❑ 20028	Mexicali Rose/You're the Only Star (In My Blue Heaven)	1948	3.75	7.50	15.00
—Reissue of 37002					
❑ 20029	Sail Along Silvery Moon/There's a Gold Mine in the Sky	1948	3.75	7.50	15.00
—Reissue of 37003					
❑ 20030	I Want a Pardon for Daddy/The End of My Round-Up Days	1948	3.75	7.50	15.00
—Reissue of 37004					
❑ 20036	Back in the Saddle Again/Little Old Band of Gold	1948	3.75	7.50	15.00
—Reissue of 37010					
❑ 20037	Goodbye Little Darlin' Goodbye/When I'm Gone You'll Soon Forget	1948	3.75	7.50	15.00
—Reissue of 37011					
❑ 20042	That Little Kid Sister of Mine/You Waited Too Long	1948	3.75	7.50	15.00
—Reissue of 37016					
❑ 20044	Be Honest with Me/What's Gonna Happen to Me	1948	3.75	7.50	15.00
—Reissue of 37018					
❑ 20047	You Are My Sunshine/It Makes No Difference Now	1948	3.75	7.50	15.00
—Reissue of 37021					
❑ 20049	I'm Thinking Tonight of My Blue Eyes/I'll Be True While You're Gone	1948	3.75	7.50	15.00
—Reissue of 37023					
❑ 20050	Tweedle-O-Twill/Take Me Back Into Your Heart	1948	3.75	7.50	15.00
—Reissue of 37024					
❑ 20052	Private Buckaroo/Rainbows on the Rio Colorado	1948	3.75	7.50	15.00
—Reissue of 37026					
❑ 20053	Call Me and I'll Be There/Yesterday's Roses	1948	3.75	7.50	15.00
—Reissue of 37027					
❑ 20061	Purple Sage in the Twilight/If You Only Believed in Me	1948	3.75	7.50	15.00
—Reissue of 37036					
❑ 20066	Darlin' What More Can I Do?/I Guess I've Been Asleep	1948	3.75	7.50	15.00
—Reissue of 37043					
❑ 20075	Have I Told You Lately That I Love You/Someday You'll Want Me to Want You	1948	3.75	7.50	15.00
—Reissue of 37079					
❑ 20084	Back in the Saddle Again/Tumbling Tumbleweeds	1948	3.00	6.00	12.00
—Reissue of 37183					
❑ 20085	Home on the Range/Red River Valley	1948	3.00	6.00	12.00
—Reissue of 37184					
❑ 20086	Mexicali Rose/South of the Border (Down Mexico Way)	1948	3.00	6.00	12.00
—Reissue of 37185					
❑ 20087	Twilight on the Trail/Ridin' Down the Canyon	1948	3.00	6.00	12.00
—Reissue of 37186					
❑ 20089	You're Not My Darlin' Anymore/Here's to the Ladies	1948	3.75	7.50	15.00
—Reissue of 37201					
❑ 20114	Ages and Ages Ago/You Laughed and I Cried	1948	3.75	7.50	15.00
—Reissue of 37322					
❑ 20125	The Angel Song/When the Snowbirds Cross the Rockies	1948	3.75	7.50	15.00
—Reissue of 37390					
❑ 20129	Gonna Build a Big Fence Around Texas/Don't Fence Me In	1948	3.75	7.50	15.00
—Reissue of 37402					
❑ 20133	Jingle, Jangle, Jingle/I'm a Cow Poke Pokin' Along	1948	3.75	7.50	15.00
—Reissue of 37406					
❑ 20137	Keep Rollin' Lazy Longhorns/Deep in the Heart of Texas	1948	3.75	7.50	15.00
—Reissue of 37410					
❑ 20139	I'll Hang My Head and Cry/You'll Be Sorry	1948	3.75	7.50	15.00
—Reissue of 37412					
❑ 20150	You Are the Light of My Life/Sweethearts or Strangers	1948	3.75	7.50	15.00
—Reissue of 37423					
❑ 20152	Too Late/Blue-Eyed Elaine	1948	3.75	7.50	15.00
—Reissue of 37425					
❑ 20157	I'll Wait for You/Lonely River	1948	3.75	7.50	15.00
—Reissue of 37430					
❑ 20164	I Wish All My Children Were Babies Again/I'm Comin' Home Darlin'	1948	3.75	7.50	15.00
—Reissue of 37437					
❑ 20242	South of the Border (Down Mexico Way)/A Gold Mine in Your Heart	1948	3.75	7.50	15.00
—Reissue of 37643					
❑ 20251	The Call of the Canyon/Broomstick Buckaroo	1948	3.75	7.50	15.00
—Reissue of 37652					
❑ 20254	A Face I See at Evening/There Ain't No Use in Crying Now	1948	3.75	7.50	15.00
—Reissue of 37655					
❑ 20259	There'll Never Be Another Pal Like You/Tears on My Pillow	1948	3.75	7.50	15.00
—Reissue of 37660					
❑ 20262	Don't Bite the Hand That's Feeding You/God Must Have Loved America	1948	3.75	7.50	15.00
—Reissue of 37663					
❑ 20281	The One Rose (That's Left in My Heart)/I Hate to Say Goodbye to the Prairie	1948	3.75	7.50	15.00
—Reissue of 37702					
❑ 20355	The Leap of Love/The Last Mile	1948	3.75	7.50	15.00
—Reissue of 37816					
❑ 20371	Gallivantin' Galveston Gal/Cowboy Blues	1948	3.75	7.50	15.00
—Reissue of 37923					
❑ 20377	Here Comes Santa Claus (Down Santa Claus Lane)/An Old Fashioned Tree	1948	3.75	7.50	15.00
—Reissue of 37942					
❑ 20386	Dixie Cannonball/Pretty Mary	1948	3.75	7.50	15.00
—Reissue of 37963					
❑ 20400	Loaded Pistols and Loaded Dice/Serenade of the Bells	1948	3.75	7.50	15.00
—Reissue of 38076					
❑ 20416	Fair Play/Lone Star Moon	1948	3.75	7.50	15.00
—Reissue of 38148					
❑ 20439	A Broken Promise Means a Broken Heart/Don't Take Your Spite Out on Me	1948	5.00	10.00	20.00
❑ 20448	Blue Shadows on the Trail/Boy from Texas, Girl from Tennessee	1948	5.00	10.00	20.00
❑ 20451	Rolling Along/They Warned Me About You	1948	5.00	10.00	20.00
❑ 20453	Don't Waste Your Tears on Me/Nobody's Darling But Mine	1948	5.00	10.00	20.00
❑ 20469	Buttons and Bows/Can't Shake the Sands of Texas from My Shoes	1948	5.00	10.00	20.00
❑ 20485	Blueberry Hill/Sycamore Lane	1948	5.00	10.00	20.00
❑ 20495	If Today Were the End of the World/Last Letter	1948	5.00	10.00	20.00
❑ 20524	Kentucky Babe/Missouri Babe	1948	5.00	10.00	20.00
❑ 20539	Bible on the Table/I Lost My Little Darlin'	1949	5.00	10.00	20.00
❑ 20541	The Last Round-Up/Take Me Back to My Saddle and Boots	1949	3.75	7.50	15.00
❑ 20542	There's a Gold Mine in the Sky/Roundup in Glory	1949	3.75	7.50	15.00
❑ 20543	When It's Roundup Time in Heaven/Old Faithful	1949	3.75	7.50	15.00
❑ 20544	Cowboy's Heaven/There's an Empty Cot in the Bunkhouse Tonight	1949	3.75	7.50	15.00
❑ 36587	Tweedle-O-Twill/Take Me Back Into Your Heart	1942	6.25	12.50	25.00
—We're not sure if this or Okeh 6680 is the original					
❑ 36840	Don't Hang Around Me Anymore/Address Unknown	1945	5.00	10.00	20.00
❑ 36880	Don't Live a Lie/I Want to Be Sure	1945	5.00	10.00	20.00
❑ 36904	Silver Spurs (On the Golden Stairs)/Good Old Fashioned Hoedown	1946	5.00	10.00	20.00
❑ 36970	I Wish I Had Never Met Sunshine/You Only Want Me When You're Lonely	1946	5.00	10.00	20.00
❑ 36984	Wave to Me, My Lady/Over and Over Again	1946	5.00	10.00	20.00
❑ 37000	Tumbling Tumbleweeds/Old Missouri Moon	1946	5.00	10.00	20.00
—Reissue					
❑ 37001	Don't Waste Your Tears on Me/Nobody's Darling But Mine	1946	5.00	10.00	20.00
—Reissue of Okeh 3070					

Had there been a country & western chart in the 1930s, Gene Autry probably would have ruled it. Even so, he still made the chart 25 times from 1944 through 1951. (Top left) His biggest chart hit was his wartime ode "At Mail Call Today," which spent eight weeks at No. 1 in 1945, just as World War II was finally winding down. (Top right) Today, Autry's many Christmas tunes are better known than the rest of his music. The first one he recorded, "Here Comes Santa Claus (Down Santa Claus Lane)," he also co-wrote. This is a scarce early 45 rpm pressing of the 20377 release of the disc. The original 78 was on Columbia 37942, then was reissued on 20377 in 1948. This 45 came out in the early 1950s. (Bottom left) The biggest long-term success of Autry's music career was his 1949 recording of "Rudolph, the Red-Nosed Reindeer." It's said to have sold more copies than any other Christmas recording except for "White Christmas" by Bing Crosby. Here's a 1950 45 rpm pressing with its original catalog number, before it was changed to the same number as on the 78. (Bottom right) None of his later Christmas songs had quite the same impact as "Rudolph." The closest he came was the very next Christmas season, 1950, when he did the definitive hit version of "Frosty the Snowman." Here is a Columbia Children's Series issue.

Number	Title (A Side/B Side)	Yr	VG	VG+	NM
❑ 37002	Mexicali Rose/You're the Only Star (In My Blue Heaven)	1946	5.00	10.00	20.00
—Reissue of Okeh 03097					
❑ 37003	Sail Along Silvery Moon/There's a Gold Mine in the Sky	1946	5.00	10.00	20.00
—Reissue of Okeh 03358					
❑ 37004	I Want a Pardon for Daddy/The End of My Round-Up Days	1946	5.00	10.00	20.00
—Reissue of Okeh 04146					
❑ 37010	Back in the Saddle Again/Little Old Band of Gold	1946	5.00	10.00	20.00
—Reissue of Okeh 05080					
❑ 37011	Goodbye Little Darlin' Goodbye/When I'm Gone You'll Soon Forget	1946	5.00	10.00	20.00
—Reissue of Okeh 05463					
❑ 37016	That Little Kid Sister of Mine/You Waited Too Long	1946	5.00	10.00	20.00
—Reissue of Okeh 05781					
❑ 37018	Be Honest with Me/What's Gonna Happen to Me	1946	5.00	10.00	20.00
—Reissue of Okeh 05980					
❑ 37021	You Are My Sunshine/It Makes No Difference Now	1946	5.00	10.00	20.00
—Reissue of Okeh 06274					
❑ 37023	I'm Thinking Tonight of My Blue Eyes/I'll Be True While You're Gone	1946	5.00	10.00	20.00
—Reissue of Okeh 6648					
❑ 37024	Tweedle-O-Twill/Take Me Back Into Your Heart	1946	5.00	10.00	20.00
—Reissue of Okeh 6680					
❑ 37026	Private Buckaroo/Rainbows on the Rio Colorado	1946	5.00	10.00	20.00
—Reissue of Okeh 6682					
❑ 37027	Call Me and I'll Be There/Yesterday's Roses	1946	5.00	10.00	20.00
—Reissue of Okeh 6684					
❑ 37036	Purple Sage in the Twilight/If You Only Believed in Me	1946	5.00	10.00	20.00
—Reissue of Okeh sides					
❑ 37041	At Mail Call Today/I'll Be Back	1946	5.00	10.00	20.00
—Reissue of Okeh 6737					
❑ 37043	Darlin' What More Can I Do?/I Guess I've Been Asleep	1946	5.00	10.00	20.00
—Reissue of Okeh 6743					
❑ 37079	Have I Told You Lately That I Love You/Someday You'll Want Me to Want You	1946	5.00	10.00	20.00
❑ 37183	Back in the Saddle Again/Tumbling Tumbleweeds	1947	3.75	7.50	15.00
❑ 37184	Home on the Range/Red River Valley	1947	3.75	7.50	15.00
❑ 37185	Mexicali Rose/South of the Border (Down Mexico Way)	1947	3.75	7.50	15.00
❑ 37186	Twilight on the Trail/Ridin' Down the Canyon	1947	3.75	7.50	15.00
❑ 37201	You're Not My Darlin' Anymore/Here's to the Ladies	1947	5.00	10.00	20.00
❑ 37322	Ages and Ages Ago/You Laughed and I Cried	1947	5.00	10.00	20.00
❑ 37390	The Angel Song/When the Snowbirds Cross the Rockies	1947	5.00	10.00	20.00
❑ 37402	Gonna Build a Big Fence Around Texas/Don't Fence Me In	1947	5.00	10.00	20.00
—Reissue of Okeh 6728					
❑ 37406	Jingle, Jangle, Jingle/I'm a Cow Poke Pokin' Along	1947	5.00	10.00	20.00
—Reissue					
❑ 37410	Keep Rollin' Lazy Longhorns/Deep in the Heart of Texas	1947	5.00	10.00	20.00
❑ 37412	I'll Hang My Head and Cry/You'll Be Sorry	1947	5.00	10.00	20.00
❑ 37423	You Are the Light of My Life/Sweethearts or Strangers	1947	5.00	10.00	20.00
❑ 37425	Too Late/Blue-Eyed Elaine	1947	5.00	10.00	20.00
❑ 37430	I'll Wait for You/Lonely River	1947	5.00	10.00	20.00
❑ 37437	I Wish All My Children Were Babies Again/I'm Comin' Home Darlin'	1947	5.00	10.00	20.00
❑ 37643	South of the Border (Down Mexico Way)/A Gold Mine in Your Heart	1947	5.00	10.00	20.00
—Reissue					
❑ 37652	The Call of the Canyon/Broomstick Buckaroo	1947	5.00	10.00	20.00
❑ 37655	A Face I See at Evening/There Ain't No Use in Crying Now	1947	5.00	10.00	20.00
❑ 37660	There'll Never Be Another Pal Like You/Tears on My Pillow	1947	5.00	10.00	20.00
❑ 37663	Don't Bite the Hand That's Feeding You/God Must Have Loved America	1947	5.00	10.00	20.00
—Reissue of Okeh 06359					
❑ 37702	The One Rose (That's Left in My Heart)/I Hate to Say Goodbye to the Prairie	1947	5.00	10.00	20.00
❑ 37816	The Leap of Love/The Last Mile	1947	5.00	10.00	20.00
❑ 37923	Gallivantin' Galveston Gal/Cowboy Blues	1947	5.00	10.00	20.00
❑ 37942	Here Comes Santa Claus (Down Santa Claus Lane)/An Old Fashioned Tree	1947	5.00	10.00	20.00
❑ 37963	Dixie Cannonball/Pretty Mary	1947	5.00	10.00	20.00
❑ 38076	Loaded Pistols and Loaded Dice/Serenade of the Bells	1948	5.00	10.00	20.00
❑ 38148	Fair Play/Lone Star Moon	1948	5.00	10.00	20.00
❑ 38610	Rudolph, the Red-Nosed Reindeer/If It Doesn't Snow On Christmas	1949	5.00	10.00	20.00

CONQUEROR

Number	Title (A Side/B Side)	Yr	VG	VG+	NM
❑ 7702	Dad in the Hills/(B-side unknown)	193?	17.50	35.00	70.00
❑ 7704	A Gangster's Warning/Don't Send My Boy to Prison	193?	17.50	35.00	70.00
—B-side by Frankie Wallace					
❑ 7843	True Blue Bill/Pictures of My Mother	193?	17.50	35.00	70.00
❑ 7999	Back to Old Smoky/(B-side unknown)	193?	17.50	35.00	70.00
❑ 8297	Eleven Months in Leavenworth/After Twenty-One Years	193?	17.50	35.00	70.00
❑ 8465	Tumbling Tumbleweeds/(B-side unknown)	193?	17.50	35.00	70.00
❑ 8629	Mexicali Rose/Nobody's Darling But Mine	193?	17.50	35.00	70.00
❑ 8685	The Answer to Nobody's Darling/Guns and Guitars	193?	17.50	35.00	70.00
❑ 8686	The Old Gray Mare/I'll Go Riding Down That Texas Trail	193?	17.50	35.00	70.00
❑ 8808	The Convict's Dream/That's Why I'm Nobody's Darling	193?	17.50	35.00	70.00
❑ 9098	You're the Only Star/(B-side unknown)	193?	15.00	30.00	60.00
❑ 9305	There's a Gold Mine in the Sky/Sail Along Silvery Moon	193?	15.00	30.00	60.00
❑ 9450	The Rhythm of the Hoof Beats/(B-side unknown)	193?	15.00	30.00	60.00

DECCA

Number	Title (A Side/B Side)	Yr	VG	VG+	NM
❑ 5426	Blue Days/(B-side unknown)	1937	12.50	25.00	50.00
❑ 5464	In the Shadow of the Pine/(B-side unknown)	1937	12.50	25.00	50.00
❑ 5488	Bear Cat Papa Blues/(B-side unknown)	1938	12.50	25.00	50.00
❑ 5501	My Carolina Sunshine Girl/(B-side unknown)	1938	12.50	25.00	50.00
❑ 5517	T.B. Blues/(B-side unknown)	1938	12.50	25.00	50.00
❑ 5527	Yodeling Hobo/(B-side unknown)	1938	12.50	25.00	50.00
❑ 5544	Pistol Packin' Papa/(B-side unknown)	1938	12.50	25.00	50.00
—Decca 78s are either reissues or re-recordings of earlier material					

DIVA

Number	Title (A Side/B Side)	Yr	VG	VG+	NM
❑ 6030	Hobo Yodel/(B-side unknown)	193?	17.50	35.00	70.00
❑ 6031	Slue-Foot Lue/Waiting for a Train	193?	17.50	35.00	70.00
❑ 6032	Blue Yodel No. 4/(B-side unknown)	193?	17.50	35.00	70.00
❑ 6033	Lullaby Yodel/(B-side unknown)	193?	17.50	35.00	70.00
❑ 6035	No One to Call Me Darling/(B-side unknown)	193?	17.50	35.00	70.00
❑ 6037	Frankie and Johnny/(B-side unknown)	193?	17.50	35.00	70.00
❑ 6049	My Rough and Rowdy Ways/(B-side unknown)	193?	17.50	35.00	70.00
❑ 6057	Cowboy Yodel/(B-side unknown)	193?	17.50	35.00	70.00

GENNETT

Number	Title (A Side/B Side)	Yr	VG	VG+	NM
❑ 7243	Cowboy Yodel/(B-side unknown)	193?	62.50	125.00	250.00
❑ 7265	In the Shadow of the Pine/(B-side unknown)	193?	62.50	125.00	250.00
❑ 7290	Hobo Bill's Last Ride/(B-side unknown)	193?	62.50	125.00	250.00
❑ 7310	Train Whistle Blues/(B-side unknown)	193?	75.00	150.00	300.00

MELOTONE

Number	Title (A Side/B Side)	Yr	VG	VG+	NM
❑ 12392	My Old Pal of Yesterday/(B-side unknown)	193?	15.00	30.00	60.00
❑ 12832	The Last Round-Up/(B-side unknown)	1933	15.00	30.00	60.00
❑ 13315	Tumbling Tumbleweeds/Old Missouri Moon	1934	15.00	30.00	60.00
❑ 13316	Texas Plains/Hold On, Little Dogies, Hold On	1934	15.00	30.00	60.00
❑ 13354	Ole Faithful/(B-side unknown)	1934	15.00	30.00	60.00

MONTGOMERY WARD

Number	Title (A Side/B Side)	Yr	VG	VG+	NM
❑ M-4242	Bear Cat Papa Blues/(B-side unknown)	193?	37.50	75.00	150.00
❑ M-4243	My Carolina Sunshine Girl/Don't Do Me That Way	193?	37.50	75.00	150.00
❑ M-4244	High-Steppin' Mama Blues/(B-side unknown)	193?	37.50	75.00	150.00
❑ M-4245	Rheumatism Blues/(B-side unknown)	193?	37.50	75.00	150.00
❑ M-4275	Wildcat Mama/(B-side unknown)	193?	37.50	75.00	150.00
❑ M-4326	That Ramshackle Shack/(B-side unknown)	193?	37.50	75.00	150.00
❑ M-4333	I'm Always Dreaming of You/(B-side unknown)	193?	37.50	75.00	150.00
❑ M-4767	Left My Gal in the Mountains/The Old Woman and the Cow	193?	50.00	100.00	200.00
❑ M-4768	She's a Low Down Mama/She Wouldn't Do It	193?	50.00	100.00	200.00
❑ M-4931	Pictures of My Mother/(B-side unknown)	193?	37.50	75.00	150.00
❑ M-4932	Yodeling Hobo/(B-side unknown)	193?	37.50	75.00	150.00
❑ M-4933	In the Shadow of the Pine/(B-side unknown)	193?	37.50	75.00	150.00
❑ M-4975	In the Jailhouse Now No. 2/T.B. Blues	193?	37.50	75.00	150.00
❑ M-4976	True Blue Bill/(B-side unknown)	193?	37.50	75.00	150.00
❑ M-4977	Jail House Blues/Pistol Packin' Papa	193?	37.50	75.00	150.00
❑ M-4978	Whisper Your Mother's Name/My Carolina Sunshine Girl	193?	37.50	75.00	150.00
❑ M-8016	Money Ain't No Use Anyway/(B-side unknown)	193?	30.00	60.00	120.00
❑ M-8017	Cowboy Yodel/Yodeling Hobo	193?	30.00	60.00	120.00
❑ M-8034	Train Whistle Blues/Texas Blues	193?	30.00	60.00	120.00

OKEH

Number	Title (A Side/B Side)	Yr	VG	VG+	NM
❑ 03070	Don't Waste Your Tears on Me/Nobody's Darling But Mine	194?	6.25	12.50	25.00
❑ 03097	Mexicali Rose/You're the Only Star (In My Blue Heaven)	194?	6.25	12.50	25.00
❑ 03262	I Hate to Say Goodbye to the Prairie/(B-side unknown)	194?	6.25	12.50	25.00
❑ 03358	Sail Along Silvery Moon/There's a Gold Mine in the Sky	194?	6.25	12.50	25.00
❑ 04146	I Want a Pardon for Daddy/The End of My Round-Up Days	194?	6.25	12.50	25.00
❑ 04246	As Long As I've Got My Horse/(B-side unknown)	194?	6.25	12.50	25.00
❑ 04262	Ride Tenderfoot Ride/The Old Trail	194?	6.25	12.50	25.00
❑ 04340	Good Bye Pinto/(B-side unknown)	194?	6.25	12.50	25.00
❑ 04375	Louisiana Moon/(B-side unknown)	194?	6.25	12.50	25.00
❑ 04485	The Last Round-Up/Way Out West in Texas	194?	6.25	12.50	25.00
❑ 04998	The Yellow Rose of Texas/(B-side unknown)	194?	6.25	12.50	25.00
❑ 05080	Back in the Saddle Again/Little Old Band of Gold	194?	6.25	12.50	25.00
❑ 05190	Little Pardner/(B-side unknown)	194?	6.25	12.50	25.00
❑ 05463	Goodbye Little Darlin' Goodbye/When I'm Gone You'll Soon Forget	194?	6.25	12.50	25.00
❑ 05599	There's Only One Love in a Lifetime/Mary Dear	1940	6.25	12.50	25.00
❑ 05781	That Little Kid Sister of Mine/You Waited Too Long	1941	6.25	12.50	25.00
❑ 05980	Be Honest with Me/What's Gonna Happen to Me	1941	6.25	12.50	25.00
❑ 06089	There Ain't No Use in Crying Now/(B-side unknown)	1941	6.25	12.50	25.00
❑ 06239	There'll Never Be Another Pal/(B-side unknown)	1941	6.25	12.50	25.00
❑ 06274	You Are My Sunshine/It Makes No Difference Now	1941	6.25	12.50	25.00

Number	Title (A Side/B Side)	Yr	VG	VG+	NM
❑ 06359	Don't Bite the Hand That's Feeding You/God Must Have Loved America	1941	6.25	12.50	25.00
❑ 06549	Blue Eyed Elaine/(B-side unknown)	194?	6.25	12.50	25.00
❑ 6627	I Hang My Head and Cry/You'll Be Sorry	1942	6.25	12.50	25.00
❑ 6648	I'm Thinking Tonight of My Blue Eyes/I'll Be True While You're Gone	1942	6.25	12.50	25.00
❑ 6680	Tweedle-O-Twill/Take Me Back Into Your Heart	1942	6.25	12.50	25.00
❑ 6682	Private Buckaroo/Rainbows on the Rio Colorado	1942	6.25	12.50	25.00
❑ 6684	Call Me and I'll Be There/Yesterday's Roses	1942	6.25	12.50	25.00
❑ 6690	Jingle, Jangle, Jingle/I'm a Cow Poke Pokin' Along	1942	6.25	12.50	25.00
❑ 6728	Gonna Build a Big Fence Around Texas/Don't Fence Me In	1944	6.25	12.50	25.00
❑ 6737	At Mail Call Today/I'll Be Back	1945	6.25	12.50	25.00
❑ 6743	Darlin' What More Can I Do?/I Guess I've Been Asleep	1945	7.50	15.00	30.00
PERFECT					
❑ 12952	The Last Round-Up/(B-side unknown)	1933	17.50	35.00	70.00
QRS					
❑ 1044	Living in the Mountains/I'll Be Thinking of You, Little Gal	1929	1000.	2000.	4000.
❑ 1047	Blue Yodel No. 6/(B-side unknown)	1929	250.00	500.00	1000.
❑ 1048	That's Why I Left the Mountains/(B-side unknown)	1929	250.00	500.00	1000.
ROMEO					
❑ 5109	That Silver Haired Daddy of Mine/(B-side unknown)	193?	75.00	150.00	300.00
❑ 5110	Jailhouse Blues/(B-side unknown)	193?	75.00	150.00	300.00
SUPERIOR					
❑ 2561	The Girl I Left Behind/(B-side unknown)	193?	75.00	150.00	300.00
❑ 2596	Dad in the Hills/(B-side unknown)	193?	50.00	100.00	200.00
❑ 2637	Pistol Packin' Papa/(B-side unknown)	193?	50.00	100.00	200.00
❑ 2660	Mean Mama Blues/(B-side unknown)	193?	50.00	100.00	200.00
❑ 2681	That's How I Got My Start/(B-side unknown)	193?	50.00	100.00	200.00
❑ 2710	Blue Days/(B-side unknown)	193?	50.00	100.00	200.00
❑ 2732	Money Ain't No Use Anyway/(B-side unknown)	193?	50.00	100.00	200.00
❑ 2769	Hobo Bill's Last Ride/(B-side unknown)	193?	50.00	100.00	200.00
SUPERTONE					
❑ 9702	Hobo Bill's Last Ride/(B-side unknown)	193?	17.50	35.00	70.00
❑ 9704	They Cut Down the Old Pine Tree/In the Shadow of the Pine	193?	17.50	35.00	70.00
❑ 9705	Whisper Your Mother's Name/(B-side unknown)	193?	17.50	35.00	70.00
❑ 9706	Train Whistle Blues/(B-side unknown)	193?	17.50	35.00	70.00
VELVET TONE					
❑ 2338-V	True Blue Bill/(B-side unknown)	193?	15.00	30.00	60.00
❑ 2374-V	A Gangster's Warning/(B-side unknown)	193?	15.00	30.00	60.00
❑ 7056-V	Hobo Yodel/(B-side unknown)	193?	15.00	30.00	60.00
❑ 7057-V	Waiting for a Train/(B-side unknown)	193?	15.00	30.00	60.00
❑ 7058-V	Blue Yodel No. 4/(B-side unknown)	193?	15.00	30.00	60.00
❑ 7059-V	Lullaby Yodel/(B-side unknown)	193?	15.00	30.00	60.00
❑ 7061-V	No One to Call Me Darling/(B-side unknown)	193?	15.00	30.00	60.00
❑ 7063-V	Frankie and Johnny/(B-side unknown)	193?	15.00	30.00	60.00
❑ 7075-V	My Rough and Rowdy Ways/(B-side unknown)	193?	15.00	30.00	60.00
❑ 7083-V	Cowboy Yodel/Why Don't You Come Back to Me	193?	15.00	30.00	60.00
VICTOR					
❑ 23530	Bear Cat Papa/(B-side unknown)	1931	50.00	100.00	200.00
❑ 23548	Do Right Daddy/(B-side unknown)	1931	50.00	100.00	200.00
❑ 23561	There's a Good Gal in the Mountains/(B-side unknown)	1931	50.00	100.00	200.00
❑ 23589	High Steppin' Mama/(B-side unknown)	1931	50.00	100.00	200.00
❑ 23617	She's a Low Down Mamma/(B-side unknown)	1931	50.00	100.00	200.00
❑ 23630	Rheumatism Blues/(B-side unknown)	1931	50.00	100.00	200.00
❑ 23642	Wild Cat Mama/(B-side unknown)	1932	62.50	125.00	250.00
❑ 23673	I'm Always Dreaming of You/(B-side unknown)	1932	62.50	125.00	250.00
❑ 23707	Black Bottom Blues/(B-side unknown)	1932	62.50	125.00	250.00
❑ 23720	Kentucky Lullaby/(B-side unknown)	1932	62.50	125.00	250.00
❑ 23725	The Gangster's Warning/(B-side unknown)	1932	62.50	125.00	250.00
❑ 23726	Back to the Old Smoky Mountains/(B-side unknown)	1932	62.50	125.00	250.00
❑ 23783	Cowboy's Heaven/(B-side unknown)	1933	62.50	125.00	250.00
❑ 23792	Louisiana Moon/(B-side unknown)	1933	62.50	125.00	250.00
❑ 23810	Your Voice Is Calling/(B-side unknown)	1933	75.00	150.00	300.00
❑ V40200	My Alabama Home/My Dreaming of You	1930	50.00	100.00	200.00
VOCALION					
❑ 02991	That Silver Haired Daddy of Mine/(B-side unknown)	1935	12.50	25.00	50.00
❑ 03007	titles unknown	1935	12.50	25.00	50.00
❑ 03070	Don't Waste Your Tears on Me/Nobody's Darling But Mine	1935	12.50	25.00	50.00
❑ 03097	Mexicali Rose/You're the Only Star (In My Blue Heaven)	1935	12.50	25.00	50.00
❑ 03101	The Answer to Red River Valley/(B-side unknown)	193?	12.50	25.00	50.00
❑ 03138	titles unknown	1936	12.50	25.00	50.00
❑ 03229	titles unknown	1936	12.50	25.00	50.00
❑ 03262	I Hate to Say Goodbye to the Prairie/(B-side unknown)	193?	12.50	25.00	50.00
❑ 03291	titles unknown	193?	12.50	25.00	50.00
❑ 03317	titles unknown	193?	12.50	25.00	50.00
❑ 03358	Sail Along Silvery Moon/There's a Gold Mine in the Sky	1936	12.50	25.00	50.00
❑ 03448	titles unknown	193?	12.50	25.00	50.00
❑ 04091	titles unknown	193?	10.00	20.00	40.00
❑ 04146	I Want a Pardon for Daddy/The End of My Round-Up Days	1938	10.00	20.00	40.00
❑ 04172	Dust/(B-side unknown)	1938	10.00	20.00	40.00
❑ 04246	As Long As I've Got My Horse/(B-side unknown)	1938	10.00	20.00	40.00
❑ 04262	Ride Tenderfoot Ride/The Old Trail	1938	10.00	20.00	40.00
❑ 04267	titles unknown	1938	10.00	20.00	40.00
❑ 04274	titles unknown	1938	10.00	20.00	40.00
❑ 04340	Good Bye Pinto/(B-side unknown)	193?	10.00	20.00	40.00
❑ 04375	Louisiana Moon/(B-side unknown)	193?	10.00	20.00	40.00
❑ 04415	titles unknown	1939	10.00	20.00	40.00
❑ 04485	The Last Round-Up/Way Out West in Texas	1939	10.00	20.00	40.00
❑ 04998	The Yellow Rose of Texas/(B-side unknown)	1939	10.00	20.00	40.00
❑ 05080	Back in the Saddle Again/Little Old Band of Gold	1939	15.00	30.00	60.00
❑ 05122	South of the Border (Down Mexico Way)/(B-side unknown)	1939	10.00	20.00	40.00
❑ 05190	Little Pardner/(B-side unknown)	1940	10.00	20.00	40.00
❑ 05463	Goodbye Little Darlin' Goodbye/When I'm Gone You'll Soon Forget	1940	10.00	20.00	40.00
❑ 05513	The Singing Hills/(B-side unknown)	1940	10.00	20.00	40.00
Albums					
CHALLENGE					
❑ CHL-600 [M]	Christmas with Gene Autry	1958	12.50	25.00	50.00
COLUMBIA					
❑ CL 677 [M]	Gene Autry and Champion — Western Adventures	1955	30.00	60.00	120.00
❑ CL 1575 [M]	Gene Autry's Greatest Hits	1961	7.50	15.00	30.00
—Red and black label with six "eye" logos					
❑ CL 2547 [10]	Merry Christmas with Gene Autry	1954	30.00	60.00	120.00
—"House Party Series" release					
❑ CL 2568 [10]	Gene Autry Sings Peter Cottontail	1955	30.00	60.00	120.00
❑ CL 6020 [10]	Easter Favorites	1949	37.50	75.00	150.00
❑ CL 6137 [10]	Merry Christmas	1950	37.50	75.00	150.00
❑ JL 8001 [10]	Gene Autry at the Rodeo	1949	37.50	75.00	150.00
❑ JL 8009 [10]	Stampede	1949	37.50	75.00	150.00
❑ JL 8012 [10]	Champion	1950	37.50	75.00	150.00
❑ CL 9001 [10]	Western Classics, Volume 1	1949	37.50	75.00	150.00
❑ CL 9002 [10]	Western Classics, Volume 2	1949	37.50	75.00	150.00
COLUMBIA SPECIAL PRODUCTS					
❑ P 15766	Christmas Favorites	1981	3.00	6.00	12.00
GRAND PRIX					
❑ KX-11 [M]	The Original Gene Autry Sings Rudolph the Red-Nosed Reindeer and Other Christmas Favorites	1961	3.75	7.50	15.00
❑ KS-X11 [S]	The Original Gene Autry Sings Rudolph the Red-Nosed Reindeer and Other Christmas Favorites	1961	5.00	10.00	20.00
GUSTO					
❑ 1038	Christmas Classics	19??	2.50	5.00	10.00
HARMONY					
❑ HL 7332 [M]	Gene Autry's Great Western Hits	1965	7.50	15.00	30.00
❑ HL 7376 [M]	Back in the Saddle Again	1966	5.00	10.00	20.00
❑ HL 7399 [M]	Gene Autry Sings	1966	5.00	10.00	20.00
❑ HL 9505 [M]	Gene Autry and Champion — Western Adventures	1959	7.50	15.00	30.00
❑ HL 9550 [M]	The Original Rudolph the Red-Nosed Reindeer and Other Children's Christmas Favorites	1964	6.25	12.50	25.00
❑ HS 14450 [R]	The Original Rudolph the Red-Nosed Reindeer and Other Children's Christmas Favorites	1964	3.00	6.00	12.00
MELODY RANCH					
❑ 101 [M]	Melody Ranch	1965	10.00	20.00	40.00
MURRAY HILL					
❑ 897296 [(4)]	Melody Ranch Radio Show	197?	15.00	30.00	60.00
—Compilation of some of Gene's radio shows in a box set					
RCA VICTOR					
❑ LPM-2623 [M]	Gene Autry's Golden Hits	1962	7.50	15.00	30.00
❑ LSP-2623 [S]	Gene Autry's Golden Hits	1962	10.00	20.00	40.00
REPUBLIC					
❑ 6011	South of the Border, All American Cowboy	1976	5.00	10.00	20.00
❑ 6012	Cowboy Hall of Fame	1976	5.00	10.00	20.00
❑ RLP 6018 [M]	Christmas with Gene Autry	1976	3.00	6.00	12.00

AXTON, HOYT

45s

Number	Title (A Side/B Side)	Yr	VG	VG+	NM
20TH FOX					
❑ 6648	Five Dollar Bill/Smoky	1966	2.50	5.00	10.00
A&M					
❑ 1437	Sweet Misery/Less Than the Song	1973	—	2.50	5.00
❑ 1497	When the Morning Comes/Billie's Theme	1974	—	2.50	5.00
❑ 1607	Boney Fingers/Life Machine	1974	—	2.50	5.00
❑ 1657	Nashville/Speed Trap	1974	—	2.50	5.00
❑ 1683	Lion in the Winter/No No Song	1975	—	2.50	5.00
❑ 1713	In a Young Girl's Mind/Southbound	1975	—	2.50	5.00
❑ 1811	Flash of Fire/Paid in Advance	1976	—	2.00	4.00
BRIAR					
❑ 100	Georgia Hoss Soldier/Drinking Gourd	1961	3.75	7.50	15.00
CAPITOL					
❑ 3121	Alice in Wonderland/Have a Nice Day	1971	—	3.00	6.00
❑ 3167	California Women/Ease Your Pain	1971	—	3.00	6.00
❑ 3259	Speed Traps/Hey, Mr. Pilot Man	1972	—	3.00	6.00
COLGEMS					
❑ 66-1005	San Fernando/Ten Thousand Sunsets	1967	2.50	5.00	10.00
COLUMBIA					
❑ 44810	Snowblind Friend/It's All Right Now	1969	—	3.50	7.00
❑ 44850	Way Before the Time of Towns/It's All Right Now	1969	—	3.50	7.00
ELEKTRA					
❑ 47133	Flo's Yellow Rose/Lion in the Winter	1981	—	2.00	4.00

Number	Title (A Side/B Side)	Yr	VG	VG+	NM
HORIZON					
❑ 2	Grizzly Bear/Gypsy Woman	1963	2.50	5.00	10.00
❑ 6	The Happy Song/We'll Sing in the Sunshine	1963	2.50	5.00	10.00
❑ 351	Greenback Dollar/Crawdad Song	1962	3.75	7.50	15.00
❑ 360	Grizzly Bear/Gypsy Woman	1963	3.00	6.00	12.00
❑ 361	This Little Light/Thunder 'N' Lightnin'	1963	3.00	6.00	12.00
❑ 362	One More Round/Greenback Dollar	1963	3.00	6.00	12.00
JEREMIAH					
❑ 1000	Della and the Dealer/A Young Girl's Mind	1979	—	2.00	4.00
❑ 1001	A Rusty Old Halo/Keep Rollin'	1979	—	2.00	4.00
❑ 1003	Wild Bull Rider/Torpedo	1979	—	2.00	4.00
❑ 1005	Evangelina/So Hard to Give It All Up	1980	—	2.00	4.00
❑ 1006	Boozers Are Losers (When the Benders Don't End)/Politicians	1980	—	2.00	4.00
❑ 1008	Where Did the Money Go/Smile As You Go By	1980	—	2.00	4.00
❑ 1011	The Devil/Jealous Man	1981	—	2.00	4.00
❑ 1012	Win This One/Ease Your Pain	1981	—	2.00	4.00
❑ 1014	She's Too Lazy to Be Crazy/You Do Not Tango	1982	—	2.00	4.00
❑ 1015	There Stands the Glass/James Dean and the Junkman	1982	—	2.00	4.00
❑ 1016	Pistol Packin' Mama/Fearless the Wonderdog	1982	—	2.00	4.00
❑ 1017	Warm Storms and Wild Flowers/Don't Fence Me In	1983	—	2.00	4.00
❑ 1018	If You're a Cowboy/I Collect Hearts	1983	—	2.00	4.00
MCA					
❑ 40711	You're the Hangnail in My Life/Never Been to Spain	1977	—	2.00	4.00
❑ 40731	Little White Moon/Funeral of the King	1977	—	2.50	5.00
VEE JAY					
❑ 604	L.A. Town/Double Double Dare	1964	3.00	6.00	12.00
❑ 619	Bring Your Lovin'/Tiger in the Closet	1964	3.00	6.00	12.00
❑ 659	Hush Hush Sweet Charlotte/After You've Gone	1965	2.50	5.00	10.00
Albums					
ACCORD					
❑ SN-7197	Heartbreak Hotel	1982	2.50	5.00	10.00
ALLEGIANCE					
❑ AV-5023	Down and Out	1984	2.50	5.00	10.00
A&M					
❑ SP-3155	Life Machine	198?	2.00	4.00	8.00
—Budget-line reissue					
❑ SP-3182	Road Songs	198?	2.00	4.00	8.00
—Budget-line reissue					
❑ SP-4376	Less Than a Song	1973	2.50	5.00	10.00
❑ SP-4402	Life Machine	1974	2.50	5.00	10.00
❑ SP-4510	Southbound	1975	2.50	5.00	10.00
❑ SP-4571	Fearless	1976	2.50	5.00	10.00
❑ SP-4669	Road Songs	1977	2.50	5.00	10.00
BRYLEN					
❑ BN 4400	Double Dare	1982	3.00	6.00	12.00
CAPITOL					
❑ ST-788	Joy to the World	1971	3.00	6.00	12.00
❑ SMAS-850	Country Anthem	1971	3.00	6.00	12.00
COLUMBIA					
❑ CS 9766	My Griffin Is Gone	1969	3.75	7.50	15.00
❑ KC 33103	My Griffin Is Gone	1975	2.50	5.00	10.00
❑ PC 33103	My Griffin Is Gone	1979	2.00	4.00	8.00
—Budget-line reissue					
EXODUS					
❑ EX-301 [M]	Hoyt Axton Sings Bessie Smith	1966	5.00	10.00	20.00
❑ EXS-321 [M]	Saturday's Child	1966	5.00	10.00	20.00
—Cover says stereo, record plays mono					
HORIZON					
❑ WP-1601 [M]	The Balladeer	1962	6.25	12.50	25.00
—Black label					
❑ WP-1601 [M]	Greenback Dollar	1963	5.00	10.00	20.00
—Black label; two fewer songs than "The Balladeer"					
❑ WP-1601 [S]	The Balladeer	1962	7.50	15.00	30.00
—Same number as mono, but with blue label					
❑ WP-1601 [S]	Greenback Dollar	1963	6.25	12.50	25.00
—Blue label; two fewer songs than "The Balladeer"					
❑ SWP-1613 [S]	Thunder 'N Lightnin'	1963	7.50	15.00	30.00
❑ WP-1613 [M]	Thunder 'N Lightnin'	1963	6.25	12.50	25.00
❑ SWP-1621 [S]	Saturday's Child	1963	7.50	15.00	30.00
❑ WP-1621 [M]	Saturday's Child	1963	6.25	12.50	25.00
JEREMIAH					
❑ JH-5000	A Rusty Old Halo	1979	3.00	6.00	12.00
❑ JH-5001	Where Did the Money Go?	1980	3.00	6.00	12.00
MCA					
❑ 647	Snow Blind Friend	198?	2.00	4.00	8.00
—Budget-line reissue					
❑ 648	Free Sailin'	198?	2.00	4.00	8.00
—Budget-line reissue					
❑ 2263	Snow Blind Friend	1977	2.50	5.00	10.00
❑ 2319	Free Sailin'	1978	2.50	5.00	10.00
SURREY					
❑ S-1005 [M]	Mr. Greenback Dollar Man	1965	5.00	10.00	20.00
❑ SS-1005 [S]	Mr. Greenback Dollar Man	1965	6.25	12.50	25.00
VEE JAY					
❑ LP-1098 [M]	Hoyt Axton Explodes!	1964	6.25	12.50	25.00
❑ LPS-1098 [R]	Hoyt Axton Explodes!	1964	5.00	10.00	20.00
❑ LP-1118 [M]	The Best of Hoyt Axton	1965	5.00	10.00	20.00
❑ LPS-1118 [S]	The Best of Hoyt Axton	1965	6.25	12.50	25.00
❑ LP-1126 [M]	Greenback Dollar	1965	5.00	10.00	20.00
❑ LPS-1126 [S]	Greenback Dollar	1965	6.25	12.50	25.00
❑ LP-1127 [M]	Saturday's Child	1965	5.00	10.00	20.00
❑ LPS-1127 [S]	Saturday's Child	1965	6.25	12.50	25.00
—Reissue of Horizon 1621					
❑ LP-1128 [M]	Thunder 'N Lightnin'	1965	5.00	10.00	20.00
❑ LPS-1128 [S]	Thunder 'N Lightnin'	1965	6.25	12.50	25.00
—Reissue of Horizon 1613					
VEE JAY INTERNATIONAL					
❑ VJS-2-1005 [(2)]	Gold	1974	5.00	10.00	20.00
—Compilation of older Vee Jay material					
❑ LP-6001	Long Old Road	1977	3.75	7.50	15.00
VEE JAY/DYNASTY					
❑ VJS-7306	Bessie Smith... My Way	1974	3.75	7.50	15.00

B

BACKROADS

Number	Title (A Side/B Side)	Yr	VG	VG+	NM
45s					
SOUNDWAVES					
❑ 4698	So Close/Gonna Stay at Night	1983	—	2.50	5.00
❑ 4718	He's a Runner/So Close	1983	—	2.50	5.00

BACKTRACK FEATURING JOHN HUNT

Number	Title (A Side/B Side)	Yr	VG	VG+	NM
45s					
GOLDMINE					
❑ 11	Mexico/I'm On the Outside	1985	—	3.00	6.00

BADALE, ANDY

Number	Title (A Side/B Side)	Yr	VG	VG+	NM
45s					
GP					
❑ 577	Nashville Beer Garden/Finger Pickin' Good	1980	—	3.00	6.00

BAGWELL, WENDY

Number	Title (A Side/B Side)	Yr	VG	VG+	NM
Albums					
CANAAN					
❑ 8331	And That's a Fact With My Hand Up	196?	3.75	7.50	15.00
❑ 9679	This, That and the Other	1971	3.75	7.50	15.00
❑ 9699	You Won't Believe This	197?	3.75	7.50	15.00
❑ 9765	Bust Out Laffin'	197?	3.00	6.00	12.00
❑ 9869	The Known Comic	197?	3.00	6.00	12.00

BAILES, EDDY

Number	Title (A Side/B Side)	Yr	VG	VG+	NM
45s					
CIN KAY					
❑ 101	Love Isn't Love (Till You Give It Away)/Houston	1976	—	2.50	5.00
❑ 104	Woman, Woman/Down in Texas	1976	—	2.50	5.00
❑ 112	Ohio/Honky Tonk Away	1976	—	2.50	5.00

BAILEY, GLEN

Number	Title (A Side/B Side)	Yr	VG	VG+	NM
45s					
YATAHEY					
❑ 1221	Stompin' on My Heart/(B-side unknown)	1982	—	2.50	5.00
❑ 3024	Designer Jeans/(B-side unknown)	1982	—	2.50	5.00
❑ 3024 [PS]	Designer Jeans/(B-side unknown)	1982	2.00	4.00	8.00

BAILEY, JOHNNY

Number	Title (A Side/B Side)	Yr	VG	VG+	NM
45s					
SOUNDWAVES					
❑ 4695	What's She Doing to My Mind/This Country Music's Driving Me Crazy	1983	—	2.50	5.00

BAILEY, JUDY

Also see MOE BANDY.

Number	Title (A Side/B Side)	Yr	VG	VG+	NM
45s					
COLUMBIA					
❑ 11-0 2045	Slow Country Dancin'/Anything You Can Do (I Can Do Worse)	1981	—	2.00	4.00
❑ 18-02505	The Best Bedroom in Town/I'm Guilty of Loving You	1981	—	2.00	4.00
WARNER BROS.					
❑ 29799	Tender Lovin' Lies/Tryin' Hard Not to Be Easy	1983	—	2.00	4.00
WHITE GOLD					
❑ 22249	There's a Lot of Good About Goodbye/Comfort	1985	—	2.50	5.00

BAILEY, LYNN

Number	Title (A Side/B Side)	Yr	VG	VG+	NM
45s					
E&R					
❑ 8101	Too Much, Too Little, Too Late/(B-side unknown)	1981	—	3.00	6.00
FRATERNITY					
❑ 3376	A Little Light Shines/Love, Peace and Music	1975	—	2.50	5.00
❑ 3379	An Orange in a Bag/Ivory Tower	197?	—	2.50	5.00
❑ 3389	Jimmy/Mama Don't Be Blue	197?	—	2.50	5.00
❑ 3396	Messin'/Letters	197?	—	2.50	5.00
❑ 3415	This World/Tupelo Travelin' Show	1977	—	2.50	5.00

Number	Title (A Side/B Side)	Yr	VG	VG+	NM
WARTRACE					
❑ 613	Cheater Fever/Small Talk	1980	—	3.00	6.00

BAILEY, RAZZY

Number	Title (A Side/B Side)	Yr	VG	VG+	NM
45s					
ABC					
❑ 10939	Stolen Moments/Re-Enlistment Papers	1967	3.00	6.00	12.00
AQUARIAN					
❑ 601	I Hate Hate/Singing Other People's Songs	1974	3.00	6.00	12.00
—As "Razzy"					
CAPRICORN					
❑ 0238	Grits and Gravy/Peanut Butter	1975	—	3.00	6.00
ERASTUS					
❑ 526	Keepin' Rosie Proud of Me/Candy Store	1976	—	3.00	6.00
❑ 528	Sweet Memories/Love Bump	1977	—	3.00	6.00
MCA					
❑ 52421	Knock on Wood/If You Happen to See My Baby	1984	—	—	3.00
❑ 52500	Touchy Situation/Music Takes Me Past the Point	1984	—	—	3.00
❑ 52547	Modern Day Marriages/New Orleans When It Rains	1985	—	—	3.00
❑ 52628	Fightin' Fire with Fire/To Write a Sad Song	1985	—	—	3.00
❑ 52701	Old Blue Yodeler/To Write a Sad Song	1985	—	—	3.00
❑ 52851	Rockin' in the Parkin' Lot/Baby My Baby	1986	—	—	3.00
MGM					
❑ 14754	Quarter to Three/Old No Homer	1974	—	2.50	5.00
—As "Razzy"					
RCA					
❑ PB-11226	Anywhere There's a Jukebox/Is It Over	1978	—	2.00	4.00
❑ PB-11338	What Time Do You Have to Be Back in Heaven/That's the Way a Cowboy Rocks and Rolls	1978	—	2.00	4.00
❑ PB-11446	Tonight She's Gonna Love Me (Like There Was No Tomorrow)/Old Love Letters	1978	—	2.00	4.00
❑ PB-11536	If Love Had a Face/Natural Love	1979	—	2.00	4.00
❑ PB-11682	I Ain't Got No Business Doin' Business Today/Conchita	1979	—	2.00	4.00
❑ PB-11885	I Can't Get Enough of You/The North Won the War Again Last Night	1979	—	2.00	4.00
❑ PB-11954	Too Old to Play Cowboy/9,999,999 Tears	1980	—	2.00	4.00
❑ GB-11990	What Time Do You Have to Be Back in Heaven/If Love Had a Face	1980	—	—	3.00
—"Gold Standard Series" reissue					
❑ PB-12062	Lovin' Up a Storm/What's a Little Love Between Friends	1980	—	2.00	4.00
❑ PB-12062 [PS]	Lovin' Up a Storm/What's a Little Love Between Friends	1980	—	3.00	6.00
❑ JB-12120 [DJ]	I Keep Coming Back/True Life Country Music	1980	3.00	6.00	12.00
—Promo only on green vinyl					
❑ PB-12120	I Keep Coming Back/True Life Country Music	1980	—	2.00	4.00
❑ PB-12120 [PS]	I Keep Coming Back/True Life Country Music	1980	—	2.50	5.00
❑ PB-12199	Friends/Anywhere There's a Jukebox	1981	—	2.00	4.00
❑ JB-12268 [DJ]	Midnight Hauler (same on both sides)	1981	3.00	6.00	12.00
—Promo only on blue vinyl					
❑ PB-12268	Midnight Hauler/Scratch My Back (And Whisper in My Ear)	1981	—	2.00	4.00
❑ GB-12311	Friends/Lovin' Up a Storm	1981	—	—	3.00
—"Gold Standard Series" reissue					
❑ PB-13007	She Left Love All Over Me/Blaze of Glory	1981	—	2.00	4.00
❑ JB-13084	Everytime You Cross My Mind (You Break My Heart) (same on both sides)	1982	3.00	6.00	12.00
—Promo only on red vinyl					
❑ PB-13084	Everytime You Cross My Mind (You Break My Heart)/Tonight She's Gonna Love Me (Like There Was No Tomorrow)	1982	—	2.00	4.00
❑ PB-13290	Love's Gonna Fall Here Tonight/Singin' Other People's Songs	1982	—	2.00	4.00
❑ JK-13359 [DJ]	Peace on Earth (same on both sides)	1982	2.50	5.00	10.00
—Promo only on green vinyl					
❑ PB-13359	Peace on Earth/Let It Snow, Let It Snow, Let It Snow	1982	—	2.50	5.00
—B-side by Charley Pride					
❑ JK-13383 [DJ]	Poor Boy (same on both sides)	1982	2.50	5.00	10.00
—Promo only on blue vinyl					
❑ PB-13383	Poor Boy/What Time Do You Have to Be Back to Heaven	1982	—	2.00	4.00
❑ JK-13512 [DJ]	After the Great Depression (same on both sides)	1983	2.50	5.00	10.00
—Promo only on red vinyl					
❑ PB-13512	After the Great Depression/Guess Who's Gonna Be a Dad	1983	—	2.00	4.00
❑ PB-13630	This Is Just the First Day/Night Life	1983	—	2.00	4.00
❑ PB-13718	In the Midnight Hour/Mr. Melody Man	1984	—	2.00	4.00
SOA					
❑ 001	If Love Ever Made a Fool/(B-side unknown)	1987	—	2.50	5.00
❑ 002	Unattended Fire/Lover Please	1988	—	2.50	5.00
❑ 003	Starting All Over Again/(B-side unknown)	1988	—	2.50	5.00
❑ 006	But You Will/(B-side unknown)	1989	—	2.50	5.00
Albums					
MCA					
❑ 5544	Cut from a Different Stone	1985	2.00	4.00	8.00
❑ 5615	Arrival	1986	2.00	4.00	8.00
RCA VICTOR					
❑ AHL1-3391	If Love Had a Face	1979	2.50	5.00	10.00
❑ AHL1-3688	Razzy	1980	2.00	4.00	8.00
❑ AHL1-4026	Makin' Friends	1981	2.00	4.00	8.00
❑ AHL1-4228	Feelin' Right	1982	2.00	4.00	8.00
❑ AHL1-4423	A Little More Razz	1982	2.00	4.00	8.00
❑ AHL1-4679	Greatest Hits	1983	2.00	4.00	8.00
❑ AHL1-4936	The Midnight Hour	1984	2.00	4.00	8.00

BAILLIE AND THE BOYS

Number	Title (A Side/B Side)	Yr	VG	VG+	NM
45s					
RCA					
❑ 2500-7-R	Perfect/Lovin' By Numbers	1990	—	—	3.00
❑ 2641-7-R	Fool Such as I/(B-side unknown)	1990	—	2.00	4.00
❑ 2720-7-R	Treat Me Like a Stranger/I'd Love To	1990	—	—	3.00
❑ 5130-7-R	Oh Heart/Waitin' Out the Storm	1987	—	—	3.00
❑ 5130-7-R [PS]	Oh Heart/Waitin' Out the Storm	1987	2.00	4.00	8.00
—Sleeve is promo only					
❑ 5227-7-R	He's Letting Go/Heartless Night	1987	—	—	3.00
❑ 5327-7-R	Wilder Days/You Fool	1987	—	—	3.00
❑ 8631-7-R	Long Shot/You Fool	1988	—	—	3.00
❑ 8796-7-R	She Deserves You/The Only Lonely One	1989	—	—	3.00
❑ 8944-7-R	(I Wish I Had a) Heart of Stone/Heartache in Motion	1989	—	—	3.00
❑ 9076-7-R	I Can't Turn the Tide/The Only Lonely One	1989	—	—	3.00
Albums					
RCA					
❑ 6272-1-R	Baillie and the Boys	1987	2.00	4.00	8.00
❑ 8454-1-R	Turn the Tide	1989	2.50	5.00	10.00

BAKER, ADAM

Number	Title (A Side/B Side)	Yr	VG	VG+	NM
45s					
AVISTA					
❑ 8601	In Love with Her/They Come and They Go	1986	—	2.50	5.00
❑ 8602	Weren't You Listening/Dixie Nightlife	1986	—	2.50	5.00
❑ 8703	You've Got a Right/(B-side unknown)	1987	—	2.50	5.00
❑ 8704	Standing Invitation/Dixie Nightlife	1987	—	2.50	5.00
SIGNATURE					
❑ 22484	I Can See Him in Her Eyes/(B-side unknown)	1985	—	3.00	6.00

BAKER, BUTCH

Number	Title (A Side/B Side)	Yr	VG	VG+	NM
45s					
MERCURY					
❑ 818379-7	Breakin' In a Broken Heart/Torture	1984	—	2.00	4.00
❑ 870486-7	Party People/After Losing You	1988	—	—	3.00
❑ 874746-7	Our Little Corner/Party People	1989	—	—	3.00
❑ 876226-7	Wonderful Tonight/Party People	1989	—	—	3.00
❑ 880020-7	Burn Georgia Burn (There's a Fire in Your Soul)/Bury My Heart (In the Smoky Mountains)	1984	—	—	3.00
❑ 880256-7	Thinkin' 'Bout Leaving/Bury My Heart (In the Smoky Mountains)	1984	—	—	3.00
❑ 880653-7	Lady Loves Her Job/Breakin' In a Broken Heart	1985	—	—	3.00
❑ 880836-7	They Ain't Like You Girl/Lady Loves Her Job	1985	—	—	3.00
❑ 884857-7	That's What Her Memory Is For/After Losing You	1986	—	—	3.00
❑ 888133-7	Your Loving Side/After Losing You	1986	—	—	3.00
❑ 888543-7	Don't It Make You Wanta Go Home/Your Loving Side	1987	—	—	3.00
❑ 888926-7	I'll Fall in Love Again/After Losing You	1987	—	—	3.00
Albums					
MERCURY					
❑ 834777-1	We Will	1989	2.50	5.00	10.00

BAKER, CARROLL

Number	Title (A Side/B Side)	Yr	VG	VG+	NM
45s					
EXCELSIOR					
❑ 1013	Mama What Does Cheatin' Mean/Lover on the Shelf	1981	—	3.00	6.00
❑ 1021	Ain't Nothin' Like a Rainy Night/(B-side unknown)	1981	—	3.00	6.00
TEMBO					
❑ 8520	It Always Hurts Like the First Time/(B-side unknown)	1985	—	3.00	6.00

BAKER, GEORGE, SELECTION

Not a country act, this Dutch group made the country charts with the below record.

Number	Title (A Side/B Side)	Yr	VG	VG+	NM
45s					
WARNER BROS.					
❑ 8115	Paloma Blanca/Dreamboat	1975	—	2.00	4.00

BAKER AND MYERS

Number	Title (A Side/B Side)	Yr	VG	VG+	NM
45s					
CURB					
❑ 76967	These Arms/Years from Here	1995	—	2.00	4.00

BALL, DAVID

Number	Title (A Side/B Side)	Yr	VG	VG+	NM
45s					
RCA					
❑ 6899-7-R	Steppin' Out/I Wish He Was Me (And She Was You)	1988	—	2.00	4.00
❑ 8636-7-R	You Go, You're Gone/I Wish He Was Me (And She Was You)	1988	—	2.00	4.00
❑ 8975-7-R	Gift of Love/I Wish He Was Me (And She Was You)	1989	—	2.00	4.00
WARNER BROS.					
❑ 16927	I Want To with You/When I Get Lonely	1999	—	—	3.00
❑ 16982	Watching My Baby Not Coming Back/Going Someplace to Forget	1999	—	—	3.00
❑ 17445	I'd Never Make It Through This Fall/What Kind of Hold	1996	—	—	3.00
❑ 17574	Hangin' In and Hangin' On/If You'd Like Some Lovin'	1996	—	—	3.00

Number	Title (A Side/B Side)	Yr	VG	VG+	NM
❑ 17639	Circle of Friends/No More Lonely	1996	—	—	3.00
❑ 17785	Honky Tonk Healin'/Blowin' Smoke	1995	—	2.00	4.00
❑ 17977	Look What Followed Me Home/What Do You Want with His Love	1994	—	2.00	4.00
❑ 18081	When the Thought of You Catches Up with Me/ Don't Think Twice	1994	—	2.00	4.00
❑ 18250	Thinkin' Problem/Down at the Bottom of a Broken Heart	1994	—	2.00	4.00

BALL, MARCIA

45s

CAPITOL

Number	Title (A Side/B Side)	Yr	VG	VG+	NM
❑ 4591	Good Times, Good Music, Good Friends/Train to Dixie	1978	—	2.50	5.00
❑ 4633	I'm a Fool to Care/50 Words or Less	1978	—	2.50	5.00

Albums

CAPITOL

Number	Title (A Side/B Side)	Yr	VG	VG+	NM
❑ ST-11752	Circuit Queen	1978	3.00	6.00	12.00

BALLARD, LARRY

45s

CAPITOL

Number	Title (A Side/B Side)	Yr	VG	VG+	NM
❑ 4247	Booze the Blues Away/I'm Gone	1976	—	2.50	5.00
❑ 4309	Send Her On Home to Me/The Silver Eagle	1976	—	2.50	5.00
❑ 4352	Honky Tonk Heaven/Someone That I Can Forget	1976	—	2.50	5.00
❑ 4391	Mother Texas/One More Hurtin' Song	1977	—	2.50	5.00

ELEKTRA

Number	Title (A Side/B Side)	Yr	VG	VG+	NM
❑ 45216	Youngblood and Sweet Country Music/I Think I'd Like to Love Again	1974	—	2.50	5.00

BALLARD, ROGER

45s

ATLANTIC

Number	Title (A Side/B Side)	Yr	VG	VG+	NM
❑ 87313	Two Steps in the Right Direction/A Little Piece of Heaven	1993	—	2.00	4.00

BALLEW, MICHAEL

45s

LIBERTY

Number	Title (A Side/B Side)	Yr	VG	VG+	NM
❑ 1447	Pretending Fool/Ain't No Future in Loving You	1982	—	2.00	4.00

BAMA BAND

45s

CAPITOL

Number	Title (A Side/B Side)	Yr	VG	VG+	NM
❑ 7PRO-79476	My Reckless Heart (same on both sides)	1990	—	2.50	5.00

—Vinyl is promo only

COMPLEAT

Number	Title (A Side/B Side)	Yr	VG	VG+	NM
❑ 144	What Used to Be Crazy/White Cadillac	1985	—	2.00	4.00
❑ 144 [PS]	What Used to Be Crazy/White Cadillac	1985	—	2.50	5.00
❑ 150	Shop Shop/Too Voodoo	1985	—	2.50	5.00
❑ 152	I've Changed My Mind/Stone Cold Country	1986	—	2.00	4.00
❑ 163	Suddenly Single/Save the Dress	1987	—	2.00	4.00

MERCURY

Number	Title (A Side/B Side)	Yr	VG	VG+	NM
❑ 870603-7	Southern Accent/It's Gotta Be Love	1988	—	—	3.00
❑ 872048-7	I Got a Rocket in My Pocket/Ellen B.	1988	—	—	3.00
❑ 872150-7	Real Old-Fashioned Broken Heart/Ellen B.	1988	—	—	3.00
❑ 872650-7	When We Get Back to the Farm/(B-side unknown)	1989	—	2.00	4.00

OASIS

Number	Title (A Side/B Side)	Yr	VG	VG+	NM
❑ 1	Dallas/A Cowboy's Welcome Home	1982	—	3.00	6.00
❑ 2	Tijuana Sunrise/It Sure Feels Like Love Tonight	1983	—	3.00	6.00

SOUNDWAVES

Number	Title (A Side/B Side)	Yr	VG	VG+	NM
❑ 4707	Tijuana Sunrise/It Sure Feels Like Love Tonight	1983	—	2.50	5.00

Albums

COMPLEAT

Number	Title (A Side/B Side)	Yr	VG	VG+	NM
❑ 671013	The Bama Band	1985	2.00	4.00	8.00

MERCURY

Number	Title (A Side/B Side)	Yr	VG	VG+	NM
❑ 834627-1	Solid Ground	1988	2.00	4.00	8.00

BANDANA

45s

WARNER BROS.

Number	Title (A Side/B Side)	Yr	VG	VG+	NM
❑ 28721	Touch Me/Heat of the Night	1986	—	2.00	4.00
❑ 28939	Lovin' Up a Storm/Good Groove	1985	—	2.00	4.00
❑ 29029	It's Just Another Heartache/Heat of the Night	1985	—	2.00	4.00
❑ 29226	All I Wanna Do (Is Make Love to You)/Outside Lookin' In	1984	—	2.00	4.00
❑ 29315	Better Our Hearts Should Bend (Than Break)/ Ocean of Love	1984	—	2.00	4.00
❑ 29524	Outside Lookin' In/Ocean of Love	1983	—	2.00	4.00
❑ 29831	I Can't Get Over You (Gettin' Over Me)/Come to Me	1982	—	2.00	4.00
❑ 29936	The Killin' Kind/Whatta I Gotta Do	1982	—	2.00	4.00
❑ 49872	Guilty Eyes/Whatta I Gotta Do	1981	—	2.00	4.00
❑ 50045	Cheatin' State of Mind/They Call It Love	1982	—	2.00	4.00

Albums

WARNER BROS.

Number	Title (A Side/B Side)	Yr	VG	VG+	NM
❑ 25115	Bandana	1985	2.00	4.00	8.00

BANDIT BAND, THE

45s

MCA

Number	Title (A Side/B Side)	Yr	VG	VG+	NM
❑ 41294	Deliverance of the Wildwood Flower/Ride Concrete Cowboy Ride	1980	—	2.50	5.00

—B-side by Roy Rogers and the Sons of the Pioneers

Number	Title (A Side/B Side)	Yr	VG	VG+	NM
❑ 51004	Rockin' Lone Star Style/Let's Do Something Cheap and Superficial	1980	—	2.50	5.00

—B-side by Clint Eastwood

PEGASUS

Number	Title (A Side/B Side)	Yr	VG	VG+	NM
❑ 108	Do You Wanna Fall in Love/(B-side unknown)	1987	—	3.00	6.00

BANDIT BROTHERS

45s

CURB

Number	Title (A Side/B Side)	Yr	VG	VG+	NM
❑ NR-76867	Women/(Instrumental)	1991	—	2.00	4.00

BANDY, CHARLIE

45s

RCI

Number	Title (A Side/B Side)	Yr	VG	VG+	NM
❑ 2379	I Better Go Home (While I Still Got a Home)/(B-side unknown)	1984	—	3.00	6.00
❑ 2386	Tenamock Georgia/All I See Is You	1984	—	3.00	6.00
❑ 2391	Love You Right Out of My Mind/(B-side unknown)	1984	—	3.00	6.00

SOUNDWAVES

Number	Title (A Side/B Side)	Yr	VG	VG+	NM
❑ 4596	Talk Back Trembling Lips/From Cotton to Satin	1981	—	2.50	5.00
❑ 4611	It Was Love What It Was/Somewhere in Kentucky	1981	—	2.50	5.00
❑ 4629	Pyramid of Cans/Till You Can Make It on Your Own	1981	—	2.50	5.00
❑ 4674	To Make a Short Story Long/Divorce Looks Good on You	1982	—	2.50	5.00

BANDY, MOE

45s

COLUMBIA

Number	Title (A Side/B Side)	Yr	VG	VG+	NM
❑ 11-02039	My Woman Loves the Devil Out of Me/Today I Almost Stopped Loving You	1981	—	2.00	4.00
❑ 18-0 2532	Rodeo Romeo/There's Nothing More Desperate (Than An Old Desperado)	1981	—	2.00	4.00
❑ 18-02735	Someday Soon/She's Playing Hard to Forget	1982	—	2.00	4.00
❑ 18-02966	She's Not Really Cheatin' (She's Just Gettin' Even)/The All American Dream	1982	—	2.00	4.00
❑ 38-03309	Only If There Is Another You/Your Memory Is Showing All Over Me	1982	—	2.00	4.00
❑ 38-03625	I Still Love You in the Same Ol' Way/Drivin' Me Back to You	1983	—	2.00	4.00
❑ 38-03970	Let's Get Over Them Together/In Love	1983	—	2.00	4.00

—A-side with Becky Hobbs

Number	Title (A Side/B Side)	Yr	VG	VG+	NM
❑ 38-04204	You're Gonna Lose Her Like That/One More Port	1983	—	2.00	4.00
❑ 38-04353	It Took a Lot of Drinkin' (To Get That Woman Over Me)/In Mexico	1984	—	2.00	4.00
❑ 38-04466	Woman Your Love/Texas Saturday Night	1984	—	2.00	4.00
❑ 38-04742	Your Memory Always Finds Its Way Back to Me/ Lovin' It Up (Livin' It Down)	1984	—	2.00	4.00
❑ 38-05438	Barroom Roses/That's All She Needed to Hear	1985	—	2.00	4.00
❑ 38-05689	Can't Leave That Woman Alone/Where Do You Take a Broken Heart	1985	—	2.00	4.00
❑ 10265	Hank Williams, You Wrote My Life/I'm the Honky-Tonk on Losers Avenue	1975	—	2.50	5.00
❑ 10313	The Biggest Airport in the World/I Think I've Got a Love On for You	1976	—	2.50	5.00
❑ 10361	Here I Am Drunk Again/What Happened to Our Love	1978	—	2.50	5.00
❑ 10428	She Took More Than Her Share/Then You Can Let Me Go (Out of Your Mind)	1976	—	2.50	5.00
❑ 10487	I'm Sorry for You, My Friend/A Four Letter Fool	1977	—	2.50	5.00
❑ 10558	Cowboys Ain't Supposed to Cry/Till I Stop Needing You	1977	—	2.50	5.00
❑ 10619	She Just Loved the Cheatin' Out of Me/Up to Now I've Wanted Everything But You	1977	—	2.50	5.00
❑ 10671	Soft Lights and Hard Country Music/There's Nobody Home on the Range Anymore	1978	—	2.50	5.00
❑ 10735	That's What Makes the Juke Box Play/Are We Making Love or Just Making Friends	1978	—	2.50	5.00
❑ 10820	Two Lonely People/I Never Miss a Day (Missing You)	1978	—	2.50	5.00
❑ 10889	It's a Cheating Situation/Try My Love On for Size	1979	—	2.50	5.00
❑ 10974	Barstool Mountain/To Cheat or Not to Cheat	1979	—	2.50	5.00
❑ 11090	I Cheated Me Right Out of You/Honky Tonk Merry-Go-Round	1979	—	2.50	5.00
❑ 11184	One of a Kind/The Bitter with the Sweet	1980	—	2.00	4.00
❑ 11255	The Champ/She Took Out the Outlaw in Me	1980	—	2.00	4.00
❑ 11305	Yesterday Once More/I Just Can't Leave Those Honky Tonks Alone	1980	—	2.00	4.00
❑ 11395	Following the Feeling/Mexico Winter	1980	—	2.00	4.00

—A-side with Judy Bailey

CURB

Number	Title (A Side/B Side)	Yr	VG	VG+	NM
❑ 10504	Americana/What Goes Around	1988	—	—	3.00
❑ 10510	Ashes in the Wind/Hittin' Close to Home	1988	—	—	3.00
❑ 10513	I Just Can't Say No to You/Nobody Gets Off in This Town	1988	—	—	3.00
❑ 10524	Many Mansions/Yuppie Love	1989	—	—	3.00
❑ 10537	Brotherly Love/Charlie	1989	—	—	3.00

Number	Title (A Side/B Side)	Yr	VG	VG+	NM
❑ 10555	This Night Won't Last Forever/Ain't Nothin' Gonna Slow This Train Down	1989	—	—	3.00
❑ B-76814	Back in My Roarin' Days/Nobody Gets Off in This Town	1990	—	2.00	4.00
FOOTPRINT					
❑ 1006	I Just Started Hatin' Cheatin' Songs Today/How Far Do You Think We Would Go	1974	2.50	5.00	10.00
GRC					
❑ 2006	I Just Started Hatin' Cheatin' Songs Today/How Far Do You Think We Would Go	1974	—	3.00	6.00
❑ 2024	Honky Tonk Amnesia/Cowboys and Playboys	1974	—	3.00	6.00
❑ 2036	It Was Always So Easy (To Find an Unhappy Woman)/I Wouldn't Cheat on Her If She Was Mine	1974	—	3.00	6.00
❑ 2055	Don't Anyone Make Love at Home Anymore/Somebody That Good	1975	—	3.00	6.00
❑ 2070	Bandy the Rodeo Clown/I'm Looking for a New Way to Love You	1975	—	3.00	6.00
MCA					
❑ 52950	One Man Band/Ridin' Her Memory Down	1986	—	—	3.00
❑ 53033	Till I'm Too Old to Die Young/You Can't Straddle the Fence	1987	—	—	3.00
❑ 53132	You Haven't Heard the Last of Me/I Forgot That I Don't Live Here Anymore	1987	—	—	3.00
SHANNON					
❑ 804	Hanging On to One/Rain Making Baby of Mine	1972	2.00	4.00	8.00
❑ 806	Somebody Nobody Knows/Sweet Memory	1972	2.00	4.00	8.00
Albums					
COLUMBIA					
❑ PC 34091	Hank Williams, You Wrote My Life	1976	3.00	6.00	12.00
—No bar code on back cover					
❑ PC 34091	Hank Williams, You Wrote My Life	198?	2.00	4.00	8.00
—With bar code on back cover					
❑ PC 34285	Here I Am Drunk Again	1976	3.00	6.00	12.00
—No bar code on back cover					
❑ PC 34443	I'm Sorry for You, My Friend	1977	3.00	6.00	12.00
—No bar code on back cover					
❑ PC 34715	The Best of Moe Bandy Volume One	1977	3.00	6.00	12.00
—No bar code on back cover					
❑ PC 34715	The Best of Moe Bandy Volume One	198?	2.00	4.00	8.00
—With bar code on back cover					
❑ PC 34874	Cowboys Ain't Supposed to Cry	1977	3.00	6.00	12.00
—No bar code on back cover					
❑ KC 35288	Soft Lights and Hard Country Music	1978	3.00	6.00	12.00
❑ KC 35534	Love Is What Life's All About	1978	3.00	6.00	12.00
❑ KC 35779	It's a Cheating Situation	1979	2.50	5.00	10.00
❑ PC 35779	It's a Cheating Situation	198?	2.00	4.00	8.00
—Budget-line reissue					
❑ JC 36228	One of a Kind	1980	2.50	5.00	10.00
❑ JC 36487	The Champ	1980	2.50	5.00	10.00
❑ JC 36789	Following the Feeling	1980	2.50	5.00	10.00
❑ PC 37350	Encore	1981	2.00	4.00	8.00
❑ FC 37568	Rodeo Romeo	1981	2.00	4.00	8.00
❑ PC 37568	Rodeo Romeo	198?	—	3.00	6.00
—Budget-line reissue					
❑ FC 38009	She's Not Really Cheatin' (She's Just Gettin' Even)	1982	2.00	4.00	8.00
❑ PC 38009	She's Not Really Cheatin' (She's Just Gettin' Even)	198?	—	3.00	6.00
—Budget-line reissue					
❑ FC 38199	I Still Love You in the Same Ol' Way	1982	2.00	4.00	8.00
❑ FC 38315	Greatest Hits	1983	2.00	4.00	8.00
❑ PC 38652	Moe Bandy Sings the Songs of Hank Williams	1983	2.00	4.00	8.00
❑ FC 38726	Devoted to Your Memory	1983	2.00	4.00	8.00
❑ FC 39275	Motel Matches	1984	2.00	4.00	8.00
❑ FC 39906	Barroom Roses	1985	2.00	4.00	8.00
❑ FC 40140	Keepin' It Country	1986	2.00	4.00	8.00
CURB					
❑ 10600	No Regrets	1988	2.50	5.00	10.00
❑ 10609	Many Mansions	1989	2.50	5.00	10.00
GRC					
❑ 10005	I Just Started Hatin' Cheatin' Songs Today	1974	3.75	7.50	15.00
❑ 10007	It Was Always So Easy (To Find an Unhappy Woman)	1975	3.75	7.50	15.00
❑ 10016	Bandy the Rodeo Clown	1975	3.75	7.50	15.00
MCA					
❑ 5914	You Haven't Heard the Last of Me	1987	2.00	4.00	8.00

BANDY, MOE, AND JOE STAMPLEY

Number	Title (A Side/B Side)	Yr	VG	VG+	NM
45s					
COLUMBIA					
❑ 18-02198	Honky Tonk Queen/Partners in Rhyme	1981	—	2.00	4.00
❑ 38-04477	Where's the Dress/Wildlife Sanctuary	1984	—	2.00	4.00
❑ 38-04601	The Boy's Night Out/Alive and Well	1984	—	2.00	4.00
❑ 38-04601 [PS]	The Boy's Night Out/Alive and Well	1984	—	2.50	5.00
❑ 38-04756	Daddy's Honky Tonk/Wild and Crazy Guys	1985	—	2.00	4.00
❑ 38-04843	Still on a Roll/He's Back in Texas	1985	—	2.00	4.00
❑ 11027	Just Good Ol' Boys/Make a Little Love Each Day	1979	—	2.50	5.00
—As "Moe and Joe"					
❑ 11147	Holding the Bag/When It Comes to Cowgirls	1979	—	2.50	5.00
—As "Moe and Joe"					
❑ 11244	Tell Ole I Ain't Here, He Better Get On Home/Only the Names Have Been Changed	1980	—	2.00	4.00
❑ 60508	Hey Joe (Hey Moe)/Two Beers Away	1981	—	2.00	4.00
Albums					
COLUMBIA					
❑ JC 36202	Just Good Ol' Boys	1979	2.50	5.00	10.00
❑ PC 36202	Just Good Ol' Boys	198?	2.00	4.00	8.00
—Budget-line reissue					
❑ FC 37003	Hey Joe!/Hey Moe!	1981	2.00	4.00	8.00
❑ PC 37003	Hey Joe!/Hey Moe!	198?	—	3.00	6.00
—Budget-line reissue					
❑ FC 38316	Greatest Hits	1983	2.00	4.00	8.00
❑ FC 39426	The Good Ol' Boys — Alive and Well	1984	2.00	4.00	8.00
❑ PC 39426	The Good Ol' Boys — Alive and Well	1986	—	3.00	6.00
—Budget-line reissue					
❑ FC 39955	Live from Bad Bob's, Memphis	1985	2.00	4.00	8.00

BANNON, R.C.

Also see LOUISE MANDRELL AND R.C. BANNON.

Number	Title (A Side/B Side)	Yr	VG	VG+	NM
45s					
CAPITOL					
❑ 3966	Freedom/I Don't Want to Play Games	1974	—	3.00	6.00
COLUMBIA					
❑ 10570	Southbound/You Make All the Difference in the World	1977	—	2.50	5.00
❑ 10612	Rainbows and Horseshoes/You Make All the Difference in the World	1977	—	2.50	5.00
❑ 10655	It Doesn't Matter Anymore/All of the Best	1977	—	2.50	5.00
❑ 10714	(The Truth Is) We're Livin' a Lie/Love at First Sight	1978	—	2.50	5.00
❑ 10771	Loveless Hotel/Nightbird	1978	—	2.50	5.00
❑ 10847	Somebody's Gonna Do It Tonight/Got That Lookin' Feelin'	1978	—	2.50	5.00
❑ 11081	Winners and Losers/Cheatin' on Him, Lovin' on Me	1979	—	2.50	5.00
❑ 11210	Lovely Lonely Lady/I've Never Gone to Bed with an Ugly Woman	1980	—	2.00	4.00
❑ 11267	If You're Serious About Cheatin'/What's a Nice Girl Like You Doing (Living in a Place Like This)	1980	—	2.00	4.00
❑ 11346	Never Be Anyone Else/What's a Nice Girl Like You Doing (Living in a Place Like This)	1980	—	2.00	4.00
RCA					
❑ PB-13029	Til Something Better Comes Along/You're Bringing Out the Fool in Me	1981	—	2.00	4.00
Albums					
COLUMBIA					
❑ KC 35346	R.C. Bannon Arrives	1978	3.00	6.00	12.00

BARBER, AVA

Number	Title (A Side/B Side)	Yr	VG	VG+	NM
45s					
OAK					
❑ 1029	I Think I Could Love You Better Than She Did/That's How Much I Love You	1981	—	2.50	5.00
RANWOOD					
❑ 1013	Goodie Man/(B-side unknown)	1975	—	2.50	5.00
❑ 1043	That's What Your Love Means to Me/More Than I Love You (When You've Hurt Me)	1976	—	2.50	5.00
❑ 1071	Waitin' at the End of Your Run/Blue Eyes Crying in the Rain-Remember Me	1977	—	2.50	5.00
❑ 1077	Your Love Is My Refuge/I'll Do It All Over Again	1977	—	2.50	5.00
❑ 1080	Don't Take My Sunshine Away/There's More Love Where That Came From	1977	—	2.50	5.00
❑ 1083	Bucket to the South/There's More Love Where That Came From	1978	—	2.50	5.00
❑ 1085	You're Gonna Love Love/I'm Gonna Make It After All	1978	—	2.50	5.00
❑ 1087	Healin'/I Never Will Get Over You	1978	—	2.50	5.00
❑ 1089	The Wayward Wind/Even a Fool Would Let Go	1979	—	2.50	5.00
Albums					
RANWOOD					
❑ 8170	Grits	1977	3.00	6.00	12.00
❑ 8180	You're Gonna Love Love	1978	3.00	6.00	12.00

BARBER, GLENN

Number	Title (A Side/B Side)	Yr	VG	VG+	NM
45s					
CENTURY 21					
❑ 100	What's the Name of That Song?/I Can't Find a Way (To Be Free)	1978	—	3.00	6.00
❑ 101	Love Songs Just for You/Go Home Little Girl	1978	—	3.00	6.00
D					
❑ 1017	Hello Sadness/Same Old Fool Tomorrow	1958	10.00	20.00	40.00
❑ 1069	Your Heart Don't Love/Most Beautiful	1959	10.00	20.00	40.00
❑ 1098	New Girl in School/Go Home Letter	1959	10.00	20.00	40.00
❑ 1128	The Window/Another You	1960	10.00	20.00	40.00
GROOVY					
❑ 102	(You Better Be) One Hell of a Woman/Is Another Man's Woman Worth Another Man's Life	1977	—	3.50	7.00
❑ 103	Cry, Cry Baby/Has It Been So Long	1977	—	3.50	7.00
GRT					
❑ 071	It Took a Drunk (To Drive God's Message Home)/If I Thought for One Moment	1976	—	3.00	6.00
HICKORY					
❑ 1494	Go Home Letter (I Wish That I Were You)/Who Made You That Way	1968	2.50	5.00	10.00
❑ 1517	Don't Worry 'Bout the Mule (Just Load the Wagon)/Reflex Reaction	1968	2.00	4.00	8.00
❑ 1527	I Don't Want No More of the Cheese/Motor Mouth Harry	1969	2.00	4.00	8.00

Number	Title (A Side/B Side)	Yr	VG	VG+	NM
❑ 1533	Gonna Make My Mama Proud of Me/You Can't Get Here from There	1969	2.00	4.00	8.00
❑ 1545	Kissed by the Rain, Warmed by the Sun/My World Is Square	1969	2.00	4.00	8.00
❑ 1557	She Cheats on Me/Who's Taking the Picture	1969	2.00	4.00	8.00
❑ 1568	Poison Red Berries/Abilene	1970	2.00	4.00	8.00
❑ 1576	Where There's Smoke/Al	1970	2.00	4.00	8.00
❑ 1585	Yes, Dear, There Is a Virginia/I'm Only Company	1970	2.00	4.00	8.00
❑ 1593	I Committed the Crime/Six Years and a Day	1971	2.00	4.00	8.00
❑ 1605	Blue Eyes Crying in the Rain/The World You Live In	1971	2.00	4.00	8.00
❑ 1618	Fat Albert/Betty Ann	1971	2.00	4.00	8.00
❑ 1626	I'm the Man on Susie's Mind/Satan's Painted Woman	1972	2.00	4.00	8.00
❑ 1645	Unexpected Goodbye/Blue Bayou	1972	2.00	4.00	8.00
❑ 1653	Yes Ma'am (I Found Her in a Honky Tonk)/Who in the World	1972	2.00	4.00	8.00
❑ 1666	It's a Beautiful Thing/That's How a Coward Tells an Angel	1973	2.00	4.00	8.00
HICKORY/MGM					
❑ 302	Country Girl (I Love You Still)/Watching You Go	1973	—	3.50	7.00
❑ 311	Daddy Number Two/We Let That Lovely Flame Die	1973	—	3.50	7.00
❑ 316	You Only Live Once (In Awhile)/Sweet on My Mind	1974	—	3.50	7.00
❑ 323	Blue Eyes Crying in the Rain/Almost	1974	—	3.50	7.00
❑ 333	You're Gettin' Heavy on My Mind/Sweet on My Mind	1974	—	3.50	7.00
❑ 340	She's No Ordinary Woman/We've Got It All Together This Time	1975	—	3.50	7.00
KIK					
❑ 912	A Woman's Touch/(B-side unknown)	1981	—	3.00	6.00
MMI					
❑ 1029	Everybody Wants to Disco/Most Wanted Man in Tennessee	1979	—	3.00	6.00
❑ 1031	Woman's Touch/Most Wanted Man in Tennessee	1979	—	3.00	6.00
SIMS					
❑ 148	How Can I Forget You/Rain Check	1963	3.75	7.50	15.00
STARDAY					
❑ 166	Ice Water/Ring Around the Moon	1954	37.50	75.00	150.00
❑ 196	Married Man/Poor Man's Baby	1955	12.50	25.00	50.00
❑ 214	Ain't It Funny/Livin' High and Wide	1955	12.50	25.00	50.00
❑ 249	Shadow My Baby/Feeling No Pain	1956	75.00	150.00	300.00
❑ 676	Stronger Than Dirt/If Anyone Can Show Cause	1964	3.00	6.00	12.00
❑ 699	Dancing Shoes/Knock Knock	1964	3.00	6.00	12.00
❑ 722	Loneliest Man in Town/She's Out of Our World	1965	3.00	6.00	12.00
❑ 741	Happy Birthday Broken Heart/Let's Take the Fear (Out of Being Close)	1965	3.00	6.00	12.00
SUNBIRD					
❑ 7551	First Love Feelings/What's the Name of That Song	1980	—	2.50	5.00
UNITED ARTISTS					
❑ 337	Most Beautiful/Night Without End	1961	5.00	10.00	20.00
❑ 512	I Can't Stop Part 1/I Can't Stop Part 2	1962	5.00	10.00	20.00
Albums					
HICKORY					
❑ LPS-152	New Star	1970	3.75	7.50	15.00
❑ LPS-167	The Best of Glenn Barber	1973	3.75	7.50	15.00
HICKORY/MGM					
❑ H3F-4510	Glenn Barber	1974	3.75	7.50	15.00

BARBRA AND NEIL

Barbra Streisand and NEIL DIAMOND.

45s

Number	Title (A Side/B Side)	Yr	VG	VG+	NM
COLUMBIA					
❑ 3-10840	You Don't Bring Me Flowers/(Instrumental)	1978	—	2.50	5.00

BARE, BOBBY

By record-company accident, he also recorded as BILL PARSONS. Also see DONNIE BOWSER.

45s

Number	Title (A Side/B Side)	Yr	VG	VG+	NM
AMI					
❑ 1328	America's Missing Children/(B-side unknown)	198?	—	2.50	5.00
CAPITOL					
❑ F3557	Down on the Corner of Love/Another Love Has Ended	1956	7.50	15.00	30.00
❑ F3686	Darling Don't/Life of a Fool	1957	7.50	15.00	30.00
❑ F3771	The Livin' End/Beggar	1957	7.50	15.00	30.00
COLUMBIA					
❑ 02038	Learning to Live Again/Appaloosa Rider	1981	—	2.00	4.00
❑ 0 2414	Take Me As I Am (Or Let Me Go)/White Freight Liner Blues	1981	—	2.00	4.00
❑ 02577	Dropping Out of Sight/She Is Gone	1981	—	2.00	4.00
❑ 02690	New Cut Road/Let Him Roll	1982	—	2.00	4.00
❑ 02895	If You Ain't Got Nothing (You've Got Nothing To Lose)/Golden Memories	1982	—	2.00	4.00
❑ 03135	New Cut Road/Numbers	1982	—	—	3.00
—Reissue					
❑ 03149	(I'm Not) A Candle in the Wind/Cold Day in Hell	1982	—	2.00	4.00
❑ 03334	Praise the Lord and Send Me the Money/I've Been Rained On Too	1982	—	2.00	4.00
❑ 03628	It's a Dirty Job/Caught in the Spotlight	1983	—	2.00	4.00
—A-side with Lacy J. Dalton					
❑ 03809	The Jogger/Gravy Train	1983	—	2.00	4.00
❑ 04092	Diet Song/Stacy Brown Got Two	1983	—	2.00	4.00

Number	Title (A Side/B Side)	Yr	VG	VG+	NM
❑ 10690	Too Many Nights Alone/A Yard Full of Rusty Cars	1978	—	2.50	5.00
❑ 10831	Sleep Tight, Good Night Man/Hot Afternoon	1978	—	2.50	5.00
❑ 10891	Healin'/Love Is a Cold Wind	1979	—	2.00	4.00
❑ 10998	Till I Gain Control Again/I'll Feel a Whole Lot Better	1979	—	2.00	4.00
❑ 11045	No Memories Hangin' Round/This Has Happened Before	1979	—	2.00	4.00
—With Roseanne Cash					
❑ 11170	Numbers/When Hippies Get Older	1980	—	2.00	4.00
❑ 11259	Tequila Sheila/Quaaludes Again	1980	—	2.00	4.00
❑ 11365	Food Blues/Used Cars	1980	—	2.00	4.00
❑ 11408	Willie Jones/If That Ain't Love	1980	—	2.00	4.00
EMI AMERICA					
❑ 8279	When I Get Home/Party of the First Part	1985	—	—	3.00
❑ 8296	Reno and Me/Party of the First Part	1985	—	—	3.00
❑ 8317	Better Not Look Down/Wait Until Tomorrow	1986	—	—	3.00
❑ 8333	Real Good/Wait Until Tomorrow	1986	—	—	3.00
EPIC					
❑ 10652	My God and I/In the Quiet of Your Love	1970	—	3.00	6.00
—B-side by Keith Barbour					
FRATERNITY					
❑ 861	I'm Hanging Up My Rifle/That's Where I Wanna Be	1959	10.00	20.00	40.00
❑ 867	Sweet Singing Sam/More Than a Poor Boy Could Give	1960	7.50	15.00	30.00
❑ 871	No Letter from My Baby/Lynchin' Party	1960	5.00	10.00	20.00
❑ 878	Book of Love/Lorena	1961	5.00	10.00	20.00
❑ 885	Sailor Man/Island of Love	1961	5.00	10.00	20.00
❑ 890	Zigzag Twist/Brooklyn Bridge	1961	5.00	10.00	20.00
❑ 892	The Day My Rainbow Fell/That Mean Old Clock	1961	5.00	10.00	20.00
MERCURY					
❑ 73097	How I Got to Memphis/It's Freezing in El Paso	1970	—	3.00	6.00
❑ 73148	Come Sundown/Woman You Have Been a Friend to Me	1970	—	3.00	6.00
❑ 73203	Please Don't Tell Me How the Story Ends/Where Have All the Seasons Gone	1971	—	3.00	6.00
❑ 73236	Short and Sweet/A Million Miles to the City	1971	—	3.00	6.00
❑ 73279	What Am I Gonna Do/Love Forever	1972	—	3.00	6.00
❑ 73317	Sylvia's Mother/Music City U.S.A.	1972	—	3.00	6.00
RCA					
❑ PB-10718	Put a Little Lovin' on Me/Those City Lights	1976	—	2.50	5.00
❑ PB-10790	Drop Kick Me, Jesus/Baby Wants to Boogie	1976	—	3.00	6.00
❑ PB-10852	Vegas/The Shelter of Your Eyes	1976	—	2.50	5.00
—A-side by Bobby and Jeannie Bare					
❑ PB-10902	Look Who I'm Cheatin' On Tonight/If You Think I'm Crazy Now (You Should Have Seen Me When I Was a Kid)	1977	—	2.50	5.00
❑ PB-11037	Red Neck Hippie Romance/Bottom Dollar	1977	—	2.50	5.00
❑ PB-11673	Hurricane Shirley/Crazy Arms	1979	—	2.50	5.00
—B-side by Willie Nelson					
RCA VICTOR					
❑ APBO-0063	You Know Who/Send Tomorrow to the Moon	1973	—	2.50	5.00
❑ AMAO-0119	Shame on Me/Above and Beyond	1973	—	2.50	5.00
❑ APBO-0197	Daddy What If/Restless Wind	1973	—	2.50	5.00
❑ APBO-0261	Marie Laveau/Mermaid	1974	—	2.50	5.00
❑ PB-10037	Where'd I Come From/Scarlet Ribbons	1974	—	2.50	5.00
—By "Bobby Bare, Jr., and Mommy"					
❑ PB-10096	Singin' in the Kitchen/You Are	1974	—	2.50	5.00
—As "Bobby Bare and the Family"					
❑ GB-10166	Daddy What If/Ride Me Down Easy	1975	—	—	3.00
—Gold Standard Series issue					
❑ PB-10223	Back in Huntsville Again/Warm and Free	1975	—	2.50	5.00
❑ PB-10318	Alimony/Daddy's Been Around the House Too Long	1975	—	2.50	5.00
❑ PB-10409	Cowboys and Daddys/High Plains Jamboree	1975	—	2.50	5.00
❑ GB-10495	Singin' in the Kitchen/You Are	1975	—	—	3.00
—Gold Standard Series issue					
❑ GB-10496	Marie Laveau/Mermaid	1975	—	—	3.00
—Gold Standard Series issue					
❑ GB-10497	Where'd I Come From/Scarlet Ribbons	1975	—	—	3.00
—Gold Standard Series issue					
❑ PB-10556	The Winner/Up Against the Wall Redneck Mother	1976	—	2.50	5.00
❑ 47-8032	Shame on Me/Above and Beyond	1962	3.00	6.00	12.00
❑ 47-8083	I Don't Believe I'll Fall in Love Today/To Whom It May Concern	1962	3.00	6.00	12.00
❑ 47-8083 [PS]	I Don't Believe I'll Fall in Love Today/To Whom It May Concern	1962	6.25	12.50	25.00
❑ 47-8146	Dear Waste Basket/I'd Fight the World	1963	3.00	6.00	12.00
❑ 47-8183	Detroit City/Heart of Ice	1963	3.75	7.50	15.00
❑ 47-8183 [PS]	Detroit City/Heart of Ice	1963	6.25	12.50	25.00
❑ 47-8238	500 Miles Away from Home/It All Depends On Linda	1963	3.75	7.50	15.00
❑ 47-8294	Miller's Cave/Jeannie's Last Kiss	1963	3.00	6.00	12.00
❑ 47-8358	Have I Stayed Away Too Long/More Than a Poor Boy Can Give	1964	3.00	6.00	12.00
❑ 47-8395	He Was a Friend of Mine/When I'm Gone	1964	3.00	6.00	12.00
❑ 47-8443	Four Strong Winds/Take Me Home	1964	3.00	6.00	12.00
❑ 47-8509	Times Are Gettin' Hard/One Day at a Time	1965	2.50	5.00	10.00
❑ 47-8571	It's Alright/She Picked a Perfect Day	1965	2.50	5.00	10.00
❑ 47-8654	Just to Satisfy You/Memories	1965	2.50	5.00	10.00
❑ 47-8699	Talk Me Some Sense/Delia's Gone	1965	2.50	5.00	10.00
❑ 47-8758	In the Same Old Way/Long Black Veil	1965	2.50	5.00	10.00
❑ 47-8851	The Streets of Baltimore/She Took My Sunshine Away	1966	2.50	5.00	10.00
❑ 47-8988	Homesick/Guess I'll Move On Down the Line	1966	2.50	5.00	10.00

Number	Title (A Side/B Side)	Yr	VG	VG+	NM
❑ 47-9098	Charleston Railroad Tavern/Vincennes	1967	2.00	4.00	8.00
❑ 47-9191	Come Kiss Me Love/Sandy's Crying Again	1967	2.00	4.00	8.00
❑ 47-9314	The Piney Wood Hills/They Covered Up the Old Swimmin' Hole	1967	2.00	4.00	8.00
❑ 47-9450	Find Out What's Happening/When Am I Ever Gonna Settle Down	1968	2.00	4.00	8.00
❑ 47-9568	A Little Bit Later On Down the Line/Don't Do Like I Done, Son (Do What I Say)	1968	2.00	4.00	8.00
❑ 47-9643	The Town That Broke My Heart/My Baby	1968	2.00	4.00	8.00
❑ 74-0110	(Margie's At) The Lincoln Park Inn/Rainy Day in Richmond	1969	—	3.00	6.00
❑ 74-0202	Which One Will It Be/My Frame of Mind	1969	—	3.00	6.00
❑ 74-0264	God Bless America Again/Baby, What Else Can I Do	1969	—	3.00	6.00
❑ 74-0866	I Hate Goodbyes/Fallin' Apart	1973	—	3.00	6.00
❑ 74-0918	Ride Me Down Easy/A Train That Never Runs	1973	—	3.00	6.00
RICE					
❑ 5057	Christian Soldier/Dropping Out of Sight	1973	—	2.50	5.00
❑ 5060	Love Forever/A Million Miles to the City	1973	—	2.50	5.00
❑ 5066	I Took a Memory to Lunch/It's Freezing in St. Paul	1974	—	2.50	5.00
Albums					
COLUMBIA					
❑ KC 35314	Bare	1977	2.50	5.00	10.00
❑ JC 36323	Down & Dirty	1978	2.50	5.00	10.00
❑ PC 36323	Down & Dirty	198?	2.00	4.00	8.00
—Budget-line reissue					
❑ JC 36785	Drunk & Crazy	1980	2.50	5.00	10.00
❑ FC 37157	As Is	1981	2.50	5.00	10.00
❑ FC 37351	Encore	1981	2.50	5.00	10.00
❑ PC 37351	Encore	198?	2.00	4.00	8.00
—Budget-line reissue					
❑ FC 37719	Ain't Got Nothin' to Lose	1982	2.50	5.00	10.00
❑ FC 38311	Biggest Hits	1982	2.50	5.00	10.00
❑ FC 38670	Drinkin' from the Bottle, Singin' from the Heart	1983	2.50	5.00	10.00
HILLTOP					
❑ 6026	Tender Years	196?	3.00	6.00	12.00
MERCURY					
❑ SR-61290	This Is Bare Country	1970	5.00	10.00	20.00
❑ SR-61316	Where Have All the Seasons Gone	1971	5.00	10.00	20.00
❑ SR-61363	What Am I Gonna Do?	1972	5.00	10.00	20.00
RCA CAMDEN					
❑ ACL1-0150	Memphis, Tennessee	1973	3.00	6.00	12.00
❑ CAS-2290	Folsom Prison Blues	1969	3.00	6.00	12.00
❑ CAS-2465	I'm a Long Way from Home	1971	3.00	6.00	12.00
RCA VICTOR					
❑ APL1-0040	I Hate Goodbyes/Ride Me Down Easy	1973	3.75	7.50	15.00
❑ CPL2-0290 [(2)]	Bobby Bare Sings Lullabys, Legends and Lies	1973	5.00	10.00	20.00
❑ ANL1-0560	Sunday Morning	1974	2.50	5.00	10.00
❑ APL1-0700	Singin' in the Kitchen	1974	3.75	7.50	15.00
❑ APL1-0906	Hard Time Hungrys	1975	3.00	6.00	12.00
❑ APL1-1222	Cowboys and Daddys	1975	3.00	6.00	12.00
❑ APL1-1786	The Winner and Other Losers	1976	3.00	6.00	12.00
❑ APL1-2179	Me and McDill	1977	3.00	6.00	12.00
❑ LPM-2776 [M]	"Detroit City" and Other Hits	1963	5.00	10.00	20.00
❑ LSP-2776 [S]	"Detroit City" and Other Hits	1963	6.25	12.50	25.00
❑ LPM-2835 [M]	500 Miles Away from Home	1964	5.00	10.00	20.00
❑ LSP-2835 [S]	500 Miles Away from Home	1964	6.25	12.50	25.00
❑ LPM-2955 [M]	The Travelin' Bare	1964	5.00	10.00	20.00
❑ LSP-2955 [S]	The Travelin' Bare	1964	6.25	12.50	25.00
❑ LPM-3395 [M]	Constant Sorrow	1965	5.00	10.00	20.00
❑ LSP-3395 [S]	Constant Sorrow	1965	6.25	12.50	25.00
❑ LPM-3479 [M]	The Best of Bobby Bare	1965	5.00	10.00	20.00
❑ LSP-3479 [S]	The Best of Bobby Bare	1965	6.25	12.50	25.00
❑ LPM-3515 [M]	Talk Me Some Sense	1966	5.00	10.00	20.00
❑ LSP-3515 [S]	Talk Me Some Sense	1966	6.25	12.50	25.00
❑ LPM-3618 [M]	The Streets of Baltimore	1966	5.00	10.00	20.00
❑ LSP-3618 [S]	The Streets of Baltimore	1966	6.25	12.50	25.00
❑ LPM-3688 [M]	This I Believe	1966	5.00	10.00	20.00
❑ LSP-3688 [S]	This I Believe	1966	6.25	12.50	25.00
❑ LPM-3831 [M]	A Bird Named Yesterday	1967	6.25	12.50	25.00
❑ LSP-3831 [S]	A Bird Named Yesterday	1967	5.00	10.00	20.00
❑ LPM-3896 [M]	The English Country Side	1967	10.00	20.00	40.00
❑ LSP-3896 [S]	The English Country Side	1967	5.00	10.00	20.00
❑ LPM-3994 [M]	The Best of Bobby Bare — Volume 2	1968	10.00	20.00	40.00
❑ LSP-3994 [S]	The Best of Bobby Bare — Volume 2	1968	5.00	10.00	20.00
❑ AYL1-4118	Greatest Hits	1982	2.00	4.00	8.00
❑ LSP-4177	(Margie's At) The Lincoln Park Inn (And Other Controversial Country Songs)	1969	5.00	10.00	20.00
❑ LSP-4422	Real Thing	1970	3.75	7.50	15.00
❑ AHL1-5469	Collector's Series	1985	2.50	5.00	10.00
❑ VPS-6090 [(2)]	This Is Bobby Bare	1972	5.00	10.00	20.00
UNITED ARTISTS					
❑ UA-LA621-G	Bare Country	1977	3.00	6.00	12.00

BARE, BOBBY, AND SKEETER DAVIS

Also see each artist's individual listings.

Number	Title (A Side/B Side)	Yr	VG	VG+	NM
45s					
RCA VICTOR					
❑ 47-8496	A Dear John Letter/Too Used to Being with You	1965	2.50	5.00	10.00
❑ 47-9789	Your Husband, My Wife/Before the Sunshine	1969	—	3.00	6.00
Albums					
RCA VICTOR					
❑ LPM-3336 [M]	Tunes for Two	1965	5.00	10.00	20.00
❑ LSP-3336 [S]	Tunes for Two	1965	6.25	12.50	25.00
❑ LSP-4335	Your Husband, My Wife	1970	3.75	7.50	15.00

BARE, BOBBY, NORMA JEAN, & LIZ ANDERSON

Also see each artist's individual listings.

Number	Title (A Side/B Side)	Yr	VG	VG+	NM
45s					
RCA VICTOR					
❑ 47-8963	The Game of Triangles/Bye Bye Bye	1966	2.50	5.00	10.00
Albums					
RCA VICTOR					
❑ LPM-3764 [M]	The Game of Triangles	1967	6.25	12.50	25.00
❑ LSP-3764 [S]	The Game of Triangles	1967	5.00	10.00	20.00

BARKLEY, BRUCE

Number	Title (A Side/B Side)	Yr	VG	VG+	NM
45s					
COLUMBIA					
❑ 4-21210	Red Pepper/Carolina in the Morning	1954	5.00	10.00	20.00
❑ 4-21267	Memphis Blues/Jumpin' Jack	1954	5.00	10.00	20.00
❑ 4-21330	Wild Honey/Tantalizin' Rhythm	1954	6.25	12.50	25.00
❑ 4-21409	My Blue Heaven/Pretty Baby	1955	5.00	10.00	20.00
❑ 4-21468	Fingertip Rhythm/Lookin' Around	1955	5.00	10.00	20.00

BARLOW, JACK

Number	Title (A Side/B Side)	Yr	VG	VG+	NM
45s					
ANTIQUE					
❑ 106	The Man on Page 602/Vinegar in My Wine	1975	2.00	4.00	8.00
—As "Zoot Fenster"					
DIAL					
❑ 4012	I Love Country Music/Number One in the Nation	1965	3.00	6.00	12.00
❑ 4024	Dear Ma/I Love Her Still	1965	3.00	6.00	12.00
DOT					
❑ 17139	Baby, Ain't That Love/It Ain't No Big Thing	1968	2.00	4.00	8.00
❑ 17212	Birmingham Blues/Papa Didn't Give Me No Love	1969	2.00	4.00	8.00
❑ 17287	Pauline/Singing Country Fool	1969	2.00	4.00	8.00
❑ 17317	Nobody Wants to Hear It Like It Is/No Time for Roses	1969	2.00	4.00	8.00
❑ 17343	Child Bride/A Little Friendly Advice	1970	2.00	4.00	8.00
❑ 17366	Dayton, Ohio/Where There Ain't No Fools	1970	2.00	4.00	8.00
❑ 17381	Somewhere in Texas/You Make My World	1971	2.00	4.00	8.00
❑ 17396	Catch the Wind/Tonight I'm Wantin' You Again	1971	2.00	4.00	8.00
❑ 17414	They Call the Wind Maria/It's a Long Way Back to Georgia	1972	2.00	4.00	8.00
❑ 17433	Baby, Don't You Cry None/You've Still Got a Hold on Me	1972	2.00	4.00	8.00
❑ 17446	How Much Love Will It Take/That's Enough	1973	2.00	4.00	8.00
❑ 17468	Oh Woman/That's Enough	1973	2.00	4.00	8.00
EPIC					
❑ 10072	Jack of All Trades/Smile on My Face	1966	3.00	6.00	12.00
❑ 10185	El Dorado/Long Green	1967	3.00	6.00	12.00
SOMA					
❑ 1175	Step Down/House of Stone	1962	3.75	7.50	15.00
❑ 1420	After All/49-51	1964	3.75	7.50	15.00

BARLOW, RANDY

Number	Title (A Side/B Side)	Yr	VG	VG+	NM
45s					
CAPITOL					
❑ 3762	Whiskey River/Nobody Likes to See a Big Man Cry	1973	—	3.00	6.00
❑ 3883	Throw Away the Pages/Hello Pawnshop	1974	—	3.00	6.00
GAZELLE					
❑ 001	Don't Leave Me Lonely Loving You/For a Few Dollars More	1983	—	2.50	5.00
❑ 153	Johnny Orphan/We're Crazy	1976	—	3.00	6.00
❑ 217	Goodnight My Love/Don't Worry I'm Okay	1976	—	3.00	6.00
❑ 280	Lonely Eyes/One Night Stand	1976	—	3.00	6.00
❑ 330	Twenty-Four Hours from Tulsa/The Bottle Took His Mother (And My Wife)	1976	—	3.00	6.00
❑ 381	Kentucky Woman/I'm a Swinger	1977	—	3.00	6.00
❑ 413	California Lady/We're Crazy	1977	—	3.00	6.00
❑ 427	Walk Away with Me/Johnny Orphan	1977	—	3.00	6.00
JAMEX					
❑ 002	Love Was Born/Chester's Eyes	1981	—	3.00	6.00
MERCURY					
❑ 72808	Color Blind/St. Clair	1968	2.50	5.00	10.00
PAID					
❑ 110	Willow Run/Can;t Believe I Fell for That Line	1980	—	2.50	5.00
❑ 116	Dixie Man/Don't Give Up on Me	1980	—	2.50	5.00
❑ 133	Love Dies Hard/New York City Cowboys-Deep in the Heart of Texas	1981	—	2.50	5.00
❑ 144	Try Me/Why Go Searchin' for Something More	1981	—	2.50	5.00
REPUBLIC					
❑ 017	Slow and Easy/Stranger I'm Married	1978	—	2.50	5.00
❑ 024	No Sleep Tonight/Burning Bridges	1978	—	2.50	5.00
❑ 034	Fall in Love with Me Tonight/One More Time	1978	—	2.50	5.00
❑ 039	Sweet Melinda/Heaven Here We Come	1979	—	2.50	5.00
❑ 044	Another Easy Lovin' Night/Louisiana Delta	1979	—	2.50	5.00
❑ 049	Lay Back in the Arms of Someone/Musical Hearts	1979	—	2.50	5.00
Albums					
GAZELLE					
❑ 6021	Arrival	1976	3.75	7.50	15.00
PAID					
❑ 2002	Dimensions	1981	3.00	6.00	12.00
REPUBLIC					
❑ RLP 6023	Fall in Love with Me	1978	3.00	6.00	12.00
❑ RLP 6024	Randy Barlow Featuring Sweet Melinda	1979	3.00	6.00	12.00

BARMBY, SHANE

45s

MERCURY

Number	Title (A Side/B Side)	Yr	VG	VG+	NM
❑ 874168-7	Let's Talk About Us/(B-side unknown)	1989	—	—	3.00
❑ 874670-7	Ridin' and Ropin'/(B-side unknown)	1989	—	—	3.00
❑ 876020-7	A Rainbow of Our Own/(B-side unknown)	1989	—	—	3.00
❑ 878828-7	One and One and One/Love's Back in Style	1990	—	2.00	4.00

BARNES, BENNY

45s

D

Number	Title (A Side/B Side)	Yr	VG	VG+	NM
❑ 1052	Gold Records in the Snow/Happy Little Blue Bird	1959	15.00	30.00	60.00

HALL-WAY

Number	Title (A Side/B Side)	Yr	VG	VG+	NM
❑ 1203	A Bar with No Beer/Headed for Heartbreak	1964	2.50	5.00	10.00
❑ 1207	It's Good to Be Home/For a Minute There	1965	2.50	5.00	10.00

KAPP

Number	Title (A Side/B Side)	Yr	VG	VG+	NM
❑ 859	A Bar with No Beer/Headed for Heartbreak	1967	2.00	4.00	8.00
❑ 912	Sweet Suzannah/It's My Mind That's Broken	1968	2.00	4.00	8.00

MEGA

Number	Title (A Side/B Side)	Yr	VG	VG+	NM
❑ 0071	Woman, Leave My Mind Alone/I'm Just Here to Get My Baby Off My Mind	1972	—	2.50	5.00

MERCURY

Number	Title (A Side/B Side)	Yr	VG	VG+	NM
❑ 71048	Poor Man's Riches/Those Who Know	1957	5.00	10.00	20.00
❑ 71057	Poor Old Me/Penalty	1957	5.00	10.00	20.00
❑ 71119	Nickels Worth of Dreams/Mine All Mine	1957	5.00	10.00	20.00
❑ 71188	King for a Day/Your Old Stand By	1957	5.00	10.00	20.00
❑ 71284	Moon Over My Shoulder/Lonely Street	1958	6.25	12.50	25.00
❑ 71552	Beggar to a King/The Fastest Gun Alive	1959	5.00	10.00	20.00
❑ 71600	That-a Boy Willie/Token of Love	1960	5.00	10.00	20.00
❑ 71637	Pretty Little Girl/Message in the Wind	1960	5.00	10.00	20.00
❑ 71717	You're Still on My Mind/I Think I'll Take a Walk and Disappear	1960	5.00	10.00	20.00
❑ 71806	Yearning/Go On, Go On	1961	5.00	10.00	20.00
❑ 71896	The World's Worst Loser/I Changed My Mind	1961	5.00	10.00	20.00

MUSICOR

Number	Title (A Side/B Side)	Yr	VG	VG+	NM
❑ 1100	Let Me Live As Long As I Can/Tea Leaves Don't Lie	1965	2.00	4.00	8.00
❑ 1127	Have We Really Tried/Heartache's Comin'	1965	2.00	4.00	8.00
❑ 1169	Diesel Smoke/That's How I Need You	1966	2.00	4.00	8.00
❑ 1194	Stand By Your Window/You're Not There	1966	2.00	4.00	8.00
❑ 1223	What's the Matter with Me/Third Time Down	1966	2.00	4.00	8.00
❑ 1247	I'm Her Lover/Same Old Boat	1967	2.00	4.00	8.00
❑ 1277	Let One Call Do It All/Rosanna Martin	1967	2.00	4.00	8.00

PLAYBOY

Number	Title (A Side/B Side)	Yr	VG	VG+	NM
❑ 5808	I've Got Some Gettin' Over You to Do/I'll Drink to That	1977	2.00	4.00	8.00
❑ 6084	Little Brown Paper Bag Blues/(B-side unknown)	1976	2.00	4.00	8.00

RCA VICTOR

Number	Title (A Side/B Side)	Yr	VG	VG+	NM
❑ 47-9830	An Old Memory Got in My Eye/You're Everywhere	1970	—	3.00	6.00
❑ 74-0271	Pressure Cooker/To the Ones I Love	1969	—	3.00	6.00

STARDAY

Number	Title (A Side/B Side)	Yr	VG	VG+	NM
❑ 236	Once Again/No Fault of Mine	1956	7.50	15.00	30.00
❑ 262	Poor Man's Riches/Those Who Know	1956	7.50	15.00	30.00
❑ 401	You Gotta Pay/Heads You Win	1958	6.25	12.50	25.00

BARNES, KATHY

45s

MGM

Number	Title (A Side/B Side)	Yr	VG	VG+	NM
❑ 14797	I'm Available (For You to Hold Me Tight)/Come to Me	1975	—	3.00	6.00
❑ 14816	I Will/I Started Livin' Today	1975	—	—	—
—Canceled?					
❑ 14822	Shhh/I Will	1975	—	3.00	6.00
❑ 14836	Be Honest with Me/Paper Cups	1975	—	3.00	6.00

REPUBLIC

Number	Title (A Side/B Side)	Yr	VG	VG+	NM
❑ 005	The Sun in Dixie/Can't Make It Without You	1977	—	2.50	5.00
❑ 012	Something's Burning/Take It and Go	1977	—	2.50	5.00
❑ 018	That Silver Haired Daddy of Mine/(B-side unknown)	1978	—	2.50	5.00
❑ 021	I'm in Love with Love/Mr. Dream Weaver	1978	—	2.50	5.00
❑ 032	You Make Me Feel It Again/Off	1978	—	2.50	5.00
❑ 037	Body Talkin'/(B-side unknown)	1979	—	2.50	5.00
❑ 046	Love at First Touch/Looking for Someone to Love	1979	—	2.50	5.00
❑ 223	Sleeping with a Memory/Hang My Head	1976	—	2.50	5.00
❑ 223 [PS]	Sleeping with a Memory/Hang My Head	1976	2.50	5.00	10.00
❑ 293	Someday Soon/Your Love (Makes Our Love So Easy)	1976	—	2.50	5.00
❑ 338	Good 'n' Country/One a Day Heartaches	1976	—	2.50	5.00
❑ 376	Catch the Wind/Starve a Fever	1977	—	2.50	5.00
❑ 389	Tweedle-O-Twill/There You Go Doin' It Again	1977	—	2.50	5.00

BARNES, KATHY AND LARRY

45s

REPUBLIC

Number	Title (A Side/B Side)	Yr	VG	VG+	NM
❑ 369	If We Can't Do It Right/(B-side unknown)	1977	—	2.50	5.00

BARNES, LARRY

45s

REPUBLIC

Number	Title (A Side/B Side)	Yr	VG	VG+	NM
❑ 232	You and Me Alone/Rainbows and Sunshine	1976	—	2.50	5.00

SMASH

Number	Title (A Side/B Side)	Yr	VG	VG+	NM
❑ 2004	I Feel Love Comin' On/Rags Is Rags	1965	3.00	6.00	12.00

BARNES, MAX D.

45s

OVATION

Number	Title (A Side/B Side)	Yr	VG	VG+	NM
❑ 1139	Dear Mr. President/Patricia	1979	—	2.50	5.00
❑ 1142	Mean Woman Blues/Too Far Gone to Find	1980	—	2.50	5.00
❑ 1149	Cowboys Are Common As Sin/Only for You	1980	—	2.50	5.00
❑ 1158	Heaven on a Freight Train/Patricia	1980	—	2.50	5.00
❑ 1164	Don't Ever Leave Me Again/Singer of Sad Songs	1981	—	2.50	5.00

POLYDOR

Number	Title (A Side/B Side)	Yr	VG	VG+	NM
❑ 14386	Rain All Over You/Bordertown Woman Blues	1977	—	3.00	6.00
❑ 14419	Allegheny Lady/All the Way In	1977	—	3.00	6.00
❑ 14466	She Loves My Troubles Away/This Workin' Man's Got You	1978	—	3.00	6.00

BARNETT, BOBBY

45s

CIN KAY

Number	Title (A Side/B Side)	Yr	VG	VG+	NM
❑ 128	Burn Atlanta Down/Pody and Barbara	1978	—	2.50	5.00

COLUMBIA

Number	Title (A Side/B Side)	Yr	VG	VG+	NM
❑ 4-44589	Love Me, Love Me/The End of the Lyin'	1968	2.00	4.00	8.00
❑ 4-44716	Your Sweet Love Lifted Me/You'll Fly Away	1968	2.00	4.00	8.00
❑ 4-44861	Drink Canada Dry/Image on Your Mind	1969	2.00	4.00	8.00

K-ARK

Number	Title (A Side/B Side)	Yr	VG	VG+	NM
❑ 741	Down, Down Came the World/Too Tough to Die	1967	2.50	5.00	10.00
❑ 766	The Losing Kind/A Long Way to Go	1967	2.50	5.00	10.00
❑ 804	Please Come Home/I Have No Conscience (When Passion Commands)	1968	2.50	5.00	10.00
❑ 839	Home Away from Home/New World Tomorrow	1968	2.50	5.00	10.00
❑ 877	Rise and Fall of a Man/Thin Line	1968	2.50	5.00	10.00
❑ 915	Stepping Stone/Little Black Cloud	1969	2.50	5.00	10.00

PRESTA

Number	Title (A Side/B Side)	Yr	VG	VG+	NM
❑ 1011	Just Gotta Be Love/Have I Won Enough to Win	197?	2.00	4.00	8.00
❑ 1014	Break Your Habit/Worst Thing	197?	2.00	4.00	8.00

RAZORBACK

Number	Title (A Side/B Side)	Yr	VG	VG+	NM
❑ 306	This Old Heart/(B-side unknown)	1960	5.00	10.00	20.00

REPRISE

Number	Title (A Side/B Side)	Yr	VG	VG+	NM
❑ 20099	Crazy Little Lover/Last of the Angels	1962	3.75	7.50	15.00
❑ 20133	Same Old Love/Temptation's Calling	1962	3.75	7.50	15.00

SIMS

Number	Title (A Side/B Side)	Yr	VG	VG+	NM
❑ 135	I Fall in Love with Every Pretty Girl I See/She Looks Good to the Crowd	1963	3.75	7.50	15.00
❑ 159	Worst of Luck/Working Man	1963	3.75	7.50	15.00
❑ 177	John Said/Hold My Hurt for Awhile	1964	3.75	7.50	15.00
❑ 198	Mismatch/Moaning the Blues	1964	3.75	7.50	15.00
❑ 231	Cheatin' Kathleen/Best Man	1965	3.75	7.50	15.00

BARNETT, MANDY

45s

ASYLUM

Number	Title (A Side/B Side)	Yr	VG	VG+	NM
❑ 64280	Maybe/Wayfaring Stranger	1996	—	2.50	5.00
❑ 64308	Now That's All Right with Me/What's Good for You	1996	—	2.50	5.00

BARNHILL, JOE

45s

CAPITOL

Number	Title (A Side/B Side)	Yr	VG	VG+	NM
❑ 7PRO-79181	Tell Me Why (I'm Still Crying Over You) (same on both sides)	1990	—	2.50	5.00
—Vinyl is promo only					

UNIVERSAL

Number	Title (A Side/B Side)	Yr	VG	VG+	NM
❑ UVL-66000	Becky Morgan (Cotton Pickin' Time)/For Cryin' Out Loud	1989	—	2.00	4.00
❑ UVL-66014	Your Old Flame's Goin' Out Tonight/For Cryin' Out Loud	1989	—	—	3.00
❑ UVL-66032	Good As Gone/Becky Morgan (Cotton Pickin' Time)	1989	—	—	3.00

BARNHILL, LESLEE

45s

REPUBLIC

Number	Title (A Side/B Side)	Yr	VG	VG+	NM
❑ 014	Let's Call It a Day (And Get On with the Night)/I Love the Way You Do What You Do	1978	—	2.50	5.00
❑ 022	By Your Side/(B-side unknown)	1978	—	2.50	5.00
❑ 026	Someday I'd Like to Love You When You're Mine/(B-side unknown)	1978	—	2.50	5.00
❑ 040	Bad Day for a Breakup/I'm Still in Love with You	1979	—	2.50	5.00

BASS, SAM D.

45s

3J

Number	Title (A Side/B Side)	Yr	VG	VG+	NM
❑ 1002	Dumbest Heart in Time/I Just Forgot for Awhile	1980	—	3.00	6.00
❑ 1003	How Could I Do This to Me/Get Ready for the Blues	1980	—	3.00	6.00
❑ 1005	She Don't Live Here Anymore/On My Mind	1980	—	3.00	6.00

BAUER, KATHY

45s

NSD

Number	Title (A Side/B Side)	Yr	VG	VG+	NM
❑ 158	I'll Get As Much of You As I Can Get/Sweet Southern Man	1983	—	2.50	5.00
❑ 164	Hold Me Till the Last Waltz Is Over/What's a Couple More	1983	—	2.50	5.00
❑ 171	Hand Over Your Heart/Softest Touch in Town	1983	—	2.50	5.00

BAUGH, PHIL

Number	Title (A Side/B Side)	Yr	VG	VG+	NM
45s					
ERA					
❑ 3202	Girl Watcher/Jesse's Theme	1969	2.50	5.00	10.00
❑ 3208	Dizzy/Those Were the Days	1969	2.50	5.00	10.00
LONGHORN					
❑ 559	Country Guitar/Chattanooga	1965	3.75	7.50	15.00
❑ 563	One Man Band/Live Wire	1965	3.75	7.50	15.00
Albums					
ERA					
❑ ES-801	California Guitar	1969	6.25	12.50	25.00
LONGHORN					
❑ LP-02 [M]	Country Guitar	1965	12.50	25.00	50.00
TORO					
❑ T-502 [M]	Country Guitar II	1965	10.00	20.00	40.00

BAXTER, BAXTER AND BAXTER

Number	Title (A Side/B Side)	Yr	VG	VG+	NM
45s					
AMI					
❑ 1315	D.W. Washburn/(B-side unknown)	1983	—	2.50	5.00
SUN					
❑ 1160	Take Me Back to the Country/John	1981	—	2.00	4.00
❑ 1167	Lying/Want to Love You More	1981	—	2.00	4.00

BEAN, JIM

Number	Title (A Side/B Side)	Yr	VG	VG+	NM
45s					
HUB					
❑ 47	Lay, Lady, Lay/(B-side unknown)	1988	—	3.00	6.00

BEAR CREEK BAND FEATURING LEONDA

Number	Title (A Side/B Side)	Yr	VG	VG+	NM
45s					
BEAR CREEK					
❑ 103	Falling in Love Right & Left/I've Had Enough (Of Romance)	1988	—	3.00	6.00

BEARDS, THE

Number	Title (A Side/B Side)	Yr	VG	VG+	NM
45s					
BEARDO					
❑ 001/002	Stone Cold Love/Fearless Heart	1988	—	3.00	6.00

BEATTY, SUSI

Number	Title (A Side/B Side)	Yr	VG	VG+	NM
45s					
STARWAY					
❑ 1205	Hard Baby to Rock/Down Home Jubilee	1989	—	3.00	6.00
❑ 1206	Heart from a Stone/Down Home Jubilee	1989	—	3.00	6.00

BEAVERS, CLYDE

Number	Title (A Side/B Side)	Yr	VG	VG+	NM
45s					
DECCA					
❑ 31173	Here I Am Drunk Again/My Love Is Real	1960	3.75	7.50	15.00
❑ 31314	Ain't Gonna Drink No More/I Wanted Heaven	1961	3.75	7.50	15.00
DOT					
❑ 17382	Last Call for Alcohol/How Can Anything Be So Wrong	1971	—	3.00	6.00
❑ 17416	Clyde/Truck Stop Wall	1972	—	3.00	6.00
❑ 17438	I Will Love You Until I Die/Broken Wings Can't Fly	1972	—	3.00	6.00
HICKORY					
❑ 1346	That's You (And What's Left of Me)/Old Tree	1966	2.00	4.00	8.00
❑ 1376	Thirty-Two Years/Train from North to South	1966	2.00	4.00	8.00
TEMPWOOD V					
❑ 1039	Still Loving You/Happy Times	1963	2.50	5.00	10.00
❑ 1044	Sukiyaki (I Look Up When I Walk)/Handprints on the Window	1963	2.50	5.00	10.00

BECKHAM, BOB

Number	Title (A Side/B Side)	Yr	VG	VG+	NM
45s					
DECCA					
❑ 30617	Tomorrow/I'm Tired of Everyone But You	1958	3.00	6.00	12.00
❑ 30861	Just As Much As Ever/Your Sweet Love	1959	3.00	6.00	12.00
❑ 31029	Crazy Arms/Beloved	1959	3.00	6.00	12.00
❑ 31089	Only the Broken Hearted/Mais Oui	1960	2.50	5.00	10.00
❑ 31132	Two Wrongs Don't Make a Right/Nothing Is Forever	1960	2.50	5.00	10.00
❑ 31163	Meet Me Halfway/One More Time	1960	2.50	5.00	10.00
❑ 31239	Forget It/Like a Fool	1961	2.50	5.00	10.00
❑ 31285	How Soon (Will I Be Seeing You)/I'm Wondering	1961	2.50	5.00	10.00
❑ 31337	10,000 Teardrops (And One Broken Heart)/Just Friends	1961	2.50	5.00	10.00
❑ 31391	I Cry Like a Baby/I'll Take My Chances	1962	2.00	4.00	8.00
❑ 31432	Building Memories/Memory Mountain	1962	2.00	4.00	8.00
❑ 31493	Footprints/Midnight	1963	2.00	4.00	8.00
❑ 31547	Grabbing at Rainbows/My Heart Would Know	1963	2.00	4.00	8.00
❑ 31607	Helpless/I'll Be Around	1964	2.00	4.00	8.00
MONUMENT					
❑ 1018	Cherokee Strip/You Really Know How to Hurt a Guy	1967	—	3.00	6.00
❑ 1030	Lily White/Look at Them	1967	—	3.00	6.00
SMASH					
❑ 1990	Slowly Dying/It's My Heart	1965	2.00	4.00	8.00

BECKHAM, CHARLIE

Number	Title (A Side/B Side)	Yr	VG	VG+	NM
45s					
OAK					
❑ 1048	Think I'll Go Home/(B-side unknown)	1988	—	3.00	6.00

BEE, KATHY

Number	Title (A Side/B Side)	Yr	VG	VG+	NM
45s					
LILAC					
❑ 1213	Let's Go Party/(B-side unknown)	1988	—	3.00	6.00

BEE, MOLLY

Also see TENNESSEE ERNIE FORD.

Number	Title (A Side/B Side)	Yr	VG	VG+	NM
45s					
CAPITOL					
❑ F2258	Tennessee Tango/Kids Who Pay	1952	6.25	12.50	25.00
❑ F2285	I Saw Mommy Kissing Santa Claus/Willy Claus (Little Son of Santa Claus)	1952	5.00	10.00	20.00
❑ F2339	Honky Tonk Mountain/Nobody's Lonesome for Me	1953	5.00	10.00	20.00
❑ F2396	What'll He Do/Dancing with Someone	1953	5.00	10.00	20.00
❑ F2494	Doggie on the Highway/I'll Tell My Mommy	1953	5.00	10.00	20.00
❑ F2567	God Bless Us All/This Is My Dog	1953	5.00	10.00	20.00
❑ F2741	Remember Me/Pine Tree Pine Over Me	1954	5.00	10.00	20.00
❑ F2790	Stuffy/In the Pyrenees	1954	5.00	10.00	20.00
❑ F3865	Magic Mirror/I'm Going Steady with a Dream	1957	3.75	7.50	15.00
❑ F3968	Don't Look Back/Please Don't Talk About Me When I'm Gone	1958	3.75	7.50	15.00
❑ F4064	Five Points of a Star/After You've Gone	1958	3.75	7.50	15.00
CORAL					
❑ 9-61357	I Won't Grow Up/False Alarm	1955	5.00	10.00	20.00
DOT					
❑ 15453	Sweet Shoppe Sweetheart/From the Wrong Side of Town	1956	5.00	10.00	20.00
❑ 15517	Since I Met You Baby/I'll Be Waiting for You	1956	5.00	10.00	20.00
GRANITE					
❑ 509	She Kept On Talkin'/Baby You Got It	1974	—	3.50	7.00
❑ 515	Right or Left at Oak Street/I Got a Man	1975	—	3.50	7.00
❑ 524	California Country/(B-side unknown)	1975	—	3.50	7.00
❑ 531	I Can't Live in the Dark Anymore/(B-side unknown)	1975	—	3.50	7.00
LIBERTY					
❑ 55438	Just for the Record/Lyin' Again	1962	3.00	6.00	12.00
❑ 55543	All My Love, All My Life/She's New to You	1963	3.00	6.00	12.00
❑ 55569	I Was Only Kidding/He's My True Love	1963	3.00	6.00	12.00
❑ 55631	Some Tears Fall Dry/Johnny Liar	1963	3.00	6.00	12.00
❑ 55691	Our Secret/He Doesn't Want You	1964	3.00	6.00	12.00
MGM					
❑ 13356	Keep It a Secret/Single Girl Again	1965	2.50	5.00	10.00
❑ 13411	Together Again/I'm Gonna Change Everything	1965	2.50	5.00	10.00
❑ 13491	Losing You/Miserable Me	1966	2.50	5.00	10.00
❑ 13537	How's the World Treating You/It Keeps Right On a-Hurtin'	1966	2.50	5.00	10.00
❑ 13694	Almost Persuaded/Heartbreak U.S.A.	1967	2.50	5.00	10.00
❑ 13770	You Win Again/I Hate to See Me Go	1967	2.50	5.00	10.00
❑ 13864	Sinner's Wine/Fresh Out of Tryin'	1967	2.50	5.00	10.00
Albums					
ACCORD					
❑ 7901	Sounds Fine to Me	1982	2.50	5.00	10.00
CAPITOL					
❑ T 1097 [M]	Young Romance	1958	10.00	20.00	40.00
GRANITE					
❑ 1002	Good Golly Ms. Molly	1974	3.00	6.00	12.00
MGM					
❑ E-4303 [M]	It's Great, It's Molly Bee	1965	5.00	10.00	20.00
❑ SE-4303 [S]	It's Great, It's Molly Bee	1965	6.25	12.50	25.00
❑ E-4423 [M]	Swingin' Country	1967	5.00	10.00	20.00
❑ SE-4423 [S]	Swingin' Country	1967	6.25	12.50	25.00

BEE GEES

The Brothers Gibb placed the B-side of the below single into the top 40 of the country charts in 1979. The track was also later remade by CONWAY TWITTY.

Number	Title (A Side/B Side)	Yr	VG	VG+	NM
45s					
RSO					
❑ 913	Too Much Heaven/Rest Your Love on Me	1978	—	2.00	4.00

BEEFEATERS, THE

Early version of THE BYRDS.

Number	Title (A Side/B Side)	Yr	VG	VG+	NM
45s					
ELEKTRA					
❑ 45013	Please Let Me Love You/It Won't Be Long	1964	125.00	250.00	500.00
❑ 45013 [DJ]	Please Let Me Love You/It Won't Be Long	1964	62.50	125.00	250.00

BEESON, MARC

Also see BURNIN' DAYLIGHT.

Number	Title (A Side/B Side)	Yr	VG	VG+	NM
45s					
BNA					
❑ 62794	A Wing and a Prayer/We'll Get By	1994	—	—	3.00

BELEW, CARL

Number	Title (A Side/B Side)	Yr	VG	VG+	NM
45s					
4 STAR					
❑ 1715	I Can't Forget/Stop the World	1958	5.00	10.00	20.00
❑ 1721	Everytime I'm Kissing You/24 Hour Night	1958	5.00	10.00	20.00
❑ 1726	No Love Tonight/My Baby's Not Here	1958	5.00	10.00	20.00

Number	Title (A Side/B Side)	Yr	VG	VG+	NM
BRUNSWICK					
❑ 9-55071	Everytime I'm Kissing You/Now We're One	1958	5.00	10.00	20.00
COLUMBIA					
❑ 4-44758	Move Over/Get Behind Life	1969	—	3.50	7.00
DECCA					
❑ 30842	Am I That Easy to Forget/Such Is Life	1959	3.00	6.00	12.00
❑ 30947	No Regrets/Cool Gater Shoes	1959	10.00	20.00	40.00
❑ 31012	I Wish I'd Never/I Know, But Tell Me Dear It Didn't Happen	1959	3.00	6.00	12.00
❑ 31086	Too Much to Lose/That's What I Get for Loving You	1960	3.00	6.00	12.00
❑ 31140	The End of Time/My Baby's Not Here	1960	3.00	6.00	12.00
❑ 31200	Another Lonely Night/I Can't Lose Something (That I Never Had)	1961	3.00	6.00	12.00
❑ 31273	Stop the World (And Let Me Off)/I Can't Take a Chance	1961	3.00	6.00	12.00
❑ 31325	I'm So Lonesome/Do I Have To	1961	3.00	6.00	12.00
❑ 31427	Can't You Hear Me Call Your Name/I Don't Know How I'll Live (And Feel This Way)	1962	3.00	6.00	12.00
❑ 32747	The Fastest Man Alive/Mary	1970	2.00	4.00	8.00
❑ 32789	Stay Close to Me/I Can Give You What You Want Now	1971	2.00	4.00	8.00
❑ 32885	God Is Alive/Buss 22	1971	2.00	4.00	8.00
❑ 32952	I Won't Care/Happy Harry's Honky Tonk	1972	2.00	4.00	8.00
❑ 33043	Who Are You saving It For/I'm Taking Care of Your Roses	1973	—	3.50	7.00
RCA VICTOR					
❑ 47-8010	Odd Man Out/Second Chance	1962	2.50	5.00	10.00
❑ 47-8058	Hello Out There/Together We Stand	1962	2.50	5.00	10.00
❑ 47-8132	Pretty Brown Eyes/The Masquerade Party	1963	2.50	5.00	10.00
❑ 47-8199	My Pride Won't Let Me/I Can't Stand to Look	1963	2.50	5.00	10.00
❑ 47-8270	Speak to Me/Big City Girls	1963	2.50	5.00	10.00
❑ 47-8352	Before I Go to Bed/Anna Louise	1964	2.50	5.00	10.00
❑ 47-8406	In the Middle of a Memory/Cheaters Never Prosper	1964	2.50	5.00	10.00
❑ 47-8527	She Reads Me Like a Book/Silent Partner	1965	2.50	5.00	10.00
❑ 47-8633	Crystal Chandelier/Lonely Hearts Do Foolish Things	1965	2.50	5.00	10.00
❑ 47-8744	Boston Jail/I Spent a Week There One Day	1966	2.50	5.00	10.00
❑ 47-8835	Possum Holler/Pick Up My Marbles and Run Home	1966	2.50	5.00	10.00
❑ 47-8996	Walking Shadow, Talking Memory	1966	2.50	5.00	10.00
❑ 47-9078	Help Stamp Out Loneliness/I Dream Too Big	1967	2.50	5.00	10.00
❑ 47-9272	Girl Crazy/Turnabout	1967	2.50	5.00	10.00
❑ 47-9351	Home Away from Home/Too Much to Lose	1967	2.50	5.00	10.00
❑ 47-9446	Mary's Little Lamb/Once	1968	2.50	5.00	10.00
Albums					
BUCKBOARD					
❑ BBS 1014	Singing My Song	197?	2.50	5.00	10.00
DECCA					
❑ DL 4074 [M]	Carl Belew	1960	6.25	12.50	25.00
❑ DL 74074 [S]	Carl Belew	1960	7.50	15.00	30.00
HILLTOP					
❑ JM-6013 [M]	Another Lonely Night	1965	5.00	10.00	20.00
❑ JS-6013 [S]	Another Lonely Night	1965	5.00	10.00	20.00
PICCADILLY					
❑ 3356	Big Time Gambling Man	198?	2.50	5.00	10.00
RCA VICTOR					
❑ LPM-2848 [M]	Hello Out There	1964	5.00	10.00	20.00
❑ LSP-2848 [S]	Hello Out There	1964	6.25	12.50	25.00
❑ LPM-3381 [M]	Am I That Easy to Forget?	1965	5.00	10.00	20.00
❑ LSP-3381 [S]	Am I That Easy to Forget?	1965	6.25	12.50	25.00
❑ LPM-3919 [M]	Twelve Shades of Belew	1968	12.50	25.00	50.00
❑ LSP-3919 [S]	Twelve Shades of Belew	1968	5.00	10.00	20.00
VOCALION					
❑ VL 3774 [M]	Country Songs	196?	3.00	6.00	12.00
❑ VL 3791 [M]	Lonely Street	1967	3.75	7.50	15.00
❑ VL 73774 [S]	Country Songs	196?	3.00	6.00	12.00
❑ VL 73791 [S]	Lonely Street	1967	3.00	6.00	12.00
WRANGLER					
❑ WR 1007 [M]	Carl Belew	1962	7.50	15.00	30.00
❑ WRS 31007 [S]	Carl Belew	1962	10.00	20.00	40.00

BELEW, CARL, AND BETTY JEAN ROBINSON

Also see each artist's individual listings.

Number	Title (A Side/B Side)	Yr	VG	VG+	NM
45s					
DECCA					
❑ 32802	All I Need Is You/Funny What a Pair of Fools Will Do	1971	2.00	4.00	8.00
❑ 32871	Hung Up on Lovin' You/Living Under Pressure	1971	2.00	4.00	8.00
❑ 32916	When My Baby Sings His Song/Don't Let That Happen to Us	1972	2.00	4.00	8.00
❑ 32970	You're the One/Lucky Ol' Me	1972	2.00	4.00	8.00
Albums					
DECCA					
❑ DL 75337	When My Baby Sings His Song	1972	3.75	7.50	15.00

BELL, DELIA

Number	Title (A Side/B Side)	Yr	VG	VG+	NM
45s					
WARNER BROS.					
❑ 29550	Coyote Song/Love Pilgrim	1983	—	2.00	4.00
❑ 29653	Flame in My Heart/Good Lord A'Mighty	1983	—	2.00	4.00
Albums					
WARNER BROS.					
❑ 23838	Delia Bell	1983	2.50	5.00	10.00

BELL, JAMES

Number	Title (A Side/B Side)	Yr	VG	VG+	NM
45s					
BELL					
❑ 710	He Ain't Country/A Friendly Place to Cry	1968	2.00	4.00	8.00

BELL, TOMMY

Number	Title (A Side/B Side)	Yr	VG	VG+	NM
45s					
GOLD SOUND					
❑ 8013	Georgiana/Untangle My Mind	1982	—	3.00	6.00
❑ 8013 [PS]	Georgiana/Untangle My Mind	1982	2.50	5.00	10.00
❑ 8016	Honky Tonk Crazy/(B-side unknown)	1983	—	3.00	6.00

BELL, VIVIAN

Number	Title (A Side/B Side)	Yr	VG	VG+	NM
45s					
GRT					
❑ 118	The Angel in Your Arms/What in the Name of Love	1977	—	2.50	5.00

BELLAMY, DAVID

One-half of THE BELLAMY BROTHERS.

Number	Title (A Side/B Side)	Yr	VG	VG+	NM
45s					
WARNER BROS.					
❑ 8123	Baby, You're Not a Legend/Nothin' Heavy	1975	—	2.50	5.00

BELLAMY BROTHERS, THE

Also see DAVID BELLAMY; THE FORESTER SISTERS.

Number	Title (A Side/B Side)	Yr	VG	VG+	NM
45s					
ATLANTIC					
❑ 87650	All in the Name of Love/Anyway I Can	1991	—	2.00	4.00
❑ 87748	She Don't Know That She's Perfect/I Make Her Laugh	1991	—	2.00	4.00
ELEKTRA					
❑ 47431	For All the Wrong Reasons/This Time	1982	—	2.00	4.00
❑ 69850	When I'm Away from You/Long Distance Love Affair	1983	—	2.00	4.00
❑ 69999	Get Into Reggae Cowboy/We're Just a Little Ole Country Band	1982	—	2.00	4.00
MCA CURB					
❑ 52380	Forget About Me/We're Having Some Fun Now	1984	—	—	3.00
❑ 52446	The World's Greatest Lover/Rock-A-Dash	1984	—	—	3.00
❑ 52518	I Need More of You/Diesel Cafe	1984	—	—	3.00
❑ 52579	Old Hippie/Wheels	1985	—	—	3.00
❑ 52668	Lie to You for Your Love/Season of the Wind	1985	—	—	3.00
❑ 52747	Feelin' the Feelin'/The Single Man and His Wife	1985	—	—	3.00
❑ 52747 [DJ]	Feelin' the Feelin' (same on both sides)	1985	3.00	6.00	12.00
—Promo only on yellow vinyl					
❑ 52834	Country Rap/One Too Many Times	1986	—	—	3.00
❑ 52834 [DJ]	Country Rap (same on both sides)	1986	3.00	6.00	12.00
—Promo only on yellow vinyl					
❑ 52917	Too Much Is Not Enough/Restless	1986	—	—	3.00
—A-side with The Forester Sisters					
❑ 52917 [DJ]	Too Much Is Not Enough (same on both sides)	1986	3.00	6.00	12.00
—With The Forester Sisters; promo only on red vinyl					
❑ 53018	Kids of the Baby Boom/Hard on a Heart	1987	—	—	3.00
❑ 53154	Crazy from the Heart/White Trash	1987	—	—	3.00
❑ 53222	Santa Fe/White Trash	1987	—	—	3.00
❑ 53310	I'll Give You All My Love Tonight/Ying Yang	1988	—	—	3.00
❑ 53399	Rebels Without a Clue/A Little Naive	1988	—	—	3.00
❑ 53478	Big Love/The Courthouse	1988	—	—	3.00
❑ 53642	Hillbilly Hell/You're My Favorite Star	1989	—	—	3.00
❑ 53672	You'll Never Be Sorry/Hillbilly Hell	1989	—	—	3.00
❑ 53719	The Center of My Universe/Hillbilly Hell	1989	—	—	3.00
❑ 79019	I Could Be Persuaded/What's This World Coming To	1990	—	—	3.00
WARNER BROS.					
❑ 8169	Let Your Love Flow/Inside My Guitar	1975	—	2.50	5.00
❑ 8220	Hell Cat/I'm the Only Man Left Alive	1976	—	2.00	4.00
❑ 8248	Rainy, Windy, Sunshine (Roadeo Road)/Satin Sheets	1976	—	2.00	4.00
❑ 8284	Livin' in the West/Highway 2-18 (Hang On to Your Dreams)	1976	—	2.00	4.00
❑ 8350	Crossfire/Tiger Lily Lover	1977	—	2.00	4.00
❑ 8401	Can Somebody Hear Me Now/You Made Me	1977	—	2.00	4.00
❑ 8462	Hard Rockin'/Memorabilia	1977	—	2.00	4.00
❑ 8521	Bird Dog/Make Me Over	1978	—	2.00	4.00
❑ 8558	Let's Give Love a Try/Slipping Away	1978	—	2.00	4.00
❑ 8627	Tumbleweed and Rosalee/Wild Honey	1978	—	2.00	4.00
❑ 8692	Lovin' on/My Shy Anne	1978	—	2.00	4.00
❑ 8790	If I Said You Have a Beautiful Body Would You Hold It Against Me/Make Me Over	1979	—	2.00	4.00
❑ 29514	Strong Weakness/Doin' It the Hard Way	1983	—	2.00	4.00
❑ 29645	I Love Her Mind/Lazy Eyes	1983	—	2.00	4.00
❑ 29923	Redneck Girl/Let Your Love Flow	1982	—	2.00	4.00
❑ 49032	You Ain't Just Whistlin' Dixie/Blue Ribbons	1979	—	2.00	4.00
❑ 49160	Sugar Daddy/I Could Be Makin' Love to You	1980	—	2.00	4.00
❑ 49241	Dancin' Cowboys/Dead Aim	1980	—	2.00	4.00
❑ 49573	Classic Case of the Blues/Lovers Live Longer	1980	—	2.00	4.00
❑ 49639	Do You Love As Good As You Look/Givin' In to Love Again	1980	—	2.00	4.00
❑ 49729	They Could Put Me in Jail/Endangered Species	1981	—	2.00	4.00

Number	Title (A Side/B Side)	Yr	VG	VG+	NM
❑ 49815	You're My Favorite Star/It's Hard to Be a Cowboy These Days	1981	—	2.00	4.00
❑ 49875	It's So Close to Christmas/Let Me Waltz Into Your Heart	1981	—	2.00	4.00

Albums

ELEKTRA

Number	Title	Yr	VG	VG+	NM
❑ 60099	When We Were Boys	1982	2.50	5.00	10.00
❑ 60210	Strong Weakness	1982	2.50	5.00	10.00

MCA CURB

Number	Title	Yr	VG	VG+	NM
❑ 1441	Restless	1985	2.00	4.00	8.00
—Reissue of MCA 5489					
❑ 1462	Greatest Hits	1985	2.00	4.00	8.00
—Reissue of Warner Bros. 23697					
❑ 5489	Restless	1984	2.50	5.00	10.00
❑ 5586	Howard & David	1985	2.50	5.00	10.00
❑ 5721	Country Rap	1987	2.50	5.00	10.00
❑ 5812	Greatest Hits Volume Two	1986	2.50	5.00	10.00
❑ 42039	Crazy from the Heart	1987	2.50	5.00	10.00
❑ 42224	Rebels Without a Clue	1988	2.50	5.00	10.00
❑ 42298	Greatest Hits Volume III	1989	2.50	5.00	10.00

WARNER BROS.

Number	Title	Yr	VG	VG+	NM
❑ BS 2941	Let Your Love Flow	1976	2.50	5.00	10.00
❑ BS 3034	Plain & Fancy	1977	2.50	5.00	10.00
❑ BSK 3176	Friends	1978	2.50	5.00	10.00
❑ BSK 3347	The Two and Only	1979	2.50	5.00	10.00
❑ BSK 3408	You Can Get Crazy	1980	2.50	5.00	10.00
❑ BSK 3491	Sons of the Sun	1980	2.50	5.00	10.00
❑ 23697	Greatest Hits	1982	2.50	5.00	10.00
❑ 60210	Strong Weakness	1983	2.00	4.00	8.00
—Reissue of Elektra 60210					

BENEDICT, ERNIE

45s

RCA VICTOR

Number	Title	Yr	VG	VG+	NM
❑ 48-0059	Polka Dots and Polka Dreams/Tzigane Polka	1949	6.25	12.50	25.00
—Original on green vinyl					
❑ 48-0106	When I Comb My Hands (Through the Sands of Texas)/Big and Beautiful	1949	7.50	15.00	30.00
—Original on green vinyl					

Selected 78s

RCA VICTOR

Number	Title	Yr	VG	VG+	NM
❑ 20-3389	Over Three Hills/Red Lips and Red Wine	1949	5.00	10.00	20.00

—His only charted hit, this should exist on 45 rpm, as other RCA 78s of the same era do, but we can't confirm that it does. Can anyone out there help?

BENONI, ARNE

45s

ROUND ROBIN

Number	Title	Yr	VG	VG+	NM
❑ 1879	Southern Lady/Those Evening Bells	1989	—	3.00	6.00
❑ 1879 [PS]	Southern Lady/Those Evening Bells	1989	2.00	4.00	8.00
❑ 1881	If I Live to Be a Hundred (I'll Die Young)/(B-side unknown)	1989	—	3.00	6.00

BENSON, MATT

45s

STEP ONE

Number	Title	Yr	VG	VG+	NM
❑ 406	When Will the Fires End/America	1989	—	2.00	4.00

BENSON, RAY

Also see ASLEEP AT THE WHEEL.

45s

ARISTA

Number	Title	Yr	VG	VG+	NM
❑ 2340	Four Scores and Seven Beers Ago/Eyes	1991	—	2.00	4.00

BENTLEY, STEPHANIE

45s

EPIC

Number	Title	Yr	VG	VG+	NM
❑ 34-78234	Who's That Girl/The Hopechest Song	1996	—	2.00	4.00
❑ 34-78336	Once I Was the Light of Your Life/What's Wrong with You (Is You Ain't Got Me)	1996	—	2.00	4.00
❑ 34-78431	Dead Ringer/Think of Me	1996	—	2.00	4.00

BENTON, BARBI

Also see MICKEY GILLEY.

45s

PLAYBOY

Number	Title	Yr	VG	VG+	NM
❑ 5802	Take Some and Give Some (And Leave Some Behind)/Ain't That Just the Way (That Life Goes Down)	1977	—	2.50	5.00
❑ 6008	Welcome Stranger/That Country Boy of Mine	1974	—	2.50	5.00
❑ 6018	Now I Lay Me Down to Sleep with You/If You Can't Do It, That's Alright	1974	—	2.50	5.00
❑ 6032	Brass Buckles/Put a Little Bit on Me	1975	—	2.50	5.00
❑ 6043	Movie Magazine, Stars in Her Eyes/He Looks Just Like His Daddy	1975	—	2.50	5.00
❑ 6056	The Reverend Bob/Ain't That Just the Way (That Life Goes Down)	1975	—	2.50	5.00
❑ 6078	Staying Power/San Diego Serenade	1976	—	2.50	5.00
❑ 6094	Needing You/In the Winter	1976	—	2.50	5.00

Albums

PLAYBOY

Number	Title	Yr	VG	VG+	NM
❑ PB 404	Barbi Doll	1974	3.75	7.50	15.00
❑ PB 406	Barbi Benton	1975	3.75	7.50	15.00
❑ PB 411	Something New	1976	3.75	7.50	15.00

BERG, MATRACA

45s

RCA

Number	Title	Yr	VG	VG+	NM
❑ 2504-7-R	Baby Walk On/(B-side unknown)	1990	—	2.00	4.00
❑ 2644-7-R	The Things You Left Undone/Dancin' on the Wire	1990	—	2.00	4.00
❑ 2710-7-R	I Got It Bad/Calico Plains	1990	—	2.00	4.00
❑ 2827-7-R	I Must Have Been Crazy/Alice in the Looking Glass	1991	—	2.00	4.00
❑ 62060	It's Easy to Tell/Baby, Walk On	1991	—	2.00	4.00

RISING TIDE

Number	Title	Yr	VG	VG+	NM
❑ 56047	That Train Don't Run/Here You Come Raining on My Parade	1997	—	2.50	5.00

BERRY, JOHN

45s

CAPITOL NASHVILLE

Number	Title	Yr	VG	VG+	NM
❑ S7-18843	If I Had Any Pride Left at All/What Are We Fighting For	1995	—	2.00	4.00
❑ S7-18910	O Holy Night/O Come Emmanuel	1995	—	2.00	4.00
❑ S7-19251	Change My Mind/Time to Be a Man	1996	—	2.00	4.00
❑ S7-19451	She's Taken a Shine/Time to Be a Man	1997	—	2.00	4.00
❑ S7-19511	I Will, If You Will/Love Is Everything	1997	—	2.00	4.00
❑ S7-19724	The Stone/Livin' On Love	1997	—	2.00	4.00
❑ S7-19975	Over My Shoulder/I Got to Know	1998	—	2.00	4.00
❑ S7-58707	Better Than a Biscuit/Mr. Jones	1998	—	—	3.00

LIBERTY

Number	Title	Yr	VG	VG+	NM
❑ S7-17518	Kiss Me in the Car/More Than Just a Little	1993	—	2.50	5.00
❑ S7-18022	Your Love Amazes Me/What's In It for Me	1994	—	3.00	6.00
—Colored vinyl					
❑ S7-18137	You and Only You/More Sorry Than You'll Ever Know	1994	—	2.00	4.00
❑ S7-18557	The Long and Winding Road/Come Together	1995	—	2.50	5.00
—B-side by Delbert McClinton					

PATRIOT

Number	Title	Yr	VG	VG+	NM
❑ S7-18401	Standing on the Edge of Goodbye/Ninety Miles an Hour	1995	—	2.00	4.00

BICKHARDT, CRAIG

Also see SCHUYLER, KNOBLOCH & BICKHARDT.

45s

LIBERTY

Number	Title	Yr	VG	VG+	NM
❑ B-1518	You Are What Love Means to Me/Overnight Sensations	1984	—	—	3.00

BIG HOUSE

45s

MCA

Number	Title	Yr	VG	VG+	NM
❑ 55253	Cold Outside/(B-side unknown)	1996	—	—	3.00
❑ 72005	You Ain't Lonely Yet/The Tables Are Turned	1997	—	—	3.00
❑ 72020	Love Ain't Easy/Blue Train	1997	—	—	3.00
❑ 72052	Faith/Travelin' Kind	1998	—	—	3.00

BILLY HILL

DENNIS ROBBINS was in this group.

45s

REPRISE

Number	Title	Yr	VG	VG+	NM
❑ 7-19738	No Chance to Dance/Too Much Month at the End of the Money	1990	—	2.00	4.00
❑ 7-22746	I Can't Help Myself (Sugar Pie, Honey Bunch)/Just in Case You Want to Know	1989	—	—	3.00
❑ 7-22942	Too Much Month at the End of the Money/Rollin' Dice	1989	—	—	3.00

Albums

REPRISE

Number	Title	Yr	VG	VG+	NM
❑ 25915	I Am Just a Rebel	1989	2.50	5.00	10.00

BILLY THE KID

45s

CYCLONE

Number	Title	Yr	VG	VG+	NM
❑ 103	What I Feel Is You/Songpainter	1979	—	3.00	6.00

BIRD, VICKI

45s

16TH AVENUE

Number	Title	Yr	VG	VG+	NM
❑ 70405	I've Got Ways of Making You Talk/I Need a Real Good Love Real Bad	1987	—	2.00	4.00
❑ 70413	A Little Bit of Lovin' (Goes a Long Long Way)/I've Got Ways of Making You Talk	1988	—	2.00	4.00
❑ 70421	Mem'ries/A Little Bit of Lovin' (Goes a Long, Long Way)	1989	—	2.00	4.00
❑ 70431	Moanin' the Blues/Mem'ries	1989	—	2.00	4.00

AVCO

Number	Title	Yr	VG	VG+	NM
❑ 604	Louisiana Swamp Rat/The Devil Gets His Nights	1974	—	3.00	6.00
❑ 611	The Spelling Game/Should I Stay at Home	1975	—	3.00	6.00

BISHOP, BOB

45s

ABC

Number	Title	Yr	VG	VG+	NM
❑ 11132	Roses to Reno/It's Gonna Hurt You More Than Me	1968	—	3.50	7.00
❑ 11200	Another Man's World/Somewhere in the Country	1969	—	3.50	7.00
❑ 11243	Man Walks Among Us/If Your Sweet Love Don't Find Me	1969	—	3.50	7.00

WAYSIDE

Number	Title (A Side/B Side)	Yr	VG	VG+	NM
❑ 1004	I Hate to Sing and Run/My Crying Chair	1967	2.00	4.00	8.00
—As "Bobby Bishop"					

BISHOP, JONI

45s

COLUMBIA

Number	Title (A Side/B Side)	Yr	VG	VG+	NM
❑ 38-07225	Heart Out of Control/Walls, Doors, Windows and Floors	1987	—	—	3.00

BISHOP, TERRI

45s

UNITED ARTISTS

Number	Title (A Side/B Side)	Yr	VG	VG+	NM
❑ XW1194	One More Kiss/My Memories	1978	—	3.00	6.00

BLACK, BILL, 'S COMBO

45s

COLUMBIA

Number	Title (A Side/B Side)	Yr	VG	VG+	NM
❑ 44867	But It's Alright/Slow Action	1969	—	2.50	5.00
❑ 44983	California Dreamin'/Funky Train	1969	—	2.50	5.00
❑ 45092	Heaven Knows/One Five One Eight Chelsea	1970	—	2.50	5.00
❑ 45162	Keep the Customer Satisfied/One Five One Eight Chelsea	1970	—	2.50	5.00

HI

Number	Title (A Side/B Side)	Yr	VG	VG+	NM
❑ 2018	Smokie (Part 2)/Smokie (Part 1)	1959	5.00	10.00	20.00
❑ 2021	White Silver Sands/The Wheel	1960	5.00	10.00	20.00
❑ 2022	Josephine/Dry Bones	1960	3.75	7.50	15.00
❑ 2022 [PS]	Josephine/Dry Bones	1960	6.25	12.50	25.00
❑ 2026	Don't Be Cruel/Rollin'	1960	3.75	7.50	15.00
❑ 2026 [PS]	Don't Be Cruel/Rollin'	1960	6.25	12.50	25.00
❑ 2027	Blue Tango/Willie	1960	3.75	7.50	15.00
❑ 2027 [PS]	Blue Tango/Willie	1960	6.25	12.50	25.00
❑ 2028	Hearts of Stone/Royal Blue	1961	3.00	6.00	12.00
❑ 2029	Old Time Religion/He's Got the Whole World in His Hands	1961	10.00	20.00	40.00
—Stereo single, small hole, plays at 33 1/3 rpm					
❑ 2030	Do Lord/When the Roll Is Called Up Yonder	1961	10.00	20.00	40.00
—Stereo single, small hole, plays at 33 1/3 rpm					
❑ 2031	Down by the Riverside/It Is No Secret (What God Can Do)	1961	10.00	20.00	40.00
—Stereo single, small hole, plays at 33 1/3 rpm					
❑ 2032	When the Saints Go Marching In/(B-side unknown)	1961	10.00	20.00	40.00
—Stereo single, small hole, plays at 33 1/3 rpm					
❑ 2033	Just a Closer Walk with Thee/This Old House	1961	10.00	20.00	40.00
—Stereo single, small hole, plays at 33 1/3 rpm					
❑ 2036	Ole Buttermilk Sky/Yogi	1961	3.00	6.00	12.00
❑ 2036 [PS]	Ole Buttermilk Sky/Yogi	1961	6.25	12.50	25.00
❑ 2038	Movin'/Honky Train	1961	3.00	6.00	12.00
❑ 2042	Twist-Her/My Girl Josephine	1961	3.00	6.00	12.00
❑ 2045	Twist-Her/Night Train	1962	10.00	20.00	40.00
—Stereo single, small hole, plays at 33 1/3 rpm					
❑ 2046	The Hucklebuck/Corrina, Corrina	1962	10.00	20.00	40.00
—Stereo single, small hole, plays at 33 1/3 rpm					
❑ 2047	Johnny B. Goode/(B-side unknown)	1962	10.00	20.00	40.00
—Stereo single, small hole, plays at 33 1/3 rpm					
❑ 2048	Josephine/My Girl Josephine	1962	10.00	20.00	40.00
—Stereo single, small hole, plays at 33 1/3 rpm					
❑ 2049	Slippin' and Slidin'/Twist with Me, Baby	1962	10.00	20.00	40.00
—Stereo single, small hole, plays at 33 1/3 rpm					
❑ 2052	Twistin' — White Silver Sands/My Babe	1962	3.00	6.00	12.00
❑ 2052 [PS]	Twistin' — White Silver Sands/My Babe	1962	6.25	12.50	25.00
❑ 2055	So What/Blues for the Red Boy	1962	3.00	6.00	12.00
❑ 2059	Joey's Song/Hot Taco	1962	3.00	6.00	12.00
❑ 2064	Do It — Rat Now/Little Jasper	1963	3.00	6.00	12.00
❑ 2069	Monkey-Shine/Love Gone	1963	3.00	6.00	12.00
❑ 2072	Comin' On/Soft Winds	1964	3.00	6.00	12.00
❑ 2077	Tequila/Raunchy	1964	3.00	6.00	12.00
❑ 2079	Little Queenie/Boo Ray	1964	3.00	6.00	12.00
❑ 2085	Come On Home/He'll Have to Go	1964	2.50	5.00	10.00
❑ 2094	Spootin'/Crazy Feeling	1965	2.50	5.00	10.00
❑ 2106	Hey, Good Lookin'/Mountain of Love	1966	2.50	5.00	10.00
❑ 2115	Rambler/You Call Everybody Darling	1966	2.50	5.00	10.00
❑ 2124	Son of Smokie/Peg Leg	1967	2.00	4.00	8.00
❑ 2145	Turn On Your Love Life/Ribbon of Darkness	1968	—	3.00	6.00
❑ 2153	Red Light/Bright Lights, Big City	1968	—	3.00	6.00
❑ 2168	Creepin' Around/The Son of Hickory Holler's Tramp	1969	—	3.00	6.00
❑ 2185	No More/Closin' Time	1971	—	2.50	5.00
❑ 2208	Daylite/Four A.M.	1972	—	2.50	5.00
❑ 2234	Smokey Bourbon Street/Mighty Fine	1973	—	2.50	5.00
❑ 2277	Soul Serenade/Pickin'	1974	—	2.00	4.00
❑ 2283	Truck Stop/Boilin' Cabbage	1975	—	2.00	4.00
❑ 2291	Almost Persuaded/Back Up and Push	1975	—	2.00	4.00
❑ 2301	Fire on the Bayou/Memphis Soul	1976	—	2.00	4.00
❑ 2311	I Can Help/Jump Back Joe	1976	—	2.00	4.00
❑ 2317	Redneck Rock/Yakety Sax	1976	—	2.00	4.00
❑ 78508	Cashin' In (A Tribute to Luther Perkins)/L.A. Blues	1978	—	2.00	4.00

MEGA

Number	Title (A Side/B Side)	Yr	VG	VG+	NM
❑ 0036	Rings/Cotton Carnival	1971	—	2.50	5.00
❑ 0052	Oh Happy Day/Sugar Cured	1971	—	2.50	5.00
❑ 0070	Harlem Nocturne/Sassy Parts	1972	—	2.50	5.00
❑ 0086	Night Train/Bluff City	1972	—	2.50	5.00
❑ 0113	Listen to the Music/Memphis Shuffle	1973	—	2.50	5.00
❑ 0117	Satin Sheets/Memphis Shuffle	1973	—	2.50	5.00
❑ 201	Smokie Part 2/Tequila	1973	—	2.50	5.00
❑ 207	Oh Happy Day/Listen to the Music	1974	—	2.00	4.00

7-Inch Extended Plays

HI

Number	Title (A Side/B Side)	Yr	VG	VG+	NM
❑ HSP 2 [PS]	(title unknown)	1962	3.75	7.50	15.00
❑ HSP 2 [S]	My Babe/40 Miles of Bad Road/Ain't That Lovin' You Baby//What'd I Say/The Walk/Witchcraft	1962	3.75	7.50	15.00
—33 1/3 rpm jukebox single, small hole					
❑ SBG 26 [PS]	Bill Black's Combo Goes Big Band	196?	2.50	5.00	10.00
❑ SBG 26 [S]	T.D.'s Boogie Woogie/Tuxedo Junction/Canadian Sunset//Leap Frog/In the Mood/So Rare	196?	2.50	5.00	10.00
—33 1/3 rpm jukebox single, small hole					
❑ HE 22002	Honky Tonk/Cherry Pink//Singing the Blues/You Win Again	1961	10.00	20.00	40.00
❑ HE 22002 [PS]	Solid and Raunchy	1961	10.00	20.00	40.00

Albums

COLUMBIA

Number	Title (A Side/B Side)	Yr	VG	VG+	NM
❑ CS 1055	Basic Black	1970	3.00	6.00	12.00
❑ CS 9848	Black with Sugar	1969	3.00	6.00	12.00
❑ CS 9957	Raindrops Keep Fallin' on My Head	1970	3.00	6.00	12.00

HI

Number	Title (A Side/B Side)	Yr	VG	VG+	NM
❑ 6005	Award Winners	1978	2.50	5.00	10.00
❑ 8004	Memphis Tennessee	1977	2.50	5.00	10.00
❑ HL-12001 [M]	Smokie	1960	15.00	30.00	60.00
—Black label with red and silver logo					
❑ HL-12001 [M]	Smokie	1960	10.00	20.00	40.00
—Orange and white label					
❑ HL-12002 [M]	Saxy Jazz	1960	10.00	20.00	40.00
❑ HL-12003 [M]	Solid and Raunchy	1960	10.00	20.00	40.00
❑ HL-12004 [M]	That Wonderful Feeling	1961	5.00	10.00	20.00
❑ HL-12005 [M]	Movin'	1961	5.00	10.00	20.00
❑ HL-12006 [M]	Bill Black's Record Hop	1961	6.25	12.50	25.00
❑ HL-12006 [M]	Let's Twist Her	1961	3.75	7.50	15.00
—Retitled version of above					
❑ HL-12009 [M]	The Untouchable Sound of Bill Black	1962	3.75	7.50	15.00
❑ HL-12012 [M]	Bill Black's Greatest Hits	1963	3.75	7.50	15.00
❑ HL-12013 [M]	Bill Black's Combo Goes West	1963	3.75	7.50	15.00
❑ HL-12015 [M]	Bill Black Plays the Blues	1964	3.75	7.50	15.00
❑ HL-12017 [M]	Bill Black Plays Tunes by Chuck Berry	1964	3.75	7.50	15.00
❑ HL-12020 [M]	Bill Black's Combo Goes Big Band	1964	3.75	7.50	15.00
❑ HL-12023 [M]	More Solid and Raunchy	1965	3.75	7.50	15.00
❑ HL-12027 [M]	Mr. Beat	1965	3.75	7.50	15.00
❑ HL-12032 [M]	All Timers	1966	3.00	6.00	12.00
❑ HL-12033 [M]	Black Lace	1966	3.00	6.00	12.00
❑ HL-12036 [M]	King of the Road	1966	3.00	6.00	12.00
❑ HL-12041 [M]	The Beat Goes On	1967	3.75	7.50	15.00
❑ HL-12044 [M]	Turn Your Lovelight On	1967	3.75	7.50	15.00
❑ HL-12047 [M]	Soulin' the Blues	1968	3.75	7.50	15.00
❑ SHL-32001 [R]	Smokie	1964	5.00	10.00	20.00
❑ SHL-32002 [R]	Saxy Jazz	1964	5.00	10.00	20.00
❑ SHL-32003 [R]	Solid and Raunchy	1964	5.00	10.00	20.00
❑ SHL-32004 [S]	That Wonderful Feeling	1961	6.25	12.50	25.00
❑ SHL-32005 [S]	Movin'	1961	6.25	12.50	25.00
❑ SHL-32006 [S]	Bill Black's Record Hop	1961	7.50	15.00	30.00
❑ SHL-32006 [S]	Let's Twist Her	1961	5.00	10.00	20.00
—Retitled version of above					
❑ SHL-32009 [S]	The Untouchable Sound of Bill Black	1962	5.00	10.00	20.00
❑ SHL-32012 [S]	Bill Black's Greatest Hits	1963	5.00	10.00	20.00
❑ SHL-32013 [S]	Bill Black's Combo Goes West	1963	5.00	10.00	20.00
❑ SHL-32015 [S]	Bill Black Plays the Blues	1964	5.00	10.00	20.00
❑ SHL-32017 [S]	Bill Black Plays Tunes by Chuck Berry	1964	5.00	10.00	20.00
❑ SHL-32020 [S]	Bill Black's Combo Goes Big Band	1964	5.00	10.00	20.00
❑ SHL-32023 [S]	More Solid and Raunchy	1965	5.00	10.00	20.00
❑ SHL-32027 [S]	Mr. Beat	1965	5.00	10.00	20.00
❑ SHL-32032 [S]	All Timers	1966	3.75	7.50	15.00
❑ SHL-32033 [S]	Black Lace	1966	3.75	7.50	15.00
❑ SHL-32036 [S]	King of the Road	1966	3.75	7.50	15.00
❑ SHL-32041 [S]	The Beat Goes On	1967	3.75	7.50	15.00
❑ SHL-32044 [S]	Turn Your Lovelight On	1967	3.75	7.50	15.00
❑ SHL-32047 [S]	Soulin' the Blues	1968	3.75	7.50	15.00
❑ SHL-32052	Solid and Raunchy The 3rd	1969	3.75	7.50	15.00
❑ SHL-32061	More Magic	1971	3.00	6.00	12.00
❑ XSHL-32078	Bill Black's Greatest Hits, Vol. 2	1973	3.00	6.00	12.00
❑ XSHL-32088	Solid and Country	1974	3.00	6.00	12.00
❑ SHL-32093	The World's Greatest Honky Tonk Band	1975	3.00	6.00	12.00
❑ SHL-32104	It's Honky Tonk Time	1976	3.00	6.00	12.00

MEGA

Number	Title (A Side/B Side)	Yr	VG	VG+	NM
❑ MLPS-600	Bill Black Is Back	1973	3.00	6.00	12.00
❑ 31-1008	The Memphis Scene	1971	3.00	6.00	12.00
❑ 31-1014	Juke Box Favorites	1972	3.00	6.00	12.00
❑ 51-5008	Rock 'n' Roll Forever	1973	3.00	6.00	12.00

BLACK, CLINT

45s

RCA

Number	Title (A Side/B Side)	Yr	VG	VG+	NM
❑ 2520-7-R	Walkin' Away/Straight from the Factory	1990	—	—	3.00
❑ 2596-7-R	Nothing's News/Live and Learn	1990	—	—	3.00
❑ 2678-7-R	Put Yourself in My Shoes/Live and Learn	1990	—	—	3.00
❑ 2749-7-R	Loving Blind/Muddy Water	1990	—	—	3.00
❑ 2819-7-R	One More Payment/You're Gonna Leave Me Again	1991	—	—	3.00
❑ 3709-7-R	'Til Santa's Gone (I Just Can't Wait) (same on both sides)	1990	—	2.00	4.00

Number	Title (A Side/B Side)	Yr	VG	VG+	NM
❑ 8781-7-R	A Better Man/Winding Down	1989	2.50	5.00	10.00

—Mysteriously, this seems to be quite scarce as a stock 45. Promos (with "A Better Man" on both sides) go for less than half this amount.

Number	Title (A Side/B Side)	Yr	VG	VG+	NM
❑ 8945-7-R	Killin' Time/A Better Man	1989	—	—	3.00
❑ 9078-7-R	Nobody's Home/Winding Down	1989	—	—	3.00
❑ 9126-7-R	Walkin' Away/Straight from the Factory	1989	—	—	3.00
❑ 62016	Where Are You Now?/Muddy Water	1991	—	—	3.00
❑ 62194	We Tell Ourselves/There Never Was a Train	1992	—	—	3.00
❑ 62337	Burn One Down/Wake Up Yesterday	1992	—	—	3.00
❑ 62429	When My Ship Comes In/Buying Time	1993	—	—	3.00
❑ 62609	No Time to Kill/Happiness Alone	1993	—	—	3.00
❑ 62700	State of Mind/Tuckered Out	1993	—	—	3.00
❑ 62762	A Good Run of Bad Luck/Half the Man	1994	—	—	3.00
❑ 62878	Half the Man/Back to Back	1994	—	—	3.00
❑ 62933	Untanglin' My Mind/I Can Get By	1994	—	—	3.00
❑ 64267	Wherever You Go/You Walked By	1994	—	—	3.00
❑ 64281	Summer's Comin'/Hey Hot Rod	1995	—	2.00	4.00
❑ 64381	One Emotion/You Made Me Feel	1995	—	—	3.00
❑ 64442	Life Gets Away/The Kid	1995	—	—	3.00
❑ 64603	Like the Rain/Desperado	1996	—	2.00	4.00
❑ 64724	Half Way Up/Cadillac Jack Favor	1996	—	—	3.00
❑ 64961	Something That We Do/Bitter Side of Sweet	1997	—	—	3.00
❑ 65350	Nothin' but the Taillights (edit)/Cadillac Jack Favor	1998	—	—	3.00

—With a-side typo of three L's in "Taillights"

Number	Title (A Side/B Side)	Yr	VG	VG+	NM
❑ 65454	The Shoes You're Wearing/Nothin' But the Taillights (Edit)	1998	—	—	3.00
❑ 65585	Loosen Up My Strings/The Shoes You're Wearing	1998	—	—	3.00
❑ 65897	When I Said I Do/You Don't Need Me Now	1999	—	—	3.00

—A-side with Lisa Hartman Black

Number	Title (A Side/B Side)	Yr	VG	VG+	NM
❑ 65966	Been There (Duet with Steve Wariner)/When I Said I Do (with Lisa Hartman Black)	2000	—	—	3.00
❑ 69005	Love She Can't Live Without/Galaxy Song	2000	—	—	3.00

Albums

RCA

Number	Title (A Side/B Side)	Yr	VG	VG+	NM
❑ 9668-1-R	Killin' Time	1989	3.75	7.50	15.00
❑ R 124690	Put Yourself in My Place	1990	5.00	10.00	20.00

—Released on vinyl only through BMG Direct Marketing

BLACK, CLINT, AND MARTINA MCBRIDE

Also see each artist's individual listings.

45s

RCA

Number	Title (A Side/B Side)	Yr	VG	VG+	NM
❑ 64850	Still Holding On (4:28)/Still Holding On (3:56)	1997	—	—	3.00

BLACK, CLINT, AND WYNONNA

Also see CLINT BLACK; WYNONNA JUDD.

45s

RCA

Number	Title (A Side/B Side)	Yr	VG	VG+	NM
❑ 62503	A Bad Goodbye/The Hard Way	1993	—	2.00	4.00

—B-side: Clint Black solo

BLACK, JEANNE

45s

CAPITOL

Number	Title (A Side/B Side)	Yr	VG	VG+	NM
❑ 4368	He'll Have to Stay/Under Your Spell Again	1960	3.00	6.00	12.00
❑ 4396	Lisa/Journey of Love	1960	2.50	5.00	10.00
❑ 4456	Sleep Walkin'/You'll Find Out	1960	2.50	5.00	10.00
❑ 4492	Oh How I Miss You Tonight/Just a Little Bit Lonely	1960	2.50	5.00	10.00
❑ 4535	Don't Speak to Me/When You're Alone	1961	2.50	5.00	10.00
❑ 4566	Commandments of Love/Jimmy Love	1961	2.50	5.00	10.00
❑ 4654	Heartbreak U.S.A./His Own Little Island	1961	2.50	5.00	10.00
❑ 4685	Letter to Anya/Guessin' Again	1962	2.50	5.00	10.00

Albums

CAPITOL

Number	Title (A Side/B Side)	Yr	VG	VG+	NM
❑ ST 1513 [S]	A Little Bit Lonely	1961	6.25	12.50	25.00
❑ T 1513 [M]	A Little Bit Lonely	1961	5.00	10.00	20.00

BLACK BROTHERS, THE

45s

LITTLE DARLIN'

Number	Title (A Side/B Side)	Yr	VG	VG+	NM
❑ 0061	Some of My Best Friends Are Women/Little Girl Blue	1969	2.50	5.00	10.00

BLACK TIE

Members: Jimmy Griffin of THE REMINGTONS (also of Bread, which is outside the realm of this book); Randy Meisner of EAGLES and POCO; and BILLY SWAN.

45s

BENCH

Number	Title (A Side/B Side)	Yr	VG	VG+	NM
❑ 27	Learning the Game/(B-side unknown)	1990	2.00	4.00	8.00

BLACKHAWK

45s

ARISTA

Number	Title (A Side/B Side)	Yr	VG	VG+	NM
❑ 12568	Goodbye Says It All/Let 'Em Whirl	1993	—	2.00	4.00
❑ 12668	Every Once in a While/One More Heartache	1994	—	2.00	4.00
❑ 12718	I Sure Can Smell the Rain/Stone by Stone	1994	—	2.00	4.00
❑ 12769	Down in Flames/Between Ragged and Wrong	1994	—	2.00	4.00
❑ 12813	That's Just About Right/Love Like This	1995	—	—	3.00
❑ 12857	I'm Not Strong Enough to Say No/A Kiss Is Worth a Thousand Words	1995	—	2.00	4.00
❑ 12897	Like There Ain't No Yesterday/A Kiss Is Worth a Thousand Words	1995	—	—	3.00
❑ 12975	Almost a Memory Now/Cast Iron Heart	1996	—	—	3.00

ARISTA NASHVILLE

Number	Title (A Side/B Side)	Yr	VG	VG+	NM
❑ 13017	Big Guitar/Any Man with a Heartbeat	1996	—	—	3.00
❑ 13049	King of the World/Bad Love Gone Good	1996	—	—	3.00
❑ 13060	We Three Kings (Star of Wonder)/Rudolph the Red-Nosed Reindeer	1996	—	2.00	4.00

—B-side by Alan Jackson

Number	Title (A Side/B Side)	Yr	VG	VG+	NM
❑ 13082	Hole in My Heart/She Dances with Her Shadow	1997	—	—	3.00
❑ 13109	Postmarked Birmingham/It Ain't About Love Anymore	1997	—	—	3.00
❑ 13134	There You Have It/When I Find It, I'll Know It	1998	—	—	3.00
❑ 13158	Your Own Little Corner of My Heart/Nobody Knows What to Say	1999	—	—	3.00

BLACKWELL, DEWAYNE

45s

RANWOOD

Number	Title (A Side/B Side)	Yr	VG	VG+	NM
❑ 967	Mama Come 'n Get Your Baby Boy/Lady	1974	—	2.50	5.00
❑ 979	I Got Your Number/Lady	1974	—	2.50	5.00

WARNER BROS.

Number	Title (A Side/B Side)	Yr	VG	VG+	NM
❑ 29573	You're Just a Little Too Young to Be a Good Ole Girl/Corpus Christi Blue	1983	—	2.00	4.00

—As "Dewayne and Jill Blackwell"

BLACKWELL, KARON

45s

BLACKLAND

Number	Title (A Side/B Side)	Yr	VG	VG+	NM
❑ 254	Blue Skies and Roses/I Wanna Love You	1976	—	3.50	7.00

BLACKWOOD, R.W.

45s

CAPITOL

Number	Title (A Side/B Side)	Yr	VG	VG+	NM
❑ 4302	Sunday Afternoon Boatride in the Park on the Lake/Lookin' at the World Through the Eyes of Love	1976	—	3.00	6.00
❑ 4346	Memory Go Round/Freedom Lives in a Country Song	1976	—	3.00	6.00
❑ 4408	We Mighta' Come Over in Different Ships/I Can Feel Love	1977	—	3.00	6.00

SCORPION

Number	Title (A Side/B Side)	Yr	VG	VG+	NM
❑ 0561	Dolly/Counterfeit Cowboy	1978	—	3.00	6.00

Albums

CAPITOL

Number	Title (A Side/B Side)	Yr	VG	VG+	NM
❑ ST-11563	We Can Feel Love	1976	2.50	5.00	10.00

BLAIR, KENNY

45s

AWESOME

Number	Title (A Side/B Side)	Yr	VG	VG+	NM
❑ 118	She's Too Good to Be Treated Like This/(B-side unknown)	1988	—	3.00	6.00
❑ 119	Lost in Austin/(B-side unknown)	1988	—	3.00	6.00

BLAKE & BRIAN

45s

CURB

Number	Title (A Side/B Side)	Yr	VG	VG+	NM
❑ D7-73024	Another Perfect Day/Straight to You	1997	—	—	3.00

BLAKER, CLAY, AND THE TEXAS HONKY-TONK BAND

45s

RAIN FOREST

Number	Title (A Side/B Side)	Yr	VG	VG+	NM
❑ 120187	A Honky Tonk Heart (And a Hillbilly Soul)/The Only Thing I Have Left	1987	—	3.50	7.00

TEXAS MUSIK

Number	Title (A Side/B Side)	Yr	VG	VG+	NM
❑ 6153	South of the Border/Lonesome Rodeo Cowboy	1987	—	3.50	7.00

BLANCH, ARTHUR

45s

MC

Number	Title (A Side/B Side)	Yr	VG	VG+	NM
❑ 5015	The Little Man's Got the Biggest Smile in Town/Another Pretty Country Song	1978	—	2.50	5.00

RIDGETOP

Number	Title (A Side/B Side)	Yr	VG	VG+	NM
❑ 00479	Maybe I'll Cry Over You/(B-side unknown)	1979	—	3.00	6.00

BLANCHARD, JACK

Also see JACK BLANCHARD AND MISTY MORGAN.

45s

EPIC

Number	Title (A Side/B Side)	Yr	VG	VG+	NM
❑ 50245	Hands/Molasses in the Moonlight	1976	—	2.00	4.00

BLANCHARD, JACK, AND MISTY MORGAN

45s

EPIC

Number	Title (A Side/B Side)	Yr	VG	VG+	NM
❑ 11030	Cockroach Stomp/Carolina Sundown Red	1973	—	2.00	4.00
❑ 11058	Just One More Song/Why Did I Sleep So Long	1973	—	2.00	4.00
❑ 11097	Something on Your Mind/Here Today and Gone Tomorrow	1974	—	2.00	4.00
❑ 50023	Down to the End of the Wine/You Can't Say I Didn't Try	1974	—	2.00	4.00
❑ 50082	Chorus/House	1975	—	2.00	4.00
❑ 50122	Because We Love/It's Me	1975	—	2.00	4.00
❑ 50181	I'm High on You/Let's Pretend	1975	—	2.00	4.00
❑ 50205	47 Miles (to the Georgia Line)/Motel Time	1976	—	2.00	4.00

MEGA

Number	Title (A Side/B Side)	Yr	VG	VG+	NM
❑ 0031	There Must Be More to Life/Fire Hydrant #79	1971	—	2.00	4.00

Number	Title (A Side/B Side)	Yr	VG	VG+	NM
❑ 0046	Somewhere in Virginia in the Rain/If Eggs Had Legs	1971	—	2.00	4.00
❑ 0063	The Legendary Chicken Fairy/The Night We Heard the Voice	1972	—	2.00	4.00
❑ 0082	Miami Sidewalks/Washin' Harry Down the Sink	1972	—	2.00	4.00
❑ 0089	Second Tuesday in December/Don't It Make You Want to Go Home	1972	—	2.00	4.00
❑ 0101	A Handful of Dimes/It Seems Like There Ain't No Going Home	1973	—	2.00	4.00
❑ 0114	Shadows of the Leaves/Sweet Memories	1973	—	2.00	4.00
UNITED ARTISTS					
❑ XW1004	Tennessee Birdwalk/Living Together	1977	—	2.00	4.00
❑ XW1067	Heartaches/You Come So Easy to Me	1977	—	2.00	4.00
WAYSIDE					
❑ 000	Big Black Bird (Spirit of Our Love)/Autumn Song (On a Yellow Day)	1969	—	2.50	5.00
—Reissue of 1028					
❑ 007	Changin' Times/Poor Jody	1969	—	2.50	5.00
❑ 010	Tennessee Bird Walk/The Clock of St. James	1970	—	2.50	5.00
❑ 013	Humphrey the Camel/A Place in My Mind	1970	—	2.50	5.00
❑ 015	You've Got Your Troubles (I've Got Mine)/How I Lost 31 Pounds in 17 Days	1970	—	2.50	5.00
❑ 1024	Bethlehem Steel/No Sign of Love	1969	—	3.00	6.00
❑ 1028	Big Black Bird (Spirit of Our Love)/Autumn Song (On a Yellow Day)	1969	—	3.00	6.00
Albums					
MEGA					
❑ 31-1009	Two Sides	1972	3.00	6.00	12.00
WAYSIDE					
❑ 33-1	Birds of a Feather	1970	3.75	7.50	15.00

BLANTON, LOY

45s

Number	Title (A Side/B Side)	Yr	VG	VG+	NM
SOUNDWAVES					
❑ 4744	Christmas at the Jersey Lily Lounge/Ghost Story	1984	—	3.00	6.00
❑ 4750	California Sleeping/I Wrote the Book	1985	—	2.50	5.00
❑ 4760	Sailing Home to Me/Run for Your Life Love Affair	1985	—	2.50	5.00

BLIXSETH, TIM, AND KATHY WALKER

45s

Number	Title (A Side/B Side)	Yr	VG	VG+	NM
COMPLEAT					
❑ 141	It Can't Be Done/Sometimes I Wish You Didn't Love Me	1985	—	2.50	5.00

BLOCK, DOUG

45s

Number	Title (A Side/B Side)	Yr	VG	VG+	NM
DOOR KNOB					
❑ 132	You're Still the One (Who Makes My Life Complete)/You Can Count on Me	1980	—	3.00	6.00
—As "Douglas"					
❑ 143	Have Another Drink/It's Only a Matter of Time	1980	—	3.00	6.00
—As "Douglas"					
REVOLVER					
❑ 005	Have Another Drink/It's Only a Matter of Time	1984	—	3.00	6.00

BLUE, BOBBY

45s

Number	Title (A Side/B Side)	Yr	VG	VG+	NM
NITE					
❑ 108	Once Upon a Time/(B-side unknown)	1986	—	3.00	6.00
❑ 108 [PS]	Once Upon a Time/(B-side unknown)	1986	2.00	4.00	8.00

BLUE BOYS, THE

Backing group for JIM REEVES. Also see BUD LOGAN.

45s

Number	Title (A Side/B Side)	Yr	VG	VG+	NM
RCA VICTOR					
❑ 47-8609	I Hear Little Rock Calling/I'll Follow Each Rainbow	1965	3.00	6.00	12.00
❑ 47-8687	Evening Bells/Over and Over Again	1965	3.00	6.00	12.00
❑ 47-8777	Love Struck Me Down/Pin a Tail on a Donkey and Call Me Jack	1965	3.00	6.00	12.00
❑ 47-8878	Soakin' Up Suds/Nobody Going Nowhere	1966	2.50	5.00	10.00
❑ 47-9039	What Makes That/Gonna Change Everything	1966	2.50	5.00	10.00
❑ 47-9131	Rum Dum/Brand New World	1967	2.50	5.00	10.00
❑ 47-9201	My Cup Runneth Over/One for the Lady	1967	2.50	5.00	10.00
❑ 47-9322	Without Love (There Is Nothing)/She's Wild as the Wind	1967	2.50	5.00	10.00
❑ 47-9418	I'm Not Ready Yet/My Heart's with You	1968	2.50	5.00	10.00
Albums					
RCA VICTOR					
❑ LPM-3331 [M]	We Remember Jim	1965	6.25	12.50	25.00
❑ LSP-3331 [S]	We Remember Jim	1965	7.50	15.00	30.00
❑ LPM-3529 [M]	Sounds of Jim Reeves	1966	5.00	10.00	20.00
❑ LSP-3529 [S]	Sounds of Jim Reeves	1966	6.25	12.50	25.00
❑ LPM-3696 [M]	The Blue Boys in Person	1967	5.00	10.00	20.00
❑ LSP-3696 [S]	The Blue Boys in Person	1967	6.25	12.50	25.00
❑ LPM-3794 [M]	Hit After Hit	1967	6.25	12.50	25.00
❑ LSP-3794 [S]	Hit After Hit	1967	5.00	10.00	20.00

BLUE RIDGE RANGERS, THE

See JOHN FOGERTY.

BLUE SKY BOYS, THE

45s

Number	Title (A Side/B Side)	Yr	VG	VG+	NM
RCA VICTOR					
❑ 48-0036	Dust on the Bible/Speak to Me Little Darling	1949	12.50	25.00	50.00
—Originals on green vinyl					
❑ 48-0072	Alabama/You've Branded Your Name	1949	12.50	25.00	50.00
—Originals on green vinyl					
❑ 48-0111	Little Mother of the Hills/Shake Hands with Your Mother	1949	12.50	25.00	50.00
—Originals on green vinyl					
❑ 48-0163	One Cold Winter's Eve/When Heaven Comes Down	1949	12.50	25.00	50.00
—Originals on green vinyl					
❑ 48-0317	The Unfinished Rug/Tears on Her Bridal Bouquet	1950	10.00	20.00	40.00
—Originals on green vinyl					
❑ 48-0318	The New Golden Rule/Lord Be With Us	1950	10.00	20.00	40.00
—Originals on green vinyl					
❑ 48-0370	Drop Your Net/Sunny Side of Life	1950	10.00	20.00	40.00
—Originals on green vinyl					
STARDAY					
❑ 652	Kentucky/Don't Trade	1963	3.00	6.00	12.00
❑ 667	Satisfied Mind/Why Not Confess	1964	3.00	6.00	12.00
Selected 78s					
BLUEBIRD					
❑ B-6457	Sunny Side of Life/Where the Soul Never Dies	193?	6.25	12.50	25.00
❑ B-6480	Down the Banks of the Ohio/Midnight on the Stormy Sea	193?	6.25	12.50	25.00
❑ B-6538	There'll Come a Time/I'm Troubled, I'm Troubled	193?	6.25	12.50	25.00
❑ B-6567	Take Up Thy Cross/Row Us Over the Tide	193?	6.25	12.50	25.00
❑ B-6621	The Dying Boy's Prayer/I'm Just Here to Get My Baby Out of Jail	193?	6.25	12.50	25.00
❑ B-6669	No One to Welcome Me Home/Only Let Me Walk with Thee	193?	6.25	12.50	25.00
❑ B-6714	titles unknown	193?	6.25	12.50	25.00
❑ B-6764	Didn't They Crucify My Lord?/When the Ransomed Get Home	193?	6.25	12.50	25.00
❑ B-6808	titles unknown	193?	6.25	12.50	25.00
❑ B-6854	titles unknown	193?	6.25	12.50	25.00
❑ B-6901	An Old Account Was Settled/Not Turning Back	193?	6.25	12.50	25.00
—B-side by the Dixon Brothers					
❑ B-7113	Within the Circle/No Disappointment in Heaven	193?	5.00	10.00	20.00
❑ B-7411	The Prisoner's Dream/The Answer to "The Prisoner's Dream"	193?	5.00	10.00	20.00
❑ B-7661	Who Wouldn't Be Lonely?/Katie Dear	193?	5.00	10.00	20.00
❑ B-7755	Beautiful, Beautiful Brown Eyes/Story of the Knoxville Girl	193?	5.00	10.00	20.00
❑ B-7803	Heaven Holds All to Me/I Need the Prayers	193?	5.00	10.00	20.00
❑ B-7878	My Last Letter/Last Night While Standing By My Window	193?	5.00	10.00	20.00
❑ B-8017	Little Bessie/We Buried Her	193?	3.75	7.50	15.00
❑ B-8110	Hang Out the Front Door Key/There Was a Time	193?	3.75	7.50	15.00
❑ B-8143	In My Little Home in Tennessee/Sing a Song for the Blind	193?	3.75	7.50	15.00
❑ B-8294	When the Roses Bloom in Dixieland/Are You from Dixie?	193?	3.75	7.50	15.00
❑ B-8308	Give Me My Roses Now/The House Where We Were Wed	193?	3.75	7.50	15.00
❑ B-8339	There's No Other Love for Me/God Sent My Little Girl	193?	3.75	7.50	15.00
❑ B-8356	Someone's Last Day/She'll Be There	193?	3.75	7.50	15.00
❑ B-8369	The Lightning Express/The Royal Telephone	193?	3.75	7.50	15.00
❑ B-8401	I'm S-A-V-E-D/Whispering Hope	193?	3.75	7.50	15.00
❑ B-8446	Mary of the Wild Moor/She's Somebody's Darling Once More	193?	3.75	7.50	15.00
❑ B-8482	Butcher's Boy/We Parted by the Riverside	193?	3.75	7.50	15.00
❑ B-8522	The Convict and the Rose/Father, Dear Father, Come Home	193?	3.75	7.50	15.00
❑ B-8552	East Bound Train/Only One Step More	193?	3.75	7.50	15.00
❑ B-8597	The Last Mile of the Way/The Evening Light	194?	3.75	7.50	15.00
❑ B-8646	A Picture on the Wall/Pictures from Life's Other Side	194?	3.75	7.50	15.00
❑ B-8693	In the Hills of Roane County/Brown Eyes	1941	3.75	7.50	15.00
❑ B-8829	Don't Say Goodbye If You Love Me/Short Life of Trouble	1941	3.75	7.50	15.00
❑ B-8843	Kneel at the Cross/Turn Your Radio On	1942	3.75	7.50	15.00
❑ 33-0516	Why Not Confess/Since the Angels Took My Mother Away	1945	3.75	7.50	15.00
RCA VICTOR					
❑ WCDJ-58 [DJ]	One Cold Winter's Eve/When Heaven Comes Down	1949	12.50	25.00	50.00
—White label "Special Purpose Series" promo					
❑ 20-2151	I Love Her More, Now Mother's Old/Have You Seen My Daddy Here	1947	3.00	6.00	12.00
❑ 20-2296	I'm Going to Write to Heaven/Kentucky	1947	3.00	6.00	12.00
Albums					
CAPITOL					
❑ ST 2483 [S]	Presenting the Blue Sky Boys	1966	6.25	12.50	25.00
❑ T 2483 [M]	Presenting the Blue Sky Boys	1966	5.00	10.00	20.00
PINE MOUNTAIN					
❑ PMR 257	Together Again	198?	3.00	6.00	12.00
RCA CAMDEN					
❑ CAL-797 [M]	The Blue Sky Boys	1963	5.00	10.00	20.00
❑ CAS-797(e) [R]	The Blue Sky Boys	1963	3.75	7.50	15.00
ROUNDER					
❑ 0236	1964	198?	3.75	7.50	15.00

Number	Title (A Side/B Side)	Yr	VG	VG+	NM
STARDAY					
❑ SLP-205 [M]	Rare Treasury of Old Song Gems	1962	10.00	20.00	40.00
❑ SLP-257 [M]	Together Again	1963	10.00	20.00	40.00
❑ SLP-269 [M]	The Blue Sky Boys	1964	10.00	20.00	40.00

BLUESTONE
Also see JERRY McBEE; RAY PENNINGTON

45s

Number	Title (A Side/B Side)	Yr	VG	VG+	NM
DIMENSION					
❑ 1002	Haven't I Loved You Somewhere Before/A Little Thing Like a Golden Ring	1980	—	2.50	5.00

BOARDO, LIZ
45s

Number	Title (A Side/B Side)	Yr	VG	VG+	NM
MASTER					
❑ 02	There's Still Enough of Us/Hangin' On by a Heartache	1987	—	2.50	5.00
❑ 03	I Need to Be Loved Again/(B-side unknown)	1987	—	2.50	5.00

BOB AND LUCILLE
Also recorded as THE CANADIAN SWEETHEARTS.

45s

Number	Title (A Side/B Side)	Yr	VG	VG+	NM
DITTO					
❑ 121	What's the Password/Demon Lover	1962	20.00	40.00	80.00
❑ 126	Eeny-Meeny-Miney-Moe/The Big Kiss	1962	20.00	40.00	80.00
DOT					
❑ 17327	Dream Baby/Southbound Plane	1969	2.00	4.00	8.00
—As "Bob Regan and Lucille Starr"					
KING					
❑ 5631	Eeny-Meeny-Miney-Moe/The Big Kiss	1962	7.50	15.00	30.00

BOCEPHUS
See HANK WILLIAMS, JR.

BOGGS, NOEL
45s

Number	Title (A Side/B Side)	Yr	VG	VG+	NM
COLUMBIA					
❑ 4-21220	Stealin' Home/Day Sleeper	1954	5.00	10.00	20.00
❑ 4-21274	How Long/Make Believe Heart	1954	5.00	10.00	20.00

BOGGUSS, SUZY
45s

Number	Title (A Side/B Side)	Yr	VG	VG+	NM
CAPITOL					
❑ B-5669	I Don't Want to Set the World on Fire/Hopeless Romantic	1987	—	2.00	4.00
❑ B-44045	Love Will Never Slip Away/True North	1987	—	2.00	4.00
❑ B-44167	I Want to Be a Cowboy's Sweetheart/I Still Love You	1988	—	2.00	4.00
❑ B-44270	Somewhere Between/I'm at Home on the Range	1989	—	2.00	4.00
❑ B-44399	Cross My Broken Heart/Hopeless Romantic	1989	—	2.00	4.00
❑ B-44503	Mr. Santa/I'm at Home on the Range	1989	—	2.50	5.00
❑ 7PRO-79788	My Sweet Love Ain't Around (same on both sides)	1989	—	3.00	6.00
—Vinyl is promo only					
CAPITOL NASHVILLE					
❑ S7-19252	No Way Out/Letting Go	1996	—	2.00	4.00
❑ S7-19349	Two-Step Around the Christmas Tree/I Heard the Bells on Christmas Day	1996	—	2.00	4.00
—Slightly altered A-side title from original on Liberty					
❑ S7-19508	She Said, He Heard/Feeling 'Bout You	1997	—	2.00	4.00
❑ NR-44772	Someday Soon/Fear of Flying	1991	—	2.50	5.00
❑ 58720	Nobody Love, Nobody Gets Hurt/When I Run	1998	—	2.00	4.00
❑ 58755	From Where I Stand/I Wish Hearts Would Break	1999	—	2.00	4.00
❑ 7PRO-79190	Under the Gun (same on both sides)	1990	—	3.00	6.00
—Vinyl is promo only					
❑ 7PRO-79380	All Things Made New Again (same on both sides)	1990	—	3.00	6.00
—Vinyl is promo only					
LIBERTY					
❑ S7-17495	Just Like the Weather/No Greem Eyes	1993	—	2.50	5.00
❑ S7-17641	Hey Cinderella/You'd Be the One	1993	—	2.50	5.00
❑ S7-17650	I'll Be Home for Christmas/Mr. Santa	1993	—	3.00	6.00
—Green vinyl					
❑ S7-17907	You Wouldn't Say That to a Stranger/Something Up My Sleeve	1994	—	2.00	4.00
—B-side with Billy Dean					
❑ S7-18091	Souvenirs/You'd Be the One	1994	—	2.00	4.00
❑ S7-56786	Drive South/In the Day	1992	—	3.00	6.00
❑ S7-56805	Two-Step 'Round the Christmas Tree/I Heard the Bells on Christmas Day	1992	—	3.00	6.00
❑ S7-56972	Heartache/Lovin' a Hurricane	1993	—	2.50	5.00
❑ S7-57753	Outbound Plane/Yellow River Road	1992	—	2.50	5.00
❑ S7-57764	Aces/Hopelessly Yours	1992	2.00	4.00	8.00
—B-side: Lee Greenwood with Suzy Bogguss					
❑ S7-57801	Letting Go/Music on the Wind	1992	—	3.50	7.00

Albums

Number	Title (A Side/B Side)	Yr	VG	VG+	NM
CAPITOL					
❑ C1-90237	Somewhere Between	1989	3.75	7.50	15.00
❑ C1-590237	Somewhere Between	1989	3.75	7.50	15.00
—Columbia House edition					

BOLT, AL
45s

Number	Title (A Side/B Side)	Yr	VG	VG+	NM
CIN KAY					
❑ 102	I'm in Love with My Pet Rock/Paint Your World Happy	1976	—	2.50	5.00
❑ 103	Family Man/If Today Were a Fish	1976	—	2.50	5.00
❑ 109	Wait a Minute/Cowboy	1976	—	2.50	5.00

BONAMY, JAMES
45s

Number	Title (A Side/B Side)	Yr	VG	VG+	NM
EPIC					
❑ 34-78090	Dog on a Toolbox/She's Got a Mind of Her Own	1995	—	2.00	4.00
❑ 34-78220	She's Got a Mind of Her Own/Amy Jane	1996	—	—	3.00
❑ 34-78298	I Don't Think I Will/Heartbreak School	1996	—	2.00	4.00
❑ 34-78396	All I Do Is Love Her/Jimmy and Jesus	1996	—	—	3.00

BOND, BOBBY
45s

Number	Title (A Side/B Side)	Yr	VG	VG+	NM
HICKORY					
❑ 1566	Houston Blues/Looking for My Tracks	1970	2.00	4.00	8.00
❑ 1594	Call of the Blues/Nothing New in Oklahoma	1971	2.00	4.00	8.00
❑ 1610	Put Me on the Road to the Country/If You're Goin' Girl	1971	2.00	4.00	8.00
❑ 1630	One More Mile, One More Town/Six White Horses	1972	2.00	4.00	8.00
❑ 1649	You Don't Mess Around with Jim/Looking for My Tracks	1972	2.00	4.00	8.00
❑ 1656	You Can Close Your Eyes/Next Time Around	1972	2.00	4.00	8.00
HICKORY/MGM					
❑ 305	I'll Sing for You/John Martin	1973	—	3.50	7.00
MGM					
❑ 13951	Anyway/Mr. and Mrs. Brown	1968	3.00	6.00	12.00
WARNER BROS.					
❑ 7292	If You're Leaving Me/One More Mile, One More Town	1969	2.50	5.00	10.00
❑ 7341	Jennifer, It's Goodbye/Pack My Suitcase	1969	2.50	5.00	10.00

Albums

Number	Title (A Side/B Side)	Yr	VG	VG+	NM
SOMERSET					
❑ P 24400 [M]	Bobby Bond Sings the Roger Miller Songbook	1966	3.00	6.00	12.00
❑ SF 24400 [S]	Bobby Bond Sings the Roger Miller Songbook	1966	3.75	7.50	15.00
TIME					
❑ S-2122 [S]	On the Country Side	1964	3.75	7.50	15.00
❑ 52122 [M]	On the Country Side	1964	3.00	6.00	12.00

BOND, JOHNNY
45s

Number	Title (A Side/B Side)	Yr	VG	VG+	NM
20TH FOX					
❑ 156	Gold Rush/The Long Tall Shadow	1959	3.00	6.00	12.00
❑ 231	Jealous Lad/A Kid Named Bell	1960	3.00	6.00	12.00
COLUMBIA					
❑ 2-100 (?)	Tennessee Saturday Night/A Heart Full of Love	1949	6.25	12.50	25.00
—Microgroove 7-inch, 33 1/3 rpm single					
❑ 2-100 (?)	Take It or Leave It Baby/Till the End of the World	1949	6.25	12.50	25.00
—Microgroove 7-inch, 33 1/3 rpm single					
❑ 2-200 (?)	Read It and Weep/Somebody Loves You	1950	6.25	12.50	25.00
—Microgroove 7-inch, 33 1/3 rpm single					
❑ 2-210 (?)	I'm Biting My Fingernails/I Wish I Had a Nickel	1949	6.25	12.50	25.00
—Microgroove 7-inch, 33 1/3 rpm single					
❑ 2-300 (?)	Drowning My Sorrows/Women Make a Fool Out of Me	1950	6.25	12.50	25.00
—Microgroove 7-inch, 33 1/3 rpm single					
❑ 2-400 (?)	A Petal from a Faded Rose/Put Me to Bed #2	1950	6.25	12.50	25.00
—Microgroove 7-inch, 33 1/3 rpm single					
❑ 2-532	Love Song in 32 Bars/Tennessee Kentucky & Alabam'	1950	6.25	12.50	25.00
—Microgroove 7-inch, 33 1/3 rpm single					
❑ 2-600 (?)	Cherokee Waltz/Mean Mama Boogie	1950	6.25	12.50	25.00
—Microgroove 7-inch, 33 1/3 rpm single					
❑ 20726	Under the Red, White and Blue/Star Spangled Waltz	1950	5.00	10.00	20.00
❑ 20734	Barrel House Bessie/It Ain't Gonna Happen to Me	1950	5.00	10.00	20.00
❑ 20738	There's a Gold Moon Shining/Cream of Kentucky	1950	5.00	10.00	20.00
❑ 20756	I Wanna Do Something For Santa/Jingle Bell Boogie	1950	5.00	10.00	20.00
❑ 20787	Set 'Em Up Joe/Glad Rags	1951	5.00	10.00	20.00
❑ 20808	Sick, Sober and Sorry/Tennessee Walking Horse	1951	5.00	10.00	20.00
❑ 20844	Ten Trips to the Altar/Keep Your Cotton Pickin' Hands	1951	5.00	10.00	20.00
❑ 20876	Broke, Disgusted and Sad/In Old New Mexico	1952	3.75	7.50	15.00
❑ 20909	I Found You Out/Alabama Boogie Boy	1952	3.75	7.50	15.00
❑ 20948	Louisiana Lucy/The Man Behind the Throttle	1952	3.75	7.50	15.00
❑ 21007	I Went to Your Wedding/Our Love Isn't Legal	1952	3.75	7.50	15.00
❑ 21041	Back Street Affair/Our Love Isn't Legal	1952	3.75	7.50	15.00
❑ 21042	Born to Be Bad/#9 Blues	1952	3.75	7.50	15.00
❑ 21066	Wildcat Boogie/Let Me Go, Devil	1953	3.75	7.50	15.00
❑ 21082	Anybody's Baby/Hills of Kentucky	1953	3.75	7.50	15.00
❑ 21113	Peace Be Still/Ninety & Nine	1953	3.75	7.50	15.00
❑ 21150	Live and Let Live/I Wonder Where You Are Tonight	1953	3.75	7.50	15.00
❑ 21160	Wildcat Boogie/Let Me Go, Devil	1953	3.75	7.50	15.00
❑ 21186	Sweet Mama Tree Top Tall/Put a Little Sweetness in Your Love	1953	3.75	7.50	15.00
❑ 21187	Thanks/I Dreamed I Searched Heaven	1953	3.75	7.50	15.00
❑ 21222	10 Little Bottles/They Got Me	1954	3.75	7.50	15.00
❑ 21243	Firewater/Old Man Blues	1954	3.75	7.50	15.00
❑ 21294	Stealin'/My Darling Lola Lee	1954	3.75	7.50	15.00
❑ 21335	I Lose Again/Everybody Knew the Truth But Me	1954	3.75	7.50	15.00
❑ 21369	Cherokee Waltz/Glad Rags	1955	3.75	7.50	15.00
❑ 21383	Jim, Johnny & Jonas/Louisiana Swing	1955	3.75	7.50	15.00
❑ 21424	Somebody's Pushin'/Carolina Waltz	1955	3.75	7.50	15.00

Number	Title (A Side/B Side)	Yr	VG	VG+	NM
❑ 21448	Remember the Alamo/Livin' It Up	1955	3.75	7.50	15.00
❑ 21494	Loaded for Bear/Six of One, Half a Dozen of the Other	1956	3.75	7.50	15.00
❑ 21521	Little Rock and Roll/I'll Be Here	1956	12.50	25.00	50.00
❑ 21565	Lonesome Train/Laughing Back the Heartaches	1956	3.75	7.50	15.00
❑ 40080	Santa Got Stuck in the Chimney/I Said a Prayer for Santa Claus	1953	3.75	7.50	15.00
—With Jimmy Boyd					
❑ 40842	Honky Tonk Fever/Lay It on the Line	1957	3.75	7.50	15.00
❑ 40973	All I Can Do Is Cry/Sale of Broken Hearts	1957	3.75	7.50	15.00
❑ 41034	That's Just What I'll Do/Broken Doll	1957	3.75	7.50	15.00
DITTO					
❑ 120	The Tijuana Jail/Fools Paradise	1959	3.00	6.00	12.00
MGM					
❑ 10627	Rag Mop/Music! Music! Music!	1950	10.00	20.00	40.00
❑ 10751	Heart of Gold/Hey Ho Virginia Reel	1950	10.00	20.00	40.00
❑ 14596	Rose of Reynosa/Who Stole the Juke Box	1973	—	2.50	5.00
REPUBLIC					
❑ 2005	Hot Rod Lincoln/Five Minute Love Affair	1960	3.00	6.00	12.00
❑ 2008	X-15/The Way a Star Is Born	1960	3.00	6.00	12.00
❑ 2010	Side Car Cycle/Like Nothin' Man	1961	3.00	6.00	12.00
❑ 2022	Sadie Was a Lady/Buck Private's Lament	1961	3.00	6.00	12.00
SMASH					
❑ 1761	I'll Step Aside/Mister Sun	1962	2.50	5.00	10.00
STARDAY					
❑ 618	How to Succeed with Girls (Without Half-Way Trying)/Don't Mention Her Name	1963	2.00	4.00	8.00
❑ 635	True Love (Is Hard to Find)/Cimarron	1963	2.00	4.00	8.00
❑ 649	Three Sheets in the Wind/Let the Tears Begin	1963	2.00	4.00	8.00
❑ 665	Have You Seen My Baby/What Have You Done for Me Lately	1964	2.00	4.00	8.00
❑ 678	Hot Rod Surfin' Hootlebeatnanny/Don't Mama Count Anymore	1964	3.75	7.50	15.00
❑ 690	My Wicked, Wicked Ways/Bachelor Bill	1964	2.00	4.00	8.00
❑ 704	10 Little Bottles/Let It Be Me	1964	2.00	4.00	8.00
❑ 721	Sick, Sober & Sorry/The Man Who Comes Around	1965	2.00	4.00	8.00
❑ 731	The Great Figure Eight Race/Sadie Was a Lady	1965	2.00	4.00	8.00
❑ 749	They Got Me/Silent Walls	1966	2.00	4.00	8.00
❑ 758	Fireball/Over the Hill	1966	2.00	4.00	8.00
❑ 776	Hell's Angels/A Way of Life	1966	2.00	4.00	8.00
❑ 803	Your Old Love Letters/Si Si	1967	2.00	4.00	8.00
❑ 813	I Ain't Gonna Go/Don't Bite the Hand That's Feeding You	1967	2.00	4.00	8.00
❑ 826	Bottom of the Bottle/I'm Gonna Raise Cain (While I'm Able)	1968	2.00	4.00	8.00
❑ 847	Down to Your Last Fool/Invitation to the Blues	1968	2.00	4.00	8.00
❑ 893	It Only Hurts When I Cry/The Girl Who Carried the Torch for Me	1970	—	3.00	6.00
❑ 916	Here Come the Elephants/Take Me Back to Tulsa	1970	—	3.00	6.00
❑ 931	The Bottle's Empty/The Late and Great Myself	1971	—	3.00	6.00
❑ 951	Put the Country Back in Country Music/Fly Me, Try Me	1972	—	3.00	6.00
❑ 7021	Hot Rod Lincoln/Barrel House Betsy	197?	—	2.50	5.00
❑ 7027	Divorce Me C.O.D./Three Sheets in the Wind	197?	—	2.50	5.00
❑ 7033	Tennessee, Kentucky and Alabam'/Glad Rags	197?	—	2.50	5.00
Selected 78s					
COLUMBIA					
❑ 20006	Gotta Make Up for Lost Time/Baby You Gotta Quit That Noise	1948	3.75	7.50	15.00
—Reissue of 36876					
❑ 20082	The First Rose/I'll Step Aside	1948	3.75	7.50	15.00
—Reissue of 37159					
❑ 20096	Divorce Me C.O.D./Rainbow at Midnight	1948	3.75	7.50	15.00
—Reissue of 37217					
❑ 20102	So Round, So Firm, So Fully Packed/You Brought Sorrow to My Heart	1948	3.75	7.50	15.00
—Reissue of 37255					
❑ 20127	Love Gone Cold/You Don't Care	1948	3.75	7.50	15.00
—Reissue of 37400					
❑ 20154	I've Had Blues Before/Those Gone and Left Me Blues	1948	3.75	7.50	15.00
—Reissue of 374??					
❑ 20162	The Road Is Way Too Long/Don't You Weep Anymore Darlin'	1948	3.75	7.50	15.00
—Reissue of 374??					
❑ 20167	Down in the Dumps/Baby You're Through Foolin' Me	1948	3.75	7.50	15.00
—Reissue of 374??					
❑ 20183	Don't Look Now/Rock My Cradle Once Again	1948	3.75	7.50	15.00
—Reissue of 37529					
❑ 20190	The Daughter of Jole Blon/It's a Sin	1948	3.75	7.50	15.00
—Reissue of 37566					
❑ 20361	Smoke! Smoke! Smoke! (That Cigarette)/Wasted Tears	1948	3.75	7.50	15.00
—Reissue of 37831					
❑ 20362	Too Many Years Too Late/Fat Girl	1948	3.75	7.50	15.00
—Reissue of 37856					
❑ 20380	Put Me to Bed/I Like My Chicken Fryin' Size	1948	3.75	7.50	15.00
—Reissue of 37949					
❑ 20398	What's Been Going On/Blind Alley	1948	3.75	7.50	15.00
—Reissue of 38063					
❑ 20419	Oklahoma Waltz/John's Other Wife	1948	3.75	7.50	15.00
—Reissue of 38160					
❑ 20442	That's Right/So Sad and Blue	1948	5.00	10.00	20.00
❑ 20502	Cimarron/What Would You Do	1948	5.00	10.00	20.00
❑ 20545	Tennessee Saturday Night/A Heart Full of Love (For a Handful of Kisses)	1949	5.00	10.00	20.00
❑ 20549	Till the End of the World/Take It or Leave It Baby	1949	5.00	10.00	20.00
❑ 36876	Gotta Make Up for Lost Time/Baby You Gotta Quit That Noise	1945	5.00	10.00	20.00
❑ 37159	The First Rose/I'll Step Aside	1946	5.00	10.00	20.00
❑ 37217	Divorce Me C.O.D./Rainbow at Midnight	1946	5.00	10.00	20.00
❑ 37255	So Round, So Firm, So Fully Packed/You Brought Sorrow to My Heart	1947	5.00	10.00	20.00
❑ 37400	Love Gone Cold/You Don't Care	1947	5.00	10.00	20.00
—Reissue of Okeh 6732					
❑ 37529	Don't Look Now/Rock My Cradle Once Again	1947	5.00	10.00	20.00
❑ 37566	The Daughter of Jole Blon/It's a Sin	1947	5.00	10.00	20.00
❑ 37831	Smoke! Smoke! Smoke! (That Cigarette)/Wasted Tears	1947	5.00	10.00	20.00
❑ 37856	Too Many Years Too Late/Fat Girl	1948	5.00	10.00	20.00
❑ 37949	Put Me to Bed/I Like My Chicken Fryin' Size	1948	5.00	10.00	20.00
❑ 38063	What's Been Going On/Blind Alley	1948	5.00	10.00	20.00
❑ 38160	Oklahoma Waltz/John's Other Wife	1948	5.00	10.00	20.00
OKEH					
❑ 6732	Love Gone Cold/You Don't Care	1945	6.25	12.50	25.00
7-Inch Extended Plays					
COLUMBIA					
❑ B-2820	(contents unknown)	1958	7.50	15.00	30.00
❑ B-2820 [PS]	Johnny Bond and His Red River Boys	1958	7.50	15.00	30.00
REPUBLIC					
❑ 100	(contents unknown)	1960	5.00	10.00	20.00
❑ 100 [PS]	Hot Rod Lincoln	1960	5.00	10.00	20.00
Albums					
CMH					
❑ 6212	The Singing Cowboy Again	1981	2.50	5.00	10.00
❑ 6213	The Return of the Singing Cowboy	1981	2.50	5.00	10.00
HARMONY					
❑ HL 7308 [M]	Johnny Bond's Best	1964	5.00	10.00	20.00
❑ HL 7353 [M]	Bottled in Bond	1965	5.00	10.00	20.00
NASHVILLE					
❑ 2054	Three Sheets to the Wind	196?	3.75	7.50	15.00
STARDAY					
❑ SLP-147 [M]	That Wild, Wicked But Wonderful West	1961	12.50	25.00	50.00
❑ SLP-227 [M]	Songs That Made Him Famous	1963	10.00	20.00	40.00
❑ SLP-298 [M]	Hot Rod Lincoln	1964	12.50	25.00	50.00
❑ 333 [M]	Ten Little Bottles	1965	10.00	20.00	40.00
❑ SLP-333 [S]	Ten Little Bottles	1965	7.50	15.00	30.00
❑ 354 [M]	Famous Hot Rodders I Have Known	1965	20.00	40.00	80.00
❑ SLP-354 [S]	Famous Hot Rodders I Have Known	1965	10.00	20.00	40.00
❑ 368 [M]	The Man Who Comes Around	1966	5.00	10.00	20.00
❑ SLP-368 [S]	The Man Who Comes Around	1966	6.25	12.50	25.00
❑ 378 [M]	Bottles Up	1966	5.00	10.00	20.00
❑ SLP-378 [S]	Bottles Up	1966	6.25	12.50	25.00
❑ 388 [M]	The Branded Stock of Johnny Bond	1966	3.75	7.50	15.00
❑ SLP-388 [S]	The Branded Stock of Johnny Bond	1966	5.00	10.00	20.00
❑ 402 [M]	Ten Nights in a Barroom	1967	3.75	7.50	15.00
❑ SLP-402 [S]	Ten Nights in a Barroom	1967	5.00	10.00	20.00
❑ SLP-416	Drink Up and Go Home	1968	3.75	7.50	15.00
❑ SLP-444	The Best of Johnny Bond	1969	3.75	7.50	15.00
❑ SLP-456	Old, New, Patriotic and Blue	1970	3.75	7.50	15.00
❑ SLP-472	Here Come the Elephants	1971	3.75	7.50	15.00
❑ 954	The Best of Johnny Bond	1976	2.50	5.00	10.00

BOND, JOHNNY, AND LEFTY FRIZZELL

Also see each artist's individual listings.

45s

Number	Title (A Side/B Side)	Yr	VG	VG+	NM
COLUMBIA					
❑ 40934	Sick, Sober and Sorry/Lover By Appointment	1957	3.75	7.50	15.00

BOND, JOHNNY, AND RED SOVINE

Also see each artist's individual listings.

45s

Number	Title (A Side/B Side)	Yr	VG	VG+	NM
STARDAY					
❑ 790	The Gearjammer and the Hobo/Sweet Nellie	1966	2.50	5.00	10.00

BONNERS, THE

45s

Number	Title (A Side/B Side)	Yr	VG	VG+	NM
OL					
❑ 110	Ordinary Hero/(B-side unknown)	1988	—	3.00	6.00
—As "The Bonner Family"					
❑ 126	Way Beyond the Blue/You Haven't Tried Me	1988	—	3.00	6.00

BONNIE AND BUDDY

See BONNIE GUITAR.

BONNIE LOU

45s

Number	Title (A Side/B Side)	Yr	VG	VG+	NM
FRATERNITY					
❑ 808	No One Ever Lost More/Have You Ever Been Lonely	1958	3.75	7.50	15.00
❑ 812	Friction Heat/I Give My Love to You	1958	3.75	7.50	15.00
KING					
❑ 1192	Seven Lonely Days/Just Out of Reach	1953	7.50	15.00	30.00
❑ 1213	Scrap of Paper/Dancin' with Someone	1953	7.50	15.00	30.00
❑ 1237	Tennessee Wig Walk/Hand Me Down Heart	1953	7.50	15.00	30.00
❑ 1272	Papaya Mama/Since You Said Goodbye	1953	7.50	15.00	30.00
❑ 1279	Texas Polka/No Heart at All	1953	7.50	15.00	30.00

Number	Title (A Side/B Side)	Yr	VG	VG+	NM
❑ 1318	Welcome Mat/Don't Stop Kissing Me Goodnight	1954	6.25	12.50	25.00
❑ 1341	Huckleberry Pie/No One	1954	6.25	12.50	25.00
❑ 1365	Wait for Me Darling/Blue Tennessee Rain	1954	3.00	6.00	25.00
❑ 1373	Two-Step Side Step/Please Don't Laugh When I Cry	1954	6.25	12.50	25.00
❑ 1384	Tell the World/Darlin' Why	1954	6.25	12.50	25.00
❑ 1414	Tennessee Mambo/Train Whistle Blues	1955	6.25	12.50	25.00
❑ 1436	Tweedle Dee/Finger of Suspicion	1955	6.25	12.50	25.00
❑ 1445	Danger, Heartbreak Ahead/A Rusty Old Halo	1955	6.25	12.50	25.00
❑ 1476	Drop Me a Line/Old Faithful	1955	6.25	12.50	25.00
❑ 1506	Barnyard Hop/Miss the Love	1955	6.25	12.50	25.00
❑ 4835	Daddy-O/Dancing in My Socks	1955	6.25	12.50	25.00
❑ 4864	Daddy-O/Miss the Love	1956	5.00	10.00	20.00
❑ 4895	Little Miss Bobby Sox/Beyond the Shadow of a Doubt	1956	5.00	10.00	20.00
❑ 4900	Bo Weevil/Chaperon	1956	5.00	10.00	20.00
❑ 4919	I Turn to You/Lonesome Lover	1956	5.00	10.00	20.00
❑ 4948	No Rock 'N' Roll Tonight/One Track Love	1956	6.25	12.50	25.00
❑ 5009	I Want You/Easy Love, Easy Kisses	1957	5.00	10.00	20.00
❑ 5033	Kit 'N Caboodle/Takes Two	1957	5.00	10.00	20.00
❑ 5063	Teeange Wedding/Runnin' Away	1957	5.00	10.00	20.00
❑ 5094	I'm Available/Waiting in Vain	1957	5.00	10.00	20.00
❑ 5425	Tweedle Dee/Daddy-O	1960	3.75	7.50	15.00
❑ 5865	Seven Lonely Days/Tennessee Wig Walk	1964	3.00	6.00	12.00
TODD					
❑ 1073	24 Hours of Loneliness/Be Tender	1962	3.00	6.00	12.00
Albums					
KING					
❑ 595 [M]	Bonnie Lou Sings	1958	35.00	70.00	140.00

BONOFF, KARLA, AND THE NITTY GRITTY DIRT BAND

Bonoff, a California singer-songwriter, is otherwise outside the scope of this book. Also see NITTY GRITTY DIRT BAND.

45s

MCA

Number	Title (A Side/B Side)	Yr	VG	VG+	NM
❑ 55182	You Believed in Me/Atlanta Reel '96	1996	—	—	3.00
—B-side by Michael Omartian					

BOOKER, JAY

45s

EMI AMERICA

Number	Title (A Side/B Side)	Yr	VG	VG+	NM
❑ B-8379	Hot Red Sweater/Mary Mandolin	1987	—	—	3.00
❑ B-43045	The Mule Won't Move/Brand New Outlaw	1987	—	—	3.00

BOONE, DEBBY

45s

WARNER BROS.

Number	Title (A Side/B Side)	Yr	VG	VG+	NM
❑ 8446	You Light Up My Life/He's a Rebel	1977	—	3.00	6.00
—B-side by The Boones					
❑ 8455	You Light Up My Life/Hasta Manana	1977	—	2.00	4.00
❑ 8511	California/Hey Everybody	1978	—	2.00	4.00
❑ 8511 [PS]	California/Hey Everybody	1978	—	2.00	4.00
❑ 8554	God Knows/Baby, I'm Yours	1978	—	2.00	4.00
❑ 8554 [PS]	God Knows/Baby, I'm Yours	1978	—	2.00	4.00
❑ 8633	Oh, No, Not My Baby/When You're Loved	1978	—	2.00	4.00
❑ 8700	In Memory of Your Love/When You're Loved	1978	—	2.00	4.00
❑ 8739	My Heart Has a Mind of Its Own/I'd Rather Leave While I'm in Love	1979	—	2.00	4.00
❑ 8814	Breakin' In a Brand New Broken Heart/When You're Loved	1979	—	2.00	4.00
❑ 49042	See You in September/Jamie	1979	—	2.00	4.00
❑ 49107	Everybody's Somebody's Fool/I'll Never Say Goodbye	1979	—	2.00	4.00
❑ 49176	Are You On the Road to Lovin' Me Again/When It's Just You and Me	1980	—	2.00	4.00
❑ 49281	Free to Be Lonely Again/Love Put a Song in My Heart	1980	—	2.00	4.00
❑ 49585	Take It Like a Woman/I Wish That I Could Hurt That Way Again	1980	—	2.00	4.00
❑ 49652	Perfect Fool/Every Day I Have to Cry	1981	—	2.00	4.00
❑ 49720	It'll Be Him/Too Many Rivers	1981	—	2.00	4.00
Albums					
CAPITOL					
❑ ST-41005	Choose Life	198?	2.50	5.00	10.00
❑ ST-41029	Surrender	198?	2.50	5.00	10.00
LAMB & LION					
❑ 1046	With My Song	1980	3.00	6.00	12.00
❑ LLR 3008	Choose Life	1985	3.00	6.00	12.00
❑ 83011	Friends for Life	198?	3.00	6.00	12.00
MCA					
❑ 962	You Light Up My Life	198?	2.00	4.00	8.00
—Reissue of Warner Bros. 3118					
❑ 1457	Best of Debby Boone	198?	2.00	4.00	8.00
WARNER BROS.					
❑ BS 3118	You Light Up My Life	1977	2.50	5.00	10.00
❑ BSK 3130	Midstream	1978	2.50	5.00	10.00
❑ BSK 3301	Debby Boone	1979	2.50	5.00	10.00
❑ BSK 3419	Love Has No Reason	1980	2.50	5.00	10.00
❑ BSK 3501	Savin' It Up	1981	2.50	5.00	10.00

BOONE, LARRY

45s

COLUMBIA

Number	Title (A Side/B Side)	Yr	VG	VG+	NM
❑ 38-73710	I Need a Miracle/Rock on the Road	1991	—	—	3.00
❑ 38-73813	To Be with You/I Still Do	1991	—	—	3.00
❑ 38-73992	It Wouldn't Kill Me/Keeper of My Heart	1991	—	—	3.00
❑ 38-74913	Get in Line/Watermelon Time in Georgia	1993	—	—	3.00
❑ 38-74994	Hotel Coupe de Ville/King of the Mountain	1993	—	—	3.00
MERCURY					
❑ 870086-7	Roses in December/It's Too Late Now	1987	—	—	3.00
❑ 870086-7 [PS]	Roses in December/It's Too Late Now	1987	—	2.00	4.00
❑ 870267-7	Stop Me (If You've Heard This One Before)/Back in the Swing of Things Again	1988	—	—	3.00
❑ 870454-7	Don't Give Candy to a Stranger/Back in the Swing of Things Again	1988	—	—	3.00
❑ 872046-7	I Just Called to Say Goodbye Again/Reason for the Rain	1988	—	—	3.00
❑ 872728-7	Wine Me Up/Old Coyote Town	1989	—	—	3.00
❑ 874538-7	Fool's Paradise/Under a Lone Star Moon	1989	—	—	3.00
❑ 875320-7	Too Blue to Be True/Hard Time Taking the Easy Way Out	1990	—	—	3.00
❑ 876426-7	Everybody Wants to Be Hank Williams/Lovesick Blues	1990	—	2.00	4.00
❑ 884858-7	Stranger Things Have Happened/Old Paths May Never Cross	1986	—	—	3.00
❑ 888044-7	She's the Trip That I've Been On/Honky Tonk Sons	1986	—	—	3.00
❑ 888427-7	Back in the Swing of Things Again/Bottom Dollar	1987	—	—	3.00
❑ 888598-7	I Talked a Lot About Leaving/Cowboy Tonight	1987	—	—	3.00
Albums					
MERCURY					
❑ 834377-1	Larry Boone	1988	2.00	4.00	8.00
❑ 836710-1	Swingin' Doors, Sawdust Floors	1989	2.50	5.00	10.00

BOONE, PAT

Generally not considered a country artist, the below either charted country or were issued on country labels.

45s

HITSVILLE

Number	Title (A Side/B Side)	Yr	VG	VG+	NM
❑ 6037	Texas Woman/It's Gone	1976	—	2.50	5.00
❑ 6042	Oklahoma Sunshine/Won't Be Home Tonight	1976	—	2.50	5.00
❑ 6047	Country Days and Country Nights/Lovelight Comes a-Shining	1976	—	2.50	5.00
❑ 6054	Colorado Country Morning/Don't Want to Fall Away from You	1977	—	2.50	5.00
LAMB & LION					
❑ 818	It's OK to Be a Kid at Christmas/Don't Let the Season Pass You By	1979	—	2.50	5.00
MC					
❑ 5001	Whatever Happened to the Good Old Honky Tonk/Ain't Going Down in the Ground Before My Time	1977	—	2.50	5.00
MELODYLAND					
❑ 6001	Candy Lips/Young Girl	1974	—	2.50	5.00
❑ 6005	Indiana Girl/Young Girl	1975	—	2.50	5.00
❑ 6018	I'd Do It with You/Yester-Me, Yester-You, Yesterday	1975	—	2.50	5.00
—A-side with Shirley Boone					
❑ 6029	Glory Train/U.F.O.	1976	—	2.50	5.00
REPUBLIC					
❑ 7049	My Heart Belongs to You/Until You Tell Me So	1953	6.25	12.50	25.00
❑ 7062	Remember to Be Mine/Half Way Chance with You	1953	6.25	12.50	25.00
❑ 7084	I Need Someone/Loving You Madly	1954	6.25	12.50	25.00
❑ 7119	My Heart Belongs to You/I Need Someone	1955	5.00	10.00	20.00
WARNER BROS.					
❑ 49097	Midnight/Can You Feel the Love	1979	—	2.00	4.00
—By "Pat and Shirley Boone"					
❑ 49255	Hostage Prayer/Love's Got a Way of Hanging On	1980	—	2.00	4.00
❑ 49596	Colorado Country Morning/Whatever Happened to the Good Old Honky Tonk	1980	—	2.00	4.00
❑ 49691	Won't Be Home Tonight/Throw It Away	1981	—	2.00	4.00
Albums					
HITSVILLE					
❑ H6-405	Texas Woman	1976	3.00	6.00	12.00
MELODYLAND					
❑ 6-501	The Country Side of Pat Boone	1975	3.00	6.00	12.00

BOOTH, LARRY

45s

CREAM

Number	Title (A Side/B Side)	Yr	VG	VG+	NM
❑ 7823	I See Love in Your Eyes/Cheater	1978	—	3.50	7.00

BOOTH, TONY

45s

CAPITOL

Number	Title (A Side/B Side)	Yr	VG	VG+	NM
❑ 3214	Cinderella/Somebody Called L.A.	1971	—	3.00	6.00
❑ 3269	The Key's in the Mailbox/The Devil Made Me Do That	1972	—	3.00	6.00
❑ 3356	A Whole Lot of Somethin'/Nobody's Fool But Yours	1972	—	3.00	6.00
❑ 3441	Lonesome 7-7203/Congratulations, You're Absolutely Right	1972	—	3.00	6.00
❑ 3515	When a Man Loves a Woman (The Way That I Love You)/Just a Man	1973	—	2.50	5.00
❑ 3582	Loving You/What a Liar I Am	1973	—	2.50	5.00
❑ 3639	Old Faithful/Don't Let True Love Slip Away	1973	—	2.50	5.00
❑ 3723	Secret Love/Someday I'm Gonna Go to Mexico	1973	—	2.50	5.00
❑ 3795	Happy Hour/Midnight Race	1973	—	2.50	5.00

Number	Title (A Side/B Side)	Yr	VG	VG+	NM
❑ 3853	Lonely Street/It Never Will Be Over for Me	1974	—	2.50	5.00
❑ 3899	There Ain't Enough of Love to Go Around/ Someone Who Really Does	1974	—	2.50	5.00
❑ 3943	Workin' at the Car Wash Blues/That Loving Feeling	1974	—	2.50	5.00
❑ 3994	Watch Out for Lucy/Good As Gone	1974	—	2.50	5.00
❑ 4058	Down at the Corner Bar/Someone Who Really Does	1975	—	2.50	5.00
❑ 4123	Fanny Lee (The Burlesque Queen)/How's Everything	1975	—	2.50	5.00
MGM					
❑ 14112	Irma Jackson/One Too Many Times	1970	2.00	4.00	8.00
❑ 14156	Give Me One Last Kiss and Go/Las Virgenes Road	1970	2.00	4.00	8.00
UNITED ARTISTS					
❑ XW906	Somethin' 'Bout You Baby I Like/Lady Alone	1976	—	2.00	4.00
❑ XW962	Letting Go/Nothing Seems to Work Anymore	1977	—	2.00	4.00
❑ XW1028	All Night Long/Fading Tail Lights	1977	—	2.00	4.00
Albums					
CAPITOL					
❑ ST-11076	The Key's in the Mailbox	1972	3.75	7.50	15.00
❑ ST-11126	Lonesone 7-7203	1972	3.75	7.50	15.00
❑ ST-11160	When a Man Loves a Woman (The Way That I Love You)	1973	3.75	7.50	15.00
❑ ST-11210	This Is Tony Booth	1973	3.75	7.50	15.00
❑ ST-11270	Happy Hour	1974	3.75	7.50	15.00
❑ ST-11352	Workin' at the Car Wash Blues	1974	3.75	7.50	15.00
MGM					
❑ SE-4704	On the Right Track	1970	5.00	10.00	20.00

BORCHERS, BOBBY

Number	Title (A Side/B Side)	Yr	VG	VG+	NM
45s					
ABC					
❑ 12075	We've Come As Far As We Can Go Together/ Revelation	1975	—	3.00	6.00
ABC DOT					
❑ 17578	God Bless Robert E. Lee/The Temptation Is Gone	1975	—	3.00	6.00
EPIC					
❑ 11073	When Johnny Cash Comes Back to Folsom/I'll Still Be Loving You This Much	1973	—	3.00	6.00
❑ 11093	Alabama Dream Girl/I'll Still Be Loving You This Much	1974	—	3.00	6.00
❑ 50585	Sweet Fantasy/You Are Yesterday	1978	—	2.00	4.00
❑ 50650	Wishing I Had Listened to Your Song/I've Had a Lovely Time	1979	—	2.00	4.00
❑ 50687	I Just Wanna Feel the Magic/Old Emotional Me	1979	—	2.00	4.00
LONGHORN					
❑ 3002	It Was Love What It Was/(B-side unknown)	1987	—	2.50	5.00
❑ 3003	(I Remember When I Thought) Whiskey Was a River/It Was Love What It Was	1987	—	2.50	5.00
PLAYBOY					
❑ 5803	Cheap Perfume and Candlelight/Hobo's Delight	1977	—	2.50	5.00
❑ 5816	What a Way to Go/Lunch-Time Lovers	1977	—	2.50	5.00
❑ 5823	I Promised Her a Rainbow/Brass Buckles	1977	—	2.50	5.00
❑ 5827	I Like Ladies in Long Black Dresses/Shawn	1978	—	2.50	5.00
❑ 6065	Someone's with Your Wife Tonight, Mister/ Hobo's Delight	1976	—	2.50	5.00
❑ 6083	They Don't Make 'Em Like That Anymore/I Can't Keep My Hands Off of You	1976	—	2.50	5.00
❑ 6092	Whispers/Just for a Minute	1976	—	2.50	5.00
Albums					
PLAYBOY					
❑ KZ 34829	Bobby Borchers	1977	3.00	6.00	12.00
❑ KZ 35027	Denim and Rhinestones	1977	3.00	6.00	12.00

BOTTOMS, DENNIS

Number	Title (A Side/B Side)	Yr	VG	VG+	NM
45s					
WARNER BROS.					
❑ 28898	Honky Tonk Heaven/Gone But Not Forgotten	1985	—	—	3.00
❑ 28944	Bring On the Sunshine/Gone But Not Forgotten	1985	—	—	3.00
❑ 29035	Did I Stay Too Long/Pick a Little Boogie	1985	—	—	3.00

BOUCHER, JESSICA

Also see MERRILL AND JESSICA; JOE STAMPLEY.

Number	Title (A Side/B Side)	Yr	VG	VG+	NM
45s					
MERCURY					
❑ 866654-7	Your Lies Ain't Working/What a Friday Night Is For	1992	—	—	3.00

BOWEN, JIMMY

Number	Title (A Side/B Side)	Yr	VG	VG+	NM
45s					
CAPEHART					
❑ 5005	Teenage Dreamworld/It's Against the Law	1962	5.00	10.00	20.00
❑ 5005 [PS]	Teenage Dreamworld/It's Against the Law	1962	12.50	25.00	50.00
CREST					
❑ 1085	Don't Drop It/Somebody to Love	1961	5.00	10.00	20.00
REPRISE					
❑ 0264	The Biggest Lover in Town/The Big Bus	1964	2.50	5.00	10.00
❑ 0358	The Golden Eagle/Spanish Cricket	1965	2.50	5.00	10.00
❑ 0450	Wonder Mother/Captain Gorgeous	1966	2.50	5.00	10.00
❑ 0592	Raunchy/It's Such a Pretty World Today	1967	2.50	5.00	10.00
ROULETTE					
❑ 4001	I'm Stickin' With You/Ever Lovin' Fingers	1957	5.00	10.00	20.00
—With the Rhythm Orchids					
❑ 4010	Warm Up to Me Baby/I Trusted You	1957	5.00	10.00	20.00
❑ 4017	Ever Since That Night/Don't Tell Me Your Troubles	1957	5.00	10.00	20.00
❑ 4023	Cross Over/It's Shameful	1957	5.00	10.00	20.00
❑ 4057	Can She Kiss/Keeping You	1958	5.00	10.00	20.00
❑ 4083	By the Light of the Silvery Moon/The Two Step	1958	5.00	10.00	20.00
❑ 4102	My Kind of Woman/Blue Moon	1958	5.00	10.00	20.00
❑ 4122	Always Faithful/Wish I Were Tied to You	1958	5.00	10.00	20.00
❑ 4175	You're Just Wasting Your Time/Walkin' on Air	1959	5.00	10.00	20.00
❑ 4224	Oh Yeah! Oh Yeah! Mm Mm/Your Loving Arms	1960	5.00	10.00	20.00
TRIPLE D					
❑ 798	I'm Stickin' With You/Party Doll	1956	250.00	500.00	1000.
—B-side by Buddy Knox					
7-Inch Extended Plays					
ROULETTE					
❑ 302	(contents unknown)	1957	50.00	100.00	200.00
❑ 302 [PS]	Jimmy Bowen	1957	50.00	100.00	200.00
Albums					
DECCA					
❑ DL 4816 [M]	Margie Bowes Sings	1967	5.00	10.00	20.00
REPRISE					
❑ R-6210 [M]	Sunday Morning with the Comics	1966	7.50	15.00	30.00
❑ RS-6210 [S]	Sunday Morning with the Comics	1966	10.00	20.00	40.00
ROULETTE					
❑ R 25004 [M]	Jimmy Bowen	1957	75.00	150.00	300.00
—Black and silver label					
❑ R 25004 [M]	Jimmy Bowen	1958	37.50	75.00	150.00
—Red label					
❑ R 25004 [M]	Jimmy Bowen	198?	3.00	6.00	12.00
—Reissue for Publishers Central Bureau (it says so on the jacket)					

BOWES, MARGIE

Number	Title (A Side/B Side)	Yr	VG	VG+	NM
45s					
DECCA					
❑ 31557	Our Things/There's Gotta Be a Way	1963	2.00	4.00	8.00
❑ 31606	Understand Your Gal/You Can Be Replaced	1964	2.00	4.00	8.00
❑ 31644	What In This World (Am I Gonna Do)/Overnight	1964	2.00	4.00	8.00
❑ 31708	Big City/Watch Me Fall	1964	2.00	4.00	8.00
❑ 31838	Lost/I Can't Love That Way	1965	2.00	4.00	8.00
❑ 31907	Look Who's Lonely/This Completely Destroys My Plans	1966	2.00	4.00	8.00
❑ 32014	Part Time Baby, Full Time Fool/It's Enough to Make a Woman Lose Her Mind	1966	2.00	4.00	8.00
❑ 32158	Making Believe/Man Around the House	1967	2.00	4.00	8.00
❑ 32301	Billy Christian/Broken Hearted, Too	1968	—	3.50	7.00
❑ 32395	Lonesome Woman/Gatherin' Dust	1968	—	3.50	7.00
❑ 32538	I Have What It Takes/Go Woman Go	1969	—	3.50	7.00
HICKORY					
❑ 1084	Won'cha Come Back to Me/One Broken Heart	1958	5.00	10.00	20.00
❑ 1087	Violets and Cheap Perfume/One Time Too Many	1958	5.00	10.00	20.00
❑ 1094	Poor Old Heartsick Me/Blue Dream	1959	3.75	7.50	15.00
❑ 1102	My Love and Little Me/Sweet Night of Love	1959	3.75	7.50	15.00
❑ 1112	Make a Wish/They Just Don't Know You	1960	3.75	7.50	15.00
❑ 1124	Day After Day/Don't Turn On the Light	1960	3.75	7.50	15.00
❑ 1135	Are You Teasing Me/Judge Not	1960	3.75	7.50	15.00
MERCURY					
❑ 71845	Little Miss Belong to No One/Bitter Sweet Kisses	1961	2.50	5.00	10.00
❑ 71897	Always Remember/Lonely Pillow	1961	2.50	5.00	10.00
❑ 71971	You're Still a Part of Me/Hammer and Nails	1962	2.50	5.00	10.00
❑ 72090	Think It Over/Within Your Crowd	1963	2.50	5.00	10.00
Albums					
DECCA					
❑ DL 4816 [M]	Margie Bowes Sings	1967	5.00	10.00	20.00
❑ DL 74816 [S]	Margie Bowes Sings	1967	3.75	7.50	15.00

BOWLING, ROGER

Number	Title (A Side/B Side)	Yr	VG	VG+	NM
45s					
LOUISIANA HAYRIDE					
❑ 783	Dance with Me Molly/(B-side unknown)	1978	—	3.50	7.00
❑ 784	A Loser's Just a Learner (On His Way to Better Things)/Lucille	1978	—	3.50	7.00
MERCURY					
❑ 57042	Yellow Pages/I Don't Feel at Home (At Home Anymore)	1981	—	2.00	4.00
❑ 57049	A Little Bit of Heaven/She Can't Break It to Her Heart	1981	—	2.00	4.00
❑ 76135	More Than I Used To/(B-side unknown)	1982	—	2.00	4.00
NSD					
❑ 37	Friday Night Fool/There'll Never Be a Love Song	1980	—	2.50	5.00
❑ 46	The Diplomat/I'm Looking for a Lonely Woman	1980	—	2.50	5.00
❑ 50	I Can't Get Over You/Dig a Little Deeper in the Well	1980	—	2.50	5.00
❑ 58	Long Arm of the Law/I Can't Get Over You	1980	—	2.50	5.00
❑ 71	Yellow Pages/I Don't Feel at Home (At Home Anymore)	1980	—	3.00	6.00
❑ 144	Good Bartender/I've Got to Break the Bottle	1983	—	2.50	5.00
❑ 149	Hangout for Your Memory/Then I'll Stop Loving You	1983	—	2.50	5.00
UNITED ARTISTS					
❑ XW715	I Want to See You One More Time/Juke Box Girl	1975	—	2.50	5.00
❑ XW803	I Don't Stand a Chance Anyway/You've Got a Lovin' Comin'	1976	—	2.50	5.00

BOWLING, SHELL

45s

SOUNDWAVES

Number	Title (A Side/B Side)	Yr	VG	VG+	NM
❑ 4690	Christmas Time Is Coming/Born on Christmas Day	1982	—	2.50	5.00

BOWMAN, BILLY BOB, AND THE BEAUMONT BAG & BURLAP COMPANY

45s

UNITED ARTISTS

Number	Title (A Side/B Side)	Yr	VG	VG+	NM
❑ 50957	Miss Pauline/Showers	1972	—	3.00	6.00

BOWMAN, CECIL

45s

D

Number	Title (A Side/B Side)	Yr	VG	VG+	NM
❑ 1048	Justice of Love/Man Awaitin'	1959	5.00	10.00	20.00
❑ 1085	Curse of Wine/Cotton	1959	5.00	10.00	20.00
❑ 1110	Sweet Cakes and Kisses/Tea Leaves Don't Lie	1960	5.00	10.00	20.00
❑ 1145	Whispering Lips/Most Beautiful	1960	5.00	10.00	20.00

BOWMAN, DON

Also see SKEETER DAVIS AND DON BOWMAN.

45s

LAGREE

Number	Title (A Side/B Side)	Yr	VG	VG+	NM
❑ 704	Coward at the Alamo/TV Commercials	197?	—	3.00	6.00

LONE STAR

Number	Title (A Side/B Side)	Yr	VG	VG+	NM
❑ 701	Willon and Waylee/The Power Tool Song	197?	—	3.00	6.00

MEGA

Number	Title (A Side/B Side)	Yr	VG	VG+	NM
❑ 0062	Hello D.J. (Part 1)/Hello D.J. (Part 2)	1972	—	3.00	6.00

RCA VICTOR

Number	Title (A Side/B Side)	Yr	VG	VG+	NM
❑ 47-8384	Chit Atkins, Make Me a Star/I Never Did Finish That Song	1964	2.50	5.00	10.00
❑ 47-8506	I Fell Out of Love with Love/The World's Worst Guitar Picker	1965	2.50	5.00	10.00
❑ 47-8588	Graduation Day/The Wrong House	1965	2.50	5.00	10.00
❑ 47-8670	Dear Harlan Howard/Freddy Four Toes	1965	2.50	5.00	10.00
❑ 47-8811	Giddyup Do-nut/Freda on the Freeway	1966	2.00	4.00	8.00
❑ 47-8916	The All American Boy/I Get the Feeling We're Through	1966	2.00	4.00	8.00
❑ 47-8990	Surely Not/Dear Sister	1966	2.00	4.00	8.00
❑ 47-9176	What Kind of Fool Am I/My Voice Is Changing	1967	2.00	4.00	8.00
❑ 47-9290	Tijuana Drum and Bugle Corps/Little Leroy	1967	2.00	4.00	8.00
❑ 47-9576	San Francisco Scene/Messin' Up My Mind	1968	2.00	4.00	8.00
❑ 47-9617	Folsom Prison Blues #2/House of the Setting Sun	1968	2.00	4.00	8.00
❑ 47-9706	Jole Blon/Little Diesel Drivin' Devil	1969	2.00	4.00	8.00
❑ 47-9783	Top Ten/How Come It Is	1969	2.00	4.00	8.00
❑ 47-9823	Roy Raisin/Still	1969	2.00	4.00	8.00
❑ 47-9949	I Owe It All to Chet Atkins/Another Puff	1971	2.00	4.00	8.00
❑ 74-0133	Poor Old Ugly Gladys Jones/The Boll Weevil Air Lives	1969	2.00	4.00	8.00
❑ 74-0233	A Boy Named Sue/How Come It Is	1969	—	—	—
—Unreleased					

Albums

LONE STAR

Number	Title (A Side/B Side)	Yr	VG	VG+	NM
❑ 4605	Still Fighting Mental Health	1979	3.75	7.50	15.00

RCA VICTOR

Number	Title (A Side/B Side)	Yr	VG	VG+	NM
❑ LPM-2831 [M]	Our Man in Trouble	1964	5.00	10.00	20.00
❑ LSP-2831 [S]	Our Man in Trouble	1964	6.25	12.50	25.00
❑ LPM-3345 [M]	Fresh from the Funny Farm	1965	5.00	10.00	20.00
❑ LSP-3345 [S]	Fresh from the Funny Farm	1965	6.25	12.50	25.00
❑ LPM-3495 [M]	Funny Way to Make an Album	1966	5.00	10.00	20.00
❑ LSP-3495 [S]	Funny Way to Make an Album	1966	6.25	12.50	25.00
❑ LPM-3646 [M]	Don Bowman Recorded Almost Live	1966	5.00	10.00	20.00
❑ LSP-3646 [S]	Don Bowman Recorded Almost Live	1966	6.25	12.50	25.00
❑ LPM-3795 [M]	From Mexico with Laughs Featuring the Tijuana Drum and Bugle Corps	1967	6.25	12.50	25.00
❑ LSP-3795 [S]	From Mexico with Laughs Featuring the Tijuana Drum and Bugle Corps	1967	5.00	10.00	20.00
❑ LPM-3920 [M]	Funny Folk Flops	1968	12.50	25.00	50.00
❑ LSP-3920 [S]	Funny Folk Flops	1968	5.00	10.00	20.00

BOWSER, DONNIE

45s

BAMBOO

Number	Title (A Side/B Side)	Yr	VG	VG+	NM
❑ 508	Talk to Me Baby/Tomorrow	1961	3.75	7.50	15.00

DESS

Number	Title (A Side/B Side)	Yr	VG	VG+	NM
❑ 7002	Rock and Roll Joys/Stone Heart	1957	75.00	150.00	300.00
—As "Little Donnie Bowshier"					
❑ 7004	I Love You Baby/Love So Rare	1957	10.00	20.00	40.00
—As "Little Donnie Bowshier"					

ERA

Number	Title (A Side/B Side)	Yr	VG	VG+	NM
❑ 3029	I Love You Baby/Stone Heart	1960	3.75	7.50	15.00

FRATERNITY

Number	Title (A Side/B Side)	Yr	VG	VG+	NM
❑ 801	I Love You Baby/Stone Heart	1958	20.00	40.00	80.00

PLAYBACK

Number	Title (A Side/B Side)	Yr	VG	VG+	NM
❑ 1342	Another One of My Near Mrs./(B-side unknown)	1989	—	3.00	6.00
—With Bobby Bare					

RIDGEWOOD

Number	Title (A Side/B Side)	Yr	VG	VG+	NM
❑ 3002	Falling for You/You've Got My Arms to Come Back To	1989	—	3.00	6.00

ROBBINS

Number	Title (A Side/B Side)	Yr	VG	VG+	NM
❑ 1009	I Love You Baby/Stone Heart	1958	50.00	100.00	200.00

SAGE

Number	Title (A Side/B Side)	Yr	VG	VG+	NM
❑ 259	I Love You Baby/Love So Rare	1958	6.25	12.50	25.00
—As "Donnie Bowshier"					
❑ 265	I Love You Baby/Stone Heart	1958	5.00	10.00	20.00
❑ 274	Got the Best of Me/It's Our Secret	1959	5.00	10.00	20.00

BOXCAR WILLIE

45s

COLUMN ONE

Number	Title (A Side/B Side)	Yr	VG	VG+	NM
❑ 1004	They're Living It Up/I Remember Roy Rogers	197?	3.00	6.00	12.00
❑ 1012	Train Medley/Lonesome Hobo	1980	2.00	4.00	8.00

ELEKTRA

Number	Title (A Side/B Side)	Yr	VG	VG+	NM
❑ 69937	The Stage/Fireball Mail	1982	—	2.50	5.00
—B-side by Roy Acuff					

GEM

Number	Title (A Side/B Side)	Yr	VG	VG+	NM
❑ NR 17677	Hey Hey Sobrino/I Shout Hooray	198?	—	3.00	6.00
❑ NR 17677 [PS]	Hey Hey Sobrino/I Shout Hooray	198?	2.00	4.00	8.00

MAIN STREET

Number	Title (A Side/B Side)	Yr	VG	VG+	NM
❑ 950	Boxcar Blues/Don't Let the Stars Get in Your Eyes	1981	—	2.50	5.00
❑ 951	Bad News/Lefty Left Us Lonely	1982	—	2.50	5.00
❑ 952	We Made Memories/To My Baby I'm a Big Star All the Time	1982	—	2.50	5.00
—A-side with Penny DeHaven					
❑ 953	Last Train to Heaven/Keep On Rollin' Down the Line	1982	—	2.50	5.00
❑ 954	Country Music Nightmare/Train Medley	1983	—	2.50	5.00
❑ 93017	The Man I Used to Be/No More Trains to Ride	1983	—	2.50	5.00
❑ 93020	Not on the Bottom Yet/It Ain't No Record	1984	—	2.50	5.00
❑ 93021	Luther/Luther (Long Version)	1984	—	2.50	5.00
❑ 93023	Whine, Whistle, Whine/Hobo's Lament	1984	—	2.50	5.00
❑ (# unk)	T for Texas/Hobo's Lament	1983	2.00	4.00	8.00
—Gold vinyl					
❑ (# unk) [PS]	T for Texas/Hobo's Lament	1983	2.50	5.00	10.00
—Sleeve calls this "Tribute to Jimmie Rodgers"					

ROTO

Number	Title (A Side/B Side)	Yr	VG	VG+	NM
❑ 7493-1	Boxcar Willie/(B-side unknown)	1976	7.50	15.00	30.00
—As "Marty Martin and the Rangers"; the song from which he took his stage name					

Albums

AHMC

Number	Title (A Side/B Side)	Yr	VG	VG+	NM
❑ AA 118	Marty Martin Sings Country Music	1976	12.50	25.00	50.00
—As "Marty Martin"; he changed his name to "Boxcar Willie" after one of his early songs					

MAIN STREET

Number	Title (A Side/B Side)	Yr	VG	VG+	NM
❑ 9309	... Not the Man I Used to Be	1984	2.50	5.00	10.00
❑ 73000	King of the Road	1981	3.00	6.00	12.00
❑ 73001	Last Train to Heaven	1982	3.00	6.00	12.00
❑ 73002	Best of Boxcar, Vol. 1	1982	3.00	6.00	12.00

BOY HOWDY

45s

CURB

Number	Title (A Side/B Side)	Yr	VG	VG+	NM
❑ D7-76934	True to His Word/I'm Already Lovin' You Too Much	1995	—	2.00	4.00
❑ D7-76940	Bigger Fish to Fry/She Can't Love You	1995	—	2.00	4.00

BOYD, BILL, AND HIS COWBOY RAMBLERS

45s

RCA VICTOR

Number	Title (A Side/B Side)	Yr	VG	VG+	NM
❑ 48-0067	Blue Danube Waltz/Varsoviana	1949	10.00	20.00	40.00
—Originals on green vinyl					
❑ 48-0112	Poison Ivy/Pass the Turnip Greens	1949	10.00	20.00	40.00
—Originals on green vinyl					
❑ 48-0129	Jingle Bells/Up on the House Top	1949	12.50	25.00	50.00
—Originals on green vinyl					
❑ 48-0129	Jingle Bells/Up on the House Top	1950	6.25	12.50	25.00
—Later issues on black vinyl					
❑ 48-0172	Texas Blues/Yes You Did	1950	10.00	20.00	40.00
—Originals on green vinyl					
❑ 48-0208	Bandera Waltz/Letters Have No Arms	1950	10.00	20.00	40.00
—Originals on green vinyl					
❑ 48-0335	Come and Get It/Red River Rag	1950	10.00	20.00	40.00
—Originals on green vinyl					
❑ 48-0351	Why Don't You Love Me/Red Lips Kiss My Blues Away	1950	10.00	20.00	40.00
—Originals on green vinyl					
❑ 48-0375	Yes I Do, Yes I Do, Yes I Do/Bill Boyd Rag	1950	10.00	20.00	40.00
—Originals on green vinyl					
❑ 48-0410	Mean, Mean, Mean/Cuckoo Waltz	1950	7.50	15.00	30.00
❑ 48-0449	Drifting Texas Sand/Stop Polka	1951	7.50	15.00	30.00
❑ 48-0482	Why Do You Punish Me/Gladiola Waltz	1951	7.50	15.00	30.00

STARDAY

Number	Title (A Side/B Side)	Yr	VG	VG+	NM
❑ 289	Big D/Texas Star	1957	6.25	12.50	25.00
❑ 303	Lone Star Rag/Ramblers March	1957	6.25	12.50	25.00

Selected 78s

BLUEBIRD

Number	Title (A Side/B Side)	Yr	VG	VG+	NM
❑ B-5608	On the Texas Plains/Ridin' on a Humpback Mule	193?	6.25	12.50	25.00
❑ B-5667	Ridin' Old Paint and Leadin' Old Ball/The Strawberry Roan	193?	6.25	12.50	25.00
❑ B-5740	titles unknown	193?	6.25	12.50	25.00
❑ B-5788	titles unknown	193?	6.25	12.50	25.00
❑ B-5945	Lulu Wall/Sweet Fern	193?	6.25	12.50	25.00
❑ B-6109	titles unknown	193?	6.25	12.50	25.00
❑ B-6119	titles unknown	193?	6.25	12.50	25.00
❑ B-6161	The Sweetest Girl/Rio Grande Waltz	193?	6.25	12.50	25.00
❑ B-6177	Barn Dance Rag/Old-Fashoned Love	193?	6.25	12.50	25.00

Number	Title (A Side/B Side)	Yr	VG	VG+	NM
❑ B-6235	titles unknown	193?	6.25	12.50	25.00
❑ B-6308	titles unknown	193?	6.25	12.50	25.00
❑ B-6323	Mam's Gettin' Hot and Papa's Gettin' Cold/Oh, No She Don't	193?	6.25	12.50	25.00
❑ B-6328	titles unknown	193?	6.25	12.50	25.00
❑ B-6346	Tumbling Tumbleweeds/When It's Twilight in Sweetheart's Lane	193?	6.25	12.50	25.00
❑ B-6351	Cheatin' on Your Baby/Must I Hesitate	193?	6.25	12.50	25.00
❑ B-6384	The Eyes of Texas/Lone Star	193?	6.25	12.50	25.00
❑ B-6420	titles unknown	193?	6.25	12.50	25.00
❑ B-6486	titles unknown	193?	6.25	12.50	25.00
❑ B-6492	Floatin' Down/Beale Street Blues	193?	6.25	12.50	25.00
❑ B-6523	titles unknown	193?	6.25	12.50	25.00
❑ B-6599	titles unknown	193?	6.25	12.50	25.00
❑ B-6670	Put Me in Your Pocket/'Way Out There	193?	6.25	12.50	25.00
❑ B-6694	titles unknown	193?	6.25	12.50	25.00
❑ B-6715	Old Water Mill by a Waterfall/Show Me the Way to Go Home	193?	6.25	12.50	25.00
❑ B-6731	titles unknown	193?	6.25	12.50	25.00
❑ B-6772	titles unknown	193?	6.25	12.50	25.00
❑ B-6807	titles unknown	193?	6.25	12.50	25.00
❑ B-6889	She's Doggin' Me/She's Killin' Me	193?	6.25	12.50	25.00
❑ B-6959	titles unknown	193?	6.25	12.50	25.00
❑ B-7004	titles unknown	193?	6.25	12.50	25.00
❑ B-7006	titles unknown	193?	6.25	12.50	25.00
❑ B-7053	titles unknown	193?	6.25	12.50	25.00
❑ B-7088	Yellow Rose of Texas/Pretty Little Dream Girl	193?	6.25	12.50	25.00
❑ B-7128	New Six or Seven Times/Fan It	193?	6.25	12.50	25.00
❑ B-7189	Sister Lucy Lee/If I Can Count on You	193?	6.25	12.50	25.00
❑ B-7260	I Saw Your Face/My Wonderful One	193?	6.25	12.50	25.00
❑ B-7299	titles unknown	193?	6.25	12.50	25.00
❑ B-7347	Jungle Town/Can't Use Each Other	193?	6.25	12.50	25.00
❑ B-7435	That's Why I'm Jealous of You/An Ace	193?	6.25	12.50	25.00
❑ B-7507	titles unknown	193?	6.25	12.50	25.00
❑ B-7521	titles unknown	193?	6.25	12.50	25.00
❑ B-7531	titles unknown	193?	6.25	12.50	25.00
❑ B-7573	titles unknown	193?	6.25	12.50	25.00
❑ B-7624	titles unknown	193?	6.25	12.50	25.00
❑ B-7662	titles unknown	193?	6.25	12.50	25.00
❑ B-7691	New Steel Guitar Rag/Jig	193?	6.25	12.50	25.00
❑ B-7739	titles unknown	1938	6.25	12.50	25.00
❑ B-7754	titles unknown	1938	6.25	12.50	25.00
❑ B-7788	titles unknown	1938	6.25	12.50	25.00
❑ B-7867	titles unknown	1938	6.25	12.50	25.00
❑ B-7880	titles unknown	1938	6.25	12.50	25.00
❑ B-7910	titles unknown	1938	6.25	12.50	25.00
❑ B-7921	New Spanish Two-Step/Spanish Fandango	1939	6.25	12.50	25.00
❑ B-7940	Tom-Cat Rag/Here Comes Pappy	1939	6.25	12.50	25.00
❑ B-7971	titles unknown	1939	6.25	12.50	25.00
❑ B-7989	Boyd's Kelly Waltz/Weeping Blues	1939	6.25	12.50	25.00
❑ B-8070	La Golondrina/I Want to Go Back	1939	6.25	12.50	25.00
❑ B-8198	That Makes Me Give In/Hold On Little Doggies	1940	6.25	12.50	25.00
❑ B-8246	By a Window/Somebody's Been Using It	1940	6.25	12.50	25.00
❑ B-8394	Drink the Barrel Dry/The Sunset Trail to Texas	1940	6.25	12.50	25.00
❑ B-8409	Down at Polka Joe's/The Zenda Waltz	1940	6.25	12.50	25.00
❑ B-8414	Pussy, Pussy, Pussy/You Better Stop That Cattin' 'Round	1940	6.25	12.50	25.00
❑ B-8458	I Wish You Knew the Way I Feel/You Take It	1940	6.25	12.50	25.00
❑ B-8498	I Want a Feller/I'll Take You Back Again	194?	6.25	12.50	25.00
❑ B-8533	If You'll Come Back/There's a Light Shining Bright	194?	6.25	12.50	25.00
❑ B-8721	Swing Steel, Swing/I'll Be Back in a Year, Little Darlin'	1941	6.25	12.50	25.00
❑ B-8728	Sweethearts or Strangers/Now I Feel the Way You Do	1941	6.25	12.50	25.00
❑ B-8769	Flower of Texas/I Can't Forget	1941	6.25	12.50	25.00
❑ B-8787	Jitter Bug Jive/I Guess You Don't Care Any More	1941	6.25	12.50	25.00
❑ B-8823	No Dice/Hold On to That Thing	1941	6.25	12.50	25.00
❑ B-8885	(Wish I Had) My Pony on the Range/Rollin' Down the Great Divide	1942	6.25	12.50	25.00
❑ B-8900	Home Coming Waltz/Over the Waves Waltz	1942	6.25	12.50	25.00
❑ B-8910	Tell Me Why My Daddy Don't Come Home/The Letter I Never Did Mail	1942	6.25	12.50	25.00
❑ B-9014	Tumble Weed Trail/My Birmingham Rose	1942	6.25	12.50	25.00
❑ 33-0530	Shame on You/Home Coming Waltz	1945	5.00	10.00	20.00
❑ 33-0533	No Time for Tears/Highways Are Happy Ways	1945	5.00	10.00	20.00

MONTGOMERY WARD

Number	Title (A Side/B Side)	Yr	VG	VG+	NM
❑ M-4789	Tumbling Tumbleweeds/(B-side unknown)	193?	6.25	12.50	25.00

RCA VICTOR

Number	Title (A Side/B Side)	Yr	VG	VG+	NM
❑ 20-1793	These Tears Are Not for You/Roadside Rag	1945	5.00	10.00	20.00
❑ 20-1907	New Steel Guitar Rag/New Spanish Two-Step	1946	3.75	7.50	15.00
❑ 20-2050	Oklahoma Bound/Jim's Polka	1947	3.75	7.50	15.00
❑ 20-2145	Lone Star Rag/Without a Woman	1947	3.75	7.50	15.00
❑ 20-2562	Out in the Rain Again/Don't Turn My...	1948	3.75	7.50	15.00
❑ 20-2833	Closed for Repairs/American Patrol	1948	3.75	7.50	15.00

Albums

BLUEBIRD

Number	Title (A Side/B Side)	Yr	VG	VG+	NM
❑ AXM2-5503 [(2)]	Bill Boyd and His Cowboy Ramblers	197?	5.00	10.00	20.00

BOYD, JIM

45s

RCA VICTOR

Number	Title (A Side/B Side)	Yr	VG	VG+	NM
❑ 47-4263	Boogie Woogie Square Dance/Texas Moon Waltz	1951	6.25	12.50	25.00
❑ 48-0031	We Were Married/Mule Boogie	1949	10.00	20.00	40.00
—Originals on green vinyl					
❑ 48-0047	Dear John/One Heart, One Love	1949	10.00	20.00	40.00
—Originals on green vinyl					
❑ 48-0093	Dust on My Telephone/Save the Next Waltz for Me	1949	10.00	20.00	40.00
—Originals on green vinyl					
❑ 48-0159	Sweetheart of Hawaii/Truck Driver's Boogie	1950	10.00	20.00	40.00
—Originals on green vinyl					
❑ 48-0301	Mule Boogie/We Were Married	1950	7.50	15.00	30.00
—Originals on green vinyl					
❑ 48-0353	Bear Creek Boogie/The Girl in the Picture	1950	7.50	15.00	30.00
—Originals on green vinyl					
❑ 48-0383	Dixieland Boogie/I Got Along Without You	1950	7.50	15.00	30.00
—Originals on green vinyl					
❑ 48-0418	The Big D Boogie/From Here On	1951	6.25	12.50	25.00
❑ 48-0443	Boogie Bottom Boogie/Dear John	1951	6.25	12.50	25.00
❑ 48-0455	Waxamachie Dishwasher Boy/When I'm Beside You	1951	6.25	12.50	25.00
❑ 48-0475	Take Time to Pray/Will You Be Mine	1951	6.25	12.50	25.00

BOYD, JIMMY

45s

CAPITOL

Number	Title (A Side/B Side)	Yr	VG	VG+	NM
❑ 4967	Day Dreamer/I've Got It Made	1963	2.50	5.00	10.00

COLUMBIA

Number	Title (A Side/B Side)	Yr	VG	VG+	NM
❑ 4-152	I Saw Mommy Kissing Santa Claus/Thumbelina	1952	5.00	10.00	20.00
—Yellow-label Children's Series issue; alternate number is 90174					
❑ 4-152 [PS]	I Saw Mommy Kissing Santa Claus/Thumbelina	1952	6.25	12.50	25.00
❑ 4-183	Santa Got Stuck In The Chimney/I Said A Prayer For Santa Claus	1953	3.75	7.50	15.00
—Yellow-label Children's Series issue					
❑ 4-183 [PS]	Santa Got Stuck In The Chimney/I Said A Prayer For Santa Claus	1953	5.00	10.00	20.00
❑ 21571	Rockin' Down the Mississippi/Crazy Mixed Up Blues	1956	12.50	25.00	50.00
❑ 39696	God's Little Candles/Owl Lullaby	1952	3.75	7.50	15.00
❑ 39733	Little Train A-Chuggin'/Needle In, Needle Out	1952	3.75	7.50	15.00
❑ 39871	I Saw Mommy Kissing Santa Claus/Thumbelina	1952	3.75	7.50	15.00
❑ 39927	Early Bird/I'll Stay in the House	1953	3.75	7.50	15.00
❑ 39955	My Bunny and My Sister Sue/Two Easter Sunday Sweethearts	1953	3.75	7.50	15.00
❑ 40007	Playmates/Shoo Fly Pie and Apple Pan Dowdy	1953	3.75	7.50	15.00
❑ 40049	Marco, the Polo Pony/God Bless Us All	1953	3.75	7.50	15.00
❑ 40070	I Saw Mommy Kissing Santa Claus/Santa Claus Is Coming to Town	1953	3.00	6.00	12.00
❑ 40071	Winter Wonderland/Here Comes Santa Claus	1953	3.00	6.00	12.00
❑ 40072	Silent Night, Holy Night/Frosty the Snowman	1953	3.00	6.00	12.00
❑ 40073	The Little Match Girl/Rudolph, the Red-Nosed Reindeer	1953	3.00	6.00	12.00
❑ 40080	Santa Got Stuck in the Chimney/I Said a Prayer for Santa Claus	1953	3.75	7.50	15.00
—With Johnny Bond					
❑ 40138	I've Got Those "Wake Up Seven-Thirty, Wash Your Ears They're Dirty, Eat Your Eggs and Oatmeal, Rush to School" Blues/Jelly on My Head	1954	5.00	10.00	20.00
❑ 40181	Little Bonny Bunny/Jimmy, Roll Me Gently	1954	3.75	7.50	15.00
❑ 40218	I'm So Glad (I'm a Little Boy and You're a Little Girl)/Kitty in the Basket	1954	3.75	7.50	15.00
—With Gayla Peevey					
❑ 40253	Ma I Miss Your Apple Pie/Shepherd Boy	1954	3.75	7.50	15.00
❑ 40304	Little Sir Echo/The Little White Duck	1954	3.75	7.50	15.00
❑ 40365	I Saw Mommy Do the Mambo (With You Know Who)/Santa Claus Blues	1954	3.75	7.50	15.00
❑ 40504	I Want a Haircut with a Moon on Top/How Come	1955	3.00	6.00	12.00
❑ 40601	Reindeer Rock/A Kiss for Christmas	1955	5.00	10.00	20.00
❑ 40756	Don't Forget to Say Your Prayers/Little Dog	1956	3.00	6.00	12.00
❑ 40881	I Wanna Go Steady/Gonna Take My Heart on a Hayride	1957	3.00	6.00	12.00
❑ 41547	Dennis the Menace/Little Josey	1960	5.00	10.00	20.00
—With Rosemary Clooney					

DOT

Number	Title (A Side/B Side)	Yr	VG	VG+	NM
❑ 16126	Dusty/Jambalaya	1960	3.00	6.00	12.00

IMPERIAL

Number	Title (A Side/B Side)	Yr	VG	VG+	NM
❑ 66166	I Would Never Do That/Lazy Me	1966	2.00	4.00	8.00
❑ 66206	She Chased Me/Will I Cry	1966	2.00	4.00	8.00
❑ 66233	So Young and So Fine/I Would Never Do That	1967	2.00	4.00	8.00

MGM

Number	Title (A Side/B Side)	Yr	VG	VG+	NM
❑ 12788	Cream Puff/I Love You So Much	1959	15.00	30.00	60.00

VEE JAY

Number	Title (A Side/B Side)	Yr	VG	VG+	NM
❑ 620	All Alone/In Love In Vain	1964	2.50	5.00	10.00
❑ 686	That's What I'll Give to You/My Home Town	1965	2.50	5.00	10.00

7-Inch Extended Plays

COLUMBIA

Number	Title (A Side/B Side)	Yr	VG	VG+	NM
❑ B-1913	I Saw Mommy Kissing Santa Claus/Jingle Bells/ /I Said A Prayer For Santa Claus/Santa Got Stuck In The Chimney	195?	3.00	6.00	12.00
❑ B-1913 [PS]	Jimmy Boyd	195?	3.75	7.50	15.00

Albums

COLUMBIA

Number	Title (A Side/B Side)	Yr	VG	VG+	NM
❑ CL 2543 [10]	I Saw Mommy Kissing Santa Claus	1955	10.00	20.00	40.00
—"House Party Series" reissue					
❑ CL 6270 [10]	Christmas with Jimmy Boyd	1953	25.00	50.00	100.00

BOYD, MIKE

45s

Number	Title (A Side/B Side)	Yr	VG	VG+	NM
CLARIDGE					
❑ 413	Deep South Carnival Show/Main Street Mission Home	1976	—	3.00	6.00
❑ 417	The Leaving Was Easy/Time Wounds All Heels	1976	—	3.00	6.00
INERGI					
❑ 305	Love and Hate/Birds and Bees	1978	—	3.00	6.00
MBI					
❑ 4815	I'll Always Love You/One Kiss for Old Times' Sake	1977	—	3.00	6.00
❑ 4816	Stop and Think It Over/Whiskey	1977	—	3.00	6.00
❑ 4817	Whiskey/April's Fool	1977	—	3.00	6.00

BOYER TWINS, THE

45s

Number	Title (A Side/B Side)	Yr	VG	VG+	NM
GUSTO					
❑ 9008	Margaritaville/Oh Ain't It a Beauty	1979	—	2.50	5.00
SABRE					
❑ 4516	Three Little Words/(B-side unknown)	1980	—	3.00	6.00

BR5-49

45s

Number	Title (A Side/B Side)	Yr	VG	VG+	NM
ARISTA NASHVILLE					
❑ 13039	Cherokee Boogie/I Ain't Never	1996	—	2.00	4.00
❑ 13046	Little Ramona (Gone Hillbilly Nuts)/Hickory Wind	1996	—	2.00	4.00
❑ 13061	Even If It's Wrong/Hickory Wind	1996	—	2.00	4.00

Albums

Number	Title (A Side/B Side)	Yr	VG	VG+	NM
ARISTA NASHVILLE					
❑ 10800 [EP]	Live from Robert's	1999	2.50	5.00	10.00
—Originally issued on CD and cassette in 1996					
❑ 18818	BR5-49	1999	3.00	6.00	12.00
—Originally issued on CD and cassette in 1996					
❑ 18862	Big Backyard Beat Show	1999	3.00	6.00	12.00
—Originally issued on CD and cassette in 1998					

BRADDOCK, BOBBY

45s

Number	Title (A Side/B Side)	Yr	VG	VG+	NM
COLUMBIA					
❑ 4-45265	Born and Raised in Your Arms/Revelation	1970	2.00	4.00	8.00
ELEKTRA					
❑ 46038	Between the Lines/Happy Hour	1979	—	2.50	5.00
❑ 46507	I Did the Right Thing/Moon Fever	1979	—	2.50	5.00
❑ 46585	Nag, Nag, Nag/Rainy Florida Afternoon	1980	—	2.50	5.00
❑ 46650	I Love You Whoever You Are/Burnin' Down	1980	—	2.50	5.00
MERCURY					
❑ 73757	My Better Half/Ruby Is a Groupie	1976	—	3.00	6.00
❑ 73816	Gloria the Magnificent/Splidene	1976	—	3.00	6.00
❑ 73868	Big Black Telephone/Twiddle	1976	—	3.00	6.00
MGM					
❑ 13737	I Know How to Do It/Get Along	1967	2.00	4.00	8.00
❑ 13843	I'm a Good Girl/Old Faithful	1967	2.00	4.00	8.00
❑ 14017	The Girls in Country Music/Put Me Back Together Again	1968	2.00	4.00	8.00
❑ 14042	Every Man's a King/Trash Man	1969	2.00	4.00	8.00
❑ 14078	Crying at the Mirror/Successful Story	1969	2.00	4.00	8.00
RCA					
❑ PB-13529	Dolly Parton's Hits/It Took a Long Time (To Get Me Over You)	1983	—	2.50	5.00
❑ PB-13871	Willie Where Are You/Avalanche of Romance	1984	—	2.00	4.00

Albums

Number	Title (A Side/B Side)	Yr	VG	VG+	NM
ELEKTRA					
❑ 6E-187	Between the Lines	1979	3.00	6.00	12.00
❑ 6E-224	Love Bomb	1980	3.00	6.00	12.00
RCA VICTOR					
❑ MHL1-8524 [EP]	Hardpore Cornography	1984	2.00	4.00	8.00

BRADFORD, KEITH

45s

Number	Title (A Side/B Side)	Yr	VG	VG+	NM
MU-SOUND					
❑ 421	Lonely People/A Whole Lot of Crying	1978	—	3.00	6.00
SCORPION					
❑ 0572	Lonely Coming Down/A Whole Lot of Crying	1979	—	3.00	6.00

BRADING, SUSIE

45s

Number	Title (A Side/B Side)	Yr	VG	VG+	NM
RIDDLE					
❑ 1010	Dream Lover/Standing on the Outside	1984	—	3.00	6.00

BRADLEY, OWEN

45s

Number	Title (A Side/B Side)	Yr	VG	VG+	NM
CORAL					
❑ 9-60208	Remember Me/Let's Go to Church (Next Sunday Morning)	1950	5.00	10.00	20.00
❑ 9-60236	Sit Down and Tell Me Where I Stand with You/Black and White Rag	1950	5.00	10.00	20.00
❑ 9-60240	Close Your Pretty Eyes/Say When	1950	5.00	10.00	20.00
❑ 9-60241	I Wanna Be Loved/La Vie En Rose	1950	5.00	10.00	20.00
❑ 9-60273	Silent Night/Oh Holy Night	1950	5.00	10.00	20.00
❑ 9-60274	The FIrst Nowell/Joy to the World	1950	5.00	10.00	20.00
❑ 9-60275	Deck the Halls/Ring Out the Bells	1950	5.00	10.00	20.00
❑ 9-60276	O Come All Ye Faithful/The Birthday of the King	1950	5.00	10.00	20.00
❑ 9-60293	Is There Somebody Else/I'll Never Be Free	1950	5.00	10.00	20.00
❑ 9-60294	Boulevard of Broken Dreams/Petite Waltz	1950	5.00	10.00	20.00
❑ 9-60314	Wabash Blues/Written Guarantee	1950	5.00	10.00	20.00
❑ 9-60360	I Give You My Love/Little Small Town Girl	1951	5.00	10.00	20.00
❑ 9-60373	Be My Love/Sentimental Music	1951	5.00	10.00	20.00
❑ 9-60378	Blue Danube Waltz/Wine, Women and Song	1951	3.75	7.50	15.00
❑ 9-60379	Voices of Spring/Vienna Life	1951	3.75	7.50	15.00
❑ 9-60380	Tales from the Vienna Woods/An Artist's Life	1951	3.75	7.50	15.00
❑ 9-60381	You and You/The Emperor Waltz	1951	3.75	7.50	15.00
❑ 9-60428	Just Live for Today/Goodnight, Sweet Princess	1951	3.75	7.50	15.00
❑ 9-60434	Blue Eyes Cryin' in the Rain/Strange Little Girl	1951	5.00	10.00	20.00
❑ 9-60443	Vienna Life/Voices of Spring	1951	3.75	7.50	15.00
❑ 9-60458	Black Maria/Satins and Lace	1951	3.75	7.50	15.00
❑ 9-60464	Lazy River/Rose of Rio Grande	1951	3.75	7.50	15.00
❑ 9-60465	Missouri Waltz/Beautiful Ohio	1951	3.75	7.50	15.00
❑ 9-60466	Swanee River/Down the River of Golden Dreams	1951	3.75	7.50	15.00
❑ 9-60467	Moonlight on the Colorado/On the Banks of the Wabash	1951	3.75	7.50	15.00
❑ 9-60507	Mister Honky Tonk/Didn't Yer Mother Ever Tell Ya Nothin'	1951	5.00	10.00	20.00
❑ 9-60539	The Girls We Never Did Wed/Dreamy Melody	1951	3.75	7.50	15.00
❑ 9-60564	Uncle Mistletoe/Merry Christmas Rhumba	1951	5.00	10.00	20.00
❑ 9-60565	Tennessee Blues/Aboard the Sentimental Train	1951	5.00	10.00	20.00
❑ 9-60594	Santa Claus Looks Like My Daddy/Uncle Mistletoe	1951	5.00	10.00	20.00
❑ 9-60601	Singin' in the Rain/The Wedding of the Painted Doll	1951	3.75	7.50	15.00
❑ 9-60602	You Are My Lucky Star/All I Do Is Dream of You	1951	3.75	7.50	15.00
❑ 9-60603	I've Got a Feelin' You're Foolin'/Should I?	1951	3.75	7.50	15.00
❑ 9-60604	Fit as a Fiddle/Beautiful Girl	1951	3.75	7.50	15.00
❑ 9-60734	Horse and Buggy/Phantom Regiment	1952	3.00	6.00	12.00
❑ 9-60735	The Penny-Whistle Song/Plink, Plank, Plunk	1952	3.00	6.00	12.00
❑ 9-60836	O Come All Ye Faithful/Blest Be the Tie That Binds	1952	3.75	7.50	15.00
❑ 9-60837	The Church's One Foundation/My Faith Looks Up to Thee	1952	3.75	7.50	15.00
❑ 9-60838	Holy, Holy, Holy/Fight the Good Fight	1952	3.75	7.50	15.00
❑ 9-60839	Come Thou Almighty King/Now the Day Is Over	1952	3.75	7.50	15.00
❑ 9-60892	I Will Still Love You/Beyond the Border	1952	3.00	6.00	12.00
❑ 9-60908	Baby, I'm Lost Without You/My Heart's Desire	1953	3.00	6.00	12.00
DECCA					
❑ 28732	Granada/Breeze	1953	3.00	6.00	12.00
❑ 29216	Happy Days and Lonely Nights/Friends and Neighbors	1954	3.00	6.00	12.00
❑ 29233	Melancholy Serenade/I'm Afraid to Say Goodbye	1954	3.00	6.00	12.00
❑ 29816	Moritat/Lights of Vienna	1956	3.00	6.00	12.00
❑ 30083	The Italian Theme/Polka Dots and Moonbeams	1956	3.00	6.00	12.00
❑ 30363	White Silver Sands/Midnight Blues	1957	3.00	6.00	12.00
❑ 30450	Dansero/The Hour of Parting	1957	3.00	6.00	12.00
—With the Anita Kerr Singers					
❑ 30564	Sentimental Dream/Big Guitar	1958	3.00	6.00	12.00
❑ 30702	Trudie/Warwind	1958	3.00	6.00	12.00
❑ 30848	Simple Simon/Little Beaver	1959	3.00	6.00	12.00

Selected 78s

Number	Title (A Side/B Side)	Yr	VG	VG+	NM
CORAL					
❑ 60107	Blues, Stay Away from Me/Fairy Tales	1949	3.75	7.50	15.00
❑ 60129	Pickin' 'Em Up/There's a Little White House	1949	3.75	7.50	15.00
❑ 60138	You're Just a Flower/Greatest Mistake of My Life	1949	3.75	7.50	15.00
❑ 60152	The Gods Were Angry with Me/When I Take My Vacation in Heaven	1950	3.75	7.50	15.00
❑ 60159	The Third Man Theme/The Cafe Mozart Waltz	1950	3.75	7.50	15.00

Albums

Number	Title (A Side/B Side)	Yr	VG	VG+	NM
CORAL					
❑ CRL 56012 [10]	Christmas Time	1950	20.00	40.00	80.00
❑ CRL 56022 [10]	Strauss Waltzes	195?	15.00	30.00	60.00
❑ CRL 56035 [10]	Lazy River	195?	15.00	30.00	60.00
❑ CRL 56047 [10]	Singin' in the Rain	195?	15.00	30.00	60.00
❑ CRL 56065 [10]	Cherished Hymns	195?	15.00	30.00	60.00
❑ CRL 57071 [M]	Organ and Chimes Played by Owen Bradley	1956	7.50	15.00	30.00
DECCA					
❑ DL 4078 [M]	Paradise Island	1960	5.00	10.00	20.00
❑ DL 8652 [M]	Joyous Bells of Christmas	1957	7.50	15.00	30.00
❑ DL 8724 [M]	Bandstand Hop	1958	7.50	15.00	30.00
❑ DL 8868 [M]	Big Guitar	1958	7.50	15.00	30.00
❑ DL 74078 [S]	Paradise Island	1960	6.25	12.50	25.00
❑ DL 78868 [S]	Big Guitar	1958	10.00	20.00	40.00

BRADSHAW, CAROLYN

45s

Number	Title (A Side/B Side)	Yr	VG	VG+	NM
ABBOTT					
❑ 141	Marriage of Mexican Joe/Baby, Then You're Catching On	1953	7.50	15.00	30.00
❑ 151	Say No, No, No/It's Still the Same	1954	6.25	12.50	25.00
❑ 153	A Man on the Loose/Flavor of the Rio	1954	6.25	12.50	25.00

BRADSHAW, TERRY

45s

Number	Title (A Side/B Side)	Yr	VG	VG+	NM
BENSON					
❑ 2001	Until You/Dimestore Jesus	1980	—	3.00	6.00
❑ 2001 [PS]	Until You/Dimestore Jesus	1980	2.50	5.00	10.00
HEART WARMING					
❑ 5395	Getting Free/Less and Less	1983	—	3.00	6.00
MERCURY					
❑ 73760	I'm So Lonesome I Could Cry/Making Plans	1976	—	2.50	5.00
❑ 73808	The Last Word in Lonesome Is Me/Less and Less	1976	—	2.50	5.00
❑ 73856	Take These Chains from My Heart/Here Comes My Baby Back Again	1976	—	2.50	5.00

Number	Title (A Side/B Side)	Yr	VG	VG+	NM
Albums					
BENSON					
❑ R-3702	Until You	1980	3.75	7.50	15.00
HEART WARMING					
❑ 3735	Here in My Heart	1983	3.75	7.50	15.00
MERCURY					
❑ SRM-1-1073	I'm So Lonesome I Could Cry	1976	5.00	10.00	20.00

BRANDON, T.C.

Number	Title (A Side/B Side)	Yr	VG	VG+	NM
45s					
BEAR					
❑ 2006	You Belong to Me/(B-side unknown)	1989	—	3.00	6.00
❑ 2006 [PS]	You Belong to Me/(B-side unknown)	1989	2.00	4.00	8.00

BRANDT, PAUL

Number	Title (A Side/B Side)	Yr	VG	VG+	NM
45s					
REPRISE					
❑ 7-16926	It's a Beautiful Thing/Add 'Em All Up	1999	—	—	3.00
❑ 7-16985	That's the Truth/Let's Live It Up	1999	—	—	3.00
❑ 7-17381	Take It from Me/12-Step Recovery	1997	—	2.00	4.00
❑ 7-17493	I Meant to Do That/All Over Me	1996	—	2.00	4.00
❑ 7-17616	I Do/One and Only Love	1996	2.00	4.00	8.00
❑ 7-17683	My Heart Has a History/Calm Before the Storm	1996	—	2.50	5.00

BRANE, SHERRY

Number	Title (A Side/B Side)	Yr	VG	VG+	NM
45s					
E.I.O.					
❑ 1129	Falling in Trouble Again/I'm Gonna Make You Love Me	1980	—	3.00	6.00
MMI					
❑ 1030	Stop! In the Name of Love/(B-side unknown)	1979	—	3.00	6.00
OAK					
❑ 1013	It's My Party/(B-side unknown)	1978	—	3.00	6.00
TEJAS					
❑ 1015	Little Girls Need Daddies/I'm Gonna Make You Love Me	1980	—	3.00	6.00

BRANNON, KIPPI

Number	Title (A Side/B Side)	Yr	VG	VG+	NM
45s					
CURB/UNIVERSAL					
❑ 56092	I'd Be with You/Daddy's Little Girl	1997	—	—	3.00
MCA					
❑ 51166	Dreamin'/Slowly	1982	—	2.00	4.00
❑ 52023	If I Could See You Tonight/I'm So Afraid of Losing You Again	1982	—	2.00	4.00
❑ 52096	He Don't Make Me Cry/Piece of My Heart	1982	—	2.00	4.00
❑ 52202	B.Y.O.B./In My Dreams	1983	—	2.00	4.00

BREAKFAST BARRY

See BARRY GRANT.

BRENNAN, WALTER

Number	Title (A Side/B Side)	Yr	VG	VG+	NM
45s					
DOT					
❑ 16066	Dutchman's Gold/Back to the Farm	1960	3.00	6.00	12.00
❑ 16066 [PS]	Dutchman's Gold/Back to the Farm	1960	5.00	10.00	20.00
❑ 16136	Space Mice/The Thievin' Stranger	1960	3.00	6.00	12.00
❑ 16348	Tribute to a Dog/Life Gets Tee-Jus Don't It	1962	3.00	6.00	12.00
EVEREST					
❑ 19365	Noah's Ark (Part 1)/Noah's Ark (Part 2)	1960	3.00	6.00	12.00
KAPP					
❑ 2126	Grandad/Man Needs to Know	1971	—	3.00	6.00
LIBERTY					
❑ 55436	Old Rivers/The Epic Ride of John B. Glenn	1962	3.00	6.00	12.00
❑ 55477	Houdini/The Old Kelly Place	1962	3.00	6.00	12.00
❑ 55477 [PS]	Houdini/The Old Kelly Place	1962	5.00	10.00	20.00
❑ 55508	Mama Sang a Song/Who Will Take Gramma	1962	3.00	6.00	12.00
❑ 55518	Henry Had A Merry Christmas/White Christmas	1962	3.00	6.00	12.00
❑ 55518 [PS]	Henry Had A Merry Christmas/White Christmas	1962	5.00	10.00	20.00
❑ 55617	Keep a-Movin' Old Man/Waiting for a Train	1963	3.00	6.00	12.00
LONDON					
❑ 141	Yesterday, When I Was Young/Time	1970	—	3.00	6.00
RPC					
❑ 502	Knight in Bright Armor/The Soul of Big Jack Dunn	1961	3.00	6.00	12.00
UNITED ARTISTS					
❑ 0055	Old Rivers/Mama Sang a Song	1973	—	2.00	4.00
—Silver Spotlight Series issue					
Albums					
DOT					
❑ DLP-3309 [M]	Dutchman's Gold	1960	6.25	12.50	25.00
❑ DLP-25309 [S]	Dutchman's Gold	1960	7.50	15.00	30.00
EVEREST					
❑ SDBR-1103 [S]	World of Miracles	1960	7.50	15.00	30.00
❑ SDBR-1123 [S]	The President: A Musical Biography of Our Chief Executive	1960	7.50	15.00	30.00
❑ LPBR-5103 [M]	World of Miracles	1960	6.25	12.50	25.00
❑ LPBR-5123 [M]	The President: A Musical Biography of Our Chief Executive	1960	6.25	12.50	25.00
HAMILTON					
❑ HLP-159 [M]	Dutchman's Gold	1965	3.00	6.00	12.00
❑ HLP-12159 [S]	Dutchman's Gold	1965	3.00	6.00	12.00
LIBERTY					
❑ LRP-3233 [M]	Old Rivers	1962	5.00	10.00	20.00
❑ LRP-3241 [M]	The President: A Musical Biography of Our Chief Executive	1962	3.75	7.50	15.00
—Reissue of Everest 5123					
❑ LRP-3244 [M]	World of Miracles	1962	3.75	7.50	15.00
—Reissue of Everest 5103					
❑ LRP-3257 [M]	'Twas the Night Before Christmas Back Home	1962	5.00	10.00	20.00
❑ LRP-3266 [M]	Mama Sang a Song	1963	5.00	10.00	20.00
❑ LRP-3317 [M]	Talkin' from the Heart	1964	5.00	10.00	20.00
❑ LRP-3372 [M]	Gunfight at the O.K. Corral	1964	5.00	10.00	20.00
❑ LST-7233 [S]	Old Rivers	1962	6.25	12.50	25.00
❑ LST-7241 [S]	The President: A Musical Biography of Our Chief Executive	1962	5.00	10.00	20.00
—Reissue of Everest 1123					
❑ LST-7244 [S]	World of Miracles	1962	5.00	10.00	20.00
—Reissue of Everest 1103					
❑ LST-7257 [S]	'Twas the Night Before Christmas Back Home	1962	6.25	12.50	25.00
❑ LST-7266 [S]	Mama Sang a Song	1963	6.25	12.50	25.00
❑ LST-7317 [S]	Talkin' from the Heart	1964	6.25	12.50	25.00
❑ LST-7372 [S]	Gunfight at the O.K. Corral	1964	6.25	12.50	25.00
LONDON					
❑ PS 577	Yesterday, When I Was Young	1970	3.75	7.50	15.00
R.P.C.					
❑ 108S [S]	By the Fireside	1961	10.00	20.00	40.00
❑ 108 [M]	By the Fireside	1961	7.50	15.00	30.00
SUNSET					
❑ SUM-1100 [M]	Country Heart	1966	3.00	6.00	12.00
❑ SUS-5100 [S]	Country Heart	1966	3.00	6.00	12.00
❑ SUS-5269	God and Country	1970	2.50	5.00	10.00
UNITED ARTISTS					
❑ UA-LA438-E	The Very Best of Walter Brennan	1975	3.00	6.00	12.00

BRENNEN, JOHN

Number	Title (A Side/B Side)	Yr	VG	VG+	NM
45s					
MERCURY					
❑ 862012-7	Moonlight and Magnolias/Wild Horses in Her Eyes	1993	—	—	3.00
❑ 862344-7	Savin' the Best for Last/Never Say Never Again	1993	—	—	3.00

BRENTWOOD

Number	Title (A Side/B Side)	Yr	VG	VG+	NM
45s					
HOT SCHATZ					
❑ 0051	Love the One You're With/(B-side unknown)	1983	—	3.00	6.00
❑ 0052	Anything for Your Love/(B-side unknown)	1984	—	3.00	6.00

BRESH, THOM, AND LANE BRODY

Also see TOM BRESH; LANE BRODY.

Number	Title (A Side/B Side)	Yr	VG	VG+	NM
45s					
LIBERTY					
❑ 1487	When It Comes to Love/Somebody Like You	1982	—	2.00	4.00

BRESH, TOM

He sometimes recorded as "Thom Bresh"; except for his duet with Lane Brody, which is above, they are included below.

Number	Title (A Side/B Side)	Yr	VG	VG+	NM
45s					
ABC					
❑ 12352	Ways of a Woman in Love/Huckleberry Week-End	1978	—	2.00	4.00
❑ 12389	First Encounter of a Close Kind/A Woman Who Will	1978	—	2.00	4.00
ABC DOT					
❑ 17703	Until I Met You/Wonder What It's Like	1977	—	2.00	4.00
❑ 17720	That Old Cold Shoulder/Start All Over Again	1977	—	2.00	4.00
❑ 17738	Smoke, Smoke, Smoke (That Cigarette)/My Lickskillet, Indiana Home	1977	—	2.00	4.00
FARR					
❑ 004	Home Made Love/California Old Time Song	1976	—	3.00	6.00
❑ 009	Sad Country Love Song/While We Make Love Together	1976	—	3.00	6.00
❑ 012	Hey Daisy (Where Have All the Good Times Gone)/Where Was I	1976	—	3.00	6.00
KAPP					
❑ 2160	Apple Pie/Where Are You	1972	2.00	4.00	8.00
—B-side by D.B. Cooper					
LIBERTY					
❑ B-1502	I'd Love You to Want Me/Somebody Like You	1983	—	2.00	4.00
❑ B-1510	Whatever Blows Your Dress Up/Somebody Like You	1983	—	2.00	4.00
MGM					
❑ 14783	You're the Best Daddy in the World/(B-side unknown)	1975	—	2.50	5.00
❑ 14824	Soda Pop and Gumball Days/(B-side unknown)	1975	—	2.50	5.00
Albums					
ABC					
❑ AB- 1055	Portrait	1978	3.00	6.00	12.00
ABC DOT					
❑ DO-2084	Kicked Back	1977	3.00	6.00	12.00
FARR					
❑ FL 1000	Homemade Love	1976	3.75	7.50	15.00

BRILEY, JEBRY LEE

Also see HILKA AND JEBRY.

45s

PAID

Number	Title (A Side/B Side)	Yr	VG	VG+	NM
❑ 141	Let Your Fingers Do the Walkin'/Riders and Drivers	1982	—	3.00	6.00

BRITT, ELTON

45s

Number	Title (A Side/B Side)	Yr	VG	VG+	NM
ABC					
❑ 10819	I Still Believe/It Just Happened That Way	1966	2.50	5.00	10.00
ABC-PARAMOUNT					
❑ 10080	The Convict and the Rose/Lost Highway	1960	3.75	7.50	15.00
❑ 10121	Sioux City Sue/Taller Than Trees	1960	3.75	7.50	15.00
❑ 10677	Home Sweet Homesick Blues/Now Is the Hour	1965	3.00	6.00	12.00
❑ 10743	There's a Star Spangled Banner Waving Somewhere/Red Wing	1965	3.00	6.00	12.00
CERTRON					
❑ 10019	Step Into My Soul/Three Things I'm Not	1970	2.50	5.00	10.00
DECCA					
❑ 31568	Christmas in November/Jingle Bell Polka	1963	3.00	6.00	12.00
RCA VICTOR					
❑ 47-4324	Kiss by Kiss/The Tale the Sailor Told	1951	6.25	12.50	25.00
❑ 47-4472	Summer Kisses/Jackass Blues	1952	6.25	12.50	25.00
❑ 47-4531	The Little Boy I Knew/Don't Ever Be Afraid to Go Home	1952	6.25	12.50	25.00
❑ 47-4532	Five Glasses on a Texas Bar/(B-side unknown)	1952	6.25	12.50	25.00
❑ 47-4630	Fooling Around/I May Hate Myself in the Morning	1952	6.25	12.50	25.00
❑ 47-4694	Red Red Rose/One Drink Makes Me Happy	1952	6.25	12.50	25.00
❑ 47-4786	God's Little Candles/I'm Gonna Walk and Talk with My Lord	1952	6.25	12.50	25.00
❑ 47-4833	Rovin' Gambler/One for the Wonder	1952	6.25	12.50	25.00
❑ 47-4988	Merry Texas Christmas, Y'All/Christmas Will Be Here	1952	6.25	12.50	25.00
❑ 47-5140	Unknown Soldier/Korean Mud	1953	6.25	12.50	25.00
❑ 47-5251	Broken Wings/Cannonball Yodel	1953	6.25	12.50	25.00
❑ 47-5402	Maybe I Was Wrong/I Feel the Blues Comin' On	1953	6.25	12.50	25.00
❑ 47-5509	That's How the Yodel Was Born/My Heart Was Made for You	1953	6.25	12.50	25.00
❑ 47-5620	Sweet Leilani/If You Should Change Your Mind	1954	5.00	10.00	20.00
❑ 47-5640	Nuevo Laredo/Blue Guitar	1954	5.00	10.00	20.00
❑ 47-5795	One Way Ticket/Trailing Arbutus	1954	5.00	10.00	20.00
❑ 47-5868	To You Sweetheart Aloha/Singing Hills	1954	5.00	10.00	20.00
❑ 47-5937	Hurts Me to My Heart/Goodnight Mrs. Jones	1954	5.00	10.00	20.00
❑ 47-5996	Skater's Yodel/St. Louis Blues Yodel	1955	5.00	10.00	20.00
❑ 47-6093	I Almost Lost My Mind/Absent Minded Heart	1955	5.00	10.00	20.00
❑ 47-6232	The Alpine Milkman/Shame	1955	5.00	10.00	20.00
❑ 47-6325	Uranium Fever/St. James Avenue	1955	5.00	10.00	20.00
❑ 47-6429	One Life, Two Loves/Lonesome River	1956	5.00	10.00	20.00
❑ 47-6520	If You Should Change Your Mind/(B-side unknown)	1956	5.00	10.00	20.00
❑ 47-9503	The Jimmie Rodgers Blues/Singin' in the Pines	1968	2.00	4.00	8.00
❑ 47-9658	The Bitter Taste/My California Sunshine Girl	1968	2.00	4.00	8.00
❑ 48-0044	Maybe I'll Cry Over You/In a Swiss Chalet	1949	10.00	20.00	40.00
—Originals on green vinyl					
❑ 48-0049	Lorelie/Rainbow in My Heart	1949	10.00	20.00	40.00
—Originals on green vinyl					
❑ 48-0091	Reaching for the Moon/Two Hearts Are Better Than One	1949	10.00	20.00	40.00
—Originals on green vinyl					
❑ 48-0125	Driftwood on the River/Tears from the Sky	1949	10.00	20.00	40.00
—Originals on green vinyl					
❑ 48-0143	Chime Bells/Put My Little Shoes Away	1949	10.00	20.00	40.00
—Originals on green vinyl; reissue of 78					
❑ 48-0164	Blueberry Lane/Wave to Me My Lady	1950	10.00	20.00	40.00
—Originals on green vinyl					
❑ 48-0218	Candy Kisses/You'll Be Sorry from Now On	1950	7.50	15.00	30.00
—Originals on green vinyl; reissue of 78					
❑ 48-0339	The Stars and Stripes Forever/The Last Straw	1950	7.50	15.00	30.00
—Originals on green vinyl					
❑ 48-0378	I'm the One Who Loves You/I'll Find You	1950	7.50	15.00	30.00
—Originals on green vinyl					
❑ 48-0381	The Red We Want Is the Red We've Got (In the Red, White and Blue)/There's a Star Spangled Banner Waving Somewhere	1950	10.00	20.00	40.00
—Originals on green vinyl					
❑ 48-0408	Lost and Found Blues/My Dearest, My Darling	1950	7.50	15.00	30.00
—Originals on green vinyl					
❑ 48-0452	It Takes Two of a Kind/Then I'll Grow Tired of You	1951	7.50	15.00	30.00
❑ 48-0473	Lonely Little Robin/Lookin' Around	1951	7.50	15.00	30.00
❑ 48-0494	Rotation Blues/Cowpoke	1951	7.50	15.00	30.00

Selected 78s

Number	Title (A Side/B Side)	Yr	VG	VG+	NM
BLUEBIRD					
❑ B-8166	Just Because You're in Deep Elem/Chime Bells	1940	7.50	15.00	30.00
❑ B-8175	They're Burning Down the House (I Was Brung Up In)/Patent Leather Boots	1940	6.25	12.50	25.00
❑ B-8223	Two More Years (And I'll Be Free)/Driftwood on the River	1940	6.25	12.50	25.00
❑ B-8245	Missouri Joe/Mistook in the Woman I Loved	1940	6.25	12.50	25.00
❑ B-8430	Why Did You Leave Me Alone?/Over the Trail	194?	6.25	12.50	25.00
❑ B-8461	Dreamy Land Bay/They're Positively Wrong	194?	6.25	12.50	25.00
❑ B-8511	I'll Never Smile Again/Goodbye, Little Darlin', Goodbye	194?	6.25	12.50	25.00
❑ B-8523	Sierra Sue/Darling, What Do You Care	194?	6.25	12.50	25.00
❑ B-8666	New Worried Mind/The Precious Jewel	1941	6.25	12.50	25.00
❑ B-8701	There's So Much That I Forgot/I'll Die Before I Tell You	1941	6.25	12.50	25.00
❑ B-8777	Too Many Tears/Darlin', I've Loved Much Too Much	1941	6.25	12.50	25.00
❑ B-8818	Rocky Mountain Lullaby/Everybody Has the Right to Be Screwy	1941	6.25	12.50	25.00
❑ B-8912	Will You Wait for Me, Little Darlin'?/I'll Be in the Army for a Stretch	1942	6.25	12.50	25.00
❑ B-8946	Where Are You Now?/She Taught Me to Yodel	1942	6.25	12.50	25.00
❑ B-9000	There's a Star Spangled Banner Waving Somewhere/When the Roses Bloom Again	1942	7.50	15.00	30.00
❑ B-9023	I Hung My Head and Cried/Buddy Boy	1942	6.25	12.50	25.00
❑ 33-0517	I'm a Convict with Old Glory in My Soul/The Best Part of Travel	1944	7.50	15.00	30.00
❑ 33-0521	Someday/Weep No More, My Darlin'	1945	7.50	15.00	30.00
❑ 33-0524	Soldier's Last Letter/Goodbye, May God Take Care of You	1946	6.25	12.50	25.00
❑ 33-0529	Darling, What More Can I Do?/Don't Weep, Don't Mourn, Don't Worry	1946	6.25	12.50	25.00
CONQUEROR					
❑ 8809	New London Texas School Tragedy/(B-side unknown)	1937	12.50	25.00	50.00
RCA VICTOR					
❑ 20-1789	Wave to Me, My Lady/Blueberry Lane	1946	5.00	10.00	20.00
❑ 20-1817	Detour/Make Room in Your Heart for a Friend	1946	5.00	10.00	20.00
❑ 20-1864	Someday/The Best Part of Travel	1946	5.00	10.00	20.00
❑ 20-1873	Blue Texas Moonlight/Thanks for the Heartaches	1946	5.00	10.00	20.00
❑ 20-1927	Gotta Get Together with My Gal/Rogue River Valley	1946	5.00	10.00	20.00
❑ 20-2027	Too Tired to Care/I Get the Blues When It Rains	1946	5.00	10.00	20.00
❑ 20-2269	Candlelight and Roses/(B-side unknown)	1947	5.00	10.00	20.00
❑ 20-2367	Castle in the Apple Tree/After We Say Goodbye	1947	5.00	10.00	20.00
❑ 20-2772	Born to Lose/Peace of Mind	1948	5.00	10.00	20.00
❑ 20-3090	Chime Bells/Put My Little Shoes Away	1948	5.00	10.00	20.00
❑ 21-0006	Candy Kisses/You'll Be Sorry from Now On	1949	5.00	10.00	20.00

Albums

Number	Title (A Side/B Side)	Yr	VG	VG+	NM
ABC-PARAMOUNT					
❑ ABC-293 [M]	The Wandering Cowboy	1959	6.25	12.50	25.00
❑ ABCS-293 [S]	The Wandering Cowboy	1959	10.00	20.00	40.00
❑ ABC-322 [M]	Beyond the Sunset	1960	6.25	12.50	25.00
❑ ABCS-322 [S]	Beyond the Sunset	1960	10.00	20.00	40.00
❑ ABC-331 [M]	I Heard a Forest Praying	1960	6.25	12.50	25.00
❑ ABCS-331 [S]	I Heard a Forest Praying	1960	10.00	20.00	40.00
❑ ABC-521 [M]	The Singing Hills	1965	6.25	12.50	25.00
❑ ABCS-521 [S]	The Singing Hills	1965	10.00	20.00	40.00
❑ ABC-566 [M]	Somethin' for Everybody	1966	6.25	12.50	25.00
❑ ABCS-566 [S]	Somethin' for Everybody	1966	10.00	20.00	40.00
RCA VICTOR					
❑ LPM-1288 [M]	Yodel Songs	1956	15.00	30.00	60.00
❑ LPM-2669 [M]	The Best of Elton Britt	1963	6.25	12.50	25.00
❑ LPM-3222 [10]	Yodel Songs	1954	30.00	60.00	120.00

BRITT, ELTON, AND ROSALIE ALLEN

Also see each artist's individual listings; THE THREE SUNS.

45s

Number	Title (A Side/B Side)	Yr	VG	VG+	NM
RCA VICTOR					
❑ 47-4752	Fiddlin' Fool/Wallflower Waltz	1952	6.25	12.50	25.00
❑ 47-5178	Side by Side/Home Came a Sailor	1953	6.25	12.50	25.00
❑ 47-5322	Just for You/On and On with You	1953	6.25	12.50	25.00
❑ 48-0064	Tennessee Yodel Polka/Swiss Lullaby	1949	10.00	20.00	40.00
—Originals on green vinyl					
❑ 48-0168	Quicksilver/The Yodel Blues	1950	10.00	20.00	40.00
—Originals on green vinyl					
❑ 48-0302	Prairie Land Polka/Acres of Diamonds	1950	7.50	15.00	30.00
—Originals on green vinyl					
❑ 48-0312	Tell Her You Love Her/Written Guarantee	1950	7.50	15.00	30.00
—Originals on green vinyl					
❑ 48-0346	Ashes of Roses/Cotton Candy and a Toy Balloon	1950	7.50	15.00	30.00
—Originals on green vinyl					
❑ 48-0396	Mocking Bird Hill/Tomorrow You'll Be Married	1950	7.50	15.00	30.00
—Originals on green vinyl					
❑ 48-0405	It Is No Secret (What God Can Do)/A Little Bit Blue	1950	7.50	15.00	30.00
—Originals on green vinyl					
❑ 48-0430	Let's Sail Away to Heaven/You Missed Your Chance	1951	7.50	15.00	30.00

BROCK, CHAD

45s

Number	Title (A Side/B Side)	Yr	VG	VG+	NM
WARNER BROS.					
❑ 7-16876	Yes!/Tell Me Your Secret	2000	—	2.00	4.00
❑ 7-16895	A Country Boy Can Survive/Going the Distance	1999	—	—	3.00
—A-side with Hank Williams Jr. and George Jones					
❑ 7-16984	Lightning Does the Work/Evangeline	1999	—	—	3.00
❑ 7-17136	Ordinary Life/My Memory Ain't What It Used to Be	1999	—	—	3.00
❑ 7-17169	Evangeline/Til I Fell for You	1998	—	—	3.00

BROCK, JOE

45s

Number	Title (A Side/B Side)	Yr	VG	VG+	NM
RONNIE					
❑ 7601	Everything You'd Never Want to Be/That's the Way My Woman Loves Me	1976	—	3.50	7.00

BRODY, LANE

Also see THOM BRESH AND LANE BRODY; JOHNNY LEE AND LANE BRODY.

45s

EMI AMERICA

Number	Title (A Side/B Side)	Yr	VG	VG+	NM
❑ B-8218	Alibis/One Heart Away	1984	—	2.00	4.00
❑ B-8266	He Burns Me Up/Memory Now	1985	—	2.00	4.00
❑ B-8266 [PS]	He Burns Me Up/Memory Now	1985	—	2.50	5.00
❑ B-8283	Baby's Eyes/Anything But My Baby	1985	—	2.00	4.00

LIBERTY

Number	Title (A Side/B Side)	Yr	VG	VG+	NM
❑ B-1457	He's Taken/My Side of the Bed	1982	—	2.00	4.00
❑ B-1470	More Nights/My Side of the Bed	1982	—	2.00	4.00
❑ B-1498	Over You/My Side of the Bed	1983	—	2.00	4.00
❑ B-1498 [PS]	Over You/My Side of the Bed	1983	—	2.50	5.00
❑ B-1509	It's Another Silent Night/It's a Bad Night for Good Girls	1983	—	2.00	4.00
❑ B-1519	Hanging On/If I Were Loving You Now	1984	—	2.00	4.00

Albums

EMI AMERICA

Number	Title (A Side/B Side)	Yr	VG	VG+	NM
❑ ST-17160	Lane Brody	1985	2.50	5.00	10.00

BROKOP, LISA

45s

PATRIOT

Number	Title (A Side/B Side)	Yr	VG	VG+	NM
❑ S7-18094	Give Me a Ring Sometime/Let Me Live Another Day	1994	—	2.00	4.00
❑ S7-18585	Take That/One of Those Nights	1995	—	2.00	4.00
❑ S7-18732	Whe Needs You/Never Did Say Goodbye	1995	—	2.00	4.00

BROOKS, GARTH

Also see STEVE WARINER; TRISHA YEARWOOD. Note: The prices for the below records fluctuate wildly; they sometimes sell for a lot more than these prices, but they also can sell for less.

12-Inch Singles

CAPITOL

Number	Title (A Side/B Side)	Yr	VG	VG+	NM
❑ 13890 [DJ]	Right Now (Jason's You Want It You Got It Club Mix/Jason's Dub of Doom/You Want It You Got It Instrumental)	1999	5.00	10.00	20.00

—"Garth Brooks as Chris Gaines"

45s

CAPITOL

Number	Title (A Side/B Side)	Yr	VG	VG+	NM
❑ S7-19851	Longneck Bottle/Rollin'	1998	—	2.00	4.00
❑ B-44342	Much Too Young (To Feel This Damn Old)/Alabama Clay	1989	2.00	4.00	8.00
❑ B-44430	If Tomorrow Never Comes/Nobody Gets Off in This Town	1989	2.50	5.00	10.00
❑ B-44492	Not Counting You/Cowboy Bill	1989	—	3.00	6.00
❑ 58788	Lost in You/It Don't Matter to the Sun	1999	—	2.00	4.00

—"Garth Brooks as Chris Gaines"

Number	Title (A Side/B Side)	Yr	VG	VG+	NM
❑ 7PRO-79024	The Dance (same on both sides)	1990	3.00	6.00	12.00

—Promo-only issue; later released as stock copy on 44629

CAPITOL NASHVILLE

Number	Title (A Side/B Side)	Yr	VG	VG+	NM
❑ S7-18842	She's Every Woman/The Cowboy Song	1995	—	3.00	6.00
❑ S7-18948	The Fever/The Night Will Only Know	1995	—	3.00	6.00
❑ S7-19022	The Beaches of Cheyenne/Ireland	1996	—	3.00	6.00
❑ NR-44629	The Dance (same on both sides)	1990	2.00	4.00	8.00
❑ NR-44647	Friends in Low Places/Nobody Gets Off in This Town	1990	2.50	5.00	10.00
❑ NR-44650	Unanswered Prayers/Alabama Clay	1990	2.00	4.00	8.00
❑ NR-44701	Two of a Kind, Workin' on a Full House/The Dance	1991	—	3.00	6.00
❑ NR-44727	The Thunder Rolls/Victim of the Game	1991	2.00	4.00	8.00
❑ NR-44771	Rodeo/New Way to Fly	1991	2.00	4.00	8.00
❑ NR-44800	Shameless/Against the Grain	1991	2.00	4.00	8.00
❑ 58845	Do What You Gotta Do/A Friend to Me	2000	—	2.00	4.00
❑ 58899	It's the Most Wonderful Time of the Year/Sleigh Ride	2000	—	2.00	4.00
❑ 7PRO-79216/39	Friends in Low Places (Edited Version)/Friends in Low Places (LP Version)	1990	3.00	6.00	12.00

—Promo-only issue; the two versions were later released on 44647 (edit) and Liberty 57733 (LP version)

LIBERTY

Number	Title (A Side/B Side)	Yr	VG	VG+	NM
❑ S7-17324	That Summer/Dixie Chicken	1993	—	2.50	5.00
❑ S7-17440	Every Now and Then/Face to Face	1993	—	2.50	5.00
❑ S7-17441	The Dance/If Tomorrow Never Comes	1993	—	2.50	5.00
❑ S7-17496	Ain't Going Down (Til the Sun Comes Up)/Kickin' and Screamin'	1993	2.00	4.00	8.00
❑ S7-17639	American Honky-Tonk Bar Association/Everytime That It Rains	1993	—	3.00	6.00
❑ S7-17649	Silent Night/White Christmas	1993	2.00	4.00	8.00

—Red vinyl

Number	Title (A Side/B Side)	Yr	VG	VG+	NM
❑ S7-17802	Standing Outside the Fire/Cold Shoulder	1994	—	3.00	6.00
❑ S7-17972	One Night a Day/Mr. Blue	1994	—	2.50	5.00
❑ S7-18136	Callin' Baton Rouge/Same Old Story	1994	—	3.00	6.00

—Red vinyl

Number	Title (A Side/B Side)	Yr	VG	VG+	NM
❑ S7-18399	Much Too Young (To Feel This Damn Old)/Rodeo	1995	—	3.00	6.00

—Green vinyl

Number	Title (A Side/B Side)	Yr	VG	VG+	NM
❑ S7-18400	Two of a Kind, Workin' On a Full House/Unanswered Prayers	1995	—	2.00	4.00
❑ S7-18554	The Red Strokes/Burning Bridges	1995	—	2.50	5.00
❑ S7-56824	Somewhere Other Than the Night/Mr. Right	1992	—	3.00	6.00
❑ S7-56973	Learning to Live Again/Walking After Midnight	1993	2.50	5.00	10.00

—Red vinyl

Number	Title (A Side/B Side)	Yr	VG	VG+	NM
❑ S7-56973	Learning to Live Again/Walking After Midnight	1993	—	2.50	5.00

—Black vinyl

Number	Title (A Side/B Side)	Yr	VG	VG+	NM
❑ S7-57733	What She's Doing Now/Friends in Low Places	1992	—	3.00	6.00
❑ S7-57734	Papa Loved Mama/New Way to Fly	1992	—	3.00	6.00
❑ S7-57744	The Thunder Rolls/Shameless	1992	—	3.00	6.00
❑ S7-57765	The River/We Bury the Hatchet	1992	—	3.00	6.00
❑ S7-57883	Friends in Low Places (Live Version)/Thunder Rolls (Live Version)	1992	—	3.00	6.00
❑ S7-57892	God Rest Ye Merry Gentlemen/White Christmas	1992	—	2.50	5.00
❑ S7-57893	The Old Man's Back in Town/Santa Looked a Lot Like Daddy	1992	—	2.50	5.00
❑ S7-57894	Go Tell It on the Mountain/The Friendly Beast	1992	—	2.50	5.00
❑ S7-57994	We Shall Be Free/Night Rider's Lament	1992	—	3.00	6.00

Albums

CAPITOL

Number	Title (A Side/B Side)	Yr	VG	VG+	NM
❑ 1P-8042	No Fences	1990	10.00	20.00	40.00

—Columbia House version; cover photo is the size of CD cover

Number	Title (A Side/B Side)	Yr	VG	VG+	NM
❑ C1-90897	Garth Brooks	1989	6.25	12.50	25.00

—Non-record club edition

Number	Title (A Side/B Side)	Yr	VG	VG+	NM
❑ C1-590897	Garth Brooks	1989	5.00	10.00	20.00

—Columbia House edition

CAPITOL NASHVILLE

Number	Title (A Side/B Side)	Yr	VG	VG+	NM
❑ R 173266	No Fences	1990	12.50	25.00	50.00

—BMG Direct Marketing version has a large cover photo

Number	Title (A Side/B Side)	Yr	VG	VG+	NM
❑ C1-596330	Ropin' the Wind	1991	12.50	25.00	50.00

—Only released on U.S. vinyl by Columbia House

BROOKS, KAREN

Also see T.G. SHEPPARD.

45s

WARNER BROS.

Number	Title (A Side/B Side)	Yr	VG	VG+	NM
❑ 29154	A Simple I Love You/Give It Up	1984	—	2.00	4.00
❑ 29225	Tonight I'm Here with Someone Else/Give It Up	1984	—	2.00	4.00
❑ 29302	Born to Love You/A Little Common Kindness	1984	—	2.00	4.00
❑ 29644	Walk On/Every Beat of My Heart	1983	—	2.00	4.00
❑ 29789	If That's What You're Thinking/Every Beat of My Heart	1983	—	2.00	4.00
❑ 29958	Country Girl/New Way Out	1982	—	2.00	4.00

Albums

WARNER BROS.

Number	Title (A Side/B Side)	Yr	VG	VG+	NM
❑ 23676	Walk On	1983	2.00	4.00	8.00
❑ 25051	Hearts of Fire	1984	2.00	4.00	8.00
❑ 25277	I Will Dance with You	1985	2.00	4.00	8.00

BROOKS, KAREN, AND JOHNNY CASH

Also see each artist's individual listings.

45s

WARNER BROS.

Number	Title (A Side/B Side)	Yr	VG	VG+	NM
❑ 28979	I Will Dance with You/Too Bad for Love	1985	—	2.00	4.00

BROOKS, KAREN, AND RANDY SHARP

45s

MERCURY

Number	Title (A Side/B Side)	Yr	VG	VG+	NM
❑ 866834-7	Baby I'm the One/The Search Goes On	1992	—	2.00	4.00

BROOKS, KIX

Also see BROOKS AND DUNN.

45s

AVION

Number	Title (A Side/B Side)	Yr	VG	VG+	NM
❑ 103	Baby, When Your Heart Breaks Down/(B-side unknown)	1983	2.00	4.00	8.00

CAPITOL

Number	Title (A Side/B Side)	Yr	VG	VG+	NM
❑ B-44217	I'm On to You/River Don't Roll	1988	—	2.50	5.00
❑ B-44275	Sacred Ground/Story of My Life	1988	—	2.50	5.00
❑ B-44352	She Does the Walk On By/(B-side unknown)	1989	—	3.00	6.00

BROOKS, TED

45s

DECCA

Number	Title (A Side/B Side)	Yr	VG	VG+	NM
❑ 9-46374	The Hot Guitar/Entitled	1951	7.50	15.00	30.00

BROOKS & DUNN

45s

ARISTA

Number	Title (A Side/B Side)	Yr	VG	VG+	NM
❑ 2232	Brand New Man/I'm No Good	1991	—	2.00	4.00
❑ 12337	My Next Broken Heart/Boot Scootin' Boogie	1991	—	2.00	4.00
❑ 12388	Neon Moon/Cheating on the Blues	1991	—	2.00	4.00
❑ 12440	Boot Scootin' Boogie/Lost & Found	1992	—	2.00	4.00
❑ 12460	Lost and Found/Cool Drink of Water	1992	—	2.00	4.00
❑ 12513	Hard Workin' Man/Texas Women	1993	—	2.00	4.00
❑ 12540	Brand New Man/Neon Moon	1993	—	—	3.00

—Reissue with "Collectables" logo on label

Number	Title (A Side/B Side)	Yr	VG	VG+	NM
❑ 12563	We'll Burn That Bridge/Heartbroke Out of My Mind	1993	—	2.00	4.00
❑ 12602	She Used to Be Mine/That Ain't No Way to Go	1993	—	2.00	4.00
❑ 12636	Rock My World (Little Country Girl)/Our Time Is Coming	1993	—	2.00	4.00
❑ 12669	That Ain't No Way to Go/Can't Put Out This Fire	1994	—	2.00	4.00
❑ 12740	She's Not the Cheatin' Kind/She's the Kind of Trouble	1994	—	2.00	4.00
❑ 12770	Whiskey Under the Bridge/My Kind of Crazy	1995	—	2.00	4.00
❑ 12779	I'll Never Forgive My Heart/A Few Good Rides Away	1994	—	2.00	4.00
❑ 12790	Little Miss Honky Tonk/Silver and Gold	1995	—	2.00	4.00
❑ 12831	You're Gonna Miss Me When I'm Gone/If That's the Way You Want It	1995	—	2.00	4.00
❑ 12993	My Maria/Mama Don't Get Dressed Up for Nothing	1996	—	2.00	4.00
❑ 13018	I Am That Man/More Than a Margarita	1996	—	2.00	4.00

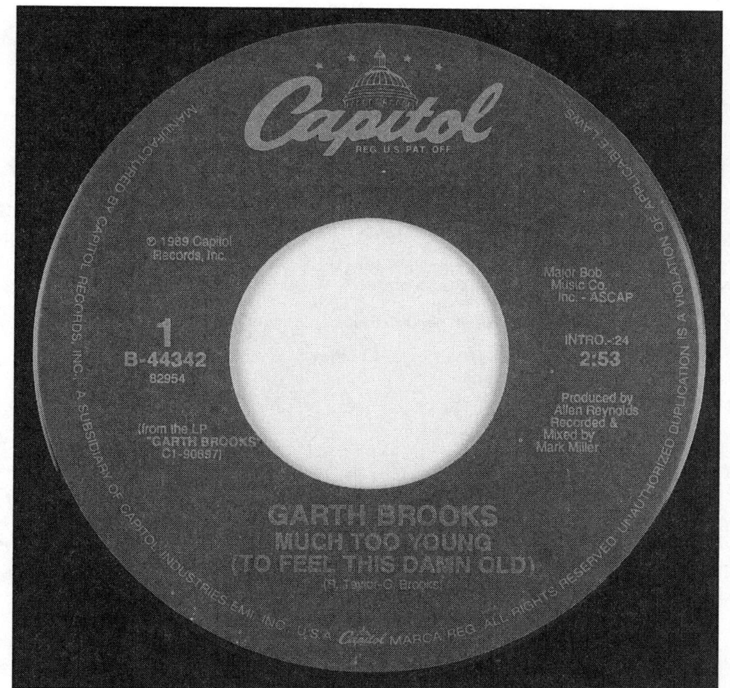

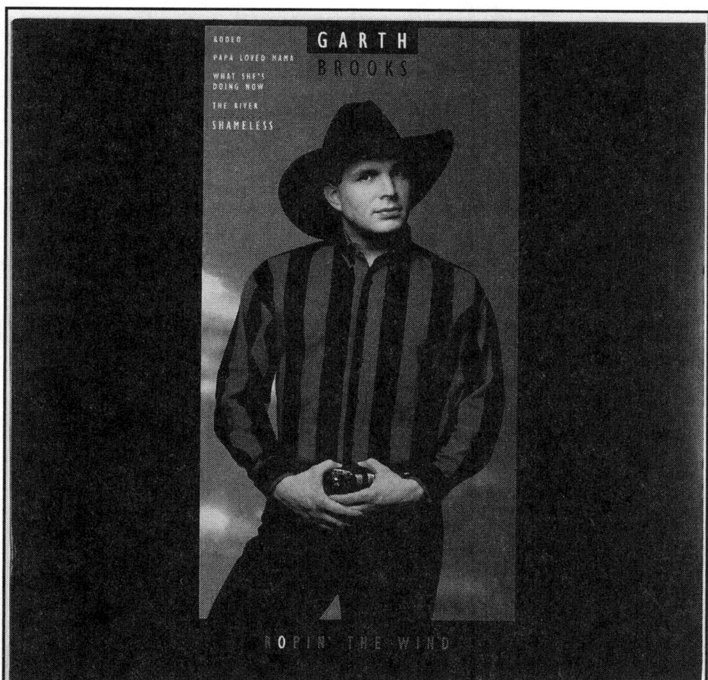

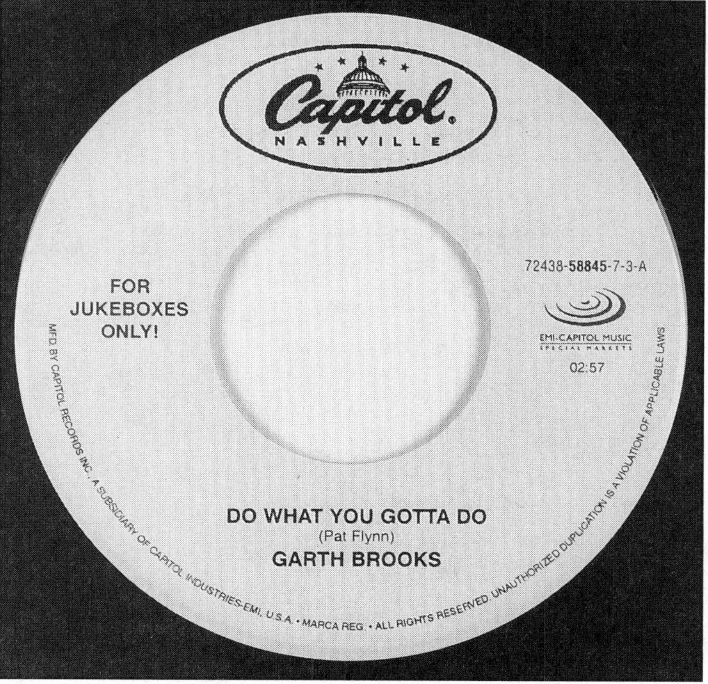

Love him or hate him, Garth Brooks' success paved the way for the phenomenal growth in country music through most of the 1990s. (Top left) His first single, issued in 1989, was "Much Too Young (To Feel This Damn Old)," a rodeo ode that also helped make Chris LeDoux a household name by mentioning the then-obscure singer in the lyrics. (Top right) His first album, released in 1989, was the only one issued on vinyl other than through record clubs. It also remains his only non-holiday project not to top the country LP chart. (Bottom left) Using the graphics from the compact disc longbox, Columbia House concocted this vinyl release of *Ropin' the Wind* in 1991. Oddly, its 10 songs are not arranged five per side, but six on side 1 and four on side 2. (Bottom right) For a couple years, no new Garth Brooks singles (other than one from the Chris Gaines project) were issued on 45. But early 2000 saw the release of "Do What You Gotta Do."

ARISTA NASHVILLE

Number	Title (A Side/B Side)	Yr	VG	VG+	NM
❑ 13043	Mama Don't Get Dressed Up for Nothing/Tequila Town	1996	—	—	3.00
❑ 13066	A Man This Lonely/One Heartache at a Time	1996	—	—	3.00
❑ 13073	Why Would I Say Goodbye/White Line Casanova	1997	—	—	3.00
❑ 13101	Honky Tonk Truth/He's Got You	1997	—	—	3.00
❑ 13116	If You See Him/If You See Her (same on both sides)	1998	—	—	3.00
—B-side listed as MCA Nashville 72051					
❑ 13143	How Long Gone/Husbands and Wives	1998	—	—	3.00
❑ 13152	I Can't Get Over You/Way Gone	1999	—	—	3.00
❑ 13164	South of Santa Fe/Your Love Don't Take a Backseat to Nothing	1999	—	—	3.00
❑ 13179	Missing You/The Trouble with Angels	1999	—	—	3.00
❑ 13188	Beer Thirty/The Trouble with Angels	1999	—	—	3.00
❑ 13198	You'll Always Be Loved by Me/Don't Look Back Now	2000	—	—	3.00

BROOKS BROTHERS BAND, THE

45s

BUCKBOARD

Number	Title (A Side/B Side)	Yr	VG	VG+	NM
❑ 115	Hurry On Home/(B-side unknown)	1984	—	3.00	6.00

BROTHER PHELPS

Also see KENTUCKY HEADHUNTERS.

45s

ASYLUM

Number	Title (A Side/B Side)	Yr	VG	VG+	NM
❑ 64436	Not So Different After All/Johnny	1995	—	2.00	4.00
❑ 64461	Anyway the Wind Blows/Lookout Mountain	1995	—	2.00	4.00
❑ 64517	Ever-Changing Woman/Watch Your Step	1994	—	2.00	4.00
❑ 64558	Eagle Over Angel/Let Go	1994	—	2.00	4.00
❑ 64598	Were You Really Livin'/Playin' House	1993	—	2.00	4.00
❑ 64614	Let Go/Everything Will Work Out Fine	1993	—	2.00	4.00

BROWN, BILLY

45s

BERNES

Number	Title (A Side/B Side)	Yr	VG	VG+	NM
❑ 101	What It Means to Be an American/Star Spangled Banner	1979	—	3.00	6.00

BROWN, COOTER

45s

REPRISE

Number	Title (A Side/B Side)	Yr	VG	VG+	NM
❑ 7-17711	Pure Bred Redneck/My Apologies	1995	—	2.00	4.00

BROWN, FLOYD

45s

Number	Title (A Side/B Side)	Yr	VG	VG+	NM
ABC DOT					
❑ 17702	Let's Get Acquainted Again/But I Do	1977	—	2.50	5.00
MAGNUM					
❑ 1002	Kiss Me Just One More Time/Fools Like Me	1983	—	3.00	6.00
MCA					
❑ 52445	Kiss Me One More Time/Just Between the Two of Us	1984	—	2.00	4.00

BROWN, GEORGIA

45s

MERCURY

Number	Title (A Side/B Side)	Yr	VG	VG+	NM
❑ 884991-7	George Jones on the Jukebox/I Hear You Knocking	1986	—	2.00	4.00
—B-side by D.J. Fontana Band					

BROWN, JIM ED

Also see THE BROWNS.

45s

Number	Title (A Side/B Side)	Yr	VG	VG+	NM
RCA					
❑ PB-10619	Let Me Love You Where It Hurts/I Love You All Over Again	1976	—	2.00	4.00
❑ PB-10786	I've Rode with the Best/Close the Door	1976	—	2.00	4.00
❑ PB-11134	When I Touch Her There/Mexican Joe	1977	—	2.00	4.00
❑ PB-11742	You're the Part of Me/Changes	1979	—	2.00	4.00
RCA VICTOR					
❑ APBO-0059	Broad-Minded Man/Helpin' You Get Over Him	1973	—	2.50	5.00
❑ APBO-0180	Sometime Sunshine/Louisiana Woman	1973	—	2.50	5.00
❑ APBO-0267	It's That Time of Night/If Wishes Were Horses	1974	—	2.50	5.00
❑ PB-10047	Get Up I Think I Love You/A Nickel for the Fiddler	1974	—	2.50	5.00
❑ PB-10131	Don Junior/Who's Gonna Love Me	1974	—	2.50	5.00
❑ PB-10233	Barroom Pal, Goodtime Gals/Nearer My Love to You	1975	—	2.50	5.00
❑ PB-10370	Fine Time to Get the Blues/Sweet Song	1975	—	2.50	5.00
❑ PB-10531	Another Morning/An Old Flame Never Dies	1975	—	2.50	5.00
❑ 47-8566	I Heard from a Memory Last Night/Just to Satisfy You	1965	2.00	4.00	8.00
❑ 47-8644	I'm Just a Country Boy/To Be or Not to Be	1965	2.00	4.00	8.00
❑ 47-8766	Regular on My Mind/The Mounties	1966	2.00	4.00	8.00
❑ 47-8867	A Taste of Heaven/Paint Me the Color of Your Wall	1966	2.00	4.00	8.00
❑ 47-8997	The Last Laugh/Party Girl	1966	2.00	4.00	8.00
❑ 47-9077	You Can Have Her/If You Were Mine, Mary	1967	2.00	4.00	8.00
❑ 47-9192	Pop a Top/Too Good to Be True	1967	2.00	4.00	8.00
❑ 47-9329	Bottle, Bottle/It Doesn't Know Any Better	1967	2.00	4.00	8.00
❑ 47-9434	The Cajun Stripper/You'll Never Know	1968	2.00	4.00	8.00
❑ 47-9518	The Enemy/I Just Came from There	1968	2.00	4.00	8.00
❑ 47-9616	Jack and Jill/Honey Tonkin'	1968	2.00	4.00	8.00
❑ 47-9677	Longest Beer of the Night/What's a Girl Like You	1968	—	3.00	6.00
❑ 47-9810	Lift Ring, Pull Open/Going Up the Country	1970	—	3.00	6.00
❑ 47-9858	Baby, I Tried/The City Cries at Night	1970	—	3.00	6.00
❑ 47-9909	Morning/How to Lose a Good Woman	1970	—	3.00	6.00
❑ 47-9965	Angel's Sunday/Every Mile of the Way	1971	—	3.00	6.00
❑ 74-0114	Man and Wife Time/Healing Hands of Time	1969	—	3.00	6.00
❑ 74-0190	The Three Bells/Beyond the Shadow	1969	—	3.00	6.00
❑ 74-0274	Ginger Is Gentle and Waiting for Me/Drink Boys Drink	1969	—	3.00	6.00
❑ 74-0509	She's Leavin' (Bonnie, Please Don't Go)/Love Is Worth the Tryin'	1971	—	3.00	6.00
❑ 74-0642	Evening/You Keep Right On Loving Me	1972	—	3.00	6.00
❑ 74-0712	How I Love Them Old Songs/Close	1972	—	3.00	6.00
❑ 74-0785	All I Had to Do/Triangle	1972	—	3.00	6.00
❑ 74-0846	Unbelievable Love/If Her Blue Eyes Don't Get You	1972	—	3.00	6.00
❑ 74-0928	Southern Loving/How Long Does It Take a Memory to Drown	1973	—	3.00	6.00

Albums

Number	Title	Yr	VG	VG+	NM
RCA CAMDEN					
❑ ACL1-0197	Hey Good Lookin'	1973	2.50	5.00	10.00
❑ ACL1-0618	The Three Bells	1974	2.50	5.00	10.00
❑ CAS-2496	Gentle on My Mind	1971	2.50	5.00	10.00
❑ CAS-2549	Country Cream	1972	2.50	5.00	10.00
RCA VICTOR					
❑ APL1-0172	Bar-Rooms & Pop-A-Tops	1973	3.75	7.50	15.00
❑ APL1-0324	Best of Jim Ed Brown	1973	3.75	7.50	15.00
❑ APL1-0572	It's That Time of Night	1974	3.75	7.50	15.00
❑ ANL1-1215	It's That Time of Night	1975	2.50	5.00	10.00
—Reissue of 0572					
❑ LPM-3569 [M]	Alone with You	1966	5.00	10.00	20.00
❑ LSP-3569 [S]	Alone with You	1966	6.25	12.50	25.00
❑ LPM-3744 [M]	Just Jim	1967	6.25	12.50	25.00
❑ LSP-3744 [S]	Just Jim	1967	5.00	10.00	20.00
❑ LPM-3853 [M]	Gems by Jim	1967	6.25	12.50	25.00
❑ LSP-3853 [S]	Gems by Jim	1967	5.00	10.00	20.00
❑ LPM-3942 [M]	Bottle, Bottle	1968	10.00	20.00	40.00
❑ LSP-3942 [S]	Bottle, Bottle	1968	5.00	10.00	20.00
❑ LSP-4011	Country's Best on Record	1968	5.00	10.00	20.00
❑ LSP-4130	This Is My Best!	1968	5.00	10.00	20.00
❑ LSP-4175	Jim Ed Sings the Browns	1969	5.00	10.00	20.00
❑ LSP-4262	Going Up the Country	1970	3.75	7.50	15.00
❑ LSP-4366	Just for You	1970	3.75	7.50	15.00
❑ LSP-4461	Morning	1971	3.75	7.50	15.00
❑ LSP-4525	Angel's Sunday	1971	3.75	7.50	15.00
❑ LSP-4614	She's Leavin'	1971	3.75	7.50	15.00
❑ LSP-4713	Evening	1972	3.75	7.50	15.00
❑ LSP-4755	Brown Is Blue	1972	3.75	7.50	15.00

BROWN, JIM ED, AND HELEN CORNELIUS

Also see each artist's individual listings.

45s

RCA

Number	Title (A Side/B Side)	Yr	VG	VG+	NM
❑ PB-10711	I Don't Want to Have to Marry You/Have I Told You Lately That I Love You	1976	—	2.50	5.00
❑ PB-10822	Saying Hello, Saying I Love You, Saying Goodbye/My Heart Cries for You	1976	—	2.50	5.00
❑ PB-10967	Born Believer/Here Today and Gone Tomorrow	1977	—	2.50	5.00
❑ PB-11044	If It Ain't Love By Now/It Takes So Long	1977	—	2.50	5.00
❑ PB-11162	Fall Softly Snow/Natividad (The Nativity)	1977	—	3.00	6.00
❑ PB-11220	I'll Never Be Free/Baby You Know How I Love You	1978	—	2.50	5.00
❑ PB-11304	If the World Ran Out of Love Tonight/Blue Ridge Mountains Turning Green	1978	—	2.50	5.00
❑ GB-11332	I Don't Want to Have to Marry You/Saying Hello, Saying I Love You, Saying Goodbye	1978	—	2.00	4.00
—"Gold Standard Series" reissue					
❑ PB-11435	You Don't Bring Me Flowers/Dear Memory	1978	—	2.50	5.00
❑ PB-11532	Lying in Love with You/Let's Take the Long Way Around the World	1979	—	2.50	5.00
❑ PB-11672	Fools/I Think About You	1979	—	2.50	5.00
❑ PB-11927	Morning Comes Too Early/Emotions	1980	—	2.50	5.00
❑ PB-12037	The Bedroom/Everything Is Changing	1980	—	2.50	5.00
❑ PB-12220	Don't Bother to Knock/Dear Memory	1981	—	2.50	5.00

Albums

RCA VICTOR

Number	Title	Yr	VG	VG+	NM
❑ APL1-2024	I Don't Want to Have to Marry You	1976	3.00	6.00	12.00
❑ APL1-2399	Born Believer	1977	3.00	6.00	12.00
❑ AHL1-2781	I'll Never Be Free	1978	3.00	6.00	12.00
❑ AHL1-3258	You Don't Bring Me Flowers	1979	2.50	5.00	10.00
❑ AHL1-3562	One Man, One Woman	1980	2.50	5.00	10.00
❑ AHL1-3999	Greatest Hits	1981	2.50	5.00	10.00
❑ AYL1-4392	Greatest Hits	1982	2.00	4.00	8.00
—Reissue of 3999					

BROWN, JOSIE

45s

RCA VICTOR

Number	Title (A Side/B Side)	Yr	VG	VG+	NM
❑ APBO-0042	Precious Memories Follow Me/After You've Had Me	1973	—	2.50	5.00
❑ APBO-0209	Both Sides of the Line/Pour a Little Water on the Flowers	1974	—	2.50	5.00
❑ APBO-0266	Satisfy Me and I'll Satisfy You/Crackerbox Mansion	1974	—	2.50	5.00
❑ PB-10002	The Man They Sweep Up Off the Floor/Delta Queen	1974	—	2.50	5.00

Number	Title (A Side/B Side)	Yr	VG	VG+	NM
❑ PB-10144	He Just Loved You Out of Me/I Can Feel Love	1974	—	2.50	5.00
❑ PB-10337	I Break Easy/Lonely Made Me Do It	1975	—	2.50	5.00

BROWN, JUNIOR

45s

Number	Title (A Side/B Side)	Yr	VG	VG+	NM
CURB					
❑ D7-76995	Venom Wearin' Denom/Surf Medley	1996	—	2.00	4.00
MGC CURB					
❑ D7-76953	Highway Patrol/Lovely Hula Hands	1995	—	2.50	5.00
❑ D7-76983	My Wife Thinks You're Dead/Sugarfoot Rag	1996	—	2.00	4.00

BROWN, MARTI

45s

Number	Title (A Side/B Side)	Yr	VG	VG+	NM
ATLANTIC					
❑ 4003	Let My Love Shine/Love Me Back to Sleep	1973	—	2.50	5.00
❑ 4011	The Single Girl and a Married Man/No Rings, No Strings	1973	—	2.50	5.00

Albums

Number	Title (A Side/B Side)	Yr	VG	VG+	NM
ATLANTIC					
❑ SD 7278	Ms. Marti Brown	1973	3.75	7.50	15.00

BROWN, MARTY

45s

Number	Title (A Side/B Side)	Yr	VG	VG+	NM
MCA					
❑ 54118	Every Now and Then/(B-side unknown)	1991	—	—	3.00
❑ 54177	High and Dry/Ole King Kong	1991	—	—	3.00
❑ 54252	Wildest Dreams/Your Sugar Daddy's Long Gone	1991	—	—	3.00
❑ 54612	It Must Be the Rain/Honky Tonk Special	1993	—	—	3.00
❑ 54727	I Don't Want to See You Again/She's Gone	1993	—	—	3.00

BROWN, MAX

45s

Number	Title (A Side/B Side)	Yr	VG	VG+	NM
DOOR KNOB					
❑ 056	If I May/Hey Cowboy	1978	—	2.50	5.00
❑ 065	Give Me a Chance to Love You/I Could Write a Book	1978	—	2.50	5.00
❑ 077	In My Little Corner of the World/Maybe	1978	—	2.50	5.00
❑ 095	Take Time to Smell the Flowers/Love Away on Me	1979	—	2.50	5.00
❑ 105	Take Good Care of My Love/Call Me Silly	1979	—	2.50	5.00
❑ 118	Reach Out to Me/(B-side unknown)	1979	—	2.50	5.00

BROWN, MAXINE

Also see THE BROWNS. Not to be confused with the R&B singer of the same name, whose biggest hit was "All in My Mind."

45s

Number	Title (A Side/B Side)	Yr	VG	VG+	NM
CHART					
❑ 1024	Never Love Again/Under the Influence of Love	1968	2.00	4.00	8.00
❑ 1046	Take Time to Know Him/I Want to Thank You	1968	2.00	4.00	8.00
❑ 1061	Sugar Cane Country/My Biggest Mistake	1968	2.00	4.00	8.00
❑ 5006	Broke Up/I'm in the Arms of a Heartache	1969	—	3.50	7.00
❑ 5169	Take It Out in Trade/Daddy, I Never Saw You Cry	1972	—	3.50	7.00

Albums

Number	Title (A Side/B Side)	Yr	VG	VG+	NM
CHART					
❑ 1012	Sugar Cane Country	1969	5.00	10.00	20.00

BROWN, MAXINE, AND GORDON TERRY

Also see each artist's individual listings.

45s

Number	Title (A Side/B Side)	Yr	VG	VG+	NM
CHART					
❑ 5020	Just Between the Two of Us/Two of a Kind	1969	—	3.50	7.00

BROWN, ROY

Best known as an R&B singer, the below single made the Billboard country charts.

Selected 78s

Number	Title (A Side/B Side)	Yr	VG	VG+	NM
DELUXE					
❑ 3198	'Fore Day in the Morning/Rainy Weather Blues	1948	12.50	25.00	50.00

BROWN, SHANNON

45s

Number	Title (A Side/B Side)	Yr	VG	VG+	NM
ARISTA NASHVILLE					
❑ 13144	I Won't Lie/A Tour of My Heart	1998	—	—	3.00

BROWN, T. GRAHAM

45s

Number	Title (A Side/B Side)	Yr	VG	VG+	NM
CAPITOL					
❑ B-5499	Drowning in Memories/Stop, You're Killing Me	1985	—	—	3.00
❑ B-5524	I Tell It Like It Used to Be/Quittin' Time	1985	—	—	3.00
❑ B-5571	I Wish That I Could Hurt That Way Again/You're Trying Too Hard	1986	—	—	3.00
❑ B-5621	Hell and High Water/Don't Make a Liar Out of Me	1986	—	—	3.00
❑ B-5621 [PS]	Hell and High Water/Don't Make a Liar Out of Me	1986	—	2.00	4.00
❑ B-5664	Don't Go to Strangers/Rock It, Billy	1987	—	—	3.00
❑ B-5664 [PS]	Don't Go to Strangers/Rock It, Billy	1987	—	2.00	4.00
❑ B-44008	Brilliant Conversationalist/Takin' To It	1987	—	—	3.00
❑ B-44008 [PS]	Brilliant Conversationalist/Takin' To It	1987	—	2.00	4.00
❑ B-44061	She Couldn't Love Me Anymore/R.F.D. 30529	1987	—	—	3.00
❑ B-44061 [PS]	She Couldn't Love Me Anymore/R.F.D. 30529	1987	—	2.00	4.00
❑ B-44125	The Last Resort/Sittin' on the Dock of the Bay	1988	—	—	3.00
❑ B-44205	Darlene/Best Love I Never Had	1988	—	—	3.00
❑ B-44273	Come As You Were/The Time Machine	1988	—	—	3.00
❑ B-44349	Never Say Never/I Read a Letter Today	1989	—	—	3.00
❑ NR-44534	If You Could Only See Me Now/We Tote the Note	1990	—	2.00	4.00
CAPITOL NASHVILLE					
❑ 7PRO-79269	Moonshadow Road (same on both sides)	1990	—	3.00	6.00
—Vinyl is promo only					
❑ 7PRO-79477	I'm Sending One Up for You (same on both sides)	1991	—	3.00	6.00
—Vinyl is promo only					
❑ 7PRO-79641	With This Ring (same on both sides)	1991	—	3.00	6.00
—Vinyl is promo only					

Albums

Number	Title (A Side/B Side)	Yr	VG	VG+	NM
CAPITOL					
❑ ST-12487	I Tell It Like It Used to Be	1986	2.00	4.00	8.00
❑ ST-12552	Brilliant Conversationalist	1987	2.00	4.00	8.00
❑ C1-48621	Come As You Were	1988	2.00	4.00	8.00

BROWNE, JANN

45s

Number	Title (A Side/B Side)	Yr	VG	VG+	NM
CURB					
❑ 10530	You Ain't Down Home/I'll Never Get Tired of You	1989	—	—	3.00
❑ 10568	Tell Me Why/There Ain't No Train	1989	—	—	3.00
❑ 76815	Mexican Wind/The One You Slip Around With	1990	—	2.00	4.00
❑ 76835	Louisville/Lovebird	1990	—	2.00	4.00
❑ 76858	Better Love Next Time/Where the Sidewalk Ends	1990	—	2.00	4.00
❑ 76879	It Only Hurts When I Laugh/Who's Gonna Be Your Next Love	1991	—	2.50	5.00

BROWNS, THE

Also see JIM ED BROWN; MAXINE BROWN.

45s

Number	Title (A Side/B Side)	Yr	VG	VG+	NM
FABOR					
❑ 107	Rio De Janeiro/Lookin' Back to See	1954	6.25	12.50	25.00
—All on Fabor as "Jim Edward and Maxine Brown"					
❑ 112	Why Am I Falling/Itsy Witsy Bitsy Me	1954	6.25	12.50	25.00
❑ 118	Here Today and Gone Tomorrow/Draggin' Main Street	1955	6.25	12.50	25.00
❑ 122	Do Memories Haunt You/Jungle Magic	1955	6.25	12.50	25.00
❑ 126	You Thought I Thought/Here Today and Gone Tomorrow	1955	6.25	12.50	25.00
RCA VICTOR					
❑ 37-7866	Ground Hog/Angel's Dolly	1961	6.25	12.50	25.00
—"Compact Single 33" (small hole, plays at LP speed)					
❑ 37-7917	Whispering Wine/My Baby's Gone	1961	6.25	12.50	25.00
—"Compact Single 33" (small hole, plays at LP speed)					
❑ 37-7969	Foolish Pride/Alpha and Omega	1961	6.25	12.50	25.00
—"Compact Single 33" (small hole, plays at LP speed)					
❑ 47-6480	I Take the Chance/Goo Goo Da Da	1956	5.00	10.00	20.00
—As "Jim Edward and Maxine Brown"					
❑ 47-6628	Here Today and Gone Tomorrow/Looking Back to See	1956	5.00	10.00	20.00
❑ 47-6629	Do Memories Haunt You/Draggin' Main Street	1956	5.00	10.00	20.00
❑ 47-6631	Just As Long As You Love Me/Don't Tell Me Your Troubles	1956	5.00	10.00	20.00
—As "Jim Edward, Maxine and Bonnie Brown"					
❑ 47-6730	A Man with a Plan/Just a Lot of Sweet Talk	1956	5.00	10.00	20.00
—As "Jim, Maxine and Bonnie Brown"					
❑ 47-6823	Money/It Takes a Long Train with a Red Caboose	1957	3.75	7.50	15.00
❑ 47-6918	I'm in Heaven/Getting Used to Being Lonely	1957	3.75	7.50	15.00
—As "Jim, Maxine and Bonnie Brown"					
❑ 47-6995	I Heard the Bluebirds Sing/The Last Thing I Want	1957	3.75	7.50	15.00
—As "Jim, Maxine and Bonnie Brown"					
❑ 47-7110	The Man in the Moon/True Love Goes Far Beyond	1957	3.75	7.50	15.00
❑ 47-7208	Crazy Dreams/Ain't No Way in the World	1958	3.75	7.50	15.00
❑ 47-7311	Would You Care?/The Trot	1958	3.75	7.50	15.00
❑ 47-7427	Beyond the Shadow/This Time I Would Know	1958	3.75	7.50	15.00
❑ 47-7555	The Three Bells/Heaven Fell Last Night	1959	3.00	6.00	12.00
❑ 47-7614	Scarlet Ribbons (For Her Hair)/Blue Bells Ring	1959	3.00	6.00	12.00
❑ 47-7700	The Old Lamplighter/Teen-Ex	1960	3.00	6.00	12.00
❑ 47-7700 [PS]	The Old Lamplighter/Teen-Ex	1960	6.25	12.50	25.00
❑ 47-7755	Lonely Little Robin/Margo (The Ninth of May)	1960	3.00	6.00	12.00
❑ 47-7755 [PS]	Lonely Little Robin/Margo (The Ninth of May)	1960	6.25	12.50	25.00
❑ 47-7780	The Whiffenpoof Song/Brighten the Corner Where You Are	1960	3.00	6.00	12.00
❑ 47-7780 [PS]	The Whiffenpoof Song/Brighten the Corner Where You Are	1960	6.25	12.50	25.00
❑ 47-7804	Send Me the Pillow You Dream On/You're So Much a Part of Me	1960	3.00	6.00	12.00
❑ 47-7820	Blue Christmas/Greenwillow Christmas	1960	3.00	6.00	12.00
❑ 47-7866	Ground Hog/Angel's Dolly	1961	2.50	5.00	10.00
❑ 47-7917	Whispering Wine/My Baby's Gone	1961	2.50	5.00	10.00
❑ 47-7969	Foolish Pride/Alpha and Omega	1961	2.50	5.00	10.00
❑ 47-7997	Buttons and Bows/Remember Me	1962	2.50	5.00	10.00
❑ 47-8066	It's Just a Little Heartache/The Old Master Painter	1962	2.50	5.00	10.00
❑ 47-8198	The Twelfth Rose/Watching My World Fall Apart	1963	2.50	5.00	10.00
❑ 47-8242	Oh, No!/Dear Teresa	1963	2.50	5.00	10.00
❑ 47-8348	Then I'll Stop Loving You/I Know My Place	1964	2.00	4.00	8.00
❑ 47-8423	Everybody's Darlin', Plus Mine/The Outskirts of Town	1964	2.00	4.00	8.00
❑ 47-8495	I Feel Like Crying/No Sad Songs for Me	1965	2.00	4.00	8.00
❑ 47-8603	You Can't Grow Peaches on a Cherry Tree/A Little Too Much to Dream	1965	2.00	4.00	8.00
❑ 47-8714	Meadowgreen/One Take Away One	1965	2.00	4.00	8.00
❑ 47-8838	I'd Just Be Fool Enough/Springtime	1966	2.00	4.00	8.00
❑ 47-8942	Coming Back to You/Gigawachem	1966	2.00	4.00	8.00
❑ 47-9153	I Hear It Now/He Will Set Your Fields on Fire	1967	2.00	4.00	8.00
❑ 47-9364	Big Daddy/I Will Bring You Water	1967	2.00	4.00	8.00

Number	Title (A Side/B Side)	Yr	VG	VG+	NM
❑ 61-7555 [S]	The Three Bells/Heaven Fell Last Night	1959	6.25	12.50	25.00
—"Living Stereo" (large hole, plays at 45 rpm)					
❑ 61-7614 [S]	Scarlet Ribbons (For Her Hair)/Blue Bells Ring	1959	6.25	12.50	25.00
—"Living Stereo" (large hole, plays at 45 rpm)					
❑ 61-7700 [S]	The Old Lamplighter/Teen-Ex	1960	6.25	12.50	25.00
—"Living Stereo" (large hole, plays at 45 rpm)					
❑ 61-7755 [S]	Lonely Little Robin/Margo (The Ninth of May)	1960	6.25	12.50	25.00
—"Living Stereo" (large hole, plays at 45 rpm)					
❑ 61-7780 [S]	The Whiffenpoof Song/Brighten the Corner Where You Are	1960	6.25	12.50	25.00
—"Living Stereo" (large hole, plays at 45 rpm)					
❑ 61-7804 [S]	Send Me the Pillow You Dream On/You're So Much a Part of Me	1960	6.25	12.50	25.00
—"Living Stereo" (large hole, plays at 45 rpm)					

7-Inch Extended Plays

Number	Title (A Side/B Side)	Yr	VG	VG+	NM
RCA VICTOR					
❑ EPA-4347	The Three Bells/Be My Love//The Man in the Moon/This Time I Would Know	1959	3.75	7.50	15.00
❑ EPA-4347 [PS]	The Browns Sing The 3 Bells	1959	3.75	7.50	15.00
❑ EPA-4352	Scarlet Ribbons/I Still Do//Love Me Tender/We Should Be Together	1959	3.75	7.50	15.00
❑ EPA-4352 [PS]	Scarlet Ribbons	1959	3.75	7.50	15.00
❑ EPA-4364	The Old Lamplighter/Oh! My Pa-Pa//True Love/The Enchanted Sea	1960	3.75	7.50	15.00
❑ EPA-4364 [PS]	The Old Lamplighter	1960	3.75	7.50	15.00

Albums

Number	Title (A Side/B Side)	Yr	VG	VG+	NM
RCA CAMDEN					
❑ CAL-885 [M]	I Heard the Bluebirds Sing	1965	3.00	6.00	12.00
❑ CAS-885 [S]	I Heard the Bluebirds Sing	1965	3.00	6.00	12.00
❑ CAL-2142 [M]	Big Ones from the Country	1967	3.00	6.00	12.00
❑ CAS-2142 [S]	Big Ones from the Country	1967	2.50	5.00	10.00
❑ CAS-2262	The Browns Sing a Harvest of Country Songs	1968	2.50	5.00	10.00
RCA VICTOR					
❑ ANL1-1083	The Best of the Browns	1975	2.50	5.00	10.00
❑ LPM-1438 [M]	Jim Edward, Maxine and Bonnie Brown	1957	12.50	25.00	50.00
❑ LPM-2144 [M]	Sweet Sounds by the Browns	1959	7.50	15.00	30.00
❑ LSP-2144 [S]	Sweet Sounds by the Browns	1959	10.00	20.00	40.00
❑ LPM-2174 [M]	Town and Country	1960	5.00	10.00	20.00
❑ LSP-2174 [S]	Town and Country	1960	6.25	12.50	25.00
❑ LPM-2260 [M]	The Browns Sing Their Hits	1960	5.00	10.00	20.00
❑ LSP-2260 [S]	The Browns Sing Their Hits	1960	6.25	12.50	25.00
❑ LPM-2333 [M]	Our Favorite Folk Songs	1961	5.00	10.00	20.00
❑ LSP-2333 [S]	Our Favorite Folk Songs	1961	6.25	12.50	25.00
❑ LPM-2345 [M]	The Little Brown Church Hymnal	1961	5.00	10.00	20.00
❑ LSP-2345 [S]	The Little Brown Church Hymnal	1961	6.25	12.50	25.00
❑ LPM-2784 [M]	Grand Ole Opry Favorites	1963	3.75	7.50	15.00
❑ LSP-2784 [S]	Grand Ole Opry Favorites	1963	5.00	10.00	20.00
❑ LPM-2860 [M]	This Young Land	1964	3.75	7.50	15.00
❑ LSP-2860 [S]	This Young Land	1964	5.00	10.00	20.00
❑ LPM-2987 [M]	Three Shades of Brown	1964	3.75	7.50	15.00
❑ LSP-2987 [S]	Three Shades of Brown	1964	5.00	10.00	20.00
❑ LPM-3423 [M]	When Love Is Gone	1965	3.75	7.50	15.00
❑ LSP-3423 [S]	When Love Is Gone	1965	5.00	10.00	20.00
❑ LPM-3561 [M]	The Best of the Browns	1966	3.75	7.50	15.00
❑ LSP-3561 [S]	The Best of the Browns	1966	5.00	10.00	20.00
❑ LPM-3668 [M]	Our Kind of Country	1966	3.75	7.50	15.00
❑ LSP-3668 [S]	Our Kind of Country	1966	5.00	10.00	20.00
❑ LPM-3798 [M]	The Old Country Church	1967	5.00	10.00	20.00
❑ LSP-3798 [S]	The Old Country Church	1967	3.75	7.50	15.00

BRUCE, ED

45s

Number	Title (A Side/B Side)	Yr	VG	VG+	NM
EPIC					
❑ 50424	When I Die, Just Let Me Go to Texas/I've Not Forgotten Marie	1977	—	2.00	4.00
❑ 50475	Star Studded Nights/Wedding Dress	1977	—	2.00	4.00
❑ 50503	Love Somebody to Death/I Can't Seem to Get the Hang of Telling Her Goodbye	1977	—	2.00	4.00
❑ 50544	Man Made of Glass/Never Take Candy from a Stranger	1978	—	2.00	4.00
❑ 50613	The Man That Turned My Mama On/Give My Old Memory a Call	1978	—	2.00	4.00
❑ 50645	Angeline/Give My Old Memory a Call	1978	—	2.00	4.00
MCA					
❑ 41201	Diane/Blue Umbrella	1980	—	—	3.00
❑ 41273	The Last Cowboy Song/The Outlaw and the Stranger	1980	—	—	3.00
❑ 51018	Girls, Women & Ladies/The Last Thing She Said	1980	—	—	3.00
❑ 51076	Evil Angel/Easy Temptations	1981	—	—	3.00
❑ 51139	(When You Fall in Love) Everything's a Waltz/Thirty-Nine and Holding	1982	—	—	3.00
❑ 51210	You're the Best Break This Old Heart Ever Had/It Just Makes Me Want You More	1982	—	—	3.00
❑ 52036	Love's Found You and Me/I Take the Chance	1982	—	—	3.00
❑ 52109	Ever, Never Lovin' You/Theme from "Bret Maverick"	1982	—	—	3.00
❑ 52156	My First Taste of Texas/One More Shot of "Old Back Home Again"	1983	—	—	3.00
❑ 52210	You're Not Leaving Here Tonight/I Think I'm in Love	1983	—	—	3.00
❑ 52251	If It Was Easy/You've Got Her Eyes	1983	—	—	3.00
❑ 52295	After All/It Would Take a Fool	1983	—	—	3.00
❑ 52433	Tell 'Em I've Gone Crazy/Birds of Paradise	1984	—	—	3.00
MONUMENT					
❑ 1118	Song for Jenny/Puzzles	1968	—	3.00	6.00
❑ 1138	Everybody Wants to Get to Heaven/When a Man Becomes a Man	1969	—	3.00	6.00
❑ 1155	Hey Porter/The Love of My Heart	1969	—	3.00	6.00
RCA					
❑ 5005-7-R	Fools for Each Other/Memphis Roots	1986	—	—	3.00
—A-side with Lynn Anderson					
❑ 5077-7-R	Quietly Crazy/Memphis Routes	1986	—	—	3.00
❑ PB-13937	You Turn Me On Like a Radio/If It Ain't Love	1984	—	—	3.00
❑ PB-14037	When Givin' Up Was Easy/Texas Girl, I'm Closing In on You	1985	—	—	3.00
❑ PB-14150	If It Ain't Love/The Migrant	1985	—	—	3.00
❑ PB-14305	Nights/Fifteen to Forty-Three (Man in the Middle)	1986	—	—	3.00
RCA VICTOR					
❑ 47-7842	Flight 303/Spun Gold	1961	3.75	7.50	15.00
❑ 47-9044	Walker's Woods/Lonesome Is Me	1966	2.00	4.00	8.00
❑ 47-9155	Last Train to Clarksville/I'm Getting Better	1967	2.00	4.00	8.00
❑ 47-9315	The Price I Pay to Stay/If I Could Just Go Home	1967	2.00	4.00	8.00
❑ 47-9394	Shadows of Her Mind/Her Sweet Love and the Baby	1967	2.00	4.00	8.00
❑ 47-9475	I'll Take You Away/Give More Than You Take	1968	2.00	4.00	8.00
❑ 47-9553	Painted Girls and Wine/Ninety-Seven More to Go	1968	2.00	4.00	8.00
❑ 61-7842 [S]	Flight 303/Spun Gold	1961	7.50	15.00	30.00
—"Living Stereo" (large hole, plays at 45 rpm)					
SUN					
❑ 276	Rock Boppin' Baby/More Than Yesterday	1957	7.50	15.00	30.00
—As "Edwin Bruce"					
❑ 292	Sweet Woman/Part of My Life	1958	10.00	20.00	40.00
—As "Edwin Bruce"					
UNITED ARTISTS					
❑ XW204	A House in New Orleans/Good Jelly Jones	1973	—	2.00	4.00
❑ XW353	July, You're a Woman/The Rain in Baby's Life	1973	—	2.00	4.00
❑ XW403	It's Not What She Done/The Devil Ain't a Lonely Woman's Friend	1974	—	2.00	4.00
❑ XW732	Mammas Don't Let Your Babies Grow Up to Be Cowboys/It's Not What She's Done (It's What You Didn't Do)	1975	—	2.50	5.00
❑ XW774	The Littlest Cowboy Rides Again/The Feel of Being Gone	1976	—	2.00	4.00
❑ XW811	Sleep All Mornin'/Working Man's Prayer	1976	—	2.00	4.00
❑ XW862	For Love's Own Sake/When Wide Open Spaces and Cowboys Are Gone	1976	—	2.00	4.00
WAND					
❑ 136	It's Coming to Me/The Greatest Man	1963	3.00	6.00	12.00
❑ 156	I'm Gonna Have a Party/Half a Love	1964	3.00	6.00	12.00

Albums

Number	Title (A Side/B Side)	Yr	VG	VG+	NM
EPIC					
❑ KE 35043	Tennesseean	1977	2.50	5.00	10.00
❑ KE 35541	Cowboys and Dreamers	1978	2.50	5.00	10.00
MCA					
❑ 3242	Ed Bruce	1980	2.50	5.00	10.00
❑ 5188	One to One	1981	2.50	5.00	10.00
❑ 5323	I Write It Down	1982	2.50	5.00	10.00
❑ 5416	You're Not Leaving Here Tonight	1983	2.50	5.00	10.00
❑ 5511	Tell 'Em I've Gone Crazy	1984	2.50	5.00	10.00
❑ 5577	Greatest Hits	1985	2.50	5.00	10.00
❑ 27068	Ed Bruce	198?	2.00	4.00	8.00
—Reissue of 3242					
MONUMENT					
❑ SLP-18118	Shades	1969	5.00	10.00	20.00
RCA VICTOR					
❑ LPM-3948 [M]	If I Could Just Go Home	1968	12.50	25.00	50.00
❑ LSP-3948 [S]	If I Could Just Go Home	1968	6.25	12.50	25.00
❑ AHL1-5324	Homecoming	1985	2.50	5.00	10.00
❑ AHL1-5808	Night Things	1986	2.50	5.00	10.00
UNITED ARTISTS					
❑ UA-LA613-G	Ed Bruce	1976	3.00	6.00	12.00

BRUCE, VIN

45s

Number	Title (A Side/B Side)	Yr	VG	VG+	NM
COLUMBIA					
❑ 4-20923	Danse La Louisianne/Fille	1952	6.25	12.50	25.00
❑ 4-20973	Sweet Love/I Trusted You	1952	6.25	12.50	25.00
❑ 4-21027	Are You Forgetting/Knocking on the Door	1952	6.25	12.50	25.00
❑ 4-21077	Clair de Lune/Je Laissez Mon Coeur	1953	5.00	10.00	20.00
❑ 4-21120	My Mama Said/I'll Stay Single	1953	5.00	10.00	20.00
❑ 4-21157	Goodbye to a Sweetheart/I'm Gonna Steal My Baby Back	1953	5.00	10.00	20.00
❑ 4-21189	Oh Ma Belle/La Valse de St. Marie	1953	5.00	10.00	20.00
❑ 4-21271	Here Is the Bottle/I Tried	1954	5.00	10.00	20.00
❑ 4-21336	Too Many Girls/Over an Ocean of Golden Dreams	1954	5.00	10.00	20.00
SWALLOW					
❑ 10137	Christmas with a Broken Heart/Christmas on the Bayou	196?	3.00	6.00	12.00

BRUSH ARBOR

45s

Number	Title (A Side/B Side)	Yr	VG	VG+	NM
CAPITOL					
❑ 3468	Proud Mary/Denver Woman	1972	—	2.50	5.00
❑ 3538	Brush Arbor Meeting/Bear Creek Dam	1973	—	2.50	5.00
❑ 3672	Alone Again (Naturally)/Washington County	1973	—	2.50	5.00
❑ 3733	Trucker and the U.F.O./Song to Mary Anne	1973	—	2.50	5.00
❑ 3733	Now That It's Over/Song to Mary Anne	1973	—	2.50	5.00
❑ 3838	On the Road to Julian/Mary's Barn Door	1974	—	2.50	5.00

Number	Title (A Side/B Side)	Yr	VG	VG+	NM
❑ 3901	Carpenter of Wood/Daddy Was a Preacher	1974	—	2.50	5.00
❑ 3968	Folk, Rock, Pop, Middle of the Road Country Singer/We Need Rain	1974	—	2.50	5.00
❑ 4118	Billy Ray/Old Fashioned Few	1975	—	2.50	5.00
MONUMENT					
❑ 45-207	Dreamin'/(B-side unknown)	1977	—	2.50	5.00
❑ 45-230	Get Down Country Music/Don't Play That Song Again	1977	—	2.50	5.00
❑ 45-247	Learn How to Love Her/Waiting for a Miracle	1978	—	2.50	5.00
❑ 45-265	This Magic Moment/All These Feelings	1978	—	2.50	5.00
❑ 8702	Emmylou/One Woman's Man	1976	—	2.50	5.00
Albums					
CAPITOL					
❑ ST-11158	Brush Arbor	1973	3.75	7.50	15.00
❑ ST-11209	Brush Arbor 2	1973	3.75	7.50	15.00
LIGHT					
❑ LS-5873	Live	1985	3.00	6.00	12.00
MONUMENT					
❑ 6637	Page One	1977	3.00	6.00	12.00
—Reissue of 34251					
❑ 7613	Straight	1978	3.00	6.00	12.00
❑ KZ 34251	Page One	1977	3.75	7.50	15.00
MYRRH					
❑ MSB-6624	Hide Away	1979	3.00	6.00	12.00
❑ MSB-6664	Hero	198?	3.00	6.00	12.00

BRYANT, JIMMY

Also see ORVILLE AND IVY.

Number	Title (A Side/B Side)	Yr	VG	VG+	NM
45s					
BIG J					
❑ 162	Ha-So/Tobacco Worm	196?	12.50	25.00	50.00
CAPITOL					
❑ F1765	Liberty Bell Polka/T-Bone Rag	1951	6.25	12.50	25.00
❑ F2057	Bryant's Shuffle/Yodelling Guitar	1952	6.25	12.50	25.00
❑ F2160	Georgia Steel Guitar/Midnight Ramble	1952	6.25	12.50	25.00
❑ F2310	Comin' On/Pickin' the Chicken	1952	6.25	12.50	25.00
❑ F2675	Sunset/This Ain't the Blues	1953	6.25	12.50	25.00
❑ F2762	Hometown Polka/Jammin' with Jimmy	1954	5.00	10.00	20.00
IMPERIAL					
❑ 66235	Lazy Guitar/Tobacco Road	1967	2.50	5.00	10.00
Albums					
CAPITOL					
❑ ST 1314 [S]	Country Cabin Jazz	1960	25.00	50.00	100.00
❑ T 1314 [M]	Country Cabin Jazz	1960	20.00	40.00	80.00
DOLTON					
❑ BLP-16505 [M]	Play Country Guitar with Jimmy Bryant	196?	6.25	12.50	25.00
❑ BST-17505 [S]	Play Country Guitar with Jimmy Bryant	196?	7.50	15.00	30.00
IMPERIAL					
❑ LP-9310 [M]	Bryant's Back in Town	1966	5.00	10.00	20.00
❑ LP-9315 [M]	Laughing Guitar, Crying Guitar	1966	5.00	10.00	20.00
❑ LP-9338 [M]	We Are Young	1967	5.00	10.00	20.00
❑ LP-9360 [M]	That Fastest Guitar in the Country	1967	6.25	12.50	25.00
❑ LP-12310 [S]	Bryant's Back in Town	1966	6.25	12.50	25.00
❑ LP-12315 [S]	Laughing Guitar, Crying Guitar	1966	6.25	12.50	25.00
❑ LP-12338 [S]	We Are Young	1967	6.25	12.50	25.00
❑ LP-12360 [S]	That Fastest Guitar in the Country	1967	5.00	10.00	20.00

BRYANT, RONNIE

Number	Title (A Side/B Side)	Yr	VG	VG+	NM
45s					
EVERGREEN					
❑ 1102	Neither One of Us/(B-side unknown)	1989	—	2.50	5.00

BRYCE, SHERRY

Also see MEL TILLIS AND SHERRY BRYCE.

Number	Title (A Side/B Side)	Yr	VG	VG+	NM
45s					
MCA					
❑ 40562	Pretty Lies/Honky Tonk Bands	1976	—	2.50	5.00
❑ 40630	Everything's Coming Up Love/Let Your Body Speak Your Mind	1976	—	2.50	5.00
MGM					
❑ 14409	One More Time/That's What Loving You Has Done for Me	1972	—	3.00	6.00
❑ 14548	Leaving's Heavy on My Mind/Coffee and Tears	1973	—	3.00	6.00
❑ 14695	Don't Stop Now/Saying What You're Spending It For	1974	—	3.00	6.00
❑ 14726	Treat Me Like a Lady/Where Love Has Died	1974	—	3.00	6.00
❑ 14747	Oh, How Happy/Come On Down to Our House	1974	—	3.00	6.00
❑ 14793	Love Song/I Love Loving You	1975	—	3.00	6.00
❑ 14812	Congratulations/Hang On Feelin'	1975	—	3.00	6.00
❑ 14842	Hang On Feelin'/This Song's for You	1976	—	3.00	6.00
PILOT					
❑ 45100	The Lady Ain't for Sale/Gone, Baby Gone	1977	—	2.50	5.00
Albums					
MGM					
❑ M3G-4967	Treat Me Like a Lady	1974	3.75	7.50	15.00
❑ M3G-5000	This Song's for You	1975	3.75	7.50	15.00

BUCHANAN, WES

Number	Title (A Side/B Side)	Yr	VG	VG+	NM
45s					
COLUMBIA					
❑ 4-44686	Warm Red Wine/Letting Me Down	1968	2.00	4.00	8.00
❑ 4-44760	A Heel That Time Will Wound/Working My Way Through a Heartache	1969	2.00	4.00	8.00
❑ 4-44878	Never Forget/Time Is Endless	1969	2.00	4.00	8.00
PEP					
❑ 114	Give Some Love My Way/Only Fools	1958	12.50	25.00	50.00

BUCHANAN BROTHERS, THE

Number	Title (A Side/B Side)	Yr	VG	VG+	NM
Selected 78s					
RCA VICTOR					
❑ 20-1850	Atomic Power/Singing an Old Hymn	1946	5.00	10.00	20.00
❑ 20-1953	Shut That Gate/Long White Robe	1946	3.75	7.50	15.00
❑ 20-2106	Left by the Wayside/Am I Still Part of Your Heart	1947	3.75	7.50	15.00

BUCK, GARY

Number	Title (A Side/B Side)	Yr	VG	VG+	NM
45s					
CAPITOL					
❑ 2316	Mister Brown/Winds Don't Blow That Strong	1968	2.50	5.00	10.00
❑ 2518	Little White Picket Fences/Love Away My Lovely	1969	2.50	5.00	10.00
❑ 2804	Wayward Woman of the World/Wildflower	1970	2.50	5.00	10.00
DIMENSION					
❑ 1029	Midnight Magic/Kentucky Lady	1982	—	2.50	5.00
PETAL					
❑ 1011	Happy to Be Unhappy/Saving All My Love for You	1963	5.00	10.00	20.00
❑ 1310	As Close As We'll Ever Be/Leave My Baby Alone	1963	5.00	10.00	20.00
❑ 1500	The Wheel Song/Suite of Sorrow	1964	5.00	10.00	20.00
❑ 1740	You're Welcome to the Club/I've Fouled Up Again	1964	5.00	10.00	20.00
❑ 1750	Back Streets of Love/Night Hawk	1964	5.00	10.00	20.00
RCA VICTOR					
❑ APBO-0151	National Pastime/Sunday's Gonna Stay	1973	2.00	4.00	8.00
❑ PB-10137	What'll I Do/Knowing That She's Leaving	1974	—	3.00	6.00
❑ 74-0479	It Takes Time/I Saw the Light	1971	2.00	4.00	8.00
❑ 74-0720	R.R. No. 2/When the Final Change Is Made	1972	2.00	4.00	8.00
❑ 74-0826	The Fool/If I'm a Fool for Leaving	1972	2.00	4.00	8.00
TOWER					
❑ 252	Before You Die/Stepping Out of the Picture	1966	3.75	7.50	15.00
❑ 292	Weather Man/Whatever's Right	1966	3.75	7.50	15.00
Albums					
TOWER					
❑ DT 5054 [R]	Country Scene	1967	3.75	7.50	15.00
❑ T 5054 [M]	Country Scene	1967	5.00	10.00	20.00

BUCKAROOS, THE

Also see BUDDY ALAN; DOYLE HOLLY; BUCK OWENS; DON RICH.

Number	Title (A Side/B Side)	Yr	VG	VG+	NM
45s					
CAPITOL					
❑ 2010	Chicken Pickin'/Apple Jack	1967	2.00	4.00	8.00
❑ 2010 [PS]	Chicken Pickin'/Apple Jack	1967	3.75	7.50	15.00
❑ 2173	I'm Coming Back Home to Stay/I Can't Stop (My Loving You)	1968	2.00	4.00	8.00
❑ 2173 [PS]	I'm Coming Back Home to Stay/I Can't Stop (My Loving You)	1968	3.75	7.50	15.00
❑ 2264	I'm Goin' Back Home Where I Belong/Too Many Chiefs (Not Enough Indians)	1968	2.00	4.00	8.00
❑ 2420	Anywhere U.S.A./Gathering Dust	1969	2.00	4.00	8.00
❑ 2629	Nobody But You/Lay a Little Light on Me	1969	2.00	4.00	8.00
—As "Don Rich and the Buckaroos"					
❑ 2750	The Night They Drove Old Dixie Down/One More Time	1970	2.00	4.00	8.00
—As "Don Rich and the Buckaroos"					
❑ 2861	Up on Cripple Creek/Guitar Pickin' Man	1970	2.00	4.00	8.00
—As "Don Rich and the Buckaroos"					
Albums					
CAPITOL					
❑ ST-194	Anywhere U.S.A.	1969	6.25	12.50	25.00
❑ ST-321	Roll Your Own with Buck Owens' Buckaroos	1969	6.25	12.50	25.00
❑ ST-440	Rompin' and Stompin'	1970	5.00	10.00	20.00
❑ ST-767	The Buckaroos Play the Hits	1971	5.00	10.00	20.00
❑ ST-860	The Buckaroos Play the Songs of Merle Haggard	1971	6.25	12.50	25.00
❑ ST 2436 [S]	The Buck Owens Song Book	1966	6.25	12.50	25.00
❑ T 2436 [M]	The Buck Owens Song Book	1966	5.00	10.00	20.00
❑ ST 2722 [S]	America's Most Wanted Band	1967	6.25	12.50	25.00
❑ T 2722 [M]	America's Most Wanted Band	1967	5.00	10.00	20.00
❑ ST 2828 [S]	The Buck Owens' Buckaroos Strike Again!	1968	6.25	12.50	25.00
❑ T 2828 [M]	The Buck Owens' Buckaroos Strike Again!	1968	10.00	20.00	40.00
❑ ST 2902	A Night on the Town with Buck Owens' Buckaroos	1968	6.25	12.50	25.00
❑ ST 2973	Meanwhile Back at the Ranch	1968	6.25	12.50	25.00

BUDDE, RUSTY

Number	Title (A Side/B Side)	Yr	VG	VG+	NM
45s					
BPC					
❑ 1002	Misty Mississippi/(B-side unknown)	1986	—	3.00	6.00

BUFF, BEVERLY

Number	Title (A Side/B Side)	Yr	VG	VG+	NM
45s					
BETHLEHEM					
❑ 3027	I'll Sign/Used to Be Sweethearts	1962	3.75	7.50	15.00
❑ 3065	Forgive Me/No Part-Time Love	1963	3.75	7.50	15.00
❑ 3078	From One Set of Arms to Another/Puzzle of Love	1963	3.75	7.50	15.00

BUFFALO CLUB, THE

Number	Title (A Side/B Side)	Yr	VG	VG+	NM
45s					
RISING TIDE					
❑ 56043	If She Don't Love You/We Lose	1997	—	2.00	4.00
❑ 56053	Heart Hold On/We Lose	1997	—	—	3.00

BUFFETT, JIMMY

45s

ABC

Number	Title (A Side/B Side)	Yr	VG	VG+	NM
❑ 11399	You Went to Paris/Peanut Butter Conspiracy	1973	—	—	—
—Unreleased? (Assigned by mistake?)					
❑ 12113	Door Number Three/Dallas	1975	—	2.50	5.00
❑ 12143	Big Red/Havana Daydreamin'	1975	—	2.50	5.00
❑ 12175	The Captain and the Kid/Cliches	1976	—	2.50	5.00
❑ 12200	Something So Feminine About a Mandolin/ Woman Goin' Crazy on Caroline Street	1976	—	2.50	5.00
❑ 12254	Margaritaville/Miss You So Badly	1977	—	2.00	4.00
❑ 12305	Changes in Latitudes, Changes in Attitudes/ Landfall	1977	—	2.00	4.00
❑ 12305 [PS]	Changes in Latitudes, Changes in Attitudes/ Landfall	1977	—	3.00	6.00
❑ 12358	Cheeseburger in Paradise/African Friend	1978	—	2.00	4.00
❑ 12391	Livingston Saturday Night/Cowboy in the Jungle	1978	—	2.00	4.00
❑ 12428	Manana/The Coast of Marsailles	1978	—	2.00	4.00

ABC DUNHILL

Number	Title (A Side/B Side)	Yr	VG	VG+	NM
❑ 4348	The Great Filling Station Hold Up/Why Don't We Get Drunk	1973	2.00	4.00	8.00
❑ 4353	The Great Filling Station Hold Up/They Can't Dance Like Carmen No More	1973	—	2.00	4.00
❑ 4359	Grapefruit-Juicy Fruit/I Found Me a Home	1973	—	2.00	4.00
❑ 4372	You Went to Paris/Peanut Butter Conspiracy	1973	—	2.00	4.00
❑ 4378	Ringling: Ringling/Saxophones	1974	—	2.00	4.00
❑ 4385	Come Monday/The Wino and I Know	1974	—	2.50	5.00
❑ 15008	Come Monday/The Wino and I Know	1974	—	2.00	4.00
❑ 15011	Brand New Country Star/Pencil Thin Moustache	1974	—	2.00	4.00
❑ 15029	Presents to Send You/A Pirate Looks at Forty	1975	—	2.00	4.00

ASYLUM

Number	Title (A Side/B Side)	Yr	VG	VG+	NM
❑ 69890	I Don't Know (Spicoli's Theme)/She's My Baby (And She's Out of Control)	1982	—	2.00	4.00
—B-side by Palmer & Jost					

BARNABY

Number	Title (A Side/B Side)	Yr	VG	VG+	NM
❑ 2013	The Christian/Richard Frost	1970	2.50	5.00	10.00
❑ 2019	He Ain't Free/There Ain't Nothing Soft About Hard Times	1970	2.50	5.00	10.00
❑ 2023	Captain America/Truckstop Salvation	1970	2.50	5.00	10.00

FULL MOON

Number	Title (A Side/B Side)	Yr	VG	VG+	NM
❑ 49659	Survive/Send Me Somebody to Love	1981	—	2.00	4.00
—B-side by Kathy Walker					

FULL MOON/ASYLUM

Number	Title (A Side/B Side)	Yr	VG	VG+	NM
❑ 47073	Hello Texas/Lyin' Eyes [by the Eagles]	1980	—	2.50	5.00

ISLAND

Number	Title (A Side/B Side)	Yr	VG	VG+	NM
❑ 562144-7	Pacing the Cage/I Will Play for Gumbo	1999	—	—	3.00

MCA

Number	Title (A Side/B Side)	Yr	VG	VG+	NM
❑ S45-17084 [DJ]	Christmas In The Caribbean (same on both sides)	1985	—	2.50	5.00
❑ 41109	Fins/Dreamsicle	1979	—	2.00	4.00
❑ 41161	Volcano/Stranded on a Sandbar	1979	—	2.00	4.00
❑ 41199	Boat Drinks/Survive	1980	—	2.00	4.00
❑ 51061	It's My Job/Little Miss Magic	1981	—	2.00	4.00
❑ 51105	Stars Fell on Alabama/Growing Older But Not Up	1981	—	2.00	4.00
❑ 52013	It's Midnight And I'm Not Famous Yet/When Salome Plays the Drum	1982	—	2.00	4.00
❑ 52050	If I Could Just Get It on Paper/Where's the Party	1982	—	2.00	4.00
❑ 52298	One Particular Harbour/Distantly in Love	1983	—	2.00	4.00
❑ 52333	Brown Eyed Girl/Twelve Volt Man	1984	—	2.00	4.00
❑ 52438	When the Wild Life Betrays Me/Ragtop Day	1984	—	2.00	4.00
❑ 52499	Come to the Moon/Bigger Than the Both of Us	1984	—	2.00	4.00
❑ 52550	Who's the Blond Stranger/She's Going Out of My Mind	1985	—	—	3.00
❑ 52607	Gypies in the Palace/Jolly Mon Sing	1985	—	—	3.00
❑ 52664	If the Phone Doesn't Ring, It's Me/Frank and Lola	1985	—	—	3.00
❑ 52752	Please Bypass This Heart/Beyond the End	1986	—	—	3.00
❑ 52849	I Love the Now/No Plane on Sunday	1986	—	—	3.00
❑ 52932	Creola/You'll Never Work in Dis Bidness Again	1986	—	—	3.00
❑ 53035	Take It Back/Floridays	1987	—	—	3.00
❑ 53360	Homemade Music/L'air de la Louisiane	1988	—	—	3.00
❑ 53396	Bring Back the Magic/That's What Living Is to Me	1988	—	—	3.00
❑ 53675	Take Another Road/Off to See the Lizard	1989	—	—	3.00
❑ 54680	Another Saturday Night/Souvenirs	1993	—	—	3.00

Albums

ABC

Number	Title	Yr	VG	VG+	NM
❑ SPDJ-43 [DJ]	Special Jimmy Buffett Sampler	1978	5.00	10.00	20.00
❑ D-914	Havana Daydreamin'	1976	3.00	6.00	12.00
❑ AB-990	Changes in Latitudes, Changes in Attitudes	1977	3.00	6.00	12.00
❑ AK-1008 [(2)]	You Had to Be There	1978	3.75	7.50	15.00
❑ AA-1046	Son of a Son of a Sailor	1978	3.00	6.00	12.00

ABC DUNHILL

Number	Title	Yr	VG	VG+	NM
❑ DS-50132	Living and Dying in 3/4 Time	1973	3.75	7.50	15.00
❑ DSX-50150	A White Sport Coat and a Pink Crustaceon	1974	3.75	7.50	15.00
❑ DS-50183	A1A	1975	3.75	7.50	15.00

BARNABY

Number	Title	Yr	VG	VG+	NM
❑ BR-6014	High Cumberland Jubilee	1975	10.00	20.00	40.00
❑ Z 30093	Down to Earth	1970	25.00	50.00	100.00

MCA

Number	Title	Yr	VG	VG+	NM
❑ 5102	Volcano	1979	2.50	5.00	10.00
❑ 5169	Coconut Telegraph	1981	2.50	5.00	10.00
❑ 5285	Somewhere Over China	1982	2.50	5.00	10.00
❑ 5447	One Particular Harbour	1983	2.50	5.00	10.00
❑ 5512	Riddles in the Sand	1984	2.50	5.00	10.00
❑ 5600	Last Mango in Paris	1985	2.50	5.00	10.00
❑ 5633	Songs You Know By Heart — Jimmy Buffett's Greatest Hit(s)	1985	2.50	5.00	10.00
❑ 5730	Floridays	1986	2.50	5.00	10.00
❑ 2-6005 [(2)]	You Had to Be There	1981	2.50	5.00	10.00
❑ 6314	Off to See the Lizard	1989	2.50	5.00	10.00
❑ 37023	Havana Daydreamin'	1981	2.00	4.00	8.00
❑ 37024	Son of a Son of a Sailor	1981	2.00	4.00	8.00
❑ 37025	Living and Dying in 3/4 Time	1981	2.00	4.00	8.00
❑ 37026	A White Sport Coat and a Pink Crustaceon	1981	2.00	4.00	8.00
❑ 37027	A1A	1981	2.00	4.00	8.00
❑ 37150	Changes in Latitudes, Changes in Attitudes	1982	2.00	4.00	8.00
❑ 37156	Volcano	1982	2.00	4.00	8.00
❑ 37246	Somewhere Over China	1984	2.00	4.00	8.00
❑ 42093	Hot Water	1988	2.50	5.00	10.00

BURBANK, GARY

45s

OVATION

Number	Title (A Side/B Side)	Yr	VG	VG+	NM
❑ 1150	Who Shot J.R.?/Honkin'	1980	—	2.50	5.00
—B-side by Tennessee Valley Authority					

BURBANK STATION

45s

PRAIRIE DUST

Number	Title (A Side/B Side)	Yr	VG	VG+	NM
❑ 112	Get Out of My Way/(B-side unknown)	1989	—	2.50	5.00
❑ 8841	Divided/Over Women	1988	—	2.50	5.00

BURCH SISTERS, THE

45s

MERCURY

Number	Title (A Side/B Side)	Yr	VG	VG+	NM
❑ 870362-7	Everytime You Go Outside I Hope It Rains/Open Arms	1988	—	—	3.00
❑ 870687-7	What Do Lonely People Do/Open Arms	1988	—	—	3.00
❑ 870687-7 [PS]	What Do Lonely People Do/Open Arms	1988	—	2.00	4.00
❑ 872324-7	I Don't Want to Mention Any Names/The Only Love You Need	1989	—	—	3.00
❑ 872730-7	Old Flame, New Fire/What We Don't Know Won't Hurt Us	1989	—	—	3.00

BURGESS, FRANK

45s

TRUE

Number	Title (A Side/B Side)	Yr	VG	VG+	NM
❑ 94	American Man/(B-side unknown)	1988	—	3.00	6.00
❑ 96	What It Boils Down To/(B-side unknown)	1989	—	3.00	6.00

BURGESS, WILMA

Also see BUD LOGAN AND WILMA BURGESS.

45s

DECCA

Number	Title (A Side/B Side)	Yr	VG	VG+	NM
❑ 31653	Raining on My Pillow/This Time Tomorrow	1964	2.50	5.00	10.00
❑ 31759	You Can't Stop My Heart from Breaking/Happy Fool	1965	2.50	5.00	10.00
❑ 31826	When You're Not Around/The Closest Thing to Love	1965	2.50	5.00	10.00
❑ 31862	Baby/Wait Till the Sun Comes Up	1965	2.00	4.00	8.00
❑ 31941	Don't Touch Me/Turn Around Teardrops	1966	2.00	4.00	8.00
❑ 32027	Misty Blue/Ain't Got No Man	1966	2.50	5.00	10.00
❑ 32105	Fifteen Days/Two Little Rivers of Tears	1967	2.00	4.00	8.00
❑ 32178	Tear Time/(How Can I Write on Paper) What I Feel in My Heart	1967	2.00	4.00	8.00
❑ 32273	Only a Fool Keeps Hangin' On/Watch the Roses Grow	1968	2.00	4.00	8.00
❑ 32359	Look at the Laughter/Sweet Promises	1968	2.00	4.00	8.00
❑ 32437	Parting (Is Such Sweet Sorrow)/Shine a Little Sun on Me	1969	2.00	4.00	8.00
❑ 32522	The Woman in Your Life/Happiness Is So Hard to Forget	1969	2.00	4.00	8.00
❑ 32593	The Sun's Gotta Shine/Only Mama That'll Walk the Line	1969	2.00	4.00	8.00
❑ 32684	Lonely for You/I Don't See Me in Your Eyes Anymore	1970	2.00	4.00	8.00
❑ 32811	Everything's Gonna Be Alright/Until My Dreams Come True	1971	2.00	4.00	8.00
❑ 32868	I See Love All Over You/A Handful of Stars	1971	—	3.50	7.00

RCA

Number	Title (A Side/B Side)	Yr	VG	VG+	NM
❑ PB-11057	Use Me/Darlin'	1977	—	2.50	5.00
❑ PB-11179	Once You Were Mine/I'm Turning You Loose	1977	—	2.50	5.00

SHANNON

Number	Title (A Side/B Side)	Yr	VG	VG+	NM
❑ 810	Feeling the Way a Woman Should/I'll Always Love the Days	1973	—	3.00	6.00
❑ 813	I'll Be Your Bridge (Just Lay Me Down)/I'll Always Love the Days	1973	—	3.00	6.00
❑ 821	Love Is Here/Sweet Lovin' Baby	1974	—	3.00	6.00
❑ 835	Baby's Not Forgotten/(B-side unknown)	1975	—	3.00	6.00
❑ 839	A Satisfied Man/(B-side unknown)	1975	—	3.00	6.00

UNITED ARTISTS

Number	Title (A Side/B Side)	Yr	VG	VG+	NM
❑ 523	Confused/Something Tells Me	1962	5.00	10.00	20.00

Albums

DECCA

Number	Title	Yr	VG	VG+	NM
❑ DL 4788 [M]	Don't Touch Me	1966	3.75	7.50	15.00
❑ DL 4852 [M]	Wilma Burgess Sings Misty Blue	1967	3.75	7.50	15.00
❑ DL 4935 [M]	Tear Time	1967	6.25	12.50	25.00
❑ DL 74788 [S]	Don't Touch Me	1966	5.00	10.00	20.00
❑ DL 74852 [S]	Wilma Burgess Sings Misty Blue	1967	5.00	10.00	20.00
❑ DL 74935 [S]	Tear Time	1967	5.00	10.00	20.00
❑ DL 75024	The Tender Lovin' Country Sound	1968	5.00	10.00	20.00
❑ DL 75090	Parting Is Such Sweet Sorrow	1968	5.00	10.00	20.00

BURKE, FIDDLIN' FRENCHIE

Number	Title (A Side/B Side)	Yr	VG	VG+	NM
45s					
20TH CENTURY					
❑ 2152	Big Mamou/There'll Be Love Tonight in My House	1974	—	2.50	5.00
—As "Fiddlin' Frenchie Bourque and the Outlaws"					
❑ 2182	Colinda/Pride, You Wouldn't Listen	1975	—	2.50	5.00
❑ 2225	The Fiddlin' of Jacques Pierre Bordeaux/ Frenchie's Cotton-Eyed Joe	1975	—	2.50	5.00
CHERRY					
❑ 644	Knock Knock Knock/(B-side unknown)	1978	—	3.00	6.00
DELTA					
❑ 11332	(Frenchie Burke's) Fire on the Mountain/Let's Go Get Drunk and Be Somebody	1981	—	3.00	6.00

BURNETTE, BILLY

Number	Title (A Side/B Side)	Yr	VG	VG+	NM
45s					
A&M					
❑ 743	Just Because We're Kids/Little Girl, Big Love	1964	6.25	12.50	25.00
—As "Young Billy Bean"; A-side written by Dr. Seuss!					
❑ 1794	Baby/Just Another Love Song	1976	—	2.50	5.00
CAPRICORN					
❑ 18525	I Still Remember (How to Miss You)/I Recovered, I Survived	1993	—	—	3.00
❑ 18751	Tangled Up in Texas/Into the Storm	1992	—	—	3.00
COLUMBIA					
❑ 02527	Let the New Love Begin/I Don't Know Why	1981	—	2.00	4.00
❑ 02699	The Bigger the Love/I Don't Know Why	1982	—	2.00	4.00
❑ 11380	Don't Say No/Rockin' L.A.	1980	—	2.00	4.00
❑ 11432	Oh Susan/Sittin' On Ready	1981	—	2.00	4.00
ENTRANCE					
❑ 7515	Broken Hearted/I'm Always Wondering	1972	—	2.50	5.00
MCA CURB					
❑ 52626	Ain't It Just Like Love/Guitar Bug	1985	—	—	3.00
❑ 52710	Who's Using Your Heart Tonight/It Ain't Over	1985	—	—	3.00
❑ 52749	It's Not Easy/Try Me	1985	—	—	3.00
❑ 52852	Soldier of Love/Guitar Bug	1986	—	—	3.00
POLYDOR					
❑ 2024	What's a Little Love Between Friends/Precious Times	1979	—	2.00	4.00
❑ 14530	Dreamin' My Way Back to You/Shoo-Be-Doo	1979	—	2.00	4.00
❑ 14549	Believe What You Say/Mississippi Line	1979	—	2.00	4.00
WARNER BROS.					
❑ 7327	Frog Prince/One Extreme to the Other	1969	2.00	4.00	8.00
❑ 19042	Nothin' to Do (And All Night to Do It)/Can't Get Over You	1992	—	—	3.00
Albums					
COLUMBIA					
❑ JC 36792	Billy Burnette	1980	2.50	5.00	10.00
❑ FC 37460	Gimme You	1981	2.50	5.00	10.00
ENTRANCE					
❑ Z 31228	Billy Burnette	1972	5.00	10.00	20.00
MCA CURB					
❑ 5604	Try Me	1985	2.50	5.00	10.00
POLYDOR					
❑ PD-1-6187	Billy Burnette	1979	2.50	5.00	10.00

BURNETTE, BILLY JOE

Number	Title (A Side/B Side)	Yr	VG	VG+	NM
45s					
BADGER					
❑ 1004	Three Flags/(B-side unknown)	1989	—	3.00	6.00
❑ 2003	Help Me Make It Through the Night/(B-side unknown)	198?	—	3.00	6.00
❑ 2005	Anything to Keep from Going Home/(B-side unknown)	198?	—	3.00	6.00
❑ 2008	Our Last Goodbye/(B-side unknown)	198?	—	3.00	6.00
GUSTO					
❑ 167	Welcome Home Elvis/Haven't Seen Mama in Years	1977	2.00	4.00	8.00
❑ 9009	The Colonel and the King/Walk Again in the Hills	1978	3.00	6.00	12.00
—May be promo only					
K-ARK					
❑ 961	Blow Smoke on a Kangaroo/Have I Told You Lately	1970	2.00	4.00	8.00
❑ 968	Sufferin'/Fickle Hearted Fool	1970	2.00	4.00	8.00

BURNETTE, DORSEY

Also see DORSEY AND JOHNNY BURNETTE.

Number	Title (A Side/B Side)	Yr	VG	VG+	NM
45s					
ABBOTT					
❑ 188	Let's Fall in Love/The Devil's Queen	1956	12.50	25.00	50.00
❑ 190	At a Distance/Jungle Magic	1957	12.50	25.00	50.00
CALLIOPE					
❑ 8004	Things I Treasure/One Mornin'	1977	—	3.00	6.00
❑ 8012	Soon As I Touched Her/Dear Hearted Children	1977	—	3.00	6.00
CAPITOL					
❑ 3073	New Orleans Woman/After the Long Drive Home	1971	—	2.50	5.00
❑ 3190	Shelby County Penal Farm/Children of the Universe	1971	—	2.50	5.00
❑ 3307	In the Spring (The Roses Always Turn Red)/The Same Old You, The Same Old Me	1972	—	2.50	5.00
❑ 3404	I Just Couldn't Let Her Walk Away/Church Bells	1972	—	2.50	5.00
❑ 3463	Cry Mama/Lonely to Be Alone	1972	—	2.50	5.00
❑ 3529	I Let Another Good One Get Away/Take Your Weapons, Lay 'Em Down	1973	—	2.50	5.00
❑ 3588	Keep Out of My Dreams/Mama, Mama	1973	—	2.50	5.00
❑ 3678	Darlin' (Don't Come Back)/Sweet Lovin' Woman	1973	—	2.50	5.00
❑ 3796	It Happens Every Time/Mr. Jukebox, Sing a Lullaby	1973	—	2.50	5.00
❑ 3829	Bob, All the Playboys, and Me/The Bootleggers	1974	—	2.50	5.00
❑ 3887	Daddy Loves You Honey/True Love Means Forgiving	1974	—	2.50	5.00
❑ 3963	What Ladies Can Do (When They Want To)/ Tangerine	1974	—	2.50	5.00
CEE-JAM					
❑ 16	Bertha Lou/'Til the Law Says Stop	1957	20.00	40.00	80.00
DOT					
❑ 16230	Rainin' in My Heart/A Full House	1961	4.00	8.00	16.00
❑ 16265	The Feminine Touch/Sad Boy	1961	4.00	8.00	16.00
❑ 16305	A Country Boy in the Army/A Dying Ember	1961	4.00	8.00	16.00
ELEKTRA					
❑ 46513	Here I Go Again/What Would It Profit Me	1979	—	2.00	4.00
❑ 46586	B.J. Kick-a-Beaux/What Would It Profit Me	1980	—	2.00	4.00
ERA					
❑ 3012	(There Was a)Tall Oak Tree/Juarez Town	1960	5.00	10.00	20.00
❑ 3019	Hey Little One/Big Rock Candy Mountain	1960	4.00	8.00	16.00
❑ 3025	The Ghost of Billy Malloo/Red Roses	1960	4.00	8.00	16.00
❑ 3033	The River and the Mountain/This Hotel	1960	4.00	8.00	16.00
❑ 3033 [PS]	The River and the Mountain/This Hotel	1960	10.00	20.00	40.00
❑ 3041	Hard Rock Mine/(It's No) Sin	1961	4.00	8.00	16.00
❑ 3045	Great Shakin' Fever/That's Me Without You	1961	4.00	8.00	16.00
HAPPY TIGER					
❑ 546	To Be a Man/Fly Away and Hurry Home	1970	—	3.00	6.00
❑ 563	One Lump Sum/Call Me Lowdown	1970	—	3.00	6.00
HICKORY					
❑ 1458	The House That Jack Built/Ain't That Fine	1967	2.00	4.00	8.00
IMPERIAL					
❑ 5561	Try/You Came as a Miracle	1959	6.25	12.50	25.00
❑ 5597	Lonely Train/Misery	1959	6.25	12.50	25.00
❑ 5668	Way in the Middle of the Night/Your Love	1960	6.25	12.50	25.00
❑ 5756	House with a Tin Roof Top/Circle Rock	1961	6.25	12.50	25.00
❑ 5987	House with a Tin Roof Top/Circle Rock	1963	3.75	7.50	15.00
LIBERTY					
❑ 56087	The Greatest Love/Thin Little Simple Little Plain Little Girl	1969	—	3.00	6.00
MEL-O-DY					
❑ 113	Little Acorn/Cold As Usual	1964	3.75	7.50	15.00
❑ 116	Jimmy Brown/Everybody's Angel	1964	3.75	7.50	15.00
❑ 118	Long Long Time Ago/Ever Since the World Began	1964	3.75	7.50	15.00
MELODYLAND					
❑ 6007	Molly (I Ain't Gettin' Any Younger)/She's Feeling Low	1975	—	2.50	5.00
❑ 6019	Lyin' in Her Arms Again/Doggone the Dogs	1975	—	2.50	5.00
❑ 6031	Ain't No Heartbreak/I Dreamed I Saw	1976	—	2.50	5.00
MERCURY					
❑ 72546	To Remember/In the Morning	1966	—	—	—
—Unreleased?					
MUSIC FACTORY					
❑ 417	I'll Walk Away/Son, You've Got to Make It Alone	1968	2.00	4.00	8.00
REPRISE					
❑ 0246	Four for Texas/Foolish Pride	1963	3.75	7.50	15.00
❑ 0246 [PS]	Four for Texas/Foolish Pride	1963	10.00	20.00	40.00
❑ 20093	Castle in the Sky/Boys Keep Hanging Around	1962	3.75	7.50	15.00
❑ 20121	Darling Jane/I'm a Waitin' For Ya Baby	1962	3.75	7.50	15.00
❑ 20177	Invisible Chains/Pebbles	1963	3.75	7.50	15.00
❑ 20208	One of the Lonely/Where's the Girl	1963	3.75	7.50	15.00
SMASH					
❑ 2029	To Remember/In the Morning	1966	2.50	5.00	10.00
❑ 2039	If You Want to Love Somebody/Teach Me Little Children	1966	2.50	5.00	10.00
❑ 2062	Tall Oak Tree/I Just Can't Be Tamed	1966	2.50	5.00	10.00
U.S. NAVY					
❑ (# unknown)	Be a Navy Man	196?	10.00	20.00	40.00
❑ (# unknown) [PS]	Be a Navy Man	196?	5.00	10.00	20.00
Albums					
CALLIOPE					
❑ CAL 7006	Things I Treasure	1977	3.00	6.00	12.00
CAPITOL					
❑ ST-11094	Here and Now	1972	3.75	7.50	15.00
❑ ST-11219	Dorsey Burnette	1973	3.75	7.50	15.00
DOT					
❑ DLP-3456 [M]	Dorsey Burnette Sings	1963	10.00	20.00	40.00
❑ DLP-25456 [S]	Dorsey Burnette Sings	1963	12.50	25.00	50.00
ERA					
❑ EL-102 [M]	Tall Oak Tree	1960	37.50	75.00	150.00
❑ ES-102 [S]	Tall Oak Tree	1960	75.00	150.00	300.00
❑ ES-800 [M]	Dorsey Burnette's Greatest Hits	1969	6.25	12.50	25.00
GUSTO					
❑ 0050	The Golden Hits of Dorsey Burnette	197?	3.00	6.00	12.00

BURNETTE, DORSEY AND JOHNNY

Also see each artist's individual listings.

Number	Title (A Side/B Side)	Yr	VG	VG+	NM
45s					
CORAL					
❑ 62190	Blues Stay Away from Me/Midnight Train	1960	50.00	100.00	200.00
—As "Johnny and Dorsey Burnette"					
IMPERIAL					
❑ 5509	Warm Love/My Honey	1958	25.00	50.00	100.00
—As "Burnette Brothers"					

Number	Title (A Side/B Side)	Yr	VG	VG+	NM
REPRISE					
❑ 20153	It Don't Take Much/Hey Sue	1963	5.00	10.00	20.00
Albums					
SOLID SMOKE					
❑ SS-8005	Together Again	1978	3.75	7.50	15.00

BURNETTE, JOHNNY

Includes the Rock 'N' Roll Trio. Also see DORSEY AND JOHNNY BURNETTE.

Number	Title (A Side/B Side)	Yr	VG	VG+	NM
45s					
CAPITOL					
❑ 5023	All Week Long/It Isn't There	1963	3.75	7.50	15.00
❑ 5114	You Taught Me the Way to Love You/The Opposite	1964	3.75	7.50	15.00
❑ 5176	Walkin' Talkin' Doll/Sweet Suzie	1964	3.75	7.50	15.00
CHANCELLOR					
❑ 1116	I Wanna Thank Your Folks/The Giant	1962	3.75	7.50	15.00
❑ 1123	Party Girl/Tag Along	1962	3.75	7.50	15.00
❑ 1129	Remember Me/Time Is Not Enough	1962	3.75	7.50	15.00
CORAL					
❑ 61651	Tear It Up/You're Undecided	1956	75.00	150.00	300.00
❑ 61675	Midnight Train/Oh Baby Babe	1956	75.00	150.00	300.00
❑ 61719	The Train Kept a-Rollin'/Honey Hush	1956	62.50	125.00	250.00
❑ 61758	Lonesome Train/I Just Found Out	1956	75.00	150.00	300.00
❑ 61829	Eager Beaver Baby/Touch Me	1957	75.00	150.00	300.00
❑ 61869	Drinkin' Wine Spo-Dee-O-Dee/Butterfingers	1957	75.00	150.00	300.00
❑ 61918	Rock Billy Boogie/If You Want It Enough	1957	75.00	150.00	300.00
FREEDOM					
❑ 44001	I'm Restless/Kiss Me	1958	20.00	40.00	80.00
❑ 44011	Gumbo/Me and the Bear	1959	20.00	40.00	80.00
❑ 44017	Sweet Baby Doll/I'll Never Love Again	1959	20.00	40.00	80.00
LIBERTY					
❑ 55222	Settin' the Woods on Fire/Kentucky Waltz	1959	5.00	10.00	20.00
❑ 55243	Don't Do It/Patrick Henry	1959	5.00	10.00	20.00
❑ 55258	Dreamin'/Cincinnati Fireball	1960	5.00	10.00	20.00
❑ 55285	You're Sixteen/I Beg Your Pardon	1960	5.00	10.00	20.00
❑ 55285 [PS]	You're Sixteen/I Beg Your Pardon	1960	12.50	25.00	50.00
❑ 55298	Little Boy Sad/(I Go) Down to the River	1961	3.75	7.50	15.00
❑ 55298 [PS]	Little Boy Sad/(I Go) Down to the River	1961	10.00	20.00	40.00
❑ 55318	Big Big World/Ballad of the One Eyed Jacks	1961	3.75	7.50	15.00
❑ 55318 [PS]	Big Big World/Ballad of the One Eyed Jacks	1961	10.00	20.00	40.00
❑ 55345	Girls/I've Got a Lot of Things to Do	1961	3.75	7.50	15.00
❑ 55377	Honestly I Do/Fools Like Me	1961	3.75	7.50	15.00
❑ 55379	God, Country and My Baby/Honestly I Do	1961	3.75	7.50	15.00
❑ 55416	Clown Shoes/The Way I Am	1962	3.75	7.50	15.00
❑ 55448	The Fool of the Year/The Poorest Boy in Town	1962	3.75	7.50	15.00
❑ 55489	Damn the Defiant/Lonesome Waters	1962	3.75	7.50	15.00
MAGIC LAMP					
❑ 515	Bigger Man/Less Than a Heartache	1964	12.50	25.00	50.00
❑ 515 [PS]	Bigger Man/Less Than a Heartache	1964	75.00	150.00	300.00
SAHARA					
❑ 512	Fountain of Love/What a Summer Day	1964	3.75	7.50	15.00
UNITED ARTISTS					
❑ 0018	Dreamin'/Little Boy Sad	1973	—	2.00	4.00
—Silver Spotlight Series issue					
❑ 0019	You're Sixteen/God, Country and My Baby	1973	—	2.00	4.00
—Silver Spotlight Series issue					
VON					
❑ 1006	You're Undecided/Go, Mule, Go	1954	1500.	2250.	3000.
7-Inch Extended Plays					
LIBERTY					
❑ LSX-1004	(contents unknown)	1960	25.00	50.00	100.00
❑ LSX-1004 [PS]	Dreamin'	1960	37.50	75.00	150.00
❑ LSX-1011	Little Boy Sad/Don't Do It//You're Sixteen/I Go Down to the River	1961	25.00	50.00	100.00
❑ LSX-1011 [PS]	Johnny Burnette's Hits	1961	37.50	75.00	150.00
Albums					
CORAL					
❑ CRL 57080 [M]	Johnny Burnette & the Rock 'N' Roll Trio	1956	2000.	4000.	6000.
—Originals have maroon labels, printing on jacket's spine and "Made in U.S.A." in lower right of back cover					
LIBERTY					
❑ LRP-3179 [M]	Dreamin'	1960	10.00	20.00	40.00
❑ LRP-3183 [M]	Johnny Burnette	1961	10.00	20.00	40.00
❑ LRP-3190 [M]	Johnny Burnette Sings	1961	10.00	20.00	40.00
❑ LRP-3206 [M]	Johnny Burnette's Hits and Other Favorites	1962	10.00	20.00	40.00
❑ LRP-3255 [M]	Roses Are Red	1962	10.00	20.00	40.00
❑ LRP-3389 [M]	The Johnny Burnette Story	1964	10.00	20.00	40.00
❑ LST-7179 [S]	Dreamin'	1960	15.00	30.00	60.00
❑ LST-7183 [S]	Johnny Burnette	1961	15.00	30.00	60.00
❑ LST-7190 [S]	Johnny Burnette Sings	1961	15.00	30.00	60.00
❑ LST-7206 [S]	Johnny Burnette's Hits and Other Favorites	1962	12.50	25.00	50.00
❑ LST-7255 [S]	Roses Are Red	1962	12.50	25.00	50.00
❑ LST-7389 [S]	The Johnny Burnette Story	1964	12.50	25.00	50.00
MCA					
❑ 1513	Listen to Johnny Burnette and the Rock 'N' Roll Trio	1982	2.50	5.00	10.00
SOLID SMOKE					
❑ SS-8001	Tear It Up	1978	7.50	15.00	30.00
—Blue vinyl					
❑ SS-8001	Tear It Up	1978	3.75	7.50	15.00
—Black viinyl					
SUNSET					
❑ SUM-1179 [M]	Dreamin'	1967	3.75	7.50	15.00
❑ SUS-5179 [S]	Dreamin'	1967	5.00	10.00	20.00
UNITED ARTISTS					
❑ UA-LA432-G	The Very Best of Johnny Burnette	1975	2.50	5.00	10.00

BURNETTE, SMILEY

Number	Title (A Side/B Side)	Yr	VG	VG+	NM
45s					
ABBOTT					
❑ 154	Chuggin' On Down "66"/Mucho Gusto	1954	7.50	15.00	30.00
❑ 161	That Long White Line/Lazy Locomotive	1954	7.50	15.00	30.00
CAPITOL					
❑ F1165	Catfish/Jackass Mail	1950	5.00	10.00	20.00
❑ F1304	Rosie the Elephant/You Put Me on My Feet	1950	5.00	10.00	20.00
❑ F1347	Hominy Grits/My Lazy Day	1950	5.00	10.00	20.00
❑ F1520	Do the Pines Grow Green in the Valley/I Can't Be Honest	1951	5.00	10.00	20.00
❑ F1746	Can't Go On/I Ain't Done Nothin' to You	1951	5.00	10.00	20.00
❑ F32110	Rudolph the Red-Nosed Reindeer/The Swiss Boy	195?	5.00	10.00	20.00
—From "Album CASF-3160"					
STARDAY					
❑ 586	Old Fishin' Pole/It's My Last Day	1962	3.75	7.50	15.00
Albums					
CRICKET					
❑ CR-11 [M]	Rodeo Songaree	1959	7.50	15.00	30.00
STARDAY					
❑ SLP-191 [M]	Ole Frog	1962	10.00	20.00	40.00

BURNETTE BROTHERS

See DORSEY AND JOHNNY BURNETTE.

BURNIN' DAYLIGHT

Also see MARC BEESON.

Number	Title (A Side/B Side)	Yr	VG	VG+	NM
45s					
CURB					
❑ D7-73005	Love Worth Fighting For/Say Yes	1996	—	2.00	4.00

BURNS, BRENT

Number	Title (A Side/B Side)	Yr	VG	VG+	NM
45s					
PANTHEON DESERT					
❑ 79	I Hear You Coming Back/Come Away with Me	1978	2.00	4.00	8.00

BURNS, GEORGE

Number	Title (A Side/B Side)	Yr	VG	VG+	NM
45s					
COMPLEAT					
❑ 112	How to Live to Be a Hundred/Katie	1983	—	2.50	5.00
MERCURY					
❑ 57011	I Wish I Was Eighteen Again/One of the Mysteries of Life	1979	—	2.00	4.00
❑ 57011 [PS]	I Wish I Was Eighteen Again/One of the Mysteries of Life	1979	—	3.00	6.00
❑ 57021	The Arizona Whiz/A Real Good Cigar	1980	—	2.00	4.00
❑ 57039	Using Things and Loving People/It's Good to See You Smiling Again	1980	—	2.00	4.00
❑ 57045	Willie, Won't You Sing a Song with Me/Just Send Me One	1981	—	2.00	4.00
❑ 76149	Young at Heart/Whatever Happened to Randolph Scott	1982	—	2.00	4.00
❑ 870286-7	I Wish I Was Eighteen Again/(B-side unknown)	1988	—	—	3.00
—Reissue					
Albums					
BUDDAH					
❑ BDS-5025	George Burns Sings	1969	3.75	7.50	15.00
❑ BDS-5127	A Musical Trip with George Burns	1972	3.00	6.00	12.00
—Reissue of 5027					
MERCURY					
❑ SRM-1-4061	Young at Heart	1982	2.50	5.00	10.00
❑ SRM-1-5025	I Wish I Was Eighteen Again	1980	2.50	5.00	10.00
❑ SRM-1-6001	George Burns in Nashville	1981	2.50	5.00	10.00
PRIDE					
❑ PRD-00 11 [(2)]	An Evening with George Burns	1974	5.00	10.00	20.00

BURNS, HUGHIE

Number	Title (A Side/B Side)	Yr	VG	VG+	NM
45s					
C-S-I					
❑ 002	The Family Inn/Tell Me a Good One	1980	—	3.00	6.00

BURNS, JACKIE

Number	Title (A Side/B Side)	Yr	VG	VG+	NM
45s					
HONOR BRIGADE					
❑ 3	That's What I Get for Being a Woman/I'll Be Your Woman	1969	2.50	5.00	10.00
❑ 5	Something's Missing (It's You)/What's a Daddy	1969	2.50	5.00	10.00
JMI					
❑ 8	(If Loving You Is Wrong) I Don't Want to Be Right/A World of Lonely Men	1972	2.00	4.00	8.00
❑ 17	One Big Unhappy Family/Gonna Miss Me	1973	2.00	4.00	8.00
❑ 23	You're All That Matters to Me/Gonna Miss Me	1973	2.00	4.00	8.00

BURNS, JETHRO

Also see HOMER AND JETHRO.

Number	Title (A Side/B Side)	Yr	VG	VG+	NM
45s					
RCA VICTOR					
❑ APBO-0199	Mama Was a Truck Driving Man/Magic Fingers	1973	2.00	4.00	8.00
❑ 74-0751	Dolly Parton's Sweet on Me/Don't Shoot the Mandolin Player	1972	2.00	4.00	8.00

BURRIS, NEAL

45s

COLUMBIA

Number	Title (A Side/B Side)	Yr	VG	VG+	NM
❑ 4-20917	There's No Reason/River of Love	1952	6.25	12.50	25.00
❑ 4-20972	I Broke a Heart/My Heart Needs Yours	1952	6.25	12.50	25.00
❑ 4-21026	Honey Baby Blues/Poison Kisses	1952	6.25	12.50	25.00
❑ 4-21081	I Bet My Heart/That's Time for Love	1953	5.00	10.00	20.00
❑ 4-21114	Don't Give Me Kisses/You're Stepping Out	1953	5.00	10.00	20.00
❑ 4-21152	For You Alone/What Does It Mean	1953	5.00	10.00	20.00
❑ 4-21234	Bonita Chiquita/Put a Little Sweetnin'	1954	5.00	10.00	20.00
❑ 4-21285	Start the Music/Why Life If Life Is Not	1954	5.00	10.00	20.00

KING

Number	Title (A Side/B Side)	Yr	VG	VG+	NM
❑ 967	Life's Been So Beautiful/Please Excuse My Manners	1951	10.00	20.00	40.00

BURRITO BROTHERS, THE

See THE FLYING BURRITO BROTHERS.

BUSH, JOHNNY

45s

ALLSTAR

Number	Title (A Side/B Side)	Yr	VG	VG+	NM
❑ 7166	You Said That Before/In My World	1958	20.00	40.00	80.00
❑ 7172	Your Kind of Love/I Should Have Known	1958	25.00	50.00	100.00

DELTA

Number	Title (A Side/B Side)	Yr	VG	VG+	NM
❑ 10041	Whiskey River/When My Conscience Hurts the Most	1981	—	3.00	6.00

GUSTO

Number	Title (A Side/B Side)	Yr	VG	VG+	NM
❑ 165	You'll Never Leave Me Completely/Put Me Out of My Memory	1977	—	2.50	5.00
❑ 9006	She Just Made Me Love You More/Hands Can Say a Lot	1978	—	2.50	5.00

MILLION

Number	Title (A Side/B Side)	Yr	VG	VG+	NM
❑ 1	I'll Be There/I Can Feel You in His Arms	1972	2.00	4.00	8.00
❑ 21	Rake Me Over the Coals/Jealously Insane	1972	2.00	4.00	8.00

RCA VICTOR

Number	Title (A Side/B Side)	Yr	VG	VG+	NM
❑ APBO-0041	Green Snakes on the Ceiling/Drinkin' My Baby Right Out of My Mind	1973	—	2.50	5.00
❑ APBO-0164	We're Back in Love Again/(Wine Friend of Mine) Stand By Me	1973	—	2.50	5.00
❑ APBO-0240	Toy Telephone/From Tennessee to Texas	1974	—	2.50	5.00
❑ APBO-0306	Wasted Wine/When It's Midnight in Dallas	1974	—	2.50	5.00
❑ PB-10070	Home in San Antone/I Can Feel Him Touching You	1974	—	2.50	5.00
❑ 74-0745	Whiskey River/Right Back in Your Arms Again	1972	—	2.50	5.00
❑ 74-0867	There Stands the Glass/These Lips Don't Know How to Say Goodbye	1973	—	2.50	5.00
❑ 74-0931	Here Comes the World Again/That Rain Makin' Baby of Mine	1973	—	2.50	5.00

STARDAY

Number	Title (A Side/B Side)	Yr	VG	VG+	NM
❑ 114	My Mind Is a Bridge/Conscience Turn Your Back	1975	—	3.00	6.00
❑ 128	You'll Never Leave Me Completely/(B-side unknown)	1975	—	3.00	6.00

STEP ONE

Number	Title (A Side/B Side)	Yr	VG	VG+	NM
❑ 369	The Twenty-Fourth Hour/I Can't See Texas from Here	1987	—	2.50	5.00

—With Darrell McCall

STOP

Number	Title (A Side/B Side)	Yr	VG	VG+	NM
❑ 126	You Oughta Hear Me Cry/Jealously Insane	1967	2.00	4.00	8.00
❑ 160	What a Way to Live/I Can Feel You in His Arms	1968	2.00	4.00	8.00
❑ 193	Undo the Right/Conscience Turn Your Back	1968	2.00	4.00	8.00
❑ 232	Each Time/Tonight We Steal Heaven Again	1968	2.00	4.00	8.00
❑ 257	You Gave Me a Mountain/Back from the Wine	1969	2.50	5.00	10.00
❑ 310	My Cup Runneth Over/Tonight I'm Going Home to an Angel	1969	2.00	4.00	8.00
❑ 354	Jim, Jack and Rose/I'll Go to a Stranger	1969	2.00	4.00	8.00
❑ 371	Warmth of the Wine/Daddy Lived in Houston	1970	2.00	4.00	8.00
❑ 380	My Joy/I'm Warm by the Flame	1970	2.00	4.00	8.00
❑ 392	City Lights/The Joy of Loving You	1971	2.00	4.00	8.00
❑ 396	Mama's Hands/It's All in the Game	1971	2.00	4.00	8.00
❑ 405	Rake Me Over the Coals/Jealously Insane	1971	2.50	5.00	10.00

WARNER BROS.

Number	Title (A Side/B Side)	Yr	VG	VG+	NM
❑ 8141	Loud Music and Strong Wine/Sunday Morning	1975	—	2.50	5.00

WHISKEY RIVER

Number	Title (A Side/B Side)	Yr	VG	VG+	NM
❑ 791	When My Conscience Hurts the Most/Drivin' Nails in My Coffin	1979	—	3.00	6.00

Albums

HILLTOP

Number	Title (A Side/B Side)	Yr	VG	VG+	NM
❑ JS-6081	You Ought to Hear Me Cry	197?	3.75	7.50	15.00

MILLION

Number	Title (A Side/B Side)	Yr	VG	VG+	NM
❑ 1001	The Best of Johnny Bush	1972	6.25	12.50	25.00

POWER PAK

Number	Title (A Side/B Side)	Yr	VG	VG+	NM
❑ PO-217	Bush Country	197?	3.00	6.00	12.00

RCA VICTOR

Number	Title (A Side/B Side)	Yr	VG	VG+	NM
❑ APL1-0216	Here Comes the World Again	1973	3.75	7.50	15.00
❑ APL1-0369	Texas Dance Hall Girl	1974	3.75	7.50	15.00
❑ LSP-4817	Whiskey River/There Stands the Glass	1973	3.75	7.50	15.00

STOP

Number	Title (A Side/B Side)	Yr	VG	VG+	NM
❑ 1028	The Greatest Hits of Johnny Bush	1972	5.00	10.00	20.00
❑ 10002	Sound of a Heartache	1968	6.25	12.50	25.00
❑ 10005	Undo the Night	1968	5.00	10.00	20.00
❑ 10008	You Gave Me a Mountain	1969	5.00	10.00	20.00
❑ 10014	Johnny Bush	1970	5.00	10.00	20.00

WHISKEY RIVER

Number	Title (A Side/B Side)	Yr	VG	VG+	NM
❑ 8024 [(2)]	Live at Dance Town USA	1979	3.75	7.50	15.00

BUTLER, BOBBY "SOFINE"

45s

IBC

Number	Title (A Side/B Side)	Yr	VG	VG+	NM
❑ 0001	Cheaper Crude or No More Food/Bobby's (Nervous) Breakdown	1979	—	3.00	6.00

PANTHEON DESERT

Number	Title (A Side/B Side)	Yr	VG	VG+	NM
❑ 77	Teddy Toad/Theme from Teddy Toad	1976	—	3.00	6.00

BUTLER, CARL

Also see CARL BUTLER AND PEARL.

45s

CAPITOL

Number	Title (A Side/B Side)	Yr	VG	VG+	NM
❑ F1335	Heartbreak Express/White Rose	1950	7.50	15.00	30.00
❑ F1399	Plastic Man/Country Mile	1951	6.25	12.50	25.00
❑ F1454	Shake, Rattle & Roll/No Guarantee on My Heart	1951	6.25	12.50	25.00
❑ F1541	Our Last Rendezvous/I Live My Life Alone	1951	5.00	10.00	20.00
❑ F1701	Linda Lou/No Trespassing	1951	5.00	10.00	20.00
❑ F1813	A String of Empties/You Plus Me	1951	5.00	10.00	20.00
❑ F1891	Blue Million Tears/River of Love	1951	5.00	10.00	20.00
❑ F1996	Alone Without You/Vicious Lies	1952	5.00	10.00	20.00
❑ F2084	Penny for Your Thoughts/Everything Will Be the Same	1952	5.00	10.00	20.00
❑ F2158	Stepping on My Heart/I Need You So	1952	5.00	10.00	20.00

COLUMBIA

Number	Title (A Side/B Side)	Yr	VG	VG+	NM
❑ 4-21353	Angel Band/Hallelujah We Shall Rise	1955	5.00	10.00	20.00
❑ 4-21407	Wedding Day/If I Could Spend My Heartaches	1955	5.00	10.00	20.00
❑ 4-21455	It's My Sin/Borrowed Love	1955	5.00	10.00	20.00
❑ 4-40874	Your Cold Heart Told Me So/I Know What It Means to Be Lonesome	1957	3.75	7.50	15.00
❑ 40994	River of Tears/Cry, You Fool, Cry	1957	3.00	6.00	12.00
❑ 41119	If You've Got the Money (I've Got the Time)/Nothing I'd Rather Do	1958	2.50	5.00	10.00
❑ 41205	Jealous Heart/So Close	1958	2.50	5.00	10.00
❑ 41263	Baby I'm a-Waitin'/My Cajun Baby	1958	2.50	5.00	10.00
❑ 41368	I Like to Pretend/Oh, How I Miss You	1959	2.50	5.00	10.00
❑ 41475	Remember the Alamo/Grief in My Heart	1959	2.50	5.00	10.00
❑ 41560	You Jes' Don't Steal from a Poor Man/Cry, You Fool, Cry	1960	2.50	5.00	10.00
❑ 41674	The Door/I Know Why I Cry	1960	2.50	5.00	10.00
❑ 41869	I'm a Prisoner of Love/For the First Time	1960	2.50	5.00	10.00
❑ 41997	Honky Tonkitis/You Were the Orchid	1961	2.50	5.00	10.00
❑ 42306	Have You Run Out of Lies/If I Had Only Met You First	1962	2.50	5.00	10.00
❑ 42593	Don't Let Me Cross Over/Wonder Drug	1962	2.50	5.00	10.00

OKEH

Number	Title (A Side/B Side)	Yr	VG	VG+	NM
❑ 18003	Just for Fooling Around/You Can't Insure a House of Dreams	1954	3.75	7.50	15.00
❑ 18012	Crowded Out/My Heart Tells Me	1954	3.75	7.50	15.00
❑ 18018	So Close/It's Wrong to Be Jealous	1954	3.75	7.50	15.00
❑ 18032	A Victim of Lies/I Just Said Goodbye to My Dreams	1955	3.75	7.50	15.00
❑ 18039	That's All Right/I'll Go Steppin' Too	1955	5.00	10.00	20.00
❑ 18052	Kisses Don't Lie/I Wouldn't Change You If I Could	1955	3.75	7.50	15.00

Albums

COLUMBIA

Number	Title (A Side/B Side)	Yr	VG	VG+	NM
❑ CL 2002 [M]	Don't Let Me Cross Over	1963	5.00	10.00	20.00
❑ CS 8802 [S]	Don't Let Me Cross Over	1963	6.25	12.50	25.00

HARMONY

Number	Title (A Side/B Side)	Yr	VG	VG+	NM
❑ HL 7385 [M]	The Great Carl Butler Sings	1966	3.00	6.00	12.00
❑ HS 11185 [S]	The Great Carl Butler Sings	1966	3.75	7.50	15.00
❑ H 30674	For the First Time	1971	3.00	6.00	12.00

BUTLER, CARL, AND PEARL

Also see CARL BUTLER.

45s

CHART

Number	Title (A Side/B Side)	Yr	VG	VG+	NM
❑ 5145	Temptation Keeps Twisting Her Arm/I'm So Close to Loving You	1972	—	2.00	4.00
❑ 5160	She Didn't Come Home/Two of a Kind	1972	—	2.00	4.00
❑ 5191	Heartaches for Lunch/Fifteen Years Ago	1973	—	2.00	4.00

COLUMBIA

Number	Title (A Side/B Side)	Yr	VG	VG+	NM
❑ 42778	Loving Arms/You'll Be Next	1963	2.00	4.00	8.00
❑ 42892	Too Late to Try Again/My Tears Don't Show	1963	2.00	4.00	8.00
❑ 43030	I'm Hanging Up the Phone/Just a Message	1964	2.00	4.00	8.00
❑ 43102	Forbidden Street/When the Door Swings Shut	1964	2.00	4.00	8.00
❑ 43210	Just Thought I'd Let You Know/We'd Destroy Each Other	1965	2.00	4.00	8.00
❑ 43335	Beers and Tears/Can I Draw the Line	1965	2.00	4.00	8.00
❑ 43433	Our Ship of Love/It's Called Cheating	1965	2.00	4.00	8.00
❑ 43536	Little Mac/Wrong Generation	1966	2.00	4.00	8.00
❑ 43685	Little Pedro/Cell 29	1966	2.00	4.00	8.00
❑ 43869	Same Old Me Lovin' Same Old You/Dreaming of a Little Cabin	1966	2.00	4.00	8.00
❑ 44043	Wild Goose Chase/Lost	1967	—	3.00	6.00
❑ 44252	Guilty of Love/For a Minute	1967	—	3.00	6.00
❑ 44447	If You Should Ever Stop Loving Me/If I'd Only Met You First	1968	—	3.00	6.00
❑ 44587	Punish Me Tomorrow/Goodbye Tennessee	1968	—	3.00	6.00
❑ 44694	I Never Got Over You/I Started Loving You Again	1968	—	3.00	6.00
❑ 44862	We'll Sweep Out the Ashes in the Morning/Your Way of Life	1969	—	3.00	6.00

Number	Title (A Side/B Side)	Yr	VG	VG+	NM
❑ 45112	Used to Own This Train/Caution	1970	—	2.50	5.00
❑ 45228	Bottoms Up/Let the Sun Shine on the People	1970	—	2.50	5.00

Albums

CHART

Number	Title (A Side/B Side)	Yr	VG	VG+	NM
❑ 1051	Temptation Keeps Twistin' Her Arm	1972	3.75	7.50	15.00

COLUMBIA

Number	Title (A Side/B Side)	Yr	VG	VG+	NM
❑ CS 1039	Carl and Pearl Butler's Greatest Hits	1970	3.75	7.50	15.00
❑ CL 2125 [M]	Loving Arms	1964	5.00	10.00	20.00
❑ CL 2308 [M]	The Old and the New	1965	3.75	7.50	15.00
❑ CL 2640 [M]	Avenue of Prayer	1967	5.00	10.00	20.00
❑ CS 8925 [S]	Loving Arms	1964	6.25	12.50	25.00
❑ CS 9108 [S]	The Old and the New	1965	5.00	10.00	20.00
❑ CS 9440 [S]	Avenue of Prayer	1967	3.75	7.50	15.00
❑ CS 9651	Our Country World	1968	3.75	7.50	15.00
❑ CS 9769	Honky Tonkin'	1969	3.75	7.50	15.00

HARMONY

Number	Title (A Side/B Side)	Yr	VG	VG+	NM
❑ H 31182	Watch and Pray	1972	3.00	6.00	12.00

BUTLER, LARRY

45s

ALLSTAR

Number	Title (A Side/B Side)	Yr	VG	VG+	NM
❑ 7186	Echoes Fade and Die/Foolish Affair	1959	5.00	10.00	20.00
❑ 7193	Stay Out of My Life/The 13th Notch	1960	5.00	10.00	20.00
❑ 7201	I Could Never Be Untrue/I've Got a Right to Cry	1960	5.00	10.00	20.00
❑ 7214	Another Heartache/I Can't Stand It Anymore	1960	5.00	10.00	20.00
❑ 7225	For Goodness Sake/I Walked Away	1961	5.00	10.00	20.00
❑ 7242	Same Old Way/I'm Crying All the Day	1961	5.00	10.00	20.00
❑ 7255	What Right Have I/Love Me	196?	3.75	7.50	15.00
❑ 7283	Blue Tears/City Sounds	196?	3.75	7.50	15.00
❑ 7295	I Love You Baby/Echoes Fade and Die	196?	3.00	6.00	12.00
❑ 7300	Walked Out/Zackly Like You	196?	3.00	6.00	12.00

DOT

Number	Title (A Side/B Side)	Yr	VG	VG+	NM
❑ 16767	Ol' Man River/How Do You Say I'm Sorry	1965	2.50	5.00	10.00

IMPERIAL

Number	Title (A Side/B Side)	Yr	VG	VG+	NM
❑ 66239	Lonesome/Sandy	1967	2.00	4.00	8.00
❑ 66277	Funny Familiar Forgotten Feelings/Break My Mind	1968	2.00	4.00	8.00
❑ 66296	Lady Madonna/Honey	1968	2.00	4.00	8.00

MCA

Number	Title (A Side/B Side)	Yr	VG	VG+	NM
❑ 51086	Tess (Love Theme)/The Journey	1981	—	2.00	4.00

UNITED ARTISTS

Number	Title (A Side/B Side)	Yr	VG	VG+	NM
❑ XW819	Theme from Stay Hungry/Til October	1976	—	2.50	5.00
❑ XW895	Misty Blue/Nashville P.M.	1976	—	2.50	5.00
❑ XW1017	Another Somebody Done Somebody Wrong Song/High Noon	1977	—	2.50	5.00

Albums

IMPERIAL

Number	Title (A Side/B Side)	Yr	VG	VG+	NM
❑ LP-9354 [M]	Take Me	1967	5.00	10.00	20.00
❑ LP-12354 [S]	Take Me	1967	3.75	7.50	15.00
❑ LP-12410	A Thing Called Love	1968	3.75	7.50	15.00

UNITED ARTISTS

Number	Title (A Side/B Side)	Yr	VG	VG+	NM
❑ UA-LA739-G	Larry Butler and Friends	1977	3.00	6.00	12.00

BUZZI, RUTH

45s

UNITED ARTISTS

Number	Title (A Side/B Side)	Yr	VG	VG+	NM
❑ XW951	You Oughta Hear the Song/'57 Chevrolet	1977	—	2.50	5.00

BYERS, BRENDA

45s

MTA

Number	Title (A Side/B Side)	Yr	VG	VG+	NM
❑ 102	Call Him Back/Voice in the Wind	1966	2.50	5.00	10.00
❑ 108	Follow the Stars/Rush	1966	2.50	5.00	10.00
❑ 116	Don't Remind Me/Rainbows and Roses	1967	2.50	5.00	10.00
❑ 146	The House That Jack Built/Nobody Knows You When You're Down and Out	1968	2.00	4.00	8.00
❑ 160	The Auctioneer/Rainbows and Roses	1968	2.00	4.00	8.00
❑ 167	Empty/(B-side unknown)	1969	2.00	4.00	8.00
❑ 171	California in a Dream/Wear My Shoes	1969	2.00	4.00	8.00
❑ 176	Thank You for Loving Me/Night Life	1969	2.00	4.00	8.00
❑ 177	Homeward Bound/The Other Side of Me	1969	2.00	4.00	8.00
❑ 183	I Can't Go On Loving You/Photographs	1970	2.00	4.00	8.00
❑ 189	Little Boys/Oh, It's Gonna Rain	1970	2.00	4.00	8.00
❑ 193	Homeward Bound/The Other Side of Me	1971	—	3.00	6.00

Albums

MTA

Number	Title (A Side/B Side)	Yr	VG	VG+	NM
❑ 5013	The Auctioneer	1968	5.00	10.00	20.00
❑ 5016	Thank You for Loving Me	1969	5.00	10.00	20.00

BYRAM, JUDY

45s

F&L

Number	Title (A Side/B Side)	Yr	VG	VG+	NM
❑ 554	No More One More Time/(B-side unknown)	1987	—	2.50	5.00

REGAL

Number	Title (A Side/B Side)	Yr	VG	VG+	NM
❑ 001	One Fire Between Us/(B-side unknown)	1988	—	2.50	5.00

BYRD, TRACY

45s

MCA

Number	Title (A Side/B Side)	Yr	VG	VG+	NM
❑ 54426	That's the Thing About a Memory/Back in the Swing of Things	1992	—	2.00	4.00
❑ 54497	Someone to Give My Love To/Talk to Me Texas	1992	—	—	3.00
❑ 54659	Holdin' Heaven/Edge of a Memory	1993	—	2.00	4.00
❑ 54735	Why Don't That Telephone Ring/An Out of Control Raging Fire	1993	—	—	3.00
❑ 54778	Lifestyles of the Not So Rich and Famous/You Never Know Just How Good You've Got It	1994	—	2.00	4.00
❑ 54889	Watermelon Crawl/You Never Know Just How Good You've Got It	1994	—	2.00	4.00
❑ 54945	The First Step/No Ordinary Man	1994	—	—	3.00
❑ 54988	The Keeper of the Stars/Pink Flamingos	1995	2.00	4.00	8.00
❑ 55049	Walking to Jerusalem/Down on the Bottom	1995	—	2.00	4.00
❑ 55102	Love Lessons/Don't Need That Heartache	1995	—	—	3.00
❑ 55155	Heaven in My Woman's Eyes/Walkin' In	1995	—	—	3.00
❑ 55201	4 to 1 in Atlanta/Have a Good One	1996	—	—	3.00
❑ 55230	Big Love/Big Love (Club Mix)	1996	—	—	3.00
❑ 55292	Don't Take Her She's All I Got/I Love You, That's All	1997	—	2.00	4.00
❑ 72002	Don't Love Make a Diamond Shine/Tuscon Too Soon	1997	—	—	3.00
❑ 72011	Good Ol' Fashioned Love/Driving Me Out of Your Mind	1997	—	—	3.00
❑ 72037	On Again, Off Again/Gettin' Me Over Mountains	1998	—	—	3.00
❑ 72040	I'm from the Country/For Me It's You	1998	—	2.00	4.00

MCA NASHVILLE

Number	Title (A Side/B Side)	Yr	VG	VG+	NM
❑ 72058	I Wanna Feel That Way Again/Gettin' Me Over Mountains	1998	—	—	3.00
❑ 72083	When Mama Ain't Happy/(B-side unknown)	1998	—	2.00	4.00

RCA

Number	Title (A Side/B Side)	Yr	VG	VG+	NM
❑ 60210	Love, You Ain't Seen the Last of Me/Put Your Hand in Mine	2000	—	—	3.00
❑ 65907	Put Your Hand in Mine/It's About Time	1999	—	—	3.00
❑ 69006	Take Me With You When You Go/Love, You Ain't Seen the Last of Me	2000	—	—	3.00

BYRDS, THE

Never made the country charts, but were highly influential on country music both collectively and individually. Members later were in CROSBY, STILLS AND NASH; DESERT ROSE BAND; THE FLYING BURRITO BROTHERS. Also see CHRIS HILLMAN; ROGER McGUINN; GRAM PARSONS.

45s

ASYLUM

Number	Title (A Side/B Side)	Yr	VG	VG+	NM
❑ 11016	Full Circle/Long Live the King	1973	—	2.50	5.00
❑ 11019	Cowgirl in the Sand/Long Live the King	1973	—	2.50	5.00

COLUMBIA

Number	Title (A Side/B Side)	Yr	VG	VG+	NM
❑ 43271	Mr. Tambourine Man/I Knew I'd Want You	1965	3.75	7.50	15.00
❑ 43271 [DJ]	Mr. Tambourine Man (same on both sides)	1965	37.50	75.00	150.00
—Red vinyl promo					
❑ 43271 [PS]	Mr. Tambourine Man	1965	75.00	150.00	300.00
—Promo-only sleeve promoting the Byrds' appeance on the TV show Hullabaloo					
❑ 43332	All I Really Want to Do/I'll Feel a Whole Lot Better	1965	3.75	7.50	15.00
❑ 43332 [DJ]	All I Really Want to Do (same on both sides)	1965	25.00	50.00	100.00
—Red vinyl promo					
❑ 43332 [DJ]	I'll Feel a Whole Lot Better (same on both sides)	1965	30.00	60.00	120.00
—Red vinyl promo					
❑ 43424	Turn! Turn! Turn! (To Everything There Is a Season)/She Don't Care About Time	1965	3.75	7.50	15.00
❑ 43424 [DJ]	Turn! Turn! Turn! (To Everything There Is a Season) (same on both sides)	1965	25.00	50.00	100.00
—Red vinyl promo					
❑ 43501	It Won't Be Wrong/Set You Free This Time	1965	3.00	6.00	12.00
❑ 43578	Eight Miles High/Why	1966	3.00	6.00	12.00
❑ 43578 [PS]	Eight Miles High/Why	1966	15.00	30.00	60.00
❑ 43702	5 D (Fifth Dimension)/Captain Soul	1966	3.00	6.00	12.00
❑ 43766	Mr. Spaceman/What's Happening	1966	3.00	6.00	12.00
❑ 43987	So You Want to Be a Rock 'N' Roll Star/Everybody's Been Burned	1967	3.00	6.00	12.00
❑ 44054	My Back Pages/Renaissance Fair	1967	3.00	6.00	12.00
❑ 44157	Have You Seen Her Face/Don't Make Waves	1967	2.50	5.00	10.00
❑ 44157 [PS]	Have You Seen Her Face/Don't Make Waves	1967	10.00	20.00	40.00
❑ 44230	Lady Friend/Old John Robertson	1967	2.50	5.00	10.00
❑ 44362	Goin' Back/Change Is Now	1967	2.00	4.00	8.00
❑ 44499	Artificial Energy/You Ain't Going Nowhere	1968	2.00	4.00	8.00
❑ 44643	Pretty Boy Floyd/I Am a Pilgrim	1968	2.00	4.00	8.00
❑ 44746	Drug Store Truck Drivin' Man/Bad Night at the Whiskey	1969	2.00	4.00	8.00
❑ 44868	Lay Lady Lay/Old Blue	1969	2.00	4.00	8.00
❑ 44990	Ballad of Easy Rider/Oil in My Lamp	1969	2.50	5.00	10.00
❑ 44990	Wasn't Born to Follow/Ballad of Easy Rider	1969	2.00	4.00	8.00
❑ 45071	Jesus Is Just Alright/It's All Over Now, Baby Blue	1970	2.00	4.00	8.00
❑ 45259	Chestnut Mare/Just a Season	1970	—	3.00	6.00
❑ 45440	Glory Glory/Citizen Kane	1971	—	3.00	6.00
❑ 45514	America's Great National Pastime/Farther Along	1971	—	3.00	6.00
❑ 45761	Jesus Is Just Alright/Mr. Spaceman	1973	2.50	5.00	10.00
❑ JZSP 116476 [DJ]	He Was a Friend of Mine (same on both sides)	1966	10.00	20.00	40.00

7-Inch Extended Plays

COLUMBIA/SCHOLASTIC

Number	Title (A Side/B Side)	Yr	VG	VG+	NM
❑ CV 10287	Lover of the Bayou/So You Want to Be a Rock and Roll Star//Chimes of Freedom/Goin' Back	1971	7.50	15.00	30.00
❑ CV 10287 [PS]	The Byrds	1971	7.50	15.00	30.00

Albums

ASYLUM

Number	Title (A Side/B Side)	Yr	VG	VG+	NM
❑ SD 5058	Byrds	1973	3.00	6.00	12.00

COLUMBIA

Number	Title (A Side/B Side)	Yr	VG	VG+	NM
❑ CL 2372 [M]	Mr. Tambourine Man	1965	10.00	20.00	40.00
—"Guaranteed High Fidelity" on label					

Number	Title (A Side/B Side)	Yr	VG	VG+	NM
❑ CL 2372 [M]	Mr. Tambourine Man	1966	7.50	15.00	30.00
—"360 Sound Mono" on label					
❑ CL 2454 [M]	Turn! Turn! Turn!	1965	7.50	15.00	30.00
❑ CL 2549 [M]	Fifth Dimension (5D)	1966	7.50	15.00	30.00
❑ CL 2642 [M]	Younger Than Yesterday	1967	7.50	15.00	30.00
❑ CL 2716 [M]	The Byrds' Greatest Hits	1967	7.50	15.00	30.00
❑ CL 2775 [M]	The Notorious Byrd Brothers	1968	12.50	25.00	50.00
❑ CS 9172 [S]	Mr. Tambourine Man	1965	10.00	20.00	40.00
—Red label, "360 Sound" in black					
❑ CS 9172 [S]	Mr. Tambourine Man	1966	6.25	12.50	25.00
—Red label, "360 Sound" in white					
❑ CS 9172 [S]	Mr. Tambourine Man	1971	2.50	5.00	10.00
—Orange label					
❑ PC 9172 [S]	Mr. Tambourine Man	198?	2.00	4.00	8.00
—Reissue with new prefix					
❑ CS 9254 [S]	Turn! Turn! Turn!	1965	6.25	12.50	25.00
—Red "360 Sound" label					
❑ CS 9254 [S]	Turn! Turn! Turn!	1971	2.50	5.00	10.00
—Orange label					
❑ PC 9254 [S]	Turn! Turn! Turn!	198?	2.00	4.00	8.00
—Reissue with new prefix					
❑ CS 9349 [S]	Fifth Dimension (5D)	1966	6.25	12.50	25.00
—Red "360 Sound" label					
❑ CS 9349 [S]	Fifth Dimension (5D)	1971	2.50	5.00	10.00
—Orange label					
❑ PC 9349 [S]	Fifth Dimension (5D)	198?	2.00	4.00	8.00
—Reissue with new prefix					
❑ CS 9442 [S]	Younger Than Yesterday	1967	6.25	12.50	25.00
—Red "360 Sound" label					
❑ CS 9442 [S]	Younger Than Yesterday	1971	2.50	5.00	10.00
—Orange label					
❑ PC 9442 [S]	Younger Than Yesterday	198?	2.00	4.00	8.00
—Reissue with new prefix					
❑ CS 9516 [S]	The Byrds' Greatest Hits	1967	5.00	10.00	20.00
—Red "360 Sound" label					
❑ KCS 9516 [S]	The Byrds' Greatest Hits	1971	2.50	5.00	10.00
—Orange label					
❑ PC 9516 [S]	The Byrds' Greatest Hits	197?	2.00	4.00	8.00
—Reissue with another new prefix					
❑ CS 9575 [S]	The Notorious Byrd Brothers	1968	5.00	10.00	20.00
—Red "360 Sound" label					
❑ CS 9575 [S]	The Notorious Byrd Brothers	1971	2.50	5.00	10.00
—Orange label					
❑ PC 9575 [S]	The Notorious Byrd Brothers	198?	2.00	4.00	8.00
—Reissue with new prefix					
❑ CS 9670 [M]	Sweetheart of the Rodeo	1968	25.00	50.00	100.00
—"Special Mono Radio Station Copy" with white label					
❑ CS 9670 [S]	Sweetheart of the Rodeo	1968	5.00	10.00	20.00
—Red "360 Sound" label					
❑ CS 9670 [S]	Sweetheart of the Rodeo	1971	2.50	5.00	10.00
—Orange label					
❑ PC 9670 [S]	Sweetheart of the Rodeo	198?	2.00	4.00	8.00
—Reissue with new prefix					
❑ CS 9755 [S]	Dr. Byrds and Mr. Hyde	1969	5.00	10.00	20.00
—Red "360 Sound" label					
❑ CS 9755 [S]	Dr. Byrds and Mr. Hyde	1971	2.50	5.00	10.00
—Orange label					
❑ PC 9755 [S]	Dr. Byrds and Mr. Hyde	198?	2.00	4.00	8.00
—Reissue with new prefix					
❑ CS 9942 [S]	Ballad of Easy Rider	1969	5.00	10.00	20.00
—Red "360 Sound" label					
❑ CS 9942 [S]	Ballad of Easy Rider	1971	2.50	5.00	10.00
—Orange label					
❑ PC 9942	Ballad of Easy Rider	1984	2.00	4.00	8.00
—Reissue with new prefix					
❑ G 30127 [(2)]	The Byrds (Untitled)	1970	5.00	10.00	20.00
—With "Kathleen" listed on back cover (it is not on the set)					
❑ G 30127 [(2)]	The Byrds (Untitled)	1970	3.75	7.50	15.00
—Without "Kathleen" listed on back cover					
❑ KC 30640	Byrdmaniax	1971	3.00	6.00	12.00
❑ C 31050	Farther Along	1971	3.00	6.00	12.00
❑ C 31795	The Best of the Byrds (Greatest Hits, Volume II)	197?	2.50	5.00	10.00
—Reissue with new prefix					
❑ KC 31795	The Best of the Byrds (Greatest Hits, Volume II)	1972	3.00	6.00	12.00
❑ PC 31795	The Best of the Byrds (Greatest Hits, Volume II)	198?	2.00	4.00	8.00
—Reissue with another new prefix					
❑ C 32183	Preflyte	197?	2.50	5.00	10.00
—Reissue with new prefix					
❑ KC 32183	Preflyte	1973	3.00	6.00	12.00
—Reissue of Together LP					
❑ CG 33645 [(2)]	Mr. Tambourine Man/Turn! Turn! Turn!	1976	3.75	7.50	15.00
❑ PC 36293	The Byrds Play Dylan	1980	2.50	5.00	10.00
❑ FC 37335	The Original Singles Volume 1 (1965-1967)	1981	2.50	5.00	10.00
❑ PC 37335	The Original Singles Volume 1 (1965-1967)	1985	2.00	4.00	8.00
—Budget-line reissue					

PAIR

Number	Title (A Side/B Side)	Yr	VG	VG+	NM
❑ PDL2-1040 [(2)]	The Very Best of the Byrds	1986	3.00	6.00	12.00

RE-FLYTE

Number	Title (A Side/B Side)	Yr	VG	VG+	NM
❑ MH-70318	Never Before	1987	3.00	6.00	12.00
—Released by Muuray Hill Records via mail order					

RHINO

Number	Title (A Side/B Side)	Yr	VG	VG+	NM
❑ R1-70244	In the Beginning	1988	2.50	5.00	10.00

SUNDAZED

Number	Title (A Side/B Side)	Yr	VG	VG+	NM
❑ LP 5057	Mr. Tambourine Man	1999	3.75	7.50	15.00
—Reissue on 180-gram vinyl					
❑ LP 5058	Turn! Turn! Turn!	1999	3.75	7.50	15.00
—Reissue on 180-gram vinyl					
❑ LP 5059	Fifth Dimension	1999	3.75	7.50	15.00
—Reissue on 180-gram vinyl					
❑ LP 5060	Younger Than Yesterday	1999	3.75	7.50	15.00
—Reissue on 180-gram vinyl					
❑ LP 5061	Sanctuary	2000	3.00	6.00	12.00

TOGETHER

Number	Title (A Side/B Side)	Yr	VG	VG+	NM
❑ ST-1-1001	Preflyte	1969	6.25	12.50	25.00

C

C COMPANY FEATURING TERRY NELSON

45s

PLANTATION

Number	Title (A Side/B Side)	Yr	VG	VG+	NM
❑ 73	Battle Hymn of Lt. Calley/Routine Patrol	1971	—	2.50	5.00

CACTUS CHOIR

45s

CURB/UNIVERSAL

Number	Title (A Side/B Side)	Yr	VG	VG+	NM
❑ 56098	Step Right Up/Hark the Herald Angels Sing	1997	—	—	3.00

CAGLE, BUDDY

Also see PENNY DeHAVEN AND BUDDY CAGLE.

45s

CAPITOL

Number	Title (A Side/B Side)	Yr	VG	VG+	NM
❑ 4924	Your Mother's Prayer/Once Again	1963	3.00	6.00	12.00
❑ 5043	Sing a Sad Song/Love Inside My Door	1963	3.00	6.00	12.00
❑ 5154	The Gold Cup/Afraid to Go	1964	3.00	6.00	12.00

IMPERIAL

Number	Title (A Side/B Side)	Yr	VG	VG+	NM
❑ 66161	Tonight I'm Coming Home/Honky Tonk College	1966	2.00	4.00	8.00
❑ 66187	Be Nice to Everybody/Too Many Mountains	1966	2.00	4.00	8.00
❑ 66187	Be Nice to Everybody/The Wild Side of Life	1966	2.00	4.00	8.00
❑ 66218	Apologize/Help's on the Way	1966	2.00	4.00	8.00
❑ 66245	Longtime Traveling/Camptown Girl	1967	2.00	4.00	8.00
❑ 66263	Cincinnati Stranger/Waikiki Sand	1967	2.00	4.00	8.00
❑ 66331	I'll Get Over You/I've Wondered Where She's Been	1968	2.00	4.00	8.00
❑ 66357	As If I Needed to Be Reminded/Daddy Please	1969	2.00	4.00	8.00
❑ 66407	Gutar Player (The Ballad of James Burton)/Mud Is to Jump In	1969	2.00	4.00	8.00

MERCURY

Number	Title (A Side/B Side)	Yr	VG	VG+	NM
❑ 72452	Honky Tonkin' Again/We the People (The Great Society)	1965	2.50	5.00	10.00

UNITED ARTISTS

Number	Title (A Side/B Side)	Yr	VG	VG+	NM
❑ 50709	Happy-Go-Lucky Me/The Kid from Whiskey Hill	1970	—	3.50	7.00

Albums

IMPERIAL

Number	Title (A Side/B Side)	Yr	VG	VG+	NM
❑ LP-9318 [M]	The Way You Like It	1966	5.00	10.00	20.00
❑ LP-9348 [M]	Mi Casa, Tu Casa	1967	5.00	10.00	20.00
❑ LP-9361 [M]	Longtime Traveling	1967	7.50	15.00	30.00
❑ LP-12318 [S]	The Way You Like It	1966	6.25	12.50	25.00
❑ LP-12348 [S]	Mi Casa, Tu Casa	1967	6.25	12.50	25.00
❑ LP-12361 [S]	Longtime Traveling	1967	6.25	12.50	25.00
❑ LP-12374	Through a Crack in a Boxcar Door	1968	6.25	12.50	25.00

CAGLE, CHRIS

45s

VIRGIN

Number	Title (A Side/B Side)	Yr	VG	VG+	NM
❑ 58867	My Love Goes On and On/Play It Loud	2000	—	2.00	4.00

CAIN, HUNTER

45s

DISCOVERY

Number	Title (A Side/B Side)	Yr	VG	VG+	NM
❑ 4587	Hollywood Heroes/She's Too Good to Be Cheated This Way	1988	—	3.50	7.00

CALAMITY JANE

Also see PAM ROSE.

45s

COLUMBIA

Number	Title (A Side/B Side)	Yr	VG	VG+	NM
❑ 18-02503	Send Me Somebody to Love/Don't You Leave Love Alone Too Long	1981	—	2.00	4.00
❑ 18-02715	I've Just Seen a Face/Midnight Bandit	1982	—	2.00	4.00
❑ 18-02958	Walkin' After Midnight/Lover to Lover	1982	—	2.00	4.00
❑ 38-03229	Love Wheel/Pick Me Up (And Let Me Love Again)	1982	—	2.00	4.00

Albums

COLUMBIA

Number	Title (A Side/B Side)	Yr	VG	VG+	NM
❑ FC 37626	Calamity Jane	1981	2.50	5.00	10.00

CALHOUN, LINDA

45s

GRAPE

Number	Title (A Side/B Side)	Yr	VG	VG+	NM
❑ 2004	I Can Feel Love/Our Tune of Yesterday	1979	2.00	4.00	8.00

MGM

Number	Title (A Side/B Side)	Yr	VG	VG+	NM
❑ 14778	Swinging Songs/(B-side unknown)	1975	—	3.00	6.00
❑ 14810	Momma, Let Me Find Shelter (In Your Lovin' Arms)/He Kinda Reminds Me of a Song	1975	—	3.00	6.00

CALICO

45s

UNITED ARTISTS

Number	Title (A Side/B Side)	Yr	VG	VG+	NM
❑ XW723	Jody, It's Still You/Help Yourself (Duff's Dilemma)	1975	—	2.50	5.00
❑ XW806	Great American Dream/September Tears	1976	—	2.50	5.00
❑ XW907	Lyin' Again/Summertime Lovin'	1976	—	2.50	5.00

Albums

UNITED ARTISTS

Number	Title (A Side/B Side)	Yr	VG	VG+	NM
❑ UA-LA454-G	Calico	1975	3.75	7.50	15.00
❑ UA-LA659-G	Calico, Vol. 2	1976	3.75	7.50	15.00

CAMERON, BART

45s

REVOLVER

Number	Title (A Side/B Side)	Yr	VG	VG+	NM
❑ 011	What's Your Name/(B-side unknown)	1986	—	2.50	5.00
❑ 013	Dark Eyed Lady/(B-side unknown)	1986	—	2.50	5.00
❑ 015	Do It for the Love of It/(B-side unknown)	1987	—	2.50	5.00

CAMP, COLLEEN

45s

MOON PICTURES

Number	Title (A Side/B Side)	Yr	VG	VG+	NM
❑ 0001	One Day Since Yesterday/I Would Like to See You Again	1981	—	3.50	7.00

CAMP, SHAWN

45s

REPRISE

Number	Title (A Side/B Side)	Yr	VG	VG+	NM
❑ 7-18331	Confessin' My Love/K-I-S-S-I-N-G	1993	—	2.00	4.00
❑ 7-18465	Fallin' Never Felt So Good/Turn Loose of My Pride	1993	—	2.00	4.00

CAMPBELL, ARCHIE

45s

ELEKTRA

Number	Title (A Side/B Side)	Yr	VG	VG+	NM
❑ 45316	Don't Be Born a Man/More or Less	1976	—	2.50	5.00
❑ 45452	I Just Found This Hat/The Night Miss Nancy Ann's Hotel for Single Girls Got Burned Down	1977	—	2.50	5.00

RCA VICTOR

Number	Title (A Side/B Side)	Yr	VG	VG+	NM
❑ APBO-0155	Freedom Ain't the Same As Bein' Free/The House	1973	—	3.00	6.00
❑ 47-7660	Trouble in the Amen Corner/Black Is the Color of My True Love's Hair	1960	3.00	6.00	12.00
❑ 47-7757	Make Friends/The Twelfth Rose	1960	3.00	6.00	12.00
❑ 47-7807	Ol' Man Mose/Don't Jump from the Bridge	1960	3.00	6.00	12.00
❑ 47-8422	Most Richly Blessed/Do Lord	1964	2.50	5.00	10.00
❑ 47-8546	Rindercella/Hockey Here Tonight	1965	2.50	5.00	10.00
❑ 47-8658	Beeping Sleauty/The Drunk	1965	2.50	5.00	10.00
❑ 47-8741	The Men in My Little Girl's Life/Abe Lincoln Comes Home	1965	2.50	5.00	10.00
❑ 47-8866	Golf, Golf, Golf/Mommy's Little Angel	1966	2.50	5.00	10.00
❑ 47-8976	Life Gets Tee-Jus Don't It/The Martins and the Coys	1966	2.50	5.00	10.00
❑ 47-9028	Christmas at the Opry/Christmas Eve in Heaven	1966	2.50	5.00	10.00
❑ 47-9081	The Cockfight/Red Silk	1967	2.50	5.00	10.00
❑ 47-9257	We Never Get Hungry on Sunday/Roho and the Black Bantam	1967	2.50	5.00	10.00
❑ 47-9888	As the Twig Is Bent/Walking on Fire	1970	—	3.50	7.00
❑ 47-9954	Get It at the General Store/The Cockfight	1971	—	3.50	7.00
❑ 47-9987	When the Roll Is Called Up Yonder/Didn't He Shine	1971	—	3.50	7.00
❑ 74-0232	Pfft, You Were Gone/Rindercella	1969	2.00	4.00	8.00
❑ 74-0663	Daddy Don't You Walk So Fast/Carry Me Back	1972	—	3.50	7.00
❑ 74-0766	People's Choice/Bean and the Jackstalk	1972	—	3.50	7.00
❑ 74-0959	A Light in the Window/Today I'm Bringing Daddy's Letter Home	1973	—	3.50	7.00

STARDAY

Number	Title (A Side/B Side)	Yr	VG	VG+	NM
❑ 557	Sergeant York/Grab a Little Sunshine	1961	3.00	6.00	12.00
❑ 568	Settin' My Tears to Music/Woman's Work Is Never Done	1961	3.00	6.00	12.00
❑ 600	Fools Side of Town/Root Beer	1962	3.00	6.00	12.00
❑ 609	Don't You Ever Fret/The Master's Hand	1962	3.00	6.00	12.00
❑ 624	A World Full of Women/My Baby's Home	1963	3.00	6.00	12.00
❑ 643	Crying in My Pillow/Don't Let Love Die	1963	3.00	6.00	12.00
❑ 727	Green Stamps/Three Little Pigs	1965	2.50	5.00	10.00

Albums

RCA VICTOR

Number	Title (A Side/B Side)	Yr	VG	VG+	NM
❑ LPM-3504 [M]	Have a Laugh on Me	1966	5.00	10.00	20.00
❑ LSP-3504 [S]	Have a Laugh on Me	1966	6.25	2.50	25.00
❑ LPM-3699 [M]	The Cockfight and Other Tall Tales	1967	5.00	10.00	20.00
❑ LSP-3699 [S]	The Cockfight and Other Tall Tales	1967	6.25	12.50	25.00
❑ LPM-3780 [M]	Kids I Love 'Em	1967	6.25	12.50	25.00
❑ LSP-3780 [S]	Kids I Love 'Em	1967	5.00	10.00	20.00
❑ LPM-3892 [M]	The Golden Years	1967	6.25	12.50	25.00
❑ LSP-3892 [S]	The Golden Years	1967	5.00	10.00	20.00

STARDAY

Number	Title (A Side/B Side)	Yr	VG	VG+	NM
❑ SLP-162 [M]	Make Friends with Archie Campbell	1962	7.50	15.00	30.00
❑ SLP-167 [M]	Bedtime Stories for Adults	1962	7.50	15.00	30.00
❑ SLP-223 [M]	The Joker Is Wild	1963	7.50	15.00	30.00
❑ SLP-377 [M]	The Grand Ole Opry's Good Humor Man	1966	6.25	12.50	25.00

CAMPBELL, ARCHIE, AND LITTLE BONNIE

45s

RCA VICTOR

Number	Title (A Side/B Side)	Yr	VG	VG+	NM
❑ 74-0147	Poor Daddy/Old Shep	1969	2.00	4.00	8.00

CAMPBELL, ARCHIE, AND LORENE MANN

Also see each artist's individual listings.

45s

RCA VICTOR

Number	Title (A Side/B Side)	Yr	VG	VG+	NM
❑ 47-9401	The Dark End of the Street/The Gettin' Place	1967	2.00	4.00	8.00
❑ 47-9549	Tell It Like It Is/If That's the Only Way	1968	2.00	4.00	8.00
❑ 47-9615	Warm and Tender Love/Pledging My Love	1968	2.00	4.00	8.00
❑ 47-9691	My Special Prayer/What Am I Living For	1968	2.00	4.00	8.00

Albums

RCA VICTOR

Number	Title (A Side/B Side)	Yr	VG	VG+	NM
❑ LSP-4068	Tell It Like It Is	1968	5.00	10.00	20.00

CAMPBELL, ARCHIE, AND MINNIE PEARL

45s

RCA VICTOR

Number	Title (A Side/B Side)	Yr	VG	VG+	NM
❑ PB-10077	As Soon As I Hang Up the Phone/Nobody's Business	1974	—	3.00	6.00

CAMPBELL, CECIL

45s

MGM

Number	Title (A Side/B Side)	Yr	VG	VG+	NM
❑ 12118	Steel Guitar Waltz/Comango	1955	5.00	10.00	20.00
❑ 12245	Dixieland Rock/Fog Rising on the Mountain	1956	15.00	30.00	60.00
❑ 12482	Rock and Roll Fever/Rocking Guitar	1957	37.50	75.00	150.00

RCA VICTOR

Number	Title (A Side/B Side)	Yr	VG	VG+	NM
❑ 47-4325	No Wedding Bells for Me/Carolina Steel	1951	6.25	12.50	25.00
❑ 48-0014	Steel Guitar Ramble/Left All Alone with a Broken Heart	1949	10.00	20.00	40.00
—Originals on green vinyl					
❑ 48-0076	Tropical Island/Tar Heel Rag	1949	10.00	20.00	40.00
—Originals on green vinyl					
❑ 48-0126	Tear Drops/No Where, No Time, No Place	1949	10.00	20.00	40.00
—Originals on green vinyl					
❑ 48-0169	No Blues for Me/One Little Flower	1950	10.00	20.00	40.00
—Originals on green vinyl					
❑ 48-0219	Steel Guitar Ramble/Left All Alone with a Broken Heart	1950	7.50	15.00	30.00
—Reissue of 48-0014; originals on green vinyl					
❑ 48-0340	Steel Guitar Swing/Catawba River	1950	7.50	15.00	30.00
—Originals on green vinyl					
❑ 48-0376	Serenade of the Winds/Proud Papa Polka	1950	7.50	15.00	30.00
—Originals on green vinyl					
❑ 48-0409	Steel Guitar Dig/Spookie Boogie	1951	7.50	15.00	30.00
❑ 48-0445	Steel Guitar Wiggle/Coconut Island	1951	7.50	15.00	30.00
❑ 48-0472	Tennessee Steel Guitar/Paper Roses	1951	7.50	15.00	30.00
❑ 48-0499	Steel Guitar Jamboree/You Kept Makin' Eyes at Me	1951	7.50	15.00	30.00

Albums

STARDAY

Number	Title (A Side/B Side)	Yr	VG	VG+	NM
❑ SLP-254 [M]	Steel Guitar Jamboree	1963	10.00	20.00	40.00

CAMPBELL, GLEN

45s

ATLANTIC AMERICA

Number	Title (A Side/B Side)	Yr	VG	VG+	NM
❑ 99525	Call Home/Sweet 16	1986	—	—	3.00
❑ 99559	Cowpoke/Rag Doll	1986	—	—	3.00
❑ 99600	It's Just a Matter of Time/Gene Autry, My Hero	1985	—	—	3.00
❑ 99600 [PS]	It's Just a Matter of Time/Gene Autry, My Hero	1985	—	2.00	4.00
❑ 99647	(Love Always) Letter to Home/An American Trilogy	1985	—	—	3.00
❑ 99691	A Lady Like You/Tennessee	1984	—	—	3.00
❑ 99768	Faithless Love/Scene of the Crime	1984	—	—	3.00
❑ 99893	On the Wings of My Victory/A Few Good Men	1983	—	—	3.00
❑ 99930	I Love How You Love Me/Hang On Baby (Ease My Mind)	1983	—	—	3.00
❑ 99967	Old Home Town/Heartache #3	1982	—	2.00	4.00
❑ 99967 [PS]	Old Home Town/Heartache #3	1982	—	2.00	4.00

CAPEHART

Number	Title (A Side/B Side)	Yr	VG	VG+	NM
❑ 5008	Death Valley/Nothin' Better Than a Pretty Woman	1961	6.25	12.50	25.00

CAPITOL

Number	Title (A Side/B Side)	Yr	VG	VG+	NM
❑ 2015	By the Time I Get to Phoenix/You've Still Got a Place in My Heart	1967	—	3.50	7.00
❑ 2076	Hey Little One/My Baby's Gone	1968	—	3.50	7.00
❑ 2076 [PS]	Hey Little One/My Baby's Gone	1968	3.00	6.00	12.00
❑ 2146	I Wanna Live/That's All That Matters	1968	—	3.50	7.00
❑ 2224	Dreams of the Everyday Housewife/Kelli Ho-Down	1968	—	3.50	7.00
❑ 2302	Wichita Lineman/Fate of Man	1968	—	3.00	6.00
❑ 2336	Christmas Is for Children/There's No Place Like Home	1968	2.00	4.00	8.00
❑ 2428	Galveston/How Come Every Time I Itch I Wind Up Scratchin' You	1969	—	3.00	6.00
❑ 2494	Where's the Playground Susie/Arkansas	1969	—	3.00	6.00
❑ 2573	True Grit/Hava Nagila	1969	—	3.00	6.00
❑ 2659	Try a Little Kindness/Lonely My Lonely Friend	1969	—	3.00	6.00
❑ 2718	Honey Come Back/Where Do You Go	1970	—	3.00	6.00
❑ 2787	Oh Happy Day/Someone Above	1970	—	3.00	6.00
❑ 2843	Everything a Man Could Ever Need/Norwood (Me and My Guitar)	1970	—	3.00	6.00

Number	Title (A Side/B Side)	Yr	VG	VG+	NM
❑ 2905	It's Only Make Believe/Pave Your Way Into Tomorrow	1970	—	3.00	6.00
❑ 3062	Dream Baby (How Long Must I Dream)/Here and Now	1971	—	3.00	6.00
❑ 3123	The Last Time I Saw Her/Bach Talk	1971	—	3.00	6.00
❑ 3254	Oklahoma Sunday Morning/Everybody's Got to Go There Sometime	1972	—	3.00	6.00
❑ 3305	Manhattan, Kansas/Wayfaring Stranger	1972	—	3.00	6.00
❑ 3382	We All Pull the Load/Wherefore and Why	1972	—	3.50	7.00
❑ 3411	I Will Never Pass This Way Again/We All Pull the Load	1972	—	3.00	6.00
❑ 3483	One Last Time/All My Tomorrows	1972	—	3.00	6.00
❑ 3509	I Believe in Christmas/New Snow on the Roof	1972	—	3.00	6.00
❑ 3548	I Knew Jesus (Before He Was a Star)/On This Road	1973	—	2.50	5.00
❑ 3669	Bring Back My Yesterday/Beautiful Love Song	1973	—	2.50	5.00
❑ 3735	Wherefore and Why/Give Me Back That Old Familiar Feeling	1973	—	2.50	5.00
❑ 3808	Houston (I'm Coming to See You)/Honestly Love	1973	—	2.50	5.00
❑ 3926	Bonaparte's Retreat/Too Many Mornings	1974	—	2.50	5.00
❑ 3988	It's a Sin When You Love Somebody/If I Were Loving You	1974	—	2.50	5.00
❑ 4095	Rhinestone Cowboy/Lovelight	1975	—	2.00	4.00
❑ 4155	Country Boy (You Got Your Feet in L.A.)/Record Collector's Dream	1975	—	2.00	4.00
❑ 4245	Then You Can Tell Me Goodbye-Don't Pull Your Love/I Miss You Tonight	1976	—	2.00	4.00
❑ 4288	See You on Sunday/Bloodline	1976	—	2.00	4.00
❑ 4376	Southern Nights/William Tell Overture	1976	—	2.00	4.00
❑ 4445	Sunflower/How High Did We Go	1977	—	2.00	4.00
❑ 4515	God Must Have Blessed America/Amazing Grace	1977	—	2.00	4.00
❑ 4584	Another Fine Mess/Can You Fool	1978	—	2.00	4.00
❑ 4638	Can You Fool/Let's All Sing a Song About It	1978	—	2.00	4.00
❑ 4682	I'm Gonna Love You/Love Takes You Higher	1979	—	2.00	4.00
❑ 4715	California/Never Tell You No Lies	1979	—	2.00	4.00
❑ 4769	Hound Dog Man/Tennessee Home	1979	—	2.00	4.00
❑ 4783	Too Late to Worry — Too Blue to Cry/How Do I Tell My Heart Not to Break	1962	3.75	7.50	15.00
❑ 4799	My Prayer/Don't Lose Me in the Confusion	1979	—	2.00	4.00
❑ 4856	Long Black Limousine/Here I Am	1962	2.50	5.00	10.00
❑ 4856 [PS]	Long Black Limousine/Here I Am	1962	5.00	10.00	20.00
❑ 4865	Somethin' 'Bout You Baby I Like/Late Night Confession	1980	—	2.00	4.00
—With Rita Coolidge					
❑ 4867	Kentucky Means Paradise/Truck Driving Man	1962	3.75	7.50	15.00
—As "The Green River Boys Featuring Glen Campbell"					
❑ 4909	Hollywood Smiles/Hooked on Love	1980	—	2.00	4.00
❑ 4925	Oh My Darling/Prima Donna	1963	3.00	6.00	12.00
❑ 4959	I Don't Want to Know Your Name/Daisy a Day	1981	—	2.00	4.00
❑ 4986	Why Don't We Just Sleep on It Tonight/It's Your World	1981	—	2.00	4.00
—With Tanya Tucker					
❑ 4990	Divorce Me C.O.D./Dark As a Dungeon	1963	3.00	6.00	12.00
❑ 5037	As Far As I'm Concerned/Same Old Places	1963	3.00	6.00	12.00
❑ 5172	Let Me Tell You About Mary/Through the Eyes of a Child	1964	3.00	6.00	12.00
❑ 5279	Summer, Winter, Spring and Fall/Heartaches Can Be Fun	1964	3.00	6.00	12.00
❑ 5279 [PS]	Summer, Winter, Spring and Fall/Heartaches Can Be Fun	1964	6.25	12.50	25.00
❑ 5360	It's a Woman's World/Tomorrow Never Comes	1965	3.00	6.00	12.00
❑ 5441	Guess I'm Dumb/That's All Right	1965	30.00	60.00	120.00
—A Brian Wilson "Pet Sounds"-like production					
❑ 5504	The Universal Soldier/Spanish Shades	1965	2.50	5.00	10.00
❑ 5545	Less of Me/Private John Q	1965	2.50	5.00	10.00
❑ 5638	Can't You See I'm Tryin'/Satisfied Mind	1966	2.50	5.00	10.00
❑ 5773	Burning Bridges/Only the Lonely	1966	2.50	5.00	10.00
❑ 5854	I Gotta Have My Baby Back/Just to Satisfy You	1967	2.50	5.00	10.00
❑ 5939	Gentle on My Mind/Just Another Man	1967	2.00	4.00	8.00
—Orange and yellow swirl, without "A Subsidiary Of"... in perimeter label print					
❑ 5939	Gentle on My Mind/Just Another Man	1968	—	3.00	6.00
—Orange and yellow swirl label with "A Subsidiary Of" in perimeter print					
❑ 7PRO-79107	On a Good Night (same on both sides)	1990	—	3.00	6.00
—Vinyl is promo only					
❑ 7PRO-79279	Somebody's Leavin' (same on both sides)	1990	—	3.00	6.00
—Vinyl is promo only					
❑ 7PRO-79966	Walkin' in the Sun (same on both sides)	1990	—	3.00	6.00
—Vinyl is promo only					
CENECO					
❑ 1324	Dreams for Sale/I've Got to Win	1961	6.25	12.50	25.00
❑ 1356	I Wonder/You, You, You	1961	5.00	10.00	20.00
COMPLEAT					
❑ 113	Letting Go/(Instrumental)	1983	—	2.00	4.00
CREST					
❑ 1087	Turn Around, Look at Me/Brenda	1961	5.00	10.00	20.00
❑ 1096	The Miracle of Love/Once More	1962	3.75	7.50	15.00
EVEREST					
❑ 2500	Delight, Arkansas/Walk Right In	1969	—	3.00	6.00
LIBERTY					
❑ S7-18214	Blue Christmas/Feliz Navidad	1994	—	2.50	5.00
—B-side on EMI Latin by Jose Feliciano; red vinyl					
MCA					
❑ 41323	Dream Lover/Bronco	1980	—	2.00	4.00
—A-side with Tanya Tucker					

Number	Title (A Side/B Side)	Yr	VG	VG+	NM
❑ 53108	The Hand That Rocks the Cradle/Arkansas	1987	—	—	3.00
—A-side with Steve Wariner					
❑ 53172	Still Within the Sound of My Voice/In My Life	1987	—	—	3.00
❑ 53218	I Have You/I'm a One Woman Man	1987	—	—	3.00
❑ 53245	I Remember You/For Sure, For Certain, Forever, For Always	1988	—	—	3.00
❑ 53426	Heart of the Matter/Light Years	1988	—	—	3.00
❑ 53493	More Than Enough/Our Movie	1989	—	—	3.00
MIRAGE					
❑ 3845	I Love My Truck/Melody's Melody	1981	—	2.00	4.00
STARDAY					
❑ 853	For the Love of a Woman/Smokey Blue Eyes	1968	2.00	4.00	8.00
UNIVERSAL					
❑ UVL-66024	She's Gone, Gone, Gone/William Tell Overture	1989	—	2.00	4.00
WARNER BROS.					
❑ 49609	Any Which Way You Can/Medley from Any Which Way You Can	1980	—	2.00	4.00
—B-side by Texas Opera Company					

Albums

Number	Title	Yr	VG	VG+	NM
ATLANTIC AMERICA					
❑ 90016	Old Home Town	1983	2.00	4.00	8.00
❑ 90164	Letter to Home	1984	2.00	4.00	8.00
❑ 90483	It's Just a Matter of Time	1985	2.00	4.00	8.00
CAPITOL					
❑ SM-103	Wichita Lineman	1977	2.00	4.00	8.00
—Reissue with new prefix					
❑ ST-103	Wichita Lineman	1968	3.75	7.50	15.00
❑ ST-210	Galveston	1969	3.75	7.50	15.00
❑ STBO-268	Glen Campbell — "Live"	1969	5.00	10.00	20.00
❑ SM-389	Try a Little Kindness	1977	2.00	4.00	8.00
—Reissue with new prefix					
❑ SW-389	Try a Little Kindness	1970	3.00	6.00	12.00
❑ SW-443	Oh Happy Day	1970	3.00	6.00	12.00
❑ SW-493	The Glen Campbell Goodtime Album	1970	3.00	6.00	12.00
❑ SM-733	The Last Time I Saw Her	1977	2.00	4.00	8.00
—Reissue with new prefix					
❑ SW-733	The Last Time I Saw Her	1971	3.00	6.00	12.00
❑ SW-752	Glen Campbell's Greatest Hits	1971	3.00	6.00	12.00
❑ ST 1810 [S]	Big Bluegrass Special	1962	25.00	50.00	100.00
—As "The Green River Boys Featuring Glen Campbell"					
❑ T 1810 [M]	Big Bluegrass Special	1962	20.00	40.00	80.00
—As "The Green River Boys Featuring Glen Campbell"					
❑ ST 1881 [S]	Too Late to Worry, Too Blue to Cry	1963	6.25	12.50	25.00
❑ T 1881 [M]	Too Late to Worry, Too Blue to Cry	1963	5.00	10.00	20.00
❑ ST 2023 [S]	The Astounding 12-String Guitar of Glen Campbell	1964	5.00	10.00	20.00
❑ T 2023 [M]	The Astounding 12-String Guitar of Glen Campbell	1964	3.75	7.50	15.00
❑ ST 2392 [S]	The Big Bad Rock Guitar of Glen Campbell	1965	5.00	10.00	20.00
❑ T 2392 [M]	The Big Bad Rock Guitar of Glen Campbell	1965	3.75	7.50	15.00
❑ ST 2679 [S]	Burning Bridges	1967	3.75	7.50	15.00
❑ T 2679 [M]	Burning Bridges	1967	3.75	7.50	15.00
❑ ST 2809 [S]	Gentle on My Mind	1967	3.75	7.50	15.00
❑ T 2809 [M]	Gentle on My Mind	1967	3.75	7.50	15.00
❑ ST 2851 [S]	By the Time I Get to Phoenix	1967	3.75	7.50	15.00
❑ T 2851 [M]	By the Time I Get to Phoenix	1967	3.75	7.50	15.00
❑ ST 2878	Hey, Little One	1968	3.75	7.50	15.00
❑ ST 2907	A New Place in the Sun	1968	3.75	7.50	15.00
❑ ST 2978	That Christmas Feeling	1968	3.75	7.50	15.00
❑ SW-11117	Glen Travis Campbell	1972	2.50	5.00	10.00
❑ SW-11185	I Knew Jesus (Before He Was a Star)	1973	2.50	5.00	10.00
❑ SW-11253	I Remember Hank Williams	1973	2.50	5.00	10.00
❑ SW-11293	Hosuton (I'm Comin' to See You)	1974	2.50	5.00	10.00
❑ SW-11336	Reunion (The Songs of Jimmy Webb)	1974	2.50	5.00	10.00
❑ SM-11407	Arkansas	1977	2.00	4.00	8.00
—Reissue with new prefix					
❑ SW-11407	Arkansas	1975	2.50	5.00	10.00
❑ SW-11430	Rhinestone Cowboy	1975	2.50	5.00	10.00
❑ SW-11516	Bloodline	1976	2.50	5.00	10.00
❑ ST-11577	The Best of Glen Campbell	1976	2.50	5.00	10.00
❑ SO-11601	Southern Nights	1977	2.50	5.00	10.00
❑ SWBC-11707 [(2)]	Live at the Royal Festival Hall	1977	3.00	6.00	12.00
❑ SW-11722	Basic	1978	2.50	5.00	10.00
❑ SM-11960	Gentle on My Mind	1979	2.00	4.00	8.00
—Reissue of 2809					
❑ SOO-12008	Highwayman	1979	2.50	5.00	10.00
❑ SM-12040	By the Time I Get to Phoenix	1979	2.00	4.00	8.00
—Reissue of 2851					
❑ SOO-12075	Somethin' 'Bout You Baby I Like	1980	2.50	5.00	10.00
❑ SOO-12124	It's the World Gone Crazy	1981	2.50	5.00	10.00
❑ SN-16029	Rhinestone Cowboy	1980	—	3.00	6.00
—Budget-line reissue					
❑ SN-16030	Southern Nights	1980	—	3.00	6.00
—Budget-line reissue					
❑ SN-16031	Glen Travis Campbell	1980	—	3.00	6.00
—Budget-line reissue					
❑ SN-16160	Wichita Lineman	1981	—	3.00	6.00
—Budget-line reissue					
❑ SN-16258	Hey Little Girl	1982	—	3.00	6.00
—Budget-line reissue					
❑ SN-16259	Galveston	1982	—	3.00	6.00
—Budget-line reissue					
❑ SN-16297	Glen Campbell's Greatest Hits	1984	—	3.00	6.00
—Budget-line reissue					

Number	Title (A Side/B Side)	Yr	VG	VG+	NM
❑ SN-16335	The Best of Glen Campbell	1984	—	3.00	6.00
—Budget-line reissue					
❑ SWAK-93157	Limited Collector's Edition	1970	5.00	10.00	20.00
—Capitol Record Club exclusive; includes tour program					

MCA

Number	Title (A Side/B Side)	Yr	VG	VG+	NM
❑ 42009	Still Within the Sound of My Voice	1987	2.00	4.00	8.00
❑ 42210	Light Years	1988	2.00	4.00	8.00

PAIR

Number	Title (A Side/B Side)	Yr	VG	VG+	NM
❑ PDL2-1089 [(2)]	All-Time Favorites	1986	3.00	6.00	12.00

PICKWICK

Number	Title (A Side/B Side)	Yr	VG	VG+	NM
❑ PTP-2048 [(2)]	Only the Lonely	197?	2.50	5.00	10.00
❑ SPC-3052	The 12 Strings of Glen Campbell	196?	2.50	5.00	10.00
❑ SPC-3134	A Satisfied Mind	197?	2.00	4.00	8.00
❑ SPC-3274	The Glen Campbell Album	197?	2.00	4.00	8.00
❑ SPC-3346	I'll Paint You a Song	197?	2.00	4.00	8.00

STARDAY

Number	Title (A Side/B Side)	Yr	VG	VG+	NM
❑ 424	Country Soul	1968	3.75	7.50	15.00
❑ 437	Country Music Star #1	1969	3.75	7.50	15.00

CAMPBELL, GLEN, AND BOBBIE GENTRY

Also see each artist's individual listings.

45s

CAPITOL

Number	Title (A Side/B Side)	Yr	VG	VG+	NM
❑ 2314	Less of Me/Morning Glory	1968	—	3.00	6.00
❑ 2387	Let It Be Me/Little Green Apples	1969	—	3.00	6.00
❑ 2745	All I Have to Do Is Dream/Less of Me	1970	—	3.00	6.00

Albums

CAPITOL

Number	Title (A Side/B Side)	Yr	VG	VG+	NM
❑ ST 2928	Bobbie Gentry & Glen Campbell	1968	3.75	7.50	15.00

CAMPBELL, JO ANN

Also see JO ANN AND TROY.

45s

ABC-PARAMOUNT

Number	Title (A Side/B Side)	Yr	VG	VG+	NM
❑ 10134 [M]	A Kookie Little Paradise/Bobby, Bobby, Bobby	1960	6.25	12.50	25.00
❑ S-10134 [S]	A Kookie Little Paradise/Bobby, Bobby, Bobby	1960	12.50	25.00	50.00
❑ 10172	But Maybe This Year/Crazy Daisy	1960	5.00	10.00	20.00
❑ 10200	Motorcycle Michael/Puka Puka Pants	1961	5.00	10.00	20.00
❑ 10224	Eddie My Love/It Wasn't Right	1961	5.00	10.00	20.00
❑ 10258	Mama Don't Wait/Duane	1961	5.00	10.00	20.00
❑ 10300	I Changed My Mind Jack/You Made Me Love You	1962	5.00	10.00	20.00
❑ 10335	Amateur Night/I Wish It Would Rain All Summer	1962	5.00	10.00	20.00

CAMEO

Number	Title (A Side/B Side)	Yr	VG	VG+	NM
❑ 223	I'm the Girl from Wolverton Mountain/Sloppy Joe	1962	5.00	10.00	20.00
❑ 237	Let Me Do It My Way/Mr. Fix-It Man	1962	5.00	10.00	20.00
❑ 249	Mother Please/Waitin' for Love	1963	5.00	10.00	20.00

EL DORADO

Number	Title (A Side/B Side)	Yr	VG	VG+	NM
❑ 504	Forever Young/Come On Baby	1957	10.00	20.00	40.00
❑ 509	Funny Thing/I Can't Give You Anything But Love	1957	10.00	20.00	40.00

GONE

Number	Title (A Side/B Side)	Yr	VG	VG+	NM
❑ 5014	Wait a Minute/It's True	1957	10.00	20.00	40.00
❑ 5014	Wait a Minute/I'm in Love with You	1957	7.50	15.00	30.00
❑ 5021	You're Driving Me Mad/Rock and Roll Love	1958	7.50	15.00	30.00
❑ 5027	Whassa Matter with You/You-Oo	1958	7.50	15.00	30.00
❑ 5037	I Really, Really Love You/I'm Nobody's Baby Now	1958	7.50	15.00	30.00
❑ 5049	Happy New Year Baby/Tall Boy	1958	7.50	15.00	30.00
❑ 5055	Mama/Nervous	1959	7.50	15.00	30.00
❑ 5068	Beach Comber/I Ain't Got No Steady Date	1959	7.50	15.00	30.00

POINT

Number	Title (A Side/B Side)	Yr	VG	VG+	NM
❑ 4	I'm Coming Home Late Tonight/Wherever You Go	1956	10.00	20.00	40.00

RORI

Number	Title (A Side/B Side)	Yr	VG	VG+	NM
❑ 711	Jim Dandy/Five Minutes More	1962	5.00	10.00	20.00

Albums

ABC-PARAMOUNT

Number	Title (A Side/B Side)	Yr	VG	VG+	NM
❑ 393 [M]	Twistin' and Listenin'	1962	20.00	40.00	80.00
❑ S-393 [S]	Twistin' and Listenin'	1962	25.00	50.00	100.00

CAMEO

Number	Title (A Side/B Side)	Yr	VG	VG+	NM
❑ C-1026 [M]	All the Hits of Jo Ann Campbell	1962	12.50	25.00	50.00
❑ SC-1026 [S]	All the Hits of Jo Ann Campbell	1962	25.00	50.00	100.00

CORONET

Number	Title (A Side/B Side)	Yr	VG	VG+	NM
❑ CX-199 [M]	Starring Jo Ann Campbell	196?	5.00	10.00	20.00
❑ CXS-199 [R]	Starring Jo Ann Campbell	196?	3.00	6.00	12.00

END

Number	Title (A Side/B Side)	Yr	VG	VG+	NM
❑ LP-306 [M]	I'm Nobody's Baby	1959	37.50	75.00	150.00

CAMPBELL, MIKE

45s

COLUMBIA

Number	Title (A Side/B Side)	Yr	VG	VG+	NM
❑ 18-02622	Barroom Games/All My Cloudy Days Are Gone	1981	—	2.00	4.00
❑ 18-02810	Just to Get to Your Love/Lonely Game	1982	—	2.00	4.00
❑ 18-03154	No Room to Cry/Just the Way I Am	1982	—	2.00	4.00
❑ 38-03488	Do You Wanna Make Love/Just to Get Your Love	1983	—	2.00	4.00
❑ 38-03838	Don't Say You Love Me (Just Love Me Again)/Barroom Games	1983	—	2.00	4.00
❑ 38-04225	Sweet and Easy to Love/Nothing Shines Brighter Than You	1983	—	2.00	4.00
❑ 38-04387	One Sided Love Affair/Sweet and Easy to Love	1984	—	2.00	4.00
❑ 38-04488	You're the Only Star (In My Blue Heaven)/Sweet and Easy to Love	1984	—	2.00	4.00

CAMPBELL, STACY DEAN

45s

COLUMBIA

Number	Title (A Side/B Side)	Yr	VG	VG+	NM
❑ 38-74357	Rosalee/Would You Run	1992	—	2.00	4.00
❑ 38-74491	Baby Don't You Know/One Little Teardrop	1992	—	2.00	4.00
❑ 38-74803	Poor Man's Rose/I Won't	1992	—	2.00	4.00
❑ 38-77891	Eight Feet High/A Blue Guitar	1995	—	2.00	4.00
❑ 38-77942	Honey I Do/Midnight Angel	1995	—	2.00	4.00

CANADIAN SWEETHEARTS, THE

Also see BOB AND LUCILLE.

45s

A&M

Number	Title (A Side/B Side)	Yr	VG	VG+	NM
❑ 713	Freight Train/Out for Fun	1963	3.00	6.00	12.00
❑ 727	Hootenanny Express/Half-Breed	1964	3.00	6.00	12.00
❑ 737	Love/Mountain Special	1964	3.00	6.00	12.00
❑ 752	Yodel Love Call/(B-side unknown)	1964	3.00	6.00	12.00
❑ 758	Blowin' in the Wind/We're Gonna Stand on the Mountain	1965	2.50	5.00	10.00
❑ 768	Lookin' Back to See/The Wayward Wind	1965	2.50	5.00	10.00
❑ 778	Don't Knock on My Door/Torture Me	1965	2.50	5.00	10.00
❑ 786	Haunting Me/Soldier Boy	1965	2.50	5.00	10.00
❑ 798	Adios, Aloha/Too Far Between Kisses	1966	2.50	5.00	10.00

EPIC

Number	Title (A Side/B Side)	Yr	VG	VG+	NM
❑ 5-10258	Let's Wait a Little Longer/More Than Money Can Buy	1968	2.00	4.00	8.00
❑ 5-10377	Hey Sue/You Were Worth the Wait	1968	2.00	4.00	8.00

SOMA

Number	Title (A Side/B Side)	Yr	VG	VG+	NM
❑ 1156	No Help Wanted/Flirtin' Kind	1961	15.00	30.00	60.00

Albums

A&M

Number	Title (A Side/B Side)	Yr	VG	VG+	NM
❑ LP-106 [M]	Introducing the Canadian Sweethearts	1964	10.00	20.00	40.00
❑ SP-4106 [S]	Introducing the Canadian Sweethearts	1964	12.50	25.00	50.00

CANNON, ACE

45s

FERNWOOD

Number	Title (A Side/B Side)	Yr	VG	VG+	NM
❑ 117	Big Shot/Rest	1960	7.50	15.00	30.00
—As "Johnny Cannon"					
❑ 135	Summertime/Hoe Down Rock	1963	5.00	10.00	20.00
❑ 137	Big Shot/Tie Me to Your Apron Strings Again	1964	5.00	10.00	20.00

HI

Number	Title (A Side/B Side)	Yr	VG	VG+	NM
❑ 2040	Tuff/Sittin' Tight	1961	4.00	8.00	16.00
❑ 2051	Blues (Stay Away from Me)/Blues in My Heart	1962	3.75	7.50	15.00
❑ 2057	Volare/Looking Back	1962	3.00	6.00	12.00
❑ 2063	Love Letters/Since I Met You Baby	1963	3.00	6.00	12.00
❑ 2065	Cottonfields/Mildew	1963	3.00	6.00	12.00
❑ 2065 [PS]	Cottonfields/Mildew	1963	5.00	10.00	20.00
❑ 2070	Swanee River/Moanin' the Blues	1963	3.00	6.00	12.00
❑ 2070 [PS]	Swanee River/Moanin' the Blues	1963	5.00	10.00	20.00
❑ 2074	Searchin'/Love Letters in the Sand	1964	2.50	5.00	10.00
❑ 2078	The Great Pretender/Gone	1964	2.50	5.00	10.00
❑ 2081	Empty Arms/Sunday Blues	1964	2.50	5.00	10.00
❑ 2084	Blue Christmas/Here Comes Santa Claus	1964	2.50	5.00	10.00
❑ 2089	Sea Cruise/Gold Coins	1965	2.00	4.00	8.00
❑ 2096	Up Shore/Ishapan	1965	2.00	4.00	8.00
❑ 2101	Funny (How Time Slips Away)/Saxy Lullaby	1966	2.00	4.00	8.00
❑ 2107	Mockingbird Hill/Dedicated to the One I Love	1966	2.00	4.00	8.00
❑ 2111	More/Spanish Eyes	1966	2.00	4.00	8.00
❑ 2117	Wonderland by Night/As Time Goes By	1966	2.00	4.00	8.00
❑ 2127	I Walk the Line/Memory	1967	2.00	4.00	8.00
❑ 2136	White Silver Sands/San Antonio Rose	1967	2.00	4.00	8.00
❑ 2144	Sleep Walk/By the Time I Get to Phoenix	1968	—	3.00	6.00
❑ 2148	Alley Cat/Cannonball	1968	—	3.00	6.00
❑ 2155	If I Had a Hammer/Soul for Sale	1969	—	3.00	6.00
❑ 2166	Amen/Down By the Riverside	1969	—	3.00	6.00
❑ 2174	Ruby, Don't Take Your Love to Town/I Can't Stop Loving You	1970	—	3.00	6.00
❑ 2180	Rainy Night in Georgia/Lodi	1970	—	3.00	6.00
❑ 2187	Chicken Fried Soul/Chunck	1971	—	2.50	5.00
❑ 2192	Me and Bobby McGee/Sweet Caroline	1971	—	2.50	5.00
❑ 2199	Easy Loving/Misty Blue	1971	—	2.50	5.00
❑ 2210	Lovesick Blues/Cold, Cold Heart	1972	—	2.50	5.00
❑ 2220	Wabash Cannonball/To Get to You	1972	—	2.50	5.00
❑ 2231	Tuffer Than Tuff/The Green Door	1973	—	2.00	4.00
❑ 2238	Ruff/Baby Don't Get Hooked on Me	1973	—	2.00	4.00
❑ 2256	Country Comfort/Closin' Time's a Downer	1973	—	2.00	4.00
❑ 2261	Last Date/Methilda	1974	—	2.00	4.00
❑ 2273	There Goes My Everything/Tennessee Saturday Night	1974	—	2.00	4.00
❑ 2286	Peace in the Valley/Raunchy	1975	—	2.00	4.00
❑ 2299	Walk On By/Malt Liquor	1975	—	2.00	4.00
❑ 2313	Blue Eyes Crying in the Rain/I'll Fly Away	1976	—	2.00	4.00
❑ 78516	It Was Almost Like a Song/(B-side unknown)	1978	—	2.00	4.00
❑ 78526	Don't It Make My Brown Eyes Blue/Blanket on the Ground	1978	—	2.00	4.00

LOUIS (LOUISE?)

Number	Title (A Side/B Side)	Yr	VG	VG+	NM
❑ 2001	Tuff/Sittin' Tight	1961	7.50	15.00	30.00

SANTO

Number	Title (A Side/B Side)	Yr	VG	VG+	NM
❑ 503	Sugar Blues/38 Special	1962	3.75	7.50	15.00
❑ 506	Big Shot/Rest	1962	3.75	7.50	15.00

Albums

ALLEGIANCE

Number	Title (A Side/B Side)	Yr	VG	VG+	NM
❑ AV-5024	Ace in the Whole	1986	2.00	4.00	8.00

Number	Title (A Side/B Side)	Yr	VG	VG+	NM
HI					
❑ 6006	After Hours	1978	2.50	5.00	10.00
❑ 8003	Sax Man	1977	2.50	5.00	10.00
❑ 8008	Cannon Country	1979	2.50	5.00	10.00
❑ HL-12007 [M]	Tuff Sax	1962	6.25	12.50	25.00
❑ HL-12008 [M]	Looking Back	1962	6.25	12.50	25.00
❑ HL-12014 [M]	The Moanin' Sax of Ace Cannon	1963	6.25	12.50	25.00
❑ HL-12016 [M]	Aces Hi	1964	5.00	10.00	20.00
❑ HL-12019 [M]	The Great Show Tunes	1964	5.00	10.00	20.00
❑ HL-12022 [M]	Christmas Cheer	1964	5.00	10.00	20.00
❑ HL-12025 [M]	Ace Cannon Live	1965	3.75	7.50	15.00
❑ HL-12028 [M]	Nashville Hits	1965	3.75	7.50	15.00
❑ HL-12030 [M]	Sweet and Tuff	1966	3.75	7.50	15.00
❑ HL-12035 [M]	The Misty Sax of Ace Cannon	1967	5.00	10.00	20.00
❑ HL-12040 [M]	Memphis Golden Hits	1967	5.00	10.00	20.00
❑ SHL-32007 [S]	Tuff Sax	1962	7.50	15.00	30.00
❑ SHL-32008 [S]	Looking Back	1962	7.50	15.00	30.00
❑ SHL-32014 [S]	The Moanin' Sax of Ace Cannon	1963	7.50	15.00	30.00
❑ SHL-32016 [S]	Aces Hi	1964	6.25	12.50	25.00
❑ SHL-32019 [S]	The Great Show Tunes	1964	6.25	12.50	25.00
❑ SHL-32022 [S]	Christmas Cheer	1964	6.25	12.50	25.00
❑ SHL-32025 [S]	Ace Cannon Live	1965	5.00	10.00	20.00
❑ SHL-32028 [S]	Nashville Hits	1965	5.00	10.00	20.00
❑ SHL-32030 [S]	Sweet and Tuff	1966	5.00	10.00	20.00
❑ SHL-32035 [S]	The Misty Sax of Ace Cannon	1967	3.75	7.50	15.00
❑ SHL-32040 [S]	Memphis Golden Hits	1967	3.75	7.50	15.00
❑ SHL-32043	The Incomparable Sax of Ace Cannon	1968	3.75	7.50	15.00
❑ SHL-32046	In the Spotlight	1968	3.75	7.50	15.00
❑ SHL-32051	The Ace of Sax	1969	3.75	7.50	15.00
❑ SHL-32057	The Happy and Mellow Sax of Ace Cannon	1970	3.00	6.00	12.00
❑ SHL-32060	Cool 'n Saxy	1971	3.00	6.00	12.00
❑ SHL-32067	Blowing Wild	1971	3.00	6.00	12.00
❑ SHL-32071	Cannon Country	1972	3.00	6.00	12.00
❑ SHL-32072/3 [(2)]	Aces Back to Back	1972	3.75	7.50	15.00
❑ SHL-32076	Baby Don't Get Hooked on Me	1973	2.50	5.00	10.00
❑ SHL-32080	Country Comfort	1974	2.50	5.00	10.00
❑ SHL-32086	That Music City Feeling	1974	2.50	5.00	10.00
❑ SHL-32090	Super Sax Country Style	1975	2.50	5.00	10.00
❑ SHL-32101	Peace in the Valley	1976	2.50	5.00	10.00

CANNON, JIMMI

45s

Number	Title (A Side/B Side)	Yr	VG	VG+	NM
WARNER BROS.					
❑ 29949	Fool's Gold/Heartache by Heartache	1982	—	2.00	4.00
❑ 49806	Whole Lot of Cheatin' Goin' On/He Just Said Goodbye	1981	—	2.00	4.00
❑ 50024	Even If It's Wrong/Stealin' Feelin's	1982	—	2.00	4.00

CANNON, JOHNNY

See ACE CANNON.

CANNONS, THE

45s

Number	Title (A Side/B Side)	Yr	VG	VG+	NM
COMPLEAT					
❑ 105	All Things Made New Again/Watch My Lips	1983	—	2.50	5.00
❑ 116	One Step Closer/Strangers Again	1983	—	2.50	5.00
MERCURY					
❑ 888048-7	Do You Mind If I Step Into Your Dreams/How Can I Love Now	1986	—	—	3.00
❑ 888048-7 [PS]	Do You Mind If I Step Into Your Dreams/How Can I Love Now	1986	—	2.00	4.00
❑ 888548-7	Love'll Come Looking for You/I'll Save My Love for You	1987	—	—	3.00
❑ 888869-7	Bet Your Heart (On a Sure Thing)/I'll Save My Love for You	1987	—	—	3.00

CANYON

45s

Number	Title (A Side/B Side)	Yr	VG	VG+	NM
16TH AVENUE					
❑ 70410	Overdue/In the Middle of the Night	1988	—	2.00	4.00
❑ 70415	In the Middle of the Night/Overdue	1988	—	2.00	4.00
❑ 70419	I Guess I Just Missed You/Love Wins	1988	—	2.00	4.00
❑ 70423	Love Is on the Line/Love Wins	1988	—	2.00	4.00
❑ 70426	Right Track, Wrong Train/Hitch a Ride	1989	—	2.00	4.00
❑ 70433	Hot Nights/Oh, Help Me	1989	—	2.00	4.00
❑ 70437	Radio Romance/Streamline	1989	—	2.00	4.00
❑ 70439	Carryin' On/Streamline	1990	—	2.00	4.00
❑ 70445	Dam These Tears/Carryin' On	1990	—	2.50	5.00

Albums

Number	Title (A Side/B Side)	Yr	VG	VG+	NM
16TH AVENUE					
❑ D1-70552	I Guess I Just Missed You	1988	2.50	5.00	10.00
❑ D1-70556	Radio Romance	1989	2.50	5.00	10.00

CAPITALS, THE

45s

Number	Title (A Side/B Side)	Yr	VG	VG+	NM
RIDGETOP					
❑ 00779	Me Touchin' You/If I Was Still Sinnin'	1979	—	2.50	5.00
❑ 01080	A Little Ground in Texas/Bridge Over Broadway	1980	—	2.50	5.00
❑ 01281	Bridge Over Broadway/Love Him Out of Your Mind	1981	—	2.50	5.00

CAPPS, HANK

45s

Number	Title (A Side/B Side)	Yr	VG	VG+	NM
CAPITOL					
❑ 3416	Bowling Green/Roll Mississippi Roll	1972	—	3.50	7.00
❑ 3545	Breakdown/Homeward Bound	1973	—	3.50	7.00

CAPTAIN AND TENNILLE

The below record was this pop duo's only country hit.

45s

Number	Title (A Side/B Side)	Yr	VG	VG+	NM
A&M					
❑ 2027	I'm On My Way/We Never Really Said Goodbye	1978	—	2.00	4.00
❑ 2027 [PS]	I'm On My Way/We Never Really Said Goodbye	1978	—	3.00	6.00

CAPTAIN STUBBY

Most of these were with the Buccaneers. Also see BURL IVES.

45s

Number	Title (A Side/B Side)	Yr	VG	VG+	NM
DECCA					
❑ 9-46240	Roses/Little Buffalo Bill	1950	7.50	15.00	30.00
❑ 9-46265	Beautiful Morning Glory/Hilegged Hilegged	1950	7.50	15.00	30.00
❑ 9-46282	At the Rainbow's End/You Never Say I Love You	1951	6.25	12.50	25.00
❑ 9-46315	Bogle to Boogle to Boone/The Hokey Pokey	1951	6.25	12.50	25.00
❑ 9-46321	The Gentle Carpenter of Bethlehem/God Put a Rainbow	1951	6.25	12.50	25.00
❑ 9-46371	It's Hard to Be Loved/I Was the Last One to Know	1951	6.25	12.50	25.00
❑ 9-46384	The Girl in the Gilded Picture Frame/Every Time I Want	1951	6.25	12.50	25.00
JANIE					
❑ 45-3/4	Cryin' Wine/Love Is My Prison	195?	5.00	10.00	20.00

Selected 78s

Number	Title (A Side/B Side)	Yr	VG	VG+	NM
DECCA					
❑ 46149	Money, Marbles and Chalk/Tennessee Tears	1949	5.00	10.00	20.00
❑ 46169	Come Wet Your Mustache with Me/Country Boy	1949	5.00	10.00	20.00
❑ 46193	He's a Chubby Little Fellow/Jolly Old Saint Nicholas	1949	5.00	10.00	20.00
—Unknown on 45 rpm; if one exists on the early-1950s label, it would be worth about double this value					
❑ 46196	Beyond the Sunset/Grandma Got to California	1948	5.00	10.00	20.00
—Unknown on 45 rpm; if one exists on the early-1950s label, it would be worth about double this value					
❑ 49196	Beyond the Sunset/Grandma Got to California	1949	5.00	10.00	20.00

CARDWELL, JACK

45s

Number	Title (A Side/B Side)	Yr	VG	VG+	NM
KING					
❑ 1163	You Hid Your Cheatin' Heart/My Love for You Would Fill Ten Pots	1953	6.25	12.50	25.00
❑ 1172	The Death of Hank Williams/Two Arms	1953	7.50	15.00	30.00
❑ 1203	Can I/Lonesome Midnight	1953	6.25	12.50	25.00
❑ 1241	I'm Not Lazy, I'm Just Tired/Stop Laughing at Me	1953	6.25	12.50	25.00
❑ 1262	I'm Gonna Write a Song/A Vitamin Called Love	1953	6.25	12.50	25.00
❑ 1269	Dear Joan/You're Looking for Something	1953	7.50	15.00	30.00
❑ 1292	I Can't Make Up My Mind/Walking My Blues Away	1953	6.25	12.50	25.00
❑ 1339	Diddle Diddle Dumpling/Blue Cave	1954	6.25	12.50	25.00
❑ 1357	Whiskey, Women and Loaded Dice/Slap-Ka-Dab	1954	6.25	12.50	25.00
❑ 1381	Will Our Love Fade and Die/There's a Train Leaving	1954	6.25	12.50	25.00
❑ 1396	No More/I Discovered You	1954	6.25	12.50	25.00
❑ 1442	Ko Ko Mo/Are You Mine	1955	5.00	10.00	20.00
❑ 1454	Whadya/Day Done Broke Too Soon	1955	5.00	10.00	20.00
SANDY					
❑ 1023	All Alone/Blue Lifetime	1959	3.75	7.50	15.00
STARDAY					
❑ 310	Hey, Hey Baby/Once Every Day	1957	50.00	100.00	200.00

CARGILL, HENSON

45s

Number	Title (A Side/B Side)	Yr	VG	VG+	NM
ARCO					
❑ 6605	Big Town/How Long Is Never	1967	2.00	4.00	8.00
ATLANTIC					
❑ 4007	Some Old California Memory/A Writer of Verses and a Singer of Songs	1973	—	2.00	4.00
❑ 4016	She Still Comes to Me (To Pour the Wine)/But You Know I Love You	1974	—	2.00	4.00
❑ 4021	Stop and Smell the Roses/Strawberry Wine	1974	—	2.00	4.00
COPPER MOUNTAIN					
❑ 201	Silence on the Line/Forever in Blue Jeans	1979	—	2.00	4.00
❑ 589	Have a Good Day/(B-side unknown)	1980	—	2.00	4.00
ELEKTRA					
❑ 45234	Deep in the Heart of Dixie/It Hurts the Man	1975	—	2.00	4.00
❑ 45273	Something to Hold On To/Now and Then	1975	—	2.00	4.00
MEGA					
❑ 0030	Pencil Marks on the Wall/Momma's Waiting	1971	—	2.50	5.00
❑ 0043	Naked and Crying/Afraid to Rock the Boat	1971	—	2.50	5.00
❑ 0060	I Can't Face the Bed Alone/Daddy Don't You Walk So Fast	1972	—	2.50	5.00
❑ 0074	Oklahoma Hell/She Likes Warm Summer Days	1972	—	2.50	5.00
❑ 0090	Red Skies Over Georgia/1932	1972	—	2.50	5.00
❑ 0100	Running from the Rain/My '47 Chevy, My Honky Tonk Guitar, and Me	1973	—	2.50	5.00
MONUMENT					
❑ 1041	Skip a Rope/Very Well Traveled Man	1967	—	3.00	6.00
❑ 1065	Row Row Row/Six White Horses	1968	—	3.00	6.00
❑ 1084	She Thinks I'm On That Train/It Just Don't Take Me Long to Say Goodbye	1968	—	3.00	6.00

Number	Title (A Side/B Side)	Yr	VG	VG+	NM
❑ 1106	A Candle for Amy/Wild Flower	1968	—	3.00	6.00
❑ 1122	None of My Business/So Many Ways of Saying She's Gone	1969	—	3.00	6.00
❑ 1142	This Generation Shall Not Pass/Little Girls and Little Boys	1969	—	3.00	6.00
❑ 1158	Then the Baby Came/Hemphill, Kentucky, Consolidated Coal Mine	1969	—	3.00	6.00
❑ 1178	Silver Bells/The Little Drummer Boy	1969	2.00	4.00	8.00
❑ 1184	Me & Bobby McGee/What's My Name	1970	—	3.00	6.00
❑ 1198	The Most Uncomplicated Goodbye I've Ever Heard/Four Shades of Love	1970	—	3.00	6.00
❑ 1209	Bless 'Em All/How Much Do Memories Cost	1970	—	3.00	6.00
TOWER					
❑ 400	Picking White Cotton/Joe, Jesse and I	1968	2.00	4.00	8.00
Albums					
ATLANTIC					
❑ SD 7279	This Is Henson Cargill Country	1973	3.00	6.00	12.00
HARMONY					
❑ KH 31397	Welcome to My World	1972	2.50	5.00	10.00
MEGA					
❑ 31-1016	On the Road	1972	3.75	7.50	15.00
MONUMENT					
❑ SLP-18094	Skip a Rope	1968	5.00	10.00	20.00
❑ SLP-18103	Coming On Strong	1968	5.00	10.00	20.00
❑ SLP-18117	None of My Business	1969	5.00	10.00	20.00
❑ SLP-18137	Uncomplicated	1970	5.00	10.00	20.00

CARLETTE

45s

Number	Title (A Side/B Side)	Yr	VG	VG+	NM
LUV					
❑ 106	Showdown/(B-side unknown)	1985	—	2.50	5.00
❑ 107	You Can't Measure My Love/(B-side unknown)	1985	—	2.50	5.00
❑ 109	Tonight's the Night/You Know What I Need (When I Need It)	1985	—	2.50	5.00
❑ 116	Two Steps from the Blues/(B-side unknown)	1986	—	2.50	5.00
❑ 118	Sugar Shack/You Know What I Need (When I Need It)	1986	—	2.50	5.00
❑ 125	We Belong Together/Tennessee	1986	—	2.50	5.00
❑ 125 [PS]	We Belong Together/Tennessee	1986	2.00	4.00	8.00
❑ 137	Waltzin' with Daddy/Tennessee	1987	—	2.50	5.00
❑ 142	You've Lost That Loving Feeling/(B-side unknown)	1987	—	2.50	5.00
OAK					
❑ 1079	Any Way That You Want Me/Oh Boy	1985	—	3.00	6.00

CARLILE, TOM

45s

Number	Title (A Side/B Side)	Yr	VG	VG+	NM
COLUMBIA					
❑ 4-44372	I Saw the Light/Nightingale	1967	2.50	5.00	10.00
DOOR KNOB					
❑ 157	Gold Cadillac/Lay Down Sally	1981	—	2.50	5.00
❑ 162	Get It While You Can/M.D. 20/20 High	1981	—	2.50	5.00
❑ 167	Catch Me if You Can/Get It While You Can	1981	—	2.50	5.00
❑ 167 [PS]	Catch Me if You Can/Get It While You Can	1981	2.00	4.00	8.00
❑ 170	Lover (Right Where I Want You)/Walk Around the Block, Deanna	1981	—	2.50	5.00
❑ 170 [PS]	Lover (Right Where I Want You)/Walk Around the Block, Deanna	1981	2.00	4.00	8.00
❑ 172	Feel/Walk Around the Block, Deanna	1981	—	2.50	5.00
❑ 172 [PS]	Feel/Walk Around the Block, Deanna	1981	2.00	4.00	8.00
❑ 176	Hurtin' for Your Love/The Man Who Loved to Drink	1982	—	2.50	5.00
❑ 176 [PS]	Hurtin' for Your Love/The Man Who Loved to Drink	1982	2.00	4.00	8.00
❑ 180	Back in Debbie's Arms/Twenty Years Ago	1982	—	2.50	5.00
❑ 180 [PS]	Back in Debbie's Arms/Twenty Years Ago	1982	2.00	4.00	8.00
❑ 187	Green Eyes/No One to Tell My Heartache To	1982	—	2.50	5.00
❑ 187 [PS]	Green Eyes/No One to Tell My Heartache To	1982	2.00	4.00	8.00
❑ 191	Rainin' Down in Nashville/(I Went to) Heaven with the Devil	1982	—	2.50	5.00
Albums					
DOOR KNOB					
❑ 1006	The Tom Carlile Feel	198?	3.75	7.50	15.00

CARLISLE, BILL

Also see CLIFF CARLISLE; THE CARLISLE BROTHERS.

45s

Number	Title (A Side/B Side)	Yr	VG	VG+	NM
CHART					
❑ 5044	I'm Movin'/Everything Will Be Alright	1969	2.00	4.00	8.00
❑ 5065	Dirty Old Mine/Big Wheel from Boston	1970	2.00	4.00	8.00
❑ 5092	Daddy Won the War on Poverty/Too Many Dollars, Not Enough Sense	1970	2.00	4.00	8.00
❑ 5117	Can't Get Enough/(B-side unknown)	1971	2.00	4.00	8.00
COLUMBIA					
❑ 4-41679	Air Brakes/Home Sweet Home	1960	3.00	6.00	12.00
❑ 4-42049	Too Old to Cut the Mustard/Have a Drink on Me	1961	2.50	5.00	10.00
❑ 4-42263	Woman Driver/Monkey Business	1962	2.50	5.00	10.00
❑ 4-42609	Hand Me Down My Walking Cane/It Takes All Kinds to Make a World	1962	2.50	5.00	10.00
HICKORY					
❑ 1254	Big John Henry's Girl/Shanghai Rooster	1964	2.00	4.00	8.00
❑ 1280	The Great Snow Man/Before She Knows I'm Gone	1964	2.00	4.00	8.00
❑ 1348	What Kinda Deal Is This/Shot Gun	1965	2.00	4.00	8.00
❑ 1383	Take This Country Music and Shove It/No Help Wanted	1966	2.00	4.00	8.00
❑ 1418	If It Were You Instead of Me (What Would You Do)/Doctor R.D.	1966	2.00	4.00	8.00
❑ 1483	Th' Wife/Wouldn't Take Your Pistol	1967	2.00	4.00	8.00
❑ 1502	All of This for Sally/My Name Is Jones	1968	2.00	4.00	8.00
❑ 1518	Do You Love Me, Honey/Don't Hit My Friend	1968	2.00	4.00	8.00
❑ 1611	Man of the Lord/I'm Going Home Last Summer	1971	—	3.50	7.00
RCA VICTOR					
❑ 47-7017	Uncle Bud/I've Waited Too Long	1957	5.00	10.00	20.00
❑ 47-7132	The Tiny Space Man/How Will I Know	1958	5.00	10.00	20.00
❑ 47-7214	Dumb Bunny/Who's-a Gonna Stop Me	1958	3.75	7.50	15.00
VANGUARD					
❑ 35165	I Wanna Be a Country Singer/That's What I Shoulda Said	1972	2.00	4.00	8.00
Selected 78s					
BLUEBIRD					
❑ B-6478	Rattlin' Daddy/I'm Wearin' the Britches Now	193?	12.50	25.00	50.00
❑ B-6568	titles unknown	193?	5.00	10.00	20.00
❑ B-6600	titles unknown	193?	5.00	10.00	20.00
❑ B-6608	titles unknown	193?	5.00	10.00	20.00
❑ B-6775	titles unknown	193?	5.00	10.00	20.00
❑ B-6938	Still There's a Spark of Love, Part 2/I'll Be All Smiles, Love	193?	5.00	10.00	20.00
❑ B-7019	The Heavenly Train/He Will Be Your Saviour, Too	193?	5.00	10.00	20.00
❑ B-7087	titles unknown	193?	5.00	10.00	20.00
❑ B-7153	titles unknown	193?	5.00	10.00	20.00
❑ B-7414	titles unknown	193?	5.00	10.00	20.00
❑ B-7613	titles unknown	193?	5.00	10.00	20.00
DECCA					
❑ 5626	No Letter in the Mail Today/Drifting	1939	5.00	10.00	20.00
❑ 5713	Sparkling Blue Eyes/(B-side unknown)	1939	5.00	10.00	20.00
❑ 46045	Wabash Cannonball/Sparkling Blue Eyes	1947	3.75	7.50	15.00
KING					
❑ 504	Maggie Get the Hammer/I Paid with a Broken Heart	1946	5.00	10.00	20.00
❑ 515	What Does It Matter to You/You Wouldn't Understand	1946	5.00	10.00	20.00
❑ 541	Dreamy Eyes/She Won't Be My Baby No More	1946	5.00	10.00	20.00
❑ 567	Rockin' Chair Money/When Snowflakes Fall	1947	5.00	10.00	20.00
❑ 608	Dollar Bill Mama Blues (Part 1)/Dollar Bill Mama Blues (Part 2)	1947	5.00	10.00	20.00
❑ 638	Girl in the Blue Velvet Band/Shine Your Light to Another	1947	5.00	10.00	20.00
❑ 657	Wedding Bells/Sparkling Blue Eyes	1947	5.00	10.00	20.00
❑ 663	The Answer to Rainbow at Midnight/You Laughed When I Cried	1948	5.00	10.00	20.00
❑ 679	When the Old Cow Went Dry/Love in the First Degree	1948	5.00	10.00	20.00
❑ 697	Tramp on the Street/Don't Be Ashamed of Your Mother	1948	5.00	10.00	20.00
❑ 709	I Never See My Baby Alone/That Guy's Out Gunnin'	1948	5.00	10.00	20.00
❑ 738	I Hope You See the Same Star/I Saw My Future in a Rainbow	1948	5.00	10.00	20.00
❑ 758	Old Joe Clark/Skip to My Lou	1949	5.00	10.00	20.00
❑ 805	Empty Arms/I'm Crying Tonight Over You	1949	5.00	10.00	20.00
VOCALION					
❑ 02520	Rattle Snake Daddy/(B-side unknown)	193?	12.50	25.00	50.00
❑ 02946	I'm Gonna Kill Myself/(B-side unknown)	193?	12.50	25.00	50.00
Albums					
HICKORY					
❑ LPM-129 [M]	The Best of Bill Carlisle	1967	6.25	12.50	25.00
❑ LPS-129 [S]	The Best of Bill Carlisle	1967	6.25	12.50	25.00

CARLISLE, BOB

45s

Number	Title (A Side/B Side)	Yr	VG	VG+	NM
JIVE/DIADEM					
❑ 42456	Butterfly Kisses (Album Version)/Butterfly Kisses (The Country Remix)	1997	—	2.50	5.00

CARLISLE, CLIFF

Also see BILL CARLISLE; THE CARLISLE BROTHERS.

Selected 78s

Number	Title (A Side/B Side)	Yr	VG	VG+	NM
BLUEBIRD					
❑ B-6350	Rambling Yodeler/Wild Cat Woman and a Tom Cat Man	193?	5.00	10.00	20.00
❑ B-6405	A Stretch of 28 Years/(B-side unknown)	193?	5.00	10.00	20.00
❑ B-6439	Cowboy Johnny's Last Ride/(B-side unknown)	193?	5.00	10.00	20.00
❑ B-6458	You'll Miss Me When I'm Gone/(B-side unknown)	193?	5.00	10.00	20.00
❑ B-6493	When I Feel Froggie, I'm Gonna Hop/(B-side unknown)	193?	5.00	10.00	20.00
❑ B-6524	Wigglin' Mama/(B-side unknown)	193?	5.00	10.00	20.00
❑ B-6540	titles unknown	193?	5.00	10.00	20.00
❑ B-6631	titles unknown	193?	5.00	10.00	20.00
❑ B-6647	titles unknown	193?	5.00	10.00	20.00
❑ B-6754	titles unknown	193?	5.00	10.00	20.00
❑ B-6791	titles unknown	193?	5.00	10.00	20.00
❑ B-6830	titles unknown	193?	5.00	10.00	20.00
❑ B-6855	Just a Wayward Boy/Shine on Me	193?	5.00	10.00	20.00
❑ B-6980	titles unknown	193?	5.00	10.00	20.00
❑ B-7031	titles unknown	193?	5.00	10.00	20.00
❑ B-7094	titles unknown	193?	5.00	10.00	20.00
❑ B-7147	titles unknown	193?	5.00	10.00	20.00

Number	Title (A Side/B Side)	Yr	VG	VG+	NM
❑ B-7290	Two Little Sweethearts/The Gal I Left Behind	193?	5.00	10.00	20.00
❑ B-7702	titles unknown	193?	3.75	7.50	15.00
❑ B-7717	titles unknown	193?	3.75	7.50	15.00
❑ B-7740	New Memories of You That Haunt Me/Ridin' the Blinds to the Call of the Pines	193?	3.75	7.50	15.00
❑ B-7790	Your Saddle Is Empty To-Night/Cowboy's Dying Dream	1938	3.75	7.50	15.00
❑ B-7817	titles unknown	1938	3.75	7.50	15.00
❑ B-8199	titles unknown	1940	3.75	7.50	15.00
❑ B-8220	Hobo's Fate/Where My Memory Lies	1940	3.75	7.50	15.00
CHAMPION					
❑ 15969	Memphis Yodel/(B-side unknown)	193?	7.50	15.00	30.00
❑ 15992	Desert Blues/(B-side unknown)	193?	7.50	15.00	30.00
❑ 16028	Virginia Blues/(B-side unknown)	193?	7.50	15.00	30.00
❑ 16140	Crazy Blues/(B-side unknown)	193?	7.50	15.00	30.00
❑ 16165	No Daddy Blues/(B-side unknown)	193?	7.50	15.00	30.00
❑ 16212	Box Car Blues/(B-side unknown)	193?	10.00	20.00	40.00
❑ 16239	High Steppin' Mama/(B-side unknown)	193?	10.00	20.00	40.00
❑ 16270	Hobo Jack's Last Ride/(B-side unknown)	193?	10.00	20.00	40.00
❑ 16329	Nobody Wants Me/(B-side unknown)	193?	10.00	20.00	40.00
❑ 16419	Memories That Haunt Me/(B-side unknown)	193?	17.50	35.00	70.00
❑ 16434	She's Waiting for Me/(B-side unknown)	193?	17.50	35.00	70.00
❑ 16447	The Fatal Run/(B-side unknown)	193?	17.50	35.00	70.00
CONQUEROR					
❑ 7968	Dear Old Daddy/Memories That Make Me Cry	193?	5.00	10.00	20.00
DECCA					
❑ 46105	Footprints in the Snow/Makes No Difference You See	1947	3.75	7.50	15.00
GENNETT					
❑ 7153	Down in the Jailhouse on My Knees/(B-side unknown)	193?	15.00	30.00	60.00
❑ 7187	Desert Blues/(B-side unknown)	193?	15.00	30.00	60.00
❑ 7206	Memphis Yodel/(B-side unknown)	193?	20.00	40.00	80.00
❑ 7244	Virginia Blues/(B-side unknown)	193?	25.00	50.00	100.00
❑ 7288	I'm Lonely and Blue/(B-side unknown)	193?	25.00	50.00	100.00
KING					
❑ 529	It's All Over Now/Stay Away Don't Bother Me	1946	5.00	10.00	20.00
PERFECT					
❑ 12816	Birmingham Jail No. 2/(B-side unknown)	193?	5.00	10.00	20.00
RCA VICTOR					
❑ 20-2248	Scars Upon My Heart/(B-side unknown)	1947	3.00	6.00	12.00
Albums					
OLD TIMEY					
❑ 103	Cliff Carlisle, Volume 1	198?	3.00	6.00	12.00
❑ 104	Cliff Carlisle, Volume 2	198?	3.00	6.00	12.00

CARLISLE BROTHERS, THE

Includes records as "The Carlisles." Also see BILL CARLISLE; CLIFF CARLISLE.

Number	Title (A Side/B Side)	Yr	VG	VG+	NM
45s					
COLUMBIA					
❑ 4-41873	John Came Home/Skin 'Im Quick	1960	3.00	6.00	12.00
KING					
❑ 5714	Empty Arms/Rainbow at Midnight	1963	3.00	6.00	12.00
MERCURY					
❑ 6348	Too Old to Cut the Mustard/My Happiness Belongs to Someone Else	1951	7.50	15.00	30.00
❑ 6371	I Would If I Could/Patch Up Your Old Love Affair	1952	7.50	15.00	30.00
❑ 6388	Tennessee Memories/True Love	1952	7.50	15.00	30.00
❑ 6403	Love, Love, Love/Woman Driver	1952	7.50	15.00	30.00
❑ 70028	No Help Wanted/My Heart Is Not for Sale	1952	6.25	12.50	25.00
❑ 70109	Knothole/Leave That Liar Alone	1953	5.00	10.00	20.00
❑ 70174	Is Zat You, Myrtle/Something Different	1953	5.00	10.00	20.00
❑ 70232	Tain't Nice (To Talk Like That)/Unpucker	1953	5.00	10.00	20.00
❑ 70306	I'll Never Love Again/I Need a Little Help	1954	5.00	10.00	20.00
❑ 70351	Shake-A-Leg/Let Me Hold Your Little Hand	1954	5.00	10.00	20.00
❑ 70435	Honey Love/Female Hercules	1954	5.00	10.00	20.00
❑ 70484	Busy Body Boogie/The Mainest Thing	1954	5.00	10.00	20.00
❑ 70544	It's Bedtime Bill/Rusty Old Hale	1955	5.00	10.00	20.00
❑ 70604	Bargain Day, Half Off/Nine Have Tried	1955	5.00	10.00	20.00
❑ 70665	Lil' Liza Jane/Teletouch	1955	5.00	10.00	20.00
❑ 70712	Middle Age Spread/On My Way to the Show	1955	5.00	10.00	20.00
❑ 70754	Dangerous Crossing/Run, Boy	1955	5.00	10.00	20.00
❑ 70828	Pickin' Peas/Goo-Goo Da Da	1956	3.75	7.50	15.00
❑ 70887	Knock Knock (You Can't Come In)/Money Tree	1956	3.75	7.50	15.00
❑ 70951	A Poor Man's Riches/Rainbow at Midnight	1956	3.75	7.50	15.00
❑ 71035	I'm Rough Stuff/Business Man	1957	3.75	7.50	15.00
❑ 71110	Wouldn't You Like To/Ladder of Love	1957	3.75	7.50	15.00
Selected 78s					
BLUEBIRD					
❑ B-8862	I'm Sorry Now/You'll Never Know	1942	5.00	10.00	20.00
❑ B-8936	No Wedding Bells/I Believe I'm Entitled to You	1942	3.75	7.50	15.00
❑ B-8996	Sugar Cane Mama/She Waits for Me There	1942	3.75	7.50	15.00
DECCA					
❑ 5774	Gonna Raise a Ruckus Tonight/There Is No More That I Can Say	1939	5.00	10.00	20.00
KING					
❑ 510	Roll On Your Weary Way/Baby You Done Flubbed Your Dub with Me	1946	5.00	10.00	20.00
❑ 535	Rainbow at Midnight/Don't Tell Me Your Worries	1946	5.00	10.00	20.00
Albums					
KING					
❑ 643 [M]	Fresh from the Country	1959	12.50	25.00	50.00
MERCURY					
❑ MG-20359 [M]	On Stage with the Carlisles	1958	12.50	25.00	50.00

CARLISLES, THE

See BILL CARLISLE; THE CARLISLE BROTHERS.

CARLLILE, KATHY

Number	Title (A Side/B Side)	Yr	VG	VG+	NM
45s					
FRONTLINE					
❑ 705	Stay Until the Rain Stops/In Front of the Line	1980	—	3.00	6.00
❑ 705 [PS]	Stay Until the Rain Stops/In Front of the Line	1980	2.00	4.00	8.00

CARLSON, PAULETTE

Also see HIGHWAY 101.

Number	Title (A Side/B Side)	Yr	VG	VG+	NM
45s					
LIBERTY					
❑ S7-57737	Not with My Heart You Don't/It's Too Bad	1992	—	2.50	5.00
RCA					
❑ JK-13546 [DJ]	You Gotta Get to My Heart (Before You Lay a Hand on Me) (same on both sides)	1983	2.50	5.00	10.00
—Promo only on red vinyl					
❑ PB-13546	You Gotta Get to My Heart (Before You Lay a Hand on Me)/With a Friend Like You (Who Needs a Lover)	1983	—	2.00	4.00
❑ JK-13599 [DJ]	I'd Say Yes (same on both sides)	1983	2.50	5.00	10.00
—Promo only on yellow vinyl					
❑ PB-13599	I'd Say Yes/Sweeten the Love	1983	—	2.00	4.00
❑ JK-13745 [DJ]	Can You Fool (same on both sides)	1984	2.50	5.00	10.00
—Promo only on yellow vinyl					
❑ PB-13745	Can You Fool/I Go to Pieces	1984	—	2.00	4.00

CARMACK, HAROLD

Number	Title (A Side/B Side)	Yr	VG	VG+	NM
45s					
DECCA					
❑ 9-46362	Down Yonder/Margie	1951	6.25	12.50	25.00

CARMAN, JENKS (TEX)

Number	Title (A Side/B Side)	Yr	VG	VG+	NM
45s					
CAPITOL					
❑ F1571	Ten Thousand Miles/I Could Love You Baby	1951	6.25	12.50	25.00
❑ F1822	Another Dream/Hilo March	1951	6.25	12.50	25.00
❑ F2067	My Trusting Heart/Don't Feel Sorry for Me	1952	5.00	10.00	20.00
❑ F2345	Hillbilly Hula/I'm a Poor Lonesome Fellow	1953	5.00	10.00	20.00
❑ F2534	Locust Hill Rag/My Lonely Heart and I	1953	5.00	10.00	20.00
❑ F2621	Blue Memories/The Caissons Go Rolling Along	1953	5.00	10.00	20.00
❑ F2752	Samba Stomp/Sweet Luwanna	1954	5.00	10.00	20.00
❑ F2886	Dixie Cannon Ball/Indian Polka	1954	5.00	10.00	20.00
DECCA					
❑ 9-28771	Hillbilly Hula/New Waikiki Beach	1953	6.25	12.50	25.00
REM					
❑ 329	Bamboo Love/Blackjack David	196?	3.75	7.50	15.00
SAGE					
❑ 218	They Had to Say Goodbye/You'll Come a-Crawlin' Back	195?	3.75	7.50	15.00
❑ 246	Krish-a-Boom-Ba/Walking and Crying for You	195?	3.75	7.50	15.00
❑ 251	My Broken Heart Won't Let Me/Wolf Creek	195?	3.75	7.50	15.00
❑ 272	Wildwood Flower/Honk, Honk, Honk	1960	3.00	6.00	12.00
❑ 289	Beverly Ann/I Feel Like I Feel	196?	3.00	6.00	12.00
❑ 300	Little May/This Lonely Road	196?	3.00	6.00	12.00
❑ 337	Amo Mia/Ozark Rose	196?	3.00	6.00	12.00
❑ 351	Fire in the Teepee/Learning to Do Without You	1962	3.00	6.00	12.00
❑ 352	Maggie's Twist/I'll Go On Loving You	1962	3.00	6.00	12.00
❑ 398	Custer's Massacre/Little Black Jack Davey	196?	3.00	6.00	12.00

CARNES, JANIS

Also see RICK AND JANIS CARNES.

Number	Title (A Side/B Side)	Yr	VG	VG+	NM
45s					
RCA					
❑ PB-12104	Smoky Places/Midnight Revival	1980	—	2.50	5.00

CARNES, KIM

Other than as a duet partner, she did not record country music until she went to MCA in 1988. Also see GENE COTTON; KENNY ROGERS.

Number	Title (A Side/B Side)	Yr	VG	VG+	NM
45s					
MCA					
❑ 53387	Speed of the Sound of Loneliness/Blood from the Bandit	1988	—	—	3.00
❑ 53433	Crazy in Love/Blood from the Bandit	1988	—	—	3.00
❑ 53433 [PS]	Crazy in Love/Blood from the Bandit	1988	—	2.00	4.00
❑ 53494	Fantastic Fire of Love/Brass and Batons	1989	—	—	3.00
Albums					
MCA					
❑ 42200	View from the House	1988	2.00	4.00	8.00

CARNES, RICK AND JANIS

Also see JANIS CARNES.

Number	Title (A Side/B Side)	Yr	VG	VG+	NM
45s					
ELEKTRA					
❑ 69928	Have You Heard/Blue, Only Blue	1982	—	2.00	4.00
MCA					
❑ 52414	Long Lost Causes/Standing in the Need of Love	1984	—	2.00	4.00
WARNER BROS.					
❑ 29448	Does He Ever Mention My Name/Silver Eagle	1983	—	2.00	4.00
❑ 29656	Poor Girl/Am I Wastin' My Time	1983	—	2.00	4.00

CARPENTER, KRIS

45s

DOOR KNOB

Number	Title (A Side/B Side)	Yr	VG	VG+	NM
❑ 146	My Song Don't Sing the Same/Cheap Wine and Watered Down Whiskey	1981	—	2.50	5.00
❑ 156	Take Care of Texas/(B-side unknown)	1981	—	2.50	5.00
❑ 178	Never Gonna Have to Hurt Again/Take Care of Texas	1982	—	2.50	5.00
❑ 189	You're Leavin' Me/(B-side unknown)	1982	—	2.50	5.00
❑ 203	Oklahoma Heartaches and California Dreams/ You're Leavin' Me	1983	—	2.50	5.00

CARPENTER, MARY CHAPIN

45s

COLUMBIA

Number	Title (A Side/B Side)	Yr	VG	VG+	NM
❑ 07598	A Lot Like Me/Family Hands	1987	—	2.50	5.00
❑ 07681	Downtown Train/Just Because	1988	—	2.50	5.00
❑ 68677	How Do/It Don't Bring You	1989	—	2.00	4.00
❑ 69051	Never Had It So Good/Other Streets in Other Towns	1989	—	2.00	4.00
❑ 73202	Quittin' Time/Heroes and Heroines	1990	—	2.00	4.00
❑ 73361	Something of a Dreamer/Slow Country Dance	1990	—	2.00	4.00
❑ 73567	You Win Again/The Moon and St. Christopher	1990	—	2.00	4.00
❑ 73699	Right Now/What You Didn't Say	1991	—	2.00	4.00
❑ 73838	Down at the Twist and Shout/Halley Came to Jackson	1991	—	3.00	6.00

—Original copies were pressed on styrene (the record is translucent dark red when held to a light)

Number	Title (A Side/B Side)	Yr	VG	VG+	NM
❑ 73838	Down at the Twist and Shout/Halley Came to Jackson	199?	—	—	3.00

—Reissues were pressed on non-translucent vinyl

Number	Title (A Side/B Side)	Yr	VG	VG+	NM
❑ 74038	Going Out Tonight/When She's Gone	1991	—	2.00	4.00
❑ 74345	I Feel Lucky/Middle Ground	1992	—	2.00	4.00
❑ 74485	Not Too Much to Ask/I Am a Town	1992	—	—	3.00

—A-side with Joe Diffie

Number	Title (A Side/B Side)	Yr	VG	VG+	NM
❑ 74795	Passionate Kisses/Middle Ground	1993	—	2.00	4.00
❑ 74930	The Hard Way/Goodbye Again	1993	—	—	3.00
❑ 77134	The Bug/Rhythm of the Blues	1993	—	—	3.00
❑ 77316	He Thinks He'll Keep Her/Only a Dream	1993	—	—	3.00
❑ 77476	I Take My Chances/Come On Come On	1994	—	—	3.00
❑ 77696	Shut Up and Kiss Me/The End of My Pirate Days	1994	—	2.00	4.00
❑ 77780	Tender When I Want to Be/John Doe No. 24	1994	—	—	3.00
❑ 77826	House of Cards/Jubilee	1995	—	—	3.00
❑ 77955	Why Walk When You Can Fly/Stones in the Road	1995	—	—	3.00
❑ 78453	Let Me Into Your Heart/Downtown	1996	—	—	3.00
❑ 78511	I Want to Be Your Girlfriend/Quittin' Time (Live)	1997	—	—	3.00

Albums

COLUMBIA

Number	Title (A Side/B Side)	Yr	VG	VG+	NM
❑ FC 40758	Hometown Girl	1987	2.50	5.00	10.00
❑ FC 44228	State of the Heart	1989	2.50	5.00	10.00

CARPENTERS

The pop duo had one country hit, listed below. Written by JUICE NEWTON, it actually made the top 10 country.

45s

A&M

Number	Title (A Side/B Side)	Yr	VG	VG+	NM
❑ 2008	Sweet, Sweet Smile/I Have You	1978	—	2.00	4.00

CARR, EDDIE LEE

45s

EVERGREEN

Number	Title (A Side/B Side)	Yr	VG	VG+	NM
❑ 1092	Big Bad Mama/(B-side unknown)	1989	—	2.50	5.00

CARR, KENNY

45s

KOTTAGE

Number	Title (A Side/B Side)	Yr	VG	VG+	NM
❑ 0090	The Writing on the Wall/(B-side unknown)	1988	—	3.00	6.00
❑ 0091	Tell Me/(B-side unknown)	1989	—	3.00	6.00

CARRINGTON, RODNEY

45s

MERCURY

Number	Title (A Side/B Side)	Yr	VG	VG+	NM
❑ 566056-7	Dancing with a Man/Fred	1998	—	—	3.00

CARSON, JEFF

45s

CURB

Number	Title (A Side/B Side)	Yr	VG	VG+	NM
❑ D7-73023	Butterfly Kisses/Here's the Deal	1997	—	2.00	4.00
❑ D7-73064	Shine On/It Wouldn't Kill Me	1998	—	—	3.00

MCG CURB

Number	Title (A Side/B Side)	Yr	VG	VG+	NM
❑ D7-76946	Yeah Buddy/Betty's Takin' Judo	1995	—	2.00	4.00
❑ D7-76954	Not on Your Love/Betty's Takin' Judo	1995	—	2.00	4.00
❑ D7-76970	The Car/Holdin' On to Somethin'	1995	—	2.00	4.00

CARSON, JOE

45s

LIBERTY

Number	Title (A Side/B Side)	Yr	VG	VG+	NM
❑ 55547	Shoot the Buffalo/Three Little Words Too Late	1963	2.50	5.00	10.00
❑ 55578	I Gotta Get Drunk (And I Shore Do Dread It)/Who Will Buy My Memories	1963	2.50	5.00	10.00
❑ 55614	Helpless/The Last Song (I'm Ever Gonna Sing)	1963	2.50	5.00	10.00
❑ 55664	Double Life/Fort Worth Jail	1964	2.50	5.00	10.00

CARSON, MARTHA

Also see STUART HAMBLEN.

45s

CAPITOL

Number	Title (A Side/B Side)	Yr	VG	VG+	NM
❑ F1900	Satisfied/Hide Me Rock of Ages	1951	3.75	7.50	15.00
❑ F1982	Weighed the Balance/You Sure Do Need Him Now	1952	3.75	7.50	15.00
❑ F2077	I Wanna Rest/Old Blind Barnabas	1952	3.75	7.50	15.00
❑ F2145	Beyond the Shadow/I'm Gonna Walk and Talk with the Lord	1952	3.75	7.50	15.00
❑ F2180	He Will Set Your Fields on Fire/When God Dips His Love	1952	3.75	7.50	15.00
❑ F2252	Fear Not/Cryin' Holy Unto the Lord	1952	3.75	7.50	15.00
❑ F2342	There's a Higher Power/Inspiration from Above	1953	3.75	7.50	15.00
❑ F2477	Ask and You Shall Receive/I Feel It in My Soul	1953	3.75	7.50	15.00
❑ F2634	Singing on the Other Side/I've Got a Better Place to Go	1953	3.75	7.50	15.00
❑ F2740	Lazarus/Bye & Bye	1954	3.75	7.50	15.00
❑ F2825	I Bowed Down/He'll Part the Water	1954	3.75	7.50	15.00
❑ F2969	Christmas Time Is Here/Peace On Earth (At Christmas Time)	1954	3.75	7.50	15.00
❑ F3045	It's Alright/Counting My Blessings	1955	3.75	7.50	15.00
❑ 4437	Everything's All Right/High on the Hill	1960	3.00	6.00	12.00

RCA VICTOR

Number	Title (A Side/B Side)	Yr	VG	VG+	NM
❑ 47-6293	Laugh a Little More/Let the Light Shine on Me	1955	5.00	10.00	20.00
❑ 47-6413	David and Goliath/I Want to Rest a Little While	1956	5.00	10.00	20.00
❑ 47-6510	Dixieland Roll/Music Drives Me Crazy	1956	5.00	10.00	20.00
❑ 47-6603	All These Things/Faith Is the Key	1956	5.00	10.00	20.00
❑ 47-6724	Get That Golden Key/He Was There	1956	5.00	10.00	20.00
❑ 47-6861	Satisfied/Let the Light Shine on Me	1957	3.75	7.50	15.00
❑ 47-6948	Now Stop/Just Whistle or Call	1957	3.75	7.50	15.00

SIMS

Number	Title (A Side/B Side)	Yr	VG	VG+	NM
❑ 144	Everybody Needs Somebody/It Takes a Lot of Lovin'	1963	2.50	5.00	10.00

Albums

CAPITOL

Number	Title (A Side/B Side)	Yr	VG	VG+	NM
❑ ST 1507 [S]	Satisfied	1960	7.50	15.00	30.00
❑ T 1507 [M]	Satisfied	1960	6.25	12.50	25.00
❑ ST 1607 [S]	A Talk with the Lord	1961	7.50	15.00	30.00
❑ T 1607 [M]	A Talk with the Lord	1961	6.25	12.50	25.00

RCA VICTOR

Number	Title (A Side/B Side)	Yr	VG	VG+	NM
❑ LPM-1145 [M]	Journey to the Sky	1955	10.00	20.00	40.00
❑ LPM-1490 [M]	Rock-a My Soul	1957	12.50	25.00	50.00

SIMS

Number	Title (A Side/B Side)	Yr	VG	VG+	NM
❑ LP-100 [M]	Martha Carson	196?	6.25	12.50	25.00

CARSON, WAYNE

45s

DECCA

Number	Title (A Side/B Side)	Yr	VG	VG+	NM
❑ 31531	There's No In Between/The Traveler	1963	3.00	6.00	12.00
❑ 31621	Blue Feeling/It's You, Always It's You	1964	3.00	6.00	12.00

ELEKTRA

Number	Title (A Side/B Side)	Yr	VG	VG+	NM
❑ 45348	The Girl That I'm Hung Up On/Keep On	1976	—	2.50	5.00
❑ 45358	Barstool Mountain/Keep On	1976	—	2.50	5.00
❑ 45407	Bugle Ann/Down to the Riverq	1977	—	2.50	5.00

EMH

Number	Title (A Side/B Side)	Yr	VG	VG+	NM
❑ 0001	Lovin' You Ain't All I Got to Do/Mr. Coachman	1982	—	2.50	5.00
❑ 0017	1 Yr 2 Mo 11 Days/The Timing's All Wrong	1983	—	2.50	5.00

MGM

Number	Title (A Side/B Side)	Yr	VG	VG+	NM
❑ 13772	Rainmaker/Salty Water Man	1967	2.50	5.00	10.00

MONUMENT

Number	Title (A Side/B Side)	Yr	VG	VG+	NM
❑ 1152	Soul Deep/Don't Let the Sun Set on You in Tulsa	1969	2.00	4.00	8.00
❑ 1192	No Love at All/She's Got Everything I Need	1970	2.00	4.00	8.00
❑ 8501	Straight/King's Hideaway	1971	—	3.00	6.00
❑ 8524	Mexican Divorce/Just as Gone	1971	—	3.00	6.00
❑ 8543	All Night Feeling/No Love at All	1972	—	3.00	6.00
❑ 8547	Neon Rainbow/The Grass Was Green	1972	—	3.00	6.00
❑ 8581	You're Gonna Love Yourself in the Morning/ Laurel Canyon	1973	—	3.00	6.00

Albums

MONUMENT

Number	Title (A Side/B Side)	Yr	VG	VG+	NM
❑ Z 30906	Life Lines	1972	3.75	7.50	15.00

CARTEE, ALAN

Also see THE CARTEE BROTHERS.

45s

GROOVY

Number	Title (A Side/B Side)	Yr	VG	VG+	NM
❑ 101	Let My Fingers Do the Walking (I'm Your Telephone Man)/Twenty-Five Women	1977	2.00	4.00	8.00

CARTEE BROTHERS, THE

Also see ALAN CARTEE.

45s

QUALLA

Number	Title (A Side/B Side)	Yr	VG	VG+	NM
❑ 03	Cindy/My Little Jeep	196?	2.50	5.00	10.00

REPRISE

Number	Title (A Side/B Side)	Yr	VG	VG+	NM
❑ 0528	Four Quarters on the Football Field/Don't Say Goodbye	1966	2.00	4.00	8.00

CARTER, ANITA

Also see THE CARTER FAMILY; THE CARTER SISTERS; JOHNNY DARRELL; WAYLON JENNINGS; HANK SNOW.

45s

CADENCE

Number	Title (A Side/B Side)	Yr	VG	VG+	NM
❑ 1333	Blue Doll/Go Away Johnny	1957	10.00	20.00	40.00

CAPITOL

Number	Title (A Side/B Side)	Yr	VG	VG+	NM
❑ 2994	Tulsa County/Where Is the Start of Lonely	1970	—	3.00	6.00
❑ 3194	A Whole Lotta Lovin'/Loving Him Was Easier	1971	—	3.00	6.00

COLUMBIA

Number	Title (A Side/B Side)	Yr	VG	VG+	NM
❑ 3-10009	Sweet Memories/Pictures on the Wall	1974	—	2.50	5.00
❑ 4-21063	Keep It Secret/Cold, Cold, Colder	1953	5.00	10.00	20.00
❑ 4-21198	Don Juan/There'll Be No Teardrops	1954	5.00	10.00	20.00
❑ 4-21242	Heartless Romance/Faithless Johnny Lee	1954	5.00	10.00	20.00

JAMIE

Number	Title (A Side/B Side)	Yr	VG	VG+	NM
❑ 1154	Mama Don't Cry at My Wedding/Moon Girl	1960	3.75	7.50	15.00
❑ 1167	Tryin' to Forget About You/That's All I Want from You	1960	3.75	7.50	15.00

MERCURY

Number	Title (A Side/B Side)	Yr	VG	VG+	NM
❑ 72073	Ring of Fire/Voice of the Bayou	1963	2.50	5.00	10.00
❑ 72179	Running Back/Brian	1963	2.50	5.00	10.00
❑ 72364	Little Things Mean a Lot/Stop (Being Mean to Your Baby)	1965	2.50	5.00	10.00

RCA VICTOR

Number	Title (A Side/B Side)	Yr	VG	VG+	NM
❑ 47-6017	I Dreamed of a Hill-Billy Heaven/Making Believe	1955	5.00	10.00	20.00
❑ 47-6129	That's What Makes the Jukebox Play/I'm Sorry If That's the Way You Feel	1955	5.00	10.00	20.00
❑ 47-6228	Mask on Your Heart/Here We Are Again	1955	5.00	10.00	20.00
❑ 47-6364	False Hearted/I Wear Dark Glasses	1955	5.00	10.00	20.00
❑ 47-6482	A Tear Fell/One Heartache at a Time	1956	3.75	7.50	15.00
❑ 47-6737	Believe It or Not/If I Had a Needle and Thread	1956	3.75	7.50	15.00
❑ 47-6805	He's a Real Gone Guy/Maybe	1957	3.75	7.50	15.00
❑ 47-8674	Twelve O'Clock High/Is It for Me	1965	2.50	5.00	10.00
❑ 47-8809	I've Been Loving You Too Long/Heard the Wind Blow Before	1966	2.00	4.00	8.00
❑ 47-8923	I'm Gonna Leave You/You Couldn't Get My Love Back	1966	2.00	4.00	8.00
❑ 47-9156	I Don't Need You Anymore/You Weren't Ashamed to Kiss Me (Last Night)	1967	2.00	4.00	8.00
❑ 47-9307	Love Me Now (While I Am Living)/It's My Life (And I'll Live It)	1967	2.00	4.00	8.00
❑ 48-0387	Somebody's Cryin'/Johnny's Got a Sweetheart	1950	10.00	20.00	40.00
—Originals on green vinyl					
❑ 48-0426	Freight Train Blues/Someone Else, Not Me	1951	6.25	12.50	25.00
❑ 48-0461	I'm Cryin'/Right Way, Wrong Way	1951	6.25	12.50	25.00
❑ 48-0493	Just You and I/I Want to Be Blue	1951	6.25	12.50	25.00

UNITED ARTISTS

Number	Title (A Side/B Side)	Yr	VG	VG+	NM
❑ 50444	To Be a Child Again/Too Many Rivers	1968	—	3.50	7.00
❑ 50555	Cry Softly/The Sound of Different Drums	1969	—	3.50	7.00

Albums

CAPITOL

Number	Title (A Side/B Side)	Yr	VG	VG+	NM
❑ ST-11085	So Much Love	1972	3.75	7.50	15.00

MERCURY

Number	Title (A Side/B Side)	Yr	VG	VG+	NM
❑ MG-20770 [M]	Folk Songs Old and New	1963	6.25	12.50	25.00
❑ MG-20847 [M]	Anita of the Carter Family	1964	6.25	12.50	25.00
❑ SR-60770 [S]	Folk Songs Old and New	1963	7.50	15.00	30.00
❑ SR-60847 [S]	Anita of the Carter Family	1964	7.50	15.00	30.00

CARTER, BENNY

Jazz multi-instrumentalist and bandleader. Of his hundreds of recordings, only the following single made the country charts.

Selected 78s

CAPITOL

Number	Title (A Side/B Side)	Yr	VG	VG+	NM
❑ 144	Hurry, Hurry/Poinciana	1944	3.75	7.50	15.00

CARTER, BRENDA

Also see GEORGE JONES AND BRENDA CARTER.

45s

MUSICOR

Number	Title (A Side/B Side)	Yr	VG	VG+	NM
❑ 1353	Everything's Found a Home with Me But You/Mama and the Teacher	1969	—	3.50	7.00
❑ 1386	Miss Nosy Brown/Shadow from Her Eyes	1969	—	3.50	7.00
❑ 1399	Life of Riley's/While You're Forgetting Me	1970	—	3.50	7.00

CARTER, CARLENE

45s

EPIC

Number	Title (A Side/B Side)	Yr	VG	VG+	NM
❑ 38-03952	Heart to Heart/One Way Ticket	1983	—	2.00	4.00

GIANT

Number	Title (A Side/B Side)	Yr	VG	VG+	NM
❑ 7-17853	Love Like This/One Tender Night	1995	—	—	3.00
❑ 7-17962	Hurricane/One Tender Night	1995	—	—	3.00
❑ 7-18006	Rockin' Little Christmas/The Working Elf Blues	1994	—	2.00	4.00
—B-side by Daron Norwood					
❑ 7-18265	I Love You 'Cause I Want To/Nowhere Train	1994	—	2.00	4.00
❑ 7-18373	Unbreakable Heart/Wastin' Time with You	1993	—	—	3.00
❑ 7-18527	Every Little Thing/Long Hard Fall	1993	—	2.50	5.00

REPRISE

Number	Title (A Side/B Side)	Yr	VG	VG+	NM
❑ 7-19255	One Love/Easy from Now On	1991	—	2.00	4.00
❑ 7-19398	The Sweetest Thing/Goodnight Dallas	1991	—	2.00	4.00
❑ 7-19564	Come On Back/The Leavin' Side	1990	—	2.00	4.00
❑ 7-19915	I Fell in Love/Guardian Angel	1990	—	2.00	4.00

WARNER BROS.

Number	Title (A Side/B Side)	Yr	VG	VG+	NM
❑ 8576	Never Together But Close Sometimes/Who Needs Words	1978	—	2.50	5.00
❑ 8658	Love Is Gone/Smoke Dreams	1978	—	2.50	5.00
❑ 49083	Do It in a Heartbeat/Swap-Meet Rag	1979	—	2.00	4.00
❑ 49155	Old Photographs/Two Sides to Every Woman	1980	—	2.00	4.00

Albums

EPIC

Number	Title (A Side/B Side)	Yr	VG	VG+	NM
❑ BFE 38663	C'est C Bon	1983	2.50	5.00	10.00

WARNER BROS.

Number	Title (A Side/B Side)	Yr	VG	VG+	NM
❑ BSK 3204	Carlene Carter	1979	2.50	5.00	10.00
❑ BSK 3616	Blue Nun	1981	2.50	5.00	10.00

CARTER, CARLENE, AND DAVE EDMUNDS

45s

WARNER BROS.

Number	Title (A Side/B Side)	Yr	VG	VG+	NM
❑ 49572	Baby Ride Easy/Too Bad About Sandy	1980	—	2.00	4.00

CARTER, DEANA

45s

CAPITOL NASHVILLE

Number	Title (A Side/B Side)	Yr	VG	VG+	NM
❑ S7-19223	Strawberry Wine/Before We Ever Heard Goodbye	1996	—	2.50	5.00
❑ S7-19450	We Danced Anyway/Did I Shave My Legs for This?	1997	—	2.00	4.00
❑ S7-19510	Count Me In/Did I Shave My Legs for This?	1997	—	2.00	4.00
❑ S7-19646	How Do I Get There/Did I Shave My Legs for This?	1997	—	2.00	4.00
❑ 58738	Absence of the Heart/Dickson County	1998	—	—	3.00
❑ 58744	Angels Working Overtime/Everything's Gonna Be Alright	1999	—	—	3.00
❑ 58760	You Still Shake Me/The Train Song	1999	—	—	3.00
❑ 58818	Carol of the Bells/Boogie Woogie Santa	1999	—	—	3.00

CARTER, FRED, JR.

45s

MONUMENT

Number	Title (A Side/B Side)	Yr	VG	VG+	NM
❑ 993	I Don't Know Why I Keep Loving You/Coffee Cup	1967	2.00	4.00	8.00
❑ 1022	And You Wonder Why/It's a Rough Old Road	1967	2.00	4.00	8.00
❑ 1067	Every Stop of the Way/Turn It Around in Your Mind	1968	2.00	4.00	8.00

CARTER, HELEN

Also see THE CARTER FAMILY; THE CARTER SISTERS.

45s

HICKORY

Number	Title (A Side/B Side)	Yr	VG	VG+	NM
❑ 1053	Heart Full of Shame/Sweet Talkin' Man	1956	5.00	10.00	20.00
❑ 1062	No, No, It's Not So/There Ain't No Future for Me	1957	5.00	10.00	20.00
❑ 1069	I'd Like to Be/He Made You for Me	1957	5.00	10.00	20.00
—With Wiley Barkdull					
❑ 1076	Set the Wedding/What's to Become of Me Now	1958	5.00	10.00	20.00

OKEH

Number	Title (A Side/B Side)	Yr	VG	VG+	NM
❑ 18023	I Like My Lovin' Overtime/You're Right	195?	6.25	12.50	25.00
❑ 18036	Like All Get Out/Unfit Mother	195?	6.25	12.50	25.00

CARTER, JUNE

Includes records as "June Carter Cash." Also see THE CARTER FAMILY; THE CARTER SISTERS; JOHNNY CASH AND JUNE CARTER; FLATT AND SCRUGGS; HOMER AND JETHRO.

45s

COLUMBIA

Number	Title (A Side/B Side)	Yr	VG	VG+	NM
❑ 3-10149	Losin' You/The Shadow of a Lady	1975	—	2.50	5.00
—As "June Carter Cash"					
❑ 4-21074	Juke Box Blues/No Swallering Place	1953	5.00	10.00	20.00
❑ 4-21128	You Flopped When You Got/We've Got Things to Do	1953	5.00	10.00	20.00
❑ 4-21343	Let Me Go Lover/Left Over Mambo	1955	5.00	10.00	20.00
❑ 4-21380	He Don't Love Me Anymore/Leftover Loving	1955	5.00	10.00	20.00
❑ 4-21535	Strange Woman/Honey Look What You've Got	1956	5.00	10.00	20.00
❑ 4-40797	Baby I Tried/I'm All Right Now	1956	3.75	7.50	15.00
❑ 4-42864	I Pitched My Tent (On the Old Campground)/Sweet Flowers	1963	2.50	5.00	10.00
❑ 4-43059	Tall Loverman/Without a Love to Call My Own	1964	2.50	5.00	10.00
❑ 4-43156	Go Away Stranger/I Want You Again	1964	2.50	5.00	10.00
❑ 4-43441	Everything Ain't Been Said/A Long Way from the Cotton Fields	1965	2.50	5.00	10.00
❑ 4-45338	A Good Man/Straw Upon the Wind	1971	2.00	4.00	8.00
—As "June Carter Cash"					
❑ 4-45789	Follow Me/The Lights of Magdala	1973	—	3.50	7.00
—As "June Carter Cash"					

LIBERTY

Number	Title (A Side/B Side)	Yr	VG	VG+	NM
❑ 55385	The Heel/If I Ever See Him Again	1961	2.50	5.00	10.00
❑ 55440	Mama Teach Me/Money	1962	2.50	5.00	10.00
❑ 55504	Overalls and Dungarees/Waving from the Hill	1962	2.50	5.00	10.00

RCA VICTOR

Number	Title (A Side/B Side)	Yr	VG	VG+	NM
❑ 48-0146	Crocodile Tears/Grandma Told Me So	1950	10.00	20.00	40.00
—Originals on green vinyl					
❑ 48-0355	Root Hog or Die/Bald Headed End of a Broom	1950	10.00	20.00	40.00
—Originals on green vinyl					
❑ 48-0401	Bashful Rascal/For Crying Out Loud	1950	7.50	15.00	30.00
❑ 48-0411	The Thing/Winkin' and a Blinkin'	1950	7.50	15.00	30.00
❑ 48-0450	Mommie's Real Pecooliar/A Bucket of Love	1951	7.50	15.00	30.00

Albums

COLUMBIA

Number	Title (A Side/B Side)	Yr	VG	VG+	NM
❑ KC 33686	Appalachian Pride	1975	3.75	7.50	15.00
—As "June Carter Cash"					

CARTER, MOTHER MAYBELLE

45s

COLUMBIA

Number	Title (A Side/B Side)	Yr	VG	VG+	NM
❑ 4-43521	I Told Them What You're Fighting For/San Antonio Rose	1966	2.50	5.00	10.00

Albums

AMBASSADOR

Number	Title (A Side/B Side)	Yr	VG	VG+	NM
❑ 98069 [M]	Mother Maybelle Carter	195?	37.50	75.00	150.00

COLUMBIA

Number	Title (A Side/B Side)	Yr	VG	VG+	NM
❑ CL 2475 [M]	A Living Legend	1965	5.00	10.00	20.00
❑ CS 9275 [S]	A Living Legend	1965	6.25	12.50	25.00
❑ KG 32436 [(2)]	Mother Maybelle Carter	1973	6.25	12.50	25.00

KAPP

Number	Title (A Side/B Side)	Yr	VG	VG+	NM
❑ KL-1413 [M]	Queen of the Autoharp	1964	5.00	10.00	20.00
❑ KS-3413 [S]	Queen of the Autoharp	1964	6.25	12.50	25.00

SMASH

Number	Title (A Side/B Side)	Yr	VG	VG+	NM
❑ MGS-27025 [M]	Mother Maybelle Carter and Her Autoharp	1963	5.00	10.00	20.00
❑ MGS-27041 [M]	Pickin' and Singin'	1963	5.00	10.00	20.00
❑ SRS-67025 [S]	Mother Maybelle Carter and Her Autoharp	1963	6.25	12.50	25.00
❑ SRS-67041 [S]	Pickin' and Singin'	1963	6.25	12.50	25.00

CARTER, WILF

See MONTANA SLIM.

CARTER, WOODY

Selected 78s

MACY'S

Number	Title (A Side/B Side)	Yr	VG	VG+	NM
❑ 100	Sittin' on the Doorstop/Slippin' Around	1949	12.50	25.00	50.00
❑ 101	Who's Gonna Chop My Baby's Firewood/Only You	1949	12.50	25.00	50.00

CARTER FAMILY, THE

Considered "The First Family of Country Music." Also see ANITA CARTER; HELEN CARTER; JUNE CARTER; THE CARTER SISTERS; JOHNNY CASH.

45s

COLUMBIA

Number	Title (A Side/B Side)	Yr	VG	VG+	NM
❑ 3-10387	Papa's Sugar/In the Pines (The Longest Train I Ever Saw)	1976	—	2.50	5.00
❑ 3-10502	My Father's Fiddle/My Ship Will Sail	1977	—	2.50	5.00
❑ 4-20920	Fair and Tender Ladies/Foggy Mountain Top	1952	6.25	12.50	25.00
❑ 4-20974	I Never Will Marry/The Sun's Gonna Shine in My Back Door	1952	6.25	12.50	25.00
❑ 4-20986	Amazing Grace/Softly and Tenderly	1952	6.25	12.50	25.00
❑ 4-21184	You Are My Flower/I Ain't Gonna Work Tomorrow	1953	6.25	12.50	25.00
❑ 4-21233	Love, Oh Crazy Love/Time's a Wastin'	1954	6.25	12.50	25.00
❑ 4-21316	Are You Afraid to Remember Me/He Went Slippin' Around	1954	6.25	12.50	25.00
❑ 4-43004	Keep on the Sunny Side/Fair and Tender Ladies	1964	2.50	5.00	10.00
❑ 4-43235	Farewell/You Win Again	1965	2.50	5.00	10.00
❑ 4-43579	I Walk the Line/For Lovin' Me	1966	2.00	4.00	8.00
❑ 4-44136	Once Around the Briar Patch/Bye Bye	1967	2.00	4.00	8.00
❑ 4-44982	If I Live Long Enough/Break My Mind	1969	2.00	4.00	8.00
❑ 4-45428	A Song to Mama/One More Summer in Virginia	1971	2.00	4.00	8.00
❑ 4-45581	Travelin' Minstrel Band/2001 (Ballad to the Future)	1972	—	3.50	7.00
❑ 4-45679	The World Needs a Melody/A Bird with Broken Wings Can't Fly	1972	—	3.50	7.00

—As "The Carter Family with Johnny Cash"

LIBERTY

Number	Title (A Side/B Side)	Yr	VG	VG+	NM
❑ 55501	Fourteen Carat Nothing/Get Up Early in the Morning	1962	3.00	6.00	12.00

MERCURY

Number	Title (A Side/B Side)	Yr	VG	VG+	NM
❑ 870397-7	Dixie Darlin'/Ain't Gonna Work Tomorrow	1988	—	2.00	4.00

Selected 78s

BANNER

Number	Title (A Side/B Side)	Yr	VG	VG+	NM
❑ 33465	Can the Circle Be Unbroken/(B-side unknown)	1935	5.00	10.00	20.00

BLUEBIRD

Number	Title (A Side/B Side)	Yr	VG	VG+	NM
❑ B-5006	Keep on the Sunny Side/When the World's On Fire	193?	5.00	10.00	20.00
❑ B-5058	Where We'll Never Grow Old/River of Jordan	193?	5.00	10.00	20.00
❑ B-5096	Meet Me by the Moonlight Alone/(B-side unknown)	193?	5.00	10.00	20.00
❑ B-5122	When the Springtime Comes Again/I'm Thinking Tonight of My Blue Eyes	193?	5.00	10.00	20.00
❑ B-5161	Will the Roses Bloom in Heaven?/We Will March Through the Streets of the City	193?	5.00	10.00	20.00
❑ B-5185	Amber Tresses/Picture on the Wall	193?	5.00	10.00	20.00
❑ B-5243	'Mid the Green Fields of Virginia/The Spirit of Love Watches Over Me	193?	5.00	10.00	20.00
❑ B-5272	God Gave Noah the Rainbow Sign/No Telephone in Heaven	193?	5.00	10.00	20.00
❑ B-5301	My Clinch Mountain Home/Little Darling, Pal of Mine	193?	5.00	10.00	20.00
❑ B-5356	Wildwood Flower/I Have No One to Love Me (But the Sailor on the Sea)	193?	5.00	10.00	20.00
❑ B-5406	Anchored in Love/Tell Me That You Love Me	193?	5.00	10.00	20.00
❑ B-5468	Sow 'Em on the Mountain/Sunshine in the Shadows	193?	5.00	10.00	20.00
❑ B-5529	I'll Be All Smiles Tonight/Hello Central! Give Me Heaven	193?	5.00	10.00	20.00
❑ B-5543	A Distant Land to Roam/The Sun of the Soul	193?	5.00	10.00	20.00
❑ B-5586	Darling Daisies/Love's Return	193?	5.00	10.00	20.00
❑ B-5650	Happy or Lonesome/The East Virginia Blues	193?	5.00	10.00	20.00
❑ B-5716	I'm Working on a Building/(B-side unknown)	193?	5.00	10.00	20.00
❑ B-5771	One Little Word/You've Been Fooling Me, Baby	193?	5.00	10.00	20.00
❑ B-5817	I'll Aggravate Your Soul/(B-side unknown)	193?	5.00	10.00	20.00
❑ B-5856	Longing for Old Virginia/(B-side unknown)	193?	5.00	10.00	20.00
❑ B-5908	My Heart's Tonight in Texas/Cowboy's Wild Song to His Herd	193?	5.00	10.00	20.00
❑ B-5911	I'll Be Home Some Day/There'll Be Joy, Joy, Joy	193?	5.00	10.00	20.00
❑ B-5924	Little Moses/Motherless Children	193?	5.00	10.00	20.00
❑ B-5927	Lulu Wall/Sweet Fern	193?	5.00	10.00	20.00
❑ B-5956	Are You Tired of Me, My Darling?/The Mountains of Tennessee	193?	5.00	10.00	20.00
❑ B-5961	On a Hill Lone and Gray/There's No Hiding Place Down Here	193?	5.00	10.00	20.00
❑ B-5974	Faded Coat of Blue/Sailor Boy	193?	5.00	10.00	20.00
❑ B-5990	Kitty Waltz/March Winds Goin' to Blow My Blues Away	193?	5.00	10.00	20.00
❑ B-5993	The Church in the Wildwood (By and By)/Room in Heaven for Me	193?	5.00	10.00	20.00
❑ B-6000	Lonesome for You/(B-side unknown)	193?	3.75	7.50	15.00
❑ B-6020	Worried Man Blues/The Cannon-Ball	193?	3.75	7.50	15.00
❑ B-6033	Diamonds in the Rough/John Hardy Was a Desperate Little Man	193?	3.75	7.50	15.00
❑ B-6036	Carter's Blues/The Lovers' Farewell	193?	3.75	7.50	15.00
❑ B-6053	Bury Me Under the Weeping Willow/When I'm Gone	193?	3.75	7.50	15.00
❑ B-6055	Where Shall I Be?/On the Rock Where Moses Stood	193?	3.75	7.50	15.00
❑ B-6106	Two Sweethearts/(B-side unknown)	193?	3.75	7.50	15.00
❑ B-6117	Lonesome Valley/The Birds Were Singing of You	193?	3.75	7.50	15.00
❑ B-6176	Fond Affection/(B-side unknown)	193?	3.75	7.50	15.00
❑ B-6223	Enging One-Forty-Three/Western Hobo	193?	3.75	7.50	15.00
❑ B-6257	Can't Feel at Home/I Never Loved But One	193?	3.75	7.50	15.00
❑ B-6271	Little Log Cabin by the Sea/Bring Back My Blue-Eyed Boy to Me	193?	3.75	7.50	15.00
❑ B-8167	On My Way to Canaan's Land/Cowboy Jack	193?	3.75	7.50	15.00
❑ B-8350	Wabash Cannon Ball/I Never Will Marry	193?	3.75	7.50	15.00
❑ B-8868	In the Valley of the Shenandoah/Dark and Stormy Weather	1941	3.75	7.50	15.00
❑ 33-0512	The Rambling Boy/The Wave on the Sea	1945	3.75	7.50	15.00

CONQUEROR

Number	Title (A Side/B Side)	Yr	VG	VG+	NM
❑ 8636	Don't Forget Me Little Darling/Gathering Flowers from the Hillside	193?	5.00	10.00	20.00
❑ 8692	Keep on the Sunny Side/Gospel Ship	193?	5.00	10.00	20.00

DECCA

Number	Title (A Side/B Side)	Yr	VG	VG+	NM
❑ 5240	My Dixie Darling/(B-side unknown)	1936	3.75	7.50	15.00
❑ 5241	My Native Home/Jealous Hearted Me	1936	3.75	7.50	15.00
❑ 5242	No Depression/(B-side unknown)	1936	3.75	7.50	15.00
❑ 5254	Just Another Broken Heart/(B-side unknown)	1936	3.75	7.50	15.00
❑ 5263	My Honey Lou/(B-side unknown)	1936	3.75	7.50	15.00
❑ 5283	You've Been a Friend to Me/(B-side unknown)	1937	3.75	7.50	15.00
❑ 5304	Bonnie Blue Eyes/(B-side unknown)	1937	3.75	7.50	15.00
❑ 5318	Sweet Heaven in My View/(B-side unknown)	1937	3.75	7.50	15.00
❑ 5359	In the Shadow of the Pines/(B-side unknown)	1937	3.75	7.50	15.00
❑ 5386	The Last Move for Me/(B-side unknown)	1937	3.75	7.50	15.00
❑ 5411	The Only Girl/(B-side unknown)	1937	3.75	7.50	15.00
❑ 5430	Lover's Lane/(B-side unknown)	1937	3.75	7.50	15.00
❑ 5447	He Never Came Back/(B-side unknown)	1937	3.75	7.50	15.00
❑ 5452	Honey in the Rock/(B-side unknown)	1937	3.75	7.50	15.00
❑ 5467	Jim Blake's Message/(B-side unknown)	1938	3.00	6.00	12.00
❑ 5479	Hello Stranger/(B-side unknown)	1938	3.00	6.00	12.00
❑ 5494	Lord I'm In Your Care/(B-side unknown)	1938	3.00	6.00	12.00
❑ 5518	Broken Down Tramp/(B-side unknown)	1938	3.00	6.00	12.00
❑ 5532	Goodbye to the Plains/(B-side unknown)	1938	3.00	6.00	12.00
❑ 5565	The Stern Old Bachelor/(B-side unknown)	1938	3.00	6.00	12.00
❑ 5579	Happy in the Prison/(B-side unknown)	1938	3.00	6.00	12.00
❑ 5596	Coal Miner's Blues/(B-side unknown)	1938	3.00	6.00	12.00
❑ 5612	Who's That Knockin' on My Window/Young Freda Bolt	1938	3.00	6.00	12.00
❑ 5632	Little Joe/(B-side unknown)	1939	3.00	6.00	12.00
❑ 5649	Bring Back My Boy/(B-side unknown)	1939	3.00	6.00	12.00
❑ 5662	Cuban Soldiers/(B-side unknown)	1939	3.00	6.00	12.00
❑ 5677	Farewell Nellie/(B-side unknown)	1939	3.00	6.00	12.00
❑ 5692	You Are My Flower/(B-side unknown)	1939	3.00	6.00	12.00
❑ 5702	Charlie and Nelly/(B-side unknown)	1939	3.00	6.00	12.00
❑ 46005	Lay My Head Beneath the Rose/Jealous Hearted Me	1946	3.00	6.00	12.00
❑ 46086	Coal Miner's Blues/My Dixie Darling	1948	3.00	6.00	12.00

MONTGOMERY WARD

Number	Title (A Side/B Side)	Yr	VG	VG+	NM
❑ M-4320	My Lover on the Deep Blue Sea/Sunny Tennessee	193?	5.00	10.00	20.00

—B-side by the Floyd County Ramblers

Number	Title (A Side/B Side)	Yr	VG	VG+	NM
❑ M-4433	Two Sweethearts/Broken-Hearted Lover	193?	5.00	10.00	20.00
❑ M-4546	Are You Tired of Me, My Darling/One Little Word	193?	5.00	10.00	20.00
❑ M-4549	My Heart's Tonight in Texas/Cowboy's Wild Song to His Herd	193?	5.00	10.00	20.00
❑ M-4732	Where We'll Never Grow Old/We Will March Through the Streets of the City	193?	5.00	10.00	20.00
❑ M-4734	Forsaken Love/I Never Loved But One	193?	5.00	10.00	20.00
❑ M-4737	Lonesome Pine Special/'Mid the Green Fields of Virginia	193?	5.00	10.00	20.00

VICTOR

Number	Title (A Side/B Side)	Yr	VG	VG+	NM
❑ 20877	The Poor Orphan Child/The Wandering Boy	1927	5.00	10.00	20.00
❑ 20937	Storms Are On the Ocean/Single Girl, Married Man	1927	5.00	10.00	20.00
❑ 21074	Bury Me Under the Weeping Willow/Little Log Cbin by the Sea	1928	5.00	10.00	20.00

Number	Title (A Side/B Side)	Yr	VG	VG+	NM
❑ 21434	Keep on the Sunny Side/River of Jordan	1928	5.00	10.00	20.00
❑ 21517	Chewing Gum/I Ain't Goin' to Work Tomorrow	1928	5.00	10.00	20.00
❑ 21638	Little Darling, Pal of Mine/Will You Miss Me When I'm Gone?	1928	5.00	10.00	20.00
❑ 23513	On the Rock/(B-side unknown)	1931	17.50	35.00	70.00
❑ 23523	Where Shall I Be?/(B-side unknown)	1931	17.50	35.00	70.00
❑ 23541	Lonesome Valley/(B-side unknown)	1931	17.50	35.00	70.00
❑ 23554	There's Someone a-Waiting for Me/(B-side unknown)	1931	20.00	40.00	80.00
❑ 23569	Can't Feel at Home/(B-side unknown)	1931	20.00	40.00	80.00
❑ 23585	Sow 'Em on the Mountain/(B-side unknown)	1931	17.50	35.00	70.00
❑ 23599	My Old Cottage Home/(B-side unknown)	1931	17.50	35.00	70.00
❑ 23618	Let the Church Roll On/(B-side unknown)	1931	17.50	35.00	70.00
❑ 23626	Weary Prodigal Son/(B-side unknown)	1932	20.00	40.00	80.00
❑ 23641	Dying Soldier/(B-side unknown)	1932	20.00	40.00	80.00
❑ 23656	I Have Never Loved But One/(B-side unknown)	1932	20.00	40.00	80.00
❑ 23672	Where We'll Never Grow Old/(B-side unknown)	1932	20.00	40.00	80.00
❑ 23686	'Mid the Green Fields of Virginia/(B-side unknown)	1932	25.00	50.00	100.00
❑ 23701	Amber Tresses/(B-side unknown)	1932	25.00	50.00	100.00
❑ 23716	Carter's Blues/(B-side unknown)	1932	25.00	50.00	100.00
❑ 23731	Wabash Cannon Ball/(B-side unknown)	1933	30.00	60.00	120.00
❑ 23748	Will the Roses Bloom in Heaven?/(B-side unknown)	1933	30.00	60.00	120.00
❑ 23761	Sweet as the Flowers in May Time/(B-side unknown)	1933	30.00	60.00	120.00
❑ 23776	The Church in the Wildwood/(B-side unknown)	1933	30.00	60.00	120.00
❑ 23791	Two Sweet Hearts/(B-side unknown)	1933	30.00	60.00	120.00
❑ 23807	I Wouldn't Mind Dying/The Winding Stream	1933	37.50	75.00	150.00
❑ 23821	Gold Watch and Chain/(B-side unknown)	1933	37.50	75.00	150.00
❑ 23835	I Loved You Better Than I Know/(B-side unknown)	1933	50.00	100.00	200.00
❑ 23845	On the Sea of Galilee/(B-side unknown)	1933	50.00	100.00	200.00
❑ V40000	Wildwood Flower/Forsaken Love	1928	10.00	20.00	40.00
❑ V40036	I Have No One/(B-side unknown)	1928	10.00	20.00	40.00
❑ V40058	Foggy Mountain Top/My Clinch Mountain Home	1929	15.00	30.00	60.00
❑ V40089	I'm Thinking Tonight of My Blue Eyes/Engine One-Forty-Three	1929	15.00	30.00	60.00
❑ V40110	Little Moses/(B-side unknown)	1929	15.00	30.00	60.00
❑ V40126	Sweet Fern/(B-side unknown)	1929	15.00	30.00	60.00
❑ V40150	Diamonds in the Rough/The Grave on the Green Hillside	1929	15.00	30.00	60.00
❑ V40190	Bring Back My Blue-Eyed Boy/John Hardy Was a Desperate Little Man	1930	15.00	30.00	60.00
❑ V40207	The Homestead on the Farm/(B-side unknown)	1930	20.00	40.00	80.00
❑ V40229	When the Roses Bloom in Dixieland/(B-side unknown)	1930	20.00	40.00	80.00
❑ V40255	Western Hobo/(B-side unknown)	1930	20.00	40.00	80.00
❑ V40277	The Lover's Farewell/Kitty Waltz	1930	20.00	40.00	80.00
❑ V40293	When the World's on Fire/(B-side unknown)	1930	20.00	40.00	80.00
❑ V40317	Worried Man Blues/(B-side unknown)	1930	25.00	50.00	100.00
❑ V40328	Don't Forget This Song/(B-side unknown)	1930	25.00	50.00	100.00

VOCALION

Number	Title (A Side/B Side)	Yr	VG	VG+	NM
❑ 02990	Broken Hearted Lover/(B-side unknown)	1935	12.50	25.00	50.00
❑ 03027	Can the Circle Be Unbroken (By and By)/Glory to the Lamb	1935	10.00	20.00	40.00
❑ 03112	Lonesome Valley/(B-side unknown)	1935	10.00	20.00	40.00
❑ 03160	The Storms Are On the Ocean/(B-side unknown)	1935	10.00	20.00	40.00
❑ 04390	Don't Forget Me Little Darling/(B-side unknown)	193?	7.50	15.00	30.00

Albums

ACME

Number	Title (A Side/B Side)	Yr	VG	VG+	NM
❑ LP-1 [M]	All Time Favorites	1960	50.00	100.00	200.00
❑ LP-2 [M]	In Memory of A.P. Carter	1960	50.00	100.00	200.00

COLUMBIA

Number	Title (A Side/B Side)	Yr	VG	VG+	NM
❑ CL 2319 [M]	The Best of the Carter Family	1965	3.75	7.50	15.00
❑ CL 2617 [M]	Country Album	1967	6.25	12.50	25.00
❑ CS 9119 [S]	The Best of the Carter Family	1965	5.00	10.00	20.00
❑ CS 9417 [S]	Country Album	1967	5.00	10.00	20.00
❑ KC 31454	Travelin' Minstrel Band	1972	5.00	10.00	20.00
❑ KC 33084	Three Generations	1974	5.00	10.00	20.00
❑ KC 34266	Country's First Family	1976	5.00	10.00	20.00

DECCA

Number	Title (A Side/B Side)	Yr	VG	VG+	NM
❑ DL 4404 [M]	A Collection of Favorites by the Carter Family	1963	7.50	15.00	30.00
❑ DL 4557 [M]	More Favorites by the Carter Family	1964	7.50	15.00	30.00

LIBERTY

Number	Title (A Side/B Side)	Yr	VG	VG+	NM
❑ LRP-3230 [M]	The Carter Family Album	1962	7.50	15.00	30.00
❑ LST-7230 [S]	The Carter Family Album	1962	10.00	20.00	40.00

RCA VICTOR

Number	Title (A Side/B Side)	Yr	VG	VG+	NM
❑ LPM-2772 [M]	'Mid the Green Fields of Virginia	1963	10.00	20.00	40.00
❑ LSP-2772 [R]	'Mid the Green Fields of Virginia	1963	5.00	10.00	20.00

STARDAY

Number	Title (A Side/B Side)	Yr	VG	VG+	NM
❑ SLP-248 [M]	Echoes of the Carter Family	1963	10.00	20.00	40.00

CARTER SISTERS, THE

Members: ANITA CARTER; HELEN CARTER; JUNE CARTER. Also see CHET ATKINS; THE CARTER FAMILY.

45s

COLUMBIA

Number	Title (A Side/B Side)	Yr	VG	VG+	NM
❑ 4-21138	Wildwood Flower/He's Solid Gone	1953	6.25	12.50	25.00
❑ 4-21262	My Destiny/Well I Guess I Told You Off	1954	6.25	12.50	25.00

RCA VICTOR

Number	Title (A Side/B Side)	Yr	VG	VG+	NM
❑ 48-0050	Someone's Last Way/Why Do You Weep Dear Willow	1949	10.00	20.00	40.00
—Originals on green vinyl					
❑ 48-0105	Walk Closer to Me/A Picture, a Ring, and a Curl	1949	10.00	20.00	40.00
—Originals on green vinyl					
❑ 48-0153	The Day of Wrath/I've Got a Home in Glory	1950	10.00	20.00	40.00
—Originals on green vinyl					
❑ 48-0319	Don't Wait/Down on My Knees	1950	10.00	20.00	40.00
—Originals on green vinyl					
❑ 48-0372	Little Orphan Girl/God Sent My Little Girl	1950	10.00	20.00	40.00
—Originals on green vinyl					
❑ 48-0394	Willow Weep for Me/Gotta Find Somebody to Love	1950	10.00	20.00	40.00
—Originals on green vinyl					
❑ 48-0433	Columbus, Ga./I've Got My Share of Trouble	1951	7.50	15.00	30.00

CARTWRIGHT, LIONEL

45s

MCA

Number	Title (A Side/B Side)	Yr	VG	VG+	NM
❑ 53444	You're Gonna Make Her Mine/In My Eyes	1988	—	—	3.00
❑ 53498	Like Father, Like Son/A Little Lesser Blue	1989	—	—	3.00
❑ 53651	Give Me His Last Chance/Let the Hard Times Roll	1989	—	—	3.00
❑ 53723	In My Eyes/That's Why They Call It Falling	1989	—	—	3.00
❑ 53779	I Watched It All (On My Radio)/Hard Act to Follow	1989	—	2.00	4.00
❑ 53955	Say It's Not True/In the Long Run	1990	—	—	3.00
❑ 54078	Leap of Faith/Smack Dab in the Middle of Love	1991	—	2.00	4.00
❑ 54237	What Kind of Fool/I'm Your Man	1991	—	—	3.00
❑ 54366	Family Tree/30 Nothin'	1992	—	—	3.00
❑ 54440	Be My Angel/Sleep Walking	1992	—	—	3.00
❑ 54514	Standing on the Promises/She Will	1992	—	2.00	4.00
❑ 79046	My Heart Is Set on You/True Believer	1990	—	—	3.00

Albums

MCA

Number	Title (A Side/B Side)	Yr	VG	VG+	NM
❑ 42276	Lionel Cartwright	1989	3.00	6.00	12.00

CARVER, JOHNNY

45s

ABC

Number	Title (A Side/B Side)	Yr	VG	VG+	NM
❑ 11357	Yellow Ribbon/Since My Baby Left Me	1973	—	2.50	5.00
❑ 11374	You Really Haven't Changed/Treat a Lady Like a Tramp	1973	—	2.50	5.00
❑ 11403	Tonight Someone's Falling in Love/Frank and Don, Howard Too, Broadway Joe and You and Me	1973	—	2.50	5.00
❑ 11425	Country Lullabye/Pass Me By	1974	—	2.50	5.00
❑ 12017	Don't Tell (That Sweet Ole Lady of Mine)/'Til We Find It All Again	1974	—	2.50	5.00
❑ 12052	January Jones/Did We Even Try	1975	—	2.50	5.00
❑ 12097	Strings/Double Exposure	1975	—	2.50	5.00

ABC DOT

Number	Title (A Side/B Side)	Yr	VG	VG+	NM
❑ 17576	Start All Over Again/Love Signs	1975	—	2.50	5.00
❑ 17614	Snap, Crackle and Pop/I Can't Go Swimming in Muddy Water	1976	—	2.50	5.00
❑ 17640	Afternoon Delight/Double Exposure	1976	—	2.50	5.00
❑ 17661	Love Is Only Love (When Shared by Two)/It Don't Hurt to Be a Dreamer	1976	—	2.50	5.00
❑ 17675	Sweet City Woman/'Till We Find It All Again	1976	—	2.50	5.00
❑ 17685	Living Next Door to Alice/Treat a Lady Like a Tramp	1977	—	2.50	5.00
❑ 17707	Down at the Pool/Double Exposure	1977	—	2.50	5.00
❑ 17729	Apartment/Frank and Don, Howard, Too, Broadway Joe and You and Me	1977	—	2.50	5.00

DOT

Number	Title (A Side/B Side)	Yr	VG	VG+	NM
❑ 16823	Poverty Stricken Heart/My Future	1966	3.75	7.50	15.00

EPIC

Number	Title (A Side/B Side)	Yr	VG	VG+	NM
❑ 5-10760	If You Think That It's All Right/This Town's Not Big Enough	1971	—	3.00	6.00
❑ 5-10813	I Start Thinking About You/Preserving Wildlife	1971	—	3.00	6.00
❑ 5-10872	I Want You/I'm Talking About You Baby	1972	—	3.00	6.00

EQUITY

Number	Title (A Side/B Side)	Yr	VG	VG+	NM
❑ 1902	Fingertips/Caribbean Nights	1980	—	3.00	6.00

IMPERIAL

Number	Title (A Side/B Side)	Yr	VG	VG+	NM
❑ 66173	One Way or the Other/Think About Her All the Time	1966	3.00	6.00	12.00
❑ 66213	Fools' Names, Fools' Faces/What If It Happened to You	1966	3.00	6.00	12.00
❑ 66234	I Gotta Go Home/You Are That Something	1967	3.00	6.00	12.00
❑ 66268	Your Lily White Hands/What If It Happened to You	1967	2.00	4.00	8.00
❑ 66297	I Still Didn't Have the Sense to Go/Feelin' Kinda Sunday in My Thinkin'	1968	2.00	4.00	8.00
❑ 66316	Leaving Again/Does She Still Get Her Way	1968	2.00	4.00	8.00
❑ 66341	Hold Me Tight/My Heart's Been Marching	1968	2.00	4.00	8.00
❑ 66361	Sweet Wine/With Every Heartbeat	1969	2.00	4.00	8.00
❑ 66389	That's Your Hang Up/Mother-in-Law	1969	2.00	4.00	8.00
❑ 66423	Willie and the Hand Jive/Take Sadie Out to the Country	1969	2.00	4.00	8.00
❑ 66442	Harvey Harrington IV/Sybil's Rights	1970	2.00	4.00	8.00

MCA

Number	Title (A Side/B Side)	Yr	VG	VG+	NM
❑ 51072	Tie a Yellow Ribbon Round the Ole Oak Tree/You Really Haven't Changed	1981	—	2.00	4.00

MONUMENT

Number	Title (A Side/B Side)	Yr	VG	VG+	NM
❑ WS4-03667	Shed a Little Light/Somewhere	1983	—	2.00	4.00

TANGLEWOOD

Number	Title (A Side/B Side)	Yr	VG	VG+	NM
❑ 1905	S.O.S./Fingertips	1980	—	3.00	6.00

UNITED ARTISTS

Number	Title (A Side/B Side)	Yr	VG	VG+	NM
❑ 50713	If You See My Baby/Paint Your Pretty Pictures	1970	—	3.50	7.00
❑ 50767	Our Old Love Song/Three Little Words	1971	—	3.50	7.00

Albums

ABC

Number	Title (A Side/B Side)	Yr	VG	VG+	NM
❑ ABCX-792	Tie a Yellow Ribbon Around the Ole Oak Tree	1973	3.00	6.00	12.00
❑ ABCX-812	Double Exposure	1974	3.00	6.00	12.00
❑ ABCD-843	Please Don't Tell (That Sweet Ole Lady of Mine)	1974	3.00	6.00	12.00
❑ ABCD-864	Strings	1975	3.00	6.00	12.00

ABC DOT

Number	Title (A Side/B Side)	Yr	VG	VG+	NM
❑ DO-2042	Afternoon Delight	1976	3.00	6.00	12.00
❑ DO-2083	The Best of Johnny Carver	1977	3.00	6.00	12.00

HARMONY

Number	Title (A Side/B Side)	Yr	VG	VG+	NM
❑ KH 32476	I Start Thinking About You	1973	3.00	6.00	12.00

IMPERIAL

Number	Title (A Side/B Side)	Yr	VG	VG+	NM
❑ LP-9347 [M]	Really Country	1967	7.50	15.00	30.00
❑ LP-12347 [S]	Really Country	1967	5.00	10.00	20.00
❑ LP-12380	You're in Good Hands with Johnny Carver	1968	5.00	10.00	20.00
❑ LP-12412	Leaving Again	1968	5.00	10.00	20.00

CASEY, KAREN

45s

WESTERN PRIDE

Number	Title (A Side/B Side)	Yr	VG	VG+	NM
❑ 112	Leavin' on Your Mind/Are You Lonesome Tonight?	1980	—	3.00	6.00

CASH, JOHNNY

12-Inch Singles

COLUMBIA

Number	Title (A Side/B Side)	Yr	VG	VG+	NM
❑ AS 921 [DJ]	Without Love (one-sided)	1980	3.75	7.50	15.00

—Black B-side has etched autographs of Johnny Cash and Nick Lowe

45s

AMERICAN

Number	Title (A Side/B Side)	Yr	VG	VG+	NM
❑ 18091	Drive On/Delia's Gone	1994	—	2.00	4.00

A&M

Number	Title (A Side/B Side)	Yr	VG	VG+	NM
❑ 2291	The Death of Me/One More Shot	1980	—	2.00	4.00

—With Levon Helm

CACHET

Number	Title (A Side/B Side)	Yr	VG	VG+	NM
❑ 4504	Wings in the Morning/What on Earth	1980	—	2.50	5.00
❑ 4504 [PS]	Wings in the Morning/What on Earth	1980	—	2.50	5.00

COLUMBIA

Number	Title (A Side/B Side)	Yr	VG	VG+	NM
❑ 02189	Mobile Bay/The Hard Way	1981	—	2.00	4.00
❑ 02669	The Reverend Mr. Black/Chattanooga City Limit Sign	1982	—	2.00	4.00
❑ 03058	Georgia on a Fast Train/Sing a Song	1982	—	2.00	4.00
❑ 03317	Fair Weather Friends/Ain't Gonna Hobo No More	1982	—	2.00	4.00
❑ 03524	I'll Cross Over Jordan Some Day/We Must Believe in Magic	1983	—	2.00	4.00
❑ 04060	I'm Ragged, But I'm Right/Brand New Dance	1983	—	2.00	4.00
❑ 04227	Johnny 99/New Cut Road	1983	—	—	3.00
❑ 04428	That's the Truth/Joshua Gone Barbados	1984	—	—	3.00
❑ 04513	The Chicken in Black/The Battle of Nashville	1984	—	—	3.00
❑ 04740	They Killed Him/The Three Bells	1985	—	—	3.00

—With the Carter Family

Number	Title (A Side/B Side)	Yr	VG	VG+	NM
❑ 04860	Crazy Old Soldier/It Ain't Gonna Worry My Mind	1985	—	—	3.00

—A-side: Ray Charles and Johnny Cash; B-side: Ray Charles and Mickey Gilley

Number	Title (A Side/B Side)	Yr	VG	VG+	NM
❑ 04881	Highwayman/The Human Condition	1985	—	—	3.00

—A-side: Willie Nelson/Waylon Jennings/Johnny Cash/Kris Kristofferson; B-side: Nelson, Cash

Number	Title (A Side/B Side)	Yr	VG	VG+	NM
❑ 04881 [PS]	Highwayman/The Human Condition	1985	—	2.50	5.00

—A-side: Willie Nelson/Waylon Jennings/Johnny Cash/Kris Kristofferson; B-side: Nelson, Cash

Number	Title (A Side/B Side)	Yr	VG	VG+	NM
❑ 05594	Desperadoes Waiting for a Train/The Twentieth Century Is Almost Over	1985	—	—	3.00

—A-side: Willie Nelson/Waylon Jennings/Johnny Cash/Kris Kristofferson; B-side: Nelson, Cash

Number	Title (A Side/B Side)	Yr	VG	VG+	NM
❑ 05672	I'm Leaving Now/Easy Street	1985	—	—	3.00
❑ 08406	Highwayman/Desperadoes Waiting for a Train	1988	—	—	3.00

—Waylon Jennings/Willie Nelson/Johnny Cash/Kris Kristofferson; reissue

Number	Title (A Side/B Side)	Yr	VG	VG+	NM
❑ 10011	The Junkie and the Juicehead/Crystal Chandeliers and Burgundy	1974	—	2.50	5.00
❑ 10048	Father and Daughter, Father and Son/Don't Take Your Love to Town	1974	—	2.50	5.00

—With Rosey Nix

Number	Title (A Side/B Side)	Yr	VG	VG+	NM
❑ 10066	The Lady Came from Baltimore/Lonesome to the Bone	1974	—	2.50	5.00
❑ 10116	My Old Kentucky Home (Turpentine and Dandelion Wine)/Hard Times Comin'	1975	—	2.50	5.00
❑ 10177	Look at Them Beans/All Around Cowboy	1975	—	2.50	5.00
❑ 10237	Texas — 1947/I Hardly Ever Sing Beer Drinking Songs	1975	—	2.50	5.00
❑ 10279	Strawberry Cake/I Got Stripes	1975	—	2.50	5.00
❑ 10321	One Piece at a Time/Go On Blues	1976	—	2.50	5.00
❑ 10381	Sold Out of Flagpoles/Mountain Lady	1976	—	2.50	5.00
❑ 10424	It's All Over/Ridin' on the Cotton Belt	1976	—	2.50	5.00
❑ 10483	The Last Gunfighter Ballad/City Jail	1977	—	2.50	5.00
❑ 10587	Lady/Hit the Road and Go	1977	—	2.50	5.00
❑ 10623	After the Ball/Calilou	1977	—	2.50	5.00
❑ 10681	I Would Like to See You Again/Lately	1978	—	2.50	5.00
❑ 10817	Gone Girl/I'm Alright Now	1978	—	2.50	5.00
❑ 10855	It'll Be Her/It Comes and Goes	1978	—	2.50	5.00
❑ 10888	I Will Rock and Roll with You/A Song for the Life	1979	—	2.50	5.00
❑ 10961	(Ghost) Riders in the Sky/I'm Gonna Sit on the Porch and Pick on My Guitar	1979	—	2.50	5.00
❑ 10961 [PS]	(Ghost) Riders in the Sky/I'm Gonna Sit on the Porch and Pick on My Guitar	1979	—	3.00	6.00
❑ 11103	I'll Say It's True/Cocaine Blues	1979	—	2.50	5.00
❑ 11237	Bull Rider/Lonesome to the Bone	1980	—	2.00	4.00
❑ 11283	Song of a Patriot/She's a Go-er	1980	—	2.00	4.00
❑ 11340	Cold Lonesome Morning/The Cowboy Who Started the Fight	1980	—	2.00	4.00
❑ 11399	The Last Time/Rockabilly Blues (Texas 1965)	1980	—	2.00	4.00
❑ 11424	Without Love/It Ain't Nothing New Babe	1981	—	2.00	4.00
❑ 30843 [S]	Loading Coal/Slow Rider	1960	7.50	15.00	30.00
❑ 30844 [S]	Lumberjack/Dorrance of Ponchartrain	1960	7.50	15.00	30.00
❑ 30845 [S]	When Papa Played the Dobro/Going to Memphis	1960	7.50	15.00	30.00
❑ 30846 [S]	Old Doc Brown/Boss Jack	1960	7.50	15.00	30.00

—The above four are "Stereo Seven" 33 1/3 rpm jukebox singles from "JS 7-12" and the album "Ride This Train"

Number	Title (A Side/B Side)	Yr	VG	VG+	NM
❑ 30847 [S]	One More Ride/Run Softly, Blue River	1960	7.50	15.00	30.00

—"Stereo Seven" 33 1/3 rpm jukebox single from "JS 7-12," but from the album "The Fabulous Johnny Cash"

Number	Title (A Side/B Side)	Yr	VG	VG+	NM
❑ 31109 [S]	Seasons of My Heart/I Couldn't Keep from Crying	1961	7.50	15.00	30.00
❑ 31110 [S]	My Shoes Keep Walking Back to You/Time Changes Everything	1961	7.50	15.00	30.00
❑ 31111 [S]	Transfusion Blues/I'd Just Be Fool Enough (To Fall)	1961	7.50	15.00	30.00
❑ 31112 [S]	I'm So Lonesome I Could Cry/I Will Miss You When You Go	1961	7.50	15.00	30.00
❑ 31113 [S]	Just One More/Honky Tonk Girl	1961	7.50	15.00	30.00

—The above five are "Stereo Seven" 33 1/3 rpm jukebox singles from "JS 7-29" and the album "Now There Was a Song"

Number	Title (A Side/B Side)	Yr	VG	VG+	NM
❑ 3-38990	Hey Porter/Big River	1964	7.50	15.00	30.00

—Stereo jukebox single, plays at 33 1/3 rpm; rather than the usual rainbow "target" label of Columbia "Stereo Seven" singles, this one has green labels

Number	Title (A Side/B Side)	Yr	VG	VG+	NM
❑ 41251	All Over Again/What Do I Care	1958	3.75	7.50	15.00
❑ 41251 [PS]	All Over Again/What Do I Care	1958	10.00	20.00	40.00
❑ 41313	Don't Take Your Guns to Town/I Still Miss Someone	1959	3.75	7.50	15.00
❑ 41313 [PS]	Don't Take Your Guns to Town/I Still Miss Someone	1959	10.00	20.00	40.00
❑ 41371	Frankie's Man, Johnny/You, Dreamer, You	1959	3.75	7.50	15.00
❑ 41427	I Got Stripes/Five Feet High and Rising	1959	3.75	7.50	15.00
❑ 41481	The Little Drummer Boy/I'll Remember You	1959	3.75	7.50	15.00
❑ 41481 [PS]	The Little Drummer Boy/I'll Remember You	1959	10.00	20.00	40.00
❑ 41618	Seasons of My Heart/Smiling Bill McCall	1960	3.75	7.50	15.00
❑ 41707	Second Honemoon/Honky Tonk Girl	1960	3.75	7.50	15.00
❑ 41804	Going to Memphis/Loading Coal	1960	3.75	7.50	15.00
❑ 41920	Girl in Saskatoon/Locomotive Man	1960	3.75	7.50	15.00
❑ 41995	The Rebel-Johnny Yuma/Forty Shades of Green	1961	3.00	6.00	12.00
❑ 41995 [PS]	The Rebel-Johnny Yuma/Forty Shades of Green	1961	6.25	12.50	25.00
❑ 42147	Tennessee Flat Top Box/Tall Men	1961	3.00	6.00	12.00
❑ 42147 [PS]	Tennessee Flat Top Box/Tall Men	1961	6.25	12.50	25.00
❑ 42301	The Big Battle/What I've Learned	1962	3.00	6.00	12.00
❑ 42301 [PS]	The Big Battle/What I've Learned	1962	6.25	12.50	25.00
❑ 42425	In the Jailhouse Now/A Little at a Time	1962	3.00	6.00	12.00
❑ 42425 [PS]	In the Jailhouse Now/A Little at a Time	1962	6.25	12.50	25.00
❑ 42512	Bonanza!/Pick a Bale o' Cotton	1962	3.00	6.00	12.00
❑ 42615	Peace in the Valley/Were You There	1962	3.00	6.00	12.00

—With the Carter Family

Number	Title (A Side/B Side)	Yr	VG	VG+	NM
❑ 42665	Busted/Send a Picture of Mother	1963	2.50	5.00	10.00
❑ 42665 [PS]	Busted/Send a Picture of Mother	1963	6.25	12.50	25.00
❑ 42788	Ring of Fire/I'd Still Be There	1963	2.50	5.00	10.00
❑ 42788 [DJ]	Ring of Fire (same on both sides)	1963	10.00	20.00	40.00

—Red vinyl promo

Number	Title (A Side/B Side)	Yr	VG	VG+	NM
❑ 42788 [PS]	Ring of Fire/I'd Still Be There	1963	7.50	15.00	30.00
❑ 42880	The Matador/Still in Town	1963	2.50	5.00	10.00
❑ 42880 [PS]	The Matador/Still in Town	1963	5.00	10.00	20.00
❑ 42964	Understand Your Man/Dark as a Dungeon	1964	2.50	5.00	10.00
❑ 43058	The Ballad of Ira Hayes/Bad News	1964	2.50	5.00	10.00
❑ 43145	It Ain't Me, Babe/Time and Time Again	1964	2.50	5.00	10.00
❑ 43206	Orange Blossom Special/All of God's Children Ain't Free	1965	2.00	4.00	8.00
❑ 43313	Mister Garfield/Streets or Laredo	1965	2.00	4.00	8.00
❑ 43342	The Sons of Katie Elder/A Certain Kinda Hurtin'	1965	2.00	4.00	8.00
❑ 43420	Happy to Be with You/Pickin' Time	1965	2.00	4.00	8.00
❑ 43496	The One on the Right Is On the Left/Cotton Pickin' Hands	1965	2.00	4.00	8.00
❑ 43673	Everybody Loves a Nut/Austin Prison	1966	—	3.00	6.00
❑ 43763	Boa Constrictor/Bottom of a Mountain	1966	—	3.00	6.00
❑ 43921	You Beat All I Ever Saw/Put the Sugar to Bill	1966	—	3.00	6.00
❑ 44288	The Wind Changes/Red Velvet	1967	—	3.00	6.00
❑ 44373	Rosanna's Going Wild/Roll Call	1967	—	3.00	6.00
❑ 44373 [PS]	Rosanna's Going Wild/Roll Call	1967	2.50	5.00	10.00
❑ 44513	Folsom Prison Blues/The Folk Singer	1968	—	3.00	6.00
❑ 44513 [PS]	Folsom Prison Blues/The Folk Singer	1968	2.50	5.00	10.00
❑ 44689	Daddy Sang Bass/He Turned the Water Into Wine	1968	—	3.00	6.00
❑ 44944	A Boy Named Sue/San Quentin	1969	—	3.00	6.00
❑ 45020	Blistered/See Ruby Fall	1969	—	3.00	6.00
❑ 45134	What Is Truth/Sing a Traveling Song	1970	—	2.50	5.00
❑ 45211	Sonday Morning Coming Down/I'm Gonna Try to Be That Way	1970	—	2.50	5.00
❑ 45269	Flesh and Blood/This Side of the Law	1970	—	2.50	5.00
❑ 45339	Man in Black/Little Bit of Yesterday	1971	—	2.50	5.00
❑ 45393	Singing in Viet Nam Talking Blues/You've Got a New Light Shining	1971	—	2.50	5.00
❑ 45460	Papa Was a Good Man/I Promise You	1971	—	2.50	5.00
❑ 45534	A Thing Called Love/Daddy	1972	—	2.50	5.00
❑ 45590	Kate/Miracle Man	1972	—	2.50	5.00
❑ 45660	Oney/Country Trash	1972	—	2.50	5.00
❑ 45740	Any Old Wind That Blows/Kentucky Straight	1972	—	2.50	5.00
❑ 45786	Children/Last Summer	1973	—	2.50	5.00
❑ 45938	Pick the Wildwood Flower/Diamonds in the Rough	1973	—	2.50	5.00

—With Mother Maybelle and the Carter Family

Number	Title (A Side/B Side)	Yr	VG	VG+	NM
❑ 45979	Christmas As I Knew It/That Christmasy Feeling	1973	—	2.50	5.00
—With Tommy Cash					
❑ 45997	Orleans Parish Prison/Jacob Green	1974	—	2.50	5.00
❑ 46028	Ragged Old Flag/Don't Go Near the Water	1974	—	2.50	5.00
❑ 60516	The Baron/I Will Dance with You	1981	—	2.00	4.00
❑ 69067	Ragged Old Flag/I'm Leaving Now	1989	—	—	3.00
❑ 73233	America Remains/Silver Stallion	1990	—	—	3.00
—Waylon Jennings/Willie Nelson/Johnny Cash/Kris Kristofferson					
❑ 73381	Born and Raised in Black and White/Texas	1990	—	—	3.00
—The Highwaymen (Waylon Jennings/Willie Nelson/Johnny Cash/Kris Kristofferson)					
❑ 73572	American Remains/Texas	1990	—	—	3.00
—The Highwaymen (Waylon Jennings/Willie Nelson/Johnny Cash/Kris Kristofferson)					
EPIC					
❑ 50778	There Ain't No Good Chain Gang/I Wish I Was Crazy Again	1979	—	2.50	5.00
—Johnny Cash/Waylon Jennings					
LIBERTY					
❑ S7-18486	It Is What It Is/The Devil's Right Hand	1995	—	—	3.00
—By The Highwaymen					
MERCURY					
❑ 870010-7	W. Lee O'Daniel (And the Light Crust Dough Boys)/Letters from Homes	1987	—	—	3.00
❑ 870237-7	Cry, Cry, Cry/Get Rhythm	1988	—	—	3.00
❑ 870688-7	Tennessee Flat Top Box/That Old Wheel	1988	—	—	3.00
—A-side with Hank Williams, Jr.					
❑ 872420-7	Ballad of a Teenage Queen/Get Rhythm	1988	—	—	3.00
—With Roseanne Cash and the Everly Brothers					
❑ 874562-7	The Last of the Drifters/(B-side unknown)	1989	—	—	3.00
—With Tom T. Hall					
❑ 875626-7	Cat's in the Cradle/I Love You, Love You	1990	—	—	3.00
❑ 878292-7	Goin' By the Book/Beans for Breakfast	1990	—	—	3.00
❑ 878710-7	The Greatest Cowboy of Them All/Hey Porter	1990	—	—	3.00
❑ 878968-7	The Mystery of Life/I'm an Easy Rider	1990	—	—	3.00
❑ 888459-7	The Night Hank Williams Came to Town/I'd Rather Have You	1987	—	—	3.00
❑ 888719-7	Sixteen Tons/The Ballad of Barbara	1987	—	—	3.00
❑ 888838-7	Let Him Roll/My Ship Will Sail	1987	—	—	3.00
SCOTTI BROS.					
❑ 02803	The General Lee/Duelin' Dukes	1982	—	2.00	4.00
—Narration on B-side: Sorrell Booke					
SMASH					
❑ 884934-7	Sixteen Candles/Rock & Roll (Fais-Do-Do)	1986	—	2.00	4.00
—With Jerry Lee Lewis, Roy Orbison and Carl Perkins					
❑ 888142-7	We Remember the King/Class of '55	1987	—	2.00	4.00
—With Jerry Lee Lewis, Roy Orbison and Carl Perkins; B-side by Carl Perkins solo					
SUN					
❑ 221	Hey Porter/Cry, Cry, Cry	1955	10.00	20.00	40.00
❑ 232	Folsom Prison Blues/So Doggone Lonesome	1956	7.50	15.00	30.00
❑ 241	I Walk the Line/Get Rhythm	1956	10.00	20.00	40.00
❑ 258	Train of Love/There You Go	1956	7.50	15.00	30.00
❑ 266	Next in Line/Don't Make Me Go	1957	7.50	15.00	30.00
❑ 279	Home of the Blues/Give My Love to Rose	1957	7.50	15.00	30.00
❑ 283	Ballad of a Teenage Queen/Big River	1958	6.25	12.50	25.00
❑ 295	Guess Things Happen That Way/Come In Stranger	1958	6.25	12.50	25.00
❑ 295 [PS]	Guess Things Happen That Way/Come In Stranger	1958	10.00	20.00	40.00
❑ 302	The Ways of a Woman in Love/The Nearest Thing to Heaven	1958	6.25	12.50	25.00
❑ 309	It's Just About Time/Just Thought You'd Like to Know	1958	6.25	12.50	25.00
❑ 316	Luther Played the Boogie/Thanks a Lot	1959	5.00	10.00	20.00
❑ 321	Katy Too/I Forgot to Remember to Forget	1959	5.00	10.00	20.00
❑ 331	Goodbye Little Darlin'/You Tell Me	1959	5.00	10.00	20.00
❑ 334	Straight A's in Love/I Love You Because	1960	5.00	10.00	20.00
❑ 343	Story of a Broken Heart/Down the Street to 301	1960	5.00	10.00	20.00
❑ 347	Mean Eyed Cat/Port of Lonely Hearts	1960	5.00	10.00	20.00
❑ 355	Oh Lonesome Me/Life Goes On	1961	5.00	10.00	20.00
❑ 363	Sugartime/My Treasurer	1961	5.00	10.00	20.00
❑ 376	Born to Lose/Blue Train	1962	5.00	10.00	20.00
❑ 392	Wide Open Road/Belshazar	1964	5.00	10.00	20.00
❑ 1103	Get Rhythm/Hey Porter	1969	—	3.00	6.00
❑ 1111	Rock Island Line/Next in Line	1970	—	3.00	6.00
❑ 1121	Big River/Come In Stranger	1971	—	2.50	5.00
7-Inch Extended Plays					
COLUMBIA					
❑ B-2155	The Rebel — Johnny Yuma/Remember the Alamo//The Ballad of Boot Hill/Lorena	1961	3.75	7.50	15.00
❑ B-2155 [PS]	The Rebel — Johnny Yuma	1961	3.75	7.50	15.00
❑ B-12531	Run Softly, Blue River/That's All Over//I Still Miss Someone/Supper-Time	1958	3.00	6.00	12.00
❑ B-12531 [PS]	The Fabulous Johnny Cash, Vol. I	1958	3.00	6.00	12.00
❑ B-12532	Frankie's Man, Johnny/The Troubadour//Don't Take Your Guns to Town/That's Enough	1958	3.00	6.00	12.00
❑ B-12532 [PS]	The Fabulous Johnny Cash, Vol. II	1958	3.00	6.00	12.00
❑ B-12533	(A-side unknown)//Pickin' Time/Shepherd of My Heart	1958	3.00	6.00	12.00
❑ B-12533 [PS]	The Fabulous Johnny Cash, Vol. III	1958	3.00	6.00	12.00
❑ B-12861	It Was Jesus/I Saw a Man//Are All the Children In?/The Old Account	1959	3.00	6.00	12.00
❑ B-12861 [PS]	Hymns by Johnny Cash, Vol. I	1959	3.00	6.00	12.00
❑ B-12862	Lead Me Gently Home/Swing Low, Sweet Chariot//Snow in His Hair/Lead Me Father	1959	3.00	6.00	12.00
❑ B-12862 [PS]	Hymns by Johnny Cash, Vol. II	1959	3.00	6.00	12.00
❑ B-12863	I Call Him/These Things Shall Pass//He'll Be a Friend/God Will	1959	3.00	6.00	12.00
❑ B-12863 [PS]	Hymns by Johnny Cash, Vol. III	1959	3.00	6.00	12.00
❑ B-13391	(contents unknown)	1959	3.00	6.00	12.00
❑ B-13391 [PS]	Songs of Our Soil, Vol. I	1959	3.00	6.00	12.00
❑ B-13392	(contents unknown)	1959	3.00	6.00	12.00
❑ B-13392 [PS]	Songs of Our Soil, Vol. II	1959	3.00	6.00	12.00
❑ B-13393	Old Apache Squaw/Don't Step on Mother's Roses//My Grandfather's Clock/It Could Be You	1959	3.00	6.00	12.00
❑ B-13393 [PS]	Songs of Our Soil, Vol. III	1959	3.00	6.00	12.00
❑ B-14631	Seasons of My Heart/I Feel Better All Over//I Couldn't Keep from Crying/Time Changes Everything	1960	3.00	6.00	12.00
❑ B-14631 [PS]	Now, There Was a Song, Vol. I	1960	3.00	6.00	12.00
❑ B-14632	My Shoes Just Keep Walking Back to You/I'd Just Be Fool Enough (To Fall)//Transfusion Blues/Why Do You Punish Me	1960	3.00	6.00	12.00
❑ B-14632 [PS]	Now, There Was a Song, Vol. II	1960	3.00	6.00	12.00
❑ B-14633	I Will Miss You When You Go/I'm So Lonesome I Could Cry//Just One More/Honky Tonk Girl	1960	3.00	6.00	12.00
❑ B-14633 [PS]	Now, There Was a Song, Vol. III	1960	3.00	6.00	12.00
SUN					
❑ EPA-111	I Can't Help It/You Win Again//Hey Good Lookin'/I Could Never Be Ashamed	1956	10.00	20.00	40.00
❑ EPA-111 [PS]	Johnny Cash Sings Hank Williams	1956	15.00	30.00	60.00
❑ EPA-112	Rock Island Line/I Heard That Lonesome Whistle//Country Boy/If the Good Lord's Willin'	1956	7.50	15.00	30.00
❑ EPA-112 [PS]	Country Boy	1956	12.50	25.00	50.00
❑ EPA-113	I Walk the Line/The Wreck of the Old '97//Folsom Prison Blues/Doin' My Time	1958	7.50	15.00	30.00
❑ EPA-113 [PS]	I Walk the Line	1958	12.50	25.00	50.00
❑ EPA-114	The Ways of a Woman in Love/Next in Line//Guess Things Happen That Way/Train of Love	1958	7.50	15.00	30.00
❑ EPA-114 [PS]	His Top Hits	1958	12.50	25.00	50.00
❑ SEP-116	Home of the Blues/Big River//You're the Nearest Thing to Heaven/I Can't Help It	1959	7.50	15.00	30.00
❑ SEP-116 [PS]	Home of the Blues	1959	12.50	25.00	50.00
❑ SEP-117	So Doggone Lonesome/I Was There When It Happened//Cry, Cry, Cry/Remember Me	1958	7.50	15.00	30.00
❑ SEP-117 [PS]	Johnny Cash	1958	12.50	25.00	50.00
Albums					
ACCORD					
❑ SN-7134	I Walk the Line	1983	2.50	5.00	10.00
❑ SN-7208	Years Gone By	1983	2.50	5.00	10.00
ALLEGIANCE					
❑ AV-5017	The First Years	1986	2.50	5.00	10.00
AMERICAN					
❑ 43097	Unchained	1996	3.00	6.00	12.00
❑ 45220	American Recordings	1994	3.00	6.00	12.00
❑ C 69691	American III: Solitary Man	2000	3.00	6.00	12.00
ARCHIVE OF FOLK MUSIC					
❑ 278	Johnny Cash	198?	3.00	6.00	12.00
CACHET					
❑ 9001	A Believer Sings the Truth	1979	3.75	7.50	15.00
COLUMBIA					
❑ GP 29 [(2)]	The World of Johnny Cash	1970	3.75	7.50	15.00
❑ C2L 38 [(2) M]	Ballads of the True West	1965	6.25	12.50	25.00
❑ C2S 838 [(2) S]	Ballads of the True West	1965	6.25	12.50	25.00
❑ CL 1253 [M]	The Fabulous Johnny Cash	1958	5.00	10.00	20.00
❑ CL 1284 [M]	Hymns by Johnny Cash	1959	6.25	12.50	25.00
❑ CL 1339 [M]	Songs of Our Soil	1959	6.25	12.50	25.00
❑ CL 1463 [M]	Now, There Was a Song!	1960	6.25	12.50	25.00
❑ CL 1464 [M]	Ride This Train	1960	6.25	12.50	25.00
❑ CL 1622 [M]	The Lure of the Grand Canyon	1961	10.00	20.00	40.00
—Cash narrates; with Andre Kostelanetz and His Orchestra					
❑ CL 1722 [M]	Hymns from the Heart	1962	5.00	10.00	20.00
❑ CL 1802 [M]	The Sound of Johnny Cash	1962	5.00	10.00	20.00
❑ CL 1930 [M]	Blood, Sweat & Tears	1963	5.00	10.00	20.00
❑ CL 2052 [M]	Ring of Fire (The Best of Johnny Cash)	1963	5.00	10.00	20.00
❑ CL 2117 [M]	The Christmas Spirit	1963	6.25	12.50	25.00
❑ CL 2190 [M]	I Walk the Line	1964	3.75	7.50	15.00
❑ CL 2248 [M]	Bitter Tears (Ballads of the American Indian)	1964	3.75	7.50	15.00
❑ CL 2309 [M]	Orange Blossom Special	1965	3.75	7.50	15.00
❑ CL 2446 [M]	Mean as Hell	1965	3.75	7.50	15.00
❑ CL 2492 [M]	Everybody Loves a Nut	1966	3.75	7.50	15.00
❑ CL 2537 [M]	That's What You Get for Lovin' Me	1966	3.75	7.50	15.00
❑ CL 2647 [M]	From Sea to Shining Sea	1967	5.00	10.00	20.00
❑ CL 2678 [M]	Johnny Cash's Greatest Hits, Volume 1	1967	5.00	10.00	20.00
❑ CS 8122 [S]	The Fabulous Johnny Cash	1959	10.00	20.00	40.00
❑ CS 8125 [S]	Hymns by Johnny Cash	1959	10.00	20.00	40.00
❑ CS 8148 [S]	Songs of Our Soil	1959	10.00	20.00	40.00
❑ CS 8254 [S]	Now, There Was a Song!	1960	10.00	20.00	40.00
❑ CS 8255 [S]	Ride This Train	1960	10.00	20.00	40.00
❑ CS 8422 [S]	The Lure of the Grand Canyon	1961	12.50	25.00	50.00
—Cash narrates; with Andre Kostelanetz and His Orchestra					
❑ CS 8522 [S]	Hymns from the Heart	1962	7.50	15.00	30.00
❑ CS 8602 [S]	The Sound of Johnny Cash	1962	7.50	15.00	30.00
❑ CS 8730 [S]	Blood, Sweat & Tears	1963	6.25	12.50	25.00
❑ CS 8852 [S]	Ring of Fire (The Best of Johnny Cash)	1963	6.25	12.50	25.00
❑ CS 8917 [S]	The Christmas Spirit	1963	7.50	15.00	30.00
❑ CS 8990 [S]	I Walk the Line	1964	5.00	10.00	20.00
❑ CS 9048 [S]	Bitter Tears (Ballads of the American Indian)	1964	5.00	10.00	20.00
❑ CS 9109 [S]	Orange Blossom Special	1965	5.00	10.00	20.00
❑ CS 9246 [S]	Mean as Hell	1965	5.00	10.00	20.00
❑ CS 9292 [S]	Everybody Loves a Nut	1966	5.00	10.00	20.00

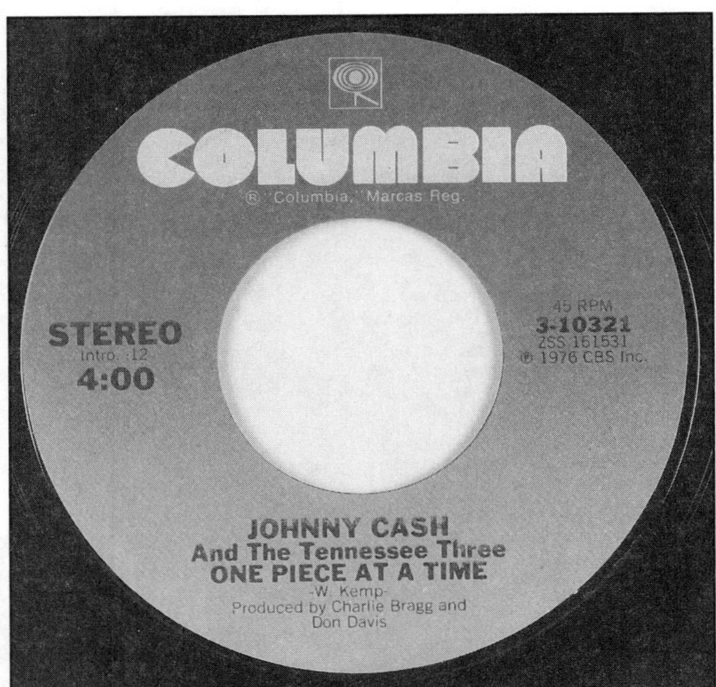

He's a rock and roll, country music and songwriters Hall of Famer, but Johnny Cash continues to make vital music, just as he has since 1955. (Top left) The first Cash single to make the country top 10 was a double-sided pairing of "So Doggone Lonesome" and "Folsom Prison Blues" in 1956. The latter track, issued from his famous live concert at Folsom Prison, would hit the top in its 1968 live version. (Top right) Sun Records began doing some extended-play singles around 1957. This is the cover from *Country Boy*, one of the Sun Johnny Cash EPs. (Bottom left) Cash's last solo No. 1 on the country charts was "One Piece at a Time," an amusing song about a guy who steals parts of a car over time, then tries to put it all together. It also made the top 40 on the pop charts. (Bottom right) Three of the most amazing records Johnny Cash has done are the three he has recorded for the American Recordings label. The first of these, *American Recordings,* features, for the most part, only Cash and his guitar and even got some airplay on college radio stations.

Number	Title (A Side/B Side)	Yr	VG	VG+	NM
❑ CS 9337 [S]	That's What You Get for Lovin' Me	1966	5.00	10.00	20.00
❑ CS 9447 [S]	From Sea to Shining Sea	1967	5.00	10.00	20.00
❑ CS 9478 [S]	Johnny Cash's Greatest Hits, Volume 1	1967	5.00	10.00	20.00
❑ CS 9639	Johnny Cash at Folsom Prison	1968	5.00	10.00	20.00
❑ KCS 9726	The Holy Land	1969	3.75	7.50	15.00
❑ CS 9827	Johnny Cash at San Quentin	1969	3.00	6.00	12.00
❑ KCS 9943	Hello, I'm Johnny Cash	1970	3.00	6.00	12.00
❑ C 30100	The Johnny Cash Show	1970	3.00	6.00	12.00
❑ S 30397	I Walk the Line	1970	3.00	6.00	12.00
—Soundtrack from movie					
❑ KC 30550	Man in Black	1971	3.00	6.00	12.00
❑ KC 30887	The Johnny Cash Collection (His Greatest Hits, Volume II)	1971	3.00	6.00	12.00
❑ CQ 30961 [Q]	Johnny Cash at San Quentin	1971	5.00	10.00	20.00
❑ KC 31256	Give My Love to Rose	1972	3.00	6.00	12.00
❑ KC 31332	A Thing Called Love	1972	3.00	6.00	12.00
❑ KC 31645	Johnny Cash: America (A 200-Year Salute in Story and Song)	1972	3.00	6.00	12.00
❑ KC 32091	Any Old Wind That Blows	1973	3.00	6.00	12.00
❑ C 32240	Sunday Morning Coming Down	1973	3.00	6.00	12.00
❑ C 32253	The Gospel Road	1973	3.00	6.00	12.00
❑ CG 32253 [(2)]	The Gospel Road	1973	6.25	12.50	25.00
❑ KC 32898	Children's Album	1974	3.00	6.00	12.00
❑ C 32917	The Ragged Old Flag	1974	3.00	6.00	12.00
❑ C 32951	Five Feet High and Rising	1974	3.00	6.00	12.00
❑ KC 33086	The Junkie and the Juicehead	1974	3.00	6.00	12.00
❑ C 33087	Johnny Cash Sings Precious Memories	1974	3.00	6.00	12.00
❑ KC 33370	John R. Cash	1975	3.00	6.00	12.00
❑ CG 33639 [(2)]	Johnny Cash at Folsom Prison/Johnny Cash at San Quentin	1974	3.75	7.50	15.00
❑ KC 33814	Look at Them Beans	1975	3.00	6.00	12.00
❑ KC 34088	Strawberry Cake	1976	3.00	6.00	12.00
❑ KC 34193	One Piece at a Time	1976	3.00	6.00	12.00
❑ JC 34314	The Last Gunfighter Ballad	1977	3.00	6.00	12.00
❑ JC 34833	The Rambler	1977	3.00	6.00	12.00
❑ KC 35313	I Would Like to See You Again	1978	2.50	5.00	10.00
❑ JC 35637	Johnny Cash's Greatest Hits, Volume 3	1978	3.00	6.00	12.00
❑ JC 36086	Silver	1979	3.00	6.00	12.00
❑ JC 36779	Rockabilly Blues	1980	2.50	5.00	10.00
❑ JC 36866	Classic Christmas	1980	3.00	6.00	12.00
❑ FC 37179	The Baron	1981	2.50	5.00	10.00
❑ FC 37355	Encore	1981	2.50	5.00	10.00
❑ PC 38074	A Believer Sings the Truth	1985	2.00	4.00	8.00
—Reissue of Priority 38074					
❑ FC 38094	The Adventures of Johnny Cash	1982	2.50	5.00	10.00
❑ FC 38317	Johnny Cash's Biggest Hits	1982	2.50	5.00	10.00
❑ FC 38696	Johnny 99	1983	2.50	5.00	10.00
❑ PC 38696	Johnny 99	1986	2.00	4.00	8.00
—Budget-line reissue					
❑ FC 39951	Rainbow	1985	2.50	5.00	10.00

COLUMBIA SPECIAL PRODUCTS

Number	Title (A Side/B Side)	Yr	VG	VG+	NM
❑ 363	Legends and Love Songs	196?	5.00	10.00	20.00
❑ P 13832	Hello, I'm Johnny Cash	1977	3.00	6.00	12.00

DORAL/CSP

Number	Title (A Side/B Side)	Yr	VG	VG+	NM
❑ (# unknown)	Doral Presents Johnny Cash	1972	10.00	20.00	40.00
—Mail-order offer from Doral cigarettes					

EVEREST

Number	Title (A Side/B Side)	Yr	VG	VG+	NM
❑ 276	Johnny Cash	19??	3.00	6.00	12.00

HARMONY

Number	Title (A Side/B Side)	Yr	VG	VG+	NM
❑ HS 11249	Golden Sounds of Country Music	1968	3.00	6.00	12.00
❑ HS 11342	Johnny Cash	1969	3.00	6.00	12.00
❑ KH 30916	Understand Your Man	1971	3.00	6.00	12.00
❑ KH 31602	The Johnny Cash Songbook	1972	3.00	6.00	12.00
❑ KH 32388	Ballads of the American Indian	1973	3.00	6.00	12.00

MERCURY

Number	Title (A Side/B Side)	Yr	VG	VG+	NM
❑ 832031-1	Johnny Cash Is Coming to Town	1987	2.50	5.00	10.00
❑ 834778-1	Water from the Wells of Home	1988	2.50	5.00	10.00

PAIR

Number	Title (A Side/B Side)	Yr	VG	VG+	NM
❑ PDL2-1107 [(2)]	Classic Cash	1986	3.75	7.50	15.00

POWER PAK

Number	Title (A Side/B Side)	Yr	VG	VG+	NM
❑ 246	Country Gold	198?	2.50	5.00	10.00

PRIORITY

Number	Title (A Side/B Side)	Yr	VG	VG+	NM
❑ UG 32253 [(2)]	The Gospel Road	1981	3.75	7.50	15.00
—Reissue of Columbia album of the same name					
❑ PU 33087	Johnny Cash Sings Precious Memories	1982	3.00	6.00	12.00
—Reissue of Columbia album of the same name					
❑ PU 38074	A Believer Sings the Truth	1982	3.00	6.00	12.00
—Reissue of Cachet album					

RHINO

Number	Title (A Side/B Side)	Yr	VG	VG+	NM
❑ RNLP 70229	The Vintage Years	1987	3.00	6.00	12.00

SHARE

Number	Title (A Side/B Side)	Yr	VG	VG+	NM
❑ 5000	I Walk the Line	197?	3.00	6.00	12.00
❑ 5001	Folsom Prison Blues	197?	3.00	6.00	12.00
❑ 5002	The Blue Train	197?	3.00	6.00	12.00
❑ 5003	Johnny Cash Sings the Greatest Hits	197?	3.00	6.00	12.00

SUN

Number	Title (A Side/B Side)	Yr	VG	VG+	NM
❑ LP-100	Original Golden Hits, Volume I	1969	3.00	6.00	12.00
❑ LP-101	Original Golden Hits, Volume II	1969	3.00	6.00	12.00
❑ LP-104	Story Songs of the Trains and Rivers	1969	3.00	6.00	12.00
❑ LP-105	Get Rhythm	1969	3.00	6.00	12.00
❑ LP-106	Showtime	1969	3.00	6.00	12.00
❑ LP-115	The Singing Story Teller	1970	3.00	6.00	12.00
❑ LP-118 [(2)]	Johnny Cash — The Legend	1970	5.00	10.00	20.00
❑ LP-122	Rough Cut King of Country	1971	3.00	6.00	12.00
❑ LP-126 [(2)]	Johnny Cash: The Man, The World, His Music	1971	5.00	10.00	20.00
❑ LP-127	Original Golden Hits, Volume III	1972	3.00	6.00	12.00
❑ LP-139	I Walk the Line	1979	2.50	5.00	10.00
❑ LP-140	Folsom Prison Blues	1979	2.50	5.00	10.00
❑ LP-141	The Blue Train	1979	2.50	5.00	10.00
❑ LP-142	Johnny Cash Sings the Greatest Hits	1979	2.50	5.00	10.00
❑ 1002	Superbilly (1955-58)	198?	2.50	5.00	10.00
❑ 1006	The Original Johnny Cash	1980	2.50	5.00	10.00
❑ SLP-1220 [M]	Johnny Cash with His Hot and Blue Guitar	1956	25.00	50.00	100.00
❑ SLP-1235 [M]	The Songs That Made Him Famous	1958	25.00	50.00	100.00
❑ SLP-1240 [M]	Johnny Cash's Greatest!	1959	12.50	25.00	50.00
❑ SLP-1245 [M]	Johnny Cash Sings Hank Williams	1960	12.50	25.00	50.00
❑ SLP-1255 [M]	Now Here's Johnny Cash	1961	12.50	25.00	50.00
❑ SLP-1270 [M]	All Aboard the Blue Train	1963	12.50	25.00	50.00
❑ SLP-1275 [M]	The Original Sun Sound of Johnny Cash	1965	12.50	25.00	50.00

WORD

Number	Title (A Side/B Side)	Yr	VG	VG+	NM
❑ WR-8333	Believe in Him	1986	3.00	6.00	12.00

CASH, JOHNNY, AND JUNE CARTER

Also see each artist's individual listings.

45s

COLUMBIA

Number	Title (A Side/B Side)	Yr	VG	VG+	NM
❑ 10436	Old Time Feeling/Far Side Banks of Jordan	1976	—	2.50	5.00
❑ 44011	Jackson/Pack Up Your Sorrows	1967	—	3.00	6.00
❑ 44158	Long-Legged Guitar Pickin' Man/You'll Be All Right	1967	—	3.00	6.00
❑ 45064	If I Were a Carpenter/'Cause I Love You	1970	—	2.50	5.00
❑ 45431	No Need to Worry/I'll Be Loving You	1971	—	2.50	5.00
❑ 45631	If I Had a Hammer/I Gotta Go	1972	—	2.50	5.00
❑ 45758	The Loving Gift/Help Me Make It Through the Night	1973	—	2.50	5.00
❑ 45890	Praise the Lord and Pass the Soup/The Ballad of Barbara	1973	—	2.50	5.00
❑ 45929	Allegheny/We're for Love	1973	—	2.50	5.00

Albums

COLUMBIA

Number	Title (A Side/B Side)	Yr	VG	VG+	NM
❑ CL 2728 [M]	Carryin' On with Johnny Cash and June Carter	1967	5.00	10.00	20.00
❑ CS 9528 [S]	Carryin' On with Johnny Cash and June Carter	1967	5.00	10.00	20.00

CASH, JOHNNY, AND WAYLON JENNINGS

Also see each artist's individual listings.

45s

COLUMBIA

Number	Title (A Side/B Side)	Yr	VG	VG+	NM
❑ 05896	Even Cowgirls Get the Blues/American by Birth	1986	—	—	3.00
❑ 06287	The Ballad of $40/Field of Diamonds	1986	—	—	3.00
❑ 10742	There Ain't No Good Chain Gang/I Wish I Was Crazy Again	1978	—	2.50	5.00

CASH, ROSEANNE

45s

COLUMBIA

Number	Title (A Side/B Side)	Yr	VG	VG+	NM
❑ 02463	My Baby Thinks He's a Train/I Can't Resist	1981	—	2.00	4.00
❑ 02659	Blue Moon with Heartache/Only Human	1981	—	2.00	4.00
❑ 02937	Ain't No Money/The Feelin'	1982	—	—	3.00
❑ 03131	Seven Year Ache/My Baby Thinks He's a Train	1982	—	—	3.00
—"Golden Oldies" reissue					
❑ 03283	I Wonder/Oh Yes I Can	1982	—	—	3.00
❑ 03705	It Hasn't Happened Yet/Somewhere in the Stars	1983	—	—	3.00
❑ 03868	Blue Moon with Heartache/Ain't No Money	1983	—	—	3.00
—"Golden Oldies" reissue					
❑ 04809	I Don't Know Why You Don't Want Me/What You Gonna Do About It	1985	—	—	3.00
❑ 04809 [PS]	I Don't Know Why You Don't Want Me/What You Gonna Do About It	1985	—	—	3.00
❑ 05621	Never Be You/Closing Time	1985	—	—	3.00
❑ 05794	Hold On/Never Gonna Hurt	1986	—	—	3.00
❑ 06159	Second to No One/Never Alone	1986	—	—	3.00
❑ 07200	The Way We Make a Broken Heart/707	1987	—	—	3.00
❑ 07624	Tennessee Flat Top Box/Why Don't You Quit Leaving Me Alone	1987	—	—	3.00
❑ 07693	It's Such a Small World/Crazy Baby	1988	—	—	3.00
—Rodney Crowell and Roseanne Cash; B-side by Crowell					
❑ 07746	If You Change Your Mind/Somewhere Sometime	1988	—	—	3.00
❑ 07988	Runaway Train/Seven Year Ache	1988	—	—	3.00
❑ 08399	Hold On/Second to No One	1988	—	—	3.00
—Reissue					
❑ 08401	I Don't Know Why You Don't Want Me/Never Be You	1988	—	—	3.00
—Reissue					
❑ 11045	No Memories Hangin' Round/This Has Happened Before	1979	—	2.00	4.00
—Duet with Bobby Bare					
❑ 11188	Couldn't Do Nothin' Right/Seeing Is Believing	1980	—	2.00	4.00
❑ 11268	Right or Wrong/Take Me, Take Me	1980	—	2.00	4.00
❑ 11426	Seven Year Ache/Blue Moon with Heartache	1981	—	2.00	4.00
❑ 68599	I Don't Want to Spoil the Party/Look What Our Love Is Coming To	1989	—	—	3.00
❑ 68599 [PS]	I Don't Want to Spoil the Party/Look What Our Love Is Coming To	1989	—	—	3.00
❑ 73054	Black and White/Never Be You	1989	—	—	3.00
❑ 73517	What We Really Want/Portrait	1990	—	—	3.00
❑ 74973	The Wheel/Private Moments	1993	—	—	3.00

The daughter of Johnny, Roseanne Cash was one of the most successful female artists of the 1980s. By the late 1990s she was recording much more sporadically than during her hit period. (Top left) Her first big hit, which even crossed over to the top 30 of the pop charts, was "Seven Year Ache." (Top right) "I Don't Know Why You Don't Want Me," which Cash co-wrote with her then-husband Rodney Crowell, features a pre-fame Vince Gill on backing male vocals. (Bottom left) "Runaway Train," written by John Stewart of Kingston Trio and "Gold" fame, was the fourth of four No. 1 singles from Cash's *King's Record Shop* LP. (Bottom right) Thanks to this 1989 recording of "I Don't Want to Spoil the Party," the songwriting team of John Lennon and Paul McCartney earned their first-ever No. 1 country song.

Number	Title (A Side/B Side)	Yr	VG	VG+	NM
Albums					
COLUMBIA					
❑ AS 1527 [DJ]	Interview with Martha Hume	1982	7.50	15.00	30.00
—Generic cover with sticker					
❑ JC 36155	Right or Wrong	1980	2.50	5.00	10.00
❑ PC 36155	Right or Wrong	1984	2.00	4.00	8.00
—Budget-line reissue with new prefix and "02" added to bar code					
❑ JC 36965	Seven Year Ache	1981	2.50	5.00	10.00
❑ PC 36965	Seven Year Ache	1984	2.00	4.00	8.00
—Budget-line reissue with new prefix and "02" added to bar code					
❑ FC 37570	Somewhere in the Stars	1982	2.50	5.00	10.00
❑ PC 37570	Somewhere in the Stars	1984	2.00	4.00	8.00
—Budget-line reissue with new prefix and "02" added to bar code					
❑ FC 39463	Rhythm and Romance	1985	2.50	5.00	10.00
❑ FC 40777	King's Record Shop	1987	2.50	5.00	10.00
❑ OC 45054	Hits 1979-1989	1989	3.00	6.00	12.00
❑ HC 46965	Seven Year Ache	1981	12.50	25.00	50.00
—Half-speed mastered edition					

CASH, TOMMY

Also see JOHNNY CASH.

Number	Title (A Side/B Side)	Yr	VG	VG+	NM
45s					
20TH CENTURY					
❑ 2263	Broken Bones/The Ballad of Jack and Lucille	1975	—	2.50	5.00
ELEKTRA					
❑ 45241	The One I Sing My Love Songs To/Goodbye Ringin' in My Ear	1975	—	2.50	5.00
❑ 45258	The Lady Is a Woman/Only a Stone	1975	—	2.50	5.00
EPIC					
❑ 5-10469	Your Lovin' Takes the Leavin' Out of Me/That Lucky Old Sun	1969	2.00	4.00	8.00
❑ 5-10540	Six White Horses/I Owe the World to You	1969	2.00	4.00	8.00
❑ 5-10590	Rise and Shine/The Honest Truth	1970	2.00	4.00	8.00
❑ 5-10630	One Song Away/The Ramblin' Kind	1970	2.00	4.00	8.00
❑ 5-10673	The Tears on Lincoln's Face/Only Place for Me	1970	2.00	4.00	8.00
❑ 5-10700	So This Is Love/Love Is Gone	1971	2.00	4.00	8.00
❑ 5-10756	I'm Gonna Write a Song/I'm Nowhere Without You	1971	2.00	4.00	8.00
❑ 5-10795	Roll Truck Roll/The Song Belongs to You	1971	2.00	4.00	8.00
❑ 5-10838	You're Everything/Someday When All My Dreams Come True	1972	2.00	4.00	8.00
❑ 5-10885	That Certain One/A Free Man	1972	2.00	4.00	8.00
❑ 5-10915	Listen/Fool Maker	1972	2.00	4.00	8.00
❑ 5-10964	Workin' on a Feelin'/Tomorrow Will Be a New Day	1973	—	3.50	7.00
❑ 5-11026	I Recall a Gypsy Woman/You'll Need the Love (I Have for You One Day)	1973	—	3.50	7.00
❑ 5-11057	She Met a Stranger, I Met a Train/The Only Place for Me	1973	—	3.50	7.00
❑ 5-11101	The Farmer and the Lord/Will the Circle Be Unbroken	1974	—	3.50	7.00
❑ 5-11148	Roller Coaster Ride/Singing My Song	1974	—	3.50	7.00
MONUMENT					
❑ 45-222	The Cowboy and the Lady/Lady I Love You	1977	—	2.50	5.00
❑ 45-229	Reach Out/There's More to Her Than Meets the Eye	1977	—	2.50	5.00
❑ 45-238	Take My Love to Rita/We Finally Got It Right	1978	—	2.50	5.00
❑ 45-250	The In Crowd/A Lot of Catching Up to Do	1978	—	2.50	5.00
❑ 45-274	I'll Be Better Off Alone/Six Feet Tall and Handsome	1979	—	2.50	5.00
❑ 45-286	Don't Give Up on Me/When the Lovin' Starts	1979	—	2.50	5.00
MUSICOR					
❑ 1060	I Guess I'll Love/Why'd She Gone	1965	3.00	6.00	12.00
❑ 1109	I Didn't Walk the Line/Where You Came From	1965	3.00	6.00	12.00
❑ 1137	Along the Way/Freedom of Livin'	1965	3.00	6.00	12.00
UNITED ARTISTS					
❑ XW863	King for a Day/Temptation	1976	—	2.50	5.00
❑ 50068	All I've Got to Show (For Loving You)/Down, Down, Down	1966	2.50	5.00	10.00
❑ 50127	Jailbirds Can't Fly/That's Where My Baby Used to Be	1967	2.50	5.00	10.00
❑ 50185	Tobacco Road/Wave Goodbye to Me	1967	2.50	5.00	10.00
❑ 50246	I'm Not the Boy I Used to Be/Leaving Your World (A Better Place to Live)	1968	2.50	5.00	10.00
❑ 50337	The Sounds of Goodbye/Easy Woman	1968	2.50	5.00	10.00
Albums					
ELEKTRA					
❑ CM-5	Only a Stone	1975	3.75	7.50	15.00
EPIC					
❑ BN 26484	Your Lovin' Takes the Leavin' Out of Me	1969	5.00	10.00	20.00
❑ BN 26535	Six White Horses	1970	3.75	7.50	15.00
❑ E 30107	Rise and Shine	1970	3.75	7.50	15.00
❑ E 30556	Cash Country	1971	3.75	7.50	15.00
❑ E 30860	American Way of Life	1971	3.75	7.50	15.00
❑ KE 31747	That Certain One	1972	3.75	7.50	15.00
❑ KE 31995	The Best of Tommy Cash, Volume I	1972	3.75	7.50	15.00
MONUMENT					
❑ 7619	The New Spirit	1978	3.00	6.00	12.00
UNITED ARTISTS					
❑ UAS-6628	Here Comes Tommy Cash	1968	5.00	10.00	20.00

CASHMAN AND WEST

This pop duo put the below record into the country charts.

Number	Title (A Side/B Side)	Yr	VG	VG+	NM
45s					
ABC DUNHILL					
❑ 4333	Songman/If You Were a Rainbow	1972	—	2.50	5.00

CASSADY, LINDA

Number	Title (A Side/B Side)	Yr	VG	VG+	NM
45s					
CIN KAY					
❑ 107	C.B. Widow/Do You Still Want What's Left of Me	1976	—	2.50	5.00
❑ 111	If It's Your Song You Sing It/This Isn't Just Another Love Song	1976	—	2.50	5.00
❑ 115	Little Things Mean a Lot/Sounds of Love	1977	—	2.50	5.00
❑ 116	I Don't Hurt Anymore/Baby There's Nothing Wrong with Me	1977	—	2.50	5.00
❑ 118	Do You Still Want What's Left of Me/(B-side unknown)	1977	—	2.50	5.00
❑ 127	Little Teardrops (Are Smarter Than You Think)/(B-side unknown)	1978	—	2.50	5.00
❑ 129	(There's Nothing Like the Love) Between a Woman and a Man/Finer Side of Life	1978	—	2.50	5.00
—With Bobby Spears					
❑ 131	Lonely Side of the Bed/That's the Way It Is	1978	—	3.00	6.00
DOOR KNOB					
❑ 002	Tell It to Someone Who'll Believe It/Jolene	1975	2.00	4.00	8.00
❑ 004	C.B. Widow/Do You Still Want What's Left of Me	1975	2.00	4.00	8.00
❑ 158	Tell It to Someone/(B-side unknown)	1981	—	2.50	5.00
METRO COUNTRY					
❑ 2010	Is Santa Claus a Hippie?/What Do You Do?	1969	2.50	5.00	10.00
SOUNDWAVES					
❑ 4584	Dusty Raven/Walk a Mile to a Country School	1980	—	2.50	5.00
❑ 4594	Out You Go/Can You Keep a Secret	1980	—	2.50	5.00
❑ 4602	Hit Man/Don't Stop Before You Get There	1981	—	2.50	5.00
❑ 4636	Is That Mountain Worth Climbing/We Can Touch, But We Don't Feel	1981	—	2.50	5.00

CATES SISTERS, THE

Number	Title (A Side/B Side)	Yr	VG	VG+	NM
45s					
CAPRICE					
❑ 2024	Mr. Guitar/Love Is a Beautiful Thing	1976	—	2.50	5.00
❑ 2030	Out of My Mind/Run Your Sweet Love By Me	1976	—	2.50	5.00
—As "The Cates"					
❑ 2032	Can't Help It/(B-side unknown)	1977	—	2.50	5.00
❑ 2036	I'll Always Love You/Second Chance	1977	—	2.50	5.00
❑ 2038	Throw Out Your Loveline/West Virginia Smile	1977	—	2.50	5.00
❑ 2041	I've Been Loved/Faded Love	1977	—	2.50	5.00
❑ 2047	Long Gone Blues/San Antonio Rose	1978	—	2.50	5.00
❑ 2051	Lovin' You Off My Mind/Amazing Grace	1978	—	2.50	5.00
MCA					
❑ 40032	He Fiddled His Way Into My Heart/Crazy Dreams	1973	2.00	4.00	8.00
—As "Marcy and Margie"					
❑ 40211	Uncle Pen/Double Your Pleasure	1974	—	3.00	6.00
OVATION					
❑ 1123	Going Down Slow/Can I See You Tonight	1979	—	2.50	5.00
—All on Ovation as "The Cates"					
❑ 1126	Make Love to Me/Day After Day	1979	—	2.50	5.00
❑ 1126 [PS]	Make Love to Me/Day After Day	1979	2.00	4.00	8.00
❑ 1134	Let's Go Through the Motions/Don't Say Love	1979	—	2.50	5.00
❑ 1144	Gonna Get Along Without You Now/I've Been Lovin' You Too Long	1980	—	2.50	5.00
❑ 1155	Lightnin' Strikin'/Touch and Go	1980	—	2.50	5.00
Albums					
OVATION					
❑ 1740	Steppin' Out	1979	3.00	6.00	12.00
—As "The Cates"					

CATO, CONNIE

Number	Title (A Side/B Side)	Yr	VG	VG+	NM
45s					
CAPITOL					
❑ 3580	How Come You Struck the Match/Love Makes Big Things Small	1973	—	3.00	6.00
❑ 3679	Four on the Floor/Don't Let the Good Times Roll Away	1973	—	3.00	6.00
❑ 3788	Superskirt/Big Stick of Dynamite	1973	—	2.50	5.00
❑ 3858	Lincoln Autry/After Midnight	1974	—	2.50	5.00
❑ 3908	Super Kitten/We'd Better Stop	1974	—	2.50	5.00
❑ 4035	Hurt/He'll Be Lovin' Her	1975	—	2.50	5.00
❑ 4113	Yes/Good Hearted Woman	1975	—	2.50	5.00
❑ 4169	Who Wants a Slightly Used Woman/Somewhere South of Macon	1975	—	2.50	5.00
❑ 4243	I Love a Beautiful Guy/Plastic Saddle	1976	—	2.50	5.00
❑ 4303	Here Comes That Rainy Day Feeling Again/I'll Be a Lady Tomorrow	1976	—	2.50	5.00
❑ 4345	I'm Sorry/Evil on Your Mind	1976	—	2.50	5.00
❑ 4379	Don't You Ever Get Tired (Of Hurting Me)/I've Been Loved by You Today	1976	—	2.50	5.00
❑ 4419	I'll Be a Lady Tomorrow (But I'm Gonna Be Your Woman Tonight)/Here Comes That Rainy Day Feeling Again	1977	—	2.00	4.00
❑ 4547	Yellow House of Love/Then Give Him Back to Me	1978	—	2.00	4.00
❑ 4603	I Won't Take It Lyin' Down/I'll Love Her Right Out of Your Mind	1978	—	2.00	4.00

MCA

Number	Title (A Side/B Side)	Yr	VG	VG+	NM
❑ 41287	You Better Hurry Home (Somethin's Burnin')/ Hangin' On My Heart	1980	—	2.00	4.00
❑ 51012	Somebody's Leavin'/Sweet Love Power	1980	—	2.00	4.00
❑ 51071	What About My Heart/(B-side unknown)	1981	—	2.50	5.00
❑ 51140	Roses for Sale/Where You Gonna Be Tonight	1981	—	2.00	4.00

Albums

CAPITOL

Number	Title (A Side/B Side)	Yr	VG	VG+	NM
❑ ST-11312	Super Connie Cato	1974	3.00	6.00	12.00
❑ ST-11387	Good Hearted Woman	1975	3.00	6.00	12.00
❑ ST-11606	Whoever Finds This, I Love You	1977	3.00	6.00	12.00

CAUDELL, LANE

45s

16TH AVENUE

Number	Title (A Side/B Side)	Yr	VG	VG+	NM
❑ 70403	Souvenirs/The Honeymoon Is Over	1987	—	2.00	4.00
❑ 70411	I Need a Good Woman Bad/Souvenirs	1988	—	2.00	4.00

CAPITOL

Number	Title (A Side/B Side)	Yr	VG	VG+	NM
❑ 3389	Let Our Love Ride/You, Him and Her	1972	2.00	4.00	8.00
❑ 3526	And Then We Danced/Play On, Play On	1973	2.00	4.00	8.00

MCA

Number	Title (A Side/B Side)	Yr	VG	VG+	NM
❑ 40901	Banging on a Star/I Love You Girl	1978	—	2.50	5.00
❑ 40935	Those Eyes/I'm an Empty Man	1978	—	2.50	5.00
❑ 40996	Love, Hit and Run/Destiny	1979	—	2.50	5.00

METROMEDIA

Number	Title (A Side/B Side)	Yr	VG	VG+	NM
❑ BMBO-0017	Mama, You Know Me Well/Should I Care	1973	—	3.00	6.00

PRIVATE STOCK

Number	Title (A Side/B Side)	Yr	VG	VG+	NM
❑ 45,122	Alabama Boy/(B-side unknown)	1976	—	3.00	6.00

Albums

MCA

Number	Title (A Side/B Side)	Yr	VG	VG+	NM
❑ 3039	Hanging on a Star	1978	2.50	5.00	10.00
❑ 3074	Midnight Hunter	1979	2.50	5.00	10.00

CEDAR CREEK

45s

MOON SHINE

Number	Title (A Side/B Side)	Yr	VG	VG+	NM
❑ 3001	Looks Like a Set-Up to Me/This Old Heart (Is Gonna Rise Again)	1981	—	2.50	5.00
❑ 3003	Took It Like a Man, Cried Like a Baby/Dreamin' Thru Another Day	1982	—	2.50	5.00
❑ 3008	Take a Ride on a Riverboat/(B-side unknown)	1982	—	2.50	5.00
❑ 3013	Lonely Heart/(B-side unknown)	1983	—	2.50	5.00
❑ 3016	Georgia Mules and Country Boys/(B-side unknown)	1983	—	2.50	5.00

CERRITO

45s

SOUNDWAVES

Number	Title (A Side/B Side)	Yr	VG	VG+	NM
❑ 4814	My Baby Left Me/(B-side unknown)	1989	—	2.50	5.00
❑ 4818	Daydream/(B-side unknown)	1989	—	2.50	5.00
❑ 4826	Bad Moon Rising/Born to Hurt Me	1989	—	2.50	5.00

CHAMBERLAIN, DAVID

45s

COUNTRY INT'L.

Number	Title (A Side/B Side)	Yr	VG	VG+	NM
❑ 214	I Owe, I Owe (It's Off to Work I Go)/Love Me Tonight (Like There's No Tomorrow)	1988	—	3.00	6.00
❑ 215	How Do You Like My Memories/(B-side unknown)	1988	—	3.00	6.00
❑ 217	Too Late for the Show/(B-side unknown_	1988	—	3.00	6.00
❑ 228	I Finally Made It (Where You Told Me to Go)/ Friends in Low Places	1989	—	3.00	6.00

CHAMBERS, CARL

45s

PRAIRIE DUST

Number	Title (A Side/B Side)	Yr	VG	VG+	NM
❑ 8001	Take Me Home with You/(B-side unknown)	1981	—	3.00	6.00

CHANCE

Also see JEFF CHANCE.

45s

MERCURY

Number	Title (A Side/B Side)	Yr	VG	VG+	NM
❑ 880555-7	To Be Lovers/Call It What You Want To (It's Still Love)	1985	—	—	3.00
❑ 880959-7	You Could Be the One Woman/Free Sailin'	1985	—	—	3.00
❑ 884178-7	She Told Me Yes/Two Hearts Are Better Than One	1986	—	—	3.00
❑ 884545-7	I Need Some Good News Bad/She Needs a Man Like Me	1986	—	—	3.00
❑ 884918-7	What Did You Do with My Heart/One Too Many Heartaches	1986	—	—	3.00

Albums

MERCURY

Number	Title (A Side/B Side)	Yr	VG	VG+	NM
❑ 826029-1	Chance	1986	2.00	4.00	8.00

CHANCE, JEFF

Also see CHANCE.

45s

CURB

Number	Title (A Side/B Side)	Yr	VG	VG+	NM
❑ 10506	So Far Not So Good/Hopelessly Falling	1988	—	—	3.00
❑ 10516	Let It Burn/She Loves Me	1988	—	—	3.00

MERCURY

Number	Title (A Side/B Side)	Yr	VG	VG+	NM
❑ 878748-7	Strangers on the Street/She Loves Me	1991	—	—	3.00

CHANEY, HANK

45s

CMI

Number	Title (A Side/B Side)	Yr	VG	VG+	NM
❑ 04	Be-Bop-A-Lula "86"/(B-side unknown)	1986	2.00	4.00	8.00

CHANTILLY

45s

F&L

Number	Title (A Side/B Side)	Yr	VG	VG+	NM
❑ 519	Right Back Loving You Again/Better Off Blue	1982	—	2.50	5.00
❑ 520	Better Off Blue/Right Back Loving You Again	1982	—	2.50	5.00
❑ 523	Storm of Love/Whatever Turns You On	1983	—	2.50	5.00
❑ 527	Have I Got a Heart for You/Reached	1983	—	2.50	5.00
❑ 534	Baby's Walkin'/Have I Got a Heart for You	1984	—	2.50	5.00

JAROCO

Number	Title (A Side/B Side)	Yr	VG	VG+	NM
❑ 31082	Whatever Turns You On/Storm of Love	1982	—	2.50	5.00
❑ 51282	Stumblin' In/Better Off Blue	1982	—	2.50	5.00

CHAPARRAL BROTHERS, THE

45s

CAPITOL

Number	Title (A Side/B Side)	Yr	VG	VG+	NM
❑ 2096	He's Looking at You/Leave	1968	2.00	4.00	8.00
❑ 2153	Standing in the Rain/Just One More Time	1968	2.00	4.00	8.00
❑ 2323	Follow Your Dream/The Rain	1968	2.00	4.00	8.00
❑ 2540	I'm Not Even Missing You/Maybe I Could Find My Way Back Home Again	1969	2.00	4.00	8.00
❑ 2625	Jesus Loves You, Rosemary/Then Darling I Could Forget You	1969	2.00	4.00	8.00
❑ 2708	Running from a Memory/Curly Brown	1970	2.00	4.00	8.00
❑ 2772	Hello L.A., Bye Bye Birmingham/I Must Have Been Out of My Mind	1970	2.00	4.00	8.00
❑ 2866	Foolin' Around/Life Has Its Little Ups and Downs	1970	2.00	4.00	8.00
❑ 2977	I Believe in You/Let Somebody Love You	1970	2.00	4.00	8.00

MGM

Number	Title (A Side/B Side)	Yr	VG	VG+	NM
❑ 14501	Another Piece of the Puzzle/Hell and Half of Georgia	1973	—	3.00	6.00

Albums

CAPITOL

Number	Title (A Side/B Side)	Yr	VG	VG+	NM
❑ ST-551	Just for the Record	1970	3.75	7.50	15.00
❑ ST 2922	Introducing the Chaparral Brothers	1968	5.00	10.00	20.00

CHAPARRO, TAMMY

45s

COMPASS

Number	Title (A Side/B Side)	Yr	VG	VG+	NM
❑ 60	Stay with Me/(B-side unknown)	1983	—	3.00	6.00

CHAPMAN, CEE CEE

45s

CAPITOL

Number	Title (A Side/B Side)	Yr	VG	VG+	NM
❑ 7PRO-79277	Everything (same on both sides)	1990	—	2.50	5.00
—Vinyl is promo only					
❑ 7PRO-79479	Exit 99 (same on both sides)	1990	—	2.50	5.00
—Vinyl is promo only					

CURB

Number	Title (A Side/B Side)	Yr	VG	VG+	NM
❑ 10518	Gone But Not Forgotten/Love Is a Liar	1988	—	—	3.00
❑ 10529	Frontier Justice/Love Is a Liar	1989	—	—	3.00
❑ 10547	Twist of Fate/Back to Santa Fe	1989	—	—	3.00

CHAPMAN, GARY

45s

RCA

Number	Title (A Side/B Side)	Yr	VG	VG+	NM
❑ 5285-7-R	When We're Together/Your Love Stays with Me	1987	—	2.00	4.00
❑ 7601-7-R	Everyday Man/Cecil (Love Goes On)	1987	—	2.00	4.00

Albums

RCA

Number	Title (A Side/B Side)	Yr	VG	VG+	NM
❑ 6375-1-R	Everyday Man	1988	2.50	5.00	10.00

CHAPMAN, MARSHALL

45s

EPIC

Number	Title (A Side/B Side)	Yr	VG	VG+	NM
❑ 8-50307	Somewhere South of Macon/Sweet Carolina and Texas	1976	—	2.50	5.00
❑ 8-50376	Know My Needs/Next Time	1977	—	2.50	5.00
❑ 50799	Don't Make Me Pregnant/Rock 'n' Roll Clothes	1979	—	2.50	5.00

Albums

EPIC

Number	Title (A Side/B Side)	Yr	VG	VG+	NM
❑ PE 34422	Me, I'm Feelin' Free	1977	2.50	5.00	10.00
❑ JE 35341	Jaded Virgin	1978	2.50	5.00	10.00
❑ JE 36192	Marshall	1979	2.50	5.00	10.00

ROUNDER

Number	Title (A Side/B Side)	Yr	VG	VG+	NM
❑ 3069	Take It On Home	1982	3.00	6.00	12.00

CHARLENE

45s

ARIOLA AMERICA

Number	Title (A Side/B Side)	Yr	VG	VG+	NM
❑ 7696	Are You Free/We Know	1977	—	2.50	5.00

MOTOWN

Number	Title (A Side/B Side)	Yr	VG	VG+	NM
❑ 1262	Give It One More Try/Relove	1973	2.00	4.00	8.00
❑ 1285	All That Love Went to Waste/Give It One More Try	1973	2.00	4.00	8.00
❑ 1492	Hungry/I Won't Remember Ever Loving You	1980	—	2.00	4.00
❑ 1611	I've Never Been to Me/Somewhere in My Life	1982	—	—	3.00
❑ 1621	Nunca He Ido A Mi/If I Could See Myself	1982	—	2.00	4.00
❑ 1663	I Want to Go Back There Again/Richie's Song	1983	—	—	3.00

Number	Title (A Side/B Side)	Yr	VG	VG+	NM
❑ 1734	We're Both in Love with You/I Want the World to Know He's Mine	1984	—	—	3.00
❑ 1761	Hit and Run Lover/Last Song	1984	—	—	3.00
PRODIGAL					
❑ 0632	It Ain't Easy Coming Down/On My Way to You	1977	—	2.50	5.00
❑ 0633	Freddie/(B-side unknown)	1977	—	2.50	5.00
❑ 0633 [PS]	Freddie/(B-side unknown)	1977	2.00	5.00	10.00
❑ 0636	I've Never Been to Me/It's Really Nice to Be in Love Again	1977	5.00	10.00	20.00
Albums					
MOTOWN					
❑ 6007 ML	Charlene	1981	2.50	5.00	10.00
❑ 6027 ML	Used to Be	1982	2.50	5.00	10.00
❑ 6090 ML	Hit and Run Lover	1985	2.50	5.00	10.00
PRODIGAL					
❑ P6-10015	Charlene	1976	5.00	10.00	20.00
❑ P6-10018	Songs of Love	1977	5.00	10.00	20.00

CHARLES, KIM

45s

MCA

Number	Title (A Side/B Side)	Yr	VG	VG+	NM
❑ 40987	Want to Thank You/By Any Chance	1979	—	2.00	4.00
❑ 41045	Release Me/Hold Me Like a Baby	1979	—	2.00	4.00

CHARLES, RAY

One of America's great performers, he recorded several country-oriented albums in the 1960s, then began making the country charts fairly regularly in the 1980s. The below listings are selective.

45s

Number	Title (A Side/B Side)	Yr	VG	VG+	NM
ABC					
❑ 10808	Let's Go Get Stoned/At the Train	1966	2.00	4.00	8.00
❑ 10840	I Chose to Sing the Blues/Hopelessly	1966	2.00	4.00	8.00
❑ 10865	Please Say You're Fooling/I Don't Need No Doctor	1966	2.00	4.00	8.00
❑ 10901	I Want to Talk About You/Something Inside Me	1967	2.00	4.00	8.00
❑ 10938	Here We Go Again/Somebody Ought to Write a Book About It	1967	2.00	4.00	8.00
❑ 10970	In the Heat of the Night/Somebody's Got to Change	1967	2.00	4.00	8.00
❑ 11009	Yesterday/Never Had Enough of Nothing Yet	1967	2.00	4.00	8.00
❑ 11045	That's a Lie/Go On Home	1968	2.00	4.00	8.00
❑ 11045 [PS]	That's a Lie/Go On Home	1968	3.75	7.50	15.00
❑ 11090	Eleanor Rigby/Understanding	1968	2.00	4.00	8.00
❑ 11133	Sweet Young Thing Like You/Listen, They're Playing Our Song	1968	2.00	4.00	8.00
❑ 11170	If It Wasn't for Bad Luck/When I Stop Dreaming	1969	2.00	4.00	8.00
—With Jimmy Lewis					
❑ 11193	I'll Be Your Servant/I Don't Know What Time It Was	1969	2.00	4.00	8.00
❑ 11213	Let Me Love You/I'm Satisfied	1969	2.00	4.00	8.00
❑ 11239	We Can Make It/I Can't Stop Loving You Baby	1969	2.00	4.00	8.00
❑ 11251	Someone to Watch Over Me/Claudie Mae	1969	2.00	4.00	8.00
❑ 11259	Laughin' and Clownin'/That Thing Called Love	1970	2.00	4.00	8.00
❑ 11271	If You Were Mine/Till I Can't Take It Anymore	1970	2.00	4.00	8.00
❑ 11291	Don't Change on Me/Sweet Memories	1971	2.00	4.00	8.00
❑ 11308	Feel So Bad/Your Love Is So Doggone Good	1971	—	3.00	6.00
❑ 11317	What Am I Living For/Tired of My Tears	1971	—	3.00	6.00
❑ 11329	Look What They've Done to My Song, Ma/America the Beautiful	1972	—	3.00	6.00
❑ 11337	Hey Mister/There'll Be No Peace Without All Men as One	1972	—	3.00	6.00
❑ 11344	Every Saturday Night/Take Me Home, Country Roads	1973	—	3.00	6.00
❑ 11351	I Can Make It Through the Days (But Oh Those Lonely Nights)/Ring of Fire	1973	—	3.00	6.00
ABC-PARAMOUNT					
❑ 4801 [S]	Don't Cry Baby/Teardrops from My Eyes	1964	5.00	10.00	20.00
❑ 4802 [S]	Baby, Don't You Cry/Cry Me a River	1964	5.00	10.00	20.00
❑ 4803 [S]	I Cried for You/Cry	1964	5.00	10.00	20.00
❑ 4804 [S]	A Tear Fell/No One to Cry To	1964	5.00	10.00	20.00
❑ 4805 [S]	You've Got Me Crying Again/After My Laughter Came Tears	1964	5.00	10.00	20.00
—The above five are 33 1/3 rpm, small hole jukebox singles excerpted from the LP "Sweet and Sour Tears"					
❑ 10081	My Baby/Who You Gonna Love	1960	3.75	7.50	15.00
❑ 10118	Sticks and Stones/Worried Life Blues	1960	3.00	6.00	12.00
❑ 10135	Georgia on My Mind/Carry Me Back to Old Virginny	1960	3.75	7.50	15.00
❑ 10141	Them That Got/I Wonder	1960	3.00	6.00	12.00
❑ 10164	Ruby/Heard Hearted Woman	1960	3.00	6.00	12.00
❑ 10244	Hit the Road Jack/The Danger Zone	1961	3.75	7.50	15.00
❑ 10266	Unchain My Heart/But on the Other Hand, Baby	1961	3.75	7.50	15.00
❑ 10314	Hide 'Nor Hair/At the Club	1962	3.00	6.00	12.00
❑ 10330	I Can't Stop Loving You/Born to Lose	1962	3.75	7.50	15.00
❑ 10345	You Don't Know Me/Careless Love	1962	3.75	7.50	15.00
❑ 10375	You Are My Sunshine/Your Cheating Heart	1962	3.00	6.00	12.00
❑ 10405	Don't Set Me Free/The Brightest Smile in Town	1963	3.00	6.00	12.00
❑ 10435	Take These Chains from My Heart/No Letter Today	1963	3.75	7.50	15.00
❑ 10453	No One/Without Love (There Is Nothing)	1963	3.00	6.00	12.00
❑ 10481	Busted/Making Believe	1963	3.75	7.50	15.00
❑ 10509	That Lucky Old Sun/Old Man Time	1963	2.50	5.00	12.00
❑ 10530	Baby Don't You Cry/My Heart Cries for You	1964	3.00	6.00	12.00
❑ 10557	My Baby Don't Dig Me/Something's Wrong	1964	3.00	6.00	12.00
❑ 10571	No One to Cry To/A Tear Fell	1964	3.00	6.00	12.00
❑ 10588	Smack Dab in the Middle/I Wake Up Crying	1964	3.00	6.00	12.00
❑ 10609	Makin' Whoopee/(Instrumental)	1964	3.00	6.00	12.00
❑ 10615	Cry/Teardrops from My Eyes	1965	3.00	6.00	12.00
❑ 10649	I Gotta Woman (Part 1)/I Gotta Woman (Part 2)	1965	3.00	6.00	12.00
❑ 10663	Without a Song (Part 1)/Without a Song (Part 2)	1965	3.00	6.00	12.00
❑ 10700	I'm a Fool to Care/Love's Gonna Live Here	1965	3.00	6.00	12.00
❑ 10720	The Cincinnati Kid/That's All I Am to You	1965	3.00	6.00	12.00
❑ 10739	Crying Time/When My Dreamboat Comes Home	1965	3.75	7.50	15.00
❑ 10785	Together Again/You're Just About to Lose Your Clown	1966	3.00	6.00	12.00
COLUMBIA					
❑ 03429	String Bean/Born to Love Me	1982	—	2.00	4.00
❑ 03810	You Feel Good All Over/ 3/4 Time	1983	—	—	3.00
❑ 04083	Ain't Your Memory Got No Pride at All/I Don't Want No Strangers Sleeping in My Bed	1983	—	—	3.00
❑ 04297	We Didn't See a Thing/I Wish You Were Here Tonight	1983	—	—	3.00
—A-side with George Jones and Chet Atkins					
❑ 04420	Do I Ever Cross Your Mind/They Call It Love	1984	—	—	3.00
❑ 04500	Woman (Sensuous Woman)/I Was On Georgia Time	1984	—	—	3.00
❑ 04531	Rock and Roll Shoes/Then I'll Be Over You	1984	—	—	3.00
—Ray Charles and B.J. Thomas					
❑ 04715	Seven Spanish Angels/Who Cares	1984	—	—	3.00
—A-side with Willie Nelson; B-side with Janie Frickie					
❑ 04860	It Ain't Gonna Worry My Mind/Crazy Old Soldier	1985	—	—	3.00
—A-side with Mickey Gilley; B-side with Johnny Cash					
❑ 05575	Two Old Cats Like Us/Little Hotel Room	1985	—	—	3.00
—A-side with Hank Williams, Jr.					
❑ 06172	Pages of My Mind/Slip Away	1986	—	—	3.00
❑ 06370	Dixie Moon/A Little Bit of Heaven	1986	—	—	3.00
❑ 08393	Seven Spanish Angels/It Ain't Gonna Worry My Mind	1988	—	—	3.00
—Reissue; A-side with Willie Nelson, B-side with Mickey Gilley					
WARNER BROS.					
❑ 18611	A Song for You/I Can't Get Enough	1993	—	—	3.00
❑ 49608	Beers to You/Cotton-Eyed Clint	1980	—	2.50	5.00
—A-side with Clint Eastwood; B-side by Texas Opera Company					

Albums

Number	Title (A Side/B Side)	Yr	VG	VG+	NM
ABC					
❑ S-335 [S]	The Genius Hits the Road	1967	3.00	6.00	12.00
❑ S-355 [S]	Dedicated to You	1967	3.00	6.00	12.00
❑ S-410 [S]	Modern Sounds in Country and Western Music	1967	3.00	6.00	12.00
❑ S-415 [S]	Ray Charles' Greatest Hits	1967	3.00	6.00	12.00
❑ S-435 [S]	Modern Sounds in Country and Western Music (Volume Two)	1967	3.00	6.00	12.00
❑ S-465 [S]	Ingredients in a Recipe for Soul	1967	3.00	6.00	12.00
❑ S-480 [S]	Sweet & Sour Tears	1967	3.00	6.00	12.00
❑ S-495 [S]	Have a Smile with Me	1967	3.00	6.00	12.00
❑ S-500 [S]	Ray Charles Live in Concert	1967	3.00	6.00	12.00
❑ S-520 [S]	Together Again	1967	3.00	6.00	12.00
—Retitled version of "Country and Western Meets Rhythm and Blues"					
❑ S-544 [S]	Crying Time	1967	3.00	6.00	12.00
❑ 550 [M]	Ray's Moods	1966	3.00	6.00	12.00
❑ S-550 [S]	Ray's Moods	1966	3.75	7.50	15.00
❑ 590X [(2) M]	A Man and His Soul	1967	3.75	7.50	15.00
❑ S-590X [(2) S]	A Man and His Soul	1967	5.00	10.00	20.00
❑ 595 [M]	Ray Charles Invites You to Listen	1967	5.00	10.00	20.00
❑ S-595 [S]	Ray Charles Invites You to Listen	1967	3.75	7.50	15.00
❑ S-625	A Portrait of Ray	1968	3.00	6.00	12.00
❑ S-675	I'm All Yours — Baby!	1969	3.00	6.00	12.00
❑ S-695	Doing His Thing	1969	3.00	6.00	12.00
❑ S-707	Love Country Style	1971	3.00	6.00	12.00
❑ S-726	Volcanic Action of My Soul	1971	3.00	6.00	12.00
❑ H-731 [(2)]	A 25th Anniversary in Show Business Salute to Ray Charles	1971	3.75	7.50	15.00
❑ X-755	A Message from the People	1972	3.00	6.00	12.00
❑ X-765	Through the Eyes of Love	1972	3.00	6.00	12.00
❑ X-781/2 [(2)]	All-Time Great Country & Western Hits	1973	3.75	7.50	15.00
❑ SQBO-91036 [(2)]	The Ray Charles Story	1967	6.25	12.50	25.00
—Capitol Record Club exclusive					
❑ ST-91233 [S]	Ray Charles Invites You to Listen	1967	3.75	7.50	15.00
—Capitol Record Club edition					
ABC-PARAMOUNT					
❑ 335 [M]	The Genius Hits the Road	1960	5.00	10.00	20.00
❑ S-335 [S]	The Genius Hits the Road	1960	7.50	15.00	30.00
❑ 355 [M]	Dedicated to You	1961	5.00	10.00	20.00
❑ S-355 [S]	Dedicated to You	1961	7.50	15.00	30.00
❑ 410 [M]	Modern Sounds in Country and Western Music	1962	6.25	12.50	25.00
❑ S-410 [S]	Modern Sounds in Country and Western Music	1962	7.50	15.00	30.00
❑ 415 [M]	Ray Charles' Greatest Hits	1962	5.00	10.00	20.00
❑ S-415 [S]	Ray Charles' Greatest Hits	1962	6.25	12.50	25.00
❑ 435 [M]	Modern Sounds in Country and Western Music (Volume Two)	1962	5.00	10.00	20.00
❑ S-435 [S]	Modern Sounds in Country and Western Music (Volume Two)	1962	6.25	12.50	25.00
❑ 465 [M]	Ingredients in a Recipe for Soul	1963	5.00	10.00	20.00
❑ S-465 [S]	Ingredients in a Recipe for Soul	1963	6.25	12.50	25.00
❑ 480 [M]	Sweet & Sour Tears	1964	5.00	10.00	20.00
❑ S-480 [S]	Sweet & Sour Tears	1964	6.25	12.50	25.00
❑ 495 [M]	Have a Smile with Me	1964	5.00	10.00	20.00
❑ S-495 [S]	Have a Smile with Me	1964	6.25	12.50	25.00
❑ 500 [M]	Ray Charles Live in Concert	1965	3.75	7.50	15.00
❑ S-500 [S]	Ray Charles Live in Concert	1965	5.00	10.00	20.00
❑ 520 [M]	Country & Western Meets Rhythm & Blues	1965	3.75	7.50	15.00
❑ S-520 [S]	Country & Western Meets Rhythm & Blues	1965	5.00	10.00	20.00

Number	Title (A Side/B Side)	Yr	VG	VG+	NM
❑ 544 [M]	Crying Time	1966	3.75	7.50	15.00
❑ S-544 [S]	Crying Time	1966	5.00	10.00	20.00
❑ ST-90144 [S]	Ray Charles Live in Concert	1965	5.00	10.00	20.00
—Capitol Record Club edition					
❑ T-90144 [M]	Ray Charles Live in Concert	1965	5.00	10.00	20.00
—Capitol Record Club edition					
❑ ST-90625 [S]	Crying Time	1966	5.00	10.00	20.00
—Capitol Record Club edition					
❑ T-90625 [M]	Crying Time	1966	5.00	10.00	20.00
—Capitol Record Club edition					
COLUMBIA					
❑ AS 1920 [DJ]	Friendship Radio Show	1984	5.00	10.00	20.00
❑ FC 38293	Wish You Were Here Tonight	1983	2.50	5.00	10.00
❑ PC 38293	Wish You Were Here Tonight	1985	2.00	4.00	8.00
—Budget-line reissue					
❑ FC 38990	Do I Ever Cross Your Mind	1984	2.50	5.00	10.00
❑ FC 39415	Friendship	1985	2.50	5.00	10.00
❑ FC 40125	The Spirit of Christmas	1985	2.50	5.00	10.00
❑ FC 40338	From the Pages of My Mind	1986	2.50	5.00	10.00
❑ FC 45062	Seven Spanish Angels and Other Hits (1982-1986)	1989	3.00	6.00	12.00
DCC COMPACT CLASSICS					
❑ LPZ-2012	Greatest Country and Western Hits	1995	17.50	35.00	70.00
—Audiophile vinyl					
RHINO					
❑ R1-70097	Greatest Hits, Volume 1	1988	2.50	5.00	10.00
❑ R1-70098	Greatest Hits, Volume 2	1988	2.50	5.00	10.00
❑ R1-70099	Modern Sounds in Country and Western Music	1988	2.50	5.00	10.00
WARNER BROS.					
❑ 26343	Would You Believe?	1990	3.75	7.50	15.00

CHARLES RIVER VALLEY BOYS, THE

45s

Number	Title (A Side/B Side)	Yr	VG	VG+	NM
ELEKTRA					
❑ 45642	I've Just Seen a Face/Ticket to Ride	1968	2.50	5.00	10.00

Albums

Number	Title (A Side/B Side)	Yr	VG	VG+	NM
ELEKTRA					
❑ EKL-4006 [M]	Beatle Country	1967	5.00	10.00	20.00
❑ EKS-74006 [S]	Beatle Country	1967	6.25	12.50	25.00

CHARLESTON EXPRESS

45s

Number	Title (A Side/B Side)	Yr	VG	VG+	NM
SOUNDWAVES					
❑ 4743	Sweet Love, Don't Cry/We Start Our Lives Again Today	1984	—	2.50	5.00
❑ 4749	Leaving/Take Me by Surprise	1985	—	2.50	5.00
❑ 4762	Behind the Shining Badge/(B-side unknown)	1985	—	2.50	5.00
❑ 4763	Swallow Your Pride/Red Bathtub	1985	—	2.50	5.00
❑ 4770	Call to Me/Moonlight Express	1986	—	2.50	5.00

CHASE, BECKY

45s

Number	Title (A Side/B Side)	Yr	VG	VG+	NM
SPIRIT HORSE					
❑ 102	Until the Music Is Gone/(B-side unknown)	1984	—	3.00	6.00

CHASE, CAROL

Also see JIM WEST.

45s

Number	Title (A Side/B Side)	Yr	VG	VG+	NM
CASABLANCA					
❑ 2301	Regrets/So Sad	1980	—	2.00	4.00
❑ 2321	If You Don't Know Me by Now/Morning Glory	1981	—	2.00	4.00
❑ 4501	This Must Be My Ship/It Always Takes a Fool to Fool Around	1979	—	2.50	5.00
❑ 4502	Sexy Song/Disco Devil	1980	—	2.50	5.00
JANUS					
❑ 256	No Time/One Woman Band	1975	—	3.00	6.00
MCA					
❑ 52296	Love in the Shadows/You're Here to Remember	1983	—	2.00	4.00

Albums

Number	Title (A Side/B Side)	Yr	VG	VG+	NM
CASABLANCA					
❑ CAC-6001	Sexy Songs	1980	3.00	6.00	12.00
❑ NBLP-7237	Chase Is On	1980	3.00	6.00	12.00

CHASE, CHARLIE

45s

Number	Title (A Side/B Side)	Yr	VG	VG+	NM
EPIC					
❑ 34-77309	Christmas Is for Kids/My Wife	1993	—	2.00	4.00

CHASTAIN, DAWN

45s

Number	Title (A Side/B Side)	Yr	VG	VG+	NM
OAK					
❑ 1018	Me Plus You Equals Love/(B-side unknown)	1978	—	3.00	6.00
PHONO					
❑ 2646	Boogie Woogie Rock 'n Roll/All I Have to Do Is Dream	1977	2.00	4.00	8.00
PRAIRIE DUST					
❑ 7622	Hey Mister/Ain't No Doubt About It	1978	—	3.00	6.00
❑ 7623	Never Knew (How Much I Loved You 'Till I Lost You)/Ain't No Doubt About It	1978	—	3.00	6.00
❑ 7624	How Can You Say You Don't Love Me No More/You and I	1978	—	3.00	6.00
SCR					
❑ 164	Love Talks/(B-side unknown)	1979	—	2.50	5.00
❑ 178	That's You, That's Me/(B-side unknown)	1979	—	2.50	5.00

Number	Title (A Side/B Side)	Yr	VG	VG+	NM
SOUNDWAVES					
❑ 4555	You Can Love Me Till My Cowboy Comes Home/Boogie Woogie, Rock and Roll	1980	—	3.00	6.00

CHER

The below single was a country Top 100 hit.

45s

Number	Title (A Side/B Side)	Yr	VG	VG+	NM
CASABLANCA					
❑ 987	It's Too Late to Love Me Now/Wasn't It Good	1979	—	2.00	4.00

CHERRY, DON

Pop singer who went country in the 1960s.

45s

Number	Title (A Side/B Side)	Yr	VG	VG+	NM
COLUMBIA					
❑ 40421	Tell It To Me Again/Clean Break	1955	3.00	6.00	12.00
❑ 40492	Be My Darling Once Again/You Still Mean the Same to Me	1955	3.00	6.00	12.00
❑ 40544	What Am I Trying to Forget/Fifty Million Salty Kisses	1955	3.00	6.00	12.00
❑ 40597	Band of Gold/Rumble Boogie	1955	3.75	7.50	15.00
❑ 40665	Wild Cherry/I'm Still a King to You	1956	2.50	5.00	10.00
❑ 40705	Ghost Town/I'll Be Around	1956	2.50	5.00	10.00
❑ 40746	Namely You/If I Had My Druthers	1956	2.50	5.00	10.00
❑ 40804	Give Me More/The Story of Sherry	1956	2.50	5.00	10.00
❑ 40828	The Last Dance/Don't You Worry Your Pretty Little Head	1957	2.50	5.00	10.00
❑ 40885	Mr. Teardrop/April Age	1957	2.50	5.00	10.00
❑ 40958	There's a Place Called Heaven/Fourteen Carat Gold	1957	2.50	5.00	10.00
❑ 41014	I Keep Running Away from You/A Ferryboat Named Minerva	1957	2.50	5.00	10.00
❑ 41077	It'll Be Me/Love Me, If You Will	1957	2.50	5.00	10.00
❑ 41134	The Glide/Another Time, Another Place	1958	2.50	5.00	10.00
❑ 41259	Big Bad Wolf/I Look for a Love	1958	2.50	5.00	10.00
❑ 41351	Hasty Heart/The Golden Age	1959	2.50	5.00	10.00
DECCA					
❑ 27244	I'll Always Love You/Maybe on Sunday	1950	3.75	7.50	15.00
—With Eileen Wilson					
❑ 27245	I Need You So/Can't Seem to Laugh Anymore	1950	3.75	7.50	15.00
❑ 27435	Seven Wonders of the World/When You Return	1951	3.00	6.00	12.00
❑ 27475	Chapel of the Roses/Beautiful Madness	1951	3.00	6.00	12.00
❑ 27484	I Apologize/Bring Back the Thrill	1951	3.00	6.00	12.00
❑ 27535	Don't Cry/Don't Leave Me Now	1951	3.00	6.00	12.00
❑ 27618	Powder Blue/Vanity	1951	3.00	6.00	12.00
❑ 27626	My Life's Desire/I Can See You	1951	3.00	6.00	12.00
❑ 27633	Far, Far Away/Star of Hope	1951	3.00	6.00	12.00
—With Elieen Wilson					
❑ 27717	Belle, Belle, My Liberty Belle/Cara Cara Bella Bella	1951	3.00	6.00	12.00
❑ 27755	The Sweetest Waltz/I Will Never Change	1951	3.00	6.00	12.00
❑ 27807	The Lamp of Faith/Sin Ain't Nothing	1951	3.00	6.00	12.00
❑ 27836	I Can't Help It/Grievin' My Heart Out for You	1951	3.00	6.00	12.00
❑ 27904	Neither Am I/Take Me Back	1951	3.00	6.00	12.00
❑ 27944	I'll Sing to You/Your Sentimental Heart	1952	3.00	6.00	12.00
❑ 28050	It Doesn't Matter Where I Go/Sentimental Tears	1952	3.00	6.00	12.00
❑ 28153	Wonder/My Mother's Pearl	1952	3.00	6.00	12.00
❑ 28292	My Name Is Morgan, But It Ain't J.P./Pretty Girl	1952	3.00	6.00	12.00
❑ 28368	It's Been So Long, Darling/Silver Dew on the Blue Grass Tonight	1952	3.00	6.00	12.00
❑ 28452	I Don't Want to Set the World on Fire/From Your Lips Only	1952	3.00	6.00	12.00
❑ 28477	How Long/Second Star to the Right	1952	3.00	6.00	12.00
❑ 28548	Lover's Quarrel/Changeable	1953	3.00	6.00	12.00
❑ 28635	All By Myself/If They Should Ask Me	1953	3.00	6.00	12.00
❑ 28768	If You See Sally/I Got to Pass Your House to Get to My House	1953	3.00	6.00	12.00
❑ 28789	No Stone Unturned/Till the Moon Turns Green	1953	3.00	6.00	12.00
❑ 28844	Too Long/For Now and Always	1953	3.00	6.00	12.00
❑ 29005	I'm Through with Love/You Didn't Have to Tell Me	1954	2.50	5.00	10.00
❑ 29142	Lulu's Back in Town/Anyplace, Anytime, Anywhere	1954	2.50	5.00	10.00
❑ 29322	Where Can You Be/I'm Just a Country Boy	1954	2.50	5.00	10.00
❑ 29444	Home Again/Sip of Moonlight	1955	2.50	5.00	10.00
❑ 29807	The Thrill Is Gone/Wanted, Someone to Love Me	1956	2.50	5.00	10.00
MONUMENT					
❑ 880	More I Cannot Do/Sweet Sugar	1965	2.00	4.00	8.00
❑ 898	The Story of My Life/Things Called Sadness	1965	2.00	4.00	8.00
❑ 930	Don't Change/I Love You Drops	1966	2.00	4.00	8.00
❑ 947	Tip of My Fingers/After I'm Number One	1966	2.00	4.00	8.00
❑ 971	I Know Love/Married	1966	2.00	4.00	8.00
❑ 989	There Goes My Everything/I Don't Wanna Go Home	1966	2.00	4.00	8.00
❑ 1008	I Live to Love You/I Run to the Door	1967	—	3.00	6.00
❑ 1027	That Lucky Old Sun/No Hearts and Flowers	1967	—	3.00	6.00
❑ 1045	Theme from "Will Penny" (Lonely Rider)/Here Comes the Rain	1967	—	3.00	6.00
❑ 1062	Good Morning/Let Me Lead the Way	1968	—	3.00	6.00
❑ 1088	Take a Message to Mary/In My Youth	1968	—	3.00	6.00
❑ 1130	Whippoorwill/To Think You've Chosen Me	1969	—	3.00	6.00
❑ 1147	Days of Sand and Shovels/That Woman's Coming Home	1969	—	3.00	6.00
❑ 1156	I'll Catch the Sun/Ain't You Glad You're Living, Joe	1969	—	3.00	6.00
❑ 1185	Lilacs in Winter/Look for Me Tomorrow	1970	—	3.00	6.00

Number	Title (A Side/B Side)	Yr	VG	VG+	NM
❑ 1201	Between Winston-Salem and Nashville, Tennessee/Just a Drop of Rain	1970	—	3.00	6.00
❑ 1222	Statue of a Fool/Ev'ry Body Else	1970	—	3.00	6.00
❑ 8530	Freedom Come, Freedom Go/Have You Ever Been to Georgia	1971	—	2.50	5.00
❑ 8542	For a Moment You Slipped My Mind/Is It Any Wonder	1972	—	2.50	5.00
❑ 8557	The Riddle Song/Wonder Where They're Going	1972	—	2.50	5.00
❑ 8578	When You Leave Amarillo, Turn Out the Lights/Cajun Fiddler	1973	—	2.50	5.00
❑ 8603	Going Away Party/The Old Rugged Cross	1974	—	2.50	5.00
❑ 8704	The Good Old Days Are Right Now/Pleasing You (As Long As I Live)	1976	—	2.50	5.00
❑ 45232	Come Sundown/Love Is Gone for Good	1977	—	2.50	5.00
❑ 45269	Six Weeks Every Summer, Christmas Every Day/Play Her Back to Yesterday	1978	—	2.50	5.00
STRAND					
❑ 25005	Vanity/Summer School Blues	1959	2.50	5.00	10.00
VERVE					
❑ 10270	Then You Can Tell Me Goodbye/When I Found I'd Lost	1962	2.50	5.00	10.00
WARWICK					
❑ 597	Hair of Gold/Somebody Cares for Me	1960	2.50	5.00	10.00
7-Inch Extended Plays					
COLUMBIA					
❑ B-8931	When the Sun Comes Out/Love Is Just Around the Corner//For You/I'll String Along with You	195?	3.00	6.00	12.00
❑ B-8931 [PS]	Swingin' for Two, Part 1	195?	3.00	6.00	12.00
❑ B-8932	I Didn't Know About You/So Rare//I'm Yours/I'm Gonna Sit Right Down and Write Myself a Letter	195?	3.00	6.00	12.00
❑ B-8932 [PS]	Swingin' for Two, Part 2	195?	3.00	6.00	12.00
Albums					
COLUMBIA					
❑ CL 893 [M]	Swingin' for Two	1956	6.25	12.50	25.00
MONUMENT					
❑ MLP-8049 [M]	Don Cherry Smashes	1966	3.00	6.00	12.00
❑ MLP-8075 [M]	There Goes My Everything	1967	3.75	7.50	15.00
❑ 8601 [(2)]	The World of Don Cherry	197?	3.00	6.00	12.00
—Reissue of 32334					
❑ SLP-18049 [S]	Don Cherry Smashes	1966	3.75	7.50	15.00
❑ SLP-18075 [S]	There Goes My Everything	1967	3.00	6.00	12.00
❑ SLP-18088	Let It Be Me	1968	3.00	6.00	12.00
❑ SLP-18109	Take a Message to Mary	1969	3.00	6.00	12.00
❑ SLP-18124	Don Cherry	1970	3.00	6.00	12.00
❑ KZG 32334 [(2)]	The World of Don Cherry	1972	3.75	7.50	15.00

CHESNEY, KENNY

45s

Number	Title (A Side/B Side)	Yr	VG	VG+	NM
BNA					
❑ 64278	Fall in Love/Something About You and a Dirt Road	1995	—	2.00	4.00
❑ 64347	All I Need to Know/Someone Else's Hog	1995	—	2.00	4.00
❑ 64352	Grandpa Told Me So/Whatever It Takes	1995	—	2.00	4.00
❑ 64523	Back in Your Arms Again/Honey Would You Stand by Me	1996	—	—	3.00
❑ 64589	Me and You/I Finally Found Someone	1996	—	—	3.00
❑ 64726	When I Close My Eyes/My Poor Old Heart	1996	—	2.00	4.00
❑ 64987	A Chance/When I Close My Eyes	1997	—	2.00	4.00
❑ 65399	That's Why I'm Here/A Chance	1998	—	—	3.00
❑ 65570	I Will Stand/She Always Said It First	1998	—	—	3.00
❑ 65666	How Forever Feels/You Win, I Win, We Lose	1999	—	2.00	4.00
❑ 65756	You Had Me from Hello/Everywhere We Go	1999	—	2.00	4.00
❑ 65934	She Thinks My Tractor's Sexy/You Had Me from Hello	1999	—	—	3.00
❑ 65964	What I Need to Do/She Thinks My Tractor's Sexy	2000	—	—	3.00
❑ 69007	I Lost It/The Tin Man	2000	—	—	3.00
CAPRICORN					
❑ 7-18323	Whatever It Takes/I'd Love to Change Your Name	1993	—	2.50	5.00

CHESNUT, JIM

45s

Number	Title (A Side/B Side)	Yr	VG	VG+	NM
ABC HICKORY					
❑ 54003	She's My Woman/Tell Me, Tell Me That You Love Me	1976	—	2.50	5.00
❑ 54007	California Lady/What Got in the Way	1977	—	2.50	5.00
❑ 54013	Let Me Love You Now/A Loaf of Bread (A Jug of Wine)	1977	—	2.50	5.00
❑ 54021	The Wrong Side of the Rainbow/I'm So Lonely for Your Baby	1977	—	2.50	5.00
❑ 54027	The Ninth of September/I Love You Babe (For All the Little Things)	1978	—	2.50	5.00
❑ 54033	Show Me a Sign/Whiskey Lady	1978	—	2.50	5.00
❑ 54038	Get Back to Loving Me/Kinder Than the Last One	1978	—	2.50	5.00
❑ 54044	Just Let Me Make Believe/Let Me Just Say I Love You	1979	2.50	5.00	10.00
—Quickly reissued on MCA 41015					
HICKORY/MGM					
❑ 369	Country Love Song/Good Lord, What Happened to the Trains	1976	—	3.00	6.00
LIBERTY					
❑ 1405	Bedtime Stories/Pick Up the Pieces	1981	—	2.00	4.00
❑ 1434	The Rose Is for Today/Dark Eyed Lady	1981	—	2.00	4.00
MCA					
❑ 41015	Just Let Me Make Believe/Let Me Just Say I Love You	1979	—	2.00	4.00
❑ 41106	Let's Take the Time to Fall in Love Again/A Loaf of Bread (A Jug of Wine)	1979	—	2.00	4.00
UNITED ARTISTS					
❑ 1372	Out Run the Sun/Pick Up the Pieces	1980	—	2.00	4.00
Albums					
ABC HICKORY					
❑ AH-44004	Let Me Love You Now	1977	3.00	6.00	12.00
❑ AH-44012	Show Me a Sign	1978	3.00	6.00	12.00

CHESNUTT, MARK

45s

Number	Title (A Side/B Side)	Yr	VG	VG+	NM
AXBAR					
❑ 6010	Full Blooded Texan/Heaven on My Mind	198?	3.75	7.50	15.00
❑ 6035	Let's Make a Memory One More Time/Welcome Fool	1985	3.75	7.50	15.00
❑ 6041	Rodeo Cowboy/The Price of Getting High	1986	3.75	7.50	15.00
❑ 6046	Country Girl/Running Out of Ways to Say I Love You	1986	3.75	7.50	15.00
❑ 6061	Since I Drank My Way to Houston/Heartache County	1988	3.75	7.50	15.00
DECCA					
❑ 54941	Goin' Through the Big D/It's Almost Like You're Here	1994	—	2.00	4.00
❑ 54978	Gonna Get a Life/Half of Everything (And All of My Heart)	1994	—	2.00	4.00
❑ 55050	Down in Tennessee/This Side of the Door	1995	—	—	3.00
❑ 55103	Trouble/Strangers	1995	—	—	3.00
❑ 55164	It Wouldn't Hurt to Have Wings/I May Be a Fool	1995	—	2.00	4.00
❑ 55199	Wrong Place, Wrong Time/As the Honky Tonk Turns	1996	—	—	3.00
❑ 55231	It's a Little Too Late/The King of Broken Hearts	1996	—	—	3.00
❑ 55293	Let It Rain/Going Through the Big D	1997	—	—	3.00
❑ 72014	Thank God for Believers/Hello Honky Tonk	1997	—	—	3.00
❑ 72031	I Might Even Quit Lovin' You/Numbers on the Jukebox	1998	—	—	3.00
❑ 72032	It's Not Over/Useless	1997	—	—	3.00
❑ 72066	Wherever You Are/Goodbye Heartache	1998	—	—	3.00
❑ 72078	I Don't Want to Miss a Thing/Wherever You Are	1998	—	2.00	4.00
❑ 72090	This Heartache Never Sleeps/That's the Way You Make an Ex	1999	—	—	3.00
MCA					
❑ 53965	Brother Jukebox/Life of a Lonely Man	1990	—	2.00	4.00
❑ 54053	Blame It on Texas/Danger at My Door	1991	—	2.00	4.00
❑ 54136	Your Love Is a Miracle/Too Good a Memory	1991	—	2.00	4.00
❑ 54256	Broken Promise Land/Friends in Low Places	1991	—	2.00	4.00
❑ 54334	Old Flames Have New Names/Postpone the Pain	1992	—	2.00	4.00
❑ 54395	I'll Think of Something/Uptown, Downtown (Misery's All the Same)	1992	—	2.50	5.00
❑ 54471	Bubba Shot the Jukebox/It's Not Over (If I'm Not Over You)	1992	—	2.50	5.00
❑ 54539	Ol' Country/Talking to Hank	1992	—	2.00	4.00
❑ 54630	It Sure Is Monday/I'm Not Getting Any Better at Goodbyes	1993	—	2.00	4.00
❑ 54718	Almost Goodbye/Texas Is Bigger Than It Used to Be	1993	—	2.00	4.00
❑ 54768	I Just Wanted You to Know/April's Fool	1993	—	2.00	4.00
❑ 54822	Woman, Sensuous Woman/Till a Better Memory Comes Along	1994	—	2.00	4.00
❑ 54887	She Dreams/What a Way to Live	1994	—	2.00	4.00
❑ 79054	Too Cold at Home/Life of a Lucky Man	1990	—	2.50	5.00
MCA NASHVILLE					
❑ 088 172162 7	Fallin' Never Felt So Good/Love in the Hot Afternoon	2000	—	—	3.00

CHEVALIER, JAY, AND SHELLEY FORD

45s

Number	Title (A Side/B Side)	Yr	VG	VG+	NM
CREOLE GOLD					
❑ 1114	Disco Blues/Super Country USA	1979	—	3.00	6.00

CHICK AND HIS HOT RODS

See RENO AND SMILEY.

CHILDRESS, LISA

45s

Number	Title (A Side/B Side)	Yr	VG	VG+	NM
AMI					
❑ 1941	This Time It's You/(B-side unknown)	1986	—	2.50	5.00
❑ 1947	It's Goodbye and So-Long to You/Touch My Heart	1986	—	2.50	5.00
TRUE					
❑ 89	(I Wanna Hear You) Say You Love Me Again/It Don't Get Better Than This	1988	—	2.50	5.00
❑ 91	You Didn't Have to Jump the Fence/I Never Will Outgrow My Love for You	1988	—	2.50	5.00
❑ 95	(Here Comes) That Old Familiar Feeling/I Should Have Known You'd Come Around	1988	—	2.50	5.00
❑ 97	Maybe There/I Should Have Known You'd Come Around	1989	—	2.50	5.00

CHILDS, ANDY

45s

Number	Title (A Side/B Side)	Yr	VG	VG+	NM
RCA					
❑ 62545	I Wouldn't Know/Let the Good Times Roll	1993	—	—	3.00
❑ 62641	Broken/Your Love Amazes Me	1993	—	—	3.00
❑ 62763	Simple Life/Mine All Mine	1994	—	—	3.00

CHINNOCK, BILLY

45s

CBS ASSOCIATED

Number	Title (A Side/B Side)	Yr	VG	VG+	NM
❑ ZS4-06673	Just a Matter of Time/Another No-Win Situation	1987	—	2.00	4.00

PARADISE

Number	Title (A Side/B Side)	Yr	VG	VG+	NM
❑ 630	The Way She Makes Love/Rock n' Roll Cowboy	1984	—	2.50	5.00

CHIPMUNKS, THE

This is the second version of the cartoon group, re-created in 1980 by Ross Bagdasarian, Jr. The first version never had any country crossovers.

12-Inch Singles

EXCELSIOR

Number	Title (A Side/B Side)	Yr	VG	VG+	NM
❑ XEP-2000 [DJ]	Call Me (Disco Version) (same on both sides)	1980	2.50	5.00	10.00

45s

EPIC

Number	Title (A Side/B Side)	Yr	VG	VG+	NM
❑ 74776	Achy Breaky Heart/I Ain't No Dang Cartoon	1992	—	2.00	4.00
—As "Alvin and the Chipmunks"; with Billy Ray Cyrus on A-side					
❑ 77768	Rockin' Around the Christmas Tree/Rudolph the Red-Nosed Reindeer	1994	—	2.00	4.00
—As "Alvin and the Chipmunks"					

EXCELSIOR

Number	Title (A Side/B Side)	Yr	VG	VG+	NM
❑ SIS 1001	You May Be Right/Crazy Little Thing Called Love	1980	—	2.50	5.00
❑ SIS 1002	Call Me/Refugee	1980	—	2.50	5.00
❑ SIS 1002 [PS]	Call Me/Refugee	1980	—	3.00	6.00

RCA

Number	Title (A Side/B Side)	Yr	VG	VG+	NM
❑ PB-12247	On the Road Again/Coward of the County	1981	—	2.00	4.00
❑ PB-12301	Mamas Don't Let Your Babies Grow Up to Be Chipmunks/Lunchbox	1981	—	2.00	4.00
—With Jerry Reed					
❑ PB-12354	The Chipmunk Song/Sleigh Ride	1981	—	2.00	4.00
❑ PB-12354 [PS]	The Chipmunk Song/Sleigh Ride	1981	—	2.50	5.00
❑ PB-13098	Bette Davis Eyes/Heartbreaker	1982	—	2.00	4.00
❑ PB-13098 [PS]	Bette Davis Eyes/Heartbreaker	1982	—	2.00	4.00
❑ PB-13374	E.T. and Me/Tomorrow (Theme from "Annie")	1982	—	2.00	4.00
❑ PB-13374 [PS]	E.T. and Me/Tomorrow (Theme from "Annie")	1982	—	2.00	4.00

Albums

EXCELSIOR

Number	Title (A Side/B Side)	Yr	VG	VG+	NM
❑ X-6008	Chipmunk Punk	1980	3.75	7.50	15.00

RCA VICTOR

Number	Title (A Side/B Side)	Yr	VG	VG+	NM
❑ AFL1-4027	Urban Chipmunk	1981	2.50	5.00	10.00
❑ AQL1-4041	A Chipmunk Christmas	1981	3.75	7.50	15.00
—With booklet					
❑ AFL1-4304	Chipmunk Rock	1982	2.50	5.00	10.00
❑ AFL1-4376	The Chipmunks Go Hollywood	1983	2.50	5.00	10.00

CHOATES, HARRY

45s

D

Number	Title (A Side/B Side)	Yr	VG	VG+	NM
❑ 1023	Allons A. Lafayette/Draggin' the Fiddle	1958	5.00	10.00	20.00
❑ 1024	Jole Blon/Draggin' the Bow	1958	5.00	10.00	20.00
❑ 1025	Jole Blon/Corpus Christi Waltz	1958	5.00	10.00	20.00
❑ 1043	Opelousas Waltz/Poor Hobo	1959	5.00	10.00	20.00
❑ 1044	Port Arthur Waltz/Honky Tonk Boogie	1959	5.00	10.00	20.00
❑ 1132	Tondelay/Basil Waltz	1960	3.75	7.50	15.00

STARDAY

Number	Title (A Side/B Side)	Yr	VG	VG+	NM
❑ 187	The Original New Jole Blon (English)/The Original New Jole Blon (French)	1955	7.50	15.00	30.00
❑ 212	Opelousas Waltz/Poor Hobo	1955	6.25	12.50	25.00
❑ 224	Port Arthur Waltz/Honky Tonk Boogie	1956	6.25	12.50	25.00
❑ 273	Allons a Lafayette/Draggin' the Fiddle	1956	6.25	12.50	25.00
❑ 284	Basile Waltz/Tondellay	1957	6.25	12.50	25.00

Selected 78s

GOLD STAR

Number	Title (A Side/B Side)	Yr	VG	VG+	NM
❑ 1314	Jole Blon/Dragging the Bow	1946	12.50	25.00	50.00

MACY'S

Number	Title (A Side/B Side)	Yr	VG	VG+	NM
❑ 124	Cat'n Around/Gra Mamou	1950	10.00	20.00	40.00
❑ 134	Louisiana Boogie/What's the Use	1951	10.00	20.00	40.00
❑ 141	Korea Here We Come/Do You Still Love Me	1951	10.00	20.00	40.00
❑ 147	I've Quit My Cattin' Around/Fiddle Polka	1951	10.00	20.00	40.00
❑ 158	Harry's Blues/She's Sweet Sweet	195?	7.50	15.00	30.00
❑ 159	My Pretty Brunette/Corpus Christi Waltz	195?	7.50	15.00	30.00

MODERN MOUNTAIN

Number	Title (A Side/B Side)	Yr	VG	VG+	NM
❑ 511	Jole Blon/Dragging the Bow	1946	10.00	20.00	40.00
—All copies have his name misspelled "Harry Coates" on label					

Albums

D

Number	Title (A Side/B Side)	Yr	VG	VG+	NM
❑ 7000 [M]	Jole Blon	196?	10.00	20.00	40.00

CHRIS AND LENNY

45s

HAPPY MAN

Number	Title (A Side/B Side)	Yr	VG	VG+	NM
❑ 821	When Daddy Did the Driving/(B-side unknown)	1989	—	3.00	6.00
❑ 821 [PS]	When Daddy Did the Driving/(B-side unknown)	1989	2.00	4.00	8.00

CHUCK WAGON GANG, THE

45s

COLUMBIA

Number	Title (A Side/B Side)	Yr	VG	VG+	NM
❑ 4-20768	Somebody Called My Name/Help Me to Be Ready Lord	1950	6.25	12.50	25.00
❑ 4-20788	Camping in Canaan's Land/Happy Day	1951	5.00	10.00	20.00
❑ 4-20806	Stormy Waters/Travellin' On	1951	5.00	10.00	20.00
❑ 4-20832	He Said If I Be Lifted Up/I'm Telling the World About His Love	1951	5.00	10.00	20.00
❑ 4-20887	Help Me Lord to Stand/Side by Side	1952	5.00	10.00	20.00
❑ 4-20916	Is Your Name in the Book of Life/I've Changed My Mind	1952	5.00	10.00	20.00
❑ 4-20964	Way Up in Glory/Walk and Talk with Jesus	1952	5.00	10.00	20.00
❑ 4-20966	When the Saints Go Marching In/I'm Telling the World About His Love	1952	5.00	10.00	20.00
❑ 4-20967	On and On We Walk Together/Travelling On	1952	5.00	10.00	20.00
❑ 4-20968	Camping in Canaan's Land/My Home Sweet Home	1952	5.00	10.00	20.00
❑ 4-20969	Come Unto Me/Shall We Gather at the River	1952	5.00	10.00	20.00
—The above four comprise a box set					
❑ 4-20998	Blessed Light Shine On/I Know My Saviour Cares	1952	5.00	10.00	20.00
❑ 4-21021	After Awhile/All God's Children Gonna Rise	1952	5.00	10.00	20.00
❑ 4-21058	We'll Be Happy All the Time/Just a Veil Between	1952	5.00	10.00	20.00
❑ 4-21097	At the Dawning/When He Calls I'll Fly Away	1953	5.00	10.00	20.00
❑ 4-21133	Hide Me Rock of Ages/There's Glory on the Winning Side	1953	5.00	10.00	20.00
❑ 4-21153	Love Leads the Way/Home of the Soul	1953	5.00	10.00	20.00
❑ 4-21185	Jesus Calls You Workers/I'm Finding New Joy	1953	5.00	10.00	20.00
❑ 4-21212	A Soul Winner for Jesus/God Put a Rainbow in the Cloud	1954	5.00	10.00	20.00
❑ 4-21254	Angels Rock Me to Sleep/As the Life of a Flower	1954	5.00	10.00	20.00
❑ 4-21286	Joy to the World/While Shepherds Watched Their Flock by Night	1954	3.75	7.50	15.00
❑ 4-21287	It Came Upon a Midnight Clear/Silent Night	1954	3.75	7.50	15.00
❑ 4-21288	The First Noel/It Came Upon a Midnight Clear	1954	3.75	7.50	15.00
❑ 4-21289	Hark the Herald Angels Sing/O Little Town of Bethlehem	1954	3.75	7.50	15.00
—The above four comprise a box set					
❑ 4-21293	Tattler's Wagon/O Why Not Tonight	1954	5.00	10.00	20.00
❑ 4-21338	I'm a Precious Friend/I Want to Be Ready to Meet Him	1955	5.00	10.00	20.00
❑ 4-21379	In the Garden/In My New Home	1955	5.00	10.00	20.00
❑ 4-21410	Wonderful Saviour/I'll Shout and Shine	1955	5.00	10.00	20.00
❑ 4-21452	In the Sweet Forever/I've Got Old Time Religion in My Heart	1955	5.00	10.00	20.00
❑ 4-21480	There's Gonna Be Shouting and Singing/I'm Gonna See Heaven	1956	5.00	10.00	20.00
❑ 4-21509	I'm Glory Bound/I've Been with Jesus	1956	5.00	10.00	20.00
❑ 4-21542	When the Sun Shines Over Jordan/A Lot of Heaven	1956	5.00	10.00	20.00
❑ 4-21567	I'm Bound for the Kingdom/I'm Gonna Take a Ride	1956	5.00	10.00	20.00
❑ 4-40834	I'll Walk and Talk with My Lord/When I Looked Up and He Looked Down	1957	3.75	7.50	15.00
❑ 4-40912	Sing on the Way/I Know	1957	3.75	7.50	15.00
❑ 4-40954	He's My Lord and King/Inside the Gate	1957	3.75	7.50	15.00
❑ 4-41031	There's Gonna Be Singing/I'm Headed for the Promised Land	1957	3.75	7.50	15.00
❑ 4-41135	He Will Answer Prayer/He's a Friend I Can Tell My Troubles To	1958	3.75	7.50	15.00
❑ 4-41219	Hallelujah, What a Promise/I Want My Light to Shine	1958	3.75	7.50	15.00
❑ 4-41324	Endless Joy Is Waiting/My Cathedral of Dreams	1959	3.00	6.00	12.00
❑ 4-41426	I'll Live in Glory/The Lord Is My Shepherd	1959	3.00	6.00	12.00
❑ 4-43048	Open Up Them Pearly Gates/That We Might Know	1964	2.50	5.00	10.00
❑ 4-43234	He Gave Me That Old Time Religion/I'll Never More Stray	1965	2.50	5.00	10.00

Albums

HARMONY

Number	Title (A Side/B Side)	Yr	VG	VG+	NM
❑ HL 7355	Christmas with the Chuck Wagon Gang	196?	3.00	6.00	12.00
❑ HS 11155 [R]	Christmas with the Chuck Wagon Gang	196?	3.00	6.00	12.00

CHURCH, CLAUDIA

45s

REPRISE

Number	Title (A Side/B Side)	Yr	VG	VG+	NM
❑ 16959	Home in My Heart (North Carolina)/Just As Long As You Love Me	1999	—	—	3.00
❑ 17112	What's the Matter with You Baby/Small Town Girl	1999	—	—	3.00

CLANTON, DARRELL

45s

AUDIOGRAPH

Number	Title (A Side/B Side)	Yr	VG	VG+	NM
❑ 474	Lonesome 7-7203/Me-Oh-My	1983	—	3.00	6.00
❑ 479	I'll Take As Much of You As I Can Get/That's What Cheaters Do	1984	—	3.00	6.00

WARNER BROS.

Number	Title (A Side/B Side)	Yr	VG	VG+	NM
❑ 29185	I Forgot That I Don't Live Here Anymore/I Told You So	1984	—	2.00	4.00

Albums

AUDIOGRAPH

Number	Title (A Side/B Side)	Yr	VG	VG+	NM
❑ 6012	Alive	1983	3.00	6.00	12.00

CLAPTON, ERIC

The below two singles charted country, with the former making the top 40.

45s

RSO

Number	Title (A Side/B Side)	Yr	VG	VG+	NM
❑ 886	Lay Down Sally/Next Time You See Her	1978	—	2.00	4.00
❑ 910	Promises/Watch Out for Lucy	1978	—	2.00	4.00

CLARK, GUY

45s

RCA

Number	Title (A Side/B Side)	Yr	VG	VG+	NM
❑ PB-10781	The Last Gunfighter Ballad/Texas Cookin'	1976	—	3.00	6.00
❑ PB-10858	Virginia's Real/Anyhow, I Love You	1976	—	3.00	6.00
❑ PB-13688	Texas Cookin'/Broken Hearted People	1983	—	2.00	4.00

Number	Title (A Side/B Side)	Yr	VG	VG+	NM
RCA VICTOR					
❑ PB-10188	The Ballad of Laverne and Cpt. Flint/Like a Coat from the Cold	1975	2.00	4.00	8.00
❑ PB-10581	Let Him Roll/Rita Ballou	1976	—	3.00	6.00
WARNER BROS.					
❑ 8714	Fools for Each Other/Fool on the Roof	1978	—	2.50	5.00
❑ 29456	Better Days/Heartbroke	1983	—	2.00	4.00
❑ 29595	Homegrown Tomatoes/Fool in a Mirror	1983	—	2.00	4.00
❑ 49542	Heartbroke/Who Do You Think You Are	1980	—	2.50	5.00
❑ 49740	The Partner Nobody Chose/Heartbroke	1981	—	2.50	5.00
❑ 49853	She's Crazy for Leavin'/South Coast of Texas	1981	—	2.50	5.00
❑ 50016	New Cut Road/The South Coast of Texas	1982	—	2.50	5.00
Albums					
RCA VICTOR					
❑ AHL1-1303	Old No. 1	198?	2.50	5.00	10.00
—Reissue with new prefix					
❑ APL1-1303	Old No. 1	1976	5.00	10.00	20.00
❑ APL1-1944	Texas Cookin'	1976	5.00	10.00	20.00
SUGAR HILL					
❑ SH-1025	Old Friends	198?	3.00	6.00	12.00
WARNER BROS.					
❑ WBMS-105 [DJ]	On the Road, Live!	198?	15.00	30.00	60.00
—Part of "The Warner Bros. Music Show" series; promo only					
❑ BSK 3241	Guy Clark	1978	3.75	7.50	15.00
❑ BSK 3381	South Coast of Texas	1981	3.75	7.50	15.00
❑ 23880	Better Days	1983	3.00	6.00	12.00

CLARK, JAY

45s

Number	Title (A Side/B Side)	Yr	VG	VG+	NM
CONCORDE					
❑ 301	Love Gone Bad/Modern Day Cowboy	1985	—	2.50	5.00
❑ 302	Modern Day Cowboy/Love Gone Bad	1986	—	2.50	5.00

CLARK, KEN, AND DON ANTHONY

Albums

Number	Title (A Side/B Side)	Yr	VG	VG+	NM
STARDAY					
❑ SLP-114 [M]	Fiddlin' Country Style	1959	10.00	20.00	40.00

CLARK, LUCKY

45s

Number	Title (A Side/B Side)	Yr	VG	VG+	NM
POLYDOR					
❑ 14317	Sing Me a Sad Song/The Guy with the Girl	1976	—	3.00	6.00
❑ 14343	Amy/Lonely Hearts Women	1976	—	3.00	6.00
❑ 14393	Everytime Two Fools Collide/Another Honky Tonk Tonight	1977	—	3.00	6.00

CLARK, MICKEY

45s

Number	Title (A Side/B Side)	Yr	VG	VG+	NM
EVERGREEN					
❑ 1051	When I'm Over You (What You Gonna Do)/(B-side unknown)	1987	—	2.50	5.00
❑ 1051 [PS]	When I'm Over You (What You Gonna Do)/(B-side unknown)	1987	2.00	4.00	8.00
❑ 1058	You Take the Leavin' Out of Me/She's Gone to L.A. Again	1987	—	2.50	5.00
MONUMENT					
❑ WS4-03519	She's Gone to L.A. Again/The Tequila Express	1983	—	2.50	5.00

CLARK, PETULA

Most of her output was pop, but the below were country records.

45s

Number	Title (A Side/B Side)	Yr	VG	VG+	NM
SCOTTI BROS.					
❑ 02676	Natural Love/Because I Love Him	1982	—	2.00	4.00
❑ 02979	Blue Eyes Crying in the Rain/Love Won't Always Pass You By	1982	—	2.00	4.00
❑ 03171	Dreamin' with My Eyes Wide Open/Afterglow	1982	—	2.00	4.00

CLARK, ROY

45s

Number	Title (A Side/B Side)	Yr	VG	VG+	NM
ABC					
❑ 12328	Must You Throw Dirt in My Face/Lazy River	1978	—	2.00	4.00
❑ 12365	Where Have You Been All of My Life/Near You	1978	—	2.00	4.00
❑ 12402	The Happy Days/Shoulder to Shoulder (Arm and Arm)	1978	—	2.00	4.00
❑ 12437	Is It Hot in Here (Or Is It Me)/Jolly Ho (Happy Hour)	1978	—	2.00	4.00
—With Buck Trent					
ABC DOT					
❑ 17530	Dear God/Take Good Care of Her	1974	—	2.00	4.00
❑ 17545	You're Gonna Love Yourself in the Morning/Banjoy	1975	—	2.00	4.00
❑ 17565	Heart to Heart/Someone Cares for You	1975	—	2.00	4.00
❑ 17605	If I Had to Do It All Over Again/It Sure Looks Good on You	1976	—	2.00	4.00
❑ 17626	Think Summer/Whatever Happened to Gauze	1976	—	2.00	4.00
❑ 17647	I Have a Dream, I Have a Love/Half a Love	1976	—	2.00	4.00
❑ 17712	We Can't Build a Fire in the Rain/I'm So Lonesome I Could Cry	1977	—	2.00	4.00
CAPITOL					
❑ 4595	Under the Double Eagle/Black Sapphire	1961	3.00	6.00	12.00
❑ 4670	Texas Twist/Wildwood Twist	1961	3.00	6.00	12.00
❑ 4794	Talk About a Party/As Long As I'm Movin'	1962	3.00	6.00	12.00
❑ 4956	Tips of My Fingers/Spooky Movies	1963	2.50	5.00	10.00
❑ 5047	Good Time Charlie/Application for Love	1963	2.50	5.00	10.00
❑ 5099	Through the Eyes of a Fool/Sweet Violets	1964	2.50	5.00	10.00
❑ 5163	Take Me As I Am/If You'll Pardon Me	1964	2.50	5.00	10.00
❑ 5233	It's My Way/I'm Forgetting Now	1964	2.50	5.00	10.00
❑ 5300	Alabama Jubilee/Down Yonder	1964	2.50	5.00	10.00
❑ 5350	When the Wind Blows In Chicago/Live Fast Love Hard	1965	2.50	5.00	10.00
❑ 5445	The Color of Her Love Is Blue/Too Pooped to Pop	1965	2.50	5.00	10.00
❑ 5512	So Much to Remember/Turn Around and Look Again	1965	2.50	5.00	10.00
❑ 5565	Malaguena/Overdue Blues	1965	2.50	5.00	10.00
❑ 5619	Rose Colored Glasses/Everybody Watches Me	1966	2.50	5.00	10.00
❑ 5664	Hey Sweet Thing/If You Want It, Come and Get It	1966	2.50	5.00	10.00
—With Mary Taylor					
❑ 5770	St. Louis Blues/Just a Closer Walk with Thee	1966	2.50	5.00	10.00
CHURCHILL					
❑ 52469	Another Lonely Night With You/(Instrumental)	1984	—	2.00	4.00
❑ 94002	Paradise Knife and Gun Club/I Don't Care	1982	—	2.50	5.00
❑ 94007	Tennessee Saturday Night/Tumbling Tumbleweeds	1982	—	2.50	5.00
❑ 94007 [PS]	Tennessee Saturday Night/Tumbling Tumbleweeds	1982	—	3.00	6.00
❑ 94011	Here We Go Again/Early in the Morning	1982	—	2.50	5.00
❑ 94016	Christmas Wouldn't Be Christmas Without You/A Way Without Words	1982	—	3.00	6.00
❑ 94017	I'm a Booger/A Way Without Words	1983	—	2.50	5.00
❑ 94025	Wildwood Flower/Southern Nights	1983	—	2.50	5.00
DOT					
❑ 17117	Do You Believe This Town/It Just Happened That Way	1968	—	3.00	6.00
❑ 17187	Love Is Just a State of Mind/Look to the Sky	1968	—	3.00	6.00
❑ 17246	Yesterday, When I Was Young/Just Another Man	1969	—	2.50	5.00
❑ 17299	September Song/For the Life of Me	1969	—	2.50	5.00
❑ 17324	Right or Left at Oak Street/I Need to Be Needed	1969	—	2.50	5.00
❑ 17335	Then She's a Lover/Say Amen	1969	—	2.50	5.00
❑ 17349	I Never Picked Cotton/Lonesome Too Long	1970	—	2.50	5.00
❑ 17355	Thank God and Greyhound/Strangers	1970	—	2.50	5.00
❑ 17368	A Simple Thing As Love/I'd Fight the World	1971	—	2.50	5.00
❑ 17370	(Where Do I Begin) Love Story/Theme from "Love Story"	1971	—	2.50	5.00
❑ 17386	She Cried/Back in the Race	1971	—	2.50	5.00
❑ 17395	Magnificent Sanctuary Bird/Be Ready	1971	—	2.50	5.00
❑ 17413	I'll Take the Time/Ode to a Critter	1972	—	2.50	5.00
❑ 17426	The Lawrence Welk—Hee Haw Counter-Revolution Polka/When the Wind Blows	1972	—	2.50	5.00
❑ 17449	Come Live with Me/Darby's Castle	1973	—	2.50	5.00
❑ 17458	Riders in the Sky/Roy's Guitar Boogie	1973	—	2.50	5.00
❑ 17480	Somewhere Between Love and Tomorrow/I'll Paint You a Song	1973	—	2.50	5.00
❑ 17498	Honeymoon Feelin'/I Really Don't Want to Know	1974	—	2.50	5.00
❑ 17518	The Great Divide/Chomp'n	1974	—	2.50	5.00
HALLMARK					
❑ 0001	What a Wonderful World/(Instrumental)	1989	—	2.50	5.00
❑ 0004	But, She Loves Me/(B-side unknown)	1989	—	2.50	5.00
MCA					
❑ 41122	Caldonia/Four O'Clock in the Morning	1979	—	2.00	4.00
❑ 41153	Chain Gang of Love/Why Don't We Go Somewhere and Love	1979	—	2.00	4.00
❑ 41208	If There Were Only Time for Love/Then I'll Be Over You	1980	—	2.00	4.00
❑ 41288	For Love's Own Sake/They'll Never Take Her Love from Me	1980	—	2.00	4.00
❑ 51031	I Ain't Got Nobody/Play Me a Little Traveling Music	1980	—	2.00	4.00
❑ 51079	She Can't Give It Away/Dig a Little Deeper in the Well	1981	—	2.00	4.00
❑ 51111	Love Takes Two/Come Sundown	1981	—	2.00	4.00
SILVER DOLLAR					
❑ 0001	Tobacco Road/Black Sapphire	1986	—	2.50	5.00
❑ 0001 [PS]	Tobacco Road/Black Sapphire	1986	2.00	4.00	8.00
❑ 0004	Juke Box Saturday Night/Night Life	1986	—	2.50	5.00
SONGBIRD					
❑ 51167	The Last Word in Jesus Is Us/Shinin' Face	1981	—	2.00	4.00
TOWER					
❑ 331	Orange Blossom Special/The Great Pretender	1967	2.00	4.00	8.00
Albums					
ABC					
❑ AB-1053	Labor of Love	1978	2.50	5.00	10.00
ABC DOT					
❑ 2001	Roy Clark/The Entertainer	1974	2.50	5.00	10.00
❑ 2005	Roy Clark, Family & Friends	1974	2.50	5.00	10.00
❑ 2010	Classic Clark	1974	2.50	5.00	10.00
❑ 2030	Roy Clark's Greatest Hits — Volume 1	1975	2.50	5.00	10.00
❑ 2041	Heart to Heart	1975	2.50	5.00	10.00
❑ 2054	Roy Clark In Concert	1976	2.50	5.00	10.00
❑ 2072 [(2)]	My Music and Me/Vocal & Instrumental	1977	3.00	6.00	12.00
❑ 2099	Hookin' It	1977	2.50	5.00	10.00
—Reissue of Record 2 of 2072					
CAPITOL					
❑ SKAO-369	The Greatest!	1969	3.00	6.00	12.00
❑ SM-369	The Greatest!	197?	2.50	5.00	10.00
—Reissue with new prefix					
❑ ST 1780 [S]	The Lightning Fingers of Roy Clark	1962	6.25	12.50	25.00
❑ T 1780 [M]	The Lightning Fingers of Roy Clark	1962	5.00	10.00	20.00
❑ ST 1972 [S]	The Tip of My Fingers	1963	6.25	12.50	25.00
❑ T 1972 [M]	The Tip of My Fingers	1963	5.00	10.00	20.00
❑ ST 2031 [S]	Happy to Be Unhappy	1964	6.25	12.50	25.00

Number	Title (A Side/B Side)	Yr	VG	VG+	NM
❑ T 2031 [M]	Happy to Be Unhappy	1964	5.00	10.00	20.00
❑ SM-2425	The Roy Clark Guitar Spectacular	197?	2.50	5.00	10.00
—Reissue with new prefix					
❑ ST 2425 [S]	The Roy Clark Guitar Spectacular	1965	6.25	12.50	25.00
❑ T 2425 [M]	The Roy Clark Guitar Spectacular	1965	5.00	10.00	20.00
❑ ST 2452 [S]	Roy Clark Sings Lonesome Love Ballads	1966	6.25	12.50	25.00
❑ T 2452 [M]	Roy Clark Sings Lonesome Love Ballads	1966	5.00	10.00	20.00
❑ ST 2535 [S]	Stringing Along with the Blues	1966	6.25	12.50	25.00
❑ T 2535 [M]	Stringing Along with the Blues	1966	5.00	10.00	20.00
❑ SABB-11264 [(2)]	The Entertainer of the Year	1974	3.75	7.50	15.00
❑ SM-11412	So Much to Remember	1975	2.50	5.00	10.00
❑ SM-12032	The Tip of My Fingers	1980	2.00	4.00	8.00
❑ SN-16161	The Greatest!	198?	2.00	4.00	8.00
❑ SN-16227	The Lightning Fingers of Roy Clark	198?	2.00	4.00	8.00
CHURCHILL					
❑ 9421	The Roy Clark Show Live from Austin City Limits	1982	2.50	5.00	10.00
❑ 9425	Turned Loose	1982	2.50	5.00	10.00
DOT					
❑ DLP-25863	Urban, Suburban	1968	3.00	6.00	12.00
❑ DLP-25895	Do You Believe This Roy Clark	1968	3.00	6.00	12.00
❑ DLP-25953	Yesterday, When I Was Young	1969	3.00	6.00	12.00
❑ DLP-25972	The Everlovin' Soul of Roy Clark	1969	3.00	6.00	12.00
❑ DLP-25977	The Other Side of Roy Clark	1970	3.00	6.00	12.00
❑ DLP-25980	I Never Picked Cotton	1970	3.00	6.00	12.00
❑ DLP-25986	The Best of Roy Clark	1971	3.00	6.00	12.00
❑ DLP-25990	The Incredible Roy Clark	1971	3.00	6.00	12.00
❑ DLP-25993	The Magnificent Sanctuary Band	1971	3.00	6.00	12.00
❑ DLP-25997	Roy Clark Country!	1972	3.00	6.00	12.00
❑ DLP-26005	Roy Clark Live!	1972	3.00	6.00	12.00
❑ DLP-26008	Roy Clark/Superpicker	1973	3.00	6.00	12.00
❑ DLP-26010	Come Live with Me	1973	3.00	6.00	12.00
❑ DLP-26018	Roy Clark's Family Album	1973	3.00	6.00	12.00
HILLTOP					
❑ 6046	Roy Clartk	196?	3.75	7.50	15.00
❑ 6080	Silver Threads and Golden Needles	1970	2.50	5.00	10.00
❑ 6094	He'll Have to Go	1970	2.50	5.00	10.00
❑ 6135	Take Me As I Am	197?	2.50	5.00	10.00
❑ 6154	Honky Tonk	197?	2.50	5.00	10.00
MCA					
❑ 675	Labor of Love	1980	2.00	4.00	8.00
❑ 676	Heart to Heart	1980	2.00	4.00	8.00
❑ 677	Hookin' It	1980	2.00	4.00	8.00
❑ 678	Yesterday, When I Was Young	198?	2.00	4.00	8.00
❑ 679	Roy Clark/Superpicker	198?	2.00	4.00	8.00
❑ 811	Back to the Country	198?	2.00	4.00	8.00
❑ 3161	Makin' Music	1980	2.50	5.00	10.00
—With Gatemouth Brown					
❑ 27015	The Best of Roy Clark	198?	2.00	4.00	8.00
❑ 27050	Roy Clark's Greatest Hits — Volume 1	198?	2.00	4.00	8.00
❑ 37130	Banjo Bandits	198?	2.00	4.00	8.00
—With Buck Trent					
❑ 37131	A Pair of Fives (Banjos, That Is)	198?	2.00	4.00	8.00
❑ 37132	Roy Clark In Concert	198?	2.00	4.00	8.00
❑ 37134	Roy Clark Live!	198?	2.00	4.00	8.00
❑ 37142	My Music	198?	2.00	4.00	8.00
PAIR					
❑ PDL2-1088 [(2)]	Country Standard Time	1986	3.00	6.00	12.00
PICKWICK					
❑ PTP-2043 [(2)]	Roy Clark	1973	3.00	6.00	12.00
SONGBIRD					
❑ 5260	The Last Word in Jesus Is Us	1981	2.50	5.00	10.00
TOWER					
❑ ST 5055 [S]	Roy Clark Live	1967	5.00	10.00	20.00
❑ T 5055 [M]	Roy Clark Live	1967	3.75	7.50	15.00
❑ DT 5118 [R]	In the Mood	1968	3.75	7.50	15.00
WORD					
❑ 8654	Roy Clark Sings Gospel	1975	3.00	6.00	12.00

CLARK, ROY, AND BUCK TRENT

Also see each artist's individual listings.

Albums

Number	Title (A Side/B Side)	Yr	VG	VG+	NM
ABC					
❑ AY-1084	Banjo Bandits	1978	2.50	5.00	10.00
ABC DOT					
❑ 2015	A Pair of Fives (Banjos, That Is)	1975	2.50	5.00	10.00

CLARK, SANFORD

45s

Number	Title (A Side/B Side)	Yr	VG	VG+	NM
DOT					
❑ 15481	The Fool/Lonesome for a Letter	1956	12.50	25.00	50.00
—Originals have maroon labels					
❑ 15481	The Fool/Lonesome for a Letter	1956	6.25	12.50	25.00
—Second pressings have black labels					
❑ 15516	A Cheat/Usta Be My Baby	1956	6.25	12.50	25.00
❑ 15534	Oooo Baby/9 Lb. Hammer	1957	6.25	12.50	25.00
❑ 15556	The Glory of Love/Darling Dear	1957	6.25	12.50	25.00
❑ 15585	Love Charms/Loo-Be-Doo	1957	6.25	12.50	25.00
❑ 15646	Swanee River Rock/The Man Who Made an Angel Cry	1957	6.25	12.50	25.00
❑ 15738	Modern Romance/Travelin' Man	1958	37.50	75.00	150.00
JAMIE					
❑ 1107	Sing 'Em Some Blues/Still as the Night	1958	5.00	10.00	20.00
❑ 1120	Bad Luck/My Jealousy	1959	5.00	10.00	20.00
❑ 1129	Run Boy Run/New Kind of Fool	1959	5.00	10.00	20.00
❑ 1153	Go On Home/Pledging My Love	1960	5.00	10.00	20.00
LHI					
❑ 1203	The Son of Hickory Holler's Tramp/Black Widow Spider	1968	2.00	4.00	8.00
❑ 1213	Love Me Till Then/Farm Labor Camp No. 2	1968	2.00	4.00	8.00
MCI					
❑ 1003	The Fool/Lonesome for a Letter	1956	50.00	100.00	200.00
RAMCO					
❑ 1972	The Fool '66/Step Aside	1966	3.75	7.50	15.00
❑ 1976	Shades/Once Upon a Time	1966	3.00	6.00	12.00
❑ 1979	They Call Me Country/Climbin' the Walls	1967	3.00	6.00	12.00
❑ 1987	It's Nothing to Me/Calling All Hearts	1967	3.00	6.00	12.00
❑ 1992	The Big Lie/Where's the Floor	1967	3.00	6.00	12.00
TREY					
❑ 3016	It Hurts Me Too/Guess It's Love	1961	5.00	10.00	20.00
WARNER BROS.					
❑ 5473	She Taught Me/Just Blessin'	1964	3.75	7.50	15.00
❑ 5624	Houston/Hard Feelings	1965	3.75	7.50	15.00

Albums

Number	Title (A Side/B Side)	Yr	VG	VG+	NM
LHI					
❑ 12003	Return of the Fool	1968	15.00	30.00	60.00

CLARK, STEVE

45s

Number	Title (A Side/B Side)	Yr	VG	VG+	NM
MERCURY					
❑ 812922-7	It's Not the Fall/Breakin' Up's Supposed to Break Your Heart	1983	—	2.00	4.00
❑ 818058-7	That It's All Over Feeling (All Over Again)/Margarita, You're No Lady	1984	—	—	3.00
❑ 880234-7	A Place Out in the Country/We're So Close	1984	—	—	3.00

CLARK, TERRI

45s

Number	Title (A Side/B Side)	Yr	VG	VG+	NM
MERCURY					
❑ 172114-7	Unsung Hero/Not Getting Over You	1999	—	—	3.00
❑ 088 172178-7	A Little Gasoline/Empty	2000	—	—	3.00
❑ 566218-7	You're Easy on the Eyes/That's Me Not Loving You	1998	—	2.00	4.00
❑ 566848-7	Everytime I Cry/Till I Get There	1999	—	—	3.00
❑ 568644-7	Poor, Poor Pitiful Me/Something You Should've Said	1996	—	—	3.00
❑ 568746-7	Now That I Found You/Getting Even with the Blues	1998	—	—	3.00
❑ 574016-7	Emotional Girl/Something in the Water	1996	—	—	3.00
❑ 574456-7	Just the Same/Hold Your Horses	1997	—	—	3.00
❑ 578280-7	Suddenly Single/Catch 22	1996	—	—	3.00
❑ 852046-7	Better Things to Do/Tyin' a Heart to a Tumbleweed	1995	—	2.00	4.00
❑ 852388-7	When Boy Meets Girl/Flowers After the Fact	1995	—	2.00	4.00
❑ 852708-7	If I Were You/Something You Should've Said	1996	—	—	3.00

CLARK, YODELING SLIM

Albums

Number	Title (A Side/B Side)	Yr	VG	VG+	NM
CONTINENTAL					
❑ C-1505 [M]	Cowboy and Yodel Songs	1962	10.00	20.00	40.00
MASTERSEAL					
❑ MS-57 [M]	Cowboy Songs	1963	6.25	12.50	25.00
❑ MS-112 [M]	Songs by Yodeling Slim Clark	1964	6.25	12.50	25.00
❑ MS-135 [M]	Cowboy Songs Vol. 2	1964	6.25	12.50	25.00
PALOMINO					
❑ 300 [M]	Yodeling Slim Clark Sings the Legendary Jimmie Rodgers Songs	1966	15.00	30.00	60.00
❑ 301 [M]	Yodeling Slim Clark Sings and Yodels Favorite Montana Slim Songs of the Mountains and Plains, Vol. 1	1966	15.00	30.00	60.00
❑ 303 [M]	Yodeling Slim Clark Sings and Yodels Favorite Montana Slim Songs of the Mountains and Plains, Vol. 2	1966	10.00	20.00	40.00
❑ 306 [M]	I Feel a Trip Coming On	1966	10.00	20.00	40.00
❑ 307 [M]	Old Chestnuts	1967	10.00	20.00	40.00
❑ 310 [M]	Yodeling Slim Clark Happens Again	1967	10.00	20.00	40.00
❑ 311 [M]	The Ballad of Billy Venero	1968	10.00	20.00	40.00
❑ 314 [M]	Yodeling Slim Clark's 50th Anniversary Album	1968	12.50	25.00	50.00
—Gold vinyl					
PLAYHOUSE					
❑ 2017 [10]	Western Songs and Dances	1954	12.50	25.00	50.00

CLAYPOOL, PHILIP

45s

Number	Title (A Side/B Side)	Yr	VG	VG+	NM
CURB					
❑ D7-73058	Looking Up from a Long Way Down/Richest Man I Know	1998	—	—	3.00
❑ D7-76952	Swinging on My Baby's Chain/She Kicked My Dog	1995	—	2.00	4.00
❑ D7-76966	Feel Like Makin' Love/Circus Leaving Town	1995	—	2.00	4.00

CLAYTON, LEE

45s

Number	Title (A Side/B Side)	Yr	VG	VG+	NM
MCA					
❑ 40151	Bottles of Booze/Lonesome Whiskey	1973	—	3.00	6.00

CLEARY, DON

Albums

Number	Title (A Side/B Side)	Yr	VG	VG+	NM
PALOMINO					
❑ 302 [M]	Don Cleary Sings Traditional Cowboy Songs	1966	12.50	25.00	50.00

CLEMENT, JACK

45s

Number	Title (A Side/B Side)	Yr	VG	VG+	NM
ELEKTRA					
❑ 45397	Just Because You Ask Me To/When I Dream	1977	—	2.00	4.00
❑ 45474	We Must Believe in Magic/When I Dream	1978	—	2.00	4.00
❑ 45518	All I Want to Do in Life/It'll Be Her	1978	—	2.00	4.00
❑ 45547	Gone Girl/There She Goes	1978	—	2.00	4.00
HALLWAY					
❑ 1796	Time After Time After Time/My Voice Is Changing	1963	3.75	7.50	15.00
JMI					
❑ 10	The One on the Right Is the One on the Left/The Child That's in the Manger	1972	—	3.00	6.00
❑ 14	She Thinks I Still Care/Never Give a Heartache a Place to Go	1973	—	3.00	6.00
❑ 20	Steal Away/(B-side unknown)	1973	—	3.00	6.00
❑ 43	The One on the Right Is on the Left/Feet	1974	—	3.00	6.00
RCA VICTOR					
❑ 47-7602	Whole Lotta Lookin'/Edge of Town	1959	3.75	7.50	15.00
SUN					
❑ 291	Ten Years/Your Lover Boy	1958	6.25	12.50	25.00
❑ 311	The Black Haired Man/Wrong	1958	6.25	12.50	25.00

Albums

Number	Title (A Side/B Side)	Yr	VG	VG+	NM
ELEKTRA					
❑ 6E-122	All I Want to Do in Life	1978	3.00	6.00	12.00

CLEMENTS, BOOTS

45s

Number	Title (A Side/B Side)	Yr	VG	VG+	NM
WEST					
❑ 705	Back to You/(Instrumental)	1984	—	3.00	6.00
—As "George Clements"					
❑ 709	Morning Love/(I Guess I'm) On the Road Again	1984	—	3.00	6.00
—As "George Clements"					
❑ 711	Back to You/Morning Love	1985	—	3.00	6.00
❑ 715	So Long Lady/My World's Just Made for You	1985	—	3.00	6.00
❑ 716	Ghost Riders in the Sky/Ghost Rider's Symphony	1985	—	3.00	6.00
❑ 718	I Can't Find Me/I Keep Thinkin' Bout You Everyday	1986	—	3.00	6.00
❑ 719	Sukiyaki "My First Lonely Night"/The Other Side of Love	1986	—	3.00	6.00
❑ 721	You Can Have Her/So Long Lady	1986	—	3.00	6.00
❑ 728	The Night Has a Thousand Eyes/So Long Lady	1987	—	3.00	6.00

CLEMENTS, VASSAR

45s

Number	Title (A Side/B Side)	Yr	VG	VG+	NM
FLYING FISH					
❑ 4004	There'll Be No Teardrops Tonight/Move	1980	—	3.00	6.00
MCA					
❑ 40776	Jessica/Don't Mess with My Funk	1977	—	2.50	5.00
MERCURY					
❑ 73677	Night Train/Listen to the Mockingbird	1975	—	2.50	5.00
❑ 73748	Barnyard Boogie/Yakety Bow	1975	—	2.50	5.00
SHIKATA					
❑ 10102	I Hear the South/(B-side unknown)	1988	—	3.00	6.00

Albums

Number	Title (A Side/B Side)	Yr	VG	VG+	NM
FLYING FISH					
❑ 038	Bluegrass Session	197?	2.50	5.00	10.00
❑ 073	Nashville Jam	197?	3.00	6.00	12.00
❑ 101 [(2)]	Hillbilly Jazz	197?	3.75	7.50	15.00
❑ 232	Vassar	1980	2.50	5.00	10.00
❑ 385	Hillbilly Jazz Rides Again	1986	2.50	5.00	10.00
MCA					
❑ 695	Vassar Clements Band	198?	2.00	4.00	8.00
—Budget-line reissue of 2270					
❑ 2270	Vassar Clements Band	1977	3.75	7.50	15.00
MERCURY					
❑ SRM-1-1022	Vassar Clements	1975	3.00	6.00	12.00
❑ SRM-1-1058	Superbow	1975	3.00	6.00	12.00
MIND DUST					
❑ MDM 1002	Westport Drive	1984	3.00	6.00	12.00
ROUNDER					
❑ 0016	Crossing the Catskills	198?	3.00	6.00	12.00

CLIFFORD, BUZZ

45s

Number	Title (A Side/B Side)	Yr	VG	VG+	NM
A&M					
❑ 878	Just Can't Wait/On My Way	1967	2.50	5.00	10.00
CAPITOL					
❑ 5880	Bored to Tears/Swing in My Back Yard	1967	2.50	5.00	10.00
COLUMBIA					
❑ 41774	Hello, Mr. Moonlight/Blue Lagoon	1960	5.00	10.00	20.00
❑ 41876	Baby Sitter Boogie/Driftwood	1960	6.25	12.50	25.00
❑ 41876	Baby Sittin' Boogie/Driftwood	1960	5.00	10.00	20.00
❑ 41876 [PS]	Baby Sittin' Boogie/Driftwood	1960	12.50	25.00	50.00
❑ 41979	Three Little Fishes/Just Because	1961	5.00	10.00	20.00
❑ 41979 [PS]	Three Little Fishes/Just Because	1961	12.50	25.00	50.00
❑ 42019	I'll Never Forget/The Awakening	1961	12.50	25.00	50.00
❑ 42019 [PS]	I'll Never Forget/The Awakening	1961	20.00	40.00	80.00
❑ 42177	Moving Day/Loneliness	1961	5.00	10.00	20.00
❑ 42177 [PS]	Moving Day/Loneliness	1961	12.50	25.00	50.00
❑ 42290	Forever/Magic Circle	1962	6.25	12.50	25.00
❑ 42290 [PS]	Forever/Magic Circle	1962	12.50	25.00	50.00
DOT					
❑ 17329	(Baby I Could Be) So Good At Loving You/Children Are Crying Aloud	1970	—	3.00	6.00
❑ 17344	Procter and Gunther/I Am the River	1971	—	3.00	6.00
RCA VICTOR					
❑ 47-8935	Until Then/Let Her Go (It's All Right)	1966	3.00	6.00	12.00
ROULETTE					
❑ 4451	No One Loves Me Like You Do/More Dead Than Alive	1962	3.75	7.50	15.00

CLINE, PATSY

45s

Number	Title (A Side/B Side)	Yr	VG	VG+	NM
4 STAR					
❑ 1033	Life's Railway to Heaven/If I Could See the World	1978	—	2.50	5.00
CORAL					
❑ 61464	A Church, a Courtroom, Then Goodbye/Honky Tonk Merry-Go-Round	1955	7.50	15.00	30.00
❑ 61523	Turn the Cards Slowly/Hidin' Out	1955	7.50	15.00	30.00
❑ 61583	I Love You Honey/Come Right In	1956	6.25	12.50	25.00
DECCA					
❑ 29963	Stop, Look and Listen/I've Loved and Lost Again	1956	5.00	10.00	20.00
❑ 30221	Walkin' After Midnight/A Poor Man's Roses (Or a Rich Man's Gold)	1957	5.00	10.00	20.00
❑ 30221 [PS]	Walkin' After Midnight/A Poor Man's Roses (Or a Rich Man's Gold)	1957	20.00	40.00	80.00
❑ 30339	Try Again/Today, Tomorrow and Forever	1957	3.75	7.50	15.00
❑ 30406	Three Cigarettes in an Ashtray/A Stranger in My Arms	1957	3.75	7.50	15.00
❑ 30504	I Don't Wanta/Then You'll Know	1957	3.75	7.50	15.00
❑ 30542	Stop the World/Walking Dream	1958	3.75	7.50	15.00
❑ 30659	Come On In/Let the Teardrops Fall	1958	3.75	7.50	15.00
❑ 30706	Never No More/I Can See an Angel	1958	3.75	7.50	15.00
❑ 30746	Just Out of Reach (Of My Two Open Arms)/If I Could See The World	1958	3.75	7.50	15.00
❑ 30794	Dear God/He Will Do for You	1958	3.75	7.50	15.00
❑ 30846	Yes, I Understand/Cry Not for Me	1959	3.75	7.50	15.00
❑ 30929	Got a Lot of Rhythm in My Soul/I'm Blue Again	1959	5.00	10.00	20.00
❑ 31061	Lovesick Blues/How Can I Face Tomorrow	1960	3.00	6.00	12.00
❑ 31128	There He Goes/Crazy Dream	1960	3.00	6.00	12.00
❑ 31205	I Fall to Pieces/Lovin' in Vain	1961	3.00	6.00	12.00
❑ 31317	Crazy/Who Can I Count On	1961	3.00	6.00	12.00
❑ 31354	She's Got You/Strange	1962	3.00	6.00	12.00
❑ 31377	When I Get Thru with You (You'll Love Me Too)/Imagine That	1962	3.00	6.00	12.00
❑ 31377 [PS]	When I Get Thru with You (You'll Love Me Too)/Imagine That	1962	6.25	12.50	25.00
❑ 31406	So Wrong/You're Stronger Than Me	1962	3.00	6.00	12.00
❑ 31429	Heartaches/Why Can't He Be You	1962	3.00	6.00	12.00
❑ 31455	Leavin' On Your Mind/Tra Le La Le La Triangle	1963	2.50	5.00	10.00
❑ 31455 [PS]	Leavin' On Your Mind/Tra Le La Le La Triangle	1963	6.25	12.50	25.00
❑ 31483	Sweet Dreams (Of You)/Back in Baby's Arms	1963	2.50	5.00	10.00
❑ 31522	Faded Love/Blue Moon of Kentucky	1963	2.50	5.00	10.00
❑ 31552	When You Need a Laugh/I'll Sail My Ship Alone	1963	2.50	5.00	10.00
❑ 31588	Your Kinda Love/Someday You'll Want Me to Love You	1964	2.50	5.00	10.00
❑ 31616	Love Letters in the Sand/That's How a Heartache Begins	1964	2.50	5.00	10.00
❑ 31671	He Called Me Baby/Bill Bailey Won't You Please Come Home	1964	2.50	5.00	10.00
❑ 31754	Your Cheatin' Heart/I Can't Help It (If I'm Still in Love with You)	1965	2.50	5.00	10.00
❑ 34130 [S]	Foolin' 'Round/The Wayward Wind	1962	5.00	10.00	20.00
❑ 34131 [S]	South of the Border (Down Mexico Way)/I Love You So Much It Hurts	1962	5.00	10.00	20.00
❑ 34132 [S]	Crazy/Seven Lonely Days	1962	6.25	12.50	25.00
❑ 34133 [S]	San Antonio Rose/True Love	1962	5.00	10.00	20.00
—The above four are 33 1/3, small hole jukebox singles					
EVEREST					
❑ 2011	Then You'll Know/Hungry for Love	1963	3.00	6.00	12.00
❑ 2020	Walking After Midnight/That Wonderful Someone	1963	3.00	6.00	12.00
❑ 2031	I Can See an Angel/Just Out of Reach	1963	3.00	6.00	12.00
❑ 2039	I've Loved and Lost Again/I Love You Honey	1964	2.50	5.00	10.00
❑ 2045	In Care of the Blues/If I Could See the World (Through the Eyes of a Child)	1964	2.50	5.00	10.00
❑ 2052	Got a Lot of Rhythm (In My Soul)/Love Me, Love Me, Honey Do	1964	2.50	5.00	10.00
❑ 2060	Crazy Dream/There He Goes	1965	2.50	5.00	10.00
❑ 20005	I Don't Wanta/I Can't Forget	1962	3.75	7.50	15.00
KAPP					
❑ 659	Just a Closer Walk with Thee	1965	3.75	7.50	15.00
—One-sided release, possibly promo only					
MCA					
❑ 41303	Always/I Sail My Ship Alone	1980	—	2.00	4.00
❑ 51038	I Fall to Pieces/True Love	1980	—	2.00	4.00
❑ 52052	So Wrong/I Fall to Pieces	1982	—	—	3.00
—A-side: With Jim Reeves (electronically created duet)					
❑ 52684	Sweet Dreams/Blue Moon of Kentucky	1985	—	—	3.00
RCA					
❑ PB-12346	Have You Ever Been Lonely (Have You Ever Been Blue)/Welcome to My World	1981	—	—	3.00
—With Jim Reeves (electronically created duet)					
STARDAY					
❑ 7030	Walking After Midnight/Lovesick Blues	1965	2.50	5.00	10.00
❑ 8024	Walking After Midnight/Lovesick Blues	1971	—	3.00	6.00

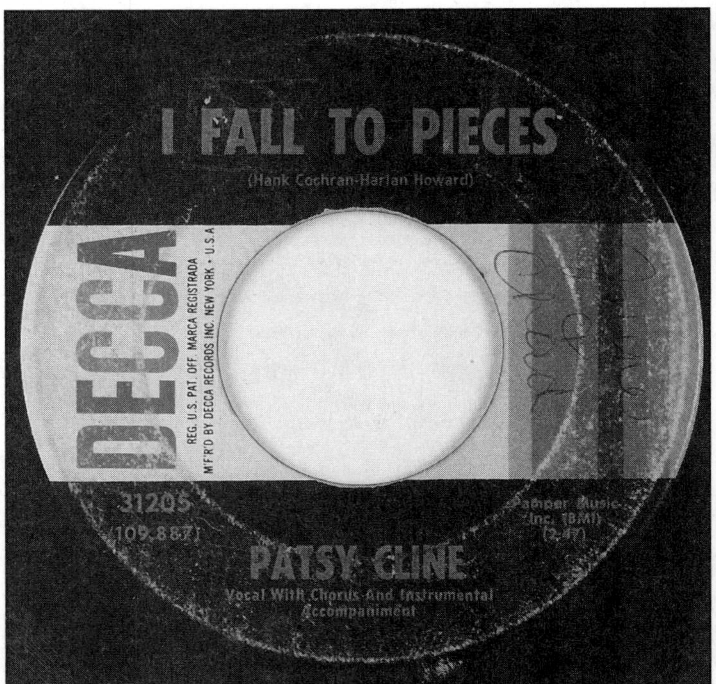

During her short life, which ended in a plane crash on March 5, 1963, Patsy Cline had only nine hits make the country charts. But the public fascination with her continues unabated; she's been immortalized in film (*Sweet Dreams*) and is one of the few country acts with a truly worthy U.S.-produced CD box set of her career. (Top left) Patsy's first album, a collection of material Decca leased from the 4 Star label, is quite rare in its original pressing on the black label with all-silver print. (Top right) Some of her earliest singles were issued on the Coral label. In 1957, after she had her first hit, "Walkin' After Midnight," Coral compiled this tough-to-find EP of older material. (Bottom left) Finally, in 1961, Patsy broke through in a big way once she was signed directly to Decca rather than 4 Star. "I Fall to Pieces" was a massive hit, as it hit No. 1 on the country charts and No. 12 pop. She would continue to cross over until her death. (Bottom right) Her biggest pop hit, which peaked at No. 9, was "Crazy," written by Willie Nelson. On the country charts, it "only" got as high as No. 2.

Selected 78s

DECCA

Number	Title (A Side/B Side)	Yr	VG	VG+	NM
❑ 30221	Walkin' After Midnight/A Poor Man's Roses (Or a Rich Man's Gold)	1957	25.00	50.00	100.00

7-Inch Extended Plays

CORAL

Number	Title (A Side/B Side)	Yr	VG	VG+	NM
❑ EC 81159	(contents unknown)	1958	6.25	12.50	25.00
❑ EC 81159 [PS]	Songs by Patsy Cline	1958	7.50	15.00	30.00

DECCA

Number	Title (A Side/B Side)	Yr	VG	VG+	NM
❑ ED 2542	(contents unknown)	1958	5.00	10.00	20.00
❑ ED 2542 [PS]	Patsy Cline	1958	5.00	10.00	20.00
❑ ED 2703	(contents unknown)	1961	3.75	7.50	15.00
❑ ED 2703 [PS]	Patsy Cline	1961	3.75	7.50	15.00
❑ ED 2707	(contents unknown)	1961	3.75	7.50	15.00
❑ ED 2707 [PS]	Patsy Cline	1961	3.75	7.50	15.00
❑ ED 2719	(contents unknown)	1962	3.75	7.50	15.00
❑ ED 2719 [PS]	Patsy Cline	1962	3.75	7.50	15.00
❑ ED 2729	So Wrong/You're Stronger Than Me//Heartaches/Your Cheatin' Heart	1962	3.75	7.50	15.00
❑ ED 2729 [PS]	Patsy Cline	1962	3.75	7.50	15.00
❑ ED 2757	(contents unknown)	1963	3.75	7.50	15.00
❑ ED 2757 [PS]	Patsy Cline	1963	3.75	7.50	15.00
❑ ED 2759	Just a Closer Walk with Thee/Life's Railroad to Heaven//Dear God/He Will Do for You	1963	3.75	7.50	15.00
❑ ED 2759 [PS]	Dear God	1963	3.75	7.50	15.00
❑ ED 2768	I'm Blue Again/How Can I Face Tomorrow//I'm Moving Along/Love Love Love Me Honey Do	1964	3.75	7.50	15.00
❑ ED 2768 [PS]	Patsy Cline	1964	3.75	7.50	15.00
❑ ED 2770	Someday You'll Want Me to Want You/Faded Love//When You Need a Laugh/I'll Sail My Ship Alone	1964	3.75	7.50	15.00
❑ ED 2770 [PS]	Someday You'll Want Me to Want You	1964	3.75	7.50	15.00
❑ ED 2794	(contents unknown)	1965	3.75	7.50	15.00
❑ ED 2794 [PS]	Portrait of Patsy Cline	1965	3.75	7.50	15.00
❑ ED 2802	(contents unknown)	1965	3.75	7.50	15.00
❑ ED 2802 [PS]	Love Letters in the Sand	1965	3.75	7.50	15.00

PATSY CLINE

Number	Title (A Side/B Side)	Yr	VG	VG+	NM
❑ EPF-16	Try Again/Turn the Cards Slowly//Come On In/Stop Look and Listen	195?	10.00	20.00	40.00
❑ EPF-16 [PS]	(title unknown)	195?	10.00	20.00	40.00
❑ EP-21	Three Cigarettes/Hungry for Love//Fingerprints/That Wonderful Someone	195?	10.00	20.00	40.00
❑ EP-21 [PS]	(title unknown)	195?	10.00	20.00	40.00

Albums

ACCORD

Number	Title (A Side/B Side)	Yr	VG	VG+	NM
❑ SN-7153	Let the Teardrops Fall	1981	2.50	5.00	10.00

ALLEGIANCE

Number	Title (A Side/B Side)	Yr	VG	VG+	NM
❑ AV-5021	Stop, Look and Listen	198?	2.50	5.00	10.00

DECCA

Number	Title (A Side/B Side)	Yr	VG	VG+	NM
❑ DXB 176 [(2) M]	The Patsy Cline Story	1963	10.00	20.00	40.00
❑ DL 4202 [M]	Patsy Cline Showcase	1961	10.00	20.00	40.00
❑ DL 4282 [M]	Sentimentally Yours	1962	7.50	15.00	30.00
❑ DL 4508 [M]	A Portrait of Patsy Cline	1964	7.50	15.00	30.00
❑ DL 4586 [M]	That's How a Heartache Begins	1964	7.50	15.00	30.00
❑ DL 4854 [M]	Patsy Cline's Greatest Hits	1967	5.00	10.00	20.00
❑ DXSB 7176 [(2) S]	The Patsy Cline Story	1963	12.50	25.00	50.00
❑ DL 8611 [M]	Patsy Cline	1957	25.00	50.00	100.00
—Black label with silver print					
❑ DL 8611 [M]	Patsy Cline	1960	12.50	25.00	50.00
—Black label with color bars					
❑ DL 74202 [S]	Patsy Cline Showcase	1961	12.50	25.00	50.00
❑ DL 74282 [S]	Sentimentally Yours	1962	10.00	20.00	40.00
❑ DL 74508 [S]	A Portrait of Patsy Cline	1964	10.00	20.00	40.00
❑ DL 74586 [S]	That's How a Heartache Begins	1964	10.00	20.00	40.00
❑ DL 74854 [S]	Patsy Cline's Greatest Hits	1967	6.25	12.50	25.00

EVEREST

Number	Title (A Side/B Side)	Yr	VG	VG+	NM
❑ 1200 [R]	Golden Hits	1962	3.00	6.00	12.00
❑ 1204 [R]	Encores	1962	3.00	6.00	12.00
❑ 1217 [R]	In Memoriam	1963	3.00	6.00	12.00
❑ 1229 [R]	Reflections	1964	3.00	6.00	12.00
❑ 5200 [M]	Golden Hits	1962	5.00	10.00	20.00
❑ 5204 [M]	Encores	1962	5.00	10.00	20.00
❑ 5217 [M]	In Memoriam	1963	5.00	10.00	20.00
❑ 5223 [M]	Legend	1963	5.00	10.00	20.00
❑ 5229 [M]	Reflections	1964	5.00	10.00	20.00

HILLTOP

Number	Title (A Side/B Side)	Yr	VG	VG+	NM
❑ 6001 [M]	Today, Tomorrow, Forever	1965	3.00	6.00	12.00
❑ S-6001 [R]	Today, Tomorrow, Forever	1965	2.50	5.00	10.00
❑ 6016 [M]	I Can't Forget You	1966	3.00	6.00	12.00
❑ S-6016 [R]	I Can't Forget You	1966	2.50	5.00	10.00
❑ S-6039	Stop the World	1968	2.50	5.00	10.00
❑ S-6072	In Care of the Blues	1969	2.50	5.00	10.00
❑ 6148	Country Music Hall of Fame	197?	2.50	5.00	10.00

MCA

Number	Title (A Side/B Side)	Yr	VG	VG+	NM
❑ 12	Patsy Cline's Greatest Hits	1973	3.00	6.00	12.00
—Reissue of Decca 74854; black label with rainbow					
❑ 12	Patsy Cline's Greatest Hits	1977	2.50	5.00	10.00
—Tan label					
❑ 12	Patsy Cline's Greatest Hits	1980	2.00	4.00	8.00
—Blue label with rainbow					
❑ 87	Patsy Cline Showcase	1973	3.00	6.00	12.00
—Reissue of Decca 74202; black label with rainbow					
❑ 90	Sentimentally Yours	1973	3.00	6.00	12.00
—Reissue of Decca 74282; black label with rainbow					
❑ 224	A Portrait of Patsy Cline	1973	3.00	6.00	12.00
—Reissue of Decca 74508; black label with rainbow					
❑ 736	The Great Patsy Cline	198?	2.50	5.00	10.00
—Reissue of Vocalion 73872					
❑ 738	Here's Patsy Cline	198?	2.50	5.00	10.00
—Reissue of Vocalion 73753					
❑ 1440	Stop, Look and Listen	198?	2.00	4.00	8.00
❑ 1463	Today, Tomorrow and Forever	198?	2.00	4.00	8.00
❑ 3263	Always	1980	3.75	7.50	15.00
❑ 4038 [(2)]	The Patsy Cline Story	1974	3.75	7.50	15.00
—Reissue of Decca 7176;; black labels with rainbow					
❑ 6149	Sweet Dreams — The Life and Times of Patsy Cline	1985	2.50	5.00	10.00
❑ 27069	Always	198?	2.00	4.00	8.00
❑ 42142	Live at the Opry	1988	2.50	5.00	10.00
❑ 42284	Live Volume 2	1989	3.00	6.00	12.00

METRO

Number	Title (A Side/B Side)	Yr	VG	VG+	NM
❑ M-540 [M]	Gotta Lot of Rhythm in My Soul	1965	3.00	6.00	12.00
❑ MS-540 [R]	Gotta Lot of Rhythm in My Soul	1965	2.50	5.00	10.00

RHINO

Number	Title (A Side/B Side)	Yr	VG	VG+	NM
❑ R1-70048	Her First Recordings, Vol. 1: Walkin' Dreams	1989	3.00	6.00	12.00
❑ R1-70049	Her First Recordings, Vol. 2: Hungry for Love	1989	3.00	6.00	12.00
❑ R1-70050	Her First Recordings, Vol. 3: The Rockin' Side	1989	3.00	6.00	12.00

SEARS

Number	Title (A Side/B Side)	Yr	VG	VG+	NM
❑ SPS-127	In Care of the Blues	1968	6.25	12.50	25.00

VOCALION

Number	Title (A Side/B Side)	Yr	VG	VG+	NM
❑ VL 3753 [M]	Here's Patsy Cline	1965	3.00	6.00	12.00
❑ VL 73753 [R]	Here's Patsy Cline	1965	2.50	5.00	10.00
❑ VL 73872	Country Great!	1969	2.50	5.00	10.00

CLOONEY, ROSEMARY

Curiously, this single by the pop singer came out on Columbia's country series.

45s

COLUMBIA

Number	Title (A Side/B Side)	Yr	VG	VG+	NM
❑ 4-21423	Go On By/I Whsiper Your Name	1955	6.25	12.50	25.00

CLOWER, JERRY

45s

DECCA

Number	Title (A Side/B Side)	Yr	VG	VG+	NM
❑ 32844	Coon Huntin' City/Marcel's Talking Chainsaw/Homecomin' Steaks	1971	—	3.00	6.00
❑ 32899	A Bully Has Done Flung a Cravin' On Me/The Chauffeur and the Professor	1971	—	3.00	6.00
❑ 32993	Knock Him Out John/The Meek Shall Inherit the Earth	1972	—	3.00	6.00

MCA

Number	Title (A Side/B Side)	Yr	VG	VG+	NM
❑ 40077	I'm That Country//Marcel Says No School Today/Marcel Wins a Bet/Three Footballs and the Game Ain't Fair	1973	—	3.00	6.00
❑ 40292	New Bull/She Cow of Women's Lib	1974	—	3.00	6.00
❑ 40423	Bird Huntin' at Uncle Versies/Coon Huntin' Monkey	1975	—	3.00	6.00
❑ 40599	Wanna Buy a Possum/The House I Live In	1976	—	2.50	5.00
❑ 40774	Steel Marbles/Tar Baby-New Gene and the Lion	1977	—	2.50	5.00
❑ 41261	The Ike and Mike Contest/Udell and Ole Skeets	1980	—	2.50	5.00

Albums

DECCA

Number	Title (A Side/B Side)	Yr	VG	VG+	NM
❑ DL 75286	From Yazoo City, Mississippi Talkin'	1971	3.00	6.00	12.00
❑ DL 75342	Mouth of Mississippi	1972	3.00	6.00	12.00

MCA

Number	Title (A Side/B Side)	Yr	VG	VG+	NM
❑ 33	From Yazoo City, Mississippi Talkin'	1973	2.50	5.00	10.00
—Reissue of Decca 75286					
❑ 47	Mouth of Mississippi	1973	2.50	5.00	10.00
—Reissue of Decca 75342					
❑ 317	Clower Power	1973	2.50	5.00	10.00
❑ 417	Country Ham	1974	2.50	5.00	10.00
❑ 486	Live in Picayune	1975	2.50	5.00	10.00
❑ 2205	The Ambassador of Goodwill	1976	2.50	5.00	10.00
❑ 2281	On the Road	1978	2.50	5.00	10.00
❑ 3062	Live from the Stage of the Grand Ole Opry!	1979	2.50	5.00	10.00
❑ 3152	Greatest Hits	1979	2.50	5.00	10.00
❑ 3247	The Ledbetter Olympics	1980	2.50	5.00	10.00
❑ 5215	More Good 'Uns	1981	2.50	5.00	10.00
❑ 5321	Dogs I Have Known	1982	2.50	5.00	10.00
❑ 5422	Live at Cleburne, Texas	1983	2.50	5.00	10.00
❑ 5491	Starke Raving	1984	2.50	5.00	10.00
❑ 5602	An Officer and a Ledbetter	1985	2.50	5.00	10.00
❑ 5773	Runaway Truck	1986	2.50	5.00	10.00
❑ 42034	Top Gum	1987	2.50	5.00	10.00
❑ 42178	Classic Clower	1988	2.50	5.00	10.00

WORD

Number	Title (A Side/B Side)	Yr	VG	VG+	NM
❑ WSB-8737	Ain't God Good!	197?	3.00	6.00	12.00

COCHRAN, ANITA

45s

WARNER BROS.

Number	Title (A Side/B Side)	Yr	VG	VG+	NM
❑ 7-16872	Good Times/Girls Like Fast Cars	2000	—	—	3.00
❑ 7-16939	For Crying Out Loud/What If I Said (duet with Steve Wariner)	1999	—	—	3.00
❑ 7-17263	What If I Said (duet with Steve Wariner)/Daddy Can You See Me	1997	—	2.50	5.00
❑ 7-17486	I Could Love a Man Like That/Wrong Side of Town	1997	—	—	3.00

COCHRAN, CLIFF

45s

ENTERPRISE

Number	Title (A Side/B Side)	Yr	VG	VG+	NM
❑ 9103	The Way I'm Needing You/Hearts Are Like That, Yes They Are	1974	—	3.00	6.00
❑ 9109	All the Love You'll Ever Need/I'd Do As Much for You	1974	—	3.00	6.00
❑ 9112	She's Only Lonely/Summer Song	1975	—	3.00	6.00

RCA

Number	Title (A Side/B Side)	Yr	VG	VG+	NM
❑ PB-11562	Love Me Like a Stranger/The Rose Is for Today	1979	—	2.00	4.00
❑ PB-11711	First Thing Each Morning (Last Thing at Night)/100% Chance of Love Tonight	1979	—	2.00	4.00

COCHRAN, HANK

Also see COCHRAN BROTHERS.

45s

CAPITOL

Number	Title (A Side/B Side)	Yr	VG	VG+	NM
❑ 4585	Willie/Uphill All the Way	1978	—	2.00	4.00

DOT

Number	Title (A Side/B Side)	Yr	VG	VG+	NM
❑ 17361	One Night for Willie/Back to His	1970	—	3.00	6.00

ELEKTRA

Number	Title (A Side/B Side)	Yr	VG	VG+	NM
❑ 46596	Make the World Go Away/I Don't Do Windows	1980	—	2.00	4.00
❑ 47062	A Little Bitty Tear/He's Got You	1980	—	2.00	4.00

GAYLORD

Number	Title (A Side/B Side)	Yr	VG	VG+	NM
❑ 6426	Yesterday's Memories/When You Gotta Go	1963	3.00	6.00	12.00
❑ 6431	A Good Country Song/Same Old Hurt	1963	3.00	6.00	12.00

LIBERTY

Number	Title (A Side/B Side)	Yr	VG	VG+	NM
❑ 55402	Lonely Little Mansion/Has Anybody Seen Me Lately	1962	3.00	6.00	12.00
❑ 55461	Sally Was a Good Old Girl/The Picture Behind the Picture	1962	3.00	6.00	12.00
❑ 55498	I'd Fight the World/Lucy, Let Your Lovelight Shine	1962	3.00	6.00	12.00
❑ 55520	I Remember/Private John Q	1963	2.50	5.00	10.00
❑ 55644	Tootsie's Orchid Lounge/Go On Home	1963	2.50	5.00	10.00

MONUMENT

Number	Title (A Side/B Side)	Yr	VG	VG+	NM
❑ 994	All of Me Belongs to You/I Just Burned a Dream	1967	—	3.00	6.00
❑ 1012	It Couldn't Happen to a Nicer Guy/Tootsie's Orchid Lounge	1967	—	3.00	6.00
❑ 1033	A Happy Goodbye/Speak Well of Me to the Kids	1967	—	3.00	6.00
❑ 1051	Has Anybody Seen Me Lately/I Woke Up	1968	—	3.00	6.00

RCA VICTOR

Number	Title (A Side/B Side)	Yr	VG	VG+	NM
❑ 47-8329	My Baby's His Baby Now/What Kind of Bird Is That	1964	2.50	5.00	10.00
❑ 47-8375	She Always Comes Back to Me/Your Country Boy	1964	2.50	5.00	10.00
❑ 47-8457	I Want to Go with You/Sad Songs and Waltzes	1964	2.50	5.00	10.00
❑ 47-8528	Somewhere in My Dreams/Going in Training	1965	2.50	5.00	10.00
❑ 47-8616	Who's Gonna/Let's Be Different	1965	2.50	5.00	10.00
❑ 47-8694	Hank Today and Him Tomorrow/I'm Alone	1965	2.50	5.00	10.00
❑ 47-8827	The Crying Section/Only You Can Make Me Well	1966	2.00	4.00	8.00
❑ 47-8955	That's What I'll Say/I Lie a Lot	1966	2.00	4.00	8.00

Albums

CAPITOL

Number	Title (A Side/B Side)	Yr	VG	VG+	NM
❑ ST-11807	With a Little Help from His Friends	1978	3.00	6.00	12.00

ELEKTRA

Number	Title (A Side/B Side)	Yr	VG	VG+	NM
❑ 6E-277	Make the World Go Away	1980	2.50	5.00	10.00

MONUMENT

Number	Title (A Side/B Side)	Yr	VG	VG+	NM
❑ SLP-18089	The Heart of Hank	1968	5.00	10.00	20.00

RCA VICTOR

Number	Title (A Side/B Side)	Yr	VG	VG+	NM
❑ LPM-3303 [M]	Hits from the Heart	1965	5.00	10.00	20.00
❑ LSP-3303 [S]	Hits from the Heart	1965	6.25	12.50	25.00
❑ LPM-3431 [M]	Going in Training	1965	5.00	10.00	20.00
❑ LSP-3431 [S]	Going in Training	1965	6.25	12.50	25.00

COCHRAN, HANK, AND WILLIE NELSON

Also see each artist's individual listings.

45s

CAPITOL

Number	Title (A Side/B Side)	Yr	VG	VG+	NM
❑ 4635	Ain't Life Hell/I'm Going With You This Time	1978	—	2.50	5.00

COCHRAN BROTHERS

Also see HANK COCHRAN.

45s

EKKO

Number	Title (A Side/B Side)	Yr	VG	VG+	NM
❑ 1003	Mr. Fiddle/Two Blue Singing Stars	1955	62.50	125.00	250.00
❑ 1005	Guilty Conscience/Your Tomorrow Never Comes	1955	62.50	125.00	250.00
❑ 3001	Tired and Sleepy/Fool's Paradise	1956	75.00	150.00	300.00

CODY, BETTY

45s

RCA VICTOR

Number	Title (A Side/B Side)	Yr	VG	VG+	NM
❑ 47-5263	Jealous Love/I'm Talkin', Start Walkin'	1953	5.00	10.00	20.00
—With Hal Lone Pine					
❑ 47-5376	Pale Moon/I Hate Myself for Loving You So Much	1953	5.00	10.00	20.00
❑ 47-5462	I Found Out More Than You'll Ever Know/Don't Believe Everything You Read	1953	5.00	10.00	20.00
❑ 47-5519	Keep Your Promise Willie Thomas/Phonograph Record	1953	5.00	10.00	20.00
❑ 47-5600	Please Throw Away the Glass/You Can't Feel the Way I Do	1954	5.00	10.00	20.00
❑ 47-5705	A Letter I Never Should Have Mailed/The Kiss That Made a Fool of Me	1954	5.00	10.00	20.00
❑ 47-5811	Dear Sister/Can You Live with Yourself	1954	5.00	10.00	20.00
❑ 47-5869	Heart to Heart/How to Get Married	1954	5.00	10.00	20.00
—With Hal Lone Pine					
❑ 47-5926	Always a Bridesmaid/You Want More of Me	1954	5.00	10.00	20.00
❑ 47-5991	Tell It Right/Butterfly Heart	1955	5.00	10.00	20.00
—With Hal Lone Pine					

COE, DAVID ALLAN

45s

COLUMBIA

Number	Title (A Side/B Side)	Yr	VG	VG+	NM
❑ 11-02118	Tennessee Whiskey/The Bottle (In My Hand)	1981	—	2.00	4.00
❑ 18-02492	(Sittin' On) The Dock of the Bay/I Love Robbin's Trains	1981	—	2.00	4.00
❑ 18-02612	Juanita/I'll Always Be a Fool for You	1981	—	2.00	4.00
❑ 18-02678	Now I Lay Me Down to Cheat/If I Knew	1981	—	2.00	4.00
❑ 18-02815	Take Time to Know Her/London Homesick Blues	1982	—	2.00	4.00
❑ 18-03022	What Made You Change Your Mind/Pouring Water on a Drowning Man	1982	—	2.00	4.00
❑ 13-03129	Jack Daniel's, If You Please/Tennessee Whiskey	1982	—	—	3.00
—Hall of Fame Series reissue					
❑ 38-03343	Whiskey, Whiskey (Take My Mind)/Those Low Down Blues	1982	—	2.00	4.00
❑ 38-03778	The Ride/Son of a Rebel Son	1983	—	2.00	4.00
❑ 38-03997	Cheap Thrills/You Never Even Call Me by My Name	1983	—	2.00	4.00
❑ 38-03997 [PS]	Cheap Thrills/You Never Even Call Me by My Name	1983	—	3.00	6.00
❑ 38-04136	Crazy Old Soldier/Drinkin' to Forget	1983	—	2.00	4.00
❑ 38-04396	Mona Lisa Lost Her Smile/Someone Special	1984	—	2.00	4.00
❑ 38-04553	It's Great to Be Single Again/Sweet Angeline	1984	—	2.00	4.00
❑ 38-04688	She Used to Love Me a Lot/For Lovers Only (Part IV)	1984	—	2.00	4.00
❑ 38-04846	Don't Cry Darlin'/You're the Only Song I Sing Today	1985	—	2.00	4.00
❑ 38-05451	My Elusive Dreams/Call Me the Breeze	1985	—	2.00	4.00
❑ 38-05631	I'm Gonna Hurt Her on the Radio/He Has to Pay (For What I Get for Free)	1985	—	2.00	4.00
❑ 38-05876	A Country Boy (Who Rolled the Rock Away)/Take My Advice	1986	—	2.00	4.00
❑ 38-06227	I've Already Cheated on You/Take My Advice	1986	—	2.00	4.00
—A-side with Willie Nelson					
❑ 38-06394	Son of the South/Gemini Girl	1986	—	2.00	4.00
❑ 38-06661	Need a Little Time Off for Bad Behavior/It's a Matter of Life and Death	1987	—	2.00	4.00
❑ 38-07129	Tanya Montana/The Ten Commandments of Love	1987	—	2.00	4.00
❑ 38-08527	Love Is a Never Ending War/Action Speaks Louder Than Words	1989	—	2.00	4.00
❑ 3-10024	(If I Could Climb) The Walls of the Bottle/Another Pretty Country Song	1974	—	2.50	5.00
❑ 3-10093	Would You Be My Lady/Rock and Roll Holiday	1975	—	2.50	5.00
❑ 3-10159	You Never Even Call Me By My Name/Would You Lay with Me (In a Field of Stone)	1975	—	3.00	6.00
❑ 3-10254	Longhaired Redneck/Family Reunion	1975	—	2.50	5.00
❑ 3-10323	When She's Got Me (Where She Wants Me)/Living on the Run	1976	—	2.50	5.00
❑ 3-10395	Willie, Waylon and Me/Please Come to Boston	1976	—	2.50	5.00
❑ 3-10475	Lately I've Been Thinking Too Much Lately/Under Rachel's Wings	1977	—	2.50	5.00
❑ 3-10583	Just to Prove My Love for You/Play Me a Sad Song	1977	—	2.50	5.00
❑ 3-10621	Face to Face/Play Me a Sad Song	1977	—	2.50	5.00
❑ 3-10701	Divers Do It Deeper/Million Dollar Memories	1978	—	2.50	5.00
❑ 3-10753	You Can Count on Me/Bad Impressions	1978	—	2.50	5.00
❑ 3-10816	If This Is Just a Game/Tomorrow's Another Day	1978	—	2.50	5.00
❑ 3-10860	Bright Morning Light/Suicide	1978	—	2.50	5.00
❑ 3-10911	Jack Daniel's, If You Please/Human Emotions	1979	—	2.50	5.00
❑ 1-11098	X's and O's (Kisses and Hugs)/Gone (Like)	1979	—	2.50	5.00
❑ 1-11167	Loving You Comes So Natural/Lost	1979	—	2.50	5.00
—With Johnny Rodriguez					
❑ 1-11277	Get a Little Dirt on Your Hands/What Can I Do	1980	—	2.50	5.00
—A-side with Bill Anderson					
❑ 1-11352	Hank Williams Jr., Jr./I've Got Something to Say	1980	—	2.50	5.00
❑ 4-46012	Sad Country Song/Atlantic Song	1974	—	3.00	6.00
❑ 11-60501	Stand By Your Man/Take This Job and Shove It	1981	—	2.00	4.00

KAT FAMILY

Number	Title (A Side/B Side)	Yr	VG	VG+	NM
❑ ZS4-04258	Ride 'Em Cowboy/Yesterday's Wine	1983	—	2.00	4.00

PLANTATION

Number	Title (A Side/B Side)	Yr	VG	VG+	NM
❑ 99	How High's the Watergate, Martha/Tricky Dicky, The Only Son of King Fu	1973	2.00	4.00	8.00
❑ 104	Keep Those Big Wheels Rolling/Memphis in My Blood	1973	2.00	4.00	8.00

SSS INTERNATIONAL

Number	Title (A Side/B Side)	Yr	VG	VG+	NM
❑ 825	Tobacco Road/Death Row	1971	2.50	5.00	10.00
❑ 864	Two-Tone Brown/Funeral Parlor Blues	1972	2.50	5.00	10.00

Albums

COLUMBIA

Number	Title (A Side/B Side)	Yr	VG	VG+	NM
❑ KC 32942	Mysterious Rhinestone Cowboy	1974	3.00	6.00	12.00
❑ PC 32942	Mysterious Rhinestone Cowboy	197?	2.50	5.00	10.00
—Early reissue with new prefix and no bar code					
❑ KC 33085	Once Upon a Rhyme	1975	3.00	6.00	12.00
❑ PC 33085	Once Upon a Rhyme	197?	2.50	5.00	10.00
—Early reissue with new prefix and no bar code					
❑ PC 33916	Longhaired Redneck	1976	2.50	5.00	10.00
❑ PC 34310	David Allan Coe Rides Again	1977	2.50	5.00	10.00
❑ PC 34780	Tattoo	1977	2.50	5.00	10.00

Number	Title (A Side/B Side)	Yr	VG	VG+	NM
❑ KC 35306	Family Album	1978	2.50	5.00	10.00
❑ KC 35535	Human Emotions — Happy Side/Su-I-Side	1978	2.50	5.00	10.00
❑ KC 35627	Greatest Hits	1978	2.50	5.00	10.00
❑ PC 35627	Greatest Hits	198?	2.00	4.00	8.00
—Budget-line reissue					
❑ KC 35789	Spectrum, VII	1979	2.50	5.00	10.00
❑ JC 36277	Compass Point	1980	2.50	5.00	10.00
❑ PC 36277	Compass Point	198?	2.00	4.00	8.00
—Budget-line reissue with new prefix					
❑ JC 36489	I've Got Something to Say	1980	2.50	5.00	10.00
❑ PC 36489	I've Got Something to Say	198?	2.00	4.00	8.00
—Budget-line reissue with new prefix					
❑ JC 36970	Invictus (Means) Unconquered	1981	2.50	5.00	10.00
❑ PC 36970	Invictus (Means) Unconquered	198?	2.00	4.00	8.00
—Budget-line reissue with new prefix					
❑ FC 37352	Encore	1981	2.50	5.00	10.00
❑ PC 37352	Encore	198?	2.00	4.00	8.00
—Budget-line reissue with new prefix					
❑ FC 37454	Tennessee Whiskey	1981	2.50	5.00	10.00
❑ PC 37454	Tennessee Whiskey	198?	2.00	4.00	8.00
—Budget-line reissue with new prefix					
❑ FC 37736	Rough Rider	1982	2.50	5.00	10.00
❑ PC 37736	Rough Rider	198?	2.00	4.00	8.00
—Budget-line reissue with new prefix					
❑ FC 38093	D.A.C.	1982	2.50	5.00	10.00
❑ FC 38318	Biggest Hits	1982	2.50	5.00	10.00
❑ FC 38535	Castles in the Sand	1983	2.50	5.00	10.00
❑ PC 38535	Castles in the Sand	1985	2.00	4.00	8.00
—Budget-line reissue with new prefix					
❑ FC 38926	Hello In There	1983	2.50	5.00	10.00
❑ FC 39269	Just Divorced	1984	2.50	5.00	10.00
❑ PC 39269	Just Divorced	1986	2.00	4.00	8.00
—Budget-line reissue with new prefix					
❑ KC2 39585 [(2)]	For the Record — The First 10 Years	1984	3.00	6.00	12.00
❑ FC 39617	Darlin', Darlin'	1985	2.50	5.00	10.00
❑ FC 40195	Unchained	1985	2.50	5.00	10.00
❑ FC 40346	Son of the South	1986	2.50	5.00	10.00
❑ FC 40571	A Matter of Life... And Death	1987	2.50	5.00	10.00
❑ FC 45057	Crazy Daddy	1989	2.50	5.00	10.00
PAIR					
❑ PDL2-1075 [(2)]	Best of David Allan Coe	1986	3.00	6.00	12.00
PLANTATION					
❑ 507	Texas Moon	197?	3.75	7.50	15.00
SSS INTERNATIONAL					
❑ 9	Penitentiary Blues	1977	20.00	40.00	80.00

COHN, MARC

45s

ATLANTIC OLDIES SERIES

Number	Title (A Side/B Side)	Yr	VG	VG+	NM
❑ 7-84882	Walking in Memphis/Ghost Train	1993	—	2.50	5.00

—First U.S. issue of these tracks on 45 (they were from a 1991 album)

COHRON, PHIL

45s

AIR

Number	Title (A Side/B Side)	Yr	VG	VG+	NM
❑ 182	Across the Room from You/(B-side unknown)	1989	—	3.00	6.00

COIN, R.C.

45s

BGM

Number	Title (A Side/B Side)	Yr	VG	VG+	NM
❑ 82087	Bed of Roses/Confidential	1987	—	3.00	6.00

COLDER, BEN

See SHEB WOOLEY.

COLE, BRENDA

45s

MELODY DAWN

Number	Title (A Side/B Side)	Yr	VG	VG+	NM
❑ 77701	But I Never Do/Barefoot Lady	1987	—	2.50	5.00
❑ 77701 [PS]	But I Never Do/Barefoot Lady	1987	—	3.00	6.00
❑ 77702	Gone, Gone, Gone/(B-side unknown)	1987	—	2.50	5.00
❑ 77702 [PS]	Gone, Gone, Gone/(B-side unknown)	1987	—	3.00	6.00
❑ 77703	Boots (These Boots Are Made for Walkin')/Gone, Gone, Gone	1988	—	2.50	5.00

COLE, KING, TRIO

Interestingly, the below 78 made the country charts — and the A-side hit number 1!

Selected 78s

CAPITOL

Number	Title (A Side/B Side)	Yr	VG	VG+	NM
❑ 154	Straighten Up and Fly Right/I Can't See for Lookin'	1944	3.00	6.00	12.00

COLE, PATSY

45s

TRA-STAR

Number	Title (A Side/B Side)	Yr	VG	VG+	NM
❑ 1225	I Never Had a Chance with You/Morning Train	1989	—	2.50	5.00
❑ 1226	Death and Taxes (And Me Lovin' You)/Lead Me On	1989	—	2.50	5.00
❑ 1227	You and the Horse (That You Rode In On)/Lot of Getting Over You	1989	—	2.50	5.00

COLE, SAMI JO

See SAMI JO.

COLEMAN, ALBERT, 'S ATLANTA POPS

45s

Number	Title (A Side/B Side)	Yr	VG	VG+	NM
EPIC					
❑ 14-02938	Just Hooked on Country (Part I)/Just Hooked on Country (Part II)	1982	—	2.00	4.00
❑ 34-03215	Just Hooked on Country (Part III)/Rock Around the Country	1982	—	2.00	4.00
❑ 34-03362	Pop Goes the Country (Part I)/Old Cowboys Never Die	1982	—	2.00	4.00
❑ 34-03973	Classic Country (Part 1)/Boots' Yakety	1983	—	2.00	4.00
RCA VICTOR					
❑ 74-0502	Foggy Mountain Breakdown/Lonely Trumpet	1971	2.00	4.00	8.00
—As "Albert Coleman and the Music City Pops"					
SOUTHERN TRACKS					
❑ 1004	Just Hooked on Country (Part I)/Just Hooked on Country (Part II)	1982	2.50	5.00	10.00
❑ 1039	Old Time Religion (Part 1)/Old Time Religion (Part 2)	1985	—	2.50	5.00

Albums

EPIC

Number	Title (A Side/B Side)	Yr	VG	VG+	NM
❑ FE 38154	Just Hooked on Country	1982	2.00	4.00	8.00
❑ FE 38630	Classic Country	1983	2.00	4.00	8.00

COLLIE, MARK

45s

Number	Title (A Side/B Side)	Yr	VG	VG+	NM
COLUMBIA					
❑ 38-78236	Love to Burn/Oh King Richard	1996	—	2.00	4.00
—B-side by Kyle Petty					
GIANT					
❑ 7-17762	Steady As She Goes/Memories (Still Missing Her)	1995	—	—	3.00
❑ 7-17855	Three Words, Two Hearts, One Night/Tunica Motel	1995	—	—	3.00
MCA					
❑ 53778	Something with a Ring to It/Another Old Soldier	1989	—	2.00	4.00
❑ 53971	Let Her Go/Where There's Smoke	1991	—	2.00	4.00
❑ 54079	Calloused Hands/Johnny Was a Rebel	1991	—	—	3.00
❑ 54224	It Don't Take a Lot/Ballad of Thunder Road	1991	—	—	3.00
❑ 54244	She's Never Comin' Back/Lucky Dog	1991	—	2.00	4.00
❑ 54448	Even the Man in the Moon Is Crying/Trouble's Comin' Like a Train	1992	—	2.00	4.00
❑ 54515	Born to Love You/The Heart of the Matter	1992	—	—	3.00
❑ 54668	Shame Shame Shame Shame/Keep It Up	1993	—	2.00	4.00
❑ 54720	Something's Gonna Change Her Mind/Linda Lou	1993	—	—	3.00
❑ 54832	It Is No Secret/Rainy Day Woman	1994	—	—	3.00
❑ 54907	Hard Lovin' Woman/Ring of Fire	1994	—	—	3.00
❑ 79023	Looks Aren't Everything/Something with a Ring to It	1990	—	2.00	4.00
❑ 79078	Hardin County Line/Bound to Ramble	1990	—	2.00	4.00

COLLIE, SHIRLEY

Also see WILLIE NELSON; WARREN SMITH.

45s

LIBERTY

Number	Title (A Side/B Side)	Yr	VG	VG+	NM
❑ 55268	My Charlie/Didn't Work Out, Did It	1960	3.75	7.50	15.00
❑ 55291	I'd Rather Hear Lies/Sad Singin' and Slow Ridin'	1960	3.75	7.50	15.00
❑ 55324	Dime a Dozen/Oh Yes, Darling	1961	3.75	7.50	15.00
❑ 55391	If I Live Long Enough/Keeping My Fingers Crossed	1961	3.75	7.50	15.00
❑ 55472	No Wonder I Sing/We're Going Back Together	1962	3.75	7.50	15.00

COLLINS, BRIAN

45s

Number	Title (A Side/B Side)	Yr	VG	VG+	NM
ABC DOT					
❑ 17527	That's the Way Love Should Be/Come a Little Bit Closer	1974	—	2.50	5.00
❑ 17546	I'd Still Be in Love with You/Sweet Memories	1975	—	2.50	5.00
❑ 17564	Faithless Love/You Won't Get Away with Mine	1975	—	2.50	5.00
❑ 17593	Queen of Temptation/Before You Close the Door	1975	—	2.50	5.00
❑ 17613	To Show You That I Love You/My Heart Would Know	1976	—	2.50	5.00
❑ 17694	If You Love Me (Let Me Know)/Round and Round	1977	—	2.50	5.00
DOT					
❑ 17466	I Wish (You Had Stayed)/Hand in Hand with Love	1973	—	2.50	5.00
❑ 17483	I Don't Plan on Losing You/Lonely Too Long	1973	—	2.50	5.00
❑ 17499	Statue of a Fool/How Can I Tell Her	1974	—	2.50	5.00
MEGA					
❑ 0012	Walkin'/Your Kind of Man	1970	—	3.00	6.00
❑ 0022	New Way to Live/What Are You Gonna Do	1971	—	3.00	6.00
❑ 0038	All I Want to Do Is Say I Love You/Time to Try My Wings	1971	—	3.00	6.00
❑ 0058	There's a Kind of Hush (All Over the World)/Ain't Gonna Be Your Fool No More	1972	—	3.00	6.00
❑ 0078	Spread It Around/Let's Give It a Try	1972	—	3.00	6.00
PRIMERO					
❑ 1001	Before I Got to Know Her/Something Very Special	1982	—	2.50	5.00
❑ 1010	I'll Be Around/(B-side unknown)	1983	—	2.50	5.00
❑ 1018	Nickel's Worth of Heaven/Something Very Special	1983	—	2.50	5.00
RCA					
❑ PB-11277	Old Flames (Can't Hold a Candle to You)/Falsely Accused	1978	—	2.50	5.00
❑ PB-11350	Moonlight and Magnolias/Crazy You, Crazy Me	1978	—	2.50	5.00
❑ PB-11478	Hello Texas/Barefoot Angels	1979	—	2.50	5.00

Number	Title (A Side/B Side)	Yr	VG	VG+	NM
Albums					
ABC					
❑ AC-1029	The ABC Collection	1977	3.75	7.50	15.00
ABC DOT					
❑ DOSD-2008	That's the Way Love Should Be	1974	3.75	7.50	15.00
DOT					
❑ DLP-26017	This Is Brian Collins	1973	3.75	7.50	15.00

COLLINS, DUGG

Number	Title (A Side/B Side)	Yr	VG	VG+	NM
45s					
CERTRON					
❑ 10029	I Just Want to Be Alone/Play Me Some Heart Songs	1971	2.00	4.00	8.00
LITTLE DARLIN'					
❑ 7912	I Think I'll Wait Awhile/No Easy Way to Do	1979	—	3.00	6.00
SCR					
❑ 143	I'm the Man/If I Don't Love You	1977	—	3.00	6.00
❑ 147	How Do You Talk to a Baby/Hurt Me One More Time	1977	—	3.00	6.00
❑ 154	Someday I'd Like to Love You in Your Mind/Hurt Mw One More Time	1978	—	3.00	6.00

COLLINS, GWEN

Also see GWEN AND JERRY COLLINS.

Number	Title (A Side/B Side)	Yr	VG	VG+	NM
45s					
BRAGG					
❑ 218	Beneath the Green Green Grass of Home/Before I Learned to Live	196?	2.50	5.00	10.00
NEW WORLD					
❑ 80002	Juke Box Blueboy/Read All About It	196?	2.50	5.00	10.00

COLLINS, GWEN AND JERRY

Also see GWEN COLLINS.

Number	Title (A Side/B Side)	Yr	VG	VG+	NM
45s					
BRAGG					
❑ 223	It'll Be Me/Walk On Boy	196?	2.50	5.00	10.00
CAPITOL					
❑ 2710	Get Together/We're Not Bad	1969	—	3.00	6.00
❑ 2835	One Tin Soldier/We've Gotta Give	1970	—	3.00	6.00
NEW WORLD					
❑ 80005	Living for Each Other/Wait for the Sun to Shine	196?	2.50	5.00	10.00

COLLINS, JIM

Number	Title (A Side/B Side)	Yr	VG	VG+	NM
45s					
ARISTA NASHVILLE					
❑ 13107	The Next Step/Not Me	1997	—	—	3.00
❑ 13119	My First, Last, One and Only/I Can Let Go Now	1998	—	—	3.00
TKM					
❑ 111216	The Things I've Done to Me/(B-side unknown)	1986	—	2.50	5.00
❑ 111217	Romance/(B-side unknown)	1986	—	2.50	5.00
WHITE GOLD					
❑ 22250	You Can Always Say Good-Bye in the Morning/(B-side unknown)	1985	—	2.50	5.00
❑ 22251	What a Memory You'd Make/(B-side unknown)	1985	—	2.50	5.00
❑ 22252	I Wanna Be a Cowboy 'Til I Die/(B-side unknown)	1985	—	2.50	5.00

COLLINS, LARRY

Also see THE COLLINS KIDS.

Number	Title (A Side/B Side)	Yr	VG	VG+	NM
45s					
COLUMBIA					
❑ 4-41727	The Rebel — Johnny Yuma/Spur of the Moment	1960	3.75	7.50	15.00
❑ 4-41953	Get Along Home Cindy/What About Tomorrow	1960	3.75	7.50	15.00
❑ 4-42131	One Step Down/There She Stands, The One	1961	3.75	7.50	15.00
❑ 4-42394	T-Bone/Wild and Wicked Love	1962	3.75	7.50	15.00
❑ 4-42534	Hey Mama Boom-a-Lacka/More Than a Friend	1962	3.75	7.50	15.00
MONUMENT					
❑ 1148	New York City, R.F.D./Say Goodbye	1969	2.00	4.00	8.00
❑ 1196	The Outcast/Shake Hands with the Devil	1970	2.00	4.00	8.00

COLLINS, LORRIE

Also see THE COLLINS KIDS.

Number	Title (A Side/B Side)	Yr	VG	VG+	NM
45s					
COLUMBIA					
❑ 4-41541	The Lonesome Road/Another Man Done Gone	1959	5.00	10.00	20.00
❑ 4-41673	Blues in the Night/That's Your Affair	1960	5.00	10.00	20.00
❑ 4-42242	Home of the Blues/Waitin' and Watchin'	1961	3.75	7.50	15.00

COLLINS, TOMMY

Number	Title (A Side/B Side)	Yr	VG	VG+	NM
45s					
CAPITOL					
❑ F2584	You Gotta Have a License/There'll Be No Other	1953	6.25	12.50	25.00
❑ F2701	You Better Not Do That/High on a Hilltop	1954	6.25	12.50	25.00
❑ F2806	I Always Get a Souvenir/Let Me Love You	1954	6.25	12.50	25.00
❑ F2891	Whatcha Gonna Do Now/You're for Me	1954	6.25	12.50	25.00
❑ F3017	Untied/Boob-I-Lak	1955	6.25	12.50	25.00
❑ F3082	It Tickles/Let Down	1955	6.25	12.50	25.00
❑ F3190	I Guess I'm Crazy/You Oughta See Pickles Now	1955	6.25	12.50	25.00
❑ F3289	I'll Be Gone/I Love You More and More Each Day	1955	6.25	12.50	25.00
❑ F3370	What Kind of a Sweetheart Are You/Wait a Little Longer	1956	5.00	10.00	20.00
❑ F3466	No Love Have I/That's the Way Love Is	1956	5.00	10.00	20.00
❑ F3591	I Wish I Had Died in My Cradle/I'll Never Let You Go	1956	5.00	10.00	20.00
❑ F3665	All of the Monkeys Ain't in the Zoo/Don't You Love Me Anymore	1957	5.00	10.00	20.00
❑ F3789	A Love Is Born/I'm Nobody's Fool But Yours	1957	5.00	10.00	20.00
❑ F4263	Little June/A Hundred Years from Now	1959	5.00	10.00	20.00
❑ F4327	The Wreck of the Old 97/You Belong in My Arms	1959	5.00	10.00	20.00
❑ 4421	Summer's Almost Gone/Keep Dreaming	1960	3.75	7.50	15.00
❑ 4495	Black Cat/My Last Chance with You	1961	12.50	25.00	50.00
❑ 4962	Take Me Back to the Good Old Days/When Did Right Become Wrong	1963	3.75	7.50	15.00
❑ 5051	I Can Do That/You'd Better Be Nice	1963	3.75	7.50	15.00
—As "Tommy and Wanda Collins"					
❑ 5117	If I Could Just Go Back/I Got Mine	1964	3.00	6.00	12.00
❑ 5345	All of the Monkeys Ain't in the Zoo/Don't Let Me Stand in His Footsteps	1965	3.00	6.00	12.00
COLUMBIA					
❑ 4-43489	If You Can't Bite, Don't Growl/Man Machine	1965	2.50	5.00	10.00
❑ 4-43628	Shindig in the Barn/Be Serious Ann	1966	2.50	5.00	10.00
❑ 4-43724	There's No Girl in My Life Anymore/A Man Gotta Do What a Man Gotta Do	1966	2.50	5.00	10.00
❑ 4-43972	Birmingham/Don't Wipe the Tears That You Cry for Him (On My Good White Shirt)	1967	2.50	5.00	10.00
❑ 4-44113	Roll Truck Roll/Wine, Take Me Away	1967	2.50	5.00	10.00
❑ 4-44260	Big Dummy/What-Cha Gonna Do Now?	1967	2.50	5.00	10.00
❑ 4-44386	I Made the Prison Band/No Love Have I	1967	2.50	5.00	10.00
❑ 4-44498	He's Gonna Have to Catch Me First/Sunny Side of My Life	1968	2.50	5.00	10.00
❑ 4-44664	High on a Hilltop/Woman You Have Been Told	1968	2.50	5.00	10.00
TOWER					
❑ 213	Take Me Back to the Good Old Days/Oh What a Dream	1966	3.00	6.00	12.00
Albums					
CAPITOL					
❑ T 776 [M]	Words and Music Country Style	1957	25.00	50.00	100.00
❑ T 1125 [M]	Light of the Lord	1959	25.00	50.00	100.00
❑ T 1196 [M]	This Is Tommy Collins	1959	15.00	30.00	60.00
❑ ST 1436 [S]	Songs I Love to Sing	1961	15.00	30.00	60.00
❑ T 1436 [M]	Songs I Love to Sing	1961	12.50	25.00	50.00
COLUMBIA					
❑ CL 2510 [M]	The Dynamic Tommy Collins	1966	7.50	15.00	30.00
❑ CL 2778 [M]	Tommy Collins On Tour — His Most Requested Songs	1968	15.00	30.00	60.00
❑ CS 9310 [S]	The Dynamic Tommy Collins	1966	10.00	20.00	40.00
❑ CS 9578 [S]	Tommy Collins On Tour — His Most Requested Songs	1968	7.50	15.00	30.00
STARDAY					
❑ SLP-474	Tommy Collins Callin'	1972	5.00	10.00	20.00
TOWER					
❑ DT 5021 [R]	Let's Live a Little	1966	5.00	10.00	20.00
❑ T 5021 [M]	Let's Live a Little	1966	7.50	15.00	30.00
❑ DT 5107 [R]	Shindig	1967	5.00	10.00	20.00
❑ T 5107 [M]	Shindig	1967	10.00	20.00	40.00

COLLINS KIDS, THE

Also see LARRY COLLINS; LORRIE COLLINS.

Number	Title (A Side/B Side)	Yr	VG	VG+	NM
45s					
COLUMBIA					
❑ 4-21470	Beetle Bug Bop/Hush Money	1955	7.50	15.00	30.00
❑ 4-21514	The Rockaway/Make Him Behave	1956	7.50	15.00	30.00
❑ 4-21543	I'm in My Teens/They're Still in Love	1956	7.50	15.00	30.00
❑ 4-21560	Rock and Roll Polka/My First Love	1956	7.50	15.00	30.00
❑ 4-40760	You Are My Sunshine/Nobody's Darling But Mine	1956	5.00	10.00	20.00
—With Carl Smith, Rosemary Clooney and Gene Autry					
❑ 4-40824	Move a Little Closer/Go Away, Don't Bother Me	1957	7.50	15.00	30.00
❑ 4-40921	Hop, Skip and Jump/Young Heart	1957	7.50	15.00	30.00
❑ 4-41012	Party/Heartbeat	1957	20.00	40.00	80.00
❑ 4-41087	Hoy Hoy/Mama Worries	1958	12.50	25.00	50.00
❑ 4-41149	Mercy/Sweet Talk	1958	12.50	25.00	50.00
❑ 4-41225	Rock Boppin' Baby/Whistle Bait	1958	15.00	30.00	60.00
—As "Lorrie and Larry Collins"					
❑ 4-41329	Sugar Plum/Kinda Like Love	1959	6.25	12.50	25.00

COLTER, JESSI

Also see DUANE AND MIRRIAM EDDY; WAYLON JENNINGS; WAYLON AND JESSI.

Number	Title (A Side/B Side)	Yr	VG	VG+	NM
45s					
CAPITOL					
❑ 4009	I'm Not Lisa/For the First Time	1974	—	2.00	4.00
❑ 4087	What's Happened to Blue Eyes/You Ain't Never Been Loved (Like I'm Gonna Love You)	1975	—	2.00	4.00
❑ 4200	It's Morning (And I Still Love You)/Would You Walk with Me (To the Lilies)	1975	—	2.00	4.00
❑ 4252	Without You/All My Life I've Been Your Love	1976	—	2.00	4.00
❑ 4325	I Thought I Heard You Calling My Name/You Hung the Moon (Didn't You Waylon)	1976	—	2.00	4.00
❑ 4472	I Belong to Him/There Ain't No Rain	1977	—	2.00	4.00
❑ 4641	Maybe You Should've Been Listening/My Cowboy's Last Ride	1978	—	2.00	4.00
❑ 4696	Love Me Back to Sleep/Don't You Think I Felt It Too	1979	—	2.00	4.00
❑ 5073	Holdin' On/(B-side unknown)	1981	—	2.00	4.00
❑ 5113	Nobody Else But You/Ain't Makin' No Headlines	1982	—	2.00	4.00
JAMIE					
❑ 1181	Lonesome Road/Young and Innocent	1961	7.50	15.00	30.00
—As "Mirriam Johnson"					
❑ 1193	I Cried Long Enough/Making Believe	1961	7.50	15.00	30.00
—As "Mirriam Johnson"					

Number	Title (A Side/B Side)	Yr	VG	VG+	NM
RCA VICTOR					
❑ PB-10309	He Called Me Baby/Take a Message to Laura	1975	—	2.50	5.00
❑ 47-9826	Cry Softly/If She's Where You Like Livin'	1970	—	2.50	5.00
❑ 47-9962	The Golden Rocket/You Mean to Say	1971	—	2.50	5.00
❑ 74-0280	Take a Message to Laura/I Ain't the One	1969	—	2.50	5.00
❑ 74-0780	You Don't Need Me, Do You/I Don't Wanna Be a One-Night Stand	1972	—	2.50	5.00
Albums					
CAPITOL					
❑ ST-11363	I'm Jessi Colter	1975	2.50	5.00	10.00
❑ ST-11477	Jessi	1976	2.50	5.00	10.00
❑ ST-11543	Diamond in the Rough	1976	2.50	5.00	10.00
❑ ST-11583	Mirriam	1977	2.50	5.00	10.00
❑ ST-11863	That's the Way a Cowboy Rocks and Rolls	1978	2.50	5.00	10.00
❑ ST-12185	Ridin' Shotgun	1981	2.50	5.00	10.00
❑ ST-511863	That's the Way a Cowboy Rocks and Rolls	1978	3.00	6.00	12.00
—Columbia House edition					
RCA VICTOR					
❑ LSP-4333	Country Star	1970	5.00	10.00	20.00

COMEAUX, AMIE

Number	Title (A Side/B Side)	Yr	VG	VG+	NM
45s					
POLYDOR					
❑ 851208-7	Who's She to You/Written in the Stars	1994	—	2.50	5.00
❑ 851890-7	Blue/One Step Ahead of You	1995	—	2.50	5.00
❑ 853780-7	Moving Out/Oh No, Not Love Again	1994	—	2.50	5.00

COMMANDER CODY AND HIS LOST PLANET AIRMEN

Number	Title (A Side/B Side)	Yr	VG	VG+	NM
45s					
ARISTA					
❑ 0271	Seven-Eleven/You Snooze You Lose	1977	—	2.00	4.00
❑ 0344	Thank You Lone Ranger/My Day	1978	—	2.00	4.00
DOT					
❑ 17487	Daddy's Drinking Up Our Christmas/ Honeysuckle Honey	1973	—	3.00	6.00
❑ 17500	Diggy Liggy Lo/Outgoing Person	1974	—	2.50	5.00
PARAMOUNT					
❑ 0130	Lost in the Ozone/Midnight Shift	1971	—	3.00	6.00
❑ 0146	Hot Rod Lincoln/My Home in My Hand	1972	—	3.00	6.00
❑ 0169	Beat Me Daddy, Eight to the Bar/Daddy's Gonna Treat You Right	1972	—	3.00	6.00
❑ 0178	Truck Stop Rock/Mama Hated Diesels	1972	—	3.00	6.00
❑ 0193	Semi-Truck/Watch My .38	1973	—	3.00	6.00
❑ 0216	Smoke! Smoke! Smoke! (That Cigarette)/Rock That Boogie	1973	—	3.00	6.00
❑ 0216 [PS]	Smoke! Smoke! Smoke! (That Cigarette)/Rock That Boogie	1973	2.50	5.00	10.00
❑ 0278	Riot in Cell Block No. 9/Oh, Momma Momma	1974	—	3.00	6.00
WARNER BROS.					
❑ 8073	Don't Let Go/Keep On Lovin' Her	1975	—	2.00	4.00
❑ 8164	It's Gonna Be One of Those Nights/Roll Your Own	1975	—	2.00	4.00
Albums					
ARISTA					
❑ AL 4125	Rock 'N' Roll Again	1977	2.50	5.00	10.00
❑ AL 4183	Flying Dreams	1978	—	—	—
—Canceled?					
BLIND PIG					
❑ BP-2086	Let's Rock	1986	2.50	5.00	10.00
MCA					
❑ 659	Live from Deep in the Heart of Texas	1980	2.00	4.00	8.00
—Reissue of Paramount 1017					
❑ 660	Country Casanova	1980	2.00	4.00	8.00
—Reissue of Paramount 6054					
❑ 661	Hot Licks, Cold Steel & Truckers Favorites	1980	2.00	4.00	8.00
—Reissue of Paramount 6031					
❑ 37101	Lost in the Ozone	1980	2.00	4.00	8.00
—Reissue of Paramount 6017					
PARAMOUNT					
❑ PAS-1017	Live from Deep in the Heart of Texas	1974	3.00	6.00	12.00
❑ PAS-6017	Lost in the Ozone	1971	3.75	7.50	15.00
❑ PAS-6031	Hot Licks, Cold Steel & Truckers Favorites	1972	3.00	6.00	12.00
❑ PAS-6054	Country Casanova	1973	3.00	6.00	12.00
WARNER BROS.					
❑ BS 2847	Commander Cody and His Lost Planet Airmen	1975	2.50	5.00	10.00
❑ BS 2883	Tales from the Ozone	1975	2.50	5.00	10.00
❑ 2LS 2939 [(2)]	We've Got a Live One Here!	1976	3.00	6.00	12.00

COMO, PERRY

The famous pop crooner put the following records on the country charts.

Number	Title (A Side/B Side)	Yr	VG	VG+	NM
45s					
RCA VICTOR					
❑ PB-10402	Just Out of Reach/Love Put a Song in My Heart	1975	—	2.00	4.00
Albums					
RCA VICTOR					
❑ APD1-0863 [Q]	Just Out of Reach	1975	3.75	7.50	15.00
❑ APL1-0863	Just Out of Reach	1975	2.50	5.00	10.00

COMPTON BROTHERS, THE

Number	Title (A Side/B Side)	Yr	VG	VG+	NM
45s					
ABC DOT					
❑ 17538	Cat's in the Cradle/A Bird with Broken Wings Can't Fly	1974	—	2.50	5.00
❑ 17563	My Music/By the Time I Get Over You	1975	—	2.50	5.00
COLUMBIA					
❑ 4-43244	Jailer Bring Me Water/Still Away	1965	2.50	5.00	10.00
DOT					
❑ 16948	Pickin' Up the Mail/Feathers to Stone	1966	2.00	4.00	8.00
❑ 17024	I Look a Lot Like Bill/If It's All the Same to You	1967	2.00	4.00	8.00
❑ 17070	Honey/Poor Side of Town	1968	2.00	4.00	8.00
❑ 17110	Two Little Hearts/Money	1968	2.00	4.00	8.00
❑ 17167	Everybody Needs Somebody/Loneliness Was Made by Man	1968	2.00	4.00	8.00
❑ 17231	Earthquakes/Step Up Walk with Me	1969	2.00	4.00	8.00
❑ 17294	Haunted House/Sound of an Angel's Wings	1969	2.00	4.00	8.00
❑ 17336	Charlie Brown/Just a Dream Away	1970	—	3.00	6.00
❑ 17352	That Ain't No Stuff/I Wanna Sing a Country Song	1970	—	3.00	6.00
❑ 17362	Nadine/Living on a Prayer, a Hope, and a Hand-Me-Down	1970	—	3.00	6.00
❑ 17378	Pine Grove/Old Memories	1971	—	3.00	6.00
❑ 17391	May Auld Acquaintance Be Forgot (Before I Lose My Mind)/Learning the Hard Way	1971	—	3.00	6.00
❑ 17408	Yellow River/Sometimes It Ain't No Fun to Love	1972	—	3.00	6.00
❑ 17427	Claudette/It Happens All the Time	1972	—	3.00	6.00
❑ 17454	Daddies Doin' Life/Some of Shelly's Blues	1973	—	3.00	6.00
❑ 17477	California Blues (Blue Yodel No. 4)/Direct Distance Dialing	1973	—	3.00	6.00
❑ 17511	Secret Memories/Sweet Honky Tonk Music	1974	—	3.00	6.00
Albums					
DOT					
❑ DLP-25867	Off the Top of...	1968	5.00	10.00	20.00
❑ DLP-25974	Haunted House/Charlie Brown	1970	5.00	10.00	20.00
❑ DLP-25998	Yellow River	1972	5.00	10.00	20.00

CONCRETE COWBOY BAND

Number	Title (A Side/B Side)	Yr	VG	VG+	NM
45s					
EXCELSIOR					
❑ 1006	Concrete Cowboys/(B-side unknown)	1981	—	3.00	6.00
❑ 1011	Country Is the Closest Thing to Heaven (You Can Hear)/San Antonio Rose	1981	—	2.50	5.00
Albums					
EXCELSIOR					
❑ 88007	Concrete Cowboys	1981	3.00	6.00	12.00

CONFEDERATE RAILROAD

Also see DANNY SHIRLEY.

Number	Title (A Side/B Side)	Yr	VG	VG+	NM
45s					
ATLANTIC					
❑ 84193	Keep On Rockin'/'Tween Sunday Morning and Saturday Night	1998	—	—	3.00
❑ 84441	I Hate Rap/The Big One	1999	—	—	3.00
❑ 84464	Cowboy Cadillac (Album Version)/same (Dance Mix)	1999	—	—	3.00
❑ 87104	When and Where/Bill's Laundromat, Bar and Grill	1995	—	—	3.00
❑ 87229	Elvis and Andy/Three Verses	1994	—	2.00	4.00
❑ 87273	Daddy Never Was the Cadillac Kind/Jesus and Mama	1994	—	2.00	4.00
❑ 87357	Trashy Women/When You Leave That Way You Can Never Go Back	1993	—	2.50	5.00
❑ 87404	Queen of Memphis/Jesus and Mama	1992	—	2.50	5.00

CONLEE, JOHN

Number	Title (A Side/B Side)	Yr	VG	VG+	NM
45s					
16TH AVENUE					
❑ 70424	Hit the Ground Runnin'/Hopelessly Yours	1988	—	2.00	4.00
❑ 70427	Fellow Travelers/Knowin' You Were Leavin'	1989	—	2.00	4.00
❑ 70432	Hopelessly Yours/I Love You	1989	—	2.00	4.00
❑ 70436	Don't Get Me Started/Knowin' You Were Leavin'	1989	—	2.00	4.00
❑ 70447	Doghouse/Love Stands Tall	1990	—	2.50	5.00
ABC					
❑ 12356	Rose Colored Glasses/I'll Be Easy	1978	—	2.50	5.00
❑ 12420	Lady Lay Down/Something Special	1978	—	2.50	5.00
❑ 12455	Backside of Thirty/Hold On	1979	—	2.50	5.00
ABC DOT					
❑ 17671	Backside of Thirty/Hold On	1976	—	3.50	7.00
❑ 17689	Let Your Love Fall Back on Me/Hold On	1977	—	3.00	6.00
❑ 17714	The "In" Crowd/You Made a Believer Out of Me	1977	—	3.00	6.00
COLUMBIA					
❑ 38-05778	Harmony/She Told Me So	1986	—	—	3.00
❑ 38-06104	Got My Heart Set on You/You've Got a Right	1986	—	—	3.00
❑ 38-06311	The Carpenter/I'll Be Seeing You	1986	—	—	3.00
❑ 38-06707	Domestic Life/I Can Sail to China	1987	—	—	3.00
❑ 38-07203	Mama's Rockin' Chair/Faded Brown Eyes	1987	—	—	3.00
❑ 38-07643	Living Like There's No Tomorrow (Finally Got to Me Tonight)/Slow Passin' Time	1987	—	—	3.00
MCA					
❑ 12455	Backside of Thirty/Hold On	1979	—	2.00	4.00
❑ 41072	Before My Time/Forever	1979	—	2.00	4.00
❑ 41163	Baby, You're Something/The In Crowd	1979	—	2.00	4.00
❑ 41233	Friday Night Blues/When I'm Out of You	1980	—	2.00	4.00
❑ 41321	She Can't Say That Anymore/Always True	1980	—	2.00	4.00
❑ 51008	Let's Get Married Again/We Belong in Love Tonight	1980	—	—	—
—Unreleased?					
❑ 51044	What I Had with You/We Belong in Love Tonight	1981	—	2.00	4.00
❑ 51112	Could You Love Me (One More Time)/When It Hurts You Most	1981	—	2.00	4.00
❑ 51164	Miss Emily's Picture/Love Is What You Need	1981	—	2.00	4.00

Number	Title (A Side/B Side)	Yr	VG	VG+	NM
❑ 52008	Busted/I'd Rather Have What We Have	1982	—	2.00	4.00
❑ 52070	Nothing Behind You, Nothing in Sight/Shame	1982	—	2.00	4.00
❑ 52116	I Don't Remember Loving You/Two Hearts	1982	—	2.00	4.00
❑ 52178	Common Man/Rose Colored Glasses	1983	—	2.00	4.00
❑ 52231	I'm Only In It for the Love/Lay Down Sally	1983	—	2.00	4.00
❑ 52282	In My Eyes/Don't Count the Rainy Days	1983	—	2.00	4.00
❑ 52351	As Long As I'm Rockin' with You/An American Trilogy	1984	—	2.00	4.00
❑ 52403	Way Back/Together Alone	1984	—	2.00	4.00
❑ 52470	Years After You/But She Loves Me	1984	—	2.00	4.00
❑ 52543	Working Man/Radio Lover	1985	—	2.00	4.00
❑ 52625	Blue Highway/De Island	1985	—	2.00	4.00
❑ 52695	Old School/She Loves My Troubles Away	1985	—	2.00	4.00
❑ 52695 [PS]	Old School/She Loves My Troubles Away	1985	—	2.50	5.00

Albums

Number	Title (A Side/B Side)	Yr	VG	VG+	NM
16TH AVENUE					
❑ D1-70555	Fellow Travelers	1989	2.50	5.00	10.00
ABC					
❑ AY-1105	Rose Colored Glasses	1978	3.00	6.00	12.00
COLUMBIA					
❑ FC 40257	Harmony	1986	2.00	4.00	8.00
❑ FC 40442	American Travelers	1987	2.00	4.00	8.00
MCA					
❑ 948	In My Eyes	1986	—	3.00	6.00
—Budget-line reissue					
❑ AY-1105	Rose Colored Glasses	1979	2.50	5.00	10.00
—Reissue of ABC 1105					
❑ 3174	Forever	1979	2.50	5.00	10.00
❑ 3246	Friday Night Blues	1980	2.50	5.00	10.00
❑ 3281	Rose Colored Glasses	1980	2.00	4.00	8.00
—Reissue of 1105					
❑ 5213	With Love...	1981	2.50	5.00	10.00
❑ 5310	Busted	1982	2.50	5.00	10.00
❑ 5405	John Conlee's Greatest Hits	1983	2.50	5.00	10.00
❑ 5434	In My Eyes	1983	2.00	4.00	8.00
❑ 5521	Blue Highway	1984	2.00	4.00	8.00
❑ 5642	Greatest Hits Volume 2	1985	2.00	4.00	8.00
❑ 5699	Songs for the Working Man	1986	2.00	4.00	8.00
❑ 5818	Conlee Country	1986	2.00	4.00	8.00
❑ 27029	Friday Night Blues	198?	2.00	4.00	8.00
—Budget-line reissue					

CONLEY, EARL THOMAS

45s

Number	Title (A Side/B Side)	Yr	VG	VG+	NM
GRT					
❑ 015	When I'm Under the Table/The Greenest Grass	1975	—	3.00	6.00
—As "Earl Conley"					
❑ 027	I Have Loved You Girl (But Not Like This Before)/ Tryin' to Beat the Morning Home	1975	—	2.50	5.00
—As "Earl Conley"					
❑ 032	It's the Bible Against the Bottle (In the Battle for Daddy's Soul)/I Have Loved You Girl (But Not Like This Before)	1975	—	2.50	5.00
—As "Earl Conley"					
❑ 041	High and Wild/The Weeds Outlived the Roses	1976	—	2.50	5.00
—As "Earl Conley"					
❑ 064	Queen of New Orleans/I Have Loved You Girl (But Not Like This Before)	1976	—	2.50	5.00
—As "Earl Conley"					
PRIZE					
❑ 22	The Night They Drove Old Dixie Down/River of Teardrops	1972	2.50	5.00	10.00
—As "Earl T. Conley"					
RCA					
❑ 2511-7-R	Who's Gonna Tell Her Goodbye/Love Don't Care (Whose Heart)	1990	—	—	3.00
❑ 2826-7-R	Shadow of a Doubt/I Wanna Be Loved Back	1991	—	2.00	4.00
❑ 5064-7-R	I Can't Win for Losing You/Love's on the Move Again	1986	—	—	3.00
❑ 5129-7-R	That Was a Close One/Right from the Start	1987	—	—	3.00
❑ 5226-7-R	Right from the Start/Attracted to Pain	1987	—	—	3.00
❑ 6894-7-R	What She Is (Is a Woman in Love)/Carol	1988	—	—	3.00
❑ 8632-7-R	We Believe in Happy Endings/No Chance, No Dance	1988	—	—	3.00
—A-side with Emmylou Harris					
❑ 8717-7-R	What I'd Say/Carol	1988	—	—	3.00
❑ 8824-7-R	Love Out Loud/No Chance, No Dance	1989	—	—	3.00
❑ 8973-7-R	Love Out Loud/No Chance, No Dance	1989	—	—	3.00
❑ 8973-7-R	You Must Not Be Drinking Enough/Too Far from the Heart of It All	1989	—	—	3.00
❑ 9121-7-R	Bring Back Your Love to Me/Chance of Lovin' You	1990	—	—	3.00
❑ PB-12286	You Don't Have to Go Too Far/Too Much Noise (Trucker's Waltz)	1981	—	2.50	5.00
❑ PB-12344	Tell Me Why/Too Much Noise (Trucker's Waltz)	1981	—	—	3.00
❑ JB-13053 [DJ]	Smokey Mountain Memories (same on both sides)	1982	2.50	5.00	10.00
—Promo only on red vinyl					
❑ PB-13053	After the Love Slips Away/Smokey Mountain Memories	1982	—	—	3.00
❑ PB-13246	Heavenly Bodies/The Highway Home	1982	—	—	3.00
❑ JB-13320 [DJ]	Somewhere Between Right and Wrong (same on both sides)	1982	2.50	5.00	10.00
—Promo only on blue vinyl					
❑ PB-13320	Somewhere Between Right and Wrong/Fire and Smoke	1982	—	—	3.00
❑ PB-13414	I Have Loved You, Girl (But Not Like This Before)/ Bottled Up Blues	1982	—	—	3.00
❑ JK-13525 [DJ]	Your Love's on the Line (same on both sides)	1983	2.50	5.00	10.00
—Promo only on gold vinyl					
❑ PB-13525	Your Love's on the Line/Under Control	1983	—	—	3.00
❑ PB-13596	Holding Her and Loving You/Home So Fine	1983	—	—	3.00
❑ PB-13596 [PS]	Holding Her and Loving You/Home So Fine	1983	—	2.50	5.00
❑ PB-13688	White Christmas/Home So Fine	1983	—	2.00	4.00
❑ PB-13702	Don't Make It Easy for Me/You Can't Go On (Like a Rolling Stone)	1983	—	—	3.00
❑ JK-13758 [DJ]	Angel in Disguise (same on both sides)	1984	2.50	5.00	10.00
—Promo only on red vinyl					
❑ PB-13758	Angel in Disguise/Coward Around the Corner	1984	—	—	3.00
❑ PB-13758 [PS]	Angel in Disguise/Coward Around the Corner	1984	—	2.00	4.00
❑ GB-13787	Holding Her and Loving You/Your Love's on the Line	1984	—	—	3.00
—"Gold Standard Series" reissue					
❑ GB-13788	Somewhere Between Right and Wrong/Heavenly Bodies	1984	—	—	3.00
—"Gold Standard Series" reissue					
❑ PB-13877	Chance of Lovin' You/Feels Like a Saturday Night	1984	—	—	3.00
❑ JK-13960 [DJ]	Honor Bound (same on both sides)	1984	2.50	5.00	10.00
—Promo only on blue vinyl					
❑ PB-13960	Honor Bound/Too Hot to Handle	1984	—	—	3.00
❑ PB-13960 [PS]	Honor Bound/Too Hot to Handle	1984	—	2.00	4.00
❑ PB-14060	Love Don't Care (Whose Heart It Breaks)/Turn This Bus Around	1985	—	—	3.00
❑ GB-14066	Chance of Lovin' You/Don't Make It Easy on Me	1985	—	—	3.00
—"Gold Standard Series" reissue					
❑ PB-14172	Nobody Falls Like a Fool/Silent Treatment	1985	—	—	3.00
❑ PB-14282	Once in a Blue Moon/I Have Loved You, Girl (But Not Like This Before)	1986	—	—	3.00
❑ GB-14345	Honor Bound/Love Don't Care (Whose Heart It Breaks)	1986	—	—	3.00
—"Gold Standard Series" reissue					
❑ GB-14351	Nobody Falls Like a Fool/Don't Make It Easy for Me	1986	—	—	3.00
—"Gold Standard Series" reissue					
❑ PB-14380	Too Many Times/Changes of Love	1986	—	—	3.00
—A-side with Anita Pointer					
❑ PB-14380 [PS]	Too Many Times/Changes of Love	1986	—	2.00	4.00
—A-side with Anita Pointer					
❑ 62167	Hard Days and Honky Tonk Nights/Borrowed Honey	1991	—	2.00	4.00
❑ 62252	If Only Your Eyes Could Lie/One of Those Days	1992	—	2.00	4.00
SUNBIRD					
❑ 7556	Silent Treatment/This Time I've Hurt Her More (Than She Loves Me)	1980	—	2.50	5.00
❑ 7561	Fire and Smoke/I Have Loved You Girl	1981	—	2.50	5.00
—Blue label					
❑ 7561	Fire and Smoke/I Have Loved You Girl	1981	—	2.00	4.00
—Multicolor label					
WARNER BROS.					
❑ 8717	Dreamin's All I Do/My Love	1978	—	2.50	5.00
—As "Earl Conley"					
❑ 8798	Middle-Age Madness/When You Were Blue and I Was Green	1979	—	2.00	4.00
❑ 49072	Stranded on a Dead-End Street/My Love	1979	—	2.50	5.00
—As "The ETC Band"					

Albums

Number	Title (A Side/B Side)	Yr	VG	VG+	NM
RCA					
❑ 5619-1-R	Too Many Times	1986	2.00	4.00	8.00
❑ 6824-1-R	The Heart of It All	1988	2.00	4.00	8.00
RCA VICTOR					
❑ AHL1-4135	Fire & Smoke	1981	2.00	4.00	8.00
❑ AHL1-4348	Somewhere Between Right and Wrong	1982	2.00	4.00	8.00
❑ AHL1-4713	Don't Make It Easy for Me	1983	2.00	4.00	8.00
❑ AYL1-5118	Fire & Smoke	1984	—	3.00	6.00
—"Best Buy Series" reissue					
❑ AYL1-5156	Somewhere Between Right and Wrong	1984	—	3.00	6.00
—"Best Buy Series" reissue					
❑ AHL1-5175	Treadin' Water	1984	2.00	4.00	8.00
❑ AHL1-7032	Greatest Hits	1985	2.00	4.00	8.00
SUNBIRD					
❑ 50105	Blue Pearl	1980	3.75	7.50	15.00

CONWAY, DAVE

45s

Number	Title (A Side/B Side)	Yr	VG	VG+	NM
TEDDY BEAR					
❑ (no #)	Jingle Bears (same on both sides)	197?	—	3.00	6.00
TRUE					
❑ 105	If You're Gonna Love (You're Gonna Hurt)/Too Late for Words	1977	—	3.00	6.00
❑ 114	I'll Go On Loving You/Too Late for Words	1978	—	3.00	6.00
❑ 115	Lookin' Back on Lovin' You/Please Don't Go	1978	—	3.00	6.00

COOK, STEVEN LEE

45s

Number	Title (A Side/B Side)	Yr	VG	VG+	NM
GRINDER'S SWITCH					
❑ 1709	Please Play More Kenny Rogers/(B-side unknown)	1979	—	3.00	6.00

COOLEY, SPADE

Also see ROY ROGERS.

45s

DECCA

Number	Title (A Side/B Side)	Yr	VG	VG+	NM
❑ 9-28253	Crazy 'Cause I Love You/Swingin' the Devil's Dreams	1952	5.00	10.00	20.00
❑ 9-28344	Carmen's Boogie/One Sweet Letter from You	1952	5.00	10.00	20.00
❑ 9-29309	Break Up Down/You Clobbered Me	1954	5.00	10.00	20.00
❑ 9-29788	Seasons of My Heart/No Need to Cry Anymore	1956	3.75	7.50	15.00
❑ 9-46310	Rhumba Boogie/Chew Tobacco Rag	1951	6.25	12.50	25.00
❑ 9-46339	Hittsitty Hottsitty/Lucky Leather Britches	1951	6.25	12.50	25.00
❑ 9-46355	Down Yonder/Horse Hair Boogie	1951	6.25	12.50	25.00
❑ 9-46376	Cowboy Waltz/My Heart Is Broken in Three	1951	6.25	12.50	25.00

RCA VICTOR

Number	Title (A Side/B Side)	Yr	VG	VG+	NM
❑ 47-3195	The Last Roundup/Wagon Wheels	1949	6.25	12.50	25.00
❑ 47-3196	Lights Out/In the Chapel in the Moonlight	1949	6.25	12.50	25.00
❑ 47-3197	Empty Saddles/The Old Spinning Wheel	1949	6.25	12.50	25.00
❑ 48-0027	The Best Deal in Town/Spanish Fandango	1949	10.00	20.00	40.00
—Originals on green vinyl					
❑ 48-0032	Call Me Darlin' Do/Four Fiddle Polka	1949	10.00	20.00	40.00
—Originals on green vinyl					
❑ 48-0043	Texas Playboy Rag/Lord Nottingham's War Dance	1949	10.00	20.00	40.00
—Originals on green vinyl					
❑ 48-0063	The Gal I Left Behind Me/Arkansas Traveler	1949	10.00	20.00	40.00
—Originals on green vinyl					
❑ 48-0077	The Wagoner/Wake Up Susan	1949	10.00	20.00	40.00
—Originals on green vinyl					
❑ 48-0078	Flop Eared Mule/The Eighth of January	1949	10.00	20.00	40.00
—Originals on green vinyl					
❑ 48-0079	Ida Red/Six Eight to the Barn	1949	10.00	20.00	40.00
—Originals on green vinyl					
❑ 48-0157	Foolish Tears/Send Ten Pretty Flowers	1950	7.50	15.00	30.00
—Originals on green vinyl					
❑ 48-0309	Texas Star/Pretty Please Love Me	1950	7.50	15.00	30.00
—Originals on green vinyl					
❑ 48-0330	Hillbilly Fever/Honky Tonkin'	1950	7.50	15.00	30.00
—Originals on green vinyl					
❑ 48-0348	Longing/Little Liza Jane	1950	7.50	15.00	30.00
—Originals on green vinyl					
❑ 48-0467	Tuesday Two-Step/Three Fiddle Rag	1951	6.25	12.50	25.00

Selected 78s

COLUMBIA

Number	Title (A Side/B Side)	Yr	VG	VG+	NM
❑ 20017	Detour/You Can't Break My Heart	1948	3.75	7.50	15.00
—Reissue of 36935					
❑ 20069	I've Taken All I'm Gonna Take from You/Forgive Me One More Time	1948	3.75	7.50	15.00
—Reissue of 37046					
❑ 20071	Shame on You/A Pair of Broken Hearts	1948	3.75	7.50	15.00
—Reissue of 37057					
❑ 20072	Crazy 'Cause I Love You/Three Way Boogie	1948	3.75	7.50	15.00
—Reissue of 37058					
❑ 20099	Oklahoma Stomp/You Better Do It Now	1948	3.75	7.50	15.00
—Reissue of 37237					
❑ 20193	You Never Miss the Water/Spadella	1948	3.75	7.50	15.00
—Reissue of 37585					
❑ 20375	Cow Bell Polka/Troubled Over You	1948	3.75	7.50	15.00
—Reissue of 37937					
❑ 20397	Steel Guitar Rag/I Guess I've Been Dreaming Again	1948	3.75	7.50	15.00
—Reissue of 38054					
❑ 20431	Hide Your Face/Yodelling Polka	1948	5.00	10.00	20.00
❑ 20490	Devil's Dream/You'll Rue the Day	1948	5.00	10.00	20.00
❑ 20571	Devil's Dream/Yodelling Polka	1949	3.75	7.50	15.00
❑ 20572	Cow Bell Polka/Steel Guitar Rag	1949	3.75	7.50	15.00
❑ 20573	Oklahoma Stomp/Shame on You	1948	3.75	7.50	15.00
❑ 20574	Spadella/Three Way Boogie	1949	3.75	7.50	15.00
❑ 36935	Detour/You Can't Break My Heart	1946	5.00	10.00	20.00
❑ 37046	I've Taken All I'm Gonna Take from You/Forgive Me One More Time	1947	5.00	10.00	20.00
—Reissue of Okeh 6746					
❑ 37057	Shame on You/A Pair of Broken Hearts	1947	5.00	10.00	20.00
—Reissue of Okeh 6731					
❑ 37058	Crazy 'Cause I Love You/Three Way Boogie	1946	5.00	10.00	20.00
❑ 37237	Oklahoma Stomp/You Better Do It Now	1947	5.00	10.00	20.00
❑ 37585	You Never Miss the Water/Spadella	1947	5.00	10.00	20.00
❑ 37937	Cow Bell Polka/Troubled Over You	1947	5.00	10.00	20.00
❑ 38054	Steel Guitar Rag/I Guess I've Been Dreaming Again	1948	5.00	10.00	20.00

OKEH

Number	Title (A Side/B Side)	Yr	VG	VG+	NM
❑ 6731	Shame on You/A Pair of Broken Hearts	1945	6.25	12.50	25.00
❑ 6746	I've Taken All I'm Gonna Take from You/Forgive Me One More Time	1945	6.25	12.50	25.00

Albums

COLUMBIA

Number	Title (A Side/B Side)	Yr	VG	VG+	NM
❑ CL 9007 [10]	Sagebrush Swing	1949	50.00	100.00	200.00

DECCA

Number	Title (A Side/B Side)	Yr	VG	VG+	NM
❑ DL 5563 [10]	Dance-O-Rama	1955	75.00	150.00	300.00

RAYNOTE

Number	Title (A Side/B Side)	Yr	VG	VG+	NM
❑ R-5007 [M]	Fidoolin'	1959	10.00	20.00	40.00
❑ RS-5007 [S]	Fidoolin'	1959	12.50	25.00	50.00

ROULETTE

Number	Title (A Side/B Side)	Yr	VG	VG+	NM
❑ R 25145 [M]	Fidoolin'	1961	7.50	15.00	30.00
❑ SR 25145 [S]	Fidoolin'	1961	10.00	20.00	40.00

COOLIDGE, RITA

Also see GLEN CAMPBELL; KRIS KRISTOFFERSON AND RITA COOLIDGE.

45s

A&M

Number	Title (A Side/B Side)	Yr	VG	VG+	NM
❑ 1256	Crazy Love/Mountains	1971	—	2.50	5.00
❑ 1271	Mud Island/I Believe in You	1971	—	2.50	5.00
❑ 1324	Lay My Burden Down/Nice Feelin'	1972	—	2.00	4.00
❑ 1353	Most Likely You Go Your Way/Family Full of Soul	1972	—	2.00	4.00
❑ 1398	Fever/My Crew	1972	—	2.00	4.00
❑ 1398 [PS]	Fever/My Crew	1972	—	3.00	6.00
❑ 1414	Donut Man/Whiskey, Whiskey	1973	—	2.00	4.00
❑ 1545	Hold an Old Friend's Hand/Mama Lou	1974	—	2.00	4.00
❑ 1642	Love Has No Pride/Heaven's Dream	1974	—	2.00	4.00
❑ 1792	Am I Blue/Star	1976	—	2.00	4.00
❑ 1816	Late Again/Keep the Candle Burning	1976	—	2.00	4.00
❑ 1922	(Your Love Has Lifted Me) Higher and Higher/Who's to Bless and Who's to Blame	1977	—	2.00	4.00
❑ 1922 [PS]	(Your Love Has Lifted Me) Higher and Higher/Who's to Bless and Who's to Blame	1977	—	3.00	6.00
❑ 1965	We're All Alone/Southern Lady	1977	—	2.00	4.00
❑ 1965 [PS]	We're All Alone/Southern Lady	1977	—	2.00	4.00
❑ 2004	The Way You Do the Things You Do/I Feel the Burden (Being Lifted Off My Shoulders)	1977	—	2.00	4.00
❑ 2004 [PS]	The Way You Do the Things You Do/I Feel the Burden (Being Lifted Off My Shoulders)	1977	—	2.00	4.00
❑ 2058	You/Only You Know and I Know	1978	—	2.00	4.00
❑ 2058 [PS]	You/Only You Know and I Know	1978	—	2.00	4.00
❑ 2090	Love Me Again/The Jealous Kind	1978	—	2.00	4.00
❑ 2169	One Fine Day/Sweet Emotions	1979	—	2.00	4.00
❑ 2199	I'd Rather Leave While I'm in Love/Sweet Emotions	1979	—	2.00	4.00
❑ 2281	Fool That I Am/Can She Keep You Satisfied	1980	—	2.00	4.00
❑ 2318	Words/Born Under a Bad Sign	1981	—	2.00	4.00
❑ 2361	The Closer You Get/Take It Home	1981	—	2.00	4.00
❑ 2385	Wishin' and Hopin'/I Did My Part	1981	—	2.00	4.00
❑ 2541	I'll Never Let You Go/Shadow in the Night	1983	—	—	3.00
❑ 2546 [DJ]	I Will Never Let You Go (same on both sides)	1983	—	2.00	4.00
—Stock copies do not exist					
❑ 2551	All Time High/(Instrumental)	1983	—	—	3.00
❑ 2551 [PS]	All Time High/(Instrumental)	1983	—	2.50	5.00
❑ 2586	Only You/Shadow in the Night	1983	—	—	3.00
❑ 2634	Something Said Love/Survivor	1984	—	—	3.00

PEPPER

Number	Title (A Side/B Side)	Yr	VG	VG+	NM
❑ 442	Rainbow Child/Secret Places, Hiding Faces	1969	2.00	4.00	8.00
❑ 443	Turn Around and Love You/Walking in the Morning	1969	2.00	4.00	8.00

Albums

A&M

Number	Title (A Side/B Side)	Yr	VG	VG+	NM
❑ SP-3107	Rita Coolidge	198?	2.00	4.00	8.00
—Budget-line reissue					
❑ SP-3130	Nice Feelin'	198?	2.00	4.00	8.00
—Budget-line reissue					
❑ SP-3163	Anytime...Anywhere	198?	2.00	4.00	8.00
—Budget-line reissue					
❑ SP-3238	Rita Coolidge/Greatest Hits	198?	2.00	4.00	8.00
—Budget-line reissue					
❑ SP-3627	Fall Into Spring	1974	2.50	5.00	10.00
❑ SP-3727	Heartbreak Radio	1981	2.50	5.00	10.00
❑ SP-4291	Rita Coolidge	1971	2.50	5.00	10.00
❑ SP-4325	Nice Feelin'	1971	2.50	5.00	10.00
❑ AP-4370	The Lady's Not for Sale	1972	2.50	5.00	10.00
❑ SP-4531	It's Only Love	1975	2.50	5.00	10.00
❑ SP-4616	Anytime...Anywhere	1977	2.50	5.00	10.00
❑ SP-4669	Love Me Again	1978	2.50	5.00	10.00
❑ SP-4781	Satisfied	1979	2.50	5.00	10.00
❑ SP-4836	Rita Coolidge/Greatest Hits	1981	2.50	5.00	10.00
❑ SP-4914	Never Let You Gp	1983	2.50	5.00	10.00
❑ SP-5003	Inside the Fire	1984	2.50	5.00	10.00

NAUTILUS

Number	Title (A Side/B Side)	Yr	VG	VG+	NM
❑ NR-16	Anytime...Anywhere	1981	6.25	12.50	25.00
—Audiophile vinyl					

COOPER, JERRY

45s

BEAR

Number	Title (A Side/B Side)	Yr	VG	VG+	NM
❑ 178	I'l Forget You/(B-side unknown)	1987	—	3.00	6.00
❑ 187	As Long As There's Women Like You/(B-side unknown)	1988	—	3.00	6.00
❑ 191	Code of Honor/(B-side unknown)	1988	—	3.00	6.00

COOPER, MARTY

45s

MC

Number	Title (A Side/B Side)	Yr	VG	VG+	NM
❑ 5003	Like a Gypsy/$10 Room	1977	—	2.50	5.00

COOPER, WILMA LEE

Also see WILMA LEE AND STONEY COOPER.

45s

DECCA

Number	Title (A Side/B Side)	Yr	VG	VG+	NM
❑ 32136	The Birds Are Back/Never Too Far from My Mind	1967	2.50	5.00	10.00
❑ 32210	Darling, How Could You/Time Keeps Standing Still	1967	2.50	5.00	10.00

COOPER, WILMA LEE AND STONEY

Also see WILMA LEE COOPER.

45s

COLUMBIA

Number	Title (A Side/B Side)	Yr	VG	VG+	NM
❑ 2-310 (?)	Moonlight on West Virginia/On the Banks of the River	1949	10.00	20.00	40.00
—Microgroove 33 1/3 rpm 7-inch single, small hole					
❑ 2-370 (?)	Thirty Pieces of Silver/What's the Matter with This World	1949	10.00	20.00	40.00
—Microgroove 33 1/3 rpm 7-inch single, small hole					
❑ 2-440 (?)	I Dreamed About Mama Last Night/No One Now	1949	10.00	20.00	40.00
—Microgroove 33 1/3 rpm 7-inch single, small hole					
❑ 2-600 (?)	I Ain't Gonna Work Tomorrow/The Message Came Special	1950	10.00	20.00	40.00
—Microgroove 33 1/3 rpm 7-inch single, small hole					
❑ 4-20713	The Legend of the Dogwood Tree/White Rose	1950	7.50	15.00	30.00
❑ 4-20781	Faded Love/Golden Rocket	1951	7.50	15.00	30.00
❑ 4-20801	Ghost Train/Mother's Prayer	1951	6.25	12.50	25.00
❑ 4-20861	West Virginia Polka/Sunny Side of the Mountain	1951	6.25	12.50	25.00
❑ 4-20898	All on Account of You/You Tried to Ruin My Name	1952	6.25	12.50	25.00
❑ 4-20949	I'm Taking My Audition/Walking My Lord Up Calvary Hill	1952	6.25	12.50	25.00
❑ 4-21000	Will the Lord Let You In/My Lord's Gonna Share My Hand	1952	6.25	12.50	25.00
❑ 4-21010	I Cried Again/Have Mercy on Me	1952	6.25	12.50	25.00
❑ 4-21049	Stoney/Clinch Mountain Waltz	1952	6.25	12.50	25.00
❑ 4-21088	Don't Play That Song/You Belong to Someone Else	1953	6.25	12.50	25.00
❑ 4-21221	Bamboozled/You Can't Feel the Way I Do	1954	6.25	12.50	25.00
❑ 4-21265	Brand New Baby/Can You Forget	1954	6.25	12.50	25.00

DECCA

Number	Title (A Side/B Side)	Yr	VG	VG+	NM
❑ 31891	It's Started Again/Wedding Bells	1966	2.50	5.00	10.00
❑ 31971	Each Season Changes You/It's Easier to Say Than Do	1966	2.50	5.00	10.00
❑ 32032	Three Windows/A Hero's Death	1966	2.50	5.00	10.00
❑ 32482	Don't Let Your Sweet Love Die/Guide Me Home, My Georgia Moon	1969	2.50	5.00	10.00
❑ 32581	Not My Kind/Right to Love What's Love	1969	2.50	5.00	10.00

HICKORY

Number	Title (A Side/B Side)	Yr	VG	VG+	NM
❑ 1028	How It Hurts to Cry Alone/Just for a While	1955	5.00	10.00	20.00
❑ 1035	Please Help Me to Be Wrong/Each Season Changes You	1955	5.00	10.00	20.00
❑ 1043	I Want to Be Loved/Row No. 2	1956	5.00	10.00	20.00
❑ 1051	Cheated Too/This Crazy Crazy World	1956	5.00	10.00	20.00
❑ 1058	Loving You/Tramp on the Street	1957	5.00	10.00	20.00
❑ 1064	This Thing Called Love/My Hearts Keep Crying	1957	5.00	10.00	20.00
❑ 1070	Diamond Joe/I Tell My Heart	1957	5.00	10.00	20.00
❑ 1078	He Taught Them How/Walking My Lord Up Calvary Hill	1958	5.00	10.00	20.00
❑ 1085	Come Walk with Me/Is It Right	1958	3.75	7.50	15.00
❑ 1098	Big Midnight Special/X Marks the Spot	1959	3.75	7.50	15.00
❑ 1107	There's a Big Wheel/Rachel's Guitar	1959	3.75	7.50	15.00
❑ 1118	Johnny, My Love (Grandma's Diary)/More Love	1960	3.75	7.50	15.00
❑ 1126	This Ole House/Heartbreak Street	1960	3.75	7.50	15.00
❑ 1147	Wreck on the Highway/Night After Night	1961	3.75	7.50	15.00
❑ 1157	Heartaches Don't Lie/The Mighty Battle Cry	1961	3.75	7.50	15.00
❑ 1167	Have Faith in Me/Matthew 24	1962	3.75	7.50	15.00
❑ 1179	Philadelphia Lawyer/Trouble Ahead	1962	3.00	6.00	12.00
❑ 1193	Doing My Time/Singing Waterfall	1962	3.00	6.00	12.00
❑ 1208	Glory Land March/Satisfied	1963	3.00	6.00	12.00
❑ 1225	There's a Higher Power/This World Can't Stand Long	1963	3.00	6.00	12.00
❑ 1257	Big John's Wife/Pirate King	1964	3.00	6.00	12.00
❑ 1279	This Train/I Couldn't Care Less	1964	3.00	6.00	12.00

STARDAY

Number	Title (A Side/B Side)	Yr	VG	VG+	NM
❑ 151	Sweet Fern/Hello Central, Give Me Heaven	1977	—	2.50	5.00
❑ 8005	Wreck on the Highway/This Ole House	197?	—	2.50	5.00

Albums

DECCA

Number	Title (A Side/B Side)	Yr	VG	VG+	NM
❑ DL 4784 [M]	Wilma Lee and Stoney Cooper Sing	1966	5.00	10.00	20.00
❑ DL 74784 [S]	Wilma Lee and Stoney Cooper Sing	1966	6.25	12.50	25.00

HARMONY

Number	Title (A Side/B Side)	Yr	VG	VG+	NM
❑ HL 7233 [M]	Sacred Songs	1960	6.25	12.50	25.00

HICKORY

Number	Title (A Side/B Side)	Yr	VG	VG+	NM
❑ LP-100 [M]	There's a Big Wheel	1960	12.50	25.00	50.00
❑ LP-106 [M]	Family Favorites	1962	10.00	20.00	40.00
❑ LP-112 [M]	New Songs of Inspiration	1962	10.00	20.00	40.00

COPAS, COWBOY

45s

DOT

Number	Title (A Side/B Side)	Yr	VG	VG+	NM
❑ 15668	Blue Kimono/Breeze	1957	5.00	10.00	20.00
❑ 15735	Circle Rock/My Little Red Wagon	1958	15.00	30.00	60.00
❑ 15847	A World That's Real/Looking for an Angel	1958	5.00	10.00	20.00

KING

Number	Title (A Side/B Side)	Yr	VG	VG+	NM
❑ 951	The Strange Little Girl/You'll Never See Me Cry	1951	10.00	20.00	40.00
❑ 964	Tennessee Flat Guitar/I Love You	1951	7.50	15.00	30.00
❑ 980	I'm Glad I'm On the Inside/Four Books in the Bible	1951	7.50	15.00	30.00
❑ 1000	'Tis Sweet to Be Remembered/Because of You	1951	7.50	15.00	30.00
❑ 1003	O Little Town of Bethlehem/It Came Upon the Midnight Clear	1951	7.50	15.00	30.00
❑ 1004	White Christmas/Jingle Bells	1951	7.50	15.00	30.00
❑ 1034	Copy Cat/Those Gone and Left Me Blues	1952	7.50	15.00	30.00
❑ 1040	I'll Pay the Price/'Tis Sweet to Be Remembered	1951	7.50	15.00	30.00
❑ 1046	Four Bare Walls and a Ceiling/I Can't Stop Loving You	1952	7.50	15.00	30.00
❑ 1064	Boomerang/It's Enough to Make Anyone Cry	1952	7.50	15.00	30.00
❑ 1080	Golden Moon/I Can't Remember to Forget	1952	7.50	15.00	30.00
❑ 1136	I've Grown So Used to You/It's No Sin to Love You	1952	7.50	15.00	30.00
❑ 1139	Purple Rose/Some Fine Morning	1952	7.50	15.00	30.00
❑ 1151	Feelin' Low/Love Me Now	1952	7.50	15.00	30.00
❑ 1166	Doll of Clay/If Wishes Were Horses	1953	6.25	12.50	25.00
❑ 1200	I Can't Go On/A Wreath at the Door of My Heart	1953	6.25	12.50	25.00
❑ 1234	Tennessee Senorita/If You Will Let Me Be Your Love	1953	6.25	12.50	25.00
❑ 1253	Look What I Got/Will You Forget	1953	6.25	12.50	25.00
❑ 1274	Blue Waltz/A Heartache Ago	1953	6.25	12.50	25.00
❑ 1306	He Stands By His Window/The Man Upstairs	1954	6.25	12.50	25.00
❑ 1313	Unwanted Alone/Sorry	1954	6.25	12.50	25.00
❑ 1329	I'll Be There/I'm a Stranger in My Home	1954	6.25	12.50	25.00
❑ 1359	Return to Sender/I'll Waltz with You	1954	6.25	12.50	25.00
❑ 1386	Carbon Copy/I'm Glad for Your Sake	1954	6.25	12.50	25.00
❑ 1407	When I Lost You/Why Should I Want Her	1954	6.25	12.50	25.00
❑ 1424	Hello Darling/The Talking Mule	1955	6.25	12.50	25.00
❑ 1444	The Stone Was Rolled Away/The Silver That Nailed Him to the Cross	1955	6.25	12.50	25.00
❑ 1456	Pledging My Love/Shamed of Myself	1955	6.25	12.50	25.00
❑ 1464	The Party's Over/Summer Kisses	1955	6.25	12.50	25.00
❑ 1486	Tragic Romance/Listen to My Heart	1955	6.25	12.50	25.00
❑ 1507	Blue Yesterday/Tell Me More	1955	6.25	12.50	25.00
❑ 4865	Any Old Time/Don't Shake Hands with the Devil	1956	5.00	10.00	20.00
❑ 5270	Tennessee Waltz/Signed, Sealed and Delivered	1959	3.75	7.50	15.00
—As "Lloyd Copas"					
❑ 5392	Carolina Sunshine Girl/Rose of Tennessee	1960	3.75	7.50	15.00
❑ 5437	A Stranger in My Home/Old Faithful and True Love	1960	3.75	7.50	15.00
❑ 5479	It's a Shame/You Walked Right Out of My Dreams	1961	3.75	7.50	15.00
❑ 5544	It's a Lonely World/Don't Let Them Change Your Mind	1961	3.75	7.50	15.00
❑ 5571	Sweet Thing/Signed, Sealed, Then Forgotten	1961	3.75	7.50	15.00
❑ 5638	I Built a Fence Around My Heart/My Blues Are Gone	1962	3.75	7.50	15.00
❑ 5676	When Jesus Beckons Me Home/I Saw the Light	1962	3.75	7.50	15.00
❑ 5733	Signed, Sealed and Delivered/The Hopes of a Broken Heart	1963	3.00	6.00	12.00
❑ 5734	Breeze/The Road of Broken Hearts	1963	3.00	6.00	12.00

STARDAY

Number	Title (A Side/B Side)	Yr	VG	VG+	NM
❑ 476	Mom and Dad's Affair/Black Cloud Risin'	1959	3.75	7.50	15.00
❑ 493	South Pacific Shore/That's All I Can Remember	1960	3.75	7.50	15.00
❑ 501	Alabam/I Can	1960	5.00	10.00	20.00
❑ 524	I Have a Friend/The Hem of His Garment	1960	3.75	7.50	15.00
❑ 528	Sittin' Flat on Ready/Midnight in Heaven	1960	3.75	7.50	15.00
❑ 542	Flat Top/True Love (Is the Greatest Thing)	1961	3.75	7.50	15.00
❑ 552	Sunny Tennessee/Dreaming	1961	3.75	7.50	15.00
❑ 559	Signed, Sealed and Delivered/New Filipino Baby	1961	3.75	7.50	15.00
❑ 573	Sal/A Thousand Miles of Ocean	1961	3.75	7.50	15.00
❑ 585	There'll Come a Time Someday/Seven Seas from You	1962	3.75	7.50	15.00
❑ 595	Sold the Farm/Table in the Corner	1962	3.75	7.50	15.00
❑ 606	Bury Me Face Down/Heart on the Run	1962	3.75	7.50	15.00
❑ 612	Family Reunion/Smoke on the Water	1962	3.75	7.50	15.00
❑ 621	Goodbye Kisses/The Gypsy Girl	1963	3.00	6.00	12.00
❑ 641	Louisiana/Break Away, Break Away	1963	3.00	6.00	12.00
❑ 658	Autobiography/The Rainbow and the Rose	1963	3.00	6.00	12.00
❑ 685	Old Man's Story/Pretty Diamonds	1964	3.00	6.00	12.00
❑ 708	Ride in My Little Red Wagon/Black Eyed Susie	1965	2.50	5.00	10.00
❑ 729	Waltzing with Sin/Blue Kimono	1965	2.50	5.00	10.00
❑ 750	Cowboy's Deck of Cards/Beyond the Sunset	1966	2.50	5.00	10.00
❑ 7000	Alabam/Goodbye Kisses	197?	—	2.50	5.00
❑ 7001	Signed, Sealed and Delivered/New Filipino Baby	197?	—	2.50	5.00
❑ 7015	I Dreamed of a Hillbilly Heaven/Tragic Romance	197?	—	2.50	5.00
❑ 8006	Signed, Sealed and Delivered/Hillbilly Heaven	197?	—	2.50	5.00
❑ 8029	Alabam/Filipino Baby	197?	—	2.50	5.00

Selected 78s

KING

Number	Title (A Side/B Side)	Yr	VG	VG+	NM
❑ 505	Filipino Baby/I Don't Blame You	1946	5.00	10.00	20.00
❑ 511	You Live in a World All Your Own/There Ain't Nobody Gonna Miss You	1946	5.00	10.00	20.00
❑ 516	Gun Totin' Mama/Please Answer My Letter	1946	5.00	10.00	20.00
❑ 537	Tragic Romance/You Will Find Me Here	1946	5.00	10.00	20.00
❑ 553	You're Living a Lie/Sundown and Sorrow	1947	5.00	10.00	20.00
❑ 566	No More Roamin'/Juke Box Blues	1947	5.00	10.00	20.00
❑ 591	In My Merry Oldsmobile/Breeze	1947	5.00	10.00	20.00
❑ 598	Kentucky Waltz/Heartaches	1947	5.00	10.00	20.00
❑ 605	Three Strikes and You're Out/Things Are Gonna Be Different	1947	5.00	10.00	20.00
❑ 618	Breeze/Dolly Dear	1947	5.00	10.00	20.00
❑ 630	Texas Red/Sweet Thing	1947	5.00	10.00	20.00
❑ 647	Honky Tonkin'/Roly Poly	1947	5.00	10.00	20.00
❑ 657	Are You Honest/Honky Tonkin'	1947	5.00	10.00	20.00
❑ 658	Signed, Sealed and Delivered/Opportunity Is Knocking	1947	5.00	10.00	20.00
❑ 666	As Advertised/Would Be Better for Us Both	1947	5.00	10.00	20.00
❑ 675	White Christmas/Jingle Bells	1947	5.00	10.00	20.00
❑ 688	Jamboree/I'm Tired of Playing Santa Claus to You	1947	5.00	10.00	20.00
❑ 696	Tennessee Waltz/How Much Do I Owe You	1948	5.00	10.00	20.00
❑ 714	Tennessee Moon/The Hope of a Broken Heart	1948	5.00	10.00	20.00
❑ 737	Rose of Oklahoma/Believe It or Not	1948	5.00	10.00	20.00
❑ 743	Too Many Teardrops/Peaches and Cream	1948	5.00	10.00	20.00

Number	Title (A Side/B Side)	Yr	VG	VG+	NM
❑ 755	An Old Farm for Sale/Where You Goin'	1948	5.00	10.00	20.00
❑ 767	I Love You So Much It Hurts/Down in Nashville Tennessee	1948	5.00	10.00	20.00
❑ 775	I'm Waltzing with Tears in My Eyes/Down in Nashville Tennessee	1949	5.00	10.00	20.00
❑ 777	Candy Kisses/Forever	1949	5.00	10.00	20.00
❑ 787	It's Wrong to Love You/A Package of Lies Tied in Blue	1949	5.00	10.00	20.00
❑ 802	Oceans of Love/Waltz with Me	1949	5.00	10.00	20.00
❑ 811	Hangman's Boogie/Blue Pacific Waltz	1949	5.00	10.00	20.00
❑ 825	Crazy Over You/A Gypsy Told Me	1949	5.00	10.00	20.00
❑ 846	Open Door, Open Arms/More Precious Than Silver and Gold	1950	5.00	10.00	20.00
❑ 855	Heartbroken/Blues in the Moonlight	1950	5.00	10.00	20.00
❑ 870	The Postman Just Passes Me By/Road of Broken Hearts	1950	5.00	10.00	20.00
❑ 885	I'm Stepping Out/My True Confession	1950	5.00	10.00	20.00
❑ 895	Signed, Sealed, Then Forgotten/My Hula Baby	1950	5.00	10.00	20.00
❑ 904	From the Manger to the Cross/King of Kings	1950	5.00	10.00	20.00
❑ 919	Tennessee Waltz/I'll Never More Be Shackled	1950	3.75	7.50	15.00
❑ 928	Goodnite Sweetheart Goodnite/Why Do the Stormy Winds Blow	1951	5.00	10.00	20.00
❑ 937	If I Should Come Back/If You But Care	1951	5.00	10.00	20.00
Albums					
KING					
❑ 553 [M]	Cowboy Copas Sings His All-Time Hits	1957	25.00	50.00	100.00
❑ 556 [M]	Favorite Sacred Songs	1957	20.00	40.00	80.00
❑ 619 [M]	Sacred Songs by Cowboy Copas	1959	20.00	40.00	80.00
❑ 714 [M]	Tragic Tales of Love and Life	1960	20.00	40.00	80.00
❑ 720 [M]	Broken Hearted Melodies	1960	20.00	40.00	80.00
❑ 817 [M]	Country Gentleman of Song	1963	10.00	20.00	40.00
❑ 824 [M]	As You Remember Cowboy Copas	1963	10.00	20.00	40.00
❑ 894 [M]	Cowboy Copas Hymns	1964	10.00	20.00	40.00
STARDAY					
❑ SLP-118 [M]	All Time Country Music Great	1960	10.00	20.00	40.00
❑ SLP-133 [M]	Inspirational Songs	1961	10.00	20.00	40.00
❑ SLP-144 [M]	Cowboy Copas	1961	10.00	20.00	40.00
❑ SLP-157 [M]	Opry Star Spotlight on Cowboy Copas	1962	10.00	20.00	40.00
❑ SLP-175 [M]	Mister Country Music	1962	10.00	20.00	40.00
❑ SLP-184 [M]	Songs That Made Him Famous	1962	10.00	20.00	40.00
❑ SLP-208 [M]	Country Music Entertainer #1	1963	10.00	20.00	40.00
❑ SLP-212 [M]	Beyond the Sunset	1963	10.00	20.00	40.00
❑ SLP-234 [M]	The Unforgettable Cowboy Copas	1963	10.00	20.00	40.00
❑ SLP-247 [M]	Star of the Grand Ole Opry	1963	10.00	20.00	40.00
❑ SLP-268 [M]	Cowboy Copas and His Friends	1964	10.00	20.00	40.00
❑ SLP-317 [M]	The Legend Lives On	1965	7.50	15.00	30.00
❑ SLP-347 [(2) M]	The Cowboy Copas Story	1965	7.50	15.00	30.00

COPAS, COWBOY, AND HAWKSHAW HAWKINS

Also see each artist's individual listings.

Number	Title (A Side/B Side)	Yr	VG	VG+	NM
Albums					
KING					
❑ 835 [M]	In Memory	1963	10.00	20.00	40.00
❑ 850 [M]	The Legend of Cowboy Copas and Hawkshaw Hawkins	1964	10.00	20.00	40.00
❑ 984 [M]	24 Great Hits	1968	6.25	12.50	25.00

COPAS, COWBOY/HAWKSHAW HAWKINS/PATSY CLINE

Also see each artist's individual listings.

Number	Title (A Side/B Side)	Yr	VG	VG+	NM
Albums					
STARDAY					
❑ SLP-346 [M]	Gone But Not Forgotten	1965	7.50	15.00	30.00

COPAS, COWBOY, AND GRANDPA JONES

Also see each artist's individual listings.

Number	Title (A Side/B Side)	Yr	VG	VG+	NM
Selected 78s					
KING					
❑ 665	Move It On Over/(B-side unknown)	1947	5.00	10.00	20.00
❑ 835	Mule Train/Feudin' Boogie	1949	5.00	10.00	20.00
❑ 844	Raggin' the Banjo/Feudin' Boogie	1950	5.00	10.00	20.00

CORBIN, RAY

Number	Title (A Side/B Side)	Yr	VG	VG+	NM
45s					
COLUMBIA					
❑ 4-44943	I'm Letting You Go/The Wild One	1969	—	3.50	7.00
❑ 4-45076	Hurricane Shirley/When You Fall As Hard As I Did	1970	—	3.50	7.00
MONUMENT					
❑ 1002	In Baby's Eyes/Mama, Don't Cry for Me	1967	2.00	4.00	8.00
❑ 1050	Absence/In My City	1968	2.00	4.00	8.00
❑ 1082	Mission of Loneliness/Sing the Blues to Daddy	1968	2.00	4.00	8.00
❑ 1102	Passin' Through/Life Doesn't Move Me	1968	2.00	4.00	8.00
TREND					
❑ 104	Just for Tonight/The Whole Night Long	196?	3.75	7.50	15.00

CORBIN/HANNER

Number	Title (A Side/B Side)	Yr	VG	VG+	NM
45s					
ALFA					
❑ 7001	Time Has Treated You Well/On the Wings of My Victory	1981	—	2.50	5.00
—As "Corbin-Hanner Band"					
❑ 7010	Oklahoma Crude/Too Lazy for Love	1981	—	2.50	5.00
—As "Corbin-Hanner Band"					
❑ 7015	Son of America/Regular Joe	1982	—	2.50	5.00
—As "Corbin-Hanner Band"					
❑ 7022	Everyone Knows I'm Yours//Son of America/Let Her Go/One Fine Morning	1982	—	2.50	5.00
—As "Corbin-Hanner Band"					
LIFESONG					
❑ 1773	Broken Man/Caribbean Nights	1978	—	2.50	5.00
—As "Corbin and Hanner"					
❑ 1783	America's Sweetheart/Like I Used To	1978	—	2.50	5.00
—As "Corbin and Hanner"					
❑ 45120	One Fine Morning/Lord, I Hope This Day Is Good	1982	—	2.50	5.00
—As "Corbin-Hanner Band"					
MERCURY					
❑ 864146-7	Just Another Hill/Wild Winds	1992	—	—	3.00
❑ 875688-7	Work Song/Wild Winds	1990	—	2.00	4.00
❑ 878746-7	Concrete Cowboy/Wild Winds	1990	—	2.00	4.00
Albums					
ALFA					
❑ AAA-10003	For the Sake of the Song	1981	3.00	6.00	12.00
—As "Corbin-Hanner Band"					
❑ AAA-11008	Son of America	1982	3.00	6.00	12.00
—As "Corbin-Hanner Band"					

CORNELIUS, HELEN

Number	Title (A Side/B Side)	Yr	VG	VG+	NM
45s					
AMERI-CAN					
❑ 1011	If Your Heart's a Rolling Stone/(B-side unknown)	1983	—	3.00	6.00
CAPITOL					
❑ 3116	You're Too Much for Me/Your Love Must Be Free	1971	—	3.00	6.00
COLUMBIA					
❑ 4-45921	If I Go On/Tweedle Dee Dee	1973	—	3.00	6.00
❑ 4-45980	Little Sugar Plum/Patchwork Girl	1973	—	3.00	6.00
ELEKTRA					
❑ 47190	Where Did Our Love Go/Spending Time	1981	—	2.50	5.00
—B-side by Joe Sun					
❑ 47232 [DJ]	Oh Holy Night/Silent Night	1981	—	3.00	6.00
—B-side by Joe Sun					
❑ 47237	Love Never Comes Easy/Losing You	1981	—	2.50	5.00
RCA					
❑ PB-10795	There's Always a Goodbye/Only Road Worth Taking	1976	—	2.50	5.00
❑ PB-11150	Everybody Everywhere Needs Somebody Sometime/Lincoln Audrey	1977	—	2.50	5.00
❑ PB-11375	What Cha Doin' After Midnight, Baby/Oh What a Night for Love	1978	—	2.50	5.00
❑ PB-11753	It Started with a Smile/I'm Changing	1979	—	2.50	5.00
RCA VICTOR					
❑ PB-10451	I'd Love You All Over/We Still Sing Love Songs in Missouri	1975	—	2.50	5.00
❑ PB-10629	Only Lovers/A Mornin' Made for Lovin'	1976	—	2.50	5.00
Albums					
MCA DOT					
❑ 39034	Helen Cornelius	198?	2.00	4.00	8.00

CORNOR, RANDY

Number	Title (A Side/B Side)	Yr	VG	VG+	NM
45s					
ABC DOT					
❑ 17592	Sometimes I Talk in My Sleep/Used to Be	1975	—	2.50	5.00
❑ 17625	Heart Don't Fail Me Now/Sugar Foot Rag	1976	—	2.50	5.00
❑ 17655	I Guess You Never Loved Me Anyway/Rocky Top	1976	—	2.50	5.00
❑ 17676	Love Doesn't Live Here Anymore/(Play That Song Again) About the Loser	1976	—	2.50	5.00
❑ 17711	Free and Easy/Love Me Like the Morning	1977	—	2.50	5.00
CHERRY					
❑ 643	Ring Telephone Ring (Damn Telephone)/If You'd Love Me Like You Loved Me	1978	—	3.00	6.00
❑ 783	Hurt As Big As Texas/Maybe You Should've Been Listenin	1978	—	3.00	6.00

COSTELLO, ELVIS

The below single and album were remakes of classic country songs.

Number	Title (A Side/B Side)	Yr	VG	VG+	NM
45s					
COLUMBIA					
❑ 02629	A Good Year for the Roses/The Angel Steps Out of Heaven	1981	—	2.00	4.00
Albums					
COLUMBIA					
❑ FC 37562	Almost Blue	1981	2.50	5.00	10.00
❑ PC 37562	Almost Blue	1984	2.00	4.00	8.00
—Reissue					

COTTON, GENE

Number	Title (A Side/B Side)	Yr	VG	VG+	NM
45s					
ABC					
❑ 12087	Country Spirit/Damn It All	1975	—	2.50	5.00
❑ 12137	Let Your Love Flow/Keepin' It on the Road	1975	—	2.50	5.00
❑ 12227	You've Got Me Runnin'/It's Over, Goodbye	1976	—	2.50	5.00
❑ 12250	Rain On/A Song for You	1977	—	2.50	5.00
❑ 12282	My Love Comes Alive/Sweet Destiny	1977	—	2.50	5.00
ARIOLA AMERICA					
❑ 7675	Before My Heart Finds Out/Like a Sunday in Salem	1977	—	2.50	5.00
❑ 7723	Like a Sunday in Salem (The Amos and Andy Song)/Shine On (You Got to Shine On)	1978	—	2.00	4.00
❑ 7778	Michael/Ocean of Love	1979	—	2.00	4.00

Number	Title (A Side/B Side)	Yr	VG	VG+	NM
KNOLL					
❑ 5002	If I Could Get You (Into My Life)/Rained On Before	1982	—	2.50	5.00
MYRRH					
❑ 116	American Indian Blues/Lessons of History	1973	—	3.00	6.00
❑ 117	Lean On One Another/(B-side unknown)	1973	—	3.00	6.00
❑ 123	Great American Noel/Mrs. Oliver	1973	—	3.00	6.00
❑ 137	Sunshine Roses/Mrs. Oliver	1974	—	3.00	6.00
(NO LABEL)					
❑ NR-16361 [DJ]	Child Of Peace (same on both sides)	1981	2.00	4.00	8.00
Albums					
ABC					
❑ D-933	For All the Young Writers	1975	2.50	5.00	10.00
❑ D-983	Rain On	1977	2.50	5.00	10.00
ARIOLA AMERICA					
❑ SW-50031	Save the Dancer	1978	2.50	5.00	10.00
❑ SW-50070	No Strings Attached	1979	2.50	5.00	10.00
KNOLL					
❑ 1001	Eclipse of the Blue Moon	1981	2.50	5.00	10.00
MYRRH					
❑ MSB-6517	In the Gray of the Morning	1973	3.00	6.00	12.00
❑ MSB-6524	Liberty	1974	3.00	6.00	12.00

COTTON, GENE, AND KIM CARNES

Also see each artist's individual listings.

45s

Number	Title (A Side/B Side)	Yr	VG	VG+	NM
ARIOLA AMERICA					
❑ 7704	You're a Part of Me/Shine On (You Got to Shine On)	1978	—	2.50	5.00

COTTON PICKERS, THE

Albums

Number	Title (A Side/B Side)	Yr	VG	VG+	NM
PHILIPS					
❑ PHM 200025 [M]	Country Guitar	1962	5.00	10.00	20.00
❑ PHS 600025 [S]	Country Guitar	1962	6.25	12.50	25.00

COTY, NEAL

45s

Number	Title (A Side/B Side)	Yr	VG	VG+	NM
MERCURY					
❑ 088 172183-7	Legacy/Breathin'	2000	—	—	3.00

COUCH, ORVILLE

45s

Number	Title (A Side/B Side)	Yr	VG	VG+	NM
CUSTOM					
❑ 101	Hello Trouble/Anywhere There's a Crowd	1962	7.50	15.00	30.00
MERCURY					
❑ 71718	Downtown/Big Jim Sandy	1960	5.00	10.00	20.00
MONUMENT					
❑ 915	Down Here Where the Hurt Begins/Permanent Wave	1966	3.00	6.00	12.00
❑ 949	The Best Things in Life/Farmington, New Mexico	1966	3.00	6.00	12.00
STARDAY					
❑ 305	You're Dreamin'/King for a Day	1957	7.50	15.00	30.00
❑ 326	Five Cent Candy/I Will If You Will	1957	7.50	15.00	30.00
VEE JAY					
❑ 470	Hello Trouble/Anywhere There's a Crowd	1962	5.00	10.00	20.00
❑ 528	Did I Miss You?/The Lonesomes	1963	5.00	10.00	20.00
❑ 589	Strike a Match/Dance Her By Me	1964	5.00	10.00	20.00
❑ 631	Hello Doll/Uncle Red	1964	5.00	10.00	20.00
❑ 693	Greenville Diner/Big Daddy of the Bayou	1965	5.00	10.00	20.00
❑ 706	Color Me Gone/You're a Little Heartache	1965	5.00	10.00	20.00

COULTERS, THE

45s

Number	Title (A Side/B Side)	Yr	VG	VG+	NM
DOLPHIN					
❑ 45003	Caroline's Still in Georgia/Free to Love You	1983	—	3.50	7.00
❑ 45003 [PS]	Caroline's Still in Georgia/Free to Love You	1983	2.00	4.00	8.00
EPIC					
❑ 50855	Crazy Old World/Love	1980	—	2.50	5.00
❑ 50905	Ozark Mountain Lullaby/For Me You're All There Is	1980	—	2.50	5.00

COUNT ROCKIN' SIDNEY

See ROCKIN' SIDNEY.

COUNTRY ALL-STARS, THE

Albums

Number	Title (A Side/B Side)	Yr	VG	VG+	NM
RCA VICTOR					
❑ LPM-3167 [10]	String Dustin'	1953	37.50	75.00	150.00

COUNTRY BOYS, THE

45s

Number	Title (A Side/B Side)	Yr	VG	VG+	NM
COLUMBIA					
❑ 4-21551	Country Boy Bounce/Red Wing	1956	6.25	12.50	25.00
❑ 4-40810	Buddy's Boogie/Raisin' the Dickens	1956	7.50	15.00	30.00

COUNTRY CAVALEERS, THE

45s

Number	Title (A Side/B Side)	Yr	VG	VG+	NM
COUNTRY SHOWCASE					
❑ 156	Call Back Operator/We Were Made for Each Other	1975	—	3.00	6.00
❑ 158	Everett the Evergreen/A Sing Along Christmas Song	1975	—	3.00	6.00
❑ 160	Lady on the Run/We Were Made for Each Other	1976	—	3.00	6.00
❑ 166	(Remember Those) Sweet Yesterdays/(B-side unknown)	1976	—	3.00	6.00
❑ 169	If I Love You/I've Got My Mind Satisfied	1976	—	3.00	6.00
❑ 171	Te Quiero (I Love You in Many Ways)/I've Got My Mind Satisfied	1976	—	3.00	6.00
MGM					
❑ 14606	Humming Bird/Hang On to What	1973	—	2.50	5.00

COUNTRY CHOIR, THE

45s

Number	Title (A Side/B Side)	Yr	VG	VG+	NM
COLUMBIA					
❑ 4-21193	Who at My Door Is Standing/Now the Day Is Over	1953	5.00	10.00	20.00
❑ 4-21235	Rock of Ages/God Be With You	1954	5.00	10.00	20.00

COUNTRY CUT-UPS, THE

Albums

Number	Title (A Side/B Side)	Yr	VG	VG+	NM
TOWN HOUSE					
❑ 1000 [M]	The Country Cut-Ups Go to College	195?	20.00	40.00	80.00

COUNTRY GENTLEMEN, THE

45s

Number	Title (A Side/B Side)	Yr	VG	VG+	NM
BRENT					
❑ 7058	For You/Saturday Night	1967	7.50	15.00	30.00
RCA VICTOR					
❑ 47-6673	A Rose and a Baby Ruth/Why Did You Go	1956	5.00	10.00	20.00
❑ 47-6764	My Heart's Desire/Right Around the Corner	1956	5.00	10.00	20.00
REBEL					
❑ 250	Bringing Mary Home/Northbound	1965	3.75	7.50	15.00
STARDAY					
❑ 344	Dixie/Backwoods Blues	1958	6.25	12.50	25.00
❑ 347	It's the Blues/Backwoods Blues	1958	6.25	12.50	25.00
❑ 367	Hey Little Girl/Hi Lonesome	1958	6.25	12.50	25.00
❑ 415	Rollin' Stone/The Devil's Own	1959	5.00	10.00	20.00
❑ 434	I'll Never Marry/Travelin' Dobro Blues	1959	5.00	10.00	20.00
❑ 455	New Freedom Bell/The Hills and Home	1959	5.00	10.00	20.00
❑ 558	Red Rockin' Chair/I Know I've Lost You	1961	5.00	10.00	20.00
❑ 628	Copper Kettle/Sunrise	1963	5.00	10.00	20.00
Albums					
CIMARRON					
❑ 2001 [M]	Songs of the Pioneers	1962	10.00	20.00	40.00
MERCURY					
❑ MG-20858 [M]	Folk Session Inside	1963	5.00	10.00	20.00
❑ SR-60858 [S]	Folk Session Inside	1963	6.25	12.50	25.00
STARDAY					
❑ SLP-109 [M]	Traveling Dobro Blues	1959	12.50	25.00	50.00
❑ SLP-174 [M]	Bluegrass at Carnegie Hall	1962	10.00	20.00	40.00
❑ SLP-311 [M]	Songs of the Pioneers	1965	6.25	12.50	25.00

COUNTRY HAMS, THE

See PAUL McCARTNEY.

COUNTRY LADS, THE

45s

Number	Title (A Side/B Side)	Yr	VG	VG+	NM
COLUMBIA					
❑ 4-41062	I Won't Beg Your Pardon/Alone in Love	1957	3.75	7.50	15.00
❑ 4-41212	Lonely Lover/Anything	1958	3.00	6.00	12.00

COUNTRY SQUIRRELS, THE

45s

Number	Title (A Side/B Side)	Yr	VG	VG+	NM
METROMEDIA COUNTRY					
❑ BMBO-0166	How I Love Those Christmas Songs/Country Christmas	1973	—	2.50	5.00
❑ 903	How I Love Those Christmas Songs/Country Christmas	1972	—	3.00	6.00

COX, DEANNA

45s

Number	Title (A Side/B Side)	Yr	VG	VG+	NM
WARNER BROS.					
❑ 7-18815	Never Gonna Be Your Fool Again/Texas Sidestep	1992	—	2.00	4.00
❑ 7-18995	Texas Sidestep/Wildest Dreams	1992	—	2.00	4.00

COX, DON (1)

45s

Number	Title (A Side/B Side)	Yr	VG	VG+	NM
ARC					
❑ 5902	Smooth Southern Highway/The Prophet and the Saint	1979	—	2.50	5.00

COX, DON (2)

Also see SUPER GRIP COWBOY BAND.

45s

Number	Title (A Side/B Side)	Yr	VG	VG+	NM
STEP ONE					
❑ 474	All Over Town/Chase the Moon	1994	—	2.00	4.00

CRABTREE, RILEY

45s

Number	Title (A Side/B Side)	Yr	VG	VG+	NM
COLUMBIA					
❑ 4-20901	Between the Pages of the Bible/Information Please	1952	6.25	12.50	25.00
❑ 4-20970	I Live with Memories/I Stood and Watched	1952	6.25	12.50	25.00
❑ 4-21030	Love Song of the Hills/If I Had Someone to Call My Very Own	1952	6.25	12.50	25.00
❑ 4-21073	An Orchid in My Bouquet/Tonight	1953	6.25	12.50	25.00

Number	Title (A Side/B Side)	Yr	VG	VG+	NM
❑ 4-21218	When Hank Williams Met Jimmie Rodgers/I'll Make You Want Me	1954	6.25	12.50	25.00
❑ 4-21268	When This World Changes Hands/Let Me Walk Through the Valley	1954	5.00	10.00	20.00

CRADDOCK, BILLY "CRASH"

Also recorded as "Bill Craddock" and "Crash Craddock," both included below.

45s

Number	Title (A Side/B Side)	Yr	VG	VG+	NM
ABC					
❑ 11342	Afraid I'll Want to Love Her One More Time/Treat Her Right	1972	—	3.00	6.00
❑ 11349	Don't Be Angry/I'm a White Boy	1973	—	3.00	6.00
❑ 11364	Slippin' and Slidin'/Living Example	1973	—	3.00	6.00
❑ 11379	'Till the Water Stops Runnin'/What Does a Loser Say	1973	—	3.00	6.00
❑ 11412	Sweet Magnolia Blossom/Home Is Such a Lonely Place to Go	1973	—	3.00	6.00
❑ 11437	Rub It In/It's Hard to Love a Hungry, Worried Man	1974	—	3.00	6.00
❑ 12013	Rub It In/It's Hard to Love a Hungry, Worried Man	1974	—	2.00	4.00
❑ 12036	Ruby, Baby/Walk When Love Walks	1974	—	2.50	5.00
❑ 12068	Still Thinkin' 'Bout You/Stay a Little Longer in Your Bed	1975	—	2.50	5.00
❑ 12104	I Love the Blues and the Boogie Woogie/No Deposit, No Return	1975	—	2.50	5.00
❑ 12335	Another Woman/The Words Still Rhyme	1978	—	2.00	4.00
❑ 12357	Think I'll Go Somewhere (And Cry Myself to Sleep)/It All Came Back	1978	—	2.00	4.00
❑ 12384	Don Juan/Things Are Mostly Fine	1978	—	2.00	4.00
ABC DOT					
❑ 17584	Easy As Pie/She's Mine	1975	—	2.50	5.00
❑ 17619	Walk Softly/She's About a Mover	1976	—	2.50	5.00
❑ 17635	You Rubbed It In All Wrong/I Need Somebody to Love Me	1976	—	2.50	5.00
❑ 17659	Broken Down in Tiny Pieces/Shake It Easy	1976	—	2.50	5.00
❑ 17682	Just a Little Thing/The First Time	1977	—	2.50	5.00
❑ 17701	A Tear Fell/A Piece of the Rock	1977	—	2.50	5.00
❑ 17723	The First Time/Walk When Love Walks	1977	—	2.50	5.00
ATLANTIC					
❑ 88851	Just Another Miserable Day (Here in Paradise)/Softly Diana	1989	—	—	3.00
❑ 88851 [PS]	Just Another Miserable Day (Here in Paradise)/Softly Diana	1989	—	2.00	4.00
CAPITOL					
❑ 4545	I Cheated on a Good Woman's Love/Not a Day Goes By	1978	—	2.00	4.00
❑ 4575	I've Been Too Long Lonely Baby/Jailhouse Rock	1978	—	2.00	4.00
❑ 4624	Hubba Hubba/Let's Go Back to the Beginning	1978	—	2.00	4.00
❑ 4672	If I Could Write a Song As Beautiful As You/Never Ending	1978	—	2.00	4.00
❑ 4707	My Mama Never Heard Me Sing/As Long As I Live	1979	—	2.00	4.00
❑ 4753	Robinhood/We Never Made It to Chicago	1979	—	2.00	4.00
❑ 4792	Till I Stop Shaking/Sneak Out of Love with You	1979	—	2.00	4.00
❑ 4838	I Just Had You on My Mind/You Just Wanta Be Mine	1980	—	2.00	4.00
❑ 4875	Sea Cruise/She's Got Legs	1980	—	2.00	4.00
❑ 4935	A Real Cowboy (You Say You're)/One Dream Coming, One Dream Going	1980	—	2.00	4.00
❑ 4972	It Was You/Betty Ruth	1981	—	2.00	4.00
❑ 5011	I Just Need You For Tonight/Leave Your Love A-Smokin'	1981	—	2.00	4.00
❑ 5051	Now That the Feeling's Gone/She's Good to Me	1981	—	2.00	4.00
❑ 5139	Love Busted/Darlin' Take Care of Yourself	1982	—	2.00	4.00
❑ 5170	The New Will Never Wear Off on You/Hold Me Tight	1982	—	2.00	4.00
CARTWHEEL					
❑ 193	Knock Three Times/The Best I Ever Had	1971	—	3.50	7.00
❑ 196	Dream Lover/I Ran Out of Time	1971	—	3.50	7.00
❑ 201	You Better Move On/Confidence and Common Sense	1971	—	3.50	7.00
❑ 210	Ain't Nothin' Shakin' (But the Leaves on the Trees)/She's My Angel	1972	—	3.50	7.00
❑ 216	I'm Gonna Knock on Your Door/What He Don't Know	1972	—	3.50	7.00
❑ 222	Afraid I'll Want to Love Her One More Time/Treat Her Right	1972	3.00	6.00	12.00
CEE CEE					
❑ 5400	Tell Me When I'm Hot/When the Feeling Is Right	1983	—	2.50	5.00
CHART					
❑ 1004	Go On Home Girl/Learning to Live Without You	1967	2.00	4.00	8.00
❑ 1025	Your Love Is What Is/Anything That's Part of You	1968	2.00	4.00	8.00
❑ 1415	There Ought to Be a Law/Two Arms Full of Lonely	1966	2.50	5.00	10.00
❑ 1450	Whipping Boy/The Love We Live Without	1967	2.50	5.00	10.00
❑ 5126	Go On Home Girl/Whipping Boy	1971	2.00	4.00	8.00
❑ 5154	Your Love Is What Is/Whipping Boy	1972	2.00	4.00	8.00
COLONIAL					
❑ 721	Bird Doggin'/Millionaire	1958	10.00	20.00	40.00
COLUMBIA					
❑ 41316	Am I to Be the One/I Miss You So Much	1959	6.25	12.50	25.00
❑ 41367	Sweetie Pie/Blabbermouth	1959	7.50	15.00	30.00
❑ 41470	Don't Destroy Me/Boom Boom Baby	1959	6.25	12.50	25.00
❑ 41470 [PS]	Don't Destroy Me/Boom Boom Baby	1959	12.50	25.00	50.00
❑ 41536	I Want That/Since She Turned Seventeen	1960	7.50	15.00	30.00
❑ 41619	All I Want Is You/Letter of Love	1960	6.25	12.50	25.00
❑ 41619 [PS]	All I Want Is You/Letter of Love	1960	12.50	25.00	50.00
❑ 41677	One Last Kiss/Is It True or False	1960	5.00	10.00	20.00
❑ 41822	Heavenly Love/Good Time Billy	1961	5.00	10.00	20.00
DATE					
❑ 1007	Lulu Lee/Ah, Poor Little Baby	1958	10.00	20.00	40.00
KING					
❑ 5912	Betty, Betty/Right Around the Corner	1964	6.25	12.50	25.00
❑ 5924	My Baby's Got Flat Feet/One Heartache Too Many	1964	6.25	12.50	25.00
❑ 5964	Teardrops on Your Letter/Love You More Everyday	1964	5.00	10.00	20.00
MERCURY					
❑ 71811	Truly True/How Lonely He Must Be	1961	5.00	10.00	20.00
❑ 71862	A Diamond Is Forever/Old King Cole	1962	6.25	12.50	25.00

Albums

Number	Title	Yr	VG	VG+	NM
ABC					
❑ X-777	Afraid I'll Want to Love Her One More Time	1973	6.25	12.50	25.00
❑ X-777	Two Sides of "Crash"	1973	3.75	7.50	15.00
—Retitled version of above					
❑ X-788	Mr. Country Rock	1973	3.75	7.50	15.00
❑ X-817	Rub It In	1974	3.75	7.50	15.00
—Black label					
❑ X-817	Rub It In	1974	3.00	6.00	12.00
—Multicolor label					
❑ X-850	Greatest Hits — Volume One	1975	3.00	6.00	12.00
❑ X-875	Still Thinkin' Bout You	1975	3.00	6.00	12.00
❑ AB-1078	Billy "Crash" Craddock Sings His Greatest Hits	1978	2.50	5.00	10.00
ABC DOT					
❑ 2040	Easy as Pie	1976	3.00	6.00	12.00
❑ 2063	Crash	1976	3.00	6.00	12.00
❑ 2082	Live!	1977	3.00	6.00	12.00
ATLANTIC					
❑ 82012	Back on Track	1989	3.00	6.00	12.00
CAPITOL					
❑ ST-11758	Billy "Crash" Craddock	1978	2.50	5.00	10.00
❑ SW-11853	Turning Up and Turning On	1978	2.50	5.00	10.00
❑ ST-11946	Laughing and Crying, Living and Dying	1979	2.50	5.00	10.00
❑ ST-12054	Changes	1980	2.50	5.00	10.00
❑ ST-12249	The New Will Never Wear Off	1981	2.50	5.00	10.00
❑ ST-12304	Greatest Hits	1983	2.50	5.00	10.00
CARTWHEEL					
❑ 193	Knock Three Times	1971	5.00	10.00	20.00
❑ 05001	You Better Move On	1972	5.00	10.00	20.00
CHART					
❑ 1053	The Best of Billy Crash Craddock	1973	3.75	7.50	15.00
HARMONY					
❑ KH 32186	Billy "Crash" Craddock	1973	3.00	6.00	12.00
KING					
❑ 912 [M]	I'm Tore Up	1964	25.00	50.00	100.00
MCA					
❑ 662	Greatest Hits — Volume One	1981	2.00	4.00	8.00
—Reissue of ABC 850					
❑ 663	Billy "Crash" Craddock Sings His Greatest Hits	1981	2.00	4.00	8.00
—Reissue of ABC 1078					
❑ 664	Easy as Pie	1981	2.00	4.00	8.00
—Reissue of ABC Dot 2040					
❑ 665	Live!	1981	2.00	4.00	8.00
—Reissue of ABC Dot 2082					
❑ 666	The First Time	1981	2.00	4.00	8.00
❑ 4165 [(2)]	The Best of Billy "Crash" Craddock	198?	3.00	6.00	12.00
MCA DOT					
❑ 39054	Crash Craddock	1986	2.50	5.00	10.00
STARDAY					
❑ 3005	16 Favorite Hits	1978	2.50	5.00	10.00

CRAFT, PAUL

45s

Number	Title (A Side/B Side)	Yr	VG	VG+	NM
RCA					
❑ PB-10971	We Know Better/Dropkick Me, Jesus	1977	—	2.50	5.00
❑ PB-11078	Lean On Jesus "Before He Leans On You"/Daddy Please Don't Go to Vegas	1977	—	2.50	5.00
❑ PB-11211	Teardrops in My Tequila/Rise Up	1978	—	2.50	5.00
❑ PB-11321	Brother Juke Box/One-Track Mine	1978	—	2.00	4.00
TRUTH					
❑ 3205	It's Me Again, Margaret/For Linda (Child in the Cradle)	1974	—	3.00	6.00

CRAMER, FLOYD

45s

Number	Title (A Side/B Side)	Yr	VG	VG+	NM
ABBOTT					
❑ 142	Little Brown Jug/Dancin' Diane	1953	3.75	7.50	15.00
❑ 146	Fancy Pants/Five Foot Two, Eyes of Blue	1953	3.75	7.50	15.00
—Black vinyl					
❑ 146	Fancy Pants/Five Foot Two, Eyes of Blue	1953	5.00	10.00	20.00
—Red vinyl					
❑ 159	Jolly Cholly/Oh! Suzanna	1954	3.75	7.50	15.00
❑ 181	Rag-a-tag/Aunt Dinah's Quilting Party	1955	3.75	7.50	15.00
MGM					
❑ 11990	Sweet Adeline/Howdy Ma'm	1955	3.00	6.00	12.00
❑ 12059	Piano Rag/Jealous, Cold, Cheatin' Heart	1955	3.00	6.00	12.00
❑ 12161	Battle Hymn of the Republic/Dixie	1955	3.00	6.00	12.00
❑ 12242	Succotash/Tennessee Central (#9)	1956	3.00	6.00	12.00
❑ 12306	Pretty Blue Jeans/Good Time Cakewalk	1956	3.00	6.00	12.00
❑ 12442	Rio Grande Valley/Slap Happy	1957	3.00	6.00	12.00
❑ 12520	Waltz with Cramer/Funny Face	1957	3.00	6.00	12.00
❑ 12619	Herman's Theme/Country Gentleman	1958	3.00	6.00	12.00

RCA

Number	Title (A Side/B Side)	Yr	VG	VG+	NM
❑ PB-10761	I'm Thinking Tonight of My Blue Eyes/Hang On Sloopy	1976	—	2.00	4.00
❑ PB-10901	La Chicana/Four in the Morning	1977	—	2.00	4.00

—With Chet Atkins and Danny Davis

Number	Title (A Side/B Side)	Yr	VG	VG+	NM
❑ PB-10908	Prelude to Love/Rhythm of the Rain	1977	—	2.00	4.00
❑ PB-11065	Coming Home/The Hurt	1977	—	2.00	4.00
❑ PB-11163	Looking for Mr. Goodbar/Father Time	1977	—	2.00	4.00
❑ PB-11284	Root Beer Rag/Morning Dew	1978	—	2.00	4.00
❑ PB-11394	The Main Street Electrical Parade/Singing in the Country Rain	1978	—	2.00	4.00
❑ PB-11432	Our Winter Love/For Lovers' Sake	1978	—	2.00	4.00
❑ PB-11576	Georgia on My Mind/Boogie Woogie	1979	—	2.00	4.00
❑ PB-11715	A Never Ending Love/Last Date	1979	—	2.00	4.00
❑ PB-11916	Dallas/Lover's Minuet	1980	—	—	3.00
❑ PB-12195	Sleepy Shores/Help Me Make It Through the Night	1981	—	—	3.00
❑ PB-12272	High Noon/Lone Ranger	1981	—	—	3.00

RCA VICTOR

Number	Title (A Side/B Side)	Yr	VG	VG+	NM
❑ APBO-0012	Lonely Street/The Battle of New Orleans	1973	—	2.00	4.00
❑ APBO-0214	Theme from "The Young and the Restless"/Boogie, Boogie, Boogie	1974	—	2.00	4.00
❑ PB-10076	Forever/Flip, Flop and Fly	1974	—	2.00	4.00
❑ PB-10336	The Last Farewell/My Melody of Love	1975	—	2.00	4.00
❑ PB-10533	Eres Tu (Touch the Wind)/Faded Love	1975	—	2.00	4.00
❑ PB-10597	Tonight's the Night/Candy Pants	1976	—	2.00	4.00
❑ 47-7156	Flip, Flop and Fly/Sophisticated Swing	1958	2.50	5.00	10.00
❑ 47-7250	Mumble Jumble/Cryin'	1958	2.50	5.00	10.00
❑ 47-7388	Rumpus/The Big Chihuahua	1958	2.50	5.00	10.00
❑ 47-7775	Last Date/Sweetie Baby	1960	3.00	6.00	12.00
❑ 47-7840	On the Rebound/Mood Indigo	1961	3.00	6.00	12.00
❑ 47-7840 [PS]	On the Rebound/Mood Indigo	1961	5.00	10.00	20.00
❑ 47-7893	San Antonio Rose/I Just Can't Imagine	1961	2.50	5.00	10.00
❑ 47-7907	Your Last Goodbye/Hang On	1961	2.50	5.00	10.00
❑ 47-7907 [PS]	Your Last Goodbye/Hang On	1961	5.00	10.00	20.00
❑ 47-7978	Chattanooga Choo Choo/Let's Go	1962	2.00	4.00	8.00
❑ 47-8013	Lovesick Blues/The First Hurt	1962	2.00	4.00	8.00
❑ 47-8041	Hot Pepper/For Those That Cry	1962	2.00	4.00	8.00
❑ 47-8084	Swing Low/Losers Weepers	1962	2.00	4.00	8.00
❑ 47-8116	Java/Melissa	1962	2.00	4.00	8.00
❑ 47-8171	(These Are) The Young Years/Kaapsedri	1963	2.00	4.00	8.00
❑ 47-8217	How High the Moon/Satan's Doll	1963	2.00	4.00	8.00
❑ 47-8265	The Hucklebuck/Heartless Heart	1963	2.00	4.00	8.00
❑ 47-8325	Want Me/Naomi	1964	2.00	4.00	8.00
❑ 47-8414	Tomorrow's Gone/Shrum	1964	2.00	4.00	8.00
❑ 47-8541	Town Square/Long Walk Home	1965	2.00	4.00	8.00
❑ 47-8899	Strangers in the Night/You've Lost That Lovin' Feelin'	1966	—	3.00	6.00
❑ 47-9065	Stood Up/Good Vibrations	1967	—	3.00	6.00
❑ 47-9157	I Wanna Be Free/Papa Gene's Blues	1967	—	3.00	6.00
❑ 47-9237	Theme for Sam/For No One	1967	—	3.00	6.00
❑ 47-9396	Gentle on My Mind/By the Time I Get to Phoenix	1967	—	3.00	6.00
❑ 47-9841	Theme from Room 222/Leaving on a Jet Plane	1970	—	2.00	4.00
❑ 47-9874	Fancy Free/Is This Tomorrow	1970	—	2.00	4.00
❑ 47-9940	For the Good Times/Everything Is Beautiful	1971	—	2.00	4.00
❑ 47-9978	Makin' Up/Theme from "Flight of the Doves"	1971	—	2.00	4.00
❑ 74-0152	Games People Play/Ob-La-Di, Ob-La-Da	1969	—	2.50	5.00
❑ 74-0209	Seattle/Lovin' Season	1969	—	2.50	5.00
❑ 74-0621	Corn Crib Symphony/Your Last Goodbye	1971	—	2.00	4.00
❑ 74-0674	Hony Tonk (Part 2)/Detour	1972	—	2.00	4.00
❑ 74-0821	Quiet Girl/Smile	1972	—	2.00	4.00
❑ 74-0869	Tonight's the Night/Crystal Chandelier	1973	—	2.00	4.00

SIMS

Number	Title (A Side/B Side)	Yr	VG	VG+	NM
❑ 121	Fancy Pants/Five Foot Two, Eyes of Blue	1961	2.00	4.00	8.00

STEP ONE

Number	Title (A Side/B Side)	Yr	VG	VG+	NM
❑ 454	Christmas Medley//We Wish You A Merry Christmas/I'll Be Home For Christmas	1992	—	2.50	5.00

—Red vinyl

7-Inch Extended Plays

RCA VICTOR

Number	Title (A Side/B Side)	Yr	VG	VG+	NM
❑ DJEO-0272 [DJ]	Behind Closed Doors/The Most Beautiful Girl//Star Spangled Banner/Top of the World	1974	2.50	5.00	10.00
❑ EPA-4377	Last Date/San Antonio Rose//Flip, Flop and Bop/Chattanooga Choo Choo	1961	2.50	5.00	10.00
❑ EPA-4377 [PS]	Last Date	1961	2.50	5.00	10.00

Albums

MGM

Number	Title (A Side/B Side)	Yr	VG	VG+	NM
❑ E-3502 [M]	That Honky-Tonk Piano	1957	10.00	20.00	40.00
❑ E-4223 [M]	Floyd Cramer Goes Honky Tonkin'	1964	3.75	7.50	15.00
❑ SE-4223 [R]	Floyd Cramer Goes Honky Tonkin'	1964	3.00	6.00	12.00
❑ SE-4666	Floyd Cramer Goes Honky Tonkin'	1970	3.00	6.00	12.00

—Reissue of 4223

PAIR

Number	Title (A Side/B Side)	Yr	VG	VG+	NM
❑ PDL2-1049 [(2)]	Country Classics	1986	3.00	6.00	12.00

RCA

Number	Title (A Side/B Side)	Yr	VG	VG+	NM
❑ 5621-1-R	Our Class Reunion	1987	2.50	5.00	10.00

RCA CAMDEN

Number	Title (A Side/B Side)	Yr	VG	VG+	NM
❑ ACL2-0128 [(2)]	Floyd Cramer Plays the Big Hits	1973	3.00	6.00	12.00
❑ ACL1-0563	Spotlight On Floyd Cramer	1974	2.50	5.00	10.00
❑ CAL-874 [M]	The Magic Touch	1965	3.00	6.00	12.00
❑ CAS-874 [S]	The Magic Touch	1965	3.00	6.00	12.00
❑ CAL-2104 [M]	Distinctive Piano Styling	196?	3.00	6.00	12.00
❑ CAS-2104 [S]	Distinctive Piano Styling	196?	3.00	6.00	12.00
❑ CAL-2152 [M]	Night Train	1967	3.00	6.00	12.00
❑ CAS-2152 [S]	Night Train	1967	3.00	6.00	12.00
❑ CAS-2508	Almost Persuaded	1971	3.00	6.00	12.00
❑ CXS-9016 [(2)]	A Date with Floyd Cramer	1972	3.75	7.50	15.00

RCA VICTOR

Number	Title (A Side/B Side)	Yr	VG	VG+	NM
❑ APD1-0155 [Q]	Super Country Hits	1973	3.75	7.50	15.00
❑ APL1-0155	Super Country Hits	1973	3.00	6.00	12.00
❑ APD1-0299 [Q]	Class of '73	1973	3.75	7.50	15.00
❑ APL1-0299	Class of '73	1973	3.00	6.00	12.00
❑ APD1-0469 [Q]	The Young and the Restless	1974	3.75	7.50	15.00
❑ APL1-0469	The Young and the Restless	1974	3.00	6.00	12.00
❑ APL1-0661	Floyd Cramer In Concert	1974	3.00	6.00	12.00
❑ APD1-0893 [Q]	Piano Masterpieces (1900-75)	1975	3.75	7.50	15.00
❑ APL1-0893	Piano Masterpieces (1900-75)	1975	2.50	5.00	10.00
❑ APD1-1191 [Q]	Class of '74 and '75	1975	3.75	7.50	15.00
❑ APL1-1191	Class of '74 and '75	1975	2.50	5.00	10.00
❑ APD1-1541 [Q]	Floyd Cramer Country	1976	3.75	7.50	15.00
❑ APL1-1541	Floyd Cramer Country	1976	2.50	5.00	10.00
❑ LPM-2151 [M]	Hello Blues	1960	3.75	7.50	15.00
❑ LSP-2151 [S]	Hello Blues	1960	5.00	10.00	20.00
❑ APL1-2278	Floyd Cramer & the Keyboard Kick Band	1977	2.50	5.00	10.00
❑ ANL1-2344	Hits from Country Hall	1977	2.50	5.00	10.00
❑ LPM-2350 [M]	Last Date	1961	5.00	10.00	20.00
❑ LSP-2350 [S]	Last Date	1961	6.25	12.50	25.00
❑ LPM-2359 [M]	On the Rebound	1961	3.75	7.50	15.00
❑ LSP-2359 [S]	On the Rebound	1961	5.00	10.00	20.00
❑ LPM-2428 [M]	Floyd Cramer Gets Organ-ized	1962	3.75	7.50	15.00
❑ LSP-2428 [S]	Floyd Cramer Gets Organ-ized	1962	5.00	10.00	20.00
❑ LPM-2466 [M]	America's Biggest Selling Pianist	1962	3.75	7.50	15.00
❑ LSP-2466 [S]	America's Biggest Selling Pianist	1962	5.00	10.00	20.00
❑ LPM-2544 [M]	I Remember Hank Williams	1962	3.75	7.50	15.00
❑ LSP-2544 [S]	I Remember Hank Williams	1962	5.00	10.00	20.00
❑ LPM-2642 [M]	Swing Along	1963	3.75	7.50	15.00
❑ LSP-2642 [S]	Swing Along	1963	5.00	10.00	20.00
❑ AHL1-2644	Looking for Mr. Goodbar	1978	2.50	5.00	10.00
❑ LPM-2701 [M]	Comin' On	1963	3.75	7.50	15.00
❑ LSP-2701 [S]	Comin' On	1963	5.00	10.00	20.00
❑ LPM-2800 [M]	Country Piano — City Strings	1964	3.75	7.50	15.00
❑ LSP-2800 [S]	Country Piano — City Strings	1964	5.00	10.00	20.00
❑ LPM-2883 [M]	Cramer at the Console	1964	3.75	7.50	15.00
❑ LSP-2883 [S]	Cramer at the Console	1964	5.00	10.00	20.00
❑ LPM-2888 [M]	The Best of Floyd Cramer	1964	3.00	6.00	12.00
❑ LSP-2888 [S]	The Best of Floyd Cramer	1964	3.75	7.50	15.00
❑ AHL1-3209	Super Hits	1979	2.50	5.00	10.00
❑ LPM-3318 [M]	Hits from the Country Hall of Fame	1965	3.75	7.50	15.00
❑ LSP-3318 [S]	Hits from the Country Hall of Fame	1965	5.00	10.00	20.00
❑ LPM-3405 [M]	Class of '65	1965	3.00	6.00	12.00
❑ LSP-3405 [S]	Class of '65	1965	3.75	7.50	15.00
❑ ANL1-3469	Floyd Cramer In Concert	1979	2.00	4.00	8.00
❑ AHL1-3487	Last Date	1979	2.50	5.00	10.00
❑ LPM-3533 [M]	The Big Ones	1966	3.00	6.00	12.00
❑ LSP-3533 [S]	The Big Ones	1966	3.75	7.50	15.00
❑ AHL1-3613	Dallas	1980	2.50	5.00	10.00
❑ LPM-3650 [M]	Class of '66	1966	3.00	6.00	12.00
❑ LSP-3650 [S]	Class of '66	1966	3.75	7.50	15.00
❑ AYL1-3745	Piano Masterpieces (1900-75)	1980	2.00	4.00	8.00
❑ LPM-3746 [M]	Here's What's Happening!	1967	3.75	7.50	15.00
❑ LSP-3746 [S]	Here's What's Happening!	1967	3.75	7.50	15.00
❑ LPM-3811 [M]	Floyd Cramer Plays the Monkees	1967	3.75	7.50	15.00
❑ LSP-3811 [S]	Floyd Cramer Plays the Monkees	1967	3.75	7.50	15.00
❑ LPM-3827 [M]	Class of '67	1967	3.75	7.50	15.00
❑ LSP-3827 [S]	Class of '67	1967	3.75	7.50	15.00
❑ LPM-3828 [M]	We Wish You a Merry Christmas	1967	7.50	15.00	30.00
❑ LSP-3828 [S]	We Wish You a Merry Christmas	1967	3.00	6.00	12.00
❑ AYL1-3900	The Best of Floyd Cramer	1981	2.00	4.00	8.00
❑ LPM-3925 [M]	Floyd Cramer Plays Country Classics	1968	5.00	10.00	20.00
❑ LSP-3925 [S]	Floyd Cramer Plays Country Classics	1968	3.75	7.50	15.00
❑ AYL1-4008	Great Country Hits	1981	2.00	4.00	8.00
❑ LPM-4025 [M]	Class of '68	1968	—	—	—

—Canceled?

Number	Title (A Side/B Side)	Yr	VG	VG+	NM
❑ LSP-4025 [S]	Class of '68	1968	3.75	7.50	15.00
❑ LSP-4070	MacArthur Park	1968	3.75	7.50	15.00
❑ LSP-4091	The Best of Floyd Cramer, Volume 2	1969	3.75	7.50	15.00
❑ AHL1-4119	Best of the West	1982	2.50	5.00	10.00
❑ LSP-4162	Class of '69	1969	3.75	7.50	15.00
❑ LSP-4220	Floyd Cramer Plays More Country Classics	1969	3.75	7.50	15.00
❑ LSP-4312	The Big Ones, Volume II	1970	3.75	7.50	15.00
❑ LSP-4367	Floyd Cramer with the Music City Pops	1970	3.75	7.50	15.00
❑ LSP-4437	Class of '70	1970	3.75	7.50	15.00
❑ LSP-4500	Sounds of Sunday	1971	3.75	7.50	15.00
❑ LSP-4590	Class of '71	1971	3.75	7.50	15.00
❑ LSP-4676	Detours	1972	3.75	7.50	15.00
❑ LSP-4772	Class of '72	1972	3.75	7.50	15.00
❑ LSP-4821	Best of the Class of...	1973	3.75	7.50	15.00
❑ AHL1-5452	Collector's Series	1985	2.50	5.00	10.00
❑ VPS-6031 [(2)]	This Is Floyd Cramer	1970	5.00	10.00	20.00

CRAWFORD/WEST

45s

WARNER BROS.

Number	Title (A Side/B Side)	Yr	VG	VG+	NM
❑ 17358	Summertime Girls/Hard to Stop a Train	1997	—	—	3.00

CREECH, ALICE

45s

TARGET

Number	Title (A Side/B Side)	Yr	VG	VG+	NM
❑ 0138	The Night They Drove Old Dixie Down/When I'm Not with You	1971	—	3.50	7.00
❑ 0144	We'll Sing in the Sunshine/I Used to Cry Over You	1972	—	3.50	7.00
❑ 0152	Born a Woman/Close to Me	1972	—	3.50	7.00
❑ 00313	The Hunter/Isn't It a Shame About Jeannie	1971	2.00	4.00	8.00

CREEDENCE CLEARWATER REVIVAL

OK, they weren't a country group. But their version of "Cotton Fields" did make the country charts, and it's not unheard of to hear certain CCR songs on country stations today. Also see JOHN FOGERTY.

12-Inch Singles

FANTASY

Number	Title (A Side/B Side)	Yr	VG	VG+	NM
❑ 759-D-LP [DJ]	I Heard It Through the Grapevine (11:05) (same on both sides)	1976	5.00	10.00	20.00

45s

FANTASY

Number	Title (A Side/B Side)	Yr	VG	VG+	NM
❑ 616	Suzie Q (Part One)/Suzie Q (Part Two)	1968	—	3.00	6.00
❑ 617	I Put a Spell on You/Walk on the Water	1968	2.00	4.00	8.00
❑ 619	Proud Mary/Born on the Bayou	1969	—	3.00	6.00
❑ 622	Bad Moon Rising/Lodi	1969	—	3.00	6.00
❑ 625	Green River/Commotion	1969	—	3.00	6.00
❑ 634	Down on the Corner/Fortunate Son	1969	—	3.00	6.00
❑ 634 [PS]	Down on the Corner/Fortunate Son	1969	3.00	6.00	12.00
❑ 637	Travelin' Band/Who'll Stop the Rain	1970	—	3.00	6.00
❑ 637 [PS]	Travelin' Band/Who'll Stop the Rain	1970	3.00	6.00	12.00
❑ 641	Up Around the Bend/Run Through the Jungle	1970	—	3.00	6.00
❑ 641 [PS]	Up Around the Bend/Run Through the Jungle	1970	3.00	6.00	12.00
❑ 645	Lookin' Out My Back Door/Long As I Can See the Light	1970	—	3.00	6.00
❑ 645 [PS]	Lookin' Out My Back Door/Long As I Can See the Light	1970	3.00	6.00	12.00
❑ 655	Have You Ever Seen the Rain/Hey Tonight	1971	—	3.00	6.00
❑ 665	Sweet Hitch-Hiker/Door to Door	1971	—	3.00	6.00
❑ 665 [PS]	Sweet Hitch-Hiker/Door to Door	1971	3.00	6.00	12.00
❑ 676	Someday Never Comes/Tearin' Up the Country	1972	—	3.00	6.00
❑ 759	I Heard It Through the Grapevine/Good Golly Miss Molly	1976	—	2.00	4.00
❑ 759 [PS]	I Heard It Through the Grapevine/Good Golly Miss Molly	1976	—	2.50	5.00
❑ 908	Tombstone Shadow/Commotion	1981	—	2.00	4.00
❑ 917	Medley U.S.A./Bad Moon Rising	1981	—	2.00	4.00
❑ 920	Cotton Fields/Lodi	1981	—	2.00	4.00
❑ 957	Medley (from "I Heard It Through the Grapevine" to "Up Around the Bend")/Medley (from "Proud Mary" to "Lodi")	1985	2.50	5.00	10.00
❑ 2832/3 [DJ]	45 Revolutions Per Minute (Part 1)/45 Revolutions Per Minute (Part 2)	1970	10.00	20.00	40.00
❑ 2832/3 [PS]	45 Revolutions Per Minute (Part 1)/45 Revolutions Per Minute (Part 2)	1970	15.00	30.00	60.00

SCORPIO

Number	Title (A Side/B Side)	Yr	VG	VG+	NM
❑ 412	Porterville/Call It Pretending	1968	20.00	40.00	80.00

Albums

DCC COMPACT CLASSICS

Number	Title (A Side/B Side)	Yr	VG	VG+	NM
❑ LPZ-2019	Willie and the Poor Boys	1996	5.00	10.00	20.00
—Audiophile vinyl					

FANTASY

Number	Title (A Side/B Side)	Yr	VG	VG+	NM
❑ CCR-1 [(2)]	Live in Europe	1973	3.00	6.00	12.00
❑ CCR-2 [(2)]	Chronicle (The 20 Greatest Hits)	1976	3.75	7.50	15.00
—Brown labels					
❑ CCR-2 [(2)]	Chronicle (The 20 Greatest Hits)	1979	3.00	6.00	12.00
—Whitish or light blue labels					
❑ CCR-3 [(2)]	Chronicle, Volume 2	1987	3.75	7.50	15.00
❑ CCR-68 [(2)]	Creedence Clearwater Revival 1968/69	1981	3.00	6.00	12.00
—Compilation of 8382 and 8387					
❑ CCR-69 [(2)]	Creedence Clearwater Revival 1969	1981	3.00	6.00	12.00
—Compilation of 8393 and 8397					
❑ CCR-70 [(2)]	Creedence Clearwater Revival 1970	1981	3.00	6.00	12.00
—Compilation of 8402 and 8410					
❑ FPM-4001 [Q]	Creedence Gold	197?	12.50	25.00	50.00
❑ MPF-4501	The Royal Albert Hall Concert	1980	3.75	7.50	15.00
—Album withdrawn and changed when it was discovered this didn't come from the Royal Albert Hall					
❑ MPF-4501	The Concert	1981	2.50	5.00	10.00
—Retitled version					
❑ MPF-4509	Creedence Country	1981	2.50	5.00	10.00
❑ ORC-4512	Creedence Clearwater Revival	1981	2.00	4.00	8.00
—Reissue of 8382					
❑ ORC-4513	Bayou Country	1981	2.00	4.00	8.00
—Reissue of 8387					
❑ ORC-4514	Green River	1981	2.00	4.00	8.00
—Reissue of 8393					
❑ ORC-4515	Willy and the Poor Boys	1981	2.00	4.00	8.00
—Reissue of 8397					
❑ ORC-4516	Cosmo's Factory	1981	2.00	4.00	8.00
—Reissue of 8402					
❑ ORC-4517	Pendulum	1981	2.00	4.00	8.00
—Reissue of 8410					
❑ ORC-4518	Mardi Gras	1981	2.00	4.00	8.00
—Reissue of 9404					
❑ MPF-4522	The Movie Album	1985	2.00	4.00	8.00
❑ ORC-4526 [(2)]	Live in Europe	1986	2.50	5.00	10.00
❑ F-8382	Creedence Clearwater Revival	1968	6.25	12.50	25.00
—With no reference to "Susie Q" on the front cover					
❑ F-8382	Creedence Clearwater Revival	1968	3.75	7.50	15.00
—With "Susie Q" mentioned on the front cover; dark blue label					
❑ F-8382	Creedence Clearwater Revival	1973	2.50	5.00	10.00
—Brown label					
❑ F-8382 [DJ]	Creedence Clearwater Revival	1968	20.00	40.00	80.00
—White label promo					
❑ F-8387	Bayou Country	1969	3.75	7.50	15.00
—Dark blue label					
❑ F-8387	Bayou Country	1973	2.50	5.00	10.00
—Brown label					
❑ F-8387 [DJ]	Bayou Country	1969	20.00	40.00	80.00
—White label promo					
❑ F-8393	Green River	1969	3.75	7.50	15.00
—Dark blue label					
❑ F-8393	Green River	1973	2.50	5.00	10.00
—Brown label					
❑ F-8393 [DJ]	Green River	1969	20.00	40.00	80.00
—White label promo					
❑ F-8397	Willy and the Poor Boys	1969	3.75	7.50	15.00
—Dark blue label					
❑ F-8397	Willy and the Poor Boys	1973	2.50	5.00	10.00
—Brown label					
❑ F-8397 [DJ]	Willy and the Poor Boys	1969	20.00	40.00	80.00
—White label promo					
❑ F-8402	Cosmo's Factory	1970	3.75	7.50	15.00
—Dark blue label					
❑ F-8402	Cosmo's Factory	1973	2.50	5.00	10.00
—Brown label					
❑ F-8402 [DJ]	Cosmo's Factory	1970	20.00	40.00	80.00
—White label promo					
❑ F-8410	Pendulum	1970	3.75	7.50	15.00
—Dark blue label					
❑ F-8410	Pendulum	1973	2.50	5.00	10.00
—Brown label					
❑ F-9404	Mardi Gras	1972	3.75	7.50	15.00
—Dark blue label					
❑ F-9404	Mardi Gras	1973	2.50	5.00	10.00
—Brown label					
❑ F-9418	Creedence Gold	1972	2.50	5.00	10.00
❑ F-9430	More Creedence Gold	1973	2.50	5.00	10.00
❑ F-9621	Chooglin'	1982	2.00	4.00	8.00

HEARTLAND

Number	Title (A Side/B Side)	Yr	VG	VG+	NM
❑ HR 2039 [(3)]	Creedence Clearwater Revival	1990	3.75	7.50	15.00

K-TEL

Number	Title (A Side/B Side)	Yr	VG	VG+	NM
❑ NU 9360	The Best of Creedence Clearwater Revival — 20 Super Hits	1978	3.75	7.50	15.00

MOBILE FIDELITY

Number	Title (A Side/B Side)	Yr	VG	VG+	NM
❑ 1-037	Cosmo's Factory	1979	17.50	35.00	70.00
—Audiophile vinyl					

TIME-LIFE

Number	Title (A Side/B Side)	Yr	VG	VG+	NM
❑ SCLR-18 [(2)]	Creedence Clearwater Revival	1989	3.75	7.50	15.00
—Part of Time-Life's "Classic Rock" series					

CREWS, DWAYNE

45s

KILLER

Number	Title (A Side/B Side)	Yr	VG	VG+	NM
❑ 124	Selfish Man/(B-side unknown)	1989	2.00	4.00	8.00

CRICKETS, THE

Also see BUDDY HOLLY.

45s

BARNABY

Number	Title (A Side/B Side)	Yr	VG	VG+	NM
❑ 2061	Rockin' 50's Rock 'N' Roll/True Love Ways	1972	5.00	10.00	20.00

BRUNSWICK

Number	Title (A Side/B Side)	Yr	VG	VG+	NM
❑ 55009	That'll Be the Day/I'm Lookin' for Someone to Love	1957	12.50	25.00	50.00
❑ 55035	Oh, Boy!/Not Fade Away	1957	12.50	25.00	50.00
❑ 55053	Maybe Baby/Tell Me How	1958	12.50	25.00	50.00
❑ 55072	Think It Over/Fool's Paradise	1958	12.50	25.00	50.00
❑ 55094	It's So Easy/Lonesome Tears	1958	12.50	25.00	50.00
❑ 55124	Love's Made a Fool of You/Someone, Someone	1959	10.00	20.00	40.00
❑ 55153	When You Ask About Love/Deborah	1959	10.00	20.00	40.00

CORAL

Number	Title (A Side/B Side)	Yr	VG	VG+	NM
❑ 62198	More Than I Can Say/Baby, My Heart	1960	10.00	20.00	40.00
❑ 62238	Peggy Sue Got Married/Don't Cha Know	1960	10.00	20.00	40.00
❑ 62407	Maybe Baby/Not Fade Away	1964	7.50	15.00	30.00

EPIC

Number	Title (A Side/B Side)	Yr	VG	VG+	NM
❑ 34-08028	T-Shirt/Hollywould	1988	—	2.50	5.00
❑ 34-08028 [PS]	T-Shirt/Hollywould	1988	—	2.50	5.00

LIBERTY

Number	Title (A Side/B Side)	Yr	VG	VG+	NM
❑ 55392	He's Old Enough to Know Better/I'm Feeling Better	1961	6.25	12.50	25.00
❑ 55441	Don't Ever Change/I'm Not a Bad Boy	1962	6.25	12.50	25.00
❑ 55492	I Believe in You/Parisian Girl	1962	6.25	12.50	25.00
❑ 55495	Little Hollywood Girl/Parisian Girl	1962	6.25	12.50	25.00
❑ 55540	My Little Girl/Teardrops Fall Like Rain	1963	6.25	12.50	25.00
❑ 55603	Don't Say You Love Me/April Avenue	1963	6.25	12.50	25.00
❑ 55660	Lonely Avenue/You Can't Be In-Between	1964	6.25	12.50	25.00
❑ 55668	Please, Please Me/From Me to You	1964	12.50	25.00	50.00
❑ 55696	(They Call Her) La Bomba/All Over You	1964	6.25	12.50	25.00
❑ 55742	We Gotta Get Together/I Think I've Caught the Blues	1964	6.25	12.50	25.00
❑ 55767	Everybody's Got a Little Problem/Now Hear This	1965	6.25	12.50	25.00

MGM

Number	Title (A Side/B Side)	Yr	VG	VG+	NM
❑ 14541	Hayride/Wasn't It Nice	1973	3.75	7.50	15.00

MUSIC FACTORY

Number	Title (A Side/B Side)	Yr	VG	VG+	NM
❑ 415	Million Dollar Movie/A Million Miles Apart	1968	5.00	10.00	20.00

7-Inch Extended Plays

BRUNSWICK

Number	Title (A Side/B Side)	Yr	VG	VG+	NM
❑ EB 71036	*I'm Looking for Someone to Love/That'll Be the Day/Not Fade Away/Oh! Boy	1957	75.00	150.00	300.00
❑ EB 71036 [PS]	The Chirping Crickets	1957	75.00	150.00	300.00
❑ EB 71038	*Maybe Baby/Rock Me My Baby/Send Me Some Lovin'/Tell Me How	1958	62.50	125.00	250.00
❑ EB 71038 [PS]	The Sound of the Crickets	1958	62.50	125.00	250.00

Albums

BARNABY

Number	Title (A Side/B Side)	Yr	VG	VG+	NM
❑ Z 30268	Rockin' 50's Rock 'N' Roll	1970	6.25	12.50	25.00

BRUNSWICK

Number	Title (A Side/B Side)	Yr	VG	VG+	NM
❑ BL 54038 [M]	The "Chirping" Crickets	1957	200.00	400.00	800.00
—Textured cover					
❑ BL 54038 [M]	The "Chirping" Crickets	1958	150.00	300.00	600.00
—Regular cover					

CORAL

Number	Title (A Side/B Side)	Yr	VG	VG+	NM
❑ CRL 57230 [M]	In Style with the Crickets	1960	50.00	100.00	200.00
❑ CRL 757230 [S]	In Style with the Crickets	1960	100.00	200.00	400.00

EPIC

Number	Title (A Side/B Side)	Yr	VG	VG+	NM
❑ FE 44446	T-Shirt	1988	3.75	7.50	15.00

LIBERTY

Number	Title (A Side/B Side)	Yr	VG	VG+	NM
❑ LRP-3272 [M]	Something Old, Something New, Something Blue, Somethin' Else	1962	37.50	75.00	150.00
❑ LRP-3351 [M]	California Sun/She Loves You	1964	25.00	50.00	100.00
❑ LST-7272 [S]	Something Old, Something New, Something Blue, Somethin' Else	1962	50.00	100.00	200.00
❑ LST-7351 [S]	California Sun/She Loves You	1964	37.50	75.00	150.00

VERTIGO

Number	Title (A Side/B Side)	Yr	VG	VG+	NM
❑ VEL-1020	Remnants	1973	5.00	10.00	20.00

CROCE, JIM

Not marketed as a country artist, but his "I'll Have to Say I Love You in a Song" made the country charts after his death, and some of his others would fit in on country radio today.

45s

21 RECORDS

Number	Title (A Side/B Side)	Yr	VG	VG+	NM
❑ 94969	Workin' at the Car Wash Blues/Rapid Roy (The Stock Car Boy)	1987	—	—	3.00
❑ 94970	It Doesn't Have to Be That Way/Time in a Bottle	1987	—	—	3.00
❑ 94971	I'll Have to Say I Love You in a Song/I Got a Name	1987	—	—	3.00
❑ 94972	You Don't Mess Around with Jim/Photographs and Memories	1987	—	—	3.00
❑ 94973	Bad, Bad Leroy Brown/Operator (That's Not the Way It Feels)	1987	—	—	3.00

ABC

Number	Title (A Side/B Side)	Yr	VG	VG+	NM
❑ 11328	You Don't Mess Around with Jim/Photographs and Memories	1972	—	2.00	4.00
❑ 11335	Operator (That's Not the Way It Feels)/Rapid Roy (The Stock Car Boy)	1972	—	2.00	4.00
❑ 11346	One Less Set of Footsteps/It Doesn't Have to Be That Way	1973	—	2.00	4.00
❑ 11359	Bad, Bad Leroy Brown/A Good Time Man Like Me Ain't Got No Business (Singin' the Blues)	1973	—	2.50	5.00
—ABC logo in children's building blocks					
❑ 11359	Bad, Bad Leroy Brown/A Good Time Man Like Me Ain't Got No Business (Singin' the Blues)	1973	—	2.00	4.00
—Regular ABC logo					
❑ 11389	I Got a Name/Alabama Rain	1973	—	2.00	4.00
❑ 11405	Time in a Bottle/Hard Time Losin' Man	1973	—	2.00	4.00
❑ 11413	It Doesn't Have to Be That Way/Roller Derby Queen	1973	—	2.00	4.00
❑ 11413 [PS]	It Doesn't Have to Be That Way/Roller Derby Queen	1973	—	2.50	5.00
❑ 11424	I'll Have to Say I Love You in a Song/Salon and Saloon	1974	—	2.00	4.00
❑ 11447	Workin' at the Car Wash Blues/Thursday	1974	—	2.00	4.00
❑ 12015	Workin' at the Car Wash Blues/Thursday	1974	—	2.50	5.00

LIFESONG

Number	Title (A Side/B Side)	Yr	VG	VG+	NM
❑ 45001	Chain Gang Medley/Stone Walls	1975	—	2.00	4.00
❑ 45005	Maybe Tomorrow/Mississippi Lady	1976	—	2.00	4.00
❑ 45018 [DJ]	It Doesn't Have to Be That Way (mono/stereo)	1976	—	2.50	5.00
—Promo-only release; Lifesong sleeve has custom sticker (add $4)					

Albums

21 RECORDS

Number	Title (A Side/B Side)	Yr	VG	VG+	NM
❑ 90467	Photographs & Memories/His Greatest Hits	1985	2.00	4.00	8.00
❑ 90468	Time in a Bottle — Jim Croce's Greatest Love Songs	1985	2.00	4.00	8.00
❑ 90469	Down the Highway	1985	2.50	5.00	10.00

ABC

Number	Title (A Side/B Side)	Yr	VG	VG+	NM
❑ ABCX-756	You Don't Mess Around with Jim	1972	5.00	10.00	20.00
—Original covers have no green box advertising "Time in a Bottle"					
❑ ABCX-756	You Don't Mess Around with Jim	1973	3.75	7.50	15.00
—Posthumous covers have a green box advertising "Time in a Bottle"					
❑ ABCX-769	Life and Times	1973	3.75	7.50	15.00
❑ ABCX-797	I Got a Name	1973	3.75	7.50	15.00
❑ ABCD-835	Photographs & Memories/His Greatest Hits	1974	3.75	7.50	15.00

CAPITOL

Number	Title (A Side/B Side)	Yr	VG	VG+	NM
❑ SMAS-315	Jim and Ingrid Croce	1970	7.50	15.00	30.00

COMMAND

Number	Title (A Side/B Side)	Yr	VG	VG+	NM
❑ QD-40006 [Q]	You Don't Mess Around with Jim	1974	6.25	12.50	25.00
❑ QD-40007 [Q]	Life and Times	1974	6.25	12.50	25.00
❑ QD-40008 [Q]	I Got a Name	1974	6.25	12.50	25.00
❑ QD-40020 [Q]	Photographs & Memories/His Greatest Hits	1974	6.25	12.50	25.00

CROCE

Number	Title (A Side/B Side)	Yr	VG	VG+	NM
❑ 101	Facets	1966	75.00	150.00	300.00

DCC COMPACT CLASSICS

Number	Title (A Side/B Side)	Yr	VG	VG+	NM
❑ LPZ-2054	His Greatest Recordings	1998	5.00	10.00	20.00
—Audiophile vinyl					

LIFESONG

Number	Title (A Side/B Side)	Yr	VG	VG+	NM
❑ LS 900 [(2)]	The Faces I've Been	1975	3.75	7.50	15.00
❑ LS 6007	Time in a Bottle — Jim Croce's Greatest Love Songs	1976	3.00	6.00	12.00
❑ JZ 34993	You Don't Mess Around with Jim	1978	2.50	5.00	10.00
❑ JZ 35000	Time in a Bottle — Jim Croce's Greatest Love Songs	1978	2.50	5.00	10.00
❑ JZ 35008	Life and Times	1978	2.50	5.00	10.00
❑ JZ 35009	I Got a Name	1978	2.50	5.00	10.00
❑ JZ 35010	Photographs & Memories/His Greatest Hits	1978	2.50	5.00	10.00
❑ JZ 35571	Bad, Bad Leroy Brown: Jim Croce's Greatest Character Songs	1978	2.50	5.00	10.00

MOBILE FIDELITY

Number	Title (A Side/B Side)	Yr	VG	VG+	NM
❑ 1-079	You Don't Mess Around with Jim	1981	10.00	20.00	40.00
—Audiophile vinyl					

PICKWICK

Number	Title (A Side/B Side)	Yr	VG	VG+	NM
❑ SPC-3332	Another Day, Another Town	1973	2.50	5.00	10.00
—Reissue of Capitol LP					

CROCKETT, HOWARD

45s

DOT

Number	Title (A Side/B Side)	Yr	VG	VG+	NM
❑ 15593	If You'll Let Me/You've Got Me Lyin'	1957	12.50	25.00	50.00
❑ 15701	The Night Rider/Branded	1958	10.00	20.00	40.00
❑ 17457	The House Where Momma Lived/Last Will and Testament (Of a Drinking Man)	1973	—	3.00	6.00
❑ 17482	I Feel More Like Myself Than I Did a While Ago/I'd Like to Be Everybody for Just One Day	1973	—	3.00	6.00
❑ 17509	The Calling/Pictures and Memories	1974	—	3.00	6.00

MANCO

Number	Title (A Side/B Side)	Yr	VG	VG+	NM
❑ 1002	Sluefoot the Bear/Polly Ann	1960	12.50	25.00	50.00
❑ 1012	That Old Juke Box/Steamboat Bill	1961	7.50	15.00	30.00
❑ 1023	Just a Poor Man/I've Got You Worried Too	1961	7.50	15.00	30.00

MEL-O-DY

Number	Title (A Side/B Side)	Yr	VG	VG+	NM
❑ 109	The Big Wheel/That Silver-Haired Daddy of Mine	1963	6.25	12.50	25.00
❑ 111	Bringing In the Gold/I've Been a Long Time Leaving	1963	6.25	12.50	25.00
❑ 115	My Lil's Run Off/Spanish Lace and Memories	1964	6.25	12.50	25.00
❑ 119	Put Me in Your Pocket/The Miles	1964	6.25	12.50	25.00
❑ 121	All the Good Times Are Gone/The Great Titanic	1965	6.25	12.50	25.00

SMASH

Number	Title (A Side/B Side)	Yr	VG	VG+	NM
❑ 1721	Deep Elm Dave/Going Down to Soldiers	1961	10.00	20.00	40.00
❑ 1750	Break Away Billy Boy/Out of Bounds Again	1962	10.00	20.00	40.00
❑ 1782	Jessie and the Glendale Train/Trail of Tears	1962	20.00	40.00	80.00

STOP

Number	Title (A Side/B Side)	Yr	VG	VG+	NM
❑ 136	The Big Cat/You're Messin' Up My Mind	1968	2.00	4.00	8.00
❑ 172	The Big Day/You Can't Get to All of 'Em Jack	1968	2.00	4.00	8.00
❑ 210	Soap and Water/A Man with No Face	1969	2.00	4.00	8.00
❑ 238	Where Were You/The Story of Bango	1969	2.00	4.00	8.00
❑ 250	The Law Says/Ask Little Brother	1969	2.00	4.00	8.00

CROFT, SANDY

45s

ANGELSONG

Number	Title (A Side/B Side)	Yr	VG	VG+	NM
❑ 1821	Easier/If I Was As Pretty As You	1982	—	3.00	6.00
❑ 1821 [PS]	Easier/If I Was As Pretty As You	1982	2.00	4.00	8.00

CAPITOL

Number	Title (A Side/B Side)	Yr	VG	VG+	NM
❑ B-5363	Easier/If I Was As Pretty As You	1984	—	2.00	4.00
—Reissue of Angelsong 1821					
❑ B-5471	Piece of My Heart/Heart Stealer	1985	—	2.00	4.00
❑ B-5471 [PS]	Piece of My Heart/Heart Stealer	1985	—	2.50	5.00

CROSBY, BING

The following single by the legendary pop crooner made the country charts.

45s

DECCA

Number	Title (A Side/B Side)	Yr	VG	VG+	NM
❑ 28265	Till the End of the World/Just a Little Lovin'	1952	2.50	5.00	10.00
—With Grady Martin					

CROSBY, BING, AND THE ANDREWS SISTERS

The below single by the crooner and vocal group made the country charts.

Selected 78s

DECCA

Number	Title (A Side/B Side)	Yr	VG	VG+	NM
❑ 23277	Pistol Packin' Mama/Vict'ry Polka	1943	3.00	6.00	12.00

CROSBY, EDDIE

Also see MERVIN SHINER.

45s

DECCA

Number	Title (A Side/B Side)	Yr	VG	VG+	NM
❑ 9-46279	Feelin' Sorry/Tears of St. Anne	1950	7.50	15.00	30.00
❑ 9-46287	Poor Beggar Boy/Be Good to Your Father and Mother	1951	6.25	12.50	25.00
❑ 9-46333	Six Feet Deep/Meet Me at the Station	1951	6.25	12.50	25.00

Selected 78s

DECCA

Number	Title (A Side/B Side)	Yr	VG	VG+	NM
❑ 46180	Blues Stay Away from Me/Foolish Notion	1949	5.00	10.00	20.00

Number	Title (A Side/B Side)	Yr	VG	VG+	NM

CROSBY, ROB

45s

ARISTA

Number	Title (A Side/B Side)	Yr	VG	VG+	NM
❑ 2124	Love Will Bring Her Around/Nobody's Gonna Hurt My Heart	1990	—	2.00	4.00
❑ 2180	She's a Natural/Somewhere Down the Line	1991	—	2.00	4.00
❑ 12336	Still Burnin' for You/Higher Ground	1991	—	—	3.00
❑ 12397	Working Woman/The Woman in You	1992	—	—	3.00
❑ 12443	She Wrote the Book/One Night Down	1992	—	—	3.00
❑ 12481	In the Blood/Cold Day in Tennessee	1992	—	—	3.00

CROSBY, STILLS AND NASH

"Wasted on the Way" made the country charts. Some of the other songs below would fit in on today's country radio as well.

45s

ATLANTIC

Number	Title (A Side/B Side)	Yr	VG	VG+	NM
❑ 2652	Marrakesh Express/Helplessly Hoping	1969	—	3.00	6.00
❑ 2676	Suite: Judy Blue Eyes/Long Time Gone	1969	—	3.00	6.00
❑ 3401	Just a Song Before I Go/Dark Star	1977	—	2.00	4.00
❑ 3401 [PS]	Just a Song Before I Go/Dark Star	1977	—	2.50	5.00
❑ 3432	Fair Game/Anything at All	1977	—	2.00	4.00
❑ 3453	I Give You Give Blind/Carried Away	1978	—	2.00	4.00
❑ 3784	Carry On/Shadow Captain	1980	—	2.50	5.00
❑ 4058	Wasted on the Way/Delta	1982	—	—	3.00
❑ 4058 [PS]	Wasted on the Way/Delta	1982	—	2.00	4.00
❑ 87909	Live It Up/Chuck's Lament	1990	—	2.00	4.00
❑ 89775	Raise a Voice/For What It's Worth	1983	—	—	3.00
❑ 89812	War Games/Shadow Captain	1983	—	—	3.00
❑ 89812 [PS]	War Games/Shadow Captain	1983	—	2.00	4.00
❑ 89888	Too Much Love to Hide/Song for Susan	1983	—	—	3.00
❑ 89969	Southern Cross/Into the Darkness	1982	—	—	3.00
❑ 89969 [PS]	Southern Cross/Into the Darkness	1982	—	2.00	4.00

Albums

ATLANTIC

Number	Title (A Side/B Side)	Yr	VG	VG+	NM
❑ SD 8229	Crosby, Stills & Nash	1969	5.00	10.00	20.00
❑ SD 16026	Replay	1980	3.00	6.00	12.00
—Also has solo cuts by Stephen Stills					
❑ SD 19104	CSN	1977	3.00	6.00	12.00
❑ SD 19117	Crosby, Stills & Nash	1977	2.50	5.00	10.00
—Reissue of 8229					
❑ SD 19360	Daylight Again	1982	3.00	6.00	12.00
❑ 80075	Allies	1983	3.00	6.00	12.00
❑ 82107	Live It Up	1990	3.75	7.50	15.00

NAUTILUS

Number	Title (A Side/B Side)	Yr	VG	VG+	NM
❑ NR-48	Crosby, Stills and Nash	1982	37.50	75.00	150.00
—Audiophile vinyl					

CROSBY, STILLS, NASH & YOUNG

"This Old House" made the country charts, and certainly "Teach Your Children" is more "country" than many other country songs of the past 20 years (thanks to Jerry Garcia on the steel guitar). Also see NEIL YOUNG.

45s

ATLANTIC

Number	Title (A Side/B Side)	Yr	VG	VG+	NM
❑ 2723	Woodstock/Helpless	1970	—	3.00	6.00
❑ 2735	Teach Your Children/Carry On	1970	—	3.00	6.00
❑ 2740	Ohio/Find the Cost of Freedom	1970	—	3.00	6.00
❑ 2740 [PS]	Ohio/Find the Cost of Freedom	1970	3.00	6.00	12.00
❑ 2760	Our House/Deja Vu	1970	—	3.00	6.00
❑ 88966	Got It Made/This Old House	1989	—	—	3.00
❑ 88966 [PS]	Got It Made/This Old House	1989	—	—	3.00
❑ 89003	American Dream/Compass	1988	—	—	3.00
❑ 89003 [PS]	American Dream/Compass	1988	—	—	3.00

Albums

ATLANTIC

Number	Title (A Side/B Side)	Yr	VG	VG+	NM
❑ PR 165 [M-DJ]	Celebration/CSNY Month	1974	25.00	50.00	100.00
—Promo-only LP in mono					
❑ PR 165 [S-DJ]	Celebration/CSNY Month	1974	12.50	25.00	50.00
—Promo-only LP in stereo					
❑ 2-902 [(2) M]	4 Way Street	1971	25.00	50.00	100.00
—White label promo; no stock copies are mono					
❑ SD 2-902 [(2)]	4 Way Street	1971	5.00	10.00	20.00
❑ SD 2-902 [(2) DJ]	4 Way Street	1971	12.50	25.00	50.00
—White label stereo promo					
❑ 7200 [M]	Deja Vu	1970	37.50	75.00	150.00
—White label promo; no stock copies are mono					
❑ SD 7200	Deja Vu	1970	3.75	7.50	15.00
—Pasted-on front cover photo must still be intact					
❑ SD 7200 [DJ]	Deja Vu	1970	15.00	30.00	60.00
—White label stereo promo					
❑ SD 18100	So Far	1974	3.00	6.00	12.00
❑ PR 18102 [DJ]	A Rap with C, S, N & Y	1974	12.50	25.00	50.00
—Promo-only interview album					
❑ SD 19118	Deja Vu	1977	2.50	5.00	10.00
—Reissue of 7200					
❑ SD 19119	So Far	1977	2.50	5.00	10.00
—Reissue of 18100					
❑ 81888	American Dream	1988	2.50	5.00	10.00

MOBILE FIDELITY

Number	Title (A Side/B Side)	Yr	VG	VG+	NM
❑ 1-088	Deja Vu	198?	50.00	100.00	200.00
—Audiophile vinyl					

CROSTON, JILL

See LACY J. DALTON.

CROW, ALVIN

45s

POLYDOR

Number	Title (A Side/B Side)	Yr	VG	VG+	NM
❑ 14387	Yes She Do, No She Don't (I'm Satisfied with My Gal)/Retirement Run	1977	—	2.50	5.00
❑ 14410	Crazy Little Mama (At My Front Door)/You're the One I Thought I'd Never Love	1977	—	2.50	5.00
❑ 14437	Nyquil Blues/Fiddler's Lady	1977	—	2.50	5.00

Albums

POLYDOR

Number	Title (A Side/B Side)	Yr	VG	VG+	NM
❑ PD-1- 6102	High Riding	1977	3.75	7.50	15.00

CROWELL, RODNEY

45s

COLUMBIA

Number	Title (A Side/B Side)	Yr	VG	VG+	NM
❑ 06102	Let Freedom Ring/The Best I Can	1986	—	—	3.00
❑ 06415	When I'm Free Again/The Best I Can	1986	—	—	3.00
❑ 06584	She Loves the Jerk/Passed Like a Mask	1987	—	—	3.00
❑ 07137	Looking for You/Stay (Don't Be Cruel)	1987	—	—	3.00
❑ 07693	It's Such a Small World/Crazy Baby	1988	—	—	3.00
—A-side: With Roseanne Cash					
❑ 07918	I Couldn't Leave You If I Tried/The Blue Hour Comes	1988	—	—	3.00
❑ 08080	She's Crazy for Leavin'/Brand New Rag	1988	—	—	3.00
❑ 68585	After All This Time/Oh King Richard	1989	—	2.00	4.00
—Originals were pressed on styrene (record appears translucent dark red when held to a light)					
❑ 68585	After All This Time/Oh King Richard	199?	—	—	3.00
—Reissues were pressed on vinyl					
❑ 68948	Above and Beyond/She Loves the Jerk	1989	—	—	3.00
❑ 73042	Many a Long & Lonesome Highway/I Know You're Married	1989	—	—	3.00
❑ 73254	If Looks Could Kill/I Didn't Know I Could Lose You	1990	—	—	3.00
❑ 73423	My Past Is Present/You Been On My Mind	1990	—	—	3.00
❑ 73569	Now That We're Alone/I Guess We've Been Together for Too Long	1990	—	—	3.00
❑ 73760	Things I Wish I'd Said/Soul Searchin'	1991	—	—	3.00
❑ 74250	Lovin' All Night/I Didn't Know I Could Lose You	1992	—	—	3.00
❑ 74360	What Kind of Love/Nobody's Gonna Tear My Playhouse Down	1992	—	—	3.00
❑ 77240	Even Cowgirls Get the Blues/Standing on a Rock	1993	—	—	3.00

MCA

Number	Title (A Side/B Side)	Yr	VG	VG+	NM
❑ 54821	Let the Picture Paint Itself/The Rose of Memphis	1994	—	—	3.00
❑ 54880	Big Heart/The Best Years of Our Lives	1994	—	—	3.00
❑ 54946	I Don't Fall in Love So Easy/That Ol' Door	1994	—	—	3.00
❑ 55024	Please Remember Me/Give My Heart a Rest	1995	—	—	3.00

REPRISE

Number	Title (A Side/B Side)	Yr	VG	VG+	NM
❑ 7-17149	I Walk the Line Revisited/Stars on the Water	1998	—	—	3.00
—A-side with Johnny Cash					

WARNER BROS.

Number	Title (A Side/B Side)	Yr	VG	VG+	NM
❑ 8637	Elvira/Ashes By Now	1978	—	2.50	5.00
❑ 8693	Song for the Life/Baby, Better Start Turnin' 'Em Down	1978	—	2.50	5.00
❑ 8794	(Now and Then There's) A Fool Such As I/Voila, An American Dream	1979	—	2.50	5.00
❑ 49224	Ashes By Now/Blues in the Daytime	1980	—	2.50	5.00
❑ 49535	Ain't No Money/One About England	1980	—	2.00	4.00
❑ 49591	Heartbroke/Here Come the 80's	1980	—	2.00	4.00
❑ 49810	Stars on the Water/Don't Need No Other Now	1981	—	2.00	4.00
❑ 50008	Victim or a Fool/Only Two Hearts	1982	—	2.00	4.00

Albums

COLUMBIA

Number	Title (A Side/B Side)	Yr	VG	VG+	NM
❑ CAS 2001 [DJ]	Dialog with T-Bone Burnett	1989	7.50	15.00	30.00
—Promo-only interview record					
❑ FC 40116	Street Language	1986	2.00	4.00	8.00
❑ FC 44076	Diamonds and Dirt	1988	2.50	5.00	10.00
❑ FC 45242	Keys to the Highway	1989	3.00	6.00	12.00

WARNER BROS.

Number	Title (A Side/B Side)	Yr	VG	VG+	NM
❑ BSK 3228	Ain't Living Long Like This	1978	3.75	7.50	15.00
❑ BSK 3407	But What Will the Neighbors Think	1980	2.50	5.00	10.00
❑ BSK 3587	Rodney Crowell	1981	2.50	5.00	10.00

CROWLEY, J.C.

45s

RCA

Number	Title (A Side/B Side)	Yr	VG	VG+	NM
❑ 8634-7-R	Boxcar 109/Living for the Fire	1988	—	—	3.00
❑ 8747-7-R	Paint the Town and Hang the Moon Tonight/ Serenade	1988	—	—	3.00
❑ 8822-7-R	I Know What I've Got/Living for the Fire	1989	—	—	3.00
❑ 9012-7-R	Beneath the Texas Moon/Living for the Fire	1989	—	—	3.00

Albums

RCA

Number	Title (A Side/B Side)	Yr	VG	VG+	NM
❑ 8370-1-R	Beneath the Texas Moon	1988	2.50	5.00	10.00

CRUM, SIMON

See FERLIN HUSKY.

CRYNER, BOBBIE

45s

EPIC

Number	Title (A Side/B Side)	Yr	VG	VG+	NM
❑ 34-77044	Daddy Laid the Blues on Me/I'm Through Waitin' on You	1993	—	—	3.00

Number	Title (A Side/B Side)	Yr	VG	VG+	NM
❑ 34-77195	He Feels Guilty/This Heart Speaks for Itself	1993	—	—	3.00
❑ 34-77487	You Could Steal Me/Leavin' Houston Blues	1994	—	—	3.00
MCA					
❑ 55099	I Can't Stand to Be Unhappy/Nobody Leaves	1995	—	—	3.00
❑ 55167	You'd Think He'd Know Me Better/Oh to Be the One	1996	—	—	3.00
❑ 55202	I Didn't Know My Own Strength/Oh to Be the One	1996	—	—	3.00

CUMMINGS, BARBARA

45s

Number	Title (A Side/B Side)	Yr	VG	VG+	NM
LONDON					
❑ 104	She's the Woman/There's Something Funny Going On	1966	2.50	5.00	10.00
❑ 109	A Good Guy Like You/Love's on Duty (24 Hours a Day)	1967	2.50	5.00	10.00
❑ 117	Three Little Fools/Anything She'll Do for You (I'll Do Better)	1967	2.50	5.00	10.00

CUMMINGS, BURTON

The below record by the ex-lead singer of the Guess Who made the country charts.

45s

Number	Title (A Side/B Side)	Yr	VG	VG+	NM
PORTRAIT					
❑ 70024	Takes a Fool to Love a Fool/I Will Play a Rhapsody	1978	—	2.50	5.00

CUMMINGS, CHRIS

45s

Number	Title (A Side/B Side)	Yr	VG	VG+	NM
WARNER BROS.					
❑ 17230	I Wanted/Lonesomeville	1998	—	—	3.00
❑ 17267	The Kind of Heart That Breaks/Almost Always	1997	—	—	3.00

CUNHA, RICK

45s

Number	Title (A Side/B Side)	Yr	VG	VG+	NM
COLUMBIA					
❑ 3-10174	Best Friends/Moving Picture Theme	1975	—	2.00	4.00
GRC					
❑ 2016	(I'm a) Yo Yo Man/Wild Side of Life	1974	—	2.50	5.00
❑ 2028	I'm Ashamed/Jesse James (Is an Outlaw, Honey)	1974	—	2.50	5.00

Albums

Number	Title (A Side/B Side)	Yr	VG	VG+	NM
GRC					
❑ GA-5004	Cunha Songs	1974	3.00	6.00	12.00
SIERRA					
❑ 8707	Moving Pictures	1980	3.00	6.00	12.00

CUNNINGHAM, J.C.

45s

Number	Title (A Side/B Side)	Yr	VG	VG+	NM
CAPITOL					
❑ 3489	I Can Feel the Heartache Comin' On/You Take the Blame for the Roses	1972	2.00	4.00	8.00
—As "Johnny Cunningham"					
❑ 3686	Wonder What I'm Doin' in Tennessee/Over and Over Again	1973	2.00	4.00	8.00
—As "Collins Cunningham"					
SCOTTI BROTHERS					
❑ 601	The Pyramid Song/I'm a Lover Not a Fighter	1980	—	2.00	4.00
VIVA					
❑ 29108	Settin' the Night on Fire/You Better Run to Him	1985	—	2.00	4.00
❑ 29168	Love Was Made to Be Made/If It Hadn't Been for Planes	1984	—	2.00	4.00
❑ 29220	Heaven Ain't What It Used to Be/Body Talk	1984	—	2.00	4.00
❑ 29311	Light Up/The Greatest Love	1984	—	2.00	4.00

Albums

Number	Title (A Side/B Side)	Yr	VG	VG+	NM
VIVA					
❑ 25173	J.C. Cunningham	1984	2.00	4.00	8.00

CURLESS, DICK

45s

Number	Title (A Side/B Side)	Yr	VG	VG+	NM
ALLAGASH					
❑ 101	A Tombstone Every Mile/Heart Talk	1964	6.25	12.50	25.00
BELMONT					
❑ 007	The Great Race/Wine	197?	2.00	4.00	8.00
❑ 009	Andre the Seal/Wintertime in Maine	197?	2.00	4.00	8.00
❑ 030	Night Train to Memphis/Then I'll Get Over You	197?	2.00	4.00	8.00
CAPITOL					
❑ 2780	Big Wheel Cannonball/I Miss a Lot of Trains	1970	2.00	4.00	8.00
❑ 2848	Hard, Hard Travelin' Man/Winter's Comin' On Again	1970	2.00	4.00	8.00
❑ 2949	Drag 'Em Off the Interstate, Sock It to 'Em, J.P. Blues/Drop Some Silver in the Juke Box	1970	2.00	4.00	8.00
❑ 3034	Juke Box Man/Please Buy My Flowers	1971	2.00	4.00	8.00
❑ 3105	Loser's Cocktail/Hot Springs	1971	2.00	4.00	8.00
❑ 3182	Snap Your Fingers/Bully of the Town	1971	2.00	4.00	8.00
❑ 3267	January, April and Me/Lay Your Hands on Me (And Heal Me)	1972	2.00	4.00	8.00
❑ 3354	Stonin' Around/For the Life of Me	1972	2.00	4.00	8.00
❑ 3470	She Called Me Baby/Wait a Little Longer	1972	2.00	4.00	8.00
❑ 3541	Chick Inspector (That's Where My Money Goes)/Travelin' Light	1973	—	3.00	6.00
❑ 3630	China Nights (Shina No Yoru)/Old Bob Burton	1973	—	3.00	6.00
❑ 3698	The Last Blues Song/Room Full of Roses	1973	—	3.00	6.00
❑ 3818	Swingin' Preacher/Get on Board My Wagon	1974	—	3.00	6.00
❑ 3879	A Brand New Bed of Roses/Pinch o' Powder	1974	—	3.00	6.00
TOWER					
❑ 124	A Tombstone Every Mile/Heart Talk	1965	3.75	7.50	15.00
❑ 135	Six Times a Day (The Trains Came Down)/Down by the Old River	1965	3.75	7.50	15.00
❑ 161	'Tater Raisin' Man/The Friend Who Makes It Four	1965	3.75	7.50	15.00
❑ 193	Travelin' Man/Rocky Mountain Queen	1965	3.75	7.50	15.00
❑ 219	Highway Man/Please Don't Make Me Go	1966	3.75	7.50	15.00
❑ 255	The Baron/A Good Job-Huntin' and Fishin'	1966	3.75	7.50	15.00
❑ 255 [PS]	The Baron/A Good Job-Huntin' and Fishin'	1966	5.00	10.00	20.00
❑ 306	All of Me Belongs to You/My Side of the Night	1967	3.00	6.00	12.00
❑ 335	House of Memories/Standing on the Outside Looking In	1967	3.00	6.00	12.00
❑ 362	Big Foot/Tornado Tillie	1967	3.00	6.00	12.00
❑ 399	Bury the Bottle with Me/Bummin' on Track "E"	1968	3.00	6.00	12.00
❑ 415	I Ain't Got Nobody/Shoes	1968	3.00	6.00	12.00
❑ 444	All I Need Is You/Tears Instead of Cheers	1968	3.00	6.00	12.00
❑ 471	Wild Side of Town/The Secret of Your Heart	1969	3.00	6.00	12.00

Albums

Number	Title (A Side/B Side)	Yr	VG	VG+	NM
CAPITOL					
❑ ST-552	Hard, Hard Travelin' Man	1970	5.00	10.00	20.00
❑ ST-689	Doggin' It	1971	5.00	10.00	20.00
❑ ST-792	Comin' On Country	1971	5.00	10.00	20.00
❑ ST-11011	Tombstone Every Mile	1972	3.75	7.50	15.00
—Reissue of Tower DT 5005					
❑ ST-11087	Stonin' Around	1972	5.00	10.00	20.00
❑ ST-11119	Live at the Wheeling Truck Driver's Jamboree	1973	5.00	10.00	20.00
❑ ST-11211	The Last Blues Song	1973	7.50	15.00	30.00
—First cover shows Dick Curless with an eye patch					
❑ ST-11211	The Last Blues Song	1973	5.00	10.00	20.00
—Second cover shows Dick Curless with no eye patch					
TIFFANY					
❑ 1016 [M]	Dick Curless Sings Songs of the Open Country	1958	25.00	50.00	100.00
❑ 1028 [M]	Singing Just for Fun	1959	25.00	50.00	100.00
❑ 1033 [M]	I Love to Tell a Story	1960	25.00	50.00	100.00
TOWER					
❑ DT 5005 [R]	Tombstone Every Mile	1965	5.00	10.00	20.00
❑ T 5005 [M]	Tombstone Every Mile	1965	7.50	15.00	30.00
❑ DT 5012 [R]	Hymns	1965	5.00	10.00	20.00
❑ T 5012 [M]	Hymns	1965	7.50	15.00	30.00
❑ DT 5013 [R]	The Soul of Dick Curless	1966	5.00	10.00	20.00
❑ T 5013 [M]	The Soul of Dick Curless	1966	7.50	15.00	30.00
❑ DT 5015 [R]	Travelin' Man	1966	5.00	10.00	20.00
❑ T 5015 [M]	Travelin' Man	1966	7.50	15.00	30.00
❑ DT 5016 [R]	At Home with Dick Curless	1966	5.00	10.00	20.00
❑ T 5016 [M]	At Home with Dick Curless	1966	7.50	15.00	30.00
❑ ST 5066 [S]	All of Me Belongs to You	1967	7.50	15.00	30.00
❑ T 5066 [M]	All of Me Belongs to You	1967	7.50	15.00	30.00
❑ ST 5089 [S]	Ramblin' Country	1967	7.50	15.00	30.00
❑ T 5089 [M]	Ramblin' Country	1967	7.50	15.00	30.00
❑ ST 5108	The Long Lonesome Road	1968	7.50	15.00	30.00
❑ ST 5139	The Wild Side of Town	1969	7.50	15.00	30.00

CURLESS, DICK, AND KAY ADAMS

Also see each artist's individual listings.

45s

Number	Title (A Side/B Side)	Yr	VG	VG+	NM
TOWER					
❑ 226	A Devil Like Me (Needs an Angel Like You)/No Fool Like an Old Fool	1966	3.75	7.50	15.00

Albums

Number	Title (A Side/B Side)	Yr	VG	VG+	NM
TOWER					
❑ DT 5025 [R]	A Devil Like Me Needs an Angel Like You	1966	5.00	10.00	20.00
❑ T 5025 [M]	A Devil Like Me Needs an Angel Like You	1966	7.50	15.00	30.00

CURREY, DIANA SICILY

45s

Number	Title (A Side/B Side)	Yr	VG	VG+	NM
CONDOR					
❑ 13	Longneck Lone Star (And Two Step Dancin')/(B-side unknown)	1989	—	3.00	6.00

CURTIS, LARRY

45s

Number	Title (A Side/B Side)	Yr	VG	VG+	NM
SCRIMSHAW					
❑ 1315	It Feels Like Love for the First Time/(B-side unknown)	1978	2.00	4.00	8.00

CURTIS, MAC

45s

Number	Title (A Side/B Side)	Yr	VG	VG+	NM
DOT					
❑ 16315	You're the One/Dance Her By Me (One More Time)	1962	2.50	5.00	10.00
EPIC					
❑ 10257	Too Close to Home/Too Good to Be True	1967	—	3.00	6.00
❑ 10324	The Quiet Kind/Love's Been Good to Me	1968	—	3.00	6.00
❑ 10385	The Sunshine Man/It's My Way	1968	—	3.00	6.00
❑ 10438	Almost Persuaded/The Friendly City	1969	—	3.00	6.00
❑ 10468	Happiness Lives in This House/Little Ole Wine Drinker Me	1969	—	3.00	6.00
❑ 10530	Don't Make Love/Us	1969	—	3.00	6.00
❑ 10574	Honey Don't/Today's Teardrops	1970	—	3.00	6.00

Number	Title (A Side/B Side)	Yr	VG	VG+	NM
FELSTED					
❑ 8592	Come Back Baby/No, Never Alone	1959	5.00	10.00	20.00
GRT					
❑ 26	Early in the Morning/When the Hurt Moves In	1970	—	2.50	5.00
❑ 41	Gulf Stream Line/I'd Run a Mile	1971	—	2.50	5.00
KING					
❑ 4927	If I Had Me a Woman/Just So You Call Me	1956	37.50	75.00	150.00
❑ 4949	Grandaddy's Rockin'/Half Hearted Love	1956	37.50	75.00	150.00
❑ 4965	You Ain't Treatin' Me Right/The Low Road	1956	37.50	75.00	150.00
❑ 4995	That Ain't Nothin' But Right/Don't You Love Me	1956	37.50	75.00	150.00
❑ 5007	What You Want/To Protect the Innocent	1957	25.00	50.00	100.00
❑ 5059	Say So/I'll Be Gentle	1957	10.00	20.00	40.00
❑ 5107	What You Want/You Are My Special Baby	1958	15.00	30.00	60.00
❑ 5121	Missy Ann/Little Miss Linda	1958	15.00	30.00	60.00
RANWOOD					
❑ 1017	Pistol Packin' Mama/Asphalt Cowboy, Parking Lot Lover	1975	—	2.50	5.00
❑ 1033	Keep Doin' What You're Doin' Now/She Knows All the Good Ways to Be Bad	1975	—	2.50	5.00
❑ 1041	More Like I Do Now/Nine Times Out of Ten	1975	—	2.50	5.00
❑ 1050	We Made It All the Way/West Texas Women	1976	—	2.50	5.00
TOWER					
❑ 319	Ties That Bind/Stepping Out on You	1967	—	3.00	6.00
Albums					
EPIC					
❑ BN 26419	The Sunshine Man	1969	5.00	10.00	20.00
HMG/HIGHTONE					
❑ HT 6601	Rockabilly Uprising: The Best of Mac Curtis	1997	2.50	5.00	10.00
ROLLIN' ROCK					
❑ LP-002	Ruffabilly	197?	2.50	5.00	10.00
❑ LP-007	Good Rockin' Tomorrow	197?	2.50	5.00	10.00

CURTIS, SONNY

45s

Number	Title (A Side/B Side)	Yr	VG	VG+	NM
'STEEM					
❑ 110185	Now I've Got a Heart of Gold/(B-side unknown)	1985	—	3.00	6.00
A&M					
❑ 1359	Lights of L.A./Sunny Mornin'	1972	7.50	15.00	30.00
❑ 1408	Love Is All Around/Last Days of Childhood	1973	—	—	—
—Unreleased?					
CAPITOL					
❑ 4158	Lovesick Blues/It's Only a Question of Time	1975	3.00	6.00	12.00
❑ 4227	It's Only a Question of Time/When It's Just You and Me	1976	3.00	6.00	12.00
❑ 4240	Where's Patricia Now/When It's Just You and Me	1976	3.00	6.00	12.00
CORAL					
❑ 60954	Someday You're Gonna Be Sorry/Forever Yours	1953	6.25	12.50	25.00
❑ 61023	No More Tears/The Best Way to Hold a Girl	1953	6.25	12.50	25.00
❑ 62207	Red Headed Stranger/Talk About My Baby	1960	10.00	20.00	40.00
DIMENSION					
❑ 1017	So Used to Loving You/The Last Song I'm Ever Gonna Sing	1963	5.00	10.00	20.00
❑ 1024	A Beatle I Want to Be/So Used to Loving You	1964	6.25	12.50	25.00
DOT					
❑ 15754	Wrong Again/Laughing Stock	1958	10.00	20.00	40.00
❑ 15799	A Pretty Girl/Willa May Jones	1958	7.50	15.00	30.00
ELEKTRA					
❑ 46526	The Cowboy Singer/Cheatin' Clouds	1979	—	2.50	5.00
❑ 46568	Do You Remember Roll Over Beethoven/Walk Right Back	1979	—	2.50	5.00
❑ 46616	The Real Buddy Holly Story/Ain't Nobody Honest	1980	—	3.00	6.00
❑ 46643	Love Is All Around/The Clone Song	1980	—	2.50	5.00
❑ 47048	You Made My Life a Song/50 Ways to Leave Your Lover	1980	—	2.50	5.00
❑ 47129	Good Ol' Girls/So Used to Loving You	1981	—	2.50	5.00
❑ 47176	Married Woman/I Live Your Music	1981	—	2.50	5.00
❑ 47231 [DJ]	The Christmas Song/Little Drummer Boy	1981	2.00	4.00	8.00
—B-side by Hank Williams, Jr.					
❑ 69942	Together Alone/Dream Well All of You Children	1982	—	2.50	5.00
LIBERTY					
❑ 55710	Bo Diddley Bach/I Pledge My Love to You	1964	5.00	10.00	20.00
MERCURY					
❑ 73438	Rock and Rol (I Gave You the Best Years of My Life)/My Mama Sure Left Me Some Good Old Days	1973	3.75	7.50	15.00
OVATION					
❑ 1006	Love Is All Around/Here, There and Everywhere	1970	5.00	10.00	20.00
❑ 1023	Unsaintly Judy/You Don't Belong in This Place	1970	3.75	7.50	15.00
VIVA					
❑ 602	My Way of Life/Last Call	1966	3.75	7.50	15.00
❑ 607	The Collection/Destiny's Child	1966	3.75	7.50	15.00
❑ 617	I'm a Gypsy Man/I Wanna Go Bummin' Around	1967	3.75	7.50	15.00
❑ 626	Day Drinker/Atlanta, Georgia Stray	1968	3.75	7.50	15.00
❑ 630	The Straight Life/How Little Men Care	1968	3.75	7.50	15.00
❑ 634	Holiday for Clowns/Day Gig	1969	3.75	7.50	15.00
❑ 636	Girl of the North/Hung Up in Your Eyes	1969	3.75	7.50	15.00
Albums					
ELEKTRA					
❑ 6E-227	Sonny Curtis	1979	2.50	5.00	10.00
❑ 6E-283	Love Is All Around	1980	2.50	5.00	10.00
❑ 6E-349	Rollin'	1981	2.50	5.00	10.00
IMPERIAL					
❑ LP-9276 [M]	Beatle Hits Flamenco Style	1964	10.00	20.00	40.00
❑ LP-12276 [S]	Beatle Hits Flamenco Style	1964	12.50	25.00	50.00
VIVA					
❑ V-36012	The First of Sonny Curtis	1968	6.25	12.50	25.00
❑ V-36021	The Sonny Curtis Style	1969	6.25	12.50	25.00

CYRUS, BILLY RAY

45s

Number	Title (A Side/B Side)	Yr	VG	VG+	NM
COLUMBIA					
❑ 77971	Fastest Horse in a One-Horse Town/Cadillac Ranch	1995	—	—	3.00
—B-side by Rick Trevino					
MERCURY					
❑ 566582-7	Busy Man/Touchy Subject	1998	—	—	3.00
❑ 568794-7	Time for Letting Go/Cover to Cover (Remix)	1998	—	—	3.00
❑ 574638-7	It's All the Same to Me/Achy Breaky Heart	1997	—	—	3.00
❑ 578304-7	Trail of Tears/Harper Valley P.T.A.	1996	—	—	3.00
❑ 856482-7	Deja Blue/A Heart with Your Name on It	1995	—	—	3.00
❑ 858132-7	Words by Heart/Throwin' Stones	1994	—	—	3.00
❑ 858746-7	Talk Some/Ain't Your Dog No More	1994	—	—	3.00
❑ 862094-7	Some Gave All/Star Spangled Banner	1993	—	—	3.00
❑ 862448-7	In the Heart of a Woman/Right Face Wrong Time	1993	—	—	3.00
❑ 862754-7	Somebody New/Only Time Will Tell	1993	—	—	3.00
❑ 864502-7	Where'm I Gonna Live/Some Gave All	1992	—	—	3.00
❑ 864778-7	She's Not Cryin' Anymore/Someday, Somewhere, Somehow	1992	—	—	3.00
❑ 865260-7	Storm in the Heartland/I Ain't Even Left	1994	—	—	3.00
❑ 866522-7	Achy Breaky Heart/Where'm I Gonna Live	1992	—	2.00	4.00
❑ 866998-7	Could've Been Me/I'm So Miserable	1992	—	—	3.00
❑ 870796-7	Give My Heart to You/Rock This Planet	1999	—	—	3.00
MONUMENT					
❑ 31 79528	You Won't Be Lonely Now/We the People	2000	—	—	3.00
Albums					
MERCURY					
❑ 1P-8218	Some Gave All	1992	6.25	12.50	25.00
—Only released on vinyl through Columbia House					

D

DAFFAN, TED

45s

Number	Title (A Side/B Side)	Yr	VG	VG+	NM
COLUMBIA					
❑ 2-360 (?)	Take That Leash Off Me/That's a Dad Blamed Lie	1949	10.00	20.00	40.00
—Microgroove 7-inch 33 1/3 rpm single					
❑ 2-500 (?)	So Dissatisfied/Strangers Passing By	1950	10.00	20.00	40.00
—Microgroove 7-inch 33 1/3 rpm single					
❑ 2-560 (?)	I've Got $5 And It's Saturday Night/I'm Gonna Leave This Darned Old Town	1950	10.00	20.00	40.00
—Microgroove 7-inch 33 1/3 rpm single					
❑ 2-750 (?)	Ain't Got No Name Rag/Kiss Me Goodnight	1950	10.00	20.00	40.00
—Microgroove 7-inch 33 1/3 rpm single					
❑ 4-21400	No Letter Today/Born to Lose	1955	5.00	10.00	20.00
—45 rpm reissue of Okeh 6706					
DAFFAN					
❑ 102	Bottom of the List/Tangled Mind	1955	7.50	15.00	30.00
Selected 78s					
COLUMBIA					
❑ 20015	Beyond the Shadow of a Doubt/Troubles Keep Hangin' 'Round My Door	1948	3.75	7.50	15.00
—Reissue of 36917					
❑ 20039	Blue Steel Blues/Worried Mind	1948	3.75	7.50	15.00
—Reissue of 37013					
❑ 20058	Look Who's Talkin'/Bluest Blues	1948	3.75	7.50	15.00
—Reissue of 37033					
❑ 20063	You're Breaking My Heart/Time Won't Heal My Broken Heart	1948	3.75	7.50	15.00
—Reissue of 37038					
❑ 20067	Headin' Down the Wrong Highway/Shadow on My Heart	1948	3.75	7.50	15.00
—Reissue of 37044					
❑ 20077	Shut That Gate/Broken Vows	1948	3.75	7.50	15.00
—Reissue of 37087					
❑ 20103	You Better Change/Baby, You Can't Get Me Down	1948	3.75	7.50	15.00
—Reissue of 37267					
❑ 20158	I Lost My Sunshine/I'll Travel Alone	1948	3.75	7.50	15.00
—Reissue of 37431					
❑ 20165	Car Hops Blues/Breakin' My Heart Over You	1948	3.75	7.50	15.00
—Reissue of 37438					
❑ 20181	My Fallen Star/Are You Satisfied Now?	1948	3.75	7.50	15.00
—Reissue of 37501					
❑ 20247	I'm a Fool to Care/Put Your Little Arms Around Me	1948	3.75	7.50	15.00
—Reissue of 37648					
❑ 20250	Let Her Go/Rainy Day Blues	1948	3.75	7.50	15.00
—Reissue of 37651					
❑ 20256	Because/Those Blue Eyes Don't Sparkle Anymore	1948	3.75	7.50	15.00
—Reissue of 37657					

Number	Title (A Side/B Side)	Yr	VG	VG+	NM
❑ 20260	Too Late Little Girl/Weary Worried and Blue	1948	3.75	7.50	15.00
—Reissue of 37661					
❑ 20261	Weary Steel Blues/Always Alone	1948	3.75	7.50	15.00
—Reissue of 37662					
❑ 20266	No Letter Today/Born to Lose	1948	3.75	7.50	15.00
—Reissue of 37667					
❑ 20358	Long John/Lonesome Highway	1948	3.75	7.50	15.00
—Reissue of 37823					
❑ 20383	Go On-Go On/Poor Little Bar Fly	1948	3.75	7.50	15.00
—Reissue of 37959					
❑ 20407	Bury Me Deep/Straight and Narrow Way	1948	3.75	7.50	15.00
—Reissue of 38092					
❑ 20427	Deep Down Inside/Too Far Gone	1948	5.00	10.00	20.00
❑ 20462	Just Born That Way/Two of a Kind	1948	5.00	10.00	20.00
❑ 20506	Now I Must Reap/You'll Always Be Around	1949	5.00	10.00	20.00
❑ 20530	Among Your Souvenirs/Got Money on My Mind	1949	5.00	10.00	20.00
❑ 36917	Beyond the Shadow of a Doubt/Troubles Keep Hangin' 'Round My Door	1946	5.00	10.00	20.00
❑ 37013	Blue Steel Blues/Worried Mind	1946	5.00	10.00	20.00
❑ 37033	Look Who's Talkin'/Bluest Blues	1946	5.00	10.00	20.00
—Reissue of Okeh 6719					
❑ 37038	You're Breaking My Heart/Time Won't Heal My Broken Heart	1946	5.00	10.00	20.00
—Reissue of Okeh 6729					
❑ 37044	Headin' Down the Wrong Highway/Shadow on My Heart	1946	5.00	10.00	20.00
—Reissue of Okeh 6744					
❑ 37087	Shut That Gate/Broken Vows	1946	5.00	10.00	20.00
❑ 37267	You Better Change/Baby, You Can't Get Me Down	1947	5.00	10.00	20.00
❑ 37431	I Lost My Sunshine/I'll Travel Alone	1947	5.00	10.00	20.00
❑ 37438	Car Hops Blues/Breakin' My Heart Over You	1947	5.00	10.00	20.00
❑ 37501	My Fallen Star/Are You Satisfied Now?	1947	5.00	10.00	20.00
❑ 37648	I'm a Fool to Care/Put Your Little Arms Around Me	1947	5.00	10.00	20.00
❑ 37651	Let Her Go/Rainy Day Blues	1947	5.00	10.00	20.00
❑ 37657	Because/Those Blue Eyes Don't Sparkle Anymore	1947	5.00	10.00	20.00
❑ 37661	Too Late Little Girl/Weary Worried and Blue	1947	5.00	10.00	20.00
❑ 37662	Weary Steel Blues/Always Alone	1947	5.00	10.00	20.00
❑ 37667	No Letter Today/Born to Lose	1947	3.75	7.50	15.00
—Reissue of Okeh 6706					
❑ 37823	Long John/Lonesome Highway	1947	5.00	10.00	20.00
❑ 37959	Go On-Go On/Poor Little Bar Fly	1947	5.00	10.00	20.00
❑ 38092	Bury Me Deep/Straight and Narrow Way	1948	5.00	10.00	20.00
OKEH					
❑ 05668	Blue Steel Blues/Worried Mind	194?	6.25	12.50	25.00
❑ 6706	No Letter Today/Born to Lose	194?	6.25	12.50	25.00
❑ 6719	Look Who's Talkin'/Bluest Blues	194?	6.25	12.50	25.00
❑ 6729	You're Breaking My Heart/Time Won't Heal My Broken Heart	1944	6.25	12.50	25.00
❑ 6744	Headin' Down the Wrong Highway/Shadow on My Heart	1945	6.25	12.50	25.00

DAISY, PAT

45s

RCA VICTOR

Number	Title (A Side/B Side)	Yr	VG	VG+	NM
❑ APBO-0087	My Love Is Deep, My Love Is Wide/You've Got Everything	1973	—	3.00	6.00
❑ 47-9972	You're the Reason/I Come Running to You	1971	—	3.50	7.00
❑ 48-1005	Are You Really Leaving Baby/One More Night of Crying	1971	—	3.50	7.00
❑ 48-1006	These Hands/Who Put the Leaving in Your Eyes	1971	—	3.50	7.00
❑ 74-0637	Everybody's Reaching Out for Someone/I'll Be There	1972	—	3.00	6.00
❑ 74-0743	Beautiful People/I Think I'm Falling	1972	—	3.00	6.00
❑ 74-0932	The Lonesomest Lonesome/I Was Meant for You and You Were Meant for Me	1973	—	3.00	6.00

DALE, KENNY

45s

Number	Title (A Side/B Side)	Yr	VG	VG+	NM
AXBAR					
❑ 6053	When I Be Five/(B-side unknown)	1987	2.00	4.00	8.00
❑ 6056	Perfect Angel/You Have My Heart	1987	2.00	4.00	8.00
❑ 6058	Two Will Be One/I Know I Love You	1987	2.00	4.00	8.00
❑ 6060	Daylight/Share All My Memories	1988	2.00	4.00	8.00
❑ 6065	John James/Getting Better at Forgetting	1988	2.00	4.00	8.00
BGM					
❑ 30186	I'm Going Crazy/Macon Georgia Love	1986	—	3.00	6.00
CAPITOL					
❑ 4389	Bluest Heartache of the Year/I'll Believe Every Word That You Lie	1977	—	2.50	5.00
❑ 4457	Shame, Shame on Me (I Had Planned to Be Your Man)/Love Walked In Again	1977	—	2.50	5.00
❑ 4528	Red Hot Memory/This Is a Sad Song	1978	—	2.50	5.00
❑ 4570	The Loser/For Love	1978	—	2.50	5.00
❑ 4619	Two Hearts Tangled in Love/Let's Make Love	1978	—	2.50	5.00
❑ 4704	Down to Earth Woman/Every Other Word Is You	1979	—	2.50	5.00
❑ 4746	Only Love Can Break a Heart/Child of the Wind	1979	—	2.50	5.00
❑ 4788	Sharing/Child of the Wind	1979	—	2.50	5.00
❑ 4829	Let Me In/Rainbow Man	1980	—	2.50	5.00
❑ 4882	Thank You, Ever-Lovin'/There Are Women (Then There's My Woman)	1980	—	2.50	5.00
❑ 4943	When It's Just You and Me/If the World Should Ever Run Out of Love	1980	—	2.50	5.00
FUNDERBURG					
❑ 5001	Moanin' the Blues/(B-side unknown)	1982	2.00	4.00	8.00
REPUBLIC					
❑ 8301	Two Will Be One/One of a Kind	1983	—	3.00	6.00
❑ 8403	Take It Slow/(B-side unknown)	1984	—	3.00	6.00
SABA					
❑ 9214	Look What Love Did to Me/I'm In Over My Heart	1985	—	3.00	6.00

Albums

CAPITOL

Number	Title (A Side/B Side)	Yr	VG	VG+	NM
❑ ST-11673	Bluest Heartache	1977	3.00	6.00	12.00
❑ ST-11762	Red Hot Memory	1978	3.00	6.00	12.00
❑ ST-12126	When It's Just You and Me	1980	3.00	6.00	12.00

DALE, TERRY

45s

LANEDALE

Number	Title (A Side/B Side)	Yr	VG	VG+	NM
❑ 711	Loving You Is Always on My Mind/(B-side unknown)	1982	—	3.50	7.00
❑ 1001	Intimate Strangers/(B-side unknown)	1981	—	3.50	7.00

DALHART, VERNON

Attempting to compile a complete discography of Dalhart, possibly America's most popular singer before Bing Crosby, is a daunting task. He recorded at least 3,000 sides for dozens of labels and under many pseudonyms. For now, we mention only the below 78, as it was the first truly popular recording in country & western music.

Selected 78s

VICTOR

Number	Title (A Side/B Side)	Yr	VG	VG+	NM
❑ 19427	The Prisoner's Song/Wreck of the Old 97	1924	5.00	10.00	20.00

—This was the original recording of the first country and western hit song. Dalhart would record "The Prisoner's Song" for at least 50 different labels!

DALICE

45s

COUNTRY PRIDE

Number	Title (A Side/B Side)	Yr	VG	VG+	NM
❑ 0021	Crazy Driver/(B-side unknown)	1989	—	3.00	6.00

DALLAS, JOHNNY

45s

LITTLE DARLIN'

Number	Title (A Side/B Side)	Yr	VG	VG+	NM
❑ 0013	Heart Full of Love/Grey Flannel World	1966	2.50	5.00	10.00
❑ 0026	If You Got Problems in Your Home/Little Folks	1967	2.50	5.00	10.00

DALLAS COUNTY LINE

45s

CURB

Number	Title (A Side/B Side)	Yr	VG	VG+	NM
❑ D7-76949	Honk If You Love to Honky Tonk/Honk If You Love to Honky Tonk (Club Mix)	1995	—	2.00	4.00

DALTON, BOB

45s

MEGA

Number	Title (A Side/B Side)	Yr	VG	VG+	NM
❑ 0003	Mama, Call Me Home/Papa's Home	1970	—	3.00	6.00
❑ 0003 [PS]	Mama, Call Me Home/Papa's Home	1970	2.50	5.00	10.00
❑ 0017	Blue Skies, Sunshine, My Rain/Tunnel #2	1970	—	3.00	6.00

DALTON, LACY J.

Also see BOBBY BARE; GEORGE JONES.

45s

Number	Title (A Side/B Side)	Yr	VG	VG+	NM
CAPITOL					
❑ NR-44519	Black Coffee/I'm Right Here	1990	—	2.00	4.00
❑ 7PRO-79126	Where Did We Go Right (same on both sides)	1990	—	3.00	6.00
—Vinyl is promo only					
❑ 7PRO-79370	Lonesome (same on both sides)	1990	—	3.00	6.00
—Vinyl is promo only					
❑ 7PRO-79616	Forever in My Heart (same on both sides)	1991	—	3.00	6.00
—Vinyl is promo only					
❑ 7PRO-79962	Black Coffee (same on both sides)	1990	—	2.50	5.00
—Promo version; stock copy is on 44519					
COLUMBIA					
❑ 11-01036	Whisper/China Doll	1981	—	—	3.00
❑ 18-02188	Takin' It Easy/Golden Memories	1981	—	—	3.00
❑ 18-02637	Everybody Makes Mistakes/Wild Turkey	1981	—	—	3.00
❑ 18-02847	Slow Down/One of the Unsatisfied	1982	—	—	3.00
❑ 18-03184	16th Avenue/You Can't Take the Texas Out of Me	1982	—	—	3.00
❑ 38-03926	Dream Baby (How Long Must I Dream)/Hold Me Again	1983	—	—	3.00
❑ 38-04133	Windin' Down/Dixie Devil	1983	—	—	3.00
❑ 38-04696	If That Ain't Love/Too Many Miles	1984	—	—	3.00
❑ 38-04884	You Can't Run Away from Your Heart/The Night Has a Heart of Its Own	1985	—	—	3.00
❑ 38-05644	The Night Has a Heart of Its Own/Adios and Run	1985	—	—	3.00
❑ 38-05759	Don't Fall in Love with Me/Over You	1985	—	—	3.00
❑ 38-06098	Working Class Man/Can't See Me Without You	1986	—	—	3.00
❑ 38-06360	This Ol' Town/Up with the Wind	1986	—	—	3.00
❑ 11107	Crazy Blue Eyes/Late Night Kind of Lonesome	1979	—	2.00	4.00
❑ 11190	Tennessee Waltz/Beer Drinkin' Song	1980	—	2.00	4.00
❑ 11253	Losing Kind of Love/Carolina Come-On	1980	—	2.00	4.00
❑ 11343	Hard Times/Old Soldier	1980	—	2.00	4.00
❑ 11410	Hillbilly Girl with the Blues/Me 'n' You	1980	—	2.00	4.00
UNIVERSAL					
❑ 53487	The Heart/Hard Luck Ace	1989	—	—	3.00
❑ UVL-66007	I'm a Survivor/Walkin' Wounded	1989	—	—	3.00
❑ UVL-66015	Hard Luck Ace/Turn to the One	1989	—	—	3.00

Number	Title (A Side/B Side)	Yr	VG	VG+	NM
Albums					
COLUMBIA					
❑ JC 36322	Lacy J. Dalton	1980	2.50	5.00	10.00
❑ PC 36322	Lacy J. Dalton	198?	—	3.00	6.00
—Budget-line reissue with new prefix					
❑ JC 36763	Hard Times	1980	2.50	5.00	10.00
❑ PC 36763	Hard Times	1985	—	3.00	6.00
—Budget-line reissue with new prefix					
❑ FC 37327	Takin' It Easy	1981	2.00	4.00	8.00
❑ PC 37327	Takin' It Easy	1985	—	3.00	6.00
—Budget-line reissue with new prefix					
❑ FC 37975	16th Avenue	1982	2.00	4.00	8.00
❑ FC 38604	Dream Baby	1983	2.00	4.00	8.00
❑ FC 38883	Greatest Hits	1984	2.00	4.00	8.00
❑ FC 40028	Can't Run Away from Your Heart	1985	2.00	4.00	8.00
❑ FC 40393	Highway Diner	1986	2.00	4.00	8.00
HARBOR					
❑ 001	Jill Croston	1978	6.25	12.50	25.00
—As "Jill Croston"					
UNIVERSAL					
❑ 42294	Survivor	1989	2.50	5.00	10.00

DALTON, LARRY, AND THE DALTON GANG

Number	Title (A Side/B Side)	Yr	VG	VG+	NM
45s					
SOUNDWAVES					
❑ 4645	Cowboy/Too Many Nights	1981	—	2.50	5.00
❑ 4672	Tomorrow/Ain't It Funny	1982	—	2.50	5.00

DANDY

Number	Title (A Side/B Side)	Yr	VG	VG+	NM
45s					
COLUMBIA					
❑ 11355	Who Were You Thinkin' Of/Arizona Highways	1980	—	2.50	5.00
—As "Dandy and the Doolittle Band"					
❑ 11355	Who Were You Thinkin' Of/Arizona Highways	1980	—	2.00	4.00
—As "The Doolittle Band"					
WARNER BROS.					
❑ 8771	Stay with Me/Come and Love Me	1979	—	2.00	4.00
❑ 8880	I Don't Want to Love You Anymore/Early Morning Love	1979	—	2.00	4.00
❑ 49111	I'm Just Your Yesterday/Number One Fan	1979	—	2.00	4.00

DANIEL

Number	Title (A Side/B Side)	Yr	VG	VG+	NM
45s					
LS					
❑ 122	But Tonight I'm Gonna Love You/Knight in Faded Blue Jeans	1977	—	3.50	7.00
❑ 132	Honky Tonk Happiness/Knight in Faded Blue Jeans	1977	—	3.50	7.00
❑ 136	Stolen Moments/Knight in Faded Blue Jeans	1977	—	3.50	7.00
❑ 145	Oh Boy/Where Does Love Go	1978	—	3.50	7.00
❑ 166	I Bow My Head (When They Say Grace)/Where Does Love Go	1978	—	3.50	7.00
❑ 187	She Pretended We Married/But Tonight I'm Gonna Love You	1979	—	3.50	7.00

DANIEL, COOTER

Number	Title (A Side/B Side)	Yr	VG	VG+	NM
45s					
CONNECTION					
❑ 1	Where Are We Going from Here/One More Time Southern Style	1980	—	3.00	6.00

DANIEL, DALE

Number	Title (A Side/B Side)	Yr	VG	VG+	NM
45s					
BNA					
❑ 62734	You Gave Her Your Name/A Little Luck of Our Own	1994	—	—	3.00

DANIEL, DAVIS

Number	Title (A Side/B Side)	Yr	VG	VG+	NM
45s					
A&M					
❑ 576078-7	I'm Not Listening Anymore/I Can't Blame Her	1996	—	2.00	4.00
MERCURY					
❑ 858568-7	I Miss Her Missing Me/Out Here Sits the King	1994	—	—	3.00
❑ 866132-7	Fighting Fire with Fire/Across the Room to You	1991	—	—	3.00
❑ 866822-7	Still Got a Crush on You/Down on My Knees	1992	—	—	3.00
❑ 868544-7	For Crying Out Loud/No Place to Go	1991	—	—	3.00
❑ 878972-7	Picture Me/No Place to Go	1991	—	—	3.00
POLYDOR					
❑ 851398-7	Tyler/Shame on Me	1995	—	—	3.00
❑ 856032-7	William and Mary/Out Here Sits the King	1994	—	—	3.00

DANIEL, PEBBLE

Number	Title (A Side/B Side)	Yr	VG	VG+	NM
45s					
ELEKTRA					
❑ 46643	Goodbye Eyes/Next to You	1980	—	2.00	4.00

DANIELLE, TINA

Number	Title (A Side/B Side)	Yr	VG	VG+	NM
45s					
CHARTA					
❑ 202	Standing Too Close to the Moon/Treat Him Like a Dog	1986	—	2.50	5.00
❑ 204	Burned Out/Lady Blue	1987	—	2.50	5.00
❑ 206	Warmed Over Romance/Maybe Maybe	1987	—	2.50	5.00

DANIELS, CHARLIE, BAND

Number	Title (A Side/B Side)	Yr	VG	VG+	NM
45s					
EPIC					
❑ 02154	In America/The Legend of Wooley Swamp	1981	—	—	3.00
—Reissue					
❑ 02185	Sweet Home Alabama/Falling in Love for the Night	1981	—	2.00	4.00
❑ 02828	Still in Saigon/Blowing Along with the Wind	1982	—	2.00	4.00
❑ 02995	Ragin' Cajun/Universal Hand	1982	—	2.00	4.00
❑ 03251	We Had It All One Time/Makes You Want to Go Home	1982	—	2.00	4.00
❑ 03918	Stroker's Theme/(B-side unknown)	1983	—	2.00	4.00
❑ 05638	American Farmer/Runnin' with That Crowd	1985	—	—	3.00
❑ 05699	Still Hurtin' Me/American Rock and Roll	1985	—	—	3.00
❑ 05835	Drinkin' My Baby Goodbye/Ever Changing Lady	1986	—	—	3.00
❑ 08002	Boogie Woogie Fiddle Country Blues/Working Man You Got It All	1988	—	—	3.00
❑ 08519	Uneasy Rider '88/Boogie Woogie Fiddle	1988	—	2.00	4.00
❑ 50243	Wichita Jail/It's My Life	1976	—	2.00	4.00
❑ 50278	Sweet Louisiana/Sweetwater, Texas	1976	—	2.00	4.00
❑ 50322	Billy the Kid/Slow Song	1976	—	2.00	4.00
❑ 50456	Heaven Can Be Anywhere (Twin Pines Theme)/Good Ole Boy	1977	—	2.00	4.00
❑ 50516	Sugar Hill Saturday Night/Maria Teresa	1977	—	2.00	4.00
❑ 50637	Sweet Lousiana/Trudy	1978	—	2.00	4.00
❑ 50700	The Devil Went Down to Georgia/Rainbow Ride	1979	—	2.00	4.00
❑ 50768	Mississippi/Passing Lane	1979	—	2.00	4.00
❑ 50806	Behind Your Eyes/Blue Star	1979	—	2.00	4.00
❑ 50845	Long Haired Country Boy/Sweet Lousiana	1980	—	2.00	4.00
❑ 50888	In America/Blue Star	1980	—	2.00	4.00
❑ 50921	The Legend of Wooley Swamp/Money	1980	—	2.00	4.00
❑ 50955	Carolina (I Remember You)/South Sea Song	1980	—	2.00	4.00
❑ 68542	Cowboy Hat in Dallas/Easy Rider	1988	—	—	3.00
❑ 68738	Midnight Train/Back to Dixie	1989	—	—	3.00
❑ 73030	Simple Man/Ill Wind	1989	—	—	3.00
❑ 73236	Mister DJ/It's My Life	1990	—	—	3.00
❑ 73426	(What This World Needs Is) A Few More Rednecks/It's My Life	1990	—	—	3.00
❑ 73577	Oh Atlanta/What Is 26	1990	—	—	3.00
❑ 73768	Honky Tonk Life/Willie Jones	1991	—	—	3.00
❑ 74061	Little Folks/Let Freedom Ring	1991	—	—	3.00
❑ 74866	The Twang Factor/Old Rock 'n Roll	1991	—	2.00	4.00
HANOVER					
❑ 4541	Robot Bomp/Rover Had a Party	1959	7.50	15.00	30.00
KAMA SUTRA					
❑ 553	Great Big Bunches of Love/(B-side unknown)	1972	—	3.00	6.00
❑ 576	Uneasy Rider/Funky Junky	1973	—	3.00	6.00
❑ 590	Whiskey/(B-side unknown)	1974	—	2.50	5.00
❑ 593	Way Down Yonder/I've Been Down	1974	—	2.50	5.00
❑ 595	Land of Opportunity/(B-side unknown)	1974	—	2.50	5.00
❑ 598	The South's Gonna Do It/King Size Rosewood Bed	1974	—	2.50	5.00
❑ 601	Long Haired Country Boy/I've Been Down	1975	—	2.50	5.00
❑ 606	Birmingham Blues/Damn Good Cowboy	1975	—	2.50	5.00
❑ 607	Texas/Everything Is Kinda Alright	1975	—	2.50	5.00
LIBERTY					
❑ S7-17398	All Night Long/America, I Believe in You	1993	—	2.50	5.00
PAULA					
❑ 246	The Middle of a Heartache/Skip It	1966	3.75	7.50	15.00
❑ 418	The Middle of a Heartache/Skip It	1976	—	2.00	4.00
Albums					
CAPITOL					
❑ ST-11414	Charlie Daniels	1975	3.00	6.00	12.00
❑ SN-16039	Charlie Daniels	1979	2.00	4.00	8.00
—Budget-line reissue					
EPIC					
❑ AS 586 [DJ]	Interchords	1979	3.75	7.50	15.00
—Music and interviews; promo only					
❑ EAS 1780 [DJ]	The Charlie Daniels Story	1990	3.75	7.50	15.00
—Promo-only interview/radio show					
❑ PE 34150	Saddle Tramp	1976	2.50	5.00	10.00
—Orange label, no bar code on cover					
❑ PE 34150	Saddle Tramp	198?	2.00	4.00	8.00
—With bar code on cover					
❑ JE 34365	Fire on the Mountain	1976	2.50	5.00	10.00
—Reissue of Kama Sutra 2603 without bonus EP; orange label, no bar code on cover					
❑ PE 34365	Fire on the Mountain	198?	2.00	4.00	8.00
—Budget-line reissue					
❑ JE 34369	Uneasy Rider	1976	2.50	5.00	10.00
—Reissue of Kama Sutra 2071 with new name; orange label, no bar code on cover					
❑ PE 34369	Uneasy Rider	198?	2.00	4.00	8.00
—Budget-line reissue					
❑ JE 34377	High Lonesome	1976	2.50	5.00	10.00
—Orange label, no bar code on cover					
❑ PE 34377	High Lonesome	198?	2.00	4.00	8.00
—Budget-line reissue					
❑ JE 34402	Nightrider	1977	2.50	5.00	10.00
—Reissue of Kama Sutra 2607; orange label, no bar code on cover					
❑ PE 34402	Nightrider	198?	2.00	4.00	8.00
—Budget-line reissue					
❑ JE 34664	Whiskey	1977	2.50	5.00	10.00
—Reissue of Kama Sutra 2076 with new name; orange label, no bar code on cover					
❑ PE 34664	Whiskey	198?	2.00	4.00	8.00
—Budget-line reissue					

Number	Title (A Side/B Side)	Yr	VG	VG+	NM
❑ JE 34665	Te John, Grease and Wolfman	1977	2.50	5.00	10.00
—Reissue of Kama Sutra 2060; orange label, no bar code on cover					
❑ PE 34665	Te John, Grease and Wolfman	198?	2.00	4.00	8.00
—Budget-line reissue					
❑ JE 34970	Midnight Wind	1977	2.50	5.00	10.00
—Orange label, no bar code on cover					
❑ PE 34970	Midnight Wind	198?	2.00	4.00	8.00
—Budget-line reissue					
❑ JE 35751	Million Mile Reflections	1979	2.50	5.00	10.00
❑ PE 35751	Million Mile Reflections	198?	2.00	4.00	8.00
—Budget-line reissue					
❑ FE 36571	Full Moon	1980	2.50	5.00	10.00
❑ PE 36571	Full Moon	198?	2.00	4.00	8.00
—Budget-line reissue					
❑ FE 37694	Windows	1982	2.50	5.00	10.00
❑ PE 37694	Windows	198?	2.00	4.00	8.00
—Budget-line reissue					
❑ FE 38795	A Decade of Hits	1983	2.50	5.00	10.00
❑ FE 39878	Me and the Boys	1985	2.50	5.00	10.00
❑ PE 39878	Me and the Boys	198?	2.00	4.00	8.00
—Budget-line reissue					
❑ FE 40760	Powder Keg	1987	2.00	4.00	8.00
❑ FE 44324	Homesick Man	1988	2.00	4.00	8.00
❑ HE 44365	Fire on the Mountain	1982	10.00	20.00	40.00
—Half-speed mastered edition					
❑ FE 45316	Simple Man	1989	3.00	6.00	12.00
❑ HE 45751	Million Mile Reflections	1982	10.00	20.00	40.00
—Half-speed mastered edition					

KAMA SUTRA

Number	Title (A Side/B Side)	Yr	VG	VG+	NM
❑ KSBS 2060	Te John, Grease and Wolfman	1972	3.75	7.50	15.00
❑ KSBS 2071	Honey in the Rock	1973	3.75	7.50	15.00
❑ KSBS 2076	Way Down Yonder	1974	3.75	7.50	15.00
❑ KSBS 2603	Fire on the Mountain	1974	3.75	7.50	15.00
—Includes bonus EP, "Volunteer Jam" (deduct 20% if missing)					
❑ KSBS 2607	Nightrider	1975	3.75	7.50	15.00

MOBILE FIDELITY

Number	Title (A Side/B Side)	Yr	VG	VG+	NM
❑ 1-176	Million Mile Reflections	1984	7.50	15.00	30.00
—Audiophile vinyl					

DANIELS, CLINT

45s

ARISTA NASHVILLE

Number	Title (A Side/B Side)	Yr	VG	VG+	NM
❑ 13126	A Fool's Progress/Swing Through Dallas	1998	—	—	3.00
❑ 13137	When I Grow Up/Long Way Down	1998	—	—	3.00

DANNY AND HAROLD

45s

COLUMBIA

Number	Title (A Side/B Side)	Yr	VG	VG+	NM
❑ 4-21436	My Heart's Hunting a New Home/Teardrop Waltz	1955	5.00	10.00	20.00

DARIN, BOBBY

Rock and pop singer; this was his only record to cross over to the country charts.

45s

ATCO

Number	Title (A Side/B Side)	Yr	VG	VG+	NM
❑ 6117	Splish Splash/Judy, Don't Be Moody	1958	5.00	10.00	20.00

DARLING, HELEN

45s

DECCA

Number	Title (A Side/B Side)	Yr	VG	VG+	NM
❑ 55060	Jenny Come Back/When the Butterflies Have Flown Away	1995	—	—	3.00
❑ 55129	I Haven't Found It Yet/Next to Love	1995	—	—	3.00
❑ 55212	Full Deck of Cards/Married in Mexico	1996	—	—	3.00

DARRELL, JOHNNY

45s

CAPRICORN

Number	Title (A Side/B Side)	Yr	VG	VG+	NM
❑ 0207	Orange Blossom Special/Glendale, Arizona	1974	—	2.00	4.00
❑ 0223	Pieces of My Life/Glendale, Arizona	1975	—	2.00	4.00
❑ 0234	Rose Colored Gin/Glendale, Arizona	1975	—	2.00	4.00

CARTWHEEL

Number	Title (A Side/B Side)	Yr	VG	VG+	NM
❑ 203	Don't It Seem to Rain a Lot/I'll Never Get Up This Slow	1971	—	2.50	5.00
❑ 209	Mr. Tambourine Man/Let Me Stay Awhile	1972	—	2.50	5.00

GUSTO

Number	Title (A Side/B Side)	Yr	VG	VG+	NM
❑ 9001	Hard to Be Friends/These Days	1978	—	2.00	4.00
❑ 9011	Was Yesterday That Long Ago/Spanish Song	1978	—	2.00	4.00

MONUMENT

Number	Title (A Side/B Side)	Yr	VG	VG+	NM
❑ 8570	Crazy Daddy/Uncle Veneer	1973	—	2.50	5.00
❑ 8579	Dakota the Dancing Bear/Just a Memory	1973	—	2.50	5.00

UNITED ARTISTS

Number	Title (A Side/B Side)	Yr	VG	VG+	NM
❑ 869	Green, Green Grass of Home/Deepening Snow	1965	2.00	4.00	8.00
❑ 943	As Long As the Wind Blows/Beggars Can't Be Choosers	1965	2.00	4.00	8.00
❑ 50008	Johnny Lose It All/For Old Times' Sake	1966	2.00	4.00	8.00
❑ 50047	She's Mighty Gone/Baby Sitter	1966	2.00	4.00	8.00
❑ 50126	Ruby, Don't Take Your Love to Town/Little Things I Love	1967	2.00	4.00	8.00
❑ 50183	My Elusive Dreams/Pickin' with Gold	1967	2.00	4.00	8.00
❑ 50207	Come See What's Left of Your Man/Passin' Through	1967	2.00	4.00	8.00
❑ 50235	The Son of Hickory Holler's Tramp/But That's Alright	1967	2.00	4.00	8.00
❑ 50235 [PS]	The Son of Hickory Holler's Tramp/But That's Alright	1967	3.75	7.50	15.00
❑ 50292	With Pen in Hand/Poetry of Love	1968	—	3.00	6.00
❑ 50442	I Ain't Buying/Little Things	1968	—	3.00	6.00
❑ 50481	Woman Without Love/I Fought the Law	1968	—	3.00	6.00
❑ 50503	The Coming of the Roads/The Other Side of the Coin	1969	—	3.00	6.00
—With Anita Carter					
❑ 50518	Why You Been Gone So Long/You're Always the One	1969	—	3.00	6.00
❑ 50572	River Bottom/Ain't That Living	1969	—	3.00	6.00
❑ 50610	She's Headed for the Country/Trouble Maker	1969	—	3.00	6.00
❑ 50629	Mama Come'n Get Your Baby Boy/These Days	1970	—	3.00	6.00
❑ 50675	Brother River/Bed of Roses	1970	—	3.00	6.00
❑ 50716	They'll Never Take Her Love from Me/One Love, Two Hearts, Three Lives	1970	—	3.00	6.00
❑ 50739	Look Out Cleveland/Winter's Comin' On	1971	—	3.00	6.00

Albums

CAPRICORN

Number	Title (A Side/B Side)	Yr	VG	VG+	NM
❑ CP 0154	Water Glass Full of Whiskey	1975	2.50	5.00	10.00

SUNSET

Number	Title (A Side/B Side)	Yr	VG	VG+	NM
❑ SUS-5232	The Johnny Darrell Sound	1969	2.50	5.00	10.00

UNITED ARTISTS

Number	Title (A Side/B Side)	Yr	VG	VG+	NM
❑ UAL 3594 [M]	Ruby, Don't Take Your Love to Town	1967	6.25	12.50	25.00
❑ UAS 6594 [S]	Ruby, Don't Take Your Love to Town	1967	5.00	10.00	20.00
❑ UAS 6634	The Son of Hickory Holler's Tramp	1968	5.00	10.00	20.00
❑ UAS 6660	With Pen in Hand	1968	5.00	10.00	20.00
❑ UAS 6707	Why You Been Gone So Long	1969	5.00	10.00	20.00
❑ UAS 6752	California Stop-Over	1970	5.00	10.00	20.00
❑ UAS 6759	The Best of Johnny Darrell, Volume 1	1970	3.75	7.50	15.00

DARREN, JAMES

The early 1960s teen idol goes country with these later releases, one of which charted.

45s

PRIVATE STOCK

Number	Title (A Side/B Side)	Yr	VG	VG+	NM
❑ 45050	Love on the Screen/Losing You	1975	—	2.00	4.00
❑ 45064	One Has My Name, The Other Has My Heart/Sleepin' in a Bed of Lies	1975	—	2.00	4.00
❑ 45136	You Take My Heart Away/You Take My Heart Away (Disco)	1977	—	2.00	4.00
❑ 45152 [DJ]	Only a Dream Away (mono/stereo)	1977	—	2.50	5.00
—Stock copies may not exist					

RCA

Number	Title (A Side/B Side)	Yr	VG	VG+	NM
❑ PB-11316	Let Me Take You in My Arms Again/California	1978	—	2.00	4.00
❑ PB-11419	Next Time/Something Like Nothing Before	1978	—	2.00	4.00

DAVE & SUGAR

Also see DAVE ROWLAND.

45s

RCA

Number	Title (A Side/B Side)	Yr	VG	VG+	NM
❑ PB-10768	I'm Gonna Love You/I'm Leavin' the Leavin' to You	1976	—	2.00	4.00
❑ PB-10876	Don't Throw It All Away/Queen of My Heart	1977	—	2.00	4.00
❑ GB-10930	The Door Is Always Open/Queen of the Silver Dollar	1977	—	—	3.00
—"Gold Standard Series" reissue					
❑ PB-11034	That's the Way Love Should Be/It's a Beautiful Morning with You	1977	—	2.00	4.00
❑ PB-11141	I'm Knee Deep in Loving You/Livin' at the End of the Rainbow	1977	—	2.00	4.00
❑ PB-11251	Gotta Quit Lookin' at You Baby/We Are the One	1978	—	2.00	4.00
❑ PB-11322	Tear Time/Easy to Love	1978	—	2.00	4.00
❑ PB-11322 [PS]	Tear Time/Easy to Love	1978	—	2.50	5.00
❑ PB-11427	Golden Tears/Feel Like a Little Love	1978	—	2.00	4.00
❑ GB-11497	Gotta Quit Lookin' at You Baby/I'm Knee Deep in Loving You	1979	—	—	3.00
—"Gold Standard Series" reissue					
❑ PB-11654	Stay with Me/What I Feel Is You	1979	—	2.00	4.00
❑ PB-11749	My World Begins and Ends with You/Why Did You Have to Be So Good	1979	—	2.00	4.00
❑ PB-11947	New York Wine and Tennessee Shine/Learnin' to Feel Love Again	1980	—	2.00	4.00
❑ GB-11989	Tear Time/Golden Tears	1980	—	—	3.00
—"Gold Standard Series" reissue					
❑ PB-12063	A Love Song/Things to Do (Without You)	1980	—	2.00	4.00
❑ PB-12168	It's a Heartache/It Ain't Easy Lovin' Me	1981	—	2.00	4.00

RCA VICTOR

Number	Title (A Side/B Side)	Yr	VG	VG+	NM
❑ PB-10425	Queen of the Silver Dollar/Fools	1975	—	2.00	4.00
❑ PB-10625	The Door Is Always Open/Late Nite Country Lovin' Music	1976	—	2.00	4.00

Albums

RCA VICTOR

Number	Title (A Side/B Side)	Yr	VG	VG+	NM
❑ APL1-1818	Dave & Sugar	1976	2.50	5.00	10.00
❑ APL1-2477	That's the Way Love Should Be	1976	2.50	5.00	10.00
❑ APL1-2861	Tear Time	1978	2.50	5.00	10.00
❑ AHL1-3360	Stay with Me/Golden Tears	1979	2.50	5.00	10.00
❑ AHL1-3823	New York Wine Tennessee Shine	1980	2.50	5.00	10.00
❑ AHL1-3915	Dave & Sugar/Greatest Hits	1981	2.50	5.00	10.00

DAVIES, GAIL

Also see WILD CHOIR.

45s

Number	Title (A Side/B Side)	Yr	VG	VG+	NM
CAPITOL					
❑ 7PRO-79255	The Other Side of Love (same on both sides)	1990	—	3.00	6.00
—Vinyl is promo only					
❑ 7PRO-79985	Happy Ever After (same on both sides)	1990	—	3.00	6.00
—Vinyl is promo only					
LIFESONG					
❑ 1771	No Love Have I/It's No Wonder I Feel Blue	1978	—	2.50	5.00
❑ 1777	Poison Love/Bucket to the South	1978	—	2.50	5.00
❑ 1784	Someone Is Looking for Someone Like You/Soft Spoken Man	1979	—	2.50	5.00
MCA					
❑ 53442	Hearts in the Wind/I Will Rise and Shine Again	1988	—	—	3.00
❑ 53505	Waiting Here for You/Meet Me Halfway	1989	—	—	3.00
RCA					
❑ 5011-7-R	Heart to Heart/I Don't Wanta Hold Your Hand	1986	—	—	3.00
—As "Wild Choir featuring Gail Davies"					
❑ PB-13912	Jagged Edge of a Broken Heart/Lion in the Winter	1984	—	—	3.00
❑ PB-13912 [PS]	Jagged Edge of a Broken Heart/Lion in the Winter	1984	—	2.00	4.00
❑ PB-14017	Nothing Can Hurt Me Now/Lovin' Me Too	1985	—	—	3.00
❑ PB-14095	Unwed Fathers/Different Train of Thought	1985	—	—	3.00
❑ PB-14184	Break Away/Not a Day Goes By	1985	—	—	3.00
WARNER BROS.					
❑ 29219	It's You Alone/Following You Around	1984	—	2.00	4.00
❑ 29374	Boys Like You/What Can I Say	1984	—	2.00	4.00
❑ 29472	You're a Hard Dog (To Keep Under the Porch)/ The Boy in You Is Showing	1983	—	2.00	4.00
❑ 29726	Singing the Blues/Movin'	1983	—	2.00	4.00
❑ 29892	Hold On/Dawn	1982	—	2.00	4.00
❑ 29972	You Turn Me On I'm a Radio/All the Fire Is Gone	1982	—	2.00	4.00
❑ 49108	Blue Heartache/When I Had You in My Arms	1979	—	2.00	4.00
❑ 49199	Like Strangers/Love Is Living Around Us	1980	—	2.00	4.00
❑ 49263	Good Lovin' Man/Careless Love	1980	—	2.00	4.00
❑ 49592	I'll Be There (If You Ever Want Me)/Farewell Song	1980	—	2.00	4.00
❑ 49694	It's a Lovely, Lovely World/I'm Hungry, I'm Tired	1981	—	2.00	4.00
❑ 49790	Grandma's Song/Mama's Gonna Give You Sweet Things	1981	—	2.00	4.00
❑ 50004	'Round the Clock Lovin'/It's Amazing What a Little Love Can Do	1982	—	2.00	4.00

Albums

Number	Title (A Side/B Side)	Yr	VG	VG+	NM
LIFESONG					
❑ KZ 35504	Gail Davies	1978	3.75	7.50	15.00
MCA					
❑ 42274	Pretty Words	1989	2.50	5.00	10.00
RCA VICTOR					
❑ AHL1-5187	Where Is a Woman to Go	1984	2.00	4.00	8.00
WARNER BROS.					
❑ BSK 3395	The Game	1980	2.50	5.00	10.00
❑ BSK 3509	I'll Be There	1981	2.50	5.00	10.00
❑ BSK 3636	Givin' Herself Away	1982	2.50	5.00	10.00
❑ 23972	What Can I Say	1983	2.50	5.00	10.00

DAVIS, CARRIE

45s

Number	Title (A Side/B Side)	Yr	VG	VG+	NM
FOUNTAIN HILLS					
❑ 130	Another Heart to Break the Fall/I'm Just Looking for the Real Thing	1989	—	3.00	6.00

DAVIS, DANNY, AND THE NASHVILLE BRASS

Also includes Danny Davis credited alone. Also see HANK LOCKLIN.

45s

Number	Title (A Side/B Side)	Yr	VG	VG+	NM
HICKORY					
❑ 1005	Can't You Feel It in Your Heart/Second Hand Dreams for Sale	1954	3.00	6.00	12.00
JAROCO					
❑ 8742	Green Eyes (Cryin' Those Blue Tears)/Little Pink Cloud	1987	—	2.50	5.00
LIBERTY					
❑ 55213	Beauty and the Beast/Glory Bugle	1959	2.50	5.00	10.00
MGM					
❑ 11103	Crazy Heart/I'm Not Alone	1951	3.75	7.50	15.00
❑ 11175	Please Bring Back the Sunshine/Deep Water	1952	3.75	7.50	15.00
❑ 11244	Always/Do You Ever Think of Me	1952	3.75	7.50	15.00
❑ 11286	Forget/Love Came Out of the Night	1952	3.75	7.50	15.00
❑ 11443	I Don't Want Your Kisses/Come to the Wedding	1953	3.75	7.50	15.00
❑ 13077	Pots 'N' Pans/Travelin' Trumpets	1962	2.00	4.00	8.00
❑ 13106	Little Bandits of Juarez/Theme from "Kill Or Cure"	1962	2.00	4.00	8.00
❑ 13270	Circus World/There Goes My Heart	1964	—	3.00	6.00
❑ 13295	Night Train from Jamaica/Ska Dee Wah	1964	—	3.00	6.00
—With Byron Lee					
❑ 13368	Ballad of Cat Ballou/Theme from "The Saint"	1965	—	3.00	6.00
❑ 13374	I'm Henry VIII, I Am/The End of the World	1965	—	3.00	6.00
RCA					
❑ PB-10871	Country Disco/Disco Dante	1977	—	2.00	4.00
❑ PB-11278	Old Fashioned Love Song/Falsely Accused	1978	—	2.00	4.00
❑ PB-11466	Sugarfoot Rag/Let Your Lovelight Shine	1979	—	2.00	4.00
❑ PB-11612	Ain't Misbehavin'/I'm Gonna Sit Right Down and Write Myself a Letter	1979	—	2.00	4.00
❑ PB-12070	Cotton Eyed Joe/Colinda	1980	—	2.00	4.00
RCA VICTOR					
❑ APBO-0019	Superstar/Come See Us	1973	—	2.00	4.00
❑ APBO-0301	Ruby, Are You Mad at Your Man/Rollin' in My Sweet Baby's Arms	1974	—	2.00	4.00
❑ PB-10232	Singing the Blues/Stay a Little Longer	1975	—	2.00	4.00
❑ PB-10255	Branigan/Peppy Time Tune	1975	—	2.00	4.00
❑ PB-10375	Running Bear/Nashville Brass Hoedown	1975	—	2.00	4.00
❑ PB-10570	Paloma Blanca/Nashville Express	1976	—	2.00	4.00
❑ PB-10814	Why Don't You Love Me/He'll Have to Go	1976	—	2.00	4.00
❑ PB-11073	How I Love Them Old Songs/Tara Jeanne	1977	—	2.00	4.00
❑ 47-9785	Wabash Cannon Ball/Sweet Dreams	1969	—	2.00	4.00
❑ 47-9847	Columbus Stockade Blues/Wings of a Dove	1970	—	2.00	4.00
❑ 47-9905	Down Yonder/May the Circle Be Unbroken	1970	—	2.00	4.00
❑ 47-9936	Jingling Brass/Silent Night	1970	—	3.00	6.00
❑ 47-9936 [DJ]	Jingling Brass/Silent Night	1970	—	3.00	6.00
—Promos available on either yellow or green labels					
❑ 74-0439	I Can't Stop Loving You/Rose Garden	1971	—	2.00	4.00
❑ 74-0506	Highland Brass/Ruby, Don't Take Your Love to Town	1971	—	2.00	4.00
❑ 74-0560	Wait for the Light to Shine/Blue Bayou	1971	—	2.00	4.00
❑ 74-0649	Java/Flowers on the Wall	1972	—	2.00	4.00
❑ 74-0760	From Dixie with Love/Under the Double Eagle	1972	—	2.00	4.00
❑ 74-0847	I'll Fly Away/Woman	1972	—	2.00	4.00
❑ 74-0858	White Christmas/Winter Wonderland	1972	—	2.50	5.00
VERVE					
❑ 10233	Theme from "Carnival"/Stardust	1961	2.50	5.00	10.00
WARTRACE					
❑ 730	I Dropped Your Name/(B-side unknown)	1985	—	2.00	4.00

Albums

Number	Title (A Side/B Side)	Yr	VG	VG+	NM
PICKWICK					
❑ ACL1-7034	Down Yonder	197?	2.00	4.00	8.00
RCA SPECIAL PRODUCTS					
❑ DPL1-0176	America 200 Years Young	1976	3.75	7.50	15.00
—Available only at Amana dealers					
RCA VICTOR					
❑ APD1-0034 [Q]	Travelin'	1973	3.00	6.00	12.00
❑ APL1-0232	Cairbbean Cruise	1973	2.50	5.00	10.00
❑ APL1-0425	The Best of Danny Davis and the Nashville Brass	1973	2.50	5.00	10.00
❑ APL1-0565	Bluegrass Country	1974	2.50	5.00	10.00
❑ APL1-0774	The Latest and Greatest	1974	2.50	5.00	10.00
❑ ANL1-0902	Orange Blossom Special	1974	2.50	5.00	10.00
❑ APD1-1043 [Q]	Dream Country	1975	3.00	6.00	12.00
❑ APL1-1043	Dream Country	1975	2.50	5.00	10.00
❑ APD1-1240 [Q]	Gold	1975	3.00	6.00	12.00
❑ APL1-1240	Gold	1975	2.50	5.00	10.00
❑ APD1-1578 [Q]	Texas	1976	3.00	6.00	12.00
❑ APL1-1578	Texas	1976	2.50	5.00	10.00
❑ ANL1-1930	Christmas with Danny Davis and the Nashville Brass	1976	2.00	4.00	8.00
—Reissue of LSP-4377					
❑ APL1-1986	Super	1976	2.50	5.00	10.00
❑ APL1-2310	Live Vegas	1977	2.50	5.00	10.00
❑ APL1-2721	How I Love Them Ol' Songs	1977	2.50	5.00	10.00
❑ APL1-2980	Cookin' Country	1978	2.50	5.00	10.00
❑ AHL1-3405	Great Songs of the Big Band Era	1979	2.50	5.00	10.00
❑ AHL1-4022	Cotton Eyed Joe	1981	2.50	5.00	10.00
❑ LSP-4059	The Nashville Sound	1969	2.50	5.00	10.00
❑ LSP-4176	More Nashville Sounds	1969	2.50	5.00	10.00
❑ LSP-4232	Movin' On	1969	2.50	5.00	10.00
❑ LSP-4334	You Ain't Heard Nothin' Yet	1970	2.50	5.00	10.00
❑ LSP-4377	Christmas with Danny Davis and the Nashville Brass	1970	2.50	5.00	10.00
❑ LSP-4424	Down Homers	1970	2.50	5.00	10.00
❑ LSP-4475	Somethin' Else	1971	2.50	5.00	10.00
❑ LSP-4571	Super Country	1971	2.50	5.00	10.00
❑ LSP-4627	Turns to Gold	1972	2.50	5.00	10.00
❑ LSP-4720	Live — In Person	1972	2.50	5.00	10.00
❑ LSP-4803	Turn On Some Happy!	1972	2.50	5.00	10.00

DAVIS, DANNY, AND WILLIE NELSON

Also see each artist's individual listings.

45s

Number	Title (A Side/B Side)	Yr	VG	VG+	NM
RCA VICTOR					
❑ PB-11893	Night Life/December Day	1980	—	2.00	4.00
❑ PB-11999	Funny How Time Slips Away/The Local Memory	1980	—	2.00	4.00

DAVIS, DIANNE

45s

Number	Title (A Side/B Side)	Yr	VG	VG+	NM
16TH AVENUE					
❑ 70430	Baby Don't Go/(B-side unknown)	1989	—	2.00	4.00
❑ 70441	I've Lost You to Her/Will You Miss Me When I'm Gone	1990	—	2.00	4.00
❑ 70448	Darlin'/Baby, Sweet Baby	1990	—	2.00	4.00

DAVIS, GAIL

45s

Number	Title (A Side/B Side)	Yr	VG	VG+	NM
COLUMBIA					
❑ 4-21469	Tomboy/I'm a Female Through and Through	1955	6.25	12.50	25.00

DAVIS, GENE

45s

Number	Title (A Side/B Side)	Yr	VG	VG+	NM
MAVERICK					
❑ 301	Oh Those Texas Women/She Says It with Love	1976	—	3.00	6.00

Number	Title (A Side/B Side)	Yr	VG	VG+	NM
DAVIS, JIMMIE					
45s					
CAPITOL					
❑ F1025	You Are My Sunshine/Nobody's Darlin' But Mine	1950	7.50	15.00	30.00
❑ F1210	Cickle Cackle Song/Poodle Dog Song	1950	7.50	15.00	30.00
❑ F1510	As Long As You Believe in Me/White Petals	1951	7.50	15.00	30.00
❑ F40251	My Bucket's Got a Hole in It/Gotta Have My Baby Back	1949	12.50	25.00	50.00
❑ F40281	White Lace, Red Clay and a Black Coffin/ Sometimes Late at Night	1950	10.00	20.00	40.00
DECCA					
❑ 9-28110	When We All Get Together/Thirty Pieces of Silver	1952	7.50	15.00	30.00
❑ 9-28259	I Heard You Talking in Your Sleep/Like the Waves Upon the River	1952	7.50	15.00	30.00
❑ 9-28438	Talkin' to the Wall/Please, Please	1952	7.50	15.00	30.00
❑ 9-28555	Lord, I'm Comin' Home/When Do I Remember	1953	7.50	15.00	30.00
❑ 9-28656	Big Mamou/Neon Love	1953	7.50	15.00	30.00
❑ 9- 28748	When the Train Comes Rollin' In/Lord, I'm Coming Home	1953	7.50	15.00	30.00
❑ 9-28799	To My Mansion in the Sky/Supper-Time	1953	7.50	15.00	30.00
❑ 9-28909	I Can't Stand the Pain/You Took	1953	7.50	15.00	30.00
❑ 9-28912	Christmas Choo Choo/I Love to Ride with Santa Claus	1953	7.50	15.00	30.00
❑ 9-29082	I Don't Care What the World Might Do/ Somewhere There's a Friend	1954	7.50	15.00	30.00
❑ 9-29157	Just Between You and Me/I Don't Know Why	1954	7.50	15.00	30.00
❑ 9-29278	Near the Cross/Taller Than Trees	1954	7.50	15.00	30.00
❑ 9-29445	Sometimes Late at Night/I Might Even Lose My Mind	1955	6.25	12.50	25.00
❑ 9-29613	When the Savior Reached Down His Hand/I Was There When It Happened	1955	6.25	12.50	25.00
❑ 9-29801	Where No One Stands Alone/My Lord Will Lead Me Home	1956	6.25	12.50	25.00
❑ 9-29965	How Long Has It Been/Dear Son	1956	6.25	12.50	25.00
❑ 9-30257	Do You Ever Think to Pray/I Know What He Meant	1957	6.25	12.50	25.00
❑ 9-30517	No Room at the Inn/Gently Rock His Cradle	1957	6.25	12.50	25.00
❑ 9-30668	Sweet Mystery/I'm Bound for the Kingdom	1958	6.25	12.50	25.00
❑ 9-30748	How Great Thou Art/I'll Meet You in the Morning	1958	6.25	12.50	25.00
❑ 9-30899	Lost Love/My Mary	1959	6.25	12.50	25.00
❑ 9-30960	You Are My Sunshine/Nobody's Darlin' But Mine	1959	6.25	12.50	25.00
❑ 9-31009	If You Can Get Along with Me/Gonna Let the Good Times Roll	1959	6.25	12.50	25.00
❑ 31270	Git On Board, Little Children/Twenty-One	1961	5.00	10.00	20.00
❑ 31327	Sitting on Top of the World/Time Changes Everything	1961	5.00	10.00	20.00
❑ 31368	Where the Old Red River Flows/Lonesome Whistle (See, I Heard That Lonesome Whistle)	1962	5.00	10.00	20.00
❑ 31509	Rocks in the Mountain/There Won't Be a Wedding	1963	5.00	10.00	20.00
❑ 31602	Don't Close the Door/The Beginning of the End	1964	3.75	7.50	15.00
❑ 31637	My Room of Prayer/When I Lay My Burdens Down	1964	3.75	7.50	15.00
❑ 31686	Go Tell It on the Mountain/It's Christmas Time Again	1964	3.75	7.50	15.00
❑ 31739	I Wouldn't Take Nothing for My Journey/You Can Have Him	1965	3.75	7.50	15.00
❑ 31797	He's Able/The Safety of His Arms	1965	3.75	7.50	15.00
❑ 31870	(Here's My) Buryin' Ground/I'm Nearer Home (Than I Was Yesterday)	1965	3.75	7.50	15.00
❑ 31906	Will the Circle Be Unbroken/Who Am I	1966	3.00	6.00	12.00
❑ 32062	Forgive Me Santa/Take Me Back to Babyland	1966	3.00	6.00	12.00
❑ 32192	The Chair That Rocked Us All/Haven't Been to Church for Some Time	1967	3.00	6.00	12.00
❑ 32236	Going Home for Christmas/Sniffles (Santa's Pet)	1967	2.50	5.00	10.00
❑ 32331	Bury Me Beneath the Willows/You'll Be My Last Love	1968	2.50	5.00	10.00
❑ 32472	Now I Have Everything/I Know a Man Who Can	1969	2.50	5.00	10.00
❑ 32559	Mary Let Your Bangs Hang Down/Today I'm Giving You Away	1969	3.00	6.00	12.00
❑ 32677	Going Home/Three Nails	1970	2.50	5.00	10.00
❑ 32843	Crumbs from the Table/My Boy Is Going Home	1971	2.50	5.00	10.00
❑ 32867	Put Your Hand in the Hand/Won't You Take Me Back and Try Me One More Time	1971	2.50	5.00	10.00
❑ 32941	If That Isn't Love/Lord, Have You Forgotten Me	1972	2.50	5.00	10.00
❑ 9-46356	Cherokee Boogie/I Wish I'd Never Met Sunshine	1951	10.00	20.00	40.00
❑ 9-46381	Fifteen Miles from Dallas/Bayou for You	1951	10.00	20.00	40.00
❑ 9-46396	Forever's a Long, Long Time/I Ain't Gonna Give	1952	10.00	20.00	40.00
❑ 9-46408	Touch the Hand of the Lord/How Great Thou Art	1952	10.00	20.00	40.00
❑ 9-46410	When the World's on Fire/You're Not Home Yet	1952	10.00	20.00	40.00
MCA					
❑ 40072	Let's All Go Down to the River/God's Last Altar Call	1973	—	3.00	6.00
❑ 53107	Over the Top/Kick the Wall	1987	—	2.00	4.00
PAULA					
❑ 406	Don't Let the Green Grass Fool You/Souvenirs of Yesterday	1974	—	3.00	6.00
❑ 414	Lay It on the Line/I Can't Stand the Pain	1975	—	3.00	6.00
❑ 416	Dating a Memory/Walking My Blues Away	1976	—	3.00	6.00
PLANTATION					
❑ 163	Hold Me/Where the Old Red River Flows	1977	—	2.50	5.00
❑ 174	Pretending She's You/It Makes No Difference Now	1978	—	2.50	5.00
Selected 78s					
BLUEBIRD					
❑ B-5005	Bear Cat Mama from Horner's Corners/She's a Hum Dum Dinger	193?	12.50	25.00	50.00
❑ B-5156	The Keyhole in the Door/It's All Coming Home to You	193?	20.00	40.00	80.00
❑ B-5187	I Wonder If She's Blue/(B-side unknown)	193?	5.00	10.00	20.00
❑ B-5359	I Want Her Tailor-Made/(B-side unknown)	193?	20.00	40.00	80.00
❑ B-5394	Beautiful Texas/The Tramp's Mother	193?	3.75	7.50	15.00
—B-side by Girls of the Golden West					
❑ B-5425	Alimony Blues/(B-side unknown)	193?	20.00	40.00	80.00
❑ B-5496	Arabella Blues/(B-side unknown)	193?	12.50	25.00	50.00
❑ B-5570	Easy Rider Blues/(B-side unknown)	193?	12.50	25.00	50.00
❑ B-5635	Triflin' Mama Blues/(B-side unknown)	193?	12.50	25.00	50.00
❑ B-5697	I'll Get Mine Bye and Bye/(B-side unknown)	193?	12.50	25.00	50.00
❑ B-5699	Red Nightgown Blues/(B-side unknown)	193?	25.00	50.00	100.00
❑ B-5751	Sewing Machine Blues/(B-side unknown)	193?	15.00	30.00	60.00
❑ B-5806	I'll Be Happy Today/(B-side unknown)	193?	15.00	30.00	60.00
❑ B-5965	Minute Man — Part 1/Minute Man — Part 2	193?	15.00	30.00	60.00
❑ B-6040	Dentist Blues/(B-side unknown)	193?	15.00	30.00	60.00
❑ B-6167	Moonlight/(B-side unknown)	193?	10.00	20.00	40.00
❑ B-6236	Sweet Sixteen/(B-side unknown)	193?	7.50	15.00	30.00
❑ B-6249	The Davis Limited/(B-side unknown)	193?	7.50	15.00	30.00
❑ B-6272	Organ Grinder Blues/(B-side unknown)	193?	7.50	15.00	30.00
❑ B-6437	Yo Yo Mama/(B-side unknown)	193?	7.50	15.00	30.00
❑ B-7071	My Dixie Sweetheart/(B-side unknown)	193?	7.50	15.00	30.00
CAPITOL					
❑ 40157	There's a Smile on the Face of the Moon Tonight/ I Got News for You	1949	6.25	12.50	25.00
❑ 40219	Moonlight Millionaire/Don't Lock Your Heart and Throw Away the Key	1949	6.25	12.50	25.00
DECCA					
❑ 1504	Nobody's Darling But Mine/(B-side unknown)	1934	7.50	15.00	30.00
❑ 5090	When It's Round-Up Time in Heaven/Nobody's Darlin' But Mine	1935	6.25	12.50	25.00
❑ 5238	My Blue Bonnet Girl/Ridin' Down the Arizona Trail	1936	5.00	10.00	20.00
❑ 5270	When It's Peach Pickin' Time in Georgia/(B-side unknown)	1936	5.00	10.00	20.00
❑ 5400	Honky Tonk Blues/Do You Ever Think of Me	1937	6.25	12.50	25.00
❑ 5435	Jimmie's Travelin' Blues/I Wonder Where You Are	1937	5.00	10.00	20.00
❑ 5616	Meet Me Tonight in Dreamland/(B-side unknown)	1938	6.25	12.50	25.00
❑ 5620	It Makes No Difference Now/The Curse of an Aching Heart	1939	6.25	12.50	25.00
❑ 5813	You Are My Sunshine/Old Timer	1940	10.00	20.00	40.00
❑ 5878	I Hung My Head and Cried/Just Because of You Little Girl	194?	6.25	12.50	25.00
❑ 5989	Pay Me No Mind/I'm Knocking at Your Door Again	1941	5.00	10.00	20.00
❑ 6009	I Wish I Had a Sweetheart/Tears on My Pillow	194?	5.00	10.00	20.00
❑ 6062	You Told Me a Lie/Don't You Cry Over Me	194?	5.00	10.00	20.00
❑ 6100	It's Too Late Now/There's a Chill on the Hill Tonight	1944	5.00	10.00	20.00
❑ 6105	There's a New Moon Over My Shoulder/Love Please Don't Let Me Down	1945	6.25	12.50	25.00
❑ 18756	Grievin' My Heart Out for You/I'm Sorry If That's the Way You Feel	1946	5.00	10.00	20.00
❑ 46003	Nobody's Darlin' But Mine/Sweethearts or Strangers	1946	5.00	10.00	20.00
❑ 46004	I Wish I Had Never Met Sunshine/My Brown Eyed Texas Rose	1946	5.00	10.00	20.00
❑ 46016	Bang Bang/I'm Gonna Write Myself a Letter	1946	5.00	10.00	20.00
❑ 46037	You Are My Sunshine/My Mary	1947	3.75	7.50	15.00
❑ 46037	Let's Be Sweethearts Again/I've Learned My Lesson	1947	3.75	7.50	15.00
❑ 46038	What's the Matter with You Darling/What Happened	1947	3.75	7.50	15.00
❑ 46039	I'm Hurt Too Much to Cry/All Because You Said Goodbye	1947	3.75	7.50	15.00
❑ 46066	You Won't Be Satisfied That Way/I Just Dropped In	1947	5.00	10.00	20.00
❑ 46085	Plant Some Flowers By My Grave/There's a Chill on the Hill Tonight	1947	5.00	10.00	20.00
❑ 46100	I'm Only in the Way/Just Thinking of You	1948	5.00	10.00	20.00
❑ 46121	Golden Curls/You Are My Sweetheart	1948	5.00	10.00	20.00
❑ 46137	Honky Tonk Blues/Columbus Stockade Blues	1948	5.00	10.00	20.00
❑ 46154	No Good for Nothin'/I'm Hating Myself	1949	5.00	10.00	20.00
❑ 46159	Do You Ever Think of Me/Shackles and Chains	1949	5.00	10.00	20.00
❑ 46211	I Wish I Had a Sweetheart/I'm Drifting Back	1950	3.75	7.50	15.00
❑ 46226	My Heart Belongs to You/Take Care of My Heart	1950	3.75	7.50	15.00
MONTGOMERY WARD					
❑ M-4283	Bear Cat Mama/(B-side unknown)	193?	10.00	20.00	40.00
❑ M-4449	The Keyhole in the Door/It's All Coming Home to You	193?	10.00	20.00	40.00
SUNRISE					
❑ S-3128	Bear Cat Mama from Horner's Corners/She's a Hum Dum Dinger	193?	50.00	100.00	200.00
❑ S-3237	The Keyhole in the Door/It's All Coming Home to You	193?	50.00	100.00	200.00
❑ S-3267	I Wonder If She's Blue/(B-side unknown)	193?	50.00	100.00	200.00
❑ S-3400	There's Evil in Ye Children Gather 'Round/(B-side unknown)	193?	50.00	100.00	200.00
❑ S-3440	I Want Her Tailor-Made/(B-side unknown)	193?	50.00	100.00	200.00
VICTOR					
❑ 23517	Arabella Blues/(B-side unknown)	1931	25.00	50.00	100.00
❑ 23525	In Arkansas/(B-side unknown)	1931	25.00	50.00	100.00
❑ 23544	Penitentiary Blues/(B-side unknown)	1931	25.00	50.00	100.00
❑ 23559	Before You Say Farewell/(B-side unknown)	1931	25.00	50.00	100.00
❑ 23573	Pea Pickin' Papa/(B-side unknown)	1931	25.00	50.00	100.00
❑ 23587	She's a Hum-Dinger/(B-side unknown)	1931	25.00	50.00	100.00

Number	Title (A Side/B Side)	Yr	VG	VG+	NM
❑ 23601	The Davis Limited/(B-side unknown)	1931	25.00	50.00	100.00
❑ 23620	Market House Blues/(B-side unknown)	1931	37.50	75.00	150.00
❑ 23628	Wild and Reckless John/(B-side unknown)	1931	37.50	75.00	150.00
❑ 23648	Lonely Hobo/(B-side unknown)	1932	37.50	75.00	150.00
❑ 23659	Red Nightgown Blues/(B-side unknown)	1932	50.00	100.00	200.00
❑ 23674	Davis' Salty Dog/(B-side unknown)	1932	50.00	100.00	200.00
❑ 23688	1982 Blues/(B-side unknown)	1932	50.00	100.00	200.00
❑ 23703	High Behind Blues/(B-side unknown)	1932	50.00	100.00	200.00
❑ 23718	Cowboy's Home Sweet Home/(B-side unknown)	1932	50.00	100.00	200.00
❑ 23746	Shotgun Wedding/(B-side unknown)	1933	50.00	100.00	200.00
❑ 23752	Bury Me in Old Kentucky/(B-side unknown)	1933	50.00	100.00	200.00
❑ 23752	Hold 'Er Newt/(B-side unknown)	1933	37.50	75.00	150.00
❑ 23763	Organ Grinder Blues/(B-side unknown)	1933	50.00	100.00	200.00
❑ 23778	The Gambler's Return/(B-side unknown)	1933	50.00	100.00	200.00
❑ V40154	The Barroom Message/(B-side unknown)	1929	37.50	75.00	150.00
❑ V40215	Out of Town Blues/(B-side unknown)	1930	37.50	75.00	150.00
❑ V40286	Doggone That Train/(B-side unknown)	1930	37.50	75.00	150.00
❑ V40302	My Louisiana Girl/(B-side unknown)	1930	37.50	75.00	150.00
❑ V40332	Settling Down for Life/(B-side unknown)	1930	37.50	75.00	150.00

Albums

DECCA

Number	Title (A Side/B Side)	Yr	VG	VG+	NM
❑ DL 4587 [M]	It's Christmas Time Again	1964	3.00	6.00	12.00
❑ DL 4868 [M]	Going Home for Christmas	1967	3.00	6.00	12.00
❑ DL 8174 [M]	Near the Cross	1955	6.25	12.50	25.00
❑ DL 8572 [M]	Hymn Time	1957	6.25	12.50	25.00
❑ DL 8729 [M]	The Door Is Always Open	1958	6.25	12.50	25.00
❑ DL 8786 [M]	Hail Him with a Song	1958	6.25	12.50	25.00
❑ DL 8896 [M]	You Are My Sunshine	1959	5.00	10.00	20.00
❑ DL 8953 [M]	Suppertime	1960	5.00	10.00	20.00
❑ DL 74587 [S]	It's Christmas Time Again	1964	3.75	7.50	15.00
❑ DL 74868 [S]	Going Home for Christmas	1967	3.00	6.00	12.00
❑ DL 78896 [S]	You Are My Sunshine	1959	6.25	12.50	25.00
❑ DL 78953 [S]	Suppertime	1960	6.25	12.50	25.00

DAVIS, JOEY

45s

MRC

Number	Title (A Side/B Side)	Yr	VG	VG+	NM
❑ 1017	Why Don't You Leave Me Alone/(B-side unknown)	1978	2.00	4.00	8.00
❑ 1023	Takin' It Easy/Got My Throttle Wide Open	1978	—	3.50	7.00

DAVIS, LINDA

Also see SKIP AND LINDA.

45s

ARISTA

Number	Title (A Side/B Side)	Yr	VG	VG+	NM
❑ 12664	Company Time/How Can I Make You Love Me	1994	—	—	3.00
❑ 12701	Love Didn't Do It/He's in Dallas	1994	—	—	3.00
❑ 12896	Some Things Are Meant to Be/There Isn't One	1995	—	—	3.00
❑ 12991	A Love Story in the Making/What Do I Know	1996	—	—	3.00
❑ 13037	Walk Away/Always Will	1996	—	—	3.00

CAPITOL NASHVILLE

Number	Title (A Side/B Side)	Yr	VG	VG+	NM
❑ NR-44684	In a Different Light (same on both sides)	1991	—	2.00	4.00
❑ 7PRO-79282	In a Different Light (same on both sides)	1991	—	2.50	5.00

—Promo-only number; stock copy is on 44684

Number	Title (A Side/B Side)	Yr	VG	VG+	NM
❑ 7PRO-79646	Some Kinda Woman (same on both sides)	1991	—	2.50	5.00

—Vinyl is promo only

EPIC

Number	Title (A Side/B Side)	Yr	VG	VG+	NM
❑ 34-08057	All the Good Ones Are Taken/Cry Baby	1988	—	—	3.00
❑ 34-68544	Back in the Swing Again/All the Good Ones Are Taken	1989	—	—	3.00
❑ 34-68919	Weak Nights/All the Good Ones Are Taken	1989	—	—	3.00

DAVIS, LINK

45s

ALLSTAR

Number	Title (A Side/B Side)	Yr	VG	VG+	NM
❑ 7171	Bon-Ta-Ru-La/Memories	195?	6.25	12.50	25.00
❑ 7185	Ballad of Jole Blon/Visions	1959	5.00	10.00	20.00
❑ 7203	Little People/Tee Mamou	1960	5.00	10.00	20.00
❑ 7305	Louisiana Waltz/Big Mamou	196?	3.75	7.50	15.00

COLUMBIA

Number	Title (A Side/B Side)	Yr	VG	VG+	NM
❑ 4-21350	Kajalena/Va Tchacher	1955	6.25	12.50	25.00
❑ 4-21431	Cajun Love/Everytime I Pass Your Door	1955	6.25	12.50	25.00

OKEH

Number	Title (A Side/B Side)	Yr	VG	VG+	NM
❑ 18001	Big Mamou/Pretty Little Demon	195?	10.00	20.00	40.00
❑ 18011	Lonely Heart/Time Will Tell	195?	7.50	15.00	30.00
❑ 18025	Mamou Waltz/Hey Garcon	195?	7.50	15.00	30.00
❑ 18035	Falling for You/Gumbo Ya Ya	195?	7.50	15.00	30.00
❑ 18048	Crawfish Crawl/You're Little But You're Cute	195?	7.50	15.00	30.00
❑ 18057	Mama Say No/You Show Up Missing	195?	7.50	15.00	30.00

Albums

MERCURY

Number	Title (A Side/B Side)	Yr	VG	VG+	NM
❑ SR-61243	Cajun Crawdaddy	1969	5.00	10.00	20.00

DAVIS, MAC

45s

CAPITOL

Number	Title (A Side/B Side)	Yr	VG	VG+	NM
❑ 5554	Bad Scene/I Protest	1965	2.00	4.00	8.00

CASABLANCA

Number	Title (A Side/B Side)	Yr	VG	VG+	NM
❑ 2244	It's Hard to Be Humble/Greatest Gift of All	1980	—	2.00	4.00
❑ 2286	Let's Keep It That Way/I Know You're Out There Somewhere	1980	—	—	3.00
❑ 2305	Texas in My Rear View Mirror/Sad Songs	1980	—	—	3.00
❑ 2327	Hooked On Music/Me and Fat Boy	1981	—	—	3.00
❑ 2336	Secrets/Remember When Beverly	1981	—	—	3.00
❑ 2341	You're My Bestest Friend/You Are So Lovely	1981	—	—	3.00
❑ 2346	Midnight Crazy/I Got the Hots for You	1981	—	—	3.00
❑ 2350	Rodeo Clown/Dammit Girl	1982	—	—	3.00
❑ 2355	The Beer Drinkin' Song/You Are So Lovely	1982	—	—	3.00
❑ 2363	Lying Here Lying/Quiet Times	1982	—	—	3.00
❑ 818168-7	Most of All/Springtime Down in Dixie	1984	—	—	3.00
❑ 818929-7	Caroline's Still in Georgia/I've Got a Dream	1984	—	—	3.00

COLUMBIA

Number	Title (A Side/B Side)	Yr	VG	VG+	NM
❑ 10018	Stop and Smell the Roses/Poor Boy Boogie	1974	—	2.00	4.00
❑ 10070	Rock 'n' Roll (I Gave You the Best Years of My Life)/Emily Suzanne	1974	—	2.00	4.00
❑ 10111	(If You Add) All the Love in the World/Smiley	1975	—	2.00	4.00
❑ 10148	Burnin' Thing/A Special Place in Heaven	1975	—	2.00	4.00
❑ 10187	I Still Love You (You Still Love Me)/The Hits Just Keep On Comin'	1975	—	2.00	4.00
❑ 10304	Forever Lovers/The Love Lamp	1976	—	2.00	4.00
❑ 10418	Every Now and Then/I'm Just in Love	1976	—	2.00	4.00
❑ 10535	Picking Up the Pieces of My Life/Do It (With Someone You Love)	1977	—	2.00	4.00
❑ 10745	Music in My Life/You Are	1978	—	2.00	4.00
❑ 45117	Whoever Finds This, I Love You/Half and Half	1970	—	2.50	5.00
❑ 45192	I'll Paint You a Song/The Closest I Ever Came	1970	—	2.50	5.00
❑ 45245	I Believe in Music/Poor Man's Gold	1970	—	2.50	5.00
❑ 45302	Beginning to Feel the Pain/Butterfly Girl	1971	—	2.50	5.00
❑ 45355	Lucas Was a Red-Neck/Fall in Love with Your Wife	1971	—	2.50	5.00
❑ 45404	Sweet Dreams and Sarah/Poem for My Little Lady	1971	—	2.50	5.00
❑ 45456	I Believe in Music/Hollywood Humpty Dumpty	1971	—	2.50	5.00
❑ 45576	Beginning to Feel the Pain/Butterfly Girl	1972	—	2.00	4.00
❑ 45618	Baby Don't Get Hooked on Me/Poem for My Little Lady	1972	—	2.00	4.00
❑ 45727	Everybody Loves a Love Song/Friend, Lover, Woman, Wife	1972	—	2.00	4.00
❑ 45773	Dream Me Home/Spread Your Love on Me	1973	—	2.00	4.00
❑ 45839	Your Side of the Bed/(Hope You Didn't) Chop No Wood	1973	—	2.00	4.00
❑ 45911	Kiss It and Make It Better/Sunshine	1973	—	2.00	4.00
❑ 46004	One Hell of a Woman/A Poor Man's Gold	1974	—	2.00	4.00

JAMIE

Number	Title (A Side/B Side)	Yr	VG	VG+	NM
❑ 1227	I'm a Poor Loser/Let Him Try	1962	2.50	5.00	10.00

MCA

Number	Title (A Side/B Side)	Yr	VG	VG+	NM
❑ 52573	I Never Made Love (Till I Made Love to You)/I Think I'm Gonna Rain	1985	—	—	3.00
❑ 52669	I Feel the Country Callin' Me/Rainy Day Lovin'	1985	—	—	3.00
❑ 52765	Sexy Young Girl/Special Place in Heaven	1986	—	—	3.00
❑ 52826	Somewhere in America/I Need a Hug	1986	—	—	3.00

VEE JAY

Number	Title (A Side/B Side)	Yr	VG	VG+	NM
❑ 492	A Little Dutch Town/Looking at Linda	1963	2.50	5.00	10.00

Albums

ACCORD

Number	Title (A Side/B Side)	Yr	VG	VG+	NM
❑ SN-7165	Little Touch of Love	1981	2.00	4.00	8.00
❑ SN-7189	With Love	1981	2.00	4.00	8.00

ALLEGIANCE

Number	Title (A Side/B Side)	Yr	VG	VG+	NM
❑ AV-5019	Volume XC	198?	2.00	4.00	8.00
❑ AV-5031	Losers	198?	2.00	4.00	8.00

CASABLANCA

Number	Title (A Side/B Side)	Yr	VG	VG+	NM
❑ NBLP 7207	It's Hard to Be Humble	1980	2.00	4.00	8.00
❑ NBLP 7239	Texas in My Rear View Mirror	1980	2.00	4.00	8.00
❑ NBLP 7257	Midnight Crazy	1981	2.00	4.00	8.00
❑ 822638-1	The Very Best and More	1984	2.00	4.00	8.00

COLUMBIA

Number	Title (A Side/B Side)	Yr	VG	VG+	NM
❑ CS 9969	Song Painter	1970	3.75	7.50	15.00

—Red "360 Sound" label

Number	Title (A Side/B Side)	Yr	VG	VG+	NM
❑ CS 9969	Song Painter	1974	2.50	5.00	10.00

—Orange label

Number	Title (A Side/B Side)	Yr	VG	VG+	NM
❑ C 30926	I Believe in Music	1971	2.50	5.00	10.00
❑ CQ 31770 [Q]	Baby Don't Get Hooked on Me	1972	3.75	7.50	15.00
❑ KC 31770	Baby Don't Get Hooked on Me	1972	2.50	5.00	10.00
❑ KC 32206	Mac Davis	1973	2.50	5.00	10.00
❑ KC 32582	Stop and Smell the Roses	1974	2.50	5.00	10.00
❑ PC 32582	Stop and Smell the Roses	1986	—	3.00	6.00

—Budget-line reissue

Number	Title (A Side/B Side)	Yr	VG	VG+	NM
❑ PC 32927	All the Love in the World	1975	2.50	5.00	10.00
❑ PCQ 32927 [Q]	All the Love in the World	1975	3.75	7.50	15.00
❑ PC 33551	Burnin' Thing	1975	2.50	5.00	10.00
❑ PC 34105	Forever Lovers	1976	2.50	5.00	10.00
❑ PCQ 34105 [Q]	Forever Lovers	1976	3.75	7.50	15.00
❑ PC 34313	Thunder in the Afternoon	1976	2.50	5.00	10.00
❑ PCQ 34313 [Q]	Thunder in the Afternoon	1976	3.75	7.50	15.00
❑ JC 35284	Fantasy	1978	2.50	5.00	10.00
❑ JC 36317	Greatest Hits	1979	2.50	5.00	10.00
❑ PC 36317	Greatest Hits	198?	—	3.00	6.00

—Budget-line reissue

Number	Title (A Side/B Side)	Yr	VG	VG+	NM
❑ FC 38950	Who's Lovin' You	1983	2.00	4.00	8.00
❑ PC 38950	Who's Lovin' You	198?	—	3.00	6.00

—Budget-line reissue

MCA

Number	Title (A Side/B Side)	Yr	VG	VG+	NM
❑ 5590	Till I Made It with You	1985	2.00	4.00	8.00
❑ 5718	Somewhere in America	1986	2.00	4.00	8.00

SPRINGBOARD

Number	Title (A Side/B Side)	Yr	VG	VG+	NM
❑ SPB-4024	Mac Davis	197?	2.00	4.00	8.00

TRIP

Number	Title (A Side/B Side)	Yr	VG	VG+	NM
❑ 9502	Mac Davis	1973	2.00	4.00	8.00

DAVIS, PAUL

Also see MARIE OSMOND; TANYA TUCKER.

45s

ARISTA

Number	Title (A Side/B Side)	Yr	VG	VG+	NM
❑ 0645	Cool Night/One More Time for the Lonely	1981	—	2.00	4.00
❑ 0661	'65 Love Affair/We're Still Together	1982	—	2.00	4.00
❑ 0697	Love or Let Me Be Lonely/Oriental Eyes	1982	—	2.00	4.00

BANG

Number	Title (A Side/B Side)	Yr	VG	VG+	NM
❑ 568	If I Wuz a Magician/Mississippi River	1969	—	3.00	6.00
❑ 576	A Little Bit of Soap/Three Little Words	1970	—	3.00	6.00
❑ 579	I Just Wanna Keep It Together/Pollyanna	1970	2.00	4.00	8.00
❑ 581	Can't You/Gonna Keep On Loving You	1970	—	3.00	6.00
❑ 587	I Feel Better/When My Little Girl Is Smiling	1971	—	3.00	6.00
❑ 590	Got to Find My Way Back/I Can't Get Her Off My Mind	1971	—	3.00	6.00
❑ 593	Come On Honey/Livin' On Your Love	1972	—	2.50	5.00
❑ 597	Simple Man/What Would We Do Without Music	1972	—	2.50	5.00
❑ 599	Boogie Woogie Man/Johnny Poverty	1972	—	2.50	5.00
❑ 702	Broken Hearted and Free/Mississippi River	1973	—	2.50	5.00
❑ 705	Daydreamer/Love Don't Come Easy	1973	—	2.50	5.00
❑ 712	Ride 'Em Cowboy/I'm the Only Sinner (In Salt Lake City)	1974	—	2.50	5.00
❑ 717	Make Her My Baby/Can't Get Back to Alabama	1975	—	2.00	4.00
❑ 718	Keep Our Love Alive/I Got a Yearning	1975	—	2.00	4.00
❑ 724	Thinking of You/Karma Baby	1976	—	2.00	4.00
❑ 726	Superstar/Magnolia Blues	1976	—	2.00	4.00
❑ 729	Medicine Woman/Hallelujah, Thank You, Jesus	1976	—	2.00	4.00
❑ 733	I Go Crazy/Reggae Kinda Way	1977	—	2.00	4.00
❑ 736	Darlin'/You're Not Just a Rose	1978	—	2.00	4.00
❑ 738	Sweet Life/Bad Dream	1978	—	2.00	4.00
❑ 4808	Do Right/He Sang Our Love Songs	1980	—	2.00	4.00
❑ 4811	Cry Just a Little/Do You Believe in Love	1980	—	2.00	4.00

Albums

ARISTA

Number	Title	Yr	VG	VG+	NM
❑ AL 8376	Cool Night	198?	2.00	4.00	8.00
—Reissue of 9578					
❑ AL 9578	Cool Night	1981	2.50	5.00	10.00

BANG

Number	Title	Yr	VG	VG+	NM
❑ BLPS-223	A Little Bit of Paul Davis	1970	10.00	20.00	40.00
❑ 401	Ride 'Em Cowboy	1974	3.00	6.00	12.00
❑ 405	Southern Tracks and Fantasies	1976	3.00	6.00	12.00
❑ 410	Singer of Songs — Teller of Tales	1977	3.00	6.00	12.00
❑ JZ 36094	Paul Davis	1980	2.50	5.00	10.00
❑ PZ 37973	The Best of Paul Davis	1982	2.50	5.00	10.00

DAVIS, PAUL (2)

45s

DOKE

Number	Title (A Side/B Side)	Yr	VG	VG+	NM
❑ 107	One of Her Fools/When You Fall	1960	6.25	12.50	25.00

DAVIS, SAMMY, JR.

The following record by this popular entertainer made the country charts.

45s

APPLAUSE

Number	Title (A Side/B Side)	Yr	VG	VG+	NM
❑ 100	Smoke, Smoke, Smoke (That Cigarette)/We Could Have Been the Closest of Friends	1982	—	2.50	5.00

DAVIS, SKEETER

Also see THE DAVIS SISTERS.

45s

MERCURY

Number	Title (A Side/B Side)	Yr	VG	VG+	NM
❑ 73818	I Love Us/It Feels So Good	1976	—	2.00	4.00
❑ 73898	If You Loved Me Now/It's Love That I Feel	1977	—	2.00	4.00

RCA VICTOR

Number	Title (A Side/B Side)	Yr	VG	VG+	NM
❑ APBO-0188	Don't Forget to Remember/Baby Get That Leavin' Off Your Mind	1973	—	2.00	4.00
❑ APBO-0277	One More Time/Stay Awhile with Me	1974	—	2.00	4.00
❑ PB-10048	Come Mornin'/Lovin' Touch	1974	—	2.00	4.00
❑ 47-7034	He Left His Heart for Me/Don't Let Your Lips Say Yes	1957	3.75	7.50	15.00
❑ 47-7084	Lost to a Geisha Girl/I'm Going Steady with a Heartache	1957	3.75	7.50	15.00
❑ 47-7189	Walk Softly Darling/I Need You All the Time	1958	3.75	7.50	15.00
❑ 47-7293	Wave Bye Bye/I Forgot More Than You'll Ever Know	1958	3.75	7.50	15.00
❑ 47-7401	I Ain't A-Talkin'/Slave	1958	3.75	7.50	15.00
❑ 47-7471	Set Him Free/The Devil's Doll	1959	3.00	6.00	12.00
❑ 47-7570	Homebreaker/Give Me Death	1959	3.00	6.00	12.00
❑ 47-7671	Am I That Easy to Forget/Wishful Thinking	1960	3.00	6.00	12.00
❑ 47-7767	(I Can't Help You) I'm Falling Too/No, Never	1960	3.00	6.00	12.00
❑ 47-7825	My Last Date (With You)/Someone I'd Like to Forget	1960	3.00	6.00	12.00
❑ 47-7863	The Hand You're Holding Now/Someday Someday	1961	3.00	6.00	12.00
❑ 47-7928	Optimistic/Blueberry Hill	1961	3.00	6.00	12.00
❑ 47-7979	Where I Ought to Be/Something Precious	1962	2.50	5.00	10.00
❑ 47-8055	The Little Music Box/The Final Stop	1962	2.50	5.00	10.00
❑ 47-8098	The End of the World/Somebody Loves You	1962	3.00	6.00	12.00
❑ 47-8176	I'm Saving My Love/Somebody Else on Your Mind	1963	2.50	5.00	10.00
❑ 47-8219	I Can't Stay Mad at You/It Was Only a Heart	1963	2.50	5.00	10.00
❑ 47-8219 [PS]	I Can't Stay Mad at You/It Was Only a Heart	1963	5.00	10.00	20.00
❑ 47-8288	He Says the Same Things to Me/How Much Can a Lonely Heart Stand	1963	2.50	5.00	10.00
❑ 47-8347	Gonna Get Along Without You Now/Now You're Gone	1964	2.50	5.00	10.00
❑ 47-8397	Let Me Get Close to You/Face of a Clown	1964	2.50	5.00	10.00
❑ 47-8450	What Am I Going to Do with You/Don't Let Me Stand in Your Way	1964	2.50	5.00	10.00
❑ 47-8496	A Dear John Letter/Too Used to Being with You	1965	2.50	5.00	10.00
—With Bobby Bare					
❑ 47-8543	You Taught Me Everything I Know/I Can't Help It	1965	2.00	4.00	8.00
❑ 47-8642	Sun Glasses/He Loved Me Too Little	1965	2.00	4.00	8.00
❑ 47-8765	I Can't See Me Without You/Don't Anybody Need My Love	1965	2.00	4.00	8.00
❑ 47-8837	If I Ever Get to Heaven/If I Had Wheels	1966	2.00	4.00	8.00
❑ 47-8932	Goin' Down the Road/I Can't Stand the Sight of You	1966	2.00	4.00	8.00
❑ 47-9058	Fuel to the Flame/You Call This Love	1966	2.00	4.00	8.00
❑ 47-9242	What Does It Take (To Keep a Man Satisfied)/What I Go Through	1967	—	3.00	6.00
❑ 47-9371	Set Him Free/Is It Worth It to You	1967	—	3.00	6.00
❑ 47-9459	How in the World/Instinct for Survival	1968	—	3.00	6.00
❑ 47-9543	There's a Fool Born Every Minute/I Can't See Past the Tears	1968	—	3.00	6.00
❑ 47-9625	I Look Up (And See You on My Mind)/Timothy	1968	—	3.00	6.00
❑ 47-9695	The Closest Thing to Love/Mama Your Big Girl's About to Cry	1968	—	3.00	6.00
❑ 47-9789	Your Husband, My Wife/Before the Sunshine	1969	—	3.00	6.00
—With Bobby Bare					
❑ 47-9818	It's Hard to Be a Woman/What a Little Girl Don't Know	1969	—	3.00	6.00
❑ 47-9871	We Need a Lot More Jesus/When You Gonna Bring Our Soldiers Home	1970	—	2.50	5.00
❑ 47-9893	Let's Get Together/Everything Is Beautiful	1970	—	3.00	6.00
—With George Hamilton IV					
❑ 47-9896	Bridge Over Troubled Water/How in the World Do You Kill a Memory	1970	—	2.50	5.00
❑ 47-9961	Bus Fare to Kentucky/From Her Arms Into Mine	1971	—	2.50	5.00
❑ 47-9997	Love Takes a Lot of Time/Love, Love, Love	1971	—	2.50	5.00
❑ 74-0148	Baby Sweet Baby/Keep Baltimore Beautiful	1969	—	3.00	6.00
❑ 74-0203	Teach Me to Love You/Bobby Blows a Blue Note	1969	—	3.00	6.00
❑ 74-0292	I Didn't Cry Today/I'm a Lover (Not a Fighter)	1969	—	3.00	6.00
❑ 74-0608	One Tin Soldier/Rachel	1971	—	2.50	5.00
❑ 74-0681	Sad Situation/All I Ever Wanted Was Love	1972	—	2.00	4.00
❑ 74-0827	Hillbilly Song/Once	1972	—	2.00	4.00
❑ 74-0968	I Can't Believe That It's All Over/Try Jesus	1973	—	2.00	4.00

Albums

GUSTO

Number	Title	Yr	VG	VG+	NM
❑ 0014	Best of the Best	1978	2.50	5.00	10.00

RCA CAMDEN

Number	Title	Yr	VG	VG+	NM
❑ ACL1-0622	He Wakes Me with a Kiss	1974	2.50	5.00	10.00
❑ CAL-818 [M]	I Forgot More Than You'll Ever Know	196?	3.00	6.00	12.00
❑ CAS-818 [S]	I Forgot More Than You'll Ever Know	196?	3.75	7.50	15.00
❑ CAL-899 [M]	Blueberry Hill and Other Favorites	1965	3.00	6.00	12.00
❑ CAS-899 [S]	Blueberry Hill and Other Favorites	1965	3.75	7.50	15.00
❑ CAS-2367	Easy to Love	1970	3.00	6.00	12.00
❑ CAS-2517	Foggy Mountain Top	1971	3.00	6.00	12.00
❑ CAS-2607	The End of the World	1972	2.50	5.00	10.00

RCA VICTOR

Number	Title	Yr	VG	VG+	NM
❑ APL1-0190	The Best of Skeeter Davis, Volume 2	1973	3.00	6.00	12.00
❑ APL1-0322	I Can't Believe It's All Over	1974	3.00	6.00	12.00
❑ LPM-2197 [M]	I'll Sing You a Song and Harmonize, Too	1960	6.25	12.50	25.00
❑ LSP-2197 [S]	I'll Sing You a Song and Harmonize, Too	1960	7.50	15.00	30.00
❑ LPM-2327 [M]	Here's the Answer	1961	6.25	12.50	25.00
❑ LSP-2327 [S]	Here's the Answer	1961	7.50	15.00	30.00
❑ LPM-2699 [M]	The End of the World	1963	6.25	12.50	25.00
❑ LSP-2699 [S]	The End of the World	1963	7.50	15.00	30.00
❑ LPM-2736 [M]	Cloudy, With Occasional Tears	1963	6.25	12.50	25.00
❑ LSP-2736 [S]	Cloudy, With Occasional Tears	1963	7.50	15.00	30.00
❑ LPM-2980 [M]	Let Me Get Close to You	1964	5.00	10.00	20.00
❑ LSP-2980 [S]	Let Me Get Close to You	1964	6.25	12.50	25.00
❑ LPM-3374 [M]	The Best of Skeeter Davis	1965	5.00	10.00	20.00
❑ LSP-3374 [S]	The Best of Skeeter Davis	1965	6.25	12.50	25.00
❑ LPM-3382 [M]	Written by the Stars	1965	5.00	10.00	20.00
❑ LSP-3382 [S]	Written by the Stars	1965	6.25	12.50	25.00
❑ LPM-3463 [M]	Skeeter Sings Standards	1965	5.00	10.00	20.00
❑ LSP-3463 [S]	Skeeter Sings Standards	1965	6.25	12.50	25.00
❑ LPM-3567 [M]	Singin' in the Summer Sun	1966	5.00	10.00	20.00
❑ LSP-3567 [S]	Singin' in the Summer Sun	1966	6.25	12.50	25.00
❑ LPM-3667 [M]	My Heart's in the Country	1966	5.00	10.00	20.00
❑ LSP-3667 [S]	My Heart's in the Country	1966	6.25	12.50	25.00
❑ LSP-3667 [S]	Hand in Hand with Jesus	1967	5.00	10.00	20.00
❑ LPM-3763 [M]	Hand in Hand with Jesus	1967	7.50	15.00	30.00
❑ LPM-3790 [M]	Skeeter Davis Sings Buddy Holly	1967	12.50	25.00	50.00
❑ LSP-3790 [S]	Skeeter Davis Sings Buddy Holly	1967	10.00	20.00	40.00
❑ LPM-3876 [M]	What Does It Take (To Keep a Man Like You Satisfied)	1967	7.50	15.00	30.00
❑ LSP-3876 [S]	What Does It Take (To Keep a Man Like You Satisfied)	1967	5.00	10.00	20.00
❑ LPM-3960 [M]	Why So Lonely?	1968	12.50	25.00	50.00
❑ LSP-3960 [S]	Why So Lonely?	1968	5.00	10.00	20.00
❑ LSP-4055	I Love Flatt & Scruggs	1968	5.00	10.00	20.00
❑ LSP-4124	The Closest Thing to Love	1969	5.00	10.00	20.00
❑ LSP-4200	Maryfrances	1969	5.00	10.00	20.00
❑ LSP-4310	A Place in the Country	1970	3.75	7.50	15.00
❑ LSP-4382	It's Hard to Be a Woman	1970	3.75	7.50	15.00
❑ LSP-4486	Skeeter	1971	3.75	7.50	15.00
❑ LSP-4557	Love Takes a Lot	1971	3.75	7.50	15.00

Number	Title (A Side/B Side)	Yr	VG	VG+	NM
❑ LSP-4642	Bring It on Home	1972	3.75	7.50	15.00
❑ LSP-4732	Skeeter Sings Dolly	1972	3.75	7.50	15.00
❑ LSP-4818	Hillbilly Singer	1972	3.75	7.50	15.00

DAVIS, SKEETER, AND DON BOWMAN

45s

RCA VICTOR

Number	Title (A Side/B Side)	Yr	VG	VG+	NM
❑ 47-9415	For Loving You/Baby, It's Cold Outside	1967	2.00	4.00	8.00

DAVIS, SKEETER, AND NRBQ

Albums

ROUNDER

Number	Title (A Side/B Side)	Yr	VG	VG+	NM
❑ 3092	She Sings, They Play	1986	3.00	6.00	12.00

DAVIS, STEPHANIE

45s

ASYLUM

Number	Title (A Side/B Side)	Yr	VG	VG+	NM
❑ 64582	Moonlighter/Lone Star Swing	1993	—	2.00	4.00
❑ 64616	It's All in the Heart/Summer Nights in Dixie	1993	—	2.00	4.00

DAVIS SISTERS, THE

Also see SKEETER DAVIS.

45s

FORTUNE

Number	Title (A Side/B Side)	Yr	VG	VG+	NM
❑ 170	Jealous Love/Going Down the Road	1952	10.00	20.00	40.00
—B-side by Roy Hall					
❑ 174	Kaw-Liga/Sorrow and Pain	1952	6.25	12.50	25.00
❑ 175	Heartbreak Ahead/Steelwood	1952	6.25	12.50	25.00

RCA VICTOR

Number	Title (A Side/B Side)	Yr	VG	VG+	NM
❑ 47-5345	I Forgot More Than You'll Ever Know/Rock-a-Bye Boogie	1953	6.25	12.50	25.00
❑ 47-5460	You're Gone/Sorrow and Pain	1953	3.75	7.50	15.00
❑ 47-5607	Takin' Time Out for Tears/Gotta Get a-Goin'	1954	3.75	7.50	15.00
❑ 47-5701	You Weren't Ashamed to Kiss Me Last Night/ Foggy Mountain Top	1954	3.75	7.50	15.00
❑ 47-5843	Show Me/Just Like Me	1954	3.75	7.50	15.00
❑ 47-5906	The Christmas Boogie/Tomorrow I'll Cry	1954	3.75	7.50	15.00
❑ 47-5966	Everlovin'/Tomorrow's Just Another Day to Cry	1954	3.75	7.50	15.00
❑ 47-6086	Fiddle Diddle Diddle/Come Back to Me	1955	3.75	7.50	15.00
❑ 47-6187	I'll Get Him Back/I've Closed the Door	1955	3.75	7.50	15.00
❑ 47-6291	Baby Be Mine/It's the Girl Who Gets the Blame	1955	3.75	7.50	15.00
❑ 47-6409	Don't Take HIm for Granted/Blues for Company	1956	3.75	7.50	15.00
❑ 47-6490	Lonely and Blue/Lying Brown Eyes	1956	3.75	7.50	15.00

DAY, JENNIFER

45s

BNA

Number	Title (A Side/B Side)	Yr	VG	VG+	NM
❑ 60239	What If It's Me/Fearless	2000	—	—	3.00
❑ 65939	The Fun of Your Love/What If It's Me	1999	—	—	3.00

DAYSPRING

45s

CON BRIO

Number	Title (A Side/B Side)	Yr	VG	VG+	NM
❑ 143	Elfie, the Littlest Elf/Christmas, Christmas (Comes But Once a Year)	1978	—	2.00	4.00
❑ 143 [PS]	Elfie, the Littlest Elf/Christmas, Christmas (Comes But Once a Year)	1978	—	2.50	5.00

DEAL, DON

45s

DONJIM

Number	Title (A Side/B Side)	Yr	VG	VG+	NM
❑ 1008	Second Best (Is Too Far Down the Line)/When	1979	—	3.50	7.00

DEAN, BILLY

Also see SUZY BOGGUSS.

45s

CAPITOL NASHVILLE

Number	Title (A Side/B Side)	Yr	VG	VG+	NM
❑ S7-19038	It's What I Do/The Mountain Moved	1996	—	2.00	4.00
❑ S7-19168	That Girl's Been Spyin' on Me/Don't Threaten Me with a Good Time	1996	—	2.00	4.00
❑ S7-19345	I Still Believe in Christmas/Blue Christmas	1996	—	2.00	4.00
—B-side by the Oak Ridge Boys					
❑ S7-19509	In the Name of Love/When Our Backs Are Against the Wall	1997	—	—	3.00
❑ NR-44773	You Don't Count the Cost/She's Taken	1991	—	2.50	5.00
❑ NR-44803	Only the Wind/Simple Things	1992	—	2.50	5.00
❑ 58736	Real Man/She Gets What She Wants	1998	—	—	3.00
❑ 58754	Innocent Bystander/A Fall in Tennessee	1999	—	—	3.00
❑ 7PRO-79247	Lowdown Lonely (same on both sides)	1990	—	3.00	6.00
—Vinyl is promo only					

COLLECTABLES

Number	Title (A Side/B Side)	Yr	VG	VG+	NM
❑ COL- 6096	Only Here for a Little While/Somewhere in My Broken Heart	199?	—	—	3.00
—First issue on stock 45 for these 1990-91 hits					
❑ COL-6291	We Just Disagree/Feed Jake	1995	—	—	3.00
—First issue on stock 45 for the 1993 hit A-side; B-side by Pirates of the Mississippi					

LIBERTY

Number	Title (A Side/B Side)	Yr	VG	VG+	NM
❑ S7-18406	Cowboy Band/Indian Head Penny	1994	—	2.00	4.00
❑ S7-56804	Tryin' to Hide a Fire in the Dark/Steam Roller	1992	—	2.00	4.00
❑ S7-56984	I Wanna Take Care of You/I'm Not Built That Way	1993	—	2.00	4.00
❑ S7-57745	Billy the Kid/Simple Things	1992	—	2.50	5.00
❑ S7-57884	If There Hadn't Been You/Small Favors	1992	—	2.00	4.00

DEAN, EDDIE

45s

CAPITOL

Number	Title (A Side/B Side)	Yr	VG	VG+	NM
❑ F1362	My Life with You/Will They Open Up That Door	1951	6.25	12.50	25.00
❑ F1389	All That I'm Asking Is Sympathy/If I Should Come Back	1951	6.25	12.50	25.00
❑ F1424	Please Don't Cry/I'll Be Back	1951	6.25	12.50	25.00
❑ F1497	I'm the Old Friend/My Sweetheart, My Own	1951	6.25	12.50	25.00
❑ F1590	I Married the Girl/Let Me Hold You	1951	6.25	12.50	25.00
❑ F1729	I'm Not in Love, Just Involved/Roses Remind Me of You	1951	6.25	12.50	25.00
❑ F1842	Beloved Enemy/The Lord's Prayer	1951	6.25	12.50	25.00
❑ F1915	Blue Wedding Bells/Tears on My Guitar	1952	6.25	12.50	25.00
❑ F2086	Gold, Yellow Gold/Poor Little Swallow	1952	6.25	12.50	25.00
❑ 4900	Run, Jimmy, Run/She Doesn't Know I'm Alive	1963	3.00	6.00	12.00

COMMERCE

Number	Title (A Side/B Side)	Yr	VG	VG+	NM
❑ 559	Don't Take Advantage of Me/Stop Me If You've Heard This One Before	196?	2.50	5.00	10.00
❑ 559 [PS]	Don't Take Advantage of Me/Stop Me If You've Heard This One Before	196?	3.75	7.50	15.00

CORAL

Number	Title (A Side/B Side)	Yr	VG	VG+	NM
❑ 9-60740	Raindrops/I Understand	1952	6.25	12.50	25.00

INTRO

Number	Title (A Side/B Side)	Yr	VG	VG+	NM
❑ 6087	I'm a Stranger in My Home/Put a Little Sweetnin' in Your Love	1953	6.25	12.50	25.00

MERCURY

Number	Title (A Side/B Side)	Yr	VG	VG+	NM
❑ 6282	On the Banks of the Sunny San Juan/Cowboy	1950	10.00	20.00	40.00

MOSRITE

Number	Title (A Side/B Side)	Yr	VG	VG+	NM
❑ 270	One More Time Around/Playing Both Ends Against the Middle	196?	3.75	7.50	15.00

ODE

Number	Title (A Side/B Side)	Yr	VG	VG+	NM
❑ 1701	I'm a Stranger in My Home/Put a Little Sweetnin' in Your Love	1953	6.25	12.50	25.00
❑ 1710	Bimbo/No, No, Not Grandma	1953	6.25	12.50	25.00

SAGE

Number	Title (A Side/B Side)	Yr	VG	VG+	NM
❑ 325	I Took the Blues Out of Tomorrow/Seeds of Doubt	1960	5.00	10.00	20.00
❑ 332	If Dreams Could Come True/Somewhere Along the Line	1960	5.00	10.00	20.00
❑ 338	Rocket to Heaven/Smoke Signals	1961	5.00	10.00	20.00
❑ 342	I Can't Go On Alone/Salesman	1961	3.75	7.50	15.00

SAGE AND SAND

Number	Title (A Side/B Side)	Yr	VG	VG+	NM
❑ 180	I Dreamed of a Hill-Billy Heaven/Stealing	1954	7.50	15.00	30.00
❑ 186	Impatient Blues/Second Hand Romance	1955	6.25	12.50	25.00
❑ 188	Impatient Blues/Cry of a Broken Heart	1955	6.25	12.50	25.00
❑ 199	Walk Beside Me/Blessed Are We	1956	6.25	12.50	25.00
❑ 200	Orphan's Prayer/Once-a-While	1956	6.25	12.50	25.00
❑ 207	Open Up the Door, Baby/Sign on the Door	1956	6.25	12.50	25.00
—With Joanie Hall					
❑ 208	The First Christmas Bell/Somebody Great	1956	6.25	12.50	25.00
❑ 215	Look Homeward Angel/Downgrade	1957	5.00	10.00	20.00
❑ 226	Rock and Roll Cowboy/The Banks of the Old Rio Grande	1957	7.50	15.00	30.00
❑ 231	Walkin' After Midnight/Fingerprints	1957	6.25	12.50	25.00
❑ 235	Lonesome Guitar/Tags	1957	6.25	12.50	25.00
❑ 236	Night Train/Got One Foot Caught in Quicksand	1957	6.25	12.50	25.00
❑ 249	Iowa Rose/Nothing But Echoes	1958	5.00	10.00	20.00
❑ 270	Green Grass/Your Wayward Heart	1958	5.00	10.00	20.00

Selected 78s

CRYSTAL

Number	Title (A Side/B Side)	Yr	VG	VG+	NM
❑ 132	One Has My Name, The Other Has My Heart/(B-side unknown)	1948	10.00	20.00	40.00
❑ 156	Gravedigger's Lament/A Million Tears Ago	1949	7.50	15.00	30.00
❑ 211	California Waltz/Lady You Should Live So Long	1949	7.50	15.00	30.00

DECCA

Number	Title (A Side/B Side)	Yr	VG	VG+	NM
❑ 5023	Tell Mother I'll Be There/(There's) No Disappointment in Heaven	1934	10.00	20.00	40.00
❑ 5024	There Shall Be Showers of Blessing/Happy in Him	1934	10.00	20.00	40.00
❑ 5988	On the Banks of the Sunny San Juan/When It's Harvest Time in Peaceful Valley	1942	6.25	12.50	25.00
❑ 6026	Little Grey Home in the West/Where the Silv'ry Colorado Wends Its Way	1942	6.25	12.50	25.00
❑ 46135	How Can You Say You Love Me/Sleepy Time in Caroline	1948	5.00	10.00	20.00

MAJESTIC

Number	Title (A Side/B Side)	Yr	VG	VG+	NM
❑ 11000	Missouri/No Vacancy	194?	5.00	10.00	20.00
❑ 11001	I Was Wrong/There's a Rose That Grows in the Ozarks	194?	5.00	10.00	20.00
❑ 11004	Rainbow at Midnight/Kentucky Waltz	194?	5.00	10.00	20.00
❑ 11007	I'll Cry on My Pillow Tonight/Ain't It a Shame, Love, Ain't It a Shame?	194?	5.00	10.00	20.00
❑ 11018	Spring Has Come to Old Missouri/Toodle-Oo My Darling	194?	5.00	10.00	20.00
❑ 11019	On the Banks of the Sunny San Juan/Let's Go Sparkin'	194?	5.00	10.00	20.00
❑ 11020	It's a Boy/I'm a Kansas Man	194?	5.00	10.00	20.00
❑ 11026	The Midnight Train/Rosanne of San Juan	194?	5.00	10.00	20.00

MERCURY

Number	Title (A Side/B Side)	Yr	VG	VG+	NM
❑ 6170	Careless Hands/Don't Tell Me Stories	1949	5.00	10.00	20.00
❑ 6195	One You Must Choose/On the Banks of the Sunny San Juan	1949	5.00	10.00	20.00
❑ 6210	'Neath Texas Skies/One You Must Choose	1949	5.00	10.00	20.00
❑ 6219	Fool's Gold/I Wish I Knew	1949	5.00	10.00	20.00
❑ 6251	Devil's Desert Isle/You Want to Divorce Me	1950	5.00	10.00	20.00

Number	Title (A Side/B Side)	Yr	VG	VG+	NM
VARSITY					
❑ 8021	Rainbow at Midnight/Kentucky Waltz	195?	2.50	5.00	10.00
Albums					
SAGE AND SAND					
❑ C-1 [M]	Greatest Westerns	1956	12.50	25.00	50.00
❑ C-5 [M]	Hi-Country	1957	12.50	25.00	50.00
❑ C-16 [M]	Hillbilly Heaven	1961	7.50	15.00	30.00
SOUND					
❑ LP-603 [M]	Greatest Westerns	1957	7.50	15.00	30.00

DEAN, JIMMY

Number	Title (A Side/B Side)	Yr	VG	VG+	NM
45s					
4 STAR					
❑ 1613	Bumming Around/Picking Sweethearts	1953	6.25	12.50	25.00
❑ 1640	Queen of Hearts/I'm Feeling For You	1953	5.00	10.00	20.00
❑ 1654	Release Me/Sweet Darling	1954	5.00	10.00	20.00
❑ 1732	Bumming Around/Release Me	1959	3.00	6.00	12.00
CASINO					
❑ 052	I.O.U./Let's Pick Up the Pieces	1976	—	2.00	4.00
❑ 074	To a Sleeping Beauty/I Didn't Have Time	1976	—	2.00	4.00
❑ 108	Where Is That Man/(B-side unknown)	1976	—	2.00	4.00
CHURCHILL					
❑ 94024	I.O.U./To a Sleeping Beauty	1983	—	2.00	4.00
COLUMBIA					
❑ 31550 [S]	Basin Street Blues/Please Pass the Biscuits	1962	5.00	10.00	20.00
❑ 31551 [S]	Have You Ever Been Lonely/Nobody	1962	5.00	10.00	20.00
❑ 31552 [S]	I Was Just Walking Out the Door/The Dark Town Poker Club	1962	5.00	10.00	20.00
❑ 31553 [S]	You're Nobody Until Somebody Loves You/ Kentucky Means Paradise	1962	5.00	10.00	20.00
❑ 31554 [S]	Little Black Book/Old Pappy's New Banjo	1962	5.00	10.00	20.00
—The above five are "Stereo Seven" 33 1/3 rpm jukebox singles from set "JS 7-63"					
❑ 40995	Deep Blue Sea/Love Me So I'll Know	1957	3.00	6.00	12.00
❑ 41025	Little Sandy Sleighfoot/When They Ring the Golden Bells	1957	3.75	7.50	15.00
❑ 41025 [PS]	Little Sandy Sleighfoot/When They Ring the Golden Bells	1957	6.25	12.50	25.00
❑ 41118	Starlight, Starbright/Makin' My Mind Up	1958	3.00	6.00	12.00
❑ 41196	School of Love/You Should See Tennessee, Mam'selle	1958	3.00	6.00	12.00
❑ 41265	My Heart Is An Open Book/Shark in the Bathtub	1958	3.00	6.00	12.00
❑ 41395	Sing Along/Weekend Blues	1959	3.00	6.00	12.00
❑ 41453	Stay a Little Longer/Counting Tears	1959	3.00	6.00	12.00
❑ 41543	Thanks for the Dream/There's Still Time, Brother	1959	3.00	6.00	12.00
❑ 41710	Little Boy Lost/There'll Be No Teardrops Tonight	1960	3.00	6.00	12.00
❑ 41956	Give Me Back My Heart/It's Been a Long, Long Time	1961	2.50	5.00	10.00
❑ 42175	Big John/I Won't Go Huntin' with You Jake (But I'll Go Chasin' Wimmin)	1961	5.00	10.00	20.00
—Lyrics say: "At the bottom of this mine lies one hell of a man."					
❑ 42175	Big Bad John/I Won't Go Huntin' with You Jake (But I'll Go Chasin' Wimmin)	1961	2.50	5.00	10.00
—Lyrics say: "At the bottom of this mine lies a big, big man." We think the song title was changed with the lyric, but we're not 100 percent sure. In other words, this title may exist with the "hell of a man" lyrics.					
❑ 42175 [PS]	Big Bad John/I Won't Go Huntin' with You Jake (But I'll Go Chasin' Wimmin)	1961	3.75	7.50	15.00
❑ 42248	Oklahoma Bill/To a Sleeping Beauty	1961	2.50	5.00	10.00
❑ 42259	Dear Ivan/Smoke, Smoke, Smoke That Cigarette	1962	2.50	5.00	10.00
❑ 42259 [PS]	Dear Ivan/Smoke, Smoke, Smoke That Cigarette	1962	3.75	7.50	15.00
❑ 42282	To a Sleeping Beauty/The Cajun Queen	1962	2.50	5.00	10.00
❑ 42282 [PS]	To a Sleeping Beauty/The Cajun Queen	1962	3.75	7.50	15.00
❑ 42338	P.T. 109/Walk On, Boy	1962	2.50	5.00	10.00
❑ 42338 [PS]	P.T. 109/Walk On, Boy	1962	3.75	7.50	15.00
❑ 42483	Steel Men/Little Bitty Big John	1962	2.50	5.00	10.00
❑ 42483 [PS]	Steel Men/Little Bitty Big John	1962	3.75	7.50	15.00
❑ 42529	Little Black Book/Please Pass the Biscuits	1962	2.50	5.00	10.00
❑ 42529 [PS]	Little Black Book/Please Pass the Biscuits	1962	3.75	7.50	15.00
❑ 42600	Gonna Raise a Rukus Tonight/A Day That Changed the World	1962	2.50	5.00	10.00
❑ 42600 [PS]	Gonna Raise a Rukus Tonight/A Day That Changed the World	1962	3.75	7.50	15.00
❑ 42738	Mile Long Train/This Ole House	1963	2.00	4.00	8.00
❑ 42861	The Funniest Thing I Ever Heard/Thumb Pick Pete	1963	2.00	4.00	8.00
❑ 42934	Mind Your Own Business/I Really Don't Want to Know	1963	2.00	4.00	8.00
❑ 43021	Shenandoah/Waitin' for the Wagon	1964	2.00	4.00	8.00
❑ 43159	Sam Hill/When I Grow Too Old to Dream	1964	2.00	4.00	8.00
❑ 43172	Yes, Patricia, There Is a Santa Claus/Little Sandy Sleighfoot	1964	2.50	5.00	10.00
❑ 43263	The First Thing Ev'ry Morning (And the Last Thing Ev'ry Night)/Awkward Situation	1965	—	3.00	6.00
❑ 43382	Harvest of Sunshine/Under the Sun	1965	—	3.00	6.00
❑ 43457	Blue Christmas/Yes, Patricia, There Is a Santa Claus	1965	2.00	4.00	8.00
❑ 43540	Things Have Gone to Pieces/Striker Bill	1966	—	3.00	6.00
❑ 43754	Once a Day/Let's Pretend	1966	—	3.00	6.00
❑ 45922	Your Sweet Love (Keeps Me Homeward Bound)/ I'm Gonna Be Gone	1973	—	2.50	5.00
❑ 45981	Who's Gonna Love Me Tomorrow/The Days When Jim Liked Jimmy	1973	—	2.50	5.00
❑ 46039	I've Been Down Some Road/Your Sweet Love	1974	—	2.50	5.00
❑ JZSP 111915/6 [DJ]	Blue Christmas/Yes, Patricia, There Is a Santa Claus	1965	5.00	10.00	20.00
—Promo only on green vinyl					
KING					
❑ 5862	There Stands the Glass/Bumming Around	1964	2.00	4.00	8.00
MERCURY					
❑ 70691	False Pride/Big Blue Diamonds	1955	3.75	7.50	15.00
❑ 70745	Find 'Em, Fool 'Em, and Leave 'Em Alone/My World Is You	1955	3.75	7.50	15.00
❑ 70786	Freight Train Blues/Glad Rags	1956	3.75	7.50	15.00
❑ 70855	Hello Mr. Blues/I Found Out	1956	3.75	7.50	15.00
❑ 71120	Losing Game/Happy Child	1957	3.75	7.50	15.00
❑ 71172	Look on the Good Side/Do You Love Me	1957	3.75	7.50	15.00
❑ 71240	Bumming Around/Nothing Can Stop My Love	1957	3.75	7.50	15.00
❑ 71313	What This Old World Needs/A Fool in Love	1958	3.75	7.50	15.00
RCA VICTOR					
❑ 47-8971	Stand Beside Me/A Tiny Drop of Sadness	1966	2.00	4.00	8.00
❑ 47-9091	Sweet Misery/When Someone Mentions Your Name	1967	2.00	4.00	8.00
❑ 47-9241	Ninety Days/In the Same Old Way	1967	2.00	4.00	8.00
❑ 47-9350	I'm a Swinger/Your Country Boy	1967	2.00	4.00	8.00
❑ 47-9454	A Thing Called Love/One Last Time	1968	2.00	4.00	8.00
❑ 47-9567	Born to Be By Your Side/Read 'Em and Weep	1968	2.00	4.00	8.00
❑ 47-9652	A Hammer and Nails/I Taught Her Everything She Knows	1968	2.00	4.00	8.00
❑ 47-9800	When Judy Smiled/My Hometown Sweetheart	1969	—	3.00	6.00
❑ 47-9859	Down Comes the Rain/Us	1970	—	3.00	6.00
❑ 47-9915	Weakness in a Man/Aunt Maudie's Fun Garden	1970	—	3.00	6.00
❑ 47-9947	Slowly/Sweet Thang	1971	—	3.00	6.00
—With Dottie West					
❑ 47-9966	Everybody Knows/Ain't Life Sweet	1971	—	3.00	6.00
❑ 74-0122	A Rose Is a Rose Is a Rose/She's Mine	1969	—	3.00	6.00
❑ 74-0600	And I'm Still Missing You/The One You Say Good Mornin' To	1971	—	3.00	6.00
Albums					
COLUMBIA					
❑ CL 1025 [M]	Jimmy Dean's Hour of Prayer	1957	10.00	20.00	40.00
❑ CL 1735 [M]	Big Bad John and Other Fabulous Songs and Tales	1961	5.00	10.00	20.00
—It's possible that two different editions exist, one with the "hell of a man" lyrics of "Big Bad John" and the other with the "big, big man" lyrics, but this has not been confirmed.					
❑ CL 1894 [M]	Portrait of Jimmy Dean	1962	5.00	10.00	20.00
❑ CL 2027 [M]	Everybody's Favorite	1963	3.75	7.50	15.00
❑ CL 2188 [M]	Songs We All Love Best	1964	3.75	7.50	15.00
❑ CL 2401 [M]	The First Thing Every Morning	1965	3.75	7.50	15.00
❑ CL 2404 [M]	Jimmy Dean's Christmas Card	1965	3.75	7.50	15.00
❑ CL 2485 [M]	Jimmy Dean's Greatest Hits	1966	3.75	7.50	15.00
❑ CL 2538 [M]	The Big Ones	1966	3.75	7.50	15.00
❑ CS 8535 [S]	Big Bad John and Other Fabulous Songs and Tales	1961	6.25	12.50	25.00
—It's possible that two different editions exist, one with the "hell of a man" lyrics of "Big Bad John" and the other with the "big, big man" lyrics, but this has not been confirmed.					
❑ CS 8694 [S]	Portrait of Jimmy Dean	1962	6.25	12.50	25.00
❑ CS 8827 [S]	Everybody's Favorite	1963	5.00	10.00	20.00
❑ CS 8988 [S]	Songs We All Love Best	1964	5.00	10.00	20.00
❑ CS 9201 [S]	The First Thing Every Morning	1965	5.00	10.00	20.00
❑ CS 9204 [S]	Jimmy Dean's Christmas Card	1965	3.00	6.00	12.00
❑ CS 9285 [S]	Jimmy Dean's Greatest Hits	1966	3.75	7.50	15.00
❑ PC 9285	Jimmy Dean's Greatest Hits	198?	2.00	4.00	8.00
—Budget-line reissue					
❑ CS 9338 [S]	The Big Ones	1966	3.75	7.50	15.00
❑ CS 9424 [R]	Jimmy Dean's Hour of Prayer	1966	3.00	6.00	12.00
❑ CS 9677	Dean's List	1968	3.75	7.50	15.00
CROWN					
❑ 291	Jimmy Dean and the Western Gentlemen	196?	3.00	6.00	12.00
GRT					
❑ 8014	I.O.U.	1977	2.50	5.00	10.00
HARMONY					
❑ HL 7268 [M]	Hymns	1960	3.75	7.50	15.00
❑ HL 7408 [M]	Mr. Country Music	1967	3.00	6.00	12.00
❑ HS 11042 [R]	Hymns	1960	3.00	6.00	12.00
❑ HS 11208 [S]	Mr. Country Music	1967	3.00	6.00	12.00
❑ HS 11270	The Country's Favorite Son	1968	3.00	6.00	12.00
HILLTOP					
❑ 6004	Golden Favorites	196?	3.00	6.00	12.00
KING					
❑ 686 [M]	Favorites of Jimmy Dean	1961	15.00	30.00	60.00
MERCURY					
❑ MG-20319 [M]	Jimmy Dean Sings His Television Favorites	1957	10.00	20.00	40.00
RCA VICTOR					
❑ LPM-3727 [M]	Jimmy Dean Is Here	1967	3.75	7.50	15.00
❑ LSP-3727 [S]	Jimmy Dean Is Here	1967	3.75	7.50	15.00
❑ LPM-3824 [M]	Most Richly Blesed	1967	5.00	10.00	20.00
❑ LSP-3824 [S]	Most Richly Blesed	1967	3.75	7.50	15.00
❑ LPM-3890 [M]	The Jimmy Dean Show	1967	5.00	10.00	20.00
❑ LSP-3890 [S]	The Jimmy Dean Show	1967	3.75	7.50	15.00
❑ LPM-3999 [M]	A Thing Called Love	1968	7.50	15.00	30.00
❑ LSP-3999 [S]	A Thing Called Love	1968	3.75	7.50	15.00
❑ LSP-4035	Speaker of the House	1968	3.75	7.50	15.00
❑ LSP-4323	Dean of Country	1970	3.75	7.50	15.00
❑ LSP-4434	Country Boy and Country Girl	1970	3.75	7.50	15.00
❑ LSP-4511	Everybody Knows	1971	3.75	7.50	15.00
❑ LSP-4618	These Hands	1972	3.75	7.50	15.00

Number	Title (A Side/B Side)	Yr	VG	VG+	NM
SEARS					
❑ 105	Jimmy Dean's Golden Favorites	196?	3.75	7.50	15.00
SPIN-O-RAMA					
❑ 108	Featuring the Coutnry Singing of Jimmy Dean	196?	3.00	6.00	12.00
❑ 137	Coutnry Round-Up Featuring Jimmy Dean	196?	3.00	6.00	12.00
WING					
❑ MGW-12292 [M]	Jimmy Dean Sings His Television Favorites	196?	3.75	7.50	15.00
❑ SRW-16292 [R]	Jimmy Dean Sings His Television Favorites	196?	3.00	6.00	12.00
WYNCOTE					
❑ 9032	Country Favorites	196?	3.00	6.00	12.00

DEAN, JIMMY / JOHNNY HORTON

Albums

Number	Title (A Side/B Side)	Yr	VG	VG+	NM
LA BREA					
❑ L 8014 [M]	Bummin' Around with Jimmy Dean and Johnny Horton	1961	20.00	40.00	80.00
STARDAY					
❑ SLP-325 [M]	Bummin' Around with Jimmy Dean and Johnny Horton	1965	7.50	15.00	30.00

DEAN, JIMMY / MARVIN RAINWATER

Albums

Number	Title (A Side/B Side)	Yr	VG	VG+	NM
PREMIER					
❑ 9054	Nashville Showtime	196?	3.00	6.00	12.00

DEAN, LARRY

45s

Number	Title (A Side/B Side)	Yr	VG	VG+	NM
USA					
❑ 620	Outside Chance/(B-side unknown)	1989	—	3.00	6.00
❑ 620 [PS]	Outside Chance/(B-side unknown)	1989	2.00	4.00	8.00

DEANNA MARIE

45s

Number	Title (A Side/B Side)	Yr	VG	VG+	NM
LITTLE DARLIN'					
❑ 0021	Fight It with Love/I Dropped My Tater Chips	1967	2.50	5.00	10.00

DEBONAIRES, THE

45s

Number	Title (A Side/B Side)	Yr	VG	VG+	NM
MTM					
❑ B-72051	I'm on Fire/Loving You's All That's On My Mind	1985	—	3.00	6.00

DEE, DUANE

45s

Number	Title (A Side/B Side)	Yr	VG	VG+	NM
ABC					
❑ 11417	Morning Girl/She's My Woman	1974	—	2.50	5.00
❑ 12018	Lovin' Naturally/She Was the Woman and the Lady	1974	—	2.50	5.00
CAPITOL					
❑ 2125	Precious/That Was My Shining Hour	1968	2.00	4.00	8.00
❑ 2250	We're the Kind of People (That Make the Jukebox Play)/It Won't Matter Much	1968	2.00	4.00	8.00
❑ 2332	True Love Travels on a Gravel Road/Have a Little Faith	1968	2.00	4.00	8.00
❑ 2519	Blessed Are the Poor/Carmelita's House	1969	2.00	4.00	8.00
❑ 2686	So Afraid/A Mighty Fortress Is Our Love	1969	2.00	4.00	8.00
❑ 2760	Ramblin' Man/Listen, They're Playing My Song	1970	2.00	4.00	8.00
❑ 5887	Why Didn't I Think of That/When the Devil Rides the Wind	1967	2.50	5.00	10.00
❑ 5986	Before the Next Teardrop Falls/You're Not Painting the Town	1967	2.50	5.00	10.00
CARTWHEEL					
❑ 192	I've Got to Sing/There Will Be an Answer	1971	—	3.00	6.00
❑ 195	Little Garden of Love/That's How I Feel	1971	—	3.00	6.00
❑ 200	How Can You Mend a Broken Heart/Georgeanna	1971	—	3.00	6.00
❑ 207	Sweet Apple Wine/I Can't Get Over You	1972	—	3.00	6.00
❑ 215	Mary in the Morning/Cold January Morning	1972	—	3.00	6.00

Albums

Number	Title (A Side/B Side)	Yr	VG	VG+	NM
CAPITOL					
❑ ST 2931	My Shining Hour	1968	3.75	7.50	15.00

DEE, GORDON

45s

Number	Title (A Side/B Side)	Yr	VG	VG+	NM
SOUTHERN TRACKS					
❑ 1002	They Just Don't Make Time Like They Used To/Happy Endings	1982	—	2.50	5.00
—With Carol Lee					
❑ 1029	(Nothing Left Between Us) But Alabama/Slowly Going Out of My Mind	1984	—	2.50	5.00
❑ 1035	I Forgot That I Don't Live Here Anymore/The Paradise Knife and Gun Club	1985	—	2.50	5.00
❑ 1047	We Don't Make Love Anymore (We Just Make Believe)/(B-side unknown)	1985	—	3.00	6.00
❑ 1057	Those Old Songs/(B-side unknown)	1986	—	3.00	6.00
❑ 1064	Starlite Drive-In Movie Queen/Those Old Songs	1986	—	2.50	5.00
❑ 1070	Beam Me Up Scotty/You'll Never Know How Much (I Needed You Today)	1986	—	3.00	6.00
❑ 1078	You're Slowly Going Out of My Mind/(B-side unknown)	1987	—	3.00	6.00

DEE, JOHNNY

See JOHN D. LOUDERMILK.

DEE, KATHY

45s

Number	Title (A Side/B Side)	Yr	VG	VG+	NM
B/W					
❑ 611/12	Trail of Tears/The Ways of a Heart	1963	3.75	7.50	15.00
❑ 619/20	If I Never Get to Heaven/Teardrops in My Heart	1963	3.75	7.50	15.00
❑ 619/20 [PS]	If I Never Get to Heaven/Teardrops in My Heart	1963	5.00	10.00	20.00
DECCA					
❑ 32372	Funny How Time Slips Away/Shadow of a Girl	1968	2.00	4.00	8.00
UNITED ARTISTS					
❑ 627	Unkind Words/Only As Far As the Door	1963	2.50	5.00	10.00
❑ 687	Don't Leave Me Lonely Too Long/I Promise Not to Cry	1964	2.50	5.00	10.00

Albums

Number	Title (A Side/B Side)	Yr	VG	VG+	NM
GUEST STAR					
❑ G-1445 [M]	Teardrops in My Heart	1964	3.75	7.50	15.00
❑ GS-1445 [S]	Teardrops in My Heart	1964	3.75	7.50	15.00

DEER, JOHN

45s

Number	Title (A Side/B Side)	Yr	VG	VG+	NM
ROYAL AMERICAN					
❑ 21	Waxahachie Woman/Big Train	1970	2.00	4.00	8.00
❑ 34	The Battle Hymn of Lt. Calley/Sitting in Atlanta Station	1971	2.00	4.00	8.00

DEHAVEN, PENNY

Also see BOXCAR WILLIE; DEL REEVES.

45s

Number	Title (A Side/B Side)	Yr	VG	VG+	NM
BAND BOX					
❑ 372	A Grain of Salt/Thing of Pleasure	1966	3.75	7.50	15.00
—As "Penny Starr"					
❑ 375	One More Like You/You've Taken All the Woman Out of Me	1967	3.75	7.50	15.00
—As "Penny Starr"					
ELEKTRA					
❑ 46645	Bayou Lullaby/How Many Teardrops	1980	—	2.50	5.00
IMPERIAL					
❑ 66294	Old Faithful/Big City Men	1968	2.00	4.00	8.00
❑ 66321	I Am the Woman/Loving You Again	1968	2.00	4.00	8.00
❑ 66367	You're Never Gonna See My Face Again/I'm Going Home	1969	2.00	4.00	8.00
❑ 66388	Mama Lou/That's Just the Way I Am	1969	2.00	4.00	8.00
❑ 66421	Down in the Boondocks/When the Sun Sets in Jackson	1969	2.00	4.00	8.00
❑ 66437	I Feel Fine/Stop & Go	1970	2.00	4.00	8.00
MAIN STREET					
❑ 93015	Only the Names Have Been Changed/Waltz Me Once Again	1983	—	2.50	5.00
❑ 93019	Friendly Game of Hearts/(B-side unknown)	1984	—	2.50	5.00
❑ 93022	Yes I Do/(B-side unknown)	1984	—	2.50	5.00
MERCURY					
❑ 73384	The Lovin' of Your Life/When You Get Home	1973	—	3.00	6.00
❑ 73434	I'll Be Doggone/Love Me to Sleep	1973	—	3.00	6.00
❑ 73468	Play with Me/Shine on Me	1974	—	3.00	6.00
❑ 73504	I Gotta Stand Tall/I'll Never Stop	1974	—	3.00	6.00
STARCREST					
❑ 066	(The Great American) Classic Cowboy/Thank God I'm a Country Girl	1976	—	3.00	6.00
❑ 080	Hit Parade of Love/(B-side unknown)	1976	—	3.00	6.00
❑ 080 [PS]	Hit Parade of Love/(B-side unknown)	1976	2.50	5.00	10.00
UNITED ARTISTS					
❑ 50703	Awful Lotta Lovin'/Tomorrow Never Comes	1970	—	3.50	7.00
❑ 50742	The First Love/The Price I Had to Pay	1971	—	3.50	7.00
❑ 50787	Don't Change on Me/That's Just the Way I Am	1971	—	3.50	7.00
❑ 50854	Another Day of Loving/Mama, Have All the Good Guys Gone?	1971	—	3.50	7.00
❑ 50894	Gone/It's As Easy As Singing	1972	—	3.50	7.00

Albums

Number	Title (A Side/B Side)	Yr	VG	VG+	NM
MAIN STREET					
❑ 9310	Penny DeHaven	1984	2.50	5.00	10.00
UNITED ARTISTS					
❑ UAS-6821	Penny DeHaven	1972	3.75	7.50	15.00

DEHAVEN, PENNY, AND BUDDY CAGLE

Also see each artist's individual listings.

45s

Number	Title (A Side/B Side)	Yr	VG	VG+	NM
IMPERIAL					
❑ 66315	Kid Games and Nursery Rhymes/So Sad (To Watch Good Love Go Bad)	1968	2.00	4.00	8.00

DEHAVEN, PENNY, AND DEL REEVES

Also see each artist's individual listings.

45s

Number	Title (A Side/B Side)	Yr	VG	VG+	NM
UNITED ARTISTS					
❑ 50669	Land Mark Tavern/So Sad	1970	—	3.50	7.00
❑ 50829	Crying in the Rain/Time	1972	—	3.00	6.00

DEKLE, MIKE

45s

Number	Title (A Side/B Side)	Yr	VG	VG+	NM
NSD					
❑ 181	Closer to the Moon/Scarlet Fever	1984	—	2.50	5.00

Number	Title (A Side/B Side)	Yr	VG	VG+	NM
❑ 188	Hanky Panky/Lady Luck (Can Be a Bitch Sometimes)	1984	—	2.50	5.00
❑ 195	The Minstrel/April's Fool	1984	—	2.50	5.00

DELEVANTES, THE

45s

CAPITOL NASHVILLE

Number	Title (A Side/B Side)	Yr	VG	VG+	NM
❑ S7-19708	I'm Your Man/My Daddy's Cadillac	1997	—	2.00	4.00

DELICATO, PAUL

45s

ARTISTS OF AMERICA

Number	Title (A Side/B Side)	Yr	VG	VG+	NM
❑ 101	Lean on Me/Ice Cream Sodas and Lollipops and a Red Hot Spinning Top	1975	—	2.50	5.00
❑ 105	Those Were the Days/Ice Cream Sodas and Lollipops and a Red Hot Spinning Top	1976	—	2.50	5.00
❑ 110	I Can't Make It All Alone/(B-side unknown)	1976	—	2.50	5.00
❑ 111	Cara Mia/Ice Cream Sodas and Lollipops and a Red Hot Spinning Top	1976	—	2.50	5.00
❑ 120	It's the Same Old Song/I Can't Make It All Alone	1976	—	2.50	5.00
❑ 122	I'll Be There/(B-side unknown)	1976	—	2.50	5.00
❑ 127	I Take a Lot of Pride in What I Am/Country Star	1976	—	2.50	5.00
❑ 1976	Spirit of America/Ice Cream Sodas and Lollipops and a Red Hot Spinning Top	1976	—	2.50	5.00

AVI

Number	Title (A Side/B Side)	Yr	VG	VG+	NM
❑ 139	I'll Show You Tomorrow/Come On Priscilla	1977	—	3.00	6.00
❑ 155	All Alone and Crying/Darling All I Need Is You	1978	—	3.00	6.00
❑ 267	Everything Good Reminds Me of You/Hell of a Woman	1979	—	3.00	6.00

Albums

ARTISTS OF AMERICA

Number	Title (A Side/B Side)	Yr	VG	VG+	NM
❑ AOA 5001	Ice Cream Sodas and Lollipops	1975	3.00	6.00	12.00
❑ AOA 5002	Cara Mia	1976	3.00	6.00	12.00

AVI

Number	Title (A Side/B Side)	Yr	VG	VG+	NM
❑ 6029	Off on an Island	1978	3.00	6.00	12.00

DELMORE BROTHERS, THE

45s

KING

Number	Title (A Side/B Side)	Yr	VG	VG+	NM
❑ 570	Freight Train Boogie/Somebody Else's Darling	1952	10.00	20.00	40.00
—Reissue of 78 issued in 1946					
❑ 826	Pan American Boogie/Troubles Ain't Nothin' but the Blues	1952	10.00	20.00	40.00
—Reissue of 78 first issued in 1949					
❑ 946	Lonesome Day/Everybody Loves Her	1951	10.00	20.00	40.00
❑ 966	Tennessee Choo Choo/Who's Gonna Be Lonesome for Me	1951	7.50	15.00	30.00
❑ 981	Girl by the River/There's Something 'Bout Love	1951	7.50	15.00	30.00
❑ 1005	Heartbreak Ridge/Kentucky Woman	1951	7.50	15.00	30.00
❑ 1023	I'll Be There/Steamboat Bill Boogie	1951	7.50	15.00	30.00
❑ 1053	I Won't Be Worried Long/Good Time Saturday Night	1952	7.50	15.00	30.00
❑ 1084	Muddy Water/Got No Way of Knowing	1952	7.50	15.00	30.00
❑ 1113	How You Gonna Get Your Lovin' Done/I Said Goodnight My Darling	1952	7.50	15.00	30.00
❑ 1141	That Old Train/I Needed You	1952	7.50	15.00	30.00
❑ 1158	What'cha Gonna Give Me/Trail of Time	1953	6.25	12.50	25.00
❑ 5224	Blues Stay Away from Me/Muddy Water	1959	3.75	7.50	15.00
❑ 5407	Silver Threads Among the Gold/Let Your Conscience Be Your Guide	1960	3.75	7.50	15.00
❑ 5675	Blues Stay Away from Me/Trouble Ain't Nothing But the Blues	1962	3.00	6.00	12.00
❑ 5866	Freight Train Boogie/Sweet, Sweet Thing	1964	3.00	6.00	12.00

Selected 78s

BLUEBIRD

Number	Title (A Side/B Side)	Yr	VG	VG+	NM
❑ B-5299	Lonesome Yodel Blues/Gonna Lay Down My Old Guitar	193?	6.25	12.50	25.00
❑ B-5338	The Frozen Girl/Bury Me Out on the Prairie	193?	6.25	12.50	25.00
❑ B-5358	I'm Leaving You/(B-side unknown)	193?	6.25	12.50	25.00
❑ B-5403	Brown's Ferry Blues/A New Salty Dog	193?	5.00	10.00	20.00
—B-side by the Allen Brothers					
❑ B-5467	Ramblin' Minded Blues/(B-side unknown)	193?	5.00	10.00	20.00
❑ B-5531	Blue Railroad Train/I've Got the Big River Blues	193?	5.00	10.00	20.00
❑ B-5589	Smoky Mountain Bill and His Song/The Girls Don't Worry My Mind	193?	5.00	10.00	20.00
❑ B-5653	I'm Mississippi Bound/(B-side unknown)	193?	5.00	10.00	20.00
❑ B-5741	Lonesome Jailhouse Blues/(B-side unknown)	193?	5.00	10.00	20.00
❑ B-5857	Hey Hey! I'm Memphis Bound/(B-side unknown)	193?	5.00	10.00	20.00
❑ B-5893	Brown's Ferry Blues, Part 2/(B-side unknown)	193?	5.00	10.00	20.00
❑ B-5925	Lorena, The Slave/Blow Yo' Whistle, Freight Train	193?	5.00	10.00	20.00
❑ B-5957	I Long to See My Mother/(B-side unknown)	193?	5.00	10.00	20.00
❑ B-6002	I Got the Kansas City Blues/(B-side unknown)	193?	5.00	10.00	20.00
❑ B-6019	The Fugitive's Lament/(B-side unknown)	193?	5.00	10.00	20.00
❑ B-6034	Alabama Lullaby/(B-side unknown)	193?	5.00	10.00	20.00
❑ B-6312	The Nashville Blues/It's Taken Me Down	193?	5.00	10.00	20.00
❑ B-6349	I'm Worried Now/(B-side unknown)	193?	5.00	10.00	20.00
❑ B-6386	Lonesome Yodel Blues No. 2/(B-side unknown)	193?	5.00	10.00	20.00
❑ B-6401	Carry Me Back to Alabama/(B-side unknown)	193?	5.00	10.00	20.00
❑ B-6522	The Lover's Warning/(B-side unknown)	193?	5.00	10.00	20.00
❑ B-6841	Southern Moon/I Don't Know Why I Love Her	193?	5.00	10.00	20.00
❑ B-6915	No Drunkard Can Enter There/Blind Child	193?	5.00	10.00	20.00
❑ B-6949	False Hearted Girl/(B-side unknown)	193?	5.00	10.00	20.00
❑ B-6998	No One/(B-side unknown)	193?	5.00	10.00	20.00
❑ B-7029	Don't Forget Me, Darling/Are You Marching with the Saviour	193?	5.00	10.00	20.00
❑ B-7129	Singing My Troubles Away/(B-side unknown)	193?	5.00	10.00	20.00
❑ B-7192	They Say It's Sinful to Flirt/(B-side unknown)	193?	5.00	10.00	20.00
❑ B-7262	The Budded Rose/Til the Roses Bloom Again	193?	5.00	10.00	20.00
❑ B-7300	The Weary Lonesome Blues/I've Got the Railroad Blues	193?	5.00	10.00	20.00
❑ B-7337	Lead Me/(B-side unknown)	193?	5.00	10.00	20.00
❑ B-7383	The Farmer's Girl/(B-side unknown)	193?	5.00	10.00	20.00
❑ B-7436	Goodbye Booze/Careless Love	193?	5.00	10.00	20.00
❑ B-7496	'Cause I Don't Mean to Cry When You're Gone/In That Vine Covered Chapel in the Valley	193?	5.00	10.00	20.00
❑ B-7560	Big Ball in Texas/(B-side unknown)	193?	5.00	10.00	20.00
❑ B-7672	Wonderful There/(B-side unknown)	193?	5.00	10.00	20.00
❑ B-7741	Brother, Take Warning/Bury Me Under the Weeping Willow	1938	5.00	10.00	20.00
❑ B-7778	Alcatraz Island Blues/My Smoky Mountain Gal	1938	5.00	10.00	20.00
❑ B-7913	Leavin' on That Train/(B-side unknown)	1938	5.00	10.00	20.00
❑ B-7957	Where Is My Sailor Boy?/(B-side unknown)	1939	5.00	10.00	20.00
❑ B-7991	The Cannon Ball/The Only Star	1939	5.00	10.00	20.00
❑ B-8031	Fifteen Miles from Birmingham/Quit Treatin' Me Mean	1939	5.00	10.00	20.00
❑ B-8052	Home on the River/(B-side unknown)	1939	5.00	10.00	20.00
❑ B-8177	Baby, You're Throwing Me Down/Don't Let My Ramblin' Bother Your Mind	1939	5.00	10.00	20.00
❑ B-8204	Wabash Blues/Go Easy, Mabel	1939	5.00	10.00	20.00
❑ B-8215	Gonna Lay Down My Old Guitar (Part 2)/I Loved You Better Than You Knew	1939	5.00	10.00	20.00
❑ B-8230	Gambler's Yodel/Brown's Ferry Blues (Part 3)	1939	5.00	10.00	20.00
❑ B-8247	Nothing But the Blues/(B-side unknown)	1939	5.00	10.00	20.00
❑ B-8264	I'm Alabama Bound/Goin' Back to Georgia	1940	5.00	10.00	20.00
❑ B-8290	A Better Range Is Home/(B-side unknown)	1940	5.00	10.00	20.00
❑ B-8404	Scatterbrain Mamma/The Wabash Cannon-Ball Blues	1940	5.00	10.00	20.00
❑ B-8418	Back to Birmingham/See That Coon in a Hickory Tree	1940	5.00	10.00	20.00
❑ B-8451	Over the Hills/The Dying Truckdriver	1940	5.00	10.00	20.00
❑ B-8488	The Eastern Gate/God Put a Rainbow in the Clouds	1940	5.00	10.00	20.00
❑ B-8557	Rainin' on the Mountain/That's How I Feel, So Goodbye	1941	5.00	10.00	20.00
❑ B-8613	The Storms Are On the Ocean/Happy on the Mississippi Shore	1941	5.00	10.00	20.00
❑ B-8637	Heart of Sorrow/Promise Me You'll Always Be Faithful	1941	5.00	10.00	20.00
❑ B-8687	Take Me Back to the Range/That Yodelin' Gal, Miss Julie	1941	5.00	10.00	20.00

COLUMBIA

Number	Title (A Side/B Side)	Yr	VG	VG+	NM
❑ 15724-D	Got the Kansas City Blues/Alamama Lullaby	1931	50.00	100.00	200.00

DECCA

Number	Title (A Side/B Side)	Yr	VG	VG+	NM
❑ 5878	titles unknown	1941	5.00	10.00	20.00
❑ 5890	titles unknown	1941	5.00	10.00	20.00
❑ 5907	titles unknown	194?	5.00	10.00	20.00
❑ 5925	titles unknown	194?	5.00	10.00	20.00
❑ 5970	Gospel Cannonball/(B-side unknown)	194?	5.00	10.00	20.00
❑ 6000	titles unknown	194?	5.00	10.00	20.00
❑ 6051	titles unknown	194?	5.00	10.00	20.00
❑ 6080	New False Hearted Girl/I'll Never Fall in Love Again	194?	5.00	10.00	20.00
❑ 46043	Honey I'm Ramblin' Away/I'm Leavin' You	1947	3.75	7.50	15.00
❑ 46049	Gospel Cannonball/Precious Jewel	1947	3.75	7.50	15.00

KING

Number	Title (A Side/B Side)	Yr	VG	VG+	NM
❑ 503	Prisoner's Farewell/Sweet, Sweet Thing	1946	6.25	12.50	25.00
❑ 509	Last Old Shovel/Remember I Feel Lonesome	1946	6.25	12.50	25.00
❑ 514	Midnite Special/Why Did You Leave Me Dear	1946	6.25	12.50	25.00
❑ 518	Lonely Moon/Be My Little Pet	1946	6.25	12.50	25.00
❑ 525	Fast Express/I've Found an Angel	1946	6.25	12.50	25.00
❑ 527	Hillbilly Boogie/I'm Sorry I Caused You to Cry	1946	6.25	12.50	25.00
❑ 533	I'm Lonesome Without You/She Left Me Standing on the Mountain	1946	6.25	12.50	25.00
❑ 548	Don't Forget Me/Midnite Train	1946	6.25	12.50	25.00
❑ 570	Freight Train Boogie/Somebody Else's Darling	1946	6.25	12.50	25.00
❑ 592	Mississippi Shore/Brown's Ferry Blues	1947	5.00	10.00	20.00
❑ 599	Boogie Woogie Baby/Born to Be Blue	1947	5.00	10.00	20.00
❑ 643	Harmonica Blues/Rounders Blues	1947	5.00	10.00	20.00
❑ 664	Used Car Blues/Barnyard Boogie	1947	5.00	10.00	20.00
❑ 680	Mobile Boogie/Waitin' for That Train	1948	5.00	10.00	20.00
❑ 708	Take It On Out the Door/Darby's Ram	1948	5.00	10.00	20.00
❑ 718	Take It to the Captain/Peach Tree Street Boogie	1948	5.00	10.00	20.00
❑ 739	Now I'm Free/Fifty Miles to Travel	1948	5.00	10.00	20.00
❑ 751	Shame on Me/Stop That Boogie	1949	5.00	10.00	20.00
❑ 769	Wrath of God/Calling to That Other Shore	1949	5.00	10.00	20.00
❑ 784	Weary Day/Down Home Boogie	1949	5.00	10.00	20.00
❑ 803	Blues Stay Away from Me/Going Back to the Blue Ridge Mountains	1949	6.25	12.50	25.00
❑ 826	Pan American Boogie/Troubles Ain't Nothin' but the Blues	1949	6.25	12.50	25.00
❑ 848	Sand Mountain Blues/I Swear by the Stars	1950	5.00	10.00	20.00
❑ 873	Some Day You'll Pay/My Heart Will Be Crying	1950	5.00	10.00	20.00
❑ 911	Blues You Never Lose/Life's Too Short	1951	5.00	10.00	20.00
❑ 927	I Let the Freight Train Carry Me On/Please Be My Sunshine	1951	5.00	10.00	20.00
❑ 935	Gotta Have Some Lovin'/Field Hand Man	1951	5.00	10.00	20.00

Albums

KING

Number	Title (A Side/B Side)	Yr	VG	VG+	NM
❑ 589 [M]	Songs by the Delmore Brothers	1958	37.50	75.00	150.00
❑ 785 [M]	30th Anniversary Album	1962	20.00	40.00	80.00
❑ 910 [M]	In Memory	1964	10.00	20.00	40.00
❑ 920 [M]	In Memory, Volume 2	1964	10.00	20.00	40.00
❑ 983 [M]	24 Great Country Songs	1966	7.50	15.00	30.00
❑ KS-983 [R]	24 Great Country Songs	1966	5.00	10.00	20.00

DELRAY, MARTIN

45s

ATLANTIC

Number	Title (A Side/B Side)	Yr	VG	VG+	NM
❑ 87584	One in a Row/Someone to Love You	1991	—	2.00	4.00
❑ 87680	Lillies White Lies/I Let Love Do My Talkin'	1991	—	2.00	4.00

COMPLEAT

Number	Title (A Side/B Side)	Yr	VG	VG+	NM
❑ 125	Holding a Woman in Love/Old Friends Over Night	1984	—	2.50	5.00
—As "Mike Martin"					
❑ 139	Temptation/What My Mind's Been On All Day	1985	—	2.50	5.00
—As "Mike Martin"					
❑ 143	Sweet Nothings (Whispered in My Ear)/Break Someone Else's Heart	1985	—	2.50	5.00
—As "Mike Martin"					

DENNIS, WESLEY

45s

MERCURY

Number	Title (A Side/B Side)	Yr	VG	VG+	NM
❑ 852286-7	Who's Counting/It Ain't Fair	1995	—	—	3.00
❑ 856486-7	I Don't Know (But I've Been Told)/Borrowed Angel	1995	—	—	3.00
❑ 856834-7	Don't Make Me Feel at Home/This Hat Ain't No Act	1995	—	—	3.00

DENNY, BURCH

45s

OAK

Number	Title (A Side/B Side)	Yr	VG	VG+	NM
❑ 1068	Yesterday Is Too Far Away/(B-side unknown)	1989	—	2.50	5.00

DENTON, JACK

45s

M.V.P.

Number	Title (A Side/B Side)	Yr	VG	VG+	NM
❑ 10001	Anna (Go With Him)/Something About You	1989	—	3.50	7.00

DENVER, JOHN

Also see DENVER, BOISE & JOHNSON.

12-Inch Singles

RCA VICTOR

Number	Title (A Side/B Side)	Yr	VG	VG+	NM
❑ JD-11189 [DJ]	Bet On the Blues (same on both sides)	1977	3.00	6.00	12.00

45s

COLUMBIA

Number	Title (A Side/B Side)	Yr	VG	VG+	NM
❑ 02679	Perhaps Love/Annie's Song	1982	—	2.00	4.00
—With Placido Domingo					
❑ 03148	Perhaps Love/Annie's Song	1982	—	—	3.00
—With Placido Domingo; reissue					

LEGACY

Number	Title (A Side/B Side)	Yr	VG	VG+	NM
❑ 77993	For You/Rocky Mountain High (Live)	1995	—	—	2.00
❑ 77993 [PS]	For You/Rocky Mountain High (Live)	1995	—	—	3.00

RCA

Number	Title (A Side/B Side)	Yr	VG	VG+	NM
❑ 5086-7-R	Love Again/Let Us Begin (What Are We Making Weapons For)	1987	—	—	3.00
❑ PB-10774	Like a Sad Song/Pegasus	1976	—	2.00	4.00
❑ PB-10854	Baby, You Look Good to Me Tonight/Wrangle Mountain Song	1976	—	2.00	4.00
❑ PB-10911	My Sweet Lady/Welcome to My Morning	1977	—	2.00	4.00
❑ GB-10940	I'm Sorry/Fly Away	1977	—	—	3.00
—Gold Standard Series					
❑ PB-11036	How Can I Leave You Again/To the Wild Country	1977	—	2.00	4.00
❑ PB-11214	It Amazes Me/Druthers	1978	—	2.00	4.00
❑ PB-11267	I Want to Live/Tradewinds	1978	—	2.00	4.00
❑ GB-11327	My Sweet Lady/Like a Sad Song	1978	—	—	3.00
—Gold Standard Series					
❑ PB-11479	Downhill Stuff/Life Is So Good	1979	—	2.00	4.00
❑ PB-11535	Sweet Melinda/What's On Your Mind	1979	—	2.00	4.00
❑ PB-11637	Garden Song/Berkeley Woman	1979	—	2.00	4.00
❑ PB-11915	Autograph/The Mountain Song	1980	—	2.00	4.00
❑ PB-11915 [PS]	Autograph/The Mountain Song	1980	—	2.00	4.00
❑ PB-12017	Dancing with the Mountains/American Child	1980	—	2.00	4.00
❑ PB-12246	Some Days Are Diamonds (Some Days Are Stone)/Country Love	1981	—	2.00	4.00
❑ PB-12345	The Cowboy and the Lady/Till You Opened My Eyes	1981	—	2.00	4.00
❑ PB-13071	Shanghai Breezes/What One Man Can Do	1982	—	2.00	4.00
❑ PB-13270	Seasons of the Heart/Islands	1982	—	2.00	4.00
❑ PB-13371	Opposite Tables/Relatively Speaking	1982	—	2.00	4.00
❑ PB-13562	Wild Montana Skies/I Remember Romance	1983	—	2.00	4.00
—A-side with Emmylou Harris					
❑ PB-13642	Flight (The Higher We Fly)/Hold On Tightly	1983	—	2.00	4.00
❑ PB-13740	World Games/It's About Time	1984	—	—	3.00
❑ PB-13782	The Way I Am/The Gold and Beyond	1984	—	—	3.00
❑ PB-13931	Love Again/It's About Time	1984	—	—	3.00
—A-side: With Sylvie Vartan					
❑ GB-14075	Calypso/Some Days Are Diamonds (Some Days Are Stone)	1985	—	—	3.00
—Gold Standard Series					
❑ PB-14115	Don't Close Your Eyes Tonight/A Wild Heart Looking for Home	1985	—	—	3.00
❑ PB-14227	Dreamland Express/African Sunrise	1985	—	—	3.00
❑ PB-14227 [PS]	Dreamland Express/African Sunrise	1985	—	2.00	4.00
❑ PB-14366 [DJ]	Flying for Me (same on both sides)	1986	—	2.00	4.00
—No stock copies were issued					
❑ PB-14406	Along for the Ride ('56 T-Bird)/Let Us Begin (What Are We Making Weapons For)	1986	—	—	3.00

RCA VICTOR

Number	Title (A Side/B Side)	Yr	VG	VG+	NM
❑ APBO-0067	Farewell Andromeda (Welcome to My Morning)/Whiskey Basin Blues	1973	—	2.00	4.00
❑ APBO-0182	Please, Daddy (Don't Get Drunk This Christmas)/Rocky Mountain High	1973	—	2.50	5.00
❑ APBO-0213	Sunshine on My Shoulders/Around and Around	1974	—	2.00	4.00
❑ APBO-0295	Annie's Song/Cool An' Green An' Shady	1974	—	2.00	4.00
❑ PB-10065	Back Home Again/It's Up to You	1974	—	2.00	4.00
❑ PB-10148	Sweet Surrender/Summer	1974	—	2.00	4.00
❑ PB-10239	Thank God I'm a Country Boy/My Sweet Lady	1975	—	2.00	4.00
❑ PB-10353	I'm Sorry/Calypso	1975	—	2.00	4.00
❑ PB-10464	Christmas for Cowboys/Silent Night, Holy Night	1975	—	2.00	4.00
❑ GB-10472	Annie's Song/Cool An' Green An' Shady	1975	—	—	3.00
—Gold Standard Series					
❑ GB-10473	Back Home Again/It's Up to You	1975	—	—	3.00
—Gold Standard Series					
❑ GB-10474	Sunshine on My Shoulders/Around and Around	1975	—	—	3.00
—Gold Standard Series					
❑ GB-10475	Farewell Andromeda (Welcome to My Morning)/Whiskey Basin Blues	1975	—	—	3.00
—Gold Standard Series					
❑ GB-10476	Thank God I'm a Country Boy/My Sweet Lady	1975	—	—	3.00
—Gold Standard Series					
❑ GB-10477	Rocky Mountain High/Spring	1975	—	—	3.00
—Gold Standard Series					
❑ GB-10478	Sweet Surrender/Summer	1975	—	—	3.00
—Gold Standard Series					
❑ PB-10517	Fly Away/Two Shots	1975	—	2.00	4.00
❑ PB-10586	Looking for Space/Windsong	1976	—	2.00	4.00
❑ PB-10687	It Makes Me Giggle/Spirit	1976	—	2.00	4.00
❑ 74-0275	Daydream/I Wish I Knew How It Would Feel to Be Free	1969	2.50	5.00	10.00
❑ 74-0305	Anthem (Revelation)/Sticky Summer Weather	1970	2.50	5.00	10.00
❑ 74-0332	Follow Me/Isabel	1970	2.50	5.00	10.00
❑ 74-0376	Sail Away Home/I Wish I Could Have Been There	1970	2.50	5.00	10.00
❑ 74-0391	Whose Garden Is This/Mr. Bojangles	1970	2.50	5.00	10.00
❑ 74-0445	Take Me Home, Country Roads/Poems, Prayers and Promises	1971	2.00	4.00	8.00
—With Fat City					
❑ 74-0567	Friends with You/Starwood in Aspen	1971	—	3.00	6.00
❑ 74-0647	Everyday/City of New Orleans	1972	—	3.00	6.00
❑ 74-0737	Goodbye Again/The Eagle and the Hawk	1972	—	3.00	6.00
❑ 74-0801	Late Winter, Early Spring/Hard Life Hard Times	1972	—	3.00	6.00
❑ 74-0829	Rocky Mountain High/Spring	1972	—	2.50	5.00
❑ 74-0955	I'd Rather Be a Cowboy/Sunshine on My Shoulders	1973	—	2.00	4.00

WINDSTAR

Number	Title (A Side/B Side)	Yr	VG	VG+	NM
❑ 75720	Country Girl in Paris/Bread and Roses	1988	—	2.50	5.00
❑ 75720 [PS]	Country Girl in Paris/Bread and Roses	1988	—	3.00	6.00

Albums

HJD

Number	Title (A Side/B Side)	Yr	VG	VG+	NM
❑ 66	John Denver Sings	1966	125.00	250.00	500.00
—Private issue of 300 or so, made by JD as Christmas gifts to friends.					

MERCURY

Number	Title (A Side/B Side)	Yr	VG	VG+	NM
❑ SRM-1-704	Beginnings	1972	5.00	10.00	20.00
—With illustration on cover					
❑ SRM-1-704	Beginnings	1974	3.00	6.00	12.00
—With mountain scene on cover					

RCA

Number	Title (A Side/B Side)	Yr	VG	VG+	NM
❑ 7624-1-R	Back Home Again	1988	2.50	5.00	10.00
—Last vinyl reissue					
❑ 7631-1-R	Poems, Prayers and Promises	1988	2.50	5.00	10.00
—Last vinyl reissue					
❑ 7632-1-R	Rocky Mountain High	1988	2.50	5.00	10.00
—Last vinyl reissue					

RCA VICTOR

Number	Title (A Side/B Side)	Yr	VG	VG+	NM
❑ DJL1-0075 [DJ]	The John Denver Radio Show	1973	7.50	15.00	30.00
❑ APL1-0101	Farewell Andromeda	1973	3.00	6.00	12.00
—Orange label					
❑ APL1-0101	Farewell Andromeda	1975	2.50	5.00	10.00
—Tan label or black label, dog near top					
❑ APL1-0374	John Denver's Greatest Hits	197?	2.00	4.00	8.00
—Reissue					
❑ AQL1-0374	John Denver's Greatest Hits	197?	2.00	4.00	8.00
—Later reissue					
❑ CPL1-0374	John Denver's Greatest Hits	1974	2.50	5.00	10.00
—Orange label					
❑ CPL1-0374	John Denver's Greatest Hits	1975	2.00	4.00	8.00
—Tan label or black label, dog near top					
❑ AFL1-0548	Back Home Again	197?	2.00	4.00	8.00
—Reissue					
❑ AQL1-0548	Back Home Again	197?	2.00	4.00	8.00
—Later reissue					
❑ CPL1-0548	Back Home Again	1974	2.50	5.00	10.00
—Orange or tan label					
❑ CPL1-0548	Back Home Again	1976	2.00	4.00	8.00
—Black label, dog near top					
❑ DJL1-0683 [DJ]	The Second John Denver Radio Show	1974	7.50	15.00	30.00
❑ CPL2-0764 [(2)]	An Evening with John Denver	1975	3.00	6.00	12.00
—Orange or tan labels					

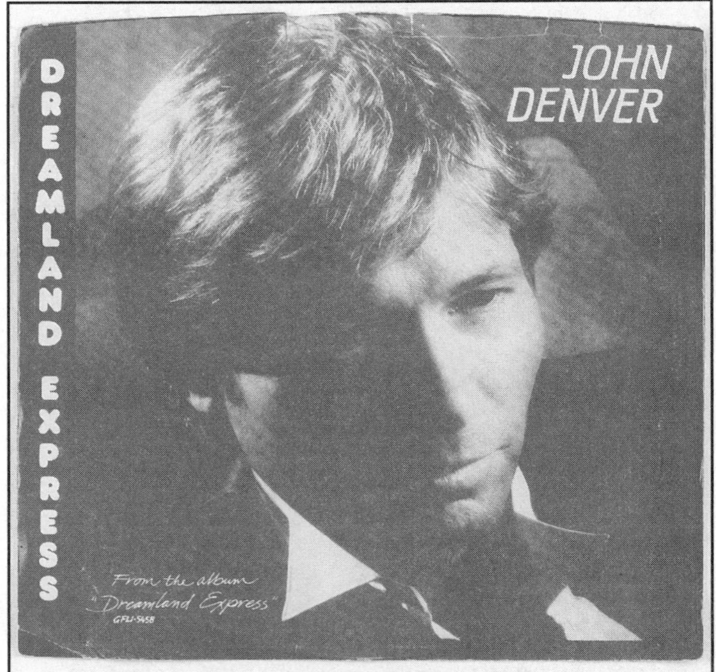

Former folkie John Denver – he had replaced Chad Mitchell in the Chad Mitchell Trio – was a country phenomenon in 1974 and 1975, with three chart-topping hits and two more in the top 10. Though his country hits tended to come sporadically after that, he didn't stop hitting the charts until 1989. (Top left) His first country chart hit, "Take Me Home, Country Roads," is today considered part of the country canon, but at the time it only got to No. 50 country, a far cry from its No. 2 pop standing. (Top right) In 1975, Denver had back-to-back chart toppers on both the country *and* pop charts, a feat that hadn't been done since 1957. The second of these was "I'm Sorry." (Bottom left) In early 1986, John Denver had one final top-10 country hit with "Dreamland Express." Reflecting changes in the music scene, the song didn't even make the pop charts. (Bottom right) The last Denver 45 was this live version of "For You," which came from the CD *The Wildlife Concert* and was issued by Sony Legacy.

Number	Title (A Side/B Side)	Yr	VG	VG+	NM
❑ CPL2-0764 [(2)]	An Evening with John Denver	1976	2.50	5.00	10.00
—Black label, dog near top					
❑ AFL1-1183	Windsong	197?	2.00	4.00	8.00
—Reissue					
❑ APL1-1183	Windsong	1975	2.50	5.00	10.00
—Tan label					
❑ APL1-1183	Windsong	1976	2.00	4.00	8.00
—Black label, dog near top					
❑ AQL1-1183	Windsong	197?	2.00	4.00	8.00
—Later reissue					
❑ AFL1-1201	Rocky Mountain Christmas	197?	2.00	4.00	8.00
—Reissue					
❑ APL1-1201	Rocky Mountain Christmas	1975	2.50	5.00	10.00
—Tan label					
❑ APL1-1201	Rocky Mountain Christmas	1976	2.00	4.00	8.00
—Black label, dog near top					
❑ APL2-1263 [(2)]	The John Denver Gift Pak	1974	7.50	15.00	30.00
—Contains "Rocky Mountain Christmas" and "Windsong" in a special Christmas sleeve.					
❑ AFL1-1694	Spirit	197?	2.00	4.00	8.00
—Reissue					
❑ APL1-1694	Spirit	1976	2.50	5.00	10.00
—Originals are black label, dog near top					
❑ AQL1-2195	John Denver's Greatest Hits, Volume 2	197?	2.00	4.00	8.00
—Reissue					
❑ CPL1-2195	John Denver's Greatest Hits, Volume 2	1977	2.50	5.00	10.00
❑ AFL1-2521	I Want to Live	1977	2.00	4.00	8.00
❑ AQL1-3075	John Denver	1979	2.00	4.00	8.00
❑ AQL1-3449	Autograph	1980	2.00	4.00	8.00
❑ AFL1-4055	Some Days Are Diamonds	1981	2.00	4.00	8.00
❑ LSP-4207	Rhymes & Reasons	1969	3.75	7.50	15.00
—Orange label, non-flexible vinyl					
❑ AFL1-4256	Seasons of the Heart	1982	2.00	4.00	8.00
❑ LSP-4278	Take Me to Tomorrow	1970	3.75	7.50	15.00
—Orange label, non-flexible vinyl					
❑ AFL1-4499	Poems, Prayers and Promises	197?	2.00	4.00	8.00
—Reissue					
❑ LSP-4499	Poems, Prayers and Promises	1971	3.00	6.00	12.00
—Orange label					
❑ LSP-4499	Poems, Prayers and Promises	1975	2.50	5.00	10.00
—Tan label or black label, dog near top					
❑ AFL1-4607	Aerie	197?	2.00	4.00	8.00
—Reissue					
❑ LSP-4607	Aerie	1971	3.00	6.00	12.00
—Orange label					
❑ LSP-4607	Aerie	1975	2.50	5.00	10.00
—Tan label or black label, dog near top					
❑ AFL1-4683	It's About Time	1983	2.00	4.00	8.00
❑ AFL1-4731	Rocky Mountain High	197?	2.00	4.00	8.00
—Reissue					
❑ AQL1-4731	Rocky Mountain High	197?	2.00	4.00	8.00
—Later reissue					
❑ LSP-4731	Rocky Mountain High	1972	3.00	6.00	12.00
—Orange label					
❑ LSP-4731	Rocky Mountain High	1975	2.50	5.00	10.00
—Tan label or black label, dog near top					
❑ AYL1-5189	Poems, Prayers and Promises	198?	—	3.00	6.00
—"Best Buy Series" reissue					
❑ AYL1-5190	Rocky Mountain High	198?	—	3.00	6.00
—"Best Buy Series" reissue					
❑ AYL1-5191	Windsong	198?	—	3.00	6.00
—"Best Buy Series" reissue					
❑ AYL1-5192	I Want to Live	198?	—	3.00	6.00
—"Best Buy Series" reissue					
❑ AYL1-5193	Back Home Again	198?	—	3.00	6.00
—"Best Buy Series" reissue					
❑ AYL1-5194	Spirit	198?	—	3.00	6.00
—"Best Buy Series" reissue					
❑ AYL1-5195	Farewell Andromeda	198?	—	3.00	6.00
—"Best Buy Series" reissue					
❑ AJL1-5313	John Denver's Greatest Hits, Volume 3	1984	2.00	4.00	8.00
❑ DJL1-5398 [DJ]	The John Denver Holiday Radio Show	1984	5.00	10.00	20.00
❑ AFL1-5458	Dreamland Express	1985	2.00	4.00	8.00
❑ AFL1-5811	One World	1986	2.00	4.00	8.00

DENVER, JOHN, AND THE MUPPETS

45s

RCA

Number	Title (A Side/B Side)	Yr	VG	VG+	NM
❑ PB-11767	Have Yourself a Merry Little Christmas//We Wish You a Merry Christmas/A Baby Just Like You	1979	—	2.50	5.00
❑ PB-11767 [PS]	Have Yourself a Merry Little Christmas//We Wish You a Merry Christmas/A Baby Just Like You	1979	—	2.50	5.00

Albums

RCA

Number	Title (A Side/B Side)	Yr	VG	VG+	NM
❑ AFL1-3451	A Christmas Together	1979	3.00	6.00	12.00

DENVER, JOHN, AND THE NITTY GRITTY DIRT BAND

Also see each artist's individual listings.

45s

UNIVERSAL

Number	Title (A Side/B Side)	Yr	VG	VG+	NM
❑ UVL-66008	And So It Goes/Amazing Grace	1989	—	2.00	4.00

DENVER, BOISE, & JOHNSON

Also see JOHN DENVER; MICHAEL JOHNSON.

45s

REPRISE

Number	Title (A Side/B Side)	Yr	VG	VG+	NM
❑ 0695	Take Me to Tomorrow/'68 Nixon (This Year's Model)	1968	3.00	6.00	12.00

DESERT ROSE BAND, THE

Featuring CHRIS HILLMAN, formerly of THE BYRDS.

45s

MCA

Number	Title (A Side/B Side)	Yr	VG	VG+	NM
❑ 53048	Leave This Town/Ashes of Love	1987	—	—	3.00
❑ 53142	Love Reunited/Hard Times	1987	—	—	3.00
❑ 53201	One Step Forward/Glass Hearts	1987	—	—	3.00
❑ 53274	He's Back and I'm Blue/The One That Got Away	1988	—	—	3.00
❑ 53354	Our Songs/Summer Wind	1988	—	—	3.00
❑ 53454	I Still Believe in You/Livin' in the House	1988	—	—	3.00

MCA CURB

Number	Title (A Side/B Side)	Yr	VG	VG+	NM
❑ 53616	She Don't Love Nobody/Step On Out	1989	—	—	3.00
❑ 53671	Hello Trouble/Homeless	1989	—	—	3.00
❑ 53746	Start All Over Again/Fooled Again	1989	—	—	3.00
❑ 53804	In Another Lifetime/Just a Memory	1990	—	—	3.00
❑ 54002	Will This Be the Day/Our Baby's Gone	1991	—	—	3.00
❑ 54107	Come a Little Closer/Everybody's Hero	1991	—	—	3.00
❑ 54188	You Can Go Home/Glory and Power	1991	—	—	3.00
❑ 54316	Twilight Is Gone/Shades of Blue	1991	—	—	3.00
❑ 79052	Story of Love/Darkness on the Playground	1990	—	—	3.00

Albums

MCA

Number	Title (A Side/B Side)	Yr	VG	VG+	NM
❑ 5991	The Desert Rose Band	1987	2.00	4.00	8.00
❑ 42169	Running	1988	2.00	4.00	8.00

DEWITT, LEW

Also see THE STATLER BROTHERS.

45s

COLUMBIA

Number	Title (A Side/B Side)	Yr	VG	VG+	NM
❑ 4-44160	She Went a Little Bit Farther/Brown Eyes	1967	2.50	5.00	10.00

COMPLEAT

Number	Title (A Side/B Side)	Yr	VG	VG+	NM
❑ 147	You'll Never Know/Wanda Glen	1985	—	3.00	6.00
❑ 151	I Love Virginia/She Must Have Lovin' Eyes	1986	—	3.00	6.00
❑ 160	Hello Houston/Don't Our Love Look	1986	—	3.00	6.00
❑ 172	Slow Dance/(B-side unknown)	1987	—	3.00	6.00

Albums

COMPLEAT

Number	Title (A Side/B Side)	Yr	VG	VG+	NM
❑ 671018-1	On My Own	1986	3.00	6.00	12.00

DEXTER, AL

45s

ALDEX

Number	Title (A Side/B Side)	Yr	VG	VG+	NM
❑ 116	Move Over, Rover/(B-side unknown)	196?	3.75	7.50	15.00
❑ 117	Bye, Bye Blue Eyes/Don't You Love Me Anymore	196?	3.75	7.50	15.00

ALLSTAR

Number	Title (A Side/B Side)	Yr	VG	VG+	NM
❑ 7306	Country Guitar/My Careless Heart	196?	3.75	7.50	15.00

CAPITOL

Number	Title (A Side/B Side)	Yr	VG	VG+	NM
❑ 4724	My Little Heartache/I Won't Be Number Two	1962	3.00	6.00	12.00

COLUMBIA

Number	Title (A Side/B Side)	Yr	VG	VG+	NM
❑ 2-280 (?)	Saturday Night Boogie/There'll Come a Time	1949	12.50	25.00	50.00
—Microgroove 7-inch 33 1/3 rpm single					
❑ 2-400 (?)	Always in My Heart/I'm Startin' Sweetheartin' Again	1949	12.50	25.00	50.00
—Microgroove 7-inch 33 1/3 rpm single					
❑ 2-470 (?)	Each Night I Cry Over Your Picture/I Don't Suppose	1950	10.00	20.00	40.00
—Microgroove 7-inch 33 1/3 rpm single					
❑ 2-660 (?)	New Pistol Packin' Mama/Barrel House Polka	1950	10.00	20.00	40.00
—Microgroove 7-inch 33 1/3 rpm single					

DECCA

Number	Title (A Side/B Side)	Yr	VG	VG+	NM
❑ 9-28137	Hotfoot Shuffle/Fisherman's Boogie	1952	5.00	10.00	20.00
—With Aubrey Grass					
❑ 9-28345	Counting My Teardrops/Honeymoon Waltz	1952	5.00	10.00	20.00
❑ 9-28508	Rosa/Guitar Polka	1952	5.00	10.00	20.00
❑ 9-28739	My Careless Heart/Move Over Rover	1953	5.00	10.00	20.00

DOT

Number	Title (A Side/B Side)	Yr	VG	VG+	NM
❑ 16842	Pistol Packin' Mama/Rosalita	1966	2.50	5.00	10.00
❑ 16977	Down at the Roadside Inn/My Careless Heart	1966	2.50	5.00	10.00

EKKO

Number	Title (A Side/B Side)	Yr	VG	VG+	NM
❑ 1020	Pistol Packin' Mama/I Won't Be Number Two	1955	6.25	12.50	25.00

Selected 78s

COLUMBIA

Number	Title (A Side/B Side)	Yr	VG	VG+	NM
❑ 20010	Guitar Polka/Honey Do You Think It's Wrong	1948	3.75	7.50	15.00
—Reissue of 36898					
❑ 20062	I'm Losing My Mind Over You/I'll Wait for You Dear	1948	3.75	7.50	15.00
—Reissue of 37037					
❑ 20065	Triflin' Gal/I'm Lost Without You	1948	3.75	7.50	15.00
—Reissue of 3704?					
❑ 20073	Wine, Women and Song/It's Up to You	1948	3.75	7.50	15.00
—Reissue of 37062					
❑ 20088	Kokomo Island/I Learned About Love	1948	3.75	7.50	15.00
—Reissue of 37200					
❑ 20108	Down at the Roadside Inn/My Love Goes With You	1948	3.75	7.50	15.00
—Reissue of 37303					

Number	Title (A Side/B Side)	Yr	VG	VG+	NM
❑ 20121	Who's Gonna Love You When I'm Gone/Am I to Blame?	1948	3.75	7.50	15.00
—Reissue of 37352					
❑ 20131	So Long Pal/Too Late to Worry	1948	3.75	7.50	15.00
—Reissue of Columbia 37404					
❑ 20144	Sundown Polka/Honky Tonk Chinese Dime	1948	3.75	7.50	15.00
—Reissue of Columbia 37417					
❑ 20161	All I Want Is You/Meet Me Down in Honky Tonk Town	1948	3.75	7.50	15.00
—Reissue of Columbia 37434					
❑ 20168	Who's Been Here/Darling It's All Over Now	1948	3.75	7.50	15.00
—Reissue of Columbia 37441					
❑ 20184	Maybe, Baby It's Me/Love Lanes of Yesterday	1948	3.75	7.50	15.00
—Reissue of 37538					
❑ 20194	New Broom Boogie/Remember You're Mine	1948	3.75	7.50	15.00
—Reissue of 37594					
❑ 20240	Jelly Roll Special/Sunshine	1948	3.75	7.50	15.00
—Reissue of 37641					
❑ 20267	Pistol Packin' Mama/Rosalita	1948	3.75	7.50	15.00
—Reissue of 37668					
❑ 20365	Why Did She Have to Be/I Waited Too Long	1948	3.75	7.50	15.00
—Reissue of 37880					
❑ 20366	Texas Waltz/Two Broken Hearts	1948	3.75	7.50	15.00
—Reissue of 37881					
❑ 20367	Can This Love Be Real/I Told My Heart	1948	3.75	7.50	15.00
—Reissue of 37882					
❑ 20395	Texas Rose/Barrel House Boogie	1948	3.75	7.50	15.00
—Reissue of 38038					
❑ 20422	Rock and Rye Rag/I'm Leaving My Troubles Behind	1948	5.00	10.00	20.00
—Reissue of 38168					
❑ 20438	Calico Rag/Rose of Mexico	1948	5.00	10.00	20.00
❑ 20461	I Cry When I'm Blue/It's Just Because of You	1948	5.00	10.00	20.00
❑ 20492	High Price for Love/Just Take a Little Time	1948	5.00	10.00	20.00
❑ 20518	I'll Always Love You/Is That the Way to Treat a Friend	1948	5.00	10.00	20.00
❑ 20540	Calamity Jane/A Good Man Is Hard to Find	1949	5.00	10.00	20.00
❑ 20569	New Guitar Polka/At the End of Each Day	1949	5.00	10.00	20.00
❑ 36898	Guitar Polka/Honey Do You Think It's Wrong	1946	5.00	10.00	20.00
❑ 37037	I'm Losing My Mind Over You/I'll Wait for You Dear	1946	5.00	10.00	20.00
—Reissue of Okeh 6727					
❑ 37040or 37042	Triflin' Gal/I'm Lost Without You	1946	5.00	10.00	20.00
—Reissue of Okeh 6740					
❑ 37062	Wine, Women and Song/It's Up to You	1946	5.00	10.00	20.00
❑ 37200	Kokomo Island/I Learned About Love	1946	5.00	10.00	20.00
❑ 37303	Down at the Roadside Inn/My Love Goes With You	1947	5.00	10.00	20.00
❑ 37352	Who's Gonna Love You When I'm Gone/Am I to Blame?	1947	5.00	10.00	20.00
❑ 37404	So Long Pal/Too Late to Worry	1947	5.00	10.00	20.00
—Reissue of Okeh 6718					
❑ 37417	Sundown Polka/Honky Tonk Chinese Dime	1947	5.00	10.00	20.00
❑ 37434	All I Want Is You/Meet Me Down in Honky Tonk Town	1947	5.00	10.00	20.00
❑ 37441	Who's Been Here/Darling It's All Over Now	1947	5.00	10.00	20.00
❑ 37538	Maybe, Baby It's Me/Love Lanes of Yesterday	1947	5.00	10.00	20.00
❑ 37594	New Broom Boogie/Remember You're Mine	1947	5.00	10.00	20.00
❑ 37641	Jelly Roll Special/Sunshine	1947	5.00	10.00	20.00
❑ 37668	Pistol Packin' Mama/Rosalita	1947	5.00	10.00	20.00
—Reissue of Okeh 6708					
❑ 37880	Why Did She Have to Be/I Waited Too Long	1947	5.00	10.00	20.00
❑ 37881	Texas Waltz/Two Broken Hearts	1947	5.00	10.00	20.00
❑ 37882	Can This Love Be Real/I Told My Heart	1947	5.00	10.00	20.00
❑ 38038	Texas Rose/Barrel House Boogie	1948	5.00	10.00	20.00
❑ 38168	Rock and Rye Rag/I'm Leaving My Troubles Behind	1948	6.25	12.50	25.00
KING					
❑ 875	I'm Setting You Free/Blow That Lonesome Whistle Casey	1950	5.00	10.00	20.00
❑ 884	Hi De Ho Boogie/Walking with the Blues	1950	5.00	10.00	20.00
❑ 899	Santa's on His Way/Merry Christmas to All	1950	5.00	10.00	20.00
❑ 913	Daddy Wah Boogie/You've Been Cheatin' Baby	1950	5.00	10.00	20.00
OKEH					
❑ 6708	Pistol Packin' Mama/Rosalita	1943	6.25	12.50	25.00
❑ 6718	So Long Pal/Too Late to Worry	1944	6.25	12.50	25.00
❑ 6727	I'm Losing My Mind Over You/I'll Wait for You Dear	1944	6.25	12.50	25.00
❑ 6740	Triflin' Gal/I'm Lost Without You	1945	6.25	12.50	25.00
VOCALION					
❑ 03435	New Jelly Roll Blues/(B-side unknown)	1936	6.25	12.50	25.00
❑ 03569	titles unknown	193?	6.25	12.50	25.00
❑ 03719	titles unknown	193?	6.25	12.50	25.00
❑ 03927	titles unknown	193?	6.25	12.50	25.00
❑ 03988	titles unknown	193?	6.25	12.50	25.00
❑ 04174	titles unknown	193?	6.25	12.50	25.00
❑ 04277	titles unknown	193?	6.25	12.50	25.00
❑ 04327	titles unknown	193?	6.25	12.50	25.00
❑ 04405	titles unknown	193?	6.25	12.50	25.00
❑ 04988	titles unknown	193?	6.25	12.50	25.00
❑ 05042	titles unknown	193?	6.25	12.50	25.00
Albums					
CAPITOL					
❑ ST 1701 [S]	Al Dexter Sings and Plays His Greatest Hits	1962	10.00	20.00	40.00
❑ T 1701 [M]	Al Dexter Sings and Plays His Greatest Hits	1962	7.50	15.00	30.00
COLUMBIA					
❑ CL 9005 [10]	Songs of the Southwest	195?	12.50	25.00	50.00
HARMONY					
❑ HL 7293 [M]	Pistol Packin' Mama	1961	5.00	10.00	20.00

DIAMOND, NEIL

This popular singer had the below singles make the country charts. Also see BARBRA AND NEIL.

45s

Number	Title (A Side/B Side)	Yr	VG	VG+	NM
COLUMBIA					
❑ 10897	Forever in Blue Jeans/Remember Me	1979	—	2.00	4.00
❑ 78242	One Good Love/Kentucky Woman	1996	—	—	3.00
—A-side: Duet with Waylon Jennings					

DIAMOND RIO

45s

Number	Title (A Side/B Side)	Yr	VG	VG+	NM
ARISTA					
❑ 2182	Meet in the Middle/The Ballad of Conley and Billy (The Proof's in the Pickin')	1991	—	2.50	5.00
❑ 2258	Mama Don't Forget to Pray for Me/Norma Jean Riley	1991	—	2.00	4.00
❑ 2262	Mirror Mirror/The Ballad of Conley and Billy (The Proof's in the Pickin')	1991	—	2.00	4.00
❑ 12407	Norma Jean Riley/Pick Me Up	1992	—	2.00	4.00
❑ 12441	Nowhere Bound/They Don't Make Hearts Like They Used To	1992	—	2.00	4.00
❑ 12457	In a Week or Two/Close to the Edge	1992	—	2.00	4.00
❑ 12464	Oh Me, Oh My, Sweet Baby/Nothing in This World	1993	—	2.00	4.00
❑ 12541	Meet in the Middle/Mama Don't Forget to Pray for Me	1993	—	—	3.00
—Reissue; "Collectables" logo on Arista label					
❑ 12542	Norma Jean Riley/Mirror Mirror	1993	—	—	3.00
—Reissue; "Collectables" logo on Arista label					
❑ 12580	This Romeo Ain't Got Julie Yet/I Was Meant to Be with You	1993	—	2.00	4.00
❑ 12610	Sawmill Road/I Was Meant to Be with You	1993	—	2.00	4.00
❑ 12696	Love a Little Stronger/It Does Get Better Than This	1994	—	2.00	4.00
❑ 12739	Finish What We Started/Appalachian Dream	1995	—	2.00	4.00
❑ 12764	Night Is Fallin' in My Heart/Down by the Riverside	1994	—	2.00	4.00
❑ 12787	Bubba Hyde/Norma Jean Riley	1995	—	2.00	4.00
❑ 12934	Walkin' Away/It's All in Your Head	1995	—	2.00	4.00
❑ 12991	That's What I Get for Lovin' You/Big	1996	—	—	3.00
❑ 13019	It's All in Your Head/Is That Asking Too Much	1996	—	—	3.00
ARISTA NASHVILLE					
❑ 13067	Holdin'/She Sure Did Like to Run	1996	—	—	3.00
❑ 13091	How Your Love Makes Me Feel/Imagine That	1997	—	2.00	4.00
❑ 13138	Unbelievable/You're Gone	1998	—	2.00	4.00
❑ 13153	I Know How the River Feels/What More Do You Want from Me	1999	—	—	3.00

DIAMONDS, THE

Direct descendant of the1950s white cover group of the same name. By the time these records charted, the group's membership had evolved to the point where there was no one in common.

45s

Number	Title (A Side/B Side)	Yr	VG	VG+	NM
CHURCHILL					
❑ 94101	Just a Little Bit/(B-side unknown)	1987	—	3.00	6.00
❑ 94102	Two Kinds of Woman/(B-side unknown)	1987	—	3.00	6.00

DIANA

45s

Number	Title (A Side/B Side)	Yr	VG	VG+	NM
ADAMAS					
❑ 103	Who's Been Sleeping in My Bed/(B-side unknown)	1982	—	3.00	6.00
❑ 103 [PS]	Who's Been Sleeping in My Bed/(B-side unknown)	1982	2.00	4.00	8.00
ELEKTRA					
❑ 46061	Just When I Needed You Most/Tie Me Down	1979	—	2.50	5.00
❑ 46539	Lonely Together/This Is the Way a Woman Wants to Feel	1979	—	2.50	5.00
SUNBIRD					
❑ 7564	He's the Fire/What a Fool I Was (To Fall in Love with You)	1981	—	2.50	5.00

DICKENS, JIMMY

Includes records as "Little Jimmy Dickens."

45s

Number	Title (A Side/B Side)	Yr	VG	VG+	NM
COLUMBIA					
❑ 2-238	Country Boy/I'm Fading Fast with the Time	1949	12.50	25.00	50.00
—Microgroove 7-inch 33 1/3 rpm single					
❑ 2-292	My Heart's Bouquet/I'll Be Back a-Sunday	1949	12.50	25.00	50.00
—Microgroove 7-inch 33 1/3 rpm single					
❑ 2-400 (?)	A-Sleeping at the Foot of the Bed/I'm in Love Up to My Ears	1949	12.50	25.00	50.00
—Microgroove 7-inch 33 1/3 rpm single					
❑ 2-472	Lovin' Lies/A Rose from the Bride's Bouquet	1950	10.00	20.00	40.00
—Microgroove 7-inch 33 1/3 rpm single					
❑ 2-550 (?)	Hillbilly Fever/Then I Had to Turn Around and Get Married	1950	10.00	20.00	40.00
—Microgroove 7-inch 33 1/3 rpm single					
❑ 2-600 (?)	Foolish Me/If It Ain't One Thing	1950	10.00	20.00	40.00
—Microgroove 7-inch 33 1/3 rpm single					
❑ 3-10426	The Preacherman/We're Gonna Make It	1976	—	2.50	5.00
❑ 4-20722	Walk Chicken Walk/Just When I Needed You	1950	7.50	15.00	30.00
❑ 4-20744	When the Love Bug Bites You/Out of Business	1950	7.50	15.00	30.00
❑ 4-20769	Bible on the Table/I'm Little But I'm Loud	1950	7.50	15.00	30.00

Number	Title (A Side/B Side)	Yr	VG	VG+	NM
❑ 4-20786	Bessie the Heifer/Cold Feet	1951	7.50	15.00	30.00
❑ 4-20809	It May Be Silly/What About You	1951	7.50	15.00	30.00
❑ 4-20835	Sign on the Highway/Galvanized Wash Tub	1951	7.50	15.00	30.00
❑ 4-20866	I've Just Got to See You Once More/Poor Little Darlin'	1952	7.50	15.00	30.00
❑ 4-20905	Brother Do You Take Time to Pray/They Locked God Outside	1952	7.50	15.00	30.00
❑ 4-20930	Hot Diggety Dog/Lola Lee	1952	7.50	15.00	30.00
❑ 4-20976	Waitress, Waitress/They Don't Know Nothing at All	1952	7.50	15.00	30.00
❑ 4-20987	Take Up Thy Cross/Just a Closer Walk	1952	7.50	15.00	30.00
❑ 4-21033	No Tears in Heaven/He Spoke Not a Word	1952	7.50	15.00	30.00
❑ 4-21038	Wedding Bell Waltz/You Don't Have Love at All	1952	7.50	15.00	30.00
❑ 4-21068	Take My Hand, Precious Lord/I Shall Not Be Moved	1953	7.50	15.00	30.00
❑ 4-21093	Sidemeat and Cabbage/Teardrops	1953	7.50	15.00	30.00
❑ 4-21132	I'll Dance at Your Wedding/I'm Making Love to a Stranger	1953	7.50	15.00	30.00
❑ 4-21159	Thick and Thin/Tomorrow Is Too Long	1953	7.50	15.00	30.00
❑ 4-21167	No Place Like Home on Christmas/Barefooted Little Cowboy	1953	7.50	15.00	30.00
❑ 4-21203	Old Country Preacher/Little Ole Country Churchhouse	1954	6.25	12.50	25.00
❑ 4-21206	You All Come/Rock Me	1954	6.25	12.50	25.00
❑ 4-21216	You Better Not Do That/Love Song on the Bayou	1954	6.25	12.50	25.00
❑ 4-21247	Out Behind the Barn/Closing Time	1954	6.25	12.50	25.00
❑ 4-21296	Black Eyed Joes/Take Me As I Am	1954	6.25	12.50	25.00
❑ 4-21341	Conscience/Stinky, Pass the Hat Around	1955	5.00	10.00	20.00
❑ 4-21384	Salty Boogie/A Ribbon and a Rose	1955	5.00	10.00	20.00
❑ 4-21434	We Could/When They Get Too Rough	1955	5.00	10.00	20.00
❑ 4-21464	I'm Braver Now/Are You Insured Beyond the Grave	1955	5.00	10.00	20.00
❑ 4-21491	Hey Worm/Where Did the Sunshine Go	1956	5.00	10.00	20.00
❑ 4-21515	Big Sandy/It Scares Me	1956	6.25	12.50	25.00
❑ 4-21555	Cornbread and Buttermilk/I Never Thought It Would Happen	1956	6.25	12.50	25.00
❑ 4-40801	I'm Coming Over Tonight/Say It Now	1956	5.00	10.00	20.00
❑ 4-40890	I Never Had the Blues/Happy Heartaches	1957	5.00	10.00	20.00
❑ 4-40961	Let's Quit Before We Start/Making the Rounds	1957	5.00	10.00	20.00
❑ 4-41080	Family Reunion/Whatever You Were	1957	5.00	10.00	20.00
❑ 4-41173	I Got a Hole in My Pocket/Me and My Big Mouth	1958	12.50	25.00	50.00
❑ 4-41340	When Your House Is Not a Home/The Honeymoon Is Over	1959	3.75	7.50	15.00
❑ 4-41436	Hannah/Country Ways and City Ideas	1959	3.75	7.50	15.00
❑ 4-41529	Hey Ma/Hot Tears	1959	3.75	7.50	15.00
❑ 4-41670	I'm Just Blue Enough (To Do Most Anything)/We Lived It Up (Now We've Got to Live It Down)	1960	3.75	7.50	15.00
❑ 4-41916	Fire Ball Mail/John Henry	1960	3.00	6.00	12.00
❑ 4-42013	Talking to the Wall/Farewell Party	1961	3.00	6.00	12.00
❑ 4-42278	Eight More Miles/Twenty Cigarettes	1962	3.00	6.00	12.00
❑ 4-42485	The Violet and a Rose/Honky Tonk Troubles	1962	3.00	6.00	12.00
❑ 4-42663	Police Police/Running Into Memories of You	1963	3.00	6.00	12.00
❑ 4-42845	Another Bridge to Burn/I'll Sit This One Out	1963	3.00	6.00	12.00
❑ 4-43040	Too Many Irons in the Fire/I Leaned Over Backwards	1964	2.50	5.00	10.00
❑ 4-43123	I'll Sit This One Out/Is Goodbye That Easy to Say	1964	2.50	5.00	10.00
❑ 4-43243	He Stands Real Tall/Life Turned Her That Way	1965	2.50	5.00	10.00
❑ 4-43388	May the Bird of Paradise Fly Up Your Nose/My Eyes Are Jealous	1965	3.00	6.00	12.00
❑ 4-43514	When the Ship Hit the Sand/Truck Load of Starvin' Kangaroos	1966	2.50	5.00	10.00
❑ 4-43701	Who Licked the Red Off Your Candy/You Don't Have Time for Me	1966	2.50	5.00	10.00
❑ 4-43804	Where the Buffalo Trod/Butter Beans	1966	2.00	4.00	8.00
❑ 4-44025	Country Music Lover/You've Destroyed Me	1967	2.00	4.00	8.00
❑ 4-44162	Jenny Needs a G String/He Knocked Me Right Out of the Box	1967	2.00	4.00	8.00
DECCA					
❑ 32187	Daddy and the Wine/They're Gonna Have Me Committed	1967	—	3.50	7.00
❑ 32253	I Came So Close to Failure/I Love Lucy Brown	1968	—	3.50	7.00
❑ 32326	How to Catch an African Skeeter Alive/Can You Build Your House (On Another Man's Grave)	1968	—	3.50	7.00
❑ 32384	They Stole My Steel Guitar/Someday You'll Call My Name	1968	—	3.50	7.00
❑ 32426	When You're Seventeen/She Never Likes Nothing for Long	1968	—	3.50	7.00
❑ 32523	Times Are Gonna Get Better/A Death in the Family	1969	—	3.50	7.00
❑ 32644	(You've Been Quite a Doll) Raggedy Ann/I'd Rather Sleep in Peace	1970	—	3.50	7.00
STARDAY					
❑ 979	Dead Skunk/Alabam	1973	—	3.00	6.00
UNITED ARTISTS					
❑ 50730	Everyday Family Man/One More Time	1970	—	3.00	6.00
❑ 50781	Here It Comes Again/There'll Be Love	1971	—	3.00	6.00
❑ 50834	What Will I Do Then/You Only Want Me for My Baby	1971	—	3.00	6.00
❑ 50889	Try It, You'll Like It/Helpless	1972	—	3.00	6.00
❑ 50941	Alabam/Someone to Care	1972	—	3.00	6.00
Selected 78s					
COLUMBIA					
❑ 20548	Take an Old Cold 'Tater (And Wait)/Pennies for Papa	1949	5.00	10.00	20.00
Albums					
COLUMBIA					
❑ CL 1047 [M]	Raisin' the Dickens	1957	20.00	40.00	80.00
❑ CL 1545 [M]	Big Songs by Little Jimmy Dickens	1960	7.50	15.00	30.00
❑ CL 1887 [M]	Little Jimmy Dickens Sings Out Behind the Barn	1962	7.50	15.00	30.00
❑ CL 2288 [M]	Handle with Care	1964	6.25	12.50	25.00
❑ CL 2442 [M]	May the Bird of Paradise Fly Up Your Nose	1965	6.25	12.50	25.00
❑ CL 2551 [M]	Little Jimmy Dickens' Greatest Hits	1966	6.25	12.50	25.00
❑ CS 8345 [S]	Big Songs by Little Jimmy Dickens	1960	10.00	20.00	40.00
❑ CS 8687 [S]	Little Jimmy Dickens Sings Out Behind the Barn	1962	10.00	20.00	40.00
❑ CL 9053 [10]	The Old Country Church	1954	30.00	60.00	120.00
❑ CS 9088 [S]	Handle with Care	1964	7.50	15.00	30.00
❑ CS 9242 [S]	May the Bird of Paradise Fly Up Your Nose	1965	7.50	15.00	30.00
❑ CS 9351 [S]	Little Jimmy Dickens' Greatest Hits	1966	7.50	15.00	30.00
DECCA					
❑ DL 4967 [M]	Jimmy Dickens Sings	1967	7.50	15.00	30.00
❑ DL 74967 [S]	Jimmy Dickens Sings	1967	5.00	10.00	20.00
❑ DL 75091	Jimmy Dickens Comes Callin'	1968	5.00	10.00	20.00
❑ DL 75133	Jimmy Dickens' Greatest Hits	1969	5.00	10.00	20.00

DICKERSON, DUB

Number	Title (A Side/B Side)	Yr	VG	VG+	NM
45s					
CAPITOL					
❑ F2504	The Bells of Monterrey/Sweet Bunch of Bitterreeds	1953	6.25	12.50	25.00
❑ F2605	One Night Stand/Dear Love	1953	6.25	12.50	25.00
❑ F2719	Mama Laid the Law Down/Everything Depends on You	1954	6.25	12.50	25.00
❑ F2821	Count Me In/You Started It All	1954	6.25	12.50	25.00
❑ F2947	My Gal Gertie/Look, Look, Look	1954	6.25	12.50	25.00
❑ F3099	Under the Heading of Business/I Must've Drove My Mules Too Hard	1955	5.00	10.00	20.00
DECCA					
❑ 9-46329	Money Talks/Chinchie Hotel	1951	6.25	12.50	25.00
❑ 9-46353	If I Had You Back/Just in Time to Be Too Late	1951	6.25	12.50	25.00
SIMS					
❑ 106	Shot Gun Wedding/Each Time	1956	6.25	12.50	25.00
❑ 127	It's About to Get Me Down/Name Your Price	1962	3.75	7.50	15.00
TODD					
❑ 1053	The Bottle/Mama Laid the Law Down	1960	3.75	7.50	15.00

DICKEY, DAN

Number	Title (A Side/B Side)	Yr	VG	VG+	NM
45s					
CHARTWHEEL					
❑ 123	Hot Mama/Close the Door	1979	—	3.00	6.00
❑ 126	Bye, Bye, Baby/(B-side unknown)	1979	—	3.00	6.00

DICKINSON, HAL

Number	Title (A Side/B Side)	Yr	VG	VG+	NM
45s					
CORAL					
❑ 9-61536	Merry Christmas Baby/Tenderly	1955	3.75	7.50	15.00
GRASS					
❑ 3301	You're Cheatin' on Me Again/Cowboy Blues	1966	3.00	6.00	12.00

DIFFIE, JOE

Also see MARY CHAPIN CARPENTER.

Number	Title (A Side/B Side)	Yr	VG	VG+	NM
45s					
COLUMBIA					
❑ 38-78284	Tearin' It Up/White Knuckle Ride	1996	—	2.00	4.00
—B-side by Lynyrd Skynyrd					
EPIC					
❑ 34-73447	Home/Liquid Heartache	1990	—	2.00	4.00
❑ 34-73637	If You Want Me To/Home	1990	—	2.00	4.00
❑ 34-73747	If the Devil Danced (In Empty Pockets)/I Ain't Leavin' 'Til She's Gone	1991	—	2.50	5.00
—Original copies were pressed on styrene (the record is translucent dark red when held to a light)					
❑ 34-73747	If the Devil Danced (In Empty Pockets)/I Ain't Leavin' 'Til She's Gone	199?	—	—	3.00
—Reissues were pressed on non-translucent vinyl					
❑ 34-73935	New Way (To Light Up an Old Flame)/Coolest Fool in Town	1991	—	2.00	4.00
❑ 34-74123	Is It Cold in Here/Back to Back Heartache	1991	—	2.00	4.00
❑ 34-74285	Ships That Don't Come In/Startin' Over Blues	1992	—	2.00	4.00
❑ 34-74415	Next Thing Smokin'/I Just Don't Know	1992	—	2.00	4.00
❑ 34-74796	Startin' Over Blues/Just a Regular Joe	1992	—	2.00	4.00
❑ 34-74911	Honky Tonk Attitude/Just a Regular Joe	1993	—	2.00	4.00
❑ 34-77071	Prop Me Up Beside the Jukebox (If I Die)/I Can Walk the Line	1993	—	2.00	4.00
❑ 34-77235	John Deere Green/Somewhere Under the Rainbow	1993	—	2.00	4.00
❑ 34-77380	In My Own Backyard/Here Comes That Train	1994	—	2.00	4.00
❑ 34-77577	Third Rock from the Sun/From Here on Out	1994	—	2.50	5.00
❑ 34-77715	Pickup Man/From Here on Out	1994	—	2.50	5.00
❑ 34-77808	So Help Me Girl/The Cows Came Home	1995	—	2.00	4.00
❑ 34-77902	I'm in Love with a Capital "U"/Wild Blue Yonder	1995	—	2.00	4.00
❑ 34-77978	That Road Not Taken/The Cows Came Home	1995	—	2.00	4.00
❑ 34-78201	Leroy the Redneck Reindeer/Wrap Me in Your Love	1995	—	2.00	4.00
❑ 34-78202	Bigger Than the Beatles/Whole Lotta Gone	1995	—	2.50	5.00
❑ 34-78246	C-O-U-N-T-R-Y/Third Rock from the Sun (Extended Mix)	1996	—	2.00	4.00
❑ 34-78333	Whole Lotta Gone/Back to the Cave	1996	—	2.00	4.00
❑ 34-78638	Somethin' Like That/This Is Your Brain	1997	—	2.00	4.00
❑ 34-79048	Texas Size Heartache/Poor Me	1998	—	2.00	4.00
❑ 34-79118	A Night to Remember/Texas Size Heartache	1999	—	2.00	4.00

Number	Title (A Side/B Side)	Yr	VG	VG+	NM

DILLARD, DOUG
Albums

Number	Title (A Side/B Side)	Yr	VG	VG+	NM
TOGETHER					
STT-1003	The Banjo Album	1970	20.00	40.00	80.00

DILLARD AND CLARK
Albums

Number	Title (A Side/B Side)	Yr	VG	VG+	NM
A&M					
SP-4158	The Fantastic Expedition of Dillard and Clark	1968	5.00	10.00	20.00
—Brown label					

DILLARDS, THE
45s

Number	Title (A Side/B Side)	Yr	VG	VG+	NM
ANTHEM					
101	It's About Time/One A.M.	1971	—	2.50	5.00
51014	Billy Jack/America	1971	—	2.50	5.00
CAPITOL					
5494	Nobody Knows/Ebo Walker	1965	2.00	4.00	8.00
5524	Lemon Chimes/The Last Thing on My Mind	1965	2.00	4.00	8.00
ELEKTRA					
45003	Dooley/Dong's Love	1964	2.50	5.00	10.00
45006	Hootin' Banjo/Polly Vaughn	1964	2.50	5.00	10.00
45641	Reason to Believe/Nobody Knows	1968	2.00	4.00	8.00
45661	Listen to the Sound/The Biggest Whatever	1969	2.00	4.00	8.00
45679	Rain Maker/West Montana Hanna	1970	2.00	4.00	8.00
45681	Close the Door Lightly/Touch Her If You Can	1970	2.00	4.00	8.00
K-ARK					
619	My Only True Love/Doug's Breakdown	196?	5.00	10.00	20.00
—As "The Dillard Brothers"; recorded in 1958, but probably not issued until the Dillards were recording for Elektra					
UNITED ARTISTS					
XW382	Hot Rod Banjo/Love Has Gone Away	1974	—	2.50	5.00
WHITE WHALE					
351	One Too Many Mornings/Turn It Around	1970	—	3.00	6.00
359	Comin' Home Again	1970	—	3.00	6.00

Albums

Number	Title (A Side/B Side)	Yr	VG	VG+	NM
ANTHEM					
ANS-5901	Roots and Branches	1972	3.75	7.50	15.00
CRYSTAL CLEAR					
CCS-5007	Mountain Rock	1979	6.25	12.50	25.00
—Direct-to-disc recording					
ELEKTRA					
EKL-232 [M]	Back Porch Bluegrass	1963	6.25	12.50	25.00
EKL-265 [M]	The Dillards, Live!!! Almost!!!	1964	5.00	10.00	20.00
EKL-285 [M]	Pickin' and Fiddlin'	1965	5.00	10.00	20.00
EKS-7232 [S]	Back Porch Bluegrass	1963	7.50	5.00	30.00
—Mandolin-player label					
EKS-7265 [S]	The Dillards, Live!!! Almost!!!	1964	6.25	12.50	25.00
—Mandolin-player label					
EKS-7285 [S]	Pickin' and Fiddlin'	1965	6.25	12.50	25.00
—Mandolin-player label					
EKS-74035	Wheatstraw Suite	1968	5.00	10.00	20.00
—Tan label with large stylized "E" on top					
EKS-74054	Copperfields	1969	5.00	10.00	20.00
—Red label with large stylized "E" on top					
FLYING FISH					
FF 040	The Dillards Vs. the Incredible L.A. Time Machine	1977	3.00	6.00	12.00
FF 082	Decade Waltz	1979	3.00	6.00	12.00
FF 215	Homecoming and Family Reunion	1979	3.00	6.00	12.00
POPPY					
PP-LA175-F	Tribute to the American Duck	1973	3.75	7.50	15.00

DILLINGHAM, CRAIG
Also see TISH HINOJOSA.

45s

Number	Title (A Side/B Side)	Yr	VG	VG+	NM
GRANNY WHITE					
10004	Memories Are Made of This/(B-side unknown)	1977	—	3.50	7.00
MCA CURB					
52301	Have You Loved Your Woman Today/Every Man Should Have One	1983	—	2.00	4.00
52352	Honky Tonk Women Make Honky Tonk Men/ Slow Dancin' with Fast Women	1984	—	2.00	4.00
52406	1984/Neon Light Idea	1984	—	2.00	4.00
52647	Next to You/Brand New Blues	1985	—	2.00	4.00

DILLON, DEAN
Also see GARY STEWART.

45s

Number	Title (A Side/B Side)	Yr	VG	VG+	NM
ATLANTIC					
7-87356	Hot, Country and Single/Holding My Own	1993	—	2.50	5.00
—Red vinyl					
7-87606	Don't You Even (Think About Leavin')/She Knows What She Wants	1991	—	2.00	4.00
7-87774	Holed Up in Some Honky Tonk/All Out of Love	1991	—	2.00	4.00
7-87794	Friday Night's Woman/Her Thinkin' I'm Doing Her Wrong (Ain't Doin' Me Right)	1991	—	2.00	4.00
CAPITOL					
B-44179	The New Never Wore Off My Sweet Baby/ Appalachia Got to Have You Feelin' in My Bones	1988	—	—	3.00
B-44239	I Go to Pieces/Hard Time for Lovers	1988	—	—	3.00
B-44294	Hey Heart/Appalachia Got to Have You Feelin' in My Bones	1988	—	—	3.00
B-44400	It's Love That Makes You Sexy/Appalachia Got to Have You Feelin' in My Bones	1989	—	2.00	4.00
7PRO-79827	Back in the Swing of Things (same on both sides)	1989	—	2.50	5.00
—Vinyl is promo only					
RCA					
PB-11881	I'm Into the Bottle (To Get You Out of My Mind)/ Tonight	1979	—	2.00	4.00
PB-12003	What Good Is a Heart/He's Number One	1980	—	2.00	4.00
PB-12109	Nobody in His Right Mind (Would've Left Her)/ Smelling Like a Rose	1980	—	2.00	4.00
PB-12234	They'll Never Take Me Alive/Tonight One of Us Is Going Out of My Mind	1981	—	2.00	4.00
PB-12319	Jesus Let Me Slide/If You're Goin' Crazy	1981	—	2.00	4.00
PB-13208	Play This Old Working Day Away/You to Come Home To	1982	—	2.00	4.00
PB-13295	You to Come Home To/I'm Into the Bottle (To Get You Off My Mind)	1982	—	2.00	4.00
PB-13628	Famous Last Words of a Fool/Ten Years and Two Babies Later	1983	—	2.00	4.00

Albums

Number	Title (A Side/B Side)	Yr	VG	VG+	NM
CAPITOL					
C1-48920	Slick Nickel	1988	2.00	4.00	8.00

DIRKSEN, SENATOR EVERETT MCKINLEY
45s

Number	Title (A Side/B Side)	Yr	VG	VG+	NM
CAPITOL					
2034	The First Time the Christmas Story Was Told/I Heard the Bells on Christmas Day	1967	2.00	4.00	8.00
5805	Gallant Men/The New Colossus	1966	—	3.00	6.00
5805 [PS]	Gallant Men/The New Colossus	1966	2.00	4.00	8.00
5912	Man Is Not Alone/The Shepherd and His Flock	1967	—	2.50	5.00

Albums

Number	Title (A Side/B Side)	Yr	VG	VG+	NM
CAPITOL					
ST 2643 [S]	Gallant Men	1966	3.75	7.50	15.00
T 2643 [M]	Gallant Men	1966	3.75	7.50	15.00
ST 2754 [S]	Man Is Not Alone	1967	3.75	7.50	15.00
T 2754 [M]	Man Is Not Alone	1967	5.00	10.00	20.00
ST 2792 [S]	Everett McKinley Dirksen at Christmas Time	1967	5.00	10.00	20.00

DIRT BAND, THE
See NITTY GRITTY DIRT BAND.

DIXIANA
45s

Number	Title (A Side/B Side)	Yr	VG	VG+	NM
AMI					
1909	Somebody Broke Into My Heart/(B-side unknown)	198?	—	3.00	6.00
EPIC					
34-74221	Waitin' for the Deal to Go Down/It Comes and It Goes	1992	—	2.00	4.00
34-74361	That's What I'm Working On Tonight/If I Can't Have You	1992	—	2.00	4.00
34-74713	I Know Where There's One/A Little in Love	1992	—	2.00	4.00
34-74936	Now You're Talkin'/Love Gone Good	1993	—	2.00	4.00
GRAND PRIZE					
5200	Dixie Anna/Livin' in the Country	1982	—	3.00	6.00
5204	Bein' Here with You/Livin' in the Country	1983	—	3.00	6.00
5209	Second Fiddle in the Band/Bein' Here with You	1983	—	3.00	6.00
SOUNDWAVES					
4779	Spirit of the Land (The Hay Song)/I Surrender	1987	—	3.00	6.00

DIXIE CHICKS
45s

Number	Title (A Side/B Side)	Yr	VG	VG+	NM
DIXIE CHICKS					
(# unknown)	Christmas Swing/The Flip Side	1991	12.50	25.00	50.00
(# unknown) [PS]	Home on the Radar Range	1991	12.50	25.00	50.00
—Sleeve for above record					
MONUMENT					
31-79047	Wide Open Spaces/There's Your Trouble	1998	—	2.00	4.00
31-79204	Tonight the Heartache's on Me/Give It Up or Let Me Go	1999	—	2.00	4.00
31-79352	Goodbye Earl/Cowboy Take Me Away	2000	—	2.00	4.00

DR. HOOK
Includes records as "Dr. Hook and the Medicine Show." Also see RAY SAWYER.

45s

Number	Title (A Side/B Side)	Yr	VG	VG+	NM
CAPITOL					
4081	Levitate/Cooky and Lila	1975	—	2.00	4.00
4104	The Millionaire/Cooky and Lila	1975	—	2.00	4.00
4171	Only Sixteen/Let Me Be Your Lover	1975	—	2.50	5.00
4280	A Little Bit More/A Couple More Years	1976	—	2.50	5.00
4364	If Not You/Bad Eye Bill	1976	—	2.00	4.00
4423	Walk Right In/Sexy Energy	1977	—	2.00	4.00
4534	Making Love and Music/Who Dat	1978	—	2.00	4.00
4615	I Don't Want to Be Alone Tonight/You Make My Pants Want to Get Up and Dance	1978	—	2.00	4.00
4621	Sharing the Night Together/You Make My Pants Want to Get Up and Dance	1978	—	2.00	4.00
4677	All the Time in the World/Dooley Jones	1979	—	2.00	4.00
4705	When You're in Love with a Beautiful Woman/ Knowing She's There	1979	—	2.00	4.00
4785	Better Love Next Time/Mountain Mary	1979	—	2.00	4.00
4831	Sexy Eyes/Help Me Mama	1980	—	2.00	4.00
4885	Years from Now/I Don't Feel Much Like Smilin'	1980	—	2.00	4.00
4885 [PS]	Years from Now/I Don't Feel Much Like Smilin'	1980	—	2.50	5.00

Number	Title (A Side/B Side)	Yr	VG	VG+	NM
CASABLANCA					
❑ 2314	Girls Can Get It/Doin' It	1980	—	2.00	4.00
❑ 2325	S.O.S. For Love/99 and Me	1981	—	2.00	4.00
❑ 2347	Baby Makes Her Blue Jeans Talk/The Turn On	1981	—	2.00	4.00
❑ 2347 [PS]	Baby Makes Her Blue Jeans Talk/The Turn On	1981	—	2.50	5.00
❑ 2351	Loveline/Pity the Fool	1981	—	2.00	4.00
COLUMBIA					
❑ 3-10032	Make It Easy/Ballad of Lucy Jordan	1974	—	3.00	6.00
—All as "Dr. Hook and the Medicine Show"					
❑ 4-45392	Last Morning/One More Ride (Lucille and Bunky)	1971	—	3.00	6.00
❑ 4-45562	Sylvia's Mother/Makin' It Natural	1972	—	3.00	6.00
—Orange label with "Columbia" background print					
❑ 4-45562	Sylvia's Mother/Makin' It Natural	1972	—	2.50	5.00
—Gray label					
❑ 4-45667	Carry Me, Carrie/Call That True Love	1972	—	2.50	5.00
❑ 4-45667 [PS]	Carry Me, Carrie/Call That True Love	1972	—	3.00	6.00
❑ 4-45732	The Cover of "Rolling Stone"/Queen of the Silver Dollar	1972	—	3.00	6.00
—Gray label					
❑ 4-45732	The Cover of "Rolling Stone"/Queen of the Silver Dollar	1972	—	2.50	5.00
—Orange label					
❑ 4-45878	Roland the Roadie and Gertrude the Groupie/Put a Little Bit on Me	1973	—	2.50	5.00
❑ 4-45925	Life Ain't Easy/Wonderful Stone Soup	1973	—	2.50	5.00
❑ 4-46026	Monterey Jack/Cops and Robbers	1974	—	2.50	5.00
Albums					
CAPITOL					
❑ ST-11397	Bankrupt	1975	2.50	5.00	10.00
❑ ST-11522	A Little Bit More	1976	2.50	5.00	10.00
❑ ST-11632	Makin' Love and Music	1977	2.50	5.00	10.00
❑ SW-11859	Pleasure and Pain	1978	2.50	5.00	10.00
❑ SOO-12018	Sometimes You Win...	1979	2.50	5.00	10.00
❑ ST-12114	Live	1981	2.50	5.00	10.00
❑ SOO-12122	Dr. Hook/Greatest Hits	1980	2.50	5.00	10.00
❑ ST-12325	The Best of Dr. Hook	1984	2.00	4.00	8.00
❑ SN-16179	Bankrupt	198?	2.00	4.00	8.00
—Budget-line reissue					
❑ SN-16180	A Little Bit More	198?	2.00	4.00	8.00
—Budget-line reissue					
❑ SN-16181	Pleasure and Pain	198?	2.00	4.00	8.00
—Budget-line reissue					
❑ SN-16228	Makin' Love and Music	198?	2.00	4.00	8.00
—Budget-line reissue					
❑ SN-16229	Sometimes You Win...	198?	2.00	4.00	8.00
—Budget-line reissue					
❑ SN-16325	Dr. Hook/Greatest Hits	198?	2.00	4.00	8.00
—Budget-line reissue					
CASABLANCA					
❑ NBLP-7251	Rising	1980	2.50	5.00	10.00
❑ NBLP-7264	Players in the Dark	1982	2.50	5.00	10.00
COLUMBIA					
❑ KC 30898	Dr. Hook & The Medicine Show	1972	3.75	7.50	15.00
❑ PC 30898	Dr. Hook & The Medicine Show	198?	2.00	4.00	8.00
—Budget-line reissue					
❑ KC 31622	Sloppy Seconds	1972	3.75	7.50	15.00
❑ PC 31622	Sloppy Seconds	198?	2.00	4.00	8.00
—Budget-line reissue					
❑ KC 32270	Belly Up!	1973	3.75	7.50	15.00
❑ C 34147	Dr. Hook and the Medicine Show Revisited	1976	2.50	5.00	10.00
❑ PC 34147	Dr. Hook and the Medicine Show Revisited	198?	2.00	4.00	8.00
—Budget-line reissue					
MERCURY					
❑ 800054-1	Players in the Dark	1983	2.00	4.00	8.00
—Reissue of Casablanca 7264					

DR. HOOK AND THE MEDICINE SHOW

See DR. HOOK.

DODD, DERYL

45s

Number	Title (A Side/B Side)	Yr	VG	VG+	NM
COLUMBIA					
❑ 38-78437	Friends Don't Drive Friends.../That's Just Me	1996	—	2.00	4.00
❑ 38-78478	That's How I Got to Memphis//Movin' Out to the Country/13 MWZ/This Ol' World (snippets)	1996	—	2.00	4.00

DODSON, DARRELL

45s

Number	Title (A Side/B Side)	Yr	VG	VG+	NM
SCR					
❑ 135	Lone Star Cowboy/(B-side unknown)	1977	2.00	4.00	8.00
❑ 139	Love Song Sing Along/One More Time	1977	2.00	4.00	8.00

DOLAN, MADONNA

45s

Number	Title (A Side/B Side)	Yr	VG	VG+	NM
TRUE					
❑ 92	The Home Team/(B-side unknown)	1988	—	3.00	6.00

DOLAN, RAMBLIN' JIMMIE

45s

Number	Title (A Side/B Side)	Yr	VG	VG+	NM
CAPITOL					
❑ F952	I'll Sail My Ship Alone/It Had to Come	1950	10.00	20.00	40.00
❑ F1150	Wham Bam/I'll Hate Myself Tomorrow	1950	7.50	15.00	30.00
❑ F1245	No Load of Trouble/I've Got the Craziest Feeling	1950	7.50	15.00	30.00
❑ F1302	R.F.D. Blues/I'll Make Believe	1950	7.50	15.00	30.00
❑ F1322	Hot Rod Race/Walking with the Blues	1950	7.50	15.00	30.00
❑ F1371	Many's the Time/Lost Love Blues	1951	7.50	15.00	30.00
❑ F1423	Wine, Women and Pink Elephants/I Always Play a Losing Hand	1951	7.50	15.00	30.00
❑ F1487	The Spider and the Fly/I'm Alone Because I Love You	1951	7.50	15.00	30.00
❑ F1633	Hot Rod Race/I'll Sail My Ship Alone	195?	5.00	10.00	20.00
—Early reissue					
❑ F1720	Juke Box Boogie/Sailor's Blues	1951	7.50	15.00	30.00
❑ F1832	Until I Die/Last Love Letter	1951	7.50	15.00	30.00
❑ F1970	Stingy/Trade Winds Never Lie	1952	6.25	12.50	25.00
❑ F2006	Got My Heart Set on You/There's a Blue Sky Way	1952	6.25	12.50	25.00
❑ F2118	Rubber Ball Heart/Rack Up the Balls, Boys	1952	6.25	12.50	25.00
❑ F2244	Hot Rod Mama/Nicotine Fits	1952	6.25	12.50	25.00
❑ F2367	Playin' Dominoes and Shootin' Dice/Memories and Heartaches	1953	6.25	12.50	25.00
❑ F2482	The Wheel That Does the Squeaking/I Can't Run Away	1953	6.25	12.50	25.00
❑ F2713	Tool Pusher on a Rotary Rig/If I Could Look Inside You	1954	6.25	12.50	25.00
❑ F2830	I'll Never Go Sailing Again/Looka Here Baby	1954	6.25	12.50	25.00
❑ F2977	A Sailor's Letter/I Wonder If I Can Lose the Blues This Way	1954	6.25	12.50	25.00
❑ F3157	Jolly Captain Huddlestead/What's Another Broken Heart	1955	5.00	10.00	20.00
❑ F3254	Black Denim Trousers and Motorcycle Boots/You Don't Love Me	1955	5.00	10.00	20.00
❑ F40261	All Alone in Texas/I'm Gonna Whittle You Down to My Size	1950	10.00	20.00	40.00
❑ F40287	Who's Kiddin' Who/I Ain't Gonna Bring My Bacon Home to You	1950	10.00	20.00	40.00
Selected 78s					
CAPITOL					
❑ 40213	Tennessee Baby/Good-Bye My One and Only	1949	5.00	10.00	20.00

DOLLAR, JOHNNY

45s

Number	Title (A Side/B Side)	Yr	VG	VG+	NM
CHART					
❑ 1057	Big Rig Rollin' Man/I've Gotta Stay High	1968	2.00	4.00	8.00
❑ 1070	Big Wheels Sing for Me/Wild Cherry	1969	2.00	4.00	8.00
❑ 5019	If I Get Low/Meeting of the Bored	1969	2.00	4.00	8.00
❑ 5035	Other Seeds to Sow/Rain Falls in Denver	1969	2.00	4.00	8.00
❑ 5049	Truck Driver's Lament/Changing Her Thinking	1969	2.00	4.00	8.00
❑ 5089	No More Truck Stops/Just a Swallow Away	1970	2.00	4.00	8.00
❑ 5116	Highway in the Sky/Gold Colored Glasses	1971	2.00	4.00	8.00
❑ 5135	If I Make the Front Door Woman/Rain Falls in Denver	1971	2.00	4.00	8.00
COLUMBIA					
❑ 4-43343	Tear Talk/Big Red (The Hound)	1965	2.50	5.00	10.00
❑ 4-43537	Stop the Start (Of Tears in My Heart)/You Ain't Wrong	1966	2.50	5.00	10.00
D					
❑ 1011	Walking Away/No Memories	1958	6.25	12.50	25.00
❑ 1185	Crawling Back to You/(B-side unknown)	1961	5.00	10.00	20.00
❑ 1229	Lonesome Trains/West Texas	1962	5.00	10.00	20.00
DATE					
❑ 1566	The Wheels Fell Off the Wagon Again/Watching Me Losing You	1967	2.00	4.00	8.00
❑ 1585	Everybody's Got to Be Somewhere/Did You Talk to Him Today	1967	2.00	4.00	8.00
❑ 1600	Do-Die/Forever Is Over	1968	2.00	4.00	8.00
DOT					
❑ 16961	Crazy Eyes/Windburn	1966	2.00	4.00	8.00
❑ 16990	Your Hands/Don't Take My Future from Me	1967	2.00	4.00	8.00
GEMINI					
❑ 1200	Do the Reindeer/Ringo	1964	3.75	7.50	15.00
Albums					
DATE					
❑ TEM 3009 [M]	Johnny Dollar	1967	6.25	12.50	25.00
❑ TES 4009 [S]	Johnny Dollar	1967	5.00	10.00	20.00

DOMINO, FATS

The legendary New Orleans piano-playing R&B and rock 'n' roll pioneer actually made the country charts with the below single.

45s

Number	Title (A Side/B Side)	Yr	VG	VG+	NM
WARNER BROS.					
❑ 49610	Whiskey Heaven/Beers to You	1980	—	2.00	4.00
—B-side by Texas Opera Company					

DON JUAN

45s

Number	Title (A Side/B Side)	Yr	VG	VG+	NM
MAXX					
❑ 821	We're Gonna Love Tonight/(B-side unknown)	1988	—	3.50	7.00
❑ 827	Let It Go/(B-side unknown)	1988	—	3.50	7.00

DONALDSON, CRAIG

45s

Number	Title (A Side/B Side)	Yr	VG	VG+	NM
GREAT AMERICAN					
❑ 281	I Believe He's Gonna Drive That Rig to Glory/I Believe He's Gonna Drive That Rig to Glory (Long Version)	1976	—	3.50	7.00

DOOLITTLE BAND, THE

See DANDY.

Number	Title (A Side/B Side)	Yr	VG	VG+	NM

DORSEY, GERRY
See ENGELBERT HUMPERDINCK.

DOTTSY
45s

RCA

Number	Title (A Side/B Side)	Yr	VG	VG+	NM
❑ PB-10766	Love Is a Two-Way Street/Lying in My Arms	1976	—	2.50	5.00
❑ PB-10982	(After Sweet Memories) Play Born to Lose Again/ Send Me the Pillow You Dream On	1977	—	2.50	5.00
❑ PB-11138	It Should Have Been Easy/Everybody's Reaching Out for Someone	1977	—	2.50	5.00
❑ PB-11203	Here in Love/A Good Love Is Like a Good Song	1978	—	2.50	5.00
❑ PB-11293	I Just Had You on My Mind/Just Remember Who Your Friends Are	1978	—	2.50	5.00
❑ PB-11448	Tryin' to Satisfy You/If I Only Had the Words (To Tell You)	1979	—	2.50	5.00
❑ PB-11610	Slip Away/Love Is a Two-Way Street	1979	—	2.50	5.00
❑ PB-11743	When I'm Gone/Storms Never Last	1979	—	2.50	5.00
RCA VICTOR					
❑ PB-10280	Storms Never Last/Follow Me	1975	—	2.50	5.00
❑ PB-10423	I'll Be Your San Antone Rose/If You Say It's So	1975	—	2.50	5.00
❑ PB-10666	The Sweetest Thing (I've Ever Known)/We Still Sing Love Songs Here in Texas	1976	—	2.50	5.00
TANGLEWOOD					
❑ 1908	Somebody's Darling, Somebody's Wife/Sing Me a Love Song	1981	—	3.00	6.00
❑ 1910	Let the Little Bird Fly/Love in My Baby's Eyes	1981	—	3.00	6.00
❑ 1912	Mama/Healing Hands of Time	1981	—	3.00	6.00

Albums

Number	Title (A Side/B Side)	Yr	VG	VG+	NM
RCA VICTOR					
❑ APL1-1358	The Sweetest Thing	1976	3.00	6.00	12.00
❑ AHL1-3380	Tryin' to Satisfy You	1979	3.00	6.00	12.00

DOUGLAS
See DOUG BLOCK.

DOUGLAS, JOE
45s

Number	Title (A Side/B Side)	Yr	VG	VG+	NM
D					
❑ 1315	You're Still on My Mind/Wine Flows Free	1978	2.00	4.00	8.00
FOXY CAJUN					
❑ 1001	Back Street Affair/Bollweevil	1980	—	3.50	7.00
❑ 1005	Leavin' You Is Easier (Than Wishing You Were Gone)/Louisiana Joe	1981	—	3.50	7.00

DOUGLAS, STEVE
45s

Number	Title (A Side/B Side)	Yr	VG	VG+	NM
DEMON					
❑ 1954	This Is True/Saying I'm Sorry	1980	—	3.50	7.00
DORMAN					
❑ 98915	To a San Antone Rose/Texas, I'm in Love with You	1989	—	3.50	7.00
❑ 981101	Funny Ways of Loving Me/Little Daughters	1989	—	3.50	7.00
TEXAS OPRY					
❑ 588	Tyke (The Christmas Elf)/(Instrumental)	198?	2.00	4.00	8.00

DOUGLAS, TONY
45s

Number	Title (A Side/B Side)	Yr	VG	VG+	NM
20TH CENTURY					
❑ 2257	If I Can Make It (Through the Mornin')/Honky-Tonk Man	1975	—	2.50	5.00
COCHISE					
❑ 100	Walkin' Over Yonder/Thank You for Touching My Life	1980	—	3.00	6.00
❑ 105	Her House/The Last Time I Saw Laura	1980	—	3.00	6.00
❑ 106	Waitin' for a Train/She Loves the Devil Out of Me	1980	—	3.00	6.00
❑ 110	Leanna/Layin' in the Sunshine	1980	—	3.00	6.00
❑ 113	Meridian/I'll Fight Every Step of the Way	1981	—	3.00	6.00
❑ 115	Walkin' Over Yonder/Thank You Lord for Makin' Her Mine	1981	—	3.00	6.00
❑ 116	That's Allright/Back to the Wind	1981	—	3.00	6.00
❑ 117	Let It Ride/(B-side unknown)	1981	—	3.00	6.00
❑ 118	His 'n' Hers/Shrimpin'	1981	—	3.00	6.00
❑ 119	Is Love Enough/Back to the Wind	1982	—	3.00	6.00
❑ 121	Angola Chains/Camp Meetin' Song	1982	—	3.00	6.00
DOT					
❑ 17443	Thank You for Touching My Life/Walkin' Over Yonder	1972	—	3.00	6.00
❑ 17464	My Last Day/I'll Fight Every Step of the Way	1973	—	3.00	6.00
❑ 17503	Love Her When She's Lonely/Rainbows, Wishing Wells	1974	—	3.00	6.00
PAULA					
❑ 268	Driven by Loneliness/The Fastest Gun Alive	1967	2.50	5.00	10.00
❑ 278	Heart/Keep Your Little Eyes on Me	1967	2.50	5.00	10.00
❑ 290	I'm a One Woman Man/Mention My Name	1968	2.50	5.00	10.00
❑ 304	Love Is the Reason/Me and My Lonely	1968	2.50	5.00	10.00
❑ 395	His and Hers/There Stands the Man	1974	—	2.50	5.00
❑ 1203	Did I Say Something Wrong/In the Time It Takes to Leave	1968	2.50	5.00	10.00
❑ 1212	That's What I Get/Family Bouquet	1969	2.50	5.00	10.00
❑ 1220	His and Hers/Your Goodbye	1970	2.00	4.00	8.00
❑ 1225	There Stands the Man/State Trooper Sammy Young	1970	2.00	4.00	8.00
❑ 1234	The Man/No Joy in My World	1970	2.00	4.00	8.00
SIMS					
❑ 160	It's Just About Time/Home Away from Home	1964	3.75	7.50	15.00
❑ 187	Your Love for Me Is Losing Light/Hey Waiter	1964	3.75	7.50	15.00
❑ 221	Big Ache of the Year/I'm Happy	1965	3.75	7.50	15.00
❑ 236	Take the Hands Off the Clock/(B-side unknown)	1965	3.75	7.50	15.00
❑ 255	Itsy Bitsy Heartache/It Didn't Help Much	1965	3.75	7.50	15.00
❑ 271	Empty Crowded Room/Poor Little Darling	1966	3.75	7.50	15.00
❑ 286	Thanks a Lot/(B-side unknown)	1966	3.75	7.50	15.00
❑ 294	Don't Piddle 'Round the Puddle/I Can't Forget Your Memory	1966	3.75	7.50	15.00
VEE JAY					
❑ 481	His and Hers/Gabby Abby	1963	5.00	10.00	20.00

Albums

Number	Title (A Side/B Side)	Yr	VG	VG+	NM
DOT					
❑ DLP-26009	Thank You for Touching My Life	1973	3.75	7.50	15.00
PAULA					
❑ LP 2198	Heart	1967	5.00	10.00	20.00

DOVE, RONNIE
45s

Number	Title (A Side/B Side)	Yr	VG	VG+	NM
DECCA					
❑ 31288	Yes Darling, I'll Be Around/Party Doll	1961	5.00	10.00	20.00
❑ 32853	Just the Other Side of Nowhere/If I Cried	1971	—	3.00	6.00
❑ 32919	Kiss the Hurt Away/He Cries Like a Baby	1972	—	3.00	6.00
❑ 32997	It's No Sin/My World of Memories	1972	—	3.00	6.00
❑ 33038	Lilacs in Winter/Is It Wrong	1972	—	3.00	6.00
DIAMOND					
❑ 163	Sweeter Than Sugar/I Believe in You	1964	2.50	5.00	10.00
❑ 167	Say You/Let Me Stay Today	1964	2.50	5.00	10.00
❑ 173	Right or Wrong/Baby Put Your Arms Around Me	1964	2.00	4.00	8.00
❑ 176	Hello Pretty Girl/Keep It a Secret	1965	2.00	4.00	8.00
❑ 179	One Kiss for Old Times' Sake/No Greater Love	1965	2.00	4.00	8.00
❑ 179	One Kiss for Old Times' Sake/Bluebird	1965	2.00	4.00	8.00
❑ 184	A Little Bit of Heaven/If I Live to Be a Hundred	1965	2.00	4.00	8.00
❑ 188	I'll Make All Your Dreams Come True/I Had to Lose You	1965	2.00	4.00	8.00
❑ 191	Kiss Away/Where in the World	1965	2.00	4.00	8.00
❑ 195	When Liking Turns to Loving/I'm Learning How to Smile Again	1965	2.00	4.00	8.00
❑ 198	Let's Start All Over Again/That Empty Feeling	1966	2.00	4.00	8.00
❑ 205	Happy Summer Days/Long After	1966	2.00	4.00	8.00
❑ 205 [PS]	Happy Summer Days/Long After	1966	3.75	7.50	15.00
❑ 208	I Really Don't Want to Know/Years of Tears	1966	2.00	4.00	8.00
❑ 214	Cry/Autumn Rhapsody	1966	2.00	4.00	8.00
❑ 217	One More Mountain to Climb/All	1967	2.00	4.00	8.00
❑ 221	My Babe/Put My Mind at Ease	1967	2.50	5.00	10.00
—A-side written and produced by Neil Diamond					
❑ 227	I Want to Love You for What You Are/I Thank You for Your Love	1967	2.00	4.00	8.00
❑ 233	Dancin' Out of My Heart/Back from Baltimore	1967	5.00	10.00	20.00
—B-side written and produced by Neil Diamond, who also supplies backing vocals					
❑ 240	In Some Time/Livin' for Your Lovin'	1968	2.00	4.00	8.00
❑ 244	Mountain of Love/Never Gonna Cry	1968	2.00	4.00	8.00
❑ 249	Tomboy/Tell Me Tomorrow	1968	2.00	4.00	8.00
❑ 256	What's Wrong with My World/That Empty Feeling	1969	—	3.00	6.00
❑ 260	I Need You Now/Bluebird	1969	—	3.00	6.00
❑ 271	Chains of Love/If I Live to Be a Hundred	1970	—	3.00	6.00
❑ 378	Heart/(B-side unknown)	1987	—	2.50	5.00
❑ 378 [PS]	Heart/(B-side unknown)	1987	—	2.50	5.00
❑ 379	Rise and Shine/(B-side unknown)	1987	—	2.50	5.00
DOVE					
❑ 1021	Lover Boy/(B-side unknown)	1955	250.00	500.00	1000.
HITSVILLE					
❑ 6038	Tragedy/Songs We Sang As Children	1976	—	2.50	5.00
❑ 6045	The Morning After the Night Before/Why Daddy	1976	—	2.50	5.00
JALO					
❑ 1406	No Greater Love/Saddest Hour	1962	6.25	12.50	25.00
MCA					
❑ 40106	So Long Dixie/Take My Love	1973	—	2.50	5.00
MELODYLAND					
❑ 6004	Please Come to Nashville/Pictures on Paper	1975	—	2.50	5.00
❑ 6011	Things/Here We Go Again	1975	—	2.50	5.00
❑ 6021	Drina (Take Your Lady Off for Me)/Your Sweet Love	1975	—	2.50	5.00
❑ 6030	Right or Wrong/Guns	1976	—	2.50	5.00
M.C.					
❑ 5013	The Angel in Your Eyes (Brings Out the Devil in Me)/Songs We Sang As Children	1978	—	3.00	6.00

Albums

Number	Title (A Side/B Side)	Yr	VG	VG+	NM
DIAMOND					
❑ D 5002 [M]	Right Or Wrong	1964	5.00	10.00	20.00
❑ DS 5002 [S]	Right Or Wrong	1964	6.25	12.50	25.00
❑ D 5003 [M]	One Kiss for Old Times' Sake	1965	5.00	10.00	20.00
❑ DS 5003 [S]	One Kiss for Old Times' Sake	1965	6.25	12.50	25.00
❑ D 5004 [M]	I'll Make All Your Dreams Come True	1965	5.00	10.00	20.00
❑ DS 5004 [S]	I'll Make All Your Dreams Come True	1965	6.25	12.50	25.00
❑ D 5005 [M]	The Best of Ronnie Dove	1966	3.75	7.50	15.00
❑ DS 5005 [S]	The Best of Ronnie Dove	1966	5.00	10.00	20.00
❑ D 5006 [M]	Ronnie Dove Sings the Hits for You	1966	3.75	7.50	15.00
❑ DS 5006 [S]	Ronnie Dove Sings the Hits for You	1966	5.00	10.00	20.00
❑ D 5007 [M]	Cry	1967	3.75	7.50	15.00
❑ DS 5007 [S]	Cry	1967	5.00	10.00	20.00
❑ D-5008 [M]	Ronne Dove's Greatest Hits, Vol. 2	1968	7.50	15.00	30.00
❑ DS-5008 [S]	Ronne Dove's Greatest Hits, Vol. 2	1968	3.75	7.50	15.00

Number	Title (A Side/B Side)	Yr	VG	VG+	NM
POWER PAK					
❑ 286	Greatest Hits	1975	3.00	6.00	12.00

DOWN HOMERS, THE

Also see KENNY ROBERTS. According to Roberts himself in an address at the 1999 Association of Vogue Picture Record Collectors convention, Bill Haley does NOT appear on these records. Haley had left the group to start his own band shortly before they were recorded. The values quoted here reflect this new evidence.

Selected 78s

Number	Title (A Side/B Side)	Yr	VG	VG+	NM
VOGUE					
❑ R736	Out Where the West Winds Blow/Who's Gonna Kiss You When I'm Gone	1946	20.00	40.00	80.00
—Picture record; A-side co-credited to Kenny Roberts					
❑ R786	Baby I Found Out All About You/Boogie Woogie Yodel	1947	25.00	50.00	100.00
—Picture record					

DOWNEY, MORTON, JR.

45s

Number	Title (A Side/B Side)	Yr	VG	VG+	NM
ARTISTS OF AMERICA					
❑ 109	He Played a Yo-Yo in Nashville/You'll Never Have to Ask Me If I Love You	1976	—	2.50	5.00
—As "Sean Morton Downey"					
❑ 123	He Played a Yo-Yo in Nashville/You'll Never Have to Ask Me If I Love You	1976	—	2.00	4.00
—As "Sean Morton Downey"					
❑ 124	You Made Me Love You/As Time Goes By	1976	—	2.00	4.00
—As "Sean Morton Downey"					
BULLDOG					
❑ 105	A Tear Fell in the Chapel/Tender Years	1959	3.75	7.50	15.00
—As "Sean Downey"					
CADENCE					
❑ 1407	The Ballad of Billy Brown/Flattery	1961	2.50	5.00	10.00
CONTENDER					
❑ 1317	Love Bug/Rags to Riches	1959	3.75	7.50	15.00
CUB					
❑ 9004	You Let Go/Hearts Are Wild	1958	3.00	6.00	12.00
—As "Sean Downey"					
ESO					
❑ 932	Green Eyed Girl/(B-side unknown)	1981	2.00	4.00	8.00
—As "Sean Morton Downey"					
IMPERIAL					
❑ 5556	Boulevard of Broken Dreams/Proud Possession	1958	2.50	5.00	10.00
LAKE ERIE					
❑ (# unknown)	Cleveland's Coming Back Again/(B-side unknown)	197?	2.00	4.00	8.00
MAGIC LAMP					
❑ 517	The Ballad of Billy Brown/Flattery	1964	2.00	4.00	8.00
NRLC					
❑ 1977	Got a Right to Live/Theme for Life	197?	—	3.00	6.00
PERSONALITY					
❑ 3506	Little Miss U.S.A./Football Freddy	1959	3.00	6.00	12.00
PRIVATE STOCK					
❑ 45168	Family Tree/Spanish Harlem	1977	—	2.00	4.00
SCEPTER					
❑ 12316	Love Theme from Christine/Christine's a Lady	1971	—	3.00	6.00
—As "Sean Morton Downey, Jr."					
❑ 12360	Break the Habit of Hate/Second Chance Lord	1972	—	3.00	6.00
—As "Sean Downey"					
STAX					
❑ 0195	I Believe in America/My Last Day on Earth	1974	—	2.00	4.00
—As "Sean Downey"					
WYE					
❑ 1010	I Beg Your Pardon/Three Steps to the Phone	1961	3.00	6.00	12.00

Albums

Number	Title (A Side/B Side)	Yr	VG	VG+	NM
ARTISTS OF AMERICA					
❑ AOA-5005	You'll Never Ask Me If I Love You	1976	3.00	6.00	12.00
COMPOSE					
❑ 9901	Morton Downey Jr. Sings!	1989	3.75	7.50	15.00

DOWNEY, PAUL

45s

Number	Title (A Side/B Side)	Yr	VG	VG+	NM
HICKORY					
❑ 1632	Camp Meeting, U.S.A./Love	1972	—	3.50	7.00

DOWNEY, SEAN; DOWNEY, SEAN MORTON

See MORTON DOWNEY, JR.

DOWNING, BIG AL

45s

Number	Title (A Side/B Side)	Yr	VG	VG+	NM
CARLTON					
❑ 489	Miss Lucy/Just Around the Corner	1959	12.50	25.00	50.00
❑ 507	It Must Be Love/When My Blue Moon Turns to Gold Again	1959	10.00	20.00	40.00
CHALLENGE					
❑ 59006	Down on the Farm/Oh Babe	1958	12.50	25.00	50.00
CHESS					
❑ 1817	The Story of My Life/I'd Love to Be Loved	1962	3.00	6.00	12.00
❑ 2158	I'll Be Holding On/Baby Let's Talk It Over	1974	—	2.50	5.00
COLUMBIA					
❑ 43028	I'm Just Nobody/All I Want Is You	1964	2.50	5.00	10.00
❑ 43185	I Feel Good/Georgia Slop	1964	2.50	5.00	10.00
DOOR KNOB					
❑ 328	I Guess By Now/(B-side unknown)	1989	—	2.50	5.00
❑ 340	Bound for Baltimore/(B-side unknown)	1989	—	2.50	5.00
❑ 345	Father #1/(B-side unknown)	1989	—	2.50	5.00
JANUS					
❑ 211	Thank You Baby/(B-side unknown)	1974	—	3.00	6.00
❑ 234	I'll Be Holding On/Hands	1974	—	3.00	6.00
LENOX					
❑ 5565	You Never Miss Your Water (Till the Well Runs Dry)/If You Want It (I Got It)	1963	3.00	6.00	12.00
—As "Little Esther Phillips and Big Al Downing"					
❑ 5572	Mr. Hurt Walked In/If I Had Our Love to Live Over	1963	3.00	6.00	12.00
POLYDOR					
❑ 14311	I Love to Love/I'm Just Nobody	1976	—	2.50	5.00
SILVER FOX					
❑ 3	Cornbreak Row/The Saints	1969	2.00	4.00	8.00
❑ 11	Medley of Soul/These Arms You Push Away	1969	2.00	4.00	8.00
TEAM					
❑ 1001	I'll Be Loving You/Don't Mess with an Angel	1982	—	2.50	5.00
❑ 1002	Darlene/(B-side unknown)	1982	—	2.50	5.00
❑ 1003	Let's Sing About Love/We Can Only Say Goodbye	1983	—	2.50	5.00
❑ 1004	It Takes Love/If You're Leaving	1983	—	2.50	5.00
❑ 1007	The Best of Families/Fool of the Year	1983	—	2.50	5.00
❑ 1008	There'll Never Be a Better Night for Bein' Wrong/(B-side unknown)	1984	—	2.50	5.00
V-TONE					
❑ 215	Yes, I'm Loving You/Please Come Home	1960	3.00	6.00	12.00
❑ 220	If I Had Our Love to Live Over/Words of Love	1961	3.00	6.00	12.00
❑ 230	So Many Memories/There'll Come a Time	1961	3.00	6.00	12.00
VINE ST.					
❑ 103	How Beautiful You Are (To Me)/The Only Thing Missing Is You	1986	—	3.00	6.00
❑ 105	Just One Night Won't Do/How Beautiful You Are (To Me)	1987	—	3.00	6.00
❑ 106	How Ya Gonna Do It/The Only Thing Missing Is You	1987	—	3.00	6.00
WARNER BROS.					
❑ 8716	Mr. Jones/I Don't Cry (The Onion Song)	1978	—	2.50	5.00
❑ 8787	Touch Me (I'll Be Your Fool Once More)/I Ain't No Fool	1979	—	2.50	5.00
❑ 49034	Midnight Lace/Counting Highway Signs	1979	—	2.00	4.00
❑ 49141	I Ain't No Fool/Mr, Jones	1979	—	2.00	4.00
❑ 49161	The Story Behind the Story/Daddy Played the Banjo	1980	—	2.00	4.00
❑ 49270	Bring It On Home/Beer Drinking People	1980	—	2.00	4.00
WHITE ROCK					
❑ 1111	Down on the Farm/Oh Babe	1958	37.50	75.00	150.00
❑ 1113	Miss Lucy/Just Around the Corner	1958	37.50	75.00	150.00

Albums

Number	Title (A Side/B Side)	Yr	VG	VG+	NM
TEAM					
❑ 2001	Big Al Downing	1982	3.00	6.00	12.00

DOWNS, LAVERNE

45s

Number	Title (A Side/B Side)	Yr	VG	VG+	NM
PEACH					
❑ 735	But You Used To/What Have I Done	1960	5.00	10.00	20.00

DOYLE, BOBBY, THREE

KENNY ROGERS was in this group.

Albums

Number	Title (A Side/B Side)	Yr	VG	VG+	NM
COLUMBIA					
❑ CL 1858 [M]	In a Most Unusual Way	1962	10.00	20.00	40.00
❑ CS 8658 [S]	In a Most Unusual Way	1962	12.50	25.00	50.00

DRAKE, GUY

45s

Number	Title (A Side/B Side)	Yr	VG	VG+	NM
ROYAL AMERICAN					
❑ 1	Welfare Cadillac/Keep Off My Grass	1970	—	3.50	7.00
❑ 15	Politickin' Pete/Born to Be an Opry Star	1970	—	3.50	7.00

Albums

Number	Title (A Side/B Side)	Yr	VG	VG+	NM
ROYAL AMERICAN					
❑ 1001	Welfare Cadillac	1970	6.25	12.50	25.00

DRAKE, PETE

45s

Number	Title (A Side/B Side)	Yr	VG	VG+	NM
SMASH					
❑ 1867	Forever/Sleepwalk	1964	2.00	4.00	8.00
❑ 1888	Midnight in Amarillo/Forever	1964	2.00	4.00	8.00
❑ 1910	I'm Sorry/I'm Just a Guitar (Everybody Picks On Me)	1964	2.00	4.00	8.00
❑ 1935	I'm Walkin'/Are You Sincere	1964	2.00	4.00	8.00
❑ 1978	Dream/Am I That Easy to Forget	1965	2.00	4.00	8.00
❑ 2046	I'm a Fool to Care/Mystic Dream	1966	2.00	4.00	8.00
STARDAY					
❑ 751	My Abilene/Y'All Come	1966	2.00	4.00	8.00
STOP					
❑ 222	Joggin'/Mama's Talkin' Guitar	1968	—	3.00	6.00
❑ 349	Lay Lady Lay/For Pete's Sake	1970	—	3.00	6.00

Number	Title (A Side/B Side)	Yr	VG	VG+	NM
DRAPER, RUSTY					
45s					
KL					
❑ 001	Harbor Lights/(B-side unknown)	1979	—	2.00	4.00
MERCURY					
❑ 5820	Just Because/How Could You (Blue Eyes)	1952	3.75	7.50	15.00
❑ 5851	Devil of a Woman/Bouncing on the Bayou	1952	3.75	7.50	15.00
❑ 5894	Sing Baby Sing/I Gotta Have My Baby Back	1952	3.75	7.50	15.00
❑ 70004	Angry/Blue Tears	1952	3.00	6.00	12.00
❑ 70077	No Help Wanted/Texarkana Baby	1953	3.00	6.00	12.00
❑ 70167	Gambler's Guitar/Free Home Demonstration	1953	3.00	6.00	12.00
❑ 70178	Lazy River/Bummin' Around	1953	3.00	6.00	12.00
❑ 70256	Native Dancer/Lonesome Song	1953	3.00	6.00	12.00
❑ 70300	Peter Rabbit/Easter Morning	1954	3.00	6.00	12.00
❑ 70327	The Train with a Rhumba Beat/Melancholy Baby	1954	3.00	6.00	12.00
❑ 70365	It Ain't Me Baby/Knock on Wood	1954	3.00	6.00	12.00
❑ 70415	Please, Please/Workshop of the Lord	1954	3.00	6.00	12.00
❑ 70446	Muskrat Ramble/The Magic Circle	1954	3.00	6.00	12.00
❑ 70526	Lookin' Back to See/Shame on You	1955	3.00	6.00	12.00
❑ 70555	The Ballad of Davy Crockett/I've Been Thinkin'	1955	3.75	7.50	15.00
❑ 70619	Eating Goober Peas/That's All I Need	1955	3.00	6.00	12.00
❑ 70651	Seventeen/Can't Live Without Them Anymore	1955	3.00	6.00	12.00
❑ 70696	The Shifting, Whispering Sands/Time	1955	2.50	5.00	10.00
❑ 70757	Are You Satisfied/Wabash Cannonball	1955	2.50	5.00	10.00
❑ 70818	Held for Questioning/Forty-Two	1956	2.50	5.00	10.00
❑ 70853	Sometimes You Win, Sometimes You Lose/The Gun of Billy the Kid	1956	2.50	5.00	10.00
❑ 70879	Rock and Roll Baby/House of Cards	1956	3.75	7.50	15.00
❑ 70921	In the Middle of the House/Pink Cadillac	1956	2.50	5.00	10.00
❑ 70938	Giant/Old Buttermilk Sky	1956	3.75	7.50	15.00
❑ 71039	Let's Go Calypso/Should I Ever Love Again	1957	2.50	5.00	10.00
❑ 71102	Freight Train/Seven Come Eleven	1957	2.50	5.00	10.00
❑ 71162	No Hu Hu/Good Golly	1957	2.50	5.00	10.00
❑ 71221	Buzz Buzz Buzz/I Get the Blues When It Rains	1957	2.50	5.00	10.00
❑ 71298	Gamblin' Gal/That's My Doll	1958	2.50	5.00	10.00
❑ 71336	June, July and August/Chicken-Pluckin' Hawk	1958	2.50	5.00	10.00
❑ 71351	Hip Monkey/Can You Depend on Me	1958	2.50	5.00	10.00
❑ 71388	With This Ring/Shopping Around	1958	2.50	5.00	10.00
❑ 71418	Hey Li Lee Li Lee Li/The Sun Will Always Shine	1959	2.50	5.00	10.00
❑ 71463	Next Stop Paradise/Don't Forget Your Shoes	1959	2.50	5.00	10.00
❑ 71545	I Get So Jealous/But For the Flow of Flo	1959	2.50	5.00	10.00
❑ 71564	Two of a Kind/If My Mother'd Only Let Me Cross the Street	1960	2.00	4.00	8.00
❑ 71581	That Lucky Old Sun/Any Time	1960	2.00	4.00	8.00
❑ 71634	Please Help Me, I'm Falling/Mule Skinner Blues	1960	2.00	4.00	8.00
❑ 71664	It's a Little More Like Heaven/Luck of the Irish	1960	2.00	4.00	8.00
❑ 71706	Jealous Heart/Ten Thousand Years Ago	1960	2.00	4.00	8.00
❑ 71784	Another/The Meadow	1961	2.00	4.00	8.00
❑ 71854	Signed, Sealed and Delivered/Scared to Go Home	1961	2.00	4.00	8.00
❑ 71914	Well I've Learned/Tongue Tied Over You	1961	2.00	4.00	8.00
❑ 71976	Beggar to a King/Deep Roots	1962	2.00	4.00	8.00
MONUMENT					
❑ 823	Night Life/That's Why I Love You Like I Do	1963	—	3.50	7.00
❑ 832	It Should Be Easier Now/Lady of the House	1964	—	3.50	7.00
❑ 843	The Puppeteer/My Baby's Not Here (In Town Tonight)	1964	—	3.50	7.00
❑ 858	I'm Worried About Me/When I've Learned	1964	—	3.50	7.00
❑ 871	I Got What I Wanted/Love Don't Grow on Trees	1965	—	3.50	7.00
❑ 894	Folsom Prison Blues/You Can't Be True, Dear	1965	—	3.50	7.00
❑ 944	Mystery Train/The Shifting, Whispering Sands	1966	—	3.00	6.00
❑ 969	Love Is Gone for Good/You Call Everybody Darling	1966	—	3.00	6.00
❑ 1019	My Elusive Dreams/Memory Lane	1967	—	3.00	6.00
❑ 1044	California Sunshine/The Gypsy	1968	—	3.00	6.00
❑ 1074	Buffalo Nickel/Make Believe I'm Him	1968	—	3.00	6.00
❑ 1116	Love Is Just a Game/Something Old, Something New	1968	—	3.00	6.00
❑ 1137	Don't Build No Fences for Me/Am I That Easy to Forget	1969	—	3.00	6.00
❑ 1157	I Walk Alone/Sunshine Man	1969	—	3.00	6.00
❑ 1188	Two Little Boys/It Don't Mean a Thing to Me	1970	—	2.50	5.00
❑ 1202	Every Man Has a Prison/Tie Me to Your Apron Strings Again	1970	—	2.50	5.00
❑ 1223	There She Goes/Travelling Song	1970	—	2.50	5.00
❑ 8628	Walking on New Grass/You Were Right	1974	—	2.00	4.00
Albums					
GOLDEN CREST					
❑ 31029	The Rusty Draper Show	1973	3.00	6.00	12.00
❑ 31030	Tour the USA	1973	3.00	6.00	12.00
MERCURY					
❑ MG-20068 [M]	Music for a Rainy Night	1956	7.50	15.00	30.00
❑ MG-20117 [M]	Encores	1957	7.50	15.00	30.00
❑ MG-20118 [M]	Rusty Draper Sings	1957	7.50	15.00	30.00
❑ MG-20173 [M]	Rusty Meets Hoagy	1957	7.50	15.00	30.00
❑ MG-20499 [M]	Hits That Sold a Million	1960	7.50	15.00	30.00
❑ MG-20657 [M]	Country and Western Golden Greats	1961	7.50	15.00	30.00
❑ SR-60176 [S]	Hits That Sold a Million	1960	10.00	20.00	40.00
❑ SR-60657 [S]	Country and Western Golden Greats	1961	10.00	20.00	40.00
MONUMENT					
❑ 6638	Greatest Hits	1977	3.00	6.00	12.00
❑ MLP-8005 [M]	Greatest Hits	1964	3.75	7.50	15.00
❑ MLP-8018 [M]	Night Life	1964	3.75	7.50	15.00
❑ MLP-8026 [M]	Rusty Draper Plays Guitar	1965	3.75	7.50	15.00
❑ SLP-18005 [S]	Greatest Hits	1964	5.00	10.00	20.00
❑ SLP-18018 [S]	Night Life	1964	5.00	10.00	20.00
❑ SLP-18026 [S]	Rusty Draper Plays Guitar	1965	5.00	10.00	20.00
❑ SLP-18105	Something Old, Something New	1969	3.75	7.50	15.00
❑ ZG 33870 [(2)]	Swingin' Country/Something Old, Something New	1976	3.75	7.50	15.00
WING					
❑ MGW-12243 [M]	Hits That Sold a Million	196?	3.75	7.50	15.00
❑ MGW-12274 [M]	Country Classics	196?	3.75	7.50	15.00
❑ SRW-16243 [S]	Hits That Sold a Million	196?	3.75	7.50	15.00
❑ SRW-16274 [S]	Country Classics	196?	3.75	7.50	15.00
DRESSER, LEE					
45s					
AIR INT'L.					
❑ 10021	The Hero/All I Have to Do	1983	—	2.50	5.00
❑ 10022	Feelings Feelin' Right/(B-side unknown)	1983	—	2.50	5.00
CAPITOL					
❑ 4529	You're All the Woman I'll Ever Need/Fallin'	1978	—	2.50	5.00
❑ 4613	A Beautiful Song (For a Beautiful Lady)/The Man Up in the Mansion	1978	—	2.50	5.00
❑ 4708	Let's Love Tonight/Someone Who Loved You Just Like Me	1979	—	2.50	5.00
DRIFTING COWBOYS, THE					
Backing band for HANK WILLIAMS. Also see JIM OWEN.					
45s					
EPIC					
❑ 8-50543	Rag Mop/Mud Hut	1978	—	3.00	6.00
MGM					
❑ K11497	Mud Hut/Corn Crib	1953	6.25	12.50	25.00
❑ K11590	Canal Street Parade/Swing Shift Boogie	1953	6.25	12.50	25.00
❑ K11691	Fish Tail/Rock Point	1954	6.25	12.50	25.00
Albums					
MGM					
❑ SE-4626	We Remember Hank Williams	1968	5.00	10.00	20.00
DRIFTWOOD, JIMMIE					
45s					
MONUMENT					
❑ 825	Lonesome Ape/What Is the Color of the Soul of Man	1963	3.00	6.00	12.00
RCA VICTOR					
❑ 47-7534	The Battle of New Orleans/Damyankee Lad	1959	3.75	7.50	15.00
❑ 47-7571	The Answer to The Battle of New Orleans/Sal's Got a Sugar Lip	1959	3.75	7.50	15.00
❑ 47-7603	John Paul Jones/The Bear Flew Over the Ocean	1959	3.75	7.50	15.00
Albums					
MONUMENT					
❑ MLP-8006 [M]	Voice of the People	1963	5.00	10.00	20.00
❑ MLP-8019 [M]	Down in the Arkansas	1965	5.00	10.00	20.00
❑ SLP-18006 [S]	Voice of the People	1963	6.25	12.50	25.00
❑ SLP-18019 [S]	Down in the Arkansas	1965	6.25	12.50	25.00
RCA VICTOR					
❑ LPM-1635 [M]	Newly Discovered Early American Folk Songs	1958	12.50	25.00	50.00
❑ LPM-1994 [M]	Jimmie Driftwood and the Wilderness Road	1959	7.50	15.00	30.00
❑ LSP-1994 [S]	Jimmie Driftwood and the Wilderness Road	1959	10.00	20.00	40.00
❑ LPM-2171 [M]	The Westward Movement	1960	7.50	15.00	30.00
❑ LSP-2171 [S]	The Westward Movement	1960	10.00	20.00	40.00
❑ LPM-2228 [M]	Tall Tales in Song	1960	7.50	15.00	30.00
❑ LSP-2228 [S]	Tall Tales in Song	1960	10.00	20.00	40.00
❑ LPM-2316 [M]	Songs of Billy Yank and Johnny Reb	1961	7.50	15.00	30.00
❑ LSP-2316 [S]	Songs of Billy Yank and Johnny Reb	1961	10.00	20.00	40.00
❑ LPM-2443 [M]	Driftwood at Sea	1962	7.50	15.00	30.00
❑ LSP-2443 [S]	Driftwood at Sea	1962	10.00	20.00	40.00
DRUMM, DON					
45s					
CASINO					
❑ 106	Lonely Hours Lady/(B-side unknown)	1976	—	2.50	5.00
CHART					
❑ 5223	In at Eight and Out at Ten/Baby's Gone	1974	—	3.00	6.00
CHURCHILL					
❑ 7704	Bedroom Eyes/Stormy	1977	—	2.50	5.00
❑ 7710	Just Another Rhinestone/If Her Love Was a Window	1978	—	2.50	5.00
❑ 7717	Something to Believe In/Sad Songs	1978	—	2.50	5.00
DRUSKY, ROY					
Also see KITTY WELLS.					
45s					
CAPITOL					
❑ 3859	Close to Home/One Day at a Time	1974	—	3.00	6.00
❑ 3942	Dixie Lily/If I Could Paint the World	1974	—	3.00	6.00
❑ 4028	I'm Knee Deep in Loving You/The Baptism of Jesse Taylor	1975	—	3.00	6.00
❑ 4132	Sunrise/Warm, Warm Bed	1975	—	3.00	6.00
❑ 4232	When My Room Gets Dark Again/This Life of Mine	1976	—	3.00	6.00
❑ 4281	Battle for Daddy's Soul/Never Before	1976	—	3.00	6.00
COLUMBIA					
❑ 4-21478	Come On Back and Love Me/What Am I Worth	1955	5.00	10.00	20.00
❑ 4-21516	I Just Can't Help Me Lovin' You/So in Love Again	1956	5.00	10.00	20.00

Number	Title (A Side/B Side)	Yr	VG	VG+	NM
❑ 4-21537	Three Blind Mice/I'll Make Amends	1956	5.00	10.00	20.00
❑ 4-40830	That's When My Heartaches Began/God Planned It That Way	1957	5.00	10.00	20.00
❑ 4-40964	Walkin'/I Walk to Heaven	1957	5.00	10.00	20.00

DECCA

Number	Title (A Side/B Side)	Yr	VG	VG+	NM
❑ 30793	Wait and See/Just About That Time	1958	3.75	7.50	15.00
❑ 30943	Such a Fool/Our Church — Your Wedding	1959	3.75	7.50	15.00
❑ 31024	Another/The Same Corner	1959	3.75	7.50	15.00
❑ 31109	Anymore/I'm So Helpless	1960	3.75	7.50	15.00
❑ 31193	Three Hearts in a Tangle/I'd Rather Loan You Out	1961	3.00	6.00	12.00
❑ 31297	I Went Out of My Way (To Make You Happy)/I've Got Some	1961	3.00	6.00	12.00
❑ 31366	There's Always One (Who Loves a Lot)/Marking Time	1962	3.00	6.00	12.00
❑ 31411	After You Turn Out Your Light/I'm Not Getting Over You	1962	3.00	6.00	12.00
❑ 31443	Second Hand Rose/It Worries Me	1962	3.00	6.00	12.00
❑ 31486	Divided Love/She Never Cried When She Was Mine	1963	2.50	5.00	10.00
❑ 31717	Summer, Winter, Spring and Fall/Almost Can't	1964	2.50	5.00	10.00

MERCURY

Number	Title (A Side/B Side)	Yr	VG	VG+	NM
❑ 72204	Peel Me a Nanner/The Room Across the Hall	1963	2.50	5.00	10.00
❑ 72204 [PS]	Peel Me a Nanner/The Room Across the Hall	1963	5.00	10.00	20.00
❑ 72265	Pick of the Week/Yesterday	1964	2.50	5.00	10.00
❑ 72325	All for the Love of a Girl/So Much Got Lost	1964	2.50	5.00	10.00
❑ 72376	(From Now On All My Friends Are Gonna Be) Strangers/Birmingham Jail	1964	2.50	5.00	10.00
❑ 72471	White Lightnin' Express/Lonely Thing Called Me	1965	2.00	4.00	8.00
❑ 72532	Rainbows and Roses/A Thing Called Sadness	1966	2.00	4.00	8.00
❑ 72561	Rainbows and Roses/Too Many Dollars	1966	2.00	4.00	8.00
❑ 72586	The World Is Round/Unless You Make His Set You Free	1966	2.00	4.00	8.00
❑ 72627	If the Whole World Stopped Lovin'/Too Many Fingerprints	1966	2.00	4.00	8.00
❑ 72689	New Lips/Now	1967	2.00	4.00	8.00
❑ 72742	Weakness in a Man/I've Got a Right to the Blues	1967	2.00	4.00	8.00
❑ 72784	You Better Sit Down Kids/Let's Put Our World Back Together	1968	2.00	4.00	8.00
❑ 72823	Jody and the Kid/Your Little Deeds of Kindness	1968	2.00	4.00	8.00
❑ 72865	I Wouldn't Be Alone/Memphis Morning	1968	2.00	4.00	8.00
❑ 72886	Where the Blue and Lonely Go/I'm Gonna Get You Off My Mind	1969	2.00	4.00	8.00
❑ 72928	My Grass Is Green/Alone with You	1969	2.00	4.00	8.00
❑ 72964	Such a Fool/All Over My Mind	1969	2.00	4.00	8.00
❑ 73007	I'll Make Amends/Our Everlasting Love Has Died	1970	—	3.50	7.00
❑ 73056	Long Long Texas Road/Emotion — Devotion	1970	—	3.50	7.00
❑ 73111	All My Hard Times/At Times Everybody's Blind	1970	—	3.50	7.00
❑ 73178	I Love the Way That You've Been Lovin' Me/On and On and On	1971	—	3.50	7.00
❑ 73212	I Can't Go On Loving You/You're Shaking the Hand	1971	—	3.50	7.00
❑ 73252	Red Red Wine/Without You Baby	1971	—	3.50	7.00
❑ 73293	Sunshine and Rainbows/The Night's Not Over Yet	1972	—	3.50	7.00
❑ 73314	The Last Time I Called Somebody Darlin'/Long Way Back to Love	1972	—	3.50	7.00
❑ 73356	I Must Be Doin' Something Right/Always You, Always Me	1972	—	3.50	7.00
❑ 73376	That Rain Makin' Baby of Mine/This Time of the Year	1973	—	3.50	7.00
❑ 73405	Satisfied Mind/I'll Take Care of You	1973	—	3.50	7.00

PLANTATION

Number	Title (A Side/B Side)	Yr	VG	VG+	NM
❑ 183	Beautiful Sunday/You've Got Your Troubles	1979	—	2.50	5.00
❑ 187	The Last Farewell/Welcome Home	1979	—	2.50	5.00
❑ 194	What a Difference a Day Makes/(B-side unknown)	1980	—	2.50	5.00

SCORPION

Number	Title (A Side/B Side)	Yr	VG	VG+	NM
❑ 154	I Used to Be a Cowboy/Don't Touch Me	1978	—	2.00	4.00
❑ 0515	Deep in the Heart of Dixie/Last Call for Alcohol	1976	—	2.50	5.00
❑ 0521	Night Flying/Lifetime in a Week	1976	—	2.50	5.00
❑ 0527	Lovers, Friends and Strangers/Five String Hero	1977	—	2.50	5.00
❑ 0540	Betty's Song/Naked Truth	1977	—	2.50	5.00

STARDAY

Number	Title (A Side/B Side)	Yr	VG	VG+	NM
❑ 185	Such a Fool/Mumbling to Myself	1955	10.00	20.00	40.00

Albums

DECCA

Number	Title (A Side/B Side)	Yr	VG	VG+	NM
❑ DL 4160 [M]	Anymore with Roy Drusky	1961	6.25	12.50	25.00
❑ DL 4340 [M]	It's My Way	1962	5.00	10.00	20.00
❑ DL 74160 [S]	Anymore with Roy Drusky	1961	7.50	15.00	30.00
❑ DL 74340 [S]	It's My Way	1962	6.25	12.50	25.00

MERCURY

Number	Title (A Side/B Side)	Yr	VG	VG+	NM
❑ MG-20883 [M]	Songs of the Cities	1963	5.00	10.00	20.00
❑ MG-20919 [M]	Yesterday's Gone	1964	5.00	10.00	20.00
❑ MG-20973 [M]	The Pick of the Country	1964	5.00	10.00	20.00
❑ MG-21006 [M]	Country Music All Around the World	1965	5.00	10.00	20.00
❑ MG-21052 [M]	Roy Drusky's Greatest Hits	1965	5.00	10.00	20.00
❑ MG-21083 [M]	In a New Dimension	1966	5.00	10.00	20.00
❑ MG-21097 [M]	If the Whole World Stopped Lovin'	1966	5.00	10.00	20.00
❑ MG-21118 [M]	Now Is a Lonely Time	1967	6.25	12.50	25.00
❑ SR-60883 [S]	Songs of the Cities	1963	6.25	12.50	25.00
❑ SR-60919 [S]	Yesterday's Gone	1964	6.25	12.50	25.00
❑ SR-60973 [S]	The Pick of the Country	1964	6.25	12.50	25.00
❑ SR-61006 [S]	Country Music All Around the World	1965	6.25	12.50	25.00
❑ SR-61052 [S]	Roy Drusky's Greatest Hits	1965	6.25	12.50	25.00
❑ SR-61083 [S]	In a New Dimension	1966	6.25	12.50	25.00
❑ SR-61097 [S]	If the Whole World Stopped Lovin'	1966	6.25	12.50	25.00
❑ SR-61118 [S]	Now Is a Lonely Time	1967	5.00	10.00	20.00
❑ SR-61145	Roy Drusky's Greatest Hits Vol. 2	1968	5.00	10.00	20.00
❑ SR-61173	Jody and the Kid	1968	5.00	10.00	20.00
❑ SR-61206	Portrait of Roy Drusky	1969	5.00	10.00	20.00
❑ SR-61233	My Grass Is Green	1969	5.00	10.00	20.00
❑ SR-61260	I'll Make Amends	1970	5.00	10.00	20.00
❑ SR-61266	The Best of Roy Drusky	1970	5.00	10.00	20.00
❑ SR-61306	All My Hard Times	1970	5.00	10.00	20.00
❑ SR-61336	I Love the Way That You've Been Lovin' Me	1971	5.00	10.00	20.00

DRUSKY, ROY, AND PRISCILLA MITCHELL

Also see each artist's individual listings.

45s

MERCURY

Number	Title (A Side/B Side)	Yr	VG	VG+	NM
❑ 72416	Yes, Mr. Peters/More Than We Deserve	1965	2.00	4.00	8.00
❑ 72497	Slippin' Around/Trouble on Our Line	1965	2.00	4.00	8.00
❑ 72650	I'll Never Tell on You/Bed of Roses	1967	2.00	4.00	8.00

Albums

MERCURY

Number	Title (A Side/B Side)	Yr	VG	VG+	NM
❑ MG-21078 [M]	Together Again	1966	5.00	10.00	20.00
❑ SR-61078 [S]	Together Again	1966	6.25	12.50	25.00

DUCAS, GEORGE

45s

CAPITOL NASHVILLE

Number	Title (A Side/B Side)	Yr	VG	VG+	NM
❑ S7-18845	Kisses Don't Lie/My World Stopped Turning	1995	—	2.00	4.00
❑ S7-19169	Every Time She Passes By/Lipstick Promises	1996	—	2.00	4.00
❑ S7-19512	Long Trail of Tears/The Invisible Man	1997	—	2.00	4.00

LIBERTY

Number	Title (A Side/B Side)	Yr	VG	VG+	NM
❑ S7-18093	Teardrops/Waiting and Wishing	1994	—	2.00	4.00
❑ S7-18306	Lipstick Promises/In No Time at All	1995	—	2.50	5.00
❑ S7-18731	Hello Cruel World/Waiting and Wishing	1995	—	2.00	4.00

DUDLEY, DAVE

45s

GOLDEN RING

Number	Title (A Side/B Side)	Yr	VG	VG+	NM
❑ 3030	Cowboy Boots/I Think I'll Cheat (A Little Tonight)	1963	3.75	7.50	15.00
	—"Golden Ring" straight across top of label				
❑ 3030	Cowboy Boots/I Think I'll Cheat (A Little Tonight)	1963	3.00	6.00	12.00
	—"Golden Ring" on two lines, curved at top of label				

GOLDEN WING

Number	Title (A Side/B Side)	Yr	VG	VG+	NM
❑ 3020	Six Days on the Road/I Feel a Cry Coming On	1963	3.00	6.00	12.00

JUBILEE

Number	Title (A Side/B Side)	Yr	VG	VG+	NM
❑ 5436	Under Cover of the Night/Please Let Me Prove (My Love for You)	1962	5.00	10.00	20.00

KING

Number	Title (A Side/B Side)	Yr	VG	VG+	NM
❑ 1508	Cry Baby Cry/This Is the Last Time	1955	10.00	20.00	40.00
❑ 4866	Ink Dries Quicker Than Tears/I'll Be Waiting for You	1956	10.00	20.00	40.00
❑ 4933	Rock and Roll Nursery/I Guess You Know You're Right	1956	10.00	20.00	40.00
❑ 5792	Ink Dries Quicker Than Tears/I'll Be Waiting for You	1963	5.00	10.00	20.00

MERCURY

Number	Title (A Side/B Side)	Yr	VG	VG+	NM
❑ 72212	Last Day in the Mines/Last Year's Heartaches	1963	2.50	5.00	10.00
❑ 72254	Big Ole House/If I Had One	1964	2.50	5.00	10.00
❑ 72308	Mad/Don't Be Surprised	1964	2.50	5.00	10.00
❑ 72384	Two Six Packs Away/Hiding Behind the Curtain	1965	2.50	5.00	10.00
❑ 72442	Truck Drivin' Son-of-a-Gun/I Got Lost	1965	2.50	5.00	10.00
❑ 72500	What We're Fighting For/Coffee, Coffee, Coffee	1965	2.50	5.00	10.00
❑ 72550	Viet Nam Blues/Then I'll Come Home Again	1966	2.00	4.00	8.00
❑ 72585	Lonelyville/Time and Place	1966	2.00	4.00	8.00
❑ 72618	Long Time Gone/I Feel a Cry Comin' On	1966	2.00	4.00	8.00
❑ 72655	My Kind of Love/Subject to Change	1967	2.00	4.00	8.00
❑ 72697	Trucker's Prayer/Don't Come Cryin' to Me	1967	2.00	4.00	8.00
❑ 72741	Anything Leaving Town Today/I'd Rather Be Forgotten	1967	2.00	4.00	8.00
❑ 72779	There Ain't No Easy Run/Why I Can't Be With You (Is a Shame)	1968	2.00	4.00	8.00
❑ 72818	I Keep Coming Back for More/Where Does a Little Boy Go	1968	2.00	4.00	8.00
❑ 72856	Please Let Me Prove (My Love for You)/I'll Be Moving Along	1968	2.00	4.00	8.00
❑ 72902	One More Mile/Angel	1969	2.00	4.00	8.00
❑ 72952	George (And the North Woods)/It's Not a Very Pleasant Day Today	1969	2.00	4.00	8.00
❑ 73029	The Pool Shark/The Bigger They Come, The Harder They Fall	1970	2.00	4.00	8.00
❑ 73089	This Night (Ain't Fit for Nothing But Drinking)/I'm Not So Easy Anymore	1970	—	3.50	7.00
❑ 73138	Listen Betty (I'm Singing Your Song)/I Hope My Kind of Love	1970	—	3.50	7.00
❑ 73142	Six Tons of Toys/Old Time Merry Christmas	1970	2.00	4.00	8.00
❑ 73193	Comin' Down/Six-O-One	1971	—	3.50	7.00
❑ 73225	Fly Away Again/There You Are Again	1971	—	3.50	7.00
❑ 73274	If It Feels Good Do It/Sometime in the Future	1972	—	3.50	7.00
❑ 73309	You've Gotta Cry Girl/Arms of a Satisfied Woman	1972	—	3.50	7.00
❑ 73367	Keep On Truckin'/It Won't Hurt As Much Tomorrow	1973	—	3.50	7.00
❑ 73404	It Takes Time/I Almost Didn't Make It Through the Door	1973	—	3.50	7.00

Number	Title (A Side/B Side)	Yr	VG	VG+	NM
NEW STAR					
❑ 6420	Under Cover of the Night/Please Let Me Prove (My Love for You)	1962	7.50	15.00	30.00
NRC					
❑ 024	Where There's a Will There's a Way/I Won't Be Just Your Friend	1959	6.25	12.50	25.00
RICE					
❑ 5064	Rollin' Rig/Six Days on the Road	1973	2.00	4.00	8.00
❑ 5067	Have It Your Way/Blue Bedroom Eyes	1974	2.00	4.00	8.00
❑ 5069	Counterfeit Cowboy/That's How Cold	1974	2.00	4.00	8.00
❑ 5070	Devils in Heaven Bound Machines/Farewell to Arms	1974	2.00	4.00	8.00
❑ 5074	Rollin' On, We Gone/Farewell Two Arms	197?	—	3.50	7.00
❑ 5077	One A.M. Alone/If Seeing Is Believing	1978	—	3.50	7.00
—B-side by Billy D. Smith					
❑ 5078	Fly Away Again/Tavern Telephone	1978	—	3.50	7.00
—B-side by Paul Click					
❑ 5083	I Do/Farewell, Two Arms	1981	—	3.50	7.00
❑ 5084	I Was Country Before Barbara Mandrell/(B-side unknown)	1981	—	3.50	7.00
STARDAY					
❑ 364	Cry Baby/Careless Fool	1958	10.00	20.00	40.00
❑ 499	It's Gotta Be That Way/Where Do I Go from Here	1960	5.00	10.00	20.00
SUN					
❑ 1140	Moonlight in Vermont/Moritat	1979	—	3.00	6.00
❑ 1150	White Line Fever/The Last Run	1980	—	3.00	6.00
❑ 1154	Rolaids, Doan's Pills and Preparation H/Maybe I Can	1980	—	3.00	6.00
❑ 1155	Big Fanny/Where's the Truck	1980	—	3.00	6.00
—With Charlie Douglas					
❑ 1158	Cowboy, You're America/The Driver	1980	—	3.00	6.00
❑ 1166 [DJ]	The Eagle (same on both sides)	1981	—	3.50	7.00
—Unknown on stock copy					
❑ 1180	I Wish I Had a Nickel/Fools Rush In	1982	—	3.00	6.00
UNITED ARTISTS					
❑ XW585	How Come It Took So Long (To Say Goodbye)/I've Lived Like a Piece of Grass	1974	—	3.00	6.00
❑ 613	Six Days on the Road/I Feel a Cry Coming On	1963	—	—	—
—Canceled					
❑ XW630	Fireball Rolled a Seven/Blue Bedroom Eyes	1975	—	3.00	6.00
❑ XW693	Where Did All the Cowboys Go/Wave At 'Em Billy Boy	1975	—	3.00	6.00
❑ XW722	Me and Ole C.B./I Can't Remember You	1975	—	3.00	6.00
❑ XW766	Sentimental Journey/The Night You Broke the News	1976	—	3.00	6.00
❑ XW773	Seventeen Seventy-Six (1776)/I Don't See the Rain	1976	—	3.00	6.00
❑ XW836	38 and Lonely/Texas Ruby	1976	—	3.00	6.00
❑ XW882	Where Does a Little Boy Go/Rooster Hill	1977	—	3.00	6.00
VEE					
❑ 7003	Maybe I Do/Your Only One	1961	7.50	15.00	30.00

Albums

Number	Title (A Side/B Side)	Yr	VG	VG+	NM
GOLDEN RING					
❑ GR 110 [M]	Dave Dudley Sings Six Days on the Road	1963	20.00	40.00	80.00
MERCURY					
❑ MG-20899 [M]	Songs About the Working Man	1964	5.00	10.00	20.00
❑ MG-20927 [M]	Travelin' with Dave Dudley	1964	5.00	10.00	20.00
❑ MG-20970 [M]	Talk of the Town	1964	5.00	10.00	20.00
❑ MG-20999 [M]	Rural Route #1	1965	5.00	10.00	20.00
❑ MG-21028 [M]	Truck Drivin' Son-of-a-Gun	1965	5.00	10.00	20.00
❑ MG-21046 [M]	Dave Dudley's Greatest Hits	1965	5.00	10.00	20.00
❑ MG-21057 [M]	There's a Star Spangled Banner Waving Somewhere	1966	5.00	10.00	20.00
❑ MG-21074 [M]	Lonelyville	1966	5.00	10.00	20.00
❑ MG-21098 [M]	Free and Easy	1966	5.00	10.00	20.00
❑ MG-21133 [M]	Dave Dudley Country	1967	6.25	12.50	25.00
❑ MG-21144 [M]	Greatest Hits Vol. 2	1968	7.50	15.00	30.00
❑ SR-60899 [S]	Songs About the Working Man	1964	6.25	12.50	25.00
❑ SR-60927 [S]	Travelin' with Dave Dudley	1964	6.25	12.50	25.00
❑ SR-60970 [S]	Talk of the Town	1964	6.25	12.50	25.00
❑ SR-60999 [S]	Rural Route #1	1965	6.25	12.50	25.00
❑ SR-61028 [S]	Truck Drivin' Son-of-a-Gun	1965	6.25	12.50	25.00
❑ SR-61046 [S]	Dave Dudley's Greatest Hits	1965	6.25	12.50	25.00
❑ SR-61057 [S]	There's a Star Spangled Banner Waving Somewhere	1966	6.25	12.50	25.00
❑ SR-61074 [S]	Lonelyville	1966	6.25	12.50	25.00
❑ SR-61098 [S]	Free and Easy	1966	5.00	10.00	20.00
❑ SR-61133 [S]	Dave Dudley Country	1967	5.00	10.00	20.00
❑ SR-61144 [S]	Greatest Hits Vol. 2	1968	5.00	10.00	20.00
❑ SR-61172	Thanks for All the Miles	1968	5.00	10.00	20.00
❑ SR-61215	One More Mile	1969	5.00	10.00	20.00

DUDLEY, DAVE, AND TOM T. HALL

Also see each artist's individual listings.

45s

Number	Title (A Side/B Side)	Yr	VG	VG+	NM
MERCURY					
❑ 73139	Day Drinkin'/Get On with the Show	1970	—	3.50	7.00

DUDLEY, DAVE, AND KAREN O'DONNAL

45s

Number	Title (A Side/B Side)	Yr	VG	VG+	NM
MERCURY					
❑ 73345	We Know It's Over/Gettin' Back Together	1972	—	3.50	7.00

DUFF, ARLIE

45s

Number	Title (A Side/B Side)	Yr	VG	VG+	NM
DECCA					
❑ 9-29243	Courtin' in the Rain/She's a Housewife	1954	6.25	12.50	25.00
❑ 9-29428	I Dreamed of a Hill-Billy Heaven/Lie Detector	1955	6.25	12.50	25.00
❑ 9-29589	Pass the Plate of Happiness Around/Take It Easy on Me	1955	6.25	12.50	25.00
❑ 9-29866	Home Boy/Oh, How I Cried	1956	6.25	12.50	25.00
❑ 9-29987	Alligator Came Across/So Close and Yet So Far	1956	6.25	12.50	25.00
STARDAY					
❑ 103	You All Come/Poor Ole Teacher	1953	10.00	20.00	40.00
❑ 105	Stuck-in-a-Mud Hole/A Million Tears	1953	7.50	15.00	30.00
❑ 132	Let Me Be Your Salty Dog/Back to the Country	1954	15.00	30.00	60.00
❑ 176	Courtin's Here to Stay/Fifteen Cents a Pop	1955	7.50	15.00	30.00
❑ 302	What a Way to Die/You've Done It Right	1957	25.00	50.00	100.00

DUGAN, JEFF

45s

Number	Title (A Side/B Side)	Yr	VG	VG+	NM
WARNER BROS.					
❑ 27995	I Wish It Was That Easy Going Home/That Won't Ever Stop Me Loving You	1988	—	—	3.00
❑ 28376	Once a Fool, Always a Fool/Somebody Killed the Jukebox	1987	—	—	3.00

DUNCAN, JOHNNY

Also see J.D. SOUTHER.

45s

Number	Title (A Side/B Side)	Yr	VG	VG+	NM
ABC-PARAMOUNT					
❑ 10775	Forgive Me and Forget Me/Who Do They Think They Are	1966	3.75	7.50	15.00
CAPITOL					
❑ F3814	Last Train to San Fernando/Jig Along Home	1957	12.50	25.00	50.00
COLUMBIA					
❑ 18-02570	All Night Long/My Heart's Not In It	1981	—	2.00	4.00
❑ 3-10007	Scarlet Water/We're Not Fooling Our Hearts	1974	—	2.50	5.00
❑ 3-10085	Charley Is My Name/Gentle Fire	1975	—	2.50	5.00
❑ 3-10182	Jo and the Cowboy/Taking a Chance on You	1975	—	2.50	5.00
❑ 3-10262	Gentle Fire/Good Morning Love	1975	—	2.50	5.00
❑ 3-10302	Stranger/Flashing, Screaming, Silent Neon Sign	1976	—	2.50	5.00
❑ 3-10417	Thinkin' of a Rendezvous/Love Should Be Easy	1976	—	2.50	5.00
❑ 3-10474	It Couldn't Have Been Any Better/Denver Woman	1977	—	2.50	5.00
❑ 3-10554	A Song in the Night/Use My Love	1977	—	2.50	5.00
❑ 3-10634	Come a Little Bit Closer/Loneliness (Can Break a Good Man Down)	1977	—	2.50	5.00
❑ 3-10694	She Can Put Her Shoes Under My Bed (Anytime)/Maybe I Just Crossed Your Mind	1978	—	2.50	5.00
❑ 3-10783	Hello Mexico (And Adios Baby to You)/I Watched an Angel (Going Through Hell)	1978	—	2.50	5.00
❑ 3-10915	Slow Dancing/One Night of Love	1979	—	2.50	5.00
❑ 1-11097	The Lady in the Blue Mercedes/Too Far Gone	1979	—	2.00	4.00
❑ 1-11185	Play Another Slow Song/My Woman's Good to Me	1979	—	2.00	4.00
❑ 1-11280	I'm Gonna Love You Tonight (In My Dreams)/Wine Oh Wine	1980	—	2.00	4.00
❑ 1-11385	Acapulco/Am I That Easy to Forget	1980	—	2.00	4.00
❑ 4-43988	Looking for Someone Lonely/Rainbow Road	1967	2.50	5.00	10.00
❑ 4-44196	Hard Luck Joe/Gotta Get Back (On the Right Track)	1967	2.00	4.00	8.00
❑ 4-44383	Baby Me Baby/Mystery	1967	2.00	4.00	8.00
❑ 4-44484	I'm the One/Solo Soul	1968	2.00	4.00	8.00
❑ 4-44580	To My Sorrow/I'm in This Town for Good	1968	2.00	4.00	8.00
❑ 4-44693	I Live to Love You/Louisville Nashville Southbound Train	1968	2.00	4.00	8.00
❑ 4-44864	When She Touches Me/Shreveport to L.A.	1969	2.00	4.00	8.00
❑ 4-45006	Window Number Five/Day Drinker	1969	2.00	4.00	8.00
❑ 4-45124	You're Gonna Need a Man/Long Tall Drawn Out Day	1970	—	3.50	7.00
❑ 4-45201	My Woman's Love/(There's Still) Someone I Can't Forget	1970	—	3.50	7.00
❑ 4-45227	Let Me Go (Set Me Free)/What I Don't Know	1970	—	3.50	7.00
❑ 4-45319	There's Something About a Lady/I Don't Know Why I Keep Loving You	1971	—	3.50	7.00
❑ 4-45418	One Night of Love/(A Whole Lot of) Peaches in Georgia	1971	—	3.50	7.00
❑ 4-45479	Baby's Smile, Woman's Kiss/I'd Rather Love You	1971	—	3.50	7.00
❑ 4-45556	Fools/Tiny Fingers	1972	—	3.50	7.00
❑ 4-45674	Here We Go Again/When We Loved	1972	—	3.50	7.00
❑ 4-45818	Sweet Country Woman/The Look in Baby's Eyes	1973	—	3.00	6.00
❑ 4-45917	Talkin' with My Lady/You're My Woman	1973	—	3.00	6.00
❑ 4-46018	The Pillow/Ain't No Way That I Can Forget You	1974	—	3.00	6.00
LEADER					
❑ 807	Bring Your Heart/Hot Sunshine	1960	10.00	20.00	40.00
❑ 812	Hello Mary Lou, Goodbye Heart/Freddie and His Go-Cart	1960	7.50	15.00	30.00
❑ 814	Raindrops/Wheels	1961	7.50	15.00	30.00
PHAROAH					
❑ 2502	The Look of a Lady in Love/(B-side unknown)	1986	—	2.50	5.00
❑ 2503	Texas Moon/(B-side unknown)	1986	—	2.50	5.00

Albums

Number	Title (A Side/B Side)	Yr	VG	VG+	NM
COLUMBIA					
❑ CS 9824	Johnny One Time	1969	5.00	10.00	20.00
❑ C 30618	There's Something About a Lady	1971	3.75	7.50	15.00
❑ KC 32440	Sweet Country Woman	1973	3.75	7.50	15.00
❑ PC 34243	The Best of Johnny Duncan	1976	3.00	6.00	12.00

Number	Title (A Side/B Side)	Yr	VG	VG+	NM
❑ PC 34442	Johnny Duncan	1977	3.00	6.00	12.00
❑ KC 35039	Come a Little Bit Closer	1977	3.00	6.00	12.00
❑ KC 35451	The Best Is Yet to Come	1978	3.00	6.00	12.00
❑ KC 35628	Greatest Hits	1978	3.00	6.00	12.00
❑ KC 35775	See You When the Sun Goes Down	1979	3.00	6.00	12.00
❑ JC 36260	Straight from Texas	1980	2.50	5.00	10.00
❑ JC 36508	In My Dreams	1980	2.50	5.00	10.00
❑ JC 36829	You're On My Mind	1981	2.50	5.00	10.00
HARMONY					
❑ KH 32477	You're Gonna Need a Man	1973	3.00	6.00	12.00

DUNCAN, JOHNNY, AND JANIE FRICKE

45s

Number	Title (A Side/B Side)	Yr	VG	VG+	NM
COLUMBIA					
❑ 1-11312	He's Out of My Life/Loving Arms	1980	—	2.00	4.00
Albums					
COLUMBIA					
❑ JC 36780	Nice 'n' Easy	1980	2.50	5.00	10.00

DUNCAN, JOHNNY, AND JUNE STEARNS

45s

Number	Title (A Side/B Side)	Yr	VG	VG+	NM
COLUMBIA					
❑ 4-44656	Jackson Ain't a Very Big Town/The True and Lasting Kind	1968	2.00	4.00	8.00
❑ 4-44752	Back to Back (We're Strangers)/If That's the Only Way	1969	2.00	4.00	8.00
❑ 4-44992	Now I Lay Me Down to Dream (With a Nightmare By My Side)/We'll Get Married or Nothing	1969	2.00	4.00	8.00
Albums					
COLUMBIA					
❑ CS 9910	Back to Back	1969	3.75	7.50	15.00

DUNCAN, TOMMY

45s

Number	Title (A Side/B Side)	Yr	VG	VG+	NM
CAPITOL					
❑ F895	In the Jailhouse Now/I Don't Believe	1950	7.50	15.00	30.00
❑ F40282	Chattanoogie Shoe Shine Boy/Never No Mo' Blues	1950	10.00	20.00	40.00
CORAL					
❑ 9-61391	San Antonio Rose/Time Changes Everything	1955	5.00	10.00	20.00
❑ 9-61474	Somebody's Pushin'/I'll Never Worry You	1955	5.00	10.00	20.00
❑ 9-64173	The Parting of the Wa/Wastin' Your Life Away	1954	6.25	12.50	25.00
❑ 9-64182	I Just Can't Take It Anymore/Walkin' in the Shadow of the Blues	1954	6.25	12.50	25.00
INTRO					
❑ 6065	Where Oh Where Has My Little Love Gone/Beneath a Neon Star in a Honky Tonk	195?	5.00	10.00	20.00
❑ 6071	Hound Dog/I Guess You Were Right	195?	5.00	10.00	20.00
❑ 6073	Grits 'n' Gravy Blues/May Take a Long Time	195?	5.00	10.00	20.00
❑ 6080	Stars Over San Antoine/I Reckon I'm a Texan	195?	5.00	10.00	20.00
❑ 6086	The Tennessee Churchbells/That Uncertain Feeling	195?	5.00	10.00	20.00
SMASH					
❑ 2073	I Brought It On Myself/Let Me Take You Out	1967	2.50	5.00	10.00
Selected 78s					
CAPITOL					
❑ 40178	Gamblin' Polka Dot Blues/September	1949	5.00	10.00	20.00
❑ 40247	You Put Me on My Feet (When You Took Her Off My Hands)/Just a Plain Old Country Boy	1949	5.00	10.00	20.00

DUNN, HOLLY

Also see MICHAEL MURPHEY; KENNY ROGERS.

45s

Number	Title (A Side/B Side)	Yr	VG	VG+	NM
MTM					
❑ B-72052	Playing for Keeps/I'm Not Through Loving You Yet	1985	—	2.50	5.00
❑ B-72057	My Heart Holds On/Shot in the Dark	1985	—	2.50	5.00
❑ B-72064	Two Too Many/You	1986	—	2.50	5.00
❑ B-72075	Daddy's Hands/Hideaway	1986	2.00	4.00	8.00
❑ B-72082	Love Someone Like Me/Burnin' Wheel	1987	—	3.50	7.00
❑ B-72091	Only When I Love/Little Prairie House	1987	—	2.50	5.00
❑ B-72093	Strangers Again/Wrap Me Up	1987	—	2.50	5.00
❑ B-72108	That's What Your Love Does to Me/Lonesome Highway	1988	—	2.50	5.00
❑ B-72116	(It's Always Gonna Be) Someday/On the Wings of an Angel	1988	—	2.50	5.00
WARNER BROS.					
❑ 18831	As Long As You Belong to Me/You Can Have Him	1992	—	2.00	4.00
❑ 18956	No Love Have I/Love Someone Like Me	1992	—	2.00	4.00
❑ 19149	No One Takes the Train Anymore/Two Too Many	1991	—	2.00	4.00
❑ 19266	Maybe I Mean Yes/Daddy's Hands	1991	—	2.50	5.00
❑ 19472	Heart Full of Love/Temporary Loss of Memory	1990	—	2.00	4.00
❑ 19756	You Really Had Me Going/When No Place Is Home	1990	—	2.00	4.00
❑ 19847	My Anniversary for Being a Fool/The Light in the Window Went Out	1990	—	2.00	4.00
❑ 22796	There Goes My Heart Again/Blue Rose of Texas	1989	—	—	3.00
❑ 22957	Are You Ever Gonna Love Me/If I'd Never Loved You	1989	—	—	3.00
Albums					
MTM					
❑ ST-71052	Holly Dunn	1986	3.00	6.00	12.00
❑ ST-71063	Cornerstone	1987	3.00	6.00	12.00
❑ ST-71070	Across the Rio Grande	1988	3.00	6.00	12.00
WARNER BROS.					
❑ PRO-A-3692 [DJ]	Blue Rose of Texas Radio Special	1989	7.50	15.00	30.00
—Promo-only interview record					
❑ 25939	The Blue Rose of Texas	1989	2.50	5.00	10.00

DUNN, RONNIE

Also see BROOKS AND DUNN.

45s

Number	Title (A Side/B Side)	Yr	VG	VG+	NM
CHURCHILL					
❑ 52383	She Put the Sad in All His Songs/Change of Attitude	1984	—	3.00	6.00
❑ 52459	Jessie/Come Back to Me	1984	—	3.00	6.00
❑ 94008	She Put the Sad in All His Songs/Change of Attitude	1983	2.00	4.00	8.00
❑ 94018	It's Written All Over Your Face/You Never Crossed My Mind	1983	2.00	4.00	8.00
❑ 94018 [PS]	It's Written All Over Your Face/You Never Crossed My Mind	1983	3.00	6.00	12.00

DURHAM, BOBBY

45s

Number	Title (A Side/B Side)	Yr	VG	VG+	NM
CAPITOL					
❑ 5202	My Past Is Present/Queen of Snob Hill	1964	3.00	6.00	12.00
❑ 5511	Let the Sad Times Roll On/Let That Be a Lesson to You, Heartache	1965	3.00	6.00	12.00
❑ 5616	Why Don't You Just Be You/Home Is Where I Hang My Head	1966	2.50	5.00	10.00
HIGHTONE					
❑ 501	Where I Grew Up/(B-side unknown)	1988	—	3.00	6.00
❑ 502	Let's Start a Rumor Today/(B-side unknown)	1988	—	3.00	6.00
Albums					
HIGHTONE					
❑ 8010	Where I Grew Up	1987	2.50	5.00	10.00

DURRENCE, SAM

45s

Number	Title (A Side/B Side)	Yr	VG	VG+	NM
RIVER					
❑ 3873	Living Wild, Living Free/(Instrumental)	1973	2.00	4.00	8.00
❑ 3875	Last Days of Childhood/She Almost Believed Me	1973	2.00	4.00	8.00
❑ 3877	You've Given Me a Feeling to Believe In/Don't Have the Time	1973	2.00	4.00	8.00
❑ 3880	Temporary/(B-side unknown)	1974	2.00	4.00	8.00
❑ 3885	And I Love You, Babe/(B-side unknown)	1974	2.00	4.00	8.00

DYCKE, JERRY

45s

Number	Title (A Side/B Side)	Yr	VG	VG+	NM
CHURCHILL					
❑ 7757	Daddy Played Harmonica/I Never Said Goodbye	1980	—	3.00	6.00
❑ 7762	There's Nobody Home on the Range No More/(B-side unknown)	1980	—	3.00	6.00
❑ 7766	Beethoven Was Before My Time/My Shoes Keep Walking Back to You	1981	—	3.00	6.00
❑ 7775	Oh Pretty Woman/(B-side unknown)	1981	—	3.00	6.00
SUN					
❑ 1109	Will the Circle Be Unbroken/A Little More, A Little Less	1970	2.00	4.00	8.00
❑ 1123	Come In Mr. Lonely/School Children	1971	2.00	4.00	8.00

DYLAN, BOB

Dylan, a musical chameleon, recorded one of the most influential country recordings of its time. Here was an ex-folkie and rock star doing country, and doing it sincerely! Among the performers who appeared with Dylan on the below are JOHNNY CASH and CHARLIE DANIELS.

45s

Number	Title (A Side/B Side)	Yr	VG	VG+	NM
COLUMBIA					
❑ 44826	I Threw It All Away/Drifter's Escape	1969	2.00	4.00	8.00
❑ 44926	Lay Lady Lay/Peggy Day	1969	2.00	4.00	8.00
❑ 45004	Tonight I'll Be Staying Here with You/Country Pie	1969	2.50	5.00	10.00
Albums					
COLUMBIA					
❑ JC 9825	Nashville Skyline	197?	2.50	5.00	10.00
❑ KCS 9825	Nashville Skyline	1969	7.50	15.00	30.00
—"360 Sound Stereo" label					
❑ KCS 9825	Nashville Skyline	1970	3.00	6.00	12.00
—Orange label					
❑ PC 9825	Nashville Skyline	198?	2.00	4.00	8.00
—Budget-line reissue					

E

E.W.B.

Also see ELLIOTT, WALTER & BENNETT. This is the same group, except Clark Walter was replaced by Richard Wesley.

Number	Title (A Side/B Side)	Yr	VG	VG+	NM
45s					
PAID					
❑ 142	We Could Go On Forever/(B-side unknown)	1981	—	2.50	5.00
Albums					
PAID					
❑ 2007	We Could Go On Forever	1981	3.00	6.00	12.00

EAGLES

Members of this group had been in THE FLYING BURRITO BROTHERS and POCO.

Number	Title (A Side/B Side)	Yr	VG	VG+	NM
12-Inch Singles					
ASYLUM					
❑ 11402 [DJ]	Please Come Home for Christmas/Funky New Year (both mono)//Please Come Home for Christmas/Funky New Year (both stereo)	1978	5.00	10.00	20.00
45s					
ASYLUM					
❑ 11005	Take It Easy/Get You in the Mood	1972	—	2.50	5.00
❑ 11008	Witchy Woman/Early Bird	1972	—	2.00	4.00
❑ 11013	Peaceful Easy Feeling/Trying	1973	—	2.00	4.00
❑ 11013	Tequila Sunrise/21	1973	—	2.00	4.00
❑ 11025	Outlaw Man/Certain Kind of Fool	1973	—	2.00	4.00
❑ 11036	Already Gone/Is It True	1974	—	2.00	4.00
❑ 45202	James Dean/Good Day in Hell	1974	—	2.00	4.00
❑ 45218	Best of My Love/Ol' 55	1974	—	2.00	4.00
❑ 45257	One of These Nights/Visions	1975	—	2.00	4.00
❑ 45279	Lyin' Eyes/Too Many People	1975	—	2.00	4.00
❑ 45293	Take It to the Limit/After the Thrill Is Gone	1975	—	2.00	4.00
❑ 45373	New Kid in Town/Victim of Love	1976	—	2.00	4.00
❑ 45386	Hotel California/Pretty Maids All in a Row	1977	—	2.00	4.00
❑ 45403	Life in the Fast Lane/The Last Resort	1977	—	2.00	4.00
❑ 45555	Please Come Home for Christmas/Funky New Year	1978	—	2.00	4.00
—Original with "clouds" label					
❑ 45555	Please Come Home for Christmas/Funky New Year	1984	—	—	3.00
—Reissue with black and yellow label					
❑ 45555 [PS]	Please Come Home for Christmas/Funky New Year	1978	—	2.00	4.00
—Sleeve was available with both original and reissue					
❑ 46545	Heartache Tonight/Teenage Jail	1979	—	2.00	4.00
❑ 46569	The Long Run/The Disco Strangler	1979	—	2.00	4.00
❑ 46608	I Can't Tell You Why/The Greeks Don't Want No Freaks	1980	—	2.00	4.00
❑ 47100	Seven Bridges Road/The Long Run	1980	—	2.00	4.00
FULL MOON					
❑ 49654	I Can't Tell You Why/Outside	1981	—	2.50	5.00
—B-side by Ambrosia					
FULL MOON/ASYLUM					
❑ 47004	Lyin' Eyes/Looking for Love	1980	—	2.00	4.00
—B-side by Johnny Lee; contains the full-length version of "Lyin' Eyes"					
❑ 47004 [PS]	Lyin' Eyes/Looking for Love	1980	—	2.50	5.00
❑ 47073	Lyin' Eyes/Hello Texas	1980	—	2.50	5.00
—B-side by Jimmy Buffett					
GEFFEN					
❑ 19376	Get Over It/Get Over It (Live)	1994	—	2.50	5.00
Albums					
ASYLUM					
❑ 6E-103	Hotel California	1977	2.00	4.00	8.00
❑ 6E-105	Eagles — Their Greatest Hits 1971-1975	1977	2.00	4.00	8.00
❑ 5E-508	The Long Run	1979	2.00	4.00	8.00
❑ BB-705 [(2)]	Eagles Live	1980	3.00	6.00	12.00
❑ 7E-1004	On the Border	1974	3.00	6.00	12.00
—Clouds label					
❑ EQ 1004 [Q]	On the Border	1974	5.00	10.00	20.00
❑ 7E-1039	One of These Nights	1975	2.50	5.00	10.00
—Clouds label					
❑ EQ 1039 [Q]	One of These Nights	1975	5.00	10.00	20.00
❑ 7E-1052	Eagles — Their Greatest Hits 1971-1975	1976	2.50	5.00	10.00
❑ 7E-1084	Hotel California	1976	2.50	5.00	10.00
❑ SD 5054	Eagles	1972	3.75	7.50	15.00
—Gatefold cover; white label with door-in-a-circle logo at top					
❑ SD 5054	Eagles	1973	3.00	6.00	12.00
—Regular cover; clouds label					
❑ SD 5068	Desperado	1973	3.00	6.00	12.00
—Clouds label					
❑ 60205	Eagles Greatest Hits, Volume 2	1982	2.50	5.00	10.00
DCC COMPACT CLASSICS					
❑ LPZ-2043	Hotel California	1997	6.25	12.50	25.00
—Audiophile vinyl					
❑ LPZ-2051	Eagles — Their Greatest Hits 1971-1975	1998	6.25	12.50	25.00
—Audiophile vinyl					
ELEKTRA					
❑ 60422	Anthology of the Eagles	1985	—	—	—
—Canceled					
MOBILE FIDELITY					
❑ 1-126	Hotel California	1984	25.00	50.00	100.00
—Audiophile vinyl					

EANES, JIM

Number	Title (A Side/B Side)	Yr	VG	VG+	NM
45s					
DECCA					
❑ 9-46403	I Cried Again/They Locked God Outside the Iron Curtain	1952	6.25	12.50	25.00
STARDAY					
❑ 414	Christmas Doll/It Won't Seem Like Christmas	1958	5.00	10.00	20.00

EARL, KENNY

Also see THE WOLFPACK.

Number	Title (A Side/B Side)	Yr	VG	VG+	NM
45s					
CINNAMON					
❑ 751	Once More/North of Sally	1973	—	3.00	6.00
KARI					
❑ 124	Wasn't It Supposed to Be Me/Raindrops	1981	—	3.00	6.00
KIK					
❑ 904	We Have to Start Meeting Like This/Raindrops	1981	—	3.00	6.00
LOBO					
❑ II	Raindrops/(B-side unknown)	1982	—	3.00	6.00
MGM					
❑ 14787	Use Me Up/(B-side unknown)	1975	—	2.50	5.00
❑ 14815	Just Walkin' in the Rain/(B-side unknown)	1975	—	2.50	5.00

EARLE, STEVE

Number	Title (A Side/B Side)	Yr	VG	VG+	NM
12-Inch Singles					
MCA					
❑ 17129 [DJ]	Someday/Fearless Heart/Good Ol' Boy	1986	—	3.00	6.00
❑ 17327 [DJ]	I Ain't Ever Satisfied (same on both sides)	1987	—	3.00	6.00
❑ 23693	Someday/State Trooper (Live)/Good Ol' Boy (Live)	1986	2.00	4.00	8.00
45s					
EPIC					
❑ 34-04070	Nothin' But You/Continental Trailways Blues	1983	—	2.50	5.00
❑ 34-04307	Squeeze Me In/The Devil's Right Hand	1984	—	2.50	5.00
❑ 34-04666	What'll You Do About Me/Cry Myself to Sleep	1984	—	2.50	5.00
❑ 34-04784	A Little Bit in Love/The Crush	1985	—	2.00	4.00
❑ 34-04784 [PS]	A Little Bit in Love/The Crush	1985	—	2.00	4.00
❑ 34-04784 [PS]	A Little Bit in Love	1985	2.00	4.00	8.00
—"Demonstration -- Not for Sale" on back					
MCA					
❑ 52785	Hillbilly Highway/Down the Road	1986	—	—	3.00
❑ 52856	Guitar Town/Little Rock 'N' Roller	1986	—	—	3.00
❑ 52920	Someday/Hillbilly Highway	1986	—	—	3.00
❑ 53011	Goodbye's All We Got Left/Good Ol' Boy (Gettin' Tough)	1987	—	—	3.00
❑ 53103	Nowhere Road/I Ain't Ever Satisfied	1987	—	—	3.00
❑ 53182	Sweet Little '66/Angry Young Man	1987	—	—	3.00
❑ 53249	Six Days on the Road/The Week of Living Dangerously	1988	—	—	3.00
❑ 53532	Guitar Town/Hillbilly Highway	1988	—	—	3.00
—"Double Hit" reissue					
❑ 53608	Someday/Goodbye's All We Got Left to Say	1988	—	—	3.00
—"Double Hit" reissue					
UNI					
❑ 55018	Back to the Wall/Little Sister (Live)	1988	—	2.00	4.00
7-Inch Extended Plays					
LSI					
❑ 8209	*Nothin' But You/Continental Trailways Blues/ Squeeze Me In/My Baby Worships Me	1982	6.25	12.50	25.00
❑ 8209 [PS]	Pink and Black	1982	6.25	12.50	25.00
Albums					
EPIC					
❑ FE 39226	Early Tracks	1987	3.50	7.00	14.00
MCA					
❑ 5713	Guitar Town	1986	2.50	5.00	10.00
❑ 5998	Exit 0	1987	2.50	5.00	10.00
❑ R 143506	Exit 0	1987	3.00	6.00	12.00
—BMG Direct Marketing edition					
❑ R 154072	Guitar Town	1986	3.00	6.00	12.00
—RCA Music Service edition					
UNI					
❑ 7	Copperhead Road	1988	2.50	5.00	10.00
❑ R 100679	Copperhead Road	1988	3.00	6.00	12.00
—BMG Direct Marketing edition					

EARWOOD, MUNDO

Number	Title (A Side/B Side)	Yr	VG	VG+	NM
45s					
EPIC					
❑ 8-50141	She Brings Her Lovin' Home to Me/Life Has Its Little Ups and Downs	1975	—	2.50	5.00
—As "Mundo Ray"					
❑ 8-50181	I Can't Quit Cheatin' on You/That's My Desire	1976	—	2.50	5.00
❑ 8-50232	Lonesome Is a Cowboy/(Don't Give Your Love to Any Man) Who Buys the Wine	1976	—	2.50	5.00
EXCELSIOR					
❑ 1005	Blue Collar Blues/Softer Place to Fall	1981	—	2.50	5.00
❑ 1010	Angela/Pyramid of Cans	1981	—	2.50	5.00
❑ 1019	I'll Still Be Loving You/Pyramid of Cans	1981	—	2.50	5.00
GMC					
❑ 102	When I Get You Alone/Let Me Down Easy	1978	—	2.50	5.00
❑ 104	Things I'd Do for You/Breaking Up Is Hard to Do	1978	—	2.50	5.00
❑ 105	Fooled Around and Fell in Love/Love Me Now	1978	—	2.50	5.00

Number	Title (A Side/B Side)	Yr	VG	VG+	NM
❑ 106	My Heart Is Not My Own/My Weakness Is Stronger Than I Am	1979	—	2.50	5.00
❑ 107	We Got Love/It's Magic	1979	—	2.50	5.00
❑ 108	Sometimes Love/Philodendron	1979	—	2.50	5.00
❑ 109	You're in Love with the Wrong Man/Before We Call It Love	1980	—	2.50	5.00
❑ 109 [PS]	You're in Love with the Wrong Man/Before We Call It Love	1980	2.00	4.00	8.00
❑ 111	Can't Keep My Mind Off Her/Just Another One of Them	1980	—	2.50	5.00
GRT					
❑ 003	Let's Hear It for Loneliness/Angeline	1974	—	3.00	6.00
❑ 011	Let Me Down Easy/Just Another One of Those Days	1974	—	3.00	6.00
PEGASUS					
❑ 110	A Woman's Way/Love Me Now	1989	—	2.50	5.00
PRIMERO					
❑ 1002	All My Lovin/Breaking Up Is Hard to Do	1982	—	3.00	6.00
❑ 1009	Pyramid of Cans/Breaking Up Is Hard to Do	1982	—	3.00	6.00
ROYAL AMERICAN					
❑ 65	Behind Blue Eyes/Breaking Up Is Hard to Do	1972	2.00	4.00	8.00
TRUE					
❑ 101	I Can Give You Love/Let's Get Naked	1977	—	2.50	5.00
❑ 104	Behind Blue Eyes/Let's Get Naked	1977	—	2.50	5.00
❑ 111	Angelene/Just Another One of Those Days	1977	—	2.50	5.00

Albums

Number	Title	Yr	VG	VG+	NM
EXCELSIOR					
❑ 88006	Mundo Earwood	1981	2.50	5.00	10.00

EAST, LYNDEL

45s

Number	Title (A Side/B Side)	Yr	VG	VG+	NM
NSD					
❑ 2	Why Do You Come Around/All She Ever Wanted	1978	—	3.00	6.00
❑ 8	Oklahoma Music/Easy As Pie	1978	—	3.00	6.00
❑ 20	Giving Her the State of West Virginia/There's Still a Lot of Love in San Antone	1979	—	3.00	6.00

EASTON, SHEENA

This Scottish pop singer had one country hit. Also see KENNY ROGERS.

45s

Number	Title (A Side/B Side)	Yr	VG	VG+	NM
EMI AMERICA					
❑ 8196	Almost Over You/I Don't Need Your Word	1983	—	2.00	4.00

EASTWOOD, CLINT

Yep, the renowned actor sang some, too! Also see RAY CHARLES; MERLE HAGGARD; T.G. SHEPPARD; RANDY TRAVIS.

45s

Number	Title (A Side/B Side)	Yr	VG	VG+	NM
CAMEO					
❑ 240	Rowdy/Cowboy Wedding Song	1963	5.00	10.00	20.00
❑ 240 [PS]	Rowdy/Cowboy Wedding Song	1963	12.50	25.00	50.00
CERTRON					
❑ 10010	Burning Bridges/When I Loved Her	1970	2.50	5.00	10.00
❑ 10010 [PS]	Burning Bridges/When I Loved Her	1970	6.25	12.50	25.00
GNP CRESCENDO					
❑ 177	Get Yourself Another Fool/For You, For Me, Forevermore	1962	10.00	20.00	40.00
❑ 177 [PS]	Get Yourself Another Fool/For You, For Me, Forevermore	1962	25.00	50.00	100.00
GOTHIC					
❑ 005	Unknown Girl of My Dreams/For All We Know	1961	6.25	12.50	25.00
❑ 005 [PS]	Unknown Girl of My Dreams/For All We Know	1961	12.50	25.00	50.00
PARAMOUNT					
❑ 0010	Best Things/Wand'rin' Star	1969	3.00	6.00	12.00
—B-side by Lee Marvin					
WARNER BROS.					
❑ 49760	Cowboy in a Three-Piece Business Suit/Dark Blue Feeling	1981	—	2.50	5.00

Albums

Number	Title	Yr	VG	VG+	NM
CAMEO					
❑ C-1056 [M]	Clint Eastwood Sings Cowboy Favorites	1963	25.00	50.00	100.00
❑ SC-1056 [S]	Clint Eastwood Sings Cowboy Favorites	1963	37.50	75.00	150.00

EATON, CONNIE

45s

Number	Title (A Side/B Side)	Yr	VG	VG+	NM
ABC					
❑ 12098	If I Knew Enough to Come Out of the Rain/Magic Mystery	1975	—	2.50	5.00
ABC DOT					
❑ 17571	It Was the Thing to Do/Who's Gonna Love Me Now	1975	—	2.50	5.00
ABC DUNHILL					
❑ 15022	Lonely Men, Lonely Women/Midnight Train to Georgia	1974	—	2.50	5.00
CHART					
❑ 1048	Too Many Dollars, Not Enough Sense/Bonnie	1968	2.00	4.00	8.00
❑ 1067	He's a Night Owl/Something's Wrong in California	1969	2.00	4.00	8.00
❑ 5009	And Say Good-Bye/Raining Blue	1969	—	3.50	7.00
❑ 5027	I've Got Life to Live/A Million Shades of Blue	1969	—	3.50	7.00
❑ 5048	Angel of the Morning/One Time Too Many	1969	—	3.50	7.00
❑ 5056	Tennessee Bird Walk/If You Can't Bring It Home	1970	—	3.50	7.00
—With Tony Martin					
❑ 5084	Memories/Tomorrow My Babies Are Coming Home	1970	—	3.50	7.00
❑ 5094	These Hills/The Best of Everything	1970	—	3.50	7.00
❑ 5110	Sing a Happy Song/Glad to Be Your Woman	1971	—	3.00	6.00
❑ 5120	And Say Goodbye/Leave Me	1971	—	3.00	6.00
❑ 5138	Don't Hang No Halos on Me/These Hills	1971	—	3.00	6.00
❑ 5148	Let Me Be the One/You May Wonder	1972	—	3.00	6.00
❑ 5162	Tar and Cement/Angel of the Morning	1972	—	3.00	6.00
❑ 5182	Love Is So Elusive/These Hills	1973	—	3.00	6.00
❑ 5196	The Other Side of Town/God Paints Pictures	1973	—	3.00	6.00
ENTERPRISE					
❑ 9096	Love Is So Elusive/It's You	1974	—	3.00	6.00
❑ 9105	I Wanna Be Wrong Right Now/Let's Get Together	1974	—	3.00	6.00
MUSICTOWN					
❑ 002	Davy Jones' Locker/A Million Shades of Blue	197?	—	3.00	6.00

EATON, CONNIE, AND DAVE PEEL

Also see each artist's individual listings.

45s

Number	Title (A Side/B Side)	Yr	VG	VG+	NM
CHART					
❑ 5066	Hit the Road Jack/The Question	1970	—	3.00	6.00
❑ 5099	It Takes Two/No Rest for the Weary	1970	—	3.00	6.00
❑ 5132	In the Shadows of the Night/Our Divorce Was a Failure	1971	—	3.00	6.00

Albums

Number	Title	Yr	VG	VG+	NM
CHART					
❑ 1034	Hit the Road Jack	1970	3.75	7.50	15.00

EBERLY, BOB

Big-band vocalist who crossed over to the country chart with the below recording.

Selected 78s

Number	Title (A Side/B Side)	Yr	VG	VG+	NM
DECCA					
❑ 24492	One Has My Name, The Other Has My Heart/Just a Little Lovin' (Will Go a Long Way)	1948	3.75	7.50	15.00

EBSEN, BUDDY

Albums

Number	Title	Yr	VG	VG+	NM
REPRISE					
❑ R-6174 [M]	Buddy Ebsen Sings Howdy!	1965	7.50	15.00	30.00
❑ RS-6174 [S]	Buddy Ebsen Sings Howdy!	1965	10.00	20.00	40.00

EDDY, DUANE

45s

Number	Title (A Side/B Side)	Yr	VG	VG+	NM
BIG TREE					
❑ 157	Renegade/Nightly News	1972	2.00	4.00	8.00
CAPITOL					
❑ B-44018	Spies/Rockabilly Holiday	1987	—	2.50	5.00
❑ B-44018 [PS]	Spies/Rockabilly Holiday	1987	—	2.50	5.00
CHINA					
❑ 42986	Peter Gunn/Something Always Happens	1986	—	—	3.00
—With Art of Noise; B-side does not feature Eddy					
❑ 42986 [PS]	Peter Gunn/Something Always Happens	1986	—	—	3.00
COLPIX					
❑ 779	Trash/South Phoenix	1965	3.75	7.50	15.00
❑ 788	Don't Think Twice, It's All Right/House of the Rising Sun	1965	3.75	7.50	15.00
❑ 788 [PS]	Don't Think Twice, It's All Right/House of the Rising Sun	1965	12.50	25.00	50.00
❑ 795	El Rancho Grande/Poppa's Movin' On	1966	3.75	7.50	15.00
CONGRESS					
❑ 6010	Freight Train/Put a Little Love in Your Heart	1970	3.75	7.50	15.00
ELEKTRA					
❑ 45359	You Are My Sunshine/From 8 to 7	1977	—	2.50	5.00
FORD					
❑ 500	Ramrod/Caravan	1957	500.00	1000.	1500.
—As "Duane Eddy and His Rock-A-Billies"					
GREGMARK					
❑ 5	Caravan (Part 1)/Caravan (Part 2)	1961	3.75	7.50	15.00
—Credited to Duane Eddy, but is actually Al Casey					
GUSTO					
❑ 2047	Rebel Rouser/40 Miles of Bad Road	1979	—	2.00	4.00
—Re-recordings					
JAMIE					
❑ JLP-71 [S]	Lonesome Road/I Almost Lost My Mind	1960	6.25	12.50	25.00
❑ JLP-72 [S]	Loving You/Anything	1960	6.25	12.50	25.00
❑ JLP-73 [S]	Peter Gunn/Along the Navaho Trail	1960	6.25	12.50	25.00
❑ JLP-74 [S]	Hard Times/Along Came Linda	1960	6.25	12.50	25.00
❑ JLP-75 [S]	The Battle/You Are My Sunshine	1960	6.25	12.50	25.00
—The above five are 33 1/3 rpm singles with small holes					
❑ 1101	Moovin N' Groovin'/Up and Down	1958	12.50	25.00	50.00
—Originals have pink labels					
❑ 1101	Moovin N' Groovin'/Up and Down	1958	6.25	12.50	25.00
—All-yellow label, "Jamie" at top					
❑ 1104	Rebel-'Rouser/Stalkin'	1958	6.25	12.50	25.00
❑ 1109	Ramrod/The Walker	1958	6.25	12.50	25.00
❑ 1111	Cannonball/Mason Dixon Line	1958	5.00	10.00	20.00
❑ 1117 [M]	The Lonely One/Detour	1959	5.00	10.00	20.00
❑ 1117 [S]	The Lonely One/Detour	1959	12.50	25.00	50.00
❑ 1122	Yep!/Three-30-Blues	1959	5.00	10.00	20.00
❑ 1122 [PS]	Yep!/Three-30-Blues	1959	12.50	25.00	50.00
❑ 1126 [M]	Forty Miles of Bad Road/The Quiet Three	1959	5.00	10.00	20.00
❑ 1126 [PS]	Forty Miles of Bad Road/The Quiet Three	1959	12.50	25.00	50.00
❑ 1126 [S]	Forty Miles of Bad Road/The Quiet Three	1959	12.50	25.00	50.00
❑ 1130 [M]	Some Kind-a Earthquake/First Love, First Tears	1959	5.00	10.00	20.00
❑ 1130 [PS]	Some Kind-a Earthquake/First Love, First Tears	1959	10.00	20.00	40.00
❑ 1130 [S]	Some Kind-a Earthquake/First Love, First Tears	1959	12.50	25.00	50.00

Number	Title (A Side/B Side)	Yr	VG	VG+	NM
❑ 1144	Bonnie Came Back/Lost Island	1959	5.00	10.00	20.00
❑ 1144 [PS]	Bonnie Came Back/Lost Island	1959	10.00	20.00	40.00
❑ 1151	Shazam!/The Secret Seven	1960	3.75	7.50	15.00
❑ 1151 [PS]	Shazam!/The Secret Seven	1960	7.50	15.00	30.00
❑ 1156	Because They're Young/Rebel Walk	1960	3.75	7.50	15.00
❑ 1156 [PS]	Because They're Young/Rebel Walk	1960	7.50	15.00	30.00
❑ 1163	Kommotion/Theme from Moon Children	1960	3.75	7.50	15.00
❑ 1163 [PS]	Kommotion/Theme from Moon Children	1960	7.50	15.00	30.00
❑ 1168	Peter Gunn/Along the Navaho Trail	1960	3.75	7.50	15.00
❑ 1168 [PS]	Peter Gunn/Along the Navaho Trail	1960	7.50	15.00	30.00
❑ 1175	"Pepe"/Lost Friend	1960	3.75	7.50	15.00
❑ 1175 [PS]	"Pepe"/Lost Friend	1960	10.00	20.00	40.00
—Red sleeve					
❑ 1175 [PS]	"Pepe"/Lost Friend	1960	7.50	15.00	30.00
—Yellow sleeve					
❑ 1183	Theme from Dixie/Gidget Goes Hawaiian	1961	3.75	7.50	15.00
❑ 1183 [PS]	Theme from Dixie/Gidget Goes Hawaiian	1961	7.50	15.00	30.00
❑ 1187	Ring of Fire/Bobbie	1961	3.75	7.50	15.00
❑ 1187 [PS]	Ring of Fire/Bobbie	1961	7.50	15.00	30.00
❑ 1195	Drivin' Home/Tammy	1961	3.75	7.50	15.00
❑ 1195 [PS]	Drivin' Home/Tammy	1961	7.50	15.00	30.00
❑ 1200	My Blue Heaven/Along Came Linda	1961	3.75	7.50	15.00
❑ 1200 [PS]	My Blue Heaven/Along Came Linda	1961	7.50	15.00	30.00
❑ 1206	The Avenger/Londonderry Air	1961	3.75	7.50	15.00
❑ 1209	The Battle/Trambone	1962	3.75	7.50	15.00
❑ 1224	Runaway Pony/Just Because	1962	3.75	7.50	15.00
❑ 1303	Rebel Rouser/Movin' N' Groovin'	1965	3.00	6.00	12.00
RCA VICTOR					
❑ 47-7999	Deep in the Heart of Texas/Saints and Sinners	1962	3.00	6.00	12.00
❑ 47-7999 [PS]	Deep in the Heart of Texas/Saints and Sinners	1962	6.25	12.50	25.00
❑ 47-8047	The Ballad of Paladin/The WIld Westerner	1962	3.00	6.00	12.00
❑ 47-8047 [PS]	The Ballad of Paladin/The WIld Westerner	1962	6.25	12.50	25.00
❑ 47-8087	(Dance with the) Guitar Man/Stretchin' Out	1962	3.75	7.50	15.00
❑ 47-8087 [PS]	(Dance with the) Guitar Man/Stretchin' Out	1962	7.50	15.00	30.00
❑ 47-8131	Boss Guitar/Desert Rat	1963	3.00	6.00	12.00
❑ 47-8131 [PS]	Boss Guitar/Desert Rat	1963	6.25	12.50	25.00
❑ 47-8180	Lonely Boy, Lonely Guitar/Joshin'	1963	3.00	6.00	12.00
❑ 47-8180 [PS]	Lonely Boy, Lonely Guitar/Joshin'	1963	6.25	12.50	25.00
❑ 47-8214	Your Baby's Gone Surfin'/Shuckin'	1963	3.75	7.50	15.00
❑ 47-8214 [PS]	Your Baby's Gone Surfin'/Shuckin'	1963	7.50	15.00	30.00
❑ 47-8276	The Son of Rebel Rouser/The Story of Three Loves	1963	3.00	6.00	12.00
❑ 47-8276 [PS]	The Son of Rebel Rouser/The Story of Three Loves	1963	6.25	12.50	25.00
❑ 47-8335	Guitar Child/Jerky Jalopy	1964	3.00	6.00	12.00
❑ 47-8376	Water Skiing/Theme from A Summer Place	1964	3.00	6.00	12.00
❑ 47-8442	Guitar Star/The Iguana	1964	3.00	6.00	12.00
❑ 47-8507	Moonshot/Roughneck	1965	3.00	6.00	12.00
REPRISE					
❑ 0504	Daydream/This Guitar Was Made for Twangin'	1966	2.50	5.00	10.00
❑ 0557	Roarin'/Monsoon	1967	2.50	5.00	10.00
❑ 0662	There Is a Mountain/This Town	1968	2.50	5.00	10.00
❑ 0690	Niki-Hoeky/Velvet Nights	1968	2.50	5.00	10.00
UNI					
❑ 55237	The Five-Seventeen/Something	1970	3.75	7.50	15.00
7-Inch Extended Plays					
JAMIE					
❑ JEP-100	Cannonball/Moovin' N' Groovin'//Mason-Dixon Lion/The Lonely One	1958	12.50	25.00	50.00
❑ JEP-100 [PS]	Duane Eddy	1958	12.50	25.00	50.00
❑ JEP-301	Lonesome Road/I Almost Lost My Mind//Detour/Loving You	1959	12.50	25.00	50.00
❑ JEP-301 [PS]	Detour	1959	12.50	25.00	50.00
❑ JEP-302	Yep/Three-30 Blues//Anytime/Stalkin'	1959	12.50	25.00	50.00
❑ JEP-302 [PS]	Yep!	1959	12.50	25.00	50.00
❑ JEP-303	Shazam/Tiger Love//My Blue Heaven/Night Train To Memphis	1960	12.50	25.00	50.00
❑ JEP-303 [PS]	Shazam!	1960	12.50	25.00	50.00
❑ JEP-304	Because They're Young/Easy//Rebel Walk/The Battle	1960	12.50	25.00	50.00
❑ JEP-304 [PS]	Because They're Young	1960	12.50	25.00	50.00
Albums					
CAPITOL					
❑ ST-12567	Duane Eddy	1987	3.00	6.00	12.00
COLPIX					
❑ CP-490 [M]	Duane A-Go-Go	1965	7.50	15.00	30.00
❑ CPS-490 [S]	Duane A-Go-Go	1965	10.00	20.00	40.00
❑ CP-494 [M]	Duane Eddy Does Bob Dylan	1965	7.50	15.00	30.00
❑ CPS-494 [S]	Duane Eddy Does Bob Dylan	1965	10.00	20.00	40.00
JAMIE					
❑ JLP-3000 [M]	Have "Twangy" Guitar — Will Travel	1958	30.00	60.00	120.00
—Duane sitting with guitar case, title on cover in white (1st)					
❑ JLP-3000 [M]	Have "Twangy" Guitar — Will Travel	1959	25.00	50.00	100.00
—Duane sitting with guitar case, title on cover in green and red (2nd)					
❑ JLP-3000 [M]	Have "Twangy" Guitar — Will Travel	1959	12.50	25.00	50.00
—Duane standing with guitar (3rd)					
❑ JLPS-3000 [R]	Have "Twangy" Guitar — Will Travel	196?	12.50	25.00	50.00
—Duane standing with guitar (3rd), album plays fake stereo					
❑ JLPS-3000 [S]	Have "Twangy" Guitar — Will Travel	1958	100.00	200.00	400.00
—Duane sitting with guitar case, title on cover in white (1st)					
❑ JLPS-3000 [S]	Have "Twangy" Guitar — Will Travel	1959	75.00	150.00	300.00
—Duane sitting with guitar case, title on cover in green and red (2nd)					
❑ JLPS-3000 [S]	Have "Twangy" Guitar — Will Travel	1959	25.00	50.00	100.00
—Duane standing with guitar (3rd), album plays true stereo					
❑ JLPM-3006 [M]	Especially for You...	1959	10.00	20.00	40.00

Number	Title (A Side/B Side)	Yr	VG	VG+	NM
❑ JLPS-3006 [S]	Especially for You...	1959	15.00	30.00	60.00
❑ JLPM-3009 [M]	The "Twangs" The "Thang"	1959	10.00	20.00	40.00
❑ JLPS-3009 [S]	The "Twangs" The "Thang"	1959	15.00	30.00	60.00
❑ JLPM-3011 [M]	Songs of Our Heritage	1960	20.00	40.00	80.00
—Gatefold cover					
❑ JLPM-3011 [M]	Songs of Our Heritage	196?	7.50	15.00	30.00
—Regular cover					
❑ JLPS-3011 [S]	Songs of Our Heritage	1960	25.00	50.00	100.00
—Gatefold cover					
❑ JLPS-3011 [S]	Songs of Our Heritage	1960	125.00	250.00	500.00
—Gatefold cover, red vinyl					
❑ JLPS-3011 [S]	Songs of Our Heritage	1960	125.00	250.00	500.00
—Gatefold cover, blue vinyl					
❑ JLPS-3011 [S]	Songs of Our Heritage	196?	10.00	20.00	40.00
—Regular cover					
❑ JLPM-3014 [M]	$1,000,000.00 Worth of Twang	1960	10.00	20.00	40.00
❑ JLPS-3014 [S]	$1,000,000.00 Worth of Twang	1960	17.50	35.00	70.00
—All but one song -- "Up and Down" -- is in true stereo					
❑ JLPM-3019 [M]	Girls! Girls! Girls!	1961	10.00	20.00	40.00
❑ JLPS-3019 [R]	Girls! Girls! Girls!	1961	7.50	15.00	30.00
❑ JLPM-3021 [M]	$1,000,000.00 Worth of Twang, Volume 2	1962	10.00	20.00	40.00
❑ JLPS-3021 [R]	$1,000,000.00 Worth of Twang, Volume 2	1962	7.50	15.00	30.00
❑ JLPM-3022 [M]	Twistin' with Duane Eddy	1962	10.00	20.00	40.00
❑ JLPS-3022 [P]	Twistin' with Duane Eddy	1962	10.00	20.00	40.00
❑ JLPM-3024 [M]	Surfin'	1963	12.50	25.00	50.00
❑ JLPS-3024 [S]	Surfin'	1963	20.00	40.00	80.00
❑ JLPM-3025 [M]	Duane Eddy & The Rebels — In Person	1963	7.50	15.00	30.00
❑ JLPS-3025 [S]	Duane Eddy & The Rebels — In Person	1963	10.00	20.00	40.00
❑ JLPM-3026 [M]	16 Greatest Hits	1964	10.00	20.00	40.00
❑ JLPS-3026 [R]	16 Greatest Hits	1964	7.50	15.00	30.00
❑ ST-90663 [S]	Duane Eddy & The Rebels — In Person	1965	12.50	25.00	50.00
—Capitol Record Club edition					
❑ T-90663 [M]	Duane Eddy & The Rebels — In Person	1965	10.00	20.00	40.00
—Capitol Record Club edition					
❑ ST-90682 [S]	Have "Twangy" Guitar — Will Travel	1965	20.00	40.00	80.00
—Capitol Record Club edition					
❑ T-90682 [M]	Have "Twangy" Guitar — Will Travel	1965	15.00	30.00	60.00
—Capitol Record Club edition					
❑ ST-91301 [S]	The "Twangs" The "Thang"	1966	15.00	30.00	60.00
—Capitol Record Club edition					
❑ T-91301 [M]	The "Twangs" The "Thang"	1966	15.00	30.00	60.00
—Capitol Record Club edition					
RCA VICTOR					
❑ LPM-2525 [M]	Twistin' 'N' Twangin'	1962	6.25	12.50	25.00
❑ LSP-2525 [S]	Twistin' 'N' Twangin'	1962	10.00	20.00	40.00
❑ LPM-2576 [M]	Twangy Guitar — Silky Strings	1962	6.25	12.50	25.00
❑ LSP-2576 [S]	Twangy Guitar — Silky Strings	1962	10.00	20.00	40.00
❑ LPM-2648 [M]	Dance with the Guitar Man	1962	6.25	12.50	25.00
❑ LSP-2648 [S]	Dance with the Guitar Man	1962	10.00	20.00	40.00
❑ ANL1-2671	Pure Gold	1978	2.50	5.00	10.00
❑ LPM-2681 [M]	Twang a Country Song	1963	6.25	12.50	25.00
❑ LSP-2681 [S]	Twang a Country Song	1963	10.00	20.00	40.00
❑ LPM-2700 [M]	"Twangin' " Up a Storm!	1963	6.25	12.50	25.00
❑ LSP-2700 [S]	"Twangin' " Up a Storm!	1963	10.00	20.00	40.00
❑ LPM-2798 [M]	Lonely Guitar	1964	5.00	10.00	20.00
❑ LSP-2798 [S]	Lonely Guitar	1964	7.50	15.00	30.00
❑ LPM-2918 [M]	Water Skiing	1964	5.00	10.00	20.00
❑ LSP-2918 [S]	Water Skiing	1964	7.50	15.00	30.00
❑ LPM-2993 [M]	Twangin' the Golden Hits	1965	5.00	10.00	20.00
❑ LSP-2993 [S]	Twangin' the Golden Hits	1965	7.50	15.00	30.00
❑ LPM-3432 [M]	Twangsville	1965	5.00	10.00	20.00
❑ LSP-3432 [S]	Twangsville	1965	7.50	15.00	30.00
❑ LPM-3477 [M]	The Best of Duane Eddy	1965	5.00	10.00	20.00
❑ LSP-3477 [P]	The Best of Duane Eddy	1965	6.25	12.50	25.00
—Black "Stereo" label					
❑ LSP-3477 [P]	The Best of Duane Eddy	1969	3.75	7.50	15.00
—Orange label					
REPRISE					
❑ R-6218 [M]	The Biggest Twang of Them All	1966	7.50	15.00	30.00
❑ RS-6218 [S]	The Biggest Twang of Them All	1966	10.00	20.00	40.00
❑ R-6240 [M]	The Roaring Twangies	1967	7.50	15.00	30.00
❑ RS-6240 [S]	The Roaring Twangies	1967	10.00	20.00	40.00
SIRE					
❑ SASH-3702 [(2)]	The Vintage Years	1975	6.25	12.50	25.00

EDDY, DUANE AND MIRRIAM

Also see JESSI COLTER, DUANE EDDY.

45s

REPRISE

Number	Title (A Side/B Side)	Yr	VG	VG+	NM
❑ 0622	Guitar on My Mind/Wicked Women from Wickenborg	1967	2.50	5.00	10.00

EDGE, KATHY

45s

NSD

Number	Title (A Side/B Side)	Yr	VG	VG+	NM
❑ 221	When You Love Me Like You Do/I Need a Friend	1986	—	2.50	5.00
❑ 228	I Take the Chance/You Always Come Back to Hurting Me	1987	—	2.50	5.00
❑ 233	I'm Not Just Another Cheatin' Heart/(B-side unknown)	1987	—	2.50	5.00
❑ 242	Nobody's Bride/(B-side unknown)	1987	—	3.00	6.00

EDWARDS, BOBBY

45s

Number	Title (A Side/B Side)	Yr	VG	VG+	NM
CAPITOL					
❑ 4674	What's the Reason/Walk Away Slowly	1961	2.00	4.00	8.00
❑ 4726	Singing the Blues/What'll I Do Without You	1962	2.00	4.00	8.00
❑ 4789	Someone New/Here's My Heart	1962	2.00	4.00	8.00
❑ 4874	Remember Who Brought You Here/The Way I Am	1962	2.00	4.00	8.00
❑ 5006	Don't Pretend/Help Me	1963	2.00	4.00	8.00
CHART					
❑ 1020	I'm Sorry to See You Go/Once a Fool (Always a Fool)	1968	—	2.50	5.00
❑ 1045	Each Time You Cross My Mind/Just Ain't My Day	1968	—	2.50	5.00
❑ 5016	Bring My Baby Home/Loving You Is Killing Me	1969	—	2.50	5.00
❑ 5061	You're the Reason/Don't Pretend	1970	—	2.50	5.00
CREST					
❑ 1075	You're the Reason/I'm a Fool for Loving You	1961	2.50	5.00	10.00
MANCO					
❑ 1026	Jealous Heart/I've Lost Everything But the Memories	1962	2.00	4.00	8.00
MUSICOR					
❑ 1101	A Little Less Heartache/Within Your Arms	1965	—	3.00	6.00

EDWARDS, JIMMY

45s

Number	Title (A Side/B Side)	Yr	VG	VG+	NM
MERCURY					
❑ 71209	Love Bug Crawl/Honey Lovin'	1957	7.50	15.00	30.00
❑ 71272	My Honey/Golden Ruby Blue	1958	7.50	15.00	30.00
❑ 71348	Do That Again/Wedding Band	1958	7.50	15.00	30.00
RCA VICTOR					
❑ 47-7597	A Favor for a Friend/Your Love Is a Good Love	1959	6.25	12.50	25.00
❑ 47-7717	Rosie Lee/Live and Let Live	1960	5.00	10.00	20.00
❑ 47-7773	Silver Slippers/What Do You Want from Me	1960	5.00	10.00	20.00

EDWARDS, JONATHAN

45s

Number	Title (A Side/B Side)	Yr	VG	VG+	NM
ATCO					
❑ 6881	Train of Glory/Everybody Knows Her	1972	—	2.50	5.00
❑ 6911	That's What Our Life Is/Stop and Start It All Again	1972	—	2.50	5.00
❑ 6920	Honky-Tonk Stardust Cowboy/(B-side unknown)	1973	—	2.50	5.00
❑ 6952	Rollin' Alone/The Place I've Been	1974	—	2.50	5.00
CAPRICORN					
❑ 8021	Sunshine/Emma	1971	—	2.50	5.00
MCA CURB					
❑ 53390	We Need to Be Locked Away/Back Up Grinnin'	1988	—	—	3.00
❑ 53467	Look What We Made (When We Made Love)/ Fewer Threads Than These	1988	—	—	3.00
❑ 53613	My Baby's a Country Song/It's a Natural Thing	1989	—	—	3.00
REPRISE					
❑ 1358	White Line/Favorite Song	1976	—	2.00	4.00
WARNER BROS.					
❑ 8364	Carolina Caroline/Never Together (But Close Sometimes)	1977	—	2.00	4.00

Albums

Number	Title (A Side/B Side)	Yr	VG	VG+	NM
ATCO					
❑ SD 36-104	Lucky Day	1974	3.00	6.00	12.00
❑ SD 7015	Honky-Tonk Stardust Cowboy	1972	3.00	6.00	12.00
❑ SD 7036	Have a Good Time for Me	1973	3.00	6.00	12.00
CAPRICORN					
❑ SD 862	Jonathan Edwards	1971	3.00	6.00	12.00
—Original has green label					
❑ SD 862	Jonathan Edwards	198?	2.00	4.00	8.00
—Reissue with tan label					
CHRONIC					
❑ 1001	Live!	1982	3.00	6.00	12.00
MCA CURB					
❑ 42256	The Natural Thing	1989	2.50	5.00	10.00
REPRISE					
❑ MS 2238	Rockin' Chair	1976	2.50	5.00	10.00
SUGAR HILL					
❑ SH-3747	Blue Ridge	1985	2.50	5.00	10.00
—With the Seldom Scene					
WARNER BROS.					
❑ BS 3020	Sailboat	1977	2.50	5.00	10.00

EDWARDS, STONEY

45s

Number	Title (A Side/B Side)	Yr	VG	VG+	NM
CAPITOL					
❑ 3005	A Two Dollar Toy/An Old Mule's Hip	1970	—	3.00	6.00
❑ 3061	Poor Folks Stick Together/Mama's Love	1971	—	3.00	6.00
❑ 3131	The Cute Little Waitress/Please Bring a Bottle	1971	—	3.00	6.00
❑ 3191	Odd-Job Dollar-Bill Man/The Fishin' Song	1971	—	3.00	6.00
❑ 3270	Daddy Did His Best/I Bought the Shoes That Just Walked Out on Me	1972	—	3.00	6.00
❑ 3347	You Can't Call Yourself Country/All She Made of Me	1972	—	3.00	6.00
❑ 3462	She's My Rock/I Won't Make It Through the Day	1972	—	2.50	5.00
❑ 3550	You're a Believer/She's Helping Me Get Over You	1973	—	2.50	5.00
❑ 3671	Hank and Lefty Raised My Country Soul/A Few of the Reasons	1973	—	2.50	5.00
❑ 3766	Daddy Bluegrass/It's Rainin' on My Sunny Day	1973	—	2.50	5.00
❑ 3878	I Will Never Get Over You/Honey	1974	—	2.50	5.00
❑ 3949	Our Garden of Love/Talk About a Woman	1974	—	2.50	5.00
❑ 4015	Clean Your Own Tables/Do You Know the Man	1974	—	2.50	5.00
❑ 4051	Mississippi You're on My Mind/A Two Dollar Toy	1975	—	2.50	5.00
❑ 4124	Moon Over Morocco/Partners on the Road	1975	—	2.50	5.00
❑ 4188	Blackbird (Hold Your Head High)/Pickin' Wildflowers	1975	—	2.50	5.00
❑ 4246	Love Still Makes the World Go 'Round/(I Want) The Real Thing	1976	—	2.50	5.00
❑ 4337	Don't Give Up on Me/July 12, 1939	1976	—	2.50	5.00
❑ 4433	Yankee Lady/Pickin' Wildflowers	1977	—	2.50	5.00
HILL COUNTRY					
❑ 901	Our Little Christmas Tree/Silent Night - Holy Night	198?	—	3.00	6.00
JMI					
❑ 47	If I Had to Do It All Over Again/I Feel Chained	1978	—	2.50	5.00
❑ 49	My Olkahome/Someone Like You	1979	—	2.50	5.00
MUSIC AMERICA					
❑ 107	No Way to Drown a Memory/Reverend Leroy	1980	—	2.50	5.00
❑ 109	One Bar at a Time/Stranger in My Arms	1980	—	2.50	5.00

Albums

Number	Title (A Side/B Side)	Yr	VG	VG+	NM
CAPITOL					
❑ ST-741	Country Singer	1970	6.25	12.50	25.00
❑ ST-834	Down Home in the Country	1971	5.00	10.00	20.00
❑ ST-11090	Stoney Edwards	1972	5.00	10.00	20.00
❑ ST-11173	She's My Rock	1973	5.00	10.00	20.00
❑ ST-11401	Mississippi on My Mind	1975	5.00	10.00	20.00
❑ ST-11499	Blackbird	1976	5.00	10.00	20.00

ELLEDGE, JIMMY

45s

Number	Title (A Side/B Side)	Yr	VG	VG+	NM
4 STAR					
❑ 1003	One By One/After You	1975	—	2.00	4.00
❑ 1015	Lady Lover/(B-side unknown)	1976	—	2.00	4.00
HICKORY					
❑ 1313	Follow Every Rainbow/I Just Walked In (Your Heart Last Night)	1965	2.00	4.00	8.00
❑ 1341	A Good Woman's Love (Not Easy to Find)/World of Lavender Lace	1965	2.00	4.00	8.00
❑ 1363	A Legend in My Time/Pink Dally Rue	1966	2.00	4.00	8.00
❑ 1393	Time Is a Thief/I Just Walked In (Your Heart Last Night)	1966	2.00	4.00	8.00
❑ 1420	Let Me Love You a Little (So I Can Love You a Lot)/She Should Save Some Loving (For a Rainy Day)	1966	2.00	4.00	8.00
❑ 1452	The Darkest Part of Night (Is Dawn)/She Should Save Some Loving (For a Rainy Day)	1967	2.00	4.00	8.00
LITTLE DARLIN'					
❑ 0047	Florence Jean/No One Ever Lost More	1968	—	3.00	6.00
RCA VICTOR					
❑ 47-7910	Send Me a Letter/Swanee River Rocket	1961	3.00	6.00	12.00
❑ 47-7946	Funny How Time Slips Away/Hey Jimmy Joe John Jim Jack	1961	2.50	5.00	10.00
❑ 47-8012	Can't You See It in My Eyes/What a Laugh	1962	5.00	10.00	20.00
❑ 47-8042	Bo Diddley/Diamonds	1962	2.00	4.00	8.00
❑ 47-8081	A Golden Tear/I'll Get By (Don't Worry)	1962	2.00	4.00	8.00
❑ 47-8136	You Can Have Her/I Miss Her Already	1963	2.00	4.00	8.00
❑ 47-8191	Please Love Me Forever/A Penny's Worth of Happiness	1963	2.00	4.00	8.00
❑ 47-8241	I Had to Run Away/There's Nothing There for Me	1963	2.00	4.00	8.00
❑ 47-8355	Dream of the Year/Gonna Turn My Voodoo On	1964	2.00	4.00	8.00
SIMS					
❑ 204	I Gotta Live Here/Hold My Heart for Awhile	1964	2.00	4.00	8.00

ELLIOTT, ALECIA

45s

Number	Title (A Side/B Side)	Yr	VG	VG+	NM
MCA NASHVILLE					
❑ 72121	I'm Diggin' It (2:40)/I'm Diggin' It (3:33)	1999	—	—	3.00
❑ 088-172159-7	You Wanna What?/That's the Only Way	2000	—	—	3.00

ELLIOTT, WALTER & BENNETT

Also see E.W.B.

45s

Number	Title (A Side/B Side)	Yr	VG	VG+	NM
PAID					
❑ DAL 1	The Twelve Days of a Dallas Cowboy Christmas/ It	1980	2.00	4.00	8.00
❑ OAK 2	The Twelve Days of an Oakland Raider Christmas/It	1980	2.00	4.00	8.00
❑ ATL 3	The Twelve Days of a Atlanta Falcon Christmas/It	1980	2.00	4.00	8.00
—Label is ungrammatical as above					
❑ PIT 4	The Twelve Days of a Pittsburg Steelers Christmas/It	1980	2.00	4.00	8.00
—The label misspells "Pittsburgh"					
❑ NEP 5	The Twelve Days of a New England Patriot Christmas/It	1980	2.00	4.00	8.00
❑ BBS 6	The Twelve Days of a Buffalo Bill Christmas/It	1980	2.00	4.00	8.00
❑ PES 7	The Twelve Days of a Philadelphia Eagle Christmas/It	1980	2.00	4.00	8.00
❑ LAX 8	The Twelve Days of a Los Angeles Ram Christmas/It	1980	2.00	4.00	8.00
❑ COB 9	The Twelve Days of a Cleveland Brown Christmas/It	1980	2.00	4.00	8.00
❑ SDC 10	The Twelve Days of a San Diego Charger Christmas/It	1980	2.00	4.00	8.00
❑ 120	We Love the Atlanta Falcons/The Race Is On	1981	2.50	5.00	10.00
❑ 121	We Love the (team unknown)/The Race Is On	1981	2.50	5.00	10.00
❑ 122	We Love the San Diego Chargers/The Race Is On	1981	2.50	5.00	10.00
❑ 123	We Love the Dallas Cowboys/The Race Is On	1981	2.50	5.00	10.00

Number	Title (A Side/B Side)	Yr	VG	VG+	NM
❑ 124	We Love the Oakland Raiders/The Race Is On	1981	2.50	5.00	10.00
❑ 125	We Love the (team unknown)/The Race Is On	1981	2.50	5.00	10.00
❑ 126	We Love the (team unknown)/The Race Is On	1981	2.50	5.00	10.00
❑ 127	We Love the Minnesota Vikings/The Race Is On	1981	2.50	5.00	10.00

—We know of at least eight in this series. The contents of Paid 119, 128 and 129 are not known, so there may be even more that eight in the series. Any help in filling in the gaps would be appreciated.

Albums

JAM

Number	Title (A Side/B Side)	Yr	VG	VG+	NM
❑ 104/105 [(2)]	Elliott, Walter & Bennett	197?	5.00	10.00	20.00
❑ 106	Zeti Reticuli	197?	20.00	40.00	80.00
❑ (# unknown)	Save a Piece of the World	1975	12.50	25.00	50.00

—As "Elliott and Walter"

ELLIS, DARRYL AND DON

45s

EPIC

Number	Title (A Side/B Side)	Yr	VG	VG+	NM
❑ 34-74325	Goodbye Highway/I Knew You'd Come Around	1992	—	—	3.00
❑ 34-74454	No Sir/I Knew You'd Come Around	1992	—	—	3.00
❑ 34-74758	Something Moving in Me/You Know Why	1992	—	—	3.00
❑ 34-74951	10 Minutes Till/You Know Why	1993	—	—	3.00
❑ 34-77212	Walk On Out of My Mind/When It Rains	1993	—	—	3.00

ELLIS, JIMMY

Also see ORION.

45s

BOBLO

Number	Title (A Side/B Side)	Yr	VG	VG+	NM
❑ 526	Tupelo Woman/The Closer He Gets	1976	—	2.00	4.00
❑ 531	There You Go/Here Comes That Wonderful Feeling	1977	—	2.00	4.00
❑ 532	Movin' On/My Baby's Out of Sight	1977	—	2.00	4.00
❑ 536	I'm Not Trying to Be Like Elvis/Games You've Been Playing	1978	—	2.00	4.00
❑ 536 [PS]	I'm Not Trying to Be Like Elvis/Games You've Been Playing	1978	2.50	5.00	10.00

DRADCO

Number	Title (A Side/B Side)	Yr	VG	VG+	NM
❑ 1892	Don't Count Your Chickens/Love Is But Love	1964	3.75	7.50	15.00

GOLDBAND

Number	Title (A Side/B Side)	Yr	VG	VG+	NM
❑ 1191	Woman in the Picture/What Swinging Doors Did to Me	196?	2.50	5.00	10.00

KRIS

Number	Title (A Side/B Side)	Yr	VG	VG+	NM
❑ 8115	Outskirts of Town (Part 1)/Outskirts of Town (Part 2)	196?	2.00	4.00	8.00

MCA

Number	Title (A Side/B Side)	Yr	VG	VG+	NM
❑ 40060	There Ya Go/Here Comes That Feeling Again	1973	—	2.00	4.00

RIDE

Number	Title (A Side/B Side)	Yr	VG	VG+	NM
❑ 146	Baby I Love You/Kiddio	196?	2.00	4.00	8.00

—As "Jimmie Ellis"; may not be the same performer as the others

SOUTHERN TRACKS

Number	Title (A Side/B Side)	Yr	VG	VG+	NM
❑ 1069	I Make the Livin' (You Make the Livin' Worthwhile)/Thank God for America	1986	—	2.00	4.00
❑ 1080	Sunday Fathers/Thank God for America	1987	—	2.00	4.00

SUN

Number	Title (A Side/B Side)	Yr	VG	VG+	NM
❑ 1129	That's All Right/Blue Moon of Kentucky	1973	—	2.50	5.00

—Originals have no artist on label in an attempt to make people believe these were lost Elvis Presley outtakes

Number	Title (A Side/B Side)	Yr	VG	VG+	NM
❑ 1129	That's All Right/Blue Moon of Kentucky	1973	—	2.00	4.00

—Second pressings credit Jimmy Ellis

Number	Title (A Side/B Side)	Yr	VG	VG+	NM
❑ 1131	I Use Her to Remind Me of You/Changing	1974	—	2.00	4.00
❑ 1136	D.O.A./Misty/That's All Right/Blue Moon of Kentucky	1977	—	2.00	4.00

Albums

BOBLO

Number	Title (A Side/B Side)	Yr	VG	VG+	NM
❑ 78-829	By Request Jimmy Sings Elvis	1978	25.00	50.00	100.00

ELLIS, MIKE

45s

CIN KAY

Number	Title (A Side/B Side)	Yr	VG	VG+	NM
❑ 130	I Never Meant to Harm You/West Virginian	1978	—	2.50	5.00

ELLWANGER, SANDY

45s

DOOR KNOB

Number	Title (A Side/B Side)	Yr	VG	VG+	NM
❑ 326	I Just Came In Here (To Let a Little Love Out)/(B-side unknown)	1989	—	2.50	5.00
❑ 334	What Kind of Girl Do You Think I Am/(B-side unknown)	1989	—	2.50	5.00
❑ 350	Walkin' in My Shoes/(B-side unknown)	1990	—	3.00	6.00
❑ 358	Change of Heart/(B-side unknown)	1990	—	3.00	6.00
❑ 363	I Don't Need Flowers/(B-side unknown)	1990	—	3.00	6.00

ELMO AND PATSY

45s

ELMO 'N' PATSY

Number	Title (A Side/B Side)	Yr	VG	VG+	NM
❑ KP-2984	Grandma Got Run Over by a Reindeer/Christmas	1979	5.00	10.00	20.00

—Original pressing of this Christmas classic; cream label, brown print

EPIC

Number	Title (A Side/B Side)	Yr	VG	VG+	NM
❑ 34-04703	Grandma Got Run Over by a Reindeer/Percy, the Puny Poinsettia	1984	—	2.00	4.00

—First issue of new recording

Number	Title (A Side/B Side)	Yr	VG	VG+	NM
❑ 34-04703 [PS]	Grandma Got Run Over by a Reindeer/Percy, the Puny Poinsettia	1984	—	2.00	4.00

—Picture sleeve known to exist with either 04703 or 05479 records inside

Number	Title (A Side/B Side)	Yr	VG	VG+	NM
❑ 34-05479	Grandma Got Run Over by a Reindeer/Percy, the Puny Poinsettia	1985	—	—	3.00

—Gray label reissue

OINK

Number	Title (A Side/B Side)	Yr	VG	VG+	NM
❑ 2984	Grandma Got Run Over by a Reindeer/Christmas	1979	2.00	4.00	8.00

—Second issue of original recording; white label, red print

SOUNDWAVES

Number	Title (A Side/B Side)	Yr	VG	VG+	NM
❑ 4658	Grandma Got Run Over by a Reindeer/Christmas	1979	—	3.00	6.00

—Third issue of original recording; white label, red print

Albums

EPIC

Number	Title (A Side/B Side)	Yr	VG	VG+	NM
❑ 5E 39931	Grandma Got Run Over by a Reindeer	1984	2.50	5.00	10.00
❑ PE 39931	Grandma Got Run Over by a Reindeer	1985	2.00	4.00	8.00

—reissue of 5E 39931

ELY, JOE

12-Inch Singles

HIGHTONE

Number	Title (A Side/B Side)	Yr	VG	VG+	NM
❑ 1001 [DJ]	Lord of the Highway (same on both sides)	1987	—	3.00	6.00
❑ 1002 [DJ]	My Baby Thinks She's French (same on both sides)	1987	—	2.50	5.00

SOUTH COAST

Number	Title (A Side/B Side)	Yr	VG	VG+	NM
❑ L33 1168 [DJ]	What's Shakin' Tonight (same on both sides)	1984	—	3.00	6.00

45s

MCA

Number	Title (A Side/B Side)	Yr	VG	VG+	NM
❑ 40666	All My Love/Mardi Gras Waltz	1976	—	2.00	4.00
❑ 40709	Gambler's Bride/Tennessee's Not the State I'm In	1977	—	2.00	4.00
❑ 40870	Fingernails/Because of the Wind	1978	—	2.00	4.00
❑ 40906	Honky Tonk Masquerade/Johnny Blues	1978	—	2.00	4.00
❑ 40956	Cornbread Moon/She Never Spoke Spanish to Me	1978	—	2.00	4.00

SOUTH COAST

Number	Title (A Side/B Side)	Yr	VG	VG+	NM
❑ 51102	Musta Notta Gotta Lotta/Rock Me My Baby	1981	—	2.00	4.00

Albums

HIGHTONE

Number	Title (A Side/B Side)	Yr	VG	VG+	NM
❑ 8008	Lord of the Highway	1987	2.50	5.00	10.00
❑ 8015	Dig All Night	1988	2.50	5.00	10.00

MCA

Number	Title (A Side/B Side)	Yr	VG	VG+	NM
❑ 2242	Joe Ely	1977	4.00	8.00	16.00
❑ 2333	Honky Tonk Masquerade	1978	4.00	8.00	16.00
❑ 3080	Down on the Drag	1979	4.00	8.00	16.00

—Originals have a gatefold sleeve

Number	Title (A Side/B Side)	Yr	VG	VG+	NM
❑ 5262	Live Shots	1981	3.00	6.00	12.00
❑ 5480	Hi-Res	1984	3.00	6.00	12.00
❑ R 124826	Live at Liberty Lunch	1990	3.75	7.50	15.00

—BMG Music Service edition

SOUTHCOAST

Number	Title (A Side/B Side)	Yr	VG	VG+	NM
❑ 5183	Musta Notta Gotta Lotta	1981	3.00	6.00	12.00

EME

45s

EPI

Number	Title (A Side/B Side)	Yr	VG	VG+	NM
❑ 1541	Every Breath I Take/Goodbye to Love	1981	2.00	4.00	8.00

EMERSON, LEE

45s

COLUMBIA

Number	Title (A Side/B Side)	Yr	VG	VG+	NM
❑ 4-21435	You Call That Waitin'/A Pair of Broken Hearts	1955	5.00	10.00	20.00
❑ 4-21487	So Little Time/Thank You My Darling	1956	5.00	10.00	20.00
❑ 4-21570	I Thought I Heard You Callin' My Name/It's So Easy for You to Be Mean	1956	5.00	10.00	20.00

EMERY, RALPH

45s

ABC

Number	Title (A Side/B Side)	Yr	VG	VG+	NM
❑ 10920	In the Misty Moonlight/Last Night Morning Sidewalks	1967	2.50	5.00	10.00
❑ 11001	One More for the Road/Yodelin' Jim	1967	2.50	5.00	10.00

ELEKTRA

Number	Title (A Side/B Side)	Yr	VG	VG+	NM
❑ 46010	Daddy, Is She Pretty As Mama/Wrestling Matches	1979	—	2.50	5.00
❑ 46033	Jesus Was a Country Boy/Kiss and Say Goodbye	1979	—	2.50	5.00

LIBERTY

Number	Title (A Side/B Side)	Yr	VG	VG+	NM
❑ 55352	Hello Fool/It's Not a Lot	1961	3.75	7.50	15.00
❑ 55383	I'll Take Good Care of Your Baby/Legend of Sleepy Hollow	1961	3.75	7.50	15.00
❑ 55429	Tough Top Cat/Two Minutes to Live	1962	3.75	7.50	15.00
❑ 55524	Christmas Dinner/Christmas Can't Be Far Away	1962	3.75	7.50	15.00
❑ 55546	Poor Boy/The Touch of the Master's Hand	1963	3.75	7.50	15.00

MERCURY

Number	Title (A Side/B Side)	Yr	VG	VG+	NM
❑ 72295	Sit Down and Write a Letter to Me, Won'tcha Baby/I Cry at Ball Games	1964	3.00	6.00	12.00

ORLANDO

Number	Title (A Side/B Side)	Yr	VG	VG+	NM
❑ 101	Daddy, Is She Pretty As Mama/Wrestling Matches	1979	2.50	5.00	10.00

EMILIO

45s

CAPITOL NASHVILLE

Number	Title (A Side/B Side)	Yr	VG	VG+	NM
❑ S7-18846	It's Not the End of the World/I Think We're On to Something	1995	—	2.00	4.00
❑ S7-19514	I'd Love You to Love Me/Any Little Lie	1997	—	—	3.00
❑ S7-19603	She Gives/The Bottom of Your Heart	1997	—	—	3.00

ENDEAVORS, THE

45s

STOP

Number	Title (A Side/B Side)	Yr	VG	VG+	NM
❑ 372	Shattered Dreams/I Know You Don't Want Me	1971	2.50	5.00	10.00

ENGLAND, TY

45s

RCA

Number	Title (A Side/B Side)	Yr	VG	VG+	NM
❑ 64280	Should've Asked Her Faster/A Swing Like That	1995	—	2.00	4.00
❑ 64405	Smoke in Her Eyes/Redneck Son	1995	—	—	3.00
❑ 64496	Redneck Son/It's Lonesome Everywhere	1996	—	—	3.00
❑ 64598	Irresistible You/You'll Find Somebody New	1996	—	—	3.00
❑ 64676	All of the Above/Sure	1996	—	—	3.00

ENGLAND DAN AND JOHN FORD COLEY

"England Dan" would later record as DAN SEALS.

45s

A&M

Number	Title (A Side/B Side)	Yr	VG	VG+	NM
❑ 1278	New Jersey/Tell Her Hello	1971	—	3.00	6.00
❑ 1354	Casey/Simone	1972	—	2.50	5.00
❑ 1369	Carolina/Free the People	1972	—	2.50	5.00
❑ 1465	I Hear the Music/Miss You Song	1973	—	2.50	5.00
❑ 1871	I Hear the Music/Simone	1976	—	2.00	4.00

BIG TREE

Number	Title (A Side/B Side)	Yr	VG	VG+	NM
❑ 16069	I'd Really Love to See You Tonight/It's Not the Same	1976	—	2.00	4.00
❑ 16079	Nights Are Forever Without You/Showboat Gambler	1976	—	2.00	4.00
❑ 16088	It's Sad to Belong/The Time Has Come	1977	—	2.00	4.00
❑ 16102	Gone Too Far/Where Do I Go from Here	1977	—	2.00	4.00
❑ 16110	We'll Never Have to Say Goodbye Again/Calling for You Again	1978	—	2.00	4.00
❑ 16117	You Can't Dance/Wantin' You Desperately	1978	—	2.00	4.00
❑ 16125	If the World Ran Out of Love Tonight/Lovin' Somebody on a Rainy Night	1978	—	2.00	4.00
❑ 16130	Westward Wind/Some Things Don't Come Easy	1979	—	2.00	4.00
❑ 16131	Love Is the Answer/Running After You	1979	—	2.00	4.00
❑ 16135	Hollywood Heckle and Jive/Rolling Fever	1979	—	2.00	4.00
❑ 17000	What Can I Do with My Broken Heart/Caught Up in the Middle	1979	—	2.00	4.00
❑ 17002	In It for Love/Who's Lonely Now	1980	—	2.00	4.00

MCA

Number	Title (A Side/B Side)	Yr	VG	VG+	NM
❑ 51027	Part of Me, Part of You/Just Tell Me You Love Me	1980	—	2.00	4.00

Albums

A&M

Number	Title (A Side/B Side)	Yr	VG	VG+	NM
❑ SP-4305	England Dan and John Ford Coley	1971	3.75	7.50	15.00
❑ SP-4350	Fables	1972	3.75	7.50	15.00
❑ SP-4613	I Hear Music	1976	3.00	6.00	12.00

BIG TREE

Number	Title (A Side/B Side)	Yr	VG	VG+	NM
❑ BT 76000	Dowdy Ferry Road	1977	2.50	5.00	10.00
❑ BT 76006	Some Things Don't Come Easy	1978	2.50	5.00	10.00
❑ BT 76015	Dr. Heckle & Mr. Jive	1979	2.50	5.00	10.00
❑ BT 76018	Best of England Dan & John Ford Coley	1980	2.50	5.00	10.00
❑ BT 89517	Nights Are Forever	1976	2.50	5.00	10.00

ENGLISH, MICHAEL

45s

CURB

Number	Title (A Side/B Side)	Yr	VG	VG+	NM
❑ D7- 76991	Your Love Amazes Me/Freedom	1996	—	2.00	4.00

ENGVALL, BILL

45s

WARNER BROS.

Number	Title (A Side/B Side)	Yr	VG	VG+	NM
❑ 17491	Here's Your Sign (Get the Picture)/Things Have Changed	1997	—	—	3.00

—A-side "With special guest Travis Tritt"

ERICKSON, JUDD

45s

REPRISE

Number	Title (A Side/B Side)	Yr	VG	VG+	NM
❑ 7-18515	Toys and Games/Forget About You	1993	—	2.00	4.00

ERVIN, SENATOR SAM

45s

COLUMBIA

Number	Title (A Side/B Side)	Yr	VG	VG+	NM
❑ 4-45956	Bridge Over Troubled Water/Zeke and the Snake	1973	—	3.00	6.00

Albums

COLUMBIA

Number	Title (A Side/B Side)	Yr	VG	VG+	NM
❑ KC 32756	Senator Sam at Home	1973	6.25	12.50	25.00

ESMERELDY

45s

MGM

Number	Title (A Side/B Side)	Yr	VG	VG+	NM
❑ K10739	Whoopin' in the Holler/Good Man in Memphis	1950	7.50	15.00	30.00

Selected 78s

MGM

Number	Title (A Side/B Side)	Yr	VG	VG+	NM
❑ 10413	I Didn't Know thw Gun Was Loaded/Hollywood Square Dance	1949	5.00	10.00	20.00

—This may exist on 45

MUSICRAFT

Number	Title (A Side/B Side)	Yr	VG	VG+	NM
❑ 524	Slap Her Down Again Paw/Red Wing	1948	5.00	10.00	20.00
❑ 536	I'm My Own Grandmaw/Ain't Nature Grand	1948	5.00	10.00	20.00
❑ 545	Put Down Your Shootin' Iron Pappy/Clementine	1948	5.00	10.00	20.00
❑ 571	Naughty Girl/Skip to My Lou	1949	5.00	10.00	20.00

ETC BAND, THE

See EARL THOMAS CONLEY.

ETHEL AND THE SHAMELESS HUSSIES

Also see GAYLE ZEILER.

45s

MCA

Number	Title (A Side/B Side)	Yr	VG	VG+	NM
❑ 53323	One Night Stan/Smokin' in Bed	1988	—	—	3.00
❑ 53382	I Thought He Was Mr. Right, But Then He Left/Last Night I Really Laid Down the Law	1988	—	—	3.00
❑ 53472	It's Just the Whiskey Talkin'/Mr. Cadillac	1988	—	—	3.00

Albums

MCA

Number	Title (A Side/B Side)	Yr	VG	VG+	NM
❑ 42191	Born to Burn	1988	2.50	5.00	10.00

EVANGELINE

45s

MCA

Number	Title (A Side/B Side)	Yr	VG	VG+	NM
❑ 54408	Bayou Boy/Bon Temps La Louisianne	1992	—	2.00	4.00
❑ 54488	Am I a Fool/Hurricane	1992	—	2.00	4.00
❑ 54598	If I Had a Heart/Who's Gonna Love You	1993	—	2.00	4.00
❑ 54747	I'm Still Lovin' You/Elvis of the Night	1993	—	2.50	5.00
❑ 54787	Let's Go Spend Your Money Honey/On the Levee	1994	—	2.00	4.00

EVANS, ASHLEY

45s

DOOR KNOB

Number	Title (A Side/B Side)	Yr	VG	VG+	NM
❑ 338	I'm So Afraid of Losing You Again/(B-side unknown)	1989	—	2.50	5.00
❑ 342	That Old Bridge/(B-side unknown)	1990	—	3.00	6.00

EVANS, DALE

Also see ROY ROGERS AND DALE EVANS; SONS OF THE PIONEERS.

45s

RCA VICTOR

Number	Title (A Side/B Side)	Yr	VG	VG+	NM
❑ 47-4308	Thirty-Two Feet and Eight Little Tails/Fuzzy Wuzzy	1951	6.25	12.50	25.00
❑ 48-0073	Don't Ever Fall in Love with a Cowboy/Nothin' in My Letter Box	1949	12.50	25.00	50.00
—Originals on green vinyl					
❑ 48-0148	It's Saturday Night/Saddle on My Heart	1950	10.00	20.00	40.00
—Originals on green vinyl					
❑ 48-0310	Lock, Stock and Barrel/A Heart of Stone	1950	10.00	20.00	40.00
—Originals on green vinyl					
❑ 48-0360	A Two Seated Saddle/Hawaii No	1950	10.00	20.00	40.00
—Originals on green vinyl					
❑ 48-0395	Cowgirl Polka/San Angelo	1950	10.00	20.00	40.00
—Originals on green vinyl					
❑ 48-0465	Please Send Me Someone to Love/Last Night My Heart Crossed the Ocean	1951	7.50	15.00	30.00

Selected 78s

MAJESTIC

Number	Title (A Side/B Side)	Yr	VG	VG+	NM
❑ 11025	Under a Texas Moon/His Hat Cost More Than Mine	194?	5.00	10.00	20.00
❑ 11031	I'm the Rage of the Sage/When the Roses Bloom in Red River Valley	194?	5.00	10.00	20.00

Albums

CAPITOL

Number	Title (A Side/B Side)	Yr	VG	VG+	NM
❑ ST 2772 [S]	It's Real	1967	6.25	12.50	25.00
❑ T 2772 [M]	It's Real	1967	6.25	12.50	25.00

EVANS, MAUREEN

45s

LITTLE DARLIN'

Number	Title (A Side/B Side)	Yr	VG	VG+	NM
❑ 0019	Touch My Heart/(B-side unknown)	1967	2.50	5.00	10.00

EVANS, PAUL

45s

ATCO

Number	Title (A Side/B Side)	Yr	VG	VG+	NM
❑ 6138	At My Party/Beat Generation	1959	3.75	7.50	15.00
❑ 6170	Long Gone/Mickey, My Love	1960	3.75	7.50	15.00

BIG TREE

Number	Title (A Side/B Side)	Yr	VG	VG+	NM
❑ 16050	Happy Birthday. America/You Made Me Over	1975	—	2.50	5.00

CARLTON

Number	Title (A Side/B Side)	Yr	VG	VG+	NM
❑ 539	Show Folk/I Love to Make Love to You	1961	3.75	7.50	15.00
❑ 543	After the Hurricane/Not Me	1961	3.75	7.50	15.00
❑ 554	Just Because I Love You/This Pullover	1961	3.75	7.50	15.00
❑ 558	Over the Mountain, Across the Sea/Sisal Twine	1961	3.75	7.50	15.00

CINNAMON

Number	Title (A Side/B Side)	Yr	VG	VG+	NM
❑ 604	One Night Led to Two/Hangin' Out and Hangin' In	1980	—	2.50	5.00

COLUMBIA

Number	Title (A Side/B Side)	Yr	VG	VG+	NM
❑ 44472	One Red Rose/Bound to Silence	1968	—	3.00	6.00

DECCA

Number	Title (A Side/B Side)	Yr	VG	VG+	NM
❑ 30680	I Think About You All the Time/Oh No	1958	5.00	10.00	20.00

DOT

Number	Title (A Side/B Side)	Yr	VG	VG+	NM
❑ 17463	That's What Loving You Is All About/Do You Remember	1973	—	2.50	5.00

EPIC

Number	Title (A Side/B Side)	Yr	VG	VG+	NM
❑ 9726	Bewitched/I Think I'm Gonna Kill Myself	1964	2.50	5.00	10.00
—By Paul & Mimi Evans					
❑ 9751	Little Miss Tease/Gina Marina Petunia	1964	2.50	5.00	10.00
❑ 9842	I Wonder What to Do/Always Thinking of the Roses	1965	2.50	5.00	10.00

Number	Title (A Side/B Side)	Yr	VG	VG+	NM
GUARANTEED					
❑ 200	Seven Little Girls Sitting in the Back Seat/ Worshipping an Idol	1959	5.00	10.00	20.00
❑ 205	Midnite Special/Since I Met You Baby	1960	3.75	7.50	15.00
❑ 208	Happy-Go-Lucky Me/Fish in the Ocean	1960	3.75	7.50	15.00
❑ 210	The Brigade of Broken Hearts/Twins	1960	3.75	7.50	15.00
❑ 213	Hushabye Little Guitar/Blind Boy	1960	3.75	7.50	15.00
KAPP					
❑ 473	A Picture of You/Feelin' No Pain	1962	3.00	6.00	12.00
❑ 486	D-Darling/Gonna Build a Mountain	1962	3.00	6.00	12.00
❑ 499	The Bell That Couldn't Jingle/Gilding the Lily	1962	3.00	6.00	12.00
❑ 520	(Mama and Papa) We've Got Something On You/ What Are the Lips of Janet	1963	3.00	6.00	12.00
❑ 527	Ten Thousand Years/Evan Tan	1963	3.00	6.00	12.00
LAURIE					
❑ 3571	Think Summer/For Old Times Sake	1971	—	3.00	6.00
❑ 3581	The Man in a Row Boat/Here We Go Around Again	1971	—	3.00	6.00
MERCURY					
❑ 73499	But I Was Born in New York City/Just As Long As You Are There	1974	—	2.50	5.00
❑ 73650	All My Children/Move In with Me	1975	—	2.50	5.00
MUSICOR					
❑ 6305	Roses Are Red Medley/If I Had My Life to Live Over	1977	—	2.00	4.00
RANWOOD					
❑ 928	Try It, You'll Like It/We Liked It	1972	—	3.00	6.00
RCA VICTOR					
❑ 47-6806	What Do You Know/Dorothy	1957	5.00	10.00	20.00
❑ 47-6924	Looking for a Sweetie/Any Little Thing	1957	5.00	10.00	20.00
❑ 47-6992	Caught/Poor Broken Heart	1957	5.00	10.00	20.00
SPRING					
❑ 183	Hello, This Is Joanie (The Telephone Answering Machine Song)/Lullabye Tissue Paper Company	1978	—	2.00	4.00
❑ 187	Down at the Bluebird/I'm Givin' Up My Baby	1978	—	2.00	4.00
❑ 193	Disneyland Daddy/Build An Ark	1979	—	2.00	4.00

Albums

Number	Title	Yr	VG	VG+	NM
CARLTON					
❑ STLP-129 [S]	Hear Paul Evans in Your Home Tonight	1961	15.00	30.00	60.00
❑ TLP-129 [M]	Hear Paul Evans in Your Home Tonight	1961	10.00	20.00	40.00
❑ STLP-130 [S]	Folk Songs of Many Lands	1961	15.00	30.00	60.00
❑ TLP-130 [M]	Folk Songs of Many Lands	1961	10.00	20.00	40.00
GUARANTEED					
❑ GUL-1000 [M]	Fabulous Teens	1960	17.50	35.00	70.00
❑ GUS-1000 [S]	Fabulous Teens	1960	20.00	40.00	80.00
KAPP					
❑ KL-1346 [M]	21 Years in a Tennessee Jail	1964	6.25	12.50	25.00
❑ KL-1475 [M]	Another Town, Another Jail	1966	6.25	12.50	25.00
❑ KS-3346 [S]	21 Years in a Tennessee Jail	1964	10.00	20.00	40.00
❑ KS-3475 [S]	Another Town, Another Jail	1966	7.50	15.00	30.00

EVANS, PAULA KAY

45s

Number	Title	Yr	VG	VG+	NM
AUTUMN					
❑ 368	Runnin' Out Again/Hangin' Out Again	1977	—	3.00	6.00

EVANS, SARA

45s

Number	Title	Yr	VG	VG+	NM
RCA					
❑ 64784	True Lies/The Week the River Raged	1997	—	2.00	4.00
❑ 64876	Three Chords and the Truth/The Week the River Raged	1997	—	2.00	4.00
❑ 65324	Shame About That/Shame About That (Remix)	1997	—	2.00	4.00
❑ 65517	Cryin' Game/Wait a Minute	1998	—	2.00	4.00
❑ 65584	No Place That Far/Cryin' Game	1998	—	3.00	6.00
❑ 69008	Born to Fly/I Could Not Ask for More	2000	—	—	3.00

Albums

Number	Title	Yr	VG	VG+	NM
RCA					
❑ 66995-1 [DJ]	Three Chords and the Truth	1997	3.75	7.50	15.00
—Vinyl is promo only					

EVERETTE, LEON

45s

Number	Title	Yr	VG	VG+	NM
MERCURY					
❑ 880611-7	Too Good to Say No To/It Never Felt Like This Before	1985	—	2.00	4.00
❑ 880829-7	A Good Love Died Tonight/(You're Never Guilty) When Love Is Your Alibi	1985	—	2.00	4.00
❑ 884040-7	'Til a Tear Becomes a Rose/It Never Felt Like This Before	1985	—	2.00	4.00
ORLANDO					
❑ 100	We Let Love Fade Away/Never Ending Crowded Circle	1979	—	2.50	5.00
❑ 102	Giving Up Easy/Mama Rocked Us to Sleep (With Country Music)	1979	—	2.50	5.00
❑ 103	Don't Feel Like the Lone Ranger/We Let Love Fade Away	1979	—	2.50	5.00
❑ 103 [PS]	Don't Feel Like the Lone Ranger/We Let Love Fade Away	1979	2.00	4.00	8.00
❑ 104	The Sun Went Down in My World Tonight/ Cheater's Trap	1979	—	2.50	5.00
❑ 105	I Love That Woman (Like the Devil Loves Sin)/ Never Ending Crowded Circle	1979	—	2.50	5.00
❑ 106	I Don't Want to Lose/Mama Rocked Us to Sleep	1980	—	2.50	5.00
❑ 107	Over/Let Me Apologize	1980	—	2.50	5.00
❑ 112	Danger List (Give Me Someone I Can Love)/Over	1986	—	2.50	5.00
❑ 114	Sad State of Affairs/Danger List (Give Me Someone I Can Love)	1986	—	2.50	5.00
❑ 115	Still in the Picture/Danger List (Give Me Someone I Can Love)	1986	—	2.50	5.00
RCA					
❑ PB-12111	Giving Up Easy/Setting Me Up	1980	—	2.00	4.00
❑ PB-12177	If I Keep On Going Crazy/The Sun Went Down in My World Tonight	1981	—	2.00	4.00
❑ PB-12270	Hurricane/Make Me Stop Loving Her	1981	—	2.00	4.00
❑ PB-12355	Midnight Rodeo/Don't Be Angry	1981	—	2.00	4.00
❑ PB-13079	Just Give Me What You Think Is Fair/Over	1982	—	2.00	4.00
❑ JK-13282 [DJ]	Soul Searchin' (same on both sides)	1982	2.50	5.00	10.00
—Promo only on red vinyl					
❑ PB-13282	Soul Searchin'/Misery	1982	—	2.00	4.00
❑ JK-13391 [DJ]	Shadows of My Mind (same on both sides)	1982	2.50	5.00	10.00
—Promo only on blue vinyl					
❑ PB-13391	Shadows of My Mind/I Keep On Going Crazy	1982	—	2.00	4.00
❑ JK-13466 [DJ]	My Lady Loves Me (Just As I Am) (same on both sides)	1983	2.50	5.00	10.00
—Promo only on yellow vinyl					
❑ PB-13466	My Lady Loves Me (Just As I Am)/Somebody Killed Dewey Jones' Daughter	1983	—	2.00	4.00
❑ JK-13584 [DJ]	The Lady, She's Right (same on both sides)	1983	2.50	5.00	10.00
—Promo only on blue vinyl					
❑ PB-13584	The Lady, She's Right/Knocking on Her Door	1983	—	2.00	4.00
❑ PB-13676	I Wanna Know Your Name/Anita, You're Dreaming	1983	—	—	—
—Canceled					
❑ JK-13717 [DJ]	I Could'a Had You (same on both sides)	1984	2.50	5.00	10.00
—Promo only on green vinyl					
❑ PB-13717	I Could'a Had You/I Wanna Know Your Name	1984	—	2.00	4.00
❑ PB-13834	Shot in the Dark/I Want to Be in Pictures	1984	—	2.00	4.00
❑ PB-13978	The Rock I'm Leaning On/I Wanna Know Your Name	1984	—	—	—
—Canceled					
TRUE					
❑ 107	Goodbye King of Rock 'n' Roll/Where the Daisies Grow Wild	1977	3.75	7.50	15.00
❑ 110	I Love That Woman (Like the Devil Loves Sin)/ Still Loving You	1977	—	3.00	6.00
❑ 112	Put It Out of Your Mind Babe/Still Loving You	1978	—	3.00	6.00

Albums

Number	Title	Yr	VG	VG+	NM
MERCURY					
❑ 824309-1	Where's the Fire	1985	2.00	4.00	8.00
ORLANDO					
❑ 1101	I Don't Want to Lose	1980	3.00	6.00	12.00
RCA VICTOR					
❑ AHL1-3916	If I Keep On Going Crazy	1981	2.50	5.00	10.00
❑ AHL1-4152	Hurricane	1981	2.50	5.00	10.00
❑ MHL1-8513 [EP]	Doin' What I Feel	1984	2.00	4.00	8.00
❑ MHL1-8600 [EP]	Leon Everette	1983	2.00	4.00	8.00
TRUE					
❑ 1002	Goodbye King of Rock and Roll	1977	6.25	12.50	25.00
—Deduct 40% if poster of Elvis Presley is missing					

EVERLY, DON

Also see THE EVERLY BROTHERS.

45s

Number	Title	Yr	VG	VG+	NM
ABC HICKORY					
❑ 54002	Love at Last Sight/Oh I'd Like to Go Away	1976	—	3.00	6.00
❑ 54005	Since You Broke My Heart/Deep Water	1977	—	3.00	6.00
❑ 54012	Brother Juke-Box/Oh, What a Feeling	1977	—	3.00	6.00
HICKORY/MGM					
❑ 368	Yesterday Just Passed My Way Again/Never Like This	1976	—	3.00	6.00
ODE					
❑ 66009	Only Me/Tumbling Tumbleweeds	1970	2.00	4.00	8.00
❑ 66046	Warming Up the Band/Evelyn Swing	1974	2.00	4.00	8.00

Albums

Number	Title	Yr	VG	VG+	NM
ABC HICKORY					
❑ AH-44003	Brother Juke-Box	1977	3.00	6.00	12.00
ODE					
❑ SP-77005	Don Everly	1970	3.75	7.50	15.00
❑ SP-77023	Sunset Towers	1974	3.75	7.50	15.00

EVERLY, PHIL

Also see THE EVERLY BROTHERS.

45s

Number	Title	Yr	VG	VG+	NM
CAPITOL					
❑ B-5197	One Way Love/Who's Gonna Keep Me Warm	1983	2.50	5.00	10.00
CURB					
❑ 02116	Sweet Southern Love/In Your Eyes	1981	2.50	5.00	10.00
❑ 5401	Dare to Dream Again/Lonely Days, Lonely Nights	1980	2.50	5.00	10.00
ELEKTRA					
❑ 46007	Don't Say You Don't Love Me No More/I Seek the Night	1979	—	2.50	5.00
—A-side: With Sondra Locke; B-side: Sondra Locke solo					
❑ 46519	Living Alone/I Just Don't Feel Like Dancing	1979	—	2.50	5.00
❑ 46556	Buy Me a Beer/You Broke It	1979	—	2.50	5.00
PYE					
❑ 71014	Old Kentucky River/Summershine	1975	2.00	4.00	8.00

Number	Title (A Side/B Side)	Yr	VG	VG+	NM
❑ 71036	New Old Song/Better Than Now	1975	2.00	4.00	8.00
❑ 71050	You and I Are a Song/Better Than Now	1975	2.00	4.00	8.00
❑ 71055	Words in Your Eyes/Back When the Bands Played in Rag Time	1976	2.00	4.00	8.00
❑ 71056	God Bless Older Ladies/Sweet Grass Country	1976	—	3.00	6.00
RCA VICTOR					
❑ APBO-0064	God Bless Older Ladies/Sweet Grass Country	1973	2.00	4.00	8.00
Albums					
ELEKTRA					
❑ 6E-213	Living Alone	1979	2.50	5.00	10.00
PYE					
❑ 12104	Phil's Diner	1975	3.00	6.00	12.00
❑ 12121	Mystic Line	1976	3.00	6.00	12.00
RCA VICTOR					
❑ APL1-0092	Star Spangled Springer	1973	3.75	7.50	15.00

EVERLY BROTHERS, THE

Also see DON EVERLY; PHIL EVERLY.

Number	Title (A Side/B Side)	Yr	VG	VG+	NM
45s					
BARNABY					
❑ 500	('Til) I Kissed You/Oh, What a Feeling	197?	—	2.50	5.00
❑ 501	Wake Up Little Susie/Maybe Tomorrow	197?	—	2.50	5.00
❑ 502	Bye, Bye Love/I Wonder If I Care As Much	197?	—	2.50	5.00
❑ 503	This Little Girl of Mine/Should We Tell Him?	197?	—	2.50	5.00
❑ 504	Problems/Love of My Life	197?	—	2.50	5.00
❑ 505	Take a Message to Mary/Poor Jenny	197?	—	2.50	5.00
❑ 506	Let It Be Me/Since You Broke My Heart	197?	—	2.50	5.00
❑ 507	When Will I Be Loved/Be Bop A-Lula	197?	—	2.50	5.00
❑ 508	Like Strangers/Brand New Heartache	197?	—	2.50	5.00
❑ 509	All I Have to Do Is Dream/Claudette	197?	—	2.50	5.00
❑ 510	Bird Dog/Devoted to You	197?	—	2.50	5.00
❑ 511	I'm Here to Get My Baby Out of Jail/Lightning Express	197?	—	2.50	5.00
—All Barnaby records are reissues of original Cadence recordings					
CADENCE					
❑ 1315	Bye, Bye Love/I Wonder If I Care As Much	1957	6.25	12.50	25.00
❑ 1337	Wake Up Little Susie/Maybe Tomorrow	1957	7.50	15.00	30.00
❑ 1337 [PS]	Wake Up Little Susie/Maybe Tomorrow	1957	62.50	125.00	250.00
❑ 1342	This Little Girl of Mine/Should We Tell Him?	1958	6.25	12.50	25.00
❑ 1348	All I Have to Do Is Dream/Claudette	1958	6.25	12.50	25.00
❑ 1348	All I Have to Do Is Dream/Claudette	1961	5.00	10.00	20.00
—Reissue with red and black label; scarcer than original					
❑ 1350	Bird Dog/Devoted to You	1958	6.25	12.50	25.00
❑ 1355	Problems/Love of My Life	1958	6.25	12.50	25.00
❑ 1355 [PS]	Problems/Love of My Life	1958	12.50	25.00	50.00
❑ 1364	Take a Message to Mary/Poor Jenny	1959	6.25	12.50	25.00
❑ 1369	('Til) I Kissed You/Oh, What a Feeling	1959	6.25	12.50	25.00
❑ 1369 [PS]	('Til) I Kissed You/Oh, What a Feeling	1959	12.50	25.00	50.00
❑ 1376	Let It Be Me/Since You Broke My Heart	1959	6.25	12.50	25.00
❑ 1376 [PS]	Let It Be Me/Since You Broke My Heart	1959	12.50	25.00	50.00
❑ 1380	When Will I Be Loved/Be Bop A-Lula	1960	6.25	12.50	25.00
❑ 1388	Like Strangers/Brand New Heartache	1960	6.25	12.50	25.00
❑ 1429	I'm Here to Get My Baby Out of Jail/Lightning Express	1962	5.00	10.00	20.00
❑ 1429 [PS]	I'm Here to Get My Baby Out of Jail/Lightning Express	1962	10.00	20.00	40.00
CAPITOL					
❑ B-44297	Don't Worry Baby/Tequila Dreams	1989	—	2.00	4.00
—A-side: With the Beach Boys; B-side by Dave Grusin					
❑ B-44297 [PS]	Don't Worry Baby/Tequila Dreams	1989	2.50	5.00	10.00
COLUMBIA					
❑ 4-21496	Keep A Lovin' Me/The Sun Keeps Shining	1956	150.00	300.00	600.00
—Maroon label					
❑ 4-21496 [DJ]	Keep A Lovin' Me/The Sun Keeps Shining	1956	62.50	125.00	250.00
—White label					
MERCURY					
❑ 872098-7	Ride the Wind/Don't Worry Baby	1988	—	—	3.00
❑ 872420-7	Ballad of a Teenage Queen/Get Rhythm	1988	—	—	3.00
—With Johnny Cash and Roseanne Cash					
❑ 880213-7	On the Wings of a Nightingale/Asleep	1984	—	2.50	5.00
—A-side written and produced by Paul McCartney					
❑ 880423-7	The Story of Me/First in Line	1984	—	2.00	4.00
❑ 884428-7	Don't Say Goodnight/Born Yesterday	1986	—	2.00	4.00
❑ 884694-7	I Know Love/These Shoes	1986	—	2.00	4.00
❑ 884694-7 [PS]	I Know Love/These Shoes	1986	—	2.00	4.00
RCA VICTOR					
❑ SP-45-409 [DJ]	Pass the Chicken and Listen	1971	7.50	15.00	30.00
—Promo-only interview record					
❑ 74-0717	Stories We Could Tell/Ridin' High	1972	2.50	5.00	10.00
❑ 74-0849	Lay It Down/Paradise	1972	2.50	5.00	10.00
❑ 74-0901	Not Fade Away/Ladies Love Outlaws	1973	2.50	5.00	10.00
WARNER BROS.					
❑ GWB 0311	That's Old Fashioned/Bowling Green	197?	—	2.00	4.00
—"Back to Back Hits" series; originals have palm-tree labels					
❑ GWB 0314	Ebony Eyes/Walk Right Back	197?	—	2.00	4.00
—"Back to Back Hits" series; originals have palm-tree labels					
❑ 5151 [DJ]	Cathy's Clown/Always It's You	1960	25.00	50.00	100.00
—Promo-only gold vinyl pressing					
❑ 5151 [M]	Cathy's Clown/Always It's You	1960	5.00	10.00	20.00
—Original stock copies have pink labels					
❑ 5151 [M]	Cathy's Clown/Always It's You	1960	3.75	7.50	15.00
—Second-pressing stock copies have red labels with arrows					
❑ 5151 [PS]	Cathy's Clown/Always It's You	1960	12.50	25.00	50.00
❑ S-5151 [S]	Cathy's Clown/Always It's You	1960	12.50	25.00	50.00
❑ 5163	So Sad (To Watch Good Love Go Bad)/Lucille	1960	3.75	7.50	15.00
❑ 5163 [DJ]	So Sad (To Watch Good Love Go Bad)/Lucille	1960	25.00	50.00	100.00
—Promo-only gold vinyl pressing					
❑ 5163 [PS]	So Sad (To Watch Good Love Go Bad)/Lucille	1960	12.50	25.00	50.00
❑ 5199	Ebony Eyes/Walk Right Back	1961	3.75	7.50	15.00
❑ 5199 [DJ]	Ebony Eyes/Walk Right Back	1961	25.00	50.00	100.00
—Promo-only gold vinyl pressing					
❑ 5199 [PS]	Ebony Eyes/Walk Right Back	1961	6.25	12.50	25.00
❑ 5220	Temptation/Stick With Me, Baby	1961	3.75	7.50	15.00
❑ 5220 [PS]	Temptation/Stick With Me, Baby	1961	7.50	15.00	30.00
❑ 5250	Crying in the Rain/I'm Not Angry	1961	3.75	7.50	15.00
❑ 5250 [PS]	Crying in the Rain/I'm Not Angry	1961	5.00	10.00	20.00
❑ 5273	That's Old Fashioned (That's the Way Love Should Be)/How Can I Meet Her?	1962	3.75	7.50	15.00
❑ 5273 [PS]	That's Old Fashioned (That's the Way Love Should Be)/How Can I Meet Her?	1962	7.50	15.00	30.00
❑ 5297	Don't Ask Me to Be Friends/No One Can Make My Sunshine Smile	1962	5.00	10.00	20.00
❑ 5297 [PS]	Don't Ask Me to Be Friends/No One Can Make My Sunshine Smile	1962	7.50	15.00	30.00
❑ 5346	(So It Was...So It Is...) So It Always Will Be/Nancy's Minuet	1963	3.75	7.50	15.00
❑ 5362	I'm Afraid/It's Been Nice	1963	3.75	7.50	15.00
❑ 5389	Love Her/The Girl Sang the Blues	1963	3.75	7.50	15.00
❑ 5422	Hello, Amy/Ain't That Loving You, Baby	1964	3.75	7.50	15.00
❑ 5441	The Ferris Wheel/Don't Forget to Cry	1964	3.75	7.50	15.00
❑ 5466	You're the One I Love/Ring Around My Rosie	1964	3.75	7.50	15.00
❑ 5478	Gone, Gone, Gone/Torture	1964	3.75	7.50	15.00
❑ 5501	Don't Blame Me/Walk Right Back//Muskrat/Lucille	1961	5.00	10.00	20.00
❑ 5501 [PS]	Don't Blame Me/Walk Right Back//Muskrat/Lucille	1961	10.00	20.00	40.00
—Part of Warner Bros. "+2" series, with two new songs and excerpts of two prior hits					
❑ 5600	You're My Girl/Don't Let the World Know	1965	3.00	6.00	12.00
❑ 5611	That'll Be the Day/Give Me a Sweetheart	1965	3.00	6.00	12.00
❑ 5628	The Price of Love/It Only Costs a Dime	1965	3.00	6.00	12.00
❑ 5639	I'll Never Get Over You/Follow Me	1965	3.00	6.00	12.00
❑ 5649	Love Is Strange/A Man with Money	1965	3.00	6.00	12.00
❑ 5649 [PS]	Love Is Strange/A Man with Money	1965	7.50	15.00	30.00
❑ 5682	It's All Over/I Used to Love You	1965	3.00	6.00	12.00
❑ 5698	The Doll House Is Empty/Lovey Kravezit	1966	3.00	6.00	12.00
❑ 5808	The Power of Love/Leave My Girl Alone	1966	3.00	6.00	12.00
❑ 5833	Somebody Help Me/Hard, Hard Year	1966	3.00	6.00	12.00
❑ 5857	Fifi the Flea/Like Every Time Before	1966	5.00	10.00	20.00
—A-side listed as "Don Everly Brother," B-side as "Phil Everly Brother"					
❑ 5901	She Never Smiles Anymore/Devil Child	1967	3.00	6.00	12.00
❑ 7020	Bowling Green/I Don't Want to Love You	1967	3.00	6.00	12.00
❑ 7062	Mary Jane/Talking to the Flowers	1967	3.00	6.00	12.00
❑ 7088	Love of the Common People/The Voice Within	1967	3.00	6.00	12.00
❑ 7110	Cathy's Clown/So Sad	1968	2.00	4.00	8.00
—"Back to Back Hits" series; originals have green "W7" label					
❑ 7111	Crying in the Rain/Lucille	1968	2.00	4.00	8.00
—"Back to Back Hits" series; originals have green "W7" label					
❑ 7120	Wake Up Little Susie/Bird Dog	1969	2.00	4.00	8.00
—"Back to Back Hits" series; originals have green "W7" label; re-recordings					
❑ 7121	Bye Bye Love/All I Have to Do Is Dream	1969	2.00	4.00	8.00
—"Back to Back Hits" series; originals have green "W7" label; re-recordings					
❑ 7192	Empty Boxes/It's My Time	1968	3.00	6.00	12.00
❑ 7226	Lord of the Manor/Milk Train	1968	3.00	6.00	12.00
❑ 7262	T for Texas/I Wonder If I Care As Much	1969	3.00	6.00	12.00
❑ 7290	I'm On My Way Home Again/Cuckoo Bird	1969	3.00	6.00	12.00
❑ 7326	Carolina on My Mind/My Little Yellow Bird	1969	3.75	7.50	15.00
❑ 7425	Yves/The Human Race	1970	3.75	7.50	15.00
7-Inch Extended Plays					
CADENCE					
❑ CEP-104	Wake Up Little Susie/Maybe Tomorrow//Bye Bye Love/I Wonder If I Care As Much	1957	12.50	25.00	50.00
❑ CEP-104 [PS]	The Everly Brothers	1957	12.50	25.00	50.00
❑ CEP-105	This Little Girl of Mine/Leave My Woman Alone//Should We Tell Him/Be-Bop-a-Lula	1957	12.50	25.00	50.00
❑ CEP-105 [PS]	The Everly Brothers	1957	12.50	25.00	50.00
❑ CEP-107	Brand New Heartache/Keep a Knockin'//Rip It Up/Hey Doll Baby	1957	12.50	25.00	50.00
❑ CEP-107 [PS]	The Everly Brothers	1957	12.50	25.00	50.00
❑ CEP-108	Roving Gambler/Oh So Many Years//Put My Little Shoes Away/That Silver Haired Daddy Of Mine	1958	12.50	25.00	50.00
❑ CEP-108 [PS]	Songs Our Daddy Taught Us, Vol. 1	1958	12.50	25.00	50.00
❑ CEP-109	Barbara Allen/Long Time Gone//Lightning Express/Who's Gonna Shoe Your Pretty Little Feet	1958	12.50	25.00	50.00
❑ CEP-109 [PS]	Songs Our Daddy Taught Us, Vol. 2	1958	12.50	25.00	50.00
❑ CEP-110	*Down in the Willow Garden/Kentucky/I'm Here to Get My Baby Out of Jail/Rockin' Alone in My Old Rockin' Chair	1958	12.50	25.00	50.00
❑ CEP-110 [PS]	Songs Our Daddy Taught Us, Vol. 3	1958	12.50	25.00	50.00
❑ CEP-111	Bird Dog/Devoted to You//All I Have to Do Is Dream/Claudette	1959	12.50	25.00	50.00
❑ CEP-111 [PS]	The Everly Brothers	1959	12.50	25.00	50.00
❑ CEP-118	(contents unknown)	1959	12.50	25.00	50.00
❑ CEP-118 [PS]	The Everly Brothers	1959	12.50	25.00	50.00
❑ CEP-121	(contents unknown)	1960	6.25	12.50	25.00
❑ CEP-121 [PS]	The Very Best of the Everly Brothers	1960	6.25	12.50	25.00
WARNER BROS.					
❑ EA 1381	So Sad (To Watch Good Love Go Bad)/You Thrill Me (Through and Through)//Memories Are Made of This/Oh, True Love	1960	10.00	20.00	40.00

Number	Title (A Side/B Side)	Yr	VG	VG+	NM
❑ EA 1381 [PS]	Foreverly Yours	1960	10.00	20.00	40.00
❑ EB 1381	Sleepless Nights/Carol Jane//Nashville Blues/That's What You Do to Me	1960	10.00	20.00	40.00
❑ EB 1381 [PS]	Especially for You	1960	10.00	20.00	40.00
Albums					
ARISTA					
❑ AL9-8207 [(2)]	24 Original Classics	1985	3.75	7.50	15.00
BARNABY					
❑ BGP-350 [(2)]	The Everly Brothers' Original Golden Hits	1970	5.00	10.00	20.00
❑ 4004	Greatest Hits, Vol. 1	1977	2.50	5.00	10.00
❑ 4005	Greatest Hits, Vol. 2	1977	2.50	5.00	10.00
❑ 4006	Greatest Hits, Vol. 3	1977	2.50	5.00	10.00
❑ BR-6006 [(2)]	The Everly Brothers' Greatest Hits	1974	3.75	7.50	15.00
❑ BR-15008 [(2)]	History of the Everly Brothers	1973	3.75	7.50	15.00
❑ ZG 30260 [(2)]	End of an Era	1971	3.75	7.50	15.00
CADENCE					
❑ CLP-3003 [M]	The Everly Brothers	1958	25.00	50.00	100.00
—Maroon label with metronome logo					
❑ CLP-3003 [M]	The Everly Brothers	1962	15.00	30.00	60.00
—Red label with black border					
❑ CLP-3016 [M]	Songs Our Daddy Taught Us	1958	25.00	50.00	100.00
—Maroon label with metronome logo					
❑ CLP-3016 [M]	Songs Our Daddy Taught Us	1962	15.00	30.00	60.00
—Red label with black border					
❑ CLP-3025 [M]	The Everly Brothers' Best	1959	22.50	45.00	90.00
—Maroon label with metronome logo					
❑ CLP-3025 [M]	The Everly Brothers' Best	1962	15.00	30.00	60.00
—Red label with black border					
❑ CLP-3040 [M]	The Fabulous Style of the Everly Brothers	1960	20.00	40.00	80.00
—Maroon label with metronome logo					
❑ CLP-3040 [M]	The Fabulous Style of the Everly Brothers	1962	12.50	25.00	50.00
—Red label with black border					
❑ CLP-3059 [M]	Folk Songs of the Everly Brothers	1963	12.50	25.00	50.00
—Reissue of 3016					
❑ CLP-3062 [M]	15 Everly Hits 15	1963	10.00	20.00	40.00
❑ CLP-25040 [P]	The Fabulous Style of the Everly Brothers	1960	30.00	60.00	120.00
—Maroon label with metronome logo					
❑ CLP-25040 [P]	The Fabulous Style of the Everly Brothers	1962	15.00	30.00	60.00
—Red label with black border					
❑ CLP-25059 [R]	Folk Songs of the Everly Brothers	1963	10.00	20.00	40.00
❑ CLP-25062 [P]	15 Everly Hits 15	1963	12.50	25.00	50.00
HARMONY					
❑ HS 11304	Wake Up Little Susie	1969	3.00	6.00	12.00
❑ HS 11350	Christmas with the Everly Brothers and the Boys Town Choir	1969	5.00	10.00	20.00
❑ KH 11388	Chained to a Memory	1970	3.00	6.00	12.00
MERCURY					
❑ 822431-1	EB 84	1984	2.50	5.00	10.00
❑ 826142-1	Born Yesterday	1986	2.50	5.00	10.00
❑ 832520-1	Some Hearts	1989	3.00	6.00	12.00
PAIR					
❑ PDL1-1063 [(2)]	Living Legends	1986	3.00	6.00	12.00
PASSPORT					
❑ 11001 [(2)]	The Everly Brothers Reunion Concert	1984	3.75	7.50	15.00
RCA VICTOR					
❑ LSP-4620	Stories We Could Tell	1972	3.75	7.50	15.00
❑ LSP-4781	Pass the Chicken and Listen	1972	3.75	7.50	15.00
❑ AFL1-5401	Home Again	1985	2.50	5.00	10.00
RHINO					
❑ RNLP-211	The Everly Brothers	1985	2.50	5.00	10.00
❑ RNLP-212	Songs Our Daddy Taught Us	1985	2.50	5.00	10.00
❑ RNLP-213	The Fabulous Style of the Everly Brothers	1985	2.50	5.00	10.00
❑ RNLP-214	All They Had to Do Was Dream	1985	2.50	5.00	10.00
❑ RNDF-258 [PD]	Heartaches and Harmonies	1985	5.00	10.00	20.00
❑ RNLP-70173	The Best of the Everly Brothers (Golden Archive Series)	1987	2.50	5.00	10.00
TIME-LIFE					
❑ SRNR-09 [(2)]	The Everly Brothers: 1957-1962	1986	5.00	10.00	20.00
—Part of "The Rock 'n' Roll Era" series; box set with insert					
WARNER BROS.					
❑ PRO 134 [10]	It's Everly Time!	1960	150.00	300.00	600.00
—Promo "souvenir sampler" from their debut on WB					
❑ W 1381 [M]	It's Everly Time!	1960	7.50	15.00	30.00
❑ WS 1381 [S]	It's Everly Time!	1960	10.00	20.00	40.00
❑ W 1395 [M]	A Date with the Everly Brothers	1960	12.50	25.00	50.00
—Gatefold edition with poster and wallet-size photos					
❑ W 1395 [M]	A Date with the Everly Brothers	1960	10.00	20.00	40.00
—Gatefold edition without poster or photos					
❑ W 1395 [M]	A Date with the Everly Brothers	1961	7.50	15.00	30.00
—Regular edition					
❑ WS 1395 [S]	A Date with the Everly Brothers	1960	18.75	37.50	75.00
—Gatefold edition with poster and wallet-size photos					
❑ WS 1395 [S]	A Date with the Everly Brothers	1960	12.50	25.00	50.00
—Gatefold edition without poster or photos					
❑ WS 1395 [S]	A Date with the Everly Brothers	1961	10.00	20.00	40.00
—Regular edition					
❑ W 1418 [M]	Both Sides of an Evening	1961	7.50	15.00	30.00
❑ WS 1418 [S]	Both Sides of an Evening	1961	10.00	20.00	40.00
❑ W 1430 [M]	Instant Party!	1962	7.50	15.00	30.00
❑ WS 1430 [S]	Instant Party!	1962	10.00	20.00	40.00
❑ W 1471 [M]	The Golden Hits of the Everly Brothers	1962	7.50	15.00	30.00
❑ WS 1471	The Golden Hits of the Everly Brothers	1967	5.00	10.00	20.00
—Green "W7" label					
❑ WS 1471	The Golden Hits of the Everly Brothers	1970	3.75	7.50	15.00
—Green "WB" label					
❑ WS 1471	The Golden Hits of the Everly Brothers	1973	3.00	6.00	12.00
—"Burbank" palm-tree label					
❑ WS 1471	The Golden Hits of the Everly Brothers	1979	2.50	5.00	10.00
—White or tan label					
❑ WS 1471 [S]	The Golden Hits of the Everly Brothers	1962	10.00	20.00	40.00
—Gold label					
❑ W 1483 [M]	Christmas with the Everly Brothers and the Boys Town Choir	1962	10.00	20.00	40.00
❑ WS 1483 [S]	Christmas with the Everly Brothers and the Boys Town Choir	1962	12.50	25.00	50.00
❑ W 1513 [M]	Great Country Hits	1963	10.00	20.00	40.00
❑ WS 1513 [S]	Great Country Hits	1963	12.50	25.00	50.00
❑ W 1554 [M]	The Very Best of the Everly Brothers	1964	7.50	15.00	30.00
—Originals have yellow covers					
❑ W 1554 [M]	The Very Best of the Everly Brothers	1965	5.00	10.00	20.00
—Later pressings have white covers					
❑ WS 1554	The Very Best of the Everly Brothers	1967	5.00	10.00	20.00
—Green "W7" label					
❑ WS 1554	The Very Best of the Everly Brothers	1970	3.75	7.50	15.00
—Green "WB" label					
❑ WS 1554	The Very Best of the Everly Brothers	1973	3.00	6.00	12.00
—"Burbank" palm-tree label					
❑ WS 1554	The Very Best of the Everly Brothers	1979	2.50	5.00	10.00
—White or tan label					
❑ WS 1554 [S]	The Very Best of the Everly Brothers	1964	10.00	20.00	40.00
—Originals have yellow covers					
❑ WS 1554 [S]	The Very Best of the Everly Brothers	1965	6.25	12.50	25.00
—White cover; gold label					
❑ W 1578 [M]	Rock & Soul	1964	10.00	20.00	40.00
❑ WS 1578 [S]	Rock & Soul	1964	12.50	25.00	50.00
❑ W 1585 [M]	Gone, Gone, Gone	1965	10.00	20.00	40.00
❑ WS 1585 [S]	Gone, Gone, Gone	1965	12.50	25.00	50.00
❑ W 1605 [M]	Beat & Soul	1965	10.00	20.00	40.00
❑ WS 1605 [S]	Beat & Soul	1965	12.50	25.00	50.00
❑ W 1620 [M]	In Our Image	1966	10.00	20.00	40.00
❑ WS 1620 [S]	In Our Image	1966	12.50	25.00	50.00
❑ W 1646 [M]	Two Yanks in London	1966	10.00	20.00	40.00
❑ WS 1646 [S]	Two Yanks in London	1966	12.50	25.00	50.00
❑ W 1676 [M]	The Hit Sound of the Everly Brothers	1967	12.50	25.00	50.00
❑ WS 1676 [S]	The Hit Sound of the Everly Brothers	1967	10.00	20.00	40.00
❑ W 1708 [M]	The Everly Brothers Sing	1967	12.50	25.00	50.00
❑ WS 1708 [S]	The Everly Brothers Sing	1967	10.00	20.00	40.00
❑ WS 1752	Roots	1968	10.00	20.00	40.00
❑ WS 1858	The Everly Brothers Show	1970	7.50	15.00	30.00
❑ ST-91343 [S]	The Very Best of the Everly Brothers	1967	10.00	20.00	40.00
—Capitol Record Club edition					
❑ ST-91601	Roots	1968	12.50	25.00	50.00
—Capitol Record Club edition					
❑ STAO-93286	The Everly Brothers Show	1970	10.00	20.00	40.00
—Capitol Record Club edition					

EWING, SKIP

Number	Title (A Side/B Side)	Yr	VG	VG+	NM
45s					
MCA					
❑ 53271	Your Memory Wins Again/Burnin' a Hole in My Heart	1988	—	—	3.00
❑ 53271 [PS]	Your Memory Wins Again/Burnin' a Hole in My Heart	1988	—	2.00	4.00
❑ 53353	I Don't Have Far to Fall/Still Under the Weather	1988	—	—	3.00
❑ 53435	Burnin' a Hole in My Heart/Autumn's Not That Cold	1988	—	—	3.00
❑ 53481	The Gospel According to Luke/Dad	1988	—	—	3.00
❑ 53663	The Coast of Colorado/Dad	1989	—	—	3.00
❑ 53732	It's You Again/Ain't That the Way It Always Ends	1989	—	—	3.00
❑ 53777	If a Man Could Live on Love Alone/She's Makin' Plans	1989	—	—	3.00
❑ 53916	The Dotted Line/A Healin' Fire	1990	—	2.00	4.00
❑ 79050	I'm Your Man/The Will to Love	1990	—	—	3.00
Albums					
MCA					
❑ 42128	The Coast of Colorado	1988	2.50	5.00	10.00
❑ 42301	The Will to Love	1989	2.50	5.00	10.00

EXILE

Number	Title (A Side/B Side)	Yr	VG	VG+	NM
45s					
ARISTA					
❑ 2009	Nobody's Talking/Don't Hang Up (Girl)	1990	—	—	3.00
❑ 2075	Yet/Show Me	1990	—	—	3.00
❑ 2139	There You Go/I'm Still Standing	1990	—	—	3.00
❑ 2228	Even Now/One Too Many Times	1991	—	—	3.00
❑ 9911	Keep It in the Middle of the Road/Yet	1989	—	—	3.00
❑ 12351	Nothing at All/What You See	1991	—	—	3.00
ATCO					
❑ 7072	Try It On/Show Me What You Got	1977	—	2.50	5.00
COLUMBIA					
❑ 4-44972	Church Street Soul Revival/Your Day Is Comin'	1969	2.00	4.00	8.00
—As "The Exiles"					
❑ 4-45210	Put Your Hands Together/Your Day Is Comin'	1970	2.00	4.00	8.00
—As "The Exiles"					
EPIC					
❑ 34-04041	High Cost of Leaving/Like a Fool's Supposed to Do	1983	—	—	3.00
❑ 34-04247	Woke Up in Love/First Things First	1983	—	2.00	4.00
❑ 34-04421	I Don't Want to Be a Memory/After All These Years (I'm Still Chasing You)	1984	—	—	3.00

Number	Title (A Side/B Side)	Yr	VG	VG+	NM
❑ 34-04567	Give Me One More Chance/Ain't That a Pity	1984	—	—	3.00
❑ 34-04567 [PS]	Give Me One More Chance/Ain't That a Pity	1984	—	2.00	4.00
❑ 34-04722	Crazy for Your Love/Just in Case	1984	—	—	3.00
❑ 34-04864	She's a Miracle/I've Never Seen Anything	1985	—	—	3.00
❑ 34-05580	Hang On to Your Heart/She Loves Her Lovin'	1985	—	—	3.00
❑ 34-05723	I Could Get Used to You/Practice Makes Perfect	1985	—	—	3.00
❑ 34-05860	Super Love/Proud to Be Your Man	1986	—	—	3.00
❑ 34-06229	It'll Be Me/Music	1986	—	—	3.00
❑ 34-07135	She's Too Good to Be True/Promises, Promises	1987	—	—	3.00
❑ 34-07597	I Can't Get Close Enough/As Long As I Have Your Memory	1987	—	—	3.00
❑ 34-07710	Feel Like Foolin' Around/Showdown	1988	—	—	3.00
❑ 34-0 7775	Just One Kiss/As Long As I Have Your Memory	1988	—	—	3.00
❑ 34-08020	It's You Again/The Girl Can't Help It	1988	—	—	3.00
MCA CURB					
❑ 52551	Stay with Me/Kiss You All Over	1985	—	—	3.00
❑ 52596	Dixie Girl/Someone Like You	1985	—	—	3.00
SSS INTERNATIONAL					
❑ 848	Got to Be All Right/Second Hand Lady	197?	2.00	4.00	8.00
—As "The Exiles"					
WARNER BROS.					
❑ 8589	Kiss You All Over/Don't Do It	1978	—	2.00	4.00
❑ 8711	You Thrill Me/One Step at a Time	1978	—	2.00	4.00
❑ 8796	How Could This Go Wrong/Being in Love with You Is Easy	1979	—	2.00	4.00
❑ 8848	Part of Me That Needs You Most/Let's Do It All Over Again	1979	—	2.00	4.00
❑ 49048	Too Proud to Cry/Destiny	1979	—	2.00	4.00
❑ 49245	You're Gone for Me/Let's Do It All Over Again	1980	—	2.00	4.00
❑ 49548	Take Me Down/It Takes Love to Make Love	1980	—	3.00	6.00
—A-side was later a hit for Alabama					
❑ 49794	Heart and Soul/Your Love Is Everything	1981	—	2.00	4.00
❑ 49863	Till the Very End/What Kind of Love Is This	1981	—	2.00	4.00
WOODEN NICKEL					
❑ BWBO-0006	Do What You Think You Should/Hold Tight Sweet Woman	1973	—	3.50	7.00
❑ 65-0115	Devil's Rite/Mabel	1973	—	3.50	7.00
Albums					
ARISTA					
❑ AL-9624	Still Standing	1990	3.75	7.50	15.00
EPIC					
❑ B6E 39154	Exile	1983	2.00	4.00	8.00
❑ FE 39424	Kentucky Hearts	1984	2.00	4.00	8.00
❑ BFE 40000	Hang On to Your Heart	1985	2.00	4.00	8.00
❑ FE 40401	Greatest Hits	1986	2.00	4.00	8.00
❑ FE 40901	Shelter from the Night	1987	2.00	4.00	8.00
MCA CURB					
❑ 946	All There Is	1986	2.00	4.00	8.00
❑ 947	Heart and Soul	1986	2.00	4.00	8.00
❑ 963	Mixed Emotions	1986	2.00	4.00	8.00
❑ 964	Don't Leave Me This Way	1986	2.00	4.00	8.00
❑ 1456	More of the Best of Exile	1986	2.00	4.00	8.00
❑ 5581	Best of Exile	1985	2.00	4.00	8.00
RCA VICTOR					
❑ AFL1-3086	Exile	1978	3.00	6.00	12.00
❑ AFL1-3087	Stage Pass	1978	3.00	6.00	12.00
WARNER BROS.					
❑ BSK 3205	Mixed Emotions	1978	2.50	5.00	10.00
❑ BSK 3323	All There Is	1979	2.50	5.00	10.00
❑ BSK 3437	Don't Leave Me This Way	1980	2.50	5.00	10.00
❑ BSK 3588	Heart and Soul	1981	2.50	5.00	10.00
WOODEN NICKEL					
❑ BWL1-0120	Exile	1973	3.75	7.50	15.00

F

FAIRBURN, WERLY

45s

Number	Title (A Side/B Side)	Yr	VG	VG+	NM
CAPITOL					
❑ F2770	Good Deal Lucille/Baby He's a Wolf	1954	7.50	15.00	30.00
❑ F2844	Love Spelled Backwards Is Evol/Nothing But Lovin'	1954	7.50	15.00	30.00
❑ F2963	Prison Cell of Love/I Feel Like Cryin'	1954	7.50	15.00	30.00
❑ F3101	It's a Cold, Weary World/Spiteful Heart	1955	7.50	15.00	30.00
COLUMBIA					
❑ 4-21432	I Guess I'm Crazy/That Sweet Love of Mine	1955	7.50	15.00	30.00
❑ 4-21483	Broken Hearted Me/Stay Close to Me	1956	7.50	15.00	30.00
❑ 4-21528	Everybody's Rockin'/It's Heaven	1956	25.00	50.00	100.00
SAVOY					
❑ 1503	All the Time/I'm a Fool About Your Love	1956	6.25	12.50	25.00
❑ 1509	My Heart's on Fire/Speak to Me Baby	1957	6.25	12.50	25.00
❑ 1521	Telephone Baby/No Blues Tomorrow	1957	6.25	12.50	25.00
TRUMPET					
❑ 195	Camping with Marie/Let's Think It Over	195?	10.00	20.00	40.00
❑ 196	Baby, Call on Me/I Feel Like Crying	195?	—	—	—
—Canceled					

FAIRCHILD, BARBARA

Also see BILLY WALKER AND BARBARA FAIRCHILD.

45s

Number	Title (A Side/B Side)	Yr	VG	VG+	NM
AUDIOGRAPH					
❑ 443	The Biggest Hurt/Every Flower Has to Have a Seed	1982	—	3.00	6.00
CAPITOL					
❑ B-5582	Just Out Riding Around/You Burn Me So Bad	1986	—	2.00	4.00
❑ B-5607	All My Cloudy Days Are Gone/You Burned Me So Bad	1986	—	2.00	4.00
❑ B-5688	Too Much Love/Bluebird	1987	—	2.00	4.00
COLUMBIA					
❑ 3-10047	Little Girl Feeling/His Green Eyes	1974	—	2.50	5.00
❑ 3-10128	Let's Love While We Can/Tara	1975	—	2.50	5.00
❑ 3-10195	You've Lost That Lovin' Feelin'/Singing Your Way Out of My Life	1975	—	2.50	5.00
❑ 3-10261	I Just Love Being a Woman/Your Good Girl's Gonna Go Bad	1975	—	2.50	5.00
❑ 3-10314	Under Your Spell Again/Too Far Gone	1976	—	2.50	5.00
❑ 3-10378	Mississippi/Over the Rainbow	1976	—	2.50	5.00
❑ 3-10423	Cheatin' Is/Touch of My Heart	1976	—	2.50	5.00
❑ 3-10485	Let Me Love You Once Before You Go/You Are Always There	1977	—	2.50	5.00
❑ 3-10607	For All the Right Reasons/The Other Side of the Morning	1977	—	2.50	5.00
❑ 3-10686	She Can't Give It Away/Painted Faces	1978	—	2.50	5.00
❑ 3-10825	It's Sad to Go to the Funeral (Of a Good Love That Has Died)/Good Time Days	1978	—	2.50	5.00
❑ 4-44797	Love Is a Gentle Thing/You Can't Stop My Heart from Breaking	1969	—	3.50	7.00
❑ 4-44925	A Woman's Hand/Got a Chance and I Took It	1969	—	3.50	7.00
❑ 4-45063	A Girl Who'll Satisfy Her Man/Chains of Love	1970	—	3.00	6.00
❑ 4-45173	Find Out What's Happenin'/(When You Close Your Eyes) I'll Make You See	1970	—	3.00	6.00
❑ 4-45272	(Loving You Is) Sunshine/Whatever Happened to Happiness	1970	—	3.00	6.00
❑ 4-45344	What Do You Do/Break Away	1971	—	3.00	6.00
❑ 4-45422	Love's Old Song/Back Then	1971	—	3.00	6.00
❑ 4-45522	Color My World/Tell Me Again	1972	—	3.00	6.00
❑ 4-45589	Thanks for the Mem'ries/Let Me Be Your Queen	1972	—	3.00	6.00
❑ 4-45690	A Sweeter Love (I'll Never Know)/That's Loving You	1972	—	3.00	6.00
❑ 4-45743	Teddy Bear Song/(You Make Me Feel Like) Singing a Song	1972	2.00	4.00	8.00
—Gray label					
❑ 4-45743	Teddy Bear Song/(You Make Me Feel Like) Singing a Song	1973	—	2.50	5.00
—Orange label					
❑ 4-45903	Kid Stuff/Make No Mistakes	1973	—	2.50	5.00
❑ 4-45988	Baby Doll/Color Them with Love	1974	—	2.50	5.00
❑ 4-46053	Standing in Your Line/You're the One I'm Living For	1974	—	2.50	5.00
KAPP					
❑ 925	Something Different/Remember the Alamo	1968	2.00	4.00	8.00
❑ 943	Lonely Old Man/Breakin' In a Brand New Man	1968	2.00	4.00	8.00
NORMAN					
❑ 574	Brand New Bed of Roses/(B-side unknown)	196?	2.50	5.00	10.00
❑ 586	The Telegram/It Gets Kind of Lonesome at Night	196?	2.50	5.00	10.00
Albums					
COLUMBIA					
❑ C 30123	Someone Special	1970	3.75	7.50	15.00
❑ C 31092	Love's Old Song	1971	3.00	6.00	12.00
❑ KC 31720	A Sweeter Love	1973	3.00	6.00	12.00
❑ KC 32711	Kid Stuff	1974	3.00	6.00	12.00
❑ KC 32960	Love Is a Gentle Thing	1974	3.00	6.00	12.00
❑ KC 33058	Standing in Yoru Line	1974	3.00	6.00	12.00
❑ PC 34307	Mississippi	1976	3.00	6.00	12.00
❑ PC 34868	Free & Easy	1977	3.00	6.00	12.00
❑ KC 35311	Greatest Hits	1978	3.00	6.00	12.00
❑ KC 35536	This Is Me	1978	3.00	6.00	12.00

FAIRGROUND ATTRACTION

Number	Title (A Side/B Side)	Yr	VG	VG+	NM
45s					
RCA					
❑ 8789-7-R	Perfect/Mythology	1988	—	—	3.00
❑ 8789-7-R [PS]	Perfect/Mythology	1988	—	2.00	4.00
Albums					
RCA					
❑ 8596-1-R	The First of a Million Kisses	1988	2.50	5.00	10.00

FALLS, RUBY

Number	Title (A Side/B Side)	Yr	VG	VG+	NM
45s					
50 STATES					
❑ 31	Sweet Country Music/Love Away the Wrong I'm About to Do	1975	—	2.50	5.00
❑ 33	He Loves Me All to Pieces/Let's Spend Summer in the Country	1975	—	2.50	5.00
❑ 39	Show Me Where/Somewhere There's a Rainbow Over Texas	1976	—	2.50	5.00
❑ 43	Beware of the Woman (Before She Gets to Your Man)/Jump in a River of Tears	1976	—	2.50	5.00
❑ 50	Do the Buck Dance/Too Many Hurts, Too Many Heartaches	1977	—	2.50	5.00
❑ 56	You've Got to Mend This Heartache/Loves Sweeter Than Sugar	1977	—	2.50	5.00
❑ 60	Three Nights a Week/Give Me Some Lovin'	1978	—	2.50	5.00
❑ 63	If That's Not Loving You (You Can't Say I Didn't Try)/Nobody's Baby But Mine	1978	—	2.50	5.00
❑ 67	Song of the Season/There's a Holiday Feeling in the Air	1978	—	3.00	6.00
❑ 70	I'm Gettin' Into Your Love/Midnight Rendezvous	1979	—	2.50	5.00
❑ 71	Empty Arms and Teardrops (Sure Go Together)/Rainy Rainy Day	1979	—	2.50	5.00
❑ 77	Bringing Home That Feeling/(B-side unknown)	1980	—	2.50	5.00

FAMILY BROWN

Number	Title (A Side/B Side)	Yr	VG	VG+	NM
45s					
OVATION					
❑ 1174	It's Really Love This Time/Nothing Really Changes	1981	—	2.50	5.00
RCA					
❑ PB-13015	But It's Cheating/No One's Gonna Love Me (Like You Do)	1981	—	2.00	4.00
❑ PB-13285	Some Never Stand a Chance/Arkansas Traveler	1982	—	2.00	4.00
❑ PB-13565	We Really Got a Hold on Love/Mister and Misbehavin'	1983	—	2.00	4.00
❑ PB-13734	Repeat After Me/Everyday People	1984	—	2.00	4.00
❑ PB-50837	Feel the Fire/Comin' from a Blue Place	1985	—	2.50	5.00
—Canadian number issued in U.S.					
❑ PB-50851	What If It's Right/Guess Who	1986	—	2.50	5.00
—Canadian number issued in U.S.					
UNITED ARTISTS					
❑ XW1090	Crossing Over/I Can't Get Used to Being Alone	1977	—	3.00	6.00
Albums					
UNITED ARTISTS					
❑ UA-LA828-G	Imaginary World	1978	3.00	6.00	12.00

FARGO, DONNA

Number	Title (A Side/B Side)	Yr	VG	VG+	NM
45s					
ABC/DOT					
❑ 17523	U.S. of A./A Woman's Prayer	1974	—	2.50	5.00
❑ 17541	If Do Feel Good/Only the Strong	1974	—	2.50	5.00
❑ 17557	Hello Little Bluebird/2 Sweet 2 Be 4 Gotten	1975	—	2.50	5.00
❑ 17579	Whatever I Say/Rain Song	1975	—	2.50	5.00
❑ 17586	What Will the New Year Bring/A Woman's Prayer	1975	—	2.50	5.00
❑ 17609	You're Not Charlie Brown (And I'm Not Raggedy Ann)/Sing, Sing, Sing	1976	—	2.00	4.00
❑ 17660	Don't Be Angry/You Don't Mess Around with Jim	1976	—	2.00	4.00
❑ 17692	I'd Love You to Want Me/How Close You Came (To Being Gone)	1977	—	2.00	4.00
CHALLENGE					
❑ 59387	Daddy/Sticks and Stones	1968	2.50	5.00	10.00
❑ 59391	Wishful Thinking/All That's Keeping Me Alive	1968	2.50	5.00	10.00
CLEVELAND INTERNATIONAL					
❑ 1	My Heart Will Always Belong to You/Reasons to Be	1984	—	2.00	4.00
❑ 10	Soldier Boy/Stand Tall	1991	—	2.50	5.00
COLUMBIA					
❑ 04097	The Sign of the Times/Reasons to Be	1983	—	2.00	4.00
COUNTRY HEARTS					
❑ CH-001 [DJ]	My Side of the Bed/Country Singer's Wife	1970	7.50	15.00	30.00
—Promo-only release					
DECCA					
❑ 33001	Daddy/Sticks and Stones	1972	2.00	4.00	8.00
DOT					
❑ 17409	The Happiest Girl in the Whole U.S.A./The Awareness of Nothing	1972	—	3.00	6.00
❑ 17429	Funny Face/How Close You Came (To Being Gone)	1972	—	3.00	6.00
❑ 17444	Superman/Forever Is As Far As I Could Go	1973	—	2.50	5.00
❑ 17460	You Were Always There/He Can Have All He Wants	1973	—	2.50	5.00
❑ 17476	Little Girl Gone/Just Call Me	1973	—	2.50	5.00
❑ 17491	I'll Try a Little Bit Harder/All About a Feeling	1973	—	2.50	5.00
❑ 17506	You Can't Be a Beacon (If Your Light Don't Shine)/Just a Friend of Mine	1974	—	2.50	5.00
MCA					
❑ 51209	Say "I Do"/All About a Feeling	1981	—	2.00	4.00
MERCURY					
❑ 884712-7	Woman of the 80's/You Were Always There	1986	—	—	3.00
❑ 888043-7	Winners/I've Laid Too Many Eggs	1986	—	—	3.00
❑ 888093-7	Me and You/I've Laid Too Many Eggs	1986	—	—	3.00
❑ 888680-7	Members Only/Funny Face	1987	—	—	3.00
—A-side: With Billy Joe Royal					
RAMCO					
❑ 1982	You Make Me Feel Like a Woman/Would You Believe a Lifetime	1967	3.75	7.50	15.00
❑ 1988	Who's Been Playin' House/You Reach for the Bottle	1967	3.75	7.50	15.00
❑ 1991	Kind of Glad I'm Me/Then You Haven't Lied	1967	3.75	7.50	15.00
RCA					
❑ PB-13264	It's Hard to Be the Dreamer/I Just Saw My Reflection in You	1982	—	2.00	4.00
❑ PB-13329	Did We Have to Go This Far (To Say Goodbye)/All I Need to Know	1982	—	2.00	4.00
WARNER BROS.					
❑ 8186	Mr. Doodles/If You Can't Love All of Me	1976	—	2.50	5.00
❑ 8227	I've Loved You All the Way/One of God's Children	1976	—	2.50	5.00
❑ 8305	Mockingbird Hill/Second Chance	1976	—	2.50	5.00
❑ 8375	That Was Yesterday/Cricket Song	1977	—	2.50	5.00
❑ 8431	Shame on Me/Hey, Mister Music Man	1977	—	2.50	5.00
❑ 8509	Do I Love You (Yes in Every Way)/Dee Dee	1977	—	2.50	5.00
❑ 8578	Ragamuffin Girl/Everybody's Girl	1978	—	2.00	4.00
❑ 8643	Another Goodbye/Changes in My Life	1978	—	2.00	4.00
❑ 8722	Somebody Special/Changes in My Life	1978	—	2.00	4.00
❑ 8867	Daddy/For the Rest of My Life	1979	—	2.00	4.00
❑ 49093	Preacher Berry/I Don't Know What to Do	1979	—	2.00	4.00
❑ 49183	Walk On By/I Wrote This Song Just for You	1980	—	2.00	4.00
❑ 49514	Land of Cotton/I Still Believe in You	1980	—	2.00	4.00
❑ 49575	Seeing Is Believing/Look What You've Done	1980	—	2.00	4.00
❑ 49757	Lonestar Cowboy/Utah Song	1981	—	2.00	4.00
❑ 49852	Jacamo/Song to Celebrate Life	1981	—	2.00	4.00
Albums					
ABC/DOT					
❑ DOSD-2002	Miss Donna Fargo	1974	3.00	6.00	12.00
❑ DOSD-2029	Whatever I Say Means I Love You	1975	3.00	6.00	12.00
❑ DO-2075	The Best of Donna Fargo	1977	3.00	6.00	12.00
DOT					
❑ DLP-26000	The Happiest Girl in the Whole U.S.A.	1972	3.00	6.00	12.00
❑ DLP-26006	My Second Album	1973	3.00	6.00	12.00
❑ DLP-26019	All About a Feeling	1973	3.00	6.00	12.00
MCA					
❑ 667	The Happiest Girl in the Whole U.S.A.	198?	2.00	4.00	8.00
—Budget-line reissue					
❑ 37108	The Best of Donna Fargo	198?	2.00	4.00	8.00
—Budget-line reissue					
MERCURY					
❑ 830236-1	Winners	1986	3.00	6.00	12.00
❑ 832507-1	Winners	1987	2.00	4.00	8.00
—Reissue with two songs deleted and one added from above					
PICKWICK					
❑ 6187	Superman	197?	2.00	4.00	8.00
SONGBIRD					
❑ 5203	Brotherly Love	1982	2.50	5.00	10.00
WARNER BROS.					
❑ BS 2926	On the Move	1976	2.50	5.00	10.00
❑ BS 2996	Donna Fargo Country	1977	2.50	5.00	10.00
❑ BS 3099	Shame on Me	1977	2.50	5.00	10.00
❑ BS 3191	Dark Eyed Lady	1978	2.50	5.00	10.00
❑ BSK 3377	Just for You	1979	2.50	5.00	10.00
❑ BSK 3470	Fargo	1980	2.50	5.00	10.00

FARMER BOYS, THE

Number	Title (A Side/B Side)	Yr	VG	VG+	NM
45s					
CAPITOL					
❑ F3077	You're a Humdinger/I'm Just Too Lazy	1955	5.00	10.00	20.00
❑ F3162	Lend a Helping Hand/Onions, Onions	1955	5.00	10.00	20.00
❑ F3246	You Lied/It Pays to Advertise	1955	5.00	10.00	20.00
❑ F3322	Flip Flop/Charming Betsy	1956	5.00	10.00	20.00
❑ F3476	My Baby Done Left Me/Somehow, Someway, Someday	1956	5.00	10.00	20.00
❑ F3569	Cool Down Mame/Oh How It Hurts	1956	5.00	10.00	20.00
❑ F3732	Flash, Crash and Thunder/Someone to Love	1957	5.00	10.00	20.00
❑ F3827	Yearning, Burning Heart/No One	1957	5.00	10.00	20.00

FAUCETT, DAWNETT

Number	Title (A Side/B Side)	Yr	VG	VG+	NM
45s					
STEP ONE					
❑ 399	This Bus Won't Be Stopping on Memory Lane/The Most I've Ever Hurt Before	1989	—	2.50	5.00
❑ 407	Money Don't Make a Man a Lover/Cross My Broken Heart	1989	—	2.50	5.00
❑ 412	As Far as Love Can Throw Me/The Most I've Ever Hurt Before	1989	—	2.50	5.00
❑ 417	Slow Dancin'/Dusty Road	1990	—	2.50	5.00
❑ 421	Taking My Time/Cheap Perfume	1990	—	2.50	5.00

Number	Title (A Side/B Side)	Yr	VG	VG+	NM
FELICIANO, JOSE					
The famous Puerto Rican-born singer/guitarist had this one entry on the country charts.					
45s					
MOTOWN					
❑ 1674	Let's Find Each Other Tonight/Cuidado	1983	—	2.00	4.00
FELL, TERRY					
45s					
RCA VICTOR					
❑ 47-6256	That's What I Like/I Really Go Crazy	1955	5.00	10.00	20.00
❑ 47-6353	That's the Way the Big Ball Bounces/What Am I Worth	1955	6.25	12.50	25.00
❑ 47-6444	Over and Over/If I Didn't Have You	1956	5.00	10.00	20.00
❑ 47-6515	Wham Bam! Hot Ziggity Zam/Consolation Prize	1956	5.00	10.00	20.00
❑ 47-6621	I Can Hear You Cluckin'/Don't Do It, Joe	1956	5.00	10.00	20.00
❑ 47-6707	Caveman/Play the Music Louder	1956	5.00	10.00	20.00
"X"					
❑ 0010	Don't Drop It/Truck Driving Man	1954	7.50	15.00	30.00
❑ 0069	We Wanna See Santa Do the Mambo/Let's Stay Together Till After Christmas	1954	7.50	15.00	30.00
❑ 0078	Get Aboard My Wagon/You Don't Give a Hang About Me	1955	6.25	12.50	25.00
❑ 0114	Mississippi River Shuffle/He's in Love with You	1955	6.25	12.50	25.00
❑ 0149	I'm Hot to Trot/Fa-So-La	1955	6.25	12.50	25.00
FELLER, DICK					
45s					
ASYLUM					
❑ 11037	Makin' the Best of a Bad Situation/She's Taken a Gentle Lover	1974	—	2.50	5.00
❑ 45220	Cry for Lori/Doin' the Best I Can	1974	—	2.50	5.00
❑ 45290	Uncle Hiram and the Homemade Beer/Let It Ride	1975	—	2.50	5.00
❑ 45306	Some Days Are Diamonds (Some Days Are Stone)/Doin' the Best I Can	1976	—	3.00	6.00
UNITED ARTISTS					
❑ XW236	Daisy Hill/Any Old Wind That Blows	1973	—	2.50	5.00
❑ XW316	Biff, The Friendly Purple Bear/Goodbye California	1973	—	2.50	5.00
❑ XW535	The Credit Card Song/Just Short of the Line	1974	—	2.50	5.00
❑ X1357	The Credit Card Song/Biff, The Friendly Purple Bear	1980	—	2.00	4.00
❑ 50984	The Sum of Margie's Blues/Any Old Wind That Blows	1972	—	2.50	5.00
Albums					
ASYLUM					
❑ CM-1	No Word on Me	1974	3.00	6.00	12.00
❑ 7E-1044	Some Days Are Diamonds	1975	2.50	5.00	10.00
UNITED ARTISTS					
❑ UA-LA349-R	Dick Feller Wrote	1974	2.50	5.00	10.00
FELTS, NARVEL					
Also see THE WOLFPACK.					
45s					
ABC					
❑ 12338	Runaway/Free	1978	—	2.50	5.00
❑ 12374	Just Keep It Up/Lonely Lady	1978	—	2.50	5.00
❑ 12414	One Run for the Roses/Lie to Me (Darling)	1978	—	2.50	5.00
❑ 12441	Everlasting Love/Small Enough to Crawl	1978	—	2.50	5.00
ABC DOT					
❑ 17549	Reconsider Me/Foggy Misty Morning	1975	—	2.50	5.00
❑ 17569	Funny How Time Slips Away/No One Knows	1975	—	2.50	5.00
❑ 17598	Somebody Hold Me (Until She Passes By)/Away	1975	—	2.50	5.00
❑ 17620	Lonely Teardrops/I Remember You	1976	—	2.50	5.00
❑ 17643	My Prayer/If Ever Two Were One (Then Surely We Are)	1976	—	2.50	5.00
❑ 17664	My Good Thing's Gone/I'm Afraid to Be Alone	1976	—	2.50	5.00
❑ 17680	The Feeling's Right/Another Crazy Dream	1977	—	2.50	5.00
❑ 17700	I Don't Hurt Anymore/When We Were Together	1977	—	2.50	5.00
❑ 17715	To Love Somebody/Remember	1977	—	2.50	5.00
❑ 17731	Please/Blue Darlin'	1977	—	2.50	5.00
ARA					
❑ 203	Four Seasons of Life/All That Heaven Sent	1964	5.00	10.00	20.00
❑ 207	You Were Mine/You Didn't Tell Me, I Didn't Know	1965	5.00	10.00	20.00
❑ 211	Night Creature/One Boy and One Night	1965	5.00	10.00	20.00
❑ 213	Welcome Home Mr. Blues/Your True Love	1965	5.00	10.00	20.00
CELEBRITY CIRCLE					
❑ 6903	Welcome Home Mr. Blues/Back Street	1965	3.00	6.00	12.00
❑ 6905	What's Wrong with Me/It All Depends	1965	3.00	6.00	12.00
CINNAMON					
❑ 756	Rockin' Little Angel/The Twelfth of Never	1973	—	3.00	6.00
❑ 763	Drift Away/Foggy Misty Morning	1973	—	3.00	6.00
❑ 771	All in the Name of Love/Before You Have to Go	1973	—	3.00	6.00
❑ 779	When Your Good Love Was Mine/Fraulein	1973	—	3.00	6.00
❑ 798	I Want to Stay/Wrap My Arms Around the World	1974	—	3.00	6.00
❑ 809	Raindrops/Tilted Cup of Love	1974	—	3.00	6.00
COLLAGE					
❑ 101	Because of Losing You/After You	1979	—	3.00	6.00
COMPLEAT					
❑ 101	Smoke Gets in Your Eyes/You're the Reason	1982	—	2.50	5.00
❑ 104	Cry Baby/Now I Don't Have to Love You	1983	—	2.50	5.00
EVERGREEN					
❑ 1011	Anytime You're Ready/Nobody's Fool	1983	—	2.50	5.00
❑ 1014	Fool/Anytime You're Ready	1983	—	2.50	5.00
❑ 1017	You Lay So Easy on My Mind/Nobody's Fool	1984	—	2.50	5.00
❑ 1022	Let's Live This Dream Together/Nobody's Fool	1984	—	2.50	5.00
❑ 1025	I'm Glad You Couldn't Sleep Last Night/It Amazes Me	1984	—	2.50	5.00
❑ 1027	Hey Lady/Anytime You're Ready	1984	—	2.50	5.00
❑ 1030	If It Was Any Better (I Couldn't Stand It)/Nobody's Fool	1985	—	2.50	5.00
❑ 1034	Out of Sight Out of Mind/It Amazes Me	1985	—	2.50	5.00
❑ 1041	Rockin' My Angel/Anytime You're Ready	1986	—	2.50	5.00
❑ 1054	When a Man Loves a Woman/Hey Lady	1987	—	2.50	5.00
❑ 1083	I Need Somebody Bad/(B-side unknown)	1988	—	3.00	6.00
GMC					
❑ 114	Louisiana Lonely/Look What Love Has Done	1981	—	2.50	5.00
❑ 115	Fire in the Night/Look What Love Has Done	1981	—	2.50	5.00
GROOVE					
❑ 58-0029	Mountain of Love/The End of My World Is Near	1963	5.00	10.00	20.00
HI					
❑ 2110	The Greatest Gift/I'll Trade All My Tomorrows	1966	3.75	7.50	15.00
❑ 2118	Bells/86 Miles	1967	3.00	6.00	12.00
❑ 2126	Don't Let Me Cross Over/Like Magic	1967	3.00	6.00	12.00
❑ 2137	Starry Eyes/Dee-Dee	1968	3.00	6.00	12.00
❑ 2141	Since I Met You Baby/I Had to Cry Again	1968	3.00	6.00	12.00
❑ 2305	This Time/I Had to Cry Again	1976	—	2.50	5.00
HI COUNTRY					
❑ 8001	Endless Love/Walkin' to the Pearly Gates	1972	2.00	4.00	8.00
❑ 8002	A Little Bit of Soap/You're Out of My Reach	1972	2.00	4.00	8.00
❑ 8003	Butterfly/Closed by a Dream	1973	2.00	4.00	8.00
KARI					
❑ 110	Love the One You're With/When There's a Will (There's a Way)	1980	—	3.00	6.00
LOBO					
❑ III	I'd Love You to Want Me/The First Time We Made Love	1982	—	3.00	6.00
❑ VIII	Sweet Southern Moonlight/The First Time We Made Love	1982	—	3.00	6.00
❑ XI	Roll Over Beethoven/I'd Love You to Want Me	1982	—	3.00	6.00
MCA					
❑ 41011	Moment by Moment/Never Again	1979	—	2.50	5.00
❑ 41055	Tower of Strength/You're a Heartbreaker	1979	—	2.50	5.00
MERCURY					
❑ 71140	Kiss-a-Me Baby/Foolish Thoughts	1957	7.50	15.00	30.00
❑ 71190	Cry, Cry, Cry/Lonesome Feeling	1957	7.50	15.00	30.00
❑ 71249	Rocket Ride/Dream World	1957	7.50	15.00	30.00
❑ 71275	Rocket Ride Stroll/Dream World	1958	7.50	15.00	30.00
❑ 71347	Little Girl Step This Way/Vadalou	1958	7.50	15.00	30.00
PINK					
❑ 701	Three Thousand Miles/Cutie Baby	1959	10.00	20.00	40.00
❑ 702	Honey Love/Genavee	1959	10.00	20.00	40.00
❑ 706	Darling Sue/Tony	1960	10.00	20.00	40.00
Albums					
ABC					
❑ 1080	Inside Love	1978	2.50	5.00	10.00
❑ 1115	One Run for the Roses	1979	2.50	5.00	10.00
ABC DOT					
❑ DOSD-2025	Narvel Felts	1975	3.00	6.00	12.00
❑ 2033	Narvel the Marvel	1976	3.00	6.00	12.00
❑ 2036	Greatest Hits Vol. 1	1975	3.00	6.00	12.00
❑ DO-2065	Doin' What I Feel	1976	3.00	6.00	12.00
❑ DO-2070	The Touch of Felts	1977	3.00	6.00	12.00
❑ DO-2095	Narvel	1977	3.00	6.00	12.00
CINNAMON					
❑ 5000	Drift Away	1973	3.75	7.50	15.00
❑ 5002	When Your Good Love Was Mine	1974	3.75	7.50	15.00
HI					
❑ 32098	This Time	1976	3.00	6.00	12.00
MCA					
❑ 634	The Touch of Felts	198?	2.00	4.00	8.00
—Reissue of ABC Dot 2070					
❑ 635	Narvel	198?	2.00	4.00	8.00
—Reissue of ABC Dot 2095					
❑ 699	Inside Love	198?	2.00	4.00	8.00
—Reissue of ABC 1080					
❑ 799	One Run for the Roses	198?	2.00	4.00	8.00
—Reissue of ABC 1115					
❑ 27020	The Very Best of Narvel Felts	198?	2.00	4.00	8.00
POWER PAK					
❑ PO-237	Live!	197?	2.50	5.00	10.00
FELTS, NARVEL, AND SHARON VAUGHN					
Also see each artist's individual listings.					
45s					
CINNAMON					
❑ 793	Until the End of Time/Someone to Give My Love To	1974	—	3.00	6.00
FENDER, FREDDY					
45s					
ABC					
❑ 12339	Louisiana Woman/If You're Looking for a Fool	1978	—	2.00	4.00
❑ 12370	Talk to Me/Please Mr. Sun	1978	—	2.00	4.00
❑ 12415	I'm Leaving It All Up to You/Whe It Rains It Really Pours	1978	—	2.00	4.00
❑ 12453	Sweet Summer Day/Walking Piece of Heaven	1979	—	2.00	4.00

Number	Title (A Side/B Side)	Yr	VG	VG+	NM
ABC/DOT					
❑ 17540	Before the Next Teardrop Falls/Waiting for Your Love	1974	—	2.50	5.00
❑ 17558	Wasted Days and Wasted Nights/I Love My Rancho Grande	1975	—	2.50	5.00
❑ 17585	Secret Love/Loving Cajun Style	1975	—	2.00	4.00
❑ 17607	You'll Lose a Good Thing/I'm to Blame	1976	—	2.00	4.00
❑ 17627	Vaya Con Dios/My Happiness	1976	—	2.00	4.00
❑ 17652	Living It Down/Take Her a Message, I'm Lonely	1976	—	2.00	4.00
❑ 17686	The Rains Came/Sugar Coated Love	1977	—	2.00	4.00
❑ 17713	If You Don't Love Me (Why Don't You Just Leave Me Alone)/Thank You, My Love	1977	—	2.00	4.00
❑ 17730	Think About Me/If That's the Way You Want It	1977	—	2.00	4.00
❑ 17734	Christmas Time in the Valley/Please Come Home for Christmas	1977	—	2.50	5.00
ARGO					
❑ 5375	A Man Can Cry/You're Something Else for Me	1960	3.75	7.50	15.00
ARV INTERNATIONAL					
❑ 5083	Crazy Arms/She Thinks I Still Care	196?	2.50	5.00	10.00
❑ 5102	Un Dia de Sol/La Costumbre	196?	2.50	5.00	10.00
❑ 5146	El Rock de la Carcel/No Seasa Cruel	196?	2.50	5.00	10.00
❑ 5216	Crazy Arms/She Thinks I Still Care	198?	—	2.50	5.00
CRAZY CAJUN					
❑ 2002	Before the Next Teardrop Falls/Waiting for Your Love	198?	—	2.50	5.00
❑ 2002	Before the Next Teardrop Falls/Crazy, Crazy Baby	198?	—	2.50	5.00
❑ 2006	Esta Noche Mia Sera/(B-side unknown)	198?	—	2.50	5.00
❑ 2014	No Toquen Ya/I Love My Rancho Grande	198?	—	2.50	5.00
❑ 2019	Vaya Con Dios/No Say El Mismo	198?	—	2.50	5.00
❑ 2037	Fannie Mae/Going Out with the Tide	198?	—	2.50	5.00
—With Tommy McLain					
❑ 2060	My Confession/Goin' Honky Tonkin'	198?	—	2.00	4.00
DUNCAN					
❑ 1000	Mean Woman/Holy One	1959	10.00	20.00	40.00
❑ 1001	Wasted Days and Wasted Nights/San Antonio Walk	1959	6.25	12.50	25.00
❑ 1002	Wild Side of Life/Crazy Baby	1959	6.25	12.50	25.00
❑ 1004	Since I Met You Baby/Little Mama	1959	6.25	12.50	25.00
GOLDBAND					
❑ 1214	My Tears of Love/Carmelia	197?	2.50	5.00	10.00
❑ 1264	Bye, Bye, Little Angel/Oh My Love	1975	—	2.50	5.00
❑ 1272	Three Wishes/Me and My Bottle of Rum	1975	—	2.50	5.00
GRT					
❑ 031	Since I Met You Baby/Little Mama	1975	—	2.50	5.00
❑ 039	Wild Side of Life/Go On Baby	1975	—	2.50	5.00
IMPERIAL					
❑ 5659	Mean Woman/Holy One	1960	5.00	10.00	20.00
❑ 5670	Wasted Days and Wasted Nights/I Can't Remember When I Didn't Love You	1960	5.00	10.00	20.00
INSTANT					
❑ 3332	Some People Say/Today's Your Wedding Day	1972	2.00	4.00	8.00
MCA					
❑ 12453	Sweet Summer Day/Walking Piece of Heaven	1979	—	2.00	4.00
❑ 52003	Across the Borderline/Before the Next Teardrop Falls	1982	—	2.00	4.00
NORCO					
❑ 100	Love's Light Is an Ember/The New Stroll	1963	2.50	5.00	10.00
❑ 102	You Made Me Cry/Never Trust a Cheating Woman	1963	2.50	5.00	10.00
❑ 103	Coming Home Soon/Going Out with the Tide	1964	2.50	5.00	10.00
❑ 104	Just a Little Bit/You Made Me a Fool	1964	2.50	5.00	10.00
❑ 106	Ooh Poo Pah Doo/Three Wishes	1964	2.50	5.00	10.00
❑ 107	Magic of Love/Bony Moronie	1965	2.50	5.00	10.00
—With Noel Vill					
❑ 108	In the Still of the Night/You Don't Have to Go	1965	2.50	5.00	10.00
❑ 111	Donna/Lover's Quarrel	1965	2.50	5.00	10.00
PA GO GO					
❑ 115	Cool Mary Lou/You Are My Sunshine	1967	2.50	5.00	10.00
PACEMAKER					
❑ 1973	Wasted Days and Wasted Nights/Bidin' My Time	197?	—	2.50	5.00
REPRISE					
❑ 19143	It's All in the Game/Before the Next Teardrop Falls	1992	—	—	3.00
STARFLITE					
❑ 4900	Yours/Rock Down in My Shoe	1979	—	2.00	4.00
❑ 4904	Squeeze Box/Turn Around	1979	—	2.00	4.00
❑ 4906	My Special Prayer/(B-side unknown)	1979	—	2.00	4.00
❑ 4908	Please Talk to My Heart/(B-side unknown)	1980	—	2.00	4.00
WARNER BROS.					
❑ 29794	Chokin' Kind/I Might As Well Forget You	1983	—	2.00	4.00
Albums					
ABC					
❑ AA-1062	Swamp Gold	1978	2.50	5.00	10.00
❑ AA-1132	Tex-Mex	1979	3.00	6.00	12.00
ABC/DOT					
❑ DOSD-2020	Before the Next Teardrop Falls	1975	3.00	6.00	12.00
❑ DOSD-2044	Are You Ready for Freddy	1975	3.00	6.00	12.00
❑ DOSD-2050	Rock 'n Country	1976	3.00	6.00	12.00
❑ DOSD-2061	If You're Ever in Texas	1976	3.00	6.00	12.00
❑ DO-2079	The Best of Freddy Fender	1977	3.00	6.00	12.00
❑ DP-2090	If You Don't Love Me	1977	3.00	6.00	12.00
❑ DO-2101	Merry Christmas — Feliz Navidad	1977	3.00	6.00	12.00
ACCORD					
❑ SN-7121	Since I Met You Baby	1981	2.50	5.00	10.00
GRT					
❑ 8005	Since I Met You Baby	1975	3.00	6.00	12.00
INTERMEDIA					
❑ QS-5035	Before the Next Teardrop Falls	198?	2.00	4.00	8.00
MCA					
❑ 639	Are You Ready for Freddy	1980	2.00	4.00	8.00
—Reissue of ABC/Dot 2044					
❑ 668	Swamp Gold	1980	2.00	4.00	8.00
—Reissue of ABC 1062					
❑ 669	If You Don't Love Me	1980	2.00	4.00	8.00
—Reissue of ABC/Dot 2090					
❑ 835	The Best of Freddy Fender	198?	2.00	4.00	8.00
—Reissue of MCA 3285					
❑ AA-1132	Tex-Mex	1979	2.50	5.00	10.00
—Reissue of ABC 1132					
❑ 3285	The Best of Freddy Fender	1979	2.50	5.00	10.00
—Reissue of ABC/Dot 2079					
❑ 15025	Merry Christmas	198?	2.00	4.00	8.00
❑ 15037	Christmas Time in the Valley	198?	2.50	5.00	10.00
❑ 37109	Tex-Mex	1980	2.00	4.00	8.00
—Reissue of MCA 1132					
❑ 37110	Before the Next Teardrop Falls	1980	2.00	4.00	8.00
—Reissue of ABC/Dot 2020					
PICCADILLY					
❑ 3589	Enter My Heart	1981	2.50	5.00	10.00
PICKWICK					
❑ JS-6178	Freddy Fender	1975	2.50	5.00	10.00
POWER PAK					
❑ PO-280	Recorded Inside Louisiana State Prison	1975	2.50	5.00	10.00
STARFLITE					
❑ JZ 36073	Balladeer	1980	2.50	5.00	10.00
❑ JZ 36284	Together We Drifted Apart	1980	2.50	5.00	10.00

FENDERMEN, THE

Number	Title (A Side/B Side)	Yr	VG	VG+	NM
45s					
CUCA					
❑ 1003	Mule Skinner Blues/Torture	1960	50.00	100.00	200.00
SOMA					
❑ 1137	Mule Skinner Blues/Torture	1960	6.25	12.50	25.00
❑ 1142	Don't You Just Know It/Beach Party	1960	5.00	10.00	20.00
❑ 1155	Heartbreakin' Special/Can't You Wait	1960	5.00	10.00	20.00
Albums					
SOMA					
❑ MG-1240 [M]	Mule Skinner Blues	1960	2000.	3000.	4000.
—Blue vinyl					
❑ MG-1240 [M]	Mule Skinner Blues	1960	300.00	600.00	1200.
—Black vinyl					

FENSTER, ZOOT

See JACK BARLOW.

FERRARI, C.W.

Number	Title (A Side/B Side)	Yr	VG	VG+	NM
45s					
SOUTHERN SOUND					
❑ 1001	Country Highways/(B-side unknown)	1988	—	2.50	5.00

FINNEY, MAURY

Number	Title (A Side/B Side)	Yr	VG	VG+	NM
45s					
SOUNDWAVES					
❑ 4516	Jambalaya/My Elusive Dreams	1975	—	3.00	6.00
❑ 4525	Maiden's Prayer/San Antonio Stroll	1975	—	2.50	5.00
❑ 4531	Rollin' in My Sweet Baby's Arms/Wild Side of Life	1976	—	2.50	5.00
❑ 4536	Waltz Across Texas/Off and Running	1976	—	2.50	5.00
❑ 4541	Everybody's Had the Blues/Too Pretty for Words	1976	—	2.50	5.00
❑ 4548	Coconut Grove/It's Such a Pretty World Today	1977	—	2.50	5.00
❑ 4557	Poor People of Paris/Almost Persuaded	1977	—	2.50	5.00
❑ 4566	I Don't Wanna Cry/Happy Sax	1978	—	2.50	5.00
❑ 4572	Whispering/Send Me the Pillow	1978	—	2.50	5.00
❑ 4578	Happy Sax/Faded Love	1979	—	2.50	5.00
❑ 4585	Your Love Takes Me So High/I Want to Play My Horn on the Grand Ole' Opry	1979	—	2.50	5.00
❑ 4613	Lonely Wine/Misery and Gin	1980	—	2.50	5.00
❑ 4637	Doodle De Doo Song/San Antonio Stroll	1981	—	2.50	5.00
Albums					
SOUNDWAVES					
❑ 3301	Sax Life in Nashville	1976	3.75	7.50	15.00

FIRST EDITION, THE

Includes "Kenny Rogers and the First Edition." Also see KENNY ROGERS; KIN VASSY.

Number	Title (A Side/B Side)	Yr	VG	VG+	NM
45s					
JOLLY ROGERS					
❑ 1001	Lady, Play Your Symphony/There's An Old Man in Our Town	1973	—	2.50	5.00
❑ 1003	(Do You Remember) The First Time/Indian Joe	1973	—	2.50	5.00
❑ 1004	Today I Started Loving You Again/She Thinks I Still Care	1973	—	2.50	5.00
❑ 1006	Whatcha Gonna Do/Something About Your Song	1973	—	2.50	5.00
❑ 1007	A Stranger in My Place/Makin' Music for Money	1974	—	2.50	5.00
—All of the above as "Kenny Rogers and the First Edition"					
REPRISE					
❑ 0628	Ticket to Nowhere/I Found a Reason	1967	2.00	4.00	8.00

Number	Title (A Side/B Side)	Yr	VG	VG+	NM
❑ 0655	Just Dropped In (To See What Condition My Condition Was In)/Shadow in the Corner of Your Mind	1967	3.00	6.00	12.00

—Original pressing has orange and brown label

Number	Title (A Side/B Side)	Yr	VG	VG+	NM
❑ 0655	Just Dropped In (To See What Condition My Condition Was In)/Shadow in the Corner of Your Mind	1967	2.50	5.00	10.00

—Second pressing has lighter orange "steamboat" Reprise/W7 label

Number	Title (A Side/B Side)	Yr	VG	VG+	NM
❑ 0683	Dream On/Only Me	1968	—	3.00	6.00
❑ 0693	Look Around, I'll Be There/Charlie the Fer-De-Lance	1968	—	3.00	6.00
❑ 0737	Just Dropped In (To See What Condition My Condition Was In)/But You Know I Love You	1971	—	2.00	4.00

—As "Kenny Rogers and the First Edition"; "Back to Back Hits" series

Number	Title (A Side/B Side)	Yr	VG	VG+	NM
❑ 0738	Ruby, Don't Take Your Love to Town/Reuben James	1971	—	2.00	4.00

—As "Kenny Rogers and the First Edition"; "Back to Back Hits" series

Number	Title (A Side/B Side)	Yr	VG	VG+	NM
❑ 0747	Something's Burning/Someone Who Cares	1972	—	2.00	4.00

—As "Kenny Rogers and the First Edition"; "Back to Back Hits" series

Number	Title (A Side/B Side)	Yr	VG	VG+	NM
❑ 0748	Tell It All Brother/Heed the Call	1972	—	2.00	4.00

—As "Kenny Rogers and the First Edition"; "Back to Back Hits" series

Number	Title (A Side/B Side)	Yr	VG	VG+	NM
❑ 0773	If I Could Only Change Your Mind/Are My Thoughts With You	1968	—	3.00	6.00
❑ 0799	But You Know I Love You/Homemade Lies	1968	—	3.00	6.00
❑ 0822	Good Time Liberator/Once Again She's All Alone	1969	—	2.50	5.00

—Starting above, by "Kenny Rogers and the First Edition"

Number	Title (A Side/B Side)	Yr	VG	VG+	NM
❑ 0829	Ruby, Don't Take Your Love to Town/Girl Get a Hold of Yourself	1969	—	2.50	5.00
❑ 0854	Ruben James/Sunshine	1969	—	2.50	5.00
❑ 0854	Reuben James/Sunshine	1969	—	2.50	5.00
❑ 0888	Something's Burning/Mama's Waiting	1970	—	2.50	5.00
❑ 0923	Tell It All Brother/Just Remember You're My Sunshine	1970	—	2.50	5.00
❑ 0953	Heed the Call/A Stranger in My Place	1970	—	2.50	5.00
❑ 0999	Someone Who Cares/Mission of San Mohera	1971	—	2.50	5.00
❑ 1018	Take My Hand/All God's Lonely Children	1971	—	2.50	5.00
❑ 1053	Where Does Rosie Go/What Am I Gonna Do	1971	—	2.50	5.00
❑ 1069	School Teacher/Trigger Happy Kid	1972	—	2.50	5.00

Albums

JOLLY ROGERS

Number	Title (A Side/B Side)	Yr	VG	VG+	NM
❑ 5001	Backroads	1973	3.75	7.50	15.00
❑ 5003	Rollin'	1974	3.75	7.50	15.00
❑ 5004	Monumental	1974	3.75	7.50	15.00

—All the above as "Kenny Rogers and the First Edition"

MCA

Number	Title (A Side/B Side)	Yr	VG	VG+	NM
❑ 913	Country Songs	1984	2.00	4.00	8.00
❑ 942	Hits and Pieces	1985	2.00	4.00	8.00
❑ 943	The 60's Revisited	1985	2.00	4.00	8.00
❑ 944	Pieces of Calico Silver	1985	2.00	4.00	8.00
❑ 1460	Greatest Hits	1985	2.00	4.00	8.00

—Reissue of Reprise 6437

REPRISE

Number	Title (A Side/B Side)	Yr	VG	VG+	NM
❑ MS 2039	Transition	1971	5.00	10.00	20.00

—As "Kenny Rogers and the First Edition"

Number	Title (A Side/B Side)	Yr	VG	VG+	NM
❑ R-6276 [M]	The First Edition	1967	7.50	15.00	30.00
❑ RS-6276 [S]	The First Edition	1967	6.25	12.50	25.00
❑ RS-6302	The First Edition's Second	1968	6.25	12.50	25.00
❑ RS-6328	The First Edition '69	1969	6.25	12.50	25.00
❑ RS-6352	Ruby, Don't Take Your Love to Town	1969	5.00	10.00	20.00

—Starting above, as "Kenny Rogers and the First Edition"

Number	Title (A Side/B Side)	Yr	VG	VG+	NM
❑ RS-6385	Something's Burning	1970	5.00	10.00	20.00
❑ RS-6412	Tell It All Brother	1970	5.00	10.00	20.00
❑ RS-6437	Greatest Hits	1971	5.00	10.00	20.00
❑ 2SX 6476 [(2)]	The Ballad of Calico	1972	6.25	12.50	25.00

FISCHOFF, GEORGE

45s

AVALANCHE

Number	Title (A Side/B Side)	Yr	VG	VG+	NM
❑ XW231	That Summer Night/For Gladys	1973	—	3.00	6.00

DRIVE

Number	Title (A Side/B Side)	Yr	VG	VG+	NM
❑ 6273	The Piano Picker/Love Dust	1979	—	2.50	5.00

GNP CRESCENDO

Number	Title (A Side/B Side)	Yr	VG	VG+	NM
❑ 491	That Great Old Song/Blue Night	1975	—	2.50	5.00

HERITAGE

Number	Title (A Side/B Side)	Yr	VG	VG+	NM
❑ 300	Little Ballerina Blue/Foxy	197?	—	3.00	6.00

LISA

Number	Title (A Side/B Side)	Yr	VG	VG+	NM
❑ 1	That Great Old Song/Blue Night	1975	—	3.50	7.00
❑ 17315	Starry Night/(B-side unknown)	198?	—	2.50	5.00

MOSS

Number	Title (A Side/B Side)	Yr	VG	VG+	NM
❑ 13365	Summer Love/(B-side unknown)	198?	—	2.50	5.00

P.I.P.

Number	Title (A Side/B Side)	Yr	VG	VG+	NM
❑ 6503	New Kingston/Waterflower	1975	—	3.00	6.00

RANWOOD

Number	Title (A Side/B Side)	Yr	VG	VG+	NM
❑ 1053	Funky Doodle/Quiet Time	1976	—	2.50	5.00

REWARD

Number	Title (A Side/B Side)	Yr	VG	VG+	NM
❑ WS4-04354	Boogie Piano Man/Blues for the Boogie Man	1984	—	2.00	4.00

UNITED ARTISTS

Number	Title (A Side/B Side)	Yr	VG	VG+	NM
❑ XW410	Georgia Porcupine/I'll Never Forget You	1974	—	3.00	6.00

FITZGERALD, ELLA

One of America's greatest jazz vocalists, her rendition of the below A-side spent a week at number 2 on the country charts.

Selected 78s

DECCA

Number	Title (A Side/B Side)	Yr	VG	VG+	NM
❑ 18587	When My Sugar Walks Down the Street/Cow-Cow Boogie	1944	5.00	10.00	20.00

FIVE RED CAPS, THE

The below single by the R&B-styled vocal group made the country chart in 1944.

Selected 78s

BEACON

Number	Title (A Side/B Side)	Yr	VG	VG+	NM
❑ 7120	I Learned a Lesson I'll Never Forget/Words Can't Explain	1944	10.00	20.00	40.00

FIVE STRINGS, THE

See SID KING.

FLATT, LESTER

Also see FLATT AND SCRUGGS.

45s

COLUMBIA

Number	Title (A Side/B Side)	Yr	VG	VG+	NM
❑ 4-45050	Great Big Woman/Life of Reilly	1969	2.00	4.00	8.00
❑ 4-45122	Reuben James/Regina	1970	2.00	4.00	8.00

NUGGET

Number	Title (A Side/B Side)	Yr	VG	VG+	NM
❑ 1056	Drink That Mash and Talk That Trash/Sunny Side of Me	1971	2.50	5.00	10.00

RCA VICTOR

Number	Title (A Side/B Side)	Yr	VG	VG+	NM
❑ APBO-0113	I've Been Away So Long/This Man Jesus	1973	—	3.50	7.00
❑ APBO-0228	Before You Go/Love's Come Over Me	1974	—	3.50	7.00
❑ 47-9953	Everybody Has One (But You)/I Can't Tell the Boys from the Girls	1971	2.00	4.00	8.00
❑ 74-0541	Don't Take It So Hard, Mr. Webster/Father's Table Grace	1971	2.00	4.00	8.00
❑ 74-0589	Kentucky Ridge Runner/Roll in My Sweet Baby's Arms	1971	2.00	4.00	8.00
❑ 74-0680	Backin' to Birmingham/You're Still Mine Tonight	1972	2.00	4.00	8.00
❑ 74-0796	Foggy Mountain Breakdown/February Snow	1972	—	3.50	7.00

Albums

COLUMBIA

Number	Title (A Side/B Side)	Yr	VG	VG+	NM
❑ CS 1006	Flatt Out	1970	5.00	10.00	20.00

NUGGET

Number	Title (A Side/B Side)	Yr	VG	VG+	NM
❑ 104	The One and Only	1971	5.00	10.00	20.00

RCA VICTOR

Number	Title (A Side/B Side)	Yr	VG	VG+	NM
❑ APL1-0131	Country Boy	1973	3.75	7.50	15.00
❑ LSP-4495	Lester Flatt on Victor	1971	5.00	10.00	20.00
❑ LSP-4633	Kentucky Ridgerunner	1972	5.00	10.00	20.00
❑ LSP-4789	Foggy Mountain Breakdown	1972	5.00	10.00	20.00

FLATT, LESTER, AND MAC WISEMAN

Also see each artist's individual listings.

45s

RCA VICTOR

Number	Title (A Side/B Side)	Yr	VG	VG+	NM
❑ 47-9989	Will You Be Loving Another Man/Jimmie Brown the Newsboy	1971	2.00	4.00	8.00
❑ 74-0576	Bluebirds Singing for Me/We'll Meet Again Sweetheart	1971	—	3.50	7.00
❑ 74-0664	Salty Dog's Blues/Mama's and Daddy's Little Girl	1972	—	3.50	7.00
❑ 74-0736	Me and Your Memory/On the Southbound Train	1972	—	3.50	7.00
❑ 74-0922	Blue Ridge Cabin Home/Waiting for the Boys to Come Home	1973	—	3.50	7.00

Albums

RCA VICTOR

Number	Title (A Side/B Side)	Yr	VG	VG+	NM
❑ LSP-4547	Lester 'n' Mac	1971	5.00	10.00	20.00
❑ LSP-4688	On the South Bound	1972	5.00	10.00	20.00

FLATT AND SCRUGGS

Includes records credited to "Lester Flatt and Earl Scruggs." Also see LESTER FLATT; EARL SCRUGGS.

45s

COLUMBIA

Number	Title (A Side/B Side)	Yr	VG	VG+	NM
❑ 20777	Come Back Darling/I'm Waiting to Hear You Call Me Darling	1951	5.00	10.00	20.00
❑ 20805	We Can't Be Darlings/I'm Head Over Heels in Love	1951	5.00	10.00	20.00
❑ 20830	Jimmy Brown the Newsboy/Somehow Tonight	1951	5.00	10.00	20.00
❑ 20854	Don't Get Above Your Raisin'/I've Lost You	1951	5.00	10.00	20.00
❑ 20886	'Tis Sweet to Be Remembered/Earl's Breakdown	1952	5.00	10.00	20.00
❑ 20915	Brother I'm Getting Ready to Go/Get in Line Brother	1952	5.00	10.00	20.00
❑ 20957	I'll Stay Around/Old Home Town	1952	5.00	10.00	20.00
❑ 21002	Over the Hills to the Poorhouse/My Darling's Last Goodbye	1952	5.00	10.00	20.00
❑ 21043	I'm Gonna Settle Down/I'm Lonesome and Blue	1952	5.00	10.00	20.00
❑ 21054	Dim Lights Thick Smoke/Flint Hill Special	1952	5.00	10.00	20.00
❑ 21091	Why Did You Wander/Thinking About You	1953	5.00	10.00	20.00
❑ 21125	Dear Old Dixie/If I Should Wander Back	1953	5.00	10.00	20.00
❑ 21147	I'm Workin' on a Road/He Took Your Place	1953	5.00	10.00	20.00
❑ 21179	Foggy Mountain Chimes/I'll Go Steppin' Too	1953	5.00	10.00	20.00
❑ 21209	Be Ready/Mother Prays Loud	1954	5.00	10.00	20.00
❑ 21248	Somebody Took My Place with You/I'd Rather Be Alone	1954	5.00	10.00	20.00
❑ 21295	Foggy Mountain Breakdown/You're Not a Drop in the Bucket	1954	5.00	10.00	20.00

Number	Title (A Side/B Side)	Yr	VG	VG+	NM
❑ 21334	Till the End of the World Rolls Around/Don't This Road Look Rough	1954	5.00	10.00	20.00
❑ 21370	You Can Feel It in Your Soul/Old Fashioned Preacher	1955	3.75	7.50	15.00
❑ 21412	I'm Gonna Sleep with One Eye Open/Before I Met You	1955	3.75	7.50	15.00
❑ 21460	Gone Home/Bubbling in My Soul	1955	3.75	7.50	15.00
❑ 21501	Randy Lynn Rag/On My Mind	1956	3.75	7.50	15.00
❑ 21536	Joy Bells/Give Mother My Crown	1956	3.75	7.50	15.00
❑ 21561	No Doubt About It/What's Good for You	1956	3.75	7.50	15.00
❑ 30904 [S]	(contents unknown)	1960	3.75	7.50	15.00
❑ 30905 [S]	(contents unknown)	1960	3.75	7.50	15.00
❑ 30906 [S]	(contents unknown)	1960	3.75	7.50	15.00
❑ 30907 [S]	(contents unknown)	1960	3.75	7.50	15.00
❑ 30908 [S]	(contents unknown)	1960	3.75	7.50	15.00

—Anyone who can fill in these gaps -- the above five all are Columbia "Stereo 7" singles -- please let us know.

Number	Title (A Side/B Side)	Yr	VG	VG+	NM
❑ 40853	Shuckin' the Corn/Six White Horses	1957	3.75	7.50	15.00
❑ 40928	Give Me Flowers While I'm Living/Is There Room for Me?	1957	3.75	7.50	15.00
❑ 40990	Don't Let Your Deal Go Down/Let Those Brown Eyes Smile at Me	1957	3.75	7.50	15.00
❑ 41064	A Hundred Years from Now/I Won't Be Hanging Around	1957	3.75	7.50	15.00
❑ 41125	Big Black Train/Crying Alone	1958	3.75	7.50	15.00
❑ 41184	Building on Sand/Heaven	1958	3.75	7.50	15.00
❑ 41244	Mama's and Daddy's Little Girl/I Don't Care Anymore	1958	3.75	7.50	15.00
❑ 41336	A Million Years in Glory/Jesus Savior, Pilot Me	1959	3.75	7.50	15.00
❑ 41389	Cabin in the Hills/Someone You Have Forgotten	1959	3.75	7.50	15.00
❑ 41518	Crying My Heart Out Over You/Foggy Mountain Rock	1959	3.75	7.50	15.00
❑ 41708	The Great Historical Bum/All I Want Is You	1960	3.75	7.50	15.00
❑ 41786	Polka on a Banjo/Shuckin' the Corn	1960	3.75	7.50	15.00
❑ 41983	I Ain't Going to Work Tomorrow/I Should Wander Back Tonight	1961	3.75	7.50	15.00
❑ 42141	Go Home/Where Will I Shelter My Sheep	1961	3.00	6.00	12.00
❑ 42280	Just Ain't/Cold, Cold Loving	1962	3.00	6.00	12.00
❑ 42413	The Legend of the Johnson Boys/Hear the Whistle Blow a Hundred Miles	1962	3.00	6.00	12.00
❑ 42606	The Ballad of Jed Clampett/Coal Loadin' Johnny	1962	3.75	7.50	15.00
❑ 42606 [PS]	The Ballad of Jed Clampett/Coal Loadin' Johnny	1962	5.00	10.00	20.00
❑ 42755	Pearl Pearl Pearl/Hard Travelin'	1963	3.00	6.00	12.00
❑ 42755 [PS]	Pearl Pearl Pearl/Hard Travelin'	1963	3.75	7.50	15.00
❑ 42840	New York Town/Mama Don't Allow It	1963	3.00	6.00	12.00
❑ 42954	You Are My Flower/My Saro Jane	1964	2.50	5.00	10.00
❑ 42982	Petticoat Junction/Have You Seen My Dear Companion	1964	3.75	7.50	15.00
❑ 43080	Workin' It Out/Fireball	1964	2.50	5.00	10.00
❑ 43135	Sally Don't You Grieve/Little Birdie	1964	2.50	5.00	10.00
❑ 43204	I Still Miss Someone/Father's Table Grace	1964	2.50	5.00	10.00
❑ 43259	Rock Salt and Nails/Gonna Have Myself a Ball	1965	2.50	5.00	10.00
❑ 43412	Memphis/Foggy Mountain Breakdown	1965	2.50	5.00	10.00
❑ 43497	Green Acres/I Had a Dream	1965	3.75	7.50	15.00

—With June Carter

Number	Title (A Side/B Side)	Yr	VG	VG+	NM
❑ 43627	For Lovin' Me/Colours	1966	2.50	5.00	10.00
❑ 43803	The Last Thing on My Mind/Mama You Been on My Mind	1966	2.50	5.00	10.00
❑ 43973	It Was Only the Wind/Why Can't I Find Myself with You	1967	2.50	5.00	10.00
❑ 44040	Nashville Cats/Roust-A-Bout	1967	2.50	5.00	10.00
❑ 44194	California Up Tight Band/Last Train to Clarksville	1967	2.50	5.00	10.00
❑ 44194 [PS]	California Up Tight Band/Last Train to Clarksville	1967	3.75	7.50	15.00
❑ 44380	Foggy Mountain Breakdown/Down in the Flood	1967	3.00	6.00	12.00
❑ 44380 [PS]	Foggy Mountain Breakdown/Down in the Flood	1967	3.00	6.00	12.00
❑ 44623	Like a Rolling Stone/I'd Like to Say a Word About Texas	1968	2.50	5.00	10.00
❑ 44731	I'll Be Your Baby Tonight/Universal Soldier	1969	2.50	5.00	10.00
❑ 45030	Maggie's Farm/Tonight We'll Be Fine	1969	2.50	5.00	10.00

MERCURY

Number	Title (A Side/B Side)	Yr	VG	VG+	NM
❑ 6161	God Loves His Children/I'm Going to Make Heaven My Home	1950	7.50	15.00	30.00

—Note: Earlier Mercury 45s by Flatt and Scruggs may exist

Number	Title (A Side/B Side)	Yr	VG	VG+	NM
❑ 6211	Down the Road/Why Don't You Tell Me So	1950	7.50	15.00	30.00
❑ 6268	Is It Too Late Now/So Happy I'll Be	1950	7.50	15.00	30.00
❑ 6287	I'll Never Love Another/My Little Girl in Tennessee	1950	7.50	15.00	30.00
❑ 6302	That Little Old Country Church House/Cora Is Gone	1951	6.25	12.50	25.00
❑ 6317	Pain in My Heart/Take Me in a Lifeboat	1951	6.25	12.50	25.00
❑ 6333	Doin' My Time/Farewell Blues	1951	6.25	12.50	25.00
❑ 6372	Roll in My Sweet Baby's Arms/I'll Just Pretend	1952	6.25	12.50	25.00
❑ 6396	Pike County Breakdown/Old Salty Dog Blues	1952	6.25	12.50	25.00
❑ 70016	Preachin', Prayin', Singin'/Will Roses Bloom	1952	5.00	10.00	20.00
❑ 70064	God Loves His Children/Back to the Cross	1953	5.00	10.00	20.00
❑ 72739	Foggy Mountain Breakdown (Theme from Bonnie & Clyde)/My Cabin in Caroline	1967	2.50	5.00	10.00
❑ 72739 [PS]	Foggy Mountain Breakdown (Theme from Bonnie & Clyde)/My Cabin in Caroline	1967	3.75	7.50	15.00

Selected 78s

MERCURY

Number	Title (A Side/B Side)	Yr	VG	VG+	NM
❑ 6181	We'll Meet Again Sweetheart/My Cabin in Caroline	1949	5.00	10.00	20.00
❑ 6200	Baby Blue Eyes/Bouquet in Heaven	1949	5.00	10.00	20.00
❑ 6230	I'll Be Going to Heaven Sometime/I'll Never Shed Another Tear	1950	3.75	7.50	15.00
❑ 6247	Foggy Mountain Breakdown/No Mother or Dad	1950	5.00	10.00	20.00

—Original 78 rpm issue of this popular bluegrass song; if a 45 on Mercury exists on this number, it would probably be worth at least $40 near mint

7-Inch Extended Plays

COLUMBIA

Number	Title (A Side/B Side)	Yr	VG	VG+	NM
❑ B-2823	Jimmy Brown, The Newsboy/Mother Prays Loud in Her Sleep//I'll Go Stepping Too/Randy Lynn Rag	195?	6.25	12.50	25.00
❑ B-2823 [PS]	(title unknown)	195?	6.25	12.50	25.00

Albums

ARCHIVE OF FOLK AND JAZZ

Number	Title	Yr	VG	VG+	NM
❑ 259	Lester Flatt & Earl Scruggs	197?	2.50	5.00	10.00

COLUMBIA

Number	Title	Yr	VG	VG+	NM
❑ GP 30 [(2)]	20 All-Time Great Recordings	1970	5.00	10.00	20.00
❑ CL 1019 [M]	Foggy Mountain Jamboree	1957	12.50	25.00	50.00
❑ CL 1424 [M]	Songs of Glory	1960	5.00	10.00	20.00
❑ CL 1564 [M]	Foggy Mountain Banjo	1961	5.00	10.00	20.00
❑ CL 1664 [M]	Songs of the Famous Carter Family	1961	5.00	10.00	20.00
❑ CL 1830 [M]	Folk Songs of Our Land	1962	5.00	10.00	20.00
❑ CL 1951 [M]	Hard Travelin' Featuring The Ballad of Jed Clampett	1963	5.00	10.00	20.00
❑ CL 2045 [M]	Flatt and Scruggs at Carnegie Hall	1963	5.00	10.00	20.00
❑ CL 2134 [M]	Recorded Live at Vanderbilt University	1964	5.00	10.00	20.00
❑ CL 2255 [M]	The Fabulous Sound of Flatt & Scruggs	1964	5.00	10.00	20.00
❑ CL 2354 [M]	Pickin' Strummin' and Singin'	1965	3.75	7.50	15.00
❑ CL 2443 [M]	Town and Country	1966	3.75	7.50	15.00
❑ CL 2513 [M]	When the Saints Go Marching In	1966	3.75	7.50	15.00
❑ CL 2570 [M]	Flatt and Scruggs' Greatest Hits	1966	3.75	7.50	15.00
❑ CL 2643 [M]	Strictly Instrumental	1967	5.00	10.00	20.00
❑ CL 2686 [M]	Hear the Whistle Blow	1967	5.00	10.00	20.00
❑ CS 8221 [S]	Songs of Glory	1960	6.25	12.50	25.00
❑ CS 8364 [S]	Foggy Mountain Banjo	1961	6.25	12.50	25.00
❑ CS 8464 [S]	Songs of the Famous Carter Family	1961	6.25	12.50	25.00
❑ CS 8630 [S]	Folk Songs of Our Land	1962	6.25	12.50	25.00
❑ CS 8751 [S]	Hard Travelin' Featuring The Ballad of Jed Clampett	1963	6.25	12.50	25.00
❑ CS 8845 [S]	Flatt and Scruggs at Carnegie Hall	1963	6.25	12.50	25.00
❑ PC 8845	Flatt and Scruggs at Carnegie Hall	198?	2.00	4.00	8.00

—Budget-line reissue

Number	Title	Yr	VG	VG+	NM
❑ CS 8934 [S]	Recorded Live at Vanderbilt University	1964	6.25	12.50	25.00
❑ CS 9055 [S]	The Fabulous Sound of Flatt & Scruggs	1964	6.25	12.50	25.00
❑ CS 9154 [S]	Pickin' Strummin' and Singin'	1965	5.00	10.00	20.00
❑ CS 9243 [S]	Town and Country	1966	5.00	10.00	20.00
❑ CS 9313 [S]	When the Saints Go Marching In	1966	5.00	10.00	20.00
❑ CS 9370 [S]	Flatt and Scruggs' Greatest Hits	1966	5.00	10.00	20.00
❑ PC 9370	Flatt and Scruggs' Greatest Hits	198?	2.00	4.00	8.00

—Budget-line reissue

Number	Title	Yr	VG	VG+	NM
❑ CS 9443 [S]	Strictly Instrumental	1967	5.00	10.00	20.00
❑ CS 9486 [S]	Hear the Whistle Blow	1967	5.00	10.00	20.00
❑ CS 9596	Changin' Times Featuring Foggy Mountain Breakdown	1968	5.00	10.00	20.00
❑ CS 9649	The Story of Bonnie & Clyde	1968	5.00	10.00	20.00
❑ CS 9741	Nashville Airplane	1969	5.00	10.00	20.00
❑ CS 9945	Final Fling	1970	3.75	7.50	15.00
❑ LE 10149	Breaking Out	197?	2.50	5.00	10.00

—Brown label "Limited Edition"

Number	Title	Yr	VG	VG+	NM
❑ C 30347	Breaking Out	1971	3.00	6.00	12.00
❑ CG 31964 [(2)]	The World of Flatt and Scruggs	1972	3.75	7.50	15.00
❑ C 32244	A Boy Named Sue	1973	3.00	6.00	12.00
❑ FC 37469	Lester Flatt & Earl Scruggs	1981	2.50	5.00	10.00

COLUMBIA MUSICAL TREASURY

Number	Title	Yr	VG	VG+	NM
❑ DS 493	Detroit City	1969	3.75	7.50	15.00

COUNTY

Number	Title	Yr	VG	VG+	NM
❑ CCS-111	You Can Feel It in Your Soul	1988	2.50	5.00	10.00

HARMONY

Number	Title	Yr	VG	VG+	NM
❑ HL 7250 [M]	Lester Flatt & Earl Scruggs	1960	3.75	7.50	15.00
❑ HL 7340 [M]	Great Original Recordings	1965	3.75	7.50	15.00
❑ HL 7402 [M]	Sacred Songs	1967	3.75	7.50	15.00
❑ HL 7465 [M]	Songs to Cherish	1968	3.75	7.50	15.00
❑ HS 11202 [S]	Sacred Songs	1967	3.00	6.00	12.00
❑ HS 11265 [S]	Songs to Cherish	1968	3.00	6.00	12.00
❑ HS 11401	Foggy Mountain Chimes	1970	3.00	6.00	12.00

MERCURY

Number	Title	Yr	VG	VG+	NM
❑ MG-20358 [M]	Country Music	1958	10.00	20.00	40.00
❑ MG-20542 [M]	Lester Flatt & Earl Scruggs	1959	10.00	20.00	40.00
❑ MG-20773 [M]	The Original Sound of Flatt & Scruggs	1963	6.25	12.50	25.00
❑ SR-60773 [R]	The Original Sound of Flatt & Scruggs	1963	3.75	7.50	15.00
❑ SR-61162	Original Theme from Bonnie & Clyde	1968	5.00	10.00	20.00

NASHVILLE

Number	Title	Yr	VG	VG+	NM
❑ 2087	The Best of Flatt and Scruggs	1970	3.00	6.00	12.00

PICKWICK

Number	Title	Yr	VG	VG+	NM
❑ 6093	Foggy Mountain Breakdown	197?	3.00	6.00	12.00
❑ 6140	Blue Grass Banjos	197?	2.50	5.00	10.00

POWER PAK

Number	Title	Yr	VG	VG+	NM
❑ 297	Golden Hits	197?	2.50	5.00	10.00

ROUNDER

Number	Title	Yr	VG	VG+	NM
❑ SS-5	The Golden Era	198?	2.50	5.00	10.00
❑ SS-8	Don't Get Above Your Raisin'	198?	2.50	5.00	10.00
❑ SS-18	The Mercury Sessions, Volume 1	1985	2.50	5.00	10.00
❑ SS-19	The Mercury Sessions, Volume 2	1985	2.50	5.00	10.00

STARDAY

Number	Title	Yr	VG	VG+	NM
❑ SLP-365 [M]	Stars of the Grand Ol' Opry	1966	6.25	12.50	25.00

—With Jim and Jesse

Number	Title (A Side/B Side)	Yr	VG	VG+	NM
WING					
❑ SRW-16376	The Original Foggy Mountain Breakdown	1968	3.00	6.00	12.00

FLETCHER, VICKY

45s

Number	Title (A Side/B Side)	Yr	VG	VG+	NM
COLUMBIA					
❑ 3-10040	Little Boy Blue/That's the Way We Fall in Love	1974	—	2.50	5.00
❑ 4-46043	Touching Me, Touching You/That's the Way We Fall in Love	1974	—	2.50	5.00
MUSIC ROW					
❑ 213	Ain't It Good to Be in Love Again/Countin' Charlie's Ribs	1976	—	3.00	6.00

FLORES, ROSIE

45s

Number	Title (A Side/B Side)	Yr	VG	VG+	NM
REPRISE					
❑ 27980	He Cares/One-Track Mem'ry	1988	—	—	3.00
❑ 28134	Somebody Loses, Somebody Wins/Heart Beats to a Different Drum	1987	—	—	3.00
❑ 28250	Crying Over You/Midnight to Moonlight	1987	—	—	3.00
❑ 28250 [PS]	Crying Over You/Midnight to Moonlight	1987	—	2.00	4.00
❑ 28645	I'm Walkin'/The End of the World	1986	—	2.00	4.00

Albums

Number	Title (A Side/B Side)	Yr	VG	VG+	NM
REPRISE					
❑ 25626	Rosie Flores	1987	2.00	4.00	8.00

FLYING BURRITO BROTHERS, THE

Also includes records as "Burrito Brothers." Also see GRAM PARSONS; EARL SCRUGGS.

45s

Number	Title (A Side/B Side)	Yr	VG	VG+	NM
A&M					
❑ 1067	Train Song/Hot Burrito #1	1969	2.00	4.00	8.00
❑ 1166	If You Gotta Go, Go Now/Cody, Cody	1970	2.00	4.00	8.00
❑ 1189	Down in the Churchyard/Older Guys	1970	2.00	4.00	8.00
❑ 1277	White Line Fever/Colorado	1971	2.00	4.00	8.00
COLUMBIA					
❑ 10229	Building Fires/Hot Burrito No. 3	1975	—	2.50	5.00
❑ 10287	Bon Soir Blues/Hot Burrito No. 3	1976	—	2.50	5.00
❑ 10389	Big Bayou/Waiting for Love to Begin	1976	—	2.50	5.00
CURB					
❑ 01011	Does She Wish She Was Single Again/Oh Lonesome Me	1981	—	2.00	4.00
—As "Burrito Brothers"					
❑ 02243	She Belongs to Everyone But Me/Why Must the Ending Always Be So Sad	1981	—	2.00	4.00
—As "Burrito Brothers"					
❑ 02641	If Something Should Come Between Us/Damned If I'll Be Lonely Tonight	1981	—	2.00	4.00
—As "Burrito Brothers"					
❑ 02667	If Something Should Come Between Us	1982	—	2.00	4.00
—As "Burrito Brothers"					
❑ 02835	Closer to You/Coast to Coast	1982	—	2.00	4.00
—As "Burrito Brothers"					
❑ 03023	I'm Drinkin' Canada Dry/How'd We Ever Get This Way	1982	—	2.00	4.00
—As "Burrito Brothers"					
❑ 03314	Blue and Broken Hearted Me/Our Roots Are Country Music	1982	—	2.00	4.00
—As "Burrito Brothers"					
❑ 5402	She's a Friend of a Friend/(B-side unknown)	1981	—	2.00	4.00
—As "Burrito Brothers"					
MCA CURB					
❑ 52329	Almost Saturday Night/Juke Box Kind of Night	1983	—	—	3.00
—As "Burrito Brothers"					
❑ 52379	My Kind of Lady/Dream Chaser	1984	—	—	3.00
—As "Burrito Brothers"					
REGENCY					
❑ 45001	White Line Fever/(B-side unknown)	1980	—	3.00	6.00

Albums

Number	Title (A Side/B Side)	Yr	VG	VG+	NM
A&M					
❑ SP-3122	The Gilded Palace of Sin	198?	2.00	4.00	8.00
—Budget-line reissue					
❑ SP-3631 [(2)]	Close Up the Honky-Tonks	1974	3.75	7.50	15.00
❑ SP-4175	The Gilded Palace of Sin	1969	5.00	10.00	20.00
—Brown label					
❑ SP-4175	The Gilded Palace of Sin	1974	3.00	6.00	12.00
—Silvery label					
❑ SP-4258	Burrito Deluxe	1970	3.75	7.50	15.00
—Brown label					
❑ SP-4258	Burrito Deluxe	1974	3.00	6.00	12.00
—Silvery label					
❑ SP-4295	The Flying Burrito Bros.	1971	3.75	7.50	15.00
—Brown label					
❑ SP-4295	The Flying Burrito Bros.	1974	3.00	6.00	12.00
—Silvery label					
❑ SP-4343	Last of the Red Hot Burritos	1972	3.75	7.50	15.00
—Brown label					
❑ SP-4343	Last of the Red Hot Burritos	1974	3.00	6.00	12.00
—Silvery label					
❑ SP-4578	Sleepless Nights	1976	3.00	6.00	12.00
—As "Gram Parsons/The Flying Burrito Bros."					
❑ SP-6510 [(2)]	Close Up the Honky-Tonks	198?	3.00	6.00	12.00
—Reissue of 3631					
❑ SP-8070 [DJ]	Hot Burrito	1975	10.00	20.00	40.00
—Promo-only issue with poster					
COLUMBIA					
❑ PC 33817	Flying Again	1975	3.00	6.00	12.00
❑ PC 34222	Airborne	1976	3.00	6.00	12.00
CURB					
❑ JZ 37004	Hearts on the Line	1981	2.50	5.00	10.00
—As "Burrito Brothers"					
❑ FZ 37705	Sunset Sundown	1982	2.50	5.00	10.00
—As "Burrito Brothers"					
REGENCY					
❑ REG-79001	Live from Tokyo	1980	2.50	5.00	10.00

FOGELBERG, DAN

Not generally considered country, but three of his singles did make the country charts, and most of his music would not sound out of place in a country context.

45s

Number	Title (A Side/B Side)	Yr	VG	VG+	NM
COLUMBIA					
❑ 45764	Anyway I Love You/Looking for a Lady	1973	—	3.00	6.00
FULL MOON/EPIC					
❑ 02488	Hard to Say/The Innocent Age	1981	—	2.00	4.00
❑ 02647	Leader of the Band/Times Like These	1981	—	2.00	4.00
❑ 02821	Run for the Roses/The Sand and the Foam	1982	—	2.00	4.00
❑ 03087	Same Old Lang Syne/Hard to Say	1982	—	—	3.00
—Reissue					
❑ 03289	Missing You/Hearts and Crafts	1982	—	2.00	4.00
❑ 03323	Missing You	1982	—	3.00	6.00
—One-sided budget release					
❑ 03525	Make Love Stay/Hearts and Crafts	1983	—	2.00	4.00
❑ 03570	Make Love Stay	1983	—	3.00	6.00
—One-sided budget release					
❑ 03843	Leader of the Band/Run for the Roses	1983	—	—	3.00
—Reissue					
❑ 04314	The Language of Love/Windows and Walls	1984	—	—	3.00
❑ 04314 [PS]	The Language of Love/Windows and Walls	1984	—	—	3.00
❑ 04447	Believe in Me/Windows and Walls	1984	—	—	3.00
❑ 04660	Sweet Magnolia and the Traveling Salesman/The Loving Cup	1984	—	—	3.00
❑ 04835	Go Down Easy/High Country Snows	1985	—	—	3.00
❑ 05446	Down the Road-Mountain Pass/High Country Snows	1985	—	—	3.00
❑ 07044	She Don't Look Back/It Doesn't Matter	1987	—	—	3.00
❑ 07044 [PS]	She Don't Look Back/It Doesn't Matter	1987	—	—	3.00
❑ 07275	Lonely in Love/Beyond the Edge	1987	—	—	3.00
❑ 07640	Hearts in Decline/Seeing You Again	1987	—	—	3.00
❑ 07756	The Way It Must Be/What You're Doing	1988	—	—	3.00
❑ 50055	Part of the Plan/Song from Half Mountain	1974	—	2.50	5.00
❑ 50108	Changing Horses/Morning Sky	1975	—	2.00	4.00
❑ 50165	Captured Angel/Next Time	1975	—	2.00	4.00
❑ 50189	Below the Surface/Comes and Goes	1976	—	2.00	4.00
❑ 50234	Old Tennessee/The Crow	1976	—	2.00	4.00
❑ 50412	Scarecrow's Dream/Love Gone By	1977	—	2.00	4.00
❑ 50462	Nether Lands/False Faces	1977	—	2.00	4.00
❑ 50536	Sketches/Promises Made	1978	—	2.00	4.00
❑ 50577	There's a Place in the World for a Gambler/Souvenirs	1978	—	2.50	5.00
❑ 50824	Longer/Along the Road	1980	—	2.00	4.00
❑ 50862	Heart Hotels/Beggar's Game	1980	—	2.00	4.00
❑ 50961	Same Old Lang Syne/Hearts and Crafts	1980	—	2.00	4.00
❑ 50961 [PS]	Same Old Lang Syne/Hearts and Crafts	1980	—	3.00	6.00
❑ 73513	Rhythm of the Rain-Rain/Ever On	1990	—	2.00	4.00

Albums

Number	Title (A Side/B Side)	Yr	VG	VG+	NM
COLUMBIA					
❑ KC 31751	Home Free	1972	3.00	6.00	12.00
❑ PC 31751	Home Free	197?	2.00	4.00	8.00
—Reissue with new prefix					
FULL MOON/EPIC					
❑ A2S 1335 [(2) DJ]	Interchords	1982	6.25	12.50	25.00
—Promo-only release					
❑ QE 28208	Dan Fogelberg/Greatest Hits	1982	2.50	5.00	10.00
❑ KE 33137	Souvenirs	1974	3.00	6.00	12.00
—First pressings have orange Epic label with small Full Moon logo					
❑ KE 33137	Souvenirs	1975	2.50	5.00	10.00
—Second pressings have dark blue/black Full Moon label					
❑ PE 33137	Souvenirs	197?	2.00	4.00	8.00
—Reissue with new prefix					
❑ PE 33499	Captured Angel	1975	2.50	5.00	10.00
—No bar code on cover					
❑ PE 33499	Captured Angel	198?	2.00	4.00	8.00
—With bar code on cover					
❑ PEQ 33499 [Q]	Captured Angel	1975	5.00	10.00	20.00
❑ PE 34185	Nether Lands	1977	2.50	5.00	10.00
—No bar code on cover					
❑ PE 34185	Nether Lands	198?	2.00	4.00	8.00
—With bar code on cover					
❑ PE 35364	Phoenix	198?	2.00	4.00	8.00
—Budget-line reissue					
❑ FE 35634	Phoenix	1979	2.50	5.00	10.00
❑ KE2 37393 [(2)]	The Innocent Age	1981	3.00	6.00	12.00
❑ QE 39004	Windows and Walls	1984	2.50	5.00	10.00
❑ FE 39616	High Country Snows	1985	2.50	5.00	10.00
❑ OE 40271	Exiles	1987	2.50	5.00	10.00
❑ HE 45634	Phoenix	1981	7.50	15.00	30.00
—Half-speed mastered edition					
❑ HE 48308	Dan Fogelberg/Greatest Hits	1983	7.50	15.00	30.00
—Half-speed mastered edition					

FOGELBERG, DAN, AND TIM WEISBERG

45s

FULL MOON/EPIC

Number	Title (A Side/B Side)	Yr	VG	VG+	NM
❑ 50605	Tell Me to My Face/Hurtwood Alley	1978	—	2.50	5.00
❑ 50606	The Power of Gold/Lahaina Luna	1978	—	2.00	4.00

Albums

FULL MOON/EPIC

Number	Title (A Side/B Side)	Yr	VG	VG+	NM
❑ JE 35339	Twin Sons of Different Mothers	1978	2.50	5.00	10.00
❑ PE 35339	Twin Sons of Different Mothers	198?	2.00	4.00	8.00
—Budget-line reissue					
❑ HE 45339	Twin Sons of Different Mothers	198?	7.50	15.00	30.00
—Half-speed mastered edition					

FOGERTY, JOHN

Includes records as "The Blue Ridge Rangers." Also see CREEDENCE CLEARWATER REVIVAL.

12-Inch Singles

WARNER BROS.

Number	Title (A Side/B Side)	Yr	VG	VG+	NM
❑ PRO-A-2234 [DJ]	The Old Man Down the Road (same on both sides)	1984	2.00	4.00	8.00
❑ PRO-A-2267 [DJ]	Rock and Roll Girls/Centerfield	1985	2.00	4.00	8.00
❑ PRO-A-2337 [DJ]	I Can't Help Myself (same on both sides)	1985	2.00	4.00	8.00
❑ PRO-A-2362 [DJ]	Vanz Kant Danz (edit)/Vanz Kant Danz (LP)	1985	2.00	4.00	8.00
❑ PRO-A-2514 [DJ]	Eye of the Zombie (same on both sides)	1986	2.00	4.00	8.00
❑ PRO-A-2595 [DJ]	Change in the Weather (edit)/(LP)	1986	2.00	4.00	8.00
❑ PRO-A-2637 [DJ]	Knockin' on Your Door (same on both sides)	1986	2.00	4.00	8.00

45s

ASYLUM

Number	Title (A Side/B Side)	Yr	VG	VG+	NM
❑ 45274	Rockin' All Over the World/The Wall	1975	—	2.50	5.00
❑ 45293	Almost Saturday Night/Sea Cruise	1975	—	2.50	5.00
❑ 45309	You Got the Magic/Evil Thing	1976	—	2.50	5.00

ELEKTRA

Number	Title (A Side/B Side)	Yr	VG	VG+	NM
❑ 45309 [DJ]	You Got the Magic (stereo/mono)	1976	2.50	5.00	10.00
—Promo-only version with wrong label					

FANTASY

Number	Title (A Side/B Side)	Yr	VG	VG+	NM
❑ 683	Blue Ridge Mountain Blues/Have Thine Own Way, Lord	1972	—	2.50	5.00
—As "The Blue Ridge Rangers"					
❑ 683 [PS]	Blue Ridge Mountain Blues/Have Thine Own Way, Lord	1972	3.75	7.50	15.00
—As "The Blue Ridge Rangers"					
❑ 689	Jambalaya (On the Bayou)/Workin' on a Building	1972	—	3.00	6.00
—As "The Blue Ridge Rangers"; green, red and orange label					
❑ 689	Jambalaya (On the Bayou)/Workin' on a Building	1972	—	2.50	5.00
—As "The Blue Ridge Rangers"; brown label					
❑ 700	Hearts of Stone/Somewhere Listening	1973	—	2.50	5.00
—As "The Blue Ridge Rangers"					
❑ 710	Back in the Hills/You Don't Own Me	1973	—	2.50	5.00
—As "The Blue Ridge Rangers"					
❑ 717	Coming Down the Road/Ricochet	1973	—	2.50	5.00

REPRISE

Number	Title (A Side/B Side)	Yr	VG	VG+	NM
❑ 17191	Premonition/Born on the Bayou	1998	—	—	3.00
❑ 17192	Almost Saturday Night/Who'll Stop the Rain	1998	—	—	3.00

WARNER BROS.

Number	Title (A Side/B Side)	Yr	VG	VG+	NM
❑ 17283	Blueboy/Bad Bad Boy	1997	—	—	3.00
❑ 28535	Change in the Weather/My Toot Toot	1986	—	2.00	4.00
❑ 28535 [PS]	Change in the Weather/My Toot Toot	1986	—	2.00	4.00
❑ 28657	Eye of the Zombie/I Confess	1986	—	2.00	4.00
❑ 28657 [PS]	Eye of the Zombie/I Confess	1986	—	2.00	4.00
❑ 29053	Rock and Roll Girls/Centerfield	1985	—	2.00	4.00
❑ 29053 [PS]	Rock and Roll Girls/Centerfield	1985	—	2.00	4.00
❑ 29100	The Old Man Down the Road/Big Train (From Memphis)	1985	—	2.00	4.00
❑ 29100 [PS]	The Old Man Down the Road/Big Train (From Memphis)	1985	—	2.00	4.00

Albums

ASYLUM

Number	Title (A Side/B Side)	Yr	VG	VG+	NM
❑ 7E-1046	John Fogerty	1975	3.00	6.00	12.00
❑ 7E-1081	Hoodoo	1976	—	—	—
—Canceled; poor quality bootleg cassettes exist					

FANTASY

Number	Title (A Side/B Side)	Yr	VG	VG+	NM
❑ MPF-4502	John Fogerty: The Blue Ridge Rangers	1981	2.50	5.00	10.00
—Reissues prominently place John Fogerty's name on the cover					
❑ F-9415	The Blue Ridge Rangers	1973	3.75	7.50	15.00
—As "The Blue Ridge Rangers"					

WARNER BROS.

Number	Title (A Side/B Side)	Yr	VG	VG+	NM
❑ 25203	Centerfield	1985	3.75	7.50	15.00
—Originals have the last song on side 2 as "Zanz Kant Danz"					
❑ 25203	Centerfield	1985	2.50	5.00	10.00
—Later editions have the last song on side 2 re-recorded and listed as "Vanz Kant Danz"					
❑ 25203 [DJ]	Centerfield	1985	5.00	10.00	20.00
—Promo versions on Quiex II audiophile vinyl					
❑ 25449	Eye of the Zombie	1986	2.50	5.00	10.00

FOLEY, BETTY

45s

BANDERA

Number	Title (A Side/B Side)	Yr	VG	VG+	NM
❑ 1304	Old Moon/Magic Love	1959	6.25	12.50	25.00
❑ 1308	Do You Wonder at All/I'm Not Surprised	1959	6.25	12.50	25.00

FOLEY, RED

Also see KITTY WELLS AND RED FOLEY.

45s

DECCA

Number	Title (A Side/B Side)	Yr	VG	VG+	NM
❑ 25652	Moonlight Bay/Smiles	196?	3.00	6.00	12.00
❑ 25689	Goodnight Irene/Sleepy Time Gal	196?	3.00	6.00	12.00
❑ 25762	Peace in the Valley/Where Could I Go But to the Lord	196?	3.00	6.00	12.00
❑ 9-27378	My Heart Cries for You/Tater Pie	1951	6.25	12.50	25.00
—With Evelyn Knight					
❑ 9-27763	Night Train to Memphis/If I Had-a Knowed, You Could-a Goed	1950	7.50	15.00	30.00
—With Roberta Lee					
❑ 9-27810	Alabama Jubilee/Dixie	1951	6.25	12.50	25.00
❑ 9-27856	Say a Little Prayer/Peace in the Valley	1951	6.25	12.50	25.00
❑ 9-27929	Whistle While You Work/Who's Afraid of the Big Bad Wolf	1952	7.50	15.00	30.00
❑ 9-27981	Milk Bucket Boogie/Salty Dog Rag	1952	6.25	12.50	25.00
❑ 9-28147	I'm Bound For Christmas/I'd Rather Have Jesus	1952	6.25	12.50	25.00
❑ 9-28252	Somebody Bigger Than You and I/God's Little Candle	1952	6.25	12.50	25.00
❑ 9-28288	Are You Trying to Tell Me Goodbye/Kisses on Paper	1952	6.25	12.50	25.00
❑ 9-28420	Midnight/Deep Blues	1952	6.25	12.50	25.00
❑ 9-28447	My God Is Real/The Mocking Bird	1952	6.25	12.50	25.00
❑ 9-28460	Don't Let the Stars Get In Your Eyes/Sally	1952	5.00	10.00	20.00
❑ 9-28567	Slaves of a Hopeless Love Affair/Blue Letter	1953	5.00	10.00	20.00
❑ 9-28587	Hot Toddy/Playin' Dominoes and Shootin' Dice	1953	5.00	10.00	20.00
❑ 9-28694	I Believe/Mansion Over the Hilltop	1953	5.00	10.00	20.00
❑ 9-28695	I'm Sorry We Met/Treasure Untold	1953	5.00	10.00	20.00
❑ 9-28759	Hot Dog Rag/That Old River Line	1953	5.00	10.00	20.00
❑ 9-28767	Unless You're Free/Baby Blues	1953	5.00	10.00	20.00
—With Patti Andrews					
❑ 9-28796	The Keys to the Kingdom/Last Mile of the Way	1953	6.25	12.50	25.00
❑ 9-28839	Shake a Hand/Stranded in Deep Water	1953	5.00	10.00	20.00
❑ 9-28940	Put Christ Back in Christmas/The Gentle Carpenter of Bethlehem	1953	5.00	10.00	20.00
❑ 9-28944	Goodbye, Bobby Boy/Peace of Mind	1953	5.00	10.00	20.00
❑ 9-29044	The Rose of Calvary/Consideration	1954	5.00	10.00	20.00
❑ 9-29100	Jilted/Pin Ball Boogie	1954	5.00	10.00	20.00
❑ 9-29159	My Friend/Lady of Guadaloupe	1954	5.00	10.00	20.00
❑ 9-29222	She'll Never Know/Bury Me Beneath the Willow	1954	5.00	10.00	20.00
—With the Andrews Sisters					
❑ 9-29339	Lookin' Glass/Walkin' in the Cold, Cold Rain	1954	5.00	10.00	20.00
❑ 9-29375	Hearts of Stone/Never	1954	5.00	10.00	20.00
❑ 9-29494	Nobody/Hominy Grits	1955	5.00	10.00	20.00
❑ 9-29505	Have a Little Talk with Jesus/Strange Things Happen	1955	5.00	10.00	20.00
—With Sister Rosetta Tharpe					
❑ 9-29517	Plantation Boogie/You Little So-and-So	1955	5.00	10.00	20.00
❑ 9-29626	Just Call Me Lonesome/Blue Guitar	1955	5.00	10.00	20.00
❑ 9-29667	When You Come to the End of the Day/The Night Watch	1955	5.00	10.00	20.00
❑ 9-29775	I See God/Someone to Care	1956	5.00	10.00	20.00
❑ 9-29894	The Hoot Owl Boogie/A Handful of Love	1956	5.00	10.00	20.00
❑ 9-30010	Take My Hand, Precious Lord/Someday, Somewhere	1956	5.00	10.00	20.00
❑ 9-30067	Rock 'n Reelin'/Don't Blame It on the Girl	1956	7.50	15.00	30.00
❑ 9-30080	(There'll Be) Peace in the Valley/A Servant	1956	5.00	10.00	20.00
❑ 9-30177	Passing By (Just Passing By)/His Arms	1957	5.00	10.00	20.00
❑ 9-30249	Come a Little Closer/One Life, Two Loves	1957	5.00	10.00	20.00
❑ 9-30334	Sweet Innocence/Why Ask for the Moon	1957	5.00	10.00	20.00
❑ 9-30452	This Could Very Well Be It/Strike While the Iron Is Hot	1957	5.00	10.00	20.00
❑ 9-30470	Steal Away/Just a Closer Walk with Thee	1957	5.00	10.00	20.00
❑ 9-30639	Strolling the Blues/With You Beside Me	1958	5.00	10.00	20.00
❑ 9-30674	Crazy Little Guitar Man/Fate	1958	7.50	15.00	30.00
❑ 9-30710	Good Night, Dear Lord/If I Can Help Somebody	1958	5.00	10.00	20.00
❑ 9-30802	Love Is Love/Smiles	1959	5.00	10.00	20.00
❑ 9-30882	Travelin' Man/Just This Side of Memphis	1959	5.00	10.00	20.00
❑ 9-30924	God Walks These Hills with Me/God Forgive Me When I Whine	1959	5.00	10.00	20.00
❑ 9-30975	Crazy 'Bout Banjos/Living Is a Lonesome Thing	1959	3.75	7.50	15.00
❑ 31056	Rockin' Chair/Blues in My Red Wagon Blues	1960	3.75	7.50	15.00
❑ 31194	End of the World/Georgia Town Blues	1961	3.75	7.50	15.00
❑ 31254	Another Heartache (For Me)/Just Before Dawn	1961	3.75	7.50	15.00
❑ 31302	The South/Dear Young Lovers	1961	3.75	7.50	15.00
❑ 31369	A Wasted Year/Happy Song	1962	3.75	7.50	15.00
❑ 31408	Mountain Boy/Polka on a Banjo	1962	3.75	7.50	15.00
❑ 31437	Hang Your Head in Shame/That's What's Wrong with Me	1962	3.75	7.50	15.00
❑ 31482	Lights Across the Bay/One True Love	1963	3.00	6.00	12.00
❑ 31530	Goodnight Mama, Goodnight Papa/Poor Jack	1963	3.00	6.00	12.00
❑ 31727	Chained to a Memory/Shame on You	1965	2.50	5.00	10.00
❑ 31776	(Remember Me) I'm the One Who Loves You/Sugar Moon	1965	2.50	5.00	10.00
❑ 31831	River of Regret/So Long Baby	1965	2.50	5.00	10.00
❑ 32044	My Gal Country Style/How's the World Treating You	1966	2.50	5.00	10.00
❑ 32063	Is There Really a Santa Claus/From Our House to Your House	1966	3.00	6.00	12.00
❑ 9-46052	Old Shep/Honey Be My Honey Bee	1950	10.00	20.00	40.00
—Lines on either side of "Decca"					
❑ 9-46052	Old Shep/Honey Be My Honey Bee	1955	5.00	10.00	20.00
—Star under "Decca"					
❑ 9-46185	Our Christmas Waltz/Here Comes Santa Claus	1950	10.00	20.00	40.00
—With Judy Martin					
❑ 9-46205	Chattanoogie Shoe Shine Boy/Sugarfoot Rag	1950	10.00	20.00	40.00
—The 45 was released later than the 78 by a few months					
❑ 9-46234	Birmingham Bounce/Choc'late Ice Cream Cone	1950	7.50	15.00	30.00
❑ 9-46235	Let's Go to Church/Remember Me	1950	7.50	15.00	30.00

Number	Title (A Side/B Side)	Yr	VG	VG+	NM
❑ 9-46241	Mississippi/Old Kentucky Fox Chase	1950	7.50	15.00	30.00
❑ 9-46261	Cincinnati Dancing Pig/Somebody's Cryin'	1950	7.50	15.00	30.00
❑ 9-46267	Frosty the Snowman/Rudolph the Red-Nosed Reindeer	1950	7.50	15.00	30.00
❑ 9-46277	I Won't Be Home/Dear Little Girls	1950	7.50	15.00	30.00
❑ 9-46285	Someone Else Not Me/Music by the Angels (Lyrics by the Lord)	1951	7.50	15.00	30.00
❑ 9-46286	Hot Rod Race/Smoke on the Water No. 2	1951	7.50	15.00	30.00
❑ 9-46291	Old Shep/Just a Man and His Dog	1951	6.25	12.50	25.00
❑ 9-46292	Tennessee Polka/Tennessee Saturday Night	1951	6.25	12.50	25.00
❑ 9-46293	Back to Tennessee/Sunday Down in Tennessee	1951	6.25	12.50	25.00
❑ 9-46294	That Little Boy of Mine/Don't Make Me Go to Bed	1951	6.25	12.50	25.00

—The above four comprise a box set

Number	Title (A Side/B Side)	Yr	VG	VG+	NM
❑ 9-46297	The Chicken Song/So Long	1951	6.25	12.50	25.00
❑ 9-46304	Hobo Boogie/Heska Holka	1951	6.25	12.50	25.00
❑ 9-46317	Tennessee Hillbilly Ghost/Giles County Pulaski Post Office	1951	6.25	12.50	25.00
❑ 9-46319	There'll Be Peace in the Valley for Me/Old Soldiers Never Die	1951	6.25	12.50	25.00
❑ 9-46320	Hill Top Rag/Steelin' the Theme	1951	6.25	12.50	25.00
❑ 9-46349	Cock-a-Doodle-Doo/Sugar Foot Rag Square Dance	1951	6.25	12.50	25.00
❑ 9-46357	Jesus and the Atheist/The Weapon of Prayer	1951	6.25	12.50	25.00
❑ 9-46411	When the Saints Go Marching In/Lonely Mile	1952	6.25	12.50	25.00
❑ 9-88030	The Prettiest Song in the World/(B-side unknown)	1950	10.00	20.00	40.00

—Yellow label "Chidren's Series" issue

Number	Title (A Side/B Side)	Yr	VG	VG+	NM
❑ 9-88060	Frosty the Snowman/Rudolph the Red-Nosed Reindeer	1950	10.00	20.00	40.00

—Yellow label "Chidren's Series" issue

Number	Title (A Side/B Side)	Yr	VG	VG+	NM
❑ 9-88137	Jesus Loves Me/I'll Be a Sunbeam	195?	7.50	15.00	30.00

—Yellow label "Chidren's Series" issue

DECCA FAITH SERIES

Number	Title (A Side/B Side)	Yr	VG	VG+	NM
❑ 9-14505	Steal Away/Just a Closer Walk with Thee	1950	10.00	20.00	40.00
❑ 9-14526	Our Lady of Fatima/The Rosary	1950	10.00	20.00	40.00
❑ 9-14537	I Hear a Choir/The Place Where I Worship	1951	7.50	15.00	30.00
❑ 9-14553	He'll Understand and Say Well Done/Milky White Way	1951	7.50	15.00	30.00
❑ 9-14566	He Bought My Soul at Calvary/It Is No Secret (What God Can Do)	1951	7.50	15.00	30.00
❑ 9-14573	Peace in the Valley/Where Could I Go But to the Lord	1951	7.50	15.00	30.00

Selected 78s

CONQUEROR

Number	Title (A Side/B Side)	Yr	VG	VG+	NM
❑ 8163	The Lone Cowboy/The Single Life Is Good Enough	193?	6.25	12.50	25.00
❑ 8676	The 1936 Floods/The Mailman's Warning	1936	7.50	15.00	30.00

DECCA

Number	Title (A Side/B Side)	Yr	VG	VG+	NM
❑ 6102	Smoke on the Water/There's a Blue Star Shining Bright (In a Window Tonight)	1944	5.00	10.00	20.00
❑ 6108	Hang Your Head in Shame/I'll Never Let You Worry My Mind	1945	5.00	10.00	20.00
❑ 9003	Harriet/My Poor Little Heart Is Broken	1946	5.00	10.00	20.00
❑ 18698	Shame on You/At Mail Call Today	1945	5.00	10.00	20.00

—As "Lawrence Welk and His Orchestra With Red Foley"

Number	Title (A Side/B Side)	Yr	VG	VG+	NM
❑ 46014	Have I Told You Lately That I Love You/Atomic Power	1946	5.00	10.00	20.00
❑ 46024	Foggy River/Lay Down Your Load	1946	5.00	10.00	20.00
❑ 46028	That's How Much I Love You/Rye Whiskey	1947	5.00	10.00	20.00
❑ 46034	New Jolie Blonde (New Pretty Blonde)/A Pillow of Sighs and Tears	1947	5.00	10.00	20.00
❑ 46035	Freight Train Boogie/Rockin' Chair Money	1947	5.00	10.00	20.00
❑ 46052	Old Shep/Honey Be My Honey Bee	1947	6.25	12.50	25.00
❑ 46058	Too Many Blues/I'll Be True to My Darling	1947	5.00	10.00	20.00
❑ 46068	Open Up That Door/Love to You Is Just a Game	1947	5.00	10.00	20.00
❑ 46074	Never Trust a Woman/A Smile Will Chase Away a Tear	1947	5.00	10.00	20.00
❑ 46081	Back to Tennessee/Easy to Please	1948	5.00	10.00	20.00
❑ 46115	Ride On King Jesus/Everybody's Gonna Have a Wonderful Time	1948	5.00	10.00	20.00
❑ 46123	I'm Picking Up the Pieces/Last Thing I Want	1948	5.00	10.00	20.00
❑ 46124	Ruby Red Lips/Television	1948	5.00	10.00	20.00
❑ 46126	I'm Waltzing with a Broken Heart/Don't Make Me Go to Bed	1948	5.00	10.00	20.00
❑ 46136	Tennessee Saturday Night/Blues in My Heart	1948	5.00	10.00	20.00
❑ 46143	Just a Man and His Dog/Tit for Tat	1948	5.00	10.00	20.00
❑ 46151	Candy Kisses/Tennessee Border	1949	5.00	10.00	20.00
❑ 46158	There's a Light Guiding Me/Cleanse Me	1949	5.00	10.00	20.00
❑ 46165	Two Cents, Three Eggs and a Postcard/I Wish I Had a Nickel	1949	5.00	10.00	20.00
❑ 46170	Tennessee Polka/I'm Throwing Rice (At the Girl I Love)	1949	5.00	10.00	20.00
❑ 46185	Our Christmas Waltz/Here Comes Santa Claus	1949	5.00	10.00	20.00

—With Judy Martin

Number	Title (A Side/B Side)	Yr	VG	VG+	NM
❑ 46197	Sunday Down in Tennessee/Every Step of the Way	1949	5.00	10.00	20.00
❑ 46201	Careless Kisses/I Gotta Have My Baby Back	1949	5.00	10.00	20.00
❑ 46205	Chattanoogie Shoe Shine Boy/Sugarfoot Rag	1950	3.75	7.50	15.00
❑ 46206	Church Music/Have I Told You Lately That I Love You	1950	3.75	7.50	15.00

7-Inch Extended Plays

DECCA

Number	Title (A Side/B Side)	Yr	VG	VG+	NM
❑ ED 2090	(contents unknown)	195?	6.25	12.50	25.00
❑ ED 2090 [PS]	Sing a Song of Christmas	195?	6.25	12.50	25.00
❑ ED 2207	Beyond the Sunset-Should You Go First/(There'll Be) Peace in the Valley (For Me)//Old Pappy's New Banjo/Someone to Care	1955	6.25	12.50	25.00
❑ ED 2207 [PS]	Beyond the Sunset	1955	6.25	12.50	25.00

Albums

DECCA

Number	Title (A Side/B Side)	Yr	VG	VG+	NM
❑ DXB 177 [(2) M]	The Red Foley Story	1964	6.25	12.50	25.00
❑ DL 4107 [M]	Red Foley's Golden Favorites	1961	5.00	10.00	20.00
❑ DL 4140 [M]	Company's Comin'	1961	5.00	10.00	20.00
❑ DL 4198 [M]	Songs of Devotion	1961	5.00	10.00	20.00
❑ DL 4290 [M]	Dear Hearts and Gentle People	1962	5.00	10.00	20.00
❑ DL 4341 [M]	The Red Foley Show	1963	5.00	10.00	20.00
❑ DL 4603 [M]	Songs Everybody Knows	1965	5.00	10.00	20.00
❑ DL 4849 [M]	Songs for the Soul	1967	6.25	12.50	25.00
❑ DL 5303 [10]	Red Foley Souvenir Album	1951	20.00	40.00	80.00
❑ DL 5338 [10]	Lift Up Your Voice	1952	20.00	40.00	80.00
❑ DXSB 7177 [(2) S]	The Red Foley Story	1964	7.50	15.00	30.00
❑ DL 8294 [M]	Red Foley Souvenir Album	1956	12.50	25.00	50.00
❑ DL 8296 [M]	Beyond the Sunset	1956	12.50	25.00	50.00
❑ DL 8767 [M]	He Walks with Thee	1958	12.50	25.00	50.00
❑ DL 8806 [M]	My Keepsake Album	1958	12.50	25.00	50.00
❑ DL 8847 [M]	Let's All Sing with Red Foley	1959	10.00	20.00	40.00
❑ DL 8903 [M]	Let's All Sing to Him	1959	10.00	20.00	40.00
❑ DL 38068 [M]	Gratefully	1958	25.00	50.00	100.00

—Special-products issue for Dickies clothing

Number	Title (A Side/B Side)	Yr	VG	VG+	NM
❑ DL 74107 [S]	Red Foley's Golden Favorites	1961	6.25	12.50	25.00
❑ DL 74140 [S]	Company's Comin'	1961	6.25	12.50	25.00
❑ DL 74198 [S]	Songs of Devotion	1961	6.25	12.50	25.00
❑ DL 74290 [S]	Dear Hearts and Gentle People	1962	6.25	12.50	25.00
❑ DL 74341 [S]	The Red Foley Show	1963	6.25	12.50	25.00
❑ DL 74603 [S]	Songs Everybody Knows	1965	6.25	12.50	25.00
❑ DL 74849 [S]	Songs for the Soul	1967	5.00	10.00	20.00
❑ DL 78847 [S]	Let's All Sing with Red Foley	1959	12.50	25.00	50.00
❑ DL 78903 [S]	Let's All Sing to Him	1959	12.50	25.00	50.00

FOLEY, RED AND BETTY

45s

DECCA

Number	Title (A Side/B Side)	Yr	VG	VG+	NM
❑ 9-29000	As Far As I'm Concerned/Tennessee Whistling Man	1954	5.00	10.00	20.00
❑ 9-29526	Satisfied Mind/How About Me	1955	5.00	10.00	20.00
❑ 9-29704	Croce di Oro (Cross of Gold)/Sweet Kentucky Rose	1955	5.00	10.00	20.00

FOLEY, RED, AND GRADY MARTIN

45s

DECCA

Number	Title (A Side/B Side)	Yr	VG	VG+	NM
❑ 9-29059	My Window Faces South/Pork Chop Stomp	1954	5.00	10.00	20.00

FOLEY, RED, AND ERNEST TUBB

45s

DECCA

Number	Title (A Side/B Side)	Yr	VG	VG+	NM
❑ 9-28634	No Help Wanted #2/You're a Real Good Friend	1953	5.00	10.00	20.00
❑ 9-28911	Too Old to Tango/Doctor Ketchum	1953	5.00	10.00	20.00
❑ 9-29195	Double-Datin'/It's the Mileage That's Slowin' Us Down	1954	5.00	10.00	20.00
❑ 9-46255	Goodnight Irene/Hillbilly Fever No. 2	1950	10.00	20.00	40.00
❑ 9-46278	The Love Bug Itch/Texas vs. Kentucky	1950	7.50	15.00	30.00
❑ 9-46311	The Strange Little Girl/Kentucky Waltz	1951	6.25	12.50	25.00
❑ 9-46387	Too Old to Cut the Mustard/I'm in Love with Molly	1952	6.25	12.50	25.00

Selected 78s

DECCA

Number	Title (A Side/B Side)	Yr	VG	VG+	NM
❑ 46200	Tennessee Border No. 2/Don't Be Ashamed of Your Age	1949	5.00	10.00	20.00

FORD, JOY

Also see DAVID HOUSTON AND JOY FORD.

45s

COUNTRY INT'L.

Number	Title (A Side/B Side)	Yr	VG	VG+	NM
❑ 100	It's Your Turn to Cry/Just Listen to Your Heart	1975	—	3.00	6.00
❑ 102	One Foot in Alabama/You'll Get Over It	1975	—	3.00	6.00
❑ 105	Tears on My Pillow/Till the End of the World	1976	—	3.00	6.00
❑ 107	Her Bridal Bouquet/White Gardenia	1976	—	3.00	6.00
❑ 113	Breaker, Breaker, Breaker, Lies and Kisses/(B-side unknown)	1976	—	3.00	6.00
❑ 117	Walking After Midnight/You'll Get Over It	1977	—	3.00	6.00
❑ 119	My Heart Is an Open Book/(B-side unknown)	1977	—	3.00	6.00
❑ 123	Remember the Good Times/(B-side unknown)	1977	—	3.00	6.00
❑ 133	Listening for the Wind/Thirty Days Hath September	1978	—	2.50	5.00

—With Herb Oscar Anderson

Number	Title (A Side/B Side)	Yr	VG	VG+	NM
❑ 134	Love Isn't Love (Till You Give It Away)/Another Favour	1978	—	2.50	5.00
❑ 138	I Love the Way You Love on Me/(B-side unknown)	1979	—	2.50	5.00
❑ 142	Take My Love/I Love the Way You Love on Me	1979	—	2.50	5.00
❑ 143	Nearer My Love to You/(B-side unknown)	1979	—	2.50	5.00
❑ 144	Give Me Something to Hold On To/I Love the Way You Love on Me	1980	—	2.50	5.00
❑ 150	Pretend/(B-side unknown)	1981	—	2.50	5.00
❑ 153	Luziana River/(B-side unknown)	1981	—	2.50	5.00
❑ 163	Love Me Again/Luziana River	1982	—	2.50	5.00
❑ 176	Christmas Card/(B-side unknown)	1982	—	2.50	5.00

—With John Krondes

Number	Title (A Side/B Side)	Yr	VG	VG+	NM
❑ 179	Carousel/Luziana River	1982	—	2.50	5.00
❑ 188	Kentucky Blues/(B-side unknown)	1983	—	2.50	5.00

Number	Title (A Side/B Side)	Yr	VG	VG+	NM
❑ 190	You Are the Music in Time with My Heart/ Carousel	1983	—	2.50	5.00
❑ 193	The Hand That Rocks the Cradle Rules the World/ (B-side unknown)	1983	—	2.50	5.00
❑ 195	Baby Have a Baby with Me/(B-side unknown)	1983	—	2.50	5.00
❑ 197	Big City Turn Me Loose/(B-side unknown)	1984	—	2.50	5.00
❑ 198	Heartaches/Big City Turn Me Loose	1984	—	2.50	5.00
❑ 200	Deeper in Love/(B-side unknown)	1984	—	2.50	5.00
❑ 202	#1 with a Heartache/(B-side unknown)	1985	—	2.50	5.00
❑ 203	String Around His Finger/(B-side unknown)	1985	—	2.50	5.00
❑ 206	Melted Down Memories/Big City Turn Me Loose	1985	—	2.50	5.00
❑ 207	Blues, Stay Away from Me/Carousel	1985	—	2.50	5.00
❑ 209	Lovin' Dangerously/(B-side unknown)	1986	—	2.50	5.00
❑ 211	Love Makes the Livin' Worthwhile/(B-side unknown)	1986	—	2.50	5.00
❑ 212	Crazy Arms/(B-side unknown)	1987	—	2.50	5.00
❑ 213	Only Six Feet Away/Look What Love Can Do	1987	—	2.50	5.00
❑ 216	Yesterday's Rain/(B-side unknown)	1988	—	2.50	5.00
❑ 218	There's a Fire in Our Bedroom/(B-side unknown)	1988	—	3.00	6.00
—With Eddie Moore					
❑ 222	Always in My Heart/Can I Believe	1989	—	3.00	6.00
❑ 224	Crystal Chandelier/(B-side unknown)	1989	—	3.00	6.00
❑ 227	The Promise/(B-side unknown)	1990	—	3.00	6.00

FORD, TENNESSEE ERNIE

Includes records issued as "Tennessee Ernie."

45s

CANADA DRY

Number	Title (A Side/B Side)	Yr	VG	VG+	NM
❑ 72-6596 [DJ]	The Real Story Of Christmas from St. Luke, Chapter 2	1972	—	2.50	5.00
—Special promo for his 1972 Christmas TV special					
❑ 72-6596 [PS]	The Real Story Of Christmas from St. Luke, Chapter 2	1972	—	2.50	5.00
—Special promo for his 1972 Christmas TV special					

CAPITOL

Number	Title (A Side/B Side)	Yr	VG	VG+	NM
❑ F-985	I've Got to Feed 'Em in the Morning/My Hobby	1950	3.75	7.50	15.00
❑ F-1124	I'll Never Be Free/Ain't Nobody's Business But My Own	1950	3.75	7.50	15.00
—With Kay Starr					
❑ F-1174	Bright Lights/The Cincinnati Dancing Pig	1950	3.75	7.50	15.00
❑ F-1205	Mama Goes Everywhere Papa Goes/Please Love Me	1950	3.75	7.50	15.00
—With Kay Starr					
❑ F-1275	Bryant's Boogie/Little Juan Pedro	1950	5.00	10.00	20.00
❑ F-1295	The Shot Gun Boogie/I Ain't Gonna Let It Happen No More	1950	5.00	10.00	20.00
❑ F-1349	Tailor Made Woman/Stack-O-Lee	1951	3.75	7.50	15.00
❑ F-1470	Kentucky Waltz/Strange Little Girl	1951	3.75	7.50	15.00
❑ F-1521	Mr. and Mississippi/She's My Baby	1951	3.75	7.50	15.00
❑ F-1567	Oceans of Tears/You're My Sugar	1951	3.75	7.50	15.00
—With Kay Starr					
❑ F-1623	I'll Never Be Free/Ain't Nobody's Business But My Own	1951	3.00	6.00	12.00
—With Kay Starr; reissue					
❑ F1626	The Shot Gun Boogie/Anticipation Blues	1951	3.00	6.00	12.00
❑ F1695	Mule Train/The Cry of the Wild Goose	1951	3.00	6.00	12.00
❑ F1775	Kissin' Bug Boogie/Woman Is a Five-Letter Word	1951	5.00	10.00	20.00
❑ F1809	Hey, Good Lookin'/Cool, Cool Kisses	1951	3.75	7.50	15.00
❑ F1830	A Rootin' Tootin' Santa Claus/Christmas Dinner	1951	3.75	7.50	15.00
❑ F1911	Rock City Boogie/Streamline Cannonball	1951	5.00	10.00	20.00
—With the Dinning Sisters					
❑ F2017	Hambone/Candy Dancers' Ball	1952	3.75	7.50	15.00
❑ F2042	Put Your Arms Around Me/Everybody's Got a Girl But Me	1952	3.75	7.50	15.00
❑ F2066	Snowshoe Thompson/Fatback Louisiana USA	1952	3.75	7.50	15.00
❑ 2145	Talk to the Animals/What a Wonderful World	1968	—	3.00	6.00
❑ F2170	Blackberry Boogie/Tennessee Local	1952	5.00	10.00	20.00
❑ F2179	Smokey Mountain Boogie/Country Junction	1952	5.00	10.00	20.00
❑ F2215	I'm Hog Tied Over You/False Hearted Girl	1952	3.75	7.50	15.00
—With Ella Mae Morse					
❑ 2334	The Little Boy King/Bring a Torch, Jeanette, Isabella	1968	—	3.00	6.00
❑ F2338	Sweet Temptation/I Don't Know	1953	3.75	7.50	15.00
❑ F2443	Hey, Mr. Cotton Picker/Three Things (A Man Must Do)	1953	3.75	7.50	15.00
❑ 2522	Honey-Eyed Girl (That's You That's You)/Good Morning, Dear	1969	—	3.00	6.00
❑ F2602	Catfish Boogie/Kiss Me Big	1953	5.00	10.00	20.00
❑ F2809	The Honeymoon's Over/This Must Be the Place	1954	3.00	6.00	12.00
—With Betty Hutton					
❑ F2810	River of No Return/Give Me Your Word	1954	3.00	6.00	12.00
❑ F2876	Losing You/Eins, Zwei, Drei	1954	3.00	6.00	12.00
❑ 2918	Rainy Night in Georgia/Let the Lovelight in Your Eyes Lead Me On	1970	—	2.50	5.00
❑ F2939	Somebody Bigger Than You and I/There Is Beauty in Everything	1954	3.00	6.00	12.00
❑ F3058	Ballad of Davy Crockett/Farewell	1955	3.75	7.50	15.00
❑ 3079	Happy Songs of Love/Don't Let the Good Life Pass You By	1971	—	2.50	5.00
❑ F3135	I Am a Pilgrim/His Hands	1955	3.00	6.00	12.00
❑ F3262	Sixteen Tons/You Don't Have to Be a Baby to Cry	1955	3.75	7.50	15.00
❑ F-3343	Bright Lights and Blonde Haired Women/That's All	1956	5.00	10.00	20.00
❑ F3421	John Henry/Rovin' Gambler	1956	3.00	6.00	12.00
❑ 3422	Pea-Pickin' Cook/The Song	1972	—	2.50	5.00
❑ F3474	Rock Roll Boogie/Call Me Darling, Call Me Sweetheart	1956	5.00	10.00	20.00
❑ F3553	First Born/Have You Seen Her	1956	3.00	6.00	12.00
❑ 3556	Printers' Alley Stars/Baby	1973	—	2.00	4.00
❑ 3631	Farther Down the River (Where the Fishin's Good)/You've Still Got Love All Over You	1973	—	2.00	4.00
❑ F3649	The Watermelon Song/One Suit	1957	3.00	6.00	12.00
❑ F3700	Lonely Man/False Hearted Girl	1957	3.00	6.00	12.00
❑ 3704	Colorado Country Morning/Daddy Usta Say	1973	—	2.00	4.00
❑ F3762	In the Middle of An Island/Ivy League	1957	3.00	6.00	12.00
❑ 3783	She Picked Up the Pieces/Sweet Child of Sunshine	1973	—	2.00	4.00
❑ 3848	I've Got Confidence/I'd Like to Be	1974	—	2.00	4.00
❑ F3868	Bless Your Pea Pickin' Heart/Down Deep	1957	3.00	6.00	12.00
❑ 3916	Come On Down/Bits and Pieces of Life	1974	—	2.00	4.00
❑ F3997	Love Makes the World Go Round/Sunday Barbecue	1958	2.50	5.00	10.00
❑ 4044	Baby/I'd Like to Be	1975	—	2.00	4.00
—With Andra Willis					
❑ F4107	Sleepin' at the Foot of the Bed/Glad Rags	1958	2.50	5.00	10.00
❑ 4160	The Devil Ain't a Lonely Woman's Friend/Smokey Taverns, Bar Room Girls	1975	—	2.00	4.00
❑ F4173	Code of the Mountains/Black-Eyed Susie	1959	2.50	5.00	10.00
❑ 4285	I Been to Georgia on a Fast Train/Baby's Home	1976	—	2.00	4.00
❑ 4302	Love Is the Only Thing/Sunny Side of Heaven	1959	2.00	4.00	8.00
❑ 4333	Sweet Feelin's/Dogs and Sheriff John	1976	—	2.00	4.00
❑ 4416	Joshua Fit De Battle/Oh Mary, Don't You Weep	1960	2.00	4.00	8.00
❑ 4446	Little Klinker/Jingle-O-The-Brownie	1960	3.00	6.00	12.00
❑ 4446 [PS]	Little Klinker/Jingle-O-The-Brownie	1960	5.00	10.00	20.00
❑ 4468	Bless This Land/Lord of All Creation	1960	2.00	4.00	8.00
❑ 4531	Dark As a Dungeon/His Love (Makes the World Go Round)	1961	2.00	4.00	8.00
❑ 4577	Litttle Red Rockin' Hood/I Gotta Have My Baby Back	1961	2.00	4.00	8.00
❑ 4734	Take Your Girlie to the Movies/There'll Be No New Tunes	1962	2.00	4.00	8.00
❑ 4793	The Work Song/Rags and Old Iron	1962	2.00	4.00	8.00
❑ 4838	How Great Thou Art/Eternal Life	1962	2.00	4.00	8.00
❑ 5425	Sixteen Tons/Hicktown	1965	—	3.00	6.00
❑ 5520	Girl Don't You Know/Now It's All Over	1965	—	3.00	6.00
❑ 5534	Sing We Now of Christmas/The Little Drummer Boy	1965	2.00	4.00	8.00
❑ 5757	God Lives/How Great Thou Art	1966	—	3.00	6.00
❑ 5900	Pearly Shells/Lahaina Luna	1967	—	3.00	6.00
❑ 5996	The Road/Hand Me Down Things	1967	—	3.00	6.00
❑ F40280	The Cry of the Wild Goose/The Donkey Serenade	1950	5.00	10.00	20.00

Selected 78s

CAPITOL

Number	Title (A Side/B Side)	Yr	VG	VG+	NM
❑ 15400	Tennessee Border/I Got the Milk 'Em in the Morning Blues	1949	5.00	10.00	20.00
❑ 15430	Country Junction/Philadelphia Lawyer	1949	5.00	10.00	20.00
❑ 40212	Smokey Mountain Boogie/You'll Find Her Name Written There	1949	5.00	10.00	20.00
❑ 40258	Mule Train/Anticipation Blues	1949	5.00	10.00	20.00

7-Inch Extended Plays

CAPITOL

Number	Title (A Side/B Side)	Yr	VG	VG+	NM
❑ EAP-413	(contents unknown)	1953	5.00	10.00	20.00
❑ EAP-413 [PS]	Backwoods Boogie and Blues	1953	5.00	10.00	20.00
❑ EAP 1-639	His Hands/Somebody Bigger Than You and I//I Am a Pilgrim/There Is Beauty in Everything	195?	3.75	7.50	15.00
❑ EAP 1-639 [PS]	Tennessee Ernie Ford	195?	3.75	7.50	15.00
❑ EAP-693	(contents unknown)	1956	3.75	7.50	15.00
❑ EAP-693 [PS]	Sixteen Tons	1956	3.75	7.50	15.00
❑ EAP 1-700	John Henry/Trouble in Mind//Gaily the Troubadour/The Lost Letter	1956	3.75	7.50	15.00
❑ EAP 1-700 [PS]	This Lusty Land! Part 1	1956	3.75	7.50	15.00
❑ EAP 2-700	Dark as a Dungeon/False Hearted Girl//I Gave My Love a Cherry/Nine Pound Hammer	1956	3.75	7.50	15.00
❑ EAP 2-700 [PS]	This Lusty Land! Part 2	1956	3.75	7.50	15.00
❑ EAP 3-700	Chicken Road/Who Will Shoe Your Pretty Little Foot//The Rovin' Gambler/In the Pines	1956	3.75	7.50	15.00
❑ EAP 3-700 [PS]	This Lusty Land! Part 3	1956	3.75	7.50	15.00
❑ EAP 1-756	The Ninety and Nine/Softly and Tenderly//Who at My Door Is Standing/Rock of Ages	1956	3.75	7.50	15.00
❑ EAP 1-756 [PS]	Hymns, Part 1	1956	3.75	7.50	15.00
❑ EAP 2-756	When They Ring the Golden Bells/In the Garden//Sweet Hour of Prayer/The Old Rugged Cross	1956	3.75	7.50	15.00
❑ EAP 2-756 [PS]	Hymns, Part 2	1956	3.75	7.50	15.00
❑ EAP 3-756	Let the Lower Lights Be Burning/Others//My Task/Ivory Palaces	1956	3.75	7.50	15.00
❑ EAP 3-756 [PS]	Hymns, Part 3	1956	3.75	7.50	15.00
❑ EAP 1-818	Just a Closer Walk with Thee/Peace in the Valley//Wayfaring Pilgrim/Were You There	195?	3.75	7.50	15.00
❑ EAP 1-818 [PS]	Spirituals, Part 1	195?	3.75	7.50	15.00
❑ EAP 2-818	He'll Understand and Say "Well Done"/I Know the Lord Laid His Hands on Me//Noah Found Grace in the Eyes of the Lord/I Want to Be Ready	195?	3.75	7.50	15.00
❑ EAP 2-818 [PS]	Spirituals, Part 2	195?	3.75	7.50	15.00
❑ EAP 3-818	Take My Hand, Precious Lord/Stand By Me//When God Dips His Love in My Heart/Get On Board, Little Children	195?	3.75	7.50	15.00
❑ EAP 3-818 [PS]	Spirituals, Part 3	195?	3.75	7.50	15.00
❑ EAP 1-888	(contents unknown)	1956	3.75	7.50	15.00
❑ EAP 1-888 [PS]	Ol' Rockin' Ern, Part 1	1956	3.75	7.50	15.00
❑ EAP 2-888	(contents unknown)	1956	3.75	7.50	15.00

Deep-voiced country singer and popular TV host Tennessee Ernie Ford had a few hits in his day, too. (Top left) His 1950-51 hit single "The Shot Gun Boogie," when he still went as simply "Tennessee Ernie," was his biggest country hit, as it spent an incredible 14 weeks at the No. 1 spot. (Top right) Ford was one of many artists to cover the popular Walt Disney theme "Ballad of Davy Crockett." It made the top 5 both on the pop and country charts. (Bottom left) If Ford is best known for only one song, it's "Sixteen Tons." Written and originally recorded by Merle Travis, this coal miner's lament was a huge across-the-board hit as it spent two months atop both the country and pop charts in 1955-56. (Bottom right) For many years after his biggest success was behind him, Tennessee Ernie recorded albums of favorite hymns. Original copies of this one, a 1960 release called *Sing a Hymn with Me*, actually had a hymnal attached.

Number	Title (A Side/B Side)	Yr	VG	VG+	NM
❑ EAP 2-888 [PS]	Ol' Rockin' Ern, Part 2	1956	3.75	7.50	15.00
❑ EAP 3-888	(contents unknown)	1956	3.75	7.50	15.00
❑ EAP 3-888 [PS]	Ol' Rockin' Ern, Part 3	1956	3.75	7.50	15.00
❑ EAP 1-1005	*What a Friend We Have in Jesus/Jesus, Savior, Pilot Me/His Eye Is on the Sparrow/Beautiful Isle of Somewhere	1958	2.50	5.00	10.00
❑ EAP 1-1005 [PS]	Nearer the Cross, Part 1	1958	2.50	5.00	10.00
❑ EAP 2-1005	Now the Day Is Over/Nearer My God to Thee//Sweet Peace the Gift of God's Love/Whispering Hope	1958	2.50	5.00	10.00
❑ EAP 2-1005 [PS]	Nearer the Cross, Part 2	1958	2.50	5.00	10.00
❑ EAP 3-1005	(contents unknown)	1958	2.50	5.00	10.00
❑ EAP 3-1005 [PS]	Nearer the Cross, Part 3	1958	2.50	5.00	10.00
❑ EAP 1-1071	*Joy to the World/O Little Town of Bethlehem/The Star Carol/Hark! The Herald Angels Sing	1958	3.00	6.00	12.00
❑ EAP 1-1071 [PS]	The Star Carol, Part 1	1958	3.00	6.00	12.00
❑ EAP 2-1071	(contents unknown)	1958	3.00	6.00	12.00
❑ EAP 2-1071 [PS]	The Star Carol, Part 2	1958	3.00	6.00	12.00
❑ EAP 3-1071	(contents unknown)	1958	3.00	6.00	12.00
❑ EAP 3-1071 [PS]	The Star Carol, Part 3	1958	3.00	6.00	12.00

GREEN GIANT

Number	Title (A Side/B Side)	Yr	VG	VG+	NM
❑ PB-2565 [DJ]	Down in the Valley/Medley: The More We Get Together-Dear Evalina-Keep on the Sunny Side of Life-How Many Biscuits Can We Eat-For He's a Jolly Green Giant/How the Green Giant Found His Song (And Almost Lost His Ho-Ho-Ho)/Good Things from the Garden	1963	2.50	5.00	10.00
—Promotional item for the Green Giant Company/Le Sueur Peas					
❑ PB-2565 [PS]	When Pea-Pickers Get Together	1963	2.50	5.00	10.00
—Promotional item for the Green Giant Company/Le Sueur Peas					

Albums

ARCHIVE OF FOLK AND JAZZ

Number	Title (A Side/B Side)	Yr	VG	VG+	NM
❑ 279	Tennessee Ernie Ford	197?	2.50	5.00	10.00

CAPITOL

Number	Title (A Side/B Side)	Yr	VG	VG+	NM
❑ ST-127	Songs I Like to Sing	1969	3.00	6.00	12.00
❑ ST-334	Holy, Holy, Holy	1969	3.00	6.00	12.00
❑ SM-412	America the Beautiful	197?	2.00	4.00	8.00
—Reissue with new prefix					
❑ STAO-412	America the Beautiful	1970	3.00	6.00	12.00
❑ STBB-485 [(2)]	Christmas Special	1970	3.75	7.50	15.00
❑ STBB-506 [(2)]	Sweet Hour of Prayer/Let Me Walk with Thee	1971	3.75	7.50	15.00
❑ ST-583	Everything Is Beautiful	1971	3.00	6.00	12.00
❑ DT 700 [R]	This Lusty Land!	196?	3.00	6.00	12.00
❑ T 700 [M]	This Lusty Land	1956	6.25	12.50	25.00
—Turquoise or gray label					
❑ T 700 [M]	This Lusty Land	1959	5.00	10.00	20.00
—Black label with colorband, logo at left					
❑ T 700 [M]	This Lusty Land!	1963	3.75	7.50	15.00
—Black label with colorband, logo at top					
❑ ST-730	Abide with Me	1971	3.00	6.00	12.00
❑ ST 756 [S]	Hymns	196?	3.75	7.50	15.00
❑ T 756 [M]	Hymns	1956	6.25	12.50	25.00
—Turquoise or gray label					
❑ T 756 [M]	Hymns	1959	5.00	10.00	20.00
—Black label with colorband, logo at left					
❑ T 756 [M]	Hymns	1962	3.75	7.50	15.00
—Black label with colorband, logo at top					
❑ ST 818 [S]	Spirituals	195?	3.75	7.50	15.00
❑ T 818 [M]	Spirituals	1957	6.25	12.50	25.00
—Turquoise or gray label					
❑ T 818 [M]	Spirituals	1959	5.00	10.00	20.00
—Black label with colorband, logo at left					
❑ T 818 [M]	Spirituals	1962	3.75	7.50	15.00
—Black label with colorband, logo at top					
❑ ST-831 [S]	C-H-R-I-S-T-M-A-S	1971	3.00	6.00	12.00
❑ ST-833	The Folk Album	1971	3.00	6.00	12.00
❑ DT 841 [R]	Tennessee Ernie Ford Favorites	196?	3.00	6.00	12.00
❑ T 841 [M]	Tennessee Ernie Ford Favorites	1958	5.00	10.00	20.00
—Black label with colorband, logo at left					
❑ T 841 [M]	Tennessee Ernie Ford Favorites	1962	3.75	7.50	15.00
—Black label with colorband, logo at top					
❑ T 888 [M]	Ol' Rockin' Ern	1957	12.50	25.00	50.00
—Turquoise or gray label					
❑ ST 1005 [S]	Nearer the Cross	1959	6.25	12.50	25.00
—Black label with colorband, logo at left					
❑ ST 1005 [S]	Nearer the Cross	1962	5.00	10.00	20.00
—Black label with colorband, logo at top					
❑ T 1005 [M]	Nearer the Cross	1958	5.00	10.00	20.00
—Black label with colorband, logo at left					
❑ T 1005 [M]	Nearer the Cross	1962	3.75	7.50	15.00
—Black label with colorband, logo at top					
❑ ST 1071 [S]	The Star Carol	1958	7.50	15.00	30.00
—Same contents as above, but in stereo; originals have black labels with colorband and "Capitol" logo on left					
❑ ST 1071 [S]	The Star Carol	1962	5.00	10.00	20.00
—Black label with colorband, "Capitol" logo on top. This was also likely reissued on later Capitol labels into the 1970s with values no more than half the above.					
❑ T 1071 [M]	The Star Carol	1958	6.25	12.50	25.00
—Originals have black labels with colorband and "Capitol" logo on left					
❑ T 1071 [M]	The Star Carol	1962	3.75	7.50	15.00
—Later pressings have black label with colorband, "Capitol" logo on top					
❑ ST 1227 [S]	Gather 'Round	1959	5.00	10.00	20.00
❑ T 1227 [M]	Gather 'Round	1959	3.75	7.50	15.00
❑ ST 1272 [S]	A Friend We Have	1959	5.00	10.00	20.00
❑ T 1272 [M]	A Friend We Have	1959	3.75	7.50	15.00
❑ STAO 1332 [S]	Sing a Hymn with Me	1960	6.25	12.50	25.00
—With hymnal					
❑ TAO 1332 [M]	Sing a Hymn with Me	1960	5.00	10.00	20.00
—With hymnal					
❑ DT 1380 [R]	Sixteen Tons	196?	3.00	6.00	12.00
❑ T 1380 [M]	Sixteen Tons	1960	3.75	7.50	15.00
❑ ST 1539 [S]	Civil War Songs of the North	1961	5.00	10.00	20.00
❑ T 1539 [M]	Civil War Songs of the North	1961	3.75	7.50	15.00
❑ ST 1540 [S]	Civil War Songs of the South	1961	5.00	10.00	20.00
❑ T 1540 [M]	Civil War Songs of the South	1961	3.75	7.50	15.00
❑ ST 1679 [S]	Sing a Hymn with Me	1962	3.75	7.50	15.00
—Reissue of 1332 with standard cover?					
❑ T 1679 [M]	Sing a Hymn with Me	1962	3.00	6.00	12.00
—Reissue of 1332 with standard cover?					
❑ T 1680 [M]	Sing a Spiritual with Me	1962	3.00	6.00	12.00
❑ ST 1684 [S]	Here Comes the Mississippi Showboat	1962	3.75	7.50	15.00
❑ T 1684 [M]	Here Comes the Mississippi Showboat	1962	3.00	6.00	12.00
❑ ST 1689 [S]	Sing a Spiritual with Me	1962	3.75	7.50	15.00
❑ ST 1694 [S]	Hymns at Home	1962	3.75	7.50	15.00
❑ T 1694 [M]	Hymns at Home	1962	3.00	6.00	12.00
❑ ST 1751 [S]	I Love to Tell the Story	1962	3.75	7.50	15.00
❑ T 1751 [M]	I Love to Tell the Story	1962	3.00	6.00	12.00
❑ ST 1794 [S]	Book of Favorite Hymns	1962	5.00	10.00	20.00
❑ T 1794 [M]	Book of Favorite Hymns	1962	3.75	7.50	15.00
❑ ST 1875 [S]	Long Long Ago	1963	3.75	7.50	15.00
❑ T 1875 [M]	Long Long Ago	1963	3.00	6.00	12.00
❑ ST 1937 [S]	We Gather Together	1963	3.75	7.50	15.00
❑ T 1937 [M]	We Gather Together	1963	3.00	6.00	12.00
❑ ST 1994 [S]	The Story of Christmas	1963	5.00	10.00	20.00
❑ T 1994 [M]	The Story of Christmas	1963	3.75	7.50	15.00
—With the Roger Wagner Chorale					
❑ SM-2026	Great Gospel Songs	197?	2.00	4.00	8.00
—Reissue with new prefix					
❑ ST 2026 [S]	Great Gospel Songs	1964	3.75	7.50	15.00
❑ T 2026 [M]	Great Gospel Songs	1964	3.00	6.00	12.00
❑ SM-2097	Country Hits...Feelin' Blue	197?	2.00	4.00	8.00
—Reissue with new prefix					
❑ ST 2097 [S]	Country Hits...Feelin' Blue	1964	3.75	7.50	15.00
❑ T 2097 [M]	Country Hits...Feelin' Blue	1964	3.00	6.00	12.00
❑ ST 2144 [S]	My Favorite Things	1966	3.75	7.50	15.00
❑ STBL 2183 [(2) S]	The World's Best Loved Hymns	1964	6.25	12.50	25.00
❑ TBL 2183 [(2) M]	The World's Best Loved Hymns	1964	5.00	10.00	20.00
❑ ST 2296 [S]	Let Me Walk with Thee	1965	3.75	7.50	15.00
❑ T 2296 [M]	Let Me Walk with Thee	1965	3.00	6.00	12.00
❑ ST 2394 [S]	Sing We Now of Christmas	1965	3.75	7.50	15.00
—Same as above, but in stereo					
❑ T 2394 [M]	Sing We Now of Christmas	1965	3.00	6.00	12.00
❑ T 2444 [M]	My Favorite Things	1966	3.00	6.00	12.00
❑ ST 2557 [S]	Wonderful Peace	1966	3.75	7.50	15.00
❑ T 2557 [M]	Wonderful Peace	1966	3.00	6.00	12.00
❑ ST 2618 [S]	God Lives	1966	3.75	7.50	15.00
❑ T 2618 [M]	God Lives	1966	3.00	6.00	12.00
❑ ST 2681 [S]	Aloha from Tennessee Ernie Ford	1967	3.00	6.00	12.00
❑ T 2681 [M]	Aloha from Tennessee Ernie Ford	1967	3.75	7.50	15.00
❑ SM-2761	Faith of Our Fathers	197?	2.00	4.00	8.00
—Reissue with new prefix					
❑ ST 2761 [S]	Faith of Our Fathers	1967	3.00	6.00	12.00
❑ T 2761 [M]	Faith of Our Fathers	1967	3.75	7.50	15.00
❑ ST 2845 [S]	Our Garden of Hymns	1968	3.00	6.00	12.00
❑ T 2845 [M]	Our Garden of Hymns	1968	5.00	10.00	20.00
❑ ST 2896	The World of Pop and Country Hits	1968	3.00	6.00	12.00
❑ STCL 2942 [(3)]	The Tennessee Ernie Ford Deluxe Set	1968	5.00	10.00	20.00
❑ SKAO 2949	Best Hymns	1968	3.00	6.00	12.00
❑ ST 2968	O Come All Ye Faithful	1968	3.00	6.00	12.00
❑ ST-11001	Mr. Words and Music	1972	2.50	5.00	10.00
❑ ST-11092	It's Tennessee Ernie Ford	1973	2.50	5.00	10.00
❑ ST-11232	Tennessee Ernie Ford Sings About Jesus	1973	2.50	5.00	10.00
❑ ST-11290	Make a Joyful Noise	1974	2.50	5.00	10.00
❑ SVBB-11325 [(2)]	25th Anniversary/Yesterday and Today	1974	3.00	6.00	12.00
❑ SVBB-11326 [(2)]	25th Anniversary/Hymns & Gospel	1974	3.00	6.00	12.00
❑ SVBB-11382 [(2)]	Precious Memories	1975	3.00	6.00	12.00
❑ ST-11495	Tennessee Ernie Ford Sings His Great Love Songs	1975	2.50	5.00	10.00
❑ SM-12033	Book of Favorite Hymns	1980	2.50	5.00	10.00
❑ SN-16040	Yesterday	1981	2.00	4.00	8.00
❑ SN-16042	Gospel	1981	2.00	4.00	8.00
❑ SN-16043	Hymns	1981	2.00	4.00	8.00
❑ SN-16173	Hymns	1981	2.00	4.00	8.00
❑ SN-16174	Spirituals	1981	2.00	4.00	8.00
❑ SN-16289	The Star Carol	1982	2.00	4.00	8.00
—Budget-line reissue					

PICKWICK

Number	Title (A Side/B Side)	Yr	VG	VG+	NM
❑ PTP-2016 [(2)]	Tennessee Ernie Ford	197?	3.00	6.00	12.00
❑ PTP-2050 [(2)]	Hymns	197?	3.00	6.00	12.00
❑ SPC-3047	Bless Your Pea-Pickin' Heart	196?	3.00	6.00	12.00
❑ SPC-3066	I Love You So Much	196?	3.00	6.00	12.00
❑ SPC-3222	The Need for Prayer	197?	2.50	5.00	10.00
❑ SPC-3268	Sixteen Tons	197?	2.50	5.00	10.00
❑ SPC-3273	Jesus Loves Me	197?	2.50	5.00	10.00
❑ SPC-3308	Amazing Grace	197?	2.50	5.00	10.00
❑ SPC-3353	Rock of Ages	197?	2.50	5.00	10.00

RANWOOD

Number	Title (A Side/B Side)	Yr	VG	VG+	NM
❑ RLP-7026 [(2)]	Tennessee Ernie Ford Sings 22 Favorite Hymns	198?	3.00	6.00	12.00

WORD

Number	Title (A Side/B Side)	Yr	VG	VG+	NM
❑ 8764	He Touched Me	1978	2.50	5.00	10.00

Number	Title (A Side/B Side)	Yr	VG	VG+	NM
❑ 8798	Swing Wide Your Golden Gate	198?	2.50	5.00	10.00
❑ 8841	Tell Me the Old Story	1979	2.50	5.00	10.00
❑ 8841	Tell Me the Old Story	198?	2.50	5.00	10.00
❑ 8858	There's a Song in My Heart	198?	2.50	5.00	10.00

FORD, TENNESSEE ERNIE, AND MOLLY BEE
Also see each artist's individual listings.

45s

CAPITOL

Number	Title (A Side/B Side)	Yr	VG	VG+	NM
❑ F2473	Don't Start Courtin' in a Hot Rod/We're a-Growin' Up	1953	5.00	10.00	20.00

FORESTER SISTERS, THE
45s

WARNER BROS.

Number	Title (A Side/B Side)	Yr	VG	VG+	NM
❑ 18906	I Got a Date/Show Me a Woman	1992	—	—	3.00
❑ 19047	What'll You Do About Me/Men	1992	—	—	3.00
❑ 19177	Let Not Your Heart Be Troubled/What About Tonight	1991	—	—	3.00
❑ 19291	Too Much Fun/The Blues Don't Stand a Chance	1991	—	—	3.00
❑ 19450	Men/Just in Case	1991	—	2.00	4.00
❑ 19744	Nothing's Gonna Bother Me Tonight/Born to Give My Love to You	1990	—	—	3.00
❑ 19766	Old Enough to Know/Between My Heart and Me	1990	—	—	3.00
❑ 19874	Drive South/You Can't Have a Good Time Without Me	1990	—	—	3.00
—A-side with the Bellamy Brothers					
❑ 22773	Leave It Alone/I Fell in Love Again Last Night	1989	—	—	3.00
❑ 22943	Don't You/All I Need	1989	—	—	3.00
❑ 22943 [PS]	Don't You/All I Need	1989	—	2.50	5.00
❑ 27575	Love Will/You Love Me	1989	—	—	3.00
❑ 27686	Sincerely/On the Other Side of the Gate	1988	—	—	3.00
❑ 27839	Letter Home/These Lips Don't Know How to Say Goodbye	1988	—	—	3.00
❑ 28207	The First Noel/This Old White Doorway	1987	—	2.00	4.00
❑ 28208	Lyin' in His Arms Again/Wrap Me Up	1987	—	—	3.00
❑ 28368	You Again/Whatever You Do, Don't	1987	—	—	3.00
❑ 28442	Too Many Rivers/If I'm Gonna Fall (I'm Gonna Fall in Love)	1987	—	—	3.00
❑ 28687	Lonely Alone/Heartless Night	1986	—	—	3.00
❑ 28795	Mama's Never Seen Those Eyes/Something Tells Me	1986	—	—	3.00
❑ 28875	Just in Case/Reckless Night	1985	—	—	3.00
❑ 28988	I Fell in Love Again Last Night/Dixie Man	1985	—	—	3.00
❑ 29114	(That's What You Do) When You're in Love/Yankee Don't Go Home	1985	—	—	3.00

Albums

WARNER BROS.

Number	Title (A Side/B Side)	Yr	VG	VG+	NM
❑ 25314	The Forester Sisters	1985	2.50	5.00	10.00
❑ 25411	Perfume, Ribbons & Pearls	1986	2.50	5.00	10.00
❑ 25571	You Again	1987	2.50	5.00	10.00
❑ 25623	A Christmas Card	1987	2.50	5.00	10.00
❑ 25746	Sincerely	1988	2.50	5.00	10.00
❑ 25897	Greatest Hits	1989	2.50	5.00	10.00
❑ R 110671	Talkin' About Men	1991	5.00	10.00	20.00
—BMG Direct Marketing edition (no regular vinyl version)					

FORMAN, PEGGY
45s

DIMENSION

Number	Title (A Side/B Side)	Yr	VG	VG+	NM
❑ 1006	There Ain't Nothing Like a Rainy Night/Sugar on Your Lies	1980	—	2.50	5.00
❑ 1008	Burnin' Up Your Memory/Sugar on Your Lies	1980	—	2.50	5.00
❑ 1012	Hard Luck Lady/Old Time Feeling	1980	—	2.50	5.00
❑ 1020	You're More to Me (Than He's Ever Been)/Steppin' Aside Ain't My Style	1981	—	2.50	5.00
❑ 1023	I Wish You Could Have Turned My Head (And Left My Heart Alone)/Falling Out of Love	1981	—	2.50	5.00
❑ 1027	That's What Your Lovin' Does to Me/Foolish Talkin'	1982	—	2.50	5.00

MCA

Number	Title (A Side/B Side)	Yr	VG	VG+	NM
❑ 40757	The Danger Zone/Yours to Hurt Tomorrow	1977	—	2.50	5.00
❑ 40823	Dance Girl/Georgia Love Affair	1977	—	2.50	5.00
❑ 40874	You Can't Lose 'Em All/Yours to Hurt Tomorrow	1978	—	2.50	5.00

FORREST, SYLVIA
45s

DOOR KNOB

Number	Title (A Side/B Side)	Yr	VG	VG+	NM
❑ 319	The Nights Are Never Long Enough with You/(B-side unknown)	1989	—	2.50	5.00

FORRESTER, HOWDY
Albums

CUB

Number	Title (A Side/B Side)	Yr	VG	VG+	NM
❑ 8008 [M]	Fancy Fiddlin' Country Style	1960	10.00	20.00	40.00

MGM

Number	Title (A Side/B Side)	Yr	VG	VG+	NM
❑ E-4035 [M]	Fancy Fiddlin' Country Style	1962	7.50	15.00	30.00
—Reissue of Cub LP					

UNITED ARTISTS

Number	Title (A Side/B Side)	Yr	VG	VG+	NM
❑ UAL-3295 [M]	Fiddlin' Country Style	1963	5.00	10.00	20.00
❑ UAS-6295 [S]	Fiddlin' Country Style	1963	6.25	12.50	25.00

FOSTER, DARLA
45s

MELODYLAND

Number	Title (A Side/B Side)	Yr	VG	VG+	NM
❑ 6017	Say Love (Or Don't Say Anything at All)/He Makes the World Seem Right	1975	—	2.50	5.00

FOSTER, JERRY
45s

BACK BEAT

Number	Title (A Side/B Side)	Yr	VG	VG+	NM
❑ 520	What Would I Do/Your Love	1958	3.75	7.50	15.00
❑ 529	My First Love/I'm Here to Tell You	1959	3.00	6.00	12.00
❑ 534	Lonely One/Romeo	1961	3.00	6.00	12.00

CINNAMON

Number	Title (A Side/B Side)	Yr	VG	VG+	NM
❑ 757	I Won't Ever Love Again/Turn It Over in Your Mind	1973	—	3.00	6.00
❑ 764	Copperhead/Ain't It Sad	1973	—	3.00	6.00
❑ 774	Looking Back/Hard to Handle	1973	—	3.00	6.00
❑ 789	New Orleans Blue/The Easy Part's Over	1974	—	3.00	6.00

HITSVILLE

Number	Title (A Side/B Side)	Yr	VG	VG+	NM
❑ 6043	I Knew You When/One	1976	—	2.50	5.00
❑ 6052	Family Man/Just Another Song Away	1977	—	2.50	5.00

KARI

Number	Title (A Side/B Side)	Yr	VG	VG+	NM
❑ 106	Giving Up Easy/I Wonder If You'll Ever Learn to Cry	1980	—	2.50	5.00
❑ 109	Matchbox/Don't Let Go	1980	—	2.50	5.00
❑ 112	That's Alright/Hard to Handle	1980	—	2.50	5.00
❑ 116	When My Blue Moon Turns to Gold Again/Looking Back	1981	—	2.50	5.00

METROMEDIA

Number	Title (A Side/B Side)	Yr	VG	VG+	NM
❑ 160	Mississippi Bound/One-Thirty Lonesome	1970	—	3.50	7.00
❑ 184	I Forgot to Remember to Forget/When My Blue Moon Turns to Gold Again	1970	—	3.50	7.00
❑ 201	Don't Be Cruel/You're Right, I'm Left, She's Gone	1970	—	3.50	7.00

MONUMENT

Number	Title (A Side/B Side)	Yr	VG	VG+	NM
❑ 45-242	Don't Take Your Sunshine From My Life/The Fifties	1978	—	2.50	5.00
❑ 45-256	I Want to Love You/My Baby Left Me	1978	—	2.50	5.00

SUN

Number	Title (A Side/B Side)	Yr	VG	VG+	NM
❑ 1176 [DJ]	The 50's (same on both sides)	1982	—	3.00	6.00
—Promo only					

TCF HALL

Number	Title (A Side/B Side)	Yr	VG	VG+	NM
❑ 115	The Fight/Here Comes the Loser	1966	2.00	4.00	8.00

FOSTER, LLOYD DAVID
45s

COLUMBIA

Number	Title (A Side/B Side)	Yr	VG	VG+	NM
❑ 38-04670	I'm Gonna Love You Right Out of the Blues/Wishful Drinkin'	1984	—	—	3.00
❑ 38-04836	I Can Feel the Fire Goin' Out/Anywhere You Want to Go	1985	—	—	3.00
❑ 38-05601	I'm As Over You As I'm Ever Gonna Get/Anywhere You Want to Go	1985	—	—	3.00

MCA

Number	Title (A Side/B Side)	Yr	VG	VG+	NM
❑ 52061	Blue Rendezvous/Love at First Sight	1982	—	2.00	4.00
❑ 52123	Honky Tonk Magic/The First Time I Saw Her (Was the Last Time)	1982	—	2.00	4.00
❑ 52173	Unfinished Business/It Takes One to Know One	1983	—	2.00	4.00
❑ 52248	You've Got That Touch/Just One	1983	—	2.00	4.00

FOSTER, RADNEY
45s

ARISTA

Number	Title (A Side/B Side)	Yr	VG	VG+	NM
❑ 12448	Just Call Me Lonesome/Louisiana Blue	1992	—	2.00	4.00
❑ 12512	Nobody Wins/Don't Say Goodbye	1993	—	2.00	4.00
❑ 12564	Easier Said Than Done/Don't Say Goodbye	1993	—	—	3.00
❑ 12608	Hammer and Nails/A Fine Line	1993	—	—	3.00
❑ 12652	Closing Time/Old Silver	1994	—	—	3.00
❑ 12661	If It Were Me/Walkin' Talkin' Woman	1995	—	—	3.00
❑ 12716	Labor of Love/Jesse's Soul	1994	—	—	3.00
❑ 12752	Willin' to Walk/Last Chance for Love	1995	—	—	3.00
❑ 12758	The Runnin' Kind/Silver Wings	1994	—	2.00	4.00
—B-side by Pam Tillis					
❑ 12861	If It Were Me/Walkin' Talkin' Woman	1995	—	—	3.00

FOSTER AND LLOYD
45s

RCA

Number	Title (A Side/B Side)	Yr	VG	VG+	NM
❑ 2502-7-R	Is It Love/Workin' on Me	1990	—	—	3.00
❑ 2635-7-R	Can't Have Nothin'/Workin' on Me	1990	—	—	3.00
❑ 5218-7-R	Crazy Over You/The Part I Know by Heart	1987	—	2.00	4.00
❑ 5218-7-R [PS]	Crazy Over You/The Part I Know by Heart	1987	—	3.00	6.00
—Sleeve is promo only					
❑ 5281-7-R	Sure Thing/Hard to Say No	1987	—	—	3.00
❑ 5281-7-R [PS]	Sure Thing/Hard to Say No	1987	—	2.00	4.00
❑ 6900-7-R	Texas in 1880/Token of Love	1988	—	—	3.00
❑ 8633-7-R	What Do You Want from Me This Time/Don't Go Out with Him	1988	—	—	3.00
❑ 8795-7-R	Fair Shake/After I'm Gone	1989	—	—	3.00
❑ 8942-7-R	Before the Heartache Rolls In/Happy for a While	1989	—	—	3.00
❑ 9028-7-R	Suzette/I'll Always Be Here Loving You	1989	—	—	3.00

Albums

RCA

Number	Title (A Side/B Side)	Yr	VG	VG+	NM
❑ 6372-1-R	Foster and Lloyd	1987	2.00	4.00	8.00
❑ 9587-1-R	Faster & Llouder	1989	2.50	5.00	10.00

FOUR GUYS, THE

Members of the Grand Ole Opry from 1967 to 2000. The Mercury and Wing singles might be by a different group!

45s

Number	Title (A Side/B Side)	Yr	VG	VG+	NM
AUDIOGRAPH					
❑ 453	Ruby Red/(B-side unknown)	1983	—	2.50	5.00
❑ 463	Whiskey and Water/(B-side unknown)	1983	—	2.50	5.00
❑ 478	Fanny Mae/If You Don't Lose It	1984	—	2.50	5.00
CINNAMON					
❑ 791	Streakin' with My Baby/Girl of Mine	1974	—	3.00	6.00
COLLAGE					
❑ 102	Mama Rocked Us to Sleep (With Country Music)/ Forever in Blue Jeans	1979	—	3.00	6.00
CUTLASS					
❑ 134	Sweet Yesterday/(B-side unknown)	197?	—	3.00	6.00
GARPAX/GRT					
❑ 139	I Remember (Edit)/I Remember (Complete)	1978	—	2.50	5.00
❑ 143	Mother Country/The Only Fool Is Me	1978	—	2.50	5.00
J&B					
❑ 1001	Made in the U.S.A./Pretty Lady	1982	—	3.00	6.00
MERCURY					
❑ 70452	Tonight's the Night/Not As a Stranger	1955	5.00	10.00	20.00
❑ 70908	Drive-In Rock/Do Unto Others	1956	6.25	12.50	25.00
MYRTLE					
❑ 1001	Stealing the Feeling/(B-side unknown)	1982	—	3.00	6.00
RCA VICTOR					
❑ PB-10055	Too Late to Turn Back Now/Gatherin' Dust	1974	—	2.50	5.00
STOP					
❑ 202	Half a Man/Labor of Love	1968	2.50	5.00	10.00
WING					
❑ 90036	Bye Bye for Just a While/May This Be Your Life	1956	5.00	10.00	20.00

4 RUNNER

45s

Number	Title (A Side/B Side)	Yr	VG	VG+	NM
A&M					
❑ 581650-7	That Was Him (This Is Now)/Let the Good Times Roll	1996	—	—	3.00
POLYDOR					
❑ 577040-7	Home Alone/You Make the Moonlight	1995	—	—	3.00
❑ 577730-7	Ripples/Oh No	1996	—	—	3.00
❑ 579450-7	A Heart with 4 Wheel Drive/Southern Wind	1995	—	—	3.00
❑ 851622-7	Cain's Blood/Ten Pound Hammer	1995	—	2.00	4.00

FOWLER, KEN

45s

Number	Title (A Side/B Side)	Yr	VG	VG+	NM
DEJA VU					
❑ 111	You're a Heartache to Follow/The Way That I Remember You	1986	—	3.00	6.00
❑ 111 [PS]	You're a Heartache to Follow/The Way That I Remember You	1986	2.00	4.00	8.00

FOWLER, WALLY

Also see THE TENNESSEE VALLEY BOYS.

45s

Number	Title (A Side/B Side)	Yr	VG	VG+	NM
DOVE					
❑ 100	A New Star in Heaven/(B-side unknown)	1977	2.50	5.00	10.00

Albums

Number	Title (A Side/B Side)	Yr	VG	VG+	NM
DECCA					
❑ DL 8560 [M]	Call of the Cross	1958	10.00	20.00	40.00
DOVE					
❑ 1000	A Tribute to Elvis Presley	1977	5.00	10.00	20.00
KING					
❑ 702 [M]	Gospel Song Festival	1960	25.00	50.00	100.00
STARDAY					
❑ SLP-112 [M]	All Nite Singing Gospel Concert	1960	10.00	20.00	40.00
❑ SLP-301 [M]	All Nite Singing Concert	1964	7.50	15.00	30.00

FOX, DOLLY

45s

Number	Title (A Side/B Side)	Yr	VG	VG+	NM
ARTIC					
❑ 1025	I've Got a Reason for Living/Who's Gonna Love Me (When You're Gone)	1978	—	3.00	6.00

FOX, KENT

45s

Number	Title (A Side/B Side)	Yr	VG	VG+	NM
MCA					
❑ 40038	New York Callin' Miami/Have Patience ('Til I Learn to Love You)	1973	—	2.50	5.00

FOXFIRE

45s

Number	Title (A Side/B Side)	Yr	VG	VG+	NM
ELEKTRA					
❑ 46625	I Can See Forever Loving You/Dreaming Won't Take Me That Far	1980	—	2.00	4.00
❑ 47021	What's a Nice Girl Like You (Doin' in a Love Like This)/Do That To Me Again	1980	—	2.00	4.00
❑ 47070	Whatever Happened to Those Drinking Songs/ Do That to Me Again	1980	—	2.00	4.00
NSD					
❑ 24	Fell Into Love/Head Over Heels in Love with You	1979	—	2.50	5.00

FOXTON, KELLY

Also see HANK SNOW AND KELLY FOXTON.

45s

Number	Title (A Side/B Side)	Yr	VG	VG+	NM
COMPLEAT					
❑ 117	Backfield in Motion/Sixteen Tons	1983	—	2.50	5.00

FOXWORTHY, JEFF

45s

Number	Title (A Side/B Side)	Yr	VG	VG+	NM
WARNER BROS.					
❑ 17526	Redneck 12 Days of Christmas/'Twas the Night After Christmas	1996	—	2.50	5.00
—Green vinyl					
❑ 17648	Redneck Games/NASA & Alabama & Fishing Shows	1996	—	2.00	4.00
—A-side with Alan Jackson					
❑ 17806	Party All Night/Southern Accent	1995	—	2.00	4.00
—A-side with Little Texas					
❑ 18116	Redneck Stomp/Words in the South	1994	—	2.00	4.00

FRADY, GARLAND

45s

Number	Title (A Side/B Side)	Yr	VG	VG+	NM
COUNTRYSIDE					
❑ 45104	The Barrooms Have Found You/Silver Moon	1973	2.00	4.00	8.00
GNP CRESCENDO					
❑ 500	The Way the World Is Going Now (You Need Country Music)/I Think of Her	1975	—	3.00	6.00
❑ 806	J.C. Is Here/Room Full of Mirrors	1976	—	3.00	6.00
PAULA					
❑ 1242	Mr. Bojangles/Fort Worth, I Love You	1971	—	3.50	7.00

FRANCIS, CLEVE

45s

Number	Title (A Side/B Side)	Yr	VG	VG+	NM
LIBERTY					
❑ S7-57728	Love Light/Happy	1992	—	2.00	4.00
PLAYBACK					
❑ 1334	Lovelight/(B-side unknown)	1989	—	3.00	6.00
SOUTHERN TRACKS					
❑ 1050	Martin (same on both sides)	1985	2.50	5.00	10.00

FRANCIS, CONNIE

Diverse singer who did a little bit of everything — and even had several country hits. Her country-oriented material is listed below.

45s

Number	Title (A Side/B Side)	Yr	VG	VG+	NM
MGM					
❑ 12899	Everybody's Somebody's Fool/Jealous of You	1960	3.75	7.50	15.00
❑ 12899 [PS]	Everybody's Somebody's Fool/Jealous of You	1960	5.00	10.00	20.00
❑ 14034	The Wedding Cake/Over Hill, Under Ground	1969	2.00	4.00	8.00
POLYDOR					
❑ 810087-7	There's Still a Few Good Love Songs Left in Me/ Let's Make It Love Tonight	1983	—	2.50	5.00

7-Inch Extended Plays

Number	Title (A Side/B Side)	Yr	VG	VG+	NM
MGM					
❑ X-1694	(contents unknown)	1960	7.50	15.00	30.00
❑ X-1694 [PS]	Country & Western Golden Hits (Part 1)	1960	7.50	15.00	30.00
❑ X-1695	(contents unknown)	1960	7.50	15.00	30.00
❑ X-1695 [PS]	Country & Western Golden Hits (Part 2)	1960	7.50	15.00	30.00
❑ X-1696	(contents unknown)	1960	7.50	15.00	30.00
❑ X-1696 [PS]	Country & Western Golden Hits (Part 3)	1960	7.50	15.00	30.00

Albums

Number	Title (A Side/B Side)	Yr	VG	VG+	NM
MGM					
❑ E-3795 [M]	Country and Western Golden Hits	1960	7.50	15.00	30.00
❑ SE-3795 [S]	Country and Western Golden Hits	1960	10.00	20.00	40.00
❑ E-4079 [M]	Country Music Connie Style	1962	6.25	12.50	25.00
❑ SE-4079 [S]	Country Music Connie Style	1962	7.50	15.00	30.00

FRANCIS, CONNIE, AND MARVIN RAINWATER

Also see each artist's individual listings.

45s

Number	Title (A Side/B Side)	Yr	VG	VG+	NM
MGM					
❑ 12555	You, My Darlin', You/The Majesty of Love	1957	6.25	12.50	25.00

FRANKS, TILLMAN

45s

Number	Title (A Side/B Side)	Yr	VG	VG+	NM
STARDAY					
❑ 651	Tadpole/Pretty Little Girls	1963	3.75	7.50	15.00
❑ 670	When the World's on Fire/Uncle Eph	1964	3.75	7.50	15.00

FRAZIER, BRENDA

45s

Number	Title (A Side/B Side)	Yr	VG	VG+	NM
TYRO					
❑ 1004	I've Given Up Giving In to the Blues/Steppin' Out Tonight	1980	2.00	4.00	8.00

FRAZIER, DALLAS

45s

Number	Title (A Side/B Side)	Yr	VG	VG+	NM
20TH CENTURY					
❑ 2171	Cash on Delivery/Watching My World Walk Away	1975	—	3.00	6.00
❑ 2199	Liberal Acres/Heaven Hangin' Over My Head	1975	—	3.00	6.00
❑ 2233	I'm Sorry If My Love Got In Your Way/Harvey, Where'd You Get That Yellow Yo-Yo	1975	—	3.00	6.00
CAPITOL					
❑ 2011	Everybody Oughta Sing a Song/Only a Fool	1967	2.50	5.00	10.00

Number	Title (A Side/B Side)	Yr	VG	VG+	NM
❑ 2133	The Sunshine of My World/Lonelier and More in Love	1968	2.50	5.00	10.00
❑ 2257	I Hope I Like Mexico Blues/I Just Thought That I Love Her ('Till I Lost You)	1968	2.50	5.00	10.00
❑ 2402	The Conspiracy of Homer Jones/Sundown of My Mind	1969	2.50	5.00	10.00
❑ F2813	Space Command/Ain't You Had No Bringin' Up at All	1954	5.00	10.00	20.00
❑ F2895	Love Life at 14/I'm Gonna Move Over Yonder	1954	5.00	10.00	20.00
❑ F2956	My Birthday Comes on Christmas/Jingle o' the Brownie	1954	5.00	10.00	20.00

—With Joe "Fingers" Carr

Number	Title (A Side/B Side)	Yr	VG	VG+	NM
❑ 5444	King of the Jungle/Make Believe You're Here with Me	1965	3.00	6.00	12.00
❑ 5560	Elvira/That Ain't No Stuff	1966	3.75	7.50	15.00
❑ 5670	Walkin' Wonder/Just a Little Bit of You	1966	3.00	6.00	12.00
❑ 5728	Tennessee Sue/Especially for You	1966	3.00	6.00	12.00
❑ 5862	My Woman Up't and Gone/Clawhammer Clyde	1967	3.00	6.00	12.00

JAMIE

Number	Title (A Side/B Side)	Yr	VG	VG+	NM
❑ 1135	Can't Go On/Without Your Love	1959	5.00	10.00	20.00

MERCURY

Number	Title (A Side/B Side)	Yr	VG	VG+	NM
❑ 72279	My Little Swing Broke Down/Money Greases the Wheels	1964	3.00	6.00	12.00

RCA VICTOR

Number	Title (A Side/B Side)	Yr	VG	VG+	NM
❑ 47-9881	The Birthmark Henry Thompson Talks About/If My Heart Had Windows	1970	2.00	4.00	8.00
❑ 47-9950	Big Mable Murphy/White Fences and Evergreen Trees	1971	2.00	4.00	8.00
❑ 47-9991	My Baby Packed Up My Mind and Left Me/I'm Finally Over You	1971	2.00	4.00	8.00
❑ 74-0259	California Cotton Fields/Sweetheart Don't Throw Yourself Away	1969	2.00	4.00	8.00
❑ 74-0569	Common, Broke Elastic, Rotten Cotton, Hound Dog Snoopin', Ankle Droopin', Funky Fuzzy, White Sock Blues No. 2/High Steppin' Mama	1971	2.00	4.00	8.00
❑ 74-0748	North Carolina/The Last Time I Called Somebody Darlin'	1972	2.00	4.00	8.00
❑ 74-0903	This Time the Hurtin's on Me/Lonesome Fiddle Man	1973	2.00	4.00	8.00

Albums

CAPITOL

Number	Title (A Side/B Side)	Yr	VG	VG+	NM
❑ ST 2552 [S]	Elvira	1966	6.25	12.50	25.00
❑ T 2552 [M]	Elvira	1966	5.00	10.00	20.00
❑ ST 2764 [S]	Tell It Like It Is	1967	5.00	10.00	20.00
❑ T 2764 [M]	Tell It Like It Is	1967	6.25	12.50	25.00

FRAZIER RIVER

45s

DECCA

Number	Title (A Side/B Side)	Yr	VG	VG+	NM
❑ 55101	Tangled Up in Texas/Last Request	1995	—	2.00	4.00
❑ 55173	She Got What She Deserves/Heaven Is Smiling	1996	—	2.00	4.00

FREE, JOHNNY

45s

SABRE

Number	Title (A Side/B Side)	Yr	VG	VG+	NM
❑ 4509	Borrowed Time/(B-side unknown)	1979	2.00	4.00	8.00

FREEMAN, ERNIE

The R&B pianist and organist had one country hit.

45s

IMPERIAL

Number	Title (A Side/B Side)	Yr	VG	VG+	NM
❑ 5474	Raunchy/Puddin'	1957	6.25	12.50	25.00

FRICKE, JANIE

Includes records as "Janie Frickie." Also see JOHNNY DUNCAN; LARRY GATLIN; MERLE HAGGARD; CHARLIE RICH.

45s

COLUMBIA

Number	Title (A Side/B Side)	Yr	VG	VG+	NM
❑ 18-02197	I'll Need Someone to Hold Me (When I Cry)/It's Raining Too	1981	—	—	3.00
❑ 18-02644	Do Me with Love/If You Could See Me Now	1981	—	—	3.00
❑ 18-02859	Don't Worry 'Bout Me Baby/Always	1982	—	—	3.00
❑ 38-03214	It Ain't Easy Bein' Easy/A Little More Love	1982	—	—	3.00
❑ 38-03498	You Don't Know Love/Heart to Heart Talk	1983	—	—	3.00
❑ 38-03899	He's a Heartache (Looking for a Place to Happen)/Tryin' to Fool a Fool	1983	—	—	3.00
❑ 38-04091	Tell Me a Lie/Love Have Mercy	1983	—	—	3.00
❑ 38-04317	Let's Stop Talkin' About It/I've Had All the Love I Can Stand	1984	—	—	3.00
❑ 38-04454	If the Fall Don't Get You/Where's the Fire	1984	—	—	3.00
❑ 38-04578	Your Heart's Not In It/Take It from the Top	1984	—	—	3.00
❑ 38-04731	The First Word in Memory Is Me/One Way Ticket	1984	—	—	3.00
❑ 38-04896	She's Single Again/The Only Thing She Took Away	1985	—	—	3.00
❑ 38-05617	Somebody Else's Fire/My Heart's Hearing Footsteps	1985	—	—	3.00
❑ 38-05781	Easy to Please/Party Shoes	1986	—	—	3.00
❑ 38-06144	Always Have Always Will/Don't Put It Past My Heart	1986	—	—	3.00
❑ 38-06144 [PS]	Always Have Always Will/Don't Put It Past My Heart	1986	—	2.00	4.00
❑ 38-06417	When a Woman Cries/Nothing Left to Say	1986	—	—	3.00
❑ 38-06985	Are You Satisfied/Till I Can't Take It Anymore	1987	—	—	3.00
❑ 38-07353	Baby You're Gone/I Don't Like Being Lonely	1987	—	—	3.00
❑ 38-07770	Where Does Love Go (When It's Gone)/The Last Thing	1988	—	—	3.00
❑ 38-07927	I'll Walk Before I Crawl/The Healing Hands of Time	1988	—	—	3.00
❑ 38-08031	Heart/The Healing Hands of Time	1988	—	—	3.00
❑ 3-10605	What're You Doing Tonight/We're a Love Song	1977	—	2.50	5.00
❑ 3-10695	Baby It's You/I Loved You All the Way	1978	—	2.00	4.00
❑ 3-10743	Please Help Me, I'm Falling (In Love with You)/Get Ready for My World	1978	—	2.00	4.00
❑ 3-10849	Playin' Hard to Get/Let Me Love You Goodbye	1978	—	2.00	4.00
❑ 3-10910	I'll Love Away Your Troubles for Awhile/River Blue	1979	—	2.00	4.00
❑ 3-11029	Let's Try Again/Love Is Worth It All	1979	—	2.00	4.00
❑ 1-11139	But Love Me/One Piece at a Time	1979	—	2.00	4.00
❑ 1-11223	Pass Me By (If You're Only Passing Through)/This Ain't Tennessee and He Ain't You	1980	—	2.00	4.00
❑ 1-11384	Down to My Last Broken Heart/Every Time a Teardrop Falls	1980	—	2.00	4.00
❑ 11-60509	Pride/Going Through the Motions	1981	—	2.00	4.00
❑ 38-68758	Love Is One of Those Words/No Ordinary Memory	1989	—	—	3.00
❑ 38-69057	Give 'Em My Number/Walking on the Moon	1989	—	—	3.00

Albums

COLUMBIA

Number	Title (A Side/B Side)	Yr	VG	VG+	NM
❑ AS99 1535 [DJ]	Janie Fricke On Tour	1982	15.00	30.00	60.00
—Promo-only picture disc					
❑ KC 35315	Singer of Songs	1978	3.00	6.00	12.00
❑ PC 35315	Singer of Songs	198?	2.00	4.00	8.00
—Budget-line reissue with new prefix					
❑ KC 35774	Love Notes	1979	3.00	6.00	12.00
❑ PC 35774	Love Notes	198?	2.00	4.00	8.00
—Budget-line reissue with new prefix					
❑ JC 36268	From the Heart	1980	3.00	6.00	12.00
❑ JC 36820	I'll Need Someone to Hold Me When I Cry	1980	2.50	5.00	10.00
❑ PC 36820	I'll Need Someone to Hold Me When I Cry	198?	2.00	4.00	8.00
—Budget-line reissue with new prefix					
❑ FC 37535	Sleeping with Your Memory	1981	2.50	5.00	10.00
❑ PC 37535	Sleeping with Your Memory	198?	2.00	4.00	8.00
—Budget-line reissue with new prefix					
❑ FC 38214	It Ain't Easy	1982	2.50	5.00	10.00
❑ FC 38310	Greatest Hits	1982	2.50	5.00	10.00
❑ FC 38730	Love Lies	1983	2.50	5.00	10.00
❑ PC 38730	Love Lies	1985	2.00	4.00	8.00
—Budget-line reissue with new prefix					
❑ FC 39338	The First Word in Memory	1984	2.50	5.00	10.00
❑ FC 39975	Somebody Else's Fire	1985	2.50	5.00	10.00
❑ FC 40165	The Very Best of Janie	1985	2.50	5.00	10.00
❑ FC 40383	Black & White	1986	2.50	5.00	10.00
❑ FC 40666	After Midnight	1987	2.50	5.00	10.00
❑ C2 40684 [(2)]	Celebration	1987	3.00	6.00	12.00
❑ FC 44143	Saddle the Wind	1988	2.50	5.00	10.00
❑ FC 45087	Labor of Love	1989	3.00	6.00	12.00

FRIEDMAN, KINKY

45s

ABC

Number	Title (A Side/B Side)	Yr	VG	VG+	NM
❑ 12073	Lover Please/Autograph	1975	—	3.00	6.00
❑ 12107	Wild Man from Borneo/Popeye the Sailor Man	1975	—	3.00	6.00

EPIC

Number	Title (A Side/B Side)	Yr	VG	VG+	NM
❑ 50299	Catfish/Dear Abby	1976	—	2.50	5.00

SUNRISE

Number	Title (A Side/B Side)	Yr	VG	VG+	NM
❑ 41932	Twirl/Hello, Good Mornin'	1983	—	3.00	6.00

—B-side with Ronee Blakely

VANGUARD

Number	Title (A Side/B Side)	Yr	VG	VG+	NM
❑ 35173	Sold American/Western Union Wire	1973	2.00	4.00	8.00

Albums

ABC

Number	Title (A Side/B Side)	Yr	VG	VG+	NM
❑ X-829	Kinky Friedman	1974	2.50	5.00	10.00

EPIC

Number	Title (A Side/B Side)	Yr	VG	VG+	NM
❑ PE 34304	Lasso from El Paso	1976	2.50	5.00	10.00

VANGUARD

Number	Title (A Side/B Side)	Yr	VG	VG+	NM
❑ VSD-79333	Sold American	1973	3.00	6.00	12.00

FRIZZELL, ALLEN

45s

ABC DOT

Number	Title (A Side/B Side)	Yr	VG	VG+	NM
❑ 17696	Honky Tonk Toys/Leave My Chapter Out	1977	—	3.00	6.00
❑ 17727	Lunch-Time Lovers/Till the Fiddle Comes Off That Wall	1977	—	3.00	6.00

EPIC

Number	Title (A Side/B Side)	Yr	VG	VG+	NM
❑ 34-04870	It'll Be Love by Morning/Mystery	1985	—	2.00	4.00
❑ 34-05567	Where the Cheaters Go/Everybody Misses You	1985	—	2.00	4.00

SOUND FACTORY

Number	Title (A Side/B Side)	Yr	VG	VG+	NM
❑ 429	Beer Joint Fever/Look What Thoughts Will Do	1981	—	3.00	6.00
❑ 447	She's Livin' It Up (And I'm Drinkin' 'Em Down)/Every Night I Take Her Memory to Bed	1981	—	3.00	6.00

FRIZZELL, DAVID

45s

CAPITOL

Number	Title (A Side/B Side)	Yr	VG	VG+	NM
❑ 3537	Last Night Was the First Night/Get Out of Town Before Sundown	1973	—	3.00	6.00
❑ 3589	Words Don't Come Easy/It's Too Late to Keep from Losing You	1973	—	3.00	6.00

Number	Title (A Side/B Side)	Yr	VG	VG+	NM
❑ 3684	Take Me One More Ride/The Bottle, Me, and Joann	1973	—	3.00	6.00
❑ 3787	I've Been Satisfied/Jesus and Joe	1973	—	3.00	6.00
❑ 3934	I'm the Bartender's Best Friend/You Won't Be Happy 'Til I'm Sad	1974	—	3.00	6.00
❑ 3983	I Gave Her Mine/She's Loved Me Away from You	1974	—	3.00	6.00
CARTWHEEL					
❑ 197	Country Pride/Kicking Sand	1971	2.00	4.00	8.00
❑ 202	Goodbye/500 Times	1971	2.00	4.00	8.00
❑ 211	Shake Hands with the Devil/(B-side unknown)	1972	2.00	4.00	8.00
COLUMBIA					
❑ 4-41425	Tag Along/I Hang My Head and Cry	1959	5.00	10.00	20.00
❑ 4-41460	Love Baby/My Kind of Love	1959	5.00	10.00	20.00
❑ 4-44995	Marley Purt Drive/Little Toy Trains	1969	2.50	5.00	10.00
❑ 4-45139	L.A. International Airport/Just Passing Through	1970	2.00	4.00	8.00
❑ 4-45238	I Just Can't Help Believing/Carmen Jones	1970	2.00	4.00	8.00
❑ 4-45325	In the Arms of Love/Hungry Row	1971	2.00	4.00	8.00
COMPLEAT					
❑ 168	Beautiful Body/All That I Am	1987	—	2.50	5.00
MCA					
❑ 40736	The Oleander/Lifetime Woman	1977	—	2.50	5.00
❑ 40786	Why You Been Gone So Long/Lifetime Woman	1977	—	2.50	5.00
❑ 40844	Jessie/The Oleander	1977	—	2.50	5.00
❑ 40877	Brand New Tennessee Waltz/Red, Red Wine	1978	—	2.50	5.00
NASHVILLE AMERICA					
❑ 1001	She Ain't Whistlin' Dixie/(B-side unknown)	1985	—	3.00	6.00
RSO					
❑ 856	A Case of You/Forever (And Always)	1976	—	2.50	5.00
VIVA					
❑ 29066	Country Music Love Affair/Maybe There's Love After All	1985	—	—	3.00
❑ 29158	No Way Jose/Who Dat (Messin' with That Woman of Mine)	1984	—	—	3.00
❑ 29232	When We Get Back to the Farm (That's When We Really Go to Town)/Settin' the Night on Fire	1984	—	—	3.00
❑ 29332	Who Dat/Honest Man	1984	—	—	3.00
❑ 29388	Black and White/All the King's Memories	1983	—	—	3.00
❑ 29498	A Million Light Beers Ago/Sweet Sweet Sin	1983	—	—	3.00
❑ 29617	Where Are You Spending Your Nights These Days/We're Back in Love Again	1983	—	—	3.00
WARNER BROS.					
❑ 29901	Lost My Baby Blues/Single and Alone	1982	—	2.00	4.00
❑ 49778	Lefty/Three Blind Hearts	1981	—	2.00	4.00
—B-side with Shelly West					
❑ 50063	I'm Gonna Hire a Wino to Decorate Our Home/She's Up to All Her Old Tricks Again	1982	—	2.00	4.00
Albums					
MCA					
❑ 27093	David Frizzell	1983	2.00	4.00	8.00
VIVA					
❑ 23907	On My Own Again	1983	2.00	4.00	8.00
❑ 25112	Solo	1984	2.00	4.00	8.00
WARNER BROS.					
❑ 23688	The Family's Fine, But This One's All Mine	1982	2.00	4.00	8.00

FRIZZELL, DAVID, AND SHELLY WEST

Also see each artist's individual listings.

Number	Title (A Side/B Side)	Yr	VG	VG+	NM
45s					
VIVA					
❑ 29048	Do Me Right/Easy, Soft and Slow	1985	—	—	3.00
❑ 29187	It's a Be Together Night/Straight from the Heart	1984	—	—	3.00
❑ 29404	Silent Partners/Confidential	1983	—	—	3.00
❑ 29544	Pleasure Island/Betcha Can't Cry Just One	1983	—	—	3.00
WARNER BROS.					
❑ 29756	Cajun Invitation/Yesterday's Lovers	1983	—	2.00	4.00
❑ 29850	Please Surrender/Being a Man, Being a Woman	1982	—	2.00	4.00
❑ 29980	I Just Came Here to Dance/Our Day Will Come	1982	—	2.00	4.00
❑ 49650	You're the Reason God Made Oklahoma/That's Where Lovers Go Wrong	1980	—	2.00	4.00
❑ 49745	A Texas State of Mind/Let's Duel	1981	—	2.00	4.00
❑ 49825	Husbands and Wives/Yours for the Asking	1981	—	2.00	4.00
❑ 50007	Another Honky Tonk Night on Broadway/Three Act Play	1982	—	2.00	4.00
Albums					
VIVA					
❑ 23907	In Session	1984	2.00	4.00	8.00
❑ 25148	Golden Duets (The Best of Frizzell & West)	1984	2.00	4.00	8.00
WARNER BROS.					
❑ BSK 3555	Carryin' On the Family Names	1981	2.50	5.00	10.00
❑ BSK 3643	The David Frizzell & Shelly West Album	1982	2.50	5.00	10.00
❑ 23754	Our Best to You	1983	2.50	5.00	10.00

FRIZZELL, LEFTY

Number	Title (A Side/B Side)	Yr	VG	VG+	NM
45s					
ABC					
❑ 11350	I Buy the Wine/Let Me Give Her the Flowers	1973	2.00	4.00	8.00
❑ 11387	I Can't Get Over You to Save My Life/Somebody's Words	1973	—	3.50	7.00
❑ 11416	I Never Go Around Mirrors/That's the Way It Goes	1974	—	3.50	7.00
❑ 11442	Railroad Lady/If I Had Half the Sense (A Fool Was Born With)	1974	—	3.50	7.00
❑ 12023	Lucky Arms/If She Just Helps Me Get Over You	1974	—	3.50	7.00
❑ 12061	Life's Like Poetry/Sittin' and Thinkin'	1975	—	3.50	7.00
❑ 12103	Falling/I Love You a Thousand Ways	1975	—	3.50	7.00
COLUMBIA					
❑ 38-04264	Get This Stranger Out of Me/This Just Ain't No Good Day for Leaving	1983	—	2.50	5.00
❑ 38-04480	Watermelon Time in Georgia/Everything Keeps Coming Back to You	1984	—	2.50	5.00
❑ 4-20739	If You've Got the Money, I've Got the Time/I Love You a Thousand Ways	1950	10.00	20.00	40.00
❑ 4-20772	Look What Thoughts Will Do/Shine, Shave, Shower (It's Saturday)	1951	6.25	12.50	25.00
❑ 4-20799	I Want to Be With You Always/My Baby's Just Like Money	1951	6.25	12.50	25.00
❑ 4-20837	Always Late (With Your Kisses)/Mom and Dad's Waltz	1951	6.25	12.50	25.00
❑ 4-20840	Blue Yodel #2/Treasures Untold	1951	5.00	10.00	20.00
❑ 4-20841	Brakeman's Blues/My Old Pal	1951	5.00	10.00	20.00
❑ 4-20842	Travellin' Blues/Blue Yodel #6	1951	6.25	12.50	25.00
❑ 4-20843	My Rough and Rowdy Ways/Lullaby Yodel	1951	5.00	10.00	20.00
—The above four comprise a box set (20842 was also available separately)					
❑ 4-20885	Give Me More, More, More (Of Your Kisses)/How Long Will It Take (To Stop Loving You)	1951	6.25	12.50	25.00
❑ 4-20911	Don't Stay Away (Till Love Grows Cold)/You're Here, So Everything's All Right	1952	6.25	12.50	25.00
❑ 4-20941	Don't Stay Away (Till Love Grows Cold)/Sad Singin', Slow Ridin'	1952	5.00	10.00	20.00
—B-side by Polly Possum; part of a 4-record various-artists box set					
❑ 4-20950	If You Can Spare the Time/It's Just You	1952	6.25	12.50	25.00
❑ 4-20958	If You've Got the Money, I've Got the Time/Look What Thoughts Will Do	1952	5.00	10.00	20.00
❑ 4-20959	I Love You a Thousand Ways/I Want to Be with You Always	1952	5.00	10.00	20.00
❑ 4-20960	Always Late (With Your Kisses)/Mom and Dad's Waltz	1952	5.00	10.00	20.00
❑ 4-20961	Don't Stay Away (Till Love Grows Cold)/If You Can Spare the Time	1952	5.00	10.00	20.00
—The above four comprise a box set					
❑ 4-20997	Forever (And Always)/I Know You're Lonesome While Waiting for Me	1952	6.25	12.50	25.00
❑ 4-21034	I'm an Old, Old Man (Tryin' to Live While I Can)/You're Just Mine (Only in My Dreams)	1952	6.25	12.50	25.00
❑ 4-21084	(Honey, Baby, Hurry) Bring Your Sweet Self Back to Me/Time Changes Things	1953	6.25	12.50	25.00
❑ 4-21100	Never No More Blues/Sleep Baby Sleep	1953	6.25	12.50	25.00
❑ 4-21101	California Blues/I'm Lonely and Blue	1953	6.25	12.50	25.00
❑ 4-21118	We Crucified Our Jesus/When It Comes to Measuring Love	1953	6.25	12.50	25.00
❑ 4-21142	Two Friends of Mine/Before You Go	1953	6.25	12.50	25.00
❑ 4-21169	Hopeless Love/Then I'll Come Back to You	1953	6.25	12.50	25.00
❑ 4-21194	Run 'Em Off/Darkest Moment	1953	6.25	12.50	25.00
❑ 4-21208	My Little Her and Him/I've Been Away Way Too Long	1954	6.25	12.50	25.00
❑ 4-21241	King Without a Queen/You Can Always Count on Me	1954	6.25	12.50	25.00
❑ 4-21284	You're Too Late/Two Hearts Broken Now	1954	6.25	12.50	25.00
❑ 4-21328	I Love You Mostly/Mama	1954	6.25	12.50	25.00
❑ 4-21366	Making Believe/A Forest Fire	1955	6.25	12.50	25.00
❑ 4-21393	I'll Sit Alone and Cry/Moonlight Darling and You	1955	6.25	12.50	25.00
❑ 4-21433	Sweet Lies/I'm Lost Between Right and Wrong	1955	6.25	12.50	25.00
❑ 4-21458	It Gets Late So Early/Your Tomorrows Will Never Come	1955	6.25	12.50	25.00
❑ 4-21488	First to Have a Second Chance/These Hands	1956	6.25	12.50	25.00
❑ 4-21506	Promises Promises/Today Is That Tomorrow	1956	6.25	12.50	25.00
❑ 4-21530	Just Can't Live That Fast/Waltz of the Angels	1956	6.25	12.50	25.00
❑ 4-21554	Heart's Highway/I'm a Boy Left Alone	1956	6.25	12.50	25.00
❑ 4-40818	Glad I Found You/Lullaby Waltz	1957	5.00	10.00	20.00
❑ 4-40867	From an Angel to a Devil/Now That You Are Gone	1957	5.00	10.00	20.00
❑ 4-40938	Is It Only That You're Lonely/No One to Talk To	1957	5.00	10.00	20.00
❑ 4-41080	Time Out for the Blues/Tell Me Dear	1957	5.00	10.00	20.00
❑ 4-41161	Silence/The Torch Within My Heart	1958	5.00	10.00	20.00
❑ 4-41268	Cigarettes and Coffee Blues/You're Humbuggin' Me	1958	5.00	10.00	20.00
❑ 4-41384	The Long Black Veil/Knock Again, True Love	1959	5.00	10.00	20.00
❑ 4-41455	Farther Than My Eyes Can See/Ballad of the Blue and Gray	1959	5.00	10.00	20.00
❑ 4-41635	She's Gone/My Blues Will Pass	1960	3.75	7.50	15.00
❑ 4-41751	What You Gonna Do Leroy/That's All I Can Remember	1960	3.75	7.50	15.00
❑ 4-41984	Looking for You/Heaven's Plan	1961	3.75	7.50	15.00
❑ 4-42253	I Feel Sorry for Me/So What, Let It Rain	1961	3.75	7.50	15.00
❑ 4-42521	Stranger/Just Passing Through	1962	3.75	7.50	15.00
❑ 4-42676	Forbidden Lovers/A Few Steps Away	1963	3.00	6.00	12.00
❑ 4-42839	Don't Let Her See Me Cry/James River	1963	3.00	6.00	12.00
❑ 4-42924	Saginaw, Michigan/When It Rains the Blues	1963	3.00	6.00	12.00
❑ 4-43051	The Nester/The Rider	1964	3.00	6.00	12.00
❑ 4-43169	'Gator Hollow/Make That One for the Road a Cup of Coffee	1964	3.00	6.00	12.00
❑ 4-43256	She's Gone Gone Gone/Confused	1965	2.50	5.00	10.00
❑ 4-43364	A Little Unfair/Love Looks Good on You	1965	2.50	5.00	10.00
❑ 4-43590	Writing on the Wall/Mama	1966	2.50	5.00	10.00
❑ 4-43747	I Just Couldn't See the Forest (For the Trees)/Everything Keeps Coming Back (But You)	1966	2.50	5.00	10.00
❑ 4-44023	You Gotta Be Puttin' Me On/A Song from a Lonely Heart	1967	2.50	5.00	10.00
❑ 4-44205	Get This Stranger Out of Me/Hobo's Pride	1967	2.50	5.00	10.00
❑ 4-44390	Anything You Can Spare/A Prayer on Your Lips	1967	2.50	5.00	10.00
❑ 4-44563	The Marriage Bit/When the Grass Grows Green Again	1968	2.50	5.00	10.00

Number	Title (A Side/B Side)	Yr	VG	VG+	NM
❑ 4-44692	Wasted Way of Life/Keep the Flowers Watered When I'm Gone	1968	2.50	5.00	10.00
❑ 4-44738	An Article from Life/Only Way to Fly	1969	2.50	5.00	10.00
❑ 4-44984	Honky Tonk Hill/Wasted Way of Life	1969	2.50	5.00	10.00
❑ 4-45145	My Baby Is a Tramp/She Brought Love, Sweet Love	1970	2.50	5.00	10.00
❑ 4-45197	Watermelon Time in Georgia/Out of You	1970	2.50	5.00	10.00
❑ 4-45310	Three Cheers for the Good Guys/I Must Be Getting Over You	1971	2.50	5.00	10.00
❑ 4-45347	Honyk Tonk Stardust Cowboy/What Am I Gonna Do	1971	2.50	5.00	10.00
❑ 4-45652	You, Babe/When It Rains the Blues	1972	2.50	5.00	10.00
❑ 4-52019	If You've Got the Money, I've Got the Time/I Love You a Thousand Ways	195?	3.75	7.50	15.00

—Early "Hall of Fame Series" issue with maroon label

Albums

ABC

Number	Title	Yr	VG	VG+	NM
❑ ABCX-799	Lefty	1974	7.50	15.00	30.00
—Original title					
❑ ABCX-799	The Legendary Lefty Frizzell	1974	5.00	10.00	20.00
—Revised title					
❑ AC-30035	The ABC Collection	1976	5.00	10.00	20.00

COLUMBIA

Number	Title	Yr	VG	VG+	NM
❑ CL 1342 [M]	The One and Only Lefty Frizzell	1959	30.00	60.00	120.00
❑ CL 2169 [M]	Saginaw, Michigan	1964	7.50	15.00	30.00
❑ CL 2386 [M]	The Sad Side of Love	1965	7.50	15.00	30.00
❑ CL 2488 [M]	Lefty Frizzell's Greatest Hits	1966	7.50	15.00	30.00
❑ CL 2772 [M]	Puttin' On	1967	12.50	25.00	50.00
❑ CS 8969 [S]	Saginaw, Michigan	1964	10.00	20.00	40.00
❑ CL 9019 [10]	Lefty Frizzell Sings the Songs of Jimmie Rodgers	1951	62.50	125.00	250.00
❑ CL 9021 [10]	Listen to Lefty	1952	62.50	125.00	250.00
❑ CS 9186 [S]	The Sad Side of Love	1965	10.00	20.00	40.00
❑ CS 9288 [S]	Lefty Frizzell's Greatest Hits	1966	10.00	20.00	40.00
—Red label, "360 Sound Stereo" at bottom					
❑ CS 9572 [S]	Puttin' On	1967	10.00	20.00	40.00
❑ C 32249	Lefty Frizzell Sings the Songs of Jimmie Rodgers	1973	5.00	10.00	20.00
❑ PC 33882	Remembering...The Greatest Hits of Lefty Frizzell	1975	5.00	10.00	20.00

HARMONY

Number	Title	Yr	VG	VG+	NM
❑ HL 7241 [M]	Lefty Frizzell Sings the Songs of Jimmie Rodgers	1960	7.50	15.00	30.00

FRUSHAY, RAY

45s

PARAMOUNT

Number	Title	Yr	VG	VG+	NM
❑ 0030	Santa Ana Winds/(B-side unknown)	1970	2.00	4.00	8.00
❑ 0069	Let the Heartaches Begin/(B-side unknown)	1970	2.00	4.00	8.00

WESTERN PRIDE

Number	Title	Yr	VG	VG+	NM
❑ 105	I Got Western Pride/Woman, Quit Walking Around in My Mind	1979	—	3.50	7.00
❑ 113	Pickin' Up Love/Dreamer's Room	1980	—	3.50	7.00

FUHRMAN, MICKI

45s

LOUISIANA HAYRIDE

Number	Title	Yr	VG	VG+	NM
❑ 785	Leave While I'm Sleeping/Big Bright Rainbow	1978	—	3.50	7.00

MCA

Number	Title	Yr	VG	VG+	NM
❑ 41057	Blue River of Tears/I Need You	1979	—	2.00	4.00
❑ 41220	Who Will Answer/I Want to Dance All Night Forever	1980	—	2.00	4.00
❑ 51005	Hold Me, Thrill Me, Kiss Me/Holding Me	1980	—	2.00	4.00
❑ 51057	Two Minus One/I Can't Find a Rope	1981	—	2.00	4.00
❑ 52012	You Win, I Lose/Never Gonna Fall in Love Again	1982	—	2.00	4.00
❑ 52059	How Do I Get to Wherever You Are/Never Gonna Fall in Love Again	1982	—	2.00	4.00
❑ 52321	I Bet You Never Thought I'd Go This Far/I Don't Want to Go Too Far	1983	—	2.00	4.00

Albums

CANAAN

Number	Title	Yr	VG	VG+	NM
❑ CAS 9855	Angels Watching Over Me	1979	2.50	5.00	10.00

DAYSPRING

Number	Title	Yr	VG	VG+	NM
❑ DST-4021	Look Again	1981	2.50	5.00	10.00

FULLER, JERRY

45s

ABC

Number	Title	Yr	VG	VG+	NM
❑ 12436	Salt on the Wound/No Time	1978	—	2.00	4.00

BELL

Number	Title	Yr	VG	VG+	NM
❑ 45233	Rhyme/Thumb Tripping	1972	—	2.50	5.00
❑ 45295	Bookends/(B-side unknown)	1972	—	2.50	5.00
❑ 45349	Lazy Susan/How Do We Stand	1973	—	2.50	5.00
❑ 45433	Arianne/(B-side unknown)	1974	—	2.50	5.00

CHALLENGE

Number	Title	Yr	VG	VG+	NM
❑ 9114	Guilty of Loving You/First Love Never Dies	1961	5.00	10.00	20.00
❑ 9128	The Place Where I Cry/Poor Little Heart	1961	5.00	10.00	20.00
❑ 9132	Wake Up Sleeping Beauty/Trust Me	1962	5.00	10.00	20.00
❑ 9148	Too Many People/Willingly, I'll Let You Go	1962	5.00	10.00	20.00
❑ 9161	Why Do They Say Goodbye/Let Me Be with You	1962	5.00	10.00	20.00
❑ 9184	Give My Love to Christy/Dear Teresa	1963	5.00	10.00	20.00
❑ 59052	Betty My Angel/Memories of You	1959	7.50	15.00	30.00
❑ 59057	Tennessee Waltz/Charlene	1959	5.00	10.00	20.00
❑ 59068	Two Loves Have I/I Dreamed About My Lover	1960	5.00	10.00	20.00
❑ 59074	Above and Beyond/One Heart	1960	5.00	10.00	20.00
—With Diane Maxwell					
❑ 59085	Gone for the Summer/Anna from Louisiana	1960	5.00	10.00	20.00
❑ 59104	Shy Away/Heavenly	1961	5.00	10.00	20.00
❑ 59217	I Only Came to Dance with You/Young Land	1963	5.00	10.00	20.00
❑ 59235	Footprints in the Snow/Hollywood Star	1964	3.75	7.50	15.00
❑ 59252	Don't Let Go/Roses Love Sunshine	1964	3.75	7.50	15.00
❑ 59269	The Killer/Mi Amora Mi Vidor	1965	3.75	7.50	15.00
❑ 59279	I Get Carried Away/Am I That Easy to Forget	1965	7.50	15.00	30.00
❑ 59307	Don't Look at Me Like That/What Happened to the Music	1965	3.75	7.50	15.00
❑ 59315	Man in Black/Master Plan	1965	3.75	7.50	15.00
❑ 59329	Double Life/Turn to Me	1966	6.25	12.50	25.00

COLUMBIA

Number	Title	Yr	VG	VG+	NM
❑ 4-45131	Could It Be/I Know We Can Make It	1970	2.00	4.00	8.00
❑ 4-45209	Go/If I Had a Mind To	1970	2.00	4.00	8.00

LIN

Number	Title	Yr	VG	VG+	NM
❑ 5011	Blue Memories/I Found a New Love	1958	7.50	15.00	30.00
❑ 5012	Do You Love Me/Teenage Love	1958	7.50	15.00	30.00
❑ 5015	A Certain Smile/Angel from Above	1958	7.50	15.00	30.00
❑ 5016	The Door Is Open/Through Eternity	1958	7.50	15.00	30.00
❑ 5019	Lipstick and Rouge/Mother Goose at the Bandstand	1959	7.50	15.00	30.00

MCA

Number	Title	Yr	VG	VG+	NM
❑ 41022	Lines/Over You	1979	—	2.00	4.00
❑ 41114	Don't Do Anything/Don't Tell Me	1979	—	2.00	4.00

Albums

LIN

Number	Title	Yr	VG	VG+	NM
❑ 100 [M]	Teenage Love	1960	62.50	125.00	250.00

MCA

Number	Title	Yr	VG	VG+	NM
❑ 3170	My Turn Now	1979	3.00	6.00	12.00

G

GABRIEL

45s

NSD

Number	Title	Yr	VG	VG+	NM
❑ 70	I Think I Could Love You (Better Than He Did)/Til I Stop Falling In	1980	—	3.00	6.00

RIDGETOP

Number	Title	Yr	VG	VG+	NM
❑ 01381	Friends Before Lovers/(B-side unknown)	1981	—	3.00	6.00

GALLIMORE, BYRON

45s

LITTLE GIANT

Number	Title	Yr	VG	VG+	NM
❑ 025	No Ordinary Woman/Simple Ways	1980	2.00	4.00	8.00

GALLION, BOB

Also see PATTI POWELL.

45s

HICKORY

Number	Title	Yr	VG	VG+	NM
❑ 1130	Loving You (Was Worth This Broken Heart)/Start All Over	1960	3.00	6.00	12.00
❑ 1145	One Way Street/Six Pallbearers	1961	3.00	6.00	12.00
❑ 1154	Sweethearts Again/You Don't Know (Or You Don't Care)	1961	3.00	6.00	12.00
❑ 1164	Honky Tonk World/Small Town Girl	1962	3.00	6.00	12.00
❑ 1181	Wall to Wall Love/Happy Birthday, My Darlin'	1962	3.00	6.00	12.00
❑ 1207	Him and Her/Two Out of Three	1963	3.00	6.00	12.00
❑ 1220	Ain't Got Time for Nothin'/Wrong Side of Town	1963	3.00	6.00	12.00
❑ 1239	The Biggest Break/Much Too Young to Die	1964	2.50	5.00	10.00
❑ 1276	You Really Know How to Hurt a Guy/Goin' Back to the Philippines	1964	2.50	5.00	10.00
❑ 1300	I Don't Have the Heart (To Disagree)/Thank the Devil for Hideaways	1965	2.50	5.00	10.00
❑ 1339	Hauling the Boys Around/Federal Aid	1965	2.50	5.00	10.00
❑ 1367	World by the Tail/Not Once But a Hundred Times	1966	2.50	5.00	10.00
❑ 1421	Happy Birthday, My Darling/I've Got Better at Home	1966	2.50	5.00	10.00
❑ 1455	I'll Do That Again/I Can't Get Love at Home	1967	2.50	5.00	10.00

MGM

Number	Title	Yr	VG	VG+	NM
❑ 12195	My Square Dancin' Mama/Your Wild Life's Gonna...	1956	30.00	60.00	120.00
❑ 12327	A Fool in Love/Trademark on What I've Found	1956	5.00	10.00	20.00
❑ 12407	Hey, Mr. Bartender/You've Gotta Have a Heartbreak	1957	5.00	10.00	20.00
❑ 12466	Out of a Honky Tonk/I Want Her Blues	1957	5.00	10.00	20.00
❑ 12628	I Miss You/Baby, Love Me	1958	7.50	15.00	30.00
❑ 12700	That's What I Tell My Heart/Run Boy	1958	3.75	7.50	15.00
❑ 12777	You Take the Table and I'll Take the Chairs/Out of a Honky Tonk	1959	3.75	7.50	15.00
❑ 12858	Hey Joe/Froggy Went a-Courtin'	1959	3.75	7.50	15.00

UNITED ARTISTS

Number	Title	Yr	VG	VG+	NM
❑ 50309	Pick a Little Happy Song/Happy Anniversary	1968	2.00	4.00	8.00
❑ 50557	Pretty Womanitis/Heartbreak Analysis	1969	2.00	4.00	8.00

Number	Title (A Side/B Side)	Yr	VG	VG+	NM

GALWAY, JAMES, AND SYLVIA

Galway, a renowned classical flutist, is otherwise outside the scope of this book. Also see SYLVIA (2).

45s

RCA

Number	Title (A Side/B Side)	Yr	VG	VG+	NM
❑ PB-13441	The Wayward Wind/Shenandoah	1983	—	—	3.00

GARDNER, BROTHER DAVE

45s

Number	Title (A Side/B Side)	Yr	VG	VG+	NM
DECCA					
❑ 30548	Hop Along Rock/All By Myself	1958	5.00	10.00	20.00
❑ 30627	Slick Slacks/Wild Streak	1958	10.00	20.00	40.00
OJ					
❑ 1002	White Silver Sands/Fat Charlie	1957	3.75	7.50	15.00
❑ 1006	Love Is My Business/Mad Witch	1958	3.75	7.50	15.00
RCA VICTOR					
❑ 47-7876	Coward at the Alamo/You Are My Love	1961	2.50	5.00	10.00

Albums

Number	Title (A Side/B Side)	Yr	VG	VG+	NM
4 STAR					
❑ 4S 75003	Brother Dave Gardner's New Comedy Album	1976	5.00	10.00	20.00
CAPITOL					
❑ ST 1867 [S]	It Don't Make No Difference	1963	6.25	12.50	25.00
❑ T 1867 [M]	It Don't Make No Difference	1963	5.00	10.00	20.00
❑ ST 2055 [S]	It's All in How You Look at It	1964	6.25	12.50	25.00
❑ T 2055 [M]	It's All in How You Look at It	1964	5.00	10.00	20.00
RCA VICTOR					
❑ LPM-2083 [M]	Rejoice, Dear Hearts!	1960	5.00	10.00	20.00
❑ LSP-2083(e) [S]	Rejoice, Dear Hearts!	196?	6.25	12.50	25.00
❑ LPM-2239 [M]	Kick Thy Own Self	1960	5.00	10.00	20.00
❑ LSP-2239(e) [S]	Kick Thy Own Self	196?	6.25	12.50	25.00
❑ LPM-2335 [M]	Ain't That Weird?	1961	5.00	10.00	20.00
❑ LSP-2335 [S]	Ain't That Weird?	1961	6.25	12.50	25.00
❑ LPM-2498 [M]	Did You Ever?	1962	5.00	10.00	20.00
❑ LSP-2498 [S]	Did You Ever?	1962	6.25	12.50	25.00
❑ LPM-2628 [M]	All Seriousness Aside	1963	5.00	10.00	20.00
❑ LSP-2628 [S]	All Seriousness Aside	1963	6.25	12.50	25.00
❑ LPM-2761 [M]	It's Bigger Than Both of Us	1963	5.00	10.00	20.00
❑ LSP-2761 [S]	It's Bigger Than Both of Us	1963	6.25	12.50	25.00
❑ LPM-2852 [M]	Best of Dave Gardner	1964	5.00	10.00	20.00
❑ LSP-2852 [S]	Best of Dave Gardner	1964	6.25	12.50	25.00
TONKA					
❑ TLP 713	Out Front	1969	5.00	10.00	20.00
TOWER					
❑ ST 5050 [S]	Hip-ocracy	1966	5.00	10.00	20.00
❑ T 5050 [M]	Hip-ocracy	1966	3.75	7.50	15.00
❑ ST 5075 [S]	It Don't Make No Difference	1967	5.00	10.00	20.00
❑ T 5075 [M]	It Don't Make No Difference	1967	3.75	7.50	15.00

GARLAND, HANK

45s

Number	Title (A Side/B Side)	Yr	VG	VG+	NM
DECCA					
❑ 9-46368	I'm Crying/Seventh and Union	1951	6.25	12.50	25.00
❑ 9-46382	Hillbilly Express/E String Rag	1951	6.25	12.50	25.00

Albums

Number	Title (A Side/B Side)	Yr	VG	VG+	NM
COLUMBIA					
❑ CL 1572 [M]	Jazz Winds from a New Direction	1961	7.50	15.00	30.00
❑ CL 1913 [M]	The Unforgettable Guitar of Hank Garland	1962	7.50	15.00	30.00
❑ CS 8372 [S]	Jazz Winds from a New Direction	1961	10.00	20.00	40.00
❑ CS 8713 [S]	The Unforgettable Guitar of Hank Garland	1962	10.00	20.00	40.00
HARMONY					
❑ HL 7231 [M]	Velvet Guitar	196?	5.00	10.00	20.00
❑ HS 11028 [S]	Velvet Guitar	196?	6.25	12.50	25.00
SESAC					
❑ SN-2301/2 [M]	Subtle Swing	196?	25.00	50.00	100.00

GARNETT, GALE

45s

Number	Title (A Side/B Side)	Yr	VG	VG+	NM
COLUMBIA					
❑ 44479	Breaking Through/Fall in Love Again	1968	—	2.50	5.00
RCA VICTOR					
❑ 47-8388	We'll Sing in the Sunshine/Prism Song	1964	2.50	5.00	10.00
❑ 47-8472	Lovin' Place/I Used to Live Here	1964	2.00	4.00	8.00
❑ 47-8472 [PS]	Lovin' Place/I Used to Live Here	1964	2.00	4.00	8.00
❑ 47-8549	I'll Cry Alone/Where Do You Go to Go Away	1965	2.00	4.00	8.00
❑ 47-8668	I'm Gonna Sit Right Down and Write Myself a Letter/Why Am I Standing in the Window	1965	2.00	4.00	8.00
❑ 47-8824	This Kind of Love/Oh There'll Be Laughter	1966	—	3.00	6.00
❑ 47-8961	It's Been a Lonely Summer/You've Got to Fall in Love Again	1966	—	3.00	6.00
❑ 47-9020	The Sun Is Gray/I Make Him Fly	1966	—	3.00	6.00
❑ 47-9196	Over the Rainbow/The Cats I Know	1967	—	3.00	6.00

Albums

Number	Title (A Side/B Side)	Yr	VG	VG+	NM
COLUMBIA					
❑ CL 2825 [M]	An Audience with the King of Wands	1968	5.00	10.00	20.00
❑ CS 9625 [S]	An Audience with the King of Wands	1968	3.75	7.50	15.00
❑ CS 9760	Sausalito Heliport	1969	3.75	7.50	15.00
RCA VICTOR					
❑ LPM-2833 [M]	My Kind of Folk Songs	1964	10.00	20.00	40.00
—Black and white/blueish cover					
❑ LPM-2833 [M]	My Kind of Folk Songs	1965	3.75	7.50	15.00
—Color photo on cover					
❑ LSP-2833 [S]	My Kind of Folk Songs	1964	12.50	25.00	50.00
—Black and white/blueish cover					
❑ LSP-2833 [S]	My Kind of Folk Songs	1965	5.00	10.00	20.00
—Color photo on cover					
❑ LPM-3305 [M]	Lovin' Place	1965	3.75	7.50	15.00
❑ LSP-3305 [S]	Lovin' Place	1965	5.00	10.00	20.00
❑ LPM-3325 [M]	The Many Faces of Gale Garnett	1965	3.75	7.50	15.00
❑ LSP-3325 [S]	The Many Faces of Gale Garnett	1965	5.00	10.00	20.00
❑ LPM-3498 [M]	Variety Is the Spice of Gale Garnett	1966	3.75	7.50	15.00
❑ LSP-3498 [S]	Variety Is the Spice of Gale Garnett	1966	5.00	10.00	20.00
❑ LPM-3586 [M]	New Adventures	1966	3.75	7.50	15.00
❑ LSP-3586 [S]	New Adventures	1966	5.00	10.00	20.00
❑ LPM-3747 [M]	Flying and Rainbows and Love	1967	6.25	12.50	25.00
❑ LSP-3747 [S]	Flying and Rainbows and Love	1967	5.00	10.00	20.00

GARRETT, PAT

45s

Number	Title (A Side/B Side)	Yr	VG	VG+	NM
COMPLEAT					
❑ 157	Rockin' My Country Heart/Daddy What Did I Do Wrong	1986	—	2.50	5.00
GOLD DUST					
❑ 101	Sexy Ole Lady/Humpty Dumpty	1980	—	3.00	6.00
❑ 102	Your Magic Touch/How Can I Please You	1980	—	3.00	6.00
❑ 104	Everlovin' Woman/(B-side unknown)	1981	—	3.00	6.00
KANSA					
❑ 608	Coldest Toes in Town/I've Gotta Touch You	1977	—	3.50	7.00
❑ 609	A Little Something on the Side/So Alone Again	1977	—	3.50	7.00
—May also exist as Kansa 3000					
MDJ					
❑ 73087	Suck It In/(B-side unknown)	1987	—	3.00	6.00

GARRETT, SNUFF, 'S TEXAS OPERA COMPANY

Albums

Number	Title (A Side/B Side)	Yr	VG	VG+	NM
RANWOOD					
❑ 8158	Classical Country	1976	2.50	5.00	10.00

GARRISON, AL

45s

Number	Title (A Side/B Side)	Yr	VG	VG+	NM
MOTION					
❑ 1032	Where Do I Go from Here/(B-side unknown)	1987	—	3.00	6.00

GARRISON, GLEN

45s

Number	Title (A Side/B Side)	Yr	VG	VG+	NM
CREST					
❑ 1047	Lovin' Lorene/You're My Darling	1958	15.00	30.00	60.00
IMPERIAL					
❑ 66191	Green to Blue/You Can't Win 'Em All	1966	2.50	5.00	10.00
❑ 66215	Where Do I Go from Here/Strong and Handsome, Sweet and Simple Side	1966	2.50	5.00	10.00
❑ 66230	Listen, They're Playing My Song/My New Creation	1967	2.50	5.00	10.00
❑ 66257	Goodbye Swingers/Hello Mama	1967	2.50	5.00	10.00
❑ 66279	Your Side of Me/If I Lived Here (I'd Be Home Now)	1968	2.00	4.00	8.00
❑ 66300	I'll Be Your Baby Tonight/You Know I Love You	1968	2.00	4.00	8.00
❑ 66333	That Lucky Old Sun/She Thinks I Still Care	1968	2.00	4.00	8.00
❑ 66401	Goodnight Irene/Change Me	1969	2.00	4.00	8.00
LODE					
❑ 106	Pony Tail Girl/Ballad of Hank Gordon	1959	15.00	30.00	60.00

Albums

Number	Title (A Side/B Side)	Yr	VG	VG+	NM
IMPERIAL					
❑ LP-9346 [M]	Country Country	1967	3.75	7.50	15.00
❑ LP-12346 [S]	Country Country	1967	3.75	7.50	15.00
❑ LP-12378	If I Lived Here	1968	3.75	7.50	15.00

GARRON, JESS

45s

Number	Title (A Side/B Side)	Yr	VG	VG+	NM
CHARTA					
❑ 131	Lo Que Sea (What Ever May the Future Be)/Those Good Times Are Over	1979	—	3.00	6.00
❑ 136	It's Summer Time/You Can't Love a Woman (Who Doesn't Want to Be Loved)	1979	—	3.00	6.00
❑ 140	That Old Piano Man/Tomorrow's a Brand New Day	1979	—	3.00	6.00
❑ 146	Sunshine Girl/Weary Lonesome Song	1980	—	3.00	6.00
❑ 152	Why Did You Do It to Me/You'll Never Do It Again	1980	—	3.00	6.00
❑ 158	Get Down Country Music/Weary Lonesome Song	1981	—	3.00	6.00

GATLIN, LARRY, AND THE GATLIN BROTHERS BAND

Includes records issued as "Larry Gatlin"; "Larry Gatlin with Family and Friends"; "The Gatlins: Larry, Steve, Rudy"; "The Gatlin Quartet."

45s

Number	Title (A Side/B Side)	Yr	VG	VG+	NM
CAPITOL					
❑ 7PRO-79053	Boogie and Beethoven (same on both sides)	1990	—	2.50	5.00
—Vinyl is promo only					
❑ 7PRO-79378	Country Girl Heart (same on both sides)	1991	—	2.50	5.00
—Vinyl is promo only					
COLUMBIA					
❑ 02123	Wind Is Bound to Change/Help Yourself to Me	1981	—	—	3.00
❑ 02522	What Are We Doin' Lonesome/You Wouldn't Know Love	1981	—	—	3.00
❑ 02698	In Like With Each Other/Hard Workin' Hands	1982	—	—	3.00
❑ 02910	She Used to Sing on Sunday/Can't Take It With You	1982	—	—	3.00
❑ 03159	Sure Feels Like Love/Home Is Where the Healin' Is	1982	—	—	3.00
❑ 03356	Steps/Sweet Baby Jesus	1982	—	2.00	4.00

Number	Title (A Side/B Side)	Yr	VG	VG+	NM
❑ CNR-03364	Sure Feels Like Love	1982	—	2.50	5.00
—One-sided budget release					
❑ 03517	Almost Called Her Baby By Mistake/Somethin' Like Each Other's Arms	1983	—	—	3.00
❑ 03885	Easy on the Eye/Anything But Leavin'	1983	—	—	3.00
❑ 04105	Houston (Means I'm One Day Closer to You)/The Whole Wide World Stood Still	1983	—	—	3.00
❑ 04395	Denver/A Dream That Got Out of Hand	1984	—	—	3.00
❑ 04533	The Lady Takes the Cowboy Everytime/It's Me	1984	—	—	3.00
❑ 05632	Runaway Go Home/Nothing But Your Love Matters	1985	—	—	3.00
❑ 05764	Nothing But Your Love Matters/When the Night Closes In	1985	—	—	3.00
❑ 06252	She Used to Be Somebody's Baby/Being Alone	1986	—	—	3.00
❑ 06592	Talkin' to the Moon/Give Me a Chance	1986	—	—	3.00
❑ 07088	From Time to Time (It Feels Like Love Again)/ Texas (Is What Life Is All About)	1987	—	—	3.00
—With Janie Frickie					
❑ 07320	Changin' Partners/Got a Lot of Women on His Hands	1987	—	—	3.00
❑ 07747	Love of a Lifetime/Don't Blame Me for Colorado	1988	—	—	3.00
❑ 07998	Alive and Well/One on One	1988	—	—	3.00
❑ 11066	All the Gold in California/How Much Is Man Supposed to Take	1979	—	2.00	4.00
❑ 11169	The Midnight Choir/Hold Me Closer	1980	—	2.00	4.00
❑ 11219	Taking Somebody With Me When I Fall/Piece by Piece	1980	—	2.00	4.00
❑ 11282	We're Number One/Can't Cry Anymore	1980	—	2.00	4.00
❑ 11369	Take Me to Your Lovin' Place/Straight to My Heart	1980	—	2.00	4.00
❑ 11438	It Don't Get No Better Than This/Straight to My Heart	1981	—	2.00	4.00
MONUMENT					
❑ 8550	Look to the Sunrise/N.Y.C.	1972	—	3.50	7.00
—As "The Gatlins"					
❑ 8568	Come On In/The Way I Did Before	1973	—	3.00	6.00
—As "The Gatlins"					
❑ 8569	My Mind's Gone to Memphis/Try to Win a Friend	1973	—	2.50	5.00
❑ 8584	Sweet Becky Walker/You've Been Handed Down to Me	1973	—	2.50	5.00
❑ 8602	Bitter They Are Harder They Fall/Silver Threads and Golden Needles	1974	—	2.50	5.00
❑ 8622	Delta Dirt/Those Also Love	1974	—	2.50	5.00
❑ 8643	Jannie/Penny Annie	1975	—	2.50	5.00
❑ 8657	Let's Turn the Lights On/Takin' a Chance on You	1975	—	2.50	5.00
❑ 8680	Broken Lady/Heart	1975	—	2.50	5.00
❑ 8696	Warm and Tender/The Heart Is Quicker Than the Eye	1976	—	2.50	5.00
❑ 45201	Statues Without Hearts/What Will I Do Now	1976	—	2.00	4.00
❑ 45212	Anything But Leavin'/Take Back "It's Over"	1977	—	2.00	4.00
❑ 45221	I Don't Wanna Cry/Mercy River	1977	—	2.00	4.00
❑ 45226	Love Is Just a Game/Everytime a Plane Flies Over Our House	1977	—	2.00	4.00
❑ 45234	I Just Wish You Were Someone I Love/Kiss It All Goodbye	1977	—	2.00	4.00
❑ 45249	Night Time Magic/It's Love at Last	1978	—	2.00	4.00
❑ 45259	Do It Again Tonight/Cold Day in Hell	1978	—	2.00	4.00
❑ 45270	I've Done Enough Dyin' Today/Nothin' You Do	1978	—	2.00	4.00
UNIVERSAL					
❑ 53501	When She Holds Me/Go or Stay	1989	—	—	3.00
❑ UVL-66005	I Might Be What You're Looking For/Rain	1989	—	—	3.00
❑ UVL-66021	#1 Heartache Place/Your Door	1989	—	—	3.00
Albums					
COLUMBIA					
❑ JC 36250	Straight Ahead	1979	2.50	5.00	10.00
❑ JC 36488	Larry Gatlin's Greatest Hits, Volume 1	1980	2.00	4.00	8.00
—Reissue of Monument 7628					
❑ PC 36541	The Pilgrim	1980	2.00	4.00	8.00
—Reissue of Monument 6632					
❑ JC 36582	Help Yourself	1980	2.50	5.00	10.00
❑ PC 36582	Help Yourself	198?	2.00	4.00	8.00
—Budget-line reissue					
❑ PC 36582	Help Yourself	198?	2.00	4.00	8.00
—Budget-line reissue					
❑ FC 37464	Not Guilty	1981	2.50	5.00	10.00
❑ PC 37464	Not Guilty	198?	2.00	4.00	8.00
—Budget-line reissue					
❑ FC 38135	Sure Feels Like Love	1982	2.50	5.00	10.00
❑ PC 38135	Sure Feels Like Love	198?	2.00	4.00	8.00
—Budget-line reissue					
❑ FC 38183	A Gatlin Family Christmas	1982	3.00	6.00	12.00
❑ PC 38183	A Gatlin Family Christmas	198?	2.00	4.00	8.00
—Budget-line reissue					
❑ PC 38336	Love Is Just a Game	1982	2.00	4.00	8.00
—Reissue of Monument 7616					
❑ PC 38337	Larry Gatlin with Family and Friends	1982	2.00	4.00	8.00
—Reissue of Monument 6634					
❑ PC 38338	High Time	1982	2.00	4.00	8.00
—Reissue of Monument 6644					
❑ PC 38339	Rain-Rainbow	1982	2.00	4.00	8.00
—Reissue of Monumnet 6633					
❑ PC 38340	Oh! Brother	1982	2.00	4.00	8.00
—Reissue of Monumnet 7626					
❑ FC 38923	Larry Gatlin's Greatest Hits, Volume 2	1983	2.50	5.00	10.00
❑ FC 39291	Houston to Denver	1984	2.50	5.00	10.00
❑ FC 40068	Smile!	1985	2.50	5.00	10.00
❑ FC 40431	Partners	1986	2.50	5.00	10.00
❑ FC 40905	Alive and Well...Living in the Land of Dreams	1988	2.50	5.00	10.00
❑ FC 44471	The Gatlin Brothers' Biggest Hits (1984-88)	1989	2.50	5.00	10.00
❑ HC 48135	Sure Feels Like Love	1982	62.50	125.00	250.00
—Half-speed mastered edition					
MONUMENT					
❑ 6632	The Pilgrim	1976	3.00	6.00	12.00
—Reissue of KZ 32571					
❑ 6633	Rain-Rainbow	1976	3.00	6.00	12.00
—Reissue of KZ 33069					
❑ 6634	Larry Gatlin with Family and Friends	1976	3.00	6.00	12.00
❑ 6644	High Time	1977	3.00	6.00	12.00
❑ 7616	Love Is Just a Game	1978	3.00	6.00	12.00
❑ 7626	Oh! Brother	1978	3.00	6.00	12.00
❑ 7628	Larry Gatlin's Greatest Hits	1978	3.00	6.00	12.00
❑ KZ 32571	The Pilgrim	1974	3.75	7.50	15.00
❑ KZ 33069	Rain-Rainbow	1974	3.75	7.50	15.00
SWORD & SHIELD					
❑ 9009 [M]	The Old Country Church	1961	25.00	50.00	100.00
—As "The Gatlin Quartet" (wisth sister Donna joining Larry, Rudy and Steve)					

GATTIS, KEITH

45s

Number	Title (A Side/B Side)	Yr	VG	VG+	NM
RCA					
❑ 64488	Little Drops of My Heart/Only Lonely Fool	1996	—	—	3.00
❑ 64574	Real Deal/Little Drops of My Heart	1996	—	—	3.00
❑ 65310	Titanic/Real Deal	1997	—	—	3.00

GAULT, LENNY

45s

Number	Title (A Side/B Side)	Yr	VG	VG+	NM
KING COAL					
❑ 03	The Honky-Tonks Are Calling Me Again/I'm Gonna Leave	1979	—	3.00	6.00
MRC					
❑ 1020	Turn On the Bright Lights/When a Woman Cries	1978	—	3.00	6.00
❑ 1024	I Just Need a Coke (To Get the Whiskey Down)/ Steppin' Aside Just Ain't My Style	1978	—	3.00	6.00

GAYLE, CRYSTAL

45s

Number	Title (A Side/B Side)	Yr	VG	VG+	NM
CAPITOL NASHVILLE					
❑ 7PRO-79054	Everybody's Reaching Out for Someone (same on both sides)	1990	—	2.50	5.00
—Vinyl is promo only					
❑ 7PRO-79256	Never Ending Song of Love (same on both sides)	1990	—	2.50	5.00
—Vinyl is promo only					
COLUMBIA					
❑ 02078	Too Many Lovers/Help Yourself to Each Other	1981	—	2.00	4.00
❑ 02523	The Woman in Me/Crying in the Rain	1981	—	2.00	4.00
❑ 02718	You Never Gave Up on Me/Tennessee	1982	—	2.00	4.00
❑ 03048	Livin' in These Troubled Times/Ain't No Sunshine	1982	—	2.00	4.00
❑ 04093	Keepin' Power/Half the Way	1983	—	2.00	4.00
❑ 11087	Half the Way/Room for One More	1979	—	2.00	4.00
❑ 11198	It's Like We Never Said Goodbye/Don't Go My Love	1980	—	2.00	4.00
❑ 11270	The Blue Side/The Danger Zone	1980	—	2.00	4.00
❑ 11359	If You Ever Change Your Mind/I Just Can't Leave Your Love Alone	1980	—	2.00	4.00
❑ 11436	Take It Easy/Ain't No Love in the Heart of the City	1981	—	2.00	4.00
DECCA					
❑ 32721	I've Cried (The Blue Right Out of My Eyes)/ Sparkling Look of Love	1970	2.00	4.00	8.00
❑ 32925	Everybody Oughta Cry/MRS Degree	1972	2.00	4.00	8.00
❑ 32969	I Hope You're Havin' Better Luck Than Me/Too Far	1972	2.00	4.00	8.00
ELEKTRA					
❑ 69893	'Til I Gain Control Again/Easier Said Than Done	1982	—	2.00	4.00
❑ 69893 [PS]	'Til I Gain Control Again/Easier Said Than Done	1982	—	2.00	4.00
❑ 69936	You and I/All My Life, All My Love	1982	—	2.00	4.00
—A-side: With Eddie Rabbitt; B-side by Eddie Rabbitt solo					
MCA					
❑ 40016	Clock on the Wall/Show Me How	1973	—	3.00	6.00
❑ 40837	I've Cried (The Blue Right Out of My Eyes)/ Sparklin' Look of Love	1977	—	3.00	6.00
UNITED ARTISTS					
❑ XW428	Restless/Layback Lover	1974	—	2.50	5.00
❑ XW555	Wrong Road Again/They Come Out at Night	1974	—	2.50	5.00
❑ XW600	Beyond You/Loving You So Long Now	1975	—	2.50	5.00
❑ XW680	This Is My Year for Mexico/When I Dream	1975	—	2.50	5.00
❑ XW740	Somebody Loves You/Coming Closer	1975	—	2.50	5.00
❑ XW781	I'll Get Over You/High Time	1976	—	2.50	5.00
❑ XW838	One More Time/Oh My Soul	1976	—	2.50	5.00
❑ XW883	You Never Miss a Real Good Thing (Till He Says Goodbye)/Forgetting About You	1976	—	2.50	5.00
❑ XW948	I'll Do It All Over Again/I'm Not So Far Away	1977	—	2.50	5.00
❑ XW1016	Don't It Make My Brown Eyes Blue/It's All Right with Me	1977	—	2.00	4.00
❑ XW1136	Ready for the Times to Get Better/Beyond You	1978	—	2.00	4.00
❑ XW1146	I'll Get Over You/The Wrong Road Again	1978	—	2.00	4.00
—Reissue					
❑ XW1147	Somebody Loves You/You Never Miss a Real Good Thing (Till He Says Goodbye)	1978	—	2.00	4.00
—Reissue					
❑ XW1148	Don't It Make My Brown Eyes Blue/The Green Door	1978	—	2.00	4.00
—Reissue					

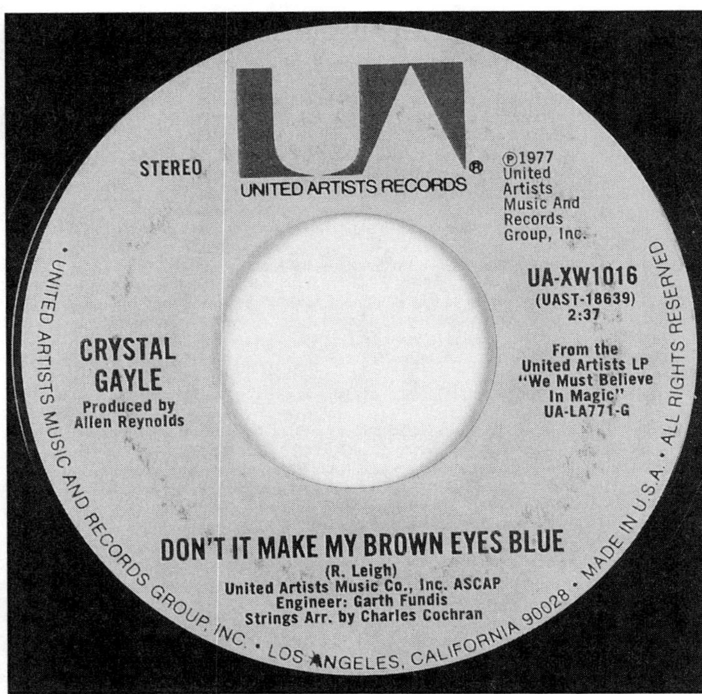

Highly recognizable for her extremely long hair, Crystal Gayle – a younger sister of Loretta Lynn – was a consistent hitmaker from 1976-87, and also made the pop charts with some consistency. (Top left) Her first No. 1 single was in 1976 with "I'll Get Over You." (Top right) Far and away the biggest hit of Gayle's career was "Don't It Make My Brown Eyes Blue." It peaked at No. 1 on the country charts and got to No. 2 on the pop charts, kept out of the top spot only by Debby Boone's "You Light Up My Life." (Bottom left) For someone as successful as she was, Gayle did a fair amount of label-hopping. Her first solo single on Elektra, after about three years on Columbia, was "'Til I Gain Control Again," which hit the top in early 1983. (Bottom right) Some time after all the Elektra country artists were re-assigned to Warner Bros., Gayle recorded "Makin' Up for Lost Time" with labelmate Gary Morris for a No. 1 duet. It was the hit song from an album inspired by the "Dallas" prime-time soap opera.

Number	Title (A Side/B Side)	Yr	VG	VG+	NM
❑ XW1149	I Wanna Come Back to You/One More Time	1978	—	2.00	4.00
—Reissue					
❑ XW1150	I'll Do It All Over Again/This Is My Year for Mexico	1978	—	2.00	4.00
—Reissue					
❑ XW1214	Talking in Your Sleep/Paintin' This Old Town Blue	1978	—	2.00	4.00
❑ XW1259	Why Have You Left the One You Left Me For/Cry Me a River	1978	—	2.00	4.00
❑ XW1288	When I Dream/Hello I Love You	1979	—	2.00	4.00
❑ XW1306	Your Kisses Will/Time Will Prove I'm Right	1979	—	2.00	4.00
❑ 1329	Your Old Cold Shoulder/We Should Be Together	1979	—	2.00	4.00
❑ 1347	Come Home Daddy/River Road	1980	—	2.00	4.00
❑ 1362	Heart Mender/This Is My Year for Mexico	1980	—	2.00	4.00
WARNER BROS.					
❑ 27682	Tennessee Nights/When Love Is New	1988	—	—	3.00
❑ 27811	Nobody's Angel/When Love Is New	1988	—	—	3.00
❑ 28209	Only Love Can Save Me Now/Till I Gain Control Again	1987	—	—	3.00
❑ 28210	Oh Holy Night/I'll Be Home for Christmas	1987	—	2.00	4.00
❑ 28409	Nobody Should Have to Love You This Way/A Little Bit Closer	1987	—	—	3.00
❑ 28499	I Still Hear the Music of Nashville/I Still Hear the Music of Nashville (Part 2)	1987	—	—	3.00
❑ 28518	Straight to the Heart/Do I Have to Say Goodbye	1986	—	—	3.00
❑ 28555	Have Yourself a Merry Little Christmas/Silver Bells	1986	—	2.00	4.00
❑ 28689	Cry/Crazy in the Heart	1986	—	—	3.00
❑ 28963	A Long and Lasting Love/Someone Like You	1985	—	—	3.00
❑ 29050	Nobody Wants to Be Alone/Coming to the Dance	1985	—	—	3.00
❑ 29151	Me Against the Night/You Made a Fool of Me	1984	—	2.00	4.00
❑ 29254	Turning Away/On Our Way to Love	1984	—	2.00	4.00
❑ 29356	I Don't Wanna Lose Your Love/Victim or a Fool	1984	—	2.00	4.00
❑ 29452	The Sound of Goodbye/Take Me Home	1983	—	2.00	4.00
❑ 29582	Baby, What About You/He Is Beautiful to Me	1983	—	2.00	4.00
❑ 29719	Our Love Is On the Faultline/Deeper in the Fire	1983	—	2.00	4.00
Albums					
COLUMBIA					
❑ JC 36203	Miss the Mississippi	1979	2.50	5.00	10.00
❑ PC 36203	Miss the Mississippi	198?	2.00	4.00	8.00
—Budget-line reissue					
❑ JC 36512	These Days	1980	2.50	5.00	10.00
❑ PC 36512	These Days	198?	2.00	4.00	8.00
—Budget-line reissue					
❑ FC 37438	Hollywood, Tennessee	1981	2.50	5.00	10.00
❑ PC 37438	Hollywood, Tennessee	198?	2.00	4.00	8.00
—Budget-line reissue					
❑ FC 38803	Crystal Gayle's Greatest Hits	1983	2.50	5.00	10.00
ELEKTRA					
❑ 60200	True Love	1982	2.50	5.00	10.00
LIBERTY					
❑ LMAS-858	When I Dream	1981	2.00	4.00	8.00
—Reissue of UA 858					
❑ LOO-1034	Favorites	1981	2.00	4.00	8.00
—Reissue of UA 1034					
❑ LOO-1080	A Woman's Heart	1981	2.50	5.00	10.00
❑ LN-10002	Crystal Gayle	1981	2.00	4.00	8.00
❑ LN-10003	Somebody Loves You	1981	2.00	4.00	8.00
—Budget-line reissue of UA 543					
❑ LN-10004	Crystal	1981	2.00	4.00	8.00
—Budget-line reissue of UA 614					
❑ LN-10005	We Must Believe in Magic	1981	2.00	4.00	8.00
—Budget-line reissue of UA 771					
❑ LN-10006	We Should Be Together	1980	2.00	4.00	8.00
—Budget-line reissue					
❑ LN-10150	Classic Crystal	1982	2.00	4.00	8.00
—Budget-line reissue of UA 982					
❑ LN-10227	When I Dream	1984	2.00	4.00	8.00
—Budget-line reissue					
❑ LN-10229	Favorites	1984	2.00	4.00	8.00
—Budget-line reissue					
MCA					
❑ 2334	I've Cried the Blue Right Out of My Eyes	1977	2.50	5.00	10.00
—Reissue of Decca material					
❑ 37077	I've Cried the Blue Right Out of My Eyes	198?	2.00	4.00	8.00
—Budget-line reissue					
MOBILE FIDELITY					
❑ 1-043	We Must Believe in Magic	1981	5.00	10.00	20.00
—Audiophile vinyl					
NAUTILUS					
❑ NR-36	When I Dream	198?	7.50	15.00	30.00
—Audiophile vinyl					
PAIR					
❑ PDL2-1083 [(2)]	Country Pure	1986	3.00	6.00	12.00
❑ PDL2-1126 [(2)]	Musical Jewels	1986	3.00	6.00	12.00
UNITED ARTISTS					
❑ UA-LA543-G	Somebody Loves You	1975	3.00	6.00	12.00
❑ UA-LA614-G	Crystal	1976	3.00	6.00	12.00
❑ UA-LA771-G	We Must Believe in Magic	1977	2.50	5.00	10.00
❑ UA-LA858-H	When I Dream	1978	2.50	5.00	10.00
❑ UA-LA969-H	We Should Be Together	1979	2.50	5.00	10.00
❑ LOO-982	Classic Crystal	1979	2.50	5.00	10.00
❑ LOO-1034	Favorites	1980	2.50	5.00	10.00
WARNER BROS.					
❑ 23958	Cage the Songbird	1983	2.50	5.00	10.00
❑ 25154	Nobody Wants to Be Alone	1984	2.50	5.00	10.00
❑ 25405	Straight to the Heart	1986	2.50	5.00	10.00
❑ 25508	A Crystal Christmas	1986	2.50	5.00	10.00
❑ 25622	The Best of Crystal Gayle	1987	2.50	5.00	10.00
❑ 25706	Nobody's Angel	1988	2.50	5.00	10.00
❑ 60200	True Love	1983	2.00	4.00	8.00
—Reissue of Elektra 60200					

GAYLE, CRYSTAL, AND GARY MORRIS

Number	Title (A Side/B Side)	Yr	VG	VG+	NM
45s					
WARNER BROS.					
❑ 28106	All of This And More/Makin' Up for Lost Time	1988	—	—	3.00
❑ 28373	Another World/Makin' Up for Lost Time	1987	—	—	3.00
❑ 28856	Makin' Up for Lost Time (The Dallas Lovers' Song)/A Few Good Men	1985	—	—	3.00
❑ 28856 [PS]	Makin' Up for Lost Time (The Dallas Lovers' Song)/A Few Good Men	1985	—	—	3.00
Albums					
WARNER BROS.					
❑ 25507	What If We Fell in Love?	1987	2.50	5.00	10.00

GEEZINSLAW BROTHERS, THE

Includes records (on Step One) as "The Geezinslaws."

Number	Title (A Side/B Side)	Yr	VG	VG+	NM
45s					
CAPITOL					
❑ 2002	Chubby (Please Take Your Love to Town)/Tender-Hearted Me	1967	2.50	5.00	10.00
❑ 2086	I Couldn't Spell Ywuk/We Split the Blanket	1968	2.50	5.00	10.00
❑ 2184	Boney and Claude/Sugar	1968	2.50	5.00	10.00
❑ 2356	Don't Blow Your Horn/My Bluebird Flew Away	1968	2.50	5.00	10.00
❑ 5722	You Wouldn't Put the Shuck on Me/Snook Is the Only Town for Me	1966	2.50	5.00	10.00
❑ 5918	Change of Wife/Brooklyn Bridge	1967	2.50	5.00	10.00
COLUMBIA					
❑ 4-42829	Cool It in Outer Space/My Old Buddy	1963	3.75	7.50	15.00
LONE STAR					
❑ 709	The Diet Song/If You Think I'm Crazy Now	1979	—	3.00	6.00
STEP ONE					
❑ 401	Yabby, Dabby, Doo/Nobody Doesn't Love Lucy	1989	—	2.50	5.00
❑ 425	Unchained Melody/My Pocket's Got a Hole in It	1990	—	2.50	5.00
❑ 442	Help, I'm White and I Can't Get Down/You Belong to Me	1992	—	2.50	5.00
❑ 451	Copenhagen/Someone Sweet to Love	1992	—	2.50	5.00
❑ 453	Lighten Up It's Christmas/Merry Christmas Baby	1992	—	2.50	5.00
—Red vinyl					
❑ 471	I Wish I Had a Job to Shove/Self Made Man	1994	—	2.50	5.00
Albums					
CAPITOL					
❑ ST-130	The Geezinslaw Brothers Are Alive	1969	5.00	10.00	20.00
❑ ST 2570 [S]	Can You Believe...The Geezinslaw Brothers!	1966	6.25	12.50	25.00
❑ T 2570 [M]	Can You Believe...The Geezinslaw Brothers!	1966	5.00	10.00	20.00
❑ ST 2771 [S]	My Dirty, Lowdown, Rotten, Cotton-Pickin' Little Darlin'	1967	6.25	12.50	25.00
❑ T 2771 [M]	My Dirty, Lowdown, Rotten, Cotton-Pickin' Little Darlin'	1967	5.00	10.00	20.00
❑ ST 2885	The Geezinslaw Brothers & "Chubby"	1968	6.25	12.50	25.00
COLUMBIA					
❑ CL 2100 [M]	The Kooky World of the Geezinslaw Brothers	1963	6.25	12.50	25.00
❑ CS 8900 [S]	The Kooky World of the Geezinslaw Brothers	1963	7.50	15.00	30.00

GENE AND DEBBE

Also see GENE THOMAS.

Number	Title (A Side/B Side)	Yr	VG	VG+	NM
45s					
HICKORY					
❑ 1643	Lovin' Season/Then You Can Tell Me Goodbye	1972	—	3.50	7.00
SAN					
❑ 1519	Go with Me/The Torch I Carry	1967	5.00	10.00	20.00
TRX					
❑ 5002	Go with Me/The Torch I Carry	1967	2.00	4.00	8.00
❑ 5006	Playboy/I'll Come Running	1967	2.50	5.00	10.00
❑ 5010	Lovin' Season/Love Will Give Us Wings	1968	2.00	4.00	8.00
❑ 5014	Rings of Gold/Make a Noise Like Love	1968	2.00	4.00	8.00
❑ 5017	Memories Are Made of This/The Sun Won't Shine Again	1969	2.00	4.00	8.00
❑ 5021	I'm Only Human/Loan Some	1969	2.00	4.00	8.00
Albums					
TRX					
❑ 1001	Here and Now	1968	6.25	12.50	25.00

GENTRY, BOBBIE

Number	Title (A Side/B Side)	Yr	VG	VG+	NM
45s					
BRUNSWICK					
❑ 55517	Another Place — Another Time/I Think I'll Cry Out Loud	1975	—	3.00	6.00
CAPITOL					
❑ 2044	Okolona River Bottom Band/Penduli Pendulum	1967	2.00	4.00	8.00
❑ 2044 [PS]	Okolona River Bottom Band/Penduli Pendulum	1967	3.75	7.50	15.00
❑ 2147	Louisiana Man/Courtyard	1968	2.00	4.00	8.00
❑ 2295	Hushabye Mountain/Sweet Peony	1968	2.00	4.00	8.00
❑ 2501	Touch 'Em With Love/Casket Vignette	1969	—	3.00	6.00
❑ 2675	Fancy/Courtyard	1969	—	3.00	6.00
❑ 2788	He Made a Woman Out of Me/Billy the Kid	1970	—	3.00	6.00
❑ 2849	Apartment 21/Seasons Come, Seasons Go	1970	—	3.00	6.00
❑ 3071	But I Can't Get Back/Marigolds and Tangerines	1971	—	3.00	6.00
❑ 3413	Girl from Cincinnati/You and Me Together	1972	—	3.00	6.00
❑ 4294	Ode to Billie Joe/Mississippi Delta	1976	—	2.50	5.00

Number	Title (A Side/B Side)	Yr	VG	VG+	NM
❑ 5950	Ode to Billie Joe/Mississippi Delta	1967	2.50	5.00	10.00
❑ 5992	I Saw An Angel Die/Poppa, Won'tcha Let Me Go to Town with You	1967	2.00	4.00	8.00
TITAN					
❑ 1736	Requiem for Love/Stranger in the Mirror	1963	3.75	7.50	15.00
—With Jody Reynolds					
WARNER BROS.					
❑ 8210	Ode to Billie Joe/There'll Be a Time	1976	—	2.50	5.00
—B-side by Michel Legrand					
❑ 8210 [PS]	Ode to Billie Joe/There'll Be a Time	1976	2.50	5.00	10.00
❑ 8532	Steal Away/He Did Me Wrong But He Did It Right	1978	—	2.00	4.00
Albums					
CAPITOL					
❑ ST-155	Touch 'Em with Love	1969	3.75	7.50	15.00
❑ SKAO-381	Bobbie Gentry's Greatest!	1969	3.75	7.50	15.00
❑ SM-381	Bobbie Gentry's Greatest!	197?	2.00	4.00	8.00
❑ ST-428	Fancy	1970	3.75	7.50	15.00
❑ ST-494	Patchwork	1970	3.75	7.50	15.00
❑ STBB-704 [(2)]	Sittin' Pretty/Tobacco Road	1971	3.75	7.50	15.00
❑ SM-2830	Ode to Billie Joe	197?	2.00	4.00	8.00
❑ ST 2830 [S]	Ode to Billie Joe	1967	3.75	7.50	15.00
❑ T 2830 [M]	Ode to Billie Joe	1967	5.00	10.00	20.00
❑ ST 2842	The Delta Sweete	1968	3.75	7.50	15.00
❑ ST 2964	The Local Gentry	1968	3.75	7.50	15.00

GENTRY, BOBBIE, AND GLEN CAMPBELL

See GLEN CAMPBELL AND BOBBIE GENTRY.

GENTRY, GARY

45s

Number	Title (A Side/B Side)	Yr	VG	VG+	NM
ELEKTRA					
❑ 47122	I Sold All of Tom T.'s Songs Last Night/Because of You	1981	—	2.00	4.00
❑ 47238	(S.O.B.) Same Old Boy/The Devil Offered More	1981	—	2.00	4.00

GEORGE AND LOUIS

45s

Number	Title (A Side/B Side)	Yr	VG	VG+	NM
SUN					
❑ 301	The Return of Jerry Lee/Lewis Boogie	1958	7.50	15.00	30.00
—B-side by Jerry Lee Lewis					
❑ 301	The Return of Jerry Lee/The Return of Jerry Lee, Part 2	1958	6.25	12.50	25.00

GIBBS, TERRI

45s

Number	Title (A Side/B Side)	Yr	VG	VG+	NM
HORIZON					
❑ 2963	Turn Around/(B-side unknown)	1987	—	2.00	4.00
MCA					
❑ 41309	Somebody's Knockin'/Some Days It Rains All Night Long	1980	—	2.00	4.00
❑ 51119	Rich Man/I Won't Cry in Dallas Anymore	1981	—	2.00	4.00
❑ 51180	I Wanna Be Around/Rocky Top	1981	—	2.00	4.00
❑ 51225	Mis'ry River/Too Long	1982	—	2.00	4.00
❑ 52040	Ashes to Ashes/Plans	1982	—	2.00	4.00
❑ 52088	Some Days It Rains All Night Long/All I Wanna Do in Life	1982	—	2.00	4.00
❑ 52134	Baby I'm Gone/I Don't Need You	1982	—	2.00	4.00
❑ 52252	Anybody Else's Heart But Mine/What a Night	1983	—	2.00	4.00
❑ 52308	Tell Mama/Bells	1983	—	2.00	4.00
❑ 52440	I Wanna Be Around/Rocky Top	1984	—	2.00	4.00
WARNER BROS.					
❑ 28895	Somebody Must Be Missing You Tonight/Here I Go Again	1985	—	—	3.00
❑ 28993	Rockin' in a Brand New Cradle/You Can't Run Away from Your Heart	1985	—	—	3.00
❑ 29056	A Few Good Men/Ain't Nobody	1985	—	—	3.00
Albums					
CANAAN					
❑ 80398	Comfort the People	198?	3.00	6.00	12.00
HORIZON					
❑ SP 759	Turn Around	1987	2.50	5.00	10.00
MCA					
❑ 1575	The Best of Terri Gibbs	198?	2.00	4.00	8.00
❑ 5173	Somebody's Knockin'	1981	2.50	5.00	10.00
❑ 5255	I'm a Lady	1981	2.50	5.00	10.00
❑ 5315	Some Days It Rains All Night Long	1982	2.00	4.00	8.00
❑ 5443	Over Easy	1983	2.00	4.00	8.00
❑ 37178	Somebody's Knockin'	198?	2.00	4.00	8.00
—Budget-line reissue of 5173					
WARNER BROS.					
❑ 25309	Old Friends	1985	2.00	4.00	8.00

GIBSON, DON

Also see DOTTIE WEST.

45s

Number	Title (A Side/B Side)	Yr	VG	VG+	NM
ABC HICKORY					
❑ 54001	I'm All Wrapped Up in You/We Live in Two Different Worlds	1976	—	2.50	5.00
❑ 54010	Fan the Flame, Feed the Fire/Bringin' In the Georgia Mail	1977	—	2.50	5.00
❑ 54014	If You Ever Get to Houston (Look Me Down)/It's All Over	1977	—	2.50	5.00
❑ 54019	When Do We Stop Starting Over/Love Is Not the Way (You Told Me)	1977	—	2.50	5.00
❑ 54024	Starting All Over Again/I'd Rather Die Young (Than Grow Old Without You)	1978	—	2.50	5.00
❑ 54029	The Fool/Every Song I Sang Would Be Blue	1978	—	2.50	5.00
❑ 54036	Oh, Such a Stranger/I Love You Because	1978	—	2.50	5.00
❑ 54039	Any Day Now/Baby's Not Home	1978	—	2.50	5.00
COLUMBIA					
❑ 20999	No Shoulder to Cry On/We're Stepping Out	1952	5.00	10.00	20.00
❑ 21060	Sample Kisses/Let Me Stay in Your Arms	1952	5.00	10.00	20.00
❑ 21109	Just Walkin' in the Moonlight/I Just Love the Way You Tell a Lie	1953	5.00	10.00	20.00
❑ 21156	You Cast Me Out/Waitin' Down the Road	1953	5.00	10.00	20.00
❑ 21231	Symptoms of Love/Many Times I've Waited	1954	5.00	10.00	20.00
❑ 21281	Selfish with Your Kisses/Ice Cold Heart	1954	5.00	10.00	20.00
HICKORY					
❑ 1559	Don't Take All Your Loving/Pretending Every Day	1970	—	2.50	5.00
❑ 1571	A Perfect Mountain/Would You Believe	1970	—	2.50	5.00
❑ 1579	Someway/Comfort for Your Mind	1970	—	2.50	5.00
❑ 1588	Guess Away the Blues/I Wanna Live	1970	—	2.50	5.00
❑ 1598	(I Heard That) Lonesome Whistle/Window Shopping	1971	2.00	4.00	8.00
❑ 1614	Country Green/Move It On Over	1971	2.00	4.00	8.00
❑ 1623	Far, Far Away/What's Happened to Me	1972	2.00	4.00	8.00
❑ 1638	Woman (Sensuous Woman)/If You Want Me To I'll Go	1972	2.00	4.00	8.00
❑ 1651	Is This the Best I'm Gonna Feel/Watching It Go	1972	2.00	4.00	8.00
❑ 1661	If You're Goin' Girl/Lonesome Number One	1973	2.00	4.00	8.00
❑ 1671	Touch the Morning/Too Much to Know	1973	2.00	4.00	8.00
HICKORY/MGM					
❑ 301	Touch the Morning/Too Much to Know	1973	—	3.00	6.00
❑ 306	That's What I'll Do/Sweet Dreams	1973	—	3.00	6.00
❑ 312	Snap Your Fingers/Love Is a Lonesome Thing	1973	—	3.00	6.00
❑ 318	One Day at a Time/Rainbow Love	1974	—	3.00	6.00
❑ 327	Bring Back Your Love to Me/Drinking Champagne	1974	—	3.00	6.00
❑ 338	I'll Sing for You/Pocatello	1974	—	3.00	6.00
❑ 345	(There She Goes) I Wish Her Well/Funny Familiar Forgotten Feelings	1975	—	3.00	6.00
❑ 353	Don't Stop Loving Me/Somebody's Words	1975	—	3.00	6.00
❑ 361	I Don't Think I'll Ever (Get Over You)/It Can't Last Always	1975	—	3.00	6.00
❑ 365	You've Got to Stop Hurting Me, Darling/Blues in My Mind	1976	—	3.00	6.00
❑ 372	Doing My Time/The World Is Waiting for the Sunrise	1976	—	3.00	6.00
MCA					
❑ 41031	Forever One Day at a Time/Look Who's Blue	1979	—	2.00	4.00
MGM					
❑ 12109	Run Boy/I Must Forget You	1955	7.50	15.00	30.00
❑ 12194	Sweet Dreams/The Road of Life Alone	1956	7.50	15.00	30.00
❑ 12290	I Ain't Gonna Waste My Time/Ah-Ha	1956	10.00	20.00	40.00
❑ 12331	I Believed in You/What a Fool I Was to Fall	1956	7.50	15.00	30.00
❑ 12494	I Ain't a-Studying You Baby/It's Hoppin'	1957	10.00	20.00	40.00
RCA VICTOR					
❑ 37-7841	What About Me/The World Is Waiting for the Sunrise	1961	5.00	10.00	20.00
—"Compact Single 33" (small hole, plays at LP speed)					
❑ 47-4364	Red Lips, White Lies and Blue Hours/Just Let Me Love You	1951	6.25	12.50	25.00
❑ 47-4473	Dark Future/Blue Million Tears	1952	6.25	12.50	25.00
❑ 47-6860	I Can't Leave/I Love You Still	1957	5.00	10.00	20.00
❑ 47-6942	Everything Turns Out for the Best/Sittin' Here Cryin'	1957	5.00	10.00	20.00
❑ 47-7010	Blue Blue Day/Too Soon to Know	1957	3.75	7.50	15.00
❑ 47-7133	Oh Lonesome Me/I Can't Stop Lovin' You	1958	3.75	7.50	15.00
❑ 47-7330	Give Myself a Party/Look Who's Blue	1958	3.75	7.50	15.00
❑ 47-7437	Who Cares/A Stranger to Me	1959	3.75	7.50	15.00
❑ 47-7505	Lonesome Old House/I Couldn't Care Less	1959	3.75	7.50	15.00
❑ 47-7566	Don't Tell Me Your Troubles/Heartbreak Avenue	1959	3.75	7.50	15.00
❑ 47-7629	I'm Movin' On/Big Hearted Man	1959	3.75	7.50	15.00
❑ 47-7690	Just One Time/I May Never Get to Heaven	1960	3.00	6.00	12.00
❑ 47-7762	Far, Far Away/A Legend in My Time	1960	3.00	6.00	12.00
❑ 47-7805	Sweet Dreams/The Same Street	1960	3.00	6.00	12.00
❑ 47-7841	What About Me/The World Is Waiting for the Sunrise	1961	3.00	6.00	12.00
❑ 47-7890	Sea of Heartbreak/I Think It's Best (To Forget Me)	1961	3.00	6.00	12.00
❑ 47-7959	Lonesome Number One/Same Old Trouble	1961	3.00	6.00	12.00
❑ 47-8017	I Can Mend Your Broken Heart/I Let Her Get Lonely	1962	2.50	5.00	10.00
❑ 47-8085	So How Come (No One Loves Me)/Baby We're Really in Love	1962	2.50	5.00	10.00
❑ 47-8085 [PS]	So How Come (No One Loves Me)/Baby We're Really in Love	1962	3.75	7.50	15.00
❑ 47-8144	Head Over Heels in Love with You/It Was Worth It All	1963	2.50	5.00	10.00
❑ 47-8144 [PS]	Head Over Heels in Love with You/It Was Worth It All	1963	3.75	7.50	15.00
❑ 47-8192	Anything New Gets Old (Except My Love for You)/After the Heartache	1963	2.50	5.00	10.00
❑ 47-8192 [PS]	Anything New Gets Old (Except My Love for You)/After the Heartache	1963	3.75	7.50	15.00
❑ 47-8367	Fireball Mail/Oh, Such a Stranger	1964	2.50	5.00	10.00
❑ 47-8456	Cause I Believe in You/A Love That Can't Be	1964	2.50	5.00	10.00
❑ 47-8589	Again/You're Going Away	1965	2.00	4.00	8.00
❑ 47-8678	Watch Where You're Going/There's a Big Wheel	1965	2.00	4.00	8.00
❑ 47-8732	A Born Loser/All the World Is Lonely Now	1965	2.00	4.00	8.00

Number	Title (A Side/B Side)	Yr	VG	VG+	NM
❑ 47-8812	(Yes) I'm Hurting/My Whole World Is Hurt	1966	2.00	4.00	8.00
❑ 47-8975	Funny, Familiar, Forgotten, Feelings/Forget Me	1966	2.00	4.00	8.00
❑ 47-9177	Lost Highway/Around the Town	1967	2.00	4.00	8.00
❑ 47-9266	All My Love/No Doubt About It	1967	2.00	4.00	8.00
❑ 47-9395	Satisfied/Where No Man Stands Alone	1967	2.00	4.00	8.00
❑ 47-9460	Ashes of Love/Good Morning, Dear	1968	—	3.00	6.00
❑ 47-9563	It's a Long, Long Way to Georgia/Low and Lonely	1968	—	3.00	6.00
❑ 47-9663	Ever Changing Mind/Thoughts	1968	—	3.00	6.00
❑ 47-9906	Montego Bay/If My Heart Had Windows	1970	—	3.00	6.00
❑ 48-0424	I Love No One But You/Carolina Breakdown	1951	6.25	12.50	25.00
❑ 48-0460	Roses Are Red/Wiggle Wag	1951	6.25	12.50	25.00
❑ 61-7762 [S]	Far, Far Away/A Legend in My Time	1960	6.25	12.50	25.00
—"Living Stereo" (large hole, plays at 45 rpm)					
❑ 74-0143	Solitary/I Just Said Goodbye to My Dreams	1969	—	3.00	6.00
❑ 74-0219	I Will Always/Half As Much	1969	—	3.00	6.00
WARNER BROS.					
❑ 49193	Sweet Sensuous Sensations/Stranger to Me	1980	—	2.00	4.00
❑ 49504	I'd Be Crazy Over You/Somewhere Between Yesterday	1980	—	2.00	4.00
❑ 49602	Love Fires/Come Back and Love Me	1980	—	2.00	4.00
7-Inch Extended Plays					
COLUMBIA					
❑ B-2146	(contents unknown)	1957	5.00	10.00	20.00
❑ B-2146 [PS]	Don Gibson	1957	5.00	10.00	20.00
RCA VICTOR					
❑ EPA-4323	(contents unknown)	1958	3.75	7.50	15.00
❑ EPA-4323 [PS]	Blue, Blue Day	1958	3.75	7.50	15.00
❑ EPA-4335	(contents unknown)	1958	3.75	7.50	15.00
❑ EPA-4335 [PS]	That Lonesome Valley	1958	3.75	7.50	15.00
❑ EPA-5114	Oh Lonesome Me/Look Who's Blue//Who Cares/Blue, Blue Day	1959	3.75	7.50	15.00
❑ EPA-5114 [PS]	Blue and Lonesome	1959	3.75	7.50	15.00
Albums					
ABC HICKORY					
❑ 44001	All Wrapped Up in You	1976	3.00	6.00	12.00
❑ 44007	If You Ever	1977	3.00	6.00	12.00
❑ 44010	Starting All Over	1978	3.00	6.00	12.00
❑ 44014	Look Who's Blue	1978	3.00	6.00	12.00
HARMONY					
❑ HL 7358 [M]	Don Gibson Sings	196?	3.00	6.00	12.00
❑ HS 11158 [S]	Don Gibson Sings	196?	3.75	7.50	15.00
❑ KH 31765	Sample Kisses	1972	2.50	5.00	10.00
HICKORY					
❑ LPS-153	Hits, The Don Gibson Way	1970	3.75	7.50	15.00
❑ LPS-155	Perfect Mountain	1971	3.75	7.50	15.00
❑ LPS-157	Don Gibson Sings Hank Williams	1971	3.75	7.50	15.00
❑ LPS-160	Country Green	1971	3.75	7.50	15.00
❑ LPS-166	Woman (Sensuous Woman)	1972	3.75	7.50	15.00
HICKORY/MGM					
❑ H3F-4501	Touch the Morning/That's What I'll Do	1973	3.75	7.50	15.00
❑ H3F-4502	The Very Best of Don Gibson	1974	3.75	7.50	15.00
❑ H3G-4509	Snap Your Fingers	1974	3.75	7.50	15.00
❑ H3G-4516	Bring Back Your Love to Me	1974	3.00	6.00	12.00
❑ H3G-4519	I'm the Loneliest Man	1975	3.00	6.00	12.00
LION					
❑ L-70069 [M]	Songs by Don Gibson	1958	20.00	40.00	80.00
MGM					
❑ GAS-138	Don Gibson (Golden Archive Series)	1970	3.75	7.50	15.00
RCA CAMDEN					
❑ ACL1-0328	Just Call Me Lonesome	1973	2.50	5.00	10.00
❑ ACL1-0758	Just One Time	1974	2.50	5.00	10.00
❑ CAL-852 [M]	Blue Million Tears	196?	3.00	6.00	12.00
❑ CAS-852 [S]	Blue Million Tears	196?	3.75	7.50	15.00
❑ CAL-2101 [M]	Hurtin' Inside	1966	3.00	6.00	12.00
❑ CAS-2101 [S]	Hurtin' Inside	1966	3.75	7.50	15.00
❑ CAS-2246	I Love You So Much	1968	3.00	6.00	12.00
❑ CAS-2317	My God Is Real	1969	3.00	6.00	12.00
❑ CAS-2392	Lovin' Lies	1970	3.00	6.00	12.00
❑ CAS-2502	I Walk Alone	1971	3.00	6.00	12.00
❑ CAS-2592	Am I That Easy to Forget	1972	3.00	6.00	12.00
RCA VICTOR					
❑ LPM-1743 [M]	Oh Lonesome Me	1958	12.50	25.00	50.00
❑ LPM-1918 [M]	No One Stands Alone	1959	7.50	15.00	30.00
❑ LSP-1918 [S]	No One Stands Alone	1959	10.00	20.00	40.00
❑ LPM-2038 [M]	That Gibson Boy	1959	7.50	15.00	30.00
❑ LSP-2038 [S]	That Gibson Boy	1959	10.00	20.00	40.00
❑ LPM-2184 [M]	Look Who's Blue	1960	7.50	15.00	30.00
❑ LSP-2184 [S]	Look Who's Blue	1960	10.00	20.00	40.00
❑ LPM-2269 [M]	Sweet Dreams	1960	7.50	15.00	30.00
❑ LSP-2269 [S]	Sweet Dreams	1960	10.00	20.00	40.00
❑ LPM-2361 [M]	Girls, Guitars and Gibson	1961	7.50	15.00	30.00
❑ LSP-2361 [S]	Girls, Guitars and Gibson	1961	10.00	20.00	40.00
❑ LPM-2448 [M]	Some Favorites of Mine	1962	7.50	15.00	30.00
❑ LSP-2448 [S]	Some Favorites of Mine	1962	10.00	20.00	40.00
❑ LPM-2702 [M]	I Wrote a Song	1963	7.50	15.00	30.00
❑ LSP-2702 [S]	I Wrote a Song	1963	10.00	20.00	40.00
❑ LPM-2878 [M]	God Walks These Hills	1964	5.00	10.00	20.00
❑ LSP-2878 [S]	God Walks These Hills	1964	6.25	12.50	25.00
❑ LPM-3376 [M]	The Best of Don Gibson	1965	5.00	10.00	20.00
❑ LSP-3376 [S]	The Best of Don Gibson	1965	6.25	12.50	25.00
❑ LPM-3470 [M]	Too Much Hurt	1965	5.00	10.00	20.00
❑ LSP-3470 [S]	Too Much Hurt	1965	6.25	12.50	25.00
❑ LPM-3594 [M]	Don Gibson with Spanish Guitars	1966	5.00	10.00	20.00
❑ LSP-3594 [S]	Don Gibson with Spanish Guitars	1966	6.25	12.50	25.00

Number	Title (A Side/B Side)	Yr	VG	VG+	NM
❑ LPM-3680 [M]	Great Country Songs	1966	5.00	10.00	20.00
❑ LSP-3680 [S]	Great Country Songs	1966	6.25	12.50	25.00
❑ LPM-3843 [M]	All My Love	1967	5.00	10.00	20.00
❑ LSP-3843 [S]	All My Love	1967	6.25	12.50	25.00
❑ LPM-3974 [M]	The King of Country Soul	1968	12.50	25.00	50.00
❑ LSP-3974 [S]	The King of Country Soul	1968	5.00	10.00	20.00
❑ LSP-4053	More Country Soul	1968	5.00	10.00	20.00
❑ LSP-4169	All-Time Country Gold	1969	3.75	7.50	15.00
❑ LSP-4281	The Best of Don Gibson, Vol. 2	1970	3.75	7.50	15.00
❑ CPL1-7052	Collector's Series	1985	2.50	5.00	10.00

GIBSON, DON, AND SUE THOMPSON

Also see each artist's individual listings.

Number	Title (A Side/B Side)	Yr	VG	VG+	NM
45s					
HICKORY					
❑ 1607	The Two of Us Together/Oh Yes, I Love You	1971	2.00	4.00	8.00
❑ 1629	Did You Ever Think/Love Garden	1972	2.00	4.00	8.00
❑ 1646	I Think They Call It Love/Over There's the Door	1972	2.00	4.00	8.00
❑ 1654	Cause I Love You/My Tears Don't Show	1972	2.00	4.00	8.00
❑ 1665	Go with Me/Two of Us Together	1973	2.00	4.00	8.00
HICKORY/MGM					
❑ 303	Warm Love/Fly the Friendly Skies with Jesus	1973	—	3.00	6.00
❑ 324	Good Old Fashioned Country Love/Ages and Ages Ago	1974	—	3.00	6.00
❑ 342	No One Will Ever Know/Put It Off Till Tomorrow	1975	—	3.00	6.00
❑ 350	Oh, How Love Changes/Sweet and Tender Times	1975	—	3.00	6.00
❑ 360	Maybe Tomorrow/I Can't Tell My Heart That	1975	—	3.00	6.00
❑ 367	Get Ready, Here I Come/Once More	1976	—	3.00	6.00
❑ 373	You've Still Got a Place in My Heart/Let's Get Together	1976	—	3.00	6.00
Albums					
HICKORY/MGM					
❑ H3G-4520	Oh How Love Changes	1975	3.00	6.00	12.00

GIBSON, HAL

Number	Title (A Side/B Side)	Yr	VG	VG+	NM
45s					
SUNDIAL					
❑ 163	The Love She Found in Me/(B-side unknown)	1989	—	3.50	7.00
❑ 170	A Man of Dust/(B-side unknown)	1990	—	3.50	7.00
❑ 173	A Party of One/(B-side unknown)	1990	—	3.50	7.00
❑ 178	Quietly Crazy/(B-side unknown)	1990	—	3.50	7.00
❑ 187	Cajun Christmas/(B-side unknown)	199?	—	3.50	7.00

GIBSON/MILLER BAND, THE

Number	Title (A Side/B Side)	Yr	VG	VG+	NM
45s					
EPIC					
❑ 34-74739	Big Heart (7" Mix)/Big Heart (Turbo Twang Mix)	1992	—	2.00	4.00
❑ 34-74856	High Rollin'/Stone Cold Country	1993	—	2.00	4.00
❑ 34-74991	Texas Tattoo/Southern Man	1993	—	—	3.00
❑ 34-77169	Small Price/Where There's Smoke	1993	—	—	3.00
❑ 34-77355	Stone Cold Country/Thank Virginia	1994	—	—	3.00
❑ 34-77488	Mammas Don't Let Your Babies Grow Up to Be Cowboys/Right Off the Top of My Head	1994	—	—	3.00
❑ 34-77651	Red, White and Blue Collar/Johnny Get Your Gun	1994	—	—	3.00

GIESE, JIMMY

Number	Title (A Side/B Side)	Yr	VG	VG+	NM
45s					
DECCA					
❑ 9-46334	Heading for Glory Land/There's Gonna Be a Jubilee	1951	6.25	12.50	25.00

GILL, VINCE

Number	Title (A Side/B Side)	Yr	VG	VG+	NM
45s					
MCA					
❑ 53717	Never Alone/Oh Girl (You Know Where to Find Me)	1989	—	2.00	4.00
❑ 53780	Oklahoma Swing/We Could Have Been	1989	—	2.00	4.00
❑ 53892	Never Knew Lonely/Riding the Rodeo	1990	—	2.00	4.00
❑ 54026	Pocket Full of Gold/A Little Left Over	1991	—	2.00	4.00
❑ 54123	Liza Jane/What's a Man to Do	1991	—	2.00	4.00
❑ 54179	Look at Us/I Quit	1991	—	2.00	4.00
❑ 54282	Take Your Memory With You/Sparkle	1992	—	2.00	4.00
❑ 54406	I Still Believe in You/One More Last Chance	1992	—	3.00	6.00
❑ 54489	Don't Let Our Love Start Slippin' Away/Love Never Broke Anyone's Heart	1992	—	2.00	4.00
❑ 54540	No Future in the Past/Pretty Words	1993	—	2.00	4.00
❑ 54706	Tryin' to Get Over You/Nothing Like a Woman	1993	—	2.00	4.00
❑ 54715	One More Last Chance/Under These Conditions	1993	—	2.00	4.00
❑ 54833	Whenever You Come Around/South Side of Dixie	1994	—	2.00	4.00
❑ 54879	What the Cowgirls Do/Go Rest High on That Mountain	1994	—	2.00	4.00
❑ 54937	When Love Finds You/If I Had My Way	1994	—	2.00	4.00
❑ 54976	Which Bridge to Cross (Which Bridge to Burn)/If There's Anything I Can Do	1994	—	2.00	4.00
❑ 55035	You Better Think Twice/A Real Lady's Man	1995	—	2.00	4.00
❑ 55098	Go Rest High on That Mountain/Maybe Tonight	1995	—	2.00	4.00
❑ 55188	High Lonesome Sound/High Lonesome Sound (Bluegrass Version featuring Alison Krauss)	1996	—	2.00	4.00
❑ 55213	Worlds Apart/Down to New Orleans	1996	—	2.00	4.00
❑ 55251	Pretty Little Adriana/Tell Me Lover	1997	—	—	3.00
❑ 55307	A Little More Love/Jenny Dreamed of Trains	1997	—	—	3.00
❑ 72010	You and You Alone/Given More Time	1997	—	—	3.00

Number	Title (A Side/B Side)	Yr	VG	VG+	NM
❑ 72055	If You Ever Have Forever in Mind/Given More Time	1998	—	—	3.00
❑ 79011	When I Call Your Name/Rita Ballou	1990	2.00	4.00	8.00
MCA NASHVILLE					
❑ 72072	Kindly Keep It Country/I Never Really Knew You	1998	—	—	3.00
❑ 72085	Don't Come Cryin' to Me/I'll Take Texas	1999	—	—	3.00
❑ 72107	My Kind of Woman-My Kind of Man/All Those Years	1999	—	—	3.00
—A-side with Patty Loveless					
❑ 088-172148	Let's Make Sure We Kiss Goodbye/Let Her In	2000	—	—	3.00
❑ 088 172168-7	When I Look Into Your Heart (a Duet with Amy Grant)/Feels Like Love	2000	—	—	3.00
RCA					
❑ 5131-7-R	Cinderella/Something's Missing	1987	—	2.00	4.00
❑ 5131-7-R [PS]	Cinderella/Something's Missing	1987	2.00	4.00	8.00
—Sleeve is promo only					
❑ 5257-7-R	Let's Do Something/It Doesn't Matter Anymore	1987	—	2.00	4.00
❑ 5331-7-R	Everybody's Sweetheart/The Way Back Home	1987	—	2.00	4.00
❑ 8301-7-R	The Radio/The Way Back Home	1988	—	2.00	4.00
❑ PB-13701	If It Weren't for Him/Don't Say That You Love Me	1983	—	—	—
—Canceled					
❑ PB-13731	Victim of Life's Circumstances/Don't Say That You Love Me	1984	—	2.00	4.00
❑ PB-13809	Oh Carolina/Half a Chance	1984	—	2.00	4.00
❑ PB-13860	Turn Me Loose/'Til the Best Comes Along	1984	—	2.00	4.00
❑ PB-14020	True Love/Livin' the Way I Do	1985	—	2.00	4.00
❑ PB-14020	True Love/Livin' the Way I Do	1985	—	2.00	4.00
❑ PB-14140	If It Weren't for Him/Savannah (Do You Ever Think of Me)	1985	—	2.00	4.00
❑ PB-14216	Oklahoma Borderline/She Don't Know	1985	—	2.00	4.00
❑ PB-14371	With You/Colder Than Winter	1986	—	2.00	4.00
Albums					
MCA					
❑ 42321	When I Call Your Name	1989	5.00	10.00	20.00
❑ R 173599	Pocket Full of Gold	1991	5.00	10.00	20.00
—Only released on vinyl through BMG Direct Marketing					
RCA					
❑ 5923-1-R	The Way Back Home	1987	3.75	7.50	15.00
RCA VICTOR					
❑ CPL1-5348	The Things That Matter	1985	3.75	7.50	15.00
❑ MHL1-8517 [EP]	Turn Me Loose	1984	2.50	5.00	10.00

GILLETTE, STEVE

45s

Number	Title (A Side/B Side)	Yr	VG	VG+	NM
REGENCY					
❑ 45002	Lost the Good Thing/Three Lines	1980	—	2.50	5.00
—A-side with Jennifer Warnes					

GILLEY, MICKEY

Also see RAY CHARLES; CHARLY McCLAIN.

45s

Number	Title (A Side/B Side)	Yr	VG	VG+	NM
ACT 1					
❑ 101	Say No More/Make Me Believe	1966	2.50	5.00	10.00
AIRBORNE					
❑ 10002	I'm Your Puppet/Don't Show Me Your Memories (And I Won't Show You Mine)	1988	—	2.00	4.00
❑ 10008	She Reminded Me of You/Easy Climb	1988	—	2.00	4.00
❑ 10016	You Still Got a Way with My Heart/It's Killing Me to Watch Love Die	1989	—	2.00	4.00
❑ 75740	There I've Said It Again/It's Killing Me to Watch Love Die	1989	—	2.00	4.00
ASTRO					
❑ 102	Down the Line/Lonely Wine	196?	25.00	50.00	100.00
❑ 103	Is It Wrong/Turn Around	196?	6.25	12.50	25.00
❑ 104	Night After Night/Susie Q	196?	6.25	12.50	25.00
❑ 106	Lotta Lovin'/I Miss You So	196?	6.25	12.50	25.00
❑ 110	A Certain Smile/If I Didn't Have a Dime	196?	6.25	12.50	25.00
❑ 112	Little Egypt/If I Didn't Have a Dime	196?	6.25	12.50	25.00
❑ 5002	Everything Is Yours That Once Was Mine/Don't Throw a Good Love Away	1971	2.00	4.00	8.00
❑ 5003	You Touch My Life/Toast to Mary Ann	1971	2.00	4.00	8.00
❑ 10003	Room Full of Roses/She Called Me Baby	1973	2.50	5.00	10.00
DARYL					
❑ 101	What Have I Done/Three's a Crowd	1963	2.50	5.00	10.00
DOT					
❑ 15706	Call Me Shorty/Come On Baby	1958	50.00	100.00	200.00
EPIC					
❑ AE7 1356 [DJ]	Mickey Gilley's Christmas Medley (2:51)/Mickey Gilley's Christmas Medley (3:34)	1981	2.50	5.00	10.00
❑ AE7 1774	Home to Texas for Christmas/I'm Spending Christmas with You	1982	—	2.50	5.00
❑ 02172	You Don't Know Me/Juke Box Argument	1981	—	—	3.00
❑ 02578	Lonely Nights/We've Watched Another Evening Waste Away	1981	—	—	3.00
❑ 02774	Tears of the Lonely/Ladies Night	1982	—	—	3.00
❑ 03055	Put Your Dreams Away/If I Can't Hold Her on the Outside	1982	—	—	3.00
❑ 03326	Talk to Me/Honky Tonkin' (I Guess I Done Some)	1982	—	—	3.00
❑ 03332	Blue Christmas/Jingle Bell Rock	1982	—	2.00	4.00
❑ 03783	Fool for Your Love/Shakin' a Heartache	1983	—	—	3.00
❑ 04018	Your Love Shines Through/Wish You Were Mine Again	1983	—	—	3.00
❑ 04269	You've Really Got a Hold on Me/Giving Up Getting Over You	1983	—	—	3.00
❑ 04563	Too Good to Stop Now/A Shoulder to Cry On	1984	—	—	3.00
❑ 04746	I'm the One Mama Warned You About/You Can Lie to Me Tonight	1985	—	—	3.00
❑ 05460	You've Got Something on Your Mind/I Feel Good About Lovin' You	1985	—	—	3.00
❑ 05744	Your Memory Ain't What It Used to Be/Lonely Nights, Lonely Heartaches	1985	—	—	3.00
❑ 05895	Play, Ruby, Play/After She's Gone	1986	—	—	3.00
❑ 06184	Doo-Wah Days/After She's Gone	1986	—	—	3.00
❑ 07009	Full Grown Fool/To My One and Only	1987	—	—	3.00
❑ 50580	Here Comes the Hurt Again/I Hate It, But I Drink It Anyway	1978	—	2.00	4.00
❑ 50631	The Song We Made Love To/Memphis Memories	1978	—	2.00	4.00
❑ 50672	Just Long Enough to Say Goodbye/Tying One On	1979	—	2.00	4.00
❑ 50740	My Silver Lining/Picture of Our Love	1979	—	2.00	4.00
❑ 50801	A Little Getting Used To/Can't Nobody Love You	1979	—	2.00	4.00
❑ 50876	True Love Ways/The More I Turn the Bottle	1980	—	2.00	4.00
❑ 50940	That's All That Matters/The Blues Don't Care Who's Got 'Em	1980	—	2.00	4.00
❑ 50973	A Headache Tomorrow (Or a Heartache Tonight)/Million Dollar Memories	1981	—	2.00	4.00
❑ 51003	Mamas Don't Let Your Babies Grow Up to Be Cowboys/Cotton-Eyed Joe	1981	—	2.00	4.00
—A-side with Johnny Lee; B-side by Bayou City Beats					
FULL MOON/ASYLUM					
❑ 46640	Stand By Me/Cotton Eyed Joe	1980	—	2.00	4.00
—B-side by the Unstrung Heroes					
❑ 46640 [PS]	Stand By Me/Cotton Eyed Joe	1980	—	2.50	5.00
—"Urban Cowboy" sleeve (John Travolta pictured)					
GOLDBAND					
❑ 1223	I Ain't Goin' Home/No Greater Love	1964	2.50	5.00	10.00
GRT					
❑ 27	I'm Nobody Today (But I Was Somebody Last Night)/She's Not Yours Anymore	1970	2.00	4.00	8.00
❑ 45	Time to Tell Another Lie/Because I Love You	1970	2.00	4.00	8.00
KHOURY'S					
❑ 712	Drive In Movie/Give Me a Chance	1959	75.00	150.00	300.00
LYNN					
❑ 503	Your Selfish Pride/Everything Turned to Love	1960	6.25	12.50	25.00
❑ 508	My Baby's Been Cheating Again/Turn Around	1960	6.25	12.50	25.00
❑ 512	Slippin' and Slidin'/End of the Line	1961	6.25	12.50	25.00
❑ 515	Long Lonely Nights/My Babe	1961	6.25	12.50	25.00
MINOR					
❑ 106	Oo-Ee Baby/Tell Me Why	1957	150.00	300.00	600.00
PAULA					
❑ 256	Make Me Believe/Say No to You	1966	2.50	5.00	10.00
❑ 269	A World of My Own/Love in the Want Ads	1967	2.00	4.00	8.00
❑ 280	Blame It on the Moon/Sounds Like Trouble	1967	2.00	4.00	8.00
❑ 281	One Way Street/Tears in My Eyes	1967	2.00	4.00	8.00
❑ 301	A New Way to Live/That Heart Belongs to Me	1968	2.00	4.00	8.00
❑ 402	Night After Night/I'm to Blame	1974	—	2.50	5.00
❑ 441	She Cheats on Me/You Can Count Me Missing	1983	—	2.00	4.00
❑ 1200	Now I Can Live Again/Without You	1968	2.00	4.00	8.00
❑ 1208	She's Still Got a Hold on You/There's No One Like You	1969	2.00	4.00	8.00
❑ 1215	Watching the Way/It's Just a Matter of Making Up My Mind	1969	2.00	4.00	8.00
PLAYBOY					
❑ 5807	Honky Tonk Memories/Five Foot Two, Eyes of Blue	1977	—	2.00	4.00
❑ 5818	Chains of Love/No. 1 Rock 'n Roll C & W Boogie Blues Man	1977	—	2.00	4.00
❑ 5826	The Power of Positive Drinkin'/Playing My Old Piano	1978	—	2.00	4.00
❑ 6004	I Overlooked an Orchid/Swinging Doors	1974	—	2.50	5.00
❑ 6015	City Lights/Fraulein	1974	—	2.50	5.00
❑ 6031	Window Up Above/I'm Movin' On	1975	—	2.50	5.00
❑ 6041	Bouquet of Roses/If You Were Mine to Lose	1975	—	2.50	5.00
❑ 6045	Roll You Like a Wheel/Let's Sing a Song Together	1975	—	2.50	5.00
—With Barbi Benton					
❑ 6045 [PS]	Roll You Like a Wheel/Let's Sing a Song Together	1975	—	3.00	6.00
—With Barbi Benton					
❑ 6055	Overnight Sensation/I'll Sail My Ship Alone	1975	—	2.50	5.00
❑ 6063	Don't All the Girls Get Prettier at Closing Time/Where Do You Go to Lose a Heartache	1976	—	2.50	5.00
❑ 6075	Bring It On Home to Me/How's My Ex Treating You	1976	—	2.50	5.00
❑ 6089	Lawdy Miss Clawdy/What Is It	1976	—	2.50	5.00
❑ 6095	Pretty Paper/Lonely Christmas Call	1976	—	2.50	5.00
❑ 6100	She's Pulling Me Back Again/Sweet Mama Goodtime	1977	—	2.50	5.00
❑ 50056	Room Full of Roses/She Called Me Baby	1974	—	2.50	5.00
POTOMAC					
❑ 901	Is It Wrong/No Greater Love	1960	3.75	7.50	15.00
PRINCESS					
❑ 4004	Drive-In Movie/Your First Time	1962	10.00	20.00	40.00
❑ 4006	Wild Side of Life/Caught in the Middle	1962	10.00	20.00	40.00
❑ 4011	I'll Keep On Dancing/I'll Keep On Searching	196?	3.75	7.50	15.00
❑ 4015	A World of My Own/I Still Care	196?	3.75	7.50	15.00
RESCO					
❑ 617	You Touch My Life/Toast to Mary Ann	1974	—	3.00	6.00
❑ 622	She Gives Me Love/Quittin' Time	1974	—	3.00	6.00
REX					
❑ 1007	Grapevine/That's How It's Got to Be	1959	7.50	15.00	30.00

Number	Title (A Side/B Side)	Yr	VG	VG+	NM
SABRA					
❑ 518	Valley of Tears/I Need Your Love	1961	5.00	10.00	20.00
SAN					
❑ 1513	I Ain't No Bo Diddley/I'm to Blame	1966	2.50	5.00	10.00
SUPREME					
❑ 101	Now That I Have You/Happy Birthday	1962	3.75	7.50	15.00
❑ 102	Everything Turned to Love/No One Will Ever Know	1962	3.75	7.50	15.00
TCF HALL					
❑ 126	When Two Worlds Collide/Let's Hurt Together	1965	2.00	4.00	8.00
Albums					
ACCORD					
❑ SN-7151	Suburban Cowboy	1981	2.50	5.00	10.00
ASTRO					
❑ 101 [M]	Lonely Wine	1964	75.00	150.00	300.00
COLUMBIA SPECIAL PRODUCTS					
❑ P 16198	All My Best	1982	2.50	5.00	10.00
EPIC					
❑ PE 34736	Room Full of Roses	198?	2.00	4.00	8.00
—Budget-line reissue					
❑ PE 34749	Smokin'	198?	2.00	4.00	8.00
—Budget-line reissue					
❑ PE 34776	First Class	198?	2.00	4.00	8.00
—Budget-line reissue					
❑ KE 35174	Songs We Made Love To	1979	2.50	5.00	10.00
❑ JE 36201	Mickey Gilley	1980	2.50	5.00	10.00
❑ JE 36492	That's All That Matters to Me	1980	2.50	5.00	10.00
❑ PE 36492	That's All That Matters to Me	198?	2.00	4.00	8.00
—Budget-line reissue					
❑ JE 36851	Encore	1981	2.50	5.00	10.00
❑ FE 37416	You Don't Know Me	1981	2.50	5.00	10.00
❑ PE 37416	You Don't Know Me	198?	2.00	4.00	8.00
—Budget-line reissue					
❑ PE 37595	Christmas at Gilley's	1981	2.50	5.00	10.00
—Some labels have "FE" prefix					
❑ FE 38082	Put Your Dreams Away	1982	2.50	5.00	10.00
❑ PE 38082	Put Your Dreams Away	198?	2.00	4.00	8.00
—Budget-line reissue					
❑ FE 38320	Mickey Gilley's Biggest Hits	1982	2.50	5.00	10.00
❑ FE 38583	Fool for Your Love	1983	2.50	5.00	10.00
❑ PE 38583	Fool for Your Love	1985	2.00	4.00	8.00
—Budget-line reissue					
❑ FE 39000	You've Really Got a Hold on Me	1983	2.50	5.00	10.00
❑ FE 39324	Too Good to Stop Now	1983	2.50	5.00	10.00
❑ KE2 39867 [(2)]	Ten Years of Hits	1984	3.00	6.00	12.00
❑ FE 39900	Live at Gilley's	1984	2.50	5.00	10.00
❑ FE 40115	I Feel Good (About Lovin' You)	1985	2.50	5.00	10.00
❑ FE 40353	The One and Only	1986	2.50	5.00	10.00
INTERMEDIA					
❑ QS-5024	With Love from Pasadena, Texas	198?	2.50	5.00	10.00
J.M.					
❑ 8127	Norwegian Wood	1981	3.00	6.00	12.00
PAIR					
❑ PDL2-1072 [(2)]	The Best of Mickey Gilley	1986	3.00	6.00	12.00
PAULA					
❑ LP-2195 [M]	Down the Line	1967	10.00	20.00	40.00
❑ LPS-2195 [S]	Down the Line	1967	10.00	20.00	40.00
❑ LPS-2224	Mickey Gilley at His Best	1974	3.75	7.50	15.00
❑ LPS-2234	Mickey Gilley	1978	3.00	6.00	12.00
PICKWICK					
❑ SPC-6180	Wild Side of Life	197?	2.50	5.00	10.00
PLAYBOY					
❑ PB-128	Room Full of Roses	1974	5.00	10.00	20.00
❑ PB-403	City Lights	1974	5.00	10.00	20.00
❑ PB-405	Mickey's Movin' On	1975	3.75	7.50	15.00
❑ PB-408	Overnight Sensation	1976	3.75	7.50	15.00
❑ PB-409	Gilley's Greatest Hits Vol. 1	1976	3.75	7.50	15.00
❑ PZ 34736	Room Full of Roses	1977	2.50	5.00	10.00
—Reissue of 128					
❑ PZ 34742	Overnight Sensation	1977	2.50	5.00	10.00
—Reissue of 408					
❑ PZ 34743	Gilley's Greatest Hits Vol. 1	1977	2.50	5.00	10.00
—Reissue of 409					
❑ PZ 34749	Smokin'	1977	3.00	6.00	12.00
❑ PZ 34776	First Class	1977	3.00	6.00	12.00
❑ KZ 34881	Gilley's Greatest Hits, Vol. 2	1977	3.00	6.00	12.00
❑ KZ 35099	Flyin' High	1978	3.00	6.00	12.00

GILMAN, BILLY

Number	Title (A Side/B Side)	Yr	VG	VG+	NM
45s					
EPIC					
❑ 34 79527	One Voice/Oklahoma	2000	—	2.00	4.00

GILMORE, JIMMIE DALE

Also see JIMMIE DALE AND THE FLATLANDERS.

Number	Title (A Side/B Side)	Yr	VG	VG+	NM
45s					
HIGHTONE					
❑ 504	White Freight Liner Blues/Trying to Get to You	1988	—	2.50	5.00
❑ 510	Honky Tonk Song/(B-side unknown)	1989	—	2.50	5.00
Albums					
HIGHTONE					
❑ HT-8011	Fair and Square	1988	2.50	5.00	10.00
❑ HT-8018	Jimmie Dale Gilmore	1989	2.50	5.00	10.00

GIRLS NEXT DOOR

Number	Title (A Side/B Side)	Yr	VG	VG+	NM
45s					
ATLANTIC					
❑ 87868	How 'Bout Us/Last Goodbye	1990	—	2.00	4.00
❑ 88791	He's Gotta Have Me/Wasn't It You	1989	—	2.00	4.00
MTM					
❑ B-72059	Love Will Get You Through Times with No Money/Ruins of Love	1985	—	2.00	4.00
❑ B-72068	Slow Boat to China/Pretty Boy's Cadillac	1986	—	2.00	4.00
❑ B-72078	Baby I Want It/(Sing-Along Version)	1986	—	2.00	4.00
❑ B-72084	Walk Me in the Rain/The Fool in Me	1987	—	2.00	4.00
❑ B-72088	What a Girl Next Door Could Do/I Think I'm Gonna Fall (In Love with You)	1987	—	2.00	4.00
❑ B-72095	Easy to Find/Message from My Heart	1987	—	2.00	4.00
❑ B-72106	Love and Other Fairy Tales/I Can Hear My Heart Begin to Cry	1988	—	2.00	4.00
Albums					
MTM					
❑ ST-71053	The Girls Next Door	1986	2.50	5.00	10.00
❑ ST-71062	What a Girl Next Door Could Do	1987	2.50	5.00	10.00

GLASER, CHUCK

Also see TOMPALL AND THE GLASER BROTHERS.

Number	Title (A Side/B Side)	Yr	VG	VG+	NM
45s					
MGM					
❑ 14663	Gypsy Queen/That's When I Love You the Most	1973	—	2.50	5.00

GLASER, JIM

Also see TOMPALL AND THE GLASER BROTHERS.

Number	Title (A Side/B Side)	Yr	VG	VG+	NM
45s					
MCA					
❑ 40636	She's Free But She's Not Easy/Lonely Bein' Free	1976	—	2.00	4.00
❑ 40742	Chasin' My Tail/Sleeping Beauty	1977	—	2.00	4.00
❑ 40813	Don't Let My Love Stand in Your Way/Honky Tonk Lady	1977	—	2.00	4.00
❑ 52619	I'll Be Your Fool Tonight/Tough Act to Follow	1985	—	—	3.00
❑ 52672	In Another Minute/Merry-Go-Round	1985	—	—	3.00
❑ 52748	If I Don't Love You/It's Not Easy	1985	—	—	3.00
❑ 52808	The Lights of Albuquerque/Waltzing Through a Rock and Roll Life	1986	—	—	3.00
MGM					
❑ 14590	I See His Love All Over You/It's Still a Long Way	1973	—	2.50	5.00
❑ 14713	Fool Passin' Through/If It Pleases You	1974	—	2.50	5.00
❑ 14758	Forgettin' 'Bout You/If It Pleases You	1974	—	2.50	5.00
❑ 14798	One, Two, Three (Never Gonna Fall in Love Again)/One Night Man	1975	—	2.50	5.00
❑ 14834	Woman, Woman/Turn to Me	1975	—	2.50	5.00
MONUMENT					
❑ 909	I'd Rather Not Know/The Outcast	1965	3.00	6.00	12.00
❑ 924	My Mind and Me/Wonderful World of Love	1966	3.00	6.00	12.00
❑ 985	A Pair of Loaded Dice/Thanks a Lot for Trying Anyway	1966	3.00	6.00	12.00
NOBLE VISION					
❑ 101	When You're Not a Lady/I Don't Wanna Make Love	1982	—	2.00	4.00
❑ 102	You Got Me Running/I'd Love to See You Again	1983	—	2.00	4.00
❑ 103	The Man in the Mirror/Pretend	1983	—	2.00	4.00
❑ 104	If I Could Only Dance with You/Woman, Woman	1984	—	2.00	4.00
❑ 105	You're Gettin' to Me Again/Stand by the Road	1984	—	2.00	4.00
❑ 107	Let Me Down Easy/I'd Love to See You Again	1984	—	2.00	4.00
RCA VICTOR					
❑ 47-9587	God Help You Woman/She Was Too Good to Me	1968	2.00	4.00	8.00
❑ 47-9696	Please Take Me Back/Kiss Her Once for Me	1968	2.00	4.00	8.00
❑ 74-0142	I'm Not Through Loving You/Can't Keep My Mind on the Game	1969	—	3.50	7.00
❑ 74-0231	Molly/Permanent Kind of Lovin' (From a Temporary Man)	1969	—	3.50	7.00
Albums					
MCA					
❑ 5612	Past the Point of No Return	1985	2.00	4.00	8.00
❑ 5723	Everybody Knows I'm Yours	1986	2.00	4.00	8.00
NOBLE VISION					
❑ 2001	The Man in the Mirror	1983	2.50	5.00	10.00
STARDAY					
❑ SLP-149 [M]	Old Time Christmas Singing	1960	17.50	35.00	70.00
❑ SLP-158 [M]	Just Looking for a Home	1961	15.00	30.00	60.00

GLASER, TOMPALL

Also see TOMPALL AND THE GLASER BROTHERS.

Number	Title (A Side/B Side)	Yr	VG	VG+	NM
45s					
ABC					
❑ 12261	It'll Be Her/Sweethearts or Strangers-I Will Always Love You	1977	—	2.00	4.00
❑ 12309	It Never Crossed My Mind/Easy on My Mind	1977	—	2.00	4.00
❑ 12329	Drinking Them Beers/Duncan and Brady	1978	—	2.00	4.00
❑ 12366	Bad Times/Carry Me On	1978	—	2.00	4.00
MGM					
❑ 14622	Bad, Bad, Bad Cowboy/Let It Be Pretty	1973	—	3.00	6.00
❑ 14701	Texas Law Sez/Pass Me On By	1974	—	3.00	6.00
❑ 14740	Musical Chairs/Grab a Hold	1974	—	3.00	6.00
❑ 14800	Put Another Log on the Fire (Male Chauvinist National Anthem)/Mendocino	1975	—	3.00	6.00
—As "Tompall"					
❑ 14843	The Hunger/Wild Side of Life	1976	—	3.00	6.00
—As "Tompall"					

Number	Title (A Side/B Side)	Yr	VG	VG+	NM
POLYDOR					
❑ 14314	T for Texas/Broken Down Momma	1976	—	2.50	5.00
ROBBINS					
❑ 1001	Five Penny Nickel/You're in My Heart	1957	7.50	15.00	30.00
❑ 1003	Baby Be Good/I Want You	1957	7.50	15.00	30.00
Albums					
ABC					
❑ AB-978	Tompall Glaser and His Outlaw Band	1977	2.50	5.00	10.00
❑ AB-1036	The Wonder of It All	1977	2.50	5.00	10.00
MGM					
❑ M3G-4977	Tompall	1974	3.00	6.00	12.00
❑ M3G-5014	The Great Tompall and His Outlaw Band	1976	3.00	6.00	12.00

GLASER BROTHERS, THE

See CHUCK GLASER; JIM GLASER; TOMPALL GLASER; TOMPALL AND THE GLASER BROTHERS.

GLENN, DARRELL

45s

Number	Title (A Side/B Side)	Yr	VG	VG+	NM
COLUMBIA					
❑ 4-43643	I Believe/Once in a While	1966	2.50	5.00	10.00
❑ 4-43775	I Can't Say Goodbye/I Waited a Long Time	1966	2.50	5.00	10.00
❑ 4-43934	You Don't Need Me Anymore/Born, St. Louis	1967	2.50	5.00	10.00
❑ 4-44146	But She's Untrue/The Meaning of Blue	1967	2.50	5.00	10.00
❑ 4-44291	Everybody Wins Sometime/You Only Used Me	1967	2.50	5.00	10.00
DOT					
❑ 15471	Send This Wanderer Home/Your Little Red Wagon	1956	5.00	10.00	20.00
LONGHORN					
❑ 539	A Matter of Fact/Bonnie Sue	1964	3.00	6,00	12.00
❑ 546	I Know I've Lost You/The Ways of the World	1965	3.00	6.00	12.00
NRC					
❑ 004	Congratulations to Me/Make Me Smile Again	1958	5.00	10.00	20.00
❑ 007	Mr. Moonlight/So I've Been Told	1958	5.00	10.00	20.00
POMPEII					
❑ 66680	The Message/I've Been Too Long	1968	2.50	5.00	10.00
❑ 66697	Nancy Loves Me/Older Man and Younger Girl	1969	2.50	5.00	10.00
RCA VICTOR					
❑ 47-5798	In the Chapel in the Moonlight/Once and Only Once	1954	6.25	12.50	25.00
❑ 47-5859	We'll Be Married/Then and Only Then	1954	6.25	12.50	25.00
❑ 47-5927	No Greater Thing/Take Back the Heart	1954	6.25	12.50	25.00
❑ 47-6031	Bye Bye Young Girls/No Tears, No Regrets	1955	6.25	12.50	25.00
❑ 47-6107	Banjo Mambo/Run Little Echo	1955	6.25	12.50	25.00
ROBBEE					
❑ 101	Hoo Doo the Voo Doo/(B-side unknown)	1960	3.75	7.50	15.00
TWINKLE					
❑ 505	That's Right/(B-side unknown)	195?	15.00	30.00	60.00
VALLEY					
❑ 105	Crying in the Chapel/Hang Up That Telephone	1953	10.00	20.00	40.00
—Original version of this classic, which was written by his father, Artie Glenn					
❑ 109	Only a Pastime/I Think I'm Falling in Love with You	1953	7.50	15.00	30.00
❑ 119	Christmas Is Just Around the Corner/(B-side unknown)	1954	7.50	15.00	30.00
Albums					
NRC					
❑ LPA-5 [M]	Crying in the Chapel	1959	6.25	12.50	25.00
❑ SLPA-5 [S]	Crying in the Chapel	1959	7.50	15.00	30.00

GLENN, HOWDY

45s

Number	Title (A Side/B Side)	Yr	VG	VG+	NM
WARNER BROS.					
❑ 8402	Don't Take Pretty to the City/White Line Fever	1977	—	2.00	4.00
❑ 8447	Touch Me/White Line Fever	1977	—	2.00	4.00
❑ 8546	Don't Take Pretty to the City/That Lucky Old Sun	1978	—	2.00	4.00
❑ 8616	You Mean the World to Me/That Lucky Old Sun	1978	—	2.00	4.00
❑ 8704	When You Were Blue and I Was Green/Don't Take Pretty to the City	1978	—	2.00	4.00

GLOSSON, LONNIE

45s

Number	Title (A Side/B Side)	Yr	VG	VG+	NM
DECCA					
❑ 9-46361	I Want You to Know That I Love You/Till the Cows Come Home	1951	6.25	12.50	25.00

GODFREY, RAY

45s

Number	Title (A Side/B Side)	Yr	VG	VG+	NM
ABC					
❑ 10999	I Can't Go On Living Like This/Right Straight in the Eye	1967	2.50	5.00	10.00
COLUMBIA					
❑ 4-43398	Old Love/There's Always Room (For One More Fool Like Me)	1965	2.50	5.00	10.00
❑ 4-43618	I Can Live It Down/Keep Your Chin Up, Soldier	1966	2.50	5.00	10.00
❑ 4-43785	Winner Take All/Please Don't Mention My Name	1966	2.50	5.00	10.00
❑ 4-44071	Three Little Words from You/The Difference in Me	1967	2.50	5.00	10.00
J&J					
❑ 001	The Picture/The Overall Song	1960	10.00	20.00	40.00
PEACH					
❑ 757	Let's Move to the City/Wait, Weep and Wonder	1961	5.00	10.00	20.00
SAVOY					
❑ 3021	The Picture/The Overall Song	1960	6.25	12.50	25.00
SIMS					
❑ 130	Better Times a-Comin'/Ten Silver Dollars	1962	5.00	10.00	20.00
SPRING					
❑ 104	I Gotta Get Away/Sherry Washington	1970	2.00	4.00	8.00
❑ 135	Candy Clown/I Want to Be Your Only Love	1973	—	3.00	6.00
TOLLIE					
❑ 9030	Count Me Out/If the Good Lord's Willing	1964	3.75	7.50	15.00

GOLDEN, JEFF

45s

Number	Title (A Side/B Side)	Yr	VG	VG+	NM
MGA					
❑ 104	Singing the Blues/(B-side unknown)	1989	—	3.00	6.00
❑ 30274	Southern and Proud of It/(B-side unknown)	1988	—	3.00	6.00
❑ 30275	This Old World Ain't the Same/(B-side unknown)	1988	—	3.00	6.00
SOUNDWAVES					
❑ 4816	That New Song (They're Playing)/(B-side unknown)	1989	—	2.50	5.00

GOLDEN, WILLIAM LEE

Also see THE OAK RIDGE BOYS.

45s

Number	Title (A Side/B Side)	Yr	VG	VG+	NM
MCA					
❑ 52819	Love Is the Only Way Out/Music for My Soul	1986	—	2.00	4.00
❑ 52944	You Can't Take It With You/Somebody Gotta Pay	1986	—	2.00	4.00
MERCURY					
❑ 875876-7	Keep Lookin' Up/Louisiana Red Dirty Highway	1990	—	—	3.00
Albums					
MCA					
❑ 5749	American Vagabond	1986	2.00	4.00	8.00

GOLDENS, THE

45s

Number	Title (A Side/B Side)	Yr	VG	VG+	NM
CAPITOL NASHVILLE					
❑ 7PRO-79547	Keep the Faith (same on both sides)	1991	—	3.00	6.00
—Vinyl is promo only					
EPIC					
❑ 34-07716	Put Us Together Again/Country Comfort	1988	—	—	3.00
❑ 34-07928	Sorry Girls/Best Friend's Baby	1988	—	—	3.00

GOLDSBORO, BOBBY

Also see DEL REEVES.

45s

Number	Title (A Side/B Side)	Yr	VG	VG+	NM
BUENA VISTA					
❑ 561	These Are the Best Times/(B-side unknown)	1979	—	2.50	5.00
CURB					
❑ 02117	Love Ain't Never Hurt Nobody/Wings of an Angel	1981	—	2.00	4.00
❑ 02583	The Round-Up Saloon/Green-Eyed Woman, Nashville Blues	1981	—	2.00	4.00
❑ 02726	Lucy and the Stranger/Outrun the Sun	1982	—	2.00	4.00
❑ 5400	Goodbye Marie/Love Has Made a Woman Out of You	1980	—	2.00	4.00
❑ 70052	Alice Doesn't Love Here Anymore/Green-Eyed Woman, Nashville Blues	1981	—	2.00	4.00
EPIC					
❑ 50342	Me and the Elephants/I Love Music	1977	—	2.00	4.00
❑ 50413	The Cowboy and the Lady/Me and Millie	1977	—	2.00	4.00
❑ 50480	He'll Have to Go/Too Hot to Handle	1977	—	2.00	4.00
❑ 50535	Life Gets Hard on Easy Street/Black Fool's Gold	1978	—	2.00	4.00
LAURIE					
❑ 3130	Lonely Traveler/You Better Go Home	1962	3.75	7.50	15.00
❑ 3148	Molly/Honey Baby	1962	3.75	7.50	15.00
❑ 3159	The Letter/The Runaround	1963	3.75	7.50	15.00
❑ 3168	Light the Candles/That's What Love Will Do	1963	3.75	7.50	15.00
UNITED ARTISTS					
❑ 0044	See the Funny Little Clown/Little Things	1973	—	2.00	4.00
❑ 0045	It's Too Late/Voodoo Woman	1973	—	2.00	4.00
❑ 0046	Honey/Autumn of My Life	1973	—	2.00	4.00
❑ 0047	Watching Scotty Grow/I'm a Drifter	1973	—	2.00	4.00
—0044 through 0047 are "Silver Spotlight Series" reissues					
❑ XW251	Summer (The First Time)/Childhood 1949	1973	—	2.50	5.00
❑ XW251 [PS]	Summer (The First Time)/Childhood 1949	1973	—	3.00	6.00
❑ XW371	Marlena/Sing Me a Smile	1973	—	2.50	5.00
❑ XW422	I Believe the South Is Gonna Rise Again/She	1974	—	2.00	4.00
❑ XW451	And Then There Was Gina/Quicksand	1974	—	2.00	4.00
❑ XW517	Summer (The First Time)/Marlena	1974	—	2.00	4.00
—Reissue					
❑ XW529	Hello Summertime/And Then There Was Gina	1974	—	2.00	4.00
❑ XW633	And Then There Was Gina/You Pull Me Down (Into Sweet, Sweet Love)	1975	—	2.00	4.00
❑ 672	See the Funny Little Clown/Hello Loser	1963	2.50	5.00	10.00
❑ XW681	I Wrote a Song (Sing Along)/You Pull Me Down (Into Sweet, Sweet Love)	1975	—	2.00	4.00
❑ 710	Whenever He Holds You/If She Was Mine	1964	2.00	4.00	8.00
❑ 710 [PS]	Whenever He Holds You/If She Was Mine	1964	3.75	7.50	15.00
❑ 742	Me Japanese Boy, I Love You/Everyone But Me	1964	2.00	4.00	8.00
❑ 781	I Don't Know You Anymore/Little Drops of Water	1964	2.00	4.00	8.00
❑ XW793	A Butterfly for Bucky/Another Night Alone	1976	—	2.00	4.00
❑ 810	Little Things/I Can't Go On Pretending	1965	2.50	5.00	10.00
❑ 862	Voodoo Woman/It Breaks My Heart	1965	2.00	4.00	8.00
❑ XW866	She Taught Me How to Live Again/Reunion	1976	—	2.00	4.00
❑ 908	If You Wait for Love/If You've Got a Heart	1965	2.00	4.00	8.00
❑ 952	Broomstick Cowboy/Ain't Got Time for Happy	1965	2.00	4.00	8.00
❑ 980	It's Too Late/I'm Goin' Home	1966	2.00	4.00	8.00

Number	Title (A Side/B Side)	Yr	VG	VG+	NM
❑ 50018	I Know You Better Than That/When Your Love Has Gone	1966	2.00	4.00	8.00
❑ 50018 [PS]	I Know You Better Than That/When Your Love Has Gone	1966	3.75	7.50	15.00
❑ 50044	Longer Than Forever/Take Your Love	1966	2.00	2.00	8.00
❑ 50056	It Hurts Me/Pity the Fool	1966	2.00	2.00	8.00
❑ 50087	Blue Autumn/I Just Don't Love You Anymore	1966	2.00	2.00	8.00
❑ 50138	Love Is/Goodbye to All You Women	1967	2.00	2.00	8.00
❑ 50186	Three in the Morning/Trusty Little Herbert	1967	2.00	2.00	8.00
❑ 50224	Pledge of Love/Jo-Jo's Place	1967	2.00	2.00	8.00
❑ 50283	Honey/Danny	1968	2.50	5.00	10.00
—Black label					
❑ 50283	Honey/Danny	1968	2.00	4.00	8.00
—Orange and pink label					
❑ 50318	Autumn of My Life/She Chased Me	1968	—	3.00	6.00
❑ 50318 [PS]	Autumn of My Life/She Chased Me	1968	3.75	7.50	15.00
❑ 50321	Autumn of My Life/She Chased Me	1968	—	—	—
—Unreleased; these were edits of the versions on UA 50318					
❑ 50461	The Straight Life/Tomorrow Is Forgotten	1968	—	3.00	6.00
❑ 50470	A Christmas Wish/Look Around You (It's Christmas Time)	1968	2.50	5.00	10.00
❑ 50497	Glad She's a Woman/Letter to Emily	1969	—	3.00	6.00
❑ 50525	I'm a Drifter/Hobos and Kings	1969	—	3.00	6.00
❑ 50565	Muddy Mississippi Line/A Richer Man Than I	1969	—	3.00	6.00
❑ 50614	Mornin' Mornin'/Requiem	1969	—	3.00	6.00
❑ 50650	Can You Feel It/Time Good, Time Bad	1970	—	2.50	5.00
❑ 50696	Down on the Bayou/It's Gonna Change	1970	—	2.50	5.00
❑ 50715	My God and I/The World Beyond	1970	—	2.50	5.00
❑ 50727	Watching Scotty Grow/Water Color Days	1970	—	2.50	5.00
❑ 50776	And I Love You So/Gentle of a Man	1971	—	2.50	5.00
❑ 50807	I'll Remember You/Come Back Home	1971	—	2.50	5.00
❑ 50846	Poem for the Little Lady/Danny Is a Mirror to Me	1971	—	2.50	5.00
❑ 50891	California Wine/To Be with You	1972	—	2.50	5.00
❑ 50938	With Pen in Hand/Southern Fried Singin' Sunday Mornin'	1972	—	2.50	5.00
❑ 51107	Country Feelin's/Brand New Kind of Love	1973	—	2.50	5.00

Albums

CURB

Number	Title (A Side/B Side)	Yr	VG	VG+	NM
❑ JZ 36822	Bobby Goldsboro	1980	3.00	6.00	12.00
❑ FZ 37734	Round-Up Saloon	1982	2.50	5.00	10.00

EPIC

Number	Title (A Side/B Side)	Yr	VG	VG+	NM
❑ PE 34703	Goldsboro	1977	3.00	6.00	12.00

LIBERTY

Number	Title (A Side/B Side)	Yr	VG	VG+	NM
❑ LMAS-5502	Bobby Goldsboro's Greatest Hits	1981	2.00	4.00	8.00
—Reissue of United Artists 5502					
❑ LN-10007	Bobby Goldsboro's 10th Anniversary Album, Volume 1	1981	2.00	4.00	8.00
❑ LN-10047	Bobby Goldsboro's 10th Anniversary Album, Volume 2	1981	2.00	4.00	8.00
❑ LN-10114	The Best of Bobby Goldsboro	1981	2.00	4.00	8.00

SUNSET

Number	Title (A Side/B Side)	Yr	VG	VG+	NM
❑ SUS-5236	This Is Bobby Goldsboro	1969	3.00	6.00	12.00
❑ SUS-5284	Pledge of Love	1970	3.00	6.00	12.00
❑ SUS-5313	Autumn of My Life	1971	3.00	6.00	12.00

UNITED ARTISTS

Number	Title (A Side/B Side)	Yr	VG	VG+	NM
❑ UA-LA019-F	Brand New Kind of Love	1972	3.75	7.50	15.00
❑ SP-58 [DJ]	The Bobby Goldsboro Family Album	1971	12.50	25.00	50.00
—Promo-only compilation					
❑ UA-LA124-F	Summer (The First Time)	1973	3.75	7.50	15.00
❑ UA-LA311-H2 [(2)]	Bobby Goldsboro's 10th Anniversary Album	1974	5.00	10.00	20.00
❑ UA-LA424-G	Through the Eyes of a Man	1975	3.00	6.00	12.00
❑ UA-LA639-G	Butterfly for Bucky	1976	3.00	6.00	12.00
❑ UAL 3358 [M]	The Bobby Goldsbob Album	1964	5.00	10.00	20.00
❑ UAL 3381 [M]	I Can't Stop Loving You	1964	5.00	10.00	20.00
❑ UAL 3425 [M]	Little Things	1965	5.00	10.00	20.00
❑ UAL 3471 [M]	Broomstick Cowboy	1966	5.00	10.00	20.00
❑ UAL 3486 [M]	It's Too Late	1966	5.00	10.00	20.00
❑ UAL 3552 [M]	Blue Autumn	1967	5.00	10.00	20.00
❑ UAL 3561 [M]	Sold Goldsboro/Bobby Goldsboro's Greatest Hits	1967	5.00	10.00	20.00
❑ UAL 3599 [M]	Romantic, Soulful, Wacky	1967	5.00	10.00	20.00
❑ UAS 5502	Bobby Goldsboro's Greatest Hits	1970	5.00	10.00	20.00
❑ UAS 5516	Come Back Home	1971	3.75	7.50	15.00
❑ UAS-5578	California Wine	1972	3.75	7.50	15.00
❑ UAS 6358 [S]	The Bobby Goldsbob Album	1964	6.25	12.50	25.00
❑ UAS 6358 [S]	I Can't Stop Loving You	1964	6.25	12.50	25.00
❑ UAS 6425 [S]	Little Things	1965	6.25	12.50	25.00
❑ UAS 6471 [S]	Broomstick Cowboy	1966	6.25	12.50	25.00
❑ UAS 6486 [S]	It's Too Late	1966	6.25	12.50	25.00
❑ UAS 6552 [S]	Blue Autumn	1967	6.25	12.50	25.00
❑ UAS 6561 [S]	Sold Goldsboro/Bobby Goldsboro's Greatest Hits	1967	5.00	10.00	20.00
❑ UAS 6599 [S]	Romantic, Soulful, Wacky	1967	5.00	10.00	20.00
❑ UAS 6642	Honey	1968	5.00	10.00	20.00
❑ UAS 6657	Word Pictures Featuring Autumn of My Life	1968	5.00	10.00	20.00
❑ UAS 6704	Today	1969	5.00	10.00	20.00
❑ UAS 6735	Muddy Mississippi Line	1969	5.00	10.00	20.00
❑ UAS 6777	We Gotta Start Lovin'	1970	5.00	10.00	20.00
❑ UAS 6777	Watching Scotty Grow	1971	3.75	7.50	15.00
—Retitled version of above					

GOODNIGHT, GARY

45s

AWESOME

Number	Title (A Side/B Side)	Yr	VG	VG+	NM
❑ 102	I Got a Thing About You Baby/(B-side unknown)	1984	—	3.00	6.00

DOOR KNOB

Number	Title (A Side/B Side)	Yr	VG	VG+	NM
❑ 133	Texas Let Me In/Ladies Don't Marry Cowboys	1980	—	2.50	5.00
❑ 138	I Have to Break the Chains That Bind Me/(B-side unknown)	1980	—	2.50	5.00
❑ 141	Make Me Believe/Back Door Slam	1981	—	2.50	5.00
❑ 149	Get Me High, Off This Low/(B-side unknown)	1981	—	2.50	5.00
❑ 155	Tell Me So/There'll Be a Blue Moon Tonight	1981	—	2.50	5.00
❑ 159	Let Me Fill for You a Fantasy/(B-side unknown)	1981	—	2.50	5.00
❑ 166	Losin' Myself in You/Vagabond Cowboy	1981	—	2.50	5.00
❑ 169	Lady Lay Down (Lay Down on My Pillow)/(B-side unknown)	1981	—	2.50	5.00

SOUNDWAVES

Number	Title (A Side/B Side)	Yr	VG	VG+	NM
❑ 4675	Bringing Out the Fool in Me/Texas Let Me In	1982	—	2.50	5.00
❑ 4689	Goodnight My Love/These Magic Feelings	1982	—	2.50	5.00
❑ 4703	My Baby's Gone/Goodnight My Love	1983	—	2.50	5.00

GOODSON, C.L.

45s

ISLAND

Number	Title (A Side/B Side)	Yr	VG	VG+	NM
❑ 030	18 Yellow Roses/The More She Thinks About Him	1975	—	3.50	7.00

GOODSON, LLOYD

45s

MERCURY

Number	Title (A Side/B Side)	Yr	VG	VG+	NM
❑ 57028	Dreamin' Dreams and Wishin' Rain/There's No Such Thing as a Cheap Motel	1980	—	2.00	4.00

UNITED ARTISTS

Number	Title (A Side/B Side)	Yr	VG	VG+	NM
❑ XW891	Jesus Is the Same in California/Wearin' Out the Patches in My Jeans	1976	—	3.00	6.00
❑ XW952	Down Home Upbringin'/Wishin' I Could Change the Kind of Fool I've Been	1977	—	3.00	6.00

GOODSON, MITCH

45s

PARTRIDGE

Number	Title (A Side/B Side)	Yr	VG	VG+	NM
❑ 002	Draggin' Leather/She Loves It (As Much As Me)	1980	—	3.00	6.00
❑ 011	Do You Wanna Spend the Night/(B-side unknown)	1980	—	3.00	6.00

GOODWIN, BILL

45s

BAND BOX

Number	Title (A Side/B Side)	Yr	VG	VG+	NM
❑ 287	Revenuer Man/Too Many Heartaches	196?	3.75	7.50	15.00
❑ 293	Those Same Old Things/Pardon My Tears	196?	3.75	7.50	15.00
❑ 309	Heartaches/Don't Take My World Away	196?	3.75	7.50	15.00
❑ 323	You Did This to Me/Making It Easy on Yourself	196?	3.75	7.50	15.00

VEE JAY

Number	Title (A Side/B Side)	Yr	VG	VG+	NM
❑ 501	Shoes of a Fool/It Keeps Right On a-Hrtin'	1963	3.75	7.50	15.00
❑ 564	I Won't Wait Up Tonight/The Stand-In	1963	3.75	7.50	15.00
❑ 602	The Saddest Eyes/The House at 103	1964	3.75	7.50	15.00

GORDON, LUKE

45s

ISLAND

Number	Title (A Side/B Side)	Yr	VG	VG+	NM
❑ 0640	Dark Hollow/You May Be Someone (Where You Came From)	1958	5.00	10.00	20.00

NASHVILLE

Number	Title (A Side/B Side)	Yr	VG	VG+	NM
❑ 5271	Love's Fantasy/Threshold to Heaven	196?	2.50	5.00	10.00

GORDON, ROBERT

45s

PRIVATE STOCK

Number	Title (A Side/B Side)	Yr	VG	VG+	NM
❑ 45156	Red Hot/Sweet Surrender	1977	—	3.00	6.00
❑ 45191	Sea Cruise/If This Is Wrong	1978	—	3.00	6.00
—With Link Wray					
❑ 45203	Fire/If This Is Wrong	1979	—	3.00	6.00
❑ 45203 [PS]	Fire/If This Is Wrong	1979	3.00	6.00	12.00

RCA

Number	Title (A Side/B Side)	Yr	VG	VG+	NM
❑ JH-11452 [DJ]	Blue Christmas (mono/stereo)	1978	—	3.00	6.00
❑ PB-11452	Blue Christmas/Fire	1978	—	2.50	5.00
—With Link Wray					
❑ PB-11471	It's Only Make Believe/Rock Billy Boogie	1979	—	2.50	5.00
❑ PB-11608	Walk On By/Black Slacks	1979	—	2.50	5.00
❑ PB-11919	Born to Lose/Need You	1980	—	2.50	5.00
❑ PB-12239	Someday, Someway/Drivin' Wheel	1981	—	2.50	5.00
❑ PB-13399	Something's Gonna Happen/Flying Saucers Rock and Roll	1982	—	2.50	5.00

Albums

PRIVATE STOCK

Number	Title (A Side/B Side)	Yr	VG	VG+	NM
❑ PS-2030	Robert Gordon with Link Wray	1977	4.00	8.00	16.00
—Formerly with Tuff Darts					
❑ PS-7008	Fresh Fish Special	1978	4.00	8.00	16.00

RCA VICTOR

Number	Title (A Side/B Side)	Yr	VG	VG+	NM
❑ AFL1-3294	Rock Billy Boogie	1979	5.00	10.00	20.00
—Original pressing on white vinyl					
❑ AFL1-3294	Rock Billy Boogie	1979	3.00	6.00	12.00
❑ AFL1-3296	Robert Gordon with Link Wray	1979	3.00	6.00	12.00
—Reissue					
❑ AFL1-3299	Fresh Fish Special	1979	3.00	6.00	12.00
—Reissue					
❑ DJL1-3411 [DJ]	Essential Robert Gordon	1979	7.50	15.00	30.00
—Promo-only live album with tracks from Tuff Darts					
❑ AFL1-3523	Bad Boy	1980	3.00	6.00	12.00
❑ AFL1-3773	Are You Gonna Be the One	1981	3.00	6.00	12.00
❑ AFL1-4380	Too Fast to Live, Too Young to Die	1982	3.00	6.00	12.00

GORME, EYDIE

The pop singer, also well known for her duets with Steve Lawrence, saw the below single make the country charts.

45s

MGM

Number	Title (A Side/B Side)	Yr	VG	VG+	NM
❑ 14563	Take One Step/The Garden	1973	—	2.50	5.00

GOSDIN, REX

Also see THE GOSDIN BROTHERS.

45s

Number	Title (A Side/B Side)	Yr	VG	VG+	NM
GRAPE VINE					
❑ 12046	Lovin' You Is Music to My Mind/How Can Anything That Sounds So Good	1980	—	3.50	7.00
GRC					
❑ 2074	How Can Anything That Sounds So Good (Make Me Feel So Bad)/Things I Remember	1975	—	3.00	6.00
METROMEDIA					
❑ 68-0110	Has Anybody Here Seen My Margie/Sarah Lee	1973	—	3.50	7.00
METROMEDIA COUNTRY					
❑ 904	Sarah Lee/(B-side unknown)	1973	2.00	4.00	8.00
MRC					
❑ 10589	We're Making Up for Lost Time/(B-side unknown)	1979	—	3.50	7.00
SABRE					
❑ 4520	Just Give Me What You Think Is Fair/Things I Remember	1980	—	3.50	7.00
—A-side with Tommy Jennings					
SUN					
❑ 1178	That Old Time Feelin'/Morning, Noon and Night	1982	—	3.50	7.00

GOSDIN, VERN

Also see THE GOSDIN BROTHERS.

45s

Number	Title (A Side/B Side)	Yr	VG	VG+	NM
AMI					
❑ 1302	Don't Ever Leave Me Again/Love Is All We Had to Share	1982	—	2.50	5.00
❑ 1307	Your Bedroom Eyes/Love Is All We Had to Share	1982	—	2.50	5.00
❑ 1310	Today My World Slipped Away/Ain't It Been Love	1982	—	2.50	5.00
❑ 1312	Friday Night Feelin'/Lovin' You Is Music to My Mind	1983	—	2.50	5.00
COLUMBIA					
❑ 38-07627	Do You Believe Me Now/Nobody Calls from Vegas Just to Say Hello	1987	—	—	3.00
❑ 38-07762	Set 'Em Up Joe/There Ain't Nothing Wrong (Just Ain't Nothing Right)	1988	—	2.00	4.00
❑ 38-08003	Chiseled in Stone/Tight as Twin Fiddles	1988	—	—	3.00
❑ 38-08528	Who You Gonna Blame It On This Time/It's Not Over Yet	1988	—	—	3.00
❑ 38-68888	I'm Still Crazy/Paradise '83	1989	—	—	3.00
❑ 38-69084	That Just About Does It/Set 'Em Up Joe	1989	—	—	3.00
❑ 38-73221	Right in the Wrong Direction/Tanqueray	1990	—	—	3.00
❑ 38-73350	Tanqueray/You're Not by Yourself	1990	—	—	3.00
❑ 38-73491	This Ain't My First Rodeo/If You're Gonna Do Me Wrong (Do It Right)	1990	—	—	3.00
❑ 38-73632	Is It Raining at Your House/Today My World Slipped Away	1990	—	—	3.00
❑ 38-73814	I Knew My Day Would Come/Love Will Keep Your Hand on the Wheel	1991	—	—	3.00
❑ 38-73946	The Garden/I'd Better Write It Down	1991	—	—	3.00
❑ 38-74103	A Month of Sundays/The Bridge I'm Still Building On	1991	—	—	3.00
❑ 38-74905	Back When/What Are We Gonna Do About Me	1993	—	2.00	4.00
COMPLEAT					
❑ 102	If You're Gonna Do Me Wrong (Do It Right)/Favorite Fool of All	1983	—	2.50	5.00
❑ 108	Way Down Deep/Today My World Slipped Away	1983	—	2.50	5.00
❑ 115	I Wonder Where We'd Be Tonight/I Feel Love Closin' In	1983	—	2.50	5.00
❑ 122	I Can Tell by the Way You Dance (You're Gonna Love Me Tonight)/My Heart Is in Good Hands	1984	—	2.50	5.00
❑ 126	What Would Your Memories Do/Lovely Right to the End	1984	—	2.50	5.00
❑ 135	Slow Burning Memory/I've Got a Heart Full of You	1984	—	2.50	5.00
❑ 142	Dim Lights, Thick Smoke (And Loud, Loud Music)/For a Minute There	1985	—	2.50	5.00
❑ 145	I Know the Way to You By Heart/Rainbows and Roses	1985	—	2.50	5.00
❑ 149	It's Only Love Again/What a Price I've Paid	1985	—	2.50	5.00
❑ 153	It's Only Love Again/Today My World Slipped Away	1986	—	2.50	5.00
❑ 155	Was It Just the Wine/Way Down Deep	1986	—	2.50	5.00
❑ 158	Time Stood Still/Slow Burning Memory	1986	—	2.50	5.00
ELEKTRA					
❑ 45353	Hangin' On/Yesterday's Gone	1976	—	2.50	5.00
❑ 45411	Till the End/It Started All Over Again	1977	—	2.50	5.00
❑ 45436	Mother Country Music/We Make Beautiful Music Together	1977	—	2.50	5.00
❑ 45483	Never My Love/I Sure Can Love You	1978	—	2.50	5.00
❑ 45532	Break My Mind/Without You There's a Sadness in My Song	1978	—	2.50	5.00
❑ 46021	You've Got Somebody, I've Got Somebody/Till I'm Over Gettin' Over You	1979	—	2.50	5.00
❑ 46052	All I Want and Need Forever/Fifteen Hundred Times a Day	1979	—	2.50	5.00
❑ 46550	Sarah's Eyes/She's Gone	1979	—	2.50	5.00
OVATION					
❑ 1163	Too Long Gone/She's Just a Place to Fall	1981	—	2.50	5.00
❑ 1171	Dream of Me/Ain't It Been Love	1981	—	2.50	5.00

Albums

Number	Title (A Side/B Side)	Yr	VG	VG+	NM
AMI					
❑ 1502	Today My World Slipped Away	1983	3.00	6.00	12.00
COLUMBIA					
❑ 1P 8037	10 Years of Greatest Hits — Newly Recorded	1990	5.00	10.00	20.00
—Columbia House vinyl edition (only U.S. version)					
❑ FC 40982	Chiseled in Stone	1988	2.00	4.00	8.00
❑ FC 45104	Alone	1989	3.00	6.00	12.00
COMPLEAT					
❑ 1004	If You're Gonna Do Me Wrong (Do It Right)	1983	2.50	5.00	10.00
❑ 1008	There Is a Season	1984	2.50	5.00	10.00
❑ 671012	Time Stood Still	1984	2.50	5.00	10.00
❑ 671022	Greatest Hits	1986	2.50	5.00	10.00
ELEKTRA					
❑ 6E-124	Never My Love	1978	2.50	5.00	10.00
❑ 6E-180	You've Got Somebody	1979	2.50	5.00	10.00
❑ 6E-228	The Best of Vern Gosdin	1979	2.50	5.00	10.00
❑ 7E-1112	Till the End	1977	2.50	5.00	10.00

GOSDIN BROTHERS, THE

Also see REX GOSDIN; VERN GOSDIN.

45s

Number	Title (A Side/B Side)	Yr	VG	VG+	NM
BAKERSFIELD INT'L.					
❑ 1002	Hangin' On/Multiple Heartache	1967	3.75	7.50	15.00
❑ 1006	She Still Wishes I Was You/There Must Be Someone	1968	3.75	7.50	15.00
CAPITOL					
❑ 2265	Sounds of Goodbye/The Victim	1968	2.50	5.00	10.00
❑ 2412	Louisiana Man/Till the End	1969	2.50	5.00	10.00
❑ 2553	The Day the Rains Came/My Love Keeps Reaching Out for You	1969	2.50	5.00	10.00
❑ 3074	I Remember/Just Like the Wind	1971	2.00	4.00	8.00
METROMEDIA					
❑ BMBO-0105	I Have Everything I Need in You/You Love Me Just Enough	1973	—	3.50	7.00
WORLD PACIFIC					
❑ 77835	Love at First Sight/To Ramona	1966	3.00	6.00	12.00

Albums

Number	Title (A Side/B Side)	Yr	VG	VG+	NM
CAPITOL					
❑ ST 2852	Sounds of Goodbye	1968	5.00	10.00	20.00

GRAHAM, TAMMY

45s

Number	Title (A Side/B Side)	Yr	VG	VG+	NM
CAREER					
❑ 12953	Tell Me Again/Cool Water	1996	—	—	3.00
❑ 13075	A Dozen Red Roses/Tell Me Again	1997	—	—	3.00
❑ 13089	Cool Water/More About Love	1997	—	—	3.00

GRAMMER, BILLY

45s

Number	Title (A Side/B Side)	Yr	VG	VG+	NM
DECCA					
❑ 31226	Columbus Stockade Blues/There's a Rainbow 'Round My Shoulder	1961	2.50	5.00	10.00
❑ 31274	Have a Drink on Me/Finger	1961	2.50	5.00	10.00
❑ 31321	Save Your Tears/I'd Like to Know You	1961	2.50	5.00	10.00
❑ 31396	He Ain't My Buddy No More/Blue Roller Rink	1962	2.50	5.00	10.00
❑ 31449	I Wanna Go Home (Detroit City)/Bottom of the Glass	1962	2.50	5.00	10.00
❑ 31514	Love Gets Better with Time/Lonesome Life	1963	2.50	5.00	10.00
❑ 31562	Old Foolish Me/I'll Leave the Porch Lights a-Burning	1963	2.50	5.00	10.00
❑ 31618	Don't Drop It/I Saw Your Face in the Moon	1964	2.00	4.00	8.00
❑ 31669	Wabash Cannonball/Gonna Lay Down My Old Guitar	1964	2.00	4.00	8.00
❑ 31757	Little Bit of Happiness/I'm Letting You Go (Goodbye)	1965	2.00	4.00	8.00
❑ 31892	Brown's Ferry Blues/Souvenirs of Sorrow	1966	2.00	4.00	8.00
EPIC					
❑ 10052	Bottles/Temporarily	1966	2.00	4.00	8.00
❑ 10103	Heaven Help This Heart of Mine/The Real Thing	1966	2.00	4.00	8.00
❑ 10169	I've Seen That Look on Me (A Thousand Times)/Written on a Jailhouse	1967	2.00	4.00	8.00
EVEREST					
❑ 19353	Unknown Soldier/Princess of Persia	1960	2.50	5.00	10.00
❑ 19384	Big Big Dream/River of Regret	1960	2.50	5.00	10.00
JMI					
❑ 9	Nobody's Listening to the Preacher Anymore/(B-side unknown)	1972	2.00	4.00	8.00
MERCURY					
❑ 72785	Money, Love and War/Last of My Future	1968	2.00	4.00	8.00
❑ 72836	The Ballad of John Dillinger/Do You Still Believe	1968	2.00	4.00	8.00
❑ 72893	The Hour of Separation/The Changing Scene	1969	—	3.00	6.00
MONUMENT					
❑ 400	Gotta Travel On/Chasing a Dream	1958	3.75	7.50	15.00
❑ 403	Bonaparte's Retreat/The Kissing Tree	1959	3.00	6.00	12.00
❑ 407	It Takes You/Willie, Quit Your Playing	1959	3.00	6.00	12.00
❑ 413	Loveland/On the Job Too Long	1960	3.00	6.00	12.00
❑ 8653	Family Man/What We Have in Common Is Love	1975	—	2.00	4.00
❑ 8665	Steppin' Out/Mom and Dad's Waltz	1975	—	2.00	4.00
❑ 8685	That's Life/Who's Gonna Buy You the Ribbons	1976	—	2.00	4.00

Number	Title (A Side/B Side)	Yr	VG	VG+	NM
RICE					
❑ 5025	Mabel (You Have Been a Friend to Me)/Papa and Mama	1967	2.00	4.00	8.00
STONEWAY					
❑ 1129	Tie Me to Your Apron Strings Again/Blue Jay Rag	197?	—	3.00	6.00
STOP					
❑ 321	Jesus Is a Soul Man/Peace on Earth Begins Today	1969	—	3.00	6.00
7-Inch Extended Plays					
DECCA					
❑ ED 2767	Detroit City/Old Foolish Me//Love Gets Better with Time/Have a Drink on Me	196?	3.00	6.00	12.00
❑ ED 2767 [PS]	Billy Grammer	196?	3.00	6.00	12.00
Albums					
DECCA					
❑ DL 4212 [M]	Gospel Guitar	1962	3.75	7.50	15.00
❑ DL 4460 [M]	Golden Gospel Favorites	1964	3.00	6.00	12.00
❑ DL 4542 [M]	Gotta Travel On	1965	3.00	6.00	12.00
❑ DL 4642 [M]	Country Guitar	1965	3.00	6.00	12.00
❑ DL 74212 [S]	Gospel Guitar	1962	5.00	10.00	20.00
❑ DL 74460 [S]	Golden Gospel Favorites	1964	3.75	7.50	15.00
❑ DL 74542 [S]	Gotta Travel On	1965	3.75	7.50	15.00
❑ DL 74642 [S]	Country Guitar	1965	3.75	7.50	15.00
EPIC					
❑ LN 24233 [M]	Sunday Guitar	1967	3.75	7.50	15.00
❑ BN 26233 [S]	Sunday Guitar	1967	3.75	7.50	15.00
MONUMENT					
❑ MLP-4000 [M]	Travelin' On	1959	10.00	20.00	40.00
❑ MLP-8039 [M]	Travelin' On	1965	6.25	12.50	25.00
❑ SLP-18039 [P]	Travelin' On	1965	7.50	15.00	30.00
VOCALION					
❑ VL 73826	Favorites	1968	3.00	6.00	12.00

GRANT, BARRY

Number	Title (A Side/B Side)	Yr	VG	VG+	NM
45s					
COUNTRYSTOCK					
❑ 1602	We're In for Hard Times/Most Wanted Outlaw	1979	—	3.00	6.00
—As "Breakfast Barry"					
CSI					
❑ 001	Out with the Boys/Pretty Poison	1979	—	3.00	6.00
NSD					
❑ 72	That's the Way My Woman Loves/Pretty Poison	1980	—	2.50	5.00
—As "Amarillo"					
❑ 81	How Long Has This Been Going On/Somehow, Someway and Someday	1981	—	2.50	5.00
—As "Amarillo"					
❑ 104	A Little Bit Crazy/Out with the Boys	1981	—	2.50	5.00
—As "Amarillo"					

GRANT, TOM

Also see MARGO SMITH; TRINITY LANE.

Number	Title (A Side/B Side)	Yr	VG	VG+	NM
45s					
ELEKTRA					
❑ 69961	I'm Gonna Love You Right Out of This World/Sundown Lady	1982	—	2.50	5.00
REPUBLIC					
❑ 036	If You Could See Me Through My Eyes/You're Easy to Love	1979	—	3.00	6.00
❑ 043	We've Gotta Get Away From It All/Catching Up on Love	1979	—	3.00	6.00
❑ 045	Sail On/Meet You in Paradise	1979	—	3.00	6.00

GRAY, BILLY

Also see WANDA JACKSON.

Number	Title (A Side/B Side)	Yr	VG	VG+	NM
45s					
DECCA					
❑ 29489	Okie Blondie/I've Had At My Heart	1955	7.50	15.00	30.00
❑ 29678	Harbor of Love/Girls, Girls, Girls	1955	7.50	15.00	30.00
❑ 29800	Tennessee Toddy/It Could Have Been Me	1956	10.00	20.00	40.00
LIBERTY					
❑ 55599	I'll Never Live Long Enough/I Left My Heart in San Francisco	1963	3.00	6.00	12.00
❑ 55712	Last Call for Alcohol/Late Last Night	1964	2.50	5.00	10.00

GRAY, CLAUDE

Number	Title (A Side/B Side)	Yr	VG	VG+	NM
45s					
COLUMBIA					
❑ 4-43150	Too Many Rivers/House of Tears	1964	2.50	5.00	10.00
❑ 4-43294	Thank You Neighbor/Kinderhook Bill	1965	2.50	5.00	10.00
❑ 4-43443	For Losing You/Thank You for the Ride	1965	2.50	5.00	10.00
❑ 4-43614	Mean Old Woman/Then Cry You Away	1966	2.50	5.00	10.00
COUNTRY INT'L.					
❑ 158	Every Night Sensation/(B-side unknown)	1980	—	3.00	6.00
❑ 164	Pride Goes Before a Fall/Every Night Sensation	1980	—	3.00	6.00
❑ 169	He's Just an Illusion/Every Night Sensation	1981	—	3.00	6.00
❑ 208	Sweet Caroline/Half a Mind	1986	—	3.00	6.00
D					
❑ 1059	Letter Overdue/I'm Not Supposed	1959	6.25	12.50	25.00
❑ 1093	Best Part of Me/Loneliness	1959	6.25	12.50	25.00
❑ 1118	Family Bible/Crying in the Night	1960	6.25	12.50	25.00
❑ 1144	My Party's Over/Leave Alone	1960	5.00	10.00	20.00
❑ 1154	When the Light Shines in the Valley/Homecoming in Heaven	1960	5.00	10.00	20.00
DECCA					
❑ 32039	I Never Had the One I Wanted/Effects Your Leaving Had on Me	1966	2.00	4.00	8.00
❑ 32122	Because of Him/If I Ever Need a Lady (I'll Call You)	1967	—	3.50	7.00
❑ 32180	How Fast Them Trucks Can Go/Next Time You See Me	1967	—	3.50	7.00
❑ 32266	Easy Way Out/Your Devil Memory	1968	—	3.00	6.00
❑ 32312	Night Life/Just Between Us Tears	1968	—	3.00	6.00
❑ 32393	The Love of a Woman/The Kind You Find Tonight Forget Tomorrow	1968	—	3.00	6.00
❑ 32456	Don't Give Me a Chance/Once in Every Lifetime	1969	—	3.00	6.00
❑ 32566	Take Off Time/Sherry Ann	1969	—	3.00	6.00
❑ 32648	The Cleanest Man in Cincinnati/Crazy Arms	1970	—	3.00	6.00
❑ 32697	Everything Will Be Alright/Apartment No. 9	1970	—	3.00	6.00
❑ 32786	Angel/Save My Mind	1971	—	3.00	6.00
❑ 32852	Baton Rouge/Your Devil Memory	1971	—	3.00	6.00
GRANNY WHITE					
❑ 10001	Rockin' My Memories (To Sleep)/But That's All Right	1976	—	3.50	7.00
❑ 10002	We Fell in Love That Way/That's My Baby	1976	—	3.50	7.00
❑ 10003	It'll Do/Vin Rose	1977	—	3.50	7.00
❑ 10005	Slow Dancing/Late Cup of Coffee	1977	—	3.50	7.00
❑ 10006	If I Ever Need a Lady/The Bar	1978	—	3.50	7.00
❑ 10007	I Never Had the One I Wanted/Late Cup of Coffee	1978	—	3.50	7.00
❑ 10009	Let's Go All the Way/We Climbed a Mountain Last Night	1982	—	3.50	7.00
—With Norma Jean					
❑ 10010	So Sad (To Watch Good Love Go Bad)/Who Sent My Ex to Texas	1982	—	3.50	7.00
❑ 10011	Old Flames Can't Hold a Candle to You/How Fast Them Trucks Can Go	198?	—	3.50	7.00
LITTLE DARLIN'					
❑ 7924	It Ain't the Wakin' Up/The Effects Your Leaving Had on Me	1979	—	3.50	7.00
MERCURY					
❑ 71732	I'll Just Have a Cup of Coffee (Then I'll Go)/I Just Want to Be Alone	1960	3.00	6.00	12.00
❑ 71826	My Ears Should Burn (When Fools Are Talked About)/Crying in the Night	1961	3.00	6.00	12.00
❑ 71898	Let's End It Before It Begins/Talk to Me Old Lonesome Heart	1961	3.00	6.00	12.00
❑ 71936	You Take the Table (I'll Take the Chairs)/Stone Heart	1962	3.00	6.00	12.00
❑ 72001	Daddy Stopped In/Three Times	1962	3.00	6.00	12.00
❑ 72063	Knock Again, True Love/Call of the Wild	1962	3.00	6.00	12.00
❑ 72088	First Love Never Dies/Heartbreak Eve	1963	3.00	6.00	12.00
❑ 72156	Go Home Cheater/I'm Gonna Lie Again	1963	3.00	6.00	12.00
❑ 72236	Eight Years (And Two Children Later)/Lonesome	1964	3.00	6.00	12.00
MILLION					
❑ 3	Straight Down to Heaven/Jeannie	1972	2.00	4.00	8.00
❑ 18	What Every Woman Wants to Hear/There's You	1972	2.00	4.00	8.00
❑ 31	Woman Ease My Mind/Don't Fight the Feeling	1972	2.00	4.00	8.00
❑ 36	Loving You Is a Habit I Can't Break/We Could	1973	2.00	4.00	8.00
Albums					
DECCA					
❑ DL 4882 [M]	Claude Gray Sings	1967	6.25	12.50	25.00
❑ DL 74882 [S]	Claude Gray Sings	1967	5.00	10.00	20.00
❑ DL 74963	The Easy Way of Claude Gray	1968	5.00	10.00	20.00
HILLTOP					
❑ JM-6051 [M]	Treasure of Love	1967	3.75	7.50	15.00
❑ JS-6051 [S]	Treasure of Love	1967	3.00	6.00	12.00
MERCURY					
❑ MG-20658 [M]	Songs of Broken Love Affairs	1962	5.00	10.00	20.00
❑ MG-20718 [M]	Country Goes to Town	1962	5.00	10.00	20.00
❑ SR-60658 [S]	Songs of Broken Love Affairs	1962	6.25	12.50	25.00
❑ SR-60718 [S]	Country Goes to Town	1962	6.25	12.50	25.00

GRAY, DOBIE

He didn't make the country charts for the first time until 1986, but many of his earlier records have a country feel.

Number	Title (A Side/B Side)	Yr	VG	VG+	NM
12-Inch Singles					
INFINITY					
❑ INF-16001	You Can Do It/Thank You for Tonight	1979	3.00	6.00	12.00
45s					
ANTHEM					
❑ 200	Guess Who?/Bits and Pieces	1972	—	2.50	5.00
ARISTA					
❑ 1047	One Can Fake It/(B-side unknown)	1983	—	2.00	4.00
CAPITOL					
❑ 2241	We the People/Funny and Groovy	1968	2.50	5.00	10.00
❑ B-5562	Gonna Be a Long Night/That's One to Grown On	1986	—	—	3.00
❑ B-5596	The Dark Side of Life/A Night in the Life of a Country Boy	1986	—	—	3.00
❑ B-5647	From Where I Stand/So Far So Good	1986	—	—	3.00
❑ 5853	River Deep, Mountain High/Tennessee Waltz	1967	3.75	7.50	15.00
❑ B-44087	Take It Real Easy/You Must Have Been Reading My Heart	1987	—	—	3.00
❑ B-44126	Love Letters/Steady As She Goes	1988	—	—	3.00
CAPRICORN					
❑ 0249	If Love Must Go/Lover's Sweat	1975	—	2.00	4.00
❑ 0259	Find 'Em, Fool 'Em and Forget 'Em/Mellow Man	1976	—	2.00	4.00
❑ 0267	Let Go/Mellow Man	1976	—	2.00	4.00

Number	Title (A Side/B Side)	Yr	VG	VG+	NM
CHARGER					
❑ 105	The "In" Crowd/To Be a Man	1964	3.00	6.00	12.00
❑ 107	See You at the "Go-Go"/Walk with Love	1965	2.50	5.00	10.00
❑ 109	In Hollywood/Mr. Engineer	1965	2.50	5.00	10.00
❑ 113	Monkey Jerk/My Baby	1965	2.50	5.00	10.00
❑ 115	No Room to Cry/Out on the Floor	1966	2.50	5.00	10.00
CORDAK					
❑ 1602	Look at Me/Walkin' and Whistlin'	1962	3.75	7.50	15.00
DECCA					
❑ 33057	Drift Away/City Stars	1973	—	2.50	5.00
INFINITY					
❑ 50003	You Can Do It/Sharing the Night Together	1978	—	2.00	4.00
❑ 50010	Who's Lovin' You/Thank You for Tonight	1979	—	2.00	4.00
❑ 50020	Spending Time, Making Love, and Going Crazy/ Let This Man Take Hold of Your Life	1979	—	2.00	4.00
❑ 50043	The In Crowd/Let This Man Take Hold of Your Life	1979	—	2.00	4.00
MCA					
❑ 40100	Loving Arms/Now That I'm Without You	1973	—	2.00	4.00
❑ 40153	Good Old Song/Reachin' for the Feelin'	1973	—	2.00	4.00
❑ 40188	Rose/Lovin' the Easy Way	1974	—	2.00	4.00
❑ 40201	There's a Honky Tonk Angel (Who'll Take Me Back In)/Lovin' the Easy Way	1974	—	2.00	4.00
❑ 40268	Watch Out for Lucy/Turning On You	1974	—	2.00	4.00
❑ 40315	The Music's Real/Roll On Sweet Mississippi	1974	—	2.00	4.00
ROBOX					
❑ RRS-117	Decorate the Night (same on both sides)	1979	—	2.50	5.00
WHITE WHALE					
❑ 300	Rose Garden/Where's the Girl Gone	1969	2.50	5.00	10.00
❑ 330	What a Way to Go/Do You Really Have a Heart	1969	50.00	100.00	200.00
❑ 342	Honey, You Can't Take It Back	1970	15.00	30.00	60.00
Albums					
CAPITOL					
❑ ST-12489	From Where I Stand	1986	2.50	5.00	10.00
CAPRICORN					
❑ CP 0163	New Ray of Sunshine	1976	2.50	5.00	10.00
CHARGER					
❑ CHR-M-2002 [M]	Dobie Gray Sings for "In" Crowders That Go "Go Go"	1965	10.00	20.00	40.00
❑ CHR-S-2002 [S]	Dobie Gray Sings for "In" Crowders That Go "Go Go"	1965	30.00	60.00	120.00
DECCA					
❑ DL 75397	Drift Away	1973	3.00	6.00	12.00
INFINITY					
❑ INF-9001	Midnight Diamond	1979	2.50	5.00	10.00
MCA					
❑ 371	Loving Arms	1973	2.50	5.00	10.00
❑ 449	Hey Dixie	1974	2.50	5.00	10.00
❑ 515	Drift Away	1974	2.50	5.00	10.00
—Reissue of Decca 75397					
ROBOX					
❑ RBX 8102	Welcome Home	1981	2.50	5.00	10.00
STRIPE					
❑ LPM 2001 [M]	Look — Dobie Gray	1963	25.00	50.00	100.00

GRAY, JAN

45s

Number	Title (A Side/B Side)	Yr	VG	VG+	NM
CYPRESS					
❑ 8510	Cross My Heart/(B-side unknown)	1986	—	3.50	7.00
JAMEX					
❑ 006	There I Go Dreamin' Again/(B-side unknown)	1982	—	2.50	5.00
❑ 008	Closer to Crazy/It's About Time	1982	—	2.50	5.00
❑ 010	No Fair Fallin' in Love/Win Some, Lose Some, Lonesome	1983	—	2.50	5.00
❑ 011	Before We Knew It/The Heart	1983	—	2.50	5.00
❑ 012	Bad Night for Good Girls/Dear Me	1983	—	2.50	5.00
PAID					
❑ 106	No Love at All/There's No Way We Can Go Wrong	1980	—	2.50	5.00
❑ 140	Have You Hugged Your Kids Today/Don't It Make You Wanna Dance	1981	—	2.50	5.00

GRAY, MARK

45s

Number	Title (A Side/B Side)	Yr	VG	VG+	NM
COLUMBIA					
❑ 38-03893	It Ain't Real (If It Ain't You)/Whatever Happened to Old Fashioned Love	1983	—	2.00	4.00
❑ 38-04137	Wounded Hearts/Till You and Your Lover Are Lovers Again	1983	—	2.00	4.00
❑ 38-04324	Left Side of the Bed/Fire from a Friend	1984	—	—	3.00
❑ 38-04464	If All the Magic Is Gone/Til Her Heartache Is Over	1984	—	—	3.00
❑ 38-04610	Diamond in the Dust/I Guess You Must Have Touched Me Just Right	1984	—	—	3.00
❑ 38-04610 [PS]	Diamond in the Dust/I Guess You Must Have Touched Me Just Right	1984	—	2.50	5.00
❑ 38-04782	Sometimes When We Touch/You're Gonna Be the Last One	1985	—	—	3.00
—A-side with Tammy Wynette					
❑ 38-05403	Smooth Sailing (Rock in the Road)/Dixie Girl	1985	—	—	3.00
❑ 38-05695	Please Be Love/I Need You Again	1985	—	—	3.00
❑ 38-05857	Back When Love Was Enough/Dance with Me	1986	—	—	3.00
Albums					
COLUMBIA					
❑ FC 39143	Magic	1984	2.00	4.00	8.00
❑ PC 39143	Magic	1985	—	3.00	6.00
—Budget-line reissue with new prefix					
❑ FC 39518	This Ol' Piano	1984	2.00	4.00	8.00
❑ PC 39518	This Ol' Piano	1986	—	3.00	6.00
—Budget-line reissue with new prefix					
❑ FC 40126	That Feeling Inside	1986	2.00	4.00	8.00

GRAY, MARK, AND BOBBI LACE

Also see each artist's individual listings.

45s

Number	Title (A Side/B Side)	Yr	VG	VG+	NM
615					
❑ 1014	Song in My Heart/(B-side unknown)	1988	—	3.00	6.00
❑ 1016	It's Gonna Be Love/(B-side unknown)	1988	—	3.00	6.00

GRAYGHOST

45s

Number	Title (A Side/B Side)	Yr	VG	VG+	NM
COMPLEAT					
❑ 166	As Long As I've Been Loving You/Out of Control	1987	—	2.50	5.00
—As "Razorback"					
❑ 174	Make a Living Out of Loving You/(B-side unknown)	1987	—	2.50	5.00
❑ 184	This Ole House/(B-side unknown)	1987	—	2.50	5.00
—As "Razorback"					
ICR					
❑ 184	This Ole House/(B-side unknown)	1987	—	3.00	6.00
—As "Razorback"					
MERCURY					
❑ 870633-7	Where Were You When I Was Blue/Something So Hot	1988	—	2.00	4.00
—As "Razorback"					
❑ 874194-7	Let's Sleep on It/(B-side unknown)	1989	—	—	3.00
❑ 874770-7	If This Ain't Love (There Ain't No Such Thing)/ Take a Little Time	1989	—	—	3.00

GRAYSON, JACK

45s

Number	Title (A Side/B Side)	Yr	VG	VG+	NM
ABC DOT					
❑ 17699	Mind Over Matter/Waiting Room	1977	—	3.00	6.00
—As "Jack Lebsock"					
AMI					
❑ 1318	Lean on Me/(B-side unknown)	1983	—	2.50	5.00
CAPITOL					
❑ 3579	For the Love of a Woman Like That/Heavy on My Mind	1973	—	3.00	6.00
—As "Jack Lebsock"					
❑ 3665	For Lovers Only/World That Cannot See	1973	—	3.00	6.00
—As "Jack Lebsock"					
❑ 3751	Lovin' Comes Easy/I'll Be Damned If I Do (Damned If I Don't)	1973	—	3.00	6.00
—As "Jack Lebsock"					
CHURCHILL					
❑ 7729	I Ain't Never Been to Heaven (But I've Spent the Night with You)/Tonight I'm Feeling You (All Over Again)	1979	—	2.50	5.00
HITBOUND					
❑ 4501	Tonight I'm Feelin' You (All Over Again)/Free to Love	1979	—	2.50	5.00
❑ 4503	The Stores Are Full of Roses/(B-side unknown)	1980	—	2.50	5.00
❑ 4504	The Devil Stands Only Five Foot Five/Free to Love	1980	—	2.50	5.00
JOE-WES					
❑ 81000	Tonight I'm Feeling You (All Over Again)/Let's Hold Hands	1982	—	2.50	5.00
❑ 81006	I Ain't Giving Up on Her Yet/Mama's Secret	1982	—	2.50	5.00
KOALA					
❑ 328	A Loser's Night Out/Devil Stands Only 5 Foot 5	1980	—	2.50	5.00
❑ 328 [PS]	A Loser's Night Out/Devil Stands Only 5 Foot 5	1980	2.00	4.00	8.00
❑ 331	Magic Eyes/The Stores Are Full of Roses	1981	—	2.50	5.00
❑ 334	My Beginning Was You/Hanging On by a Heartstring	1981	—	2.50	5.00
❑ 340	When a Man Loves a Woman/A Little Tear	1981	—	2.50	5.00
❑ 346	Tonight I'm Feeling You (All Over Again)/(B-side unknown)	1982	—	3.00	6.00
MONUMENT					
❑ 8693	She Took My Words Away/Country Music Is a Lady	1976	—	3.00	6.00
—As "Jack Lebsock"					
Albums					
JOE-WES					
❑ 8100	Jack Grayson Sings	1982	3.00	6.00	12.00
KOALA					
❑ 15751	When a Man Loves a Woman	1981	3.00	6.00	12.00

GRAYSON, KIM

45s

Number	Title (A Side/B Side)	Yr	VG	VG+	NM
SOUNDWAVES					
❑ 4787	Love's Slippin' Up on Me/(B-side unknown)	1987	—	2.50	5.00
❑ 4787 [PS]	Love's Slippin' Up on Me/(B-side unknown)	1987	—	3.00	6.00
❑ 4795	If You Only Knew/Love's Slippin' Up on Me	1987	—	2.50	5.00
❑ 4795 [PS]	If You Only Knew/Love's Slippin' Up on Me	1987	—	3.00	6.00
❑ 4800	Missin' Texas/(B-side unknown)	1988	—	2.50	5.00
❑ 4800 [PS]	Missin' Texas/(B-side unknown)	1988	—	3.00	6.00

GREAT DIVIDE, THE

45s

ATLANTIC

Number	Title (A Side/B Side)	Yr	VG	VG+	NM
❑ 84102	Never Could/Pour Me a Vacation	1998	—	—	3.00
❑ 84159	Pour Me a Vacation/Dodgers Were in Brooklyn	1998	—	—	3.00

GREAT PLAINS

45s

COLUMBIA

Number	Title (A Side/B Side)	Yr	VG	VG+	NM
❑ 38-73961	A Picture of You/Give It Some Time	1991	—	—	3.00
❑ 38-74137	Faster Gun/Oh Sweetness	1991	—	—	3.00
❑ 38-74310	Iola/Take Me to Topeka	1992	—	—	3.00

GREBEL, DEBBIE

45s

CON BRIO

Number	Title (A Side/B Side)	Yr	VG	VG+	NM
❑ 111	Grandma Was the Motor (But She Let My Grandpa Drive)/You Won't Remember Her Name	1976	—	3.00	6.00
❑ 123	He Always Writes Me (When He's Done Me Wrong)/If You Wanna Love Me	1977	—	3.00	6.00
❑ 128	Please Take Me With You/If You Wanna Love Me	1977	—	3.00	6.00

GREEN, BILL

45s

Number	Title (A Side/B Side)	Yr	VG	VG+	NM
NSD					
❑ 11	Fool Such As I/Let's Cheat Again	1978	—	2.50	5.00
❑ 15	Free Born Man/Texas Greats	1979	—	2.50	5.00
❑ 30	I Hang Around/I Don't Know Why I Keep Loving You	1979	—	2.50	5.00
❑ 39	Big Fat Mama/Rainy Day Song	1980	—	2.50	5.00
PHONO					
❑ 2629	Texas on a Saturday Night/Let's Cheat Again	1976	2.00	4.00	8.00
❑ 2641	Rainbow Over Texas/Texas Greats	1977	2.00	4.00	8.00

GREEN, JERRY

45s

CONCORDE

Number	Title (A Side/B Side)	Yr	VG	VG+	NM
❑ 152	I Know the Feeling/How Sweet It Is	1977	—	3.00	6.00
❑ 154	Genuine Texas Good Guy/(B-side unknown)	1977	—	3.00	6.00

GREEN, LLOYD

45s

Number	Title (A Side/B Side)	Yr	VG	VG+	NM
CHART					
❑ 1029	Woman, Woman/Mr. Nashville Sound	1968	2.00	4.00	8.00
❑ 1071	Bar Hoppin'/Greenblue	1969	2.00	4.00	8.00
❑ 5014	Orbit/Robin	1969	2.00	4.00	8.00
❑ 5043	Tell Ya What/Steel Blue	1969	2.00	4.00	8.00
❑ 5072	Ride, Ride, Ride/Not Another Time	1970	2.00	4.00	8.00
LITTLE DARLIN'					
❑ 007	Skillet Lickin'/Green Strings	1966	6.25	12.50	25.00
❑ 0023	Pedal Pattle/Little Darlin'	1967	6.25	12.50	25.00
❑ 0050	Sweet Cheeks/Green Strings	1968	2.50	5.00	10.00
MONUMENT					
❑ 8549	Morning Has Broken/Phase Phive	1972	—	3.00	6.00
❑ 8562	I Can See Clearly Now/Steelin' Away	1973	—	3.00	6.00
❑ 8574	Here Comes the Sun/Peace	1973	—	3.00	6.00
❑ 8592	Sleep Walk/Dixie Drive-In	1973	—	3.00	6.00
❑ 8608	Atlantis/San Antonio Rose	1974	—	3.00	6.00
❑ 8615	Seaside/Summer Clouds	1974	—	3.00	6.00
❑ 8624	Canadian Sunset/Spirit of '49	1974	—	3.00	6.00
❑ 8635	Sally G/Lucretia	1974	—	3.00	6.00
❑ 8648	I Can Help/Theme from A Summer Place	1975	—	2.50	5.00
—With Charlie McCoy					
OCTOBER					
❑ 1002	You and Me/Edgewater Beach	1976	—	3.00	6.00
❑ 1009	Feelings/Stainless Steel	1977	—	3.00	6.00
PRIZE					
❑ 01	Midnight Silence/Wide Awake	1971	—	3.50	7.00
❑ 09	Soundwaves/Tom's Tavern Blues	1971	—	3.50	7.00
SOUNDWAVES					
❑ 4560	The Whistler/Afterglow	1977	—	2.50	5.00

Albums

Number	Title	Yr	VG	VG+	NM
CHART					
❑ CHM-1006 [M]	Mr. Nashville Sound	1968	12.50	25.00	50.00
❑ CHS-1006 [S]	Mr. Nashville Sound	1968	6.25	12.50	25.00
❑ CHS-1010	Cool Steel Man	1969	6.25	12.50	25.00
❑ 1024	Moody River	1970	6.25	12.50	25.00
GRT					
❑ 8018	Feelings	1977	3.00	6.00	12.00
LITTLE DARLIN'					
❑ LD-4002	Day for Decision	196?	6.25	12.50	25.00
❑ LD 4005	The Hit Sounds of Lloyd Green	196?	6.25	12.50	25.00
MONUMENT					
❑ KZ 32532	Shades of Steel	1973	3.75	7.50	15.00
❑ KZ 33368	Steel Rides	1975	3.75	7.50	15.00
TIME					
❑ ST-2152 [S]	Big Steel Guitar	1964	10.00	20.00	40.00
❑ T-2152 [M]	Big Steel Guitar	1964	7.50	15.00	30.00

GREENE, JACK

45s

Number	Title (A Side/B Side)	Yr	VG	VG+	NM
DECCA					
❑ 31768	Don't You Ever Get Tired/The Hurt's On Me	1965	2.50	5.00	10.00
❑ 31856	Ever Since My Baby Went Away/Room for One More Heartache	1965	2.00	4.00	8.00
❑ 32023	There Goes My Everything/The Hardest Easy Thing	1966	2.00	4.00	8.00
❑ 32123	All the Time/Wanting You But Never Having You	1967	2.00	4.00	8.00
❑ 32190	What Locks the Door/Left Over Feelings	1967	2.00	4.00	8.00
❑ 32261	You Are My Treasure/If God Can Forgive You, So Can I	1968	2.00	4.00	8.00
❑ 32352	Love Takes Care of Me/Your Favorite Fool	1968	2.00	4.00	8.00
❑ 32423	Until My Dreams Come True/We'll Try a Little Bit Harder	1968	2.00	4.00	8.00
❑ 32490	Statue of a Fool/There's More to Love	1969	2.00	4.00	8.00
❑ 32558	Back in the Arms of Love/The Key That Fits Her Door	1969	2.00	4.00	8.00
❑ 32631	Lord Is That Me/Just a Little While Ago	1970	—	3.50	7.00
❑ 32699	The Whole World Comes to Me/If This Is Love	1970	—	3.50	7.00
❑ 32755	Something Unseen/What's the Use	1970	—	3.50	7.00
❑ 32823	There's a Whole Lot About a Woman (A Man Don't Know)/Makin' Up His Mind	1971	—	3.50	7.00
❑ 32863	Hanging Over Me/The Birth of Our Love	1971	—	3.50	7.00
❑ 32939	If You Ever Need My Love/Ask Me to Stay	1972	—	3.50	7.00
❑ 33008	Satisfaction/From Here On Out	1972	—	3.50	7.00
EMH					
❑ 0015	I'd Be Home On Christmas Day/(B-side unknown)	1982	—	3.00	6.00
❑ 0016	The Jukebox Never Plays Home Sweet Home/I Don't Want to Be Alone Tonight	1983	—	2.50	5.00
❑ 0019	From Cotton to Satin/I'd Be Home on Christmas Day	1983	—	2.50	5.00
❑ 0025	Midnight Tennessee Woman/Goin' Through Hell for an Angel	1983	—	2.50	5.00
❑ 0028	I'd Do As Much for You/Singing My Heart Out for You	1984	—	2.50	5.00
❑ 0031	Dying to Believe/There Goes My Everything	1984	—	2.50	5.00
❑ 0035	If It's Love (Then Bet It All)/Statue of a Fool	1984	—	2.50	5.00
FIRSTLINE					
❑ 709	Devil's Den/It's Not the End of the World	1980	—	2.50	5.00
FRONTLINE					
❑ 704	Yours for the Taking/Sixty Days	1979	—	2.50	5.00
❑ 706	The Rock I'm Leaning On/I'll Do It Better Next Time	1980	—	2.50	5.00
MCA					
❑ 40035	The Fool I've Been Today/You Left Me	1973	—	2.50	5.00
❑ 40108	I Need Somebody Bad/Joyride	1973	—	2.50	5.00
❑ 40179	It's Time to Cross That Bridge/Half That Much	1974	—	2.50	5.00
❑ 40263	Sing for the Good Times/Something Seems to Fall Apart Inside	1974	—	2.50	5.00
❑ 40354	This Time The Hurtin's On Me/Sawmill Depot	1974	—	2.50	5.00
❑ 40415	Cheatin' River/On the Way Home	1975	—	2.50	5.00
❑ 40481	He Little Thing'd Her Out of His Arms/Let Me Love You Back Together Again	1975	—	2.50	5.00
❑ 40526	Birmingham/My Long Gone Reason	1976	—	2.50	5.00

Albums

Number	Title	Yr	VG	VG+	NM
DECCA					
❑ DL 4845 [M]	There Goes My Everything	1967	5.00	10.00	20.00
❑ DL 4904 [M]	All the Time	1967	5.00	10.00	20.00
❑ DL 4939 [M]	What Locks the Door	1968	6.25	12.50	25.00
❑ DL 4979 [M]	You Are My Treasure	1968	7.50	15.00	30.00
❑ DL 74845 [S]	There Goes My Everything	1967	3.75	7.50	15.00
❑ DL 74904 [S]	All the Time	1967	3.75	7.50	15.00
❑ DL 74939 [S]	What Locks the Door	1968	3.75	7.50	15.00
❑ DL 74979 [S]	You Are My Treasure	1968	3.75	7.50	15.00
❑ DL 75080	I Am Not Alone	1969	3.75	7.50	15.00
❑ DL 75124	Statue of a Fool	1969	3.75	7.50	15.00
❑ DL 75188	Lord Is That Me	1970	3.75	7.50	15.00
❑ DL 75208	Greatest Hits	1970	3.75	7.50	15.00
❑ DL 75283	There's a Whole Lot About a Woman	1971	3.75	7.50	15.00
❑ DL 75308	Greene Country	1972	3.75	7.50	15.00
MCA					
❑ 291	Greatest Hits	1973	3.00	6.00	12.00
—Reissue of Decca 75208					
❑ 295	Greene Country	1973	3.00	6.00	12.00
—Reissue of Decca 75308					
PICKWICK					
❑ SPC-6173	I Never Had It So Good	197?	2.50	5.00	10.00

GREENE, JACK, AND JEANNIE SEELY

45s

DECCA

Number	Title (A Side/B Side)	Yr	VG	VG+	NM
❑ 32580	Wish I Didn't Have to Miss You/My Tears Don't Show	1969	—	3.50	7.00
❑ 32898	Much Oblige/First Day	1971	—	3.50	7.00
❑ 32991	What in the World Has Gone Wrong with Our Love/Willingly	1972	—	3.00	6.00

Albums

Number	Title	Yr	VG	VG+	NM
DECCA					
❑ DL 75171	Jack Greene and Jeannie Seely	1970	3.75	7.50	15.00
❑ DL 75392	Two for the Show	1972	3.75	7.50	15.00
MCA					
❑ 77	Two for the Show	1973	3.00	6.00	12.00
—Reissue of Decca 75392					

GREENE, LORNE

45s

ARTISTS OF AMERICA

Number	Title (A Side/B Side)	Yr	VG	VG+	NM
1776	National Glass Casket Company/Spirit of America	1976	2.00	4.00	8.00

COLUMBIA

Number	Title (A Side/B Side)	Yr	VG	VG+	NM
44971	The Perfect Woman/It's All in the Game	1969	—	3.00	6.00

GRT

Number	Title (A Side/B Side)	Yr	VG	VG+	NM
32	Daddy (I'm Proud to Be Your Son)/I Love a Rainbow	1969	—	3.00	6.00
37	The First Word/I Love a Rainbow	1970	—	3.00	6.00

RCA VICTOR

Number	Title (A Side/B Side)	Yr	VG	VG+	NM
47-8113	My Sons, My Sons/The Place Where I Worship	1962	2.50	5.00	10.00
47-8229	I'm the Same Old Me/Love Finds a Way	1963	2.50	5.00	10.00
47-8444	Ringo/Bonanza	1964	2.00	4.00	8.00
47-8490	The Man/Pop Goes the Hammer	1964	2.00	4.00	8.00
47-8554	An Ol' Tin Cup/Sand	1965	2.00	4.00	8.00
47-8757	Five Card Stud/Shadow of the Cactus	1965	2.00	4.00	8.00
47-8819	Daddy's Little Girl/I Love a Rainbow	1966	2.00	4.00	8.00
47-8901	Waco/All But the Remembering	1966	2.00	4.00	8.00
47-9037	Must Be Santa/One Solitary Life	1966	2.50	5.00	10.00

Albums

RCA CAMDEN

Number	Title (A Side/B Side)	Yr	VG	VG+	NM
CAS-2391	Five Card Stud	1970	6.25	12.50	25.00

RCA VICTOR

Number	Title (A Side/B Side)	Yr	VG	VG+	NM
SP-33-327 [DJ]	Palaver with The Man	1965	12.50	25.00	50.00
—Promo-only interview record with script					
LPM-2661 [M]	Young at Heart	1963	6.25	12.50	25.00
LSP-2661 [S]	Young at Heart	1963	7.50	15.00	30.00
LPM-2843 [M]	Welcome to the Ponderosa	1964	6.25	12.50	25.00
LSP-2843 [S]	Welcome to the Ponderosa	1964	7.50	15.00	30.00
LPM-3302 [M]	The Man	1965	6.25	12.50	25.00
LSP-3302 [S]	The Man	1965	7.50	15.00	30.00
LPM-3409 [M]	Lorne Greene's American West	1965	6.25	12.50	25.00
LSP-3409 [S]	Lorne Greene's American West	1965	7.50	15.00	30.00
LPM-3410 [M]	Have a Happy Holiday	1965	6.25	12.50	25.00
LSP-3410 [S]	Have a Happy Holiday	1965	7.50	15.00	30.00
LPM-3678 [M]	Portrait of the West	1966	6.25	12.50	25.00
LSP-3678 [S]	Portrait of the West	1966	7.50	15.00	30.00

RCA VICTOR RED SEAL

Number	Title (A Side/B Side)	Yr	VG	VG+	NM
LM-2783 [M]	Peter and the Wolf	1964	6.25	12.50	25.00
LSC-2783 [S]	Peter and the Wolf	1964	7.50	15.00	30.00
—Above with the London Symphony Orchestra					

GREENE, LORNE; MICHAEL LANDON; DAN BLOCKER

Albums

RCA VICTOR

Number	Title (A Side/B Side)	Yr	VG	VG+	NM
LPM-2583 [M]	Bonanza — Ponderosa Party Time!	1962	7.50	15.00	30.00
LSP-2583 [S]	Bonanza — Ponderosa Party Time!	1962	10.00	20.00	40.00
LPM-2757 [M]	Christmas on the Ponderosa	1963	6.25	12.50	25.00
LSP-2757 [S]	Christmas on the Ponderosa	1963	7.50	15.00	30.00

GREENWOOD, LEE

45s

CAPITOL NASHVILLE

Number	Title (A Side/B Side)	Yr	VG	VG+	NM
7PRO-79530	Just Like Me (same on both sides)	1991	—	3.00	6.00
—Vinyl is promo only					

DOT

Number	Title (A Side/B Side)	Yr	VG	VG+	NM
17271	Love Is Not Enough/Someone to Watch Over Me	1969	3.75	7.50	15.00
17312	Maria/Turn It Over	1969	3.00	6.00	12.00

MCA

Number	Title (A Side/B Side)	Yr	VG	VG+	NM
51159	It Turns Me Inside Out/Thank You for Changing My Life	1981	—	2.00	4.00
52026	Ring on Her Finger, Time on Her Hands/Doncha Hear Me Callin'	1982	—	2.00	4.00
52087	She's Lying/Home Away from Home	1982	—	2.00	4.00
52150	Ain't No Trick (It Takes Magic)/Broken Pieces of My Heart	1982	—	2.00	4.00
52199	I.O.U./Another You	1983	—	2.00	4.00
52199 [PS]	I.O.U./Another You	1983	—	2.50	5.00
52257	Somebody's Gonna Love You/You're the Woman I Love	1983	—	2.00	4.00
52322	Going, Going, Gone/Come On Back and Love Me Some More	1983	—	2.00	4.00
52386	God Bless the U.S.A./This Old Bed	1984	—	2.00	4.00
—Reissued in 1991 with the same catalog number, but without a picture sleeve					
52386 [PS]	God Bless the U.S.A./This Old Bed	1984	—	2.50	5.00
52426	Fool's Gold/Worth It for the Ride	1984	—	2.00	4.00
52509	You've Got a Good Love Comin'/Even Love Can't Save Us Now	1984	—	2.00	4.00
52564	Dixie Road/(I Found) Love in Time	1985	—	—	3.00
52564 [PS]	Dixie Road/(I Found) Love in Time	1985	—	2.00	4.00
52656	I Don't Mind the Thorns (If You're the Rose)/Same Old Song	1985	—	—	3.00
52733	Christmas to Christmas (Loving You)/Lone Star Christmas	1987	—	2.00	4.00
52733 [PS]	Christmas to Christmas (Loving You)/Lone Star Christmas	1987	—	2.50	5.00
52741	Don't Underestimate My Love for You/Leave My Heart the Way You Found It	1985	—	—	3.00
52741 [PS]	Don't Underestimate My Love for You/Leave My Heart the Way You Found It	1985	—	2.00	4.00
52807	Hearts Aren't Made to Break (They're Made to Love)/The Will to Love	1986	—	—	3.00
52896	Didn't We/Heartbreak Radio	1986	—	—	3.00
52984	Mornin' Ride/Little Red Caboose	1986	—	—	3.00
53096	Someone/Let's Make the Most of Love	1987	—	—	3.00
53156	If There's Any Justice/We Could Have Been	1987	—	—	3.00
53234	Touch and Go Crazy/Silver Dollar	1987	—	—	3.00
53312	I Still Believe/I'll Be Lovin' You	1988	—	—	3.00
53386	You Can't Fall in Love When You're Cryin'/I'll Still Be Lovin' You	1988	—	—	3.00
53475	I'll Be Lovin' You/Do That to Me One More Time	1988	—	—	3.00
53655	I Love the Way He Left You/Home to Alaska	1989	—	—	3.00
53716	I Go Crazy/Any Way the Law Allows	1989	—	—	3.00

PARAMOUNT

Number	Title (A Side/B Side)	Yr	VG	VG+	NM
0102	Touch and Go/My First Night Alone Without You	1971	2.50	5.00	10.00

Albums

MCA

Number	Title (A Side/B Side)	Yr	VG	VG+	NM
1451	You've Got a Good Love Comin'	1985	—	3.00	6.00
—Reissue of 5488					
1452	Inside Out	1985	—	3.00	6.00
—Reissue of second version of 5305					
1573	Somebody's Gonna Love You	1986	—	3.00	6.00
—Reissue of 5488					
5305	Inside and Out	1982	3.00	6.00	12.00
—Original title					
5305	Inside Out	1982	2.00	4.00	8.00
—Corrected title					
5403	Somebody's Gonna Love You	1983	2.00	4.00	8.00
5488	You've Got a Good Love Comin'	1984	2.00	4.00	8.00
5582	Greatest Hits	1985	2.00	4.00	8.00
5622	Streamline	1985	2.00	4.00	8.00
5623	Christmas to Christmas	1985	2.50	5.00	10.00
5770	Love Will Find Its Way to You	1986	2.00	4.00	8.00
5999	If There's Any Justice	1987	2.00	4.00	8.00
42167	This Is My Country	1988	2.00	4.00	8.00
42219	Greatest Hits — Volume Two	1988	2.00	4.00	8.00
42300	If Only for One Night	1989	2.50	5.00	10.00

GREENWOOD, LEE, WITH SUZY BOGGUSS

Also see each artist's individual listings.

45s

CAPITOL NASHVILLE

Number	Title (A Side/B Side)	Yr	VG	VG+	NM
7PRO-79690	Hopelessly Yours (same on both sides)	1991	—	3.00	6.00
—Vinyl is promo only					

GREGG, RICKY LYNN

45s

CAPITOL NASHVILLE

Number	Title (A Side/B Side)	Yr	VG	VG+	NM
S7-18911	Santa Claus Is Coming to Town/What Child Is This	1995	—	2.00	4.00

LIBERTY

Number	Title (A Side/B Side)	Yr	VG	VG+	NM
S7-17323	If I Had a Cheatin' Heart/Three Nickels and a Dime	1993	—	2.50	5.00
S7-17399	Can You Feel It/Bring On the Neon	1993	—	2.00	4.00
S7-18092	Get a Little Closer/If I Had a Cheatin' Heart	1994	—	2.00	4.00

GREGORY, CLINTON

45s

POLYDOR

Number	Title (A Side/B Side)	Yr	VG	VG+	NM
579088-7	A-11/No Relief in Sight	1995	—	—	3.00
851566-7	You Don't Miss a Thing/Hacksaw	1995	—	—	3.00
853990-7	The Gulf and the Shell/I've Got a Double	1994	—	—	3.00

STEP ONE

Number	Title (A Side/B Side)	Yr	VG	VG+	NM
405	Nobody's Darling But Mine/Watermelon Time in Georgia	1989	—	2.50	5.00
415	Made for Lovin' You/Nobody's Darling But Mine	1990	—	2.00	4.00
418	She Put the Music in Me/Lovin' on Backstreets	1990	—	2.00	4.00
422	Couldn't Love Have Picked a Better Place to Die/You Can't Take It With You	1990	—	2.00	4.00
427	(If It Weren't for Country Music) I'd Go Crazy/Darlin' Does He	1991	—	2.00	4.00
430	One Shot at a Time/There's Never Been a Honky Tonk	1991	—	2.00	4.00
434	Satisfy Me and I'll Satisfy You/Your Uncharted Mind	1991	—	2.00	4.00
437	Play, Ruby, Play/She Can't Believe My Eyes	1992	—	2.00	4.00
439	She Takes the Sad Out of Saturday Night/Blue Country Frame of Mind	1992	—	2.00	4.00
443	Christmas in Virginia/Blue Christmas	1992	—	2.50	5.00
444	Who Needs It/The Jukebox Has a 45	1992	—	2.00	4.00
457	Look Who's Needing Who/I'll Never Always Love You	1993	—	2.00	4.00
461	Standing on the Edge of Love/Till This Ring Turns Green	1993	—	2.00	4.00
466	Master of Illusion/Watermelon Time in Georgia	1993	—	2.00	4.00

GREGORY, TERRY

45s

HANDSHAKE

Number	Title (A Side/B Side)	Yr	VG	VG+	NM
WS9-02442	Cinderella/We Better Talk It Over	1981	—	2.00	4.00
WS9-02563	I Can't Say Goodbye to You/We Had All It Takes to Fall in Love	1981	—	2.00	4.00
WS9-02736	I Never Knew the Devil's Eyes Were Blue/I Need Another Lover (Like a Hole in the Heart)	1982	—	2.00	4.00
WS9-02959	I'm Takin' a Heart Break/After You've Shopped Around	1982	—	2.00	4.00
WS8-70071	Just Like Me/Love Left Over	1981	—	2.00	4.00

Number	Title (A Side/B Side)	Yr	VG	VG+	NM
SCOTTI BROTHERS					
❑ ZS4-04410	Cowgirl in a Coupe de Ville/The Old Songs	1984	—	—	3.00
❑ ZS4-04735	Pardon Me, But This Heart's Taken/Fallin'	1985	—	—	3.00
Albums					
HANDSHAKE					
❑ 12196	Just Like Me	1981	2.50	5.00	10.00
❑ FW 37131	Just Like Me	1981	2.00	4.00	8.00
—Reissue of 12196					
❑ FW 37907	From the Heart	1982	2.00	4.00	8.00

GRIFF, RAY

Number	Title (A Side/B Side)	Yr	VG	VG+	NM
45s					
ABC DOT					
❑ 17542	If That's What It Takes/Adam's Child	1974	—	3.00	6.00
CAPITOL					
❑ 4126	You Ring My Bell/Dear Jesus	1975	—	2.50	5.00
❑ 4208	If I Let Her Come In/Runnin'	1976	—	2.50	5.00
❑ 4266	I Love the Way That You Love Me/Wrapped Around Your Finger	1976	—	2.50	5.00
❑ 4320	That's What I Get (For Doin' My Own Thinkin')/Falling	1976	—	2.50	5.00
❑ 4368	The Last of the Winfield Amateurs/You Put the Bounce Back Into My Step	1976	—	2.50	5.00
❑ 4415	A Passing Thing/Piano Man	1977	—	2.50	5.00
❑ 4446	A Cold Day in July/Rusty	1977	—	2.50	5.00
❑ 4492	Raymond's Place/Goodbye Baby	1977	—	2.50	5.00
DOT					
❑ 17082	The Sugar from My Candy/Till the Right One Comes Along	1968	2.00	4.00	8.00
❑ 17124	Ray of Sunshine/Baby	1968	2.00	4.00	8.00
❑ 17171	Sweet Bird of Youth/A Lean Horse	1968	2.00	4.00	8.00
❑ 17206	Move a Little Farther Along/Wanderin' Through the Valley	1969	2.00	4.00	8.00
❑ 17252	Miracles Do Happen/Pebbles on the Beach	1969	2.00	4.00	8.00
❑ 17288	The Entertainer/Caution to the Wind	1969	2.00	4.00	8.00
❑ 17440	It Rains Just the Same in Missouri/Somewhere Between Atlanta and Mobile	1972	—	3.00	6.00
❑ 17456	A Song for Everyone/Another Sad Affair	1973	—	3.00	6.00
❑ 17471	What Got to You (Before It Got to Me)/Darlin'	1973	—	3.00	6.00
❑ 17501	That Doesn't Mean (I Don't Love My God)/Lost Love of Mine	1974	—	3.00	6.00
❑ 17519	The Hill/All Loved Out	1974	—	3.00	6.00
MGM					
❑ 13855	Your Lily White Hands/One of the Chosen Few	1967	2.50	5.00	10.00
RCA					
❑ PB-50722	If Tomorrow Never Comes/Draw Me a Line	1983	—	2.50	5.00
—Canadian number issued in U.S.					
❑ PB-50846	What My Woman Does to Me/(B-side unknown)	1986	—	2.50	5.00
—Canadian number issued in U.S.					
ROYAL AMERICAN					
❑ 16	My Everlasting Love/Ain't Nowhere to Go	1970	2.00	4.00	8.00
❑ 19	Patches/Dixie	1970	2.00	4.00	8.00
❑ 30	Don't Look at Me/(B-side unknown)	1971	2.00	4.00	8.00
❑ 38	What Can I Say/Wait a Little Longer	1971	2.00	4.00	8.00
❑ 46	The Mornin' After Baby Let Me Down/I'll Love You Enough for Both of Us	1971	2.00	4.00	8.00
❑ 56	It's the First Day/Waxamachie Woman	1972	2.00	4.00	8.00
VISION					
❑ 440	Draw Me a Line/Heaven	1981	—	2.50	5.00
❑ 442	Things That Songs Are Made Of/Light as a Feather	1982	—	2.50	5.00
❑ 442 [PS]	Things That Songs Are Made Of/Light as a Feather	1982	2.00	4.00	8.00
Albums					
ABC DOT					
❑ DOSD-2011	Expressions	1974	3.00	6.00	12.00
CAPITOL					
❑ ST-11486	Ray Griff	1976	2.50	5.00	10.00
❑ ST-11566	The Last of the Winfield Amateurs	1976	2.50	5.00	10.00
❑ ST-11718	Raymond's Place	1977	2.50	5.00	10.00
DOT					
❑ DLP-25868	A Ray of Sunshine	1968	5.00	10.00	20.00
❑ DLP-26013	Songs for Everyone	1973	3.75	7.50	15.00
ROYAL AMERICAN					
❑ RAS 1007	Ray Griff Sings	1972	3.75	7.50	15.00

GRIFFITH, ANDY

Number	Title (A Side/B Side)	Yr	VG	VG+	NM
45s					
CAPITOL					
❑ 2571	Romeo and Juliet (Part 1)/Romeo and Juliet (Part 2)	1969	2.00	4.00	8.00
❑ F2693	What It Was, Was Football (Part 1)/What It Was, Was Football (Part 2)	1953	7.50	15.00	30.00
—Original pressings as "Deacon Andy Griffith"					
❑ F2693	What It Was, Was Football (Part 1)/What It Was, Was Football (Part 2)	195?	6.25	12.50	25.00
—Later pressings (purple Capitol label, large logo at top) as "Andy Griffith"					
❑ F2696	Romeo and Juliet (Part 1)/Romeo and Juliet (Part 2)	1954	7.50	15.00	30.00
—Original pressings as "Deacon Andy Griffith"					
❑ F2696	Romeo and Juliet (Part 1)/Romeo and Juliet (Part 2)	195?	6.25	12.50	25.00
—Later pressings (purple label, large Capitol logo at top) as "Andy Griffith"					
❑ F2855	Swan Lake (Part 1)/Swan Lake (Part 2)	1954	6.25	12.50	25.00
❑ F3057	Ko Ko Mo (I Love You So)/Make Yourself Comfortable	1955	5.00	10.00	20.00
❑ F3402	Opera Carmen (Part 1)/Opera Carmen (Part 2)	1956	6.25	12.50	25.00
❑ F3498	Standing on the Corner/No Time for Sergeants	1956	5.00	10.00	20.00
❑ F3705	Mama Guitar/A Face in the Crowd	1957	5.00	10.00	20.00
❑ F3706	Free Man in the Morning/Just a Closer Walk with Thee	1957	5.00	10.00	20.00
❑ F3872	Silhouettes/Conversation with a Mule	1958	5.00	10.00	20.00
❑ F3938	Andy's Lament/Thank Heaven for Little Girls	1958	5.00	10.00	20.00
❑ F3990	Love Poems: To the Lovely Juanita Beasley/Togetherness	1958	5.00	10.00	20.00
❑ F4052	Midnight Special/She's Bad, Bad Business	1958	5.00	10.00	20.00
❑ F4157	Hamlet (Part 1)/Hamlet (Part 2)	1959	5.00	10.00	20.00
❑ F4204	Once Knew a Fella/Don't Look Back	1959	3.75	7.50	15.00
❑ 4236	Look at the Son-Shine/My Dog Underdog	1976	—	3.00	6.00
❑ 4539	New River Train/(B-side unknown)	1961	3.75	7.50	15.00
❑ 4684	Flop Eared Mule/A Good Man Is Hard to Find	1962	3.75	7.50	15.00
❑ 4848	The Pool Table/Whistling Ping Pong Game	1962	3.75	7.50	15.00
❑ 5073	Andy and Cleopatra (Part 1)/Andy and Cleopatra (Part 2)	1963	3.75	7.50	15.00
COLONIAL					
❑ E3	What It Was, Was Football (Part 1)/What It Was, Was Football (Part 2)	1953	15.00	30.00	60.00
COLUMBIA					
❑ 4-45711	Lead Me to That Rock/Somebody Bigger Than You and I	1972	2.00	4.00	8.00

GRIFFITH, GLENDA

Number	Title (A Side/B Side)	Yr	VG	VG+	NM
45s					
ARIOLA AMERICA					
❑ 7680	Don't Worry ('Bout Me)/Heavenly Island	1977	—	2.00	4.00
❑ 7695	Angel, Spread Your Wings/Heavenly Island	1978	—	2.00	4.00
❑ 7698	Oh, Boy!/Angel, Spread Your Wings	1978	—	2.00	4.00

GRIFFITH, NANCI

Number	Title (A Side/B Side)	Yr	VG	VG+	NM
45s					
MCA					
❑ 53009	Lone Star State of Mind/There's a Light Beyond the Woods (Mary Margaret)	1987	—	2.00	4.00
❑ 53082	Trouble in the Fields/Love in a Memory	1987	—	2.00	4.00
❑ 53147	Cold Heart, Closed Minds/Ford Econoline	1987	—	2.00	4.00
❑ 53184	Never Mind/From a Distance	1987	—	2.50	5.00
❑ 53306	I Knew Love/So Long Ago	1988	—	2.00	4.00
❑ 53374	Anyone Can Be Someone's Fool/Love Wore a Halo (Back Before the War)	1988	—	2.00	4.00
❑ 53700	It's a Hard Life Wherever You Go/From a Distance	1989	—	2.00	4.00
❑ 53761	I Don't Want to Talk About Love/Drive-In Movies and Dashboard Lights	1989	—	2.00	4.00
PHILO					
❑ 1096	Once in a Very Blue Moon/(B-side unknown)	1986	—	3.00	6.00
Albums					
B.F. DEAL					
❑ BFD 9	There's a Light Beyond These Woods	1978	12.50	25.00	50.00
ELEKTRA					
❑ 62015	Blue Roses from the Moons	1997	3.00	6.00	12.00
FEATHERBED					
❑ FB 902	Poet in My Window	1982	5.00	10.00	20.00
❑ FB 903	There's a Light Beyond These Woods	1982	5.00	10.00	20.00
MCA					
❑ 5927	Lone Star State of Mind	1987	2.00	4.00	8.00
❑ 6319	Storms	1989	2.50	5.00	10.00
❑ 42102	Little Love Affairs	1988	2.00	4.00	8.00
❑ 42255	One Fair Summer Evening	1988	2.00	4.00	8.00
PHILO					
❑ PH-1096	Once in a Very Blue Moon	1984	3.00	6.00	12.00
❑ PH-1097	There's a Light Beyond These Woods	1986	3.00	6.00	12.00
❑ PH-1098	Poet in My Window	1986	3.00	6.00	12.00
❑ PH-1109	Last of the True Believers	1986	3.00	6.00	12.00

GRIGGS, ANDY

Number	Title (A Side/B Side)	Yr	VG	VG+	NM
45s					
RCA					
❑ 65936	She's More/I'll Go Crazy	2000	—	—	3.00

GRISSOM, RICH

Number	Title (A Side/B Side)	Yr	VG	VG+	NM
45s					
MERCURY					
❑ 866378-7	I Don't Do Floors/Emotional Blackmail	1992	—	—	3.00
❑ 875226-7	It Must Be Love/(B-side unknown)	1990	—	—	3.00
❑ 875880-7	Tell Me I'm Wrong/Remains	1990	—	—	3.00
❑ 878504-7	Hillbilly Boy with the R&R Blues/Remains	1990	—	—	3.00

GROCE, LARRY

Number	Title (A Side/B Side)	Yr	VG	VG+	NM
45s					
DISNEYLAND					
❑ 564	Winnie the Pooh for President (Campaign Song)/(B-side unknown)	1976	5.00	10.00	20.00
MGM					
❑ 14621	Muddy Boggy Banjo Man/Sweet Sweet Love	1973	—	2.50	5.00
PEACEABLE					
❑ 3	Junk Food Junkie/Muddy Boggy Banjo Man	1975	2.50	5.00	10.00
❑ 3 [PS]	Junk Food Junkie/Muddy Boggy Banjo Man	1975	2.50	5.00	10.00

Number	Title (A Side/B Side)	Yr	VG	VG+	NM
WARNER BROS.					
❑ 8165	Junk Food Junkie/Muddy Boggy Banjo Man	1975	—	2.50	5.00
❑ 8221	We've Been Malled/Old Fashioned Girl	1976	—	2.00	4.00
❑ 8327	The Ballad of Billy Don Rice/Big White House in Indiana	1977	—	2.00	4.00
❑ 8442	Turn On Your TV/Hog and Dog Factory	1977	—	2.00	4.00
Albums					
DAYBREAK					
❑ 2000	The Wheat Lies Low	1971	3.00	6.00	12.00
❑ 2010	Crescentville	1972	3.00	6.00	12.00
WARNER BROS.					
❑ BS 2933	Junkfood Junkie	1976	2.50	5.00	10.00

GROOMS, SHERRY

Also see EVEN STEVENS.

Number	Title (A Side/B Side)	Yr	VG	VG+	NM
45s					
ABC					
❑ 10812	The Girls' Song/Call of the Wild One	1966	5.00	10.00	20.00
❑ 10875	Night Fall/Take Away the Memories (Of a Love So Fine)	1966	7.50	15.00	30.00
❑ 10987	Forever Is a Long Time/That Same Old Song	1967	5.00	10.00	20.00
PARACHUTE					
❑ 514	Me/Mama's Boys	1978	—	2.50	5.00

GROVES, EDGEL

Number	Title (A Side/B Side)	Yr	VG	VG+	NM
45s					
SILVER STAR					
❑ 20	Footprints in the Sand/(Instrumental)	1981	—	3.00	6.00

GUITAR, BONNIE

Number	Title (A Side/B Side)	Yr	VG	VG+	NM
45s					
4 STAR					
❑ 1006	I Wanna Spend My Life with You/Maggie	1975	—	2.50	5.00
❑ 1041	Honey on the Moon/Lonely Eyes	1980	—	2.50	5.00
—Number also listed as 1003. Which is correct? Or are both?					
COLUMBIA					
❑ 4-45643	Just As Soon As I Get Over Loving You/Happy Everything	1972	—	2.50	5.00
DOLTON					
❑ 10	Candy Apple Red/Come to Me, I Love You	1959	3.00	6.00	12.00
❑ 19	Candy Apple Red/Come to Me, I Love You	1960	2.50	5.00	10.00
DOT					
❑ 15550	Dark Moon/Big Mile	1957	3.75	7.50	15.00
❑ 15587	Half Your Heart/If You See My Love Dancing	1957	3.00	6.00	12.00
❑ 15612	There's a New Moon Over My Shoulder/Mister Fire Eyes	1957	3.00	6.00	12.00
❑ 15678	Making Believe/I Saw Your Face in the Moon	1957	3.00	6.00	12.00
❑ 15708	A Very Precious Love/Johnny Vagabond	1958	3.00	6.00	12.00
❑ 15776	I Found You Out/If You'll Be the Teacher	1958	3.00	6.00	12.00
❑ 15862	Rocky Mountain Moon/Whispering Hope	1958	3.00	6.00	12.00
❑ 15894	Baby Moon/Solitude	1959	3.00	6.00	12.00
❑ 16811	I'm Living in Two Worlds/Goodtime Charlie	1965	—	3.00	6.00
❑ 16872	Would You Believe/Get Your Life the Way You Want It	1966	—	3.00	6.00
❑ 16919	Are You SIncere/The Tallest Tree	1966	—	3.00	6.00
❑ 16968	I'll Be Missing You (Under the Mistletoe)/Blue Christmas	1966	5.00	10.00	20.00
❑ 16987	The Kickin' Tree/Only I	1967	—	3.00	6.00
❑ 17007	You Can Steal Me/Ramblin' Man	1967	—	3.00	6.00
❑ 17029	I Want My Baby/Woman in Love	1967	—	3.00	6.00
❑ 17057	Wings of a Dove/Stop the Sun	1967	—	3.00	6.00
❑ 17097	Faded Love/I Believe in Love	1968	—	2.50	5.00
❑ 17150	Almost Like Being with You/Leaves Are the Tears of Autumn	1968	—	2.50	5.00
❑ 17249	Perfect Strangers/I'll Meet You in Denver	1969	—	2.50	5.00
❑ 17276	I'll Pick Up My Heart/That See Me Later Look	1969	—	2.50	5.00
FABOR					
❑ 138	Ra Ta Ta Ta/Leave Weeping to the Willow Tree	1964	2.00	4.00	8.00
❑ 4013	If You See My Love Dancing/Hello, Hello, Please Answer	1956	6.25	12.50	25.00
❑ 4017	Clinging VIne/Dream Dreamers	1956	6.25	12.50	25.00
❑ 4018	Dark Moon/Big Mile	1957	10.00	20.00	40.00
JERDEN					
❑ 707	There'll Be No Teardrops Tonight/The Fool	1963	2.50	5.00	10.00
MCA					
❑ 40192	The Bed I Love In/Wishing Star	1974	—	2.00	4.00
❑ 40306	From This Moment On/Shine	1974	—	2.00	4.00
PARAMOUNT					
❑ 0004	A Truer Love You'll Never Find (Than Mine)/That's When	1969	—	3.50	7.00
—As "Bonnie and Buddy"					
❑ 0045	Allegheny/Red Checkered Blazer	1970	—	3.50	7.00
PLAYBACK					
❑ 1304	Things Songs Are Made Of/Here We Lie	1988	—	3.00	6.00
❑ 1309	Paradise/Wine from My Table	1988	—	3.00	6.00
❑ 1326	What Can I Say/What's In It for Me	1989	—	3.00	6.00
❑ 1341	Lonely Eyes/Honey on the Moon	1989	—	3.00	6.00
❑ 75714	Still the Same/If You Were Here	1989	—	2.50	5.00
RADIO					
❑ 101	Please, My Love/Love Is Over, Love Is Done	1958	3.00	6.00	12.00
❑ 110	Shanty Boat/Only the Moon Man Knows	1958	3.00	6.00	12.00
RCA VICTOR					
❑ 47-7951	I'll Step Down/Tell Her Bye	1961	2.50	5.00	10.00
❑ 47-8063	Broken Hearted Girl/Who Is She	1962	2.50	5.00	10.00
Albums					
DOT					
❑ DLP-3069 [M]	Moonlight and Shadows	1957	12.50	25.00	50.00
❑ DLP-3151 [M]	Whispering Hope	1958	10.00	20.00	40.00
❑ DLP-3335 [M]	Dark Moon	1961	6.25	12.50	25.00
❑ DLP-3696 [M]	Two Worlds	1966	5.00	10.00	20.00
❑ DLP-3737 [M]	Miss Bonnie Guitar	1966	5.00	10.00	20.00
❑ DLP-3746 [M]	Merry Christmas from Bonnie Guitar	1966	5.00	10.00	20.00
❑ DLP-3793 [M]	Award Winner	1967	5.00	10.00	20.00
❑ DLP-25069 [R]	Moonlight and Shadows	196?	3.75	7.50	15.00
❑ DLP-25151 [S]	Whispering Hope	1958	12.50	25.00	50.00
❑ DLP-25335 [R]	Dark Moon	196?	3.75	7.50	15.00
❑ DLP-25696 [S]	Two Worlds	1966	6.25	12.50	25.00
❑ DLP-25737 [S]	Miss Bonnie Guitar	1966	6.25	12.50	25.00
❑ DLP-25746 [S]	Merry Christmas from Bonnie Guitar	1966	6.25	12.50	25.00
❑ DLP-25793 [S]	Award Winner	1967	5.00	10.00	20.00
❑ DLP-25840	Bonnie Guitar	1968	5.00	10.00	20.00
❑ DLP-25947	Bonnie Guitar Affair!	1969	5.00	10.00	20.00
PARAMOUNT					
❑ PAS-5018	Allegheny	1970	3.75	7.50	15.00
PICKWICK					
❑ SPC-3086	Favorite Lady of Song	196?	3.00	6.00	12.00
RCA CAMDEN					
❑ CAS-2339	Night Train to Memphis	1969	3.75	7.50	15.00

GUNN, J.W.

Number	Title (A Side/B Side)	Yr	VG	VG+	NM
45s					
PRIMERO					
❑ 1013	Love Me Today, Love Me Forever/Bessie, Jane & I	1982	—	3.00	6.00

GUNTER, HARDROCK

Number	Title (A Side/B Side)	Yr	VG	VG+	NM
45s					
DECCA					
❑ 9-46300	Boogie Woogie on a Saturday Night/Honky Tonk	1951	10.00	20.00	40.00
❑ 9-46350	I've Done Gone Hog Wild/I Believe That Mountain Music	1951	6.25	12.50	25.00
❑ 9-46363	Sixty Minute Man/Tennessee Blues	1951	6.25	12.50	25.00
❑ 9-46367	Dixieland Boogie/If I Could Only Live My Dreams	1951	6.25	12.50	25.00
❑ 9-46383	Hesitation Boogie/Don't You Agree	1951	6.25	12.50	25.00
❑ 9-46401	Silver and Gold/Senator from Tennessee	1952	6.25	12.50	25.00
KING					
❑ 4858	Turn the Other Cheek/Before My Time	1955	5.00	10.00	20.00
MGM					
❑ K-11520	Like the Lovers Do/Naptown, Indiana	1953	6.25	12.50	25.00
❑ K-11596	Sunday Angel/Where Have You Been	1953	6.25	12.50	25.00
SUN					
❑ 201	Fallen Angel/Gonna Dance All Night	1954	500.00	1000.	2000.

GURLEY, RANDY

Number	Title (A Side/B Side)	Yr	VG	VG+	NM
45s					
ABC					
❑ 12392	True Love Ways/I'll Never Get Over Loving You	1978	—	2.00	4.00
ABC DOT					
❑ 17728	Heartbreaker/Louisville	1977	—	2.50	5.00
RCA					
❑ PB-11611	Don't Treat Me Like a Stranger/Every Night	1979	—	2.00	4.00
❑ PB-11726	If I Ever/How Long	1979	—	2.00	4.00

GUTHRIE, JACK

Number	Title (A Side/B Side)	Yr	VG	VG+	NM
45s					
CAPITOL					
❑ F2128	Oklahoma Hills/Oakie Boogie	1952	10.00	20.00	40.00
CAPITOL STARLINE					
❑ 6085	Oklahoma Hills/Oakie Boogie	1966	2.50	5.00	10.00
—Originals on green swirl label					
Selected 78s					
CAPITOL					
❑ 201	Oklahoma Hills/I'm a-Brandin' My Darlin' with My Heart	1945	3.75	7.50	15.00
❑ 246	When the Cactus Is in Bloom/I Loved You Once	1946	3.75	7.50	15.00
❑ 309	Chained to a Memory/I'm Telling You	1946	3.75	7.50	15.00
❑ 341	Oakie Boogie/Clouds Rained Trouble Down	1947	3.75	7.50	15.00
❑ 406	It's Too Late to Change Your Mind/You Laughed and I Cried	1947	3.75	7.50	15.00
❑ 15251	Answer to Moonlight and Skies/In the Shadows of My Heart	1948	3.75	7.50	15.00
❑ 15266	Oakie Boogie/Oklahoma Hills	1948	3.75	7.50	15.00
❑ 40012	This Troubled Mind o' Mine/I'm Building a Stairway to Heaven	1947	3.75	7.50	15.00
❑ 40032	Oklahoma's Calling/Please, Oh Please	1947	3.75	7.50	15.00
❑ 40075	Ida Red/Next to the Soil	1948	3.75	7.50	15.00
❑ 40118	Bow Down Brother/You're Gonna Be Sorry (Some of These Days)	1948	3.75	7.50	15.00
❑ 40131	Look Out for the Crossing/No Need to Knock	1948	3.75	7.50	15.00
❑ 40222	Welcome Home Stranger/Colorado Blues	1949	3.75	7.50	15.00
Albums					
CAPITOL					
❑ T 2456 [M]	Jack Guthrie's Greatest Songs	1966	6.25	12.50	25.00

GUY & RALNA

45s

RANWOOD

Number	Title (A Side/B Side)	Yr	VG	VG+	NM
897	I've Confessed to the Breeze/Where Has My Hubby Gone Blues	1971	—	3.00	6.00
948	Have I Told You Lately That I Love You/Cowboy Buckaroo	1973	—	2.50	5.00
1000	Loving You/You're the One	1974	—	2.50	5.00
1016	I'd Like to Share Your Life/Red River Valley	1975	—	2.50	5.00
1029	We've Got It All Together Now/Red River Valley	1975	—	2.50	5.00
1037	Lovelight/Until the End of Time	1975	—	2.50	5.00
1070	If I Didn't Love You/She Knows Me Better	1977	—	2.50	5.00
1074	Listen to My Smile/Old Fashioned Love Song	1977	—	2.50	5.00

Albums

RANWOOD

Number	Title (A Side/B Side)	Yr	VG	VG+	NM
8110	Country Songs We Love to Sing	1973	2.50	5.00	10.00
8120	Give Me That Old Time Religion	1974	2.50	5.00	10.00
8148	How Great Thou Art	1975	2.50	5.00	10.00

H

HADDOCK, DURWOOD

45s

CAPRICE

Number	Title (A Side/B Side)	Yr	VG	VG+	NM
2004	Angel in an Apron/Truck Driver's Turn	1974	—	3.00	6.00
2008	It Sure Looks Good on You/(B-side unknown)	1975	—	3.00	6.00

COUNTRY INT'L.

Number	Title (A Side/B Side)	Yr	VG	VG+	NM
132	The Perfect Love Song/You Loved Me So Good (That's Why I Miss You So Bad)	1978	—	2.50	5.00
140	Low Down Time/Everynight Sensation	1979	—	2.50	5.00

EAGLE INT'L.

Number	Title (A Side/B Side)	Yr	VG	VG+	NM
1137	Low Down Time/She Gave Me Good Love	1977	—	2.50	5.00
1138	You Loved Me So Good (That's Why I Miss You So Bad)/(B-side unknown)	1977	—	2.50	5.00
1144	The Perfect Love Song/(B-side unknown)	1978	—	2.50	5.00
1148	Everynight Sensation/Low Down Time	1978	—	2.50	5.00
1161	It Sure Looks Good on You/(B-side unknown)	1980	—	2.50	5.00
1162	Baby One More Time/(B-side unknown)	1981	—	2.50	5.00
1179	Big Night at My House/Baby One More Time	198?	—	2.50	5.00

MONUMENT

Number	Title (A Side/B Side)	Yr	VG	VG+	NM
1080	I'm Gonna Quit Drinking/Wait Till I Get My Hands on You	1968	2.00	4.00	8.00
1112	Mac the Merchant/The Newest Thing in Night Life	1968	2.00	4.00	8.00

HAGER, CHARLIE

45s

KILLER

Number	Title (A Side/B Side)	Yr	VG	VG+	NM
114	Men with Broken Hearts/(B-side unknown)	1988	—	3.00	6.00

HAGERS, THE

45s

BARNABY

Number	Title (A Side/B Side)	Yr	VG	VG+	NM
2056	Ain't No Sunshine/Mammy Blue	1972	—	3.00	6.00
2062	The Cost of Love Is Getting Higher/Cynthia Daye	1972	—	3.00	6.00
5002	I Just Don't Feel at Home/Summer Only Needs Its Autumn	1972	—	3.00	6.00
5016	A Fool Such As I/Summer Only Needs Its Autumn	1973	—	3.00	6.00

CAPITOL

Number	Title (A Side/B Side)	Yr	VG	VG+	NM
2533	Tracks (Running Through the City)/With Lonely	1969	—	3.50	7.00
2647	Gotta Get to Oklahoma ('Cause California's Gettin' To Me)/Your Tender Loving Care	1969	—	3.50	7.00
2740	Loneliness Without You/Give It Time	1970	—	3.50	7.00
2803	Goin' Home to Your Mother/I'm Not Going Back to Jackson	1970	—	3.50	7.00
2887	Silver Wings/Flowers Need Sun, Too	1970	—	3.50	7.00
3012	I'm Miles Away/Lonely Caboose	1971	—	3.50	7.00
3101	Motherhood, Apple Pie and the Flag/White Line Fever	1971	—	3.50	7.00

ELEKTRA

Number	Title (A Side/B Side)	Yr	VG	VG+	NM
45209	Love My Life Away/You Can't Get There from Here	1974	—	2.00	4.00
45219	Cherry Pie/All Your Love	1974	—	2.00	4.00
45239	Heartaches by the Number/Take Me	1975	—	2.00	4.00
45266	Hot Lips/Old Fashioned Girl	1975	—	2.00	4.00

Albums

BARNABY

Number	Title (A Side/B Side)	Yr	VG	VG+	NM
BR 15002	Country Side	1972	3.75	7.50	15.00

CAPITOL

Number	Title (A Side/B Side)	Yr	VG	VG+	NM
ST-438	The Hagers	1970	3.75	7.50	15.00
ST-553	Two Hagers Are Better Than One	1970	3.75	7.50	15.00
ST-783	Apple Pie, Motherhood and the Flag	1971	3.75	7.50	15.00

ELEKTRA

Number	Title (A Side/B Side)	Yr	VG	VG+	NM
7E-1021	The Hagers	1974	3.00	6.00	12.00

HAGGARD, MARTY

45s

DIMENSION

Number	Title (A Side/B Side)	Yr	VG	VG+	NM
1009	Music, Red Wine and Honky Tonk Angels/Lookin'	1980	—	2.50	5.00
1016	Charleston Cotton Mill/Rain	1981	—	2.50	5.00

MTM

Number	Title (A Side/B Side)	Yr	VG	VG+	NM
B-72073	Talkin' Blue Eyes/I Broke the Rules Today	1986	—	2.00	4.00
B-72085	Weekend Cowboys/Forget He's Your Husband	1987	—	2.00	4.00
B-72103	Trains Make Me Lonesome/By the Dawn's Early Light	1988	—	2.00	4.00
B-72107	Now You See 'Em, Now You Don't/Missing California Blues	1988	—	2.00	4.00

HAGGARD, MERLE

Also see PAYCHECK AND HAGGARD.

45s

CAPITOL

Number	Title (A Side/B Side)	Yr	VG	VG+	NM
2017	Sing Me Back Home/Good Times	1967	2.00	4.00	8.00
2017 [PS]	Sing Me Back Home/Good Times	1967	2.00	4.00	8.00
2123	The Legend of Bonnie and Clyde/Today I Started Loving You Again	1968	2.00	4.00	8.00
2219	Mama Tried/You'll Never Love Me Now	1968	2.00	4.00	8.00
2219 [PS]	Mama Tried/You'll Never Love Me Now	1968	2.00	4.00	8.00
2289	I Take a Lot of Pride in What I Am/Keep Me from Cryin' Today	1968	2.00	4.00	8.00
2289 [PS]	I Take a Lot of Pride in What I Am/Keep Me from Cryin' Today	1968	2.00	4.00	8.00
2383	Hungry Eyes/California Blues	1969	2.00	4.00	8.00
2383 [PS]	Hungry Eyes/California Blues	1969	2.00	4.00	8.00
2503	Workin' Man Blues/Silver Wings	1969	2.00	4.00	8.00
2503 [PS]	Workin' Man Blues/Silver Wings	1969	2.00	4.00	8.00
2626	Okie from Muskogee/If I Had Left It Up to You	1969	2.00	4.00	8.00
2626 [PS]	Okie from Muskogee/If I Had Left It Up to You	1969	2.00	4.00	8.00
2719	The Fightin' Side of Me/Every Fool Has a Rainbow	1970	2.00	4.00	8.00
2719 [PS]	The Fightin' Side of Me/Every Fool Has a Rainbow	1970	2.00	4.00	8.00
2778	Street Singer/Mexicali Rose	1970	2.00	4.00	8.00
2838	Jesus, Take a Hold/No Reason to Quit	1970	2.00	4.00	8.00
2891	I Can't Be Myself/Sidewalks of Chicago	1970	2.00	4.00	8.00
2891 [PS]	I Can't Be Myself/Sidewalks of Chicago	1970	2.00	4.00	8.00
3024	Soldier's Last Letter/The Farmer's Daughter	1971	—	3.00	6.00
3024 [PS]	Soldier's Last Letter/The Farmer's Daughter	1971	2.00	4.00	8.00
3112	Someday We'll Look Back/It's Great to Be Alive	1971	—	3.00	6.00
3144	Song from Sleepwalk/Slow 'n Easy *—By "Merle Haggard's Strangers"*	1971	2.00	4.00	8.00
3198	Daddy Frank (The Guitar Man)/My Heart Would Know	1971	—	3.00	6.00
3222	Carolyn/When the Feelin' Goes Away	1971	—	3.00	6.00
3294	Grandma Harp/Turnin' Off a Memory	1972	—	3.00	6.00
3376	I'm a Light Boy/Shoulder to Cry On	1972	2.50	5.00	10.00
3419	It's Not Love (But It's Not Bad)/My Woman Keeps Lovin' Her Man	1972	—	3.00	6.00
3488	I Wonder If They Ever Think of Me/I Forget You Every Day	1972	—	3.00	6.00
3552	The Emptiest Arms in the World/Radiator Man from Waco	1973	—	2.50	5.00
3641	Everybody's Had the Blues/Nobody Knows I'm Hurtin'	1973	—	2.50	5.00
3746	If We Make It Through December/Bobby Wants a Puppy Dog for Christmas	1973	—	2.50	5.00
3830	Things Aren't Funny Anymore/Honky Tonk Night Time Man	1974	—	2.50	5.00
3900	Old Man from the Mountain/Holding Things Together	1974	—	2.50	5.00
3974	Kentucky Gambler/I've Got a Darlin' (For a Wife)	1974	—	2.50	5.00
3989	Santa Claus and Popcorn/If We Make It Through December	1974	—	2.50	5.00
4027	Always Wanting You/I've Got a Yearning	1975	—	2.50	5.00
4085	Movin' On/Here in Frisco	1975	—	2.50	5.00
4141	It's All in the Movies/Living with the Shades Pulled Down	1975	—	2.50	5.00
4204	The Roots of My Raising/The Way It Was in '51	1975	—	2.50	5.00
4267	Here Comes the Freedom Train/I Won't Give Up My Train	1976	—	2.50	5.00
4326	Cherokee Maiden/What Have You Got Planned Tonight Diana	1976	—	2.50	5.00
4477	A Workin' Man Can't Get Nowhere Today/Blues Stay Away from Me	1977	—	2.50	5.00
4525	Running Kind/Making Believe	1978	—	2.50	5.00
4636	The Way It Was in '51/Moanin' the Blues	1978	—	2.50	5.00
5460	I'm Gonna Break Every Heart I Can/Falling for You	1965	2.50	5.00	10.00
5523	This Town's Not Big Enough/Shade Tree	1965	2.50	5.00	10.00
5600	Swinging Doors/The Girl Turned Ripe	1966	2.50	5.00	10.00
5704	The Bottle Let Me Down/The Longer You Wait	1966	2.50	5.00	10.00
5803	The Fugitive/Someone Told My Story	1966	3.00	6.00	12.00
5803	I'm a Lonesome Fugitive/Someone Told My Story *—Retitled A-side*	1967	2.00	4.00	8.00
5844	I Threw Away the Rose/Loneliness Is Eating Me Alive	1967	2.00	4.00	8.00
5844 [PS]	I Threw Away the Rose/Loneliness Is Eating Me Alive	1967	2.00	4.00	8.00
5931	Branded Man/You Don't Have Very Far to Go	1967	2.00	4.00	8.00
5931 [PS]	Branded Man/You Don't Have Very Far to Go	1967	2.00	4.00	8.00

Number	Title (A Side/B Side)	Yr	VG	VG+	NM
CAPITOL NASHVILLE					
❑ S7-19346	White Christmas/Silver Bells	1996	—	2.00	4.00
CURB					
❑ 76832	When It Rains It Pours/Me and Crippled Soldiers	1990	—	2.00	4.00
❑ 76846	Blue Jungle/Me and Crippled Soldiers	1990	—	2.00	4.00
❑ 76854	A Bar in Bakersfield/Lucky Old Colorado	1991	—	2.00	4.00
ELEKTRA					
❑ 46634	Bar Room Buddies/The Not So Great Train Robbery	1980	—	2.00	4.00
—With Clint Eastwood					
❑ 46634 [PS]	Bar Room Buddies/The Not So Great Train Robbery	1980	—	2.50	5.00
EPIC					
❑ AE7 1777 [DJ]	Santa Claus and Popcorn/Grandma's Homemade Christmas Card	1982	—	2.50	5.00
❑ 02504	My Favorite Memory/Texas Fiddle Song	1981	—	—	3.00
❑ 02686	Big City/I Think I'm Gonna Live Forever	1981	—	—	3.00
❑ 02894	Are the Good Times Really Over (I Wish a Buck Was Still Silver)/I Always Get Lucky with You	1982	—	—	3.00
❑ 03315	Going Where the Lonely Go/Someday You're Gonna Need Your Friends Again	1982	—	—	3.00
❑ 03365	Going Where the Lonely Go	1982	2.00	4.00	8.00
—One-sided budget release					
❑ 03406	Goin' Home for Christmas/If We Make It Through December	1982	—	2.00	4.00
❑ 03723	You Take Me for Granted/I Won't Give Up My Train	1983	—	—	3.00
❑ 04006	What Am I Gonna Do (With the Rest of My Life)/ I Think I'll Stay	1983	—	—	3.00
❑ 04226	That's the Way Love Goes/Don't Seem Like We've Been Together All Our Lives	1983	—	—	3.00
❑ 04402	Someday When Things Are Good/If You Hated Me	1984	—	—	3.00
❑ 04512	Let's Chase Each Other Around the Room/All I Want to Do Is Sing My Song	1984	—	—	3.00
❑ 04830	Natural High/I Won't Go Home Anymore	1985	—	—	3.00
❑ 05426	Kern River/The Old Water Mill	1985	—	—	3.00
❑ 05659	Amber Waves of Grain/I Wish Things Were Simple Again	1985	—	—	3.00
❑ 05734	American Waltz/The Farmer's Daughter	1985	—	—	3.00
❑ 05782	I Had a Beautiful Time/This Time I Really Do	1986	—	—	3.00
❑ 06097	A Friend in California/Mama's Prayers	1986	—	—	3.00
❑ 06344	Out Among the Stars/Suzie	1986	—	—	3.00
❑ 07036	Almost Persuaded/Love Don't Hurt Everytime	1987	—	—	3.00
❑ 07631	Twinkle, Twinkle, Lucky Star/I Don't Have Any Love Around	1987	—	—	3.00
❑ 07754	Chill Factor/Thanking the Good Lord	1988	—	—	3.00
❑ 07944	We Never Touch at All/Man from Another Time	1988	—	—	3.00
❑ 08111	You Babe/Thirty Again	1988	—	—	3.00
❑ 68598	5:01 Blues/Man from Another Time	1989	—	—	3.00
❑ 68979	A Better Love Next Time/Me and Crippled Soldiers	1989	—	—	3.00
❑ 73076	If You Want to Be My Woman/Someday We'll Know	1989	—	—	3.00
❑ 73303	Broken Friend/Wouldn't That Be Something	1990	—	2.00	4.00
MCA					
❑ 40700	If We're Not Back in Love By Monday/I Think It's Gone Forever	1977	—	2.00	4.00
❑ 40743	Ramblin' Fever/When My Blue Moon Turns to Gold Again	1977	—	2.00	4.00
❑ 40804	From Graceland to the Promised Land/Are You Lonesome Tonight	1977	—	3.00	6.00
❑ 40869	I'm Always on a Mountain When I Fall/The Life of a Rodeo Cowboy	1978	—	2.00	4.00
❑ 40936	It's Been a Great Afternoon/Love Me When You Can	1978	—	2.00	4.00
❑ 41007	Red Bandana/I Must Have Done Something Bad	1979	—	2.00	4.00
❑ 41112	My Own Kind of Hat/Heaven Was a Drink of Wine	1979	—	2.00	4.00
❑ 41168	If We Make It Through December/The Fightin' Side of Me	1979	—	2.50	5.00
❑ 41200	The Way I Am/Wake Up	1980	—	2.00	4.00
❑ 41255	Misery and Gin/No One to Sing For	1980	—	2.00	4.00
❑ 41255 [PS]	Misery and Gin/No One to Sing For	1980	—	2.50	5.00
❑ 51014	I Think I'll Just Stay Here and Drink/Back to the Barrooms	1980	—	2.00	4.00
❑ 51048	Leonard/Our Paths May Never Cross	1981	—	2.00	4.00
❑ 51120	Rainbow Stew/Blue Yodel No. 9	1981	—	2.00	4.00
❑ 52020	Dealing with the Devil/Fiddle Breakdown	1982	—	2.00	4.00
❑ 52276	It's All in the Game/New Cocaine Blues	1983	—	—	3.00
❑ 52595	Make-Up and Faded Blue Jeans/Love Me When You Can	1985	—	—	3.00
TALLY					
❑ 152	Singin' My Heart Out/Skid Row	1963	5.00	10.00	20.00
❑ 155	Sing a Sad Song/You Don't Even Try	1963	3.75	7.50	15.00
❑ 178	Sam Hill/You Don't Have Far to Go	1964	3.75	7.50	15.00
❑ 179	(My Friends Are Gonna Be) Strangers/Please Mr. D.J.	1964	3.75	7.50	15.00
Albums					
CAPITOL					
❑ SKAO-168	Pride In What I Am	1969	6.25	12.50	25.00
❑ SM-168	Pride in What I Am	197?	2.50	5.00	10.00
—Reissue with new prefix					
❑ SWBB-223 [(2)]	Same Train, A Different Time	1969	7.50	15.00	30.00
❑ SWBB-259 [(2)]	Close-Up	1969	7.50	15.00	30.00
—Reissue in one package of "Strangers" and "Swinging Doors"					

Number	Title (A Side/B Side)	Yr	VG	VG+	NM
❑ ST-319	A Portrait of Merle Haggard	1969	5.00	10.00	20.00
❑ ST-384	Okie from Muskogee	1970	5.00	10.00	20.00
❑ ST-451	The Fightin' Side of Me	1970	5.00	10.00	20.00
❑ ST-638	A Tribute to the Best Damn Fiddle Player in the World (Or, My Salute to Bob Wills)	1970	6.25	12.50	25.00
❑ STBB-707 [(2)]	Sing a Sad Song/High on a Hilltop	1971	7.50	15.00	30.00
❑ ST-735	Hag	1971	3.75	7.50	15.00
❑ SWBO-803 [(2)]	The Land of Many Churches	1971	15.00	30.00	60.00
❑ ST-823	Truly the Best of Merle Haggard	1971	10.00	20.00	40.00
❑ ST-835	Someday We'll Look Back	1971	5.00	10.00	20.00
❑ ST-882	Let Me Tell You About a Song	1972	5.00	10.00	20.00
❑ ST 2373 [S]	Strangers	1965	7.50	15.00	30.00
❑ T 2373 [M]	Strangers	1965	6.25	12.50	25.00
❑ SM-2585	Swinging Doors	197?	2.50	5.00	10.00
—Reissue with new prefix					
❑ ST 2585 [S]	Swinging Doors	1966	7.50	15.00	30.00
❑ T 2585 [M]	Swinging Doors	1966	6.25	12.50	25.00
❑ SM-2702	I'm a Lonesome Fugitive	197?	2.50	5.00	10.00
—Reissue with new prefix					
❑ ST 2702 [S]	I'm a Lonesome Fugitive	1967	7.50	15.00	30.00
❑ T 2702 [M]	I'm a Lonesome Fugitive	1967	6.25	12.50	25.00
❑ ST 2789 [S]	Branded Man	1967	7.50	15.00	30.00
❑ T 2789 [M]	Branded Man	1967	6.25	12.50	25.00
❑ ST 2848 [S]	Sing Me Back Home	1968	6.25	12.50	25.00
❑ T 2848 [M]	Sing Me Back Home	1968	7.50	15.00	30.00
❑ ST 2912	The Legend of Bonnie and Clyde	1968	6.25	12.50	25.00
❑ SKAO 2951	The Best of Merle Haggard	1968	6.25	12.50	25.00
❑ ST 2972	Mama Tried	1968	6.25	12.50	25.00
❑ ST-11082	The Best of the Best of Merle Haggard	1972	3.75	7.50	15.00
❑ ST-11127	It's Not Love	1972	3.00	6.00	12.00
❑ ST-11141	Totally Instrumental with One Exception	1973	3.75	7.50	15.00
❑ ST-11200	I Love Dixie Blues...So I Recorded "Live" in New Orleans	1973	3.00	6.00	12.00
❑ ST-11230	Merle Haggard's Christmas Present (Something Old, Something New)	1973	3.00	6.00	12.00
❑ ST-11276	If We Make It Through December	1974	3.00	6.00	12.00
❑ ST-11331	Merle Haggard Presents His 30th Album	1974	3.00	6.00	12.00
❑ ST-11365	Keep Movin' On	1975	3.00	6.00	12.00
❑ ST-11483	It's All in the Movies	1975	3.00	6.00	12.00
❑ SABB-11531 [(2)]	Songs I'll Always Sing	1976	3.75	7.50	15.00
❑ ST-11544	My Love Affair with Trains	1976	3.00	6.00	12.00
❑ ST-11586	The Roots of My Raising	1976	3.00	6.00	12.00
❑ ST-11693	A Working Man Can't Get Nowhere Today	1977	3.00	6.00	12.00
❑ ST-11745	Eleven Winners	1977	3.00	6.00	12.00
❑ SM-11823	My Love Affair with Trains	1978	2.50	5.00	10.00
—Reissue					
❑ SW-11839	The Way It Was	1978	3.00	6.00	12.00
❑ SM-12036	It's All in the Movies	1979	2.50	5.00	10.00
—Reissue					
❑ SN-16052	Sing a Sad Song	1979	2.00	4.00	8.00
—Budget-line reissue					
❑ SN-16053	High on a Hilltop	1979	2.00	4.00	8.00
—Budget-line reissue					
❑ SN-16054	The Best of Merle Haggard	1979	2.00	4.00	8.00
—Budget-line reissue					
❑ SN-16277	Okie from Muskogee	1982	2.00	4.00	8.00
—Budget-line reissue					
❑ SN-16278	The Fightin' Side of Me	1982	2.00	4.00	8.00
—Budget-line reissue					
❑ SN-16279	A Tribute to the Best Damn Fiddle Player in the World (Or, My Salute to Bob Wills)	1982	2.00	4.00	8.00
—Budget-line reissue					
❑ SN-16303	Eleven Winners	1984	2.00	4.00	8.00
—Budget-line reissue					
CAPITOL SPECIAL MARKETS					
❑ SL-8086 [(2)]	Songs I'll Always Sing	1977	5.00	10.00	20.00
EPIC					
❑ FE 37593	Big City	1981	2.50	5.00	10.00
❑ PE 37593	Big City	1985	2.00	4.00	8.00
—Budget-line reissue					
❑ FE 38092	Going Where the Lonely Go	1982	2.50	5.00	10.00
❑ PE 38092	Going Where the Lonely Go	1985	2.00	4.00	8.00
—Budget-line reissue					
❑ PE 38307	Goin' Home for Christmas	1982	2.50	5.00	10.00
❑ FE 38815	That's the Way Love Goes	1983	2.50	5.00	10.00
❑ FE 39159	The Epic Collection	1983	2.50	5.00	10.00
❑ PE 39159	The Epic Collection	1985	2.00	4.00	8.00
—Budget-line reissue					
❑ FE 39364	It's All in the Game	1984	2.50	5.00	10.00
❑ FE 39545	His Epic Hits: The First 11	1985	2.50	5.00	10.00
❑ FE 39602	Kern River	1985	2.50	5.00	10.00
❑ FE 40107	Out Among the Stars	1986	2.50	5.00	10.00
❑ PE 40107	Out Among the Stars	1986	2.00	4.00	8.00
—Budget-line reissue					
❑ FE 40224	Amber Waves of Grain	1985	2.50	5.00	10.00
❑ FE 40286	A Friend in California	1986	2.50	5.00	10.00
❑ FE 40986	Chill Factor	1988	2.50	5.00	10.00
❑ FE 44283	5:01 Blues	1989	2.50	5.00	10.00
MCA					
❑ 2267	Ramblin' Fever	1977	3.00	6.00	12.00
❑ 2314	My Farewell to Elvis	1977	3.75	7.50	15.00
❑ 2375	I'm Always on a Mountain	1978	3.00	6.00	12.00
❑ 3089	Serving 190 Proof	1979	3.00	6.00	12.00
❑ 3229	The Way I Am	1980	3.00	6.00	12.00
❑ 5139	Back to the Barrooms	1980	3.00	6.00	12.00

For 20 years, from 1966 through 1985, every new Merle Haggard single (not including cash-ins from former labels and holiday tunes) made the top 10 on the country charts. (Top left) The first time Haggard made the top 10 was with "(My Friends Are Gonna Be) Strangers," when he was still on the Bakersfield, Calif.-based Tally Records. The song became so closely associated with Merle that he named his backing band after it. (Top right) In 1969, Haggard became a hero to the "counter-counterculture" with his reactionary ode, "Okie from Muskogee." A live album, recorded in Muskogee, resulted. Over time, Haggard, feeling his song had been misunderstood, treated his biggest hit as a joke. (Bottom left) The follow-up single to "Okie" was another song that hit home with the "silent majority," "The Fightin' Side of Me." (Bottom right) Haggard was signed with MCA from 1977 through 1980. During that time, he still made the top 10 consistently, but only one of his hits got to No. 1, "I Think I'll Just Stay Here and Drink," which features an unusually long instrumental fade at the end.

Number	Title (A Side/B Side)	Yr	VG	VG+	NM
❑ 5250	Songs for the Mamma	1981	3.00	6.00	12.00
❑ 5386	Greatest Hits	1982	3.00	6.00	12.00
❑ 5573	His Best	1985	2.50	5.00	10.00
❑ 37138	Ramblin' Fever	1980	2.00	4.00	8.00
—Budget-line reissue					
❑ 37139	My Farewell to Elvis	1980	2.00	4.00	8.00
—Budget-line reissue					
❑ 37140	I'm Always on a Mountain	1980	2.00	4.00	8.00
—Budget-line reissue					
❑ 37141	Serving 190 Proof	1980	2.00	4.00	8.00
—Budget-line reissue					
❑ 37207	The Way I Am	1982	2.00	4.00	8.00
—Budget-line reissue					

HAGGARD, MERLE, AND JANIE FRICKE

Also see each artist's individual listings.

45s

EPIC

Number	Title (A Side/B Side)	Yr	VG	VG+	NM
❑ 04663	A Place to Fall Apart/All I Want to Do Is Sing My Song	1984	—	—	3.00

HAGGARD, MERLE, AND JEWEL

45s

BNA

Number	Title (A Side/B Side)	Yr	VG	VG+	NM
❑ 65895	That's the Way Love Goes/Silver Wings	1999	—	—	3.00

HAGGARD, MERLE, AND GEORGE JONES

Also see each artist's individual listings.

45s

EPIC

Number	Title (A Side/B Side)	Yr	VG	VG+	NM
❑ 03072	Yesterday's Wine/I Haven't Found Her Yet	1982	—	—	3.00
❑ 03405	C.C. Waterback/After I Sing All My Songs	1982	—	—	3.00

Albums

EPIC

Number	Title (A Side/B Side)	Yr	VG	VG+	NM
❑ FE 38203	A Taste of Yesterday's Wine	1982	2.50	5.00	10.00

HAGGARD, MERLE, AND WILLIE NELSON

Also see each artist's individual listings.

45s

EPIC

Number	Title (A Side/B Side)	Yr	VG	VG+	NM
❑ 03494	Reasons to Quit/Half a Man	1983	—	2.00	4.00
❑ ENR-03495	Reasons to Quit	1983	2.00	4.00	8.00
—One-sided budget release					
❑ 03842	Pancho and Lefty/Opportunity to Cry	1983	—	2.00	4.00
❑ 34-07400	If I Could Only Fly/Without You on My Side	1987	—	—	3.00

Albums

EPIC

Number	Title (A Side/B Side)	Yr	VG	VG+	NM
❑ FE 37958	Poncho and Lefty	1983	3.75	7.50	15.00
—Note misspelled LP title					
❑ FE 37958	Pancho and Lefty	1983	2.50	5.00	10.00
—Reissue corrects spelling of LP title					
❑ FE 40293	Seashores of Old Mexico	1987	2.50	5.00	10.00

HAGGARD, MERLE, AND BONNIE OWENS

Also see each artist's individual listings.

45s

TALLY

Number	Title (A Side/B Side)	Yr	VG	VG+	NM
❑ 181	Just Between the Two of Us/Slowly But Sure	1964	5.00	10.00	20.00

Albums

CAPITOL

Number	Title (A Side/B Side)	Yr	VG	VG+	NM
❑ ST 2453 [S]	Just Between the Two of Us	1966	7.50	15.00	30.00
❑ T 2453 [M]	Just Between the Two of Us	1966	6.25	12.50	25.00

HAGGARD, MERLE, AND LEONA WILLIAMS

Also see each artist's individual listings.

45s

MCA

Number	Title (A Side/B Side)	Yr	VG	VG+	NM
❑ 40962	The Bull and the Beaver/I'm Gettin' High	1978	—	2.00	4.00

MERCURY

Number	Title (A Side/B Side)	Yr	VG	VG+	NM
❑ 812214-7	We're Strangers Again/Sally Let Your Bangs Hang Down	1983	—	—	3.00
❑ 880139-7	Don't Ever Let Your Lover Sleep Alone/It's Cold in California	1984	—	2.00	4.00

Albums

MERCURY

Number	Title (A Side/B Side)	Yr	VG	VG+	NM
❑ 812183-1	Heart to Heart	1983	2.50	5.00	10.00

HAGGARD, NOEL

45s

ATLANTIC

Number	Title (A Side/B Side)	Yr	VG	VG+	NM
❑ 84867	Once You Learn/Cowgirl Blues	1997	—	—	—
—As best as can be determined, this 45 was never issued					

HALEY, BILL, AND HIS COMETS

After leaving THE DOWN HOMERS (though he was NOT on the Vogue picture records done by that group), Haley formed the Four Aces of Western Swing, who were later known as the Saddlemen, and still later as the Comets.

45s

APT

Number	Title (A Side/B Side)	Yr	VG	VG+	NM
❑ 25081	Stop, Look, and Listen/Burn That Candle	1965	5.00	10.00	20.00
❑ 25087	Haley A-Go-Go/Tongue Tied Tony	1965	6.25	12.50	25.00

ARZEE

Number	Title (A Side/B Side)	Yr	VG	VG+	NM
❑ 4677	Yodel Your Blues Away/Within This Broken Heart of Mine	1978	6.25	12.50	25.00
❑ 4677 [PS]	Yodel Your Blues Away/Within This Broken Heart of Mine	1978	6.25	12.50	25.00

BUDDAH

Number	Title (A Side/B Side)	Yr	VG	VG+	NM
❑ 169	Rock Around the Clock/Framed	1970	3.75	7.50	15.00

DECCA

Number	Title (A Side/B Side)	Yr	VG	VG+	NM
❑ 29124	(We're Gonna) Rock Around the Clock/Thirteen Women (And Only One Man in Town)	1954	15.00	30.00	60.00
—With lines on either side of "Decca"					
❑ 29124	(We're Gonna) Rock Around the Clock/Thirteen Women (And Only One Man in Town)	1955	5.00	10.00	20.00
—With star under "Decca"					
❑ 29204	Shake, Rattle and Roll/A.B.C. Boogie	1954	10.00	20.00	40.00
—With lines on either side of "Decca"					
❑ 29204	Shake, Rattle and Roll/A.B.C. Boogie	1954	5.00	10.00	20.00
—With star under "Decca"					
❑ 29317	Dim, Dim the Lights (I Want Some Atmosphere)/ Happy Baby	1954	10.00	20.00	40.00
—With lines on either side of "Decca"					
❑ 29317	Dim, Dim the Lights (I Want Some Atmosphere)/ Happy Baby	1954	5.00	10.00	20.00
—With star under "Decca"					
❑ 29418	Mambo Rock/Birth of the Boogie	1955	6.25	12.50	25.00
❑ 29552	Razzle-Dazzle/Two Hound Dogs	1955	6.25	12.50	25.00
❑ 29713	Burn That Candle/Rock-a-Beatin' Boogie	1955	6.25	12.50	25.00
❑ 29791	See You Later, Alligator/The Paper Boy (On Main Street, U.S.A.)	1956	6.25	12.50	25.00
❑ 29870	R-O-C-K/The Saints Rock 'N' Roll	1956	6.25	12.50	25.00
❑ 29948	Hot Dog Buddy Buddy/Rockin' Through the Rye	1956	6.25	12.50	25.00
❑ 30028	Rip It Up/Teenager's Mother (Are You Right?)	1956	6.25	12.50	25.00
❑ 30085	Rudy's Rock/Blue Comet Blues	1956	6.25	12.50	25.00
❑ 30148	Don't Knock the Rock/Choo Choo Ch'Boogie	1956	6.25	12.50	25.00
❑ 30214	Forty Cups of Coffeee/Hook, Line and Sinker	1957	6.25	12.50	25.00
❑ 30314	(You Hit the Wrong Note) Billy Goat/Rockin' Rollin' Rover	1957	6.25	12.50	25.00
❑ 30314 [PS]	(You Hit the Wrong Note) Billy Goat/Rockin' Rollin' Rover	1957	30.00	60.00	120.00
❑ 30394	The Dipsy Doodle/Miss You	1957	6.25	12.50	25.00
❑ 30461	Rock the Joint/How Many	1957	6.25	12.50	25.00
❑ 30530	It's a Sin/Mary, Mary Lou	1957	6.25	12.50	25.00
❑ 30530 [PS]	It's a Sin/Mary, Mary Lou	1957	20.00	40.00	80.00
❑ 30592	Skinny Minnie/Sway with Me	1958	7.50	15.00	30.00
❑ 30681	Lean Jean/Don't Nobody Move	1958	6.25	12.50	25.00
❑ 30741	Chiquita Linda/Whoa Mabel	1958	6.25	12.50	25.00
❑ 30781	Corrine, Corrina/B.B. Betty	1958	6.25	12.50	25.00
❑ 30844	Charmaine/I Got a Woman	1959	6.25	12.50	25.00
❑ 30873	(Now and Then, There's) A Fool Such As I/Where Did You Go Last Night	1959	6.25	12.50	25.00
❑ 30926	Caldonia/Shakey	1959	6.25	12.50	25.00
❑ 30956	Joey's Song/Ooh, Look-a-There, Ain't She Pretty	1959	6.25	12.50	25.00
❑ 31030	Skokiaan (South African Song)/Puerto Rican Peddler	1959	6.25	12.50	25.00
❑ 31080	Music, Music, Music/Strictly Instrumental	1960	6.25	12.50	25.00
❑ 31649	The Green Door/Yeah, She's Evil	1964	3.00	6.00	12.00

ESSEX

Number	Title (A Side/B Side)	Yr	VG	VG+	NM
❑ 102	Rock Around the Clock/Crazy Man, Crazy	1955	12.50	25.00	50.00
—Actually a bootleg, but highly sought-after nonetheless					
❑ 303	Rock the Joint/Icy Heart	1952	25.00	50.00	100.00
—Black vinyl, block logo ("ESSEX" in all caps)					
❑ 303	Rock the Joint/Icy Heart	1952	15.00	30.00	60.00
—Black vinyl, script logo ("Essex" not in all caps)					
❑ 303	Rock the Joint/Icy Heart	1952	900.00	1350.	1800.
—Red vinyl					
❑ 305	Rocking Chair on the Moon/Dance with a Dolly (With a Hole in Her Stocking)	1952	25.00	50.00	100.00
—Essex 303 and 305 credit "Bill Haley and the Saddlemen"					
❑ 310	Real Rock Drive/Stop Beatin' Round the Mulberry Bush	1952	37.50	75.00	150.00
—Blue label					
❑ 310	Real Rock Drive/Stop Beatin' Round the Mulberry Bush	1952	20.00	40.00	80.00
—Orange label					
❑ 321	Crazy Man, Crazy/Whatcha Gonna Do	1953	15.00	30.00	60.00
❑ 327	Pat-a-Cake/Fractured	1953	10.00	20.00	40.00
❑ 332	Live It Up/Farewell, So Long, Goodbye	1953	10.00	20.00	40.00
❑ 340	Ten Little Indians/I'll Be True	1953	10.00	20.00	40.00
❑ 348	Chattanooga Choo Choo/Straight Jacket	1954	10.00	20.00	40.00
❑ 374	Sundown Boogie/Jukebox Cannonball	1954	18.75	37.50	75.00
❑ 381	Rocket 88/Green Tree Boogie	1955	31.25	62.50	125.00
❑ 399	Rock the Joint/Farewell, So Long, Goodbye	1955	18.75	37.50	75.00

GNP CRESCENDO

Number	Title (A Side/B Side)	Yr	VG	VG+	NM
❑ 475	I'm Walkin'/Crazy Man, Crazy	1974	3.00	6.00	12.00

GONE

Number	Title (A Side/B Side)	Yr	VG	VG+	NM
❑ 5111	Spanish Twist/My Kind of Woman	1961	6.25	12.50	25.00
❑ 5116	Riviera/War Paint	1961	6.25	12.50	25.00

HOLIDAY

Number	Title (A Side/B Side)	Yr	VG	VG+	NM
❑ 113	Sundown Boogie/Jukebox Cannonball	1951	125.00	250.00	500.00
—As "Bill Haley and the Saddlemen"; the only Holiday single known to exist on a 45. Earlier Holiday singles only exist on 78s.					

JANUS

Number	Title (A Side/B Side)	Yr	VG	VG+	NM
❑ 162	Travelin' Band/A Little Piece at a Time	1971	3.00	6.00	12.00

KAMA SUTRA

Number	Title (A Side/B Side)	Yr	VG	VG+	NM
❑ 508	Rock Around the Clock/Framed	1970	5.00	10.00	20.00

Number	Title (A Side/B Side)	Yr	VG	VG+	NM
KASEY					
❑ 7006	A.B.C. Boogie/Rock Around the Clock	1961	5.00	10.00	20.00
—B-side by Phil Flowers					
MCA					
❑ 60025	(We're Gonna) Rock Around the Clock/Thirteen Women (And Only One Man in Town)	1973	—	2.50	5.00
—Reissue on black label with rainbow; made the Top 40 in 1974					
NEWTOWN					
❑ 5013	Tenor Man/Up Goes My Love	1962	5.00	10.00	20.00
❑ 5024	Dance Around the Clock/What Can I Say After I Say I'm Sorry	1963	5.00	10.00	20.00
NICETOWN					
❑ 5025	You Call Everybody Darling/Tandy	1963	5.00	10.00	20.00
TRANS WORLD					
❑ 718	Real Rock Drive/Yes, Indeed	1954	50.00	100.00	200.00
UNITED ARTISTS					
❑ 50483	Ain't Love Funny, Ha Ha Ha/That's How I Got to Memphis	1969	3.00	6.00	12.00
WARNER BROS.					
❑ 5145	Candy Kisses/Tamiami	1960	6.25	12.50	25.00
❑ 5145 [DJ]	Candy Kisses/Tamiami	1960	12.50	25.00	50.00
—Promo only on yellow vinyl					
❑ 5154	Hawk/Chick Safari	1960	6.25	12.50	25.00
❑ 5171	Let the Good Times Roll, Creole/So Right Tonight	1960	6.25	12.50	25.00
❑ 5228	Flip, Flop and Fly/Honky Tonk	1961	6.25	12.50	25.00
❑ 7124	Rock Around the Clock/Shake, Rattle and Roll	1969	3.75	7.50	15.00
Selected 78s					
ATLANTIC					
❑ 727	Why Do I Cry Over You?/I'm Gonna Dry Ev'ry Tear with a Kiss	1950	100.00	200.00	400.00
—As "Bill Haley and His Saddle Men"					
COWBOY					
❑ 1201	Four Leaf Clover/Too Many Parties, Too Many Pals	1948	125.00	250.00	500.00
—As "Bill Haley and the Four Aces of Western Swing"					
❑ 1202	Candy Kisses/Tennessee Border	1948	125.00	250.00	500.00
—As "Bill Haley and the Four Aces of Western Swing"					
❑ 1701	My Palomino and I/My Sweet Little Girl from Nevada	1950	75.00	150.00	300.00
—As "Bill Haley with Reno Browne and Her Buckaroos"					
HOLIDAY					
❑ 105	Rocket 88/Tearstains on My Heart	1951	37.50	75.00	150.00
—As "Bill Haley and the Saddlemen"					
❑ 108	Green Tree Boogie/Down Deep in My Heart	1951	37.50	75.00	150.00
—As "Bill Haley and the Saddlemen"					
❑ 110	I'm Crying/Pretty Baby	1951	37.50	75.00	150.00
—As "Bill Haley and the Saddlemen"					
❑ 111	A Year Ago This Christmas/I Don't Want to Be Alone This Holiday	1951	37.50	75.00	150.00
—As "Bill Haley and the Saddlemen"					
KEYSTONE					
❑ 5101	Deal Me a Hand/Ten Gallon Stetson	1950	250.00	500.00	1000.
—As "Bill Haley and His Saddle Men"					
❑ 5102	Susan Van Dusan/I'm Not to Blame	1950	250.00	500.00	1000.
—As "Bill Haley and His Saddle Men"					
7-Inch Extended Plays					
CLAIRE					
❑ 4779	*All I Need Is Some More Lovin'/Trouble in Mind/Life of the Party/I Should Write a Song About You	1978	3.75	7.50	15.00
❑ 4779 [PS]	Bill Haley and the Comets	1978	3.75	7.50	15.00
DECCA					
❑ ED 2168	Shake, Rattle and Roll/A.B.C. Boogie//(We're Gonna) Rock Around the Clock/Thirteen Women (And Only One Man in Town)	1954	15.00	30.00	60.00
❑ ED 2168 [PS]	Shake, Rattle and Roll	1954	15.00	30.00	60.00
❑ ED 2209	Dim, Dim the Lights/Happy Baby//Birth of the Boogie/Mambo Rock	1955	15.00	30.00	60.00
❑ ED 2209 [PS]	Dim, Dim the Lights	1955	15.00	30.00	60.00
❑ ED 2322	Razzle-Dazzle/Two Hound Dogs//Burn That Candle/Rock-a-Beatin' Boogie	1956	15.00	30.00	60.00
❑ ED 2322 [PS]	Rock and Roll	1956	15.00	30.00	60.00
❑ ED 2398	See You Later Alligator/R-O-C-K//The Saints Rock 'n Roll/Burn That Candle	1956	12.50	25.00	50.00
❑ ED 2398 [PS]	He Digs Rock 'n' Roll, Part 1	1956	12.50	25.00	50.00
❑ ED 2399	(contents unknown)	1956	12.50	25.00	50.00
❑ ED 2399 [PS]	He Digs Rock 'n' Roll, Part 2	1956	12.50	25.00	50.00
❑ ED 2400	(contents unknown)	1956	12.50	25.00	50.00
❑ ED 2400 [PS]	He Digs Rock 'n' Roll, Part 3	1956	12.50	25.00	50.00
❑ ED 2416	(contents unknown)	1956	12.50	25.00	50.00
❑ ED 2416 [PS]	Rock 'n' Roll Stage Show, Part 1	1956	12.50	25.00	50.00
❑ ED 2417	A Rockin' Little Tune/Hide and Seek//Choo Choo Ch' Boogie/Blue Comet Blues	1956	12.50	25.00	50.00
❑ ED 2417 [PS]	Rock 'n' Roll Stage Show, Part 2	1956	12.50	25.00	50.00
❑ ED 2418	Hey Then, There Now/Goofin' Around//Hot Dog Buddy Buddy/Tonight's the Night	1956	12.50	25.00	50.00
❑ ED 2418 [PS]	Rock 'n' Roll Stage Show, Part 3	1956	12.50	25.00	50.00
❑ ED 2532	(contents unknown)	1957	12.50	25.00	50.00
❑ ED 2532 [PS]	Rockin' the Oldies	1957	12.50	25.00	50.00
❑ ED 2533	(contents unknown)	1957	12.50	25.00	50.00
❑ ED 2533 [PS]	Rock 'n' Roll Party	1957	12.50	25.00	50.00
❑ ED 2534	(contents unknown)	1957	12.50	25.00	50.00
❑ ED 2534 [PS]	Rockin' & Rollin'	1957	12.50	25.00	50.00
❑ ED 2564	(contents unknown)	1957	12.50	25.00	50.00
❑ ED 2564 [PS]	Rockin' Around the World	1957	12.50	25.00	50.00

Number	Title (A Side/B Side)	Yr	VG	VG+	NM
❑ ED 2576	(contents unknown)	1957	12.50	25.00	50.00
❑ ED 2576 [PS]	Rockin' Around Europe	1957	12.50	25.00	50.00
❑ ED 2577	(contents unknown)	1957	12.50	25.00	50.00
❑ ED 2577 [PS]	Rockin' Around the Americas	1957	12.50	25.00	50.00
❑ ED 2615	Rock Lomond/It's a Sin//Move It On Over/New Rock the Joint	1958	10.00	20.00	40.00
❑ ED 2615 [PS]	Rockin' the Joint, Part 1	1958	10.00	20.00	40.00
❑ ED 2616	(contents unknown)	1958	10.00	20.00	40.00
❑ ED 2616 [PS]	Rockin' the Joint, Part 2	1958	10.00	20.00	40.00
❑ ED 2638 [M]	(contents unknown)	1958	10.00	20.00	40.00
❑ ED 2638 [PS]	Bill Haley's Chicks	1958	10.00	20.00	40.00
❑ ED 7-2638 [PS]	Bill Haley's Chicks	1959	20.00	40.00	80.00
❑ ED 7-2638 [S]	(contents unknown)	1959	20.00	40.00	80.00
❑ ED 2670 [M]	Joe's Song/Ooh Look-a There Ain't She Pretty//Shakey/Caledonia	1959	10.00	20.00	40.00
❑ ED 2670 [PS]	Bill Haley and His Comets	1959	10.00	20.00	40.00
❑ ED 7-2670 [PS]	Bill Haley and His Comets	1959	20.00	40.00	80.00
❑ ED 7-2670 [S]	Joe's Song/Ooh Look-a There Ain't She Pretty//Shakey/Caledonia	1959	20.00	40.00	80.00
❑ ED 2671 [M]	Strictly Instrumental/South Africa Song//Mack the Knife/In a Little Spanish Town	1959	10.00	20.00	40.00
❑ ED 2671 [PS]	Strictly Instrumental	1959	10.00	20.00	40.00
❑ ED 7-2671 [PS]	Strictly Instrumental	1959	20.00	40.00	80.00
❑ ED 7-2671 [S]	Strictly Instrumental/South Africa Song//Mack the Knife/In a Little Spanish Town	1959	20.00	40.00	80.00
ESSEX					
❑ TWEP-102	Rock the Joint/Rockin' Chair on the Moon//Crazy Man, Crazy/Pat-a-Cake	1954	25.00	50.00	100.00
❑ TWEP-102 [PS]	For Your Dance Party	1954	30.00	60.00	120.00
❑ EP-117	*Live It Up/Farewell, So Long, Goodbye/Real Rock Drive/Fractured	1954	25.00	50.00	100.00
❑ EP-117 [PS]	Rock with Bill Haley and His Comets, Volume 1	1954	30.00	60.00	120.00
❑ EP-118	*Stop Beatin' Round the Mulberry Bush/Watcha Gonna Do/I'll Be True/Juke Box Cannon Ball	1954	25.00	50.00	100.00
❑ EP-118 [PS]	Rock with Bill Haley and His Comets, Volume 2	1954	30.00	60.00	120.00
❑ EP-119	(contents unknown)	1954	25.00	50.00	100.00
❑ EP-119 [PS]	Rock with Bill Haley and His Comets, Volume 3	1954	30.00	60.00	120.00
SOMERSET					
❑ 460	(contents unknown)	1955	20.00	40.00	80.00
❑ 460 [PS]	Rock with Bill Haley and His Comets	1955	20.00	40.00	80.00
TRANS WORLD					
❑ TWEP-117	(contents unknown)	1955	20.00	40.00	80.00
❑ TWEP-117 [PS]	Rock with Bill Haley and His Comets, Volume 1	1955	20.00	40.00	80.00
❑ TWEP-118	(contents unknown)	1955	20.00	40.00	80.00
❑ TWEP-118 [PS]	Rock with Bill Haley and His Comets, Volume 2	1955	20.00	40.00	80.00
❑ TWEP-119	(contents unknown)	1955	20.00	40.00	80.00
❑ TWEP-119 [PS]	Rock with Bill Haley and His Comets, Volume 3	1955	20.00	40.00	80.00
Albums					
ACCORD					
❑ SN-7125	Rockin' and Rollin'	1981	2.50	5.00	10.00
DECCA					
❑ DL 5560 [10]	Shake, Rattle and Roll	1955	200.00	400.00	800.00
❑ DXSE-7211 [(2)]	Bill Haley's Golden Hits	1972	3.75	7.50	15.00
❑ DL 8225 [M]	Rock Around the Clock	1955	37.50	75.00	150.00
—All-black label with silver print					
❑ DL 8225 [M]	Rock Around the Clock	1960	12.50	25.00	50.00
—Black label with colorband, no mention of MCA on label					
❑ DL 8225 [M]	Rock Around the Clock	1967	7.50	15.00	30.00
—Black label with colorband, "A Division of MCA" on label					
❑ DL 8315 [M]	Music for the Boyfriend	1956	37.50	75.00	150.00
❑ DL 8345 [M]	Rock 'n Roll Stage Show	1956	37.50	75.00	150.00
❑ DL 8569 [M]	Rockin' the Oldies	1957	37.50	75.00	150.00
❑ DL 8692 [M]	Rockin' Around the World	1958	37.50	75.00	150.00
❑ DL 8775 [M]	Rockin' the Joint	1958	37.50	75.00	150.00
❑ DL 8821 [M]	Bill Haley's Chicks	1959	25.00	50.00	100.00
❑ DL 8964 [M]	Strictly Instrumental	1960	25.00	50.00	100.00
❑ DL 75027	Bill Haley's Greatest Hits	1968	3.75	7.50	15.00
❑ DL 78225 [R]	Rock Around the Clock	1959	18.75	37.50	75.00
—All-black label with silver print					
❑ DL 78225 [R]	Rock Around the Clock	1960	6.25	12.50	25.00
—Black label with colorband, no mention of MCA on label					
❑ DL 78225 [R]	Rock Around the Clock	1967	3.75	7.50	15.00
—Black label with colorband, "A Division of MCA" on label					
❑ DL 78821 [S]	Bill Haley's Chicks	1959	37.50	75.00	150.00
❑ DL 78964 [S]	Strictly Instrumental	1960	37.50	75.00	150.00
ESSEX					
❑ LP 202 [M]	Rock with Bill Haley and the Comets	1955	125.00	250.00	500.00
GNP CRESCENDO					
❑ GNPS-2077	Rock 'N' Roll	1973	3.00	6.00	12.00
❑ GNPS-2097	Rock Around the Country	1976	3.00	6.00	12.00
GREAT NORTHWEST					
❑ GNW 4015	Interviewed by Red Robinson	1981	3.00	6.00	12.00
JANUS					
❑ 3035	Travelin' Band	1972	6.25	12.50	25.00
❑ 7003 [(2)]	Razzle-Dazzle	1972	3.75	7.50	15.00
KAMA SUTRA					
❑ KLPS-2014	Scrapbook	1970	7.50	15.00	30.00
MCA					
❑ 161	Bill Haley's Greatest Hits	1973	2.50	5.00	10.00
—Reissue of Decca 75027					
❑ 4010 [(2)]	Bill Haley's Golden Hits	1973	3.00	6.00	12.00
—Reissue of Decca 7211					
❑ 5539 [(2)]	From the Original Master Tapes	1987	3.00	6.00	12.00

PAIR

Number	Title (A Side/B Side)	Yr	VG	VG+	NM
❑ MSM2-35069 [(2)]	Rock and Roll Giant	1986	3.00	6.00	12.00

PICCADILLY

Number	Title (A Side/B Side)	Yr	VG	VG+	NM
❑ PIC-3408	Greatest Hits	1980	2.50	5.00	10.00

PICKWICK

Number	Title (A Side/B Side)	Yr	VG	VG+	NM
❑ PTP-2077 [(2)]	Rock 'N' Roll	197?	3.00	6.00	12.00
❑ SPC-3256	Bill Haley and the Comets	1970	2.50	5.00	10.00
❑ SPC-3280	Rock 'N' Roll Revival	197?	2.50	5.00	10.00

ROULETTE

Number	Title (A Side/B Side)	Yr	VG	VG+	NM
❑ R 25174 [M]	Twistin' Knights at the Roundtable	1962	20.00	40.00	80.00
❑ SR 25174 [S]	Twistin' Knights at the Roundtable	1962	25.00	50.00	100.00

SOMERSET

Number	Title (A Side/B Side)	Yr	VG	VG+	NM
❑ P-4600 [M]	Rock with Bill Haley and the Comets	1958	37.50	75.00	150.00

TRANS WORLD

Number	Title (A Side/B Side)	Yr	VG	VG+	NM
❑ LP 202 [M]	Rock with Bill Haley and the Comets	1956	75.00	150.00	300.00

VOCALION

Number	Title (A Side/B Side)	Yr	VG	VG+	NM
❑ VL 3696 [M]	Bill Haley and the Comets	1963	6.25	12.50	25.00

WARNER BROS.

Number	Title (A Side/B Side)	Yr	VG	VG+	NM
❑ W 1378 [M]	Bill Haley and His Comets	1959	12.50	25.00	50.00
❑ WS 1378 [S]	Bill Haley and His Comets	1959	17.50	35.00	70.00
❑ W 1391 [M]	Bill Haley's Jukebox	1960	12.50	25.00	50.00
❑ WS 1391 [S]	Bill Haley's Jukebox	1960	17.50	35.00	70.00
❑ WS 1831	Rock 'N' Roll Revival	1970	3.75	7.50	15.00
❑ ST-93103	Rock 'N' Roll Revival	1970	6.25	12.50	25.00

—Capitol Record Club edition

HALL, BUCK

45s

TRACK

Number	Title (A Side/B Side)	Yr	VG	VG+	NM
❑ 206	Swinging Doors/I Like My Whiskey Chased with Women	1989	—	3.00	6.00

HALL, CONNIE

45s

DECCA

Number	Title (A Side/B Side)	Yr	VG	VG+	NM
❑ 31130	It's Not Wrong/The Poison in Your Hand	1960	2.50	5.00	10.00
❑ 31208	Sleep, Baby, Sleep/Sittin' Out the Last Dance	1961	2.50	5.00	10.00
❑ 31277	Fools Like Me/I'm As Lonely As Anyone Can Be	1961	2.50	5.00	10.00
❑ 31310	What a Pleasure/The Key to Your Heart	1961	2.50	5.00	10.00
❑ 31386	Half the Time/Yes, There's a Reason	1962	2.50	5.00	10.00
❑ 31438	Fool Me Once/We Don't Have Much in Common (Anymore)	1962	2.50	5.00	10.00
❑ 31484	Don't Tempt Me/It's Not Revenge I Want	1963	2.00	4.00	8.00
❑ 31542	Mark on My Finger/Second Best	1963	2.00	4.00	8.00
❑ 31587	Daddy Doesn't Live Here Anymore/I Reserve the Right	1964	2.00	4.00	8.00
❑ 31652	Yellow Roses/Back to Loneliness	1964	2.00	4.00	8.00

MERCURY

Number	Title (A Side/B Side)	Yr	VG	VG+	NM
❑ 71285	I'm the Girl in the U.S.A./Dixie Strut	1958	3.75	7.50	15.00
❑ 71420	A Hundred Hearts or More/You Deserved Your Invitation to the Blues	1959	3.00	6.00	12.00
❑ 71471	Heartache Avenue/Third Party at the Table	1959	3.00	6.00	12.00
❑ 71540	The Bottle or Me/After Date Rendezvous	1959	3.00	6.00	12.00

Albums

DECCA

Number	Title (A Side/B Side)	Yr	VG	VG+	NM
❑ DL 4217 [M]	Connie Hall	1962	6.25	12.50	25.00
❑ DL 74217 [S]	Connie Hall	1962	7.50	15.00	30.00

VOCALION

Number	Title (A Side/B Side)	Yr	VG	VG+	NM
❑ VL 3752 [M]	Country Songs	1965	5.00	10.00	20.00
❑ VL 3801 [M]	Country Style	1968	5.00	10.00	20.00
❑ VL 73752 [S]	Country Songs	1965	6.25	12.50	25.00
❑ VL 73801 [S]	Country Style	1968	5.00	10.00	20.00

HALL, DICKSON

45s

EPIC

Number	Title (A Side/B Side)	Yr	VG	VG+	NM
❑ 9262	Cowboy/It's a Long Walk Home	1958	3.75	7.50	15.00
❑ 9262 [PS]	Cowboy/It's a Long Walk Home	1958	6.25	12.50	25.00

Albums

EPIC

Number	Title (A Side/B Side)	Yr	VG	VG+	NM
❑ LN 3427 [M]	25 All-Time Country and Western Hits	1958	6.25	12.50	25.00

KAPP

Number	Title (A Side/B Side)	Yr	VG	VG+	NM
❑ KL-1067 [M]	Fabulous Country Hits Way Out West	1957	7.50	15.00	30.00
❑ KL-1464 [M]	24 Fabulous Country Hits	1966	5.00	10.00	20.00
❑ KS-3464 [S]	24 Fabulous Country Hits	1966	6.25	12.50	25.00

MGM

Number	Title (A Side/B Side)	Yr	VG	VG+	NM
❑ E-329 [10]	Outlaws of the Old West	1954	15.00	30.00	60.00
❑ E-3263 [M]	Outlaws of the Old West	1956	10.00	20.00	40.00

PERFECT

Number	Title (A Side/B Side)	Yr	VG	VG+	NM
❑ P-14016 [M]	Country & Western Million Sellers	1960	5.00	10.00	20.00
❑ PS-14016 [S]	Country & Western Million Sellers	1960	6.25	12.50	25.00

HALL, JOANIE

Albums

SAGE AND SAND

Number	Title (A Side/B Side)	Yr	VG	VG+	NM
❑ C-34 [M]	Western Meets Country	1962	6.25	12.50	25.00

HALL, REBECCA

45s

CAPITOL

Number	Title (A Side/B Side)	Yr	VG	VG+	NM
❑ B-5486	Heartbeat/Melted Down Memories	1985	—	—	3.00

HALL, SAMMY

45s

DREAM

Number	Title (A Side/B Side)	Yr	VG	VG+	NM
❑ 300	Anything for Your Love/(B-side unknown)	1984	—	3.00	6.00

HALL, TOM T.

Also see DAVE DUDLEY AND TOM T. HALL.

45s

MERCURY

Number	Title (A Side/B Side)	Yr	VG	VG+	NM
❑ 55001	It's All in the Game/The Little Green Flowers	1977	—	2.00	4.00
❑ 72700	I Wish My Face in the Morning Dew/Picture of Your Mother	1967	2.00	4.00	8.00
❑ 72749	Beauty Is a Fading Flower/Your Love Is Mine Again	1967	2.00	4.00	8.00
❑ 72786	The World the Way I Want It/Shame on the Rain	1968	2.00	4.00	8.00
❑ 72835	Ain't Got the Time/Hope	1968	2.00	4.00	8.00
❑ 72863	Ballad of Forty Dollars/Highways	1968	—	3.00	6.00
❑ 72913	Strawberry Farms/3	1969	—	3.00	6.00
❑ 72951	Homecoming/Myra	1969	—	3.00	6.00
❑ 72998	A Week in a Country Jail/Flat-Footin' It	1969	—	3.00	6.00
❑ 73039	Shoeshine Man/Kentucky in the Morning	1970	—	3.00	6.00
❑ 73078	Salute to a Switchblade/That'll Be Alright with Me	1970	—	3.00	6.00
❑ 73140	One Hundred Children/I Took a Memory to Lunch	1970	—	3.00	6.00
❑ 73189	Ode to a Half Pound of Ground Round/Pinto the Wonder Horse Is Dead	1971	—	3.00	6.00
❑ 73221	The Year That Clayton Delaney Died/Second Handed Flowers	1971	—	2.50	5.00
❑ 73278	Me and Jesus/Coot Marseilles Blues	1972	—	2.50	5.00
❑ 73297	The Monkey That Became President/She Gave Her Heart to Jethro	1972	—	2.50	5.00
❑ 73327	More About John Henry/Windy City Anne	1972	—	2.50	5.00
❑ 73346	(Old Dogs-Children and) Watermelon Wine/Grandma Whistled	1972	—	2.50	5.00
❑ 73377	Ravishing Ruby/I Flew Over Our House Last Night	1973	—	2.50	5.00
❑ 73394	Watergate Blues/Spokane Motel Blues	1973	—	2.50	5.00
❑ 73436	I Love/Back When We Were Young	1973	—	2.00	4.00
❑ 73488	That Song Is Driving Me Crazy/Forget It	1974	—	2.00	4.00
❑ 73617	Country Is/God Came Through Bellville, Ga.	1974	—	2.00	4.00
❑ 73641	I Care/Sneaky Snake	1974	—	2.00	4.00
❑ 73686	Deal/It Rained in Every Town Except Paducah	1975	—	2.00	4.00
❑ 73704	I Like Beer/From a Mansion to a Honky Tonk	1975	—	2.00	4.00
❑ 73755	Faster Horses (The Cowboy and the Poet)/No New Friends Please	1975	—	2.00	4.00
❑ 73795	Negatory Romance/It's Got to Be Kentucky for Me	1976	—	2.00	4.00
❑ 73850	Fox on the Run/Bluegrass Festival in the Sky	1976	—	2.00	4.00
❑ 73899	Your Man Loves You Honey/One of the Mysteries of Life	1977	—	2.00	4.00
❑ 812835-7	Everything from Jesus to Jack Daniels/(Old Dogs-Children and) Watermelon Wine	1983	—	—	3.00
❑ 814560-7	How'd You Get Home So Soon/The Year That Clayton Delaney Died	1983	—	—	3.00
❑ 870669-7	Let's Play Remember/Fox Hollow's Animal Train	1988	—	—	3.00
❑ 872180-7	Let's Spend Christmas at My House/Let's Go Shopping Today	1988	—	—	3.00
❑ 880030-7	Famous in Missouri/I Only Think About You When I'm Drunk	1984	—	—	3.00
❑ 880216-7	P.S. I Love You/My Heroes Have Always Been Cowboys	1984	—	—	3.00
❑ 880690-7	A Bar with No Beer/Red Sails in the Sunset	1985	—	—	3.00
❑ 884017-7	Down in the Florida Keys/Song in a Seashell	1985	—	—	3.00
❑ 884850-7	Susie's Beauty Shop/Love Letters in the Sand	1986	—	—	3.00
❑ 888155-7	Dowm at the Mall/We're All Through Dancing	1986	—	—	3.00

RCA

Number	Title (A Side/B Side)	Yr	VG	VG+	NM
❑ PB-11158	May the Force Be With You Always/No One Feels My Heart	1977	—	2.50	5.00
❑ PB-11253	I Wish I Loved Somebody Else/Whiskey	1978	—	2.00	4.00
❑ PB-11376	What Have You Got to Lose/The Three Sofa Story	1978	—	2.00	4.00
❑ PB-11453	Son of Clayton Delaney/The Great East Breadway Onion Championship of 1978	1978	—	2.00	4.00
❑ PB-11568	There Is a Miracle in You/Saturday Morning Show	1979	—	2.00	4.00
❑ PB-11713	You Show Me Your Heart (And I'll Show You Mine)/Old Habits Die Hard	1979	—	2.00	4.00
❑ PB-11765	Christmas Is/Thanksgiving Is	1979	—	2.00	4.00
❑ PB-11888	The Old Side of Town/Jesus on the Radio (Daddy on the Phone)	1979	—	2.00	4.00
❑ PB-12005	Soldier of Fortune/The World According to Raymond	1980	—	—	3.00
❑ PB-12066	Back When Gas Was Thirty Cents a Gallon/Texas Never Fell in Love with Me	1980	—	—	3.00
❑ PB-12219	The All New Me/Pour Me (Pour Me Another Drink)	1981	—	—	3.00

Albums

MERCURY

Number	Title (A Side/B Side)	Yr	VG	VG+	NM
❑ SRM-1-500	Songs of Fox Hollow	1975	3.00	6.00	12.00
❑ SRM-1-668	The Rhymer and Other Five and Dimers	1973	3.00	6.00	12.00
❑ SRM-1-687	For the People in the Last Hard Town	1974	3.00	6.00	12.00
❑ SRM-1-1009	Country Is	1974	3.00	6.00	12.00
❑ SRM-1-1033	I Wrote	1975	3.00	6.00	12.00
❑ SRM-1-1044	Greatest Hits, Volume 2	1975	3.00	6.00	12.00
❑ SRM-1-1076	Faster Horses	1976	3.00	6.00	12.00
❑ SRM-1-1111	Magnificent Music	1977	3.00	6.00	12.00
❑ SRM-1-1139	About Love	1977	3.00	6.00	12.00
❑ SRM-1-5008	Greatest Hits, Volume 3	1978	3.00	6.00	12.00
❑ SR-61211	Ballad of Forty Dollars	1969	5.00	10.00	20.00
❑ SR-61247	Homecoming	1969	5.00	10.00	20.00

Number	Title (A Side/B Side)	Yr	VG	VG+	NM
❑ SR-61277	Witness Life	1970	5.00	10.00	20.00
❑ SR-61307	100 Children	1970	5.00	10.00	20.00
❑ SR-61350	In Search of a Song	1971	3.75	7.50	15.00
❑ SR-61362	We All Got Together And...	1972	3.75	7.50	15.00
❑ SR-61369	Greatest Hits	1972	3.75	7.50	15.00
❑ 814025-1	Jesus to Jack Daniels	1983	2.00	4.00	8.00
❑ 822425-1	Natural Dreams	1984	2.00	4.00	8.00
❑ 822500-1	In Search of a Song	1987	2.00	4.00	8.00
❑ 824143-1	Greatest Hits	1985	2.00	4.00	8.00
—Reissue					
❑ 824144-1	Greatest Hits, Volume 2	1985	2.00	4.00	8.00
—Reissue					
❑ 824145-1	Greatest Hits, Volume 3	1985	2.00	4.00	8.00
—Reissue					
❑ 824508-1	Song in a Seashell	1985	2.00	4.00	8.00
❑ 832350-1	Songs of Fox Hollow	1987	2.00	4.00	8.00
—Reissue					
❑ 834779-1	Country Songs for Children	1988	2.00	4.00	8.00
—Reissue					
PICCADILLY					
❑ 3558	I Like Beer	198?	2.00	4.00	8.00
RCA VICTOR					
❑ AHL1-2622	New Train	1978	2.50	5.00	10.00
❑ AHL1-3018	Places I've Been	1979	2.50	5.00	10.00
❑ AHL1-3495	T's in Town	1979	2.50	5.00	10.00
❑ AHL1-3685	Soldier of Fortune	1980	2.50	5.00	10.00
❑ AHL1-4749	In Concert: Recorded Live at the Grand Ole Opry	1983	2.50	5.00	10.00
❑ AYL1-5432	In Concert: Recorded Live at the Grand Ole Opry	1985	2.00	4.00	8.00
—"Best Buy Series" reissue					

HALL, TOM T., AND EARL SCRUGGS

Also see each artist's individual listings.

Number	Title (A Side/B Side)	Yr	VG	VG+	NM
45s					
COLUMBIA					
❑ 18-02858	There Ain't No Country Music on This Jukebox/ Don't This Road Look Rough and Rocky	1982	—	2.00	4.00
❑ 18-03033	Song of the South/Shackles and Chains	1982	—	2.00	4.00
Albums					
COLUMBIA					
❑ FC 37953	Storyteller and Banjo Man	1982	2.50	5.00	10.00

HALLMAN, VICTORIA

Number	Title (A Side/B Side)	Yr	VG	VG+	NM
45s					
EVERGREEN					
❑ 1055	Next Time I Marry/Don't You Think It's Time	1987	—	2.50	5.00

HALLMARK, ROGER

See THE THRASHER BROTHERS.

HAMBLEN, STUART

Number	Title (A Side/B Side)	Yr	VG	VG+	NM
45s					
COLUMBIA					
❑ 2-351	(I Won't Go Huntin', Jake) But I'll Go Chasin' Women/Let's See You Fix It	1949	10.00	20.00	40.00
—Microgroove 33 1/3 rpm 7-inch record, small hole					
❑ 2-430 (?)	Pony Express/Blue Bonnets in Her Golden Hair	1950	10.00	20.00	40.00
—Microgroove 33 1/3 rpm 7-inch record, small hole					
❑ 2-550 (?)	Condemnation/Sheepskin Corn and a Wrinkle on a Horn	1950	10.00	20.00	40.00
—Microgroove 33 1/3 rpm 7-inch record, small hole					
❑ 4-20714	(Remember Me) I'm the One Who Loves You/I'll Find You	1950	7.50	15.00	30.00
❑ 4-20724	It Is No Secret (What God Can Do)/Blood on Your Hands	1950	7.50	15.00	30.00
❑ 4-20733	Good Mornin' Y'all/I Whisper Your Name	1950	7.50	15.00	30.00
❑ 4-20754	You Can't Kiss Santa Goodnight/Three Little Dwarfs	1950	7.50	15.00	30.00
❑ 4-20779	Old Glory/My Life with You	1951	6.25	12.50	25.00
❑ 4-20795	King of All Kings/He Bought My Soul at Calvary	1951	6.25	12.50	25.00
❑ 4-20827	Our Old Captain/Don't Fool Around with Calico	1951	6.25	12.50	25.00
❑ 4-20848	I Believe/These Things Shall Pass	1951	6.25	12.50	25.00
❑ 4-20880	Just Let Me Love You/You're Always Brand New	1952	6.25	12.50	25.00
❑ 4-20938	Black Diamond/This Ship of Mine	1952	6.25	12.50	25.00
❑ 4-20988	Got So Many Million Years (I Can't Count 'Em)/ Lord, I Pray	1952	6.25	12.50	25.00
❑ 4-21012	Is He Satisfied/Known Only to Him	1952	5.00	10.00	20.00
❑ 4-21013	I Get Lonesome/Our Love Affair	1952	5.00	10.00	20.00
❑ 4-21014	Grasshopper MacClain/Oklahoma Bill	1952	5.00	10.00	20.00
❑ 4-21061	A Million Wild Horses/My Mary	1953	6.25	12.50	25.00
❑ 4-21079	Friends I Know/Old Pappy's New Banjo	1953	6.25	12.50	25.00
❑ 4-21116	Daddy's Cutie Pie/The Hidden You	1953	6.25	12.50	25.00
❑ 4-21124	I Believe/Teach Me Lord to Wait	1953	6.25	12.50	25.00
❑ 4-21158	Partners with God/You Must Be Born Again	1953	6.25	12.50	25.00
❑ 4-21190	My Religion's Not Old Fashioned/He Made a Way	1953	6.25	12.50	25.00
❑ 4-21211	Robe of Calvary/Workshop of the Lord	1954	5.00	10.00	20.00
❑ 4-21277	Beyond the Sun/Please Tell Me	1954	5.00	10.00	20.00
❑ 4-21428	I've Got So Many Million Years (I Can't Count 'Em)/Lord, I Pray	1955	5.00	10.00	20.00
❑ 4-41780	The Foreman/Golden River	1960	3.00	6.00	12.00
❑ 4-42198	Good Old Days/What Can I Do for My Country	1961	3.00	6.00	12.00
❑ 4-42363	Across the Great Divide/My Home	1962	2.50	5.00	10.00
CORAL					
❑ 9-62089	Remember Me (I'm the One Who Loves You)/ Indiana	1959	3.00	6.00	12.00
KAPP					
❑ 733	This Old House Has Got to Go/Tho' Autumn's Comin' On	1965	2.00	4.00	8.00
RCA VICTOR					
❑ 47-5739	This Ole House/When My Lord Picks Up the 'Phone	1954	5.00	10.00	20.00
❑ 47-5810	I Am Persuaded/Heavenly Cannonball	1954	5.00	10.00	20.00
❑ 47-5918	Old Pappy Time Is a-Pickin' Pockets/Toy Violin	1954	5.00	10.00	20.00
❑ 47-5990	If We All Said a Prayer/My Brother	1955	3.75	7.50	15.00
❑ 47-6042	Just a Man/Go On By	1955	3.75	7.50	15.00
❑ 47-6152	Lord, I'll Try/Lonesome Valley	1955	3.75	7.50	15.00
❑ 47-6250	I've Got So Many Million Years (I Can't Count 'Em)/Lord, I Can't Come Now	1955	3.75	7.50	15.00
—With Martha Carson					
❑ 47-6333	A Handful of Sunshine/You'll Always Be Mine	1955	3.75	7.50	15.00
❑ 47-6465	Hell Train/A Few Things to Remember	1956	3.75	7.50	15.00
❑ 47-6581	This Book/The Rock	1956	3.75	7.50	15.00
❑ 47-6714	Desert Sunrise/Whistler's Dream	1956	3.75	7.50	15.00
❑ 47-6736	God Is a Good God/The Sweetest Story Ever Told	1956	3.75	7.50	15.00
❑ 47-6759	Beyond the Sun/Dear Lord, Be My Shepherd	1956	3.75	7.50	15.00
❑ 47-6911	The Lonesome Cowboy's Prayer/My Father	1957	3.75	7.50	15.00
❑ 47-7052	The Old Rugged Cross/Old Time Religion	1957	3.75	7.50	15.00
❑ 47-7111	This Ole World/Don't Mess Around with Calico	1957	3.75	7.50	15.00
❑ 74-0525	What Can I Do for My Country/When Earth's Last Picture Is Painted	1971	—	3.50	7.00
Selected 78s					
BLUEBIRD					
❑ B-5242	Boy in Blue/(B-side unknown)	193?	6.25	12.50	25.00
DECCA					
❑ 5001	Texas Plains/(B-side unknown)	1934	6.25	12.50	25.00
❑ 5077	titles unknown	1934	6.25	12.50	25.00
❑ 5109	titles unknown	1935	6.25	12.50	25.00
❑ 5145	titles unknown	1935	6.25	12.50	25.00
VICTOR					
❑ 23685	My Brown-Eyed Texas Rose/My Mary	1932	25.00	50.00	100.00
❑ V40109	Boy in Blue/(B-side unknown)	1929	20.00	40.00	80.00
❑ V40242	Wrong Keyhole/(B-side unknown)	1930	20.00	40.00	80.00
❑ V40306	Standin' on the Pier in the Rain/(B-side unknown)	1930	20.00	40.00	80.00
❑ V40311	Sailor's Farewell/(B-side unknown)	1930	20.00	40.00	80.00
❑ V40319	Drifting Back to Dixie/(B-side unknown)	1930	20.00	40.00	80.00
Albums					
COLUMBIA					
❑ CL 1769 [M]	Of God I Sing	1962	5.00	10.00	20.00
❑ CS 8388 [S]	The Spell of the Yukon	1961	6.25	12.50	25.00
❑ CS 8569 [S]	Of God I Sing	1962	6.25	12.50	25.00
CORAL					
❑ CRL 57254 [M]	Remember Me	1960	6.25	12.50	25.00
HARMONY					
❑ HL 7009 [M]	Hymns	1957	6.25	12.50	25.00
RCA CAMDEN					
❑ CAL-537 [M]	Beyond the Sun	1959	6.25	12.50	25.00
RCA VICTOR					
❑ LPM-1253 [M]	It Is No Secret	1956	10.00	20.00	40.00
❑ LPM-1436 [M]	Grand Old Hymns	1957	10.00	20.00	40.00
❑ LPM-3265 [10]	It Is No Secret	1954	15.00	30.00	60.00

HAMILTON, GEORGE, IV

Number	Title (A Side/B Side)	Yr	VG	VG+	NM
45s					
ABC					
❑ 12342 [DJ]	Only the Best (mono/stereo)	1978	—	2.50	5.00
—May be promo only					
❑ 12376	One Day at a Time/Take This Heart	1978	—	2.00	4.00
ABC-PARAMOUNT					
❑ 9765	A Rose and a Baby Ruth/If You Don't Know	1956	7.50	15.00	30.00
❑ 9782	Only One Love/If I Possessed a Printing Press	1957	7.50	15.00	30.00
❑ 9838	High School Romance/Everybody's Baby	1957	7.50	15.00	30.00
❑ 9862	Why Don't They Understand/Even Tho'	1957	7.50	15.00	30.00
❑ 9898	Now and For Always/One Heart	1958	6.25	12.50	25.00
❑ 9924	I Know Where I'm Goin'/Who's Taking You to the Prom	1958	6.25	12.50	25.00
❑ 9946	When Will I Know/Your Cheatin' Heart	1958	6.25	12.50	25.00
❑ 9966	Lucy, Lucy/The Two of Us	1958	6.25	12.50	25.00
❑ 10009	The Steady Game/Can You Blame Us	1959	5.00	10.00	20.00
❑ 10028	Gee/I Know Your Sweetheart	1959	5.00	10.00	20.00
❑ 10059	One Little Acre/Little Tom	1959	5.00	10.00	20.00
❑ 10090	Why I'm Walkin'/Tremble	1960	5.00	10.00	20.00
❑ 10125	Before This Day Ends/Loneliness All Around Me	1960	5.00	10.00	20.00
❑ 10167	A Walk on the Wild Side of Life/It's Just the Idea	1960	5.00	10.00	20.00
ABC/DOT					
❑ 17687	I Wonder Who's Kissing Her Now/In the Palm of Her Hand	1977	—	2.00	4.00
❑ 17708	Cornbread, Beans and Sweet Potato Pie/May the Wind Be Always at Your Back	1977	—	2.00	4.00
❑ 17723	Everlasting (Everlasting Love)/In the Palm of Your Hand	1977	—	2.00	4.00
COLONIAL					
❑ 420	A Rose and a Baby Ruth/If You Don't Know	1956	20.00	40.00	80.00
❑ 451	I've Got a Secret/Sam	1956	10.00	20.00	40.00
GRT					
❑ 063	Blue Jeans, Ice Cream and Saturday Shoes/Bad Romancer	1976	—	2.50	5.00
MCA					
❑ 41149	Forever Young/'Rangement Blues	1979	—	2.00	4.00
❑ 41215	I'll Be Here in the Morning/Spin Spin	1980	—	2.00	4.00
❑ 41282	Catfish Bates/Mose Rankin	1980	—	2.00	4.00

Number	Title (A Side/B Side)	Yr	VG	VG+	NM
RCA					
❑ 2722-7-R	Abilene/Oh So Many Tears	1990	—	2.00	4.00
RCA VICTOR					
❑ APBO-0084	Second Cup of Coffee/Farmer's Song	1973	—	2.00	4.00
❑ APBO-0203	Claim on Me/Early Mornin' Rain	1973	—	2.00	4.00
❑ APBO-0314	The Ways of a Country Girl/Pictou County Jail	1974	—	2.00	4.00
❑ 47-7881	Three Steps to the Picnic/The Ballad of Widder Jones	1961	3.75	7.50	15.00
❑ 47-7934	To You and Yours (From Me and Mine)/I Want a Girl	1961	3.75	7.50	15.00
❑ 47-8001	China Doll/Commerce Street and Sixth Avenue North	1962	3.75	7.50	15.00
❑ 47-8062	If You Don't Know, I Ain't Gonna Tell You/Where Nobody Knows Me	1962	3.75	7.50	15.00
❑ 47-8118	In This Very Same Room/If You Want Me To	1962	3.75	7.50	15.00
❑ 47-8181	Abilene/Oh So Many Years	1963	3.00	6.00	12.00
❑ 47-8250	There's More Pretty Girls Than One/If You Don't, Somebody Else Will	1963	3.00	6.00	12.00
❑ 47-8304	Linda with the Lonely Eyes/Fair and Tender Ladies	1963	3.00	6.00	12.00
❑ 47-8392	Fort Worth, Dallas or Houston/Life's Railway to Heaven	1964	3.00	6.00	12.00
❑ 47-8462	Truck Driving Man/The Little Grave	1964	3.00	6.00	12.00
❑ 47-8537	The Last Mister Jones/Anymore	1965	2.50	5.00	10.00
❑ 47-8608	Walking the Floor Over You/Driftwood on the River	1965	2.50	5.00	10.00
❑ 47-8690	Write Me a Picture/Twist of the Wrist	1965	2.50	5.00	10.00
❑ 47-8797	Steel Rail Blues/Tobacco	1966	2.50	5.00	10.00
❑ 47-8924	Early Morning Rain/Slightly Used	1966	2.50	5.00	10.00
❑ 47-9059	Urge for Going/Changes	1966	2.50	5.00	10.00
❑ 47-9239	Break My Mind/Something Special to Me	1967	2.00	4.00	8.00
❑ 47-9385	Little World Girl/Song for a Winter's Night	1967	2.00	4.00	8.00
❑ 47-9519	It's My Time/Canadian Railroad Trilogy	1968	2.00	4.00	8.00
❑ 47-9637	Take My Hand for Awhile/Wonderful World of My Dreams	1968	2.00	4.00	8.00
❑ 47-9775	Natividad (The Nativity)/The Little Grave	1969	2.00	4.00	8.00
❑ 47-9829	She's a Little Bit Country/My Nova Scotia Home	1970	—	3.00	6.00
❑ 47-9886	Back Where It's At/Then I Miss You	1970	—	3.00	6.00
❑ 47-9893	Let's Get Together/Everything Is Beautiful	1970	—	3.00	6.00
—With Skeeter Davis					
❑ 47-9937	Natividad (The Nativity)/The Little Grave	1970	—	3.00	6.00
❑ 47-9945	Anyway/The Best That I Can Do	1971	—	3.00	6.00
❑ 74-0100	Back to Denver/Suzanne	1969	2.00	4.00	8.00
❑ 74-0171	Canadian Pacific/Sisters of Mercy	1969	2.00	4.00	8.00
❑ 74-0256	Carolina in My Mind/I'm Gonna Be a Country Boy Again	1969	2.00	4.00	8.00
❑ 74-0469	Countryfied/My North Country Home	1971	—	3.00	6.00
❑ 74-0531	West Texas Highway/There's No Room in This Rat Race	1971	—	3.00	6.00
❑ 74-0622	10 Degrees and Getting Colder/Tumbleweed	1971	—	3.00	6.00
❑ 74-0697	Country Music in My Soul/Child's Song	1972	—	2.50	5.00
❑ 74-0776	Travelin' Light/Alberta Bound	1972	—	2.50	5.00
❑ 74-0854	Blue Train (Of the Heartbreak Line)/Maritime Farewell	1972	—	2.50	5.00
❑ 74-0948	Dirty Old Man/Abilene	1973	—	2.50	5.00
7-Inch Extended Plays					
ABC-PARAMOUNT					
❑ A-220	Clementine/When I Grow Too Old to Dream//Tell Me Why/Let Me Call You Sweetheart	1958	5.00	10.00	20.00
❑ A-220 [PS]	On Campus	1958	5.00	10.00	20.00
Albums					
ABC					
❑ X-750	16 Greatest Hits	1972	2.50	5.00	10.00
❑ AC-30032	The ABC Collection	1975	3.00	6.00	12.00
ABC-PARAMOUNT					
❑ 220 [M]	On Campus	1958	10.00	20.00	40.00
❑ S-220 [S]	On Campus	1958	12.50	25.00	50.00
❑ 251 [M]	Sing Me a Sad Song (A Tribute to Hank Williams)	1958	10.00	20.00	40.00
❑ S-251 [S]	Sing Me a Sad Song (A Tribute to Hank Williams)	1958	12.50	25.00	50.00
❑ 461 [M]	George Hamilton IV's Big 15	1963	7.50	15.00	30.00
❑ S-461 [P]	George Hamilton IV's Big 15	1963	10.00	20.00	40.00
ABC/DOT					
❑ DO-2081	Fine Lace	1977	2.50	5.00	10.00
DOT					
❑ 39033	George Hamilton IV	1985	2.50	5.00	10.00
HARMONY					
❑ HS 11379	Your Cheatin' Heart	1970	2.50	5.00	10.00
LAMB AND LION					
❑ 1015	Bluegrass Gospel	1974	3.00	6.00	12.00
MCA					
❑ 705	Forever Young	198?	2.00	4.00	8.00
—Reissue of 3206					
❑ 3206	Forever Young	1980	2.50	5.00	10.00
RCA CAMDEN					
❑ ACL1-0242	Singin' on the Mountains	1973	2.50	5.00	10.00
❑ CAL-2200 [M]	A Rose and a Baby Ruth	1967	3.75	7.50	15.00
❑ CAS-2200 [S]	A Rose and a Baby Ruth	1967	2.50	5.00	10.00
❑ CAS-2468	Early Morning Rain	1971	2.50	5.00	10.00
RCA VICTOR					
❑ APL1-0455	Greatest Hits	1974	3.00	6.00	12.00
❑ LPM-2373 [M]	To You and Yours from Me and Mine	1961	6.25	12.50	25.00
❑ LSP-2373 [S]	To You and Yours from Me and Mine	1961	7.50	15.00	30.00
❑ LPM-2778 [M]	Abilene	1963	6.25	12.50	25.00
❑ LSP-2778 [S]	Abilene	1963	7.50	15.00	30.00

Number	Title (A Side/B Side)	Yr	VG	VG+	NM
❑ LPM-2972 [M]	Fort Worth, Dallas or Houston	1964	6.25	12.50	25.00
❑ LSP-2972 [S]	Fort Worth, Dallas or Houston	1964	7.50	15.00	30.00
❑ LPM-3371 [M]	Mister Sincerity... A Tribute to Ernest Tubb	1965	6.25	12.50	25.00
❑ LSP-3371 [S]	Mister Sincerity... A Tribute to Ernest Tubb	1965	7.50	15.00	30.00
❑ LPM-3510 [M]	Coast Country	1966	6.25	12.50	25.00
❑ LSP-3510 [S]	Coast Country	1966	7.50	15.00	30.00
❑ LPM-3601 [M]	Steel Rail Blues	1966	5.00	10.00	20.00
❑ LSP-3601 [S]	Steel Rail Blues	1966	5.00	10.00	20.00
❑ LPM-3752 [M]	Folk Country Classics	1967	6.25	12.50	25.00
❑ LSP-3752 [S]	Folk Country Classics	1967	5.00	10.00	20.00
❑ LPM-3854 [M]	Folksy	1967	6.25	12.50	25.00
❑ LSP-3854 [S]	Folksy	1967	5.00	10.00	20.00
❑ LPM-3962 [M]	The Gentle Country Sound of George Hamilton IV	1968	10.00	20.00	40.00
❑ LSP-3962 [S]	The Gentle Country Sound of George Hamilton IV	1968	5.00	10.00	20.00
❑ LSP-4066	In the 4th Dimension	1968	5.00	10.00	20.00
❑ LSP-4164	Canadian Pacific	1969	3.75	7.50	15.00
❑ LSP-4265	The Best of George Hamilton IV	1970	3.75	7.50	15.00
❑ LSP-4342	Back Where It's At	1970	3.75	7.50	15.00
❑ LSP-4435	Down Home in the Country	1971	3.75	7.50	15.00
❑ LSP-4517	North Country	1971	3.75	7.50	15.00
❑ LSP-4609	West Texas Highway	1971	3.75	7.50	15.00
❑ LSP-4700	Country Music in My Soul	1972	3.00	6.00	12.00
❑ LSP-4772	Travelin' Light	1972	3.00	6.00	12.00
❑ LSP-4826	International Ambassador	1973	3.00	6.00	12.00

HAMILTON, GEORGE, V

45s

Number	Title (A Side/B Side)	Yr	VG	VG+	NM
MTM					
❑ B-72101	She Says/Grass Grows Greener	1988	—	2.00	4.00

HAMILTON, PENNY

45s

Number	Title (A Side/B Side)	Yr	VG	VG+	NM
DOOR KNOB					
❑ 096	You Lit the Fire, Now Fan the Flame/(B-side unknown)	1979	—	2.50	5.00

HANDY, CHERYL

45s

Number	Title (A Side/B Side)	Yr	VG	VG+	NM
AUDIOGRAPH					
❑ 475	Here I Go Again/(B-side unknown)	1984	—	3.00	6.00
COMPLEAT					
❑ 176	Will You Still Love Me Tomorrow/Don't Take My Heart Away	1987	—	3.00	6.00
RCM					
❑ 00105	One of the Boys/(B-side unknown)	1986	—	3.00	6.00

HANK FLAMINGO

45s

Number	Title (A Side/B Side)	Yr	VG	VG+	NM
GIANT					
❑ 7-18248	White Lightnin'/Grandaddy's Place	1994	—	2.00	4.00
❑ 7-18384	Baby It's You/Tennessee Plates	1993	—	2.00	4.00

HANKINS, ESCO

Albums

Number	Title (A Side/B Side)	Yr	VG	VG+	NM
AUDIO LAB					
❑ AL-1547 [M]	Country Style	1961	50.00	100.00	200.00

HANKS, KAMRYN

45s

Number	Title (A Side/B Side)	Yr	VG	VG+	NM
COUNTRY PRIDE					
❑ 0025	Eyes Never Lie/(B-side unknown)	1989	—	3.00	6.00

HANSON, CONNIE

45s

Number	Title (A Side/B Side)	Yr	VG	VG+	NM
SOUNDWAVES					
❑ 4682	Honky Tonk for Woman/Muffy's Going Crazy	1982	—	3.00	6.00
❑ 4692	There's Still a Lot of Love in San Antone/Muffy's Going Crazy	1982	—	3.00	6.00
—As "Connie Hanson and Friend"					
❑ 4692 [PS]	There's Still a Lot of Love in San Antone/Muffy's Going Crazy	1982	2.00	4.00	8.00
—As "Connie Hanson and Friend"					
❑ 4700	Close All the Honky Tonks/Never Get It Right	1983	—	3.00	6.00

HARDEN, ARLENE

45s

Number	Title (A Side/B Side)	Yr	VG	VG+	NM
CAPITOL					
❑ 3911	Leave Me Alone (Ruby Red Dress)/It's So Good with You	1974	—	2.50	5.00
—As "Arleen Harden"					
❑ 4014	I Could Almost Say Goodbye/Papa's Sugar	1974	—	2.50	5.00
—As "Arleen Harden"					
❑ 4088	Country Sunday/Teddy Bear's Picnic	1975	—	2.50	5.00
—As "Arleen Harden"					
❑ 4148	Roll On Sweet Mississippi/Crazy	1975	—	2.50	5.00
—As "Arleen Harden"					
❑ 4217	Misty Mountain Rain/You Just Loved the Leavin' Out of Me	1976	—	2.50	5.00
—As "Arleen Harden"					
COLUMBIA					
❑ 4-44001	You and Only You/Money, Money, Money	1967	2.50	5.00	10.00
❑ 4-44133	Fair Weather Love/Don't Ask for Tomorrow	1967	2.00	4.00	8.00

Number	Title (A Side/B Side)	Yr	VG	VG+	NM
❑ 4-44310	You're Easy to Love/What Has the World Done to My Baby	1967	2.00	4.00	8.00
❑ 4-44461	He's a Good Ole Boy/When	1968	—	3.50	7.00
❑ 4-44581	What Can I Say/Like You Love Me Now	1968	—	3.50	7.00
❑ 4-44783	Too Much of a Man (To Be Tied Down)/When True Love Walks In	1969	—	3.50	7.00
❑ 4-45016	My Friend/Baby	1969	—	3.50	7.00
❑ 4-45120	Lovin' Man (Oh Pretty Woman)/My World Walked Away with a Blond	1970	—	3.00	6.00
❑ 4-45203	Crying/It's Over	1970	—	3.00	6.00
❑ 4-45203 [PS]	Crying/It's Over	1970	2.50	5.00	10.00
❑ 4-45275	Coming Home Soldier/Funny Familiar Forgotten Feelings	1970	2.00	4.00	8.00
❑ 4-45287	True Love Is Greater Than Friendship/Funny Familiar Forgotten Feeling	1970	—	3.00	6.00
❑ 4-45365	Married to a Memory/Coming Home Soldier	1971	—	3.00	6.00
❑ 4-45420	Congratulations (You Sure Made a Man Out of Him)/Sing Me Some Sunshine	1971	—	3.00	6.00
❑ 4-45489	Ruby Gentry's Daughter/With Pen in Hand	1971	—	3.00	6.00
❑ 4-45577	A Special Day/What a Woman in Love Won't Do	1972	—	3.00	6.00
❑ 4-45708	It Takes a Lot of Tenderness/It's Over	1972	—	3.00	6.00
❑ 4-45845	Would You Walk with Me Jimmy/You Can Always Have Me	1973	—	3.00	6.00

ELEKTRA

Number	Title (A Side/B Side)	Yr	VG	VG+	NM
❑ 45401	Southern Belle/Lady in Waiting	1977	—	2.00	4.00
—As "Arleen Harden"					
❑ 45434	A Place Where Love Has Been/Lady in Waiting	1977	—	2.00	4.00
—As "Arleen Harden"					
❑ 45463	You're Not Free and I'm Not Easy/Do You Ever Dream	1978	—	2.00	4.00

Albums

COLUMBIA

Number	Title	Yr	VG	VG+	NM
❑ CL 2833 [M]	Sing Me Back Home	1967	7.50	15.00	30.00
❑ CS 9633 [S]	Sing Me Back Home	1967	5.00	10.00	20.00
❑ CS 9674	What Can I Say	1968	5.00	10.00	20.00

HARDEN, BOBBY

Also see THE HARDEN TRIO.

45s

COLUMBIA

Number	Title (A Side/B Side)	Yr	VG	VG+	NM
❑ 4-44322	After Having You/My Heart's Caught in the Door	1967	2.50	5.00	10.00
❑ 4-44543	Don't Drive Me/The Texarkana	1968	2.50	5.00	10.00

MEGA

Number	Title (A Side/B Side)	Yr	VG	VG+	NM
❑ 0006	Little Boy Wonder/Tulsa	1970	2.00	4.00	8.00
❑ 0018	I Wanted Love from You, Mary/Mama's Song	1971	2.00	4.00	8.00
❑ 0028	Just Because He Loved Her/St. Vincent Motor Hotel	1971	2.00	4.00	8.00
❑ 0053	Except for Love/Someone Write a Perfect Melody	1971	2.00	4.00	8.00

METROMEDIA

Number	Title (A Side/B Side)	Yr	VG	VG+	NM
❑ BMBO-0068	Greenest Grass in Town/Mrs. Willingham	1973	—	3.00	6.00

STARDAY

Number	Title (A Side/B Side)	Yr	VG	VG+	NM
❑ 875	The Wild Ones/Except for One	1969	2.50	5.00	10.00
❑ 879	We Got Each Other/Love for a Child	1969	2.50	5.00	10.00
—A-side with Karen Wheeler					

UNITED ARTISTS

Number	Title (A Side/B Side)	Yr	VG	VG+	NM
❑ XW459	Please Come to Boston/It's a Long Way Back to Little Rock	1974	—	2.50	5.00
❑ XW597	One Step/Holding On	1975	—	2.50	5.00
❑ XW662	All the King's Horses (And All the King's Men)/A Song I Couldn't Write	1975	—	2.50	5.00
❑ XW714	Flashing, Screaming, Silent Neon Sign/A Song I Couldn't Write	1975	—	2.50	5.00
❑ XW859	Rainbow Man/White Silver Sands	1976	—	2.50	5.00

Albums

STARDAY

Number	Title	Yr	VG	VG+	NM
❑ SLP-443	Nashville Sensation	1969	3.75	7.50	15.00

HARDEN, ROBBIE

Also see THE HARDEN TRIO.

45s

PLANTATION

Number	Title (A Side/B Side)	Yr	VG	VG+	NM
❑ 58	The Service/Still Wanting You	1970	2.00	4.00	8.00

HARDEN TRIO, THE

Also see ARLENE HARDEN; BOBBY HARDEN; ROBBIE HARDEN; THE HARDENS.

45s

COLUMBIA

Number	Title (A Side/B Side)	Yr	VG	VG+	NM
❑ 43229	Poor Boy/Let It Be Me	1965	2.00	4.00	8.00
❑ 43463	Tippy Toeing/Don't Remind Me	1965	2.00	4.00	8.00
❑ 43710	Little Boy Walk Like a Man/Dear Brother	1966	—	3.00	6.00
❑ 43844	Seven Days of Crying (Makes One Weak)/ Husbands and Wives	1966	—	3.00	6.00
❑ 44059	Sneaking 'Cross the Border/Childhood Place	1967	—	3.00	6.00
❑ 44249	Forbidden/Manana (Is Soon Enough for Me)	1967	—	3.00	6.00
❑ 44420	He Looks a Lot Like You/My Friend Mr. Echo	1968	—	2.50	5.00
❑ 44552	Everybody Wants to Be Somebody Else/Diddle Diddle Dumplin'	1968	—	2.50	5.00

Albums

COLUMBIA

Number	Title	Yr	VG	VG+	NM
❑ CL 2506 [M]	Tippy Toeing	1966	5.00	10.00	20.00
❑ CS 9306 [S]	Tippy Toeing	1966	6.25	12.50	25.00

HARDENS, THE

Also see ARLENE HARDEN; ROBBIE HARDEN.

45s

COLUMBIA

Number	Title (A Side/B Side)	Yr	VG	VG+	NM
❑ 4-44675	Who Loves You/This Is Where You Get Off	1968	—	3.00	6.00

HARDIN, GUS

45s

RCA

Number	Title (A Side/B Side)	Yr	VG	VG+	NM
❑ PB-13445	After the Last Goodbye/I've Been Loving You Too Long	1983	—	2.00	4.00
❑ PB-13532	If I Didn't Love You/You Can Call Me Blue	1983	—	2.00	4.00
❑ PB-13597	Loving You Hurts/Since I Don't Have You	1983	—	2.00	4.00
❑ PB-13704	Fallen Angel (Flyin' High Tonight)/Not Tonight, I've Got a Heartache	1983	—	2.00	4.00
❑ PB-13751	I Pass/Night Light	1984	—	2.00	4.00
❑ PB-13751 [PS]	I Pass/Night Light	1984	—	2.50	5.00
❑ PB-13814	How Are You Spending My Nights/Night Lights	1984	—	2.00	4.00
❑ PB-13938	All Tangled Up in Love/More or Less	1984	—	2.00	4.00
—A-side with Earl Thomas Conley					
❑ PB-14040	My Mind Is on You/What About When It Rains	1985	—	2.00	4.00
❑ PB-14255	What We Gonna Do/What About When It Rains	1985	—	2.00	4.00

Albums

RCA VICTOR

Number	Title	Yr	VG	VG+	NM
❑ CPL1-4937	Fallen Angel	1984	2.00	4.00	8.00
❑ CPL1-5358	Wall of Tears	1985	2.00	4.00	8.00
❑ CPL1-7033	Wall of Tears	1985	2.00	4.00	8.00
❑ MHL1-8603 [EP]	Gus Hardin	1983	—	3.00	6.00

HARDIN, GUS, AND DAVE LOGGINS

45s

RCA

Number	Title (A Side/B Side)	Yr	VG	VG+	NM
❑ PB-14159	Just As Long As I Have You/More or Less	1985	—	2.00	4.00

HARDING, GAYLE

45s

ROBCHRIS

Number	Title (A Side/B Side)	Yr	VG	VG+	NM
❑ 1008	Sexy Eyes/(B-side unknown)	1978	—	3.00	6.00
❑ 1009	I'm Lovin' the Lovin' Out of You/I Fooled Around Behind You	1978	—	3.00	6.00

HARDY, JOHNNY

45s

ACE

Number	Title (A Side/B Side)	Yr	VG	VG+	NM
❑ 624	In Memory of Johnny Horton/Wasting My Time	1961	5.00	10.00	20.00

J&J

Number	Title (A Side/B Side)	Yr	VG	VG+	NM
❑ 003	In Memory of Johnny Horton/Wasting My Time	1961	6.25	12.50	25.00

HARGROVE, DANNY

45s

50 STATES

Number	Title (A Side/B Side)	Yr	VG	VG+	NM
❑ 61	Sweet Mary/Four Strong Winds	1978	—	3.00	6.00
❑ 64	I Wanna Be Her #1/She Belongs to the Man at the Bar	1978	—	3.00	6.00

HARGROVE, LINDA

45s

CAPITOL

Number	Title (A Side/B Side)	Yr	VG	VG+	NM
❑ 4153	Love Was (Once Around the Dance Floor)/Half My Heart's in Texas	1975	—	2.50	5.00
❑ 4228	Love, You're the Teacher/Save the Children	1976	—	2.50	5.00
❑ 4283	Fire at First Sight/20-20 Hindsight	1976	—	2.50	5.00
❑ 4355	Most of All/The Only Man-Made Thing in Heaven Are the Scars on Jesus' Hands	1976	—	2.50	5.00
❑ 4390	Down to My Pride/Old Fashioned Love	1977	—	2.50	5.00
❑ 4447	Mexican Love Songs/Not Even for Love	1977	—	2.50	5.00

ELEKTRA

Number	Title (A Side/B Side)	Yr	VG	VG+	NM
❑ 45204	Blue Jean Country Queen/Where Do I Begin	1974	—	3.00	6.00
❑ 45215	I've Never Loved Anyone More/Grandma Was the Motor	1974	—	3.00	6.00
❑ 45854	Fallen Angel/My Secret Life	1973	—	3.50	7.00
❑ 45870	Let It Shine/The Farmer's Former Wife	1973	—	3.50	7.00
❑ 45877	What If We're Running Out of Love/New York City Song	1974	—	3.50	7.00

RCA

Number	Title (A Side/B Side)	Yr	VG	VG+	NM
❑ PB-11378	You Are Still the One/I Forgave (But I Forgot to Forget)	1978	—	2.50	5.00
❑ PB-11493	You're the Only One of You I Got/Carnival of Love	1979	—	2.50	5.00

Albums

CAPITOL

Number	Title	Yr	VG	VG+	NM
❑ ST-11463	Love, You're the Teacher	1975	3.00	6.00	12.00
❑ ST-11564	Just Like You	1976	3.00	6.00	12.00
❑ ST-11685	Impressions	1977	3.00	6.00	12.00

ELEKTRA

Number	Title	Yr	VG	VG+	NM
❑ 7E-1013	Blue Jean Country Queen	1974	3.00	6.00	12.00
❑ EKS-75063	Music Is Your Mistress	1973	3.75	7.50	15.00

HARLESS, OGDEN

45s

DOOR KNOB

Number	Title (A Side/B Side)	Yr	VG	VG+	NM
❑ 268	The Richest Poor Man Alive/(B-side unknown)	1987	—	2.50	5.00
❑ 272	How Many More Like Me/(B-side unknown)	1987	—	2.50	5.00
❑ 283	Somebody Ought to Tell Him That She's Gone/ (B-side unknown)	1987	—	2.50	5.00

Number	Title (A Side/B Side)	Yr	VG	VG+	NM
❑ 287	Walk On Boy/(B-side unknown)	1987	—	2.50	5.00
❑ 293	I Wish We Were Strangers/(B-side unknown)	1988	—	2.50	5.00
❑ 297	Down on the Bayou/(B-side unknown)	1988	—	2.50	5.00

MSC

Number	Title (A Side/B Side)	Yr	VG	VG+	NM
❑ 188	Together Alone/(B-side unknown)	1988	—	2.50	5.00

HARLING, KEITH

45s

GIANT

Number	Title (A Side/B Side)	Yr	VG	VG+	NM
❑ 16900	Bring It On/Heartaches and Honky Tonks	1999	—	—	3.00

MCA

Number	Title (A Side/B Side)	Yr	VG	VG+	NM
❑ 72042	Papa Bear/Right in the Middle	1998	—	—	3.00

MCA NASHVILLE

Number	Title (A Side/B Side)	Yr	VG	VG+	NM
❑ 72064	Coming Back for You/I Never Go Around Mirrors	1998	—	—	3.00
❑ 72081	Write It in Stone/There Goes the Neighborhood	1998	—	—	3.00
❑ 72093	There Goes the Neighborhood/I Never Go Around Mirrors	1999	—	—	3.00

HARMS, DALLAS

45s

CON BRIO

Number	Title (A Side/B Side)	Yr	VG	VG+	NM
❑ 157	Legend of the Duke/In the Loving Arms of Marie	1979	—	3.00	6.00

HARMS, JONI

45s

UNIVERSAL

Number	Title (A Side/B Side)	Yr	VG	VG+	NM
❑ 53492	I Need a Wife/The Only Thing Bluer Than His Eyes	1989	—	—	3.00
❑ UVL-66012	The Only Thing Bluer Than His Eyes/A Woman Knows	1989	—	2.00	4.00

HARRELL & SCOTT

45s

ASSOCIATED ARTISTS

Number	Title (A Side/B Side)	Yr	VG	VG+	NM
❑ 503	Weak Men Break/(B-side unknown)	1989	—	3.00	6.00
❑ 505	Darkness of the Light/(B-side unknown)	1989	—	3.00	6.00

HARRINGTON, CARLY

45s

OAK

Number	Title (A Side/B Side)	Yr	VG	VG+	NM
❑ 1055	Badland Preacher/(B-side unknown)	1988	—	3.00	6.00

HARRIS, DONNA

45s

ABC

Number	Title (A Side/B Side)	Yr	VG	VG+	NM
❑ 10839	He Was Almost Persuaded/I'm Sending Hin Back to You	1966	2.50	5.00	10.00
❑ 10886	Masquerade Party/If You Think You've Reached the Bottom	1966	2.00	4.00	8.00
❑ 10921	I Just Now Remembered I Forgot/My Hi-Fi to Cry By	1967	2.00	4.00	8.00

HARRIS, EMMYLOU

Also see EARL THOMAS CONLEY; JOHN DENVER; CHARLIE LOUVIN; BUCK OWENS; DOLLY PARTON/LINDA RONSTADT/EMMYLOU HARRIS; LINDA RONSTADT.

45s

ASYLUM

Number	Title (A Side/B Side)	Yr	VG	VG+	NM
❑ 64570	Thanks to You/Lovin' You Again	1993	—	—	3.00
❑ 64610	High Powered Love/Ballad of a Runaway Horse	1992	—	—	3.00

A&M

Number	Title (A Side/B Side)	Yr	VG	VG+	NM
❑ 2290	Wish We Were Back in Missouri/Riding with Jesse James	1980	—	2.00	4.00

—B-side by Charlie Daniels

HUGHES

Number	Title (A Side/B Side)	Yr	VG	VG+	NM
❑ 53236	I Still Dream of You/Back in Baby's Arms	1988	—	—	3.00

JUBILEE

Number	Title (A Side/B Side)	Yr	VG	VG+	NM
❑ 5679	I'll Be Your Baby Tonight/I'll Never Fall in Love Again	1969	5.00	10.00	20.00
❑ 5697	Paddy/Fugue for the Ox	1970	5.00	10.00	20.00

REPRISE

Number	Title (A Side/B Side)	Yr	VG	VG+	NM
❑ 1326	Too Far Gone/Boulder to Birmingham	1975	—	2.50	5.00
❑ 1332	If I Could Only Win Your Love/Boulder to Birmingham	1975	—	2.50	5.00
❑ 1341	Light of the Stable/Bluebird Wine	1975	2.50	5.00	10.00

—A-side is a longer version than later releases

Number	Title (A Side/B Side)	Yr	VG	VG+	NM
❑ 1341 [PS]	Light of the Stable/Bluebird Wine	1975	3.00	6.00	12.00
❑ 1346	Together Again/Here, There and Everywhere	1976	—	2.50	5.00
❑ 1353	Till I Gain Control Again/One of These Days	1976	—	2.50	5.00
❑ 1371	Sweet Dreams/Amarillo	1976	—	2.50	5.00
❑ 1379	Light of the Stable/Boulder to Birmingham	1976	—	2.50	5.00
❑ 19281	Rollin' and Ramblin'/Sweet Dreams Of You	1991	—	—	3.00
❑ 19510	Wheels of Love/Better Off Without You	1991	—	—	3.00
❑ 19707	Never Be Anyone Else But You/Red, Red Rose	1990	—	—	3.00
❑ 19870	Gulf Coast Highway/Evangeline	1990	—	—	3.00

—A-side: With Willie Nelson

Number	Title (A Side/B Side)	Yr	VG	VG+	NM
❑ 22850	I Still Miss Someone/No Regrets	1989	—	—	3.00
❑ 22999	Heaven Only Knows/A River for Him	1989	—	—	3.00
❑ 27635	Heartbreak Hill/Icy Blue Heart	1989	—	—	3.00

WARNER BROS.

Number	Title (A Side/B Side)	Yr	VG	VG+	NM
❑ PRO-S-2872 [DJ]	Light of the Stable/It Came Upon a Midnight Clear	1987	2.50	5.00	10.00

—B-side by Highway 101

Number	Title (A Side/B Side)	Yr	VG	VG+	NM
❑ 8329	C'est La Vie (You Never Can Tell)/You're Supposed to Be Feeling Good	1977	—	2.50	5.00
❑ 8388	Making Believe/I'll Be Your San Antone Rose	1977	—	2.50	5.00
❑ 8498	To Daddy/Tulsa Queen	1977	—	2.50	5.00
❑ 8553	Two More Bottles of Wine/I Ain't Living Long Like This	1978	—	2.50	5.00
❑ 8623	Easy from Now On/You're Supposed to Be Feeling Good	1978	—	2.50	5.00
❑ 8732	Too Far Gone/Tulsa Queen	1979	—	2.00	4.00
❑ 8815	Save the Last Dance for Me/Even Cowgirls Get the Blues	1979	—	2.50	5.00
❑ 28302	Someday My Ship Will Sail/When He Calls	1987	—	—	3.00
❑ 28714	Today I Started Loving You Again/When I Was Young	1986	—	—	3.00
❑ 28770	I Had My Heart Set on You/Your Long Journey	1986	—	—	3.00
❑ 28852	Timberline/Sweet Chariot	1985	—	2.00	4.00
❑ 28952	Rhythm Guitar/Diamond in My Crown	1985	—	—	3.00
❑ 29041	White Line/Long Tall Sally Rose	1985	—	2.00	4.00
❑ 29138	Someone Like You/Light of the Stable	1984	—	2.00	4.00
❑ 29218	Pledging My Love/Baby, Better Start Turnin' 'Em Down	1984	—	2.00	4.00
❑ 29329	In My Dreams/Like an Old Fashioned World	1984	—	2.00	4.00
❑ 29443	Drivin' Wheel/Good News	1983	—	2.00	4.00
❑ 29583	So Sad (To Watch Good Love Go Bad)/Amarillo	1983	—	2.00	4.00
❑ 29729	I'm Movin' On/Maybe Tonight	1983	—	2.00	4.00
❑ 29898	(Lost His Love) On Our Last Date/Another Pot O' Tea	1982	—	2.00	4.00
❑ 29993	Born to Run/Colors of My Heart	1982	—	2.00	4.00
❑ 49056	Blue Kentucky Girl/Leaving Louisiana in the Broad Daylight	1979	—	2.00	4.00
❑ 49164	Beneath Still Waters/'Til I Gain Control Again	1980	—	2.00	4.00
❑ 49239	Wayfaring Stranger/Green Pastures	1980	—	2.00	4.00
❑ 49262	That Lovin' You Feeling Again/Lola	1980	—	2.50	5.00

—A-side: With Roy Orbison; B-side by Craig Hundley

Number	Title (A Side/B Side)	Yr	VG	VG+	NM
❑ 49551	The Boxer/Precious Love	1980	—	2.00	4.00
❑ 49633	Beautiful Star of Bethlehem/The Little Drummer Boy	1980	—	2.00	4.00
❑ 49645	Light of the Stable/The Little Drummer Boy	1980	—	2.00	4.00
❑ 49684	Mister Sandman/Fools' Thin Air	1981	—	2.00	4.00
❑ 49739	I Don't Have to Crawl/Colors of Your Heart	1981	—	2.00	4.00
❑ 49809	If I Needed You/Ashes By Now	1981	—	2.00	4.00

—A-side with Don Williams

Number	Title (A Side/B Side)	Yr	VG	VG+	NM
❑ 49892	Tennessee Rose/Mama Help	1982	—	2.00	4.00

Albums

JUBILEE

Number	Title (A Side/B Side)	Yr	VG	VG+	NM
❑ JGS-8031	Gliding Bird	1969	30.00	60.00	120.00

—Originals have color covers; counterfeit covers are black and white

MOBILE FIDELITY

Number	Title (A Side/B Side)	Yr	VG	VG+	NM
❑ 1-015	Quarter Moon in a Ten Cent Town	1979	10.00	20.00	40.00

—Audiophile vinyl

REPRISE

Number	Title (A Side/B Side)	Yr	VG	VG+	NM
❑ MS 2213	Pieces of the Sky	1975	2.50	5.00	10.00
❑ MS 2236	Elite Hotel	1976	2.50	5.00	10.00
❑ MSK 2284	Pieces of the Sky	1977	2.00	4.00	8.00

—Reissue of 2213

Number	Title (A Side/B Side)	Yr	VG	VG+	NM
❑ MSK 2286	Elite Hotel	1977	2.00	4.00	8.00

—Reissue of 2236

Number	Title (A Side/B Side)	Yr	VG	VG+	NM
❑ 25776	Bluebird	1989	2.50	5.00	10.00

WARNER BROS.

Number	Title (A Side/B Side)	Yr	VG	VG+	NM
❑ BSK 3115	Luxury Liner	1977	2.50	5.00	10.00
❑ BSK 3141	Quarter Moon in a Ten Cent Town	1978	2.50	5.00	10.00
❑ BSK 3258	Profile/Best of Emmylou Harris	1978	2.50	5.00	10.00
❑ BSK 3318	Blue Kentucky Girl	1979	2.50	5.00	10.00
❑ BSK 3422	Roses in the Snow	1980	2.50	5.00	10.00
❑ BSK 3484	Light of the Stable: The Christmas Album	1980	2.50	5.00	10.00
❑ BSK 3508	Evangeline	1981	2.50	5.00	10.00
❑ BSK 3603	Cimarron	1981	2.50	5.00	10.00
❑ 23740	Last Date	1982	2.50	5.00	10.00
❑ 23961	White Shoes	1983	2.50	5.00	10.00
❑ 25161	Profile II — The Best of Emmylou Harris	1984	2.50	5.00	10.00
❑ 25205	The Ballad of Sally Rose	1985	2.50	5.00	10.00
❑ 25352	Thirteen	1986	2.50	5.00	10.00
❑ 25585	Angel Band	1987	2.50	5.00	10.00

HARRISON, B.J.

45s

TELESONIC

Number	Title (A Side/B Side)	Yr	VG	VG+	NM
❑ 801	I Need a Little More Time/(B-side unknown)	1980	2.00	4.00	8.00

HARRISON, DIXIE

45s

AIR INT'L.

Number	Title (A Side/B Side)	Yr	VG	VG+	NM
❑ 10078	Yes Man (He Found Me in a Honky Tonk)/Careless Kinda Heart	1982	—	3.00	6.00

HART, CLAY

45s

METROMEDIA

Number	Title (A Side/B Side)	Yr	VG	VG+	NM
❑ 119	Spring/Child of the Wind	1969	—	3.00	6.00
❑ 140	Another Day, Another Mile, Another Highway/Penny	1969	—	3.00	6.00
❑ 158	Face of a Dear Friend/Gotta Be Free	1970	—	3.00	6.00
❑ 172	If I'd Only Come and Gone/Take Your Precious Love from Me	1970	—	3.00	6.00
❑ 207	Depend on Me/Mobile Blues	1970	—	3.00	6.00
❑ 221	Poor Man's Gold/Reach Out and Touch One Another	1971	—	3.00	6.00

Number	Title (A Side/B Side)	Yr	VG	VG+	NM
RANWOOD					
❑ 959	Another New Day/Smiles of Joy	1974	—	2.50	5.00
❑ 1007	Travelin' Minstrel Man/Someone to Give My Love To	1975	—	2.50	5.00
❑ 1018	Sing Me a Love Song/You're My Rainy Day Woman	1975	—	2.50	5.00
Albums					
METROMEDIA					
❑ 1008	Spring	1969	3.75	7.50	15.00
RANWOOD					
❑ 8122	Most Requested Country Favorites	1973	2.50	5.00	10.00
❑ 8135	Travelin' Minstrel Man	1974	2.50	5.00	10.00

HART, FREDDIE

Number	Title (A Side/B Side)	Yr	VG	VG+	NM
45s					
CAPITOL					
❑ F2524	Butterfly Love/My Heart Is a Playground	1953	6.25	12.50	25.00
❑ F2588	Secret Kisses/Whole Hog or None	1953	5.00	10.00	20.00
❑ 2692	The Whole World Holding Hands/Without You	1969	2.00	4.00	8.00
❑ F2726	Loose Talk/The Curtain Never Falls	1954	5.00	10.00	20.00
❑ 2768	One More Mountain to Climb/Just Another Girl	1970	2.00	4.00	8.00
❑ 2839	Fingerprints/I Can't Keep My Hands Off of You	1970	2.00	4.00	8.00
❑ F2873	Caught at Last/It Just Don't Seem Like Home	1954	5.00	10.00	20.00
❑ 2933	California Grapevine/What's Wrong with Your Head, Fred	1970	2.00	4.00	8.00
❑ F2991	I'm Going Out on the Front Porch and Cry/Please Don't Tell Her	1954	5.00	10.00	20.00
❑ F3090	Miss Lonely Heart/Oh Heart Let Her Go	1955	5.00	10.00	20.00
❑ 3115	Easy Loving/Brother Bluebird	1971	—	3.00	6.00
❑ F3203	Canada to Tennessee/No Thanks to You	1955	5.00	10.00	20.00
❑ 3261	My Hang-Up Is You/Big Bad Wolf	1972	—	3.00	6.00
❑ F3299	Hiding in Darkness/That's What You Gave to Me	1955	5.00	10.00	20.00
❑ 3353	Bless Your Heart/Conscience Makes Cowards (Of Us All)	1972	—	3.00	6.00
❑ 3453	Got the All Overs for You (All Over Me)/Just Another Girl	1972	—	3.00	6.00
❑ 3524	Super Kind of Woman/Mother Nature Made a Believer Out of Me	1973	—	3.00	6.00
❑ 3612	Trip to Heaven/Look-a Here	1973	—	3.00	6.00
❑ 3730	If You Can't Feel It (It Ain't There)/Skid Row Street	1973	—	3.00	6.00
❑ 3789	Blue Christmas/I Believe in Santa Claus	1973	—	3.50	7.00
❑ 3827	Hang In There Girl/You Belong to Me	1974	—	3.00	6.00
❑ 3898	The Want-To's/Phenix City, Alabama	1974	—	3.00	6.00
❑ 3970	My Woman's Man/Let's Clean Up the Country	1974	—	3.00	6.00
❑ 4031	I'd Like to Sleep Til I Get Over You/Nothing's Better Than That	1975	—	3.00	6.00
❑ 4099	The First Time/Sexy	1975	—	3.00	6.00
❑ 4152	Warm Side of You/I Love You, I Just Don't Like You	1975	—	3.00	6.00
❑ 4210	You Are the Song (Inside of Me)/I Can Almost See Houston from Here	1976	—	3.00	6.00
❑ 4251	She'll Throw Stones at You/Love Makes It Alright	1976	—	3.00	6.00
❑ 4313	That Look in Her Eyes/Try My Love for Size	1976	—	3.00	6.00
❑ 4363	Why Lovers Turn to Strangers/Paper Sack Full of Memories	1976	—	3.00	6.00
❑ 4409	Thank God She's Mine/Falling All Over Me	1977	—	2.00	4.00
❑ 4448	The Pleasure's Been All Mine/It's Heaven Loving You	1977	—	2.00	4.00
❑ 4498	The Search/Honky Tonk Toys	1977	—	2.50	5.00
❑ 4530	So Good, So Rare, So Fine/There's an Angel Living There	1978	—	2.50	5.00
❑ 4561	Only You/I Love You, I Just Don't Like You	1978	—	2.50	5.00
❑ 4609	Toe to Toe/And Then Some	1978	—	2.50	5.00
❑ 4684	My Lady/Guilty	1979	—	2.50	5.00
❑ 4720	Wasn't It Easy Baby/My Lady Loves	1979	—	2.50	5.00
COLUMBIA					
❑ 21512	Dig Boy Dig/Two of a Kind	1956	12.50	25.00	50.00
❑ 21550	Snatch It and Grab It/Human Thing to Do	1956	3.75	7.50	15.00
❑ 21558	Drink Up and Go Home/Blue	1956	3.75	7.50	15.00
❑ 40821	On the Prowl/Extra	1957	3.75	7.50	15.00
❑ 40896	Fraulein/Baby Don't Leave	1957	3.75	7.50	15.00
❑ 41005	Say No More/The Outside World	1957	3.75	7.50	15.00
❑ 41081	You Are My World/Heaven Only Knows	1957	3.75	7.50	15.00
❑ 41144	I Won't Be Home Tonight/Love, Come to Me	1958	3.75	7.50	15.00
❑ 41269	I'm No Angel/Midnight Date	1958	3.75	7.50	15.00
❑ 41345	The Wall/Davy Jones	1959	3.00	6.00	12.00
❑ 41439	Farther Than My Eyes Can See/My Kind of Love	1959	—	—	—
—Unreleased					
❑ 41456	Chain Gang/Rock Bottom	1959	3.00	6.00	12.00
❑ 41597	The Key's in the Mailbox/Starvation Days	1960	3.00	6.00	12.00
❑ 41805	Lying Again/Do My Heart a Favor	1960	3.00	6.00	12.00
❑ 42146	What a Laugh!/Heart Attack	1961	3.00	6.00	12.00
❑ 42285	Some Do, Some Don't, Some Will, Some Won't/Like You Are	1962	3.00	6.00	12.00
❑ 42491	Stand Up/Ugly Duckling	1962	3.00	6.00	12.00
❑ 42679	I'll Hit It with a Stick/Stranger Drive Away	1963	3.00	6.00	12.00
❑ 42769	Angels Like You/Mary Ann	1963	3.00	6.00	12.00
EL DORADO					
❑ 101	I Don't Want to Lose You/My Favorite Entertainer	1985	—	3.50	7.00
FIFTH ST.					
❑ 1091	Best Love I Never Had/I'm Not Going Hungry	1987	—	3.00	6.00
KAPP					
❑ 632	Love Can Make or Break a Heart/Hurts Feel So Good	1964	2.50	5.00	10.00
❑ 661	Moon Gal/You've Got It Coming To Ya	1965	2.50	5.00	10.00
❑ 694	Hank Williams' Guitar/I Created a Monster	1965	2.50	5.00	10.00
❑ 743	Why Should I Cry Over You/Keys in the Mailbox	1966	2.50	5.00	10.00
❑ 765	Together Again/Waiting for a Train	1966	2.50	5.00	10.00
❑ 794	Misty Blue/Elm Street Pawn Shop	1966	2.50	5.00	10.00
❑ 820	I'll Hold You in My Heart/Too Much of You (Left of Me)	1967	2.50	5.00	10.00
❑ 841	Anna Maria/Leon and the Rain	1967	2.50	5.00	10.00
❑ 879	Togetherness/Portrait of a Lonely Man	1967	2.50	5.00	10.00
❑ 879 [PS]	Togetherness/Portrait of a Lonely Man	1967	3.75	7.50	15.00
❑ 910	Born a Fool/Hands of a Man	1968	2.50	5.00	10.00
❑ 944	Don't Cry Baby/Here Lies a Heart	1968	2.50	5.00	10.00
❑ 976	Why Leave Something I Can't Use/Hang On to Her	1969	2.50	5.00	10.00
❑ 993	I Lost All My Tomorrows/That's How High a Man Can Go	1969	2.50	5.00	10.00
❑ 2183	Don't Cry Baby/Loving You Again	1972	—	3.50	7.00
MCA					
❑ 40011	Born a Fool/My Anna Maria	1973	—	3.00	6.00
MONUMENT					
❑ 826	For a Second There/The Almighty Dollar	1963	3.00	6.00	12.00
❑ 838	First You Go Through Me/Valentino	1964	3.00	6.00	12.00
SUNBIRD					
❑ 110	Sure Thing/Makin' Love to a Memory	1980	—	3.00	6.00
❑ 7550	Sure Thing/Makin' Love to a Memory	1980	—	2.50	5.00
❑ 7553	Roses Are Red/Battle of the Sexes	1980	—	2.50	5.00
❑ 7560	You're Crazy Man/Playboy's Centerfolk	1981	—	2.50	5.00
❑ 7565	You Were There/The Weaker Sex	1981	—	2.50	5.00
Albums					
CAPITOL					
❑ ST-469	New Sounds	1970	3.00	6.00	12.00
❑ ST-593	California Grapevine	1970	3.00	6.00	12.00
❑ ST-838	Easy Loving	1971	3.00	6.00	12.00
❑ ST-11014	My Hang-Up Is You	1972	3.00	6.00	12.00
❑ ST-11073	Bless Your Heart	1972	3.00	6.00	12.00
❑ ST-11107	Got the All-Overs	1972	3.00	6.00	12.00
❑ ST-11156	Super Kind of Woman	1973	3.00	6.00	12.00
❑ ST-11197	Trip to Heaven	1973	3.00	6.00	12.00
❑ ST-11252	If You Can't Feel It	1974	3.00	6.00	12.00
❑ ST-11296	Hang In There Girl	1974	3.00	6.00	12.00
❑ ST-11353	Country Heart 'N' Soul	1975	3.00	6.00	12.00
❑ ST-11374	Greatest Hits	1975	3.00	6.00	12.00
❑ ST-11449	The First Time	1975	2.50	5.00	10.00
❑ ST-11504	People Put to Music	1976	2.50	5.00	10.00
❑ ST-11568	That Look in Her Eyes	1976	2.50	5.00	10.00
❑ ST-11626	The Pleasure's Been All Mine	1977	2.50	5.00	10.00
❑ ST-11724	Only You	1978	2.50	5.00	10.00
COLUMBIA					
❑ CL 1792 [M]	The Spirited Freddie Hart	1962	10.00	20.00	40.00
❑ G 31550 [(2)]	The World of Freddie Hart	1972	3.75	7.50	15.00
HARMONY					
❑ HL 7412 [M]	The Best of Freddie Hart	1967	3.00	6.00	12.00
❑ HS 11212 [S]	The Best of Freddie Hart	1967	3.00	6.00	12.00
❑ KH 31165	Lonesome Love	1972	2.50	5.00	10.00
❑ KH 32467	You Are My World	1973	2.50	5.00	10.00
HILLTOP					
❑ 6117	From Canada to Tennessee	1972	2.50	5.00	10.00
KAPP					
❑ KL-1456 [M]	The Hart of Country Music	1966	3.75	7.50	15.00
❑ KL-1492 [M]	Straight from the Heart	1966	3.75	7.50	15.00
❑ KL-1513 [M]	Hurtin' Man	1967	5.00	10.00	20.00
❑ KL-1539 [M]	The Neon and the Rain	1967	5.00	10.00	20.00
❑ KS-3456 [S]	The Hart of Country Music	1966	5.00	10.00	20.00
❑ KS-3492 [S]	Straight from the Heart	1966	5.00	10.00	20.00
❑ KS-3513 [S]	Hurtin' Man	1967	5.00	10.00	20.00
❑ KS-3539 [S]	The Neon and the Rain	1967	5.00	10.00	20.00
❑ KS-3546	Togetherness	1968	5.00	10.00	20.00
❑ KS-3568	Born a Fool	1968	5.00	10.00	20.00
❑ KS-3592	Greatest Hits	1969	3.75	7.50	15.00
MCA					
❑ 4088 [(2)]	The Best of Freddie Hart	1975	3.75	7.50	15.00
SUNBIRD					
❑ ST-50100	Sure Thing	1980	3.00	6.00	12.00

HART, J.D.

Number	Title (A Side/B Side)	Yr	VG	VG+	NM
45s					
UNIVERSAL					
❑ UVL-66017	Come Back Brenda/Love Still Lives	1989	—	2.00	4.00

HART, ROD

Number	Title (A Side/B Side)	Yr	VG	VG+	NM
45s					
LITTLE RICHIE					
❑ 1010	C.B. Savage/Better Off Gone	1976	2.00	4.00	8.00
PLANTATION					
❑ 144	C.B. Savage/Better Off Gone	1976	—	2.50	5.00
❑ 152	Arizona Flash and Cloudy/She Never Cried Like That for Me	1977	—	2.50	5.00
Albums					
PLANTATION					
❑ 500	Breakeroo!	1976	3.00	6.00	12.00

HART, SALLY JUNE
45s
BUDDAH

Number	Title (A Side/B Side)	Yr	VG	VG+	NM
❑ 479	Takin' What I Can Get/Beautiful Love Song Melodies	1975	—	2.50	5.00
❑ 510	This Is My Love Song/(B-side unknown)	1975	—	2.50	5.00

HARTFORD, CHAPIN
45s
LS

Number	Title (A Side/B Side)	Yr	VG	VG+	NM
❑ 165	I Knew the Mason/Rio Grande	1978	—	3.00	6.00
❑ 171	Puttin' the Lady Back Together/I Knew the Mason	1978	—	3.00	6.00
❑ 177	Hit and Run/Rio Grande	1979	—	3.00	6.00

HARTFORD, JOHN
45s

Number	Title (A Side/B Side)	Yr	VG	VG+	NM
AMPEX					
❑ 11019	One Too Many Mornings/(B-side unknown)	1971	—	2.50	5.00
FLYING FISH					
❑ 4013	Piece of My Heart/(B-side unknown)	1984	—	2.00	4.00
MCA DOT					
❑ 53104	Ohio River Rag/Love Wrote This Song	1987	—	2.00	4.00
RCA VICTOR					
❑ 47-8987	Tall Tall Grass/Jack's in the Sack	1966	2.00	4.00	8.00
❑ 47-9175	Gentle on My Mind/Electric Washing Machine	1967	2.00	4.00	8.00
❑ 47-9345	A Simple Thing As Love/Landscape Grown Cold	1967	2.00	4.00	8.00
❑ 47-9451	Big Blue Balloon/Six O'Clock Train and a Girl with Green Eyes	1968	2.00	4.00	8.00
❑ 47-9507	Shiny Rails of Steel/Natural to Be Gone	1968	2.00	4.00	8.00
❑ 47-9611	I Didn't Know the World Would Last This Long/The Category Stomp	1968	—	3.00	6.00
❑ 47-9668	California Earthquake/Mouth to Mouth Resuscitation	1968	—	3.00	6.00
❑ 47-9753	I Didn't Know the World Would Last This Long/Orphan of World War II	1969	—	3.00	6.00
❑ 47-9772	Like Unto a Mockingbird/Natural to Be Gone	1969	—	3.00	6.00

Albums

Number	Title (A Side/B Side)	Yr	VG	VG+	NM
FLYING FISH					
❑ FF-020	Mark Twang	1976	2.50	5.00	10.00
❑ FF-028	Nobody Knows What You Do	1977	2.50	5.00	10.00
❑ FF-044	All in the Name of Love	1983	2.50	5.00	10.00
❑ FF-063	Headin' Down Into the Mystery Below	1978	2.50	5.00	10.00
❑ FF-095	Slumberin' on the Cumberland	1979	2.50	5.00	10.00
—With Pat Burton and Benny Martin					
❑ FF-228	You and Me at Home	1980	2.50	5.00	10.00
❑ FF-259	Catalogue	1982	2.50	5.00	10.00
❑ FF-289	Gum Tree Canoe	1984	2.50	5.00	10.00
❑ FF-440	Me Oh My, How Time Flies	1987	2.50	5.00	10.00
MCA					
❑ 5861	Annual Waltz	1987	2.00	4.00	8.00
RCA VICTOR					
❑ LPM-3687 [M]	John Hartford Looks at Life	1966	5.00	10.00	20.00
❑ LSP-3687 [S]	John Hartford Looks at Life	1966	3.75	7.50	15.00
❑ LPM-3796 [M]	Earthwords and Music	1967	6.25	12.50	25.00
❑ LSP-3796 [S]	Earthwords and Music	1967	3.75	7.50	15.00
❑ LPM-3884 [M]	The Love Album	1967	6.25	12.50	25.00
❑ LSP-3884 [S]	The Love Album	1967	3.75	7.50	15.00
❑ LSP-3998	Housing Project	1968	3.75	7.50	15.00
❑ LSP-4068	Gentle on My Mind and Other Originals	1968	3.75	7.50	15.00
❑ LSP-4156	John Hartford	1969	3.75	7.50	15.00
❑ LSP-4337	Iron Mountain Depot	1970	3.75	7.50	15.00
WARNER BROS.					
❑ WS 1916	Aereo-Plain	1971	3.00	6.00	12.00
❑ BS 2651	Morning Bugle	1972	3.00	6.00	12.00

HARTSOOK, JIMMY
45s
RCA VICTOR

Number	Title (A Side/B Side)	Yr	VG	VG+	NM
❑ APBO-0202	Anything to Prove My Love to You/Dreamin' Again	1973	—	3.00	6.00
❑ APBO-0202	Anything to Prove My Love to You/Dreamin' Again	1973	2.00	4.00	8.00
❑ PB-10011	I Keep Loving You on My Mind/Making Believe	1974	—	3.00	6.00

HARTT, DOLLY
45s
KASS

Number	Title (A Side/B Side)	Yr	VG	VG+	NM
❑ 1015	Here Comes the Night/(B-side unknown)	1988	—	3.00	6.00

HARVELL, NATE
45s
REPUBLIC

Number	Title (A Side/B Side)	Yr	VG	VG+	NM
❑ 019	Another Worn Out Rhinestone/(B-side unknown)	1978	—	2.50	5.00
❑ 025	Three Times a Lady/Happy Ending	1978	—	2.50	5.00
❑ 033	One in a Million/Silver Rails	1978	—	2.50	5.00
❑ 265	Wine and Weakness/(B-side unknown)	1976	—	2.50	5.00
❑ 372	Just Another Man/(B-side unknown)	1977	—	2.50	5.00

HARVESTERS, THE
45s
COLUMBIA

Number	Title (A Side/B Side)	Yr	VG	VG+	NM
❑ 4-21457	Let God Abide/I Just Telephone Upstairs	1955	6.25	12.50	25.00
❑ 4-21495	I Want You to Be More Like Jesus/When I'm Alone	1956	6.25	12.50	25.00
❑ 4-21511	Jacob's Ladder/He's Everywhere	1956	6.25	12.50	25.00
❑ 4-40897	These Are the Things That Matter/That Will Be a Great Day	1957	5.00	10.00	20.00
❑ 4-41074	I Shall Not Be Moved/Closer Than a Brother	1957	5.00	10.00	20.00

HARVEY, ALEX
Not to be confused with the British artist of the same name, the below is an American country singer.

45s

Number	Title (A Side/B Side)	Yr	VG	VG+	NM
CAPITOL					
❑ 3172	To Make My Life Beautiful/Lady	1971	—	2.00	4.00
❑ 3336	Delta Dawn/Momma's Waiting	1972	—	2.00	4.00
❑ 3469	Angeline/Devil on My Shoulder	1972	—	2.00	4.00
❑ 3493	Good Time Christmas/Someone Who Cares	1972	—	2.00	4.00
—With Son Lex					
❑ 3649	Right On/Summer Days	1973	—	2.00	4.00
❑ 3703	You Don't Need a Reason/Goodbye Miss Carolina	1973	—	2.00	4.00
❑ 3847	Tangerine/Jody's Face	1974	—	2.00	4.00
METROMEDIA					
❑ 143	Louisiana River Bay/King of Oak Street	1969	—	3.00	6.00
❑ 173	Tell It All Brother/Mama Tried	1970	—	3.00	6.00
UNITED ARTISTS					
❑ 50494	It Takes a Lot of Tenderness/I'll Be Your Tomorrow	1969	2.00	4.00	8.00

Albums
CAPITOL

Number	Title (A Side/B Side)	Yr	VG	VG+	NM
❑ ST-789	Alex Harvey	1972	3.00	6.00	12.00
❑ ST-11128	Souvenirs	1973	3.00	6.00	12.00

HATFIELD, VINCE & DIANNE
45s
SOUNDWAVES

Number	Title (A Side/B Side)	Yr	VG	VG+	NM
❑ 4638	I Won't Last a Day Without You/Divided Love	1981	—	2.50	5.00
❑ 4649	You Show Me Yours/I'm the Dreamer, You're the Dream	1981	—	2.50	5.00
❑ 4668	Back in My Baby's Arms/Travelin' Man	1982	—	2.50	5.00
❑ 4704	Love Has Made a Woman Out of You/Texas, I Dream of You	1983	—	2.50	5.00
❑ 4730	Let's Fan the Flame/Today I Started Loving You Again	1984	—	2.50	5.00

HAUSER, BRUCE, AND SAWMILL CREEK
45s
COWBOY

Number	Title (A Side/B Side)	Yr	VG	VG+	NM
❑ 200	I Just Came Back (To Break My Heart Again)/(B-side unknown)	1985	—	3.00	6.00
❑ 202	Bidding America Goodbye (The Auction)/(B-side unknown)	1986	—	3.00	6.00
❑ 1045	Barely Gettin' By/Friends	1981	—	3.00	6.00
—As "Sawmill Creek"					

HAVENS, BOBBY
45s
CIN KAY

Number	Title (A Side/B Side)	Yr	VG	VG+	NM
❑ 043	Hey You/Typical Saturday Night	1978	—	3.00	6.00

HAWKINS, DEBI
45s
WARNER BROS.

Number	Title (A Side/B Side)	Yr	VG	VG+	NM
❑ 7746	He's My Walkin' Love/Someday I'll Leave You	1973	—	3.00	6.00
❑ 7792	Standing Room Only/Teach Me How to Love You	1974	—	2.50	5.00
❑ 7838	Mama Never Told Me/Take Me Home and Love Me	1974	—	—	—
—Unreleased?					
❑ 8017	Mama Never Told Me/Take Me Home and Love Me	1974	—	2.50	5.00
—Unreleased?					
❑ 8076	Making Believe/The Man in My Life	1975	—	2.50	5.00
❑ 8104	What I Keep Sayin', Is a Lie/A Beautiful Memory Tonight	1975	—	2.50	5.00
❑ 8140	When I Stop Dreaming/I Want to Hold You in My Arms	1975	—	2.50	5.00
❑ 8188	Walnut Street Wrangler/Magic Cloud of Love	1976	—	2.50	5.00
❑ 8269	I'll Be There (If You Ever Want Me)/Jojo's Wagon	1976	—	2.50	5.00
❑ 8394	Love Letters/Hey Mister Train	1977	—	2.50	5.00

HAWKINS, ERSKINE
The jazz trumpeter and his band had the following hit on the Billboard country charts.

Selected 78s
BLUEBIRD

Number	Title (A Side/B Side)	Yr	VG	VG+	NM
❑ 30-0813	Don't Cry, Baby/Bear-Mash Blues	1943	5.00	10.00	20.00

HAWKINS, HAWKSHAW
45s
COLUMBIA

Number	Title (A Side/B Side)	Yr	VG	VG+	NM
❑ 4-41419	Soldier's Joy/Big Red Benson	1959	5.00	10.00	20.00
❑ 4-41574	Alaska Lil and Texas Bill/Patanio	1960	5.00	10.00	20.00
❑ 4-41714	Put a Nickel in the Jukebox/Your Conscience	1960	5.00	10.00	20.00
❑ 4-41811	You Know Me Too Well/My Story	1960	5.00	10.00	20.00
❑ 4-42002	No Love for Me/The Love I Have for You	1961	3.75	7.50	15.00
❑ 4-42223	Twenty Miles from Shore/Big Ole Heartache	1961	3.75	7.50	15.00
❑ 4-42441	I Can't Seem to Say Goodbye/Darkness on the Face of the Earth	1962	3.75	7.50	15.00

Number	Title (A Side/B Side)	Yr	VG	VG+	NM
KING					
❑ 969	I'm Waiting Just for You/A Heartache to Recall	1951	10.00	20.00	40.00
❑ 997	Sunny Side of the Mountain/Blue Skies in Your Eyes	1951	10.00	20.00	40.00
❑ 998	Slow Poke/Two Roads	1951	10.00	20.00	40.00
❑ 1039	Be My Life's Companion/Everybody's Got a Girl But Me	1952	7.50	15.00	30.00
❑ 1047	Over the Hill/I Am Slowly Dying of a Broken Heart	1952	7.50	15.00	30.00
❑ 1062	Unwanted/Got You on My Mind	1952	7.50	15.00	30.00
❑ 1081	Loaded with Love/I Love the Way You Say Goodnight	1952	7.50	15.00	30.00
❑ 1133	Heavenly Road/An Empty Mansion	1952	7.50	15.00	30.00
❑ 1134	I'm a Lone Wolf/I Hope You're Cryin' Too	1952	7.50	15.00	30.00
❑ 1154	Tangled Heart/Betty Lorraine	1953	7.50	15.00	30.00
❑ 1174	The Life Story of Hank Williams/Picking Sweethearts	1953	10.00	20.00	40.00
❑ 1175	Kaw-Liga/If I Ever Get Rich Mom	1953	7.50	15.00	30.00
❑ 1190	Barbara Allen/The Life Story of Hank Williams	1953	7.50	15.00	30.00
❑ 5404	Nothing More to Say/Between the Lines	1960	3.75	7.50	15.00
❑ 5692	Silver Threads and Golden Needles/Girl Without a Name	1962	3.75	7.50	15.00
❑ 5695	Bad News Travels Fast/Let Them Talk	1962	3.75	7.50	15.00
❑ 5712	Lonesome 7-7203/Everything Has Changed	1963	3.75	7.50	15.00
❑ 5765	Love Died Tonight/Sunny Side of the Mountain	1963	3.75	7.50	15.00
❑ 5810	Caught in the Middle of Two Hearts/If I Ever Get Rich Mom	1963	3.75	7.50	15.00
❑ 5871	I'm Beginning to Forget/Teardrops on Your Letter	1964	3.75	7.50	15.00
❑ 5909	This Particular Baby/The Shadows	1964	3.75	7.50	15.00
❑ 6047	The Last Letter/Never Mind the Tears	1967	3.00	6.00	12.00
❑ 6074	Jealous Fate/It's Easy to Remember	1967	3.00	6.00	12.00
RCA VICTOR					
❑ 47-5333	I'll Trade Yours for Mine/Long Way	1953	6.25	12.50	25.00
❑ 47-5444	A Heap of Lovin'/Mark Round My Finger	1953	6.25	12.50	25.00
❑ 47-5549	I'll Never Close My Heart to You/When You Say Yes	1953	6.25	12.50	25.00
❑ 47-5623	Flashing Lights/Waitin' for My Baby	1954	6.25	12.50	25.00
❑ 47-5702	Rebound/Why Didn't I Hear It from You	1954	6.25	12.50	25.00
❑ 47-5808	One White Rose/I Wanna Be Hugged to Death	1954	6.25	12.50	25.00
❑ 47-5890	I'll Take a Chance with You/Why Don't You Leave This Town	1954	6.25	12.50	25.00
❑ 47-6022	Ling Ting Tong/Ko Ko Mo, I Love You So	1955	6.25	12.50	25.00
—With Rita Robbins					
❑ 47-6103	How Can Anything So Pretty Be So Doggone Mean/Pedro Gonzalez Tennessee Lopez	1955	6.25	12.50	25.00
❑ 47-6211	Car Hoppin' Mama/The Love You Steal	1955	6.25	12.50	25.00
❑ 47-6298	I Gotta Have You/Standing at the End of My World	1955	6.25	12.50	25.00
❑ 47-6396	If It Ain't on the Menu/Borrowing	1956	6.25	12.50	25.00
❑ 47-6509	It Would Be a Doggone Lie/Sunny Side of the Mountain	1956	6.25	12.50	25.00
❑ 47-6716	I'll Be Gone/My Fate Is In Your Hands	1956	6.25	12.50	25.00
❑ 47-6794	Action/Oh How I Cried	1957	5.00	10.00	20.00
❑ 47-6910	Dark Moon/With This Pen	1957	5.00	10.00	20.00
❑ 47-7054	Is My Ring on Your Finger/Sensation	1957	5.00	10.00	20.00
❑ 47-7145	Guilty of Dreaming/It's Easier Said Than Done	1958	5.00	10.00	20.00
❑ 47-7222	I Don't Apologize/I'll Get Even with You	1958	5.00	10.00	20.00
❑ 47-7389	I've Got It Again/Freedom	1958	5.00	10.00	20.00
❑ 47-7486	Are You Happy/She Was Here	1959	5.00	10.00	20.00
Selected 78s					
KING					
❑ 544	After All We Have Meant to Each Other/The Way I Love You	1946	7.50	15.00	30.00
❑ 557	I'll Never Cry Over You/I Ain't Goin' Honky Tonkin' Anymore	1946	6.25	12.50	25.00
❑ 558	Soldier's Last Letter/There's a Little Bit of Everything	1946	6.25	12.50	25.00
❑ 559	Blue-Eyed Elaine/Try Me One More Time	1946	6.25	12.50	25.00
❑ 560	You Nearly Lost My Mind/Are You Waiting Just for Me	1946	6.25	12.50	25.00
❑ 561	It's Been So Long Darling/I Wonder Why You Said Goodbye	1946	6.25	12.50	25.00
❑ 562	Walking the Floor Over You/I'll Get Along Somehow	1946	6.25	12.50	25.00
❑ 563	Mean Mama Blues/Mean Old Bed Bug Blues	1946	6.25	12.50	25.00
❑ 564	I'm Wondering How/That's When It's Coming Home to You	1946	6.25	12.50	25.00
❑ 611	When They Found the Atomic Power/Since You Went Away	1947	6.25	12.50	25.00
❑ 625	Moonlight on Your Cabin/Blue Skies in Your Eyes	1947	6.25	12.50	25.00
❑ 667	Sunny Side of the Mountain/After Yesterday	1947	6.25	12.50	25.00
❑ 686	Secrets of My Heart/Never Say Goodbye	1948	6.25	12.50	25.00
❑ 689	Pan American/I Suppose	1948	6.25	12.50	25.00
❑ 720	Dog House Boogie/I Can't Tell My Broken Heart a Lie	1948	6.25	12.50	25.00
❑ 742	Some of These Nights/I Didn't Have the Heart	1948	6.25	12.50	25.00
❑ 756	Somebody Lied/Memories Always Linger On	1949	5.00	10.00	20.00
❑ 776	Life Lost Its Color/All Because of My Jealous Heart	1949	5.00	10.00	20.00
❑ 793	The Longer We're Together/Would You Like to Have a Broken Heart	1949	5.00	10.00	20.00
❑ 821	I Wasted a Nickel/I'm Kissing Your Picture Counting Tears	1949	5.00	10.00	20.00
❑ 838	Wanted: Someone to Love Me/There's a Teardrop in Your Eye	1950	5.00	10.00	20.00
❑ 859	Back to the Dog House/Pardon Me for Loving You	1950	5.00	10.00	20.00
❑ 876	Yesterday's Kisses/That's All She Wrote	1950	5.00	10.00	20.00
❑ 897	Stop, Please Stop/Handcuffed to Love	1950	5.00	10.00	20.00
❑ 918	I Love You a Thousand Ways/Teardrops from My Eyes	1951	5.00	10.00	20.00
❑ 932	Shot Gun Boogie/You Don't Belong to Me	1951	5.00	10.00	20.00
❑ 944	Rattlesnakin' Daddy/I Hate Myself	1951	5.00	10.00	20.00
Albums					
GLADWYNNE					
❑ G-2006 [M]	Country Western Cavalcade with Hawkshaw Hawkins	195?	30.00	60.00	120.00
HARMONY					
❑ HL 7301 [M]	The Great Hawkshaw Hawkins	1963	5.00	10.00	20.00
❑ HS 11044 [R]	The Great Hawkshaw Hawkins	1963	3.75	7.50	15.00
KING					
❑ 587 [M]	Hawkshaw Hawkins	1958	25.00	50.00	100.00
❑ 592 [M]	Grand Ole Opry Favorites	1958	25.00	50.00	100.00
❑ 599 [M]	Hawkshaw Hawkins	1959	25.00	50.00	100.00
❑ 808 [M]	The All New Hawkshaw Hawkins	1963	20.00	40.00	80.00
❑ KS-808 [S]	The All New Hawkshaw Hawkins	1963	25.00	50.00	100.00
❑ 858 [M]	Taken From Our Vaults, Volume 1	1963	10.00	20.00	40.00
❑ 870 [M]	Taken From Our Vaults, Volume 2	1963	10.00	20.00	40.00
❑ 873 [M]	Taken From Our Vaults, Volume 3	1964	10.00	20.00	40.00
LABREA					
❑ 8020 [M]	Hawkshaw Hawkins	195?	25.00	50.00	100.00
RCA CAMDEN					
❑ CAL-808 [M]	Hawkshaw Hawkins Sings	1964	5.00	10.00	20.00
❑ CAS-808 [R]	Hawkshaw Hawkins Sings	1964	3.75	7.50	15.00
❑ CAL-931 [M]	The Country Gentleman	1966	5.00	10.00	20.00
❑ CAS-931 [R]	The Country Gentleman	1966	3.75	7.50	15.00

HAWKINS, RONNIE

Number	Title (A Side/B Side)	Yr	VG	VG+	NM
45s					
COTILLION					
❑ 44060	Matchbox/Down in the Alley	1970	—	3.00	6.00
❑ 44067	Forty Days/Bitter Green	1970	—	3.00	6.00
❑ 44076	Little Bird/One More Night	1970	—	3.00	6.00
MONUMENT					
❑ 8548	Lawdy Miss Clawdy/Cora Mae	1972	—	2.50	5.00
❑ 8561	Lonesome Town/Kinky	1973	—	2.50	5.00
❑ 8573	Diddley Daddy/Cora Mae	1973	—	2.50	5.00
❑ 8583	Bo Diddley/Lonely Hours	1973	—	2.50	5.00
ROULETTE					
❑ 4154 [M]	Forty Days/One of These Days	1959	6.25	12.50	25.00
❑ SSR-4154 [S]	Forty Days/One of These Days	1959	12.50	25.00	50.00
❑ 4177 [M]	Mary Lou/Need Your Lovin'	1959	7.50	15.00	30.00
❑ SSR-4177 [S]	Mary Lou/Need Your Lovin'	1959	12.50	25.00	50.00
❑ 4209	Southern Love/Love Me Like You Can	1959	5.00	10.00	20.00
❑ 4228	Lonely Hours/Clara	1960	5.00	10.00	20.00
❑ 4231	The Ballad of Caryl Chessman/The Tale of Floyd Collins	1960	5.00	10.00	20.00
❑ 4249	Ruby Baby/Hayride	1960	5.00	10.00	20.00
❑ 4267	Sumemrtime/Mister and Mississippi	1960	5.00	10.00	20.00
❑ 4311	Cold, Cold Heart/Nobody's Lonesome for Me	1960	5.00	10.00	20.00
❑ 4400	Come Love/I Feel Good	1961	5.00	10.00	20.00
❑ 4483	Bo Diddley/Who Do You Love	1963	5.00	10.00	20.00
❑ 4502	High Blood Pressure/There's a Screw Loose	1963	5.00	10.00	20.00
Albums					
ACCORD					
❑ SN-7213	Premonition	1983	2.50	5.00	10.00
COTILLION					
❑ SD 9019	Ronnie Hawkins	1970	3.75	7.50	15.00
❑ SD 9039	The Hawk	1971	3.75	7.50	15.00
MONUMENT					
❑ KZ 31330	Rock and Roll Resurrection	1972	3.00	6.00	12.00
❑ KZ 32940	The Ghost of Rock and Roll	1973	3.00	6.00	12.00
❑ ZG 33855 [(2)]	Rock and Roll Resurrection/The Ghost of Rock and Roll	1976	3.75	7.50	15.00
ROULETTE					
❑ R 25078 [M]	Ronnie Hawkins	1959	37.50	75.00	150.00
—White label with spokes					
❑ R 25078 [M]	Ronnie Hawkins	1964	12.50	25.00	50.00
—Orange/yellow label					
❑ SR 25078 [S]	Ronnie Hawkins	1959	50.00	100.00	200.00
—White label with spokes; black vinyl					
❑ SR 25078 [S]	Ronnie Hawkins	1959	150.00	300.00	600.00
—White label with spokes; red vinyl					
❑ SR 25078 [S]	Ronnie Hawkins	1964	15.00	30.00	60.00
—Orange/yellow label					
❑ R 25102 [M]	Mr. Dynamo	1960	37.50	75.00	150.00
❑ SR 25102 [S]	Mr. Dynamo	1960	50.00	100.00	200.00
—Black vinyl					
❑ SR 25102 [S]	Mr. Dynamo	1960	150.00	300.00	600.00
—Red vinyl					
❑ R 25120 [M]	The Folk Ballads of Ronnie Hawkins	1960	25.00	50.00	100.00
❑ SR 25120 [S]	The Folk Ballads of Ronnie Hawkins	1960	37.50	75.00	150.00
❑ R 25137 [M]	The Songs of Hank Williams	1960	25.00	50.00	100.00
❑ SR 25137 [S]	The Songs of Hank Williams	1960	37.50	75.00	150.00
❑ SR 42045	The Best of Ronnie Hawkins and His Band	1970	6.25	12.50	25.00
UNITED ARTISTS					
❑ UA-LA968-H	The Hawk	1979	2.50	5.00	10.00

HAWKS, MICKEY

Number	Title (A Side/B Side)	Yr	VG	VG+	NM
45s					
C-HORSE					
❑ 589	Me and My Harley-Davidson/The Good Old Days	1989	2.50	5.00	10.00

Number	Title (A Side/B Side)	Yr	VG	VG+	NM
HUNCH					
❑ 347	Hidi Hidi Hidi/(B-side unknown)	1961	25.00	50.00	100.00
PROFILE					
❑ 4002	Bip Bop Boom/Rock 'n' Roll Rhythm	1958	200.00	400.00	800.00
❑ 4007	Hidi Hidi Hidi/Cottonpickin'	1959	200.00	400.00	800.00
❑ 4010	Screamin' Mini Jeanie/I'm Lost	1959	250.00	500.00	1000.

HAYES, BILL

45s

Number	Title (A Side/B Side)	Yr	VG	VG+	NM
ABC-PARAMOUNT					
❑ 9785	Wringle, Wrangle/Westward Ho the Wagons	1957	3.00	6.00	12.00
❑ 9785 [PS]	Wringle, Wrangle/Westward Ho the Wagons	1957	5.00	10.00	20.00
❑ 9809	Ramshackle Daddy/On the Outside	1957	3.00	6.00	12.00
❑ 9895	Bop Boy/Uh Huh Oh Yeah	1958	15.00	30.00	60.00
CADENCE					
❑ 1245	I Knew an Old Lady/(B-side unknown)	1954	3.00	6.00	12.00
❑ 1256	The Ballad of Davy Crockett/Farewell	1955	3.75	7.50	15.00
❑ 1261	The Berry Tree/Blue Back Hair	1955	3.00	6.00	12.00
❑ 1274	That Do Make It Nice/Kwela Kwela	1955	3.00	6.00	12.00
❑ 1275	The Legend of Wyatt Earp/White Buffalo	1955	3.75	7.50	15.00
❑ 1294	I Knew an Old Lady/Das Ist Music	1956	3.00	6.00	12.00
❑ 1301	A Message from James Dean/The Trail's End	1956	3.75	7.50	15.00
KAPP					
❑ 258	Wimoweh/Goin' Down the Road Feelin' Bad	1959	2.50	5.00	10.00
❑ 298	Choppin' Mountains/Tall Teller of Tall Tales	1959	2.50	5.00	10.00
MERCURY					
❑ 5599	Too Young/Shenandoah Waltz	1951	5.00	10.00	20.00
MGM					
❑ 11006	Waltz of the Wind/Mine	1951	3.75	7.50	15.00
❑ 11042	The Love of a Gypsy/I've Got an Idea for a Song	1951	3.75	7.50	15.00
❑ 11064	I Love You/Never	1951	3.75	7.50	15.00
❑ 11112	Charmaine/For All We Know	1951	3.75	7.50	15.00
❑ 11142	We Won't Live in A.../Tulips and Heather	1952	3.75	7.50	15.00
❑ 11205	April Sings/Golden Haired Boy	1952	3.75	7.50	15.00
❑ 11210	When I Dream/Don't Send Me Home	1952	3.75	7.50	15.00
—With Judy Johnson					
❑ 11266	High Noon/Padam Padam	1952	3.75	7.50	15.00
❑ 11296	Say You'll Wait for Me/My Search for You	1952	3.75	7.50	15.00
❑ 11384	My Ever Lovin'/As Long As You Care	1952	3.75	7.50	15.00
❑ 11394	How Do You Speak to An Angel/The Donkey Song	1953	3.75	7.50	15.00
❑ 11492	I'm So Lonesome/There's Music in You	1953	3.75	7.50	15.00
❑ 11556	A Little Kiss Each Morning/Love You	1953	3.75	7.50	15.00
—With Judy Johnson					
❑ 12004	Wanderin'/You're Nearer	1955	3.00	6.00	12.00

Albums

Number	Title (A Side/B Side)	Yr	VG	VG+	NM
ABC-PARAMOUNT					
❑ 194 [M]	Bill Hayes Sings the Best of Disney	1957	10.00	20.00	40.00
DAYBREAK					
❑ DR-2020	The Look of Love	1972	6.25	12.50	25.00
KAPP					
❑ KL-1106 [M]	Jimmy Crack Corn	1958	6.25	12.50	25.00

HAYES, WADE

45s

Number	Title (A Side/B Side)	Yr	VG	VG+	NM
COLUMBIA					
❑ 38-77739	Old Enough to Know Better/Family Reunion	1994	—	2.00	4.00
❑ 38- 77842	I'm Still Dancin' with You/It's Gonna Take a Miracle	1995	—	—	3.00
❑ 38-77954	Don't Stop/Someone Had to Teach You	1995	—	—	3.00
❑ 38-78087	What I Meant to Say/Kentucky Bluebird	1995	—	—	3.00
❑ 38-78312	On a Good Night/Steady As She Goes	1996	—	2.00	4.00
❑ 38-78369	Where Do I Go to Start All Over/My Side of Town	1996	—	—	3.00
❑ 38-78486	It's Over My Head/Hurts Don't It	1996	—	—	3.00
❑ 38-78674	Wichita Lineman/On a Good Night	1997	—	2.00	4.00

HAZARD

45s

Number	Title (A Side/B Side)	Yr	VG	VG+	NM
WARNER BROS.					
❑ 29755	Love Letters/Island	1983	—	2.00	4.00
❑ 29914	On the Radio Tonight/You've Got That Look	1982	—	2.00	4.00

HAZARD, DONNA

45s

Number	Title (A Side/B Side)	Yr	VG	VG+	NM
EXCELSIOR					
❑ 1004	My Turn/I Don't Want to Dance with You (No More)	1980	—	2.50	5.00
❑ 1009	Go Home and Go to Pieces/(B-side unknown)	1981	—	2.50	5.00
❑ 1016	Love Never Hurt So Good/I'm Your Lady	1981	—	2.50	5.00
❑ 1020	Slow Texas Dancing/Tailwinds	1981	—	2.50	5.00

Albums

Number	Title (A Side/B Side)	Yr	VG	VG+	NM
EXCELSIOR					
❑ 88008	My Turn	1981	2.50	5.00	10.00

HEAD, ROY

45s

Number	Title (A Side/B Side)	Yr	VG	VG+	NM
ABC					
❑ 12346	How You See 'Em, Now You Don't/Smooth Whiskey	1978	—	2.00	4.00
❑ 12383	Tonight's the Night/A Lady in My Room	1978	—	2.00	4.00
❑ 12418	Dixie/Love Survived	1978	—	2.00	4.00
❑ 12462 [DJ]	Kiss You and Make It Better (mono/stereo)	1979	—	2.00	4.00
—May be promo only					
ABC DOT					
❑ 17608	Lady Luck and Mother Nature/The Door I Used to Close	1976	—	2.00	4.00
❑ 17629	Ain't It Funny (How Times Haven't Changed)/A Bridge for Crawling Back	1976	—	2.00	4.00
❑ 17650	One Night/Deep Elem Blues	1976	—	2.00	4.00
❑ 17669	Just Because/Angel with a Broken Wing	1976	—	2.00	4.00
❑ 17706	Julianne/Velvet Strings	1977	—	2.00	4.00
❑ 17722	Come to Me/Georgia on My Mind	1977	—	2.00	4.00
ABC DUNHILL					
❑ 4240	I'm Not a Fool Anymore/Mama Mama	1970	—	3.00	6.00
ATLANTIC AMERICA					
❑ 99529	There's Something on Your Mind/Everything A Man Can Do (And I Love You)	1986	—	—	3.00
AVION					
❑ 105	Where Did He Go Right/(B-side unknown)	1983	—	3.50	7.00
BACK BEAT					
❑ 543	Teenage Letter/Pain	1965	3.00	6.00	12.00
❑ 546	Treat Her Right/So Long, My Love	1965	4.00	8.00	16.00
❑ 555	Apple of My Eye/I Pass the Day	1965	3.00	6.00	12.00
❑ 560	My Babe/Pain	1966	3.00	6.00	12.00
❑ 563	Driving Wheel/Wigglin' and Gigglin'	1966	3.00	6.00	12.00
❑ 571	Don't Cry No More/To Make a Big Man Cry	1966	3.00	6.00	12.00
❑ 576	You're (Almost) Tough/Tush Hog	1966	3.00	6.00	12.00
❑ 582	Nobody But Me/A Good Man Is Hard to Find	1967	2.50	5.00	10.00
CHURCHILL					
❑ 7778	After Texas/California Day	1981	—	2.50	5.00
ELEKTRA					
❑ 46549	In Our Room/Things I Never Could Have Left Behind	1979	—	2.00	4.00
❑ 46582	The Fire of Two Old Flames/Under Suspicion	1980	—	2.00	4.00
❑ 46653	Long Drop/Gonna Save It for My Baby	1980	—	2.00	4.00
❑ 47029	Drinking Them Long Necks/Baby's Found Another Way to Love Me	1980	—	2.00	4.00
❑ 47081	I've Never Gone to Bed With an Ugly Woman/All Night Long Is Gone	1981	—	2.00	4.00
MEGA					
❑ 1219	Baby's Not Home/Do What You Can Do	1974	—	2.50	5.00
MERCURY					
❑ 72750	Got Down on Saturday (Sunday in the Rain)/The Grass Was Green	1967	2.00	4.00	8.00
❑ 72799	Broadway Walk/Turn Out the Lights	1968	2.00	4.00	8.00
❑ 72848	Ain't Goin' Down Right/Lovin' Man on Your Hands	1968	2.00	4.00	8.00
❑ 72922	I Miss You Baby/I Want Some Action	1969	2.00	4.00	8.00
NSD					
❑ 129	Play Another Gettin' Drunk and Take Somebody Home Song/Your Next One and Only	1982	—	2.50	5.00
❑ 146	The Trouble with Hearts/Naughty Smile	1982	—	2.50	5.00
❑ 156	Your Mama Don't Dance/Party Time	1982	—	2.50	5.00
SCEPTER					
❑ 12116	Just a Little Bit/Treat Me Right	1965	2.50	5.00	10.00
❑ 12117	Won't Be Blue/One More Time	1965	2.50	5.00	10.00
❑ 12124	Get Back — Part 1/Get Back — Part 2	1965	2.50	5.00	10.00
❑ 12138	Convicted/One More Time	1966	2.50	5.00	10.00
SHANNON					
❑ 829	The Most Wanted Woman in Town/Gingerbread Man	1975	—	2.50	5.00
❑ 833	Help Yourself to Me/To Make a Big Man Cry	1975	—	2.50	5.00
❑ 838	I'll Take It/The One That Got Away	1975	—	2.50	5.00
TEXAS CRUDE					
❑ 614	Break Out the Good Stuff/She Needs Time	1985	2.00	4.00	8.00
TMI					
❑ 75-0103	Rock and Roll Mood/You Got the Power	1972	—	2.50	5.00
❑ 75-0106	Why Don't We Go Somewhere and Love/Smell-A-Woman	1972	—	2.50	5.00
❑ BTBO-0111	Small Town Girl/Chug All Night	1973	—	2.50	5.00
❑ 75-0113	Carol/Clyde O'Riley	1973	—	2.50	5.00
❑ 9000	Puff of Smoke/Lord Take a Bow	1971	—	3.00	6.00
❑ 9010	Bit By Bit/Wait Till I Arrive	1972	—	3.00	6.00
TNT					
❑ 194	Don't Be Blue/One More Time	1965	3.75	7.50	15.00

Albums

Number	Title (A Side/B Side)	Yr	VG	VG+	NM
ABC					
❑ AB-1054	Tonight's the Night	1978	2.50	5.00	10.00
ABC DOT					
❑ DO-2051	Head First	1976	3.00	6.00	12.00
❑ DO-2066	A Head of His Time	1977	3.00	6.00	12.00
ABC DUNHILL					
❑ DS-50080	Same People	1970	5.00	10.00	20.00
ELEKTRA					
❑ 6E-234	In Our Room	1979	2.50	5.00	10.00
❑ 6E-298	The Many Sides of Roy Head	1980	2.50	5.00	10.00
MCA					
❑ 796	Tonight's the Night	1980	2.00	4.00	8.00
—Reissue of ABC album					
SCEPTER					
❑ S-532 [M]	Treat Me Right	1965	7.50	15.00	30.00
❑ SS-532 [S]	Treat Me Right	1965	10.00	20.00	40.00
TMI					
❑ 1000	Dismal Prisoner	1972	3.75	7.50	15.00
TNT					
❑ 101 [M]	Roy Head and the Traits	1965	37.50	75.00	150.00
—Counterfeit alert: Authentics do NOT contain the hit "Treat Her Right."					

HEAP, JIMMY

45s

CAPITOL

Number	Title (A Side/B Side)	Yr	VG	VG+	NM
❑ F1958	True or False/A Lifetime of Shame	1952	7.50	15.00	30.00
❑ F2035	You're in Love with You/Girl with a Past	1952	7.50	15.00	30.00
❑ F2142	You Don't Kiss Me/That One I Won	1952	7.50	15.00	30.00
❑ F2294	Heartbreaker/That One I Won	1952	7.50	15.00	30.00
❑ F2425	Let's Do It Just Once/This Night Won't Last Forever	1953	6.25	12.50	25.00
❑ F2518	Release Me/Just to Be with You	1953	6.25	12.50	25.00
❑ F2636	Cat'n Around/Make Me Live Again	1953	6.25	12.50	25.00
❑ F2767	Cry, Cry Darling/Then I'll Be Happy	1954	6.25	12.50	25.00
❑ F2866	Ethyl in My Gas Tank/You Oughta Know	1954	6.25	12.50	25.00
❑ F2990	Sharp Shooter/I Told You So	1954	6.25	12.50	25.00
❑ F3071	Seven Come Eleven/That's All I Want from You	1955	6.25	12.50	25.00
❑ F3156	Go Ahead On/Love Can Move Mountains	1955	6.25	12.50	25.00
❑ F3252	Rovin' Girl/Riches on Rags	1955	6.25	12.50	25.00
❑ F3253	Just for Tonight/My First Love Affair	1955	6.25	12.50	25.00
❑ F3333	Butternut/It Takes a Heap of Lovin'	1956	6.25	12.50	25.00
❑ F3434	A Heap o' Boogie/Conscience, I'm Guilty	1956	6.25	12.50	25.00
❑ F3543	This Song Is Just for You/Mingling	1956	6.25	12.50	25.00

D

Number	Title (A Side/B Side)	Yr	VG	VG+	NM
❑ 1050	Someone Else Is Filling Your Shoes/Born to Love You	1959	5.00	10.00	20.00

DART

Number	Title (A Side/B Side)	Yr	VG	VG+	NM
❑ 119	Gismo/Meanwhile	1959	3.75	7.50	15.00

FAME

Number	Title (A Side/B Side)	Yr	VG	VG+	NM
❑ 501	Alone at a Phone/I'm One of Those	196?	5.00	10.00	20.00
❑ 509	Summit Ridge Rock/Night Cap	196?	5.00	10.00	20.00
❑ 510	Wild Side of Life/Go Get 'Em	196?	5.00	10.00	20.00
❑ 511	Forever Rock/Forever Yours	196?	5.00	10.00	20.00

IMPERIAL

Number	Title (A Side/B Side)	Yr	VG	VG+	NM
❑ 8325	Wild Side of Life/When They Operated on Papa	1960	3.75	7.50	15.00

Selected 78s

IMPERIAL

Number	Title (A Side/B Side)	Yr	VG	VG+	NM
❑ 8064	That's My Baby/Today, Tonight and Tomorrow	1949	6.25	12.50	25.00
❑ 8066	Bermuda Grass Waltz/Snakes in My Boots	1950	5.00	10.00	20.00
❑ 8069	You Were Meant to Ruin My Dreams/There's a Broken Pane in the Window of My Heart	1950	5.00	10.00	20.00
❑ 8074	Mean Old Blues/Haunted Hungry Heart	1950	5.00	10.00	20.00
❑ 8077	Love for Sale/The Yegua Waltz	1950	5.00	10.00	20.00
❑ 8082	A Million Tears/If Mama Wasn't Here	1950	5.00	10.00	20.00
❑ 8084	I Hope You're Satisfied/Sunset Send a Sorrow	1950	5.00	10.00	20.00
❑ 8089	Ethyl in My Gas Tank/My Heart's Turned to Stone	1950	5.00	10.00	20.00
❑ 8090	I've Got a Cause to Be Lonesome/The Woods Are Full of Them	1950	5.00	10.00	20.00
❑ 8093	Honk Your Horn/Carbon Copy	1951	5.00	10.00	20.00
❑ 8098	Don't Steal My Dreams/It's One Thing to Forgive, Another to Forget	1951	5.00	10.00	20.00
❑ 8101	Morning, Noon and Night/A Coffee Built for Two	1951	5.00	10.00	20.00
❑ 8103	Butter Ball Bounce/Drop in the Bucket	1951	5.00	10.00	20.00
❑ 8105	Wild Side of Life/When They Operated on Papa	1951	5.00	10.00	20.00
❑ 8112	Honky Tonkin' Woman/Curtain of Tears	1951	5.00	10.00	20.00
❑ 8122	Somebody's Blues/More Than Friends	1951	5.00	10.00	20.00
❑ 8129	That's That/Till Death Do You Part	1951	5.00	10.00	20.00
❑ 8133	My Angel Isn't On My Christmas Tree/Don't Baby Your Baby	1951	5.00	10.00	20.00
❑ 8136	Easy Way Out/If Tomorrow Would Be Yesterday	1951	5.00	10.00	20.00

HEART OF NASHVILLE

Country-music equivalent of USA FOR AFRICA — an all-star group raising funds to help the hungry and homeless.

45s

COMPLEAT

Number	Title (A Side/B Side)	Yr	VG	VG+	NM
❑ 679001	One Big Family/(Instrumental)	1985	—	2.50	5.00
❑ 679001 [PS]	One Big Family/(Instrumental)	1985	—	2.50	5.00

HEARTLAND

45s

TRA-STAR

Number	Title (A Side/B Side)	Yr	VG	VG+	NM
❑ 1221	New River/Way Down	1988	—	3.00	6.00
❑ 1222	Making Love to Dixie/(B-side unknown)	1988	—	3.00	6.00
❑ 1223	Keep the Faith/(B-side unknown)	1989	—	3.00	6.00

HEATH, BOYD

Selected 78s

BLUEBIRD

Number	Title (A Side/B Side)	Yr	VG	VG+	NM
❑ 33-0522	Smoke on the Water/Dreamy Rio Grande	1945	6.25	12.50	25.00

HEATHERLY, ERIC

45s

MERCURY

Number	Title (A Side/B Side)	Yr	VG	VG+	NM
❑ 088 172152-7	Flowers on the Wall/Someone Else's Cadillac	2000	—	—	3.00
❑ 088 172176-7	Swimming in Champagne/Freedom Chain	2000	—	—	3.00
❑ 088 172191-7	Wrong Five O'Clock/WhyDon'tCha	2000	—	—	3.00

HEAVENER, DAVID

45s

BRENT

Number	Title (A Side/B Side)	Yr	VG	VG+	NM
❑ 1017	Cheat on Him Tonight/Please Help Me Lord	1981	—	2.50	5.00
❑ 1019	Honky Tonk Tonight/Jesus Is Coming to Town	1982	—	2.50	5.00
❑ 1020	I Am the Fire/(B-side unknown)	1982	—	2.50	5.00

HECKEL, BEVERLY

Also see THE HECKELS.

45s

RCA

Number	Title (A Side/B Side)	Yr	VG	VG+	NM
❑ PB-10981	Don't Hand Me No Hand Me Down Love/Halfway to Paradise	1977	—	2.00	4.00
❑ PB-11161	I'm Not Blind/Room Without a Door	1977	—	2.00	4.00
❑ PB-11237	Borrowing/Living Without	1978	—	2.00	4.00
❑ PB-11360	Bluer Than Blue/Living Without	1978	—	2.00	4.00

HECKELS, THE

Also see BEVERLY HECKEL.

45s

RCA VICTOR

Number	Title (A Side/B Side)	Yr	VG	VG+	NM
❑ PB-10685	A Cowboy Like You/The Devil's Way of Tempting Me	1976	—	2.00	4.00

HELMS, BOBBY

45s

CAPITOL

Number	Title (A Side/B Side)	Yr	VG	VG+	NM
❑ 3003	The Only Thing That Matters/Just Hold My Hand and Sing	1970	2.00	4.00	8.00

CERTRON

Number	Title (A Side/B Side)	Yr	VG	VG+	NM
❑ 10002	Mary Goes 'Round/Cold Winds Blow on Me	1970	2.00	4.00	8.00
❑ 10021	Jingle Bell Rock/The Old Year Is Gone	1970	2.00	4.00	8.00
❑ 10023	I Wouldn't Take the World for You/Look What You've Done	1970	2.00	4.00	8.00

COLUMBIA

Number	Title (A Side/B Side)	Yr	VG	VG+	NM
❑ 4-42801	Fraulein/My Special Angel	1963	2.50	5.00	10.00
❑ 4-43031	It's a Girl/Put Your Arms Around Him	1964	2.50	5.00	10.00

DECCA

Number	Title (A Side/B Side)	Yr	VG	VG+	NM
❑ 9-29947	Tennessee Rock 'N' Roll/I Don't Owe You Nothing	1956	12.50	25.00	50.00
❑ 9-30194	Fraulein/(Got a) Heartsick Feeling	1957	5.00	10.00	20.00
❑ 9-30194 [PS]	Fraulein/(Got a) Heartsick Feeling	1957	12.50	25.00	50.00
❑ 9-30423	My Special Angel/Standing at the End of My World	1957	6.25	12.50	25.00
❑ 9-30513	Jingle Bell Rock/Captain Santa Claus	1957	6.25	12.50	25.00
—Black label with star					
❑ 9-30513	Jingle Bell Rock/Captain Santa Claus	1960	3.00	6.00	12.00
—Black label with color bars					
❑ 9-30513 [PS]	Jingle Bell Rock/Captain Santa Claus	1957	12.50	25.00	50.00
❑ 9-30557	Just a Little Lonesome/Love My Baby	1958	5.00	10.00	20.00
❑ 9-30619	Jacqueline/Living in the Shadow of the Past	1958	5.00	10.00	20.00
❑ 9-30682	Schoolboy Crush/Borrowed Dreams	1958	5.00	10.00	20.00
❑ 9-30749	A Hundred Hearts/The Fool and the Angel	1958	5.00	10.00	20.00
❑ 9-30831	New River Train/Miss Memory	1959	3.75	7.50	15.00
❑ 9-30886	Soon It Can Be Told/I Guess I'll Miss the Prom	1959	3.75	7.50	15.00
❑ 9-30928	No Other Baby/You're No Longer Mine	1959	3.75	7.50	15.00
❑ 9-30976	My Lucky Day/Hurry Baby	1959	3.75	7.50	15.00
❑ 9-31041	To My Sorrow/Someone Was Already There	1960	3.75	7.50	15.00
❑ 31103	Let Me Be the One/I Wanna Be with You	1960	3.75	7.50	15.00
❑ 31148	Lonely River Rhine/Guess We Thought the World Would End	1960	3.75	7.50	15.00
❑ 31230	Sad-Eyed Baby/You're the One	1961	3.00	6.00	12.00
❑ 31287	How Can You Divide a Little Child/My Greatest Weakness	1961	3.00	6.00	12.00
❑ 31356	One Deep Love/Once in a Lifetime	1962	3.00	6.00	12.00
❑ 31403	Then Came You/Yesterday's Champagne	1962	3.00	6.00	12.00

GUSTO

Number	Title (A Side/B Side)	Yr	VG	VG+	NM
❑ 116	That Heart Belongs to Me/With Jenny on My Mind	1974	—	3.00	6.00
❑ 119	Work Things Out with Annie/With Jenny on My Mind	1974	—	3.00	6.00

KAPP

Number	Title (A Side/B Side)	Yr	VG	VG+	NM
❑ 708	I'm the Man/Have This Love on Me	1965	2.50	5.00	10.00
❑ 719	Jingle Bell Rock/The Bell That Couldn't Jingle	1965	3.00	6.00	12.00
❑ 732	Those Snowy Glowy Blowy Days of Winter/Sailor	1965	2.50	5.00	10.00
❑ 777	The Things I Remember Most/Sorry, My Name Isn't Fred	1966	2.50	5.00	10.00
❑ 876	I Miss My Fraulein/Where Does a Shadow Go	1967	2.00	4.00	8.00

LITTLE DARLIN'

Number	Title (A Side/B Side)	Yr	VG	VG+	NM
❑ 0030	He Thought He'd Die Laughing/You'd Better Make Up Your Mind	1967	2.50	5.00	10.00
❑ 0034	The Day You Stop Loving Me/You Can Tell the World	1967	2.50	5.00	10.00
❑ 0038	Jingle Bell Rock/I Wanta Go to Santa Claus Land	1967	3.00	6.00	12.00
❑ 0041	I Feel You, I Love You/The Day You Stop Loving Me	1968	2.50	5.00	10.00
❑ 0049	Or Is It Love/Touch My Heart	1968	2.50	5.00	10.00
❑ 0054	My Special Angel/Expressing My Love	1968	2.50	5.00	10.00
❑ 0062	So Long/Just Do the Best You Can	1969	2.50	5.00	10.00
❑ 0073	Echoes and Shadows/Step Into My Soul	1969	2.50	5.00	10.00
❑ 7801	I'm Gonna Love the Devil Out of You/I Can't Promise You	1978	—	3.00	6.00
❑ 7807	The Things I Remember Most/I'm Not Sorry	1978	—	3.00	6.00
❑ 7809	Jingle Bell Rock/I Wanta Go to Santa Claus Land	1978	—	3.00	6.00
❑ 7916	One More Dollar for the Band/Touch My Heart	1979	—	3.00	6.00

MCA

Number	Title (A Side/B Side)	Yr	VG	VG+	NM
❑ 65026	Jingle Bell Rock/Captain Santa Claus	1973	—	2.50	5.00
—Black label with rainbow					
❑ 65026	Jingle Bell Rock/Captain Santa Claus	1980	—	—	3.00
—Blue label with rainbow					
❑ 65029	Jingle Bell Rock/The Bell That Couldn't Jingle	1973	—	2.50	5.00
—Black label with rainbow; this contains the 1965 Kapp re-recording of the A-side					
❑ 65029	Jingle Bell Rock/The Bell That Couldn't Jingle	1980	—	—	3.00
—Blue label with rainbow					

Number	Title (A Side/B Side)	Yr	VG	VG+	NM
MILLION					
❑ 5	It's the Little Things/Love's Sweet Mystery	1972	—	3.50	7.00
❑ 22	It's Starting to Rain Again/Wouldn't Give Up on You	1972	—	3.50	7.00
MISTLETOE					
❑ 802	Jingle Bell Rock/Jingle Bells	197?	—	2.50	5.00
❑ 802 [PS]	Jingle Bell Rock/Jingle Bells	197?	2.00	4.00	8.00
PLAYBACK					
❑ 1305	Lay Me Down Look/Dance with Me	1988	—	3.00	6.00
❑ 1322	Somebody Wrong Is Looking Right/This Song for You	1988	—	3.00	6.00
❑ 1328	Southern Belle/Troubles Wall to Wall	1989	—	3.00	6.00
❑ 75709	Southern Belle/Troubles Wall to Wall	1989	—	2.50	5.00
SPEED					
❑ 45-114	Yesterday's Lovin'/Hanging Around	1957	7.50	15.00	30.00
7-Inch Extended Plays					
DECCA					
❑ ED 2555	If Only I Knew/Far Away Heart//My Shoes Keep Walking Back to You/Sugar Moon	1957	5.00	10.00	20.00
❑ ED 2555 [PS]	(title unknown)	1957	5.00	10.00	20.00
❑ ED 2586	Plaything/Magic Song//Tonight's the Night/Just a Little Lonesome	1957	5.00	10.00	20.00
❑ ED 2586 [PS]	Tonight's the Night	1957	5.00	10.00	20.00
❑ ED 2629	Jacqueline/My Special Angel//Borrowed Dreams/Schoolboy Crush	1957	5.00	10.00	20.00
❑ ED 2629 [PS]	Bobby Helms	1957	5.00	10.00	20.00
Albums					
COLUMBIA					
❑ CL 2060 [M]	The Best of Bobby Helms	1963	6.25	12.50	25.00
❑ CS 8860 [S]	The Best of Bobby Helms	1963	7.50	15.00	30.00
DECCA					
❑ DL 8638 [M]	Bobby Helms Sings to My Special Angel	1957	30.00	60.00	120.00
HARMONY					
❑ HL 7409 [M]	Fraulein	1967	3.00	6.00	12.00
❑ HS 11209 [S]	Fraulein	1967	3.00	6.00	12.00
KAPP					
❑ KL 1463 [M]	I'm the Man	1966	3.75	7.50	15.00
❑ KL 1505 [M]	Sorry My Name Isn't Fred	1966	3.75	7.50	15.00
❑ KS 3463 [S]	I'm the Man	1966	5.00	10.00	20.00
❑ KS 3505 [S]	Sorry My Name Isn't Fred	1966	5.00	10.00	20.00
LITTLE DARLIN'					
❑ 8088	All New Just for You	1968	6.25	12.50	25.00
MISTLETOE					
❑ MLP-1206	Jingle Bell Rock	197?	3.00	6.00	12.00
POWER PAK					
❑ 283	Greatest Hits	197?	2.50	5.00	10.00
VOCALION					
❑ VL 3743 [M]	Someone Already There	1965	3.75	7.50	15.00
❑ VL 73743 [R]	Someone Already There	1965	3.00	6.00	12.00
❑ VL 73874	My Special Angel	1969	3.00	6.00	12.00

HELMS, DORI

45s

Number	Title (A Side/B Side)	Yr	VG	VG+	NM
LITTLE DARLIN'					
❑ 0029	Ruby's Answer/I'll Keep Them Laughing	1967	2.50	5.00	10.00
❑ 0058	Neglected/A Touch of Yesterday	1969	2.50	5.00	10.00

HENDERSON, BRICE

45s

Number	Title (A Side/B Side)	Yr	VG	VG+	NM
UNION STATION					
❑ 1000	Lonely Eyes/She Still Has That Hold on Me	1982	—	3.00	6.00
❑ 1001	Lovers Again/She Still Has That Hold on Me	1983	—	3.00	6.00
❑ 1003	Flames/Crossing the Love Line	1983	—	3.00	6.00

HENDERSON, MIKE

45s

Number	Title (A Side/B Side)	Yr	VG	VG+	NM
RCA					
❑ 62730	Hillbilly Jitters/That Train Don't Stop Here Anymore	1994	—	—	3.00
❑ 62831	The Want To/Wishful Thinkin'	1994	—	—	3.00
❑ 62939	If the Jukebox Took Teardrops/Country Music Made Me Do It	1994	—	2.00	4.00

HENHOUSE FIVE PLUS TOO

See RAY STEVENS.

HENRY, AUDIE

45s

Number	Title (A Side/B Side)	Yr	VG	VG+	NM
CANYON CREEK					
❑ 2008	Being a Fool Again/(B-side unknown)	1985	—	2.50	5.00
❑ 2025	You'll Never Find a Good Man (Playing in a Country Band)/(B-side unknown)	1984	—	2.50	5.00
❑ 5020	Heaven Knows/I Knew the First Time I Saw You	1985	—	2.50	5.00
❑ 8019	Sweet Salvation/A Step in the Right Direction	1985	—	2.50	5.00

HENSLEY, TARI

45s

Number	Title (A Side/B Side)	Yr	VG	VG+	NM
MERCURY					
❑ 76197	Falling in Love/Down to My Last Time	1982	—	2.00	4.00
❑ 814431-7	Once the Fire Is Gone/I'll Take Your Love Anytime	1983	—	—	3.00
❑ 880054-7	Love Isn't Love ('Til You Give It Away)/Sweet Nights	1984	—	—	3.00
❑ 880424-7	I'm the One Who's Breaking Up/It's the Nights That Drive Me Crazy	1984	—	—	3.00
❑ 880801-7	Hard Baby to Rock/Down to My Last Time	1985	—	—	3.00
❑ 884484-7	Oh Yes I Can/Sweet Nights	1986	—	—	3.00
❑ 884852-7	I've Cried a Mile/We Can't Communicate	1986	—	—	3.00

HERNDON, TY

45s

Number	Title (A Side/B Side)	Yr	VG	VG+	NM
EPIC					
❑ 34-77843	What Mattered Most/You Don't Mess Around with Jim	1995	—	2.00	4.00
❑ 34-77946	I Want My Goodbye Back/Heart Half Empty	1995	—	—	3.00
❑ 34-78073	Heart Half Empty/Love at 90 Miles an Hour	1995	—	—	3.00
❑ 34-78247	In Your Face/What Mattered Most	1996	—	—	3.00
❑ 34-78364	Living in a Moment/Returning the Faith	1996	—	2.00	4.00
❑ 34-78482	She Wants to Be Wanted Again/Before There Was You	1996	—	—	3.00
❑ 34-79049	It Must Be Love/A Man Holdin' On (To a Woman Lettin' Go)	1998	—	—	3.00
❑ 34-79345	No Mercy/Steam	2000	—	—	3.00

HERRING, RED

45s

Number	Title (A Side/B Side)	Yr	VG	VG+	NM
COUNTRY JUBILEE					
❑ 533	Wasted Love/(B-side unknown)	1960	5.00	10.00	20.00

HESTER, HOOT

45s

Number	Title (A Side/B Side)	Yr	VG	VG+	NM
LITTLE DARLIN'					
❑ 7911	I Still Love Her Memory/Forever Ended Yesterday	1979	—	3.50	7.00
❑ 7920	If You're Gonna Love You Gotta Hurt/Gotta Honky Tonk Woman	1979	—	3.50	7.00

HEWITT, DOLPH

45s

Number	Title (A Side/B Side)	Yr	VG	VG+	NM
JANIE					
❑ 45-1/2	You're the Keeper of My Heart/There's Somebody Else on Your Mind	195?	6.25	12.50	25.00
—number may be 7593					
❑ 455	Last Night Was the End of My World/Autumn Love	1959	6.25	12.50	25.00
❑ 460	If You Are Present at Christmas/Look Into Your Heart	1959	6.25	12.50	25.00
❑ 461	Half a Chance/Look Into Your Heart	1960	6.25	12.50	25.00
RCA VICTOR					
❑ 48-0107	I Wish I Knew/I Would Send You Roses	1949	10.00	20.00	40.00
—Originals on green vinyl					
❑ 48-0162	Waltzing My Blues Away/Check My Heart	1950	10.00	20.00	40.00
—Originals on green vinyl					
❑ 48-0311	When a Dream Is Broken Into/An Empty Promise	1950	7.50	15.00	30.00
—Originals on green vinyl					
❑ 48-0369	I Hurt Inside/For Every Kiss	1950	7.50	15.00	30.00
—Originals on green vinyl					
❑ 48-0416	You Gave Me Back My Ring/End of the Rainbow	1951	7.50	15.00	30.00
❑ 48-0462	Don't Tell Me Goodbye/Tear Drops on the Roses	1951	7.50	15.00	30.00

HICKEY, SARA "HONEYBEAR"

45s

Number	Title (A Side/B Side)	Yr	VG	VG+	NM
PCM					
❑ 203	This Ain't Tennessee and He Ain't You/(B-side unknown)	1983	2.00	4.00	8.00

HICKS, JEANETTE

Also see GEORGE JONES.

45s

Number	Title (A Side/B Side)	Yr	VG	VG+	NM
COLUMBIA					
❑ 4-21064	No Wild Side of Life/Pick Up Blues	1953	7.50	15.00	30.00
❑ 4-21135	I Swear/Too Late To	1953	6.25	12.50	25.00
❑ 4-21177	You All Come/Sippin' Cider	1953	6.25	12.50	25.00
❑ 4-21240	Nueve Laredo/Hey Now Honey	1954	6.25	12.50	25.00
❑ 4-21374	Just Like in the Movies/Such a Wonderful Feeling	1955	6.25	12.50	25.00
OKEH					
❑ 18008	I Think of You/Still I Lost You	195?	6.25	12.50	25.00
❑ 18021	He Knows Why/All I Care About	195?	6.25	12.50	25.00
❑ 18055	Lipstick on a Glass/Kingless Hand	195?	6.25	12.50	25.00
STARDAY					
❑ 271	Extra Extra/Cry, Cry, It's Good for You	1956	5.00	10.00	20.00

HICKS, LANEY

See LANEY SMALLWOOD.

HIGGINS, BERTIE

45s

Number	Title (A Side/B Side)	Yr	VG	VG+	NM
CBS ASSOCIATED					
❑ ZS4-05465	The Wall/(B-side unknown)	1985	—	2.00	4.00
KAT FAMILY					
❑ WS9-02524	Key Largo/White Line Fever	1981	—	2.00	4.00
❑ ZS5-02839	Just Another Day in Paradise/She's Going to Live on the Mountain	1982	—	2.00	4.00
❑ ZS5-03066	The Heart Is the Hunter/Port o' Call	1982	—	2.00	4.00
❑ ZS5-03256	Casablanca/She's Gone to Live on the Mountain	1982	—	2.00	4.00
❑ ZS4-03782	Tokyo Joe/Beneath the Island Lights	1983	—	2.00	4.00
❑ ZS4-03869	Only Yesterday/Pirates and Poets	1983	—	2.00	4.00
❑ ZS4-04164	When You Fall in Love/Beneath the Island Light	1983	—	2.00	4.00

SOUTHERN TRACKS

Number	Title (A Side/B Side)	Yr	VG	VG+	NM
❑ 1056	Gone with the Wind/Cannonball	1986	—	2.50	5.00
❑ 1084	Don't Show Me Your Memories Again/Florida	1988	—	2.50	5.00
❑ 2000	You Blossom Me/Florida	1988	—	2.50	5.00
❑ 2005	Homeless People/Cannonball	1988	—	2.50	5.00
❑ 2010	Leah/Key Largo	1989	2.00	4.00	8.00

—A-side with Roy Orbison

Number	Title (A Side/B Side)	Yr	VG	VG+	NM
❑ 2015	Miami Moon/Back to the Island	1989	—	2.50	5.00

Albums

KAT FAMILY

Number	Title (A Side/B Side)	Yr	VG	VG+	NM
❑ FZ 37901	Just Another Day in Paradise	1982	2.50	5.00	10.00
❑ PZ 37901	Just Another Day in Paradise	198?	2.00	4.00	8.00

—Budget-line reissue with new prefix

Number	Title (A Side/B Side)	Yr	VG	VG+	NM
❑ FZ 38587	Pirates and Poets	1983	2.50	5.00	10.00

HIGHFILL, GEORGE

45s

WARNER BROS.

Number	Title (A Side/B Side)	Yr	VG	VG+	NM
❑ 7-28177	Mad Money/Nickels and Dimes	1987	—	—	3.00
❑ 7-28312	Waitin' Up/West Texas	1987	—	—	3.00

Albums

WARNER BROS.

Number	Title (A Side/B Side)	Yr	VG	VG+	NM
❑ 25618	Waitin' Up	1987	3.00	6.00	12.00

HIGHWAY 101

Also see PAULETTE CARLSON.

45s

LIBERTY

Number	Title (A Side/B Side)	Yr	VG	VG+	NM
❑ S7-17497	You Baby You/You Are What You Do	1993	—	2.00	4.00

WARNER BROS.

Number	Title (A Side/B Side)	Yr	VG	VG+	NM
❑ PRO-S-2872 [DJ]	It Came Upon a Midnight Clear/Light of the Stable	1987	2.50	5.00	10.00

—B-side by Emmylou Harris

Number	Title (A Side/B Side)	Yr	VG	VG+	NM
❑ 7-18878	Honky Tonk Baby/Storm of Love	1992	—	2.00	4.00
❑ 7-19043	Baby, I'm Missing You/Desperate	1991	—	2.00	4.00
❑ 7-19203	The Blame/River of Tears	1991	—	2.00	4.00
❑ 7-19346	Bing Bang Boom/Baby I'm Missing You	1991	—	2.00	4.00
❑ 7-19593	Someone Else's Trouble Now/The Bed You Made for Me	1990	—	2.00	4.00
❑ 7-19829	This Side of Goodbye/If Love Had a Heart	1990	—	2.00	4.00
❑ 7-19968	Walkin', Talkin', Cryin', Barely Beatin' Broken Heart/Sweet Baby James	1990	—	—	3.00
❑ 7-22779	Who's Lonely Now/Don't It Make Your Mama Cry	1989	—	—	3.00
❑ 7-22955	Honky Tonk Heart/Desperate Road	1989	—	—	3.00
❑ 7-27581	Setting Me Up/Long Way Down	1989	—	—	3.00
❑ 7-27735	All the Reasons Why/Higher Ground	1988	—	—	3.00
❑ 7-27867	(Do You Love Me) Just Say Yes/I'll Be Missing You	1988	—	—	3.00
❑ 7-27867 [PS]	(Do You Love Me) Just Say Yes/I'll Be Missing You	1988	—	2.00	4.00
❑ 7-28105	Cry, Cry, Cry/One Step Closer	1988	—	—	3.00
❑ 7-28105 [PS]	Cry, Cry, Cry/One Step Closer	1988	—	2.00	4.00
❑ 7-28223	Somewhere Tonight/Are You Still Mine	1987	—	—	3.00
❑ 7-28223 [PS]	Somewhere Tonight/Are You Still Mine	1987	—	2.00	4.00
❑ 7-28372	Whiskey, If You Were a Woman/I'll Take You (Heartache and All)	1987	—	—	3.00
❑ 7-28483	The Bed You Made for Me/I'm Gonna Run Through the Wind	1986	—	—	3.00
❑ 7-28646	Some Find Love/What a Lonely Night Can Be	1986	—	2.00	4.00

Albums

WARNER BROS.

Number	Title (A Side/B Side)	Yr	VG	VG+	NM
❑ 1P 8076	Greatest Hits	1990	3.75	7.50	15.00

—Columbia House edition (no regular vinyl version)

Number	Title (A Side/B Side)	Yr	VG	VG+	NM
❑ 25608	Highway 101	1987	2.00	4.00	8.00
❑ 25742	101 (2)	1988	2.00	4.00	8.00
❑ 25992	Paint the Town	1989	2.50	5.00	10.00
❑ R 183480	Greatest Hits	1990	5.00	10.00	20.00

—BMG Direct Marketing edition (no regular vinyl version)

HIGHWAYMEN, THE (2)

See JOHNNY CASH; WAYLON JENNINGS; KRIS KRISTOFFERSON; WILLIE NELSON.

HILKA AND JEBRY

Also see JEBRY LEE BRILEY.

45s

IBC

Number	Title (A Side/B Side)	Yr	VG	VG+	NM
❑ 0004	I Just Wonder Where He Could Be Tonight/(And) Robin Danced	1979	—	3.00	6.00
❑ 0006	(I'm Just the) Cuddle Up Kind/Here Comes the Dawn	1979	—	2.50	5.00

—As "Hilka"

HILL, EDDIE

45s

COLUMBIA

Number	Title (A Side/B Side)	Yr	VG	VG+	NM
❑ 4-21556	I'm Worried/Unredeemed Diamonds	1956	6.25	12.50	25.00
❑ 4-40829	I'm Gonna Be a Loser Again/I Cried in My Dream Last Night	1957	5.00	10.00	20.00

MERCURY

Number	Title (A Side/B Side)	Yr	VG	VG+	NM
❑ 6347	The Hot Guitar/Steamboat Stomp	1951	7.50	15.00	30.00
❑ 6375	Cold, Cold Woman/Educated Fool	1952	7.50	15.00	30.00
❑ 6383	Stolen Love/Salty Dog Rag	1952	7.50	15.00	30.00
❑ 6392	Baby My Heart/Mountain Jam	1952	7.50	15.00	30.00
❑ 6410	Fire Ball Eight/A Full Time Job	1952	7.50	15.00	30.00
❑ 70142	Live While You're Young, Dream When You're Old/Buckshot	1953	6.25	12.50	25.00
❑ 70195	Hit and Run Lover/High, Wide and Handsome	1953	6.25	12.50	25.00

RCA VICTOR

Number	Title (A Side/B Side)	Yr	VG	VG+	NM
❑ 47-5641	I Changed My Mind/Presswood the Giant Killer	1954	6.25	12.50	25.00
❑ 47-5642	Who Wrote That Letter to Old John/Lovin' Spree	1954	6.25	12.50	25.00
❑ 47-5706	My Sugar Booger/Slender, Tender and Sweet	1954	6.25	12.50	25.00
❑ 47-5809	Same Old Dream (About You)/Whittlin' on a Piece of Wood	1954	6.25	12.50	25.00
❑ 47-5893	I Did, It Does and I Do/Knock It Off	1954	6.25	12.50	25.00
❑ 47-5978	The Gottalotta Song/I Don't Think I'm Gonna Like It	1955	6.25	12.50	25.00
❑ 47-6136	Smack Dab in the Middle/'Cause I Have You	1955	6.25	12.50	25.00
❑ 47-6279	Black Denim Trousers and Motorcycle Boots/Someday You'll Call My Name	1955	6.25	12.50	25.00

HILL, FAITH

Also see TIM McGRAW.

45s

WARNER BROS.

Number	Title (A Side/B Side)	Yr	VG	VG+	NM
❑ 7-16792	Let's Make Love/There Will Come a Day	2000	—	—	3.00

—A-side with Tim McGraw

Number	Title (A Side/B Side)	Yr	VG	VG+	NM
❑ 7-16818	The Way You Love Me/Never Gonna Be Your Lady	2000	—	—	3.00
❑ 7-16884	Breathe/It All Comes Down to Love	2000	—	2.00	4.00
❑ 7-17247	This Kiss/Better Days	1998	—	2.00	4.00
❑ 7-17531	I Can't Do That Anymore/Take Me As I Am	1996	—	2.00	4.00
❑ 7-17718	It Matters to Me/Keep Walkin' On	1995	—	2.00	4.00
❑ 7-17817	Let's Go to Vegas/You Will Be Mine	1995	—	2.00	4.00
❑ 7-18179	But I Will/Love's Too Short to Love Like That	1994	—	—	3.00
❑ 7-18261	Piece of My Heart/I Would Be Stronger Than That	1994	—	2.00	4.00
❑ 7-18411	Wild One/Go the Distance	1993	—	2.00	4.00

HILL, GOLDIE

Also see RED SOVINE; JUSTIN TUBB.

45s

DECCA

Number	Title (A Side/B Side)	Yr	VG	VG+	NM
❑ 9-28355	Don't Send No More Roses/Why Talk to My Heart	1952	6.25	12.50	25.00
❑ 9-28473	I Let the Stars Get In My Eyes/Waiting for a Letter	1952	6.25	12.50	25.00
❑ 9-28685	I'm Yvonne (On the Bayou)/Say Big Boy	1953	6.25	12.50	25.00
❑ 9-28769	I'm the Loneliest Gal in Town/My Love Is Aflame	1953	6.25	12.50	25.00
❑ 9-28898	I'm Yesterday's Girl/Let Me Be the One	1953	6.25	12.50	25.00
❑ 9-29045	Liquor and Women/Am I Still Your Baby	1954	5.00	10.00	20.00
❑ 9-29069	Make Love to Me/Young Heart	1954	5.00	10.00	20.00
❑ 9-29161	Cry, Cry Darling/Call Off the Wedding	1954	5.00	10.00	20.00
❑ 9-29224	Please Don't Betray Me/Treat Me Kind	1954	5.00	10.00	20.00
❑ 9-29602	Ain't Gonna Wash My Face/Why Don't You Let Me Go	1955	5.00	10.00	20.00
❑ 9-29771	Second Chance/Steel Guitar	1956	5.00	10.00	20.00
❑ 9-29955	Sample My Kissin'/I'm Beginning to Feel Mistreated	1956	5.00	10.00	20.00
❑ 9-30142	Footsteps/New Names, New Faces	1956	5.00	10.00	20.00
❑ 9-30290	A Wasted Love Affair/Cleanin' House	1957	3.75	7.50	15.00
❑ 9-30460	It's Only a Matter of Time/Till I Said It to You	1957	3.75	7.50	15.00
❑ 9-30826	Yankee, Go Home/What's Happened to Us	1959	3.75	7.50	15.00
❑ 9-30918	Honky Tonk Hill/It's Here to Stay	1959	3.75	7.50	15.00
❑ 9-31083	Living Alone/Twice As Blue	1960	3.75	7.50	15.00
❑ 31172	Baby Blue/Your Love Came Into My Heart	1960	3.75	7.50	15.00
❑ 31221	It's a Lovely, Lovely World/Loved and Lost	1961	3.75	7.50	15.00
❑ 31261	Lonely Heartaches/I'm the One Who Loves You	1961	3.75	7.50	15.00
❑ 31342	Many Lies Ago/Live for Tomorrow	1961	3.75	7.50	15.00
❑ 31389	I'm Afraid/Door Step to Heaven	1962	3.00	6.00	12.00
❑ 31434	Little Boy Blue/Come Back to Me	1962	3.00	6.00	12.00
❑ 31466	Baby Go Slow/Pretending I'm a Fool	1963	3.00	6.00	12.00
❑ 31496	If I Could Hold Back the Dawn/I'm Gonna Bring You Down	1963	3.00	6.00	12.00
❑ 31535	Closer/Still Wanting You	1963	3.00	6.00	12.00
❑ 31620	Put Yourself in My Place/Don't Let Him	1964	3.00	6.00	12.00
❑ 31675	Three's a Crowd/You're Free to Go	1964	3.00	6.00	12.00

EPIC

Number	Title (A Side/B Side)	Yr	VG	VG+	NM
❑ 5-10245	There's Gotta Be More to Life (Than Loving a Man)/Almost Enough	1967	2.50	5.00	10.00

—As "Goldie Hill Smith"

Number	Title (A Side/B Side)	Yr	VG	VG+	NM
❑ 5-10296	Lovable Fool/Making Plans	1968	2.50	5.00	10.00

—As "Goldie Hill Smith"

Number	Title (A Side/B Side)	Yr	VG	VG+	NM
❑ 5-10423	Got Me Sumpin' Goin'/Tell It to Your Lonely Walls	1968	2.50	5.00	10.00

—As "Goldie Hill Smith"

Albums

DECCA

Number	Title (A Side/B Side)	Yr	VG	VG+	NM
❑ DL 4034 [M]	Goldie Hill	1960	6.25	12.50	25.00
❑ DL 4148 [M]	Lonely Heartaches	1961	5.00	10.00	20.00
❑ DL 4219 [M]	According to My Heart	1962	5.00	10.00	20.00
❑ DL 4492 [M]	Country Hit Parade	1964	5.00	10.00	20.00
❑ DL 74034 [S]	Goldie Hill	1960	7.50	15.00	30.00
❑ DL 74148 [S]	Lonely Heartaches	1961	6.25	12.50	25.00
❑ DL 74219 [S]	According to My Heart	1962	6.25	12.50	25.00
❑ DL 74492 [S]	Country Hit Parade	1964	6.25	12.50	25.00

HILL, KIM

45s

BNA

Number	Title (A Side/B Side)	Yr	VG	VG+	NM
❑ 62768	Janie's Gone Fishin'/Natural Thing	1994	—	—	3.00
❑ 62871	Wise Beyond Her Tears/When We're Home	1994	—	—	3.00

HILL, TINY

45s

MERCURY

Number	Title (A Side/B Side)	Yr	VG	VG+	NM
❑ 5508	I'll Sail My Ship Alone/Back in Your Own Back Yard	1950	7.50	15.00	30.00
❑ 5524	I'm Moving On/Just a Girl That Men Forget	1950	7.50	15.00	30.00
❑ 5543	Don't Make Love to Me/Everybody Loves That Hadocol	1950	7.50	15.00	30.00
❑ 5546	Handcuffed to Love/(B-side unknown)	1950	7.50	15.00	30.00
❑ 5547	Hot Rod Race/Lovebug Itch	1950	7.50	15.00	30.00
❑ 5552	Mocking Bird Hill/If You've Got the Money (I've Got the Time)	1950	7.50	15.00	30.00
❑ 5557	Country Wedding Day/Melanae in "F"	1950	7.50	15.00	30.00
❑ 5582	Old Fashioned Love/Stingy	1951	6.25	12.50	25.00
❑ 5598	Hot Rod Race #2/Let's Live a Little	1951	7.50	15.00	30.00
❑ 5605	Please Don't Talk About Me When I'm Gone/You're a Sweetheart	1951	6.25	12.50	25.00
❑ 5635	Pick Up Truck/Two Letters	1951	6.25	12.50	25.00
❑ 5664	Take Back Your Paper Heart/Three Handed Woman	1951	6.25	12.50	25.00
❑ 5691	Dancing My Fanny Around/How'm I Doin'	1951	6.25	12.50	25.00
❑ 5726	Battle with the Bottle/Something I Et	1951	6.25	12.50	25.00
❑ 5740	Slow Poke/Don't Put a Tax on Love	1951	6.25	12.50	25.00
❑ 5765	Find 'Em — Fool 'Em/Cryin'	1951	6.25	12.50	25.00
❑ 5789	Milk Bucket Boogie/Silver and Gold	1952	6.25	12.50	25.00
❑ 5830	The Wild Side of Life/Just Lookin'	1952	6.25	12.50	25.00
❑ 5840	Busybody/Diesel Smoke, Dangerous Curves	1952	6.25	12.50	25.00
❑ 5876	Omaha/After I Say I'm Sorry	1952	6.25	12.50	25.00
❑ 70005	It's Enough to Make a Preacher Cuss/That's Where I Came In	1952	5.00	10.00	20.00
❑ 70029	Move It On Over/Five Foot Two	1953	5.00	10.00	20.00
❑ 70079	Dew Dew Dewy Day/I'm Alone Because I Love You	1953	5.00	10.00	20.00
❑ 70249	Two Ton Tessie/Don't Bring Lulu	1953	5.00	10.00	20.00
❑ 70395	Don't Do It Darling/On the Uppermost Branch	1954	5.00	10.00	20.00
❑ 70448	I Get the Blues/Someday You'll Be Sorry	1954	5.00	10.00	20.00

Selected 78s

MERCURY

Number	Title (A Side/B Side)	Yr	VG	VG+	NM
❑ 2024	Sioux City Sue/I'll Keep On Lovin' You	1945	5.00	10.00	20.00
❑ 5163	That Silver Haired Daddy of Mine/Your Key Don't Fit My Lock Anymore	1948	3.75	7.50	15.00
❑ 5205	You're Just a Butterfly/I Don't Care What You	1948	3.75	7.50	15.00
❑ 5277	I Don't Care/Never Knew I'd Be So Blue	1949	3.75	7.50	15.00
❑ 5308	Ain't She Sweet/Me, Myself and I	1949	3.75	7.50	15.00
❑ 5375	Tuck Me to Sleep/It Serves You Right	1950	3.75	7.50	15.00
❑ 6001	Angry/He's Coming Home to Stay	1946	5.00	10.00	20.00
❑ 6007	I Can Read Between the Lines/Lips That Touch Liquor Shall Never Touch Mine	194?	5.00	10.00	20.00
❑ 6011	The Darling Song/I Had Someone Else	194?	5.00	10.00	20.00
❑ 6022	I Need Lovin'/Pretty Baby	194?	5.00	10.00	20.00
❑ 6027	Somebody Stole My Gal/Ain'tcha Tired	194?	5.00	10.00	20.00
❑ 6044	You're a Real Sweetheart/Please Don't Talk About Me When I'm Gone	1947	5.00	10.00	20.00
❑ 6050	What's the Reason?/You'll Live to Regret It	1947	5.00	10.00	20.00
❑ 6062	Never Trust a Woman/Behind the Eight Ball	1947	5.00	10.00	20.00
❑ 6070	Send Me Your Love for Christmas/Auld Lang Syne	1947	5.00	10.00	20.00
❑ 6076	If You Knew Susie/San	1948	5.00	10.00	20.00
❑ 6087	I'm My Own Grandpaw/The Eyes of Texas	1948	5.00	10.00	20.00
❑ 6098	I Wasn't Born Yesterday/It Makes No Difference	1948	5.00	10.00	20.00
❑ 6110	That's the Last Straw/Baby Won't	1948	5.00	10.00	20.00

Albums

MERCURY

Number	Title (A Side/B Side)	Yr	VG	VG+	NM
❑ MG-20630 [M]	Dancin' and Singin' with Tiny Hill	195?	6.25	12.50	25.00
❑ MG-20631 [M]	Golden Hits	195?	6.25	12.50	25.00
❑ MG-25126 [10]	Tiny Hill	1952	12.50	25.00	50.00
❑ SR-60631 [R]	Golden Hits	196?	3.75	7.50	15.00

HILL CITY

45s

MOON SHINE

Number	Title (A Side/B Side)	Yr	VG	VG+	NM
❑ 3040	I'd Do It in a Heartbeat/The Ghost of Brandy Jones	1985	—	2.50	5.00

HILLMAN, CHRIS

Also see THE BYRDS; DESERT ROSE BAND; McGUINN AND HILLMAN.

45s

ASYLUM

Number	Title (A Side/B Side)	Yr	VG	VG+	NM
❑ 45330	Step On Out/Take It on the Run	1976	—	2.00	4.00
❑ 45350	Falling Again/Love Is the Sweetest Amnesty	1976	—	2.00	4.00
❑ 45428	Heartbreaker/Lucky in Love	1977	—	2.00	4.00

SUGAR HILL

Number	Title (A Side/B Side)	Yr	VG	VG+	NM
❑ 4105	Somebody's Back in Town/Desert Rose	1984	—	2.50	5.00
❑ 4106	Running the Roadblocks/Turn Your Radio On	1985	—	2.50	5.00

Albums

ASYLUM

Number	Title (A Side/B Side)	Yr	VG	VG+	NM
❑ 7E-1062	Slippin' Away	1976	3.00	6.00	12.00
❑ 7E-1104	Clear Sailin'	1977	3.00	6.00	12.00

SUGAR HILL

Number	Title (A Side/B Side)	Yr	VG	VG+	NM
❑ SH 3729	Morning Sky	1982	3.00	6.00	12.00
❑ SH 3743	Desert Rose	1984	3.00	6.00	12.00

HILLMAN, CHRIS, AND ROGER MCGUINN

See McGUINN AND HILLMAN.

HILTON, DENNY

45s

OAK

Number	Title (A Side/B Side)	Yr	VG	VG+	NM
❑ 1027	Layin' Low/Delores	1981	—	3.00	6.00

ROSEBRIDGE

Number	Title (A Side/B Side)	Yr	VG	VG+	NM
❑ 010	Sharing the Night Together/(B-side unknown)	1983	—	3.00	6.00
❑ 0014	How'd You Get So Good/(B-side unknown)	1982	—	3.00	6.00

HINOJOSA, TISH

45s

A&M

Number	Title (A Side/B Side)	Yr	VG	VG+	NM
❑ 1468	Til U Love Me Again/(B-side unknown)	1989	—	2.50	5.00

HINOJOSA, TISH, AND CRAIG DILLINGHAM

Also see each artist's individual listings.

45s

MCA CURB

Number	Title (A Side/B Side)	Yr	VG	VG+	NM
❑ 52823	I'll Pull You Through/Too Soon to Say It's Too Late	1986	—	2.00	4.00

HITCHCOCK, STAN

45s

CINNAMON

Number	Title (A Side/B Side)	Yr	VG	VG+	NM
❑ 750	I Did It All for You/Love Don't Live Here	1973	—	3.00	6.00
❑ 754	Let Me Roll/The Shadow of Your Smile	1973	—	3.00	6.00
❑ 759	The Same Old Way/Lonely Wine	1973	—	3.00	6.00
❑ 770	Half-Empty Bed/When Love Was At Its Best	1973	—	3.00	6.00
❑ 782	I'm Free/Oklahoma Wind	1974	—	3.00	6.00

EPIC

Number	Title (A Side/B Side)	Yr	VG	VG+	NM
❑ 5-9581	I Had Heaven in My Arms/Somebody Had to Lose	1963	3.00	6.00	12.00
❑ 5-9634	This Town (Just Ain't Big Enough)/Someone to Be Lonesome For	1963	3.00	6.00	12.00
❑ 5-9699	Ole Bad/Looking Through a Teardrop	1964	3.00	6.00	12.00
❑ 5-9733	Lonely Wine/Candy Apple Red	1964	3.00	6.00	12.00
❑ 5-9802	Thumbing My Way Back Home/Back in My Baby's Arms	1965	2.50	5.00	10.00
❑ 5-9854	Imitation of a Man/Swiss-Made Heart	1965	2.50	5.00	10.00
❑ 5-10022	Hello World/Hush-a-Bye	1966	2.50	5.00	10.00
❑ 5-10081	To Tell the Truth/He Took My Place	1966	2.50	5.00	10.00
❑ 5-10182	She's Looking Good/Have I Stayed Away Too Long	1967	2.00	4.00	8.00
❑ 5-10246	Rings/Such a Little Teardrop	1967	2.00	4.00	8.00
❑ 5-10307	I'm Easy to Love/Don't Do Like I've Done (Do What I Say)	1968	2.00	4.00	8.00
❑ 5-10388	The Phoenix Flash/My Memory	1968	2.00	4.00	8.00
❑ 5-10432	Test of Time/Someday You'll Call My Name	1969	2.00	4.00	8.00
❑ 5-10464	Golden Slipper Rose/I Don't Know When That Will Be	1969	2.00	4.00	8.00
❑ 5-10525	Honey, I'm Home/Slip-Up And She'll Slip Away	1969	2.00	4.00	8.00
❑ 5-10586	Call Me Gone/Your Kind of Man	1970	2.00	4.00	8.00

GRT

Number	Title (A Side/B Side)	Yr	VG	VG+	NM
❑ 23	Dixie Belle/I Did It All for You	1970	—	3.50	7.00
❑ 39	At Least Part of the Way/The Shadow of Your Smile	1971	—	3.50	7.00

MMI

Number	Title (A Side/B Side)	Yr	VG	VG+	NM
❑ 1023	Slowly Turning to Love/Kiss Away	1978	—	3.00	6.00
❑ 1024	Falling/Only One	1978	—	3.00	6.00
❑ 1028	Finders Keepers, Losers Weepers/(B-side unknown)	1979	—	3.00	6.00

—A-side with Sue Richards

RAMBLIN'

Number	Title (A Side/B Side)	Yr	VG	VG+	NM
❑ 1711	She Sings Amazing Grace/(B-side unknown)	1981	—	2.50	5.00

Albums

AUDIOGRAPH

Number	Title (A Side/B Side)	Yr	VG	VG+	NM
❑ 6004	Stan Hitchcock	1982	2.50	5.00	10.00

CINNAMON

Number	Title (A Side/B Side)	Yr	VG	VG+	NM
❑ 5001	Stan Hitchcock Country	1973	3.75	7.50	15.00

EPIC

Number	Title (A Side/B Side)	Yr	VG	VG+	NM
❑ LN 24138 [M]	Just Call Me Lonesome	1965	5.00	10.00	20.00
❑ BN 26138 [S]	Just Call Me Lonesome	1965	6.25	12.50	25.00
❑ BN 26408	I'm Easy to Love	1968	5.00	10.00	20.00
❑ BN 26438	Softly and Tenderly	1969	5.00	10.00	20.00
❑ BN 26530	Honey, I'm Home	1969	3.75	7.50	15.00

GRT

Number	Title (A Side/B Side)	Yr	VG	VG+	NM
❑ 20001	Dixie Belle	1970	3.75	7.50	15.00

HOBBS, BECKY

Also see MOE BANDY.

45s

CURB

Number	Title (A Side/B Side)	Yr	VG	VG+	NM
❑ 76758	A Little Bit of Heaven/Are You Gonna Let Me	1990	—	2.00	4.00

EMI AMERICA

Number	Title (A Side/B Side)	Yr	VG	VG+	NM
❑ B-8224	Pardon Me (Haven't We Loved Somewhere Before)/Anyway	1984	—	—	3.00
❑ B-8247	Wheels in Emotion/Slow Dancin' Lines	1984	—	—	3.00
❑ B-8273	Hottest "Ex" in Texas/The Lover of You	1985	—	—	3.00
❑ B-8273 [PS]	Hottest "Ex" in Texas/The Lover of You	1985	—	2.50	5.00

LIBERTY

Number	Title (A Side/B Side)	Yr	VG	VG+	NM
❑ B-1520	Oklahoma Heart/Fool Me Once, Fool Me Twice	1984	—	2.00	4.00

MCA

Number	Title (A Side/B Side)	Yr	VG	VG+	NM
❑ 40281	I'll Be Your Audience/Paradise Is In Your Mind	1974	—	3.00	6.00

MERCURY

Number	Title (A Side/B Side)	Yr	VG	VG+	NM
❑ 55049	The More I Get the More I Want/I Feel Like Breakin' Somebody's Heart Tonight	1978	—	2.00	4.00

Number	Title (A Side/B Side)	Yr	VG	VG+	NM
❑ 55062	I Can't Say Goodbye to You/What Love Is All About	1979	—	2.00	4.00
❑ 57010	Just What the Doctor Ordered/You Can't Tie a Ramblin' Man Down	1979	—	2.00	4.00
❑ 57020	I'm Gonna Love You Tonight (Like There's No Tomorrow)/Good-for-Nothin' Guitar Pickin' Man	1980	—	2.00	4.00
❑ 57033	I Learned All About Cheatin' from You/Stay Away from Married Men	1980	—	2.00	4.00
❑ 57041	Honky-Tonk Saturday Night/Old Memories	1981	—	2.00	4.00
❑ 74049	The More I Get The More I Want/I Feel Like Breakin' Somebody's Heart Tonight	1978	—	—	—

—Unreleased?

MTM

Number	Title (A Side/B Side)	Yr	VG	VG+	NM
❑ B-72104	Jones on the Jukebox/I'm Gonna Get to You	1988	—	2.00	4.00
❑ B-72109	They Always Look Better When They're Leavin'/Mama Was a Working Man	1988	—	2.00	4.00
❑ B-72114	Are There Any More Like You (Where You Came From)/Cowgirl's Heart	1988	—	2.00	4.00

RCA

Number	Title (A Side/B Side)	Yr	VG	VG+	NM
❑ 8974-7-R	Do You Feel the Same Way Too?/Jones on the Jukebox	1989	—	—	3.00

TATTOO

Number	Title (A Side/B Side)	Yr	VG	VG+	NM
❑ TB-10725	I'm in Love Again/No Friends Like Old Friends	1976	—	2.50	5.00
❑ TB-10919	Everyday/I Don't Know Why (I Love That Guy)	1977	—	2.50	5.00
❑ TB-11026	Someone to Watch Over Me/I Don't Know Why	1977	—	2.50	5.00

Albums

MCA

Number	Title	Yr	VG	VG+	NM
❑ 434	Becky Hobbs	1974	3.75	7.50	15.00

MTM

Number	Title	Yr	VG	VG+	NM
❑ ST-71067	All Keyed Up	1988	2.50	5.00	10.00

TATTOO

Number	Title	Yr	VG	VG+	NM
❑ BJL1-1673	Heartland	1976	3.00	6.00	12.00
❑ BJL1-2169	Everyday	1977	3.00	6.00	12.00

HOBBS, BUD

45s

MGM

Number	Title (A Side/B Side)	Yr	VG	VG+	NM
❑ 11579	Goose Rock/Rightfully Yours	1953	20.00	40.00	80.00

Selected 78s

MGM

Number	Title (A Side/B Side)	Yr	VG	VG+	NM
❑ 10163	Enough Is Enough/Honey There Ain't No Pleasin' You	1948	5.00	10.00	20.00
❑ 10206	Lazy Mary/You're Mine Tonight (But Will You Be Mine Tomorrow)	1948	5.00	10.00	20.00
❑ 10305	I Heard About You/Oklahoma Sweetheart	1948	5.00	10.00	20.00
❑ 10366	Candy Kisses/Tennessee Border	1949	5.00	10.00	20.00
❑ 10428	Too Proud to Cry/Broken Fences and Broken Dreams	1949	5.00	10.00	20.00
❑ 10571	Alabama Moon/For the Sake of an Old Memory	1949	5.00	10.00	20.00

HOBBS, LOU

45s

CINNAMON

Number	Title (A Side/B Side)	Yr	VG	VG+	NM
❑ 792	What's Wrong with Me/Mission Bell	1974	2.00	4.00	8.00

—As "Louis Hobbs"

KIK

Number	Title (A Side/B Side)	Yr	VG	VG+	NM
❑ 902	Loving You Was All I Ever Needed/It's All Your Fault	1981	2.00	4.00	8.00
❑ 911	We're Building Our Love on a Rock/Run Right Back	1981	2.00	4.00	8.00

LOBO

Number	Title (A Side/B Side)	Yr	VG	VG+	NM
❑ X	There Ain't No Way/A Simple Man	1982	—	3.00	6.00
❑ XIII	Somebody Shot the Jukebox/(B-side unknown)	1982	—	3.00	6.00

HOBBS, PAM

45s

50 STATES

Number	Title (A Side/B Side)	Yr	VG	VG+	NM
❑ 79	Have You Ever Seen the Rain/(B-side unknown)	1980	—	2.50	5.00
❑ 81	I Thought I Heard You Calling My Name/Love Is Not a Game	1981	—	2.50	5.00
❑ 84	You're the Only Dancer/(B-side unknown)	1981	—	2.50	5.00
❑ 87	Love Me or Leave Me Alone/(B-side unknown)	1981	—	2.50	5.00

HOGSED, ROY

45s

CAPITOL

Number	Title (A Side/B Side)	Yr	VG	VG+	NM
❑ F1201	The Red We Want/Don't Bite the Hand That's Feeding You	1950	7.50	15.00	30.00
❑ F1529	Shuffleboard Shuffle/Poco Tempo	1951	6.25	12.50	25.00
❑ F1635	Cocaine Blues/Fishtail Boogie	195?	5.00	10.00	20.00

—Reissue

Number	Title (A Side/B Side)	Yr	VG	VG+	NM
❑ F1721	Free Samples/I Wish I Wuz	1951	6.25	12.50	25.00
❑ F1854	Snake Dance Boogie/I'm Gonna Get Along Without Ya	1951	6.25	12.50	25.00
❑ F1987	Mean, Mean Woman/Let Your Pendulum Swing	1952	6.25	12.50	25.00
❑ F2083	Stretchin' a Point or Two/Put Some Sugar in Your Shoes	1952	6.25	12.50	25.00
❑ F2350	Roll 'Em Dice/Ain't a Bump in the Road	1953	6.25	12.50	25.00
❑ F2468	Red Wing/It's More Fun That Way	1953	6.25	12.50	25.00
❑ F2720	Who Wrote That Letter to John/Babies and Bacon	1954	5.00	10.00	20.00
❑ F2807	You're Just My Style/Too Many Chiefs and Not Enough Indians	1954	5.00	10.00	20.00
❑ F3007	I'm Hurtin' Again/Do You Call That a Sweetheart	1955	5.00	10.00	20.00
❑ F40274	Cocaine Blues/Fishtail Boogie	1950	10.00	20.00	40.00
❑ F40286	Rag Mop/Rainbow Polka	1950	10.00	20.00	40.00

Selected 78s

CAPITOL

Number	Title (A Side/B Side)	Yr	VG	VG+	NM
❑ 40120	Cocaine Blues/Fishtail Boogie	1948	6.25	12.50	25.00
❑ 40133	Easy Payment Blues/The Short Cut Cutie Polka	1948	5.00	10.00	20.00
❑ 40141	Slow Train to Arkansas/Twenty-Five Chickens	1949	5.00	10.00	20.00
❑ 40220	Dill Pickles/Let's Go Dancing	1949	5.00	10.00	20.00

HOKUM, SUZI JANE

Also see VIRGIL WARNER AND SUZI JANE HOKUM.

45s

LHI

Number	Title (A Side/B Side)	Yr	VG	VG+	NM
❑ 14	Reason to Believe/I'll Never Fall in Love Again	1969	2.00	4.00	8.00
❑ 19	Alone/The Same Old Songs	1969	—	3.50	7.00
❑ 21	Califia (Stone Rider)/Nobody Like You	1970	—	3.50	7.00
❑ 17014	Good Time Music/Little War	1967	2.00	4.00	8.00

HOLDEN, REBECCA

45s

TRA-STAR

Number	Title (A Side/B Side)	Yr	VG	VG+	NM
❑ 1229	The Truth Doesn't Always Rhyme/If You Ever Wanna Try Again	1989	—	3.00	6.00
❑ 1234	License to Steal/(B-side unknown)	1989	—	3.00	6.00

HOLLADAY, DAVE

45s

STEP ONE

Number	Title (A Side/B Side)	Yr	VG	VG+	NM
❑ 356	Pull Up a Pillow/I.O. Blues	1986	—	2.50	5.00
❑ 365	Now She's in Paris/I.O. Blues	1986	—	2.50	5.00
❑ 368	What Cheatin' Is Today/I.O. Blues	1987	—	2.50	5.00
❑ 375	(My Heart Won't Let Me Love) No One But You/You Should Still Be Mine	1987	—	2.50	5.00
❑ 389	Ramona from Daytona/Excuse Me for Loving You	1988	—	2.50	5.00

HOLLAND, GREG

45s

WARNER BROS.

Number	Title (A Side/B Side)	Yr	VG	VG+	NM
❑ 18033	When I Come Back (I Wanna Be My Dog)/Oh to Be the One	1994	—	2.00	4.00
❑ 18152	Let Me Drive/Up to Feelin' Down	1994	—	2.00	4.00

HOLLIER, JILL

45s

WARNER BROS.

Number	Title (A Side/B Side)	Yr	VG	VG+	NM
❑ 22700	Mama's Daily Bread/Cry So Easy	1989	—	—	3.00
❑ 22966	If It Wasn't for the Heartache/Empty Arms	1989	—	—	3.00
❑ 27881	If You're Gonna Be Dumb, You Gotta Be Tough/I've Come a Long Way (But I've Got a Long Way to Go)	1988	—	—	3.00
❑ 28559	Sweet Time/Magic of the Moment	1986	—	—	3.00
❑ 28796	You Can't Take the Telephone to Bed/Baby Don't Stop	1986	—	2.00	4.00

HOLLOWELL, TERRI

45s

CON BRIO

Number	Title (A Side/B Side)	Yr	VG	VG+	NM
❑ 134	Happy Go Lucky Morning/Say What I Feel Tonight	1978	—	3.00	6.00
❑ 139	Strawberry Fields Forever/If You Wanna	1978	—	3.00	6.00
❑ 144	Just Stay with Me/Virginia Morning	1978	—	3.00	6.00
❑ 150	May I/I Wasn't There	1979	—	3.00	6.00
❑ 156	It's Too Soon to Say Goodbye/Holding It Back	1979	—	3.00	6.00

HOLLY, BUDDY

Also see THE CRICKETS.

45s

CORAL

Number	Title (A Side/B Side)	Yr	VG	VG+	NM
❑ 61852	Words of Love/Mailman, Bring Me No More Blues	1957	150.00	250.00	400.00

—Promos for any Coral title valued at $50 or under Near Mint are worth 2-4 times the stock copy value.

Number	Title (A Side/B Side)	Yr	VG	VG+	NM
❑ 61885	Peggy Sue/Everyday	1957	12.50	25.00	50.00

—Orange label

Number	Title (A Side/B Side)	Yr	VG	VG+	NM
❑ 61885	Peggy Sue/Everyday	196?	6.25	12.50	25.00

—Black color bars label

Number	Title (A Side/B Side)	Yr	VG	VG+	NM
❑ 61947	I'm Gonna Love You Too/Listen to Me	1958	12.50	25.00	50.00
❑ 61985	Rave On/Take Your Time	1958	12.50	25.00	50.00
❑ 62006	Early in the Morning/Now We're One	1958	12.50	25.00	50.00
❑ 62051	Heartbeat/Well...All Right	1958	12.50	25.00	50.00
❑ 62074	It Doesn't Matter Anymore/Raining in My Heart	1959	10.00	20.00	40.00
❑ 62134	Peggy Sue Got Married/Crying, Waiting, Hoping	1959	15.00	30.00	60.00
❑ 62210	True Love Ways/That Makes It Tough	1960	12.50	25.00	50.00
❑ 62283	You're So Square (Baby I Don't Care)/Valley of Tears	1961	40.00	80.00	160.00

—Evidently only released in Canada

Number	Title (A Side/B Side)	Yr	VG	VG+	NM
❑ 62329	Reminiscing/Wait Till the Sun Shines, Nellie	1962	7.50	15.00	30.00
❑ 62352	True Love Ways/Bo Diddley	1963	15.00	30.00	60.00
❑ 62369	Brown Eyed Handsome Man/Wishing	1963	10.00	20.00	40.00
❑ 62390	Rock Around with Ollie Vee/I'm Gonna Love You Too	1963	10.00	20.00	40.00
❑ 62448	Slippin' and Slidin'/What to Do	1965	25.00	50.00	100.00
❑ 62554	Rave On/Early in the Morning	1968	7.50	15.00	30.00
❑ 62558	Love Is Strange/You're the One	1969	5.00	10.00	20.00
❑ 62558 [PS]	Love Is Strange/You're the One	1969	7.50	15.00	30.00

Number	Title (A Side/B Side)	Yr	VG	VG+	NM
DECCA					
❑ 29854	Blue Days, Black Nights/Love Me	1956	150.00	300.00	600.00
—With lines on either side of "Decca"					
❑ 29854	Blue Days, Black Nights/Love Me	1956	75.00	150.00	300.00
—With star under "Decca"					
❑ 29854 [DJ]	Blue Days, Black Nights/Love Me	1956	100.00	200.00	400.00
—Promos have pink labels					
❑ 30166	Modern Don Juan/You Are My One Desire	1956	125.00	250.00	500.00
—With lines on either side of "Decca"					
❑ 30166	Modern Don Juan/You Are My One Desire	1956	62.50	125.00	250.00
—With star under "Decca"					
❑ 30166 [DJ]	Modern Don Juan/You Are My One Desire	1956	75.00	150.00	300.00
—Promos have pink labels					
❑ 30434	That'll Be the Day/Rock Around with Ollie Vee	1957	62.50	125.00	250.00
—With star under "Decca"					
❑ 30434	That'll Be the Day/Rock Around with Ollie Vee	1957	100.00	200.00	400.00
—With lines on either side of "Decca"					
❑ 30434 [DJ]	That'll Be the Day/Rock Around with Ollie Vee	1957	62.50	125.00	250.00
—Promos have pink labels					
❑ 30543	Love Me/You Are My One Desire	1958	75.00	150.00	300.00
❑ 30543 [DJ]	Love Me/You Are My One Desire	1958	75.00	150.00	300.00
—Green label promos					
❑ 30543 [DJ]	Love Me/You Are My One Desire	1958	50.00	100.00	200.00
—Pink label promos					
❑ 30650	Ting-a-Ling/Girl on My Mind	1958	75.00	150.00	300.00
❑ 30650 [DJ]	Ting-a-Ling/Girl on My Mind	1958	50.00	100.00	200.00
—Promos have pink labels					
MCA					
❑ 40905	It Doesn't Matter Anymore/Peggy Sue	1978	—	2.50	5.00
❑ 40905 [PS]	It Doesn't Matter Anymore/Peggy Sue	1978	—	2.50	5.00

7-Inch Extended Plays

Number	Title (A Side/B Side)	Yr	VG	VG+	NM
CORAL					
❑ EC 81169	Listen to Me/Peggy Sue//I'm Gonna Love You Too/Everyday	1958	75.00	150.00	300.00
❑ EC 81169 [PS]	Listen to Me	1958	75.00	150.00	300.00
❑ EC 81182	It Doesn't Matter Anymore/Heartbeat//Raining in My Heart/Early in the Morning	1959	75.00	150.00	300.00
❑ EC 81182 [PS]	The Buddy Holly Story	1959	75.00	150.00	300.00
❑ EC 81191	Peggy Sue Got Married/Crying, Waiting, Hoping//Learning the Game/That Makes It Tough	1961	62.50	125.00	250.00
❑ EC 81191 [PS]	Buddy Holly	1961	62.50	125.00	250.00
❑ EC 81193	Brown Eyed Handsome Man/Wishing//Bo Diddley/True Love Ways	1961	62.50	125.00	250.00
❑ EC 81193 [PS]	Brown Eyed Handsome Man	1961	62.50	125.00	250.00
DECCA					
❑ ED 2575	*That'll Be the Day/Blue Days — Black Nights/Ting-a-Ling/You Are My One Desire	1958	150.00	300.00	600.00
❑ ED 2575 [PS]	That'll Be the Day	1958	500.00	1000.	2000.
—Sleeve has liner notes on back					
❑ ED 2575 [PS]	That'll Be the Day	1958	150.00	300.00	600.00
—Sleeve has other EP ads on back					

Albums

Number	Title (A Side/B Side)	Yr	VG	VG+	NM
CORAL					
❑ CXB 8 [(2) M]	The Best of Buddy Holly	1966	20.00	40.00	80.00
❑ CXSB 8 [(2) R]	The Best of Buddy Holly	1966	12.50	25.00	50.00
❑ CRL 57210 [M]	Buddy Holly	1958	100.00	200.00	400.00
—Maroon label					
❑ CRL 57210 [M]	Buddy Holly	1964	25.00	50.00	100.00
—Black label with color bars					
❑ CRL 57279 [M]	The Buddy Holly Story	1959	75.00	150.00	300.00
—Maroon label; back color print in black and red					
❑ CRL 57279 [M]	The Buddy Holly Story	1959	37.50	75.00	150.00
—Maroon label; back color print in all black					
❑ CRL 57279 [M]	The Buddy Holly Story	1963	20.00	40.00	80.00
—Black label with color bars					
❑ CRL 57326 [M]	The Buddy Holly Story, Vol. 2	1959	50.00	100.00	200.00
—Maroon label					
❑ CRL 57326 [M]	The Buddy Holly Story, Vol. 2	1963	20.00	40.00	80.00
—Black label with color bars					
❑ CRL 57405 [M]	Buddy Holly and the Crickets	1962	37.50	75.00	150.00
—Reissue of the Crickets LP on Brunswick 54038					
❑ CRL 57426 [M]	Reminiscing	1963	50.00	100.00	200.00
—Maroon label					
❑ CRL 57426 [M]	Reminiscing	1964	20.00	40.00	80.00
—Black label with color bars					
❑ CRL 57450 [M]	Buddy Holly Showcase	1964	25.00	50.00	100.00
❑ CRL 57463 [M]	Holly in the Hills	1965	30.00	60.00	120.00
❑ CRL 57492 [M]	Buddy Holly's Greatest Hits	1967	20.00	40.00	80.00
❑ CRL 757279 [R]	The Buddy Holly Story	1963	10.00	20.00	40.00
❑ CRL 757326 [R]	The Buddy Holly Story, Vol. 2	1963	10.00	20.00	40.00
❑ CRL 757405 [R]	Buddy Holly and the Crickets	1963	10.00	20.00	40.00
❑ CRL 757426 [R]	Reminiscing	1964	10.00	20.00	40.00
❑ CRL 757450 [R]	Buddy Holly Showcase	1964	20.00	40.00	80.00
❑ CRL 757463 [R]	Holly in the Hills	1965	25.00	50.00	100.00
❑ CRL 757492 [P]	Buddy Holly's Greatest Hits	1967	12.50	25.00	50.00
❑ CRL 757504 [S]	Giant	1969	12.50	25.00	50.00
CRICKET					
❑ C001000	Buddy Holly Live — Volume 1	197?	5.00	10.00	20.00
❑ C001001	Buddy Holly Live — Volume 1	197?	5.00	10.00	20.00
DECCA					
❑ DXSE 7207 [(2)]	A Rock 'n' Roll Collection	1972	10.00	20.00	40.00
❑ DL 8707 [M]	That'll Be the Day	1958	375.00	750.00	1500.
—Black label with silver print					
❑ DL 8707 [M]	That'll Be the Day	1961	75.00	150.00	300.00
—Black label with color bars					
GREAT NORTHWEST					
❑ GNW-4014	Visions of Buddy	197?	2.50	5.00	10.00
—Interview album					
MCA					
❑ 737	The Great Buddy Holly	197?	2.50	5.00	10.00
—Reissue of MCA Coral LP					
❑ 1484	Buddy Holly/The Crickets 20 Golden Greats	198?	2.00	4.00	8.00
—Reissue of 3040					
❑ 3040	Buddy Holly/The Crickets 20 Golden Greats	1978	3.75	7.50	15.00
❑ 4009 [(2)]	A Rock 'n' Roll Collection	1973	5.00	10.00	20.00
—Black labels with rainbow					
❑ 4009 [(2)]	A Rock 'n' Roll Collection	1978	3.00	6.00	12.00
—Later pressings on tan or blue/rainbow labels					
❑ 4184 [(2)]	Legend	1985	5.00	10.00	20.00
❑ 5540 [(2)]	From the Original Master Tapes	1986	6.25	12.50	25.00
❑ 11161	Buddy Holly	1995	10.00	20.00	40.00
—Audiophile "Heavy Vinyl" reissue with gatefold cover					
❑ 25239	Buddy Holly	1989	3.00	6.00	12.00
—Reissue of Coral 57210					
❑ 27059	For the First Time Anywhere	1983	2.50	5.00	10.00
❑ 80000 [(6)]	The Complete Buddy Holly	1981	12.50	25.00	50.00
—Box set with booklet and custom innersleeves					
MCA CORAL					
❑ CD-20101	The Great Buddy Holly	1973	3.00	6.00	12.00
VOCALION					
❑ VL 3811 [M]	The Great Buddy Holly	1967	20.00	40.00	80.00
❑ VL 73811 [R]	The Great Buddy Holly	1967	12.50	25.00	50.00
❑ VL 73923	Good Rockin'	1971	30.00	60.00	120.00

HOLLY, DOYLE

45s

Number	Title (A Side/B Side)	Yr	VG	VG+	NM
50 STATES					
❑ 46	Senorita Del Noche/Hey Ginny	1976	—	3.00	6.00
❑ 48	Somebody to Love/Heaven Help the Poor Man	1977	—	3.00	6.00
❑ 55	Takin' a Chance/Goodbye Rose	1977	—	3.00	6.00
BARNABY					
❑ 602	A Rainbow in My Hand/Free Love	1974	—	2.50	5.00
❑ 605	Just Another Cowboy Song/January Bittersweet Jones	1974	—	2.50	5.00
❑ 608	Richard and the Cadillac Kings/She Can't Make the Hurt Go Away	1974	—	2.50	5.00
❑ 612	Funky Water/Watch Out Woman	1975	—	2.50	5.00
❑ 2064	Vanishing Breed/Richer Than I Am	1972	—	3.00	6.00
❑ 5004	My Heart Cries for You/All the Way from Alabama	1972	—	2.50	5.00
❑ 5010	Headed for the Country/Slow Poke	1973	—	2.50	5.00
❑ 5018	Queen of the Silver Dollar/Take a Walk in the Country	1973	—	2.50	5.00
❑ 5027	Lila/Darling, Are You Ever Coming Home	1973	—	2.50	5.00
❑ 5030	Lord How Long Has This Been Going On/January Bittersweet Jones	1974	—	2.50	5.00
CAPITOL					
❑ 2637	I'm a Natural Loser/The Biggest Storm of All	1969	2.00	4.00	8.00
❑ 2756	Cinderella/I'll Be Alright Tomorrow	1970	2.00	4.00	8.00
MOSRITE					
❑ 160	The Dumb Thing/The Best Girl	196?	3.00	6.00	12.00
WARNER BROS.					
❑ 8125	Jesse California/Skid Row Today	1975	—	2.50	5.00

Albums

Number	Title (A Side/B Side)	Yr	VG	VG+	NM
BARNABY					
❑ BR-15010	Doyle Holly	1973	3.75	7.50	15.00
❑ BR-15011	Just Another Cowboy Song	1973	3.75	7.50	15.00

HOLM, JOHNNY

45s

Number	Title (A Side/B Side)	Yr	VG	VG+	NM
ASI					
❑ 1012	Lightnin' Bar Blues/Ain't It a Beauty	1977	—	3.00	6.00

HOLMES, MONTY

45s

Number	Title (A Side/B Side)	Yr	VG	VG+	NM
ASHLEY					
❑ 1001	A Way to Survive/(B-side unknown)	1989	—	3.00	6.00

HOLMES, SALTY

45s

Number	Title (A Side/B Side)	Yr	VG	VG+	NM
DECCA					
❑ 9-46313	Harmonica Boogie/Blue Eyes Crying in the Rain	1951	6.25	12.50	25.00

HOLT, DARRELL

Also see SWEETWATER.

45s

Number	Title (A Side/B Side)	Yr	VG	VG+	NM
ANOKA					
❑ 221	I Can't Take Her Anywhere/(B-side unknown)	1988	—	3.00	6.00
❑ 222	Catch 22/(B-side unknown)	1987	—	3.00	6.00
❑ 224	I'd Throw It All Away/(B-side unknown)	1988	—	3.00	6.00
❑ 225	Only the Strong Survive/(B-side unknown)	1989	—	3.00	6.00

HOLY, STEVE

45s

Number	Title (A Side/B Side)	Yr	VG	VG+	NM
CURB					
❑ D7-73087	Don't Make Me Beg/Blue Moon	2000	—	—	3.00

HOMER AND JETHRO

Also see JETHRO BURNS.

45s

KING

Number	Title (A Side/B Side)	Yr	VG	VG+	NM
❑ 1216	Don't Let Your Sweet Love Die/Long Handle Line	1953	7.50	15.00	30.00
❑ 5747	Five Minutes More/Tell a Woman	1963	3.00	6.00	12.00

RCA VICTOR

Number	Title (A Side/B Side)	Yr	VG	VG+	NM
❑ 47-4239	Sound Off #2/I Love You 1,000 Ways	1951	6.25	12.50	25.00
❑ 47-4290	Too Young/Too Old to Cut the Mustard	1951	7.50	15.00	30.00
❑ 47-4397	Cold, Cold Heart #2/Alabama Jubilee	1951	6.25	12.50	25.00
❑ 47-4557	Slow Poke #2/When It's Tooth Pickin' Time in False Teeth Valley	1952	6.25	12.50	25.00
❑ 47-4770	Li'l Ole Kiss of Fire/I'm Torn	1952	6.25	12.50	25.00
❑ 47-4936	The Billboard Song/Child Psychology	1952	6.25	12.50	25.00
❑ 47-5043	Jam Bowl Liar/You Belong to Me No. 2	1952	6.25	12.50	25.00
❑ 47-5099	A Screwball's Love Song/Settin' the Woods on Fire No. 2	1952	6.25	12.50	25.00
❑ 47-5214	Don't Let the Stars Get In Your Eyeballs/Unhappy Day	1953	6.25	12.50	25.00
❑ 47-5280	(How Much Is) That Hound Dog in the Window/Pore Ol' Koo-Liger	1953	7.50	15.00	30.00
❑ 47-5372	I'm Walking Behind You-All/Mexican Joe #6 7/8	1953	6.25	12.50	25.00
❑ 47-5429	Your Clobbered Heart/Gamblers Git Box	1953	6.25	12.50	25.00
❑ 47-5456	I Saw Mommy Smoochin' Santa Claus/(All I Want for Christmas Is) My Upper Plate	1953	5.00	10.00	20.00
❑ 47-5456 [PS]	I Saw Mommy Smoochin' Santa Claus/(All I Want for Christmas Is) My Upper Plate	1953	7.50	15.00	30.00
❑ 47-5555	You-Ewe-U/Hey Shmo!	1953	6.25	12.50	25.00
❑ 47-5633	Oh My Pappy/Swappin' Partners	1954	5.00	10.00	20.00
❑ 47-5708	Crazy Mixed Up Song/That Tired Run Down Feeling	1954	5.00	10.00	20.00
❑ 47-5788	Hernando's Hideaway/Wanted	1954	5.00	10.00	20.00
❑ 47-5903	The Night After Christmas/Santy Baby	1954	5.00	10.00	20.00
❑ 47-6029	Mister Sandman/The Nutty Lady of Shady Lane	1955	5.00	10.00	20.00
❑ 47-6053	Let Me Go, Blubber/Over the Rainbow	1955	5.00	10.00	20.00
❑ 47-6178	The Ballad of Davy Crew-Cut/Pickin' and Singin' (Medley)	1955	6.25	12.50	25.00
❑ 47-6241	The Yellow Rose of Texas, You All/Listen to the Gooney Bird	1955	5.00	10.00	20.00
❑ 47-6322	Nuttin' for Christmas/Santy's Movin' On	1955	5.00	10.00	20.00
❑ 47-6342	The Sifting, Whimpering Sands/They Laid Him in the Ground	1955	5.00	10.00	20.00
❑ 47-6374	Love and Marriage/This Is a Wife?	1955	5.00	10.00	20.00
❑ 47-6542	Two Tone Shoes/Heartbreak Hotel	1956	6.25	12.50	25.00
❑ 47-6651	Where Is That Doggone Gal of Mine/Just Be Here	1956	5.00	10.00	20.00
❑ 47-6706	Houn' Dawg/Screen Door (Green Door)	1956	6.25	12.50	25.00
❑ 47-6765	I'm My Own Grand Paw/Mama from the Train	1956	5.00	10.00	20.00
❑ 47-6954	Gone/Ramblin' Rose	1957	3.75	7.50	15.00
❑ 47-7030	My Dog Likes Your Dog/Kentucky	1957	3.75	7.50	15.00
❑ 47-7162	At the Flop/My Special Angel	1958	3.75	7.50	15.00
❑ 47-7342	Lullaby of Bird Dog/I Guess Things Happen That Way	1958	3.75	7.50	15.00
❑ 47-7493	Don't Sing Along (On Top of Old Smoky)/Middle Aged Teenager	1959	3.75	7.50	15.00
❑ 47-7585	The Battle of Kookamonga/Waterloo	1959	3.75	7.50	15.00
❑ 47-7704	El Paso (Numero Dos)/That's Good, That's Bad	1960	3.75	7.50	15.00
❑ 47-7744	Sink the Bismarck/He'll Have to Go	1960	3.75	7.50	15.00
❑ 47-7790	Itsy Bitsy Teenie Weenie Yellow Polka Dot Bikini/Please Help Me, I'm Falling	1960	3.75	7.50	15.00
❑ 47-7852	Are You Lonesome Tonight/I Love Your Pizza	1961	3.75	7.50	15.00
❑ 47-8075	She Thinks I Don't Care/Are You Kissing More Now (But Enjoying It Less)	1962	3.00	6.00	12.00
❑ 47-8305	Joe Bean/Freda on the Freeway	1963	3.00	6.00	12.00
❑ 47-8345	I Want to Hold Your Hand/She Loves You	1964	3.75	7.50	15.00
❑ 47-8345 [PS]	I Want to Hold Your Hand/She Loves You	1964	7.50	15.00	30.00
❑ 47-8604	Misty/Tenderly	1965	3.00	6.00	12.00
❑ 47-8664	King of the Camp/Camp Runamuck	1965	3.00	6.00	12.00
❑ 47-8874	Act Naturally/Finished Musicians	1966	2.50	5.00	10.00
❑ 47-9130	Nashville Cats/Winchester Cathedral	1967	2.50	5.00	10.00
❑ 47-9299	Somethin' Stupid/The Ballad of Roger Miller	1967	2.50	5.00	10.00
❑ 47-9581	Hill Billy Boogie/I Crept Into the Crypt and Cried	1968	2.50	5.00	10.00
❑ 47-9674	The Gal from Possum Holler/There Ain't a Chicken Safe in Tennessee	1968	2.50	5.00	10.00
❑ 47-9866	Daddy Played First Base/You Smell Like Turtles	1970	2.00	4.00	8.00
❑ 47-9922	Hello Darlin' No. 2/Funny Farm	1970	2.00	4.00	8.00
❑ 48-0075	Baby, It's Cold Outside/Country Girl	1949	12.50	25.00	50.00
—With June Carter; originals on green vinyl					
❑ 48-0086	Waltz with Me/Roll Along Kentucky Moon	1949	10.00	20.00	40.00
—Originals on green vinyl					
❑ 48-0113	Tennessee Border — No. 2/I'm Gettin' Older Every Day	1949	10.00	20.00	40.00
—Originals on green vinyl					
❑ 48-0144	The Wedding of Hillbilly Lilli Marlene/The Hucklebuck	1950	10.00	20.00	40.00
—With June Carter; originals on green vinyl					
❑ 48-0170	She Made Toothpicks Out of the Timber of My Heart/I've Got Tears in My Ears	1950	10.00	20.00	40.00
—Originals on green vinyl					
❑ 48-0181	I Said My Nightshirt (And Put On My Prayers)/Music, Music, Music	1950	10.00	20.00	40.00
—Originals on green vinyl					
❑ 48-0308	You Tell Her I Stutter/Does the Spearmint Lose Its Flavor	1950	10.00	20.00	40.00
—Originals on green vinyl					
❑ 48-0349	Pistol Pete/Put That Knife Away Nellie	1950	10.00	20.00	40.00
—Originals on green vinyl					
❑ 48-0404	Oh Babe/Disc Jockey Nightmare	1951	7.50	15.00	30.00
❑ 48-0446	So Long — No. 2/I'm Movin' On — No. 2	1951	7.50	15.00	30.00
❑ 48-0468	King Sized Baby/That Texas Land	1951	7.50	15.00	30.00
❑ 48-0484	Knock-Kneed Susy/She Loves to Cry	1951	7.50	15.00	30.00
—With June Carter					
❑ 74-0566	We Didn't Make It Through the Night/Fer the Good Times	1971	2.00	4.00	8.00

Selected 78s

KING

Number	Title (A Side/B Side)	Yr	VG	VG+	NM
❑ 571	Five Minutes More/Rye Whiskey	1946	7.50	15.00	30.00
❑ 583	Boll Weevil/Don't Let Your Sweet Love Die	1947	6.25	12.50	25.00
❑ 596	Over the Rainbow/Groundhog	1947	6.25	12.50	25.00
❑ 615	For Sentimental Reasons/Cielito Lindo	1947	6.25	12.50	25.00
❑ 620	Managua, Nicaragua/Bill Bailey	1947	6.25	12.50	25.00
❑ 623	I'll Close My Eyes/Symphony	1947	6.25	12.50	25.00
❑ 659	Fly, Birdie, Fly/Donkey Serenade	1947	6.25	12.50	25.00
❑ 682	I Wonder Who's Kissing Her Now/Three Nights Experience	1948	6.25	12.50	25.00
❑ 695	Oh You Beautiful Doll/Tell a Woman	1948	6.25	12.50	25.00
❑ 701	Gotta See Mama Every Night/It Bruised Her Somewhat	1948	6.25	12.50	25.00
❑ 721	Glow Worm/It's a Bloody War	1948	6.25	12.50	25.00
❑ 749	I Feel That Old Age Creeping On/Goodbye Old Booze	1949	6.25	12.50	25.00
❑ 751	Blue Tail Fly/All Night Long	1949	6.25	12.50	25.00
❑ 773	The Girl on Police Gazette/Poor Little Liza, Poor Girl	1949	6.25	12.50	25.00
❑ 809	Always/Poor Little Liza, Poor Girl	1949	6.25	12.50	25.00

7-Inch Extended Plays

RCA VICTOR

Number	Title (A Side/B Side)	Yr	VG	VG+	NM
❑ EPA 534	Randolph the Flat-Nosed Reindeer/(All I Want for Christmas Is) My Upper Plate//I Saw Mommy Smoochin' Santa Claus/Frosty the De-Frosted Snow Man	195?	3.75	7.50	15.00
❑ EPA 534 [PS]	Seasoned Greetings	195?	3.75	7.50	15.00

Albums

AUDIO LAB

Number	Title (A Side/B Side)	Yr	VG	VG+	NM
❑ AL-1513 [M]	Musical Madness	1958	25.00	50.00	100.00

KING

Number	Title (A Side/B Side)	Yr	VG	VG+	NM
❑ 639 [M]	They Sure Are Corny	1959	25.00	50.00	100.00
❑ 848 [M]	Cornier Than Corn	1963	17.50	35.00	70.00
❑ KS-1005	24 Great Songs in the Homer & Jethro Style	1967	5.00	10.00	20.00

RCA VICTOR

Number	Title (A Side/B Side)	Yr	VG	VG+	NM
❑ LPM-1412 [M]	Barefoot Ballads	1957	12.50	25.00	50.00
❑ LPM-1560 [M]	The Worst of Homer & Jethro	1958	12.50	25.00	50.00
❑ LPM-1880 [M]	Life Can Be Miserable	1958	7.50	15.00	30.00
❑ LSP-1880 [S]	Life Can Be Miserable	1958	12.50	25.00	50.00
❑ LPM-2181 [M]	Homer and Jethro at the Country Club	1960	6.25	12.50	25.00
❑ LSP-2181 [S]	Homer and Jethro at the Country Club	1960	10.00	20.00	40.00
❑ LPM-2286 [M]	Songs My Mother Never Sang	1961	6.25	12.50	25.00
❑ LSP-2286 [S]	Songs My Mother Never Sang	1961	7.50	15.00	30.00
❑ LPM-2455 [M]	Zany Songs of the '30s	1962	6.25	12.50	25.00
❑ LSP-2455 [S]	Zany Songs of the '30s	1962	7.50	15.00	30.00
❑ LPM-2459 [M]	Playing It Straight	1962	6.25	12.50	25.00
❑ LSP-2459 [S]	Playing It Straight	1962	7.50	15.00	30.00
❑ LPM-2492 [M]	Homer and Jethro at the Convention	1962	6.25	12.50	25.00
❑ LSP-2492 [S]	Homer and Jethro at the Convention	1962	7.50	15.00	30.00
❑ LPM-2674 [M]	Homer and Jethro Go West	1963	6.25	12.50	25.00
❑ LSP-2674 [S]	Homer and Jethro Go West	1963	7.50	15.00	30.00
❑ LPM-2743 [M]	Ooh, That's Corny	1963	6.25	12.50	25.00
❑ LSP-2743 [S]	Ooh, That's Corny	1963	7.50	15.00	30.00
❑ LPM-2928 [M]	Cornfucius Say	1964	6.25	12.50	25.00
❑ LSP-2928 [S]	Cornfucius Say	1964	7.50	15.00	30.00
❑ LPM-2954 [M]	Fractured Folk Songs	1964	6.25	12.50	25.00
❑ LSP-2954 [S]	Fractured Folk Songs	1964	7.50	15.00	30.00
❑ LPM-3112 [10]	Homer & Jethro Fracture Frank Loesser	1953	37.50	75.00	150.00
❑ LPM-3357 [M]	Homer and Jethro Sing Tenderly	1965	6.25	12.50	25.00
❑ LSP-3357 [S]	Homer and Jethro Sing Tenderly	1965	7.50	15.00	30.00
❑ LPM-3462 [M]	The Old Crusty Minstrels	1965	6.25	12.50	25.00
❑ LSP-3462 [S]	The Old Crusty Minstrels	1965	7.50	15.00	30.00
❑ LPM-3474 [M]	The Best of Homer and Jethro	1966	6.25	12.50	25.00
❑ LSP-3474 [S]	The Best of Homer and Jethro	1966	7.50	15.00	30.00
❑ LPM-3538 [M]	Any News from Nashville?	1966	6.25	12.50	25.00
❑ LSP-3538 [S]	Any News from Nashville?	1966	7.50	15.00	30.00
❑ LPM-3673 [M]	Wanted for Murder	1966	6.25	12.50	25.00
❑ LSP-3673 [S]	Wanted for Murder	1966	7.50	15.00	30.00
❑ LPM-3701 [M]	It Ain't Necessarily Square	1967	7.50	15.00	30.00
❑ LSP-3701 [S]	It Ain't Necessarily Square	1967	6.25	12.50	25.00
❑ LPM-3822 [M]	Nashville Cats	1967	10.00	20.00	40.00
❑ LSP-3822 [S]	Nashville Cats	1967	6.25	12.50	25.00
❑ LPM-3877 [M]	Somethin' Stupid	1967	12.50	25.00	50.00
❑ LSP-3877 [S]	Somethin' Stupid	1967	6.25	12.50	25.00
❑ LPM-3973 [M]	There's Nothing Like an Old Hippie	1968	25.00	50.00	100.00
❑ LSP-3973 [S]	There's Nothing Like an Old Hippie	1968	6.25	12.50	25.00
❑ LSP-4001	Cool, Crazy Christmas	1968	5.00	10.00	20.00
❑ LSP-4024	Homer and Jethro at Vanderbilt U.	1969	5.00	10.00	20.00
❑ LSP-4148	Homer and Jethro's Next Album	1969	5.00	10.00	20.00

HOMESTEADERS, THE

45s

LITTLE DARLIN'

Number	Title (A Side/B Side)	Yr	VG	VG+	NM
❑ 0010	Show Me the Way to the Circus/The Country Joined the Country Club	1966	2.50	5.00	10.00

Number	Title (A Side/B Side)	Yr	VG	VG+	NM
❑ 0018	Love, Love, Love (Makes the World Go Round)/It's a Woman	1967	2.50	5.00	10.00
❑ 0033	Homesteadin'/If You Should Come Back Today	1967	2.50	5.00	10.00
❑ 0036	Lovin' Time/Making Believe	1967	2.50	5.00	10.00
❑ 0045	Gonna Miss Me/Homewrecker	1968	2.50	5.00	10.00
❑ 0053	Sleep/In Magnolia Blossoms	1968	2.50	5.00	10.00

HOOD, BOBBY

45s

CHUTE

Number	Title (A Side/B Side)	Yr	VG	VG+	NM
❑ 004	Slow Tunes and Promises/You Gotta Go Down	1979	—	2.50	5.00
❑ 008	Easy/No Love Lost	1979	—	2.50	5.00
❑ 009	It Takes One to Know One/After the Rain	1979	—	2.50	5.00
❑ 010	When She Falls/(B-side unknown)	1980	—	3.00	6.00
❑ 015	Mexico Winter/(B-side unknown)	1980	—	3.00	6.00
❑ 016	Pick Up the Pieces Joanne/(B-side unknown)	1980	—	3.00	6.00
❑ 018	Woman in My Heart/(B-side unknown)	1981	—	3.00	6.00
❑ 101	I've Got an Angel (That Loves Me Like the Devil)/Tennessee Frost	1978	—	2.50	5.00
❑ 102	Come to Me/(B-side unknown)	1978	—	2.50	5.00

PLANTATION

Number	Title (A Side/B Side)	Yr	VG	VG+	NM
❑ 169	Come On In/Southern Ladies Kind of Man	1978	—	2.50	5.00
❑ 177	Got You on My Mind/(B-side unknown)	1978	—	3.00	6.00

HOOSIER HOT SHOTS

Selected 78s

BANNER

Number	Title (A Side/B Side)	Yr	VG	VG+	NM
❑ 6-05-57	Bow-Wow Blues/Wah-Hoo	1936	5.00	10.00	20.00
❑ 33312	Four Thousand Years Ago/Whistlin' Joe from Kokomo	193?	5.00	10.00	20.00
❑ 33358	Hoosier Stomp/Oakville Twister	193?	5.00	10.00	20.00
❑ 33403	Sentimental Gentleman from Georgia/Farmer Gray	193?	5.00	10.00	20.00
❑ 33420	Yes She Do — No She Don't/I'm Looking for a Girl	193?	5.00	10.00	20.00

COLUMBIA

Number	Title (A Side/B Side)	Yr	VG	VG+	NM
❑ 20287	Goofus/Runnin' Wild	1948	3.00	6.00	12.00
—Reissue of 37710					
❑ 20290	Hoosier Stomp/Oakvile Twister	1948	3.00	6.00	12.00
—Reissue of 37713					
❑ 20291	Black Eyed Susan Brown/Back in Indiana	1948	3.00	6.00	12.00
—Reissue of 37714					
❑ 20292	Alexander's Ragtime Band/Margie	1948	3.00	6.00	12.00
—Reissue of 37715					
❑ 20293	Pick That Bass/Everybody Stomp	1948	3.00	6.00	12.00
—Reissue of 37716					
❑ 20294	I Want a Girl/I Like Mountain Music	1948	3.00	6.00	12.00
—Reissue of 37717					
❑ 20432	Bye Bye Blues/Take Me Out to the Ball Game	1948	3.75	7.50	15.00
—Reissue					
❑ 20472	Jingle Bells/I'll Soon Be Rolling Home	1948	3.75	7.50	15.00
—Reissue					
❑ 37710	Runnin' Wild/Goofus	1947	3.75	7.50	15.00
—Reissue of Vocalion 03683					
❑ 37713	Hoosier Stomp/Oakvile Twister	1947	3.75	7.50	15.00
—Reissue of Vocalion 03725					
❑ 37714	Black Eyed Susan Brown/Back in Indiana	1947	3.75	7.50	15.00
—Reissue of Vocalion 03730					
❑ 37715	Alexander's Ragtime Band/Margie	1947	3.75	7.50	15.00
—Reissue					
❑ 37716	Pick That Bass/Everybody Stomp	1947	3.75	7.50	15.00
—Reissue					
❑ 37717	I Want a Girl/I Like Mountain Music	1947	3.75	7.50	15.00
—Reissue of Vocalion 03853					

CONQUEROR

Number	Title (A Side/B Side)	Yr	VG	VG+	NM
❑ 8445	Four Thousand Years Ago/Whistlin' Joe from Kokomo	193?	5.00	10.00	20.00
❑ 8480	Hoosier Stomp/Oakville Twister	193?	5.00	10.00	20.00
❑ 8494	Sentimental Gentleman from Georgia/Farmer Gray	193?	5.00	10.00	20.00
❑ 8513	Yes She Do — No She Don't/I'm Looking for a Girl	193?	5.00	10.00	20.00
❑ 8601	Ha-Cha-Nan/Limehouse Blues	193?	5.00	10.00	20.00
❑ 8615	They Go Wild Simply Wild Over Me/At the Old Maids Ball	193?	5.00	10.00	20.00
❑ 8635	Wah-Hoo/The Hill-Billies Are Mountain Williams Now	193?	5.00	10.00	20.00
❑ 8655	This Is the Chorus/Ida	193?	5.00	10.00	20.00
❑ 8661	At the Darktown Strutter's Ball/You're Driving Me Crazy	193?	5.00	10.00	20.00
❑ 8745	Take Me Out to the Ball Game/Bye Bye Blues	193?	5.00	10.00	20.00
❑ 8792	Alexander's Ragtime Band/Margie	193?	5.00	10.00	20.00
❑ 9191	Ferdinand the Bull/When Paw Was Courtin' Maw	193?	5.00	10.00	20.00
❑ 9246	Three Little Fishes/Beer Barrel Polka	193?	5.00	10.00	20.00
❑ 9395	I'm Just Wild About Harry/Ma, She's Making Eyes at Me	193?	5.00	10.00	20.00
❑ 9399	Careless/In an Old Dutch Garden (By an Old Dutch Mill)	193?	5.00	10.00	20.00
❑ 9402	Who's Sorry Now/Beer Barrel Polka	193?	5.00	10.00	20.00
❑ 9581	Down by the O-Hi-O/Way Down in Arkansaw	193?	5.00	10.00	20.00
❑ 9583	Poor Papa/My Wife Is On a Diet	193?	5.00	10.00	20.00
❑ 9917	Tiger Rag/The Guy Who Stole My Wife	193?	5.00	10.00	20.00
❑ 9918	Lazy River/No Romance in Your Soul	193?	5.00	10.00	20.00

DECCA

Number	Title (A Side/B Side)	Yr	VG	VG+	NM
❑ 4442	She Broke My Heart in Three Places/Don't Change Horses	1944	5.00	10.00	20.00
❑ 4453	The Barn Dance Polka/This Is the Chorus	1944	5.00	10.00	20.00
❑ 4455	Dummy Song/Somedays You Can't Make a Nickel	1944	5.00	10.00	20.00
❑ 18738	Someday (You'll Want Me to Want You)/You Two-Timed Me One Time Too Often	1945	5.00	10.00	20.00
❑ 18745	Sioux City Sue/There's a Tear in My Beer Tonight	1946	5.00	10.00	20.00
❑ 46020	The First Thing I Do Every Mornin'/When Johnny Brings Lelahani Home	1946	5.00	10.00	20.00
❑ 46023	Them Hillbillies Are Mountain Williams Now/Divorce Me C.O.D.	1946	5.00	10.00	20.00
❑ 46062	You Kissed Me Once/The Musket Came Down from the Door	1948	5.00	10.00	20.00
❑ 46131	Someday (You'll Want Me to Want You)/There's a Tear in My Beer Tonight	1949	3.75	7.50	15.00

MELOTONE

Number	Title (A Side/B Side)	Yr	VG	VG+	NM
❑ 5-12-55	Black Eyed Susan Brown/Back in Indiana	1935	5.00	10.00	20.00
❑ 6-02-62	San/Them Hill-Billies Are Mountain Williams Now	1936	5.00	10.00	20.00
❑ 6-04-58	Ida/I Like Bananas. Because They Have No Bones	1936	5.00	10.00	20.00
❑ 6-05-53	Nobody's Sweetheart/At the Dark-Town Strutter's Ball	1936	5.00	10.00	20.00
❑ 6-05-57	Wah-Hoo/Bow Wow Blues	1936	5.00	10.00	20.00
❑ 6-09-51	Is It True What They Say About Dixie/Where Are You Going Honey	1936	5.00	10.00	20.00
❑ 6-10-51	Bye Bye Blues/Take Me Out to the Ball Game	1936	5.00	10.00	20.00
❑ 6-11-57	Hold 'Er Eb'ner/Some of These Days	1936	5.00	10.00	20.00
❑ 6-12-72	Shake Your Dogs/That's What I Learned in College	1936	5.00	10.00	20.00
❑ 7-01-68	Toot, Toot, Tootsie, Goo'bye/You're Driving Me Crazy	1937	5.00	10.00	20.00
❑ 7-03-63	Alexander's Ragtime Band/Margie	1937	5.00	10.00	20.00
❑ 7-05-51	When You Wore a Tulip/The Coat and the Pants Do All of the Work	1937	5.00	10.00	20.00
❑ 7-06-60	Sweet Sue Just You/Hot Lips	1937	5.00	10.00	20.00
❑ 7-08-51	Ain't She Sweet/I've Got a Bimbo Down on the Bamboo Isle	1937	5.00	10.00	20.00
❑ 35-09-14	Ha-Cha-Nan/This Is the Chorus	1935	5.00	10.00	20.00
❑ 35-10-30	Down in the Valley/Meet Me by the Ice House Lizzie	1935	5.00	10.00	20.00
❑ M 13279	Whistlin' Joe from Kokomo/Four Thousand Years Ago	193?	5.00	10.00	20.00
❑ M 13325	Hoosier Stomp/Oakville Twister	193?	5.00	10.00	20.00
❑ M 13370	Farmer Gray/Sentimental Gentlemen from Georgia	193?	5.00	10.00	20.00
❑ M 13387	Yes She Do — No She Don't/I'm Looking for a Girl	193?	5.00	10.00	20.00

OKEH

Number	Title (A Side/B Side)	Yr	VG	VG+	NM
❑ 03734	Nobody's Sweetheart/At the Dark-Town Strutter's Ball	1940	3.75	7.50	15.00
—Reissue of Vocalion 03734					
❑ 03740	Jingle Bells/I'll Soon Be Rolling Home	1940	3.75	7.50	15.00
—Reissue of Vocalion 03740					
❑ 03744	Sweet Sue Just You/Hot Lips	1940	3.75	7.50	15.00
—Reissue of Vocalion 03744					
❑ 04946	Moving Day in Jungle Town/From the Indies to the Andes in His Undies	1940	5.00	10.00	20.00
—Reissue of Vocalion 04946					
❑ 05665	Diga Diga Doo/The Kitten with the Big Green Eyes	1940	6.25	12.50	25.00
❑ 05708	Poor Papa/My Wife Is on a Diet	1940	6.25	12.50	25.00
❑ 05754	Big Noise from Kokomo/Who's Sorry Now	1940	6.25	12.50	25.00
❑ 05809	Okay Baby/The Poor Little Country Maid	1940	6.25	12.50	25.00
❑ 05853	When There's Tears in the Eyes of a Potato/Beatrice Fairfax, Tell Me What to Do	1940	6.25	12.50	25.00
❑ 05891	Way Down in Arkansaw/Noah's Wife	1940	6.25	12.50	25.00
❑ 06065	With a Twist of the Wrist/Keep an Eye on Your Heart	1941	6.25	12.50	25.00
❑ 06114	There'll Be Some Changes Made/Let's Not and Say We Did	1941	6.25	12.50	25.00
❑ 06173	The Streets of New York/Swing Little Indians, Swing	1941	6.25	12.50	25.00
❑ 06217	The Guy Who Stole My Wife/St. Louis Blues	1941	6.25	12.50	25.00
❑ 06273	The Band Played On/The Hut-Sut Song	1941	6.25	12.50	25.00
❑ 06348	He's a Hillbilly Gaucho/Windmill Tillie	1941	6.25	12.50	25.00
❑ 6425	When Lightnin' Struck the Coon Creek Party Line/Since We Put a Radio Out in the Henhouse	1941	6.25	12.50	25.00
❑ 6503	Dude Cowboy/Bull Frog Serenade	1942	6.25	12.50	25.00
❑ 6599	Rhyme Your Sweetheart/Blues	1942	6.25	12.50	25.00

ORIOLE

Number	Title (A Side/B Side)	Yr	VG	VG+	NM
❑ 8418	Four Thousand Years Ago/Whistlin' Joe from Kokomo	193?	5.00	10.00	20.00

PERFECT

Number	Title (A Side/B Side)	Yr	VG	VG+	NM
❑ 7-01-68	Toot, Toot, Tootsie, Goo'bye/You're Driving Me Crazy	1937	5.00	10.00	20.00
❑ 7-05-51	When You Wore a Tulip/The Coat and the Pants Do All of the Work	1937	5.00	10.00	20.00
❑ 7-09-61	Breezin' Along with the Breeze/I Wish I Could Shimmy Like My Sister Kate	1937	5.00	10.00	20.00

VOCALION

Number	Title (A Side/B Side)	Yr	VG	VG+	NM
❑ 03644	Breezin' Along with the Breeze/I Wish I Could Shimmy Like My Sister Kate	1937	6.25	12.50	25.00
❑ 03683	Runnin' Wild/Goofus	1937	6.25	12.50	25.00
❑ 03724	Whistlin' Joe from Kokomo/Four Thousand Years Ago	1937	5.00	10.00	20.00
—Reissue					
❑ 03725	Hoosier Stomp/Oakville Twister	1937	5.00	10.00	20.00
—Reissue					

Number	Title (A Side/B Side)	Yr	VG	VG+	NM
❑ 03726	Farmer Gray/Sentimental Gentlemen from Georgia	1937	5.00	10.00	20.00
—Reissue					
❑ 03727	Yes She Do — No She Don't/I'm Looking for a Girl	1937	5.00	10.00	20.00
—Reissue					
❑ 03728	Ha-Cha-Nan/This Is the Chorus	1937	5.00	10.00	20.00
—Reissue					
❑ 03729	Down in the Valley/Meet Me by the Ice House Lizzie	1937	5.00	10.00	20.00
—Reissue					
❑ 03730	Black Eyed Susan Brown/Back in Indiana	1937	5.00	10.00	20.00
—Reissue					
❑ 03731	San/Them Hill-Billies Are Mountain Williams Now	1937	5.00	10.00	20.00
—Reissue					
❑ 03732	Ida/I Like Bananas. Because They Have No Bones	1937	5.00	10.00	20.00
—Reissue					
❑ 03733	Wah-Hoo/Bow Wow Blues	1937	5.00	10.00	20.00
—Reissue					
❑ 03734	Nobody's Sweetheart/At the Dark-Town Strutter's Ball	1937	5.00	10.00	20.00
—Reissue					
❑ 03735	Is It True What They Say About Dixie/Where Are You Going Honey	1937	5.00	10.00	20.00
—Reissue					
❑ 03736	Bye Bye Blues/Take Me Out to the Ball Game	1937	5.00	10.00	20.00
—Reissue					
❑ 03737	Hold 'Er Eb'ner/Some of These Days	1937	5.00	10.00	20.00
—Reissue					
❑ 03738	Shake Your Dogs/That's What I Learned in College	1937	5.00	10.00	20.00
—Reissue					
❑ 03739	Toot, Toot, Tootsie, Goo'bye/You're Driving Me Crazy	1937	5.00	10.00	20.00
—Reissue					
❑ 03740	Jingle Bells/I'll Soon Be Rolling Home	1937	5.00	10.00	20.00
—Presumably a reissue					
❑ 03741	Alexander's Ragtime Band/Margie	1937	5.00	10.00	20.00
—Reissue					
❑ 03742	Pick That Bass/Everybody Stomp	1937	5.00	10.00	20.00
—Presumably a reissue					
❑ 03743	When You Wore a Tulip/The Coat and the Pants Do All of the Work	1937	5.00	10.00	20.00
—Reissue					
❑ 03744	Sweet Sue Just You/Hot Lips	1937	5.00	10.00	20.00
—Reissue					
❑ 03745	Ain't She Sweet/I've Got a Bimbo Down on the Bamboo Isle	1937	5.00	10.00	20.00
—Reissue					
❑ 03853	I Want a Girl/I Like Mountain Music	1938	6.25	12.50	25.00
❑ 03901	It Ain't Nobody's Biz'ness What I Do/No More	1938	5.00	10.00	20.00
❑ 03949	Virginia Blues/I Ain't Got Nobody	1938	5.00	10.00	20.00
❑ 04090	Down Home Rag/Meet Me Tonight in the Cow Shed	1938	5.00	10.00	20.00
❑ 04215	After You've Gone/You Said Something When You Said Dixie	1938	5.00	10.00	20.00
❑ 04289	Red Hot Fannie/Swinging with Dora	1938	6.25	12.50	25.00
❑ 04352	Milenberg Joys/How Ya Gonna Keep 'Em Down on the Farm	1938	6.25	12.50	25.00
❑ 04426	A Hot Dog, a Blanket, and You/The Flat Foot Floogie	1938	6.25	12.50	25.00
❑ 04481	The Sheik of Araby/Tit Willow	1938	6.25	12.50	25.00
❑ 04502	The Man with the Whiskers/The Girl Friend of the Whirling Dervish	1938	6.25	12.50	25.00
❑ 04614	Wabash Blues/Oh By Jingo!	1939	6.25	12.50	25.00
❑ 04688	Like a Monkey Likes Cocoanuts/Where Has My Little Dog Gone	1939	6.25	12.50	25.00
❑ 04697	It's a Lonely Trail/Annabelle	1939	6.25	12.50	25.00
❑ 04824	Beer Barrel Polka/Ever So Quiet	1939	5.00	10.00	20.00
❑ 04893	When You're Smiling/Skeede-Waddle-Dee-Waddle-Do	1939	6.25	12.50	25.00
❑ 04946	Moving Day in Jungle Town/From the Indies to the Andes in His Undies	1939	6.25	12.50	25.00
❑ 05013	Limehouse Blues/Look on the Bright Side	1939	6.25	12.50	25.00
❑ 05119	Willie, Willie Will Ya!/The Merry Go Roundup	1939	6.25	12.50	25.00
❑ 05132	Sam the College Leader Man/Put On Your Old Red Flannels	1939	6.25	12.50	25.00
❑ 05145	Are You Havin' Any Fun/Start the Day Right	1939	6.25	12.50	25.00
❑ 05214	The Martins and the Coys/Rural Rhythm	1939	6.25	12.50	25.00
❑ 05295	In an Old Dutch Garden/Careless	1939	6.25	12.50	25.00
❑ 05345	He'd Have to Get Under, Get Out and Get Under/Oh You Beautiful Doll	1940	6.25	12.50	25.00
❑ 05390	Ma, She's Making Eyes at Me/I'm Just Wild About Harry	1940	6.25	12.50	25.00
❑ 05485	Sam, the College Leader Man/The Pants That My Pappy Gave to Me	1940	6.25	12.50	25.00
❑ 05547	No, No, Nora/O-Hi-O	1940	6.25	12.50	25.00
7-Inch Extended Plays					
TOPS					
❑ 45-R261-49	Humming Bird/The Man from Laramie//The Kentuckian/Daniel Boone	1955	5.00	10.00	20.00
—We're not sure about the existence of a cover; if it does, add another $20					

HOPE (COUNTRY MUSIC'S QUEST FOR A CURE)

All-star group performing a benefit for the T.J. Martell Foundation (cancer and AIDS research).

Number	Title (A Side/B Side)	Yr	VG	VG+	NM
45s					
GIANT					
❑ 7-17669	Hope (All Star Version A)/Hope (All Star Version B)	1996	—	2.00	4.00

HORN, DEANNE

Number	Title (A Side/B Side)	Yr	VG	VG+	NM
45s					
CHARTWHEEL					
❑ 102	I Just Want to Love You/I'm a Country Girl (Livin' in a City World)	1978	—	3.00	6.00
❑ 108	I Know/(B-side unknown)	1978	—	3.00	6.00

HORN, JAMES T.

Number	Title (A Side/B Side)	Yr	VG	VG+	NM
45s					
CURB/UNIVERSAL					
❑ 56096	Texas Diary/Geronimo	1997	—	—	3.00

HORNSBY, BRUCE, AND THE RANGE

"Mandolin Rain" made the top 40 of the country charts. As it doesn't sound much different than most of his other material, we've included his complete vinyl discography.

Number	Title (A Side/B Side)	Yr	VG	VG+	NM
45s					
RCA					
❑ 2621-7-R	Across the River/Fire on the Cross	1990	—	—	3.00
❑ 2704-7-R	Lost Soul/Stranger on the Mountain	1990	—	—	3.00
❑ 2846-7-R	Set Me in Motion/Excerpts	1991	—	—	3.00
❑ 5023-7-R	The Way It Is/The Wild Frontier	1986	—	—	3.00
❑ 5087-7-R	Mandolin Rain/The Red Plains (Live)	1987	—	—	3.00
❑ 5087-7-R [PS]	Mandolin Rain/The Red Plains (Live)	1987	—	—	3.00
❑ 5165-7-R	Every Little Kiss (Remix)/Mandolin Rain (Live)	1987	—	—	3.00
❑ 7645-7-R	The Valley Road/The Long Race (Live)	1988	—	—	3.00
❑ 7645-7-R [PS]	The Valley Road/The Long Race (Live)	1988	—	—	3.00
❑ 8340-7-R	The Way It Is/Mandolin Rain	1988	—	—	3.00
—Gold Standard Series					
❑ 8678-7-R	Look Out Any Window/The Way It Is	1988	—	—	3.00
❑ 8678-7-R [PS]	Look Out Any Window/The Way It Is	1988	—	—	3.00
❑ 8776-7-R	Defenders of the Flag/On the Western Skyline	1988	—	—	3.00
❑ PB-14361	Every Little Kiss/The Red Plains	1986	—	2.50	5.00
❑ 64382	Walk in the Sun/Cruise Control	1995	—	—	3.00
Albums					
RCA					
❑ 2041-1-R	A Night on the Town	1990	3.00	6.00	12.00
❑ 6686-1-R	Scenes from the Southside	1988	2.00	4.00	8.00
RCA VICTOR					
❑ 5904-1-RX	The Way It Is	1986	2.00	4.00	8.00
—Revised edition; cover is dark with a photo of the whole band					
❑ NFL1-8058	The Way It Is	1986	3.75	7.50	15.00
—Original edition; cover is light brown with blurry picture of Hornsby in the middle					

HORTON, BILLIE JEAN

Number	Title (A Side/B Side)	Yr	VG	VG+	NM
45s					
20TH FOX					
❑ 238	I'd Give the World (To Have You Back Again)/Angel Eyes	1961	3.75	7.50	15.00
❑ 266	Ocean of Tears/Don't Take His Love	1961	3.75	7.50	15.00
❑ 291	Devoted to You/Octopus	1961	3.75	7.50	15.00
ABC-PARAMOUNT					
❑ 10332	Tell Him I Can't See Him Anymore/I'd Rather You Didn't Love Me	1962	3.75	7.50	15.00
ATLANTIC					
❑ 2249	I Know I'll Never See Him Again/Johnny Come Lately	1964	3.75	7.50	15.00

HORTON, JOHNNY

Number	Title (A Side/B Side)	Yr	VG	VG+	NM
45s					
ABBOTT					
❑ 100	Candy Jones/Devilish Lovelight	1951	10.00	20.00	40.00
❑ 101	Happy Millionaire/Mean Mean Son of a Gun	1951	10.00	20.00	40.00
❑ 102	Plaid and Calico/Done Roving	1951	10.00	20.00	40.00
—B-side by Bill Thompson's Westerners					
❑ 103	Birds and Butteflies/Coal Smoke, Valve Oil and Steam	1951	10.00	20.00	40.00
❑ 104	Go and Wash (Those Dirty Feet)/In My Home in Shelby County	1951	10.00	20.00	40.00
❑ 105	Shadows on the Old Bayou/Talk Gobbler Talk	1951	10.00	20.00	40.00
❑ 106	Smokey Joe's Barbeque/Words	1951	10.00	20.00	40.00
❑ 107	Long Rocky Road/On the Banks of the Beautiful Nile	1952	10.00	20.00	40.00
❑ 108	Somebody Rocking in My Broken Chair/Betty Lorraine	1952	10.00	20.00	40.00
—With Hillbilly Barton					
❑ 109	Rhythm in My Baby's Walk/Bowlin' Baby	1952	10.00	20.00	40.00
❑ 135	Plaid and Calico/Shadows on the Old Bayou	1953	7.50	15.00	30.00
COLUMBIA					
❑ 21504	Honky Tonk Man/I'm Ready If You're Willing	1956	7.50	15.00	30.00
❑ 21538	I'm a One Woman Man/I Don't Like I Did	1956	6.25	12.50	25.00
❑ 30568 [S]	Sink the Bismarck/The Same Old Tale the Crow Told Me	1960	6.25	12.50	25.00
—"Stereo Single 33"; small hole, plays at 33 1/3 rpm					
❑ 31104 [S]	North to Alaska/Whispering Pines	1961	5.00	10.00	20.00
❑ 31105 [S]	Johnny Reb/The Mansion You Stole	1961	5.00	10.00	20.00
❑ 31106 [S]	When It's Springtime in Alaska/The Battle of New Orleans	1961	5.00	10.00	20.00

Number	Title (A Side/B Side)	Yr	VG	VG+	NM
❑ 31107 [S]	All for the Love of a Girl/Sink the Bismarck	1961	5.00	10.00	20.00
❑ 31108 [S]	The Brave Comanche/Jim Bridger	1961	5.00	10.00	20.00

—The above five all are Columbia "Stereo 7" singles with small center holes

Number	Title (A Side/B Side)	Yr	VG	VG+	NM
❑ 40813	I'm Coming Home/I Got a Hole in My Picture	1957	7.50	15.00	30.00
❑ 40919	She Knows Why/The Woman I Need	1957	5.00	10.00	20.00
❑ 40986	I'll Do It Every Time/Let's Take the Long Way Home	1957	5.00	10.00	20.00
❑ 41043	You're My Baby/Lover's Rock	1957	7.50	15.00	30.00
❑ 41110	Honky Tonk Hardwood Floor/The Wild One	1958	15.00	30.00	60.00
❑ 41210	All Grown Up/Counterfeit Love	1958	5.00	10.00	20.00
❑ 41308	When It's Springtime in Alaska (It's Forty Below)/ Whispering Pines	1958	3.75	7.50	15.00
❑ 41308 [PS]	When It's Springtime in Alaska (It's Forty Below)/ Whispering Pines	1958	7.50	15.00	30.00

—Promo-only black and white sleeve

Number	Title (A Side/B Side)	Yr	VG	VG+	NM
❑ 41339	The Battle of New Orleans/All for the Love of a Girl	1959	3.75	7.50	15.00
❑ 41339 [PS]	The Battle of New Orleans/All for the Love of a Girl	1959	5.00	10.00	20.00
❑ 41437	Johnny Reb/Sal's Got a Sugar Lip	1959	3.75	7.50	15.00
❑ 41502	I'm Ready If You're Willing/Take Me Like I Am	1959	3.75	7.50	15.00
❑ 41522	They Shined Up Rudolph's Nose/The Electrified Donkey	1959	3.75	7.50	15.00
❑ 41568	Sink the Bismarck/The Same Old Tale the Crow Told Me	1960	3.00	6.00	12.00
❑ 41568 [PS]	Sink the Bismarck/The Same Old Tale the Crow Told Me	1960	5.00	10.00	20.00
❑ 41685	Johnny Freedom/Comanche	1960	3.00	6.00	12.00
❑ 41685 [PS]	Johnny Freedom/Comanche	1960	5.00	10.00	20.00
❑ 41782	North to Alaska/The Mansion You Stole	1960	3.00	6.00	12.00
❑ 41782 [PS]	North to Alaska/The Mansion You Stole	1960	5.00	10.00	20.00
❑ 41963	Sleepy Eyed John/They'll Never Take Her Love from Me	1961	3.00	6.00	12.00
❑ 41963 [PS]	Sleepy Eyed John/They'll Never Take Her Love from Me	1961	5.00	10.00	20.00
❑ 42063	Ole Slewfoot/Miss Marcy	1961	3.00	6.00	12.00
❑ 42063 [PS]	Ole Slewfoot/Miss Marcy	1961	5.00	10.00	20.00
❑ 42302	Honky Tonk Man/Words	1962	3.75	7.50	15.00
❑ 42302 [PS]	Honky Tonk Man/Words	1962	5.00	10.00	20.00
❑ 42653	All Grown Up/I'm a One Woman Man	1962	3.00	6.00	12.00
❑ 42653 [PS]	All Grown Up/I'm a One Woman Man	1962	5.00	10.00	20.00
❑ 42774	Sugar Coated Baby/When It's Springtime in Alaska (It's Forty Below)	1963	2.50	5.00	10.00
❑ 42993	Hooray for That Little Difference/Tell My Baby I Love Her	1964	2.50	5.00	10.00
❑ 42993 [PS]	Hooray for That Little Difference/Tell My Baby I Love Her	1964	5.00	10.00	20.00
❑ 43143	Lost Highway/The Same Old Tale the Crow Told Me	1964	2.50	5.00	10.00
❑ 43228	Rock Island Line/I Just Don't Like This Kind of Lovin'	1965	2.50	5.00	10.00
❑ 43719	Sam Magee/All for the Love of a Girl	1966	2.00	4.00	8.00
❑ 44156	The Battle of New Orleans/All for the Love of a Girl	1967	—	3.00	6.00

CORMAC

Number	Title (A Side/B Side)	Yr	VG	VG+	NM
❑ 1193	Plaid and Calico/Done Roving	1951	30.00	60.00	120.00
❑ 1197	Birds and Butteflies/Coal Smoke, Valve Oil and Steam	1951	30.00	60.00	120.00

DOT

Number	Title (A Side/B Side)	Yr	VG	VG+	NM
❑ 15966	Plaid and Calico/Shadows on the Old Bayou	1959	3.00	6.00	12.00

MERCURY

Number	Title (A Side/B Side)	Yr	VG	VG+	NM
❑ 6412	The Devil Sent Me You/First Train Headin' South	1952	7.50	15.00	30.00
❑ 6418	The Rest of Your Life/This Won't Be the First Time	1952	7.50	15.00	30.00
❑ 70014	I Won't Forget/The Child's Side of Life	1952	7.50	15.00	30.00
❑ 70100	Tennessee Jive/The Mansion You Stole	1953	7.50	15.00	30.00
❑ 70156	S.S. Loveline/I Won't Get Dreamy-Eyed	1953	7.50	15.00	30.00
❑ 70198	You, You, You/Red Lips and Warm Red Wine	1953	7.50	15.00	30.00
❑ 70227	All for the Love of a Girl/Broken Hearted	1953	7.50	15.00	30.00
❑ 70325	Move On Down the Line/Train with the Rhumba Beat	1954	7.50	15.00	30.00
❑ 70399	The Door of Your Mansion/Ha Ha and Moonface	1954	7.50	15.00	30.00
❑ 70462	No True Love/There'll Never Be Another Mary	1954	7.50	15.00	30.00
❑ 70636	Journey with No End/Ridin' the Sunshine Special	1955	7.50	15.00	30.00
❑ 70707	Big Wheels Rollin'/Hey Sweet, Sweet Thing	1955	7.50	15.00	30.00

7-Inch Extended Plays

COLUMBIA

Number	Title (A Side/B Side)	Yr	VG	VG+	NM
❑ B-13621	The Battle of New Orleans/Whispering Pines// The First Train Heading South/Lost Highway	1960	3.00	6.00	12.00
❑ B-13621 [PS]	The Spectacular Johnny Horton, Vol. 1	1960	4.00	8.00	16.00
❑ B-13622	Joe's Been a-Gettin' There/Sam Magee//When It's Springtime in Alaska/Cherokee Boogie	1960	3.00	6.00	12.00
❑ B-13622 [PS]	The Spectacular Johnny Horton, Vol. 2	1960	4.00	8.00	16.00
❑ B-13623	All for the Love of a Girl/The Golden Rocket//Mr. Moonlight/Got the Bull by the Horns	1960	3.00	6.00	12.00
❑ B-13623 [PS]	The Spectacular Johnny Horton, Vol. 3	1960	4.00	8.00	16.00

Albums

BRIAR

Number	Title (A Side/B Side)	Yr	VG	VG+	NM
❑ 104 [M]	Done Rovin'	196?	37.50	75.00	150.00

COLUMBIA

Number	Title (A Side/B Side)	Yr	VG	VG+	NM
❑ CL 1362 [M]	The Spectacular Johnny Horton	1959	7.50	15.00	30.00
❑ CL 1478 [M]	Johnny Horton Makes History	1960	7.50	15.00	30.00
❑ 1596/8396	Johnny Horton's Greatest Hits Bonus Photo	1961	2.50	5.00	10.00
❑ CL 1596 [M]	Johnny Horton's Greatest Hits	1961	6.25	12.50	25.00
❑ CL 1721 [M]	Honky-Tonk Man	1962	7.50	15.00	30.00
❑ CL 2299 [M]	I Can't Forget You	1965	6.25	12.50	25.00
❑ CL 2566 [M]	Johnny Horton on Stage at the Louisiana Hayride	1966	5.00	10.00	20.00
❑ CS 8167 [S]	The Spectacular Johnny Horton	1959	10.00	20.00	40.00
❑ CS 8269 [S]	Johnny Horton Makes History	1960	10.00	20.00	40.00
❑ CS 8396 [S]	Johnny Horton's Greatest Hits	1961	7.50	15.00	30.00
❑ PC 8396	Johnny Horton's Greatest Hits	198?	2.00	4.00	8.00

—Budget-line reissue

Number	Title (A Side/B Side)	Yr	VG	VG+	NM
❑ CS 8779 [R]	Honky-Tonk Man	1962	3.75	7.50	15.00
❑ CS 9099 [R]	I Can't Forget You	1965	3.75	7.50	15.00
❑ CS 9366 [S]	Johnny Horton on Stage at the Louisiana Hayride	1966	6.25	12.50	25.00
❑ CS 9940	Johnny Horton On the Road	1969	3.75	7.50	15.00
❑ G 30884 [(2)]	The World of Johnny Horton	1971	3.75	7.50	15.00

DOT

Number	Title (A Side/B Side)	Yr	VG	VG+	NM
❑ DLP 3221 [M]	Johnny Horton	1962	7.50	15.00	30.00
❑ DLP 25221 [R]	Johnny Horton	1962	3.75	7.50	15.00

HARMONY

Number	Title (A Side/B Side)	Yr	VG	VG+	NM
❑ HS 11291	The Unforgettable Johnny Horton	196?	3.00	6.00	12.00
❑ HS 11384	The Legendary Johnny Horton	1970	3.00	6.00	12.00
❑ KH 30394	The Battle of New Orleans	1971	3.00	6.00	12.00

HILLTOP

Number	Title (A Side/B Side)	Yr	VG	VG+	NM
❑ 6012	The Voice of Johnny Horton	196?	3.00	6.00	12.00
❑ 6060	All for the Love of a Girl	196?	3.00	6.00	12.00

MERCURY

Number	Title (A Side/B Side)	Yr	VG	VG+	NM
❑ MG-20478 [M]	The Fantastic Johnny Horton	1959	12.50	25.00	50.00

SESAC

Number	Title (A Side/B Side)	Yr	VG	VG+	NM
❑ 1201 [M]	Free and Easy Songs	1959	37.50	75.00	150.00

HORTON, STEVEN WAYNE

45s

CAPITOL

Number	Title (A Side/B Side)	Yr	VG	VG+	NM
❑ B-44350	Roll Over/I've Been Stung	1989	—	2.00	4.00
❑ B-44482	Tennessee Plates/Nothin' Shakin'	1989	—	2.00	4.00

Albums

CAPITOL

Number	Title (A Side/B Side)	Yr	VG	VG+	NM
❑ C1-91983	Steven Wayne Horton	1989	3.00	6.00	12.00

HOSFORD, LARRY

45s

SHELTER

Number	Title (A Side/B Side)	Yr	VG	VG+	NM
❑ 40312	Long Distance Kisses/Long Line to Chicago	1974	—	2.50	5.00
❑ 40381	Everything's Broken Down/Long Line to Chicago	1975	—	2.50	5.00
❑ 40434	A King Takes a Queen/Singers and Dancers	1975	—	2.50	5.00
❑ 62001	Nobody Remembers the Loser/Wishing I Could	1976	—	2.50	5.00

WARNER BROS.

Number	Title (A Side/B Side)	Yr	VG	VG+	NM
❑ 8445	Home Run Willie/Salinas	1977	—	2.50	5.00

Albums

SHELTER

Number	Title (A Side/B Side)	Yr	VG	VG+	NM
❑ 2132	A.K.A. Lorenzo	1975	3.75	7.50	15.00
❑ SRL-52003	Crosswords	1976	3.00	6.00	12.00

HOUSE, DAVID

45s

DOOR KNOB

Number	Title (A Side/B Side)	Yr	VG	VG+	NM
❑ 177	Everything's All Right/Should've Been Chasin' My Dreams	1982	—	2.50	5.00
❑ 183	Little White Lies/Maybe Now We Can Be Friends	1982	—	2.50	5.00

HOUSE, JAMES

45s

EPIC

Number	Title (A Side/B Side)	Yr	VG	VG+	NM
❑ 34-77610	A Real Good Way to Wind Up Lonesome/That's Something (You Don't See Every Day)	1994	—	—	3.00
❑ 34-77752	Little by Little/Take Me Away	1994	—	—	3.00
❑ 34-77870	This Is Me Missing You/Take Me Away	1995	—	2.00	4.00
❑ 34-77982	Anything for Love/Silence Makes a Lonesome Sound	1995	—	—	3.00
❑ 34-78458	Until You Set Me Free/Days Gone By	1996	—	—	3.00

MCA

Number	Title (A Side/B Side)	Yr	VG	VG+	NM
❑ 53510	Don't Quit Me Now/Call It in the Air	1989	—	—	3.00
❑ 53669	That'll Be the Last Thing/Lucinda	1989	—	—	3.00
❑ 53731	Hard Times for an Honest Man/Born Ready	1989	—	—	3.00
❑ 53934	You Just Get Better All the Time/I Ain't Like That Anymore	1990	—	2.00	4.00
❑ 79039	Southern Belles/Take It	1990	—	2.00	4.00

HOUSTON, DAVID

45s

COLONIAL

Number	Title (A Side/B Side)	Yr	VG	VG+	NM
❑ 101	Waltz of the Angels/(B-side unknown)	1978	2.00	4.00	8.00

COUNTRY INT'L.

Number	Title (A Side/B Side)	Yr	VG	VG+	NM
❑ 145	You're the Perfect Reason/We Couldn't Make It Love	1980	—	3.00	6.00
❑ 148	Sad Love Song Lady/Thanks for Being You and Loving Me	1980	—	3.00	6.00
❑ 149	The Bottom Line/We Couldn't Make It Love	1980	—	3.00	6.00
❑ 155	Bandera Waltz/(B-side unknown)	1981	—	3.00	6.00
❑ 220	A Penny for Your Thoughts Tonight Virginia/(B-side unknown)	1989	—	3.00	6.00

DERRICK

Number	Title (A Side/B Side)	Yr	VG	VG+	NM
❑ 126	Let Your Love Fall Back on Me/Take Me to Your Heart	1979	—	3.00	6.00
❑ 127	Here's to All the Hard Working Husbands (In the World)/Next Sunday I'm Gonna Be Saved	1979	—	3.00	6.00

ELEKTRA

Number	Title (A Side/B Side)	Yr	VG	VG+	NM
❑ 45513	Sunday I'm Gonna Be Saved/Waltz of the Angels	1978	—	2.00	4.00
❑ 45552	Best Friends Make the Worst Enemies/There Won't Be a Wedding	1978	—	2.00	4.00
❑ 46028	Faded Love and Winter Roses/Beyond the Blue Horizon	1979	—	2.00	4.00

EPIC

Number	Title (A Side/B Side)	Yr	VG	VG+	NM
❑ 9625	Mountain of Love/Angeline	1963	2.00	4.00	8.00
❑ 9658	Chickashay/Passing Through	1964	2.00	4.00	8.00
❑ 9690	One If For Him, Two If For Me/Your Memories	1964	2.00	4.00	8.00
❑ 9720	Love Looks Good on You/My Little Lady	1964	2.00	4.00	8.00
❑ 9746	Sweet, Sweet Judy/Too Many Times (Away from You)	1964	2.00	4.00	8.00
❑ 9782	Rose Colored Glasses/Ballad of the Fool Killer	1965	2.50	5.00	10.00
❑ 9831	Livin' in a House Full of Love/Cowpoke	1965	2.00	4.00	8.00
❑ 9884	Sammy/I'll Take You Home Again, Kathleen	1966	2.00	4.00	8.00
❑ 9884 [PS]	Sammy/I'll Take You Home Again, Kathleen	1966	2.50	5.00	10.00
❑ 10025	Almost Persuaded/We Got Love	1966	2.00	4.00	8.00
❑ 10102	A Loser's Cathedral/Where Could I Go? (But to Her)	1966	—	3.00	6.00
❑ 10102 [PS]	A Loser's Cathedral/Where Could I Go? (But to Her)	1966	2.50	5.00	10.00
❑ 10154	With One Exception/Sweet, Sweet Judy	1967	—	3.00	6.00
❑ 10154 [PS]	With One Exception/Sweet, Sweet Judy	1967	2.50	5.00	10.00
❑ 10224	You Mean the World to Me/Don't Mention Tomorrow	1967	—	3.00	6.00
❑ 10224 [PS]	You Mean the World to Me/Don't Mention Tomorrow	1967	2.50	5.00	10.00
❑ 10291	Have a Little Faith/Too Far Gone	1968	—	3.00	6.00
❑ 10291 [PS]	Have a Little Faith/Too Far Gone	1968	2.50	5.00	10.00
❑ 10338	Already It's Heaven/Lighter Shade of Pale	1968	—	3.00	6.00
❑ 10338 [PS]	Already It's Heaven/Lighter Shade of Pale	1968	2.50	5.00	10.00
❑ 10394	Where Love Used to Live/I Love a Rainbow	1968	—	3.00	6.00
❑ 10430	My Woman's Good to Me/Lullaby to a Little Girl	1968	—	3.00	6.00
❑ 10488	I'm Down to My Last "I Love You"/Watching My World Walk Away	1969	—	3.00	6.00
❑ 10539	Baby, Baby (I Know You're a Lady)/True Love's a Lasting Thing	1969	—	3.00	6.00
❑ 10596	I Do My Swinging at Home/Then I'll Know You Care	1970	—	3.00	6.00
❑ 10643	Wonders of the Wine/If God Can Forgive Me	1970	—	3.00	6.00
❑ 10696	A Woman Always Knows/The Rest of My Life	1970	—	3.00	6.00
❑ 10748	Nashville/That's Why I Cry	1971	—	3.00	6.00
❑ 10778	Maiden's Prayer/Home Sweet Home	1971	—	3.00	6.00
❑ 10830	The Day That Love Walked In/Sweet Lovin'	1972	—	3.00	6.00
❑ 10870	Soft, Sweet and Warm/The Rest of My Life	1972	—	3.00	6.00
❑ 10911	I Wonder How John Felt (When He Baptized Jesus)/Will the Circle Be Unbroken	1972	2.00	4.00	8.00
❑ 10939	Good Things/The Love She Gives	1973	—	3.00	6.00
❑ 10995	She's All Woman/Sweet Lovin'	1973	—	2.50	5.00
❑ 11048	The Lady of the Night/Thank You Teardrop	1973	—	2.50	5.00
❑ 11096	That Same Ol' Look of Love/Clinging Vine	1974	—	2.50	5.00
❑ 50009	Can't You Feel It/I Walk and I Walk and I Walk	1974	—	2.50	5.00
❑ 50066	A Man Needs Love/Flower of Love	1975	—	2.50	5.00
❑ 50113	I'll Be Your Steppin' Stone/Then I'll Know You Care	1975	—	2.50	5.00
❑ 50134	Sweet Molly/Old Blind Fiddler	1975	—	2.50	5.00
—With Calvin Crawford					
❑ 50156	The Woman on My Mind/I Can't Sit Still	1975	—	2.50	5.00
❑ 50186	What a Night/From the Bottom of My Heart	1976	—	2.50	5.00
❑ 50241	Lullaby Song/White Circle	1976	—	2.50	5.00
❑ 50275	Come On Down (To Our Favorite Forget-About-Her Place)/Me and Susan Wright	1976	—	2.50	5.00

EXCELSIOR

Number	Title (A Side/B Side)	Yr	VG	VG+	NM
❑ 1007	My Lady/Something You've Never Heard	1981	—	2.50	5.00
❑ 1012	Texas Ida Red/(B-side unknown)	1981	—	3.00	6.00
❑ 1015	After All/(B-side unknown)	1981	—	2.00	4.00

GUSTO

Number	Title (A Side/B Side)	Yr	VG	VG+	NM
❑ 156	So Many Ways/Touch My World	1977	—	3.00	6.00
❑ 161	Amazing Grace/Return to Me	1977	—	—	—
—Canceled					
❑ 162	Ain't That Lovin' You Baby/Love Is a Mystery	1977	—	3.00	6.00
❑ 168	The Twelfth of Never/Barroom Champagne	1977	—	3.00	6.00
❑ 172	It Started All Over Again/Touch My World	1977	—	3.00	6.00
❑ 184	No Tell Motel/Hate to Tell Baby a Lie	1978	—	3.00	6.00

IMPERIAL

Number	Title (A Side/B Side)	Yr	VG	VG+	NM
❑ 8291	I'm Sorry I Made You Cry/Blue Prelude	1955	10.00	20.00	40.00

NRC

Number	Title (A Side/B Side)	Yr	VG	VG+	NM
❑ 005	Waited So Long/All I Do Is Dream of You	1958	5.00	10.00	20.00
❑ 012	The Key/So Young, So Unknowing	1958	5.00	10.00	20.00
❑ 047	It's Been So Long/Kalua	1959	5.00	10.00	20.00

PHILLIPS INTERNATIONAL

Number	Title (A Side/B Side)	Yr	VG	VG+	NM
❑ 3583	Sherry's Lips/Miss Brown	1961	7.50	15.00	30.00

RCA VICTOR

Number	Title (A Side/B Side)	Yr	VG	VG+	NM
❑ 47-6611	Sugar Sweet/Hasta Luego	1956	7.50	15.00	30.00
❑ 47-6696	Blue Prelude/I'll Always Have It on My Mind	1956	7.50	15.00	30.00
❑ 47-6837	Someone Else's Arms/Ain't Going There No More	1957	7.50	15.00	30.00
❑ 47-6927	One and Only/Hackin' Around	1957	12.50	25.00	50.00
❑ 47-7001	The Teenage Frankie and Johnny/I'll Follow	1957	7.50	15.00	30.00

SOUNDWAVES

Number	Title (A Side/B Side)	Yr	VG	VG+	NM
❑ 4712	E.T. Still Means Ernest Tubb to Me/One Good Cry Away from Happiness	1982	—	2.00	4.00

SUN

Number	Title (A Side/B Side)	Yr	VG	VG+	NM
❑ 403	Sherry's Lips/Miss Brown	1966	5.00	10.00	20.00
❑ 1127	Sherry's Lips/Miss Brown	1972	2.00	4.00	8.00

Albums

EPIC

Number	Title (A Side/B Side)	Yr	VG	VG+	NM
❑ EGP 502 [(2)]	The World of David Houston	1970	5.00	10.00	20.00
❑ LN 24112 [M]	New Voice from Nashville	1964	3.75	7.50	15.00
❑ LN 24156 [M]	12 Great Country Hits	1965	3.75	7.50	15.00
❑ LN 24213 [M]	Almost Persuaded	1966	3.75	7.50	15.00
❑ LN 24303 [M]	A Loser's Cathedral	1967	5.00	10.00	20.00
❑ LN 24320 [M]	Golden Hymns	1967	5.00	10.00	20.00
❑ LN 24338 [M]	You Mean the World to Me	1967	5.00	10.00	20.00
❑ LN 24342 [M]	David Houston's Greatest Hits	1968	7.50	15.00	30.00
❑ BN 26112 [S]	New Voice from Nashville	1964	5.00	10.00	20.00
❑ BN 26156 [S]	12 Great Country Hits	1965	5.00	10.00	20.00
❑ BN 26213 [S]	Almost Persuaded	1966	5.00	10.00	20.00
❑ BN 26303 [S]	A Loser's Cathedral	1967	3.75	7.50	15.00
❑ BN 26320 [S]	Golden Hymns	1967	3.75	7.50	15.00
❑ BN 26338 [S]	You Mean the World to Me	1967	3.75	7.50	15.00
❑ BN 26342 [S]	David Houston's Greatest Hits	1968	3.75	7.50	15.00
❑ BN 26391	Already It's Heaven	1968	3.75	7.50	15.00
❑ BN 26432	Where Love Used to Live	1969	3.75	7.50	15.00
❑ BN 26482	David	1969	3.75	7.50	15.00
❑ BN 26539	Baby, Baby	1970	3.75	7.50	15.00
❑ E 30108	Wonders of the Wine	1970	3.75	7.50	15.00
❑ E 30437	Sweet Lovin'	1971	3.75	7.50	15.00
❑ E 30602	David Houston's Greatest Hits, Volume 2	1971	3.75	7.50	15.00
❑ E 30657	A Woman Always Knows	1971	3.75	7.50	15.00
❑ KE 31385	The Day Love Walked In	1972	3.00	6.00	12.00
❑ KE 32189	Good Things	1973	3.00	6.00	12.00
❑ KE 33948	What a Night	1976	3.00	6.00	12.00

GUSTO

Number	Title (A Side/B Side)	Yr	VG	VG+	NM
❑ 0012	The Best of David Houston	1978	2.50	5.00	10.00

HARMONY

Number	Title (A Side/B Side)	Yr	VG	VG+	NM
❑ HS 11412	David Houston	1970	2.50	5.00	10.00
❑ KH 31778	The Many Sides of David Houston	1972	2.50	5.00	10.00
❑ KH 32287	Old Time Religion	1973	2.50	5.00	10.00

RCA CAMDEN

Number	Title (A Side/B Side)	Yr	VG	VG+	NM
❑ CAL-2126 [M]	David Houston Sings	1966	3.75	7.50	15.00
❑ CAS-2126 [R]	David Houston Sings	1966	2.50	5.00	10.00

STARDAY

Number	Title (A Side/B Side)	Yr	VG	VG+	NM
❑ 990	David Houston	1978	2.50	5.00	10.00

HOUSTON, DAVID, AND JOY FORD

Also see each artist's individual listings.

45s

COUNTRY INT'L.

Number	Title (A Side/B Side)	Yr	VG	VG+	NM
❑ 146	(Making the Best of) A Bad Situation/(B-side unknown)	1980	—	2.50	5.00

HOUSTON, DAVID, AND BARBARA MANDRELL

Also see each artist's individual listings.

45s

EPIC

Number	Title (A Side/B Side)	Yr	VG	VG+	NM
❑ 10656	After Closing Time/My Song of Love	1970	2.00	4.00	8.00
❑ 10779	We've Got Everything But Love/Try a Little Harder	1971	2.00	4.00	8.00
❑ 10908	A Perfect Match/Almost Persuaded	1972	2.00	4.00	8.00
❑ 11068	I Love You, I Love You/Let's Go Down Together	1973	—	3.00	6.00
❑ 11120	Lovin' You Is Worth It/How Can It Be Wrong	1974	—	3.00	6.00
❑ 20005	Ten Commandments of Love/Try a Little Harder	1974	—	3.00	6.00

Albums

EPIC

Number	Title (A Side/B Side)	Yr	VG	VG+	NM
❑ KE 31705	A Perfect Match	1972	3.00	6.00	12.00
❑ KE 32915	The Best of David Houston and Barbara Mandrell	1974	3.00	6.00	12.00

HOUSTON, DAVID, AND TAMMY WYNETTE

Also see each artist's individual listings.

45s

EPIC

Number	Title (A Side/B Side)	Yr	VG	VG+	NM
❑ 10194	My Elusive Dreams/Marriage on the Rocks	1967	2.50	5.00	10.00
❑ 10274	It's All Over/Together We Stand	1967	2.50	5.00	10.00

Albums

EPIC

Number	Title (A Side/B Side)	Yr	VG	VG+	NM
❑ LN 24325 [M]	My Elusive Dreams	1967	5.00	10.00	20.00
❑ BN 26325 [S]	My Elusive Dreams	1967	3.75	7.50	15.00

HOWARD, CHUCK

45s

ABC

Number	Title (A Side/B Side)	Yr	VG	VG+	NM
❑ 11105	Great Dreams/What the Robin Gonna Do	1968	2.50	5.00	10.00

BOONE

Number	Title (A Side/B Side)	Yr	VG	VG+	NM
❑ 1049	Easy to Say, Hard to Do/You Don't Have Time for Me	1966	3.75	7.50	15.00
❑ 1057	Anywhere the Wind Blows/Please Stay with Me	1967	3.75	7.50	15.00

COLUMBIA

Number	Title (A Side/B Side)	Yr	VG	VG+	NM
❑ 4-43194	After My Laughter Came Tears/I Hope You Hear Sad Songs	1964	3.75	7.50	15.00
❑ 4-43329	I Want to Hear It from You/Searching for Baby	1965	3.75	7.50	15.00

ESV

Number	Title (A Side/B Side)	Yr	VG	VG+	NM
❑ 1017	Joy Gray/Don't Let It Bother You	1957	20.00	40.00	80.00

FLAME

Number	Title (A Side/B Side)	Yr	VG	VG+	NM
❑ 1020	Gossip/(B-side unknown)	1959	50.00	100.00	200.00

FRATERNITY

Number	Title (A Side/B Side)	Yr	VG	VG+	NM
❑ 923	Don't Let Them Move/Thing Called Sadness	1964	3.00	6.00	12.00

GARRETT

Number	Title (A Side/B Side)	Yr	VG	VG+	NM
❑ 4001	Johnny Be Good/Don't Let Them Move	1963	6.25	12.50	25.00

JOY

Number	Title (A Side/B Side)	Yr	VG	VG+	NM
❑ 238	Let Me Walk You Home, Jeanette/Congratulations to You	1960	3.75	7.50	15.00

MONUMENT

Number	Title (A Side/B Side)	Yr	VG	VG+	NM
❑ 916	Someone Please Cry/What Does He Do	1966	5.00	10.00	20.00

Number	Title (A Side/B Side)	Yr	VG	VG+	NM
NEW STAR					
❑ 120	Don't Let Them Move/Thing Called Sadness	1964	6.25	12.50	25.00
PORT					
❑ 70002	Crazy Crazy Baby/Can't You Tell	1958	15.00	30.00	60.00
SAND					
❑ 266	Crazy Crazy Baby/Can't You Tell	1958	25.00	50.00	100.00
VIVA					
❑ 29499	Suddenly Single/Wedding Prayer	1983	—	2.00	4.00
WARNER BROS.					
❑ 49509	I've Come Back (To Say I Love You One More Time)/Everyone But Me	1980	—	2.00	4.00
❑ 49625	Easy to Say, Hard to Do/Love Won't Work	1980	—	2.00	4.00
❑ 49719	Thing Called Sadness/Beginnings	1981	—	2.00	4.00
Albums					
BRYLEN					
❑ BN 4478	The Fire Behind His Eyes	198?	2.50	5.00	10.00

HOWARD, EDDY

A pop singer of the 1940s and 1950s, he had this one charted country hit.

Number	Title (A Side/B Side)	Yr	VG	VG+	NM
Selected 78s					
MAJESTIC					
❑ 1155	Ragtime Cowboy Joe/On the Old Spanish Trail	1947	3.00	6.00	12.00

HOWARD, HARLAN

Number	Title (A Side/B Side)	Yr	VG	VG+	NM
45s					
CAPITOL					
❑ 4612	Legion of the Lost/We're Proud to Call Him Son	1961	5.00	10.00	20.00
❑ 4682	She Called Me Baby/Wishin' She Was Here	1962	5.00	10.00	20.00
❑ 4813	I Ain't Got Nobody/Ramblin' Son of a Gun	1962	5.00	10.00	20.00
❑ 4928	My Baby's His Baby Now/Someday Sweetheart	1963	3.75	7.50	15.00
MONUMENT					
❑ 833	I Can't Stand It/It's All in Your Mind	1964	3.75	7.50	15.00
❑ 849	Time to Run Again/Previews of Coming Attractions	1964	3.75	7.50	15.00
❑ 864	Hobo Jungle/The Deepening Snow	1964	3.75	7.50	15.00
❑ 883	How Slow Time Goes/What's Left of Me	1965	3.00	6.00	12.00
❑ 907	Busted/The Everglades	1965	3.00	6.00	12.00
❑ 919	Another Bridge to Burn/Baby, That Would Sure Go Good	1966	3.00	6.00	12.00
❑ 1207	Look Behind You/Too Many Rivers	1970	2.50	5.00	10.00
NUGGET					
❑ 1058	Sunday Morning Christian/That Little Boy Who Follows Me	1971	2.50	5.00	10.00
❑ 1060	Uncle Sam/Better Get Your Pride Back Boy	1971	2.50	5.00	10.00
RCA VICTOR					
❑ 47-9252	I'd Rather Be a Fool/Take It and Go	1967	2.50	5.00	10.00
❑ 47-9352	It's Nothin' to Me/Home from the Forest	1967	2.50	5.00	10.00
❑ 47-9535	Where Were You When I Was Young/Old Podner	1968	2.50	5.00	10.00
Albums					
CAPITOL					
❑ ST 1631 [S]	Harlan Howard Sings Harlan Howard	1961	10.00	20.00	40.00
❑ T 1631 [M]	Harlan Howard Sings Harlan Howard	1961	7.50	15.00	30.00
MONUMENT					
❑ MLP-8038 [M]	All-Time Favorite Country Songwriter	1965	6.25	12.50	25.00
❑ SLP-18038 [S]	All-Time Favorite Country Songwriter	1965	7.50	15.00	30.00
RCA VICTOR					
❑ LPM-3729 [M]	Mr. Songwriter	1967	6.25	12.50	25.00
❑ LSP-3729 [S]	Mr. Songwriter	1967	5.00	10.00	20.00
❑ LPM-3886 [M]	Down to Earth	1968	12.50	25.00	50.00
❑ LSP-3886 [S]	Down to Earth	1968	5.00	10.00	20.00

HOWARD, JAN

Also see BILL ANDERSON; WYNN STEWART.

Number	Title (A Side/B Side)	Yr	VG	VG+	NM
45s					
AVI					
❑ 347	My Friend/Tainted Love	198?	—	3.00	6.00
CAPITOL					
❑ 4744	Please Pass the Kisses/Tomorrow You Won't Even Know My Name	1962	3.00	6.00	12.00
❑ 4817	The Real Me/What'cha Gonna Do for an Encore	1962	3.00	6.00	12.00
❑ 4869	Looking Back/See One Broken Heart	1962	3.00	6.00	12.00
❑ 4918	Wind Me Up (I Cry)/You've Got Me Where You Want Me	1963	3.00	6.00	12.00
❑ 4987	Dime a Dozen/I Can't Stop Crying	1963	3.00	6.00	12.00
❑ 5035	I Wish I Was a Single Girl Again/The Saddest Part of All	1963	3.00	6.00	12.00
❑ 5122	I Walked a Hundred Miles/I'm Here to Get My Baby Out of Jail	1964	3.00	6.00	12.00
CHALLENGE					
❑ 9112	Careless Hands/Let Me Know	1961	3.75	7.50	15.00
❑ 9125	Bring It On Back to Me/My Baby's in Berlin	1961	3.75	7.50	15.00
❑ 59059	The One You Slip Around With/I Wish I Could Fall in Love Again	1959	3.75	7.50	15.00
❑ 59080	If Your Conscience Can't Stop You/Many Dreams Ago	1960	3.75	7.50	15.00
❑ 59094	A World I Can't Live In/I've Got My Pride	1960	3.75	7.50	15.00
❑ 59106	All Alone Again/Too Many Teardrops Too Late	1961	3.75	7.50	15.00
❑ 59361	The One You Slip Around With/Jealous Love	1967	2.50	5.00	10.00
CON BRIO					
❑ 118	I'll Hold You in My Heart (Till I Can Hold You in My Arms)/Thought I Had Her	1977	—	3.00	6.00
❑ 125	Better Off Alone/My Coloring Book	1977	—	3.00	6.00
❑ 132	To Love a Rolling Stone/Thought I Had Him	1978	—	3.00	6.00
DECCA					
❑ 31701	What Makes a Man Wander?/Slipping Back to You	1964	2.50	5.00	10.00
❑ 31791	I've Got Feelings Too/What Do You Want Now	1965	2.50	5.00	10.00
❑ 31858	I Don't Mind/You Don't Find a Good Man Every Day	1965	2.50	5.00	10.00
❑ 31933	Evil on Your Mind/Crying for Love	1966	2.50	5.00	10.00
❑ 32016	Bad Seed/You Go Your Way (I'll Go Crazy)	1966	2.50	5.00	10.00
❑ 32096	Any Old Way You Do/Your Ole Handy Man	1967	2.50	5.00	10.00
❑ 32154	Roll Over and Play Dead/You and Me and Tears and Roses	1967	2.50	5.00	10.00
❑ 32269	Count Your Blessings, Woman/But Not for Love My Dear	1968	2.00	4.00	8.00
❑ 32357	I Still Believe in Love/Life's That Way	1968	2.00	4.00	8.00
❑ 32407	My Son/The Tip of My Fingers	1968	2.00	4.00	8.00
❑ 32447	When We Tried/I Hurt All Over	1969	2.00	4.00	8.00
❑ 32543	We Had All the Good Things Going/I'll Go Where You Go	1969	2.00	4.00	8.00
❑ 32636	Rock Me Back to Little Rock/Hello Stranger	1970	2.00	4.00	8.00
❑ 32743	The Soul You Never Had/I Have Your Love	1970	2.00	4.00	8.00
❑ 32778	Baby Without You/Marriage Has Ruined More Good Love Affairs	1971	2.00	4.00	8.00
❑ 32822	Dallas You've Won/Love Is a Sometimes Thing	1971	2.00	4.00	8.00
❑ 32905	Love Is Like a Spinning Wheel/I Never Once Stopped Loving You	1971	2.00	4.00	8.00
❑ 32955	Let Him Have It/Remember the Good	1972	2.00	4.00	8.00
❑ 33019	It's Your World/New York City Song	1972	—	3.50	7.00
GRT					
❑ 010	Seein' Is Believin'/My Kind of People	1974	—	3.00	6.00
❑ 019	Get It While the Gettin's Good/I'm All Right 'Til I See You	1975	—	3.00	6.00
❑ 024	Wedding Song/You'll Never Know	1975	—	3.00	6.00
MCA					
❑ 40020	Too Many Ties That Bind/Everybody Knows I Love You	1973	—	3.00	6.00
Albums					
CAPITOL					
❑ ST 1779 [S]	Sweet and Sentimental	1962	6.25	12.50	25.00
❑ T 1779 [M]	Sweet and Sentimental	1962	5.00	10.00	20.00
DECCA					
❑ DL 4793 [M]	Jan Howard Sings Evil on Your Mind	1966	3.75	7.50	15.00
❑ DL 4832 [M]	Bad Seed	1966	3.75	7.50	15.00
❑ DL 4931 [M]	This Is Jan Howard Country	1967	6.25	12.50	25.00
❑ DL 74793 [S]	Jan Howard Sings Evil on Your Mind	1966	5.00	10.00	20.00
❑ DL 74832 [S]	Bad Seed	1966	5.00	10.00	20.00
❑ DL 74931 [S]	This Is Jan Howard Country	1967	5.00	10.00	20.00
❑ DL 75012	Count Your Blessings, Woman	1968	5.00	10.00	20.00
❑ DL 75130	Jan Howard	1969	5.00	10.00	20.00
❑ DL 75166	For God and Country	1969	6.25	12.50	25.00
❑ DL 75207	Rock Me Back to Little Rock	1970	5.00	10.00	20.00
❑ DL 75293	Love Is Like a Spinning Wheel	1972	5.00	10.00	20.00
TOWER					
❑ ST 5068 [S]	Lonely Country	1967	5.00	10.00	20.00
❑ T 5068 [M]	Lonely Country	1967	5.00	10.00	20.00
❑ DT 5119 [R]	The Real Me	1968	3.75	7.50	15.00
WRANGLER					
❑ 1005 [M]	Jan Howard	1962	6.25	12.50	25.00
❑ S-1005 [S]	Jan Howard	1962	7.50	15.00	30.00

HOWARD, JIM

Number	Title (A Side/B Side)	Yr	VG	VG+	NM
45s					
DEL-MAR					
❑ 1013	Meet Me Tonight Outside of Town/Too Much Taking — Not Enough Giving	1964	3.75	7.50	15.00

HOWARD, RANDY

Number	Title (A Side/B Side)	Yr	VG	VG+	NM
45s					
ATLANTIC AMERICA					
❑ 99317	Southern Soul/Kitchen Sink	1988	—	—	3.00
❑ 99355	I Make a Motion/(B-side unknown)	1988	—	—	3.00
❑ 99387	Ring of Fire/(B-side unknown)	1987	—	—	3.00
VIVA					
❑ 29622	Johnny Walker Home/My Nose Don't Work No More	1983	—	2.00	4.00
WARNER BROS.					
❑ 29781	All American Redneck/All American Redneck (Dirty Version)	1983	—	2.00	4.00
❑ 29781 [PS]	All American Redneck/All American Redneck (Dirty Version)	1983	—	3.00	6.00
Albums					
ATLANTIC AMERICA					
❑ 90679	Randy Howard	1987	2.50	5.00	10.00
WARNER BROS.					
❑ 23820	All-American Redneck	1983	2.00	4.00	8.00

HOWARD, REBECCA LYNN

Number	Title (A Side/B Side)	Yr	VG	VG+	NM
45s					
MCA NASHVILLE					
❑ 72120	When My Dreams Come True/Out Here in the Water	1999	—	—	3.00
❑ 088-172171-7	I Don't Paint Myself Into Corners/Was It As Hard to Be Together	2000	—	—	3.00

HOWELL, LEE

45s

LITTLE DARLIN'

Number	Title (A Side/B Side)	Yr	VG	VG+	NM
❑ 0063	Don't Blow Sad Bugles/Too Light to Fight, Too Thin to Win	1969	2.50	5.00	10.00

HUBBLE, HAL

45s

50 STATES

Number	Title (A Side/B Side)	Yr	VG	VG+	NM
❑ 66	My Pulse Pumps Passions/Before I Leave This Land	1978	—	2.50	5.00

HUDSON, HELEN

45s

CYCLONE

Number	Title (A Side/B Side)	Yr	VG	VG+	NM
❑ 102	Nothing But Time/One More Guitar	1979	—	3.00	6.00

HUDSON, LARRY G.

45s

AQUARIAN

Number	Title (A Side/B Side)	Yr	VG	VG+	NM
❑ 603	Someone I Can't Forget/Which Way Is Up	1976	—	3.00	6.00
❑ 605	Singing a Happy Song/Legend in My Time	1976	—	3.00	6.00
❑ 606	You Light Up My World/The One I Wed Is Home	1976	—	3.00	6.00
❑ 609	It Looks Like Love Tonight/(B-side unknown)	1977	—	3.00	6.00

LONE STAR

Number	Title (A Side/B Side)	Yr	VG	VG+	NM
❑ 702	Just Out of Reach of My Two Open Arms/Warm and Tender Love	1978	—	2.50	5.00
❑ 706	Loving You Is a Natural High/You Don't Know Me	1978	—	2.50	5.00

MERCURY

Number	Title (A Side/B Side)	Yr	VG	VG+	NM
❑ 57015	I Can't Cheat/Just for the Heaven of It	1980	—	2.00	4.00
❑ 57029	I'm Still in Love with You/Easy Come, Easy Go	1980	—	2.00	4.00

HUDSON AND LANDRY

45s

DORE

Number	Title (A Side/B Side)	Yr	VG	VG+	NM
❑ 852	The Hippie and the Redneck/Top 40 DJ's	1971	2.50	5.00	10.00
❑ 855	Ajax Liquor Store/The Hippie and the Redneck	1971	2.50	5.00	10.00
❑ 868	Ajax Airlines/Bruiser La Rue	1972	2.50	5.00	10.00
❑ 874	Obscene Phone Bust/The Prospectors	1972	2.50	5.00	10.00
❑ 879	Soul Bowl/Friar Shuck	1972	2.50	5.00	10.00
❑ 880	Frontier Christmas (Harlowe and The Mrs.)/The Soul Bowl	1972	2.50	5.00	10.00
❑ 881	Ajax Mortuary/Ajax Pet Store	1973	2.50	5.00	10.00
❑ 891	The Chocolate Freak/The Fate of the Mightiest Nation	1973	2.50	5.00	10.00
❑ 895	The Gas Man/Sir Basil	1974	2.50	5.00	10.00
❑ 898	The Weird Kingdom/Montague for President	1974	2.50	5.00	10.00

Albums

DORE

Number	Title (A Side/B Side)	Yr	VG	VG+	NM
❑ 324	Hanging In There	1971	5.00	10.00	20.00
❑ 326	Losing Their Heads	1971	5.00	10.00	20.00
❑ 329	Right-Off!	1972	5.00	10.00	20.00
❑ 331	Weird Kingdom	1973	5.00	10.00	20.00
❑ 333	The Best of Hudson and Landry	1974	3.75	7.50	15.00
❑ 334	The Best of Hudson and Landry 2	1975	3.75	7.50	15.00

HUGHES, HOLLIE

45s

LUV

Number	Title (A Side/B Side)	Yr	VG	VG+	NM
❑ 110	It's a Bad Night for Good Girls/(B-side unknown)	1985	2.00	4.00	8.00
❑ 130	67 Miles to Cow Town/I'm in Love	1986	2.00	4.00	8.00

OAK

Number	Title (A Side/B Side)	Yr	VG	VG+	NM
❑ 1054	It's a Bad Night for Good Girls/The Pleasure's All Mine	198?	—	3.00	6.00

HUGHES, JOEL

45s

AWESOME

Number	Title (A Side/B Side)	Yr	VG	VG+	NM
❑ 100	Between Home and Motels/(B-side unknown)	1984	—	3.00	6.00
❑ 109	This Ain't No Way to Be/(B-side unknown)	1984	—	3.00	6.00

SUNBIRD

Number	Title (A Side/B Side)	Yr	VG	VG+	NM
❑ 7569	Handy Man/(B-side unknown)	1982	—	3.00	6.00

HUMMERS, THE

45s

CAPITOL

Number	Title (A Side/B Side)	Yr	VG	VG+	NM
❑ 3646	Old Betsy Goes Boing, Boing, Boing/One Good Thing About Being Down	1973	—	3.00	6.00
❑ 3870	Julianna/Daddy's Song	1974	—	3.00	6.00

HUMMON, MARCUS

45s

COLUMBIA

Number	Title (A Side/B Side)	Yr	VG	VG+	NM
❑ 38-78251	God's Country/Somebody's Leaving	1996	—	2.00	4.00
❑ 38-78330	Honky Tonk Mona Lisa/I Do	1996	—	2.00	4.00

HUMPERDINCK, ENGELBERT

His first American single was on Roy Acuff's Hickory label. He began to make the country charts upon his switch to Epic in 1976, so we have included him.

45s

EPIC

Number	Title (A Side/B Side)	Yr	VG	VG+	NM
❑ AE7 1170 [DJ]	Christmas Song/Silent Night	1978	—	2.00	4.00
❑ AE7 1170 [PS]	Christmas Song/Silent Night	1978	—	2.00	4.00
❑ 02060	Don't You Love Me Anymore/Till I Get It Right	1981	—	—	3.00
❑ 02245	Maybe This Time/When the Night Ends	1981	—	—	3.00
❑ 03817	Till You and Your Lover Are Lovers Again/What Will I Write	1983	—	—	3.00
❑ 50270	After the Lovin'/Let's Remember the Good Times	1976	—	2.50	5.00
❑ 50365	I Believe in Miracles/Goodbye My Friend	1977	—	2.00	4.00
❑ 50447	A Lover's Holiday/Look at Me	1977	—	2.00	4.00
❑ 50488	A Night to Remember/Silent Night	1977	—	2.00	4.00
❑ 50526	The Last of the Romantics/I Have Paid the Toll	1978	—	2.00	4.00
❑ 50566	Love Me Tender/This Time One Year Ago	1978	—	2.00	4.00
❑ 50579	Love's In Need of Love Today/Sweet Marjorene	1978	—	2.00	4.00
❑ 50632	This Moment in Time/And the Day Begins	1978	—	2.00	4.00
❑ 50692	Can't Help Falling in Love/You Know Me	1979	—	2.00	4.00
❑ 50732	Lovin' Too Well/Much, Much Greater Love	1979	—	2.00	4.00
❑ 50844	Love's Only Love/Burning Ember	1980	—	—	3.00
❑ 50899	A Chance to Be a Hero/Any Kind of Love at All	1980	—	—	3.00
❑ 50933	Don't Cry Out Loud/Don't Touch That Dial	1980	—	—	3.00
❑ 50958	It's Not Easy to Live Together/Royal Affair	1980	—	—	3.00

HICKORY

Number	Title (A Side/B Side)	Yr	VG	VG+	NM
❑ 1337	Baby Turn Around/If I Could Do the Things I Want to Do	1965	4.00	8.00	16.00
—As "Gerry Dorsey"					

PARROT

Number	Title (A Side/B Side)	Yr	VG	VG+	NM
❑ 40011 [M]	Release Me (And Let Me Love Again)/Ten Guitars	1967	2.00	4.00	8.00
❑ 40011 [S]	Release Me (And Let Me Love Again)/Ten Guitars	1967	5.00	10.00	20.00
—Both sides in true stereo. Letters "XDR" are stamped in run-off area before the matrix number					
❑ 40015	There Goes My Everything/You Love	1967	2.00	4.00	8.00
❑ 40019	The Last Waltz/That Promise	1967	2.00	4.00	8.00
❑ 40019 [PS]	The Last Waltz/That Promise	1967	3.00	6.00	12.00
❑ 40023	Am I That Easy to Forget/Pretty Ribbons	1967	2.00	4.00	8.00
❑ 40023 [PS]	Am I That Easy to Forget/Pretty Ribbons	1967	3.00	6.00	12.00
❑ 40027	A Man Without Love/Call on Me	1968	2.00	4.00	8.00
❑ 40032	Les Bicyclettes De Belsize/Three Little Words	1968	2.00	4.00	8.00
❑ 40032 [PS]	Les Bicyclettes De Belsize/Three Little Words	1968	3.00	6.00	12.00
❑ 40036	The Way It Used to Be/A Good Thing Going	1969	—	3.00	6.00
❑ 40036 [PS]	The Way It Used to Be/A Good Thing Going	1969	2.50	5.00	10.00
❑ 40040	I'm a Better Man/Cafe	1969	—	3.00	6.00
❑ 40044	Winter World of Love/Take My Heart	1969	—	3.00	6.00
❑ 40044 [PS]	Winter World of Love/Take My Heart	1969	2.50	5.00	10.00
❑ 40049	My Marie/Our Song (La Paloma)	1970	—	3.00	6.00
❑ 40049 [PS]	My Marie/Our Song (La Paloma)	1970	2.00	4.00	8.00
❑ 40054	Sweetheart/Born to Be Wanted	1970	—	3.00	6.00
❑ 40054 [PS]	Sweetheart/Born to Be Wanted	1970	2.00	4.00	8.00
❑ 40059	When There's No You/Stranger, Step In My World	1971	—	3.00	6.00
❑ 40059 [PS]	When There's No You/Stranger, Step In My World	1971	2.00	4.00	8.00
❑ 40065	Another Time, Another Place/You're the Window of My World	1971	—	3.00	6.00
❑ 40069	Too Beautiful to Last/A Hundred Times a Day	1972	—	2.50	5.00
❑ 40071	In Time/How Does It Feel	1972	—	2.50	5.00
❑ 40072	I Never Said Goodbye/Time After Time	1972	—	2.50	5.00
❑ 40073	I'm Leavin' You/My Summer Song	1973	—	2.00	4.00
❑ 40076	Love Is All/Lady of the Night	1973	—	2.00	4.00
❑ 40077	Free as the Wind/My Friend the Wind	1974	—	2.00	4.00
❑ 40079	Catch Me I'm Falling/Love, Oh Precious Love	1974	—	2.00	4.00
❑ 40082	Forever and Ever/Precious Love	1974	—	2.00	4.00
❑ 40085	This Is What You Mean to Me/A World Without Music	1975	—	2.00	4.00

Albums

EPIC

Number	Title (A Side/B Side)	Yr	VG	VG+	NM
❑ PE 34381	After the Lovin'	1976	2.50	5.00	10.00
—Orange label					
❑ PE 34381	After the Lovin'	198?	2.00	4.00	8.00
—Reissue with bar code; dark blue label					
❑ E 34436	The Ultimate	1977	2.50	5.00	10.00
—Orange label					
❑ PE 34436	The Ultimate	198?	2.00	4.00	8.00
—Reissue with bar code; dark blue label					
❑ E 34719	Golden Love Songs	1977	2.50	5.00	10.00
—Orange label					
❑ PE 34719	Golden Love Songs	198?	2.00	4.00	8.00
—Reissue with bar code; dark blue label					
❑ PE 34730	Miracles	1977	2.50	5.00	10.00
—Orange label					
❑ PE 34730	Miracles	198?	2.00	4.00	8.00
—Reissue with bar code; dark blue label					
❑ JE 35020	Last of the Romantics	1978	2.50	5.00	10.00
—Orange label					
❑ PE 35020	Last of the Romantics	198?	2.00	4.00	8.00
—Reissue with bar code; dark blue label					
❑ PE 35031	Christmas Tyme	1977	3.00	6.00	12.00
❑ JE 35791	This Moment in Time	1979	2.50	5.00	10.00
❑ PE 35791	This Moment in Time	198?	2.00	4.00	8.00
—Budget-line reissue					
❑ JE 36431	Love's Only Love	1980	2.50	5.00	10.00
❑ PE 36765	A Merry Christmas with Engelbert Humperdinck	1980	2.50	5.00	10.00
—Some copies of the record have a "JE" prefix					
❑ E2X 36782 [(2)]	All of Me/Live in Concert	1980	3.00	6.00	12.00
❑ FE 37128	Don't You Love Me Anymore	1981	2.50	5.00	10.00
❑ PE 37128	Don't You Love Me Anymore	1983	2.00	4.00	8.00
—Budget-line reissue					
❑ FE 38087	You and Your Lover	1983	2.50	5.00	10.00
❑ PE 39469	White Christmas	1984	2.50	5.00	10.00
❑ (no #) [PD]	Last of the Romantics	1978	6.25	12.50	25.00

LONDON

Number	Title (A Side/B Side)	Yr	VG	VG+	NM
❑ BP 688/9 [(2)]	Engelbert Humperdinck Sings for You	1977	3.75	7.50	15.00
❑ PS 709	Love Letters	1978	2.50	5.00	10.00

Number	Title (A Side/B Side)	Yr	VG	VG+	NM
PARROT					
❑ PA 61012 [M]	Release Me	1967	5.00	10.00	20.00
❑ PA 61015 [M]	The Last Waltz	1967	5.00	10.00	20.00
❑ PAS 71012 [S]	Release Me	1967	3.75	7.50	15.00
❑ PAS 71015 [S]	The Last Waltz	1967	3.75	7.50	15.00
❑ PAS 71022	A Man Without Love	1968	3.75	7.50	15.00
❑ PAS 71026	Engelbert	1969	3.75	7.50	15.00
❑ XPAS 71030	Engelbert Humperdinck	1969	3.75	7.50	15.00
❑ XPAS 71038	We Made It Happen	1970	3.75	7.50	15.00
❑ XPAS 71043	Sweetheart	1971	3.75	7.50	15.00
❑ XPAS 71048	Another Time, Another Place	1971	3.75	7.50	15.00
❑ XPAS 71051	Live at the Riviera, Las Vegas	1971	3.75	7.50	15.00
❑ XPAS 71056	In Time	1972	3.75	7.50	15.00
❑ XPAS 71061	King of Hearts	1973	3.75	7.50	15.00
❑ APAS 71065	My Love	1974	3.75	7.50	15.00
❑ PAS 71067	His Greatest Hits	1974	3.75	7.50	15.00

HUNLEY, CON

45s

Number	Title (A Side/B Side)	Yr	VG	VG+	NM
CAPITOL					
❑ B-5428	All American Country Boy/Sad But True	1984	—	—	3.00
❑ B-5457	I'd Rather Be Crazy/Sad But True	1985	—	—	3.00
❑ B-5485	Nobody Ever Gets Enough Love/Sad But True	1985	—	—	3.00
❑ B-5525	What Am I Gonna Do About You/Lord, She Sure Looks Good Tonight	1985	—	—	3.00
❑ B-5586	Blue Suede Shoes/Sad But True	1986	—	—	3.00
❑ B-5631	Quittin' Time/Late at Night	1986	—	—	3.00
MCA					
❑ 52208	Once You Get the Feel of It/It's Tearin' Me Up to Lay Your Memory Down	1983	—	2.00	4.00
❑ 52259	Satisfied Mind/Let Me Love You Once Before You Go	1983	—	2.00	4.00
PRAIRIE DUST					
❑ 7601	Misery Loves Company/Columbus Stockade	1976	—	2.50	5.00
❑ 7605	Loving You Is a Habit I Can't Break/(B-side unknown)	1976	—	3.00	6.00
❑ 7608	Pick Up the Pieces/It Looks Like a Good Night for Drinking	1976	—	2.50	5.00
❑ 7614	I'll Always Remember That Song/Never Felt More Like Dying (Than I Do Now)	1977	—	2.50	5.00
❑ 7618	Breaking Up Is Hard to Do/Woman to Man, Man to Woman	1977	—	2.50	5.00
❑ 84110	Deep in the Arms of Texas/Never Felt More Like Dying	1984	—	2.50	5.00
WARNER BROS.					
❑ 8520	Cry Cry Darling/Just Hangin' On	1978	—	2.00	4.00
❑ 8572	Week-End Friend/Only the Strong Survive	1978	—	2.00	4.00
❑ 8671	You've Still Got a Place in My Heart/Honky Tonk Heart	1978	—	2.00	4.00
❑ 8723	I've Been Waiting for You All of My Life/Just Hangin' On	1978	—	2.00	4.00
❑ 8812	Since I Fell for You/Cry Cry Darling	1979	—	2.00	4.00
❑ 29902	Confidential/I Still Have Dreamin'	1982	—	2.00	4.00
❑ 49090	I Don't Want to Lose You/That's All That Matters	1979	—	2.00	4.00
❑ 49187	You Lay a Whole Lot of Love on Me/When It Hurts You Most	1980	—	2.00	4.00
❑ 49528	They Never Lost You/Lover's Lullaby	1980	—	2.00	4.00
❑ 49613	What's New with You/This Ol' Cowboy's Goin' Home	1980	—	2.00	4.00
❑ 49800	She's Steppin' Out/Ask Any Woman	1981	—	2.00	4.00
❑ 49887	No Relief in Sight/Table for Two	1981	—	2.00	4.00
❑ 50058	Oh Girl/Tonight I Took Your Memory Off the Wall	1982	—	2.00	4.00

Albums

Number	Title (A Side/B Side)	Yr	VG	VG+	NM
MCA					
❑ 5423	Once You Get the Feel of It	1983	3.75	7.50	15.00
WARNER BROS.					
❑ BSK 3285	Con Hunley	1979	2.50	5.00	10.00
—With this title on both cover and label					
❑ BSK 3285	No Limit	1979	3.75	7.50	15.00
—Same cover as "Con Hunley," but the above title is on the label					
❑ BSK 3378	I Don't Want to Lose You	1980	2.50	5.00	10.00
❑ BSK 3474	Don't It Break Your Heart	1980	2.50	5.00	10.00
❑ BSK 3617	Ask Any Woman	1981	2.50	5.00	10.00
❑ BSK 3693	Oh Girl	1982	2.50	5.00	10.00

HUNNICUT, ED

45s

Number	Title (A Side/B Side)	Yr	VG	VG+	NM
MCA					
❑ 52207	Fade to Blue/Gettin' It Right Without You	1983	—	2.00	4.00
❑ 52262	My Angel's Got the Devil in Her Eyes/Home Is Where the Heart Is	1983	—	2.00	4.00
❑ 52353	In Real Life/There Oughta Be a Law	1984	—	2.00	4.00

HUNTER, JESSE

45s

Number	Title (A Side/B Side)	Yr	VG	VG+	NM
BNA					
❑ 62735	Born Ready/L.A. Freeway	1994	—	—	3.00
❑ 62857	By the Way She's Lookin'/Long Steady Rain	1994	—	—	3.00
❑ 62976	Long Legged Hannah (From Butte Montana)/ Logn Legged Hannah (From Butte Montana) (Dance Mix)	1994	—	2.00	4.00

HUNTER, TOMMY

45s

Number	Title (A Side/B Side)	Yr	VG	VG+	NM
COLUMBIA					
❑ 4-44104	In a Way/Cup of Disgrace	1967	2.00	4.00	8.00
❑ 4-44234	Mary in the Morning/The Battle of the Little Big Horn	1967	2.00	4.00	8.00
❑ 4-44367	Half a World Away/Charlie's Side	1967	—	3.50	7.00
❑ 4-44541	Are You Sad/Tyin' Me Down	1968	—	3.50	7.00
❑ 4-44684	I Couldn't Find a Space/Nowhere Bound with Greyhound	1968	—	3.50	7.00

HURLEY, LIBBY

45s

Number	Title (A Side/B Side)	Yr	VG	VG+	NM
EPIC					
❑ 34-07366	Don't Get Me Started/The Last One to Know	1987	—	—	3.00
❑ 34-07650	You Just Watch Me/The Last One to Know	1987	—	—	3.00
❑ 34-07771	Don't Talk to Me/I'm Turning Blue	1988	—	—	3.00
WARNER BROS.					
❑ 7-18768	Beginning of the End of the Line/Wing and a Prayer (The Rodeo Song)	1992	—	2.00	4.00

HURT, CHARLOTTE

45s

Number	Title (A Side/B Side)	Yr	VG	VG+	NM
COMPASS					
❑ 0020	The Price of Borrowed Love Is Just Too High/ Wheel of Fortune	1978	2.00	4.00	8.00

HURT, CINDY

45s

Number	Title (A Side/B Side)	Yr	VG	VG+	NM
CHURCHILL					
❑ 7767	Single Girl/Dark Moon	1981	—	2.50	5.00
❑ 7772	Headin' for a Heartache/(B-side unknown)	1981	—	2.50	5.00
❑ 7777	Dreams Can Come In Handy/Headin' for a Heartache	1981	—	2.50	5.00
❑ 94000	Don't Come Knockin'/Love Me Up	1982	—	2.50	5.00
❑ 94004	Talk to Me Loneliness/Dreams Can Come In Handy	1982	—	2.50	5.00
❑ 94010	What's Good About Goodbye/You Made It Feel Like Love	1982	—	2.50	5.00
❑ 94013	I'm in Love All Over Again/Dark Moon	1983	—	2.50	5.00
❑ 94013 [PS]	I'm in Love All Over Again/Dark Moon	1983	2.00	4.00	8.00

Albums

Number	Title (A Side/B Side)	Yr	VG	VG+	NM
CHURCHILL					
❑ 9422	Talk to Me	1982	2.50	5.00	10.00

HUSKEY, KENNI

45s

Number	Title (A Side/B Side)	Yr	VG	VG+	NM
CAPITOL					
❑ 3184	A Living Tornado/Only You Can Break My Heart	1971	—	3.00	6.00
❑ 3229	Within My Loving Arms/Peace of Mind	1971	—	3.00	6.00
❑ 3282	It's Too Late to Keep from Losing You/Number One Heel	1972	—	3.00	6.00
❑ 3337	Gonna Roll Out the Red Carpet/I'll Be Swingin' Too	1972	—	3.00	6.00
❑ 3394	Hollywood and Vine/You'll Never Miss the Water	1972	—	3.00	6.00

HUSKY, FERLIN

Includes records as "Simon Crum" and "Terry Preston." Also see JEAN SHEPARD.

45s

Number	Title (A Side/B Side)	Yr	VG	VG+	NM
4 STAR					
❑ 1516	Guilty Feeling/Road to Heaven	1950	12.50	25.00	50.00
—All 4 Star records as "Terry Preston"; it's possible that not all these exist on 45s					
❑ 1518	Let's Keep the Communists Out/The Sabbath	1950	12.50	25.00	50.00
❑ 1542	Irma/Put Me in Your Pocket	1950	12.50	25.00	50.00
❑ 1566	Wise Guy/Cross Eyed Gal from the Ozarks	1951	10.00	20.00	40.00
❑ 1571	Jezebel/Tennessee Hillbilly Ghost	1951	10.00	20.00	40.00
❑ 1572	Crying Heart Blues/If You Don't Believe I'm Leaving (Just Count the Days I'm Gone)	1951	10.00	20.00	40.00
❑ 1573	Rotation Blues/Deadly Weapon	1951	10.00	20.00	40.00
ABC					
❑ 11345	True True Lovin'/A Legend in My Time	1973	—	3.00	6.00
❑ 11360	Between Me and Blue/(B-side unknown)	1973	—	3.00	6.00
❑ 11381	Baby's Blue/One	1973	—	3.00	6.00
❑ 11395	Rosie Cries a Lot/Shoes	1973	—	3.00	6.00
❑ 11432	Freckles and Polliwog Days/Everything Is Nothing Without You	1974	—	3.00	6.00
❑ 12020	Drinkin' Man/Cuzz Yore So Sweet	1974	—	3.00	6.00
—As "Simon Crum"					
❑ 12021	A Room for a Boy...Never Used/A Ring of String	1974	—	2.50	5.00
❑ 12048	Champagne Ladies and Blue Ribbon Babies/I Feel Better All Over	1974	—	2.50	5.00
❑ 12085	Burning/A Touch of Yesterday	1975	—	2.50	5.00
ABC DOT					
❑ 17574	An Old Memory (Got in My Eye)/She's Not Yours Anymore	1975	—	2.50	5.00
CAPITOL					
❑ F1861	China Doll/Tennessee Central #9	1951	6.25	12.50	25.00
❑ F1947	I Want You So/Time	1952	5.00	10.00	20.00
—As "Terry Preston"					
❑ 2023	Christmas Dream/Christmas Is Holy	1967	2.00	4.00	8.00
❑ F2024	Words/I'm Missin' Lots of Lovin'	1952	5.00	10.00	20.00
—As "Terry Preston"					
❑ 2048	Just for You/Don't Hurt Me Anymore	1967	2.00	4.00	8.00

Number	Title (A Side/B Side)	Yr	VG	VG+	NM
❑ F2105	Counting My Heartaches/I Love You	1952	5.00	10.00	20.00
—As "Terry Preston"					
❑ 2154	I Promised You the World/You Should Live My Life	1968	2.00	4.00	8.00
❑ F2211	I'm Only Wishing/Are You Afraid	1952	5.00	10.00	20.00
—As "Terry Preston"					
❑ 2288	White Fences and Evergreen Trees/Love's Been Good to Me	1968	2.00	4.00	8.00
❑ F2298	Gone/Out of Reach	1952	7.50	15.00	30.00
—As "Terry Preston"					
❑ F2391	My Foolish Heart/Undesired	1953	5.00	10.00	20.00
—As "Terry Preston"					
❑ F2397	Hank's Song/I'll Never Have You	1953	5.00	10.00	20.00
❑ 2411	Flat River, Mo./One Life to Live	1969	2.00	4.00	8.00
❑ F2467	I've Got a Woman's Love/Watch the Company You Keep	1953	5.00	10.00	20.00
—As "Terry Preston"					
❑ F2495	Mini Ha Cha/I Lost My Love Today	1953	5.00	10.00	20.00
❑ 2512	That's Why I Love You So Much/Forever Yours	1969	2.00	4.00	8.00
❑ F2558	How Much Are You Mine/You'll Die a Thousand Deaths	1953	5.00	10.00	20.00
❑ F2627	Walkin' and Hummin'/I Wouldn't Treat a Dog Like You're Treating Me	1953	5.00	10.00	20.00
❑ 2666	Every Step of the Way/That's What I'd Do	1969	2.00	4.00	8.00
❑ F2746	Eli the Camel/Somebody Lied	1954	5.00	10.00	20.00
❑ 2793	Heavenly Sunshine/All My Little Loving Ways	1970	—	3.00	6.00
❑ F2814	Each Time You Leave/Deceived	1954	5.00	10.00	20.00
—As "Terry Preston"					
❑ F2835	The Drunken Driver/Homesick	1954	5.00	10.00	20.00
❑ 2882	Your Sweet Love Lifted Me/You're the Happy Song I Sing	1970	—	3.00	6.00
❑ F2914	King of a Lonely Castle/Very Seldom Frequently Ever	1954	5.00	10.00	20.00
❑ 2999	Sweet Misery/Because You're Mine	1970	—	3.00	6.00
❑ F3001	I Feel Better All Over (More Than Anywhere's Else)/Little Tom	1954	3.75	7.50	15.00
❑ F3063	Cuzz Yore So Sweet/My Gallina	1955	5.00	10.00	20.00
—As "Simon Crum"					
❑ 3069	One More Time/Don't Let the Good Life Pass You By	1971	—	3.00	6.00
❑ F3097	I'll Baby Sit with You/She's Always There	1955	3.75	7.50	15.00
❑ 3165	Open Up the Book (And Take a Look)/Even If It's True	1971	—	3.00	6.00
❑ F3183	Don't Blame the Children/Saith the Lord	1955	3.75	7.50	15.00
❑ F3233	Dear Mr. Brown/I'll Be Here for a Lifetime	1955	3.75	7.50	15.00
❑ F3270	A Hillbilly Deck of Cards/Ooh I Want You	1955	5.00	10.00	20.00
—As "Simon Crum"					
❑ 3308	Just Plain Lonely/Always in All Ways	1972	—	3.00	6.00
❑ F3316	A Sinful Secret/Slow Down Brother	1956	3.75	7.50	15.00
❑ 3415	How Could You Be Anything But Love/I'd Walk a Mile for a Smile	1972	—	3.00	6.00
❑ F3428	Aladdin's Lamp/That Big Old Moon	1956	3.75	7.50	15.00
❑ F3460	Bop Cat Bop/Muki Ruki	1956	5.00	10.00	20.00
—As "Simon Crum"					
❑ F3522	Nothing Looks As Good As You/Waiting	1956	3.75	7.50	15.00
❑ F3628	Gone/Missing Persons	1957	3.75	7.50	15.00
❑ F3742	A Fallen Star/Prize Possession	1957	3.00	6.00	12.00
❑ F3790	Make Me Live Again/This Moment of Love	1957	3.00	6.00	12.00
❑ F3862	What'cha Doin' After School/Wang Dang Doo	1957	3.00	6.00	12.00
❑ F3943	Kingdom of Love/Terrific Together	1958	3.00	6.00	12.00
❑ F4000	I Saw God/I Feel That Old Heartache Again	1958	3.00	6.00	12.00
❑ F4046	I Will/All of the Time	1958	3.00	6.00	12.00
❑ F4073	Country Music Is Here to Stay/Stand Up, Sit Down, Shut Your Mouth	1958	5.00	10.00	20.00
—As "Simon Crum"					
❑ F4123	My Reason for Living/Wrong	1959	3.00	6.00	12.00
❑ F4186	Draggin' the River/Sea Sand	1959	3.00	6.00	12.00
❑ F4252	Morgan Poisoned the Water Hole/I Fell Out of Love with You	1959	3.75	7.50	15.00
—As "Simon Crum"					
❑ F4278	Black Sheep/I'll Always Return	1959	3.00	6.00	12.00
❑ 4343	My Love for You/Asi Es La Vida	1960	3.00	6.00	12.00
❑ 4406	Wings of a Dove/Next to Jimmy	1960	3.00	6.00	12.00
❑ 4464	Country Music Fiddler/I Feel Better All Over	1960	3.75	7.50	15.00
—As "Simon Crum"					
❑ 4499	Enormity in Motion/Cuzz Yore So Sweet	1961	3.75	7.50	15.00
—As "Simon Crum"					
❑ 4548	Before I Lose My Mind/What Good Will I Ever Be	1961	3.00	6.00	12.00
❑ 4594	Willow Tree/Take a Look	1961	3.00	6.00	12.00
❑ 4650	The Waltz You Saved for Me/Out of a Clear Blue Sky	1961	3.00	6.00	12.00
❑ 4721	Somebody Save Me/Just Another Lonely Night	1962	2.50	5.00	10.00
❑ 4779	Stand Up/It Scares Me	1962	2.50	5.00	10.00
❑ 4853	It Was You/Near You	1962	2.50	5.00	10.00
❑ 4908	You Hurt Me/My Reason for Living	1963	2.50	5.00	10.00
❑ 4966	Don't Be Mad/Little Red Webb	1963	3.00	6.00	12.00
—As "Simon Crum"					
❑ 4977	Who's Next/As Close As We'll Ever Be	1963	2.50	5.00	10.00
❑ 5067	Face of a Clown/Love Looks Good on You	1963	2.50	5.00	10.00
❑ 5111	Timber I'm Falling/Don't Count the Diamonds	1964	2.50	5.00	10.00
❑ 5206	Up on the Mountain Top/Weaker Moments	1964	2.50	5.00	10.00
❑ 5355	True, True Lovin'/Love Built the House	1965	2.50	5.00	10.00
❑ 5438	Willie Was a Gamblin' Man/Picking Up the Pieces	1965	2.50	5.00	10.00
❑ 5522	Money Greases the Wheels/Lasting Love	1965	2.50	5.00	10.00
❑ 5615	I Could Sing All Night/What Does Your Conscience Say to You	1966	2.50	5.00	10.00
❑ 5679	I Hear Little Rock Calling/Stand Beside Me	1966	2.50	5.00	10.00
❑ 5775	Once/Why Do I Put Up with You	1966	2.50	5.00	10.00
❑ 5852	What Am I Gonna Do Now/General G	1967	2.00	4.00	8.00
❑ 5938	You Pushed Me Too Far/A Bridge I Have Never Crossed	1967	2.00	4.00	8.00

KING

Number	Title (A Side/B Side)	Yr	VG	VG+	NM
❑ 5434	Irma/Cotton Pickin' Heart	1960	3.00	6.00	12.00
❑ 5476	Electrified Donkey/Guilty Feeling	1961	3.00	6.00	12.00

7-Inch Extended Plays

CAPITOL

Number	Title (A Side/B Side)	Yr	VG	VG+	NM
❑ EAP 1-609	(contents unknown)	1955	5.00	10.00	20.00
❑ EAP 1-609 [PS]	Ferlin Husky	1955	5.00	10.00	20.00
❑ EAP 1-718	Hang Your Head in Shame/That Silver Haired Daddy of Mine//Honky-Tonkin' Party Girl/Useless	1956	3.75	7.50	15.00
❑ EAP 1-718 [PS]	Songs of the Home and Heart, Part 1	1956	3.75	7.50	15.00
❑ EAP 2-718	I Can't Go On This Way/That Little Girl of Mine//You Make Me Feel Funny, Honey/Rockin' Alone in an Old Rockin' Chair	1956	3.75	7.50	15.00
❑ EAP 2-718 [PS]	Songs of the Home and Heart, Part 2	1956	3.75	7.50	15.00
❑ EAP 3-718	Farther and Farther Apart/Never Have, Never Will//I Dreamed of an Old Love Affair/Daddy's Little Girl	1956	3.75	7.50	15.00
❑ EAP 3-718 [PS]	Songs of the Home and Heart, Part 3	1956	3.75	7.50	15.00
❑ EAP 1-880	(contents unknown)	1957	3.75	7.50	15.00
❑ EAP 1-880 [PS]	Boulevard of Broken Dreams, Part 1	1957	3.75	7.50	15.00
❑ EAP 2-880	(contents unknown)	1957	3.75	7.50	15.00
❑ EAP 2-880 [PS]	Boulevard of Broken Dreams, Part 2	1957	3.75	7.50	15.00
❑ EAP 3-880	(contents unknown)	1957	3.75	7.50	15.00
❑ EAP 3-880 [PS]	Boulevard of Broken Dreams, Part 3	1957	3.75	7.50	15.00
❑ EAP 1-921	Don't Walk Away/Somewhere There's Sunshine//My Home Town/This Whole Wide World	1958	3.00	6.00	12.00
❑ EAP 1-921 [PS]	Country Music Holiday	1958	3.00	6.00	12.00
❑ EAP 1-1280	(contents unknown)	1960	3.00	6.00	12.00
❑ EAP 1-1280 [PS]	Ferlin Favorites, Part 1	1960	3.00	6.00	12.00
❑ EAP 2-1280	(contents unknown)	1960	3.00	6.00	12.00
❑ EAP 2-1280 [PS]	Ferlin Favorites, Part 2	1960	3.00	6.00	12.00
❑ EAP 3-1280	(contents unknown)	1960	3.00	6.00	12.00
❑ EAP 3-1280 [PS]	Ferlin Favorites, Part 3	1960	3.00	6.00	12.00
❑ EAP 1-1516	(contents unknown)	1961	3.00	6.00	12.00
❑ EAP 1-1516 [PS]	Wings of a Dove	1961	3.00	6.00	12.00

Albums

ABC

Number	Title (A Side/B Side)	Yr	VG	VG+	NM
❑ X-776	True True Lovin'	1973	3.00	6.00	12.00
❑ X-818	Freckles and Polliwog Days	1974	3.00	6.00	12.00
❑ X-849	Champagne Ladies and Blue Ribbon Babies	1974	3.00	6.00	12.00
❑ X-884	The Foster-Rice Songbook	1975	3.00	6.00	12.00

CAPITOL

Number	Title (A Side/B Side)	Yr	VG	VG+	NM
❑ ST-115	White Fences and Evergreen Trees	1968	3.75	7.50	15.00
❑ SKAO-143	The Best of Ferlin Husky	1969	3.75	7.50	15.00
❑ SM-143	The Best of Ferlin Husky	197?	2.50	5.00	10.00
—Reissue with new prefix					
❑ ST-239	That's Why I Love You So Much	1969	3.75	7.50	15.00
❑ ST-433	Your Love Is Heavenly Sunshine	1970	3.75	7.50	15.00
❑ ST-591	Your Sweet Love Has Lifted Me	1970	3.75	7.50	15.00
❑ T 718 [M]	Songs of the Home and Heart	1956	15.00	30.00	60.00
—Turquoise label					
❑ T 718 [M]	Songs of the Home and Heart	1959	10.00	20.00	40.00
—Black colorband label, Capitol logo at left					
❑ T 718 [M]	Songs of the Home and Heart	1962	6.25	12.50	25.00
—Black colorband label, Capitol logo at top					
❑ ST-768	One More Time	1971	3.75	7.50	15.00
❑ T 880 [M]	Boulevard of Broken Dreams	1957	15.00	30.00	60.00
—Turquoise label					
❑ T 976 [M]	Sittin' On a Rainbow	1958	15.00	30.00	60.00
—Turquoise label					
❑ T 1204 [M]	Born to Lose	1959	10.00	20.00	40.00
—Black colorband label, Capitol logo at left					
❑ T 1204 [M]	Born to Lose	1962	6.25	12.50	25.00
—Black colorband label, Capitol logo at top					
❑ T 1280 [M]	Ferlin's Favorites	1960	10.00	20.00	40.00
—Black colorband label, Capitol logo at left					
❑ T 1280 [M]	Ferlin's Favorites	1962	6.25	12.50	25.00
—Black colorband label, Capitol logo at top					
❑ DT 1383 [R]	Gone	196?	3.00	6.00	12.00
❑ T 1383 [M]	Gone	1960	10.00	20.00	40.00
—Black colorband label, Capitol logo at left					
❑ T 1383 [M]	Gone	1962	6.25	12.50	25.00
—Black colorband label, Capitol logo at top					
❑ ST 1546 [S]	Walkin' and Hummin'	1961	7.50	15.00	30.00
—Black colorband label, Capitol logo at left					
❑ ST 1546 [S]	Walkin' and Hummin'	1962	5.00	10.00	20.00
—Black colorband label, Capitol logo at top					
❑ T 1546 [M]	Walkin' and Hummin'	1961	6.25	12.50	25.00
—Black colorband label, Capitol logo at left					
❑ T 1546 [M]	Walkin' and Hummin'	1962	3.75	7.50	15.00
—Black colorband label, Capitol logo at top					
❑ ST 1633 [S]	Memories of Home	1961	7.50	15.00	30.00
—Black colorband label, Capitol logo at left					
❑ ST 1633 [S]	Memories of Home	1962	5.00	10.00	20.00
—Black colorband label, Capitol logo at top					
❑ T 1633 [M]	Memories of Home	1961	6.25	12.50	25.00
—Black colorband label, Capitol logo at left					
❑ T 1633 [M]	Memories of Home	1962	3.75	7.50	15.00
—Black colorband label, Capitol logo at top					

Number	Title (A Side/B Side)	Yr	VG	VG+	NM
❑ ST 1720 [S]	Some of My Favorites	1962	5.00	10.00	20.00
❑ T 1720 [M]	Some of My Favorites	1962	3.75	7.50	15.00
❑ ST 1885 [S]	The Heart and Soul of Ferlin Husky	1963	5.00	10.00	20.00
❑ T 1885 [M]	The Heart and Soul of Ferlin Husky	1963	3.75	7.50	15.00
❑ DT 1991 [R]	The Hits of Ferlin Husky	1963	3.00	6.00	12.00
❑ T 1991 [M]	The Hits of Ferlin Husky	1963	3.75	7.50	15.00
❑ ST 2101 [S]	By Request	1964	5.00	10.00	20.00
❑ T 2101 [M]	By Request	1964	3.75	7.50	15.00
❑ ST 2305 [S]	True, True Lovin'	1965	5.00	10.00	20.00
❑ T 2305 [M]	True, True Lovin'	1965	3.75	7.50	15.00
❑ ST 2439 [S]	Ferlin Husky Sings the Songs of Music City, U.S.A.	1966	5.00	10.00	20.00
❑ T 2439 [M]	Ferlin Husky Sings the Songs of Music City, U.S.A.	1966	3.75	7.50	15.00
❑ ST 2548 [S]	I Could Sing All Night	1966	5.00	10.00	20.00
❑ T 2548 [M]	I Could Sing All Night	1966	3.75	7.50	15.00
❑ ST 2705 [S]	What Am I Gonna Do Now?	1967	3.75	7.50	15.00
❑ T 2705 [M]	What Am I Gonna Do Now?	1967	5.00	10.00	20.00
❑ ST 2793 [S]	Christmas All Year Long	1967	3.75	7.50	15.00
❑ T 2793 [M]	Christmas All Year Long	1967	3.75	7.50	15.00
❑ ST 2870	Just for You	1968	3.75	7.50	15.00
❑ ST 2913	Where No One Stands Alone	1968	3.75	7.50	15.00
❑ ST-11069	Just Plain Lonely	1972	3.75	7.50	15.00
HILLTOP					
❑ 6005	Ole Opry Favorites	196?	3.00	6.00	12.00
❑ 6086	Green, Green Grass of Home	1970	3.00	6.00	12.00
❑ 6099	Wings of a Dove	197?	3.00	6.00	12.00
KING					
❑ 647 [M]	Country Tunes Sung from the Heart	1959	17.50	35.00	70.00
❑ 728 [M]	Easy Livin'	1960	17.50	35.00	70.00
STARDAY					
❑ 3018	Greatest Hits	197?	3.00	6.00	12.00

HUTCHENS, THE

45s

Number	Title (A Side/B Side)	Yr	VG	VG+	NM
ATLANTIC					
❑ 7-87092	Knock, Knock/She Just Wants to Dance	1995	—	—	3.00

HUTCHINS, LONEY

45s

Number	Title (A Side/B Side)	Yr	VG	VG+	NM
ARC					
❑ 0005	Still Dancing/(B-side unknown)	1987	—	2.50	5.00
❑ 0005 [PS]	Still Dancing/(B-side unknown)	1987	—	3.00	6.00

I

IFIELD, FRANK

British singer who began having country hits when his U.S. records started coming out on Hickory Records.

45s

Number	Title (A Side/B Side)	Yr	VG	VG+	NM
CAPITOL					
❑ 5032	I'm Confessin' (That I Love You)/Waltzing Matilda	1963	2.50	5.00	10.00
❑ 5089	Please/Mule Train	1963	2.50	5.00	10.00
❑ 5134	Don't Blame Me/Say It Isn't So	1964	2.50	5.00	10.00
❑ 5170	Sweet Lorraine/You Came a Long Way from St. Louis	1964	2.50	5.00	10.00
❑ 5275	True Love Ways/I Should Care	1964	2.50	5.00	10.00
❑ 5349	Without You/Don't Make Me Laugh	1965	2.50	5.00	10.00
HICKORY					
❑ 1397	No One Will Ever Know/I'm Saving All My Love (For You)	1966	2.00	4.00	8.00
❑ 1411	Call Her Your Sweetheart/Give Myself a Party	1966	2.00	4.00	8.00
❑ 1435	I Remember You/Stranger to You	1967	2.00	4.00	8.00
❑ 1454	Kaw-Liga/Out of Nowhere	1967	2.00	4.00	8.00
❑ 1473	Just Let Me Make Believe/Fireball Mail	1967	2.00	4.00	8.00
❑ 1486	Oh, Such a Stranger/Then You Can Tell Me Goodbye	1967	2.00	4.00	8.00
❑ 1499	Adios Matador/Movin' Lover	1968	2.00	4.00	8.00
❑ 1507	Don't Forget to Cry/Morning in Your Eyes	1968	2.00	4.00	8.00
❑ 1514	Good Morning Dear/Innocent Years	1968	2.00	4.00	8.00
❑ 1525	Maurie/I'm Learning Child	1968	2.00	4.00	8.00
❑ 1540	Let Me Into Your Life/Mary in the Morning	1969	—	3.00	6.00
❑ 1550	I Love You Because/It's My Time	1969	—	3.00	6.00
❑ 1556	Lights of Home/Love Hurts	1969	—	3.00	6.00
❑ 1574	Sweet Memories/You've Still Got a Place in My Heart	1970	—	3.00	6.00
❑ 1595	Someone/One More Mile, One More Town (One More Time)	1971	—	3.00	6.00
MAM					
❑ 3612	Lonesome Jubilee/Teach Me Little Children	1971	—	2.50	5.00
VEE JAY					
❑ 457	I Remember You/I Listen to My Heart	1962	3.75	7.50	15.00
—With Frank Ifield's name spelled correctly on label					
❑ 457	I Remember You/I Listen to My Heart	1962	5.00	10.00	20.00
—With both labels misspelled "Farnk Ifield"					
❑ 477	Lovesick Blues/Anytime	1962	3.00	6.00	12.00
❑ 499	The Wayward Wind/I'm Smiling Now	1963	3.00	6.00	12.00
❑ 525	Unchained Melody/Nobody's Darlin' But Mine	1963	3.00	6.00	12.00
❑ 553	I'm Confessin' (That I Love You)/Heart and Soul	1963	3.00	6.00	12.00
WARNER BROS.					
❑ 8730	Why Don't We Leave Together/Crawling Back	1979	—	2.00	4.00
❑ 8853	Crystal/Touch the Morning	1979	—	2.00	4.00
❑ 49095	Play Born to Lose Again/Yesterday Just Passed My Way Again	1979	—	2.00	4.00

Albums

Number	Title (A Side/B Side)	Yr	VG	VG+	NM
CAPITOL					
❑ ST 10356 [S]	I'm Confessin'	1963	6.25	12.50	25.00
❑ T 10356 [M]	I'm Confessin'	1963	5.00	10.00	20.00
HICKORY					
❑ LPM-132 [M]	The Best of Frank Ifield	1966	5.00	10.00	20.00
❑ LPS-132 [P]	The Best of Frank Ifield	1966	5.00	10.00	20.00
❑ LPM-136 [M]	Tale of Two Cities	1967	3.75	7.50	15.00
❑ LPS-136 [S]	Tale of Two Cities	1967	5.00	10.00	20.00
❑ ST-90753 [S]	The Best of Frank Ifield	1966	6.25	12.50	25.00
—Capitol Record Club edition					
❑ T-90753 [M]	The Best of Frank Ifield	1966	6.25	12.50	25.00
—Capitol Record Club edition					
VEE JAY					
❑ LP 1054 [M]	I Remember You	1962	7.50	15.00	30.00
❑ SR 1054 [S]	I Remember You	1962	12.50	25.00	50.00

IGLESIAS, JULIO

The below album by the Spanish crooner made the country charts. Also see WILLIE NELSON.

Albums

Number	Title (A Side/B Side)	Yr	VG	VG+	NM
COLUMBIA					
❑ FC 38640	Julio	1984	2.00	4.00	8.00

IN PURSUIT

45s

Number	Title (A Side/B Side)	Yr	VG	VG+	NM
MTM					
❑ B-72080	Only for You/Don't Stop	1986	—	2.50	5.00
❑ B-72087	Thin Line/Don't Stop	1987	—	2.50	5.00
❑ B-72096	Getting Older/Listen	1988	—	2.50	5.00

INDIANA

45s

Number	Title (A Side/B Side)	Yr	VG	VG+	NM
KILLER					
❑ 1005	Midnite Rock/(B-side unknown)	1987	—	3.00	6.00

INGLE, RED

45s

Number	Title (A Side/B Side)	Yr	VG	VG+	NM
CAPITOL					
❑ 54-686	Temptation (Tim-Tayshun)/Cigareetes, Whuskey and Wild, Wild Women	1949	7.50	15.00	30.00
❑ 54-713	"A" Yore A-Dopey-Gal/Two Dollar Pistol	1949	6.25	12.50	25.00
❑ F1076	You Can't Be Fit as a Fiddle/Turn Your Head Little Darling	1950	6.25	12.50	25.00
❑ F1431	Chew Tobacco Rag/Let Me In	1951	6.25	12.50	25.00
❑ F1599	People Are Funny/Pool	1951	6.25	12.50	25.00
❑ F1639	Temptation (Tim-Tayshun)/Cigareetes, Whuskey and Wild, Wild Women	195?	5.00	10.00	20.00
—Reissue					
MERCURY					
❑ 70085	Don't Let the Stars Get In Your Eyes/Why Don't You Believe Me	1953	5.00	10.00	20.00

Selected 78s

Number	Title (A Side/B Side)	Yr	VG	VG+	NM
CAPITOL					
❑ 412	Temptation (Tim-Tayshun)/(I Love You) For Seventy Mental Reasons	1947	3.75	7.50	15.00
❑ 451	Song of Indians/Them Durn Fool Things	1947	3.75	7.50	15.00
❑ 476	Pagan Ninny's Keep-Er-Goin' Stomp/Nowhere	1947	3.75	7.50	15.00
❑ 15045	Cigareetes, Whuskey, and Wild, Wild Women/ Pearly Maude	1948	3.75	7.50	15.00
❑ 15123	Moe Zart's Turkey Trot/Git Up Off'n the Floor, Hannah! (A Bitter New Year's Eve)	1948	3.75	7.50	15.00
❑ 15210	Serutan Yob (A Song for Backward Boys and Girls Under 40)/Oh! Nick-O-Deemo	1948	5.00	10.00	20.00
❑ 15312	The Prisoner of Love's Song/The Traveling Salesman Polka	1949	3.75	7.50	15.00

INGLES, DAVID

45s

Number	Title (A Side/B Side)	Yr	VG	VG+	NM
CAPITOL					
❑ 2648	Johnny Let the Sunshine In/You're a Part of This Man	1969	2.00	4.00	8.00

INMAN, AUTRY

45s

Number	Title (A Side/B Side)	Yr	VG	VG+	NM
DECCA					
❑ 28290	Who Do You Love/Just Smile As You Go By	1952	5.00	10.00	20.00
❑ 28495	Does Your Sweetheart Seem Different Lately/All of a Sudden	1952	5.00	10.00	20.00
❑ 28592	I'll Miss My Heart/Stop Stallin'	1953	5.00	10.00	20.00
❑ 28629	That's All Right/Uh Huh Honey	1953	6.25	12.50	25.00
❑ 28778	Pucker Up/That's When I Need You the Most	1953	5.00	10.00	20.00
❑ 28798	A Dear John Letter/Brown Eyed Baby	1953	5.00	10.00	20.00
❑ 28960	It Hurts Too Much to Cry/Happy Go Lucky	1953	5.00	10.00	20.00
❑ 29060	Just Reminiscing/Under the Moon	1954	5.00	10.00	20.00
❑ 29170	Little One/Once More	1954	5.00	10.00	20.00

Number	Title (A Side/B Side)	Yr	VG	VG+	NM
❑ 29362	Finally I'm Free/Don't Put It Off	1954	5.00	10.00	20.00
❑ 29447	You Said Goodbye/It's a Shame	1955	5.00	10.00	20.00
❑ 29635	Tell Me Now/A Friend	1955	5.00	10.00	20.00
❑ 29690	Blue Monday/Look Over Your Shoulder	1955	6.25	12.50	25.00
❑ 29936	Be-Bop Baby/It Would Be a Doggone Lie	1956	25.00	50.00	100.00
❑ 46407	Let's Take the Long Way Home Tonight/I Hope Tomorrow Never Comes	1952	5.00	10.00	20.00
EPIC					
❑ 10232	Don't Call Me (I'll Call You)/Love Has to Die (All By Itself)	1967	2.00	4.00	8.00
❑ 10276	There Stands the Glass/This Heart Was Made for Lovin'	1968	2.00	4.00	8.00
❑ 10327	I Can See an Angel/Wish in One Hand (Cry in the Other)	1968	2.00	4.00	8.00
❑ 10389	Ballad of Two Brothers/Don't Call Me (I'll Call You)	1968	2.00	4.00	8.00
❑ 10452	Home Is Heavy on My Mind/You're the Only One in My Heart	1969	2.00	4.00	8.00
❑ 10494	I'll Be Waiting/Traveling Salesman	1969	2.00	4.00	8.00
GLAD					
❑ 1002	I'm Still in Love with Mary/Please Cut Me Down	1960	3.75	7.50	15.00
JUBILEE					
❑ 9001	The Drinks Are On Me/You Don't Live There Anymore	1964	2.00	4.00	8.00
❑ 9010	Keep Her Out of Sight/Blue Is Next in Line	1965	2.00	4.00	8.00
❑ 9016	Hurtache/Mr. Love Passed Away	1965	2.00	4.00	8.00
❑ 9023	You Don't Live There Anymore/The Drinks Are on Me	1965	2.00	4.00	8.00
KOALA					
❑ 325	That's Why You're Being Paid/(B-side unknown)	1980	—	2.50	5.00
MERCURY					
❑ 71983	Living with One and Loving Two/I Guess I'm Crazy	1962	3.00	6.00	12.00
MILLION					
❑ 4	Please Let Me Love You/Maybe This Is the Day	1972	—	3.00	6.00
❑ 24	If You Were Mine/Please Let Me Love You	1972	—	3.00	6.00
RCA VICTOR					
❑ 47-7173	Dream Boat/Remember the Night	1958	7.50	15.00	30.00
❑ 47-7260	Mary Nell/The Hard Way	1958	7.50	15.00	30.00
SIMS					
❑ 131	The Volunteer/Unlucky Am I	1963	2.50	5.00	10.00
❑ 140	Big Sam/My Word	1963	2.50	5.00	10.00
❑ 170	The Ballad of John F. Kennedy/The World's Worst Lover	1964	2.50	5.00	10.00
❑ 188	My Past/You're Welcome Dear	1964	2.50	5.00	10.00
❑ 219	Give Me 40 Acres (To Turn This Rig Around)/Six Rounds of Love and Hate	1964	2.50	5.00	10.00
UNITED ARTISTS					
❑ 278	That's All Right/Farther to Go Than I've Been	1960	3.75	7.50	15.00
❑ 303	Let's Take the Long Way Home/Too Blue to Cry	1961	3.75	7.50	15.00
Selected 78s					
BULLET					
❑ 687	Double Cross/In My Imagination	1949	10.00	20.00	40.00
Albums					
EPIC					
❑ BN 26428	Ballad of Two Brothers	1968	5.00	10.00	20.00
JUBILEE					
❑ JGM-2055 [M]	Riscotheque Saturday Night	1964	5.00	10.00	20.00
❑ JGS-2055 [S]	Riscotheque Saturday Night	1964	6.25	12.50	25.00
❑ JGM-2056 [M]	New Year's Eve with Autry Inman	1964	5.00	10.00	20.00
❑ JGS-2056 [S]	New Year's Eve with Autry Inman	1964	6.25	12.50	25.00
MOUNTAIN DEW					
❑ 7022 [M]	Autry Inman	1963	5.00	10.00	20.00
❑ S-7022 [S]	Autry Inman	1963	6.25	12.50	25.00
SIMS					
❑ 107 [M]	Autry Inman at the Frontier Club	1964	5.00	10.00	20.00
❑ S-107 [S]	Autry Inman at the Frontier Club	1964	6.25	12.50	25.00

INMAN, JERRY

Number	Title (A Side/B Side)	Yr	VG	VG+	NM
45s					
CHELSEA					
❑ 3006	You're the One/Leah	1974	—	2.50	5.00
COLUMBIA					
❑ 4-44453	From Me to You/Help!	1968	2.00	4.00	8.00
❑ 4-44619	Train of Thought/Leaves Are the Tears of Autumn	1968	2.00	4.00	8.00
❑ 4-44774	Mississippi Woman/One If for Him, Two If for Her	1969	2.00	4.00	8.00
❑ 4-44894	Spanish Eyes/Talk	1969	2.00	4.00	8.00
ELEKTRA					
❑ 45333	She's Lying Next to Me/Woman with a Gun	1976	—	2.50	5.00
❑ 45352	Single Again/Six Weeks in Alaska	1976	—	2.50	5.00
❑ 45414	Smoke on the Far Horizon/J.C.'s Country Band	1977	—	2.00	4.00
❑ 45508	Why, Baby, Why/Gonna Save It for My Baby	1978	—	2.00	4.00
❑ 46006	Why Don't We Lie Down and Talk It Over/Gonna Save It for My Baby	1979	—	2.00	4.00
HILLSIDE					
❑ 8004	Make Room for the Blues/What She Don't Know Won't Hurt Me	1980	—	3.00	6.00
❑ 8102	Take These Chains/Tulsa Turnaround	1981	—	3.00	6.00
Albums					
COLUMBIA					
❑ CL 2793 [M]	Lennon-McCartney Country Style R.F.D.	1967	7.50	15.00	30.00
❑ CS 9593 [S]	Lennon-McCartney Country Style R.F.D.	1967	5.00	10.00	20.00
ELEKTRA					
❑ 7E-1068	You Betchum!	1976	3.00	6.00	12.00

INTERNATIONAL SUBMARINE BAND, THE

Number	Title (A Side/B Side)	Yr	VG	VG+	NM
45s					
ASCOT					
❑ 2218	The Russians Are Coming/Truck Driving Man	1966	3.75	7.50	15.00
❑ 2218 [PS]	The Russians Are Coming/Truck Driving Man	1966	12.50	25.00	50.00
—Counterfeit identification: Fake copies are missing the Ascot logo and catalog number.					
COLUMBIA					
❑ 43935	Sum Up Broke/One Day Week	1966	7.50	15.00	30.00
LHI					
❑ 1205	Luxury Liner/Blue Eyes	1968	3.75	7.50	15.00
❑ 1217	Miller's Cave/I Must Be Somebody Else	1968	3.75	7.50	15.00
Albums					
LHI					
❑ 12001	Safe at Home	1968	25.00	50.00	100.00
—Counterfeits have white labels, legitimate copies have multi-color labels					

IRBY, JERRY

Number	Title (A Side/B Side)	Yr	VG	VG+	NM
45s					
4 STAR					
❑ 1578	Buy Me a Bottle of Beer/Rose	1951	6.25	12.50	25.00
❑ 1591	Standing on the Corner/The First Time I Saw That Gal	1952	6.25	12.50	25.00
DAFFAN					
❑ 106	Call for Me Darling/It's Time You Started Loving	1956	12.50	25.00	50.00
❑ 108	Clickety Clack/A Man Is a Slave	1956	25.00	50.00	100.00
❑ 111	That's Too Bad/I'd Give Anything in This World	1957	15.00	30.00	60.00
JER-RAY					
❑ 222	Chantilly Lace/(B-side unknown)	1959	7.50	15.00	30.00
MGM					
❑ 10475	By the Rio Grande/You Just Can't Be Trusted Anymore	1949	10.00	20.00	40.00
❑ 10580	Mama Don't Allow It/Memory of a Rose	1949	10.00	20.00	40.00
❑ 10595	One Way Blues/Don't Know Where I'm Goin'	1950	7.50	15.00	30.00
❑ 10771	Cuddling Baby/I'm So Disgusted	1950	7.50	15.00	30.00
❑ 10809	Hillbilly Boogie/Ball and Chain	1950	7.50	15.00	30.00
❑ 11109	There's a Moon to Love By/I've Got the Blues	1951	7.50	15.00	30.00
Selected 78s					
CIRECO					
❑ 101	Almost Every Time/(B-side unknown)	194?	6.25	12.50	25.00
GLOBE					
❑ 113	Nails in My Coffin/(B-side unknown)	194?	6.25	12.50	25.00
❑ 114	Steel Guitar Special/(B-side unknown)	194?	6.25	12.50	25.00
❑ 115	Don't You Weep/(B-side unknown)	194?	6.25	12.50	25.00
❑ 120	Super Boogie Woogie/(B-side unknown)	194?	6.25	12.50	25.00
GULF					
❑ 103	Nails in My Coffin/(B-side unknown)	194?	7.50	15.00	30.00
HUMMING BIRD					
❑ 1001	After Today/(B-side unknown)	194?	6.25	12.50	25.00
IMPERIAL					
❑ 8003	I'm Gonna Get Tight/Texas Gal Polka	194?	5.00	10.00	20.00
❑ 8005	Ball and Chain/There's Nothing Left for Me	194?	5.00	10.00	20.00
❑ 8006	Don't Lie My Darlin'/By the Rio Grande	194?	5.00	10.00	20.00
❑ 8007	Too Many Women/If I Had a Great Long Pistol	194?	5.00	10.00	20.00
❑ 8011	Uptown Swing/My Life Is Full of Sorrow	194?	5.00	10.00	20.00
❑ 8013	Super Boogie Woogie/Steel Guitar Special	194?	5.00	10.00	20.00
❑ 8014	Hillbilly Boogie/My Gal from Tennessee	194?	5.00	10.00	20.00
❑ 8017	Mama Don't Allow It/Tell Me You Care	1947	6.25	12.50	25.00
❑ 8029	Just for Tonight/A Million Times or More	1948	5.00	10.00	20.00
MGM					
❑ 10117	Roses Have Thorns/A Cup of Coffee and a Cigarette	1948	5.00	10.00	20.00
❑ 10151	Cryin' in My Beer/Answer to Drivin' Nails in My Coffin	1948	5.00	10.00	20.00
❑ 10188	Great Long Pistol/49 Women	1948	5.00	10.00	20.00
❑ 10253	Song of San Antone/The Sun Won't Shine for Me	1948	5.00	10.00	20.00
❑ 10345	Don't Count Your Chickens/Texas Gal Polka	1949	3.75	7.50	15.00
❑ 10396	Uptown Swing/A Broken Heart Is Good for You	1949	3.75	7.50	15.00

IRVING, LONNIE

Number	Title (A Side/B Side)	Yr	VG	VG+	NM
45s					
LONNIE IRVING					
❑ (# unknown)	Pinball Machine/I Got Blues on My Mind	1959	12.50	25.00	50.00
STARDAY					
❑ 486	Pinball Machine/I Got Blues on My Mind	1960	6.25	12.50	25.00
❑ 505	Gooseball Brown/An Old Fashioned Love	1960	5.00	10.00	20.00
❑ 520	I Wish I Had My Heart Back/Trucker's Vitus	1960	5.00	10.00	20.00

ISAACSON, PETER

Number	Title (A Side/B Side)	Yr	VG	VG+	NM
45s					
UNION STATION					
❑ 1002	Froze in Her Line of Fire/Baby Your Love	1983	—	3.50	7.00
❑ 1004	Don't Take Much/(B-side unknown)	1983	2.00	4.00	8.00
❑ 1005	No Survivors/(B-side unknown)	1984	2.00	4.00	8.00
❑ 1006	It's a Cover Up/(B-side unknown)	1984	2.00	4.00	8.00

IVES, BURL

Number	Title (A Side/B Side)	Yr	VG	VG+	NM
45s					
BELL					
❑ 930	Real Roses/Roll Up Some Inspiration	1970	—	2.50	5.00
❑ 943	Time/(B-side unknown)	1970	—	2.50	5.00
BIG TREE					
❑ 130	Gingerbread House/Tumbleweed Snowman	1971	—	2.50	5.00

Number	Title (A Side/B Side)	Yr	VG	VG+	NM
BUENA VISTA					
❑ 419	On the Front Porch/Ugly Bug Ball	1963	2.00	4.00	8.00
❑ 419 [PS]	On the Front Porch/Ugly Bug Ball	1963	3.00	6.00	12.00
COLUMBIA					
❑ 4-124	Grandfather Kringle/The 12 Days Of Christmas	1951	3.00	6.00	12.00
—Yellow-label "Chidren's Series" record; alternate number is 90138					
❑ 4-124 [PS]	Grandfather Kringle/The 12 Days Of Christmas	1951	3.75	7.50	15.00
❑ 1-173	Riders in the Sky (Cowboy Legend)/Wayfaring Stranger-Woolie Boogie Bee	1949	10.00	20.00	40.00
—Microgroove 33 1/3 rpm 7-inch single					
❑ 1-418	Mule Train/Greer County Bachelor	1950	7.50	15.00	30.00
—Microgroove 33 1/3 rpm 7-inch single					
❑ 1-550 (?)	John Henry/Mah Lindy Lou	1950	7.50	15.00	30.00
—Microgroove 33 1/3 rpm 7-inch single					
❑ 1-580 (?)	The Doughnut Song/I Got a Fever in My Bones	1950	7.50	15.00	30.00
—Microgroove 33 1/3 rpm 7-inch single					
❑ 1-630 (?)	Got the World by the Tail/My Momma Told Me	1950	7.50	15.00	30.00
—Microgroove 33 1/3 rpm 7-inch single					
❑ 1-780 (?)	Pig Pig/Last Night the Nightingale Woke Me	1950	7.50	15.00	30.00
—Microgroove 33 1/3 rpm 7-inch single					
❑ 6-780 (?)	Pig Pig/Last Night the Nightingale Woke Me	1950	6.25	12.50	25.00
❑ 1-910 (?)	There's a Little White House/Little White Duck	1950	7.50	15.00	30.00
—Microgroove 33 1/3 rpm 7-inch single					
❑ 6-910 (?)	There's a Little White House/Little White Duck	1950	6.25	12.50	25.00
❑ 39328	On Top of Old Smoky/The Syncopated Clock	1951	3.75	7.50	15.00
—With Percy Faith co-credited					
❑ 44508	I'll Be Your Baby Tonight/Maria	1968	—	3.00	6.00
❑ 44606	Little Green Apples/One Too Many Mornings	1968	—	3.00	6.00
❑ 44711	Santa Mouse/Oh What a Lucky Boy Am I	1968	—	3.00	6.00
❑ 44711 [PS]	Santa Mouse/Oh What a Lucky Boy Am I	1968	2.50	5.00	10.00
❑ 44974	Montego Bay/Tessie's Bar Mystery	1969	—	3.00	6.00
CYCLONE					
❑ 75014	One More Time Billy Brown/Tied Down Here at Home	1970	—	3.50	7.00
DECCA					
❑ 25524	Mockin' Bird Hill/Royal Telephone (Telephone to Glory)	196?	2.00	4.00	8.00
❑ 25585	Twelve Days of Christmas/The Indian Christmas Carol	1962	2.50	5.00	10.00
❑ 25691	You Know You Belong to Someone Else/Jealous	196?	2.00	4.00	8.00
❑ 25754	I Talk to the Trees/They Call the Wind Maria	1970	—	3.00	6.00
❑ 27079	This Time Tomorrow/One Hour Ahead of the Posse	1950	5.00	10.00	20.00
❑ 28055	Wild Side of Life/It's So Long and Goodbye to You	1952	3.75	7.50	15.00
❑ 28079	This Time Tomorrow/One Hour Ahead of the Posse	1952	3.75	7.50	15.00
❑ 28161	Diesel Smoke, Dangerous Curves/The Little Green Valley	1952	3.75	7.50	15.00
—With Grady Martin					
❑ 28299	There's a Mule Up in Tombstone, Arizona/ Lonesome, So Lonesome	1952	3.75	7.50	15.00
❑ 28347	The Friendly Beasts/There Were Three Ships	1952	3.00	6.00	12.00
❑ 28348	Jesous Anatonia/What Child Is This	1952	3.00	6.00	12.00
❑ 28349	The Seven Joys of Mary (Part 1)/The Seven Joys of Mary (Part 2)	1952	3.00	6.00	12.00
❑ 28350	King Herod and the Clock/Down in Yon Forest	1952	3.00	6.00	12.00
—The above four comprise a box set					
❑ 28708	Close the Door Richard/Left My Gal in the Mountains	1953	3.75	7.50	15.00
❑ 28849	Great White Bird/Brighten the Corner Where You Are	1953	3.75	7.50	15.00
❑ 28935	The Crawdad Song/Hound Dog	1953	3.75	7.50	15.00
❑ 29039	There's Plenty of Fish in the Ocean/The Old Red Barn	1954	3.75	7.50	15.00
❑ 29088	True Love Goes On and On/Brave Man	1954	3.75	7.50	15.00
❑ 29129	Wait for Me Darling/Casey Jones	1954	3.00	6.00	12.00
❑ 29282	The Mission San Miguel/Tangled Web	1954	3.75	7.50	15.00
❑ 29423	The Ballad of Davy Crockett/Goober Peas	1955	3.75	7.50	15.00
❑ 29533	I Wonder What's Become of Sally/Wabash Cannonball	1955	3.00	6.00	12.00
❑ 29549	Be Sure You're Right (Then Go Ahead)/Ol' Betsy	1955	3.75	7.50	15.00
❑ 29910	Jack Was Every Inch a Sailor/Harlem Man	1956	3.00	6.00	12.00
❑ 30046	The Bus Stop Song/That's My Heart Strings	1956	3.00	6.00	12.00
❑ 30217	Marianne/Pretty Girl	1957	3.00	6.00	12.00
❑ 30855	We Love Ye, Jimmy/I Never See Maggie Alone	1959	3.00	6.00	12.00
❑ 31248	Long Black Veil/Forty Hour Week	1961	2.50	5.00	10.00
❑ 31330	A Little Bitty Tear/Shanghaid	1961	2.50	5.00	10.00
❑ 31371	Funny Way of Laughin'/Mother Wouldn't Do That	1962	2.50	5.00	10.00
❑ 31405	Call Me Mr. In-Between/What You Gonna Do, Leroy	1962	2.50	5.00	10.00
❑ 31433	Mary Ann Regrets/How Do You Fall Out of Love	1962	2.50	5.00	10.00
❑ 31453	The Same Old Hurt/Curry Road	1963	2.50	5.00	10.00
❑ 31479	Roses and Orchids/Baby Come Home to Me	1963	2.50	5.00	10.00
❑ 31504	I'm the Boss/The Moon Is High	1963	2.50	5.00	10.00
❑ 31518	This Is All I Ask/There Goes Another Pal of Mine	1963	2.50	5.00	10.00
❑ 31543	It Comes and Goes/I Found My Best Friend in the Dog Pound	1963	2.50	5.00	10.00
❑ 31571	True Love Goes On and On/I Wonder What's Become of Sally	1963	2.50	5.00	10.00
❑ 31610	Four Initials on a Tree/This Is Your Day	1964	2.00	4.00	8.00
❑ 31659	Pearly Shells/What Little Tears Are Made Of	1964	2.00	4.00	8.00
❑ 31695	A Holly Jolly Christmas/Snow for Johnny	1964	2.50	5.00	10.00
❑ 31729	Call My Name/My Gal Sal	1965	2.00	4.00	8.00
❑ 31772	On the Beach at Waikiki/Some Hangin' Round You All the Time	1965	2.00	4.00	8.00
❑ 31811	Salt Water Guitar/The Story of Bobby Lee Trent	1965	2.00	4.00	8.00
❑ 31857	Frangipani/A Girl Sittin' Up in a Tree	1965	2.00	4.00	8.00

Number	Title (A Side/B Side)	Yr	VG	VG+	NM
❑ 31918	The Sixties/Don't Forget Your Paddle	1966	2.00	4.00	8.00
❑ 31981	Here She Comes (There She Goes)/Atlantic Coastal Line	1966	2.00	4.00	8.00
❑ 31997	Evil Off My Mind/Taste of Heaven	1966	2.00	4.00	8.00
❑ 32078	Lonesome 7-7203/Hollow Words	1967	2.00	4.00	8.00
❑ 32165	Funny Little Show/Holding Hands for Joe	1967	2.00	4.00	8.00
❑ 32282	Bury the Bottle/That's Where My Baby Used to Be	1968	2.00	4.00	8.00
❑ 32990	Stayin' Song/The Best Is Yet to Come	1972	—	3.00	6.00
❑ 33049	Miss Johnson's Happiness Emporium/Anytime You Say	1972	—	3.00	6.00
DISNEYLAND					
❑ F-130	Chim Chim Chiree/Lavender Blue	1964	2.00	4.00	8.00
❑ F-130 [PS]	Chim Chim Chiree/Lavender Blue	1964	3.00	6.00	12.00
MCA					
❑ 31695	A Holly Jolly Christmas/Snow For Johnny	1989	—	2.50	5.00
—Double the NM value if insert is enclosed					
❑ 40082	Payin' My Dues Again/All Around	1973	—	2.50	5.00
❑ 40175	Tale of the Comet Kohoutek/A Very Fine Lady	1974	—	2.50	5.00
MONKEY JOE					
❑ MJ-1 [DJ]	The Christmas Legend of Monkey Joe/It's Gonna Be A Mixed Up Xmas	1978	2.50	5.00	10.00
UNITED ARTISTS					
❑ 293	Alexander's Ragtime Band/Say It Isn't So	1961	2.00	4.00	8.00
❑ 429	All Alone/Always	1962	2.00	4.00	8.00
❑ 1568	Go 'Way from My House/Two Maidens Went Milking	196?	2.00	4.00	8.00
❑ 1569	Willie Boy/Irish Rover	196?	2.00	4.00	8.00
❑ 1570	Alexander's Ragtime Band/What'll I Do	196?	2.00	4.00	8.00
❑ 1571	All Alone/Always	196?	2.00	4.00	8.00
—The above four all are "Silver Spotlight Series" releases					
Selected 78s					
DECCA					
❑ 24547	Lavender Blue (Dilly Dilly)/Billy Boy	1949	3.75	7.50	15.00
—This may exist on 45. The original edition was definitely on 78.					
7-Inch Extended Plays					
DECCA					
❑ ED 2235	*The Locktender's Lament/Ox Driver's Song/The Bold Soldier/The Young Married Man (Cod Liver Oil)/Sad Man's Song (Fare Thee Well, O Honey)/ The Harlem Man	195?	3.00	6.00	12.00
❑ ED 2235 [PS]	Songs For and About Men, Part 1	195?	3.00	6.00	12.00
❑ ED 2236	The Western Settler/Waltzing Matilda (The Jolly Swagman's Song)//The Wild Rover/Frankie and Johnny/The Deceiver	195?	3.00	6.00	12.00
❑ ED 2236 [PS]	Songs For and About Men, Part 2	195?	3.00	6.00	12.00
❑ ED 2714	(contents unknown)	1961	2.50	5.00	10.00
❑ ED 2714 [PS]	Burl Ives	1961	2.50	5.00	10.00
❑ ED 2720	Funny Way of Laughin'/Mother Wouldn't Do That/ /What You Gonna Do Leroy/I Ain't Comin' Home Tonight	1962	2.50	5.00	10.00
❑ ED 2720 [PS]	It's Just My Funny Way of Laughin'	1962	2.50	5.00	10.00
❑ ED 2726	Call Me Mr. In-Between/Poor Little Jimmie//In Foggy Old London/Thumbin' Johnny Brown	1962	2.50	5.00	10.00
❑ ED 2726 [PS]	Call Me Mr. In-Between	1962	2.50	5.00	10.00
❑ ED 2741	(contents unknown)	1962	2.50	5.00	10.00
❑ ED 2741 [PS]	Mary Ann Regrets	1962	2.50	5.00	10.00
❑ ED 2771	True Love Goes On and On/This Is All I Ask//It Comes and Goes/I'm the Boss	1963	2.50	5.00	10.00
❑ ED 2771 [PS]	True Love Goes On and On	1963	2.50	5.00	10.00
Albums					
ARCHIVE OF FOLK AND JAZZ					
❑ 340	Burl Ives Live	1978	2.50	5.00	10.00
BELL					
❑ 6055	Time	1971	2.50	5.00	10.00
COLUMBIA					
❑ CL 628 [M]	The Wayfaring Stranger	1955	7.50	15.00	30.00
❑ CL 980 [M]	Burl Ives Sings Songs for All Ages	1956	7.50	15.00	30.00
❑ CL 1459 [M]	Return of the Wayfaring Stranger	1960	7.50	15.00	30.00
❑ CL 2570 [10]	Children's Favorites	1955	10.00	20.00	40.00
—"House Party Series" issue					
❑ CL 6058 [10]	The Return of the Wayfaring Stranger	1949	12.50	25.00	50.00
❑ CL 6109 [10]	The Wayfaring Stranger	1950	12.50	25.00	50.00
❑ CL 6144 [10]	More Folk Songs	1950	12.50	25.00	50.00
❑ CS 9041 [R]	The Wayfaring Stranger	1964	3.00	6.00	12.00
❑ CS 9675	The Times They Are a-Changin'	1969	3.00	6.00	12.00
❑ CS 9728	Burl Ives Christmas Album	1968	3.00	6.00	12.00
❑ CS 9925	Softly and Tenderly	1969	3.00	6.00	12.00
DECCA					
❑ DXB 167 [(2) M]	The Best of Burl Ives	1961	6.25	12.50	25.00
❑ DL 4152 [M]	The Versatile Burl Ives	1961	3.75	7.50	15.00
❑ DL 4179 [M]	Songs of the West	1961	3.75	7.50	15.00
❑ DL 4279 [M]	It's Just My Funny Way of Laughin'	1962	3.75	7.50	15.00
❑ DL 4304 [M]	Sing Out, Sweet Land	1962	3.75	7.50	15.00
❑ DL 4320 [M]	Sunshine in My Soul	1962	3.75	7.50	15.00
❑ DL 4361 [M]	Burl	1963	3.75	7.50	15.00
❑ DL 4390 [M]	The Best of Burl's for Boys and Girls	1963	3.75	7.50	15.00
❑ DL 4433 [M]	Singin' Easy	1964	3.75	7.50	15.00
❑ DL 4533 [M]	True Love	1964	3.75	7.50	15.00
❑ DL 4578 [M]	Pearly Shells	1964	3.75	7.50	15.00
❑ DL 4606 [M]	My Gal Sal	1965	3.00	6.00	12.00
❑ DL 4668 [M]	On the Beach at Waikiki	1965	3.00	6.00	12.00
❑ DL 4689 [M]	Have a Holly Jolly Christmas	1965	3.00	6.00	12.00
❑ DL 4734 [M]	Burl's Choice	1966	3.00	6.00	12.00
❑ DL 4789 [M]	Something Special	1966	3.00	6.00	12.00
❑ DL 4850 [M]	Burl Ives' Greatest Hits	1967	3.75	7.50	15.00

Number	Title (A Side/B Side)	Yr	VG	VG+	NM
❑ DL 4876 [M]	Broadway	1967	3.75	7.50	15.00
❑ DL 4972 [M]	Big Country Hits	1968	3.75	7.50	15.00
❑ DL 5013 [10]	Ballads and Folk Songs	1949	12.50	25.00	50.00
❑ DL 5080 [10]	Ballads and Folk Songs, Volume 2	1949	12.50	25.00	50.00
❑ DL 5093 [10]	Ballads, Folk and Country Songs	1949	12.50	25.00	50.00
❑ DL 5428 [10]	Christmas Day in the Morning	1952	12.50	25.00	50.00
❑ DL 5467 [10]	Folk Songs Dramatic and Dangerous	1953	12.50	25.00	50.00
❑ DL 5490 [10]	Women: Folk Songs About the Fair Sex	1954	12.50	25.00	50.00
❑ DXSB 7167 [(2) S]	The Best of Burl Ives	1961	7.50	15.00	30.00
❑ DL 8080 [M]	Coronation Concert	1953	10.00	20.00	40.00
❑ DL 8107 [M]	The Wild Side of Life	1955	6.25	12.50	25.00
❑ DL 8125 [M]	Men	1956	6.25	12.50	25.00
❑ DL 8245 [M]	Down to the Sea in Ships	1956	6.25	12.50	25.00
❑ DL 8246 [M]	Women	1956	6.25	12.50	25.00
❑ DL 8247 [M]	In the Quiet of Night	1956	6.25	12.50	25.00
❑ DL 8248 [M]	Burl Ives Sings for Fun	1956	6.25	12.50	25.00
❑ DL 8391 [M]	Christmas Eve	1957	6.25	12.50	25.00
❑ DL 8444 [M]	Songs of Ireland	1958	6.25	12.50	25.00
❑ DL 8587 [M]	Captain Burl Ives' Ark	1958	6.25	12.50	25.00
❑ DL 8637 [M]	Old Time Varieties	1958	6.25	12.50	25.00
❑ DL 8749 [M]	Australian Folk Songs	1959	6.25	12.50	25.00
❑ DL 8886 [M]	Cheers	1959	6.25	12.50	25.00
❑ DL 74152 [S]	The Versatile Burl Ives	1961	5.00	10.00	20.00
❑ DL 74179 [S]	Songs of the West	1961	5.00	10.00	20.00
❑ DL 74279 [S]	It's Just My Funny Way of Laughin'	1962	5.00	10.00	20.00
❑ DL 74304 [S]	Sing Out, Sweet Land	1962	5.00	10.00	20.00
❑ DL 74320 [S]	Sunshine in My Soul	1962	5.00	10.00	20.00
❑ DL 74361 [S]	Burl	1963	5.00	10.00	20.00
❑ DL 74390 [S]	The Best of Burl's for Boys and Girls	1963	5.00	10.00	20.00
❑ DL 74433 [S]	Singin' Easy	1964	5.00	10.00	20.00
❑ DL 74533 [S]	True Love	1964	5.00	10.00	20.00
❑ DL 74578 [S]	Pearly Shells	1964	5.00	10.00	20.00
❑ DL 74606 [S]	My Gal Sal	1965	3.75	7.50	15.00
❑ DL 74668 [S]	On the Beach at Waikiki	1965	3.75	7.50	15.00
❑ DL 74689 [S]	Have a Holly Jolly Christmas	1965	3.75	7.50	15.00
❑ DL 74734 [S]	Burl's Choice	1966	3.75	7.50	15.00
❑ DL 74789 [S]	Something Special	1966	3.75	7.50	15.00
❑ DL 74850 [S]	Burl Ives' Greatest Hits	1967	3.00	6.00	12.00
❑ DL 74876 [S]	Broadway	1967	3.00	6.00	12.00
❑ DL 74972 [S]	Big Country Hits	1968	3.00	6.00	12.00
❑ DL 78391 [R]	Christmas Eve	196?	2.50	5.00	10.00
❑ DL 78886 [S]	Cheers	1959	7.50	15.00	30.00

DISNEYLAND

Number	Title (A Side/B Side)	Yr	VG	VG+	NM
❑ ST-3927 [M]	Chim Chim Chiree and Other Children's Choices	1964	3.75	7.50	15.00
❑ STER-3927 [S]	Chim Chim Chiree and Other Children's Choices	1964	5.00	10.00	20.00

HARMONY

Number	Title (A Side/B Side)	Yr	VG	VG+	NM
❑ HL 9507 [M]	The Little White Duck	196?	3.75	7.50	15.00
❑ HL 9551 [M]	The Lollipop Tree	196?	3.75	7.50	15.00
❑ HS 11275	Got the World by the Tail	196?	2.50	5.00	10.00

MCA

Number	Title (A Side/B Side)	Yr	VG	VG+	NM
❑ 114	Burl Ives' Greatest Hits	1973	2.50	5.00	10.00
—Reissue of Decca 74850					
❑ 318	Paying My Dues Again	1973	2.50	5.00	10.00
❑ 4034 [(2)]	The Best of Burl Ives	197?	3.00	6.00	12.00
❑ 4089 [(2)]	The Best of Burl Ives Volume 2	197?	3.00	6.00	12.00
❑ 15002	Have a Holly Jolly Christmas	1973	3.00	6.00	12.00
—Reissue of Decca 74689; black label with rainbow					
❑ 15002	Have a Holly Jolly Christmas	1980	2.00	4.00	8.00
—Blue label with rainbow					
❑ 15030	Santa Claus Is Coming to Town	198?	2.50	5.00	10.00

NATIONAL GEOGRAPHIC

Number	Title (A Side/B Side)	Yr	VG	VG+	NM
❑ 7806	We Americans	1978	3.00	6.00	12.00

PICKWICK

Number	Title (A Side/B Side)	Yr	VG	VG+	NM
❑ SPC-1018	Twelve Days of Christmas	197?	2.50	5.00	10.00

STINSON

Number	Title (A Side/B Side)	Yr	VG	VG+	NM
❑ SLP-1 [10]	The Wayfaring Stranger	1949	15.00	30.00	60.00

SUNSET

Number	Title (A Side/B Side)	Yr	VG	VG+	NM
❑ SUS-5280	Favorites	1970	2.50	5.00	10.00

UNITED ARTISTS

Number	Title (A Side/B Side)	Yr	VG	VG+	NM
❑ UAL 3060 [M]	Ballads	1959	3.75	7.50	15.00
❑ UAS 6060 [S]	Ballads	1959	5.00	10.00	20.00

WORD

Number	Title (A Side/B Side)	Yr	VG	VG+	NM
❑ 3259 [M]	Faith and Joy	196?	3.75	7.50	15.00
❑ 3339 [M]	Shall We Gather at the River	1966	3.00	6.00	12.00
❑ 3391 [M]	I Do Believe	1967	3.00	6.00	12.00
❑ 8140 [S]	Faith and Joy	196?	5.00	10.00	20.00
❑ 8339 [S]	Shall We Gather at the River	1966	3.75	7.50	15.00
❑ 8391 [S]	I Do Believe	1967	3.75	7.50	15.00
❑ 8537	How Great Thou Art	1971	3.00	6.00	12.00

IVIE, ROGER

See SILVER CREEK.

IVORY JACK

45s

COUNTRY INT'L.

Number	Title (A Side/B Side)	Yr	VG	VG+	NM
❑ 154	Love Signs/I Came So Close to Calling You Last Night	1981	—	3.00	6.00
❑ 161	If It Wasn't for the Honky Tonks/Pickin' 'Em Up and Puttin' 'Em Down	1981	—	3.00	6.00
❑ 168	I'll Be More Than Just One Man/Love Signs	1982	—	3.00	6.00

NSD

Number	Title (A Side/B Side)	Yr	VG	VG+	NM
❑ 28	How I Love My Wicked Ways/Love Me Like There's No Tomorrow	1979	—	3.00	6.00
❑ 36	Made in the U.S.A./Borrowed Angel	1980	—	3.00	6.00

J

JACK AND DANIEL

45s

DECCA

Number	Title (A Side/B Side)	Yr	VG	VG+	NM
❑ 9-28467	Don't Make Love in a Buggy/Tennessee Tango	1952	5.00	10.00	20.00

JACK AND TRINK

45s

NSD

Number	Title (A Side/B Side)	Yr	VG	VG+	NM
❑ 4	I'm Tired of Being Me/Ain't No Way of Gettin'...	1978	—	3.00	6.00
❑ 12	After the Roses/I Can't See Me Without You	1978	—	3.00	6.00
❑ 48	Get Back to the Basics/I've Got a Brand New Love Song	1980	—	3.00	6.00
❑ 61	I'm Not Really Drinking, I'm Just Holding the Can/I Can't See Me Without Her	1980	—	3.00	6.00

JACKSON, ALAN

45s

ARISTA

Number	Title (A Side/B Side)	Yr	VG	VG+	NM
❑ 2032	Wanted/Dog River Blues	1990	—	2.00	4.00
❑ 2095	Chasin' That Neon Rainbow/Short Sweet Ride	1990	—	2.00	4.00
❑ 2166	I'd Love You All Over Again/Home	1990	—	2.00	4.00
❑ 2220	Don't Rock the Jukebox/Home	1991	—	2.00	4.00
❑ 9892	Blue Blooded Woman/Home	1989	2.50	5.00	10.00
—Issued on blue vinyl					
❑ 9922	Here in the Real World/Blue Blooded Woman	1989	—	2.00	4.00
❑ 12335	Someday/From a Distance	1991	—	2.00	4.00
❑ 12372	I Only Want You for Christmas/Merry Christmas to Me	1991	—	2.00	4.00
❑ 12385	Dallas/Just Playin' Possum	1991	—	2.00	4.00
❑ 12418	Midnight in Montgomery/Working Class Hero	1992	—	2.00	4.00
❑ 12447	Love's Got a Hold on You/That's All I Need to Know	1992	—	2.00	4.00
❑ 12463	She's Got the Rhythm (And I Got the Blues)/She Likes It Too	1992	—	2.00	4.00
❑ 12514	Tonight I Climbed the Wall/Up to My Ears in Tears	1993	—	—	3.00
❑ 12535	Here in the Real World/Wanted	1993	—	—	3.00
—Reissue with "Collectables" logo on label					
❑ 12536	Don't Rock the Jukebox/I'd Love You All Over Again	1993	—	—	3.00
—Reissue with "Collectables" logo on label					
❑ 12537	Chasin' That Neon Rainbow/Midnight in Montgomery	1993	—	—	3.00
—Reissue with "Collectables" logo on label					
❑ 12538	Love's Got a Hold on You/Someday	1993	—	—	3.00
—Reissue with "Collectables" logo on label					
❑ 12560	Chattahoochee/I Don't Need the Booze (To Get a Buzz On)	1993	—	2.00	4.00
❑ 12607	Mercury Blues/Chattahoochee (Club Mix)	1993	—	2.00	4.00
❑ 12611	Honky Tonk Christmas/The Angels Cried	1993	—	—	3.00
—B-side with Alison Krauss					
❑ 12649	(Who Says) You Can't Have It All/If It Ain't One Thing (It's You)	1993	—	—	3.00
❑ 12697	Summertime Blues/Hole in the Wall	1994	—	2.00	4.00
❑ 12745	Livin' on Love/Let's Get Back to Me and You	1994	—	2.00	4.00
❑ 12775	Gone Country/All American Country Boy	1994	—	2.00	4.00
❑ 12792	Song for the Life/You Can't Give Up on Love	1995	—	—	3.00
❑ 12830	I Don't Even Know Your Name/If I Had You	1995	—	—	3.00
❑ 12879	Tall, Tall Trees/Home	1995	—	—	3.00
❑ 12942	Home/I'll Try	1996	—	—	3.00

ARISTA NASHVILLE

Number	Title (A Side/B Side)	Yr	VG	VG+	NM
❑ 13048	Little Bitty/Must've Had a Ball	1996	—	—	3.00
❑ 13060	Rudolph the Red-Nosed Reindeer/We Three Kings (Star of Wonder)	1996	—	2.00	4.00
—B-side by Blackhawk					
❑ 13068	Everything I Love/It's Time You Learned About Good-Bye	1996	—	—	3.00
❑ 13069	Who's Cheatin' Who/Buicks to the Moon	1997	—	—	3.00
❑ 13070	There Goes/A House with No Curtains	1997	—	—	3.00
❑ 13106	Between the Devil and Me/Walk on the Rocks	1997	—	—	3.00
❑ 13135	I'll Go On Loving You/Chattahoochee	1998	—	—	3.00
❑ 13136	Right On the Money/A Woman's Love	1998	—	—	3.00
❑ 13145	Little Man/Hurtin' Comes Easy	1999	—	—	3.00
❑ 13155	Gone Crazy/Amarillo	1999	—	—	3.00
❑ 13183	Pop a Top/Revenooer Man	1999	—	—	3.00
❑ 13193	The Blues Man/My Own Kind of Hat	2000	—	—	3.00
❑ 69020	www.memory/It's Alright to Be a Redneck	2000	—	—	3.00

ARISTA/FOX

Number	Title (A Side/B Side)	Yr	VG	VG+	NM
❑ 10001	A Holly Jolly Christmas/I Only Want You for Christmas	1992	—	2.00	4.00

Albums

ARISTA

Number	Title (A Side/B Side)	Yr	VG	VG+	NM
❑ AS 8623	Here in the Real World	1990	5.00	10.00	20.00
❑ AS 8681	Don't Rock the Jukebox	1991	6.25	12.50	25.00
—Columbia House vinyl edition					
❑ R 143877	Don't Rock the Jukebox	1991	6.25	12.50	25.00
—BMG Direct Marketing vinyl version					

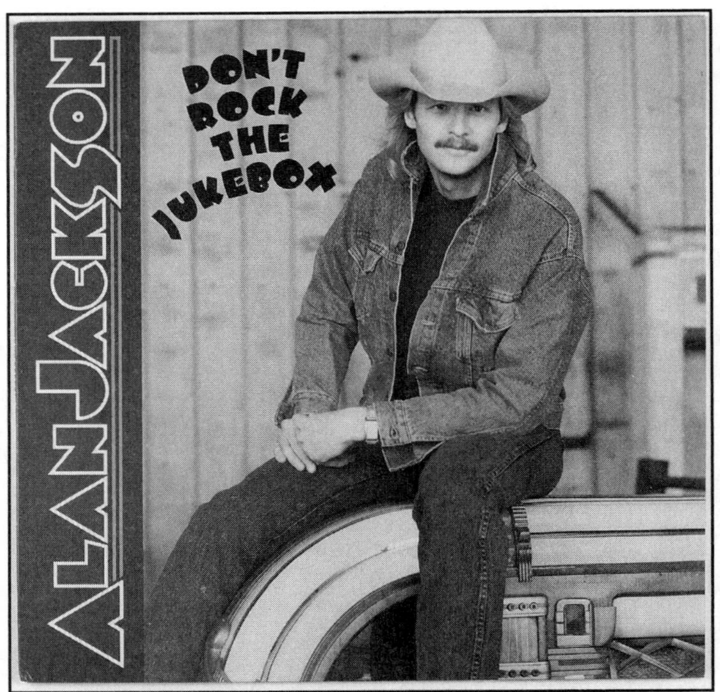

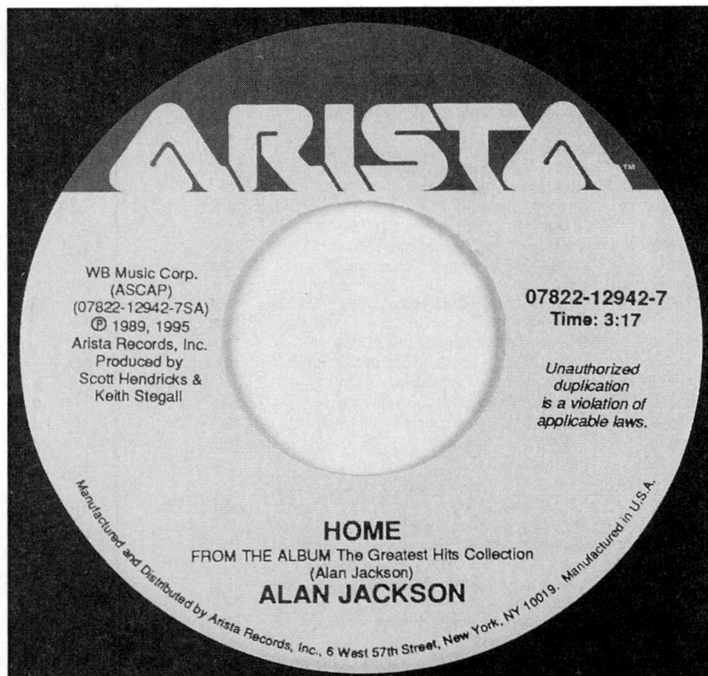

One of the 1990s' most successful country performers was Alan Jackson, who had success without ticking off the traditionalists. (Top left) *Don't Rock the Jukebox*, named after perhaps his career-defining hit, was the last of his albums to be issued on vinyl. This is the BMG pressing from 1991. (Top right) His biggest hit to date, which spent four weeks at No. 1, was "Chattahoochee," a wild, short romp from 1993 that, on sales alone, also made the top 50 of the *Billboard* pop chart. (Bottom left) After it had been the B-side of four different singles, the song "Home," which was from his first album, finally became a top-5 hit in 1996. (Bottom right) Jackson's most controversial hit was the mostly-spoken "I'll Go On Loving You," the 1998 hit that seemed to be an overt ode to seduction until you listened more closely to the lyrics.

JACKSON, CARL

45s

COLUMBIA

Number	Title (A Side/B Side)	Yr	VG	VG+	NM
❑ 38-04647	She's Gone, Gone, Gone/You Made a Memory of Me	1984	—	—	3.00
❑ 38-04786	All That's Left for Me/I'm Beside Myself	1985	—	—	3.00
❑ 38-04926	Dixie Train/I'm Beside Myself	1985	—	—	3.00
❑ 38-05645	You Are the Rock (And I'm a Rolling Stone)/ Tennessee Girl	1985	—	—	3.00

JACKSON, LOLITA

45s

OAK

Number	Title (A Side/B Side)	Yr	VG	VG+	NM
❑ 1069	Every Time You Walk in the Room/(B-side unknown)	1989	—	3.00	6.00

JACKSON, NISHA

45s

CAPITOL

Number	Title (A Side/B Side)	Yr	VG	VG+	NM
❑ B-44064	Alive and Well/Going Down Slow	1987	—	—	3.00

JACKSON, SHOT

Albums

CUMBERLAND

Number	Title (A Side/B Side)	Yr	VG	VG+	NM
❑ MGC-29513 [M]	Bluegrass Dobro	1965	5.00	10.00	20.00
❑ SRC-69513 [S]	Bluegrass Dobro	1965	6.25	12.00	25.00

STARDAY

Number	Title (A Side/B Side)	Yr	VG	VG+	NM
❑ SLP-230 [M]	The Singing Strings of Steel Guitar and Dobro	1962	7.50	15.00	30.00

JACKSON, STONEWALL

45s

COLUMBIA

Number	Title (A Side/B Side)	Yr	VG	VG+	NM
❑ 4-40883	Don't Be Angry/Knock Off Your Naggin'	1957	6.25	12.50	25.00
❑ 4-40997	I Need You Real Bad/A Broken Heart, A Wedding Band	1957	6.25	12.50	25.00
❑ 4-41114	Tears on Her Brodal Bouquet/Gettin' Older	1958	5.00	10.00	20.00
❑ 4-41199	Grieving in My Heart/I Can't Go On Living This Way	1958	5.00	10.00	20.00
❑ 4-41257	Life to Go/Misery Known As Heartache	1958	5.00	10.00	20.00
❑ 4-41393	Waterloo/Smoke Along the Track	1959	3.75	7.50	15.00
❑ 4-41393 [PS]	Waterloo/Smoke Along the Track	1959	7.50	15.00	30.00
❑ 4-41488	Igmoo (The Pride of South Central High)/Uncle Sam and Big John Bull	1959	3.75	7.50	15.00
❑ 4-41533	Mary Don't You Weep/Run	1959	3.75	7.50	15.00
❑ 4-41591	Why I'm Walkin'/Life of a Poor Boy	1960	3.75	7.50	15.00
❑ 4-41695	Thirty Links of Chain/Sixteen Fathoms	1960	3.75	7.50	15.00
❑ 4-41785	A Little Guy Called Joe/I'm Gonna Find You	1960	3.75	7.50	15.00
❑ 4-41932	Greener Pastures/Wedding Bells for You and Me	1961	3.75	7.50	15.00
❑ 4-42028	Hungry for Love/For the Last Time	1961	3.75	7.50	15.00
❑ 4-42229	A Wound Time Can't Erase/Second Choice	1961	3.75	7.50	15.00
❑ 4-42426	Leona/One Look at Heaven	1962	3.00	6.00	12.00
❑ 4-42628	Can't Hang Up the Phone/Slowly	1962	3.00	6.00	12.00
❑ 4-42765	Old Showboat/A Toast to the Bride	1963	3.00	6.00	12.00
❑ 4-42846	Wild Wind Wind/The Water's So Cold	1963	3.00	6.00	12.00
❑ 4-42889	B.J. the D.J./Big House on the Corner	1963	3.00	6.00	12.00
❑ 4-43011	Not My Kind of People/Give It Back to the Indians	1964	3.00	6.00	12.00
❑ 4-43076	Don't Be Angry/It's Not Me	1964	3.00	6.00	12.00
❑ 4-43197	I Washed My Hands in Muddy Water/I've Got to Change	1964	3.00	6.00	12.00
❑ 4-43304	Lost in the Shuffle/Trouble and Me	1965	2.50	5.00	10.00
❑ 4-43411	If This House Could Talk/Poor Red Georgia Dirt	1965	2.50	5.00	10.00
❑ 4-43552	The Minute Men (Are Turning in Their Graves)/I Wish I Had a Girl	1966	2.50	5.00	10.00
❑ 4-43552 [PS]	The Minute Men (Are Turning in Their Graves)/I Wish I Had a Girl	1966	5.00	10.00	20.00
❑ 4-43718	Blues Plus Booze (Means I Lose)/Still Awake	1966	2.50	5.00	10.00
❑ 4-43917	Mommy Look, Santa Is Crying/Blue Christmas	1966	3.00	6.00	12.00
❑ 4-43966	Stamp Out Loneliness/Road to Recovery	1967	2.50	5.00	10.00
❑ 4-44121	Promises and Hearts (Were Made to Break)/ While the Daisies Go Free	1967	2.50	5.00	10.00
❑ 4-44283	This World Means Nothing (Since You're Gone)/ Almsot Hear the Blues	1967	2.50	5.00	10.00
❑ 4-44416	Nothing Takes the Place of Loving You/If Heartaches Were Wine	1968	2.50	5.00	10.00
❑ 4-44501	I Believe in Love/Drinking and Driving	1968	2.50	5.00	10.00
❑ 4-44501 [PS]	I Believe in Love/Drinking and Driving	1968	3.75	7.50	15.00
❑ 4-44625	Angry Words/Red Roses Blooming Back Home	1968	2.50	5.00	10.00
❑ 4-44726	Somebody's Always Leaving/Recess Time	1969	2.50	5.00	10.00
❑ 4-44863	"Never More" Quoth the Raven/How Many Lies Can I Tell	1969	2.50	5.00	10.00
❑ 4-44976	Ship in the Bottle/Thoughts of a Lonely Man	1969	2.50	5.00	10.00
❑ 4-45075	Better Days for Mama/The Harm You've Done	1970	2.00	4.00	8.00
❑ 4-45151	Born That Way/Blue Field	1970	2.00	4.00	8.00
❑ 4-45217	Oh, Lonesome Me/When He Was Nine	1970	2.00	4.00	8.00
❑ 4-45291	Save a Little Place for Me/Wings of a Dove	1970	2.00	4.00	8.00
❑ 4-45381	Me and You and a Dog Named Boo/Here's to Hank	1971	2.00	4.00	8.00
❑ 4-45465	Push the Panic Button/Waitin' for Dawn 'Til Dawn	1971	2.00	4.00	8.00
❑ 4-45546	That's All This Old World Needs/Big Busy World	1972	2.00	4.00	8.00
❑ 4-45632	Torn from the Pages of Life/Waterloo	1972	2.00	4.00	8.00
❑ 4-45738	I'm Not Strong Enough (To Build Another Dream)/ I've Run Out of Reasons	1972	2.00	4.00	8.00
❑ 4-45831	True Love Is the Thing/House of Bottles and Cans	1973	2.00	4.00	8.00

GRT

Number	Title (A Side/B Side)	Yr	VG	VG+	NM
❑ 013	Read Between the Lines/Don't Be Late	1974	—	3.00	6.00
❑ 023	Waterloo/I Washed My Hands in Muddy Water	1975	—	3.00	6.00

LITTLE DARLIN'

Number	Title (A Side/B Side)	Yr	VG	VG+	NM
❑ 7800	Spirits of St. Louis/Alcohol of Fame	1978	—	3.00	6.00
❑ 7802	Walk Out on Me Before I Walk Out on You/Burned On Low	1978	—	3.00	6.00
❑ 7806	I Can't Sing a Love Song/My Favorite Sin	1978	—	3.00	6.00
❑ 7915	Come On Home/Point of No Return	1979	—	3.00	6.00
❑ 7927	Listening to Johnny Paycheck/Here's to the Ripoff	1979	—	3.00	6.00

MGM

Number	Title (A Side/B Side)	Yr	VG	VG+	NM
❑ 14569	Herman Schwartz/Lovin' the Fool Out of Me	1973	—	3.50	7.00
❑ 14675	Ol' Blue/Things to Think About	1973	—	3.50	7.00

Albums

COLUMBIA

Number	Title (A Side/B Side)	Yr	VG	VG+	NM
❑ CL 1391 [M]	The Dynamic Stonewall Jackson	1959	6.25	12.50	25.00
❑ CL 1770 [M]	Sadness in a Song	1962	5.00	10.00	20.00
❑ CL 2059 [M]	I Love a Song	1963	5.00	10.00	20.00
❑ CL 2278 [M]	Trouble & Me	1964	3.75	7.50	15.00
❑ CL 2377 [M]	Stonewall Jackson's Greatest Hits	1965	3.75	7.50	15.00
❑ CL 2509 [M]	All's Fair in Love 'n' War	1966	3.75	7.50	15.00
❑ CL 2674 [M]	Help Stamp Out Loneliness	1967	6.25	12.50	25.00
❑ CL 2762 [M]	Stonewall Jackson Country	1967	6.25	12.50	25.00
❑ CS 8186 [S]	The Dynamic Stonewall Jackson	1959	7.50	15.00	30.00
❑ CS 8570 [S]	Sadness in a Song	1962	6.25	12.50	25.00
❑ CS 8859 [S]	I Love a Song	1963	6.25	12.50	25.00
❑ CS 9078 [S]	Trouble & Me	1964	5.00	10.00	20.00
❑ CS 9177 [S]	Stonewall Jackson's Greatest Hits	1965	5.00	10.00	20.00
❑ CS 9309 [S]	All's Fair in Love 'n' War	1966	5.00	10.00	20.00
❑ CS 9474 [S]	Help Stamp Out Loneliness	1967	5.00	10.00	20.00
❑ CS 9562 [S]	Stonewall Jackson Country	1967	5.00	10.00	20.00
❑ CS 9669	Nothing Takes the Place of Loving You	1968	5.00	10.00	20.00
❑ CS 9708	The Great Old Songs	1968	5.00	10.00	20.00
❑ CS 9754	The Old Country Church	1969	6.25	12.50	25.00
❑ CS 9880	Tribute to Hank Williams	1969	5.00	10.00	20.00

JACKSON, WANDA

45s

ABC

Number	Title (A Side/B Side)	Yr	VG	VG+	NM
❑ 12116	Take a Look/I Can't Stand to Hear You Say Goodbye	1975	—	2.50	5.00

CAPITOL

Number	Title (A Side/B Side)	Yr	VG	VG+	NM
❑ 2021	A Girl Don't Have to Drink to Have Fun/My Days Are Darker Than Your Nights	1967	2.50	5.00	10.00
❑ 2085	By the Time You Get to Phoenix/Wishing Well	1968	2.00	4.00	8.00
❑ 2151	My Baby Walked Right Out on Me/No Place to Go But Home	1968	2.00	4.00	8.00
❑ 2245	Little Boy Soldier/I Talk a Pretty Story	1968	2.00	4.00	8.00
❑ 2315	I Wish I Was Your Friend/Poor Old Me	1968	2.00	4.00	8.00
❑ 2379	If I Had a Hammer/The Pain of It All	1969	2.00	4.00	8.00
❑ 2472	Your Tender Love/As the Day Wears On	1969	2.00	4.00	8.00
❑ 2524	Everything's Leaving/You Cheated Me	1969	2.00	4.00	8.00
❑ 2614	My Big Iron Skillet/The Hunter	1969	2.00	4.00	8.00
❑ 2693	Two Separate Bar Stools/Two Wrongs Don't Make a Right	1969	2.00	4.00	8.00
❑ 2761	A Woman Lives for Love/What Have We Done	1970	—	3.00	6.00
❑ 2872	Who Shot John/Stop the World	1970	—	3.00	6.00
❑ 2986	Fancy Satin Pillows/Why Don't We Love Like That Anymore	1970	—	3.00	6.00
❑ 3070	People Gotta Be Loving/Glory Hallelujah	1971	—	3.00	6.00
❑ 3143	Back Then/I'm Gonna Walk Out of Your Life	1971	—	3.00	6.00
❑ 3218	I Already Know (What I'm Gettin' for My Birthday)/ The Man You Could Have Been	1971	—	3.00	6.00
❑ 3293	I'll Be Whatever You Say/The More You See Me Less	1972	—	3.00	6.00
❑ 3385	I Wouldn't Want You Any Other Way/Song of the Wind	1972	—	3.00	6.00
❑ F3485	I Gotta Know/Half As Good a Girl	1956	10.00	20.00	40.00
❑ 3498	Roll with the Tide/Tennessee Women's Prison	1972	—	3.00	6.00
❑ F3575	The Hot Dog That Made Him Mad/Silver Threads and Golden Needles	1956	10.00	20.00	40.00
❑ 3599	I Don't Know How to Tell Him/Your Memory Comes and Gets Me	1973	—	3.00	6.00
❑ F3637	Cryin' Through the Night/Baby Loves Him	1957	12.50	25.00	50.00
❑ F3683	Don'a Wana/Let Me Explain	1957	7.50	15.00	30.00
❑ F3764	Cool Love/Did You Miss Me	1957	7.50	15.00	30.00
❑ F3843	Fujiyama Mama/No Wedding Bells for Joe	1957	7.50	15.00	30.00
❑ F3941	Just a Queen for a Day/Honey Bop	1958	7.50	15.00	30.00
❑ F4026	(Every Time They Play) Our Song/Mean, Mean Man	1958	7.50	15.00	30.00
❑ F4081	Sinful Heart/Rock Your Baby	1958	7.50	15.00	30.00
❑ F4142	Savin' My Love/I Wanna Waltz	1959	6.25	12.50	25.00
❑ F4207	A Date with Jerry/You're the One for Me	1959	6.25	12.50	25.00
❑ F4286	Reaching/I'd Rather Have You	1959	6.25	12.50	25.00
❑ 4354	My Destiny/Please Call Today	1960	6.25	12.50	25.00
❑ 4397	Let's Have a Party/Cool Love	1960	10.00	20.00	40.00
❑ 4469	Mean, Mean Man/Happy, Happy Birthday	1960	6.25	12.50	25.00
❑ 4520	Riot in Cell Black #9/Little Charm Bracelet	1961	6.25	12.50	25.00
❑ 4553	Right or Wrong/Funnel of Love	1961	6.25	12.50	25.00
❑ 4635	In the Middle of a Heartache/I'd Be Ashamed	1961	6.25	12.50	25.00
❑ 4681	A Little Bitty Tear/I Don't Wanta Go	1962	5.00	10.00	20.00
❑ 4723	If I Cried Every Time You Hurt Me/Let My Love Walk In	1962	5.00	10.00	20.00
❑ 4723 [PS]	If I Cried Every Time You Hurt Me/Let My Love Walk In	1962	7.50	15.00	30.00
❑ 4785	I Misunderstood/Between the Window and the Phone	1962	3.75	7.50	15.00
❑ 4833	The Greatest Actor/You Bug Me Bad	1962	3.75	7.50	15.00

Number	Title (A Side/B Side)	Yr	VG	VG+	NM
❑ 4884	Whirlpool/One Teardrop at a Time	1962	3.75	7.50	15.00
❑ 4917	But I Was Lying/Sympathy	1963	3.75	7.50	15.00
❑ 4973	This Should Go On Forever/We Haven't a Moment to Lose	1963	3.75	7.50	15.00
❑ 5015	Memory Mountain/Let Me Talk to You	1963	3.75	7.50	15.00
❑ 5072	Slippin'/Just for You	1963	3.75	7.50	15.00
❑ 5142	The Violet and a Rose/To Tell You the Truth	1964	3.00	6.00	12.00
❑ 5228	Leave My Baby Alone/I'm Mad at Me	1964	3.00	6.00	12.00
❑ 5287	Candy Man/Weary Blues From Waitin'	1964	3.00	6.00	12.00
❑ 5364	My Baby's Gone/If I Were You	1965	3.00	6.00	12.00
❑ 5433	Have I Grown Used to Missing You/Take Me Home	1965	3.00	6.00	12.00
❑ 5491	My First Day Without You/Send Me No Roses	1965	3.00	6.00	12.00
❑ 5559	The Box It Came In/Look Out Heart	1965	3.00	6.00	12.00
❑ 5645	Because It's You/Long As I Have You	1966	2.50	5.00	10.00
❑ 5712	This Gun Don't Care/I Wonder If She Knows	1966	2.50	5.00	10.00
❑ 5789	Tears Will Be the Chaser for Your Wine/Reckless Love Affair	1967	2.50	5.00	10.00
❑ 5863	Both Sides of the Line/Famous Last Words	1967	2.50	5.00	10.00
❑ 5960	My Heart Gets All the Breaks/You'll Always Have My Love	1967	2.50	5.00	10.00
DECCA					
❑ 29140	You Can't Have My Love/Lovin' Country Style	1954	15.00	30.00	60.00
—With Billy Gray					
❑ 29253	The Right to Love/If You Knew What I Know	1954	15.00	30.00	60.00
❑ 29267	If You Don't, Somebody Else Will/You'd Be the First One to Know	1954	12.50	25.00	50.00
—With Billy Gray					
❑ 29514	Tears at the Grand Ole Opry/Nobody's Darlin' But Mine	1955	12.50	25.00	50.00
❑ 29677	Don't Do the Things He'd Do/It's the Same World	1955	7.50	15.00	30.00
❑ 29803	Wasted/I Cried Again	1956	12.50	25.00	50.00
❑ 30153	You Won't Forget (About Me)/A Heart You Could Have Had	1956	7.50	15.00	30.00
JIN					
❑ 300	Lonely Days, Lonely Nights/My Memories	197?	—	2.50	5.00
MYRRH					
❑ 122	When It's Time to Fall in Love Again/Say "I Do"	1973	—	2.50	5.00
❑ 126	Come On Home (To This Lonely Heart)/It's a Long, Long Time to Cry	1973	—	2.50	5.00
❑ 143	Jesus Put a Yodel in My Soul/(B-side unknown)	1974	—	2.50	5.00
❑ 152	Where Do I Put His Memory/Take a Look	1975	—	2.50	5.00

Albums

Number	Title	Yr	VG	VG+	NM
CAPITOL					
❑ ST-129	The Many Moods of Wanda Jackson	1969	3.75	7.50	15.00
❑ ST-238	The Happy Side of Wanda Jackson	1969	3.75	7.50	15.00
❑ ST-345	Wanda Jackson In Person	1970	3.75	7.50	15.00
❑ ST-434	Wanda Jackson Country!	1970	3.75	7.50	15.00
❑ ST-554	A Woman Lives for Love	1970	3.75	7.50	15.00
❑ ST-669	I've Gotta Sing!	1971	3.75	7.50	15.00
❑ T 1041 [M]	Wanda Jackson	1958	75.00	150.00	300.00
—Black colorband label, Capitol logo at left					
❑ T 1041 [M]	Wanda Jackson	1962	25.00	50.00	100.00
—Black colorband label, Capitol logo at top					
❑ T 1384 [M]	Rockin' with Wanda	1960	100.00	200.00	400.00
—Black colorband label, Capitol logo at left					
❑ T 1384 [M]	Rockin' with Wanda	1962	62.50	125.00	250.00
—Gold "Star Line" label					
❑ T 1384 [M]	Rockin' with Wanda	1963	37.50	75.00	150.00
—Black "Star Line" label					
❑ ST 1511 [S]	There's a Party Goin' On	1961	100.00	200.00	400.00
—Black colorband label, Capitol logo at left					
❑ T 1511 [M]	There's a Party Goin' On	1961	62.50	125.00	250.00
—Black colorband label, Capitol logo at left					
❑ ST 1596 [S]	Right or Wrong	1961	12.50	25.00	50.00
—Black colorband label, Capitol logo at left					
❑ ST 1596 [S]	Right or Wrong	1962	6.25	12.50	25.00
—Black colorband label, Capitol logo at top					
❑ T 1596 [M]	Right or Wrong	1961	10.00	20.00	40.00
—Black colorband label, Capitol logo at left					
❑ T 1596 [M]	Right or Wrong	1962	5.00	10.00	20.00
—Black colorband label, Capitol logo at top					
❑ ST 1776 [S]	Wonderful Wanda	1962	7.50	15.00	30.00
❑ T 1776 [M]	Wonderful Wanda	1962	6.25	12.50	25.00
❑ ST 1911 [S]	Love Me Forever	1963	7.50	15.00	30.00
❑ T 1911 [M]	Love Me Forever	1963	6.25	12.50	25.00
❑ ST 2030 [S]	Two Sides of Wanda	1964	7.50	15.00	30.00
❑ T 2030 [M]	Two Sides of Wanda	1964	6.25	12.50	25.00
❑ ST 2306 [S]	Blues in My Heart	1965	7.50	15.00	30.00
❑ T 2306 [M]	Blues in My Heart	1965	6.25	12.50	25.00
❑ ST 2438 [S]	Wanda Jackson Sings Country Songs	1965	7.50	15.00	30.00
❑ T 2438 [M]	Wanda Jackson Sings Country Songs	1965	6.25	12.50	25.00
❑ ST 2606 [S]	Wanda Jackson Salutes the Country Music Hall of Fame	1966	5.00	10.00	20.00
❑ T 2606 [M]	Wanda Jackson Salutes the Country Music Hall of Fame	1966	3.75	7.50	15.00
❑ ST 2704 [S]	Reckless Love Affair	1967	3.75	7.50	15.00
❑ T 2704 [M]	Reckless Love Affair	1967	5.00	10.00	20.00
❑ ST 2812 [S]	You'll Always Have My Love	1967	3.75	7.50	15.00
❑ T 2812 [M]	You'll Always Have My Love	1967	5.00	10.00	20.00
❑ ST 2883	The Best of Wanda Jackson	1968	3.75	7.50	15.00
❑ ST 2976	Cream of the Crop	1968	3.75	7.50	15.00
❑ ST-11023	Praise the Lord	1972	3.75	7.50	15.00
❑ ST-11096	I Wouldn't Want You Any Other Way	1972	3.75	7.50	15.00
❑ ST-11161	Country Keepsakes	1973	3.75	7.50	15.00
DECCA					
❑ DL 4224 [M]	Lovin' Country Style	1962	12.50	25.00	50.00
HILLTOP					
❑ 6058	Please Help Me I'm Falling	197?	2.50	5.00	10.00
❑ 6074	Leave My Baby Alone	197?	3.00	6.00	12.00
❑ 6116	We'll Sing in the Sunshine	197?	3.00	6.00	12.00
❑ 6123	Phoenix	197?	2.50	5.00	10.00
❑ 6182	Tears at the Grand Ole Opry	197?	2.50	5.00	10.00
MYRRH					
❑ 6533	Now I Have Everything	197?	3.00	6.00	12.00
❑ 6556	Make Me Like a Child Again	197?	3.00	6.00	12.00
PICKWICK					
❑ PTP-2053 [(2)]	Wanda Jackson	197?	3.00	6.00	12.00
VARRICK					
❑ VR-025	Rock 'n' Roll Away Your Blues	1987	3.00	6.00	12.00
WORD					
❑ WST-8614	Country Gospel	197?	3.00	6.00	12.00
❑ WST-8781	Closer to Jesus	197?	3.00	6.00	12.00

JACOBS, LORI

45s

Number	Title (A Side/B Side)	Yr	VG	VG+	NM
NEOSTAT					
❑ 102	Tugboat Annie/Blue Eyes	1980	—	3.00	6.00

JACOBY BROTHERS, THE

45s

Number	Title (A Side/B Side)	Yr	VG	VG+	NM
COLUMBIA					
❑ 4-21309	Kiss Me Once More/Laredo	1954	6.25	12.50	25.00
❑ 4-21359	Who Ye Primpin' Fer/One Man's Opinion	1955	6.25	12.50	25.00

JACQUES, RICK

45s

Number	Title (A Side/B Side)	Yr	VG	VG+	NM
CAPRICE					
❑ 2046	Song Man/There Is a Slow Moving Train	1978	—	3.00	6.00

JAMES, ATLANTA

See MACK VICKERY.

JAMES, BRETT

45s

Number	Title (A Side/B Side)	Yr	VG	VG+	NM
CAREER					
❑ 12838	Female Bonding/Dark Side of the Moon	1995	—	2.00	4.00
❑ 12869	If I Could See Love/Many Tears Ago	1995	—	2.00	4.00
❑ 12935	Worth the Fall/Wake Up and Smell the Whiskey	1996	—	2.00	4.00

JAMES, DUSTY

45s

Number	Title (A Side/B Side)	Yr	VG	VG+	NM
SCR					
❑ 172	You're All the Woman I'll Ever Need/Old Flame New Fire	1979	—	3.00	6.00

JAMES, GEORGE

45s

Number	Title (A Side/B Side)	Yr	VG	VG+	NM
JANC					
❑ 103	When Our Love Began (Cowboys and Indians)/Break My Mind	1979	2.00	4.00	8.00
❑ 10417	It's Gonna Be Magic/I'm Takin' a Heartbreak	1979	2.00	4.00	8.00

JAMES, JESSECA

Includes records she made as "Kathy Twitty" (her real name).

45s

Number	Title (A Side/B Side)	Yr	VG	VG+	NM
MCA					
❑ 40613	Johnny One Time/Lying in My Arms	1976	—	3.00	6.00
❑ 40660	Give Me One Good Reason/One More Day with You	1976	—	3.00	6.00
❑ 40703	My First Country Song/Let It Ring	1977	—	3.00	6.00
❑ 40792	I Take It Back/Everybody Needs a Rainbow	1977	—	3.00	6.00
PERMIAN					
❑ 82008	Little Miss Understanding/Green Eyes	1984	—	2.50	5.00
—As "Kathy Twitty"					
❑ 82009	Green Eyes/That's What Your Lovin' Does to Me	1984	—	2.50	5.00
—As "Kathy Twitty"					

JAMES, MARY KAY

45s

Number	Title (A Side/B Side)	Yr	VG	VG+	NM
AVCO					
❑ 601	It Amazes Me (Sweet Lovin' Time)/Before I'm Fool Enough	1974	—	2.50	5.00
❑ 605	The Crossroad/Before the Curtain Falls	1974	—	2.50	5.00
❑ 610	I Think I'll Say Goodbye/Which Way Do We Go	1975	—	2.50	5.00
JMI					
❑ 31	I'm Not That Good at Goodbye/Home Is Anywhere You Are	1973	—	3.00	6.00
❑ 38	Please Help Me Say No/Before the Curtain Falls	1974	—	3.00	6.00
❑ 46	It Amazes Me (Sweet Lovin' Time)/Before I'm Fool Enough	1974	—	3.50	7.00

JAMES, SONNY

45s

Number	Title (A Side/B Side)	Yr	VG	VG+	NM
CAPITOL					
❑ 2067	A World of Our Own/An Old Sweetheart of Mine	1967	2.50	5.00	10.00
❑ 2067 [PS]	A World of Our Own/An Old Sweetheart of Mine	1967	3.75	7.50	15.00
❑ 2155	Heaven Says Hello/Fairy Tales	1968	2.50	5.00	10.00

From 1967 through 1971, Sonny James, "The Southern Gentleman," had 16 consecutive No. 1 country singles, with none of them even getting higher than 65 on the pop charts! (Top left) Long before his string began, James hit the top with the record that remained his biggest hit, "Young Love." A cover version by Tab Hunter was somewhat bigger on the pop side, but it's Sonny's version that has lived on. (Top right) After bouncing around several labels from 1958-63, he returned to Capitol in mid-1963. By the end of 1964, he was hitting No. 1, which he would do regularly for a decade. "Heaven Says Hello," a chart-topper in 1968, was one of his few hits in his 16-in-a-row run that was not previously a hit for someone else. (Bottom left) "Running Bear" topped the chart in 1969. It had originally been a pop hit for Johnny Preston in early 1960. (Bottom right) In the middle of 1972, Sonny signed with Columbia, where he continued hitting the top 10 for five years, but the No. 1 hits began to dry up. His last chart-topper was "Is It Wrong (For Loving You)" from 1974.

Number	Title (A Side/B Side)	Yr	VG	VG+	NM
❑ 2155 [PS]	Heaven Says Hello/Fairy Tales	1968	3.75	7.50	15.00
❑ F2164	Short Cut/It's So Nice to Make Up	1952	6.25	12.50	25.00
❑ F2259	That's Me Without You/Cool, Cold and Colder	1952	6.25	12.50	25.00
❑ 2271	Born to Be With You/In Waikiki	1968	2.50	5.00	10.00
❑ 2271 [PS]	Born to Be With You/In Waikiki	1968	3.00	6.00	12.00
❑ 2370	Only the Lonely/The Journey	1968	2.50	5.00	10.00
❑ 2370 [PS]	Only the Lonely/The Journey	1968	3.00	6.00	12.00
❑ F2399	The One I Can't Forget/Somebody's Heartache	1953	6.25	12.50	25.00
❑ 2486	Running Bear/Midnight Mood	1969	2.50	5.00	10.00
❑ 2486 [PS]	Running Bear/Midnight Mood	1969	3.00	6.00	12.00
❑ F2508	I Forgot More Than You'll Ever Know/Poor Boy, Rich Lovin'	1953	6.25	12.50	25.00
❑ 2595	Since I Met You, Baby/Clinging to a Hope	1969	2.50	5.00	10.00
❑ 2595 [PS]	Since I Met You, Baby/Clinging to a Hope	1969	3.00	6.00	12.00
❑ F2641	Won't Somebody Tell Me/My Greatest Thrill	1953	6.25	12.50	25.00
❑ 2700	It's Just a Matter of Time/This World of Ours	1969	2.50	5.00	10.00
❑ 2700 [PS]	It's Just a Matter of Time/This World of Ours	1969	3.00	6.00	12.00
❑ F2734	I've Always Wanted You/That's How I Need You	1954	6.25	12.50	25.00
❑ 2782	My Love/Blue for You	1970	2.00	4.00	8.00
❑ 2782 [PS]	My Love/Blue for You	1970	2.50	5.00	10.00
❑ F2829	Table Next to Mine/Believe Another's Lips	1954	6.25	12.50	25.00
❑ 2834	Don't Keep Me Hangin' On/Woodbine Valley	1970	2.00	4.00	8.00
❑ 2834 [PS]	Don't Keep Me Hangin' On/Woodbine Valley	1970	2.50	5.00	10.00
❑ F2906	She Done Give Her Heart to Me/Oceans of Tears	1954	6.25	12.50	25.00
❑ 2914	Endlessly/Happy Memories	1970	2.00	4.00	8.00
❑ 2914 [PS]	Endlessly/Happy Memories	1970	2.50	5.00	10.00
❑ F2958	Christmas in My Home Town/I Forgot to Remember Santa Claus	1954	7.50	15.00	30.00
❑ 3015	Empty Arms/Everything Begins and Ends with You	1971	2.00	4.00	8.00
❑ 3015 [PS]	Empty Arms/Everything Begins and Ends with You	1971	2.50	5.00	10.00
❑ F3025	Lovin' Season/This Kiss Must Last Forever	1955	6.25	12.50	25.00
❑ F3112	Deceive Me Once Again/Ain't Gonna Take No Chance	1955	6.25	12.50	25.00
❑ 3114	Bright Lights, Big City/True Love Lasts Forever	1971	2.00	4.00	8.00
❑ 3114 [PS]	Bright Lights, Big City/True Love Lasts Forever	1971	2.50	5.00	10.00
❑ F3163	Til the Last Leaf Shall Fall/You Don't Have to Walk Alone	1955	6.25	12.50	25.00
❑ 3174	Here Comes Honey Again/The Only Ones We Truly Hurt	1971	2.00	4.00	8.00
❑ 3174 [PS]	Here Comes Honey Again/The Only Ones We Truly Hurt	1971	2.50	5.00	10.00
❑ F3198	Too Much/Let's Go Bunny Huggin'	1955	6.25	12.50	25.00
❑ 3232	Only Love Can Break a Heart/He Has Walked This Way Before	1971	2.00	4.00	8.00
❑ 3232 [PS]	Only Love Can Break a Heart/He Has Walked This Way Before	1971	2.50	5.00	10.00
❑ F3281	Careless with My Heart/Pigtails and Ribbons	1955	6.25	12.50	25.00
❑ 3322	That's Why I Love You Like I Do/Still Water Runs Deep	1972	2.00	4.00	8.00
❑ F3357	For Rent (One Empty Heart)/My Stolen Love	1956	5.00	10.00	20.00
❑ 3398	Traces/I'm in Love with You	1972	—	3.50	7.00
❑ F3441	Twenty Feet of Muddy Water/All Mixed Up	1956	5.00	10.00	20.00
❑ 3475	Downfall of Me/I'll Follow You	1972	—	3.50	7.00
❑ F3542	The Cat Came Back/Hello, Old Broken Heart	1956	5.00	10.00	20.00
❑ 3564	Reach Out Your Hand and Touch Me/Just Keep Thinking of Me	1973	—	3.50	7.00
❑ F3602	Young Love/You're the Reason I'm in Love	1956	5.50	11.00	22.00
❑ 3653	Heaven on Earth/She Believes in Me	1973	—	3.50	7.00
❑ F3674	First Date, First Kiss, First Love/Speak to Me	1957	5.00	10.00	20.00
❑ F3734	Lovesick Blues/Dear Love	1957	5.00	10.00	20.00
❑ 3779	Surprise, Surprise/What Am I Living For	1973	—	3.50	7.00
❑ F3792	Love Conquered/Mighty Loveable Man	1957	5.00	10.00	20.00
❑ F3840	Uh Huh-mm/Why Can't They Remember	1957	5.00	10.00	20.00
❑ F3888	Kathleen/Walk to the Dance	1958	5.00	10.00	20.00
❑ 3931	All the Way Together/Clinging Vine	1974	—	3.00	6.00
❑ F3962	Are You Mine/Let's Play Love	1958	5.00	10.00	20.00
❑ F4020	You Got That Touch/I Can See It in Your Eyes	1958	5.00	10.00	20.00
❑ F4066	Let Me Be the One to Love You/I Can't Stay Away from You	1958	5.00	10.00	20.00
❑ F4127	Yo-Yo/Dream Big	1959	5.00	10.00	20.00
❑ F4178	Talk of the School/The Table	1959	5.00	10.00	20.00
❑ F4229	Pure Love/This Love of Mine	1959	5.00	10.00	20.00
❑ F4268	Who's Next in Line/Red Mud	1959	5.00	10.00	20.00
❑ F4268 [PS]	Who's Next in Line/Red Mud	1959	10.00	20.00	40.00
❑ 4307	Till Tomorrow/I Forgot More Than You'll Ever Know	1959	5.00	10.00	20.00
❑ 4969	The Minute You're Gone/Gold and Silver	1963	3.00	6.00	12.00
❑ 5057	Going Through the Motions (Of Living)/Bad Times a-Comin'	1963	3.00	6.00	12.00
❑ 5129	Baltimore/Least of All You	1964	3.00	6.00	12.00
❑ 5197	Ask Marie/Sugar Lump	1964	3.00	6.00	12.00
❑ 5280	You're the Only World I Know/Tying Pieces Together	1964	3.00	6.00	12.00
❑ 5280	You're the Only World I Know/Tying Pieces Together	1964	5.00	10.00	20.00
❑ 5375	I'll Keep Holding On (Just to Your Love)/I'm Getting Gray from Being Blue	1965	3.00	6.00	12.00
❑ 5375 [PS]	I'll Keep Holding On (Just to Your Love)/I'm Getting Gray from Being Blue	1965	5.00	10.00	20.00
❑ 5454	Behind the Tear/Runnin'	1965	3.00	6.00	12.00
❑ 5454 [PS]	Behind the Tear/Runnin'	1965	5.00	10.00	20.00
❑ 5536	True Love's a Blessing/Just Ask Your Heart	1965	3.00	6.00	12.00
❑ 5536 [PS]	True Love's a Blessing/Just Ask Your Heart	1965	5.00	10.00	20.00
❑ 5612	Take Good Care of Her/On the Fingers of One Hand	1966	3.00	6.00	12.00
❑ 5612 [PS]	Take Good Care of Her/On the Fingers of One Hand	1966	5.00	10.00	20.00
❑ 5690	Room in Your Heart/How Many Times Can a Man Be a Fool	1966	3.00	6.00	12.00
❑ 5690 [PS]	Room in Your Heart/How Many Times Can a Man Be a Fool	1966	5.00	10.00	20.00
❑ 5733	My Christmas Dream/Barefoot Santa Claus	1966	3.00	6.00	12.00
❑ 5733 [PS]	My Christmas Dream/Barefoot Santa Claus	1966	5.00	10.00	20.00
❑ 5833	Need You/On and On	1967	3.00	6.00	12.00
❑ 5833 [PS]	Need You/On and On	1967	5.00	10.00	20.00
❑ 5914	I'll Never Find Another You/Goodbye, Maggie, Goodbye	1967	3.00	6.00	12.00
❑ 5914 [PS]	I'll Never Find Another You/Goodbye, Maggie, Goodbye	1967	3.75	7.50	15.00
❑ 5987	It's the Little Things/Don't Cut Timber on a Windy Day	1967	3.00	6.00	12.00
❑ 5987 [PS]	It's the Little Things/Don't Cut Timber on a Windy Day	1967	3.75	7.50	15.00

COLUMBIA

Number	Title (A Side/B Side)	Yr	VG	VG+	NM
❑ 3-10001	A Mi Esposa Con Amor (To My Wife with Love)/Just Don't Stop Lovin' Me	1974	—	2.50	5.00
❑ 3-10001 [PS]	A Mi Esposa Con Amor (To My Wife with Love)/Just Don't Stop Lovin' Me	1974	2.00	4.00	8.00
❑ 3-10072	A Little Bit South of Saskatoon/Home Style Lovin'	1974	—	2.50	5.00
❑ 3-10072 [PS]	A Little Bit South of Saskatoon/Home Style Lovin'	1974	2.00	4.00	8.00
❑ 3-10121	Little Band of Gold/Pop and Me	1975	—	2.50	5.00
❑ 3-10121 [PS]	Little Band of Gold/Pop and Me	1975	2.00	4.00	8.00
❑ 3-10139	Indian Love Call/Maria Elena	1975	—	2.50	5.00
—As "The Guitars of Sonny James"					
❑ 3-10184	What in the World's Come Over You/Walking the Railroad Trestle	1975	—	2.50	5.00
❑ 3-10184 [PS]	What in the World's Come Over You/Walking the Railroad Trestle	1975	—	3.00	6.00
❑ 3-10249	Eres Tu (Touch the Wind)/Apache	1975	—	2.50	5.00
❑ 3-10276	The Prisoner's Song/Back in the Saddle Again	1975	—	2.50	5.00
❑ 3-10276 [PS]	The Prisoner's Song/Back in the Saddle Again	1975	—	3.00	6.00
❑ 3-10335	When Something Is Wrong with My Baby/Big Silver Bird	1976	—	2.50	5.00
❑ 3-10392	Come On In/Baby's Eyes	1976	—	2.50	5.00
❑ 3-10466	You're Free to Go/Puttin' On the Dog Tonight	1976	—	2.50	5.00
❑ 3-10551	In the Jailhouse Now/Amazing Grace	1977	—	2.50	5.00
❑ 3-10551 [PS]	In the Jailhouse Now/Amazing Grace	1977	—	2.50	5.00
❑ 3-10628	Abilene/Pistol Packin' Mama	1977	—	2.50	5.00
❑ 3-10703	This Is the Love/It'll Still Be Worth It All	1978	—	2.50	5.00
❑ 3-10703 [PS]	This Is the Love/It'll Still Be Worth It All	1978	—	3.00	6.00
❑ 3-10764	Caribbean/Each Time I Look at You	1978	—	2.50	5.00
❑ 3-10852	Building Memories/Little Band of Gold	1978	—	2.50	5.00
❑ 4-45644	When the Snow Is On the Roses/Love is a Rainbow	1972	—	3.50	7.00
❑ 4-45644 [PS]	When the Snow Is On the Roses/Love is a Rainbow	1972	2.50	5.00	10.00
❑ 4-45706	White Silver Sands/Why Is It I'm the Last to Know	1972	—	3.50	7.00
❑ 4-45770	I Love You More and More Everyday/I'll Think About That Tomorrow	1973	—	3.50	7.00
❑ 4-45770 [PS]	I Love You More and More Everyday/I'll Think About That Tomorrow	1973	2.50	5.00	10.00
❑ 4-45871	If She Just Helps Me Get Over You/I Won't Think About It Now	1973	—	3.00	6.00
❑ 4-46003	Is It Wrong (For Loving You)/Suddenly There's a Valley	1974	—	3.00	6.00

DIMENSION

Number	Title (A Side/B Side)	Yr	VG	VG+	NM
❑ 1026	Innocent Lies/Don't Let the Stars Get in Your Eyes	1981	—	2.50	5.00
❑ 1026 [PS]	Innocent Lies/Don't Let the Stars Get in Your Eyes	1981	2.00	4.00	8.00
❑ 1033	A Place in the Sun/Lean On Me Girl	1982	—	2.50	5.00
❑ 1033 [PS]	A Place in the Sun/Lean On Me Girl	1982	2.00	4.00	8.00
❑ 1036	I'm Looking Over the Rainbow/Something's Got a Hold on Me	1982	—	2.50	5.00
❑ 1036 [PS]	I'm Looking Over the Rainbow/Something's Got a Hold on Me	1982	2.00	4.00	8.00
❑ 1040	The Fool in Me/Little Rainbow	1982	—	2.50	5.00
❑ 1045	A Free Roamin' Mind/Don't Let the Stars Get In Your Eyes	1983	—	2.50	5.00

DOT

Number	Title (A Side/B Side)	Yr	VG	VG+	NM
❑ 16381	A Mile and a Quarter/Just One More Lie	1962	3.75	7.50	15.00
❑ 16419	On the Longest Day/The Only Cure	1963	3.75	7.50	15.00

GROOVE

Number	Title (A Side/B Side)	Yr	VG	VG+	NM
❑ 1	Young Love/Broken Wings	1961	5.00	10.00	20.00

MONUMENT

Number	Title (A Side/B Side)	Yr	VG	VG+	NM
❑ 45280	Hold What You've Got/Hanging On to Yesterday	1979	—	2.50	5.00
❑ 45280 [PS]	Hold What You've Got/Hanging On to Yesterday	1979	—	3.00	6.00
❑ 45288	Lorelei/If I Ever Wanted You	1979	—	2.50	5.00

NRC

Number	Title (A Side/B Side)	Yr	VG	VG+	NM
❑ 050	Jenny Lou/Passin' Through	1960	6.25	12.50	25.00
❑ 050 [PS]	Jenny Lou/Passin' Through	1960	12.50	25.00	50.00
❑ 056	Cold in the Morning/Wondering	1960	6.25	12.50	25.00
❑ 061	Bimbo/I Wish This Night Would Never End	1960	5.00	10.00	20.00

RCA VICTOR

Number	Title (A Side/B Side)	Yr	VG	VG+	NM
❑ 47-7858	Apache/Magnetism	1961	3.75	7.50	15.00
❑ 47-7919	Innocent Angel/Hey Little Ducky	1961	3.75	7.50	15.00
❑ 47-7998	The Day's Not Over Yet/The Legend of Brown Mountain Light	1962	3.75	7.50	15.00

7-Inch Extended Plays

CAPITOL

Number	Title (A Side/B Side)	Yr	VG	VG+	NM
❑ EAP 1-779	Can't Get Over Missin' You/Cold, Cold Heart//Only One Heart to Give/I Got the Feeling	1957	5.00	10.00	20.00
❑ EAP 1-779 [PS]	Southern Gentleman, Part 1	1957	5.00	10.00	20.00
❑ EAP 2-779	I Wish I Knew/Forgive Me//I'll Always Wonder (But I'll Never Know)/Lonesome	1957	5.00	10.00	20.00
❑ EAP 2-779 [PS]	Southern Gentleman, Part 2	1957	5.00	10.00	20.00
❑ EAP 3-779	'Til the Last Leaf Shall Fall/Only a Shadow Between//May God Be With You/My God and I	1957	5.00	10.00	20.00
❑ EAP 3-779 [PS]	Southern Gentleman, Part 3	1957	5.00	10.00	20.00
❑ EAP 1-827	Young Love/Twenty Feet of Muddy Water//For Rent/Hello Old Broken Heart	1957	6.25	12.50	25.00
❑ EAP 1-827 [PS]	Young Love	1957	6.25	12.50	25.00

Albums

ABC

Number	Title (A Side/B Side)	Yr	VG	VG+	NM
❑ AC-30027	The ABC Collection	1976	3.00	6.00	12.00

CAPITOL

Number	Title (A Side/B Side)	Yr	VG	VG+	NM
❑ ST-111	Born to Be with You	1968	3.75	7.50	15.00
❑ SKAO-144	The Best of Sonny James Vol. 2	1969	3.75	7.50	15.00
❑ ST-193	Only the Lonely	1969	3.75	7.50	15.00
❑ SWBB-258 [(2)]	Close-Up	1969	5.00	10.00	20.00
—Combines ST 2500 and ST 2788 in one package					
❑ ST-320	The Astrodome Presents In Person Sonny James	1969	3.75	7.50	15.00
❑ ST-432	It's Just a Matter of Time	1970	3.75	7.50	15.00
❑ ST-478	My Love/Don't Keep Me Hangin' On	1970	3.75	7.50	15.00
❑ STBB-535 [(2)]	You're the Only World I Know/I'll Never Find Another You	1970	5.00	10.00	20.00
—Combines the two listed albums in one package					
❑ ST-629	#1	1970	3.75	7.50	15.00
❑ ST-734	Empty Arms	1971	3.75	7.50	15.00
❑ T 779 [M]	The Southern Gentleman	1957	12.50	25.00	50.00
—Turquoise label					
❑ T 779 [M]	The Southern Gentleman	1964	5.00	10.00	20.00
—Black label with colorband, logo on top					
❑ ST-804	The Sensational Sonny James	1971	3.75	7.50	15.00
❑ ST-849	Here Comes Honey Again	1971	3.75	7.50	15.00
❑ T 887 [M]	Sonny	1957	12.50	25.00	50.00
—Turquoise label					
❑ T 887 [M]	Sonny	1964	5.00	10.00	20.00
—Black label with colorband, logo on top					
❑ T 988 [M]	Honey	1958	12.50	25.00	50.00
—Turquoise label					
❑ T 988 [M]	Honey	1964	5.00	10.00	20.00
—Black label with colorband, logo on top					
❑ T 1178 [M]	This Is Sonny James	1959	10.00	20.00	40.00
—Black label with colorband, logo at left					
❑ T 1178 [M]	This Is Sonny James	1964	5.00	10.00	20.00
—Black label with colorband, logo on top					
❑ ST 2017 [S]	The Minute You're Gone	1964	6.25	12.50	25.00
❑ T 2017 [M]	The Minute You're Gone	1964	5.00	10.00	20.00
❑ ST 2209 [S]	You're the Only World I Know	1965	6.25	12.50	25.00
❑ T 2209 [M]	You're the Only World I Know	1965	5.00	10.00	20.00
❑ ST 2317 [S]	I'll Keep Holding On	1965	6.25	12.50	25.00
❑ T 2317 [M]	I'll Keep Holding On	1965	5.00	10.00	20.00
❑ ST 2415 [S]	Behind the Tear	1965	6.25	12.50	25.00
❑ T 2415 [M]	Behind the Tear	1965	5.00	10.00	20.00
❑ ST 2500 [S]	True Love's a Blessing	1966	6.25	12.50	25.00
❑ T 2500 [M]	True Love's a Blessing	1966	5.00	10.00	20.00
❑ ST 2561 [S]	Till the Last Leaf Shall Fall	1966	6.25	12.50	25.00
❑ T 2561 [M]	Till the Last Leaf Shall Fall	1966	5.00	10.00	20.00
❑ ST 2589 [S]	My Christmas Dream	1966	6.25	12.50	25.00
❑ T 2589 [M]	My Christmas Dream	1966	5.00	10.00	20.00
❑ SM-2615	The Best of Sonny James	197?	2.50	5.00	10.00
❑ ST 2615 [S]	The Best of Sonny James	1966	5.00	10.00	20.00
—Black Starline label					
❑ T 2615 [M]	The Best of Sonny James	1966	3.75	7.50	15.00
❑ ST 2703 [S]	Need You	1967	3.75	7.50	15.00
❑ T 2703 [M]	Need You	1967	5.00	10.00	20.00
❑ ST 2788 [S]	I'll Never Find Another You	1967	3.75	7.50	15.00
❑ T 2788 [M]	I'll Never Find Another You	1967	5.00	10.00	20.00
❑ ST 2884 [S]	A World of Our Own	1968	3.75	7.50	15.00
❑ T 2884 [M]	A World of Our Own	1968	6.25	12.50	25.00
❑ ST 2937	Heaven Says Hello	1968	3.75	7.50	15.00
❑ SM-11013	The Biggest Hits of Sonny James	197?	2.50	5.00	10.00
❑ ST-11013	The Biggest Hits of Sonny James	1972	3.75	7.50	15.00
❑ ST-11067	That's Why I Love You Like I Do	1972	3.75	7.50	15.00
❑ ST-11108	Traces	1972	3.00	6.00	12.00
❑ ST-11144	The Gentleman from the South	1973	3.00	6.00	12.00
❑ ST-11196	Young Love	1973	3.00	6.00	12.00

COLUMBIA

Number	Title (A Side/B Side)	Yr	VG	VG+	NM
❑ KC 31646	When the Snow Is On the Roses	1972	3.00	6.00	12.00
❑ KC 32028	Sonny James Sings the Greatest Country Hits of '72	1973	3.00	6.00	12.00
❑ KC 32291	If She Just Helps Me Get Over You	1973	3.00	6.00	12.00
❑ KC 32805	Is It Wrong	1974	3.00	6.00	12.00
❑ KC 33056	A Mi Esposa Con Amor (To My Wife with Love)	1974	3.00	6.00	12.00
❑ KC 33428	A Little Bit South of Saskatoon/Little Band of Gold	1975	3.00	6.00	12.00
❑ PC 33477	The Guitars of Sonny James	1975	3.00	6.00	12.00
❑ CG 33627 [(2)]	When the Snow Is On the Roses/If She Just Helps Me Get Over You	1975	3.75	7.50	15.00
❑ PC 33846	Country Male Artist of the Decade	1975	3.00	6.00	12.00
❑ PC 34035	200 Years of Country Music	1976	3.00	6.00	12.00
❑ PC 34309	When Something Is Wrong with My Baby	1976	3.00	6.00	12.00
❑ PC 34472	You're Free to Go	1977	3.00	6.00	12.00
❑ PC 34706	Sonny James In Prison, In Person	1977	3.00	6.00	12.00
❑ KC 35379	This Is the Love	1978	3.00	6.00	12.00
❑ KC 35626	Sonny James' Greatest Hits	1978	3.00	6.00	12.00

DOT

Number	Title (A Side/B Side)	Yr	VG	VG+	NM
❑ DLP 3462 [M]	Young Love	1962	10.00	20.00	40.00
❑ DLP 25462 [S]	Young Love	1962	12.50	25.00	50.00

DOT/MCA

Number	Title (A Side/B Side)	Yr	VG	VG+	NM
❑ 39087	Sonny James	198?	2.50	5.00	10.00

HILLTOP

Number	Title (A Side/B Side)	Yr	VG	VG+	NM
❑ 6067	Invisible Tears	1969	2.50	5.00	10.00
❑ 6079	Timberline	1969	2.50	5.00	10.00

PICKWICK

Number	Title (A Side/B Side)	Yr	VG	VG+	NM
❑ SPC-3594	Young Love	1977	2.00	4.00	8.00

RCA CAMDEN

Number	Title (A Side/B Side)	Yr	VG	VG+	NM
❑ CAL-2140 [M]	Young Love	1967	3.75	7.50	15.00
❑ CAS-2140 [S]	Young Love	1967	3.00	6.00	12.00

JAMES, TOMMY

The former lead singer of Tommy James and the Shondells had this one solo country hit. And because it uses the same backing track, we've also included his recording of the same song with a Spanish vocal.

45s

MILLENNIUM

Number	Title (A Side/B Side)	Yr	VG	VG+	NM
❑ YB-11785	Three Times in Love/I Just Wanna Play the Music	1980	—	2.00	4.00
❑ YB-11787	No Hay Dos Sin Tres (Three Times in Love)/I Just Wanna Play the Music	1980	—	2.50	5.00
❑ YB-11787 [PS]	No Hay Dos Sin Tres (Three Times in Love)/I Just Wanna Play the Music	1980	2.50	5.00	10.00

JAMESON, CODY

45s

ATCO

Number	Title (A Side/B Side)	Yr	VG	VG+	NM
❑ 7073	Brooklyn/That Little Bit of Us	1977	—	2.50	5.00

JAN AND MALCOLM

45s

PAULA

Number	Title (A Side/B Side)	Yr	VG	VG+	NM
❑ 421	Rainbow in Your Eyes (Love's Got a Hold on Me)/You Are What I Am	1977	—	3.50	7.00

JANO

45s

SCR

Number	Title (A Side/B Side)	Yr	VG	VG+	NM
❑ 180	Sundown Sideshow/(B-side unknown)	1979	—	3.00	6.00

JANSKY, CLIFTON

45s

AXBAR

Number	Title (A Side/B Side)	Yr	VG	VG+	NM
❑ 6033	Will You Love Me in the Morning/Just Can't Help Believing	1985	2.00	4.00	8.00

JAYE, JERRY

45s

COLUMBIA

Number	Title (A Side/B Side)	Yr	VG	VG+	NM
❑ 10170	It's All in the Game/Love Me 'Til the Morning Comes	1975	—	2.00	4.00
❑ 10269	Maybellene/Because It's Love	1975	—	2.00	4.00

HI

Number	Title (A Side/B Side)	Yr	VG	VG+	NM
❑ 2120	My Girl Josephine/Five Miles from Home	1967	2.00	4.00	8.00
❑ 2128	Let the Four Winds Blow/Singin' the Blues	1967	2.00	4.00	8.00
❑ 2139	Brown-Eyed Handsome Man/In the Middle of Nowhere	1968	—	3.00	6.00
❑ 2150	Long Black Veil/(Today) I Started Loving You Again	1968	—	3.00	6.00
❑ 2171	Never Going Back/You've Got to Go	1969	—	3.00	6.00
❑ 2310	Honky Tonk Women Love Redneck Men/What's Left	1976	—	2.00	4.00
❑ 2318	Hot and Still Heatin'/Crazy	1976	—	2.00	4.00
❑ 2323	When Morning Comes to Memphis/(B-side unknown)	1977	—	2.00	4.00

MEGA

Number	Title (A Side/B Side)	Yr	VG	VG+	NM
❑ 0033	I Didn't Hear a Thing/Love Is a Job	1971	—	2.50	5.00
❑ 0045	Don't Bring the Rain Back Again/Tiny Praying Hands	1971	—	2.50	5.00
❑ 0066	Share Your Love with Me/When My Ship Comes In	1972	—	2.50	5.00
❑ 0116	Honky Tonk Livin'/I'm Gonna Spend My Whole Life Lovin' You	1973	—	2.50	5.00
❑ 209	Walkin' My Baby Back Home/I Slipped But I Didn't Fall	1974	—	2.00	4.00
❑ 1218	Poor Side of Town/Lay Down	1974	—	2.00	4.00

STEPHENY

Number	Title (A Side/B Side)	Yr	VG	VG+	NM
❑ 1820	Sugar Dumplin'/How Could You Lose Your Trust in Me	1958	10.00	20.00	40.00

JAYHAWKS, THE

Albums

AMERICAN

Number	Title (A Side/B Side)	Yr	VG	VG+	NM
❑ 43006	Tomorrow the Green Grass	1995	2.50	5.00	10.00
❑ 43114	Sound of Lies	1997	3.00	6.00	12.00

BUNKHOUSE

Number	Title (A Side/B Side)	Yr	VG	VG+	NM
❑ 7001	The Jayhawks	1986	20.00	40.00	80.00

TWIN/TONE

Number	Title (A Side/B Side)	Yr	VG	VG+	NM
❑ TTR 89151	Blue Earth	1989	3.75	7.50	15.00

JED ZEPPELIN

Impromptu country supergroup consisting of members of DIAMOND RIO plus LEE ROY PARNELL and STEVE WARINER.

45s

ARISTA

Number	Title (A Side/B Side)	Yr	VG	VG+	NM
❑ 12755	Workin' Man Blues/Tonight the Bottle Let Me Down	1994	—	2.00	4.00

—B-side by Brooks and Dunn

JEFFERSON, PAUL

45s

ALMO SOUNDS

Number	Title (A Side/B Side)	Yr	VG	VG+	NM
❑ 89003	Check Please/That's As Close As I'll Get to Loving You	1996	—	—	3.00
❑ 89005	Fear of a Broken Heart/Missouri	1996	—	—	3.00
❑ 89006	I Might Just Make It/Common Ground	1996	—	—	3.00

JENKINS, BOB

45s

Number	Title (A Side/B Side)	Yr	VG	VG+	NM
20TH CENTURY					
❑ 2126	Country Feelings/South of the Rio Grande	1974	—	2.50	5.00
LIBERTY					
❑ B-1448	The Cube/Sometimes I Wish	1982	—	2.00	4.00
PICAP					
❑ 009	Workin' in a Coalmine/Muscle and Blood	1983	—	3.00	6.00

JENKINS, BOBBY

45s

ZONE 7

Number	Title (A Side/B Side)	Yr	VG	VG+	NM
❑ 30185	Me and Margarita/(B-side unknown)	1985	—	2.50	5.00
❑ 40984	Blackjack Whiskey/(B-side unknown)	1984	—	2.50	5.00
❑ 61884	Louisiana Heatwave/(B-side unknown)	1984	—	2.50	5.00

JENKINS, LARRY

45s

Number	Title (A Side/B Side)	Yr	VG	VG+	NM
CAPITOL					
❑ B-5167	I'm So Tired of Going Home Drunk/I Laughed 'Till I Cried	1982	—	2.00	4.00
❑ B-5198	Women and Whiskey/Come Next Spring	1983	—	2.00	4.00
MCA					
❑ 52396	You're the Best I Never Had/When It Comes to Makin' Love	1984	—	2.00	4.00

JENNIFER

See JENNIFER WARNES.

JENNINGS, BOB

45s

SIMS

Number	Title (A Side/B Side)	Yr	VG	VG+	NM
❑ 161	The First Step Down (Is the Longest)/It Takes a Lot of Money	1964	2.50	5.00	10.00
❑ 202	Leave a Little Play (In the Chain of Love)/I'm Barely Hangin' On to Me	1964	2.50	5.00	10.00

JENNINGS, TOMMY

Also see REX GOSDIN.

45s

Number	Title (A Side/B Side)	Yr	VG	VG+	NM
MONUMENT					
❑ 45-248	Don't You Think It's Time/That's the Way It Was	1978	—	2.50	5.00
❑ 45-278	Can't Stand to Be Alone/New Orleans	1979	—	2.50	5.00
PARAGON					
❑ 102	Make It Easy on Yourself/I Almost Did	1975	—	3.00	6.00

JENNINGS, WAYLON

12-Inch Singles

RCA

Number	Title (A Side/B Side)	Yr	VG	VG+	NM
❑ WJ-01 [DJ]	Don't You Think This Outlaw Bit's Done Got Out of Hand/Medley of Buddy Holly Hits	1979	3.75	7.50	15.00
❑ WJ-0283 [DJ]	Medley of Hits (7:14) (same on both sides)	1983	3.75	7.50	15.00

45s

Number	Title (A Side/B Side)	Yr	VG	VG+	NM
ARK 21					
❑ S7-58711	I Know About Me, Don't Know About You/Closing In on the Fire	1998	—	—	3.00
A&M					
❑ 722	Rave On/Love, Denise	1963	5.00	10.00	20.00
❑ 739	Four Strong Winds/Just to Satisfy You	1964	3.75	7.50	15.00
❑ 753	The Race Is On/Sing the Girls a Song	1964	3.75	7.50	15.00
BAT					
❑ 121636	White Lightning/(B-side unknown)	1962	12.50	25.00	50.00
❑ 121639	Dream Baby/Crying	1962	10.00	20.00	40.00
BRUNSWICK					
❑ 55130	Jole Blon/When Sin Stops	1959	75.00	150.00	300.00
COLUMBIA					
❑ 04881	Highwayman/The Human Condition	1985	—	—	3.00
—A-side: Willie Nelson/Waylon Jennings/Johnny Cash/Kris Kristofferson; B-side: Nelson, Cash					
❑ 04881 [PS]	Highwayman/The Human Condition	1985	—	2.00	4.00
—A-side: Willie Nelson/Waylon Jennings/Johnny Cash/Kris Kristofferson; B-side: Nelson, Cash					
❑ 05594	Desperadoes Waiting for a Train/The Twentieth Century Is Almost Over	1985	—	—	3.00
—A-side: Willie Nelson/Waylon Jennings/Johnny Cash/Kris Kristofferson; B-side: Nelson, Cash					
❑ 08406	Highwayman/Desperadoes Waiting for a Train	1988	—	—	3.00
—Waylon Jennings/Willie Nelson/Johnny Cash/Kris Kristofferson; reissue					
❑ 73233	Silver Stallion/America Remains	1990	—	—	3.00
—Waylon Jennings/Willie Nelson/Johnny Cash/Kris Kristofferson					
❑ 73381	Born and Raised in Black and White/Texas	1990	—	—	3.00
—The Highwaymen (Waylon Jennings/Willie Nelson/Johnny Cash/Kris Kristofferson)					
❑ 73572	American Remains/Texas	1990	—	—	3.00
—The Highwaymen (Waylon Jennings/Willie Nelson/Johnny Cash/Kris Kristofferson)					
EPIC					
❑ 73352	Wrong/Waking Up with You	1990	—	—	3.00
❑ 73519	Where Corn Don't Grow/Waking Up with You	1990	—	—	3.00
❑ 73647	What Bothers Me Most/Wrong	1990	—	—	3.00
❑ 73718	The Eagle/What Bothers Me Most	1991	—	—	3.00
❑ 74403	Just Talkin'/I've Got My Faults	1992	—	—	3.00
❑ 74705	Too Dumb for New York City, Too Smart for L.A./I've Got My Faults	1992	—	—	3.00
LIBERTY					
❑ S7-18486	It Is What It Is/The Devil's Right Hand	1995	—	—	3.00
—By The Highwaymen					
MCA					
❑ 52776	Working Without a Net/They Ain't Got 'Em All	1986	—	—	3.00
❑ 52830	Will the Wolf Survive/I've Got Me a Woman	1986	—	—	3.00
❑ 52915	What You'll Do When I'm Gone/That Dog Won't Hurt	1986	—	—	3.00
❑ 53009	Rose in Paradise/Crying Don't Even Come Close	1987	—	—	3.00
❑ 53088	Fallin' Out/Deep in the West	1987	—	—	3.00
❑ 53158	My Rough and Rowdy Days/Love Song (I Can't Sing Anymore)	1987	—	—	3.00
❑ 53243	If Ole Hank Could Only See Us Now (Chapter Five...Nashville)/You Went Out with Rock 'n' Roll	1988	—	—	3.00
❑ 53314	How Much Is It Worth to Live in L.A./G.I. Joe	1988	—	—	3.00
❑ 53476	Which Way Do I Go (Now That I'm Gone)/Hey Willie	1988	—	—	3.00
❑ 53634	Trouble Man/Yoyos, Bozos, Bimbos and Heroes	1989	—	—	3.00
❑ 53710	You Put the Soul in the Song/Woman I Hate It	1989	—	—	3.00
RAMCO					
❑ 1997	My World/Another Blue Day	1968	3.00	6.00	12.00
RCA					
❑ 5034-7-R	The Broken Promise Land/I Don't Have Any More Love Songs	1986	—	2.00	4.00
❑ PB-10842	Are You Ready for the Country/So Good Woman	1976	—	2.50	5.00
❑ PB-10924	Luckenbach, Texas (Back to the Basics of Love)/Belle of the Ball	1977	—	2.50	5.00
❑ GB-10927	Dreaming My Dreams with You/Can't You See	1977	—	—	3.00
—Gold Standard Series					
❑ PB-11118	The Wurlitzer Prize (I Don't Want to Get Over You)/Lookin' for a Feeling	1977	—	2.50	5.00
❑ PB-11344	I've Always Been Crazy/I Never Said It Would Be Easy	1978	—	2.00	4.00
❑ PB-11390	Don't You Think This Outlaw Bit's Done Got Out of Hand/Girl I Can Tell (You're Trying to Work It Out)	1978	—	2.00	4.00
❑ GB-11500	Are You Ready for the Country/The Wurlitzer Prize (I Don't Want to Get Over You)	1978	—	—	3.00
—Gold Standard Series					
❑ PB-11596	Amanda/Lonesome, On'ry and Mean	1979	—	2.00	4.00
❑ PB-11596 [PS]	Amanda/Lonesome, On'ry and Mean	1979	—	2.50	5.00
❑ PB-11723	Come with Me/Mes'kin	1979	—	2.00	4.00
❑ GB-11757	Luckenbach, Texas (Back to the Basics of Love)/Belle of the Ball	1979	—	—	3.00
—Gold Standard Series					
❑ PB-11898	I Ain't Living Long Like This/The World's Crazy	1979	—	2.00	4.00
❑ GB-11991	I've Always Been Crazy/Don't You Think This Outlaw Bit's Done Got Out of Hand	1980	—	—	3.00
—Gold Standard Series					
❑ PB-12007	Clyde/I Came Here to Party	1980	—	2.00	4.00
❑ PB-12067	Theme from "The Dukes of Hazzard" (Good Ol' Boys)/It's Alright	1980	—	2.00	4.00
❑ PB-12067 [PS]	Theme from "The Dukes of Hazzard" (Good Ol' Boys)/It's Alright	1980	—	2.50	5.00
❑ GB-12187	Theme from "The Dukes of Hazzard" (Good Ol' Boys)/Come with Me	1981	—	—	3.00
—Gold Standard Series					
❑ GB-12313	Amanda/I Ain't Living Long Like This	1981	—	—	3.00
—"Gold Standard Series" reissue					
❑ PB-12367	Shine/White Water	1981	—	2.00	4.00
❑ PB-13257	Women Do Know How to Carry On/Honky Tonk Blues	1982	—	2.00	4.00
❑ PB-13465	Lucille (You Won't Do Your Daddy's Will)/Medley of Hits	1983	—	2.00	4.00
❑ PB-13543	Breakin' Down/Livin' Legends (A Dyin' Breed)	1983	—	2.00	4.00
❑ PB-13631	The Conversation/Fancy Free	1983	—	2.00	4.00
—A-side with Hank Williams, Jr.					
❑ PB-13729	I May Be Used (But Baby I Ain't Used Up)/So You Want to Be a Cowboy Singer	1984	—	2.00	4.00
❑ PB-13827	Never Could Toe the Mark/Talk Good Boogie	1984	—	2.00	4.00
❑ PB-13903	Silent Night, Holy Night/Precious Memories	1984	—	2.00	4.00
—A-side with Jessi Colter					
❑ PB-13908	America/People Up in Texas	1984	—	2.00	4.00
❑ PB-13984	Waltz Me to Heaven/Dream On	1984	—	2.00	4.00
❑ PB-14094	Drinkin' and Dreamin'/Prophets Show Up in Strange Places	1985	—	2.00	4.00
❑ PB-14215	The Devil's on the Loose/Good Morning John	1985	—	2.00	4.00
❑ PB-14291	Sweet Mother Texas/Hanging On	1985	—	2.00	4.00
RCA VICTOR					
❑ APBO-0086	You Asked Me To/Willy, the Wandering Gypsy and Me	1973	2.00	4.00	8.00

Waylon Jennings had his first charted hit in 1965, but it took almost a decade for country audiences to catch on. Once they did, he was a regular chart presence, both solo and with Willie Nelson, for over a decade. (Top left) He had a bunch of top 10 singles before he finally hit the top spot in 1974 with "This Time." (Top right) His song that immortalized a small town in the Lone Star State, "Luckenbach, Texas," was the biggest hit of his career, with six weeks at the top. (Bottom left) Few country songs have been heard as often as Waylon's theme from "The Dukes of Hazzard," thanks to weekly exposure on the CBS television network. In addition to a No. 1 placement on the country charts, it became his biggest pop hit, peaking at No. 21. (Bottom right) The last time Jennings hit No. 1 was in 1987, with "Rose in Paradise."

Number	Title (A Side/B Side)	Yr	VG	VG+	NM
❑ AMAO-0122	MacArthur Park/The Taker	1973	—	2.50	5.00
❑ APBO-0251	This Time/Mona	1974	—	3.00	6.00
❑ PB-10020	I'm a Ramblin' Man/Got a Lot Going for Me	1974	—	3.00	6.00
❑ PB-10142	Rainy Day Woman/Let's All Help the Cowboys (Sing the Blues)	1974	—	3.00	6.00
❑ GB-10169	This Time/You Asked Me To	1975	—	2.00	4.00
—Gold Standard Series					
❑ PB-10270	Dreaming My Dreams with You/Waymore's Blues	1975	—	3.00	6.00
❑ PB-10379	Are You Sure Hank Done It This Way/Bob Wills Is Still the King	1975	—	3.00	6.00
❑ GB-10498	I'm a Ramblin' Man/Got a Lot Going for Me	1975	—	2.00	4.00
—Gold Standard Series					
❑ GB-10499	Rainy Day Woman/Let's All Help the Cowboys (Sing the Blues)	1975	—	2.00	4.00
—Gold Standard Series					
❑ GB-10673	Are You Sure Hank Done It This Way/Bob Wills Is Still the King	1976	—	2.00	4.00
—Gold Standard Series					
❑ PB-10721	Can't You See/I'll Go Back to Her	1976	—	2.50	5.00
❑ 47-8572	That's the Chance I'll Have to Take/I Wonder Just Where I Went Wrong	1965	2.50	5.00	10.00
❑ 47-8652	Stop the World (And Let Me Off)/The Dark Side of Fame	1965	2.50	5.00	10.00
❑ 47-8729	Anita, You're Dreaming/Look Into My Teardrops	1965	2.50	5.00	10.00
❑ 47-8822	Time to Bum Again/Norwegian Wood	1966	2.50	5.00	10.00
❑ 47-8917	(That's What You Get) For Lovin' Me/Time Will Tell the Story	1966	2.50	5.00	10.00
❑ 47-9025	Green River/Silver Ribbons	1966	2.50	5.00	10.00
❑ 47-9146	Mental Revenge/Born to Love You	1967	2.50	5.00	10.00
❑ 47-9259	The Chokin' Kind/Love of the Common People	1967	2.50	5.00	10.00
❑ 47-9414	Walk On Out of My Mind/Julie	1967	2.50	5.00	10.00
❑ 47-9480	I Got You/No One's Gonna Miss Me	1968	2.50	5.00	10.00
—A-side with Anita Carter					
❑ 47-9561	Only Daddy That'll Walk the Line/Right Before My Eyes	1968	2.50	5.00	10.00
❑ 47-9642	Yours Love/Six Strings Away	1968	2.50	5.00	10.00
❑ 47-9819	Singer of Sad Songs/Lila	1970	2.00	4.00	8.00
❑ 47-9885	The Taker/Shadows of the Gallows	1970	2.00	4.00	8.00
❑ 47-9925	(Don't Let the Sun Set on You) Tulsa/You'll Look for Me	1970	2.00	4.00	8.00
❑ 47-9967	Mississippi Woman/Life Goes On	1971	2.00	4.00	8.00
❑ 48-1003	Cedartown, Georgia/I Think It's Time She Learned	1971	2.00	4.00	8.00
❑ 74-0105	Something's Wrong in California/Farewell Party	1969	2.00	4.00	8.00
❑ 74-0157	The Days of Sand and Shovels/Delia's Gone	1969	2.00	4.00	8.00
❑ 74-0210	MacArthur Park/But You Know I Love You	1969	2.00	4.00	8.00
❑ 74-0281	Brown Eyed Handsome Man/Sorrow (Breaks a Good Man Down)	1969	2.00	4.00	8.00
❑ 74-0615	Good Hearted Woman/It's All Over Now	1971	2.00	4.00	8.00
❑ 74-0716	Sweet Dream Woman/Sure Didn't Take Him Long	1972	2.00	4.00	8.00
❑ 74-0808	Pretend I Never Happened/Nothin' Worth Takin' or Leavin'	1972	2.00	4.00	8.00
❑ 74-0886	You Can Have Her/Gone to Denver	1973	2.00	4.00	8.00
❑ 74-0961	We Had It All/Do No Good Woman	1973	2.00	4.00	8.00

TREND

Number	Title (A Side/B Side)	Yr	VG	VG+	NM
❑ 102	Another Blue Day/Never Again	1962	7.50	15.00	30.00
❑ 106	The Stage/My Baby Walks All Over Me	1963	25.00	50.00	100.00

Albums

A&M

Number	Title (A Side/B Side)	Yr	VG	VG+	NM
❑ SP-4238	Don't Think Twice	1969	10.00	20.00	40.00

BAT

Number	Title (A Side/B Side)	Yr	VG	VG+	NM
❑ 1001 [M]	Waylon Jennings at JD's	1964	175.00	350.00	700.00
—Approximately 500 copies pressed					

MCA

Number	Title (A Side/B Side)	Yr	VG	VG+	NM
❑ 731	Waylon Jennings	198?	3.00	6.00	12.00
—Reissue of Vocalion LP					
❑ 5688	Will the Wolf Survive	1986	2.50	5.00	10.00
❑ 5911	Hangin' Tough	1987	2.50	5.00	10.00
❑ 42038	A Man Called Hoss	1987	2.50	5.00	10.00
❑ 42222	Full Circle	1988	2.50	5.00	10.00
❑ 42287	New Classic Waylon	1989	2.50	5.00	10.00

PAIR

Number	Title (A Side/B Side)	Yr	VG	VG+	NM
❑ PDL1-1005 [(2)]	Waylon!	1986	3.00	6.00	12.00
❑ PDL1-1033 [(2)]	A Couple More Years	1986	3.00	6.00	12.00
❑ PDL1-1110 [(2)]	Honly Tonk Hero	1986	3.00	6.00	12.00

RCA

Number	Title (A Side/B Side)	Yr	VG	VG+	NM
❑ 5620-1-RB	The Best of Waylon	1987	2.50	5.00	10.00
❑ 9561-1-R	The Early Years (1965-1969)	1989	2.50	5.00	10.00

RCA CAMDEN

Number	Title (A Side/B Side)	Yr	VG	VG+	NM
❑ ACL1-0306	Only Daddy That'll Walk the Line	1973	2.50	5.00	10.00
❑ CAL-2183 [M]	The One and Only Waylon Jennings	1967	3.75	7.50	15.00
❑ CAS-2183 [S]	The One and Only Waylon Jennings	1967	3.00	6.00	12.00
❑ CAS-2556	Heartaches by the Number	1972	3.00	6.00	12.00
❑ CAS-2608	Ruby, Don't Take Your Love to Town	1972	3.00	6.00	12.00

RCA VICTOR

Number	Title (A Side/B Side)	Yr	VG	VG+	NM
❑ APL1-0240	Honky Tonk Heroes	1973	3.75	7.50	15.00
❑ APL1-0539	This Time	1974	3.00	6.00	12.00
❑ APL1-0734	The Ramblin' Man	1974	3.00	6.00	12.00
❑ APL1-1062	Dreaming My Dreams	1975	2.50	5.00	10.00
❑ APL1-1108	Waylon Live	1976	2.50	5.00	10.00
❑ APL1-1816	Are You Ready for the Country	1976	2.50	5.00	10.00
❑ AAL1-2317	Ol' Waylon	198?	2.00	4.00	8.00
—Reissue					
❑ APL1-2317	Ol' Waylon	1977	2.50	5.00	10.00
❑ AFL1-2979	I've Always Been Crazy	1978	2.50	5.00	10.00
❑ AHL1-3378	Greatest Hits	1979	2.50	5.00	10.00
❑ AHL1-3493	What Goes Around Comes Around	1979	2.50	5.00	10.00
❑ LPM-3523 [M]	Folk-Country	1966	7.50	15.00	30.00
❑ LSP-3523 [S]	Folk-Country	1966	10.00	20.00	40.00
❑ AHL1-3602	Music Man	1980	2.50	5.00	10.00
❑ LPM-3620 [M]	Leavin' Town	1966	7.50	15.00	30.00
❑ LSP-3620 [S]	Leavin' Town	1966	10.00	20.00	40.00
❑ LPM-3660 [M]	Waylon Sings Ol' Harlan	1967	7.50	15.00	30.00
❑ LSP-3660 [S]	Waylon Sings Ol' Harlan	1967	10.00	20.00	40.00
❑ AYL1-3663	Are You Ready for the Country	1980	2.00	4.00	8.00
—Budget-line reissue					
❑ LPM-3736 [M]	Nashville Rebel	1967	10.00	20.00	40.00
❑ LSP-3736 [S]	Nashville Rebel	1967	12.50	25.00	50.00
❑ LPM-3825 [M]	Love of the Common People	1967	7.50	15.00	30.00
❑ LSP-3825 [S]	Love of the Common People	1967	6.25	12.50	25.00
❑ AYL1-3897	Honky Tonk Heroes	1980	2.00	4.00	8.00
—Budget-line reissue					
❑ LPM-3918 [M]	Hangin' On	1968	25.00	50.00	100.00
❑ LSP-3918 [S]	Hangin' On	1968	6.25	12.50	25.00
❑ LPM-4023 [M]	Only the Greatest	1968	—	—	—
—Canceled?					
❑ LSP-4023 [S]	Only the Greatest	1968	6.25	12.50	25.00
❑ AYL1-4072	Dreaming My Dreams	1981	2.00	4.00	8.00
—Budget-line reissue					
❑ AYL1-4073	The Ramblin' Man	1981	2.00	4.00	8.00
—Budget-line reissue					
❑ LSP-4085	Jewels	1968	6.25	12.50	25.00
❑ LSP-4137	Just to Satisfy You	1969	6.25	12.50	25.00
❑ AYL1-4163	Waylon Live	1981	2.00	4.00	8.00
—Budget-line reissue					
❑ AYL1-4164	I've Always Been Crazy	1981	2.00	4.00	8.00
—Budget-line reissue					
❑ LSP-4180	Country-Folk	1969	6.25	12.50	25.00
❑ AHL1-4247	Black On Black	1982	2.50	5.00	10.00
❑ AYL1-4250	Music Man	1982	2.00	4.00	8.00
—Budget-line reissue					
❑ LSP-4260	Waylon	1970	5.00	10.00	20.00
❑ LSP-4341	The Best of Waylon Jennings	1970	5.00	10.00	20.00
❑ LSP-4418	Singer of Sad Songs	1970	5.00	10.00	20.00
❑ LSP-4487	The Taker/Tulsa	1971	5.00	10.00	20.00
❑ LSP-4567	Cedartown, Georgia	1971	5.00	10.00	20.00
❑ LSP-4647	Good Hearted Woman	1972	5.00	10.00	20.00
❑ AFL1-4673	It's Only Rock & Roll	1983	2.50	5.00	10.00
❑ LSP-4751	Ladies Love Outlaws	1972	5.00	10.00	20.00
❑ AHL1-4826	Waylon and Company	1983	2.50	5.00	10.00
❑ AYL1-4828	The Best of Waylon Jennings	1983	2.00	4.00	8.00
—Budget-line reissue					
❑ LSP-4854	Lonesome, On'ry and Mean	1973	3.75	7.50	15.00
❑ AHL1-5017	Never Could Toe the Mark	1984	2.50	5.00	10.00
❑ AYL1-5126	Ol' Waylon	1984	2.00	4.00	8.00
—Budget-line reissue					
❑ AHL1-5325	Waylon's Greatest Hits, Vol. 2	1984	2.50	5.00	10.00
❑ AHL1-5428	Turn the Page	1985	2.50	5.00	10.00
❑ AYL1-5433	Waylon and Company	1985	2.00	4.00	8.00
—Budget-line reissue					
❑ AHL1-5473	Collector's Series	1985	2.50	5.00	10.00
❑ AYL1-7046	Never Could Toe the Mark	1985	2.00	4.00	8.00
—Budget-line reissue					
❑ AHL1-7184	Sweet Mother Texas	1986	2.50	5.00	10.00

SOUNDS

Number	Title (A Side/B Side)	Yr	VG	VG+	NM
❑ 1001 [M]	Waylon Jennings at JD's	1964	125.00	250.00	500.00
—Approximately 500 copies pressed; reissue of Bat 1001					

VOCALION

Number	Title (A Side/B Side)	Yr	VG	VG+	NM
❑ DL 73873	Waylon Jennings	1969	6.25	12.50	25.00

JENNINGS, WAYLON; WILLIE NELSON; JESSI COLTER; TOMPALL GLASER

Also see JESSI COLTER; TOMPALL GLASER; WAYLON JENNINGS; WILLIE NELSON; WAYLON AND JESSI; WAYLON AND WILLIE.

Albums

RCA VICTOR

Number	Title (A Side/B Side)	Yr	VG	VG+	NM
❑ AAL1-1321	Wanted! The Outlaws	198?	2.00	4.00	8.00
—Reissue					
❑ APL1-1321	Wanted! The Outlaws	1976	3.00	6.00	12.00
—Tan label					
❑ APL1-1321	Wanted! The Outlaws	1976	2.50	5.00	10.00
—Black label, dog near top					

JENNINGS, WAYLON, AND JERRY REED

45s

RCA

Number	Title (A Side/B Side)	Yr	VG	VG+	NM
❑ PB-13580	Hold On, I'm Comin'/Waiting On Down the Line	1983	—	2.00	4.00
❑ GB-13789	Hold On, I'm Comin'/The Conversation	1984	—	—	3.00
—Gold Standard Series; B-side by Waylon and Hank Williams, Jr.					

JEREMIAH

45s

CHARIOT

Number	Title (A Side/B Side)	Yr	VG	VG+	NM
❑ 1921	To Be Loved/(B-side unknown)	1988	2.00	4.00	8.00

JERRICO, SHERRI

45s

GUSTO

Number	Title (A Side/B Side)	Yr	VG	VG+	NM
❑ 159	Denver Rain/All Over Me	1977	—	3.00	6.00
❑ 164	Thanks for Leaving, Lucille/All Over Me	1977	—	3.00	6.00

Number	Title (A Side/B Side)	Yr	VG	VG+	NM
❑ 170	Hell Yes, I Cheated/He Drove Me Back to Loving You Again	1977	—	3.00	6.00
❑ 178	Goodbye Clothes/Party Time	1978	—	3.00	6.00
❑ 9012	I Cried a Tear/Party Time	1979	—	3.00	6.00
SOUNDWAVES					
❑ 4609	Weekends Were Made for Foolin' Around/Sofa Queen	1980	—	2.50	5.00

JIM & JESSE

45s

Number	Title (A Side/B Side)	Yr	VG	VG+	NM
CAPITOL					
❑ F2233	Are You Missing Me/I'll Wash You Love From My Heart	1952	7.50	15.00	30.00
❑ F2365	Purple Heart/I Will Always Be Waiting for You	1953	6.25	12.50	25.00
❑ F2476	Virginia Waltz/Air Mail Special	1953	6.25	12.50	25.00
❑ F2578	Is It True/My Darling's in Heaven	1953	6.25	12.50	25.00
❑ F2683	My Little Honeysuckle Rose/Just Wondering Why	1953	6.25	12.50	25.00
❑ F2798	Look for Me/Are You Lost in Sin	1954	6.25	12.50	25.00
❑ 3026	Freight Train/Just Wondering Why	1971	—	3.00	6.00
❑ 3099	I'll Always Be Waiting for You/San Quentin Quail	1971	—	3.00	6.00
❑ F3141	Memory of You/Too Many Tears	1955	5.00	10.00	20.00
❑ F3505	I'll Wear the Banner/My Garden of Love	1956	5.00	10.00	20.00
❑ 3921	Billy, Don't Be a Hero/Ain't No Place for a Country Boy	1974	—	3.00	6.00
❑ 3969	Bring Back Your Sweet Love/Love Is a Fading Rose	1974	—	3.00	6.00
COLUMBIA					
❑ 4-42180	Beautiful Moon of Kentucky/Diesel Train	1961	3.00	6.00	12.00
EPIC					
❑ 5-9508	My Empty Arms/Stormy Horizons	1962	2.50	5.00	10.00
❑ 5-9528	Pickin' and a Grinnin'/Sweet Little Miss Blue Eyes	1962	2.50	5.00	10.00
❑ 5-9568	Uncle Will Played the Fiddle/Voice of My Darling	1963	2.50	5.00	10.00
❑ 5-9635	Drifting and Dreaming of You/Lascassas, Tennessee	1963	2.50	5.00	10.00
❑ 5-9676	Cotton Mill Man/(It's a Long, Long Way) To the Top of the World	1964	2.00	4.00	8.00
❑ 5-9716	The Old Country Church/Swing Low, Sweet Chariot	1964	2.00	4.00	8.00
❑ 5-9729	Better Times a-Coming/Wild Georgia Boys	1964	2.00	4.00	8.00
❑ 5-9851	Memphis/Maybellene	1965	2.00	4.00	8.00
❑ 5-9890	Johnny B. Goode/Dancing Molly	1966	2.00	4.00	8.00
❑ 5-10040	Don't Let Nobody Tie You Down/If You've Seen One You've Seen Them All	1966	2.00	4.00	8.00
❑ 5-10138	Diesel on My Tail/All for the Love of a Girl	1967	—	3.50	7.00
❑ 5-10213	Ballad of Thunder Road/Tijuana Taxi	1967	—	3.50	7.00
❑ 5-10263	Greenwich Village Folk Song Salesman/Truck Drivin' Man	1967	—	3.50	7.00
❑ 5-10314	Pretty Girls (In Mini-Skirts)/Where the Chilly Winds Don't Blow	1968	—	3.50	7.00
❑ 5-10370	Yonder Comes a Freight Train/Banderilla	1968	—	3.50	7.00
❑ 5-10429	When the Snow Is on the Roses/(B-side unknown)	1969	2.00	4.00	8.00
❑ 5-10455	We'll Build a Bridge/Then I'll Stop Goin' for You	1969	—	3.50	7.00
❑ 5-10508	I'm Hoping That You're Hoping/When I Stop Dreaming	1969	—	3.50	7.00
❑ 5-10563	The Golden Rocket/A Freight Train in My Mind	1969	—	3.50	7.00
MSR					
❑ 198310	Oh Louisiana/(B-side unknown)	1986	—	3.00	6.00
STARDAY					
❑ 412	Hard Hearted/Pardon Me	1958	3.75	7.50	15.00
❑ 433	Let Me Whisper/Border Ride	1959	3.75	7.50	15.00
❑ 458	Nobody But You/Have You Lost Your Love for Me	1959	3.75	7.50	15.00

Albums

Number	Title	Yr	VG	VG+	NM
EPIC					
❑ LN 24031 [M]	Bluegrass Special	1963	5.00	10.00	20.00
❑ LN 24074 [M]	Bluegrass Classics	1963	5.00	10.00	20.00
❑ LN 24107 [M]	The Old Country Church	1964	5.00	10.00	20.00
❑ LN 24144 [M]	Y'All Come	1964	5.00	10.00	20.00
❑ LN 24176 [M]	Berry Pickin' the Country	1965	5.00	10.00	20.00
❑ LN 24204 [M]	Sing Unto Him	1966	5.00	10.00	20.00
❑ LN 24314 [M]	Diesel on My Tail	1967	5.00	10.00	20.00
❑ BN 26031 [S]	Bluegrass Special	1963	6.25	12.50	25.00
❑ BN 26074 [S]	Bluegrass Classics	1963	6.25	12.50	25.00
❑ BN 26107 [S]	The Old Country Church	1964	6.25	12.50	25.00
❑ BN 26144 [S]	Y'All Come	1964	6.25	12.50	25.00
❑ BN 26176 [S]	Berry Pickin' the Country	1965	6.25	12.50	25.00
❑ BN 26204 [S]	Sing Unto Him	1966	6.25	12.50	25.00
❑ BN 26314 [S]	Diesel on My Tail	1967	6.25	12.50	25.00
❑ BN 26394	All-Time Great Country Instrumentals	1968	5.00	10.00	20.00
❑ BN 26465	Saluting the Louvin Brothers	1969	5.00	10.00	20.00

JIM & JESSE AND CHARLIE LOUVIN

Also see each artist's individual listings.

45s

Number	Title (A Side/B Side)	Yr	VG	VG+	NM
SOUNDWAVES					
❑ 4671	North Wind/Sweeter Than the Flowers	1982	—	2.50	5.00
❑ 4688	Showboat Gambler/Until She Said Goodbye	1982	—	2.50	5.00

JIMMIE DALE AND THE FLATLANDERS

Also see JIMMIE DALE GILMORE.

45s

Number	Title (A Side/B Side)	Yr	VG	VG+	NM
PLANTATION					
❑ 92	Dallas/Tonight I'm Gonna Go Downtown	1972	12.50	25.00	50.00
❑ 106	Jole Blon/You've Never Seen Me Cry	1972	12.50	25.00	50.00

Albums

Number	Title	Yr	VG	VG+	NM
PLANTATION					
❑ 22	One Road More	1972	—	—	—
—May exist only as an 8-track tape. Should an LP exist, its value would be in the hundreds.					
ROUNDER					
❑ SS-34	More a Legend Than a Band	1990	3.00	6.00	12.00
—As "The Flatlanders"; reissue of Plantation material					

JIMMY AND JOHNNY

Also see COUNTRY JOHNNY MATHIS.

45s

Number	Title (A Side/B Side)	Yr	VG	VG+	NM
CHESS					
❑ 4859	If You Don't Somebody Else Will/I'm Beginning to Remember	1954	7.50	15.00	30.00
—As "Jimmy Lee and Johnny Mathis"					
❑ 4862	Can't You, Won't You/The Fun Is Over	1955	7.50	15.00	30.00
D					
❑ 1004	I Can't Find the Door Knob/Keep Telling Me	1958	5.00	10.00	20.00
❑ 1089	My Little Baby/All I Need Is Time	1959	5.00	10.00	20.00
DECCA					
❑ 9-29772	Sweet Swinging Daddy/Take Me	1956	6.25	12.50	25.00
❑ 9-29954	Another Man's Name/Til the End of the World	1956	6.25	12.50	25.00
❑ 9-30061	Sweet Love on My Mind/Imagination	1956	6.25	12.50	25.00
❑ 9-30278	Don't Give Me That Look/Here Comes My Baby	1957	6.25	12.50	25.00
❑ 9-30410	What'cha Doin' to Me/I'll Do It Every Time	1957	6.25	12.50	25.00
FEATURE					
❑ 1092	If You Don't Somebody Else Will/I'm Beginning to Remember	1954	25.00	50.00	100.00
—As "Jimmy Lee and Johnny Mathis"					
TNT					
❑ 184	Two Empty Arms/Call You	1960	3.75	7.50	15.00

JJ WHITE

45s

Number	Title (A Side/B Side)	Yr	VG	VG+	NM
CURB					
❑ NR-76852	Have a Little Faith/Love Is Back in Style	1991	—	2.00	4.00
❑ NR-76876	The Crush/Everyday	1991	—	2.00	4.00

JO ANN AND TROY

Also see JO ANN CAMPBELL; TROY SEALS.

45s

Number	Title (A Side/B Side)	Yr	VG	VG+	NM
ATLANTIC					
❑ 2256	Who Do You Love/I Found a Love, Oh What a Love	1964	3.75	7.50	15.00
❑ 2293	Same Old Feeling/Just Because	1965	3.75	7.50	15.00

JOE BOB'S NASHVILLE SOUND COMPANY

45s

Number	Title (A Side/B Side)	Yr	VG	VG+	NM
CAPITOL					
❑ 4059	In the Mood/A String of Pearls	1975	—	3.00	6.00
❑ 4182	Chattanooga Choo Choo/Take the "A" Train	1975	—	3.00	6.00

JOHNNIE AND JACK

Also see JOHNNY WRIGHT.

45s

Number	Title (A Side/B Side)	Yr	VG	VG+	NM
DECCA					
❑ 31255	I'm Always By Myself/When I'm Alone	1961	3.00	6.00	12.00
❑ 31289	Let My Heart Be Broken/Uncle John's Bongos	1961	3.00	6.00	12.00
❑ 31361	The Moon Is High and So Am I/Sweet Baby	1962	3.00	6.00	12.00
❑ 31397	Slow Poison/You'll Never Get a Better Chance Than This	1962	3.00	6.00	12.00
❑ 31423	36-22-36/What Do You Think of Her Now	1962	3.00	6.00	12.00
❑ 31472	Bye, Bye Love/I Overlooked an Orchid	1963	3.00	6.00	12.00
❑ 31517	Love Problems/Smiles and Tears	1963	3.00	6.00	12.00
RCA VICTOR					
❑ 47-4251	Hummingbird/Let Your Conscience Be Your Guide	1951	6.25	12.50	25.00
❑ 47-4389	Ashes of Love/You Tried to Ruin My Name	1951	6.25	12.50	25.00
❑ 47-4555	Three Ways of Knowing/When You Want a Little Lovin'	1952	6.25	12.50	25.00
❑ 47-4765	Slow Poison/Heart Trouble	1952	6.25	12.50	25.00
❑ 47-4878	You Can't Fool God/Shake My Mother's Hand for Me	1952	6.25	12.50	25.00
❑ 47-4949	Two Timing Blues/Gone and Done It Again	1952	6.25	12.50	25.00
❑ 47-5040	Don't Let the Stars Get in Your Eyes/The Only One I Ever Loved, I Lost	1952	6.25	12.50	25.00
❑ 47-5098	I'll Live with God/The Eastern Gate	1952	6.25	12.50	25.00
❑ 47-5164	Hank Williams Will Live Forever/Just for Tonight	1953	7.50	15.00	30.00
❑ 47-5290	South in New Orleans/Winner of Your Heart	1953	6.25	12.50	25.00
❑ 47-5375	Private Property/Don't Say Goodbye If You Love Me	1953	6.25	12.50	25.00
❑ 47-5427	Angels Rock Me to Sleep/When the Saviour Reached Down	1953	6.25	12.50	25.00
❑ 47-5483	Pig Latin Serenade/You're My Downfall	1953	6.25	12.50	25.00
❑ 47-5517	From the Manger to the Cross/God Put a Rainbow in the Clouds	1953	6.25	12.50	25.00
❑ 47-5581	Cheated Out of Love/Love Trap	1954	6.25	12.50	25.00
❑ 47-5635	You Got Me in Your Power/Dynamite Kisses	1954	6.25	12.50	25.00
❑ 47-5649	Borrowed Diamonds/But I Love You Just the Same	1954	6.25	12.50	25.00
❑ 47-5681	(Oh Baby Mine) I Get So Lonely/You're Just What the Doctor Ordered	1954	6.25	12.50	25.00
❑ 47-5775	Goodnight, Sweetheart, Goodnight/Honey, I Need You	1954	6.25	12.50	25.00

Number	Title (A Side/B Side)	Yr	VG	VG+	NM
47-5880	Kiss-Crazy Baby/Beware of "It"	1954	6.25	12.50	25.00
47-6014	Sincerely/Carry On	1955	5.00	10.00	20.00
47-6094	No One Dear But You/We Live in Two Different Worlds	1955	5.00	10.00	20.00
47-6203	Look Out/So Lovely, Baby	1955	5.00	10.00	20.00
47-6295	S.O.S./Weary Moments	1955	5.00	10.00	20.00
47-6395	I Want to Be Loved/Feet of Clay	1956	5.00	10.00	20.00
—With Ruby Wells					
47-6508	You Can't Divorce My Heart/Baby It's in the Making	1956	5.00	10.00	20.00
47-6594	I Loved You Better Than You Know/Love, Love, Love	1956	5.00	10.00	20.00
47-6680	Tom Cat's Kittens/Live and Let Live	1956	5.00	10.00	20.00
47-6777	The Banana Boat Song/Mr. Clock	1956	5.00	10.00	20.00
47-6857	All the Time/Pleasure Not a Habit in Mexico	1957	5.00	10.00	20.00
47-6932	Oh Boy, I Love Her/That's Why I'm Leavin'	1957	5.00	10.00	20.00
47-7018	Move It On Over/Love Fever	1957	5.00	10.00	20.00
47-7137	Stop the World (And Let Me Off)/Camel Walk Stroll	1958	3.75	7.50	15.00
47-7246	I've Seen This Movie Before/Yeah!	1958	3.75	7.50	15.00
47-7324	Lonely Island Pearl/Leave Our Moon Alone	1958	3.75	7.50	15.00
47-7402	That's the Way the Cookie Crumbles/Poison Love	1958	3.75	7.50	15.00
47-7478	What Do You Know About Heartaches/I Wonder If You Know?	1959	3.75	7.50	15.00
47-7545	Sailor Man/Wild and Wicked World	1959	3.75	7.50	15.00
47-7698	Sweetie Pie/Happy Lucky Love	1960	3.75	7.50	15.00
47-7749	Just Like You/Dreams Come True	1960	3.75	7.50	15.00
47-7799	Country Music Has Gone to Town/Talkin' Eyes	1960	3.75	7.50	15.00
48-0055	She Went with a Smile/Trials and Tribulations	1949	10.00	20.00	40.00
—Originals on green vinyl					
48-0109	Just When I Needed You/Buried Alive	1949	10.00	20.00	40.00
—Originals on green vinyl					
48-0160	For Old Time's Sake/I Heard My Saviour Call	1950	10.00	20.00	40.00
—Originals on green vinyl					
48-0215	What About You/Pray Together	1950	10.00	20.00	40.00
—Originals on green vinyl					
48-0314	Jesus Hits Like the Atom Bomb/Too Much Sinning	1950	10.00	20.00	40.00
—Originals on green vinyl					
48-0323	Shout/Too Far from God	1950	7.50	15.00	30.00
—Originals on green vinyl					
48-0324	Jesus Remembered Me/You Better Get Down	1950	7.50	15.00	30.00
—Originals on green vinyl					
48-0377	Poison Love/Lonesome	1950	7.50	15.00	30.00
—Originals on green vinyl					
48-0415	I Can't Tell My Heart That/A Smile on My Lips	1951	6.25	12.50	25.00
48-0448	Take My Ring from Your Finger/I'm Gonna Love You One More Time	1951	6.25	12.50	25.00
48-0478	Cryin' Heart Blues/How Can I Believe You	1951	6.25	12.50	25.00

Selected 78s

KING

Number	Title (A Side/B Side)	Yr	VG	VG+	NM
866	He Will Set Your Fields on Fire/I Heard My Name on the Radio	1950	6.25	12.50	25.00

Albums

Number	Title (A Side/B Side)	Yr	VG	VG+	NM
DECCA					
DL 4308 [M]	Smiles and Tears	1962	5.00	10.00	20.00
DL 74308 [S]	Smiles and Tears	1962	6.25	12.50	25.00
RCA CAMDEN					
CAL-747 [M]	Johnny & Jack Sing "Poison Love" and Other Country Favorites	1963	6.25	12.50	25.00
CAS-747 [R]	Johnny & Jack Sing "Poison Love" and Other Country Favorites	1963	3.00	6.00	12.00
CAL-822 [M]	Sincerely	1964	6.25	12.50	25.00
CAS-822 [R]	Sincerely	1964	3.00	6.00	12.00
RCA VICTOR					
LPM-1587 [M]	The Tennessee Mountain Boys	1957	10.00	20.00	40.00
LPM-2017 [M]	Hits by Johnnie & Jack	1959	7.50	15.00	30.00
LSP-2017 [R]	Hits by Johnnie & Jack	1959	5.00	10.00	20.00
VPM-6022 [(2)]	All the Best of Johnnie & Jack	1970	6.25	12.50	25.00

JOHNS, PORTER

45s

Number	Title (A Side/B Side)	Yr	VG	VG+	NM
DECCA					
9-46341	Angel of Peace/Each Day I Live I Love You More	1951	6.25	12.50	25.00
9-46379	This Lonely World/Just a Few	1951	6.25	12.50	25.00

JOHNS, SAMMY

Also see SAMI JO.

45s

Number	Title (A Side/B Side)	Yr	VG	VG+	NM
ELEKTRA					
47189	Common Man/Easy to Be with You	1981	—	2.00	4.00
47248	Love Me Off the Road/This Time	1981	—	2.00	4.00
GRC					
1001	Shake a Hand/(B-side unknown)	1973	—	2.00	4.00
1007	America/(B-side unknown)	1973	—	2.00	4.00
2021	Early Morning Love/Holy Mother, Aging Father	1974	—	2.00	4.00
2046	Chevy Van/Hang My Head and Moan	1975	—	2.50	5.00
2062	Rag Doll/Friends of Mine	1975	—	2.00	4.00
MCA					
53398	Chevy Van/Love Me Off the Road	1988	—	—	3.00
REAL WORLD					
7307	Falling Over You/Six Feet Tall and Handsome	1980	—	2.00	4.00
SOUTHERN TRACKS					
1010	There! I've Said It Again/All Wrapped Up in Your Love	1982	—	2.50	5.00
1031	I'd Rather Be Hurt by You/All Wrapped Up in Your Love	1984	—	2.50	5.00
1036	Desperado Love/All Wrapped Up in Your Love	1985	—	2.50	5.00
1046	You Just Made Me Up in Your Mind/Lifetime Thing	1985	—	2.50	5.00
1075	Rock You Like a Baby/Tennessee Valley Girl	1987	—	2.50	5.00
1086	Early Morning Love/(B-side unknown)	1988	—	2.50	5.00
1096	Sam's Song/Tennessee Valley Girl	1988	—	2.50	5.00
WARNER BROS.					
8224	Peas in a Pod/Friends of Mine	1976	—	2.00	4.00
8270	America/Bless Our Soul	1976	—	2.00	4.00
8335	Hey Mr. Dreamer/Female Chauvinist Sow	1977	—	2.00	4.00
8441	Chevy Van/Music of the Band	1977	—	2.00	4.00

Albums

Number	Title (A Side/B Side)	Yr	VG	VG+	NM
GRC					
5003	Sammy Johns	1975	3.00	6.00	12.00

JOHNS, SARAH

45s

Number	Title (A Side/B Side)	Yr	VG	VG+	NM
RCA					
PB-11097	I Don't Want to Get Over You/Heartaches in Heartaches	1977	—	2.50	5.00
RCA VICTOR					
PB-10203	Glory, Tennessee/I'm Makin' Love to a Memory	1975	—	3.00	6.00
PB-10333	I'm Ready to Love You Now/Love Me Back Together Again	1975	—	2.50	5.00
PB-10465	Feelings/I'm Making Love to a Memory	1975	—	2.50	5.00
PB-10590	Let the Big Wheels Roll/Glory, Tennessee	1976	—	2.50	5.00
PB-10710	Our Love/Have I Wasted My Time Loving You	1976	—	2.50	5.00
WARNER BROS.					
8260	Take Me All the Way/You Lift Me Up	1976	—	2.00	4.00

JOHNS, TRICIA

45s

Number	Title (A Side/B Side)	Yr	VG	VG+	NM
ELEKTRA					
46635	I Just Want Love/Who's Been Sleeping in My Bed	1980	—	2.00	4.00
47057	Did We Fall Out of Love/Night Romancing	1980	—	2.00	4.00
47172	Cathy's Clown/Out Among the Stars	1981	—	2.00	4.00
WARNER BROS.					
8357	The Heat Is On/You Lift Me Up	1977	—	2.50	5.00

JOHNSON, BUDDY

The popular R&B pianist and bandleader had this one record make the country charts.

Selected 78s

Number	Title (A Side/B Side)	Yr	VG	VG+	NM
DECCA					
8655	When My Man Comes Home/I'll Be with You	1944	5.00	10.00	20.00

JOHNSON, CAROLYN DAWN

45s

Number	Title (A Side/B Side)	Yr	VG	VG+	NM
ARISTA NASHVILLE					
69010	Georgia/Love Is Always Worth the Ache	2000	—	—	3.00

JOHNSON, LOIS

Also see HANK WILLIAMS, JR., AND LOIS JOHNSON.

45s

Number	Title (A Side/B Side)	Yr	VG	VG+	NM
20TH CENTURY					
2106	Come On In and Let Me Love You/If I Throw Away My Pride	1974	—	3.00	6.00
2151	Loving You Will Never Grow Old/Lonesome Number One	1974	—	3.00	6.00
2187	You Know Just What I'd Do/You're the Rock of Ages	1975	—	3.00	6.00
2223	Hope for the Flowers/Merrily We Love Along	1975	—	3.00	6.00
2242	The Door's Always Open/Bring It On Home	1975	—	3.00	6.00
COLUMBIA					
4-44646	One Drink Farther Away/Paying Dues	1968	2.00	4.00	8.00
4-44725	Softly and Tenderly/Goin' Down	1968	2.00	4.00	8.00
4-44830	You Can't Stop My Heart from Breaking/Mama, Was His Love Worth Leaving Me	1969	2.00	4.00	8.00
EMH					
0030	It Won't Be Easy/You Are the Melody	1984	—	2.50	5.00
0034	Middle of the Road/Angel in My Arms	1984	—	2.50	5.00
0036	Loveshine/Angel in My Arms	1984	—	2.50	5.00
EPIC					
5-9828	You Really Know How to Hurt a Girl/The Whole World Is Turning (Just for Us)	1965	2.50	5.00	10.00
5-9898	G.I. Joe/Heaven in My Arms	1966	2.50	5.00	10.00
5-10043	Daddy, Don't Hang Up the Pgone/Letters Have No Arms	1966	2.00	4.00	8.00
5-10143	Mr. John/Your Second Wedding Day	1967	2.00	4.00	8.00
5-10238	How Will You Hurt Me Then/To Chicago with Love	1967	2.00	4.00	8.00
5-10316	Tell Me a Lie/Turn On Your Love Light	1968	2.00	4.00	8.00
MERCURY					
55031	When I Need You/A Dreamer of Dreams	1978	—	—	—
—Unreleased?					
MGM					
14186	When He Touches Me (Nothing Else Matters)/When a Woman Stands Alone	1970	—	3.50	7.00
14217	From Warm to Cool to Cold/You Didn't Stop to Say Hello	1971	—	3.50	7.00
14260	Daughter of a Catfish Man/Good Morning Dear	1971	—	3.50	7.00

Number	Title (A Side/B Side)	Yr	VG	VG+	NM
❑ 14304	Breakin' In a Brand New Broken Heart/One Way Ride	1971	—	3.50	7.00
❑ 14401	Rain-Rain/My Heart Has a Mind of Its Own	1972	—	3.50	7.00
❑ 14523	When He Touches Me/I Ain't the Kind of Girl	1973	—	3.50	7.00
❑ 14638	Love Will Stand/Don't Be Cruel	1973	—	3.50	7.00
POLYDOR					
❑ 14328	Weep No More My Baby/Birthday Wish	1976	—	2.50	5.00
❑ 14355	Midnight/I'm Not That Good at Goodbye	1976	—	2.50	5.00
❑ 14371	Your Pretty Roses Came Too Late/Birthday Wish	1976	—	2.50	5.00
❑ 14392	I Hate Goodbyes/I'm Your Friend	1977	—	2.50	5.00
❑ 14435	All the Love We Threw Away/We Can't Make It Anymore	1977	—	2.50	5.00
—With Bill Rice					
❑ 14476	When I Need You/A Dreamer of Dreams	1978	—	2.50	5.00
Albums					
20TH CENTURY					
❑ T-465	Lois Johnson	1975	3.00	6.00	12.00

JOHNSON, MICHAEL
Also see DENVER, BOISE & JOHNSON; SYLVIA.

Number	Title (A Side/B Side)	Yr	VG	VG+	NM
45s					
ATCO					
❑ 6942	Rooty Toot Toot for the Moon/Pilot Me	1973	2.00	4.00	8.00
EMI AMERICA					
❑ 8001	Bluer Than Blue/Two in Love	1978	—	2.00	4.00
❑ 8004	Almost Like Being in Love/Ridin' in the Sky	1978	—	2.00	4.00
❑ 8004 [PS]	Almost Like Being in Love/Ridin' in the Sky	1978	—	3.00	6.00
❑ 8006	When You Come Home/Sailing Without a Sail	1978	—	2.00	4.00
❑ 8019	This Night Won't Last Forever/I Just Can't Say No to You	1979	—	2.00	4.00
❑ 8031	The Very First Time/A Drop of Water	1980	—	2.00	4.00
❑ 8054	You Can Call Me Blue/Don't Ask Why	1980	—	2.00	4.00
❑ 8062	After You/Empty Hearts	1980	—	2.00	4.00
❑ 8086	Home Free/The Love She Found in Me	1981	—	2.00	4.00
❑ 8179	Lifetime Guarantee/One Step Ahead of the Bad News	1983	—	2.00	4.00
RCA					
❑ 5091-7-R	The Moon Is Still Over Her Shoulder/That's What Your Love Does to Me	1986	—	—	3.00
❑ 5171-7-R	Ponies/Cool Me in the River of Love	1987	—	—	3.00
❑ 5279-7-R	Crying Shame/True Love	1987	—	—	3.00
❑ 5355-7-R	This Time of Year/There's a New Kid in Town	1987	—	2.00	4.00
❑ 6835-7-R	I Will Whisper Your Name/That's That	1988	—	—	3.00
❑ 8650-7-R	That's That/Some People's Lives	1988	—	—	3.00
❑ 8748-7-R	Ruller Coaster Run (Up Too Slow Down Too Fast)/Diamond Dreams	1988	—	—	3.00
❑ JK-14239 [DJ]	There's a New Kid In Town (same on both sides)	1985	—	—	3.00
❑ PB-14239	There's a New Kid in Town/Blue Colorado	1985	—	2.00	4.00
❑ PB-14294	Gotta Learn to Live Without You/River Colorado	1986	—	—	3.00
❑ PB-14412	Give Me Wings/Magic Time	1986	—	—	3.00
❑ PB-14412 [PS]	Give Me Wings/Magic Time	1986	—	2.50	5.00
—Sleeve is promo only					
Albums					
ATCO					
❑ SD 7028	There Is a Breeze	1973	3.75	7.50	15.00
EMI AMERICA					
❑ SW-17002	The Michael Johnson Album	1978	2.50	5.00	10.00
❑ SW-17010	Dialogue	1979	2.50	5.00	10.00
❑ SW-17035	Call Me Blue	1980	2.50	5.00	10.00
❑ SW-17057	Home Free	1981	2.50	5.00	10.00
❑ SW-17104	Lifetime Guarantee	1983	2.50	5.00	10.00
RCA					
❑ 6715-1-R	That's That	1988	2.00	4.00	8.00
RCA VICTOR					
❑ AEL1-9501	Wings	1986	2.00	4.00	8.00
SANSKRIT					
❑ (# unknown)	There Is a Breeze	1973	12.50	25.00	50.00

JOHNSON, MIRRIAM
See JESSI COLTER.

JOHNSON, ROLAND

Number	Title (A Side/B Side)	Yr	VG	VG+	NM
45s					
BRUNSWICK					
❑ 9-55110	I Traded Her Love (For Deep Purple Wine)/I'll Be With You	1958	5.00	10.00	20.00
DECCA					
❑ 9-28302	Deep South Rhythm/The Almanse Song	1952	6.25	12.50	25.00
❑ 9-46405	Warmed Over Love/Honest and Truly	1952	6.25	12.50	25.00

JOHNSON, TIM

Number	Title (A Side/B Side)	Yr	VG	VG+	NM
45s					
SUNDIAL					
❑ 123	Between the Sun and San Antone/(B-side unknown)	1987	—	3.00	6.00
❑ 135	Hard Headed Heart/(B-side unknown)	1987	—	3.00	6.00

JOHNSTON, DAY

Number	Title (A Side/B Side)	Yr	VG	VG+	NM
45s					
ROADRUNNER					
❑ 4639	What Cha' Doin' to Me/Little Red Heart	1988	—	3.00	6.00

JOHNSTONS, THE

Number	Title (A Side/B Side)	Yr	VG	VG+	NM
45s					
HIDDEN VALLEY					
❑ 1286	Two-Name Girl/This Time	1986	—	3.00	6.00

JON AND LYNN

Number	Title (A Side/B Side)	Yr	VG	VG+	NM
45s					
SOUNDWAVES					
❑ 4656	Let the Good Times Roll/I Want To (Do Everything for You)	1981	—	2.50	5.00
❑ 4677	(What a Day for a) Day Dream/I Never Do Get Tired of Telling You	1982	—	2.50	5.00

JONES, ANN

Number	Title (A Side/B Side)	Yr	VG	VG+	NM
45s					
CAPITOL					
❑ F1059	I Wish We Could Try All Over Again/You've Got to See Mama Ev'ry Night	1950	7.50	15.00	30.00
❑ F1303	You've Got Me Right Away/He May Be Your Man	1950	7.50	15.00	30.00
DECCA					
❑ 9-30523	Mountain Dew/Old Rattler's Pup	1957	5.00	10.00	20.00
KING					
❑ 961	Hi-Ballin' Daddy/God Gave Me You	1951	10.00	20.00	40.00
❑ 972	Secret Love/Knockin' Blues	1951	10.00	20.00	40.00
❑ 1017	Too Old to Cut the Mustard/I Carry Your Picture	1951	10.00	20.00	40.00
❑ 1028	Be Safe, Be Sure/You Won't Find Me Singing	1952	7.50	15.00	30.00
❑ 1094	Smart Alec/Out of Sight	1952	7.50	15.00	30.00
❑ 1123	Monkey Business/I Love You As Time Goes By	1952	7.50	15.00	30.00
❑ 1148	Love Bird/If I Could Buy You	1952	7.50	15.00	30.00
❑ 1232	I've Had It/Love Is a Losing Game	1953	6.25	12.50	25.00
❑ 1264	A Big Fat Gal Like You/Lonesome with You	1953	6.25	12.50	25.00
❑ 1285	A Little Bit of Nylon/How Many Times	1953	6.25	12.50	25.00
❑ 1307	Our Kind of Love/You Ain't Got It Anymore	1954	6.25	12.50	25.00
❑ 5502	Hit and Run/Pieces of My Heart	1961	3.00	6.00	12.00
SIMS					
❑ 102	Get Up and Go/What Do They Know About Being So Good	1955	12.50	25.00	50.00
Selected 78s					
CAPITOL					
❑ 15414	Give Me a Hundred Reasons/I Believe You, Baby	1949	5.00	10.00	20.00
❑ 40227	Baby Sitter's Blues/It Isn't Any Wonder	1949	5.00	10.00	20.00
❑ 40249	Post Office/Give Me Liberty	1949	5.00	10.00	20.00

JONES, ANTHONY ARMSTRONG

Number	Title (A Side/B Side)	Yr	VG	VG+	NM
45s					
AIR					
❑ 103	Those Eyes/One Night at a Time	1986	—	2.50	5.00
CHART					
❑ 1053	Breakin' Point/Be Quiet Mind	1968	2.00	4.00	8.00
❑ 5002	It's Only Lonely Me/One Good Thing About a Bad Thing	1969	2.00	4.00	8.00
❑ 5017	Proud Mary/The Only Girl I Can't Forget	1969	2.00	4.00	8.00
❑ 5033	New Orleans/And Say Goodbye	1969	2.00	4.00	8.00
❑ 5045	Take a Letter Maria/I Still Love You	1969	2.00	4.00	8.00
❑ 5064	Lead Me Not Into Temptation/One for the Road	1970	—	3.50	7.00
❑ 5083	Sugar in the Flowers/If You Gotta Go, Go Now	1970	—	3.50	7.00
❑ 5100	Sweet Caroline/Too Much of You	1970	—	3.50	7.00
❑ 5118	I Forgot to Live Today/I'm Gonna Stop Loving You	1971	—	3.50	7.00
❑ 5134	That Lucky Old Sun/Make It Hard for Me	1971	—	3.50	7.00
❑ 5139	It's Too Late/Little Deeds of Kindness	1971	—	3.50	7.00
❑ 5147	One Night to Remember/(B-side unknown)	1972	—	3.50	7.00
❑ 5157	It's a Crying Shame/Mine, Mine, Mine	1972	—	3.50	7.00
❑ 5170	Colorado Callin'/(B-side unknown)	1972	—	3.50	7.00
EPIC					
❑ 5-10970	I'm Right Where I Belong/I Can Take On the World	1973	—	3.00	6.00
❑ 5-11002	Bad, Bad Leroy Brown/There's Never Been Anyone Like You	1973	—	3.00	6.00
❑ 5-11042	I've Got Mine/Quietly Doin' My Thing	1973	—	3.00	6.00
❑ 5-11086	Born to Lose/(B-side unknown)	1974	—	3.00	6.00
Albums					
CHART					
❑ 1019	Proud Mary	1969	3.75	7.50	15.00
❑ 1027	Take a Letter Maria	1970	3.75	7.50	15.00
❑ 1036	Sugar in the Flowers	1970	3.75	7.50	15.00
❑ 1047	Greatest Hits, Vol. 1	1971	3.75	7.50	15.00

JONES, CORKY
See BUCK OWENS.

JONES, DAVID LYNN

Number	Title (A Side/B Side)	Yr	VG	VG+	NM
45s					
MERCURY					
❑ 870128-7	High Ridin' Heroes/Living in the Promiseland	1988	—	—	3.00
❑ 870128-7 [PS]	High Ridin' Heroes/Living in the Promiseland	1988	—	—	3.00
❑ 870525-7	The Rogue/Home of My Heart	1988	—	—	3.00
❑ 872054-7	Tonight in America/Valley of a Thousand Years	1988	—	—	3.00
❑ 875624-7	When Times Were Good/We Were All a Lot Older Then	1990	—	—	3.00
❑ 878254-7	I Feel a Change Comin' On/One Song	1990	—	—	3.00
❑ 888733-7	Bonnie Jean (Little Sister)/Valley of a Thousand Years	1987	—	—	3.00
❑ 888733-7 [PS]	Bonnie Jean (Little Sister)/Valley of a Thousand Years	1987	—	2.00	4.00

Albums

MERCURY

Number	Title (A Side/B Side)	Yr	VG	VG+	NM
❑ 832518-1	Hard Times on Easy Street	1987	2.00	4.00	8.00

JONES, GEORGE

Also see GENE PITNEY.

45s

D

Number	Title (A Side/B Side)	Yr	VG	VG+	NM
❑ 1226	New Baby for Christmas/Maybe Next Christmas	1961	3.00	6.00	12.00

EPIC

Number	Title (A Side/B Side)	Yr	VG	VG+	NM
❑ 02526	Still Doin' Time/Good Ones and Bad Ones	1981	—	—	3.00
❑ 02696	Same Ol' Me/Together Alone	1982	—	—	3.00
❑ 03489	Shine On (Shine All Your Sweet Love on Me)/Memories of Mama	1982	—	—	3.00
❑ 03883	I Always Get Lucky with You/I'd Rather Have What We Had	1983	—	—	3.00
❑ 04082	Tennessee Whiskey/Almost Persuaded	1983	—	—	3.00
❑ 04413	You've Still Got a Place in My Heart/I'm Ragged But Right	1984	—	—	3.00
❑ 04609	She's My Rock/(What Love Can Do) The Second Time Around	1984	—	—	3.00
❑ 04876	Size Seven Round (Made of Gold)/All I Want to Do in Life	1985	—	—	3.00
—A-side with Lacy J. Dalton; B-side with Janie Frickie					
❑ 05439	Who's Gonna Fill Their Shoes/A Whole Lot of Trouble for You	1985	—	—	3.00
❑ 05698	The One I Loved Back Then (The Corvette Song)/If Only You'd Love Me Again	1985	—	—	3.00
❑ 05862	Somebody Wants Me Out of the Way/Call the Wrecker for My Heart	1986	—	—	3.00
❑ 06296	Wine Colored Roses/These Old Eyes Have Seen It All	1986	—	—	3.00
❑ 06593	The Right Left Hand/The Very Best on Me	1986	—	—	3.00
❑ 07107	I Turn to You/Don't Leave Without Taking Your Silver	1987	—	—	3.00
❑ 07655	The Bird/I'm Goin' Home Like I Never Did Before	1987	—	—	3.00
❑ 07748	I'm a Survivor/The Real McCoy	1988	—	—	3.00
❑ 07913	The Old Man No One Loves/One Hell of a Song	1988	—	—	3.00
❑ 08011	If I Could Bottle This Up/I Always Get It Right with You	1988	—	—	3.00
—With Shelby Lynne					
❑ 08509	I'm a One Woman Man/Pretty Little Lady from Beaumont, Texas	1988	—	—	3.00
❑ 10831	We Can Make It/One of These Days	1972	—	2.50	5.00
❑ 10858	Loving You Could Never Be Better/Try It, You'll Like It	1972	—	2.50	5.00
❑ 10917	A Picture of Me (Without You)/The Man Worth Loving You	1972	—	2.50	5.00
❑ 10959	What My Woman Can't Do/My Loving Wife	1973	—	2.50	5.00
❑ 11006	Nothing Ever Hurt Me (Half As Bad As Losing You)/Wine	1973	—	2.50	5.00
❑ 11053	Once You've Had the Best/Mary Don't Go Round	1973	—	2.50	5.00
❑ 11122	The Grand Tour/Our Private Life	1974	—	2.50	5.00
❑ 50038	The Door/Wean Me	1974	—	2.50	5.00
❑ 50088	These Days (I Barely Get By)/Baby, There's Nothing Like You	1975	—	2.50	5.00
❑ 50127	Memories of Us/I Just Don't Give a Damn	1975	—	2.50	5.00
❑ 50187	The Battle/I'll Come Back	1976	—	2.50	5.00
❑ 50227	You Always Look Your Best (Here in My Arms)/Have You Seen My Chicken	1976	—	2.50	5.00
❑ 50271	Her Name Is.../Diary of My Mind	1976	—	2.50	5.00
❑ 50385	Old King Kong/It's a 10-33 (Let's Get Jesus on the Line)	1977	—	2.00	4.00
❑ 50423	If I Could Put Them All Together (I'd Have You)/You've Got the Best of Me Again	1977	—	2.00	4.00
❑ 50495	Bartender's Blues/Rest in Peace	1977	—	2.00	4.00
❑ 50564	I'll Just Take It Out in Love/Leaving Love All Over the Place	1978	—	2.00	4.00
❑ 50684	Someday My Day Will Come/We Oughta Be Ashamed	1979	—	2.00	4.00
❑ 50867	He Stopped Loving Her Today/A Hard Act to Follow	1980	—	3.00	6.00
❑ 50922	I'm Not Ready Yet/Garage Sale Today	1980	—	2.00	4.00
❑ 50968	If Drinkin' Don't Kill Me (Her Memory Will)/Brother to the Blues	1980	—	2.00	4.00
❑ 68743	Ya Ba Da Ba Do (So Are You)/Don't You Ever Get Tired (Of Hurting Me)	1989	—	2.50	5.00
❑ 68743	The King Is Gone (So Are You)/Don't You Ever Get Tired (Of Hurting Me)	1989	—	—	3.00
—Same song, different title (changed for legal reasons)					
❑ 68743 [PS]	Ya Ba Da Ba Do (So Are You)/Don't You Ever Get Tired (Of Hurting Me)	1989	—	2.50	5.00
❑ 68991	Writing on the Wall/Burning Bridges	1989	—	—	3.00
❑ 73070	Radio Lover/Burning Bridges	1989	—	—	3.00
❑ 73424	Six Foot Deep, Six Foot Down/He Never Got the Picture at All	1990	—	2.00	4.00

MCA

Number	Title (A Side/B Side)	Yr	VG	VG+	NM
❑ 54187	You Couldn't Get the Picture/Heckle and Jeckle	1991	—	2.00	4.00
❑ 54272	She Loved a Lot in Her Time/Come Home to Me	1991	—	2.00	4.00
❑ 54370	Honky Tonk Myself to Death/Where the Tall Grass Grows	1992	—	2.00	4.00
❑ 54470	I Don't Need Your Rockin' Chair/Finally Friday	1992	—	2.50	5.00
❑ 54604	Wrong's What I Do Best/The Bottle Let Me Down	1993	—	2.00	4.00
❑ 54687	Walls Can Fall/You Must Have Walked Across My Mind Again	1993	—	—	3.00
❑ 54749	High-Tech Redneck/Forever's Here to Stay	1993	—	2.00	4.00
❑ 54969	A Good Year for the Roses/I've Still Got Some Hurtin' Left to Do	1994	—	2.00	4.00
—A-side with Alan Jackson					
❑ 55228	Honky Tonk Song/The Lone Ranger	1996	—	2.00	4.00
❑ 55287	Billy B. Bad/Back Down to Hung Up on You	1996	—	2.00	4.00
❑ 72038	Wild Irish Rose/No Future for Me in Our Past	1998	—	—	3.00

MERCURY

Number	Title (A Side/B Side)	Yr	VG	VG+	NM
❑ 7045 [S]	White Lightning/Treasure of Love	196?	10.00	20.00	40.00
❑ 7046 [S]	Why Baby Why/Hearts in My Dream	196?	10.00	20.00	40.00
❑ 7047 [S]	The Window Up Above/Color of the Blues	196?	10.00	20.00	40.00
❑ 7048 [S]	Tall, Tall Trees/Don't Stop the Music	196?	10.00	20.00	40.00
❑ 7049 [S]	Who Shot Sam/Accidentally on Purpose	196?	10.00	20.00	40.00
❑ 71029	Don't Stop the Music/Uh, Uh, No	1957	6.25	12.50	25.00
❑ 71049	Just One More/Gonna Come Get You	1957	6.25	12.50	25.00
❑ 71096	Too Much Water/All I Want to Do	1957	6.25	12.50	25.00
❑ 71139	Nothing Can Stop Me/I'm With the Wrong One	1957	6.25	12.50	25.00
❑ 71176	Tall, Tall Trees/Hearts in My Dream	1957	5.00	10.00	20.00
❑ 71224	Take the Devil Out of Me/A Cup of Loneliness	1957	5.00	10.00	20.00
❑ 71225	New Baby for Christmas/Maybe Next Christmas	1957	5.00	10.00	20.00
❑ 71257	Color of the Blues/Eskimo Pie	1958	5.00	10.00	20.00
❑ 71340	Wandering Soul/Jesus Wants Me	1958	5.00	10.00	20.00
❑ 71373	Treasure of Love/If I Don't Love You (Grits Ain't Groceries)	1958	5.00	10.00	20.00
❑ 71406	White Lightning/Long Time to Forget	1959	3.75	7.50	15.00
❑ 71464	Who Shot Sam/Into My Arms Again	1959	3.75	7.50	15.00
❑ 71506	My Lord Has Called Me/If You Want to Wear a Crown	1959	5.00	10.00	20.00
❑ 71514	Money to Burn/Big Harlan Taylor	1959	3.75	7.50	15.00
❑ 71583	Accidently on Purpose/Sparkling Blue Eyes	1960	3.75	7.50	15.00
❑ 71615	Have Mercy on Me/If You Believe	1960	5.00	10.00	20.00
❑ 71636	Family Bible/Your Old Standby	1960	5.00	10.00	20.00
❑ 71641	Out of Control/Just Little Boy Blue	1960	3.75	7.50	15.00
❑ 71700	The Window Up Above/Candy Hearts	1960	3.75	7.50	15.00
❑ 71721	Family Bible/Taggin' Along	1961	3.75	7.50	15.00
❑ 71804	Tender Years/Battle of Love	1961	3.00	6.00	12.00
❑ 71804 [PS]	Tender Years/Battle of Love	1961	3.75	7.50	15.00
❑ 71910	Aching, Breaking Heart/When My Heart Hurts No More	1962	3.00	6.00	12.00
❑ 71910 [PS]	Aching, Breaking Heart/When My Heart Hurts No More	1962	3.75	7.50	15.00
❑ 72010	You're Still on My Mind/Cold, Cold Heart	1962	3.00	6.00	12.00
❑ 72010 [PS]	You're Still on My Mind/Cold, Cold Heart	1962	3.75	7.50	15.00
❑ 72087	I Love You Because/Revenoor Man	1963	3.00	6.00	12.00
❑ 72087 [PS]	I Love You Because/Revenoor Man	1963	3.75	7.50	15.00
❑ 72159	Are You Mine/I Didn't Hear You	1963	3.00	6.00	12.00
❑ 72200	Mr. Fool/One Is a Lonely Number	1963	3.00	6.00	12.00
❑ 72233	The Last Town I Painted/Tarnished Angel	1964	3.00	6.00	12.00
❑ 72233 [PS]	The Last Town I Painted/Tarnished Angel	1964	3.75	7.50	15.00
❑ 72293	Oh Lonesome Me/Life to Go	1964	3.00	6.00	12.00
❑ 72293 [PS]	Oh Lonesome Me/Life to Go	1964	3.75	7.50	15.00
❑ 72362	I Wouldn't Know About That/You Better Treat Your Man Right	1964	3.00	6.00	12.00

MUSICOR

Number	Title (A Side/B Side)	Yr	VG	VG+	NM
❑ 1067	Things Have Gone to Pieces/Wearing My Heart Away	1965	2.00	4.00	8.00
❑ 1067 [PS]	Things Have Gone to Pieces/Wearing My Heart Away	1965	3.75	7.50	15.00
❑ 1098	Love Bug/I Can't Get Used to Being Lonely	1965	2.00	4.00	8.00
❑ 1117	Take Me/Ship of Love	1965	2.00	4.00	8.00
❑ 1143	I'm a People/I Woke Up from Dreaming	1966	2.00	4.00	8.00
❑ 1174	Old Brush Arbors/Flowers for Mama	1966	2.00	4.00	8.00
❑ 1181	Four-O-Thirty Three/Don't Think I Don't	1966	2.00	4.00	8.00
❑ 1226	Walk Through This World with Me/Developing My Pictures	1967	2.00	4.00	8.00
❑ 1243	I Can't Get There from Here/A Poor Man's Riches	1967	2.00	4.00	8.00
❑ 1244	A Cup of Loneliness/That the World But Give Me Jesus	1967	3.00	6.00	12.00
❑ 1267	If My Heart Had Windows/Honky Tonk Downstairs	1967	2.00	4.00	8.00
❑ 1289	Say It's Not You/Poor Chinee	1968	2.00	4.00	8.00
❑ 1297	Small Time Laboring Man/Well It's Alright	1968	2.00	4.00	8.00
❑ 1298	As Long As I Live/Your Angel Steps Out of Heaven	1968	2.00	4.00	8.00
❑ 1333	When the Grass Grows Over Me/Heartaches and Hangovers	1968	2.00	4.00	8.00
❑ 1339	Lonely Christmas Call/My Mom and Santa Claus	1968	2.00	4.00	8.00
❑ 1351	I'll Share My World with You/I'll See You a While Ago	1969	2.00	4.00	8.00
❑ 1366	If Not for You/When the Wife Runs Off	1969	2.00	4.00	8.00
❑ 1381	She's Mine/No Blues Is Good News	1969	2.00	4.00	8.00
❑ 1392	Where Grass Won't Grow/Shoulder to Shoulder	1970	—	3.00	6.00
❑ 1404	Going Life's Way/Uncloudy Day	1970	—	3.00	6.00
❑ 1408	Tell Me My Lying Eyes Are Wrong/You've Become My Everything	1970	—	3.00	6.00
❑ 1425	A Good Year for the Roses/Let a Little Loving Come In	1970	2.00	4.00	8.00
❑ 1432	Sometimes You Just Can't Win/Brothers of a Bottle	1971	—	3.00	6.00
❑ 1440	Right Won't Touch a Hand/Someone Sweet to Love	1971	—	3.00	6.00
❑ 1446	I'll Follow You (Up to Our Cloud)/Getting Over the Storm	1971	—	3.00	6.00

RCA VICTOR

Number	Title (A Side/B Side)	Yr	VG	VG+	NM
❑ AMBO-0123	Tender Years/White Lightnin'	1973	—	2.50	5.00
❑ APBO-0218	My Favorite Lies/You Gotta Be My Baby	1974	—	2.50	5.00

Number	Title (A Side/B Side)	Yr	VG	VG+	NM
❑ PB-10052	I Can Love You Enough/Talk to Me Lonesome Heart	1974	—	2.50	5.00
❑ 74-0625	A Day in the Life of a Fool/Old, Old House	1971	—	3.00	6.00
❑ 74-0700	I Made Leaving (Easy for You)/How Proud I Would Have Been	1972	—	3.00	6.00
❑ 74-0792	Wrapped Around Her Finger/With Half a Heart	1972	—	3.00	6.00
❑ 74-0878	I Can Still See Him in Your Eyes/She's Mine	1973	—	3.00	6.00
STARDAY					
❑ 130	No Money in This Deal/You're in My Heart	1954	25.00	50.00	100.00
❑ 146	Play It Cool, Man/Wrong About You	1954	15.00	30.00	60.00
—B-side with Sonny Burns					
❑ 160	Let Him Know/Let Me Catch My Breath	1954	15.00	30.00	60.00
❑ 162	You All Goodnight/Let Him Know	1954	15.00	30.00	60.00
❑ 165	Tell Her/Heartbroken Me	1954	15.00	30.00	60.00
—B-side with Sonny Burns					
❑ 188	Hold Everything/What's Wrong with You	1955	12.50	25.00	50.00
❑ 202	Why Baby Why/Season of My Heart	1955	12.50	25.00	50.00
❑ 216	What Am I Worth/Still Hurtin'	1955	10.00	20.00	40.00
❑ 234	I'm Ragged But I'm Right/Your Heart	1956	10.00	20.00	40.00
❑ 240	Rock It/How Come It	1956	50.00	100.00	200.00
—As "Thumper Jones"					
❑ 247	You Gotta Be My Baby/It's OK	1956	10.00	20.00	40.00
❑ 256	Boat of Life/Taggin' Along	1956	10.00	20.00	40.00
❑ 264	Just One More/Gonna Come Get You	1956	10.00	20.00	40.00
❑ 7003	Seasons of My Heart/I'm Ragged But I'm Right	197?	—	2.50	5.00
❑ 7020	Wasted Words/Any Old Time	197?	—	2.50	5.00
❑ 7036	Why Baby Why/You Gotta Be My Baby	197?	—	2.50	5.00
❑ 8012	Why Baby Why/Seasons of My Heart	197?	—	2.50	5.00
UNITED ARTISTS					
❑ 424	She Thinks I Still Care/Sometimes You Just Can't Win	1962	2.50	5.00	10.00
❑ 424 [PS]	She Thinks I Still Care/Sometimes You Just Can't Win	1962	3.75	7.50	15.00
❑ 442	Beacon in the Night/He Made Me Free	1962	3.00	6.00	12.00
❑ 462	Open Pit Mine/Geronimo	1962	2.50	5.00	10.00
❑ 463	He Is So Good to Me/Magic Valley	1962	3.00	6.00	12.00
❑ 500	A Girl I Used to Know/Big Fool of the Year	1962	2.50	5.00	10.00
❑ 528	Not What I Had in Mind/I Saw Me	1962	2.50	5.00	10.00
❑ 530	Lonely Christmas Call/My Mom and Santa Claus	1962	3.75	7.50	15.00
❑ 578	You Comb Her Hair/Ain't It Funny What a Fool Will Do	1963	2.50	5.00	10.00
❑ 578 [PS]	You Comb Her Hair/Ain't It Funny What a Fool Will Do	1963	3.75	7.50	15.00
❑ 683	Your Heart Turned Left (And I Was On the Right)/ My Tears Are Overdue	1964	2.50	5.00	10.00
❑ 724	Where Does a Little Tear Come From/Something I Dreamed	1964	2.50	5.00	10.00
❑ 751	The Race Is On/She's Lonesome Again	1964	2.50	5.00	10.00
❑ 804	Least of All/Brown to Blue	1965	2.50	5.00	10.00
❑ 858	Wrong Number/Old Old House	1965	2.50	5.00	10.00
❑ 901	What's Money/I Get Lonely in a Hurry	1965	2.50	5.00	10.00
❑ 965	World's Worse Loser/I Can't Change Overnight	1965	2.50	5.00	10.00
❑ 50014	Best Guitar Picker/A Good Old Fashioned Cry	1966	2.50	5.00	10.00

Albums

Number	Title (A Side/B Side)	Yr	VG	VG+	NM
ACCORD					
❑ SN-7201	Tender Years	1982	2.50	5.00	10.00
ALLEGIANCE					
❑ AV-5015	Cold Cold Heart	198?	2.50	5.00	10.00
ARCHIVE OF FOLK AND JAZZ					
❑ 353	George Jones Sings Country Hits	198?	2.50	5.00	10.00
BULLDOG					
❑ BDL-2009	20 Golden Pieces of George Jones	198?	2.50	5.00	10.00
EPIC					
❑ KE 31321	George Jones	1972	3.75	7.50	15.00
—Yellow label					
❑ KE 31321	George Jones	1973	3.00	6.00	12.00
—Orange label					
❑ KE 31718	A Picture of Me (Without You)	1972	3.75	7.50	15.00
—Yellow label					
❑ KE 31718	A Picture of Me (Without You)	1973	3.00	6.00	12.00
—Orange label					
❑ KE 32414	Nothing Ever Hurt Me (Half As Bad As Losing You)	1973	3.75	7.50	15.00
❑ KE 32563	In a Gospel Way	1974	3.75	7.50	15.00
❑ KE 33083	The Grand Tour	1974	3.75	7.50	15.00
❑ KE 33352	The Best of George Jones	1975	3.75	7.50	15.00
❑ PE 33352	The Best of George Jones	198?	2.00	4.00	8.00
—Budget-line reissue					
❑ KE 33547	Memories of Us	1975	3.75	7.50	15.00
❑ BG 33749 [(2)]	George Jones/A Picture of Me (Without You)	1976	3.75	7.50	15.00
❑ KE 34034	The Battle	1976	3.00	6.00	12.00
❑ KE 34290	Alone Again	1976	3.00	6.00	12.00
❑ PE 34692	All-Time Greatest Hits Volume 1	1977	3.00	6.00	12.00
—Orange label					
❑ PE 34692	All-Time Greatest Hits Volume 1	198?	2.00	4.00	8.00
—Dark blue label					
❑ PE 34717	I Wanta Sing	1977	3.00	6.00	12.00
—Orange label					
❑ PE 34717	I Wanta Sing	198?	2.00	4.00	8.00
—Dark blue label					
❑ KE 35414	Bartender's Blues	1978	3.00	6.00	12.00
❑ PE 35414	Bartender's Blues	198?	2.00	4.00	8.00
—Budget-line reissue					
❑ JE 35544	My Very Special Guests	1979	3.00	6.00	12.00
❑ PE 35544	My Very Special Guests	198?	2.00	4.00	8.00
—Budget-line reissue					
❑ JE 36586	I Am What I Am	1980	3.00	6.00	12.00
❑ FE 37106	Still the Same Old Me	1981	2.50	5.00	10.00
❑ PE 37106	Still the Same Ole Me	198?	2.00	4.00	8.00
—Budget-line reissue					
❑ FE 37346	Encore	1981	2.50	5.00	10.00
❑ KE2 38323 [(2)]	Anniversary — 10 Years of Hits	1982	3.00	6.00	12.00
❑ FE 38406	Shine On	1983	2.50	5.00	10.00
❑ PE 38406	Shine On	198?	2.00	4.00	8.00
—Budget-line reissue					
❑ FE 38978	Jones Country	1983	2.50	5.00	10.00
❑ PE 38978	Jones Country	1985	2.00	4.00	8.00
—Budget-line reissue					
❑ FE 39002	You've Still Got a Place in My Heart	1984	2.50	5.00	10.00
❑ FE 39272	Ladies' Choice	1984	2.50	5.00	10.00
❑ FE 39546	By Request	1984	2.50	5.00	10.00
❑ FE 39598	Who's Gonna Fill Their Shoes	1985	2.50	5.00	10.00
❑ FE 39899	First Time Live!	1985	2.50	5.00	10.00
❑ FE 40413	Wine Colored Roses	1986	2.50	5.00	10.00
❑ FE 40776	Super Hits	1987	2.50	5.00	10.00
❑ FE 40781	Too Wild Too Long	1988	2.50	5.00	10.00
❑ FE 44078	One Woman Man	1989	2.50	5.00	10.00
HILLTOP					
❑ 6048	You're In My Heart	1968	3.75	7.50	15.00
❑ 6092	Heartaches by the Number	1969	3.75	7.50	15.00
❑ 6133	Oh Lonesome Me	1970	3.75	7.50	15.00
INTERMEDIA					
❑ QS-5044	I Can't Change Overnight	198?	2.50	5.00	10.00
❑ QS-5061	How I Love These Old Songs	198?	2.50	5.00	10.00
LIBERTY					
❑ LN-10167	Trouble in Mind	1981	2.00	4.00	8.00
❑ LN-10168	I Get Lonely in a Hurry	1981	2.00	4.00	8.00
MCA					
❑ 10398	And Along Came Jones	1991	5.00	10.00	20.00
—Vinyl issued only through Columbia House					
MERCURY					
❑ ML-8014	Greatest Hits	1980	3.00	6.00	12.00
❑ MG-20282 [M]	Hillbilly Hit Parade, Volume 1	1957	37.50	75.00	150.00
—Five tracks by George Jones, one by George Jones with Benny Barnes, and four by other artists					
❑ MG-20306 [M]	14 Country Favorites	1957	37.50	75.00	150.00
❑ MG-20462 [M]	Country Church Time	1959	50.00	100.00	200.00
❑ MG-20477 [M]	George Jones Sings White Lightning and Other Favorites	1959	37.50	75.00	150.00
❑ MG-20596 [M]	George Jones Salutes Hank Williams	1960	20.00	40.00	80.00
❑ MG-20621 [M]	George Jones' Greatest Hits	1961	10.00	20.00	40.00
❑ MG-20624 [M]	Country and Western Hits	1961	10.00	20.00	40.00
❑ MG-20694 [M]	George Jones Sings From the Heart	1962	10.00	20.00	40.00
❑ MG-20793 [M]	The Novelty Side of George Jones	1963	20.00	40.00	80.00
❑ MG-20836 [M]	The Ballad Side of George Jones	1963	10.00	20.00	40.00
❑ MG-20906 [M]	Blue and Lonesome	1964	6.25	12.50	25.00
❑ MG-20937 [M]	Country and Western No. 1 Male Singer	1964	6.25	12.50	25.00
❑ MG-20990 [M]	Heartaches and Tears	1965	6.25	12.50	25.00
❑ MG-21029 [M]	Singing the Blues	1965	6.25	12.50	25.00
❑ MG-21048 [M]	George Jones' Greatest Hits Volume 2	1965	6.25	12.50	25.00
❑ SR-60257 [S]	George Jones Salutes Hank Williams	1960	25.00	50.00	100.00
❑ SR-60621 [P]	George Jones' Greatest Hits	1961	12.50	25.00	50.00
❑ SR-60624 [P]	Country and Western Hits	1961	12.50	25.00	50.00
❑ SR-60694 [S]	George Jones Sings From the Heart	1962	12.50	25.00	50.00
❑ SR-60793 [S]	The Novelty Side of George Jones	1963	25.00	50.00	100.00
❑ SR-60836 [S]	The Ballad Side of George Jones	1963	12.50	25.00	50.00
❑ SR-60906 [S]	Blue and Lonesome	1964	7.50	15.00	30.00
❑ SR-60937 [S]	Country and Western No. 1 Male Singer	1964	7.50	15.00	30.00
❑ SR-60990 [S]	Heartaches and Tears	1965	7.50	15.00	30.00
❑ SR-61029 [S]	Singing the Blues	1965	7.50	15.00	30.00
❑ SR-61048 [S]	George Jones' Greatest Hits Volume 2	1965	7.50	15.00	30.00
❑ 822646-1	George Jones Salutes Hank Williams	1985	2.50	5.00	10.00
❑ 826095-1	Rockin' the Country	1985	2.50	5.00	10.00
❑ 826248-1	Greatest Hits	1986	2.50	5.00	10.00
MUSICOR					
❑ MM-2046 [M]	Mr. Country and Western Music	1965	7.50	15.00	30.00
❑ MM-2060 [M]	New Country Hits	1965	7.50	15.00	30.00
❑ MM-2061 [M]	Old Brush Arbors	1966	7.50	15.00	30.00
❑ MM-2088 [M]	Love Bug	1966	7.50	15.00	30.00
❑ MM-2099 [M]	I'm a People	1966	6.25	12.50	25.00
❑ MM-2106 [M]	We Found Heaven Right Here on Earth	1966	6.25	12.50	25.00
❑ MM-2116 [M]	George Jones' Greatest Hits	1967	6.25	12.50	25.00
❑ MM-2119 [M]	Walk Through This World with Me	1967	7.50	15.00	30.00
❑ MM-2124 [M]	Cup of Loneliness	1967	7.50	15.00	30.00
❑ MM-2128 [M]	Hits by George	1967	7.50	15.00	30.00
❑ MS-3046 [S]	Mr. Country and Western Music	1965	10.00	20.00	40.00
❑ MS-3060 [S]	New Country Hits	1965	10.00	20.00	40.00
❑ MS-3061 [S]	Old Brush Arbors	1966	10.00	20.00	40.00
❑ MS-3088 [S]	Love Bug	1966	10.00	20.00	40.00
❑ MS-3099 [S]	I'm a People	1966	7.50	15.00	30.00
❑ MS-3106 [S]	We Found Heaven Right Here on Earth	1966	7.50	15.00	30.00
❑ MS-3116 [S]	George Jones' Greatest Hits	1967	6.25	12.50	25.00
❑ MS-3119 [S]	Walk Through This World with Me	1967	5.00	10.00	20.00
❑ MS-3124 [S]	Cup of Loneliness	1967	5.00	10.00	20.00
❑ MS-3128 [S]	Hits by George	1967	5.00	10.00	20.00
❑ MS-3149	The Songs of Dallas Frazier	1968	5.00	10.00	20.00
❑ MS-3158	If My Heart Had Windows	1968	5.00	10.00	20.00
❑ M2S-3159 [(2)]	The George Jones Story: The Musical Loves, Life and Sorrows of America's Great Country Star	1968	7.50	15.00	30.00

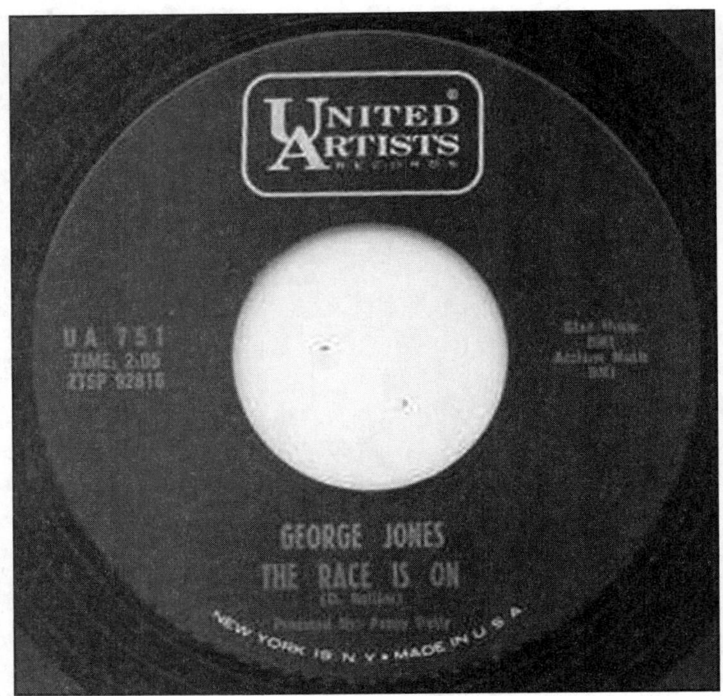

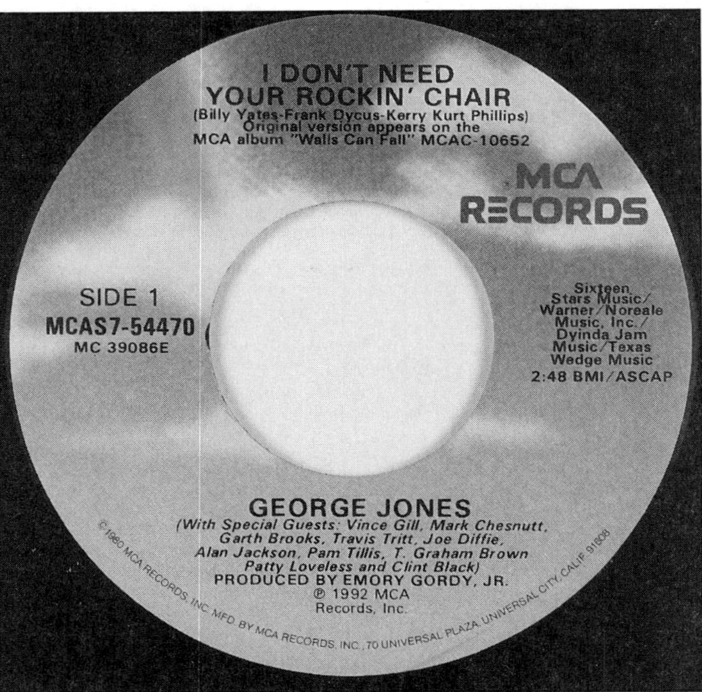

George Jones had his first hit single in 1955, and 44 years later he was back in the top 30 with his album cut "Choices." (Top left) One of the Possum's best-remembered hits from the 1960s is "The Race Is On," which got to No. 3 in 1964. It was also a pop hit in a cover by Jack Jones, and later Sawyer Brown did a hit remake of it. (Top right) Jones had had hits on Starday, Mercury, United Artists and Musicor, but his tenure on Epic from 1971-89 was by far his most consistent as a hitmaker. "The Grand Tour" hit No. 1 in 1974, his first solo chart-topper in seven years. (Bottom left) Considered by many to be the greatest country performance of all time, "He Stopped Loving Her Today" was a song that both singer and the songwriters thought little of – until it all came together. (Bottom right) Jones' hits were much less frequent in the "hot new country" 1990s. Here he gets help from a lot of his "friends" on the I-ain't-dead-yet declaration "I Don't Need Your Rockin' Chair."

Number	Title (A Side/B Side)	Yr	VG	VG+	NM
❑ M2S-3169 [(2)]	My Country	1969	7.50	15.00	30.00
❑ MS-3177	I'll Share My World with You	1969	5.00	10.00	20.00
❑ MS-3181	Where Grass Won't Grow	1969	5.00	10.00	20.00
❑ MS-3188	Will You Visit Me on Sunday?	1970	5.00	10.00	20.00
❑ MS-3191	The Best of George Jones	1970	5.00	10.00	20.00
❑ MS-3194	George Jones With Love	1971	5.00	10.00	20.00
❑ MS-3203	The Best of Sacred Music	1971	5.00	10.00	20.00
❑ MS-3204	The Great Songs of Leon Payne	1971	5.00	10.00	20.00
NASHVILLE					
❑ 2076	Seasons of My Heart	1970	3.75	7.50	15.00
PAIR					
❑ PDL2-1074 [(2)]	The Best of George Jones	1986	3.00	6.00	12.00
❑ PDL2-1080 [(2)]	Country, By George!	1986	3.00	6.00	12.00
POWER PAK					
❑ 271	The Crown Prince of Country Music	197?	2.50	5.00	10.00
QUICKSILVER					
❑ QS-1011	Frozen in Time	198?	2.50	5.00	10.00
❑ QS-1012	If My Heart Had Windows	198?	2.50	5.00	10.00
RCA CAMDEN					
❑ ACL1-0377	The Race Is On	1973	3.00	6.00	12.00
❑ CAS-2591	Flowers for Mama	1973	3.00	6.00	12.00
RCA VICTOR					
❑ APL1-0316	Best of George Jones Vol. II	1973	3.75	7.50	15.00
❑ APL1-0486	You Gotta Be My Baby	1974	3.75	7.50	15.00
❑ APL1-0612	His Songs	1974	3.75	7.50	15.00
❑ APL1-0815	I Can Love You Enough	1974	3.75	7.50	15.00
❑ APL1-1113	The Best of the Best	1975	3.75	7.50	15.00
❑ LSP-4672	First in the Hearts of Country Music Lovers	1972	3.75	7.50	15.00
❑ LSP-4716	Best of George Jones Vol. I	1972	3.75	7.50	15.00
❑ LSP-4725	Poor Man's Riches	1972	3.75	7.50	15.00
❑ LSP-4726	I Made Leaving (Easy for You)	1972	3.75	7.50	15.00
❑ LSP-4727	Country Singer	1972	3.75	7.50	15.00
❑ LSP-4733	George Jones And Friends	1972	3.75	7.50	15.00
❑ LSP-4785	Four-O Thirty-Three	1972	3.75	7.50	15.00
❑ LSP-4786	Tender Years	1972	3.75	7.50	15.00
❑ LSP-4787	Take Me	1972	3.75	7.50	15.00
❑ LSP-4801	Wrapped Around Her Finger	1973	3.75	7.50	15.00
❑ LSP-4847	I Can Still See Him	1973	3.75	7.50	15.00
ROUNDER					
❑ SS-15	Burn the Honky Tonk Down	198?	2.50	5.00	10.00
❑ SS-17	Heartaches & Hangovers	198?	2.50	5.00	10.00
SEARS					
❑ SPS-125	Maybe, Little Baby	196?	5.00	10.00	20.00
STARDAY					
❑ SLP 101 [M]	The Grand Ole Opry's New Star	1958	300.00	600.00	1200.
❑ SLP 125 [M]	The Crown Prince of Country Music	1960	40.00	80.00	160.00
❑ SLP 150 [M]	George Jones Sings His Greatest Hits	1962	12.50	25.00	50.00
❑ SLP 151 [M]	The Fabulous Country Music Sound of George Jones	1962	12.50	25.00	50.00
❑ SLP 335 [M]	George Jones	1965	10.00	20.00	40.00
❑ SLP 344 [M]	Long Live King George	1965	10.00	20.00	40.00
❑ SLP 366	The George Jones Story Bonus Photo	1966	5.00	10.00	20.00
❑ SLP 366 [(2) M]	The George Jones Story	1966	7.50	15.00	30.00
❑ SLP 401	The George Jones Song Book & Picture Album	1967	12.50	25.00	50.00
—With book					
❑ SLP 401 [M]	The George Jones Song Book & Picture Album	1967	7.50	15.00	30.00
—Without book					
❑ SLP 440 [M]	The Golden Country Hits of George Jones	1969	7.50	15.00	30.00
❑ 3021	16 Greatest Hits	197?	2.50	5.00	10.00
❑ DT-90080 [R]	George Jones Sings His Greatest Hits	1964	20.00	40.00	80.00
—Capitol Record Club edition					
UNITED ARTISTS					
❑ UXS-85 [(2)]	George Jones Superpak	1972	5.00	10.00	20.00
❑ UAL-3193 [M]	The New Favorites of George Jones	1962	7.50	15.00	30.00
❑ UAL-3218 [M]	George Jones Sings the Hits of His Country Cousins	1962	7.50	15.00	30.00
❑ UAL-3219 [M]	Homecoming in Heaven	1962	7.50	15.00	30.00
❑ UAL-3220 [M]	My Favorites of Hank Williams	1962	7.50	15.00	30.00
❑ UAL-3221 [M]	George Jones Sings Bob Wills	1962	10.00	20.00	40.00
❑ UAL-3270 [M]	I Wish the Night Would Never End	1963	6.25	12.50	25.00
❑ UAL-3291 [M]	The Best of George Jones	1963	6.25	12.50	25.00
❑ UAL-3338 [M]	More New Favorites	1964	6.25	12.50	25.00
❑ UAL-3364 [M]	George Jones Sings Like the Dickens	1964	10.00	20.00	40.00
❑ UAL-3388 [M]	I Get Lonely in a Hurry	1964	7.50	15.00	30.00
❑ UAL-3408 [M]	Trouble in Mind	1965	7.50	15.00	30.00
❑ UAL-3422 [M]	The Race Is On	1965	7.50	15.00	30.00
—With photo of George Jones on front					
❑ UAL-3422 [M]	The Race Is On	1965	5.00	10.00	20.00
—With cartoon on front					
❑ UAL-3442 [M]	King of Broken Hearts	1965	7.50	15.00	30.00
❑ UAL-3457 [M]	The Great George Jones	1966	7.50	15.00	30.00
❑ UAL-3532 [M]	George Jones' Golden Hits, Volume 1	1966	5.00	10.00	20.00
❑ UAL-3558 [M]	The Young George Jones	1967	7.50	15.00	30.00
❑ UAL-3566 [M]	George Jones' Golden Hits, Volume 2	1967	7.50	15.00	30.00
❑ UAS-6193 [S]	The New Favorites of George Jones	1962	10.00	20.00	40.00
❑ UAS-6218 [S]	George Jones Sings the Hits of His Country Cousins	1962	10.00	20.00	40.00
❑ UAS-6219 [S]	Homecoming in Heaven	1962	10.00	20.00	40.00
❑ UAS-6220 [S]	My Favorites of Hank Williams	1962	10.00	20.00	40.00
❑ UAS-6221 [S]	George Jones Sings Bob Wills	1962	12.50	25.00	50.00
❑ UAS-6270 [S]	I Wish the Night Would Never End	1963	7.50	15.00	30.00
❑ UAS-6291 [S]	The Best of George Jones	1963	7.50	15.00	30.00
❑ UAS-6328 [S]	More New Favorites	1964	7.50	15.00	30.00
❑ UAS-6364 [S]	George Jones Sings Like the Dickens	1964	12.50	25.00	50.00
❑ UAS-6388 [S]	I Get Lonely in a Hurry	1964	10.00	20.00	40.00
❑ UAS-6408 [S]	Trouble in Mind	1965	10.00	20.00	40.00
❑ UAS-6422 [S]	The Race Is On	1965	10.00	20.00	40.00
—With photo of George Jones on front					
❑ UAS-6422 [S]	The Race Is On	1965	6.25	12.50	25.00
—With cartoon on front					
❑ UAS-6442 [S]	King of Broken Hearts	1965	10.00	20.00	40.00
❑ UAS-6457 [S]	The Great George Jones	1966	10.00	20.00	40.00
❑ UAS-6532 [S]	George Jones' Golden Hits, Volume 1	1966	6.25	12.50	25.00
❑ UAS-6558 [S]	The Young George Jones	1967	5.00	10.00	20.00
❑ UAS-6566 [S]	George Jones' Golden Hits, Volume 2	1967	5.00	10.00	20.00
WING					
❑ MGW-12266 [M]	The Great George Jones	196?	3.75	7.50	15.00
❑ SRW-16266 [S]	The Great George Jones	196?	3.75	7.50	15.00

JONES, GEORGE, AND BRENDA CARTER

Also see each artist's individual listings.

45s

Number	Title (A Side/B Side)	Yr	VG	VG+	NM
MUSICOR					
❑ 1325	Milwaukee, Here I Come/Great Big Spirit of Love	1968	2.00	4.00	8.00
❑ 1375	Lonesome End of the Line/Just Your Average Couple	1969	2.00	4.00	8.00

JONES, GEORGE, AND JEANETTE HICKS

Also see each artist's individual listings.

45s

Number	Title (A Side/B Side)	Yr	VG	VG+	NM
MERCURY					
❑ 71061	Yearning/Cry, Cry	1957	6.25	12.50	25.00
STARDAY					
❑ 279	Yearning/So Near Yet So Far Away	1956	7.50	15.00	30.00

JONES, GEORGE, AND BRENDA LEE

Also see each artist's individual listings.

45s

Number	Title (A Side/B Side)	Yr	VG	VG+	NM
EPIC					
❑ 04723	Hallelujah I Love Her So/(What Love Can Do) The Second Time Around	1984	—	2.00	4.00

JONES, GEORGE, AND MELBA MONTGOMERY

Also see each artist's individual listings.

45s

Number	Title (A Side/B Side)	Yr	VG	VG+	NM
MUSICOR					
❑ 1204	Close Together (As You and Me)/Long As We're Dreaming	1966	2.00	4.00	8.00
❑ 1238	Party Pickin'/Simply Divine	1967	2.00	4.00	8.00
UNITED ARTISTS					
❑ 575	We Must Have Been Out of Our Minds/Until Then	1963	2.50	5.00	10.00
❑ 635	Let's Invite Them Over/What's In Our Hearts	1963	2.50	5.00	10.00
❑ 704	There's a Friend in the Way/Suppose Tonight Would Be Our Last	1964	2.50	5.00	10.00
❑ 732	Please Be My Love/Will There Ever Be Another	1964	2.50	5.00	10.00
❑ 784	Multiply the Heartaches/Once More	1964	2.50	5.00	10.00
❑ 828	House of Gold/I Dreamed My Baby Came Home	1965	2.50	5.00	10.00
❑ 899	Don't Go/I Let You Go	1965	2.50	5.00	10.00
❑ 941	Blue Moon of Kentucky/I Can't Get Over You	1965	2.50	5.00	10.00
❑ 50015	Afraid/Now Tell Me	1966	2.50	5.00	10.00

Albums

Number	Title (A Side/B Side)	Yr	VG	VG+	NM
LIBERTY					
❑ LN-10169	Singing What's In Our Hearts	1981	2.00	4.00	8.00
MUSICOR					
❑ MM-2109 [M]	Close Together (As You and Me)	1966	5.00	10.00	20.00
❑ MM-2127 [M]	Let's Get Together	1967	7.50	15.00	30.00
❑ MM-2127 [M]	Boy Meets Girl	1967	7.50	15.00	30.00
—Alternate title					
❑ MS-2127 [S]	Let's Get Together	1967	5.00	10.00	20.00
❑ MS-2127 [S]	Boy Meets Girl	1967	5.00	10.00	20.00
—Alternate title					
❑ MS-3109 [S]	Close Together (As You and Me)	1966	6.25	12.50	25.00
UNITED ARTISTS					
❑ UAL-3301 [M]	Singing What's In Our Heart	1963	6.25	12.50	25.00
❑ UAL-3352 [M]	Bluegrass Hootenanny	1964	6.25	12.50	25.00
❑ UAL-3472 [M]	Blue Moon of Kentucky	1966	5.00	10.00	20.00
❑ UAS-6301 [S]	Singing What's In Our Heart	1963	7.50	15.00	30.00
❑ UAS-6352 [S]	Bluegrass Hootenanny	1964	7.50	15.00	30.00
❑ UAS-6472 [S]	Blue Moon of Kentucky	1966	6.25	12.50	25.00

JONES, GEORGE; MELBA MONTGOMERY; JUDY LYNN

Albums

Number	Title (A Side/B Side)	Yr	VG	VG+	NM
UNITED ARTISTS					
❑ UAL-3367 [M]	A King and Two Queens	1964	5.00	10.00	20.00
❑ UAS-6367 [S]	A King and Two Queens	1964	6.25	12.50	25.00

JONES, GEORGE; MELBA MONTGOMERY; GENE PITNEY

Albums

Number	Title (A Side/B Side)	Yr	VG	VG+	NM
MUSICOR					
❑ MM-2079 [M]	Famous Country Duets	1965	5.00	10.00	20.00
❑ MS-3079 [S]	Famous Country Duets	1965	6.25	12.50	25.00

JONES, GEORGE, AND JOHNNY PAYCHECK

Also see each artist's individual listings.

45s

Number	Title (A Side/B Side)	Yr	VG	VG+	NM
EPIC					
❑ 50647	Mabellene/Don't Want No Stranger Sleepin' in My Bed	1978	—	2.00	4.00

Number	Title (A Side/B Side)	Yr	VG	VG+	NM
❑ 50708	You Can Have Her/Along Came Jones	1979	—	2.00	4.00
❑ 50891	When You're Ugly Like Us (You Just Naturally Got to Be Cool)/Kansas City	1980	—	2.00	4.00
❑ 50949	You Better Move On/Smack Dab in the Middle	1980	—	2.00	4.00

Albums

EPIC

Number	Title (A Side/B Side)	Yr	VG	VG+	NM
❑ JE 35783	Double Trouble	1980	2.50	5.00	10.00

JONES, GEORGE, AND MARGIE SINGLETON

Also see each artist's individual listings.

45s

MERCURY

Number	Title (A Side/B Side)	Yr	VG	VG+	NM
❑ 71856	Did I Ever Tell You/Not Even Friends	1961	3.00	6.00	12.00
❑ 71955	Waltz of the Angels/Talk About Lovin'	1962	3.00	6.00	12.00

Albums

MERCURY

Number	Title (A Side/B Side)	Yr	VG	VG+	NM
❑ MG-20747 [M]	Duets Country Style	1962	7.50	15.00	30.00
❑ SR-60747 [S]	Duets Country Style	1962	10.00	20.00	40.00

JONES, GEORGE, AND TAMMY WYNETTE

Also see each artist's individual listings; TINA WITH DADDY AND MOMMY.

45s

EPIC

Number	Title (A Side/B Side)	Yr	VG	VG+	NM
❑ 10815	Take Me/We Go Together	1971	—	2.50	5.00
❑ 10881	The Ceremony/The Great Divide	1972	—	2.50	5.00
❑ 10923	Old Fashioned Singing/We Love to Sing About Jesus	1972	—	2.50	5.00
❑ 10963	Let's Build a World Together/Touching Shoulders	1973	—	2.50	5.00
❑ 11031	We're Gonna Hold On/My Elusive Dreams	1973	—	2.50	5.00
❑ 11077	Mr. and Mrs. Santa Claus/The Greatest Christmas Gift	1973	—	2.50	5.00
❑ 11083	(We're Not) The Jet Set/The Crawdad Song	1974	—	2.50	5.00
❑ 11151	We Loved It Away/Ain't It Been Good	1974	—	2.50	5.00
❑ 50099	God's Gonna Getcha (For That)/Those Were the Good Times	1975	—	2.50	5.00
❑ 50235	Golden Ring/We're Putting It Back Together	1976	—	2.50	5.00
❑ 50314	Near You/Tattletale Eyes	1976	—	2.50	5.00
❑ 50418	Southern California/Keep the Change	1977	—	2.00	4.00
❑ 50849	Two Story House/It Sure Was Good	1980	—	2.00	4.00
❑ 50930	A Pair of Old Sneakers/We'll Talk About It Later	1980	—	2.00	4.00

MCA

Number	Title (A Side/B Side)	Yr	VG	VG+	NM
❑ 55048	One/Golden Ring	1995	—	2.00	4.00

Albums

EPIC

Number	Title (A Side/B Side)	Yr	VG	VG+	NM
❑ E 30802	We Go Together	1971	3.75	7.50	15.00
❑ KE 31554	Me and the First Lady	1972	3.75	7.50	15.00
—Yellow label					
❑ KE 31554	Me and the First Lady	1973	3.00	6.00	12.00
—Orange label					
❑ KE 31719	We Love to Sing About Jesus	1972	3.75	7.50	15.00
—Yellow label					
❑ KE 31719	We Love to Sing About Jesus	1973	3.00	6.00	12.00
—Orange label					
❑ KE 32113	Let's Build a World Together	1973	3.75	7.50	15.00
❑ KE 32757	We're Gonna Hold On	1973	3.75	7.50	15.00
❑ KE 33351	George & Tammy & Tina	1975	3.75	7.50	15.00
❑ BG 33752 [(2)]	We Go Together/Me and the First Lady	1976	3.75	7.50	15.00
❑ PE 34291	Golden Ring	1976	3.00	6.00	12.00
—Orange label					
❑ PE 34291	Golden Ring	198?	2.00	4.00	8.00
—Dark blue label					
❑ KE 34716	Greatest Hits	1977	3.00	6.00	12.00
❑ PE 34716	Greatest Hits	198?	2.00	4.00	8.00
—Budget-line reissue					
❑ JE 36764	Together Again	1980	2.50	5.00	10.00
❑ PE 36764	Together Again	198?	2.00	4.00	8.00
—Budget-line reissue					
❑ FE 37348	Encore	1981	2.50	5.00	10.00
❑ PE 37348	Encore	198?	2.00	4.00	8.00
—Budget-line reissue					

JONES, GRANDPA

Also see COWBOY COPAS AND GRANDPA JONES; HANK SNOW.

45s

DECCA

Number	Title (A Side/B Side)	Yr	VG	VG+	NM
❑ 9-30264	Eight More Miles to Louisville/Dark As a Dungeon	1957	5.00	10.00	20.00
❑ 9-30523	Mountain Dew/Old Rattler's Tip	1957	5.00	10.00	20.00
❑ 9-30655	Daylight Saving Time/Don't Look Back	1958	5.00	10.00	20.00
❑ 9-30823	The All American Boy/Pickin' Time	1959	5.00	10.00	20.00
❑ 9-30904	Don't Bring Your Banjo Home/It Takes a Lot of Livin'	1959	5.00	10.00	20.00

KING

Number	Title (A Side/B Side)	Yr	VG	VG+	NM
❑ 976	What'll I Do with the Baby-O/Chicken Don't Roost Too High	1951	10.00	20.00	40.00
❑ 992	Rain Is Still Falling/Happy Little Home in Arkansas	1951	10.00	20.00	40.00
❑ 1029	That Memphis Train/You Done Me Mean and Hateful	1952	7.50	15.00	30.00
❑ 1061	Down in Dixie/Time, Time, Time, Time	1952	7.50	15.00	30.00
❑ 1069	Fix Me a Pallet/Fifteen Cents Is All I Got	1952	7.50	15.00	30.00
❑ 1097	A Light in His Soul/There's a Hole in the Ground	1952	7.50	15.00	30.00
❑ 1301	Come Be My Rainbow/You Done Me Mean and Dirty	1954	6.25	12.50	25.00
❑ 5321	Are You from Dixie/Fast Moving Night Train	1960	3.75	7.50	15.00
❑ 5335	A Night Out/Fifteen Cents Is All I Got	1960	3.75	7.50	15.00
❑ 5397	Grandpa's Banjo Boogie/Uncle Eph's Got the Coon	1960	3.75	7.50	15.00
❑ 5489	It's Raining Here This Morning/And So You Have Come Back to Me	1961	3.75	7.50	15.00
❑ 5867	Old Rattler/Mountain Dew	1964	3.00	6.00	12.00

MONUMENT

Number	Title (A Side/B Side)	Yr	VG	VG+	NM
❑ 422	The Thing/Ladies Man	1960	3.75	7.50	15.00
❑ 430	Hip Cats' Wedding/I Don't Love Nobody	1960	3.75	7.50	15.00
❑ 440	Billy Yank and Johnny Reb/These Hills	1961	3.75	7.50	15.00
❑ 454	Banjo Sam/Count Your Blessings	1962	3.75	7.50	15.00
❑ 801	T for Texas/Tritzem Yodel	1962	3.75	7.50	15.00
❑ 811	My Carolina Sunshine/Night Train to Memphis	1963	3.75	7.50	15.00
❑ 820	Away Out on the Mountain/My Little Lady	1963	3.75	7.50	15.00
❑ 844	Going from the Cotton Field/Root Hog Root	1964	3.00	6.00	12.00
❑ 866	Falling Leaves/Here Comes the Champion	1964	3.00	6.00	12.00
❑ 903	Are You from Dixie/My Darlin's Not My Darlin' Anymore	1965	3.00	6.00	12.00
❑ 973	Eight More Miles to Louisville/As Long As We're Dreaming	1966	3.00	6.00	12.00
❑ 1000	Moon of Arizona/Everything I Had Going for Me Is Gone	1967	2.50	5.00	10.00
❑ 1043	Don't Look Back/That's All This Old World Needs	1967	2.50	5.00	10.00
❑ 1069	Bill's Gonna Be Home Soon/These Hills	1968	2.50	5.00	10.00
❑ 1108	Smoke, Smoke, Smoke (But Not Around Me)/I'll Just Keep Living Alone	1968	2.50	5.00	10.00
❑ 1143	Mountain Laurel/Old Troupe Dog	1969	2.50	5.00	10.00
❑ 1179	Christmas Guest/Christmas Roses	1969	3.00	6.00	12.00
❑ 1203	Trouble in Mind/I've Learned to Leave That to the Lord	1970	2.50	5.00	10.00
❑ 1939	Christmas Guest/Christmas Roses	1976	—	2.00	4.00
—"Golden Series" reissue					
❑ 8528	Valley of the Never Do No Good/A Dollar Short	1971	2.00	4.00	8.00
❑ 8539	Here I Am Makin' Plans/Coal Camp	1972	2.00	4.00	8.00
❑ 8556	Christmas Guest/Christmas Roses	1972	2.00	4.00	8.00
❑ 8577	Mountain Dew/Four Winds a-Blowin'	1973	2.00	4.00	8.00
❑ 8599	Nashville on My Mind/Brown Girl and Fair Eleanor	1973	2.00	4.00	8.00
❑ 8677	Christmas Guest/Christmas Roses	1975	—	3.00	6.00

RCA VICTOR

Number	Title (A Side/B Side)	Yr	VG	VG+	NM
❑ 47-4505	The Retreat/Mountain Laurel	1952	7.50	15.00	30.00
❑ 47-4660	T.V. Blues/Stop That Ticklin' Me	1952	7.50	15.00	30.00
❑ 47-4771	I'm No Communist/Pickin' on Me	1952	7.50	15.00	30.00
❑ 47-4956	Sassafrass/Closer to the Bone	1952	7.50	15.00	30.00
❑ 47-5113	Old Rattler's Son/Deal Old Sunny South by the Sea	1953	6.25	12.50	25.00
❑ 47-5234	Papa's Corn Likker Still/Bread and Gravy	1953	6.25	12.50	25.00
❑ 47-5357	You Ain't Seen Nothin' Yet/You're Never Too Old	1953	6.25	12.50	25.00
❑ 47-5475	My Heart Is Like a Train/That New Vitamine	1953	6.25	12.50	25.00
❑ 47-5576	The Trader/Y'All Come	1954	6.25	12.50	25.00
❑ 47-5685	Some More Mountain Dew/Old Blue	1954	6.25	12.50	25.00
❑ 47-5770	Back Up Buddy If You Don't Want a Whipping/Lookin' Back to See	1954	6.25	12.50	25.00
—With Ruby Wells					
❑ 47-5789	Standing in the Depot/High Silk Hat and a Gold Top Walkin' Cane	1954	6.25	12.50	25.00
❑ 47-5939	Keep On the Sunny Side of Life/Some Little Boy Is Going to Find You	1954	6.25	12.50	25.00
❑ 47-6006	Old Dan Tucker/Gooseberry Pie	1955	6.25	12.50	25.00
❑ 47-6179	Herd o' Turtles/In the Future	1955	6.25	12.50	25.00
❑ 47-6263	What Has She Got/The Champion	1955	6.25	12.50	25.00

WARNER BROS.

Number	Title (A Side/B Side)	Yr	VG	VG+	NM
❑ 8016	Time/Freedom Lives in a Country Song	1974	—	3.50	7.00

Selected 78s

KING

Number	Title (A Side/B Side)	Yr	VG	VG+	NM
❑ 502	It's Raining Here This Morning/I'll Be Around If You Need Me	1946	6.25	12.50	25.00
❑ 508	I'll Never Lose That Loneliness for You/That's a Grave in the Way	1946	6.25	12.50	25.00
❑ 513	The Steppin' Out Kind/You'll Be Lonesome Too	1946	6.25	12.50	25.00
❑ 517	Don't Sweet Talk Me/Maybe You Will Miss Me When I'm Gone	1946	6.25	12.50	25.00
❑ 524	Our Worlds Are Not the Same/I've Been All Around This World	1946	6.25	12.50	25.00
❑ 532	Tears That Make Believe/Eight More Miles to Louisville	1946	6.25	12.50	25.00
❑ 545	Get Things Ready/East Bound Freight Train	1946	6.25	12.50	25.00
❑ 575	Heart Stealin' Mama/Darling Won't You Love Me Now	1947	6.25	12.50	25.00
❑ 587	Ridin' on That Train/Are There Tears Behind Your Smiles	1947	6.25	12.50	25.00
❑ 601	Get Back on the Glory Road/She's Gone and Left Another	1947	6.25	12.50	25.00
❑ 624	Mountain Dew/My Darling's Not My Darling Anymore	1947	6.25	12.50	25.00
❑ 644	Alimony Trouble/Call Me Darling Once Again	1947	6.25	12.50	25.00
❑ 668	Old Rattler/Mountain Naw	1947	6.25	12.50	25.00
❑ 685	New Pins and Needles/Going Down the Country	1948	6.25	12.50	25.00
❑ 694	I'm My Own Grandpaw/I Often Wonder Why You Changed Your Mind	1948	6.25	12.50	25.00
❑ 717	Bald Headed End of the Broom/I'm On My Way Somewhere	1948	6.25	12.50	25.00
❑ 733	Old Rattler's Tred Again/I Guess You Don't Remember Me	1948	6.25	12.50	25.00
❑ 740	My Old Red River Home/How Many Biscuits Can You Eat	1948	6.25	12.50	25.00

Number	Title (A Side/B Side)	Yr	VG	VG+	NM
❑ 747	That Depot in the Sky/144,000 Were There	1949	6.25	12.50	25.00
❑ 772	Going Down Town/Kitty Clyde	1949	6.25	12.50	25.00
❑ 794	I Ain't Got Much to Lose/You'll Make Our Shack a Mansion	1949	6.25	12.50	25.00
❑ 812	Grandpa's Boogie/Weary Lonesome Me	1949	6.25	12.50	25.00
❑ 815	Jonah and the Whale/Our Fathers Had Religion	1949	6.25	12.50	25.00
❑ 834	Daisy Dean/I Do	1949	6.25	12.50	25.00
❑ 847	Are You from Dixie/Jesse James	1950	5.00	10.00	20.00
❑ 867	Uncle Eph's Got the Coon/Five String Banjo Boogie	1950	5.00	10.00	20.00
❑ 890	Grandpa's Getting Married Again/I Don't Know Gee from Haw	1950	5.00	10.00	20.00
❑ 896	Dark as a Dungeon/Come and Dine	1950	5.00	10.00	20.00
❑ 912	Melinda/Stay in the Wagon	1950	5.00	10.00	20.00
❑ 930	Golden Rocket/Jeannie Get Your Hoe Cakes Done	1951	5.00	10.00	20.00
❑ 934	Trouble, Trouble, Trouble/Send In Your Name and Address	1951	5.00	10.00	20.00
❑ 948	I'm Hog Wild Crazy Over You/Nobody Loves Me Anymore	1951	5.00	10.00	20.00
Albums					
DECCA					
❑ DL 4364 [M]	An Evening with Grandpa Jones	1963	6.25	12.50	25.00
❑ DL 74364 [S]	An Evening with Grandpa Jones	1963	7.50	15.00	30.00
KING					
❑ 554 [M]	Grandpa Jones Sings His Biggest Hits	1958	25.00	50.00	100.00
❑ 625 [M]	Strictly Country Tunes	1959	25.00	50.00	100.00
❑ 809 [M]	Rollin' Along with Grandpa Jones	1963	15.00	30.00	60.00
❑ 822 [M]	16 Sacred Gospel Songs	1963	15.00	30.00	60.00
❑ 845 [M]	Do You Remember?	1963	15.00	30.00	60.00
❑ 888 [M]	The Other Side of Grandpa Jones	1964	15.00	30.00	60.00
❑ KS-1042	The Living Legend of Country Music	1969	5.00	10.00	20.00
MONUMENT					
❑ MLP-4006 [M]	Grandpa Jones Makes the Rafters Ring	1962	6.25	12.50	25.00
❑ MLP-8001 [M]	Yodeling Hits	1963	5.00	10.00	20.00
❑ MLP-8021 [M]	Real Folk Songs	1964	5.00	10.00	20.00
❑ MLP-8041 [M]	Grandpa Jones Remembers the Brown's Ferry Four	1966	6.25	12.50	25.00
❑ SLP-14006 [S]	Grandpa Jones Makes the Rafters Ring	1962	7.50	15.00	30.00
❑ SLP-18001 [S]	Yodeling Hits	1963	6.25	12.50	25.00
❑ SLP-18021 [S]	Real Folk Songs	1964	6.25	12.50	25.00
❑ SLP-18041 [S]	Grandpa Jones Remembers the Brown's Ferry Four	1966	7.50	15.00	30.00
❑ SLP-18083	Everybody's Grandpa	1968	5.00	10.00	20.00
❑ SLP-18131	Grandpa Jones Sings Hits from Hee Haw	1969	5.00	10.00	20.00

JONES, GRANDPA, AND MINNIE PEARL

45s

RCA VICTOR

Number	Title (A Side/B Side)	Yr	VG	VG+	NM
❑ 47-5891	Papa Loves Mambo/Gotta Marry Off Our Daughter	1954	6.25	12.50	25.00
❑ 47-6088	Matrimony Ridge/Spring Fever	1955	6.25	12.50	25.00
❑ 47-6474	Kissin' Games/I'm Gettin' Gray Hair	1956	6.25	12.50	25.00

JONES, HARRISON

45s

GRT

Number	Title (A Side/B Side)	Yr	VG	VG+	NM
❑ 004	But Tonight I'm Gonna Love You/It's That Time Again	1974	—	3.00	6.00

JONES, KASEY

45s

CURB

Number	Title (A Side/B Side)	Yr	VG	VG+	NM
❑ D7-73030	1-900-Bubba/But I'm Not Bitter	1997	—	—	3.00

JONES, MICKEY

45s

Number	Title (A Side/B Side)	Yr	VG	VG+	NM
BAYSHORE					
❑ 100	She Loves My Troubles Away/Forever	1979	—	3.00	6.00
STOP HUNGER					
❑ 1102	A Song a Day Keeps the Blues Away/Here's a Rose	1989	—	3.50	7.00
❑ 1103	Bigger Man Than Me!/Play Another Good Old Country Song!	1989	—	3.50	7.00

JONES, NEAL

45s

COLUMBIA

Number	Title (A Side/B Side)	Yr	VG	VG+	NM
❑ 4-21236	Walkin', Plowin', Talkin', Cryin'/Who-R-O-Ee, My Life Has Just Begun	1954	7.50	15.00	30.00
❑ 4-21292	Foolin' Women/Maybe Next Week Sometime	1954	6.25	12.50	25.00
❑ 4-21356	Hot Jing Jolly/Down Boy	1955	7.50	15.00	30.00
❑ 4-21415	I'm Playin' It Cool/High Steppin' Baby	1955	7.50	15.00	30.00
❑ 4-21475	Two Wrongs/What This World Needs	1955	6.25	12.50	25.00

JONES, THUMPER

See GEORGE JONES.

JONES, TOM

He began to make the country charts upon his switch to Epic in 1976, so we have included him. In fact, he had 16 country hits from 1976-85.

12-Inch Singles

Number	Title (A Side/B Side)	Yr	VG	VG+	NM
INTERSCOPE					
❑ 2172 [DJ]	If I Only Knew (4 versions)	1994	2.50	5.00	10.00
❑ 2194 [DJ]	Situation (5 versions)	1994	2.50	5.00	10.00
MCA					
❑ 55144	She's a Lady (3 versions)	1995	2.50	5.00	10.00
45s					
CHINA					
❑ 871038-7	Kiss/E.F.L.	1989	—	—	3.00
—A-side: The Art of Noise with Tom Jones; B-side by Art of Noise					
❑ 871038-7 [PS]	Kiss/E.F.L.	1989	—	—	3.00
EPIC					
❑ 50308	Say You'll Stay Until Tomorrow/Lady Lay	1976	—	2.00	4.00
❑ 50382	Take Me Tonight/I Hope You'll Understand	1977	—	2.00	4.00
❑ 50468	What a Night/That's Where I Belong	1977	—	2.00	4.00
❑ 50506	There's Nothing Stronger Than Our Love/No One Gave Me Love	1978	—	2.00	4.00
❑ 50636	Hey Love/Baby, As You Turn Away	1978	—	2.00	4.00
MCA					
❑ 41127	Dancing Endlessly/Never Had a Lady Before	1979	—	2.00	4.00
MERCURY					
❑ 76100	Darlin'/I Don't Want to Know You That Way	1981	—	2.00	4.00
❑ 76115	What in the World's Come Over You/The Things That Matter Most to Me	1981	—	2.00	4.00
❑ 76125	Lady Lay Down/A Daughter's Question	1981	—	2.00	4.00
❑ 76172	A Woman's Touch/I'll Never Get Over You	1982	—	2.00	4.00
❑ 810445-7	Touch Me (I'll Be Your Fool Once More)/We're Wasting Our Time	1983	—	—	3.00
❑ 812631-7	It'll Be Me/If I Ever Had to Say Goodbye to You	1983	—	—	3.00
❑ 814820-7	I've Been Rained On Too/That Old Piano	1983	—	—	3.00
❑ 818801-7	This Time/Memphis, Tennessee	1984	—	—	3.00
❑ 870233-7	Things That Matter Most to Me/Green, Green Grass of Home	1988	—	—	3.00
❑ 880173-7	All the Love Is On the Radio/(B-side unknown)	1984	—	—	3.00
❑ 880402-7	I'm an Old Rock and Roller (Dancin' to a Different Beat)/My Kind of Girl	1984	—	—	3.00
❑ 880569-7	Give Her All the Roses (Don't Wait Until Tomorrow)/A Picture of You	1985	—	—	3.00
❑ 884039-7	Not Another Heart Song/Only My Heart Knows	1985	—	—	3.00
❑ 884252-7	It's Four in the Morning/I'll Never Get Over You	1985	—	—	3.00
❑ 888911-7	Lover to Lover/A Daughter's Question	1987	—	—	3.00
PARROT					
❑ 9737	It's Not Unusual/To Wait for Love (Is to Waste Your Life Away)	1965	2.50	5.00	10.00
❑ 9765	What's New Pussycat/Once Upon a Time	1965	2.50	5.00	10.00
❑ 9765 [PS]	What's New Pussycat/Once Upon a Time	1965	3.75	7.50	15.00
❑ 9787	With These Hands/Some Other Guy	1965	2.00	4.00	8.00
❑ 9787 [PS]	With These Hands/Some Other Guy	1965	3.00	6.00	12.00
❑ 9801	Thunderball/Key to My Heart	1965	2.00	4.00	8.00
❑ 9801 [PS]	Thunderball/Key to My Heart	1965	5.00	10.00	20.00
—Version 1: with a dead female and a spear gun					
❑ 9801 [PS]	Thunderball/Key to My Heart	1965	3.00	6.00	12.00
—Version 2: without the above elements on sleeve					
❑ 9809	Promise Her Anything/Little You	1966	2.00	4.00	8.00
❑ 40006	Not Responsible/Once There Was a Time	1966	2.00	4.00	8.00
❑ 40008	City Girl/What a Party	1966	2.00	4.00	8.00
❑ 40009	Green, Green Grass of Home/If I Had You	1966	2.00	4.00	8.00
❑ 40012	Detroit City/Ten Guitars	1967	2.00	4.00	8.00
❑ 40014	Funny Familiar Forgotten Feelings/I'll Never Let You Go	1967	2.00	4.00	8.00
❑ 40016	Sixteen Tons/Things I Wanna Do	1967	2.00	4.00	8.00
❑ 40018	I'll Never Fall in Love Again/Once Upon a Time	1967	3.00	6.00	12.00
—First pressings contain the full-length version of the A-side; time is listed at over four minutes					
❑ 40018	I'll Never Fall in Love Again/Once Upon a Time	1967	2.00	4.00	8.00
—Later pressings delete a verse from the A-side; time is listed at 2:55					
❑ 40020	Land of a Thousand Dances/I Can't Stop Loving You	1967	5.00	10.00	20.00
—May be promo only					
❑ 40024	I'm Coming Home/Lonely One	1967	2.00	4.00	8.00
❑ 40025	Delilah/Smile Away Your Blues	1968	2.00	4.00	8.00
❑ 40029	Help Yourself/Day by Day	1968	2.00	4.00	8.00
❑ 40035	A Minute of Your Time/Looking Out My Window	1968	2.00	4.00	8.00
❑ 40038	Love Me Tonight/Hide and Seek	1969	—	3.00	6.00
❑ 40038 [PS]	Love Me Tonight/Hide and Seek	1969	2.00	4.00	8.00
❑ 40045	Without Love (There Is Nothing)/The Man Who Knows Too Much	1969	—	3.00	6.00
❑ 40045 [PS]	Without Love (There Is Nothing)/The Man Who Knows Too Much	1969	2.00	4.00	8.00
❑ 40048	Daughter of Darkness/Tupelo Mississippi Flash	1970	—	3.00	6.00
❑ 40048 [PS]	Daughter of Darkness/Tupelo Mississippi Flash	1970	2.00	4.00	8.00
❑ 40051	I (Who Have Nothing)/Stop Breaking My Heart	1970	—	3.00	6.00
❑ 40051 [PS]	I (Who Have Nothing)/Stop Breaking My Heart	1970	2.00	4.00	8.00
❑ 40056	Can't Stop Loving You/Never Give Away Love	1970	—	3.00	6.00
❑ 40056 [PS]	Can't Stop Loving You/Never Give Away Love	1970	2.00	4.00	8.00
❑ 40058	She's a Lady/My Way	1971	—	3.00	6.00
❑ 40058 [PS]	She's a Lady/My Way	1971	2.00	4.00	8.00
❑ 40062	Puppet Man/Every Mile	1971	—	3.00	6.00
❑ 40064	Puppet Man/Resurrection Shuffle	1971	—	2.50	5.00
❑ 40067	Till/One Day Soon	1971	—	2.50	5.00
❑ 40070	The Young New Mexican Puppeteer/All That I Need Is Time	1972	—	2.50	5.00
❑ 40074	Letter to Lucille/Thank the Lord	1973	—	2.50	5.00
❑ 40078	La, La, La (Just Having You Here)/Love, Love, Love	1973	—	2.50	5.00
❑ 40080	Somethin' 'Bout You Baby I Like/Keep a-Talkin' 'Bout Love	1973	—	2.50	5.00
❑ 40081	Pledging My Love/I'm Too Far Gone	1974	—	2.50	5.00
❑ 40083	Ain't No Love/When the Band Goes Home	1974	—	2.50	5.00
❑ 40084	I Got Your Number/The Pain of Love	1974	—	2.50	5.00

Number	Title (A Side/B Side)	Yr	VG	VG+	NM
❑ 40086	Memories Don't Leave Like People Do/Helping Hand	1975	—	2.50	5.00

TOWER

Number	Title (A Side/B Side)	Yr	VG	VG+	NM
❑ 126	Little Lonely One/That's What We'll All Do	1965	3.00	6.00	12.00
❑ 126 [PS]	Little Lonely One/That's What We'll All Do	1965	5.00	10.00	20.00
❑ 176	Lonely One/I Was a Fool	1965	3.00	6.00	12.00
❑ 176 [PS]	Lonely One/I Was a Fool	1965	5.00	10.00	20.00
❑ 190	Baby I'm in Love/Chills and Fever	1966	2.50	5.00	10.00

Albums

EPIC

Number	Title (A Side/B Side)	Yr	VG	VG+	NM
❑ PE 34383	Classic Tom Jones	1976	3.00	6.00	12.00
❑ PE 34468	Say You'll Stay Until Tomorrow	1977	3.00	6.00	12.00
❑ PE 34720	Tom Is Love	1977	2.50	5.00	10.00
❑ JE 35023	What a Night	1978	2.50	5.00	10.00

JIVE

Number	Title (A Side/B Side)	Yr	VG	VG+	NM
❑ 1214-1-J	Move Closer	1989	3.00	6.00	12.00

LONDON

Number	Title (A Side/B Side)	Yr	VG	VG+	NM
❑ PS 717	The Country Side of Tom Jones	1978	2.50	5.00	10.00
❑ LC-50002	Tom Jones' Greatest Hits	1977	3.00	6.00	12.00
❑ 820234-1	This Is Tom Jones	1985	2.00	4.00	8.00
❑ 820319-1	Tom Jones' Greatest Hits	1985	2.50	5.00	10.00

MCA

Number	Title (A Side/B Side)	Yr	VG	VG+	NM
❑ 3182	Tom Jones	1979	2.50	5.00	10.00
❑ 37114	Rescue Me	1980	2.00	4.00	8.00

MERCURY

Number	Title (A Side/B Side)	Yr	VG	VG+	NM
❑ SRM-1-4010	Darlin'	1981	2.50	5.00	10.00
❑ SRM-1-4062	Tom Jones Country	1982	2.50	5.00	10.00
❑ 814448-1	Don't Let Our Dreams Die Young	1983	2.50	5.00	10.00
❑ 822701-1	Love Is on the Radio	1984	2.50	5.00	10.00
❑ 826140-1	Tender Loving Care	1985	2.50	5.00	10.00
❑ 830409-1	Things That Matter Most to Me	1987	2.50	5.00	10.00

PARROT

Number	Title (A Side/B Side)	Yr	VG	VG+	NM
❑ XPAS-1 [DJ]	Special Tom Jones Interview	1970	25.00	50.00	100.00
—Promo-only open-end interview with gatefold cover and script					
❑ PA 61004 [M]	It's Not Unusual	1965	3.75	7.50	15.00
❑ PA 61006 [M]	What's New Pussycat?	1965	3.75	7.50	15.00
❑ PA 61007 [M]	A-Tom-Ic Jones	1966	3.75	7.50	15.00
❑ PA 61009 [M]	Green, Green Grass of Home	1967	3.75	7.50	15.00
❑ PA 61011 [M]	Funny Familiar Forgotten Feelings	1967	3.75	7.50	15.00
❑ PA 61014 [M]	Tom Jones Live	1967	3.75	7.50	15.00
❑ PAS 71004 [S]	It's Not Unusual	1965	3.75	7.50	15.00
❑ PAS 71006 [S]	What's New Pussycat?	1965	3.75	7.50	15.00
❑ PAS 71007 [S]	A-Tom-Ic Jones	1966	3.75	7.50	15.00
❑ PAS 71009 [S]	Green, Green Grass of Home	1967	3.75	7.50	15.00
❑ PAS 71011 [S]	Funny Familiar Forgotten Feelings	1967	3.75	7.50	15.00
❑ PAS 71014 [S]	Tom Jones Live	1967	3.75	7.50	15.00
❑ PAS 71019	The Tom Jones Fever Zone	1968	3.00	6.00	12.00
❑ PAS 71025	Help Yourself	1969	3.00	6.00	12.00
❑ PAS 71028	This Is Tom Jones	1969	3.00	6.00	12.00
❑ PAS 71031	Live in Las Vegas	1969	3.00	6.00	12.00
❑ PAS 71037	Tom	1970	3.00	6.00	12.00
❑ PAS 71039	I (Who Have Nothing)	1970	3.00	6.00	12.00
❑ PAS 71046	She's a Lady	1971	3.00	6.00	12.00
❑ PAS 71049	Live at Caesar's Palace	1971	3.00	6.00	12.00
❑ XPAS 71055	Close Up	1972	3.00	6.00	12.00
❑ XPAS 71060	The Body and Soul of Tom Jones	197?	3.00	6.00	12.00
❑ XPAS 71062	Tom Jones' Greatest Hits	1973	3.00	6.00	12.00
❑ PAS 71066	Somethin' 'Bout You Baby I Like	1974	3.00	6.00	12.00
❑ PAS 71068	Memories Don't Leave Like People Do	197?	3.00	6.00	12.00

JORDAN, JERRY

45s

MCA

Number	Title (A Side/B Side)	Yr	VG	VG+	NM
❑ 40639	What It Was, Was Football/Phone Call from God	1976	—	2.00	4.00

Albums

MCA

Number	Title (A Side/B Side)	Yr	VG	VG+	NM
❑ 473	Phone Call from God	1975	2.50	5.00	10.00
❑ 2174	Don't Call Me... I'll Call You	1976	2.50	5.00	10.00

JORDAN, JILL

45s

MAXX

Number	Title (A Side/B Side)	Yr	VG	VG+	NM
❑ 822	Calendar Blues/(B-side unknown)	1988	—	3.00	6.00
❑ 823	I Did It for Love/(B-side unknown)	1988	—	3.00	6.00

JORDAN, LOUIS

Bandleader, R&B star and rock 'n' roll pioneer, he actually had two Number One hits on the Billboard country charts, both of which are listed below.

Selected 78s

DECCA

Number	Title (A Side/B Side)	Yr	VG	VG+	NM
❑ 8654	Ration Blues/Deacon Jones	1943	5.00	10.00	20.00
❑ 8659	Is You Is or Is You Ain't (Ma' Baby)/G.I. Jive	1944	5.00	10.00	20.00

JORDAN, PETER

45s

MC

Number	Title (A Side/B Side)	Yr	VG	VG+	NM
❑ 5006	What We Do Two by Two/Broken Bones	1978	—	2.50	5.00

JORDANAIRES, THE

45s

CAPITOL

Number	Title (A Side/B Side)	Yr	VG	VG+	NM
❑ F1254	Working on the Building/I Want to Rest	1950	7.50	15.00	30.00
❑ F1363	David and Goliath/Journey to the Sky	1951	6.25	12.50	25.00
❑ F1407	One Day/Something Within	1951	6.25	12.50	25.00
❑ F1499	He Bought My Soul/Read That Book	1951	6.25	12.50	25.00
❑ F2725	Tattler's Wagon/In My Saviour's Loving Arms	1954	5.00	10.00	20.00
❑ F2815	Bugle Call from Heaven/Oh Lord Stand By Me	1954	5.00	10.00	20.00
❑ F2915	This Ole House/Be Prepared	1954	5.00	10.00	20.00
❑ F3022	When the Saints Go Marching In/All the Way	1955	5.00	10.00	20.00
❑ F3158	Let's Make a Joyful Noise/Will You Be Ready	1955	5.00	10.00	20.00
❑ F3265	Shaking Bridges/What Will the Verdict Be	1955	5.00	10.00	20.00
❑ F3356	A House of Gold/Blow, Whistle, Blow	1956	5.00	10.00	20.00
❑ F3420	Rock 'n Roll Religion/Do Unto Others	1956	5.00	10.00	20.00
❑ F3492	Hands of God/Fighting for the Lord	1956	5.00	10.00	20.00
❑ F3610	Sugaree/Baby Won't You Please Come Home	1957	5.00	10.00	20.00
❑ F3684	Walk Away/Ridin' for a Fall	1957	5.00	10.00	20.00
❑ F3750	Summer Vacation/Each Day	1957	5.00	10.00	20.00
❑ F3807	Any Which-a-Way/Mood for the Blues	1957	5.00	10.00	20.00
❑ F3940	Little Miss Ruby/All I Need Is You	1958	3.75	7.50	15.00
❑ F4025	Wella Wella Honey/Where Many Go	1958	3.75	7.50	15.00
❑ 4431	Sit Down/Girl in the Valley	1960	3.00	6.00	12.00

COLUMBIA

Number	Title (A Side/B Side)	Yr	VG	VG+	NM
❑ 4-43283	Malibu Run/Who Does He Think He Is	1965	2.50	5.00	10.00
—Said to be a different group than the rest.					

DECCA

Number	Title (A Side/B Side)	Yr	VG	VG+	NM
❑ 9-46242	Dig a Little Deeper/I'm Free Again	1950	10.00	20.00	40.00
❑ 9-46366	Loafin' on a Lazy River/Sweet Roses of Morn	1951	6.25	12.50	25.00

DECCA FAITH SERIES

Number	Title (A Side/B Side)	Yr	VG	VG+	NM
❑ 9-14530	Peace in the Valley/(B-side unknown)	1950	7.50	15.00	30.00

RCA VICTOR

Number	Title (A Side/B Side)	Yr	VG	VG+	NM
❑ 47-4378	The Four Horsemen (Of the Apocalypse)/Mansion Over the Hilltop	1951	6.25	12.50	25.00
❑ 47-4607	Who Can He Be/Gonna Walk Those Golden Stairs	1952	6.25	12.50	25.00
❑ 47-4645	Goodbye Pharaoh/Roll, Jordan, Roll	1952	6.25	12.50	25.00
❑ 47-4943	Rag Mama/I Never Will Marry	1952	6.25	12.50	25.00
❑ 47-4948	My Rock/I'll Tell It Wherever I Go	1952	6.25	12.50	25.00
❑ 47-5021	He'll Understand and Say Well Done/I'm Moving On to Glory	1952	6.25	12.50	25.00
❑ 47-5076	Beautiful City/Stand by Me	1952	5.00	10.00	20.00
❑ 47-5077	By the River of Life/Noah	1952	5.00	10.00	20.00
❑ 47-5078	You Better Run/Dry Bones	1952	5.00	10.00	20.00
❑ 47-5079	When Dey Ring Dem Golden Bells/Didn't They Crucify My Lord	1952	5.00	10.00	20.00
❑ 47-5373	On the Jericho Road/The Lord Will Make a Way Somehow	1953	6.25	12.50	25.00
❑ 47-5458	Is He Satisfied/I Am So Glad Jesus Lifted Me	1953	6.25	12.50	25.00

STOP

Number	Title (A Side/B Side)	Yr	VG	VG+	NM
❑ 259	You're Wasting Your Time Girl/A Hundred Years of Real Estate	1969	2.00	4.00	8.00

"X"

Number	Title (A Side/B Side)	Yr	VG	VG+	NM
❑ 0034	Say It Again/I Can't Smoke You Out of My Heart	1954	5.00	10.00	20.00

Selected 78s

DECCA

Number	Title (A Side/B Side)	Yr	VG	VG+	NM
❑ 46198	Just a Little Talk with Jesus/Old Ship of Zion	1950	5.00	10.00	20.00

7-Inch Extended Plays

SESAC

Number	Title (A Side/B Side)	Yr	VG	VG+	NM
❑ AD 46	Wanderin'/John Henry//Honey Baby Mine/Twenty-One Froggies	195?	5.00	10.00	20.00
❑ AD 46 [PS]	Songs of the Plains	195?	5.00	10.00	20.00

Albums

CAPITOL

Number	Title (A Side/B Side)	Yr	VG	VG+	NM
❑ T 1011 [M]	Heavenly Spirit	1958	10.00	20.00	40.00
❑ T 1167 [M]	Gloryland	1959	10.00	20.00	40.00
❑ ST 1311 [S]	Land of Jordan	1960	10.00	20.00	40.00
❑ T 1311 [M]	Land of Jordan	1960	7.50	15.00	30.00
❑ ST 1559 [S]	To God Be the Glory	1961	6.25	12.50	25.00
❑ T 1559 [M]	To God Be the Glory	1961	5.00	10.00	20.00
❑ ST 1742 [S]	Spotlight on the Jordanaires	1962	7.50	15.00	30.00
❑ T 1742 [M]	Spotlight on the Jordanaires	1962	6.25	12.50	25.00

CLASSIC

Number	Title (A Side/B Side)	Yr	VG	VG+	NM
❑ CCR 1935	Christmas to Elvis from the Jordanaires	1978	3.00	6.00	12.00

COLUMBIA

Number	Title (A Side/B Side)	Yr	VG	VG+	NM
❑ CL 2214 [M]	This Land	1964	5.00	10.00	20.00
❑ CL 2458 [M]	The Big Country Hits	1966	5.00	10.00	20.00
❑ CS 9014 [S]	This Land	1964	6.25	12.50	25.00
❑ CS 9258 [S]	The Big Country Hits	1966	6.25	12.50	25.00

DECCA

Number	Title (A Side/B Side)	Yr	VG	VG+	NM
❑ DL 8681 [M]	Peace in the Valley	1957	12.50	25.00	50.00

RCA VICTOR

Number	Title (A Side/B Side)	Yr	VG	VG+	NM
❑ LPM-3081 [10]	Beautiful City	1953	25.00	50.00	100.00

SESAC

Number	Title (A Side/B Side)	Yr	VG	VG+	NM
❑ 1401/2 [M]	Of Rivers and Plains	195?	20.00	40.00	80.00

JOY, HOMER

45s

CAPITOL

Number	Title (A Side/B Side)	Yr	VG	VG+	NM
❑ 3767	Holdin' On/Southern California Sand	1973	—	2.50	5.00
❑ 3834	John Law/Ain't No Sunshine All the Time	1974	—	2.50	5.00
❑ 4068	I Could Never See Love in Your Eyes/Sure Didn't Take Him Long	1975	—	2.50	5.00

JOYCE, BRENDA

45s

WESTERN PACIFIC

Number	Title (A Side/B Side)	Yr	VG	VG+	NM
❑ 107	Don't Touch Me/I've Been Burned	1979	2.00	4.00	8.00

JUDD, CLEDUS T.

45s

MONUMENT

Number	Title (A Side/B Side)	Yr	VG	VG+	NM
❑ 31 79495	My Cellmate Thinks I'm Sexy/My Cellmate Thinks I'm Sexy (Dance Mix)	2000	—	—	3.00

RAZOR & TIE

Number	Title (A Side/B Side)	Yr	VG	VG+	NM
❑ 80741	Wives Do It All the Time/First Redneck on the Internet	1998	—	—	3.00
—B-side with Buck Owens					
❑ 80754	Everybody's Free (To Get Sunburned) (5:56)/ same (4:18)	1999	—	—	3.00
❑ 80764	Coronary Life/Livin' Like John Travolta	2000	—	—	3.00
❑ 80767	Christ-Mas/Grandpa Got Runned Over by a John Deere	1999	—	—	3.00

JUDD, WYNONNA

Includes records as "Wynonna." Also see THE JUDDS.

45s

CURB/MCA

Number	Title (A Side/B Side)	Yr	VG	VG+	NM
❑ 54320	She Is His Only Need/No One Else on Earth	1992	—	2.50	5.00
❑ 54407	I Saw the Light/When I Reach the Place I'm Goin'	1992	—	2.50	5.00
❑ 54449	No One Else on Earth (Dance Remix)/No One Else on Earth	1992	—	3.00	6.00
❑ 54516	My Strongest Weakness/What It Takes	1992	—	2.00	4.00
❑ 54606	Tell Me Why/A Little Bit of Love (Goes a Long, Long Way)	1993	—	2.50	5.00
❑ 54689	Only Love/Just Like New	1993	—	2.00	4.00
❑ 54754	Is It Over Yet/That Was Yesterday	1993	—	2.00	4.00
❑ 54809	Rock Bottom/Girls with Guitars	1994	—	2.00	4.00
❑ 54875	Girls with Guitars/I Just Drove By	1994	—	2.00	4.00
❑ 55084	To Be Loved by You/Freebird	1995	—	2.00	4.00
❑ 55194	Heaven Help My Heart/Heaven Help My Heart (Album Version)	1996	—	—	3.00
❑ 55252	My Angel Is Here/Change the World	1996	—	—	3.00
❑ 55286	Somebody to Love You/Somebody to Love You (Club Mix)	1996	—	—	3.00

CURB/UNIVERSAL

Number	Title (A Side/B Side)	Yr	VG	VG+	NM
❑ 56095	When Love Starts Talkin'/The Other Side	1997	—	—	3.00
—As "Wynonna"					

MERCURY

Number	Title (A Side/B Side)	Yr	VG	VG+	NM
❑ 088-172141-7	Can't Nobody Love You (Like I Do)/Help Me	1999	—	—	3.00
❑ 088-172155-7	(Without Your Love)...I'm Going Nowhere/Who Am I Trying to Fool	2000	—	—	3.00

Albums

MCA

Number	Title (A Side/B Side)	Yr	VG	VG+	NM
❑ 1P-8201	Wynonna	1992	6.25	12.50	25.00

—Only released on vinyl through Columbia House; label misspells her name as "Wyonna"!

JUDDS, THE

Also see WYNONNA JUDD.

45s

RCA

Number	Title (A Side/B Side)	Yr	VG	VG+	NM
❑ 2524-7-R	Guardian Angels/Cadillac Red	1990	—	2.00	4.00
❑ 2597-7-R	Born to Be Blue/Rompin' Stompin' Blues	1990	—	2.00	4.00
❑ 2708-7-R	Love Can Build a Bridge/This Country's Rockin'	1990	—	2.00	4.00
❑ 2782-7-R	One Hundred and Two/Are The Roses Not Blooming	1991	—	2.00	4.00
❑ 5000-7-R	Cry Myself to Sleep/Dream Chaser	1986	—	—	3.00
❑ 5048-7-R	Who Is This Babe/Light of the Stable	1986	—	—	3.00
❑ 5094-7-R	Don't Be Cruel/The Sweetest Gift	1987	—	—	3.00
❑ 5094-7-R [PS]	Don't Be Cruel/The Sweetest Gift	1987	—	3.00	6.00
—Sleeve may be promo only					
❑ 5164-7-R	I Know Where I'm Going/If I Were You	1987	—	—	3.00
❑ 5184-7-R	Rockin' with the Rhythm of the Rain/Cry Myself to Sleep	1987	—	—	3.00
—"Gold Standard Series" reissue					
❑ 5255-7-R	Maybe Your Baby's Got the Blues/My Baby's Gone	1987	—	—	3.00
❑ 5329-7-R	Turn It Loose/Cow Cow Boogie	1987	—	—	3.00
❑ 5350-7-R	Silver Bells/Away in a Manger	1987	—	—	3.00
❑ 8300-7-R	Give a Little Love/Why Don't You Believe Me	1988	—	—	3.00
❑ 8383-7-R	Turn It Loose/Maybe Your Baby's Got the Blues	1988	—	—	3.00
—Gold Standard Series					
❑ 8715-7-R	Change of Heart/I Wish She Wouldn't Treat You That Way	1988	—	—	3.00
❑ 8820-7-R	Young Love/Cow Cow Boogie	1988	—	—	3.00
❑ 8947-7-R	Let Me Tell You About Love/Water of Love	1989	—	—	3.00
❑ 9069-7-R	Silver Bells/Oh Holy Night	1989	—	2.00	4.00
❑ 9077-7-R	One Man Woman/Sleepless Nights	1989	—	—	3.00
❑ PB-13673	Had a Dream (For the Heart)/Don't You Hear Jerusalem Moan	1983	—	2.50	5.00
❑ PB-13673 [DJ]	Had a Dream (For the Heart) (same on both sides)	1983	5.00	10.00	20.00
—Promo only on red vinyl					
❑ PB-13772	Mama He's Crazy/Down Home	1984	—	2.00	4.00
❑ PB-13906	Light of the Stable/Change of Heart	1984	—	2.00	4.00
❑ PB-13923	Why Not Me/Lazy Country Evening	1984	—	2.00	4.00
❑ PB-13991	Girls Night Out/Sleeping Heart	1985	—	2.00	4.00
❑ GB-14068	Mama He's Crazy/Why Not Me	1985	—	—	3.00
—Gold Standard Series					
❑ PB-14093	Love Is Alive/Mr. Pain	1985	—	2.00	4.00
❑ PB-14193	Have Mercy/Bye Bye Blues	1985	—	2.00	4.00
❑ PB-14240	Who Is This Babe/Change of Heart	1985	—	2.00	4.00
❑ PB-14290	Grandpa (Tell Me 'Bout the Good Old Days)/ Drops of Water	1986	—	2.00	4.00
❑ GB-14348	Girls Night Out/Love Is Alive	1986	—	—	3.00
—Gold Standard Series					
❑ GB-14352	Why Not Me/Have Mercy	1986	—	—	3.00
—Gold Standard Series					
❑ PB-14362	Rockin' with the Rhythm of the Rain/River Roll On	1986	—	2.00	4.00
❑ 62038	John Deere Tractor/Calling in the Wind	1991	—	2.00	4.00

Albums

HEARTLAND

Number	Title (A Side/B Side)	Yr	VG	VG+	NM
❑ HL-2041 [(2)]	Classic Gold	1992	5.00	10.00	20.00

RCA

Number	Title (A Side/B Side)	Yr	VG	VG+	NM
❑ 5916-1-R	Heartland	1987	2.50	5.00	10.00
❑ 6422-1-R	Christmas Time with the Judds	1987	2.50	5.00	10.00
❑ 8318-1-R	Greatest Hits	1988	2.50	5.00	10.00
❑ 9595-1-R	River of Time	1989	3.00	6.00	12.00

RCA VICTOR

Number	Title (A Side/B Side)	Yr	VG	VG+	NM
❑ AHL1-5319	Why Not Me	1984	2.50	5.00	10.00
❑ AHL1-7042	Rockin' with the Rhythm	1985	2.50	5.00	10.00
❑ MHL1-8515 [EP]	The Judds	1984	2.00	4.00	8.00

JURGENS, DICK

A pop bandleader and composer, he had this one country hit.

Selected 78s

COLUMBIA

Number	Title (A Side/B Side)	Yr	VG	VG+	NM
❑ 37210	(Oh Why, Oh Why, Did I Ever Leave) Wyoming/ Bless You	1947	3.00	6.00	12.00

JUSTIS, BILL

45s

BELL

Number	Title (A Side/B Side)	Yr	VG	VG+	NM
❑ 921	Electric Dreams/Dark Continent Contribution	1970	—	2.50	5.00

MCA

Number	Title (A Side/B Side)	Yr	VG	VG+	NM
❑ 40810	Foxy Lady/Orange Blossom Special	1977	—	2.00	4.00

MONUMENT

Number	Title (A Side/B Side)	Yr	VG	VG+	NM
❑ 956	Yellow Summer/So Until I See You	1966	2.50	5.00	10.00
❑ 8699	Sea Dream/Touching, Feeling, Dreaming	1976	—	2.50	5.00

NRC

Number	Title (A Side/B Side)	Yr	VG	VG+	NM
❑ 1119	Blowing Rock/Boogie Woogie Rock	1959	5.00	10.00	20.00

PHILLIPS INTERNATIONAL

Number	Title (A Side/B Side)	Yr	VG	VG+	NM
❑ 3519	Raunchy/Midnight Man	1957	5.00	10.00	20.00
❑ 3522	College Man/The Stranger	1958	5.00	10.00	20.00
❑ 3525	Wild Ride/Scroungie	1958	5.00	10.00	20.00
❑ 3529	Cattywampus/Summer Holiday	1958	5.00	10.00	20.00
❑ 3535	Bop Train/String of Pearls	1958	5.00	10.00	20.00
❑ 3544	Flea Circus/Cloud Nine	1959	5.00	10.00	20.00

SMASH

Number	Title (A Side/B Side)	Yr	VG	VG+	NM
❑ 1812	I'm Gonna Learn to Dance/Tamoure	1963	2.50	5.00	10.00
❑ 1812 [PS]	I'm Gonna Learn to Dance/Tamoure	1963	4.00	8.00	16.00
❑ 1851	Sunday in Madrid/Satin and Velvet	1963	2.50	5.00	10.00
❑ 1902	Lavender Sax/Fia, Fia	1964	2.50	5.00	10.00
❑ 1955	How Soon/Ska-Ha	1964	2.50	5.00	10.00
❑ 1977	Late Game/Last Farewell	1965	2.50	5.00	10.00

Albums

HARMONY

Number	Title (A Side/B Side)	Yr	VG	VG+	NM
❑ KH 31189	Enchanted Sea	1972	3.00	6.00	12.00

MONUMENT

Number	Title (A Side/B Side)	Yr	VG	VG+	NM
❑ MLP 8078 [M]	The Eternal Sea	1967	3.75	7.50	15.00
❑ SLP 18078 [S]	The Eternal Sea	1967	3.75	7.50	15.00

PHILLIPS INTERNATIONAL

Number	Title (A Side/B Side)	Yr	VG	VG+	NM
❑ PLP-1950 [M]	Cloud Nine	1959	100.00	200.00	400.00

SMASH

Number	Title (A Side/B Side)	Yr	VG	VG+	NM
❑ MGS-27021 [M]	Bill Justis Plays 12 Big Instrumental Hits (Alley Cat/Green Onions)	1962	3.75	7.50	15.00
❑ MGS-27030 [M]	Bill Justis Plays 12 More Big Instrumental Hits (Telstar/The Lonely Bull)	1963	3.75	7.50	15.00
❑ MGS-27031 [M]	Bill Justis Plays 12 Smash Instrumental Hits	1963	3.75	7.50	15.00
❑ MGS-27036 [M]	Bill Justis Plays 12 Top Tunes	1963	3.75	7.50	15.00
❑ MGS-27043 [M]	Bill Justis Plays 12 Other Instrumental Hits	1964	3.75	7.50	15.00
❑ MGS-27047 [M]	Dixieland Folk Style	1964	3.75	7.50	15.00
❑ MGS-27065 [M]	More Instrumental Hits	1965	3.75	7.50	15.00
❑ MGS-27077 [M]	Taste of Honey/The "In" Crowd	1966	3.75	7.50	15.00
❑ SRS-67021 [S]	Bill Justis Plays 12 Big Instrumental Hits (Alley Cat/Green Onions)	1962	5.00	10.00	20.00
❑ SRS-67030 [S]	Bill Justis Plays 12 More Big Instrumental Hits (Telstar/The Lonely Bull)	1963	5.00	10.00	20.00
❑ SRS-67031 [S]	Bill Justis Plays 12 Smash Instrumental Hits	1963	5.00	10.00	20.00
❑ SRS-67036 [S]	Bill Justis Plays 12 Top Tunes	1963	5.00	10.00	20.00
❑ SRS-67043 [S]	Bill Justis Plays 12 Other Instrumental Hits	1964	5.00	10.00	20.00
❑ SRS-67047 [S]	Dixieland Folk Style	1964	5.00	10.00	20.00
❑ SRS-67065 [S]	More Instrumental Hits	1965	5.00	10.00	20.00
❑ SRS-67077 [S]	Taste of Honey/The "In" Crowd	1966	5.00	10.00	20.00
❑ 830898-1	Raunchy	1987	2.50	5.00	10.00

SUN

Number	Title (A Side/B Side)	Yr	VG	VG+	NM
❑ LP-109	Raunchy	1969	3.00	6.00	12.00

K

KALIN TWINS, THE

45s

AMY

Number	Title (A Side/B Side)	Yr	VG	VG+	NM
❑ 969	Thinkin' About You Baby/Sometimes It Comes	1966	2.00	4.00	8.00

DECCA

Number	Title (A Side/B Side)	Yr	VG	VG+	NM
❑ 30552	Jumpin' Jack/Walkin' to School	1958	5.00	10.00	20.00
❑ 30642	When/Three O'Clock Thrill	1958	6.25	12.50	25.00
❑ 30745	Forget Me Not/Dream of Me	1958	6.25	12.50	25.00
❑ 30807	It's Only the Beginning/Oh My Goodness	1959	5.00	10.00	20.00
❑ 30868	Cool/When I Look in the Mirror	1959	5.00	10.00	20.00
❑ 30911	Sweet Sugar Lips/Moody	1959	5.00	10.00	20.00
❑ 30977	Why Don't You Believe Me/The Meaning of the Blues	1959	5.00	10.00	20.00
❑ 30977 [PS]	Why Don't You Believe Me/The Meaning of the Blues	1959	7.50	15.00	30.00
❑ 31064	Loneliness/Chicken Thief	1960	3.75	7.50	15.00
❑ 31111	True to You/Blue, Blue Town	1960	3.75	7.50	15.00
❑ 31169	Zing! Went the Strings of My Heart/No Money Can Buy	1960	3.75	7.50	15.00
❑ 31220	Momma-Poppa/You Mean the World to Me	1961	3.75	7.50	15.00
❑ 31286	Bubbles (I'm Forever Blowing Bubbles)/One More Time	1961	3.75	7.50	15.00
❑ 31410	Trouble/A Picture of You	1962	3.75	7.50	15.00

7-Inch Extended Plays

DECCA

Number	Title (A Side/B Side)	Yr	VG	VG+	NM
❑ ED 2623	(contents unknown)	1958	15.00	30.00	60.00
❑ ED 2623 [PS]	When	1958	20.00	40.00	80.00
❑ ED 2641	(contents unknown)	1958	12.50	25.00	50.00
❑ ED 2641 [PS]	Forget Me Not	1958	15.00	30.00	60.00

Albums

DECCA

Number	Title (A Side/B Side)	Yr	VG	VG+	NM
❑ DL 8812 [M]	The Kalin Twins	1959	25.00	50.00	100.00

VOCALION

Number	Title (A Side/B Side)	Yr	VG	VG+	NM
❑ VL 3771 [M]	When	1966	3.75	7.50	15.00
❑ VL 73771 [R]	When	1966	3.00	6.00	12.00

KALLIE JEAN

45s

HICKORY

Number	Title (A Side/B Side)	Yr	VG	VG+	NM
❑ 1615	Eight Track Player Boy/All I Really Need Is You	1971	2.00	4.00	8.00
❑ 1633	Jerry Jones/I'll Come Running	1972	2.00	4.00	8.00
❑ 1657	One-Fourth Heaven, Three-Fourths Hell/ Outgrowing the Father	1973	2.00	4.00	8.00
❑ 1672	If You Care Enough/It Takes a Good Man to Keep Up with a Good Woman	1973	2.00	4.00	8.00

HICKORY/MGM

Number	Title (A Side/B Side)	Yr	VG	VG+	NM
❑ 309	If You Care Enough/I'll Come Running	1973	—	3.00	6.00

KANDY, JIM

45s

K-ARK

Number	Title (A Side/B Side)	Yr	VG	VG+	NM
❑ 635	Strangers/Looking Through a Teardrop	1965	3.75	7.50	15.00
❑ 637	Cocaine Blues/Only Girl for Me	1965	3.75	7.50	15.00
❑ 647	I'm the Man/Angelville + Sky	1965	3.75	7.50	15.00
❑ 664	How Great Thou Art/Where No One Stands Alone	1966	3.75	7.50	15.00
❑ 672	Cheaters Never Win/Flip a Coin	1966	3.75	7.50	15.00
❑ 673	Everybody But Me Wants to Go Home/Which One	1966	3.75	7.50	15.00
❑ 709	From Your House to Hers/Wake Up in the Morning	1967	3.75	7.50	15.00

KANE, KIERAN

Also see THE O'KANES.

45s

ATLANTIC

Number	Title (A Side/B Side)	Yr	VG	VG+	NM
❑ 7-87311	I'm Here to Love You/Forgive and Forget	1993	—	—	3.00

ELEKTRA

Number	Title (A Side/B Side)	Yr	VG	VG+	NM
❑ 47111	The Baby/I Don't Drink from the River	1981	—	2.00	4.00
❑ 47148	You're the Best/Finishing Touches	1981	—	2.00	4.00
❑ 47228	It's Who You Love/Doctor's Orders	1981	—	2.00	4.00
❑ 47415	I Feel It with You/She's Looking for Something New	1982	—	2.00	4.00
❑ 47478	I'll Be Your Man Around the House/Blue All Over You	1982	—	2.00	4.00
❑ 69943	Gonna Have a Party/As Long As I'm Rockin' with You	1982	—	2.00	4.00

WARNER BROS.

Number	Title (A Side/B Side)	Yr	VG	VG+	NM
❑ 29336	Dedicate/Surrender to Your Heart	1984	—	—	3.00
❑ 29711	It's You/Makin' It Up	1983	—	—	3.00

Albums

ELEKTRA

Number	Title (A Side/B Side)	Yr	VG	VG+	NM
❑ 60004	Kieran Kane	1982	2.50	5.00	10.00

KANTER, HILLARY

45s

MCA

Number	Title (A Side/B Side)	Yr	VG	VG+	NM
❑ 53225	Lonely Again/Looks Like It's Gonna Rain Today	1987	—	—	3.00

RCA

Number	Title (A Side/B Side)	Yr	VG	VG+	NM
❑ PB-13835	Good Night for Falling in Love/I Couldn't Help Myself	1984	—	—	3.00
❑ PB-13935	Hey/My Heart's Saying Yes	1984	—	—	3.00
❑ PB-14053	We Work/Harbor of Your Heart	1985	—	—	3.00
❑ PB-14185	It's Such a Heartache/(B-side unknown)	1985	—	—	3.00

KAY, MELISSA

45s

REED

Number	Title (A Side/B Side)	Yr	VG	VG+	NM
❑ 1115	Don't Forget Your Way Home/(B-side unknown)	1988	—	3.00	6.00
❑ 1119	After Lovin' You/(B-side unknown)	1988	—	3.00	6.00
❑ 1121	Angel Fire/(B-side unknown)	1988	—	3.00	6.00
❑ 1123	Poison Sugar/(B-side unknown)	1989	—	3.00	6.00

KAYE, ANGELA

45s

YATAHEY

Number	Title (A Side/B Side)	Yr	VG	VG+	NM
❑ 804	Catching Fire/(B-side unknown)	1981	—	3.00	6.00

KAYE, BARRY

45s

MCA

Number	Title (A Side/B Side)	Yr	VG	VG+	NM
❑ 40868	Easy/Life	1978	—	2.50	5.00
❑ 40939	Cheatin'/How Many Tears Will It Take	1978	—	2.50	5.00

PAID

Number	Title (A Side/B Side)	Yr	VG	VG+	NM
❑ 114	Randolph The Redneck Reindeer/The Season to Be Lonely	1980	—	3.00	6.00

KAYE, DEBBIE LORI

45s

COLUMBIA

Number	Title (A Side/B Side)	Yr	VG	VG+	NM
❑ 4-43295	What Makes You Do Me Like You Do/Pick Up My Hat	1965	2.50	5.00	10.00
❑ 4-43454	Soldier Boy/Could That Be	1965	2.50	5.00	10.00
❑ 4-43591	Every Song You Sing/You're Not There	1966	2.00	4.00	8.00
❑ 4-43730	The Iron Cross/Baby What I Mean	1966	2.00	4.00	8.00
❑ 4-43999	Lonely Clown/The Playground	1967	2.00	4.00	8.00
❑ 4-44142	Legend in My Time/Sweet Georgia Brown	1967	2.00	4.00	8.00
❑ 4-44311	Break My Mind/Ride, Ride, Ride	1967	2.00	4.00	8.00
❑ 4-44538	Come On Home/Help Me Love You	1968	2.00	4.00	8.00
❑ 4-44815	Baby's Come Home/It's Only a Daydream	1969	2.00	4.00	8.00

SSS INTERNATIONAL

Number	Title (A Side/B Side)	Yr	VG	VG+	NM
❑ 810	Taste of Tears/No Brass Band	197?	—	3.50	7.00

KAYE, LOIS

45s

OVATION

Number	Title (A Side/B Side)	Yr	VG	VG+	NM
❑ 1105	I'll Leave in the Middle of the Night/Sheltered in Your Lovin' Hideaway	1978	—	3.00	6.00
❑ 1111	One Less Set of Footsteps/I Got the Feeling	1978	—	3.00	6.00
❑ 1130	Drown in the Flood/Why'd You Have to Be So Good	1979	—	3.00	6.00

KAYE, SANDRA

45s

DOOR KNOB

Number	Title (A Side/B Side)	Yr	VG	VG+	NM
❑ 068	This Magic Moment/Baby Doesn't Live Here Anymore	1978	—	2.50	5.00
❑ 075	One More Time/My Dolly and I	1978	—	2.50	5.00
❑ 088	I'll Still Love You in My Dreams/Kiss and Run	1978	—	2.50	5.00
❑ 093	I've Seen It All/I'll Still Love You in My Dreams	1979	—	2.50	5.00
❑ 097	You Broke My Heart So Gently (It Almost Didn't Break)/Where Would I Be	1979	—	2.50	5.00
❑ 120	I'll Get By/Where Would I Be	1980	—	2.50	5.00

KEARNEY, RAMSEY

45s

CHALLENGE

Number	Title (A Side/B Side)	Yr	VG	VG+	NM
❑ 59346	Soft Lips and Sweet Perfume/Night to Away	1966	3.00	6.00	12.00

HICKORY

Number	Title (A Side/B Side)	Yr	VG	VG+	NM
❑ 1162	Keep Your Love for Me/Thinking About My Baby	1962	3.00	6.00	12.00
❑ 1176	I Never Let You Cross My Mind/Nine Little Teardrops	1962	3.00	6.00	12.00
❑ 1192	I'll Cry Myself to Sleep (Again Tonight)/But Whatcha Gonna Do	1962	3.00	6.00	12.00
❑ 1211	The Blues Keep Hangin' On/Put Away That Gun Boy	1963	3.00	6.00	12.00
❑ 1233	El Diablo/Move Over	1963	3.00	6.00	12.00
❑ 1251	Google Eyes/Take a Walk (In My Shoes)	1964	3.00	6.00	12.00

NASHCO

Number	Title (A Side/B Side)	Yr	VG	VG+	NM
❑ 51586	Let's Go Away Somewhere/Forgotten People	198?	2.00	4.00	8.00
❑ 51686	A School Teacher's Dream/Hell Yes, I'm Country	1986	2.00	4.00	8.00
❑ 121181	Rubber Legs and Gin/Just a Bikin' Along	1981	2.00	4.00	8.00

SAFARI

Number	Title (A Side/B Side)	Yr	VG	VG+	NM
❑ 101	White Man's Blues/Evergreen Love	1981	2.00	4.00	8.00
❑ 103	Don't Call Me (I'll Call You)/Something of Value	198?	2.00	4.00	8.00
❑ 104	That's How Much I Love You/My Love for You	1982	2.00	4.00	8.00
❑ 107	Put On Your Love Tonight (same on both sides)	1983	2.00	4.00	8.00
❑ 108	I Found Love (When I Found You)/Emotions	1984	2.00	4.00	8.00
❑ 111	It's Time to Go/From One Lover to Another	1984	2.00	4.00	8.00
❑ 112	Kisses and Coffee/I Think It's You	1984	2.00	4.00	8.00
❑ 114	King of Oak Street/Je T'aime Beaucoup (I Love You Very Much)	1985	2.00	4.00	8.00
❑ 115	I Wouldn't Blame Jesus/Country Music Singer	198?	2.00	4.00	8.00
❑ 117	One Time Thing/(B-side unknown)	1988	2.00	4.00	8.00
❑ 119	Ramsey's Monkey/Each Minute Seems a Million Years	1989	2.00	4.00	8.00

Number	Title (A Side/B Side)	Yr	VG	VG+	NM
❑ 1000	Joy in the Morning/(Even If It Kills Me) I'll Die Lovin' You	1975	2.50	5.00	10.00
❑ 1001	Cattle Call/Jack Benny's Fiddle	1977	2.50	5.00	10.00
❑ 9338	More Waters on the Beans/Life Begins at Forty	198?	2.00	4.00	8.00

Albums

NASHCO

Number	Title (A Side/B Side)	Yr	VG	VG+	NM
❑ 608	Together in a Song	198?	3.75	7.50	15.00
❑ 611	Lots to Look Back On	198?	3.75	7.50	15.00
❑ 613	I Write the Words	1981	3.75	7.50	15.00
❑ 615	Reflections of You	1981	3.75	7.50	15.00
❑ 616	God Made Them All	1981	3.75	7.50	15.00
❑ 646	Broken Heart	1986	3.75	7.50	15.00
❑ 654	Red White and Blue USA	1987	3.75	7.50	15.00

KEITH, TOBY

45s

A&M

Number	Title (A Side/B Side)	Yr	VG	VG+	NM
❑ 581714-7	A Woman's Touch/She's Perfect	1996	—	2.00	4.00

DREAMWORKS

Number	Title (A Side/B Side)	Yr	VG	VG+	NM
❑ 459033-7	When Love Fades/Country Comes to Town	1999	—	—	3.00
❑ 459041-7	How Do You Like Me Now?!/When Love Fades	2000	—	—	3.00

MERCURY

Number	Title (A Side/B Side)	Yr	VG	VG+	NM
❑ 566432-7	Getcha Some/Should've Been a Cowboy	1998	—	—	3.00
❑ 566912-7	If a Man Answers/You Ain't Much Fun	1999	—	—	3.00
❑ 568114-7	I'm So Happy I Can't Stop Crying/Jacky Don Tucker (Play by the Rules Miss All the Fun)	1997	—	2.00	4.00
❑ 568928-7	Double Wide Paradise/Tired	1998	—	—	3.00
❑ 574636-7	We Were in Love/Double Wide Paradise	1997	—	—	3.00
❑ 574950-7	Dream Walkin'/Strangers Again	1998	—	—	3.00
❑ 578810-7	Me Too/The Lonely	1996	—	—	3.00
❑ 858290-7	Wish I Didn't Know Now/Under the Fall	1994	—	—	3.00
❑ 862262-7	He Ain't Worth Missing/A Little Less Talk and a Lot More Action	1993	—	—	3.00
❑ 862844-7	A Little Less Talk and a Lot More Action/Mama Come Quick	1993	—	—	3.00
❑ 864990-7	Should've Been a Cowboy/Some Kinda Good Kinda Hold on Me	1993	—	2.00	4.00

POLYDOR

Number	Title (A Side/B Side)	Yr	VG	VG+	NM
❑ 576140-7	Does That Blue Moon Ever Shine on You/She's Gonna Get It	1996	—	—	3.00
❑ 579574-7	Big Ol' Truck/In Other Words	1995	—	—	3.00
❑ 851136-7	Upstairs Downtown/Woman Behind the Man	1994	—	—	3.00
❑ 851728-7	You Ain't Much Fun/Life Was a Play (The World a Stage)	1995	—	2.00	4.00
❑ 853358-7	Who's That Man/You Ain't Much Fun	1994	—	2.00	4.00

KELLEY, JOHN

45s

COMSTAR

Number	Title (A Side/B Side)	Yr	VG	VG+	NM
❑ 8201	This Morning I Woke Up in New York City/(B-side unknown)	1982	2.00	4.00	8.00

KELLUM, MURRY

45s

CINNAMON

Number	Title (A Side/B Side)	Yr	VG	VG+	NM
❑ 765	Walking Tall/Huckleberry's Ferry Boat Building Blues	1973	—	2.50	5.00
❑ 777	Lovely Lady/Alive and Doing Well	1973	—	2.50	5.00
❑ 794	Girl of My Life/Since You've Been Gone	1974	—	2.50	5.00

EPIC

Number	Title (A Side/B Side)	Yr	VG	VG+	NM
❑ 10741	Joy to the World/In a Phone Booth on My Knees	1971	—	2.50	5.00
❑ 10784	Train Train (Carry Me Away)/What's Made Milwaukee Famous	1971	—	2.50	5.00
❑ 10832	Love You to Sleep Tonight/You Do the Callin' (I'll Do the Crawlin')	1972	—	2.50	5.00

M.O.C.

Number	Title (A Side/B Side)	Yr	VG	VG+	NM
❑ 653	Long, Tall Texan/I Gotta Leave This Town	1963	3.00	6.00	12.00
—B-side by Glenn Sutton					
❑ 657	Red Ryder/Texas Lil	1964	3.00	6.00	12.00
❑ 658	I Dreamed I Was a Beatle/Oh How Sweet It Could Be	1964	5.00	10.00	20.00

PLANTATION

Number	Title (A Side/B Side)	Yr	VG	VG+	NM
❑ 176 [DJ]	Memphis Sun (mono/stereo)	1978	—	2.50	5.00
—Released only as a promo					

RANWOOD

Number	Title (A Side/B Side)	Yr	VG	VG+	NM
❑ 1047	Shoot Low Sheriff/How Long Has It Been (Since They Played Something You Could Dance To)	1976	—	2.50	5.00

Albums

PLANTATION

Number	Title (A Side/B Side)	Yr	VG	VG+	NM
❑ 531	Country Comedy	1978	3.00	6.00	12.00

KELLY, IRENE

45s

MCA

Number	Title (A Side/B Side)	Yr	VG	VG+	NM
❑ 53756	Love Is a Hard Road/Too Late (To Turn Back Now)	1989	—	2.00	4.00
❑ 53885	A Rock and a Rolling Stone/Love Is a Hard Road	1990	—	2.00	4.00

KELLY, JERRI

Also see MICK LLOYD; PRICE MITCHELL.

45s

CARRERE

Number	Title (A Side/B Side)	Yr	VG	VG+	NM
❑ ZS5-03017	Walk Me 'Cross the River/All That Shines Is Gold	1982	—	2.50	5.00

GRT

Number	Title (A Side/B Side)	Yr	VG	VG+	NM
❑ 006	Marbles/'Cause It's Easier for You	1974	2.00	4.00	8.00
❑ 026	I Don't Wanna Be Lonely Tonight/Back Sliding Man	1975	2.00	4.00	8.00
❑ 035	Knight in Faded Blue Jeans/Back Sliding Man	1975	2.00	4.00	8.00

LITTLE GIANT

Number	Title (A Side/B Side)	Yr	VG	VG+	NM
❑ 021	For a Slow Dance with You/Stop Startin' Over	1979	—	3.00	6.00
❑ 026	Fallin' for You/Guess I'd Better Be Strong (And Move Along)	1980	—	3.00	6.00
❑ 026 [PS]	Fallin' for You/Guess I'd Better Be Strong (And Move Along)	1980	2.00	4.00	8.00
❑ 030	Forsaking All the Rest/I'm As Much of a Woman (As You Care to Make Me)	1980	—	3.00	6.00
❑ 030 [PS]	Forsaking All the Rest/I'm As Much of a Woman (As You Care to Make Me)	1980	2.00	4.00	8.00

KELLY, KAREN

45s

ABC

Number	Title (A Side/B Side)	Yr	VG	VG+	NM
❑ 11369	Something Got a Hold of Me/Crying's Not a Laughing Matter	1973	—	3.00	6.00
❑ 11393	Just a New Version of an Old Song/If Fingerprints Showed Up on Skin	1973	—	3.00	6.00
❑ 11414	He's Your Baby Now/Half Empty Bed	1973	—	3.00	6.00

CAPITOL

Number	Title (A Side/B Side)	Yr	VG	VG+	NM
❑ 2771	Sunday Go to Cheatin' Dress/If Everyone Loved Like You Love	1970	—	3.50	7.00
❑ 2883	Let Me Go, Lover/Susie's Toys	1970	—	3.50	7.00
❑ 3018	I Swore I'd Fix His Wagon/Permanently Lonely	1971	—	3.50	7.00

MELODYLAND

Number	Title (A Side/B Side)	Yr	VG	VG+	NM
❑ 6008	Annie/The Dessert	1975	—	2.50	5.00

KELLY, NORVIN

45s

COLUMBIA

Number	Title (A Side/B Side)	Yr	VG	VG+	NM
❑ 4-21279	Without You/You Didn't Want a Home	1954	5.00	10.00	20.00
❑ 4-21381	I'm Back in Your Arms Again/You Can't Make Me Live with the Blues	1955	5.00	10.00	20.00

KEMP, DAVE

45s

SOUNDWAVES

Number	Title (A Side/B Side)	Yr	VG	VG+	NM
❑ 4702	Ain't That the Way It Goes/Prisoner of Honky Tonk Hell	1983	—	2.50	5.00
❑ 4713	Face Another Day/Pull Up a Pillow	1983	—	2.50	5.00

KEMP, WAYNE

45s

BOYD

Number	Title (A Side/B Side)	Yr	VG	VG+	NM
❑ 126	Little Bitty Woman/They're Tearing Our Little House Down	196?	3.75	7.50	15.00
❑ 128	One Time Too Many/The Loneliest Lonely Heart	196?	3.75	7.50	15.00
—With Opaline Bacon					

DECCA

Number	Title (A Side/B Side)	Yr	VG	VG+	NM
❑ 32422	Won't You Come Home (And Talk to a Stranger)/I Turn My Mind on You	1968	—	3.00	6.00
❑ 32534	Bar Room Habits/Here We Go Again	1969	—	3.00	6.00
❑ 32653	Too Close to the End/She Won't Live It Down	1970	—	3.00	6.00
❑ 32767	Who'll Turn Out the Lights/Burn Another Honky Tonk Down	1971	—	3.00	6.00
❑ 32824	Award to an Angel/Darling Who's the Stranger	1971	—	3.00	6.00
❑ 32891	Did We Have to Come This Far to Say Goodbye/Play Me a Cheatin' Song	1971	—	3.00	6.00
❑ 32946	Darlin'/Just to Know She'd Let Me Leave Her	1972	—	3.00	6.00
❑ 33025	Your Memory Comes and Gets Me/Touch Me with Your Eyes	1972	—	3.00	6.00

DOOR KNOB

Number	Title (A Side/B Side)	Yr	VG	VG+	NM
❑ 200	Don't Send Me No Angels/Living Off the Memories	1983	—	2.50	5.00
❑ 206	Merry Christmas, Darling/Happy Birthday, Darling	1983	—	2.50	5.00
❑ 211	I've Always Wanted To/Happy Anniversary Darling	1984	—	2.50	5.00
❑ 231	You Can't Have Your Way with a Memory/(B-side unknown)	1985	—	2.50	5.00

JAB

Number	Title (A Side/B Side)	Yr	VG	VG+	NM
❑ 9005	Babblin' Incoherently/An Image of Me	1967	2.00	4.00	8.00

MCA

Number	Title (A Side/B Side)	Yr	VG	VG+	NM
❑ 40019	Honky Tonk Wine/Pretty Mansions	1973	—	2.50	5.00
❑ 40112	Kentucky Sunshine/Hurt Me Again	1973	—	2.50	5.00
❑ 40176	Listen/She Knows When You're On My Mind Again	1974	—	2.50	5.00
❑ 40249	Harlan County/I'll Leave This World Loving You	1974	—	2.50	5.00

MERCURY

Number	Title (A Side/B Side)	Yr	VG	VG+	NM
❑ 57023	Love Goes to Hell When It Dies/She Won't Close the Book on Me	1980	—	2.00	4.00
❑ 57035	I'll Leave This World Loving You/Who Left the Door to Heaven Open	1980	—	2.00	4.00
❑ 57047	Your Wife Is Cheatin' on Us Again/God Made Her Special	1981	—	2.00	4.00
❑ 57053	Just Got Back from No Man's Land/Turn Me Loose	1981	—	2.00	4.00
❑ 57060	Why Am I Doing Without/Wrecked Up Frame of Mind	1981	—	2.00	4.00

Number	Title (A Side/B Side)	Yr	VG	VG+	NM
❑ 76139	Sloe Gin and Fast Women/I'm the Man	1982	—	2.00	4.00
❑ 76165	She Only Meant to Use Him/I Know Just How She Feels	1982	—	2.00	4.00
UNITED ARTISTS					
❑ XW678	I Can't Wait to Dream That Dream/We're Waking a Sleeping Prayer	1975	—	2.50	5.00
❑ XW805	Waiting for the Tables to Turn/I Can't Wait to Dream That Dream Again	1976	—	2.50	5.00
❑ XW850	I Should Have Watched That First Step/Tell Ole I Ain't Here to Get On Home	1976	—	2.50	5.00
❑ XW980	Leona Doesn't Live Here Anymore/Baby This and Baby That	1977	—	2.50	5.00
❑ XW1031	I Love It (When You Love All Over Me)/Love's Already Been Here and Gone	1977	—	2.50	5.00
Albums					
DECCA					
❑ DL 75290	Wayne Kemp	1971	3.75	7.50	15.00
MCA					
❑ 369	Kentucky Sunshine	1973	3.00	6.00	12.00

KEMP, WAYNE, AND BOBBY G. RICE

Also see each artist's individual listings.

Number	Title (A Side/B Side)	Yr	VG	VG+	NM
45s					
DOOR KNOB					
❑ 243	Red Neck and Over Thirty/State of the Union	1986	—	2.50	5.00
❑ 250	One More Time Around/From Housewife to Everyone's Girl	1986	—	2.50	5.00

KENDALL, JEANNIE

Also see THE KENDALLS.

Number	Title (A Side/B Side)	Yr	VG	VG+	NM
45s					
DOT					
❑ 17497	Baby Went Bye Bye/Come Back Home	1974	2.00	4.00	8.00
❑ 17513	Birmingham/(B-side unknown)	1974	2.00	4.00	8.00

KENDALLS, THE

Also see JEANNIE KENDALL.

Number	Title (A Side/B Side)	Yr	VG	VG+	NM
45s					
DOT					
❑ 17405	Two Divided by Love/Easy to Love	1972	2.00	4.00	8.00
❑ 17422	Everything I Own/Big Silver Jet	1972	2.00	4.00	8.00
❑ 17453	You and Me/You Got a Lot	1973	2.00	4.00	8.00
❑ 17473	I Wanna Live Here in Your Love/Part of My Life	1973	2.00	4.00	8.00
EPIC					
❑ 34-68933	Blue Blue Day/Temporarily Out of Order	1989	—	—	3.00
K-ARK					
❑ 903	Come Back and Love Me/Little Billy	196?	3.75	7.50	15.00
MCA CURB					
❑ 52850	Too Late/Party Line	1986	—	—	3.00
❑ 52933	Fire at First Sight/You Can't Fool Love	1986	—	—	3.00
❑ 52983	Little Doll/He Can't Make Your Kind of Love	1986	—	—	3.00
MERCURY					
❑ 57055	Teach Me to Cheat/Summer Melodies	1981	—	2.00	4.00
❑ 76131	If You're Waiting on Me (You're Backing Up)/I'm Lettin' You In (On a Feelin')	1981	—	2.00	4.00
❑ 76155	Cheater's Prayer/Borrowing Lovin'	1982	—	2.00	4.00
❑ 76178	That's What I Get for Thinking/Honey Dew	1982	—	2.00	4.00
❑ 812300-7	Precious Love/Take Me to Heaven (Before You Take Me Home)	1983	—	—	3.00
❑ 814195-7	Movin' Train/Say the Word	1983	—	—	3.00
❑ 818056-7	Thank God for the Radio/Flaming Eyes	1984	—	—	3.00
❑ 822203-7	My Baby's Gone/I'll Be Faithful to You	1984	—	—	3.00
❑ 880306-7	I'd Dance Every Dance with You/Dark End of the Street	1984	—	—	3.00
❑ 880588-7	Four Wheel Drive/This Ain't the First Time I've Fallen	1985	—	—	3.00
❑ 880828-7	If You Break My Heart/One Good-Bye from Gone	1985	—	—	3.00
❑ 884140-7	Two Heart Harmony/I Don't Know Any Better	1985	—	—	3.00
OVATION					
❑ 1101	Makin' Believe/Let the Music Play	1977	2.00	4.00	8.00
❑ 1103	Heaven's Just a Sin Away/Live and Let Live	1977	—	3.00	6.00
❑ 1106	It Don't Feel Like Sinnin' to Me/Try Me Again	1978	—	2.50	5.00
❑ 1109	Pittsburgh Stealers/When Can We Do This Again	1978	—	2.50	5.00
❑ 1112	Sweet Desire/Old Fashioned Love	1978	—	2.50	5.00
❑ 1119	I Had a Lovely Time/Love Is a Hurting Thing	1978	—	2.50	5.00
❑ 1125	Just Like Real People/Another Dream Just Came True	1979	—	2.50	5.00
❑ 1129	I Don't Do Like That No More/Never My Love	1979	—	2.50	5.00
❑ 1136	You'd Make an Angel Wanna Cheat/I Take the Chance	1979	—	2.50	5.00
❑ 1143	I'm Already Blue/I Don't Drink from the River	1980	—	2.50	5.00
❑ 1154	Put It Off Until Tomorrow/Gone Away	1980	—	2.50	5.00
❑ 1170	Heart of the Matter/Mandolin Man	1981	—	2.50	5.00
STEP ONE					
❑ 371	Routine/A Far Cry	1987	—	2.00	4.00
❑ 374	Dancin' with Myself Tonight/A Whole Lot to Lose	1987	—	2.00	4.00
❑ 379	Still Pickin' Up After You/Country Music Station	1987	—	2.00	4.00
❑ 384	The Rhythm of Romance/They Can't Stop Me	1988	—	2.00	4.00
STOP					
❑ 373	Leaving on a Jet Plane/She Thinks I Still Care	1970	2.50	5.00	10.00
❑ 379	Please Tell Me Why/You've Lost That Lovin' Feeling	1970	2.50	5.00	10.00
❑ 394	Behind That Locked Door/Love, Love, Love	1971	2.50	5.00	10.00
UNITED ARTISTS					
❑ XW645	I'd Have to Lie/Love Do or Die	1975	2.00	4.00	8.00
❑ XW721	I Can't Believe I'm Loving You Again/Diesel Gypsy	1975	2.00	4.00	8.00
❑ XW782	Imaginary Harmony/Miss Lucy's on the Juice Again	1976	2.00	4.00	8.00
Albums					
DOT					
❑ DLP-26001	Two Divided by Love	1972	3.75	7.50	15.00
EPIC					
❑ E2 45249 [(2)]	20 Favorites	1989	3.75	7.50	15.00
GUSTO					
❑ GT 0001	1978 Grammy Award Winners — Best Country Duo	1978	2.50	5.00	10.00
MCA					
❑ 27021	Never Ending Song of Love	198?	2.50	5.00	10.00
MCA CURB					
❑ 5724	Fire at First Sight	1986	2.00	4.00	8.00
MERCURY					
❑ SRM-1-4046	Stickin' Together	1982	2.50	5.00	10.00
❑ SRM-1-6005	Lettin' You In on a Feelin'	1981	2.50	5.00	10.00
❑ 812779-1	Movin' Train	1983	2.00	4.00	8.00
❑ 824250-1	Two Heart Harmony	1985	2.00	4.00	8.00
❑ 826307-1	Thank God for the Radio... And All the Hits	1986	2.00	4.00	8.00
OVATION					
❑ 1719	Heaven's Just a Sin Away	1977	3.00	6.00	12.00
❑ 1733	Old Fashioned Love	1978	3.00	6.00	12.00
❑ 1739	Just Like Real People	1979	3.00	6.00	12.00
❑ 1746	Heart of the Matter	1979	3.00	6.00	12.00
❑ 1756	The Best of the Kendalls	1980	3.00	6.00	12.00
POWER PAK					
❑ PO-216	Leavin' on a Jet Plane	197?	2.50	5.00	10.00
STEP ONE					
❑ 0023	Break the Routine	1987	2.50	5.00	10.00
STOP					
❑ 1020	Meet the Kendalls	1970	5.00	10.00	20.00

KENNARD AND JOHN

Number	Title (A Side/B Side)	Yr	VG	VG+	NM
45s					
CURB					
❑ 10563	Thrill of Love/Maria	1989	—	—	3.00
❑ 76759	Cadillac/Maria	1990	—	2.00	4.00

KENNEDY, GENE

Number	Title (A Side/B Side)	Yr	VG	VG+	NM
45s					
DOOR KNOB					
❑ 003	She Took Me Where I've Never Been Before/High Flies the Eagle	1976	—	3.00	6.00
❑ 039	When I Fall in Love/High Flies the Eagle	197?	—	3.00	6.00
❑ 205	In the Misty Moonlight/(B-side unknown)	1983	—	2.50	5.00
SOCIETY					
❑ 110	My Wife's House/(B-side unknown)	1986	—	2.50	5.00

KENNEDY, GENE, AND KAREN JEGLUM

Number	Title (A Side/B Side)	Yr	VG	VG+	NM
45s					
DOOR KNOB					
❑ 145	I Want to See Me in Your Eyes/Nothing Left to Lose	1981	—	2.50	5.00
❑ 151	I'd Rather Be the Stranger in Your Eyes/(B-side unknown)	1981	—	2.50	5.00
❑ 173	Easier to Go/A Thing or Two on My Mind	1981	—	2.50	5.00
❑ 181	What About Tonight (We Might Find Something Beautiful Tonight)/You're Still the One (Who Makes My Life Complete)	1982	—	2.50	5.00
❑ 192	Be Happy for Me/What About Tonight	1983	—	2.50	5.00
❑ 199	Will You Still Love Me Tomorrow/Today We're Gonna Get Married	1983	—	2.50	5.00
Albums					
DOOR KNOB					
❑ 1004	Gene Kennedy and Karen Jeglum	1981	3.00	6.00	12.00

KENNEDY, LARRY WAYNE

Number	Title (A Side/B Side)	Yr	VG	VG+	NM
45s					
JERE					
❑ 1001	She Almost Makes Me Forget About You/(B-side unknown)	1985	—	2.50	5.00

KENNEDY, RAY

Number	Title (A Side/B Side)	Yr	VG	VG+	NM
45s					
ATLANTIC					
❑ 87651	I Like the Way It Feels/I'm Sending One Up for You	1991	—	2.00	4.00
❑ 87743	Scars/I'm Sending One Up for You	1991	—	2.00	4.00
❑ 87930	Doin' Life Without You/Cog in a Wheel	1991	—	2.00	4.00
❑ 87960	What a Way to Go/The Storm	1990	—	2.00	4.00

KENNY O.

Number	Title (A Side/B Side)	Yr	VG	VG+	NM
45s					
RHINESTONE					
❑ 1002	Old Fangled Country Songs/Walking By My Side	1981	—	3.00	6.00

KENT, GEORGE

45s

MERCURY

Number	Title (A Side/B Side)	Yr	VG	VG+	NM
❑ 72985	Hello, I'm a Jukebox/I Always Did Like Leavenworth	1969	—	3.50	7.00
❑ 73066	Doogie Ray/The Great South State Truck Stop Disaster	1970	—	3.00	6.00
❑ 73127	Mama Bake a Pie (Daddy Kill a Chicken)/Let's Just Pretend	1970	—	3.00	6.00
❑ 73182	Hitting the Bottle/I'm in a Bad Mood Tonight	1971	—	3.00	6.00

RICE

Number	Title (A Side/B Side)	Yr	VG	VG+	NM
❑ 5004	This Is Me/How'd He Get That Way	196?	3.00	6.00	12.00
❑ 5015	She'll Wear Us Out Leavin' Town/Bad Juice	196?	3.00	6.00	12.00
❑ 5027	Hitting the Bottle/Missing You	1967	2.50	5.00	10.00
❑ 5040	Falling Apart/You Wouldn't Want Me Now	1971	2.00	4.00	8.00
❑ 5044	It Takes a Drinking Man/Running with the Wind	1972	2.00	4.00	8.00
❑ 5050	I Can't Leave Now ('Cause Someone Moved the Door)/I'm Not Gonna Fly	1972	2.00	4.00	8.00
❑ 5054	Hardscuffle Road/Doggie Ray	1972	2.00	4.00	8.00

SHANNON

Number	Title (A Side/B Side)	Yr	VG	VG+	NM
❑ 811	Sweet Lovin' Woman/I Can't Say I Love You	1973	—	2.50	5.00
❑ 815	It Takes a Fool a Time or Two/(B-side unknown)	1973	—	2.50	5.00
❑ 818	Take My Life and Shape It with Your Love/Sunshine Light	1974	—	2.50	5.00
❑ 824	Whole Lotta Difference in Love/Coming Back on My Mind	1974	—	2.50	5.00
❑ 830	Honky Tonkin' Soul/Just Because You Understand Your Woman	1975	—	2.50	5.00
❑ 834	She'll Wear It Out Leaving Town/Don't Tell It to Me	1975	—	2.50	5.00
❑ 840	Shake 'Em Up and Let 'Em Roll/Singin' Lonesome Cowboy Songs	1976	—	2.50	5.00

SOUNDWAVES

Number	Title (A Side/B Side)	Yr	VG	VG+	NM
❑ 4542	Low Class Reunion/(How Can I Write on Paper) What I Feel in My Heart	1977	—	2.50	5.00

Albums

SHANNON

Number	Title (A Side/B Side)	Yr	VG	VG+	NM
❑ 1003	George Kent	1974	5.00	10.00	20.00

KENTUCKY HEADHUNTERS, THE

Also see BROTHER PHELPS.

45s

MERCURY

Number	Title (A Side/B Side)	Yr	VG	VG+	NM
❑ 862150-7	Dixie Fried/Celina Tennessee	1993	—	—	3.00
❑ 864808-7	Honky Tonk Walkin'/Redneck Girl	1993	—	—	3.00
❑ 866134-7	Only Daddy That'll Walk the Line/Walk Softly on This Heart of Mine	1991	—	2.00	4.00
❑ 868122-7	The Ballad of Davy Crockett/Smooth	1991	—	2.00	4.00
❑ 868418-7	With Body and Soul/Some Folks Like to Steal	1991	—	2.00	4.00
❑ 868760-7	It's Chitlin' Time/Dumas Walker	1991	—	2.00	4.00
❑ 874744-7	Walk Softly on This Heart of Mine/Skip a Rope	1989	—	2.00	4.00
❑ 875450-7	Oh Lonesome Me/My Daddy Was a Milkman	1990	—	2.00	4.00
❑ 876536-7	Dumas Walker/High Steppin' Daddy	1990	—	3.00	6.00
❑ 878214-7	Rock 'n' Roll Angel/Rag Top	1990	—	2.00	4.00

Albums

MERCURY

Number	Title (A Side/B Side)	Yr	VG	VG+	NM
❑ 838744-1	Pickin' on Nashville	1989	3.75	7.50	15.00

KENYON, JOE

45s

MERCURY

Number	Title (A Side/B Side)	Yr	VG	VG+	NM
❑ 888642-7	Hymne/My Only Love	1987	—	—	3.00
❑ 888910-7	Joe's Theme/Never Say Goodbye	1987	—	—	3.00

KERSH, DAVID

45s

CURB

Number	Title (A Side/B Side)	Yr	VG	VG+	NM
❑ D7-73045	If I Never Stop Loving You/The Need	1998	—	—	3.00
❑ D7-76990	Goodnight Sweetheart/Breaking Hearts and Taking Names	1996	—	2.00	4.00

KERSHAW, DOUG

45s

BGM

Number	Title (A Side/B Side)	Yr	VG	VG+	NM
❑ 12989	Boogie Queen/Jambalaya	1989	—	2.50	5.00
❑ 81588	Cajun Baby/I Wanna Hold You	1988	—	2.50	5.00

K-ARK

Number	Title (A Side/B Side)	Yr	VG	VG+	NM
❑ 754	Fa-Do-Do/Ain't Gonna Get Me Down	1967	2.50	5.00	10.00

SCOTTI BROTHERS

Number	Title (A Side/B Side)	Yr	VG	VG+	NM
❑ ZS6-02137	Hello Woman/Sing Along	1981	—	2.00	4.00
❑ ZS5-02508	Instant Hero/Don't We Make Music	1981	—	2.00	4.00
❑ ZS5-02957	Flash/Ballad of the General Lee	1982	—	2.00	4.00
❑ ZS5-03065	Keep Between Them Ditches/Ballad of the General Lee	1982	—	2.00	4.00

WARNER BROS.

Number	Title (A Side/B Side)	Yr	VG	VG+	NM
❑ 7304	Feed It to the Fish/You Fight Your Fight (I'll Fight Mine)	1969	—	3.00	6.00
❑ 7329	Diggy Diggy Lo/Papa and Mama Had Love	1969	—	3.00	6.00
❑ 7413	Orange Blossom Special/Swamp Rat	1970	—	3.00	6.00
❑ 7432	Natural Man/You'll Never Catch Me Walking in Your Tracks	1970	—	3.00	6.00
❑ 7463	Play, Fiddle, Play/They Don't Make You No Better Than Me	1971	—	3.00	6.00
❑ 7494	Mama Said Yeah/Natural Man	1971	—	3.00	6.00
❑ 7590	Sally Jo/Swamp Grass	1972	—	3.00	6.00
❑ 7648	Devil's Elbow/Jamestown Ferry	1972	—	3.00	6.00
❑ 7763	Mama's Got the Know How/Hippy Ti Yo	1973	—	2.50	5.00
❑ 7813	Nickel in My Pocket/Swamp Dance	1974	—	2.50	5.00
❑ 8033	All You Want to Do Is Make Kids/Whatcha Gonna Do When You Can't	1974	—	2.50	5.00
❑ 8195	It Takes All Day to Get Over Night/Mon Chapeau	1976	—	2.50	5.00
❑ 8257	House Husband/I'm Just a Nobody	1976	—	2.50	5.00
❑ 8374	I'm Walkin'/Kershaw's Two Step	1977	—	2.50	5.00
❑ 8424	You Won't Let Me/Mamou Two-Step	1977	—	2.50	5.00
❑ 8594	Marie/Louisiana Sun	1978	—	2.50	5.00

Albums

SCOTTI BROTHERS

Number	Title (A Side/B Side)	Yr	VG	VG+	NM
❑ SB 7115	Instant Hero	1981	3.00	6.00	12.00
❑ FZ 37428	Instant Hero	1981	2.50	5.00	10.00

WARNER BROS.

Number	Title (A Side/B Side)	Yr	VG	VG+	NM
❑ WS 1820	Cajun Way	1969	5.00	10.00	20.00
—Green label, "W7" box logo at top					
❑ WS 1820	Cajun Way	1970	3.75	7.50	15.00
—Green label, "WB" shield logo at top					
❑ WS 1861	Spanish Moss	1970	3.75	7.50	15.00
—Green label					
❑ WS 1906	Doug Kershaw	1971	3.75	7.50	15.00
—Green label					
❑ BS 2581	Swamp Grass	1972	3.75	7.50	15.00
—Green label					
❑ BS 2649	Devil's Elbow	1973	3.75	7.50	15.00
❑ BS 2725	Douglas James Kershaw	1973	3.75	7.50	15.00
❑ BS 2793	Mama Kershaw's Boy	1974	3.75	7.50	15.00
❑ BS 2851	Alive & Pickin'	1975	3.00	6.00	12.00
❑ BS 2910	Ragin' Cajun	1976	3.00	6.00	12.00
❑ BS 3025	Flip, Flop & Fly	1977	3.00	6.00	12.00
❑ BSK 3166	Louisiana Man	1978	3.00	6.00	12.00

KERSHAW, RUSTY AND DOUG

45s

FEATURE

Number	Title (A Side/B Side)	Yr	VG	VG+	NM
❑ 2003	It's Better to Be a Has Been (Than Be a Never Was)/No, No, It's Not So	1954	25.00	50.00	100.00

HICKORY

Number	Title (A Side/B Side)	Yr	VG	VG+	NM
❑ 1027	So Lovely, Baby/Why Cry for You	1955	7.50	15.00	30.00
❑ 1036	Can I Be Dreaming/Look Around	1955	7.50	15.00	30.00
❑ 1042	Honey Honey/Let's Stay Together	1956	7.50	15.00	30.00
❑ 1048	Hey You There/Your Crazy, Crazy Heart	1956	7.50	15.00	30.00
❑ 1055	I'll Understand/Mister Love	1956	7.50	15.00	30.00
❑ 1061	If I Win, I Win/Money	1957	7.50	15.00	30.00
—B-side by Al Terry					
❑ 1063	Going Down the Road/You'll See	1957	10.00	20.00	40.00
❑ 1068	Love Me to Pieces/I Never Had the Blues	1957	10.00	20.00	40.00
❑ 1072	Dream Queen/Take My Love	1957	7.50	15.00	30.00
❑ 1077	Hey Mae/Why Don't You Love Me	1958	7.50	15.00	30.00
❑ 1083	Hey Sheriff/Sweet Thing	1958	7.50	15.00	30.00
❑ 1091	It's Too Late/We'll Do It Anyway	1958	7.50	15.00	30.00
❑ 1095	Kaw-Liga/Never Love Again	1959	15.00	30.00	60.00
❑ 1101	Dancing Shoes/I Love You Like This	1959	15.00	30.00	60.00
❑ 1110	The Love I Want/Oh Love	1959	7.50	15.00	30.00
❑ 1137	Louisiana Man/Make Me Realize	1960	12.50	25.00	50.00
❑ 1151	Diggy Liggy Lo/Hey Mae	1961	15.00	30.00	60.00
❑ 1163	Cheated Too/So Lovely Baby	1961	7.50	15.00	30.00
❑ 1177	Cajun Joe (Bully of the Bayou)/Sweet Sweet to Me	1962	7.50	15.00	30.00
❑ 1575	Louisiana Man/(Our Own) Jole Blon	1970	2.50	5.00	10.00

RCA VICTOR

Number	Title (A Side/B Side)	Yr	VG	VG+	NM
❑ 47-8266	Cajun Stripper/Half the Time	1963	3.75	7.50	15.00
❑ 47-8362	Cleopatra/Malinda	1964	3.75	7.50	15.00
❑ 47-8415	St. Louis Blues/I Can't See Myself	1964	3.75	7.50	15.00

Albums

HICKORY

Number	Title (A Side/B Side)	Yr	VG	VG+	NM
❑ LPM-103 [M]	Rusty and Doug Sing Louisiana Man	1960	30.00	60.00	120.00

HICKORY/MGM

Number	Title (A Side/B Side)	Yr	VG	VG+	NM
❑ H3G-4506	Louisiana Man	1974	5.00	10.00	20.00

KERSHAW, SAMMY

45s

MERCURY

Number	Title (A Side/B Side)	Yr	VG	VG+	NM
❑ 172112-7	Me and Maxine/Louisiana Hot Sauce	1999	—	—	3.00
❑ 566052-7	Honky Tonk America/One Day Left to Live	1998	—	—	3.00
❑ 568140-7	Love of My Life/Roamin' Love	1997	—	—	3.00
❑ 568524-7	Matches/Thank God You're Gone	1998	—	—	3.00
❑ 574182-7	Fit to Be Tied Down/For Years	1997	—	—	3.00
❑ 578612-7	Politics, Religion and Her/Here She Comes	1996	—	—	3.00
❑ 852208-7	Your Tattoo/Still Lovin' You	1995	—	—	3.00
❑ 852874-7	Meant to Be/Vidalia	1996	—	2.00	4.00
❑ 856410-7	Southbound/Better Call a Preacher	1994	—	2.00	4.00
❑ 856686-7	If You're Gonna Walk, I'm Gonna Crawl/If You Ever Come This Way Again	1995	—	—	3.00
❑ 858102-7	I Can't Reach Her Anymore/What Might Have Been	1994	—	2.00	4.00
❑ 858722-7	National Working Women's Holiday/The Heart That Time Forgot	1994	—	2.00	4.00
❑ 858922-7	Third Rate Romance/Paradise from Nine to One	1994	—	—	3.00
❑ 862096-7	Haunted Heart/Cry, Cry Darlin'	1993	—	2.00	4.00
❑ 862600-7	Queen of My Double Wide Trailer/A Memory	1993	—	2.00	4.00
❑ 864316-7	Anywhere But Here/Old-Fashioned Broken Heart	1992	—	2.00	4.00
❑ 864854-7	She Don't Know She's Beautiful/Buy Her Roses	1993	—	2.50	5.00

Number	Title (A Side/B Side)	Yr	VG	VG+	NM
❑ 866324-7	Don't Go Near the Water/Every Third Monday	1992	—	2.50	5.00
❑ 866754-7	Yard Sale/What Am I Worth	1992	—	2.00	4.00
❑ 868812-7	Cadillac Style/Harbor for a Lonely Night	1991	—	2.00	4.00

KETCHUM, HAL
45s
CURB

Number	Title (A Side/B Side)	Yr	VG	VG+	NM
❑ D7-73051	I Saw the Light/When Love Looks Back at You	1998	—	—	3.00
❑ NR-76865	Small Town Saturday Night/Don't Strike a Match (To the Book of Love)	1991	—	2.50	5.00
❑ NR-76892	I Know Where Love Lives/Long Day Comin'	1991	—	2.50	5.00
❑ D7-76929	Stay Forever/Every Little Word	1995	—	2.00	4.00
❑ D7-76965	Every Little Word/Veil of Tears	1995	—	2.00	4.00

KILGORE, JERRY
45s
VIRGIN

Number	Title (A Side/B Side)	Yr	VG	VG+	NM
❑ 38667	Love Trip/The Real Thing	1999	—	—	3.00
❑ 58851	Cactus in a Coffee Can/I Just Want My Baby Back	2000	—	—	3.00

KILGORE, MERLE
45s

Number	Title (A Side/B Side)	Yr	VG	VG+	NM
ASHLEY					
❑ 6000	Packing and Unpacking/Beyond My Conscience and the Door	1968	2.50	5.00	10.00
❑ 35007	That's Alright/God Bless the Working Man	197?	—	3.50	7.00
COLUMBIA					
❑ 4-44279	Fast Talking Louisiana Man/Avenue of Tears	1967	2.50	5.00	10.00
❑ 4-44463	Patches (Made the Change)/Wild Rose	1968	2.50	5.00	10.00
D					
❑ 1042	It'll Be My First Time/I Take a Trip to the Moon	1959	5.00	10.00	20.00
ELEKTRA					
❑ 47252	Mister Garfield/I'm a One Woman Man	1981	—	2.50	5.00
❑ 69895	The Night They Drove Old Dixie Down/She Went a Little Bit Farther	1982	—	2.50	5.00
EPIC					
❑ 5-9762	Every Day's a Holiday/It's All Over Now	1965	3.00	6.00	12.00
❑ 5-9816	Dig, Dig, Dig, Dig (There's No More)/Help Me Up Darling (All Fools Fall Down)	1965	3.00	6.00	12.00
❑ 5-9873	Baby, I Got It/Mama's Killing Daddy	1965	3.00	6.00	12.00
❑ 5-10049	Nevada Smith/Too Many Mountains	1966	3.00	6.00	12.00
❑ 5-10146	I Just Don't Care Anymore/I'd Cry Like a Baby	1967	3.00	6.00	12.00
IMPERIAL					
❑ 5379	Please, Please, Please/Teen-Ager's Holiday	1956	7.50	15.00	30.00
❑ 5409	Ernie/Trying to Find (Someone Like You)	1956	15.00	30.00	60.00
❑ 5555	Tom Dooley, Jr./Hang Doll	1958	5.00	10.00	20.00
❑ 5584	Start All Over Again/Static	1959	5.00	10.00	20.00
❑ 8256	More and More/What Makes Me Love You	1954	10.00	20.00	40.00
❑ 8266	Seeing Double, Feeling Single/It Can't Rain	1954	10.00	20.00	40.00
❑ 8300	Everybody Needs a Little Lovin'/Funny Feelin'	1955	12.50	25.00	50.00
MERCURY					
❑ 71839	Wicked City/I'll Take Ginger and Run Away	1961	5.00	10.00	20.00
❑ 71918	42 in Chicago/Lover's Hell	1962	5.00	10.00	20.00
❑ 71978	A Girl Named Liz/Trouble at the Towers	1962	5.00	10.00	20.00
❑ 72048	Ain't Nothin' but a Man/Somethin' Goin' On	1962	5.00	10.00	20.00
MGM					
❑ 13168	Five Miles Down the Road/Whiskey Road	1963	3.75	7.50	15.00
❑ 13209	Always an Apple/Johnny Zero	1964	3.75	7.50	15.00
❑ 13277	The Bell Witch/Slow Hard Way	1964	3.75	7.50	15.00
STARDAY					
❑ 469	Dear Mama/Jimmie Brings Sunshine	1959	5.00	10.00	20.00
❑ 497	Love Has Made You Beautiful/Gettin' Old Before My Time	1960	5.00	10.00	20.00
❑ 533	Daddy's Place/Just Another Song Now	1961	5.00	10.00	20.00
❑ 644	Pinball Machine/Old Smokey	1963	3.75	7.50	15.00
❑ 964	Different Kind of Pretty/My Side of Life	1973	2.00	4.00	8.00
WARNER BROS.					
❑ 7831	Montgomery Mable/Old Home Filler-Up An' Keep On-a Truckin' Cafe	1974	—	2.50	5.00
❑ 8039	Love o' Love/Baby's Comin' Home to Stay	1974	—	2.50	5.00
❑ 8081	I'm Not Responsible/Tied	1975	—	2.50	5.00
❑ 29062	Guilty/When You Leave That Way You Can Never Go Back	1985	—	2.00	4.00
❑ 29267	Just Out of Reach/Road Women	1984	—	2.00	4.00

Albums

Number	Title	Yr	VG	VG+	NM
STARDAY					
❑ SLP-251 [M]	There's Gold in Them Thar Hills	1963	7.50	15.00	30.00
WING					
❑ MGW-12316 [M]	Tall Texan	196?	3.75	7.50	15.00
❑ SRW-16316 [S]	Tall Texan	196?	3.00	6.00	12.00

KIM AND KARMEN
45s
COMPLEAT

Number	Title (A Side/B Side)	Yr	VG	VG+	NM
❑ 130	Honky Tonk Lullabys/I Had Too Much to Dream (Last Night)	1984	—	2.50	5.00

KIMBERLY SPRINGS
45s
CAPITOL

Number	Title (A Side/B Side)	Yr	VG	VG+	NM
❑ B-5366	Slow Dancin'/Temptation	1984	—	2.00	4.00
❑ B-5404	Old Memories Are Hard to Lose/That's One to Grow On	1984	—	2.00	4.00

KIMBERLYS, THE
45s
COLUMBIA

Number	Title (A Side/B Side)	Yr	VG	VG+	NM
❑ 4-43287	You Can't Roller Skate in a Buffalo Herd/Four Long Seasons	1965	2.50	5.00	10.00
❑ 4-43399	Denver/Pretty Little Children	1965	2.50	5.00	10.00
❑ 4-43601	Soldiers and Lilies/Don't Send Me Away	1965	2.50	5.00	10.00
❑ 4-44403	I Never Will Marry/Early Morning Sun	1967	2.00	4.00	8.00

KING, CLAUDE
45s

Number	Title (A Side/B Side)	Yr	VG	VG+	NM
COLUMBIA					
❑ 42043	Big River, Big Man/Sweet Lovin'	1961	2.50	5.00	10.00
❑ 42196	The Comancheros/I Can't Get Over the Way You Got Over Me	1961	2.50	5.00	10.00
❑ 42196 [PS]	The Comancheros/I Can't Get Over the Way You Got Over Me	1961	3.75	7.50	15.00
❑ 42352	Wolverton Mountain/Little Bitty Heart	1962	3.00	6.00	12.00
❑ 42352 [PS]	Wolverton Mountain/Little Bitty Heart	1962	3.75	7.50	15.00
❑ 42581	The Burning of Atlanta/Don't That Moon Look Lonesome	1962	2.50	5.00	10.00
❑ 42581 [PS]	The Burning of Atlanta/Don't That Moon Look Lonesome	1962	3.75	7.50	15.00
❑ 42630	I've Got the World by the Tail/Shopping Center	1962	2.50	5.00	10.00
❑ 42630 [PS]	I've Got the World by the Tail/Shopping Center	1962	3.75	7.50	15.00
❑ 42688	Sheepskin Valley/I Backed Out	1963	2.50	5.00	10.00
❑ 42688 [PS]	Sheepskin Valley/I Backed Out	1963	3.75	7.50	15.00
❑ 42782	Building a Bridge/What Will I Do	1963	2.50	5.00	10.00
❑ 42782 [PS]	Building a Bridge/What Will I Do	1963	3.75	7.50	15.00
❑ 42833	Hey Lucille!/Scarlett O'Hara	1963	2.50	5.00	10.00
❑ 42833 [PS]	Hey Lucille!/Scarlett O'Hara	1963	3.75	7.50	15.00
❑ 42959	That's What Makes the World Go Around/A Lace Mantilla and a Rose of Red	1964	2.00	4.00	8.00
❑ 43083	Sam Hill/Big Ole Shoulder	1964	2.00	4.00	8.00
❑ 43157	Whirlpool (Of Your Love)/This Land of Yours and Mine	1964	2.00	4.00	8.00
❑ 43298	Tiger Woman/When You Gotta Go	1965	2.00	4.00	8.00
❑ 43416	Little Buddy/Come On Home	1965	2.00	4.00	8.00
❑ 43510	Catch a Little Raindrop/Hold That Tiger	1966	2.00	4.00	8.00
❑ 43714	The Juggler/I Won't Be Long in Your Town	1966	2.50	5.00	10.00
❑ 43867	Little Things That Every Girl Should Know/The Right Place	1966	2.00	4.00	8.00
❑ 44035	The Watchman/That's the Way the Wind Blows	1967	2.00	4.00	8.00
❑ 44237	Laura (What's He Got That I Ain't Got)/Good-By My Love	1967	2.00	4.00	8.00
❑ 44340	Yellow Haired Woman/Ninety-Nine Years	1967	2.00	4.00	8.00
❑ 44504	Parchman Farm Blues/Birmingham Bus Station	1968	2.00	4.00	8.00
❑ 44642	The Power of Your Sweet Love/Beertops and Teardrops	1968	2.00	4.00	8.00
❑ 44749	Sweet Love on My Mind/Four Roses	1969	2.00	4.00	8.00
❑ 44833	All for the Love of a Girl/I Remember Johnny	1969	2.00	4.00	8.00
❑ 44833 [PS]	All for the Love of a Girl/I Remember Johnny	1969	3.00	6.00	12.00
❑ 45015	Friend, Lover, Woman, Wife/The House of the Rising Sun	1969	2.00	4.00	8.00
❑ 45142	I'll Be Your Baby Tonight/It's Good to Have My Baby Home	1970	—	3.00	6.00
❑ 45248	Mary's Vineyard/Johnny Valentine	1970	—	3.00	6.00
❑ 45340	Chip 'n' Dale's Place/Highway Lonely	1971	—	3.00	6.00
❑ 45441	When You're Twenty-One/Heart	1971	—	3.00	6.00
❑ 45515	Darlin' Raise the Shade (Let the Sun Shine In)/Sweet Mary Ann	1971	—	3.00	6.00
❑ 45614	The Lady of Our Town/Just As Soon As I Get Over Loving You	1972	—	3.00	6.00
❑ 45704	He Ain't Country/This Time I'm Through	1972	—	3.00	6.00
TRUE					
❑ 103	Cotton Dan/I'll Spend My Lifetime Loving You	1977	—	3.00	6.00
❑ 106	Sugar Baby, Candy Girl/(B-side unknown)	1977	—	3.00	6.00
❑ 124	Wobble Water/(B-side unknown)	197?	—	3.00	6.00

Albums

Number	Title	Yr	VG	VG+	NM
COLUMBIA					
❑ CS 1024	Friend, Lover, Woman, Wife	1970	3.75	7.50	15.00
❑ CL 1810 [M]	Meet Claude King	1962	6.25	12.50	25.00
—Six "eye" logos on label					
❑ CL 1810 [M]	Meet Claude King	1963	3.75	7.50	15.00
—"Guaranteed High Fidelity" or "Mono" on red label					
❑ CL 2415 [M]	Tiger Woman	1965	5.00	10.00	20.00
❑ CS 8610 [S]	Meet Claude King	1962	10.00	20.00	40.00
—Six "eye" logos on label					
❑ CS 8610 [S]	Meet Claude King	1963	5.00	10.00	20.00
—"360 Sound Stereo" on red label					
❑ CS 9215 [S]	Tiger Woman	1965	6.25	12.50	25.00
—"360 Sound Stereo" on red label					
❑ CS 9789	I Remember Johnny Horton	1968	3.75	7.50	15.00
—"360 Sound Stereo" on red label					
❑ C 30804	Chip 'n' Dale's Place	1971	3.75	7.50	15.00
HARMONY					
❑ HS 11300	The Best of Claude King	1969	3.00	6.00	12.00

KING, DON
45s

Number	Title (A Side/B Side)	Yr	VG	VG+	NM
615					
❑ 1015	Can't Stop the Music/(B-side unknown)	1988	—	2.50	5.00
BENCH MARK					
❑ 8601	All We Had Was One Another/(B-side unknown)	1986	—	2.50	5.00

Number	Title (A Side/B Side)	Yr	VG	VG+	NM
CON BRIO					
❑ 106	Days of You and Me/Diamond Red Cowboy	1976	—	3.00	6.00
❑ 108	Dancing Across My Memory/I Can See Forever in Your Eyes	1976	—	3.00	6.00
❑ 112	Cabin High (In the Blue Ridge Mountains)/Leavin' Talk	1976	—	2.50	5.00
❑ 116	I've Got You (To Come Home To)/Diamond Red Cowboy	1977	—	2.50	5.00
❑ 120	She's the Girl of My Dreams/Dancing Across My Memory	1977	—	2.50	5.00
❑ 126	I Must Be Dreaming/Truck Drivin' Lash LaRue	1977	—	2.50	5.00
❑ 129	Music Is My Woman/Drinkin' in Texas	1977	—	2.50	5.00
❑ 133	Don't Make No Promises (You Can't Keep)/Cabin High (In the Blue Ridge Mountains)	1978	—	2.50	5.00
❑ 137	The Feeling's So Right Tonight/Where Were You	1978	—	2.50	5.00
❑ 142	You Were Worth Waiting For/Don't Get Around Much	1978	—	2.50	5.00
❑ 149	Live Entertainment/I Must Be Dreaming	1979	—	2.50	5.00
❑ 153	I've Got Country Music in My Soul/She's the Girl of My Dreams	1979	—	2.50	5.00
EPIC					
❑ 19-02046	I Still Miss Someone/More Than a Memory	1981	—	2.00	4.00
❑ 14-02468	The Closer You Get/The Time of Our Lives	1981	—	2.00	4.00
❑ 14-02674	Running on Love/Lean On Jesus	1981	—	2.00	4.00
❑ 14-03155	Maximum Security (To Minimum Wage)/The Shadow of My Love	1982	—	2.00	4.00
❑ 50840	Lonely Hotel/Same Old Feeling	1980	—	2.00	4.00
❑ 50877	Here Comes That Feeling Again/My Happiness Is You	1980	—	2.00	4.00
❑ 50928	Take This Heart/Saddle the Stallion	1980	—	2.00	4.00
Albums					
CON BRIO					
❑ 052	Dreams 'n Things	1977	3.00	6.00	12.00
❑ 053	The Feelin's So Right	1978	3.00	6.00	12.00

KING, DONNY

45s

Number	Title (A Side/B Side)	Yr	VG	VG+	NM
WARNER BROS.					
❑ 8074	Mathilda/I Played That Song for You	1975	—	2.00	4.00
❑ 8145	I'm a Fool to Care/Hello Mary Lou, Goodbye Heart	1975	—	2.00	4.00
❑ 8229	Stop the World (And Let Me Off)/Wake Me Gently	1976	—	2.00	4.00

KING, HUGH

45s

Number	Title (A Side/B Side)	Yr	VG	VG+	NM
HICKORY/MGM					
❑ 307	When She's Good, She's Really Good/You're the One	1973	—	3.50	7.00
❑ 317	The Girl I Love/I Spend a Week There Last Night	1974	—	3.50	7.00
❑ 322	I'd Just Be Fool Enough/Let Me Introduce Myself	1974	—	3.50	7.00
❑ 332	Our Sun Shines at Night/Wish I Were in Love Again	1974	—	3.50	7.00

KING, MATT

45s

Number	Title (A Side/B Side)	Yr	VG	VG+	NM
ATLANTIC					
❑ 84101	A Woman's Tears/Five O'Clock Hero	1998	—	—	3.00
❑ 84160	Five O'Clock Hero/September Rain	1998	—	—	3.00

KING, PEE WEE

Many of the below feature the vocals and songwriting of REDD STEWART.

45s

Number	Title (A Side/B Side)	Yr	VG	VG+	NM
BRIAR					
❑ 120	Tennessee Waltz/Wooden Heart Polka	196?	3.00	6.00	12.00
CUCA					
❑ 1207	Guitar Polka/Wings of a Dove	1965	2.50	5.00	10.00
❑ 1247	Danny Boy/I Am Praying for the Day Peace Will Come	1965	2.50	5.00	10.00
❑ 1275	History Repeats Itself/Hope, Faith and Love	1966	2.50	5.00	10.00
❑ 1315	Too Many Years/I Want to Light a Candle	1966	2.50	5.00	10.00
❑ 1316	Night Friends/Alone in San Antone	1966	2.50	5.00	10.00
❑ 1420	I'm in Love with the Bridesmaid/(No One) Unless It's You	1966	2.50	5.00	10.00
JARO					
❑ 77025	Hi Diddle Diddle/Vagabond Waltz	1960	3.00	6.00	12.00
LANDA					
❑ 668	Looking Back to Sea/Slow Poke	1961	3.00	6.00	12.00
❑ 673	Bumming Around/When, When, When	1961	3.00	6.00	12.00
RCA VICTOR					
❑ 47-4238	Two Roads/Makin' Like a Train	1951	6.25	12.50	25.00
❑ 47-4458	Silver and Gold/Ragtime Annie Lee	1952	5.00	10.00	20.00
❑ 47-4601	Tennessee Waltz/Bullfiddle Boogie	1952	3.75	7.50	15.00
❑ 47-4602	Silver and Gold/Texas Toni Lee	1952	3.75	7.50	15.00
❑ 47-4603	Slow Poke/Ten Gallon Boogie	1952	3.75	7.50	15.00
❑ 47-4604	Kentucky Waltz/Bonaparte's Retreat	1952	3.75	7.50	15.00
—The above four comprise a box set					
❑ 47-4655	Busybody/I Don't Mind	1952	5.00	10.00	20.00
❑ 47-4883	Two Faced Clock/Mighty Pretty Waltz	1952	5.00	10.00	20.00
❑ 47-4969	My Adobe Hacienda/Spanish Two-Step	1952	3.75	7.50	15.00
❑ 47-4970	Steel Guitar Rag/Over the Waves	1952	3.75	7.50	15.00
❑ 47-4971	San Antonio Rose/Varsouviana	1952	3.75	7.50	15.00
❑ 47-4972	The One Rose/Under the Double Eagle	1952	3.75	7.50	15.00
—The above four comprise a box set					
❑ 47-5009	Tennessee Tango/Crazy Waltz	1952	5.00	10.00	20.00
❑ 47-5144	Railroad Boogie/The Crying Steel Guitar Waltz	1953	5.00	10.00	20.00
❑ 47-5260	Screwball/Last Night on the Back Porch	1953	5.00	10.00	20.00
❑ 47-5344	Your Kisses Aren't Kisses Anymore/If and When	1953	5.00	10.00	20.00
❑ 47-5454	Ricochet/Oh Mis'rable Love	1953	5.00	10.00	20.00
❑ 47-5537	Changing Partners/Bimbo	1953	5.00	10.00	20.00
❑ 47-5587	Red Deck of Cards/Deck of Cards	1954	6.25	12.50	25.00
❑ 47-5632	Why Don't Y'All Go Home/Huggin' My Pillow	1954	5.00	10.00	20.00
❑ 47-5694	Backward, Turn Backward/Indian Giver	1954	5.00	10.00	20.00
❑ 47-5782	In a Garden of Roses/How Long	1954	5.00	10.00	20.00
❑ 47-5847	Keep Your Eye on My Darling/Here Lies My Heart	1954	5.00	10.00	20.00
❑ 47-5889	Peaches and Cream/I Can't Tell a Waltz from a Tango	1954	5.00	10.00	20.00
❑ 47-6005	Tweedlee Dee/You Can't Hardly Get Them No More	1955	3.75	7.50	15.00
❑ 47-6070	Plantation Boogie/Jim, Johnny and Jonas	1955	3.75	7.50	15.00
❑ 47-6162	Nevermind/Beauty Is As Beauty Gets	1955	3.75	7.50	15.00
❑ 47-6233	Seven Come Eleven/Farewell Blues	1955	3.75	7.50	15.00
❑ 47-6302	Peek-a-Boo Waltz/You Won't Need My Love Anymore	1955	3.75	7.50	15.00
❑ 47-6450	Blue Suede Shoes/Tennessee Dancin' Doll	1956	6.25	12.50	25.00
❑ 47-6666	Ballroom Baby/Absolutely Positive	1956	3.75	7.50	15.00
❑ 47-6793	Sugar Beet/I'll Be Walking Alone in a Crowd	1957	3.75	7.50	15.00
❑ 47-7090	Congratulations Joe/Prelude to a Broken Heart	1957	3.75	7.50	15.00
❑ 47-7375	Janie/Unbreakable Heart	1958	3.75	7.50	15.00
❑ 48-0003	Tennessee Waltz/Rootie Tootie	1949	7.50	15.00	30.00
—Green vinyl original					
❑ 48-0037	Bull Fiddle Boogie/Chattanooga Bus	1949	7.50	15.00	30.00
—Green vinyl original					
❑ 48-0085	Tennessee Polka/The Nashville Waltz	1949	7.50	15.00	30.00
—Green vinyl original					
❑ 48-0114	Bonaparte's Retreat/The Waltz of Regret	1949	7.50	15.00	30.00
—Green vinyl original					
❑ 48-0118	You Call Everybody Darlin'/Shocking Rye Straw	1950	6.25	12.50	25.00
—Green vinyl original					
❑ 48-0119	The Battle Hymn of the Republic/Blackeyed Susie	1950	6.25	12.50	25.00
—Green vinyl original					
❑ 48-0120	Cornbread, Lasses and Sassafras Tea/Fire on the Mountain	1950	6.25	12.50	25.00
—Green vinyl original; the above three comprise a box set					
❑ 48-0122	Fisher's Hornpipe/Devil's Dream	1950	6.25	12.50	25.00
—Green vinyl original					
❑ 48-0123	Sally Goodin/Arkansas Traveler	1950	6.25	12.50	25.00
—Green vinyl original					
❑ 48-0124	Billy in the Low Ground/Whistling Rufus	1950	6.25	12.50	25.00
—Green vinyl original; the above three comprise a box set					
❑ 48-0179	Rag Mop/When They Played That Old Missouri Waltz	1950	7.50	15.00	30.00
—Green vinyl original					
❑ 48-0223	Kentucky Waltz/Keep Them Cold Icy Fingers Off Me	1950	7.50	15.00	30.00
—Green vinyl original					
❑ 48-0307	Blame It All on Nashville/The Kissing Dance	1950	6.25	12.50	25.00
—Green vinyl original					
❑ 48-0332	Birmingham Bounce/What, Where and When	1950	6.25	12.50	25.00
—Green vinyl original					
❑ 48-0354	Blue Grass Waltz/Get Together Polka	1950	6.25	12.50	25.00
—Green vinyl original					
❑ 48-0379	Cincinnati Dancing Pig/We're Gonna Go Fishin'	1950	6.25	12.50	25.00
—Green vinyl original					
❑ 48-0393	Mop Rag Boogie/River Road Two-Step	1950	7.50	15.00	30.00
—Green vinyl original					
❑ 48-0407	Tennessee Waltz/Hilegged, Hilegged	1951	6.25	12.50	25.00
❑ 48-0429	No One But You/Within My Heart	1951	6.25	12.50	25.00
❑ 48-0451	The Strange Little Girl/Chew Tobacco Rag	1951	6.25	12.50	25.00
❑ 48-0489	Slow Poke/Whisper Waltz	1951	6.25	12.50	25.00
STARDAY					
❑ 668	Goodbye New Orleans/Waitin'	1964	2.50	5.00	10.00
❑ 682	When the Lights Go Dim Downtown/Stay Away from Me	1964	2.50	5.00	10.00
❑ 698	Ten Thousand Crying Towels/The Urge	1964	2.50	5.00	10.00
TODD					
❑ 1009	Slow Poke Cha Cha/I Got a Wife	1959	3.00	6.00	12.00
❑ 1020	Too Tall/Slow Poke Cha Cha	1959	3.00	6.00	12.00
TOP RANK					
❑ 2087	Do You Remember/(B-side unknown)	1960	3.00	6.00	12.00
Selected 78s					
BULLET					
❑ 615	That Cheap Look in Your Eye/You Were the Cause of It All	1947	12.50	25.00	50.00
RCA VICTOR					
❑ 20-2680	Tennessee Waltz/Rootie Tootie	1948	5.00	10.00	20.00
❑ 21-0037	Tennessee Tears/Alabama Moon	1949	5.00	10.00	20.00
—Mysteriously, this does not appear to exist on a 45					
Albums					
BRIAR					
❑ 102	Golden Olde Tyme Dances	1975	15.00	30.00	60.00
LONGHORN					
❑ 1236 [M]	The Legendary Pee Wee King	1967	6.25	12.50	25.00
RCA CAMDEN					
❑ CAL-876 [M]	Country Barn Dance	1965	5.00	10.00	20.00
❑ CAS-876 [R]	Country Barn Dance	1965	3.00	6.00	12.00
RCA VICTOR					
❑ LPM-1237 [M]	Swing West	1956	10.00	20.00	40.00
❑ LPM-3028 [10]	Pee Wee King	195?	20.00	40.00	80.00
❑ LPM-3071 [10]	Western Hits	195?	20.00	40.00	80.00

Number	Title (A Side/B Side)	Yr	VG	VG+	NM
LPM-3109 [10]	Waltzes	195?	20.00	40.00	80.00
LPM-3280 [10]	Swing West	195?	20.00	40.00	80.00
STARDAY					
SLP-284 [M]	Back Again with the Songs That Made Them Famous	1964	7.50	15.00	30.00

KING, SHERRI

45s

UNITED ARTISTS

Number	Title (A Side/B Side)	Yr	VG	VG+	NM
XW855	Almost Persuaded/A Good Woman Waits on Her Man	1976	—	2.00	4.00
XW902	Take Time to Know Him/Walking on the Edge	1976	—	2.00	4.00
XW943	Your Sweet Love/A Good Woman Waits on Her Man	1977	—	2.00	4.00
XW975	Seasons of My Heart/Then Give Him Back to Me	1977	—	2.00	4.00

KING, SID

45s

COLUMBIA

Number	Title (A Side/B Side)	Yr	VG	VG+	NM
4-21361	I Like It/Put Something in the Pot Now	1955	12.50	25.00	50.00
—As "The Five Strings"					
4-21403	Drinkin' Wine Spoli-Oli/Crazy Little Heart	1955	15.00	30.00	60.00
—As "The Five Strings"					
4-21449	Sag, Drag and Fall/But I Don't Care	1955	12.50	25.00	50.00
4-21489	Mama I Want You/Purr, Kitty, Purr	1956	12.50	25.00	50.00
4-21505	Blue Suede Shoes/Let 'Er Roll	1956	15.00	30.00	60.00
4-21564	Good Rockin' Baby/Gonna Shake This	1956	15.00	30.00	60.00
4-40680	Oobie Doobie/Boozer Red	1956	12.50	25.00	50.00
4-40833	It's True, I'm Blue/When My Baby Left Me	1957	12.50	25.00	50.00
4-41019	I've Got the Blues/What Have Ya Got to Lose	1957	12.50	25.00	50.00
DOT					
16293	Hello There Rockin' Chair/Once Upon a Time	1961	7.50	15.00	30.00
SOUNDWAVES					
4612	Back Door Man/I'd Rather Hear Willie	1980	2.00	4.00	8.00

KING EDWARD IV AND THE KNIGHTS

45s

SOUNDWAVES

Number	Title (A Side/B Side)	Yr	VG	VG+	NM
4529	The Lonely Bull/In the Pines	1976	—	2.50	5.00
4540	Rabbit Run/Kentucky Flower	1976	—	2.50	5.00
4550	Greenback Shuffle/New Corena	1977	—	2.50	5.00
4563	Wipe You from My Eyes (Gettin' Over You)/No News Is Good News	1978	—	2.50	5.00
4573	Baby Blue/Rabbit Run	1978	—	2.50	5.00
4583	A Couple More Years/The Old Spinning Wheel	1979	—	2.50	5.00
4592	I'll Fly Away/Love Potion #9	1979	—	2.50	5.00
4597	A Song for Noel/Desperado	1980	—	2.50	5.00
4616	Cotton Eyed Joe/Everybody's Doin' the Cotton Eyed Joe	1980	—	2.50	5.00
4626	Dixie Road/Joyful Noise	1980	—	2.50	5.00
4635	Keep On Movin'/Kentucky Flower	1981	—	2.50	5.00

KING SISTERS, THE

Pop vocal group who had this one hit on the country charts.

Selected 78s

RCA VICTOR

Number	Title (A Side/B Side)	Yr	VG	VG+	NM
20-2018	Divorce Me C.O.D./It's a Pity to Say Goodnight	1946	3.00	6.00	12.00

KINGSTON, LARRY

45s

JMI

Number	Title (A Side/B Side)	Yr	VG	VG+	NM
37	Good Morning Loving/Make a Dream Come True	1974	—	3.00	6.00
45	The Door's Always Open/In the Palm of Your Mind	1974	—	3.00	6.00
WARNER BROS.					
8089	The Door Is Always Open/Rails to Birmingham	1975	—	2.50	5.00
8116	I Feel Chained/Bossier City	1975	—	2.50	5.00
8139	Good Morning Lovin'/Make a Dream Come True	1975	—	2.50	5.00
8230	Another Perfect Night/Wilma Lou	1976	—	2.50	5.00

KINLEYS, THE

45s

EPIC

Number	Title (A Side/B Side)	Yr	VG	VG+	NM
34-78656	Please//Just Between You and Me/Talk to Me/You Make It Seem So Easy (all snippets)	1997	—	—	3.00
34-79071	Somebody's Out There Watching/Please	1998	—	—	3.00

KIRBY, DAVE

45s

BOONE

Number	Title (A Side/B Side)	Yr	VG	VG+	NM
1078	Marie St. John/My Faults Will Fade Away	1969	2.00	4.00	8.00
1083	A Walk on the Outside/Mary and Jane	1969	2.00	4.00	8.00
CAPITOL					
4119	Colorado/Good to Be Back on the Road	1975	—	3.00	6.00
DIMENSION					
1013	Great All American Good Timin' Honky Tonk Man/Ain't Nothing Older Than That	1980	—	2.50	5.00
1019	North Alabama/How Can I Tell You Goodbye	1981	—	2.50	5.00
1022	Moccasin Man/When Will Forgetting Begin	1981	—	2.50	5.00
1030	Something New to Love/Cowboy Connection	1982	—	2.50	5.00
DOT					
17437	Lila Is My Kind of Woman/So Long Train Whistle	1972	—	3.00	6.00
17461	Charleston Cotton Mill/Is Anybody Goin' to San Antone	1973	—	3.00	6.00
MONUMENT					
1168	Her and the Car and the Mobile Home/Don't It Make You Want to Go Home	1969	—	3.00	6.00
1215	I Came Out Smelling Like a Rose/The Hobo	1970	—	3.00	6.00
ZODIAC					
1007	What Kind of Bird Is That/Gonna Ride the Santa Fe to Santa Fe	1976	—	3.00	6.00

Albums

DOT

Number	Title (A Side/B Side)	Yr	VG	VG+	NM
DLP-26014	Singer, Picker, Writer	1973	3.00	6.00	12.00

KIRK, EDDIE

45s

CAPITOL

Number	Title (A Side/B Side)	Yr	VG	VG+	NM
F877	Two Years We Were Married/Unfaithful One	1950	7.50	15.00	30.00
F974	Four Hearts/Saturday Night Blues	1950	7.50	15.00	30.00
F1048	Sugar Baby/An Armful of Great Heartaches	1950	7.50	15.00	30.00
F1175	Puppy Love/Somebody's Cryin'	1950	7.50	15.00	30.00
F1287	Blue Bonnet Blues/In the Shambles of My Heart	1950	7.50	15.00	30.00
F1445	Honey Costs Money/Sowing Teardrops	1951	6.25	12.50	25.00
F1591	Alone in a Tavern/Drifting Texas Sand	1951	6.25	12.50	25.00
F1790	I'll Save My Heart/Freight Train Breakdown	1951	6.25	12.50	25.00
F40260	Dear Hearts and Gentle People/Careless Kisses	1949	10.00	20.00	40.00
F40285	A Year of City Livin'/Away Out on the Mountain	1950	7.50	15.00	30.00
RCA VICTOR					
47-5149	Five Star President/Hit and Run Lover	1953	6.25	12.50	25.00
47-5287	Wanderin' Eyes/The Country Way	1953	6.25	12.50	25.00
47-5412	Caribbean/As God Is My Witness	1953	6.25	12.50	25.00

Selected 78s

CAPITOL

Number	Title (A Side/B Side)	Yr	VG	VG+	NM
15176	The Gods Were Angry with Me/You Sweet Little You	1948	5.00	10.00	20.00
15310	No Tears Tomorrow/You Drove Me to Another's Arms	1949	3.75	7.50	15.00
15369	I've Lived a Lifetime for You/When My Castles Come Tumbling Down	1949	5.00	10.00	20.00
15391	Candy Kisses/Save the Next Waltz for Me	1949	3.75	7.50	15.00
40046	Judy/Memories Are My Souvenirs	1947	5.00	10.00	20.00
40069	Those Dark Clouds Don't Bother Me/Sad and Blue	1947	5.00	10.00	20.00
40092	What's Another Heart to You/A Petal from a Faded Rose	1948	5.00	10.00	20.00
40116	Born to Lose/How Do You Mend a Broken Heart	1948	5.00	10.00	20.00
40127	A Little White House/Tomorrow the Sun Will Shine	1948	5.00	10.00	20.00
40188	You Can't Pick a Rose in December/Promise Me	1949	5.00	10.00	20.00
40226	I'd Rather Hear Most Anything/I Wouldn't Take a Million	1949	5.00	10.00	20.00

KIRK, RED

45s

MERCURY

Number	Title (A Side/B Side)	Yr	VG	VG+	NM
6274	Never Been So Lonesome/Church Bells Chimed	1950	7.50	15.00	30.00
6288	Can't Understand a Woman/Teardrops from My Eyes	1950	7.50	15.00	30.00
6309	Cold Steel Blues/Three's a Crowd	1951	6.25	12.50	25.00
6332	Sugar Coated Love/Mad at My Heart	1951	6.25	12.50	25.00
6358	Sentimental Journey/Train Track Shuffle	1951	6.25	12.50	25.00
6363	Gentle Hands/Only One Step More	1951	6.25	12.50	25.00
6409	Careless Mind/Knock Out the Lights and Call the Law	1952	6.25	12.50	25.00

Selected 78s

MERCURY

Number	Title (A Side/B Side)	Yr	VG	VG+	NM
6189	Lovesick Blues/A Package Tied in Blue	1949	3.75	7.50	15.00
6204	A Tear for Your Waltz/Honeymoon Waltz	1949	3.75	7.50	15.00
6223	Cry Baby Heart/I Wasted a Nickel	1950	3.75	7.50	15.00
6242	Why Do You Care/It's Raining in My Heart	1950	3.75	7.50	15.00
6257	Lose Your Blues/Over an Ocean of Golden Dreams	1950	3.75	7.50	15.00

KNIGHT, JEFF

45s

MERCURY

Number	Title (A Side/B Side)	Yr	VG	VG+	NM
862630-7	Easy Street/Four-Wheel Drive	1993	—	—	3.00
866520-7	Got Through Everything But the Door/They've Been Talkin' About Me	1992	—	—	3.00
866812-7	Walk Softly on the Bridges/Casting My Shadow on the Road	1992	—	—	3.00
866916-7	I Wish She Didn't Know Me/They've Been Talkin' About Me	1992	—	—	3.00

KNOBLOCK, FRED

Also see SCHUYLER, KNOBLOCH & BICKHARDT; SCHUYLER, KNOBLOCH & OVERSTREET.

45s

SCOTTI BROTHERS

Number	Title (A Side/B Side)	Yr	VG	VG+	NM
518	Why Not Me/Can I Get a Wish	1980	—	2.50	5.00
600	Why Not Me/Can I Get a Wish	1980	—	2.00	4.00
607	Let Me Love You/It's Over	1980	—	2.00	4.00
609	Killin' Time/Love Is No Friend to a Fool	1980	—	2.00	4.00
—A-side with Susan Anton					
ZS5-02434	Memphis/Love Isn't Easy	1981	—	2.00	4.00
ZS5-02752	I Had It All/Love, Love, Love	1982	—	2.00	4.00

Number	Title (A Side/B Side)	Yr	VG	VG+	NM
Albums					
SCOTTI BROTHERS					
❑ SB 7109	Why Not Me	1980	2.50	5.00	10.00

KNOX, BUDDY

Number	Title (A Side/B Side)	Yr	VG	VG+	NM
45s					
LIBERTY					
❑ 55290	Lovey Dovey/I Got You	1960	3.00	6.00	12.00
❑ 55305	Ling, Ting, Tong/The Kisses	1961	3.00	6.00	12.00
❑ 55305 [PS]	Ling, Ting, Tong/The Kisses	1961	7.50	15.00	30.00
❑ 55366	All By Myself/Three Eyed Man	1961	3.00	6.00	12.00
❑ 55411	Cha-Hua-Hua/Open	1962	3.00	6.00	12.00
❑ 55473	She's Gone/There's Only Me	1962	3.00	6.00	12.00
❑ 55503	Dear Abby/Three Way Love Affair	1962	3.00	6.00	12.00
❑ 55592	Shadaroom/Tomorrow Is a-Comin'	1963	2.50	5.00	10.00
❑ 55650	Thanks a Lot/Hitchhike Back to Georgia	1963	2.50	5.00	10.00
❑ 55694	Good Lovin'/All Time Loser	1964	2.50	5.00	10.00
REPRISE					
❑ 0395	Livin' in a House Full of Love/Good Time Girl	1965	2.50	5.00	10.00
❑ 0431	A Lover's Question/You Said Goodbye	1965	2.50	5.00	10.00
❑ 0463	A White Sport Coat/That Don't Do Me No Good	1966	2.50	5.00	10.00
❑ 0501	Love Has Many Ways/Sixteen Feet of Patio	1966	2.50	5.00	10.00
ROULETTE					
❑ 4002	Party Doll/My Baby's Gone	1957	12.50	25.00	50.00
—Maroon label, silver print, with roulette wheel around outside					
❑ 4002	Party Doll/My Baby's Gone	1957	7.50	15.00	30.00
—Red label, roulette wheel on top half of label					
❑ 4002	Party Doll/My Baby's Gone	1957	6.25	12.50	25.00
—Red label, no roulette wheel					
❑ 4002	Party Doll/My Baby's Gone	1957	10.00	20.00	40.00
—Red label, black print, with roulette wheel around outside					
❑ 4002	Party Doll/My Baby's Gone	1958	3.75	7.50	15.00
—White label with color spokes					
❑ 4009	Rock Your Little Baby to Sleep/Don't Make Me Cry	1957	10.00	20.00	40.00
—Red label with roulette wheel around outside					
❑ 4009	Rock Your Little Baby to Sleep/Don't Make Me Cry	1957	6.25	12.50	25.00
—Red label, roulette wheel on top half of label					
❑ 4009	Rock Your Little Baby to Sleep/Don't Make Me Cry	1957	5.00	10.00	20.00
—Red label, no roulette wheel					
❑ 4018	Hula Love/Devil Woman	1957	6.25	12.50	25.00
❑ 4042	Swingin' Daddy/Whenever I'm Lonely	1958	6.25	12.50	25.00
❑ 4082	Somebody Touched Me/C'mon Baby	1958	6.25	12.50	25.00
❑ 4120	That's Why I Cry/Teaseable, Pleaseable You	1958	6.25	12.50	25.00
❑ 4140	I Think I'm Gonna Kill Myself/To Be with You	1959	6.25	12.50	25.00
❑ 4179	Taste of the Blues/I Ain't Sharin' Sharon	1959	6.25	12.50	25.00
❑ 4262	Long Lonely Nights/Storm Clouds	1960	6.25	12.50	25.00
RUFF					
❑ 1001	Jo-Ann/Don't Make a Ripple	1965	2.50	5.00	10.00
TRIPLE D					
❑ 798	Party Doll/I'm Stickin' With You	1956	250.00	500.00	1000.
—B-side by Jimmy Bowen					
UNITED ARTISTS					
❑ 50301	This Time Tomorrow/Gypsy Man	1968	2.00	4.00	8.00
❑ 50463	Today My Sleepless Nights Came Back to Town/A Million Years or So	1968	2.00	4.00	8.00
❑ 50526	God Knows I Love You/Night Runners	1969	2.00	4.00	8.00
❑ 50596	Salt Lake City/I'm Only Rockin'	1969	2.00	4.00	8.00
❑ 50644	Yesterday Is Gone/Back to New Orleans	1970	—	3.00	6.00
❑ 50722	White Dove/Glory Train	1970	—	3.00	6.00
❑ 50789	Come Softly to Me/Travelin' Light	1971	—	3.00	6.00
Albums					
ACCORD					
❑ SN-7218	Party Doll and Other Hits	1981	2.50	5.00	10.00
LIBERTY					
❑ LRP-3251 [M]	Buddy Knox's Golden Hits	1962	7.50	15.00	30.00
❑ LST-7251 [S]	Buddy Knox's Golden Hits	1962	10.00	20.00	40.00
ROULETTE					
❑ R 25003 [M]	Buddy Knox	1957	50.00	100.00	200.00
—Black label, all silver print (original)					
❑ R 25003 [M]	Buddy Knox	1957	37.50	75.00	150.00
—Black label, red and silver print					
❑ R 25003 [M]	Buddy Knox	1959	25.00	50.00	100.00
—White label with colored spokes					
❑ R 25048 [M]	Buddy Knox and Jimmy Bowen	1959	50.00	100.00	200.00
—Black label, red and silver print					
❑ R 25048 [M]	Buddy Knox and Jimmy Bowen	1959	25.00	50.00	100.00
—White label with colored spokes					
UNITED ARTISTS					
❑ UAS 6689	Gypsy Man	1969	6.25	12.50	25.00

KRAMER, REX

Number	Title (A Side/B Side)	Yr	VG	VG+	NM
45s					
COLUMBIA					
❑ 3-10286	You Oughta Be Against the Law/Our Love Is Blooming	1976	—	2.50	5.00

KRAUSS, ALISON, AND UNION STATION

Also see ALAN JACKSON; SHENANDOAH.

Number	Title (A Side/B Side)	Yr	VG	VG+	NM
45s					
BNA					
❑ 64277	When You Say Nothing at All/Charlotte's in North Carolina	1995	—	2.00	4.00
—B-side by Keith Whitley					
ROUNDER					
❑ 4585	New Fool/Steel Rails	1992	—	3.00	6.00
Albums					
ROUNDER					
❑ 0235	Too Late to Cry	1987	3.00	6.00	12.00
❑ 0265	Two Highways	1989	3.00	6.00	12.00
❑ 0275	I've Got That Old Feeling	1990	3.00	6.00	12.00
❑ 0325	Now That I've Found You: A Collection	1995	3.00	6.00	12.00

KRISTOFFERSON, KRIS

Also see WILLIE NELSON.

Number	Title (A Side/B Side)	Yr	VG	VG+	NM
45s					
COLUMBIA					
❑ 04881	Highwayman/The Human Condition	1985	—	—	3.00
—A-side: Willie Nelson/Waylon Jennings/Johnny Cash/Kris Kristofferson; B-side: Nelson, Cash					
❑ 04881 [PS]	Highwayman/The Human Condition	1985	—	2.00	4.00
—A-side: Willie Nelson/Waylon Jennings/Johnny Cash/Kris Kristofferson; B-side: Nelson, Cash					
❑ 05594	Desperadoes Waiting for a Train/The Twentieth Century Is Almost Over	1985	—	—	3.00
—A-side: Willie Nelson/Waylon Jennings/Johnny Cash/Kris Kristofferson; B-side: Nelson, Cash					
❑ 08406	Highwayman/Desperadoes Waiting for a Train	1988	—	—	3.00
—Waylon Jennings/Willie Nelson/Johnny Cash/Kris Kristofferson; reissue					
❑ 08406	Highwayman/Desperadoes Waiting for a Train	1988	—	—	3.00
—Waylon Jennings/Willie Nelson/Johnny Cash/Kris Kristofferson; reissue					
❑ 10525	Watch Closely Now/Crippled Crow	1977	—	2.00	4.00
❑ 10731	The Fighter/Forever in Your Love	1978	—	2.00	4.00
❑ 11160	Prove It to You One More Time Again/Fallen Angel	1979	—	2.00	4.00
❑ 11383	I'll Take Any Chance I Can with You/Maybe You Heard	1980	—	2.00	4.00
❑ 60507	Nobody Loves Anybody Anymore/Maybe You Heard	1981	—	2.00	4.00
❑ 73381	Born and Raised in Black and White/Texas	1990	—	—	3.00
—The Highwaymen (Waylon Jennings/Willie Nelson/Johnny Cash/Kris Kristofferson)					
❑ 73572	American Remains/Texas	1990	—	—	3.00
—The Highwaymen (Waylon Jennings/Willie Nelson/Johnny Cash/Kris Kristofferson)					
EPIC					
❑ 10225	Golden Idol/Killing Time	1967	3.75	7.50	15.00
LIBERTY					
❑ S7-18486	It Is What It Is/The Devil's Right Hand	1995	—	—	3.00
—By The Highwaymen					
MERCURY					
❑ 888345-7	They Killed Him/Anthem '84	1987	—	—	3.00
❑ 888554-7	Love Is the Way/This Old Road	1987	—	—	3.00
❑ 888723-7	El Coyote/They Killed Him	1987	—	—	3.00
MONUMENT					
❑ 1210	Sunday Morning Comin' Down/To Beat the Devil	1970	2.00	4.00	8.00
❑ 8525	Loving Her Was Easier (Than Anything I'll Ever Do Again)/Epitaph	1971	—	3.00	6.00
❑ 8531	The Taker/Pilgrim: Chapter 33	1971	—	3.00	6.00
❑ 8536	Josie/Border Lord	1972	—	3.00	6.00
❑ 8558	Jesus Was a Capricorn/Enough for You	1972	—	3.00	6.00
❑ 8564	Jesse Younger/Give It Time to Be Tender	1973	—	3.00	6.00
❑ 8571	Why Me/Help Me	1973	—	2.50	5.00
❑ 8618	I May Smoke Too Much/Lights of Magdala	1974	—	2.50	5.00
❑ 8658	Easy, Come On/Rocket to Star	1975	—	2.00	4.00
❑ 8679	If It's All the Same to You/The Year 2000 Minus 25	1975	—	2.00	4.00
❑ 8707	The Prisoner/It's Never Gonna Be the Same Again	1976	—	2.00	4.00
❑ 21000	Here Comes That Rainbow Again/(B-side unknown)	1981	—	2.00	4.00
Albums					
COLUMBIA					
❑ PZ 30679	The Silver Tongued Devil and I	1976	2.00	4.00	8.00
—Reissue					
❑ PZ 30817	Me and Bobby McGee	1976	2.00	4.00	8.00
—Reissue					
❑ PZ 31302	Border Lord	1976	2.00	4.00	8.00
—Reissue					
❑ PZ 31909	Jesus Was a Capricorn	1976	2.00	4.00	8.00
—Reissue					
❑ PZ 32914	Spooky Lady's Sideshow	1976	2.00	4.00	8.00
—Reissue					
❑ PZ 33379	Who's to Bless…And Who's to Blame	1976	2.00	4.00	8.00
—Reissue					
❑ PZ 34254	Surreal Thing	1976	3.00	6.00	12.00
❑ PZ 34687	Songs of Kristofferson	1977	3.00	6.00	12.00
❑ JZ 35310	Easter Island	1978	3.00	6.00	12.00
❑ JZ 36135	Shake Hands with the Devil	1979	3.00	6.00	12.00
❑ JZ 36885	To the Bone	1980	3.00	6.00	12.00
MERCURY					
❑ 830406-1	Repossessed	1987	2.50	5.00	10.00
MONUMENT					
❑ SLP-18139	Kristofferson	1970	6.25	12.50	25.00
—Original label is light green with a yellow ring					
❑ Z 30679	The Silver Tongued Devil and I	1971	3.00	6.00	12.00
❑ ZQ 30679 [Q]	The Silver Tongued Devil and I	1972	5.00	10.00	20.00

Number	Title (A Side/B Side)	Yr	VG	VG+	NM
❑ Z 30817	Me and Bobby McGee	1971	3.00	6.00	12.00
—Reissue of 18139 with new title					
❑ KZ 31302	Border Lord	1972	3.00	6.00	12.00
❑ KZ 31909	Jesus Was a Capricorn	1972	3.00	6.00	12.00
❑ ZQ 31909 [Q]	Jesus Was a Capricorn	1973	5.00	10.00	20.00
❑ PZ 32914	Spooky Lady's Sideshow	1974	3.00	6.00	12.00
❑ PZQ 32914 [Q]	Spooky Lady's Sideshow	1974	5.00	10.00	20.00
❑ PZ 33379	Who's to Bless...And Who's to Blame	1975	3.00	6.00	12.00
❑ PW 38392	Songs of Kristofferson	1982	2.00	4.00	8.00
—Reissue of 34687					
PAIR					
❑ PDL2-1078 [(2)]	My Songs	1986	3.00	6.00	12.00

KRISTOFFERSON, KRIS, AND RITA COOLIDGE

Also see each artist's individual listings.

45s

Number	Title (A Side/B Side)	Yr	VG	VG+	NM
A&M					
❑ 1475	A Song I'd Like to Sing/From the Bottle to the Bottom	1973	—	2.00	4.00
❑ 1475 [PS]	A Song I'd Like to Sing/From the Bottle to the Bottom	1973	—	3.00	6.00
❑ 1498	Loving Arms/I'm Down	1974	—	2.00	4.00
❑ 2121	Not Everyone Knows/Blue As I Do	1979	—	2.00	4.00
MONUMENT					
❑ 8630	Rain/What'cha Gonna Do	1974	—	2.00	4.00
❑ 8636	Lover Please/Slow Down	1975	—	2.00	4.00
❑ 8646	We Must Have Been Out of Our Minds/Sweet Susannah	1975	—	2.00	4.00

Albums

Number	Title (A Side/B Side)	Yr	VG	VG+	NM
A&M					
❑ SP-4403	Full Moon	1973	3.00	6.00	12.00
❑ SP-4690	Natural Act	1979	2.50	5.00	10.00
MONUMENT					
❑ PZ 33278	Breakaway	1974	3.00	6.00	12.00

KUNKEL, LEAH

See LIVINGSTON TAYLOR WITH LEAH KUNKEL

L

LA COSTA

Includes records as "La Costa Tucker."

45s

Number	Title (A Side/B Side)	Yr	VG	VG+	NM
CAPITOL					
❑ 3856	I Wanta Get to You/That's What Your Love Has Done	1974	—	2.50	5.00
❑ 3945	Get On My Love Train/I Can Feel Love Growing	1974	—	2.50	5.00
❑ 4022	He Took Me for a Ride/Superman	1974	—	2.50	5.00
❑ 4082	This House Runs on Sunshine/Ain't It Good	1975	—	2.50	5.00
❑ 4139	Weatern Man/Rescue Me	1975	—	2.50	5.00
❑ 4209	I Just Got a Feeling/Let's Talk It Over	1976	—	2.50	5.00
❑ 4264	Lovin' Somebody on a Rainy Night/The Best of My Love	1976	—	2.50	5.00
❑ 4327	What'll I Do/Your Love	1976	—	2.50	5.00
❑ 4414	We're All Alone/I Second That Emotion	1977	—	2.50	5.00
❑ 4495	Jessie and the Light/I Still Love You	1977	—	2.50	5.00
❑ 4541	Even Cowgirls Get the Blues/Alice, Texas	1978	—	2.50	5.00
❑ 4577	#1 with a Heartache/Take Your Love Away	1978	—	2.50	5.00
❑ 4830	Changing All the Time/Had to Fall in Love	1980	—	2.00	4.00
❑ 4899	It Was Time/Since I Fell for You	1980	—	2.00	4.00
ELEKTRA					
❑ 47414	Love Take It Easy on Me/The Best Is Yet to Come	1982	—	2.00	4.00
—As "La Costa Tucker"					

Albums

Number	Title (A Side/B Side)	Yr	VG	VG+	NM
CAPITOL					
❑ ST-11345	Get On My Love Train	1974	3.00	6.00	12.00
❑ ST-11391	With All My Love	1975	3.00	6.00	12.00
❑ ST-11569	Lovin' Somebody	1975	3.00	6.00	12.00
❑ ST-11713	La Costa	1977	3.00	6.00	12.00
❑ ST-12090	Changin' All the Time	1980	3.00	6.00	12.00

LABEEF, SLEEPY

45s

Number	Title (A Side/B Side)	Yr	VG	VG+	NM
COLUMBIA					
❑ 43452	Everybody's Got to Have Somebody (To Love)/You Can't Catch Me	1965	3.00	6.00	12.00
❑ 43875	I Feel a Lot More Like I Do Now/I'm Too Broke	1966	3.00	6.00	12.00
❑ 44068	Sure Beats the Heck Out of Settlin' Down/Schneider	1967	2.50	5.00	10.00
❑ 44261	Completely Destroyed/Go Ahead On Baby	1967	2.50	5.00	10.00
❑ 44455	Every Day/If I'm Right I'm Wrong	1968	2.50	5.00	10.00
CRESCENT					
❑ 102	Turn Me Loose/(B-side unknown)	195?	50.00	100.00	200.00
MERCURY					
❑ 71112	I'm Through/All Alone	1957	25.00	50.00	100.00
❑ 71179	All the Time/Lonely	1957	25.00	50.00	100.00
PICTURE					
❑ 1937	Ride On Josephine/(B-side unknown)	1959	37.50	75.00	150.00
PLANTATION					
❑ 55	Too Much Monkey Business/Got You on My Mind	1970	6.25	12.50	25.00
❑ 66	Asphalt Cowboy/Got You on My Mind	1971	2.50	5.00	10.00
❑ 74	Blackland Farmer/Got You on My Mind	1971	2.50	5.00	10.00
❑ 74 [DJ]	Blackland Farmer (mono/stereo)	1971	3.00	6.00	12.00
—Promo only on green vinyl					
STARDAY					
❑ 292	I'm Through/All Alone	1957	37.50	75.00	150.00
SUN					
❑ 1132	Thunder Road/A Hundred Pounds of Lovin'	1974	—	2.00	4.00
❑ 1133 [DJ]	Ghost Riders in the Sky (same on both sides)	1975	—	2.00	4.00
—Promo only					
❑ 1134	There Ain't Much After Taxes/A Hundred Pounds of Lovin'	1976	—	2.00	4.00
❑ 1137	Good Rockin' Boogie (Part 1)/Good rockin' Boogie (Part 2)	1978	—	2.00	4.00
❑ 1145	Flying Saucers Rock and Roll/Boogie Woogie Country Girl	1979	—	2.00	4.00
WAYSIDE					
❑ 1651	Ride On Josephine/(B-side unknown)	1959	50.00	100.00	200.00
—Wayside titles as "Tommy LaBeef"					
❑ 1652	Walkin' Slowly/(B-side unknown)	1959	62.50	125.00	250.00
❑ 1654	Tore Up/Lonely	1959	75.00	150.00	300.00

Albums

Number	Title (A Side/B Side)	Yr	VG	VG+	NM
ROUNDER					
❑ 3052	It Ain't What You Eat...	198?	2.50	5.00	10.00
❑ 3070	Electricity	198?	2.50	5.00	10.00
❑ 3072	Nothin' But the Truth	198?	2.50	5.00	10.00
SUN					
❑ 130	Bull's Night Out	1974	3.00	6.00	12.00
❑ 138	Western Gold	197?	3.00	6.00	12.00
❑ 1004	Rockabilly 1977	1977	3.00	6.00	12.00
❑ 1018	Downtown Rockabilly	1978	3.00	6.00	12.00

LACE

45s

Number	Title (A Side/B Side)	Yr	VG	VG+	NM
143/WARNER BROS.					
❑ 7-16932	I Want a Man/Swept Away	1999	—	—	3.00

LACE, BOBBI

Also see MARK GRAY.

45s

Number	Title (A Side/B Side)	Yr	VG	VG+	NM
615					
❑ 1008	Skin Deep/(B-side unknown)	1987	—	2.50	5.00
❑ 1008 [PS]	Skin Deep/(B-side unknown)	1987	2.00	4.00	8.00
❑ 1010	There's a Real Woman in Me/(B-side unknown)	1987	—	2.50	5.00
❑ 1010 [PS]	There's a Real Woman in Me/(B-side unknown)	1987	2.00	4.00	8.00
❑ 1011	Another Woman's Man/(B-side unknown)	1988	—	2.50	5.00
❑ 1012	If Hearts Could Talk/(B-side unknown)	1988	—	2.50	5.00
❑ 1017	Son of a Preacher Man/(B-side unknown)	1989	—	2.50	5.00
❑ 1026	Lonesome 3 A.M./(B-side unknown)	199?	—	3.00	6.00
GBS					
❑ 730	You've Been My Rock for Ages/(B-side unknown)	1986	—	2.50	5.00

LAFLEUR, DON

45s

Number	Title (A Side/B Side)	Yr	VG	VG+	NM
WORTH					
❑ 102	Beggars Can't Be Choosers/(B-side unknown)	1988	—	3.00	6.00

LAMASTER, DON

45s

Number	Title (A Side/B Side)	Yr	VG	VG+	NM
K-ARK					
❑ 1046	My Rose Is Blue/Key's in the Mailbox	1989	—	3.00	6.00

LANCE, LYNDA K.

Also see JIMMIE PETERS AND LYNDA K. LANCE.

45s

Number	Title (A Side/B Side)	Yr	VG	VG+	NM
ABC					
❑ 10942	It Just Can't Be/King of Sorrow	1967	2.50	5.00	10.00
GARPAX					
❑ 081	Say You Love Me/Pretend My Eyes Are Brown	1976	—	3.00	6.00
NSD					
❑ 64	Backslidin' Again/Morning Sky	1980	—	2.50	5.00
ROYAL AMERICAN					
❑ 5	I'm Seeing Leaving in Your Eyes/The Power of a Woman	1970	—	3.50	7.00
❑ 17	Catch the Wind/What I Don't See	1970	—	3.50	7.00
❑ 24	My Guy/Weakness of a Woman	1970	—	3.50	7.00
❑ 35	Will You Love Me Tomorrow/Bad Water	1971	—	3.50	7.00
❑ 281	Loving Kind/The World I Used to Know	1969	2.00	4.00	8.00
❑ 287	Ain't Had No Lovin'/That's All That Matters	1969	2.00	4.00	8.00
❑ 290	A Woman's Side of Love/That's All I Want from You	1969	2.00	4.00	8.00
SUNBIRD					
❑ 7567	All I Really Need Is You/(B-side unknown)	1981	—	3.00	6.00
TRIUNE					
❑ 7202	God's Gift to Me/I've Just Gotta Feel Like a Woman Tonight	1973	—	3.00	6.00
❑ 7207	You, You, You/I've Just Gotta Feel Like a Woman Tonight	1973	—	3.00	6.00

Number	Title (A Side/B Side)	Yr	VG	VG+	NM
WARNER BROS.					
❑ 7827	It's No Laughing Matter/Long Distance Kissing	1974	—	2.50	5.00
❑ 8068	Let's Let Our Hearts Talk It Over/Love and Golden Rings	1975	—	2.50	5.00
WAYSIDE					
❑ 1015	Fool of the Year/Now That It's Over	1968	2.50	5.00	10.00
Albums					
ROYAL AMERICAN					
❑ RA 2801	A Woman's Side of Love	1969	3.75	7.50	15.00

LANDERS, DAVE

Number	Title (A Side/B Side)	Yr	VG	VG+	NM
45s					
MGM					
❑ K10682	Draw Up the Papers, Lawyer/How Many Hearts Do You Have	1950	7.50	15.00	30.00
❑ K10872	Everything That's Good/Clomp, Click, Click	1951	6.25	12.50	25.00
❑ K10933	Don't Do Anything/What's the Use to Take You Back Again	1951	6.25	12.50	25.00
❑ K11050	I Got a Cinder in My Eye/Bumble Bee	1951	6.25	12.50	25.00
Selected 78s					
MGM					
❑ 10427	Before You Call/Is There Any Need to Worry	1949	3.75	7.50	15.00
❑ 10561	It Meant So Little to You/Too Good to Be True	1949	3.75	7.50	15.00

LANDERS, RICH

Number	Title (A Side/B Side)	Yr	VG	VG+	NM
45s					
AMI					
❑ 1301	Lay Back Down and Love Me/Your Bedroom Eyes	1981	—	2.50	5.00
❑ 1305	Pull My String/Friday Night Feeling	1982	—	2.50	5.00
❑ 1311	Take It All/What Will I Do Without You	1982	—	2.50	5.00
❑ 1313	What Goes Up/(B-side unknown)	1983	—	2.50	5.00
❑ 1316	Every Breath You Take/(B-side unknown)	1983	—	2.50	5.00
❑ 1325	Don't Blame Me/(B-side unknown)	1985	—	2.50	5.00
❑ 1326	Your Sexy Ways/(B-side unknown)	1985	—	2.50	5.00
DOOR KNOB					
❑ 044	A Christmas Request/Santa's Helping Hand	1977	—	3.00	6.00
❑ 048	Hold On/Honky Tonkin' Lover	1978	—	3.00	6.00
OVATION					
❑ 1166	Friday Night Feelin'/The Lady Waiting at Home	1981	—	2.50	5.00
❑ 1173	Hold On/Honky Tonkin' Lover	1981	—	2.50	5.00

LANE, CRISTY

Number	Title (A Side/B Side)	Yr	VG	VG+	NM
45s					
K-ARK					
❑ 686	Stop Foolin' with Me/Janie Took My Place	1966	3.00	6.00	12.00
❑ 717	Let's Pretend/Subtract His Love	1966	3.00	6.00	12.00
LIBERTY					
❑ 1396	I Have a Dream/Rio Grande	1981	—	2.00	4.00
❑ 1396 [PS]	I Have a Dream/Rio Grande	1981	—	3.00	6.00
❑ 1406	Love to Love You/Everything I Own	1981	—	2.00	4.00
❑ 1432	Cheatin' Is Still on My Mind/Just a Mile from Nowhere	1981	—	2.00	4.00
❑ 1443	Lies on Your Lips/I Really Got the Blues	1981	—	2.00	4.00
❑ 1461	Fragile — Handle with Care/Tangerine	1982	—	2.00	4.00
❑ 1483	The Good Old Days/Do I Dare	1982	—	2.00	4.00
❑ 1501	I've Come Back (To Say I Love You One More Time)/Now the Day Is Over	1983	—	2.00	4.00
❑ 1508	Footprints in the Sand/Miracle Maker	1983	—	2.00	4.00
❑ 1521	Midnight Blue/Simple Little Words	1984	—	2.00	4.00
LS					
❑ 110	Tryin' to Forget About You/By the Way	1977	—	2.50	5.00
❑ 121	Sweet Deceiver/Walk On Baby	1977	—	2.50	5.00
❑ 131	Let Me Down Easy/This Is the First Time (I've Seen the Last Time on Your Face)	1977	—	2.50	5.00
❑ 148	Shake Me I Rattle/Pretty Paper	1977	—	3.00	6.00
❑ 148	Shake Me I Rattle/I Can't Tell You	1978	—	2.50	5.00
❑ 156	I'm Gonna Love You Anyway/I Can't Tell You	1978	—	2.50	5.00
❑ 167	Penny Arcade/Somebody's Baby	1978	—	2.50	5.00
❑ 169	I Just Can't Stay Married to You/Rain Song	1978	—	2.50	5.00
❑ 172	Simple Little Words/He Believes in Me	1979	—	3.00	6.00
❑ 1987	I Wanna Wake Up with You/He's Got the Whole World in His Hands	1987	—	2.50	5.00
❑ 9146	Man from Galilee/Shake Me I Rattle (Squeeze Me I Cry)	1984	—	3.00	6.00
UNITED ARTISTS					
❑ X1304	Simple Little Words/He Believes in Me	1979	—	2.00	4.00
❑ X1314	Slippin' Up, Slippin' Around/He's Back in Town	1979	—	2.00	4.00
❑ X1328	Come to My Love/Love Lies	1979	—	2.00	4.00
❑ X1342	One Day at a Time/I Knew the Mason	1980	—	2.00	4.00
❑ X1369	Sweet Sexy Eyes/Maybe I'm Thinkin'	1980	—	2.00	4.00
Albums					
ARRIVAL					
❑ NU 9640	One Day at a Time: 14 Songs of Inspiration and Harmony	1983	2.50	5.00	10.00
LANE					
❑ LPS-101	Cristy Lane Salutes the G.I.'s of Vietnam	197?	6.25	12.50	25.00
LIBERTY					
❑ LT-978	Simple Little Words	1981	2.00	4.00	8.00
—Reissue of United Artists 978					
❑ LT-1023	Ask Me to Dance	1981	2.00	4.00	8.00
—Reissue of United Artists 1023					
❑ LT-1083	I Have a Dream	1981	2.00	4.00	8.00
❑ LN-10226	Christmas with Cristy	198?	2.50	5.00	10.00
❑ LN-10239	Amazing Grace	198?	—	3.00	6.00
—Budget-line reissue					
❑ LN-10306	Footprints in the Sand	1986	—	3.00	6.00
—Budget-line reissue					
❑ LN-10309	Cristy Lane At Her Best	1986	—	3.00	6.00
—Budget-line reissue					
❑ LT-51112	Fragile — Handle with Care	1981	2.00	4.00	8.00
❑ LT-51117	Amazing Grace	1982	2.00	4.00	8.00
❑ LT-51137	Here's to Us	1982	2.00	4.00	8.00
❑ LT-51148	Footprints in the Sand	1983	2.00	4.00	8.00
❑ LT-51153	Cristy Lane At Her Best	1984	2.00	4.00	8.00
LS					
❑ 1001	Easy to Love	198?	2.50	5.00	10.00
❑ 1987	Christmas Gold	1987	2.50	5.00	10.00
❑ 2002	Country Classics Vol. 2	198?	2.50	5.00	10.00
❑ 2003	Country Classics Vol. 3	198?	2.50	5.00	10.00
❑ 8027	Cristy Lane Is the Name	1978	3.00	6.00	12.00
❑ 8028	Love Lies	1979	3.00	6.00	12.00
❑ SLL-8334	The Sweetest Voice This Side of Heaven	198?	2.50	5.00	10.00
❑ SLL-8358	Christmas Is the Man from Galilee	1983	2.50	5.00	10.00
❑ SLL-8385	Greatest Hits	198?	2.50	5.00	10.00
❑ SLL-8386	One Day at a Time	198?	2.50	5.00	10.00
❑ 9227	Cristy Lane Salutes the G.I.'s of Vietnam	198?	2.50	5.00	10.00
RIVERSONG					
❑ 2413	14 Golden Hymns	198?	2.50	5.00	10.00
SUFFOLK MARKETING					
❑ SLL-8289	One Day at a Time	198?	2.50	5.00	10.00
UNITED ARTISTS					
❑ UA-LA978-H	Simple Little Words	1979	2.50	5.00	10.00
❑ LT-1023	Ask Me to Dance	1980	2.50	5.00	10.00

LANE, JERRY "MAX"

Includes records as "Jerry Lane." Also see LYNN ANDERSON.

Number	Title (A Side/B Side)	Yr	VG	VG+	NM
45s					
ABC					
❑ 11410	The Snake/Don't Take the You Out of Us	1973	—	2.50	5.00
❑ 11444	Tearjoint/Walk Off the World	1974	—	2.50	5.00
❑ 12031	Right Out of This World/Fine As Wine	1974	—	2.50	5.00
❑ 12091	I've Got a Lotta Missin' You to Do/Back on My Feet Again	1975	—	2.50	5.00
CHART					
❑ 1012	Lover's Lane/My Mind Won't Mind Me	1967	2.00	4.00	8.00
❑ 1034	She Lives in Your World/Quietly Losing My Mind	1968	2.00	4.00	8.00
❑ 1056	It's Also New to Me/Ten Years of Life	1968	2.00	4.00	8.00
❑ 1185	Gonna Live It Up/(B-side unknown)	1965	2.50	5.00	10.00
❑ 1335	Anywhere But Gone/I Miss You Every Chance I Get	1966	2.50	5.00	10.00
❑ 1395	I've Done Wrong/The Things I Do Best	1966	2.50	5.00	10.00
❑ 5025	Crawling Back to You/The More I Think of You	1969	2.00	4.00	8.00
❑ 5060	I Hate to Sing and Run/The Sun Is Free	1970	—	3.50	7.00
STOCKYARD					
❑ 1000	When the Music Stops/(B-side unknown)	1983	—	3.00	6.00
❑ 1003	I've Got a Lot of Missin' You to Do/(B-side unknown)	1983	—	3.00	6.00
Albums					
CHART					
❑ CHS-1025	Lover's Lane	1970	3.75	7.50	15.00

LANE, RED

Number	Title (A Side/B Side)	Yr	VG	VG+	NM
45s					
RCA VICTOR					
❑ 47-9914	Arkansas Lovin' Man/You Gotta Hold On	1970	—	3.00	6.00
❑ 47-9970	The World Needs a Melody/The Barker Store	1971	—	3.00	6.00
❑ 74-0534	Set the World on Fire (With Love)/They Don't Make Love Like They Used To	1971	—	3.00	6.00
❑ 74-0616	Throw a Rope Around the Wind/Singeree	1971	—	3.00	6.00
❑ 74-0721	It Was Love While It Lasted/Lovin', Likin' Kind	1972	—	3.00	6.00
❑ 74-0843	The Day I Jump from Uncle Hardy's Plane/One Foot in the Grave	1972	—	3.00	6.00
Albums					
RCA VICTOR					
❑ LSP-4576	The World Needs a Melody	1971	3.75	7.50	15.00

LANE, TERRI

Number	Title (A Side/B Side)	Yr	VG	VG+	NM
45s					
MONUMENT					
❑ 8565	Daisy May (And Daisy May Not)/Gonna Be Alright Now	1973	—	3.00	6.00
❑ 8582	Be Certain/Brand New Woman	1973	—	3.00	6.00
❑ 8598	Auntie Katie/I Want to Lay Down Beside You	1974	—	3.00	6.00

LANE, TERRI, AND JIMMY NALL

Also see each artist's individual listings.

Number	Title (A Side/B Side)	Yr	VG	VG+	NM
45s					
MONUMENT					
❑ 8611	Mockingbird/Let It Be Me	1974	—	3.00	6.00
❑ 8620	What We've Got in Common Is Love/The Way You Do the Things You Do	1974	—	3.00	6.00

LANE BROTHERS, THE

Number	Title (A Side/B Side)	Yr	VG	VG+	NM
45s					
FXL					
❑ 0026	Marianne/(You've Gotta) Believe in America	1981	2.00	4.00	8.00

Number	Title (A Side/B Side)	Yr	VG	VG+	NM
LEADER					
❑ 804	Mimi/Two Dozen and a Half	1960	2.50	5.00	10.00
RCA VICTOR					
❑ 47-6810	Marianne/Sogni D'Oro	1957	3.75	7.50	15.00
❑ 47-6900	Ding Dang Dinglin'/Uh Uh Honey	1957	3.00	6.00	12.00
❑ 47-7107	Don't Tempt Me Baby/Lover's Heart	1957	3.00	6.00	12.00
❑ 47-7220	Boppin' in a Sack/Somebody Sweet	1958	3.00	6.00	12.00
❑ 47-7304	Little Brother/So Satisfied	1958	3.00	6.00	12.00

LANG, K.D.

Also see ROY ORBISON.

Number	Title (A Side/B Side)	Yr	VG	VG+	NM
12-Inch Singles					
SIRE					
❑ PRO-A-2697 [DJ]	Turn Me Round (same on both sides)	1987	2.50	5.00	10.00
❑ PRO-A-6052 [DJ]	Miss Chatelaine (4 remixes)	1992	3.75	7.50	15.00
❑ 41197	Just Keep Me Moving (5 versions)/In Perfect Dreams	1993	2.50	5.00	10.00
❑ 41379	Lifted by Love (4 versions)/No More Tears (3 versions)	1994	2.00	4.00	8.00
45s					
SIRE					
❑ 18289	Just Keep Me Moving/In Perfect Dreams	1994	—	2.00	4.00
❑ 18608	Miss Chatelaine/Outside Myself	1993	—	—	3.00
❑ 18942	Constant Craving/Season of Hollow Soul	1992	—	2.00	4.00
❑ 19793	Seven Lonely Days/Ridin' the Rails	1990	—	2.00	4.00
❑ 22734	Three Days/Trail of Broken Hearts	1989	—	—	3.00
❑ 22734 [PS]	Three Days/Trail of Broken Hearts	1989	—	3.00	6.00
❑ 22932	Full Moon of Love/Wallpaper Waltz	1989	—	—	3.00
❑ 22932 [PS]	Full Moon of Love/Wallpaper Waltz	1989	—	2.50	5.00
❑ 27813	Lock, Stock and Teardrop/Don't Let the Stars Get In Your Eyes	1988	—	—	3.00
❑ 27813 [PS]	Lock, Stock and Teardrop/Don't Let the Stars Get In Your Eyes	1988	—	2.00	4.00
❑ 27919	I'm Down to My Last Cigarette/Western Stars	1988	—	—	3.00
❑ 27919 [PS]	I'm Down to My Last Cigarette/Western Stars	1988	—	—	3.00
WARNER BROS.					
❑ 17747	If I Were You/Get Some	1995	—	—	3.00
Albums					
BUMSTEAD					
❑ BUM-842	A Truly Western Experience	1984	15.00	30.00	60.00
—Canadian import					
❑ BUM-862	A Truly Western Experience	1984	5.00	10.00	20.00
—Canadian import; reissue of Bumstead 842					
SIRE					
❑ PRO-A-3120 [DJ]	The Making of Shadowland	1988	6.25	12.50	25.00
❑ 25441	Angel with a Lariat	1987	2.50	5.00	10.00
❑ 25724	Shadowland	1988	2.50	5.00	10.00
❑ 25877	Absolute Torch and Twang	1989	2.50	5.00	10.00
❑ R 134567	Shadowland	1988	3.00	6.00	12.00
—BMG Direct Marketing edition					
❑ R 160100	Angel with a Lariat	1987	3.00	6.00	12.00
—BMG Direct Marketing edition					
WARNER BROS.					
❑ 46034	All You Can Eat	1995	2.50	5.00	10.00

LANG, KELLY

Number	Title (A Side/B Side)	Yr	VG	VG+	NM
45s					
SOUNDWAVES					
❑ 4681	Lady, Lady/Doctor's Orders	1982	—	2.50	5.00
❑ 4681 [PS]	Lady, Lady/Doctor's Orders	1982	—	3.00	6.00
❑ 4694	All the Losers Look the Same/Could It Be Love	1982	—	2.50	5.00

LANSDOWNE, JERRY

Number	Title (A Side/B Side)	Yr	VG	VG+	NM
45s					
STEP ONE					
❑ 400	She Had Every Right to Do You Wrong/I Will Carry You	1989	—	2.00	4.00
❑ 404	Who'll Give This Heart a Home/I Will Carry You	1989	—	2.00	4.00
❑ 411	Lessons of Love/She Had Every Right to Do You Wrong	1990	—	2.00	4.00
❑ 416	Plenty of Love/Who'll Give This Heart Love	1990	—	2.00	4.00
❑ 420	Paradise Gun and Knife Cafe/Your Lovin' Ways	1990	—	2.00	4.00
❑ 424	No Condition to Rock 'n' Roll/Hopeful Heart	1991	—	2.00	4.00
❑ 431	I Give You What You Need/While I Was Slippin' In	1991	—	2.00	4.00

LAPOINTE, PERRY

Also see BOBBY G. RICE.

Number	Title (A Side/B Side)	Yr	VG	VG+	NM
45s					
DOOR KNOB					
❑ 249	New Shade of Blue/(B-side unknown)	1986	—	2.50	5.00
❑ 252	You're a Better Man Than I/New Shade of Blue	1986	—	2.50	5.00
❑ 260	Chosen/You're a Better Man Than I	1986	—	2.50	5.00
❑ 270	Walk On By/(B-side unknown)	1987	—	2.50	5.00
❑ 281	The Power of a Woman/(B-side unknown)	1987	—	2.50	5.00
❑ 303	Open for Suggestions/(B-side unknown)	1988	—	2.50	5.00
❑ 333	Sweet Memories of You/(B-side unknown)	1989	—	2.50	5.00
❑ 341	Take It Easy on Me/(B-side unknown)	1990	—	2.50	5.00
❑ 348	Look Out Loretta/(B-side unknown)	1990	—	2.50	5.00
❑ 351	Can I Come Back to You/(B-side unknown)	1990	—	2.50	5.00

LARGE, BILLY

Number	Title (A Side/B Side)	Yr	VG	VG+	NM
45s					
COLUMBIA					
❑ 4-43741	The Goodie Wagon/Big Yellow Peaches	1966	2.50	5.00	10.00
❑ 4-43741 [PS]	The Goodie Wagon/Big Yellow Peaches	1966	3.75	7.50	15.00
❑ 4-44002	My $3.98 Plaster Mail Order Guitar/New Street to Walk On	1967	2.50	5.00	10.00

LARKIN, BILLY

Number	Title (A Side/B Side)	Yr	VG	VG+	NM
45s					
BRYAN					
❑ 1010	Leave It Up to Me/When You Left	1974	—	3.00	6.00
❑ 1018	The Devil in Mrs. Jones/No Reason Why	1975	—	3.00	6.00
❑ 1026	Indian Giver/Dig a Little Deeper	1975	—	3.00	6.00
CASINO					
❑ 053	#1 with a Heartache/If Misery Loves Company	1976	—	2.50	5.00
❑ 076	Kiss and Say Goodbye/There's a Soul Brother in a Country Band	1976	—	2.50	5.00
❑ 097	Here's to the Next Time/Lonely Woman	1976	—	2.50	5.00
MERCURY					
❑ 55040	My Side of Town/Ring in My Pocket	1978	—	2.00	4.00
❑ 55065	Every Night/Haven't I Loved You Somewhere Before	1979	—	2.00	4.00
SUNBIRD					
❑ 107	I Can't Stop Now/Lovin' a Lie	1980	—	2.00	4.00
❑ 7557	20-20 Hindsight/Lonely Woman	1981	—	2.00	4.00
❑ 7562	Longing for the High/Is There Nothing Left to Say	1981	—	2.00	4.00
Albums					
BRYAN					
❑ 105	Billy Larkin	1975	3.75	7.50	15.00
SUNBIRD					
❑ SN 50107	All My Best	1981	2.50	5.00	10.00

LARRATT, IRIS

Number	Title (A Side/B Side)	Yr	VG	VG+	NM
45s					
INFINITY					
❑ 50015	You Can't Make Love to a Memory/Country Love Song	1979	—	2.50	5.00
❑ 50045	Sorry Doesn't Always Make It Right/Surrender Your Love	1979	—	2.50	5.00

LARSON, NICOLETTE

Number	Title (A Side/B Side)	Yr	VG	VG+	NM
45s					
MCA					
❑ 52528	Only Love Will Make It Right/Blow On Chilly Wind	1985	—	2.00	4.00
❑ 52571	When You Get a Little Lonely/I Just Keep Falling in Love	1985	—	2.00	4.00
❑ 52653	Building Bridges/You Were the One	1985	—	2.00	4.00
❑ 52797	Let Me Be the First/If I Didn't Love You	1986	—	2.00	4.00
❑ 52839	That's How You Know When Love's Right/As an Eagle Stirreth Her Nest	1986	—	2.00	4.00
❑ 52937	That's More About Love (Than I Wanted to Know)/Captured by Love	1986	—	2.00	4.00
WARNER BROS.					
❑ 8664	Lotta Love/Angels Rejoiced	1978	—	2.50	5.00
❑ 8795	Rhumba Girl/Last in Love	1979	—	2.50	5.00
❑ 8851	Mexican Divorce/Give a Little	1979	—	2.50	5.00
❑ 29948	I Only Want to Be with You/Now We Can Go Home	1982	—	2.00	4.00
❑ 49130	Let Me Go, Love/Trouble	1979	—	2.00	4.00
❑ 49130 [PS]	Let Me Go, Love/Trouble	1979	—	3.00	6.00
❑ 49520	Back in My Arms/Just in the Nick of Time	1980	—	2.00	4.00
❑ 49666	Ooo-Eee/Straight from the Heart	1981	—	2.00	4.00
❑ 49710	When You Come Around/How Can We Go On	1981	—	2.00	4.00
❑ 49763	Radioland/How Can We Go On	1981	—	2.00	4.00
❑ 49820	Fool Me Again/Arthur's Theme (Instrumental)	1981	—	2.00	4.00
Albums					
MCA					
❑ 5556	... Say When	1985	2.00	4.00	8.00
❑ 5719	Rose of My Heart	1986	2.00	4.00	8.00
WARNER BROS.					
❑ BSK 3243	Nicolette	1978	2.50	5.00	10.00
❑ HS 3370	In the Nick of Time	1979	2.50	5.00	10.00
❑ BSK 3502	Radioland	1980	2.50	5.00	10.00
❑ BSK 3678	All Dressed Up & No Place to Go	1982	2.50	5.00	10.00

LATHAM, BUDDY

Number	Title (A Side/B Side)	Yr	VG	VG+	NM
45s					
PRAIRIE DUST					
❑ 8853	(She Likes) Warm Summer Days/Higher Roller	1988	—	3.00	6.00

LAUDERDALE, JIM

Number	Title (A Side/B Side)	Yr	VG	VG+	NM
45s					
EPIC					
❑ 34-08113	Stay Out of My Arms/Highways Through My Home	1988	—	—	3.00
❑ 34-68908	Lucky 13/Might Seem Like a Loser	1989	—	—	3.00
REPRISE					
❑ 7-19344	Maybe/What You Don't Know	1991	—	2.00	4.00

LAWRENCE, TRACY

Number	Title (A Side/B Side)	Yr	VG	VG+	NM
45s					
ATLANTIC					
❑ 83004	Better Man, Better Off/Any Minute Now	1997	—	—	3.00
❑ 84166	While You Sleep/Renegades, Rebels and Rogues	1998	—	—	3.00

Number	Title (A Side/B Side)	Yr	VG	VG+	NM
❑ 84414	I'll Never Pass This Way Again/Virginia	1998	—	—	3.00
—B-side by Gene Miller					
❑ 87020	Is That a Tear/Different Man	1997	—	2.00	4.00
❑ 87052	Stars Over Texas/Is That a Tear	1996	—	2.00	4.00
❑ 87119	If the World Had a Front Porch/Texas Tornado	1995	—	2.00	4.00
❑ 87180	As Any Fool Can See/Texas Tornado	1995	—	2.00	4.00
❑ 87199	I See It Now/God Made Woman on a Good Day	1994	—	2.00	4.00
❑ 87312	My Second Home/Crying Ain't Dying	1993	—	2.00	4.00
❑ 87330	Can't Break It to My Heart/I Threw the Rest Away	1993	—	2.00	4.00
❑ 87372	Alibis/Somebody Paints the Wall	1993	—	2.00	4.00
❑ 87588	Sticks and Stones/Paris, TN	1991	—	2.00	4.00

LAWRENCE, VICKI

45s

BELL

Number	Title (A Side/B Side)	Yr	VG	VG+	NM
❑ 45303	The Night the Lights Went Out in Georgia/Dime a Dance	1973	—	2.50	5.00
❑ 45362	He Did with Me/Mr. Allison	1973	—	2.00	4.00
❑ 45409	Sensual Man/Ships in the Night	1973	—	2.00	4.00
❑ 45437	Mama's Gonna Make It Better/Cameo	1974	—	2.00	4.00
ELF					
❑ 90035	And I'll Go/The Whole State of Alabama	1970	—	3.00	6.00
PRIVATE STOCK					
❑ 45036	The Other Woman/Cameo	1975	—	2.00	4.00
❑ 45067	There's a Gun Still Smokin' in Nashville	1976	—	2.00	4.00
❑ 45121	Love in the Hot Afternoon/(B-side unknown)	1976	—	2.00	4.00
SOMA					
❑ 5248	The Night the Lights Went Out in Georgia/He Did with Me	197?	—	2.50	5.00
—Original, reissue or bootleg? Please advise.					
UNITED ARTISTS					
❑ 50748	No, No/Lincoln Street Chapel	1971	—	3.00	6.00

Albums

BELL

Number	Title	Yr	VG	VG+	NM
❑ 1120	The Night the Lights Went Out in Georgia	1973	3.00	6.00	12.00

LAWSON, JANET

45s

BIG APPLE

Number	Title (A Side/B Side)	Yr	VG	VG+	NM
❑ 404	Yes My Darling There's a Santa Claus/Dear Santa (I've Been a Teensy Weensy Bad)	19??	—	2.50	5.00
UNITED ARTISTS					
❑ 50671	Two Little Rooms/Dindi	1970	—	3.00	6.00
❑ 50725	Good Enough to Be Your Wife/To Keep from Losing You	1970	—	3.00	6.00

LAY, RODNEY

45s

CHURCHILL

Number	Title (A Side/B Side)	Yr	VG	VG+	NM
❑ 94001	Happy Country Birthday Darlin'/Her Memories Faster Than Me	1982	—	2.50	5.00
❑ 94005	I Wish I Had a Job to Shove/The Way I Feel Tonight	1982	—	2.50	5.00
❑ 94005 [PS]	I Wish I Had a Job to Shove/The Way I Feel Tonight	1982	—	3.00	6.00
❑ 94012	You Could've Heard a Heart Break/Hollywood and Wine	1982	—	2.50	5.00
❑ 94020	Marylee/Blue with Envy	1983	—	2.50	5.00
❑ 94020 [PS]	Marylee/Blue with Envy	1983	—	3.00	6.00
EVERGREEN					
❑ 1046	Walk Softly on the Bridges/Ten Toes Up, Ten Toes Down	1986	—	2.50	5.00
SUN					
❑ 1144	Shenandoah/Back in the Saddle Again	1979	—	2.50	5.00
❑ 1149	Sea Cruise/Nashville Connection	1980	—	2.50	5.00
❑ 1164	Seven Days Come Sunday/Close	1981	—	2.50	5.00
❑ 1168	Silent Partners/Stolen Wine	1981	—	2.50	5.00

Albums

CHURCHILL

Number	Title	Yr	VG	VG+	NM
❑ 9423	Heartbreak	1982	2.50	5.00	10.00
SUN					
❑ 1022	Rockabilly Nuggets	1979	3.00	6.00	12.00
❑ 1027	Silent Partners	1981	3.00	6.00	12.00
—All copies on yellow vinyl					

LEAPY LEE

45s

CADET

Number	Title (A Side/B Side)	Yr	VG	VG+	NM
❑ 5635	It's All Happening/It's Great	1969	—	3.50	7.00
DECCA					
❑ 32380	Little Arrows/Time Will Tell	1968	2.00	4.00	8.00
❑ 32436	Here Comes the Rain/I'm Gonna Spend My Love	1969	—	3.50	7.00
❑ 32492	Little Yellow Aeroplane/Boom Boom (That's How My Heart Beats)	1969	—	3.50	7.00
❑ 32584	Someone's in Love/Best to Forget	1969	—	3.50	7.00
❑ 32625	Good Morning/Teresa	1970	—	3.50	7.00
❑ 32692	Tupelo Mississippi Flash/Green Green Trees	1970	—	3.00	6.00
❑ 32808	Best to Forget/I'll Be Your Baby Tonight	1971	—	3.00	6.00
MAM					
❑ 3618	Just Another Night/My Advice to You	1972	—	3.00	6.00
❑ 3622	Summer Rain/No Full Moon	1972	—	3.00	6.00
MCA					
❑ 40470	Every Road Leads Back to You/Honey Go Drift Away	1975	—	2.50	5.00

Albums

DECCA

Number	Title	Yr	VG	VG+	NM
❑ DL 75076	Little Arrows	1968	5.00	10.00	20.00
❑ DL 75237	Leapy Lee	1970	3.75	7.50	15.00

LEATHERWOOD, BILL

45s

COUNTRY JUBILEE

Number	Title (A Side/B Side)	Yr	VG	VG+	NM
❑ 539	The Long Walk/(B-side unknown)	1960	3.75	7.50	15.00

LEATHERWOOD, PATTI

45s

EPIC

Number	Title (A Side/B Side)	Yr	VG	VG+	NM
❑ 8-50303	It Should Have Been Easy/Super Lover	1976	—	2.50	5.00
❑ 8-50409	Feels So Much Better/Burning Love	1977	—	2.50	5.00

LEBEAU, TIM

45s

ROSE HILL

Number	Title (A Side/B Side)	Yr	VG	VG+	NM
❑ 001	Playing with Matches/(B-side unknown)	1988	—	3.50	7.00

LEBSOCK, JACK

See JACK GRAYSON.

LEDFORD, SUSAN

45s

PROJECT ONE

Number	Title (A Side/B Side)	Yr	VG	VG+	NM
❑ 6189	Ancient History/(B-side unknown)	1989	—	3.00	6.00

LEDOUX, CHRIS

45s

AMERICAN COWBOY SONGS

Number	Title (A Side/B Side)	Yr	VG	VG+	NM
❑ 14001	I Used to Want to Be a Cowboy/You Bring Out the Beast in Me	198?	—	3.00	6.00
CAPITOL NASHVILLE					
❑ S7-19039	Gravitational Pull/Five Dollar Fine	1996	—	2.00	4.00
❑ S7-19348	Santa Claus Is Comin' to Town/'Twas the Night Before Christmas	1996	—	2.00	4.00
❑ S7-19513	When I Say Forever/Stampede	1997	—	2.00	4.00
❑ S7-19697	This Cowboy's Hat (Live)/Copenhagen (Live)	1997	—	2.00	4.00
❑ S7-19977	Runaway Love/Life Is a Highway	1998	—	2.00	4.00
❑ 58737	Bang a Drum/One Road Man	1998	—	2.00	4.00
❑ 58780	Life Is a Highway/Hooked on an 8 Second Ride	1999	—	—	3.00
❑ 58800	Stampede/Hooked on an 8 Second Ride	1999	—	—	3.00
❑ 58817	Santa Claus Is Coming to Town/The Christmas Song	1999	—	—	3.00
—B-side by Trace Adkins					
❑ 58889	Silence on the Line/I'm Country	2000	—	2.00	4.00
LIBERTY					
❑ S7-17443	Under This Old Hat/Cowboys Like a Little Rock and Roll	1993	—	2.00	4.00
❑ S7-17638	Every Time I Roll the Dice/Wild and Wooly	1993	—	2.00	4.00
❑ S7-17714	For Your Love/Get Back on That Pony	1994	—	2.00	4.00
❑ S7-18090	Honky Tonk World/Sons of the Pioneers	1994	—	2.00	4.00
❑ S7-18555	Dallas Days and Fort Worth Nights/Big Love	1995	—	2.00	4.00
❑ S7-56787	Cadillac Ranch/Call of the Wild	1993	—	2.00	4.00
❑ S7-56952	Look at You Girl/Little Long-Haired Outlaw	1993	—	2.00	4.00
❑ S7-57736	Riding for a Fall/Cadillac Cowboy	1992	—	2.00	4.00
❑ S7-57885	Whatcha Gonna Do with a Cowboy/Western Skies	1992	—	2.50	5.00
LUCKY MAN					
❑ LMM-11	I'm Country/Time	1977	2.00	4.00	8.00
❑ 6520	Cabello Diablo or "Devil Horse"/Point Me Back Home to Wyoming	1979	—	3.00	6.00
❑ 6834	Ten Seconds in the Saddle/Dirt and Sweat Cowboy	1980	—	3.00	6.00
❑ 10270	Lean, Mean and Hungry/(B-side unknown)	1979	—	3.00	6.00

Albums

AMERICAN COWBOY SONGS

Number	Title	Yr	VG	VG+	NM
❑ ACS 17001	Thirty Dollar Cowboy	1983	6.25	12.50	25.00
❑ ACS 20001	Melodies and Memories	1984	7.50	15.00	30.00
❑ ACS 23001	Chris LeDoux and the Saddle Boogie Band	198?	5.00	10.00	20.00
LUCKY MAN					
❑ NR 4249	Rodeo Songs Old and New	1973	7.50	15.00	30.00
❑ ACS 5524	Sing Me a Song, Mr. Rodeo Man	197?	7.50	15.00	30.00
❑ NR 7648	Songs of the American West	1976	7.50	15.00	30.00
❑ NR 9175	Chris LeDoux Sings Western Country	1978	7.50	15.00	30.00
❑ LM 10193	Paint Me Back Home in Wyoming	1978	7.50	15.00	30.00
❑ LM 10194	Western Tunesmith	1980	7.50	15.00	30.00

LEE, BRENDA

45s

DECCA

Number	Title (A Side/B Side)	Yr	VG	VG+	NM
❑ 30050	Jambalaya (On the Bayou)/Bigelow 6-2000	1956	7.50	15.00	30.00
❑ 30107	Christy Christmas/I'm Gonna Lasso Santa Claus	1956	6.25	12.50	25.00
❑ 30198	One Step at a Time/Fairyland	1957	6.25	12.50	25.00
❑ 30333	Dynamite/Love You 'Til I Die	1957	6.25	12.50	25.00
❑ 30411	Ain't That Love/One Teenager to Another	1957	6.25	12.50	25.00
❑ 30535	Rock-a-Bye Baby Blues/Rock the Bop	1958	6.25	12.50	25.00
❑ 30673	Ring-a My Phone/Little Jonah	1958	7.50	15.00	30.00

Number	Title (A Side/B Side)	Yr	VG	VG+	NM
❑ 30776	Rockin' Around the Christmas Tree/Papa Noel	1958	6.25	12.50	25.00
—Originals have black labels with star under "Decca"					
❑ 30776	Rockin' Around the Christmas Tree/Papa Noel	1960	3.75	7.50	15.00
—Reissues have black labels with color bars					
❑ 30776 [PS]	Rockin' Around the Christmas Tree/Papa Noel	1960	12.50	25.00	50.00
❑ 30806	Bill Bailey Won't You Please Come Home/ Hummin' the Blues	1959	6.25	12.50	25.00
❑ 30885	Let's Jump the Broomstick/One of These Days	1959	7.50	15.00	30.00
❑ 30967	Sweet Nothin's/Weep No More My Baby	1959	5.00	10.00	20.00
❑ 30967 [PS]	Sweet Nothin's/Weep No More My Baby	1959	30.00	60.00	120.00
❑ 31093	I'm Sorry/That's All You Gotta Do	1960	5.00	10.00	20.00
❑ 31093 [PS]	I'm Sorry/That's All You Gotta Do	1960	12.50	25.00	50.00
❑ 31149	I Want to Be Wanted/Just a Little	1960	3.75	7.50	15.00
❑ 31149 [PS]	I Want to Be Wanted/Just a Little	1960	10.00	20.00	40.00
❑ 31195	Emotions/I'm Learning About Love	1961	3.75	7.50	15.00
❑ 31195 [PS]	Emotions/I'm Learning About Love	1961	7.50	15.00	30.00
❑ 31231	You Can Depend on Me/It's Never Too Late	1961	3.75	7.50	15.00
❑ 31231 [PS]	You Can Depend on Me/It's Never Too Late	1961	7.50	15.00	30.00
❑ 31272	Dum Dum/Eventually	1961	3.75	7.50	15.00
❑ 31272 [PS]	Dum Dum/Eventually	1961	—	—	—
—Rumored to exist, but without conclusive evidence, we will delete this from future editions					
❑ 31309	Fool #1/Anybody But Me	1961	3.75	7.50	15.00
❑ 31309 [PS]	Fool #1/Anybody But Me	1961	7.50	15.00	30.00
❑ 31348	Break It To Me Gently/So Deep	1962	3.75	7.50	15.00
❑ 31348 [PS]	Break It To Me Gently/So Deep	1962	6.25	12.50	25.00
❑ 31379	Everybody Loves Me But You/Here Comes That Feelin'	1962	3.75	7.50	15.00
❑ 31407	Heart in Hand/It Started All Over Again	1962	3.75	7.50	15.00
❑ 31424	All Alone Am I/Save All Your Lovin' for Me	1962	3.75	7.50	15.00
❑ 31424 [PS]	All Alone Am I/Save All Your Lovin' for Me	1962	6.25	12.50	25.00
❑ 31454	Your Used to Be/She'll Never Know	1963	3.75	7.50	15.00
❑ 31454 [PS]	Your Used to Be/She'll Never Know	1963	6.25	12.50	25.00
❑ 31478	Losing You/He's So Heavenly	1963	3.75	7.50	15.00
❑ 31478 [PS]	Losing You/He's So Heavenly	1963	6.25	12.50	25.00
❑ 31510	My Whole World Is Falling Down/I Wonder	1963	3.75	7.50	15.00
❑ 31510 [PS]	My Whole World Is Falling Down/I Wonder	1963	6.25	12.50	25.00
❑ 31539	The Grass Is Greener/Sweet Impossible You	1963	3.75	7.50	15.00
❑ 31539 [PS]	The Grass Is Greener/Sweet Impossible You	1963	6.25	12.50	25.00
❑ 31570	As Usual/Lonely Lonely Lonely Me	1963	3.75	7.50	15.00
❑ 31599	Think/The Waiting Game	1964	2.50	5.00	10.00
❑ 31599 [PS]	Think/The Waiting Game	1964	3.75	7.50	15.00
❑ 31628	Alone with You/My Dreams	1964	2.50	5.00	10.00
❑ 31628 [PS]	Alone with You/My Dreams	1964	3.75	7.50	15.00
❑ 31654	When You Loved Me/He's Sure to Remember Me	1964	2.50	5.00	10.00
❑ 31654 [PS]	When You Loved Me/He's Sure to Remember Me	1964	3.75	7.50	15.00
❑ 31687	Jingle Bell Rock/Winter Wonderland	1964	3.00	6.00	12.00
❑ 31687 [PS]	Jingle Bell Rock/Winter Wonderland	1964	4.00	8.00	16.00
❑ 31688	This Time of the Year/Christmas Will Be Just Another Lonely Day	1964	3.00	6.00	12.00
❑ 31688 [PS]	This Time of the Year/Christmas Will Be Just Another Lonely Day	1964	4.00	8.00	16.00
❑ 31690	Is It True/Just Behind the Rainbow	1964	2.50	5.00	10.00
❑ 31690 [PS]	Is It True/Just Behind the Rainbow	1964	3.75	7.50	15.00
❑ 31728	Thanks a Lot/The Crying Game	1965	2.50	5.00	10.00
❑ 31762	Truly, Truly, True/I Still Miss Someone	1965	2.50	5.00	10.00
❑ 31762 [PS]	Truly, Truly, True/I Still Miss Someone	1965	3.75	7.50	15.00
❑ 31792	Too Many Rivers/No One	1965	2.50	5.00	10.00
❑ 31849	Rusty Bells/If You Don't (Not Like You)	1965	2.50	5.00	10.00
❑ 31917	Too Little Time/Time and Time Again	1966	2.00	4.00	8.00
❑ 31970	Ain't Gonna Cry No More/It Takes One to Know One	1966	2.00	4.00	8.00
❑ 32018	Coming On Strong/You Keep Coming Back to Me	1966	2.00	4.00	8.00
❑ 32079	Ride, Ride, Ride/Lonely People Do Foolish Things	1967	2.00	4.00	8.00
❑ 32119	Born to Be By Your Side/Take Me	1967	2.00	4.00	8.00
❑ 32161	My Heart Keeps Hangin' On/Where Love Is	1967	2.00	4.00	8.00
❑ 32213	Where's the Melody/Save Me for a Rainy Day	1967	2.00	4.00	8.00
❑ 32248	That's All Right/Fantasy	1967	2.00	4.00	8.00
❑ 32299	Cabaret/Mood Indigo	1968	2.00	4.00	8.00
—With Pete Fountain					
❑ 32330	Kansas City/Each Day Is a Rainbow	1968	2.00	4.00	8.00
❑ 32428	Johnny One Time/I Must Have Been Out of My Mind	1968	2.00	4.00	8.00
❑ 32428 [PS]	Johnny One Time/I Must Have Been Out of My Mind	1968	3.75	7.50	15.00
❑ 32491	You Don't Need Me for Anything Anymore/Bring Me Sunshine	1969	—	3.00	6.00
❑ 32560	Let It Be Me/You Better Move On	1969	—	3.00	6.00
❑ 32675	I Think I Love You Again/Hello Love	1970	—	3.00	6.00
❑ 32734	Do Right Woman, Do Right Man/Sisters in Sorrow	1970	—	3.00	6.00
❑ 32848	If This Is Our Last Time/Everybody's Reaching Out for Someone	1971	—	3.00	6.00
❑ 32918	I'm a Memory/Misty Memories	1972	—	3.00	6.00
❑ 32975	Always on My Mind/That Ain't Right	1972	—	3.00	6.00
❑ 34494 [DJ]	Where's the Melody? (same on both sides)	1967	3.75	7.50	15.00
—Promo-only number, pink label					
❑ 38236 [DJ]	Voice Tracks by Brenda Lee: For Brenda Lee Day, March 29, 1961/Introduction and Station Breaks for General Use	1961	10.00	20.00	40.00
—Pink label promo					
❑ 88215	Christy Christmas/I'm Gonna Lasso Santa Claus	1956	12.50	25.00	50.00
—As "Little Brenda Lee" on Decca's Children's Series					
❑ 88215 [PS]	Christy Christmas/I'm Gonna Lasso Santa Claus	1956	20.00	40.00	80.00
ELEKTRA					
❑ 45492	Left-Over Love/Could It Be I Found Love Tonight	1978	—	2.50	5.00
MCA					
❑ 40003	Nobody Wins/We Had a Good Thing Goin'	1973	—	2.50	5.00
❑ 40107	Sunday Sunrise/Must I Believe	1973	—	2.50	5.00
❑ 40171	Wrong Ideas/Something For A Rainy Day	1973	—	2.50	5.00
❑ 40262	Big Four Poster Bed/Castles In The Sand	1974	—	2.50	5.00
❑ 40318	Rock On Baby/More Than A Memory	1974	—	2.50	5.00
❑ 40385	He's My Rock/Feel Free	1975	—	2.50	5.00
❑ 40442	Bringing It Back/Papa's Knee	1975	—	2.50	5.00
❑ 40511	Find Yourself Another Puppet/What I Had With You	1976	—	2.50	5.00
❑ 40584	Brother Shelton/Now He's Coming Home	1976	—	2.50	5.00
❑ 40640	Takin' What I Can Get/Your Favorite Wornout Nightmare's Coming Home	1976	—	2.50	5.00
❑ 40683	Ruby's Lounge/Oklahoma Superstar	1977	—	2.50	5.00
❑ 41130	Tell Me What It's Like/Let Your Love Fall Back On Me	1979	—	2.50	5.00
❑ 41187	The Cowgirl And The Dandy/Do You Wanna Spend The Night	1980	—	2.50	5.00
❑ 41262	Keeping Me Warm For You/At The Moonlight	1980	—	2.50	5.00
❑ 41270	Don't Promise Me Anything (Do It)/You Only Broke My Heart	1980	—	2.50	5.00
❑ 41322	Broken Trust/Right Behind The Rain	1980	—	2.50	5.00
—With the Oak Ridge Boys					
❑ 51047	Every Now And Then/He'll Play The Music	1981	—	2.00	4.00
❑ 51113	Fool, Fool/Right Behind The Rain	1981	—	2.00	4.00
❑ 51154	Enough For You/What Am I Gonna Do	1981	—	2.00	4.00
❑ 51195	Only When I Laugh/Too Many Nights Alone	1981	—	2.00	4.00
❑ 51230	From Levis To Calvin Klein Jeans/I Know A Lot About Love	1982	—	2.00	4.00
❑ 52060	Keeping Me Warm For You/There's More To Me Than You Can See	1982	—	2.00	4.00
❑ 52124	Just For The Moment/Love Letters	1982	—	2.00	4.00
—With the Oak Ridge Boys					
❑ 52268	Didn't We Do It Good/We're So Close	1983	—	2.00	4.00
❑ 52394	A Sweeter Love (I'll Never Know)/A Woman's Mind	1984	—	2.00	4.00
❑ 52654	I'm Takin' My Time/That's The Way It Was Then	1985	—	2.00	4.00
❑ 52720	Why You Been Gone So Long/He Can't Make Your Kind of Love	1985	—	2.00	4.00
❑ 52720 [PS]	Why You Been Gone So Long/He Can't Make Your Kind of Love	1985	—	2.00	4.00
❑ 52804	Two Hearts/Loving Arms	1986	—	2.00	4.00
❑ 52804 [DJ]	Two Hearts (same on both sides)	1986	2.50	5.00	10.00
—Promo only on red vinyl					
❑ 60069	Sweet Nothin's/I Want to Be Wanted	197?	—	2.00	4.00
—Reissue; originals have black rainbow label					
❑ 60070	I'm Sorry/All Alone Am I	197?	—	2.00	4.00
—Reissue; originals have black rainbow label					
❑ 65027	Rockin' Around the Christmas Tree/Papa Noel	1973	—	2.00	4.00
—Black label with rainbow					
❑ 65027	Rockin' Around the Christmas Tree/Papa Noel	1980	—	—	3.00
—Blue label with rainbow					
❑ 65028	Jingle Bell Rock/Winter Wonderland	1973	—	2.00	4.00
—Black label with rainbow					
❑ 65028	Jingle Bell Rock/Winter Wonderland	1980	—	—	3.00
—Blue label with rainbow					
MONUMENT					
❑ 03781	You're Gonna Love Yourself (In the Morning)/ What Do You Think About Lovin'	1983	—	2.00	4.00
—A-side: With Willie Nelson; B-side: With Dolly Parton					
WARNER BROS.					
❑ 19303	A Little Unfair/Some of These Days	1991	—	—	3.00
❑ 19397	Your One and Only/You Better Do Better	1991	—	—	3.00
7-Inch Extended Plays					
DECCA					
❑ ED 2678	(contents unknown)	1960	5.00	10.00	20.00
❑ ED 2678 [PS]	Sweet Nothin's	1960	5.00	10.00	20.00
❑ ED 2682	Be My Love Again/Just Let Me Dream// Jambalaya/Wee Wee Willie	1960	5.00	10.00	20.00
❑ ED 2682 [PS]	(title unknown)	1960	5.00	10.00	20.00
❑ ED 2683	Dynamite/Heading Home//I'm Sorry/That's All You Gotta Do	1960	5.00	10.00	20.00
❑ ED 2683 [PS]	I'm Sorry	1960	5.00	10.00	20.00
❑ ED 2695	I Want to Be Wanted/Just a Little//Teach Me Tonite/Walkin' to New Orleans	1961	5.00	10.00	20.00
❑ ED 2695 [PS]	(title unknown)	1961	5.00	10.00	20.00
❑ ED 2702	Dum Dum/Eventually//When I Fall in Love/Build a Big Fence	1961	5.00	10.00	20.00
❑ ED 2702 [PS]	(title unknown)	1961	5.00	10.00	20.00
❑ ED 2704	(contents unknown)	1961	5.00	10.00	20.00
❑ ED 2704 [PS]	Lover Come Back to Me	1961	5.00	10.00	20.00
❑ ED 2712	Fool #1/Anybody But Me//You Can Depend on Me/It's Never Too Late	1961	5.00	10.00	20.00
❑ ED 2712 [PS]	(title unknown)	1961	5.00	10.00	20.00
❑ ED 2716	Break It to Me Gently/Will You Love Me Tomorrow//Tragedy/So Deep	1962	5.00	10.00	20.00
❑ ED 2716 [PS]	Break It to Me Gently	1962	5.00	10.00	20.00
❑ ED 2725	Here Comes That Feeling/Everybody Loves Me But You//You've Got Me Crying Again/Lazy River	1962	5.00	10.00	20.00
❑ ED 2725 [PS]	Everybody Loves Me But You	1962	5.00	10.00	20.00
❑ ED 2730	It Started All Over Again/Heart in Hand//You Always Hurt the One You Love/Cry	1962	5.00	10.00	20.00
❑ ED 2730 [PS]	(title unknown)	1962	5.00	10.00	20.00
❑ ED 2738	All Alone Am I/Why Me//It's a Lonely Old Town/ Save All Your Loving for Me	1962	5.00	10.00	20.00

Number	Title (A Side/B Side)	Yr	VG	VG+	NM
❑ ED 2738 [PS]	All Alone Am I	1962	5.00	10.00	20.00
❑ ED 2745	My Coloring Book/I Left My Heart in San Francisco//What Kind of Fool Am I/Fly Me to the Moon	1962	5.00	10.00	20.00
❑ ED 2745 [PS]	Fly Me to the Moon	1962	5.00	10.00	20.00
❑ ED 2764	The Grass Is Greener/I Wonder//My Whole World Is Falling Down/Losing You	1963	5.00	10.00	20.00
❑ ED 2764 [PS]	The Grass Is Greener	1963	5.00	10.00	20.00
❑ ED 2775	As Usual/The End of the World//There Goes My Heart/Out in the Cold Again	1963	5.00	10.00	20.00
❑ ED 2775 [PS]	As Usual	1963	5.00	10.00	20.00
❑ ED 2801	Thanks a Lot/Think//Is It True/When You Love Me	1965	5.00	10.00	20.00
❑ ED 2801 [PS]	(title unknown)	1965	5.00	10.00	20.00
❑ 7-4216 [DJ]	You Always Hurt the One You Love/Lazy River/You've Got Me Crying//I Miss You So/Fools Rush In/I'll Be Seeing You	1962	5.00	10.00	20.00
—Jukebox EP, stereo, small hole, plays at 33 1/3 rpm					
❑ 7-4216 [PS]	Sincerely	1962	5.00	10.00	20.00
❑ 7-4439 [DJ]	I Wanna Be Around/Our Day Will Come/You're the Reason I'm in Love//End of the World/Losing You/Break It to Me Gently	1963	5.00	10.00	20.00
—Jukebox EP, stereo, small hole, plays at 33 1/3 rpm					
❑ 7-4439 [PS]	Let Me Sing	1963	5.00	10.00	20.00
❑ 7-4825 [DJ]	What Now My Love/You Don't Have to Say You Love Me/You've Got Your Troubles//Up Tight/Strangers in the Night/Call Me	1966	5.00	10.00	20.00
—Jukebox EP, stereo, small hole, plays at 33 1/3 rpm					
❑ 7-4825 [PS]	Coming On Strong	1966	5.00	10.00	20.00
❑ 7-34254	This Time of the Year/Blue Christmas/Jingle Bell Rock//Rockin' Around the Christmas Tree/Marshmallow World/Winter Wonderland	1964	6.25	12.50	25.00
—Jukebox EP, stereo, small hole, plays at 33 1/3 rpm					
❑ 7-34254 [PS]	Merry Christmas	1964	6.25	12.50	25.00
—Sleeve says this is "DL 74583"; price includes title strips					
❑ 7-34363 [DJ]	Bye Bye Blues/September in the Rain/What a Difference a Day Makes//The Good Life/Shadow of Your Smile/Softly As I Leave You	1966	5.00	10.00	20.00
—Jukebox EP, stereo, small hole, plays at 33 1/3 rpm					
❑ 7-34363 [PS]	Bye Bye Blues	1966	5.00	10.00	20.00

Albums

DECCA

Number	Title (A Side/B Side)	Yr	VG	VG+	NM
❑ DL 4039 [M]	Brenda Lee	1960	6.25	12.50	25.00
❑ DL 4082 [M]	This Is...Brenda	1960	6.25	12.50	25.00
❑ DL 4104 [M]	Emotions	1961	6.25	12.50	25.00
❑ DL 4176 [M]	All the Way	1961	6.25	12.50	25.00
❑ DL 4216 [M]	Sincerely	1962	6.25	12.50	25.00
❑ DL 4326 [M]	Brenda, That's All	1962	6.25	12.50	25.00
❑ DL 4370 [M]	All Alone Am I	1963	6.25	12.50	25.00
❑ DL 4439 [M]	Let Me Sing	1963	6.25	12.50	25.00
❑ DL 4509 [M]	By Request	1964	5.00	10.00	20.00
❑ DL 4583 [M]	Merry Christmas from Brenda Lee	1964	5.00	10.00	20.00
❑ DL 4626 [M]	Top Teen Hits	1965	5.00	10.00	20.00
❑ DL 4661 [M]	The Versatile Brenda Lee	1965	5.00	10.00	20.00
❑ DL 4684 [M]	Too Many Rivers	1965	5.00	10.00	20.00
❑ DL 4755 [M]	Bye Bye Blues	1966	5.00	10.00	20.00
❑ DL 4757 [M]	10 Golden Years	1966	6.25	12.50	25.00
—With gatefold cover					
❑ DL 4757 [M]	10 Golden Years	196?	3.75	7.50	15.00
—With regular cover					
❑ DL 4825 [M]	Coming On Strong	1966	3.75	7.50	15.00
❑ DL 4941 [M]	Reflections in Blue	1967	5.00	10.00	20.00
❑ DL 8873 [M]	Grandma, What Great Songs You Sang	1960	10.00	20.00	40.00
❑ DL 74039 [S]	Brenda Lee	1960	7.50	15.00	30.00
❑ DL 74082 [S]	This Is...Brenda	1960	7.50	15.00	30.00
❑ DL 74104 [S]	Emotions	1961	7.50	15.00	30.00
❑ DL 74176 [S]	All the Way	1961	7.50	15.00	30.00
❑ DL 74216 [S]	Sincerely	1962	7.50	15.00	30.00
❑ DL 74326 [S]	Brenda, That's All	1962	7.50	15.00	30.00
❑ DL 74370 [S]	All Alone Am I	1963	7.50	15.00	30.00
❑ DL 74439 [S]	Let Me Sing	1963	7.50	15.00	30.00
❑ DL 74509 [S]	By Request	1964	6.25	12.50	25.00
❑ DL 74583 [S]	Merry Christmas from Brenda Lee	1964	6.25	12.50	25.00
❑ DL 74626 [S]	Top Teen Hits	1965	6.25	12.50	25.00
❑ DL 74661 [S]	The Versatile Brenda Lee	1965	6.25	12.50	25.00
❑ DL 74684 [S]	Too Many Rivers	1965	6.25	12.50	25.00
❑ DL 74755 [S]	Bye Bye Blues	1966	6.25	12.50	25.00
❑ DL 74757 [S]	10 Golden Years	1966	7.50	15.00	30.00
—With gatefold cover					
❑ DL 74757 [S]	10 Golden Years	196?	5.00	10.00	20.00
—With regular cover					
❑ DL 74825 [S]	Coming On Strong	1966	5.00	10.00	20.00
❑ DL 74941 [S]	Reflections in Blue	1967	3.75	7.50	15.00
❑ DL 74955	For the First Time	1968	3.75	7.50	15.00
—With Pete Fountain					
❑ DL 75111	Johnny One Time	1969	3.75	7.50	15.00
❑ DL 75232	Memphis Portrait	1970	3.75	7.50	15.00
❑ DL 78873 [S]	Grandma, What Great Songs You Sang	1960	12.50	25.00	50.00
❑ ST-92062	Johnny One Time	1969	5.00	10.00	20.00
—Capitol Record Club edition					
❑ R 103619 [S]	Merry Christmas from Brenda Lee	1971	5.00	10.00	20.00
—RCA Music Service edition					

MCA

Number	Title (A Side/B Side)	Yr	VG	VG+	NM
❑ 232 [S]	Merry Christmas from Brenda Lee	1973	3.00	6.00	12.00
❑ 305	Brenda	1973	3.75	7.50	15.00
❑ 375	New Sunrise	1973	3.00	6.00	12.00
❑ 433	Brenda Lee Now	1974	3.00	6.00	12.00
❑ 477	Sincerely, Brenda Lee	1975	2.50	5.00	10.00
❑ 758	Even Better	198?	2.00	4.00	8.00
—Reissue of 3211					
❑ 824	Only When I Laugh	1982	2.00	4.00	8.00
—Reissue of 5278					
❑ 2233	L.A. Sessions	1976	2.50	5.00	10.00
❑ 3211	Even Better	1979	2.50	5.00	10.00
❑ 4012 [(2)]	The Brenda Lee Story — Her Greatest Hits	1973	5.00	10.00	20.00
❑ 5143	Take Me Back	1980	2.50	5.00	10.00
❑ 5278	Only When I Laugh	1981	2.50	5.00	10.00
❑ 5342	Greatest Country Hits	1982	2.50	5.00	10.00
❑ 5626	Feels So Right	1985	2.50	5.00	10.00
❑ 15021 [S]	Merry Christmas from Brenda Lee	197?	2.50	5.00	10.00
❑ 15038	Rockin' Around the Christmas Tree	198?	2.50	5.00	10.00

MCA CORAL

Number	Title (A Side/B Side)	Yr	VG	VG+	NM
❑ CB-20044	Let It Be Me	197?	2.50	5.00	10.00

VOCALION

Number	Title (A Side/B Side)	Yr	VG	VG+	NM
❑ VL 3795 [M]	Here's Brenda Lee	1967	3.00	6.00	12.00
❑ VL 73795 [S]	Here's Brenda Lee	1967	3.00	6.00	12.00
❑ VL 73890	Let It Be Me	1970	3.00	6.00	12.00

LEE, CHANDY

45s

ODC

Number	Title (A Side/B Side)	Yr	VG	VG+	NM
❑ 548	She's Still Around/Three Riddles	1979	—	3.00	6.00

LEE, DICKEY

45s

ATCO

Number	Title (A Side/B Side)	Yr	VG	VG+	NM
❑ 6546	Run Right Back/Red, Green, Yellow, Blue	1968	2.00	4.00	8.00
❑ 6580	All My Life/Hang-Ups	1968	2.00	4.00	8.00
❑ 6609	You're Young and You'll Forget/Waitin' for Love to Come My Way	1968	2.00	4.00	8.00

DIAMOND

Number	Title (A Side/B Side)	Yr	VG	VG+	NM
❑ 266	Ruby Baby/I Remember Barbara	1969	2.00	4.00	8.00

DOT

Number	Title (A Side/B Side)	Yr	VG	VG+	NM
❑ 16087	Life in a Teenage World/Why Don't You Write On	1960	3.75	7.50	15.00

HALLWAY

Number	Title (A Side/B Side)	Yr	VG	VG+	NM
❑ 1924	Big Brother/She's Walking Away	1964	2.50	5.00	10.00

MERCURY

Number	Title (A Side/B Side)	Yr	VG	VG+	NM
❑ 55068	I'm Just a Heartache Away/Midnight Flyer	1979	—	2.00	4.00
❑ 57005	He's an Old Rock 'N' Roller/It Hurts to Be in Love	1979	—	2.00	4.00
❑ 57017	Don't Look Back/I'm Trustin' a Feelin'	1980	—	2.00	4.00
❑ 57027	Workin' My Way to Your Heart/If You Want Me	1980	—	2.00	4.00
❑ 57036	Lost in Love/Again	1980	—	2.00	4.00
—A-side with Kathy Burdick					
❑ 57052	Honky Tonk Hearts/Best I Hit the Road	1981	—	2.00	4.00
❑ 57056	I Wonder If I Care As Much/Further Than a Country Mile	1981	—	2.00	4.00
❑ 76129	Everybody Loves a Winner/You Won't Be Here Tonight	1982	—	2.00	4.00

RCA

Number	Title (A Side/B Side)	Yr	VG	VG+	NM
❑ PB-10764	9,999,999 Tears/I Never Will Get Over You	1976	—	2.00	4.00
❑ PB-10914	If You Gotta Make a Fool of Somebody/My Love Shows Thru	1977	—	2.00	4.00
❑ GB-10929	Rocky/9,999,999 Tears	1977	—	—	3.00
—Gold Standard Series					
❑ PB-11009	Virginia, How Far Will You Go/My Love Shows Thru	1977	—	2.00	4.00
❑ PB-11125	Peanut Butter/Breezy Was Her Name	1977	—	2.00	4.00
❑ PB-11191	Love Is a Word/I'll Be Leaving Alone	1978	—	2.00	4.00
❑ PB-11294	My Heart Won't Cry Anymore/Danna	1978	—	2.00	4.00
❑ PB-11389	It's Not Easy/I've Been Honky-Tonkin' Too Long	1978	—	2.00	4.00

RCA VICTOR

Number	Title (A Side/B Side)	Yr	VG	VG+	NM
❑ APBO-0082	Sparklin' Brown Eyes/Country Song	1973	—	2.50	5.00
❑ APBO-0227	I Use the Soap/Strawberry Women	1974	—	2.50	5.00
❑ PB-10014	Give Me One Good Reason/Sweet Fever	1974	—	2.50	5.00
❑ PB-10091	The Busiest Memory in Town/Way to Go On	1974	—	2.50	5.00
❑ PB-10289	You Make It Look So Easy/The Door's Always Open	1975	—	2.00	4.00
❑ PB-10361	Rocky/The Closest Thing to You	1975	—	2.00	4.00
❑ PB-10543	Angels, Roses and Rain/Danna	1976	—	2.00	4.00
❑ PB-10684	Makin' Love Don't Always Make Love Grow/I Never Will Get Over You	1976	—	2.00	4.00
❑ 47-9862	All Too Soon/Charlie	1970	—	3.00	6.00
❑ 47-9941	Home To/Special	1971	—	3.00	6.00
❑ 47-9988	The Mahogany Pulpit/Everybody's Reaching Out for Someone	1971	—	3.00	6.00
❑ 48-1013	Never Ending Song of Love/On the Southbound	1971	—	3.00	6.00
❑ 74-0623	I Saw My Lady/What We Used to Hang On To	1971	—	3.00	6.00
❑ 74-0710	Ashes of Love/The Kingdom I Call Home	1972	—	2.50	5.00
❑ 74-0798	Baby, Bye Bye/She Thinks I Still Care	1972	—	2.50	5.00
❑ 74-0892	Crying Over You/My World Around You	1973	—	2.50	5.00
❑ 74-0980	Put Me Down Softly/If She Turns Up in Atlanta	1973	—	2.50	5.00

RENDEZVOUS

Number	Title (A Side/B Side)	Yr	VG	VG+	NM
❑ 188	Dream Boy/Stay True Baby	1962	6.25	12.50	25.00

SMASH

Number	Title (A Side/B Side)	Yr	VG	VG+	NM
❑ 1758	Patches/More or Less	1962	3.75	7.50	15.00
❑ 1791	I Saw Linda Yesterday/The Girl I Can't Forget	1962	3.00	6.00	12.00
❑ 1808	Don't Wanna Talk About Paula/Just a Friend	1963	3.00	6.00	12.00
❑ 1822	I Go Lonely/Ten Million Faces	1963	3.00	6.00	12.00
❑ 1844	She Wants to Be Bobby's Girl/The Day the Sawmill Closed Down	1963	3.00	6.00	12.00
❑ 1871	To the Aisle/Mother Nature	1964	3.00	6.00	12.00
❑ 1913	Me and My Teardrops/Only Trust in Me	1964	3.00	6.00	12.00

Number	Title (A Side/B Side)	Yr	VG	VG+	NM
SUN					
❑ 280	Good Lovin'/Memories Never Grow Old	1957	7.50	15.00	30.00
❑ 297	Dreamy Nights/Fool, Fool, Fool	1958	20.00	40.00	80.00
TAMPA					
❑ 131	Dream Boy/Stay True Baby	1957	7.50	15.00	30.00
TCF HALL					
❑ 102	Laurie (Strange Things Happen)/Party Doll	1965	2.50	5.00	10.00
❑ 111	The Girl from Peyton Place/The Girl I Used to Know	1965	2.50	5.00	10.00
❑ 118	Good Girl Goin' Bad/Pretty White Dress	1965	2.50	5.00	10.00
❑ 128	Good Guy/Annie	1966	2.50	5.00	10.00
Albums					
MERCURY					
❑ SRM-1-5020	Dickey Lee	1979	2.50	5.00	10.00
❑ SRM-1-5026	Dickey Lee Again	1980	2.50	5.00	10.00
RCA VICTOR					
❑ APL1-0311	Sparklin' Brown Eyes	1974	3.00	6.00	12.00
❑ APL1-1243	Rocky	1975	3.00	6.00	12.00
❑ APL1-1725	Angels, Roses and Rain	1976	3.00	6.00	12.00
❑ LSP-4637	Never Ending Song of Love	1971	3.00	6.00	12.00
❑ LSP-4715	Ashes of Love	1972	3.00	6.00	12.00
❑ LSP-4791	Baby, Bye Bye	1972	3.00	6.00	12.00
❑ LSP-4857	Crying Over You	1973	3.00	6.00	12.00
SMASH					
❑ MGS-27020 [M]	The Tale of Patches	1962	7.50	15.00	30.00
❑ SRS-67020 [S]	The Tale of Patches	1962	10.00	20.00	40.00
TCF HALL					
❑ ST-9001 [S]	"Laurie" and "The Girl from Peyton Place"	1965	6.25	12.50	25.00
❑ T-9001 [M]	"Laurie" and "The Girl from Peyton Place"	1965	5.00	10.00	20.00

LEE, DON

45s

Number	Title (A Side/B Side)	Yr	VG	VG+	NM
CRESCENT					
❑ 103	16 Lovin' Ounces to the Pound/All I Ever Wanted Was You (Here Lovin' Me)	1982	—	3.00	6.00

LEE, ERNIE

45s

Number	Title (A Side/B Side)	Yr	VG	VG+	NM
MGM					
❑ 11517	Hangin' My Heart Out to Dry/How Come You Never Answer	1953	6.25	12.50	25.00
RCA VICTOR					
❑ 48-0158	My Home Is the Dust of the Road/You're Next to Heaven	1950	7.50	15.00	30.00
—Originals on green vinyl					
❑ 48-0182	Second Hand Heart/Headin' Home	1950	7.50	15.00	30.00
—Originals on green vinyl					
❑ 48-0341	Tormented/I'm a Lonesome Man	1950	7.50	15.00	30.00
—Originals on green vinyl					

LEE, HAROLD

45s

Number	Title (A Side/B Side)	Yr	VG	VG+	NM
CARTWHEEL					
❑ 198	Mountain Woman/If I Never Hear Goodbye	1971	—	3.00	6.00
❑ 204	Outside of Wichita/Way Down I Think I Love You	1971	—	3.00	6.00
❑ 213	Neon Lady/The Old Mother's Locket Twist	1972	—	3.00	6.00
❑ 219	Lila/Outside of Wichita	1972	—	3.00	6.00
COLUMBIA					
❑ 4-44458	The Two Sides of Me/Bringing Daddy Home	1968	2.00	4.00	8.00
❑ 4-44649	Mother, Brother and Sweet Darlin' Now/Boys Kept Hanging Around	1968	2.00	4.00	8.00
GRT					
❑ 088	Trouble Workin' Overtime/(B-side unknown)	1976	—	2.50	5.00

LEE, JOHNNY

45s

Number	Title (A Side/B Side)	Yr	VG	VG+	NM
ABC DOT					
❑ 17603	Sometimes/Get Off My Back	1975	—	2.50	5.00
ASYLUM					
❑ 47076	One in a Million/Anni	1980	—	2.00	4.00
❑ 47105	Pickin' Up Strangers/Never Lay My Lovin' Down	1981	—	2.00	4.00
❑ 47138	Prisomer of Home/Fool for Love	1981	—	2.00	4.00
❑ 47215	Bet Your Heart on Me/Highways Run On Forever	1981	—	2.00	4.00
❑ 47301	Be There for Me Baby/Finally Fallin'	1982	—	2.00	4.00
CURB					
❑ 10536	Maybe I Won't Love You Anymore/Annie	1989	—	—	3.00
❑ 10552	I'm Not Over You/Anniversary Song	1989	—	—	3.00
❑ 10564	I Can Be a Heartbreaker, Too/Anniversary Song	1989	—	—	3.00
❑ 10573	You Can't Fly Like an Eagle/By-Pass Row	1989	—	—	3.00
❑ 76809	Heart to Heart Talk/Annie	1990	—	2.00	4.00
❑ 76827	Dangerously Lonely/Annie	1990	—	2.00	4.00
❑ 76841	Money in My Pocket/(B-side unknown)	1990	—	2.00	4.00
ELEKTRA					
❑ 47230 [DJ]	Please Come Home for Christmas/Silver Bells	1981	—	3.00	6.00
—B-side by Tompall and the Glaser Brothers					
FULL MOON					
❑ 29605	Hey Bartender/Blue Monday	1983	—	2.00	4.00
FULL MOON/ASYLUM					
❑ 47004	Looking for Love/Lyin' Eyes	1980	—	2.00	4.00
—B-side by Eagles					
❑ 47004 [PS]	Looking for Love/Lyin' Eyes	1980	—	2.50	5.00
❑ 47444	When You Fall in Love/Crossfire	1982	—	2.00	4.00
❑ 69848	Sounds Like Love/The Deeper We Fall	1983	—	2.00	4.00
❑ 69945	Cherokee Fiddle/You Know Me	1982	—	2.00	4.00
FULL MOON/EPIC					
❑ 19-02012	Rode Hard and Put Up Wet/Honky Tonk Wine	1981	—	2.00	4.00
GRT					
❑ 065	Red Sails in the Sunset/In My Own Way	1976	—	2.50	5.00
❑ 098	Ramblin' Rose/Congratulations	1976	—	2.50	5.00
❑ 125	Country Party/This Should Go On Forever	1977	—	2.50	5.00
❑ 137	Dear Alice/It's Gonna Be Me	1977	—	2.50	5.00
❑ 144	This Time/Frisco	1978	—	2.50	5.00
WARNER BROS.					
❑ 28747	I Could Get Used to This/It Ain't the Leaving	1986	—	—	3.00
—A-side with Lane Brody					
❑ 28839	The Loneliness in Lucy's Eyes (The Life Sue Ellen Is Living)/If I Knew Then What I Know Now	1985	—	—	3.00
❑ 28901	They Never Had to Get Over You/Rock 'n' Roll Money	1985	—	—	3.00
❑ 29021	Save the Last Chance/It Ain't the Leaving	1985	—	—	3.00
❑ 29110	Rollin' Lonely/Rock It, Billy	1985	—	—	3.00
❑ 29206	You Could've Heard a Heart Break/Waitin' on Ice	1984	—	—	3.00
❑ 29270	One More Shot/The Eyes of Love	1984	—	—	3.00
❑ 29375	The Yellow Rose/Say When	1984	—	—	3.00
—A-side with Lane Brody					
❑ 29486	My Baby Don't Slow Dance/You Really Got a Hold on Me	1983	—	—	3.00
Albums					
ACCORD					
❑ 7219	Country Party	1983	2.00	4.00	8.00
ASYLUM					
❑ 6E-309	Lookin' for Love	1980	2.50	5.00	10.00
CURB					
❑ 10617	New Directions	1989	2.50	5.00	10.00
FULL MOON					
❑ 23899	Hey Bartender	1983	2.00	4.00	8.00
FULL MOON/ASYLUM					
❑ 5E-541	Bet Your Heart on Me	1981	2.00	4.00	8.00
❑ 60147	Sounds Like Love	1982	2.00	4.00	8.00
PLANTATION					
❑ 45	Party Time	1981	2.50	5.00	10.00
WARNER BROS.					
❑ 6E-309	Lookin' for Love	198?	2.00	4.00	8.00
—Reissue of Asylum 6E-309					
❑ 23967	Greatest Hits	1983	2.00	4.00	8.00
❑ 25056	'Til the Bars Burn Down	1984	2.00	4.00	8.00
❑ 25125	Workin' for a Livin'	1984	2.00	4.00	8.00
❑ 25210	Keep Me Hangin' On	1985	2.00	4.00	8.00

LEE, JONI

45s

Number	Title (A Side/B Side)	Yr	VG	VG+	NM
MCA					
❑ 40501	I'm Sorry Charlie/And a Little Girl Cried	1975	—	2.50	5.00
❑ 40553	Angel on My Shoulder/Just Lead the Way	1976	—	2.50	5.00
❑ 40592	Baby Love/It Really Doesn't Matter Anymore	1976	—	2.50	5.00
❑ 40651	I've Just Got to Know (How Loving You Would Be)/Playmates	1976	—	2.50	5.00
❑ 40687	The Reason Why I'm Here/We Loved	1977	—	2.50	5.00
❑ 40766	He Sure Does Make It Hard to Go/Your Love Had Taken Me That High	1977	—	2.50	5.00
❑ 40826	I Love How You Love Me/I Think of You	1977	—	2.50	5.00
Albums					
MCA					
❑ 2194	Joni Lee	1976	3.00	6.00	12.00

LEE, ROBIN

45s

Number	Title (A Side/B Side)	Yr	VG	VG+	NM
ATLANTIC					
❑ 7-87599	Back to Bein' Blue/When I Miss You	1991	—	2.00	4.00
❑ 7-87681	Nothin' But You/Betrayed	1991	—	2.00	4.00
❑ 7-87835	Love Letter/Every Little Bit Hurts	1990	—	2.00	4.00
❑ 7-87890	How About Goodbye/Younger Love	1990	—	2.00	4.00
❑ 7-87979	Black Velvet/Stay with Me	1990	—	2.00	4.00
ATLANTIC AMERICA					
❑ 7-99264	Before You Cheat on Me Once (You Better Think Twice)/Serious Afffection	1988	—	2.00	4.00
❑ 7-99264 [PS]	Before You Cheat on Me Once (You Better Think Twice)/Serious Afffection	1988	—	2.00	4.00
❑ 7-99307	Shine a Light on a Lie/I'm Gettin' Good at Bein' Bad	1988	—	2.00	4.00
❑ 7-99307 [PS]	Shine a Light on a Lie/I'm Gettin' Good at Bein' Bad	1988	—	2.00	4.00
❑ 7-99353	This Old Flame/Maybe I Will, Maybe I Won't	1988	—	2.00	4.00
❑ 7-99353 [PS]	This Old Flame/Maybe I Will, Maybe I Won't	1988	—	2.00	4.00
EVERGREEN					
❑ 1003	Turning Back the Covers (Don't Turn Back the Time)/Angel in Your Arms	1983	—	2.50	5.00
❑ 1003 [PS]	Turning Back the Covers (Don't Turn Back the Time)/Angel in Your Arms	1983	2.00	4.00	8.00
❑ 1006	Heart for a Heart/Turning Back the Covers (Don't Turn Back the Time)	1983	—	2.50	5.00
❑ 1012	Love Always Leaves Me Lonely/(B-side unknown)	1983	—	2.50	5.00
❑ 1016	Angel in Your Arms/Turning Back the Covers (Don't Turn Back the Time)	1983	—	2.50	5.00
❑ 1018	Want Ads/Breaking the Chains	1984	—	2.50	5.00
❑ 1023	Cold in July/Breaking the Chains	1984	—	2.50	5.00
❑ 1026	I Heard It on the Radio/Angel in Your Arms	1984	—	2.50	5.00

Number	Title (A Side/B Side)	Yr	VG	VG+	NM
❑ 1026 [PS]	I Heard It on the Radio/Angel in Your Arms	1984	—	3.00	6.00
❑ 1033	Paint the Town Blue/Angel in Your Arms	1985	—	2.50	5.00
—A-side with Lobo					
❑ 1037	Safe in the Arms of Love/Between the Lies	1985	—	2.50	5.00
❑ 1039	I'll Take Your Love Anytime/Between the Lies	1986	—	2.50	5.00
❑ 1043	If You're Anything Like Your Eyes/Paint the Town Blue	1986	—	2.50	5.00
Albums					
ATLANTIC AMERICA					
❑ 90906	This Old Flame	1988	2.50	5.00	10.00
EVERGREEN					
❑ 1001	Robin Lee	1986	3.00	6.00	12.00

LEE, T.L., AND KATHY WALKER

Number	Title (A Side/B Side)	Yr	VG	VG+	NM
45s					
COMPLEAT					
❑ 164	A Silent Understanding/Hers and Mine	1987	—	2.00	4.00
❑ 164 [PS]	A Silent Understanding/Hers and Mine	1987	—	2.50	5.00

LEE, VICKI

Number	Title (A Side/B Side)	Yr	VG	VG+	NM
45s					
RUSTIC					
❑ 1027	Cry-Cry/It Don't Take Much to Make Me Happy	198?	—	3.00	6.00
❑ 1028	Heaven Help Me If I Fall/(B-side unknown)	198?	—	3.00	6.00
❑ 1029	Here Comes the Night/(B-side unknown)	198?	—	3.00	6.00
❑ 1030	Love Him Back to Georgia/(B-side unknown)	198?	—	3.00	6.00
SUNSHINE					
❑ 1400	Bluemonia/(B-side unknown)	1986	—	3.00	6.00

LEE, WOODY

Number	Title (A Side/B Side)	Yr	VG	VG+	NM
45s					
ATLANTIC					
❑ 7-87123	Get Over It/I Like the Sound of That	1995	—	—	3.00

LEGARDE TWINS, THE

Number	Title (A Side/B Side)	Yr	VG	VG+	NM
45s					
4 STAR					
❑ 1037	I Can Almost Touch the Feelin'/True Love	1979	—	2.50	5.00
—As "The LeGardes"					
BEAR					
❑ 194	Crocodile Man (From Walk-About Creek)/(B-side unknown)	1988	—	3.00	6.00
DOT					
❑ 15608	Freight Train Yodel/Poison Darts	1959	6.25	12.50	25.00
❑ 17377	Another Glass of Beer/From New South Wales to Nashville	1971	2.00	4.00	8.00
INVITATION					
❑ 101	Daddy's Makin' Records in Nashville/Grady Family Band	1980	—	3.00	6.00
KOALA					
❑ 0001	Andaleigha Mia/13 Colonies	197?	—	3.00	6.00
❑ 0001 [PS]	Andaleigha Mia/13 Colonies	197?	2.00	4.00	8.00
RAINDROP					
❑ 012	True Love/25 Years and 15 Days	1978	2.00	4.00	8.00
—As "The LeGardes"					
Albums					
KOALA					
❑ K 10001	Andaleigha Mia	197?	3.75	7.50	15.00

LEGENDARY STARDUST COWBOY, THE

Number	Title (A Side/B Side)	Yr	VG	VG+	NM
45s					
MERCURY					
❑ 72862	Paralyzed/Who's Knocking on My Door	1968	5.00	10.00	20.00
❑ 72891	Down in the Wrecking Yard/I Took a Trip on a Gemini Spaceship	1969	5.00	10.00	20.00
❑ 72912	Everything's Getting Bigger But Our Love/Kiss and Run	1969	5.00	10.00	20.00
NORTON					
❑ 012	I Hate CD's/Linda	199?	—	—	2.00
❑ 012 [PS]	I Hate CD's/Linda	199?	—	—	2.00
PSYCHO-SUAVE					
❑ 1033	Paralyzed/Who's Knocking on My Door	1968	7.50	15.00	30.00

LEHR, ZELLA

Number	Title (A Side/B Side)	Yr	VG	VG+	NM
45s					
COLUMBIA					
❑ 18-02431	Feedin' the Fire/What a Man, My Man Is	1981	—	2.00	4.00
❑ 18-02677	Blue Eyes Don't Make an Angel/Doin' a Lot	1982	—	2.00	4.00
❑ 18-02816	Didn't Mean to Fall in Love Again/He's a Gypsy	1982	—	2.00	4.00
❑ 18-03164	What a Way to Spend the Night/Ain't It Funny	1982	—	2.00	4.00
❑ 38-03593	Haven't We Loved Somewhere Before/Get Out of My Heart	1983	—	2.00	4.00
COMPLEAT					
❑ 129	All Heaven Is About to Break Loose/I'll Get You Back	1984	—	2.50	5.00
❑ 136	You Bring Out the Lover in Me/I'll Get You Back	1985	—	2.50	5.00
MEGA					
❑ 1213	Dirty Mary, Crazy Larry/(B-side unknown)	1974	—	3.50	7.00
❑ 1229	I Can't Help Myself/Red Skies Over Georgia	1975	—	3.00	6.00
❑ 1241	Just Believe in Me/Over the Rainbow	1975	—	3.00	6.00
RCA					
❑ PB-11174	Two Doors Down/Two Sides to Every Woman	1977	—	2.00	4.00
❑ PB-11265	When the Fire Gets Hot/Can't Help But Wonder	1978	—	2.00	4.00
❑ PB-11359	Danger, Heartbreak Ahead/I Can't Imagine Laying Down (With Anyone But You)	1978	—	2.00	4.00
❑ PB-11433	Play Me a Memory/Expert at Everything	1978	—	2.00	4.00
❑ PB-11543	Only Diamonds Are Forever/Music Maker	1979	—	2.00	4.00
❑ PB-11648	Once in a Blue Moon/All He Did Was Tell Me Lies (To Try to Woo Me)	1979	—	2.00	4.00
❑ PB-11754	Love Has Taken Its Time/If You Only Knew	1979	—	2.00	4.00
❑ PB-11953	Rodeo Eyes/You Look So Good on Me	1980	—	2.00	4.00
❑ PB-12073	Love Crazy Love/It Feels Good Enough to Call It Love	1980	—	2.00	4.00
Albums					
COLUMBIA					
❑ FC 37431	Feedin' the Fire	1982	2.50	5.00	10.00

LEIGH, BONNIE

Number	Title (A Side/B Side)	Yr	VG	VG+	NM
45s					
R.C.P.					
❑ 010	Runaway/(B-side unknown)	1986	—	3.00	6.00
❑ 016	That's When (You Can Call Me Your Own)/(B-side unknown)	1987	—	3.00	6.00
❑ 020	Moon Walking/(B-side unknown)	1987	—	3.00	6.00

LEIGH, DANNI

Number	Title (A Side/B Side)	Yr	VG	VG+	NM
45s					
DECCA					
❑ 72067	If the Jukebox Took Teardrops/Mixed Up Mess of a Heart	1998	—	—	3.00
❑ 72086	29 Nights/Touch Me	1999	—	—	3.00

LEIGH, RICHARD

Number	Title (A Side/B Side)	Yr	VG	VG+	NM
45s					
CAPITOL					
❑ B-5247	Ain't Gonna Worry My Mind/Whole New World	1983	—	2.00	4.00
UNITED ARTISTS					
❑ X-1351	Let's Do It Right/I've Come a Long Way	1980	—	2.00	4.00
Albums					
UNITED ARTISTS					
❑ LT-1036	Richard Leigh	1980	2.50	5.00	10.00

LEIGH, SHANNON

Number	Title (A Side/B Side)	Yr	VG	VG+	NM
45s					
AMI					
❑ 1308	Rock 'n' Roll Stories/(B-side unknown)	1982	—	3.00	6.00

LEMMON, DAVE

Number	Title (A Side/B Side)	Yr	VG	VG+	NM
45s					
SCP					
❑ 9781	Too Good to Be Through/Maggie	1983	2.00	4.00	8.00

LESTER, CHESTER

Number	Title (A Side/B Side)	Yr	VG	VG+	NM
45s					
CON BRIO					
❑ 148	Mama, Make Up My Room/High on Love	1979	—	3.00	6.00
❑ 154	If Only We Could/Woman from Kentucky	1979	—	3.00	6.00

LEWIS, BOBBY

Not to be confused with the R&B singer Bobby Lewis, who had a big pop hit in 1961 with "Tossin' and Turnin'."

Number	Title (A Side/B Side)	Yr	VG	VG+	NM
45s					
ACE OF HEARTS					
❑ 0463	Already Gone to My Heart/Mr. President	1973	—	3.00	6.00
❑ 0466	Here with You/Where Happiness Is	1973	—	3.00	6.00
❑ 0472	Too Many Memories/With Meaning	1973	—	3.00	6.00
❑ 0480	I Never Get Through Missing You/Lady Lover	1974	—	3.00	6.00
❑ 0502	Let Me Take Care of You/Where Happiness Is	1975	—	3.00	6.00
❑ 7503	It's So Nice to Be with You/(B-side unknown)	1975	—	3.00	6.00
CAPRICORN					
❑ 0318	She's Been Keeping Me Up Nights/I Keep Falling in Love with You	1979	—	2.50	5.00
❑ 0331	Love Won't Be Love Without You/This Is a Man and Woman Kind of Night	1979	—	2.50	5.00
GRT					
❑ 007	Lady Lover/I Never Get Through Missing You	1974	—	3.00	6.00
❑ 008	I See Love/Your Love	1974	—	3.00	6.00
HME					
❑ 04853	Love Is An Overload/Treat Her Like a Stranger	1985	—	2.00	4.00
RPA					
❑ 7603	For Your Love/(B-side unknown)	1976	—	3.00	6.00
❑ 7613	I'm Getting High Remembering/With Meaning	1976	—	3.00	6.00
❑ 7622	What a Diff'rence a Day Made/I Can Feel It	1977	—	3.00	6.00
UNITED ARTISTS					
❑ 842	Everybody's Baby/Perfect Example of a Fool	1965	2.50	5.00	10.00
❑ 920	Why Me/Six Days a Week, Twice on Sunday	1965	2.50	5.00	10.00
❑ 50009	You Remind Me Of Myself/I Hope You Find in Him What You Were Looking For in Me	1966	2.00	4.00	8.00
❑ 50067	How Long Has It Been/Easy to Say, Hard to Do	1966	2.00	4.00	8.00
❑ 50133	Two of the Usual/Your B.A.B.Y. Baby Don't Love You	1967	2.00	4.00	8.00
❑ 50161	Love Me and Make It All Better/My Tears Don't Care (They Fall Anywhere)	1967	2.00	4.00	8.00
❑ 50208	I Doubt It/Laughing Girl, She's Not Happy	1967	2.00	4.00	8.00
❑ 50263	Ordinary Miracle/These Are Things I Miss	1968	2.00	4.00	8.00
❑ 50327	From Heaven to Heartache/Only for Me	1968	2.00	4.00	8.00

Number	Title (A Side/B Side)	Yr	VG	VG+	NM
❑ 50476	Each and Every Part of Me/My (Is Such a Lonely Word)	1969	2.00	4.00	8.00
❑ 50528	Til Something Better Comes Along/I'm Only a Man	1969	2.00	4.00	8.00
❑ 50573	Things for You and I/Somebody Lied to Me	1969	2.00	4.00	8.00
❑ 50620	I'm Going Home/I May Never Be Free	1969	2.00	4.00	8.00
❑ 50668	Hello Mary Lou/Love, Wonderful Love	1970	—	3.50	7.00
❑ 50719	Simple Days and Simple Ways/Love's Garden	1970	—	3.50	7.00
❑ 50754	Come Sundown/He Gives Us All His Love	1971	—	3.50	7.00
❑ 50791	If I Had You/Doggone This Heartache	1971	—	3.50	7.00
❑ 50850	Today's Teardrops/Love's Satisfaction	1971	—	3.50	7.00
❑ 50885	Only Love Can Break a Heart/We Ran Out of Time	1972	—	3.50	7.00

Albums

ACE OF HEARTS

Number	Title (A Side/B Side)	Yr	VG	VG+	NM
❑ 1002	Too Many Memories	1974	3.75	7.50	15.00

RPA

Number	Title (A Side/B Side)	Yr	VG	VG+	NM
❑ 1002	Portrait in Love	1976	2.50	5.00	10.00
❑ 1013	Soul Full of Music	1977	2.50	5.00	10.00

UNITED ARTISTS

Number	Title (A Side/B Side)	Yr	VG	VG+	NM
❑ UAL-3582 [M]	How Long Has It Been	1967	6.25	12.50	25.00
❑ UAS-6582 [S]	How Long Has It Been	1967	6.25	12.50	25.00
❑ UAS-6616	A World of Love from Bobby Lewis	1967	5.00	10.00	20.00
❑ UAS-6629	An Ordinary Miracle	1968	5.00	10.00	20.00
❑ UAS-6673	From Heaven to Heartache	1968	5.00	10.00	20.00
❑ UAS-6717	Thanks for You and I	1969	5.00	10.00	20.00
❑ UAS-6760	The Best of Bobby Lewis, Vol. 1	1970	3.75	7.50	15.00

LEWIS, HUGH X.

45s

COLUMBIA

Number	Title (A Side/B Side)	Yr	VG	VG+	NM
❑ 4-45047	Everything I Love/Mr. Policeman	1969	—	3.00	6.00
❑ 4-45144	My Babysitter/When Love's Gone	1970	—	3.00	6.00

GRT

Number	Title (A Side/B Side)	Yr	VG	VG+	NM
❑ 28	Blues Sells a Lot of Booze/Help Yourself to Me	1970	—	3.00	6.00

KAPP

Number	Title (A Side/B Side)	Yr	VG	VG+	NM
❑ 622	What I Need Most/Too Late	1964	2.00	4.00	8.00
❑ 673	Out Where the Ocean Meets the Sky/Talking to a Bottle	1965	—	3.50	7.00
❑ 717	I'd Better Call the Law on Me/Take Me Out of It	1965	—	3.50	7.00
❑ 757	I'm Losing You (I Can Tell)/Just Before Dawn	1966	—	3.50	7.00
❑ 771	Wish Me a Rainbow/You Belong to My Heart	1966	—	3.50	7.00
❑ 812	Tender Hearted Me (The Bug Song)/Another Day Just Slipped Away	1967	—	3.50	7.00
❑ 830	You're So Cold (I'm Turning Blue)/No Chance for Happiness	1967	—	3.50	7.00
❑ 868	Wrong Side of the World/Your Steppin' Stone	1967	—	3.50	7.00
❑ 895	Evolution and the Bible/Gone, Gone, Gone	1968	—	3.50	7.00
❑ 921	War Is Hell/With These Hands	1968	—	3.50	7.00
❑ 939	Country Music Fever/The World Doesn't End Here	1968	—	3.50	7.00
❑ 955	Tonight We're Calling It a Day/Sittin' and Thinkin'	1968	—	3.50	7.00
❑ 978	All Heaven Broke Loose/Some Other Time	1969	—	3.50	7.00
❑ 2020	Restless Melissa/Our Angels Just Aren't Singing Anymore	1969	—	3.50	7.00

LITTLE DARLIN'

Number	Title (A Side/B Side)	Yr	VG	VG+	NM
❑ 7803	Love Don't Hide from Me/Thinking of You Thinking of Him	1978	—	3.00	6.00
❑ 7913	What Can I Do (To Make You Love Me)/Once Before I Die	1979	—	3.00	6.00

Albums

KAPP

Number	Title (A Side/B Side)	Yr	VG	VG+	NM
❑ KL-1462 [M]	The Hugh X. Lewis Album	1966	5.00	10.00	20.00
❑ KL-1494 [M]	Just Before Dawn	1966	5.00	10.00	20.00
❑ KL-1522 [M]	My Kind of Country	1967	7.50	15.00	30.00
❑ KS-3462 [S]	The Hugh X. Lewis Album	1966	6.25	12.50	25.00
❑ KS-3494 [S]	Just Before Dawn	1966	6.25	12.50	25.00
❑ KS-3522 [S]	My Kind of Country	1967	6.25	12.50	25.00
❑ KS-3545	Just a Prayer Away	1968	6.25	12.50	25.00
❑ KS-3563	Country Fever	1968	6.25	12.50	25.00

LEWIS, J.D.

45s

SING ME

Number	Title (A Side/B Side)	Yr	VG	VG+	NM
❑ 43	My Heart's on Hold/(B-side unknown)	1989	—	3.00	6.00
❑ 43 [PS]	My Heart's on Hold/(B-side unknown)	1989	2.00	4.00	8.00

LEWIS, JERRY LEE

Also see RONNIE McDOWELL.

45s

ELEKTRA

Number	Title (A Side/B Side)	Yr	VG	VG+	NM
❑ 46030	Rockin' My Life Away/I Wish I Was Eighteen Again	1979	—	2.00	4.00
❑ 46067	Who Will the Next Fool Be/Rita May	1979	—	2.00	4.00
❑ 46591	When Two Worlds Collide/Good News Travels Fast	1980	—	2.00	4.00
❑ 46642	Honky Tonk Stuff/Rockin' Jerry Lee	1980	—	2.00	4.00
❑ 47026	Over the Rainbow/Folsom Prison Blues	1980	—	2.00	4.00
❑ 47095	Thirty-Nine and Holding/Change Places with Me	1980	—	2.00	4.00
❑ 69962	I'd Do It All Again/Who Will Buy the Wine	1982	—	2.00	4.00

MCA

Number	Title (A Side/B Side)	Yr	VG	VG+	NM
❑ 52151	My Fingers Do the Talkin'/Forever Forgiving	1983	—	—	3.00
❑ 52188	Come As You Were/Circumstantial Evidence	1983	—	—	3.00
❑ 52233	She Sings Amazing Grace/Why You Been Gone So Long	1983	—	—	3.00
❑ 52369	I Am What I Am/That Was the Way It Was Then	1984	—	—	3.00

MERCURY

Number	Title (A Side/B Side)	Yr	VG	VG+	NM
❑ 55011	Middle Age Crazy/Georgia on My Mind	1977	—	3.00	6.00
❑ 55021	Come On In/Who's Sorry Now	1977	—	3.00	6.00
❑ 55028	I'll Find It Where I Can/Don't Let the Stars Get In Your Eyes	1977	—	3.00	6.00
❑ 73099	There Must Be More to Love Than This/Home Away from Home	1970	2.00	4.00	8.00
❑ 73155	I Can't Have a Merry Christmas, Mary (Without You)/In Loving Memories	1970	2.50	5.00	10.00
❑ 73192	Touching Home/Woman, Woman	1971	2.00	4.00	8.00
❑ 73227	When He Walks on You (Like You Have Walked on Me)/Foolish Kind of Man	1971	2.00	4.00	8.00
❑ 73248	Would You Take Another Chance on Me/Me and Bobby McGee	1971	2.00	4.00	8.00
❑ 73273	Chantilly Lace/Think About It Darlin'	1972	2.00	4.00	8.00
❑ 73296	Lonely Weekends/Turn On Your Love Light	1972	2.00	4.00	8.00
❑ 73328	Who's Gonna PlayThis Old Piano/No Honky Tonks in Heaven	1972	2.00	4.00	8.00
❑ 73361	No More Hanging On/Mercy of a Letter	1973	2.00	4.00	8.00
❑ 73374	Drinking Wine Spo-Dee O'Dee/Rock and Roll Medley	1973	2.00	4.00	8.00
❑ 73402	No Headstone on My Grave/Jack Daniels	1973	2.00	4.00	8.00
❑ 73423	Sometimes a Memory Ain't Enough/I Think I Need to Pray	1973	2.00	4.00	8.00
❑ 73452	I'm Left, You're Right, She's Gone/I've Fallen to the Bottom	1974	2.00	4.00	8.00
❑ 73462	Meat Man/Just a Little Bit	1974	2.00	4.00	8.00
❑ 73491	Tell Tale Signs/Cold, Cold Morning Light	1974	2.00	4.00	8.00
❑ 73618	He Can't Fill My Shoes/Tomorrow's Taking Baby Away	1974	—	3.00	6.00
❑ 73661	I Can Still Hear the Music in the Restroom/Remember Me	1975	—	3.00	6.00
❑ 73685	Boogie Woogie Country Man/I'm Still Jealous of You	1975	—	3.00	6.00
❑ 73729	A Damn Good Country Song/When I Take My Vacation in Heaven	1975	—	3.00	6.00
❑ 73763	Don't Boogie Woogie/That Kind of Fool	1976	—	3.00	6.00
❑ 73822	Let's Put It Back Together Again/Jerry Lee's Rock and Roll Revival Show	1976	—	3.00	6.00
❑ 73872	The Closest Thing to You/You Belong to Me	1976	—	3.00	6.00
❑ 76148	I'm So Lonesome I Could Cry/Pick Me Up on Your Way Down	1982	—	2.50	5.00

PHILLIPS INT'L.

Number	Title (A Side/B Side)	Yr	VG	VG+	NM
❑ 3559	In the Mood/I Get the Blues When It Rains	1960	12.50	25.00	50.00
—As "The Hawk"					

POLYDOR

Number	Title (A Side/B Side)	Yr	VG	VG+	NM
❑ 889312-7	Breathless/Great Balls of Fire	1989	—	2.00	4.00
❑ 889312-7 [PS]	Breathless/Great Balls of Fire	1989	—	2.00	4.00
❑ 889798-7	Crazy Arms/Great Balls of Fire	1989	—	2.00	4.00

SCR

Number	Title (A Side/B Side)	Yr	VG	VG+	NM
❑ 386	Get Out Your Big Roll, Daddy/Honky Tonkin' Rock 'N' Roll Piano Man	1985	—	2.50	5.00

SIRE

Number	Title (A Side/B Side)	Yr	VG	VG+	NM
❑ 19809	It Was the Whiskey Talkin' (Not Me)/same (Rock and Roll Version)	1990	—	—	3.00
❑ 64423	Goose Bumps/Crown Victoria 51	1995	—	2.50	5.00

SMASH

Number	Title (A Side/B Side)	Yr	VG	VG+	NM
❑ 1857	Pen and Paper/Hit the Road Jack	1963	3.75	7.50	15.00
❑ 1886	I'm on Fire/Bread and Butter Man	1964	10.00	20.00	40.00
❑ 1906	She Was My Baby (He Was My Friend)/The Hole He Said He'd Dig for Me	1964	3.75	7.50	15.00
❑ 1930	High Heel Sneakers/You Went Back on Your Word	1964	3.75	7.50	15.00
❑ 1969	Baby Hold Me Close/I Believe in You	1965	3.75	7.50	15.00
❑ 1992	This Must Be the Place/Rocking Pneumonia and the Boogie Woogie Flu	1965	3.75	7.50	15.00
❑ 2006	Green, Green Grass of Home/You've Got What It Takes	1965	3.75	7.50	15.00
❑ 2027	Sticks and Stones/What a Heck of a Mess	1966	3.00	6.00	12.00
❑ 2053	If I Had It All to Do Over/Memphis Beat	1966	3.00	6.00	12.00
❑ 2103	Holding On/It's a Hang-Up, Baby	1967	3.00	6.00	12.00
❑ 2122	Turn On Your Love Light/Shotgun Man	1967	3.00	6.00	12.00
❑ 2146	Another Place, Another Time/Walking the Floor Over You	1968	2.50	5.00	10.00
❑ 2164	What's Made Milwaukee Famous (Has Made a Loser Out of Me)/All the Good Is Gone	1968	2.50	5.00	10.00
❑ 2186	She Still Comes Around (To Love What's Left of Me)/Slipping Around	1968	2.50	5.00	10.00
❑ 2202	To Make Love Sweeter for You/Let's Talk About Us	1968	2.50	5.00	10.00
❑ 2224	One Has My Name (The Other Has My Heart)/I Can't Stop Loving You	1969	2.50	5.00	10.00
❑ 2244	She Even Woke Me Up to Say Goodbye/Echoes	1969	2.50	5.00	10.00
❑ 2257	Once More with Feeling/You Went Out of Your Way (To Walk on Me)	1970	2.50	5.00	10.00
❑ 884934-7	Sixteen Candles/Rock and Roll (Fais-Do-Do)	1986	—	2.00	4.00
—B-side with Roy Orbison, Carl Perkins and Johnny Cash					
❑ 888142-7	We Remember the King/Class of '55	1987	—	2.00	4.00
—With Johnny Cash, Roy Orbison and Carl Perkins; B-side by Carl Perkins solo					

SUN

Number	Title (A Side/B Side)	Yr	VG	VG+	NM
❑ 259	Crazy Arms/End of the Road	1957	25.00	50.00	100.00
—As "Jerry Lee Lewis"					
❑ 259	Crazy Arms/End of the Road	1957	12.50	25.00	50.00
—As "Jerry Lee Lewis and His Pumping Piano"					
❑ 267	Whole Lot of Shakin' Going On/It'll Be Me	1957	10.00	20.00	40.00

Number	Title (A Side/B Side)	Yr	VG	VG+	NM
❑ 281	Great Balls of Fire/You Win Again	1957	10.00	20.00	40.00
❑ 281 [PS]	Great Balls of Fire/You Win Again	1957	20.00	40.00	80.00
❑ 288	Breathless/Down the Line	1958	10.00	20.00	40.00
❑ 296	High School Confidential/Fools Like Me	1958	7.50	15.00	30.00
❑ 296 [PS]	High School Confidential/Fools Like Me	1958	20.00	40.00	80.00
❑ 301	Lewis Boogie/The Return of Jerry Lee	1958	7.50	15.00	30.00
—B-side by George and Louis					
❑ 303	I'll Make It All Up to You/Break-Up	1958	6.25	12.50	30.00
❑ 312	I'll Sail My Ship Alone/It Hurt Me So	1958	6.25	12.50	25.00
❑ 317	Lovin' Up a Storm/Big Blon' Baby	1959	6.25	12.50	25.00
❑ 324	Let's Talk About Us/Ballad of Billy Joe	1959	6.25	12.50	25.00
❑ 330	Little Queenie/I Could Never Be Ashamed of You	1959	6.25	12.50	25.00
❑ 337	Old Black Joe/Baby Baby, Bye Bye	1960	5.00	10.00	20.00
❑ 344	Hang Up My Rock and Roll Shoes/John Henry	1960	5.00	10.00	20.00
❑ 352	Love Made a Fool of Me/When I Get Paid	1960	5.00	10.00	20.00
❑ 356	What'd I Say/Livin' Lovin' Wreck	1961	5.00	10.00	20.00
❑ 364	Cold, Cold Heart/It Won't Happen with Me	1961	5.00	10.00	20.00
❑ 367	Save the Last Dance for Me/As Long As I Live	1961	5.00	10.00	20.00
❑ 371	Money/Bonnie B	1961	5.00	10.00	20.00
❑ 374	I've Been Twistin'/Ramblin' Rose	1962	5.00	10.00	20.00
❑ 379	Sweet Little Sixteen/How's My Ex Treating You	1962	5.00	10.00	20.00
❑ 382	Good Golly Miss Molly/I Can't Trust Me	1962	5.00	10.00	20.00
❑ 384	Teenage Letter/Seasons of My Heart	1963	5.00	10.00	20.00
❑ 396	Carry Me Back to Old Virginny/I Know What It Means	1965	5.00	10.00	20.00
❑ 1101	Invitation to Your Party/I Could Never Be Ashamed of You	1969	—	3.00	6.00
❑ 1107	One Minute Past Eternity/Frankie and Johnny	1969	—	3.00	6.00
❑ 1115	I Can't Seem to Say Goodbye/Goodnight Irene	1970	—	2.50	5.00
❑ 1119	Waiting for the Train (All Around the Watertank)/ Big Legged Woman	1970	—	2.50	5.00
❑ 1125	Love on Broadway/Matchbox	1971	—	2.50	5.00
❑ 1128	Your Loving Ways/I Can't Trust Me in Your Arms Anymore	1972	—	2.50	5.00
❑ 1130	Good Rockin' Tonight/I Can't Trust Me in Your Arms Anymore	1973	—	2.50	5.00
❑ 1138	Matchbox/Am I to Be the One	1978	—	2.00	4.00
❑ 1139	Save the Last Dance for Me/Am I to Be the One	1978	—	2.00	4.00
—With uncredited "duet" partner, actually Orion (Jimmy Ellis); a shameless attempt to concoct a "lost Elvis Presley duet"					
❑ 1141	Cold, Cold Heart/Hello Josephine	1979	—	2.00	4.00
❑ 1151	Be-Bop-a-Lula/The Breakup	1980	—	2.00	4.00
—B-side by Charlie Rich; both sides are duets with Orion					

7-Inch Extended Plays

SUN

Number	Title	Yr	VG	VG+	NM
❑ EPA-107	Mean Woman Blues/I'm Feelin' Sorry//Whole Lot of Shakin' Goin' On/Turn Around	1958	20.00	30.00	80.00
❑ EPA-107 [PS]	The Great Ball of Fire	1958	20.00	30.00	80.00
❑ EPA-108	Don't Be Cruel/Goodnight Irene//Put Me Down/It All Depends	1958	12.50	25.00	50.00
❑ EPA-108 [PS]	Jerry Lee Lewis	1958	12.50	25.00	50.00
❑ EPA-109	(contents unknown)	1958	12.50	25.00	50.00
❑ EPA-109 [PS]	Jerry Lee Lewis	1958	12.50	25.00	50.00
❑ EPA-110	(contents unknown)	1958	12.50	25.00	50.00
❑ EPA-110 [PS]	Jerry Lee Lewis	1958	12.50	25.00	50.00

Albums

ACCORD

Number	Title	Yr	VG	VG+	NM
❑ SN-7133	I Walk the Line	1981	2.50	5.00	10.00

DESIGN

Number	Title	Yr	VG	VG+	NM
❑ DLP-165 [M]	Rockin' with Jerry Lee Lewis	1963	6.25	12.50	25.00
❑ DST-165 [R]	Rockin' with Jerry Lee Lewis	1963	5.00	10.00	20.00

ELEKTRA

Number	Title	Yr	VG	VG+	NM
❑ 6E-184	Jerry Lee Lewis	1979	3.00	6.00	12.00
❑ 6E-254	When Two Worlds Collide	1980	3.00	6.00	12.00
❑ 6E-291	Killer Country	1980	3.00	6.00	12.00
❑ 60191	The Best of Jerry Lee Lewis Featuring 39 and Holding	1982	2.50	5.00	10.00

HILLTOP

Number	Title	Yr	VG	VG+	NM
❑ 6102	Sunday After Church	1971	2.50	5.00	10.00
❑ 6110	Roll Over Beethoven	1972	2.50	5.00	10.00
❑ 6120	Rural Route #1	1972	2.50	5.00	10.00

MCA

Number	Title	Yr	VG	VG+	NM
❑ 5387	My Fingers Do the Talkin'	1983	2.50	5.00	10.00
❑ 5478	I Am What I Am	1984	2.50	5.00	10.00

MERCURY

Number	Title	Yr	VG	VG+	NM
❑ SRM-1-637	The "Killer" Rocks On	1972	3.75	7.50	15.00
❑ SRM-1-677	Sometimes a Memory Ain't Enough	1973	3.75	7.50	15.00
❑ 690 [DJ]	A Jerry Lee Lewis Radio Special	1973	12.50	25.00	50.00
❑ SRM-1-690	Southern Roots — Back Home to Memphis	1973	3.75	7.50	15.00
❑ SRM-1-710	I-40 Country	1974	3.75	7.50	15.00
❑ SRM-2-803 [(2)]	The Session	1973	5.00	10.00	20.00
❑ SRM-1-1030	Boogie Woogie Country Man	1975	3.75	7.50	15.00
❑ SRM-1-1064	Odd Man In	1975	3.75	7.50	15.00
❑ SRM-1-1109	Country Class	1976	3.75	7.50	15.00
❑ SRM-1-5004	Country Memories	1977	3.75	7.50	15.00
❑ SRM-1-5006	The Best of Jerry Lee Lewis Volume II	1978	3.75	7.50	15.00
❑ SRM-1-5010	Jerry Lee Lewis Keeps Rockin'	1978	3.75	7.50	15.00
❑ SR-61278	Live at the International, Las Vegas	1970	3.75	7.50	15.00
❑ SR-61318	In Loving Memories	1970	7.50	15.00	30.00
❑ SR-61323	There Must Be More to Love Than This	1971	3.75	7.50	15.00
❑ SR-61343	Touching Home	1971	3.75	7.50	15.00
—With photo of Jerry Lee in front of a brick wall					
❑ SR-61343	Touching Home	1971	5.00	10.00	20.00
—With drawing on cover and small photo of Jerry Lee					
❑ SR-61346	Would You Take Another Chance on Me?	1971	3.75	7.50	15.00
❑ SR-61366	Who's Gonna Play This Old Piano... (Think About It Darlin')	1972	3.75	7.50	15.00
❑ 822789-1	The Best of Jerry Lee Lewis Volume II	198?	2.50	5.00	10.00
❑ 826251-1	Greatest Hits	198?	2.50	5.00	10.00
❑ 830399-1	Would You Take Another Chance on Me	1987	2.50	5.00	10.00
—Reissue of 61346					
❑ 836935-1	Killer: The Mercury Years Volume One, 1963-1968	1989	3.00	6.00	12.00
❑ 836938-1	Killer: The Mercury Years Volume Two, 1969-1972	1989	3.00	6.00	12.00
❑ 836941-1	Killer: The Mercury Years Volume Three, 1973-1977	1989	3.00	6.00	12.00

PAIR

Number	Title	Yr	VG	VG+	NM
❑ PDL2-1132 [(2)]	Solid Gold	1986	3.00	6.00	12.00

PICKWICK

Number	Title	Yr	VG	VG+	NM
❑ PTP-2055 [(2)]	Jerry Lee Lewis	1973	3.00	6.00	12.00
❑ SPC-3224	High Heel Sneakers	1970	2.50	5.00	10.00
❑ SPC-3344	Drinking Wine Spo-Dee-O-Dee	1973	2.50	5.00	10.00

POLYDOR

Number	Title	Yr	VG	VG+	NM
❑ 826139-1	I'm on Fire	1985	2.50	5.00	10.00
❑ 839516-1	Great Balls of Fire!	1989	3.00	6.00	12.00

POWER PAK

Number	Title	Yr	VG	VG+	NM
❑ 247	From the Vaults of Sun	1974	2.50	5.00	10.00

RHINO

Number	Title	Yr	VG	VG+	NM
❑ RNDF-255 [PD]	Original Sun Greatest Hits	1983	3.75	7.50	15.00
❑ RNDA-1499 [(2)]	Milestones	1985	3.75	7.50	15.00
❑ R1-70255	Original Sun Greatest Hits	1989	2.50	5.00	10.00
—Reissue of 255 on black vinyl					
❑ R1-70656	Jerry Lee Lewis	1989	3.00	6.00	12.00
—Reissue of Sun 1230					
❑ R1-70657	Jerry Lee's Greatest	1989	3.00	6.00	12.00
—Reissue of Sun 1265					
❑ R1-70899	Wild One: Rare Tracks from Jerry Lee Lewis	1989	3.00	6.00	12.00
❑ R1-71499 [(2)]	Milestones	1989	3.00	6.00	12.00
—Reissue of 1499					

SEARS

Number	Title	Yr	VG	VG+	NM
❑ SPS-610	Hound Dog	1970	6.25	12.50	25.00

SMASH

Number	Title	Yr	VG	VG+	NM
❑ SL-7001	Golden Hits	1980	3.00	6.00	12.00
❑ MGS-27040 [M]	The Golden Hits of Jerry Lee Lewis	1964	6.25	12.50	25.00
❑ MGS-27056 [M]	The Greatest Live Show on Earth	1964	25.00	50.00	100.00
❑ MGS-27063 [M]	The Return of Rock	1965	7.50	15.00	30.00
❑ MGS-27071 [M]	Country Songs for City Folks	1965	6.25	12.50	25.00
❑ MGS-27079 [M]	Memphis Beat	1966	6.25	12.50	25.00
❑ MGS-27086 [M]	By Request — More of the Greatest Live Show on Earth	1966	7.50	15.00	30.00
❑ MGS-27097 [M]	Soul My Way	1967	7.50	15.00	30.00
❑ SRS-67040 [S]	The Golden Hits of Jerry Lee Lewis	1964	7.50	15.00	30.00
❑ SRS-67040 [S]	The Golden Rock Hits of Jerry Lee Lewis	1969	3.75	7.50	15.00
—Retitled reissue					
❑ SRS-67056 [S]	The Greatest Live Show on Earth	1964	37.50	75.00	150.00
❑ SRS-67063 [S]	The Return of Rock	1965	10.00	20.00	40.00
❑ SRS-67071	All Country	1969	3.75	7.50	15.00
—Retitled reissue					
❑ SRS-67071 [S]	Country Songs for City Folks	1965	7.50	15.00	30.00
❑ SRS-67079 [S]	Memphis Beat	1966	7.50	15.00	30.00
❑ SRS-67086 [S]	By Request — More of the Greatest Live Show on Earth	1966	10.00	20.00	40.00
❑ SRS-67097 [S]	Soul My Way	1967	10.00	20.00	40.00
❑ SRS-67104	Another Place Another Time	1968	5.00	10.00	20.00
❑ SRS-67112	She Still Comes Around (To Love What's Left of Me)	1969	5.00	10.00	20.00
❑ SRS-67117	Jerry Lee Lewis Sings the Country Music Hall of Fame Hits, Vol. 1	1969	5.00	10.00	20.00
❑ SRS-67118	Jerry Lee Lewis Sings the Country Music Hall of Fame Hits, Vol. 2	1969	5.00	10.00	20.00
❑ SRS-67128	She Even Woke Me Up to Say Goodbye	1970	5.00	10.00	20.00
❑ SRS-67131	The Best of Jerry Lee Lewis	1970	5.00	10.00	20.00

SUN

Number	Title	Yr	VG	VG+	NM
❑ LP-102	Original Golden Hits — Volume 1	1969	3.75	7.50	15.00
❑ LP-103	Original Golden Hits — Volume 2	1969	3.75	7.50	15.00
❑ LP-107	Rockin' Rhythm and Blues	1969	3.75	7.50	15.00
❑ LP-108	The Golden Cream of the Country	1969	3.75	7.50	15.00
❑ LP-114	A Taste of Country	1970	3.75	7.50	15.00
❑ LP-124	Monsters	1971	3.75	7.50	15.00
❑ LP-128	Original Golden Hits — Volume 3	1972	3.75	7.50	15.00
❑ 1005	The Original	1978	3.00	6.00	12.00
❑ 1011	Duets	1978	3.00	6.00	12.00
—With Orion (uncredited)					
❑ 1018	Trio +	1979	3.00	6.00	12.00
—With Carl Perkins, Charlie Rich and (uncredited) Orion					
❑ SLP-1230 [M]	Jerry Lee Lewis	1958	50.00	100.00	200.00
❑ SLP-1265 [M]	Jerry Lee's Greatest	1961	62.50	125.00	250.00
❑ SLP-1265 [M-DJ]	Jerry Lee's Greatest	1961	200.00	400.00	800.00
—White label promo					

SUNNYVALE

Number	Title	Yr	VG	VG+	NM
❑ 905	The Sun Story, Vol. 5	1977	2.50	5.00	10.00

WING

Number	Title	Yr	VG	VG+	NM
❑ PKW2-125 [(2)]	The Legend of Jerry Lee Lewis	1969	6.25	12.50	25.00
❑ MGW-12340 [M]	The Return of Rock	1967	3.00	6.00	12.00
❑ SRW-16340	In Demand	1968	2.50	5.00	10.00
❑ SRW-16340 [S]	The Return of Rock	1967	3.00	6.00	12.00
❑ SRW-16406	Unlimited	1968	3.00	6.00	12.00

LEWIS, JERRY LEE, AND LINDA GAIL LEWIS

Also see each artist's individual listings.

45s

Number	Title (A Side/B Side)	Yr	VG	VG+	NM
MERCURY					
❑ 73303	Writing on the Wall/Me and Jesus	1972	—	3.50	7.00
SMASH					
❑ 2220	Don't Let Me Cross Over/We Live in Two Different Worlds	1969	2.50	5.00	10.00
❑ 2254	Roll Over Beethoven/Secret Places	1969	2.50	5.00	10.00

Albums

Number	Title (A Side/B Side)	Yr	VG	VG+	NM
SMASH					
❑ SRS-67126	Together	1969	5.00	10.00	20.00

LEWIS, LINDA GAIL

Also see JERRY LEE LEWIS.

45s

Number	Title (A Side/B Side)	Yr	VG	VG+	NM
MERCURY					
❑ 73113	Before the Snow Flies/What Is Love	1970	—	3.50	7.00
❑ 73245	Paper Roses/Working Girl	1971	—	3.50	7.00
❑ 73316	Smile, Somebody Loves You/Louisiana	1972	—	3.50	7.00
❑ 73343	Ivory Tower/He's Loved Me Much Too Much	1972	—	3.50	7.00
❑ 73463	I Wanna Be a Sensuous Woman/I Should Not Have Fallen in Love with You	1974	—	3.00	6.00
❑ 73473	The Joy and Love You Bring/A Lover and a Friend	1974	—	3.00	6.00
SMASH					
❑ 2193	Turn Back the Hands of Time/Good	1968	2.50	5.00	10.00
❑ 2211	T-H-E E-N-D/Then We Said Goodbye	1969	2.00	4.00	8.00
❑ 2240	He's Loved Me Much Too Much (Much Too Long)/Southside Soul Society Chapter No. 1	1969	2.00	4.00	8.00
❑ 2261	My Heart Was the Last One to Know/Gather Round Children	1970	2.00	4.00	8.00

Albums

Number	Title (A Side/B Side)	Yr	VG	VG+	NM
SMASH					
❑ SRS-67119	Two Sides of Linda Gail Lewis	1969	6.25	12.50	25.00

LEWIS, MARGARET

45s

Number	Title (A Side/B Side)	Yr	VG	VG+	NM
CAPITOL					
❑ 5185	Raggedy Ann/Fame and Fortune	1964	2.50	5.00	10.00
❑ 5385	If You Ever Wonder/Nobody's Darling But Mine	1965	2.50	5.00	10.00
SSS INTERNATIONAL					
❑ 743	Honey (I Miss You Too)/Milk and Honey	1968	2.00	4.00	8.00
❑ 753	Mrs. Cooper's Tea Party/Miss to Mrs. to Misery	1968	—	3.50	7.00

LEWIS, MELISSA

45s

Number	Title (A Side/B Side)	Yr	VG	VG+	NM
DOOR KNOB					
❑ 122	The First Time/When Love Finds a Place in Your Heart	1980	—	2.50	5.00
❑ 129	One Good Reason/You'll Never Know (How Close He Came to Hurting You)	1980	—	2.50	5.00
WARNER BROS.					
❑ 29242	Lookin' for a Brand New Heartache/Don't Leave Me in Love	1984	—	2.00	4.00

LEWIS, ROSS

45s

Number	Title (A Side/B Side)	Yr	VG	VG+	NM
WILD DOG					
❑ 4	Hold Your Fire/(B-side unknown)	1988	—	3.00	6.00
❑ 4 [PS]	Hold Your Fire/(B-side unknown)	1988	—	3.50	7.00
❑ 5	Love in Motion/(B-side unknown)	1988	—	3.00	6.00
❑ 5 [PS]	Love in Motion/(B-side unknown)	1988	—	3.50	7.00
❑ 6	The Chance You Take/(B-side unknown)	1989	—	3.00	6.00
❑ 6 [PS]	The Chance You Take/(B-side unknown)	1989	—	3.50	7.00
❑ 7	Of All the Foolish Things to Do/(B-side unknown)	1989	—	3.00	6.00

LEWIS, TEXAS JIM

45s

Number	Title (A Side/B Side)	Yr	VG	VG+	NM
CORAL					
❑ 60856	Sweet Face but a Cold Heart/Banjo Schottische	1952	5.00	10.00	20.00
❑ 69000	Where Did Robinson Crusoe Go with Friday on Saturday Night?/(B-side unknown)	195?	5.00	10.00	20.00

Selected 78s

Number	Title (A Side/B Side)	Yr	VG	VG+	NM
DECCA					
❑ 5874	Seven Beers with the Wrong Man/(B-side unknown)	1940	5.00	10.00	20.00
❑ 5990	Old Fashioned Hoedown/Pretty Quadroon	1941	5.00	10.00	20.00
❑ 6099	Too Late to Worry, Too Blue to Cry/'Leven Miles from Leavenworth	1944	5.00	10.00	20.00
❑ 46015	Have I Been Mean to You/Spanish Two Step	1946	5.00	10.00	20.00
❑ 46021	Rock and Rye Polka/Wine, Women and Song	1946	5.00	10.00	20.00
❑ 46063	Beaver Creek/The Covered Wagon Rolled Right Along	1947	5.00	10.00	20.00
❑ 46073	They Always Pick on Me/You've Got Me Wrapped	1947	5.00	10.00	20.00
❑ 46097	Worried Mind/New San Antonio Rose	1948	5.00	10.00	20.00
❑ 46130	No One Will Ever Know/One Little Teardrop Too Late	1948	5.00	10.00	20.00
❑ 46138	You Call Everybody Darling/Dear Odie	1948	5.00	10.00	20.00
VOCALION					
❑ 03754	titles unknown	1937	6.25	12.50	25.00
❑ 03915	titles unknown	1938	6.25	12.50	25.00
❑ 03977	titles unknown	1938	6.25	12.50	25.00

LIBBY, BRENDA

45s

Number	Title (A Side/B Side)	Yr	VG	VG+	NM
COMSTOCK					
❑ 1726	Give It Back/We Don't Make Sense Anymore	1983	2.00	4.00	8.00

LIGHTFOOT, GORDON

45s

Number	Title (A Side/B Side)	Yr	VG	VG+	NM
ABC-PARAMOUNT					
❑ 10352	Daisy-Doo/I'm the One (Remember Me)	1962	6.25	12.50	25.00
—As "Gord Lightfoot"					
❑ 10373	It's Too Late, He Wins/Negotiations	1962	6.25	12.50	25.00
CHATEAU					
❑ 142	Daisy-Doo/I'm the One (Remember Me)	1962	12.50	25.00	50.00
❑ 148	It's Too Late, He Wins/Negotiations	1962	12.50	25.00	50.00
❑ 152	I'll Meet You in Michigan/Is My Baby Blue Tonight	1962	10.00	20.00	40.00
REPRISE					
❑ 0744	If You Could Read My Mind/Me and Bobby McGee	1972	—	2.00	4.00
—"Back to Back Hits" series					
❑ 0745	Talking in Your Sleep/Summer Side of Life	1972	—	2.00	4.00
—"Back to Back Hits" series					
❑ 0926	Me and Bobby McGee/Pony Man	1970	—	2.50	5.00
❑ 0974	If You Could Read My Mind/Poor Little Allison	1970	—	3.00	6.00
❑ 1020	Talking in Your Sleep/Nous Vivons Ensemble	1971	—	2.50	5.00
❑ 1035	Summer Side of Life/Love and Maple Syrup	1971	—	2.50	5.00
❑ 1088	Beautiful/Don Quixote	1972	—	2.50	5.00
❑ 1128	You Are What I Am/The Same Old Obsession	1972	—	2.50	5.00
❑ 1145	Can't Depend on You/It's Worth Believin'	1972	—	2.50	5.00
❑ 1194	Sundown/Too Late for Prayin'	1974	—	2.00	4.00
❑ 1309	Carefree Highway/Seven Island Suite	1974	—	2.00	4.00
❑ 1328	Rainy Day People/Cherokee Bend	1975	—	2.00	4.00
❑ 1369	The Wreck of the Edmund Fitzgerald/The House You Live In	1976	—	2.00	4.00
❑ 1380	Race Among the Ruins/Protocol	1976	—	2.00	4.00
UNITED ARTISTS					
❑ 929	Just Like Tom Thumb's Blues/Ribbon of Darkness	1965	2.50	5.00	10.00
❑ 50055	For Lovin' Me/Spin, Spin	1966	2.00	4.00	8.00
❑ 50114	I'll Be Alright/Go Go Round	1967	2.00	4.00	8.00
❑ 50152	The Way I Feel/Peaceful Waters	1967	2.00	4.00	8.00
❑ 50281	Pussywillows, Cat-Tails/Black Day in July	1968	2.00	4.00	8.00
❑ 50447	Does Your Mother Know/Bitter Green	1968	2.00	4.00	8.00
❑ 50765	If I Could/Softly	1971	—	2.50	5.00
WARNER BROS.					
❑ 5621	For Lovin' Me/I'm Not Sayin'	1965	3.75	7.50	15.00
❑ 8518	The Circle Is Small/Sweet Guinevere	1978	—	2.50	5.00
—Without A-side subtitle					
❑ 8518	The Circle Is Small (I Can See It In Your Eyes)/Sweet Guinevere	1978	—	2.00	4.00
—Subtitle added to later pressings					
❑ 8579	Daylight Katy/Hangdog Hotel Room	1978	—	2.00	4.00
❑ 8644	Dreamland/Songs the Minstrel Sang	1978	—	2.00	4.00
❑ 28222	Ecstasy Made Easy/Morning Glory	1987	—	—	3.00
❑ 28422	East of Midnight/I'll Tag Along	1987	—	—	3.00
❑ 28553	Stay Loose/Morning Glory	1986	—	—	3.00
❑ 28655	Anything for Love/Let It Ride	1986	—	—	3.00
❑ 28655 [PS]	Anything for Love/Let It Ride	1986	—	2.00	4.00
❑ 29466	Someone to Believe In/Without You	1983	—	2.00	4.00
❑ 29511	Knotty Pine/Salute	1983	—	2.00	4.00
❑ 29859	Shadows/In My Fashion	1982	—	2.00	4.00
❑ 29963	Blackberry Wine/(B-side unknown)	1982	—	2.00	4.00
❑ 49230	Dream Street Rose/Make Way for the Lady	1980	—	2.00	4.00
❑ 49516	If You Need Me/Mister Rock of Ages	1980	—	2.00	4.00
❑ 50012	Baby Step Back/Thank You for the Promises	1982	—	2.00	4.00

Albums

Number	Title (A Side/B Side)	Yr	VG	VG+	NM
LIBERTY					
❑ LN-10038	The Best of Lightfoot	198?	2.00	4.00	8.00
—Budget-line reissue					
❑ LN-10039	Sunday Concert	198?	2.00	4.00	8.00
—Budget-line reissue					
❑ LN-10040	Back Here on Earth	198?	2.00	4.00	8.00
—Budget-line reissue					
❑ LN-10041	Did She Mention My Name	198?	2.00	4.00	8.00
—Budget-line reissue					
❑ LN-10043	The Way I Feel	198?	2.00	4.00	8.00
—Budget-line reissue					
❑ LN-10044	Lightfoot	198?	2.00	4.00	8.00
—Budget-line reissue					
MOBILE FIDELITY					
❑ 1-018	Sundown	1979	10.00	20.00	40.00
—Audiophile vinyl					
PAIR					
❑ PDL2-1081 [(2)]	Songbook	1986	3.00	6.00	12.00
REPRISE					
❑ MS 2037	Summer Side of Life	1971	3.00	6.00	12.00
❑ MS 2056	Don Quixote	1972	3.00	6.00	12.00
❑ MS 2116	Old Dan's Records	1972	3.00	6.00	12.00
❑ MS 2177	Sundown	1974	3.00	6.00	12.00
❑ MS 2206	Cold on the Shoulder	1975	3.00	6.00	12.00
❑ 2RS 2237 [(2)]	Gord's Gold	1975	3.75	7.50	15.00
❑ MS 2246	Summertime Dream	1976	3.00	6.00	12.00
❑ RS 6392	Sit Down Young Stranger	1970	3.75	7.50	15.00
❑ RS 6392	If You Could Read My Mind	1971	2.50	5.00	10.00
—Retitled version					
❑ ST-93228	Sit Down Young Stranger	1970	5.00	10.00	20.00
—Capitol Record Club edition					

UNITED ARTISTS

Number	Title (A Side/B Side)	Yr	VG	VG+	NM
❑ UA-LA243-G	The Very Best of Gordon Lightfoot	1974	3.00	6.00	12.00
❑ UAL-3487 [M]	Lightfoot	1966	5.00	10.00	20.00
❑ UAL-3587 [M]	The Way I Feel	1967	5.00	10.00	20.00
❑ UAS-5510	Classic Lightfoot (The Best of Lightfoot/Volume 2)	1971	3.75	7.50	15.00
❑ UAS-6487 [S]	Lightfoot	1966	6.25	12.50	25.00
❑ UAS-6587 [S]	The Way I Feel	1967	6.25	12.50	25.00
❑ UAS-6649	Did She Mention My Name	1968	5.00	10.00	20.00
❑ UAS-6672	Back Here on Earth	1969	5.00	10.00	20.00
❑ UAS-6714	Sunday Concert	1969	3.75	7.50	15.00
❑ UAS-6754	The Best of Lightfoot	1970	3.75	7.50	15.00

WARNER BROS.

Number	Title (A Side/B Side)	Yr	VG	VG+	NM
❑ BSK 3149	Endless Wire	1978	2.50	5.00	10.00
❑ HS 3426	Dream Street Rose	1980	2.50	5.00	10.00
❑ BSK 3633	Shadows	1982	2.50	5.00	10.00
❑ 23901	Salute	1983	2.50	5.00	10.00
❑ 25482	East of Midnight	1986	2.50	5.00	10.00
❑ 25784	Gord's Gold, Volume II	1989	3.00	6.00	12.00

LINCOLN COUNTY

45s

SOUNDWAVES

Number	Title (A Side/B Side)	Yr	VG	VG+	NM
❑ 4629	Making the Night the Best Part of My Day/I'm Gonna Be Strong	1981	—	2.50	5.00
❑ 4644	Hard Holding Heaven/Worst End of the Deal	1981	—	2.50	5.00

LINDSAY, REG

45s

CON BRIO

Number	Title (A Side/B Side)	Yr	VG	VG+	NM
❑ 102	Takin' a Chance/There You Go	1975	—	3.00	6.00
❑ 105	To Get to You/I'd Walk a Mile for a Smile	1976	—	2.50	5.00
❑ 119	Give Me Liberty (Or Give Me Love)/Ain't Gonna Let You Sock It to Me	1977	—	2.50	5.00
❑ 136	Would You Take Me Back Again/Gonna Live This Long	1978	—	2.50	5.00
❑ 141	Just Play Me a Simple Song/Blue	1978	—	2.50	5.00
❑ 147	Rhinestones Are Forever/Southern Bound	1979	—	2.50	5.00
❑ 155	I'd Walk a Mile for a Smile/I Just Try and Smell the Roses	1979	—	2.50	5.00

LINDSEY, BENNY

45s

PHONO

Number	Title (A Side/B Side)	Yr	VG	VG+	NM
❑ 2614	Wine, Women and Loud Happy Songs/(B-side unknown)	1976	—	3.50	7.00
❑ 2621	Bring It On Home to Me/(B-side unknown)	1976	—	3.50	7.00
❑ 2633	Save the Last Dance for Me/(B-side unknown)	1976	—	3.50	7.00

LINDSEY, GEORGE

45s

CAPITOL

Number	Title (A Side/B Side)	Yr	VG	VG+	NM
❑ 2450	96 Miles to Bakersfield/It's Such a Pretty World Today	1969	2.50	5.00	10.00
❑ 2572	Just Love Her/Remember Back When	1969	2.50	5.00	10.00
❑ 2685	Freaked Out/My Home Town	1969	2.50	5.00	10.00

COLUMBIA

Number	Title (A Side/B Side)	Yr	VG	VG+	NM
❑ 4-44215	Call Me Country/The World's Biggest Whopper	1967	3.00	6.00	12.00

Albums

CAPITOL

Number	Title (A Side/B Side)	Yr	VG	VG+	NM
❑ ST-230	96 Miles to Bakersfield	1969	6.25	12.50	25.00
❑ ST 2965	Goober Sings!	1968	6.25	12.50	25.00

LINDSEY, JUDY

45s

GYPSY

Number	Title (A Side/B Side)	Yr	VG	VG+	NM
❑ 83881	Wrong Train/From My Heart's Point of View	1988	—	3.00	6.00

LINDSEY, LAWANDA

45s

CAPITOL

Number	Title (A Side/B Side)	Yr	VG	VG+	NM
❑ 3652	Today Will Be the First Day of the Rest of My Life/Paint Me a Picture of Our Love	1973	—	2.50	5.00
❑ 3739	Sunshine Feeling/Love Makes the World Go Around	1973	—	2.50	5.00
❑ 3819	Hello Trouble/Your Tender Loving Care	1974	—	2.50	5.00
❑ 3875	Hello Out There/Top of the Morning to You	1974	—	2.50	5.00
❑ 3950	I Ain't Hangin' 'Round/Your Monkey Won't Be Home Tonight	1974	—	2.50	5.00
❑ 4048	Postcard Blues/Comin' Down with Love	1975	—	2.50	5.00
❑ 4094	Good Time Baby/We're Gonna Let the Good Times Roll	1975	—	2.50	5.00
❑ 4127	Let Your Fingers Do the Walking/You're the One I Was Born to Love	1975	—	2.50	5.00
❑ 4195	A Matter of Pride/Road, I'll Follow You Down	1975	—	2.50	5.00

CHART

Number	Title (A Side/B Side)	Yr	VG	VG+	NM
❑ 1019	Beggars Can't Be Choosers/Faded Blue	1968	2.00	4.00	8.00
❑ 1036	The Decline and Fall of Me/Wave Bye-Bye to the Man	1968	2.00	4.00	8.00
❑ 1054	I Did My Duty/What Kind of Woman	1968	2.00	4.00	8.00
❑ 5003	Take Me Home/Woman's Intuition	1969	—	3.00	6.00
❑ 5024	I'm Not Half as Strong/Strike Three You're Out	1969	—	3.00	6.00
❑ 5042	Partly Bill/Making Waves	1969	—	3.00	6.00
❑ 5076	We'll Sing in the Sunshine/I'll Just Take Your Word for It, Baby	1970	—	3.00	6.00
❑ 5107	Day of Our Love/No Matter How You Do Me	1971	—	3.00	6.00
❑ 5129	You Make My Day/Why Should I Care	1971	—	3.00	6.00
❑ 5144	Partin' of the Ways/Say It with Flowers	1971	—	3.00	6.00
❑ 5153	I WIsh I Was a Little Boy Again/Time Heals All Wounds	1972	—	3.00	6.00
❑ 5177	One Time Too Many/Partly Bill	1973	—	3.00	6.00

MERCURY

Number	Title (A Side/B Side)	Yr	VG	VG+	NM
❑ 55007	Faithless Love/Gone Forever (File Me Under Memories)	1977	—	2.00	4.00
❑ 55041	I'm a Woman in Love/Let Your Body Speak Your Mind	1978	—	2.00	4.00
❑ 73889	Walk Right Back/(Try to Love Him) A Little Bit More	1977	—	2.00	4.00

Albums

CAPITOL

Number	Title (A Side/B Side)	Yr	VG	VG+	NM
❑ ST-11306	This Is LaWanda Lindsey	1974	3.00	6.00	12.00

CHART

Number	Title (A Side/B Side)	Yr	VG	VG+	NM
❑ CHS-1015	Swingin' and Singin' My Song	1969	3.75	7.50	15.00
❑ CHS-1035	We'll Sing in the Sunshine	1970	3.75	7.50	15.00
❑ CHS-1048	LaWanda Lindsey's Greatest Hits, Volume 1	1971	3.75	7.50	15.00

LINDSEY, LAWANDA, AND KENNY VERNON

Also see each artist's individual listings.

45s

CHART

Number	Title (A Side/B Side)	Yr	VG	VG+	NM
❑ 1063	Eye to Eye/Looking Over Our Shoulders	1968	2.00	4.00	8.00
❑ 5055	Pickin' Wild Mountain Berries/We Don't Deserve Each Other	1970	—	3.00	6.00
❑ 5090	Let's Think About Where We're Going/Puzzles of My Mind	1970	—	3.00	6.00
❑ 5114	The Crawdad Song/Wrong Number	1971	—	3.00	6.00

LINTON, SHERWIN

45s

AMERICAN HOMESTEAD

Number	Title (A Side/B Side)	Yr	VG	VG+	NM
❑ AH 1882	Don't Fiddle with My Farm/Blackland Farmer	198?	3.00	6.00	12.00

BLACK GOLD

Number	Title (A Side/B Side)	Yr	VG	VG+	NM
❑ 6913	I'm Not Among the Loving/(B-side unknown)	1969	2.00	4.00	8.00
❑ 7217	Little Peace of Mind/Livin' My Life with a Cheater	1972	2.00	4.00	8.00

BREAKER

Number	Title (A Side/B Side)	Yr	VG	VG+	NM
❑ 3902	Santa Got a DWI/An Old Christmas Card	1986	—	2.00	4.00
❑ 3902 [PS]	Santa Got a DWI/An Old Christmas Card	1986	—	3.00	6.00

HICKORY

Number	Title (A Side/B Side)	Yr	VG	VG+	NM
❑ 1541	Sunshine/Working for the Man	1969	2.50	5.00	10.00
❑ 1553	Then I Miss You/I'm Leaving for Good This Time	1969	2.50	5.00	10.00

NEW WORLD

Number	Title (A Side/B Side)	Yr	VG	VG+	NM
❑ 80004	Cotton King/Innocent Rose	196?	2.50	5.00	10.00

SOMA

Number	Title (A Side/B Side)	Yr	VG	VG+	NM
❑ 1405	Remember Me/Who Besides Me	1965	6.25	12.50	25.00

SOUNDWAVES

Number	Title (A Side/B Side)	Yr	VG	VG+	NM
❑ 4556	Jesse I Wanted That Award/Men Talk	1977	—	3.00	6.00
❑ 4568	I Fell in Love with Dolly Parton/Put Another Log on the Fire	1978	—	3.00	6.00
❑ 4696	Football Junkie/Thank You to the NFL	1983	—	2.50	5.00
—With Patti Trobec					
❑ 4709	Rockabilly Is Better the Second Time Around/I Forgot to Remember to Forget	1983	3.00	6.00	12.00

TWIN TOWN

Number	Title (A Side/B Side)	Yr	VG	VG+	NM
❑ 716	House of Blue Lights/Gimme Another Bottle of Beer	1965	5.00	10.00	20.00

Albums

BLACK GOLD

Number	Title (A Side/B Side)	Yr	VG	VG+	NM
❑ 7116	I'm Not Johnny Cash	1972	6.25	12.50	25.00

BREAKER

Number	Title (A Side/B Side)	Yr	VG	VG+	NM
❑ BR-4001	Christmas Memories	1987	3.00	6.00	12.00

RE-CAR

Number	Title (A Side/B Side)	Yr	VG	VG+	NM
❑ 2108	Sherwin Linton and the Cotton Kings	1968	15.00	30.00	60.00

LIPHAM, CURLY

45s

DECCA

Number	Title (A Side/B Side)	Yr	VG	VG+	NM
❑ 9-46323	Maybe Someday/Hearts That Could Never Be True	1951	6.25	12.50	25.00
❑ 9-46347	You're Lucky That I Love You/I Know What It Means	1951	6.25	12.50	25.00
❑ 9-46372	Blue Fedora/I'm Afraid of Your Kisses	1951	6.25	12.50	25.00

LIPTON, HOLLY

45s

EVERGREEN

Number	Title (A Side/B Side)	Yr	VG	VG+	NM
❑ 1096	At This Moment/(B-side unknown)	1989	—	2.50	5.00

LITTLE, PEGGY

45s

DOT

Number	Title (A Side/B Side)	Yr	VG	VG+	NM
❑ 17199	Son of a Preacher Man/One More Nightly Cry	1969	—	3.50	7.00
❑ 17259	Sweet Baby Girl/My Heart's Not In It Anymore	1969	—	3.50	7.00
❑ 17308	Put Your Lovin' Where Your Mouth Is/Softly and Tenderly	1969	—	3.50	7.00
❑ 17338	Mama, I Won't Be Wearing a Ring/Love's Biggest Fool	1970	—	3.00	6.00
❑ 17353	I Knew You'd Be Leaving/Gentle Man	1970	—	3.00	6.00
❑ 17364	My Santa in Tennis Shoes/Ho Ho Ho	1970	2.00	4.00	8.00

Number	Title (A Side/B Side)	Yr	VG	VG+	NM
❑ 17371	I've Got to Have You/I've Got a Lot of Love (Left in Me)	1971	—	3.00	6.00
❑ 17393	He Goes Walking Through My Mind/Snap Your Fingers	1971	—	3.00	6.00
❑ 17398	Goodbye Baby/Little Henry Hurt	1971	—	3.00	6.00
❑ 17417	I Depend on You/Little Golden Band	1972	—	3.00	6.00

EPIC

Number	Title (A Side/B Side)	Yr	VG	VG+	NM
❑ 5-10968	Listen, Spot/Everything's All Right	1973	—	2.50	5.00
❑ 5-11028	Sugarman/If Lovin' You Starts Hurtin' Me	1973	—	2.50	5.00
❑ 5-11081	Just for You/One More Chance	1974	—	2.50	5.00

Albums

DOT

Number	Title (A Side/B Side)	Yr	VG	VG+	NM
❑ DLP-25948	A Little Bit of Peggy	1969	3.75	7.50	15.00
❑ DLP-25982	More Than a Little	1971	3.75	7.50	15.00

LITTLE TEXAS

Also see JEFF FOXWORTHY; BRADY SEALS.

45s

WARNER BROS.

Number	Title (A Side/B Side)	Yr	VG	VG+	NM
❑ 7-17391	Bad for Us/Long Way Down	1997	—	—	3.00
❑ 7-17770	Life Goes On/Country Crazy	1995	—	—	3.00
❑ 7-18001	Amy's Back in Austin/Excerpts from Country World Premiere Radio Show	1994	—	—	3.00
❑ 7-18103	Kick a Little/Hit Country Song	1994	—	2.00	4.00
❑ 7-18295	My Love/Only Thing I'm Sure Of	1994	—	2.50	5.00
❑ 7-18385	God Blessed Texas/Cutoff Jeans	1993	—	2.50	5.00
❑ 7-18516	What Might Have Been/Stop on a Dime	1993	—	2.50	5.00
❑ 7-18668	I'd Rather Miss You/Cry On	1993	—	2.00	4.00
❑ 7-18741	What Were You Thinkin'/Just One More Night	1992	—	2.00	4.00
❑ 7-18867	You and Forever and Me/Dance	1992	—	2.00	4.00
❑ 7-19024	First Time for Everything/Some Guys Have All the Love	1992	—	2.00	4.00

LITTLEJOHN, JIMMY

45s

COLUMBIA

Number	Title (A Side/B Side)	Yr	VG	VG+	NM
❑ 4-21259	Tequila Mama/No Parking Here	1954	5.00	10.00	20.00
❑ 4-21320	Haunted Blues/I'm Mean When I'm Mad	1954	5.00	10.00	20.00
❑ 4-21417	Never, Never, Never/Walking the Streets	1955	5.00	10.00	20.00

LLOYD, MICK, AND JERRI KELLY

Also see JERRI KELLY.

45s

LITTLE GIANT

Number	Title (A Side/B Side)	Yr	VG	VG+	NM
❑ 040	Be My Lover, Be My Friend/Drifter's Lullaby	1980	—	3.00	6.00
❑ 046	Sweet Natural Love/Forsaking All the Rest	1981	—	3.00	6.00

LOBO

45s

ATLANTIC

Number	Title (A Side/B Side)	Yr	VG	VG+	NM
❑ 3851 [DJ]	Caribbean Carnival (same on both sides)	1981	—	2.50	5.00

—May be promo only

BIG TREE

Number	Title (A Side/B Side)	Yr	VG	VG+	NM
❑ 112	Me and You and a Dog Named Boo/Walk Away from It All	1971	—	3.00	6.00
❑ 116	She Didn't Do Magic/I'm the Only One	1971	—	2.50	5.00
❑ 119	California Kid and Reemo/A Little Different	1971	—	2.50	5.00
❑ 134	The Albatross/We'll Make It, I Know We Will	1972	—	2.50	5.00
❑ 141	A Simple Man/Don't Expect Me to Be Your Friend	1972	—	2.50	5.00
❑ 147	I'd Love You to Want Me/Am I True to Myself	1972	—	2.50	5.00
❑ 158	Don't Expect Me to Be Your Friend/A Simple Man	1973	—	2.00	4.00
❑ 15001	Standing at the End of the Line/Stoney	1974	—	2.00	4.00
❑ 15008	Rings/I'm Just Dreaming	1974	—	2.00	4.00
❑ 16001	It Sure Took a Long, Long Time/Running Deer	1973	—	2.00	4.00
❑ 16004	How Can I Tell Her/Hope You're Proud of Me Girl	1973	—	2.00	4.00
❑ 16012	There Ain't No Way/Love Me for What I Am	1973	—	2.00	4.00
❑ 16033	Don't Tell Me Goodnight/My Mama Had Soul	1975	—	2.00	4.00
❑ 16040	Would I Still Have You/Morning Sun	1975	—	2.00	4.00

ELEKTRA

Number	Title (A Side/B Side)	Yr	VG	VG+	NM
❑ 47099	I Can't Believe You Anymore/Fight Fire with Fire	1980	—	2.00	4.00

EVERGREEN

Number	Title (A Side/B Side)	Yr	VG	VG+	NM
❑ 1028	Am I Going Crazy (Or Just Out of My Mind)/I Don't Want to Want You	1985	—	2.50	5.00

—Stock copies have corrected title

Number	Title (A Side/B Side)	Yr	VG	VG+	NM
❑ 1028 [DJ]	Am I Going Crazy (Or Just Out of Her Mind) (same on both sides)	1985	—	3.00	6.00

—Promo copies have incorrect title

LAURIE

Number	Title (A Side/B Side)	Yr	VG	VG+	NM
❑ 3526	Happy Days in New York City/My Friend Is Here	1969	3.75	7.50	15.00

—As "Kent LaVoie"

LOBO

Number	Title (A Side/B Side)	Yr	VG	VG+	NM
❑ I	I Don't Want to Want You/No One Will Ever Know	1981	—	2.50	5.00
❑ IV	Come Looking for Me/I Don't Want to Want You	1982	—	2.50	5.00
❑ X	Living My Life Without You/A Simple Man	1982	—	2.50	5.00

MCA

Number	Title (A Side/B Side)	Yr	VG	VG+	NM
❑ 41065	Where Were You When I Was Falling in Love/I Don't Wanna Make Love Anymore	1979	—	2.00	4.00
❑ 41152	Holdin' On for Dear Love/Gus, the Dancing Dog	1979	—	2.00	4.00

WARNER BROS.

Number	Title (A Side/B Side)	Yr	VG	VG+	NM
❑ 8493	Afterglow/Our Best Time	1977	—	2.00	4.00
❑ 8537	You Are All I'll Ever Need/Our Best Time	1978	—	2.00	4.00

Albums

BIG TREE

Number	Title (A Side/B Side)	Yr	VG	VG+	NM
❑ 2003	Introducing Lobo	1971	3.75	7.50	15.00
❑ 2013	Of a Simple Man	1972	3.75	7.50	15.00
❑ 2100	Introducing Lobo	1973	3.00	6.00	12.00

—Reissue of 2003 with new cover

Number	Title (A Side/B Side)	Yr	VG	VG+	NM
❑ 2101	Calumet	1973	3.75	7.50	15.00
❑ BT 89501	Just a Singer	1974	3.00	6.00	12.00
❑ BT 89505	A Cowboy Afraid of Horses	1975	3.00	6.00	12.00
❑ BT 89513	The Best of Lobo	1976	3.00	6.00	12.00

MCA

Number	Title (A Side/B Side)	Yr	VG	VG+	NM
❑ 3194	Lobo	1979	2.50	5.00	10.00

LOCKLIN, HANK

45s

4 STAR

Number	Title (A Side/B Side)	Yr	VG	VG+	NM
❑ 1556	I Could Love You Darling/The Song of the Whispering Leaves	1951	10.00	20.00	40.00
❑ 1564	Your House of Love Won't Stand/Who Do You Think You're Fooling	1951	10.00	20.00	40.00
❑ 1574	Send Me the Pillow You Dream On, No. 2/I Always Lose	1951	10.00	20.00	40.00
❑ 1582	Stumpy Joe/I'm Going to Copyright Your Kisses	1951	10.00	20.00	40.00
❑ 1594	Tell Me You Love Me/Tomorrow's Just Another Day to Cry	1952	10.00	20.00	40.00
❑ 1605	Could You/Down Texas Way	1952	7.50	15.00	30.00
❑ 1608	Who's Knocking at My Heart/The Harvest Is Ripe	1952	7.50	15.00	30.00
❑ 1624	Alone at a Table for Two/Golden Wristwatch	1953	7.50	15.00	30.00
❑ 1632	Won't You Change Your Mind/Crazy Over You	1953	7.50	15.00	30.00
❑ 1641	Let Me Be the One/I'm Tired of Runnin' Around	1953	7.50	15.00	30.00
❑ 1688	Who Will It Be/Empty Bottle, Empty Heart	1954	7.50	15.00	30.00
❑ 1747	The Same Sweet Girl/You Burned a Hole in My Heart	1960	3.75	7.50	15.00

DECCA

Number	Title (A Side/B Side)	Yr	VG	VG+	NM
❑ 9-28526	I Like to Play with Your Kisses/Picking Sweethearts	1953	6.25	12.50	25.00
❑ 9-28740	I Can't Run Away/Red Rose	1953	6.25	12.50	25.00
❑ 9-28826	Lessons in Love/Shadows	1953	6.25	12.50	25.00
❑ 9-29030	Queen of Hearts/Mysteries of Life	1954	6.25	12.50	25.00
❑ 9-29270	Baby You Can Count on Me/Whispering Scandal	1954	6.25	12.50	25.00
❑ 9-29599	Let Me Confess/I'll Always Be Standing By	1955	6.25	12.50	25.00

KING

Number	Title (A Side/B Side)	Yr	VG	VG+	NM
❑ 5283	Send Me the Pillow You Dream On/Let Me Be the One	1959	3.75	7.50	15.00

MGM

Number	Title (A Side/B Side)	Yr	VG	VG+	NM
❑ 14753	Send Me Your Coffee Cup/True Love Is Always Hard to Find	1974	—	2.50	5.00
❑ 14777	The Sweetest Mistake/Hang My Picture in Your Heart	1975	—	2.50	5.00
❑ 14802	Irish Eyes/Please Let Me Have You	1975	—	2.50	5.00

PLANTATION

Number	Title (A Side/B Side)	Yr	VG	VG+	NM
❑ 135	These Arms You Push Away/Baby I Need You	1976	—	2.50	5.00
❑ 142	Daytime Love Affair/You Never Miss the Water	1976	—	2.50	5.00
❑ 151	You Love Me Don't Cha/(B-side unknown)	1977	—	2.50	5.00
❑ 160	There Never Was a Time/(B-side unknown)	1977	—	2.50	5.00

RCA VICTOR

Number	Title (A Side/B Side)	Yr	VG	VG+	NM
❑ APBO-0031	Jonas P. Jones/Send Me the Pillow You Dream On	1973	—	3.00	6.00
❑ APBO-0226	Wildwood Flower/Sweet Inspiration	1974	—	3.00	6.00
❑ 47-6170	Your Heart Is an Island/You're Out of Step	1955	5.00	10.00	20.00
❑ 47-6242	Who Am I to Cast the First Stone/These Ruins Belong to You	1955	5.00	10.00	20.00
❑ 47-6347	Why Baby Why/Love or Spite	1955	5.00	10.00	20.00
❑ 47-6434	I'm a Fool/A Good Woman's Love	1956	5.00	10.00	20.00
❑ 47-6571	Seven or Eleven/You Can't Never Tell	1956	5.00	10.00	20.00
❑ 47-6672	How Much/She's Better Than Most	1956	5.00	10.00	20.00
❑ 47-6778	14 Karat Gold/By the Sweat of My Brow	1956	5.00	10.00	20.00
❑ 47-6867	Goin' Home All By Myself/The Rich and the Poor	1957	5.00	10.00	20.00
❑ 47-6967	Geisha Girl/Livin' Alone	1957	5.00	10.00	20.00
❑ 47-7127	Send Me the Pillow You Dream On/Why Don't You Haul Off and Love Me	1957	5.00	10.00	20.00
❑ 47-7203	It's a Little More Like Heaven/Blue Grass Skirt	1958	3.75	7.50	15.00
❑ 47-7317	That Inner Glow/The Upper Room	1958	3.75	7.50	15.00
❑ 47-7393	I Gotta Talk to Your Heart/The Other Side of the Door	1958	3.75	7.50	15.00
❑ 47-7472	Foreign Car/When the Band Plays the Blues	1959	3.75	7.50	15.00
❑ 47-7561	Hiding in My Heart/The Border of the Blues	1959	3.75	7.50	15.00
❑ 47-7612	Seven Days (The Humming Song)/Blues in Advance	1959	3.75	7.50	15.00
❑ 47-7692	Please Help Me, I'm Falling/My Old Home Town	1960	3.75	7.50	15.00
❑ 47-7813	One Step Ahead of My Past/Toujours Moi	1960	3.00	6.00	12.00
❑ 47-7871	From Here to There to You/This Song Is Just for You	1961	3.00	6.00	12.00
❑ 47-7921	You're the Reason/Happy Birthday to Me	1961	3.00	6.00	12.00
❑ 47-7965	Happy Journey/I Need You Now	1961	3.00	6.00	12.00
❑ 47-8034	We're Gonna Go Fishin'/Welcome Home, Mister Blues	1962	3.00	6.00	12.00
❑ 47-8106	Wabash Cannonball/Once More	1962	3.00	6.00	12.00
❑ 47-8136	Flyin' South/Behind the Footlights	1963	3.00	6.00	12.00
❑ 47-8248	Wooden Soldier/Kiss on the Door	1963	3.00	6.00	12.00
❑ 47-8318	Followed Closely by My Teardrops/You Never Want to Love Me	1964	3.00	6.00	12.00
❑ 47-8399	Hello Heartache/I Was Coming Home to You	1964	3.00	6.00	12.00
❑ 47-8497	I'm Blue/Give Your Wife a Kiss for Me	1965	2.50	5.00	10.00
❑ 47-8560	Forty Nine, Fifty One/Faith and Trust	1965	2.50	5.00	10.00
❑ 47-8695	The Girls Get Prettier (Every Day)/To Him	1965	2.50	5.00	10.00
❑ 47-8783	Insurance/I Feel a Cry Coming On	1966	2.50	5.00	10.00

Number	Title (A Side/B Side)	Yr	VG	VG+	NM
❑ 47-8891	There's More Pretty Girls Than One/A Good Woman's Love	1966	2.50	5.00	10.00
❑ 47-8928	The Best Part of Loving You/The Last Thing on My Mind	1966	2.50	5.00	10.00
❑ 47-9092	Hasta Luego (See You Later)/Wishing on a Star	1967	2.50	5.00	10.00
❑ 47-9218	Nashville Women/Behind My Back	1967	2.50	5.00	10.00
❑ 47-9323	The Country Hall of Fame/Evergreen	1967	2.50	5.00	10.00
❑ 47-9476	Love Song for You/Little Geisha Girl	1968	2.50	5.00	10.00
❑ 47-9582	Everlasting Love/I'm Slowly Going Out of Your Mind	1968	2.50	5.00	10.00
❑ 47-9646	Lovin' You (The Way I Do)/Hot Pepper Doll	1968	2.50	5.00	10.00
❑ 47-9710	Where the Blue of the Night Meets the Gold of the Day/The Girls Who Wait	1969	2.00	4.00	8.00
❑ 47-9849	Flying South/Rosalita	1970	2.00	4.00	8.00
❑ 47-9894	Bless Her Heart...I Love Her/Morning	1970	2.00	4.00	8.00
❑ 47-9955	She's As Close As I Can Get to Loving You/I Like a Woman	1971	2.00	4.00	8.00
❑ 47-9986	My Heart Needs a Friend/Only a Fool	1971	2.00	4.00	8.00
❑ 48-1014	The Devil Out of Me/Softly	1971	2.00	4.00	8.00
❑ 74-0196	Jeannie/Cuban Girl	1969	2.00	4.00	8.00
❑ 74-0287	Please Help Me, I'm Falling/Anna	1969	2.00	4.00	8.00
❑ 74-0634	Imagination Running Wild/Love Has a Mind of Its Own	1972	—	3.00	6.00
❑ 74-0772	Eventually/I Forgot to Live Today	1972	—	3.00	6.00
❑ 74-0848	Goodbye Dear Ole Ryman/Just Call Me Darling	1972	—	3.00	6.00
❑ 74-0941	Before My Time/If Loving You Means Anything	1973	—	3.00	6.00

Selected 78s

4 STAR

Number	Title (A Side/B Side)	Yr	VG	VG+	NM
❑ 1313	The Same Sweet Girl/The Last Look at Mother	1949	6.25	12.50	25.00
❑ 1337	Born to Ramble/Knocking at Your Door	1949	6.25	12.50	25.00
❑ 1360	Send Me the Pillow (That You Dream On)/I'm Lonely Darling	1949	6.25	12.50	25.00
❑ 1397	You Burned a Hole in My Heart/Our Love Will Show the Way	1950	5.00	10.00	20.00
❑ 1405	Are You Treating Your Neighbor As Yourself/Fifty Miles of Elbow Room	1950	5.00	10.00	20.00
❑ 1444	Midnight Tears/It's So Hard to Say I Love You	1950	5.00	10.00	20.00
❑ 1466	Paper Face/Pin Ball Millionaire	1950	5.00	10.00	20.00
❑ 1506	Come Share the Sunshine with Me/The Place and the Time	1950	5.00	10.00	20.00
❑ 1521	The Holy Train/Is There Room for Me	1950	5.00	10.00	20.00
❑ 1530	No One Is Sweeter Than You/Tho' I've Lost	1950	5.00	10.00	20.00
❑ 1545	To Whom It May Concern/A Year of Time	1950	5.00	10.00	20.00

—Some of the above may exist on 45, but we haven't confirmed this

GOLD STAR

Number	Title (A Side/B Side)	Yr	VG	VG+	NM
❑ 1341	Rio Grande Waltz/(B-side unknown)	194?	10.00	20.00	40.00

ROYALTY

Number	Title (A Side/B Side)	Yr	VG	VG+	NM
❑ 603	Please Come Back to Stay/I've Got a Feeling	194?	10.00	20.00	40.00
❑ 604	I Worship You/You've Been Talking in Your Sleep	194?	10.00	20.00	40.00

Albums

KING

Number	Title	Yr	VG	VG+	NM
❑ 672 [M]	The Best of Hank Locklin	1961	15.00	30.00	60.00
❑ 738 [M]	Encores	1961	15.00	30.00	60.00

RCA VICTOR

Number	Title	Yr	VG	VG+	NM
❑ LPM-1673 [M]	Foreign Love	1958	15.00	30.00	60.00
❑ LPM-2291 [M]	Please Help Me, I'm Falling	1960	7.50	15.00	30.00
❑ LSP-2291 [S]	Please Help Me, I'm Falling	1960	10.00	20.00	40.00
❑ LPM-2464 [M]	Happy Journey	1962	6.25	12.50	25.00
❑ LSP-2464 [S]	Happy Journey	1962	7.50	15.00	30.00
❑ LPM-2597 [M]	A Tribute to Roy Acuff, the King of Country Music	1962	6.25	12.50	25.00
❑ LSP-2597 [S]	A Tribute to Roy Acuff, the King of Country Music	1962	7.50	15.00	30.00
❑ LPM-2680 [M]	The Ways of Love	1963	6.25	12.50	25.00
❑ LSP-2680 [S]	The Ways of Love	1963	7.50	15.00	30.00
❑ LPM-2801 [M]	Irish Songs, Country Style	1964	5.00	10.00	20.00
❑ LSP-2801 [S]	Irish Songs, Country Style	1964	6.25	12.50	25.00
❑ LPM-2997 [M]	Hank Locklin Sings Hank Williams	1964	5.00	10.00	20.00
❑ LSP-2997 [S]	Hank Locklin Sings Hank Williams	1964	6.25	12.50	25.00
❑ LPM-3391 [M]	Hank Locklin Sings Eddy Arnold	1965	5.00	10.00	20.00
❑ LSP-3391 [S]	Hank Locklin Sings Eddy Arnold	1965	6.25	12.50	25.00
❑ LPM-3465 [M]	Once Over Lightly	1965	5.00	10.00	20.00
❑ LSP-3465 [S]	Once Over Lightly	1965	6.25	12.50	25.00
❑ LPM-3559 [M]	The Best of Hank Locklin	1966	5.00	10.00	20.00
❑ LSP-3559 [S]	The Best of Hank Locklin	1966	6.25	12.50	25.00
❑ LPM-3588 [M]	The Girls Get Prettier	1966	5.00	10.00	20.00
❑ LSP-3588 [S]	The Girls Get Prettier	1966	6.25	12.50	25.00
❑ LPM-3656 [M]	The Gloryland Way	1966	5.00	10.00	20.00
❑ LSP-3656 [S]	The Gloryland Way	1966	6.25	12.50	25.00
❑ LPM-3770 [M]	Send Me the Pillow You Dream On	1967	6.25	12.50	25.00
❑ LSP-3770 [S]	Send Me the Pillow You Dream On	1967	5.00	10.00	20.00
❑ LPM-3841 [M]	Nashville Women	1967	6.25	12.50	25.00
❑ LSP-3841 [S]	Nashville Women	1967	5.00	10.00	20.00
❑ LPM-3946 [M]	Country Hall of Fame	1968	25.00	50.00	100.00
❑ LSP-3946 [S]	Country Hall of Fame	1968	5.00	10.00	20.00
❑ LSP-4030	My Love Song for You	1968	5.00	10.00	20.00
❑ LSP-4113	Softly	1969	5.00	10.00	20.00

SEARS

Number	Title	Yr	VG	VG+	NM
❑ SPS-104	Send Me the Pillow You Dream On	196?	6.25	12.50	25.00

WRANGLER

Number	Title	Yr	VG	VG+	NM
❑ 1004 [M]	Hank Locklin	1962	6.25	12.50	25.00

LOFTIS, BOBBY WAYNE

45s

CHARTA

Number	Title (A Side/B Side)	Yr	VG	VG+	NM
❑ 100	See the Big Man Cry/Number One Lady in Town	1976	—	2.50	5.00
❑ 104	Poor Side of Town/Don't Wake Up the Children	1976	—	2.50	5.00
❑ 108	You're So Good for Me (And That's Bad)/We're Back Together Again	1977	—	2.50	5.00
❑ 111	Sunny Day Lover/California Please	1977	—	2.50	5.00
❑ 118	Can't Shake You Off My Mind/Let's Pretend We Just Got Married	1978	—	2.50	5.00
❑ 121	Welcome Back Baby/Without Your Sweet Lips on Mine	1978	—	2.50	5.00
❑ 125	The Texas Winds Are Givin' Me the Willies/Think About the Teardrops	1978	—	2.50	5.00
❑ 132	Small Time Picker/I'll Remember	1979	—	2.50	5.00
❑ 135	Red Red Rosie/Think About the Teardrops	1979	—	2.50	5.00
❑ 141	I'll Remember/Winter's Coming On	1979	—	2.50	5.00
❑ 143	My Lady/She Loves Me All to Pieces	1979	—	2.50	5.00

LOGAN, BUD

Also see THE BLUE BOYS.

45s

MERCURY

Number	Title (A Side/B Side)	Yr	VG	VG+	NM
❑ 73091	The Carter Boys/That's Just Part of Forgetting	1970	—	3.50	7.00
❑ 73157	You Can't Take It With You/If You Don't Do It	1970	—	3.50	7.00

RCA VICTOR

Number	Title (A Side/B Side)	Yr	VG	VG+	NM
❑ 47-9630	I Was Losing You/What Am I Doing Hangin' 'Round	1968	2.00	4.00	8.00
❑ 47-9678	Sock It To Me Santa/(Old Mr. Winter) Here You Come Again	1968	2.00	4.00	8.00
❑ 74-0125	In a Way/Lonely as a Seagull	1969	2.00	4.00	8.00
❑ 74-0201	Silver Bird/You'll Think of Me	1969	2.00	4.00	8.00

RICE

Number	Title (A Side/B Side)	Yr	VG	VG+	NM
❑ 5037	Sweet Caroline/There Is No Easy Way	1971	2.00	4.00	8.00
❑ 5043	A Time and a Place/I Was On My Way Before the Dawn	1971	2.00	4.00	8.00

SHANNON

Number	Title (A Side/B Side)	Yr	VG	VG+	NM
❑ 809	My Way of Life/Take a Picture of Me	1973	—	3.00	6.00
❑ 825	Gonna Find Me a Bluebird/If You Leave Me	1974	—	3.00	6.00

LOGAN, BUD, AND WILMA BURGESS

Also see each artist's individual listings.

45s

SHANNON

Number	Title (A Side/B Side)	Yr	VG	VG+	NM
❑ 816	Wake Me Into Love/Here Together	1973	—	3.00	6.00
❑ 820	The Best Day of the Rest of Our Love/It Ain't Nothing But Love	1974	—	3.00	6.00
❑ 826	Love Is the Foundation/I'm in Love with Everything	1974	—	3.00	6.00

LOGAN, JOSH

45s

CURB

Number	Title (A Side/B Side)	Yr	VG	VG+	NM
❑ 10519	Everytime I Get to Dreamin'/Easy Lovin' Kind	1988	—	—	3.00
❑ 10528	Somebody Paints the Wall/The Light of My Life	1989	—	—	3.00
❑ 10553	I Was Born with a Broken Heart/I've Learned to Lie	1989	—	—	3.00
❑ 10574	Lovin' on Back Streets/Danger Soft Shoulders	1989	—	—	—
—Unreleased?					
❑ 76752	Lovin' on Back Streets/Danger Soft Shoulders	1990	—	2.00	4.00
❑ 76813	Dallas Fort Worth Airport/Possession's Nine-Tenths of the Law	1990	—	2.00	4.00

NSD

Number	Title (A Side/B Side)	Yr	VG	VG+	NM
❑ 76	I Made You a Woman/Long Distance Lover	198?	—	3.00	6.00

LOGGINS, DAVE

Best known in country circles as a composer, he also did duets with GUS HARDIN and ANNE MURRAY.

45s

EPIC

Number	Title (A Side/B Side)	Yr	VG	VG+	NM
❑ 02152	Please Come to Boston/Someday	1981	—	—	3.00
—Reissue					
❑ 11115	Please Come to Boston/Let Me Go Now	1974	—	2.50	5.00
❑ 50035	Someday/Girl from Knoxville	1974	—	2.00	4.00
❑ 50069	Second Hand Lady/So You Couldn't Get to Me	1975	—	2.00	4.00
❑ 50221	Saviour of My Natural Life/You've Got Me to Hold On To	1976	—	2.00	4.00
❑ 50246	Movin' to the Country/Wild Millie the Country Girl	1976	—	2.00	4.00
❑ 50326	Three Little Words (I Love You)/Don't Treat Me Like a Stranger	1976	—	2.00	4.00
❑ 50491	Ship in a Bottle/The Ballad of Cowboy 20	1977	—	2.00	4.00
❑ 50509	One-Way Ticket to Paradise/Crowd of Lonely People	1978	—	2.00	4.00
❑ 50578	So Much for Dreams/You Found It Now	1978	—	2.00	4.00
❑ 50711	Pieces of April/Color of My Mood	1979	—	2.00	4.00
❑ 50783	One Way Ticket to Paradise/The Fool in Me	1979	—	2.00	4.00

VANGUARD

Number	Title (A Side/B Side)	Yr	VG	VG+	NM
❑ 35147	Claudia/Think'n of You	1972	—	2.50	5.00
❑ 35167	Pieces of April/Think'n of You	1972	—	2.50	5.00
❑ 35177	Building Condemned/Lady in an Orange Silk Blouse	1973	—	2.50	5.00

Albums

EPIC

Number	Title	Yr	VG	VG+	NM
❑ KE 32833	Apprentice (In a Musical Workshop)	1974	2.50	5.00	10.00
❑ PE 33946	Country Suite	1975	2.50	5.00	10.00
❑ PE 34713	One Way	1977	2.50	5.00	10.00
❑ JE 35792	David Loggins	1979	2.50	5.00	10.00

VANGUARD

Number	Title	Yr	VG	VG+	NM
❑ VSD-6580	Personal Belongings	1972	3.75	7.50	15.00

LOGGINS AND MESSINA

The pop duo of Kenny Loggins and Jim Messina, the B-side of the below single, plus the listed album, were country hits.

45s

COLUMBIA

Number	Title (A Side/B Side)	Yr	VG	VG+	NM
❑ 10222	A Lover's Question/Oh, Lonesome Me	1975	—	2.50	5.00

Albums

COLUMBIA

Number	Title (A Side/B Side)	Yr	VG	VG+	NM
❑ PC 33810	So Fine	1975	2.50	5.00	10.00
—Original with no bar code					
❑ PC 33810	So Fine	198?	2.00	4.00	8.00
—With bar code					

LOGSDON, JIMMIE

45s

DECCA

Number	Title (A Side/B Side)	Yr	VG	VG+	NM
❑ 9-28502	I Wanna Be Mama'd/That's When I Love You the Best	1952	7.50	15.00	30.00
❑ 9-28584	The Death of Hank Williams/Hank Williams Sings the Blues No More	1953	12.50	25.00	50.00
—Lines on either side of "Decca"					
❑ 9-28584	The Death of Hank Williams/Hank Williams Sings the Blues No More	1955	7.50	15.00	30.00
—Star under "Decca"					
❑ 9-28726	As Long As We're Together/The Love You Gave to Me	1953	7.50	15.00	30.00
❑ 9-28864	Where the Old Red River Flows/Let's Have a Happy Time	1953	7.50	15.00	30.00
❑ 9-28913	In the Mission of St. Augustine/Papaya Mama	1953	7.50	15.00	30.00
❑ 9-29075	Good Deal Lucille/Midnight Boogie	1954	6.25	12.50	25.00
❑ 9-29122	These Lonesome Blues/My Sweet French Baby	1954	6.25	12.50	25.00
❑ 9-29337	I'm Goin' Back to Tennessee/You Ain't Nothing But the Blues	1954	6.25	12.50	25.00

DOT

Number	Title (A Side/B Side)	Yr	VG	VG+	NM
❑ 1274	Cold Cold Rain/Midnight Blues	1956	7.50	15.00	30.00

KING

Number	Title (A Side/B Side)	Yr	VG	VG+	NM
❑ 5748	I Know You're Married/Mother's Flower Garden	1963	3.00	6.00	12.00
❑ 5752	The Life of Hank Williams (Part 1)/The Life of Hank Williams (Part 2)	1963	3.75	7.50	15.00
❑ 5795	Gear Jammer/Truck Drivin' Daddy	1963	3.00	6.00	12.00
❑ 5827	Making Believe/I Guess I've Let You Down	1963	3.00	6.00	12.00
❑ 5846	Daddy Don't Go/The Loneliest Guy in Town	1964	3.00	6.00	12.00
❑ 5872	I've Got Over You/I Have to Laugh	1964	3.00	6.00	12.00

STARDAY

Number	Title (A Side/B Side)	Yr	VG	VG+	NM
❑ 286	No Longer Do I Cry/Can't Make Up My Mind	1957	25.00	50.00	100.00

Albums

KING

Number	Title (A Side/B Side)	Yr	VG	VG+	NM
❑ 843 [M]	Howdy Neighbors	1963	15.00	30.00	60.00

LONDON, EDDIE

45s

RCA

Number	Title (A Side/B Side)	Yr	VG	VG+	NM
❑ 2822-7-R	If We Can't Do It Right/Business As Usual	1991	—	2.00	4.00
❑ 62103	Uninvited Memory/I Wouldn't Change a Thing About You Except Your Name	1991	—	2.00	4.00

LONE JUSTICE

12-Inch Singles

GEFFEN

Number	Title (A Side/B Side)	Yr	VG	VG+	NM
❑ PRO-A-2275 [DJ]	Ways to Be Wicked (same on both sides)	1985	—	2.50	5.00
❑ PRO-A-2329 [DJ]	Sweet Sweet Baby/Sweet Sweet Baby (Remix)	1985	—	3.00	6.00
❑ PRO-A-2596 [DJ]	Shelter (same on both sides)	1986	—	3.00	6.00
❑ PRO-A-2645 [DJ]	I Found Love (same on both sides)	1986	—	3.00	6.00
❑ 20570	Shelter/Belfry/I Can't Look Back	1988	2.00	4.00	8.00

45s

GEFFEN

Number	Title (A Side/B Side)	Yr	VG	VG+	NM
❑ 28470	I Found Love/If You Don't Like Pain	1987	—	—	3.00
❑ 28520	Shelter/Belfry	1986	—	—	3.00
❑ 28520 [PS]	Shelter/Belfry	1986	—	—	3.00
❑ 28965	Sweet Sweet Baby (I'm Falling)/Don't Toss Us Away	1985	—	—	3.00
❑ 28965 [PS]	Sweet Sweet Baby (I'm Falling)/Don't Toss Us Away	1985	—	—	3.00
❑ 29023	Ways to Be Wicked/Cactus Rose	1985	—	—	3.00
❑ 29023 [PS]	Ways to Be Wicked/Cactus Rose	1985	—	—	3.00

Albums

GEFFEN

Number	Title (A Side/B Side)	Yr	VG	VG+	NM
❑ GHS 24060	Lone Justice	1985	2.50	5.00	10.00
❑ GHS 24122	Shelter	1986	2.50	5.00	10.00

LONESOME STRANGERS, THE

45s

HIGHTONE

Number	Title (A Side/B Side)	Yr	VG	VG+	NM
❑ 508	Goodbye Lonesome, Hello Baby Doll/We Used to Fuss	1989	—	3.00	6.00
❑ 511	Just Can't Cry No More/(B-side unknown)	1989	—	3.00	6.00

Albums

HIGHTONE

Number	Title (A Side/B Side)	Yr	VG	VG+	NM
❑ 8016	The Lonesome Strangers	1989	3.00	6.00	12.00

LONESTAR

45s

BNA

Number	Title (A Side/B Side)	Yr	VG	VG+	NM
❑ 60212	What About Now/Smile	2000	—	—	3.00
❑ 64386	Tequila Talkin'/No News	1995	—	2.50	5.00
❑ 64549	Runnin' Away with My Heart/I Love the Way You Do That	1996	—	—	3.00
❑ 64638	When Cowboys Didn't Dance/Ragtop Cadillac	1996	—	—	3.00
❑ 64687	I'll Be Home for Christmas/White Christmas	1996	—	—	—
—The existence of this on 45 has been questioned					
❑ 64841	Come Cryin' to Me/What Would It Take	1997	—	2.00	4.00
❑ 64942	You Walked In/Keys to My Heart	1997	—	—	3.00
❑ 65395	Say When/Amie	1998	—	—	3.00
❑ 65755	Amazed/Tell Her	1999	—	2.50	5.00
❑ 65906	Smile/Amazed	1999	—	2.00	4.00

LONG, SHORTY

Not to be confused with the soul singer who used the same name.

45s

DOT

Number	Title (A Side/B Side)	Yr	VG	VG+	NM
❑ 1154	Pretend/Crying Street Guitar Waltz	1953	6.25	12.50	25.00

KING

Number	Title (A Side/B Side)	Yr	VG	VG+	NM
❑ 953	Goodnight Cincinnati/Just Like Two Drops of Water	1951	10.00	20.00	40.00
❑ 5605	Take Me to the Happy Land/Mary, Oh Mary	1962	6.25	12.50	25.00

RCA VICTOR

Number	Title (A Side/B Side)	Yr	VG	VG+	NM
❑ 47-6472	Hey, Doll Baby/Luscious	1956	25.00	50.00	100.00
❑ 47-6572	Vacation Rock/Burnt Toast and Black Coffee	1956	25.00	50.00	100.00
❑ 47-6804	Another Love Has Ended/Little White Horse	1957	25.00	50.00	100.00
❑ 47-6873	You Don't Have to Be a Baby to Cry/I'd Crawl Back	1957	25.00	50.00	100.00
❑ 48-0057	The Morning After/Please Daddy Forgive	1949	10.00	20.00	40.00
—Originals on green vinyl; second pressing on black vinyl is unconfirmed					
❑ 48-0098	The Warm Red Wine/I Got Mine	1949	10.00	20.00	40.00
—Originals on green vinyl; second pressing on black vinyl is unconfirmed					
❑ 48-0134	I Wasted a Nickel/This Cold War with You	1950	10.00	20.00	40.00
—Originals on green vinyl; second pressing on black vinyl is unconfirmed					
❑ 48-0347	A Bottle and a Blonde/Waltz of Colorado	1950	10.00	20.00	40.00
—Originals on green vinyl; second pressing on black vinyl is unconfirmed					

"X"

Number	Title (A Side/B Side)	Yr	VG	VG+	NM
❑ 0024	Standing in the Station/Make with Me De Love	1954	5.00	10.00	20.00

Selected 78s

DECCA

Number	Title (A Side/B Side)	Yr	VG	VG+	NM
❑ 46139	Sweeter Than the Flowers/I Love You So Much It Hurts	1948	6.25	12.50	25.00
❑ 46142	Tennessee Moon/Yesterday's Mail	1948	6.25	12.50	25.00

KING

Number	Title (A Side/B Side)	Yr	VG	VG+	NM
❑ 874	Finders Keepers, Losers Weepers/Because the One I Love	1950	5.00	10.00	20.00
❑ 889	Calm, Cool and Collected/Foolish Pride	1950	5.00	10.00	20.00
❑ 906	No Wars in Heaven/Don't Tell My Mommy	1950	5.00	10.00	20.00
❑ 923	Blinding Tears/Mama	1951	5.00	10.00	20.00

Albums

FORD

Number	Title (A Side/B Side)	Yr	VG	VG+	NM
❑ FXM-712 [M]	Country Jamboree	1963	5.00	10.00	20.00

LONZO AND OSCAR

45s

CAPITOL

Number	Title (A Side/B Side)	Yr	VG	VG+	NM
❑ F939	If Texas Told What Arkansaw/Onions, Onions	1950	7.50	15.00	30.00
❑ F1446	Pretty Little Indian Maid/Tickle Tomcats Tail	1951	6.25	12.50	25.00
❑ F40269	My Dreams Turned Into a Nightmare/I'll Go Chasing Women	1950	7.50	15.00	30.00

CHALET

Number	Title (A Side/B Side)	Yr	VG	VG+	NM
❑ 1052	Hertz Rent-a-Chick/Dolly	1969	2.50	5.00	10.00
❑ 1058	Heartaches for Fun and Profit/Wood	1969	2.50	5.00	10.00
❑ 1067	My Business Ain't Doin' So Good/Ants A-Go-Go	1970	2.50	5.00	10.00

COLUMBIA

Number	Title (A Side/B Side)	Yr	VG	VG+	NM
❑ 4-44400	Did You Have to Bring That Up/Give Me a King-Sized Cola and a Moon Pie	1967	2.00	4.00	8.00

DECCA

Number	Title (A Side/B Side)	Yr	VG	VG+	NM
❑ 9-28060	Music Makin' Mama Second Hand/Let Old Mother Nature #2	1952	5.00	10.00	20.00
❑ 9-28363	Goodbye Little Darlin' #2/Honky Tonk Sweetheart	1952	5.00	10.00	20.00
❑ 9-28510	Knock Kneed Suzy/Tell Me Was It Worth It in the End	1952	5.00	10.00	20.00
❑ 9-28624	Baby Me Baby/Skunk Skin Britches	1953	5.00	10.00	20.00
❑ 9-28961	Frosty the De-Frosted Snowman/Jangle Bells	1953	5.00	10.00	20.00
❑ 9-28972	Hey Joe #2/It Can't Be Done	1954	5.00	10.00	20.00
❑ 9-29425	See Saw Baby/One Love for Me	1955	5.00	10.00	20.00
❑ 9-30374	Gone #2/A Fallen Star	1957	5.00	10.00	20.00
❑ 9-46299	I Lithp/Metro Polka	1951	6.25	12.50	25.00
❑ 9-46312	I'm Movin' On Number Two/Give Me an RC Cola	1951	6.25	12.50	25.00
❑ 9-46340	Jezebel/It Must Have Been Somethin' I Et	1951	6.25	12.50	25.00
❑ 9-46359	I Courted the Sunshine/Extravagant Baby	1951	6.25	12.50	25.00
❑ 9-46378	Let's Live a Little Number Two/Strange Little Girl	1951	6.25	12.50	25.00
❑ 9-46393	Mona Lisa Number Two/Charming Betsy	1952	6.25	12.50	25.00

DOT

Number	Title (A Side/B Side)	Yr	VG	VG+	NM
❑ 1196	Let Me Be the One #2/Wild Oats	1954	5.00	10.00	20.00
❑ 1216	Crazy 'Bout You Baby/Got It on My Mind	1954	5.00	10.00	20.00

GRC

Number	Title (A Side/B Side)	Yr	VG	VG+	NM
❑ 1006	Traces of Life/Lubbock	1973	2.00	4.00	8.00
❑ 2013	Any Old Wind That Blows/Railroad Take Your Whistle Home	1974	2.00	4.00	8.00
❑ 2022	Catfish Dinner/Don't Want to Change It Now	1974	2.00	4.00	8.00

Number	Title (A Side/B Side)	Yr	VG	VG+	NM
❑ 2029	From Your Shoulders to Mine/God Is the Color of Love	1974	2.00	4.00	8.00
❑ 2035	He Came Back/God Is the Color of Love	1975	2.00	4.00	8.00
❑ 2054	Bitter Grapes/When I Stop Dreaming	1975	2.00	4.00	8.00
❑ 2063	When the Fields in the Valley Turn Green/He Came Back	1975	2.00	4.00	8.00
NUGGET					
❑ 201	Hand Holdin'/Uh, What's Her Name	1962	3.75	7.50	15.00
❑ 208	Grandpa's Mountain Dew/Going Up Town	196?	3.75	7.50	15.00
❑ 210	The Sound of Nashville/I Worship the Ground You Walk On	196?	3.75	7.50	15.00
❑ 223	Old Leather Saddle/All Day Singing	196?	3.75	7.50	15.00
❑ 235	Rip andf Snort/Fangers	196?	3.75	7.50	15.00
❑ 250	New River Train #2/Dormant Volcano	196?	3.75	7.50	15.00
❑ 256	Funny Way of Living/Getting the Hang of It Now	196?	3.75	7.50	15.00
STARDAY					
❑ 404	Deep Thinking/Have a Little Faith in Me	1958	5.00	10.00	20.00
❑ 436	Gotta Find Julie/Hills of East Tennessee	1959	5.00	10.00	20.00
❑ 463	Bare Faced Bird Brain/I'm My Own Grandpa	1959	5.00	10.00	20.00
❑ 491	I Lost an Angel/Blue Love	1960	5.00	10.00	20.00
❑ 523	Takin' a Chance with You/Punkin Raiser	1960	5.00	10.00	20.00
❑ 543	Country Music Time/Can't Pitch Woo (In an Igloo)	1961	5.00	10.00	20.00
❑ 563	Honey Babe/The Touch of You	1961	5.00	10.00	20.00
Selected 78s					
CAPITOL					
❑ 40236	Who Pulled the Plug from the Jug/I Wonder Why She Almost Drives Me Wild	1949	5.00	10.00	20.00
❑ 40255	Love Is Sweet But Oh How Bitter/Sheepskin Corn	1949	5.00	10.00	20.00
RCA VICTOR					
❑ 20-2563	I'm My Own Grandpa/You Blacked My Blue Eyes Once Too Often	1947	6.25	12.50	25.00
Albums					
COLUMBIA					
❑ CS 9587	Mountain Dew	1968	5.00	10.00	20.00
DECCA					
❑ DL 4363 [M]	Country Comedy Time	1963	5.00	10.00	20.00
STARDAY					
❑ SLP-119 [M]	America's Greatest Country Comedians	1960	10.00	20.00	40.00
❑ SLP-244 [M]	Country Music Time	1963	10.00	20.00	40.00

LORD, BOBBY

45s

Number	Title (A Side/B Side)	Yr	VG	VG+	NM
COLUMBIA					
❑ 21339	No More No More/Why Were You Only Fooling Me	1955	12.50	25.00	50.00
—With longer A-side title					
❑ 21339	No More/Why Were You Only Fooling Me	1955	6.25	12.50	25.00
❑ 21367	I'm the Devil Who Made Her That Way/Ain'tcha Ever Gonna	1955	6.25	12.50	25.00
❑ 21397	Something's Missing/Sittin' Home Prayin' for Rain	1955	5.00	10.00	20.00
❑ 21437	Hawk-Eye/I Can't Make My Dreams Understand	1955	7.50	15.00	30.00
❑ 21459	I Can't Do Without You Anymore/Don't Make Me Laugh	1955	5.00	10.00	20.00
❑ 21498	So Doggone Lonesome/Pie Peachie Pie Pie	1956	5.00	10.00	20.00
❑ 21539	Everybody's Rockin' But Me/Without Your Love	1956	20.00	40.00	80.00
—"Without Your Love" was the hit, but "Everybody's Rockin' But Me" is the collectible side					
❑ 40666	Fire of Love/Beautiful Baby	1956	7.50	15.00	30.00
❑ 40819	Your Sweet Love/My Baby's Not My Baby Anymore	1957	5.00	10.00	20.00
❑ 40927	High Voltage/Just Wonderful	1957	10.00	20.00	40.00
❑ 41030	Am I a Fool/I Know It Was You	1957	5.00	10.00	20.00
❑ 41155	Sack/Fire of Love	1958	6.25	12.50	25.00
❑ 41288	When I've Learned/Walking Alone	1958	5.00	10.00	20.00
❑ 41352	Party Pooper/What a Thrill	1959	6.25	12.50	25.00
❑ 41505	Too Many Miles/Swamp Fox	1959	6.25	12.50	25.00
❑ 41596	Give Me a Woman/Where Did My Woman Go	1960	5.00	10.00	20.00
❑ 41824	Before I Lose My Mind/When the Snow Falls	1960	5.00	10.00	20.00
❑ 42012	A Rose and a Thorn/Fascination	1961	5.00	10.00	20.00
DECCA					
❑ 32115	Look What You're Doing/On and On Goes the Hurt	1967	2.00	4.00	8.00
❑ 32174	Shadows on the Wall/One Day Down	1967	2.00	4.00	8.00
❑ 32277	Live Your Life Out Loud/Charlotte, North Carolina	1968	—	3.00	6.00
❑ 32373	The True and Lasting Kind/It's My Life	1968	—	3.00	6.00
❑ 32431	Yesterday's Letters/Don't Forget to Smell the Flowers (Along the Way)	1969	—	3.00	6.00
❑ 32578	Rainbow Girl/Do You Ever Think of Me	1969	—	3.00	6.00
❑ 32657	You and Me Against the World/Something Real	1970	—	3.00	6.00
❑ 32718	Wake Me Up Early in the Morning/Violets Are Red	1970	—	3.00	6.00
❑ 32797	Do It to Someone You Love/So in Love with You	1970	2.00	4.00	8.00
❑ 32797	Goodbye Jukebox/Do It to Someone You Love	1971	—	3.00	6.00
❑ 32841	They've Got Something in the Country/Peace of Mind	1971	—	3.00	6.00
❑ 32932	Everybody's Here/Sweet Inspiration	1972	—	3.00	6.00
HICKORY					
❑ 1158	I'll Go On Alone/My Heart Tells Me So	1961	3.00	6.00	12.00
❑ 1169	Precious Jewel/Trail of Tears	1962	3.00	6.00	12.00
❑ 1190	Don't Shed Any Tears for Me/Out Behind the Barn	1962	3.00	6.00	12.00
❑ 1210	Cry, Cry Darling/Shopping Center	1963	2.50	5.00	10.00
❑ 1232	Life Can Have Meaning/Pickin' White Gold	1963	2.50	5.00	10.00
❑ 1259	A Man Needs a Woman/Take a Bucket to the Wall	1964	2.50	5.00	10.00
❑ 1310	I'm Going Home Next Summer/That Room in the Corner of the House	1965	2.50	5.00	10.00
❑ 1361	Cash on the Barrelhead/That's Love	1965	2.50	5.00	10.00
❑ 1389	It Only Hurts When I'm Laughing/Losers Like Me	1966	2.00	4.00	8.00
RICE					
❑ 5056	I've Had You/Got Yourself Something	1973	2.00	4.00	8.00
❑ 5062	Hello Wine/(B-side unknown)	1973	2.00	4.00	8.00
❑ 5063	Looking for a Cold, Lonely Winter/Hello Wine	1973	2.00	4.00	8.00
❑ 5068	The Look of Love/Your Song	1974	2.00	4.00	8.00
Albums					
DECCA					
❑ DL 75246	Bobby Lord	1970	3.00	6.00	12.00
HARMONY					
❑ HL 7322 [M]	Bobby Lord's Best	1964	6.25	12.50	25.00
HICKORY					
❑ LP-126 [M]	The Bobby Lord Show	1965	5.00	10.00	20.00

LORD, MIKE

45s

Number	Title (A Side/B Side)	Yr	VG	VG+	NM
NSD					
❑ 225	I Can Read Between the Lines/We Can't Try Anymore	1987	—	2.50	5.00
❑ 230	Just Try Texas/Lying Here Lonely	1987	—	2.50	5.00

LORIE ANN

45s

Number	Title (A Side/B Side)	Yr	VG	VG+	NM
SING ME					
❑ 34	Down on Market Street/(B-side unknown)	1988	—	3.00	6.00
❑ 34 [PS]	Down on Market Street/(B-side unknown)	1988	2.00	4.00	8.00
❑ 37	Say the Part About I Love You/(B-side unknown)	1988	—	3.00	6.00
❑ 37 [PS]	Say the Part About I Love You/(B-side unknown)	1988	2.00	4.00	8.00
❑ 41	Just Because You're Leavin'/Reasons a-Plenty	1989	—	3.00	6.00
❑ 41 [PS]	Just Because You're Leavin'/Reasons a-Plenty	1989	2.00	4.00	8.00

LORRIE, MYRNA/BUDDY DEVAL

45s

Number	Title (A Side/B Side)	Yr	VG	VG+	NM
ABBOTT					
❑ 172	Are You Mine/You Bet I Kissed Him	1954	6.25	12.50	25.00
❑ 177	I'm Your Man/Underway	1955	6.25	12.50	25.00

LOS LOBOS

12-Inch Singles

Number	Title (A Side/B Side)	Yr	VG	VG+	NM
SLASH					
❑ PRO-A-2226 [DJ]	Don't Worry Baby/Will the Wolf Survive?	1984	—	3.50	7.00
❑ PRO-A-2252 [DJ]	Will the Wolf Survive? (Remix Edit)/Will the Wolf Survive? (LP Version)	1984	—	3.50	7.00
❑ PRO-A-2640 [DJ]	Shakin' Shakin' Shakes (same on both sides)	1986	2.00	4.00	8.00
❑ PRO-A-2685 [DJ]	Is That All There Is (same on both sides)	1987	—	3.50	7.00
❑ PRO-A-2690 [DJ]	Set Me Free (Rosa Lee) (same on both sides)	1987	—	2.50	5.00
❑ PRO-A-2737 [DJ]	La Bamba/La Bamba (Fade)	1987	2.00	4.00	8.00
45s					
SLASH					
❑ 21942	La Bamba/Come On, Let's Go	198?	—	—	3.00
—"Back to Back Hits" reissue					
❑ 28186	Come On, Let's Go/Ooh My Head	1987	—	—	3.00
❑ 28336	La Bamba/Charlena	1987	—	—	3.00
❑ 28336 [PS]	La Bamba/Charlena	1987	—	—	3.00
❑ 28390	Set Me Free (Rosalie)/Tears of God	1987	—	—	3.00
❑ 28464	One Time One Night/All I Wanted to Do Was Dance	1987	—	—	3.00
❑ 28464 [PS]	One Time One Night/All I Wanted to Do Was Dance	1987	—	2.00	4.00
❑ 29093	Will the Wolf Survive?/The Breakdown	1985	—	—	3.00
❑ 29093 [PS]	Will the Wolf Survive?/The Breakdown	1985	—	—	3.00
Albums					
NEW VISTAS					
❑ 1001	Just Another Band from East L.A.	1978	50.00	100.00	200.00
SLASH					
❑ 23963 [EP]	And a Time to Dance	1983	3.00	6.00	12.00
❑ 25177	How Will the Wolf Survive?	1984	3.00	6.00	12.00
❑ 25523	By the Light of the Moon	1987	3.00	6.00	12.00
❑ 25790	La Pistola y El Corazon	1988	3.00	6.00	12.00
❑ 26131	The Neighborhood	1990	3.00	6.00	12.00
❑ R 144507	By the Light of the Moon	1987	3.50	7.00	14.00
—RCA Music Service edition					

LOUDERMILK, JOHN D.

Includes records as "Johnny Dee."

45s

Number	Title (A Side/B Side)	Yr	VG	VG+	NM
COLONIAL					
❑ 430	Sittin' in the Balcony/A-Plus in Love	1957	7.50	15.00	30.00
—As "Johnny Dee"					
❑ 430 [PS]	Sittin' in the Balcony/A-Plus in Love	1957	100.00	200.00	400.00
—As "Johnny Dee"					
❑ 433	Teenage Queen/It's Gotta Be You	1957	7.50	15.00	30.00
—As "Johnny Dee"					
❑ 435	1000 Concrete Blocks/In My Simple Way	1958	7.50	15.00	30.00
—As "Johnny Dee"					
COLUMBIA					
❑ 4-41165	Yearbook/Susie's House	1958	3.75	7.50	15.00
❑ 4-41165 [PS]	Yearbook/Susie's House	1958	6.25	12.50	25.00
❑ 4-41209	Lover's Lane/Yo Yo	1958	3.75	7.50	15.00
❑ 4-41247	Goin' Away to School/This Cold War with You	1958	3.75	7.50	15.00
❑ 4-41507	The Happy Wanderer/Red Headed Stranger	1959	3.75	7.50	15.00
❑ 4-41562	Tobacco Road/Midnight Bus	1960	5.00	10.00	20.00

Number	Title (A Side/B Side)	Yr	VG	VG+	NM
DOT					
❑ 15699	Somebody Sweet/They Were Right	1958	7.50	15.00	30.00
—As "Johnny Dee"					
RCA VICTOR					
❑ 47-7938	Language of Love/Darling Jane	1961	3.00	6.00	12.00
❑ 47-7993	Thou Shalt Not Steal/Mister Jones	1962	3.00	6.00	12.00
❑ 47-8054	Callin' Doctor Casey/Oh How Sad	1962	3.00	6.00	12.00
❑ 47-8101	Road Hog/Angela Jones	1962	3.00	6.00	12.00
❑ 47-8101 [PS]	Road Hog/Angela Jones	1962	5.00	10.00	20.00
❑ 47-8154	Bad News/The Guitar Player	1963	3.00	6.00	12.00
❑ 47-8308	Blue Train (Of the Heartbreak Line)/Rhythm and Blues	1962	3.00	6.00	12.00
❑ 47-8389	Th' Wife/Nothing to Gain	1964	3.00	6.00	12.00
❑ 47-8579	That Ain't All/Then You Can Tell Me Goodbye	1965	3.00	6.00	12.00
—B-side is the original version of the future hit					
❑ 47-8826	Run On Home Baby Brother/Silver Cloud Talking Blues	1966	2.50	5.00	10.00
❑ 47-8973	I Hear It Now/You're the Guilty One	1966	2.50	5.00	10.00
❑ 47-9189	It's My Time/Bahama Mama	1967	2.50	5.00	10.00
❑ 47-9592	Sidewalks/The Odd Folks of Okracoke	1968	2.00	4.00	8.00
❑ 74-0121	Brown Girl/The Jones'	1969	2.00	4.00	8.00
WARNER BROS.					
❑ 7489	When I Was Nine/Lord Have Mercy	1971	—	3.50	7.00
Albums					
RCA VICTOR					
❑ LPM-2434 [M]	Language of Love	1961	6.25	12.50	25.00
❑ LSP-2434 [S]	Language of Love	1961	7.50	15.00	30.00
❑ LPM-2539 [M]	Twelve Sides of Loudermilk	1962	5.00	10.00	20.00
❑ LSP-2539 [S]	Twelve Sides of Loudermilk	1962	6.25	12.50	25.00
❑ LPM-3497 [M]	A Bizarre Collection of the Most Unusual Songs	1965	5.00	10.00	20.00
❑ LSP-3497 [S]	A Bizarre Collection of the Most Unusual Songs	1965	6.25	12.50	25.00
❑ LPM-3807 [M]	Suburban Attitudes in Country Music	1967	6.25	12.50	25.00
❑ LSP-3807 [S]	Suburban Attitudes in Country Music	1967	5.00	10.00	20.00
❑ LSP-4040	Country Love Songs	1968	5.00	10.00	20.00
❑ LSP-4097	The Open Mind of John D. Loudermilk	1968	5.00	10.00	20.00
WARNER BROS.					
❑ WS 1922	Volume 1, Elloree	1971	3.75	7.50	15.00

LOUVIN, CHARLIE

Also see JIM AND JESSE; THE LOUVIN BROTHERS.

Number	Title (A Side/B Side)	Yr	VG	VG+	NM
45s					
CAPITOL					
❑ 2007	The Only Way Out (Is to Walk Over Me)/Too Little and Too Late	1967	2.50	5.00	10.00
❑ 2106	Will You Visit Me on Sundays?/Tears, Wine and Flowers	1968	2.00	4.00	8.00
❑ 2231	Hey Daddy/She Will Get Lonesome	1968	2.00	4.00	8.00
❑ 2350	What Are Those Things (With Big Black Wings)/What Then	1968	2.00	4.00	8.00
❑ 2448	Let's Put Our World Back Together/Heart of Clay	1969	2.00	4.00	8.00
❑ 2612	Little Reasons/After Awhile	1969	2.00	4.00	8.00
❑ 2703	Here's a Toast to Mama/Show Me the Way Back to Your Heart	1969	2.00	4.00	8.00
❑ 2770	Tiny Wings/I Ain't Gonna Work Tomorrow	1970	2.00	4.00	8.00
❑ 2824	Come and Get It Mama/Is Home Sweet Home	1970	2.00	4.00	8.00
❑ 2972	Sittin' Bull/It Ain't No Big Thing	1970	2.00	4.00	8.00
❑ 3048	Love Has to Die All By Itself/I Wish It Had Been a Dream	1971	2.00	4.00	8.00
❑ 3243	I Placed a Call/I'm Going Home	1971	2.00	4.00	8.00
❑ 3319	Just in Time (To Watch Love Die)/She Just Wants to Be Needed	1972	2.00	4.00	8.00
❑ 3528	Bottom of the Fifth/The Roses and the Rain	1973	2.00	4.00	8.00
❑ 3607	Funny Man/Harvest Time	1973	2.00	4.00	8.00
❑ 5173	I Don't Love You Anymore/My Book of Memories	1964	2.50	5.00	10.00
❑ 5296	Less and Less/I Don't Want It	1964	2.50	5.00	10.00
❑ 5369	See the Big Man Cry/I Just Don't Understand	1965	2.50	5.00	10.00
❑ 5475	Think I'll Go Somewhere and Cry Myself to Sleep/Life Begins at Love	1965	2.50	5.00	10.00
❑ 5550	You Finally Said Something Good (When You Said Goodbye)/Something to Think About	1965	2.50	5.00	10.00
❑ 5606	To Tell the Truth (I Told a Lie)/That's What Your Leaving's Done to Me	1966	2.50	5.00	10.00
❑ 5665	Something's Wrong/I Want a Happy Life	1966	2.50	5.00	10.00
❑ 5729	The Proof Is in the Kissing/Scared of the Blues	1966	2.50	5.00	10.00
❑ 5791	Off and On/Still Loving You	1967	2.50	5.00	10.00
❑ 5872	On the Other Hand/Someone's Heartache	1967	2.50	5.00	10.00
❑ 5948	I Forgot to Cry/Drive Me Out of My Mind	1967	2.50	5.00	10.00
LITTLE DARLIN'					
❑ 7922	Love Don't Care/Who's Gonna Love Me Now	1979	—	2.50	5.00
—A-side with Emmylou Harris					
UNITED ARTISTS					
❑ XW368	You're My Wife, She's My Woman/If I Had to Build a Bridge	1973	—	3.00	6.00
❑ XW430	It Almost Felt Like Love/Until I'm Out of Sight	1974	—	3.00	6.00
❑ XW540	When Love Is Gone/I Want to See You One More Time	1974	—	3.00	6.00
❑ XW616	When You Have to Fly Alone/I Just Want a Happy Life	1975	—	3.00	6.00
❑ XW689	I Just Went Out, That's All/Is I Love You That Easy to Say	1975	—	3.00	6.00
❑ XW919	Sweet Texas/(B-side unknown)	1976	—	3.00	6.00
Albums					
CAPITOL					
❑ ST-142	Hey Daddy	1969	5.00	10.00	20.00
❑ ST-248	The Kind of Man I Am	1969	5.00	10.00	20.00
❑ ST-416	Here's a Toast to Mama	1970	5.00	10.00	20.00
❑ ST-555	Ten Times	1970	5.00	10.00	20.00
❑ ST 2208 [S]	Less and Less and I Don't Love You Anymore	1965	6.25	12.50	25.00
❑ T 2208 [M]	Less and Less and I Don't Love You Anymore	1965	5.00	10.00	20.00
❑ ST 2437 [S]	The Many Moods of Charlie Louvin	1966	6.25	12.50	25.00
❑ T 2437 [M]	The Many Moods of Charlie Louvin	1966	5.00	10.00	20.00
❑ ST 2482 [S]	Lonesome Is Me	1966	6.25	12.50	25.00
❑ T 2482 [M]	Lonesome Is Me	1966	5.00	10.00	20.00
❑ ST 2689 [S]	I'll Remember Always	1967	5.00	10.00	20.00
❑ T 2689 [M]	I'll Remember Always	1967	6.25	12.50	25.00
❑ ST 2787 [S]	I Forgot to Cry	1967	5.00	10.00	20.00
❑ T 2787 [M]	I Forgot to Cry	1967	6.25	12.50	25.00
❑ ST 2958	Will You Visit Me on Sundays	1968	5.00	10.00	20.00

LOUVIN, CHARLIE, AND ROY ACUFF

Also see each artist's individual listings.

Number	Title (A Side/B Side)	Yr	VG	VG+	NM
45s					
HAL KAT					
❑ 63058	The Precious Jewel/Buried Alive	1989	2.00	4.00	8.00

LOUVIN, CHARLIE, AND MELBA MONTGOMERY

Also see each artist's individual listings.

Number	Title (A Side/B Side)	Yr	VG	VG+	NM
45s					
CAPITOL					
❑ 2915	Something to Brag About/Let's Help Each Other to Forget	1970	2.00	4.00	8.00
❑ 3029	Did You Ever/Don't Believe Me	1971	2.00	4.00	8.00
❑ 3111	Baby, You've Got What It Takes/If We Don't Make It	1971	2.00	4.00	8.00
❑ 3208	I'm Gonna Leave You/When I Stop Dreaming	1971	2.00	4.00	8.00
❑ 3388	Baby, What's Wrong with Us/Unmatched Wedding Bands	1972	2.00	4.00	8.00
❑ 3508	A Man Likes Things Like That/That Don't Mean I Don't Love You	1973	2.00	4.00	8.00
Albums					
CAPITOL					
❑ ST-686	Somethin' to Brag About	1971	5.00	10.00	20.00
❑ ST-808	Baby, You've Got What It Takes	1971	5.00	10.00	20.00

LOUVIN, IRA

Also see THE LOUVIN BROTHERS.

Number	Title (A Side/B Side)	Yr	VG	VG+	NM
45s					
CAPITOL					
❑ 5190	Make Believe It's Me/Who Threw Dat Rock	1964	2.50	5.00	10.00
❑ 5428	Yodel, Sweet Molly/You're Looking for an Angel	1965	2.50	5.00	10.00
Albums					
CAPITOL					
❑ ST 2413 [S]	The Unforgettable Ira Louvin	1965	7.50	15.00	30.00
❑ T 2413 [M]	The Unforgettable Ira Louvin	1965	6.25	12.50	25.00

LOUVIN BROTHERS, THE

Also see CHARLIE LOUVIN; IRA LOUVIN.

Number	Title (A Side/B Side)	Yr	VG	VG+	NM
45s					
CAPITOL					
❑ F2296	The Family Who Prays Together/Let Us Travel On	1952	6.25	12.50	25.00
❑ F2381	Broadminded/I Know What You're Talking About	1953	6.25	12.50	25.00
❑ F2510	Born Again/From Mother's Arms to Korea	1952	6.25	12.50	25.00
❑ F2612	Preach the Gospel/I Love God's Way of Living	1953	6.25	12.50	25.00
❑ F2753	God Bless Her/No One to Sing for Me	1954	6.25	12.50	25.00
❑ F2852	If We Forget God/Satan Lied to Me	1954	6.25	12.50	25.00
❑ F2965	Satan and the Saint/Swing Low Sweet Chariot	1954	6.25	12.50	25.00
❑ F3083	Love Thy Neighbor As Thyself/Make Him a Soldier	1955	6.25	12.50	25.00
❑ F3177	When I Stop Dreaming/Pitfall	1955	5.00	10.00	20.00
❑ F3241	Just Rehearsing/Pray for Me	1955	5.00	10.00	20.00
❑ F3300	I Don't Believe You've Met My Baby/In the Middle of Nowhere	1955	5.00	10.00	20.00
❑ F3413	Hoping That You're Hoping/Childish Love	1956	5.00	10.00	20.00
❑ F3467	Where Will You Build/That's All He's Asking of Me	1956	5.00	10.00	20.00
❑ F3523	You're Running Wild/Cash on the Barrel Head	1956	5.00	10.00	20.00
❑ F3630	Don't Laugh/New Partner Waltz	1957	5.00	10.00	20.00
❑ F3715	Plenty of Everything But You/The First One to Love You	1957	5.00	10.00	20.00
❑ F3770	Praying/There's No Excuse	1957	5.00	10.00	20.00
❑ F3804	Call Me/I Wish You Knew	1957	5.00	10.00	20.00
❑ F3871	Dog Sled/When I Loved You	1958	3.75	7.50	15.00
❑ F3974	My Baby Came Back/She Didn't Even Know I Was Gone	1958	3.75	7.50	15.00
❑ F4055	My Baby's Gone/Lorene	1958	3.75	7.50	15.00
❑ F4112	The River of Jordan/He Can Be Found	1959	3.75	7.50	15.00
❑ F4117	Knoxville Girl/I Wish It Had Been a Dream	1959	3.75	7.50	15.00
❑ F4200	Blue from Now On/While You're Cheating on Me	1959	3.75	7.50	15.00
❑ F4255	You're Learning/My Curly Headed Baby	1959	3.75	7.50	15.00
❑ 4331	Nellie Moved to Town/Stagger	1960	3.75	7.50	15.00
❑ 4359	Just Suppose/I See a Bridge	1960	3.75	7.50	15.00
❑ 4395	Ruby's Song/If You Love Me, Stay Away	1960	3.75	7.50	15.00
❑ 4430	Love Is a Lonely Street/What a Change	1960	3.75	7.50	15.00
❑ 4473	Santa Claus Parade/It's Christmas Time	1960	3.75	7.50	15.00
❑ 4506	I Love You Best of All/Scared of the Blues	1961	3.75	7.50	15.00
❑ 4559	I Ain't Gonna Work Tomorrow/I Can't Keep You in Love with Me	1961	3.75	7.50	15.00
❑ 4628	How's the World Treating You/It Hurts Me More	1961	3.75	7.50	15.00
❑ 4686	Weapon of Prayer/Great Atomic Power	1962	3.75	7.50	15.00

Number	Title (A Side/B Side)	Yr	VG	VG+	NM
❑ 4757	Broken Engagement/Time Goes So Slow	1962	3.75	7.50	15.00
❑ 4822	Must You Throw Dirt in My Face/The First Time in Life	1962	3.75	7.50	15.00
❑ 4886	Keep Your Eyes on Jesus/Don't Let Them Take the Bible	1962	3.75	7.50	15.00
❑ 4941	Love Turns to Hate/I Cried After You Left	1963	3.00	6.00	12.00
❑ 4999	I'm Glad That I'm Not Him/Message to Your Heart	1963	3.00	6.00	12.00
❑ 5075	Every Time You Leave/There Is No Easy Way	1963	3.00	6.00	12.00

MGM

Number	Title (A Side/B Side)	Yr	VG	VG+	NM
❑ K10988	Weapon of Prayer/They've Got the Church Outnumbered	1951	7.50	15.00	30.00
❑ K11065	You'll Be Rewarded Over There/Robe of White	1951	7.50	15.00	30.00
❑ K11221	Get Acquainted/My Love Song	1952	7.50	15.00	30.00
❑ K11277	Insured Before the Grave/Great Atomic Power	1952	7.50	15.00	30.00
❑ K11392	Do You Live What You Preach/I'll Live with God	1953	7.50	15.00	30.00

Selected 78s

DECCA

Number	Title (A Side/B Side)	Yr	VG	VG+	NM
❑ 46187	Seven Year Blues/Alabama	1949	7.50	15.00	30.00

Albums

CAPITOL

Number	Title (A Side/B Side)	Yr	VG	VG+	NM
❑ DT 769 [R]	Tragic Songs of Life	196?	5.00	10.00	20.00
❑ T 769 [M]	Tragic Songs of Life	1956	25.00	50.00	100.00
—Turquoise label					
❑ T 769 [M]	Tragic Songs of Life	1959	10.00	20.00	40.00
—Black colorband label, logo at left					
❑ T 769 [M]	Tragic Songs of Life	1962	6.25	12.50	25.00
—Black colorband label, logo at top					
❑ T 825 [M]	Nearer My God to Thee	1957	25.00	50.00	100.00
—Turquoise label					
❑ T 825 [M]	Nearer My God to Thee	1959	10.00	20.00	40.00
—Black colorband label, logo at left					
❑ T 825 [M]	Nearer My God to Thee	1962	6.25	12.50	25.00
—Black colorband label, logo at top					
❑ T 910 [M]	Ira and Charlie	1958	25.00	50.00	100.00
—Turquoise label					
❑ T 910 [M]	Ira and Charlie	1959	10.00	20.00	40.00
—Black colorband label, logo at left					
❑ T 910 [M]	Ira and Charlie	1962	6.25	12.50	25.00
—Black colorband label, logo at top					
❑ DT 1061 [R]	The Family Who Prays	196?	5.00	10.00	20.00
❑ T 1061 [M]	The Family Who Prays	1958	20.00	40.00	80.00
—Black colorband label, logo at left					
❑ T 1061 [M]	The Family Who Prays	1962	6.25	12.50	25.00
—Black colorband label, logo at top					
❑ T 1106 [M]	Country Love Ballads	1959	20.00	40.00	80.00
—Black colorband label, logo at left					
❑ T 1106 [M]	Country Love Ballads	1962	6.25	12.50	25.00
—Black colorband label, logo at top					
❑ T 1277 [M]	Satan Is Real	1960	20.00	40.00	80.00
—Black colorband label, logo at left					
❑ T 1277 [M]	Satan Is Real	1962	6.25	12.50	25.00
—Black colorband label, logo at top					
❑ T 1385 [M]	My Baby's Gone	1960	20.00	40.00	80.00
—Black colorband label, logo at left					
❑ T 1385 [M]	My Baby's Gone	1962	6.25	12.50	25.00
—Black colorband label, logo at top					
❑ T 1449 [M]	A Tribute to the Delmore Brothers	1960	20.00	40.00	80.00
—Black colorband label, logo at left					
❑ T 1449 [M]	A Tribute to the Delmore Brothers	1962	6.25	12.50	25.00
—Black colorband label, logo at top					
❑ T 1547 [M]	Encore	1961	20.00	40.00	80.00
—Black colorband label, logo at left					
❑ T 1547 [M]	Encore	1962	6.25	12.50	25.00
—Black colorband label, logo at top					
❑ ST 1616 [S]	Country Christmas	1961	20.00	40.00	80.00
—Black rainbow label with "Capitol" at left					
❑ ST 1616 [S]	Country Christmas	1962	6.25	12.50	25.00
—Black rainbow label with "Capitol" at top					
❑ T 1616 [M]	Country Christmas	1961	12.50	25.00	50.00
—Black rainbow label with "Capitol" at left					
❑ T 1616 [M]	Country Christmas	1962	5.00	10.00	20.00
—Black rainbow label with "Capitol" at top					
❑ ST 1721 [S]	Weapon of Prayer	1962	12.50	25.00	50.00
❑ T 1721 [M]	Weapon of Prayer	1962	10.00	20.00	40.00
❑ ST 1834 [S]	Keep Your Eyes on Jesus	1963	12.50	25.00	50.00
❑ T 1834 [M]	Keep Your Eyes on Jesus	1963	10.00	20.00	40.00
❑ ST 2091 [S]	The Louvin Brothers Sing and Play Their Current Hits	1964	7.50	15.00	30.00
❑ T 2091 [M]	The Louvin Brothers Sing and Play Their Current Hits	1964	6.25	12.50	25.00
❑ ST 2331 [S]	Thank God for My Christian Home	1965	7.50	15.00	30.00
❑ T 2331 [M]	Thank God for My Christian Home	1965	6.25	12.50	25.00
❑ ST 2827 [S]	The Great Roy Acuff Songs	1967	7.50	15.00	30.00
❑ T 2827 [M]	The Great Roy Acuff Songs	1967	10.00	20.00	40.00

METRO

Number	Title (A Side/B Side)	Yr	VG	VG+	NM
❑ M-598 [M]	The Louvin Brothers	1966	6.25	12.50	25.00
❑ MS-598 [R]	The Louvin Brothers	1966	5.00	10.00	20.00

MGM

Number	Title (A Side/B Side)	Yr	VG	VG+	NM
❑ E-3426 [M]	The Louvin Brothers	1957	50.00	100.00	200.00

TOWER

Number	Title (A Side/B Side)	Yr	VG	VG+	NM
❑ DT 5038 [R]	Two Different Worlds	1966	5.00	10.00	20.00
❑ T 5038 [M]	Two Different Worlds	1966	7.50	15.00	30.00
❑ DT 5122	Country Heart and Soul	1968	5.00	10.00	20.00

LOVELESS, PATTY

Also see VINCE GILL; DWIGHT YOAKAM.

45s

EPIC

Number	Title (A Side/B Side)	Yr	VG	VG+	NM
❑ 34-74906	Blame It on Your Heart/What's a Broken Heart	1993	—	2.00	4.00
❑ 34-77076	Nothin' But the Wheel/Love Builds the Bridges (Pride Builds the Walls)	1993	—	2.00	4.00
❑ 34-77271	You Will/You Don't Know How Lucky You Are	1993	—	2.00	4.00
❑ 34-77416	How Can I Help You Say Goodbye/How About You	1994	—	2.00	4.00
❑ 34-77609	I Try to Think About Elvis/Ships	1994	—	2.50	5.00
❑ 34-77734	Here I Am/When the Fallen Angels Fly	1994	—	2.00	4.00
❑ 34-77856	You Don't Even Know Who I Am/Over My Shoulder	1995	—	2.00	4.00
❑ 34-77956	Halfway Down/Feelin' Good About Feelin' Bad	1995	—	2.00	4.00
❑ 34-78209	You Can Feel Bad/Feelin' Good About Feelin' Bad	1996	—	2.00	4.00
❑ 34-78309	A Thousand Times a Day/I Feel Good About Feelin' Bad	1996	—	2.00	4.00
❑ 34-78371	Lonely Too Long/Feelin' Good About Feelin' Bad	1996	—	2.00	4.00

MCA

Number	Title (A Side/B Side)	Yr	VG	VG+	NM
❑ 52694	Lonely Days, Lonely Nights/Country I'm Coming Home to You	1985	—	2.00	4.00
❑ 52694 [DJ]	Lonely Days, Lonely Nights (same on both sides)	1985	2.50	5.00	10.00
—Promo only on yellow vinyl					
❑ 52694 [PS]	Lonely Days, Lonely Nights/Country I'm Coming Home to You	1985	—	3.00	6.00
❑ 52787	I Did/Lonely Days, Lonely Nights	1986	—	3.00	6.00
❑ 52787 [DJ]	I Did (same on both sides)	1986	3.00	6.00	12.00
—Promo only on blue vinyl					
❑ 52969	Wicked Ways/Half Over You	1986	—	2.00	4.00
❑ 53040	I Did/You Are Everything	1987	—	2.00	4.00
❑ 53040 [DJ]	I Did (same on both sides)	1987	2.50	5.00	10.00
—Promo only on blue vinyl					
❑ 53097	After All/I Did	1987	—	2.00	4.00
❑ 53097 [DJ]	After All (same on both sides)	1987	2.50	5.00	10.00
—Promo only on yellow vinyl					
❑ 53179	You Saved Me/Fly Away	1987	—	2.00	4.00
❑ 53270	If My Heart Had Windows/So Good to Be in Love	1988	—	—	3.00
❑ 53333	A Little Bit in Love/I Can't Get You Off My Mind	1988	—	—	3.00
❑ 53418	Blue Side of Town/I'll Never Grow Tired of You	1988	—	—	3.00
❑ 53477	Don't Toss Us Away/After All	1989	—	—	3.00
❑ 53641	Timber, I'm Falling in Love/Go On	1989	—	2.00	4.00
❑ 53702	The Lonely Side of Love/I'll Never Grow Tired of You	1989	—	—	3.00
❑ 53764	Chains/I'm On Your Side	1989	—	2.00	4.00
❑ 53895	The Night's Too Long/Overtime	1990	—	2.00	4.00
❑ 53977	I'm That Kind of Girl/Some Morning Soon	1990	—	2.00	4.00
❑ 54075	Blue Memories/You Can't Run Away from My Heart	1991	—	2.00	4.00
❑ 54178	Hurt Me Bad (In a Real Good Way)/God Will	1991	—	2.50	5.00
❑ 54271	Jealous Bone/I Came Straight to You	1991	—	2.00	4.00
❑ 54371	Can't Stop Myself from Loving You/If You Don't Want Me	1992	—	2.50	5.00
❑ 79004	On Down the Line/Feelings of Love	1990	—	2.00	4.00

Albums

MCA

Number	Title (A Side/B Side)	Yr	VG	VG+	NM
❑ 5915	Patty Loveless	1987	2.50	5.00	10.00
❑ 42092	If My Heart Had Windows	1988	2.50	5.00	10.00
❑ 42223	Honky Tonk Angel	1988	2.50	5.00	10.00

LOVETT, LYLE

45s

MCA

Number	Title (A Side/B Side)	Yr	VG	VG+	NM
❑ 52818	Farther Down the Line/Why I Don't Know	1986	—	—	3.00
❑ 52818 [DJ]	Farther Down the Line (same on both sides)	1986	2.50	5.00	10.00
—Promo only on green vinyl					
❑ 79025	Here I Am/Nobody Knows Me	1990	—	—	3.00

MCA/CURB

Number	Title (A Side/B Side)	Yr	VG	VG+	NM
❑ 52951	Cowboy Man/The Waltzing Fool	1986	—	—	3.00
❑ 52951 [DJ]	Cowboy Man (same on both sides)	1986	3.75	7.50	15.00
—Promo only on clear vinyl					
❑ 53030	God Will/An Acceptable Level of Ecstasy (The Wedding Song)	1987	—	—	3.00
❑ 53030 [DJ]	God Will (same on both sides)	1987	2.50	5.00	10.00
—Promo only on blue vinyl					
❑ 53102	Why I Don't Know/If I Were the Man You Wanted	1987	—	—	3.00
❑ 53157	Give Back My Heart/Simple Song	1987	—	—	3.00
❑ 53246	She's No Lady/Pontiac	1988	—	—	3.00
❑ 53316	I Loved You Yesterday/L.A. County	1988	—	—	3.00
❑ 53401	If I Had a Boat/Black and Blue	1988	—	—	3.00
❑ 53471	I Married Her Just Because She Looks Like You/If I Had a Boat	1988	—	—	3.00
❑ 53611	Stand By Your Man/Wallisville Road	1989	—	—	3.00
❑ 53650	Nobody Knows Me/Here I Am	1989	—	—	3.00
❑ 53703	If I Were the Man You Wanted/Cryin' Shame	1989	—	—	3.00

SBK

Number	Title (A Side/B Side)	Yr	VG	VG+	NM
❑ S7-56996	Stand By Your Man/The Crying Game	1993	—	3.00	6.00
—B-side by Boy George; red vinyl					
❑ S7-56996	Stand By Your Man/The Crying Game	1993	—	2.00	4.00
—B-side by Boy George; black vinyl					

Albums

MCA/CURB

Number	Title (A Side/B Side)	Yr	VG	VG+	NM
❑ 5748	Lyle Lovett	1986	2.50	5.00	10.00

Number	Title (A Side/B Side)	Yr	VG	VG+	NM
❑ 17355 [EP]	Not Exactly Mr. Showbiz	1987	3.75	7.50	15.00
—Promo-only five-song EP with special sleeve					
❑ 42028	Pontiac	1988	2.50	5.00	10.00
❑ 42263	Lyle Lovett and His Large Band	1989	2.50	5.00	10.00
❑ R 100932	Lyle Lovett And His Large Band	1989	3.00	6.00	12.00
—BMG Direct Marketing edition					
❑ R 133603	Lyle Lovett	1986	3.00	6.00	12.00
—RCA Music Service edition					
❑ R 153258	Pontiac	1988	3.00	6.00	12.00
—BMG Direct Marketing edition					

LOWE, JIM

45s

Number	Title (A Side/B Side)	Yr	VG	VG+	NM
20TH CENTURY FOX					
❑ 426	Hootenanny Granny/These Bones Gonna Rise Again	1963	2.00	4.00	8.00
BUDDAH					
❑ 44	Michael J. Polalrd for President/The Ol' Racetrack	1968	—	3.00	6.00
DECCA					
❑ 31153	Someone Else's Arms/Man of the Cloth	1960	2.50	5.00	10.00
❑ 31198	That Do Make It Nice/Two Sides to Every Story	1961	2.50	5.00	10.00
DOT					
❑ 15381	Close the Door/Nuevo Laredo	1955	3.00	6.00	12.00
❑ 15407	Maybellene/Rene La Rue	1955	3.00	6.00	12.00
❑ 15429	John Jacob Jingleheimer Smith/St. James Avenue	1955	3.00	6.00	12.00
❑ 15456	The Sixty-Four Thousand Dollar Question/Blue Suede Shoes	1956	3.00	6.00	12.00
❑ 15486	The Green Door/(The Story of) The Little Man in Chinatown	1956	3.75	7.50	15.00
—Originals have maroon labels					
❑ 15486	The Green Door/(The Story of) The Little Man in Chinatown	1956	3.00	6.00	12.00
—Second pressings have black labels					
❑ 15525	By You, By You, By You/I Feel the Beat	1957	2.50	5.00	10.00
❑ 15569	Four Walls/Talkin' to the Blues	1957	3.00	6.00	12.00
❑ 15611	From a Jack to a King/Slow Train	1957	2.50	5.00	10.00
❑ 15665	Rick-a-Chickie/The Bright Light	1957	2.50	5.00	10.00
❑ 15693	Kewpie Doll/The Lady from Johannesburg	1958	2.50	5.00	10.00
❑ 15753	Take Us To Your President/Later On Tonight	1958	2.50	5.00	10.00
❑ 15832	Chapel Bells on Chapel Hill/Ja, Ja, Ja	1958	2.50	5.00	10.00
❑ 15869	Play Number Eleven/Come Away from Her Arms	1958	2.50	5.00	10.00
❑ 15954	I'm Movin' On/Without You	1959	2.50	5.00	10.00
❑ 16046	He'll Have to Go/Dress Rehearsal	1960	2.50	5.00	10.00
❑ 16074	The Midnight Ride of Paul Revere/A Tomorrow That Never Comes	1960	2.50	5.00	10.00
❑ 16636	Addis Ababa/Have You Ever Been Lonely	1964	—	3.00	6.00
MERCURY					
❑ 70163	Gambler's Guitar/The Martins and the Coys	1953	5.00	10.00	20.00
❑ 70265	Santa Claus Rides a Strawberry Roan/Love in Both Directions	1953	5.00	10.00	20.00
❑ 70319	Goodbye Little Sweetheart/River Boat	1954	5.00	10.00	20.00
❑ 71016	Prince of Peace/Santa Claus Rides a Strawberry Roan	1956	3.75	7.50	15.00
UNITED ARTISTS					
❑ 874	Mr. Moses/Make Your Back Strong	1965	—	3.00	6.00
❑ 50124	Gambler's Guitar/Blotson Bottom	1967	—	3.00	6.00

Albums

Number	Title (A Side/B Side)	Yr	VG	VG+	NM
DOT					
❑ DLP-3051 [M]	The Green Door	1956	37.50	75.00	150.00
❑ DLP-3114 [M]	Wicked Women	1958	25.00	50.00	100.00
❑ DLP-3681 [M]	Songs They Sing Behind the Green Door	1965	6.25	12.50	25.00
❑ DLP-25881 [S]	Songs They Sing Behind the Green Door	1965	7.50	15.00	30.00
MERCURY					
❑ MG-20246 [M]	The Door of Fame	1957	37.50	75.00	150.00

LOWES, THE

45s

Number	Title (A Side/B Side)	Yr	VG	VG+	NM
API					
❑ 1001	Cry Baby/(B-side unknown)	1986	—	3.00	6.00
❑ 1002	I Ain't Never/(B-side unknown)	1986	—	3.00	6.00
SOUNDWAVES					
❑ 4775	Good and Lonesome/He's Got a Heartache on His Mind	1986	—	2.50	5.00

LOWRY, RON

45s

Number	Title (A Side/B Side)	Yr	VG	VG+	NM
50 STATES					
❑ 35	I Wish I Had Someone to Love Me/Every Moment, Every Hour, Every Day	1975	—	2.50	5.00
❑ 40	Temporary/Can't Keep My Mind Off Loving You	1976	—	2.50	5.00
❑ 53	He'll Have to Go/Open Up Your Door	1977	—	2.50	5.00
REPUBLIC					
❑ 1409	Marry Me/World Champion Fool	1970	2.50	5.00	10.00
❑ 1413	River on My Mind/I Will	1970	2.50	5.00	10.00
❑ 1415	Oh How I Waited/Look at Me	1970	2.50	5.00	10.00

Albums

Number	Title (A Side/B Side)	Yr	VG	VG+	NM
REPUBLIC					
❑ 1303	Marry Me	1970	3.75	7.50	15.00

LUCAS, TAMMY

45s

Number	Title (A Side/B Side)	Yr	VG	VG+	NM
SOA					
❑ 005	9,999,999 Tears/Don't Go to Sleep	1988	2.00	4.00	8.00

LUKE THE DRIFTER

See HANK WILLIAMS.

LUKE THE DRIFTER, JR.

See HANK WILLIAMS, JR.

LULU BELLE AND SCOTTY

45s

Number	Title (A Side/B Side)	Yr	VG	VG+	NM
MERCURY					
❑ 6304	Shenandoah Waltz/My Heart Cries for You	1951	7.50	15.00	30.00
❑ 6354	Saturday Night Waltz/All Night Long	1951	7.50	15.00	30.00
❑ 6389	Ay-Round the Corner/Wishin'	1952	7.50	15.00	30.00
❑ 6400	Tied Down/I'm No Communist	1952	7.50	15.00	30.00
❑ 6414	Imagination/Honey Bunch	1952	7.50	15.00	30.00
❑ 70051	You're the Sweetest Mistake/New Love Waltz	1953	6.25	12.50	25.00
❑ 70092	That's Only Half of It/Walk Me By the River	1953	6.25	12.50	25.00
❑ 70155	Lips That Touch Liquor/God Put a Rainbow in the Cloud	1953	6.25	12.50	25.00
❑ 70824	Have I Told You Lately That I Love You/In My Heart	1956	5.00	10.00	20.00
STARDAY					
❑ 746	Try to Live Some (When You're Here)/I'll Be All Smiles Tonight	1965	3.00	6.00	12.00

Selected 78s

Number	Title (A Side/B Side)	Yr	VG	VG+	NM
MELOTONE					
❑ 6-06-53	The Farmer's Daughter/Madam, I've Come to Marry You	1936	6.25	12.50	25.00
OKEH					
❑ 05833	Did You Ever Go Sailing/Remember	1940	5.00	10.00	20.00
VOCALION					
❑ 04690	titles unknown	1939	5.00	10.00	20.00
❑ 04772	titles unknown	1939	5.00	10.00	20.00
❑ 04841	titles unknown	1939	5.00	10.00	20.00
❑ 04910	titles unknown	1939	5.00	10.00	20.00
❑ 04962	titles unknown	1939	5.00	10.00	20.00
VOGUE					
❑ R718	Some Sunday Morning/In the Dog House Now	1946	20.00	40.00	80.00
—Picture record					
❑ R719	Have I Told You Lately That I Love You/I Get a Kick Out of Corn	1946	20.00	40.00	80.00
—Picture record					
❑ R720	Grandpa's Gettin' Younger Ev'ry Day/Time Will Tell	1946	20.00	40.00	80.00
—Picture record					

Albums

Number	Title (A Side/B Side)	Yr	VG	VG+	NM
STARDAY					
❑ SLP-206 [M]	The Sweethearts of Country Music	1963	10.00	20.00	40.00
❑ SLP-285 [M]	Down Memory Lane	1964	10.00	20.00	40.00
❑ SLP-351 [M]	Lulu Belle & Scotty	1965	10.00	20.00	40.00
SUPER					
❑ 6201 [M]	Lule Belle & Scotty	1963	12.50	25.00	50.00

LUMAN, BOB

45s

Number	Title (A Side/B Side)	Yr	VG	VG+	NM
CAPITOL					
❑ F3972	Try Me/I Know My Baby Cares	1958	7.50	15.00	30.00
❑ F4059	Precious/Svengali	1958	7.50	15.00	30.00
EPIC					
❑ 10312	Ain't Got Time to Be Unhappy/I Can't Remember to Forget	1968	—	3.00	6.00
❑ 10381	I Like Trains/A World of Unhappiness	1968	—	3.00	6.00
❑ 10416	I'm In This Town for Good/A Woman Without Love	1968	—	3.00	6.00
❑ 10439	Come On Home and Sing the Blues to Daddy/Big, Big World	1969	—	3.00	6.00
❑ 10480	Every Day I Have to Cry Some/Livin' in a House Full of Love	1969	—	3.00	6.00
❑ 10535	The Gun/Cleanin' Up the Streets of Memphis	1969	—	3.00	6.00
❑ 10581	Gettin' Back to Norma/Maybelline	1970	—	3.00	6.00
❑ 10631	Honky Tonk Man/I Ain't Built That Way	1970	—	3.00	6.00
❑ 10667	What About the Hurt/The Time to Remember	1970	—	3.00	6.00
❑ 10699	Is It Any Wonder That I Love You?/Give Us One More Chance	1971	—	2.50	5.00
❑ 10755	I Got a Woman/One Hundred Songs on the Jukebox	1971	—	2.50	5.00
❑ 10786	A Chain Don't Take to Me/Don't Let Love Pass You By	1971	—	2.50	5.00
❑ 10823	When You Say Love/Have a Little Faith	1972	—	2.50	5.00
❑ 10869	It Takes You/Let's Think About Livin'	1972	—	2.50	5.00
❑ 10905	Lonely Women Make Good Lovers/Love Ought to Be a Happy Thing	1972	—	2.50	5.00
❑ 10943	Neither One of Us/Anything But Lonesome	1973	—	2.00	4.00
❑ 10994	A Good Love Is Like a Good Song/Have I Ever Said "I Love You" to a Lady	1973	—	2.00	4.00
❑ 11039	Still Loving You/I'm Gonna Write a Song	1973	—	2.00	4.00
❑ 11087	Just Enough to Make Me Stay/Baby Make It Good	1974	—	2.00	4.00
❑ 11138	Let Me Make the Bright Lights Shine for You/The Closest Thing to Heaven That I Love	1974	—	2.00	4.00
❑ 50065	Proud of You Baby/Tonight Your Baby's Coming Home	1975	—	2.00	4.00

Number	Title (A Side/B Side)	Yr	VG	VG+	NM
❑ 50136	Shame on Me/How Do You Start Over	1975	—	2.00	4.00
❑ 50183	A Satisfied Mind/Cleanin' Up the Streets of Memphis	1975	—	2.00	4.00
❑ 50216	The Man from Bowling Green/It's Only Make Believe	1976	—	2.00	4.00
❑ 50247	How Do You Start Over/Red Cadillac and Black Mustache	1976	—	2.00	4.00
❑ 50297	Labor of Love/Blond Haired Woman	1976	—	2.00	4.00
❑ 50323	He's Got a Way with Women/Here We Are Making Love Again	1976	—	2.00	4.00

HICKORY

Number	Title (A Side/B Side)	Yr	VG	VG+	NM
❑ 1201	You're Welcome/Interstate 40	1963	3.00	6.00	12.00
❑ 1219	Can't Take the Country from the Boy/I'm Gonna Write a Song of Love	1963	3.00	6.00	12.00
❑ 1221	Too Hot to Dance/I Like Your Kind of Love	1963	3.00	6.00	12.00

—With Sue Thompson

Number	Title (A Side/B Side)	Yr	VG	VG+	NM
❑ 1238	The File/Bigger Men Than I (Have Cried)	1964	3.00	6.00	12.00
❑ 1266	Lonely Room (Empty Walls)/Run On Home Baby Brother	1964	3.00	6.00	12.00
❑ 1277	Fire Engine Red/Old George Dickel	1964	3.00	6.00	12.00
❑ 1289	Bad, Bad Day/Tears from Out of Nowhere	1965	2.50	5.00	10.00
❑ 1307	Jealous Heart/Go On Home Boy	1965	2.50	5.00	10.00
❑ 1333	I Love You Because/Love Worked a Miracle	1965	2.50	5.00	10.00
❑ 1355	Five Miles from Home (Soon I'll See Mary)/(I Get So) Sentimental	1965	2.50	5.00	10.00
❑ 1382	Poor Boy Blues/(Can't Get You) Off My Mind	1966	2.50	5.00	10.00
❑ 1410	Come On and Sing/It's a Sin	1966	2.50	5.00	10.00
❑ 1430	Hardly Anymore/Freedom of Living	1967	2.00	4.00	8.00
❑ 1460	If You Don't Love Me (Then Why Don't You Leave Me Alone)/Throwin' Kisses	1967	2.00	4.00	8.00
❑ 1481	Running Scared/The Best Years of My Wife	1967	2.00	4.00	8.00
❑ 1536	It's All Over (But the Shouting)/Still Loving You	1969	—	3.00	6.00
❑ 1564	Still Loving You/Meet Mr. Mud	1970	—	3.00	6.00

IMPERIAL

Number	Title (A Side/B Side)	Yr	VG	VG+	NM
❑ 5705	A Red Cadillac and a Black Moustache/All Night Long	1960	6.25	12.50	25.00
❑ 8311	A Red Cadillac and a Black Moustache/All Night Long	1957	20.00	40.00	80.00
❑ 8313	Red Hot/Whenever You're Ready	1957	20.00	40.00	80.00
❑ 8315	Make Up Your Mind, Baby/Your Love	1958	15.00	30.00	60.00

—The same coupling was slated for Imperial 8314 but not released.

POLYDOR

Number	Title (A Side/B Side)	Yr	VG	VG+	NM
❑ 14408	I'm a Honky-Tonk Woman's Man/Lonely Women Make Good Lovers	1977	—	2.00	4.00
❑ 14431	The Pay Phone/He'll Be the One	1977	—	2.00	4.00
❑ 14444	A Christmas Tribute/Give Someone You Love (A Little Bit of Love This Year)	1977	—	2.00	4.00
❑ 14454	Proud Lady/Let Me Love Him Out of You	1978	—	2.00	4.00

ROLLIN' ROCK

Number	Title (A Side/B Side)	Yr	VG	VG+	NM
❑ 028	Stranger Than Fiction/You're the Cause of It All	1978	—	2.00	4.00

WARNER BROS.

Number	Title (A Side/B Side)	Yr	VG	VG+	NM
❑ 5081	My Baby Walks All Over Me/Class of '59	1959	6.25	12.50	25.00
❑ 5105	Dreamy Doll/Buttercup	1959	6.25	12.50	25.00
❑ 5172	Let's Think About Living/You've Got Everything	1960	5.00	10.00	20.00
❑ 5172 [PS]	Let's Think About Living/You've Got Everything	1960	10.00	20.00	40.00
❑ 5184	Why, Why, Bye, Bye/Oh Lonesome Me	1960	5.00	10.00	20.00
❑ 5184 [PS]	Why, Why, Bye, Bye/Oh Lonesome Me	1960	10.00	20.00	40.00
❑ 5204	The Great Snow Man/The Pig Latin Song	1961	5.00	10.00	20.00
❑ 5204 [PS]	The Great Snow Man/The Pig Latin Song	1961	10.00	20.00	40.00
❑ 5233	Private Eyes/You've Turned Down the Lights	1961	5.00	10.00	20.00
❑ 5233 [PS]	Private Eyes/You've Turned Down the Lights	1961	10.00	20.00	40.00
❑ 5255	Louisiana Man/Rocks of Reno	1962	5.00	10.00	20.00
❑ 5272	Big River Rose/Belonging to You	1962	5.00	10.00	20.00
❑ 5299	Hey Joe/The Fool	1962	5.00	10.00	20.00
❑ 5321	You're Everything/Envy	1962	5.00	10.00	20.00
❑ 5506	Boston Rocker/Old Friends//Bad Bad Day/Let's Think About Living	1960	25.00	50.00	100.00

—Part of Warner Bros. "+2" series, with two new songs and excerpts of two prior hits

Number	Title (A Side/B Side)	Yr	VG	VG+	NM
❑ 5506 [PS]	Boston Rocker/Old Friends//Bad Bad Day/Let's Think About Living	1960	25.00	50.00	100.00

Albums

EPIC

Number	Title (A Side/B Side)	Yr	VG	VG+	NM
❑ BN 26393	Ain't Got Time to Be Unhappy	1968	5.00	10.00	20.00
❑ BN 26463	Come On Home and Sing the Blues	1969	5.00	10.00	20.00
❑ BN 26541	Gettin' Back	1970	5.00	10.00	20.00
❑ E 30617	Is It Any Wonder	1971	5.00	10.00	20.00
❑ E 30923	Chain Don't Take to Me	1972	5.00	10.00	20.00
❑ KE 31375	When You Say Love	1972	5.00	10.00	20.00
❑ KE 31746	Lonely Women Make Good Lovers	1972	5.00	10.00	20.00
❑ KE 32191	Neither One of Us	1973	3.75	7.50	15.00
❑ KE 32759	Bob Luman's Greatest Hits	1974	3.75	7.50	15.00
❑ KE 33942	Satisfied Mind	1975	3.00	6.00	12.00
❑ KE 34445	Alive and Well!	1976	3.00	6.00	12.00

HARMONY

Number	Title (A Side/B Side)	Yr	VG	VG+	NM
❑ KH 32006	Bob Luman	1973	3.00	6.00	12.00

HICKORY

Number	Title (A Side/B Side)	Yr	VG	VG+	NM
❑ LPM-124 [M]	Livin' Lovin' Sounds	1965	6.25	12.50	25.00
❑ LPS-124 [S]	Livin' Lovin' Sounds	1965	7.50	15.00	30.00

HICKORY/MGM

Number	Title (A Side/B Side)	Yr	VG	VG+	NM
❑ H3G-4508	Still Loving You	1974	3.75	7.50	15.00

POLYDOR

Number	Title (A Side/B Side)	Yr	VG	VG+	NM
❑ PD-1-6135	Bob Luman	1978	3.00	6.00	12.00

WARNER BROS.

Number	Title (A Side/B Side)	Yr	VG	VG+	NM
❑ W 1396 [M]	Let's Think About Livin'	1960	12.50	25.00	50.00
❑ WS 1396 [S]	Let's Think About Livin'	1960	17.50	35.00	70.00

LUNSFORD, MIKE

45s

EVERGREEN

Number	Title (A Side/B Side)	Yr	VG	VG+	NM
❑ 1068	Tonight She Went Crazy Without Me/(B-side unknown)	1988	—	2.50	5.00

GUSTO

Number	Title (A Side/B Side)	Yr	VG	VG+	NM
❑ 122	Snake River Canyon/San Francisco Morning	1974	2.50	5.00	10.00
❑ 124	While the Feeling's Good/Blanket of the Blues	1975	—	3.50	7.00
❑ 9013	I Wish I'd Never Borrowed Anybody's Angel/Honky Tonk Super Star	1978	—	2.50	5.00
❑ 9018	I Still Believe in You/It's My Life	1979	—	2.50	5.00
❑ 9024	Is It Wrong/Lost Letter	1980	—	2.50	5.00

STARDAY

Number	Title (A Side/B Side)	Yr	VG	VG+	NM
❑ 129	How Can I Tell My Dreams/Stumbled 'Round	1975	—	3.00	6.00
❑ 130	Tonight My Lady Learns to Love/Proud Mary	1975	—	3.00	6.00
❑ 133	Sugar Sugar/Mumbled Round, Fumbled Round	1975	—	3.00	6.00
❑ 135	Too Hurt to Fight/If She Knocks on My Door (One More Time)	1976	—	3.00	6.00
❑ 138	Comin' Down Slow/Something to Walk On	1976	—	3.00	6.00
❑ 143	Honey Hungry/Tonight My Lady Learns to Love	1976	—	3.00	6.00
❑ 146	Stealin' Feelin'/Part Time Lovers, Full Time Fools	1976	—	3.00	6.00
❑ 149	If There Ever Comes a Day/Think About It One More Time	1977	—	3.00	6.00
❑ 157	Women Have a Feeling (same on both sides)	1977	2.00	4.00	8.00
❑ 160	I Can't Stop Now/I Haven't Seen Mama in Years	1977	—	3.00	6.00
❑ 176	I've Never Cheated on You/Brothers, Strangers and Friends	1978	—	3.00	6.00
❑ 187	The Reason Why I'm Here/I Feel Love	1978	—	3.00	6.00

Albums

STARDAY

Number	Title (A Side/B Side)	Yr	VG	VG+	NM
❑ SD 951	Mike Lunsford	1975	3.00	6.00	12.00
❑ SD 969X	Mike Lunsford	1977	3.00	6.00	12.00

LYERLY, BILL

45s

RCA

Number	Title (A Side/B Side)	Yr	VG	VG+	NM
❑ PB-12255	My Baby's Coming Home Again Today/Tryin' to Drink You Off My Mind	1981	—	2.00	4.00
❑ PB-12352	Mystery Train/Lonesome Whistle	1981	—	2.00	4.00

LYNDELL, LIZ

Also see DEL REEVES AND LIZ LYNDELL.

45s

KOALA

Number	Title (A Side/B Side)	Yr	VG	VG+	NM
❑ 326	Undercover Man/How I'd Love to Be With You Tonight	1980	—	2.50	5.00
❑ 327	I'm Gonna Ride Gilley's Bull/Rodeo Romeo	1980	—	2.50	5.00
❑ 330	I'm Gonna Let Go (And Love Somebody)/Leavin' Your Tracks on My Mind	1981	—	2.50	5.00
❑ 332	Right in the Wrong Direction/Going Back to the Country	1981	—	2.50	5.00
❑ 335	I Never Once Stopped Loving You/Kentucky Skies	1981	—	2.50	5.00
❑ 338	I'm Just the Cuddle-Up Kind/(B-side unknown)	1981	—	2.50	5.00
❑ 349	Marty (We Love You)/The Lovin' and Leavin' Man	1982	—	3.00	6.00

LYNDEN, TRACY

45s

RCA

Number	Title (A Side/B Side)	Yr	VG	VG+	NM
❑ PB-14059	Straight Laced Lady/(B-side unknown)	1985	—	2.00	4.00

LYNN, JENNY

45s

BETA

Number	Title (A Side/B Side)	Yr	VG	VG+	NM
❑ 1000	Gee! It's Christmas Day/Jingle Bells	197?	2.00	4.00	8.00

COLONIAL

Number	Title (A Side/B Side)	Yr	VG	VG+	NM
❑ 102	Taste of Love/(B-side unknown)	1978	2.00	4.00	8.00

LYNN, JUDY

45s

ABC-PARAMOUNT

Number	Title (A Side/B Side)	Yr	VG	VG+	NM
❑ 9767	I Slipped Off My Wedding Ring/Tip Toe	1956	5.00	10.00	20.00

AMARET

Number	Title (A Side/B Side)	Yr	VG	VG+	NM
❑ 131	Married to a Memory/So Natural Is My Love	1971	2.00	4.00	8.00
❑ 137	Elusive Butterfly/When the Love Starts to Come	1971	2.00	4.00	8.00
❑ 138	Parts of Love/Just to Be Kind	1971	2.00	4.00	8.00
❑ 139	Winterwood/You Make the World I Live In	1971	2.00	4.00	8.00
❑ 141	Give Me Something to Believe In/And You Love Me	1972	2.00	4.00	8.00
❑ 149	Pour Me a Little More Wine/Footprints on the Moon	1973	—	3.50	7.00
❑ 150	I'll Never Sing You a Sad Song/Posters on the Wall	1973	—	3.50	7.00
❑ 152	I've Never Been a Fool Like This Before/220 Mama	1973	—	3.50	7.00

COLUMBIA

Number	Title (A Side/B Side)	Yr	VG	VG+	NM
❑ 4-44220	Don't Play with Matches Anymore/I Lost My Wings Last Night	1967	2.00	4.00	8.00
❑ 4-44409	A Thing of Pleasure/Evil on Your Mind	1967	—	3.50	7.00
❑ 4-44489	May I Drive You Home/Green Paper	1968	—	3.50	7.00
❑ 4-44661	Bring the Woman Out in Me/Mommy, Here Comes the Judge	1968	—	3.50	7.00
❑ 4-44794	What's a Honky Tonk Woman/Bull by the Tail	1969	2.00	4.00	8.00
❑ 4-44981	America, the Beautiful/Gentle on My Mind	1969	2.00	4.00	8.00

MUSICOR

Number	Title (A Side/B Side)	Yr	VG	VG+	NM
❑ 1163	Golden Nugget/Your Picture on the Wall	1966	2.00	4.00	8.00
❑ 1183	That Was in the Deal/Transition Tape Recorder	1966	2.00	4.00	8.00
❑ 1192	Moment of Silence/The Prospector	1966	2.00	4.00	8.00
❑ 1222	Do I Look Like I Got/Honey Stuff	1966	2.00	4.00	8.00
❑ 1239	Little Shoes/My Heart Gets in the Way	1967	2.00	4.00	8.00
❑ 1266	Walk on Me/Lonely Came to Visit	1967	2.00	4.00	8.00
❑ 1283	On Smoke, Not Fire/Yellowstone	1967	2.00	4.00	8.00

UNITED ARTISTS

Number	Title (A Side/B Side)	Yr	VG	VG+	NM
❑ 472	Footsteps of a Fool/This Lonely Pillow	1962	3.00	6.00	12.00
❑ 519	My Secret/I Just Want to See You Once	1962	3.00	6.00	12.00
❑ 571	My Father's Voice/When You Thanked Me for the Roses	1963	3.00	6.00	12.00
❑ 606	Oh Why Can't He Forget Her/Slowly, Day by Day	1963	3.00	6.00	12.00
❑ 674	Calm Before the Storm/I Make Excuses	1963	3.00	6.00	12.00
❑ 723	Almost Out of Hand/My Tears Are on the Roses	1964	2.50	5.00	10.00
❑ 767	Hello Operator/I'm Making Plans	1964	2.50	5.00	10.00
❑ 818	Antique in My Closet/Unexpected Guest	1965	2.50	5.00	10.00
❑ 857	I'll Pick Up My Heart/The Letter	1965	2.50	5.00	10.00
❑ 931	Hello Mr. D.J./Royalties from Wedding Bells	1965	2.50	5.00	10.00

WARNER BROS.

Number	Title (A Side/B Side)	Yr	VG	VG+	NM
❑ 8059	Padre/Burden of Freedom	1974	—	3.00	6.00
❑ 8082	The Burden of Freedom/Dark Moon	1975	—	2.50	5.00

Albums

AMARET

Number	Title	Yr	VG	VG+	NM
❑ ST-5011	Parts of Love	1971	3.75	7.50	15.00
❑ AST-5014	Naturally	197?	3.75	7.50	15.00

COLUMBIA

Number	Title	Yr	VG	VG+	NM
❑ CS 9879	Judy Lynn Sings at Caesar's Palace	1968	3.75	7.50	15.00

MUSICOR

Number	Title	Yr	VG	VG+	NM
❑ MM-2096 [M]	The Judy Lynn Show Plays Again	1966	3.75	7.50	15.00
❑ MM-2112 [M]	Honey Stuff	1966	3.75	7.50	15.00
❑ MM-2126 [M]	Golden Nuggets	1967	3.75	7.50	15.00
❑ MS-3096 [S]	The Judy Lynn Show Plays Again	1966	5.00	10.00	20.00
❑ MS-3112 [S]	Honey Stuff	1966	5.00	10.00	20.00
❑ MS-3126 [S]	Golden Nuggets	1967	3.75	7.50	15.00

UNART

Number	Title	Yr	VG	VG+	NM
❑ 20009 [M]	Judy Lynn in Las Vegas	1967	3.75	7.50	15.00
❑ 21009 [S]	Judy Lynn in Las Vegas	1967	3.00	6.00	12.00

UNITED ARTISTS

Number	Title	Yr	VG	VG+	NM
❑ UAL-3226 [M]	Judy Lynn Sings at the Golden Nugget	1962	5.00	10.00	20.00
❑ UAL-3288 [M]	Here Is Our Gal, Judy Lynn	1963	3.75	7.50	15.00
❑ UAL-3342 [M]	Country and Western Girl Singer	1964	3.75	7.50	15.00
❑ UAL-3390 [M]	The Judy Lynn Show	1964	3.75	7.50	15.00
❑ UAL-3443 [M]	The Judy Lynn Show Act 2	1965	3.75	7.50	15.00
❑ UAL-3461 [M]	The Best of Judy Lynn	1966	3.75	7.50	15.00
❑ UAS-6226 [S]	Judy Lynn Sings at the Golden Nugget	1962	6.25	12.50	25.00
❑ UAS-6288 [S]	Here Is Our Gal, Judy Lynn	1963	5.00	10.00	20.00
❑ UAS-6342 [S]	Country and Western Girl Singer	1964	5.00	10.00	20.00
❑ UAS-6390 [S]	The Judy Lynn Show	1964	5.00	10.00	20.00
❑ UAS-6443 [S]	The Judy Lynn Show Act 2	1965	5.00	10.00	20.00
❑ UAS-6461 [S]	The Best of Judy Lynn	1966	5.00	10.00	20.00

LYNN, LORETTA

Also see DOLLY PARTON; ERNEST TUBB AND LORETTA LYNN; CONWAY TWITTY AND LORETTA LYNN.

45s

DECCA

Number	Title (A Side/B Side)	Yr	VG	VG+	NM
❑ 31323	The Girl That I Am Now/I Walked Away from the Wreck	1961	3.75	7.50	15.00
❑ 31384	Success/Hundred Proof Heartache	1962	3.00	6.00	12.00
❑ 31435	World of Forgotten People/Get Set for a Heartache	1962	3.75	7.50	15.00
❑ 31471	The Other Woman/Who'll Help Me Get Over You	1963	2.50	5.00	10.00
❑ 31541	Before I'm Over You/Where Were You	1963	2.50	5.00	10.00
❑ 31608	Wine, Women and Song/This Haunted House	1964	2.50	5.00	10.00
❑ 31707	Happy Birthday/When Lonely Hits Your Heart	1964	2.50	5.00	10.00
❑ 31769	Blue Kentucky Girl/Two Steps Forward	1965	2.50	5.00	10.00
❑ 31836	The Home You're Tearin' Down/The Farther You Go	1965	2.50	5.00	10.00
❑ 31879	When I Hear My Children Play/Everybody Wants to Go to Heaven	1965	3.00	6.00	12.00
❑ 31893	Dear Uncle Sam/Hurtin' for Certain	1966	2.50	5.00	10.00
❑ 31966	You Ain't Woman Enough/God Gave Me a Heart to Forgive	1966	2.50	5.00	10.00
❑ 32043	It Won't Seem Like Christmas/To Heck with Santa Claus	1966	2.50	5.00	10.00
❑ 32043 [PS]	It Won't Seem Like Christmas/To Heck with Santa Claus	1966	3.75	7.50	15.00
❑ 32045	Don't Come Home a-Drinkin' (With Lovin' on Your Mind)/A Saint to a Sinner	1966	2.50	5.00	10.00
❑ 32127	If You're Not Gone Too Long/A Man I Hardly Know	1967	2.50	5.00	10.00
❑ 32184	What Kind of a Girl (Do You Think I Am?)/Bargain Basement Dress	1967	2.50	5.00	10.00
❑ 32264	Fist City/Slowly Killing Me	1968	2.00	4.00	8.00
❑ 32332	You've Just Stepped In (From Stepping Out on Me)/Taking the Place of My Man	1968	2.00	4.00	8.00
❑ 32392	Your Squaw Is On the Warpath/Let Me Go, You're Hurtin' Me	1968	2.00	4.00	8.00
❑ 32439	Woman of the World (Leave My World Alone)/Sneakin' In	1969	2.00	4.00	8.00
❑ 32513	To Make a Man (Feel Like a Man)/One Little Reason	1969	2.00	4.00	8.00
❑ 32586	Wings Upon Your Horns/Let's Get Back Down to Earth	1969	2.00	4.00	8.00
❑ 32637	I Know How/The End of My World	1970	2.00	4.00	8.00
❑ 32693	You Wanna Give Me a Lift/What's the Bottle Done Today Baby	1970	2.00	4.00	8.00
❑ 32749	Coal Miner's Daughter/Man of the House	1970	2.50	5.00	10.00
❑ 32749 [PS]	Coal Miner's Daughter/Man of the House	1970	3.00	6.00	12.00
❑ 32763	I Love You/That Ain't a Woman's Way	1970	2.00	4.00	8.00
❑ 32796	I Wanna Be Free/If I Never Love Again	1971	—	3.50	7.00
❑ 32851	You're Lookin' at Country/When You're Poor	1971	—	3.50	7.00
❑ 32900	Here in Topeka/Kinfolks Holler	1971	5.00	10.00	20.00
❑ 32900	One's On the Way/Kinfolks Holler	1971	—	3.50	7.00
	—Retitled version of A-side				
❑ 32974	Here I Am Again/My Kind of Man	1972	—	3.50	7.00
❑ 33039	Rated "X"/'Til the Pain Outwears the Shame	1972	—	3.50	7.00

MCA

Number	Title (A Side/B Side)	Yr	VG	VG+	NM
❑ 40058	Love Is the Foundation/What Sundown Does to You	1973	—	2.50	5.00
❑ 40150	Hey Loretta/Turn Me Any Way But Loose	1973	—	2.50	5.00
❑ 40223	They Don't Make 'Em Like My Daddy/Nothin'	1974	—	2.50	5.00
❑ 40283	Trouble in Paradise/We've Already Tasted Love	1974	—	2.50	5.00
❑ 40358	The Pill/Will You Be There	1975	—	2.50	5.00
❑ 40438	Home/You Take Me to Heaven Every Night	1975	—	2.50	5.00
❑ 40484	When the Tingle Becomes a Chill/All I Want from You (Is Away)	1975	—	2.50	5.00
❑ 40541	Red, White and Blue/Sounds of a New Love (Being Born)	1976	—	2.50	5.00
❑ 40607	Somebody Somewhere (Don't Know What He's Missin' Tonight)/Sundown Tavern	1976	—	2.50	5.00
❑ 40679	She's Got You/The Lady That Lived Here Before	1977	—	2.50	5.00
❑ 40747	Why Can't He Be You/I Keep On Putting On	1977	—	2.50	5.00
❑ 40832	Out of My Head and Back in My Bed/Old Rooster	1977	—	2.50	5.00
❑ 40910	Spring Fever/God Bless the Children	1978	—	2.00	4.00
❑ 40954	We've Come a Long Way, Baby/I Can't Feel You Anymore	1978	—	2.00	4.00
❑ 40954 [PS]	We've Come a Long Way, Baby/I Can't Feel You Anymore	1978	—	3.00	6.00
❑ 41021	I Can't Feel You Anymore/True Love Needs to Keep in Touch	1979	—	2.00	4.00
❑ 41129	I've Got a Picture of Us on My Mind/I Don't Feel Like a Movie Tonight	1979	—	2.00	4.00
❑ 41185	Pregnant Again/You're a Cross I Can't Bear	1980	—	2.00	4.00
❑ 41250	Naked in the Rain/I Should Be Over You by Now	1980	—	2.00	4.00
❑ 51015	Cheatin' On a Cheater/Until I Met You	1980	—	2.00	4.00
❑ 51058	Somebody Led Me Away/Everybody's Lookin' for Somebody New	1981	—	2.00	4.00
❑ 51226	I Lie/If I Ain't Got It	1982	—	2.50	5.00
❑ 52005	I Lie/If I Ain't Got It	1982	—	2.00	4.00
❑ 52092	Making Love from Memory/Don't It Feel Good	1982	—	2.00	4.00
❑ 52158	Breakin' It/There's All Kinds of Smoke (In the Barroom)	1983	—	2.00	4.00
❑ 52219	Lyin', Cheatin', Woman Chasin', Honky Tonkin', Whiskey Drinkin' You/Star Light, Star Bright	1983	—	2.00	4.00
❑ 52289	Walking with My Memories/It's Gone	1983	—	2.00	4.00
❑ 52621	Heart Don't Do This to Me/Adam's Rib	1985	—	—	3.00
❑ 52706	Wouldn't It Be Great/One Man Band	1985	—	—	3.00
❑ 52766	Just a Woman/Take Me in Your Arms (And Hold Me)	1986	—	—	3.00
❑ 53320	Who Was That Stranger/Elsie Banks	1988	—	—	3.00
❑ 53397	Fly Away/Your Used to Be	1988	—	—	3.00
❑ 65034	Shadrack, the Black Reindeer/Let's Put Christ Back in Christmas	1974	—	2.00	4.00
	—Black label with rainbow				
❑ 65034	Shadrack, the Black Reindeer/Let's Put Christ Back in Christmas	1980	—	—	3.00
	—Blue label with rainbow				

ZERO

Number	Title (A Side/B Side)	Yr	VG	VG+	NM
❑ 107	I'm a Honky Tonk Girl/Whispering Sea	1960	125.00	250.00	500.00
❑ 110	New Rainbow/Heartaches Meet Mr. Blues	1960	100.00	200.00	400.00
❑ 112	The Darkest Day/Gonna Pack My Troubles	1961	100.00	200.00	400.00

7-Inch Extended Plays

DECCA

Number	Title	Yr	VG	VG+	NM
❑ ED 2762	The Other Woman/Where Were You//Success/Before I'm Over You	1964	5.00	10.00	20.00
❑ ED 2762 [PS]	The Other Woman	1964	5.00	10.00	20.00
❑ ED 2784	(contents unknown)	1965	5.00	10.00	20.00
❑ ED 2784 [PS]	Wine, Women and Song	1965	5.00	10.00	20.00
❑ ED 2793	(contents unknown)	1965	5.00	10.00	20.00
❑ ED 2793 [PS]	The End of the World	1965	5.00	10.00	20.00
❑ ED 2800	(contents unknown)	1965	5.00	10.00	20.00
❑ ED 2800 [PS]	Songs from the Heart	1965	5.00	10.00	20.00

Albums

DECCA

Number	Title	Yr	VG	VG+	NM
❑ DL 4457 [M]	Loretta Lynn Sings	1963	15.00	30.00	60.00
❑ DL 4541 [M]	Before I'm Over You	1964	7.50	15.00	30.00
❑ DL 4620 [M]	Songs from My Heart	1965	7.50	15.00	30.00
❑ DL 4665 [M]	Blue Kentucky Girl	1965	7.50	15.00	30.00
❑ DL 4695 [M]	Hymns	1965	7.50	15.00	30.00
❑ DL 4744 [M]	I Like 'Em Country	1966	6.25	12.50	25.00
❑ DL 4783 [M]	You Ain't Woman Enough	1966	6.25	12.50	25.00
❑ DL 4817 [M]	Country Christmas	1966	6.25	12.50	25.00
❑ DL 4842 [M]	Don't Come Home a-Drinkin' (With Lovin' on Your Mind)	1967	7.50	15.00	30.00
❑ DL 4928 [M]	Who Says God Is Dead!	1967	10.00	20.00	40.00
❑ DL 4930 [M]	Singin' with Feelin'	1967	7.50	15.00	30.00
❑ DL 74457 [S]	Loretta Lynn Sings	1963	20.00	40.00	80.00
❑ DL 74541 [S]	Before I'm Over You	1964	10.00	20.00	40.00

Of all women in the history of country music, only Dolly Parton has had more chart success than Loretta Lynn. (Top left) Any of Loretta's three 45s on the Zero label fetch hundreds of dollars in top condition. This was her first one, "I'm a Honky-Tonk Gal," which made the charts in 1960. (Top right) Her first 11 charted solo hits on Decca, including the No. 1 "Don't Come Home a-Drinkin' (With Lovin' on Your Mind)," were compiled on *Loretta Lynn's Greatest Hits*, from 1968. One best-of album soon would be woefully inadequate. (Bottom left) No song is more closely associated with Loretta Lynn than "Coal Miner's Daughter," which she wrote. It would also serve as the name of her autobiography and the movie based on the book. (Bottom right) She continued to have hits well into the 1980s, but her last chart-topper was "Out of My Head and Back in My Bed," from 1977.

Number	Title (A Side/B Side)	Yr	VG	VG+	NM
❑ DL 74620 [S]	Songs from My Heart	1965	10.00	20.00	40.00
❑ DL 74665 [S]	Blue Kentucky Girl	1965	10.00	20.00	40.00
❑ DL 74695 [S]	Hymns	1965	10.00	20.00	40.00
❑ DL 74744 [S]	I Like 'Em Country	1966	7.50	15.00	30.00
❑ DL 74783 [S]	You Ain't Woman Enough	1966	7.50	15.00	30.00
❑ DL 74817 [S]	Country Christmas	1966	7.50	15.00	30.00
❑ DL 74842 [S]	Don't Come Home a-Drinkin' (With Lovin' on Your Mind)	1967	6.25	12.50	25.00
❑ DL 74928 [S]	Who Says God Is Dead!	1967	6.25	12.50	25.00
❑ DL 74930 [S]	Singin' with Feelin'	1967	6.25	12.50	25.00
❑ DL 74997	Fist City	1968	6.25	12.50	25.00
❑ DL 75000	Loretta Lynn's Greatest Hits	1968	6.25	12.50	25.00
❑ DL 75084	Your Squaw Is On the Warpath	1969	10.00	20.00	40.00
—First editions had a track called "Barney"					
❑ DL 75084	Your Squaw Is On the Warpath	1969	6.25	12.50	25.00
—Later editions delete the track "Barney"					
❑ DL 75113	Woman of the World/To Make a Man	1969	6.25	12.50	25.00
❑ DL 75163	Wings Upon Your Horns	1970	6.25	12.50	25.00
❑ DL 75198	Loretta Lynn Writes 'Em and Sings 'Em	1970	6.25	12.50	25.00
❑ DL 75253	Coal Miner's Daughter	1971	5.00	10.00	20.00
❑ DL 75282	I Wanna Be Free	1971	5.00	10.00	20.00
❑ DL 75310	You're Lookin' at Country	1971	5.00	10.00	20.00
❑ DL 75334	One's On the Way	1972	5.00	10.00	20.00
❑ DL 75351	God Bless America Again	1972	5.00	10.00	20.00
❑ DL 75381	Here I Am Again	1972	5.00	10.00	20.00
MCA					
❑ 1	Loretta Lynn's Greatest Hits	1973	3.75	7.50	15.00
—Reissue of Decca 75000					
❑ 5	Hymns	1973	3.75	7.50	15.00
—Reissue of Decca 74695					
❑ 6	You Ain't Woman Enough	1973	3.75	7.50	15.00
—Reissue of Decca 74783					
❑ 7	Who Says God Is Dead!	1973	3.75	7.50	15.00
—Reissue of Decca 74928					
❑ 58	Here I Am Again	1973	3.75	7.50	15.00
—Reissue of Decca 75381					
❑ 113	Don't Come Home a-Drinkin' (With Lovin' on Your Mind)	1973	3.75	7.50	15.00
—Reissue of Decca 74842					
❑ 248	Country Christmas	1973	3.75	7.50	15.00
—First reissue of Decca LP					
❑ 300	Entertainer of the Year — Loretta	1973	3.75	7.50	15.00
❑ 355	Love Is the Foundation	1973	3.75	7.50	15.00
❑ 420	Loretta Lynn's Greatest Hits Vol. II	1974	3.75	7.50	15.00
❑ 444	They Don't Make 'Em Like My Daddy	1974	3.75	7.50	15.00
❑ 471	Back to the Country	1975	3.00	6.00	12.00
❑ 628	When the Tingle Becomes a Chill	198?	2.00	4.00	8.00
—Budget-line reissue					
❑ 630	Somebody Somewhere	198?	2.00	4.00	8.00
—Budget-line reissue					
❑ 721	We've Come a Long Way, Baby	198?	2.00	4.00	8.00
—Budget-line reissue					
❑ 735	Alone with You	198?	2.50	5.00	10.00
❑ L33-1934 [DJ]	Loretta Lynn	1974	10.00	20.00	40.00
—Promo-only compilation					
❑ 2146	Home	1975	3.00	6.00	12.00
❑ 2179	When the Tingle Becomes a Chill	1976	3.00	6.00	12.00
❑ 2228	Somebody Somewhere	1976	3.00	6.00	12.00
❑ 2265	I Remember Patsy	1977	3.00	6.00	12.00
❑ 2330	Out of My Head and Back in My Bed	1978	3.00	6.00	12.00
❑ 2341	Loretta Lynn's Greatest Hits	1978	3.00	6.00	12.00
—Reissue of MCA 1					
❑ 2342	Coal Miner's Daughter	1978	3.00	6.00	12.00
—Reissue					
❑ 2353	Loretta Lynn's Greatest Hits Vol. II	1978	3.00	6.00	12.00
—Reissue of MCA 420					
❑ 3073	We've Come a Long Way, Baby	1979	3.00	6.00	12.00
❑ 3217	Loretta	1980	2.50	5.00	10.00
❑ 5148	Lookin' Good	1980	2.50	5.00	10.00
❑ 5293	I Lie	1982	2.50	5.00	10.00
❑ 5426	Lyin', Cheatin', Woman Chasin', Honky Tonkin', Whiskey Drinkin' You	1983	2.50	5.00	10.00
❑ 5613	Just a Woman	1985	2.50	5.00	10.00
❑ 15022	Country Christmas	1974	3.00	6.00	12.00
—Second reissue of Decca LP; black rainbow label					
❑ 15022	Country Christmas	1980	2.50	5.00	10.00
—Blue rainbow label					
❑ 15032	Christmas Without Daddy	198?	3.00	6.00	12.00
❑ 35013	Allis-Chalmers Presents Loretta Lynn	1978	10.00	20.00	40.00
—Special products compilation					
❑ 35018	Crisco Presents Loretta Lynn's Country Classics	1979	10.00	20.00	40.00
—Special products compilation					
❑ 37080	I Remember Patsy Cline	198?	2.00	4.00	8.00
—Budget-line reissue					
❑ 37165	Loretta	198?	2.00	4.00	8.00
—Budget-line reissue					
❑ 37205	Loretta Lynn's Greatest Hits Vol. II	198?	2.00	4.00	8.00
—Budget-line reissue					
❑ 37235	Loretta Lynn's Greatest Hits	198?	2.00	4.00	8.00
—Budget-line reissue					
❑ 37236	Coal Miner's Daughter	198?	2.00	4.00	8.00
—Budget-line reissue					
❑ 42174	Who Was That Stranger	1988	2.50	5.00	10.00
VOCALION					
❑ VL 73853	Here's Loretta Lynn	1968	3.75	7.50	15.00

LYNN, LORETTA, AND ERNEST TUBB

See ERNEST TUBB AND LORETTA LYNN.

LYNN, LORETTA, AND CONWAY TWITTY

See CONWAY TWITTY AND LORETTA LYNN.

LYNN, MARCIA

Number	Title (A Side/B Side)	Yr	VG	VG+	NM
45s					
EVERGREEN					
❑ 1063	Don't Start the Fire/(B-side unknown)	1987	—	2.50	5.00
SOUNDWAVES					
❑ 4776	Good Ole Country Mood/Lie Left on His Finger	1986	—	2.50	5.00
❑ 4780	Just When/What You Did to Me	1986	—	2.50	5.00
❑ 4784	You've Got That Leaving Look in Your Eye/Lie Left on His Finger	1987	—	2.50	5.00
❑ 4789	Looking for a Feeling/(B-side unknown)	1987	—	2.50	5.00

LYNN, MICHELLE

Number	Title (A Side/B Side)	Yr	VG	VG+	NM
45s					
MASTER					
❑ 07	The Letter/(B-side unknown)	1988	—	3.00	6.00
❑ 11	Brand New Week/(B-side unknown)	1989	—	3.00	6.00

LYNN, REBECCA

Number	Title (A Side/B Side)	Yr	VG	VG+	NM
45s					
RANWOOD					
❑ 968	No More Tears/I'll Break the Habit	1974	—	2.50	5.00
❑ 1004	Cold Carolina Morning/He's Too Busy Working to Cheat on Me	1974	—	2.50	5.00
❑ 1012	I'll Break the Habit/He's Too Busy Working to Cheat on Me	1975	—	2.50	5.00
❑ 1028	He's That Kind of a Man/(B-side unknown)	1975	—	2.50	5.00
SCORPION					
❑ 0550	Music, Music, Music/No More Tears	1978	—	3.00	6.00
❑ 0559	Minstrel Man/He Loves Me All to Pieces	1978	—	3.00	6.00
❑ 0573	Goody Goody/My Happiness	1979	—	3.00	6.00
❑ 0581	Disco Girl Go Away/Make Believe You Love Me	1979	—	3.00	6.00
SUNBIRD					
❑ 106	Fairytale/(B-side unknown)	1980	—	3.00	6.00

LYNN, TRISHA

Number	Title (A Side/B Side)	Yr	VG	VG+	NM
45s					
OAK					
❑ 1053	I Go to Pieces/(B-side unknown)	1988	—	3.00	6.00
❑ 1062	Not Fade Away/(B-side unknown)	1989	—	3.00	6.00
—As "Trish Lynn"					
❑ 1072	Kiss Me Darling/(B-side unknown)	1989	—	3.00	6.00
❑ 1083	I Can't Help Myself/(B-side unknown)	1989	—	3.00	6.00

LYNNE, SHELBY

Also see GEORGE JONES.

Number	Title (A Side/B Side)	Yr	VG	VG+	NM
45s					
EPIC					
❑ 34-68584	Under Your Spell Again/Blue to the Bone	1989	—	—	3.00
❑ 34-68942	The Hurtin' Side/If I Could Bottle This Up	1989	—	—	3.00
❑ 34-73032	Little Bits and Pieces/Your Love Stays with Me	1989	—	—	3.00
❑ 34-73319	I'll Lie Myself to Sleep/What About This Girl	1990	—	2.00	4.00
❑ 34-73521	Things Are Tough All Over/I Walk the Line	1990	—	2.00	4.00
❑ 34-73716	What About the Love We Made/I'll Lie Myself to Sleep	1991	—	2.00	4.00
❑ 34-73904	The Very First Lasting Love/Lonely Weekends	1991	—	2.00	4.00
—A-side with Les Taylor					
❑ 34-74062	Don't Cross Your Heart/Stop Me	1991	—	2.00	4.00
MORGAN CREEK					
❑ 23018	Feelin' Kind of Lonely Tonight/Don't Cry for Me	1993	—	2.50	5.00
❑ 23019	Tell Me I'm Crazy/Rain Might Wash Your Love Away	1993	—	2.50	5.00

LYNNS, THE

Number	Title (A Side/B Side)	Yr	VG	VG+	NM
45s					
REPRISE					
❑ 17248	Woman to Woman/The Story Behind "Woman to Woman" and "Nights Like These"	1998	—	—	3.00
❑ 17276	Nights Like These/Oh My Goodness	1997	—	—	3.00

LYNYRD SKYNYRD

Number	Title (A Side/B Side)	Yr	VG	VG+	NM
12-Inch Singles					
MCA					
❑ L33-17385 [DJ]	Truck Drivin' Man/Simple Man	1987	2.00	4.00	8.00
❑ L33-17444 [DJ]	Georgia Peaches (same on both sides)	1987	2.00	4.00	8.00
❑ L33-17488 [DJ]	Swamp Music (same on both sides)	1987	2.00	4.00	8.00
❑ L33-17569 [DJ]	Gimme Back My Bullets/Comin' Home	198?	2.00	4.00	8.00
45s					
ATINA					
❑ 129	Need All My Friends/Michelle	1978	3.75	7.50	15.00
COLUMBIA					
❑ 78284	White Knuckle Ride/Tearin' It Up	1996	—	2.00	4.00
—B-side by Joe Diffie					
MCA					
❑ L45-1966 [DJ]	Gimme Back My Bullets (same on both sides)	1976	6.25	12.50	25.00
❑ 40258	Sweet Home Alabama/Take Your Time	1974	—	2.50	5.00
❑ 40328	Free Bird/Down South Jukin'	1974	—	2.50	5.00
❑ 40416	Saturday Night Special/Made in the Shade	1975	—	2.50	5.00
❑ 40532	Double Trouble/Roll Gypsy Roll	1975	—	2.50	5.00

Number	Title (A Side/B Side)	Yr	VG	VG+	NM
❑ 40565	Gimme Back My Bullets/All I Can Do Is Write About It	1976	—	2.50	5.00
❑ 40647	Gimme Three Steps/Travelin' Man	1976	—	2.50	5.00
❑ 40665	Free Bird/Searching	1976	—	2.50	5.00
❑ 40819	What's Your Name/I Know a Little	1977	—	2.50	5.00
—"What's Your Name" is a different mix than that on the Street Survivors LP.					
❑ 40888	You Got That Right/Ain't No Good Life	1978	—	2.50	5.00
❑ 40957	Down South Jukin'/Wino	1978	—	2.50	5.00
❑ 53206	When You Got Good Friends/Truck Drivin' Man	1987	—	2.00	4.00
❑ 60191	Sweet Home Alabama/Saturday Night Special	1976	—	2.00	4.00
—Reissue					

SHADE TREE

Number	Title (A Side/B Side)	Yr	VG	VG+	NM
❑ 101	Need All My Friends/Michelle	1971	375.00	750.00	1500.
—As "Lynard Skynard"; approximately 300 copies pressed					

SOUNDS OF THE SOUTH

Number	Title (A Side/B Side)	Yr	VG	VG+	NM
❑ 40158	Gimme Three Steps/Mr. Banker	1973	2.00	4.00	8.00
❑ 40231	Don't Ask Me No Questions/Take Your Time	1974	2.00	4.00	8.00
❑ 40258	Sweet Home Alabama/Take Your Time	1974	2.00	4.00	8.00

Albums

ATLANTIC

Number	Title (A Side/B Side)	Yr	VG	VG+	NM
❑ A1-82258	Lynyrd Skynyrd 1991	1991	5.00	10.00	20.00
—The only U.S. vinyl version was released through Columbia House					

MCA

Number	Title (A Side/B Side)	Yr	VG	VG+	NM
❑ 363	(pronounced leh-nerd skin-nerd)	1975	3.00	6.00	12.00
—Reissue on black rainbow label					
❑ 413	Second Helping	1975	3.00	6.00	12.00
—Reissue on black rainbow label					
❑ 1448	Best of the Rest	1985	2.00	4.00	8.00
❑ L33-1946 [(2) DJ]	One More From the Road	1976	6.25	12.50	25.00
—Promo only on black vinyl					
❑ L33-1946 [(2) DJ]	One More From the Road	1976	12.50	25.00	50.00
—Promo on blue, gold, purple or red vinyl (each has the same value)					
❑ L33-1988 [DJ]	Skynyrd's First and...Last	1978	6.25	12.50	25.00
—Promo sampler					
❑ 2137	Nuthin' Fancy	1975	3.00	6.00	12.00
❑ 3019	(pronounced leh-nerd skin-nerd)	1976	2.50	5.00	10.00
—Second reissue with new number on black rainbow label					
❑ 3020	Second Helping	1976	2.50	5.00	10.00
—Second reissue with new number on black rainbow label					
❑ 3021	Nuthin' Fancy	1976	2.50	5.00	10.00
—Reissue with new number on black rainbow label					
❑ 3022	Gimme Back My Bullets	1976	3.00	6.00	12.00
❑ 3029	Street Survivors	1977	6.25	12.50	25.00
—Originals with the band in flames on the front cover and a smaller band photo on the back cover					
❑ 3029	Street Survivors	1977	2.50	5.00	10.00
—After the band's plane crash, the "flames" photo was replaced with the back cover photo; the back cover is black with only the song titles					
❑ 3047	Skynyrd's First and...Last	1978	3.00	6.00	12.00
—Originals with tan labels and gatefold cover					
❑ 5221	(pronounced leh-nerd skin-nerd)	1980	2.00	4.00	8.00
❑ 5222	Second Helping	1980	2.00	4.00	8.00
❑ 5223	Street Survivors	1980	2.00	4.00	8.00
❑ 5370	Best of the Rest	1982	2.50	5.00	10.00
—Original version					
❑ 6001 [(2)]	One More From the Road	1976	3.75	7.50	15.00
—Originals with black rainbow label and gatefold cover					
❑ 6897 [(2)]	One More From the Road	1985	2.50	5.00	10.00
—Most, if not all, of these pressings have no gatefold					
❑ 6898 [(2)]	Gold & Platinum	1985	2.50	5.00	10.00
—Most, if not all, of these pressings have no gatefold					
❑ 8027 [(2)]	Southern by the Grace of God	1988	3.00	6.00	12.00
❑ 10014 [(2)]	One More From the Road	1980	2.50	5.00	10.00
❑ 11008 [(2)]	Gold & Platinum	1979	3.00	6.00	12.00
—Originals with embossed gatefold cover					
❑ 37069	Gimme Back My Bullets	1980	2.00	4.00	8.00
❑ 37070	Nuthin' Fancy	1980	2.00	4.00	8.00
❑ 37071	Skynyrd's First and...Last	1980	2.00	4.00	8.00
❑ 37211	(pronounced leh-nerd skin-nerd)	1985	2.00	4.00	8.00
❑ 37212	Second Helping	1985	2.00	4.00	8.00
❑ 37213	Street Survivors	1985	2.00	4.00	8.00
❑ 42084	Legend	1987	2.50	5.00	10.00
❑ 42293	Skynyrd's Innyrds	1989	3.00	6.00	12.00

SOUNDS OF THE SOUTH

Number	Title (A Side/B Side)	Yr	VG	VG+	NM
❑ 363	(pronounced leh-nerd skin-nerd)	1973	5.00	10.00	20.00
❑ 413	Second Helping	1974	5.00	10.00	20.00
—Both of the above are original pressings with yellow labels					

M

MAC, JIMMY

45s

AV

Number	Title (A Side/B Side)	Yr	VG	VG+	NM
❑ 924	You Really Know How to Break a Heart/(B-side unknown)	1984	—	3.50	7.00

MACGREGOR, BYRON

45s

CAPITOL

Number	Title (A Side/B Side)	Yr	VG	VG+	NM
❑ 4034	Thank You America/Eulogy to a Dog	1975	—	2.50	5.00
❑ 4172	Children, Do You Know Where Your Parents Are/Love, It Comes in All Colors	1975	—	2.50	5.00

WESTBOUND

Number	Title (A Side/B Side)	Yr	VG	VG+	NM
❑ 222	Americans/America the Beautiful	1973	—	2.50	5.00
❑ 225	How Good You Have It in America/The Strongest Americans	1974	—	2.50	5.00

Albums

WESTBOUND

Number	Title (A Side/B Side)	Yr	VG	VG+	NM
❑ WB-1000	Americans	1974	2.50	5.00	10.00

MACGREGOR, MARY

45s

ARIOLA AMERICA

Number	Title (A Side/B Side)	Yr	VG	VG+	NM
❑ 7638	Torn Between Two Lovers/I Just Want to Love You	1976	—	2.50	5.00
❑ 7662	This Girl (Has Turned Into a Woman)/Good Together	1977	—	2.50	5.00
❑ 7667	For a While/Lady I Am	1977	—	2.50	5.00
❑ 7677	In Your Eyes/I've Never Been to Me	1977	—	2.50	5.00
❑ 7708	Memories/Seashells on the Windows, Candles and a Magic Stone	1978	—	2.50	5.00
❑ 7726	Wedding Song (There Is Love)/Benjamin	1978	—	2.50	5.00

RSO

Number	Title (A Side/B Side)	Yr	VG	VG+	NM
❑ 938	Good Friend/Rudy and Tripper	1979	—	2.00	4.00
❑ 1025	Dancin' Like Lovers/I Can't Hold On	1980	—	2.00	4.00
❑ 1044	Dominoes/Somebody Please	1980	—	2.00	4.00

Albums

ARIOLA AMERICA

Number	Title (A Side/B Side)	Yr	VG	VG+	NM
❑ SMAS-50015	Torn Between Two Lovers	1977	3.00	6.00	12.00
❑ SW-50025	In Your Eyes	1978	3.00	6.00	12.00

RSO

Number	Title (A Side/B Side)	Yr	VG	VG+	NM
❑ RS-1-3083	Mary MacGregor	1979	3.00	6.00	12.00

MACK, BILL

45s

D

Number	Title (A Side/B Side)	Yr	VG	VG+	NM
❑ 1125	John's Back in Town/I'll Come Back	1960	7.50	15.00	30.00

HICKORY

Number	Title (A Side/B Side)	Yr	VG	VG+	NM
❑ 1601	That's Love/That's Why I Cry	1971	2.00	4.00	8.00
❑ 1628	End of the Road/La Donna	1972	2.00	4.00	8.00
❑ 1660	Today I'm Bringing You Roses/Waitin' for the River to Rise	1973	2.00	4.00	8.00

STARDAY

Number	Title (A Side/B Side)	Yr	VG	VG+	NM
❑ 231	Kitty Kat/Fat Woman	1956	62.50	125.00	250.00
❑ 252	Cat Just Got in Town/Sweet Dreams Baby	1956	50.00	100.00	200.00
❑ 280	It's Saturday Night/That's Why I Cry	1957	50.00	100.00	200.00
❑ 313	A Million Miles Away/Cheatin' on Your Mind	1957	12.50	25.00	50.00
❑ 360	Blue/Faded Rose	1958	10.00	20.00	40.00
❑ 418	I'll Still Be Here Tomorrow/Long, Long Train	1959	10.00	20.00	40.00
❑ 453	Johnny's Gal Frankie/Loneliest Fool in Town	1959	10.00	20.00	40.00

MACK, BOBBY

45s

ACE OF HEARTS

Number	Title (A Side/B Side)	Yr	VG	VG+	NM
❑ 0462	Heartaches Caused by You/It's Time to Move Along	1973	—	3.00	6.00
❑ 0467	Love Will Come Again (Just Like the Roses)/A Love Nobody Knows	1973	—	3.00	6.00
❑ 0475	Lovin' Feeling/It's Time to Move Along	1973	—	3.00	6.00
❑ 0483	The Same Old Way/Lovin' Feeling	1974	—	3.00	6.00

MACK, GARY

45s

GRAND PRIZE

Number	Title (A Side/B Side)	Yr	VG	VG+	NM
❑ 5205	I've Been Out of Love Too Long/My Most Requested Song	1983	—	3.00	6.00

SOUNDWAVES

Number	Title (A Side/B Side)	Yr	VG	VG+	NM
❑ 4522	Yesterday Is All the Future (That I'll Ever See)/Hamburger Patty and Dollar Bill	1975	—	3.00	6.00
❑ 4528	To Be with You Again/No Easy Way	1976	—	3.00	6.00
❑ 4532	One Love Down/Mister and Mississippi	1976	—	3.00	6.00
❑ 4538	Throwaway Kind of Love/The One I Dream About	1976	—	3.00	6.00

MACK, VONNIE

45s

COLUMBIA

Number	Title (A Side/B Side)	Yr	VG	VG+	NM
❑ 4-21541	Blue Mountain Waltz/Slowly I'm Losing You	1956	5.00	10.00	20.00

MACK, WARNER

45s

DECCA

Number	Title (A Side/B Side)	Yr	VG	VG+	NM
❑ 9-30301	Is It Wrong (For Loving You)/Baby, Squeeze Me	1957	5.00	10.00	20.00
❑ 9-30471	Rock-a-Chicka/Since I Lost You	1957	6.25	12.50	25.00
❑ 9-30587	That's My Heart's Desire/Falling in Love	1958	5.00	10.00	20.00
❑ 9-30645	Lonesome for You Now/Your Fool	1958	5.00	10.00	20.00
❑ 9-30714	The First Chance I Get/Going Back to School	1958	5.00	10.00	20.00
❑ 31436	Afraid to Look Back/I Wake Up Crying	1962	3.75	7.50	15.00
❑ 31506	Working Girl/I'll Step Out of the Picture	1963	3.00	6.00	12.00
❑ 31559	Surely/This Little Hurt	1963	3.00	6.00	12.00
❑ 31626	The Least Little Thing Would Make Me Stay/I'll Be Alright in the Morning	1964	3.00	6.00	12.00
❑ 31684	Sittin' in an All Nite Cafe/Blue Mood	1964	3.00	6.00	12.00
❑ 31774	The Bridge Washed Out/The Biggest Part of Me	1965	2.50	5.00	10.00
❑ 31853	Sittin' on a Rock (Cryin' in a Creek)/The Way It Feels to Die	1965	2.50	5.00	10.00
❑ 31911	Talkin' to the Wall/One Mile Tall	1966	2.50	5.00	10.00
❑ 32004	It Takes a Lot of Money/A Million Thoughts from My Mind	1966	2.50	5.00	10.00
❑ 32082	Driftin' Apart/When We Are Alone at Night	1967	2.50	5.00	10.00
❑ 32142	How Long Will It Take/As Long As I Keep Wantin' (I'll Keep Wanting You)	1967	2.50	5.00	10.00
❑ 32211	I'd Give the World (To Be Back Loving You)/It's Been a Good Life Loving You	1967	2.50	5.00	10.00
❑ 32308	I'm Gonna Move On/Tell Me to Go	1968	2.00	4.00	8.00
❑ 32365	Pray for Your Country/Be Good to Your Neighbor Every Day	1968	2.00	4.00	8.00
❑ 32394	Don't Wake Me I'm Dreaming/When the Walls Come Tumblin' Down	1968	2.00	4.00	8.00
❑ 32473	Leave My Dream Alone/You're Always Turnin' Up Again	1969	2.00	4.00	8.00
❑ 32547	I'l Still Be Missing You/Sunshine (Bring Back My Sunshine)	1969	2.00	4.00	8.00
❑ 32646	Love Hungry/Love Is Where the Heart Is	1970	2.00	4.00	8.00
❑ 32725	Live for the Good Times/Another Mountain to Climb	1970	2.00	4.00	8.00
❑ 32781	You Make Me Feel Like a Man/Changin' Your Style	1971	2.00	4.00	8.00
❑ 32858	I Wanna Be Loved Completely/Sweetie	1971	—	3.50	7.00
❑ 32926	Draggin' the River/These Arms	1972	—	3.50	7.00
❑ 32982	You're Burnin' My House Down/Your Warm Love	1972	—	3.50	7.00
❑ 33045	Some Roads Have No Ending/I've Got a Feeling	1973	—	3.50	7.00

KAPP

Number	Title (A Side/B Side)	Yr	VG	VG+	NM
❑ 392	Tears for Two/Forever We'll Walk Hand in Hand	1961	3.75	7.50	15.00
❑ 656	Wild Side of Life/Forever We'll Walk Hand in Hand	1965	2.00	4.00	8.00
❑ 903	Drinking Champagne/Waitin'	1968	—	3.50	7.00

LOST GOLD

Number	Title (A Side/B Side)	Yr	VG	VG+	NM
❑ 4	Dasher with the Light Upon His Tail (same on both sides)	1993	—	2.50	5.00

—Green vinyl

MCA

Number	Title (A Side/B Side)	Yr	VG	VG+	NM
❑ 40064	After the Lights Go Out/Then	1973	—	2.50	5.00
❑ 40137	Goodbyes Don't Come Easy/Christie, Christie	1973	—	2.50	5.00
❑ 40398	Don't Bring the Rain Down on Me/One Step Away	1975	—	2.50	5.00
❑ 40452	Baby, You've Built a Fire/Who's Makin' the Changes	1975	—	2.50	5.00
❑ 40516	I've Got a Friend (Just Over the Mountain)/Nothin' Ain't Right	1976	—	2.50	5.00

MOON SHINE

Number	Title (A Side/B Side)	Yr	VG	VG+	NM
❑ 3035	Go Around Again/(B-side unknown)	1985	—	3.00	6.00

PAGEBOY

Number	Title (A Side/B Side)	Yr	VG	VG+	NM
❑ 31	These Crazy Thoughts (Run Through My Mind)/ I Wanna Go Back	1977	—	2.50	5.00

SCARLET

Number	Title (A Side/B Side)	Yr	VG	VG+	NM
❑ 4002	My Love for You/Someone Somewhere	1960	5.00	10.00	20.00

TOP RANK

Number	Title (A Side/B Side)	Yr	VG	VG+	NM
❑ 2053	I'll Run Back to You/Prison of Love	1960	5.00	10.00	20.00

Albums

DECCA

Number	Title	Yr	VG	VG+	NM
❑ DL 4692 [M]	The Bridge Washed Out	1965	5.00	10.00	20.00
❑ DL 4766 [M]	The Country Touch	1966	5.00	10.00	20.00
❑ DL 4883 [M]	Drifting Apart	1967	6.25	12.50	25.00
❑ DL 4912 [M]	Songs We Sand in Church and Home	1967	6.25	12.50	25.00
❑ DL 74692 [S]	The Bridge Washed Out	1965	6.25	12.50	25.00
❑ DL 74766 [S]	The Country Touch	1966	6.25	12.50	25.00
❑ DL 74883 [S]	Drifting Apart	1967	5.00	10.00	20.00
❑ DL 74912 [S]	Songs We Sand in Church and Home	1967	5.00	10.00	20.00
❑ DL 74995	The Many Country Moods of Warner Mack	1968	5.00	10.00	20.00
❑ DL 75092	The Country Beat of Warner Mack	1969	5.00	10.00	20.00
❑ DL 75165	I'll Still Be Missing You	1969	5.00	10.00	20.00

KAPP

Number	Title	Yr	VG	VG+	NM
❑ KL-1255 [M]	Golden Country Hits	1961	5.00	10.00	20.00
❑ KL-1279 [M]	Golden Country Hits, Vol. 2	1962	5.00	10.00	20.00
❑ KL-1461 [M]	Everybody's Country Favorites	196?	3.75	7.50	15.00
❑ KS-3255 [S]	Golden Country Hits	1961	6.25	12.50	25.00
❑ KS-3279 [S]	Golden Country Hits, Vol. 2	1962	6.25	12.50	25.00
❑ KS-3461 [S]	Everybody's Country Favorites	196?	5.00	10.00	20.00

MACKEY, BOBBY

45s

MOON SHINE

Number	Title (A Side/B Side)	Yr	VG	VG+	NM
❑ 3007	Pepsi Man/What a Difference	1982	—	3.00	6.00

MADDOX, ROSE

Also see THE MADDOX BROTHERS AND ROSE; BUCK OWENS.

45s

CAPITOL

Number	Title (A Side/B Side)	Yr	VG	VG+	NM
❑ F4177	Gambler's Love/What Makes Me Hang Around	1959	5.00	10.00	20.00
❑ F4241	Custer's Last Stand/My Little Baby	1959	5.00	10.00	20.00
❑ F4296	I'm Happy Every Day I Live/I Lost Today	1959	5.00	10.00	20.00
❑ 4347	Please Help Me, I'm Falling/Down, Down, Down	1960	3.75	7.50	15.00
❑ 4432	Billy Cline/Shining Silver, Gleaming Gold	1960	3.75	7.50	15.00
❑ 4487	Kissing My Pillow/I Want to Live Again	1960	3.75	7.50	15.00
❑ 4598	Conscience, I'm Guilty/Lonely Street	1961	3.75	7.50	15.00
❑ 4651	There Ain't No Love/Your Kind of Lovin' Won't Do	1961	3.75	7.50	15.00
❑ 4709	Fool Me Again/Here We Go Again	1962	3.75	7.50	15.00
❑ 4771	Take Me Back Again/Let's Pretend We're Strangers	1962	3.75	7.50	15.00
❑ 4845	Sing a Little Song of Heartache/Tie a Ribbon on the Apple Tree	1962	3.75	7.50	15.00
❑ 4905	Lonely Teardrops/George Carter	1963	3.75	7.50	15.00
❑ 4975	Down to the River/I Don't Hear You	1963	3.75	7.50	15.00
❑ 5038	Somebody Told Somebody/Let Me Kiss You for Old Times	1963	3.75	7.50	15.00
❑ 5110	Alone with You/When the Sun Goes Down	1964	3.00	6.00	12.00
❑ 5186	Blue Bird Let Me Tag Along/Stand Up Fool	1964	3.00	6.00	12.00
❑ 5263	Silver Threads and Golden Needles/Tia Lisa Lynn	1964	3.00	6.00	12.00
❑ 5439	I'll Always Be Loving You/Mad at the World	1965	3.00	6.00	12.00

COLUMBIA

Number	Title (A Side/B Side)	Yr	VG	VG+	NM
❑ 4-21016	Take These Shackles/Cocquita of Laredo	1952	6.25	12.50	25.00
❑ 4-21062	Little Willie Waltz/The Hiccough Song	1953	6.25	12.50	25.00
❑ 4-21065	No Help Wanted/Hearts and Flowers	1953	6.25	12.50	25.00
❑ 4-21155	I'm a Little Red Caboose/These Wasted Years	1953	6.25	12.50	25.00
❑ 4-21171	Kiss Me Like Crazy/Just One More Time	1953	6.25	12.50	25.00
❑ 4-21215	The Birthday Card Song/Waltz of the Pines	1954	5.00	10.00	20.00
❑ 4-21253	Poor Little Heartbroken Rose/Marry Me Again	1954	5.00	10.00	20.00
❑ 4-21306	Forever Yours/You Won't Believe This	1954	5.00	10.00	20.00
❑ 4-21333	I Wonder If I Can Lose the Blues/There's No Right Way to Do Me	1954	5.00	10.00	20.00
❑ 4-21345	I Could Never Stop Loving You/Fountain of Youth	1955	5.00	10.00	20.00
❑ 4-21375	Rusty Old Halo/I Gotta Go Get My Baby	1955	5.00	10.00	20.00
❑ 4-21394	Wild Wild Young Men/Second Chance	1955	5.00	10.00	20.00
❑ 4-21419	Hummingbird/Words Are So Easy to Say	1955	5.00	10.00	20.00
❑ 4-21453	Hasty Baby/When the Sun Goes Down	1955	5.00	10.00	20.00
❑ 4-21490	Hey Little Dreamboat/Tall Men	1956	5.00	10.00	20.00
❑ 4-21533	Burrito Jo/False Hearted	1956	5.00	10.00	20.00
❑ 4-21559	The Death of Rock and Roll/Paul Bunyon Love	1956	7.50	15.00	30.00
❑ 4-40814	Looky There, Over There/Your Sweet, Mean Heart	1957	5.00	10.00	20.00
❑ 4-40873	Take a Gamble on Me/1-2-3 Anyplace Road	1957	5.00	10.00	20.00
❑ 4-40948	Old Man Blues/Tomorrow Land	1957	5.00	10.00	20.00
❑ 4-41047	I'll Go Steppin' Too/Let Those Brown Eyes Smile at me	1957	5.00	10.00	20.00

STARDAY

Number	Title (A Side/B Side)	Yr	VG	VG+	NM
❑ 895	The Bigger the Pride/Faded Love	1970	2.00	4.00	8.00
❑ 921	Two of Us/Get It Over	1971	2.00	4.00	8.00

UNI

Number	Title (A Side/B Side)	Yr	VG	VG+	NM
❑ 55040	Bottom of the Glass/Step Right In	1967	2.50	5.00	10.00

Albums

CAPITOL

Number	Title	Yr	VG	VG+	NM
❑ ST 1312 [S]	The One Rose	1960	10.00	20.00	40.00
❑ T 1312 [M]	The One Rose	1960	7.50	15.00	30.00
❑ ST 1437 [S]	Glorybound Train	1960	10.00	20.00	40.00
❑ T 1437 [M]	Glorybound Train	1960	7.50	15.00	30.00
❑ ST 1548 [S]	A Big Bouquet of Roses	1961	10.00	20.00	40.00
❑ T 1548 [M]	A Big Bouquet of Roses	1961	7.50	15.00	30.00
❑ ST 1799 [S]	Rose Maddox Sings Bluegrass	1962	12.50	25.00	50.00
❑ T 1799 [M]	Rose Maddox Sings Bluegrass	1962	10.00	20.00	40.00
❑ ST 1993 [S]	Alone with You	1963	10.00	20.00	40.00
❑ T 1993 [M]	Alone with You	1963	7.50	15.00	30.00

COLUMBIA

Number	Title	Yr	VG	VG+	NM
❑ CL 1159 [M]	Precious Memories	1958	10.00	20.00	40.00

MADDOX BROTHERS AND ROSE

45s

4 STAR

Number	Title (A Side/B Side)	Yr	VG	VG+	NM
❑ 1570	Shimmy Shakin' Daddy/No One Is Sweeter Than You	1951	10.00	20.00	40.00
❑ 1577	Rock All Our Babies to Sleep/The South	1951	10.00	20.00	40.00
❑ 1586	I Wish I Was a Single Girl Again/I Want to Live and Love	1952	7.50	15.00	30.00
❑ 1596	8:30 Blues/Your Love Light Never Shone	1952	7.50	15.00	30.00
❑ 1604	Detour #2/I'll Still Write Your Name in the Sand	1952	7.50	15.00	30.00
❑ 1618	Texas Guitar Stomp/Country Bugle Boy	1952	7.50	15.00	30.00
❑ 1626	I Just Steal Away and Pray/I'd Rather Have Jesus	1953	7.50	15.00	30.00
❑ 1633	The Meanest Man in Town/Rosalie by the Rio	1953	7.50	15.00	30.00
❑ 1639	I'll Fly Away/The Land Where We'll Never Grow Old	1953	7.50	15.00	30.00
❑ 1657	Momma Says It's Naughty/Old Pal of Yesterday	1954	5.00	10.00	20.00
❑ 1664	I'll Never Do It Again/I've Stopped My Dreaming	1954	5.00	10.00	20.00
❑ 1671	Baby You Should Live So Long/You've Been Talking in Your Sleep	1955	5.00	10.00	20.00

COLUMBIA

Number	Title (A Side/B Side)	Yr	VG	VG+	NM
❑ 4-20924	I'll Make Sweet Love to You/Coquita of Laredo	1952	6.25	12.50	25.00
❑ 4-20955	Wedding Blues/I'll Make Sweet	1952	6.25	12.50	25.00
❑ 4-21099	Green Grow the Lilacs/Empty Mansion	1953	6.25	12.50	25.00
❑ 4-21127	I'd Rather Die Young/The Nightingale Song	1953	6.25	12.50	25.00

Number	Title (A Side/B Side)	Yr	VG	VG+	NM
❑ 4-21146	A-Wooin' We Will Go/On Mexico's Beautiful Shore	1953	6.25	12.50	25.00
❑ 4-21181	Kiss Me Quick and Go/I Won't Stand in Your Way	1953	6.25	12.50	25.00
❑ 4-21217	This Is Spring/Beautiful Bouquet	1954	5.00	10.00	20.00
❑ 4-21270	Kiss from Your Lips/Poor Little Heartbroken Roses	1954	5.00	10.00	20.00
❑ 4-21297	Waltz of the Pines/The Life That You've Led	1954	5.00	10.00	20.00
❑ 4-21405	I've Got Four Big Brothers/No More Time	1955	5.00	10.00	20.00
❑ 4-21426	Just Over the Stars/Will There Be Any Stars in My Crown	1955	5.00	10.00	20.00
❑ 4-21466	Old Black Choo Choo/Let This Be the Last Time	1955	5.00	10.00	20.00
❑ 4-21513	Away This Side of Heaven/It's a Dark, Dark Place	1956	5.00	10.00	20.00
❑ 4-21546	I'll Find Her/Wish You Would	1956	5.00	10.00	20.00
❑ 4-40836	Ugly and Slouchy/By the Sweat of My Brow	1957	5.00	10.00	20.00
❑ 4-40895	Love Is Strange/My Life with You	1957	5.00	10.00	20.00
❑ 4-41020	Stop Whistlin' Wolf/Let Me Love You	1957	5.00	10.00	20.00
DECCA					
❑ 9-28478	Jingle Bells/Silent Night	1952	6.25	12.50	25.00
❑ 9-28551	Why Not Confess/Hangover Blues	1953	6.25	12.50	25.00
❑ 9-28784	I'll Be No Stranger There/The Unclouded Day	1953	6.25	12.50	25.00
❑ 9-29279	Yes, He Set Me Free/Gonna Lay My Burden Down	1954	6.25	12.50	25.00
Selected 78s					
4 STAR					
❑ 1184	Midnight Train/Careless Driver	194?	5.00	10.00	20.00
❑ 1185	Milk Cow Blues/I Couldn't Believe It Was True	194?	5.00	10.00	20.00
❑ 1209	Whoa Sailor/Navajo Maiden	194?	5.00	10.00	20.00
❑ 1210	Mean and Wicked Boogie/Sweet Little You	194?	5.00	10.00	20.00
❑ 1238	Honky Tonkin'/Brown Eyes	194?	5.00	10.00	20.00
❑ 1239	Flowers for the Master's Bouquet/Tramp on the Street	194?	5.00	10.00	20.00
❑ 1240	Move It On Over/New Muleskinner Blues	194?	5.00	10.00	20.00
❑ 1271	Time Nor Tide/Gosh, I Miss You All the Time	194?	5.00	10.00	20.00
❑ 1288	Brown Eyes/New Muleskinner Blues	194?	5.00	10.00	20.00
❑ 1289	Philadelphia Lawyer/Sunset Trail	194?	5.00	10.00	20.00
❑ 1301	When God Dips His Love in My Heart/Who at My Door Is Standing	194?	5.00	10.00	20.00
❑ 1322	Last Night I Heard You Crying in Your Sleep/ Honky Tonkin'	1949	5.00	10.00	20.00
❑ 1326	Dear Lord, Take My Hand/Gardens in the Sky	1949	5.00	10.00	20.00
❑ 1328	At the First Fall of Snow/On the Banks of the Old Ponchartrain	1949	5.00	10.00	20.00
❑ 1369	Why Don't You Haul Off and Love Me/George's Playhouse Boogie	1949	5.00	10.00	20.00
❑ 1398	Sally Let Your Bangs Hang Down/You've Been Talking in Your Sleep	1949	5.00	10.00	20.00
❑ 1399	Mule Train/I'm Sending Daffodils	1949	5.00	10.00	20.00
❑ 1400	Jingle Bells/Silent Night	1949	5.00	10.00	20.00
❑ 1440	I Love the Woman/Just One Little Kiss	1950	5.00	10.00	20.00
❑ 1473	We Are Climbing Jacob's Ladder/He Will Set Your Fields on Fire	1950	5.00	10.00	20.00
❑ 1507	Water Baby Blues/Chill in My Heart	1950	5.00	10.00	20.00
❑ 1527	It's Only Human Nature/Oklahoma Sweetheart Sally Anne	1950	5.00	10.00	20.00
❑ 1540	Dark as a Dungeon/Faded Love	1950	5.00	10.00	20.00
❑ 1549	Pay Me Alimony/Now Step It Up and Go	1951	5.00	10.00	20.00
❑ 1553	If We Never Meet Again/How Can You Refuse Him Now	1951	5.00	10.00	20.00
Albums					
KING					
❑ 669 [M]	A Collection of Standard Sacred Songs	1959	37.50	75.00	150.00
❑ 677 [M]	The Maddox Brothers and Rose	1960	30.00	60.00	120.00
❑ 752 [M]	I'll Write Your Name in the Sand	1961	30.00	60.00	120.00
WRANGLER					
❑ W-1003 [M]	The Maddox Brothers and Rose	1962	7.50	15.00	30.00
❑ WS-1003 [S]	The Maddox Brothers and Rose	1962	10.00	20.00	40.00

MAGGARD, CLEDUS

Number	Title (A Side/B Side)	Yr	VG	VG+	NM
45s					
MERCURY					
❑ 55033	The Farmer/Lovin' May Be Dangerous to Your Health	1978	—	2.00	4.00
❑ 55067	The Liquored Up Pick 'Em Up Truck/21.9	1979	—	2.00	4.00
❑ 73751	The White Knight (Short Version)/The White Knight (Long Version)	1975	—	2.00	4.00
❑ 73789	Kentucky Moonrunner/Dad I Gotta Go	1976	—	2.00	4.00
❑ 73823	Virgil and the $300 Vacation/The Banana Bowl	1976	—	2.00	4.00
❑ 73865	Poppin' 'Um/The Torn Flag	1976	—	2.00	4.00
❑ 73897	Yovnoc/Mercy Day	1977	—	2.00	4.00
Albums					
MERCURY					
❑ SRM-1-1072	The White Knight	1976	3.00	6.00	12.00

MAGIC ORGAN, THE

The easy-listening artist (real name: Jerry Smith) saw the below album make the Billboard country LP charts.

Number	Title (A Side/B Side)	Yr	VG	VG+	NM
Albums					
RANWOOD					
❑ R-8092	Street Fair	1972	2.50	5.00	10.00

MAINES BROTHERS BAND, THE

Number	Title (A Side/B Side)	Yr	VG	VG+	NM
45s					
MERCURY					
❑ 814561-7	Louisiana Anna/They Call It Love	1983	—	—	3.00
❑ 818346-7	You Are a Miracle/Dixieland Rock	1984	—	—	3.00
❑ 818944-7	Amarillo Highway/I'll Come Around	1984	—	—	3.00
❑ 880536-7	Everybody Needs Love on Saturday Night/Little Broken Pieces	1985	—	—	3.00
❑ 880995-7	When My Blue Moon Turns to Gold Again/Have You Heard the Latest Blues	1985	—	—	3.00
❑ 884228-7	Some of Shelly's Blues/Roll Truck Roll	1985	—	—	3.00
❑ 884483-7	Danger Zone/Gonna Get Well Tonight	1986	—	—	3.00
❑ 884798-7	What Cha Gonna Do When the Sun Goes Down/ You'll Never Know	1986	—	—	3.00
Albums					
MERCURY					
❑ 814985-1	High Rollin'	1984	2.00	4.00	8.00
❑ 826143-1	The Boys Are Back in Town	1986	2.00	4.00	8.00

MALCHAK, TIM

Number	Title (A Side/B Side)	Yr	VG	VG+	NM
45s					
ALPINE					
❑ 004	Easy Does It/Let Me Down Easy	1986	—	2.50	5.00
❑ 006	Colorado Moon/Let Me Down Easy	1987	—	2.50	5.00
❑ 007	Restless Angel/I Owe It All to You	1987	—	2.50	5.00
❑ 008	It Goes Without Saying/I Owe It All to You	1987	—	2.50	5.00
❑ 009	Not a Night Goes By/I Owe It All to You	1988	—	2.50	5.00
UNIVERSAL					
❑ UVL-66004	Not Like This/I Owe It All to You	1989	—	—	3.00
❑ UVL-66013	If You Had a Heart/Sweet Virginia	1989	—	—	3.00
Albums					
ALPINE					
❑ 1001	Colorado Moon	1987	3.00	6.00	12.00
UNIVERSAL					
❑ UVL-76002	Different Circles	1989	2.50	5.00	10.00

MALCHAK AND RUCKER

Number	Title (A Side/B Side)	Yr	VG	VG+	NM
45s					
ALPINE					
❑ 001	I Could Love You in a Heartbeat/(B-side unknown)	1985	—	2.50	5.00
❑ 002	Let Me Down Easy/I Could Love You in a Heartbeat	1986	—	2.50	5.00
❑ 003	Slow Motion/(B-side unknown)	1986	—	2.50	5.00
❑ 005	Christmas Is For Kids/All I Want For Christmas Is Your Love	1986	—	2.50	5.00
❑ 005 [PS]	Christmas Is for Kids/All I Want for Christmas Is Your Love	1986	—	3.00	6.00
REVOLVER					
❑ 004	Just Like That/(B-side unknown)	1984	—	2.50	5.00
❑ 006	All I Want for Christmas Is Your Love/Christmas Is for Kids	1984	—	2.50	5.00
—Red vinyl					
❑ 006 [PS]	All I Want for Christmas Is Your Love/Christmas Is for Kids	1984	—	3.00	6.00
❑ 007	Why Didn't I Think of That/(B-side unknown)	1985	—	2.50	5.00

MALENA, DON

Number	Title (A Side/B Side)	Yr	VG	VG+	NM
45s					
MAXIMA					
❑ 1256	Ready or Not/Lodi	1986	—	3.00	6.00
❑ 1277	Moonwalkin'/(B-side unknown)	1987	—	3.00	6.00
❑ 1311	Dance for Me/(B-side unknown)	1987	—	3.00	6.00

MALLIE ANN AND SLIM

Number	Title (A Side/B Side)	Yr	VG	VG+	NM
45s					
COLUMBIA					
❑ 4-21223	I Can Hear Harbor Bells/Undo Latch Strings	1954	5.00	10.00	20.00
❑ 4-21273	Love You/Hillbilly Rhumba	1954	6.25	12.50	25.00
❑ 4-21332	Love of Jesus/Better Than Gold	1954	5.00	10.00	20.00
❑ 4-21342	I'll Bear the Shame/There's No Tomorrow for Me	1955	5.00	10.00	20.00
❑ 4-21396	If You Know Where You're Going/I Want to Know More About Jesus	1955	5.00	10.00	20.00
❑ 4-21456	Light Up the Old Flame/I'll Always Love You	1955	5.00	10.00	20.00

MANDRELL, BARBARA

Also see DAVID HOUSTON AND BARBARA MANDRELL.

Number	Title (A Side/B Side)	Yr	VG	VG+	NM
45s					
ABC					
❑ 12362	Tonight/If I Were a River	1978	—	2.00	4.00
❑ 12403	Sleeping Single in a Double Bed/Just One More of Your Goodbyes	1978	—	2.00	4.00
❑ 12451	(If Loving You Is Wrong) I Don't Want to Be Right/ I Feel the Hurt Coming On	1979	—	2.50	5.00
ABC DOT					
❑ 17601	Standing Room Only/Can't Help But Wonder	1975	—	2.00	4.00
❑ 17623	Beginning of the End/That's What Friends Are For	1976	—	2.00	4.00
❑ 17644	Love Is Thin Ice/Will We Ever Make Love In Love Again	1976	—	2.00	4.00
❑ 17668	Midnight Angel/I Count on You	1976	—	2.00	4.00
❑ 17688	Married But Not to Each Other/Fools Gold	1977	—	2.00	4.00
❑ 17716	Hold Me/This Is Not Another Cheatin' Song	1977	—	2.00	4.00
❑ 17736	Woman to Woman/Let the Rain Out	1977	—	2.00	4.00
CAPITOL					
❑ B-44220	I Wish That I Could Fall in Love Today/I'll Be Your Jukebox Tonight	1988	—	—	3.00
❑ B-44276	My Train of Thought/Blanket of Love	1989	—	—	3.00
❑ B-44383	Mirror Mirror/Blanket of Love	1989	—	—	3.00
❑ B-44494	Why Do Bad Things Happen to Good People/You Wouldn't Know Love	1990	—	2.00	4.00

Number	Title (A Side/B Side)	Yr	VG	VG+	NM
CAPITOL NASHVILLE					
❑ 7PRO-79029	You've Become the Dream (same on both sides)	1990	—	2.50	5.00
—Vinyl is promo only					
❑ 7PRO-79334	Men and Trains (same on both sides)	1991	—	2.50	5.00
—Vinyl is promo only					
COLUMBIA					
❑ 10082	Wonder When My Baby's Comin' Home/Kiss the Hurt Away	1974	—	2.50	5.00
❑ 44955	I've Been Loving You Too Long (To Stop Now)/ Baby Come Home	1969	—	3.00	6.00
❑ 45143	Playin' Around with Love/I Almost Lost My Mind	1970	—	2.50	5.00
❑ 45307	Do Right Woman — Do Right Man/The Letter	1971	—	2.50	5.00
❑ 45391	Treat Him Right/Break My Mind	1971	—	2.50	5.00
❑ 45505	Tonight My Baby's Coming Home/He'll Never Take the Place of You	1971	—	2.50	5.00
❑ 45580	Show Me/Satisfied	1972	—	2.50	5.00
❑ 45702	Holdin' On (To the Love I Got)/Smile, Somebody Loves You	1972	—	2.50	5.00
❑ 45819	Give a Little, Take a Little/Ain't It Good	1973	—	2.50	5.00
❑ 45904	The Midnight Oil/In the Name of Love	1973	—	2.50	5.00
❑ 46054	This Time I Almost Made It/Son-of-a-Gun	1974	—	2.50	5.00
EMI AMERICA					
❑ 43032	Child Support/I'm Glad I Married You	1987	—	—	3.00
❑ 43042	Angels Love Bad Men/Sunshine Street	1988	—	—	3.00
EMI MANHATTAN					
❑ 50102	Sure Feels Good/Sunshine Street	1987	—	—	3.00
MCA					
❑ S45-1241 [DJ]	Santa, Bring My Baby Back Home//It Must Have Been the Mistletoe/From Our House to Yours	1984	2.50	5.00	10.00
❑ 12451	(If Loving You Is Wrong) I Don't Want to Be Right/ I Feel the Hurt Coming On	1979	—	2.00	4.00
—Reissue of ABC 12451					
❑ 41077	Fooled by a Feeling/Love Takes a Long Time to Die	1979	—	—	3.00
❑ 41162	Years/Darlin'	1979	—	—	3.00
❑ 41162 [PS]	Years/Darlin'	1979	—	2.00	4.00
❑ 41263	Crackers/Using Him to Get to You	1980	—	—	3.00
❑ 51001	The Best of Strangers/Sometime, Somewhere, Somehow	1980	—	—	3.00
❑ 51062	Love Is Fair/Sometime, Somewhere, Somehow	1981	—	—	3.00
❑ 51107	I Was Country When Country Wasn't Cool/ Woman's Got a Right	1981	—	2.00	4.00
❑ 51171	Wish You Were Here/She's Out There Dancin' Alone	1981	—	—	3.00
❑ 52038	'Till You're Gone/You're Not Supposed to Be Here	1982	—	—	3.00
❑ 52111	Operator, Long Distance Please/Black and White	1982	—	—	3.00
❑ 52206	In Times Like These/Loveless	1983	—	—	3.00
❑ 52258	One of a Kind Pair of Fools/As Well As Can Be Expected	1983	—	—	3.00
❑ 52340	Happy Birthday Dear Heartache/A Man's Not a Man ('Til He's Loved by a Woman)	1984	—	—	3.00
❑ 52397	Only a Lonely Heart Knows/I Wonder What the Rich Folk Are Doin' Tonight	1984	—	—	3.00
❑ 52465	Crossword Puzzle/If It's Not One Thing It's Another	1984	—	—	3.00
❑ 52537	There's No Love in Tennessee/Sincerely I'm Yours	1985	—	—	3.00
❑ 52537 [PS]	There's No Love in Tennessee/Sincerely I'm Yours	1985	—	—	3.00
❑ 52645	Angel in Your Arms/Don't Look in My Eyes	1985	—	—	3.00
❑ 52737	Fast Lanes and Country Roads/You Only You	1985	—	—	3.00
❑ 52737 [DJ]	Fast Lanes and Country Roads (same on both sides)	1985	2.50	5.00	10.00
—Promo only on yellow vinyl					
❑ 52737 [PS]	Fast Lanes and Country Roads/You Only You	1985	—	—	3.00
❑ 52802	When You Get to the Heart/Survivors	1986	—	—	3.00
—With the Oak Ridge Boys					
❑ 52802 [DJ]	When You Get to the Heart (same on both sides)	1986	2.50	5.00	10.00
—Promo only on red vinyl					
❑ 52900	No One Mends a Broken Heart Like You/Love Is Adventure in the Great Unknown	1986	—	—	3.00
MOSRITE					
❑ 190	Queen for a Day/Alone in the Crowd	196?	6.25	12.50	25.00
Albums					
ABC					
❑ AB-1088	Moods	1978	3.00	6.00	12.00
❑ AB-1119	The Best of Barbara Mandrell	1979	3.00	6.00	12.00
ABC DOT					
❑ DOSD-2045	This Is Barbara Mandrell	1976	3.00	6.00	12.00
❑ DOSD-2067	Midnight Angel	1976	3.00	6.00	12.00
❑ DO-2076	Lovers, Friends and Strangers	1977	3.00	6.00	12.00
❑ DO-2098	Love's Ups and Downs	1977	3.00	6.00	12.00
CAPITOL					
❑ C1-90416	I'll Be Your Jukebox Tonight	1988	2.50	5.00	10.00
❑ C1-91977	Morning Sun	1990	3.00	6.00	12.00
COLUMBIA					
❑ C 30967	Treat Him Right	1971	5.00	10.00	20.00
❑ KC 32743	The Midnight Oil	1973	3.75	7.50	15.00
❑ PC 32743	The Midnight Oil	198?	2.00	4.00	8.00
—Budget-line reissue					
❑ KC 32959	This Time I Almost Made It	1974	3.75	7.50	15.00
❑ PC 34876	The Best of Barbara Mandrell	1977	3.00	6.00	12.00
—No bar code on cover					
❑ PC 34876	The Best of Barbara Mandrell	198?	2.00	4.00	8.00
—Reissue with bar code on cover					
❑ FC 37437	Looking Back	1982	2.50	5.00	10.00
❑ PC 37437	Looking Back	198?	2.00	4.00	8.00
—Budget-line reissue					
EMI AMERICA					
❑ ET-46956	Sure Feels Good	1987	2.50	5.00	10.00
MCA					
❑ 641	Midnight Angel	198?	2.00	4.00	8.00
—Reissue of ABC Dot 2067					
❑ 672	This Is Barbara Mandrell	198?	2.00	4.00	8.00
—Reissue of ABC Dot 2045					
❑ 673	Lovers, Friends and Strangers	198?	2.00	4.00	8.00
—Reissue of ABC Dot 2076					
❑ 674	Love's Ups and Downs	198?	2.00	4.00	8.00
—Reissue of ABC Dot 2098					
❑ 3165	Just for the Record	1979	2.50	5.00	10.00
❑ 3280	Moods	1980	2.00	4.00	8.00
—Reissue of ABC 1088					
❑ 5136	Love Is Fair	1980	2.50	5.00	10.00
❑ 5243	Barbara Mandrell Live	1981	2.50	5.00	10.00
❑ 5295	...In Black and White	1982	2.50	5.00	10.00
❑ 5330	He Set My Life to Music	1982	2.50	5.00	10.00
❑ 5377	Spun Gold	1983	2.50	5.00	10.00
❑ 5474	Clean Cut	1984	2.50	5.00	10.00
❑ 5519	Christmas at Our House	1984	3.00	6.00	12.00
❑ 5566	Greatest Hits	1985	2.50	5.00	10.00
❑ 5619	Get to the Heart	1985	2.50	5.00	10.00
❑ 37173	Just for the Record	198?	2.00	4.00	8.00
—Budget-line reissue					
❑ 37202	Moods	198?	—	3.00	6.00
—Budget-line reissue					
❑ 37224	Barbara Mandrell Live	198?	2.00	4.00	8.00
—Budget-line reissue					
PAIR					
❑ PDL1-1079 [(2)]	The Best of Barbara Mandrell	1986	3.00	6.00	12.00

MANDRELL, BARBARA, AND LEE GREENWOOD

Also see each artist's individual listings.

Number	Title (A Side/B Side)	Yr	VG	VG+	NM
45s					
MCA					
❑ 52415	To Me/We Were Meant for Each Other	1984	—	—	3.00
❑ 52525	It Should Have Been Love By Now/Can't Get Too Much of a Good Thing	1985	—	2.00	4.00
Albums					
MCA					
❑ 5477	Meant for Each Other	1984	2.00	4.00	8.00

MANDRELL, LOUISE

Number	Title (A Side/B Side)	Yr	VG	VG+	NM
45s					
EPIC					
❑ 50565	Put It On Me/Yes, I Do	1978	—	2.50	5.00
❑ 50651	Everlasting Love/You Never Cross My Mind	1978	—	2.50	5.00
❑ 50682	Band of Gold/Everlasting Love	1979	—	3.00	6.00
❑ 50752	I Never Loved Anyone Like I Love You/Surrender to My Heart	1979	—	2.50	5.00
❑ 50856	Wake Me Up/That Song Called Forever	1980	—	2.00	4.00
❑ 50896	Beggin' for Mercy/Come Here	1980	—	2.00	4.00
❑ 50935	Love Insurance/When It Hurts You Most	1980	—	2.00	4.00
RCA					
❑ 5115-7-R	Do I Have to Say Goodbye/Keep What We Had Going	1987	—	—	3.00
❑ 5208-7-R	Tender Time/Take Me Back	1987	—	—	3.00
❑ PB-13039	(You Sure Know Your Way) Around My Heart/ Dance Me Around Cowboy	1982	—	2.00	4.00
❑ PB-13039 [PS]	(You Sure Know Your Way) Around My Heart/ Dance Me Around Cowboy	1982	—	3.00	6.00
❑ PB-13278	Some of My Best Friends Are Old Songs/689-Double-2-0-3	1982	—	2.00	4.00
❑ PB-13373	Romance/Better Things to Do	1982	—	2.00	4.00
❑ PB-13450	Save Me/Trust	1983	—	—	3.00
❑ PB-13567	Too Hot to Sleep/We Put On Quite a Show	1983	—	—	3.00
❑ PB-13567 [PS]	Too Hot to Sleep/We Put On Quite a Show	1983	—	2.00	4.00
❑ PB-13649	Runaway Heart/There's More to Love	1983	—	—	3.00
❑ PB-13752	I'm Not Through Loving You Yet/A New Girl in Town	1984	—	—	3.00
❑ PB-13954	This Bed's Not Big Enough/Paying Through the Heart	1984	—	—	3.00
❑ PB-13954 [PS]	This Bed's Not Big Enough/Paying Through the Heart	1984	—	2.00	4.00
❑ PB-14039	Maybe My Baby/Are You Just Playing with Me	1985	—	—	3.00
❑ PB-14151	I Wanna Say Yes/There'll Never Be Another for Me	1985	—	—	3.00
❑ PB-14251	Some Girls Have All the Luck/How Did It Get So Late, So Early	1985	—	—	3.00
❑ PB-14320	Talkin' About My Baby/(B-side unknown)	1986	—	2.00	4.00
❑ PB-14364	I Wanna Hear It from Your Lips/Summer Nights	1986	—	—	3.00
Albums					
EPIC					
❑ FE 37242	Louise Mandrell	1981	2.50	5.00	10.00
❑ PE 37242	Louise Mandrell	198?	2.00	4.00	8.00
—Budget-line reissue					
RCA					
❑ 5622-1-R	Dreamin'	1987	2.50	5.00	10.00
❑ 6714-1-R	The Best of Louise Mandrell	1988	2.00	4.00	8.00
RCA VICTOR					
❑ AHL1-4820	Too Hot to Sleep	1983	2.50	5.00	10.00
❑ AHL1-5015	I'm Not Through Loving You Yet	1984	2.50	5.00	10.00

Number	Title (A Side/B Side)	Yr	VG	VG+	NM
❑ AYL1-5434	Too Hot to Sleep	1985	2.00	4.00	8.00
—"Best Buy Series" reissue					
❑ AHL1-5454	Maybe My Baby	1985	2.50	5.00	10.00
❑ MHL1-8601 [EP]	Close Up	1983	2.00	4.00	8.00

MANDRELL, LOUISE, AND R.C. BANNON

Also see each artist's individual listings.

45s

Number	Title (A Side/B Side)	Yr	VG	VG+	NM
EPIC					
❑ 50668	I Thought You'd Never Ask/Yes, I Do	1979	—	2.00	4.00
❑ 50717	Reunited/Hello There Stranger	1979	—	2.00	4.00
❑ 50789	We Love Each Other/I Want to (Do Everything to You)	1979	—	2.00	4.00
❑ 50951	One False Move (And I'm Yours)/The Pleasure's All Mine	1980	—	2.00	4.00
RCA					
❑ PB-12359	Where There's Smoke There's Fire/Before You	1981	—	2.00	4.00
❑ PB-13095	Our Wedding Band/Just Married	1982	—	2.00	4.00
❑ PB-13321	(Remember Me) I'm the One Who Loves You/We've Got a Secret	1982	—	2.00	4.00
❑ PB-13358	Christmas Is Just a Song for Us This Year/Christmas in Dixie	1982	—	2.50	5.00
—B-side by Alabama					

Albums

Number	Title (A Side/B Side)	Yr	VG	VG+	NM
RCA VICTOR					
❑ AHL1-4059	Me and My RC	1982	2.50	5.00	10.00
❑ AHL1-4377	(You're My) Super Woman/(You're My) Incredible Man	1982	2.50	5.00	10.00

MANN, CARL

45s

Number	Title (A Side/B Side)	Yr	VG	VG+	NM
ABC					
❑ 12035	Burnin' Holes in the Eyes of Abraham Lincoln/Ballad of Johnny Clyde	1974	—	2.50	5.00
❑ 12071	Neon Lights/Just About Out	1975	—	2.50	5.00
❑ 12092	It's Not the Coffee/Cheatin' Time	1975	—	2.50	5.00
ABC/DOT					
❑ 17596	Back Loving/Annie Over Time	1975	—	2.50	5.00
❑ 17621	Twilight Time/Belly-Rubbin' Country Soul	1976	—	2.50	5.00
JAXON					
❑ 502	Gonna Rock and Roll Tonight/Rockin' Love	1957	750.00	1500.	3000.
MONUMENT					
❑ 974	Down to My Last I Forgive You/Serenade of the Bells	1966	3.75	7.50	15.00
PHILLIPS INT'L.					
❑ 3539	Mona Lisa/Foolish One	1959	6.25	12.50	25.00
❑ 3546	Pretend/Rockin' Love	1959	6.25	12.50	25.00
❑ 3550	Some Enchanted Evening/I Can't Forget	1960	6.25	12.50	25.00
❑ 3555	South of the Border/I'm Comin' Home	1960	6.25	12.50	25.00
❑ 3564	The Wayward Wind/Born to Be Bad	1961	6.25	12.50	25.00
❑ 3569	I Ain't Got No Home/If I Could Change You	1961	6.25	12.50	25.00
❑ 3579	When I Grow Too Old to Dream/Mountain Dew	1962	6.25	12.50	25.00

Albums

Number	Title (A Side/B Side)	Yr	VG	VG+	NM
PHILLIPS INT'L.					
❑ PLP-1960 [M]	Like Mann	1960	150.00	300.00	600.00

MANN, LORENE

Also see ARCHIE CAMPBELL; JUSTIN TUBB.

45s

Number	Title (A Side/B Side)	Yr	VG	VG+	NM
RCA VICTOR					
❑ 47-8469	He Gave Me That Too/So I Could Be Your Friend	1964	2.50	5.00	10.00
❑ 47-8583	One of Them/Stranger at the Funeral	1965	2.50	5.00	10.00
❑ 47-8756	Back Where I Started/Don't Take the Children from Me	1966	2.50	5.00	10.00
❑ 47-9045	Don't Put Your Hands on Me/Stay Out of My Dreams	1966	2.00	4.00	8.00
❑ 47-9183	Have You Ever Wanted To?/It Tears Me Up	1967	2.00	4.00	8.00
❑ 47-9288	You Love Me Too Little/I Couldn't Hardly	1967	2.00	4.00	8.00
❑ 47-9776	Indian Santa Claus/I Know My Man Too Well	1969	2.00	4.00	8.00
❑ 74-0184	Tell It All/You Used to Call Me Baby	1969	2.00	4.00	8.00
❑ 74-0638	Hide My Sin/There Is Always One Man	1972	—	3.00	6.00
❑ 74-0704	Hurts and Avis/Stay Out of My Dreams	1972	—	3.00	6.00

Albums

Number	Title (A Side/B Side)	Yr	VG	VG+	NM
RCA VICTOR					
❑ LSP-4243	A Mann Named Lorene	1969	3.75	7.50	15.00

MANNERS, ZEKE

45s

Number	Title (A Side/B Side)	Yr	VG	VG+	NM
CAPITOL					
❑ F1552	Satins and Lace/There's a Rainbow in the Sky	1951	6.25	12.50	25.00
❑ F1906	Piano Players/Good Humoresque Boogie	1951	6.25	12.50	25.00
RCA VICTOR					
❑ 48-0052	There Is Nothin' Like a Dame/When It's Springtime in the Rockies	1949	10.00	20.00	40.00
—Originals on green vinyl					

Selected 78s

Number	Title (A Side/B Side)	Yr	VG	VG+	NM
RCA VICTOR					
❑ 20-1797	Sioux City Sue/Don't Dog Me 'Round	1945	5.00	10.00	20.00
❑ 20-1889	Make with the Music/Nobody's Love Is Like Mine	1946	5.00	10.00	20.00
❑ 20-2013	Inflation/Missouri	1946	5.00	10.00	20.00
❑ 20-2139	Eeny Meeny Dixie Deeny/Fat Man Blues	1947	5.00	10.00	20.00

MANNING, LINDA

45s

Number	Title (A Side/B Side)	Yr	VG	VG+	NM
BULLETIN					
❑ 1000	Our World of Rock & Roll/Sweeter Than Sweet	196?	3.00	6.00	12.00
GAYLORD					
❑ 6425	Thanks a Lot for Everything/Johnny Kiss and Tell	196?	3.00	6.00	12.00
❑ 6429	Turning Back the Tables/Hello Little Lover	1963	3.00	6.00	12.00
MERCURY					
❑ 72803	Someone Up There Still Loves Me/Hurt Me Now	1968	2.00	4.00	8.00
❑ 72875	Since They Fired the Band Director (At Murphy High)/Talk of the Town	1968	2.00	4.00	8.00
❑ 72906	The Peaceful Protest of Charlie McDugg/Billy Christian	1969	2.00	4.00	8.00
❑ 73016	If There's Not a Heaven/Old Memories Don't Die	1970	—	3.50	7.00
❑ 73135	When They Burned Down the Local Motel/Riverboat Queen	1970	—	3.50	7.00
RICE					
❑ 5010	The Girl from Saginaw, Michigan/Boo on You	196?	2.50	5.00	10.00
❑ 5012	Au Revoir (Goodbye)/I Feel a Cry Coming On	196?	2.50	5.00	10.00
❑ 5020	Smoking in Bed/Only for a Moment	196?	2.50	5.00	10.00
❑ 5022	Life Keeps Movin' On/You Wouldn't Know What to Do with It	196?	2.50	5.00	10.00
❑ 5024	No Thanks to You/Bon Jour Tristesse	196?	2.50	5.00	10.00
SOUNDWAVES					
❑ 4792	Out with the Boys/(B-side unknown)	1987	—	2.50	5.00
❑ 4799	You Really Know How to Break a Heart/Out with the Boys	1988	—	2.50	5.00

MANTELLI, STEVE

45s

Number	Title (A Side/B Side)	Yr	VG	VG+	NM
PICAP					
❑ 005	You're a Keep Me Wondering Kind of Woman/(B-side unknown)	1982	2.00	4.00	8.00
❑ 008	I'll Baby You/(B-side unknown)	1982	2.00	4.00	8.00

MAPHIS, JOE

45s

Number	Title (A Side/B Side)	Yr	VG	VG+	NM
COLUMBIA					
❑ 4-21427	Your Old Love Letters/You Ain't Got the Sense (You Were Borned With)	1955	5.00	10.00	20.00
❑ 4-21518	Guitar Rock and Roll/Tennessee Two-Step	1956	7.50	15.00	30.00
❑ 4-21547	Floggin' the Banjo/Bully of the Town	1956	5.00	10.00	20.00
❑ 4-40882	Town Hall Shuffle/Sweet Fern	1957	5.00	10.00	20.00
❑ 4- 41353	Moonshot/Short Recess	1959	3.75	7.50	15.00
❑ 4-41579	Del Rio/Jubilo	1959	3.75	7.50	15.00
LARIAT					
❑ 1106	Lonesome Train Boogie/Square Dance Boogie	195?	10.00	20.00	40.00
MACGREGOR					
❑ 8505	Green River Rag/(B-side unknown)	196?	5.00	10.00	20.00
REPUBLIC					
❑ 2006	Water Baby Boogie/Black Combrero	1960	3.75	7.50	15.00
STARDAY					
❑ 683	Hot Rod Guitar/Lonesome Jailhouse Blues	1964	2.50	5.00	10.00

7-Inch Extended Plays

Number	Title (A Side/B Side)	Yr	VG	VG+	NM
COLUMBIA					
❑ B-10051	*Fire on the Strings/Guitar Rock and Roll/Flying Fingers/Twin Banjo Special	1957	6.25	12.50	25.00
❑ B-10051 [PS]	Joe Maphis	1957	6.25	12.50	25.00

Albums

Number	Title (A Side/B Side)	Yr	VG	VG+	NM
COLUMBIA					
❑ CL 1005 [M]	Fire on the Strings	1957	25.00	50.00	100.00
HARMONY					
❑ HL 7180 [M]	Hi-Fi Holiday for Banjo	1959	6.25	12.50	25.00
❑ HS 11032 [S]	Hi-Fi Holiday for Banjo	1959	7.50	15.00	30.00
KAPP					
❑ KL-1347 [M]	Hootenanny Star	1964	5.00	10.00	20.00
❑ KS-3347 [S]	Hootenanny Star	1964	6.25	12.50	25.00
MACGREGOR					
❑ MGR-1205 [M]	King of the Strings	196?	20.00	40.00	80.00
MOSRITE					
❑ MA-400 [M]	The New Sound of Joe Maphis	1967	7.50	15.00	30.00
❑ MS-400 [S]	The New Sound of Joe Maphis	1967	7.50	15.00	30.00
STARDAY					
❑ SLP-316 [M]	King of the Strings	1966	12.50	25.00	50.00
❑ SLP-373 [M]	Country Guitar Goes to the Jimmy Dean Show	1966	15.00	30.00	60.00
—Deduct 1/3 if instruction book is missing					

MAPHIS, JOE AND JODY

45s

Number	Title (A Side/B Side)	Yr	VG	VG+	NM
CHART					
❑ 5122	If I'm Gonna Have Your Lovin'/Sippin', Pickin' and Flippin'	1971	—	3.50	7.00

MAPHIS, JOE AND ROSE LEE

45s

Number	Title (A Side/B Side)	Yr	VG	VG+	NM
CAPITOL					
❑ 5077	Maple on the Hill/Whiskey Is the Devil in Liquid Form	1963	2.50	5.00	10.00
CHART					
❑ 5029	Gee, Aren't We Lucky/Guitar Happy	1969	2.00	4.00	8.00
❑ 5074	Run That By Me One More Time/I Don't Care	1970	—	3.50	7.00
CMH					
❑ 1520	Somewhere Between/Fiddle Pickin'	1979	—	3.00	6.00

Number	Title (A Side/B Side)	Yr	VG	VG+	NM
COLUMBIA					
❑ 4-21389	Honky Tonk Down Town/Parting of the Way	1955	5.00	10.00	20.00
❑ 4-21479	I Love You Deeply/Fire on the Strings	1956	5.00	10.00	20.00
❑ 4-21568	I'm Willin' to Try/Let's Pull Together	1956	5.00	10.00	20.00
❑ 4-41004	A Picture, a Ring and a Curl/I Gotta Lotta Lovin'	1957	5.00	10.00	20.00
LARIAT					
❑ 1203	Let's Fly Away/You Can't Take the Heart Out of Me	1952	10.00	20.00	40.00
MOSRITE					
❑ 150	Send Me Your Love A.P.O./Write Him a Letter	196?	2.50	5.00	10.00
❑ 290	Tunin' Up for the Blues/Lifetime of Love	1966	2.50	5.00	10.00
❑ 310	Country Girl Courtship/Pickin' and Guttin'	196?	2.50	5.00	10.00
OKEH					
❑ 18013	Black Mountain Rag/Dim Lights, Thick Smoke	195?	6.25	12.50	25.00
❑ 18024	Please Mr. Mailman/I'm a Stranger in My Home	195?	6.25	12.50	25.00
❑ 18029	Henhouse Serenade/Cold Heart of Steel	195?	6.25	12.50	25.00
❑ 18041	Dream House for Sale/The Go'Fer Song	195?	6.25	12.50	25.00
❑ 18051	Devil's Doll/Let's Talk About Love	195?	6.25	12.50	25.00
❑ 18059	Honky Tonk Love Affair/Quicksand	195?	6.25	12.50	25.00
STARDAY					
❑ 675	Hoot'n Annie/Remember, I'm Just As Close As the Phone	1964	2.50	5.00	10.00
❑ 710	Hot Time in Nashville/I've Come to Take You Home	1965	2.50	5.00	10.00
❑ 728	Your Little Black Book/Don't Pass Me By	1965	2.50	5.00	10.00
❑ 745	Ridin' Down Ole 99/Turn On the Bright Lights	1965	2.50	5.00	10.00
Albums					
CAPITOL					
❑ ST 1778 [S]	Rose Lee and Joe Maphis	1962	10.00	20.00	40.00
❑ T 1778 [M]	Rose Lee and Joe Maphis	1962	7.50	15.00	30.00
STARDAY					
❑ SLP-286 [M]	Mr. and Mrs. Country Music	1964	7.50	15.00	30.00
❑ SLP-322 [M]	Golden Gospel	1966	7.50	15.00	30.00

MAPHIS, ROSE LEE

Number	Title (A Side/B Side)	Yr	VG	VG+	NM
Albums					
COLUMBIA					
❑ CL 1598 [M]	Rose Lee Maphis	1961	7.50	15.00	30.00
❑ CS 8398 [S]	Rose Lee Maphis	1961	10.00	20.00	40.00

MARABLE, ABBY

Number	Title (A Side/B Side)	Yr	VG	VG+	NM
45s					
MCA					
❑ 40933	I Want You/Midnight	1978	—	2.50	5.00
❑ 41125	All Alone Am I/Sweet Country Music	1979	—	2.50	5.00

MARCY BROS., THE

Number	Title (A Side/B Side)	Yr	VG	VG+	NM
45s					
ATLANTIC					
❑ 7-87587	The Lady I Love/Why Not Tonight	1991	—	2.00	4.00
❑ 7-87741	She Can/One Less Lonely Heart	1991	—	2.00	4.00
WARNER BROS.					
❑ 7-22659	Missing You/Walkin' Shoes	1990	—	2.00	4.00
❑ 7-22753	You're Not Even Crying/The Things I Didn't Say	1989	—	—	3.00
❑ 7-22956	Cotton Pickin' Time/If Only Your Eyes Could Lie	1989	—	—	3.00
❑ 7-27573	Threads of Gold/You Gotta Learn to Dance	1989	—	—	3.00
❑ 7-27938	The Things I Didn't Say/Nobody Knows-Everybody's Guessin'	1988	—	—	3.00
❑ 7-27938 [PS]	The Things I Didn't Say/Nobody Knows-Everybody's Guessin'	1988	—	2.00	4.00

MARIPAT

Number	Title (A Side/B Side)	Yr	VG	VG+	NM
45s					
OAK					
❑ 1073	No One to Talk To But the Blues/(B-side unknown)	1989	—	3.00	6.00
❑ 1085	I'm Here to Forget/(B-side unknown)	1989	—	3.00	6.00

MARNEY, BEN

Number	Title (A Side/B Side)	Yr	VG	VG+	NM
45s					
SOUTHERN BISCUIT					
❑ 101	Disco Go to Hell/Circle	1981	2.00	4.00	8.00
❑ 107	Where Cheaters Go/Until the Day We Die	1981	—	3.50	7.00

MARR, LEAH

Number	Title (A Side/B Side)	Yr	VG	VG+	NM
45s					
OAK					
❑ 1060	Sealed with a Kiss/(B-side unknown)	1988	—	3.00	6.00
❑ 1071	Half Heaven Half Heartache/(B-side unknown)	1989	—	3.00	6.00
❑ 1084	I've Been a Fool/(B-side unknown)	1989	—	3.00	6.00

MARRIOTT, JOHN

Number	Title (A Side/B Side)	Yr	VG	VG+	NM
45s					
PHOENIX					
❑ 152	Modern Day Cowboy/(B-side unknown)	1989	2.00	4.00	8.00

MARSHALL, ROGER

Number	Title (A Side/B Side)	Yr	VG	VG+	NM
45s					
AVM					
❑ 17	Hocus Pocus/(B-side unknown)	1988	—	3.00	6.00
MASTER					
❑ 05	Take a Letter Maria/(B-side unknown)	1988	—	3.00	6.00

MARSHALL TUCKER BAND, THE

This "Southern rock" band has had more country chart hits (8) than pop chart hits (7).

Number	Title (A Side/B Side)	Yr	VG	VG+	NM
12-Inch Singles					
WARNER BROS.					
❑ PRO-A-816 [DJ]	Running Like the Wind (Edit)/Last of the Singing Cowboys	1979	2.50	5.00	10.00
❑ PRO-A-863 [DJ]	It Takes Time (Single Version)//Sing My Blues/Cattle Drive	1980	3.00	6.00	12.00
45s					
CAPRICORN					
❑ 0021	Can't You See/See You Later, I'm Gone	1973	—	3.00	6.00
❑ 0030	Take the Highway/Jesus Told Me So	1973	—	3.00	6.00
❑ 0049	Another Cruel Love/Blue Ridge Mountain Sky	1974	—	2.50	5.00
❑ 0228	This Ol' Cowboy/Try One More Time	1975	—	2.50	5.00
❑ 0244	Fire on the Mountain/Bop Away My Blues	1975	—	2.50	5.00
❑ 0251	Searchin' for a Rainbow/Walkin' and Talkin'	1976	—	2.50	5.00
❑ 0258	Long Hard Ride/Windy City Blues	1976	—	2.50	5.00
❑ 0270	Heard It in a Love Song/Life in a Song	1977	—	2.50	5.00
❑ 0278	Can't You See/Fly Like an Eagle	1977	—	2.50	5.00
❑ 0300	Dream Lover/A Change Is Gonna Come	1978	—	2.50	5.00
❑ 0307	I'll Be Seeing You/Everybody Needs Somebody	1978	—	2.50	5.00
MERCURY					
❑ 870050-7	Once You Get the Feel of It/Slow Down	1987	—	—	3.00
❑ 870505-7	Dancin' Shoes/I'm Glad It's Gone	1988	—	—	3.00
❑ 872096-7	Still Holdin' On/Same Old Moon	1989	—	—	3.00
❑ 888774-7	Hangin' Out in Smokey Places/He Don't Know	1987	—	—	3.00
WARNER BROS.					
❑ 8841	Last of the Singing Cowboys/Pass It On	1979	—	2.50	5.00
❑ 8841 [PS]	Last of the Singing Cowboys/Pass It On	1979	—	3.00	6.00
❑ 29355	I May Be Easy But You Make It Hard/Shot Down Where You Stand	1984	—	2.00	4.00
❑ 29619	A Place I've Never Been/8:05	1983	—	2.00	4.00
❑ 29939	Reachin' for a Little Bit More/Sweet Elaine	1982	—	2.00	4.00
❑ 29995	Mr. President/The Sea, Dreams and Fairy Tales	1982	—	2.00	4.00
❑ 49068	Running Like the Wind/(B-side unknown)	1979	—	2.50	5.00
❑ 49215	It Takes Time/Jimi	1980	—	2.50	5.00
❑ 49259	Disillusioned/Without You	1980	—	2.00	4.00
❑ 49724	This Time I Believe/Tell the Blues to Take Off the Night	1981	—	2.00	4.00
❑ 49764	Time Has Come/Love Some	1981	—	2.00	4.00
Albums					
CAPRICORN					
❑ CP 0112	The Marshall Tucker Band	1973	3.00	6.00	12.00
❑ CP 0124	A New Life	1974	3.00	6.00	12.00
❑ 2CP 0145 [(2)]	Where We All Belong	1974	3.75	7.50	15.00
❑ CP 0161	Searchin' for a Rainbow	1975	3.00	6.00	12.00
❑ CP 0170	Long Hard Ride	1976	3.00	6.00	12.00
❑ CPK 0180	Carolina Dreams	1977	3.00	6.00	12.00
❑ CP 0205	Together Forever	1978	3.00	6.00	12.00
❑ CP 0214	Greatest Hits	1978	3.00	6.00	12.00
MERCURY					
❑ 832794-1	Still Holdin' On	1988	2.50	5.00	10.00
WARNER BROS.					
❑ BSK 3317	Running Like the Wind	1979	2.50	5.00	10.00
❑ HS 3410	Tenth	1980	2.50	5.00	10.00
❑ HS 3525	Dedicated	1981	2.50	5.00	10.00
❑ BSK 3606	The Marshall Tucker Band	1982	2.50	5.00	10.00
—Reissue of Capricorn 0112					
❑ 2WS 3608 [(2)]	Where We All Belong	1982	3.00	6.00	12.00
—Reissue of Capricorn 0145					
❑ BSK 3609	Searchin' for a Rainbow	1982	2.50	5.00	10.00
—Reissue of Capricorn 0161					
❑ BSK 3610	Carolina Dreams	1982	2.50	5.00	10.00
—Reissue of Capricorn 0180					
❑ BSK 3611	Greatest Hits	1982	2.50	5.00	10.00
—Reissue of Capricorn 0214					
❑ BSK 3662	A New Life	1982	2.50	5.00	10.00
—Reissue of Capricorn 0124					
❑ BSK 3663	Long Hard Ride	1982	2.50	5.00	10.00
—Reissue of Capricorn 0170					
❑ BSK 3664	Together Forever	1982	2.50	5.00	10.00
—Reissue of Capricorn 0205					
❑ BSK 3684	Tuckerized	1982	2.50	5.00	10.00
❑ 23803	Just Us	1983	2.50	5.00	10.00

MARTEL, MARTY

Number	Title (A Side/B Side)	Yr	VG	VG+	NM
45s					
RIDGETOP					
❑ 00379	I Can Feel It/(B-side unknown)	1979	—	3.00	6.00
❑ 00679	First Step/(B-side unknown)	1979	—	3.00	6.00

MARTELL, LINDA

Number	Title (A Side/B Side)	Yr	VG	VG+	NM
45s					
PLANTATION					
❑ 24	Color Him Father/I Almost Called Your Name	1969	—	3.00	6.00
❑ 35	Before the Next Teardrop Falls/Tender Leaves of Love	1969	—	3.00	6.00
❑ 46	Bad Case of the Blues/Old Letter Song	1970	—	3.00	6.00
❑ 67	You're Crying Boy, Crying/The Wedding Cake	1971	—	3.00	6.00
Albums					
PLANTATION					
❑ 9	Color Me Country	1970	3.75	7.50	15.00

MARTIN, BENNY

Also see DON RENO AND BENNY MARTIN.

45s

Number	Title (A Side/B Side)	Yr	VG	VG+	NM
DECCA					
❑ 9-30712	Border Baby/My Fortune	1958	5.00	10.00	20.00
❑ 9-30935	Untrue You/If I Can Stay Away Long Enough	1959	5.00	10.00	20.00
❑ 9-31050	Top Gun/Going Down This Road	1960	5.00	10.00	20.00
GULF REEF					
❑ 1005	Thinking About Love/The Man Next Door	196?	5.00	10.00	20.00
JAB					
❑ 9002	I'm a Father Alone/Salvation Army	1967	2.00	4.00	8.00
MERCURY					
❑ 70476	Read Between the Lines/Secret of Your Heart	1954	7.50	15.00	30.00
❑ 70508	Me and My Fiddle/The Law of My Heart	1954	7.50	15.00	30.00
❑ 70560	Ice Cold Love/You Know That I Know	1955	7.50	15.00	30.00
❑ 70664	Take My Word/Who Put Those Tears in Your Eyes	1955	7.50	15.00	30.00
❑ 70731	Yes, It's True/I'm Right and You're Wrong	1955	7.50	15.00	30.00
❑ 70794	If I Didn't Have a Conscience/You're Guilty Darlin'	1956	7.50	15.00	30.00
❑ 70883	Lover of the Town/Whippoor-Will	1956	7.50	15.00	30.00
RCA VICTOR					
❑ 47-6855	That's the Story of My Life/Look What You've Done	1957	6.25	12.50	25.00
❑ 47-7003	I Saw Your Face in the Moon/Torch of Love	1957	6.25	12.50	25.00
❑ 47-7100	Do Me a Favor/(B-side unknown)	1957	6.25	12.50	25.00
STARDAY					
❑ 519	A Dime's Worth of Dreams/Pretty Girl	1960	5.00	10.00	20.00
❑ 536	You Are the One/No One But You	1961	3.75	7.50	15.00
❑ 623	Rosebuds and You/Sinful Cinderella	1963	3.75	7.50	15.00
❑ 646	Down in the Shinnery/Two Take Away One Equals Lonesome	1963	3.75	7.50	15.00
❑ 705	Stick Your Finger in a Glass of Water/The Other Me	1964	3.75	7.50	15.00
❑ 725	One Way or the Other/Weekend Ellie	1965	3.00	6.00	12.00
❑ 743	Hello City Limits/I'll Never Get Over Loving You	1965	3.00	6.00	12.00

Albums

Number	Title	Yr	VG	VG+	NM
STARDAY					
❑ SLP-131 [M]	Country Music's Sensational Entertainer	1961	12.50	25.00	50.00

MARTIN, BETTY

45s

Number	Title (A Side/B Side)	Yr	VG	VG+	NM
DOOR KNOB					
❑ 071	Don't You Feel It Now/I Love Being Lied To	1978	—	2.50	5.00
❑ 086	One of Us/I Love Being Lied To	1978	—	2.50	5.00

MARTIN, BOBBI

45s

Number	Title (A Side/B Side)	Yr	VG	VG+	NM
BUDDAH					
❑ 217	No Love at All/A Place for Me	1971	—	2.00	4.00
❑ 227	Devotion/A Place for Me	1971	—	2.00	4.00
❑ 253	Tomorrow/Sentimental Journey	1971	—	2.00	4.00
❑ 286	Something Tells Me (Something's Gonna Happen Tonight)/Give Me a Star to Live On	1972	—	2.00	4.00
CORAL					
❑ 62263	I Need Your Love/Cry, Cry, Cry (I Never Thought I'd Make You Cry)	1961	2.00	4.00	8.00
❑ 62285	Wooden Heart/How Should I Cry	1961	2.00	4.00	8.00
❑ 62321	Forgive Me/Tired and Blue	1962	2.00	4.00	8.00
❑ 62340	Afraid/Brenda, Brenda	1962	2.00	4.00	8.00
❑ 62351	I'll Never Stop Loving You/Why, Tell Me Why	1963	2.00	4.00	8.00
❑ 62384	"A" You're Adorable/A Girl's Prayer	1963	2.00	4.00	8.00
❑ 62410	I'm a Fool (To Go On Loving You)/Does Your Heart Hurt a Little	1964	—	3.00	6.00
❑ 62426	Don't Forget I Still Love You/On the Outside (Looking In)	1964	—	3.00	6.00
❑ 62447	I Can't Stop Thinking of You/A Million Thanks to You	1965	—	3.00	6.00
❑ 62452	I Love You So/When Will the Torch Go Out	1965	—	3.00	6.00
❑ 62452 [PS]	I Love You So/When Will the Torch Go Out	1965	2.50	5.00	10.00
❑ 62457	Holding Back the Tears/I Don't Want to Love	1965	—	3.00	6.00
❑ 62466	Auf Wiedersehn Good Bye/There Are No Rules	1965	—	3.00	6.00
❑ 62472	Just One Time/Trying to Get You Off My Mind	1965	—	3.00	6.00
❑ 62475	Don't Take It Out on Me/Something on My Mind	1965	—	3.00	6.00
❑ 62485	I Can Give You Love/Sometimes	1966	—	3.00	6.00
❑ 62488	Oh, Lonesome Me/It's a Sin to Tell a Lie	1966	—	3.00	6.00
❑ 62503	Just As Much As Ever/You Have No Idea	1966	—	3.00	6.00
❑ 62512	Anytime/How Long	1967	—	3.00	6.00
MGM					
❑ 14587	Smile for Me/Now Lonely Is Only a Word	1973	—	2.00	4.00
UNITED ARTISTS					
❑ 0148	For the Love of Him/I Think of You	1973	—	2.00	4.00
—"Silver Spotlight Series" reissue					
❑ 50253	Only You (And You Alone)/Would You Believe	1968	—	2.50	5.00
❑ 50297	A Man and a Woman/Before You	1968	—	2.50	5.00
❑ 50443	Harper Valley P.T.A./He Called Me Baby	1968	—	2.50	5.00
❑ 50456	I Love Him/I Think of You	1968	—	2.50	5.00
❑ 50523	Your Cheatin' Heart/Tennessee Waltz	1969	—	2.50	5.00
❑ 50602	For the Love of Him/I Think of You	1969	—	2.50	5.00
❑ 50687	Goin' South/Give a Woman Love	1970	—	2.50	5.00
❑ 50728	No Love at All/What Greater Love	1970	—	2.50	5.00

Albums

Number	Title	Yr	VG	VG+	NM
BUDDAH					
❑ BDS-5090	Tomorrow	1971	3.00	6.00	12.00
CORAL					
❑ CRL 57472 [M]	Don't Forget I Still Love You	1965	3.75	7.50	15.00
❑ CRL 57478 [M]	I Love You So	1965	3.75	7.50	15.00
❑ CRL 757472 [S]	Don't Forget I Still Love You	1965	5.00	10.00	20.00
❑ CRL 757478 [S]	I Love You So	1965	5.00	10.00	20.00
SUNSET					
❑ SUS-5319	Thinking of You	197?	2.50	5.00	10.00
UNITED ARTISTS					
❑ UAS-6668	Harper Valley P.T.A.	1968	3.00	6.00	12.00
❑ UAS-6700	For the Love of Him	1969	3.00	6.00	12.00
❑ UAS-6755	With Love	1970	3.00	6.00	12.00
VOCALION					
❑ VL 73906	Have You Ever Been Lonely	196?	2.50	5.00	10.00

MARTIN, DEAN

Once his career gained a second wind in 1964 with the hit "Everybody Loves Somebody," Martin frequently covered country hits. Some were authentic enough to garner attention from the country music establishment. The below list includes only his Reprise material and beyond starting with "Everybody Loves Somebody."

45s

Number	Title (A Side/B Side)	Yr	VG	VG+	NM
REPRISE					
❑ PRO 248 [DJ]	White Christmas (same on both sides)	1966	2.50	5.00	10.00
❑ 0281	Everybody Loves Somebody/A Little Voice	1964	2.50	5.00	10.00
❑ 0307	The Door Is Still Open to My Heart/Every Minute, Every Hour	1964	2.00	4.00	8.00
❑ 0333	You're Nobody Till Somebody Loves You/You'll Always Be the One I Love	1964	2.00	4.00	8.00
❑ 0344	Send Me the Pillow You Dream On/I'll Be Seeing You	1965	2.00	4.00	8.00
❑ 0369	(Remember Me) I'm the One Who Loves You/Born to Lose	1965	2.00	4.00	8.00
❑ 0393	Houston/Bumming Around	1965	2.00	4.00	8.00
❑ 0415	I Will/You're the Reason I'm in Love	1965	2.00	4.00	8.00
❑ 0443	Somewhere There's a Someone/That Old Clock on the Wall	1965	2.00	4.00	8.00
❑ 0466	Come Running Back/Bouquet of Roses	1966	—	3.00	6.00
❑ 0500	A Million and One/Shades	1966	—	3.00	6.00
❑ 0516	Nobody's Baby Again/It Just Happened That Way	1966	—	3.00	6.00
❑ 0538	(Open Up the Door) Let the Good Times In/I'm Not the Marrying Kind	1966	—	3.00	6.00
❑ 0542	Blue Christmas/A Marshmallow World	1966	—	3.00	6.00
❑ 0571	Lay Some Happiness on Me/Think About Me	1967	—	3.00	6.00
❑ 0601	In the Chapel in the Moonlight/Welcome to My World	1967	—	3.00	6.00
❑ 0608	Little Ole Wine Drinker, Me/I Can't Help Remembering You	1967	—	3.00	6.00
❑ 0640	In the Misty Moonlight/Wallpaper Roses	1967	—	3.00	6.00
❑ 0640	In the Misty Moonlight/The Glory of Love	1967	—	3.00	6.00
❑ 0672	You've Still Got a Place in My Heart/Old Yellow Line	1968	—	2.50	5.00
❑ 0703	Lay Some Happiness on Me/(Open Up the Door) Let the Good Times In	1968	—	2.50	5.00
❑ 0709	Everybody Loves Somebody/A Million and One	1968	—	2.50	5.00
❑ 0711	Somewhere There's a Someone/Come Running Back	1968	—	2.50	5.00
❑ 0714	Houston/I Will	1968	—	2.50	5.00
❑ 0717	You're Nobody Till Somebody Loves You/(Remember Me) I'm the One Who Loves You	1968	—	2.50	5.00
❑ 0718	Send Me the Pillow You Dream On/The Door Is Still Open to My Heart	1968	—	2.50	5.00
❑ 0730	In the Chapel in the Moonlight/Little Ole Wine Drinker, Me	1968	—	2.50	5.00
❑ 0735	In the Misty Moonlight/Not Enough Indians	1970	—	2.00	4.00
—0703 through 0735 are "Back to Back Hits" reissues					
❑ 0761	April Again/That Old Time Feelin'	1968	—	2.50	5.00
❑ 0765	Five Card Stud/One Lonely Boy	1968	—	2.50	5.00
❑ 0780	Not Enough Indians/Rainbows Are Back in Style	1968	—	2.50	5.00
❑ 0812	Gentle on My Mind/That's When I See the Blues	1969	—	2.50	5.00
❑ 0841	I Take a Lot of Pride in What I Am/Drowning in My Tears	1969	—	2.50	5.00
❑ 0857	Crying TIme/One Cup of Happiness	1969	—	2.50	5.00
❑ 0893	Down Home/Come On Down	1970	—	2.50	5.00
❑ 0915	For the Love of a Woman/The Tracks of My Tears	1970	—	2.50	5.00
❑ 0934	My Woman, My Woman, My Wife/Here We Go Again	1970	—	2.50	5.00
❑ 0955	Detroit City/Turn the World Around	1970	—	2.50	5.00
❑ 0973	For the Good Times/Georgia Sunshine	1970	—	2.50	5.00
❑ 1004	She's a Little Bit Country/Raining in My Heart	1971	—	2.50	5.00
❑ 1060	What's Yesterday/The Right Kind of Woman	1971	—	2.50	5.00
❑ 1085	I Can Give You What You Want Now/Guess Who	1972	—	2.50	5.00
❑ 1141	Amor Mio/You Made Me Love You	1972	—	2.50	5.00
❑ 1166	Smile/Get On With Your Livin'	1973	—	2.50	5.00
❑ 1178	You're the Best Thing That Ever Happened to Me/Free to Carry On	1973	—	2.50	5.00
WARNER BROS.					
❑ 29480	Drinking Champagne/Since I Met You Baby	1983	—	2.00	4.00
❑ 29584	My First Country Song/Hangin' Around	1983	—	2.00	4.00

Albums

Number	Title	Yr	VG	VG+	NM
REPRISE					
❑ MS 2053	Dino	1972	3.75	7.50	15.00
❑ MS 2174	You're the Best Thing That Ever Happened to Me	1973	3.75	7.50	15.00
❑ MS 2267	Once in a Lifetime	1978	3.00	6.00	12.00
❑ R-6061 [M]	Country Style	1963	3.75	7.50	15.00
❑ R9-6061 [S]	Country Style	1963	5.00	10.00	20.00
❑ R-6085 [M]	Dean "Tex" Martin Rides Again	1963	3.75	7.50	15.00

Number	Title (A Side/B Side)	Yr	VG	VG+	NM
❑ R9-6085 [S]	Dean "Tex" Martin Rides Again	1963	5.00	10.00	20.00
❑ R-6123 [M]	Dream with Dean	1964	3.00	6.00	12.00
❑ RS-6123 [S]	Dream with Dean	1964	3.75	7.50	15.00
❑ R-6130 [M]	Everybody Loves Somebody	1964	3.00	6.00	12.00
❑ RS-6130 [S]	Everybody Loves Somebody	1964	3.75	7.50	15.00
❑ R-6140 [M]	The Door Is Still Open to My Heart	1964	3.00	6.00	12.00
❑ RS-6140 [S]	The Door Is Still Open to My Heart	1964	3.75	7.50	15.00
❑ R-6146 [M]	Dean Martin Hits Again	1965	3.00	6.00	12.00
❑ RS-6146 [S]	Dean Martin Hits Again	1965	3.75	7.50	15.00
❑ R-6170 [M]	(Remember Me) I'm the One Who Loves You	1965	3.00	6.00	12.00
❑ RS-6170 [S]	(Remember Me) I'm the One Who Loves You	1965	3.75	7.50	15.00
❑ R-6181 [M]	Houston	1965	3.00	6.00	12.00
❑ RS-6181 [S]	Houston	1965	3.75	7.50	15.00
❑ R-6201 [M]	Somewhere There's a Someone	1966	3.00	6.00	12.00
❑ RS-6201 [S]	Somewhere There's a Someone	1966	3.75	7.50	15.00
❑ R-6211 [M]	The Silencers	1966	5.00	10.00	20.00
❑ RS-6211 [S]	The Silencers	1966	6.25	12.50	25.00
❑ R-6213 [M]	The Hit Sound of Dean Martin	1966	3.00	6.00	12.00
❑ RS-6213 [S]	The Hit Sound of Dean Martin	1966	3.75	7.50	15.00
❑ R 6222 [M]	The Dean Martin Christmas Album	1966	3.75	7.50	15.00
❑ RS 6222 [S]	The Dean Martin Christmas Album	1966	5.00	10.00	20.00
❑ R-6233 [M]	The Dean Martin TV Show	1966	3.00	6.00	12.00
❑ RS-6233 [S]	The Dean Martin TV Show	1966	3.75	7.50	15.00
❑ R-6242 [M]	Happiness Is Dean Martin	1967	3.75	7.50	15.00
❑ RS-6242 [S]	Happiness Is Dean Martin	1967	3.75	7.50	15.00
❑ R-6250 [M]	Welcome to My World	1967	3.75	7.50	15.00
❑ RS-6250 [S]	Welcome to My World	1967	3.75	7.50	15.00
❑ RS-6301	Dean Martin's Greatest Hits! Vol. 1	1968	3.75	7.50	15.00
❑ RS-6320	Dean Martin's Greatest Hits! Vol. 2	1968	3.75	7.50	15.00
❑ RS-6330	Gentle on My Mind	1968	3.75	7.50	15.00
❑ RS-6338	I Take a Lot of Pride in What I Am	1969	3.75	7.50	15.00
❑ RS-6403	My Woman, My Woman, My Wife	1970	3.75	7.50	15.00
❑ RS-6428	For the Good Times	1971	3.75	7.50	15.00

WARNER BROS.

Number	Title (A Side/B Side)	Yr	VG	VG+	NM
❑ 23870	The Nashville Sessions	1983	3.00	6.00	12.00

MARTIN, GRADY

Also see BING CROSBY; BURL IVES; MERVIN SHINER; DICK TODD.

45s

DECCA

Number	Title (A Side/B Side)	Yr	VG	VG+	NM
❑ 25525	Boom Boom/Somebody Stole My Gal	196?	2.00	4.00	8.00
❑ 25553	Wedding Bells/Three O'Clock in the Morning	196?	2.00	4.00	8.00
❑ 25568	City Lights/Fraulein	196?	2.00	4.00	8.00
❑ 25589	Ol' Man River/Colonel Bogey March	196?	2.00	4.00	8.00
❑ 25605	Anytime/Down the River of Golden Dreams	196?	2.00	4.00	8.00
❑ 25617	Let Me Call You Sweetheart/Beautiful Brown Eyes	196?	2.00	4.00	8.00
❑ 25629	Melody of Love/Around the World	1964	2.00	4.00	8.00
❑ 25642	Heartaches by the Number/The Velvet Glove	1964	2.00	4.00	8.00
❑ 25668	He'll Have to Go/Bully of the Town	1965	2.00	4.00	8.00
❑ 25676	Ring of Fire/Forever	1965	2.00	4.00	8.00
❑ 25688	Japanese Sandman/The South	196?	2.00	4.00	8.00
❑ 25695	That Old Gang of Mine/Wabash Blues	196?	2.00	4.00	8.00
❑ 25705	Singing the Blues/River, Stay 'Way from My Door	196?	—	3.00	6.00
❑ 25708	Lazy River/Tennessee Waltz	196?	—	3.00	6.00
❑ 25711	Swanee River/Dragnet	196?	—	3.00	6.00
❑ 25714	Mary Lou/Side by Side	196?	—	3.00	6.00
❑ 25719	Lara's Theme from Doctor Zhivago/At Sundown	196?	—	3.00	6.00
❑ 25726	Ka-Lu-A/Drifting and Dreaming	196?	—	3.00	6.00
❑ 25733	Swingin' Down the Lane/What'll I Do	196?	—	3.00	6.00
❑ 25739	Born Free/San Antonio Rose	196?	—	3.00	6.00
❑ 25749	Alley Cat/I Wanna Be Around	196?	—	3.00	6.00
❑ 9-27838	Stardust/Beer Barrel Polka	1951	6.25	12.50	25.00
❑ 9-28074	Get Up and Give/Don't Stay Away	1952	5.00	10.00	20.00
❑ 9-28231	Night and Day/You Are the Light o' My Life	1952	5.00	10.00	20.00
❑ 9-28388	I Went to Your Wedding/You Belong to Me	1952	5.00	10.00	20.00
❑ 9-28472	Anniversary Song/Happy Birthday	1952	5.00	10.00	20.00
❑ 9-28497	Sioux City Sue/September Song	1952	5.00	10.00	20.00
❑ 9-28588	A Fool Such as I/Side by Side	1953	5.00	10.00	20.00
❑ 9-28613	Shenanigans (Part 1)/Shenanigans (Part 2)	1953	5.00	10.00	20.00
❑ 9-28689	Bandera/Poor Butterfly	1953	5.00	10.00	20.00
❑ 9-28845	Dragnet/The Velvet Glove	1953	5.00	10.00	20.00
❑ 9-28987	Bimbo/Mexicali Rose	1954	5.00	10.00	20.00
❑ 9-29146	Isle of Capri/Twelfth Street Rag	1954	5.00	10.00	20.00
❑ 9-29213	Jalousie/Alexander's Ragtime Band	1954	5.00	10.00	20.00
❑ 9-29328	A Pretty Girl Is Like a Melody/What's the Use	1954	5.00	10.00	20.00
❑ 9-29468	Long John Boogie/Gorgeous	1955	3.75	7.50	15.00
❑ 9-29558	Singing the Blues Till My Daddy Comes Home/Hot Lips	1955	3.75	7.50	15.00
❑ 9-29691	Don't Take Your Love from Me/Nashville	1955	3.75	7.50	15.00
❑ 9-30022	Allegheny Moon/When My Dreamboat Comes Home	1956	3.75	7.50	15.00
❑ 9-30196	Keep It Movin'/Somebody Stole My Girl	1957	3.75	7.50	15.00
❑ 9-30453	All the Way/Chicago	1957	3.75	7.50	15.00
❑ 9-30940	Hey Chick/Tuxedo Junction	1959	3.00	6.00	12.00
❑ 9-31013	Elmer's Tune/You've Got Me Crying Again	1959	3.00	6.00	12.00
❑ 31211	The Fuzz/Tippin' In	1961	3.00	6.00	12.00
❑ 31381	Twist and Turn/Good, Good, Good	1962	2.50	5.00	10.00
❑ 31691	Theme from "Malamondo" (Funny World)/El Paso	1964	2.50	5.00	10.00
❑ 31885	May the Bird of Paradise Fly Up Your Nose/The Battle of New Orleans	1965	2.50	5.00	10.00
❑ 31990	Double-o-Dobro/Last Letter	1966	2.50	5.00	10.00
❑ 32099	Kaw-Liga/Heartless Woman	1967	2.00	4.00	8.00
❑ 32173	Ribbon of Darkness/Don't Let the Stars Get In Your Eyes	1967	2.00	4.00	8.00
❑ 9-46375	San Antonio Rose/Bully of the Town	1951	6.25	12.50	25.00

7-Inch Extended Plays

DECCA

Number	Title (A Side/B Side)	Yr	VG	VG+	NM
❑ ED 2747	*Colonel Bogey March/Fraulein/Happy Birthday/Red River Valley	1963	2.50	5.00	10.00
❑ ED 2747 [PS]	Happy Birthday	1963	2.50	5.00	10.00

Albums

DECCA

Number	Title (A Side/B Side)	Yr	VG	VG+	NM
❑ DL 4072 [M]	Big City Lights	1960	5.00	10.00	20.00
❑ DL 4286 [M]	Swingin' Down the River	1962	3.75	7.50	15.00
❑ DL 4476 [M]	Songs Everybody Knows	1963	3.75	7.50	15.00
❑ DL 5566 [10]	Dance-O-Rama	1955	50.00	100.00	200.00
❑ DL 8181 [M]	Powerhouse Dance Party	1955	7.50	15.00	30.00
❑ DL 8292 [M]	Juke Box Jamboree	1956	7.50	15.00	30.00
❑ DL 8648 [M]	The Roaring Twenties	1957	7.50	15.00	30.00
❑ DL 8883 [M]	Hot Time Tonight	1959	5.00	10.00	20.00
❑ DL 74072 [S]	Big City Lights	1960	6.25	12.50	25.00
❑ DL 74286 [S]	Swingin' Down the River	1962	5.00	10.00	20.00
❑ DL 74476 [S]	Songs Everybody Knows	1963	5.00	10.00	20.00
❑ DL 78883 [S]	Hot Time Tonight	1959	6.25	12.50	25.00

MARTIN, GYPSY

45s

OMNI

Number	Title (A Side/B Side)	Yr	VG	VG+	NM
❑ 61581	This Ain't Tennessee and He Ain't You/(B-side unknown)	1981	2.00	4.00	8.00

MARTIN, J.D.

45s

CAPITOL

Number	Title (A Side/B Side)	Yr	VG	VG+	NM
❑ B-5573	Running Out of Reasons to Run/Wrap Me Up in Your Love	1986	—	—	3.00
❑ B-5606	Wrap Me Up in Your Love/Hold On	1986	—	—	3.00

MARTIN, JIMMY

45s

DECCA

Number	Title (A Side/B Side)	Yr	VG	VG+	NM
❑ 9-30493	I'll Drink No More Wine/Skip, Hop and Wobble	1957	3.75	7.50	15.00
❑ 9-30613	Ocean of Diamonds/Sophronic	1958	3.75	7.50	15.00
❑ 9-30703	Rock Hearts/I'll Never Take No for an Answer	1958	5.00	10.00	20.00
❑ 9-30812	The Voice of My Savior/I Like to Hear 'Em Preach It	1959	3.75	7.50	15.00
❑ 9-30877	Night/It's Not Like Home	1959	3.75	7.50	15.00
❑ 9-30965	Hold Whatcha Got/She's Left Me	1959	3.75	7.50	15.00
❑ 31073	The Joke's on You/Foggy Old London	1960	3.00	6.00	12.00
❑ 31157	Bear Tracks/You Don't Know My Mind	1960	3.00	6.00	12.00
❑ 31176	An Old-Fashioned Christmas/Hold to God's Unchanging Hand	1960	3.00	6.00	12.00
❑ 31234	Hi-De Diddle/My Walking Shoes	1961	3.00	6.00	12.00
❑ 31311	I Can, I Will, I Do Believe/There Was a Love	1961	3.00	6.00	12.00
❑ 31376	God Is Always the Same/God, Guide Our Leader's Hand	1962	3.00	6.00	12.00
❑ 31414	Don't Cry to Me/Poor Little Bullfrog	1962	3.00	6.00	12.00
❑ 31442	The Shut-In's Prayer/Prayer Bell of Heaven	1962	3.00	6.00	12.00
❑ 31461	Hey Lonesome/The Old Man's Drunk Again	1963	2.50	5.00	10.00
❑ 31558	Widow Maker/Red River Valley	1963	2.50	5.00	10.00
❑ 31629	I'd Rather Have America/Leavin' Town	1964	2.50	5.00	10.00
❑ 31680	Guitar Picking President/It Takes One to Know One	1964	2.50	5.00	10.00
❑ 31748	20-20 Vision/Sunny Side of the Mountain	1965	2.50	5.00	10.00
❑ 31846	Sweet Dixie/Last Song	1965	2.50	5.00	10.00
❑ 31921	I Can't Quit Cigarettes/Run Boy Run	1966	2.00	4.00	8.00
❑ 31987	Goodbye/Who'll Sing for Me	1966	2.00	4.00	8.00
❑ 32031	Home Run Man/You're Gonna Change (Or I'm Gonna Leave)	1966	2.00	4.00	8.00
❑ 32092	Give Me the Roses Now/Pray the Clouds Away	1967	2.00	4.00	8.00
❑ 32132	Living Like a Fool/The Big Country	1967	2.00	4.00	8.00
❑ 32201	Goin' Ape/The Wild Indian	1967	2.00	4.00	8.00
❑ 32300	Tennessee/Steal Away Somewhere and Die	1968	2.00	4.00	8.00
❑ 32378	Losing You/Free Born Man	1968	2.00	4.00	8.00
❑ 32461	Red Rooster/Moonshine Hollow	1969	2.00	4.00	8.00
❑ 32517	Give Me Your Hand/Little White Church	1969	—	3.50	7.00
❑ 32553	Shackles and Chains/Milwaukee Here I Come	1969	2.00	4.00	8.00
❑ 32674	Arab Bounce/Future on Ice	1970	—	3.50	7.00
❑ 32731	Singing All Day and Dinner on the Ground/Help Thy Brother	1970	—	3.50	7.00
❑ 32750	Midnight Rambler/Between Fire and Water	1970	—	3.50	7.00
❑ 32820	Chattanooga Dog/I Cried Again	1971	—	3.50	7.00
❑ 32934	Lonesome Prison Blues/I'd Like to Be Sixteen Again	1972	—	3.50	7.00

MCA

Number	Title (A Side/B Side)	Yr	VG	VG+	NM
❑ 40076	Sunshine of the Mountain/You Don't Know My Mind	1973	—	3.00	6.00
❑ 40147	Mary Ann/Just Plain Yellow	1973	—	3.00	6.00
❑ 40237	Fly Me to Frisco/Theme Time	1974	—	3.00	6.00
❑ 40338	You Are My Sunshine/Lost to a Stranger	1974	—	3.00	6.00
❑ 40449	Better Times a-Comin'/I Buried My Future	1975	—	3.00	6.00

Albums

DECCA

Number	Title (A Side/B Side)	Yr	VG	VG+	NM
❑ DL 4016 [M]	Good 'n Country	1960	6.25	12.50	25.00
❑ DL 4285 [M]	Country Music Time	1962	6.25	12.50	25.00
❑ DL 4360 [M]	This World Is Not My Home	1963	6.25	12.50	25.00

Number	Title (A Side/B Side)	Yr	VG	VG+	NM
❑ DL 4536 [M]	Widow Maker	1964	5.00	10.00	20.00
❑ DL 4643 [M]	Sunny Side of the Mountain	1965	5.00	10.00	20.00
❑ DL 4769 [M]	Mr. Good 'n Country Music	1966	5.00	10.00	20.00
❑ DL 4891 [M]	Big and Country Instrumentals	1967	5.00	10.00	20.00
❑ DL 74016 [S]	Good 'n Country	1960	7.50	15.00	30.00
❑ DL 74285 [S]	Country Music Time	1962	7.50	15.00	30.00
❑ DL 74360 [S]	This World Is Not My Home	1963	7.50	15.00	30.00
❑ DL 74536 [S]	Widow Maker	1964	6.25	12.50	25.00
❑ DL 74643 [S]	Sunny Side of the Mountain	1965	6.25	12.50	25.00
❑ DL 74769 [S]	Mr. Good 'n Country Music	1966	6.25	12.50	25.00
❑ DL 74891 [S]	Big and Country Instrumentals	1967	5.00	10.00	20.00
❑ DL 74996	Tennessee	1968	5.00	10.00	20.00

MARTIN, JOEY

45s

DOOR KNOB

Number	Title (A Side/B Side)	Yr	VG	VG+	NM
❑ 115	Without You (same on both sides)	1979	—	3.00	6.00
MELODYLAND					
❑ 6025	Anything to Keep from Going Home/Ruby Is a Groupie	1975	—	3.00	6.00
NICKELODEON					
❑ 1002	I've Been a Long Time Leaving (But I'll Be a Long Time Gone)/Dance Hall Girl	1978	—	3.50	7.00

MARTIN, MARTY

See BOXCAR WILLIE.

MARTIN, MIKE

See MARTIN DELRAY.

MARTINDALE, WINK

45s

ABC DOT

Number	Title (A Side/B Side)	Yr	VG	VG+	NM
❑ 17606	Deck of Cards/Black Land Farmer	1976	—	2.50	5.00
DOT					
❑ 15968	Deck of Cards/Now You Know How It Feels	1959	3.00	6.00	12.00
❑ 15968 [PS]	Deck of Cards/Now You Know How It Feels	1959	6.25	12.50	25.00
❑ 16020	Life Gets Tee-Jus, Don't It/I Never See Maggie Alone	1959	2.50	5.00	10.00
❑ 16051	Blue Bobby Sox/Steal Away	1960	2.50	5.00	10.00
❑ 16083	Lincoln's Gettysburg Address/Love's Old Sweet Song	1960	2.50	5.00	10.00
❑ 16138	Glory of Love/I Wanna Play House	1960	2.50	5.00	10.00
❑ 16243	Black Land Farmer/Make Him Happy	1961	2.50	5.00	10.00
❑ 16282	A Man Needs a Woman/Three Steps to the Phone	1961	2.50	5.00	10.00
❑ 16316	Melody of Love/The Thing	1961	2.50	5.00	10.00
❑ 16347	The World's Greatest Man/Sweet Little Loveable You	1961	2.50	5.00	10.00
❑ 16435	A Vision at the Peace Table/I Saw Me	1963	2.00	4.00	8.00
❑ 16491	Deck of Cards/Black Land Farmer	1963	2.00	4.00	8.00
❑ 16531	I Heard the Bluebirds Sing/Nevertheless	1963	2.00	4.00	8.00
❑ 16555	First Kiss/Our Love Affair	1963	2.00	4.00	8.00
❑ 16597	Why Don't They Understand/Big Buildin'	1964	2.00	4.00	8.00
❑ 16628	Born Too Late/Hey Girl, Hey Boy	1964	2.00	4.00	8.00
❑ 16698	My True Love/A String, an Eraser, and a Blotter	1965	2.00	4.00	8.00
❑ 16821	Giddy-Up Go/Working Man's Prayer	1966	—	3.50	7.00
❑ 16863	To a Sleeping Beauty/A Vision at the Peace Table	1966	—	3.50	7.00
RANWOOD					
❑ 1005	America: An Affirmation/The People	1974	—	3.00	6.00

Albums

DOT

Number	Title (A Side/B Side)	Yr	VG	VG+	NM
❑ DLP-3245 [M]	Deck of Cards	1960	5.00	10.00	20.00
❑ DLP-3293 [M]	The Bible Story	1960	3.75	7.50	15.00
❑ DLP-3403 [M]	Big Bad John	1962	3.75	7.50	15.00
❑ DLP-3571 [M]	My True Love	1964	3.75	7.50	15.00
❑ DLP-3692 [M]	Giddyup Go	1966	3.75	7.50	15.00
❑ DLP-25245 [S]	Deck of Cards	1960	6.25	12.50	25.00
❑ DLP-25293 [S]	The Bible Story	1960	5.00	10.00	20.00
❑ DLP-25403 [S]	Big Bad John	1962	5.00	10.00	20.00
❑ DLP-25571 [S]	My True Love	1964	5.00	10.00	20.00
❑ DLP-25692 [S]	Giddyup Go	1966	5.00	10.00	20.00

MARTINE, LAYNG, JR.

45s

BARNABY

Number	Title (A Side/B Side)	Yr	VG	VG+	NM
❑ 2041	Rub It In/Live on the Sunshine	1971	2.00	4.00	8.00
❑ 2053	Come On Over to My House/Linda Let's Me Live	1971	2.00	4.00	8.00
❑ 2059	Find Out If She Likes Me/You and Me and the Night Time	1972	2.00	4.00	8.00
❑ 5006	Wisdom of a Child/You Don't Need a Ring (To Be My Baby)	1972	2.00	4.00	8.00
DATE					
❑ 1511	Crazy Daisy/Love Comes and Goes	1966	2.50	5.00	10.00
DECCA					
❑ 32621	The Recruit/St. Anne	1970	2.00	4.00	8.00
GENERAL INT'L.					
❑ 351	Sarubian Lament/Pick All the Flowers That You Can	196?	3.00	6.00	12.00
PLAYBOY					
❑ 6069	Don Juan/Walking Tall	1976	—	3.00	6.00
❑ 6081	Summertime Lovin'/Piece by Piece	1976	—	3.00	6.00

MARTINO, AL

The popular singer of the 1950s and 1960s had this one country hit.

45s

CAPITOL

Number	Title (A Side/B Side)	Yr	VG	VG+	NM
❑ 2674	I Started Loving You Again/Let Me Stay Awhile (With You)	1969	—	3.00	6.00

MARVELL, JAMES

45s

CAVALEER

Number	Title (A Side/B Side)	Yr	VG	VG+	NM
❑ 117	Urban Cowboys, Outlaws, Cavaliers/Love (Can Make You Happy)	1981	2.00	4.00	8.00

MASON, MILA

45s

ATLANTIC

Number	Title (A Side/B Side)	Yr	VG	VG+	NM
❑ 84116	The Strong One/Bossa' My Heart	1998	—	—	3.00
❑ 84178	This Heart/Let Me Cry	1998	—	—	3.00
❑ 84866	Dark Horse/I Do	1997	—	2.00	4.00
❑ 87047	That's Enough of That/Heart Without a Past	1996	—	2.00	4.00

MASON, SANDY

45s

HICKORY

Number	Title (A Side/B Side)	Yr	VG	VG+	NM
❑ 1442	There You Go/Give Me a Sweetheart	1967	2.00	4.00	8.00
❑ 1471	We Live in Two Different Worlds/I Forgot More Than You'll Ever Know	1967	2.00	4.00	8.00
JMI					
❑ 29	I'm Alright/Winds of Time	1973	—	3.00	6.00
MERCURY					
❑ 73090	Me and Jack Daniels/My Past	1970	—	3.50	7.00
MGM					
❑ 13393	Then You Can Tell Me Goodbye/Terry	1965	2.50	5.00	10.00
❑ 13494	Three Steps to the Phone/The Worst Mistake	1966	2.50	5.00	10.00
ROULETTE					
❑ 4485	What in the World's Come Over You/Which Way Shall I Go	1963	3.00	6.00	12.00

MASON DIXON

45s

CAPITOL

Number	Title (A Side/B Side)	Yr	VG	VG+	NM
❑ B-44189	Dangerous Road/Where Does Love Go	1988	—	—	3.00
❑ B-44249	When Karen Comes Around/Where Does Love Go	1988	—	—	3.00
❑ B-44331	Exception to the Rule/A Woman Like You	1989	—	—	3.00
❑ B-44381	A Mountain Ago/When It Hurts You Most	1989	—	—	3.00
NLT					
❑ 1989	Lone Star Lullaby/(B-side unknown)	198?	—	3.00	6.00
PREMIER ONE					
❑ 101	Home Grown/Savin' the Best for Last	1986	—	2.50	5.00
❑ 112	3935 West End Avenue/Baby's Song	1987	—	2.50	5.00
❑ 115	Don't Say No Tonight/Natchez Queen	1987	—	2.50	5.00
TEXAS					
❑ 5502 *—Black vinyl*	Every Breath You Take/Armadillo Country	1983	—	3.00	6.00
❑ 5502 *—Yellow vinyl*	Every Breath You Take/Armadillo Country	1983	2.50	5.00	10.00
❑ 5508	Houston Heartache/Mason Dixon Lines	1985	—	3.00	6.00
❑ 5510	Got My Heart Set on You/Armadillo Country	1985	—	3.00	6.00
❑ 5511	Silent Night/O Come All Ye Faithful	1985	—	3.00	6.00
❑ 5555	Mason Dixon Lines/(B-side unknown)	1983	—	3.00	6.00
❑ 5556	I Never Had a Chance with You/Circle	1984	—	3.00	6.00
❑ 5557	Gettin' Over You/(B-side unknown)	1984	—	3.00	6.00
❑ 5558	Only a Dream Away/Buried Treasure	1985	—	3.00	6.00

Albums

CAPITOL

Number	Title (A Side/B Side)	Yr	VG	VG+	NM
❑ C1-90120	Exception to the Rule	1989	2.50	5.00	10.00

MASSEY, WAYNE

Also see CHARLY McCLAIN.

45s

EPIC

Number	Title (A Side/B Side)	Yr	VG	VG+	NM
❑ 34-06249	Give It Back/That's What You Mean to Me	1986	—	—	3.00
MCA					
❑ 52019	Easin' On Back/I'd Ever Let You Go	1982	—	2.00	4.00
❑ 52082	It Should Have Been Easy/What's a Couple More	1982	—	2.00	4.00
❑ 52211	Lover in Disguise/Born to Love You	1983	—	2.00	4.00
❑ 52246	Say You'll Stay/Born to Love You	1983	—	2.00	4.00
❑ 52299	Spellbound/Straight from the Heart	1983	—	2.00	4.00
MERCURY					
❑ 870994-7	Shoot the Moon/What a Perfect Way	1988	—	—	3.00
❑ 872952-7	Heaven in a Haystack/What a Perfect Way	1989	—	—	3.00
POLYDOR					
❑ 2112	One Life to Live/Theme from "One Life to Live"	1980	—	3.00	6.00
❑ 2132 *—Canceled*	Una Vida Para/Theme from "One Life to Live"	1980	—	—	—
❑ 2147	Diamonds and Teardrops/The Best of the Rest of Our Lives	1980	—	2.00	4.00
❑ 2160 *—With Mary Murray*	Best of Friends (A Song for Judd)/Love So Right	1981	—	2.00	4.00

Albums

POLYDOR

Number	Title (A Side/B Side)	Yr	VG	VG+	NM
❑ PD-1-6309	One Life to Live	1980	3.00	6.00	12.00

MASTERS, A.J.
45s
BERMUDA DUNES

Number	Title (A Side/B Side)	Yr	VG	VG+	NM
❑ 101	They Don't Play None of Mine/Someone Else Tonight	1984	—	2.50	5.00
❑ 102	Do It on a Dare/(B-side unknown)	1984	—	2.50	5.00
❑ 104	Take a Little Bit of It Home/(B-side unknown)	1985	—	2.50	5.00
❑ 111	Lonely Together/(B-side unknown)	1985	—	2.50	5.00
❑ 112	Back Home/Lonely Together	1986	—	2.50	5.00
❑ 114	Love Keep Your Distance/Get Outta My House Blues	1987	—	2.50	5.00
❑ 115	I Don't Mean Maybe/(B-side unknown)	1986	—	2.50	5.00
❑ 116	In It Again/On a Night Like This	1987	—	2.50	5.00
❑ 117	255 Harbor Drive/Our Love Is Like the South	1987	—	2.50	5.00

MASTERS FAMILY, THE
45s
COLUMBIA

Number	Title (A Side/B Side)	Yr	VG	VG+	NM
❑ 4-20785	I'll Be Going to Heaven Sometime/Let the Spirit Descend	1951	5.00	10.00	20.00
❑ 4-20813	Just a Sinner Saved by Grace/While Ages Roll On	1951	5.00	10.00	20.00
❑ 4-20851	Hand Me Down My Trumpet/Happiness Comes	1951	5.00	10.00	20.00
❑ 4-20888	From 40 to 65/When the Wagon Was New	1952	5.00	10.00	20.00
❑ 4-20940	Cry from the Cross/Glory Land March	1952	5.00	10.00	20.00
❑ 4-20996	The Old World Is Rocking in Sin/Stop Kicking God's Children	1952	5.00	10.00	20.00
❑ 4-21044	Southbound Passenger Train/My Heart's Like a Beggar	1952	5.00	10.00	20.00
❑ 4-21094	They've Made a New Bible/Marching On to Glory	1953	5.00	10.00	20.00
❑ 4-21136	Singing in the Promised Land/I Have Changed	1953	5.00	10.00	20.00
❑ 4-21175	You Gotta Pray/Swing Wide Your Golden Gate	1953	5.00	10.00	20.00
❑ 4-21219	New World to Come/Back in the Good Old Days	1954	5.00	10.00	20.00
❑ 4-21272	God Owns It All/When He Heard My Plea	1954	5.00	10.00	20.00
❑ 4-21313	Noah and the Mighty Ark/It Takes a Lot of Lovin'	1954	5.00	10.00	20.00
❑ 4-21357	Filled with the Spirit of God/Don't You Wait to Go to Heaven	1955	5.00	10.00	20.00
❑ 4-21413	Everlasting Joy/Coming to Carry Me Home	1955	5.00	10.00	20.00
❑ 4-21549	Heaven/I Wasn't There	1956	5.00	10.00	20.00

DECCA

Number	Title (A Side/B Side)	Yr	VG	VG+	NM
❑ 31378	Great Gilded Hall/Medals for Mother	1962	3.00	6.00	12.00

MATA, BILLY
45s
BGM

Number	Title (A Side/B Side)	Yr	VG	VG+	NM
❑ 70188	Photographic Memory/(B-side unknown)	1988	—	3.00	6.00
❑ 92087	Macon Georgia Love/She Ain't Got Nothin' on You	1987	—	3.00	6.00

MATHIS, COUNTRY JOHNNY
The "original" Johnny Mathis, the "Country" prefix was added to his name after the "other" Johnny Mathis became far more popular. Also see JIMMY AND JOHNNY.
45s
D

Number	Title (A Side/B Side)	Yr	VG	VG+	NM
❑ 1027	Lonely Night/I've Been Known to Cry	1958	5.00	10.00	20.00
❑ 1054	From a Kiss to the Blues/Since I Said Goodbye to Love	1959	3.75	7.50	15.00
❑ 1078	Run Please Run/I Don't Know How I Can Live	1959	3.75	7.50	15.00
❑ 1119	Come On In/Chances Are	1960	3.75	7.50	15.00
❑ 1130	Caryl Chessman/Tears and Gold	1960	3.75	7.50	15.00
❑ 1152	When I Came Through Town/Only Time Will Tell	1960	3.75	7.50	15.00

HILLTOP

Number	Title (A Side/B Side)	Yr	VG	VG+	NM
❑ 3008	Welcome Home/Carolina Sunshine Girl	1965	2.50	5.00	10.00

LITTLE DARLIN'

Number	Title (A Side/B Side)	Yr	VG	VG+	NM
❑ 009	Black Sheep/Something in Your World	1966	2.50	5.00	10.00
❑ 0015	I Could Never Forget Your Love/Sugar Thief	1966	2.50	5.00	10.00
❑ 0037	A Heart Needs a Heart/No Place to Go	1967	2.50	5.00	10.00
❑ 0051	Big Old Heart Full of Love/Take Your Heart and Go	1968	2.50	5.00	10.00
❑ 0056	Come Here to My Heart/I'll Cry When I Call Your Name	1969	2.50	5.00	10.00
❑ 0067	Bring Back My Life/Sweet Rita	1970	2.50	5.00	10.00

MERCURY

Number	Title (A Side/B Side)	Yr	VG	VG+	NM
❑ 71202	Moonlight Magic/You Don't Care	1957	5.00	10.00	20.00
❑ 71273	Harbor of Love/One Life	1958	5.00	10.00	20.00

UNITED ARTISTS

Number	Title (A Side/B Side)	Yr	VG	VG+	NM
❑ 396	Thinking Too Far Behind/Wouldn't That Be Something	1961	3.00	6.00	12.00
❑ 460	Every Road Must Have a Turn/I'm Still in Love with Kay	1962	3.00	6.00	12.00
❑ 536	Please Talk to My Heart/Let's Go Home	1963	3.00	6.00	12.00
❑ 633	If I Could Keep You Off My Mind/Love Gone Wrong	1963	3.00	6.00	12.00
❑ 697	Was It You/Little Girl	1964	2.50	5.00	10.00

Albums
HILLTOP

Number	Title (A Side/B Side)	Yr	VG	VG+	NM
❑ 7004	Hilltop Gospel	1965	6.25	12.50	25.00

LITTLE DARLIN'

Number	Title (A Side/B Side)	Yr	VG	VG+	NM
❑ 8007	He Keeps Me Singin'	1967	5.00	10.00	20.00

MATHIS, JOEL
45s
CHART

Number	Title (A Side/B Side)	Yr	VG	VG+	NM
❑ 5217	Ann/Glasses of Beer	1974	—	3.00	6.00
❑ 5225	The Deep End/Friday We'll Be Back in Love Again	1974	—	3.00	6.00

SOUNDWAVES

Number	Title (A Side/B Side)	Yr	VG	VG+	NM
❑ 4543	Love Me, Trust Me/Our Room	1977	—	3.00	6.00
❑ 4553	Houston on My Mind/Living in Yesterday	1977	—	3.00	6.00
❑ 4562	The Farmer's Song (We Ain't Gonna Work for Peanuts)/Dirt Farming Man	1977	—	3.00	6.00
❑ 4565	Close Encounters of the Loving Kind/Looking for Something Hooking	1978	—	3.00	6.00
❑ 4574	Runnin' After Rainbows/Houston on My Mind	1978	—	3.00	6.00

MATTEA, KATHY
45s
MERCURY

Number	Title (A Side/B Side)	Yr	VG	VG+	NM
❑ 088-172160-7	Trouble with Angels/Prove That by Me	2000	—	—	3.00
❑ 088-172173-7	BFD/The Innocent Years	2000	—	—	3.00
❑ 578550-7	Love Travels/I'm On Your Side	1997	—	—	3.00
❑ 578950-7	455 Rocket/All Roads to the River	1997	—	—	3.00
❑ 814375-7	Street Talk/Heartbeat	1983	—	2.00	4.00
❑ 818289-7	Someone Is Falling in Love/That's Easy for You to Say	1984	—	2.00	4.00
❑ 822218-7	You've Got a Soft Place to Fall/Back to the Heartbreak Kid	1984	—	2.00	4.00
❑ 856262-7	Maybe She's Human/Who Turned On the Light	1994	—	—	3.00
❑ 856484-7	Clown in Your Rodeo/Who's Gonna Know	1995	—	—	3.00
❑ 858464-7	Walking Away a Winner/The Cape	1994	—	2.00	4.00
❑ 858800-7	Nobody's Gonna Rain on Our Parade/Grand Canyon	1994	—	—	3.00
❑ 862064-7	Seeds/Lonely at the Bottom	1993	—	—	3.00
❑ 862650-7	Listen to the Radio/Slow Boat	1993	—	—	3.00
❑ 864318-7	Lonesome Standard Time/Asking Us to Dance	1992	—	2.00	4.00
❑ 864810-7	Standing Knee Deep in a River (Dying of Thirst)/ Listen to the Radio	1993	—	2.00	4.00
❑ 868394-7	Whole Lotta Holes/Quarter Moon	1991	—	—	3.00
❑ 868866-7	Asking Us to Dance/Where've You Been	1991	—	2.00	4.00
❑ 870148-7	Eighteen Wheels and a Dozen Roses/Like a Hurricane	1988	—	2.00	4.00
❑ 870148-7 [PS]	Eighteen Wheels and a Dozen Roses/Like a Hurricane	1988	—	2.50	5.00
❑ 870476-7	Untold Stories/Late in the Day	1988	—	—	3.00
❑ 872082-7	Life As We Knew It/As Long As I Have a Heart	1988	—	—	3.00
❑ 872766-7	Come from the Heart/True North	1989	—	—	3.00
❑ 874672-7	Burnin' Old Memories/Hills of Alabam	1989	—	—	3.00
❑ 876262-7	Where've You Been/I'll Take Care of You	1989	—	3.00	6.00
❑ 876746-7	She Came from Fort Worth/Here's Hopin'	1990	—	—	3.00
❑ 878246-7	A Few Good Things Remain/Evenin'	1990	—	2.00	4.00
❑ 878934-7	Time Passes By/What Could Have Been	1991	—	—	3.00
❑ 880192-7	That's Easy for You to Say/Somewhere Down the Road	1984	—	2.00	4.00
❑ 880595-7	It's Your Reputation Talkin'/Never Look Back	1985	—	2.00	4.00
❑ 880867-7	He Won't Give In/I Believe I Could Fall in Love	1985	—	2.00	4.00
❑ 884177-7	Heart of the Country/Talkin' to Myself	1985	—	2.00	4.00
❑ 884573-7	Love at the Five & Dime/Can't Run Away from Your Heart	1986	—	—	3.00
❑ 884978-7	Walk the Way the Wind Blows/Come Home to West Virginia	1986	—	—	3.00
❑ 888319-7	You're the Power/Song for the Life	1987	—	—	3.00
❑ 888574-7	Train of Memories/Evenin'	1987	—	—	3.00
❑ 888874-7	Goin' Gone/Every Love	1987	—	—	3.00
❑ 888874-7 [PS]	Goin' Gone/Every Love	1987	—	2.50	5.00

Albums
MERCURY

Number	Title (A Side/B Side)	Yr	VG	VG+	NM
❑ R 110791	A Collection of Hits	1990	5.00	10.00	20.00
—Only released on vinyl by BMG Direct Marketing					
❑ 818560-1	Kathy Mattea	1984	2.50	5.00	10.00
❑ 824308-1	From My Heart	1985	2.50	5.00	10.00
❑ 830405-1	Walk the Way the Wind Blows	1986	2.50	5.00	10.00
❑ 832793-1	Untasted Honey	1987	2.50	5.00	10.00
❑ 836950-1	Willow in the Wind	1989	3.00	6.00	12.00

MATTHEWS, WRIGHT & KING
45s
COLUMBIA

Number	Title (A Side/B Side)	Yr	VG	VG+	NM
❑ 38-74275	The Power of Love/Everytime She Says Yes	1992	—	2.00	4.00
❑ 38-74400	Mother's Eyes/When the River Runs High	1992	—	2.00	4.00
❑ 38-74749	House Huntin'/Leavin' Reasons	1992	—	2.00	4.00
❑ 38-77020	I Got a Love/The Truth Is Killin' Me	1993	—	—	3.00
❑ 38-77180	One of These Days/Big Money	1993	—	—	3.00

MAVERICKS, THE
45s
MCA

Number	Title (A Side/B Side)	Yr	VG	VG+	NM
❑ 54464	This Broken Heart/Excuse Me (I Think I've Got a Heartache)	1992	—	2.00	4.00
❑ 54520	I Got You/A Better Way	1992	—	2.00	4.00
❑ 54748	What a Crying Shame/The Things You Said to Me	1993	—	2.50	5.00
❑ 54780	O What a Thrill/Ain't Found Nobody	1994	—	2.00	4.00
❑ 54975	I Should Have Been True/The Losing Side of Me	1995	—	—	3.00
❑ 55021	Missing You/Foolish Heart	1996	—	—	3.00
❑ 55026	All That Heaven Will Allow/Pretend	1995	—	2.00	4.00
❑ 55080	Here Comes the Rain/I'm Not Gonna Cry for You	1995	—	—	3.00
❑ 55154	All You Ever Do Is Bring Me Down/Volver, Volver	1996	—	2.00	4.00
❑ 55247	I Don't Care (If You Love Me Anymore)/ Something Stupid	1996	—	—	3.00
❑ 72056	Dance the Night Away/Save a Prayer	1998	—	—	3.00

Albums

MCA

Number	Title (A Side/B Side)	Yr	VG	VG+	NM
❑ 11257	Music for All Occasions	1995	2.50	5.00	10.00

MAXEDON, SMILEY

45s

COLUMBIA

Number	Title (A Side/B Side)	Yr	VG	VG+	NM
❑ 4-20910	Crazy to Care/In the Window	1952	6.25	12.50	25.00
❑ 4-21046	Your Old Love Letters/I'm Shuttin' the Door of Love	1952	6.25	12.50	25.00
❑ 4-21095	What Good Is My Love/We Can't Live Together	1953	5.00	10.00	20.00
❑ 4-21188	Give Me a Red Hot Mama/Why Can't You Look Me in the Eye	1953	5.00	10.00	20.00
❑ 4-21244	If I Should Change Your Ways/Too Late to Cry Over You	1954	5.00	10.00	20.00
❑ 4-21301	That's All Right/Blue as Blue Can Be	1954	7.50	15.00	30.00
❑ 4-21337	I Want You/Oh Why Did I Cheat	1955	5.00	10.00	20.00
❑ 4-21395	You've Lost Too Much/I'll Swear You Don't Love Me	1955	5.00	10.00	20.00
❑ 4-21451	Until Then/Give Me Your Love for a While	1955	5.00	10.00	20.00

MAY, RALPH

45s

AMI

Number	Title (A Side/B Side)	Yr	VG	VG+	NM
❑ 1901	In a Stranger's Eyes/(B-side unknown)	1982	—	3.00	6.00

EVERGREEN

Number	Title (A Side/B Side)	Yr	VG	VG+	NM
❑ 1048	Memory Attack/(B-side unknown)	1986	—	2.50	5.00

PRIMERO

Number	Title (A Side/B Side)	Yr	VG	VG+	NM
❑ 1006	Here Comes That Feelin' Again/(B-side unknown)	1982	—	3.00	6.00
❑ 1021	Angels Get Lonely Too/Keep Me from Blowin' Away	1983	—	3.00	6.00

SOUNDWAVES

Number	Title (A Side/B Side)	Yr	VG	VG+	NM
❑ 4608	Together We're Falling Apart/(B-side unknown)	1980	—	3.00	6.00
❑ 4630	Cajun Lady/Together We're Falling Apart	1981	—	3.00	6.00
❑ 4639	Roll Down Dixie Road/Cajun Lady	1981	—	3.00	6.00

MCALLISTER, BILLY JOE

45s

LITTLE DARLIN'

Number	Title (A Side/B Side)	Yr	VG	VG+	NM
❑ 0044	My Worst Is the Best/These Things I'm Not	1968	2.50	5.00	10.00

MCALYSTER

45s

MCA NASHVILLE

Number	Title (A Side/B Side)	Yr	VG	VG+	NM
❑ 088 172186 7	I Know How the River Feels/Looking Over My Shoulder	2000	—	—	3.00

MCANALLY, MAC

45s

ARIOLA AMERICA

Number	Title (A Side/B Side)	Yr	VG	VG+	NM
❑ 7665	It's a Crazy World/We Can Be Strong	1977	—	2.50	5.00
❑ 7671	Bad Boy/Let Him Go	1977	—	2.50	5.00
❑ 7688	The Lord and the Devil/Opinion on Love	1978	—	2.50	5.00

GEFFEN

Number	Title (A Side/B Side)	Yr	VG	VG+	NM
❑ 27675	History/Alien	1988	—	—	3.00
❑ 29515	On the Line/Other People Say	1983	—	2.00	4.00
❑ 29602	How Cool/Middle Man	1983	—	2.00	4.00
❑ 29736	Minimum Love/Like Your Mother	1983	—	2.00	4.00

MCA

Number	Title (A Side/B Side)	Yr	VG	VG+	NM
❑ 54372	Live and Learn/All These Years	1992	—	—	3.00
❑ 54450	The Trouble with Diamonds/Socrates	1992	—	—	3.00
❑ 54537	Junk Cars/Somewhere Nice Forever	1992	—	—	3.00
❑ 54629	Not That Long Ago/Somewhere Nice Forever	1993	—	—	3.00
❑ 54818	Down the Road/The Know	1994	—	—	3.00

RCA

Number	Title (A Side/B Side)	Yr	VG	VG+	NM
❑ PB-12026	It's My Job/Trying to Make the Lights Yellow	1980	—	2.00	4.00

WARNER BROS.

Number	Title (A Side/B Side)	Yr	VG	VG+	NM
❑ 19800	Down the Road/She's Going Out of My Mind	1990	—	2.00	4.00
❑ 22662	Back Where I Come From/Company Time	1990	—	2.00	4.00

Albums

ARIOLA AMERICA

Number	Title (A Side/B Side)	Yr	VG	VG+	NM
❑ ST-50019	Mac McAnally	1977	3.00	6.00	12.00
❑ SW-50029	No Problem	1978	3.00	6.00	12.00

GEFFEN

Number	Title (A Side/B Side)	Yr	VG	VG+	NM
❑ GHS 2033	Nothing But the Truth	1983	2.50	5.00	10.00
❑ 24191	Finish Lines	1988	2.50	5.00	10.00

RCA VICTOR

Number	Title (A Side/B Side)	Yr	VG	VG+	NM
❑ AFL1-3519	Cuttin' Corners	1980	3.00	6.00	12.00

MCANALLY, SHANE

45s

CURB

Number	Title (A Side/B Side)	Yr	VG	VG+	NM
❑ D7-73085	Are Your Eyes Still Blue/If It's Over	1999	—	—	3.00

MCAULIFFE, LEON

45s

CAPITOL

Number	Title (A Side/B Side)	Yr	VG	VG+	NM
❑ 5066	Shape Up or Ship Out/I Don't Love Nobody	1963	2.50	5.00	10.00
❑ 5168	Things to Remember/Bluesville U.S.A.	1964	2.50	5.00	10.00
❑ 5266	Next Time I Fall in Love/Don't Call Me, I'll Call You	1964	2.50	5.00	10.00

CIMARRON

Number	Title (A Side/B Side)	Yr	VG	VG+	NM
❑ 0711	Playboy Page Fourteen/Juke Box	197?	—	3.00	6.00
❑ 4039	Steel Guitar Rag/Panhandle Rag	1959	5.00	10.00	20.00
❑ 4043	Lookin' Glass/Wapanuka	1959	3.75	7.50	15.00
❑ 4046	Bear Creek Hop/Boogie on Strings	1960	3.75	7.50	15.00
❑ 4047	Water Baby Boogie/The Three Bears	1960	3.75	7.50	15.00
❑ 4049	Orange Blossom Special/Cimarron (Roll On)	1961	3.75	7.50	15.00
❑ 4050	Cozy Inn/Ain't Gonna Hurt No More	1961	3.75	7.50	15.00
❑ 4052	Choo Choo Ch'Boogie/Honky Tonk Song	1961	3.75	7.50	15.00
❑ 4054	My Ace in the Hole/Night Life	1962	3.75	7.50	15.00
❑ 4057	Faded Love/My Little Red Wagon	1962	3.75	7.50	15.00

COLUMBIA

Number	Title (A Side/B Side)	Yr	VG	VG+	NM
❑ 2-346	Panhandle Waltz/Sugar and Salt *—Microgroove 33 1/3 rpm small-holed 7-inch single*	1949	10.00	20.00	40.00
❑ 2-420 (?)	The Three Bears/Twin Fiddle Rag *—Microgroove 33 1/3 rpm small-holed 7-inch single*	1949	10.00	20.00	40.00
❑ 2-520 (?)	Chattanoogie Shoe Shine Boy/Rag Mop *—Microgroove 33 1/3 rpm small-holed 7-inch single*	1950	10.00	20.00	40.00
❑ 2-600 (?)	Cimarron Rag/Birmingham Bounce *—Microgroove 33 1/3 rpm small-holed 7-inch single*	1950	10.00	20.00	40.00
❑ 2-700 (?)	Bonaparte's Retreat/What, Where and When *—Microgroove 33 1/3 rpm small-holed 7-inch single*	1950	10.00	20.00	40.00
❑ 4-20755	Jelly Bean Rag/What've You Got	1950	10.00	20.00	40.00
❑ 4-20782	Take It Away Leon/Tulsa Straight Ahead	1951	7.50	15.00	30.00
❑ 4-20807	There's a Right Way and a Wrong Way/I've Never Lived in Tennessee	1951	7.50	15.00	30.00
❑ 4-20845	Blue Guitar Stomp/I Didn't Know How Much	1951	7.50	15.00	30.00
❑ 4-20872	Makin' Believe You're There/Search My Heart	1952	6.25	12.50	25.00
❑ 4-20907	Blacksmith Blues/I'm Going Back to Birmingham	1952	6.25	12.50	25.00
❑ 4-20952	This Side of Town/Who Took My Ring from Your Finger	1952	6.25	12.50	25.00
❑ 4-21020	Stolen Love/Hear Me Now	1952	6.25	12.50	25.00
❑ 4-21072	Redskin Rag/Bitter Tears	1953	6.25	12.50	25.00
❑ 4-21115	Eating Right Out of Your Hand/Heart Attacks	1953	6.25	12.50	25.00
❑ 4-21174	Run 'Em Off/Blue Man's Blues	1953	6.25	12.50	25.00
❑ 4-21227	Wished You Would/Tie Your Apron Strings	1954	5.00	10.00	20.00
❑ 4-21283	Sh-Boom/Smooth Sailing	1954	6.25	12.50	25.00
❑ 4-21319	One Little Dream of You/Mr. Steel Guitar	1954	5.00	10.00	20.00
❑ 4-21398	Hard Hearted Gal/Dial Love for Me	1955	5.00	10.00	20.00

DOT

Number	Title (A Side/B Side)	Yr	VG	VG+	NM
❑ 15613	Under the Double Eagle/What's the Use	1957	5.00	10.00	20.00
❑ 15741	My Love/Lone Star Rag	1958	5.00	10.00	20.00
❑ 15845	There's That Smile Again/Johnny Can Read	1958	5.00	10.00	20.00

STONEWAY

Number	Title (A Side/B Side)	Yr	VG	VG+	NM
❑ 1105	Twin Fiddle Rag/My Blue Heaven	197?	2.00	4.00	8.00

Selected 78s

COLUMBIA

Number	Title (A Side/B Side)	Yr	VG	VG+	NM
❑ 20546	Panhandle Rag/Careless Hands	1949	5.00	10.00	20.00
❑ 20565	No One for Me/Someone Else Is a-Beatin' My Time	1949	5.00	10.00	20.00

Albums

ABC-PARAMOUNT

Number	Title (A Side/B Side)	Yr	VG	VG+	NM
❑ ABC-394 [M]	Cozy Inn	1961	10.00	20.00	40.00
❑ ABCS-394 [S]	Cozy Inn	1961	15.00	30.00	60.00

CAPITOL

Number	Title (A Side/B Side)	Yr	VG	VG+	NM
❑ ST 2016 [S]	The Dancin'est Band Around	1964	10.00	20.00	40.00
❑ T 2016 [M]	The Dancin'est Band Around	1964	7.50	15.00	30.00
❑ ST 2148 [S]	Everybody Dance! Everybody Swing!	1964	10.00	20.00	40.00
❑ T 2148 [M]	Everybody Dance! Everybody Swing!	1964	7.50	15.00	30.00

CIMARRON

Number	Title (A Side/B Side)	Yr	VG	VG+	NM
❑ CLP-2002 [M]	The Swingin' Western Strings of Leon McAuliff	1960	12.50	25.00	50.00

DOT

Number	Title (A Side/B Side)	Yr	VG	VG+	NM
❑ DLP-3139 [M]	Take Off	1958	15.00	30.00	60.00
❑ DLP-3689 [M]	Golden Country Hits	1966	10.00	20.00	40.00
❑ DLP-25689 [R]	Golden Country Hits	1966	6.25	12.50	25.00

SESAC

Number	Title (A Side/B Side)	Yr	VG	VG+	NM
❑ 1601 [M]	Points West	1957	25.00	50.00	100.00
❑ (# unknown) [M]	Just a Minute	1957	25.00	50.00	100.00

STARDAY

Number	Title (A Side/B Side)	Yr	VG	VG+	NM
❑ SLP-171 [M]	Mr. Western Swing	1962	12.50	25.00	50.00
❑ SLP-280 [M]	The Swingin' West with Leon McAuliff	1964	10.00	20.00	40.00
❑ SLP-309 [M]	The Swingin' Western Strings of Leon McAuliff	1964	10.00	20.00	40.00

MCBEE, JERRY

45s

DIMENSION

Number	Title (A Side/B Side)	Yr	VG	VG+	NM
❑ 1004	That's the Chance We'll Have to Take/(B-side unknown)	1980	—	2.50	5.00

MCBRIDE, DALE

45s

CON BRIO

Number	Title (A Side/B Side)	Yr	VG	VG+	NM
❑ 109	Getting Over You Again/You Have Missed Nothing	1976	—	2.50	5.00
❑ 114	Ordinary Man/Mexicali Rose	1976	—	2.50	5.00
❑ 117	I'm Savin' Up Sunshine/She's My Heaven	1977	—	2.50	5.00
❑ 121	Love I Need You/For All Seasons	1977	—	2.50	5.00
❑ 124	My Girl/She Makes Love Feel Good	1977	—	2.50	5.00
❑ 127	Always Lovin' Her Man/I Know the Feeling	1977	—	2.50	5.00
❑ 131	A Sweet Love Song the World Can Sing/I'm Savin' Up Sunshine	1978	—	2.50	5.00
❑ 135	I Don't Like Cheatin' Songs/My Girl	1978	—	2.50	5.00
❑ 140	Let's Be Lonely Together/She Makes Me Feel Good	1978	—	2.50	5.00
❑ 145	It's Hell to Know She's Heaven/You Have Missed Nothing	1979	—	2.50	5.00

Number	Title (A Side/B Side)	Yr	VG	VG+	NM
❑ 151	Getting Over You Again/She Makes Love Feel Good	1979	—	2.50	5.00
❑ 158	Get Your Hands on Me Baby/I Knew the Feeling	1979	—	2.50	5.00

FAME

Number	Title (A Side/B Side)	Yr	VG	VG+	NM
❑ 507	Prissy Missy/Class Beyond Compare	1959	20.00	40.00	80.00

MCA

Number	Title (A Side/B Side)	Yr	VG	VG+	NM
❑ 40853	My World Is Empty Without You/Quiet Moments	1978	—	2.00	4.00

REPRISE

Number	Title (A Side/B Side)	Yr	VG	VG+	NM
❑ 0331	Barbara/I Can't Ever Free My Mind	1964	2.50	5.00	10.00

TEAR DROP

Number	Title (A Side/B Side)	Yr	VG	VG+	NM
❑ 3029	Lovely Little One/Guess Who	1964	3.00	6.00	12.00
❑ 3041	Barbara/I Can't Ever Free My Mind	1964	3.00	6.00	12.00
❑ 3062	Am I That Easy to Forget/Our Hearts Beat as One	1965	3.00	6.00	12.00
❑ 3077	Prissy Missy/Two Steps from the Blues	1965	3.00	6.00	12.00
❑ 3091	Haunted Hungry Heart/What's Happening Baby	196?	2.50	5.00	10.00
❑ 3100	I Love Only You/(B-side unknown)	196?	2.50	5.00	10.00

THUNDERBIRD

Number	Title (A Side/B Side)	Yr	VG	VG+	NM
❑ 528	Life to Me/Guess You've Made Your Mind Up	1970	2.00	4.00	8.00
❑ 539	Corpus Christi Wind/Is Anybody Going to San Antone	1971	2.00	4.00	8.00
❑ 547	A Man Without Love/(B-side unknown)	197?	2.00	4.00	8.00

Albums

CON BRIO

Number	Title (A Side/B Side)	Yr	VG	VG+	NM
❑ 051	The Ordinary Man Album	1977	3.00	6.00	12.00

MCBRIDE, MARTINA

45s

RCA

Number	Title (A Side/B Side)	Yr	VG	VG+	NM
❑ 60214	There You Are/Do What You Do	2000	—	—	3.00
❑ 62215	The Time Has Come/The Rope	1992	—	2.00	4.00
❑ 62291	That's Me/Losing You Feels Good	1992	—	2.00	4.00
❑ 62398	Cheap Whiskey/I Can't Sleep	1992	—	2.00	4.00
❑ 62599	My Baby Loves Me/A Woman Knows	1993	—	2.50	5.00
❑ 62697	Life #9/Life #9 (Extended Dance Mix)	1993	—	2.00	4.00
❑ 62828	Independence Day/True Blue Fool	1994	—	2.50	5.00
❑ 62948	Where I Used to Have a Heart/Heart Trouble	1995	—	2.00	4.00
❑ 62961	Heart Trouble/That Wasn't Me	1994	—	2.00	4.00
❑ 64345	Safe in the Arms of Love/Life #9 (Dance Mix)	1995	—	2.00	4.00
❑ 64437	Wild Angels/Two More Bottles of Wine	1995	—	2.50	5.00
❑ 64487	Phones Are Ringin' All Over Town/Beyond the Blue	1996	—	2.00	4.00
❑ 64610	Swingin' Doors/Phones Are Ringin' All Over Town	1996	—	—	3.00
❑ 64688	O Holy Night/Silver Bells	1996	—	—	—
—The existence of this on 45 has been questioned					
❑ 64728	Cry on the Shoulder of the Road/A Great Disguise	1997	—	—	3.00
❑ 64963	A Broken Wing/Valentine	1997	—	2.00	4.00
—B-side with Jim Brickman					
❑ 65456	Wrong Again/Happy Girl	1998	—	—	3.00
❑ 65730	Whatever You Say/Be That Way	1999	—	—	3.00
❑ 65896	I Love You/Whatever You Say	1999	—	—	3.00
❑ 65933	Love's the Only House/I Love You	1999	—	—	3.00

MCBRIDE AND THE RIDE

45s

MCA

Number	Title (A Side/B Side)	Yr	VG	VG+	NM
❑ 54022	Can I Count on You/Turn to Blue	1991	—	2.00	4.00
❑ 54125	Same Old Star/Stone Country	1991	—	—	3.00
❑ 54356	Sacred Ground/Your One and Only	1992	—	2.50	5.00
❑ 54413	Going Out of My Mind/Trick Rider	1992	—	2.00	4.00
❑ 54494	Just One Night/All I Have to Offer You Is Me	1992	—	2.00	4.00
❑ 54601	Love on the Loose, Heart on the Run/Hangin' In and Hangin' On	1993	—	2.00	4.00
❑ 54688	Hurry Sundown/Just the Thought of Losing You	1993	—	—	3.00
❑ 54761	No More Cryin'/Don't Be Mean to Me	1993	—	2.00	4.00
❑ 54853	Been There/He's Living My Dreams	1994	—	—	3.00
—As "Terry McBride and the Ride"					
❑ 54936	High Hopes and Empty Pockets/Teardrops	1994	—	—	3.00
—As "Terry McBride and the Ride"					
❑ 54986	Somebody Will/I'll See You Again Someday	1995	—	—	3.00
—As "Terry McBride and the Ride"					
❑ 79038	Every Step of the Way/Ain't No Big Deal	1990	—	2.00	4.00
❑ 79074	Felicia/Every Step of the Way	1990	—	2.00	4.00

MCCALL, C.W.

45s

AMERICAN GRAMAPHONE

Number	Title (A Side/B Side)	Yr	VG	VG+	NM
❑ 351	Old Home Filler-Up An' Keep On-a-Truckin' Café/Old 30	1974	3.75	7.50	15.00

MGM

Number	Title (A Side/B Side)	Yr	VG	VG+	NM
❑ 14738	Old Home Filler-Up An' Keep On-a-Truckin' Café/Old 30	1974	—	2.00	4.00
❑ 14764	Wolf Creek Pass/Sloan	1974	—	2.00	4.00
❑ 14801	Classified/I've Trucked All Over This Land	1975	—	2.00	4.00
❑ 14825	Black Bear Road/Four Wheel Drive	1975	—	2.00	4.00
❑ 14839	Convoy/Long Lonesome Road	1975	—	2.50	5.00

POLYDOR

Number	Title (A Side/B Side)	Yr	VG	VG+	NM
❑ 14310	There Won't Be No Country Music (There Won't Be No Rock 'n' Roll)/Green River	1976	—	2.00	4.00
❑ 14331	Crispy Critters/Jackson Hole	1976	—	2.00	4.00
❑ 14352	Four Wheel Cowboy/Aurora Borealis	1976	—	2.00	4.00
❑ 14365	'Round the World with the Rubber Duck/Night Rider	1976	—	2.00	4.00
❑ 14377	Audubon/Ratchetjaw	1977	—	2.00	4.00
❑ 14420	Roses for Mama/Columbine	1977	—	2.00	4.00
❑ 14445	Sing Silent Night/Old Glory	1977	—	2.50	5.00
❑ 14458	Old Glory/Watch the Wildwood Flowers	1978	—	2.00	4.00
❑ 14527	Outlaws and Lone Star Beer/Silver Cloud Breakdown	1978	—	2.00	4.00
❑ 14550	Milton/The Little Things in Life	1979	—	2.00	4.00

Albums

MGM

Number	Title (A Side/B Side)	Yr	VG	VG+	NM
❑ M3G-4989	Wolf Creek Pass	1975	2.50	5.00	10.00
❑ M3G-5008	Black Bear Road	1975	2.50	5.00	10.00

POLYDOR

Number	Title (A Side/B Side)	Yr	VG	VG+	NM
❑ PD-1-6069	Wilderness	1976	2.50	5.00	10.00
❑ PD-1-6094	Rubber Duck	1977	2.50	5.00	10.00
❑ PD-1-6125	Roses for Mama	1978	2.50	5.00	10.00
❑ PD-1-6156	Greatest Hits	1978	2.50	5.00	10.00
❑ PD-1-6190	C.W. McCall & Co.	1979	2.50	5.00	10.00
❑ 825793-1	Greatest Hits	198?	2.00	4.00	8.00
—Reissue of 6156					

MCCALL, DARRELL

Also see JOHNNY BUSH; CURTIS POTTER.

45s

ATLANTIC

Number	Title (A Side/B Side)	Yr	VG	VG+	NM
❑ 4019	There's Still a Lot of Love in San Antone/A Texas Honky Tonk	1974	—	2.50	5.00
❑ 4200	If You Don't Know Your Roses/Where Is All That Love You Talked About	1974	—	2.50	5.00

AVCO

Number	Title (A Side/B Side)	Yr	VG	VG+	NM
❑ 609	Cold Beer Signs and Country Music/Face to the Wall	1975	—	3.00	6.00
❑ 615	Helpless/If You Don't Believe I Love You	1975	—	3.00	6.00

CAPITOL

Number	Title (A Side/B Side)	Yr	VG	VG+	NM
❑ 4543	My Kind of Lovin'/Beyond Imagination	1961	3.00	6.00	12.00
❑ 4609	Call the Zoo/Lonesome	1961	3.00	6.00	12.00

COLUMBIA

Number	Title (A Side/B Side)	Yr	VG	VG+	NM
❑ 3-10296	Pins and Needles (In My Heart)/Every Girl I See	1976	—	2.50	5.00
❑ 3-10410	I Come Home to Face the Music/It's Been So Long, Darlin'	1976	—	2.50	5.00
❑ 3-10480	Lily Dale/Please Don't Leave Me	1976	—	2.50	5.00
—A-side with Willie Nelson					
❑ 3-10576	Dreams of a Dreamer/Sad Songs and Waltzes	1977	—	2.50	5.00
❑ 3-10653	Down the Roads of Daddy's Dreams/An Old Memory's Arms	1977	—	2.50	5.00
❑ 3-10723	The Weeds Outlived the Roses/Love Didn't Drive My Good Woman Wild	1978	—	2.50	5.00

INDIGO

Number	Title (A Side/B Side)	Yr	VG	VG+	NM
❑ 304	Memphis in May/(B-side unknown)	1984	—	3.00	6.00

PHILIPS

Number	Title (A Side/B Side)	Yr	VG	VG+	NM
❑ 40053	I Can Take His Baby Away/A Man Can Change	1962	2.50	5.00	10.00
❑ 40079	A Stranger Was Here/I'm a Little Bit Lonely	1962	2.50	5.00	10.00
❑ 40116	No Place to Hide/Hud	1963	2.50	5.00	10.00
❑ 40154	Keeping My Feet on the Ground/Got My Baby on My Mind	1963	2.50	5.00	10.00

RCA

Number	Title (A Side/B Side)	Yr	VG	VG+	NM
❑ PB-12033	Long Line of Empties/I Wonder Which One of Us Is to Blame	1980	—	2.00	4.00

WAYSIDE

Number	Title (A Side/B Side)	Yr	VG	VG+	NM
❑ 003	Hurry Up/Wedding Band	1969	—	3.00	6.00
❑ 005	Hide and Go Cheat/Tiny Ribbons	1969	—	3.00	6.00
❑ 008	The Arms of My Weakness/Big Oak Tree	1970	—	3.00	6.00
❑ 011	Sally Bryson/(B-side unknown)	1970	—	3.00	6.00
❑ 1011	I'd Love to Live with You Again/I Love You Baby	1968	—	3.50	7.00
❑ 1021	Wall of Pictures/I'd Die to See You Smile	1968	—	3.50	7.00

Albums

COLUMBIA

Number	Title (A Side/B Side)	Yr	VG	VG+	NM
❑ KC 34718	Lily Dale	1977	3.00	6.00	12.00

WAYSIDE

Number	Title (A Side/B Side)	Yr	VG	VG+	NM
❑ 1030	Meet Darrell McCall	1969	5.00	10.00	20.00

MCCARTERS, THE

45s

WARNER BROS.

Number	Title (A Side/B Side)	Yr	VG	VG+	NM
❑ 7-19836	Shot Full of Love/Mountain Memories	1990	—	2.00	4.00
—As "Jennifer McCarter and the McCarters"					
❑ 7-19964	Better Be Home Soon/Moving On	1990	—	2.00	4.00
—As "Jennifer McCarter and the McCarters"					
❑ 7-22763	Quit While I'm Behind/Oh Lonesome You	1989	—	—	3.00
—As "Jennifer McCarter and the McCarters"					
❑ 7-22991	Up and Gone/Letter from Home	1989	—	—	3.00
❑ 7-27721	I Give You Music/The Memories Remain	1988	—	—	3.00
❑ 7-27868	The Gift/Loving You	1988	—	—	3.00
❑ 7-27868 [PS]	The Gift/Loving You	1988	—	2.00	4.00
❑ 7-28125	Timeless and True Love/My Songbird	1987	—	—	3.00
❑ 7-28125 [PS]	Timeless and True Love/My Songbird	1987	—	2.00	4.00

Albums

WARNER BROS.

Number	Title (A Side/B Side)	Yr	VG	VG+	NM
❑ 25737	The Gift	1988	2.50	5.00	10.00

MCCARTNEY, PAUL

Only those forays into country music are included — "Country Dreamer," the B-side of "Helen Wheels"; "Sally G," the B-side of "Junior's Farm" and a Top 100 country hit; and the Country Hams sessions.

45s

Number	Title (A Side/B Side)	Yr	VG	VG+	NM
APPLE					
❑ 1869	Helen Wheels/Country Dreamer	1973	2.00	4.00	8.00
	—Paul McCartney and Wings				
❑ 1875	Junior's Farm/Sally G	1974	2.00	4.00	8.00
	—Paul McCartney and Wings				
❑ 1875	Junior's Farm/Sally G	1975	20.00	40.00	80.00
	—Paul McCartney and Wings; with "All Rights Reserved" on label				
❑ P-1875 [DJ]	Sally G (mono/stereo)	1974	20.00	40.00	80.00
	—Paul McCartney and Wings				
❑ PRO-6787 [DJ]	Country Dreamer (mono/stereo)	1973	100.00	200.00	400.00
	—Paul McCartney and Wings				
CAPITOL					
❑ 1869	Helen Wheels/Country Dreamer	1976	3.75	7.50	15.00
	—Paul McCartney and Wings; black label				
❑ 1875	Junior's Farm/Sally G	1976	3.75	7.50	15.00
	—Paul McCartney and Wings; black label				
EMI					
❑ 3977	Walking in the Park with Eloise/Bridge on the River Suite	1974	15.00	30.00	60.00
❑ 3977 [PS]	Walking in the Park with Eloise/Bridge on the River Suite	1974	20.00	40.00	80.00
	—As "The Country Hams"				

MCCLAIN, CHARLY

Also see JOHNNY RODRIGUEZ.

45s

Number	Title (A Side/B Side)	Yr	VG	VG+	NM
EPIC					
❑ 19-01045	Surround Me with Love/He's Back	1981	—	—	3.00
❑ 14-02421	Sleepin' with the Radio On/That's All a Woman Lives For	1981	—	—	3.00
❑ 14-02656	The Very Best Is You/Love Left Over	1981	—	—	3.00
❑ 14-02975	Dancing Your Memory Away/Love This Time	1982	—	—	3.00
❑ 34-03308	With You/Crazy Hearts	1982	—	—	3.00
❑ 34-03808	Fly Into Love/The Best That Never Was	1983	—	—	3.00
❑ 34-04172	Sentimental Ol' You/I'll Get You Back	1983	—	—	3.00
❑ 34-04423	Band of Gold/His Love Is Out of My Hands	1984	—	—	3.00
❑ 34-04586	Some Hearts Get All the Breaks/Someone Just Like You	1984	—	—	3.00
❑ 34-04777	Radio Heart/You Make Me Feel So Good	1985	—	—	3.00
❑ 34-06167	So This Is Love/Too Many Tears Too Late	1986	—	—	3.00
❑ 34-06980	Don't Touch Me There/I Know the Way By Heart	1987	—	—	3.00
❑ 34-07244	And Then Some/What Makes Love Go Round N' Round	1987	—	—	3.00
❑ 34-07670	Still I Stay/If You Didn't Need Me	1988	—	—	3.00
❑ 50285	Lay Down/Pride and Sorrow	1976	—	2.00	4.00
❑ 50338	Lay Something on My Bed Besides a Blanket/Love Me 'Til the Morning Comes	1977	—	2.00	4.00
❑ 50378	It's Too Late to Love Me Now/You Can Love It Away	1977	—	2.00	4.00
❑ 50436	Make the World Go Away/Leanin' on the Bottle (And Slowly Fallig Down)	1977	—	2.00	4.00
❑ 50525	Let Me Be Your Baby/Your Eyes	1978	—	2.00	4.00
❑ 50598	That's What You Do to Me/1 + 1 = Love	1978	—	2.00	4.00
❑ 50653	Take Me Back/Bedtime Comes Earlier at Our House	1978	—	2.00	4.00
❑ 50706	When a Love Ain't Right/You Can't Make Love by Yourself	1979	—	2.00	4.00
❑ 50759	You're a Part of Me/I Never Loved Nobody Like I Loved You	1979	—	2.00	4.00
❑ 50825	Men/Come Take Care of Me	1979	—	2.00	4.00
❑ 50873	Let's Put Our Love in Motion/I'm Puttin' My Love Inside You	1980	—	2.00	4.00
❑ 50916	Women Get Lonely/I'd Rather Fall in Love with You	1980	—	2.00	4.00
❑ 50948	Who's Cheatin' Who/Love Scenes	1980	—	2.00	4.00
MERCURY					
❑ 870508-7	Sometimes She Feels Like a Man/You Can Be You (And Be Mine Too)	1988	—	—	3.00
❑ 872036-7	Down the Road/You Can Be You (And Be Mine Too)	1988	—	—	3.00
❑ 872506-7	One in Your Heart One on Your Mind/You Got the Job	1989	—	—	3.00
❑ 872998-7	You Got the Job/You Can Be You (And Be Mine Too)	1989	—	—	3.00

Albums

Number	Title (A Side/B Side)	Yr	VG	VG+	NM
EPIC					
❑ PE 34447	Here's Charly McClain	1977	3.00	6.00	12.00
	—Original with orange label				
❑ PE 34447	Here's Charly McClain	1979	2.00	4.00	8.00
	—Budget-line reissue with dark blue label and bar code				
❑ KE 35448	Let Me Be Your Baby	1978	3.00	6.00	12.00
	—Original with orange label				
❑ PE 35448	Let Me Be Your Baby	198?	2.00	4.00	8.00
	—Budget-line reissue; dark blue label				
❑ JE 36090	Alone Too Long	1979	3.00	6.00	12.00
❑ JE 36408	Women Get Lonely	1980	2.50	5.00	10.00
❑ PE 36408	Women Get Lonely	198?	2.00	4.00	8.00
	—Budget-line reissue with new prefix				
❑ JE 36760	Who's Cheatin' Who	1980	2.50	5.00	10.00
❑ PE 36760	Who's Cheatin' Who	198?	2.00	4.00	8.00
	—Budget-line reissue with new prefix				
❑ FE 37108	Surround Me with Love	1981	2.50	5.00	10.00
❑ PE 37108	Surround Me with Love	198?	2.00	4.00	8.00
	—Budget-line reissue with new prefix				
❑ FE 37347	Encore	1981	2.50	5.00	10.00
❑ PE 37347	Encore	198?	2.00	4.00	8.00
	—Budget-line reissue with new prefix				
❑ FE 38064	Too Good to Hurry	1982	2.50	5.00	10.00
❑ PE 38064	Too Good to Hurry	198?	2.00	4.00	8.00
	—Budget-line reissue with new prefix				
❑ FE 38313	Greatest Hits	1982	2.50	5.00	10.00
❑ FE 38584	Paradise	1983	2.50	5.00	10.00
❑ PE 38584	Paradise	1985	2.00	4.00	8.00
	—Budget-line reissue with new prefix				
❑ FE 38979	The Woman in Me	1984	2.50	5.00	10.00
❑ PE 38979	The Woman in Me	1986	2.00	4.00	8.00
	—Budget-line reissue with new prefix				
❑ FE 39425	Charly	1984	2.00	4.00	8.00
❑ FE 39871	Radio Heart	1985	2.00	4.00	8.00
❑ FE 40186	Biggest Hits	1985	2.00	4.00	8.00
❑ FE 40534	Still I Stay	1987	2.00	4.00	8.00
❑ FE 40907	Ten Year Anniversary	1987	2.00	4.00	8.00
MERCURY					
❑ 834998-1	Charly McClain	1988	2.00	4.00	8.00

MCCLAIN, CHARLY, AND MICKEY GILLEY

Also see each artist's individual listings.

45s

Number	Title (A Side/B Side)	Yr	VG	VG+	NM
EPIC					
❑ 34-04007	Paradise Tonight/Four Seasons of Love	1983	—	—	3.00
❑ 34-04368	Candy Man/The Phone Call	1984	—	—	3.00
❑ 34-04489	The Right Stuff/We Got a Love Thing	1984	—	—	3.00

Albums

Number	Title (A Side/B Side)	Yr	VG	VG+	NM
EPIC					
❑ FE 39292	It Takes Believers	1984	2.00	4.00	8.00

MCCLAIN, CHARLY, AND WAYNE MASSEY

Also see each artist's individual listings.

45s

Number	Title (A Side/B Side)	Yr	VG	VG+	NM
EPIC					
❑ 34-05398	With Just One Look in Your Eyes/Tangled in a Tightrope	1985	—	—	3.00
❑ 34-05398 [PS]	With Just One Look in Your Eyes/Tangled in a Tightrope	1985	—	2.00	4.00
❑ 34-05693	You Are My Music, You Are My Song/We Got Love	1985	—	—	3.00
❑ 34-05842	When It's Down to Me and You/I'll Always Try Forever One More Time	1986	—	—	3.00
❑ 34-06433	When Love Is Right/Someone Like You	1986	—	—	3.00

Albums

Number	Title (A Side/B Side)	Yr	VG	VG+	NM
EPIC					
❑ FE 40249	When Love Is Right	1986	2.00	4.00	8.00

MCCLINTON, DELBERT

Also see TANYA TUCKER.

45s

Number	Title (A Side/B Side)	Yr	VG	VG+	NM
ABC					
❑ 12132	Object of My Affection/Two More Bottles of Wine	1975	—	2.50	5.00
❑ 12167	Victim of Life's Circumstances/(I Guess I Done Me Some) Honky Tonkin'	1976	—	2.50	5.00
❑ 12218	Blue Monday/Special Love Song	1976	—	2.50	5.00
BOBILL					
❑ 101	I Know She Knows/Please Help Me, I'm Falling	1967	2.50	5.00	10.00
BROWNFIELD					
❑ 303	I Know She Knows/Please Help Me, I'm Falling	1964	5.00	10.00	20.00
CAPITOL/MSS					
❑ 4948	Giving It Up for Your Love/My Sweet Baby	1980	—	2.00	4.00
❑ 4984	Shotgun Rider/Baby Ruth	1981	—	2.00	4.00
❑ 5003	Going Back to Louisiana/Jealous Kind	1981	—	2.00	4.00
❑ 5069	Sandy Beaches/I Wanna Thank You	1981	—	2.00	4.00
CAPRICORN					
❑ 0302	Take It Easy/Lovingest Man	1978	—	2.50	5.00
❑ 0328	Shot from the Saddle (mono/stereo)	1979	2.00	4.00	8.00
	—Only released as a promo				
CURB					
❑ 76823	I'm with You/My Love Is Burnin'	1990	—	2.00	4.00
❑ 76839	My Baby's Lovin'/Who's Foolin' Who	1990	—	2.50	5.00
❑ 76847	I Want to Love You/That's the Way I Feel	1991	—	2.00	4.00
JUBILEE					
❑ 9012	I Know She Knows/Please Help Me, I'm Falling	1965	3.00	6.00	12.00
LONDON					
❑ 9544	Angel Eyes/Dunkirk	1962	5.00	10.00	20.00
	—As "Del McClinton"				
MCA					
❑ 51124	Special Love Song/Let Love Come Between Us	1981	—	2.00	4.00
PARAMOUNT					
❑ 0016	Fannie Mae/I Know She Knows	1969	2.50	5.00	10.00
RISING TIDE					
❑ 56050	Sending Me Angels/Better Off with the Blues	1997	—	2.00	4.00
SOFT					
❑ 1041	100 Pounds of Honey/Zip-a-Dee-Do-Dah	1970	2.50	5.00	10.00

Number	Title (A Side/B Side)	Yr	VG	VG+	NM
Albums					
ABC					
❑ ABCD-907	Victim of Life's Circumstances	1975	5.00	10.00	20.00
❑ ABCD-959	Genuine Cowhide	1976	5.00	10.00	20.00
❑ ABCD-991	Love Rustler	1977	5.00	10.00	20.00
ACCORD					
❑ SN-7145	Wake Up Baby	198?	2.50	5.00	10.00
ALLIGATOR					
❑ AL-3902	Honky Tonkin' (I Done Me Some)	1986	2.50	5.00	10.00
❑ AL-4773	Live from Austin	1989	3.00	6.00	12.00
CAPITOL/MSS					
❑ ST-12115	The Jealous Kind	1980	3.00	6.00	12.00
❑ ST-12188	Playin' from the Heart	1981	3.00	6.00	12.00
CAPRICORN					
❑ CPN-0201	Second Wind	1978	5.00	10.00	20.00
❑ CPN-0223	Keeper of the Flame	1979	3.75	7.50	15.00
INTERMEDIA					
❑ QS-5029	Feelin' Alright!	198?	2.50	5.00	10.00
MCA					
❑ 5197	The Best of Delbert McClinton	1981	2.50	5.00	10.00

MCCLINTON, O.B.

Number	Title (A Side/B Side)	Yr	VG	VG+	NM
45s					
ABC DOT					
❑ 17704	Country Boots/PTA (Part-Time Association)	1977	—	2.50	5.00
❑ 17719	Catfish Bates/Who's Making Love	1977	—	2.50	5.00
❑ 17735	Part-Time Association (PTA)/Talk to My Children's Mama	1977	—	2.50	5.00
ENTERPRISE					
❑ 9033	Country Music's My Thing/San Bernardino	1971	—	3.50	7.00
❑ 9040	Bad Guys Don't Always Wear Black Hats/Ballad of a Stamp Licker	1971	—	3.50	7.00
❑ 9044	Deep in the Heart of Me/Slip Away	1972	—	3.50	7.00
❑ 9051	Six Pack of Trouble/You Don't Love Me	1972	—	3.00	6.00
❑ 9059	Don't Let the Green Grass Fool You/Lay a Little Lovin' on Her	1972	—	3.00	6.00
❑ 9062	My Whole World Is Falling Down/Music City, Tennessee	1973	—	3.00	6.00
❑ 9070	I Wish It Would Rain/Obie from Senatobie	1973	—	3.00	6.00
❑ 9079	You Don't Miss Your Water/Let Me Love You Like I Want To	1973	—	3.00	6.00
❑ 9084	I Want You in the Morning/The Unluckiest Songwriter in Nashville	1973	—	3.00	6.00
❑ 9091	Something Better/I'd Rather Be a Stranger	1974	—	3.00	6.00
❑ 9100	If You Loved Her That Way/Mr. Miller's Granddaughter	1974	—	3.00	6.00
❑ 9107	Lean on Me/Blind, Crippled and Crazy	1974	—	3.50	7.00
❑ 9108	Yours and Mine/Lean on Me	1974	—	3.00	6.00
❑ 9110	Little Boy Blue/Blind, Crippled and Crazy	1975	—	3.00	6.00
EPIC					
❑ 34-06682	Turn the Music On/(Country Music Is) American Soul	1987	—	—	3.00
❑ 34-07124	Still a Wanted Man/I Love Your Face	1987	—	—	3.00
❑ 50563	Hello, This Is Anna/Let's Get It On	1978	—	2.50	5.00
—A-side with Peggy Jo Adams					
❑ 50620	Natural Love/I Can't Get Over Last Night	1978	—	2.50	5.00
❑ 50698	The Real Thing/Crack of Dawn	1979	—	2.00	4.00
❑ 50749	Soap/Miss Sara Lee	1979	—	2.00	4.00
MERCURY					
❑ 73720	Just in Case/Woman, You're Dynamite	1975	—	2.50	5.00
❑ 73777	It's So Good Lovin' You/She'll Never Be That Easy Again	1976	—	2.50	5.00
❑ 73817	Happy Day Inn, North (Room 309)/Black Speck	1976	—	2.50	5.00
❑ 73861	Sweet Thang/Let's Just Celebrate the Temporary	1976	—	2.50	5.00
MOON SHINE					
❑ 3024	Honky Tonk Tan/(B-side unknown)	1984	—	2.50	5.00
❑ 3042	Last Right/(B-side unknown)	1985	—	2.50	5.00
SUNBIRD					
❑ 7554	Not Exactly Free/Walking After Kim	1980	—	2.50	5.00
Albums					
ENTERPRISE					
❑ ENS-1023	Country	1972	7.50	15.00	30.00
❑ ENS-1029	Obie from Senatobie	1973	7.50	15.00	30.00
❑ ENS-1037	Live at Randy's Rodeo	1973	7.50	15.00	30.00
❑ ENS-7506	If You Loved Her That Way	1974	6.25	12.50	25.00
EPIC					
❑ FE 40674	The Only One	1987	2.50	5.00	10.00
HOMETOWN					
❑ 104	Album No. 1	198?	3.00	6.00	12.00

MCCORD, CALI

Number	Title (A Side/B Side)	Yr	VG	VG+	NM
45s					
GAZELLE					
❑ 011	Bad Day for a Break Up/Slow Healing	1987	—	3.00	6.00
❑ 012	All in My Mind/(B-side unknown)	1988	—	3.00	6.00

MCCORISON, DAN

Number	Title (A Side/B Side)	Yr	VG	VG+	NM
45s					
MCA					
❑ 40729	That's the Way My Woman Loves Me/Don't Forget the Man	1977	—	2.50	5.00
❑ 40790	I Carry Your Smile/Don't Forget the Man	1977	—	2.50	5.00

MCCOY, CHARLIE

Number	Title (A Side/B Side)	Yr	VG	VG+	NM
45s					
CADENCE					
❑ 1390	Cherry Berry Wine/My Little Woman	1960	2.50	5.00	10.00
❑ 1415	I Just Want to Make Love to You/Rooster Blues	1962	2.50	5.00	10.00
MONUMENT					
❑ 842	My Babe/Will You Love Me Tomorrow	1964	3.00	6.00	12.00
❑ 870	I'm Ready/Harpoon Man	1965	2.00	4.00	8.00
❑ 893	Girl (Those Were the Good Old Days)/It's a Man Down There	1965	2.00	4.00	8.00
❑ 926	Let Him Go/Screamin', Shoutin', Beggin', Pleadin'	1966	2.00	4.00	8.00
❑ 975	Stubborn Kind of Fellow/My Baby's Back Again	1966	2.00	4.00	8.00
❑ 998	Cold Cold World/You've Got to Face Life	1967	2.00	4.00	8.00
❑ 1076	Gimme Some Lovin'/Boy from England	1968	—	3.00	6.00
❑ 1093	Harper Valley P.T.A./Juke	1968	—	3.00	6.00
❑ 1938	Blue Christmas/Christmas Cheer	1976	—	—	3.00
—"Golden Series" reissue					
❑ 03518	The State of Our Union/Just Doin' Nothin' with You (Is Really Somethin')	1983	—	2.00	4.00
—With Laney Hicks					
❑ 8529	I Started Loving You Again/The Real McCoy	1971	—	2.50	5.00
❑ 8546	I'm So Lonesome I Could Cry/Grade A	1972	—	2.50	5.00
❑ 8554	I Really Don't Want to Know/Minor, Minor	1972	—	2.50	5.00
❑ 8566	Orange Blossom Special/Hangin' On	1973	—	2.50	5.00
❑ 8576	Shenandoah/John Henry	1973	—	2.50	5.00
❑ 8589	Release Me/Fastest Harp in the South	1973	—	2.50	5.00
❑ 8600	Silver Threads and Golden Needles/I Just Can't Stand to See You Cry	1974	—	2.00	4.00
❑ 8611	Boogie Woogie (A/K/A T.D.'s Boogie Woogie)/ Keep On Harpin'	1974	—	2.00	4.00
—With Barefoot Jerry					
❑ 8625	The Way We Were/I Can't Help It	1974	—	2.00	4.00
❑ 8633	Blue Christmas/Christmas Cheer	1974	—	2.50	5.00
❑ 8638	Everybody Stand Up and Holler for the Union/ New River Gorge	1975	—	2.00	4.00
❑ 8650	Please Don't Tell Me How the Story Ends/Juke	1975	—	2.00	4.00
❑ 8660	Blues Stay Away from Me/Pots and Pans	1975	—	2.00	4.00
❑ 8672	Columbus Stockade Blues/(I Heard That) Lonesome Whistle	1975	—	2.00	4.00
❑ 8683	The Star-Spangled Banner/Silver Wings	1976	—	2.00	4.00
❑ 8703	Wabash Cannonball/Ode to Billie Joe	1976	—	2.00	4.00
❑ 21001	Until the Nights/I Love the Way You Love Me	1981	—	2.50	5.00
—With Laney Smallwood					
❑ 45210	Summit Ridge Drive/Play It Again Charlie	1977	—	2.50	5.00
❑ 45224	Amazing Grace/Squeezing	1977	—	2.50	5.00
❑ 45239	Foggy River/Last Letter	1977	—	2.50	5.00
❑ 45258	Fair and Tender Ladies/18th Century Rosewood Clock	1978	—	2.50	5.00
❑ 45272	Drifting Lovers/West Virginia Mountain Melody	1978	—	2.50	5.00
❑ 45282	Midnight Flyer/Cripple Creek	1979	—	2.50	5.00
❑ 45289	Ramblin' Music Man/Red Haired Boy	1979	—	2.50	5.00
❑ 45292	Carolina Morning/Appalachian Fever	1979	—	2.50	5.00
❑ 45296	Cold, Cold Heart/Station Break	1980	—	2.50	5.00
STEP ONE					
❑ 419	One O'Clock Jump/She Sure Knows How to Treat Me Right	1990	—	2.50	5.00
Albums					
CMH					
❑ 9030 [(2)]	Flat-Picking Spectacular	1984	3.00	6.00	12.00
MONUMENT					
❑ 6623	The Real McCoy	1976	2.50	5.00	10.00
—Reissue of 31359					
❑ 6624	Charlie McCoy	1976	2.50	5.00	10.00
—Reissue of 31910					
❑ 6625	Good Time Charlie	1976	2.50	5.00	10.00
—Reissue of 32215					
❑ 6626	The Fastest Harp in the South	1976	2.50	5.00	10.00
—Reissue of 32749					
❑ 6627	The Nashville Hit Man	1976	2.50	5.00	10.00
—Reissue of 32922					
❑ 6628	Charlie My Boy!	1976	2.50	5.00	10.00
—Reissue of 33384					
❑ 6629	Harpin' the Blues	1976	2.50	5.00	10.00
—Reissue of 33802					
❑ 6630	Play It Again Charlie	1976	2.50	5.00	10.00
❑ 7612	Cookin'	1977	2.50	5.00	10.00
❑ 7622	Greatest Hits	1978	2.50	5.00	10.00
❑ 7632	Appalachian Fever	1979	2.50	5.00	10.00
❑ SLP-18097	The World of Charlie McCoy	1968	3.75	7.50	15.00
❑ Z 31359	The Real McCoy	1971	3.00	6.00	12.00
❑ KZ 31910	Charlie McCoy	1972	3.00	6.00	12.00
❑ KZ 32215	Good Time Charlie	1973	3.00	6.00	12.00
❑ KZ 32749	The Fastest Harp in the South	1974	3.00	6.00	12.00
❑ KZ 32922	The Nashville Hit Man	1974	3.00	6.00	12.00
❑ PZ 33384	Charlie My Boy!	1975	3.00	6.00	12.00
❑ PZ 33802	Harpin' the Blues	1975	3.00	6.00	12.00
❑ PW 38387	The Greatest Hits of Charlie McCoy	1982	2.00	4.00	8.00

MCCOY, NEAL

Number	Title (A Side/B Side)	Yr	VG	VG+	NM
45s					
16TH AVENUE					
❑ 70417	That's How Much I Love You/Memphis Might As Well Be on the Moon	1988	—	2.50	5.00
—As "Neal McGoy"					
❑ 70428	That's America/(B-side unknown)	1989	—	2.50	5.00

ATLANTIC

Number	Title (A Side/B Side)	Yr	VG	VG+	NM
❑ 7-84158	Love Happens Like That/Broken Record	1998	—	—	3.00
❑ 7-87053	Then You Can Tell Me Goodbye/Going, Going, Gone	1996	—	2.00	4.00
❑ 7-87120	If I Was a Drinkin' Man/You Gotta Love That	1995	—	2.00	4.00
❑ 7-87213	The City Put the Country Back in Me/Why Not Tonight	1994	—	2.00	4.00
❑ 7-87247	Wink/No Doubt About It	1994	—	2.00	4.00
❑ 7-87287	No Doubt About It/The City Put the Country Back in Me	1994	—	2.50	5.00
❑ 7-87636	This Time I Hurt Her More (Than She Loves Me)/Down on the River	1991	—	2.00	4.00
❑ 7-87740	Hillbilly Blue/At This Moment	1991	—	2.00	4.00
❑ 7-87833	If I Built You a Fire/The Big Heat	1990	—	2.00	4.00

GIANT

Number	Title (A Side/B Side)	Yr	VG	VG+	NM
❑ 7-16837	Every Man for Himself/The Key to Your Heart	2000	—	—	3.00
❑ 7-16871	Forever Works for Me (Monday, Tuesday, Wednesday, Thursday)/Beatin' It In	2000	—	—	3.00

MCCRAY, MACK

45s

DECCA

Number	Title (A Side/B Side)	Yr	VG	VG+	NM
❑ 9-46327	One More Beer/That's a Horse of a Different Color	1951	6.25	12.50	25.00
❑ 9-46354	Rock All the Babies to Sleep/You're My Sweetheart	1951	6.25	12.50	25.00

MCCREADY, MINDY

45s

BNA

Number	Title (A Side/B Side)	Yr	VG	VG+	NM
❑ 64470	Ten Thousand Angels/Not Somebody's Fool	1996	—	2.50	5.00
❑ 64575	Guys Do It All the Time/Guys Do It All the Time (Dance Mix)	1996	2.00	4.00	8.00
❑ 64650	Maybe He'll Notice Her Now/Breakin' It	1996	—	2.00	4.00
❑ 64757	A Girl's Gotta Do (What a Girl's Gotta Do)/Maybe He'll Notice Her Now	1997	—	2.00	4.00
❑ 64990	What If I Do/If I Don't Stay the Night	1997	—	2.00	4.00
❑ 65394	You'll Never Know/Long, Long Time	1998	—	—	3.00
❑ 65512	The Other Side of This Kiss/If I Don't Stay the Night	1998	—	2.00	4.00

CAPITOL NASHVILLE

Number	Title (A Side/B Side)	Yr	VG	VG+	NM
❑ 58890	Scream/I Just Want Love	2000	—	2.00	4.00

MCCULLA, PAULA

45s

RIVERMARK

Number	Title (A Side/B Side)	Yr	VG	VG+	NM
❑ 1001	Thanks for Leavin' Him (For Me)/Heart Over Mind	1988	—	3.00	6.00

MCCULLOUGH, GARY

45s

SOUNDWAVES

Number	Title (A Side/B Side)	Yr	VG	VG+	NM
❑ 4783	The Cheater/I've Been Out of Love Too Long	1987	—	2.50	5.00
❑ 4786	I'd Know a Lie/Easy Way Out	1987	—	2.50	5.00

MCDANIEL, MEL

45s

CAPITOL

Number	Title (A Side/B Side)	Yr	VG	VG+	NM
❑ 4249	Have a Dream on Me/Gotta Lotta Love	1976	—	2.50	5.00
❑ 4324	I Thank God She Isn't Mine/Or I'll Keep On Lovin' You	1976	—	2.50	5.00
❑ 4373	All the Sweet/A Little More Country	1976	—	2.50	5.00
❑ 4430	Gentle to Your Senses/Honky Tonk Lady	1977	—	2.50	5.00
❑ 4481	Soul of a Honky Tonk Woman/Roll Your Own	1977	—	2.50	5.00
❑ 4520	God Made Love/I'll Just Take It Out in Love	1977	—	2.50	5.00
❑ 4569	The Farm/Every Square Has an Angle	1978	—	2.50	5.00
❑ 4597	Bordertown Woman/The Grandest Lady of Them All	1978	—	2.50	5.00
❑ 4691	Love Lies/Oklahoma Wind	1979	—	2.50	5.00
❑ 4740	Play Her Back to Yesterday/T.J.'s Last Ride	1979	—	2.50	5.00
❑ 4784	Lovin' Starts Where Friendship Ends/I Tried	1979	—	2.50	5.00
❑ 4886	Hello Daddy, Good Morning Darling/Cold Hard Facts of Love	1980	—	2.50	5.00
❑ 4949	Countryfied/Manhattan Affair	1980	—	2.50	5.00
❑ 4983	Louisiana Saturday Night/My Ship's Comin' In	1981	—	2.00	4.00
❑ 5022	Right in the Palm of Your Hand/Who's Been Sleeping in My Bed	1981	—	2.00	4.00
❑ 5059	Preaching Up a Storm/In the Heat of the Night	1981	—	2.00	4.00
❑ 5095	Take Me to the Country/10 Years, 3 Kids and 2 Loves Too Late	1982	—	2.00	4.00
❑ B-5138	Big Ole Brew/Lay Down	1982	—	2.00	4.00
❑ B-5169	I Wish I Was in Nashville/Stars	1982	—	2.00	4.00
❑ B-5218	Old Man River (I've Come to Talk Again)/The Big Time	1983	—	—	3.00
❑ B-5259	Hot Time in Old Town Tonight/Some Folks Are Dying to Live Like This	1983	—	—	3.00
❑ B-5298	I Call It Love/Goodbye Marie	1983	—	—	3.00
❑ B-5333	Where'd That Woman Go/You've Got Another Thing Comin' If You Think I'm Comin' Back to Take Another Drink of Your Wine	1984	—	—	3.00
❑ B-5349	Most of All I Remember You/The Gunfighter's Song	1984	—	—	3.00
❑ B-5371	All Around the Water Tank/Cheatin's Only Cheatin'	1984	—	—	3.00
❑ B-5418	Baby's Got Her Blue Jeans On/The Gunfighter's Song	1984	—	2.50	5.00
❑ B-5458	Let It Roll (Let It Rock)/Dreamin' with You	1985	—	—	3.00
❑ B-5513	Stand Up/I Feel a Storm Coming	1985	—	—	3.00
❑ B-5513 [PS]	Stand Up/I Feel a Storm Coming	1985	—	2.00	4.00
❑ B-5544	Shoe String/Worn Out Shoe	1985	—	—	3.00
❑ B-5544 [PS]	Shoe String/Worn Out Shoe	1985	—	2.00	4.00
❑ B-5587	Doctor's Orders/Thank You Nadine	1986	—	—	3.00
❑ B-5620	Stand on It/In Oklahoma	1986	—	—	3.00
❑ B-5620 [PS]	Stand on It/In Oklahoma	1986	—	2.00	4.00
❑ B-5682	Oh What a Night/Chain Smokin'	1987	—	—	3.00
❑ B-5705	Anger & Tears/Sunday Mornin' Preachers	1987	—	—	3.00
❑ B-44052	Love Is Everywhere/Do You Want to Say Goodbye	1987	—	—	3.00
❑ B-44106	Now You're Talkin'/Sunday Mornin' Preachers	1987	—	—	3.00
❑ B-44127	Ride This Train/Jump Into Love	1988	—	—	3.00
❑ B-44158	Real Good Feel Good Song/Chain Smokin'	1988	—	—	3.00
❑ B-44244	Henrietta/Under My Skin	1988	—	—	3.00
❑ B-44303	Walk That Way/The Tractor	1989	—	—	3.00
❑ B-44358	Blue Suede Blues/Oklahoma Shines	1989	—	—	3.00
❑ 7PRO-79791	You Can't Play the Blues (In an Air-Conditioned Room) (same on both sides)	1989	—	3.00	6.00

—Vinyl is promo only

Albums

CAPITOL

Number	Title (A Side/B Side)	Yr	VG	VG+	NM
❑ ST-11694	Gentle to Your Senses	1977	2.50	5.00	10.00
❑ ST-11779	Mello	1978	2.50	5.00	10.00
❑ ST-12116	I'm Countryfied	1980	2.50	5.00	10.00
❑ ST-12208	Take Me to the Country	1982	2.50	5.00	10.00
❑ ST-12265	Naturally Country	1983	2.00	4.00	8.00
❑ ST-12326	Mel McDaniel with Oklahoma Wind	1984	2.00	4.00	8.00
❑ ST-12402	Let It Roll	1985	2.00	4.00	8.00
❑ ST-12437	Stand Up	1985	2.00	4.00	8.00
❑ ST-12528	Just Can't Sit Down Music	1986	2.00	4.00	8.00
❑ ST-12572	Greatest Hits	1987	2.00	4.00	8.00
❑ SN-16307	I'm Countryfied	198?	2.00	4.00	8.00
—Budget-line reissue					
❑ SN-16381	Take Me to the Country	1986	2.00	4.00	8.00
—Budget-line reissue					
❑ C1-48058	Now You're Talkin'	1988	2.00	4.00	8.00
❑ C1-91133	Rock-a-Billy Boy	1989	3.00	6.00	12.00

MCDONALD, SKEETS

45s

CAPITOL

Number	Title (A Side/B Side)	Yr	VG	VG+	NM
❑ F1518	Scoot, Git and Begone/The Blues Is Bad News	1951	6.25	12.50	25.00
❑ F1570	Bless Your Little Old Heart/Today I'm Moving Out	1951	6.25	12.50	25.00
❑ F1771	I'm Hurtin'/Ridin' with the Blues	1951	6.25	12.50	25.00
❑ F1890	Baby Brown Eyes/Fuss and Fight	1951	6.25	12.50	25.00
❑ F1967	Tell Me Why/Be My Life's Companion	1952	5.00	10.00	20.00
❑ F1993	Wheel of Fortune/Love That Hurt Me So	1952	5.00	10.00	20.00
❑ F2073	Curtain of Tears/Please Come Back	1952	5.00	10.00	20.00
❑ F2216	Don't Let the Stars Get In Your Eyes/Big Family Trouble	1952	5.00	10.00	20.00
❑ F2326	Let Me Know/I'm Sorry to Say I'm Sorry	1953	5.00	10.00	20.00
❑ F2434	I Can't Last Long/I've Got to Win Your Love Again	1953	5.00	10.00	20.00
❑ F2523	Baby I'm Courtin'/It's Your Life	1953	5.00	10.00	20.00
❑ F2573	Hi Diddle Dee/Worried Mind	1953	5.00	10.00	20.00
—With Helen O'Connell					
❑ F2607	Looking at the Moon and Wishing/I Need Your Love	1953	5.00	10.00	20.00
❑ F2696	Look Who's Cryin' Now/Walkin' on Teardrops	1954	5.00	10.00	20.00
❑ F2774	I Love You Mama Mia/Remember You're Mine	1954	5.00	10.00	20.00
❑ F2885	But I Do/Your Love Is Like a Faucet	1954	5.00	10.00	20.00
❑ F2976	Smoke Comes Out My Chimney/Each Time a New Love Dies	1954	5.00	10.00	20.00
❑ F3038	Number One in Your Heart/I Can't Stand It Any Longer	1955	5.00	10.00	20.00
❑ F3117	You're Too Late/A Losing Hand	1955	5.00	10.00	20.00
❑ F3215	Strollin'/You Turned Me Down	1955	5.00	10.00	20.00
❑ F3312	Baby I'm Lost Without You/I Got a New Field to Plow	1956	3.75	7.50	15.00
❑ F3378	Fallen Angel/It'll Take Me a Long, Long Time	1956	3.75	7.50	15.00
❑ F3461	You Oughta See Grandma Rock/Heart Breakin' Mama	1956	25.00	50.00	100.00
❑ F3525	You Gotta Be My Baby/Somebody	1956	3.75	7.50	15.00
❑ F3600	Don't Push Me Too Far/You Better Not Go	1956	3.75	7.50	15.00
❑ F3679	Keep Her Off Your Mind/I Am Music	1957	3.75	7.50	15.00
❑ F3741	Welcome Home/Your Sweet Love Is Gone	1957	3.75	7.50	15.00
❑ F3778	Fingertips/Bless Your Little Ol' Heart	1957	3.75	7.50	15.00
❑ F3833	I'm Hurtin'/Love Wind	1957	3.75	7.50	15.00
❑ F4095	What I Know About Her/What Am I Doing Here	1958	3.75	7.50	15.00
❑ F4147	Baby Wait/What a Lonesome Life It's Been	1959	3.75	7.50	15.00

COLUMBIA

Number	Title (A Side/B Side)	Yr	VG	VG+	NM
❑ 4-41556	Cheek to Cheek with the Blues/Where You Go (I'll Follow)	1960	3.00	6.00	12.00
❑ 4-41667	Gotta Get Away from That Crowd/The Everglades	1960	3.00	6.00	12.00
❑ 4-41773	This Old Heart/Make Room for the Blues	1960	3.00	6.00	12.00
❑ 4-42001	You're Not Wicked, You're Just Weak/He'll Let You Live a Little	1961	3.00	6.00	12.00
❑ 4-42252	Same Old Town/I Write You Letters	1961	3.00	6.00	12.00
❑ 4-42421	You Warned Me/What a Fool I Was	1962	3.00	6.00	12.00
❑ 4-42655	Dear John/I've Gotta Show You	1962	3.00	6.00	12.00
❑ 4-42807	Call Me Mr. Brown/This Old Broken Heart	1963	2.50	5.00	10.00
❑ 4-42960	Chin Up, Chest Out/I'd Hate to See Him	1963	2.50	5.00	10.00
❑ 4-43065	Too Many Times Away from You/Think of Me	1964	2.50	5.00	10.00
❑ 4-43152	Down in Mexico/Teardrop Inn	1964	2.50	5.00	10.00

Number	Title (A Side/B Side)	Yr	VG	VG+	NM
❑ 4-43275	Me and My Heart and My Shoes/Mrs. Right's Divorcing Mr. Wrong	1965	2.50	5.00	10.00
❑ 4-43425	Big Chief Buffalo Nickel (Desert Blues)/Day Sleeper	1965	2.50	5.00	10.00
❑ 4-43573	A Member of the Blues/Polly Brown	1966	2.50	5.00	10.00
❑ 4-43791	There Sits an Angel/She's Never Gone That Route	1966	2.50	5.00	10.00
❑ 4-43946	Mabel/Too Much of Me (Walked Away with You)	1966	2.50	5.00	10.00
UNI					
❑ 55041	It's Genuine/Old Indians Never Die	1967	2.50	5.00	10.00
Albums					
CAPITOL					
❑ T 1040 [M]	Goin' Steady with the Blues	1958	20.00	40.00	80.00
❑ T 1179 [M]	The Country's Best	1959	12.50	25.00	50.00
COLUMBIA					
❑ CL 2170 [M]	Call Me Skeets	1964	6.25	12.50	25.00
❑ CS 8970 [S]	Call Me Skeets	1964	7.50	15.00	30.00
FORTUNE					
❑ 3001	The Tattooed Lady and Other Songs	1969	12.50	25.00	50.00
SEARS					
❑ SPS-116 [R]	Skeets	196?	6.25	12.50	25.00

MCDOWELL, RONNIE

Number	Title (A Side/B Side)	Yr	VG	VG+	NM
45s					
CURB					
❑ 10501	It's Only Make Believe/Baby Me Baby	1987	—	—	3.00
❑ 10508	I'm Still Missing You/Suspicion	1988	—	—	3.00
❑ 10521	Never Too Old to Rock 'n' Roll/Rock and Roll Kiss	1988	—	2.50	5.00
—A-side with Jerry Lee Lewis					
❑ 10525	Sea of Heartbreak/Ain't Love Wonderful	1989	—	—	3.00
❑ 10544	Who'll Turn Out the Lights/Hey Hey Miss Lucy	1989	—	—	3.00
❑ 10558	She's a Little Past Forty/Under These Conditions	1989	—	—	3.00
❑ 76811	Sheet Music/(B-side unknown)	1990	—	2.50	5.00
❑ 76826	Paralyzed/Sheet Music	1990	—	2.00	4.00
❑ 76850	Unchained Melody/Sheet Music	1990	—	2.00	4.00
❑ 76888	Since I Don't Have You/Just Out of Reach	1991	—	2.00	4.00
EPIC					
❑ 19-02129	Older Women/No Body's Perfect	1981	—	2.00	4.00
❑ 14-02614	Watchin' Girls Go By/Good Time Lovin' Man	1981	—	2.00	4.00
❑ 14-02884	I Just Cut Myself/World's Greatest Lover	1982	—	2.00	4.00
❑ 14-03203	Step Back/I Never Felt So Much Love (In One Bed)	1982	—	2.00	4.00
❑ 34-03526	Personally/You Make My Day Pay Off (All Night Long)	1982	—	2.00	4.00
❑ 34-03946	You're Gonna Ruin My Bad Reputation/I Should've Lied	1983	—	2.00	4.00
❑ 34-04167	You Made a Wanted Man Out of Me/This Could Take Forever	1983	—	2.00	4.00
❑ 34-04367	I Dream of Women Like You/Your Baby's Not My Baby	1984	—	2.00	4.00
❑ 34-04499	I Got a Million of 'Em/My Baby Don't Wear No Pajamas	1984	—	2.00	4.00
❑ 34-04816	In a New York Minute/Something Special	1985	—	2.00	4.00
❑ 34-05404	Love Talks/She Lays Me Down	1985	—	2.00	4.00
❑ 50696	World's Most Perfect Woman/Rockin' You Easy, Lovin' You Slow	1979	—	2.00	4.00
❑ 50753	Love Me Now/Never Seen a Mountain So High	1979	—	2.00	4.00
❑ 50813	Peaches/When the Right Time Comes	1979	—	—	—
—Canceled?					
❑ 50857	Lovin' a Livin' Dream/When the Right Time Comes	1980	—	2.00	4.00
❑ 50925	Gone/24 Hours of Love	1980	—	2.00	4.00
❑ 50962	Wandering Eyes/What Would Heaven Say	1980	—	2.00	4.00
MCA					
❑ 53126	Make Me Late for Work Today/Hold Me Tight	1987	—	—	3.00
MCA CURB					
❑ 52816	All Tied Up/Strings of Silver Satin	1986	—	—	3.00
❑ 52907	When You Hurt, I Hurt/Whoopla	1986	—	—	3.00
❑ 52994	Lovin' That Crazy Feelin'/I Don't Want to Set the World on Fire	1986	—	—	3.00
❑ 52994 [DJ]	Lovin' That Crazy Feelin' (same on both sides)	1986	2.50	5.00	10.00
—Promo only on red vinyl					
SCORPION					
❑ 135	The King Is Gone/Walking Through Georgia in the Rain	1977	—	3.00	6.00
❑ 149	I Love You, I Love You, I Love You/Fallin'	1977	—	3.50	7.00
❑ 159	Here Comes the Reason I Live/Travelin' Wanderin' Man	1978	—	3.50	7.00
❑ 0533	Only the Lonely/The Bridge Washed Out	1977	2.50	5.00	10.00
❑ 0542	Naturally/Look at the Moon	1977	2.00	4.00	8.00
❑ 0543	The King Is Gone/Walking Through Georgia in the Rain	1977	3.00	6.00	12.00
—Original issue; quickly reissued as Scorpion 135					
❑ 0553	I Just Wanted You to Know/Animal	1978	—	3.50	7.00
❑ 0560	This Is a Holdup/The Bridge Washed Out	1978	—	3.50	7.00
❑ 0569	He's a Cowboy from Texas/When It Comes to You	1978	—	3.50	7.00
❑ 0575	Kiss and Say Goodbye/Heart	1979	2.00	4.00	8.00
❑ 0584	Knight in Faded Blue Jeans/(B-side unknown)	1979	2.00	4.00	8.00
Albums					
CURB					
❑ 10602	I'm Still Missing You	1988	2.00	4.00	8.00
EPIC					
❑ JE 36142	Rockin' You Easy, Lovin' You Slow	1979	2.50	5.00	10.00
❑ PE 36142	Rockin' You Easy, Lovin' You Slow	198?	2.00	4.00	8.00
—Budget-line reissue with new prefix					
❑ JE 36336	Love So Many Ways	1980	2.50	5.00	10.00
❑ JE 36821	Going, Going ... Gone	1980	2.50	5.00	10.00
❑ PE 36821	Going, Going ... Gone	198?	2.00	4.00	8.00
—Budget-line reissue with new prefix					
❑ FE 37399	Good Time Lovin' Man	1981	2.50	5.00	10.00
❑ PE 37399	Good Time Lovin' Man	198?	2.00	4.00	8.00
—Budget-line reissue with new prefix					
❑ FE 38017	Love to Burn	1982	2.50	5.00	10.00
❑ PE 38017	Love to Burn	198?	2.00	4.00	8.00
—Budget-line reissue with new prefix					
❑ FE 38314	Greatest Hits	1983	2.50	5.00	10.00
❑ FE 38514	Personally	1983	2.50	5.00	10.00
❑ PE 38514	Personally	1985	2.00	4.00	8.00
—Budget-line reissue with new prefix					
❑ FE 38981	Country Boy's Heart	1983	2.50	5.00	10.00
❑ PE 38981	Country Boy's Heart	1985	2.00	4.00	8.00
—Budget-line reissue with new prefix					
❑ FE 39329	Willing	1984	2.50	5.00	10.00
❑ FE 39954	In a New York Minute	1985	2.50	5.00	10.00
❑ PE 40643	Older Women and Other Greatest Hits	1987	2.50	5.00	10.00
MCA CURB					
❑ 5725	All Tied Up in Love	1986	2.00	4.00	8.00
SCORPION					
❑ 0010	Live at the Fox	1978	3.75	7.50	15.00
❑ 8021	The King Is Gone	1977	5.00	10.00	20.00
❑ 8028	I Love You, I Love You, I Love You	1978	3.75	7.50	15.00

MCENTIRE, PAKE

Also see THE SINGING McENTIRES.

Number	Title (A Side/B Side)	Yr	VG	VG+	NM
45s					
NSD					
❑ 96	Matches/The World's Champion	1981	—	3.00	6.00
RCA					
❑ 5004-7-R	Bad Love/Every Night	1986	—	—	3.00
❑ 5004-7-R [PS]	Bad Love/Every Night	1986	—	2.50	5.00
—Sleeve is promo only					
❑ 5092-7-R	Heart Vs. Heart/(What I Got Is) Good for You	1987	—	—	3.00
❑ 5207-7-R	Too Old to Grow Up Now/Caroline's Still in Georgia	1987	—	—	3.00
❑ 5256-7-R	Good God, I Had It Good/Every Night	1987	—	—	3.00
❑ 5256-7-R [PS]	Good God, I Had It Good/Every Night	1987	—	2.00	4.00
❑ 5332-7-R	Life in the City/Another Place, Another Time	1988	—	—	3.00
❑ PB-14220	Every Night/Too Old to Grow Up Now	1985	—	—	3.00
❑ PB-14220 [PS]	Every Night/Too Old to Grow Up Now	1985	—	2.00	4.00
❑ PB-14336	Savin' My Love for You/I'm Having Fun	1986	—	—	3.00
Albums					
RCA					
❑ 6607-1-R	My Whole World	1988	2.00	4.00	8.00
RCA VICTOR					
❑ AEL1-5809	Too Old to Grow Up Now	1986	2.00	4.00	8.00

MCENTIRE, REBA

Also see THE SINGING McENTIRES; JACKY WARD.

Number	Title (A Side/B Side)	Yr	VG	VG+	NM
12-Inch Singles					
MCA					
❑ 55195	You Keep Me Hangin' On (Classic Paradise Mix) (Classic Paradise Instrumental)/(Deep Love Mix) (Aphrodisiac Mix)	1996	2.50	5.00	10.00
45s					
MCA					
❑ S45-17446 [DJ]	The Christmas Song (Chestnuts Roasting on an Open Fire)/O Holy Night	1987	2.50	5.00	10.00
❑ S45-17725 [DJ]	I'll Be Home for Christmas/The Christmas Guest	1987	2.50	5.00	10.00
❑ 52349	Just a Little Love/Your Heart's Not In It (What's In It for Me)	1984	—	—	3.00
❑ 52349 [PS]	Just a Little Love/Your Heart's Not In It (What's In It for Me)	1984	—	2.50	5.00
❑ 52404	He Broke Your Mem'ry Last Night/If Only	1984	—	—	3.00
❑ 52468	How Blue/That's What He Said	1984	—	—	3.00
❑ 52527	Somebody Should Leave/Don't You Believe Him	1985	—	—	3.00
❑ 52527 [PS]	Somebody Should Leave/Don't You Believe Him	1985	—	2.50	5.00
❑ 52604	Have I Got a Deal for You/Whose Heartache Is This Anyway	1985	—	—	3.00
❑ 52604 [PS]	Have I Got a Deal for You/Whose Heartache Is This Anyway	1985	—	2.50	5.00
❑ 52691	Only in My Mind/She's the Only One Loving You Now	1985	—	—	3.00
❑ 52767	Whoever's in New England/Can't Stop Now	1986	—	2.00	4.00
❑ 52848	Little Rock/If You Only Knew	1986	—	—	3.00
❑ 52922	What Am I Gonna Do About You/I Heard Her Crying	1986	—	—	3.00
❑ 52922 [DJ]	What Am I Gonna Do About You (same on both sides)	1986	3.00	6.00	12.00
—Promo only on blue vinyl					
❑ 52990	Let the Music Lift You Up/Lookin' for a New Love Story	1986	—	—	3.00
❑ 52990 [DJ]	Let the Music Lift You Up (same on both sides)	1986	2.50	5.00	10.00
—Promo only on yellow vinyl					
❑ 53092	One Promise Too Late/Why Not Tonight	1987	—	2.00	4.00
❑ 53092 [DJ]	One Promise Too Late (same on both sides)	1987	2.50	5.00	10.00
—Promo only on yellow vinyl					
❑ 53159	The Last One to Know/I Don't Want to Be Alone	1987	—	—	3.00

For over 20 years, Reba McEntire has been a consistent presence near the top of the country charts. (Top left) After six years of trying, McEntire finally had her first chart-topping hit in 1982, with "Can't Even Get the Blues." (Top right) After she left Mercury for MCA, Reba's career shot through the roof. Her second No. 1 single with her new label was "Somebody Should Leave" in 1985. (Bottom left) As was true of many other country artists, McEntire still had vinyl made for the record clubs after it was no longer made for the general public. The last of these was the stellar *For My Broken Heart.* (Bottom right) Reba's most recent chart-topping single was in 1998 with the unusual "event" record with Brooks & Dunn, "If You See Him/If You See Her." This 45 was odd because one side had an "MCA Nashville" catalog number and the other side had an "Arista Nashville" catalog number.

Number	Title (A Side/B Side)	Yr	VG	VG+	NM
❑ 53244	Love Will Find Its Way to You/Someone Else	1988	—	—	3.00
❑ 53315	Sunday Kind of Love/So, So, So Long	1988	—	—	3.00
❑ 53402	I Know How He Feels/So, So, So Long	1988	—	—	3.00
❑ 53473	New Fool at an Old Game/You're the One I Dream About	1988	—	—	3.00
❑ 53638	Cathy's Clown/Walk On	1989	—	2.00	4.00
❑ 53694	'Til Love Comes Again/You Must Really Love Me	1989	—	—	3.00
❑ 53763	Little Girl/Am I the Only One Who Cares	1989	—	2.00	4.00
❑ 53970	Rumor Has It/You Remember Me	1990	—	2.00	4.00
❑ 54042	Fancy/This Picture	1991	—	2.50	5.00
❑ 54108	Fallin' Out of Love/Now You Tell Me	1991	—	2.00	4.00
❑ 54223	For My Broken Heart/Bobby	1991	—	2.50	5.00
❑ 54319	Is There Life Out There/Buying Her Roses	1992	—	3.00	6.00
❑ 54386	The Night the Lights Went Out in Georgia/All Dressed Up (With Nowhere to Go)	1992	—	2.00	4.00
❑ 54441	The Greatest Man I Never Knew/If I Had Only Known	1992	—	2.50	5.00
❑ 54496	It's Your Call/For Herself	1992	—	2.00	4.00
❑ 54544	Take It Back/Baby's Gone Blues	1992	—	2.00	4.00
❑ 54599	The Heart Won't Lie/Will He Ever Go Away	1993	—	2.50	5.00
—A-side with Vince Gill					
❑ 54719	Does He Love You/Straight from You	1993	—	2.00	4.00
❑ 54769	They Asked About You/For Herself	1993	—	2.00	4.00
❑ 54823	Why Haven't I Heard from You/If I Had Only Known	1994	—	2.00	4.00
❑ 54888	Till You Love Me/I Wouldn't Wanna Be You	1994	—	2.00	4.00
❑ 54899	She Thinks His Name Was John/I Wish That I Could Tell You	1994	—	2.50	5.00
❑ 54987	The Heart Is a Lonely Hunter/Read My Mind	1995	—	2.00	4.00
❑ 55047	And Still/I Won't Stand in Line	1995	—	—	3.00
❑ 55100	On My Own/Read My Mind	1995	—	—	3.00
❑ 55161	Ring on Her Finger, Time on Her Hands/You Keep Me Hangin' On	1995	—	—	3.00
❑ 55183	Starting Over Again/I Won't Mention It Again	1996	—	—	3.00
❑ 55249	The Fear of Being Alone/Never Had a Reason To	1996	—	—	3.00
❑ 55290	How Was I to Know/Just Looking for Him	1997	—	2.00	4.00
❑ 72001	What If It's You/Close to Crazy	1997	—	—	3.00
❑ 72006	I'd Rather Ride Around with You/State of Grace	1997	—	—	3.00
❑ 72026	What If (same on both sides)	1997	—	—	3.00
❑ 79009	Walk On/It Always Rains on Saturday	1990	—	2.00	4.00
❑ 79071	You Lie/That's All She Wrote	1990	—	2.00	4.00

MCA NASHVILLE

Number	Title (A Side/B Side)	Yr	VG	VG+	NM
❑ 72051	If You See Him/If You See Her (same on both sides)	1998	—	2.00	4.00
—With Brooks & Dunn; B-side listed as Arista Nashville 13116					
❑ 72062	Forever Love/All This Time	1998	—	—	3.00
—As "Reba"					
❑ 72075	Wrong Night/Up and Flying	1998	—	—	3.00
❑ 72094	One Honest Heart/I'll Give You Something to Miss	1999	—	—	3.00
❑ 088 172131	What Do You Say/Nobody Dies from a Broken Heart	1999	—	—	3.00
❑ 088 172143-7	I'll Be/When You're Not Trying To	2000	—	—	3.00
❑ 088 172181 7	We're So Good Together/Nobody Dies from a Broken Heart	2000	—	—	3.00

MERCURY

Number	Title (A Side/B Side)	Yr	VG	VG+	NM
❑ 55014	I've Waited All My Life for You/One to One	1977	3.00	6.00	12.00
❑ 55036	Last Night, Ev'ry Night/Angel in Your Arms	1978	2.00	4.00	8.00
❑ 55058	Runaway Heart/Make Me Feel Like a Woman Wants to Feel	1979	2.00	4.00	8.00
❑ 57003	Sweet Dreams/I'm a Woman	1979	—	3.50	7.00
❑ 57014	(I Still Long to Hold You) Now and Then/It's Gotta Be Love	1979	—	3.50	7.00
❑ 57025	(You Lift Me) Up to Heaven/Rain Fallin'	1980	—	3.50	7.00
❑ 57034	I Can See Forever in Your Eyes/A Poor Man's Roses	1980	—	3.50	7.00
❑ 57046	I Don't Think Love Ought to Be That Way/Tears on My Pillow	1981	—	3.50	7.00
❑ 57054	Today All Over Again/Look at the One (Who's Been Looking at You)	1981	—	3.50	7.00
❑ 57062	Only You (And You Alone)/Love by Love	1981	—	3.50	7.00
❑ 57062 [PS]	Only You (And You Alone)/Love by Love	1981	2.50	5.00	10.00
❑ 73788	I Don't Want to Be a One Night Stand/I'm Not Your Kind of Girl	1976	2.50	5.00	10.00
❑ 73879	(There's Nothing Like the Love) Between a Woman and a Man/I Was Glad to Give My Everything to You	1977	2.50	5.00	10.00
❑ 73929	Glad I Waited Just for You/Invitation to the Blues	1977	2.50	5.00	10.00
❑ 76157	I'm Not That Lonely Yet/Over, Under and Around	1982	—	3.00	6.00
❑ 76180	Can't Even Get the Blues/Sweet Dreams	1982	—	3.00	6.00
❑ 810338-7	You're the First Time I've Thought About Leaving/Up to Heaven	1983	—	3.00	6.00
—Chicago skyline label					
❑ 810338-7	You're the First Time I've Thought About Leaving/Up to Heaven	1983	—	2.00	4.00
—Black label					
❑ 812632-7	Why Do We Want (What We Know We Can't Have)/I Can See Forever in Your Eyes	1983	—	2.50	5.00
❑ 814629-7	There Ain't No Future in This/Reasons	1983	—	2.50	5.00

Albums

MCA

Number	Title (A Side/B Side)	Yr	VG	VG+	NM
❑ 5475	Just a Little Love	1984	2.00	4.00	8.00
❑ 5516	My Kind of Country	1984	2.00	4.00	8.00
❑ 5585	Have I Got a Deal for You	1985	2.00	4.00	8.00
❑ 5691	Whoever's in New England	1986	2.00	4.00	8.00
❑ 5807	What Am I Gonna Do About You	1986	2.00	4.00	8.00
❑ 5979	Reba McEntire's Greatest Hits	1987	2.00	4.00	8.00
❑ 6294	Sweet Sixteen	1989	2.50	5.00	10.00
❑ 1P-8162	For My Broken Heart	1991	6.25	12.50	25.00
—Only released on vinyl through Columbia House					
❑ 10016	Rumor Has It	1990	5.00	10.00	20.00
❑ 42030	The Last One to Know	1987	2.00	4.00	8.00
❑ 42031	Merry Christmas to You	1987	2.50	5.00	10.00
❑ 42134	Reba	1988	2.00	4.00	8.00
❑ R 164184	Merry Christmas to You	1987	3.00	6.00	12.00
—BMG Direct Marketing edition					
❑ R 244602 [(2)]	Reba Live	1989	6.25	12.50	25.00
—Only released on vinyl through BMG Direct Marketing					

MERCURY

Number	Title (A Side/B Side)	Yr	VG	VG+	NM
❑ SRM-1-1177	Reba McEntire	1977	25.00	50.00	100.00
❑ SRM-1-4047	Unlimited	1982	6.25	12.50	25.00
❑ SRM-1-5002	Reba McEntire	1977	10.00	20.00	40.00
—Reissue of 1177					
❑ SRM-1-5017	Out of a Dream	1979	10.00	20.00	40.00
❑ SRM-1-5029	Feel the Fire	1980	7.50	15.00	30.00
❑ SRM-1-6003	Heart to Heart	1981	7.50	15.00	30.00
❑ 812781-1	Behind the Scene	1983	5.00	10.00	20.00
❑ 822455-1	Reba Nell McEntire	1986	2.50	5.00	10.00
❑ 822882-1	Unlimited	1986	2.50	5.00	10.00
—Reissue					
❑ 822887-1	Feel the Fire	1986	2.50	5.00	10.00
—Reissue					
❑ 824342-1	The Best of Reba McEntire	1985	2.50	5.00	10.00

MCENTIRE, REBA, AND JERRY FULLER

45s

MERCURY

Number	Title (A Side/B Side)	Yr	VG	VG+	NM
❑ 888027-7	It's Another Silent Night/Hold On	1986	—	2.50	5.00

MCEUEN, JOHN

45s

WARNER BROS.

Number	Title (A Side/B Side)	Yr	VG	VG+	NM
❑ 28983	Fly Trouble/Streetwalk	1985	—	2.00	4.00
❑ 29047	Blue Days Black Nights/John Hardy	1985	—	2.00	4.00

Albums

WARNER BROS.

Number	Title (A Side/B Side)	Yr	VG	VG+	NM
❑ 25266	John McEuen	1985	2.00	4.00	8.00

MCGILL, TONY

45s

KILLER

Number	Title (A Side/B Side)	Yr	VG	VG+	NM
❑ 1004	Like an Oklahoma Morning/(B-side unknown)	1986	—	3.00	6.00
❑ 1006	Taming My Mind/(B-side unknown)	1987	—	3.00	6.00
❑ 1008	For Your Love/(B-side unknown)	1987	—	3.00	6.00

MCGOVERN, MAUREEN

The pop singer, mostly of movie and TV songs, had the below country hit.

45s

WARNER BROS.

Number	Title (A Side/B Side)	Yr	VG	VG+	NM
❑ 8750	Can You Read My Mind/You Love Me Too Late	1979	—	2.00	4.00

MCGRAW, TIM

Also see FAITH HILL.

45s

CURB

Number	Title (A Side/B Side)	Yr	VG	VG+	NM
❑ D7-73019	It's Your Love/She Never Lets It Go to Her Heart	1997	—	2.00	4.00
—A-side with Faith Hill					
❑ D7-73056	One of These Days/Just to See You Smile	1998	—	2.00	4.00
❑ D7-73080	Please Remember Me/For a Little While	1999	—	—	3.00
❑ NR-76923	Indian Outlaw/Don't Take the Girl	1994	—	2.50	5.00
❑ D7-76931	Not a Moment Too Soon/Refried Dreams	1995	—	2.00	4.00
❑ D7-76961	I Like It, I Love It, I Want Some More of It/(Dance Mix)	1995	—	2.50	5.00
❑ D7-76971	Can't Be Really Gone/That's Just Me	1995	—	2.00	4.00

Albums

CURB

Number	Title (A Side/B Side)	Yr	VG	VG+	NM
❑ (# unknown) [DJ]	Everywhere	1997	6.25	12.50	25.00
—Promo-only picture disc					

MCGUFFEY LANE

45s

ATCO

Number	Title (A Side/B Side)	Yr	VG	VG+	NM
❑ 7319	Long Time Lovin' You/(B-side unknown)	1980	—	3.00	6.00
❑ 7345	Start It All Over/Don't You Think About Me (When I'm Gone)	1982	—	2.50	5.00
❑ 7404	Fallin' Timber/A New Beginning	1982	—	2.50	5.00
❑ 99908	Doing It Right/Too Many Days	1983	—	2.00	4.00
❑ 99959	Making a Living's Been Killing Me/You Wouldn't Give Up on Me	1982	—	2.00	4.00

ATLANTIC AMERICA

Number	Title (A Side/B Side)	Yr	VG	VG+	NM
❑ 99717	The First Time/You've Got a Right	1984	—	2.00	4.00
❑ 99778	Day by Day/Jamaica in My Mind	1984	—	2.00	4.00

Albums

ATCO

Number	Title (A Side/B Side)	Yr	VG	VG+	NM
❑ SD 38-133	McGuffey Lane	1980	2.50	5.00	10.00
❑ SD 38-144	Aqua Dream	1982	2.50	5.00	10.00
❑ 90020	Let the Hard Times Roll	1983	2.00	4.00	8.00

ATLANTIC AMERICA

Number	Title (A Side/B Side)	Yr	VG	VG+	NM
❑ 90155	Day by Day	1984	2.00	4.00	8.00

MCGUINN, ROGER
Also see THE BYRDS.

45s
COLUMBIA

Number	Title (A Side/B Side)	Yr	VG	VG+	NM
❑ 10019	Gate of Horn/Same Old Sound	1974	—	3.00	6.00
❑ 10181	Somebody Loves You/Easy Does It	1975	—	3.00	6.00
❑ 10201	Lover of the Bayou/Easy Does It	1975	—	3.00	6.00
❑ 10385	Take Me Away/Friend	1976	—	3.00	6.00
❑ 10543	American Girl/I'm Not Lonely Anymore	1977	—	3.00	6.00
❑ 45931	Draggin'/Time Cube	1973	—	3.00	6.00

Albums
ARISTA

Number	Title (A Side/B Side)	Yr	VG	VG+	NM
❑ AL 8648	Back from Rio	1991	3.75	7.50	15.00

COLUMBIA

Number	Title (A Side/B Side)	Yr	VG	VG+	NM
❑ AS 353 [DJ]	The Roger McGuinn Airplay Anthology	1977	7.50	15.00	30.00
—Promo only; also includes Byrds tracks					
❑ KC 31946	Roger McGuinn	1973	3.00	6.00	12.00
❑ KC 32956	Peace On You	1974	3.00	6.00	12.00
❑ PC 33541	Roger McGuinn & Band	1975	3.00	6.00	12.00
❑ PC 34154	Cardiff Rose	1976	3.00	6.00	12.00
❑ PC 34656	Thunderbyrd	1977	3.00	6.00	12.00

MCGUINN AND HILLMAN
Also see CHRIS HILLMAN; ROGER McGUINN.

45s
CAPITOL

Number	Title (A Side/B Side)	Yr	VG	VG+	NM
❑ 4952	Turn Your Radio On/Making Movies	1980	—	2.00	4.00
❑ 4965	Love Me Tonight/Two Lonely Nights	1981	—	2.00	4.00

UNIVERSAL

Number	Title (A Side/B Side)	Yr	VG	VG+	NM
❑ UVL-66006	You Ain't Going Nowhere/Don't You Hear Jerusalem Moan	1989	—	2.00	4.00
—As "Chris Hillman and Roger McGuinn"					

Albums
CAPITOL

Number	Title (A Side/B Side)	Yr	VG	VG+	NM
❑ SOO-12108	McGuinn and Hillman	1980	2.50	5.00	10.00

MCGUINN, CLARK, & HILLMAN
Also see CHRIS HILLMAN; ROGER McGUINN.

45s
CAPITOL

Number	Title (A Side/B Side)	Yr	VG	VG+	NM
❑ 4693	Don't You Write Her Off/Sad Boy	1979	—	2.50	5.00
❑ 4739	Surrender to Me/Little Mama	1979	—	2.00	4.00
❑ 4763	Bye Bye Baby/Backstage Pass	1979	—	2.00	4.00
❑ 4821	Street Talk/One More Chance	1980	—	2.00	4.00
❑ 4855	Deeper/City	1980	—	2.00	4.00

Albums
CAPITOL

Number	Title (A Side/B Side)	Yr	VG	VG+	NM
❑ SW-11910	McGuinn, Clark & Hillman	1979	3.00	6.00	12.00
❑ ST-12043	City	1980	3.00	6.00	12.00

MCGUIRE, DOUG

45s
MULTI-MEDIA

Number	Title (A Side/B Side)	Yr	VG	VG+	NM
❑ 7	Stranger, I'm Married/Oh What a Moment	1980	—	3.00	6.00

MCKUHEN, LANIER

45s
SOUNDWAVES

Number	Title (A Side/B Side)	Yr	VG	VG+	NM
❑ 4764	I'd Rather Be Your Lover Than Your Friend/Let It Be a Dream	1986	—	2.50	5.00
❑ 4767	Counting My Memories/Face to Face	1986	—	2.50	5.00
❑ 4777	Rockin' at the Reunion/Let It Be a Dream	1986	—	2.50	5.00
❑ 4781	Small Change/When I'm with You	1987	—	2.50	5.00
❑ 4785	Searching (For Someone Like You)/Face to Face	1987	—	2.50	5.00

MCLEAN, DON
Began making the country charts in the early 1980s.

45s
ARISTA

Number	Title (A Side/B Side)	Yr	VG	VG+	NM
❑ 0284	Prime Time/The Statue	1977	—	2.00	4.00
❑ 0379	It Doesn't Matter Anymore/If We Try	1978	—	2.00	4.00

CAPITOL

Number	Title (A Side/B Side)	Yr	VG	VG+	NM
❑ B-44098	Perfect Love/Can't Blame the Train	1987	—	—	3.00
❑ B-44186	Love in the Heart/Every Day's a Miracle	1988	—	—	3.00
❑ B-44258	Eventually/It's Not Your Fault	1988	—	—	3.00

EMI

Number	Title (A Side/B Side)	Yr	VG	VG+	NM
❑ 9100	American Pie/Vincent	1992	2.00	4.00	8.00
—Scarce reissue with entire 8:30 version of "American Pie" on one side					

EMI AMERICA

Number	Title (A Side/B Side)	Yr	VG	VG+	NM
❑ 8375	He's Got You/To Have and To Hold	1987	—	—	3.00
❑ 43025	Superman's Ghost/(B-side unknown)	1987	—	—	3.00

MEDIARTS

Number	Title (A Side/B Side)	Yr	VG	VG+	NM
❑ 108	And I Love You So/Castles in the Air	1970	2.50	5.00	10.00

MILLENNIUM

Number	Title (A Side/B Side)	Yr	VG	VG+	NM
❑ YB-11799	Crying/Genesis (In the Beginning)	1980	—	2.00	4.00
❑ YB-11803	Lloras "Crying"/Genesis (In the Beginning)	1981	—	—	—
—Unreleased					
❑ YB-11804	Since I Don't Have You/Your Cheating Heart	1981	—	2.00	4.00
❑ YB-11809	It's Just the Sun/Words and Music	1981	—	2.00	4.00
❑ YB-11819	Castles in the Air/Crazy Eyes	1981	—	2.00	4.00
❑ YB-13106	Jerusalem/Left for Dead on the Road of Love	1982	—	2.00	4.00
❑ GB-13477	Crying/Since I Don't Have You	1983	—	—	3.00
—Gold Standard Series					

UNITED ARTISTS

Number	Title (A Side/B Side)	Yr	VG	VG+	NM
❑ XW206	If We Try/The More You Pay	1973	—	2.00	4.00
❑ XW363	Fool's Paradise/Happy Trails	1973	—	2.00	4.00
❑ XW519	Vincent/Dreidel	1974	—	2.00	4.00
—Reissue					
❑ XW520	American Pie (Part 1)/American Pie (Part 2)	1974	—	2.00	4.00
—Reissue					
❑ XW541	Sitting on Top of the World/Mule Skinner Blues	1974	—	2.00	4.00
❑ XW579	Homeless Brothers/La La Love You	1974	—	2.00	4.00
❑ XW614	Wonderful Baby/Birthday Song	1975	—	2.00	4.00
❑ 50796	And I Love You So/Castles in the Air	1971	—	3.00	6.00
❑ 50856	American Pie/Empty Chairs	1971	—	—	—
—Unreleased?					
❑ 50856	American Pie — Part 1/American Pie — Part 2	1971	—	2.50	5.00
❑ 50856 [DJ]	American Pie (mono/stereo)	1971	2.00	4.00	8.00
—With a different edit than the Part 1/Part 2 stock copy					
❑ 50856 [PS]	American Pie	1971	2.50	5.00	10.00
—Comes with both promos and stock copies					
❑ 50887	Vincent/Castles in the Air	1972	—	2.50	5.00
❑ 50887 [PS]	Vincent/Castles in the Air	1972	2.50	5.00	10.00
❑ 51100	Dreidel/Bronco Bill's Lament	1973	—	2.00	4.00

Albums
ARISTA

Number	Title (A Side/B Side)	Yr	VG	VG+	NM
❑ AL 4149	Prime Time	1978	2.50	5.00	10.00

CAPITOL

Number	Title (A Side/B Side)	Yr	VG	VG+	NM
❑ C1-48080	Love Tracks	1988	2.50	5.00	10.00

CASABLANCA

Number	Title (A Side/B Side)	Yr	VG	VG+	NM
❑ NBLP 7173	Chain Lightning	1979	—	—	—
—Canceled					

EMI AMERICA

Number	Title (A Side/B Side)	Yr	VG	VG+	NM
❑ ST-17255	Don McLean's Greatest Hits, Then and Now	1987	2.50	5.00	10.00

LIBERTY

Number	Title (A Side/B Side)	Yr	VG	VG+	NM
❑ LN-10037	American Pie	1980	2.00	4.00	8.00
—Reissue of United Artists 5535					
❑ LN-10157	Tapestry	1982	2.00	4.00	8.00
—Reissue of United Artists 5522					
❑ LN-10211	Homeless Brother	198?	2.00	4.00	8.00
—Reissue of United Artists 315					

MEDIARTS

Number	Title (A Side/B Side)	Yr	VG	VG+	NM
❑ 41-4	Tapestry	1970	5.00	10.00	20.00

MILLENNIUM

Number	Title (A Side/B Side)	Yr	VG	VG+	NM
❑ BXL1-7756	Chain Lightning	1981	2.50	5.00	10.00
❑ BXL1-7762	Believers	1981	2.50	5.00	10.00

UNITED ARTISTS

Number	Title (A Side/B Side)	Yr	VG	VG+	NM
❑ UA-LA161-F	Playin' Favorites	1973	3.00	6.00	12.00
❑ UA-LA315-G	Homeless Brother	1974	3.00	6.00	12.00
❑ UA-LA652-H2 [(2)]	Solo	1976	3.75	7.50	15.00
❑ UAS-5522	Tapestry	1971	3.00	6.00	12.00
—Reissue of Mediarts LP					
❑ UAS-5535	American Pie	1971	3.00	6.00	12.00
❑ UAS-5651	Don McLean	1972	3.00	6.00	12.00

MCMILLAN, JIMMY

45s
BLUM

Number	Title (A Side/B Side)	Yr	VG	VG+	NM
❑ 001	Footsteps/I Can't Look Into Your Eyes	1980	—	3.00	6.00
❑ 767	Her Empty Pillow (Lying Next to Mine)/It Feels So Good	1981	—	3.00	6.00

MCMILLAN, TERRY

45s
RCA

Number	Title (A Side/B Side)	Yr	VG	VG+	NM
❑ PB-12300	All I Really Want to Know/Freight Train Boogie	1981	—	2.00	4.00
❑ PB-13360	Love Is a Full Time Thing/You're Bringing Out the Fool in Me	1982	—	2.00	4.00

STEP ONE

Number	Title (A Side/B Side)	Yr	VG	VG+	NM
❑ 467	I've Got a Feeling/Just As I Am	1993	—	2.00	4.00

MCPHERSON, WYLEY

45s
I.E.

Number	Title (A Side/B Side)	Yr	VG	VG+	NM
❑ 007	Jedediah Jones/Longneck Lonestar	1982	—	3.00	6.00
❑ 007 [PS]	Jedediah Jones/Longneck Lonestar	1982	2.00	4.00	8.00
❑ 009	The Devil Inside/Love Is What You Make It	1982	—	3.00	6.00
❑ 009 [PS]	The Devil Inside/Love Is What You Make It	1982	2.00	4.00	8.00

MCQUAIG, SCOTT

45s
UNIVERSAL

Number	Title (A Side/B Side)	Yr	VG	VG+	NM
❑ UVL-66001	Honky Tonk Amnesia/My Friend the Bottle	1989	—	—	3.00
❑ UVL-66028	Johnny and the Dreamers/High Friends in the Places (All Over Town)	1989	—	—	3.00

Albums
UNIVERSAL

Number	Title (A Side/B Side)	Yr	VG	VG+	NM
❑ UVL-76000	Scott McQuaig	1989	2.50	5.00	10.00

MCVICKER, DANA

45s
CAPITOL

Number	Title (A Side/B Side)	Yr	VG	VG+	NM
❑ B-44155	Rock-a-Bye Heart/It's All So New to Me	1988	—	—	3.00
❑ B-44223	I'm Loving the Wrong Man Again/I'm Lonely for You Only	1988	—	—	3.00

EMI AMERICA

Number	Title (A Side/B Side)	Yr	VG	VG+	NM
❑ B-8371	I'd Rather Be Crazy/Love Spent the Night	1987	—	—	3.00
❑ B-43017	Call Me a Fool/Love Spent the Night	1987	—	—	3.00

Albums

CAPITOL

Number	Title (A Side/B Side)	Yr	VG	VG+	NM
❑ C1-46967	Dana McVicker	1988	2.50	5.00	10.00

MEADE, DONNA

45s

MERCURY

Number	Title (A Side/B Side)	Yr	VG	VG+	NM
❑ 870283-7	Love's Last Stand/I'm Out of the Blue	1988	—	—	3.00
❑ 870575-7	Congratulations/Slow Fire	1988	—	—	3.00
❑ 872010-7	Leavin' on Your Mind/From a Distance	1988	—	—	3.00
❑ 874280-7	When He Leaves You/(B-side unknown)	1989	—	—	3.00
❑ 874806-7	Cry Baby/The Chokin' Kind	1989	—	—	3.00
❑ 888993-7	Be Serious/I'm Out of the Blue	1987	—	—	3.00

Albums

MERCURY

Number	Title (A Side/B Side)	Yr	VG	VG+	NM
❑ 834624-1	Love's Last Stand	1988	2.50	5.00	10.00

MEDLEY, BILL

45s

A&M

Number	Title (A Side/B Side)	Yr	VG	VG+	NM
❑ 1285	A Song for You/We've Only Just Begun	1971	—	2.50	5.00
❑ 1309	You've Lost That Lovin' Feeling/We've Only Just Begun	1971	—	2.50	5.00
❑ 1311	A Song for You/We've Only Just Begun	1971	—	2.00	4.00
❑ 1336	Help Me Make It Through the Night/Hung on You	1972	—	2.00	4.00
❑ 1350	Freedom for the Stallion/Damn Good Friend	1972	—	2.00	4.00
❑ 1371	A Simple Man/Missing You Too Long	1972	—	2.00	4.00
❑ 1434	Put a Little Love Away/It's Not Easy	1973	—	2.00	4.00

COLUMBIA

Number	Title (A Side/B Side)	Yr	VG	VG+	NM
❑ 38-07938	He Ain't Heavy, He's My Brother/The Bridge	1988	—	—	3.00

—B-side by Georgio Moroder

CURB

Number	Title (A Side/B Side)	Yr	VG	VG+	NM
❑ 10542	Most of All You/I'm Gonna Be Strong	1989	—	—	3.00
❑ 76890	Don't Let Go/Bridge Over Troubled Water	1990	—	—	3.00

ELEKTRA

Number	Title (A Side/B Side)	Yr	VG	VG+	NM
❑ 69281	Rude Awakening/Leave Love Behind	1989	—	—	3.00

—B-side by Jonathan Elias

LIBERTY

Number	Title (A Side/B Side)	Yr	VG	VG+	NM
❑ 1402	Don't Know Much/Woman	1981	—	2.00	4.00
❑ 1412	Stay the Night/Grandma and Grandpa	1981	—	2.00	4.00

MCA

Number	Title (A Side/B Side)	Yr	VG	VG+	NM
❑ 53443	Brown Eyed Woman/You've Lost That Lovin' Feelin'	1988	—	—	3.00

MGM

Number	Title (A Side/B Side)	Yr	VG	VG+	NM
❑ 13931	I Can't Make It Alone/One Day Girl	1968	2.00	4.00	8.00
❑ 13959	Brown Eyed Woman/Let the Good Times Roll	1968	2.00	4.00	8.00
❑ 14000	Peace Brother Peace/Winter Won't Come This Year	1968	2.00	4.00	8.00
❑ 14025	Something's So Wrong/This Is a Love Song	1969	2.00	4.00	8.00
❑ 14081	Reaching Back/Someone Is Standing Outside	1969	2.00	4.00	8.00
❑ 14099	Evie/Let Me Love Again	1969	2.00	4.00	8.00
❑ 14119	Hold On, I'm Comin'/Makin' My Way	1970	—	3.00	6.00
❑ 14145	Nobody Knows/Something's So Wrong	1970	—	3.00	6.00
❑ 14179	Gone/What Have You Got to Lose	1970	—	3.00	6.00
❑ 14202	Wasn't It Easy/Gone	1970	—	3.00	6.00

PARAMOUNT

Number	Title (A Side/B Side)	Yr	VG	VG+	NM
❑ 0089	Swing Low, Sweet Chariot/(B-side unknown)	1971	—	3.00	6.00

PLANET

Number	Title (A Side/B Side)	Yr	VG	VG+	NM
❑ YB-13317	Right Here and Now/The Best of My Life	1982	—	2.00	4.00
❑ YB-13425	I'm No Angel/I Need You in My Life	1983	—	—	3.00
❑ YB-13474	For You/I Need You in My Life	1983	—	—	3.00

RCA

Number	Title (A Side/B Side)	Yr	VG	VG+	NM
❑ 5224-7-RX	(I've Had) The Time of My Life/Love Is Strange	1987	—	—	3.00
—A-side: With Jennifer Warnes; B-side by Mickey and Sylvia					
❑ 5224-7-RX [PS]	(I've Had) The Time of My Life/Love Is Strange	1987	—	2.00	4.00
—A-side: With Jennifer Warnes; B-side by Mickey and Sylvia					
❑ PB-13692	I've Got Dreams to Remember/Till Your Memory's Gone	1983	—	—	3.00
❑ PB-13753	I Still Do/I've Got Dreams to Remember	1984	—	—	3.00
❑ PB-13851	Turn It Loose/I've Always Got the Heart to Sing the Blues	1984	—	—	3.00
❑ PB-13962	She Keeps Me in One Piece/Old Friend	1984	—	—	—
—Unreleased					
❑ PB-14021	Is There Anything I Can Do/Old Friend	1985	—	—	3.00
❑ PB-14081	Women in Love/Stand Up	1985	—	—	3.00

REPRISE

Number	Title (A Side/B Side)	Yr	VG	VG+	NM
❑ 0413	I Surrender to Your Touch/Leavin' Town	1965	3.75	7.50	15.00

UNITED ARTISTS

Number	Title (A Side/B Side)	Yr	VG	VG+	NM
❑ XW1256	Lay a Little Lovin' On Me/Wasn't That You Last Night	1978	—	2.00	4.00
❑ XW1270	Statue of a Fool/Wasn't That You Last Night	1978	—	2.00	4.00
❑ 1349	Hello Rock & Roll/Still a Fool	1980	—	2.00	4.00

VERVE

Number	Title (A Side/B Side)	Yr	VG	VG+	NM
❑ 10569	That Lucky Old Sun/My Darling Clementine	1967	2.50	5.00	10.00

Albums

A&M

Number	Title (A Side/B Side)	Yr	VG	VG+	NM
❑ SP-3505	A Song for You	1971	3.00	6.00	12.00
❑ SP-3517	Smile	1972	3.00	6.00	12.00

LIBERTY

Number	Title (A Side/B Side)	Yr	VG	VG+	NM
❑ LT-1097	Sweet Thunder	1981	2.00	4.00	8.00

—Reissue of United Artists 1097

MGM

Number	Title (A Side/B Side)	Yr	VG	VG+	NM
❑ SE-4583	Bill Medley 100%	1968	5.00	10.00	20.00
❑ SE-4603	Soft and Soulful	1969	5.00	10.00	20.00
❑ SE-4640	Someone Is Standing Outside	1969	5.00	10.00	20.00
❑ SE-4702	Nobody Knows	1970	3.75	7.50	15.00
❑ SE-4741	Gone	1970	3.75	7.50	15.00

RCA VICTOR

Number	Title (A Side/B Side)	Yr	VG	VG+	NM
❑ BXL1-4434	Right Here and Now	1982	2.50	5.00	10.00
❑ CPL1-5352	Still Hung Up on You	1984	2.50	5.00	10.00
❑ MHL1-8519 [EP]	I Still Do	1985	2.00	4.00	8.00

UNITED ARTISTS

Number	Title (A Side/B Side)	Yr	VG	VG+	NM
❑ UA-LA929-H	Lay a Little Lovin' on Me	1978	2.50	5.00	10.00
❑ LT-1097	Sweet Thunder	1980	2.50	5.00	10.00

MELLENCAMP, JOHN

The roots rocker had some crossover country success in the late 1980s. "The Lonesome Jubilee" made the country LP charts, and "Jackie Brown" made the country singles charts. In addition to those two, we've included all the singles from the former LP and the album from which the latter came (plus the other singles from it).

45s

MERCURY

Number	Title (A Side/B Side)	Yr	VG	VG+	NM
❑ 870126-7	Check It Out/We Are the People	1988	—	—	3.00
—Mercury releases starting with "870" and "888" are by "John Cougar Mellecamp"					
❑ 870126-7 [PS]	Check It Out/We Are the People	1988	—	—	3.00
❑ 870327-7	Rooty Toot Toot/Check It Out	1988	—	—	3.00
❑ 870327-7 [PS]	Rooty Toot Toot/Check It Out	1988	—	—	3.00
❑ 874012-7	Pop Singer/J.M.'s Question	1989	—	—	3.00
❑ 874012-7 [PS]	Pop Singer/J.M.'s Question	1989	—	—	3.00
❑ 874644-7	Jackie Brown/Jackie Brown (Acoustic Version)	1989	—	—	3.00
❑ 874644-7 [PS]	Jackie Brown/Jackie Brown (Acoustic Version)	1989	—	—	3.00
❑ 874932-7	Let It All Hang Out/Country Gentleman	1989	—	2.00	4.00
❑ 874932-7 [PS]	Let It All Hang Out/Country Gentleman	1989	—	2.00	4.00
❑ 888763-7	Paper in Fire/Never Too Old	1987	—	—	3.00
❑ 888763-7 [PS]	Paper in Fire/Never Too Old	1987	—	—	3.00
❑ 888934-7	Cherry Bomb/Shama Lama Ding Dong	1987	—	—	3.00
❑ 888934-7 [PS]	Cherry Bomb/Shama Lama Ding Dong	1987	—	—	3.00

Albums

MERCURY

Number	Title (A Side/B Side)	Yr	VG	VG+	NM
❑ 832465-1	The Lonesome Jubilee	1987	2.00	4.00	8.00
❑ 838220-1	Big Daddy	1989	2.50	5.00	10.00

MOBILE FIDELITY

Number	Title (A Side/B Side)	Yr	VG	VG+	NM
❑ 1-222	The Lonesome Jubilee	1995	5.00	10.00	20.00

—Audiophile vinyl

MELLONS, KEN

45s

EPIC

Number	Title (A Side/B Side)	Yr	VG	VG+	NM
❑ 34-77390	Lookin' in the Same Direction/Seven Lonely Days (Make One Weak)	1994	—	2.00	4.00
❑ 34-77579	Jukebox Junkie/The Pleasure's All Mine	1994	—	2.00	4.00
❑ 34-77764	I Can Bring Her Back/Honky Tonk Teachers	1994	—	—	3.00
❑ 34-77861	Workin' for the Weekend/Keepin' It Country	1995	—	—	3.00
❑ 34-78066	Rub-a-Dubbin'/Jukebox Junkie	1995	—	—	3.00
❑ 34-78240	Stranger in Your Eyes/Memory Remover	1996	—	—	3.00

MEMPHIS

45s

MPI

Number	Title (A Side/B Side)	Yr	VG	VG+	NM
❑ 1691	We've Got to Start Meeting Like This/Gone But Not Forgotten	1984	—	3.00	6.00

MENSY, TIM

45s

COLUMBIA

Number	Title (A Side/B Side)	Yr	VG	VG+	NM
❑ 38-68676	Hometown Advantage/I've Got to Hand It to You	1989	—	—	3.00
❑ 38-69007	Stone by Stone/I've Got to Hand It to You	1989	—	—	3.00
❑ 38-73204	You Still Love Me in My Dreams/Stone by Stone	1989	—	—	3.00
❑ 38-73332	You Can't Throw Dirt/Stone by Stone	1990	—	—	3.00
❑ 38-73446	Too Close to Tulsa/Stone by Stone	1990	—	—	3.00

GIANT

Number	Title (A Side/B Side)	Yr	VG	VG+	NM
❑ 7-18742	That's Good/The Grandpa That I Know	1992	—	—	3.00
❑ 7-18864	This Ol' Heart/The Grandpa That I Know	1992	—	—	3.00

MEREDITH, BUDDY

45s

NASHVILLE

Number	Title (A Side/B Side)	Yr	VG	VG+	NM
❑ 5015	Time/Please Stay a Little While	196?	5.00	10.00	20.00
❑ 5042	I May Fall Again/Haunted House	1962	5.00	10.00	20.00

RICE

Number	Title (A Side/B Side)	Yr	VG	VG+	NM
❑ 5003	Almost Out of My Mind/Trapper Man	1964	3.00	6.00	12.00
❑ 5011	New Girl in Town/Lonely in Person	196?	2.50	5.00	10.00
❑ 5014	Sugarland U.S.A./We Let Love Go to Sleep	196?	2.50	5.00	10.00
❑ 5017	Big Riverboat Gambler/Just Call My Name	196?	2.50	5.00	10.00
❑ 5019	For the Love of Mike/Little Black Bug	196?	2.50	5.00	10.00
❑ 5021	I Pledge Allegiance/I'm Comin' Back in Style	196?	2.50	5.00	10.00
❑ 5026	Flop Top Beer/We Let Love Go to Sleep	196?	2.50	5.00	10.00

STARDAY

Number	Title (A Side/B Side)	Yr	VG	VG+	NM
❑ 603	Secret Sin/I Miss You All Over	1963	3.75	7.50	15.00
❑ 617	The Heart Is No Plaything/Here I Am Again	1963	3.75	7.50	15.00

MERRILL AND JESSICA
Also see THE OSMONDS.

45s

EMI AMERICA

Number	Title (A Side/B Side)	Yr	VG	VG+	NM
❑ B-8388	You're Here to Remember (I'm Here to Forget)/The Price You Pay	1987	—	—	3.00

MESSINA, JO DEE
45s

CURB

Number	Title (A Side/B Side)	Yr	VG	VG+	NM
❑ D7-73034	Bye-Bye/I'm Alright	1998	—	2.00	4.00
❑ D7-76982	Heads Carolina, Tails California/Walk to the Light	1996	—	2.00	4.00

MESSNER, BUD
Selected 78s

ABBEY

Number	Title (A Side/B Side)	Yr	VG	VG+	NM
❑ 15004	Slippin' Around with Jole Blon/I Died All Over You	1950	5.00	10.00	20.00

METROS, THE
45s

MTM

Number	Title (A Side/B Side)	Yr	VG	VG+	NM
❑ B-72070	After the Passion's Gone/Don't Let Our Love Go (Baby)	1986	—	2.00	4.00

MEYERS, AUGIE
45s

Number	Title (A Side/B Side)	Yr	VG	VG+	NM
ATLANTIC AMERICA					
❑ 99382	Kep Pa So/To Nothing at All	1988	—	—	3.00
AXBAR					
❑ 6020	Release Me/Deep in the Heart of Texas	198?	—	2.50	5.00
PARAMOUNT					
❑ 0192	Sugar Blu/Five Cent Bag	1973	2.00	4.00	8.00
TEXAS RE-CORD					
❑ 103	High Texas Rider/Memories	197?	2.00	4.00	8.00
❑ 106	Why Don't We Make Love Like We Used To/Just Because	197?	2.00	4.00	8.00
—With Domingo Saldivar					
❑ 107	Down in Mexico/The Sun Shines Down on Me in Texas	197?	2.00	4.00	8.00
❑ 121	I Want to See You Again/Wedding Blues	197?	2.00	4.00	8.00
V.O.L.					
❑ 135	If You Ever Go/I've Seen the Way	196?	2.50	5.00	10.00
—As "Augie"					

Albums

Number	Title (A Side/B Side)	Yr	VG	VG+	NM
ATLANTIC AMERICA					
❑ 90856	My Main Squeeze	1988	2.50	5.00	10.00
PARAMOUNT					
❑ PAS-6065	California Blues	1973	5.00	10.00	20.00
POLYDOR					
❑ 24-4069	Western Head Music Co.	1971	5.00	10.00	20.00
TEXAS RE-CORD					
❑ 1002	Live at the Longneck	197?	7.50	15.00	30.00

MEYERS, MICHAEL
45s

MBP

Number	Title (A Side/B Side)	Yr	VG	VG+	NM
❑ 1980	I'm Just the Leavin' Kind/(B-side unknown)	1981	—	3.50	7.00

MIDDLEMAN, GEORGIA
45s

GIANT

Number	Title (A Side/B Side)	Yr	VG	VG+	NM
❑ 7-16852	No Place Like Home/Michelangelo	2000	—	—	3.00

MIDDLETON, EDDIE
45s

EPIC

Number	Title (A Side/B Side)	Yr	VG	VG+	NM
❑ 50388	Midnight Train to Georgia/I've Been Hurt	1977	—	2.00	4.00
❑ 50431	Endlessly/After the Lovin'	1977	—	2.00	4.00
❑ 50481	What Kind of Fool (Do You Think I Am)/Don't Say Let's Wait	1977	—	2.00	4.00

Albums

EPIC

Number	Title (A Side/B Side)	Yr	VG	VG+	NM
❑ PE 34882	Eddie Middleton	1977	2.50	5.00	10.00

MILES, DICK
45s

CAPITOL

Number	Title (A Side/B Side)	Yr	VG	VG+	NM
❑ 2113	The Last Goodbye/Candle-Lighted World	1968	2.50	5.00	10.00
❑ 2225	Thank You for Loving Me/Cap'n	1968	2.50	5.00	10.00
❑ 2357	This Was My World/Wake Up, Son	1968	2.50	5.00	10.00
❑ 2542	The Deal/Happiness Was	1969	2.50	5.00	10.00

Albums

CAPITOL

Number	Title (A Side/B Side)	Yr	VG	VG+	NM
❑ ST 2925	The Last Goodbye	1968	3.75	7.50	15.00

MILLER, CARL
45s

COUNTRY BACH

Number	Title (A Side/B Side)	Yr	VG	VG+	NM
❑ 0004	Life of the Party/Memories	1983	2.00	4.00	8.00

MILLER, DEAN
45s

CAPITOL NASHVILLE

Number	Title (A Side/B Side)	Yr	VG	VG+	NM
❑ S7-19648	Nowhere, U.S.A./If I Was Your Man	1997	—	—	3.00
❑ S7-19896	Wake Up and Smell the Whiskey/Broke Down in Birmingham	1998	—	—	3.00

MILLER, ELLEN LEE
45s

GOLDEN TRUMPET

Number	Title (A Side/B Side)	Yr	VG	VG+	NM
❑ 103	You Only Love Me When I'm Leavin'/(B-side unknown)	1989	—	3.00	6.00

MILLER, FRANKIE
45s

Number	Title (A Side/B Side)	Yr	VG	VG+	NM
COLUMBIA					
❑ 4-21314	It's No Big Thing to Me/Hey, Where Ya Goin'	1954	5.00	10.00	20.00
❑ 4-21378	You're Crying on My Shoulder Again/You Don't Show Me Much	1955	5.00	10.00	20.00
❑ 4-21420	Paid in Full/My Wedding Song for You	1955	5.00	10.00	20.00
❑ 4-21472	Pain, Powder and Perfume/What You Do from Now On	1955	5.00	10.00	20.00
❑ 4-21510	Day by Day/I Don't Know Why I Love You	1956	5.00	10.00	20.00
MERCURY					
❑ 884450-7	Game of Love/I'd Lie to You for Your Love	1986	—	2.00	4.00
STARDAY					
❑ 424	Black Land Farmer/True Blue	1959	3.75	7.50	15.00
❑ 457	Family Man/Poppin' Johnny	1959	3.75	7.50	15.00
❑ 481	The Money Side of Life/Reunion (With Dinner on the Ground)	1960	3.75	7.50	15.00
❑ 496	Baby Rocked Her Dolly/Rain Rain	1960	3.75	7.50	15.00
❑ 513	Strictly Nothin'/Young Widow Brown	1960	3.75	7.50	15.00
❑ 525	Out of Bounds/Two Lips Away	1960	3.75	7.50	15.00
—With Dottie Sills					
❑ 537	I'll Write to You/Richest Poor Boy	1961	3.75	7.50	15.00
❑ 550	Lookin' Around Downtown/A Little Bit Later	1961	3.75	7.50	15.00
❑ 566	The Cat and the Mouse/It's Not Easy	1961	3.75	7.50	15.00
❑ 577	Gotta Win My Baby Back Again/The Picture at St. Helene	1962	3.75	7.50	15.00
❑ 655	A Little South of Memphis/Too Hot to Handle	1963	3.00	6.00	12.00
❑ 673	Out of This World/Fifteen Acres of Peanut Land	1964	3.00	6.00	12.00
❑ 691	It Took a Lot of Love/Mean Old Greyhound	1964	3.00	6.00	12.00
❑ 709	I Can Almost Forget/Big Talk of the Town	1965	3.00	6.00	12.00
❑ 739	Country Music Who's Who/Bringing Mary Home	1965	3.00	6.00	12.00
❑ 777	Charlie's Got a Good Thing Goin'/Tough Road to Hoe	1966	3.00	6.00	12.00
❑ 793	Fickle Hand of Fate/She's My Antibiotic	1967	3.00	6.00	12.00
❑ 8021	Black Land Farmer/Too Hot to Handle	197?	—	3.00	6.00

Albums

Number	Title (A Side/B Side)	Yr	VG	VG+	NM
AUDIO LAB					
❑ AL-1562 [M]	The Fine Country Singing of Frankie Miller	1963	37.50	75.00	150.00
STARDAY					
❑ SLP-134 [M]	Country Music's Great New Star	1961	25.00	50.00	100.00
❑ SLP-199 [M]	The True Country Style of Frankie Miller	1962	25.00	50.00	100.00
❑ SLP-339 [M]	Blackland Farmer	1965	15.00	30.00	60.00

MILLER, JODY
45s

Number	Title (A Side/B Side)	Yr	VG	VG+	NM
CAPITOL					
❑ 2005	To Sir, With Love/Only When You're Lonely	1967	2.00	4.00	8.00
❑ 2066	I Knew You Well/I'm Into Lookin' for Someone to Love Me	1967	2.00	4.00	8.00
❑ 2187	It's My Time/Over the Edge	1968	2.00	4.00	8.00
❑ 2290	Long Black Limousine/Back in the Race	1968	2.00	4.00	8.00
❑ 2398	All the Crying in the World/Bon Soir Cher	1969	—	3.00	6.00
❑ 2558	Times to Come/My Daddy's Thousand Dollars	1969	—	3.00	6.00
❑ 5090	He Walks Like a Man/Looking at the World Through a Tear	1963	2.50	5.00	10.00
❑ 5162	They Call My Guy a Tiger/Wonderful Round of Indifference	1964	2.50	5.00	10.00
❑ 5192	In My Room/Fever	1964	2.50	5.00	10.00
❑ 5269	My Baby's Gone/Warm Is the Love	1964	2.50	5.00	10.00
❑ 5298	This Is the Life/Look for Small Pleasures	1964	2.50	5.00	10.00
❑ 5353	Be My Man/Never Let Him Go	1965	2.50	5.00	10.00
❑ 5402	Queen of the House/The Greatest Actor	1965	2.00	4.00	8.00
❑ 5429	Silver Threads and Golden Needles/Melody for Robin	1965	2.00	4.00	8.00
❑ 5429 [PS]	Silver Threads and Golden Needles/Melody for Robin	1965	3.00	6.00	12.00
❑ 5483	Home of the Brave/This Is the Life	1965	2.00	4.00	8.00
❑ 5483 [PS]	Home of the Brave/This Is the Life	1965	3.00	6.00	12.00
❑ 5541	Magic Town/A Lonely Queen	1965	2.00	4.00	8.00
❑ 5594	We're Gonna Let the Good Times Roll/I Don't Care	1966	2.00	4.00	8.00
❑ 5671	I Remember Mama/Something in My Eye	1966	2.00	4.00	8.00
❑ 5743	Things/Quite a Long, Long Time	1966	2.00	4.00	8.00
❑ 5768	If You Were a Carpenter/Let Me Walk with You	1966	2.00	4.00	8.00
❑ 5846	Crazy/How Do You Say Goodbye	1967	2.00	4.00	8.00
❑ 5911	Shutters and Boards/Kiss Me	1967	2.00	4.00	8.00
EPIC					
❑ 10641	Look at Mine/Safe in These Lovin' Arms of Mine	1970	—	3.00	6.00
❑ 10692	If You Think I Love You Now (I've Just Started)/Looking Out My Back Door	1970	—	3.00	6.00
❑ 10734	He's So Fine/You're Number Two	1971	—	3.00	6.00

Number	Title (A Side/B Side)	Yr	VG	VG+	NM
❑ 10785	Baby I'm Yours/Good Lovin'	1971	—	3.00	6.00
❑ 10835	Be My Baby/Your Love's Been a Long Time Comin'	1972	—	2.50	5.00
❑ 10878	There's a Party Goin' On/Love's the Answer	1972	—	2.50	5.00
❑ 10916	To Know Him Is to Love Him/Make Me Your Kind of Woman	1972	—	2.50	5.00
❑ 10960	Good News/Soul Song	1973	—	2.50	5.00
❑ 11016	Darling, You Can Always Come Back Home/We'll Sing Our Song Together	1973	—	2.50	5.00
❑ 11056	The House of the Rising Sun/In the Name of Love	1973	—	2.50	5.00
❑ 11076	Silent Night, Lonely Night/(B-side unknown)	1973	—	3.00	6.00
❑ 11094	Reflections/One More Chance	1974	—	2.50	5.00
❑ 11134	Natural Woman/Jimmy's Roses	1974	—	2.50	5.00
❑ 50042	Country Girl/Safe in These Lovin' Arms of Mine	1974	—	2.00	4.00
❑ 50079	The Best in Me/I'm Alright 'Til I See	1975	—	2.00	4.00
❑ 50117	Don't Take It Away/Long, Long Time	1975	—	2.00	4.00
❑ 50158	Will You Love Me Tomorrow/Love, You Never Had It So Good	1975	—	2.00	4.00
❑ 50203	Ashes of Love/She Calls Me Baby	1976	—	2.00	4.00
❑ 50304	When the New Wears Off Our Love/Silver and Gold	1976	—	2.00	4.00
❑ 50360	Spread a Little Love Around/Montana Cowboy	1977	—	2.00	4.00
❑ 50432	Another Lonely Night/All Night Long	1977	—	2.00	4.00
❑ 50512	Soft Lights and Slow Sexy Music/Home	1978	—	2.00	4.00
❑ 50568	(I Wanna) Love My Life Away/I'm Gonna Write a Song	1978	—	2.00	4.00
❑ 50612	Kiss Away/Hold Me, Thrill Me, Kiss Me	1978	—	2.00	4.00
❑ 50673	I'm Gonna Make You Mine/I Don't Want Nobody (To Lead Me On)	1979	—	2.00	4.00
❑ 50734	Lay a Little Lovin' On Me/Crazy on You	1979	—	2.00	4.00
Albums					
CAPITOL					
❑ ST 1913 [S]	Wednesday's Child Is Full of Woe	1963	10.00	20.00	40.00
❑ T 1913 [M]	Wednesday's Child Is Full of Woe	1963	7.50	15.00	30.00
❑ ST 2349 [S]	Queen of the House	1965	5.00	10.00	20.00
❑ T 2349 [M]	Queen of the House	1965	3.75	7.50	15.00
❑ ST 2412 [S]	Home of the Brave	1965	5.00	10.00	20.00
❑ T 2412 [M]	Home of the Brave	1965	3.75	7.50	15.00
❑ ST 2446 [S]	Jody Miller Sings the Great Hits of Buck Owens	1966	5.00	10.00	20.00
❑ T 2446 [M]	Jody Miller Sings the Great Hits of Buck Owens	1966	3.75	7.50	15.00
❑ ST 2996	The Nashville Sound of Jody Miller	1968	3.75	7.50	15.00
❑ ST-11169	The Best of Jody Miller	1973	3.00	6.00	12.00
EPIC					
❑ E 30282	Look at Mine	1971	3.00	6.00	12.00
❑ E 30659	He's So Fine	1971	3.00	6.00	12.00
❑ KE 31706	There's a Party Goin' On	1972	3.00	6.00	12.00
❑ KE 32386	Good News!	1973	3.00	6.00	12.00
❑ KE 32569	House of the Rising Sun	1974	3.00	6.00	12.00
❑ KE 33349	Country Girl	1975	3.00	6.00	12.00
❑ KE 33934	Will You Love Me Tomorrow?	1976	3.00	6.00	12.00
❑ PE 34446	Here's Jody	1977	3.00	6.00	12.00

MILLER, JODY, AND JOHNNY PAYCHECK

Also see each artist's individual listings.

45s

Number	Title (A Side/B Side)	Yr	VG	VG+	NM
EPIC					
❑ 5-10863	Let's All Go Down to the River/In the Garden	1972	—	3.50	7.00

MILLER, MARY K.

45s

Number	Title (A Side/B Side)	Yr	VG	VG+	NM
INERGI					
❑ 300	I Fall to Pieces/Just Can't Believe You're Gone	1977	—	2.50	5.00
❑ 302	You Just Don't Know/Lovesick Blues	1977	—	2.50	5.00
❑ 304	The Longest Walk/Love Is	1977	—	2.50	5.00
❑ 306	Right or Wrong/Smile Me a Song	1978	—	2.50	5.00
❑ 307	I Can't Stop Loving You/Let Me Go Lover	1978	—	2.50	5.00
❑ 310	Handcuffed to a Heartache/Over and Over	1978	—	2.50	5.00
❑ 311	Going, Going, Gone/Woman, Woman	1978	—	2.50	5.00
❑ 312	Next Best Feeling/One Woman's Heaven	1979	—	2.50	5.00
❑ 315	Say a Long Goodbye/You Asked Me To	1980	—	2.50	5.00
RCA					
❑ PB-11665	Guess Who Loves You/Georgia on My Mind	1979	—	2.00	4.00
Albums					
INERGI					
❑ ILP-1000	Mary K. Miller	197?	3.00	6.00	12.00

MILLER, NED

45s

Number	Title (A Side/B Side)	Yr	VG	VG+	NM
CAPITOL					
❑ 2074	Endless/Only a Fool	1968	—	3.00	6.00
❑ 4607	My Heart Waits at the Door/Cold Gray Bars	1961	3.00	6.00	12.00
❑ 4652	Dark Moon/Go On Back, You Fool	1961	3.00	6.00	12.00
❑ 5431	Whistle Walkin'/Two Voices, Two Shadows, Two Faces	1965	2.00	4.00	8.00
❑ 5502	Fall of the King/Down the Street	1965	2.00	4.00	8.00
❑ 5568	Lovin' Pains/If the World Turned Into Ashes	1965	2.00	4.00	8.00
❑ 5661	Right Behind These Lips/Summer Roses	1966	2.00	4.00	8.00
❑ 5742	Lorraine/Teardrop Lane	1966	2.00	4.00	8.00
❑ 5868	The Hobo/Echo of the Pines	1967	2.00	4.00	8.00
DOT					
❑ 15601	From a Jack to a King/Parade of Broken Hearts	1957	10.00	20.00	40.00
❑ 15651	Turn Back/Lights in the Street	1957	3.75	7.50	15.00
FABOR					
❑ 114	From a Jack to a King/Parade of Broken Hearts	1962	3.00	6.00	12.00
❑ 116	One Among the Many/Man Behind the Gun	1963	2.50	5.00	10.00
❑ 121	Another Fool Like Me/Magic Moon	1963	2.50	5.00	10.00
❑ 125	Big Love/Sunday Morning Tears	1964	2.50	5.00	10.00
❑ 128	Invisible Tears/Old Restless Ocean	1964	2.50	5.00	10.00
❑ 137	Do What You Do Do Well/Dusty Guitar	1964	2.00	4.00	8.00
❑ 139	What I Know/Lights in the Street	1965	2.00	4.00	8.00
JACKPOT					
❑ 48020	Girl from the Second World/Ring the Bell for Johnny	1960	3.00	6.00	12.00
—With Jan Howard					
RADIO					
❑ 105	Gypsy/With Enough Love	1958	6.25	12.50	25.00
REPUBLIC					
❑ 1404	Autumn Winds/My Last Go-Round	1969	—	2.50	5.00
❑ 1410	Breakin'/Just Walkin' in the Rain	1970	—	2.50	5.00
❑ 1411	The Lover's Song/Cold Gray Bars	1970	—	2.50	5.00
❑ 1416	Back to Oklahoma/I Hang My Head and Cry	1970	—	2.50	5.00
Albums					
CAPITOL					
❑ ST 2330 [S]	Ned Miller Sings the Songs of Ned Miller	1965	6.25	12.50	25.00
❑ T 2330 [M]	Ned Miller Sings the Songs of Ned Miller	1965	5.00	10.00	20.00
❑ ST 2414 [S]	The Best of Ned Miller	1966	5.00	10.00	20.00
❑ T 2414 [M]	The Best of Ned Miller	1966	3.75	7.50	15.00
❑ ST 2586 [S]	Teardrop Lane	1967	5.00	10.00	20.00
❑ T 2586 [M]	Teardrop Lane	1967	5.00	10.00	20.00
❑ ST 2914	In the Name of Love	1968	3.75	7.50	15.00
FABOR					
❑ FLP-1001 [M]	From a Jack to a King	1963	10.00	20.00	40.00
—Black vinyl					
❑ FLP-1001 [M]	From a Jack to a King	1963	25.00	50.00	100.00
—Colored vinyl					

MILLER, ROGER

45s

Number	Title (A Side/B Side)	Yr	VG	VG+	NM
20TH CENTURY					
❑ 2421	The Hat/Pleasing the Crowd	1979	—	2.00	4.00
BUENA VISTA					
❑ 493	Whistle Stop/Not in Nottingham	1973	—	2.50	5.00
❑ 493 [PS]	Whistle Stop/Not in Nottingham	1973	—	2.50	5.00
COLUMBIA					
❑ 02681	Old Friends/When a House Is Not a Home	1982	—	2.00	4.00
—Roger Miller/Willie Nelson/Ray Price					
❑ 10052	Our Love/Yester Waltz	1974	—	2.50	5.00
❑ 10107	I Love a Rodeo/Lovin' You Is Always on My Mind	1975	—	2.50	5.00
❑ 45873	Open Up Your Heart/Qua La Linta	1973	—	2.50	5.00
❑ 45948	I Believe in the Sunrise/Shannon's Song	1973	—	2.50	5.00
❑ 46000	Whistle Stop/The 4th of July	1974	—	2.50	5.00
DECCA					
❑ 30838	Wrong Kind of Girl/A Man Like Me	1959	3.75	7.50	15.00
❑ 30953	Sweet Ramona/Jason Fleming	1959	3.75	7.50	15.00
ELEKTRA					
❑ 47192	Everyone Gets Crazy Now and Then/Aladam Bama	1981	—	2.00	4.00
MCA					
❑ 52663	River in the Rain/Hand for the Hog	1985	—	—	3.00
❑ 52855	Some Hearts Get All the Breaks/Arkansas	1986	—	—	3.00
MERCURY					
❑ 71212	Poor Little John/My Fellow	1957	6.25	12.50	25.00
❑ 73102	South/Don't We All Have the Right	1970	—	2.50	5.00
❑ 73190	Tomorrow Night in Baltimore/A Million Years or So	1971	—	2.50	5.00
❑ 73230	Loving Her Was Easier (Than Anything I'll Ever Do Again)/Que La Linta	1971	—	2.50	5.00
❑ 73268	We Found It in Each Other's Arms/Sunny Side of My Life	1972	—	2.50	5.00
❑ 73321	Rings for Sale/Conversations	1972	—	2.50	5.00
❑ 73354	Hoppy's Gone/I Jumped from Uncle Harvey's Plane	1972	—	2.50	5.00
MUSICOR					
❑ 1102	Can't Stop Loving You/You're Forgetting Me	1965	2.50	5.00	10.00
RCA VICTOR					
❑ 47-7776	Footprints in the Snow/You Don't Want My Love	1960	3.75	7.50	15.00
❑ 47-7878	When Two Worlds Collide/Every Which-A-Way	1961	3.75	7.50	15.00
❑ 47-7958	Burma Shave/Fair Swiss Maiden	1961	3.75	7.50	15.00
❑ 47-8028	Sorry, Willie/Hitch-Hiker	1962	3.00	6.00	12.00
❑ 47-8091	Trouble on the Turnpike/Hey Little Star	1962	3.00	6.00	12.00
❑ 47-8175	Lock, Stock and Teardrops/I Know Who It Is	1963	3.00	6.00	12.00
❑ 47-8651	If You Want Me To/Hey Little Star	1965	2.50	5.00	10.00
SMASH					
❑ 1876	Less and Less/Got Two Again	1964	3.00	6.00	12.00
❑ 1881	Dang Me/Got Two Again	1964	2.50	5.00	10.00
❑ 1881 [PS]	Dang Me/Got Two Again	1964	3.75	7.50	15.00
—Red sleeve					
❑ 1881 [PS]	Dang Me/Got Two Again	1964	5.00	10.00	20.00
—Yellow sleeve					
❑ 1926	Chug-a-Lug/Reincarnation	1964	2.50	5.00	10.00
❑ 1947	Do-Wacka-Do/Love Is Not for Me	1964	2.50	5.00	10.00
❑ 1947 [PS]	Do-Wacka-Do/Love Is Not for Me	1964	3.75	7.50	15.00
❑ 1965	King of the Road/Atta Boy Girl	1965	3.00	6.00	12.00
❑ 1983	Engine, Engine #9/The Last Word in Lonesome Is Me	1965	2.00	4.00	8.00
❑ 1994	One Dyin' and a-Buryin'/It Happened Just That Way	1965	2.00	4.00	8.00

Number	Title (A Side/B Side)	Yr	VG	VG+	NM
❑ 1994 [PS]	One Dyin' and a-Buryin'/It Happened Just That Way	1965	3.75	7.50	15.00
❑ 1998	Kansas City Star/Guess I'll Pack Up My Heart (And Go Home)	1965	2.00	4.00	8.00
❑ 2010	England Swings/Good Old Days	1965	2.00	4.00	8.00
❑ 2024	Husbands and Wives/I've Been a Long Time Leavin'	1966	2.00	4.00	8.00
❑ 2043	You Can't Roller Skate in a Buffalo Herd/Train of Life	1966	2.00	4.00	8.00
❑ 2055	My Uncle Used to Love Me But She Died/You're My Kingdom	1966	2.00	4.00	8.00
❑ 2066	Heartbreak Hotel/Less and Less	1966	2.00	4.00	8.00
❑ 2081	Walkin' in the Sunshine/Home	1967	2.00	4.00	8.00
❑ 2121	The Ballad of Waterhole #3 (Code of the West)/Rainbow Valley	1967	2.00	4.00	8.00
❑ 2121 [PS]	The Ballad of Waterhole #3 (Code of the West)/Rainbow Valley	1967	3.75	7.50	15.00
❑ 2130	Old Toy Trains/Silent Night	1967	2.50	5.00	10.00
❑ 2130 [PS]	Old Toy Trains/Silent Night	1967	3.00	6.00	12.00
❑ 2148	Little Green Apples/Our Little Love	1968	2.00	4.00	8.00
❑ 2148 [PS]	Little Green Apples/Our Little Love	1968	3.00	6.00	12.00
❑ 2183	What I'd Give (To Be the Wind)/Toliver	1968	2.00	4.00	8.00
❑ 2197	Vance/Little Children Run and Play	1968	2.00	4.00	8.00
❑ 2230	Me and Bobby McGee/I'm Gonna Teach My Heart to Bend (Instead of Break)	1969	—	3.00	6.00
❑ 2246	Where Have All the Average People Gone/Boeing Boeing 707	1969	—	3.00	6.00
❑ 2258	The Tom Green County Fair/I Know Who It Is	1970	—	3.00	6.00
STARDAY					
❑ 356	Can't Stop Loving You/You're Forgetting Me	1958	5.00	10.00	20.00
❑ 718	Playboy/Poor Little John	1965	2.50	5.00	10.00
❑ 7029	Under Your Spell Again/I Ain't Never	197?	—	2.50	5.00
❑ 7032	Country Girl/Jimmy Brown, The Newsboy	197?	—	2.50	5.00
❑ 7038	Tip of My Fingers/I Wish I Could Fall in Love Today	197?	—	2.50	5.00
WINDSONG					
❑ CB-11072	Baby Me Baby/Dark Side of the Moon	1977	—	2.00	4.00
❑ CB-11166	Oklahoma Woman/There's Nobody Like You	1977	—	2.00	4.00
Albums					
20TH CENTURY					
❑ T-592	Making a Name for Myself	1979	3.00	6.00	12.00
COLUMBIA					
❑ KC 32449	Dear Folks Sorry I Haven't Written Lately	1973	3.75	7.50	15.00
HILLTOP					
❑ 6109	King of the Road	197?	2.50	5.00	10.00
❑ 6131	Little Green Apples	197?	2.50	5.00	10.00
MCA					
❑ 5722	Roger Miller	1986	2.50	5.00	10.00
MERCURY					
❑ SR-61297	A Trip in the Country	1970	3.75	7.50	15.00
❑ SR-61361	The Best of Roger Miller	1971	3.75	7.50	15.00
❑ 826261-1	Golden Hits	198?	2.00	4.00	8.00
—Reissue of Smash 67073					
NASHVILLE					
❑ 2046	The Amazing Roger Miller	196?	3.00	6.00	12.00
PICKWICK					
❑ PTP-2057 [(2)]	King High	1973	3.00	6.00	12.00
❑ SPC-3226	Engine #9	197?	2.50	5.00	10.00
RCA CAMDEN					
❑ CAL-851 [M]	Roger Miller	1964	3.00	6.00	12.00
❑ CAS-851 [S]	Roger Miller	1964	3.75	7.50	15.00
❑ CAL-903 [M]	The One and Only Roger Miller	1965	3.00	6.00	12.00
❑ CAS-903 [S]	The One and Only Roger Miller	1965	3.75	7.50	15.00
SMASH					
❑ MGS-27049 [M]	Roger and Out	1964	3.75	7.50	15.00
❑ MGS-27049 [M]	Dang Me/Chug-a-Lug	196?	3.00	6.00	12.00
—Retitled version of "Roger and Out"					
❑ MGS-27061 [M]	The Return of Roger Miller	1965	3.75	7.50	15.00
❑ MGS-27068 [M]	The 3rd Time Around	1965	3.75	7.50	15.00
❑ MGS-27073 [M]	Golden Hits	1965	3.75	7.50	15.00
❑ MGS-27075 [M]	Words and Music	1966	3.75	7.50	15.00
❑ MGS-27092 [M]	Walkin' in the Sunshine	1967	5.00	10.00	20.00
❑ MGS-27096 [M]	Waterhole #3	1967	6.25	12.50	25.00
❑ SRS-67049 [S]	Roger and Out	1964	5.00	10.00	20.00
❑ SRS-67049 [S]	Dang Me/Chug-a-Lug	196?	3.75	7.50	15.00
—Retitled version of "Roger and Out"					
❑ SRS-67061 [S]	The Return of Roger Miller	1965	5.00	10.00	20.00
❑ SRS-67068 [S]	The 3rd Time Around	1965	5.00	10.00	20.00
❑ SRS-67073 [S]	Golden Hits	1965	5.00	10.00	20.00
❑ SRS-67075 [S]	Words and Music	1966	5.00	10.00	20.00
❑ SRS-67092 [S]	Walkin' in the Sunshine	1967	5.00	10.00	20.00
❑ SRS-67096 [S]	Waterhole #3	1967	5.00	10.00	20.00
❑ SRS-67103	A Tender Look at Love	1968	5.00	10.00	20.00
❑ SRS-67123	Roger Miller	1969	5.00	10.00	20.00
❑ SRS-67129	Roger Miller 1970	1970	5.00	10.00	20.00
STARDAY					
❑ SLP-318 [M]	Wild Child Roger Miller	1965	7.50	15.00	30.00
❑ SLP-318 [M]	The Country Side of Roger Miller	196?	6.25	12.50	25.00
—Retitled version of "Wild Child"					
❑ 3011	Painted Poetry	1978	2.50	5.00	10.00
WINDSONG					
❑ BHL1-2337	Off the Wall	1977	3.00	6.00	12.00

MILLETT, LOU

Number	Title (A Side/B Side)	Yr	VG	VG+	NM
45s					
COLUMBIA					
❑ 4-20979	Just Me, My Heart and You/Weary, Worried and Blue	1952	6.25	12.50	25.00
❑ 4-21029	Worried, Lonesome and Blue/Your Own Heart You Must Mend	1952	6.25	12.50	25.00
❑ 4-21086	Bayou Pigeon/Get a Grip on Your Heart	1953	5.00	10.00	20.00
❑ 4-21143	God Only Knows/Memories from Your Cedar Chest	1953	5.00	10.00	20.00
❑ 4-21225	That's How I Need You/Since the Devil Moved In	1954	25.00	50.00	100.00

MILLINDER, LUCKY

This black bandleader, who had six pop hits and 10 R&B hits in the 1940s and early 1950s, also had two country hits, as listed below.

Number	Title (A Side/B Side)	Yr	VG	VG+	NM
Selected 78s					
DECCA					
❑ 18569	Sweet Slumber/Don't Cry Baby	1943	5.00	10.00	20.00
❑ 18609	Hurry, Hurry/I Can't See for Lookin'	1944	5.00	10.00	20.00

MILLS, FRANK

Number	Title (A Side/B Side)	Yr	VG	VG+	NM
45s					
CAPITOL					
❑ B-5455	Spanish Coffee/The Poet & I	1985	—	2.00	4.00
EPIC					
❑ 5-10490	Fredericka/Love Is On the Way	1969	—	3.50	7.00
POLYDOR					
❑ 2002	Peter Piper/Interlude	1979	—	2.00	4.00
❑ 2067	Ski Fever/Wherever You Go	1980	—	2.00	4.00
❑ 2148	Happy Song/On the Move	1980	—	2.00	4.00
❑ 14517	Music Box Dancer/The Poet & I	1979	—	2.00	4.00
SUNFLOWER					
❑ 118	Love Me, Love Me, Love/Windsong	1972	—	2.50	5.00
❑ 122	Poor Little Fool/What Do You Think of Love	1972	—	2.50	5.00
Albums					
CAPITOL					
❑ ST-12388	Music Box Dancer	1985	2.00	4.00	8.00
❑ ST-12421	Traveler	1985	2.00	4.00	8.00
❑ SN-16290	A Special Christmas	198?	2.00	4.00	8.00
POLYDOR					
❑ PD-1-6192	Music Box Dancer	1979	2.50	5.00	10.00
❑ PD-1-6225	Sunday Morning	1980	2.50	5.00	10.00
❑ PD-1-6305	The Frank Mills Album	1982	2.50	5.00	10.00

MILLS BROTHERS, THE

The famous vocal group had one single make the country charts, listed below.

Number	Title (A Side/B Side)	Yr	VG	VG+	NM
45s					
DOT					
❑ 17321	It Ain't No Big Thing/Help Yourself to Some Tomorrow	1969	—	3.00	6.00

MILSAP, RONNIE

Number	Title (A Side/B Side)	Yr	VG	VG+	NM
12-Inch Singles					
RCA					
❑ JD-11683 [DJ]	Get It Up/Hi-Heel Sneakers	1979	5.00	10.00	20.00
—Promo only on green vinyl					
45s					
BOBLO					
❑ 524	Make Love Sweet/(B-side unknown)	1977	—	2.50	5.00
CAPITOL NASHVILLE					
❑ S7-18909	The Christmas Song/Till the Season Comes 'Round Again	1995	—	—	3.00
CHIPS					
❑ 2889	Loving You Is a Natural Thing/So Hung Up on Sylvia	1970	2.00	4.00	8.00
❑ 2987	A Rose by Any Other Name (Is Still a Rose)/Sermonette	1970	2.00	4.00	8.00
FESTIVAL					
❑ 5002	Wishing You Were Here/Your Tears Leave Me Cold	1977	—	2.50	5.00
LIBERTY					
❑ S7-17595	True Believer/These Foolish Things (Remind Me of You)	1993	—	2.00	4.00
—Red vinyl					
❑ S7-17640	I'm Playing for You/Better Off with the Blues	1993	—	2.00	4.00
PACEMAKER					
❑ 245	Wishing You Were Here/A Loving Background	1967	2.00	4.00	8.00
RCA					
❑ 2509-7-R	Are You Loving Me Like I'm Loving You/Back to the Grindstone	1990	—	—	3.00
❑ 2848-7-R	Since I Don't Have You/I Ain't Gonna Cry No More	1991	—	—	3.00
❑ 5033-7-R	How Do I Turn You On/Don't Take It Tonight	1986	—	—	3.00
❑ 5049-7-R	Only One Night of the Year/It's Just Not Christmas (If I Can't Spend It With You)	1986	—	—	3.00
❑ 5169-7-R	Snap Your Fingers/This Time Last Year	1987	—	—	3.00
❑ 5209-7-R	Make No Mistake, She's Mine/You're My Love	1987	—	—	3.00
—With Kenny Rogers					
❑ 5259-7-R	Where Do the Nights Go/If You Don't Want Me To	1987	—	—	3.00
❑ 5351-7-R	Christmas Medley: Carol of the Bells/O Come, O Come Emmanuel/Silent Night/Joy to the World//I'll Be Home for Christmas	1987	—	—	3.00
❑ 6896-7-R	Old Folks/Earthquake	1988	—	—	3.00
—A-side with Mike Reid					

Number	Title (A Side/B Side)	Yr	VG	VG+	NM
❑ 6896-7-R [PS]	Old Folks/Earthquake	1988	—	2.50	5.00
—A-side with Mike Reid					
❑ 8389-7-R	Button Off My Shirt/One Night	1988	—	—	3.00
❑ 8746-7-R	Don't You Ever Get Tired (Of Hurtin' Me)/I Never Expected to See You	1988	—	—	3.00
❑ 8868-7-R	Houston Solution/If You Don't Want Me To	1989	—	—	3.00
❑ 9027-7-R	A Woman in Love/Starting Today	1989	—	—	3.00
❑ 9071-7-R	I'll Be Home for Christmas/We're Here to Love	1989	—	—	3.00
❑ 9120-7-R	Stranger Things Have Happened/Southern Roots	1989	—	—	3.00
❑ PB-10843	Let My Love Be Your Pillow/Busy Makin' Plans	1976	—	2.00	4.00
❑ GB-10931	(I'm a) Stand By My Woman Man/What Goes On When the Sun Goes Down	1977	—	2.00	4.00
—Gold Standard Series					
❑ PB-10976	It Was Almost Like a Song/It Don't Hurt to Dream	1977	—	2.00	4.00
❑ PB-11146	What a Difference You've Made in My Life/Selfish	1977	—	2.00	4.00
❑ PB-11270	Only One Live in My Life/Back on My Mind Again	1978	—	2.00	4.00
❑ PB-11333	Let My Love Be Your Pillow/Busy Makin' Plans	1978	—	2.00	4.00
❑ PB-11369	Let's Take the Long Way Around the World/Not Trying to Forget	1978	—	2.00	4.00
❑ PB-11421	Back on My Mind Again/Santa Barbara	1978	—	2.00	4.00
❑ GB-11496	It Was Almost Like a Song/Only One Love in My Life	1979	—	2.00	4.00
—Gold Standard Series					
❑ PB-11553	Nobody Likes Sad Songs/Just Because It Feels Good	1979	—	2.00	4.00
❑ PB-11695	In No Time at All/Get It Up	1979	—	2.00	4.00
❑ PB-11909	Why Don't You Spend the Night/Heads I Go, Hearts I Stay	1980	—	2.00	4.00
❑ PB-11952	My Heart/Silent Night (After the Fight)	1980	—	2.00	4.00
❑ GB-11987	What a Difference You've Made in My Life/Let's Take the Long Way Around the World	1980	—	2.00	4.00
—Gold Standard Series					
❑ GB-11994	Back on My Mind Again/Nobody Likes Sad Songs	1980	—	2.00	4.00
—Gold Standard Series					
❑ PB-12006	Cowboys and Clowns/Misery Loves Company	1980	—	2.00	4.00
❑ PB-12006 [PS]	Cowboys and Clowns/Misery Loves Company	1980	—	2.50	5.00
❑ PB-12084	Smoky Mountain Rain/Crystal Fallin' Rain	1980	—	2.00	4.00
❑ PB-12194	Am I Losing You/He'll Have to Go	1981	—	2.00	4.00
❑ PB-12264	(There's) No Gettin' Over Me/I Live My Whole Life at Night	1981	—	2.00	4.00
❑ GB-12314	Why Don't You Spend the Night/Smoky Mountain Rain	1981	—	—	3.00
—Gold Standard Series					
❑ GB-12315	My Heart/Silent Night (After the Fight)	1981	—	—	3.00
—Gold Standard Series					
❑ PB-12342	I Wouldn't Have Missed It For the World/It Happens Every Time (I Think of You)	1981	—	2.00	4.00
❑ PB-13216	Any Day Now/It's Just a Room	1982	—	2.00	4.00
❑ PB-13286	He Got You/I Love New Orleans Music	1982	—	2.00	4.00
❑ PB-13362	Inside/Carolina Dreams	1982	—	2.00	4.00
❑ PB-13470	Stranger in My House/Is It Over	1983	—	2.00	4.00
❑ GB-13491	(There's) No Gettin' Over Me/I Wouldn't Have Missed It for the World	1983	—	—	3.00
—Gold Standard Series					
❑ PB-13564	Don't You Know How Much I Love You/Feelings Change	1983	—	2.00	4.00
❑ PB-13658	Show Her/Watch Out for the Other Guy	1983	—	2.00	4.00
❑ PB-13665	It's Christmas/We're Here to Love	1983	—	2.00	4.00
❑ GB-13784	Don't You Know How Much I Love You/Show Her	1984	—	—	3.00
—Gold Standard Series					
❑ GB-13785	Any Day Now/Stranger in My House	1984	—	—	3.00
—Gold Standard Series					
❑ PB-13805	Still Losing You/I'll Take Care of You	1984	—	—	3.00
❑ PB-13847	She Loves My Car/Prisoner of the Highway	1984	—	—	3.00
❑ JD-13869 [DJ]	She Loves My Car/(Instrumental)	1984	2.00	4.00	8.00
❑ PB-13955	She's Always in Love/I Might Have Said	1984	—	—	—
—Unreleased					
❑ PB-14034	She Keeps the Home Fires Burning/Is It Over	1985	—	—	3.00
❑ PB-14135	Lost in the Fifties Tonight (In the Still of the Night)/I Might Have Said	1985	—	2.00	4.00
❑ PB-14135 [PS]	Lost in the Fifties Tonight (In the Still of the Night)/I Might Have Said	1985	—	2.00	4.00
❑ PB-14286	Happy Happy Birthday Baby/I'll Take Care of You	1986	—	—	3.00
❑ GB-14349	Lost in the Fifties Tonight (In the Still of the Night)/She Keeps the Home Fires Burning	1986	—	—	3.00
—Gold Standard Series					
❑ PB-14365	In Love/Old Fashioned Girl Like You	1986	—	—	3.00
❑ 62104	Turn That Radio On/Old Habits Are Hard to Break	1991	—	—	3.00
❑ 62217	All Is Fair in Love and War/Back to the Grindstone	1992	—	—	3.00
❑ 62332	L.A. to the Moon/When the Hurt Comes Down	1992	—	—	3.00
❑ 62370	Still Losing You/If You Really Don't Want Me	1992	—	—	3.00
RCA VICTOR					
❑ APBO-0097	That Girl Who Waits on Tables/You're Drivin' Me Out of My Mind	1973	—	3.00	6.00
❑ APBO-0237	Pure Love/Love the Second Time Around	1974	—	3.00	6.00
❑ APBO-0313	Please Don't Tell Me How the Story Ends/Streets of Gold	1974	—	3.00	6.00
❑ PB-10112	(I'd Be) A Legend in My Time/The Biggest Lie	1974	—	2.50	5.00
❑ GB-10167	That Girl Who Waits on Tables/I Hate You	1975	—	2.00	4.00
—Gold Standard Series					
❑ PB-10228	Too Late to Worry, Too Blue to Cry/Country Cookin'	1975	—	2.50	5.00
❑ PB-10335	Daydreams About Night Things/Play Born to Lose	1975	—	2.50	5.00
❑ PB-10420	Just In Case/Remember to Remind Me (I'm Leaving)	1975	—	2.50	5.00
❑ GB-10500	Please Don't Tell Me How the Story Ends/Streets of Gold	1975	—	2.00	4.00
—Gold Standard Series					
❑ GB-10501	Too Late to Worry, Too Blue to Cry/Country Cookin'	1975	—	2.00	4.00
—Gold Standard Series					
❑ GB-10502	(I'd Be) A Legend in My Time/The Biggest Lie	1975	—	2.00	4.00
—Gold Standard Series					
❑ GB-10503	Pure Love/Love the Second Time Around	1975	—	2.00	4.00
—Gold Standard Series					
❑ PB-10593	What Goes On When the Sun Goes Down/Love Takes a Long Time to Die	1976	—	2.50	5.00
❑ GB-10672	Daydreams About Night Things/Just in Case	1976	—	2.00	4.00
—Gold Standard Series					
❑ PB-10724	(I'm a) Stand By My Woman Man/Lovers, Friends and Strangers	1976	—	2.50	5.00
❑ 74-0969	I Hate You/(All Together Now) Let's Fall Apart	1973	—	3.00	6.00
SCEPTER					
❑ 12109	Let's Go Get Stoned/Never Had It So Good	1965	3.00	6.00	12.00
❑ 12127	A Thousand Miles from Nowhere/When It Comes to My Baby	1966	3.00	6.00	12.00
❑ 12145	The End of the World/I Saw Pity in the Face of a Friend	1966	3.00	6.00	12.00
❑ 12161	When the Boys Talk About the Girls/Ain't No Sole in These Old Shoes	1966	3.00	6.00	12.00
❑ 12161	When the Boys Talk About the Girls/Another Branch from the Old Branch	1966	3.00	6.00	12.00
❑ 12206	House of the Rising Sun/I Can't Tell a Lie	1967	2.50	5.00	10.00
❑ 12228	Do What You Gotta Do/Mr. Mailman	1968	2.00	4.00	8.00
❑ 12246	Nothing Is As Good As It Used to Be/Denver	1969	2.00	4.00	8.00
❑ 12272	What's Your Game/Love Will Never Pass Us By	1970	2.00	4.00	8.00
VIRGIN					
❑ 58853	Time, Love and Money/Livin' on Love	2000	—	—	3.00
WARNER BROS.					
❑ 5405	Total Disaster/It Went to Your Head	1963	3.75	7.50	15.00
❑ 7540	Sunday Rain/Why	1971	—	3.00	6.00
❑ 7629	Magic Me Again/Me and You, You and Me	1972	—	3.00	6.00
❑ 8127	She Even Woke Me Up to Say Goodbye/Loving You's a Natural Thing	1975	—	2.00	4.00
❑ 8160	A Rose by Any Other Name/Please Don't Tell Me How the Story Ends	1975	—	2.00	4.00
❑ 8218	Crying/Why	1976	—	2.00	4.00

Albums

Number	Title	Yr	VG	VG+	NM
PAIR					
❑ PDL2-1031 [(2)]	Believe It!	1986	3.00	6.00	12.00
❑ PDL2-1105 [(2)]	Back on My Mind Again	1986	3.00	6.00	12.00
PICKWICK					
❑ JS-6179	Plain and Simple	197?	2.50	5.00	10.00
RCA					
❑ 9588-1-R	Stranger Things Have Happened	1989	2.50	5.00	10.00
❑ R 183710	Back to the Grindstone	1991	5.00	10.00	20.00
—Only released on vinyl through BMG Direct Marketing					
RCA VICTOR					
❑ APL1-0338	Where My Heart Is	1973	5.00	10.00	20.00
❑ APD1-0500 [Q]	Pure Love	1974	5.00	10.00	20.00
❑ APL1-0500	Pure Love	1974	3.75	7.50	15.00
❑ APD1-0846 [Q]	A Legend in My Time	1975	5.00	10.00	20.00
❑ APL1-0846	A Legend in My Time	1975	3.75	7.50	15.00
❑ APL1-1223	Night Things	1975	3.75	7.50	15.00
❑ APL1-1666	20-20 Vision	1976	3.00	6.00	12.00
❑ APL1-2043	Ronnie Milsap Live	1976	3.00	6.00	12.00
❑ AFL1-2439	It Was Almost Like a Song	1977	3.00	6.00	12.00
❑ AFL1-2780	Only One Love in My Life	1978	3.00	6.00	12.00
❑ AHL1-3346	Images	1979	3.00	6.00	12.00
❑ AHL1-3563	Milsap Magic	1980	2.50	5.00	10.00
❑ AYL1-3760	Where My Heart Is	1980	2.00	4.00	8.00
—"Best Buy Series" reissue					
❑ AHL1-3772	Greatest Hits	1980	2.50	5.00	10.00
❑ AYL1-3899	Pure Love	1981	2.00	4.00	8.00
—"Best Buy Series" reissue					
❑ AAL1-3932	Out Where the Bright Lights Are Glowing	1981	2.50	5.00	10.00
❑ AHL1-4060	There's No Gettin' Over Me	1981	2.50	5.00	10.00
❑ AYL1-4171	Images	1981	2.00	4.00	8.00
—"Best Buy Series" reissue					
❑ AYL1-4255	Ronnie Milsap Live	1982	2.00	4.00	8.00
—"Best Buy Series" reissue					
❑ AHL1-4311	Inside Ronnie Milsap	1982	2.50	5.00	10.00
❑ AHL1-4670	Keyed Up	1983	2.50	5.00	10.00
❑ AHL1-5016	One More Try for Love	1984	2.50	5.00	10.00
❑ AYL1-5139	It Was Almost Like a Song	1984	2.00	4.00	8.00
—"Best Buy Series" reissue					
❑ AYL1-5140	There's No Gettin' Over Me	1984	2.00	4.00	8.00
—"Best Buy Series" reissue					
❑ AYL1-5142	Inside Ronnie Milsap	1984	2.00	4.00	8.00
—"Best Buy Series" reissue					
❑ AHL1-5425	Greatest Hits, Vol. 2	1985	2.50	5.00	10.00
❑ AYL1-5435	Keyed Up	1985	2.00	4.00	8.00
—"Best Buy Series" reissue					
❑ 5624-1-R	Christmas with Ronnie Milsap	1986	2.50	5.00	10.00
❑ 6425-1-R	Heart and Soul	1987	2.50	5.00	10.00
❑ CPL1-7166	Collector's Series	1986	2.00	4.00	8.00
❑ AHL1-7194	Lost in the Fifties Tonight	1986	2.50	5.00	10.00

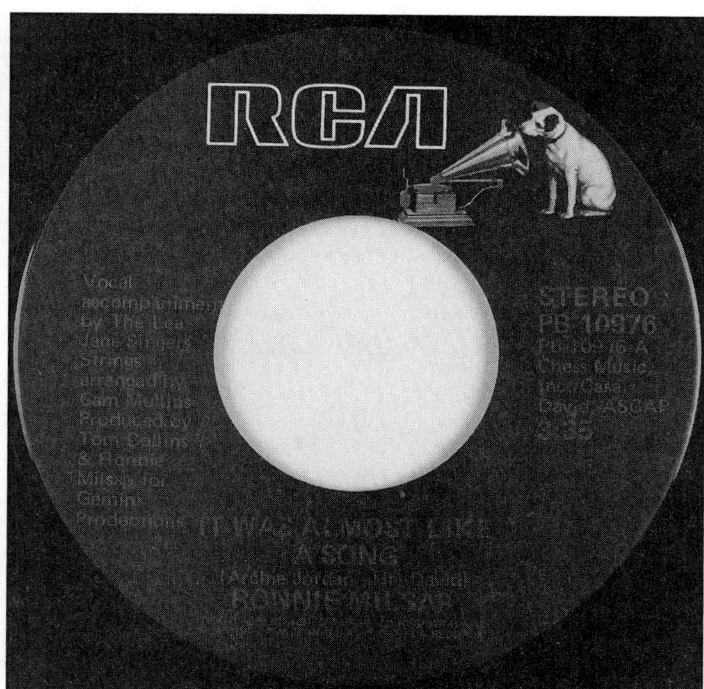

From 1974 through 1989, Ronnie Milsap had at least one chart-topping hit every year, the longest streak in country music history until it was broken by George Strait. (Top left) The first of Milsap's records to hit the top spot was "Pure Love." (Top right) In 1977, three years before *Urban Cowboy* made country crossovers fairly common, Ronnie's No. 1 country smash "It Was Almost Like a Song" actually made the top 20 of the pop charts as well. Perhaps it was the Barry Manilow-esque arrangement that did it. (Bottom left) The soundtrack of the Clint Eastwood movie *Bronco Billy* yielded two No. 1 singles, one of which was Milsap's version of "Cowboys and Clowns." (Bottom right) The last No. 1 single of 1989 turned out to be the last No. 1 single of Ronnie Milsap's career, "A Woman in Love."

Number	Title (A Side/B Side)	Yr	VG	VG+	NM
❑ 7618-1-R	Heart and Soul	1988	2.00	4.00	8.00
—Reissue of 6245					
WARNER BROS.					
❑ WS 1934	Ronnie Milsap	1971	5.00	10.00	20.00
❑ BS 2870	A Rose By Any Other Name	1975	3.75	7.50	15.00

MINNIE PEARL

Also see CHET ATKINS; GRANDPA JONES AND MINNIE PEARL.

45s

Number	Title (A Side/B Side)	Yr	VG	VG+	NM
KING					
❑ 978	On Top of Old Smoky/In the Shadow of the Pine	1951	10.00	20.00	40.00
RCA VICTOR					
❑ 47-5605	Man (Uh-Huh)/I Wish They Would	1954	5.00	10.00	20.00
❑ 47-5699	How to Catch a Man/And That's Good Enough for Me	1954	5.00	10.00	20.00
❑ 47-5812	I Wonder Where That Man of Mine Has Went/ Never Been Kissed	1954	5.00	10.00	20.00
❑ 47-5982	Me/Hurtin' Season	1955	5.00	10.00	20.00
STARDAY					
❑ 754	Giddyup Go — Answer/Road Runner	1966	2.50	5.00	10.00
❑ 764	What Is an American/Live Some While You're Here	1966	2.50	5.00	10.00
Selected 78s					
BULLET					
❑ 613	I'm Lookin' Fer a Feller/Jealous Hearted Me	1946	12.50	25.00	50.00
KING					
❑ 590	On Top of Old Smoky/In the Shadow of the Pine	1947	6.25	12.50	25.00
Albums					
STARDAY					
❑ SLP-224 [M]	Howdee!	1963	10.00	20.00	40.00
❑ SLP-380 [M]	America's Beloved Minnie Pearl	1965	10.00	20.00	40.00
❑ SLP-397 [M]	The Country Music Story	1966	7.50	15.00	30.00

MINOR, SHANE

45s

Number	Title (A Side/B Side)	Yr	VG	VG+	NM
MERCURY					
❑ 088 172151-7	I Think You're Beautiful/A Girl Like That	2000	—	—	3.00
❑ 562291-7	Ordinary Love/How Many Times	1999	—	—	3.00
❑ 870818-7	Slave to the Heart/Tell Me Now	1999	—	—	3.00

MINTER, PAT

45s

Number	Title (A Side/B Side)	Yr	VG	VG+	NM
KILLER					
❑ 121	Whiskey River You Win/(B-side unknown)	1989	—	3.00	6.00

MITCHELL, CHARLES

Selected 78s

Number	Title (A Side/B Side)	Yr	VG	VG+	NM
BLUEBIRD					
❑ 33-0508	If It's Wrong to Love You/Mean Mama Blues	1944	5.00	10.00	20.00

MITCHELL, CHARLIE

45s

Number	Title (A Side/B Side)	Yr	VG	VG+	NM
SOUNDWAVES					
❑ 4810	I'm Goin' Nowhere/(B-side unknown)	1988	—	2.50	5.00

MITCHELL, GUY

45s

Number	Title (A Side/B Side)	Yr	VG	VG+	NM
CHALICE					
❑ 711	My Angel/Bit of Love	1963	7.50	15.00	30.00
❑ 711	My Angel/Mr. Hobo	1963	7.50	15.00	30.00
❑ 712	Take Your Time/(B-side unknown)	1963	7.50	15.00	30.00
❑ 713	Your Imagination/(B-side unknown)	1963	7.50	15.00	30.00
COLUMBIA					
❑ 1-640 (?)	Giddy Up/Where in the World	1950	7.50	15.00	30.00
—Microgroove 33 1/3 rpm 7-inch single					
❑ 1-680 (?)	Me and My Imagination/To Me You're a Song	1950	7.50	15.00	30.00
—Microgroove 33 1/3 rpm 7-inch single					
❑ 1-760 (?)	Angels Cry/You're Not in My Arms Tonight	1950	7.50	15.00	30.00
—Microgroove 33 1/3 rpm 7-inch single					
❑ 6-760 (?)	Angels Cry/You're Not in My Arms Tonight	1950	6.25	12.50	25.00
❑ 1-918	My Heart Cries for You/The Roving Kind	1950	7.50	15.00	30.00
—Microgroove 33 1/3 rpm 7-inch single					
❑ 6-918	My Heart Cries for You/The Roving Kind	1950	6.25	12.50	25.00
❑ 39067	My Heart Cries for You/The Roving Kind	1950	3.75	7.50	15.00
❑ 39190	Sparrow in the Tree Top/Christopher Columbus	1951	3.70	7.50	15.00
❑ 3-39190	Sparrow in the Tree Top/Christopher Columbus	1951	7.50	15.00	30.00
—Microgroove 33 1/3 rpm 7-inch single					
❑ 39331	Unless/A Beggar in Love	1951	3.75	7.50	15.00
❑ 39415	My Truly, Truly Fair/Who Knows Love	1951	3.75	7.50	15.00
❑ 39512	Belle, Belle, My Liberty Belle/Sweetheart of Yesterday	1951	3.75	7.50	15.00
❑ 39595	There's Always Room at Our House/I Can't Help It (If I'm Still in Love with You)	1951	3.75	7.50	15.00
❑ 39639	Wimmin'/We Don't Live in a Castle	1952	5.00	10.00	20.00
❑ 39663	Pittsburgh, Pennsylvania/Doll with a Sawdust Heart	1952	3.75	7.50	15.00
❑ 39753	The Day of Jubilo/You'll Never Be Mine	1952	5.00	10.00	20.00
❑ 39822	Feet Up (Pat Him on the Po-Po)/Jenny Kissed Me	1952	3.75	7.50	15.00
❑ 39879	('Cause I Love You) That's-a Why/Train of Love	1952	3.75	7.50	15.00
—With Mindy Carson					
❑ 39886	Don't Rob Another Man's Castle/Why Should I Go Home	1952	3.75	7.50	15.00
❑ 39909	She Wears Red Feathers/Pretty Little Blackeyed Susie	1952	3.75	7.50	15.00
❑ 39950	I Want You for a Sunbeam/So Am I	1953	3.00	6.00	12.00
❑ 39992	There's Nothing As Sweet As My Baby/Tell Us Where the Good Times Are	1953	3.00	6.00	12.00
—With Mindy Carson					
❑ 40008	Hannah Lee/Look at That Girl	1953	3.00	6.00	12.00
❑ 40035	Cloud Lucky Seven/Chicka-Boom	1953	3.00	6.00	12.00
❑ 40077	Sippin' Soda/Strollin' Blues	1953	3.00	6.00	12.00
❑ 40128	Got a Hole in My Sweater/The Cuff of My Shirt	1953	3.00	6.00	12.00
❑ 40175	Tear Down the Mountains/A Dime and a Dollar	1954	3.00	6.00	12.00
❑ 40240	There Once Was a Man/My Heaven on Earth	1954	3.00	6.00	12.00
❑ 40278	What Am I Doin' in Kansas City/You've Ruined Me	1954	3.00	6.00	12.00
❑ 40389	I Met the Cutest Little Eyeful (At the Eiffel Tower)/ Gee But You Gotta Come Home	1954	3.00	6.00	12.00
❑ 40468	Nobody Home/Zoo Baby	1955	2.50	5.00	10.00
❑ 40507	Otto's Gotta Go (Otto Drives Me Crazy)/Man Overboard	1955	3.00	6.00	12.00
❑ 40531	Let Us Be Sweethearts Again/Too Late	1955	2.50	5.00	10.00
❑ 40560	When Binky Blows/Belonging	1955	2.50	5.00	10.00
❑ 40631	Ninety Nine Years (Dead or Alive)/Perfume, Candy and Flowers	1955	2.50	5.00	10.00
❑ 40672	Solo/Green Grows the Grass	1956	2.50	5.00	10.00
❑ 40700	Give Me a Carriage with Eight White Horses/I Used to Hate Ya	1956	2.50	5.00	10.00
❑ 40724	Finders Keepers/I'd Like to Say a Few Words About Texas	1956	2.50	5.00	10.00
❑ 40769	Singing the Blues/Crazy with Love	1956	2.50	5.00	10.00
❑ 40769 [PS]	Singing the Blues/Crazy with Love	1956	5.00	10.00	20.00
❑ 40820	Knee Deep in the Blues/Take Me Back Baby	1957	2.50	5.00	10.00
❑ 40820 [PS]	Knee Deep in the Blues/Take Me Back Baby	1957	3.75	7.50	15.00
❑ 40877	Rock-a-Billy/Hoot Owl	1957	2.50	5.00	10.00
❑ 40877 [PS]	Rock-a-Billy/Hoot Owl	1957	3.75	7.50	15.00
❑ 40940	Sweet Stuff/In the Middle of a Dark, Dark Night	1957	2.50	5.00	10.00
❑ 40987	A Cure for the Blues/Call Rosie on the Phone	1957	2.50	5.00	10.00
❑ 41033	C'mon Let's Go/The Unbeliever	1957	2.50	5.00	10.00
❑ 41075	One Way Street/The Lord Made a Peanut	1957	2.50	5.00	10.00
❑ 41146	Hey, Madame/Till We're Engaged	1958	2.00	4.00	8.00
❑ 41177	Hangin' Around/Honey Brown Eyes	1958	2.00	4.00	8.00
❑ 41215	Let It Shine, Let It Shine/Butterfly Doll	1958	2.00	4.00	8.00
❑ 41274	My Heart Cries for You/Under the Rainbow	1958	2.00	4.00	8.00
❑ 41311	Guilty Heart/Half As Much	1958	2.00	4.00	8.00
❑ 41359	Alias Jesse James/Pride o' Dixie	1959	2.00	4.00	8.00
❑ 41397	Loosen Up, Lucy/I'm Gonna Leave You Now	1959	2.00	4.00	8.00
❑ 41476	Heartaches By the Number/Two	1959	2.50	5.00	10.00
❑ 41476 [PS]	Heartaches By the Number/Two	1959	3.75	7.50	15.00
❑ 41576	The Same Old Me/Build Up My Gallows High	1960	2.00	4.00	8.00
❑ 41653	Symphony of Spring/Cry Hurtin' Heart	1960	2.00	4.00	8.00
❑ 41725	My Shoes Keep Walking Back to You/Silver Moon Upon the Golden Sands	1960	2.00	4.00	8.00
❑ 41853	Sunshine Guitar/Ridin' Around in the Rain	1960	2.00	4.00	8.00
❑ 41853 [PS]	Sunshine Guitar/Ridin' Around in the Rain	1960	3.00	6.00	12.00
❑ 41970	Follow Me/Your Goodnight Kiss	1961	2.00	4.00	8.00
❑ 42143	Divorce/I'll Just Pretend	1961	2.00	4.00	8.00
❑ 42231	Soft Rain/Big Big Chance	1961	2.00	4.00	8.00
JOY					
❑ 264	Rusty Old Halo/Charlie's Shoes	1962	2.00	4.00	8.00
❑ 270	Go Tiger Go/If You Ever Go Away	1962	2.00	4.00	8.00
❑ 273	Have I Told You Lately That I Love You/Blue Violet	1963	2.00	4.00	8.00
REPRISE					
❑ 0477	Best Thing That Ever Happened to Me/If I Had My Life to Live Over	1966	—	3.00	6.00
❑ 0513	Run to the Door/Foreign Love Affair	1966	—	3.00	6.00
STARDAY					
❑ 819	Traveling Shoes/Every Night Is a Lifetime	1967	—	3.00	6.00
❑ 828	Alabam/Irene Good-By	1968	—	3.00	6.00
❑ 846	Frisco Line/Singing the Blues	1968	—	3.00	6.00
❑ 866	Get It Over/Just Wish You'd Change Your Mind	1969	—	3.00	6.00
❑ 878	Smokey Blue Eyes/Heartaches by the Number	1969	—	3.00	6.00
7-Inch Extended Plays					
COLUMBIA					
❑ B-1585	My Truly, Truly Fair/The Roving Kind//Sparrow in the Treetop/My Heart Cries for You	195?	5.00	10.00	20.00
❑ B-1585 [PS]	Guy Mitchell Spotlite	195?	5.00	10.00	20.00
❑ B-2502	*My Heart Cries for You/The Roving Kind/My Truly, Truly Fair/Pittsburgh, Pennsylvania	1957	3.00	6.00	12.00
❑ B-2502 [PS]	Guy Mitchell (Hall of Fame Series)	1957	3.00	6.00	12.00
Albums					
COLUMBIA					
❑ CL 1211 [M]	Guy in Love	1958	10.00	20.00	40.00
❑ CL 1226 [M]	Guy's Greatest Hits	1959	12.50	25.00	50.00
—Red and black label with six "eye" logos					
❑ CL 1226 [M]	Guy's Greatest Hits	1962	7.50	15.00	30.00
—"Guaranteed High Fidelity" on red label					
❑ CL 1226 [M]	Guy's Greatest Hits	1965	5.00	10.00	20.00
—"360 Sound Mono" on red label					
❑ CL 1552 [M]	Sunshine Guitar	1960	7.50	15.00	30.00
❑ CL 6231 [10]	Open Spaces	1953	17.50	35.00	70.00
❑ CS 8011 [S]	Guy in Love	1959	12.50	25.00	50.00
❑ CS 8352 [S]	Sunshine Guitar	1960	10.00	20.00	40.00
KING					
❑ 644 [M]	Sincerely Yours	1959	75.00	150.00	300.00
NASHVILLE					
❑ 2074	Heartaches	1970	3.00	6.00	12.00
STARDAY					
❑ 412	Traveling Shoes	1968	5.00	10.00	20.00
❑ 432	Singin' Up a Storm	1969	5.00	10.00	20.00

MITCHELL, MARTY

45s

ATLANTIC

Number	Title (A Side/B Side)	Yr	VG	VG+	NM
❑ 4023	Midnight Man/I'd Be Your Fool Again	1974	—	2.50	5.00
❑ 4205	Juke Box Band/A Submarine Called Aspen Town	1974	—	2.50	5.00

HITSVILLE

Number	Title (A Side/B Side)	Yr	VG	VG+	NM
❑ 6044	My Eyes Adored You/Devil Woman	1976	—	2.50	5.00

MC

Number	Title (A Side/B Side)	Yr	VG	VG+	NM
❑ 5005	You Are the Sunshine of My Life/Yester-Me, Yester-You, Yesterday	1978	—	2.50	5.00
❑ 5011	All Alone in Austin/Virginia	1978	—	2.50	5.00

Albums

MC

Number	Title (A Side/B Side)	Yr	VG	VG+	NM
❑ MC6-511S1	You Are the Sunshine of My Life	1977	3.00	6.00	12.00

MITCHELL, PRICE

45s

GRT

Number	Title (A Side/B Side)	Yr	VG	VG+	NM
❑ 005	Is It Too Late to Try/(B-side unknown)	1974	2.00	4.00	8.00
❑ 020	Personality/Daddy's Going Bye Bye	1975	—	3.00	6.00
❑ 037	Seems Like I Can't Live With You, But I Can't Live Without You/(I Wanna Be) The Man Who Takes You Home	1976	—	3.00	6.00
❑ 050	Tra-La-La-La Suzy/Sweet Molly Brown	1976	—	3.00	6.00
❑ 067	You're the Reason I'm Living/Take Me Back	1976	—	3.00	6.00

METROMEDIA

Number	Title (A Side/B Side)	Yr	VG	VG+	NM
❑ BMBO-0189	Daddy's Going Bye-Bye/I'm a Fool for Leaving	1973	2.00	4.00	8.00
❑ 68-0109	Small Enough to Crawl/Somewhere in the Wee Small Hours	1973	2.00	4.00	8.00

PRIZE

Number	Title (A Side/B Side)	Yr	VG	VG+	NM
❑ 10	I Might As Well Be Home/Mr. and Mrs. Untrue	1971	2.00	4.00	8.00

Albums

BRYLEN

Number	Title (A Side/B Side)	Yr	VG	VG+	NM
❑ BN-4402	Can't Live Without You	1982	2.50	5.00	10.00

GRT

Number	Title (A Side/B Side)	Yr	VG	VG+	NM
❑ 8008	Mr. Country Soul	197?	3.75	7.50	15.00

SUNBIRD

Number	Title (A Side/B Side)	Yr	VG	VG+	NM
❑ SN-50108	The Best of Price Mitchell	1979	3.00	6.00	12.00

MITCHELL, PRICE, AND JERRI KELLY

Also see each artist's individual listings.

45s

GRT

Number	Title (A Side/B Side)	Yr	VG	VG+	NM
❑ 016	I Can't Help Myself (Sugar Pie, Honey Bunch)/Got You on My Mind	1974	—	3.50	7.00
❑ 029	Saving It All for You/(B-side unknown)	1975	—	3.50	7.00

MITCHELL, PRICE, AND RENE SLOANE

45s

SUNBIRD

Number	Title (A Side/B Side)	Yr	VG	VG+	NM
❑ 101	Mr. and Mrs. Untrue/Savin' It All for You	1979	—	2.50	5.00

MITCHELL, PRISCILLA

Also see ROY DRUSKY AND PRISCILLA MITCHELL.

45s

MERCURY

Number	Title (A Side/B Side)	Yr	VG	VG+	NM
❑ 72499	It Comes and Goes/The Teen Years	1965	2.50	5.00	10.00
❑ 72565	Almost Everything a Lonely Girl Needs/Sweet Talk	1966	2.50	5.00	10.00
❑ 72635	Acres of Heartaches/Look at the Laughter	1966	2.50	5.00	10.00
❑ 72681	He's Not for Real/Take Me Home to Your Mama	1967	2.00	4.00	8.00
❑ 72757	Your Old Handy Man/Who's Cheating Who	1967	2.00	4.00	8.00
❑ 72807	Natch'illy Ain't No Good/You're Gonna Be Sorry	1968	2.00	4.00	8.00

MITCHUM, ROBERT

45s

CAPITOL

Number	Title (A Side/B Side)	Yr	VG	VG+	NM
❑ F3672	What Is This Generation Coming To/Mama Looka Boo Boo	1957	3.75	7.50	15.00
❑ 3741	The Ballad of Thunder Road/My Baby's Lovin' Arms	1973	—	3.00	6.00
❑ 3986	The Ballad of Thunder Road/My Honey's Lovin' Arms	1962	2.00	4.00	8.00

—Orange and yellow swirl label, no "F" prefix

Number	Title (A Side/B Side)	Yr	VG	VG+	NM
❑ 3986	The Ballad of Thunder Road/My Honey's Lovin' Arms	1969	—	3.00	6.00

—Red and orange "target" label

Number	Title (A Side/B Side)	Yr	VG	VG+	NM
❑ 3986	The Ballad of Thunder Road/My Honey's Lovin' Arms	1973	—	2.00	4.00

—Orange label, "Capitol" at bottom

Number	Title (A Side/B Side)	Yr	VG	VG+	NM
❑ F3986	The Ballad of Thunder Road/My Honey's Lovin' Arms	1958	3.75	7.50	15.00

—Purple label with "F" prefix

Number	Title (A Side/B Side)	Yr	VG	VG+	NM
❑ F3986 [PS]	The Ballad of Thunder Road/My Honey's Lovin' Arms	1958	6.25	12.50	25.00

COLUMBIA

Number	Title (A Side/B Side)	Yr	VG	VG+	NM
❑ 03483	The Ballad of Thunder Road/That Little Ole Wine Drinker Me	1983	—	2.50	5.00

MONUMENT

Number	Title (A Side/B Side)	Yr	VG	VG+	NM
❑ 1006	Little Old Wine Drinker Me/Walker's Woods	1967	—	3.50	7.00
❑ 1025	You Deserve Each Other/That Man Right There	1967	—	3.50	7.00

Albums

CAPITOL

Number	Title (A Side/B Side)	Yr	VG	VG+	NM
❑ T 853 [M]	Calypso — Is Like So...	1957	25.00	50.00	100.00

MONUMENT

Number	Title (A Side/B Side)	Yr	VG	VG+	NM
❑ MLP-8066 [M]	That Man, Robert Mitchum, Sings	1967	6.25	12.50	25.00
❑ SLP-18066 [S]	That Man, Robert Mitchum, Sings	1967	6.25	12.50	25.00

MIZE, BILLY

45s

COLUMBIA

Number	Title (A Side/B Side)	Yr	VG	VG+	NM
❑ 4-43417	Terrible Tangled Web/You Don't Have Very Far to Go	1965	2.50	5.00	10.00
❑ 4-43770	You Can't Stop Me/The Bigger the Fool (The Harder the Fall)	1966	2.50	5.00	10.00
❑ 4-43982	It's Gonna Get Lonely/Imagine Me	1967	2.50	5.00	10.00
❑ 4-44339	I'd Rather Have You Than My Pride/The Lights of Albuquerque	1967	2.50	5.00	10.00
❑ 4-44621	Walking Through the Memories of My Mind/Wind (I'll Catch Up to You)	1968	2.50	5.00	10.00

IMPERIAL

Number	Title (A Side/B Side)	Yr	VG	VG+	NM
❑ 66365	Make It Rain/You Done Me Wrong	1969	2.00	4.00	8.00
❑ 66403	While I'm Thinkin' About It/The Absence of You	1969	2.00	4.00	8.00
❑ 66427	Mama, the Sparrow and the Tree/The Closest I Ever Came	1969	2.00	4.00	8.00
❑ 66447	If This Were the Last Song/I Learned to Walk	1970	2.00	4.00	8.00

MEGA

Number	Title (A Side/B Side)	Yr	VG	VG+	NM
❑ 1216	Linda's Love Stop/(B-side unknown)	1974	—	3.00	6.00
❑ 1223	Do Apples Look Like Oranges/It's a Feeling Called Love	1974	—	3.00	6.00
❑ 1232	Born to Love Me/You Can Get By	1975	—	3.00	6.00
❑ 1240	The Lady's Leavin'/(B-side unknown)	1975	—	3.00	6.00

UNITED ARTISTS

Number	Title (A Side/B Side)	Yr	VG	VG+	NM
❑ XW265	California Is Just Mississippi/Just the Other Side of Nowhere	1973	—	3.00	6.00
❑ XW372	Thank You for the Feeling/Detroit City	1973	—	3.00	6.00
❑ XW503	Lord Let It Rain/Poor Man's Hobby	1974	—	3.00	6.00
❑ 50717	Beer Drinking, Honky Tonkin' Blues/Someday When It Gets to Be Tomorrow	1970	—	3.00	6.00
❑ 50751	You're Alright with Me/I Forgot More Than You'll Ever Know	1971	—	3.00	6.00
❑ 50828	All Together Now, Cry/Blowin' on Cold Ashes	1971	—	3.00	6.00
❑ 50945	Take It Easy/Susan's Floor	1972	—	3.00	6.00
❑ 50991	Good Time Charlie's Got the Blues/Middle Tennessee Country Boy's Blues	1972	—	3.00	6.00

ZODIAC

Number	Title (A Side/B Side)	Yr	VG	VG+	NM
❑ 1006	Heaven for the Weekend/Two People Party	1976	—	2.50	5.00
❑ 1011	It Hurts to Know the Feeling's Gone/Living Her Life in a Song	1976	—	2.50	5.00
❑ 1014	Livin' Her Life in a Song/Linda's Love Stop	1977	—	2.50	5.00

Albums

IMPERIAL

Number	Title (A Side/B Side)	Yr	VG	VG+	NM
❑ LP-12441	This Time and Place	1969	5.00	10.00	20.00

UNITED ARTISTS

Number	Title (A Side/B Side)	Yr	VG	VG+	NM
❑ UAS-6781	You're Alright with Me	1971	3.75	7.50	15.00

ZODIAC

Number	Title (A Side/B Side)	Yr	VG	VG+	NM
❑ 5007	Love 'n' Stuff	1976	3.00	6.00	12.00

MOE AND JOE

See MOE BANDY AND JOE STAMPLEY.

MOEBAKKEN, DICK

45s

ASI

Number	Title (A Side/B Side)	Yr	VG	VG+	NM
❑ 1016	Heaven Is Being Good to Me/The Lord's Prayer	1978	—	3.00	6.00

MOFFATT, HUGH

45s

MERCURY

Number	Title (A Side/B Side)	Yr	VG	VG+	NM
❑ 55024	The Gambler/That Light in Your Eyes	1978	—	2.00	4.00
❑ 55059	Love and Only Love/The Morning After (The Night Before)	1978	—	2.00	4.00

Albums

PHILO

Number	Title (A Side/B Side)	Yr	VG	VG+	NM
❑ PH-1111	Loving You	1987	2.50	5.00	10.00
❑ PH-1127	Troubadour	1989	3.00	6.00	12.00

MOFFATT, KATY

45s

COLUMBIA

Number	Title (A Side/B Side)	Yr	VG	VG+	NM
❑ 3-10271	I Can Almost See Houston from Here/Take Me Back to Texas	1975	—	2.50	5.00
❑ 3-10328	Can't Help Lovin' That Man/Kansas City Morning	1976	—	2.50	5.00
❑ 3-10377	Easy Come, Easy Go/She Calls Me "Baby"	1976	—	2.50	5.00
❑ 3-10636	Um, Um, Um, Um, Um, Um/(Waitin' for) The Real Thing	1977	—	2.50	5.00
❑ 3-10692	Up on the Roof/Kansas City Morning	1978	—	2.50	5.00

PERMIAN

Number	Title (A Side/B Side)	Yr	VG	VG+	NM
❑ 82002	Under Loved and Over Lonely/Let's Make Something of It	1983	—	2.50	5.00
❑ 82004	Reynosa/Lonely But Only for You	1984	—	2.50	5.00
❑ 82005	This Ain't Tennessee and He Ain't You/Midnight Harbor	1984	—	2.50	5.00

Albums

COLUMBIA

Number	Title (A Side/B Side)	Yr	VG	VG+	NM
❑ PC 34172	Katy Moffatt	1976	3.75	7.50	15.00
❑ JC 34774	Kissin' in the California Sun	1977	3.75	7.50	15.00

PHILO

Number	Title (A Side/B Side)	Yr	VG	VG+	NM
❑ PH-1128	Walkin' on the Moon	1989	3.00	6.00	12.00
❑ PH-1133	Child Bride	1990	3.00	6.00	12.00

MOLLY AND THE HEYMAKERS

45s

REPRISE

Number	Title (A Side/B Side)	Yr	VG	VG+	NM
❑ 7-18944	Jimmy McCarthy's Truck/Milkhouse	1992	—	2.00	4.00
❑ 7-19025	Mountain of Love/If Love	1992	—	2.00	4.00
❑ 7-19332	He Comes Around/This Time	1991	—	2.00	4.00
❑ 7-19517	Chasin' Something Called Love/Gulf of Mexico	1990	—	2.00	4.00

MOM & DADS, THE

45s

GNP CRESCENDO

Number	Title (A Side/B Side)	Yr	VG	VG+	NM
❑ 439	The Rangers Waltz/Quentin's E Flat Boogie	1971	—	2.50	5.00
❑ 451	In the Blue Canadian Rockies/Blue Skirt Waltz	1972	—	2.50	5.00
❑ 455	Amazing Grace/Rippling River Waltz	1972	—	2.50	5.00
❑ 460	Jingle Bell Rock/Auld Lang Syne	1972	—	2.50	5.00
❑ 461	Angry/Anniversary Waltz	1973	—	2.00	4.00
❑ 466	The Waltz You Saved for Me/When the Saints Go Marching In	1973	—	2.00	4.00
❑ 472	Somewhere My Love/My Happiness	1973	—	2.00	4.00
❑ 478	My Blue Heaven/Your Cheatin' Heart	1974	—	2.00	4.00
❑ 485	Maiden's Prayer/Wabash Cannonball	1974	—	2.00	4.00
❑ 496	Kentucky Waltz/(B-side unknown)	1975	—	2.00	4.00
❑ 803	Silver Bells/Bill Bailey	1975	—	2.00	4.00

Albums

GNP CRESCENDO

Number	Title (A Side/B Side)	Yr	VG	VG+	NM
❑ GNP-2061	The Rangers Waltz	1971	2.50	5.00	10.00
❑ GNP-2063	In the Blue Canadian Rockies	1972	2.50	5.00	10.00
❑ GNP-2065	Souvenirs	1972	2.50	5.00	10.00
❑ GNP-2068	Again!	1973	2.50	5.00	10.00
❑ GNP-2072	Reminiscing	1973	2.50	5.00	10.00
❑ GNP-2078	Dance with the Mom & Dads	1974	2.50	5.00	10.00
❑ GNP-2082	The Mom & Dads Play Your Favorite Hymns	1974	2.50	5.00	10.00
❑ GNP-2084	Love Is a Beautiful Song	1974	2.50	5.00	10.00
❑ GNP-2087	The Best of the Mom & Dads	1975	2.50	5.00	10.00
❑ GNP-2092	Dream	1975	2.50	5.00	10.00
❑ GNP-2096	Memories	1976	2.50	5.00	10.00
❑ GNP-2102	Summertime	1976	2.50	5.00	10.00
❑ GNP-2106	Down the River of Golden Dreams	1977	2.50	5.00	10.00
❑ GNP-2108	Whispering Hope	1977	2.50	5.00	10.00
❑ GNP-2110	One Dozen Roses	1977	2.50	5.00	10.00
❑ GNP-2117	Gratefully Yours	1978	2.50	5.00	10.00
❑ 2GNP-2123 [(2)]	Golden Country	1979	3.00	6.00	12.00
❑ GNP-2125	Love Letters in the Sand	1979	2.50	5.00	10.00
❑ 2GNP-2129 [(2)]	The Very Best of the Mom & Dads	1980	3.00	6.00	12.00
❑ GNP-2130	Blue Hawaii	1980	2.50	5.00	10.00
❑ GNP-2136	To Mom & Dad With Love from the Mom & Dads	1980	2.50	5.00	10.00
❑ GNP-2139	Waltz Across Texas	1981	2.50	5.00	10.00
❑ GNP-2150	Good Night Sweetheart	1985	2.00	4.00	8.00
❑ GNP-2173	20 Favorite Waltzes	1986	2.00	4.00	8.00
❑ GNP-2189	Red Sails in the Sunset	1987	2.00	4.00	8.00

MONDAY, CARLA

45s

MCM

Number	Title (A Side/B Side)	Yr	VG	VG+	NM
❑ 001	No One Can Touch Me/(B-side unknown)	1987	—	3.00	6.00
❑ 001 [PS]	No One Can Touch Me/(B-side unknown)	1987	2.50	5.00	10.00

—Sleeve appears to be promo only

MONROE, BILL

Also see THE MONROE BROTHERS.

45s

COLUMBIA

Number	Title (A Side/B Side)	Yr	VG	VG+	NM
❑ 2-207	The Old Cross Road/Remember the Cross	1949	10.00	20.00	40.00
—Microgroove 7-inch, small hole, 33 1/3 rpm single					
❑ 2-275	Along About Daybreak/Heavy Traffic Ahead	1949	10.00	20.00	40.00
—Microgroove 7-inch, small hole, 33 1/3 rpm single					
❑ 2-323	I'm Going Back to Old Kentucky/Molly and Tenbooks	1949	10.00	20.00	40.00
—Microgroove 7-inch, small hole, 33 1/3 rpm single					
❑ 2-423	Blue Grass Stomp/Girl in the Blue Velvet Band	1950	10.00	20.00	40.00
—Microgroove 7-inch, small hole, 33 1/3 rpm single					
❑ 2-540 (?)	Travelling This Lonesome Road/Can't You Hear Me Calling	1950	10.00	20.00	40.00
—Microgroove 7-inch, small hole, 33 1/3 rpm single; With Mac Wiseman					

DECCA

Number	Title (A Side/B Side)	Yr	VG	VG+	NM
❑ 9-28183	Sailor's Plea/When the Cactus Is in Bloom	1952	6.25	12.50	25.00
❑ 9-28356	Pike County Breakdown/A Mighty Pretty Waltz	1952	6.25	12.50	25.00
❑ 9-28416	Footprints in the Snow/In the Pines	1952	6.25	12.50	25.00
❑ 9-28749	Cabin of Love/Country Waltz	1953	6.25	12.50	25.00
❑ 9-28878	The Little Girl and the Dreadful Snake/Memories of Mother and Dad	1953	6.25	12.50	25.00
❑ 9-29009	Wishing Waltz/I Hope You Have Learned	1954	6.25	12.50	25.00
❑ 9-29021	Chainging Partners/Y'All Come	1954	6.25	12.50	25.00
❑ 9-29141	Get Up John/White House Blues	1954	6.25	12.50	25.00
❑ 9-29196	Happy on My Way/We Will Set Your Fields Afire	1954	6.25	12.50	25.00
❑ 9-29289	Blue Moon of Kentucky/Close By	1954	6.25	12.50	25.00
❑ 9-29348	I'm Working on a Building/A Voice from On High	1954	6.25	12.50	25.00
❑ 9-29406	Cheyenne/Roanoke	1955	5.00	10.00	20.00
❑ 9-29436	Let the Light Shine Down on Me/Wait a Little Longer Jesus	1955	5.00	10.00	20.00
❑ 9-29645	Wheel Hoss/Put My Little Shoes Away	1955	5.00	10.00	20.00
❑ 9-29886	On and On/I Believe in You Darling	1956	5.00	10.00	20.00
❑ 9-30178	You'll Find Her Name Written There/Sittin' All Alone	1957	5.00	10.00	20.00
❑ 9-30327	Four Walls/A Fallen Star	1957	5.00	10.00	20.00
❑ 9-30486	I'm Sitting on Top of the World/Molly and Tenbrooks	1957	5.00	10.00	20.00
❑ 9-30647	Sally-Jo/Brand New Shoes	1958	3.75	7.50	15.00
❑ 9-30739	Scotland/Panhandle Country	1958	3.75	7.50	15.00
❑ 9-30809	Gotta Travel On/No One But My Darling	1959	3.75	7.50	15.00
❑ 9-30944	Dark as the Night, Blue as the Day/Tomorrow I'll Be Gone	1959	3.75	7.50	15.00
❑ 9-31031	Come Go with Me/Lonesome Wind Blues	1959	3.75	7.50	15.00
❑ 31107	Jesus Hold My Hand/Precious Memories	1960	3.75	7.50	15.00
❑ 31218	Linda Lou/Put Your Rubber Doll Away	1961	3.00	6.00	12.00
❑ 31346	Blue Grass/Flowers of Love	1962	3.00	6.00	12.00
❑ 31409	Danny Boy/Toy Heart	1962	3.00	6.00	12.00
❑ 31456	Blue Ridge Mountain Blues/How Will I Explain About You	1963	3.00	6.00	12.00
❑ 31487	Big Sandy River/There Was Nothing We Could Do	1963	3.00	6.00	12.00
❑ 31540	New John Henry Blues/Devil's Dream	1963	3.00	6.00	12.00
❑ 31596	Darling Corey/Salt Creek	1964	2.50	5.00	10.00
❑ 31658	Mary at the Home Place/Shenandoah Breakdown	1964	2.50	5.00	10.00
❑ 31802	Cindy/Jimmy Brown the Newsboy	1965	2.50	5.00	10.00
❑ 31878	I Live in the Past/Old, Old House	1965	2.50	5.00	10.00
❑ 31943	Going Home/The Master Builder	1966	2.50	5.00	10.00
❑ 32075	When My Blue Moon Turns to Gold Again/Pretty Fair Maiden in the Garden	1967	2.50	5.00	10.00
❑ 32245	Train 45/Is the Blue Moon Still Shining	1968	2.00	4.00	8.00
❑ 32404	Gold Rush/Virginia Darlin'	1968	2.00	4.00	8.00
❑ 32502	Crossing the Cumberlands/I Haven't Seen Mary in Years	1969	2.00	4.00	8.00
❑ 32574	With Body and Soul/Fireball Mail	1969	2.00	4.00	8.00
❑ 32654	McKinley's March/Walk Softly on My Heart	1970	2.00	4.00	8.00
❑ 32827	Goin' Up Caney/Tallahassee	1971	2.00	4.00	8.00
❑ 32966	Lonesome Moonlight Waltz/My Old Kentucky and You	1972	2.00	4.00	8.00
❑ 9-46222	New Muleskinner Blues/My Little Georgia Rose	1950	10.00	20.00	40.00
❑ 9-46236	The Old Fiddler/Alabama Waltz	1950	10.00	20.00	40.00
❑ 9-46254	Boat of Love/I'm Blue, I'm Lonesome	1950	10.00	20.00	40.00
❑ 9-46266	Memories of You/Blue Grass Ramble	1950	10.00	20.00	40.00
❑ 9-46283	Uncle Pen/When the Golden Leaves Begin to Fall	1951	7.50	15.00	30.00
❑ 9-46298	On the Old Kentucky Shore/Poison Love	1951	7.50	15.00	30.00
❑ 9-46305	Lord, Protect My Soul/River of Death	1951	7.50	15.00	30.00
❑ 9-46314	Kentucky Waltz/The Prisoner's Song	1951	7.50	15.00	30.00
❑ 9-46325	Swing Low, Sweet Chariot/Angels Rock Me to Sleep	1951	7.50	15.00	30.00
❑ 9-46344	Lonesome Truck Driver's Blues/Rotation Blues	1951	7.50	15.00	30.00
❑ 9-46351	Get Down on Your Knees/I'll Meet You in Church	1951	7.50	15.00	30.00
❑ 9-46369	Highway of Sorrow/Sugar Coated Love	1951	7.50	15.00	30.00
❑ 9-46380	Brake Man's Blues/Travelin' Blues	1951	7.50	15.00	30.00
❑ 9-46386	Christmas Time's A-Comin'/The First Whip-Poor-Wills	1951	7.50	15.00	30.00
❑ 9-46392	Letter from My Darlin'/Rawhide	1952	7.50	15.00	30.00

MCA

Number	Title (A Side/B Side)	Yr	VG	VG+	NM
❑ 40220	Down Yonder/Swing Low Sweet Chariot	1974	—	2.50	5.00
❑ 40675	My Sweet Blue-Eyed Darlin'/Monroe Blues	1976	—	2.50	5.00
❑ 51129	My Last Days on Earth/Go Hither to Go Yonder	1981	—	2.00	4.00

Selected 78s

BLUEBIRD

Number	Title (A Side/B Side)	Yr	VG	VG+	NM
❑ B-8568	Mule Skinner Blues/Six White Horses	1940	6.25	12.50	25.00
❑ B-8611	No Letter in the Mail/Cryin' Holy Unto My Lord	1940	5.00	10.00	20.00
❑ B-8692	Dog House Blues/Katy Hill	1941	5.00	10.00	20.00
❑ B-8813	Tennessee Blues/I Wonder If You Feel the Way I Do	1941	5.00	10.00	20.00
❑ B-8861	Blue Yodel No. 7/In the Pines	1942	5.00	10.00	20.00
❑ B-8893	The Coupon Song/Orange Blossom Special	1942	5.00	10.00	20.00
❑ B-8953	Shake My Mother's Hand for Me/Were You There?	1942	5.00	10.00	20.00
❑ B-8988	Back Up and Push/Honky Tonk Swing	1942	5.00	10.00	20.00

COLUMBIA

Number	Title (A Side/B Side)	Yr	VG	VG+	NM
❑ 20013	Kentucky Waltz/Rocky Road Blues	1948	3.75	7.50	15.00
—Reissue of 36907					
❑ 20080	Footprints in the Snow/True Life Blues	1948	3.75	7.50	15.00
—Reissue of 37151					
❑ 20107	Mansions for Me/Mother's Only Sleeping	1948	3.75	7.50	15.00
—Reissue of 37294					
❑ 20189	Blue Yodel #4/Will You Be Loving Another Man	1948	3.75	7.50	15.00
—Reissue of 37565					
❑ 20370	Blue Moon of Kentucky/Goodbye Old Pal	1948	3.75	7.50	15.00
—Reissue of 37888					
❑ 20384	Blue Grass Special/How Will I Explain About You	1948	3.75	7.50	15.00
—Reissue of 37960					
❑ 20402	I'm a-Travelling On and On/Shine, Hallelujah, Shine	1948	3.75	7.50	15.00
—Reissue of 38078					
❑ 20423	Sweetheart, You Done Me Wrong/My Rose of Old Kentucky	1948	3.75	7.50	15.00
—Reissue of 38172					

Number	Title (A Side/B Side)	Yr	VG	VG+	NM
❑ 20459	I Hear a Sweet Voice Calling/Little Cabin Home on the Hill	1948	5.00	10.00	20.00
❑ 20488	Little Community Church/That Home Above	1948	5.00	10.00	20.00
❑ 20503	Wicked Path of Sin/Summertime Is Past and Gone	1948	5.00	10.00	20.00
❑ 20526	When You Are Lonely/It's Mighty Dark to Travel	1949	5.00	10.00	20.00
❑ 20552	Toy Heart/Blue Grass Breakdown	1949	5.00	10.00	20.00
❑ 36907	Kentucky Waltz/Rocky Road Blues	1946	5.00	10.00	20.00
❑ 37151	Footprints in the Snow/True Life Blues	1946	5.00	10.00	20.00
❑ 37294	Mansions for Me/Mother's Only Sleeping	1947	5.00	10.00	20.00
❑ 37565	Blue Yodel #4/Will You Be Loving Another Man	1947	5.00	10.00	20.00
❑ 37888	Blue Moon of Kentucky/Goodbye Old Pal	1947	5.00	10.00	20.00
❑ 37960	Blue Grass Special/How Will I Explain About You	1947	5.00	10.00	20.00
❑ 38078	I'm a-Travelling On and On/Shine, Hallelujah, Shine	1948	5.00	10.00	20.00
❑ 38172	Sweetheart, You Done Me Wrong/My Rose of Old Kentucky	1948	5.00	10.00	20.00

Albums

COLUMBIA

Number	Title	Yr	VG	VG+	NM
❑ FC 38904	Columbia Historic Editions	1983	3.00	6.00	12.00

DECCA

Number	Title	Yr	VG	VG+	NM
❑ DL 4080 [M]	Mr. Bluegrass	1960	7.50	15.00	30.00
❑ DL 4266 [M]	Bluegrass Ramble	1962	7.50	15.00	30.00
❑ DL 4327 [M]	My All Time Country Favorites	1962	6.25	12.50	25.00
❑ DL 4382 [M]	Bluegrass Special	1963	6.25	12.50	25.00
❑ DL 4537 [M]	I'll Meet You in Chuch Sunday Morning	1964	6.25	12.50	25.00
❑ DL 4601 [M]	Bluegrass Instrumentals	1965	5.00	10.00	20.00
❑ DL 4780 [M]	The High Lonesome Sound of Bill Monroe	1966	5.00	10.00	20.00
❑ DL 4896 [M]	Bluegrass Time	1967	7.50	15.00	30.00
❑ DL 8731 [M]	Knee Deep in Bluegrass	1958	12.50	25.00	50.00
❑ DL 8769 [M]	I Saw the Light	1959	12.50	25.00	50.00
❑ DL 74080 [S]	Mr. Bluegrass	1960	10.00	20.00	40.00
❑ DL 74266 [S]	Bluegrass Ramble	1962	10.00	20.00	40.00
❑ DL 74327 [S]	My All Time Country Favorites	1962	7.50	15.00	30.00
❑ DL 74382 [S]	Bluegrass Special	1963	7.50	15.00	30.00
❑ DL 74537 [S]	I'll Meet You in Church Sunday Morning	1964	7.50	15.00	30.00
❑ DL 74601 [S]	Bluegrass Instrumentals	1965	6.25	12.50	25.00
❑ DL 74780 [S]	The High Lonesome Sound of Bill Monroe	1966	6.25	12.50	25.00
❑ DL 74896 [S]	Bluegrass Time	1967	5.00	10.00	20.00
❑ DL 75010	Bill Monroe's Greatest Hits	1968	5.00	10.00	20.00
❑ DL 75135	A Voice from On High	1969	5.00	10.00	20.00
❑ DL 75213	Kentucky Bluegrass	1970	5.00	10.00	20.00
❑ DL 75281	Country Music Hall of Fame	1972	5.00	10.00	20.00
❑ DL 78731 [S]	Knee Deep in Bluegrass	1958	17.50	35.00	70.00
❑ DL 78769 [S]	I Saw the Light	1959	17.50	35.00	70.00

HARMONY

Number	Title	Yr	VG	VG+	NM
❑ HL 7290 [M]	The Great Bill Monroe and His Bluegrass Boys	1961	6.25	12.50	25.00
❑ HL 7315 [M]	Bill Monroe's Best	1964	5.00	10.00	20.00
❑ HL 7338 [M]	The Original Bluegrass Sound	1965	5.00	10.00	20.00
❑ HS 11335 [R]	The Great Bill Monroe and His Bluegrass Boys	1969	3.75	7.50	15.00

MCA

Number	Title	Yr	VG	VG+	NM
❑ 17	Bill Monroe's Greatest Hits *—Reissue of Decca 75010*	1973	3.00	6.00	12.00
❑ 82	Mr. Bluegrass *—Reissue of Decca 74080*	1973	3.00	6.00	12.00
❑ 88	Bluegrass Ramble *—Reissue of Decca 74266*	1973	3.00	6.00	12.00
❑ 97	Bluegrass Special *—Reissue of Decca 74382*	1973	3.00	6.00	12.00
❑ 104	Bluegrass Instrumentals *—Reissue of Decca 74601*	1973	3.00	6.00	12.00
❑ 110	The High Lonesome Sound of Bill Monroe *—Reissue of Decca 74780*	1973	3.00	6.00	12.00
❑ 116	Bluegrass Time *—Reissue of Decca 74896*	1973	3.00	6.00	12.00
❑ 131	A Voice from On High *—Reissue of Decca 75135*	1973	3.00	6.00	12.00
❑ 136	Kentucky Bluegrass *—Reissue of Decca 75213*	1973	3.00	6.00	12.00
❑ 140	Country Music Hall of Fame *—Reissue of Decca 75281*	1973	3.00	6.00	12.00
❑ 226	I'll Meet You in Church Sunday Morning *—Reissue of Decca 74537*	1973	3.00	6.00	12.00
❑ 426	Road of Life	1974	3.75	7.50	15.00
❑ 500	Uncle Pen	197?	3.00	6.00	12.00
❑ 527	I Saw the Light *—Reissue of Decca 78769*	197?	3.00	6.00	12.00
❑ 707	Weary Traveler *—Reissue of 2173*	198?	2.50	5.00	10.00
❑ 708	Bill Monroe Sings Bluegrass, Body and Soul *—Reissue of 2251*	198?	2.50	5.00	10.00
❑ 765	Bean Blossom '79 *—Reissue of 3209*	198?	2.50	5.00	10.00
❑ 2173	Weary Traveler	1976	3.75	7.50	15.00
❑ 2251	Bill Monroe Sings Bluegrass, Body and Soul	1977	3.75	7.50	15.00
❑ 2315	Bluegrass Memories	1978	3.75	7.50	15.00
❑ 3209	Bean Blossom '79	1979	3.75	7.50	15.00
❑ 4090 [(2)]	The Best of Bill Monroe	197?	3.75	7.50	15.00
❑ 5435	Bill Monroe and Friends	1984	3.00	6.00	12.00
❑ 5625	Bill Monroe and the Stars of the Bluegrass Hall of Fame	1985	3.00	6.00	12.00
❑ 8002 [(2)]	Bean Blossom	1973	5.00	10.00	20.00

RCA CAMDEN

Number	Title	Yr	VG	VG+	NM
❑ CAL-719 [M]	Father of Bluegrass Music	1962	6.25	12.50	25.00

MONROE, CHARLIE

Also see THE MONROE BROTHERS.

45s

DECCA

Number	Title (A Side/B Side)	Yr	VG	VG+	NM
❑ 9-28281	Find 'Em, Fool 'Em and Leave 'Em Alone/These Triflin' Women	1952	6.25	12.50	25.00
❑ 9-30048	Why Did You Say Goodbye/That's What I Like About You	1956	5.00	10.00	20.00
❑ 9-30307	Weep and Cry/I'm Weary of Heartaches	1957	5.00	10.00	20.00
❑ 9-46406	I'm Old Kentucky Bound/An Angel in Disguise	1952	6.25	12.50	25.00

RCA VICTOR

Number	Title (A Side/B Side)	Yr	VG	VG+	NM
❑ 47-4291	You'll Find Her Name Written There/That Wild Black Engine	1951	6.25	12.50	25.00
❑ 48-0046	Rosa Lee McFall/They Didn't Believe It Was True *—Originals on green vinyl*	1949	10.00	20.00	40.00
❑ 48-0103	Our Mansion Is Ready/A Valley of Peace *—Originals on green vinyl*	1949	10.00	20.00	40.00
❑ 48-0149	Red Rocking Chair/Time Clock of Life *—Originals on green vinyl*	1950	10.00	20.00	40.00
❑ 48-0193	When the Angels Carry Me Home/If We Never Meet Again *—Originals on green vinyl*	1950	7.50	15.00	30.00
❑ 48-0194	Mother's Not Dead/There's No Depression in Heaven *—Originals on green vinyl*	1950	7.50	15.00	30.00
❑ 48-0195	Campin' in Canaan's Land/Don't Forget to Pray *—Originals on green vinyl*	1950	7.50	15.00	30.00
❑ 48-0222	Down in the Willow Garden/Bringin' In the Georgia Mail *—Originals on green vinyl*	1950	7.50	15.00	30.00
❑ 48-0325	You'll Find Me There/Come Shake Hands with Mother *—Originals on green vinyl*	1950	7.50	15.00	30.00
❑ 48-0326	My Saviour's Train/Springtime in Glory *—Originals on green vinyl*	1950	7.50	15.00	30.00
❑ 48-0327	I Know He's Been Dealing with Me/You'd Better Be Somewhere *—Originals on green vinyl*	1950	7.50	15.00	30.00
❑ 48-0361	So Blue/Without Me Are You Blue *—Originals on green vinyl*	1950	7.50	15.00	30.00
❑ 48-0391	Sugar Cane Mama/Down in Caroline *—Originals on green vinyl*	1950	7.50	15.00	30.00
❑ 48-0417	Good Morning to You/'Neath a Cold Gray Tomb of Stone	1951	6.25	12.50	25.00
❑ 48-0456	Gold Star Mother/I'm Gonna Sing, Sing, Sing	1951	6.25	12.50	25.00
❑ 48-0485	Jesus Is Calling/My Lord's Gonna Move This Wicked Race	1951	6.25	12.50	25.00

Selected 78s

BLUEBIRD

Number	Title (A Side/B Side)	Yr	VG	VG+	NM
❑ B-7862	The Great Speckled Bird/Every Time I Feel	1938	5.00	10.00	20.00
❑ B-7922	Farther Along/No Home, No Place to Pillow My Head	1938	5.00	10.00	20.00
❑ B-7949	You're Gonna Miss Me/(B-side unknown)	1939	5.00	10.00	20.00
❑ B-7990	When the World's on Fire/(B-side unknown)	1939	5.00	10.00	20.00
❑ B-8050	Guided by Love/Is She Praying There?	1939	5.00	10.00	20.00
❑ B-8092	Oh, Death/If You See My Saviour	1939	5.00	10.00	20.00
❑ B-8118	Joy Bells in My Soul/From Shore to Shore	1939	5.00	10.00	20.00

Albums

STARDAY

Number	Title	Yr	VG	VG+	NM
❑ SLP-361 [M]	Lord, Build Me a Cabin	1965	6.25	12.50	25.00
❑ SLP-372 [M]	Charlie Monroe Sings Again	1966	6.25	12.50	25.00

MONROE, VAUGHN

Bandleader and deep-voiced singer, his one country hit is considered a classic and is often remade to this day.

45s

RCA VICTOR

Number	Title (A Side/B Side)	Yr	VG	VG+	NM
❑ 47-2902	Riders in the Sky (A Cowboy Legend)/Single Saddle	1949	6.25	12.50	25.00

MONROE BROTHERS, THE

The most popular of the "brother" groups of the 1930s, they were a seminal act in the evolution of bluegrass music. Also see BILL MONROE; CHARLIE MONROE.

Selected 78s

BLUEBIRD

Number	Title (A Side/B Side)	Yr	VG	VG+	NM
❑ B-6309	The World Is Not My Home/What Would You Give in Exchange	193?	6.25	12.50	25.00
❑ B-6363	What Is Home Without Love?/Drifting Too Far from the Shore	193?	6.25	12.50	25.00
❑ B-6422	My Long Journey Home/Nine-Pound Hammer Is Too Heavy	193?	6.25	12.50	25.00
❑ B-6477	You've Got to Walk That Lonesome Valley/God Holds the Future in His Hands	193?	6.25	12.50	25.00
❑ B-6512	Six Months Ain't Long/Darling Corey	193?	6.25	12.50	25.00
❑ B-6552	Just a Song of Old Kentucky/Don't Forget Me	193?	6.25	12.50	25.00
❑ B-6607	On Some Foggy Mountain Top/(B-side unknown)	193?	6.25	12.50	25.00
❑ B-6645	Little Red Shoes/New River Train	193?	6.25	12.50	25.00
❑ B-6676	Old Crossroad/We Read of a Place That's Called Heaven	193?	6.25	12.50	25.00
❑ B-6729	My Saviour's Train/I Dreamed I Searched Heaven for You	193?	6.25	12.50	25.00
❑ B-6762	Where Is My Sailor Boy?/The Carter Family and Jimmie Rodgers in Texas *—B-side by Jimmie Rodgers with the Carter Family*	193?	6.25	12.50	25.00
❑ B-6773	Roll in My Sweet Baby's Arms/(B-side unknown)	193?	5.00	10.00	20.00

Number	Title (A Side/B Side)	Yr	VG	VG+	NM
❑ B-6820	Will the Circle Be Unbroken?/The Saints Go Marching In	193?	5.00	10.00	20.00
❑ B-6829	Forgotten Soldier Boy/(B-side unknown)	193?	5.00	10.00	20.00
❑ B-6866	I Am Ready to Go/(B-side unknown)	193?	5.00	10.00	20.00
❑ B-6912	What Would the Profit Be?/I Have Found the Way	193?	5.00	10.00	20.00
❑ B-6960	Katy Cline/(B-side unknown)	193?	5.00	10.00	20.00
❑ B-7007	I Am Going That Way/I'll Live On	193?	5.00	10.00	20.00
❑ B-7055	Do You Call That Religion?/(B-side unknown)	193?	5.00	10.00	20.00
❑ B-7093	Weeping Willow Tree/Oh, Hide You in the Blood	193?	5.00	10.00	20.00
❑ B-7122	What Would You Give in Exchange (Parts 2 and 3)	193?	5.00	10.00	20.00
❑ B-7145	On My Way to Glory/He Will Set Your Fields on Fire	193?	5.00	10.00	20.00
❑ B-7191	All the Good Times Are Passed and Gone/Let Us Be Lovers	193?	5.00	10.00	20.00
❑ B-7273	On That Old Gospel Ship/My Last Moving Day	193?	5.00	10.00	20.00
❑ B-7326	What Would You Give in Exchange? (Part 4)/ Sinner, You Better Get Ready	193?	5.00	10.00	20.00
❑ B-7385	On the Banks of the Ohio/Fame Apart from God's Approval	193?	5.00	10.00	20.00
—B-side by Uncle Dave Macon					
❑ B-7425	The Old Man's Story/I've Still Got Ninety-Nine	193?	5.00	10.00	20.00
❑ B-7460	On My Way Back Home/Pearly Gates	193?	5.00	10.00	20.00
❑ B-7508	Have a Feast Here Tonight/Goodbye, Maggie	193?	5.00	10.00	20.00
❑ B-7562	A Beautiful Life/When Our Lord Shall Come Again	193?	5.00	10.00	20.00
❑ B-7598	Rollin' On/Little Joe	1938	5.00	10.00	20.00
Albums					
BLUEBIRD					
❑ AXM2-5510 [(2)]	Feast Here Tonight	197?	3.75	7.50	15.00

MONTANA

45s

Number	Title (A Side/B Side)	Yr	VG	VG+	NM
WATERHOUSE					
❑ 15005	The Shoe's on the Other Foot Tonight/(B-side unknown)	1981	2.00	4.00	8.00

MONTANA, BILLY, AND THE LONG SHOTS

45s

Number	Title (A Side/B Side)	Yr	VG	VG+	NM
WARNER BROS.					
❑ 7-27809	Oh Jenny/All I Need	1988	—	—	3.00
❑ 7-28256	Baby I Was Leaving Anyhow/And So It Goes (With Everything But Love)	1987	—	—	3.00
❑ 7-28426	Crazy Blue/That's the Bottom Line	1987	—	—	3.00

MONTANA, PATSY

Selected 78s

Number	Title (A Side/B Side)	Yr	VG	VG+	NM
BANNER					
❑ 6-04-53	The She Buckaroo/Sweetheart of the Saddle	1936	6.25	12.50	25.00
❑ 6-08-52	Woman's Answer to Nobody's Darling/Gold Coast Express	1936	6.25	12.50	25.00
❑ 6-09-58	Blazin' the Trail/Montana	1936	6.25	12.50	25.00
COLUMBIA					
❑ 20201	I Wanna Be a Cowboy's Sweetheart/Ridin' Old Paint	1948	3.75	7.50	15.00
—Reissue of 37602					
❑ 37602	I Wanna Be a Cowboy's Sweetheart/Ridin' Old Paint	1946	5.00	10.00	20.00
—Reissue					
CONQUEROR					
❑ 8575	I Wanna Be a Cowboy's Sweetheart/Ridin' Old Paint	1935	7.50	15.00	30.00
❑ 8887	Ridin' the Sunset Trail/There's a Ranch in the Sky	193?	6.25	12.50	25.00
❑ 8893	I Only Want a Buddy Not a Sweetheart/Pride of the Prairie	193?	6.25	12.50	25.00
❑ 8979	Little Rose of the Prairie/My Dear Old Arizona Home	193?	6.25	12.50	25.00
❑ 8980	Out on the Lone Prairie/Someone to Go Home To	193?	6.25	12.50	25.00
❑ 9003	Rodeo Sweetheart/The Waltz of the Hills	193?	6.25	12.50	25.00
DECCA					
❑ 5947	I'll Be Waiting for You Darlin'/Shy Anne from Old Cheyenne	1941	5.00	10.00	20.00
❑ 6024	Blanket Me with Western Skies/Gallopin' to Gallup (On the Santa Fe Trail)	1941	5.00	10.00	20.00
❑ 6032	Deep in the Heart of Texas/I'll Wait for You	1941	5.00	10.00	20.00
❑ 6101	Good Night Soldier/Smile and Drive Your Blues Away	1942	5.00	10.00	20.00
MELOTONE					
❑ 6-06-58	Give Me a Home in Montana/The Wheel of the Wagon Is Broken	1936	6.25	12.50	25.00
❑ 6-07-55	Lone Star/Old Black Mountain Trail	1936	6.25	12.50	25.00
❑ 6-08-52	Woman's Answer to Nobody's Darling/Gold Coast Express	1936	6.25	12.50	25.00
❑ 7-01-52	I'm an Old Cowhand (From the Rio Grande)/ Echoes from the Hills	1937	6.25	12.50	25.00
❑ 7-04-69	I'm a Wild and Reckless Cowboy (From the West Side of Town)/With a Banjo on My Knee	1937	6.25	12.50	25.00
❑ 7-05-74	A Cowboy Honeymoon/I Wanna Be a Cowboy's Sweetheart No. 2 (I've Found My Cowboy Sweetheart)	1937	6.25	12.50	25.00
❑ M 17969	Old Black Mountain Trail/(B-side unknown)	193?	6.25	12.50	25.00
PERFECT					
❑ 6-06-58	Give Me a Home in Montana/The Wheel of the Wagon Is Broken	1936	6.25	12.50	25.00
❑ 6-07-55	Lone Star/Old Black Mountain Trail	1936	6.25	12.50	25.00
❑ 6-09-58	Blazin' the Trail/Montana	1936	6.25	12.50	25.00
❑ 7-02-52	Chuck Wagon Blues/Goin' Back to Old Montana	1937	6.25	12.50	25.00
❑ 7-05-74	A Cowboy Honeymoon/I Wanna Be a Cowboy's Sweetheart No. 2 (I've Found My Cowboy Sweetheart)	1937	6.25	12.50	25.00
RCA VICTOR					
❑ 20-2686	If I Could Only Learn to Yodel/Slap 'Er Down Ag'in Paw	1948	5.00	10.00	20.00
❑ 20-2899	Little Old Rag Doll/Mama Never Said a Word About Love	1948	5.00	10.00	20.00
VICTOR					
❑ 23760	I Love My Daddy Too/(B-side unknown)	1932	37.50	75.00	150.00
VOCALION					
❑ 03010	titles unknown	193?	6.25	12.50	25.00
❑ 03135	titles unknown	193?	6.25	12.50	25.00
❑ 03268	titles unknown	193?	6.25	12.50	25.00
❑ 03292	titles unknown	193?	6.25	12.50	25.00
❑ 03377	titles unknown	193?	6.25	12.50	25.00
❑ 03422	titles unknown	193?	6.25	12.50	25.00
❑ 04023	Cowboy Rhythm/Little Sweetheart of the Ozarks	1938	5.00	10.00	20.00
❑ 04076	titles unknown	1938	5.00	10.00	20.00
❑ 04135	Big Moon/Shine On, Rocky Mountain Moonlight	1938	5.00	10.00	20.00
❑ 04247	Little Rose of the Prairie/My Dear Old Arizona Home	1938	5.00	10.00	20.00
❑ 04291	titles unknown	1938	5.00	10.00	20.00
❑ 04469	titles unknown	1938	5.00	10.00	20.00
❑ 04482	The Strawberry Roan/High Falutin' Newton	1938	5.00	10.00	20.00
❑ 04518	Give Me a Home in Montana/The Wheel of the Wagon Is Broken	1938	5.00	10.00	20.00
❑ 04568	That's Where the West Begins/You're the Only Star (In My Blue Heaven)	1938	5.00	10.00	20.00
❑ 04689	titles unknown	1938	5.00	10.00	20.00
❑ 04742	I'm a-Ridin' Up the Old Kentucky Mountain/ Han'some Joe (From the Land of the Navaho)	1939	5.00	10.00	20.00
❑ 05081	titles unknown	1939	5.00	10.00	20.00
❑ 05217	I Wanna Be a Western Cowgirl/My Song of the West	1939	5.00	10.00	20.00
❑ 05284	I'd Love to Be a Cowgirl (But I'm Afraid of Cows)/ The Moon Hangs Low (On the Ohio)	1939	5.00	10.00	20.00
❑ 05334	Back on Montana Plains/My Poncho Pony	1940	5.00	10.00	20.00
VOGUE					
❑ R721	When I Gets to Where I'm Goin'/You're Only in My Arms (To Cry on My Shoulder)	1946	25.00	50.00	100.00
—Picture record					
Albums					
SIMS					
❑ 122 [M]	The New Sound of Patsy Montana	1964	12.50	25.00	50.00
STARDAY					
❑ SLP-376 [M]	Cowboy's Sweetheart	1966	7.50	15.00	30.00

MONTANA SKYLINE

45s

Number	Title (A Side/B Side)	Yr	VG	VG+	NM
SNOW					
❑ 2022	Full Moon — Empty Pockets/The Circle of Love	1981	2.00	4.00	8.00

MONTANA SLIM

Also recorded extensively under his real name, "Wilf Carter." Other records are billed to both names.

45s

Number	Title (A Side/B Side)	Yr	VG	VG+	NM
DECCA					
❑ 9-29384	My Mountain High Yodel Song/Shoo Shoo Shoo Sh'La La	1954	6.25	12.50	25.00
❑ 9-29535	The Sunshine Bird/Maple Leaf Rag	1955	5.00	10.00	20.00
❑ 9-29585	A Strawberry Roan/Dynamite Trail	1955	5.00	10.00	20.00
❑ 9-29671	The Alpine Milkman/There's a Tree on Every Road	1955	5.00	10.00	20.00
❑ 9-29942	I'm Ragged But I'm Right/Yodeling Song	1956	5.00	10.00	20.00
❑ 9-30079	My Little Lady/Silver Bell Yodel	1956	5.00	10.00	20.00
❑ 9-30340	Away Out on the Mountain/Padlock on Your Heart	1957	5.00	10.00	20.00
❑ 9-30633	X's from Down in Texas/Let a Little Sunshine in Your Heart	1958	5.00	10.00	20.00
❑ 9-30907	My French Canadian Girl/My Prairie Rose	1959	3.75	7.50	15.00
❑ 9-31034	Blind Boy's Prayer/There's a Bluebird on Your Windowsill	1959	3.75	7.50	15.00
RCA VICTOR					
❑ 47-4252	Wha' Hoppen/Tears Don't Always	1951	6.25	12.50	25.00
❑ 47-4303	The Night Before Christmas/Punkinhead	1951	6.25	12.50	25.00
❑ 47-4446	My Oklahoma Rose/I Wish There Were Three Days in the Year	1952	6.25	12.50	25.00
❑ 47-4523	Goodbye Maria/Driftwood on the River	1952	6.25	12.50	25.00
❑ 47-4846	Alabama Saturday Night/Manhunt	1952	6.25	12.50	25.00
❑ 47-5045	Huggin' Squeezin' Kissin' Teasin'/Sweet Little Love	1952	6.25	12.50	25.00
❑ 47-5276	Sleep, Little One, Sleep/Mockingbird Love	1953	6.25	12.50	25.00
❑ 47-8205	32 Wonderful Years/Cashbox for a Heartache	1963	3.00	6.00	12.00
❑ 48-0054	Bluebird on Your Windowsill/All I Need Is Some More Lovin'	1949	10.00	20.00	40.00
—Originals on green vinyl					
❑ 48-0090	Streamlined Yodel Song/My Swiss Moonlight Lullaby	1949	10.00	20.00	40.00
—Originals on green vinyl					
❑ 48-0139	When the Ice Warms Next Again/Shackles and Chains	1950	10.00	20.00	40.00
—Originals on green vinyl					
❑ 48-0180	Unfaithful One/Give a Little, Take a Little	1950	10.00	20.00	40.00
—Originals on green vinyl					

Number	Title (A Side/B Side)	Yr	VG	VG+	NM
❑ 48-0316	No, No, Don't Ring/A Little Shirt Mama Made for Me	1950	7.50	15.00	30.00
—Originals on green vinyl					
❑ 48-0352	Take It Easy Blues/Apple, Cherry, Mince, Chocolate	1950	7.50	15.00	30.00
—Originals on green vinyl					
❑ 48-0392	Jolly Old St. Nicholas/Rudolph the Red-Nosed Reindeer	1950	10.00	20.00	40.00
—Originals on green vinyl					
❑ 48-0397	The K.P. Blues/When That Love Bug Bites You	1950	7.50	15.00	30.00
—Originals on green vinyl					
❑ 48-0419	My Heart's Closed for Repairs/Just a Woman's Smile	1951	7.50	15.00	30.00
❑ 48-0457	Let's Go Back to the Bible/She'll Be There	1951	7.50	15.00	30.00
❑ 48-0477	My Wife Is On a Diet/Sick, Sober and Sorry	1951	7.50	15.00	30.00
STARDAY					
❑ 686	Grandad's Yodeling Song/The Little Shirt My Mother Made for Me	1964	3.00	6.00	12.00
Selected 78s					
BLUEBIRD					
❑ B-5536	titles unknown	193?	7.50	15.00	30.00
❑ B-5545	The Round-Up in the Fall/Take Me Back to Old Montana	193?	7.50	15.00	30.00
❑ B-5871	I'm Gonna Ride to Heaven on a Streamline Train/The Two-Gun Cowboy	193?	7.50	15.00	30.00
❑ B-6009	titles unknown	193?	7.50	15.00	30.00
❑ B-6107	titles unknown	193?	7.50	15.00	30.00
❑ B-6208	Lonesome for Baby Tonight/Hillbilly Valley	193?	7.50	15.00	30.00
❑ B-6380	titles unknown	193?	7.50	15.00	30.00
❑ B-6515	My Swiss Moonlight Lullaby/Midnight, the Unconquered Outlaw	193?	7.50	15.00	30.00
❑ B-6814	Prairie Sunset/(B-side unknown)	193?	7.50	15.00	30.00
❑ B-6826	Round-Up Time in Heaven/Dreamy Prairie Moon	193?	7.50	15.00	30.00
❑ B-6827	Roamin' My Whole Life Away/Yodeling Cowgirl	193?	7.50	15.00	30.00
❑ B-7618	By the Grave of Nobody's Darling/Talking to the River	1938	7.50	15.00	30.00
—B-side by Norwood Tew					
❑ B-8111	There's a Love-Knot in My Lariat/My Little Yoho Lady	1939	6.25	12.50	25.00
❑ B-8150	What Difference Does It Make?/Golden Lariat	1939	6.25	12.50	25.00
❑ B-8181	Down the Yodeling Trail at Twilight/Answer to "Swiss Moonlight Lullaby"	1939	6.25	12.50	25.00
❑ B-8202	When It's Twilight Over Texas/Memories of My Little Old Log Shack	1939	6.25	12.50	25.00
❑ B-8241	The Preacher and the Cowboy/Roll On Dreamy Texas Moon	1939	6.25	12.50	25.00
❑ B-8284	When I Say Hello in the Rockies/My Only Romance Is Memories of You	1939	6.25	12.50	25.00
❑ B-8313	I'm Only a Dude in Cowboy Clothes/My Honeymoon Bridge Broke Down	1939	6.25	12.50	25.00
❑ B-8329	The Cowboy Wedding in May/I'm Still Waiting for You	1939	6.25	12.50	25.00
❑ B-8361	Rootin' Tootin' Cowboy/The Little Red Patch on the Seat of My Pants	1939	6.25	12.50	25.00
❑ B-8374	Old Barn Dance/Broken-Down Cowboy	1940	6.25	12.50	25.00
❑ B-8389	The Fate of Old Strawberry Roan/Yodeling Hillbilly	1940	6.25	12.50	25.00
❑ B-8425	It's All Over Now/Rattin' Cannonball	1940	6.25	12.50	25.00
❑ B-8441	It's Cowboy's Night to Howl/Red River Valley Blues	1940	6.25	12.50	25.00
❑ B-8456	When the White Azaleas Start Blooming/My Ramblin' Days Are Through	1940	6.25	12.50	25.00
❑ B-8472	Why Should I Feel Sorry for You Now?/Beautiful Girl of the Prairie	1940	6.25	12.50	25.00
❑ B-8491	What a Wonderful Mother of Mine/You Are My Sunshine	1940	6.25	12.50	25.00
❑ B-8517	I Still Think of You, Sweet Nellie Dean/My True and Earnest Prayer	1940	6.25	12.50	25.00
❑ B-8531	He Left the One Who Loved Him for Another/My Old Lasso Is Headed Straight for You	1940	6.25	12.50	25.00
❑ B-8566	Back Ridin' the Old Trails Again/My Old Canadian Home	1940	6.25	12.50	25.00
❑ B-8591	Dad's Little Texas Lad/Thinking	1940	6.25	12.50	25.00
❑ B-8616	Echoing Hills Yodel Back to Me/My Texas Sweetheart	1941	5.00	10.00	20.00
❑ B-8641	You Were With Me in the Waltz of My Dreams/When That Somebody Else Was You	1941	5.00	10.00	20.00
❑ B-8661	Old Chuck Wagon Days/My Missoula Valley Moon	1941	5.00	10.00	20.00
❑ B-8696	I Bought a Rock for a Rocky Mountain Girl/Streamlined Yodel Song	1941	5.00	10.00	20.00
❑ B-8753	It's Great to Be Back in the Saddle Again/Call of the Range	1941	5.00	10.00	20.00
❑ B-8800	LaVerne, My Brown-Eyed Rose/Ride for the Open Range	1941	5.00	10.00	20.00
❑ B-8842	Why Did We Ever Part?/The Last Letter	1942	5.00	10.00	20.00
❑ B-8875	Let's Go Back to the Bible/There'll Be No Blues Up Yonder	1942	5.00	10.00	20.00
❑ B-8924	My Lulu/If You Don't Really Care	1942	5.00	10.00	20.00
❑ B-8983	West of Rainbow Trail/Headin' for That Land of Gold	1942	5.00	10.00	20.00
❑ B-9032	I'm Thinking Tonight of My Blue Eyes/Put My Little Shoes Away	1942	5.00	10.00	20.00
❑ 33-0519	Just One More Ride/(B-side unknown)	1945	5.00	10.00	20.00

Number	Title (A Side/B Side)	Yr	VG	VG+	NM
Albums					
DECCA					
❑ DL 4092 [M]	The Dynamite Trail	1960	12.50	25.00	50.00
❑ DL 8917 [M]	I'm Ragged But I'm Right	1959	15.00	30.00	60.00
❑ DL 74092 [S]	The Dynamite Trail	1960	15.00	30.00	60.00
RCA CAMDEN					
❑ CAL-527 [M]	Wilf Carter/Montana Slim	1958	10.00	20.00	40.00
❑ CAL-668 [M]	Reminiscin' with Montana Slim	1962	6.25	12.50	25.00
❑ CAL-846 [M]	32 Wonderful Years	1965	5.00	10.00	20.00
❑ CAS-846 [R]	32 Wonderful Years	1965	3.00	6.00	12.00
STARDAY					
❑ SLP-300 [M]	Wilf Carter As Montana Slim	1964	7.50	15.00	30.00
❑ SLP-389 [M]	Wilf Carter	1966	7.50	15.00	30.00

MONTGOMERY, JOHN MICHAEL

Number	Title (A Side/B Side)	Yr	VG	VG+	NM
45s					
ATLANTIC					
❑ 7-84157	Cover You in Kisses/Little Cowboy's Cry	1998	—	2.00	4.00
❑ 7-85006	The Little Girl/Brand New Me	2000	—	—	3.00
—A-side with Alison Krauss and Dan Tyminski					
❑ 7-87019	Friends/A Few Cents Short	1997	—	2.00	4.00
❑ 7-87044	Ain't Got Nothin' on Us/I Miss You a Little	1996	—	2.00	4.00
❑ 7-87105	No Man's Land/Sold (The Grundy County Auction Incident)	1995	—	2.50	5.00
❑ 7-87198	If You've Got Love/Kick It Up	1994	—	2.00	4.00
❑ 7-87236	Be My Baby Tonight/Full-Time Love	1994	—	2.00	4.00
❑ 7-87248	Rope the Moon/Friday at Five	1994	—	2.00	4.00
❑ 7-87288	I Swear/Dream On Texas Ladies	1994	—	2.50	5.00
❑ 7-87326	Beer and Bones/I Love the Way You Love Me	1993	—	2.00	4.00
❑ 7-87371	I Love the Way You Love Me/Life's a Dance	1993	—	2.50	5.00

MONTGOMERY, MELBA

Also see GEORGE JONES; CHARLIE LOUVIN; GENE PITNEY.

Number	Title (A Side/B Side)	Yr	VG	VG+	NM
45s					
CAPITOL					
❑ 2513	As Far As My Forgetting's Got/You Let Me Win	1969	2.00	4.00	8.00
❑ 2758	The Closer She Gets/Where Do We Go from Here	1970	2.00	4.00	8.00
❑ 2825	Together Again/Eloy Crossing	1970	2.00	4.00	8.00
❑ 3091	He's My Man/We Don't Live Here Anymore	1971	2.00	4.00	8.00
❑ 3297	Hope I Never Love That Way Again/Say You'll Never Leave Me	1972	2.00	4.00	8.00
❑ 4290	He Called Me Baby/Country Child	1976	—	2.00	4.00
COMPASS					
❑ 45-7	Straight Talkin'/(B-side unknown)	1986	—	3.00	6.00
ELEKTRA					
❑ 45211	If You Want the Rainbow/Love, I Need You	1974	—	2.50	5.00
❑ 45229	Don't Let the Good Times Fool You/It Sure Gets Lonely	1975	—	2.50	5.00
❑ 45247	Searchin' (For Someone Like You)/Hiding in the Darkness of My Mind	1975	—	2.50	5.00
❑ 45272	If I Ever Needed Someone/He Loved You Right Out of My Mind	1975	—	2.50	5.00
❑ 45296	Love Was the Wind/I Never Dreamed That Love Could Be This Good	1975	—	2.50	5.00
❑ 45866	Wrap Your Love Around Me/Let Me Show You How I Can	1973	—	3.00	6.00
❑ 45875	He'll Come Home/Country Written Up and Down Your Face	1973	—	3.00	6.00
❑ 45883	No Charge/Wrap Your Love Around Me	1974	—	3.00	6.00
❑ 45883	No Charge/I Love Him Because He's That Way	1974	—	3.00	6.00
❑ 45894	Your Pretty Roses Came Too Late/My Feel Good Sure Feels Fine	1974	—	3.00	6.00
KARI					
❑ 111	The Star/Carolina in My Mind	1980	—	3.00	6.00
MUSICOR					
❑ 1157	Don't Keep Me Lonely Too Long/I'm Looking for the Man	1966	2.50	5.00	10.00
❑ 1175	Crossing Over Jordan/The Dead Shall Live Again	1966	2.50	5.00	10.00
❑ 1182	He's Out There With Her Somewhere/My Tiny Music Box	1966	2.50	5.00	10.00
❑ 1209	He Stayed Away (Long As He Could)/Won't Take Long	1966	2.50	5.00	10.00
❑ 1241	What Can I Tell the Folks Back Home/The Right Time to Lose My Mind	1967	2.50	5.00	10.00
❑ 1278	The Day Your Memory Came to Town/Twilight Years	1967	2.50	5.00	10.00
❑ 1291	He Wrote Forgive Me/You Put Me Here	1968	2.50	5.00	10.00
❑ 1311	Our Little Man/Tell Me Your Troubles	1968	2.50	5.00	10.00
❑ 1324	Hallelujah Road/Life Beyond Death	1968	2.50	5.00	10.00
❑ 1344	What's to Become of What's Left of Me/Every Day's a Happy Day for Fools	1969	2.50	5.00	10.00
UNITED ARTISTS					
❑ 576	Hall of Shame/What's Bad for You Is Good for Me	1963	3.00	6.00	12.00
❑ 652	The Greatest One of All/Lies Can't Hide What's On My Mind	1963	3.00	6.00	12.00
❑ 705	The Face/I Will Always Keep Loving You	1964	3.00	6.00	12.00
❑ 768	Big City Heartaches/Why Does the Lady Cry	1964	3.00	6.00	12.00
❑ 803	I Can't Change Overnight/I Can't Get Used to Being Lonely	1965	3.00	6.00	12.00
❑ 850	White Lightning/I Saw It	1965	3.00	6.00	12.00
❑ 900	Yearning/I'll Wait Till Seven	1965	3.00	6.00	12.00
❑ 964	Big Joke/Constantly	1965	3.00	6.00	12.00
❑ XW1008	Never Ending Love Affair/You	1977	—	2.50	5.00
❑ XW1115	Angel of the Morning/Pinkerton's Flowers	1977	—	2.50	5.00
❑ XW1175	Leavin' Me in Your Mind/We've Been Lyin' Here Too Long	1978	—	2.50	5.00

Albums

Number	Title (A Side/B Side)	Yr	VG	VG+	NM
ELEKTRA					
❑ CM-2	Don't Let the Good Times Fool You	1975	2.50	5.00	10.00
❑ CM-6	The Greatest Gift of All	1975	2.50	5.00	10.00
❑ EKS-75069	Melba Montgomery	1973	3.00	6.00	12.00
❑ EKS-75079	No Charge	1974	2.50	5.00	10.00
MUSICOR					
❑ MM-2074 [M]	Country Girl	1966	3.75	7.50	15.00
❑ MM-2097 [M]	The Hallelujah Road	1966	3.75	7.50	15.00
❑ MM-2113 [M]	Melba Toast	1967	5.00	10.00	20.00
❑ MM-2114 [M]	Don't Keep Me Lonely Too Long	1967	5.00	10.00	20.00
❑ MS-3074 [S]	Country Girl	1966	5.00	10.00	20.00
❑ MS-3097 [S]	The Hallelujah Road	1966	5.00	10.00	20.00
❑ MS-3113 [S]	Melba Toast	1967	5.00	10.00	20.00
❑ MS-3114 [S]	Don't Keep Me Lonely Too Long	1967	5.00	10.00	20.00
STARDAY					
❑ SLP-352 [M]	Queen of Country Music	1965	6.25	12.50	25.00
UNITED ARTISTS					
❑ UAL-3341 [M]	America's Number One Country & Western Singer	1964	5.00	10.00	20.00
❑ UAL-3369 [M]	Down Home	1964	5.00	10.00	20.00
❑ UAL-3391 [M]	I Can't Get Used to Being Lonely	1965	5.00	10.00	20.00
❑ UAS-6341 [S]	America's Number One Country & Western Singer	1964	6.25	12.50	25.00
❑ UAS-6369 [S]	Down Home	1964	6.25	12.50	25.00
❑ UAS-6391 [S]	I Can't Get Used to Being Lonely	1965	6.25	12.50	25.00

MONTGOMERY, NANCY

45s

Number	Title (A Side/B Side)	Yr	VG	VG+	NM
OVATION					
❑ 1172	All I Have to Do Is Dream/(B-side unknown)	1981	—	2.50	5.00

MONTGOMERY GENTRY

45s

Number	Title (A Side/B Side)	Yr	VG	VG+	NM
COLUMBIA					
❑ 38-79115	Hillbilly Shoes/All Night Long	1999	—	—	3.00
❑ 38-79210	Lonely and Gone/Hillbilly Shoes	1999	—	—	3.00
❑ 38-79515	All Night Long/Merry Christmas from the Family	2000	—	—	3.00

MOODY, CLYDE

45s

Number	Title (A Side/B Side)	Yr	VG	VG+	NM
DECCA					
❑ 9-28662	Mexican Joe/The Kind of Love I Can't Forget	1953	6.25	12.50	25.00
❑ 9-28785	What a Life/Canadian Waltz	1953	6.25	12.50	25.00
KING					
❑ 968	West Virginia Waltz/You're a Real Sweetheart to Me	1951	10.00	20.00	40.00
❑ 977	Too Young/Tend to Your Business	1951	10.00	20.00	40.00
❑ 987	She Cooked My Goose/I'm Sorry If That's the Way You Feel	1951	10.00	20.00	40.00
❑ 1031	If You Only Knew/You Are the Rainbow in My Dreams	1952	15.00	30.00	60.00
—Red vinyl					
❑ 1031	If You Only Knew/You Are the Rainbow in My Dreams	1952	7.50	15.00	30.00
—Black vinyl					
❑ 1072	When You Have No One to Love You/Why Don't You Come Back to Me	1952	7.50	15.00	30.00
❑ 1125	Landslide of Love/I Love You Dear Forever	1952	7.50	15.00	30.00
❑ 1147	Forgive Me/Hard Hearted	1952	7.50	15.00	30.00
LITTLE DARLIN'					
❑ 0069	California Dream/While My Heart Is Breaking	1970	2.50	5.00	10.00
STARDAY					
❑ 653	Nobody's Business/Waltzing in the Arms of a Friend	1963	3.75	7.50	15.00
❑ 671	Where There's Smoke (There's Bound to Be Fire)/Whispering Pines	1964	3.00	6.00	12.00
❑ 702	Dark Midnight/What It Means to Be Lonely	1964	3.00	6.00	12.00

Selected 78s

Number	Title (A Side/B Side)	Yr	VG	VG+	NM
KING					
❑ 619	Shenandoah Waltz/There's a Big Rock in the Road	1947	6.25	12.50	25.00
❑ 637	If You Need Me I'll Be Around/Lonely Broken Heart	1947	6.25	12.50	25.00
❑ 671	Where the Old Red River Flows/Next Sunday Darling Is My Birthday	1948	5.00	10.00	20.00
❑ 693	Waltz of the Wind/Rockin' Alone in an Old Rockin' Chair	1948	5.00	10.00	20.00
❑ 706	Carolina Waltz/Red Roses Tied in Blue	1948	5.00	10.00	20.00
❑ 726	That Little Cabin of Mine/There's No Room in My Heart	1948	5.00	10.00	20.00
❑ 744	Little Blossom/Last Goodbye	1948	5.00	10.00	20.00
❑ 745	I Waltz Alone/I Know What It Means to Be Lonesome	1949	5.00	10.00	20.00
❑ 782	Blue Mexico Skies/Over the Hill	1949	5.00	10.00	20.00
❑ 804	Paid in Full/I Dreamed You Dreamed of Me	1949	5.00	10.00	20.00
❑ 822	Cherokee Waltz/You'll Never Know What I've Been Through	1949	5.00	10.00	20.00
❑ 837	I Love You Because/Afraid	1950	5.00	10.00	20.00
❑ 849	Tears on My Pillow/I Won't Care a Hundred Years from Now	1950	5.00	10.00	20.00
❑ 862	Angels Must Have Cried Last Night/It's Too Late to Say	1950	5.00	10.00	20.00
❑ 909	Remember Me/I've Only Myself to Blame	1950	5.00	10.00	20.00
❑ 922	Six White Horses/Ivy	1951	5.00	10.00	20.00
❑ 943	Someday You'll Remember/The Blues Came Pouring Down	1951	5.00	10.00	20.00
❑ 952	Beautiful Brown Eyes/What Can I Do	1951	5.00	10.00	20.00

Albums

Number	Title (A Side/B Side)	Yr	VG	VG+	NM
KING					
❑ 891 [M]	The Best of Clyde Moody	1964	20.00	40.00	80.00
OLD HOMESTEAD					
❑ 90013	Moody's Blues — Bluesy Bluegrass	197?	3.75	7.50	15.00

MOORE, ABRA

45s

Number	Title (A Side/B Side)	Yr	VG	VG+	NM
ARISTA AUSTIN					
❑ 13082	Four Leaf Clover/Four Leaf Clover (Alternate Version)	1997	—	2.00	4.00

MOORE, BETH

45s

Number	Title (A Side/B Side)	Yr	VG	VG+	NM
CAPITOL					
❑ 2741	Lady Can I See Your Baby/You Come First After Me	1970	—	3.00	6.00
❑ 2813	Go Go Girl/Last Days of Love	1970	—	3.00	6.00
❑ 2894	If You Ain't Lovin' (You Ain't Livin')/I Almost Let Him Win	1970	—	3.00	6.00
❑ 3012	Put Your Hand in the Hand/I'm Losin' My Man	1971	—	3.00	6.00

MOORE, JIM, AND SIDEWINDER

45s

Number	Title (A Side/B Side)	Yr	VG	VG+	NM
WILLOW WIND					
❑ 0511	Ain't She Shinin' Tonight/(B-side unknown)	1988	—	3.00	6.00

MOORE, LATTIE

45s

Number	Title (A Side/B Side)	Yr	VG	VG+	NM
ARC					
❑ 8005	Juke Joint Johnny/Pretty Woman Blues	1952	50.00	100.00	200.00
KING					
❑ 1194	Foolish Castles/I'm Gonna Tell You Something	1953	12.50	25.00	50.00
❑ 1250	I Gotta Go Home/A Brand New Case of Love	1953	12.50	25.00	50.00
❑ 1327	They're Not Worth the Paper They're Printed On/Under a Mexico Moon	1954	12.50	25.00	50.00
❑ 1350	Pull Down the Blinds/What Am I Supposed to Do	1954	12.50	25.00	50.00
❑ 4955	100,000 Women Can't Be Wrong/Lonesome Man Blues	1956	12.50	25.00	50.00
❑ 5370	Cajun Doll/Mine Again	1960	10.00	20.00	40.00
❑ 5413	Drunk Again/Driving Nails	1960	6.25	12.50	25.00
❑ 5526	Sundown and Sorrow/If the Good Lord's Willing	1961	5.00	10.00	20.00
❑ 5685	I Told You So/Heaven All Around Me	1962	3.75	7.50	15.00
❑ 5723	Out of Control/Just About Then	1963	3.75	7.50	15.00
❑ 5762	Honky Tonk Heaven/Lonesome Man Blues	1963	3.75	7.50	15.00
SPEED					
❑ 101	Juke Joint Johnny/(B-side unknown)	1952	100.00	200.00	400.00
STARDAY					
❑ 403	You Never Looked Sweeter/Why Did You Lie to Me	1958	7.50	15.00	30.00
❑ 441	Too Hot to Handle/Just a-Waitin'	1959	7.50	15.00	30.00

Albums

Number	Title (A Side/B Side)	Yr	VG	VG+	NM
AUDIO LAB					
❑ AL-1555 [M]	The Best of Lattie Moore	1960	50.00	100.00	200.00
❑ AL-1573 [M]	Country Side	1962	37.50	75.00	150.00
DERBYTOWN					
❑ 102 [M]	Lattie Moore	196?	10.00	20.00	40.00

MOORE, SCOTTY

45s

Number	Title (A Side/B Side)	Yr	VG	VG+	NM
FERNWOOD					
❑ 107	Have Guitar Will Travel/Rest	1958	7.50	15.00	30.00

Albums

Number	Title (A Side/B Side)	Yr	VG	VG+	NM
EPIC					
❑ LN 24103 [M]	The Guitar That Changed the World	1964	20.00	40.00	80.00
❑ BN 26103 [S]	The Guitar That Changed the World	1964	25.00	50.00	100.00
GUINNESS					
❑ GNS-36038	What's Left	1977	3.75	7.50	15.00

MOORER, ALLISON

45s

Number	Title (A Side/B Side)	Yr	VG	VG+	NM
MCA					
❑ 72030	A Soft Place to Fall/Big Ball's in Cowtown	1998	—	2.00	4.00
—Label credits this to "Various Artists" rather than to anyone specific; B-side is actually by Don Walser; both songs are from the soundtrack to the movie The Horse Whisperer					
MCA NASHVILLE					
❑ 72069	Set You Free/Easier to Forget	1998	—	—	3.00
❑ 72077	Alabama Song/Call My Name	1999	—	—	3.00
❑ 72087	Pardon Me/Found a Letter	1999	—	—	3.00
❑ 088-172172-7	Send Down an Angel/Day You Said Goodbye	2000	—	—	3.00

MORGAN, AL

45s

Number	Title (A Side/B Side)	Yr	VG	VG+	NM
COLUMBIA					
❑ 4-40755	I'm Paying for Yesterday's Mistakes/Let's Dance Ragtime	1956	3.75	7.50	15.00
❑ 4-40943	Easy Goin' Heart/Don't Rob Another Man's Castle	1957	3.75	7.50	15.00
❑ 4-41022	Bouquet of Roses/The Wanderer Came Home	1957	3.75	7.50	15.00

CRYSTAL

Number	Title (A Side/B Side)	Yr	VG	VG+	NM
❑ 102	It Took a Dream to Wake Me Up/(B-side unknown)	196?	3.75	7.50	15.00
❑ 104	I've Got the World on a String/When Your Lover Has Gone	196?	3.75	7.50	15.00

DECCA

Number	Title (A Side/B Side)	Yr	VG	VG+	NM
❑ 9-27794	Sin/Jealous Eyes	1951	6.25	12.50	25.00
❑ 9-27887	Too Good to Be True/Blue Smoke	1951	6.25	12.50	25.00
❑ 9-27902	I'll Never Let You Cry/The Bluest Word I Know Is "Lonesome"	1951	6.25	12.50	25.00
❑ 9-27908	Good Night, Sweet Jesus/Mother At Your Feet Is Kneeling	1951	6.25	12.50	25.00
❑ 9-28040	Mistakes/My Castle in Spain	1952	6.25	12.50	25.00
❑ 9-28229	Is It True What They Say About Dixie/Someday Sweetheart	1952	6.25	12.50	25.00
❑ 9-28585	If I Had a Penny/Things I Might Have Been	1953	6.25	12.50	25.00

LONDON

Number	Title (A Side/B Side)	Yr	VG	VG+	NM
❑ 885	If I Had My Way/You Tell Me Your Dream	1950	7.50	15.00	30.00
❑ 887	Smile, Darn Ya, Smile/Gee But It's Great	1950	7.50	15.00	30.00
❑ 30001	Jealous Heart/Turnabout Is Fair Play	1949	10.00	20.00	40.00
❑ 30006	Tears on My Pillow/(B-side unknown)	1950	7.50	15.00	30.00

RENDEZVOUS

Number	Title (A Side/B Side)	Yr	VG	VG+	NM
❑ 113	I'll Take Care of Your Cares/Me and the Moon	1959	5.00	10.00	20.00

"X"

Number	Title (A Side/B Side)	Yr	VG	VG+	NM
❑ 0004	Sweet Kentucky Sue/You Told Me to Go	1954	6.25	12.50	25.00
❑ 0015	That Silver-Haired Daddy of Mine/My Mom	1954	6.25	12.50	25.00
❑ 0052	Tell Me Now/Bells of Memory	1954	6.25	12.50	25.00

MORGAN, BILL

45s

COLUMBIA

Number	Title (A Side/B Side)	Yr	VG	VG+	NM
❑ 4-21373	Mucher We Do It/Mighty, Mighty Lonesome	1955	5.00	10.00	20.00
❑ 4-21450	Adios, So Long, Goodbye/I'm a Fool to Think You Care	1955	5.00	10.00	20.00

MORGAN, BILLIE

45s

STARDAY

Number	Title (A Side/B Side)	Yr	VG	VG+	NM
❑ 420	Life to Live/Thinking All Night	1959	3.75	7.50	15.00
❑ 464	Country Girl at Heart/Treatin' Me	1959	3.75	7.50	15.00
❑ 489	I'll Accept What I Can't Change/I Had to Talk to Someone	1960	3.75	7.50	15.00

MORGAN, CRAIG

45s

ATLANTIC

Number	Title (A Side/B Side)	Yr	VG	VG+	NM
❑ 7-84669	Something to Write Home About/302 South Maple Avenue	2000	—	—	3.00

MORGAN, GEORGE

Also see MARION WORTH.

45s

4 STAR

Number	Title (A Side/B Side)	Yr	VG	VG+	NM
❑ 1001	In the Misty Moonlight/Welcome Back to My World	1975	—	2.50	5.00
❑ 1009	From This Moment On/One Wife Five Kids Later	1975	—	2.50	5.00
❑ 1034	I Just Want You to Know/I Will Take Care of You	1978	—	2.50	5.00
❑ 1040	I'm Completely Satisfied with You/From This Moment On	1979	—	2.50	5.00

—With Lorrie Morgan

COLUMBIA

Number	Title (A Side/B Side)	Yr	VG	VG+	NM
❑ 2-280 (?)	Room Full of Roses/Put All Your Love in a Cookie Jar	1949	10.00	20.00	40.00
—Microgroove 33 1/3 rpm small hole 7-inch single					
❑ 2-355 (?)	Cry-Baby Heart/I Love Everything About You	1949	10.00	20.00	40.00
—Microgroove 33 1/3 rpm small hole 7-inch single					
❑ 2-450 (?)	Rings on Your Fingers/Why in Heaven's Name	1950	10.00	20.00	40.00
—Microgroove 33 1/3 rpm small hole 7-inch single					
❑ 2-550 (?)	Angel Mother/Lucky Seven	1950	10.00	20.00	40.00
—Microgroove 33 1/3 rpm small hole 7-inch single					
❑ 2-700 (?)	Greedy Fingers/Warm Hands, Cold Heart	1950	10.00	20.00	40.00
—Microgroove 33 1/3 rpm small hole 7-inch single					
❑ 4-20730	You Win the Bride/So Far	1950	7.50	15.00	30.00
❑ 4-20747	I Know You'll Never Change/Don't Be Afraid to Love Me	1950	7.50	15.00	30.00
❑ 4-20774	I Love No One But You/Somebody Robbed Me	1951	7.50	15.00	30.00
❑ 4-20811	I Wish I May/Broken Candy Heart	1951	7.50	15.00	30.00
❑ 4-20822	Tennessee Hillbilly Ghost/My Heart Keeps Telling Me	1951	7.50	15.00	30.00
❑ 4-20850	My Baby Lied to Me/Waltzing by the Ohio	1951	7.50	15.00	30.00
❑ 4-20870	Broken Candy Heart/I Wish I May, I Wish I Might	1952	6.25	12.50	25.00
❑ 4-20884	The Cry of the Lamb/Mansion Over the Hilltop	1952	6.25	12.50	25.00
❑ 4-20906	Almost/You're a Little Girl	1952	6.25	12.50	25.00
❑ 4-20944	Almost/There's No Reason	1952	5.00	10.00	20.00
—B-side by Neal Burris; one record of a 4-record various-artists box					
❑ 4-20945	Be Sure You Know/Whistle My Love	1952	6.25	12.50	25.00
❑ 4-21006	One Woman Man/Everything Rolled Into One	1952	6.25	12.50	25.00
❑ 4-21052	Please Believe/A Stranger in the Night	1952	6.25	12.50	25.00
❑ 4-21070	(I Just Had a Date) A Lover's Quarrel/Most of All	1953	6.25	12.50	25.00
❑ 4-21071	Withered Roses/You Love Me Just Enough to Hurt Me	1953	6.25	12.50	25.00
❑ 4-21108	Half Hearted/I Passed By Your Window	1953	6.25	12.50	25.00
❑ 4-21151	Lonesome Waltz/I'll Furnish the Shoulder You Cry On	1953	6.25	12.50	25.00
❑ 4-21170	Every Prayer Is a Flower/How Many Times	1953	6.25	12.50	25.00
❑ 4-21178	Look What Followed Me Home/No One Knows It Better Than Me	1953	6.25	12.50	25.00
❑ 4-21204	Love, Love, Love/The First Time I Told You a Lie	1954	6.25	12.50	25.00
❑ 4-21237	It's Been Nice/I Think I'm Going to Cry	1954	6.25	12.50	25.00
❑ 4-21276	Walking Shoes/Sweetheart	1954	6.25	12.50	25.00
❑ 4-21318	Whither Thou Goest/Oh Gentle Shepherd	1954	6.25	12.50	25.00
❑ 4-21321	A Shot in the Dark/Oceans of Tears	1954	6.25	12.50	25.00
❑ 4-21344	A Cheap Affair/So Lonesome	1955	6.25	12.50	25.00
❑ 4-21390	Best Mistake/I'd Like to Know	1955	6.25	12.50	25.00
❑ 4-21430	Little Pioneer/Ain't Love Grand	1955	6.25	12.50	25.00
❑ 4-21438	You Don't Have to Walk Alone/Jesus Saviour Pilot Me	1955	7.50	15.00	30.00
❑ 4-21465	Every So Often/Lonesome Record	1955	6.25	12.50	25.00
❑ 4-21517	Take a Look at Yourself/Send for My Baby	1956	6.25	12.50	25.00
❑ 4-21548	Stay Away from Me Baby/Now You Know	1956	6.25	12.50	25.00
❑ 4-40792	There Goes My Love/Can I Be Dreaming	1956	5.00	10.00	20.00
❑ 4-40859	The Tears Behind the Smile/Don't Cry, For You I Love	1957	5.00	10.00	20.00
❑ 4-40967	My House Is Divided/Late Date	1957	5.00	10.00	20.00
❑ 4-40978	Our Summer Vacation/It Always Ends Too Soon	1957	5.00	10.00	20.00
❑ 4-41063	A Perfect Romance/Sweet, Sweet Lips	1957	5.00	10.00	20.00
❑ 4-41188	I'm Not Afraid/Loveable You	1958	5.00	10.00	20.00
❑ 4-41246	Candy Kisses/Rockabilly Bungalow	1958	7.50	15.00	30.00
❑ 4-41318	I'm in Love Again/It Was All in Your Mind	1959	3.75	7.50	15.00
❑ 4-41420	Little Dutch Girl/The Last Thing I Want to Know	1959	3.75	7.50	15.00
❑ 4-41523	You're the Only Good Thing (That's Happened to Me)/Come Away from His Arms	1959	3.75	7.50	15.00
❑ 4-41701	Who Knows You the Best/Where There's a Will There's a Way	1960	3.75	7.50	15.00
❑ 4-41794	One Empty Chair/It's Best You Know	1960	3.75	7.50	15.00
❑ 4-41957	Only One Minute More/The Little Green Men	1961	3.75	7.50	15.00
❑ 4-42060	Every Day of My Life/Our Love	1961	3.75	7.50	15.00
❑ 4-42277	Lonely Room/Let Me Live and Love Today	1962	3.75	7.50	15.00
❑ 4-42505	I Can Hear My Heart Break/Across the Wide Missouri	1962	3.75	7.50	15.00
❑ 4-42650	Blue Snowfall/Mach Nichts (It Makes No Difference)	1962	3.75	7.50	15.00
❑ 4-42757	Beyond My Heart/Where Is My Love	1963	3.75	7.50	15.00
❑ 4-42882	One Dozen Roses (And Our Love)/All Right (I'll Sign the Papers)	1963	3.75	7.50	15.00
❑ 4-43098	Tears and Roses/You're Not Home Yet	1964	3.00	6.00	12.00
❑ 4-43216	Happy Endings/Dear John	1965	3.00	6.00	12.00
❑ 4-43282	Not from My World/All Coming Home to You But Me	1965	3.00	6.00	12.00
❑ 4-43393	A Picture That's New/Roses	1965	3.00	6.00	12.00
❑ 4-43653	Home Is Where the Heart Is/No Man Could Hurt As Much As I	1966	3.00	6.00	12.00
❑ 4-43899	There Goes My World/Speak Well of Me	1966	3.00	6.00	12.00

DECCA

Number	Title (A Side/B Side)	Yr	VG	VG+	NM
❑ 32886	Gentle Rains of Home/Walking Shadow, Talking Mem'ry	1971	—	3.00	6.00
❑ 32953	Running Wild/Let's Live Together Marianne	1972	—	3.00	6.00
❑ 33037	Makin' Heartaches/Sing My Blues and Birthday Song	1972	—	3.00	6.00

MCA

Number	Title (A Side/B Side)	Yr	VG	VG+	NM
❑ 40069	Mr. Ting-a-Ling (Steel Guitar Man)/Our Wedding Song	1973	—	2.50	5.00
❑ 40159	Red Rose from the Blue Side of Town/You Turn Me On	1973	—	2.50	5.00
❑ 40227	Somewhere Around Midnight/I Never Knew Love	1974	—	2.50	5.00
❑ 40298	A Candy Mountain Melody/You're That Much Woman to Me	1974	—	2.50	5.00

STARDAY

Number	Title (A Side/B Side)	Yr	VG	VG+	NM
❑ 804	I Couldn't See/Look at the Lonely	1967	2.50	5.00	10.00
❑ 814	Shiny Red Automobile/Have Some of Mine	1967	2.50	5.00	10.00
❑ 825	Barbara/Sad Bird	1967	2.50	5.00	10.00
❑ 834	Living/Rosebuds and You	1968	2.50	5.00	10.00
❑ 850	Sounds of Goodbye/Ballad of the Grand Ole Opry	1968	2.50	5.00	10.00
❑ 860	I'll Sail My Ship Alone/Live and Let Live and Be Happy	1969	2.50	5.00	10.00
❑ 8014	Candy Kisses/Room Full of Roses	197?	—	2.50	5.00

STOP

Number	Title (A Side/B Side)	Yr	VG	VG+	NM
❑ 252	Like a Bird/Left Over Feelings	1969	2.00	4.00	8.00
❑ 297	We've Done All the Lovin' We Can Do/Color of a Bird	1969	2.00	4.00	8.00
❑ 357	I Walk on the Outside/The Enemy	1970	2.00	4.00	8.00
❑ 365	Lilacs and Fire/Hardest Easy Thing	1970	2.00	4.00	8.00
❑ 378	Kansas City Stockyards/I'm Happy with You	1970	2.00	4.00	8.00
❑ 384	One and the Same/I Wouldn't Have You Any Other Way	1971	2.00	4.00	8.00
❑ 393	Rose Is Gone/Give Us One More Chance	1971	2.00	4.00	8.00

Selected 78s

COLUMBIA

Number	Title (A Side/B Side)	Yr	VG	VG+	NM
❑ 20547	Candy Kisses/Please Don't Let Me Love You	1949	5.00	10.00	20.00
—This may exist on a 45 with this number; if so, the 45 is worth at least double the above values.					
❑ 20563	Rainbow in My Heart/All I Need Is Some More Lovin'	1949	5.00	10.00	20.00

Albums

4 STAR

Number	Title (A Side/B Side)	Yr	VG	VG+	NM
❑ 002	From This Moment On	1975	3.00	6.00	12.00

COLUMBIA

Number	Title (A Side/B Side)	Yr	VG	VG+	NM
❑ CL 1044 [M]	Morgan, By George	1957	12.50	25.00	50.00
❑ CL 1631 [M]	Golden Memories	1961	6.25	12.50	25.00
❑ CL 2111 [M]	Tender Lovin' Care	1964	5.00	10.00	20.00
❑ CL 2333 [M]	Red Roses for a Blue Lady	1965	5.00	10.00	20.00
❑ CS 8431 [S]	Golden Memories	1961	7.50	15.00	30.00

Number	Title (A Side/B Side)	Yr	VG	VG+	NM
❑ CS 8911 [S]	Tender Lovin' Care	1964	6.25	12.50	25.00
❑ CS 9133 [S]	Red Roses for a Blue Lady	1965	6.25	12.50	25.00
❑ PC 33894	Remembering George Morgan	1975	3.00	6.00	12.00
MCA					
❑ 422	Red Rose from the Blue Side of Town/ Somewhere Around Midnight	1974	3.00	6.00	12.00
❑ 461	Candy Mountain Melody	1974	3.00	6.00	12.00
STARDAY					
❑ SLP-400	Candy Kisses	1967	6.25	12.50	25.00
❑ SLP-410	Country Hits by Candelight	1967	6.25	12.50	25.00
❑ SLP-413	Steal Away	1968	5.00	10.00	20.00
❑ SLP-417	Barbara	1969	5.00	10.00	20.00
STOP					
❑ 10009	George Morgan Sings Like a Bird	1969	3.75	7.50	15.00

MORGAN, JANE

Best known for the pop hit "Fascination," she recorded country music for RCA Victor.

45s

Number	Title (A Side/B Side)	Yr	VG	VG+	NM
RCA VICTOR					
❑ 47-9727	Congratulations, I Guess/All of My Laughter	1969	—	2.50	5.00
❑ 47-9839	A Girl Named Johnny Cash/Charley	1970	—	2.50	5.00
❑ 47-9901	The First Day/I'm Only a Woman	1970	—	2.50	5.00
❑ 74-0153	Marry Me, Marry Me/Three Rest Stops	1969	—	2.50	5.00
❑ 74-0194	Traces/Where Do I Go	1969	—	2.50	5.00
❑ 74-0316	He Gives Me Love/He's Never Too Busy	1970	—	2.50	5.00
❑ 74-0395	Jamie Boy/Things of Life	1970	—	2.50	5.00

Albums

Number	Title (A Side/B Side)	Yr	VG	VG+	NM
RCA VICTOR					
❑ LSP-4171	Traces of Love	1969	3.00	6.00	12.00
❑ LSP-4322	Jane Morgan in Nashville	1970	3.00	6.00	12.00

MORGAN, LORRIE

Also see GEORGE MORGAN; KEITH WHITLEY.

45s

Number	Title (A Side/B Side)	Yr	VG	VG+	NM
ABC HICKORY					
❑ 54041	Two People in Love/I Don't Care	1979	—	3.00	6.00
BNA					
❑ 62333	Watch Me/Takin' Him Back Again	1992	—	2.00	4.00
❑ 62414	What Part of No/You Leave Me Like This	1992	—	2.50	5.00
❑ 62415	I Guess You Had to Be There/Someone to Call Me Darling	1993	—	2.00	4.00
❑ 62576	Half Enough/It's a Heartache	1993	—	2.00	4.00
❑ 62707	Crying Time/I'm So Lonesome I Could Cry	1993	—	2.00	4.00
—B-side by Aaron Tippin					
❑ 62767	My Night to Howl/Evening Up the Odds	1994	—	2.00	4.00
❑ 62864	If You Came Back from Heaven/Exit 99	1994	—	2.00	4.00
❑ 62946	Heart Over Mind/The Hard Part Was Easy	1994	—	—	3.00
❑ 64287	I Didn't Know My Own Strength/War Paint	1995	—	2.00	4.00
❑ 64353	Back in Your Arms Again/My Favorite Things	1995	—	2.00	4.00
❑ 64406	Up on Santa Claus Mountain/My Favorite Things	1995	—	2.00	4.00
❑ 64608	I Just Might Be/Steppin' Stones	1996	—	—	3.00
❑ 64681	Good As I Was to You/She Walked Beside the Wagon	1997	—	2.00	4.00
❑ 64914	Go Away/I've Enjoyed As Much of This As I Can Stand	1997	—	2.00	4.00
❑ 65333	One of Those Nights Tonight/By My Side	1997	—	—	3.00
❑ 65440	I'm Not That Easy to Forget/You Can't Take That	1998	—	—	3.00
❑ 65729	Maybe Not Tonight (duet with Sammy Kershaw)/ Go Away	1999	—	—	3.00
❑ 65965	To Get to You/Maybe Not Tonight	2000	—	—	3.00
MCA					
❑ 41052	Tell Me I'm Only Dreaming/In for Rain	1979	—	2.50	5.00
❑ 52280	Someday We'll Be Together/Everything You Say	1983	—	2.00	4.00
❑ 52331	Don't Go Changing/Everything You Say	1983	—	2.00	4.00
❑ 52439	Easy Love/If You Came Back Tonight	1984	—	2.00	4.00
RCA					
❑ 2508-7-R	He Talks to Me/If I Didn't Love You	1990	—	2.00	4.00
❑ 2748-7-R	We Both Walk/Faithfully	1991	—	2.50	5.00
❑ 8638-7-R	Trainwreck of Emotion/One More Last Time	1988	—	2.00	4.00
❑ 8866-7-R	Dear Me/Eight Days a Week	1989	—	—	3.00
❑ 9016-7-R	Out of Your Shoes/One More Last Time	1989	—	2.00	4.00
❑ 9118-7-R	Five Minutes/I'll Take the Memories	1990	—	2.50	5.00
❑ 62014	A Picture of Me (Without You)/Tears on My Pillow	1991	—	2.00	4.00
❑ 62105	Except for Monday/Hand Over Your Heart	1991	—	2.00	4.00
❑ 62219	Something in Red/It's Too Late (To Love Me Now)	1992	—	2.50	5.00

Albums

Number	Title (A Side/B Side)	Yr	VG	VG+	NM
RCA					
❑ 9594-1-R	Leave the Light On	1989	3.00	6.00	12.00
❑ R 183848	Something in Red	1991	5.00	10.00	20.00
—Only available on vinyl through BMG Direct Marketing					

MORI, MIKI

45s

Number	Title (A Side/B Side)	Yr	VG	VG+	NM
NSD					
❑ 49	The Last Farewell/You Are the Answer	1980	—	3.00	6.00
OAK					
❑ 1002	The Part of Me That Needs You Most/Baby You Are the Answer	1979	—	3.00	6.00
❑ 1010	Driftin' Away/Tell All Your Troubles	1979	—	3.00	6.00
RED FEATHER					
❑ 2280	Tell All Your Troubles to Me/Driftin' Away	1979	2.00	4.00	8.00
—As "Mickie Mori"					
STARCOM					
❑ 1001	Rainin' in My Eyes/Reunion	1980	—	2.50	5.00

MORRIS, BOB

45s

Number	Title (A Side/B Side)	Yr	VG	VG+	NM
CAPITOL					
❑ 2293	Going Home to Mama/Wicked Wind	1968	2.00	4.00	8.00
❑ 2444	All I Had Going for Me/What's Wrong with Staying Home (With Julie)	1969	2.00	4.00	8.00
CHALLENGE					
❑ 59215	Silly Willy/Pur Your Arms Around Him	1963	6.25	12.50	25.00
❑ 59247	See the Monkey Walk Through the Door/I Tried to Make You Over	1964	6.25	12.50	25.00
❑ 59284	Walkin' Talkin' Livin' Doll/Don't Underestimate Me	1965	7.50	15.00	30.00
❑ 59313	Fool Enough/Something to Think About	1965	7.50	15.00	30.00
❑ 59324	I Bumped Into It/Ordinarily	1966	3.75	7.50	15.00
TOWER					
❑ 307	Fishin' on the Mississippi/Little Bit of You	1966	2.50	5.00	10.00
❑ 338	The First Thing I Think Of/Queen Bee	1967	2.50	5.00	10.00
❑ 375	That Old Letter from Home/All That's Missing Here Tonight Is You	1967	2.50	5.00	10.00

MORRIS, GARRETT

45s

Number	Title (A Side/B Side)	Yr	VG	VG+	NM
MCA					
❑ 41243	I Wanna Be a Cowboy (But I'm Too Short)/Secret Place	1980	—	2.50	5.00

MORRIS, GARY

Also see LYNN ANDERSON; CRYSTAL GAYLE.

45s

Number	Title (A Side/B Side)	Yr	VG	VG+	NM
CAPITOL					
❑ 7PRO-79968	One Fall Is All It Takes (same on both sides)	1990	—	2.50	5.00
—Vinyl is promo only					
UNIVERSAL					
❑ UVL-66011	Never Had a Love Song/Bread and Water	1989	—	—	3.00
❑ UVL-66026	The Jaws of Modern Romance/Stand My Ground	1989	—	2.00	4.00
WARNER BROS.					
❑ 27706	Every Christmas/Silver Bells	1988	—	2.00	4.00
❑ 27706 [PS]	Every Christmas/Silver Bells	1988	—	2.00	4.00
❑ 28218	Finishing Touches/Mama You Can't Give Me No Whippin'	1987	—	—	3.00
❑ 28388	Simply Meant to Be/Simply Meant to Be	1987	—	—	3.00
—A-side with Jennifer Warnes; B-side by Henry Mancini					
❑ 28468	Plain Brown Wrapper/Moonshine	1987	—	—	3.00
❑ 28542	Leave Me Lonely/Eleventh Hour	1986	—	—	3.00
❑ 28654	Honeycomb/Whoever's Watchin'	1986	—	—	3.00
❑ 28713	Anything Goes/Draggin' the Lake for the Moon	1986	—	—	3.00
❑ 28823	100% Chance of Rain/Back in Her Arms Again	1986	—	—	3.00
❑ 28947	I'll Never Stop Loving You/Heaven's Hell Without You	1985	—	—	3.00
❑ 29028	Lasso the Moon/When I Close My Eyes	1985	—	—	3.00
❑ 29131	Baby Bye Bye/West Texas Highway and Me	1984	—	—	3.00
❑ 29230	Second Hand Heart/Whoever's Watchin'	1984	—	—	3.00
❑ 29321	Between Two Fires/All She Said Was Yes	1984	—	—	3.00
❑ 29450	Why Lady Why/The Way I Love You Tonight	1983	—	—	3.00
❑ 29532	The Wind Beneath My Wings/The Way I Love You Tonight	1983	—	3.00	6.00
❑ 29683	The Love She Found in Me/That's the Way It Is	1983	—	—	3.00
❑ 29853	Velvet Chains/When I Close My Eyes	1982	—	—	3.00
❑ 29967	Dreams Die Hard/(B-side unknown)	1982	—	—	3.00
❑ 49564	May I Borrow Some Sugar for You/Sweet Red Wine	1980	—	2.50	5.00
❑ 49668	Fire in Your Eyes/Heartaches by the Number	1981	—	2.00	4.00
❑ 49829	Headed for a Heartache/I'm So Tired of Losing	1981	—	2.00	4.00
❑ 50017	Don't Look Back/She Gave Me Till Friday	1982	—	2.00	4.00

Albums

Number	Title (A Side/B Side)	Yr	VG	VG+	NM
UNIVERSAL					
❑ UVL-76005	Stones	1989	2.50	5.00	10.00
❑ UVL-76010	Every Christmas	1989	3.00	6.00	12.00
—Same as Warner Bros. 25760 with one track deleted and one added					
WARNER BROS.					
❑ BSK 3658	Gary Morris	1982	2.00	4.00	8.00
❑ 23738	Why Lady Why	1983	2.00	4.00	8.00
❑ 25069	Faded Blue	1984	2.00	4.00	8.00
❑ 25279	Anything Goes...	1985	2.00	4.00	8.00
❑ 25438	Plain Brown Wrapper	1986	2.00	4.00	8.00
❑ 25581	Hits	1987	2.00	4.00	8.00
❑ 25760	Every Christmas	1988	2.50	5.00	10.00

MORRIS, LAMAR

45s

Number	Title (A Side/B Side)	Yr	VG	VG+	NM
20TH CENTURY					
❑ 2206	Come and Sit Down at My Table/Look Back Once More	1975	—	2.50	5.00
MGM					
❑ 13586	Send Me a Box of Kleenex/Both of You	1966	2.00	4.00	8.00
❑ 13753	Baby Is Gone/Now I Can't Call My Baby, Baby Anymore	1967	2.00	4.00	8.00
❑ 13866	The Great Pretender/The World's Perfect Couple	1967	2.00	4.00	8.00
❑ 14114	She Came to Me/Only with Teardrops	1970	—	3.00	6.00
❑ 14187	You're the Reason I'm Living/Things	1970	—	3.00	6.00
❑ 14236	If You Love Me (Really Love Me)/Pour the Wine	1971	—	3.00	6.00
❑ 14289	Near You/She Came to Me	1971	—	3.00	6.00
❑ 14359	All My Lovin'/Back Stage Sue	1972	—	3.00	6.00
❑ 14417	Here We Go Again/I Don't Have Anything to Lose	1972	—	3.00	6.00
❑ 14448	You Call Everybody Darling/I Need You	1972	—	3.00	6.00

Number	Title (A Side/B Side)	Yr	VG	VG+	NM
❑ 14645	Cover Me/I Wanna Be Close to You	1973	—	3.00	6.00
❑ 14719	To Each His Own/I Need You	1974	—	3.00	6.00

MORTON, ANN J.

45s

PRAIRIE DUST

Number	Title (A Side/B Side)	Yr	VG	VG+	NM
❑ 7603	Willie I Will/Onions and Love Affairs	1976	—	3.00	6.00
❑ 7606	Poor Wilted Rose/Molly Jones (Is a Happy Hooker)	1976	—	2.50	5.00
❑ 7612	Don't Call Me No Lady/Onions and Love Affairs	1977	—	2.50	5.00
❑ 7613	You Don't Have to Be a Baby to Cry/Good Looking Cowboy	1977	—	2.50	5.00
❑ 7617	Don't Want to Take a Chance (On Loving You)/ Tainted Rose	1977	—	2.50	5.00
❑ 7619	Blueberry Hill/Onions and Love Affairs	1977	—	2.50	5.00
❑ 7621	Black and Blue Heart/Me and My Horse Named Daddy	1977	—	2.50	5.00
❑ 7627	Share Your Love Tonight/Willie I Will	1978	—	2.50	5.00
❑ 7629	I'm Not in the Mood (For Love)/Willie I Will	1978	—	2.50	5.00
❑ 7631	Don't Stay on Your Side of the Bed Tonight/It's Written All Over Your Face	1979	—	2.50	5.00
❑ 7632	My Empty Arms/Don't Stay on Your Side of the Bed Tonight	1979	—	2.50	5.00
❑ 7633	(We Used to Kiss Each Other on the Lips But It's) All Over Now/I Like Being Lonely	1979	—	2.50	5.00
❑ 7634	Hey Vern/I'll Do It 'Cause I Love You	1980	—	2.50	5.00
❑ 7636	Share Your Love Tonight/(B-side unknown)	1980	—	2.50	5.00
❑ 8004	You've Got the Devil in Your Eyes/No Strings Attached	1980	—	2.50	5.00

MOSBY, JOHNNY AND JONIE

Also see JONIE MOSBY.

45s

CAPITOL

Number	Title (A Side/B Side)	Yr	VG	VG+	NM
❑ 2087	Mr. and Mrs. John Smith/Hello There Stranger	1968	—	3.00	6.00
❑ 2179	Our Golden Wedding Day/Two Dollar Honeymoon Room	1968	—	3.00	6.00
❑ 2258	Come In the Back Door (Go 'Round, Go 'Round)/ You Be the Mama, I'll Be the Papa	1968	—	3.00	6.00
❑ 2384	Just Hold My Hand/Walkin' Papers	1969	—	3.00	6.00
❑ 2505	Hold Me, Thrill Me, Kiss Me/Comparing Him with You	1969	—	3.00	6.00
❑ 2608	I'll Never Be Free/Pattern of Our Lives	1969	—	3.00	6.00
❑ 2730	Third World/You Go Back to Your World (I'll Go Back to Mine)	1970	—	3.00	6.00
❑ 2796	I'm Leavin' It Up to You/If It's Left Up to Me	1970	—	3.00	6.00
❑ 2865	My Happiness/Let Your Sun Shine on Me	1970	—	3.00	6.00
❑ 2978	A Little of Me, A Little of You/Someone to Take My Place	1970	—	3.00	6.00
❑ 3039	Oh, Love of Mine/Closing Time Till Dawn	1971	—	3.00	6.00
❑ 3141	Let's Get This Show on the Road/Souvenirs of Love	1971	—	3.00	6.00
❑ 3219	Just One More Time/Meet Me Tonight	1971	—	3.00	6.00
❑ 3277	Music to My Ears/I'll Say It Again	1972	—	3.00	6.00
❑ 3332	My Ecstasy/Ain't You Ever	1972	—	3.00	6.00
❑ 3613	Let's Try Love Again/It's All Because of You	1973	—	3.00	6.00
❑ 5980	Make a Left and Then a Right/Take Back the World	1967	—	3.00	6.00

CHALLENGE

Number	Title (A Side/B Side)	Yr	VG	VG+	NM
❑ 59088	He Wouldn't Take Me Home to Meet His Mother/ Hard Luck and Misery	1960	3.75	7.50	15.00

COLUMBIA

Number	Title (A Side/B Side)	Yr	VG	VG+	NM
❑ 42449	I'd Fight the World/Answer to Charlie's Shoes	1962	3.00	6.00	12.00
❑ 42668	Don't Call Me from a Honky Tonk/Wrong Side of Town	1963	2.50	5.00	10.00
❑ 42841	Trouble in My Arms/Who's Been Cheatin' Who	1963	2.50	5.00	10.00
❑ 43005	Keep Those Cards and Letters Coming In/Take Me Home	1964	2.50	5.00	10.00
❑ 43100	How the Other Half Lives/Stolen Paradise	1964	2.50	5.00	10.00
❑ 43218	Strawberry Wine/Wrong Company	1965	2.00	4.00	8.00
❑ 43344	The High Cost of Loving/The Home She's Tearing Down	1965	2.00	4.00	8.00
❑ 43631	Heartbreak U.S.A./Identity	1966	2.00	4.00	8.00

TOPPA

Number	Title (A Side/B Side)	Yr	VG	VG+	NM
❑ 1034	Unreceived, Address Unknown/A Cup of Coffee	1961	3.75	7.50	15.00
❑ 1039	Making Believe/Ain't You Ever	1961	3.75	7.50	15.00
❑ 1047	Dear Okie/You Can't Hurt Me Anymore	1962	3.75	7.50	15.00

Albums

CAPITOL

Number	Title (A Side/B Side)	Yr	VG	VG+	NM
❑ ST-170	Just Hold My Hand	1969	3.75	7.50	15.00
❑ ST-286	Hold Me	1969	3.75	7.50	15.00
❑ ST-414	I'll Never Be Free	1970	3.75	7.50	15.00
❑ ST-556	My Happiness	1970	3.75	7.50	15.00
❑ ST-737	Oh, Love of Mine	1971	3.75	7.50	15.00
❑ ST 2903	Make a Left and Then a Right	1968	3.75	7.50	15.00

COLUMBIA

Number	Title (A Side/B Side)	Yr	VG	VG+	NM
❑ CL 2297 [M]	Mr. & Mrs. Country Music	1965	3.75	7.50	15.00
❑ CS 9097 [S]	Mr. & Mrs. Country Music	1965	5.00	10.00	20.00

HARMONY

Number	Title (A Side/B Side)	Yr	VG	VG+	NM
❑ HS 11389	Mr. & Mrs. Country Music	1970	2.50	5.00	10.00

STARDAY

Number	Title (A Side/B Side)	Yr	VG	VG+	NM
❑ SLP-328 [M]	The New Sweethearts of Country Music	1965	7.50	15.00	30.00

MOSBY, JONIE

Also see JOHNNY AND JONIE MOSBY.

45s

CAPITOL

Number	Title (A Side/B Side)	Yr	VG	VG+	NM
❑ 3454	I've Been There/I'll Be Leaving You Again	1972	—	2.50	5.00

MOWREY, DUDE

45s

ARISTA

Number	Title (A Side/B Side)	Yr	VG	VG+	NM
❑ 12515	Maybe You Were the One/View from the Bottom	1993	—	—	3.00
❑ 12579	Hold On, Elroy/Turn for the Worse	1993	—	—	3.00
❑ 12643	Somewhere In Between/I'll Never Listen to That Fool Again	1993	—	—	3.00

MULLEN, BRUCE

45s

CHART

Number	Title (A Side/B Side)	Yr	VG	VG+	NM
❑ 5199	Petals of My Orchids/Holiday Inn	1973	—	3.00	6.00
❑ 5215	Auctioneer Love/The Love in the Touch of Her Hand	1974	—	3.00	6.00

MULLICAN, MOON

45s

CORAL

Number	Title (A Side/B Side)	Yr	VG	VG+	NM
❑ 9-61994	Jennie Lee/That's Me	1958	6.25	12.50	25.00
❑ 9-62042	Sweet Rockin' Music/Moon's Rock	1958	6.25	12.50	25.00

DECCA

Number	Title (A Side/B Side)	Yr	VG	VG+	NM
❑ 9-30962	Writin' on the Wall/Cush Cush Ky-Yay	1960	5.00	10.00	20.00

HALLWAY

Number	Title (A Side/B Side)	Yr	VG	VG+	NM
❑ 1208	Mr. Tears/Big, Big City	1965	3.00	6.00	12.00
❑ 1907	The Coffee Song/I'll Pour the Wine	1962	3.75	7.50	15.00
❑ 1914	Fools Like Me/Make Friends	1963	3.75	7.50	15.00
❑ 1923	Colinda/I'll Pour the Wine	1964	3.75	7.50	15.00

KAPP

Number	Title (A Side/B Side)	Yr	VG	VG+	NM
❑ 2027	I'll Pour the Wine/Make Friends	1969	2.00	4.00	8.00
❑ 2055	Big Big City/Fools Like Me	1969	2.00	4.00	8.00

KING

Number	Title (A Side/B Side)	Yr	VG	VG+	NM
❑ 830	I'll Sail My Ship Alone/Moon's Tune	195?	12.50	25.00	50.00
—Not issued on 45 until 1951 or 1952 at the earliest; maroon label, gold print					
❑ 965	Cherokee Boogie (Eh-Oh-Aleena)/Love Is the Light That Leads Me Home	1951	10.00	20.00	40.00
❑ 984	Another Night Is Coming/Heartless Lover	1951	10.00	20.00	40.00
❑ 1006	Memphis Blues/Piano Breakdown	1951	10.00	20.00	40.00
❑ 1007	Country Boogie/Moonshine Blues	1951	10.00	20.00	40.00
❑ 1043	Shoot the Moon/A Million Regrets	1952	7.50	15.00	30.00
❑ 1060	My Tears Will Fall/Triflin' Woman Blues	1952	7.50	15.00	30.00
❑ 1078	Save a Little Dream for Me/Trouble, Trouble	1952	7.50	15.00	30.00
❑ 1106	Jambalaya/A Mighty Pretty Waltz	1952	7.50	15.00	30.00
❑ 1137	Sugar Beet/Pipeliner's Blues	1952	7.50	15.00	30.00
❑ 1152	1001 Sleepless Nights/A Crushed Red Rose	1952	7.50	15.00	30.00
❑ 1164	Ooglie Ooglie Ooglie/So Long	1953	7.50	15.00	30.00
❑ 1198	Rheumatism Boogie/Rocket to the Moon	1953	7.50	15.00	30.00
❑ 1221	Hey Mr. Corn Picker/Leaving You with a Worried Mind	1953	7.50	15.00	30.00
❑ 1244	I Done It/Grandpa Stole My Baby	1953	7.50	15.00	30.00
❑ 1337	Good Deal, Lucille/Wanted	1954	7.50	15.00	30.00
❑ 1343	All I Need Is You/Don't Let Temptation Turn You Round	1954	7.50	15.00	30.00
❑ 1355	End of the Rainbow/Where the Beautiful Flowers Are	1954	7.50	15.00	30.00
❑ 1366	I'm Hanging Up All My Work Clothes/No Stranger	1954	7.50	15.00	30.00
❑ 1408	Downstream/You Got the Best of Me	1954	7.50	15.00	30.00
❑ 1421	Yearning/Put Your Arms Around Me	1955	6.25	12.50	25.00
❑ 1427	Crippled for Life/There Goes the Bride	1955	6.25	12.50	25.00
❑ 1447	When Love Dies/What's the Matter with the Mill	1955	6.25	12.50	25.00
❑ 1461	San Antonio Rose/Cedarwood Blues	1955	6.25	12.50	25.00
❑ 1467	Jose the Mexican Boy/Someone More Lonesome Than You	1955	6.25	12.50	25.00
❑ 1481	Mexicali Rose/Panhandle Rag	1955	6.25	12.50	25.00
❑ 4894	Honolulu Rock-a Roll-a/Seven Nights to Rock	1956	10.00	20.00	40.00
❑ 4915	Rock and Roll Mr. Bullfrog/I'm Mad with You	1956	10.00	20.00	40.00
❑ 4937	Hey Shah/Maybe It's All for the Best	1956	5.00	10.00	20.00
❑ 4979	Keep a Light in the Window for Me/If You Don't Want No More of My Loving	1956	5.00	10.00	20.00
❑ 5172	I'll Sail My Ship Alone/Seven Nights to Rock	1959	5.00	10.00	20.00
❑ 5223	Goodnight Irene/Mona Lisa	1959	3.75	7.50	15.00
❑ 5328	New Jole Blon/Jambalaya	1960	3.75	7.50	15.00
❑ 5354	I Was Sorta Wondering/Sweeter Than the Flowers	1960	3.75	7.50	15.00
❑ 5379	Rocket to the Moon/Pipeliner	1960	3.75	7.50	15.00
❑ 5473	I Don't Know What to Do/I'll Take Your Hat Right Off My Rack	1961	3.75	7.50	15.00
❑ 5828	I'll Sail My Ship Alone/New Jole Blon	1963	3.00	6.00	12.00

MUSICOR

Number	Title (A Side/B Side)	Yr	VG	VG+	NM
❑ 1126	Love That Might Have Been/Custer's Last Stand	1965	2.50	5.00	10.00
❑ 1168	Just for Laughs/Jackson County	1965	2.50	5.00	10.00

SPAR

Number	Title (A Side/B Side)	Yr	VG	VG+	NM
❑ 9007	I'm Just One Tear Away/Mr. Honky Tonk Man	196?	3.75	7.50	15.00

STARDAY

Number	Title (A Side/B Side)	Yr	VG	VG+	NM
❑ 527	New Jole Blon/Farewell	1960	5.00	10.00	20.00
❑ 545	Ragged But Right/Bottom of the Glass	1961	5.00	10.00	20.00
❑ 556	Just Plain Lonesome/The Way You're Treatin' Me	1961	5.00	10.00	20.00
❑ 562	I'll Sail My Ship Alone/Mona Lisa	1961	5.00	10.00	20.00

Number	Title (A Side/B Side)	Yr	VG	VG+	NM
❑ 594	Ballad of Frank Clement/Good Times Gonna Roll Again	1962	3.75	7.50	15.00
❑ 596	Ain't Nothin' Like Lovin'/Good Times Gonna Roll Again	1962	3.75	7.50	15.00
❑ 7002	I'll Sail My Ship Alone/New Jole Blon	197?	—	3.00	6.00
❑ 7017	Mona Lisa/Sweeter Than the Flowers	197?	—	3.00	6.00
❑ 8035	I'll Sail My Ship Alone/New Jole Blon	197?	—	2.50	5.00
TCF HALL					
❑ 106	Quarter Mile Rows/Just to Be with You	1965	3.00	6.00	12.00
Selected 78s					
KING					
❑ 565	Lonesome Hearted Blues/It's a Sin to Love You Like I Do	1947	6.25	12.50	25.00
❑ 578	New Pretty Blonde (Jole Blon)/When a Soldier Knocks and Finds Nobody Home	1947	6.25	12.50	25.00
❑ 607	New Milk Cow Blues/Moonshine Polka	1947	6.25	12.50	25.00
❑ 613	Foggy River/Worries on My Mind	1947	6.25	12.50	25.00
❑ 632	Jole Blon's Sister/Showboy Special	1947	6.25	12.50	25.00
❑ 673	Sweeter Than the Flowers/I Left My Heart in Texas	1948	6.25	12.50	25.00
❑ 684	Over the Waves/Columbus Stockade Blues	1948	6.25	12.50	25.00
❑ 722	Wait a Minute/What My Eyes See My Heart Believes	1948	6.25	12.50	25.00
❑ 734	A Maiden's Prayer/I'm Gonna Move Home By and By	1948	6.25	12.50	25.00
❑ 745	Why Don't You Love Me/The Lie That Binds	1948	6.25	12.50	25.00
❑ 761	Jole Blon Is Gone, Amen/Oh She's Gone But Not Forgotten	1949	6.25	12.50	25.00
❑ 783	Sweeter Than the Flowers #2/There's a Chill on the Hill	1949	6.25	12.50	25.00
❑ 796	You Had Your Way/What Have I Done That Made You Go Away	1949	6.25	12.50	25.00
❑ 830	I'll Sail My Ship Alone/Moon's Tune	1949	6.25	12.50	25.00
❑ 839	Broken Dreams/Don't Ever Take My Picture Down	1950	6.25	12.50	25.00
❑ 868	Southern Hospitality/You Don't Have to Be a Baby to Cry	1950	6.25	12.50	25.00
❑ 886	Mona Lisa/Goodnight Irene	1950	6.25	12.50	25.00
❑ 894	Well Oh Well/Nine-Tenths of the Tennessee River	1950	6.25	12.50	25.00
❑ 905	Think It Over/Mona Lisa	1950	6.25	12.50	25.00
❑ 917	I Was Sorta Wonderin'/Leaves Mustn't Fall	1950	6.25	12.50	25.00
❑ 931	Short But Sweet/Too Many Irons in the Fire	1951	6.25	12.50	25.00
❑ 941	Lamp of Life/Without a Port of Love	1951	6.25	12.50	25.00
Albums					
AUDIO LAB					
❑ AL-1568 [M]	Instrumentals	1962	37.50	75.00	150.00
CORAL					
❑ CRL 57235 [M]	Moon Over Mullican	1958	125.00	250.00	500.00
HILLTOP					
❑ JS-6033	Good Times Gonna Roll Again	1966	6.25	12.50	25.00
KAPP					
❑ KS-3600	Showcase	1968	7.50	15.00	30.00
KING					
❑ 555 [M]	Moon Mullican Sings His All-Time Greatest Hits	1958	50.00	100.00	200.00
❑ 628 [M]	Moon Mullican Plays and Sings 16 of His Favorite Tunes	1959	37.50	75.00	150.00
❑ 681 [M]	The Many Moods of Moon Mullican	1960	37.50	75.00	150.00
❑ 937 [M]	Moon Mullican Sings 24 of His Favorite Tunes	1965	12.50	25.00	50.00
NASHVILLE					
❑ 2080	I'll Sail My Ship Alone	1970	5.00	10.00	20.00
SPAR					
❑ SP-3005 [M]	Mister Honky Tonk Man	1965	25.00	50.00	100.00
STARDAY					
❑ SLP-135 [M]	Playin' and Singin'	1963	25.00	50.00	100.00
❑ SLP-267 [M]	Mister Piano Man	1964	12.50	25.00	50.00
❑ SLP-398 [M]	The Unforgettable Moon Mullican	1967	10.00	20.00	40.00
STERLING					
❑ ST-601 [M]	I'll Sail My Ship Alone	1958	50.00	100.00	200.00
MULLINS, DEE					
45s					
MEL-O-DY					
❑ 117	Love Makes the World Go, But Money Greases the Wheel/Come On Back	1964	6.25	12.50	25.00
PLANTATION					
❑ 17	The Big Man/Run Willie Run	1969	—	3.00	6.00
❑ 31	Guilt Box/California, the Promised Land	1969	—	3.00	6.00
❑ 54	Irma Jackson/In a Small Time	1970	—	3.00	6.00
❑ 61	The Next Face I See/War Baby	1970	—	3.00	6.00
❑ 68	Remember Bethlehem/California, the Promised Land	1970	—	3.00	6.00
❑ 68 [DJ]	Remember Bethlehem (same on both sides)	1970	2.50	5.00	10.00
—Green vinyl					
❑ 119	Remember Bethlehem/California, the Promised Land	1974	—	2.50	5.00
SSS INTERNATIONAL					
❑ 707	War Baby/Parking for Cheaters	1967	2.00	4.00	8.00
❑ 728	I Am the Grass/The World I'm Livin' In	1968	—	3.50	7.00
❑ 745	Texas Tea/Parking for Cheaters	1968	—	3.50	7.00
❑ 749	The Continuing Story of Harper Valley P.T.A./Satisfied Old Man	1968	—	3.50	7.00
TRIUNE					
❑ 7205	Circle Me/Friday's Wine	1973	—	3.00	6.00

Number	Title (A Side/B Side)	Yr	VG	VG+	NM
❑ 7209	Rev the Engines Up High/A Little Better	1973	—	3.00	6.00
❑ 7211	Rusty Nails, Puppy Dog Tails and Little Boys/Wake Up, Town	1973	—	3.00	6.00
Albums					
PLANTATION					
❑ PLP-4	The Continuing Story	1969	3.75	7.50	15.00
MUNDY, JIM					
45s					
ABC					
❑ 11365	Swamp Witch/Run Away	1973	—	3.00	6.00
❑ 11380	Angel/I Robbed My Uncle Blind	1973	—	3.00	6.00
❑ 11400	The River's Too Wide/Run Away	1973	—	3.00	6.00
❑ 11428	Come Home/Nobody Loves You	1974	—	3.00	6.00
❑ 12001	She's No Ordinary Woman (Ordinarily)/Rosalie's Good-Eats Cafe	1974	—	2.50	5.00
❑ 12041	The Band/Little Flame a-Burnin'	1974	—	2.50	5.00
❑ 12074	She's Already Gone/While the Feeling's Good	1975	—	2.50	5.00
❑ 12120	Blue Eyes and Waltzes/Holdin' On	1975	—	2.50	5.00
ABC DOT					
❑ 17602	I Fall in Love Again/I'm a White Boy	1975	—	2.50	5.00
❑ 17617	I'm Knee Deep in Loving You/Monroe, Louisiana	1976	—	2.50	5.00
❑ 17638	I Never Met a Girl I Didn't Like/Lucy Ain't Your Loser Lookin' Good	1976	—	2.50	5.00
❑ 17678	I've Never Really Been in Love Before/Her Love for Her Man	1976	—	2.50	5.00
HICKORY					
❑ 1509	Ease of Mind/Working Man	1968	2.50	5.00	10.00
❑ 1529	Colorblind/Hurting All the Time	1969	2.00	4.00	8.00
❑ 1537	A Woman's Touch/Pull My String and Wind Me Up	1969	2.00	4.00	8.00
❑ 1563	Road Map/Have the Lonelies Ever Touched You	1970	2.00	4.00	8.00
❑ 1589	Hey Joe/That's the Way It Oughta Be	1971	2.00	4.00	8.00
❑ 1604	My Office Is a Ballpoint Pen/Genuine Cowhide Billfold	1971	2.00	4.00	8.00
❑ 1621	Bo Diddley/I Wish I Hadn't Brought My Face Home Last Night	1972	2.00	4.00	8.00
❑ 1634	Sorry/Catchin' Up Time	1972	2.00	4.00	8.00
❑ 1648	If You Got It, Flaunt It/Oh, I Love That Woman of Mine	1972	2.00	4.00	8.00
❑ 1655	She Got the Fortune/It's Gettin' Where You Can't Trust Nobody	1972	2.00	4.00	8.00
HILL COUNTRY					
❑ 778	Summertime Blues/Gibson County Sidewalks	1977	—	3.50	7.00
MUNDY, JIM, AND TERRI MELTON					
45s					
MCM					
❑ 100	If You Think I Love You Now/(B-side unknown)	1978	—	3.00	6.00
❑ 101	Kiss You All Over/(B-side unknown)	1978	—	3.00	6.00
MUNDY, MARILYN					
45s					
DOOR KNOB					
❑ 322	I Still Love You Babe/(B-side unknown)	1989	—	2.50	5.00
❑ 336	Feelings for Each Other/(B-side unknown)	1989	—	3.00	6.00
MURPHEY, MARK					
45s					
TRAVELER ENTERPRISES					
❑ 106	California Wine/(B-side unknown)	1989	2.00	4.00	8.00
MURPHEY, MICHAEL					
Also includes records as "Michael Martin Murphey."					
45s					
A&M					
❑ 1368	Geronimo's Cadillac/Boy from the Country	1972	—	2.50	5.00
❑ 1368 [PS]	Geronimo's Cadillac/Boy from the Country	1972	—	3.00	6.00
❑ 1447	Cosmic Cowboy/Temperature Train	1973	—	2.50	5.00
❑ 1459	Calico Silver/Blessing in Disguise	1973	—	2.50	5.00
❑ 1712	Geronimo's Cadillac/Blessing in Disguise	1975	—	2.00	4.00
EMI AMERICA					
❑ 8243	What She Wants/Still Taking Chances	1984	—	—	3.00
❑ 8265	Carolina in the Pines/Cherokee Fiddle	1985	—	—	3.00
EPIC					
❑ 02075	Take It As It Comes/Hard Country	1981	—	2.00	4.00
—With Katy Moffatt					
❑ 11130	Holy Roller/Rye By-The-Sea	1974	—	2.00	4.00
❑ 11130 [PS]	Holy Roller/Rye By-The-Sea	1974	—	3.00	6.00
❑ 50014	You Can Only Say So Much/Fort Worth, I Love You	1974	—	2.00	4.00
❑ 50084	Wildfire/Night Thunder	1975	—	2.50	5.00
❑ 50131	Carolina in the Pines/Without My Lady There	1975	—	2.00	4.00
❑ 50184	Mansion on the Hill/Renegade	1976	—	2.00	4.00
❑ 50214	Rhythm of the Road/Swans Against the Sun	1976	—	2.00	4.00
❑ 50319	Cherokee Fiddler/Running Wide Open	1976	—	2.00	4.00
❑ 50369	Changing Woman/A North Wind and a New Moon	1977	—	2.00	4.00
❑ 50540	Nothing Is Your Own/Song Day	1978	—	2.00	4.00
❑ 50572	Paradise Tonight/Song Dog	1978	—	2.00	4.00
❑ 50686	Lightning/Chain Gang	1979	—	2.00	4.00
❑ 50739	South Coast/Backsliders Wine	1979	—	2.00	4.00
LIBERTY					
❑ 1455	Lost River/The Two-Step Is Easy	1982	—	—	3.00
❑ 1466	What's Forever For/Crystal	1982	—	—	3.00
❑ 1486	Still Taking Chances/Lost River	1982	—	—	3.00

Number	Title (A Side/B Side)	Yr	VG	VG+	NM
❑ 1494	Crystal/Love Affairs	1983	—	—	3.00
❑ 1505	The Heart Never Lies/Don't Count the Rainy Days	1983	—	—	3.00
❑ 1514	Will It Be Love by Morning/Goodbye Money Mountain	1983	—	—	3.00
❑ 1517	Disenchanted/Sacred Heart	1984	—	—	3.00
—Starting here, as "Michael Martin Murphey"					
❑ 1523	Radio Land/The Heart Never Lies	1984	—	—	3.00
WARNER BROS.					
❑ PRO-S-2869 [DJ]	Colorado Christmas/The Cowboy's Christmas Ball	1987	—	3.00	6.00
—B-side by Nitty Gritty Dirt Band					
❑ 7-18321	Big Iron/Cowboy Logic	1993	—	2.00	4.00
❑ 18928	I Don't Do Floors/I'm Gonna Miss You Girl	1992	—	—	3.00
❑ 19290	What Am I Doin' Here/Where Do Cowboys Go When They Die-Reincarnation	1991	—	—	3.00
❑ 19412	Let the Cowboy Dance/Red River Valley	1991	—	—	3.00
❑ 19724	Cowboy Logic/Spanish Is the Lovin' Tongue	1990	—	—	3.00
❑ 22666	Route 66/Juke Box	1990	—	—	3.00
❑ 22765	Family Tree/Wood Smoke in the Wind	1989	—	—	3.00
❑ 22970	Never Givin' Up on Love/Desperation Road	1989	—	—	3.00
❑ 27668	From the Word Go/Vanishing Breed	1989	—	—	3.00
❑ 27810	Pilgrims on the Way (Matthew's Song)/Still Got the Fire	1988	—	—	3.00
❑ 27947	Talkin' to the Wrong Man/What Am I Doin' Hangin' 'Round	1988	—	—	3.00
❑ 28168	I'm Gonna Miss You, Girl/Running Blood	1987	—	—	3.00
❑ 28370	A Long Line of Love/Worlds Apart	1987	—	—	3.00
❑ 28471	A Face in the Crowd/You're History	1987	—	—	3.00
—With Holly Dunn					
❑ 28598	Fiddlin' Man/Ghost Town (Messages from the Ghost Ranch)	1986	—	—	3.00
❑ 28694	Rollin' Nowhere/Face-2-Face with the Night	1986	—	—	3.00
❑ 28797	Tonight We Ride/Santa Fe Cantina	1986	—	—	3.00

Albums

Number	Title	Yr	VG	VG+	NM
A&M					
❑ SP-3134	Geronimo's Cadillac	198?	2.00	4.00	8.00
—Budget-line reissue					
❑ SP-3137	Cosmic Cowboy Souvenir	198?	2.00	4.00	8.00
—Budget-line reissue					
❑ SP-4358	Geronimo's Cadillac	1972	3.00	6.00	12.00
❑ SP-4388	Cosmic Cowboy Souvenir	1973	3.00	6.00	12.00
EMI AMERICA					
❑ LN-10310	The Heart Never Lies	1986	2.00	4.00	8.00
—Budget-line reissue					
❑ ST-17143	The Best of Michael Martin Murphey	1984	2.50	5.00	10.00
EPIC					
❑ KE 32835	Michael Murphey	1974	3.00	6.00	12.00
❑ KE 33290	Blue Sky — Night Thunder	1975	2.50	5.00	10.00
❑ PE 33290	Blue Sky — Night Thunder	197?	2.00	4.00	8.00
—Reissue with new prefix & dark blue label					
❑ PE 33851	Swans Against the Sun	1975	2.50	5.00	10.00
❑ PEQ 33851 [Q]	Swans Against the Sun	1975	4.00	8.00	16.00
❑ PE 34220	Flowing Free Forever	1976	2.50	5.00	10.00
❑ JE 35013	Lonewolf	1978	2.50	5.00	10.00
❑ JE 35742	Peaks, Valleys, Honky-Tonks & Alleys	1979	2.50	5.00	10.00
LIBERTY					
❑ LT-51120	Michael Martin Murphey	1982	2.50	5.00	10.00
❑ LT-51150	The Heart Never Lies	1983	2.50	5.00	10.00
WARNER BROS.					
❑ 25369	Tonight We Ride	1986	2.50	5.00	10.00
❑ 25500	Americana	1987	2.50	5.00	10.00
❑ 25644	River of Time	1988	2.50	5.00	10.00
❑ 25894	Land of Enchantment	1989	3.00	6.00	12.00

MURPHY, CHUCK

45s

Number	Title (A Side/B Side)	Yr	VG	VG+	NM
COLUMBIA					
❑ 4-21258	Hocus Pocus/Hard Headed	1954	5.00	10.00	20.00
❑ 4-21305	Riding the Sunshine Special/Rhythm Hall	1954	5.00	10.00	20.00
❑ 4-21322	Santa Plays the Trombone (In the North Pole Band)/Let's Have an Old-Fashioned Christmas	1954	5.00	10.00	20.00
❑ 4-21376	Gonne Run, Not Walk/Friday Night Free-for-All	1955	5.00	10.00	20.00
CORAL					
❑ 9-60800	Who Drank My Beer While I Was in the Rear?/Oceana Roll	1952	7.50	15.00	30.00
❑ 9-61014	A 2-D Gal in a 3-D Town/One Beer	1953	7.50	15.00	30.00

MURPHY, DAVID LEE

45s

Number	Title (A Side/B Side)	Yr	VG	VG+	NM
MCA					
❑ 54794	Just Once/High Weeds and Rust	1994	—	2.00	4.00
❑ 54877	Fish Ain't Bitin'/Why Can't People Just Get Along	1994	—	—	3.00
❑ 54944	Dust on the Bottle/Mama 'n Them	1994	—	2.50	5.00
❑ 54977	Party Crowd/Can't Turn It Off	1995	—	2.00	4.00
❑ 55153	Out with a Bang/Greatest Show on Earth	1995	—	—	3.00
❑ 55186	Every Time I Get Around You/Pirates Cove	1996	—	—	3.00
❑ 55205	The Road You Leave Behind/Gettin' Out the Good Stuff	1996	—	—	3.00
❑ 55269	Genuine Rednecks/Genuine Rednecks (Club Mix)	1996	—	—	3.00
❑ 72000	Breakfast in Birmingham/100 Years Too Late	1997	—	—	3.00
❑ 72008	All Lit Up in Love/She's Really Something to See	1997	—	—	3.00
❑ 72024	Just Don't Wait Around Til She's Leavin'/Kentucky Girl	1997	—	—	3.00

MURPHY, JIMMY

45s

Number	Title (A Side/B Side)	Yr	VG	VG+	NM
ARK					
❑ 259	I Love to Hear Hank Sing the Blues/Swing Steel Blues	1963	3.75	7.50	15.00
—B-side by Paul Smith					
❑ 260	My Feet's on Solid Ground/Wake Me Up Sweet Jesus	1963	3.00	6.00	12.00
COLUMBIA					
❑ 4-21486	Here Kitty Kitty/I'm Looking for a Mustard Patch	1956	37.50	75.00	150.00
❑ 4-21534	Sixteen Tons Rock and Roll/My Gal Dottie	1956	50.00	100.00	200.00
❑ 4-21569	Baboon Boogie/Grandpaw's Cat	1956	50.00	100.00	200.00
ENCORE					
❑ 10033	Two Sides/What Would the World Be Without Music?	1986	—	2.50	5.00
❑ 10036	Keep the Faith/What Would the World Be Without Music?	1987	—	2.50	5.00
RCA VICTOR					
❑ 47-4609	That First Guitar of Mine/Love That Satisfies	1952	10.00	20.00	40.00
❑ 48-0447	Electricity/Mother, Where Is Your Daughter	1951	12.50	25.00	50.00
❑ 48-0474	Big Mama Blues/We Live a Long Time	1951	12.50	25.00	50.00
REM					
❑ 368	Half a Loaf of Bread/Take This Message to Mother	196?	7.50	15.00	30.00
REV					
❑ 3508	I'm Gone Mama/Plum Crazy	1957	12.50	25.00	50.00

Albums

Number	Title	Yr	VG	VG+	NM
SUGAR HILL					
❑ SH-3702	Electricity	1978	3.00	6.00	12.00

MURPHY, VERN

45s

Number	Title (A Side/B Side)	Yr	VG	VG+	NM
SUNSET					
❑ 0021	Blue and Lonely/Don't Cheat on Me	1973	—	3.50	7.00

MURRAY, ANNE

45s

Number	Title (A Side/B Side)	Yr	VG	VG+	NM
CAPITOL					
❑ 2738	Snowbird/Just Bidin' My Time	1970	—	3.00	6.00
❑ 2988	Sing High — Sing Low/Days of the Looking Glass	1970	—	2.50	5.00
❑ 3059	A Stranger in My Place/Sycamore Slick	1971	—	2.50	5.00
❑ 3082	Put Your Hand in the Hand/It Takes Time	1971	—	2.50	5.00
❑ 3159	Talk It Over in the Morning/Head Above the Water	1971	—	2.50	5.00
❑ 3260	Cotton Jenny/Destiny	1972	—	2.50	5.00
❑ 3352	Bobbie's Song for Jesus/You Can't Have a Hand on Me	1972	—	2.50	5.00
❑ 3481	Danny's Song/Drown Me	1972	—	2.00	4.00
❑ 3600	What About Me/Let Sunshine Have Its Day	1973	—	2.00	4.00
❑ 3648	Send a Little Love My Way/Head Above the Water	1973	—	2.00	4.00
❑ 3776	Love Song/You Can't Go Back	1973	—	2.00	4.00
❑ 3867	You Won't See Me/He Thinks I Still Care	1974	—	2.50	5.00
❑ 3955	Just One Look/Son of a Rotten Gambler	1974	—	2.00	4.00
❑ 4000	Day Tripper/Lullaby	1974	—	2.00	4.00
❑ 4025	Uproar/Lift Your Hearts to the Sun	1975	—	2.00	4.00
❑ 4072	A Stranger in My Place/Dream Lover	1975	—	2.00	4.00
❑ 4142	Sunday Sunrise/Out on the Road Again	1975	—	2.00	4.00
❑ 4207	The Call/Lady Bug	1976	—	2.00	4.00
❑ 4265	Golden Oldie/Together	1976	—	2.00	4.00
❑ 4329	Things/Caress Me Pretty Music	1976	—	2.00	4.00
❑ 4375	Sunday School to Broadway/Dancin' All Night Long	1976	—	2.00	4.00
❑ 4402	Canterbury Song/Shilo Song	1977	—	2.00	4.00
—With Gene MacLellan					
❑ 4527	Walk Right Back/A Million More	1978	—	2.00	4.00
❑ 4574	You Needed Me/I Still Wish the Very Best for You	1978	—	2.00	4.00
❑ 4675	I Just Fall in Love Again/Just to Feel This Love from You	1979	—	2.00	4.00
❑ 4675 [PS]	I Just Fall in Love Again/Just to Feel This Love from You	1979	—	2.50	5.00
❑ 4716	Shadows in the Moonlight/Yucatan Cafe	1979	—	2.00	4.00
❑ 4773	Broken Hearted Me/Why Don't You Stick Around	1979	—	2.00	4.00
❑ 4813	Daydream Believer/Do You Think of Me	1979	—	2.00	4.00
❑ 4848	Lucky Me/Somebody's Waiting	1980	—	2.00	4.00
❑ 4878	I'm Happy Just to Dance with You/What's Forever For	1980	—	2.00	4.00
❑ 4920	Could I Have This Dance/Somebody's Waiting	1980	—	2.00	4.00
❑ 4920 [PS]	Could I Have This Dance/Somebody's Waiting	1980	—	2.50	5.00
❑ 4987	Blessed Are the Believers/Only Love	1981	—	2.00	4.00
❑ 4987 [PS]	Blessed Are the Believers/Only Love	1981	—	2.50	5.00
❑ A-5013	We Don't Have to Hold Out/Call Me with the News	1981	—	2.00	4.00
❑ A-5023	It's All I Can Do/If a Heart Must Be Broken	1981	—	2.00	4.00
❑ A-5083	Another Sleepless Night/It Should Have Been Easy	1982	—	2.00	4.00
❑ B-5145	Hey! Baby!/Song for the Mira	1982	—	—	3.00
❑ B-5183	Somebody's Always Saying Goodbye/That'll Keep Me Dreamin'	1982	—	—	3.00
❑ B-5264	A Little Good News/I'm Not Afraid Anymore	1983	—	—	3.00
❑ B-5264 [PS]	A Little Good News/I'm Not Afraid Anymore	1983	—	2.50	5.00
❑ B-5305	That's Not the Way (It's S'posed to Be)/The More We Try	1983	—	—	3.00
❑ B-5344	Just Another Woman in Love/Heart Stealer	1984	—	—	3.00
❑ B-5384	Let Your Heart Do the Talking/I Don't Think I'm Ready for You	1984	—	—	3.00

Number	Title (A Side/B Side)	Yr	VG	VG+	NM
❑ B-5401	Nobody Loves Me Like You Do/Love You Out of Your Mind	1984	—	—	3.00
—A-side: With Dave Loggins					
❑ B-5436	Time Don't Run Out on Me/Let Your Heart Do the Talking	1985	—	—	3.00
❑ B-5472	I Don't Think I'm Ready for You/Take Good Care of My Baby	1985	—	—	3.00
❑ B-5472 [PS]	I Don't Think I'm Ready for You/Take Good Care of My Baby	1985	—	2.00	4.00
❑ B-5536	Go Tell It On the Mountain/O Holy Night	1985	—	2.00	4.00
❑ B-5536 [PS]	Go Tell It On the Mountain/O Holy Night	1985	—	2.50	5.00
❑ B-5547	Now and Forever (You and Me)/I Don't Wanna Spend Another Night Without You	1986	—	—	3.00
❑ B-5547 [PS]	Now and Forever (You and Me)/I Don't Wanna Spend Another Night Without You	1986	—	2.00	4.00
❑ B-5576	Who's Leaving Who/Reach for Me	1986	—	—	3.00
❑ B-5610	My Life's a Dance/Call Us Fools	1986	—	—	3.00
❑ B-5655	On and On/Gotcha	1986	—	—	3.00
❑ SPRO-9723 [DJ]	Christmas Medley: Silver Bells/I'll Be Home for Christmas/Winter Wonderland (same on both sides)	1981	2.00	4.00	8.00
❑ B-44005	Are You Still in Love with Me/Give Me Your Love	1987	—	—	3.00
❑ B-44053	Anyone Can Do the Heartbreak/Without You	1987	—	—	3.00
❑ B-44134	Perfect Strangers/It Happens All the Time	1988	—	—	3.00
—With Doug Mallory					
❑ B-44219	Flying On Your Own/Slow All Night	1988	—	—	3.00
❑ B-44272	Slow Passin' Time/Flying on Your Own	1989	—	—	3.00
❑ B-44341	Who But You/You Make Me Curious	1989	—	—	3.00
❑ B-44432	If I Ever Fall in Love Again/Just Another Woman in Love	1989	—	—	3.00
—A-side: With Kenny Rogers					
❑ B-44495	I'd Fall in Love Tonight/Now and Forever (You and Me)	1989	—	—	3.00
❑ 7PRO-79189	Feed This Fire (same on both sides)	1990	2.00	4.00	8.00
—Vinyl is promo only					

SBK

Number	Title (A Side/B Side)	Yr	VG	VG+	NM
❑ S7-18912	Winter Wonderland/The Little Drummer Boy	1995	—	—	3.00

Albums

CAPITOL

Number	Title (A Side/B Side)	Yr	VG	VG+	NM
❑ ST-579	Snowbird	1970	3.00	6.00	12.00
❑ ST-667	Anne Murray	1971	3.00	6.00	12.00
❑ ST-821	Talk It Over in the Morning	1971	3.00	6.00	12.00
❑ ST-11024	Annie	1972	2.50	5.00	10.00
❑ ST-11172	Danny's Song	1973	2.50	5.00	10.00
❑ ST-11266	Love Song	1974	2.50	5.00	10.00
❑ ST-11324	Country	1974	2.50	5.00	10.00
❑ ST-11354	Highly Prized Possession	1974	2.50	5.00	10.00
❑ ST-11433	Together	1975	2.50	5.00	10.00
❑ ST-11559	Keeping in Touch	1976	2.50	5.00	10.00
❑ ST-11743	Let's Keep It That Way	1978	2.50	5.00	10.00
❑ SW-11849	New Kind of Feeling	1979	2.50	5.00	10.00
❑ SOO-12012	I'll Always Love You	1979	2.50	5.00	10.00
❑ ST-12039	A Country Collection	1980	2.50	5.00	10.00
❑ SOO-12064	Somebody's Waiting	1980	2.50	5.00	10.00
❑ SOO-12110	Anne Murray's Greatest Hits	1980	2.50	5.00	10.00
❑ SOO-12144	Where Do You Go When You Dream	1981	2.50	5.00	10.00
❑ ST-12225	The Hottest Night of the Year	1982	2.50	5.00	10.00
❑ ST-12301	A Little Good News	1983	2.50	5.00	10.00
❑ SJ-12363	Heart Over Mind	1984	2.50	5.00	10.00
❑ SJ-12466	Something to Talk About	1986	2.50	5.00	10.00
❑ PJ-12562	Harmony	1987	2.50	5.00	10.00
❑ SN-16080	Talk It Over in the Morning	1980	2.00	4.00	8.00
—Budget-line reissue					
❑ SN-16081	Highly Prized Possession	1980	2.00	4.00	8.00
—Budget-line reissue					
❑ SN-16082	Keeping in Touch	1980	2.00	4.00	8.00
—Budget-line reissue					
❑ SN-16211	Danny's Song	1981	2.00	4.00	8.00
—Budget-line reissue					
❑ SN-16212	Love Song	1981	2.00	4.00	8.00
—Budget-line reissue					
❑ SN-16213	Country	1981	2.00	4.00	8.00
—Budget-line reissue					
❑ SN-16232	Christmas Wishes	1981	2.50	5.00	10.00
—Original issue was on the budget-line series					
❑ SN-16233	There's a Hippo in My Tub	1981	2.50	5.00	10.00
—Original issue was on the budget-line series					
❑ SN-16282	Together	1982	2.00	4.00	8.00
—Budget-line reissue					
❑ SN-16283	New Kind of Feeling	1982	2.00	4.00	8.00
—Budget-line reissue					
❑ SN-16338	A Country Collection	198?	2.00	4.00	8.00
—Budget-line reissue					
❑ SN-16341	Let's Keep It That Way	198?	2.00	4.00	8.00
—Budget-line reissue					
❑ C1-48764	As I Am	1988	2.50	5.00	10.00
❑ C1-90886	Christmas	1987	2.00	4.00	8.00
❑ C1-92072	Greatest Hits Volume II	1989	3.00	6.00	12.00

CAPITOL NASHVILLE

Number	Title (A Side/B Side)	Yr	VG	VG+	NM
❑ R 173232	You Will	1990	5.00	10.00	20.00
—Only released on vinyl through BMG Direct Marketing					

PICKWICK

Number	Title (A Side/B Side)	Yr	VG	VG+	NM
❑ SPC-3350	What About Me	197?	2.00	4.00	8.00

MURRAY, ANNE, AND GLEN CAMPBELL

Also see each artist's individual listings.

45s

CAPITOL

Number	Title (A Side/B Side)	Yr	VG	VG+	NM
❑ 3200	I Say a Little Prayer-By the Time I Get to Phoenix/All Through the Night	1971	—	2.50	5.00
❑ 3287	United We Stand/Ease Your Pain	1972	—	2.50	5.00

Albums

CAPITOL

Number	Title (A Side/B Side)	Yr	VG	VG+	NM
❑ SW-869	Anne Murray/Glen Campbell	1971	3.00	6.00	12.00
❑ SN-16144	Anne Murray/Glen Campbell	1980	2.00	4.00	8.00
—Budget-line reissue					

MUSIC CITY SOUNDS, THE

45s

MGM

Number	Title (A Side/B Side)	Yr	VG	VG+	NM
❑ 14132	My Happiness/Gotta Travel On	1970	2.00	4.00	8.00
❑ 14168	Tennessee Waltz/Release Me	1970	2.00	4.00	8.00

Albums

MGM

Number	Title (A Side/B Side)	Yr	VG	VG+	NM
❑ SE-4672	The Music City Sounds Featuring Lloyd Green and Pete Wade	1970	3.75	7.50	15.00

MUSIC ROW

45s

DEBUT

Number	Title (A Side/B Side)	Yr	VG	VG+	NM
❑ 8013	There Ain't a Song/(B-side unknown)	1980	—	3.00	6.00
❑ 8115	Lady's Man/(B-side unknown)	1981	—	3.00	6.00
❑ 8116	It's Not the Rain/(B-side unknown)	1981	—	3.00	6.00

MYERS, FRANK

45s

CAPRICE

Number	Title (A Side/B Side)	Yr	VG	VG+	NM
❑ 1999	Hangin' On to What I've Got/She'll Have Sunshine Where She Goes	1974	—	3.00	6.00
❑ 2005	Keep On Keepin' On/(B-side unknown)	1974	—	3.00	6.00
❑ 2011	I'm Going to Get Lovin' You Off My Mind/(B-side unknown)	1975	—	3.00	6.00

CARTWHEEL

Number	Title (A Side/B Side)	Yr	VG	VG+	NM
❑ 212	Talk to My Children's Mama/Make It Easy	1972	—	3.00	6.00

LITTLE DARLIN'

Number	Title (A Side/B Side)	Yr	VG	VG+	NM
❑ 7805	Half Empty Bed/I Hold the Key	1978	—	3.00	6.00
❑ 7914	Put Some Feeling in the Things You Say/My Fingers and You	1979	—	3.00	6.00

N

NAIL, LINDA

Also see DANNY WHITE.

45s

COMPLEAT

Number	Title (A Side/B Side)	Yr	VG	VG+	NM
❑ 111	Lovin', Lovin', Lovin'/Before I Started Loving You	1984	—	2.50	5.00

GRAND PRIX

Number	Title (A Side/B Side)	Yr	VG	VG+	NM
❑ 3	Reminiscing/I Go to Pieces	1983	—	3.00	6.00

PARAGON

Number	Title (A Side/B Side)	Yr	VG	VG+	NM
❑ 103	Stop in Nevada/My Love and I	198?	—	3.00	6.00

RIDGETOP

Number	Title (A Side/B Side)	Yr	VG	VG+	NM
❑ 00178	Me Touchin' You/A Woman and a Man	1978	—	3.00	6.00
❑ 00279	There Hangs His Hat/The Love Line's Slippin'	1979	—	3.00	6.00

NAILL, JERRY

45s

EL DORADO

Number	Title (A Side/B Side)	Yr	VG	VG+	NM
❑ 156	Her Cheatin' Heart (Made a Drunken Fool Out of Me)/(B-side unknown)	1979	2.00	4.00	8.00

NALL, JIMMY

Also see TERRI LANE AND JIMMY NALL.

45s

CHART

Number	Title (A Side/B Side)	Yr	VG	VG+	NM
❑ 5034	Concrete Jungle/Numbers Lie	1969	—	3.50	7.00
❑ 5057	Spell of the Freight Train/Such a Short Time	1970	—	3.00	6.00

MONUMENT

Number	Title (A Side/B Side)	Yr	VG	VG+	NM
❑ 45-213	Love Got in the Way/$2.00 Down	1977	—	2.50	5.00
❑ 1035	Face in the Mirror/Heaven Help My Soul	1967	2.00	4.00	8.00
❑ 1066	I Get So Lonesome/There's a Jim in Every Town	1968	—	3.50	7.00
❑ 1091	How Could You Do That to Me/Man Child	1968	—	3.50	7.00
❑ 1119	I'll Never Understand/Silver Ribbons	1968	—	3.50	7.00
❑ 8563	Her Arms Are Always Open/Working Man's Woman	1973	—	2.50	5.00
❑ 8575	Annie White/Face in the Mirror	1973	—	2.50	5.00
❑ 8595	Good Time Girl/I Get So Lonesome	1974	—	2.50	5.00
❑ 8626	Concrete Jungle/I Must Go Where My Heart Is	1974	—	2.50	5.00
❑ 8639	On the Rebound/When I'm Gone	1975	—	2.50	5.00

Number	Title (A Side/B Side)	Yr	VG	VG+	NM
❑ 8656	Sunday Kind of Woman/Face the Nashui Music	1975	—	2.50	5.00
❑ 8688	This Way of Mine/I Guess I'll Have to Sing About Tex	1976	—	2.50	5.00

NASH, BILL

45s

LIBERTY

Number	Title (A Side/B Side)	Yr	VG	VG+	NM
❑ B-1400	Fingertip Fever/Don't Throw Our Love to the Wind	1981	—	2.00	4.00
❑ B-1410	Burning Bridges/Saturday Night Live	1981	—	2.00	4.00
❑ B-1433	Slippin' Out, Slippin' In/Take Me As I Am	1981	—	2.00	4.00
❑ B-1463	Survivor/I Don't Want to Hear a Heartache Song Again	1982	—	2.00	4.00
❑ B-1481	Enough of Each Other/Night Talk	1982	—	2.00	4.00

NASH, LINDA

45s

ACE OF HEARTS

Number	Title (A Side/B Side)	Yr	VG	VG+	NM
❑ 0454	He's Already Gone to My Heart/Follow It	1973	—	3.00	6.00
❑ 0459	Good Things Just Don't Last/Gumbo Clay	1973	—	3.00	6.00
❑ 0473	Country Boogie Woogie/Good Things Just Don't Last	1973	—	3.00	6.00
❑ 0481	I Don't Have to Come This Far to See It Rain/(B-side unknown)	1974	—	3.00	6.00

NASHVILLE BRASS, THE

See DANNY DAVIS AND THE NASHVILLE BRASS.

NASHVILLE GUITARS, THE

45s

MONUMENT

Number	Title (A Side/B Side)	Yr	VG	VG+	NM
❑ 1105	Guantanamera/Bandido	1968	2.00	4.00	8.00

Albums

MONUMENT

Number	Title (A Side/B Side)	Yr	VG	VG+	NM
❑ MLP-8058 [M]	The Nashville Guitars	1966	3.75	7.50	15.00
❑ SLP-18058 [S]	The Nashville Guitars	1966	5.00	10.00	20.00
❑ MLP-18093	The Nashville Guitars at Home	1968	3.75	7.50	15.00

NASHVILLE NIGHTSHIFT

45s

NCA

Number	Title (A Side/B Side)	Yr	VG	VG+	NM
❑ 133737	Nightshift/(B-side unknown)	1985	—	3.50	7.00

NASHVILLE SUPERPICKERS

45s

SOUND FACTORY

Number	Title (A Side/B Side)	Yr	VG	VG+	NM
❑ 426	New York Cowboy/Sexy Southern Lady	1981	—	3.00	6.00

NAYLOR, JERRY

Also see KELLI WARREN.

45s

Number	Title (A Side/B Side)	Yr	VG	VG+	NM
COLUMBIA					
❑ 4-44809	The Chokin' Kind/Helga	1969	2.00	4.00	8.00
❑ 4-44874	Gotta Travel On/Posters on the Wall	1969	2.00	4.00	8.00
❑ 4-45106	But for Love/Angeline	1970	—	3.50	7.00
❑ 4-45170	Broken-Hearted Man/Mind Excursion	1970	—	3.50	7.00
❑ 4-45212	If I Promise/Marie	1970	—	3.50	7.00
❑ 4-45292	Come On Love/Las Virgenes Road	1970	—	3.50	7.00
HITSVILLE					
❑ 6041	The Bad Part of Me/I Hate to Drink Alone	1976	—	2.50	5.00
❑ 6046	The Last Time You Love Me/Born to Fool Around	1976	—	2.50	5.00
MC					
❑ 5004	If You Don't Want to Love Her/Love Away Her Memory Tonight	1978	—	2.50	5.00
❑ 5010	Rave On/Lady, Would You Like to Dance	1978	—	2.50	5.00
MELODYLAND					
❑ 6003	Is This All There Is to a Honky Tonk?/You're the One	1974	—	2.50	5.00
❑ 6012	He'll Have to Go/Once Again	1975	—	2.50	5.00
❑ 6020	What's a Nice Girl Like You Doing in a Honky Tonk/Prayin' for My Mind	1975	—	2.50	5.00
MGM					
❑ 14312	With This Ring/Goodtime Chariot	1971	—	3.00	6.00
❑ 14393	That'll Be the Day/Hands	1972	—	3.00	6.00
❑ 14439	Continental Highway/In This World	1972	—	3.00	6.00
❑ 14497	Bitter Memories/Love You Most of All	1973	—	3.00	6.00
❑ 14546	If You Don't Know Me by Now/Bitter Memories	1973	—	3.00	6.00
❑ 14637	Honky Tonk Women/You Are a Song	1973	—	3.00	6.00
OAK					
❑ 1014	Cheating Eyes/America, I'm Coming Home to You	1980	—	3.00	6.00
SKYLA					
❑ 1118	You're Thirteen/Stop Your Crying	1961	5.00	10.00	20.00
❑ 1123	Judee Malone/I'm Tired	1962	5.00	10.00	20.00
SMASH					
❑ 1971	I'll Take You Home/I Found You	1965	3.75	7.50	15.00
TOWER					
❑ 139	It's Only Make Believe/Leave Him and Come to My Loving Arms	1965	3.75	7.50	15.00
❑ 162	City Lights/Life	1965	3.75	7.50	15.00
❑ 214	My Special Angel/Would You Believe	1966	3.00	6.00	12.00
❑ 264	Almost Persuaded/I'll Get My Life the Way I Want It	1966	3.00	6.00	12.00
❑ 280	Drinkin' and Thinkin'/Johnny Brown	1966	3.00	6.00	12.00
❑ 327	Sweet Violets/Temptation Leads Me	1967	3.00	6.00	12.00
❑ 365	High on Happiness/Today and Tomorrow	1967	3.00	6.00	12.00
WARNER BROS.					
❑ 8767	But for Love/Part Time Lover, Part Time Fool	1979	—	2.50	5.00
❑ 8881	She Wears It Well/Part Time Lover, Full Time Heartache	1979	—	2.50	5.00
WEST					
❑ 723	For Old Time Sake/I Want to Be Loved	1986	—	3.00	6.00
❑ 726	Lean on Me/I Wanna Be Loved	1987	—	3.00	6.00

NEEL, JO ANNA

45s

Number	Title (A Side/B Side)	Yr	VG	VG+	NM
DECCA					
❑ 32817	Let's Make It a Long Night/Touch Me Like a Man	1971	2.00	4.00	8.00
❑ 32865	Daddy Was a Preacher But Mama Was a Go-Go Girl/A Perfect Stranger	1971	—	3.50	7.00
❑ 32950	One More Time/The Sparrow and Me	1972	—	3.50	7.00
❑ 33010	Lies/Still I Want to See You	1972	—	3.50	7.00
MCA					
❑ 40071	Ding-Bat/Sweet Little Singin' You	1973	—	3.00	6.00

NEELY, SAM

45s

Number	Title (A Side/B Side)	Yr	VG	VG+	NM
A&M					
❑ 1523	Come a Little Bit Closer/Sadie Take a Lover	1974	—	2.00	4.00
❑ 1612	You Can Have Her/It's a Fine Morning	1974	—	2.00	4.00
❑ 1651	I Fought the Law/Guitar Man	1974	—	2.00	4.00
❑ 1694	Sanctuary/Cajun Man	1975	—	2.00	4.00
CAPITOL					
❑ 3235	Long Road to Texas/Change a Sad to a Happy Song	1971	—	3.00	6.00
❑ 3358	Blue Time/Cry Me a Song	1972	—	3.00	6.00
❑ 3381	Loving You Just Crossed My Mind/Everyday Is the Same As Today	1972	—	2.50	5.00
❑ 3510	Rosalie/Try to Reason Why	1973	—	2.50	5.00
❑ 3586	Blue Time/Kiss the Morning Sunshine	1973	—	2.50	5.00
ELEKTRA					
❑ 45419	Sail Away/My Lover and My Friend	1977	—	2.00	4.00
❑ 45484	Your Love Is In Good Hands/Things That Lovers Do	1978	—	2.00	4.00
MCA					
❑ 52194	The Party's Over (Everybody's Gone)/What Do I Tell My Heart	1983	—	—	3.00
❑ 52226	When You Leave That Way You Can Never Go Back/Music Made Me Do It	1983	—	—	3.00
❑ 52269	Let's Fall in Love Again Tonight/You're No Ordinary Memory	1983	—	—	3.00
❑ 52323	Old Photographs/Somebody's Leaving	1983	—	—	3.00

Albums

Number	Title (A Side/B Side)	Yr	VG	VG+	NM
A&M					
❑ SP-3626	Sam Neely	1974	3.00	6.00	12.00
CAPITOL					
❑ ST-873	Long Road to Texas	1972	3.75	7.50	15.00
❑ ST-11097	Loving You Just Crossed My Mind	1972	3.00	6.00	12.00
—Reissued version of ST-873					
❑ SMAS-11143	Sam Neely — 2	1973	3.00	6.00	12.00

NELMS, JOHNNY

45s

DECCA

Number	Title (A Side/B Side)	Yr	VG	VG+	NM
❑ 9-46318	I Told My Heart/Crossroads	1951	6.25	12.50	25.00
❑ 9-46346	Should I Come Back/I've Been Lonesome Before	1951	6.25	12.50	25.00

NELSON, BONNIE

45s

DOOR KNOB

Number	Title (A Side/B Side)	Yr	VG	VG+	NM
❑ 221	Ladies' Man/You've Lost That Lovin' Feelin'	1984	—	2.50	5.00
❑ 227	You Belong to Me/Do What	1985	—	2.50	5.00
❑ 229	Ooh Lola Love/You Can't Break a Broken Heart	1985	—	2.50	5.00
❑ 233	Willie, Where Are You/(B-side unknown)	1985	—	3.00	6.00
❑ 238	You've Got What It Takes (To Take What I've Got)/Crazy	1986	—	2.50	5.00
❑ 257	Don't Let It Go to Your Heart/Willie, Where Are You	1986	—	2.50	5.00
❑ 264	More Than Friendly Persuasion/If You Want to Be Loved	1987	—	2.50	5.00

NELSON, RICKY

Also recorded as "Rick Nelson." Just as is true with ELVIS PRESLEY, Nelson had country hits both early and late in his career, so we've chosen to include his entire discography.

45s

Number	Title (A Side/B Side)	Yr	VG	VG+	NM
CAPITOL					
❑ 4962	Almost Saturday Night/The Loser Babe Is You	1981	—	2.50	5.00
❑ 4974	Call It What You Want/It Hasn't Happened Yet	1981	—	2.50	5.00
❑ 4988	Believe What You Say/The Loser Babe Is You	1981	—	2.50	5.00
❑ B-5178	No Fair Falling in Love/Give 'Em My Number	1982	—	2.50	5.00
❑ 89574	The Christmas Song (Chestnuts Roasting on an Open Fire)/Jingle Bells	2000	2.00	4.00	8.00
—Red vinyl					
DECCA					
❑ 31475	You Don't Love Me Anymore (And I Can Tell)/I Got a Woman	1963	3.75	7.50	15.00
❑ 31475 [PS]	You Don't Love Me Anymore (And I Can Tell)/I Got a Woman	1963	7.50	15.00	30.00
❑ 31495	String Along/Gypsy Woman	1963	3.75	7.50	15.00
❑ 31495 [PS]	String Along/Gypsy Woman	1963	7.50	15.00	30.00

Number	Title (A Side/B Side)	Yr	VG	VG+	NM
❑ 31533	Fools Rush In/Down Home	1963	3.75	7.50	15.00
❑ 31533 [PS]	Fools Rush In/Down Home	1963	7.50	15.00	30.00
❑ 31574	For You/That's All She Wrote	1963	3.75	7.50	15.00
❑ 31574 [PS]	For You/That's All She Wrote	1963	7.50	15.00	30.00
❑ 31612	The Very Thought of You/I Wonder (If Your Love Will Ever Belong to Me)	1964	3.00	6.00	12.00
❑ 31612 [PS]	The Very Thought of You/I Wonder (If Your Love Will Ever Belong to Me)	1964	7.50	15.00	30.00
❑ 31656	There's Nothing I Can Say/Lonely Corner	1964	3.00	6.00	12.00
❑ 31656 [PS]	There's Nothing I Can Say/Lonely Corner	1964	7.50	15.00	30.00
❑ 31703	A Happy Guy/Don't Breathe a Word	1964	3.00	6.00	12.00
❑ 31703 [PS]	A Happy Guy/Don't Breathe a Word	1964	7.50	15.00	30.00
❑ 31756	Mean Old World/When the Chips Are Down	1965	3.00	6.00	12.00
❑ 31756 [PS]	Mean Old World/When the Chips Are Down	1965	7.50	15.00	30.00
❑ 31800	Yesterday's Love/Come Out Dancin'	1965	3.00	6.00	12.00
❑ 31845	Love and Kisses/Say You Love Me	1965	3.00	6.00	12.00
❑ 31900	Your Kind of Lovin'/Fire Breathin' Dragon	1966	3.00	6.00	12.00
❑ 31900 [PS]	Your Kind of Lovin'/Fire Breathin' Dragon	1966	20.00	40.00	80.00
❑ 31956	Louisiana Man/You Jsut Can't Quit	1966	3.00	6.00	12.00
❑ 31956 [PS]	Louisiana Man/You Jsut Can't Quit	1966	15.00	30.00	60.00
❑ 32026	Alone/Things You Gave Me	1966	3.00	6.00	12.00
❑ 32026 [PS]	Alone/Things You Gave Me	1966	20.00	40.00	80.00
❑ 32055	They Don't Give Medals (To Yesterday's Heroes)/ Take a Broken Heart	1966	3.00	6.00	12.00
❑ 32120	Take a City Bride/I'm Called Lonely	1967	2.50	5.00	10.00
❑ 32120 [PS]	Take a City Bride/I'm Called Lonely	1967	15.00	30.00	60.00
❑ 32176	Moonshine/Suzanne on a Sunday Morning	1967	2.50	5.00	10.00
❑ 32222	Dream Weaver/Baby Close Your Eyes	1967	2.50	5.00	10.00
❑ 32284	Don't Blame It on Your Wife/Promenade in Green	1968	2.50	5.00	10.00
❑ 32298	Barefoot Boy/Don't Make Promises	1968	2.50	5.00	10.00
❑ 32550	She Belongs to Me/Promises	1969	2.00	4.00	8.00
❑ 32635	Easy to Be Free/Come On In	1970	2.00	4.00	8.00
❑ 32635 [PS]	Easy to Be Free/Come On In	1970	3.75	7.50	15.00
❑ 32676	I Shall Be Released/If You Gotta Go, Go Now	1970	2.00	4.00	8.00
❑ 32711	Look at Mary/We Got Such a Long Way to Go	1970	2.00	4.00	8.00
❑ 32739	How Long/Down Along the Bayou Country	1970	2.00	4.00	8.00
❑ 32779	Life/California	1971	2.00	4.00	8.00
❑ 32860	Thank You Lord/Sing Me a Song	1971	2.00	4.00	8.00
❑ 32906	Love Minus Zero-No Limit/Gypsy Pilot	1971	2.00	4.00	8.00
❑ 32980	Garden Party/So Long Mama	1972	2.50	5.00	10.00
❑ 34193/7 [PS]	Envelope, bonus photo and intact jukebox title strips for below 5 singles	1963	25.00	50.00	100.00
❑ 34193 [S]	Gypsy Woman/For Your Sweet Love	1963	25.00	50.00	100.00
❑ 34194 [S]	Pick Up the Pieces/Every Time I See You Smilin'	1963	25.00	50.00	100.00
❑ 34195 [S]	One Boy Too Late/Everytime I Think About You	1963	25.00	50.00	100.00
❑ 34196 [S]	Let's Talk the Whole Thing Over/I Got a Woman	1963	25.00	50.00	100.00
❑ 34197 [S]	I Will Follow You/What Comes Next	1963	25.00	50.00	100.00

—34193-34197 are 33 1/3 rpm, small hole jukebox singles. The set came with a package, priced separately.

EPIC

Number	Title (A Side/B Side)	Yr	VG	VG+	NM
❑ 06066	Dream Lover/Rave On	1986	—	2.00	4.00
❑ 06066 [PS]	Dream Lover/Rave On	1986	—	2.00	4.00
❑ 50458	It's Another Day/You Can't Dance	1977	—	2.50	5.00
❑ 50501	Gimme A Little Sign/Something You Can't Buy	1978	—	2.50	5.00
❑ 50674	Dream Lover/That Ain't the Way Love's Supposed to Be	1979	—	2.50	5.00

IMPERIAL

Number	Title (A Side/B Side)	Yr	VG	VG+	NM
❑ 5463	Be-Bop Baby/Have I Told You Lately That I Love You	1957	12.50	25.00	50.00
—Red label					
❑ 5463	Be-Bop Baby/Have I Told You Lately That I Love You	1957	6.25	12.50	25.00
—Black label					
❑ 5463 [PS]	Be-Bop Baby/Have I Told You Lately That I Love You	1957	20.00	40.00	80.00
❑ 5483	Stood Up/Waitin' in School	1957	10.00	20.00	40.00
—Red label					
❑ 5483	Stood Up/Waitin' in School	1957	6.25	12.50	25.00
—Black label					
❑ 5483 [PS]	Stood Up/Waitin' in School	1957	17.50	35.00	70.00
❑ 5503	Believe What You Say/My Bucket's Got a Hole in It	1958	7.50	15.00	30.00
❑ 5503 [PS]	Believe What You Say/My Bucket's Got a Hole in It	1958	17.50	35.00	70.00
❑ 5528	Poor Little Fool/Don't Leave Me This Way	1958	7.50	15.00	30.00
❑ 5545	Lonesome Town/I Got a Feeling	1958	7.50	15.00	30.00
❑ 5545	Lonesome Town/I Got a Feeling	1958	150.00	300.00	600.00
—Red vinyl					
❑ 5545 [PS]	Lonesome Town/I Got a Feeling	1958	17.50	35.00	70.00
❑ 5565	Never Be Anyone Else But You/It's Late	1959	6.25	12.50	25.00
—Black label					
❑ 5565	Never Be Anyone Else But You/It's Late	1959	10.00	20.00	40.00
—Red label					
❑ 5565 [PS]	Never Be Anyone Else But You/It's Late	1959	20.00	40.00	80.00
❑ 5595	Just a Little Too Much/Sweeter Than You	1959	6.25	12.50	25.00
❑ 5595 [PS]	Just a Little Too Much/Sweeter Than You	1959	17.50	35.00	70.00
❑ 5614	I Wanna Be Loved/Mighty Good	1959	6.25	12.50	25.00
❑ 5614 [PS]	I Wanna Be Loved/Mighty Good	1959	17.50	35.00	70.00
❑ 5663	Young Emotions/Right By My Side	1960	6.25	12.50	25.00
❑ 5663 [PS]	Young Emotions/Right By My Side	1960	17.50	35.00	70.00
❑ 5685	I'm Not Afraid/Yes Sir, That's My Baby	1960	6.25	12.50	25.00
❑ 5685 [PS]	I'm Not Afraid/Yes Sir, That's My Baby	1960	17.50	35.00	70.00
❑ 5707	You Are the Only One/Milk Cow Blues	1960	6.25	12.50	25.00
❑ 5707 [PS]	You Are the Only One/Milk Cow Blues	1960	17.50	35.00	70.00
❑ 5741	Travelin' Man/Hello Mary Lou	1961	6.25	12.50	25.00
❑ 5741	Travelin' Man/Hello Mary Lou	1961	200.00	400.00	800.00
—Red vinyl					
❑ 5741 [PS]	Travelin' Man/Hello Mary Lou	1961	17.50	35.00	70.00
❑ 5770	A Wonder Like You/Everlovin'	1961	5.00	10.00	20.00
—Starting here, Imperial singles by "Rick Nelson"					
❑ 5770 [PS]	A Wonder Like You/Everlovin'	1961	10.00	20.00	40.00
❑ 5805	Young World/Summertime	1962	5.00	10.00	20.00
❑ 5805 [PS]	Young World/Summertime	1962	10.00	20.00	40.00
❑ 5864	Teen Age Idol/I've Got My Eyes on You	1962	5.00	10.00	20.00
❑ 5864 [PS]	Teen Age Idol/I've Got My Eyes on You	1962	10.00	20.00	40.00
❑ 5901	It's Up to You/I Need You	1962	5.00	10.00	20.00
❑ 5901 [PS]	It's Up to You/I Need You	1962	10.00	20.00	40.00
❑ 5910	That's All/I'm in Love Again	1963	6.25	12.50	25.00
❑ 5935	Old Enough to Love/If You Can't Rock Me	1963	5.00	10.00	20.00
❑ 5935 [PS]	Old Enough to Love/If You Can't Rock Me	1963	10.00	20.00	40.00
❑ 5958	A Long Vacation/Mad Mad World	1963	5.00	10.00	20.00
❑ 5958	A Long Vacation/Mad Mad World	1963	75.00	150.00	300.00
—Red vinyl					
❑ 5985	Time After Time/There's Not a Minute	1963	5.00	10.00	20.00
❑ 58896	Young World/A Wonder Like You	2000	—	2.50	5.00
—EMI-Capitol jukebox issue with Imperial logo at top					
❑ 66004	Today's Teardrops/Thank You Darlin'	1963	3.75	7.50	15.00
❑ 66004 [PS]	Today's Teardrops/Thank You Darlin'	1963	10.00	20.00	40.00
❑ 66017	Congratulations/One Minute to One	1964	3.75	7.50	15.00
❑ 66039	Everybody But Me/Lucky Star	1964	3.75	7.50	15.00

MCA

Number	Title (A Side/B Side)	Yr	VG	VG+	NM
❑ 40001	Palace Guard/A Flower Opens Gently By	1973	—	3.00	6.00
❑ 40130	Evil Woman Child/Lifestream	1973	—	3.00	6.00
❑ 40187	Windfall/Legacy	1974	—	3.00	6.00
❑ 40214	One Night Stand/Lifestream	1974	—	3.00	6.00
❑ 40392	Louisiana Belle/Try (Try to Fall in Love)	1975	—	3.00	6.00
❑ 40458	Rock and Roll Lady/Fadeaway	1975	—	3.00	6.00
❑ 52781	You Know What I Mean/Don't Leave Me This Way	1986	—	2.50	5.00
❑ 52781 [PS]	You Know What I Mean/Don't Leave Me This Way	1986	—	2.50	5.00

UNITED ARTISTS

Number	Title (A Side/B Side)	Yr	VG	VG+	NM
❑ 0071	Be-Bop Baby/Stood Up	1973	—	2.50	5.00
❑ 0072	Lonesome Town/It's Up to You	1973	—	2.50	5.00
❑ 0073	Poor Little Fool/My Bucket's Got a Hole in It	1973	—	2.50	5.00
❑ 0074	Travelin' Man/Believe What You Say	1973	—	2.50	5.00
❑ 0075	Teen Age Idol/Young Emotions	1973	—	2.50	5.00
❑ 0076	Never Be Anyone Else But You/That's All	1973	—	2.50	5.00
❑ 0077	Young World/It's Late	1973	—	2.50	5.00
❑ 0078	Just a Little Too Much/Waitin' in School	1973	—	2.50	5.00
❑ 0079	Hello Mary Lou/Sweeter Than You	1973	—	2.50	5.00
❑ 0080	A Wonder Like You/Everlovin'	1973	—	2.50	5.00

—0071 through 0080 are "Silver Spotlight Series" reissues

VERVE

Number	Title (A Side/B Side)	Yr	VG	VG+	NM
❑ 10047	I'm Walkin'/A Teenager's Romance	1957	12.50	25.00	50.00
—Orange and yellow label					
❑ 10047	I'm Walkin'/A Teenager's Romance	1957	10.00	20.00	40.00
—Black and white label					
❑ 10070	You're My One and Only Love/Honey Rock	1957	10.00	20.00	40.00

—B-side by Barney Kessel

7-Inch Extended Plays

DECCA

Number	Title (A Side/B Side)	Yr	VG	VG+	NM
❑ ED 2760	I Will Follow You/Pick Up the Pieces//One Boy Too Late/Let's Talk the Whole Thing Over	1963	37.50	75.00	150.00
❑ ED 2760 [PS]	One Boy Too Late	1963	37.50	75.00	150.00
❑ 7-34319 [PS]	Best Always	1965	7.50	15.00	30.00
—With title strips					
❑ 7-34319 [S]	I'm Not Ready for You Yet/Lonely Corner/Mean Old World//I Know a Place/It's Beginning to Hurt/ When the Chips Are Down	1965	7.50	15.00	30.00

—33 1/3 rpm, small hole jukebox edition

IMPERIAL

Number	Title (A Side/B Side)	Yr	VG	VG+	NM
❑ IMP 153	Be-Bop Baby/Have I Told You Lately That I Love You//Honeycomb/Boppin' the Blues	1957	12.50	25.00	50.00
❑ IMP 153 [PS]	Ricky (Honeycomb)	1957	12.50	25.00	50.00
❑ IMP 154	Teenage Doll/If You Can't Rock Me//Whole Lotta Shakin' Goin' On/Baby I'm Sorry	1957	12.50	25.00	50.00
❑ IMP 154 [PS]	Ricky, Volume 2	1957	12.50	25.00	50.00
❑ IMP 155	Your True Love/True Love//Am I Blue/I'm Confessin'	1957	12.50	25.00	50.00
❑ IMP 155 [PS]	Ricky (True Love)	1957	12.50	25.00	50.00
❑ IMP 156	Shirley Lee/There's Good Rockin' Tonight// Someday/I'm Feelin' Sorry	1958	12.50	25.00	50.00
❑ IMP 156 [PS]	Ricky Nelson (Someday)	1958	12.50	25.00	50.00
❑ IMP 157	Down the Line/Don't Leave Me This Way//I'm in Love Again/My Babe	1958	12.50	25.00	50.00
❑ IMP 157 [PS]	Ricky Nelson (Down the Line)	1958	12.50	25.00	50.00
❑ IMP 158	Unchained Melody/I'll Walk Alone//There Goes My Baby/Poor Little Fool	1958	12.50	25.00	50.00
❑ IMP 158 [PS]	Ricky Nelson (Unchained Melody)	1958	12.50	25.00	50.00
❑ IMP 159	Be True to Me/One of These Mornings// Lonesome Town/It's Late	1959	12.50	25.00	50.00
❑ IMP 159 [PS]	Ricky Sings Again (Be True to Me)	1959	12.50	25.00	50.00
❑ IMP 160	Restless Kid/It's All in the Game//Believe What You Say/You Tear Me Up	1959	12.50	25.00	50.00
❑ IMP 160 [PS]	Ricky Sings Again (Restless Kid)	1959	12.50	25.00	50.00
❑ IMP 161	Old Enough to Love/Tryin' to Get to You//Never Be Anyone Else But You/I Can't Help It	1959	12.50	25.00	50.00
❑ IMP 161 [PS]	Ricky Sings Again (Old Enough to Love)	1959	12.50	25.00	50.00
❑ IMP 162	You'll Never Know What You're Missin'/I've Been Thinkin'//So Long/You're So Fine	1959	12.50	25.00	50.00

Number	Title (A Side/B Side)	Yr	VG	VG+	NM
IMP 162 [PS]	Songs by Ricky (You'll Never Know What You're Missin')	1959	12.50	25.00	50.00
IMP 163	One Minute To One/Blood from a Stone//Half Breed/Just a Little Too Much	1959	12.50	25.00	50.00
IMP 163 [PS]	Songs by Ricky (One Minute to One)	1959	12.50	25.00	50.00
IMP 164	Don't Leave Me/That's All//Sweeter Than You/A Long Vacation	1959	12.50	25.00	50.00
IMP 164 [PS]	Songs by Ricky (Don't Leave Me)	1959	12.50	25.00	50.00
IMP 165	Glory Train/I Bowed My Head in Shame//March with the Band of the Lord/If You Believe It	1959	25.00	50.00	100.00
IMP 165 [PS]	Ricky Sings Spirituals	1959	25.00	50.00	100.00
LP 4-2232 [PS]	Million Sellers	1964	20.00	40.00	80.00
LP 4-2232 [S]	Travelin' Man/Never Be Anyone Else But You/It's Late//Young Emotions/Hello Mary Lou/Yes Sir, That's My Baby	1964	20.00	40.00	80.00
—33 1/3 rpm, small hole, jukebox edition					

VERVE

Number	Title (A Side/B Side)	Yr	VG	VG+	NM
5048	I'm Walkin'/A Teenager's Romance//You're My One and Only Love/Honey Rock	1957	37.50	75.00	150.00
5048 [PS]	Ricky	1957	50.00	100.00	200.00

Albums

CAPITOL

Number	Title (A Side/B Side)	Yr	VG	VG+	NM
SOO-12109	Playing to Win	1981	2.50	5.00	10.00

DECCA

Number	Title (A Side/B Side)	Yr	VG	VG+	NM
DL 4419 [M]	For Your Sweet Love	1963	7.50	15.00	30.00
DL 4479 [M]	Rick Nelson Sings "For You"	1963	7.50	15.00	30.00
DL 4559 [M]	The Very Thought of You	1964	7.50	15.00	30.00
DL 4608 [M]	Spotlight on Rick	1964	7.50	15.00	30.00
DL 4660 [M]	Best Always	1965	7.50	15.00	30.00
DL 4678 [M]	Love and Kisses	1965	7.50	15.00	30.00
DL 4779 [M]	Bright Lights and Country Music	1966	6.25	12.50	25.00
DL 4827 [M]	Country Fever	1967	6.25	12.50	25.00
DL 4944 [M]	Another Side of Rick	1967	6.25	12.50	25.00
DL 5014 [M]	Perspective	1968	12.50	25.00	50.00
—Mono copies are promo only					
DL 74419 [S]	For Your Sweet Love	1963	10.00	2.00	40.00
DL 74479 [S]	Rick Nelson Sings "For You"	1963	10.00	20.00	40.00
DL 74559 [S]	The Very Thought of You	1964	10.00	20.00	40.00
DL 74608 [S]	Spotlight on Rick	1964	10.00	20.00	40.00
DL 74660 [S]	Best Always	1965	10.00	20.00	40.00
DL 74678 [S]	Love and Kisses	1965	10.00	20.00	40.00
DL 74779 [S]	Bright Lights and Country Music	1966	7.50	15.00	30.00
DL 74827 [S]	Country Fever	1967	7.50	15.00	30.00
DL 74944 [S]	Another Side of Rick	1967	7.50	15.00	30.00
DL 75014 [S]	Perspective	1968	7.50	15.00	30.00
DL 75162	Rick Nelson In Concert	1970	6.25	12.50	25.00
DL 75236	Rick Sings Nelson	1970	6.25	12.50	25.00
—Deduct 20 percent if poster is missing					
DL 75297	Rudy the Fifth	1971	6.25	12.50	25.00
DL 75391	Garden Party	1972	6.25	12.50	25.00

EPIC

Number	Title (A Side/B Side)	Yr	VG	VG+	NM
JE 34420	Intakes	1977	3.00	6.00	12.00
FE 40388	The Memphis Sessions	1986	2.50	5.00	10.00

EPIC/NU-DISK

Number	Title (A Side/B Side)	Yr	VG	VG+	NM
3E 36868 [10]	Four You	1981	3.00	6.00	12.00

IMPERIAL

Number	Title (A Side/B Side)	Yr	VG	VG+	NM
LP 9048 [M]	Ricky	1957	25.00	50.00	100.00
—Black label with stars					
LP 9048 [M]	Ricky	1964	6.25	12.50	25.00
—Black label with pink and white at left					
LP 9048 [M]	Ricky	1966	5.00	10.00	20.00
—Black label with green and white at left					
LP 9050 [M]	Ricky Nelson	1958	25.00	50.00	100.00
—Black label with stars					
LP 9050 [M]	Ricky Nelson	1964	6.25	12.50	25.00
—Black label with pink and white at left					
LP 9050 [M]	Ricky Nelson	1966	5.00	10.00	20.00
—Black label with green and white at left					
LP 9061 [M]	Ricky Sings Again	1959	25.00	50.00	100.00
—Black label with stars					
LP 9061 [M]	Ricky Sings Again	1964	6.25	12.50	25.00
—Black label with pink and white at left					
LP 9061 [M]	Ricky Sings Again	1966	5.00	10.00	20.00
—Black label with green and white at left					
LP 9082 [M]	Songs by Ricky	1959	18.75	37.50	75.00
—Black label with stars					
LP 9082 [M]	Songs by Ricky	1964	6.25	12.50	25.00
—Black label with pink and white at left					
LP 9082 [M]	Songs by Ricky	1966	5.00	10.00	20.00
—Black label with green and white at left					
LP 9122 [M]	More Songs by Ricky	1960	18.75	37.50	75.00
—Black label with stars					
LP 9122 [M]	More Songs by Ricky	1964	6.25	12.50	25.00
—Black label with pink and white at left					
LP 9122 [M]	More Songs by Ricky	1966	5.00	10.00	20.00
—Black label with green and white at left					
LP 9152 [M]	Rick Is 21	1961	10.00	20.00	40.00
—Black label with stars					
LP 9152 [M]	Rick Is 21	1964	6.25	12.50	25.00
—Black label with pink and white at left					
LP 9152 [M]	Rick Is 21	1966	5.00	10.00	20.00
—Black label with green and white at left					
LP 9167 [M]	Album Seven by Rick	1962	10.00	20.00	40.00
—Black label with stars					
LP 9167 [M]	Album Seven by Rick	1964	6.25	12.50	25.00
—Black label with pink and white at left					
LP 9167 [M]	Album Seven by Rick	1966	5.00	10.00	20.00
—Black label with green and white at left					
LP 9218 [M]	Best Sellers by Rick Nelson	1963	10.00	20.00	40.00
—Black label with stars					
LP 9218 [M]	Best Sellers by Rick Nelson	1964	6.25	12.50	25.00
—Black label with pink and white at left					
LP 9218 [M]	Best Sellers by Rick Nelson	1966	5.00	10.00	20.00
—Black label with green and white at left					
LP 9223 [M]	It's Up to You	1963	10.00	20.00	40.00
—Black label with stars					
LP 9223 [M]	It's Up to You	1964	6.25	12.50	25.00
—Black label with pink and white at left					
LP 9223 [M]	It's Up to You	1966	5.00	10.00	20.00
—Black label with green and white at left					
LP 9232 [M]	Million Sellers	1963	10.00	20.00	40.00
—Black label with stars					
LP 9232 [M]	Million Sellers	1964	6.25	12.50	25.00
—Black label with pink and white at left					
LP 9232 [M]	Million Sellers	1966	5.00	10.00	20.00
—Black label with green and white at left					
LP 9244 [M]	A Long Vacation	1963	10.00	20.00	40.00
—Black label with stars					
LP 9244 [M]	A Long Vacation	1964	6.25	12.50	25.00
—Black label with pink and white at left					
LP 9244 [M]	A Long Vacation	1966	5.00	10.00	20.00
—Black label with green and white at left					
LP 9251 [M]	Rick Nelson Sings for You	1964	10.00	20.00	40.00
—Black label with stars					
LP 9251 [M]	Rick Nelson Sings for You	1964	6.25	12.50	25.00
—Black label with pink and white at left					
LP 9251 [M]	Rick Nelson Sings for You	1966	5.00	10.00	20.00
—Black label with green and white at left					
LP 12030 [S]	Songs by Ricky	1959	50.00	100.00	200.00
—Black label with silver print					
LP 12030 [S]	Songs by Ricky	1964	10.00	20.00	40.00
—Black label with pink and white at left					
LP 12030 [S]	Songs by Ricky	1966	6.25	12.50	25.00
—Black label with green and white at left					
LP 12059 [DJ]	More Songs by Ricky	1960	250.00	500.00	1000.
—Promo copy on blue vinyl. Add 20 percent for enclosed poster.					
LP 12059 [S]	More Songs by Ricky	1960	25.00	50.00	100.00
—Black label with silver print					
LP 12059 [S]	More Songs by Ricky	1964	10.00	20.00	40.00
—Black label with pink and white at left					
LP 12059 [S]	More Songs by Ricky	1966	6.25	12.50	25.00
—Black label with green and white at left					
LP 12071 [S]	Rick Is 21	1961	25.00	50.00	100.00
—Black label with silver print					
LP 12071 [S]	Rick Is 21	1964	10.00	20.00	40.00
—Black label with pink and white at left					
LP 12071 [S]	Rick Is 21	1966	6.25	12.50	25.00
—Black label with green and white at left					
LP 12082 [S]	Album Seven by Rick	1962	25.00	50.00	100.00
—Black label with silver print					
LP 12082 [S]	Album Seven by Rick	1964	10.00	20.00	40.00
—Black label with pink and white at left					
LP 12082 [S]	Album Seven by Rick	1966	6.25	12.50	25.00
—Black label with green and white at left					
LP 12090 [S]	Ricky Sings Again	1962	37.50	75.00	150.00
—Black label with silver print					
LP 12090 [S]	Ricky Sings Again	1964	10.00	20.00	40.00
—Black label with pink and white at left					
LP 12090 [S]	Ricky Sings Again	1966	6.25	12.50	25.00
—Black label with green and white at left					
LP 12218 [R]	Best Sellers	1964	5.00	10.00	20.00
—Black label with pink and white at left					
LP 12218 [R]	Best Sellers	1966	3.75	7.50	15.00
—Black label with green and white at left					
LP 12232 [R]	Million Sellers	1964	5.00	10.00	20.00
—Black label with pink and white at left					
LP 12232 [R]	Million Sellers	1966	3.75	7.50	15.00
—Black label with green and white at left					
LP 12244 [R]	A Long Vacation	1964	5.00	10.00	20.00
—Black label with pink and white at left					
LP 12244 [R]	A Long Vacation	1966	3.75	7.50	15.00
—Black label with green and white at left					
LP 12251 [R]	Rick Nelson Sings for You	1964	6.25	12.50	25.00
—Black label with silver print					
LP 12251 [R]	Rick Nelson Sings for You	1964	5.00	10.00	20.00
—Black label with pink and white at left					
LP 12251 [R]	Rick Nelson Sings for You	1966	3.75	7.50	15.00
—Black label with green and white at left					
LP 12392 [R]	Ricky	1968	3.75	7.50	15.00
—Rechanneled reissue of 9048					
LP 12393 [R]	Ricky Nelson	1968	3.75	7.50	15.00
—Rechanneled reissue of 9050					

LIBERTY

Number	Title (A Side/B Side)	Yr	VG	VG+	NM
LM-1004	Ricky	1981	2.00	4.00	8.00
—Reissue of United Artists 1004					
LXB-9960 [(2)]	Legendary Masters	198?	3.00	6.00	12.00
—Reissue of United Artists 9960					
LN-10134	Ricky Sings Again	1982	2.50	5.00	10.00
—Reissue of Imperial 12090					
LN-10205	Souvenirs	1983	2.00	4.00	8.00
LN-10253	Teen Age Idol	1984	2.00	4.00	8.00

Number	Title (A Side/B Side)	Yr	VG	VG+	NM
❑ LN-10305	Ricky Nelson	1986	2.00	4.00	8.00
—Another reissue					
❑ LM-51004	Ricky	1983	2.00	4.00	8.00
—Reissue of Liberty 1004					
MCA					
❑ 3	Rick Nelson In Concert	1973	3.00	6.00	12.00
—Reissue of Decca 75162					
❑ 20	Rick Sings Nelson	1973	3.00	6.00	12.00
—Reissue of Decca 75236					
❑ 37	Rudy the Fifth	1973	3.00	6.00	12.00
—Reissue of Decca 75297					
❑ 62	Garden Party	1973	3.00	6.00	12.00
—Reissue of Decca 75391					
❑ 383	Windfall	1974	3.75	7.50	15.00
❑ 1517	The Decca Years	1982	2.00	4.00	8.00
❑ 2-4004 [(2)]	Rick Nelson Country	1973	3.75	7.50	15.00
❑ 6163	All My Best	1986	2.50	5.00	10.00
RHINO					
❑ RNLP 215	Greatest Hits	1985	3.00	6.00	12.00
❑ RNDF 259 [PD]	Greatest Hits	1985	3.75	7.50	15.00
❑ R1-70215	Greatest Hits	1987	2.50	5.00	10.00
❑ R1-71114	Live 1983-1985	1989	3.00	6.00	12.00
SUNSET					
❑ SUM-1118 [M]	Ricky Nelson	1966	3.75	7.50	15.00
❑ SUS-5118 [P]	Ricky Nelson	1966	5.00	10.00	20.00
❑ SUS-5205	I Need You	1968	3.75	7.50	15.00
TIME-LIFE					
❑ SRNR 31 [(2)]	Rick Nelson: 1957-1972	1989	3.75	7.50	15.00
UNITED ARTISTS					
❑ UA-LA330-E	The Very Best of Rick Nelson	1974	3.00	6.00	12.00
❑ LM-1004	Ricky	1980	2.50	5.00	10.00
—Reissue of Imperial 9048					
❑ UAS-9960 [(2)]	Legendary Masters	1971	6.25	12.50	25.00
VERVE					
❑ V 2083 [M]	Teen Time	1957	125.00	250.00	500.00
—Has three Ricky Nelson songs plus tracks by four others; usually treated as Rick's LP because of his prominence on the cover					

NELSON, TRACY

45s

Number	Title (A Side/B Side)	Yr	VG	VG+	NM
ATLANTIC					
❑ 3235	It Takes a Lot to Laugh, It Takes a Train to Cry/Lean On Me	1975	—	2.50	5.00
CAPITOL					
❑ 4442	Sad Situation/Let's Get Down to the Truth	1977	—	2.00	4.00
—With Larry Ballard					
MCA					
❑ 40479	Sweet Soul Music/Nothing I Can't Handle	1975	—	2.00	4.00
MERCURY					
❑ 72995	Sad Situation/Stay As Sweet As You Are	1970	2.00	4.00	8.00

Albums

Number	Title (A Side/B Side)	Yr	VG	VG+	NM
ADELPHI					
❑ 4119	Doin' It My Way	1981	2.50	5.00	10.00
ATLANTIC					
❑ SD 7310	Tracy Nelson	1974	3.00	6.00	12.00
COLUMBIA					
❑ KC 31759	Poor Man's Paradise	1973	3.00	6.00	12.00
FLYING FISH					
❑ FF-052	Homemade Songs	1978	2.50	5.00	10.00
❑ FF-209	Come See About Me	1980	2.50	5.00	10.00
MCA					
❑ 494	Sweet Soul Music	1975	3.00	6.00	12.00
❑ 2203	Time Is On My Side	1976	3.00	6.00	12.00
PRESTIGE					
❑ PRLP 7393 [M]	Deep Are the Roots	1965	6.25	12.50	25.00
❑ PRST 7393 [S]	Deep Are the Roots	1965	7.50	15.00	30.00
❑ PRST 7726	Deep Are the Roots	1969	3.75	7.50	15.00

NELSON, TRACY AND WILLIE

Also see each artist's individual listings.

45s

Number	Title (A Side/B Side)	Yr	VG	VG+	NM
ATLANTIC					
❑ 4028	After the Fire Is Gone/Whiskey River	1976	—	2.50	5.00

NELSON, WILLIE

Includes many duets not listed separately below. Also see HANK COCHRAN; DANNY DAVIS; MERLE HAGGARD; WAYLON JENNINGS; TRACY NELSON; WAYLON AND WILLIE.

45s

Number	Title (A Side/B Side)	Yr	VG	VG+	NM
AMERICAN GOLD					
❑ 7601	Night Life/Rainy Day Blues	1976	—	2.50	5.00
ATLANTIC					
❑ 2968	Shotgun Willie/Sad Songs and Waltzes	1973	—	2.50	5.00
❑ 2979	Devil in a Sleepin' Bag/Stay All Night	1973	—	2.50	5.00
❑ 3008	Heaven and Hell/I Still Can't Believe You're Gone	1974	—	2.50	5.00
❑ 3020	Phases and Stages/Bloody Mary Morning	1974	—	2.50	5.00
❑ 3228	Sister's Coming Home/Pick Up the Tempo	1974	—	2.50	5.00
❑ 3334	Heaven and Hell/I Still Can't Believe You're Gone	1976	—	2.50	5.00
BELLAIRE					
❑ 107	Night Life/Rainy Day Blues	1963	7.50	15.00	30.00
❑ 107	Night Life/Rainy Day Blues	1963	15.00	30.00	60.00
—Colored vinyl					
❑ 5000	Night Life '76/Man with the Blues	1976	—	2.50	5.00
BETTY					
❑ 5702	What a Way to Love/Misery Mansion	1964	5.00	10.00	20.00
❑ 5703	Man with the Blues/The Storm Has Just Begun	1964	5.00	10.00	20.00
CHALLENGE					
❑ 59280	I'm Talking About Love/I'm in Love with a Dancing Girl Working at Metropole	1965	3.75	7.50	15.00
COLUMBIA					
❑ AE7 1182 [DJ]	White Christmas/Blue Christmas	1979	6.25	12.50	25.00
—Green vinyl					
❑ AE7 1183 [DJ]	Pretty Paper/Rudolph the Red-Nosed Reindeer	1979	6.25	12.50	25.00
—Red vinyl					
❑ AE7 1775 [DJ]	Pretty Paper/White Christmas	1982	—	3.00	6.00
❑ 02000	Mona Lisa/Twinkle, Twinkle Little Star	1981	—	2.00	4.00
❑ 02166	On the Road Again/September Song	1981	—	—	3.00
—Reissue					
❑ 02187	I'm Gonna Sit Right Down and Write Myself a Letter/Over the Rainbow	1981	—	2.00	4.00
❑ 02558	Heartaches of a Fool/Uncloudy Day	1981	—	2.00	4.00
❑ 02741	Always on My Mind/The Party's Over	1982	—	2.00	4.00
❑ 03073	Let It Be Me/Permanently Lonely	1982	—	2.00	4.00
❑ 03123	Angel Flying Too Close to the Ground/Mona Lisa	1982	—	—	3.00
—Reissue					
❑ 03124	Heartache of a Fool/Midnight Rider	1982	—	—	3.00
—Reissue					
❑ 03385	Last Thing I Needed First Thing This Morning/Old Fords and a Natural Stone	1982	—	2.00	4.00
❑ 03476	Pretty Paper/White Christmas	1982	—	2.50	5.00
❑ 03674	Beer Barrel Polka/Little Old Fashioned Karma	1983	—	2.00	4.00
❑ 03965	Why Do I Have to Choose/Would You Lay with Me (In a Field of Stone)	1983	—	2.00	4.00
❑ 04217	To All the Girls I've Loved Before/I Don't Want to Wake You	1984	—	—	3.00
—Julio Iglesias & Willie Nelson; B-side by Julio Iglesias solo					
❑ 04217 [PS]	To All the Girls I've Loved Before/I Don't Want to Wake You	1984	—	2.50	5.00
—Julio Iglesias & Willie Nelson; first sleeve has artists' names in both capital and small letters					
❑ 04217 [PS]	To All the Girls I've Loved Before/I Don't Want to Wake You	1984	—	2.00	4.00
—Julio Iglesias & Willie Nelson; second sleeve has artists' names in all capital letters					
❑ 04263	Without a Song/I Can't Begin to Tell You	1983	—	—	3.00
❑ 04495	As Time Goes By/You'll Never Know	1984	6.25	12.50	25.00
—Willie Nelson and Julio Iglesias; withdrawn immediately upon release					
❑ 04495 [PS]	As Time Goes By/You'll Never Know	1984	6.25	12.50	25.00
—Willie Nelson and Julio Iglesias; withdrawn immediately upon release					
❑ 04568	City of New Orleans/Why Are You Pickin' On Me	1984	—	—	3.00
❑ 04568 [PS]	City of New Orleans/Why Are You Pickin' On Me	1984	—	2.00	4.00
❑ 04715	Seven Spanish Angels/Who Cares	1984	—	—	3.00
—A-side: Ray Charles and Willie Nelson; B-side: Ray Charles and Janie Frickie					
❑ 04847	Forgiving You Was Easy/You Wouldn't Cross the Street (To Say Goodbye)	1985	—	—	3.00
❑ 04881	Highwayman/The Human Condition	1985	—	—	3.00
—A-side: Willie Nelson/Waylon Jennings/Johnny Cash/Kris Kristofferson; B-side: Nelson, Cash					
❑ 04881 [PS]	Highwayman/The Human Condition	1985	—	2.00	4.00
—A-side: Willie Nelson/Waylon Jennings/Johnny Cash/Kris Kristofferson; B-side: Nelson, Cash					
❑ 05566	Are There Any More Real Cowboys/I'm a Memory	1985	—	—	3.00
—A-side with Neil Young					
❑ 05594	Desperadoes Waiting for a Train/The Twentieth Century Is Almost Over	1985	—	—	3.00
—A-side: Willie Nelson/Waylon Jennings/Johnny Cash/Kris Kristofferson; B-side: Nelson, Cash					
❑ 05597	Me and Paul/I Let My Mind Wander	1985	—	—	3.00
❑ 05677	Slow Movin' Outlaw/They All Went to Mexico	1985	—	—	3.00
—A-side with Lacy J. Dalton; B-side with Carlos Santana					
❑ 05749	I Told a Lie to My Heart/Slow Movin' Outlaw	1986	—	—	3.00
—A-side with Hank Williams, Jr.; B-side: with Lacy J. Dalton					
❑ 05834	Living in the Promiseland/Bach Minuet in G	1986	—	—	3.00
❑ 06246	I'm Not Trying to Forget You/I've Got the Craziest Feeling	1986	—	—	3.00
❑ 06530	Partners After All/Home Away from Home	1986	—	—	3.00
❑ 07007	Heart of Gold/So Much Like My Dad	1987	—	—	3.00
❑ 07202	Island in the Sun/There Is No Easy Way (But There Is a Way)	1987	—	—	3.00
❑ 07636	Nobody There But Me/Wake Me When It's Over	1987	—	—	3.00
❑ 08044	Spanish Eyes/Ole Buttermilk Sky	1988	—	—	3.00
—With Julio Iglesias					
❑ 08395	Living in the Promiseland/Forgiving You Was Easy	1988	—	—	3.00
—Reissue					
❑ 08406	Highwayman/Desperadoes Waiting for a Train	1988	—	—	3.00
—Waylon Jennings/Willie Nelson/Johnny Cash/Kris Kristofferson; reissue					
❑ 08541	Twilight Time/Ac-Cent-Tchu-Ate the Positive	1989	—	—	3.00
❑ 10176	Blue Eyes Cryin' in the Rain/Bandera	1975	—	2.50	5.00
❑ 10275	Remember Me/Time of the Preacher	1975	—	2.50	5.00
❑ 10327	I'd Have to Be Crazy/Amazing Grace	1976	—	2.50	5.00
❑ 10383	If You've Got the Money, I've Got the Time/The Sound in Your Mind	1976	—	2.50	5.00
❑ 10453	Uncloudy Day/Precious Memories	1976	—	2.50	5.00
❑ 10588	I Love You a Thousand Ways/Mom and Dad's Waltz	1977	—	2.50	5.00
❑ 10644	Something to Brag About/Anybody's Darlin' (Anybody But Mine)	1977	—	2.50	5.00
—With Mary Kay Place					
❑ 10704	Georgia on My Mind/On the Sunny Side of the Street	1978	—	2.50	5.00
❑ 10784	Blue Skies/Moonlight in Vermont	1978	—	2.50	5.00
❑ 10834	All of Me/Unchained Melody	1978	—	2.50	5.00
❑ 10877	Whiskey River/Under the Double Eagle	1978	—	2.50	5.00

Number	Title (A Side/B Side)	Yr	VG	VG+	NM
❑ 10929	September Song/Don't Get Around Much Anymore	1979	—	2.00	4.00
❑ 11126	Help Me Make It Through the Night/The Pilgrim: Chapter 33	1979	—	2.00	4.00
❑ 11186	My Heroes Have Always Been Cowboys/Rising Star (Love Theme)	1980	—	2.00	4.00
❑ 11257	Midnight Rider/Do You Think You're a Cowboy	1980	—	2.00	4.00
❑ 11351	On the Road Again/Jumpin' Cotton-Eyed Joe	1980	—	2.00	4.00
—B-side by Johnny Gimble					
❑ 11418	Angel Flying Too Close to the Ground/I Guess I've Come to Live Here in Your Eyes	1981	—	2.00	4.00
❑ 68923	Nothing I Can Do About It Now/If I Were a Painting	1989	—	—	3.00
❑ 73015	There You Are/Spirit	1989	—	—	3.00
❑ 73233	Silver Stallion/America Remains	1990	—	—	3.00
—Waylon Jennings/Willie Nelson/Johnny Cash/Kris Kristofferson					
❑ 73249	The Highway/Spirit	1990	—	—	3.00
❑ 73374	Is the Better Part Over/Mr. Record Man	1990	—	—	3.00
❑ 73381	Born and Raised in Black and White/Texas	1990	—	—	3.00
—The Highwaymen (Waylon Jennings/Willie Nelson/Johnny Cash/Kris Kristofferson)					
❑ 73518	It Ain't Necessarily So/I Never Cared for You	1990	—	—	3.00
❑ 73572	American Remains/Texas	1990	—	—	3.00
—The Highwaymen (Waylon Jennings/Willie Nelson/Johnny Cash/Kris Kristofferson)					
❑ 73655	The Piper Came Today/(I Don't Have a Reason) To Go to California Anymore	1991	—	—	3.00
❑ 73749	Ten with a Two/You Decide	1991	—	—	3.00
❑ 77184	Still Is Still Moving to Me/Valentine	1993	—	—	3.00
D					
❑ 1084	Man with the Blues/The Storm Has Just Begun	1959	7.50	15.00	30.00
❑ 1131	What a Way to Love/Misery Mansion	1960	7.50	15.00	30.00
ISLAND					
❑ 572414-7	The Maker/I Never Cared for You	1998	—	—	3.00
LIBERTY					
❑ S7-18486	It Is What It Is/The Devil's Right Hand	1995	—	—	3.00
—By The Highwaymen					
❑ S7-18584	One After 909/Yesterday	1995	—	—	3.00
—B-side by Billy Dean					
❑ 55155	Susie/No Dough	1958	6.25	12.50	25.00
❑ 55386	Mr. Record Man/The Part Where I Cry	1961	5.00	10.00	20.00
❑ 55403	Willingly/Chain of Love	1962	3.75	7.50	15.00
—A-side with Shirley Collie					
❑ 55439	Touch Me/Where My House Lives	1962	3.75	7.50	15.00
❑ 55468	You Dream About Me/Is This My Destiny	1962	3.75	7.50	15.00
—A-side with Shirley Collie					
❑ 55494	Wake Me When It's Over/There's Gonna Be Love in My House	1962	3.75	7.50	15.00
❑ 55532	Half a Man/The Last Letter	1963	3.00	6.00	12.00
❑ 55591	Take My Word/Feed It a Memory	1963	3.00	6.00	12.00
❑ 55638	How Long Is Forever/You Took My Happy Away	1963	3.00	6.00	12.00
❑ 55661	Am I Blue/There'll Be No Teardrops Tonight	1964	2.50	5.00	10.00
❑ 55697	River Boy/Opportunity to Cry	1964	2.50	5.00	10.00
❑ 56143	Right or Wrong/I Hope So	1969	—	3.00	6.00
LONE STAR					
❑ 703	The End of Understanding/Will You Remember Mine	1978	—	2.50	5.00
MONUMENT					
❑ 855	I Never Cared for You/You Left Me	1964	3.75	7.50	15.00
❑ 03408	Everything Is Beautiful (In Its Own Way)/Put It Off Until Tomorrow	1982	—	2.00	4.00
—A-side: Willie Nelson and Dolly Parton; B-side: Dolly Parton and Kris Kristofferson					
❑ 03781	You're Gonna Love Yourself (In the Morning)/ What Do You Think About Lovin'	1983	—	2.00	4.00
—A-side: Willie Nelson and Brenda Lee; B-side: Dolly Parton and Brenda Lee					
PARADISE					
❑ 629	Wabash Cannonball/Tennessee Waltz	1984	—	2.00	4.00
—A-side with Hank Wilson (a.k.a. Leon Russell); B-side by Wilson solo					
RCA					
❑ PB-10969	I'm a Memory/It Should Be Easier Now	1977	—	2.50	5.00
—With Darrell McCall					
❑ PB-11061	You Ought to Hear Me Cry/One in a Row	1977	—	2.50	5.00
❑ PB-11235	If You Can Touch Her at All/Rainy Day Blues	1978	—	2.50	5.00
❑ PB-11465	Sweet Memories/Little Things	1979	—	2.50	5.00
❑ PB-11673	Crazy Arms/Hurricane Shirley	1979	—	2.50	5.00
—B-side by Bobby Bare					
❑ GB-11995	Sweet Memories/If You Can Touch Her At All	1980	—	—	3.00
—Gold Standard Series					
❑ PB-12254	Good Times/Where Do You Stand	1981	—	2.00	4.00
❑ PB-12254 [PS]	Good Times/Where Do You Stand	1981	—	2.50	5.00
❑ PB-12328	Mountain Dew/Laying My Burdens Down	1981	—	2.00	4.00
RCA VICTOR					
❑ PB-10429	I'm a Memory/Fire and Rain	1975	—	2.50	5.00
❑ PB-10461	Pretty Paper/What a Merry Christmas This Could Be	1975	2.00	4.00	8.00
❑ PB-10591	Summer of Roses/I Gotta Get Drunk	1976	—	2.50	5.00
❑ 47-8484	Pretty Paper/What a Merry Christmas This Could Be	1964	3.75	7.50	15.00
❑ 47-8519	She's Not for You/Permanently Lonely	1965	3.00	6.00	12.00
❑ 47-8594	Healing Hands of Time/One Day at a Time	1965	3.00	6.00	12.00
❑ 47-8682	I Just Can't Let You Say Goodbye/And So Will You, My Love	1965	3.00	6.00	12.00
❑ 47-8801	Columbus Stockade Blues/He Sits at My Table	1966	3.00	6.00	12.00
❑ 47-8852	I'm Still Not Over You/I Love You Because	1966	3.00	6.00	12.00
❑ 47-8933	One in a Row/San Antonio Rose	1966	3.00	6.00	12.00
❑ 47-9029	Pretty Paper/What a Merry Christmas This Could Be	1966	3.00	6.00	12.00
❑ 47-9100	The Party's Over/Make Way for a Better Man	1967	2.50	5.00	10.00
❑ 47-9202	Blackjack County Chain/Some Other World	1967	2.50	5.00	10.00
❑ 47-9324	San Antonio/To Make a Long Story Short	1967	2.50	5.00	10.00
❑ 47-9427	Little Things/I'll Stay Around	1968	2.50	5.00	10.00
❑ 47-9536	Good Times/Don't You Ever Get Tired	1968	2.50	5.00	10.00
❑ 47-9605	Johnny One Time/She's Still Gone	1968	2.50	5.00	10.00
❑ 47-9684	Bring Me Sunshine/Don't Say Love or Nothing	1968	2.50	5.00	10.00
❑ 47-9778	Pretty Paper/What a Merry Christmas This Could Be	1969	—	—	—
—Unreleased					
❑ 47-9798	Who Do I Know in Dallas/Once More with Feeling	1969	2.00	4.00	8.00
❑ 47-9903	Laying My Burdens Down/Truth Number One	1970	2.00	4.00	8.00
❑ 47-9931	Pretty Paper/What a Merry Christmas This Could Be	1970	2.00	4.00	8.00
❑ 47-9951	I'm a Memory/I'm So Lonesome I Could Cry	1971	—	3.00	6.00
❑ 47-9984	Kneel at the Feet of Jesus/What Can You Do to Me Now	1971	—	3.00	6.00
❑ 74-0162	Jimmy's Road/Natural to Be Gone	1969	2.00	4.00	8.00
❑ 74-0542	Yesterday's Wine/Me and Paul	1971	—	3.00	6.00
❑ 74-0635	A Moment Isn't Very Long/Words Don't Fit the Picture	1972	—	3.00	6.00
❑ 74-0816	Mountain Dew/Phases, Stages, Circles, Cycles, and Scenes	1972	—	3.00	6.00
SARG					
❑ 260	A Storm Has Just Begun/When I Sang My Last Hillbilly Song	196?	12.50	25.00	50.00
—Some sources say this came out in 1955, but that doesn't coincide with this label's history					
SONGBIRD					
❑ 41313	Family Bible/In God's Eyes	1980	—	2.00	4.00
UNITED ARTISTS					
❑ 641	Night Life/Rainy Day Blues	1963	3.75	7.50	15.00
❑ XW771	The Last Letter/There Goes a Man	1976	—	2.50	5.00
❑ XW1165	Hello Walls/The Last Letter	1978	—	2.50	5.00
❑ XW1254	There'll Be Teardrops Tonight/Blue Must Be the Color of the Blues	1978	—	2.50	5.00
WILLIE NELSON					
❑ 628	No Place for Me/The Lumberjack	1957	75.00	150.00	300.00
Albums					
ALLEGIANCE					
❑ AV-5005	Willie or Won't He	1983	2.50	5.00	10.00
❑ AV-5010	Wild & Willie	1983	2.50	5.00	10.00
ATLANTIC					
❑ SD 7262	Shotgun Willie	1973	5.00	10.00	20.00
❑ SD 7291	Phases and Stages	1974	5.00	10.00	20.00
COLUMBIA					
❑ PC 33482	Red Headed Stranger	1975	3.75	7.50	15.00
—No bar code on back cover					
❑ PC 33482	Red Headed Stranger	1979	2.00	4.00	8.00
—With bar code on back cover; budget-line reissue					
❑ PC 34092	The Sound in Your Mind	1976	3.00	6.00	12.00
—No bar code on back cover					
❑ PC 34092	The Sound in Your Mind	1979	2.00	4.00	8.00
—With bar code on back cover; budget-line reissue					
❑ PC 34112	The Troublemaker	1976	3.00	6.00	12.00
—No bar code on back cover					
❑ PC 34112	The Troublemaker	1979	2.00	4.00	8.00
—With bar code on back cover; budget-line reissue					
❑ JC 34695	To Lefty From Willie	1977	3.00	6.00	12.00
❑ PC 34695	To Lefty From Willie	1979	2.00	4.00	8.00
—Budget-line reissue					
❑ JC 35305	Stardust	1978	2.50	5.00	10.00
❑ KC2 35642 [(2)]	Willie and Family Live	1978	3.75	7.50	15.00
❑ JC 36188	Willie Nelson Sings Kristofferson	1979	2.50	5.00	10.00
❑ PC 36188	Willie Nelson Sings Kristofferson	1980	2.00	4.00	8.00
—Budget-line reissue					
❑ JC 36189	Pretty Paper	1979	2.50	5.00	10.00
❑ JS 36327	The Electric Horseman	1979	2.50	5.00	10.00
—Side 2 by Dave Grusin					
❑ S2 36752 [(2)]	Honeysuckle Rose	1980	3.00	6.00	12.00
—Over half of the LP is by Willie					
❑ FC 36883	Somewhere Over the Rainbow	1981	2.50	5.00	10.00
❑ KC2 37542 [(2)]	Willie Nelson's Greatest Hits (& Some That Will Be)	1981	3.00	6.00	12.00
❑ FC 37951	Always on My Mind	1982	2.50	5.00	10.00
❑ PC 37951	Always on My Mind	1984	2.00	4.00	8.00
—Budget-line reissue					
❑ PC 38248	Tougher Than Leather	1984	2.00	4.00	8.00
—Budget-line reissue					
❑ QC 38248	Tougher Than Leather	1983	2.50	5.00	10.00
❑ CX 38250 [(10)]	Willie Nelson	1983	30.00	60.00	120.00
❑ FC 39110	Without a Song	1983	2.50	5.00	10.00
❑ PC 39110	Without a Song	1984	2.00	4.00	8.00
—Budget-line reissue					
❑ FC 39145	City of New Orleans	1984	2.50	5.00	10.00
❑ PC 39145	City of New Orleans	1985	2.00	4.00	8.00
—Budget-line reissue					
❑ FC 39363	Angel Eyes	1984	2.50	5.00	10.00
❑ PC 39363	Angel Eyes	1985	2.00	4.00	8.00
—Budget-line reissue					
❑ FC 39894	Partners	1986	2.50	5.00	10.00
❑ PC 39894	Partners	1987	2.00	4.00	8.00
—Budget-line reissue					
❑ 9C9 39943 [PD]	Always on My Mind	1985	5.00	10.00	20.00
❑ FC 39990	Half Nelson	1985	2.50	5.00	10.00
—Duets with 10 different artists					

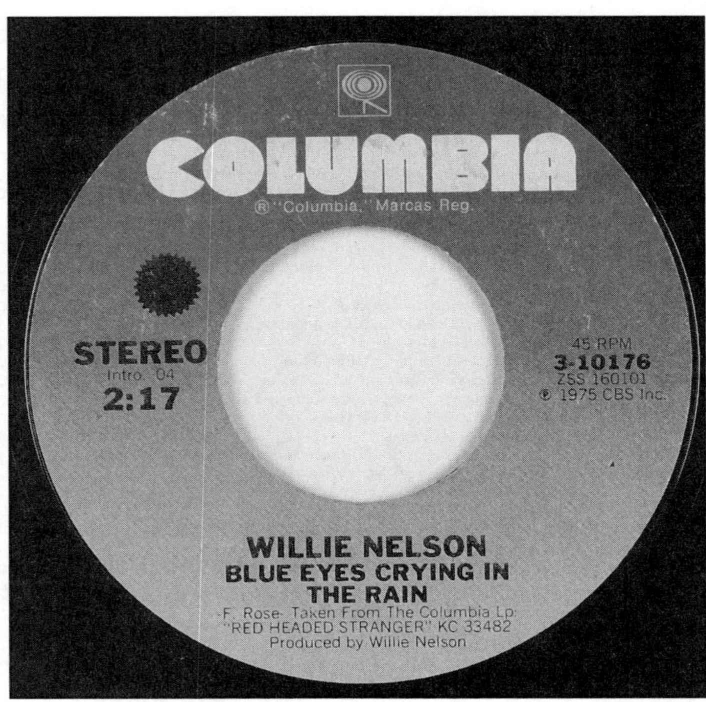

Willie Nelson originally worked within the Nashville establishment as a songwriter. But, unable to have sustained success as a singer, he left the city, and finally became big once he did. (Top left) Nelson made one 45 for the Monument label in 1964, "I Never Cared for You." His producer was Fred Foster, who crafted Roy Orbison's biggest hits, but he was unable to work his magic on Willie. (Top right) When Nelson finally started to make the charts consistently, one of the greatest ironies is that many of his biggest hits were written by others! His first No. 1 record was the 1975 version of "Blue Eyes Cryin' in the Rain." (Bottom left) In 1984, Willie did a version of Steve Goodman's "City of New Orleans." Not long after Goodman died of leukemia, this version hit the top of the country charts. (Bottom right) One of the great supergroups in country music history was Willie, Waylon Jennings, Kris Kristofferson and Johnny Cash. They teamed up for the one-off single "Highwayman," a Jim Webb song. When it became a success, the foursome made three albums' worth of material, and eventually became known as "The Highwaymen" after the hit song.

Number	Title (A Side/B Side)	Yr	VG	VG+	NM
❑ PC 39990	Half Nelson	1986	2.00	4.00	8.00
—Budget-line reissue					
❑ FC 40008	Me and Paul	1985	2.50	5.00	10.00
❑ PC 40008	Me and Paul	1986	2.00	4.00	8.00
—Budget-line reissue					
❑ FC 40327	The Promiseland	1986	2.50	5.00	10.00
❑ FC 40487	Island in the Sea	1987	2.50	5.00	10.00
❑ HC 43482	Red Headed Stranger	1982	10.00	20.00	40.00
—Half-speed mastered edition					
❑ FC 44431	What a Wonderful World	1988	2.50	5.00	10.00
❑ FC 45046	A Horse Called Music	1989	2.50	5.00	10.00
❑ HC 45305	Stardust	1981	17.50	35.00	70.00
—Half-speed mastered edition					
❑ HC 47951	Always on My Mind	1982	12.50	25.00	50.00
—Half-speed mastered edition					
❑ HC 48248	Tougher Than Leather	1983	12.50	25.00	50.00
—Half-speed mastered edition					
HEARTLAND					
❑ HL 1038/9 [(2)]	The Best of Willie Nelson	1987	3.75	7.50	15.00
LIBERTY					
❑ LRP-3239 [M]	...And Then I Wrote	1962	10.00	20.00	40.00
❑ LRP-3308 [M]	Here's Willie Nelson	1963	10.00	20.00	40.00
❑ LST-7239 [S]	...And Then I Wrote	1962	12.50	25.00	50.00
❑ LST-7308 [S]	Here's Willie Nelson	1963	12.50	25.00	50.00
❑ LN-10013	Country Willie	1980	2.00	4.00	8.00
—Budget-line reissue					
❑ LN-10118	The Best of Willie Nelson	1982	2.00	4.00	8.00
—Budget-line reissue					
PAIR					
❑ PDL2-1007 [(2)]	Country Winners	1986	3.00	6.00	12.00
❑ PDL2-1032 [(2)]	Once More with Feeling	1986	3.00	6.00	12.00
❑ PDL2-1114 [(2)]	Good Hearted Woman	1986	3.00	6.00	12.00
PICKWICK					
❑ ACL1-0326	Country Winners	1976	2.00	4.00	8.00
❑ ACL1-0705	Spotlight on Willie Nelson	1976	2.00	4.00	8.00
❑ SPC-3584	Hello Walls	197?	2.50	5.00	10.00
❑ ACL1-7018	Columbus Stockade Blues	1976	2.00	4.00	8.00
RCA CAMDEN					
❑ ACL1-0326	Country Winners	1973	3.00	6.00	12.00
❑ ACL1-705	Spotlight on Willie Nelson	1974	3.00	6.00	12.00
❑ CAS-2444	Columbus Stockade Blues	1970	3.75	7.50	15.00
❑ ACL1-7018	Columbus Stockade Blues	1975	2.50	5.00	10.00
RCA VICTOR					
❑ ANL1-1102	Yesterday's Wine	1975	2.50	5.00	10.00
❑ APL1-1234	What Can You Do to Me Now	1975	3.00	6.00	12.00
❑ APL1-1487	Willie Nelson Live	1976	3.00	6.00	12.00
❑ APL1-2210	Before His Time	1977	2.50	5.00	10.00
❑ AHL1-3243	Sweet Memories	1979	2.50	5.00	10.00
❑ LPM-3418 [M]	Country Willie — His Own Songs	1965	5.00	10.00	20.00
❑ LSP-3418 [S]	Country Willie — His Own Songs	1965	6.25	12.50	25.00
❑ LPM-3528 [M]	Country Favorites, Willie Nelson Style	1966	5.00	10.00	20.00
❑ LSP-3528 [S]	Country Favorites, Willie Nelson Style	1966	6.25	12.50	25.00
❑ AHL1-3549	Danny Davis & Willie Nelson with the Nashville Brass	1980	2.50	5.00	10.00
❑ LPM-3659 [M]	Country Music Concert	1966	5.00	10.00	20.00
❑ LSP-3659 [S]	Country Music Concert	1966	6.25	12.50	25.00
❑ AYL1-3671	Before His Time	1980	2.00	4.00	8.00
—"Best Buy Series" reissue					
❑ LPM-3748 [M]	Make Way for Willie Nelson	1967	5.00	10.00	20.00
❑ LSP-3748 [S]	Make Way for Willie Nelson	1967	6.25	12.50	25.00
❑ AYL1-3800	Yesterday's Wine	1980	2.00	4.00	8.00
—"Best Buy Series" reissue					
❑ LPM-3858 [M]	The Party's Over and Other Great Willie Nelson Songs	1967	6.25	12.50	25.00
❑ LSP-3858 [S]	The Party's Over and Other Great Willie Nelson Songs	1967	5.00	10.00	20.00
❑ LPM-3937 [M]	Texas in My Soul	1968	25.00	50.00	100.00
❑ LSP-3937 [S]	Texas in My Soul	1968	5.00	10.00	20.00
❑ AYL1-3958	What Can You Do to Me Now	1981	2.00	4.00	8.00
—"Best Buy Series" reissue					
❑ AHL1-4045	The Minstrel Man	1981	2.50	5.00	10.00
❑ LSP-4057	Good Times	1968	5.00	10.00	20.00
❑ LSP-4111	My Own Peculiar Way	1969	5.00	10.00	20.00
❑ AYL1-4165	Willie Nelson Live	1981	2.00	4.00	8.00
—"Best Buy Series" reissue					
❑ LSP-4294	Both Sides Now	1970	5.00	10.00	20.00
❑ AYL1-4300	Sweet Memories	1982	2.00	4.00	8.00
—"Best Buy Series" reissue					
❑ LSP-4404	Laying My Burdens Down	1970	5.00	10.00	20.00
❑ AHL1-4420	The Best of Willie Nelson	1982	2.50	5.00	10.00
❑ LSP-4489	Willie Nelson & Family	1971	5.00	10.00	20.00
❑ LSP-4568	Yesterday's Wine	1971	5.00	10.00	20.00
❑ LSP-4653	The Picture	1972	5.00	10.00	20.00
❑ LSP-4760	The Willie Way	1972	5.00	10.00	20.00
❑ AHL1-4819	My Own Way	1983	2.50	5.00	10.00
❑ AYL1-5143	The Best of Willie Nelson	1984	2.00	4.00	8.00
—"Best Buy Series" reissue					
❑ CPL1-5174	Don't You Ever Get Tired of Hurting Me	1984	2.50	5.00	10.00
❑ AYL1-5438	My Own Way	1985	2.00	4.00	8.00
—"Best Buy Series" reissue					
❑ AHL1-5470	Collector's Series	1985	2.50	5.00	10.00
❑ CPL1-7158	Willie	1986	2.50	5.00	10.00
SONGBIRD					
❑ 3258	Family Bible	1980	2.50	5.00	10.00
SUNSET					
❑ SUM-1138 [M]	Hello Walls	1966	3.75	7.50	15.00
❑ SUS-5138 [S]	Hello Walls	1966	5.00	10.00	20.00
TAKOMA					
❑ TAK-7104	The Legend Begins	1983	2.50	5.00	10.00
TIME-LIFE					
❑ P 16946 [(3)]	Country and Western Classics	1983	5.00	10.00	20.00
UNITED ARTISTS					
❑ UA-LA086-E	The Best of Willie Nelson	1973	3.75	7.50	15.00
—Reissue of Liberty tracks					
❑ UA-LA410-G	Country Willie	1975	3.75	7.50	15.00
❑ UA-LA574-H2 [(2)]	Texas Country	1975	4.50	9.00	18.00
❑ UA-LA930-G	There'll Be No Teardrops Tonight	1978	3.75	7.50	15.00

NELSON, WILLIE, AND KRIS KRISTOFFERSON

Also see each artist's individual listings.

Number	Title (A Side/B Side)	Yr	VG	VG+	NM
45s					
COLUMBIA					
❑ 38-04652	How Do You Feel About Foolin' Around/Eye of the Storm	1984	—	—	3.00
Albums					
COLUMBIA					
❑ FC 39531	Music from Songwriter	1984	2.50	5.00	10.00

NELSON, WILLIE, AND ROGER MILLER

Also see each artist's individual listings.

Number	Title (A Side/B Side)	Yr	VG	VG+	NM
45s					
COLUMBIA					
❑ 02681	Old Friends/When a House Is Not a Home	1982	—	2.00	4.00
—With Ray Price					
Albums					
COLUMBIA					
❑ FC 38013	Old Friends	1982	2.50	5.00	10.00
❑ PC 38013	Old Friends	198?	2.00	4.00	8.00
—Budget-line reissue					

NELSON, WILLIE, AND WEBB PIERCE

Also see each artist's individual listings.

Number	Title (A Side/B Side)	Yr	VG	VG+	NM
45s					
COLUMBIA					
❑ 03231	In the Jailhouse Now/Back Street Affair	1982	—	2.00	4.00
Albums					
COLUMBIA					
❑ FC 38095	In the Jailhouse Now	1982	2.50	5.00	10.00
❑ PC 38095	In the Jailhouse Now	198?	2.00	4.00	8.00
—Budget-line reissue					

NELSON, WILLIE, AND RAY PRICE

Also see each artist's individual listings.

Number	Title (A Side/B Side)	Yr	VG	VG+	NM
45s					
COLUMBIA					
❑ 11329	Faded Love/This Cold World with You	1980	—	2.00	4.00
❑ 11405	Don't You Ever Get Tired (Of Loving Me)/Funny How Time Slips Away	1980	—	2.00	4.00
Albums					
COLUMBIA					
❑ JC 36476	San Antonio Rose	1980	2.50	5.00	10.00
❑ PC 36476	San Antonio Rose	198?	2.00	4.00	8.00
—Budget-line reissue					

NELSON, WILLIE, AND LEON RUSSELL

Also see each artist's individual listings.

Number	Title (A Side/B Side)	Yr	VG	VG+	NM
45s					
COLUMBIA					
❑ 11023	Heartbreak Hotel/Sioux City Sue	1979	—	2.00	4.00
❑ 11119	Trouble in Mind/One for My Baby (And One More for the Road)	1979	—	2.00	4.00
Albums					
COLUMBIA					
❑ KC2 36064 [(2)]	One for the Road	1979	3.75	7.50	15.00

NELSON, WILLIE, AND HANK SNOW

Number	Title (A Side/B Side)	Yr	VG	VG+	NM
Albums					
COLUMBIA					
❑ FC 39977	Brand on My Heart	1984	2.50	5.00	10.00
❑ PC 39977	Brand on My Heart	1985	2.00	4.00	8.00
—Budget-line reissue					

NELSON, WILLIE, AND FARON YOUNG

Number	Title (A Side/B Side)	Yr	VG	VG+	NM
Albums					
COLUMBIA					
❑ FC 39484	Funny How Time Slips Away	1984	2.50	5.00	10.00
❑ PC 39484	Funny How Time Slips Away	1985	2.00	4.00	8.00
—Budget-line reissue					

NESBITT, JIM

Number	Title (A Side/B Side)	Yr	VG	VG+	NM
45s					
ACE					
❑ 621	Please Mr. Kennedy/The Horse Race	1961	5.00	10.00	20.00
CAPRICORN					
❑ 0236	Shaving Cream/Suck It Up Suds	1975	—	3.00	6.00
CHART					
❑ 1008	Quittin' Time/So Many Times	1967	2.00	4.00	8.00

Number	Title (A Side/B Side)	Yr	VG	VG+	NM
❑ 1018	Truck Drivin' Cat with Nine Wives/Social Security	1968	2.00	4.00	8.00
❑ 1043	Clean the Slate in '68/The Husband Is the Last to Know	1968	2.00	4.00	8.00
❑ 1055	Living the Life of Riley/Six Broken Hearts	1968	2.00	4.00	8.00
❑ 1065	Looking for More in '64/Cry Me a River	1964	2.00	4.00	8.00
❑ 1100	Mother-in-Law/If You Don't Love Me	1964	2.00	4.00	8.00
❑ 1165	A Tiger in My Tank/I Can't Stand This Living Alone	1965	2.00	4.00	8.00
❑ 1200	Still Alive in '65/I Laughed When You Said You Were Leaving	1965	2.00	4.00	8.00
❑ 1240	The Friendly Undertaker/Crying and Waiting for You	1965	2.00	4.00	8.00
❑ 1290	You Better Watch Your Friend/You're No Good	1965	2.00	4.00	8.00
❑ 1320	She Didn't Come Home/Working All My Life	1966	2.00	4.00	8.00
❑ 1350	Heck of a Fix in '66/I'm from the Country	1966	2.00	4.00	8.00
❑ 1410	Stranded/These Modern Things	1966	2.00	4.00	8.00
❑ 1445	Husbands-in-Law/I Want to Have My Operation on TV	1967	2.00	4.00	8.00
❑ 5004	I'm Yeller/If You See My Brother	1969	2.00	4.00	8.00
❑ 5023	It's Great to Stay in the U.S.A./Intoxicated, Frustrated Me	1969	2.00	4.00	8.00
❑ 5052	Runnin' Bare/A Good Woman Is Hard to Find	1970	2.00	4.00	8.00
❑ 5070	My Old Drinking Friends/When They Sent My Old Lady to the Moon	1970	2.00	4.00	8.00
❑ 5096	Pollution/Spiro	1970	2.00	4.00	8.00
❑ 5112	I Love Them Old Nasty Cigarettes/Nice Guys Always Finish Last	1971	2.00	4.00	8.00
❑ 5131	Having Fun in '71/Here Today and Here Tomorrow	1971	2.00	4.00	8.00
❑ 5150	Going Home to Die/I Am a Married Man	1972	2.00	4.00	8.00
DOT					
❑ 16197	Please Mr. Kennedy/The Horse Race	1961	3.00	6.00	12.00
❑ 16424	Livin' Offa Credit/I'm a Married Man	1963	3.00	6.00	12.00
SCORPION					
❑ 0500	Phone Call from the Devil/Drop in the Bucket	1975	—	3.00	6.00
❑ 0505	The Short Sheriff/Overseas by Mail	1976	—	2.50	5.00
❑ 0513	Twenty Years and Holding/Run for a Life	1976	—	2.50	5.00
—With Tammy Haney					
SMASH					
❑ 1746	New Frontier/Mother-in-Law	1962	3.75	7.50	15.00

Albums

CHART

Number	Title	Yr	VG	VG+	NM
❑ CHM-1005 [M]	Truck Drivin' Cat with Nine Wives	1968	7.50	15.00	30.00
❑ CHS-1005 [S]	Truck Drivin' Cat with Nine Wives	1968	5.00	10.00	20.00
❑ CHS-1031	Runnin' Bare	1970	5.00	10.00	20.00

NESMITH, MICHAEL

45s

Number	Title (A Side/B Side)	Yr	VG	VG+	NM
COLPIX					
❑ 787	The New Recruit/A Journey	1965	37.50	75.00	150.00
—As "Michael Blessing"					
❑ 792	Until It's Time for You to Go/What's the Trouble, Officer	1965	37.50	75.00	150.00
—As "Michael Blessing"					
EDAN					
❑ 1001	Just a Little Love/Curson Terrace	1965	30.00	60.00	120.00
PACIFIC ARTS					
❑ 084	Life, the Unsuspecting Captive/Rio	1977	2.00	4.00	8.00
❑ 101	Roll with the Flow/I've Just Begun to Care	1978	—	3.00	6.00
❑ 104	Casablanca Moonlight/Rio	1978	—	3.00	6.00
❑ 104 [PS]	Casablanca Moonlight/Rio	1978	3.00	6.00	12.00
❑ 106	Magic (This Night Is Magic)/Dance	1979	—	3.00	6.00
❑ 108	Cruisin'/Horserace	1979	—	3.00	6.00
❑ 6373	Life, the Unsuspecting Captive/Rio	1976	2.50	5.00	10.00
❑ 6398	Navajo Trail/Love's First Kiss	1976	2.50	5.00	10.00
RCA VICTOR					
❑ 47-9853	Rose City Chimes/Little Red Rider	1970	2.50	5.00	10.00
❑ 74-0368	Joanne/One Rose	1970	3.00	6.00	12.00
❑ 74-0399	Silver Moon/Lady of the Valley	1970	2.50	5.00	10.00
❑ 74-0453	Nevada Fighter/Here I Am	1971	2.00	4.00	8.00
❑ 74-0453 [PS]	Nevada Fighter/Here I Am	1971	5.00	10.00	20.00
❑ 74-0491	Tumbling Tumbleweeds/Texas Morning	1971	2.00	4.00	8.00
❑ 74-0540	Only Bound/Propinquity	1971	2.00	4.00	8.00
❑ 74-0629	Lazy Lady/Mama Rocker	1971	2.00	4.00	8.00
❑ 74-0804	Roll with the Flow/Keep On	1972	2.00	4.00	8.00

Albums

Number	Title	Yr	VG	VG+	NM
PACIFIC ARTS					
❑ 11-101A	The Prison	1975	12.50	25.00	50.00
—Boxed set with booklet					
❑ 7-101	The Prison	197?	5.00	10.00	20.00
—Standard cover					
❑ 7-106	Compilation	1976	5.00	10.00	20.00
❑ 7-107	From a Radio Engine to the Photon Wing	1977	5.00	10.00	20.00
❑ 7-116	And the Hits Just Keep On Comin'	1978	5.00	10.00	20.00
—Reissue of RCA 4695					
❑ 7-117	Pretty Much Your Standard Ranch Stash	1978	5.00	10.00	20.00
—Reissue of RCA APL1-0164					
❑ 7-118	Live at the Palais	1978	5.00	10.00	20.00
❑ 7-130	Infinite Rider on the Big Dogma	1979	5.00	10.00	20.00
❑ (no #) [DJ]	The Michael Nesmith Radio Special	1979	10.00	20.00	40.00
RCA VICTOR					
❑ APL1-0164	Pretty Much Your Standard Ranch Stash	1973	6.25	12.50	25.00
❑ LSP-4371	Magnetic South	1970	7.50	15.00	30.00
❑ LSP-4415	Loose Salute	1970	7.50	15.00	30.00
❑ LSP-4497	Nevada Fighter	1971	6.25	12.50	25.00
❑ LSP-4563	Tantamount to Treason	1971	6.25	12.50	25.00
❑ LSP-4695	And the Hits Just Keep On Comin'	1972	6.25	12.50	25.00
RHINO					
❑ R1-70168	The Newer Stuff	1989	3.00	6.00	12.00

NETTLES, BILL

45s

Number	Title (A Side/B Side)	Yr	VG	VG+	NM
MERCURY					
❑ 6350	Smiles Won't Hide an Achin' Heart/Long Road to Travel	1951	7.50	15.00	30.00
STARDAY					
❑ 174	Wine-O Boogie/Gumbo Mumbo	1955	25.00	50.00	100.00

Selected 78s

Number	Title (A Side/B Side)	Yr	VG	VG+	NM
BULLET					
❑ 637	High Falutin' Mama/Too Many Blues	194?	6.25	12.50	25.00
IMPERIAL					
❑ 8032	Ain't No Telling What a Woman Will Do/The Same Thing Could Happen to You	194?	6.25	12.50	25.00
❑ 8039	Tear Drops/Somebody's Darling	194?	6.25	12.50	25.00
MERCURY					
❑ 6190	Hadacol Boogie/I'm Footloose Now	1949	5.00	10.00	20.00
❑ 6209	Why Don't You Haul Off and Love Me/Do Right Daddy	1949	5.00	10.00	20.00
❑ 6249	I Hauled Off and Loved Her/Life's Road of Sorrow	1950	5.00	10.00	20.00
VOCALION					
❑ 03634	My Cross-Eyed Nancy Jane/(B-side unknown)	1938	5.00	10.00	20.00
❑ 03662	No Daddy Blues/(B-side unknown)	1938	5.00	10.00	20.00

NEVILLE, AARON

The well-known New Orleans singer is generally not a country artist, but the below records are (and the first one even charted).

45s

Number	Title (A Side/B Side)	Yr	VG	VG+	NM
A&M					
❑ 31458 0312 7	The Grand Tour/Don't Take Away My Heaven	1993	—	2.00	4.00
❑ 31458 0442 7	Please Come Home for Christmas/Louisiana Christmas Day	1993	—	2.50	5.00
❑ 31458 1112 7	For the Good Times/Crying in the Chapel	1995	—	2.00	4.00

NEVILLE, AARON, AND TRISHA YEARWOOD

Also see each artist's individual listings.

45s

Number	Title (A Side/B Side)	Yr	VG	VG+	NM
MCA					
❑ 54836	I Fall to Pieces/(Instrumental)	1994	—	2.00	4.00

NEW GRASS REVIVAL

45s

Number	Title (A Side/B Side)	Yr	VG	VG+	NM
CAPITOL					
❑ B-44078	Unconditional Love/I Can Talk to You	1987	—	—	3.00
❑ B-44128	Can't Stop Now/I Can Talk to You	1988	—	—	3.00
❑ B-44357	Callin' Baton Rouge/Let Me Be Your Man	1989	—	2.50	5.00
❑ B-44451	You Plant Your Fields/Friday Night in America	1989	—	2.00	4.00
❑ 7PRO-79790	You Plant Your Fields (same on both sides)	1989	—	2.50	5.00
—Promo; later issued as stock copy on 44453					
EMI AMERICA					
❑ B-8329	What You Do to Me/Sweet Release	1986	—	2.00	4.00
❑ B-8347	Ain't That Peculiar/Seven by Seven	1986	—	2.00	4.00
STARDAY					
❑ 965	Great Balls of Fire/I Wish I Said	1972	2.50	5.00	10.00
❑ 974	Prince of Peace/(B-side unknown)	1973	2.50	5.00	10.00

Albums

Number	Title	Yr	VG	VG+	NM
CAPITOL					
❑ C1-90739	Friday Night in America	1989	3.00	6.00	12.00
EMI AMERICA					
❑ ST-17216	New Grass Revival	1986	2.50	5.00	10.00
FLYING FISH					
❑ FF-016	Fly Through the Country	1975	3.75	7.50	15.00
❑ FF-032	When the Storm Is Over	1976	3.75	7.50	15.00
❑ FF-050	Too Late to Turn Back	1977	3.75	7.50	15.00
❑ FF-083	Barren County	1979	3.75	7.50	15.00
❑ FF-254	Commonwealth	198?	3.00	6.00	12.00
STARDAY					
❑ SLP-482	New Grass Revival	1973	3.75	7.50	15.00
SUGAR HILL					
❑ SH-3745	On the Boulevard	198?	2.50	5.00	10.00
❑ SH-3771	Live!	1989	3.00	6.00	12.00

NEWBURY, MICKEY

45s

Number	Title (A Side/B Side)	Yr	VG	VG+	NM
ABC HICKORY					
❑ 54006	Hand Me Another of Those/Leavin' Kentucky	1977	—	2.50	5.00
❑ 54015	Makes Me Wonder If I Ever Said Goodbye/Shenandoah	1977	—	2.50	5.00
❑ 54025	Gone to Alabama/Westphalia Texas Blues	1978	—	2.50	5.00
❑ 54034	It Don't Matter Anymore/Wish I Was	1978	—	2.50	5.00
❑ 54042	Looking for the Sunshine/A Weed Is a Weed	1979	—	2.50	5.00
AIRBORNE					
❑ 10005	An American Trilogy/San Francisco Mabel Joy	1988	—	2.50	5.00
ELEKTRA					
❑ 45206	You Only Live Once (In a While)/Baby's Not Home	1974	—	2.50	5.00
❑ 45238	Lovers/Good Night	1975	—	2.50	5.00
❑ 45256	Sail Away/If You Ever Get to Houston	1975	—	2.50	5.00
❑ 45329	An American Trilogy/Sunshine	1976	—	2.50	5.00
❑ 45750	An American Trilogy/San Francisco Mable Joy	1971	2.50	5.00	10.00
❑ 45771	Mobile Blue/Frisco Depot	1972	—	3.00	6.00

Number	Title (A Side/B Side)	Yr	VG	VG+	NM
❑ 45789	How I Love Them Old Songs/Remember the Good	1972	—	3.00	6.00
❑ 45840	Heaven Help the Child/Good Morning Dear	1973	—	2.50	5.00
❑ 45853	Sunshine/Song for Susan	1973	—	2.50	5.00
❑ 45889	If I Could Be/Love Look	1974	—	2.50	5.00
HICKORY					
❑ 1312	Lonely Place/Well I Did (Last Night)	1965	2.50	5.00	10.00
❑ 1344	There Is a Time to Die/Travelin' Man	1965	2.50	5.00	10.00
❑ 1370	Anyway You Want Me/(It May Not Take) Too Much	1966	2.50	5.00	10.00
❑ 1419	After the Rains/Baby Just Said Goodbye	1966	2.50	5.00	10.00
❑ 1463	Dreamin' in the Rain/Leavin' Makes the Rain Come Down	1967	2.50	5.00	10.00
❑ 1673	America the Beautiful/Freedom	1980	—	2.50	5.00
MCA					
❑ 41032	Blue Sky Shinin'/Darlin' Take Care of Yourself	1979	—	2.50	5.00
MERCURY					
❑ 57061	Country Boy Saturday Night/Let's Say Goodbye One More Time	1981	—	2.50	5.00
❑ 72975	Ten Tottle Tommy/San Francisco Mable Joy	1969	—	3.50	7.00
❑ 73036	Sunshine/Sad Satin Rhyme	1970	—	3.50	7.00
RCA VICTOR					
❑ 47-9570	Weeping Annaleah/Are My Thoughts with You	1968	2.00	4.00	8.00
❑ 47-9632	Got Down on Saturday/Sweet Memories	1968	2.00	4.00	8.00
❑ 47-9690	Organized Noise/The Queen	1968	2.00	4.00	8.00
Albums					
ABC HICKORY					
❑ HA-44002	Rusty Tracks	1977	2.50	5.00	10.00
❑ HA-44011	Eye on the Sparrow	1978	2.50	5.00	10.00
❑ HB-44017	The Sailor	1979	2.50	5.00	10.00
ELEKTRA					
❑ 7E-1007	I Came to Hear the Music	1974	2.50	5.00	10.00
❑ 7E-1030	Lovers	1975	2.50	5.00	10.00
❑ EQ-4107 [Q]	'Frisco Mabel Joy	1974	5.00	10.00	20.00
❑ EKS-74107	'Frisco Mabel Joy	1971	2.50	5.00	10.00
❑ EKS-75055	Heaven Help the Child	1973	2.50	5.00	10.00
MCA					
❑ 802 *—Reissue*	Rusty Tracks	198?	2.00	4.00	8.00
❑ 803 *—Reissue*	Eye on the Sparrow	198?	2.00	4.00	8.00
❑ 804 *—Reissue*	The Sailor	198?	2.00	4.00	8.00
❑ 945	Sweet Memories	1885	2.50	5.00	10.00
MERCURY					
❑ SR 61236	Looks Like Rain	1969	3.75	7.50	15.00
RCA VICTOR					
❑ LSP-4043	Harlequin Melodies	1968	3.75	7.50	15.00

NEWMAN, JACK

45s

Number	Title (A Side/B Side)	Yr	VG	VG+	NM
TNT					
❑ 160	After Night Falls/Sirens in the Distance	1959	6.25	12.50	25.00
❑ 170	House of Blue Lovers/I Didn't Think This Could Happen to Me	1959	7.50	15.00	30.00
❑ 178	I Just Can't Stand These Blues/I Could Be the One	1959	6.25	12.50	25.00
❑ 179	Candy Town/Bronco Buster	1959	6.25	12.50	25.00
❑ 183	Make Room for One More/Out in the World Alone	1960	6.25	12.50	25.00

NEWMAN, JIMMY

Also recorded as "Jimmy C. Newman" and "Jimmy 'C' Newman" (the "C" stands for "Cajun").

45s

Number	Title (A Side/B Side)	Yr	VG	VG+	NM
DECCA					
❑ 31217	Everybody's Dying for Love/Just One More Night (With You)	1961	2.50	5.00	10.00
❑ 31281	Big Mamou/Finally	1961	2.50	5.00	10.00
❑ 31324	Alligator Man/Give Me Heaven	1961	2.50	5.00	10.00
❑ 31374	Crazy Old Heart/Of All the Things (You Left)	1962	2.50	5.00	10.00
❑ 31416	After Dark Affair/You Must Be True	1962	2.50	5.00	10.00
❑ 31440	Bayou Talk/I May Fall Again	1962	2.50	5.00	10.00
❑ 31503	Already I'm Falling/Everything	1963	2.50	5.00	10.00
❑ 31553	D.J. for a Day/The Mover	1963	2.50	5.00	10.00
❑ 31609	Angel on Leave/Summer Skies and Golden Sands	1964	2.00	4.00	8.00
❑ 31677	You're Still on My Mind/Sue May Sun	1964	2.00	4.00	8.00
❑ 31745	Back in Circulation/City of the Angels	1965	2.00	4.00	8.00
❑ 31841	Artificial Rose/My Love for You	1965	2.00	4.00	8.00
❑ 31916	Back Pocket Money/For Better or For Worse	1966	2.00	4.00	8.00
❑ 31994	Bring Your Heart Home/Unwanted Feeling	1966	2.00	4.00	8.00
❑ 32067	Dropping Out of Sight/We Lose a Little Ground	1966	2.00	4.00	8.00
❑ 32130	Louisiana Saturday Night/Gentleman Loafer	1967	—	3.00	6.00
❑ 32202	Blue Lonely Winter/The Devil Was Laughing at Me	1967	—	3.00	6.00
❑ 32285	Sunshine and Bluebirds/I'm Sorry Letters	1968	—	3.00	6.00
❑ 32366	Born to Love You/Carmelita	1968	—	3.00	6.00
❑ 32440	Future Farmers of America/My Prayer for Today	1969	—	3.00	6.00
❑ 32484	Boo Dan/Surrounded by Your Love	1969	—	3.00	6.00
❑ 32549	Three/There'll Always Be a Song	1969	—	3.00	6.00
❑ 32609	Foolishly/Lousiana Dirty Rice	1970	—	3.00	6.00
❑ 32668	Be Proud of Your Man/Washington, D.C.	1970	—	3.00	6.00
❑ 32740	I'm Holding Your Memory (But He's Holding You)/ It'll Take a Lot Out of You	1970	—	3.00	6.00
❑ 32805	Is It Really Over/As Long As There's a Honky Tonk	1971	—	3.00	6.00
DOT					
❑ 1195	Cry, Cry Darling/You Didn't Have to Go	1954	5.00	10.00	20.00
❑ 1215	Night Time Is Cry Time/Diggy Liggy Love	1954	5.00	10.00	20.00
❑ 1231	Your True and Faithful One/Can It Be Right	1954	5.00	10.00	20.00
❑ 1237	Daydreamin'/Crying for a Pastime	1955	5.00	10.00	20.00
❑ 1260	Blue Darlin'/Let Me Stay in Your Arms	1955	5.00	10.00	20.00
❑ 1270	God Was So Good/I Thought I'd Fall in Love Again	1955	5.00	10.00	20.00
❑ 1278	Seasons of My Heart/Let's Stay Together	1956	5.00	10.00	20.00
❑ 1283	Come Back to Me/I Wanta Tell All the World	1956	5.00	10.00	20.00
❑ 1286	Honky Tonk Tears/Let the Whole World Talk	1956	5.00	10.00	20.00
❑ 1288	The Way That You're Living/I've Got You on My Mind	1957	5.00	10.00	20.00
❑ 1289	A Fallen Star/I Can't Go On This Way	1957	6.25	12.50	25.00
❑ 15574	A Fallen Star/I Can't Go On This Way	1957	3.75	7.50	15.00
❑ 15627	A Sweet Kind of Love/Need Me	1957	3.75	7.50	15.00
❑ 15659	Cry, Cry Darling/You're the Idol of My Dreams	1957	3.75	7.50	15.00
❑ 15704	With Tears in My Eyes/Step Aside Shallow Water	1958	3.75	7.50	15.00
❑ 15766	Carry On/Bop-a-Hula	1958	10.00	20.00	40.00
FEATURE					
❑ 1060	I Made a Big Mistake/I Don't Know What to Do	1953	12.50	25.00	50.00
GOLDBAND					
❑ 1320	Sugar Bee/Girls Over 30	198?	—	3.00	6.00
KHOURY'S					
❑ 530	Cry, Cry Darling/You Didn't Have to Go	1954	7.50	15.00	30.00
LA LOUISIANNE					
❑ 8139	Lache Pas La Patate/Grand Texas	198?	—	3.00	6.00
❑ 8141	The Go Go Song/Jolie Blonde	198?	—	3.00	6.00
❑ 8145	Vieux Cajun/Grand Mamou	198?	—	3.00	6.00
❑ 8151	When the Saints Go Marching In/Hippy Ti-Yo	198?	—	3.00	6.00
MGM					
❑ 12707	You're Makin' a Fool Out of Me/Outside Your Door	1958	3.75	7.50	15.00
❑ 12749	So Soon/What'cha Gonna Do	1959	3.00	6.00	12.00
❑ 12790	Lonely Girl/I'd Be Fool Enough	1959	3.00	6.00	12.00
❑ 12812	Grin and Bear It/The Ballad of Baby Doe	1959	3.00	6.00	12.00
❑ 12830	Walkin' Down the Road/Angels Cryin'	1959	3.00	6.00	12.00
❑ 12864	I Miss You Already/The End of the Line	1960	3.00	6.00	12.00
❑ 12894	A Lovely Work of Art/What About Me	1960	3.00	6.00	12.00
❑ 12945	Wanting You with Me Tonight/Now That You're Gone	1960	3.00	6.00	12.00
MONUMENT					
❑ 8535	Happy Cajun Man/You Have a Secret Lover	1972	—	2.50	5.00
❑ 8545	Big Bayou/Not as a Sweetheart	1972	—	2.50	5.00
PLANTATION					
❑ 140	Lafayette/Shrimp Boats	1976	—	2.50	5.00
❑ 143	Big Mamou/Diggy Liggy Lo	1976	—	2.50	5.00
❑ 153	Alligator Man/Lache Las La Patate	1977	—	2.50	5.00
❑ 155	Hello, Dolly/(B-side unknown)	1977	—	3.00	6.00
❑ 162	Billy's Brother/(B-side unknown)	1977	—	3.00	6.00
❑ 166	Louisiana Cajun Rock Band/Everywhere I Go	1978	—	2.50	5.00
❑ 175	Thibodeaux and the Cajun Band/Lousiana Saturday Night	1979	—	2.50	5.00
❑ 182	Happy Cajun/More Happy Cajun	1979	—	2.50	5.00
❑ 186	Sugar Bee/Big Texan	1980	—	2.50	5.00
❑ 188	A Cajun Man Can/Sweet Suzanna	1980	—	2.50	5.00
PLAYBACK					
❑ 1314	Louisiana Love/There Ain't No Ugly Girls	1988	—	3.00	6.00
SHANNON					
❑ 807	Good Time Charlie's Got the Blues/Wild Rose	1973	—	3.00	6.00
❑ 808	The Kind of Love I Can't Forget/Welcome to My World	1973	—	3.00	6.00
❑ 814	Just Once More/You Can't Break the Chains of Love	1973	—	3.00	6.00
SOUNDWAVES					
❑ 4788	Laissez Les Bon Temps Rouler/(B-side unknown)	1987	—	2.50	5.00
SWALLOW					
❑ 10283	Wondering/Va Dormir Avec Les Chiens	198?	—	2.50	5.00
❑ 10285	Passe Partout/So Used to Loving You	198?	—	2.50	5.00
Selected 78s					
FEATURE					
❑ 1022	H-Brown Shuffle/Dreamland Island	1950	10.00	20.00	40.00
❑ 1030	Wondering/I Thank You	195?	7.50	15.00	30.00
❑ 1039	Again in Your Arms/Words Can't Explain	195?	7.50	15.00	30.00
❑ 1043	What Will I Do (If I Can't Have You)/If You Tried As Hard to Love Me (As You Do to Break My Heart)	195?	7.50	15.00	30.00
❑ 1053	Don't Say Goodbye/If You Lose You'll Understand	195?	7.50	15.00	30.00
Albums					
DECCA					
❑ DL 4221 [M]	Jimmy Newman	1962	6.25	12.50	25.00
❑ DL 4398 [M]	Folk Songs of the Bayou Country	1963	10.00	20.00	40.00
❑ DL 4748 [M]	Artificial Rose	1966	5.00	10.00	20.00
❑ DL 4781 [M]	Jimmy Newman Sings Country Songs	1966	5.00	10.00	20.00
❑ DL 4885 [M]	The World of Country Music	1967	6.25	12.50	25.00
❑ DL 4960 [M]	The Jimmy Newman Way	1967	6.25	12.50	25.00
❑ DL 74221 [S]	Jimmy Newman	1962	7.50	15.00	30.00
❑ DL 74398 [S]	Folk Songs of the Bayou Country	1963	12.50	25.00	50.00
❑ DL 74748 [S]	Artificial Rose	1966	6.25	12.50	25.00
❑ DL 74781 [S]	Jimmy Newman Sings Country Songs	1966	6.25	12.50	25.00
❑ DL 74885 [S]	The World of Country Music	1967	5.00	10.00	20.00
❑ DL 74960 [S]	The Jimmy Newman Way	1967	5.00	10.00	20.00
❑ DL 75065	Born to Love You	1968	5.00	10.00	20.00

Number	Title (A Side/B Side)	Yr	VG	VG+	NM
DOT					
❑ DLP-3690 [M]	A Fallen Star	1965	7.50	15.00	30.00
❑ DLP-3736 [M]	Country Crossroads	1966	7.50	15.00	30.00
❑ DLP-25736 [R]	Country Crossroads	1966	5.00	10.00	20.00
MGM					
❑ E-3777 [M]	This Is Jimmy Newman	1959	6.25	12.50	25.00
❑ SE-3777 [S]	This Is Jimmy Newman	1959	7.50	15.00	30.00
❑ E-4045 [M]	Songs by Jimmy Newman	1962	6.25	12.50	25.00
❑ SE-4045 [S]	Songs by Jimmy Newman	1962	7.50	15.00	30.00

NEWMAN, RANDY

The below was this wry singer-songwriter's only country hit.

45s

Number	Title (A Side/B Side)	Yr	VG	VG+	NM
WARNER BROS.					
❑ 8630	Rider in the Rain/Sigmund Freud's Impersonation of Albert Einstein in America	1978	—	2.00	4.00

NEWMAN, TERRI SUE

45s

Number	Title (A Side/B Side)	Yr	VG	VG+	NM
TEXAS SOUL					
❑ 71378	Gypsy Eyes/Time for One More Song	1978	2.00	4.00	8.00

NEWTON, JUICE

45s

Number	Title (A Side/B Side)	Yr	VG	VG+	NM
CAPITOL					
❑ 4499	Come to Me/Save a Heart	1977	—	3.00	6.00
❑ 4552	It's a Heartache/Wouldn't Mind the Rain	1978	—	3.00	6.00
❑ 4611	Hey Baby/It's Not Impossible	1978	—	3.00	6.00
❑ 4679	Let's Keep It That Way/Tell My Baby Goodbye	1979	—	2.50	5.00
❑ 4714	Lay Back in the Arms of Someone/It's Not Impossible	1979	—	2.50	5.00
❑ 4768	Any Way That You Want Me/A Dream Never Dies	1979	—	2.50	5.00
❑ 4793	Until Tonight/Lay Back in the Arms of Someone	1979	—	2.50	5.00
❑ 4818	Sunshine/Go Easy on Me	1980	—	2.00	4.00
❑ 4856	You Fill My Life/Tear It Up	1980	—	2.00	4.00
❑ 4976	Angel of the Morning/Headin' for a Heartache	1981	—	—	3.00
❑ 4976 [PS]	Angel of the Morning/Headin' for a Heartache	1981	—	2.00	4.00
❑ 4997	Queen of Hearts/River of Love	1981	—	—	3.00
❑ 4997 [PS]	Queen of Hearts/River of Love	1981	—	2.00	4.00
❑ A-5046	The Sweetest Thing (I've Ever Known)/Ride 'Em Cowboy	1981	—	—	3.00
❑ A-5046 [PS]	The Sweetest Thing (I've Ever Known)/Ride 'Em Cowboy	1981	—	2.00	4.00
❑ B-5120	Love's Been a Little Bit Hard on Me/Ever True	1982	—	—	3.00
❑ B-5120 [PS]	Love's Been a Little Bit Hard on Me/Ever True	1982	—	2.00	4.00
❑ B-5148	Break It to Me Gently/Adios Mi Corazon	1982	—	—	3.00
❑ B-5148 [PS]	Break It to Me Gently/Adios Mi Corazon	1982	—	2.00	4.00
❑ B-5192	Heart of the Night/Love Sail Away	1982	—	—	3.00
❑ B-5192 [PS]	Heart of the Night/Love Sail Away	1982	—	2.00	4.00
❑ B-5265	Tell Her No/Stranger at My Door	1983	—	—	3.00
❑ B-5265 [PS]	Tell Her No/Stranger at My Door	1983	—	2.00	4.00
❑ B-5289	Dirty Looks/20 Years Ago	1983	—	—	3.00
❑ B-5289 [PS]	Dirty Looks/20 Years Ago	1983	—	2.00	4.00
❑ B-5379	Ride 'Em Cowboy/Love Sail Away	1984	—	—	3.00
RCA					
❑ 5068-7-R	What Can I Do with My Heart/Let Your Woman Take Care of You	1986	—	—	3.00
❑ 5170-7-R	First Time Caller/Til You Cry	1987	—	—	3.00
❑ 5283-7-R	Tell Me True/If I Didn't Love You	1987	—	—	3.00
❑ 8815-7-R	When Love Comes Around the Bend/(B-side unknown)	1989	—	—	3.00
❑ PB-10828	If I Ever/Bye, Bye Baby	1976	2.00	4.00	8.00
❑ PB-13823	A Little Love/Waiting for the Sun	1984	—	—	3.00
❑ PB-13823 [PS]	A Little Love/Waiting for the Sun	1984	—	2.00	4.00
❑ PB-13863	Can't Wait All Night/Restless Heart	1984	—	—	3.00
❑ PB-13863 [PS]	Can't Wait All Night/Restless Heart	1984	—	2.00	4.00
❑ PB-13907	Restless Heart/Eye of a Hurricane	1984	—	—	3.00
❑ PB-14139	You Make Me Want to Make You Mine/Waiting for the Sun	1985	—	—	3.00
❑ PB-14139 [PS]	You Make Me Want to Make You Mine/Waiting for the Sun	1985	—	2.00	4.00
❑ PB-14199	Hurt/Eye of a Hurricane	1985	—	—	3.00
❑ PB-14295	Old Flame/One Touch	1986	—	—	3.00
❑ GB-14355	Hurt/You Make Me Want to Make You Mine	1986	—	—	3.00
❑ PB-14377	Both to Each Other (Friends and Lovers)/A World Without Love	1986	—	—	3.00
—With Eddie Rabbitt					
❑ PB-14377 [PS]	Both to Each Other (Friends and Lovers)/A World Without Love	1986	—	2.50	5.00
❑ PB-14417	Cheap Love/Old Flame	1986	—	—	3.00
RCA VICTOR					
❑ PB-10354	Catwillow River/It's High Time	1975	2.00	4.00	8.00
—With Silver Spur					
❑ PB-10412	The Sweetest Thing (I've Ever Known)/The Shelter of Your Love	1975	2.00	4.00	8.00
—With Silver Spur					
❑ PB-10538	Love Is a Word/The Sweetest Thing (I've Ever Known)	1976	2.00	4.00	8.00
—With Silver Spur					

Albums

Number	Title (A Side/B Side)	Yr	VG	VG+	NM
CAPITOL					
❑ ST-11682	Come to Me	1977	3.75	7.50	15.00
❑ ST-11811	Well-Kept Secret	1978	3.75	7.50	15.00
❑ ST-12000	Take Heart	1980	3.75	7.50	15.00
❑ ST-12136	Juice	1981	2.50	5.00	10.00
❑ ST-12210	Quiet Lies	1982	2.50	5.00	10.00
❑ ST-12294	Dirty Looks	1983	2.50	5.00	10.00
❑ SJ-12353	Greatest Hits	1984	2.50	5.00	10.00
❑ SN-16242	Come to Me	1982	2.00	4.00	8.00
—Budget-line reissue					
❑ SN-16243	Well-Kept Secret	1982	2.00	4.00	8.00
—Budget-line reissue					
❑ SN-16244	Take Heart	1982	2.00	4.00	8.00
—Budget-line reissue					
❑ SN-16313	Juice	1984	2.00	4.00	8.00
—Budget-line reissue					
❑ SN-16314	Quiet Lies	1984	2.00	4.00	8.00
—Budget-line reissue					
❑ SN-16356	Dirty Looks	1985	2.00	4.00	8.00
—Budget-line reissue					
❑ SN-16471	Greatest Hits	1987	2.00	4.00	8.00
—Budget-line reissue					
RCA					
❑ 5646-1-R	Old Flame	1986	2.50	5.00	10.00
—Reissue of 5493 with slightly different lineup					
❑ 6371-1-R	Emotion	1987	2.50	5.00	10.00
❑ 8376-1-R	Ain't Gonna Cry	1989	2.50	5.00	10.00
RCA VICTOR					
❑ APL1-1004	Juice Newton and Silver Spur	1975	5.00	10.00	20.00
❑ APL1-1722	After Dust Settled	1977	3.75	7.50	15.00
❑ AYL1-4037	Juice Newton and Silver Spur	1982	2.00	4.00	8.00
—"Best Buy Series" reissue					
❑ AYL1-4038	After Dust Settled	1982	2.00	4.00	8.00
—"Best Buy Series" reissue					
❑ AFL1-4995	Can't Wait All Night	1984	2.50	5.00	10.00
❑ AFL1-5493	Old Flame	1985	3.00	6.00	12.00

NEWTON, WAYNE

The Las Vegas showman had his first country hit in 1972 and his second in 1989; we list all his recordings that span those dates.

45s

Number	Title (A Side/B Side)	Yr	VG	VG+	NM
20TH CENTURY					
❑ 2393	Hold Me Like You Never Had Me/Housewife	1978	—	2.00	4.00
ARIES II					
❑ 101	You Stepped Into My Life/She Believes in Me	1979	—	2.00	4.00
❑ 108	Years/Rhythm Rhapsody	1980	—	2.00	4.00
CHELSEA					
❑ BCBO-0091	May the Road Rise to Meet You/Pour Me a Little More Wine	1973	—	2.00	4.00
❑ 78-0100	Daddy Don't You Walk So Fast/Echo Valley 2-6809	1972	—	3.00	6.00
—White label (not a promo)					
❑ 78-0100	Daddy Don't You Walk So Fast/Echo Valley 2-6809	1972	—	2.50	5.00
—Mostly pink label					
❑ 78-0105	Can't You Hear the Song?/You Don't Have to Ask	1972	—	2.00	4.00
❑ 78-0109	Anthem/Fool	1972	—	2.00	4.00
❑ 78-0116	Just Yesterday/While We're Still Young	1973	—	2.00	4.00
❑ 78-0124	Help Me Help You/We Didn't Know the Time of Day	1973	—	2.00	4.00
❑ 3003	Lay Lady Lay/Walking in the Sand	1974	—	2.00	4.00
❑ 3018	All Alone Am I/You Don't Have to Ask	1975	—	2.00	4.00
❑ 3028	Run to Me/Lady Lonely	1975	—	2.00	4.00
❑ 3041	The Hungry Years/In Dreams	1976	—	2.00	4.00
❑ 3058	It Could Have Been a Wonderful Christmas/Jingle Bell Hustle	1976	—	2.50	5.00
CURB					
❑ 10520	Cowboy's Christmas/(B-side unknown)	1988	—	—	3.00
❑ 10559	While the Feeling's Good/Our Wedding Band	1989	—	—	3.00
—A-side with Tammy Wynette					
ELEKTRA					
❑ 45528	Last Exit for Love/Too Good to Be True	1978	—	2.00	4.00
RCA VICTOR					
❑ AMBO-0126	Daddy Don't You Walk So Fast/Fool	1973	—	2.00	4.00
—Gold Standard Series reissue					
WARNER BROS.					
❑ 8415	I Want You with Me/Midnight Sun	1977	—	2.00	4.00

7-Inch Extended Plays

Number	Title (A Side/B Side)	Yr	VG	VG+	NM
ARIES II					
❑ 102	White Christmas/It's the Season//I'll Be Home for Christmas/Blue Snow at Christmas	1979	—	2.00	4.00

Albums

Number	Title (A Side/B Side)	Yr	VG	VG+	NM
20TH CENTURY					
❑ T-576	Change of Heart	1979	2.50	5.00	10.00
ARIES II					
❑ WY 201	Wayne Newton Christmas	1979	2.50	5.00	10.00
CHELSEA					
❑ BCL1-0367	Pour Me a Little More Wine	1973	3.00	6.00	12.00
❑ CHL-504	The Best of Wayne Newton Live	1974	2.50	5.00	10.00
❑ CHL-507	Midnight Idol	1975	2.50	5.00	10.00
❑ CHL-512	Tomorrow	1976	2.50	5.00	10.00
❑ CHL-513	Daddy Don't You Walk So Fast	1976	2.50	5.00	10.00
—Reissue of 1001					
❑ CHE 1001	Daddy Don't You Walk So Fast	1972	3.00	6.00	12.00
❑ CHE 1003	Can't You Hear the Song?	1972	3.00	6.00	12.00
❑ CHE 1006	While We're Still Young	1973	3.00	6.00	12.00
CURB					
❑ 10607	Coming Home	1989	3.00	6.00	12.00

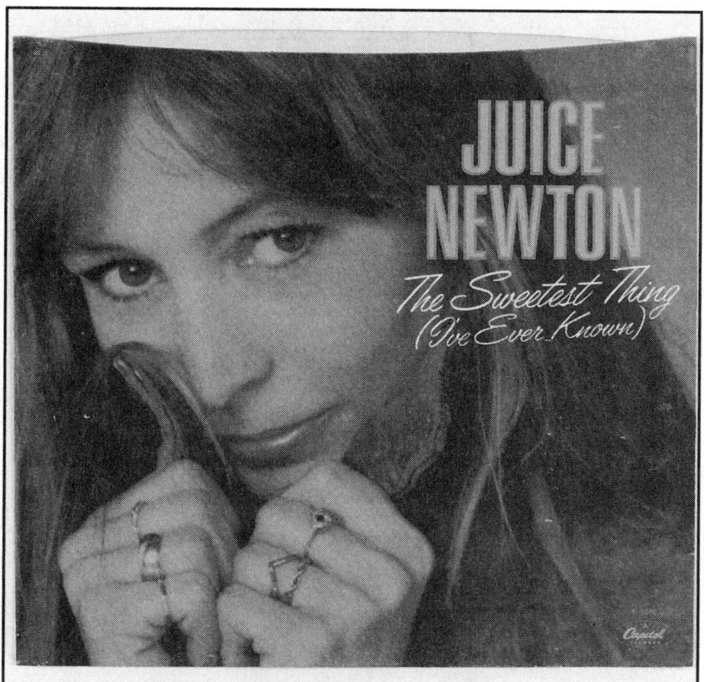

At first she hit the charts fronting a group called Silver Spur. Once she started having big hits, Juice Newton was actually more successful on the pop charts than the country charts for a time. But that situation eventually reversed itself. (Top left) "Queen of Hearts," originally performed by Dave Edmunds, was a No. 2 pop hit, but only peaked at 14 on the country charts. At the time, though, it was Newton's biggest country hit. (Top right) Newton's next single, "The Sweetest Thing (I've Ever Known)," was a new version of an old Silver Spur song, and this one became her first country chart-topper. (Bottom left) Out of what seemed like nowhere, Juice suddenly had back-to-back No. 1 songs in 1985-86. The first of these was "You Make Me Want to Make You Mine." (Bottom right) The follow-up, a remake of the Timi Yuro pop hit "Hurt," also hit the top of the charts for a week.

NEWTON, WOOD

45s

ELEKTRA

Number	Title (A Side/B Side)	Yr	VG	VG+	NM
❑ 45528	Last Exit for Love/Too Good to Be True	1978	—	2.00	4.00
❑ 46013	Lock, Stock & Barrel/Dreams of Desiree	1979	—	2.00	4.00
❑ 46059	Julie (Do I Ever Cross Your Mind?)/Cotton Pickin' Time	1979	—	2.00	4.00
❑ 46537	So Easy for You/Love the Hurt Away	1979	—	2.00	4.00

Albums

ELEKTRA

Number	Title (A Side/B Side)	Yr	VG	VG+	NM
❑ 6E-176	Wood Newton	1979	2.50	5.00	10.00

NEWTON-JOHN, OLIVIA

Also see RAYBON BROS.

12-Inch Singles

MCA

Number	Title (A Side/B Side)	Yr	VG	VG+	NM
❑ 23606	Toughen Up (Dance Remix) (Instrumental)	1986	2.00	4.00	8.00
❑ 23890	The Rumour (4 versions)	1988	2.00	4.00	8.00

45s

ATLANTIC

Number	Title (A Side/B Side)	Yr	VG	VG+	NM
❑ 89420	The Best of Me/Sage	1986	—	—	3.00
—With David Foster					
❑ 89420 [PS]	The Best of Me/Sage	1986	—	—	3.00

MCA

Number	Title (A Side/B Side)	Yr	VG	VG+	NM
❑ 40043	Take Me Home, Country Roads/Sail Into Tomorrow	1973	—	—	—
—Unreleased?					
❑ 40043 [DJ]	Take Me Home, Country Roads (mono/stereo)	1973	5.00	10.00	20.00
❑ 40101	Let Me Be There/Maybe Then I'll Think of You	1973	—	2.50	5.00
❑ 40209	If You Love Me (Let Me Know)/Brotherly Love	1974	—	2.50	5.00
❑ 40280	I Honestly Love You/Home Ain't Home Anymore	1974	—	2.50	5.00
❑ 40349	Have You Never Been Mellow/Water Under the Bridge	1974	—	2.50	5.00
❑ 40418	Please Mr. Please/And In the Morning	1975	—	2.50	5.00
❑ 40418 [PS]	Please Mr. Please/And In the Morning	1975	2.50	5.00	10.00
❑ 40459	Something Better to Do/He's My Rock	1975	—	2.50	5.00
❑ 40459 [PS]	Something Better to Do/He's My Rock	1975	—	3.00	6.00
❑ 40495	Let It Shine/He Ain't Heavy, He's My Brother	1975	—	2.50	5.00
❑ 40525	Come On Over/Small Talk and Pride	1976	—	2.00	4.00
❑ 40600	Don't Stop Believin'/Greensleeves	1976	—	2.00	4.00
—A-side not a Christmas song					
❑ 40600 [PS]	Don't Stop Believin'/Greensleeves	1976	—	2.50	5.00
❑ 40642	Every Face Tells a Story/Love You Hold the Key	1976	—	2.00	4.00
❑ 40670	Sam/I'll Bet You a Kangaroo	1976	—	2.00	4.00
❑ 40737	Making a Good Thing Better/I Think I'll Say Goodbye	1977	—	2.00	4.00
❑ 40811	I Honestly Love You/Don't Cry for Me Argentina	1977	—	2.50	5.00
❑ 40811 [PS]	I Honestly Love You/Don't Cry for Me Argentina	1977	2.50	5.00	10.00
❑ 40975	A Little More Love/Borrowed Time	1978	—	2.00	4.00
❑ 40975 [PS]	A Little More Love/Borrowed Time	1978	—	2.50	5.00
❑ 41009	Deeper Than the Night/Please Don't Keep Me Waiting	1979	—	2.00	4.00
❑ 41074	Totally Hot/Dancing Round and Round	1979	—	2.00	4.00
❑ 41074 [PS]	Totally Hot/Dancing Round and Round	1979	—	2.50	5.00
❑ 41247	Magic/Fool Country	1980	—	2.50	5.00
—Custom pink "Xanadu" label					
❑ 41247	Magic/Fool Country	1980	—	2.00	4.00
—Standard blue rainbow label					
❑ 41247 [PS]	Magic/Fool Country	1980	—	2.50	5.00
❑ 41286	Xanadu/Whenever You're Away from Me	1980	—	2.00	4.00
—A-side with Electric Light Orchestra; B-side with Gene Kelly. Persistent rumors claim existence of a U.S. picture sleeve for this record, but we've never seen one.					
❑ 41287	Suddenly/You Made Me Love You	1980	—	2.50	5.00
—A-side with Cliff Richard					
❑ 51007	Suddenly/You Made Me Love You	1980	—	2.00	4.00
—A-side with Cliff Richard					
❑ 51007 [PS]	Suddenly/You Made Me Love You	1980	—	2.50	5.00
❑ 51182	Physical/The Promise (The Dolphin Song)	1981	—	—	3.00
❑ 51182 [PS]	Physical/The Promise (The Dolphin Song)	1981	—	2.00	4.00
❑ 52000	Make a Move on Me/Falling	1982	—	—	3.00
❑ 52000 [PS]	Make a Move on Me/Falling	1982	—	2.50	5.00
❑ 52069	Landslide/Recovery	1982	—	—	3.00
❑ 52069 [PS]	Landslide/Recovery	1982	—	2.00	4.00
❑ 52100	Heart Attack/Strangers Touch	1982	—	—	3.00
❑ 52100 [PS]	Heart Attack/Strangers Touch	1982	—	—	3.00
❑ 52155	Tied Up/Silvery Rain	1983	—	—	3.00
❑ 52155 [PS]	Tied Up/Silvery Rain	1983	—	—	3.00
❑ 52284	Twist of Fate/Take a Chance	1983	—	—	3.00
❑ 52284 [PS]	Twist of Fate/Take a Chance	1983	—	—	3.00
❑ 52341	Livin' in Desperate Times/Landslide	1984	—	—	3.00
❑ 52341 [PS]	Livin' in Desperate Times/Landslide	1984	—	—	3.00
❑ 52686	Soul Kiss/Electric	1985	—	—	3.00
❑ 52686 [PS]	Soul Kiss/Electric	1985	—	—	3.00
❑ 52757	Toughen Up/Driving Music	1986	—	—	3.00
❑ 52757 [PS]	Toughen Up/Driving Music	1986	—	—	3.00
❑ 53294	The Rumour/Winter Angel	1988	—	—	3.00
❑ 53294 [PS]	The Rumour/Winter Angel	1988	—	—	3.00
❑ 53438	Can't We Talk It Over in Bed/Get Out	1988	—	—	3.00
❑ 72053	I Honestly Love You/I Honestly Love You (Remix)	1998	—	—	3.00
—New recordings					

MCA NASHVILLE

Number	Title (A Side/B Side)	Yr	VG	VG+	NM
❑ 72074	Back with a Heart/Under My Skin	1998	—	—	3.00

RSO

Number	Title (A Side/B Side)	Yr	VG	VG+	NM
❑ 903	Hopelessly Devoted to You/Love Is a Many-Splendored Thing	1978	—	2.00	4.00

UNI

Number	Title (A Side/B Side)	Yr	VG	VG+	NM
❑ 55281	If Not for You/The Biggest Clown	1971	2.50	5.00	10.00
❑ 55304	Banks of the Ohio/It's So Hard to Say Goodbye	1971	2.00	4.00	8.00
❑ 55317	What Is Life/I'm a Small and Lonely Light	1972	2.00	4.00	8.00
❑ 55348	Just a Little Too Much/My Old Man's Gotta Gun	1972	3.00	6.00	12.00

Albums

GEFFEN

Number	Title (A Side/B Side)	Yr	VG	VG+	NM
❑ GHS 24257	Warm and Tender	1989	3.00	6.00	12.00

MCA

Number	Title (A Side/B Side)	Yr	VG	VG+	NM
❑ 389	Let Me Be There	1973	3.75	7.50	15.00
❑ 411	If You Love Me Let Me Know	1974	3.75	7.50	15.00
—Originals have incorrect song title: "I Love You, I Honestly Love You"					
❑ 411	If You Love Me Let Me Know	1974	2.50	5.00	10.00
—With corrected song title: "I Honestly Love You"					
❑ 2133	Have You Never Been Mellow	1975	2.50	5.00	10.00
❑ 2148	Clearly Love	1975	2.50	5.00	10.00
❑ 2186	Come On Over	1976	2.50	5.00	10.00
❑ 2223	Don't Stop Believin'	1976	2.50	5.00	10.00
❑ 2280	Making a Good Thing Better	1977	2.50	5.00	10.00
❑ 3012	Let Me Be There	1977	2.00	4.00	8.00
—Reissue					
❑ 3013	If You Love Me Let Me Know	1977	2.00	4.00	8.00
—Reissue					
❑ 3014	Have You Never Been Mellow	1977	2.00	4.00	8.00
—Reissue					
❑ 3015	Clearly Love	1977	2.00	4.00	8.00
—Reissue					
❑ 3016	Come On Over	1977	2.00	4.00	8.00
—Reissue					
❑ 3017	Don't Stop Believin'	1977	2.00	4.00	8.00
—Reissue					
❑ 3018	Making a Good Thing Better	1977	2.00	4.00	8.00
—Reissue					
❑ 3028	Olivia Newton-John's Greatest Hits	1977	2.50	5.00	10.00
❑ 3067	Totally Hot	1978	2.50	5.00	10.00
❑ 5229	Physical	1981	2.00	4.00	8.00
❑ 5347	Olivia's Greatest Hits, Vol. 2	1982	2.00	4.00	8.00
❑ 6151	Soul Kiss	1985	2.00	4.00	8.00
❑ 6245	The Rumour	1988	2.00	4.00	8.00
❑ 16011	Physical	1982	6.25	12.50	25.00
—Audiophile edition					
❑ 37061	Clearly Love	1980	2.00	4.00	8.00
—Reissue					
❑ 37062	Come On Over	1980	2.00	4.00	8.00
—Reissue					
❑ 37063	Don't Stop Believin'	1980	2.00	4.00	8.00
—Reissue					
❑ 37123	Totally Hot	1981	2.00	4.00	8.00
—Reissue					

MOBILE FIDELITY

Number	Title (A Side/B Side)	Yr	VG	VG+	NM
❑ 1-040	Totally Hot	1980	5.00	15.00	20.00
—Audiophile vinyl					

UNI

Number	Title (A Side/B Side)	Yr	VG	VG+	NM
❑ 73117	If Not for You	1971	20.00	40.00	80.00

NEYMAN, JUNE

45s

STARSHIP

Number	Title (A Side/B Side)	Yr	VG	VG+	NM
❑ 101	He Ain't Heavy, He's My Brother/Release Me	1978	2.00	4.00	8.00
❑ 110	You're Gonna Miss Me/Kansas City	1979	2.00	4.00	8.00

NICKS, STEVIE

The Fleetwood Mac singer and solo artist saw this single make the country charts.

45s

MODERN

Number	Title (A Side/B Side)	Yr	VG	VG+	NM
❑ 7405	After the Glitter Fades/Think About It	1982	—	3.00	6.00
❑ 7405 [PS]	After the Glitter Fades/Think About It	1982	2.00	4.00	8.00

NIELSEN, SHAUN

45s

ADONDA

Number	Title (A Side/B Side)	Yr	VG	VG+	NM
❑ 79022	Lights of L.A./I've Never Loved Anyone More	1980	—	3.00	6.00

AUDIOGRAPH

Number	Title (A Side/B Side)	Yr	VG	VG+	NM
❑ 465	Lights of L.A./(B-side unknown)	1983	—	2.50	5.00

MCA

Number	Title (A Side/B Side)	Yr	VG	VG+	NM
❑ 51130	Dream Baby (How Long Must I Dream)/Give Her Thorns (And She'll Find the Roses)	1981	—	2.00	4.00

RCA

Number	Title (A Side/B Side)	Yr	VG	VG+	NM
❑ PB-11418	Let's Try and Fall in Love Again/You're Slowly Turning Me Into Your Fool	1978	—	2.50	5.00

SCORPION

Number	Title (A Side/B Side)	Yr	VG	VG+	NM
❑ 0526	Sweet Affection/I've Never Loved Anyone More	1976	—	3.00	6.00

NIELSEN WHITE BAND, THE

45s

VISION

Number	Title (A Side/B Side)	Yr	VG	VG+	NM
❑ 122574	Somethin' You Got/(B-side unknown)	1986	—	2.50	5.00
❑ 122575	I Got the One I Wanted/(B-side unknown)	1987	—	2.50	5.00

Number	Title (A Side/B Side)	Yr	VG	VG+	NM

NIGHTSTREETS

45s

EPIC

Number	Title (A Side/B Side)	Yr	VG	VG+	NM
❑ 50827	Love in the Meantime/Chasin' Like This	1980	—	2.00	4.00
—As "Streets"					
❑ 50886	Falling Together/You Never Know	1980	—	2.00	4.00
❑ 50944	If I Had It My Way/A Little Gettin' Used To	1980	—	2.00	4.00
❑ 19-51004	(Lookin' at Things) In a Different Light/Out of the Spotlight	1981	—	2.00	4.00

NILLES, LYNN

45s

GRT

Number	Title (A Side/B Side)	Yr	VG	VG+	NM
❑ 100	You're Gonna Make Love to Me/Got a Feeling	1977	—	2.50	5.00

NITTY GRITTY DIRT BAND

Includes The Dirt Band. Also see JOHN DENVER.

45s

DECCA

Number	Title (A Side/B Side)	Yr	VG	VG+	NM
❑ 55206	Maybe Baby/Crying, Waiting, Hoping	1996	—	—	3.00
—B-side by Marty Stuart and Steve Earle					

LIBERTY

Number	Title (A Side/B Side)	Yr	VG	VG+	NM
❑ 1389	High School Yearbook/Too Good to Be True	1980	—	2.00	4.00
—As "The Dirt Band"					
❑ 1398	Nazamas Nuestra Magic (Make a Little Magic)/ Jas' Moon	1981	—	2.00	4.00
—As "The Dirt Band"					
❑ 1429	Fire in the Sky/EZ Slow	1981	—	2.00	4.00
—As "The Dirt Band"					
❑ 1449	Badlands/Jealousy	1982	—	2.00	4.00
—As "The Dirt Band"					
❑ 1467	Too Close for Comfort/Circular Man	1982	—	2.00	4.00
—As "The Dirt Band"					
❑ 1499	Let's Go/Shot Full of Love	1983	—	2.00	4.00
❑ 1507	Mary Anne/Dance Little Jean	1983	—	2.00	4.00
❑ 1513	Colorado Christmas/Mr. Bojangles	1983	—	3.00	6.00
❑ 55948	Buy for Me the Rain/Candy Man	1967	2.50	5.00	10.00
❑ 55982	The Teddy Bear's Picnic/Truly Right	1967	2.00	4.00	8.00
❑ 55982 [PS]	The Teddy Bear's Picnic/Truly Right	1967	3.75	7.50	15.00
❑ 56054	These Days/Collegiana	1968	2.00	4.00	8.00
❑ 56134	Some of Shelley's Blues/Yukon Railroad	1969	—	3.00	6.00
❑ 56159	Rave On/The Cure	1970	—	3.00	6.00
❑ 56197	Mr. Bojangles/Mr. Bojangles (Prelude: Uncle Charlie and His Dog Teddy)	1970	—	3.00	6.00
❑ 56197	Mr. Bojangles (Prelude: Uncle Charlie and His Dog Teddy)/Spanish Fandango	1970	2.00	4.00	8.00
❑ S7-57766	I Fought the Law/Mr. Bojangles	1992	—	2.00	4.00

MCA

Number	Title (A Side/B Side)	Yr	VG	VG+	NM
❑ 53795	One Step Over the Line/Riding Along	1990	—	—	3.00
—A-side: With Roseanne Cash; B-side: With Emmylou Harris					
❑ 53964	The Rest of the Dream/Snowballs	1990	—	—	3.00
❑ 55182	You Believed in Me/Atlanta Reel '96	1996	—	—	3.00
—A-side by Karla Bonoff and the Nitty Gritty Dirt Band; B-side by Michael Omartian					
❑ 79013	From Small Things (Big Things One Day Come)/ Blues Berry Hill	1990	—	—	3.00
❑ 79075	You Make Life Good Again/Snowballs	1990	—	—	3.00

UNITED ARTISTS

Number	Title (A Side/B Side)	Yr	VG	VG+	NM
❑ 0061	Mr. Bojangles/Buy for Me the Rain	1973	—	2.00	4.00
—"Silver Spotlight Series" reissue					
❑ XW177	Will the Circle Be Unbroken/Honky Tonkin'	1973	—	2.50	5.00
❑ XW247	Grand Ole Opry Song/Orange Blossom Special	1973	—	2.50	5.00
❑ XW263	Cosmic Cowboy (Part 1)/Cosmic Cowboy (Part 2)	1973	—	2.50	5.00
❑ XW321	Tennessee Stud/Way Down Town	1973	—	2.50	5.00
—With Doc Watson					
❑ XW544	The Battle of New Orleans/Mountain Whipporwill	1974	—	2.50	5.00
❑ XW544 [PS]	The Battle of New Orleans/Mountain Whipporwill	1974	—	3.00	6.00
❑ XW655	(All I Have to Do Is) Dream/Raleigh-Durham Reel	1975	—	2.50	5.00
❑ XW741	Mother of Love/The Moon Just Turned Blue	1975	—	2.50	5.00
❑ XW830	Cosmic Cowboy/Stars and Stripes Forever	1976	—	2.00	4.00
—As "The Dirt Band"					
❑ XW889	Jamaica Lady/Bayou Jubilee-Sally Was a Goodun	1976	—	2.00	4.00
—As "The Dirt Band"					
❑ XW936	Buy for Me the Rain/Mother Earth (Provides for Me)	1976	—	2.00	4.00
—As "The Dirt Band"					
❑ XW1164	Orange Blossom Special/Will the Circle Be Unbroken	1978	—	2.00	4.00
❑ XW1228	Wild Nights/In for the Night	1978	—	2.00	4.00
—As "The Dirt Band"					
❑ XW1268	For a Little While/On the Loose	1978	—	2.00	4.00
—As "The Dirt Band"					
❑ 1312	In Her Eyes/Jas' Moon	1979	—	2.00	4.00
—As "The Dirt Band"					
❑ 1330	An American Dream/Take Me Back	1979	—	2.50	5.00
—As "The Dirt Band"					
❑ 1356	Make a Little Magic/Jas' Moon	1980	—	2.00	4.00
—As "The Dirt Band"					
❑ 1378	Badlands/Too Good to Be True	1980	—	2.00	4.00
—As "The Dirt Band"					
❑ 50769	House at Pooh Corner/Travelin' Mood	1971	—	3.00	6.00
❑ 50769 [PS]	House at Pooh Corner/Travelin' Mood	1971	2.00	4.00	8.00
❑ 50817	The Cure/Some of Shelly's Blues	1971	—	3.00	6.00
❑ 50849	Precious Jewel/I Saw the Light	1971	—	3.00	6.00
—With Roy Acuff					
❑ 50861	I Saw the Light/Sixteen Tracks	1971	—	3.00	6.00
❑ 50890	Jambalaya (On the Bayou)/Hoping to Say	1972	—	3.00	6.00
❑ 50890 [PS]	Jambalaya (On the Bayou)/Hoping to Say	1972	2.00	4.00	8.00
❑ 50921	Baltimore/Fish Song	1972	—	3.00	6.00
❑ 50965	Honky Tonkin'/Jamaica	1972	—	3.00	6.00

UNIVERSAL

Number	Title (A Side/B Side)	Yr	VG	VG+	NM
❑ UVL-66009	Turn of the Century/Blueberry Hill	1989	—	—	3.00
❑ UVL-66023	When It's Gone/I'm Sittin' on Top of the World	1989	—	2.00	4.00

WARNER BROS

Number	Title (A Side/B Side)	Yr	VG	VG+	NM
❑ PRO-S-2869 [DJ]	Colorado Christmas/The Cowboy's Christmas Ball	1987	—	3.00	6.00
—B-side by Michael Martin Murphey					

WARNER BROS.

Number	Title (A Side/B Side)	Yr	VG	VG+	NM
❑ 27679	Down That Road Tonight/A Lot Like Me	1989	—	—	3.00
❑ 27750	I've Been Lookin'/Must Be Love	1988	—	—	3.00
❑ 27940	Workin' Man/Brass Sky	1988	—	—	3.00
❑ 28173	Oh What a Love/America, My Sweetheart	1987	—	—	3.00
❑ 28311	Fishin' in the Dark/Keepin' the Road Hot	1987	—	—	3.00
❑ 28443	Baby's Got a Hold on Me/Oleanna	1987	—	—	3.00
❑ 28547	Cadillac Ranch/Fire in the Sky	1986	—	—	3.00
❑ 28690	Stand a Little Rain/Miner's Night Out	1986	—	—	3.00
❑ 28780	Partners, Brothers and Friends/Redneck Riviera	1986	—	—	3.00
❑ 28897	Home Again in My Heart/Telluride	1985	—	2.00	4.00
❑ 29027	Modern Day Romance/Queen of the Road	1985	—	2.00	4.00
❑ 29099	High Horse/Must Be Love	1985	—	2.00	4.00
❑ 29203	I Love Only You/Face on the Cutting Room Floor	1984	—	2.00	4.00
❑ 29282	Long Hard Road (The Sharecropper's Dream)/ Video Tape	1984	—	2.00	4.00

Albums

LIBERTY

Number	Title	Yr	VG	VG+	NM
❑ LWB-184 [(2)]	Stars and Stripes Forever	1981	2.50	5.00	10.00
❑ LKCL-670 [(3)]	Dirt, Silver and Gold	1981	3.00	6.00	12.00
❑ LO-974	An American Dream	1981	2.00	4.00	8.00
❑ LT-1042	Make a Little Magic	1981	2.00	4.00	8.00
❑ LRP-3501 [M]	The Nitty Gritty Dirt Band	1967	6.25	12.50	25.00
❑ LRP-3516 [M]	Ricochet	1967	6.25	12.50	25.00
❑ LMAS-5553	All the Good Times	1981	2.00	4.00	8.00
❑ LST-7501 [S]	The Nitty Gritty Dirt Band	1967	7.50	15.00	30.00
❑ LST-7516 [S]	Ricochet	1967	7.50	15.00	30.00
❑ LST-7540	Rare Junk	1968	6.25	12.50	25.00
❑ LST-7611	Alive	1969	6.25	12.50	25.00
❑ LST-7642	Uncle Charlie and His Dog Teddy	1970	6.25	12.50	25.00
—Standard issue of LP					
❑ LST-7642 [DJ]	Uncle Charlie and His Dog Teddy	1970	30.00	60.00	120.00
—Leatherette promo pack with LP, two other discs, photos, booklet					
❑ LTAO-7642	Uncle Charlie and His Dog Teddy	1981	2.00	4.00	8.00
❑ LT-51146	Let's Go	1982	2.50	5.00	10.00
❑ LWCL-51158 [(3)]	Will the Circle Be Unbroken	1986	3.75	7.50	15.00

MCA

Number	Title	Yr	VG	VG+	NM
❑ 6407	The Rest of the Dream	1990	3.00	6.00	12.00

UNITED ARTISTS

Number	Title	Yr	VG	VG+	NM
❑ UA-LA184-J2 [(2)]	Stars and Stripes Forever	1974	3.75	7.50	15.00
❑ UA-LA469-G	Dream	1975	3.00	6.00	12.00
❑ UA-LA670-L3 [(3)]	Dirt, Silver and Gold	1976	5.00	10.00	20.00
❑ UA-LA830-H	The Chicken Chronicles	1978	2.50	5.00	10.00
❑ UA-LA854-H	The Dirt Band	1978	2.50	5.00	10.00
❑ UA-LA974-H	An American Dream	1979	2.50	5.00	10.00
❑ LT-1042	Make a Little Magic	1980	2.50	5.00	10.00
❑ LW-1106	Jealousy	1981	2.50	5.00	10.00
❑ UAS-5553	All the Good Times	1972	3.75	7.50	15.00
❑ UAS-9801 [(3)]	Will the Circle Be Unbroken	1972	7.50	15.00	30.00

UNIVERSAL

Number	Title	Yr	VG	VG+	NM
❑ UVL2-12500 [(2)]	Will the Circle Be Unbroken, Volume Two	1989	5.00	10.00	20.00

WARNER BROS.

Number	Title	Yr	VG	VG+	NM
❑ 25113	Plain Dirt Fashion	1984	2.00	4.00	8.00
❑ 25304	Partners, Brothers and Friends	1985	2.00	4.00	8.00
❑ 25382	Twenty Years of Dirt: The Best of the Nitty Gritty Dirt Band	1986	2.00	4.00	8.00
❑ 25573	Hold On	1987	2.00	4.00	8.00
❑ 25722	Workin' Band	1988	2.00	4.00	8.00
❑ 25830	More Great Dirt: The Best of the Nitty Gritty Dirt Band, Vol. 2	1989	2.50	5.00	10.00

NIX, TOM

45s

RMA

Number	Title (A Side/B Side)	Yr	VG	VG+	NM
❑ 6009	Home Along the Highway/(B-side unknown)	1980	2.00	4.00	8.00

NIXON, NICK

45s

KAPP

Number	Title (A Side/B Side)	Yr	VG	VG+	NM
❑ 2024	Sleep Woman Sleep/Wide Place in the Road	1969	2.00	4.00	8.00
❑ 2077	Lover's Cocktail/My Darlin' Sarah	1970	—	3.50	7.00

MCA

Number	Title (A Side/B Side)	Yr	VG	VG+	NM
❑ 41030	What're We Doing, Doing This Again/Have a Heart	1979	—	2.50	5.00
❑ 41100	San Francisco Is a Lonely Town/Suspicion	1979	—	2.50	5.00

MERCURY

Number	Title (A Side/B Side)	Yr	VG	VG+	NM
❑ 55010	I'll Get Over You/Long Stemmed Rosie	1977	—	2.50	5.00
❑ 55035	She's Lying Next to Me/You Really Know My Song	1978	—	2.50	5.00
❑ 73435	The Battle of New Orleans/Leave Your Back Porch Light On	1973	—	3.00	6.00

Number	Title (A Side/B Side)	Yr	VG	VG+	NM
❑ 73467	I'm Turning You Loose/An Old Memory (Got in My Eye)	1974	—	2.50	5.00
❑ 73506	A Habit I Can't Break/Walk On By	1974	—	2.50	5.00
❑ 73654	It's Only a Barroom/You Stood By Me Through It All	1975	—	2.50	5.00
❑ 73691	I'm Too Use to Loving Her/I Just Love Her	1975	—	2.50	5.00
❑ 73726	She's Just an Old Love Turned Memory/It's Much Too Rainy	1975	—	2.50	5.00
❑ 73772	Rocking in Rosalee's Boat/I'll Get Over You	1976	—	2.50	5.00
❑ 73866	Neon Lights/Everyday	1976	—	2.50	5.00
❑ 73930	Love Songs and Romance Magazines/It's a Crying Shame (But People Change)	1977	—	2.50	5.00

Albums

MERCURY

Number	Title	Yr	VG	VG+	NM
❑ SRM-1-1175	Nick Nixon	1977	2.50	5.00	10.00

NOACK, EDDIE

45s

ALLSTAR

Number	Title (A Side/B Side)	Yr	VG	VG+	NM
❑ 7252	Too Hot to Handle/Tell Her	196?	2.00	4.00	8.00
❑ 7266	We Are the Lonely Ones/(B-side unknown)	196?	—	3.50	7.00
❑ 7296	Fall-Out Keeps On Hurting/Think of Her Now	196?	—	3.50	7.00
❑ 7299	You Can't Keep a Good Man Down/(B-side unknown)	196?	—	3.50	7.00
❑ 7322	Prisoner of Love/Two Bright Lights	196?	—	3.50	7.00
D					
❑ 1019	Have Blues — Will Travel/The Price of Love	1958	7.50	15.00	30.00
❑ 1037	Walk 'Em Off/I Don't Live There Anymore	1959	15.00	30.00	60.00
❑ 1060	A Thinking Man's Woman/Don't Look Behind	1959	6.25	12.50	25.00
❑ 1094	Relief Is Just a Swallow Away/Man on the Wall	1959	6.25	12.50	25.00
❑ 1124	Shake Hands with the Blues/Sunflower Song	1960	5.00	10.00	20.00
❑ 1148	Firewater Luke/Too Weak to Go	1960	5.00	10.00	20.00
❑ 1220	It's Hard to Tell an Old Love Goodbye/Love's Other Face	1961	5.00	10.00	20.00
❑ 1294	Raise the Taxes/We'll Still Be On Our Honeymoon	197?	2.00	4.00	8.00
K-ARK					
❑ 813	Cotton Mill/The End of the Line	1969	—	3.50	7.00
❑ 843	Psycho/Invisible Stripes	1969	—	3.50	7.00
❑ 885	House on a Mountain/Stolen Rose	1969	—	3.50	7.00
STARDAY					
❑ 159	Take It Away Lucky/Don't Trade	1954	7.50	15.00	30.00
❑ 169	Left Over Lovin'/I'll Be So Good to You	1955	7.50	15.00	30.00
❑ 201	If It Ain't on the Menu/Wind Me Up	1955	7.50	15.00	30.00
❑ 213	Fair Today, Cold Tomorrow/Don't Worry 'Bout Me Baby	1955	7.50	15.00	30.00
❑ 225	It Ain't Much But It's Home/When the Bright Lights Grow Dim	1956	7.50	15.00	30.00
❑ 246	You Done Got Me/For You I Weep	1956	7.50	15.00	30.00
❑ 276	The Worm Has Turned/She Can't Stand the Light of Day	1956	7.50	15.00	30.00
❑ 316	Scarecrow/Think of Her Now	1957	7.50	15.00	30.00
❑ 334	Dust on the River/What's the Matter, Joe?	1957	7.50	15.00	30.00
TNT					
❑ 110	Too Hot to Handle/How Does It Feel to Be the Winner	1954	7.50	15.00	30.00
WIDE WORLD					
❑ 1005	Any Old Time/Why Did You Give Me Your Love	1970	—	3.50	7.00
❑ 1009	Mother, the Queen of My Heart/(B-side unknown)	1970	—	3.50	7.00
❑ 1017	He's Getting Smaller (With Each Drink)/Your Share	197?	—	3.50	7.00

Albums

WIDE WORLD

Number	Title	Yr	VG	VG+	NM
❑ 2001	Remembering Jimmie Rodgers	1970	6.25	12.50	25.00

NOBLE, NICK

45s

20TH CENTURY FOX

Number	Title (A Side/B Side)	Yr	VG	VG+	NM
❑ 6612	The Girl with the Long Red Hair/Simple, Simple	1965	2.00	4.00	8.00
CAPITOL					
❑ 3677	It's All Up to You/Let Me Be a Man	1973	—	2.50	5.00
CHESS					
❑ 1876	Sleep Walk/Flying Over Rainbows	1963	2.50	5.00	10.00
❑ 1879	Stay with Me/Flying Over Rainbows	1963	2.00	4.00	8.00
❑ 1909	Don't Forget/Not Like I Used to Be	1964	2.00	4.00	8.00
CHURCHILL					
❑ 7701	May God Be With You/(B-side unknown)	1978	—	3.00	6.00
❑ 7713	Stay with Me/My Country Kind of Girl	1978	—	3.00	6.00
❑ 7755	Big Man's Cafe/My Country Kind of Girl	1980	—	3.00	6.00
COLUMBIA					
❑ 4-44887	I'm Gonna Make You Love Me/I'm So Busy Being Broken Hearted	1969	—	3.00	6.00
CORAL					
❑ 9-62075	How Much Can a Heart Take/My Darling's Earrings	1959	2.50	5.00	10.00
❑ 9-62124	I Need Someone/Thank Heaven for Little Girls	1959	2.50	5.00	10.00
❑ 9-62144	Somethin' Cha Cha/I Surrender Dear	1959	2.50	5.00	10.00
❑ 62169	Violino/Lemons and Cloves	1960	2.50	5.00	10.00
❑ 62213	The Tip of My Fingers/Sweet Love	1960	3.00	6.00	12.00
❑ 62233	Excuse Me (I Think I've Got a Heartache)/Island Farewell	1960	2.50	5.00	10.00
❑ 62246	Someplace to Cry/Over Someone's Shoulder	1961	2.50	5.00	10.00
❑ 62262	(I'm Gonna) Cry Some Tears/They Call Me the Fool	1961	2.50	5.00	10.00
❑ 62280	For Just a Little While Tonight/The Beat of My Soul	1961	2.50	5.00	10.00
❑ 62495	The Tip of My Fingers/Someplace to Cry	1966	2.00	4.00	8.00
DATE					
❑ 1582	Until It's Time for You to Go/You're the Right One for Me	1967	—	3.50	7.00
❑ 1616	My Marie/It Hurts to Say Goodbye	1968	—	3.50	7.00
❑ 1629	Take Me Back/Lonely As I Need You	1968	—	3.50	7.00
EPIC					
❑ 50327	Forgetting Someone/If We Could Live Our Life Away	1977	—	2.00	4.00
FRATERNITY					
❑ 817	Fountains Cry/There's a Church in Your Heart	1958	2.50	5.00	10.00
❑ 825	One Track Mind/Lonely Star	1958	2.50	5.00	10.00
LIBERTY					
❑ 55442	The Twelfth Dark Hour/My Heart Came Running Back to You	1962	2.00	4.00	8.00
❑ 55488	Hello Out There/We Could	1962	2.00	4.00	8.00
❑ 55534	A Legend in My Time/Closer to Heaven	1963	2.00	4.00	8.00
❑ 55576	Gee Little Girl/A Rose and a Star	1963	2.00	4.00	8.00
MERCURY					
❑ 70397	Right or Wrong/Maybe Today	1954	3.75	7.50	15.00
❑ 70496	Tara's Theme/Please Don't Break My Heart	1954	3.75	7.50	15.00
❑ 70821	To You, My Love/You Are My Only Love	1956	3.00	6.00	12.00
❑ 70897	Keeping Cool (With Lemonade)/You're Sensational	1956	3.00	6.00	12.00
❑ 70959	Autumn Concerto/Mom, Oh Mom	1956	3.00	6.00	12.00
❑ 70981	You Don't Know What Love Is/The Star You Wished On Last Night	1956	3.00	6.00	12.00
❑ 71031	No One Sweeter Than You/I'm a Visitor	1957	3.00	6.00	12.00
❑ 71117	A Fallen Star/They're Playing Our Song	1957	3.00	6.00	12.00
❑ 71124	A Fallen Star/Let Me Hold You in My Arms	1957	2.50	5.00	10.00
❑ 71169	Moonlight Swim/Lucy Lou	1957	2.50	5.00	10.00
❑ 71233	Halo of Love/Sweet Treat	1957	2.50	5.00	10.00
TMS					
❑ 601	The Girl on the Other Side/Why Don't You Believe Me	1979	—	3.00	6.00
❑ 612	I Wanna Go Back/(B-side unknown)	1979	—	3.00	6.00
WING					
❑ 90003	The Bible Tells Me So/Army of the Lord	1955	3.00	6.00	12.00
❑ 90028	The Best Is Yet to Come/If It Happened to You	1955	3.00	6.00	12.00
❑ 90042	Lovely Lies/Bella Bella Perzicella	1955	3.00	6.00	12.00
❑ 90045	To You My Love/You Are My Only Love	1955	3.75	7.50	15.00

Albums

COLUMBIA

Number	Title	Yr	VG	VG+	NM
❑ CS 9810	I'm Gonna Make You Love Me	1969	3.75	7.50	15.00
LIBERTY					
❑ LRP-3302 [M]	Relax	1963	5.00	10.00	20.00
❑ LST-7302 [M]	Relax	1963	6.25	12.50	25.00
MERCURY					
❑ MG-20182 [M]	You Don't Know What Love Is	1956	6.25	12.50	25.00
WING					
❑ MGW-12184 [M]	Music for Lovers	196?	3.75	7.50	15.00

NOEL

A female singer, not to be confused with the male singer whose biggest pop hit was "Silent Morning."

45s

DEEP SOUTH

Number	Title (A Side/B Side)	Yr	VG	VG+	NM
❑ 681	Lying Myself to Sleep/Lonely for Too Long	198?	—	3.00	6.00
❑ 690	Apartment #9/Lovin' the Night Away	1982	—	3.00	6.00
❑ 706	One Tear (At a Time)/Lonely Too Long	1982	—	3.00	6.00
❑ 719	Huggin', Kissin', Lovin'/Apartment #9	1983	—	3.00	6.00
❑ 1003	L-L-L-L, Love You All Night/(B-side unknown)	198?	—	3.00	6.00
❑ 1004	Someone I Used to Know/(B-side unknown)	198?	—	3.00	6.00
MADD CASH					
❑ 1045	P.S./How Sweet It Is	1985	—	3.00	6.00

NOLAN, BOB

Also see SONS OF THE PIONEERS.

45s

RCA VICTOR

Number	Title (A Side/B Side)	Yr	VG	VG+	NM
❑ 47-5127	The Mystery of His Way/An Angel in the Choir	1953	5.00	10.00	20.00
❑ 47-5241	I Can't Lie to Myself/The House of Broken Dreams	1953	5.00	10.00	20.00
❑ 47-5403	Tumbling Tumbleweeds/Manhunt	1953	5.00	10.00	20.00

NORMA JEAN

Also see BOBBY BARE; CLAUDE GRAY.

45s

COLUMBIA

Number	Title (A Side/B Side)	Yr	VG	VG+	NM
❑ 4-41400	Chapel Bells/Honolulu Queen	1959	5.00	10.00	20.00
❑ 4-41476	You Called Me Another Woman's Name/The Gambler and the Lady	1959	3.75	7.50	15.00
❑ 4-41636	What Does a Poor Girl Do/Just Like I Knew	1960	3.75	7.50	15.00
❑ 4-41795	I Didn't Mean It/Some Place to Cry	1960	3.75	7.50	15.00
RCA VICTOR					
❑ APBO-0005	I Can't Sleep with You/It's a Long Way from Heaven	1973	—	3.50	7.00
❑ 47-8261	Let's Go All the Way/Private Little World	1963	3.00	6.00	12.00
❑ 47-8328	Put Your Arms Around Her/I'm a Walkin' Advertisement (For the Blues)	1964	3.00	6.00	12.00
❑ 47-8433	Go Cat Go/Lonesome Number One	1964	3.00	6.00	12.00
❑ 47-8518	I Cried All the Way to the Bank/You Have to Be Out of Your Mind	1965	3.00	6.00	12.00

Number	Title (A Side/B Side)	Yr	VG	VG+	NM
❑ 47-8623	I Wouldn't Buy a Used Car from Him/I'm No Longer in Your Heart	1965	3.00	6.00	12.00
❑ 47-8720	You're Driving Me Out of My Mind/Then Go Home to Her	1965	3.00	6.00	12.00
❑ 47-8790	The Shirt/Please Don't Hurt Me	1966	3.00	6.00	12.00
❑ 47-8887	Pursuing Happiness/It Wasn't God Who Made Honky Tonk Angels	1966	3.00	6.00	12.00
❑ 47-8989	Don't Let That Doorknob Hit You/Company's Comin'	1966	3.00	6.00	12.00
❑ 47-9147	Conscience Keep an Eye on Me/Still	1967	2.50	5.00	10.00
❑ 47-9258	Jackson Ain't a Very Big Town/Now It's Every Night	1967	2.50	5.00	10.00
❑ 47-9362	Heaven Help the Working Girl/Your Alibi Called Today	1967	2.50	5.00	10.00
❑ 47-9466	Truck Driving Woman/Supper Time	1968	2.50	5.00	10.00
❑ 47-9558	You Changed Everything About Me But My Name/A-11	1968	2.50	5.00	10.00
❑ 47-9645	One Man Band/I Can't Leave Him	1968	2.50	5.00	10.00
❑ 47-9774	You're At Your Best/Long Ago Is Gone	1969	2.00	4.00	8.00
❑ 47-9809	Two Good Reasons/Somebody's Gonna Plow Your Field	1969	2.00	4.00	8.00
❑ 47-9854	What More Can I Do/Another Man Loved Me Last Night	1970	2.00	4.00	8.00
❑ 47-9900	Whiskey-Six Years Old/I'm Givin' Up	1970	2.00	4.00	8.00
❑ 47-9946	The Kind of Needin' I Need/A Little Unfair	1971	2.00	4.00	8.00
❑ 47-9983	Back to His-Hers/That Song Writin' Man	1971	2.00	4.00	8.00
❑ 48-1016	Chicken Every Sunday/Heavenly	1971	2.00	4.00	8.00
❑ 74-0115	Dusty Road/Love's a Woman's Job	1969	2.00	4.00	8.00
❑ 74-0214	Home-Made Love/These Flowers	1969	2.00	4.00	8.00
❑ 74-0643	If I'm a Fool for Leaving/Thank You for Loving Me	1972	—	3.50	7.00
❑ 74-0749	Hundred Dollar Funeral/Sally Trash	1972	—	3.50	7.00
❑ 74-0814	I Guess That Comes from Being Poor/I Know an Ending	1972	—	3.50	7.00
❑ 74-0935	Jersey 33/The Only Way to Hold Your Man	1973	—	3.50	7.00

Albums

HARMONY

Number	Title	Yr	VG	VG+	NM
❑ HL 7363 [M]	Country's Favorite	1966	5.00	10.00	20.00
❑ HS 11163 [R]	Country's Favorite	1966	3.75	7.50	15.00

RCA VICTOR

Number	Title	Yr	VG	VG+	NM
❑ LPM-2961 [M]	Let's Go All the Way	1964	6.25	12.50	25.00
❑ LSP-2961 [S]	Let's Go All the Way	1964	7.50	15.00	30.00
❑ LPM-3449 [M]	Pretty Miss Norma Jean	1965	6.25	12.50	25.00
❑ LSP-3449 [S]	Pretty Miss Norma Jean	1965	7.50	15.00	30.00
❑ LPM-3541 [M]	Please Don't Hurt Me	1966	6.25	12.50	25.00
❑ LSP-3541 [S]	Please Don't Hurt Me	1966	7.50	15.00	30.00
❑ LPM-3664 [M]	Norma Jean Sings a Tribute to Kitty Wells	1966	6.25	12.50	25.00
❑ LSP-3664 [S]	Norma Jean Sings a Tribute to Kitty Wells	1966	7.50	15.00	30.00
❑ LPM-3700 [M]	Norma Jean Sings Porter Wagoner	1967	7.50	15.00	30.00
❑ LSP-3700 [S]	Norma Jean Sings Porter Wagoner	1967	6.25	12.50	25.00
❑ LPM-3836 [M]	Jackson Ain't a Very Big Town	1967	7.50	15.00	30.00
❑ LSP-3836 [S]	Jackson Ain't a Very Big Town	1967	6.25	12.50	25.00
❑ LPM-3910 [M]	Heaven's Just a Prayer Away	1967	12.50	25.00	50.00
❑ LSP-3910 [S]	Heaven's Just a Prayer Away	1967	6.25	12.50	25.00
❑ LSP-3977	Body and Mind	1968	6.25	12.50	25.00
❑ LSP-4080	Love's a Woman's Job	1968	6.25	12.50	25.00
❑ LSP-4146	Country Giants	1969	6.25	12.50	25.00
❑ LSP-4227	The Best of Norma Jean	1969	6.25	12.50	25.00
❑ LSP-4446	It's Time for Norma Jean	1969	6.25	12.50	25.00

NORMALTOWN FLYERS, THE

45s

MERCURY

Number	Title	Yr	VG	VG+	NM
❑ 868088-7	Rockin' the Love Boat/Up Above the Clouds	1991	—	2.50	5.00

NORMAN, JIM

45s

OVATION

Number	Title	Yr	VG	VG+	NM
❑ 1159	The Old Songs/Worn Out Dreams and Desires	1980	—	2.50	5.00

REPUBLIC

Number	Title	Yr	VG	VG+	NM
❑ 030	The Love in Me/Love Makes the World Go Square	1978	—	2.50	5.00

NORMAN, JIMMY

45s

MERCURY

Number	Title	Yr	VG	VG+	NM
❑ 72658	Family Tree/It's Beautiful When You're Falling in Love	1967	2.50	5.00	10.00
❑ 72727	If You Love Her (Show It)/I'm Leaving (This Old Town)	1967	2.50	5.00	10.00

NORWOOD, DARON

45s

GIANT

Number	Title	Yr	VG	VG+	NM
❑ 7-17881	My Girl Friday/Break the Radio	1995	—	2.00	4.00
❑ 7-17958	Bad Dog, No Biscuit/There'll Always Be a Honky Tonk Somewhere	1995	—	2.00	4.00
❑ 7-18005	The Working Elf Blues/Rockin' Little Christmas *—B-side by Carlene Carter*	1994	—	2.00	4.00
❑ 7-18216	Cowboys Don't Cry/J.T. Miller's Farm	1994	—	2.00	4.00
❑ 7-18388	If It Wasn't for Her I Wouldn't Have You/A Little Bigger Piece of American Pie	1993	—	2.00	4.00

NUNLEY, BILL

45s

CANNERY

Number	Title	Yr	VG	VG+	NM
❑ 0402	I'll Know the Good Times/That's How Long I'll Wait for You	1988	—	3.00	6.00
❑ 0525	The Way You Got Over Me/(B-side unknown)	1988	—	3.00	6.00

NUNN, EARL

Selected 78s

SPECIALTY

Number	Title	Yr	VG	VG+	NM
❑ 701	Double Talkin' Woman/I've Loved You Too Long to Forget You	1949	7.50	15.00	30.00

NUTTER, MAYF

45s

CAPITOL

Number	Title	Yr	VG	VG+	NM
❑ 3181	Never Ending Song of Love/Okla.	1971	—	3.00	6.00
❑ 3226	Never Had a Doubt/The Litterbug Song	1971	—	3.00	6.00
❑ 3296	The Sing-Along Song/I Better Let You Be	1972	—	3.00	6.00
❑ 3447	Party Doll/Another Cup of Memories	1972	—	3.00	6.00
❑ 3532	I'll Try to Make It Home Next Sunday Night/Martin Collier Was a Gambler	1973	—	3.00	6.00
❑ 3606	Take Me, Make Me/Working for the City	1973	—	3.00	6.00
❑ 3734	Green Door/One More Lie	1973	—	3.00	6.00
❑ 3812	Chattanoogie Shoe Shine Boy/Never Had a Doubt	1974	—	3.00	6.00

GNP CRESCENDO

Number	Title	Yr	VG	VG+	NM
❑ 805	Sweet Southern Lovin'/Hitch Hike Nightmare	1976	—	2.50	5.00
❑ 809	Goin' Skinny Dippin'/(Take Me Home) Country Roads	1976	—	2.50	5.00

REPRISE

Number	Title	Yr	VG	VG+	NM
❑ 0882	Hey There Johnny/My Kind of Music	1969	—	3.50	7.00

STARDAY

Number	Title	Yr	VG	VG+	NM
❑ 910	The Other Side/Simpson Creek (Won't Never Run Free Again)	1970	2.00	4.00	8.00

STRAIGHT

Number	Title	Yr	VG	VG+	NM
❑ 103	Are My Thoughts with You/Baby You Can Fly	1969	3.00	6.00	12.00
❑ 105	Everybody's Talkin'/Long Distance	1969	3.75	7.50	15.00

Albums

CAPITOL

Number	Title	Yr	VG	VG+	NM
❑ ST-11194	The First Batch	1973	3.00	6.00	12.00

GNP CRESCENDO

Number	Title	Yr	VG	VG+	NM
❑ GNPS-2104	Goin' Skinny Dippin'	1976	3.00	6.00	12.00

O

O'CONNOR, MARK

45s

WARNER BROS

Number	Title	Yr	VG	VG+	NM
❑ PRO-S-2842 [DJ]	Sleigh Ride/White Christmas Makes Me Blue *—B-side by Randy Travis*	1987	—	3.00	6.00

WARNER BROS.

Number	Title	Yr	VG	VG+	NM
❑ 7-18342	The Devil Comes Back to Georgia/Diggy Diggy Do	1993	—	2.00	4.00
❑ 7-19354	Restless/Dance of the Ol' Swamp Rat	1991	—	—	3.00

O'DAY, TOMMY

45s

NU TRAYL

Number	Title	Yr	VG	VG+	NM
❑ 901	Frisco (I'm Going Back Home)/I'm Gonna Change My Ways Tomorrow	197?	2.00	4.00	8.00
❑ 904	The Memory Tree/Roses Are Red	197?	2.00	4.00	8.00
❑ 905	They Call the Wind Maria/Sweeter Than Mountain Water	197?	2.00	4.00	8.00
❑ 906	Portrait of My Love/Today's Woman	197?	2.00	4.00	8.00
❑ 907	Cattle Call/Billy Bayou	197?	2.00	4.00	8.00
❑ 909	The Man in Her Sleep/Up and Over Your Love	1977	—	3.00	6.00
❑ 912	Candy Bars, Lollipops/Wrote This Song for You	1977	—	3.00	6.00
❑ 916	Mr. Sandman/Winter Winds of Love	1977	—	3.00	6.00
❑ 919	Memories Are Made of This/Up and Over Your Love	1977	—	3.00	6.00
❑ 922	I Wrote This Song for You/Sweeter Than Mountain Water	1978	—	3.00	6.00
❑ 923	When a Woman Cries/Round and Round	1978	—	3.00	6.00
❑ 924	From a Jack to a King/The Wayward Wind	1978	—	3.00	6.00
❑ 926	I Heard a Song Today/Today's Woman	1978	—	3.00	6.00
❑ 929	Accentuate the Positive/Blue River	1979	—	3.00	6.00
❑ 930	Your Other Love/Painted, Tainted Rose	1979	—	3.00	6.00
❑ 931	Secretly/I'm Gonna Kiss Your Past Goodbye	1979	—	3.00	6.00
❑ 933	Daddy Went Out Walking/Don't Stepping Out Mean	1979	—	3.00	6.00
❑ 1001	Look at All the Angels/(B-side unknown)	1980	—	3.00	6.00

Albums

NU TRAYL

Number	Title	Yr	VG	VG+	NM
❑ NLP-6005	Tommy O'Day	1977	3.75	7.50	15.00
❑ NLP-6006	Tommy O'Day Sings Today's Woman	1978	3.75	7.50	15.00

O'DELL, DOYE

Number	Title (A Side/B Side)	Yr	VG	VG+	NM
45s					
BERDIE					
❑ 1003/4	Suddenly/Just Trying to Help You Out	196?	3.75	7.50	15.00
❑ 1009	I'm Picking Fights for Christmas/(B-side unknown)	196?	3.75	7.50	15.00
ERA					
❑ 1024	According to the Evidence/Bow Your Head and Pray	1956	5.00	10.00	20.00
INTRO					
❑ 6032	Ol' Tex Kringle/My Little Red Wagon	195?	5.00	10.00	20.00
❑ 6047	Diesel Smoke/If Tears Were Gold	195?	5.00	10.00	20.00
❑ 6048	The Man Behind the Throttle/Mabel, Mabel	195?	5.00	10.00	20.00
❑ 6084	Dear Oakie/When My Sunshine Goes Walking in the Rain	195?	5.00	10.00	20.00
JAN MAR					
❑ 306	Louisiana Lady/Give Someone Else the Welfare	197?	2.00	4.00	8.00
LIBERTY					
❑ 55310	Run, Thief, Run/Two Sides to Every Story	1961	3.75	7.50	15.00
❑ 55347	Dreamboat, Still Afloat/Lights in the Streets	1961	3.75	7.50	15.00
LONGHORN					
❑ 2001	Diesel Smoke, Dangerous Curves/Cheers To Ya Baby	198?	—	3.00	6.00
RADIO					
❑ 115	Strange Nights/Bring a Hammer and a Needle	1958	5.00	10.00	20.00
SAGE					
❑ 295	Uncle Happy/Andy Backer	196?	3.75	7.50	15.00
❑ 297	If the Devil Wants to Talk/Everybody Likes a Little Lovin'	196?	3.75	7.50	15.00
❑ 304	That Takes a Lot Out of Me/Half Past a Heartache	196?	3.75	7.50	15.00
❑ 314	Count Down/Shalley Belle	196?	3.75	7.50	15.00
❑ 345	Diesel Smoke/Wish I Stayed in the Wagon Yard	196?	3.75	7.50	15.00
❑ 350	Burning Bridges/Take Any Number	196?	3.75	7.50	15.00
❑ 357	Plant a Watermelon on My Grave/Someone Has to Lose	196?	3.75	7.50	15.00
SAND					
❑ 362	A Hammer and a Needle/Little Scraps of Paper	196?	3.75	7.50	15.00
❑ 367	Pretty Little Gal/A House But Not a Home	196?	3.75	7.50	15.00
❑ 376	Half Past a Heartache/White Shortguns	196?	3.75	7.50	15.00
❑ 395	Andy Bakker/Uncle Happy	196?	3.75	7.50	15.00
❑ 427	You're Lonely, He's Left, I'm Right/So What!	196?	3.75	7.50	15.00
❑ 437	Goin' to Do Some Walkin'/It's So Hard to Face Tomorrow	196?	3.75	7.50	15.00
❑ 442	Paint the Bar Stool White/Pick Me Up on Your Way Down	196?	3.75	7.50	15.00
Selected 78s					
EXCLUSIVE					
❑ 14x	Up the River/Wearing My Heart on My Sleeve	1947	5.00	10.00	20.00
❑ 15x	Old Shep/Two Eyes, Two Lips	1947	5.00	10.00	20.00
❑ 22x	Give Me Texas/The Little Shirt My Mother Made for Me	1947	5.00	10.00	20.00
❑ 25x	Bath Tub Blues/I'm Not Foolin' Now	1948	5.00	10.00	20.00
❑ 27x	Who Do You Spend Your Dreams With?/Shut Up and Drink Your Beer	1948	5.00	10.00	20.00
❑ 30x	Peekin', Peekin', Peekin'/A Million Memories	1948	5.00	10.00	20.00
❑ 33x	Dear Oakie/Lookin' Poor, But Feelin' Rich	1948	5.00	10.00	20.00
❑ 43x	The Roving Gambler/Mother, the Queen of My Heart	1948	5.00	10.00	20.00
❑ 52x	Old Boy/I Signed on the Dotted Line	1948	5.00	10.00	20.00
❑ 58x	Please My Little Darlin'/Ring Around the Moon	1948	5.00	10.00	20.00
❑ 65x	Blue Christmas/Dear Mr. Santa	1948	6.25	12.50	25.00
❑ 72x	Sally Sue from Salisaw/I Don't Call Me Daddy	1949	5.00	10.00	20.00
❑ 73x	Tennessee/Red Head Polka	1949	5.00	10.00	20.00
❑ 88x	Oakies in California/She Left Me When My Dreamboat Started Leakin'	1949	5.00	10.00	20.00
❑ 112	Horses, Women and Wine/I Want More Mustard on My Hot Dog	1949	5.00	10.00	20.00
MERCURY					
❑ 6218	Mosey On/If You Want Some Lovin'	1949	5.00	10.00	20.00
❑ 6238	Without Your Wedding Ring/There's a Shamrock (Growin' in Texas)	1950	5.00	10.00	20.00
❑ 6245	Somebody's Stealin' My Baby's Sugar/Sitting Alone at the Table	1950	5.00	10.00	20.00
❑ 6259	The Candy Man/That's Just My Hand You're Holding (Not My Heart)	1950	5.00	10.00	20.00
Albums					
ERA					
❑ EL-20004 [M]	Doye	1956	12.50	25.00	50.00
—Red vinyl					
❑ EL-20004 [M]	Doye	1956	7.50	15.00	30.00
—Black vinyl					
SAGE					
❑ C-36 [M]	Crossroads	195?	7.50	15.00	30.00

O'DELL, KENNY

Number	Title (A Side/B Side)	Yr	VG	VG+	NM
45s					
CAPRICORN					
❑ 0020	Rock and Roll Man/Ain't Gonna Study No More	1973	—	2.50	5.00
❑ 0038	You Bet Your Sweet. Sweet Love/Let's Go Find Some Country Music	1973	—	2.50	5.00
❑ 0203	I Take It On Home/I'll Find Another Way	1974	—	2.00	4.00
❑ 0219	Soulful Woman/Let's Get On the Road	1975	—	2.00	4.00
❑ 0233	My Honky Tonk Ways/Behind Closed Doors	1975	—	2.00	4.00
❑ 0247	Together This Christmas/I Can't Think When You're Doing That to Me	1975	—	2.00	4.00
❑ 0301	Let's Shake Hands and Come Out Lovin'/We Might Be All Night	1978	—	2.00	4.00
❑ 0309	As Long As I Can Wake Up in Your Arms/Soulful Woman	1978	—	2.00	4.00
❑ 0317	Medicine Woman/Who Do I Know in Denver	1979	—	2.00	4.00
EPIC					
❑ 10693	If I Was a Rambler/High on Life	1971	—	2.50	5.00
❑ 10730	I Was a Loser (But Now I've Got You)/Jubal	1971	—	2.50	5.00
❑ 10791	I Was a Loser (But Now I've Got You)/Jubal	1971	—	2.50	5.00
KAPP					
❑ 2169	Two for the Road/Why Don't We Go Somewhere and Love	1972	—	2.50	5.00
❑ 2178	Lizzie and the Rainman/Homecoming Queen	1972	—	2.50	5.00
MAR-KAY					
❑ 3696	Old Time Lovin'/Take Another Look	1966	2.50	5.00	10.00
VEGAS					
❑ 718	Beautiful People/Flower Girl	1967	2.00	4.00	8.00
❑ 722	Springfield Plane/I'm Gonna Take It	1968	—	3.00	6.00
❑ 724	Happy with You/Couldn't Love You	1968	—	3.00	6.00
WHITE WHALE					
❑ 319	No Obligation/(B-side unknown)	1969	—	3.00	6.00
❑ 331	Groovy Relationship/(B-side unknown)	1969	—	3.00	6.00
Albums					
CAPRICORN					
❑ CP 0140	Kenny O'Dell	1974	3.00	6.00	12.00
❑ CP 0211	Let's Shake Hands and Come Out Lovin'	1978	3.00	6.00	12.00
VEGAS					
❑ 401	Beautiful People	1968	6.25	12.50	25.00

O'DOSKI, GAIL

Number	Title (A Side/B Side)	Yr	VG	VG+	NM
45s					
DOOR KNOB					
❑ 258	Please Have Your Number Changed/(B-side unknown)	1987	—	2.50	5.00
❑ 265	Early Morning Love/Please Have Your Number Changed	1987	—	2.50	5.00
❑ 273	Before They Pour the Wine/(B-side unknown)	1987	—	2.50	5.00
❑ 288	First Came the Feelin'/(B-side unknown)	1987	—	2.50	5.00
❑ 300	(Just an) Old Wives' Tale/(B-side unknown)	1988	—	2.50	5.00

O'GWYNN, JAMES

Also see RITA REMINGTON.

Number	Title (A Side/B Side)	Yr	VG	VG+	NM
45s					
D					
❑ 1006	Talk to Me Lonesome Heart/Changeable	1958	7.50	15.00	30.00
❑ 1022	Blue Memories/You Don't Want to Hold Me	1958	7.50	15.00	30.00
MERCURY					
❑ 71066	Mule Skinner Blues/Who'll Be the Next One	1957	5.00	10.00	20.00
❑ 71127	I Cry/Do You Miss Me	1957	5.00	10.00	20.00
❑ 71234	Two Little Hearts/You've Always Won	1957	5.00	10.00	20.00
❑ 71419	How Can I Think of Tomorrow/Were You Ever a Stranger	1959	3.75	7.50	15.00
❑ 71452	Trying to Forget You/Take the Last Look	1959	3.75	7.50	15.00
❑ 71513	Easy Money/Tears of Tomorrow	1959	3.75	7.50	15.00
❑ 71584	Someone Sweet to Love/That's All I Got from You	1960	3.75	7.50	15.00
❑ 71640	You're Too Easy to Remember/I Won't Love You Anymore	1960	3.75	7.50	15.00
❑ 71731	House of Blue Lovers/Another Falling Tear	1960	3.75	7.50	15.00
❑ 71807	Down on the Corner of Love/I'm Getting Nowhere Fast	1961	3.75	7.50	15.00
❑ 71864	Too Much of You/Your Heart	1961	3.75	7.50	15.00
❑ 71935	My Name Is Mud/You're Getting All Over Me	1962	3.75	7.50	15.00
❑ 72008	Does He Mean That Much to You/What Do You Want from Me	1962	3.75	7.50	15.00
❑ 72053	Don't We All Have the Right/That's How It Is	1962	3.75	7.50	15.00
PLANTATION					
❑ 83	House of Blue Lovers/Tomorrow Ends Like Today	1972	2.00	4.00	8.00
❑ 94	I'm the Mail She's Waiting For/Country Song	197?	2.00	4.00	8.00
❑ 98	Shade Tree Fix-It Man/Country Song	197?	2.00	4.00	8.00
❑ 109	Queen of Every Honk-E-Tonk/Gotebo	197?	2.00	4.00	8.00
❑ 115	Singing in the Jungle/If I Could Sing a Country Song	197?	2.00	4.00	8.00
❑ 122	We Love Her/(B-side unknown)	197?	—	3.50	7.00
—With Rusty Adams					
❑ 130	Talk to Me, Lonely Heart/Tender Years	1975	—	3.00	6.00
❑ 138	One Night One/Living with a Memory	1976	—	3.50	7.00
❑ 161	Sock It To Her Song/(B-side unknown)	197?	—	3.00	6.00
❑ 164	If I Could Get One More Hit/Sock It To Her Song	197?	—	3.00	6.00
❑ 181	The Colour of the Blues/Swinging Doors	197?	—	3.00	6.00
STARDAY					
❑ 266	If I Never Get to Heaven/Losing Game	1956	7.50	15.00	30.00
Albums					
MERCURY					
❑ MG-20727 [M]	The Best of James O'Gwynn	1962	7.50	15.00	30.00
❑ SR-60727 [S]	The Best of James O'Gwynn	1962	10.00	20.00	40.00
PLANTATION					
❑ 21	Greatest Hits	197?	3.00	6.00	12.00
WING					
❑ MGW-12290 [M]	Heartaches and Memories	1964	5.00	10.00	20.00
❑ SRW-16290 [S]	Heartaches and Memories	1964	6.25	12.50	25.00

O'HARA, JAMIE
Also see THE O'KANES.

Number	Title (A Side/B Side)	Yr	VG	VG+	NM
45s					
RCA					
❑ 62610	What's a Good Ol' Boy to Do/For Reasons I've Forgotten	1993	—	2.00	4.00
❑ 62797	The Cold Hard Truth/Miles of Heartache	1994	—	2.00	4.00

O'KANES, THE
Also see KIERAN KANE; JAMIE O'HARA.

Number	Title (A Side/B Side)	Yr	VG	VG+	NM
45s					
COLUMBIA					
❑ 38-06242	Oh Darlin'/When I Found You	1986	—	—	3.00
❑ 38-06242 [PS]	Oh Darlin'/When I Found You	1986	—	2.00	4.00
❑ 38-06606	Can't Stop My Heart from Loving You/Blue Grass	1987	—	—	3.00
❑ 38-06606 [PS]	Can't Stop My Heart from Loving You/Blue Grass	1987	—	2.00	4.00
❑ 38-07187	Daddies Need to Grow Up Too/Oh Darlin'	1987	—	—	3.00
❑ 38-07611	Just Lovin' You/When We're Gone, Long Gone	1987	—	—	3.00
❑ 38-07736	One True Love/If I Could Be There	1988	—	—	3.00
❑ 38-07943	Blue Love/Highway 55	1988	—	—	3.00
❑ 38-08099	Rocky Road/All Because of You	1988	—	—	3.00
❑ 38-73216	Why Should I?/This Ain't Love	1989	—	—	3.00
❑ 38-73304	Diddy All Night Long/Why Should I	1990	—	2.00	4.00
❑ 38-73445	Tell Me I Was Dreaming/This Ain't Love	1990	—	2.00	4.00
Albums					
COLUMBIA					
❑ BFC 40459	The O'Kanes	1986	2.00	4.00	8.00
❑ FC 44066	Tired of the Runnin'	1988	2.00	4.00	8.00

O'KEEFE, DANNY

Number	Title (A Side/B Side)	Yr	VG	VG+	NM
45s					
ATLANTIC					
❑ 2978	Angel, Spread Your Wings/Mad Ruth the Babe	1973	—	2.50	5.00
❑ 3267	The Delta Queen/Quits	1975	—	2.50	5.00
JERDEN					
❑ 806	Don't Wake Me in the Morning/That Old Sweet Song	1966	2.50	5.00	10.00
PICCADILLY					
❑ 228	Don't Wake Me in the Morning/That Old Sweet Song	1967	2.00	4.00	8.00
❑ 237	Today One Day Later/Baby	1967	2.00	4.00	8.00
SIGNPOST					
❑ 70004	Good Time Charlie's Got the Blues/The Valentine Pieces	1972	—	3.00	6.00
❑ 70012	The Road/I'm Sober Now	1972	—	2.50	5.00
WARNER BROS.					
❑ 8435	You Look Just Like a Girl Again/On Discovering a Missing Person	1977	—	2.50	5.00
❑ 8489	The Runaway/Just Jones	1977	—	2.50	5.00
Albums					
ATLANTIC					
❑ SD 7264	Breezy Stories	1973	3.00	6.00	12.00
❑ SD 18125	So Long, Harry Truman	1975	3.00	6.00	12.00
COTILLION					
❑ SD 9036	Danny O'Keefe	1971	3.75	7.50	15.00
FIRST AMERICAN					
❑ 7700	The Seattle Tapes	1977	3.00	6.00	12.00
❑ 7721	The Seattle Tapes, Volume 2	1979	3.00	6.00	12.00
PANORAMA					
❑ 105	Introducing Danny O'Keefe	1966	10.00	20.00	40.00
SIGNPOST					
❑ SD 8404	O'Keefe	1972	3.00	6.00	12.00
WARNER BROS.					
❑ PRO 760 [DJ]	The O'Keefe File	1977	3.75	7.50	15.00
❑ BS 3050	American Roulette	1977	2.50	5.00	10.00
❑ BSK 3314	Global Blues	1978	2.50	5.00	10.00

O'NEAL, AUSTIN

Number	Title (A Side/B Side)	Yr	VG	VG+	NM
45s					
PROJECT ONE					
❑ 002	Nights Like Tonight/(B-side unknown)	1983	2.00	4.00	8.00

O'NEAL, COLEMAN

Number	Title (A Side/B Side)	Yr	VG	VG+	NM
45s					
CHANCELLOR					
❑ 108	Mr. Heartache, Move On/Make Him Know	1962	3.00	6.00	12.00

O'NEAL, JAMIE

Number	Title (A Side/B Side)	Yr	VG	VG+	NM
45s					
MERCURY					
❑ 088 172177-7	There Is No Arizona/Frantic	2000	—	—	3.00

O'NEAL, POLLY

Number	Title (A Side/B Side)	Yr	VG	VG+	NM
45s					
COLUMBIA					
❑ 4-21331	I've Been Cryin'/That New Girl Down the Street	1954	5.00	10.00	20.00

O'SHEA, CATHY

Number	Title (A Side/B Side)	Yr	VG	VG+	NM
45s					
MCA					
❑ 40843	Help Me Make It Through the Night/Broken Dolls Need Love Too	1977	—	2.50	5.00
❑ 40884	Love at First Sight/Strawberry Jam	1978	—	2.50	5.00
❑ 40934	Roses Ain't Red/Love Is Just a Bar Stool Away	1978	—	2.00	4.00
MONUMENT					
❑ 8587	Don't Mess with Me/Goodbye for the Last Time	1973	—	2.50	5.00
❑ 8609	Behind Every Good Woman/Thanks, I Needed That	1974	—	2.50	5.00
❑ 8637	You're Gonna Love Yourself in the Morning/Little Boy Tracks	1975	—	2.50	5.00
❑ 8668	Help Me/I Won't Be Out Playin'	1975	—	2.50	5.00

O'SHEA, SHAD

Number	Title (A Side/B Side)	Yr	VG	VG+	NM
45s					
FRATERNITY					
❑ 3372	Y-Tel Presents/Maybe the Roses	197?	—	—	—
—Canceled					
❑ 3381	Colorado Call/Bub-Bub-Bub-Boo	1975	2.00	4.00	8.00
❑ 3385	Big John D/Ginger Cookies	1976	—	3.00	6.00
❑ 3386	What Is America?/One Small Voice	1976	—	3.00	6.00
❑ 3393	The Good Ship Titanic/One Small Voice	197?	—	3.00	6.00
❑ 3410	Sweet Chastity/Big Mac and Tiny Tim	197?	—	3.00	6.00
❑ 3432	Thanks for the Ride/Y-Tel Presents	197?	—	3.00	6.00
❑ 3491	Where's the Beef/(B-side unknown)	1984	—	3.00	6.00
❑ 3494	Centerfolds Bare She Is/(B-side unknown)	1984	—	3.00	6.00
GRT					
❑ 068	What Is America?/One Small Voice	1976	—	2.50	5.00
NORMAN					
❑ 521	Hit Record Pt. 2/Shad's Tune	1963	3.00	6.00	12.00
❑ 529	The Club/The Golden Miracle	1963	3.00	6.00	12.00
PLANTATION					
❑ 101	Goodbye Sam/The Applegate Free Food Band	1973	—	3.00	6.00
❑ 210	McLove Story (same on both sides)	1982	2.00	4.00	8.00
PRIVATE STOCK					
❑ 45,071	Colorado Call/Bub-Bub-Bub-Boo	1976	—	2.50	5.00
SOUND STAGE 7					
❑ 2539	Little General/I Got the Miz-Er-Ees	1965	2.50	5.00	10.00

OAK RIDGE BOYS, THE
Includes records by the group's predecessor, The Oak Ridge Quartet. Also see WILLIAM LEE GOLDEN.

Number	Title (A Side/B Side)	Yr	VG	VG+	NM
45s					
ABC					
❑ 12350	I'll Be True to You/Old Time Family Bluegrass Band	1978	—	2.00	4.00
❑ 12397	Cryin' Again/I Can Love You	1978	—	2.00	4.00
❑ 12434	Come On In/Morning Glory Do	1978	—	2.00	4.00
❑ 12463	Sail Away/Only One	1979	—	2.00	4.00
ABC/DOT					
❑ 17710	Y'All Come Back Saloon/Emmylou	1977	—	2.00	4.00
❑ 17732	You're the One/Morning Glory Do	1977	—	2.00	4.00
CADENCE					
❑ 1362	The Mocking Bird/The House of the Lord	1959	6.25	12.50	25.00
—As "The Oak Ridge Quartet"					
CAPITOL					
❑ F2181	A Mother's Prayer/My Lord's Gonna Move This Wicked Race	1952	7.50	15.00	30.00
❑ F2182	Give Me That Old Time Religion/No Tears in Heaven	1952	7.50	15.00	30.00
❑ F2183	Her Mansion Is Higher Than Mine/I've Found a Hidin' Place	1952	7.50	15.00	30.00
—The above three as "The Oak Ridge Quartet"					
CAPITOL NASHVILLE					
❑ S7-19345	Blue Christmas/I Still Believe in Christmas	1996	—	—	3.00
—B-side by Billy Dean					
COLUMBIA					
❑ 10083	Rhythm Guitar/There Must Be a Better Way	1975	—	2.50	5.00
❑ 10226	Heaven Bound/Look Away Mama	1975	—	2.50	5.00
❑ 10320	Where the Soul Never Dies/No Earthly Good	1976	—	2.50	5.00
❑ 10349	Family Reunion/Don't Be Late	1976	—	2.50	5.00
❑ 10419	All Our Favorite Songs/Whoever Finds This, I Love You	1976	—	2.50	5.00
❑ 11009	Rhythm Guitar/All Our Favorite Songs	1979	—	2.00	4.00
❑ 46001	He's Gonna Shine on Me/Put Your Arms Around Me, Blessed Jesus	1974	—	2.50	5.00
❑ 46044	Loves Me Like a Rock/He	1974	—	2.50	5.00
HEARTWARMING					
❑ 5067	How Much Farther Can We Go/(B-side unknown)	197?	2.00	4.00	8.00
❑ 5094	Talk About the Good Times/Get Together	197?	2.00	4.00	8.00
❑ 5103	Jesus Christ, What a Man/God Is Beautiful	197?	2.00	4.00	8.00
❑ 5119	The Flowers Kissed the Shoes/(B-side unknown)	197?	2.00	4.00	8.00
MCA					
❑ S45-1154 [DJ]	Santa's Song/Happy Christmas Eve	1982	3.00	6.00	12.00
❑ S45-1250 [DJ]	Thank God for Kids/Jesus Is Born Today	1982	3.00	6.00	12.00
❑ S45-1741 [DJ]	The Boy Scout Way/Check Out the Boy Scouts	1981	3.75	7.50	15.00
—Label calls this a "Public Service Recording (Not for Sale)"					
❑ 12463	Sail Away/Only One	1979	—	—	3.00
❑ S45-17233 [DJ]	When You Give It Away/The Voices of Rejoicing Love	1986	3.75	7.50	15.00
—Promo only on green vinyl					
❑ S45-17450 [DJ]	There's a New Kid In Town/From a Distance	1986	2.50	5.00	10.00
—B-side by Nanci Griffith					
❑ 41078	Dream On/Sometimes the Rain Won't Let Me Sleep	1979	—	2.00	4.00
❑ 41154	Leaving Louisiana in the Broad Daylight/I Gotta Get Over This	1979	—	2.00	4.00
❑ 41217	Trying to Love Two Women/Hold On 'Til Sunday	1980	—	2.00	4.00
❑ 41280	Love Takes Two/Heart of Mine	1980	—	2.00	4.00

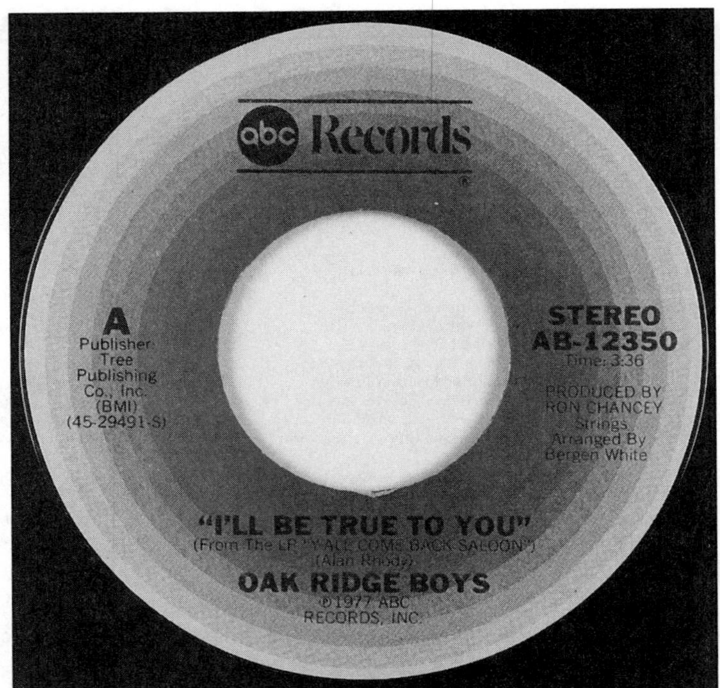

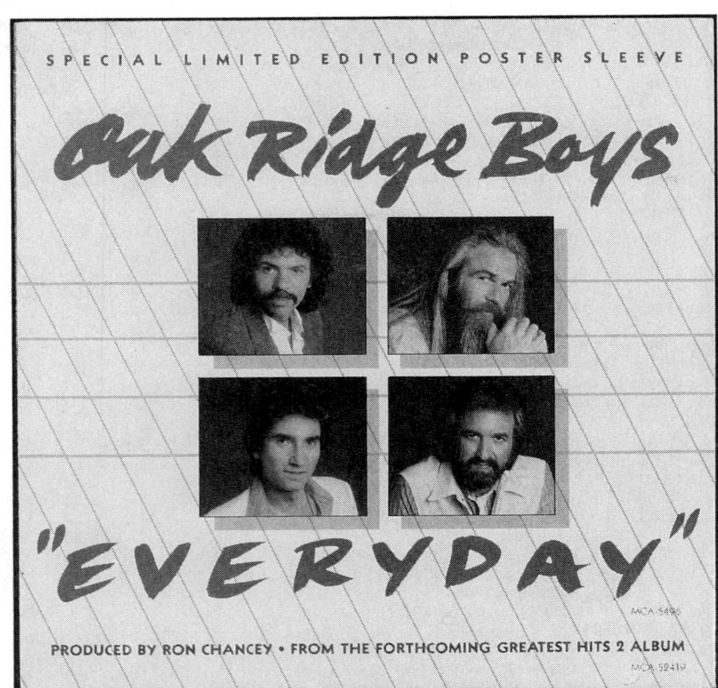

The Oak Ridge Boys were a direct descendant of the gospel group The Oak Ridge Quintet. They kept the same harmonies but sang country music instead. (Top left) Their first chart-topper was "I'll Be True to You" in 1978; it was their third straight top 10 hit. (Top right) During the height of *Urban Cowboy*-inspired country crossovers in 1981, "Elvira" became a phenomenon. Their remake of an obscure Dallas Frazier song made the top 5 of the pop charts, hit the top on the country charts, and was certified platinum. (Bottom left) "Everyday," a No. 1 song from 1984, came with a fold-out poster sleeve on some of its stock copies. (Bottom right) In 1990, the Oak Ridge Boys signed with RCA. Their last vinyl album, *Unstoppable* in 1991, was issued, appropriately, by the BMG Music Service.

Number	Title (A Side/B Side)	Yr	VG	VG+	NM
❑ 51022	Ready to Take My Chances/Beautiful You	1980	—	2.00	4.00
❑ 51084	Elvira/A Woman Like You	1981	—	2.00	4.00
❑ 51169	Fancy Free/How Long Has It Been	1981	—	2.00	4.00
❑ 51231	Bobbie Sue/Live In Love	1982	—	2.00	4.00
❑ 52006	Bobbie Sue/Live In Love	1982	—	2.00	4.00
❑ 52065	So Fine/I Wish You Were Here	1982	—	2.00	4.00
❑ 52095	Back in Your Arms Again/I Wish I Could Have Turned My Head	1982	—	2.00	4.00
❑ 52145	Thank God for Kids/Christmas Is Paintin' the Town	1982	—	2.00	4.00
❑ 52179	American Made/The Cure for My Broken Heart	1983	—	2.00	4.00
❑ 52224	Love Song/Heart on the Line	1983	—	2.00	4.00
❑ 52288	Ozark Mountain Jubilee/Down Deep Inside	1983	—	2.00	4.00
❑ 52342	I Guess It Never Hurts to Hurt Sometimes/ Through My Eyes	1984	—	—	3.00
❑ 52419	Everyday/Ain't No Cure for the Rock 'N' Roll	1984	—	—	3.00
❑ 52488	Make My Life with You/Break My Mind	1984	—	—	3.00
❑ 52556	Little Things/Secret of Love	1985	—	—	3.00
❑ 52646	Touch a Hand, Make a Friend/Only One I Love	1985	—	—	3.00
❑ 52722	Come On In (You Did the Best You Could Do)/ Roll Tennessee River	1985	—	—	3.00
❑ 52722 [DJ]	Come On In (You Did the Best You Could Do) (same on both sides)	1985	2.50	5.00	10.00
—Promo only on blue vinyl					
❑ 52722 [PS]	Come On In (You Did the Best You Could Do)/ Roll Tennessee River	1985	—	2.00	4.00
❑ 52801	Juliet/Everybody Wins	1986	—	—	3.00
❑ 52801 [DJ]	Juliet (same on both sides)	1986	3.00	6.00	12.00
—Promo only on green vinyl					
❑ 52873	You Made a Rock Out of a Rolling Stone/Hidin' Place	1986	—	—	3.00
❑ 53010	It Takes a Little Rain (To Make Love Grow)/ Looking for Love	1987	—	—	3.00
❑ 53023	This Crazy Love/Where the Fast Lane Ends	1987	—	—	3.00
❑ 53023 [DJ]	This Crazy Love (same on both sides)	1987	2.50	5.00	10.00
—Promo only on blue vinyl					
❑ 53175	Time In/A Little More Coal on the Fire	1987	—	—	3.00
❑ 53272	True Heart/Love Without Mercy	1988	—	—	3.00
❑ 53381	Gonna Take a Lot of River/Private Lives	1988	—	—	3.00
❑ 53460	Bridges and Walls/Never Together (But Close Sometimes)	1988	—	—	3.00
❑ 53625	Beyond Those Years/Too Many Heartaches	1989	—	—	3.00
❑ 53705	An American Family/Too Many Heartaches	1989	—	—	3.00
❑ 53757	No Matter How High/Bed of Roses	1989	—	—	3.00
❑ 79006	Baby, You'll Be My Baby/Cajun Girl	1990	—	—	3.00
RCA					
❑ 2665-7-R	Soul and Inspiration/(B-side unknown)	1990	—	2.00	4.00
❑ 2779-7-R	Lucky Moon/Walkin' After Midnight	1991	—	2.00	4.00
❑ 62013	Change My Mind/Our Love Is Here to Stay	1991	—	2.00	4.00
❑ 62099	Baby On Board/When It Comes to You	1991	—	2.00	4.00
❑ 62228	Fall/Wait Until You're Back in My Arms Again	1992	—	2.00	4.00
WARNER BROS.					
❑ 5359	This Ole House/Early in the Morning	1963	5.00	10.00	20.00

Albums

Number	Title	Yr	VG	VG+	NM
ABC					
❑ AA-1065	Room Service	1978	2.50	5.00	10.00
❑ AA-1135	Have Arrived	1979	3.00	6.00	12.00
ABC/DOT					
❑ DA-2093	Y'all Come Back Saloon	1977	2.50	5.00	10.00
ACCORD					
❑ SN-7138	Spiritual Jubilee	198?	2.50	5.00	10.00
❑ SN-7159	Spiritual Jubilee — Volume 2	198?	2.50	5.00	10.00
❑ SN-7199	Spiritual Jubilee — Volume 3	198?	2.50	5.00	10.00
CADENCE					
❑ CLP-3019 [M]	The Oak Ridge Quartet	1958	15.00	30.00	60.00
CANAAN					
❑ 9625	Together	1966	5.00	10.00	20.00
—With the Harvesters					
COLUMBIA					
❑ KC 32742	The Oak Ridge Boys	1974	3.00	6.00	12.00
❑ PC 32742	The Oak Ridge Boys	197?	2.00	4.00	8.00
—Reissue					
❑ KC 33057	Sky High	1975	3.00	6.00	12.00
❑ PC 33057	Sky High	197?	2.00	4.00	8.00
—Reissue					
❑ KC 33935	Old Fashioned, Down Home, Hand Clappin', Foot Stompin', Southern Style, Gospel Quartet Music	1976	3.00	6.00	12.00
❑ PC 35202	The Best of the Oak Ridge Boys	1978	2.50	5.00	10.00
❑ PC 37711	Old Fashoned Gospel Quartet Music	1984	2.00	4.00	8.00
❑ FC 37737	All Our Favorite Songs	1981	2.50	5.00	10.00
❑ PC 38467	Smoky Mountain Gospel	1984	2.00	4.00	8.00
HEARTWARMING					
❑ HWS 3036	Thanks	1971	3.75	7.50	15.00
❑ HWS 3091	International	1971	3.75	7.50	15.00
❑ HWS 3159	The Light	1972	3.75	7.50	15.00
INTERMEDIA					
❑ QS-5012	Glory Train	198?	2.50	5.00	10.00
LIBERTY					
❑ LN-10046	The Oak Ridge Boys at Their Best	1981	2.00	4.00	8.00
MCA					
❑ AA-1135	Have Arrived	1979	2.50	5.00	10.00
❑ L33-2-1276 [(2) DJ]	"Step On Out" World Premiere	1985	6.25	12.50	25.00
—Promo-only interview and music LP with no script or cover					
❑ 1446	Deliver	1985	2.00	4.00	8.00
—Budget-line reissue					
❑ 1447	American Made	1985	2.00	4.00	8.00
—Budget-line reissue					
❑ 3220	Together	1980	2.50	5.00	10.00
❑ 5150	Greatest Hits	1980	2.50	5.00	10.00
❑ 5209	Fancy Free	1981	2.50	5.00	10.00
❑ 5294	Bobbie Sue	1982	2.50	5.00	10.00
❑ 5365	Christmas	1982	2.50	5.00	10.00
❑ 5390	American Made	1983	2.50	5.00	10.00
❑ 5455	Deliver	1983	2.50	5.00	10.00
❑ 5496	Greatest Hits 2	1984	2.50	5.00	10.00
❑ 5555	Step On Out	1985	2.50	5.00	10.00
❑ 5714	Seasons	1986	2.50	5.00	10.00
❑ 5799	Christmas Again	1986	2.50	5.00	10.00
❑ 5945	Where the Fast Lane Ends	1987	2.50	5.00	10.00
❑ 37153	Room Service	198?	2.00	4.00	8.00
—Budget-line reissue					
❑ 37221	Have Arrived	1984	2.00	4.00	8.00
—Budget-line reissue					
❑ 37222	Y'all Come Back Saloon	1984	2.00	4.00	8.00
—Budget-line reissue					
❑ 37223	Together	1984	2.00	4.00	8.00
—Budget-line reissue					
❑ 42036	Heartbeat	1987	2.50	5.00	10.00
❑ 42205	Monongahela	1988	2.50	5.00	10.00
❑ 42311	American Dreams	1989	2.50	5.00	10.00
NASHVILLE					
❑ 2086	Higher Power	1970	3.75	7.50	15.00
POWER PAK					
❑ 716	The Oak Ridge Boys	197?	2.50	5.00	10.00
PRIORITY					
❑ PU 37711	Old Fashoned Gospel Quartet Music	1981	2.50	5.00	10.00
❑ PU 38467	Smoky Mountain Gospel	1983	2.50	5.00	10.00
RCA					
❑ R 164223	Unstoppable	1991	3.75	7.50	15.00
—Only released on vinyl through BMG Direct Marketing					
SKYLITE					
❑ RLP-6020 [M]	The Oak Ridge Boys Sing for You	1964	5.00	10.00	20.00
❑ SRLP-6020 [S]	The Oak Ridge Boys Sing for You	1964	6.25	12.50	25.00
❑ RLP-6030 [M]	I Wouldn't Take Nothing for My Journey Now	1965	5.00	10.00	20.00
❑ SRLP-6030 [S]	I Wouldn't Take Nothing for My Journey Now	1965	6.25	12.50	25.00
❑ RLP-6040 [M]	The Solid Gospel Sound of the Oak Ridge Boys	1966	5.00	10.00	20.00
❑ SRLP-6040 [S]	The Solid Gospel Sound of the Oak Ridge Boys	1966	6.25	12.50	25.00
❑ RLP-6045 [M]	River of Love	1967	5.00	10.00	20.00
❑ SRLP-6045 [S]	River of Love	1967	6.25	12.50	25.00
STARDAY					
❑ SLP-356 [M]	The Sensational Oak Ridge Boys	1965	6.25	12.50	25.00
UNITED ARTISTS					
❑ UAL 3554 [M]	The Oak Ridge Boys at Their Best	1966	5.00	10.00	20.00
❑ UAS 6554 [S]	The Oak Ridge Boys at Their Best	1966	6.25	12.50	25.00
❑ LN-10046	The Oak Ridge Boys at Their Best	1979	2.50	5.00	10.00
WARNER BROS.					
❑ W 1497 [M]	With Sounds of Nashville	1963	5.00	10.00	20.00
❑ WS 1497 [S]	With Sounds of Nashville	1963	6.25	12.50	25.00
❑ W 1521 [M]	Folk-Minded Spirituals for Spiritual-Minded Folks	1963	5.00	10.00	20.00
❑ WS 1521 [S]	Folk-Minded Spirituals for Spiritual-Minded Folks	1963	6.25	12.50	25.00

ODESSA

45s

Number	Title (A Side/B Side)	Yr	VG	VG+	NM
SING ME					
❑ 40	Hooked on You/(B-side unknown)	1989	—	3.00	6.00

ODOM, DONNA

45s

Number	Title (A Side/B Side)	Yr	VG	VG+	NM
DECCA					
❑ 32214	She Gets the Roses (I Get the Tears)/I'm a Woman	1967	2.00	4.00	8.00
❑ 32309	I'm Just About to Break and Tell It All/You Ain't Got a Home No More	1968	—	3.50	7.00
❑ 32548	Who's With My Baby/Rainbow in My Tears	1969	—	3.50	7.00

ORBISON, ROY

He didn't begin making the country charts until 1980, but his 1950s and 1960s material is definitely held in high regard in country circles.

12-Inch Singles

Number	Title (A Side/B Side)	Yr	VG	VG+	NM
VIRGIN					
❑ PR 2593 [DJ]	You Got It (same on both sides)	1989	2.50	5.00	10.00
❑ PR 2667 [DJ]	She's a Mystery to Me (same on both sides)	1989	2.50	5.00	10.00

45s

Number	Title (A Side/B Side)	Yr	VG	VG+	NM
ASYLUM					
❑ 46048	Tears/Easy Way Out	1979	—	2.50	5.00
❑ 46541	Poor Baby/Lay It Down	1979	—	2.50	5.00
ERIC					
❑ 7101	Pretty Paper/Oh Pretty Woman	197?	—	2.00	4.00
JE-WEL					
❑ 101	Ooby Dooby/Tryin' to Get to You	1956	1500.	2750.	4000.
—As "The Teen Kings"; with "Vocal: Roy Orbison" credit (spelled correctly)					
❑ 101	Ooby Dooby/Tryin' to Get to You	1956	1500.	2750.	4000.
—As "The Teen Kings"; with "Vocal: Roy Oribson" credit (spelled incorrectly)					
MERCURY					
❑ 73610	Sweet Mama Blue/Heartache	1974	2.00	4.00	8.00
❑ 73652	Hung Up onYou/Spanish Nights	1975	—	3.00	6.00
❑ 73705	It's Lonely/Still	1975	—	3.00	6.00

Number	Title (A Side/B Side)	Yr	VG	VG+	NM
MGM					
❑ CS9-5	Celebrity Scene: Roy Orbison	1967	25.00	50.00	100.00
—Box set of five singles (13756-13760). Price includes box, all 5 singles, jukebox title strips, bio. Records are sometimes found by themselves, so they are also listed separately.					
❑ 13386	Ride Away/Wonderin'	1965	2.50	5.00	10.00
❑ 13386 [PS]	Ride Away/Wonderin'	1965	5.00	10.00	20.00
❑ 13410	Crawling Back/If You Can't Say Something Nice	1965	2.50	5.00	10.00
❑ 13410 [PS]	Crawling Back/If You Can't Say Something Nice	1965	5.00	10.00	20.00
❑ 13446	Breakin' Up Is Breakin' My Heart/Wait	1966	2.50	5.00	10.00
❑ 13446 [PS]	Breakin' Up Is Breakin' My Heart/Wait	1966	5.00	10.00	20.00
❑ 13498	Twinkle Toes/Where Is Tomorrow	1966	2.50	5.00	10.00
❑ 13498 [PS]	Twinkle Toes/Where Is Tomorrow	1966	5.00	10.00	20.00
❑ 13549	Too Soon to Know/You'll Never Be Sixteen Again	1966	2.50	5.00	10.00
❑ 13549 [PS]	Too Soon to Know/You'll Never Be Sixteen Again	1966	5.00	10.00	20.00
❑ 13634	Communication Breakdown/Going Back to Gloria	1966	2.50	5.00	10.00
❑ 13685	So Good/Memories	1967	2.50	5.00	10.00
❑ 13756	Ride Away/Crawlin' Back	1967	3.75	7.50	15.00
—Part of Celebrity Scene CS9-5					
❑ 13757	Breakin' Up Is Breakin' My Heart/Too Soon to Know	1967	3.75	7.50	15.00
—Part of Celebrity Scene CS9-5					
❑ 13758	Twinkle Toes/Where Is Tomorrow?	1967	3.75	7.50	15.00
—Part of Celebrity Scene CS9-5					
❑ 13759	Sweet Dreams/Going Back to Gloria	1967	3.75	7.50	15.00
—Part of Celebrity Scene CS9-5					
❑ 13760	You'll Never Be Sixteen Again/There Won't Be Many Coming Home	1967	3.75	7.50	15.00
—Part of Celebrity Scene CS9-5					
❑ 13764	Cry Softly Lonely One/Pistolero	1967	2.50	5.00	10.00
❑ 13764 [PS]	Cry Softly Lonely One/Pistolero	1967	5.00	10.00	20.00
❑ 13817	She/Here Comes the Rain Baby	1967	2.50	5.00	10.00
❑ 13889	Shy Away/Born to Be Loved by You	1968	2.50	5.00	10.00
❑ 13950	Flowers/Walk On	1968	2.50	5.00	10.00
❑ 13991	Heartache/Sugar Man	1968	2.50	5.00	10.00
❑ 14039	Southbound Jericho Parkway/My Friend	1969	2.50	5.00	10.00
❑ 14079	Penny Arcade/Tennessee Own My Soul	1969	2.50	5.00	10.00
❑ 14105	How Do You Start Over/She Cheats on Me	1970	2.50	5.00	10.00
❑ 14121	So Young/If I Had a Woman Like You	1970	2.50	5.00	10.00
❑ 14293	Close Again/Last Night	1971	2.50	5.00	10.00
❑ 14358	Changes/God Loves You	1972	2.50	5.00	10.00
❑ 14413	Remember the Good/Harlem Woman	1972	2.50	5.00	10.00
❑ 14413	Remember the Good/If Only for a While	1972	2.50	5.00	10.00
❑ 14441	I Can Read Between the Lines/Memphis, Tennessee	1972	2.50	5.00	10.00
❑ 14552	Rain Rain (Coming Down)/Sooner or Later	1973	2.50	5.00	10.00
❑ 14626	I Wanna Live/You Lay So Easy on My Mind	1973	2.50	5.00	10.00
MONUMENT					
❑ 409	Paper Boy/With the Bug	1959	20.00	40.00	80.00
—White label with vertical lines					
❑ 412	Uptown/Pretty One	1959	7.50	15.00	30.00
❑ 421	Only the Lonely (Know the Way I Feel)/Here Comes That Song Again	1960	6.25	12.50	25.00
❑ 425	Blue Angel/Today's Teardrops	1960	5.00	10.00	20.00
❑ 433	I'm Hurtin'/I Can't Stop Loving You	1960	5.00	10.00	20.00
❑ 433 [PS]	I'm Hurtin'/I Can't Stop Loving You	1960	30.00	60.00	120.00
❑ 438	Running Scared/Love Hurts	1961	5.00	10.00	20.00
❑ 438 [PS]	Running Scared/Love Hurts	1961	10.00	20.00	40.00
❑ 447	Crying/Candy Man	1961	5.00	10.00	20.00
❑ 447 [PS]	Crying/Candy Man	1961	10.00	20.00	40.00
❑ 456	Dream Baby (How Long Must I Dream)/The Actress	1962	5.00	10.00	20.00
❑ 456 [PS]	Dream Baby (How Long Must I Dream)/The Actress	1962	10.00	20.00	40.00
❑ 461	The Crowd/Mama	1962	5.00	10.00	20.00
❑ 461 [PS]	The Crowd/Mama	1962	10.00	20.00	40.00
❑ 467	Leah/Workin' for the Man	1962	5.00	10.00	20.00
❑ 467 [PS]	Leah/Workin' for the Man	1962	10.00	20.00	40.00
❑ 806	In Dreams/Shahdaroba	1963	5.00	10.00	20.00
❑ 806 [PS]	In Dreams/Shahdaroba	1963	10.00	20.00	40.00
❑ 815	Falling/Distant Drums	1963	5.00	10.00	20.00
❑ 815 [PS]	Falling/Distant Drums	1963	12.50	25.00	50.00
❑ 824	Mean Woman Blues/Blue Bayou	1963	5.00	10.00	20.00
❑ 830	Pretty Paper/Beautiful Dreamer	1963	5.00	10.00	20.00
❑ 837	It's Over/Indian Wedding	1964	5.00	10.00	20.00
❑ 837 [PS]	It's Over/Indian Wedding	1964	10.00	20.00	40.00
❑ 851	Pretty Woman/Yo Te Amo Maria	1964	7.50	15.00	30.00
—Original title					
❑ 851	Oh Pretty Woman/Yo Te Amo Maria	1964	5.00	10.00	20.00
—Revised title					
❑ 873	Goodnight/Only with You	1965	3.75	7.50	15.00
❑ 891	(Say) You're My Girl/Sleepy Hollow	1965	3.75	7.50	15.00
❑ 906	Let the Good Times Roll/Distant Drums	1965	3.75	7.50	15.00
❑ 939	Lana/Our Summer Song	1966	3.75	7.50	15.00
❑ 1936	Pretty Paper/Beautiful Dreamer	1976	—	2.00	4.00
❑ 8690	Belinda/All These Chains	1976	—	2.50	5.00
❑ 45200	(I'm a) Southern Man/Born to Love Me	1976	—	2.50	5.00
❑ 45215	Drifting Away/Under Suspicion	1977	—	2.50	5.00
RCA VICTOR					
❑ 47-7381	Sweet and Innocent/Seems to Me	1958	10.00	20.00	40.00
❑ 47-7447	Almost Eighteen/Julie	1959	10.00	20.00	40.00
SUN					
❑ 242	Ooby Dooby/Go! Go! Go!	1956	25.00	50.00	100.00
❑ 251	Rockhouse/You're My Baby	1956	15.00	30.00	60.00
❑ 265	Devil Doll/Sweet and Easy to Love	1957	20.00	40.00	80.00
❑ 284	Chicken Hearted/I Like Love	1958	12.50	25.00	50.00
❑ 353	Devil Doll/Sweet and Easy to Love	1960	62.50	125.00	250.00
VIRGIN					
❑ 99159	Oh Pretty Woman/Claudette	1989	—	—	3.00
❑ 99159 [PS]	Oh Pretty Woman/Claudette	1989	—	—	3.00
❑ 99202	California Blue/In Dreams	1989	—	—	3.00
❑ 99202 [PS]	California Blue/In Dreams	1989	—	—	3.00
❑ 99227	She's a Mystery to Me/Dream Baby	1989	—	—	3.00
❑ 99227 [PS]	She's a Mystery to Me/Dream Baby	1989	—	—	3.00
❑ 99245	You Got It/The Only One	1989	—	—	3.00
❑ 99245 [PS]	You Got It/The Only One	1989	—	—	3.00
❑ 99388	Crying/Falling	1988	—	—	3.00
—A-side with k.d. lang					
❑ 99388 [PS]	Crying/Falling	1988	—	—	3.00
❑ 99434	In Dreams/Leah	1987	—	—	3.00
❑ 99434 [PS]	In Dreams/Leah	1987	—	2.00	4.00
WARNER BROS.					
❑ 49262	That Lovin' You Feeling Again/Lola	1980	—	2.50	5.00
—A-side with Emmylou Harris; B-side by Craig Hundley					
Albums					
ACCORD					
❑ SN-7150	Ooby Dooby	1981	2.00	4.00	8.00
ASYLUM					
❑ 6E-198	Laminar Flow	1979	3.00	6.00	12.00
BUCKBOARD					
❑ 5-1015	Roy Orbison's Golden Hits	197?	2.50	5.00	10.00
CANDELITE					
❑ P2 12946 [(2)]	The Living Legend of Roy Orbison	1976	3.75	7.50	15.00
DESIGN					
❑ DLP-164 [M]	Orbiting with Roy Orbison	196?	3.75	7.50	15.00
❑ DLPS-164 [R]	Orbiting with Roy Orbison	196?	2.50	5.00	10.00
HALLMARK					
❑ SHM-824	The Exciting Roy Orbison	197?	2.00	4.00	8.00
HITS UNLIMITED					
❑ 233-0	My Spell on You	1982	2.00	4.00	8.00
MERCURY					
❑ SRM-1-1045	I'm Still in Love with You	1975	3.00	6.00	12.00
MGM					
❑ E-4308 [M]	There Is Only One Roy Orbison	1965	6.25	12.50	25.00
❑ SE-4308 [S]	There Is Only One Roy Orbison	1965	8.75	17.50	35.00
❑ E-4322 [M]	The Orbison Way	1965	6.25	12.50	25.00
❑ SE-4322 [S]	The Orbison Way	1965	8.75	17.50	35.00
❑ E-4379 [M]	The Classic Roy Orbison	1966	6.25	12.50	25.00
❑ SE-4379 [S]	The Classic Roy Orbison	1966	8.75	17.50	35.00
❑ E-4424 [M]	Roy Orbison Sings Don Gibson	1967	6.25	12.50	25.00
❑ SE-4424 [S]	Roy Orbison Sings Don Gibson	1967	8.75	17.50	35.00
❑ E-4514 [M]	Cry Softly, Lonely One	1967	6.25	12.50	25.00
❑ SE-4514 [S]	Cry Softly, Lonely One	1967	8.75	17.50	35.00
❑ SE-4636	The Many Moods of Roy Orbison	1969	6.25	12.50	25.00
❑ SE-4659	The Great Songs of Roy Orbison	1970	6.25	12.50	25.00
❑ SE-4683	Hank Williams the Roy Orbison Way	1970	6.25	12.50	25.00
❑ SE-4835	Roy Orbison Sings	1972	3.75	7.50	15.00
❑ SE-4867	Memphis	1972	3.75	7.50	15.00
❑ SE-4934	Milestones	1973	3.75	7.50	15.00
❑ ST 90454 [S]	There Is Only One Roy Orbison	1965	10.00	20.00	40.00
—Capitol Record Club edition					
❑ T 90454 [M]	There Is Only One Roy Orbison	1965	10.00	20.00	40.00
—Capitol Record Club edition					
❑ ST-90631 [S]	The Orbison Way	1965	8.75	17.50	35.00
—Capitol Record Club edition					
❑ T-90631 [M]	The Orbison Way	1965	8.75	17.50	35.00
—Capitol Record Club edition					
❑ ST-90928 [S]	The Classic Roy Orbison	1966	8.75	17.50	35.00
—Capitol Record Club edition					
❑ T-90928 [M]	The Classic Roy Orbison	1966	8.75	17.50	35.00
—Capitol Record Club edition					
❑ ST-91173 [S]	Roy Orbison Sings Don Gibson	1967	8.75	17.50	35.00
—Capitol Record Club edition					
❑ T-91173 [M]	Roy Orbison Sings Don Gibson	1967	8.75	17.50	35.00
—Capitol Record Club edition					
MONUMENT					
❑ M-4002 [M]	Lonely and Blue	1961	37.50	75.00	150.00
❑ M-4007 [M]	Crying	1962	30.00	60.00	120.00
❑ M-4009 [M]	Roy Orbison's Greatest Hits	1962	12.50	25.00	50.00
❑ MC-6619	Roy Orbison's Greatest Hits	1977	3.00	6.00	12.00
❑ MC-6620	In Dreams	1977	3.00	6.00	12.00
❑ MC-6621	More of Roy Orbison's Greatest Hits	1977	3.00	6.00	12.00
❑ MC-6622	The Very Best of Roy Orbison	1977	3.00	6.00	12.00
❑ MG-7600	Regeneration	1976	3.75	7.50	15.00
❑ MLP-8000 [M]	Roy Orbison's Greatest Hits	1963	7.50	15.00	30.00
❑ MLP-8003 [M]	In Dreams	1963	12.50	25.00	50.00
—White and rainbow label					
❑ MLP-8003 [M]	In Dreams	1964	7.50	15.00	30.00
—Green and gold label					
❑ MLP-8023 [M]	Early Orbison	1964	7.50	15.00	30.00
❑ MLP-8024 [M]	More of Roy Orbison's Greatest Hits	1964	7.50	15.00	30.00
❑ MLP-8035 [M]	Orbisongs	1965	6.25	12.50	25.00
❑ MLP-8045 [M]	The Very Best of Roy Orbison	1966	6.25	12.50	25.00
❑ MP-8600 [(2)]	The All-Time Greatest Hits of Roy Orbison	1977	4.00	8.00	16.00
❑ SM-14002 [S]	Lonely and Blue	1961	150.00	300.00	600.00
❑ SM-14007 [S]	Crying	1962	150.00	300.00	600.00
❑ SM-14009 [S]	Roy Orbison's Greatest Hits	1962	20.00	40.00	80.00
❑ SLP-18000 [S]	Roy Orbison's Greatest Hits	1963	10.00	20.00	40.00
❑ SLP-18003 [S]	In Dreams	1963	25.00	50.00	100.00
—White and rainbow label					

Number	Title (A Side/B Side)	Yr	VG	VG+	NM
❑ SLP-18003 [S]	In Dreams	1964	12.50	25.00	50.00
—Green and gold label					
❑ SLP-18023 [S]	Early Orbison	1964	12.50	25.00	50.00
❑ SLP-18024 [S]	More of Roy Orbison's Greatest Hits	1964	10.00	20.00	40.00
❑ SLP-18035 [S]	Orbisongs	1965	8.75	17.50	35.00
❑ SLP-18045 [P]	The Very Best of Roy Orbison	1966	8.75	17.50	35.00
—"It's Over" is rechanneled					
❑ KZG 31484 [(2)]	The All-Time Greatest Hits of Roy Orbison	1972	6.25	12.50	25.00
❑ KWG 38384 [(2)]	The All-Time Greatest Hits of Roy Orbison	1982	2.50	5.00	10.00
RHINO					
❑ R1 70711	The Classic Roy Orbison	1989	3.00	6.00	12.00
❑ R1 70916	The Sun Years	1989	3.75	7.50	15.00
❑ R1 71493 [(2)]	For the Lonely: A Roy Orbison Anthology	1988	3.00	6.00	12.00
SUN					
❑ 113	The Original Sun Sound of Roy Orbison	1969	3.00	6.00	12.00
❑ SLP-1260 [M]	Roy Orbison at the Rockhouse	1961	150.00	300.00	600.00
TIME-LIFE					
❑ SRNR 34 [(2)]	Roy Orbison 1960-1965	1990	5.00	10.00	20.00
—Box set in "The Rock 'n' Roll Era" series					
TRIP					
❑ TLX-8505	The Best of Roy Orbison	197?	2.00	4.00	8.00
VIRGIN					
❑ 90604 [(2)]	In Dreams: The Greatest Hits	1987	3.00	6.00	12.00
—Re-recordings of his original hits					
❑ 91058	Mystery Girl	1989	2.50	5.00	10.00
❑ 91295	A Black and White Night	1990	3.75	7.50	15.00

ORDGE, JIMMY ARTHUR

Number	Title (A Side/B Side)	Yr	VG	VG+	NM
45s					
DORE					
❑ 969	Stay Away from Jim/Hard Times	1981	—	3.00	6.00

ORENDER, DEWAYNE

Number	Title (A Side/B Side)	Yr	VG	VG+	NM
45s					
NU TRAYL					
❑ 920	Brother/Standing in the Rain	1978	—	3.00	6.00
RCA					
❑ PB-10813	If You Want to Make Me Feel at Home/Don't Let Any of Her Love Get on You	1976	—	2.50	5.00
❑ PB-10936	To Make a Good Love Die/I Can't Keep My Eyes Off Her	1977	—	2.50	5.00
❑ PB-11039	Love Me Into Heaven Again/If You're Gonna Love	1977	—	2.50	5.00
VOLUNTEER					
❑ 102	Better Than Now/(B-side unknown)	1978	—	3.00	6.00

ORIGINAL TEXAS PLAYBOYS, THE

See THE TEXAS PLAYBOYS.

ORION

Also see JIMMY ELLIS.

Number	Title (A Side/B Side)	Yr	VG	VG+	NM
45s					
KRISTAL					
❑ 2292/2308	I'm Saving Up My Pennies/I'm Starting Over	1985	—	2.00	4.00
❑ 2338	100 Pounds of Clay/Because He Lived	1986	—	2.00	4.00
RADIOACTIVE					
❑ 18772-1 [DJ]	Unchained Melody (same on both sides)	1987	—	2.50	5.00
STARGEM					
❑ 2465 [DJ]	Only a Woman Like You (same on both sides)	1990	—	2.50	5.00
❑ 2469	I Want You, I Need You, I Love You/Plastic Saddle	1990	—	2.50	5.00
❑ 2502	Love It Back Together/If That Isn't Love	1990	—	2.50	5.00
—Red vinyl					
❑ 2502 [PS]	Love It Back Together/If That Isn't Love	1990	—	2.50	5.00
SUN					
❑ 1142	Honey/Ebony Eyes	1979	—	2.00	4.00
❑ 1147	Before the Next Teardrop Falls/Washing Machine	1979	—	2.00	4.00
❑ 1148	Remember Bethlehem/Silent Night	1979	—	2.00	4.00
❑ 1148 [DJ]	Remember Bethlehem (same on both sides)	1979	2.50	5.00	10.00
—Yellow vinyl promo					
❑ 1151	Be-Bop-a-Lula/The Breakup	1980	—	2.00	4.00
—A-side with Jerry Lee Lewis; B-side with Charlie Rich					
❑ 1152	It Ain't No Mystery/Stranger in My Place	1980	—	2.00	4.00
❑ 1152 [DJ]	It Ain't No Mystery (same on both sides)	1980	2.50	5.00	10.00
—Yellow vinyl promo					
❑ 1153	Texas Tea/Faded Love	1980	—	2.00	4.00
❑ 1153 [DJ]	Texas Tea (same on both sides)	1980	2.50	5.00	10.00
—Yellow vinyl promo					
❑ 1156	Am I That Easy to Forget/Crazy Arms	1980	—	2.00	4.00
❑ 1156 [DJ]	Am I That Easy to Forget (same on both sides)	1980	2.50	5.00	10.00
—Yellow vinyl promo					
❑ 1159	Rockabilly Rebel/Memphis Sun	1980	—	2.00	4.00
❑ 1159 [DJ]	Rockabilly Rebel (same on both sides)	1980	2.50	5.00	10.00
—Yellow vinyl promo					
❑ 1162	Crazy Little Thing Called Love/Matchbox	1981	—	2.00	4.00
❑ 1165	Born/If I Can't Have You	1981	—	2.00	4.00
❑ 1165 [DJ]	Born (same on both sides)	1981	2.50	5.00	10.00
—Yellow vinyl promo					
❑ 1170	Some You Win, Some You Lose/Ain't No Good	1981	—	2.00	4.00
❑ 1170 [DJ]	Some You Win, Some You Lose (same on both sides)	1981	2.50	5.00	10.00
—Yellow vinyl promo					
❑ 1172	Baby Please Say Yes/Feelings	1982	—	2.00	4.00
❑ 1175	Honky Tonk Heaven/Morning, Noon and Night	1982	—	2.00	4.00
❑ 1175 [DJ]	Honky Tonk Heaven (same on both sides)	1982	2.50	5.00	10.00
—Yellow vinyl promo					

Number	Title (A Side/B Side)	Yr	VG	VG+	NM
7-Inch Extended Plays					
SUN					
❑ 1152 [DJ]	Stranger in My Place Greetings: Wedding Anniversary/Good Music/Great Station//Favorite Station/Best Music/Birthday	1981	10.00	20.00	40.00
—Came with insert but no cover					
Albums					
SUN					
❑ 1012	Orion Reborn	1978	7.50	15.00	30.00
—White cover, also known as the "coffin cover"					
❑ 1012	Orion Reborn	1978	2.50	5.00	10.00
—Blue cover					
❑ 1017	Sunrise	1979	2.50	5.00	10.00
❑ 1019	Orion Country	1980	2.50	5.00	10.00
❑ 1021	Rockabilly	1981	2.50	5.00	10.00
❑ 1025	Glory	1982	2.50	5.00	10.00
❑ 1028	Fresh	1983	2.50	5.00	10.00

ORLEANS

By the 1980s, they had evolved into a country group.

Number	Title (A Side/B Side)	Yr	VG	VG+	NM
12-Inch Singles					
INFINITY					
❑ L33-1004 [DJ]	Love Takes Time (same on both sides)	1979	2.00	4.00	8.00
45s					
ABC					
❑ 11408	Please Be There/Mountains	1973	—	2.50	5.00
❑ 11420	If/Stoned	1974	—	2.50	5.00
ASYLUM					
❑ 45243	Let There Be Music/Give One Heart	1975	—	2.00	4.00
❑ 45261	Dance with Me/Ending of a Song	1975	—	2.50	5.00
❑ 45336	Still the One/Siam Sam	1976	—	2.50	5.00
—Clouds label					
❑ 45336	Still the One/Siam Sam	1976	—	2.50	5.00
—Dark blue cloudless label					
❑ 45375	Reach/Sweet Destiny	1976	—	2.00	4.00
❑ 45391	The Bum/Spring Fever	1977	—	2.00	4.00
❑ 45447	Business As Usual/Time Passes On	1977	—	2.00	4.00
ATLANTIC AMERICA					
❑ 99981	One of a Kind/Beatin' Around the Bush	1982	—	2.00	4.00
INFINITY					
❑ 50006	Love Takes Time/Isn't It Easy	1979	—	2.00	4.00
❑ 50017	Don't Throw Our Love Away/The Flame and the Moth	1979	—	2.00	4.00
❑ 50036	Forever/Keep On Rollin'	1979	—	2.00	4.00
MCA					
❑ 41228	Change Your Mind/When Are You Coming Home	1980	—	2.00	4.00
❑ 41283	No Ordinary Lady/Dukie's Tune	1980	—	2.00	4.00
❑ 52862	Lady Liberty/On Hold	1986	—	—	3.00
❑ 52909	Grown-Up Children/On Hold	1986	—	—	3.00
❑ 52963	You're Mine/Language of Love	1986	—	—	3.00
Albums					
ABC					
❑ ABCX-795	Orleans	1973	3.75	7.50	15.00
❑ AA-1058	Before the Dance	1977	2.50	5.00	10.00
ASYLUM					
❑ 7E-1029	Let There Be Music	1975	2.50	5.00	10.00
❑ 7E-1070	Waking and Dreaming	1976	2.50	5.00	10.00
INFINITY					
❑ INF-9006	Forever	1979	2.50	5.00	10.00
MCA					
❑ 5110	Orleans	1980	2.50	5.00	10.00
❑ 5767	Grown Up Children	1986	2.00	4.00	8.00
RADIO					
❑ 90012	One of a Kind	1982	2.50	5.00	10.00

ORRALL, ROBERT ELLIS

Also see ORRALL AND WRIGHT.

Number	Title (A Side/B Side)	Yr	VG	VG+	NM
12-Inch Singles					
RCA					
❑ PD-12327	Call the Uh-Oh Squad/(B-side unknown)	1981	2.50	5.00	10.00
❑ JD-13775 [DJ]	Walking Through Landmines (Long)/(Short)	1984	2.00	4.00	8.00
❑ JR-13822 [DJ]	Alibi (same on both sides)	1984	2.00	4.00	8.00
45s					
RCA					
❑ PB-12256	Actually/Looking for the Right Girl	1981	—	2.00	4.00
❑ PB-12326	Call the Uh-Oh Squad/(B-side unknown)	1981	—	2.00	4.00
❑ PB-13431	I Couldn't Say No/The Message	1983	—	2.00	4.00
❑ PB-13593	Tell Me If It Hurts/(You Had) Too Much to Think	1983	—	2.00	4.00
❑ PB-13820	Alibi/There's Nothing Wrong with You	1984	—	2.00	4.00
❑ 62335	Boom! It Was Over/Flying Colors	1992	—	—	3.00
❑ 62475	A Little Bit of Her Love/'Til the Tears Fall	1993	—	—	3.00
❑ 62547	Every Day When I Get Home/True Believer	1993	—	—	3.00
Albums					
RCA VICTOR					
❑ AFL1-4081	Fixation	1981	2.00	4.00	8.00
❑ AFL1-4853	Contain Yourself	1984	2.00	4.00	8.00
❑ MFL1-8502 [EP]	Special Pain	1983	2.00	4.00	8.00

ORRALL AND WRIGHT

Also see ROBERT ELLIS ORRALL; CURTIS WRIGHT.

45s

GIANT

Number	Title (A Side/B Side)	Yr	VG	VG+	NM
❑ 7-18049	If You Could Say What I'm Thinking/Pound, Pound, Pound	1994	—	2.00	4.00
❑ 7-18162	She Loves Me Like She Means It/You Saved Me	1994	—	2.00	4.00

ORTEGA, GILBERT

45s

LRJ

Number	Title (A Side/B Side)	Yr	VG	VG+	NM
❑ 1050	Is It Wrong/Is This All There Is to a Honky Tonk	1977	2.00	4.00	8.00

ORTEGA

Number	Title (A Side/B Side)	Yr	VG	VG+	NM
❑ 1050	I Don't Believe I'll Fall in Love Today/Send Me the Pillow	1978	—	3.50	7.00

ORVILLE AND IVY

See SPEEDY WEST AND JIMMY BRYANT.

OSBORNE, JIMMIE

45s

KING

Number	Title (A Side/B Side)	Yr	VG	VG+	NM
❑ 958	I Hate to Be Jealous/Tell Me Daddy	1951	10.00	20.00	40.00
❑ 971	The Arm of God/He'll Come Like a Thief in the Night	1951	10.00	20.00	40.00
❑ 988	The Voice of Free America/I'm Just a Habit with You	1951	10.00	20.00	40.00
❑ 1012	It's Me Who Has to Suffer/Love Me or Leave Me	1951	7.50	15.00	30.00
❑ 1038	Missing in Action/Give Back My Ring and Picture	1952	7.50	15.00	30.00
❑ 1048	A Million People Have Died/God Has Taken My Flower	1952	7.50	15.00	30.00
❑ 1066	We Can't Take It With Us/How Many Hearts Can You Break	1952	7.50	15.00	30.00
❑ 1117	Mama Won't Agree/Automobile Baby	1952	7.50	15.00	30.00
❑ 1144	Don't Slam the Door/This Evil Life Don't Pay	1952	7.50	15.00	30.00
❑ 1193	Nag, Nag, Nag/I'm Scared to Go Home	1953	7.50	15.00	30.00
❑ 1231	Hills of Roan County/My Main Trial Is Yet to Come	1953	6.25	12.50	25.00
❑ 1268	A Tribute to Robert A. Taft/Korean Story	1953	6.25	12.50	25.00
❑ 1295	You All Come/Come Back to Your Loved Ones	1954	6.25	12.50	25.00
❑ 1314	My Tissue Paper Heart/It Just Tears Me All to Pieces	1954	6.25	12.50	25.00
❑ 1354	I Did and I Does and I Do/A Tennessee Ocean	1954	6.25	12.50	25.00
❑ 1363	Blue Days and Lonely Nights/Invest Your Little Heart	1954	6.25	12.50	25.00
❑ 1393	The First One to Know/An Empty Old Cottage	1954	6.25	12.50	25.00
❑ 1412	Married on Paper/When You Told Me You Love Me	1954	6.25	12.50	25.00
❑ 1484	Too Many Friends/You Can't Sometimes	1955	6.25	12.50	25.00
❑ 1501	Victims of an Innocent Dance/Sinner's Love Affair	1955	6.25	12.50	25.00

Selected 78s

KING

Number	Title (A Side/B Side)	Yr	VG	VG+	NM
❑ 715	My Heart Echoes/Your Lies Have Broken My Heart	1948	5.00	10.00	20.00
❑ 725	Forever Far Apart/It's So Hard to Smile	1948	5.00	10.00	20.00
❑ 736	Mom Is Dying Tonight/A Vacant Sign Upon My Heart	1948	5.00	10.00	20.00
❑ 768	Son Please Meet Me in Heaven/Not Unloved Nor Unclaimed	1949	5.00	10.00	20.00
❑ 788	The Death of Little Kathy Fiscus/A Bundle of Kisses	1949	5.00	10.00	20.00
❑ 817	The Tears of St. Anne/Your Lovin' and Huggin'	1949	5.00	10.00	20.00
❑ 831	I'm Gonna Strut My Stuff/Forever and a Day	1949	5.00	10.00	20.00
❑ 863	You're the Only Angel/What a Price to Pay for Love	1950	5.00	10.00	20.00
❑ 878	You Get the Roses/Helpless Heart	1950	5.00	10.00	20.00
❑ 893	God Please Protect America/The Moon Is Weeping Over You	1950	5.00	10.00	20.00
❑ 908	Thank God for Victory in Korea/Old Family Bible	1950	5.00	10.00	20.00
❑ 926	No Longer an Orphan/The Door to My Heart Is Wide Open	1951	5.00	10.00	20.00
❑ 942	No Bitter Tears/My Saddest Mistake	1951	5.00	10.00	20.00

Albums

AUDIO LAB

Number	Title (A Side/B Side)	Yr	VG	VG+	NM
❑ AL-1527 [M]	Singing Songs He Wrote	1959	25.00	50.00	100.00

KING

Number	Title (A Side/B Side)	Yr	VG	VG+	NM
❑ 730 [M]	The Legendary Jimmy Osborne	1961	12.50	25.00	50.00
❑ 782 [M]	Golden Harvest	1963	12.50	25.00	50.00
❑ 892 [M]	The Very Best of Jimmie Osborne	1964	10.00	20.00	40.00
❑ 941 [M]	Jimmie Osborne's Golden Harvest	1965	10.00	20.00	40.00

OSBORNE BROTHERS, THE

45s

CMH

Number	Title (A Side/B Side)	Yr	VG	VG+	NM
❑ 1522	Shackles and Chains/(B-side unknown)	1979	—	2.00	4.00
—With Mac Wiseman					
❑ 1524	I Can Hear Kentucky Calling Me/(B-side unknown)	1980	—	2.00	4.00

DECCA

Number	Title (A Side/B Side)	Yr	VG	VG+	NM
❑ 31546	Take This Hammer/Don't Even Look at Me	1963	2.00	4.00	8.00
❑ 31595	Bluegrass Express/Cuckoo Bird	1964	2.00	4.00	8.00
❑ 31655	Charlie Cotton/This Heart of Mine	1964	2.00	4.00	8.00
❑ 31751	Hey, Hey, Bartender/Me and My Old Banjo	1965	2.00	4.00	8.00
❑ 31823	Lonesome Day/I'll Be Alright Tomorrow	1965	2.00	4.00	8.00
❑ 31886	Up This Hill and Down/Memories	1965	2.00	4.00	8.00
❑ 31977	Hard Times/A World of Unwanted	1966	2.00	4.00	8.00
❑ 32052	The Kind of Woman I Got/One Tear	1966	2.00	4.00	8.00
❑ 32137	Roll Muddy River/Making Plans	1967	2.00	4.00	8.00
❑ 32242	Rocky Top/My Favorite Memory	1967	2.00	4.00	8.00
❑ 32325	Cut the Cornbread, Mama/If I Could Count on You	1968	2.00	4.00	8.00
❑ 32382	Son of a Sawmill Man/That Was Yesterday	1968	2.00	4.00	8.00
❑ 32451	Working Man/World of Forgotten	1969	2.00	4.00	8.00
❑ 32516	Tennessee Hound Dog/Thanks for All the Yesterdays	1969	2.00	4.00	8.00
❑ 32598	Ruby, Are You Mad/Sempre	1969	2.00	4.00	8.00
❑ 32680	Listen to the Rain/Midnight Angel	1970	2.00	4.00	8.00
❑ 32746	My Old Kentucky Home (Turpentine and Dandelion Wine)/No Good Son of a Gun	1970	2.00	4.00	8.00
❑ 32794	Georgia Pineywoods/Searching for Yesterday	1971	2.00	4.00	8.00
❑ 32864	Muddy Bottom/Beneath Still Waters	1971	2.00	4.00	8.00
❑ 32908	Take Me Home, Country Roads/Tears Are No Stranger	1971	2.00	4.00	8.00
❑ 32942	Windy City/Shelly's Winter Love	1972	2.00	4.00	8.00
❑ 32979	Miss You Mississippi/Today I Started Loving You Again	1972	2.00	4.00	8.00
❑ 33028	Midnight Flyer/Tears Will Kiss the Morning Dew	1972	2.00	4.00	8.00
❑ 55274	Rocky Top (Radio Mix)/Rocky Top (Original Version)	1996	—	2.00	4.00

MCA

Number	Title (A Side/B Side)	Yr	VG	VG+	NM
❑ 40028	Lizzie Lou/Tears	1973	—	2.00	4.00
❑ 40113	Blue Heartache/You're Heavy on My Mind	1973	—	2.00	4.00
❑ 40169	Sled Ridin'/Fastest Grass Alive	1973	—	2.00	4.00
❑ 40226	Bluegrass Melodies/The Seventh of December	1974	—	2.00	4.00
❑ 40346	El Rancho/A Heartache Looking for a Home	1974	—	2.00	4.00
❑ 40509	Don't Let Smokey Mountain Smoke Get In Your Eyes/Born a Ramblin' Man	1976	—	2.00	4.00

MGM

Number	Title (A Side/B Side)	Yr	VG	VG+	NM
❑ 12308	My Aching Heart/Ruby Are You Mad	1956	3.75	7.50	15.00
—With Red Allen					
❑ 12383	Whu Dun It/Teardrops in My Eyes	1956	3.75	7.50	15.00
—With Red Allen					
❑ 12420	Ho Honey Ho/Down in the Willow Garden	1957	3.00	6.00	12.00
—With Red Allen					
❑ 12527	Della Mae/Wild Mountain Honey	1957	3.00	6.00	12.00
—With Red Allen					
❑ 12583	Once More/She's No Angel	1957	3.00	6.00	12.00
—With Red Allen					
❑ 12633	My Destiny/If You Don't Somebody Else Will	1958	3.00	6.00	12.00
—With Red Allen					
❑ 12689	Love Pains/It Hurts to Know	1958	3.00	6.00	12.00
—With Red Allen					
❑ 12762	I Love You Only/Give This Message to Your Heart	1959	3.00	6.00	12.00
❑ 12805	Lost Highway/You'll Never Know	1959	3.00	6.00	12.00
❑ 12839	Sweethearts Again/There's a Woman Behind Every Man	1959	3.00	6.00	12.00
❑ 12930	Blame Me/Lonely, Lonely Me	1960	2.50	5.00	10.00
❑ 12970	At the First Fall of Snow/Fair and Tender Ladies	1960	2.50	5.00	10.00
❑ 13045	Black Sheep Returned to the Fold/Each Season Changes You	1961	2.50	5.00	10.00
❑ 13073	Five Days of Heaven/It Ain't Gonna Rain No Mo'	1962	2.50	5.00	10.00
❑ 13098	Banjo Boys/Poor Old Cora	1962	2.50	5.00	10.00
❑ 13126	Mule Skinner Blues/Lovey Told Me Goodbye	1963	2.50	5.00	10.00

RCA

Number	Title (A Side/B Side)	Yr	VG	VG+	NM
❑ PB-13097	Rocky Top/Old Flames Can't Hold a Candle to You	1982	—	2.00	4.00

Albums

CMH

Number	Title (A Side/B Side)	Yr	VG	VG+	NM
❑ 4501	Greatest Bluegrass Hits, Vol. 1	198?	3.00	6.00	12.00
❑ 6206	#1	197?	3.00	6.00	12.00
❑ 6231	Bluegrass Concerto	197?	3.00	6.00	12.00
❑ 6244	Kentucky Calling Me	1980	3.00	6.00	12.00
❑ 6256	Bobby and His Mandolin	1981	3.00	6.00	12.00
❑ 9008 [(2)]	From Rocky Top to Muddy Bottom	1977	3.75	7.50	15.00
❑ 9011 [(2)]	Bluegrass Collection	1978	3.75	7.50	15.00
❑ 9016 [(2)]	The Essential Bluegrass Album	1979	3.75	7.50	15.00
—With MacWiseman					

DECCA

Number	Title (A Side/B Side)	Yr	VG	VG+	NM
❑ DL 4602 [M]	Voices in the Bluegrass	1965	3.75	7.50	15.00
❑ DL 4767 [M]	Up This Hill and Down	1966	3.75	7.50	15.00
❑ DL 4903 [M]	Modern Sounds of Bluegrass Music	1967	3.75	7.50	15.00
❑ DL 4993 [M]	Yesterday, Today and The Osborne Brothers	1968	6.25	12.50	25.00
❑ DL 74602 [S]	Voices in the Bluegrass	1965	5.00	10.00	20.00
❑ DL 74767 [S]	Up This Hill and Down	1966	5.00	10.00	20.00
❑ DL 74903 [S]	Modern Sounds of Bluegrass Music	1967	5.00	10.00	20.00
❑ DL 74993 [S]	Yesterday, Today and The Osborne Brothers	1968	5.00	10.00	20.00
❑ DL 75079	Favorite Hymns by the Osborne Brothers	1969	5.00	10.00	20.00
❑ DL 75128	Up to Date and Down to Earth	1969	5.00	10.00	20.00
❑ DL 75204	Ru-Beeeee	1970	5.00	10.00	20.00
❑ DL 75271	The Osborne Brothers	1971	3.75	7.50	15.00
❑ DL 75321	Country Roads	1971	3.75	7.50	15.00
❑ DL 75356	Bobby & Sonny	1972	3.75	7.50	15.00

MCA

Number	Title (A Side/B Side)	Yr	VG	VG+	NM
❑ 105	Voices in the Bluegrass	1973	3.00	6.00	12.00
—Reissue of Decca 74602					
❑ 119	Yesterday, Today and The Osborne Brothers	1973	3.00	6.00	12.00
—Reissue of Decca 74993					
❑ 125	Favorite Hymns by the Osborne Brothers	1973	3.00	6.00	12.00
—Reissue of Decca 75079					
❑ 135	Ru-Beeeee	1973	3.00	6.00	12.00
—Reissue of Decca 75204					
❑ 4086 [(2)]	The Best of the Osborne Brothers	1974	3.75	7.50	15.00

Number	Title (A Side/B Side)	Yr	VG	VG+	NM
MGM					
❑ GAS 140	The Osborne Brothers (Golden Archives Series)	1970	5.00	10.00	20.00
❑ E-3734 [M]	Country Pickin' and Hillside Singin'	1959	12.50	25.00	50.00
❑ E-4018 [M]	Bluegrass Music	1962	6.25	12.50	25.00
❑ SE-4018 [S]	Bluegrass Music	1962	7.50	15.00	30.00
❑ E-4090 [M]	Bluegrass Instrumentals	1962	6.25	12.50	25.00
❑ SE-4090 [S]	Bluegrass Instrumentals	1962	7.50	15.00	30.00
❑ E-4149 [M]	Cuttin' Grass	1963	6.25	12.50	25.00
❑ SE-4149 [S]	Cuttin' Grass	1963	7.50	15.00	30.00
RCA VICTOR					
❑ AHL1-4324	Bluegrass Spectacular	1982	2.50	5.00	10.00
❑ AYL1-5436	Bluegrass Spectacular	1985	2.00	4.00	8.00
—"Best Buy Series" reissue					
ROUNDER					
❑ SS-03	The Osborne Brothers with Red Allen	1981	3.00	6.00	12.00
❑ SS-04	The Osborne Brothers	198?	3.00	6.00	12.00
SUGAR HILL					
❑ SH-3740	Some Things I Want to Sing About	1984	2.50	5.00	10.00
❑ SH-3754	Once More, Vol. 1	1986	2.50	5.00	10.00
❑ SH-3758	Once More, Vol. 2	1987	2.50	5.00	10.00
❑ SH-3764	Singing, Shouting Praises	1988	2.50	5.00	10.00

OSLIN, K.T.

45s

Number	Title (A Side/B Side)	Yr	VG	VG+	NM
BNA					
❑ 64600	Silver Tongue and Gold Plated Lies/Miss the Mississippi and You	1996	—	—	3.00
ELEKTRA					
❑ 47132	Clean Your Own Tables/Nelda Jean Prudy	1981	—	2.50	5.00
—As "Kay T. Oslin"					
❑ 69959	Younger Men/How Many Loves Have I Got Left	1982	—	2.50	5.00
—As "Kay T. Oslin"					
RCA					
❑ 2567-7-R	Two Hearts/Jealous	1990	—	—	3.00
❑ 2667-7-R	Come Next Monday/Truly Blue	1990	—	2.00	4.00
❑ 2746-7-R	Mary and Willie/Love Is Strange	1991	—	2.00	4.00
❑ 2829-7-R	You Call Everybody Darling/Still on My Mind	1991	—	—	3.00
❑ 5066-7-R	Wall of Tears/Two Hearts Are Better Than One	1986	—	—	3.00
❑ 5066-7-R [PS]	Wall of Tears/Two Hearts Are Better Than One	1986	—	2.00	4.00
❑ 5154-7-R	80's Ladies/Old Pictures	1987	—	—	3.00
❑ 5154-7-R [PS]	80's Ladies/Old Pictures	1987	—	2.00	4.00
❑ 5239-7-R	Do Ya'/Lonely But Only for You	1987	—	—	3.00
❑ 5330-7-R	I'll Always Come Back/Old Pictures	1987	—	—	3.00
❑ 8380-7-R	Do Ya'/80's Ladies	1988	—	—	3.00
—"Gold Standard Series" reissue					
❑ 8388-7-R	Money/Dr., Dr.	1988	—	—	3.00
❑ 8725-7-R	Hold Me/She Don't Talk Like Us No More	1988	—	—	3.00
❑ 8865-7-R	Hey Bobby/Where Is a Woman to Go	1989	—	—	3.00
❑ 8943-7-R	This Woman/Younger Men	1989	—	—	3.00
❑ 9029-7-R	Didn't Expect It to Go Down This Way/Round the Clock Lovin'	1989	—	—	3.00
❑ 62053	Cornell Crawford/Two Hearts	1991	—	2.00	4.00

Albums

Number	Title (A Side/B Side)	Yr	VG	VG+	NM
RCA					
❑ 5924-1-R	80's Ladies	1987	2.50	5.00	10.00
❑ 8369-1-R	This Woman	1988	2.50	5.00	10.00

OSMOND, DONNY AND MARIE

Also see MARIE OSMOND. Donny never made the country charts on his own, nor did he try, so his solo records are not listed.

45s

Number	Title (A Side/B Side)	Yr	VG	VG+	NM
MGM					
❑ 14735	I'm Leaving It (All) Up to You/The Umbrella Song	1974	—	2.50	5.00
❑ 14765	Morning Side of the Mountain/One of Those Days	1974	—	2.00	4.00
❑ 14807	Make the World Go Away/Living on My Suspicion	1975	—	2.00	4.00
❑ 14840	Deep Purple/Take Me Back Again	1975	—	2.00	4.00
POLYDOR					
❑ 14363	Ain't Nothin' Like the Real Thing/Sing	1976	—	2.00	4.00
❑ 14439	(You're My) Soul and Inspiration/Now We're Together	1977	—	2.00	4.00
❑ 14456	Baby, I'm Sold on You/Sure Would Be Nice	1978	—	2.00	4.00
❑ 14474	May Tomorrow Be a Perfect Day/I Want to Give You My Everything	1978	—	2.00	4.00
❑ 14510	On the Shelf/Certified Honey	1978	—	2.00	4.00

Albums

Number	Title (A Side/B Side)	Yr	VG	VG+	NM
MGM					
❑ M3G-4968	I'm Leaving It All Up to You	1974	2.50	5.00	10.00
❑ M3G-4996	Make the World Go Away	1975	2.50	5.00	10.00
POLYDOR					
❑ PD-1-6068	Donny & Marie — Featuring Songs from Their Television Show	1976	2.00	4.00	8.00
❑ PD-1-6083	Donny & Marie — New Season	1976	2.00	4.00	8.00
❑ PD-1-6127	Winning Combination	1978	2.00	4.00	8.00
❑ PD-1-6169	Goin' Coconuts	1978	2.00	4.00	8.00

OSMOND, MARIE

Also see DONNY AND MARIE OSMOND.

45s

Number	Title (A Side/B Side)	Yr	VG	VG+	NM
CAPITOL					
❑ B-5445	Until I Fall in Love Again/I Don't Want to Go Too Far	1985	—	—	3.00
❑ B-5478	Meet Me in Montana/What Do Lonely People Do	1985	—	—	3.00
—With Dan Seals					
❑ B-5478 [PS]	Meet Me in Montana/What Do Lonely People Do	1985	—	2.00	4.00
❑ B-5521	There's No Stopping Your Heart/Blue Sky Shinin'	1985	—	—	3.00
❑ B-5563	Read My Lips/That Old Devil Moon	1986	—	—	3.00
❑ B-5613	You're Still New to Me/New Love	1986	—	—	3.00
—With Paul Davis					
❑ B-5613 [PS]	You're Still New to Me/New Love	1986	—	2.00	4.00
❑ B-5663	I Only Wanted You/We're Gonna Need a Love Song	1986	—	—	3.00
❑ B-5703	Everybody's Crazy 'Bout My Baby/Making Music	1987	—	—	3.00
❑ B-44044	Cry Just a Little/More Than Dancing	1987	—	—	3.00
❑ B-44176	Without a Trace/Baby's Blue Eyes	1988	—	—	3.00
❑ B-44215	Sweet Life/My Home Town Boy	1988	—	—	3.00
—A-side: With Paul Davis					
❑ B-44269	I'm in Love and He's in Dallas/My Home Town Boy	1989	—	—	3.00
❑ B-44412	Steppin' Stone/What Would You Do About Me If You Were Me	1989	—	—	3.00
❑ B-44468	Slowly But Surely/What Would You Do About You	1989	—	2.00	4.00
❑ 7PRO-79808	Slowly But Surely (same on both sides)	1989	—	2.50	5.00
—Vinyl originally was promo only					
❑ 7PRO-(# unk) [DJ]	Let Me Be the First (same on both sides)	1990	—	2.50	5.00
—Vinyl is promo only					
CURB					
❑ 76840	Like a Hurricane/I'll Be Faithful to You	1990	—	2.00	4.00
❑ 76851	Paper Roses/Think with Your Heart	1990	—	2.00	4.00
ELEKTRA					
❑ 69882	I'm Learning/Look Who's Getting Over Who	1982	—	2.00	4.00
❑ 69995	Back to Believing Again/Look Who's Getting Over Who	1982	—	2.00	4.00
MGM					
❑ 14609	Paper Roses/Least of All You	1973	—	2.50	5.00
❑ 14609 [PS]	Paper Roses/Least of All You	1973	2.00	4.00	8.00
❑ 14694	My Little Corner of the World/It's Just the Other Way Around	1974	—	2.00	4.00
❑ 14786	Who's Sorry Now/This I Promise You	1975	—	2.00	4.00
POLYDOR					
❑ 14333	"A" My Name Is Alice/Weeping Willow	1976	—	2.00	4.00
❑ 14385	This Is the Way That I Feel/Play the Music Loud	1977	—	2.00	4.00
❑ 14385 [PS]	This Is the Way That I Feel/Play the Music Loud	1977	—	2.50	5.00
❑ 14405	Cry, Baby, Cry/Please Tell Him I Said Hello	1977	—	2.00	4.00
RCA					
❑ PB-13680	Who's Counting/'Til the Best Comes Along	1983	—	2.00	4.00

Albums

Number	Title (A Side/B Side)	Yr	VG	VG+	NM
CAPITOL					
❑ ST-12414	There's No Stopping Your Heart	1985	2.00	4.00	8.00
❑ ST-12516	I Only Wanted You	1986	2.00	4.00	8.00
❑ C1-48968	All in Love	1988	2.00	4.00	8.00
❑ C1-91781	Steppin' Stone	1989	2.50	5.00	10.00
MGM					
❑ SE-4910	Paper Roses	1973	3.00	6.00	12.00
❑ M3G-4944	In My Little Corner of the World	1974	3.00	6.00	12.00
❑ M3G-4979	Who's Sorry Now	1975	3.00	6.00	12.00
POLYDOR					
❑ PD-1-6099	This Is the Way That I Feel	1977	2.00	4.00	8.00

OSMONDS, THE

The below are the records from their 1980s country years, most of which were released as "The Osmond Brothers." Also see MERRILL AND JESSICA.

45s

Number	Title (A Side/B Side)	Yr	VG	VG+	NM
ELEKTRA					
❑ 47438	I Think About Your Lovin'/Working Man's Blues	1982	—	2.00	4.00
❑ 69883	Never Ending Song of Love/You'll Be Seeing Me	1982	—	2.00	4.00
❑ 69969	It's Like Falling in Love/Your Leaving Was the Last Thing on My Mind	1982	—	2.00	4.00
EMI AMERICA					
❑ 8298	Baby When Your Heart Breaks Down/Love Burning Down	1985	—	—	3.00
❑ 8313	Baby Wants/Lovin' Proof	1986	—	—	3.00
❑ 8325	You Look Like the One I Love/It's Only a Heartache	1986	—	—	3.00
❑ 8360	Looking for Suzanne/Back in Your Arms	1986	—	—	3.00
❑ 43033	Slow Ride/Heartbreak Radio	1987	—	—	3.00
WARNER BROS.					
❑ 28982	Any Time/Desperately	1985	—	—	3.00
❑ 29312	If Every Man Had a Woman Like You/Come Back to Me	1984	—	2.00	4.00
❑ 29387	Where Does An Angel Go When She Cries/One More for Lovers	1984	—	2.00	4.00
❑ 29594	She's Ready for Someone to Love Her/You Make the Long Road Shorter with Your Love	1983	—	2.00	4.00

Albums

Number	Title (A Side/B Side)	Yr	VG	VG+	NM
ELEKTRA					
❑ 60180	The Osmond Brothers	1982	2.50	5.00	10.00
WARNER BROS.					
❑ 25070	One Way Rider	1983	2.00	4.00	8.00

OTT, PAUL

45s

Number	Title (A Side/B Side)	Yr	VG	VG+	NM
ELEKTRA					
❑ 46066	A Salute to the Duke/Listen to the Eagle	1979	—	2.50	5.00
MONUMENT					
❑ 45-291	Jody and the Kid/I Don't Want My Poor Heart to Remember	1980	—	2.50	5.00
❑ 45-293	Our First Night/Turn to Me	1980	—	2.50	5.00
❑ 8605	Ole Blue/Plant a Tree	1974	—	2.50	5.00
❑ 8655	I'm the South/Keep Me Comin' 'Round	1975	—	2.50	5.00
❑ 8691	Listen to the Eagle/Ole Blue	1976	—	2.50	5.00

Number	Title (A Side/B Side)	Yr	VG	VG+	NM
SHOW BIZ					
❑ 502	Soldier's Prayer/Danny Boy	1972	—	3.00	6.00
❑ 503	The Twenty-Second Day/Danny Boy	1972	—	3.00	6.00
THUNDER INT'L.					
❑ 1022	Kitty Kat/(B-side unknown)	1960	25.00	50.00	100.00
❑ 1024	Times Have Changed/(B-side unknown)	1960	25.00	50.00	100.00

OUTLAWS

45s

Number	Title (A Side/B Side)	Yr	VG	VG+	NM
ARISTA					
❑ 0150	There Goes Another Love Song/Keep Prayin'	1975	—	2.00	4.00
❑ 0188	Breaker-Breaker/South Carolina	1976	—	2.00	4.00
❑ 0213	Green Grass and High Tides/Prisoner	1976	—	2.50	5.00
❑ 0258	Hurry Sundown/So Afraid	1977	—	2.00	4.00
❑ 0282	Hearin' My Heart Talkin'/Holiday	1977	—	2.00	4.00
❑ 0338	Green Grass and High Tides/Holiday	1978	—	2.00	4.00
❑ 0378	Take It Anyway You Want It/Cry Some More	1978	—	2.00	4.00
❑ 0397	You Are the Show/If Dreams Came True	1979	—	2.00	4.00
❑ 0582	(Ghost) Riders in the Sky/Devil's Road	1981	—	2.00	4.00
❑ 0597	Wishing Well/I Can't Stop Loving You	1981	—	2.00	4.00
❑ 0678	Running/(B-side unknown)	1982	—	2.00	4.00
PASHA					
❑ 06550	Saved by the Bell/One Last Ride	1987	—	—	3.00

Albums

Number	Title (A Side/B Side)	Yr	VG	VG+	NM
ARISTA					
❑ AL 4042	Outlaws	1975	2.50	5.00	10.00
❑ AL 4070	Lady in Waiting	1976	2.50	5.00	10.00
❑ AL 4135	Hurry Sundown	1977	2.50	5.00	10.00
❑ AB 4205	Playin' to Win	1978	2.50	5.00	10.00
❑ A2L 8114 [(2)]	Bring It Back Alive	198?	2.50	5.00	10.00
—Second reissue					
❑ A2L 8300 [(2)]	Bring It Back Alive	1978	3.00	6.00	12.00
❑ AL 8301	Outlaws	198?	2.00	4.00	8.00
—Reissue					
❑ AL 8319	Greatest Hits of the Outlaws/High Tides Forever	198?	2.00	4.00	8.00
—Reissue					
❑ AL 8369	Hurry Sundown	198?	2.00	4.00	8.00
—Reissue					
❑ A2L 8608 [(2)]	Bring It Back Alive	198?	2.50	5.00	10.00
—Reissue					
❑ AL 9507	In the Eye of the Storm	1979	2.50	5.00	10.00
❑ AL 9542	Ghost Riders	1980	2.50	5.00	10.00
❑ AL 9584	Los Hombres Malo	1982	2.50	5.00	10.00
❑ AL 9614	Greatest Hits of the Outlaws/High Tides Forever	1982	2.50	5.00	10.00
DIRECT DISC					
❑ SD 16617	Outlaws	198?	12.50	25.00	50.00
—Audiophile vinyl					
PAIR					
❑ PDL2-1050 [(2)]	The Outlaws	1986	3.00	6.00	12.00
PASHA					
❑ BFZ 40512	Soldiers of Fortune	1986	2.00	4.00	8.00

OVERSTREET, PAUL

Also see SCHUYLER, KNOBLOCH & OVERSTREET; TANYA TUCKER.

45s

Number	Title (A Side/B Side)	Yr	VG	VG+	NM
MTM					
❑ B-72113	Love Helps Those/What God Has Joined Together	1988	—	2.00	4.00
RCA					
❑ 2505-7-R	Richest Man on Earth/Neath the Light of Your Love	1990	—	—	3.00
❑ 2707-7-R	Daddy's Come Around/The Calm at the Center of My Storm	1990	—	2.00	4.00
❑ 2780-7-R	Heroes/Straight and Narrow	1991	—	2.00	4.00
❑ 8919-7-R	Sowin' Love/Love Helps Those	1989	—	—	3.00
❑ 9015-7-R	All the Fun/Homemaker	1989	—	2.00	4.00
❑ 9116-7-R	Seein' My Father in Me/Love Never Sleeps	1989	—	2.00	4.00
❑ PB-13042	Beautiful Baby/Feels Good	1982	—	2.00	4.00
❑ 62012	Ball and Chain/Love Lives On	1991	—	2.00	4.00
❑ 62106	If I Could Bottle This Up/'Til the Mountains Disappear	1991	—	—	3.00
❑ 62193	Billy Can't Read/She Supports Her Man	1992	—	—	3.00
❑ 62254	Me and My Baby/Lord, She Sure Is Good at Loving Me	1992	—	—	3.00
❑ 62361	Still Out There Swinging/Till the Answer Comes (Gotta Keep Praying)	1992	—	—	3.00
❑ 62473	Take Another Run/Take Some Action	1993	—	—	3.00

Albums

Number	Title (A Side/B Side)	Yr	VG	VG+	NM
RCA					
❑ 9717-1-R	Sowin' Love	1989	3.00	6.00	12.00
❑ R 150526	Heroes	1991	3.75	7.50	15.00
—Only available on vinyl through BMG Direct Marketing					
RCA VICTOR					
❑ NFL1-8007	Paul Overstreet	1983	3.00	6.00	12.00

OVERSTREET, TOMMY

45s

Number	Title (A Side/B Side)	Yr	VG	VG+	NM
ABC					
❑ 12367	Better Me/Tell My Woman I Miss Her	1978	—	2.50	5.00
❑ 12408	Fadin' In, Fadin' Out/If This Is Freedom (Then I Want Out)	1978	—	2.50	5.00
❑ 12456	Cheater's Kit/Stolen Wine	1979	—	2.50	5.00
ABC DOT					
❑ 17533	I'm a Believer/This Land Is a Big Land	1974	—	2.50	5.00
❑ 17552	That's When My Woman Begins/A Small Quiet Table (In the Corner)	1975	—	2.50	5.00
❑ 17580	From Woman to Woman/Grass Don't Grow in Heaven	1975	—	2.50	5.00
❑ 17630	Here Comes That Girl Again/I'll Give Up (When You Give Up on Me)	1976	—	2.50	5.00
❑ 17657	Young Girl/90 Proof Lies	1976	—	2.50	5.00
❑ 17672	If Love Was a Bottle of Wine/I Never Really Missed You	1976	—	2.50	5.00
❑ 17697	Don't Go City Girl on Me/I'll Give Up (When You Give Up on Me)	1977	—	2.50	5.00
❑ 17721	This Time I'm In It for the Love/(Don't Make Me) A Memory Before My Time	1977	—	2.50	5.00
❑ 17737	Yes Ma'am/It's All Coming Home	1977	—	2.50	5.00
AMI					
❑ 1314	Dream Maker/More Than You Can Stand	1983	—	2.50	5.00
❑ 1317	Heart of Dixie/(B-side unknown)	1983	—	2.50	5.00
DOT					
❑ 17118	Every Day I Fall More in Love with You/Don't Get the Pain on You	1968	—	3.50	7.00
❑ 17189	Love, Love, Love/Watching the Trains Go By	1968	—	3.50	7.00
❑ 17228	Games People Play/Birmingham	1969	—	3.50	7.00
❑ 17281	Rocking a Memory (That Won't Go to Sleep)/He's Already Been There	1969	—	3.00	6.00
❑ 17331	Painted by the Wine/You Can't Walk in the Sunshine	1969	—	3.00	6.00
❑ 17350	Good Day Sunshine/Playing with Fire	1970	—	3.00	6.00
—With Peggy Little					
❑ 17357	If You're Looking for a Fool/The Smartest Fool	1970	—	3.00	6.00
❑ 17375	Gwen (Congratulations)/One Love, Two Hearts, Three Lives	1971	—	3.00	6.00
❑ 17387	I Don't Know You (Anymore)/I Still Love You Enough (To Love You All Over Again)	1971	—	3.00	6.00
❑ 17402	Ann (Don't Go Runnin')/Within This World of Mine	1971	—	3.00	6.00
❑ 17418	A Seed Before the Rose/How'd We Ever Get This Way	1972	—	3.00	6.00
❑ 17428	Heaven Is My Woman's Love/Baby's Gone	1972	—	3.00	6.00
❑ 17428 [PS]	Heaven Is My Woman's Love/Baby's Gone	1972	2.50	5.00	10.00
❑ 17455	Send Me No Roses/Your Love Controls My Life	1973	—	3.00	6.00
❑ 17474	I'll Never Break These Chains/Woman, Your Name Is My Song	1973	—	3.00	6.00
❑ 17493	(Jeannie Marie) You Were a Lady/Smile at Me Sweet Nancy	1974	—	3.00	6.00
❑ 17515	If I Miss You Again Tonight/I'm Not Ready Yet	1974	—	3.00	6.00
ELEKTRA					
❑ 46023	I'll Never Let You Down/You Needed Me	1979	—	2.00	4.00
❑ 46516	What More Could a Man Need/Only a Fool	1979	—	2.00	4.00
❑ 46564	Fadin' Renegade/Smokey Mountain Lullabye	1979	—	2.00	4.00
❑ 46600	Down in the Quarter/Forever in Blue Jeans	1980	—	2.00	4.00
❑ 46658	Sue/Her Heart Still Belongs to Me	1980	—	2.00	4.00
❑ 47041	Me and the Boys in the Band/You	1980	—	2.00	4.00
GERVASI					
❑ 665	I Still Love Your Body/(B-side unknown)	1984	—	2.50	5.00
SILVER DOLLAR					
❑ 0002	Next to You/Letting Go Was Easier	1986	—	3.00	6.00
TINA					
❑ 523	Tears (There's Nowhere Else to Hide)/Lord, If I Make It to Heaven	1978	—	3.00	6.00

Albums

Number	Title (A Side/B Side)	Yr	VG	VG+	NM
ABC					
❑ AB-1066	Better Me	1978	3.00	6.00	12.00
ABC DOT					
❑ DOSD-2016	I'm a Believer	1975	3.75	7.50	15.00
❑ DOSD-2027	Greatest Hits Vol. One	1975	3.75	7.50	15.00
❑ DOSD-2038	The Tommy Overstreet Show Live from the Silver Slipper	1975	3.75	7.50	15.00
❑ DOSD-2056	Turn On to Tommy Overstreet	1976	3.75	7.50	15.00
❑ DO-2071	Vintage '77	1977	3.00	6.00	12.00
❑ DO-2086	Hangin' 'Round	1977	3.00	6.00	12.00
DOT					
❑ DLP-25992	Gwen (Congratulations)	1971	5.00	10.00	20.00
❑ DLP-25994	This Is Tommy Overstreet	1972	5.00	10.00	20.00
❑ DLP-26003	Heaven Is My Woman's Love	1972	5.00	10.00	20.00
❑ DLP-26010	My Friends Call Me T.O.	1973	5.00	10.00	20.00
❑ DLP-26021	Woman, Your Name Is My Song	1974	5.00	10.00	20.00
ELEKTRA					
❑ 6E-178	I'll Never Let You Down	1979	2.50	5.00	10.00
❑ 6E-226	The Real Tommy Overstreet	1979	2.50	5.00	10.00
❑ 6E-292	The Best of Tommy Overstreet	1980	2.50	5.00	10.00
MCA					
❑ 645	Vintage '77	198?	2.00	4.00	8.00
—Reissue					
❑ 646	Hangin' 'Round	198?	2.00	4.00	8.00
—Reissue					
❑ 797	Better Me	198?	2.00	4.00	8.00
—Reissue					

OWEN, DOUG

45s

Number	Title (A Side/B Side)	Yr	VG	VG+	NM
ABC HICKORY					
❑ 54018	Live Wire/Stars	1977	—	2.50	5.00
❑ 54026	Baby Don't Go/Back Together	1978	—	2.50	5.00
MCA					
❑ 41049	Back Together/Highway Flyer	1979	—	2.00	4.00

Number	Title (A Side/B Side)	Yr	VG	VG+	NM

OWEN, JIM

45s

EPIC

Number	Title (A Side/B Side)	Yr	VG	VG+	NM
❑ 50498	Lovesick Blues/A Gift in the Name of Love	1977	—	3.00	6.00

—With the Drifting Cowboys

SUN

Number	Title (A Side/B Side)	Yr	VG	VG+	NM
❑ 1157	Ten Anniversary Presents/Please Don't Go Home Till Morning	1980	—	2.50	5.00
❑ 1163	Serena/Honky Tonk Heart	1981	—	2.50	5.00
❑ 1171	Hell Yes, I Cheated/Dragging These Chains	1982	—	2.50	5.00
❑ 1174	Coal Miner's Blues/Ain't No Cowboy's Blues	1982	—	2.50	5.00
❑ 1179 [DJ]	Bogalusa (same on both sides)	1982	—	3.50	7.00

—No stock copies issued

OWEN BROTHERS, THE

45s

AUDIOGRAPH

Number	Title (A Side/B Side)	Yr	VG	VG+	NM
❑ 445	Nights Out at the Days End/Love In Tonight	1982	—	3.00	6.00
❑ 470	Southern Women/(B-side unknown)	1983	—	3.00	6.00

OWENS, A.L. "DOODLE"

45s

RAINDROP

Number	Title (A Side/B Side)	Yr	VG	VG+	NM
❑ 010	Honky Tonk Toys/California Rose	1977	—	3.50	7.00
❑ 010 [PS]	Honky Tonk Toys/California Rose	1977	2.50	5.00	10.00

OWENS, BONNIE

Also see MERLE HAGGARD AND BONNIE OWENS.

45s

CAPITOL

Number	Title (A Side/B Side)	Yr	VG	VG+	NM
❑ 2029	Don't Tell Me/Somewhere Between	1967	2.00	4.00	8.00
❑ 2210	How Can Our Cheatin' Be Wrong/Yes I Love You Only	1968	2.00	4.00	8.00
❑ 2340	Lead Me On/I'll Always Be Glad to Take You Back	1968	2.00	4.00	8.00
❑ 2586	It Don't Take Much to Make Me Cry/My Hi-Fi to Cry By	1969	2.00	4.00	8.00
❑ 2716	Philadelphia Lawyer/That Little Boy of Mine	1970	2.00	4.00	8.00
❑ 5459	Number One Heel/The Longer You Wait	1965	2.50	5.00	10.00
❑ 5529	Excuse Me for Living/Souvenirs	1965	2.50	5.00	10.00
❑ 5618	Merry-Go-Round/Livin' on Your Love	1966	2.50	5.00	10.00
❑ 5688	You Don't Even Try/What's It Gonna Cost Me	1966	2.50	5.00	10.00
❑ 5755	Consider the Children/I Know He Loves Me	1966	2.50	5.00	10.00
❑ 5847	Someone Else You've Known/The Best Part of Me	1967	2.50	5.00	10.00
❑ 5977	I'd Be More of a Woman/Everything That's Fastened Down Is Coming Loose	1967	2.50	5.00	10.00

MAR-VEL

Number	Title (A Side/B Side)	Yr	VG	VG+	NM
❑ 102	A Dear John Letter/Wonderful World	1953	12.50	25.00	50.00

—With Fuzzy Owens

TALLY

Number	Title (A Side/B Side)	Yr	VG	VG+	NM
❑ 149	Why Don't Daddy Live Here Anymore/Waggin' Tongues	1963	6.25	12.50	25.00
❑ 156	Don't Take Advantage of Me/Stop the World	1964	6.25	12.50	25.00
❑ 184	Lie a Little/I'll Try Again Tomorrow	1964	6.25	12.50	25.00

"X"

Number	Title (A Side/B Side)	Yr	VG	VG+	NM
❑ 0028	I Traded My Heart for His Gold/Take Me	1954	10.00	20.00	40.00
❑ 0065	No Tomorrow/Just a Love for Someone to Steal	1954	10.00	20.00	40.00

Albums

CAPITOL

Number	Title (A Side/B Side)	Yr	VG	VG+	NM
❑ ST-195	Lead Me On	1969	6.25	12.50	25.00
❑ ST-341	Hi-Fi to Cry By	1969	6.25	12.50	25.00
❑ ST-557	Mother's Favorite Hymns	1970	6.25	12.50	25.00
❑ ST 2403 [S]	Don't Take Advantage of Me	1965	6.25	12.50	25.00
❑ T 2403 [M]	Don't Take Advantage of Me	1965	5.00	10.00	20.00
❑ ST 2600 [S]	All of Me Belongs to You	1967	6.25	12.50	25.00
❑ T 2600 [M]	All of Me Belongs to You	1967	6.25	12.50	25.00
❑ ST 2861	Somewhere Between	1968	6.25	12.50	25.00

OWENS, BUCK

Also see DWIGHT YOAKAM.

45s

CAPITOL

Number	Title (A Side/B Side)	Yr	VG	VG+	NM
❑ 2001	It Takes People Like You (To Make People Like Me)/You Left Her Lonely Too Long	1967	2.00	4.00	8.00
❑ 2001 [PS]	It Takes People Like You (To Make People Like Me)/You Left Her Lonely Too Long	1967	3.00	6.00	12.00
❑ 2080	How Long Will My Baby Be Gone/Everybody Needs Somebody	1968	2.00	4.00	8.00
❑ 2080 [PS]	How Long Will My Baby Be Gone/Everybody Needs Somebody	1968	3.00	6.00	12.00
❑ 2142	Sweet Rosie Jones/Happy Times Are Here Again	1968	2.00	4.00	8.00
❑ 2142 [PS]	Sweet Rosie Jones/Happy Times Are Here Again	1968	3.00	6.00	12.00
❑ 2237	Let the World Keep On a-Turnin'/I'll Love You Forever and Ever	1968	2.00	4.00	8.00

—With Buddy Alan

Number	Title (A Side/B Side)	Yr	VG	VG+	NM
❑ 2237 [PS]	Let the World Keep On a-Turnin'/I'll Love You Forever and Ever	1968	3.00	6.00	12.00

—As "Buck Owens and Buddy Alan and the Buckaroos"

Number	Title (A Side/B Side)	Yr	VG	VG+	NM
❑ 2300	I've Got You on My Mind Again/That's All Right with Me (If It's All Right with You)	1968	2.00	4.00	8.00
❑ 2300 [PS]	I've Got You on My Mind Again/That's All Right with Me (If It's All Right with You)	1968	3.00	6.00	12.00
❑ 2328	Christmas Shopping/One of Everything You Got	1968	2.00	4.00	8.00
❑ 2330	Turkish Holiday/Things I Saw Happening at the Fountain	1968	2.00	4.00	8.00
❑ 2377	Who's Gonna Mow Your Grass/There's Gotta Be Some Chances Made	1969	2.00	4.00	8.00
❑ 2377 [PS]	Who's Gonna Mow Your Grass/There's Gotta Be Some Chances Made	1969	3.00	6.00	12.00
❑ 2485	Johnny B. Goode/Maybe If I Close My Eyes (It'll Go Away)	1969	2.00	4.00	8.00
❑ 2485 [PS]	Johnny B. Goode/Maybe If I Close My Eyes (It'll Go Away)	1969	3.00	6.00	12.00
❑ 2570	Tall Dark Stranger/Sing That Kind of Song	1969	2.00	4.00	8.00
❑ 2570 [PS]	Tall Dark Stranger/Sing That Kind of Song	1969	3.00	6.00	12.00
❑ 2646	Big in Vegas/White Satin Bed	1969	2.00	4.00	8.00
❑ 2646 [PS]	Big in Vegas/White Satin Bed	1969	3.00	6.00	12.00
❑ 2783	The Kansas City Song/I'd Love to Be Your Man	1970	2.00	4.00	8.00
❑ 2783 [PS]	The Kansas City Song/I'd Love to Be Your Man	1970	2.50	5.00	10.00
❑ 2947	I Wouldn't Live in New York City (If They Gave Me the Whole Dang Town)/No Milk and Honey in Baltimore	1970	2.00	4.00	8.00
❑ 2947 [PS]	I Wouldn't Live in New York City (If They Gave Me the Whole Dang Town)/No Milk and Honey in Baltimore	1970	2.50	5.00	10.00
❑ 2962	Buckaroo/Okie from Muskogee	1970	3.00	6.00	12.00

—As "Buck Owens' Bakersfield Brass"

Number	Title (A Side/B Side)	Yr	VG	VG+	NM
❑ 3011	Act Naturally/My Heart Skips a Beat	1971	3.00	6.00	12.00

—As "Buck Owens' Bakersfield Brass"

Number	Title (A Side/B Side)	Yr	VG	VG+	NM
❑ 3023	Bridge Over Troubled Water/(I'm Goin') Home	1971	—	3.00	6.00
❑ 3023 [PS]	Bridge Over Troubled Water/(I'm Goin') Home	1971	2.50	5.00	10.00
❑ 3066	Cajun Brass/Waitin' in Your Welfare Line	1971	2.50	5.00	10.00

—As "Buck Owens' Bakersfield Brass"

Number	Title (A Side/B Side)	Yr	VG	VG+	NM
❑ 3096	Ruby (Are You Mad)/Heartbreak Mountain	1971	—	3.00	6.00
❑ 3164	Rollin' in My Sweet Baby's Arms/Corn Likker	1971	—	3.00	6.00
❑ 3164 [PS]	Rollin' in My Sweet Baby's Arms/Corn Likker	1971	2.50	5.00	10.00
❑ 3215	Too Old to Cut the Mustard/Wham Bam	1971	—	3.00	6.00

—As "Buck and Buddy" (Buck Owens and BUDDY ALAN)

Number	Title (A Side/B Side)	Yr	VG	VG+	NM
❑ 3215 [PS]	Too Old to Cut the Mustard/Wham Bam	1971	2.50	5.00	10.00
❑ 3262	I'll Still Be Waiting for You/Full Time Daddy	1972	—	3.00	6.00
❑ 3314	Made in Japan/Black Texas Dirt	1972	—	3.00	6.00
❑ 3429	You Ain't Gonna Have Ol' Buck to Kick Around No More/I Love You So Much It Hurts	1972	—	3.00	6.00
❑ 3504	In the Palm of Your Hand/Get Out of Town Before Sundown	1972	—	3.00	6.00
❑ 3563	Ain't It Amazing, Gracie/The Good Old Days	1973	—	3.00	6.00
❑ 3688	Arms Full of Empty/Songwriter's Lament	1973	—	3.00	6.00
❑ 3769	Big Game Hunter/That Loving Feeling	1973	—	3.00	6.00
❑ F3824	Come Back/I Know What It Means	1957	5.00	10.00	20.00
❑ 3841	On the Cover of the Music City News/Stony Mountain, West Virginia	1974	—	3.00	6.00
❑ 3907	(It's a) Monsters' Holiday/Great Expectations	1974	—	3.00	6.00
❑ F3957	Sweet Thing/I Only Know That I Love You So	1957	5.00	10.00	20.00
❑ 3976	Great Expectations/Let the Fun Begin	1974	—	3.00	6.00
❑ 4043	41st Street Lonely Hearts Club/Weekend Daddy	1975	—	3.00	6.00
❑ F4090	I'll Take a Chance on Loving You/Walk the Floor	1958	5.00	10.00	20.00
❑ 4138	The Battle of New Orleans/Run Him to the Roundhouse Nellie	1975	—	3.00	6.00
❑ F4172	Second Fiddle/Everlasting Love	1959	5.00	10.00	20.00
❑ 4181	Meanwhile Back at the Ranch/Country Singer's Prayer	1976	—	3.00	6.00
❑ F4245	Under Your Spell Again/Tired of Livin'	1959	5.00	10.00	20.00
❑ 4337	Above and Beyond/Till These Dreams Come True	1960	3.75	7.50	15.00
❑ 4412	Excuse Me (I Think I've Got a Heartache)/I've Got a Right to Know	1960	3.75	7.50	15.00
❑ 4496	Foolin' Around/High As the Mountains	1961	3.75	7.50	15.00
❑ 4602	Under the Influence of Love/Bad Dreams	1961	3.75	7.50	15.00
❑ 4679	Nobody's Fool But Yours/Mirror Mirror on the Wall	1962	3.75	7.50	15.00
❑ 4765	Save the Last Dance for Me/King of Fools	1962	3.75	7.50	15.00
❑ 4826	Kickin' Our Hearts Around/I Can't Stop (My Lovin' You)	1962	3.75	7.50	15.00
❑ 4872	You're for Me/House Down the Block	1962	3.75	7.50	15.00
❑ 4937	Act Naturally/Over and Over Again	1963	3.75	7.50	15.00
❑ 5025	Love's Gonna Live Here/Getting Used to Losing You	1963	3.00	6.00	12.00
❑ 5136	My Heart Skips a Beat/Together Again	1964	3.00	6.00	12.00
❑ 5240	I Don't Care (Just As Long As You Love Me)/Don't Let Her Know	1964	3.00	6.00	12.00
❑ 5336	I've Got a Tiger by the Tail/Cryin' Time	1965	2.50	5.00	10.00
❑ 5336 [PS]	I've Got a Tiger by the Tail/Cryin' Time	1965	3.75	7.50	15.00
❑ 5410	Before You Go/No One But You	1965	2.50	5.00	10.00
❑ 5410 [PS]	Before You Go/No One But You	1965	3.75	7.50	15.00
❑ 5465	Only You (Can Break My Heart)/Gonna Have Love	1965	2.50	5.00	10.00
❑ 5465 [PS]	Only You (Can Break My Heart)/Gonna Have Love	1965	3.75	7.50	15.00
❑ 5517	Buckaroo/If You Want a Love	1965	2.50	5.00	10.00
❑ 5537	Santa Looked a Lot Like Daddy/All I Want for Christmas Dear Is You	1965	2.50	5.00	10.00
❑ 5537	Santa Looked A Lot Like Daddy/All I Want For Christmas Dear Is You	1973	—	2.00	4.00

—Orange label, "Capitol" at bottom

Number	Title (A Side/B Side)	Yr	VG	VG+	NM
❑ 5537 [PS]	Santa Looked a Lot Like Daddy/All I Want for Christmas Dear Is You	1965	3.75	7.50	15.00
❑ 5566	Waitin' in Your Welfare Line/In the Palm of Your Hand	1965	2.50	5.00	10.00
❑ 5647	Think of Me/Heart of Glass	1966	2.50	5.00	10.00
❑ 5647 [PS]	Think of Me/Heart of Glass	1966	3.75	7.50	15.00

Number	Title (A Side/B Side)	Yr	VG	VG+	NM
5705	Open Up Your Heart/No More Me and You	1966	2.50	5.00	10.00
5705 [PS]	Open Up Your Heart/No More Me and You	1966	3.75	7.50	15.00
5811	Where Does the Good Times Go/The Way That I Love You	1967	2.00	4.00	8.00
5811 [PS]	Where Does the Good Times Go/The Way That I Love You	1967	3.00	6.00	12.00
5865	Sam's Place/Don't Ever Tell Me Goodbye	1967	2.00	4.00	8.00
5865 [PS]	Sam's Place/Don't Ever Tell Me Goodbye	1967	3.00	6.00	12.00
5942	Your Tender Loving Care/What a Liar I Am	1967	2.00	4.00	8.00
5942 [PS]	Your Tender Loving Care/What a Liar I Am	1967	3.00	6.00	12.00
B-44248	Hot Dog/Second Fiddle	1988	—	2.00	4.00
B-44248 [PS]	Hot Dog/Second Fiddle	1988	—	2.50	5.00
B-44295	A-11/Sweethearts in Heaven	1989	—	2.00	4.00
B-44356	Put a Quarter in the Jukebox/Don't Let Her Know	1989	—	2.00	4.00
B-44409	Act Naturally/The Key's in the Mailbox	1989	3.75	7.50	15.00
—A-side with Ringo Starr					
7PRO-79805 [DJ]	Gonna Have Love (same on both sides)	1989	2.50	5.00	10.00
—Vinyl is promo only					
DIXIE					
505	Hot Dog/Rhythm and Booze	1956	100.00	200.00	400.00
—As "Corky Jones"					
PEP					
105	It Don't Show on Me/Down on the Corner of Love	1956	12.50	25.00	50.00
106	The House Down the Block/Right After the Dance	1956	12.50	25.00	50.00
107	Hot Dog/Rhythm and Booze	1956	62.50	125.00	250.00
—As "Corky Jones"					
109	There Goes My Love/Sweethearts in Heaven	1957	12.50	25.00	50.00
REPRISE					
27964	Streets of Bakersfield/One More Name	1988	—	—	3.00
—With Dwight Yoakam					
27964 [PS]	Streets of Bakersfield/One More Name	1988	—	2.00	4.00
STARDAY					
571	There Goes My Love/It Don't Show on Me	1961	3.75	7.50	15.00
588	Down on the Corner of Love/Right After the Dance	1962	3.75	7.50	15.00
7010	Sweethearts in Heaven/Down on the Corner of Love	196?	—	2.50	5.00
8004	Sweethearts in Heaven/Down on the Corner of Love	197?	—	2.00	4.00
WARNER BROS.					
8223	Hollywood Waltz/Rain on Your Parade	1976	—	2.50	5.00
8255	California Okie/Child Support	1976	—	2.50	5.00
8316	World Famous Holiday Inn/He Don't Deserve You Anymore	1977	2.50	5.00	10.00
8316	World Famous Paradise Inn/He Don't Deserve You Anymore	1977	—	2.50	5.00
8395	It's Been a Long, Long Time/Rain on Your Parade	1977	—	2.50	5.00
8433	Our Old Mansion/How Come My God Don't Bark	1977	—	2.50	5.00
8486	Let the Good Times Roll/Texas Tornado	1977	—	2.50	5.00
8614	Nights Are Forever Without You/When I Need You	1978	—	2.00	4.00
8701	Do You Wanna Make Love/Seasons of My Heart	1978	—	2.00	4.00
8830	Play Together Again Again/He Don't Deserve You Anymore	1979	—	2.00	4.00
—A-side with Emmylou Harris					
49046	Hangin' In and Hangin' On/Sweet Molly Brown's	1979	—	2.00	4.00
49118	Let Jesse Rob the Train/Victim of Life's Circumstances	1979	—	2.00	4.00
49200	Love Is a Warm Cowboy/I Don't Want to Live in San Francisco	1980	—	2.00	4.00
49278	Moonlight and Magnolia/Nickels and Dimes	1980	—	2.00	4.00
49651	Without You/Love Don't Make the Bars	1981	—	2.00	4.00
7-Inch Extended Plays					
CAPITOL					
R-5446	Memphis/Let the Bad Times Roll On//Fallin' for You/If You Fall Out of Love	1965	3.75	7.50	15.00
R-5446 [PS]	4-By Buck Owens	1965	6.25	12.50	25.00
Albums					
CAPITOL					
ST-131	I've Got You on My Mind Again	1969	5.00	10.00	20.00
SKAO-145	The Best of Buck Owens, Volume 3	1969	5.00	10.00	20.00
ST-194	Anywhere U.S.A.	1969	5.00	10.00	20.00
ST-212	Tall Dark Stranger	1969	5.00	10.00	20.00
ST-232	Buck Owens in London	1969	5.00	10.00	20.00
SWBB-257 [(2)]	Close-Up	1969	5.00	10.00	20.00
—Reissue of "Together Again" and "No One But You"					
ST-439	Your Mother's Prayer	1970	5.00	10.00	20.00
ST-476	The Kansas City Song	1970	5.00	10.00	20.00
STBB-486 [(2)]	A Merry "Hee Haw" Christmas	1970	6.25	12.50	25.00
STCL-574 [(3)]	Buck Owens	1970	10.00	20.00	40.00
ST-628	I Wouldn't Live in New York City	1970	5.00	10.00	20.00
ST-685	Bridge Over Troubled Water	1971	3.75	7.50	15.00
ST 1482 [S]	Buck Owens Sings Harlan Howard	1961	12.50	25.00	50.00
T 1482 [M]	Buck Owens Sings Harlan Howard	1961	10.00	20.00	40.00
DT 1489 [R]	Under Your Spell Again	1968	6.25	12.50	25.00
T 1489 [M]	Under Your Spell Again	1961	10.00	20.00	40.00
ST 1777 [S]	You're for Me	1962	12.50	25.00	50.00
T 1777 [M]	You're for Me	1962	10.00	20.00	40.00
ST 1879 [S]	On the Bandstand	1963	12.50	25.00	50.00
T 1879 [M]	On the Bandstand	1963	10.00	20.00	40.00
ST 1989 [S]	Buck Owens Sings Tommy Collins	1963	12.50	25.00	50.00
T 1989 [M]	Buck Owens Sings Tommy Collins	1963	10.00	20.00	40.00
ST 2105 [S]	The Best of Buck Owens	1964	7.50	15.00	30.00
T 2105 [M]	The Best of Buck Owens	1964	6.25	12.50	25.00
ST 2135 [S]	Together Again/My Heart Skips a Beat	1964	7.50	15.00	30.00
T 2135 [M]	Together Again/My Heart Skips a Beat	1964	6.25	12.50	25.00
ST 2186 [S]	I Don't Care	1964	7.50	15.00	30.00
T 2186 [M]	I Don't Care	1964	6.25	12.50	25.00
ST 2283 [S]	I've Got a Tiger by the Tail	1965	7.50	15.00	30.00
T 2283 [M]	I've Got a Tiger by the Tail	1965	6.25	12.50	25.00
ST 2353 [S]	Before You Go	1965	7.50	15.00	30.00
T 2353 [M]	Before You Go	1965	6.25	12.50	25.00
ST 2367 [S]	The Instrumental Hits of Buck Owens & the Buckaroos	1965	7.50	15.00	30.00
T 2367 [M]	The Instrumental Hits of Buck Owens & the Buckaroos	1965	6.25	12.50	25.00
ST 2396 [S]	Christmas with Buck Owens and His Buckaroos	1965	7.50	15.00	30.00
T 2396 [M]	Christmas with Buck Owens and His Buckaroos	1965	5.00	10.00	20.00
ST 2443 [S]	Roll Out the Red Carpet for Buck Owens & The Buckaroos	1966	6.25	12.50	25.00
T 2443 [M]	Roll Out the Red Carpet for Buck Owens & The Buckaroos	1966	5.00	10.00	20.00
ST 2497 [S]	Dust on Mother's Bible	1966	6.25	12.50	25.00
T 2497 [M]	Dust on Mother's Bible	1966	5.00	10.00	20.00
ST 2556 [S]	Carnegie Hall Concert	1966	6.25	12.50	25.00
T 2556 [M]	Carnegie Hall Concert	1966	5.00	10.00	20.00
ST 2640 [S]	Open Up Your Heart	1967	6.25	12.50	25.00
T 2640 [M]	Open Up Your Heart	1967	5.00	10.00	20.00
ST 2715 [S]	Buck Owens and His Buckaroos in Japan	1967	6.25	12.50	25.00
T 2715 [M]	Buck Owens and His Buckaroos in Japan	1967	5.00	10.00	20.00
ST 2760 [S]	Your Tender Loving Care	1967	6.25	12.50	25.00
T 2760 [M]	Your Tender Loving Care	1967	6.25	12.50	25.00
ST 2841 [S]	It Takes People Like You to Make People Like Me	1968	6.25	12.50	25.00
T 2841 [M]	It Takes People Like You to Make People Like Me	1968	10.00	20.00	40.00
ST 2897	The Best of Buck Owens, Vol. 2	1968	6.25	12.50	25.00
ST 2902	A Night on the Town	1968	6.25	12.50	25.00
ST 2962	Sweet Rosie Jones	1968	6.25	12.50	25.00
ST 2977	Christmas Shopping	1968	6.25	12.50	25.00
SPRO 2980/1 [DJ]	Minute Masters	1966	12.50	25.00	50.00
—Promo-only excerpts of 24 songs					
ST 2994	Buck Owens, The Guitar Player	1968	6.25	12.50	25.00
ST-11105	Live at the White House	1972	3.75	7.50	15.00
ST-11136	In the Palm of Your Hand	1973	3.75	7.50	15.00
SMAS-11180	Ain't It Amazing, Gracie	1973	3.75	7.50	15.00
ST-11222	Arms Full of Empty	1972	3.75	7.50	15.00
ST-11332	Monster's Holiday	1974	3.75	7.50	15.00
ST-11390	Weekend Daddy	1974	3.75	7.50	15.00
ST-11471	The Best of Buck Owens, Volume 6	1976	3.75	7.50	15.00
C1-91132	Hot Dog!	1988	3.00	6.00	12.00
C1-92893	Act Naturally	1989	3.75	7.50	15.00
COUNTRY MUSIC FOUNDATION					
CMF-012	Live at Carnegie Hall	198?	3.00	6.00	12.00
LABREA					
1017 [M]	Buck Owens	1961	25.00	50.00	100.00
8017 [S]	Buck Owens	1961	37.50	75.00	150.00
STARDAY					
SLP-172	The Fabulous Country Music Sound of Buck Owens	1962	12.50	25.00	50.00
SLP-324	Coutnry Hit Maker #1	1964	6.25	12.50	25.00
WARNER BROS.					
BS 2952	Buck 'Em	1976	3.00	6.00	12.00
BS 3087	Our Old Mansion	1977	3.00	6.00	12.00

OWENS, BUCK, AND ROSE MADDOX

Also see each artist's individual listings.

Number	Title (A Side/B Side)	Yr	VG	VG+	NM
45s					
CAPITOL					
4550	Mental Cruelty/Loose Talk	1961	3.75	7.50	15.00
4992	We're the Talk of the Town/Sweethearts in Heaven	1963	3.75	7.50	15.00

OWENS, BUCK, AND SUSAN RAYE

Also see each artist's individual listings.

Number	Title (A Side/B Side)	Yr	VG	VG+	NM
45s					
CAPITOL					
2731	We're Gonna Get Together/Everybody Needs Somebody	1970	2.00	4.00	8.00
2731 [PS]	We're Gonna Get Together/Everybody Needs Somebody	1970	2.50	5.00	10.00
2791	Togetherness/Fallin' for You	1970	2.00	4.00	8.00
2791 [PS]	Togetherness/Fallin' for You	1970	2.50	5.00	10.00
2871	The Great White Horse/Your Tender Loving Care	1970	2.00	4.00	8.00
2871 [PS]	The Great White Horse/Your Tender Loving Care	1970	2.50	5.00	10.00
3225	Santa's Gonna Come in a Stagecoach/One of Everything You Got	1971	2.00	4.00	8.00
3368	Looking Back to See/Cryin' Time	1972	—	3.00	6.00
3368 [PS]	Looking Back to See/Cryin' Time	1972	2.50	5.00	10.00
3601	The Good Old Days (Are Here Again)/When You Get to Heaven (I'll Be There)	1973	—	3.00	6.00
4100	Love Is Strange/Sweethearts in Heaven	1975	—	3.00	6.00
Albums					
CAPITOL					
ST-448	We're Gonna Get Together	1970	5.00	10.00	20.00
ST-558	Great White Horse	1970	3.75	7.50	15.00
ST-837	Merry Christmas from Buck Owens and Susan Raye	1971	3.75	7.50	15.00
ST-11084	The Best of Buck Owens and Susan Raye	1972	3.75	7.50	15.00
ST-11207	The Good Old Days (Are Here Again)	1973	3.75	7.50	15.00

OWENS, DUSTY

45s

COLUMBIA

Number	Title (A Side/B Side)	Yr	VG	VG+	NM
❑ 4-21202	Hello Operator/The Life You Want to Live	1954	6.25	12.50	25.00
❑ 4-21260	Just Call on Me/Somewhere She's Waiting	1954	6.25	12.50	25.00
❑ 4-21310	They Didn't Know the Difference/A Love That Once Was Mine	1954	6.25	12.50	25.00
❑ 4-21362	Give Me a Little Chance/Wouldn't You	1955	6.25	12.50	25.00
❑ 4-21440	Who Do You Think They Would Blame/Forget My Broken Heart	1955	6.25	12.50	25.00

OWENS, MARIE

45s

4 STAR

Number	Title (A Side/B Side)	Yr	VG	VG+	NM
❑ 1002	Reasons a-Plenty/The Devil's Song	1975	—	3.00	6.00
❑ 1007	Will the Circle Be Unbroken/You Gave Me a Mountain	1975	—	3.00	6.00
❑ 1019	Someone Loves You Honey/The Devil's Song	1975	—	3.00	6.00

LOBO

Number	Title (A Side/B Side)	Yr	VG	VG+	NM
❑ VII	Long Loving Night/(B-side unknown)	1982	—	3.00	6.00

MCA

Number	Title (A Side/B Side)	Yr	VG	VG+	NM
❑ 40018	Love's Gonna Come to You/Why Don't You Love Me Alone	1973	—	3.50	7.00
❑ 40087	It Ain't No Little Thing/I'll Find One I Can	1973	—	3.50	7.00
❑ 40184	J. John Jones/Take It from Me	1974	—	3.00	6.00
❑ 40241	Release Me/Just Out of Reach	1974	—	3.00	6.00
❑ 40308	I Want to Lay Down Beside You/Broken Wings	1974	—	3.00	6.00

MMI

Number	Title (A Side/B Side)	Yr	VG	VG+	NM
❑ 1012	When Your Good Love Was Mine/I'll Be in His Arms Tonight	1977	—	3.50	7.00
❑ 1015	Burning/Wish You Were Here	1975	—	3.50	7.00
❑ 1022	Roller Coaster Ride/(B-side unknown)	1978	—	3.50	7.00
❑ 1026	Nickelodeon/No One's Gonna Love Me (Like You Do)	1978	—	3.50	7.00

SING ME

Number	Title (A Side/B Side)	Yr	VG	VG+	NM
❑ 12	Ease My Mind on You/Sweet Love	1977	—	3.50	7.00

OXFORD, VERNON

45s

RCA

Number	Title (A Side/B Side)	Yr	VG	VG+	NM
❑ PB-10787	Clean Your Own Tables/Baby Sister	1976	—	2.00	4.00
❑ PB-10872	A Good Old Fashioned Saturday Night Honky Tonk Barrom Brawl/One More Night to Spare	1977	—	2.00	4.00
❑ PB-10952	Only the Shadows Know/We Sure Danced Us Some Goodin's	1977	—	2.00	4.00
❑ PB-11020	Redneck Roots/Images	1977	—	2.00	4.00

RCA VICTOR

Number	Title (A Side/B Side)	Yr	VG	VG+	NM
❑ PB-10098	How High Does the Cotton Grow Mama/I've Got to Get Peter Off Your Mind	1974	—	3.00	6.00
❑ PB-10185	I Wish You Would Leave Me Alone/Soft and Warm	1975	—	3.00	6.00
❑ PB-10348	Giving the Pill/Country Singer	1975	—	3.00	6.00
❑ PB-10442	Shadows of My Mind/She's Always There	1975	—	2.50	5.00
❑ PB-10595	Your Wanting Me Is Gone/Don't Be Late	1976	—	2.50	5.00
❑ PB-10693	Redneck! (The Redneck National Anthem)/Leave Me Alone with the Blues	1976	—	3.00	6.00
❑ 47-8759	Woman, Let Me Sing You a Song/Watermelon Time in Georgia	1966	2.50	5.00	10.00
❑ 47-8843	Let's Take a Cold Shower/Hide	1966	2.50	5.00	10.00
❑ 47-8943	Baby Sitter/Goin' Home	1966	2.50	5.00	10.00
❑ 47-9117	A Field of Flowers/Stone by Stone	1967	2.50	5.00	10.00
❑ 47-9306	Little Sister Throw Your Red Shoes Away/Old Folks' Home	1967	2.50	5.00	10.00
❑ 47-9372	Roll Big Wheels Roll/That's the Way I Talk	1967	2.50	5.00	10.00
❑ 47-9467	This Woman Is Mine/The Touch of God's Hand	1968	2.50	5.00	10.00

ROUNDER

Number	Title (A Side/B Side)	Yr	VG	VG+	NM
❑ 4527	His and Hers/Lonesome Rainin' City	198?	—	3.00	6.00
❑ 4535	They'll Never Take Her Love from Me/Sad Situation	198?	—	3.00	6.00

Albums

RCA VICTOR

Number	Title (A Side/B Side)	Yr	VG	VG+	NM
❑ LPM-3704 [M]	Woman, Let Me Sing You a Song	1967	10.00	20.00	40.00
❑ LSP-3704 [S]	Woman, Let Me Sing You a Song	1967	7.50	15.00	30.00

ROUNDER

Number	Title (A Side/B Side)	Yr	VG	VG+	NM
❑ 0091	If I Had My Wife to Love Over	198?	3.75	7.50	15.00
❑ 0123	His and Hers	198?	3.75	7.50	15.00
❑ 0156	Keepin' It Country	1982	3.75	7.50	15.00

OZARK MOUNTAIN DAREDEVILS

45s

A&M

Number	Title (A Side/B Side)	Yr	VG	VG+	NM
❑ 1477	Country Girl/Within Without	1973	—	2.50	5.00
❑ 1515	If You Wanna Get to Heaven/Spaceship Orion	1974	—	2.50	5.00
❑ 1623	Look Away/It Probably Always Will	1974	—	2.00	4.00
❑ 1654	Jackie Blue/Better Days	1974	—	2.00	4.00
❑ 1654 [PS]	Jackie Blue/Better Days	1974	—	3.00	6.00
❑ 1709	Colorado Song/Thin Ice	1975	—	2.00	4.00
❑ 1772	If I Only Knew/Dreams	1975	—	2.00	4.00
❑ 1808	Keep On Churnin'/Time Warp	1976	—	2.00	4.00
❑ 1809	You Make It Right/Dreams	1976	—	2.00	4.00
❑ 1842	Journey to the Center of Your Heart/Chicken Train Stomp	1976	—	2.00	4.00
❑ 1880	Noah (Let It Rain)/Red Plum	1976	—	2.00	4.00
❑ 1888	You Know Like I Know/Arroyo	1976	—	2.00	4.00
❑ 1888 [PS]	You Know Like I Know/Arroyo	1976	—	3.00	6.00
❑ 1989	Crazy Lovin'/Stinghead	1977	—	2.00	4.00
❑ 2016	Following (The Way That I Feel)/Snowbound	1978	—	2.00	4.00

COLUMBIA

Number	Title (A Side/B Side)	Yr	VG	VG+	NM
❑ 11247	Take You Tonight/Runnin' Out	1980	—	2.00	4.00
❑ 11357	Oh Darlin'/Sailin' Around the World	1980	—	2.00	4.00

Albums

A&M

Number	Title (A Side/B Side)	Yr	VG	VG+	NM
❑ SP-3110	The Ozark Mountain Daredevils	198?	2.00	4.00	8.00
—Budget-line reissue					
❑ SP-3192	It'll Shine When It Shines	198?	2.00	4.00	8.00
—Budget-line reissue					
❑ SP-3202	The Best of Ozark Mountain Daredevils	1982	2.50	5.00	10.00
❑ SP-3654	It'll Shine When It Shines	1974	3.00	6.00	12.00
❑ SP-4411	The Ozark Mountain Daredevils	1973	3.00	6.00	12.00
❑ SP-4549	The Car Over the Lake Album	1975	3.00	6.00	12.00
❑ SP-4601	Men from Earth	1976	3.00	6.00	12.00
❑ SP-4662	Don't Look Down	1977	3.00	6.00	12.00
❑ SP-6006 [(2)]	It's Alive	1978	3.75	7.50	15.00

COLUMBIA

Number	Title (A Side/B Side)	Yr	VG	VG+	NM
❑ JC 36375	Ozark Mountain Daredevils	1980	2.50	5.00	10.00

SOUNDS GREAT

Number	Title (A Side/B Side)	Yr	VG	VG+	NM
❑ SG-5004	The Lost Cabin Sessions	1985	2.50	5.00	10.00

P

PACIFIC STEEL CO.

45s

PACIFIC ARTS

Number	Title (A Side/B Side)	Yr	VG	VG+	NM
❑ 111	Fat 'n Sassy/Rio	1980	—	3.00	6.00

PACK, BOB

45s

OAK

Number	Title (A Side/B Side)	Yr	VG	VG+	NM
❑ 1051	The Request/(B-side unknown)	1988	—	3.00	6.00

PACK, RAY

45s

HAPPY MAN

Number	Title (A Side/B Side)	Yr	VG	VG+	NM
❑ 818	Where Was I/(B-side unknown)	1989	—	3.00	6.00

PAGE, PATTI

While not as big on the country charts as she was on the pop charts, she did make the country charts in five different decades!

45s

AVCO

Number	Title (A Side/B Side)	Yr	VG	VG+	NM
❑ 603	I May Not Be Lovin' You/Whoever Finds This, I Love You	1974	—	2.00	4.00
❑ 607	Pour Your Lovin' on Me/Big Wind from Dallas	1975	—	2.00	4.00
❑ 613	Less Than the Song/Did He Ask About Me	1975	—	2.00	4.00

COLUMBIA

Number	Title (A Side/B Side)	Yr	VG	VG+	NM
❑ 42671	Pretty Boy Lonely/Just a Simple Melody	1963	2.00	4.00	8.00
❑ 42791	Say Wonderful Things/I Knew I Would See Him Again	1963	2.00	4.00	8.00
❑ 42857	Nobody/Maybe He'll Come Back to Me	1963	2.00	4.00	8.00
❑ 42963	I Adore You/I Wonder, I Wonder, I Wonder	1964	—	3.00	6.00
❑ 43019	Drive-In Movie/I'd Rather Be Sorry	1964	—	3.00	6.00
❑ 43078	Drina (Little Soldier Boy)/Promises	1964	—	3.00	6.00
❑ 43183	Don't You Pass Me By/Days of the Waltz	1964	—	3.00	6.00
❑ 43251	Hush, Hush, Sweet Charlotte/Longing to Hold You Again	1965	2.00	4.00	8.00
❑ 43345	You Can't Be True, Dear/Who's Gonna Shoe My Pretty Little Feet	1965	—	3.00	6.00
❑ 43429	Ribbons and Roses/That's What I Tell Them	1965	—	3.00	6.00
❑ 43447	Happy Birthday, Jesus (A Child's Prayer)/Christmas Bells	1965	2.00	4.00	8.00
❑ 43447 [PS]	Happy Birthday, Jesus (A Child's Prayer)/Christmas Bells	1965	2.50	5.00	10.00
❑ 43517	Till You Come Back to Me/Custody	1966	—	3.00	6.00
❑ 43647	Can I Trust You?/In This Day and Age	1966	—	3.00	6.00
❑ 43761	It's the World Outside/Detour	1966	—	3.00	6.00
❑ 43794	Almost Persuaded/It's the World Outside	1966	—	3.00	6.00
❑ 43909	The Wishing Doll/Music and Memories	1966	—	3.00	6.00
❑ 43990	Wish Me a Rainbow/This Is the Sunday	1967	—	2.50	5.00
❑ 44115	Walkin' — Just Walkin'/Same Old You	1967	—	2.50	5.00
❑ 44242	What's She Got That I Ain't Got (Darlin')/Pretty Bluebird	1967	—	2.50	5.00
❑ 44257	All the Time/Pretty Bluebird	1967	—	2.50	5.00
❑ 44353	Gentle on My Mind/Excuse Me	1967	—	2.50	5.00
❑ 44556	Little Green Apples/This House	1968	—	2.50	5.00
❑ 44666	Stand By Your Man/Red Summer Roses	1968	—	2.50	5.00
❑ 44778	A Mighty Fortress Is Our Love/The Love Song	1969	—	2.50	5.00
❑ 44989	Boy from the Country/You Don't Need a Heart	1969	—	2.50	5.00
❑ 45059	Pickin' Up the Pieces/Tied Down	1969	—	2.50	5.00

Number	Title (A Side/B Side)	Yr	VG	VG+	NM
❑ 45159	I Wish I Had a Mommy Like You/He'll Never Take the Place of You	1970	—	2.50	5.00
❑ JZSP 111907/8 [DJ]	Happy Birthday, Jesus (A Child's Prayer)/ Christmas Bells	1965	2.50	5.00	10.00
—Green vinyl					
❑ JZSP 111907/8 [DJ]	Happy Birthday, Jesus (A Child's Prayer)/ Christmas Bells	1965	2.00	4.00	8.00
—Black vinyl					

EPIC

Number	Title (A Side/B Side)	Yr	VG	VG+	NM
❑ 11032	Love Lives Again/I Can't Sit Still	1973	—	2.00	4.00
❑ 11072	You're Gonna Hurt Me/Mama Take Me Home	1973	—	2.00	4.00
❑ 11109	Someone Came to See Me/One Final Stand	1974	—	2.00	4.00

MERCURY

Number	Title (A Side/B Side)	Yr	VG	VG+	NM
❑ 505	Confess/Money, Marbles and Chalk	1950	7.50	15.00	30.00
—Reissue of her first hit from 1948					
❑ 5396	I Don't Care If the Sun Don't Shine/I'm Gonna Paper All My Walls with Your Love Letters	1950	5.00	10.00	20.00
❑ 5455	All My Love (Bolero)/Roses Remind Me of You	1950	5.00	10.00	20.00
❑ 5463	Back in Your Own Backyard/Right Kind of Love	1950	5.00	10.00	20.00
❑ 5511	Confess/That Old Feeling	1950	5.00	10.00	20.00
❑ 5512	All My Love (Bolero)/Back in Your Own Backyard	1950	5.00	10.00	20.00
❑ 5521	So in Love/Why Can't You Behave	1950	5.00	10.00	20.00
❑ 5534	The Tennessee Waltz/Boogie Woogie Santa Claus	1950	5.00	10.00	20.00
❑ 5534	The Tennessee Waltz/Long, Long Ago	1951	3.75	7.50	15.00
❑ 5571	Would I Love You (Love You, Love You)/ Sentimental Music	1951	3.75	7.50	15.00
❑ 5579	Down the Trail of Achin' Hearts/Ever True Ever More	1951	3.75	7.50	15.00
❑ 5592	Tag-a-Long/Soft and Tenderly	1951	5.00	10.00	20.00
—With Rex Allen					
❑ 5595	Mockin' Bird Hill/I Love You Because	1951	3.75	7.50	15.00
❑ 5645	Mister and Mississippi/These Things I Offer You	1951	3.75	7.50	15.00
—Black vinyl					
❑ 5645	Mister and Mississippi/These Things I Offer You	1951	10.00	20.00	40.00
—Red vinyl					
❑ 5682	Detour/Who's Gonna Shoe My Pretty Little Feet	1951	3.75	7.50	15.00
❑ 5706	And So to Sleep Again/One Sweet Letter	1951	3.75	7.50	15.00
❑ 5707	Whispering/Cabaret	1951	3.75	7.50	15.00
❑ 5715	That's All I Ask of You/I'm Glad You're Happy with Someone Else	1951	3.75	7.50	15.00
❑ 5729	Boogie Woogie Santa Claus/Christmas Bells	1951	3.75	7.50	15.00
❑ 5730	Jingle Bells/Christmas Choir	1951	3.75	7.50	15.00
❑ 5731	Santa Claus Is Coming to Town/Silent Night	1951	3.75	7.50	15.00
❑ 5732	White Christmas/The Christmas Song	1951	3.75	7.50	15.00
—The above four comprise a box set					
❑ 5751	Down in the Valley/I Want to Be a Cowboy's Sweetheart	1951	3.75	7.50	15.00
❑ 5772	Come What May/Retreat (Cries My Heart)	1952	3.75	7.50	15.00
❑ 5816	Whispering Winds/Love Where You Are	1952	3.75	7.50	15.00
❑ 5867	Once in Awhile/I'm Glad You're Happy with Someone Else	1952	3.75	7.50	15.00
❑ 5895	Release Me/Wedding Bells Will Soon Be Ringing	1952	3.75	7.50	15.00
—With Rusty Draper					
❑ 5899	I Went to Your Wedding/You Belong to Me	1952	3.75	7.50	15.00
❑ 70025	Why Don't You Believe Me/Conquest	1952	3.75	7.50	15.00
❑ 70070	The Doggie in the Window/My Jealous Eyes	1953	3.75	7.50	15.00
❑ 70127	Do What You Do to Me/Now That I'm in Love	1953	3.75	7.50	15.00
❑ 70137	Tell Me Why/Big Mamou	1953	3.75	7.50	15.00
—With Rusty Draper					
❑ 70183	Butterflies/This Is My Song	1953	3.75	7.50	15.00
❑ 70190	Arfie, the Doggie in the Window/Arfie Goes to School	1953	5.00	10.00	20.00
❑ 70222	Father, Father/The Lord's Prayer	1953	5.00	10.00	20.00
❑ 70230	My World Is You/Milwaukee Polka	1953	3.75	7.50	15.00
❑ 70260	Changing Partners/Where Did My Snowman Go	1953	3.75	7.50	15.00
❑ 70295	Changing Partners/Don't Get Around Much Anymore	1954	3.75	7.50	15.00
❑ 70302	Cross Over the Bridge/My Restless Lover	1954	3.75	7.50	15.00
❑ 70380	Steam Heat/Lonely Days	1954	3.75	7.50	15.00
❑ 70416	What a Dream/I Cried	1954	3.75	7.50	15.00
❑ 70458	The Mama Doll Song/I Can't Tell a Waltz from a Tango	1954	3.75	7.50	15.00
❑ 70506	Pretty Snowflakes/I Wanna Go Dancing with Willie	1954	3.75	7.50	15.00
❑ 70511	Let Me Go, Lover!/Hocus Pocus	1954	3.75	7.50	15.00
❑ 70528	Everlovin'/You Too Can Be a Dreamer	1955	3.00	6.00	12.00
❑ 70532	I Got It Bad/Don't Get Around Much Anymore	1955	3.00	6.00	12.00
❑ 70579	Little Crazy Quilt/Keep Me in Mind	1955	3.00	6.00	12.00
❑ 70607	Near to You/I Love to Dance with You	1955	3.00	6.00	12.00
❑ 70657	Piddily Patter Patter/Every Day	1955	3.00	6.00	12.00
❑ 70713	Croce di Oro (Cross of Gold)/Search My Heart	1955	3.00	6.00	12.00
❑ 70766	Go On with the Wedding/The Voice Inside	1955	3.00	6.00	12.00
❑ 70820	Too Young to Go Steady/My First Formal Gown	1956	3.00	6.00	12.00
❑ 70878	Allegheny Moon/The Strangest Romance	1956	3.00	6.00	12.00
❑ 70971	Mama from the Train/Every Time (I Feel His Spirit)	1956	3.00	6.00	12.00
❑ 71015	Repeat After Me/Learnin' My Latin	1956	3.00	6.00	12.00
❑ 71059	A Poor Man's Roses (Or a Rich Man's Gold)/The Wall	1957	2.50	5.00	10.00
❑ 71101	Old Cape Cod/Wondering	1957	2.50	5.00	10.00
❑ 71177	No One to Cry To/Money, Marbles and Chalk	1957	2.50	5.00	10.00
❑ 71189	I'll Remember Today/My How the Time Goes By	1957	2.50	5.00	10.00
❑ 71247	Belonging to Someone/Bring Up Together	1957	2.50	5.00	10.00
❑ 71294	Another Time, Another Place/These Worldly Wonders	1958	2.50	5.00	10.00
❑ 71331	Left Right Out of Your Heart (Hi Lee Hi Lo Hi Lup Up Up)/Longing to Hold You Again	1958	2.50	5.00	10.00
❑ 71355	Fibbin'/You Will Find Your Love (In Paris)	1958	2.50	5.00	10.00
❑ 71355 [PS]	Fibbin'/You Will Find Your Love (In Paris)	1958	5.00	10.00	20.00
❑ 71400	Trust in Me/Under the Sun Valley Moon	1958	2.50	5.00	10.00
❑ 71428	The Walls Have Ears/My Promise	1959	2.50	5.00	10.00
❑ 71469	With My Eyes Wide Open I'm Dreaming/My Mother's Eyes	1959	2.50	5.00	10.00
❑ 71510	Goodbye Charlie/Because Him Is a Baby	1959	2.50	5.00	10.00
❑ 71555	The Sound of Music/Little Donkey	1959	2.50	5.00	10.00
❑ 71597	Two Thousand, Two Hundred, Twenty-Three Miles/Promise Me, Thomas	1960	2.00	4.00	8.00
❑ 71639	One of Us (Will Weep Tonight)/What Will My Future Be	1960	2.00	4.00	8.00
❑ 71639 [PS]	One of Us (Will Weep Tonight)/What Will My Future Be	1960	3.75	7.50	15.00
❑ 71695	I Wish I'd Never Been Born/I Need You	1960	2.00	4.00	8.00
❑ 71695 [PS]	I Wish I'd Never Been Born/I Need You	1960	3.75	7.50	15.00
❑ 71745	Don't Read the Letter/That's All I Need to Know	1960	2.00	4.00	8.00
❑ 71745 [PS]	Don't Read the Letter/That's All I Need to Know	1960	3.75	7.50	15.00
❑ 71792	A City Girl Stole My Country Boy/Dondi	1961	2.00	4.00	8.00
❑ 71792 [PS]	A City Girl Stole My Country Boy/Dondi	1961	3.75	7.50	15.00
❑ 71823	You'll Answer to Me/Mom and Dad's Waltz	1961	2.00	4.00	8.00
❑ 71823 [PS]	You'll Answer to Me/Mom and Dad's Waltz	1961	3.75	7.50	15.00
❑ 71870	Broken Heart and a Pillow Filled with Tears/Dark Moon	1961	2.00	4.00	8.00
❑ 71870 [PS]	Broken Heart and a Pillow Filled with Tears/Dark Moon	1961	3.75	7.50	15.00
❑ 71906	Go On Home/Too Late to Cry	1961	2.00	4.00	8.00
❑ 71906 [PS]	Go On Home/Too Late to Cry	1961	3.75	7.50	15.00
❑ 71950	Most People Get Married/You Don't Know Me	1962	2.00	4.00	8.00
❑ 71950 [PS]	Most People Get Married/You Don't Know Me	1962	3.00	6.00	12.00
❑ 72013	The Boys' Night Out/Three Fools	1962	2.00	4.00	8.00
❑ 72013 [PS]	The Boys' Night Out/Three Fools	1962	3.00	6.00	12.00
❑ 72044	Everytime I Hear Your Name/Let's Cry Together	1962	2.00	4.00	8.00
❑ 72078	High on the Hill of Hope/By a Long Shot	1963	2.00	4.00	8.00
❑ 72123	I'm Walkin'/Invitation to the Blues	1963	2.00	4.00	8.00
❑ 73162	Give Him Love/Wish I Could Take That Little Boy Home	1970	—	2.50	5.00
❑ 73199	Make Me Your Kind of Woman/I Wish I Was a Little Boy Again	1971	—	2.50	5.00
❑ 73222	I'd Rather Be Sorry/Words	1971	—	2.50	5.00
❑ 73249	Think Again/A Woman Left Lonely	1971	—	2.50	5.00
❑ 73280	Jody and the Kid/Things We Care About	1972	—	2.50	5.00
❑ 73306	Come What May/Love Is a Friend of Mine	1972	—	2.50	5.00

PLANTATION

Number	Title (A Side/B Side)	Yr	VG	VG+	NM
❑ 197	No Aces/Everytime You Touch Me	1981	—	2.00	4.00
❑ 199	Wasn't It Good/Detour	1981	—	2.00	4.00
❑ 201	On the Inside/A Poor Man's Roses	1981	—	2.00	4.00
❑ 208	My Man Friday/Tennessee Waltz	1982	—	2.00	4.00
❑ 212	Barbara's Daughter/(B-side unknown)	1982	—	2.00	4.00

Selected 78s

MERCURY

Number	Title (A Side/B Side)	Yr	VG	VG+	NM
❑ 5061	What Every Woman Knows/Every So Often	1947	5.00	10.00	20.00
❑ 5063	Can't Help Loving That Man of Mine/I've Got Some Forgetting to Do	1947	5.00	10.00	20.00
❑ 5078	I'm Sorry I Didn't Say I'm Sorry/I Feel So Smoochie	1947	3.75	7.50	15.00
❑ 5087	There's a Man in My Life/The First Time I Kissed You	1947	3.75	7.50	15.00
❑ 5098	You Turn the Tables on Me/It's the Bluest Kind of Blues	1948	3.75	7.50	15.00
❑ 5129	Confess/Twelve O'Clock Flight	1948	3.00	6.00	12.00
❑ 5142	Gotta Have More Money/Ready, Set, Go	1948	3.00	6.00	12.00
❑ 5153	Tomorrow Night/Give Me Time	1948	3.00	6.00	12.00
❑ 5184	My Sweet Adair/5-4-3-2	1948	3.00	6.00	12.00
❑ 5187	I Can't Go On Without You/All My Love Belongs to You	1948	3.00	6.00	12.00
❑ 5199	What's Wrong with Me/Goody Goodley	1948	3.00	6.00	12.00
❑ 5230	So in Love/Where's the Man	1949	3.00	6.00	12.00
❑ 5240	Streets of Laredo/My Dream Is Yours	1949	3.00	6.00	12.00
❑ 5251	Money, Marbles and Chalk/Where Is the One	1949	3.00	6.00	12.00
❑ 5290	Cabaret/Whispering	1949	3.00	6.00	12.00
❑ 5310	I'll Keep the Love Light Burning (In My Heart)/I Love You	1949	3.00	6.00	12.00
❑ 5323	Just to Have Him Around/A Thousand Violins	1949	3.00	6.00	12.00
❑ 5336	Dear Hearts and Gentle People/Game of Broken Hearts	1949	3.00	6.00	12.00
❑ 5344	With My Eyes Wide Open I'm Dreaming/ Oklahoma Blues	1949	3.00	6.00	12.00

7-Inch Extended Plays

MERCURY

Number	Title (A Side/B Side)	Yr	VG	VG+	NM
❑ EP-1-3008	The Tennessee Waltz/And So to Sleep Again// Come What May/Down the Trail of Aching Hearts	195?	3.00	6.00	12.00
❑ EP-1-3008 [PS]	Tennessee Waltz	195?	3.00	6.00	12.00
❑ EP-1-3038	The Christmas Song/The First Noel//Christmas Choir/Christmas Bells	1956	3.00	6.00	12.00
❑ EP-1-3038 [PS]	Christmas with Patti Page	1956	3.00	6.00	12.00

Albums

ACCORD

Number	Title (A Side/B Side)	Yr	VG	VG+	NM
❑ SN-7206	Special Thoughts	1982	2.50	5.00	10.00

COLUMBIA

Number	Title (A Side/B Side)	Yr	VG	VG+	NM
❑ CL 2049 [M]	Say Wonderful Things	1963	3.75	7.50	15.00
❑ CL 2132 [M]	Love After Midnight	1964	3.75	7.50	15.00

Number	Title (A Side/B Side)	Yr	VG	VG+	NM
❑ CL 2353 [M]	Hush, Hush, Sweet Charlotte	1965	3.75	7.50	15.00
❑ CL 2414 [M]	Christmas with Patti Page	1965	3.00	6.00	12.00
❑ CL 2505 [M]	America's Favorite Hymns	1966	3.00	6.00	12.00
❑ CL 2526 [M]	Patti Page's Greatest Hits	1966	3.00	6.00	12.00
❑ CL 2761 [M]	Today My Way	1967	5.00	10.00	20.00
❑ CS 8849 [S]	Say Wonderful Things	1963	5.00	10.00	20.00
❑ CS 8932 [S]	Love After Midnight	1964	5.00	10.00	20.00
❑ CS 9153 [S]	Hush, Hush, Sweet Charlotte	1965	5.00	10.00	20.00
❑ CS 9214 [S]	Christmas with Patti Page	1965	3.75	7.50	15.00
❑ CS 9305 [S]	America's Favorite Hymns	1966	3.75	7.50	15.00
❑ CS 9326	Patti Page's Greatest Hits	1970	2.50	5.00	10.00
—Orange label					
❑ CS 9326 [S]	Patti Page's Greatest Hits	1966	3.75	7.50	15.00
—"360 Sound" label					
❑ PC 9326	Patti Page's Greatest Hits	198?	2.00	4.00	8.00
—Budget-line reissue					
❑ CS 9561 [S]	Today My Way	1967	3.75	7.50	15.00
❑ CS 9666	Gentle on My Mind	1968	3.75	7.50	15.00
❑ CS 9999	Honey Come Back	1970	3.00	6.00	12.00
EMARCY					
❑ MG-36074 [M]	In the Land of Hi-Fi	1956	12.50	25.00	50.00
❑ MG-36116 [M]	The East Side	1957	12.50	25.00	50.00
❑ MG-36136 [M]	The West Side	1957	12.50	25.00	50.00
❑ SR-60013 [S]	The West Side	1959	12.50	25.00	50.00
❑ SR-60014 [S]	The East Side	1959	12.50	25.00	50.00
❑ SR-80000 [S]	In the Land of Hi-Fi	1959	12.50	25.00	50.00
HARMONY					
❑ HS 11381	Stand By Your Man	1970	2.50	5.00	10.00
❑ KH 30407	Green, Green Grass of Home	1971	2.50	5.00	10.00
MERCURY					
❑ PKW-118 [(2)]	The Most	1969	3.75	7.50	15.00
❑ MG-20076 [M]	Romance on the Range	1955	7.50	15.00	30.00
❑ MG 20093 [M]	Christmas with Patti Page	1956	7.50	15.00	30.00
❑ MG-20095 [M]	Page I	1955	7.50	15.00	30.00
❑ MG-20096 [M]	Page II	1955	7.50	15.00	30.00
❑ MG-20097 [M]	Page III	1955	7.50	15.00	30.00
❑ MG-20098 [M]	You Go to My Head	1955	7.50	15.00	30.00
❑ MG-20099 [M]	Music for Two in Love	1955	7.50	15.00	30.00
❑ MG-20100 [M]	The Voice of Patti Page	1955	7.50	15.00	30.00
❑ MG-20101 [M]	Page IV	1955	7.50	15.00	30.00
❑ MG-20102 [M]	This Is My Song	1955	7.50	15.00	30.00
❑ MG-20226 [M]	Manhattan Tower	1956	7.50	15.00	30.00
❑ MG-20318 [M]	The Waltz Queen	1957	7.50	15.00	30.00
❑ MG-20387 [M]	Let's Get Away From it All	1957	7.50	15.00	30.00
❑ MG-20388 [M]	I've Heard That Song Before	1957	7.50	15.00	30.00
❑ MG-20398 [M]	Patti Page On Camera	1958	7.50	15.00	30.00
❑ MG-20405 [M]	Indiscretion	1959	7.50	15.00	30.00
❑ MG-20406 [M]	I'll Remember April	1959	7.50	15.00	30.00
❑ MG-20417 [M]	Three Little Words	1960	7.50	15.00	30.00
❑ MG-20495 [M]	Patti Page's Golden Hits	1960	7.50	15.00	30.00
❑ MG-20573 [M]	Just a Closer Walk with Thee	1960	7.50	15.00	30.00
❑ MG-20599 [M]	Patti Page Sings and Stars In "Elmer Gantry"	1960	6.25	12.50	25.00
❑ MG-20615 [M]	Country & Western Golden Hits	1961	5.00	10.00	20.00
❑ MG-20689 [M]	Go On Home	1962	5.00	10.00	20.00
❑ MG-20712 [M]	Golden Hits of the Boys	1962	5.00	10.00	20.00
❑ MG-20758 [M]	Patti Page On Stage	1963	5.00	10.00	20.00
❑ MG-20794 [M]	Patti Page's Golden Hits, Volume 2	1963	5.00	10.00	20.00
❑ MG-20819 [M]	The Singing Rage	1963	5.00	10.00	20.00
❑ MG-20909 [M]	Blue Dream Street	1964	5.00	10.00	20.00
❑ MG-20952 [M]	The Nearness of You	1965	3.75	7.50	15.00
❑ MG-25059 [10]	Songs	1950	10.00	20.00	40.00
❑ MG-25101 [10]	Folksong Favorites	1951	10.00	20.00	40.00
❑ MG-25109 [10]	Christmas	1951	10.00	20.00	40.00
❑ MG-25154 [10]	Tennessee Waltz	1952	10.00	20.00	40.00
❑ MG-25185 [10]	Patti Sings for Romance	1954	10.00	20.00	40.00
❑ MG-25187 [10]	Song Souvenirs	1954	10.00	20.00	40.00
❑ MG-25196 [10]	Just Patti	1954	10.00	20.00	40.00
❑ MG-25197 [10]	Patti's Songs	1954	10.00	20.00	40.00
❑ MG-25209 [10]	And I Thought About You	1954	10.00	20.00	40.00
❑ MG-25210 [10]	So Many Memories	1954	10.00	20.00	40.00
❑ SR-60010 [S]	Let's Get Away From it All	1959	10.00	20.00	40.00
❑ SR-60011 [S]	I've Heard That Song Before	1959	10.00	20.00	40.00
❑ SR-60025 [S]	Patti Page On Camera	1959	10.00	20.00	40.00
❑ SR-60037 [S]	Three Little Words	1960	10.00	20.00	40.00
❑ SR-60049 [S]	The Waltz Queen	1959	10.00	20.00	40.00
❑ SR-60059 [S]	Indiscretion	1959	10.00	20.00	40.00
❑ SR-60081 [S]	I'll Remember April	1959	10.00	20.00	40.00
❑ SR-60233 [S]	Just a Closer Walk with Thee	1960	10.00	20.00	40.00
❑ SR-60260 [S]	Patti Page Sings and Stars In "Elmer Gantry"	1960	7.50	15.00	30.00
❑ SR-60495 [S]	Patti Page's Golden Hits	196?	6.25	12.50	25.00
❑ SR-60615 [S]	Country & Western Golden Hits	1961	6.25	12.50	25.00
❑ SR-60689 [S]	Go On Home	1962	6.25	12.50	25.00
❑ SR-60712 [S]	Golden Hits of the Boys	1962	6.25	12.50	25.00
❑ SR-60758 [S]	Patti Page On Stage	1963	6.25	12.50	25.00
❑ SR-60794 [S]	Patti Page's Golden Hits, Volume 2	1963	6.25	12.50	25.00
❑ SR-60819 [S]	The Singing Rage	1963	6.25	12.50	25.00
❑ SR-60909 [S]	Blue Dream Street	1964	6.25	12.50	25.00
❑ SR-60952 [S]	The Nearness of You	1965	5.00	10.00	20.00
❑ SR-61344	I'd Rather Be Sorry	1971	3.00	6.00	12.00
❑ 822740-1	Christmas with Patti Page	1987	2.50	5.00	10.00
—Reissue					
PLANTATION					
❑ 548	Aces	1981	2.50	5.00	10.00
WING					
❑ MGW 12121 [M]	The Waltz Queen	196?	3.00	6.00	12.00
❑ MGW 12174 [M]	Christmas with Patti Page	196?	5.00	10.00	20.00
—Same contents and order as Mercury 20093					
❑ MGW 12250 [M]	Let's Get Away From It All	196?	3.00	6.00	12.00
❑ SRW 16121 [S]	The Waltz Queen	196?	3.75	7.50	15.00
❑ SRW 16250 [S]	Let's Get Away From It All	196?	3.75	7.50	15.00

PAGE, PATTI, AND TOM T. HALL

Also see each artist's individual listings.

45s

Number	Title (A Side/B Side)	Yr	VG	VG+	NM
MERCURY					
❑ 73347	Hello We're Lonely/We're Not Getting Older	1972	—	2.50	5.00

PAIN, JOE

45s

Number	Title (A Side/B Side)	Yr	VG	VG+	NM
LITTLE DARLIN'					
❑ 0025	Down at Kelly's/A Thousand Times Paid	1967	2.50	5.00	10.00
❑ 0039	Deaf, Dumb and Blind/True Love Dies	1968	2.50	5.00	10.00

PAISLEY, BRAD

45s

Number	Title (A Side/B Side)	Yr	VG	VG+	NM
ARISTA NASHVILLE					
❑ 13156	Who Needs Pictures/It Never Woulda Worked Out Anyway	1999	—	2.00	4.00
❑ 13172	Me Neither/Don't Breathe	2000	—	—	3.00
❑ 13176	He Didn't Have to Be/I've Been Better	1999	—	—	3.00
❑ 69009	We Danced/Me Neither	2000	—	—	3.00

PALMER, KEITH

45s

Number	Title (A Side/B Side)	Yr	VG	VG+	NM
EPIC					
❑ 34-73988	Don't Throw Me in the Briarpatch/My Arms Tonight	1991	—	2.00	4.00
❑ 34-74174	Forgotten But Not Gone/Memory Lane	1992	—	2.00	4.00

PALOMINO ROAD

45s

Number	Title (A Side/B Side)	Yr	VG	VG+	NM
LIBERTY					
❑ S7-56974	Why Baby Why/Over and Over	1993	—	2.50	5.00

PAPA JOE'S MUSIC BOX

See JERRY SMITH.

PARIS, JACK

45s

Number	Title (A Side/B Side)	Yr	VG	VG+	NM
2-J					
❑ 201	It Sets Me Free/A Woman Ought to Be	1976	2.00	4.00	8.00
50 STATES					
❑ 47	Run Samson Run/(B-side unknown)	1976	—	2.50	5.00
❑ 49	Gypsy River/Mountain of Love	1977	—	2.50	5.00
❑ 57	Mississippi/Heaven's Here Tonight	1977	—	2.50	5.00
❑ 58	Lay Down Sally/I Wonder Where You Are Tonight	1978	—	2.50	5.00
❑ 62	(It's Gonna Be a) Happy Day/(B-side unknown)	1978	—	2.50	5.00
❑ 65	Broken White Line/(B-side unknown)	1978	—	2.50	5.00

Albums

Number	Title (A Side/B Side)	Yr	VG	VG+	NM
2-J					
❑ 101	My Music, My Friends	197?	3.75	7.50	15.00
❑ 102	Strawberries and Butterflies	197?	3.75	7.50	15.00
50 STATES					
❑ 1002	Southern Session	197?	3.75	7.50	15.00
❑ 1005	Nashville Heart and Soul	197?	3.75	7.50	15.00

PARKER, BILLY

45s

Number	Title (A Side/B Side)	Yr	VG	VG+	NM
CANYON CREEK					
❑ 0315	It's Time for Your Dreams to Come True/You Are My Angel	1989	—	2.50	5.00
❑ 0801	She's Sittin' Pretty/(B-side unknown)	1988	—	2.50	5.00
❑ 1208	You Are My Angel/(B-side unknown)	1987	—	2.50	5.00
DECCA					
❑ 32462	The Pillow/I'll Drink to That	1969	2.00	4.00	8.00
❑ 32572	Room Full of Fools/Only a Woman Like You	1969	2.00	4.00	8.00
❑ 32652	I Get a Happy Feeling/If These Tears Could Talk	1970	2.00	4.00	8.00
❑ 32913	Ladder of Success/Looking for a Woman	1972	2.00	4.00	8.00
OAK					
❑ 47565	Better Side of Thirty/Lord If I Make It	1981	—	3.00	6.00
SCR					
❑ 118	Travelin' Truckin' Man/The Man from Galilee	1975	—	3.00	6.00
❑ 120	Average Man/(B-side unknown)	1975	—	3.00	6.00
❑ 127	More Than One Kind of Love/(B-side unknown)	1976	—	3.00	6.00
❑ 129	I'll Hold You in My Heart/These Hard Times	1976	—	3.00	6.00
❑ 133	It's Bad When You're Caught (With the Goods)/I Guess I Owe That Much to You	1976	—	3.00	6.00
❑ 136	Lord, If I Make It to Heaven Can I Bring My Own Angel Along/Jerri Again	1976	—	3.00	6.00
❑ 144	What Did I Promise Her Last Night/Let a Fool Take a Bow	1977	—	3.00	6.00
❑ 148	If You Got to Have It Your Way (I'll Go Mine)/The Line Between Love and Hate	1977	—	3.00	6.00
❑ 153	You Read Between the Lines/Trophy of Gold	1977	—	3.00	6.00
❑ 157	If There's One Angel Missing (She's Here in My Arms Tonight)/Tough Act to Follow	1978	—	2.50	5.00
❑ 157 [PS]	If There's One Angel Missing (She's Here in My Arms Tonight)/Tough Act to Follow	1978	2.00	4.00	8.00
❑ 160	Until the Next Time/Tough Act to Follow	1978	—	2.50	5.00

Number	Title (A Side/B Side)	Yr	VG	VG+	NM
❑ 162	Pleasin' My Woman/Thanks E.T. Thanks a Lot	1978	—	2.50	5.00
❑ 177	Thanks a Lot/Until the Next Time	1979	—	2.50	5.00
❑ 181	Tough Act to Follow/(B-side unknown)	1979	—	2.50	5.00
❑ 185	Lord, If I Make It to Heaven Can I Bring My Own Angel Along/(B-side unknown)	1980	—	2.50	5.00
SIMS					
❑ 146	The Line Between Love and Hate/I Hurt Me (Instead of You)	1963	3.75	7.50	15.00
❑ 184	Sounds Like a Winner/Tattooed Lover	1964	3.00	6.00	12.00
SOUNDWAVES					
❑ 4643	I'll Drink to That/One More Last Time	1981	—	2.50	5.00
❑ 4659	I See an Angel Every Day/Hello Out There	1981	—	2.50	5.00
❑ 4670	(Who's Gonna Sing) The Last Country Song/ What's a Nice Girl Like You	1982	—	2.50	5.00
—A-side as "Billy Parker and Friend"					
❑ 4678	If I Ever Need a Lady/Can I Have What's Left	1982	—	2.50	5.00
—A-side as "Billy Parker and Friend"					
❑ 4686	Too Many Irons in the Fire/Honky Tonk Girl	1982	—	2.50	5.00
—A-side with Cal Smith					
❑ 4699	Who Said Love Was Fair/Take Me Back to Tulsa	1983	—	2.50	5.00
—A-side as "Billy Parker and Friends"					
❑ 4708	Love Don't Know a Lady (From a Honky Tonk Girl)/It's Not Me	1983	—	2.50	5.00
—A-side as "Billy Parker and Friends"					
❑ 4719	Memory #1/Why Do I Keep Calling You Honey	1983	—	2.50	5.00
—A-side with Webb Pierce					
❑ 4729	When I Need Love Bad/Tomorrow Never Comes	1984	—	2.50	5.00
❑ 4746	Why Do I Keep Calling You Honey, Honey/I Believe I'm Entitled to You	1984	—	2.50	5.00
❑ 4773	Her Lovin' Already Told Me She Was Gone/I Found a Miracle in You	1986	—	2.50	5.00

PARKER, FESS

Number	Title (A Side/B Side)	Yr	VG	VG+	NM
45s					
BUENA VISTA					
❑ F-426	Ballad of Davy Crockett/Farewell	1963	3.00	6.00	12.00
❑ F-426 [PS]	Ballad of Davy Crockett/Farewell	1963	3.75	7.50	15.00
CASCADE					
❑ 5910	Eyes of an Angel/Strong Man	1959	3.75	7.50	15.00
❑ 5913	Lonely/Jayhawkers	1959	3.75	7.50	15.00
COLUMBIA					
❑ J4-242	Ballad of Davy Crockett/I Gave My Love (Riddle Song)	1955	5.00	10.00	20.00
—Yellow label "Children's Series" release					
❑ J4-242 [PS]	Ballad of Davy Crockett/I Gave My Love (Riddle Song)	1955	10.00	20.00	40.00
—Yellow label "Children's Series" release					
❑ 4-40449	Ballad of Davy Crockett/I Gave My Love (Riddle Song)	1955	3.75	7.50	15.00
❑ 4-40450	Farewell/I'm Lonely My Darlin'	1955	3.75	7.50	15.00
❑ 4-40568	Yaller Yaller Gold/King of the River	1955	6.25	12.50	25.00
DISNEYLAND					
❑ F-039	Wringle Wrangle/(Instrumental)	1957	7.50	15.00	30.00
—B-side by Camarata					
❑ F-043	Wringle Wrangle/The Ballad of John Coulter	1957	3.00	6.00	12.00
❑ F-043 [PS]	Wringle Wrangle/The Ballad of John Coulter	1957	6.25	12.50	25.00
❑ F-045	Pioneer's Prayer/The Ballad of John Coulter	1957	3.00	6.00	12.00
❑ F-045 [PS]	Pioneer's Prayer/The Ballad of John Coulter	1957	6.25	12.50	25.00
❑ F-049	A Hole in the Sky/Wedding Bell Calypso	1957	3.00	6.00	12.00
❑ F-049 [PS]	A Hole in the Sky/Wedding Bell Calypso	1957	6.25	12.50	25.00
❑ F-053	Gonna Find Me a Bluebird/Catch Me Fish	1957	6.25	12.50	25.00
GUSTO					
❑ 900	Ballad of Davy Crockett/Lonely	1963	2.50	5.00	10.00
RCA VICTOR					
❑ 47-8429	Daniel Boone/The Ballad of Davy Crockett	1964	3.00	6.00	12.00
❑ 47-8429 [PS]	Daniel Boone/The Ballad of Davy Crockett	1964	5.00	10.00	20.00
❑ 74-0249	Comin' After Jimmy/Sittin' Here Drinkin'	1969	2.50	5.00	10.00
Albums					
COLUMBIA					
❑ CL 666 [M]	Walt Disney's Davy Crockett, King of the Wild Frontier	1955	25.00	50.00	100.00
DISNEYLAND					
❑ WDL-1007 [M]	Yarns and Songs of the West	1959	7.50	15.00	30.00
—Reissue of 3006					
❑ DQ-1269 [M]	Pecos Bill and Other Stories in Song	1965	7.50	15.00	30.00
❑ DQ-1315 [M]	Three Adventures of Davy Crockett	1968	6.25	12.50	25.00
—Another reissue, this time of 1926					
❑ DQ-1336	Cowboy and Indian Songs	1969	7.50	15.00	30.00
❑ ST-1926 [M]	Three Adventures of Davy Crockett	1963	7.50	15.00	30.00
—Reissue of 3602					
❑ WDL-3006 [M]	Yarns and Songs	1957	10.00	20.00	40.00
❑ WDL-3041 [M]	Westward Ho the Wagons	1959	7.50	15.00	30.00
—Reissue of 4008					
❑ WDA-3602 [M]	Three Adventures of Davy Crockett	1958	12.50	25.00	50.00
—Reissue of Columbia 666					
❑ WDL-4006 [M]	Westward Ho the Wagons	1956	20.00	40.00	80.00
RCA VICTOR					
❑ LPM-2973 [M]	Fess Parker Sings About Daniel Boone, Davy Crockett and Abe Lincoln	1964	6.25	12.50	25.00
❑ LSP-2973 [S]	Fess Parker Sings About Daniel Boone, Davy Crockett and Abe Lincoln	1964	7.50	15.00	30.00

PARKER, FESS, AND BUDDY EBSEN

Number	Title (A Side/B Side)	Yr	VG	VG+	NM
45s					
COLUMBIA					
❑ B-2031	Davy Crockett, Indian Fighter	1955	10.00	20.00	40.00
—Cover for 40476 and 40477					
❑ B-2032	Davy Crockett Goes to Congress	1955	10.00	20.00	40.00
—Cover for 40478 and 40479					
❑ B-2033	Davy Crockett at the Alamo	1955	10.00	20.00	40.00
—Cover for 40480 and 40481					
❑ 4-40476	Davy Crockett, Indian Fighter (Part 1)/Davy Crockett, Indian Fighter (Part 4)	1955	5.00	10.00	20.00
❑ 4-40477	Davy Crockett, Indian Fighter (Part 2)/Davy Crockett, Indian Fighter (Part 3)	1955	5.00	10.00	20.00
❑ 4-40478	Davy Crockett Goes to Congress (Part 1)/Davy Crockett Goes to Congress (Part 4)	1955	5.00	10.00	20.00
❑ 4-40479	Davy Crockett Goes to Congress (Part 2)/Davy Crockett Goes to Congress (Part 3)	1955	5.00	10.00	20.00
❑ 4-40480	Davy Crockett at the Alamo (Part 1)/Davy Crockett at the Alamo (Part 4)	1955	5.00	10.00	20.00
❑ 4-40481	Davy Crockett at the Alamo (Part 2)/Davy Crockett at the Alamo (Part 3)	1955	5.00	10.00	20.00
❑ 4-40510	Be Sure You're Right (Then Go Ahead)/Old Betsy (Davy Crockett's Rifle)	1955	5.00	10.00	20.00

PARKER, GARY DALE

Number	Title (A Side/B Side)	Yr	VG	VG+	NM
45s					
615					
❑ 1022	Once and For Always/(B-side unknown)	1989	—	2.50	5.00

PARKER, LORI

Number	Title (A Side/B Side)	Yr	VG	VG+	NM
45s					
CON BRIO					
❑ 113	Steppin' Out Tonight/Empty Arms	1976	—	2.50	5.00
❑ 122	I Like Everything About Loving You/Out of Luck, Out of Love	1977	—	2.50	5.00
❑ 130	Everything You Say Tonight/Steppin' Out Tonight	1977	—	2.50	5.00
DOT					
❑ 17180	World of Children/There I Go	1968	2.00	4.00	8.00
❑ 17318	There Is Nothing More to Say/A Million Miles Away	1969	2.00	4.00	8.00
❑ 17339	The Clock/Do You Really Have a Heart	1970	—	3.50	7.00

PARKER, RONNIE

Number	Title (A Side/B Side)	Yr	VG	VG+	NM
45s					
LITTLE DARLIN'					
❑ 7921	Spent a Week There Last Night/Country Road from You	1979	—	3.00	6.00

PARKS, MICHAEL

Number	Title (A Side/B Side)	Yr	VG	VG+	NM
45s					
MGM					
❑ 14092	Tie Me to Your Apron Strings Again/Won't You Ride in My Little Red Wagon	1969	—	2.50	5.00
❑ 14104	Long Lonesome Highway/Mountain High	1970	—	3.00	6.00
❑ 14154	Sally/Save a Little, Spend a Little	1970	—	2.50	5.00
❑ 14363	Won't You Ride in My Little Red Wagon/Big "T" Water	1972	—	2.50	5.00
VERVE					
❑ 10653	Drownin' on Dry Land/River's Invitation	1971	—	2.50	5.00
Albums					
FIRST AMERICAN					
❑ 7781	You Don't Know Me	1983	2.50	5.00	10.00
MGM					
❑ SE-4646	Closing the Gap	1969	3.75	7.50	15.00
❑ SE-4662	Long Lonesome Highway	1970	3.75	7.50	15.00
❑ SE-4717	Blue	1970	3.75	7.50	15.00
❑ SE-4784	The Best of Michael Parks	1971	3.75	7.50	15.00
VERVE					
❑ V6-5079	Lost and Found	1971	3.75	7.50	15.00

PARKS, P.J.

Number	Title (A Side/B Side)	Yr	VG	VG+	NM
45s					
KIK					
❑ 901	The Way You Are/Saint of New Orleans	1980	—	3.00	6.00
❑ 903	Falling In/Saint of New Orleans	1981	—	3.00	6.00
❑ 906	The First Cowboy/(B-side unknown)	1981	—	3.00	6.00

PARNELL, LEE ROY

Number	Title (A Side/B Side)	Yr	VG	VG+	NM
45s					
ARISTA					
❑ 2028	Oughta Be a Law/Crocodile Tears	1990	—	2.00	4.00
❑ 2093	Family Tree/Red Hot	1990	—	2.00	4.00
❑ 9912	Crocodile Tears/Let's Have Some Fun	1990	—	2.50	5.00
❑ 12400	The Rock/Road Scholar	1992	—	2.00	4.00
❑ 12431	What Kind of Fool Do You Think I Am/Roller Coaster	1992	—	2.50	5.00
❑ 12462	Love Without Mercy/Done Deal	1992	—	2.00	4.00
❑ 12523	Tender Moment/The Rock	1993	—	2.00	4.00
❑ 12598	On the Road/Back in My Arms Again	1993	—	2.00	4.00
❑ 12642	I'm Holding My Own/Fresh Coat of Paint	1993	—	2.00	4.00
❑ 12695	Take These Chains from My Heart/Straight Shooter	1994	—	—	3.00
❑ 12747	The Power of Love/Straight and Narrow	1994	—	—	3.00

ARISTA NASHVILLE

Number	Title (A Side/B Side)	Yr	VG	VG+	NM
❑ 13098	All That Matters Anymore/One Foot in Front of the Other	1998	—	—	3.00
❑ 13175	She Won't Be Lonely Long/Long Way to Fall	1999	—	—	3.00

CAREER

Number	Title (A Side/B Side)	Yr	VG	VG+	NM
❑ 10503	Givin' Water to a Drowning Man/Squeeze Me In	1996	—	—	3.00
❑ 12823	A Little Bit of You/Givin' Water to a Drowning Man	1995	—	2.00	4.00
❑ 12862	When a Woman Loves a Man/The House Is Rockin'	1995	—	—	3.00
❑ 12952	Heart's Desire/Knock Yourself Out	1996	—	—	3.00
❑ 13044	We All Get Lucky Sometimes/I Had to Let It Go	1996	—	—	3.00
❑ 13078	Lucky Me, Lucky You/Every Night's a Saturday	1997	—	—	3.00
❑ 13079	You Can't Get There from Here/Mama Screw Your Wig On Right	1997	—	—	3.00

PARSONS, BILL

45s

FRATERNITY

Number	Title (A Side/B Side)	Yr	VG	VG+	NM
❑ 835	The All American Boy/Rubber Dolly	1959	10.00	20.00	40.00
—This record is actually by Bobby Bare miscredited					
❑ 838	Educated Rock and Roll/Carefree Wanderer	1959	7.50	15.00	30.00

STARDAY

Number	Title (A Side/B Side)	Yr	VG	VG+	NM
❑ 526	Hod Rod Volkswagen/Guitar Blues	1960	7.50	15.00	30.00
❑ 544	The Price We Pay for Livin'/A-Waitin'	1960	5.00	10.00	20.00

PARSONS, GRAM

An important figure in the melding of country with rock. EMMYLOU HARRIS appears on some of his solo recordings. Also see THE BYRDS; THE FLYING BURRITO BROTHERS; THE INTERNATIONAL SUBMARINE BAND.

45s

REPRISE

Number	Title (A Side/B Side)	Yr	VG	VG+	NM
❑ 1139	That's All It Took/She	1972	—	3.00	6.00
❑ 1192	Love Hurts/In My Hour of Darkness	1974	—	3.00	6.00

SIERRA

Number	Title (A Side/B Side)	Yr	VG	VG+	NM
❑ 104	Medley (Bony Moronie/40 Days/Almost Grown)/ /Conversations/Hot Burrito #1	1982	—	2.50	5.00
—Second song on side 2 by Gene Parsons					
❑ 104 [PS]	Gram Parsons and the Fallen Angels	1982	—	2.50	5.00
❑ 105	Love Hurts/The New Soft Shoe	1982	—	2.50	5.00

WARNER BROS.

Number	Title (A Side/B Side)	Yr	VG	VG+	NM
❑ 50013	Return of the Grievous Angel/Hearts on Fire	1982	—	2.50	5.00

Albums

REPRISE

Number	Title (A Side/B Side)	Yr	VG	VG+	NM
❑ MS 2123	G.P.	1973	3.75	7.50	15.00
❑ MS 2171	Grievous Angel	1974	3.75	7.50	15.00

SIERRA

Number	Title (A Side/B Side)	Yr	VG	VG+	NM
❑ SP-1963	Early Years, Volume 1 (1963-65)	198?	2.00	4.00	8.00
—Reissue of 8702					
❑ GP-1973	Gram Parsons and the Fallen Angels Live '73	1982	2.50	5.00	10.00
❑ 8702	Early Years, Volume 1 (1963-65)	1979	2.50	5.00	10.00

PARSONS, ROB

45s

MCA

Number	Title (A Side/B Side)	Yr	VG	VG+	NM
❑ 51202	Shadow of Love/Today May Be the Day	1981	—	2.00	4.00
❑ 52034	Nothing Else Can Change a Cowboy/There's Nobody Home on the Range No More	1982	—	2.00	4.00
❑ 52147	Wheel of Life/Plans	1982	—	2.00	4.00
❑ 52185	Wasted Love/The Wheel of Life	1983	—	2.00	4.00

PARTON, DOLLY

12-Inch Singles

RCA

Number	Title (A Side/B Side)	Yr	VG	VG+	NM
❑ JD-11425	Baby I'm Burning/I'm Falling in Love	1978	2.50	5.00	10.00
❑ PW-13545 [DJ]	Potential New Boyfriend (Long Version)/ (Instrumental) (Short Version)	1983	2.50	5.00	10.00
❑ PW-13712 [DJ]	Save the Last Dance for Me (Long Version)/ (Instrumetnal) (Short Version)	1983	2.00	4.00	8.00

RCA VICTOR

Number	Title (A Side/B Side)	Yr	VG	VG+	NM
❑ PD-11425	Baby I'm Burnin'/I Wanna Fall in Love	1978	3.00	6.00	12.00
—Pink vinyl					

45s

COLUMBIA

Number	Title (A Side/B Side)	Yr	VG	VG+	NM
❑ 07665	The River Unbroken/More Than I Can Say	1988	—	—	3.00
❑ 07665 [PS]	The River Unbroken/More Than I Can Say	1988	—	—	3.00
❑ 07727	I Know You by Heart/Could I Have Your Autograph	1988	—	—	3.00
—With Smokey Robinson					
❑ 07727 [PS]	I Know You by Heart/Could I Have Your Autograph	1988	—	—	3.00
❑ 07995	Make Love Mine/Two Lovers	1988	—	—	3.00
❑ 68760	Why'd You Come In Here Lookin' Like That/Wait Til I Get You Home	1989	—	—	3.00
❑ 69040	Yellow Roses/Wait Til I Get You Home	1989	—	—	3.00
❑ 73200	He's Alive/What Is It We Love	1990	—	—	3.00
❑ 73226	Time for Me to Fly/The Moon, the Stars, and Me	1990	—	—	3.00
❑ 73341	White Limozeen/The Moon, the Stars, and Me	1990	—	—	3.00
❑ 73498	Slow Healin' Heart/Take Me Back to the Country	1990	—	—	3.00
❑ 73711	Rockin' Years/What a Heartache	1991	—	—	3.00
—A-side with Ricky Van Shelton					
❑ 73826	Silver and Gold/Runaway Feelin'	1991	—	—	3.00
❑ 74011	Eagle When She Flies/Wildest Dreams	1991	—	—	3.00
❑ 74183	The Best Woman Wins/Country Road	1992	—	—	3.00
—A-side with Lorrie Morgan					
❑ 74876	Romeo/The High and the Mighty	1993	—	—	3.00
—A-side: "Dolly Parton and Friends"					
❑ 74954	More Where That Came From/I'll Make Your Bed	1993	—	—	3.00
❑ 77083	Full Circle/What Will Baby Be	1993	—	—	3.00
❑ 77294	Silver Threads and Golden Needles/Let Her Fly	1993	—	—	3.00
—Dolly Parton/Tammy Wynette/Loretta Lynn					
❑ 77723	To Daddy/PMS Blues	1994	—	—	3.00
❑ 78079	I Will Always Love You/Speakin' of the Devil	1995	—	—	3.00
—A-side: "With Special Guest Vince Gill"					

DECCA

Number	Title (A Side/B Side)	Yr	VG	VG+	NM
❑ 72061	Honky Tonk Songs/Paradise Road	1998	—	—	3.00
❑ 72080	The Salt in My Tears/Hungry Again	1998	—	—	3.00

GOLD BAND

Number	Title (A Side/B Side)	Yr	VG	VG+	NM
❑ 1086	Puppy Love/Girl Left Alone	1959	150.00	300.00	600.00

MERCURY

Number	Title (A Side/B Side)	Yr	VG	VG+	NM
❑ 71982	It's Sure Gonna Hurt/The Love You Gave	1962	75.00	150.00	300.00

MONUMENT

Number	Title (A Side/B Side)	Yr	VG	VG+	NM
❑ 869	I Wasted My Tears/What Do You Think About Lovin'	1965	3.75	7.50	15.00
❑ 897	Old Enough to Know Better (Too Young to Resist)/Happy, Happy Birthday Baby	1965	3.75	7.50	15.00
❑ 913	Busy Signal/I Took Him for Granted	1965	3.75	7.50	15.00
❑ 922	Control Yourself/Don't Drop Out	1966	3.75	7.50	15.00
❑ 948	Little Things/I'll Put It Off Until Tomorrow	1966	3.75	7.50	15.00
❑ 982	Dumb Blonde/The Giving and the Taking	1967	2.50	5.00	10.00
❑ 1007	Something Fishy/I've Lived My Life	1967	2.50	5.00	10.00
❑ 1032	Why, Why, Why/I Couldn't Wait Forever	1967	2.50	5.00	10.00
❑ 1047	I'm Not Worth the Tears/Ping Pong	1968	2.00	4.00	8.00
❑ 03408	Everything Is Beautiful (In Its Own Way)/Put It Off Until Tomorrow	1982	—	2.00	4.00
—A-side with Willie Nelson; B-side with Kris Kristofferson					
❑ 03781	What Do You Think About Lovin'/You're Gonna Love Yourself (In the Morning)	1983	—	2.00	4.00
—A-side: Dolly Parton and Brenda Lee; B-side: Willie Nelson and Brenda Lee					

RCA

Number	Title (A Side/B Side)	Yr	VG	VG+	NM
❑ 5001-7-R	Do I Ever Cross Your Mind/We Had It All	1986	—	—	3.00
❑ PB-10935	Light of a Clear Blue Morning/There	1977	—	2.00	4.00
❑ PB-11123	Here You Come Again/Me and Little Andy	1977	—	2.00	4.00
❑ PB-11240	Two Doors Down/It's All Wrong, But It's All Right	1978	—	2.00	4.00
❑ JB-11296 [DJ]	Heartbreaker (same on both sides)	1978	2.50	5.00	10.00
—Promo only on red vinyl					
❑ PB-11296	Heartbreaker/Sure Thing	1978	—	2.00	4.00
❑ JB-11420 [DJ]	Baby I'm Burning (same on both sides)	1978	2.50	5.00	10.00
—Promo only on red vinyl					
❑ PB-11420	Baby I'm Burning/I Really Got the Feeling	1978	—	2.00	4.00
❑ GB-11505	Here You Come Again/Two Doors Down	1979	—	—	3.00
—Gold Standard Series					
❑ PB-11577	You're the Only One/Down	1979	—	2.00	4.00
❑ JB-11705 [DJ]	Great Balls of Fire (same on both sides)	1979	2.50	5.00	10.00
—Promo only on red vinyl					
❑ PB-11705	Sweet Summer Lovin'/Great Balls of Fire	1979	—	2.00	4.00
❑ JH-11926 [DJ]	Starting Over Again (same on both sides)	1980	3.00	6.00	12.00
—Promo only on green vinyl					
❑ PB-11926	Starting Over Again/Sweet Agony	1980	—	2.00	4.00
❑ GB-11993	Baby I'm Burnin'/Heartbreaker	1980	—	—	3.00
—Gold Standard Series					
❑ PB-12040	Old Flames Can't Hold a Candle to You/I Knew You When	1980	—	2.00	4.00
❑ JH-12133 [DJ]	9 to 5 (same on both sides)	1980	3.75	7.50	15.00
—Prom only on blue vinyl					
❑ PB-12133	9 to 5/Sing for the Common Man	1980	—	2.00	4.00
❑ PB-12133 [PS]	9 to 5/Sing for the Common Man	1980	—	2.50	5.00
❑ PB-12200	But You Know I Love You/Poor Folks' Town	1981	—	2.00	4.00
❑ PB-12282	The House of the Rising Sun/Working Girl	1981	—	2.00	4.00
❑ GB-12316	9 to 5/Old Flames Can't Hold a Candle to You	1981	—	—	3.00
—Gold Standard Series					
❑ JK-13057 [DJ]	Single Women (same on both sides)	1982	3.00	6.00	12.00
—Promo only on red vinyl					
❑ PB-13057	Single Women/Barbara on Your Mind	1982	—	2.00	4.00
❑ PB-13234	Heartbreak Express/Act Like a Fool	1982	—	2.00	4.00
❑ PB-13260	I Will Always Love You/Do I Ever Cross Your Mind	1982	—	2.00	4.00
—A-side is the same song, but a different recording than that on APBO-0234					
❑ PB-13260 [PS]	I Will Always Love You/Do I Ever Cross Your Mind	1982	—	2.50	5.00
❑ JK-13361 [DJ]	Hard Candy Christmas (same on both sides)	1982	3.00	6.00	12.00
—Promo only on red vinyl					
❑ PB-13361	Hard Candy Christmas/Me and Little Andy	1982	—	2.00	4.00
❑ JK-13514 [DJ]	Potential New Boyfriend (Short) (same on both sides)	1983	3.00	6.00	12.00
—Promo only on yellow vinyl					
❑ JK-13514 [DJ]	Potential New Boyfriend (same on both sides)	1983	3.00	6.00	12.00
—Promo only on blue vinyl					
❑ PB-13514	Potential New Boyfriend/One of Those Days	1983	—	—	3.00
❑ PB-13619	Tennessee Homesick Blues/Butterflies	1984	—	—	3.00
❑ JK-13703 [DJ]	Save the Last Dance for Me (same on both sides)	1983	2.50	5.00	10.00
—Promo only on green vinyl					
❑ PB-13703	Save the Last Dance for Me/Elusive Butterfly	1983	—	—	3.00
❑ PB-13756	The Great Pretender/Downtown	1984	—	—	3.00
❑ PB-13756 [PS]	The Great Pretender/Downtown	1984	—	—	3.00
❑ PB-13856	Sweet Lovin' Friends/Too Much Water	1984	—	—	—
—Unreleased					
❑ PB-13883	Sweet Lovin' Friends/God Won't Get You	1984	—	—	3.00
—With Sylvester Stallone					
❑ JK-13944 [DJ]	Medley: Winter Wonderland/Sleigh Ride (same on both sides)	1984	—	2.00	4.00

A gifted singer and songwriter, Dolly Parton first began recording in the early 1960s and was still having hits into the 1990s. (Top left) Her first single, on the Goldband label, is very rare. Her second, on Mercury, is also a top country rarity. Look closely at "It's Sure Gonna Hurt," from 1962: Parton co-wrote the song. (Top right) After years in the business, Dolly finally had a chart-topping single in early 1971 with "Joshua." (Bottom left) By 1980, she was a full-fledged phenomenon, with both pop and country hits to her credit. She then appeared in the movie *9 to 5* and got good reviews for her acting. Her theme song from the movie made the top of both the pop and country charts. (Bottom right) The only song to top the country charts with two different versions by the same artist is "I Will Always Love You." Parton, who wrote the song, first took it to No. 1 in 1974. She then re-recorded it for the film version of *The Best Little Whorehouse in Texas,* and the new version also peaked at the top in 1982.

Number	Title (A Side/B Side)	Yr	VG	VG+	NM
❑ PB-13944	Medley: Winter Wonderland-Sleigh Ride/The Christmas Song	1984	—	—	3.00
—B-side by Kenny Rogers					
❑ PB-13987	Don't Call It Love/We Got Too Much	1985	—	—	3.00
❑ GB-14070	Tennessee Homesick Blues/Hard Candy Christmas	1985	—	—	3.00
—Gold Standard Series					
❑ PB-14218	Think About Love/Come Back to Me	1985	—	—	3.00
❑ PB-14297	Tie Our Love (In a Double Knot)/I Hope You're Never Happy	1986	—	—	3.00
❑ GB-14346	Don't Call It Love/Real Love	1986	—	—	3.00
—Gold Standard Series					

RCA VICTOR

Number	Title (A Side/B Side)	Yr	VG	VG+	NM
❑ APBO-0145	Jolene/Love, You're So Beautiful Tonight	1973	—	2.50	5.00
❑ APBO-0234	I Will Always Love You/Lonely Comin' Down	1974	—	2.50	5.00
❑ PB-10031	Love Is Like a Butterfly/Sacred Memories	1974	—	2.00	4.00
❑ PB-10164	The Bargain Store/I'll Never Forget	1975	—	2.00	4.00
❑ GB-10165	Jolene/My Tennessee Mountain Home	1975	—	—	3.00
—Gold Standard Series					
❑ PB-10310	The Seeker/Love with Feeling	1975	—	2.00	4.00
❑ PB-10396	We Used To/My Heart Started Breaking	1975	—	2.00	4.00
❑ GB-10504	Love Is Like a Butterfly/Sacred Memories	1975	—	—	3.00
—Gold Standard Series					
❑ GB-10505	I Will Always Love You/Lovely Comin' Down	1975	—	—	3.00
—Gold Standard Series					
❑ PB-10564	Hey, Lucky Lady/Most of All, Why	1976	—	2.00	4.00
❑ GB-10676	The Bargain Store/The Seeker	1976	—	—	3.00
—Gold Standard Series					
❑ PB-10730	All I Can Do/Falling Out of Love with Me	1976	—	2.00	4.00
❑ 47-9548	Just Because I'm a Woman/I Wish I Felt This Way at Home	1968	2.00	4.00	8.00
❑ 47-9657	In the Good Old Days (When Times Were Bad)/Try Being Lonely	1968	2.00	4.00	8.00
❑ 47-9784	Daddy Come and Get Me/Chas	1969	—	3.00	6.00
❑ 47-9863	Mule Skinner Blues/More Than Their Share	1970	—	3.00	6.00
❑ 47-9928	Joshua/I'm Doing This for Your Sake	1970	—	3.00	6.00
❑ 47-9971	Comin' For to Carry Me Home/Golden Streets of Glory	1971	—	3.00	6.00
❑ 47-9999	My Blue Tears/The Mystery of the Mystery	1971	—	3.00	6.00
❑ 74-0132	Daddy/He's a Go-Getter	1969	—	3.00	6.00
❑ 74-0192	In the Ghetto/Bridge	1969	—	3.00	6.00
❑ 74-0243	My Blue Ridge Mountain Boy/'Til Death Do Us Part	1969	—	3.00	6.00
❑ 74-0538	Coat of Many Colors/Here I Am	1971	—	3.00	6.00
❑ 74-0538 [PS]	Coat of Many Colors/Here I Am	1971	2.50	5.00	10.00
❑ 74-0662	Touch Your Woman/Mission Chapel Memories	1972	—	2.50	5.00
❑ 74-0757	Washday Blues/Just As Good As Gone	1972	—	2.50	5.00
❑ 74-0797	Lord, Hold My Hand/When I Sing for Him	1972	—	2.50	5.00
❑ 74-0868	My Tennessee Mountain Home/Better Part of Life	1973	—	2.50	5.00
❑ 74-0950	Traveling Man/I Remember	1973	—	2.50	5.00

RISING TIDE

Number	Title (A Side/B Side)	Yr	VG	VG+	NM
❑ 56041	Just When I Needed You Most/For the Good Times	1996	—	—	3.00

Albums

COLUMBIA

Number	Title (A Side/B Side)	Yr	VG	VG+	NM
❑ FC 40968	Rainbow	1987	2.50	5.00	10.00
❑ FC 44384	White Limozeen	1989	3.00	6.00	12.00
❑ C 46882	Eagle When She Flies	1991	5.00	10.00	20.00
—Available on vinyl only through Columbia House					

MONUMENT

Number	Title (A Side/B Side)	Yr	VG	VG+	NM
❑ 7623	In the Beginning	197?	3.00	6.00	12.00
❑ MLP-8085 [M]	Hello, I'm Dolly	1967	7.50	15.00	30.00
❑ SLP-18085 [S]	Hello, I'm Dolly	1967	10.00	20.00	40.00
❑ SLP-18136	As Long As I Love	1970	5.00	10.00	20.00
❑ KZG 31913 [(2)]	The World of Dolly	1972	5.00	10.00	20.00
❑ KZG 33876 [(2)]	Hello, I'm Dolly	1975	5.00	10.00	20.00

PAIR

Number	Title (A Side/B Side)	Yr	VG	VG+	NM
❑ PDL2-1009 [(2)]	Just the Way I Am	1986	3.00	6.00	12.00
❑ PDL2-1116 [(2)]	Portrait	1986	3.00	6.00	12.00

RCA

Number	Title (A Side/B Side)	Yr	VG	VG+	NM
❑ 5706-1-R	The Best of Dolly Parton, Vol. 3	1987	2.50	5.00	10.00
❑ 6497-1-R	The Best There Is	1987	2.50	5.00	10.00

RCA CAMDEN

Number	Title (A Side/B Side)	Yr	VG	VG+	NM
❑ ACL1-0307	Mine	1973	2.50	5.00	10.00
❑ CAS-2583	Just the Way I Am	1972	2.50	5.00	10.00

RCA VICTOR

Number	Title (A Side/B Side)	Yr	VG	VG+	NM
❑ APD1-0033 [Q]	My Tennessee Mountain Home	1973	5.00	10.00	20.00
❑ APL1-0033	My Tennessee Mountain Home	1973	3.00	6.00	12.00
❑ APL1-0286	Bubbling Over	1973	3.00	6.00	12.00
❑ APL1-0473	Jolene	1974	3.00	6.00	12.00
❑ APL1-0712	Love Is Like a Butterfly	1974	3.00	6.00	12.00
❑ APL1-0950	The Bargain Store	1975	3.00	6.00	12.00
❑ APL1-1117	The Best of Dolly Parton	1975	3.00	6.00	12.00
❑ APL1-1221	Dolly	1975	3.00	6.00	12.00
❑ APL1-1665	All I Can Do	1976	3.00	6.00	12.00
❑ APL1-2188	New Harvest...First Gathering	1977	3.00	6.00	12.00
❑ DJL1-2314 [DJ]	Personal Music Dialogue with Dolly Parton	1976	6.25	12.50	25.00
❑ AFL1-2544	Here You Come Again	1977	3.00	6.00	12.00
❑ AFL1-2797	Heartbreaker	1978	3.00	6.00	12.00
❑ AHL1-3361	Great Balls of Fire	1979	3.00	6.00	12.00
❑ AHL1-3546	Dolly Dolly Dolly	1980	3.00	6.00	12.00
❑ AYL1-3665	Heartbreaker	1980	2.00	4.00	8.00
—"Best Buy Series" reissue					
❑ AYL1-3764	My Tennessee Mountain Home	1980	2.00	4.00	8.00
—"Best Buy Series" reissue					
❑ AHL1-3852	9 to 5 and Odd Jobs	1980	3.00	6.00	12.00
❑ AYL1-3898	Jolene	1981	2.00	4.00	8.00
—"Best Buy Series" reissue					
❑ LPM-3949 [M]	Just Because I'm a Woman	1968	25.00	50.00	100.00
❑ LSP-3949 [S]	Just Because I'm a Woman	1968	7.50	15.00	30.00
—"Stereo" on black label					
❑ LSP-3949 [S]	Just Because I'm a Woman	1968	5.00	10.00	20.00
—Orange label					
❑ AYL1-3980	New Harvest	1981	2.00	4.00	8.00
—"Best Buy Series" reissue					
❑ LSP-4099	In the Good Old Days	1969	5.00	10.00	20.00
❑ LSP-4188	My Blue Ridge Mountain Boy	1969	5.00	10.00	20.00
❑ LSP-4288	The Fairest of Them All	1970	5.00	10.00	20.00
❑ AHL1-4289	Heartbreak Express	1982	3.00	6.00	12.00
❑ LSP-4387	A Real Live Dolly	1970	6.25	12.50	25.00
—Four songs feature Porter Wagoner					
❑ LSP-4398	Golden Streets of Glory	1971	5.00	10.00	20.00
❑ AHL1-4422	Greatest Hits	1982	2.50	5.00	10.00
—Contains one Christmas song:					
❑ AHL1-4422	Greatest Hits	1982	3.00	6.00	12.00
❑ LSP-4449	The Best of Dolly Parton	1970	5.00	10.00	20.00
❑ LSP-4507	Joshua	1971	5.00	10.00	20.00
❑ LSP-4603	Coat of Many Colors	1971	5.00	10.00	20.00
❑ LSP-4686	Touch Your Woman	1972	5.00	10.00	20.00
❑ AHL1-4691	Burlap & Satin	1983	2.50	5.00	10.00
❑ LSP-4752	My Favorite Song Writer: Porter Wagoner	1972	5.00	10.00	20.00
❑ LSP-4762	Dolly Parton Sings	1972	3.75	7.50	15.00
❑ AYL1-4829	Here You Come Again	1984	2.00	4.00	8.00
—"Best Buy Series" reissue					
❑ AYL1-4830	9 to 5 and Odd Jobs	1984	2.00	4.00	8.00
—"Best Buy Series" reissue					
❑ AHL1-4940	The Great Pretender	1984	2.50	5.00	10.00
❑ AYL1-5146	The Best of Dolly Parton	1984	2.00	4.00	8.00
—"Best Buy Series" reissue					
❑ AHL1-5414	Real Love	1985	2.50	5.00	10.00
❑ AYL1-5437	Burlap & Satin	1985	2.00	4.00	8.00
—"Best Buy Series" reissue					
❑ AHL1-5471	Collector's Series	1985	2.50	5.00	10.00
❑ AHL1-9508	Think About Love	1986	2.50	5.00	10.00

PARTON, DOLLY/GEORGE JONES

Albums

STARDAY

Number	Title (A Side/B Side)	Yr	VG	VG+	NM
❑ LP 429 [P]	Dolly Parton and George Jones	1968	10.00	20.00	40.00
—One side of Dolly in stereo, one side of "Possum" in rechanneled stereo					

PARTON, DOLLY/LINDA RONSTADT/EMMYLOU HARRIS

Also see each artist's individual listings.

45s

WARNER BROS.

Number	Title (A Side/B Side)	Yr	VG	VG+	NM
❑ 27970	Wildflowers/Hobo's Meditation	1988	—	—	3.00
❑ 28248	Those Memories of You/My Dear Companion	1987	—	—	3.00
❑ 28248 [PS]	Those Memories of You/My Dear Companion	1987	—	2.00	4.00
❑ 28371	Telling Me Lies/Rosewood Casket	1987	—	—	3.00
❑ 28492	To Know Him Is to Love Him/Farther Along	1987	—	—	3.00
❑ 28492 [PS]	To Know Him Is to Love Him/Farther Along	1987	—	2.00	4.00

Albums

WARNER BROS.

Number	Title (A Side/B Side)	Yr	VG	VG+	NM
❑ 25491	Trio	1987	2.50	5.00	10.00

PARTON, DOLLY/FAYE TUCKER

Albums

SOMERSET

Number	Title (A Side/B Side)	Yr	VG	VG+	NM
❑ S-9700 [M]	Hits Made Famous by Country Queens	1963	6.25	12.50	25.00
❑ SF-19700 [S]	Hits Made Famous by Country Queens	1963	7.50	15.00	30.00
—Dolly Parton sings songs made famous by Kitty Wells					
❑ SF-29400	Dolly Parton Sings Country Oldies	1968	3.75	7.50	15.00

TIME

Number	Title (A Side/B Side)	Yr	VG	VG+	NM
❑ 2108	Country & Western Soul	1963	10.00	20.00	40.00

PARTON, RANDY

45s

RCA

Number	Title (A Side/B Side)	Yr	VG	VG+	NM
❑ PB-10877	Down/Just As Good As Gone	1977	—	2.50	5.00
❑ PB-12137	Hold Me Like You Never Had Me/My Blue Tears	1981	—	2.00	4.00
❑ JK-12271 [DJ]	Shot Full of Love (same on both sides)	1981	2.50	5.00	10.00
—Promo only on red vinyl					
❑ PB-12271	Shot Full of Love/Please Don't Lie	1981	—	2.00	4.00
❑ PB-12351	Don't Cry Baby/Again and Again	1981	—	2.00	4.00
❑ JK-13087 [DJ]	Oh, No (same on both sides)	1982	2.50	5.00	10.00
—Promo only on yellow vinyl					
❑ JK-13087 [PS]	Oh, No	1982	2.50	5.00	10.00
—Sleeve is promo only					
❑ PB-13087	Oh, No/Hold Me Like You Never Had Me	1982	—	2.00	4.00
❑ JK-13309 [DJ]	Roll On Eighteen Wheeler (same on both sides)	1982	3.00	6.00	12.00
—Promo only on yellow vinyl					
❑ PB-13309	Roll On Eighteen Wheeler/You'll Always Get Your Way	1982	—	2.50	5.00
❑ PB-13608	A Stranger in Her Bed/Waltz Across Texas	1983	—	2.00	4.00

RCA VICTOR

Number	Title (A Side/B Side)	Yr	VG	VG+	NM
❑ PB-10261	If You Were Mine/Tennessee Born	1975	—	2.50	5.00
❑ PB-10432	In Love/Losing Everything	1975	—	2.50	5.00

PARTON, STELLA
Also see CARMOL TAYLOR.

45s

AIRBORNE

Number	Title (A Side/B Side)	Yr	VG	VG+	NM
❑ 10015	I Don't Miss You Like I Used To/(B-side unknown)	1989	—	2.50	5.00

COUNTRY SOUL

Number	Title (A Side/B Side)	Yr	VG	VG+	NM
❑ 039	I Want to Hold You in My Dreams Tonight/Ode to Olivia	1975	—	3.00	6.00

ELEKTRA

Number	Title (A Side/B Side)	Yr	VG	VG+	NM
❑ 45383	I'm Not That Good at Goodbye/Love Me to Sleep	1977	—	2.50	5.00
❑ 45410	The Danger of a Stranger/The More the Change	1977	—	2.50	5.00
❑ 45437	Standard Lie Number One/The More the Change	1977	—	2.50	5.00
❑ 45468	Four Little Letters/Fade My Blues Away	1978	—	2.50	5.00
❑ 45490	Undercover Lovers/There's a Rumor Going 'Round	1978	—	2.50	5.00
❑ 45533	Stormy Weather/Lie to Linda	1978	—	2.50	5.00
❑ 46029	Steady as the Rain/A Little Inconvenient	1979	—	2.50	5.00
❑ 46068	The Room at the Top of the Stairs (no B-side)	1979	2.50	5.00	10.00
—May never have advanced beyond the test-pressing stage; certainly no stock copies were issued; its actual release was on 46502					
❑ 46502	The Room at the Top of the Stairs/Honey Come Home	1979	—	2.50	5.00

LUV

Number	Title (A Side/B Side)	Yr	VG	VG+	NM
❑ 132	Cross My Heart/Heart Don't Fail Me Now	1987	—	2.50	5.00
❑ 132 [PS]	Cross My Heart/Heart Don't Fail Me Now	1987	2.00	4.00	8.00

RCA

Number	Title (A Side/B Side)	Yr	VG	VG+	NM
❑ PB-13924	Goin' Back to Heaven/(B-side unassigned?)	1984	—	—	—
—Canceled					

SOUL, COUNTRY & BLUES

Number	Title (A Side/B Side)	Yr	VG	VG+	NM
❑ 088	It's Not Funny Anymore/(I've Got to Get Back on) The Right Side of God	1975	—	3.00	6.00

TOWN HOUSE

Number	Title (A Side/B Side)	Yr	VG	VG+	NM
❑ 1056	I'll Miss You/I Hate the Night	1982	—	2.50	5.00
❑ 1056 [PS]	I'll Miss You/I Hate the Night	1982	2.00	4.00	8.00
❑ 1058	Young Love/Something to Go By	1982	—	2.50	5.00
❑ 1058 [PS]	Young Love/Something to Go By	1982	2.00	4.00	8.00

Albums

ELEKTRA

Number	Title (A Side/B Side)	Yr	VG	VG+	NM
❑ 6E-126	Stella Parton	1978	3.00	6.00	12.00
❑ 6E-191	Love Ya	1979	3.00	6.00	12.00
❑ 6E-229	The Best of Stella Parton	1979	3.00	6.00	12.00
❑ 7E-1111	Country Sweet	1977	3.00	6.00	12.00

SOUL, COUNTRY & BLUES

Number	Title (A Side/B Side)	Yr	VG	VG+	NM
❑ 6006	I Want to Hold You in My Dreams Tonight	1975	5.00	10.00	20.00

TOWN HOUSE

Number	Title (A Side/B Side)	Yr	VG	VG+	NM
❑ ST-7005	So Far So Good	1982	3.00	6.00	12.00

PASTELL, JAMES

45s

PAULA

Number	Title (A Side/B Side)	Yr	VG	VG+	NM
❑ 425	Hell Yes I Cheated/Woman of the World	1977	—	2.50	5.00
❑ 427	Don't Let the Stars Get in Your Eyes/Warm, Warm Woman	1977	—	2.50	5.00
❑ 433	You Know Me So Much Better (Than I Do)/Robin Hood	1978	—	2.50	5.00
❑ 434	Disco Pistol/I Can Heal	1979	—	2.50	5.00
❑ 438	Going to Gilley's/Shining Star	1982	—	2.50	5.00

PAUL, BUDDY

45s

MURCO

Number	Title (A Side/B Side)	Yr	VG	VG+	NM
❑ 1018	This Old Town/Foolish Me	1960	6.25	12.50	25.00
❑ 1022	They Stuck to Their Guns/Trust Me	1960	6.25	12.50	25.00

PAUL, JOYCE

45s

CHANCELLOR

Number	Title (A Side/B Side)	Yr	VG	VG+	NM
❑ 105	Big Girls Don't Cry/The One Who Carries the Torch	1962	3.75	7.50	15.00

DOT

Number	Title (A Side/B Side)	Yr	VG	VG+	NM
❑ 15703	Baby, You've Had It/Bad News	1958	10.00	20.00	40.00
❑ 16246	Cold, Cold Heart/Captured	1961	3.00	6.00	12.00

IMPERIAL

Number	Title (A Side/B Side)	Yr	VG	VG+	NM
❑ 66008	I'll Give You Me (If You'll Give Me You)/Don't Send Flowers	1964	2.50	5.00	10.00
❑ 66024	Lasting Love/Painted Smile	1964	2.50	5.00	10.00

REPUBLIC

Number	Title (A Side/B Side)	Yr	VG	VG+	NM
❑ 7053	I've Forgotten More Than You'll Ever Know/Caribbean	1953	6.25	12.50	25.00

UNITED ARTISTS

Number	Title (A Side/B Side)	Yr	VG	VG+	NM
❑ 902	I'm the Girl on the Billboard/Changing World	1965	2.50	5.00	10.00
❑ 50003	Just to Hurt Me/Kiss Away My Yesterday	1966	2.50	5.00	10.00
❑ 50149	Calico Doll/Been Rained On	1967	2.50	5.00	10.00
❑ 50226	I Loved Him Much Longer Than You/Mama's Gonna Fix the Baby's Wagon	1967	2.50	5.00	10.00
❑ 50315	Phone Call to Mama/Don't Keep Me Hanging On	1968	2.00	4.00	8.00
❑ 50454	Do Right Woman, Do Right Man/You Didn't Come Home Last Night	1968	2.00	4.00	8.00

Albums

UNITED ARTISTS

Number	Title (A Side/B Side)	Yr	VG	VG+	NM
❑ UAS-6684	Heartaches, Laughter and Tears	1968	3.75	7.50	15.00

PAUL, LES, AND MARY FORD
The well-known pop duo had one of their hits make the country charts. Also see CHET ATKINS AND LES PAUL.

45s

CAPITOL

Number	Title (A Side/B Side)	Yr	VG	VG+	NM
❑ F1373	Mockin' Bird Hill/Chicken Reel	1951	5.00	10.00	20.00

PAXTON, GARY
The pop-rock performer (under such names as Skip & Flip and Gary & Clyde) and producer ("Monster Mash" by Bobby "Boris" Pickett) had one country hit song.

45s

RCA VICTOR

Number	Title (A Side/B Side)	Yr	VG	VG+	NM
❑ PB-10449	Too Far Gone (To Care What You Do to Me)/Freedom Lives in a Country Song	1975	—	2.50	5.00

PAYCHECK, JOHNNY
Also includes records made under his original alter ego, "Donny Young." Also see GEORGE JONES; JODY MILLER.

45s

AMI

Number	Title (A Side/B Side)	Yr	VG	VG+	NM
❑ 1322	I Never Got Over You/Ole Pay Ain't Checked Out Yet	1984	—	2.50	5.00
❑ 1323	You're Every Step I Take/I Can't Stop Drinking	1985	—	2.50	5.00
❑ 1327	Everything Is Changing/Palimony	1985	—	2.50	5.00

CERTRON

Number	Title (A Side/B Side)	Yr	VG	VG+	NM
❑ 10003	Forever Ended Yesterday/It's For Sure I Can't Go On	1970	2.00	4.00	8.00

DAMASCUS

Number	Title (A Side/B Side)	Yr	VG	VG+	NM
❑ 2001	Scars/(B-side unknown)	1989	—	3.00	6.00

DECCA

Number	Title (A Side/B Side)	Yr	VG	VG+	NM
❑ 9-30763	On This Mountaintop/It's Been a Long, Long Time for Me	1958	7.50	15.00	30.00
—A-side as "Donny Young and Roger Miller"; B-side as "Donny Young"					
❑ 9-30881	The Old Man and the River/Pictures Can't Talk Back	1959	6.25	12.50	25.00
—As "Donny Young"					
❑ 31077	Shakin' the Blues/Miracle of Love	1960	10.00	20.00	40.00
—As "Donny Young"					
❑ 31283	Go Ring the Bells/I Guess I Had It Coming	1961	6.25	12.50	25.00
—As "Donny Young"					

DESPERADO

Number	Title (A Side/B Side)	Yr	VG	VG+	NM
❑ 1001	Out of Beer/Oklahoma Lady	1988	—	3.00	6.00

EPIC

Number	Title (A Side/B Side)	Yr	VG	VG+	NM
❑ 19-02144	Yesterday's News (Just Hit Home Today)/Someone Told My Story	1981	—	2.00	4.00
❑ 14-02684	The Highlight of '81/Sharon Rae	1982	—	2.00	4.00
❑ 14-02817	No Way Out/We've All Gone Crazy	1982	—	2.00	4.00
❑ 14-03052	D.O.A. (Drunk On Arrival)/Gonna Get Right (And Do Something Wrong)	1982	—	2.00	4.00
❑ 5-10783	She's All I Got/You Touched	1971	—	3.50	7.00
❑ 5-10836	Someone to Give My Love To/Love Sure Is Beautiful	1972	—	3.50	7.00
❑ 5-10876	Love Is a Good Thing/High on the Thought of You	1972	—	3.50	7.00
❑ 5-10912	Somebody Loves Me/Without You	1972	—	3.50	7.00
❑ 5-10947	Something About You I Love/Your Love Is the Key to It All	1973	—	3.00	6.00
❑ 5-10999	Mr. Lovemaker/Once You've Had the Best	1973	—	3.00	6.00
❑ 5-11046	Song and Dance Man/Love Is a Strange and Wonderful Thing	1973	—	3.00	6.00
❑ 5-11090	My Part of Forever/If Love Gets Any Better	1974	—	3.00	6.00
❑ 5-11142	Keep On Lovin' Me/The Ballad of Thunder Road	1974	—	3.00	6.00
❑ 8-50040	For a Minute There/She's All I Live For	1974	—	3.00	6.00
❑ 8-50073	Loving You Beats All I've Ever Seen/Touch of the Master's Hand	1975	—	3.00	6.00
❑ 8-50111	I Didn't Love Her Anymore/Loving Her Is All I Thought It Would Be	1975	—	3.00	6.00
❑ 8-50146	All-American Man/The Fool Strikes Again	1975	—	3.00	6.00
❑ 8-50193	The Feminine Touch/Rhythm Guitar	1976	—	3.00	6.00
❑ 8-50215	Gone at Last/Live with Me	1976	—	3.00	6.00
❑ 8-50249	11 Months and 29 Days/Live with Me (Till I Can Learn to Live Again)	1976	—	3.00	6.00
❑ 8-50291	I Can See Me Lovin' You Again/I Sleep with Her Memory Every Night	1976	—	3.00	6.00
❑ 8-50334	Slide Off of Your Satin Sheets/That's What the Outlaws in Texas Want to Hear	1977	—	3.00	6.00
❑ 8-50391	I'm the Only Hell (Mama Ever Raised)/She's Still Lookin' Good	1977	—	3.00	6.00
❑ 8-50469	Take This Job and Shove It/Colorado Kool-Aid	1977	2.00	4.00	8.00
❑ 8-50539	Georgia in a Jug/Me and the I.R.S.	1978	—	3.00	6.00
❑ 8-50621	Friend, Lover, Wife/Leave It to Me	1978	—	3.00	6.00
❑ 8-50655	The Outlaw's Prayer/Armed and Crazy	1979	—	3.00	6.00
❑ 9-50777	(Stay Away From) The Cocaine Train/Billy Bardo	1979	—	2.50	5.00
❑ 9-50818	Drinkin' and Drivin'/Just Makin' Love Don't Make It Love	1979	—	2.50	5.00
❑ 9-50863	Fifteen Beers/Who Was That Man Who Beat Me So	1980	—	2.50	5.00
❑ 9-50923	In Memory of a Memory/New York Town	1980	—	2.50	5.00

HILLTOP

Number	Title (A Side/B Side)	Yr	VG	VG+	NM
❑ 3002	Don't Start Countin' on Me/I'd Rather Be Your Fool	1964	5.00	10.00	20.00
❑ 3006	For Those Who Think Young/The Girl They Talk About	1965	3.75	7.50	15.00
❑ 3007	A-11/Where (In the World)	1965	3.75	7.50	15.00
❑ 3009	Heartbreak Tennessee/Help Me Hank, I'm Fallin'	1966	3.75	7.50	15.00
❑ 3015	I'm Barely Hangin' On to Me/The Real Mr. Heartache	1966	3.75	7.50	15.00

Number	Title (A Side/B Side)	Yr	VG	VG+	NM
LITTLE DARLIN'					
❑ 008	The Lovin' Machine/Pride Covered Ears	1966	2.50	5.00	10.00
❑ 0011	The Ballad of the Green Berets/A Dying Hero	1966	2.50	5.00	10.00
❑ 0014	Right Back Where We Parted/The Way Things Were Going	1966	2.50	5.00	10.00
—With Micki Evans					
❑ 0016	Motel Time Again/If You Should Come Back Today	1966	2.50	5.00	10.00
❑ 0020	Jukebox Charlie/Something in Your World	1967	2.50	5.00	10.00
❑ 0032	The Cave/Then Love Dies	1967	2.50	5.00	10.00
❑ 0035	Don't Monkey with Another Monkey's Monkey/You'll Recover in Time	1967	2.50	5.00	10.00
❑ 0042	(It Won't Be Long) And I'll Be Hating You/Fools Hall of Fame	1968	2.50	5.00	10.00
❑ 0043	The Old Year Is Gone/According to the Bible	1968	2.50	5.00	10.00
❑ 0046	My Heart Keeps Running to You/Yesterday, Today and Tomorrow	1968	2.50	5.00	10.00
❑ 0052	If I'm Gonna Sink/The Loser	1968	2.50	5.00	10.00
❑ 0055	Jingle Bells/The Old Year Is Gone	1968	2.50	5.00	10.00
❑ 0057	My World of Memories/(B-side unknown)	1969	2.50	5.00	10.00
❑ 0060	Wherever You Are/I Can't Promise You Won't Get Lonely	1969	2.50	5.00	10.00
❑ 0072	Wildfire/Basin Street Mama	1969	2.50	5.00	10.00
❑ 7804	It Won't Be Long/If I'm Gonna Sink (Might As Well Go to the Bottom)	1978	—	3.00	6.00
❑ 7808	Down on the Corner at a Bar Named Kelly's/Something He'll Have to Learn	1978	—	3.00	6.00
❑ 7810	I'll Place My Order Early/The Old Year Is Gone	1978	—	3.00	6.00
❑ 7918	California Dreams/The Loser	1979	—	3.00	6.00
❑ 7923	Gentle on My Mind/Everything You Touch Turns to Hurt	1979	—	3.00	6.00
MERCURY					
❑ 71900	On Second Thought/One Day a Week	1962	5.00	10.00	20.00
—As "Donny Young"					
❑ 71981	Not Much I Don't/I'd Come Back to Me	1962	5.00	10.00	20.00
—As "Donny Young"					
❑ 884720-7	Old Violin/Comin' Home to Baby	1986	—	2.00	4.00
❑ 888088-7	Don't Bury Me 'Til I'm Ready/Ex-Wives and Lovers	1986	—	2.00	4.00
❑ 888341-7	Come to Me/Ragtime Redneck	1987	—	2.00	4.00
❑ 888651-7	I Grow Old Too Fast (And Smart Too Slow)/Caught Between a Rock and a Soft Place	1987	—	2.00	4.00
❑ 888925-7	Modern Times/She Don't Love Me All the Time	1987	—	2.00	4.00
TODD					
❑ 1098	Don't You Get Lonesome Without Me/I'm Glad to Have Her Back Again	1964	5.00	10.00	20.00
—As "Donny Young"					
Albums					
ACCORD					
❑ SN-7173	Extra Special	1981	2.50	5.00	10.00
ALLEGIANCE					
❑ AV-435	I Don't Need to Know That Right Now	198?	2.00	4.00	8.00
CERTRON					
❑ 7002	Johnny Paycheck Again	1970	3.75	7.50	15.00
EPIC					
❑ E 31141	She's All I Got	1971	3.00	6.00	12.00
❑ KE 31449	Someone to Give My Love To	1972	3.00	6.00	12.00
❑ KE 31702	Somebody Loves Me	1972	3.00	6.00	12.00
❑ KE 32387	Something About You I Love	1973	3.00	6.00	12.00
❑ KE 32570	Song and Dance Man	1973	3.00	6.00	12.00
❑ KE 33091	Greatest Hits	1974	2.50	5.00	10.00
❑ PE 33091	Greatest Hits	198?	2.00	4.00	8.00
—Budget-line reissue					
❑ KE 33354	Loving You	1975	2.50	5.00	10.00
❑ KE 33943	11 Months and 29 Days	1975	2.50	5.00	10.00
❑ PE 34693	Slide Off of Your Satin Sheets	1976	2.50	5.00	10.00
❑ KE 35045	Take This Job and Shove It	1977	2.50	5.00	10.00
❑ PE 35045	Take This Job and Shove It	198?	2.00	4.00	8.00
—Budget-line reissue					
❑ KE 35444	Armed and Crazy	1978	2.50	5.00	10.00
❑ KE 35623	Greatest Hits, Volume 2	1978	2.50	5.00	10.00
❑ PE 35623	Greatest Hits, Volume 2	198?	2.00	4.00	8.00
—Budget-line reissue					
❑ JE 36200	Everybody's Got a Family — Meet Mine	1979	2.50	5.00	10.00
❑ JE 36496	New York Town	1980	2.50	5.00	10.00
❑ FE 36761	Mr. Hag Told My Story	1981	2.50	5.00	10.00
❑ PE 36761	Mr. Hag Told My Story	1981	2.00	4.00	8.00
—Budget-line reissue					
❑ FE 37345	Encore	1981	2.50	5.00	10.00
❑ PE 37345	Encore	198?	2.00	4.00	8.00
—Budget-line reissue					
❑ FE 37933	Lovers and Losers	1982	2.50	5.00	10.00
❑ FE 38322	Johnny Paycheck's Biggest Hits	1983	2.50	5.00	10.00
❑ PE 39943	John Austin Paycheck	1984	2.00	4.00	8.00
INTERMEDIA					
❑ QS-5018	Back On the Job	198?	2.00	4.00	8.00
LITTLE DARLIN'					
❑ LD-4001 [M]	Johnny Paycheck at Carnegie Hall	1966	5.00	10.00	20.00
❑ LD-4003 [M]	The Lovin' Machine	1966	5.00	10.00	20.00
❑ LD-4004 [M]	Gospeltime in My Fashion	1967	5.00	10.00	20.00
❑ LD-4006 [M]	Johnny Paycheck Sings Jukebox Charlie	1967	6.25	12.50	25.00
❑ SLD-8001 [S]	Johnny Paycheck at Carnegie Hall	1966	6.25	12.50	25.00
❑ SLD-8003 [S]	The Lovin' Machine	1966	6.25	12.50	25.00
❑ SLD-8004 [S]	Gospeltime in My Fashion	1967	6.25	12.50	25.00
❑ SLD-8006 [S]	Johnny Paycheck Sings Jukebox Charlie	1967	6.25	12.50	25.00

Number	Title (A Side/B Side)	Yr	VG	VG+	NM
❑ SLD-8010	Country Soul	1968	6.25	12.50	25.00
❑ SLD-8012	Johnny Paycheck's Greatest Hits	1968	6.25	12.50	25.00
❑ SLD-8023	Wherever You Are	1969	6.25	12.50	25.00
MERCURY					
❑ 830404-1	Modern Times	1987	2.50	5.00	10.00
POWER PAK					
❑ PO-284	Johnny Paycheck At His Best	197?	2.00	4.00	8.00

PAYCHECK, JOHNNY, AND MERLE HAGGARD

Also see each artist's individual listings.

Number	Title (A Side/B Side)	Yr	VG	VG+	NM
45s					
EPIC					
❑ 19-51012	I Can't Hold Myself in Line/Carolyn	1981	—	2.00	4.00

PAYNE, DENNIS

Number	Title (A Side/B Side)	Yr	VG	VG+	NM
45s					
CAPITOL					
❑ 4083	Come On Home Girl/Do You Believe in Me	1975	—	3.00	6.00
❑ 4196	Love Me Like You've Never Done Before/Remembering You	1975	—	3.00	6.00
NASHVILLE WEST					
❑ 7202	I'll Live for Today/Guitar Picker's Blues	1972	—	3.00	6.00
❑ 7304	Sing a Song/Three Faces of Eve	1973	—	3.00	6.00
❑ 7306	Blueberry Hill/For All These Things	1973	—	3.00	6.00
❑ 7407	The Last Thing on My Mind/Conscience of You	1974	—	3.00	6.00
TRUE					
❑ 87	I Know All About Her/Lovin' You Mo	1987	—	2.50	5.00
❑ 88	I Can't Hang On Anymore/(B-side unknown)	1988	—	2.50	5.00
❑ 90	California Sunny Beach/(B-side unknown)	1988	—	2.50	5.00
❑ 93	That's Why You Haven't Seen Me/Crazy Woman	1988	—	2.50	5.00

PAYNE, ERNIE

Number	Title (A Side/B Side)	Yr	VG	VG+	NM
45s					
MC					
❑ 5009	Neon Riders and Sawdust Gliders/The Very Last Love Letter	1978	—	2.50	5.00
MELODYLAND					
❑ 6026	Take Me (The Way That I Am)/Talk to Jeanette	1975	—	2.50	5.00

PAYNE, JIMMY

Number	Title (A Side/B Side)	Yr	VG	VG+	NM
45s					
CINNAMON					
❑ 772	Ramblin' Man/One Man's Woman at a Time	1973	—	3.00	6.00
❑ 780	If It Pleases You/You and Me and Love on the Open Road	1974	—	3.00	6.00
❑ 796	Sweet Fantasy/(B-side unknown)	1974	—	3.00	6.00
EPIC					
❑ 5-10027	My Most Requested Song/What Does It Take	1966	2.00	4.00	8.00
❑ 5-10173	Woman, Woman/Money Cannot Make the Man	1967	2.00	4.00	8.00
❑ 5-10222	What Does It Take (To Keep a Woman Like You Satisfied)/Woman, Woman	1967	2.00	4.00	8.00
❑ 5-10261	He Will Break Your Heart/Where Has All the Love Gone	1967	2.00	4.00	8.00
❑ 5-10301	Baby Don't Cry/Boston	1968	2.00	4.00	8.00
❑ 5-10444	L.A. Angels/A Rose Is a Rose	1969	—	3.50	7.00
❑ 5-10518	Tonight's the Night Miss Sally Testifies/Where Has All the Love Gone	1969	—	3.50	7.00
❑ 5-10588	Tallahassee/The Worst That Love Can Give	1970	—	3.50	7.00
❑ 5-10620	Give Love a Place to Begin/Cheatum	1970	—	3.50	7.00
KIK					
❑ 907	Turnin' My Love On/She's Free But She's Not Easy	1981	—	3.00	6.00
VEE JAY					
❑ 517	Why Can't We Love Each Other/Sweet Little Pretty Girl	1963	3.75	7.50	15.00
Albums					
EPIC					
❑ BN 26372	Woman, Woman! What Does It Take?	1968	5.00	10.00	20.00

PAYNE, JODY

Number	Title (A Side/B Side)	Yr	VG	VG+	NM
45s					
KARI					
❑ 117	There's a Crazy Man/(B-side unknown)	1981	—	2.00	4.00

PAYNE, LEON

Number	Title (A Side/B Side)	Yr	VG	VG+	NM
45s					
CAPITOL					
❑ F920	I'm a Lone Wolf/I Just Said Goodnight to My Dreams	1950	7.50	15.00	30.00
❑ F1093	I Couldn't Do a Thing Without You/You Still Got a Place	1950	7.50	15.00	30.00
❑ F1164	Did I Forget to Call/I Miss That Girl	1950	7.50	15.00	30.00
❑ F1321	Because You Love Me/My Daddy	1950	7.50	15.00	30.00
❑ F1338	The Great American Eagle/Fatal Letter	1950	7.50	15.00	30.00
❑ F1405	I Don't Know Why/If I Could Live My Life Over	1951	6.25	12.50	25.00
❑ F1463	Empty Dreams/Farewell Waltz	1951	6.25	12.50	25.00
❑ F1580	A Million Years Ago/Lonely and Blue Over Someone	1951	6.25	12.50	25.00
❑ F1782	It's Many a Mile Back Home/Teach Me to Forget	1951	6.25	12.50	25.00
❑ F1872	Gentle Hands/He Is the Light of the World	1951	6.25	12.50	25.00
❑ F1910	I Want You to Love Me/How Can I Help It	1951	6.25	12.50	25.00
❑ F2055	Polk Salad Green/Weeping Willow	1952	6.25	12.50	25.00
❑ F2155	Jesus Paid the Price/Golden Harvest	1952	6.25	12.50	25.00
❑ F2295	Mailman/Lying to My Heart	1952	6.25	12.50	25.00

Number	Title (A Side/B Side)	Yr	VG	VG+	NM
❑ F2454	I Need Your Love/Wouldn't It Be Wonderful	1953	6.25	12.50	25.00
❑ F2561	Sister Sue Polka/If I Took the Time	1953	6.25	12.50	25.00
❑ F40270	I Hate to Leave You/Find Them, Fool Them, and Leave Them	1950	7.50	15.00	30.00
D					
❑ 1108	Brothers of a Bottle/Mitzie McGraw	1960	3.75	7.50	15.00
❑ 1138	There's No Justice/With Half a Heart	1960	3.75	7.50	15.00
❑ 1150	Things/Blue Side of Lonesome	1960	3.75	7.50	15.00
DECCA					
❑ 9-28851	Don't Be Afraid/Pedro the Hot Tamale Man	1953	6.25	12.50	25.00
❑ 9-29046	A Face in the Crowd/You Haven't Got a Heart	1954	6.25	12.50	25.00
❑ 9-29333	A Lifetime to Regret/The Moon, Your God and You	1954	6.25	12.50	25.00
MERCURY					
❑ 71063	Lumberjack/A Million to One	1957	5.00	10.00	20.00
STARDAY					
❑ 208	We're on the Main Line/I Die 10,000 Times a Day	1955	5.00	10.00	20.00
❑ 215	Christmas Everyday/Christmas Love Song	1955	5.00	10.00	20.00
❑ 220	Doorstep to Heaven/You Are the One	1956	5.00	10.00	20.00
❑ 232	Two by Four/You Can't Lean on Me	1956	5.00	10.00	20.00
❑ 250	All the Time/One More Chance	1956	5.00	10.00	20.00
❑ 267	Sweet Sweet Love/A Prisoner's Diary	1956	5.00	10.00	20.00
❑ 620	Joe Lopez/You Stood Me Up This Morning	1963	3.00	6.00	12.00
❑ 637	Close to You/The Log Train	1963	3.00	6.00	12.00
❑ 666	September Memory/Six Foot Six	1964	3.00	6.00	12.00
TNT					
❑ 168	My Ship of Dreams/I'll Still Be Around	1959	5.00	10.00	20.00
❑ 192	We'll Break the Tie/The Walls Are Closing	196?	3.75	7.50	15.00
Selected 78s					
BLUEBIRD					
❑ B-8735	Ten Thousand Tomorrows/Down Where the Violets Grow	1941	6.25	12.50	25.00
❑ B-8788	When the Sun Sets on the Sierra/'Neath an Indian Summer Moon	1941	6.25	12.50	25.00
❑ B-8837	Let It End This Way/'Neath the Old Pine Tree	1941	6.25	12.50	25.00
BULLET					
❑ 647	Empty Arms/Lipstick Trail	194?	5.00	10.00	20.00
❑ 649	Don't Try It/Listening to Regret	194?	5.00	10.00	20.00
❑ 670	Baby Boy/Lost Highway	194?	5.00	10.00	20.00
❑ 671	What's the Need/Rollin' Stone	194?	5.00	10.00	20.00
❑ 672	I Found Someone New/They'll Never Take Her Love	194?	5.00	10.00	20.00
❑ 679	Cheaters Never Win/I'll Stick by You	194?	5.00	10.00	20.00
CAPITOL					
❑ 40238	I Love You Because/A Link in the Chain of Broken Hearts	1949	3.75	7.50	15.00

—A 45 rpm single with this number ought to exist, as this record was on the charts well into the spring of 1950. But we haven't confirmed the 45's existence.

Number	Title (A Side/B Side)	Yr	VG	VG+	NM
Albums					
STARDAY					
❑ SLP-231 [M]	Leon Payne: A Living Legend of Country Music	1963	20.00	40.00	80.00
❑ SLP-236 [M]	Americana	1963	12.50	25.00	50.00

PEARCE, KEVIN

Number	Title (A Side/B Side)	Yr	VG	VG+	NM
45s					
EVERGREEN					
❑ 1057	The Bigger the Love/(B-side unknown)	1987	—	2.50	5.00
❑ 1067	Love Ain't Made for Fools/(B-side unknown)	1988	—	2.50	5.00
❑ 1074	Took It Like a Man, Cried Like a Baby/(B-side unknown)	1988	—	2.50	5.00
❑ 1080	Love's Talkin'/(B-side unknown)	1988	—	2.50	5.00
❑ 1115	Days Like These/(B-side unknown)	1989	—	3.00	6.00
❑ 1122	Givin' Up Easy/(B-side unknown)	1990	—	3.00	6.00
ORLANDO					
❑ 108	It's Gonna Be a Heartache/(B-side unknown)	1983	—	2.50	5.00
❑ 109	Sweet Southern Woman/(B-side unknown)	1984	—	2.50	5.00
❑ 110	I Wanna Know Your Name/(B-side unknown)	1984	—	2.50	5.00
❑ 111	Pink Cadillac/(B-side unknown)	1985	—	2.50	5.00

PEARL, MINNIE

See MINNIE PEARL in the M's.

PEDERSEN, HERB

Also see DESERT ROSE BAND; THE DILLARDS.

Number	Title (A Side/B Side)	Yr	VG	VG+	NM
45s					
EPIC					
❑ 50309	Our Baby's Gone/Jesus Once Again	1976	—	2.50	5.00
❑ 50368	Paperback Writer/Younger Days	1977	—	2.50	5.00
❑ 50457	Bring Back the Smile/My Little Man	1977	—	2.50	5.00
Albums					
EPIC					
❑ PE 34225	South by Southwest	1976	3.75	7.50	15.00
❑ PE 34933	Sandman	1977	3.75	7.50	15.00
SUGAR HILL					
❑ SH-3738	Lonesome Feeling	1984	3.00	6.00	12.00

PEEK, EVERETT

Number	Title (A Side/B Side)	Yr	VG	VG+	NM
45s					
COMMERCIAL					
❑ 00016	Sea Cruise/(B-side unknown)	1977	2.00	4.00	8.00

PEEL, DAVE

Also see CONNIE EATON.

Number	Title (A Side/B Side)	Yr	VG	VG+	NM
45s					
CHART					
❑ 5037	I'm Walkin'/My Baby	1969	2.00	4.00	8.00
❑ 5054	Wax Museum/If You've Been Better Than I've Been	1970	—	3.00	6.00
❑ 5086	Sad Man's Song/You're Walking Through the Rooms	1970	—	3.00	6.00
❑ 5109	(You've Got to) Move Two Mountains/Willard Crabtree's Running	1971	—	3.00	6.00
❑ 5123	The Day/My Baby	1971	—	3.00	6.00
❑ 5143	Cracklin' Rosie/I Thought of You Today	1971	—	3.00	6.00
❑ 5159	Ordinary Day/Wax Museum	1972	—	3.00	6.00
Albums					
CHART					
❑ CHS-1039	Move Two Mountains	1971	3.75	7.50	15.00

PEGGY SUE

Number	Title (A Side/B Side)	Yr	VG	VG+	NM
45s					
DECCA					
❑ 32485	I'm Dynamite/Love Whatcha Got at Home	1969	—	3.50	7.00
❑ 32571	I'm Gettin' Tired of Babyin' You/No Woman Can Hold Him Too Long	1969	—	3.50	7.00
❑ 32640	After the Preacher's Gone/You Can't Pull the Wool Over My Eyes	1970	—	3.00	6.00
❑ 32698	All American Husband/I'm Leaving the Bottle and You	1970	—	3.00	6.00
❑ 32754	Apron Strings/You're Leaving Me for Her Again	1970	—	3.00	6.00
❑ 32812	I Say "Yes Sir"/Do it Girl Before It's Too Late	1971	—	3.00	6.00
❑ 32917	L-O-V-E, Love/You're Leavin' Me for Her Again	1972	—	3.00	6.00
❑ 32984	Coffee and Tears/Bread Upon the Waters	1972	—	3.00	6.00
DOOR KNOB					
❑ 021	Every Beat of My Heart/This Time It's Love	1976	—	2.50	5.00
❑ 029	I Just Came In Here (To Let a Little Hurt Out)/Jody Come Home	1977	—	2.50	5.00
❑ 036	Good Evening Henry/Fire in Texas	1977	—	2.50	5.00
❑ 043	Mama's Country Christmas/Donkey Without a Name	1977	—	2.50	5.00
❑ 045	To Be Loved/I've Been Close to Love (Too Many Times)	1978	—	2.50	5.00
❑ 052	Let Me Down Easy/Come and Lay Down with Me	1978	—	2.50	5.00
❑ 069	All Night Long/Good Evening Henry	1978	—	2.50	5.00
❑ 079	How I Love You in the Morning/Where Your Memories Play	1978	—	2.50	5.00
❑ 094	I Want to See Me in Your Eyes/Let Me Down Easy	1979	—	2.50	5.00
❑ 102	The Love Song and the Dream Belong to Me/Rainy Day Lovin'	1979	—	2.50	5.00
❑ 121	For as Long as You Want Me/Only One Thing Left to Do	1980	—	2.50	5.00
❑ 131	Why Don't You Go to Dallas/Only One Thing Left to Do	1980	—	2.50	5.00
❑ 137	Slow Motion/The Love Song and the Dream Belong to Me	1980	—	2.50	5.00
❑ 160	Too Late to Go Dancing/The Love Song and the Dream Belong to Me	1981	—	2.50	5.00
MCA					
❑ 40063	Rough and Ready/Home Was Never Like This	1973	—	2.50	5.00
❑ 40125	Love What 'Cha Got at Home/Kick It Again	1973	—	2.50	5.00
❑ 40189	My Heart Keeps Getting in My Way/Poverty Hill	1974	—	2.50	5.00
❑ 40267	Romeo/I Love You to Pieces	1974	—	2.50	5.00
❑ 40323	Lookin' in a Devil's Eye/Never Say Never	1974	—	2.50	5.00
Albums					
DECCA					
❑ DL 75153	Dynamite!	1969	6.25	12.50	25.00
❑ DL 75215	All American Husband	1970	6.25	12.50	25.00

PEGGY SUE AND SONNY WRIGHT

Also see each artist's individual listings.

Number	Title (A Side/B Side)	Yr	VG	VG+	NM
45s					
DOOR KNOB					
❑ 038	If This Is What Love Is All About/Someone I Can't Say No To	1977	—	2.50	5.00
❑ 113	Gently Hold Me/If This Is What Love's All About	1979	—	2.50	5.00

PENN, BOBBY

Number	Title (A Side/B Side)	Yr	VG	VG+	NM
45s					
50 STATES					
❑ 1	You Were on My Mind/Pretty Girl from Kingston Town	1971	—	3.50	7.00
❑ 4	High Heel Sneakers/You and Only You	1971	—	3.00	6.00
❑ 8	Sunshine Lady/Promise Her Anything	1972	—	3.00	6.00
❑ 14	Lay Your Sweet Lovin' on Me/(B-side unknown)	1972	—	3.00	6.00
❑ 20	Bring Your Sugar to Daddy/Blue Lady	1973	—	3.00	6.00
❑ 29	Watch Out for Lucy/The Worst I Ever Had Was Good	1974	—	2.50	5.00
❑ 30	Watch Out for Lucy (Alternate Take)/(B-side unknown)	1974	—	3.00	6.00
❑ 32	Rhythm of Love/Blue Lady	1975	—	2.50	5.00
❑ 34	Louisiana Lady/Where's the Party Tonight	1975	—	2.50	5.00
❑ 42	Little Weekend Warriors/You're All That Really Matters to Me	1976	—	2.50	5.00

PENNELL, ZAG

45s

COLUMBIA

Number	Title (A Side/B Side)	Yr	VG	VG+	NM
❑ 4-21255	Vegetable Love/I Never Hear You Say "I Love You"	1954	6.25	12.50	25.00
❑ 4-21302	Day and Night Patrol/Some Kinna	1954	5.00	10.00	20.00
❑ 4-21365	Tender Lovin' Care/I'm Doing All Right	1955	5.00	10.00	20.00
❑ 4-21408	How Could It Be Wrong/Everything Needs Something	1955	5.00	10.00	20.00

PENNINGTON, J.P.

Also see EXILE.

45s

MCA

Number	Title (A Side/B Side)	Yr	VG	VG+	NM
❑ 54047	Whatever It Takes/If I Were You	1991	—	2.00	4.00
❑ 54126	You Gotta Get Serious/Blue Highway	1991	—	2.00	4.00
❑ 54255	Old Familiar Ring/Watcha Tryin' to Do	1992	—	—	3.00

PENNINGTON, RAY

Also see BLUESTONE; THE SWING SHIFT BAND.

45s

Number	Title (A Side/B Side)	Yr	VG	VG+	NM
CAPITOL					
❑ 2006	Who's Gonna Walk the Dog (And Put Out the Cat)/You Turned the Lights On	1967	2.00	4.00	8.00
❑ 2118	Hush, Hush, Sweet Charlotte/Someday You'll Fall Back to Me	1968	2.00	4.00	8.00
❑ 5751	Who's Been Mowing the Lawn (While I Was Gone)/I Don't Feel at Home	1966	2.00	4.00	8.00
❑ 5855	Ramblin' Man/Let Go	1967	2.00	4.00	8.00
DIMENSION					
❑ 1039	For Christmas/Don't Let Me Lie Again	1982	—	2.50	5.00
❑ 1043	While I Was Slippin' In (She Was Steppin' Out)/I Can Forget About You	1983	—	2.50	5.00
EMH					
❑ 0022	The Memories That Last/Nothing to Go On	1983	—	2.50	5.00
❑ 0027	For Christmas/Dark Haired Woman	1983	—	2.50	5.00
❑ 0029	Drowning My Troubles (Till They've Learned How to Swim)/Till the Fear Slips Away	1984	—	2.50	5.00
❑ 0033	Nothing's Changed, Nothing's New/The Devil's Den	1984	—	2.50	5.00
KING					
❑ 5783	The First Step Down Is the Longest/Your Diary	1963	3.00	6.00	12.00
LEE					
❑ 502	Boogie Woogie Country Girl/(B-side unknown)	1958	62.50	125.00	250.00
❑ 504	My Steady Baby/(B-side unknown)	1958	37.50	75.00	150.00
MONUMENT					
❑ 1109	Raining in My Heart/My Mind Is No Match for Your Memory	1968	—	3.50	7.00
❑ 1134	After I'm Number One/Cold, Gray Light of Dawn	1969	—	3.50	7.00
❑ 1145	What Eva Doesn't Have/Denver	1969	—	3.50	7.00
❑ 1170	This Song Don't Care Who Sings It/I Wouldn't Treat a Doggone Dog (The Way You're Treatin' Me)	1969	—	3.50	7.00
❑ 1194	You Don't Know Me/Country Blues	1970	—	3.50	7.00
❑ 1208	The Other Woman/I Know Love	1970	—	3.50	7.00
❑ 1231	Bubbles in My Beer/Don't Build No Fences for Me	1970	—	3.50	7.00
❑ 8527	The Best Worst Thing/My Daddy Was a Travelin' Man	1971	—	3.00	6.00
❑ 8537	My Church/This Song Don't Care Who Sings It	1971	—	3.00	6.00
❑ 8540	Woman Go On Home/Dark Haired Woman	1972	—	3.00	6.00
❑ 8553	Let Them Talk/Happy Times	1972	—	3.00	6.00
MRC					
❑ 1022	She Wanted a Little Bit More/(B-side unknown)	1978	—	2.50	5.00
RUBY					
❑ 290	Fancy Free/You'll Want Me Back But I Won't Care	1957	15.00	30.00	60.00
STEP ONE					
❑ 340	Deep Water/Faded Love	198?	—	2.50	5.00
❑ 343	Cincinnati Blues/Before You Turn Me Down	198?	—	2.50	5.00
❑ 362	Good Ole Country Mood/In the Mood	1986	—	2.50	5.00
❑ 403	Blue of a Kind/Fat Boy Rag	1989	—	2.50	5.00
ZODIAC					
❑ 1003	I Can't Get Up Myself/(B-side unknown)	1976	—	3.00	6.00
❑ 1010	Steppin' Aside Just Ain't My Style/The Good Old Days Are Right Now	1976	—	3.00	6.00

Albums

Number	Title (A Side/B Side)	Yr	VG	VG+	NM
DIMENSION					
❑ DLP-5007	Memories	1983	3.00	6.00	12.00
MONUMENT					
❑ SLP-18145	Ray Pennington Sings for the Other Woman	1970	3.75	7.50	15.00

PENNY, HANK

Also see SUE THOMPSON.

45s

Number	Title (A Side/B Side)	Yr	VG	VG+	NM
DECCA					
❑ 9-29560	I Can't Get You Out of My Mind/When They Ask About You	1955	5.00	10.00	20.00
❑ 9-29597	A Letter from Home/Bloodshot Eyes	1955	5.00	10.00	20.00
❑ 9-29926	Rock of Gibraltar/Southern Fried Chicken	1956	5.00	10.00	20.00
❑ 9-30179	Wham! Bam! Thank You Ma'am/Texas Never Woulda	1957	5.00	10.00	20.00
❑ 9-30313	The Cricket Song/Big Footed Sam	1957	5.00	10.00	20.00
❑ 9-30531	A Night at the Copa/Fool's Lament	1957	5.00	10.00	20.00
KING					
❑ 957	You're So Different/You Better Save It for a Rainy Day	1951	10.00	20.00	40.00
❑ 1020	Alabama Jubilee/Back Up a Little Bit	1951	10.00	20.00	40.00
❑ 1021	Steel Guitar Polka/Won't You Ride in My Little Red Wagon	1951	10.00	20.00	40.00
❑ 1090	Back Up a Little Bit/Don't You Know It's Wrong	1952	7.50	15.00	30.00
❑ 1122	Two Timin' Mama/Low Down Woman Blues	1952	7.50	15.00	30.00
❑ 1500	Bloodshot Eyes/Wham, Bam, Thank You Ma'am	1955	6.25	12.50	25.00
RCA VICTOR					
❑ 47-4363	I Want My Rib/White Shotgun	1951	6.25	12.50	25.00
❑ 47-4414	That Mink on Her Back/My Little Red Wagon	1951	6.25	12.50	25.00
❑ 47-4633	Taxes, Taxes/You're Bound to Look Like a Monkey	1952	6.25	12.50	25.00
❑ 47-4862	Hadicillin Boogie/If I Can't Wear the Pants	1952	6.25	12.50	25.00
❑ 47-5023	Makin' Love Tennessee Style/Sweet Mama Put Him in Low	1952	6.25	12.50	25.00
❑ 47-5150	That's My Weakness Now/I Want to Live a Little	1953	6.25	12.50	25.00
❑ 47-5283	Fan It/You Can't Pull the Wool	1953	5.00	10.00	20.00
—With Jaye P. Morgan					
❑ 48-0406	Tater Pie/Just for Old Time's Sake	1950	7.50	15.00	30.00
❑ 48-0436	No Mess, No Fuss, No Bother/A Bad Penny Always Returns	1951	7.50	15.00	30.00
❑ 48-0466	What She's Got Is Mine/Hold the Phone	1951	7.50	15.00	30.00
❑ 48-0501	Catch 'Em Young, Treat 'Em Rough/I Like Molasses	1951	7.50	15.00	30.00
STARDAY					
❑ 8030	Bloodshot Eyes/The Freckle Song	197?	—	3.00	6.00

Selected 78s

Number	Title (A Side/B Side)	Yr	VG	VG+	NM
COLUMBIA					
❑ 15766-D	My Blue Ridge Mountain Bride/When It's Apple Blossom Time Up in the Berkshires	1932	50.00	100.00	200.00
—As "Old Hank Penny"					
❑ 20265	Why Did I Cry/Lonesome Train Blues	1948	3.75	7.50	15.00
—Reissue of 37666					
❑ 20310	She's Just That Kind/Cheatin' on Your Baby	1948	3.75	7.50	15.00
—Reissue of 37733					
❑ 20317	Red Hot Papa/I Told Them All About You	1948	3.75	7.50	15.00
—Reissue of 37740					
❑ 20327	Peach Tree Shuffle/Steel Guitar Hula	1948	3.75	7.50	15.00
—Reissue of 37750					
❑ 37666	Why Did I Cry/Lonesome Train Blues	1947	5.00	10.00	20.00
—Reissue					
❑ 37733	She's Just That Kind/Cheatin' on Your Baby	1947	5.00	10.00	20.00
—Reissue					
❑ 37740	Red Hot Papa/I Told Them All About You	1947	5.00	10.00	20.00
—Reissue					
❑ 37750	Peach Tree Shuffle/Steel Guitar Hula	1947	5.00	10.00	20.00
—Reissue					
KING					
❑ 507	Last Night/Tear Stains on Your Letter	1946	6.25	12.50	25.00
❑ 512	Talkin' 'Bout You/I Hope You're Satisfied	1946	6.25	12.50	25.00
❑ 519	When You Cry, You Cry Alone/I'm Singin' the Blues	1946	6.25	12.50	25.00
❑ 521	Bless Your Heart Little Girl/If You'd Only Be True	1946	6.25	12.50	25.00
❑ 528	Steel Guitar Stomp/I'm Counting the Days	1946	6.25	12.50	25.00
❑ 534	Flamin' Mamie/I Just Can't Understand	1946	6.25	12.50	25.00
❑ 540	Get Yourself a Red Head/Missouri	1946	6.25	12.50	25.00
❑ 551	Time Will Tell/These Wild, Wild Women	1946	6.25	12.50	25.00
❑ 581	Texas in My Soul/Merle's Buck Dance	1947	6.25	12.50	25.00
❑ 597	Wildcat Mama/Here Today and Gone Tomorrow	1947	6.25	12.50	25.00
❑ 606	Open the Door, Richard/The Freckle Song	1947	6.25	12.50	25.00
❑ 614	Let Me Play with Your Poodle/The Freckle Song	1947	6.25	12.50	25.00
❑ 621	Locked Out/Penny Blows His Top	1947	6.25	12.50	25.00
❑ 639	Steel Guitar Polka/Won't You Ride in My Little Red Wagon	1947	6.25	12.50	25.00
❑ 672	I'm Gonna Change Things/I'm Not Satisfied	1948	6.25	12.50	25.00
❑ 698	Hillbilly Jump/Kentucky	1948	6.25	12.50	25.00
❑ 727	Wouldn't It Be Fun/Big Fat Papa	1948	6.25	12.50	25.00
❑ 748	Someone Moved the Ladder/I'm Wasting My Time	1949	6.25	12.50	25.00
❑ 770	One Heart, One Love, One Life/Red Hot Mama	1949	6.25	12.50	25.00
❑ 771	Why Didn't I Think of That/Politics	1949	6.25	12.50	25.00
❑ 795	Hillbilly Bebop/Sweet Talkin' Mama	1949	6.25	12.50	25.00
❑ 813	We Met Too Late/My Inlaws Made an Outlaw Out of Me	1949	6.25	12.50	25.00
❑ 828	Bloodshot Eyes/I Was Satisfied	1949	6.25	12.50	25.00
❑ 842	Got the Louisiana Blues/Now Ain't You Glad Dear	1950	6.25	12.50	25.00
❑ 869	Wham, Bam, Thank You Ma'am/Jersey Bounce	1950	6.25	12.50	25.00
❑ 891	Tin Pan Polka/What've You Got	1950	6.25	12.50	25.00
❑ 902	Remington Ride/I'm Gonna Have My Picture Took	1950	6.25	12.50	25.00
❑ 924	Solitary Blues/Tell Me All About Georgia	1951	5.00	10.00	20.00
❑ 941	Riding On an Old Ferris Wheel/Guess Who Took Your Place	1951	5.00	10.00	20.00
OKEH					
❑ 5840	Just Forget/Rose's Sister	194?	6.25	12.50	25.00
VOCALION					
❑ 04543	titles unknown	193?	6.25	12.50	25.00
❑ 04640	titles unknown	193?	6.25	12.50	25.00
❑ 04741	titles unknown	193?	6.25	12.50	25.00
❑ 04826	titles unknown	193?	6.25	12.50	25.00
❑ 04922	titles unknown	193?	6.25	12.50	25.00
❑ 05067	titles unknown	193?	6.25	12.50	25.00

Number	Title (A Side/B Side)	Yr	VG	VG+	NM
Albums					
AUDIO LAB					
❑ AL-1508 [M]	Hank Penny Sings	1959	50.00	100.00	200.00

PENNY, JOE

Number	Title (A Side/B Side)	Yr	VG	VG+	NM
45s					
FEDERAL					
❑ 12322	Mercy, Mercy Percy/Bip a Little, Bop a Little	1958	50.00	100.00	200.00
SIMS					
❑ 173	Frosty Window Pane/Hatty Fatty	1964	5.00	10.00	20.00

PEPPER, BRENDA

Number	Title (A Side/B Side)	Yr	VG	VG+	NM
45s					
PLAYBOY					
❑ 6038	You Bring Out the Best in Me/Goodbye Ain't As Far Away As Gone	1975	—	2.50	5.00
❑ 6049	Son-of-a-Gun/This Is My Love Song	1975	—	2.50	5.00
❑ 6070	Southern Lady/(B-side unknown)	1976	—	2.50	5.00

PEREZ, TONY

Number	Title (A Side/B Side)	Yr	VG	VG+	NM
45s					
REPRISE					
❑ 7-22838	Take Another Run/Texarkana	1989	—	—	3.00
❑ 7-27591	Oh How I Love You (Como Te Quiero)/Bridge to Burn	1989	—	—	3.00

PERFECT STRANGER

Number	Title (A Side/B Side)	Yr	VG	VG+	NM
45s					
CURB					
❑ D7- 76956	You Have the Right to Remain Silent/It's Up to You	1995	—	2.00	4.00
❑ D7-76969	I'm a Stranger Here Myself/I Ain't Never	1995	—	—	3.00
❑ D7-76978	Remember the Ride/Cut Me Off	1996	—	—	3.00

PERKINS, CARL

Number	Title (A Side/B Side)	Yr	VG	VG+	NM
45s					
COLUMBIA					
❑ 41131	Pink Pedal Pushers/Jive After Five	1958	7.50	15.00	30.00
❑ 41131 [PS]	Pink Pedal Pushers/Jive After Five	1958	30.00	60.00	120.00
❑ 41207	Levi Jacket/Pop, Let Me Have the Car	1958	6.25	12.50	25.00
❑ 41296	Y-O-U/This Life I Live	1958	6.25	12.50	25.00
❑ 41379	Pointed Toe Shoes/Highway of Love	1959	6.25	12.50	25.00
❑ 41449	One Ticket to Loneliness/I Don't See Me in Your Eyes Anymore	1959	6.25	12.50	25.00
❑ 41651	L-O-V-E-V-I-L-L-E/Too Much for a Man to Understand	1960	6.25	12.50	25.00
❑ 41825	Honey, 'Cause I Love You/Just for You	1960	6.25	12.50	25.00
❑ 42061	Anyway the Wind Blows/The Unhappy Girls	1961	6.25	12.50	25.00
❑ 42403	Hollywood City/Forget Me Next Time Around	1962	—	—	—
—Unreleased?					
❑ 42405	Hollywood City/The Fool I Used to Be	1962	6.25	12.50	25.00
❑ 42405 [PS]	Hollywood City/The Fool I Used to Be	1962	30.00	60.00	120.00
❑ 42514	Sister Twister/Hambone	1962	6.25	12.50	25.00
❑ 42514 [PS]	Sister Twister/Hambone	1962	100.00	200.00	400.00
❑ 42753	I Just Got Back from There/Forget Me Next Time Around	1963	6.25	12.50	25.00
❑ 44723	Restless/1143	1968	2.00	4.00	8.00
❑ 44883	For Your Love/Four Letter Word	1969	2.00	4.00	8.00
❑ 44993	C.C. Rider/Soul Beat	1969	2.00	4.00	8.00
❑ 45107	All Mama's Children/Step Aside	1970	2.00	4.00	8.00
—With NRBQ					
❑ 45132	State of Confusion/My Son, My Son	1970	—	3.00	6.00
❑ 45253	What Every Little Boy Ought to Know/Just As Long	1970	—	2.50	5.00
❑ 45347	Me Without You/Red Headed Woman	1971	—	2.50	5.00
❑ 45466	Cotton Top/About All I Can Give You Is My Love	1971	—	2.50	5.00
❑ 45582	High on Love/Take Me Back to Memphis	1972	—	2.50	5.00
❑ 45694	Someday/The Trip	1972	—	2.50	5.00
DECCA					
❑ 31548	Help Me Find My Baby/For a Little While	1963	3.75	7.50	15.00
❑ 31591	After Sundown/I Wouldn't Have Told You	1964	3.75	7.50	15.00
❑ 31709	The Monkeyshine/Let My Baby Be	1964	3.75	7.50	15.00
❑ 31786	One of These Days/Mama of My Song	1965	3.75	7.50	15.00
DOLLIE					
❑ 505	Country Boy's Dream/If I Could Come Back	1966	3.00	6.00	12.00
❑ 508	Shine, Shine, Shine/Almost Love	1967	3.00	6.00	12.00
❑ 512	Without You/You Can Take the Boy Out of the Country	1967	3.00	6.00	12.00
❑ 514	My Old Home Town/Back to Tennessee	1967	3.00	6.00	12.00
❑ 516	It's You/Lake County Cotton Country	1968	3.00	6.00	12.00
FLIP					
❑ 501	Movie Magg/Turn Around	1955	250.00	500.00	1000.
JET					
❑ 5054	Blue Suede Shoes/Rock Around the World	1979	—	2.00	4.00
MERCURY					
❑ 55009	The E.P. Express/Big Bad Blues	1977	—	2.00	4.00
❑ 73425	(Let's Get) Dixiefried/One More Loser Goin' Home	1973	—	3.00	6.00
❑ 73489	Ruby, Don't Take Your Love to Town/Sing My Song	1974	—	2.50	5.00
❑ 73653	You'll Always Be a Lady to Me/Low Class	1974	—	2.50	5.00
❑ 73690	The E.P. Express/Big Bad Blues	1975	—	2.50	5.00
❑ 73993	Help Me Dream/You Tore My Heaven All to Hell	1973	—	3.00	6.00
MMI					
❑ 1016	Don't Get Off Gettin' It On/Georgia Court Room	1977	—	2.00	4.00
❑ 1019	Standing in the Need of Love/Georgia Court Room	1977	—	2.00	4.00
MUSIC MILL					
❑ 1007	Born to Boogie/Take Me Back	1976	—	2.00	4.00
SMASH					
❑ 884760-7	Birth of Rock and Roll/Rock and Roll (Fais-Do-Do)	1986	—	2.00	4.00
—B-side with Jerry Lee Lewis, Roy Orbison and Johnny Cash					
❑ 884760-7 [PS]	Birth of Rock and Roll/Rock and Roll (Fais-Do-Do)	1986	—	2.00	4.00
—B-side with Jerry Lee Lewis, Roy Orbison and Johnny Cash					
❑ 884934-7	Sixteen Candles/Rock & Roll (Fais-Do-Do)	1986	—	2.00	4.00
—B-side with Jerry Lee Lewis, Roy Orbison and Johnny Cash; A-side by Jerry Lee Lewis					
❑ 888142-7	Class of '55/We Remember the King	1987	—	2.00	4.00
—B-side with Jerry Lee Lewis, Roy Orbison and Johnny Cash					
SUEDE					
❑ 101	I Don't Want to Fall in Love Again/We Did It in '54	1978	—	2.00	4.00
❑ 102	Rock-a-Billy Fever/Till You Get Through with Me	1978	—	2.00	4.00
❑ 6777	Little Teardrops/Green Grass of Home	1977	—	2.00	4.00
SUN					
❑ 224	Gone, Gone, Gone/Let the Jukebox Keep On Playing	1955	25.00	50.00	100.00
❑ 234	Blue Suede Shoes/Honey Don't	1956	15.00	30.00	60.00
❑ 235	Sure to Fall/Tennessee	1956	—	—	—
—Unreleased					
❑ 243	Boppin' the Blues/All Mama's Children	1956	10.00	20.00	40.00
❑ 249	Dixie Fried/I'm Sorry, I'm Not Sorry	1956	7.50	15.00	30.00
❑ 261	Matchbox/Your True Love	1957	7.50	15.00	30.00
❑ 274	That's Right/Forever Yours	1957	7.50	15.00	30.00
❑ 287	Glad All Over/Lend Me Your Comb	1958	7.50	15.00	30.00
UNIVERSAL					
❑ UVL-66002	Charlene/Love Makes Dreams Come True	1989	—	2.00	4.00
❑ UVL-66019	Hambone/Love Makes Dreams Come True	1989	—	2.00	4.00
7-Inch Extended Plays					
COLUMBIA					
❑ B-12341	(contents unknown)	1958	50.00	100.00	200.00
❑ B-12341 [PS]	Whole Lotta Shakin'	1958	50.00	100.00	200.00
SUN					
❑ EPA-115	Blue Suede Shoes/Movie Magg//Sure to Fall/ Gone, Gone, Gone	1958	100.00	200.00	400.00
❑ EPA-115 [PS]	Carl Perkins	1958	100.00	200.00	400.00
Albums					
ACCORD					
❑ SN-7169	Presenting Carl Perkins	1982	2.50	5.00	10.00
ALBUM GLOBE					
❑ 8118	Country Soul	1980	2.50	5.00	10.00
❑ 9037	Goin' Back to Memphis	1980	2.50	5.00	10.00
ALLEGIANCE					
❑ AV-5001	The Heart and Soul of Carl Perkins	198?	2.50	5.00	10.00
BULLDOG					
❑ BDL-2034	Twenty Golden Pieces	198?	2.50	5.00	10.00
COLUMBIA					
❑ CL 1234 [DJ]	Whole Lotta Shakin'	1958	200.00	400.00	800.00
—White label promo					
❑ CL 1234 [M]	Whole Lotta Shakin'	1958	100.00	200.00	400.00
❑ CS 9833	Carl Perkins' Greatest Hits	1969	6.25	12.50	25.00
—Red "360 Sound Stereo" label					
❑ CS 9931	Carl Perkins On Top	1969	6.25	12.50	25.00
—Red "360 Sound Stereo" label					
❑ CS 9981	Boppin' the Blues	1970	6.25	12.50	25.00
—Red "360 Sound Stereo" label					
❑ CS 9981	Boppin' the Blues	1970	3.00	6.00	12.00
—Orange label					
❑ PC 9981	Boppin' the Blues	198?	2.00	4.00	8.00
—Budget-line reissue					
❑ LE 10117	Carl Perkins' Greatest Hits	1974	3.00	6.00	12.00
—"Limited Edition" brown label					
❑ FC 37961	The Survivors	1982	2.50	5.00	10.00
—With Johnny Cash and Jerry Lee Lewis					
❑ PC 37961	The Survivors	198?	2.00	4.00	8.00
—Budget-line reissue					
DESIGN					
❑ DLP-611 [M]	Tennessee	1963	7.50	15.00	30.00
❑ SDLP-611 [R]	Tennessee	1963	5.00	10.00	20.00
DOLLIE					
❑ 4001	Country Boy's Dream	1967	7.50	15.00	30.00
❑ ST-91428	Country Boy's Dream	1967	10.00	20.00	40.00
—Capitol Record Club edition					
DOOTO					
❑ DL- [M]	Introducing Carl Perkins	196?	3.75	7.50	15.00
DOOTONE					
❑ DL- [M]	Introducing Carl Perkins	1956	30.00	60.00	120.00
—Black vinyl					
❑ DL- [M]	Introducing Carl Perkins	1956	50.00	100.00	200.00
—Red vinyl					
HARMONY					
❑ HS 11385	Carl Perkins	1970	3.75	7.50	15.00
❑ KH 31179	Brown Eyed Handsome Man	1971	3.00	6.00	12.00
❑ KH 31792	Greatest Hits	1972	3.00	6.00	12.00
HILLTOP					
❑ 6103	Matchbox	197?	3.00	6.00	12.00

Number	Title (A Side/B Side)	Yr	VG	VG+	NM
JET					
❑ JT-LA856-H	Ol' Blue Suede's Back	1978	3.75	7.50	15.00
❑ JZ 35604	Ol' Blue Suede's Back	1978	2.50	5.00	10.00
KOALA					
❑ AW 14164	Country Soul	198?	2.50	5.00	10.00
MCA DOT					
❑ 39035	Carl Perkins	1985	2.50	5.00	10.00
MERCURY					
❑ SRM-1-691	My Kind of Country	1973	3.00	6.00	12.00
RHINO					
❑ RNLP-70221	Original Sun Greatest Hits (1955-1957)	1986	3.00	6.00	12.00
ROUNDER					
❑ SS-27	Honky Tonk Gal: Rare and Unissued Sun Masters	1989	3.00	6.00	12.00
SMASH					
❑ 830002-1	Class of '55	1986	3.00	6.00	12.00
—With Jerry Lee Lewis, Roy Orbison and Johnny Cash					
SUEDE					
❑ 002	Live at Austin City Limits	1981	2.50	5.00	10.00
SUN					
❑ LP-111	Original Golden Hits	1969	3.00	6.00	12.00
❑ LP-112	Blue Suede Shoes	1969	3.00	6.00	12.00
❑ SLP-1225 [M]	The Dance Album of Carl Perkins	1957	300.00	600.00	1200.
❑ SLP-1225 [M]	Teen Beat — The Best of Carl Perkins	1961	125.00	250.00	500.00
—Reissue with new title					
SUNNYVALE					
❑ 9330803	The Sun Story, Vol. 3	1977	3.00	6.00	12.00
TRIP					
❑ TLP-8503 [(2)]	The Best of Carl Perkins	1974	3.00	6.00	12.00
UNIVERSAL					
❑ UVL-76001	Born to Rock	1989	3.75	7.50	15.00

PERKINS, DAL

45s

Number	Title (A Side/B Side)	Yr	VG	VG+	NM
CHALLENGE					
❑ 59262	Last of the Lovers/It's So Nice to See You	1964	3.75	7.50	15.00
❑ 59288	If You Were Mine/Money Greases the Wheel	1965	3.75	7.50	15.00
❑ 59318	Second Choice/Standing in Your Shadow	1965	3.75	7.50	15.00
COLUMBIA					
❑ 4-44204	Here's to the Girls/One Day a Week	1967	2.50	5.00	10.00
❑ 4-44343	Helpless/Woman in the Darkness	1967	2.50	5.00	10.00
VIV					
❑ 102	Shy/Young Lovers	195?	6.25	12.50	25.00

PERRY, BRENDA KAYE

Also see BILLY WALKER.

45s

Number	Title (A Side/B Side)	Yr	VG	VG+	NM
MRC					
❑ 1010	Deeper Water/Home Sweet Home	1977	—	2.50	5.00
❑ 1013	I Can't Get Up by Myself/Free	1978	—	2.50	5.00
❑ 1021	My Daddy Was a Travelin' Man/I Am a Woman	1978	—	2.50	5.00
❑ 1026	Make Me Your Woman/(What a) Wonderful World	1979	—	2.50	5.00

PETERS, BEN

45s

Number	Title (A Side/B Side)	Yr	VG	VG+	NM
CAPITOL					
❑ 3687	Would You Still Love Me/This Has Got to Last	1973	—	3.00	6.00
LIBERTY					
❑ 56114	San Francisco Is a Lonely Town/You're the Happy Song I Sing	1969	2.00	4.00	8.00
❑ 56139	For My Woman's Love/It's Time for Me to Go	1969	2.00	4.00	8.00
❑ 56174	Can't Get Over You/Downtown U.S.A.	1970	2.00	4.00	8.00

PETERS, DEBBIE

45s

Number	Title (A Side/B Side)	Yr	VG	VG+	NM
OAK					
❑ 1012	It Can't Wait/I Can't Get Enough of You	1980	—	3.00	6.00
RCA					
❑ PB-11159	I'd Rather Give It Away/Feel Like a Little Love	1977	—	2.50	5.00

PETERS, DOUG

45s

Number	Title (A Side/B Side)	Yr	VG	VG+	NM
COMSTOCK					
❑ 1751	Change of Pace/(B-side unknown)	198?	—	3.00	6.00
❑ 1763	Cup of Love/(B-side unknown)	198?	—	3.00	6.00
❑ 1765	Walk Away/(B-side unknown)	198?	—	3.00	6.00
❑ 1789	The World Is Round/(B-side unknown)	198?	—	3.00	6.00
❑ 1799	Give Your New Love a Try/(B-side unknown)	198?	—	3.00	6.00
❑ 1895	My Heart's Way Behind/(B-side unknown)	1988	—	3.00	6.00
❑ 1982	Captured by Love/(B-side unknown)	1989	—	3.50	7.00

PETERS, JIMMIE

45s

Number	Title (A Side/B Side)	Yr	VG	VG+	NM
MCA					
❑ 40203	I Overlooked a Good Thing Way Too Long/What About the Good Times	1974	—	3.00	6.00
❑ 40270	Everyday with You/What's Left of Her	1974	—	3.00	6.00
❑ 40336	This Kind of Fool Again/The Farther We Go	1974	—	3.00	6.00
❑ 40361	Danger Zone/Put My Love in Your Pocket	1975	—	3.00	6.00
MERCURY					
❑ 55005	Lipstick Traces/Even If It's Wrong	1977	—	2.50	5.00
❑ 55016	634-5789/Just Because It Feels Good	1978	—	2.50	5.00
❑ 55025	I Will Always Love You/Just Because It Feels Good	1978	—	2.50	5.00
❑ 73911	Somebody Took Her Love (And Never Gave It Back)/I'm What I Am (Because You're Mine)	1977	—	2.50	5.00
SUNBIRD					
❑ 105	Hearts/Let's Write a Love Song	1980	—	2.50	5.00
❑ 105 [PS]	Hearts/Let's Write a Love Song	1980	—	3.00	6.00
❑ 7552	Keep On Playing That Country Music/No One As Married As I	1980	—	2.50	5.00

PETERS, JIMMIE, AND LYNDA K. LANCE

Also see each artist's individual listings.

45s

Number	Title (A Side/B Side)	Yr	VG	VG+	NM
VISTA					
❑ 101	I Hate the Way Our Love Is/(B-side unknown)	1978	—	3.00	6.00
❑ 106	First Class Fool/(B-side unknown)	1979	—	3.00	6.00

PETERS, RAY

Albums

Number	Title (A Side/B Side)	Yr	VG	VG+	NM
JCW					
❑ 1333	From the Heart	1968	6.25	12.50	25.00

PETERS, SUSAN

45s

Number	Title (A Side/B Side)	Yr	VG	VG+	NM
WARNER BROS.					
❑ 29873	Why'd I Hire a Wino to Decorate Our Home/Heartbreak Avenue	1982	—	2.50	5.00

PETERS AND LEE

45s

Number	Title (A Side/B Side)	Yr	VG	VG+	NM
PHILIPS					
❑ 40729	Welcome Home/Can't Keep My Mind on the Game	1974	—	3.00	6.00
❑ 40732	Don't Stay Away Too Long/The Old-Fashioned Way	1974	—	3.00	6.00

PETERSON, COLLEEN

45s

Number	Title (A Side/B Side)	Yr	VG	VG+	NM
CAPITOL					
❑ 4314	Don't It Make You Wanna Dance/Sad Songs and Waltzes	1976	—	2.50	5.00
❑ 4349	Souvenirs/Six Days on the Road	1976	—	2.50	5.00
❑ 4535	Beginning to Feel Like Home/Bucket to the South	1978	—	2.50	5.00
❑ 4567	Delaney/Dim Lights, Thick Smoke, and Loud, Loud Music	1978	—	2.50	5.00

Albums

Number	Title (A Side/B Side)	Yr	VG	VG+	NM
CAPITOL					
❑ ST-11567	Beginning to Feel Like Home	1976	3.00	6.00	12.00
❑ ST-11714	Colleen Peterson	1978	3.00	6.00	12.00

PETERSON, EARL

45s

Number	Title (A Side/B Side)	Yr	VG	VG+	NM
COLUMBIA					
❑ 21364	Boogie Blues/Believe Me	1955	12.50	25.00	50.00
❑ 21406	Be Careful of the Heart You're Going to Break/I'm Not Buying Baby	1955	12.50	25.00	50.00
❑ 21467	I Ain't Gonna Fall in Love/I'll Live My Life Alone	1955	12.50	25.00	50.00
❑ 21540	You Gotta Be My Baby/World of Make Believe	1956	10.00	20.00	40.00
SUN					
❑ 197	Boogie Blues/In the Dark	1954	125.00	250.00	500.00

PETERSON, MICHAEL

45s

Number	Title (A Side/B Side)	Yr	VG	VG+	NM
REPRISE					
❑ 7-16933	Sure Feels Real Good/Laughin' All the Way to the Bank	1999	—	—	3.00
❑ 7-16995	Somethin' 'Bout a Sunday/Lost in the Shuffle	1999	—	—	3.00
❑ 7-17379	Drink, Swear, Steal & Lie/For a Song	1997	—	2.00	4.00

PFEIFER, DIANE

45s

Number	Title (A Side/B Side)	Yr	VG	VG+	NM
CAPITOL					
❑ 4823	Free to Be Lonely Again/Oh No, Not Love Again	1980	—	2.00	4.00
❑ 4858	Roses Ain't Red/Do You Mind (If I Fall in Love with You)	1980	—	2.00	4.00
❑ 4916	Wishful Drinkin'/Just When I Needed a Love Song	1980	—	2.00	4.00
❑ 5060	Play Something We Could Love To/Sing You to Sleep	1981	—	2.00	4.00
❑ B-5116	Something to Love For Again/Missing You All By Myself	1982	—	2.00	4.00
❑ B-5154	Let's Get Crazy Again/Missing You All By Myself	1982	—	2.00	4.00

Albums

Number	Title (A Side/B Side)	Yr	VG	VG+	NM
CAPITOL					
❑ ST-12046	Diane Pfeifer	1980	2.50	5.00	10.00

PHILLIPS, BILL

Also see MEL TILLIS.

45s

Number	Title (A Side/B Side)	Yr	VG	VG+	NM
AVCO					
❑ 602	I've Loved You All Over the World/We Gave Birth to Passion	1974	—	3.00	6.00
❑ 608	Four Roses/Typical Day	1975	—	3.00	6.00
COLUMBIA					
❑ 4-41218	Lying Lips/There's a Change in Me	1958	5.00	10.00	20.00

Number	Title (A Side/B Side)	Yr	VG	VG+	NM
❑ 4-41323	Foolish Me/The Tears That Fall	1959	3.75	7.50	15.00
❑ 4-41646	Empty Hours/All Night Long	1960	3.75	7.50	15.00
❑ 4-41827	How Could You/I Found a True Love	1960	3.75	7.50	15.00
❑ 4-41954	Walk with Me Baby/The Blues Are Settin' In	1961	3.75	7.50	15.00
❑ 4-42158	Love Never Dies/The Outsider	1961	3.75	7.50	15.00
❑ 4-42353	The Yankee Trader/Pledged to Silence	1962	3.75	7.50	15.00
DECCA					
❑ 31480	Let's Walk Away Strangers/Lying to Be Together	1963	3.00	6.00	12.00
❑ 31584	I Can Stand It (As Long As She Can)/Wheeling Dealing Daddy	1964	2.50	5.00	10.00
❑ 31648	Stop Me/Stepping Out	1964	2.50	5.00	10.00
❑ 31733	I Guess You Made a Fool Out of Me/A Kiss Must Last Forever	1965	2.50	5.00	10.00
❑ 31781	I'd Be Better Off Without You/Wanted	1965	2.50	5.00	10.00
❑ 31848	Friends Tell Friends/It Happens Every Time	1965	2.50	5.00	10.00
❑ 31901	Put It Off Until Tomorrow/Lonely Lonely Boy	1966	3.75	7.50	15.00
❑ 31996	The Company You Keep/The Lies Just Can't Be True	1966	2.50	5.00	10.00
❑ 32074	The Words I'm Gonna Have to Eat/Falling Back to You	1967	2.00	4.00	8.00
❑ 32141	I Learn Something New Everyday/I Didn't Forget	1967	2.00	4.00	8.00
❑ 32207	Love's Dead End/Oh, What It Did to Me	1967	2.00	4.00	8.00
❑ 32295	I Talked About You Too/Everything Turns Out for the Best	1968	2.00	4.00	8.00
❑ 32375	I've Got a Wonderful Future Behind Me/I'm Thankful	1968	2.00	4.00	8.00
❑ 32432	I Only Regret/She's an Angel	1969	2.00	4.00	8.00
❑ 32565	Little Boy Sad/I'm Living in Two Worlds	1969	2.00	4.00	8.00
❑ 32638	She's Hungry Again/You've Still Got a Place in My Heart	1970	2.00	4.00	8.00
❑ 32707	Same Old Story, Same Old Lie/You Can't Love Me When I'm Gone	1970	2.00	4.00	8.00
❑ 32782	Big Rock Candy Mountain/I Didn't Forget	1971	2.00	4.00	8.00
SOUNDWAVES					
❑ 4570	Divorce Suit (You Were Named Co-Respondent)/I've Been Loving You Too Long	1978	—	2.50	5.00
❑ 4575	I Love My Neighbor/I'm Turning You Loose	1978	—	2.50	5.00
❑ 4579	You're Gonna Make a Cheater Out of Me/Temporarily Yours	1979	—	2.50	5.00
❑ 4587	At the Moonlite/I'm Turning You Loose	1979	—	2.50	5.00
❑ 4598	Memory Bound/When Can We Do This Again	1979	—	2.50	5.00
UNITED ARTISTS					
❑ XW266	It's Only Over Now and Then/I've Got Yesterday	1973	—	3.00	6.00
❑ XW332	Teach Your Children/New World Tomorrow	1973	—	3.00	6.00
❑ 50879	I Am, I Said/Son	1972	—	3.00	6.00
❑ 50937	We'll Make It/My Intentions	1972	—	3.00	6.00
❑ 50995	Nothing's Too Good for My Woman/When Our Love Was Young Enough	1972	—	3.00	6.00
Albums					
DECCA					
❑ DL 4792 [M]	Put It Off Until Tomorrow	1966	7.50	15.00	30.00
❑ DL 4897 [M]	Bill Phillips' Style	1967	7.50	15.00	30.00
❑ DL 74792 [S]	Put It Off Until Tomorrow	1966	10.00	20.00	40.00
❑ DL 74897 [S]	Bill Phillips' Style	1967	6.25	12.50	25.00
❑ DL 75022	Country Action	1968	5.00	10.00	20.00
❑ DL 75182	Little Boy Sad	1970	5.00	10.00	20.00
HARMONY					
❑ HL 7309 [M]	Bill Phillips' Best	1964	5.00	10.00	20.00

PHILLIPS, CHARLIE

45s

Number	Title (A Side/B Side)	Yr	VG	VG+	NM
COLUMBIA					
❑ 42035	No More Sugartime/Welcome to the Wedding	1961	3.00	6.00	12.00
❑ 42289	I Guess I'll Never Learn/Now That It's Over	1962	2.50	5.00	10.00
❑ 42526	Cancel the Call/You're Moving Away	1962	2.50	5.00	10.00
❑ 42691	No One to Love/'Til Sunday	1963	2.50	5.00	10.00
❑ 42851	Later Tonight/This Is the House	1963	2.50	5.00	10.00
❑ 43014	Street of Loneliness/Please Help Me Believe	1964	2.50	5.00	10.00
CORAL					
❑ 61970	Be My Bride/Too Many Tears	1958	6.25	12.50	25.00
K-ARK					
❑ 874	Your Going Is Coming/Just Let the Flowers Grow	197?	2.00	4.00	8.00
REPRISE					
❑ 0581	Be Careful, Go Easy, Go Slow/Souvenirs of Sorrow	1967	2.00	4.00	8.00

PHILLIPS, JOHN

45s

Number	Title (A Side/B Side)	Yr	VG	VG+	NM
ABC DUNHILL					
❑ 4236	Mississippi/April Anne	1970	—	3.00	6.00
ATCO					
❑ 6960	Green-Eyed Lady/Lion	1974	—	3.00	6.00
COLUMBIA					
❑ 45737	Cup of Tea/Revolution on Vacation	1972	—	2.50	5.00
Albums					
ABC DUNHILL					
❑ DS-50077	John Phillips (John the Wolfking of L.A.)	1970	3.75	7.50	15.00

PHILLIPS, STU

Sometimes known as "Singing Stu Phillips." Not to be confused with the soundtrack composer and orchestra leader of the same name.

45s

Number	Title (A Side/B Side)	Yr	VG	VG+	NM
CAPITOL					
❑ 3335	Outback/Seven Sharp Nine	1972	—	3.50	7.00
❑ 3448	Another Way to Say Goodbye/I Hear Your Name	1972	—	3.50	7.00
❑ 3575	Restless Woman/If Loving You Means Anything	1973	—	3.00	6.00
❑ 5466	Feels Like Lovin'/Kathy Keep Playing	1965	2.50	5.00	10.00
COLUMBIA					
❑ 4-42393	One Day Early/This Heart of Mine	1962	3.00	6.00	12.00
❑ 4-42978	Heart/Here She Comes Again	1964	3.00	6.00	12.00
RCA VICTOR					
❑ 47-8771	Bracero/Angel of Love	1966	2.00	4.00	8.00
❑ 47-8868	The Great El Tigre (The Tiger)/Another Day Has Gone	1966	2.00	4.00	8.00
❑ 47-9066	Walk Me to the Station/Guess Things Happen That Way	1967	2.00	4.00	8.00
❑ 47-9219	Vin Rose/I Wish I Had Never Seen Sunshine	1967	2.00	4.00	8.00
❑ 47-9333	Juanita Jones/A Castle, A Castle	1967	2.00	4.00	8.00
❑ 47-9481	The Note in Box Number 9/Our Last Rendezvous	1968	2.00	4.00	8.00
❑ 47-9557	The Top of the World/That Completely Destroys My Plans	1968	2.00	4.00	8.00
❑ 47-9673	Bring Love Back Into Our World/Speak Softly, My Love	1968	2.00	4.00	8.00
❑ 74-0134	Let the Guitars Play/Rings of Grass	1969	2.00	4.00	8.00
❑ 74-0227	Little Tin God/Secret of the Summer Wind	1969	2.00	4.00	8.00
Albums					
CAPITOL					
❑ ST 2356 [S]	Feels Like Lovin'	1965	7.50	15.00	30.00
❑ T 2356 [M]	Feels Like Lovin'	1965	6.25	12.50	25.00
RCA VICTOR					
❑ LPM-3619 [M]	Singin' Stu Phillips	1966	5.00	10.00	20.00
❑ LSP-3619 [S]	Singin' Stu Phillips	1966	6.25	12.50	25.00
❑ LPM-3717 [M]	Grassroots Country	1967	7.50	15.00	30.00
❑ LSP-3717 [S]	Grassroots Country	1967	6.25	12.50	25.00
❑ LSP-4012	Our Last Rendezvous	1968	6.25	12.50	25.00

PICKARD, SORRELLS

45s

Number	Title (A Side/B Side)	Yr	VG	VG+	NM
BOONE					
❑ 1061	There Ain't Enough of You to Go Around/See Ruby Fall	1967	2.00	4.00	8.00
DECCA					
❑ 32963	Marianne/Who Really Cares	1972	—	3.00	6.00
❑ 33023	Is That All San Francisco Did for You/Lovely Lady	1972	—	3.00	6.00
Albums					
DECCA					
❑ DL 75338	Sorrells Pickard	1972	3.75	7.50	15.00

PIERCE, WEBB

Also see WILLIE NELSON; RED SOVINE; MEL TILLIS; KITTY WELLS.

45s

Number	Title (A Side/B Side)	Yr	VG	VG+	NM
4 STAR					
❑ 1601	Heebie Jeebie Blues/High Geared Daddy	1952	7.50	15.00	30.00
❑ 1610	Hawaiian Echoes/I Saw Your Face in the Moon	1952	7.50	15.00	30.00
❑ 1616	Georgia Rag/Lucky Lee	1952	7.50	15.00	30.00
❑ 1629	Jilted Love/I'm Happy You Hurt Me	1953	7.50	15.00	30.00
DECCA					
❑ 9-28091	That Heart Belongs to Me/So Used to Loving You	1952	6.25	12.50	25.00
❑ 9-28369	Back Street Affair/I'll Always Take Care of You	1952	6.25	12.50	25.00
❑ 9-28431	Bow Thy Head/The Country Church	1952	7.50	15.00	30.00
❑ 9-28534	I'll Go On Alone/That's Me Without You	1953	6.25	12.50	25.00
❑ 9-28594	The Last Waltz/I Haven't Got the Heart	1953	6.25	12.50	25.00
❑ 9-28725	It's Been So Long/Don't Throw Your Life Away	1953	6.25	12.50	25.00
❑ 9-28834	There Stands the Glass/I'm Walking the Dog	1953	6.25	12.50	25.00
❑ 9-28991	Slowly/You Just Can't Be True	1954	6.25	12.50	25.00
❑ 9-29107	Even Tho/Sparkling Blue Eyes	1954	6.25	12.50	25.00
❑ 9-29155	Mother Calling My Name in Prayer/Bugle Call from Heaven	1954	7.50	15.00	30.00
❑ 9-29252	More and More/You're Not Mine Anymore	1954	6.25	12.50	25.00
❑ 9-29391	In the Jailhouse Now/I'm Gonna Fall Out of Love with You	1955	5.00	10.00	20.00
❑ 9-29480	I Don't Care/Your Good for Nothing Heart	1955	5.00	10.00	20.00
❑ 9-29662	Love, Love, Love/If You Were Me	1955	5.00	10.00	20.00
❑ 9-29805	Yes, I Know Why/'Cause I Love You	1956	5.00	10.00	20.00
❑ 9-29974	Any Old Time/We'll Find a Way	1956	5.00	10.00	20.00
❑ 9-30045	Teenage Boogie/I'm Really Glad You Hurt Me	1956	10.00	20.00	40.00
❑ 9-30155	I'm Tired/It's My Way	1956	5.00	10.00	20.00
❑ 9-30255	Honky Tonk Song/Someday	1957	5.00	10.00	20.00
❑ 9-30321	Bye Bye, Love/Missing You	1957	3.75	7.50	15.00
❑ 9-30419	Holiday for Love/Don't Do It Darlin'	1957	3.75	7.50	15.00
❑ 9-30550	New Panhandle Rag/How Long?	1958	3.75	7.50	15.00
❑ 9-30623	Cryin' Over You/You'll Come Back	1958	3.75	7.50	15.00
❑ 9-30711	Tupelo County Jail/Falling Back to You	1958	3.75	7.50	15.00
❑ 9-30789	I'm Letting You Go/Sittin' Alone	1958	3.75	7.50	15.00
❑ 9-30858	A Thousand Miles Ago/What Goes On in Your Heart	1959	3.75	7.50	15.00
❑ 9-30923	I Ain't Never/Shanghaied	1959	3.75	7.50	15.00
❑ 9-31021	No Love Have I/Whirlpool of Love	1959	3.75	7.50	15.00
❑ 31058	Is It Wrong (For Loving You)/(Doin' the) Lovers Leap	1960	3.00	6.00	12.00
❑ 31118	Drifting Texas Sand/All I Need Is You	1960	3.00	6.00	12.00
❑ 31165	Fallen Angel/Truck Driver's Blues	1960	3.00	6.00	12.00
❑ 31197	Let Forgiveness In/There's More Pretty Girls Than One	1961	3.00	6.00	12.00
❑ 31249	Sweet Lips/Last Night	1961	3.00	6.00	12.00
❑ 31298	Walking the Streets/How Do You Talk to a Baby	1961	3.00	6.00	12.00
❑ 31347	Alla My Love/You Are My Life	1962	3.00	6.00	12.00
❑ 31380	Take Time/Crazy Wild Desire	1962	3.00	6.00	12.00
❑ 31421	Cow Town/Sooner or Later	1962	3.00	6.00	12.00

Number	Title (A Side/B Side)	Yr	VG	VG+	NM
❑ 31451	Sawmill/If I Could Come Back	1963	2.50	5.00	10.00
❑ 31488	Sands of Gold/Nobody's Darlin'	1963	2.50	5.00	10.00
❑ 31544	Those Wonderful Years/If the Back Door Could Talk	1963	2.50	5.00	10.00
❑ 31582	Waiting a Lifetime/Love Come to Me	1964	2.50	5.00	10.00
❑ 31617	Memory No. 1/French Riviera	1964	2.50	5.00	10.00
❑ 31704	That's Where My Money Goes/Broken Engagement	1964	2.50	5.00	10.00
❑ 31737	Loving You Then Losing You/Let Me Live a Little	1965	2.50	5.00	10.00
❑ 31816	Who Do I Think I Am/Hobo and the Rose	1965	2.50	5.00	10.00
❑ 31867	Christmas at Home/Sweet Memories	1965	3.00	6.00	12.00
❑ 31924	You Ain't No Better Than Me/The Champ	1966	2.50	5.00	10.00
❑ 31982	Love's Something (I Can't Understand)/A Loner	1966	2.50	5.00	10.00
❑ 32033	Where'd Ya Stay Last Night/She's Twenty-One	1966	2.50	5.00	10.00
❑ 32098	Goodbye City, Goodbye Girl/That Same Old Street	1967	2.00	4.00	8.00
❑ 32167	Fool Fool Fool/Bottles and Babies	1967	2.00	4.00	8.00
❑ 32246	Luzianna/Somebody Please Kiss My Sweet Thing	1967	2.00	4.00	8.00
❑ 32339	Stranger in a Strange, Strange City/In Another World	1968	2.00	4.00	8.00
❑ 32388	Saturday Night/I Tried Everything to Please	1968	2.00	4.00	8.00
❑ 32438	If I Had Last Night to Live Over/No Tears Tonight	1969	2.00	4.00	8.00
❑ 32508	This Thing/Does My Memory Ever Cross Your Mind	1969	2.00	4.00	8.00
❑ 32577	Love Ain't Never Gonna Be No Better/The Other Side of You	1969	2.00	4.00	8.00
❑ 32641	Merry-Go-Round World/Fools Night Out	1970	2.00	4.00	8.00
❑ 32694	The Man You Want Me to Be/Too Long	1970	2.00	4.00	8.00
❑ 32762	Showing His Dollar/The Way We Were Back Then	1970	2.00	4.00	8.00
❑ 32787	Tell Him That You Love Him/Heartaches Are for Lovers, Not for Friends	1971	2.00	4.00	8.00
❑ 32855	Someone Stepped In (And Stole Me Blind)/I Miss the Little Things	1971	2.00	4.00	8.00
❑ 32924	Hey Good Lookin'/Wonderful, Wonderful, Wonderful	1972	2.00	4.00	8.00
❑ 32973	I'm Gonna Be a Swinger/Someday	1972	2.00	4.00	8.00
❑ 33015	There Stands the Glass/Valentino of the Hobos	1972	2.00	4.00	8.00
❑ 33044	Let the Children Pick the Flowers/You're Letting Me Go	1973	2.00	4.00	8.00
❑ 7-34014 [S]	Hideaway Heart/(B-side unknown)	1962	3.75	7.50	15.00
—33 1/3 rpm jukebox single, small hole					
❑ 7-34015 [S]	Cow Town/(B-side unknown)	1962	3.75	7.50	15.00
—33 1/3 rpm jukebox single, small hole					
❑ 7-34016 [S]	First to Have a Second Chance/(B-side unknown)	1962	3.75	7.50	15.00
—33 1/3 rpm jukebox single, small hole					
❑ 7-34017 [S]	Tennessee Waltz/(B-side unknown)	1962	3.75	7.50	15.00
—33 1/3 rpm jukebox single, small hole					
❑ 7-34018 [S]	I'm Walking Behind You/(B-side unknown)	1962	3.75	7.50	15.00
—33 1/3 rpm jukebox single, small hole					
❑ 7-34135 [S]	I've Got a New Heartache/(B-side unknown)	1963	3.75	7.50	15.00
—33 1/3 rpm jukebox single, small hole					
❑ 7-34136 [S]	What Good Will It Do/(B-side unknown)	1963	3.75	7.50	15.00
—33 1/3 rpm jukebox single, small hole					
❑ 7-34137 [S]	Are You Sincere?/(B-side unknown)	1963	3.75	7.50	15.00
—33 1/3 rpm jukebox single, small hole					
❑ 7-34138 [S]	I Can't Stop Loving You/(B-side unknown)	1963	3.75	7.50	15.00
—33 1/3 rpm jukebox single, small hole					
❑ 7-34139 [S]	If I Lost Your Love/(B-side unknown)	1963	3.75	7.50	15.00
—33 1/3 rpm jukebox single, small hole					
❑ 9-46322	If Crying Would Make You Care/Drifting Texas Sand	1951	7.50	15.00	30.00
❑ 9-46332	California Blues/You Scared the Love Right Out of Me	1951	7.50	15.00	30.00
❑ 9-46364	Wondering/New Silver Bells	1951	6.25	12.50	25.00
❑ 9-46385	I'm Gonna See My Baby/You Know I'm Still in Love	1952	6.25	12.50	25.00
KING					
❑ 5366	New Panhandle Rag/It's All Between the Lines	1960	3.00	6.00	12.00
❑ 5429	Jilted Love/Georgia Rag	1960	3.00	6.00	12.00
MCA					
❑ 40128	Lo-Lenna/When You're Living in Hell	1973	—	3.00	6.00
❑ 40181	I'd Be Number One/You Better Treat Her Right	1974	—	3.00	6.00
❑ 40255	Honey (Open That Door)/Take the Time It Takes	1974	—	3.00	6.00
❑ 40310	I Know, I Know, I Know/I'm Ashamed to Be Here	1974	—	3.00	6.00
PLANTATION					
❑ 131	The Good Lord Giveth (And Uncle Sam Taketh Away)/Send My Love to Me	1975	—	3.00	6.00
❑ 136	I've Got Leaving on My Mind/Shame, Shame, Shame	1976	—	3.00	6.00
❑ 141	That's Me Without You/Appleton	1976	—	3.00	6.00
❑ 145	Christmas Time's a Coming/The Family Christmas Tree	1976	—	3.00	6.00
❑ 149	Got You on My Mind/Love Brought Us Together	1977	—	2.50	5.00
—With Carol Channing					
❑ 154	Rhinestone Cowboy Club/Sparkling Brown Eyes	1977	—	3.00	6.00

Selected 78s

Number	Title (A Side/B Side)	Yr	VG	VG+	NM
4 STAR					
❑ 1359	Heebie Jeebie Blues/Sweetheart I Love You So	1949	6.25	12.50	25.00
❑ 1413	English Sweetheart/High Geared Daddy	1950	5.00	10.00	20.00
❑ 1447	Groovie Boogie Woogie Boy/New Panhandle Rag	1950	5.00	10.00	20.00
❑ 1479	Georgia Rag/I Saw Your Face in the Moon	1950	5.00	10.00	20.00
❑ 1517	Hawaiian Echoes/I've Loved You Forever It Seems	1950	5.00	10.00	20.00

7-Inch Extended Plays

Number	Title (A Side/B Side)	Yr	VG	VG+	NM
DECCA					
❑ ED 2144	Wondering/There Stands the Glass//That's Me Without You/Don't Throw Your Life Away	195?	5.00	10.00	20.00
❑ ED 2144	The Wondering Boy, Part 1	195?	5.00	10.00	20.00
❑ ED 2145	Back Street Affair/It's Been So Long//Slowly/That Heart Belongs to Me	195?	5.00	10.00	20.00
❑ ED 2145	The Wondering Boy, Part 2	195?	5.00	10.00	20.00
❑ ED 2241	(contents unknown)	195?	5.00	10.00	20.00
❑ ED 2241 [PS]	Webb Pierce, Vol. 1	195?	5.00	10.00	20.00
❑ ED 2242	(contents unknown)	195?	5.00	10.00	20.00
❑ ED 2242 [PS]	Webb Pierce, Vol. 2	195?	5.00	10.00	20.00
❑ ED 2243	(contents unknown)	195?	5.00	10.00	20.00
❑ ED 2243 [PS]	Webb Pierce, Vol. 3	195?	5.00	10.00	20.00
❑ ED 2355	(contents unknown)	1956	5.00	10.00	20.00
❑ ED 2355 [PS]	The Country Church	1956	5.00	10.00	20.00
❑ ED 2364	(contents unknown)	1956	5.00	10.00	20.00
❑ ED 2364 [PS]	The Wondering Boy, Vol. 3	1956	5.00	10.00	20.00
❑ ED 2581	*New Love Affair/I Care No More/Just Imagination/I Love	1958	5.00	10.00	20.00
❑ ED 2581 [PS]	Just Imagination	1958	5.00	10.00	20.00
❑ ED 2653 [M]	*After the Boy Gets the Girl/I Owe It to Myself/My Shoes Keep Walking Back to You/Life to Go	1959	5.00	10.00	20.00
❑ ED 2653 [PS]	Webb	1959	5.00	10.00	20.00
❑ ED 7-2653 [PS]	Webb	1959	7.50	15.00	30.00
❑ ED 7-2653 [S]	*After the Boy Gets the Girl/I Owe It to Myself/My Shoes Keep Walking Back to You/Life to Go	1959	7.50	15.00	30.00
❑ ED 2668 [M]	*I Ain't Never/Shanghaied/A Thousand Miles Ago/What Goes On in Your Heart	1959	5.00	10.00	20.00
❑ ED 2668 [PS]	I Ain't Never	1959	5.00	10.00	20.00
❑ ED 7-2668 [PS]	I Ain't Never	1959	7.50	15.00	30.00
❑ ED 7-2668 [S]	*I Ain't Never/Shanghaied/A Thousand Miles Ago/What Goes On in Your Heart	1959	7.50	15.00	30.00
❑ ED 2685	*Walking the Streets/All I Need Is You/Drifting Texas Sand/Drinking My Blues Away	1960	6.25	12.50	25.00
❑ ED 2685 [PS]	Walking the Streets	1960	6.25	12.50	25.00
❑ ED 2694	*Is It Wrong/Lover's Leap/No Love Have I/Whirlpool of Love	1961	6.25	12.50	25.00
❑ ED 2694 [PS]	Is It Wrong	1961	6.25	12.50	25.00
❑ ED 2709	*Hideaway Heart/Tender Years/Pictures on the Wall/First to Have a Second Chance	1962	6.25	12.50	25.00
❑ ED 2709 [PS]	Hideaway Heart	1962	6.25	12.50	25.00
❑ ED 2719	(contents unknown)	1962	6.25	12.50	25.00
❑ ED 2719 [PS]	Webb Pierce	1962	6.25	12.50	25.00
❑ ED 2734	*Crazy Wild Desire/Take Time/I'm Falling in Love with You/There's More Pretty Girls Than One	1962	6.25	12.50	25.00
❑ ED 2734 [PS]	Crazy Wild Desire	1962	6.25	12.50	25.00
❑ ED 2748	(contents unknown)	1963	7.50	15.00	30.00
❑ ED 2748 [PS]	Fallen Angel	1963	7.50	15.00	30.00
❑ ED 2761	*Cow Town/If I Could Come Back/Sooner or Later/Sawmill	1964	7.50	15.00	30.00
❑ ED 2761 [PS]	Cow Town	1964	7.50	15.00	30.00
❑ ED 2785	(contents unknown)	1965	10.00	20.00	40.00
❑ ED 2785 [PS]	Nobody's Darling But Mine	1965	10.00	20.00	40.00
❑ ED 2786	(contents unknown)	1965	10.00	20.00	40.00
❑ ED 2786 [PS]	Softly and Tenderly	1965	10.00	20.00	40.00
❑ ED 2799	(contents unknown)	1966	10.00	20.00	40.00
❑ ED 2799 [PS]	Loving You Then Losing You	1966	10.00	20.00	40.00

Albums

Number	Title	Yr	VG	VG+	NM
DECCA					
❑ DXB 181 [(2) M]	The Webb Pierce Story	1964	7.50	15.00	30.00
—Deduct 25% if booklet is missing					
❑ DL 4015 [M]	Webb with a Beat	1960	7.50	15.00	30.00
❑ DL 4079 [M]	Walking the Streets	1960	7.50	15.00	30.00
❑ DL 4110 [M]	Golden Favorites	1961	7.50	15.00	30.00
❑ DL 4144 [M]	Fallen Angel	1961	7.50	15.00	30.00
❑ DL 4218 [M]	Hideaway Heart	1962	7.50	15.00	30.00
❑ DL 4294 [M]	Cross Country	1962	7.50	15.00	30.00
❑ DL 4358 [M]	I've Got a New Heartache	1963	6.25	12.50	25.00
❑ DL 4384 [M]	Bow Thy Head	1963	6.25	12.50	25.00
❑ DL 4486 [M]	Sands of Gold	1964	6.25	12.50	25.00
❑ DL 4604 [M]	Memory #1	1965	6.25	12.50	25.00
❑ DL 4659 [M]	Country Music Time	1965	6.25	12.50	25.00
❑ DL 4739 [M]	Sweet Memories	1966	6.25	12.50	25.00
❑ DL 4782 [M]	Webb's Choice	1966	6.25	12.50	25.00
❑ DL 4844 [M]	Where'd Ya Stay Last Night	1967	7.50	15.00	30.00
❑ DL 4964 [M]	Fool, Fool, Fool	1968	12.50	25.00	50.00
❑ DL 5536 [10]	That Wondering Boy	1954	30.00	60.00	120.00
❑ DXSB 7181 [(2) S]	The Webb Pierce Story	1964	10.00	20.00	40.00
—Deduct 25% if booklet is missing					
❑ DL 8129 [M]	Webb Pierce	1955	15.00	30.00	60.00
—Black label, silver print					
❑ DL 8129 [M]	Webb Pierce	196?	7.50	15.00	30.00
—Black label with color bar					
❑ DL 8295 [M]	That Wondering Boy	1956	15.00	30.00	60.00
—Black label, silver print					
❑ DL 8295 [M]	That Wondering Boy	196?	7.50	15.00	30.00
—Black label with color bar					
❑ DL 8728 [M]	Just Imagination	1957	12.50	25.00	50.00
—Black label, silver print					
❑ DL 8728 [M]	Just Imagination	196?	7.50	15.00	30.00
—Black label with color bar					
❑ DL 8889 [M]	Bound for the Kingdom	1959	10.00	20.00	40.00
—Black label, silver print					

Number	Title (A Side/B Side)	Yr	VG	VG+	NM
❑ DL 8889 [M]	Bound for the Kingdom	196?	6.25	12.50	25.00
—Black label with color bar					
❑ DL 8899 [M]	Webb!	1959	10.00	20.00	40.00
—Black label, silver print					
❑ DL 8899 [M]	Webb!	196?	6.25	12.50	25.00
—Black label with color bar					
❑ DL 74015 [S]	Webb with a Beat	1960	10.00	20.00	40.00
❑ DL 74079 [S]	Walking the Streets	1960	10.00	20.00	40.00
❑ DL 74110 [S]	Golden Favorites	1961	10.00	20.00	40.00
❑ DL 74144 [S]	Fallen Angel	1961	10.00	20.00	40.00
❑ DL 74218 [S]	Hideaway Heart	1962	10.00	20.00	40.00
❑ DL 74294 [S]	Cross Country	1962	10.00	20.00	40.00
❑ DL 74358 [S]	I've Got a New Heartache	1963	7.50	15.00	30.00
❑ DL 74384 [S]	Bow Thy Head	1963	7.50	15.00	30.00
❑ DL 74486 [S]	Sands of Gold	1964	7.50	15.00	30.00
❑ DL 74604 [S]	Memory #1	1965	7.50	15.00	30.00
❑ DL 74659 [S]	Country Music Time	1965	7.50	15.00	30.00
❑ DL 74739 [S]	Sweet Memories	1966	7.50	15.00	30.00
❑ DL 74782 [S]	Webb's Choice	1966	7.50	15.00	30.00
❑ DL 74844 [S]	Where'd Ya Stay Last Night	1967	6.25	12.50	25.00
❑ DL 74964 [S]	Fool, Fool, Fool	1968	6.25	12.50	25.00
❑ DL 74999	Webb Pierce's Greatest Hits	1968	6.25	12.50	25.00
❑ DL 75071	Saturday Night	1969	6.25	12.50	25.00
❑ DL 75132	Webb Pierce Sings This Thing	1969	6.25	12.50	25.00
❑ DL 75168	Love Ain't Never Gonna Be No Better	1970	6.25	12.50	25.00
❑ DL 75210	Merry-Go-Round World	1970	5.00	10.00	20.00
❑ DL 75280	The Webb Pierce Road Show	1971	5.00	10.00	20.00
❑ DL 75393	I'm Gonna Be a Swinger	1972	5.00	10.00	20.00
❑ DL 78889 [S]	Bound for the Kingdom	1959	12.50	25.00	50.00
—Black label, silver print					
❑ DL 78889 [S]	Bound for the Kingdom	196?	7.50	15.00	30.00
—Black label with color bar					
❑ DL 78899 [M]	Webb!	196?	7.50	15.00	30.00
—Black label with color bar					
❑ DL 78899 [S]	Webb!	1959	12.50	25.00	50.00
—Black label, silver print					
KING					
❑ 648 [M]	The One and Only Webb Pierce	1959	17.50	35.00	70.00
MCA					
❑ 130	Greatest Hits	1973	3.00	6.00	12.00
❑ 513	I'm Gonna Be a Swinger	197?	3.00	6.00	12.00
—Reissue of Decca 75393					
❑ 4087 [(2)]	The Best of Webb Pierce	1974	3.75	7.50	15.00
VOCALION					
❑ VL 73830	Country Songs	1968	3.00	6.00	12.00
❑ VL 73911	Country Favorites	1970	3.75	7.50	15.00

PIERCE, WEBB AND DEBBIE

Number	Title (A Side/B Side)	Yr	VG	VG+	NM
45s					
MCA					
❑ 40048	Foreign Girl/What the People Say	1973	—	3.00	6.00
PLANTATION					
❑ 189	On My Way Out/I'm Coming Home Again	1980	—	2.50	5.00
❑ 191	Reality of Life/My Memory Remembers	1980	—	2.50	5.00
❑ 196	Happy Birthday Jesus/(B-side unknown)	1980	—	3.00	6.00

PIERCE, WEBB, AND NANCY DEE

Number	Title (A Side/B Side)	Yr	VG	VG+	NM
45s					
DECCA					
❑ 32884	Above Suspicion/I Owe It to My Heart	1971	2.00	4.00	8.00

PIERCE, WEBB; MARVIN RAINWATER; STUART HAMBLEN

Number	Title (A Side/B Side)	Yr	VG	VG+	NM
Albums					
AUDIO LAB					
❑ AL-1563 [M]	Sing for You	1960	50.00	100.00	200.00

PILLOW, RAY

Also see JEAN SHEPARD.

Number	Title (A Side/B Side)	Yr	VG	VG+	NM
45s					
ABC					
❑ 11114	Wonderful Day/If Every Man Had a Woman Like You	1968	—	3.50	7.00
❑ 11180	Stop and Drink It Over/I Ran Out of Tomorrows Today	1969	—	3.50	7.00
ABC DOT					
❑ 17526	Livin' in the Sunshine of Your Love/The Party	1974	—	2.50	5.00
❑ 17543	I Slipped But Didn't Fall/The Simple Things in Life	1975	—	2.50	5.00
❑ 17560	Dog Tired of Cattin' Around/Rita Faye	1975	—	2.50	5.00
❑ 17589	Roll On, Truckers/We've Got to Love That Other Woman Out of Me	1975	—	2.50	5.00
❑ 17628	Love Is Comin' Over Me/She Never Likes Nothing for Long	1976	—	2.50	5.00
CAPITOL					
❑ 2030	Gone with the Wine/No Milk Today	1967	2.00	4.00	8.00
❑ 5180	Left Out/What's the World Coming To	1964	2.50	5.00	10.00
❑ 5323	Take Your Hands Off My Heart/Even the Bad Times Are Good	1964	2.00	4.00	8.00
❑ 5405	I'm Here to Make a Deal/Long Way Home	1965	2.00	4.00	8.00
❑ 5518	Thank You Ma'am/"If" Is a Mighty Big Word	1965	2.00	4.00	8.00
❑ 5597	Common Colds and Broken Hearts/You've Got a Good Thing Going	1966	2.00	4.00	8.00
❑ 5735	Volkswagen/And I Like That Sort of Thing	1966	2.00	4.00	8.00
❑ 5851	The First Chance I Get/Two Minus One Leaves Blue	1967	2.00	4.00	8.00
❑ 5953	I Just Want to Be Alone/I Like a Whole Lot	1967	2.00	4.00	8.00
FIRST GENERATION					
❑ 011	One Too Many Memories/Friday Night Blues	1981	—	3.00	6.00
HILLTOP					
❑ 130	Who's Gonna Tie My Shoes/Can I Have What's Left	1978	—	3.00	6.00
MCA					
❑ 40994	Heaven Help the Tempted Man/Hungry Man's Dream	1979	—	2.50	5.00
❑ 41047	Super Lady/Nighttime Masquerade	1979	—	2.50	5.00
MEGA					
❑ 0025	She Knows What Love Can Do/The Waitress	1971	—	3.00	6.00
❑ 0040	Rock It/Haven't You Heard	1971	—	3.00	6.00
❑ 0055	Since Then/While I'm Gone	1972	—	3.00	6.00
❑ 0072	She's Doing It to Me Again/Everytime	1972	—	3.00	6.00
❑ 0088	Excuse Me/I'm Doing What I Love, Loving You	1972	—	3.00	6.00
❑ 0095	Slipping Around/Too Much One Too Many Times	1972	—	3.00	6.00
❑ 1202	Countryfied/I'm Doing What I Love, Loving You	1973	—	3.00	6.00
PLANTATION					
❑ 25	Reconsider Me/The Doors of Love	1969	—	3.00	6.00
❑ 36	It Takes All Kinds of People/They Left Me Holding the Bottle	1969	—	3.00	6.00
❑ 49	Slice of Life/House of Glass	1970	—	3.00	6.00
Albums					
ABC					
❑ ABCS-665	Ray Pillow Sings	1968	3.75	7.50	15.00
ABC DOT					
❑ DOSD-2013	Countryfied	1975	3.00	6.00	12.00
CAPITOL					
❑ ST 2417 [S]	Presenting Ray Pillow	1965	5.00	10.00	20.00
❑ T 2417 [M]	Presenting Ray Pillow	1965	3.75	7.50	15.00
❑ ST 2738 [S]	Even When It's Bad, It's Good!	1967	3.75	7.50	15.00
❑ T 2738 [M]	Even When It's Bad, It's Good!	1967	5.00	10.00	20.00
HILLTOP					
❑ JS-6164	Wonderful Day	197?	3.00	6.00	12.00
MEGA					
❑ 1017	Slippin' Around with Ray Pillow	1972	3.75	7.50	15.00
PLANTATION					
❑ PLP-6	People Music	1970	3.75	7.50	15.00

PINETOPPERS, THE

Also see KENNY ROBERTS.

Number	Title (A Side/B Side)	Yr	VG	VG+	NM
45s					
CORAL					
❑ 9-60783	The Irish Polka/Twin Mazurka	1952	3.75	7.50	15.00
❑ 9-60811	Till the End of the World/Bell Bottom Polka	1952	3.75	7.50	15.00
❑ 9-60830	My Little Girl/Tennessee Warbler	1952	3.75	7.50	15.00
❑ 9-60922	The Stars and Stripes Forever/Washington Post March	1953	3.75	7.50	15.00
❑ 9-60949	Small World/Seven Lonely Days	1953	3.75	7.50	15.00
❑ 9-61032	Blue Canary/Mama What'll I Do	1953	3.75	7.50	15.00
—With the Marlin Sisters					
❑ 9-61074	As Long As I'm Dreaming/It's Written in the Stars	1953	3.75	7.50	15.00
—With the Marlin Sisters					
❑ 9-61151	American Patrol/National Emblem March	1954	3.75	7.50	15.00
❑ 9-61192	Pretty Rainbow/Boom Boom Polka	1954	3.75	7.50	15.00
—With the Marlin Sisters					
❑ 9-61245	Blossoms in the Springtime (Melody Version)/Blossoms in the Springtime (Harmony Version)	1954	3.75	7.50	15.00
—With the Marlin Sisters					
❑ 9-61311	Notre Dame Victory March/Boola-Boola	1954	3.75	7.50	15.00
❑ 9-64061	Mockin' Bird Hill/Big Parade Polka	1950	6.25	12.50	25.00
—Note: Earlier Coral 45s in the 64000 series by the Pinetoppers may exist					
❑ 9-64074	Metro Polka/Waltz of the Roses	1951	5.00	10.00	20.00
❑ 9-64085	Jolly Little Boxer/Maple Leaf Waltz	1951	5.00	10.00	20.00
❑ 9-64095	Cherry Beer Polka/All Alone 'Neath the Blue Grass	1951	5.00	10.00	20.00
❑ 9-64106	Jolly Old Saint Nicholas/Ting-a-Ling-a-Jingle	1951	5.00	10.00	20.00
—With the Marlin Sisters					
❑ 9-64114	The Woodpecker Polka/Jolly Cop Polka	1952	5.00	10.00	20.00
DECCA					
❑ 9-29458	Home in the Hills/Roly Polka	1955	3.00	6.00	12.00
—As "Vaughn Horton's Pinetoppers"					
❑ 9-29639	A Big Stack o' Barley/A Sailor Is Always True	1955	3.00	6.00	12.00
❑ 9-29824	Bye Bye My Baby/Forgetful	1956	3.00	6.00	12.00
Albums					
CORAL					
❑ CRL 56200 [10]	Square Dances	195?	10.00	20.00	40.00
❑ CRL 57048 [M]	The Pinetoppers	195?	7.50	15.00	30.00
DECCA					
❑ DL 8348 [M]	Saturday Night Barn Dance	1956	7.50	15.00	30.00

PINK, CELINDA

Number	Title (A Side/B Side)	Yr	VG	VG+	NM
45s					
STEP ONE					
❑ 458	Pack Your Lies and Go/I've Earned the Right to Sing the Blues	1993	—	2.00	4.00
❑ 465	Victimized/I've Earned the Right to Sing the Blues	1993	—	2.00	4.00

PINKARD AND BOWDEN

Number	Title (A Side/B Side)	Yr	VG	VG+	NM
45s					
WARNER BROS.					
❑ 22987	Libyan on a Jet Plane/Don't Pet the Dog	1989	—	2.00	4.00
❑ 27909	Arab, Alabama/Satellite Dish	1988	—	2.00	4.00
❑ 28611	She Thinks I Steal Cars/Imelda's Shoes	1986	—	2.00	4.00
❑ 28837	A Christmas Gift/Noel Bon Temps Roullee	1985	—	2.50	5.00

Number	Title (A Side/B Side)	Yr	VG	VG+	NM
❑ 28942	Crumbling Stumbleweeds/Guns Made America Great	1985	—	2.00	4.00
❑ 29000	Music Industry/The Ballad of Dick and Jane	1985	—	2.00	4.00
❑ 29205	Mama She's Lazy/Shake a Snake	1984	—	2.50	5.00
❑ 29268	I Lobster But Never Flounder/Mail Order Dog	1984	—	2.50	5.00
❑ 29370	Adventures in Parodies (Part 1)/(Part 2)	1984	—	2.50	5.00

Albums

WARNER BROS.

Number	Title	Yr	VG	VG+	NM
❑ 25057	Writers in Disguise	1984	2.00	4.00	8.00
❑ 25299	PG-13	1985	2.00	4.00	8.00

PIRATES OF THE MISSISSIPPI

45s

CAPITOL NASHVILLE

Number	Title	Yr	VG	VG+	NM
❑ NR-44775	Fighting for You/Talkin' 'Bout Love	1991	—	2.50	5.00
❑ 7PRO-79529	Feed Jake (same on both sides)	1991	—	3.50	7.00
—Vinyl originally was promo only					

GIANT

Number	Title	Yr	VG	VG+	NM
❑ 7-17915	Paradise/Rodeo Queen	1995	—	—	3.00

LIBERTY

Number	Title	Yr	VG	VG+	NM
❑ S7-57704	Til I'm Holding You Again/Feed Jake	1992	—	2.50	5.00
❑ S7-57767	Too Much/Speak of the Devil	1992	—	2.50	5.00
❑ S7-57995	A Street Man Named Desire/Mystery Ship	1992	—	2.00	4.00

PITNEY, GENE, AND GEORGE JONES

Also see GEORGE JONES. (As a solo artist, Gene Pitney never made the country charts.)

45s

MUSICOR

Number	Title	Yr	VG	VG+	NM
❑ 1066	I've Got Five Dollars and It's Saturday Night/ Wreck on the Highway	1965	3.00	6.00	12.00
❑ 1071	I've Got a New Heartache/My Shoes Keep Walking Back to You	1965	—	—	—
—Unreleased?					
❑ 1097	I'm a Fool to Care/Louisiana Man	1965	3.00	6.00	12.00
❑ 1097 [PS]	I'm a Fool to Care/Louisiana Man	1965	3.75	7.50	15.00
❑ 1115	Your Old Standby/Big Job	1965	3.00	6.00	12.00
❑ 1115 [PS]	Your Old Standby/Big Job	1965	3.75	7.50	15.00
❑ 1165	Y'All Come/That's All It Took	1966	2.50	5.00	10.00

Albums

MUSICOR

Number	Title	Yr	VG	VG+	NM
❑ MM-2044 [M]	For the First Time! Two Great Singers Together: George Jones and Gene Pitney	1965	6.25	12.50	25.00
❑ MM-2065 [M]	It's Country Time Again	1965	6.25	12.50	25.00
❑ MS-3044 [S]	For the First Time! Two Great Singers Together: George Jones and Gene Pitney	1965	7.50	15.00	30.00
❑ MS-3065 [S]	It's Country Time Again	1965	7.50	15.00	30.00

PITNEY, GENE, AND MELBA MONTGOMERY

Also see MELBA MONTGOMERY. (As a solo artist, Gene Pitney never made the country charts.)

45s

MUSICOR

Number	Title	Yr	VG	VG+	NM
❑ 1135	Baby, Ain't That Fine/Everybody Knows But You and Me	1965	3.00	6.00	12.00
❑ 1173	King and Queen/Being Together	1966	2.50	5.00	10.00

Albums

MUSICOR

Number	Title	Yr	VG	VG+	NM
❑ MM-2077 [M]	Being Together	1966	6.25	12.50	25.00
❑ MS-3077 [S]	Being Together	1966	7.50	15.00	30.00

PLACE, MARY KAY

Actress who played fictional country singer Loretta Haggers on the TV soap opera "Mary Hartman, Mary Hartman"; her portrayal was convincing enough that she had some real-life country hits!

45s

COLUMBIA

Number	Title	Yr	VG	VG+	NM
❑ 3-10422	Baby Boy/Streets of This Town (Ode to Fernwood)	1976	—	2.50	5.00
—Credited to "Mary Kay Place as Loretta Haggers"					
❑ 3-10510	Vitamin L/Coke and Chips	1977	—	2.50	5.00
—Credited to "Mary Kay Place as Loretta Haggers"					
❑ 3-10644	Something to Brag About/Anybody's Darling (Anything But Mine)	1977	—	2.50	5.00
—A-side with Willie Nelson					
❑ 3-10707	Don't Make Love (To a Country Music Singer)/ Marlboro Man	1978	—	2.50	5.00

Albums

COLUMBIA

Number	Title	Yr	VG	VG+	NM
❑ KC 34353	Tonite! At the Capri Lounge Loretta Haggers	1976	2.50	5.00	10.00
❑ PC 34908	Aimin' to Please	1977	2.50	5.00	10.00

PLAINSMEN, THE

45s

HICKORY

Number	Title	Yr	VG	VG+	NM
❑ 1668	Joplin-Dallas Turn Around/I'm Gonna Walk and Talk with My Lord	1973	2.00	4.00	8.00

PLOWMAN, LINDA

45s

COLUMBIA

Number	Title	Yr	VG	VG+	NM
❑ 4-45689	If You Step Over the Line/Gonna Find Me a Bluebird	1972	—	3.00	6.00
❑ 4-45817	My Daddy Plays the Guitar/Half a Dozen Tricycle Motors	1973	—	3.00	6.00
❑ 4-45905	Nobody But You/You're the Best Thing That Ever Happened to Me	1973	—	3.00	6.00

JANUS

Number	Title (A Side/B Side)	Yr	VG	VG+	NM
❑ 146	I'm So Lonesome I Could Cry/I Would	1970	—	3.50	7.00
❑ 165	Clinging to a Saving Hand/You've Still Got a Place	1971	—	3.50	7.00

PO' BOYS, THE

Backing group for BILL ANDERSON.

45s

DECCA

Number	Title	Yr	VG	VG+	NM
❑ 31915	Dear Heart/Orange Blossom Special	1966	2.00	4.00	8.00
❑ 32170	Faded Love/Sunny-Gem	1967	2.00	4.00	8.00
❑ 32281	White Rabbit/Up & Atom	1968	2.00	4.00	8.00
❑ 32821	Louisiana Man/Sidewalkin'	1971	2.00	4.00	8.00
❑ 32944	Sunnyside Up/Guitar Boy	1972	2.00	4.00	8.00

MCA

Number	Title	Yr	VG	VG+	NM
❑ 40117	Pass Me By/Fire Ball Mail	1973	—	3.00	6.00

Albums

DECCA

Number	Title	Yr	VG	VG+	NM
❑ DL 4725 [M]	Bill Anderson Presents the Po' Boys	1966	5.00	10.00	20.00
❑ DL 4884 [M]	The Po' Boys Pick Again	1967	6.25	12.50	25.00
❑ DL 74725 [S]	Bill Anderson Presents the Po' Boys	1966	6.25	12.50	25.00
❑ DL 74884 [S]	The Po' Boys Pick Again	1967	5.00	10.00	20.00

MCA

Number	Title	Yr	VG	VG+	NM
❑ 337	The Rich Sounds of Bill Anderson's Po' Boys	1973	3.75	7.50	15.00

POCO

Pioneering country-rock group that had only two low-charting hits on the country charts. Members of this group later joined EAGLES and BLACK TIE.

12-Inch Singles

MCA

Number	Title	Yr	VG	VG+	NM
❑ 2314 [DJ]	Under the Gun (same on both sides)	1980	2.00	4.00	8.00

RCA

Number	Title	Yr	VG	VG+	NM
❑ 9039-1-RAB [DJ]	Call It Love (Edit)/Call It Love (LP)	1989	—	3.00	6.00

45s

ABC

Number	Title	Yr	VG	VG+	NM
❑ 12126	Keep On Tryin'/Georgia, Bind My Ties	1975	—	2.50	5.00
❑ 12159	Makin' Love/Flyin' Solo	1976	—	2.50	5.00
❑ 12204	Rose of Cimarron/Tulsa Turnaround	1976	—	2.50	5.00
❑ 12295	Indian Summer/Me and You	1977	—	2.50	5.00
❑ 12439	Crazy Love/Barbados	1978	—	2.50	5.00

ATLANTIC

Number	Title	Yr	VG	VG+	NM
❑ 89629 [DJ]	Save a Corner of Your Heart (same on both sides)	1984	—	—	3.00
—May be promo only					
❑ 89650	This Old Flame/The Storm	1984	—	—	3.00
❑ 89674	Days Gone By/Daylight	1984	—	—	3.00
❑ 89851 [DJ]	Break of Hearts (same on both sides)	1983	—	—	3.00
—May be promo only					
❑ 89919	Shoot for the Moon/The Midnight Rodeo	1982	—	—	3.00
❑ 89970	Ghostown/High Sierra	1982	—	—	3.00
❑ 89970 [PS]	Ghostown/High Sierra	1982	—	2.00	4.00

EPIC

Number	Title	Yr	VG	VG+	NM
❑ 10501	Pickin' Up the Pieces/First Love	1969	2.50	5.00	10.00
❑ 10543	My Kind of Love/Hard Luck	1969	2.50	5.00	10.00
❑ 10636	You Better Think Twice/Anyway, Bye Bye	1970	2.00	4.00	8.00
❑ 10714	C'Mon/I Guess You Made It	1971	2.00	4.00	8.00
❑ 10804	Just for Me and You/Ol' Forgiver	1971	2.00	4.00	8.00
❑ 10816	You Are the One/Railroad Days	1971	2.00	4.00	8.00
❑ 10890	Good Feeling to Know/Early Times	1972	—	3.00	6.00
❑ 10958	I Can See Everything/Go and Say Goodbye	1973	—	3.00	6.00
❑ 11055	Here We Go Again/Fools Gold	1973	—	3.00	6.00
❑ 11092	Magnolia/Blue Water	1974	—	3.00	6.00
❑ 11141	Rocky Mountain Breakdown/Faith in the Families	1974	—	3.00	6.00
❑ 50076	Bitter Blue/High and Dry	1975	—	3.00	6.00

MCA

Number	Title	Yr	VG	VG+	NM
❑ 41023	Heart of the Night/Last Goodbye	1979	—	2.00	4.00
❑ 41103	Legend/Indian Summer	1979	—	2.00	4.00
❑ 41269	Under the Gun/Reputation	1980	—	2.00	4.00
❑ 41269 [PS]	Under the Gun/Reputation	1980	—	3.00	6.00
❑ 41326	Midnight Rain/Fool's Paradise	1980	—	2.00	4.00
❑ 51034	Everlasting Kind/Friends in the Distance	1980	—	2.00	4.00
❑ 51172	Down on the River Again/Widowmaker	1981	—	2.00	4.00
❑ 52001	Seas of Heartbreals/Feudin'	1982	—	2.00	4.00

RCA

Number	Title	Yr	VG	VG+	NM
❑ 9038-7-R	Call It Love/Lovin' You Every Minute	1989	—	—	3.00
❑ 9038-7-R [PS]	Call It Love/Lovin' You Every Minute	1989	—	—	3.00
❑ 9131-7-R	Nothin' to Hide/If It Wasn't for You	1989	—	—	3.00
❑ 9131-7-R [PS]	Nothin' to Hide/If It Wasn't for You	1989	—	—	3.00

Albums

ABC

Number	Title	Yr	VG	VG+	NM
❑ D-890	Head Over Heels	1975	2.50	5.00	10.00
❑ D-946	Rose of Cimarron	1976	2.50	5.00	10.00
❑ D-989	Indian Summer	1977	2.50	5.00	10.00
❑ AA-1099	Legend	1978	3.00	6.00	12.00

ATLANTIC

Number	Title	Yr	VG	VG+	NM
❑ 80008	Ghost Town	1982	2.50	5.00	10.00
❑ 80148	Inamorata	1984	2.50	5.00	10.00

EPIC

Number	Title	Yr	VG	VG+	NM
❑ BN 26460	Pickin' Up the Pieces	1969	3.75	7.50	15.00
—Yellow label					
❑ BN 26460	Pickin' Up the Pieces	1973	2.50	5.00	10.00
—Orange label					
❑ BN 26522	Poco	1970	3.75	7.50	15.00
—Yellow label					

Number	Title (A Side/B Side)	Yr	VG	VG+	NM
❑ BN 26522	Poco	1973	2.50	5.00	10.00
—Orange label					
❑ EQ 30209 [Q]	Deliverin'	1972	5.00	10.00	20.00
❑ KE 30209	Deliverin'	1971	3.75	7.50	15.00
—Yellow label					
❑ KE 30209	Deliverin'	1973	2.50	5.00	10.00
—Orange label					
❑ E 30753	From the Inside	1973	2.50	5.00	10.00
—Reissue with new prefix					
❑ KE 30753	From the Inside	1971	3.75	7.50	15.00
—Yellow label					
❑ KE 30753	From the Inside	1973	2.50	5.00	10.00
—Orange label					
❑ KE 31601	A Good Feelin' to Know	1972	3.75	7.50	15.00
—Yellow label					
❑ KE 31601	A Good Feelin' to Know	1973	2.50	5.00	10.00
—Orange label					
❑ PE 31601	A Good Feelin' to Know	198?	2.00	4.00	8.00
—Budget-line reissue					
❑ EQ 32354 [Q]	Crazy Eyes	1973	5.00	10.00	20.00
❑ KE 32354	Crazy Eyes	1973	3.00	6.00	12.00
—Orange label					
❑ PE 32354	Crazy Eyes	1979	2.00	4.00	8.00
—Blue label					
❑ EQ 32895 [Q]	Seven	1974	5.00	10.00	20.00
❑ KE 32895	Seven	1974	3.00	6.00	12.00
—Orange label					
❑ PCQ 33192 [Q]	Cantamos	1974	5.00	10.00	20.00
❑ PE 33192	Cantamos	1974	3.00	6.00	12.00
—Orange label					
❑ PE 33336	Live	1976	3.00	6.00	12.00
—Orange label					
❑ PEG 33537 [(2)]	The Very Best of Poco	1975	3.75	7.50	15.00
—Orange labels					
❑ JE 36210	The Songs of Paul Cotton	1980	2.50	5.00	10.00
❑ JE 36211	The Songs of Richie Furay	1980	2.50	5.00	10.00

MCA

Number	Title (A Side/B Side)	Yr	VG	VG+	NM
❑ AA-1099	Legend	1979	2.50	5.00	10.00
—Reissue of ABC 1099					
❑ 5132	Under the Gun	1980	2.50	5.00	10.00
❑ 5227	Blue and Gray	1981	2.50	5.00	10.00
❑ 5288	Cowboys & Englishmen	1982	2.50	5.00	10.00
❑ 5363	Backtracks	1983	2.50	5.00	10.00
❑ 37009	Head Over Heels	1980	2.00	4.00	8.00
—Budget-line reissue					
❑ 37010	Rose of Cimarron	1980	2.00	4.00	8.00
—Budget-line reissue					
❑ 37011	Indian Summer	1980	2.00	4.00	8.00
—Budget-line reissue					
❑ 37117	Legend	1981	2.00	4.00	8.00
—Budget-line reissue					
❑ 37160	Under the Gun	198?	2.00	4.00	8.00
—Budget-line reissue					

MOBILE FIDELITY

Number	Title (A Side/B Side)	Yr	VG	VG+	NM
❑ 1-020	Legend	1979	5.00	10.00	20.00
—Audiophile vinyl					

RCA

Number	Title (A Side/B Side)	Yr	VG	VG+	NM
❑ 9694-1-R	Legacy	1989	2.50	5.00	10.00

POINTER SISTERS, THE

The black vocal group had one record make the country charts. Also see EARL THOMAS CONLEY.

45s

BLUE THUMB

Number	Title (A Side/B Side)	Yr	VG	VG+	NM
❑ 254	Fairytale/Love In Them Thar Hills	1974	2.50	5.00	10.00
—First pressing has a gray to white label and no reference to ABC					
❑ 254	Fairytale/Love In Them Thar Hills	1974	—	2.50	5.00
—Second pressing has a multicolor label with ABC logo					

POLLARD, CHUCK

45s

MCA

Number	Title (A Side/B Side)	Yr	VG	VG+	NM
❑ 40944	You Should Win an Oscar Every Night/Wet, Wild and Warm	1978	—	2.00	4.00
❑ 40965	The Other Side of Jeannie/Wet, Wild and Warm	1978	—	2.00	4.00

POMSL, PAT

45s

ASI

Number	Title (A Side/B Side)	Yr	VG	VG+	NM
❑ 1017	Let My Fingers Do the Walking/(B-side unknown)	1979	—	3.50	7.00

POOLE, CHERYL

45s

PAULA

Number	Title (A Side/B Side)	Yr	VG	VG+	NM
❑ 251	Every Chance You Get/Throwing In the Crying Towel	1966	2.00	4.00	8.00
❑ 263	Heart Trouble/His Wife	1967	2.00	4.00	8.00
❑ 277	Second Hand Girl/There's Got to Be a Woman Too	1967	2.00	4.00	8.00
❑ 297	Swingin' Blue/Ruby's Stool	1968	2.00	4.00	8.00
❑ 309	Three Playing Love/I'm Not Your Woman (You're Not My Man)	1968	2.00	4.00	8.00
❑ 1205	How About Your Love for Christmas/It's Christmas Every Day of the Year	1968	2.00	4.00	8.00
❑ 1207	The Skin's Gettin' Closer to the Bone/You Ain't No Friend of Mine	1969	—	3.50	7.00
❑ 1214	Walk Among the People/(I'll Always Be) Daddy's Little Girl	1969	—	3.50	7.00
❑ 1219	Everybody's Gotta Hurt/You Haven't Read the Book	1970	—	3.50	7.00
❑ 1232	Kansas City/With You	1970	—	3.50	7.00
❑ 1237	I'm So Lonesome I Could Cry/Dirty Little Four Letter Word	1971	—	3.50	7.00

PORTER, BOB

45s

LITTLE DARLIN'

Number	Title (A Side/B Side)	Yr	VG	VG+	NM
❑ 0070	There's No Easy Way to Die/I Think I'll Wait Awhile	1970	2.00	4.00	8.00

PORTER, ROCKY

45s

COLUMBIA

Number	Title (A Side/B Side)	Yr	VG	VG+	NM
❑ 4-20903	I've Fallen in Love with an Angel/Keep On Keeping On	1952	6.25	12.50	25.00
❑ 4-20980	Suppose/I'm in Love with No One	1952	6.25	12.50	25.00
❑ 4-21028	Please Say a Prayer/All Seeing Eye	1952	6.25	12.50	25.00
❑ 4-21264	The World Is a Monster/I Talked to the Man in the Moon	1954	6.25	12.50	25.00
❑ 4-21325	I Knew It All Along/Don't Forget to Remember	1954	6.25	12.50	25.00

POSEY, SANDY

45s

AUDIOGRAPH

Number	Title (A Side/B Side)	Yr	VG	VG+	NM
❑ 449	Can't Get Used to Sleeping Without You/(B-side unknown)	1983	—	2.00	4.00

COLUMBIA

Number	Title (A Side/B Side)	Yr	VG	VG+	NM
❑ 45360	Losing Out on You/You Say Beautiful Things to Me	1971	—	2.50	5.00
❑ 45458	Bring Him Safely Home To Me/A Man in Need of Love	1971	—	2.50	5.00
❑ 45596	Why Don't We Go Somewhere and Love/Together	1972	—	2.50	5.00
❑ 45703	Happy Happy Birthday Baby/Thank the Lord for New York City	1972	—	2.50	5.00
❑ 45828	Don't/Thank the Lord for New York City	1973	—	2.50	5.00
❑ 45828	Don't/Thank the Lord for New York City	1973	—	2.50	5.00

MGM

Number	Title (A Side/B Side)	Yr	VG	VG+	NM
❑ 13501	Born a Woman/Caution to the Wind	1967	2.00	4.00	8.00
❑ 13612	Single Girl/Blue Is My Best Color	1966	2.00	4.00	8.00
❑ 13612 [PS]	Single Girl/Blue Is My Best Color	1966	3.00	6.00	12.00
❑ 13702	What a Woman in Love Won't Do/Shattered	1967	2.00	4.00	8.00
❑ 13744	I Take It Back/The Boy I Love	1967	2.00	4.00	8.00
❑ 13744 [PS]	I Take It Back/The Boy I Love	1967	3.00	6.00	12.00
❑ 13824	Are You Never Coming Home/I Can Show You How to Live	1967	2.00	4.00	8.00
❑ 13892	Silly Girl, Silly Boy/Something I'll Remember	1968	—	3.00	6.00
❑ 13967	Ways of the World/Wonderful World of Summer	1968	—	3.00	6.00
❑ 14006	All Hung Up in Your Green Eyes/Your Conception of Love	1968	—	3.00	6.00

MONUMENT

Number	Title (A Side/B Side)	Yr	VG	VG+	NM
❑ 8698	Trying to Live Without You Kind of Days/Why Do We Carry On	1976	—	2.50	5.00

WARNER BROS.

Number	Title (A Side/B Side)	Yr	VG	VG+	NM
❑ 8289	It's Midnight (Do You Know Where Your Baby Is)/Long Distance Kissing	1976	—	2.00	4.00
❑ 8540	Born to Be with You/It's Not Too Late	1978	—	2.00	4.00
❑ 8610	Love, Love, Love-Chapel of Love/I Believe in Love	1978	—	2.00	4.00
❑ 8731	Love Is Sometimes Easy/I Believe in Love	1979	—	2.00	4.00
❑ 8852	Try Home/Love Is Sometimes Easy	1979	—	2.00	4.00
❑ 49104	Black Is the Night/Best Things in My Life	1979	—	2.00	4.00

Albums

COLUMBIA

Number	Title (A Side/B Side)	Yr	VG	VG+	NM
❑ KC 31594	Why Don't We Go Somewhere and Love	1972	3.00	6.00	12.00

MGM

Number	Title (A Side/B Side)	Yr	VG	VG+	NM
❑ GAS-125	Sandy Posey (Golden Archive Series)	1970	3.75	7.50	15.00
❑ E-4418 [M]	Born a Woman	1966	3.75	7.50	15.00
❑ SE-4418 [S]	Born a Woman	1966	5.00	10.00	20.00
❑ E-4455 [M]	Single Girl	1967	5.00	10.00	20.00
❑ SE-4455 [S]	Single Girl	1967	5.00	10.00	20.00
❑ E-4480 [M]	I Take It Back	1967	5.00	10.00	20.00
❑ SE-4480 [S]	I Take It Back	1967	5.00	10.00	20.00
❑ E-4509 [M]	The Best of Sandy Posey	1967	6.25	12.50	25.00
❑ SE-4509 [S]	The Best of Sandy Posey	1967	5.00	10.00	20.00
❑ E-4525 [M]	Looking at You	1968	6.25	12.50	25.00
❑ SE-4525 [S]	Looking at You	1968	3.75	7.50	15.00
❑ ST-91110	Single Girl	1967	6.25	12.50	25.00
—Capitol Record Club issue					

POSEY, SANDY/ SKEETER DAVIS

Albums

GUSTO

Number	Title (A Side/B Side)	Yr	VG	VG+	NM
❑ 0005	The Best of Sandy Posey/Skeeter Davis	198?	2.00	4.00	8.00

POSSUM, POLLY

45s

COLUMBIA

Number	Title (A Side/B Side)	Yr	VG	VG+	NM
❑ 4-20908	Sad Singin', Slow Ridin'/Don't Cry	1952	6.25	12.50	25.00
❑ 4-20947	Lord Oh Lord/Hurry	1952	6.25	12.50	25.00

Number	Title (A Side/B Side)	Yr	VG	VG+	NM
❑ 4-21048	Just Five Years/Save the Pieces	1952	6.25	12.50	25.00
❑ 4-21090	Sin Is Satin/Don't Talk to Me About Man	1953	6.25	12.50	25.00
❑ 4-21140	Castanets/Between You and the Birds	1953	5.00	10.00	20.00
❑ 4-21196	Bimbo/I'm a Stranger in My Home	1954	5.00	10.00	20.00
❑ 4-21238	Takes All Kinds of People/Something Happened to You	1954	5.00	10.00	20.00

POTTER, CURTIS

45s

DOT

Number	Title (A Side/B Side)	Yr	VG	VG+	NM
❑ 17153	Drowning Man/Dumb Dumb	1968	2.50	5.00	10.00
❑ 17247	You Comb Her Hair/You've Gone Too Far	1969	2.00	4.00	8.00
❑ 17302	Handful/Heartaches Can Be Fun	1969	2.00	4.00	8.00
❑ 17348	It's My Day/My First Stop Is Omaha	1970	2.00	4.00	8.00
❑ 17374	Devil River/Old Lovers Make Bad Friends	1971	—	3.50	7.00
❑ 17392	Change Me/One Minus Everything	1971	—	3.50	7.00

FOX

Number	Title (A Side/B Side)	Yr	VG	VG+	NM
❑ 409	I'm a Real Glad Daddy/(B-side unknown)	1958	62.50	125.00	250.00

HILLSIDE

Number	Title (A Side/B Side)	Yr	VG	VG+	NM
❑ 7903	Fraulein (The Texas National Anthem)/The Story Behind the Photograph	1979	—	3.00	6.00
❑ 7905	Part-Time Lover, Full-Time Heartache/Soft Rain	1979	—	3.00	6.00
❑ 8001	San Antonio Medley/Thank God for Country Music	1980	—	3.00	6.00
—With Darrell McCall					
❑ 8003	It's the Cheatin' She Loves/Undo the Right	1980	—	3.00	6.00
❑ 8101	Texas Proud/When My Baby Double Talks to Me	1981	—	3.00	6.00
❑ 8104	She Wears Faded Jeans/You Left a Long, Long Time Ago	1981	—	3.00	6.00

RCA VICTOR

Number	Title (A Side/B Side)	Yr	VG	VG+	NM
❑ APBO-0247	All I Need Is Time/You Can Always Come to Me	1974	—	3.00	6.00
❑ PB-10016	If She Keeps Loving Me/The Farther I Go with You	1974	—	3.00	6.00
❑ PB-10087	Too Much Woman/Am I What's the Matter with You	1974	—	3.00	6.00
❑ PB-10195	Close Every Door Behind You/I Can't Keep My Mind Off of You	1975	—	3.00	6.00

STEP ONE

Number	Title (A Side/B Side)	Yr	VG	VG+	NM
❑ 333	How Come I Didn't Cry/I'm Not Supposed to Care	198?	—	2.50	5.00
❑ 335	Time to Turn the Page/Holding On to Holding On	198?	—	2.50	5.00
❑ 338	I Used to Turn You On/Twin Fiddles Turn Me On	198?	—	2.50	5.00
❑ 348	I Wish It Was That Easy/If This Was Texas	1985	—	2.50	5.00
❑ 354	You Comb Her Hair/I Never Thought I Could	1986	—	2.50	5.00
❑ 367	Chicago Dancin' Girls/Then I Can Face Your Memory	1986	—	2.50	5.00
❑ 372	Close Your Eyes/All I Need Is Time	1987	—	2.50	5.00
❑ 376	All I Need Is Time/Am I Blue	1987	—	2.50	5.00

WINSTON

Number	Title (A Side/B Side)	Yr	VG	VG+	NM
❑ 1030	You're Not an Angel/Baby Love	1959	6.25	12.50	25.00
❑ 1042	Can I Be Sure/Who Do You Miss	1959	5.00	10.00	20.00

ZODIAC

Number	Title (A Side/B Side)	Yr	VG	VG+	NM
❑ 1009	Far Away Feeling/Let Me Love in Peace	1976	—	3.00	6.00

Albums

DOT

Number	Title (A Side/B Side)	Yr	VG	VG+	NM
❑ DLP-25988	Here Comes Curtis Potter	1971	5.00	10.00	20.00

STEP ONE

Number	Title (A Side/B Side)	Yr	VG	VG+	NM
❑ 0004	Down in Texas Today	1984	5.00	10.00	20.00
❑ 0020	All I Need Is Time	1987	5.00	10.00	20.00

POWELL, PATTI

45s

HICKORY

Number	Title (A Side/B Side)	Yr	VG	VG+	NM
❑ 1602	Long Haul Widow/To See the Kids Again	1971	2.00	4.00	8.00
❑ 1616	The Best Way to Hold a Man/Your Boots Are By the Door	1971	2.00	4.00	8.00
❑ 1642	Not Once But a Hundred Times/Please Let Him Wake Up Loving Me	1972	2.00	4.00	8.00
❑ 1659	High on Jesus/Satisfied	1973	2.00	4.00	8.00

METROMEDIA COUNTRY

Number	Title (A Side/B Side)	Yr	VG	VG+	NM
❑ BMBO-0037	Love by Appointment/If You Could Do Any Better (You'd Done Been Gone)	1973	—	3.50	7.00
—With Bob Gallion					

POWELL, SUE

45s

RCA

Number	Title (A Side/B Side)	Yr	VG	VG+	NM
❑ PB-12227	Midnite Flyer/You Keep Coming Back to Me	1981	—	2.00	4.00
❑ PB-12287	(There's No Me) Without You/Delta Queen	1981	—	2.00	4.00
❑ PB-13250	Gonna Love You (Till the Cows Come Home)/In His Eyes	1982	—	2.00	4.00

POZO-SECO SINGERS, THE

DON WILLIAMS was in this group.

45s

CERTRON

Number	Title (A Side/B Side)	Yr	VG	VG+	NM
❑ 10006	Apartment #9/Comin' Apart	1970	—	2.50	5.00
❑ 10020	Strawberry Fields & Something/There's Never Been a Time	1970	—	2.50	5.00
❑ 10033	Bringing It Down to Me/He's a Friend of Mine	1971	—	2.50	5.00

COLUMBIA

Number	Title (A Side/B Side)	Yr	VG	VG+	NM
❑ 43437	Time/Down the Road I Go	1965	2.00	4.00	8.00
❑ 43646	I'll Be Gone/It Ain't Worth the Lonely Road Back	1966	2.00	4.00	8.00
❑ 43784	I Can Make It With You/Come a Little Bit Closer	1966	2.00	4.00	8.00
❑ 43927	Look What You've Done/Almost Persuaded	1966	2.00	4.00	8.00
❑ 44041	I Believed It All/Excuse Me Dear Martha	1967	2.00	4.00	8.00
❑ 44168	It's All Right/Morning Dew	1967	2.00	4.00	8.00
❑ 44263	Louisiana Man/Tomorrow Proper	1967	2.00	4.00	8.00
❑ 44598	Gotta Come Up with Something/The Renegade	1968	—	3.00	6.00
❑ 44690	Good Morning Today/Remember Suzie	1968	—	3.00	6.00
❑ 44841	Leavin'/Creole Woman	1969	—	3.00	6.00
❑ 44979	Woman in Love/God Save the Children	1969	—	3.00	6.00
—As "Susan Taylor and Pozo Seco"					
❑ 44980	Morning Mama Memories/The Proper Mrs. Brown	1969	2.50	5.00	10.00
—As "Don Williams and Pozo Seco"; his first "solo" credit					
❑ 45065	High on Life/Till You Hear Your Mama Call	1970	—	3.00	6.00

EDMARK

Number	Title (A Side/B Side)	Yr	VG	VG+	NM
❑ 10017	Time/Down the Road I Go	1965	5.00	10.00	20.00

Albums

CERTRON

Number	Title (A Side/B Side)	Yr	VG	VG+	NM
❑ CS-7007	Spend Some Time with Me	1970	3.75	7.50	15.00

COLUMBIA

Number	Title (A Side/B Side)	Yr	VG	VG+	NM
❑ CL 2515 [M]	Time/I'll Be Gone	1966	3.75	7.50	15.00
❑ CL 2600 [M]	I Can Make It with You	1967	5.00	10.00	20.00
❑ CS 9315 [S]	Time/I'll Be Gone	1966	5.00	10.00	20.00
❑ CS 9400 [S]	I Can Make It with You	1967	3.75	7.50	15.00
❑ CS 9656	Shades of Time	1968	3.75	7.50	15.00

POWER PAK

Number	Title (A Side/B Side)	Yr	VG	VG+	NM
❑ 285	The Pozo-Seco Singers with Don Williams	198?	2.50	5.00	10.00

PRADO, PEREZ

"The King of the Mambo" actually had the below single make the Top 20 of the Billboard country chart in 1958.

45s

RCA VICTOR

Number	Title (A Side/B Side)	Yr	VG	VG+	NM
❑ 47-7245	Patricia/Why Wait	1958	2.50	5.00	10.00

PRAIRIE OYSTER

45s

RCA

Number	Title (A Side/B Side)	Yr	VG	VG+	NM
❑ 2510-7-R	I Don't Hurt Anymore/But You Said	1990	—	2.00	4.00
❑ 2569-7-R	If I Could Take My Own Advice/Goodbye, So Long, Hello	1990	—	2.00	4.00
❑ 9124-7-R	Goodbye, So Long, Hello/Different Kind of Fire	1990	—	2.00	4.00
❑ 62108	One Precious Love/Goodbye Lonesome (Hello Baby Doll)	1991	—	—	3.00
❑ 62218	Will I Do (Till the Real Thing Comes Along)/Am I That Easy to Forget	1992	—	—	3.00

PRESLEY, ELVIS

Before he was "The King of Rock 'n' Roll," Elvis was "The Hillbilly Cat," a star of the Louisiana Hayride and a charted country act when he was still on the Sun label. Later, from 1968-77 and beyond, he was rediscovered by country audiences and generally was bigger on the country charts than on the pop charts. In fact, he had two Number One country hits in 1977, including the week of his death, and a posthumous chart-topper in 1981. We have chosen to include his entire discography in this book.

12-Inch Singles

RCA

Number	Title (A Side/B Side)	Yr	VG	VG+	NM
❑ EP-0517 [DJ]	Little Sister/Rip It Up	1983	25.00	50.00	100.00

45s

COLLECTABLES

Number	Title (A Side/B Side)	Yr	VG	VG+	NM
❑ COL-4500	Good Rockin' Tonight/I Don't Care If the Sun Don't Shine	1986	—	—	3.00
—Black vinyl					
❑ COL-4500	Good Rockin' Tonight/I Don't Care If the Sun Don't Shine	1992	—	2.00	4.00
—Gold vinyl					
❑ COL-4501	You're a Heartbreaker/Milkcow Blues Boogie	1986	—	—	3.00
—Black vinyl					
❑ COL-4501	You're a Heartbreaker/Milkcow Blues Boogie	1992	—	2.00	4.00
—Gold vinyl					
❑ COL-4502	Baby Let's Play House/I'm Left, You're Right, She's Gone	1986	—	—	3.00
—Black vinyl					
❑ COL-4502	Baby Let's Play House/I'm Left, You're Right, She's Gone	1992	—	2.00	4.00
—Gold vinyl					
❑ COL-4503	I Got a Woman/I'm Counting on You	1986	—	—	3.00
—Black vinyl					
❑ COL-4503	I Got a Woman/I'm Counting on You	1992	—	2.00	4.00
—Gold vinyl					
❑ COL-4504	I'll Never Let You Go (Little Darlin')/I'm Gonna Sit Right Down and Cry (Over You)	1986	—	—	3.00
—Black vinyl					
❑ COL-4504	I'll Never Let You Go (Little Darlin')/I'm Gonna Sit Right Down and Cry (Over You)	1992	—	2.00	4.00
—Gold vinyl					
❑ COL-4505	Tryin' to Get to You/I Love You Because	1986	—	—	3.00
—Black vinyl					
❑ COL-4505	Tryin' to Get to You/I Love You Because	1992	—	2.00	4.00
—Gold vinyl					
❑ COL-4506	Money Honey/One-Sided Love Affair	1986	—	—	3.00
—Black vinyl					
❑ COL-4506	Money Honey/One-Sided Love Affair	1992	—	2.00	4.00
—Gold vinyl					
❑ COL-4507	Too Much/Playing for Keeps	1986	—	—	3.00
—Black vinyl					
❑ COL-4507	Too Much/Playing for Keeps	1992	—	2.00	4.00
—Gold vinyl					
❑ COL-4508	A Big Hunk o'Love/My Wish Came True	1986	—	—	3.00
—Black vinyl					

Number	Title (A Side/B Side)	Yr	VG	VG+	NM
❑ COL-4508	A Big Hunk o'Love/My Wish Came True	1992	—	2.00	4.00
—Gold vinyl					
❑ COL-4509	Stuck on You/Fame and Fortune	1986	—	—	3.00
—Black vinyl					
❑ COL-4509	Stuck on You/Fame and Fortune	1992	—	2.00	4.00
—Gold vinyl					
❑ COL-4510	I Feel So Bad/Wild in the Country	1986	—	—	3.00
—Black vinyl					
❑ COL-4510	I Feel So Bad/Wild in the Country	1992	—	2.00	4.00
—Gold vinyl					
❑ COL-4511	She's Not You/Jailhouse Rock	1986	—	—	3.00
—Black vinyl					
❑ COL-4511	She's Not You/Jailhouse Rock	1992	—	2.00	4.00
—Gold vinyl					
❑ COL-4512	One Broken Heart for Sale/Devil in Disguise	1986	—	—	3.00
—Black vinyl					
❑ COL-4512	One Broken Heart for Sale/Devil in Disguise	1992	—	2.00	4.00
—Gold vinyl					
❑ COL-4513	Bossa Nova Baby/Such a Night	1986	—	—	3.00
—Black vinyl					
❑ COL-4513	Bossa Nova Baby/Such a Night	1992	—	2.00	4.00
—Gold vinyl					
❑ COL-4514	Love Me/Flaming Star	1986	—	—	3.00
—Black vinyl					
❑ COL-4514	Love Me/Flaming Star	1992	—	2.00	4.00
—Gold vinyl					
❑ COL-4515	Follow That Dream/When My Blue Moon Turns to Gold Again	1986	—	—	3.00
—Black vinyl					
❑ COL-4515	Follow That Dream/When My Blue Moon Turns to Gold Again	1992	—	2.00	4.00
—Gold vinyl					
❑ COL-4516	Frankie and Johnny/Love Letters	1986	—	—	3.00
—Black vinyl					
❑ COL-4516	Frankie and Johnny/Love Letters	1992	—	2.00	4.00
—Gold vinyl					
❑ COL-4517	U.S. Male/Until It's Time for You to Go	1986	—	—	3.00
—Black vinyl					
❑ COL-4517	U.S. Male/Until It's Time for You to Go	1992	—	2.00	4.00
—Gold vinyl					
❑ COL-4518	Old Shep/You'll Never Walk Alone	1986	—	—	3.00
—Black vinyl					
❑ COL-4518	Old Shep/You'll Never Walk Alone	1992	—	2.00	4.00
—Gold vinyl					
❑ COL-4519	Poor Boy/An American Trilogy	1986	—	—	3.00
—Black vinyl					
❑ COL-4519	Poor Boy/An American Trilogy	1992	—	2.00	4.00
—Gold vinyl					
❑ COL-4520	How Great Thou Art/His Hand in Mine	1986	—	—	3.00
—Black vinyl					
❑ COL-4520	How Great Thou Art/His Hand in Mine	1992	—	2.00	4.00
—Gold vinyl					
❑ COL-4521	Big Boss Man/Paralyzed	1986	—	—	3.00
—Black vinyl					
❑ COL-4521	Big Boss Man/Paralyzed	1992	—	2.00	4.00
—Gold vinyl					
❑ COL-4522	Fools Fall in Love/Blue Suede Shoes	1986	—	—	3.00
—Black vinyl					
❑ COL-4522	Fools Fall in Love/Blue Suede Shoes	1992	—	2.00	4.00
—Gold vinyl					
❑ COL-4564	The Elvis Medley/Always on My Mind	1986	—	—	3.00
❑ COL-4738	Ask Me/The Girl of My Best Friend	1997	—	—	3.00
❑ COL-4743	Girls! Girls! Girls!/Ain't That Loving You Baby	1997	—	—	3.00
❑ COL-4744	It's Only Love/Beyond the Reef	1997	—	—	3.00
❑ 04764	Witchcraft/Spinout	1997	—	—	3.00
❑ 80000	(Now and Then There's) A Fool Such As I/I Need Your Love Tonight	1997	—	2.00	4.00
—Gray marbled vinyl					
❑ 80001	Separate Ways/Always On My Mind	1997	—	2.00	4.00
—Gray marbled vinyl					
❑ 80002	An American Trilogy/Until It's Time for You to Go	1997	—	2.00	4.00
—Gray marbled vinyl					
❑ 80003	Crying in the Chapel/I Believe in the Man in the Sky	1997	—	2.00	4.00
—Gray marbled vinyl					
❑ 80004	Don't/I Beg of You	1997	—	2.00	4.00
—Gray marbled vinyl					
❑ 80005	Don't Cry Daddy/Rubberneckin'	1997	—	2.00	4.00
—Gray marbled vinyl					
❑ 80006	Good Luck Charm/Anything That's Part of You	1997	—	2.00	4.00
—Gray marbled vinyl					
❑ 80007	Guitar Man/Hi-Heel Sneakers	1997	—	2.00	4.00
—Gray marbled vinyl					
❑ 80008	Hard Headed Woman/Don't Ask Me Why	1997	—	2.00	4.00
—Gray marbled vinyl					
❑ 80009	Heartbreak Hotel/I Was the One	1997	—	2.00	4.00
—Gray marbled vinyl					
❑ 80010	Mystery Train/I Forgot to Remember to Forget	1997	—	2.00	4.00
—Gray marbled vinyl					
❑ 80011	One Night/I Got Stung	1997	—	2.00	4.00
—Gray marbled vinyl					
❑ 80012	I Really Don't Want to Know/There Goes My Everything	1997	—	2.00	4.00
—Gray marbled vinyl					
❑ 80013	I Want You, I Need You, I Love You/My Baby Left Me	1997	—	2.00	4.00
—Gray marbled vinyl					
❑ 80014	If I Can Dream/Edge of Reality	1997	—	2.00	4.00
—Gray marbled vinyl					
❑ 80015	Kentucky Rain/My Little Friend	1997	—	2.00	4.00
—Gray marbled vinyl					
❑ 80016	Kiss Me Quick/Suspicion	1997	—	2.00	4.00
—Gray marbled vinyl					
❑ 80017	Kissin' Cousins/It Hurts Me	1997	—	2.00	4.00
—Gray marbled vinyl					
❑ 80018	Marie's the Name His Latest Flame/Little Sister	1997	—	2.00	4.00
—Gray marbled vinyl					
❑ 80019	(Let Me Be You) Teddy Bear/Loving You	1997	—	2.00	4.00
—Gray marbled vinyl					
❑ 80020	The Wonder of You/Mama Liked the Roses	1997	—	2.00	4.00
—Gray marbled vinyl					
❑ 80021	Memories/Charro	1997	—	2.00	4.00
—Gray marbled vinyl					
❑ 80022	My Boy/Thinking About You	1997	—	2.00	4.00
—Gray marbled vinyl					
❑ 80023	Way Down/My Way	1997	—	2.00	4.00
—Gray marbled vinyl					
❑ 80024	Patch It Up/You Don't Have to Say You Love Me	1997	—	2.00	4.00
—Gray marbled vinyl					
❑ 80025	Surrender/Lonely Man	1997	—	2.00	4.00
—Gray marbled vinyl					
❑ 80026	That's All Right/Blue Moon of Kentucky	1997	—	2.00	4.00
—Gray marbled vinyl					
❑ 80027	Wear My Ring Around Your Neck/Doncha' Think It's Time	1997	—	2.00	4.00
—Gray marbled vinyl					
❑ 80028	Puppet on a String/Wooden Heart	1997	—	2.00	4.00
—Gray marbled vinyl					
RCA					
❑ DME1-1803R	King of the Whole Wide World/King Creole	1997	3.75	7.50	15.00
—Red vinyl, marked as a promotional copy (about 3,000 pressed)					
❑ DME1-1803	King of the Whole Wide World/King Creole	1997	2.00	4.00	8.00
—Gold vinyl (about 7,000 pressed)					
❑ DME1-1803 [DJ]	King of the Whole Wide World/King Creole	1997	100.00	200.00	400.00
—Test pressings of above on green, blue, white and clear vinyl. Value is for any of them.					
❑ DME1-1803 [PS]	King of the Whole Wide World/King Creole	1997	2.00	4.00	8.00
—Same picture sleeve with either edition					
❑ 8760-7-R	Heartbreak Hotel/Heartbreak Hotel	1988	—	2.50	5.00
—B-side by David Keith					
❑ 8760-7-R [PS]	Heartbreak Hotel/Heartbreak Hotel	1988	—	3.00	6.00
—"Pink Cadillac" sleeve					
❑ 8760-7-R [PS]	Heartbreak Hotel/Heartbreak Hotel	1988	20.00	40.00	80.00
—Promo-only sleeve of RCA executive Butch Waugh dressed as Elvis					
❑ GB-10485	Take Good Care of Her/I've Got a Thing About You, Baby	1977	—	2.00	4.00
—Gold Standard Series; black label					
❑ GB-10486	Separate Ways/Always on My Mind	1977	—	2.00	4.00
—Gold Standard Series; black label					
❑ GB-10487	T-R-O-U-B-L-E/Mr. Songman	1977	—	2.00	4.00
—Gold Standard Series; black label					
❑ GB-10488	Promised Land/It's Midnight	1977	—	2.00	4.00
—Gold Standard Series; black label					
❑ GB-10489	My Boy/Thinking About You	1977	—	2.00	4.00
—Gold Standard Series; black label					
❑ PB-10601	Hurt/For the Heart	1976	25.00	50.00	100.00
—Second pressings (very rare) on the 1976-88 "dog near top" black label					
❑ JB-10857 [DJ]	Moody Blue/She Thinks I Still Care	1976	250.00	500.00	1000.
—Colored vinyl pressings exist in five different colors -- red, white, gold, blue green. Value is for any of them.					
❑ PB-10857	Moody Blue/She Thinks I Still Care	1976	—	2.50	5.00
❑ PB-10857 [PS]	Moody Blue/She Thinks I Still Care	1976	2.50	5.00	10.00
❑ JH-10951 [DJ]	Let Me Be There (mono/stereo)	1977	50.00	100.00	200.00
—Promo only					
❑ PB-10998	Way Down/Pledging My Love	1977	—	2.50	5.00
❑ PB-10998 [PS]	Way Down/Pledging My Love	1977	2.50	5.00	10.00
❑ PB-11099	Hound Dog/Don't Be Cruel	1977	—	2.00	4.00
❑ PB-11099 [PS]	Hound Dog/Don't Be Cruel	1977	—	2.00	4.00
—From boxes "15 Golden Records, 30 Golden Hits" and "20 Golden Hits in Full Color Sleeves"					
❑ PB-11100	In the Ghetto/Any Day Now	1977	—	2.00	4.00
❑ PB-11100 [PS]	In the Ghetto/Any Day Now	1977	—	2.00	4.00
—From boxes "15 Golden Records, 30 Golden Hits" and "20 Golden Hits in Full Color Sleeves"					
❑ PB-11101	Jailhouse Rock/Treat Me Nice	1977	—	2.00	4.00
❑ PB-11101 [PS]	Jailhouse Rock/Treat Me Nice	1977	—	2.00	4.00
—From box "15 Golden Records, 30 Golden Hits"					
❑ PB-11102	Can't Help Falling in Love/Rock-a-Hula Baby	1977	—	2.00	4.00
❑ PB-11102 [PS]	Can't Help Falling in Love/Rock-a-Hula Baby	1977	—	2.00	4.00
—From boxes "15 Golden Records, 30 Golden Hits" and "20 Golden Hits in Full Color Sleeves"					
❑ PB-11103	Suspicious Minds/You'll Think of Me	1977	—	2.00	4.00
❑ PB-11103 [PS]	Suspicious Minds/You'll Think of Me	1977	—	2.00	4.00
—From box "15 Golden Records, 30 Golden Hits"					
❑ PB-11104	Are You Lonesome To-Night?/I Gotta Know	1977	—	2.00	4.00
❑ PB-11104 [PS]	Are You Lonesome To-Night?/I Gotta Know	1977	—	2.00	4.00
—From boxes "15 Golden Records, 30 Golden Hits" and "20 Golden Hits in Full Color Sleeves"					
❑ PB-11105	Heartbreak Hotel/I Was the One	1977	—	2.00	4.00
❑ PB-11105 [PS]	Heartbreak Hotel/I Was the One	1977	—	2.00	4.00
—From boxes "15 Golden Records, 30 Golden Hits" and "20 Golden Hits in Full Color Sleeves"					
❑ PB-11106	All Shook Up/That's When Your Heartaches Begin	1977	—	2.00	4.00
❑ PB-11106 [PS]	All Shook Up/That's When Your Heartaches Begin	1977	—	2.00	4.00
—From boxes "15 Golden Records, 30 Golden Hits" and "20 Golden Hits in Full Color Sleeves"					
❑ PB-11107	Blue Suede Shoes/Tutti Frutti	1977	—	2.00	4.00

Number	Title (A Side/B Side)	Yr	VG	VG+	NM
❑ PB-11107 [PS]	Blue Suede Shoes/Tutti Frutti	1977	—	2.00	4.00
—From boxes "15 Golden Records, 30 Golden Hits" and "20 Golden Hits in Full Color Sleeves"					
❑ PB-11108	Love Me Tender/Any Way You Want Me (That's How I Will Be)	1977	—	2.00	4.00
❑ PB-11108 [PS]	Love Me Tender/Any Way You Want Me (That's How I Will Be)	1977	—	2.00	4.00
—From boxes "15 Golden Records, 30 Golden Hits" and "20 Golden Hits in Full Color Sleeves"					
❑ PB-11109	(Let Me Be Your) Teddy Bear/Loving You	1977	—	2.00	4.00
❑ PB-11109 [PS]	(Let Me Be Your) Teddy Bear/Loving You	1977	—	2.00	4.00
—From boxes "15 Golden Records, 30 Golden Hits" and "20 Golden Hits in Full Color Sleeves"					
❑ PB-11110	It's Now or Never/A Mess of Blues	1977	—	2.00	4.00
❑ PB-11110 [PS]	It's Now or Never/A Mess of Blues	1977	—	2.00	4.00
—From box "15 Golden Records, 30 Golden Hits"					
❑ PB-11111	Return to Sender/Where Do You Come From	1977	—	2.00	4.00
❑ PB-11111 [PS]	Return to Sender/Where Do You Come From	1977	—	2.00	4.00
—From boxes "15 Golden Records, 30 Golden Hits" and "20 Golden Hits in Full Color Sleeves"					
❑ PB-11112	One Night/I Got Stung	1977	—	2.00	4.00
❑ PB-11112 [PS]	One Night/I Got Stung	1977	—	2.00	4.00
—From box "15 Golden Records, 30 Golden Hits"					
❑ PB-11113	Crying in the Chapel/I Believe in the Man in the Sky	1977	—	2.00	4.00
❑ PB-11113 [PS]	Crying in the Chapel/I Believe in the Man in the Sky	1977	—	2.00	4.00
—From box "15 Golden Records, 30 Golden Hits"					
❑ PB-11165	My Way/America	1977	—	2.50	5.00
❑ PB-11165	My Way/America the Beautiful	1977	5.00	10.00	20.00
❑ PB-11165 [PS]	My Way/America	1977	2.50	5.00	10.00
❑ PB-11165 [PS]	My Way/America the Beautiful	1977	6.25	12.50	25.00
❑ PB-11212	Unchained Melody/Softly, As I Leave You	1978	2.50	5.00	10.00
—Erroneously states "Vocal Accompaniment by Sherrill Nielsen" on "Unchained Melody" side					
❑ PB-11212	Unchained Melody/Softly, As I Leave You	1978	—	2.50	5.00
—No credit to Sherrill Nielsen on the "Unchained Melody" side					
❑ PB-11212 [PS]	Unchained Melody/Softly, As I Leave You	1978	2.50	5.00	10.00
❑ PP-11301	15 Golden Records, 30 Golden Hits	1977	15.00	30.00	60.00
—Includes 15 records (11099-11113) and outer box					
❑ PB-11320	(Let Me Be Your) Teddy Bear/Puppet on a String	1978	—	2.50	5.00
❑ PB-11320 [PS]	(Let Me Be Your) Teddy Bear/Puppet on a String	1978	2.50	5.00	10.00
❑ GB-11326	Moody Blue/For the Heart	1978	—	2.00	4.00
—Gold Standard Series					
❑ PP-11340	20 Golden Hits in Full Color Sleeves	1977	20.00	40.00	80.00
—Includes 10 records (11099, 11100, 11102, 11104-11109, 11111) and outer box					
❑ GB-11504	Way Down/My Way	1979	—	2.00	4.00
—Gold Standard Series					
❑ PB-11533	Are You Sincere/Solitaire	1979	—	2.50	5.00
❑ PB-11533 [PS]	Are You Sincere/Solitaire	1979	2.50	5.00	10.00
❑ PB-11679	There's a Honky Tonk Angel (Who Will Take Me Back In)/I Got a Feelin' in My Body	1979	3.75	7.50	15.00
—Has full production credits (background vocals, strings) listed in error on both sides					
❑ PB-11679	There's a Honky Tonk Angel (Who Will Take Me Back In)/I Got a Feelin' in My Body	1979	—	2.50	5.00
—Has production credits removed; only producers are listed					
❑ PB-11679 [PS]	There's a Honky Tonk Angel (Who Will Take Me Back In)/I Got a Feelin' in My Body	1979	2.50	5.00	10.00
❑ GB-11988	Unchained Melody/Are You Sincere	1980	—	2.00	4.00
—Gold Standard Series					
❑ JH-12158 [DJ]	Guitar Man (mono/stereo)	1981	75.00	150.00	300.00
—Promo only on red vinyl					
❑ PB-12158	Guitar Man/Faded Love	1981	—	2.50	5.00
❑ PB-12158 [PS]	Guitar Man/Faded Love	1981	2.50	5.00	10.00
❑ JB-12205 [DJ]	Lovin' Arms/You Asked Me To	1981	75.00	150.00	300.00
—Promo only on green vinyl					
❑ PB-12205	Lovin' Arms/You Asked Me To	1981	—	3.00	6.00
—Not issued with picture sleeve (bootlegs exist)					
❑ PB-13058	There Goes My Everything/You'll Never Walk Alone	1982	—	2.50	5.00
❑ PB-13058 [PS]	There Goes My Everything/You'll Never Walk Alone	1982	2.50	5.00	10.00
❑ GB-13275	Suspicious Minds/You'll Think of Me	1982	—	2.00	4.00
—Gold Standard Series					
❑ JH-13302	The Impossible Dream (The Quest)/An American Trilogy	1982	25.00	50.00	100.00
❑ JH-13302 [PS]	The Impossible Dream (The Quest)/An American Trilogy	1982	25.00	50.00	100.00
—Promo only, distributed to visitors to Elvis' birthplace in Tupelo, Mississippi, in 1982.					
❑ JB-13351 [DJ]	The Elvis Medley (Long Version)/The Elvis Medley (Short Version)	1982	75.00	150.00	300.00
—Promo only on gold vinyl					
❑ PB-13351	The Elvis Medley/Always on My Mind	1982	—	2.50	5.00
❑ PB-13351 [PS]	The Elvis Medley/Always on My Mind	1982	2.50	5.00	10.00
❑ JB-13500 [DJ]	I Was the One/Wear My Ring Around Your Neck	1983	75.00	150.00	300.00
—Promo only on gold vinyl					
❑ PB-13500	I Was the One/Wear My Ring Around Your Neck	1983	—	2.50	5.00
❑ PB-13500 [PS]	I Was the One/Wear My Ring Around Your Neck	1983	2.50	5.00	10.00
❑ JB-13547 [DJ]	Little Sister/Paralyzed	1983	75.00	150.00	300.00
—Promo only on blue vinyl					
❑ PB-13547	Little Sister/Paralyzed	1983	—	2.50	5.00
❑ PB-13547 [PS]	Little Sister/Paralyzed	1983	2.50	5.00	10.00
❑ JB-13875 [DJ]	Baby Let's Play House/Hound Dog	1984	50.00	100.00	200.00
—Gold vinyl, custom label					
❑ PB-13875	Baby Let's Play House/Hound Dog	1984	10.00	20.00	40.00
—Gold vinyl, custom label					
❑ PB-13875 [PS]	Baby Let's Play House/Hound Dog	1984	10.00	20.00	40.00
❑ PB-13885	Blue Suede Shoes/Tutti Frutti	1984	—	2.00	4.00
—From box "Elvis' Greatest Hits, Golden Singles, Volume 1"; gold vinyl					
❑ PB-13885 [PS]	Blue Suede Shoes/Tutti Frutti	1984	—	2.00	4.00

Number	Title (A Side/B Side)	Yr	VG	VG+	NM
❑ PB-13886	Don't Be Cruel/Hound Dog	1984	—	2.00	4.00
—From box "Elvis' Greatest Hits, Golden Singles, Volume 1"; gold vinyl					
❑ PB-13886 [PS]	Don't Be Cruel/Hound Dog	1984	—	2.00	4.00
❑ PB-13887	I Want You, I Need You, I Love You/Love Me	1984	—	2.00	4.00
—From box "Elvis' Greatest Hits, Golden Singles, Volume 1"; gold vinyl					
❑ PB-13887 [PS]	I Want You, I Need You, I Love You/Love Me	1984	—	2.00	4.00
❑ PB-13888	All Shook Up/(Let Me Be Your) Teddy Bear	1984	—	2.00	4.00
—From box "Elvis' Greatest Hits, Golden Singles, Volume 1"; gold vinyl					
❑ PB-13888 [PS]	All Shook Up/(Let Me Be Your) Teddy Bear	1984	—	2.00	4.00
❑ PB-13889	It's Now or Never/Surrender	1984	—	2.00	4.00
—From box "Elvis' Greatest Hits, Golden Singles, Volume 1"; gold vinyl					
❑ PB-13889 [PS]	It's Now or Never/Surrender	1984	—	2.00	4.00
❑ PB-13890	In the Ghetto/If I Can Dream	1984	—	2.00	4.00
—From box "Elvis' Greatest Hits, Golden Singles, Volume 1"; gold vinyl					
❑ PB-13890 [PS]	In the Ghetto/If I Can Dream	1984	—	2.00	4.00
❑ PB-13891	That's All Right/Blue Moon of Kentucky	1984	—	2.00	4.00
—From box "Elvis' Greatest Hits, Golden Singles, Volume 2"; gold vinyl					
❑ PB-13891 [PS]	That's All Right/Blue Moon of Kentucky	1984	—	2.00	4.00
❑ PB-13892	Heartbreak Hotel/Jailhouse Rock	1984	—	2.00	4.00
—From box "Elvis' Greatest Hits, Golden Singles, Volume 2"; gold vinyl					
❑ PB-13892 [PS]	Heartbreak Hotel/Jailhouse Rock	1984	—	2.00	4.00
❑ PB-13893	Love Me Tender/Loving You	1984	—	2.00	4.00
—From box "Elvis' Greatest Hits, Golden Singles, Volume 2"; gold vinyl					
❑ PB-13893 [PS]	Love Me Tender/Loving You	1984	—	2.00	4.00
❑ PB-13894	(Marie's the Name) His Latest Flame/Little Sister	1984	—	2.00	4.00
—From box "Elvis' Greatest Hits, Golden Singles, Volume 2"; gold vinyl					
❑ PB-13894 [PS]	(Marie's the Name) His Latest Flame/Little Sister	1984	—	2.00	4.00
❑ PB-13895	Are You Lonesome Tonight/Can't Help Falling in Love	1984	—	2.00	4.00
—From box "Elvis' Greatest Hits, Golden Singles, Volume 2"; gold vinyl					
❑ PB-13895 [PS]	Are You Lonesome Tonight/Can't Help Falling in Love	1984	—	2.00	4.00
❑ PB-13896	Suspicious Minds/Burning Love	1984	—	2.00	4.00
—From box "Elvis' Greatest Hits, Golden Singles, Volume 2"; gold vinyl					
❑ PB-13896 [PS]	Suspicious Minds/Burning Love	1984	—	2.00	4.00
❑ PB-13897	Elvis' Greatest Hits, Golden Singles, Volume 1	1984	3.75	7.50	15.00
—Box set of six 45s with sleeves (13885-13890) with box					
❑ PB-13898	Elvis' Greatest Hits, Golden Singles, Volume 2	1984	3.75	7.50	15.00
—Box set of six 45s with sleeves (13891-13896) with box					
❑ PB-13929	Blue Suede Shoes/Promised Land	1984	3.75	7.50	15.00
—Blue vinyl; incorrect label -- "Blue Suede Shoes" side says "Stereo" and "Promised Land" side says "Mono"					
❑ PB-13929	Blue Suede Shoes/Promised Land	1984	3.00	6.00	12.00
—Blue vinyl; correct label -- "Blue Suede Shoes" side says "Mono" and "Promised Land" side says "Stereo"					
❑ PB-13929 [PS]	Blue Suede Shoes/Promised Land	1984	2.50	5.00	10.00
❑ PB-14090	Always on My Mind/My Boy	1985	2.50	5.00	10.00
—Purple vinyl					
❑ PB-14090 [PS]	Always on My Mind/My Boy	1985	2.50	5.00	10.00
❑ PB-14237	Merry Christmas Baby/Santa Claus Is Back in Town	1985	3.75	7.50	15.00
—"Elvis 50th Anniversary" label					
❑ PB-14237	Merry Christmas Baby/Santa Claus Is Back in Town	1985	—	2.50	5.00
—Normal black RCA label					
❑ PB-14237	Merry Christmas Baby/Santa Claus Is Back in Town	1985	3.75	7.50	15.00
—Green vinyl					
❑ PB-14237 [PS]	Merry Christmas Baby/Santa Claus Is Back in Town	1985	3.00	6.00	12.00
❑ 62402	Don't Be Cruel/Ain't That Lovin' You Baby (Fast Version)	1992	—	2.50	5.00
❑ 62402 [PS]	Don't Be Cruel/Ain't That Lovin' You Baby (Fast Version)	1992	—	2.50	5.00
—Generic white sleeve with "Elvis -- The King of Rock 'n' Roll" sticker					
❑ 62403	Blue Christmas/Love Me Tender	1992	—	2.50	5.00
❑ 62403 [PS]	Blue Christmas/Love Me Tender	1992	—	2.50	5.00
—Generic white sleeve with "Elvis -- The King of Rock 'n' Roll" sticker					
❑ 62411	Silver Bells (Unreleased Version)/Silver Bells	1993	—	2.50	5.00
❑ 62449	Heartbreak Hotel/Hound Dog	1992	—	2.50	5.00
❑ 64476	Heartbreak Hotel/I Was the One//Heartbreak Hotel (Alternate Take 5)/I Was the One (Alternate Take 2)	1996	—	—	3.00
❑ 64476 [PS]	Heartbreak Hotel/I Was the One//Heartbreak Hotel (Alternate Take 5)/I Was the One (Alternate Take 2)	1996	—	—	3.00
❑ 447-0600	I Forgot to Remember to Forget/Mystery Train	1977	—	2.00	4.00
—Note: All RCA releases with a "447" prefix are from the Gold Standard Series and are black label, dog on side					
❑ 447-0601	That's All Right/Blue Moon of Kentucky	1977	—	2.00	4.00
❑ 447-0602	Good Rockin' Tonight/I Don't Care If the Sun Don't Shine	1977	—	2.00	4.00
❑ 447-0603	Milkcow Blues Boogie/You're a Heartbreaker	1977	—	2.00	4.00
❑ 447-0604	Baby Let's Play House/I'm Left, You're Right, She's Gone	1977	—	2.00	4.00
❑ 447-0605	Heartbreak Hotel/I Was the One	1977	—	2.00	4.00
❑ 447-0607	I Want You, I Need You, I Love You/My Baby Left Me	1977	—	2.00	4.00
❑ 447-0608	Hound Dog/Don't Be Cruel	1977	—	2.00	4.00
❑ 447-0609	Blue Suede Shoes/Tutti Frutti	1977	—	2.00	4.00
❑ 447-0613	Blue Moon/Just Because	1977	—	2.00	4.00
❑ 447-0614	Money Honey/One-Sided Love Affair	1977	—	2.00	4.00
❑ 447-0615	Lawdy Miss Clawdy/Shake, Rattle, and Roll	1977	—	2.00	4.00
❑ 447-0616	Love Me Tender/Anyway You Want Me (That's How I Will Be)	1977	—	2.00	4.00
❑ 447-0617	Too Much/Playing for Keeps	1977	—	2.00	4.00

Number	Title (A Side/B Side)	Yr	VG	VG+	NM
❑ 447-0618	All Shook Up/That's When Your Heartaches Begin	1977	—	2.00	4.00
❑ 447-0619	Jailhouse Rock/Treat Me Nice	1977	—	2.00	4.00
❑ 447-0620	(Let Me Be Your) Teddy Bear/Loving You	1977	—	2.00	4.00
❑ 447-0621	Don't/I Beg of You	1977	—	2.00	4.00
❑ 447-0622	Wear My Ring Around Your Neck/Don'tcha Think It's Time	1977	—	2.00	4.00
❑ 447-0623	Hard Headed Woman/Don't Ask Me Why	1977	—	2.00	4.00
❑ 447-0624	One Night/I Got Stung	1977	—	2.00	4.00
❑ 447-0625	(Now and Then There's) A Fool Such As I/I Need Your Love Tonight	1977	—	2.00	4.00
❑ 447-0626	A Big Hunk o'Love/My Wish Came True	1977	—	2.00	4.00
❑ 447-0627	Stuck on You/Fame and Fortune	1977	—	2.00	4.00
❑ 447-0628	It's Now or Never/A Mess of Blues	1977	—	2.00	4.00
❑ 447-0629	Are You Lonesome To-Night?/I Gotta Know	1977	—	2.00	4.00
❑ 447-0630	Surrender/Lonely Man	1977	—	2.00	4.00
❑ 447-0631	I Feel So Bad/Wild in the Country	1977	—	2.00	4.00
❑ 447-0634	(Marie's the Name) His Latest Flame/Little Sister	1977	—	2.00	4.00
❑ 447-0635	Can't Help Falling in Love/Rock-a-Hula Baby	1977	—	2.00	4.00
❑ 447-0636	Good Luck Charm/Anything That's Part of You	1977	—	2.00	4.00
❑ 447-0637	She's Not You/Just Tell Her Jim Said Hello	1977	—	2.00	4.00
❑ 447-0638	Return to Sender/Where Do You Come From	1977	—	2.00	4.00
❑ 447-0639	Kiss Me Quick/Suspicion	1977	—	2.00	4.00
❑ 447-0640	One Broken Heart for Sale/They Remind Me Too Much of You	1977	—	2.00	4.00
❑ 447-0641	(You're the) Devil in Disguise/Please Don't Drag That String Around	1977	—	2.00	4.00
❑ 447-0642	Bossa Nova Baby/Witchcraft	1977	—	2.00	4.00
❑ 447-0643	Crying in the Chapel/I Believe in the Man in the Sky	1977	—	2.00	4.00
❑ 447-0644	Kissin' Cousins/It Hurts Me	1977	—	2.00	4.00
❑ 447-0645	Such a Night/Never Ending	1977	—	2.00	4.00
❑ 447-0646	Viva Las Vegas/What'd I Say	1977	—	2.00	4.00
❑ 447-0647	Blue Christmas/Santa Claus Is Back in Town	1977	—	2.00	4.00
❑ 447-0647 [PS]	Blue Christmas/Santa Claus Is Back in Town	1977	2.50	5.00	10.00
—Does not mention "Gold Standard Series" on sleeve					
❑ 447-0648	Do the Clam/You'll Be Gone	1977	—	2.00	4.00
❑ 447-0649	Ain't That Loving You Baby/Ask Me	1977	—	2.00	4.00
❑ 447-0650	Puppet on a String/Wooden Heart	1977	—	2.00	4.00
❑ 447-0651	Joshua Fit the Battle/Known Only to Him	1977	—	2.00	4.00
❑ 447-0653	(Such An) Easy Question/It Feels So Right	1977	—	2.00	4.00
❑ 447-0654	I'm Yours/(It's a) Long, Lonely Highway	1977	—	2.00	4.00
❑ 447-0655	Tell Me Why/Blue River	1977	—	2.00	4.00
❑ 447-0656	Frankie and Johnny/Please Don't Stop Loving Me	1977	—	2.00	4.00
❑ 447-0657	Love Letters/Come What May	1977	—	2.00	4.00
❑ 447-0658	Spinout/All That I Do	1977	—	2.00	4.00
❑ 447-0659	Indescribably Blue/Fools Fall in Love	1977	—	2.00	4.00
❑ 447-0661	There's Always Me/Judy	1977	—	2.00	4.00
❑ 447-0662	Big Boss Man/You Don't Know Me	1977	—	2.00	4.00
❑ 447-0663	Guitar Man/High Heel Sneakers	1977	—	2.00	4.00
❑ 447-0664	U.S. Male/Stay Away	1977	—	2.50	5.00
❑ 447-0665	You'll Never Walk Alone/We Call on Him	1977	—	2.00	4.00
❑ 447-0666	Let Yourself Go/Your Time Hasn't Come Yet, Baby	1977	—	2.00	4.00
❑ 447-0667	A Little Less Conversation/Almost in Love	1977	—	2.00	4.00
❑ 447-0668	If I Can Dream/Edge of Reality	1977	—	2.00	4.00
❑ 447-0669	Memories/Charro	1977	—	2.00	4.00
❑ 447-0670	How Great Thou Art/His Hand in Mine	1977	—	2.00	4.00
❑ 447-0671	In the Ghetto/Any Day Now	1977	—	2.00	4.00
❑ 447-0672	Clean Up Your Own Back Yard/The Fair Is Moving On	1977	—	2.00	4.00
❑ 447-0673	Suspicious Minds/You'll Think of Me	1977	—	2.00	4.00
❑ 447-0674	Don't Cry Daddy/Rubberneckin'	1977	—	2.00	4.00
❑ 447-0675	Kentucky Rain/My Little Friend	1977	—	2.00	4.00
❑ 447-0676	The Wonder of You/Mama Liked the Roses	1977	—	2.00	4.00
❑ 447-0677	I've Lost You/The Next Step Is Love	1977	—	2.00	4.00
❑ 447-0678	You Don't Have to Say You Love Me/Patch It Up	1977	—	2.00	4.00
❑ 447-0679	I Really Don't Want to Know/There Goes My Everything	1977	—	2.00	4.00
❑ 447-0680	Where Did They Go, Lord/Rags to Riches	1977	—	2.00	4.00
❑ 447-0681	If Every Day Was Like Christmas/How Would You Like to Be	1977	—	2.00	4.00
❑ 447-0682	Life/Only Believe	1977	—	2.00	4.00
❑ 447-0683	I'm Leavin'/Heart of Rome	1977	—	2.00	4.00
❑ 447-0684	It's Only Love/The Sound of Your Cry	1977	—	2.00	4.00
❑ 447-0685	An American Trilogy/Until It's Time for You to Go	1977	—	2.00	4.00
RCA VICTOR					
❑ CR-15 [DJ]	Old Shep	1956	250.00	500.00	1000.
—One-sided promo					
❑ SP-45-76 [DJ]	Don't/Wear My Ring Around Your Neck	1960	200.00	400.00	800.00
❑ SP-45-76 [PS]	Don't/Wear My Ring Around Your Neck	1960	1000.	1500.	2000.
❑ APBO-0088	Raised on Rock/For Ol' Times Sake	1973	—	3.00	6.00
❑ APBO-0088 [PS]	Raised on Rock/For Ol' Times Sake	1973	3.75	7.50	15.00
❑ 4-834-115 [DJ]	I'll Be Back	1966	4000.	6000.	8000.
—One-sided promo with designation "For Special Academy Consideration Only"					
❑ SP-45-118 [DJ]	King of the Whole Wide World/Home Is Where the Heart Is	1962	50.00	100.00	200.00
❑ SP-45-118 [PS]	King of the Whole Wide World/Home Is Where the Heart Is	1962	75.00	150.00	300.00
❑ SP-45-139 [DJ]	Roustabout/One Track Heart	1964	75.00	150.00	300.00
❑ SP-45-162 [DJ]	How Great Thou Art/So High	1967	37.50	75.00	150.00
❑ SP-45-162 [PS]	How Great Thou Art/So High	1967	50.00	100.00	200.00
❑ APBO-0196	Take Good Care of Her/I've Got a Thing About You, Baby	1973	—	3.00	6.00
❑ APBO-0196 [PS]	Take Good Care of Her/I've Got a Thing About You, Baby	1973	3.75	7.50	15.00

Number	Title (A Side/B Side)	Yr	VG	VG+	NM
❑ APBO-0280	If You Talk in Your Sleep/Help Me	1974	3.00	6.00	12.00
—On label, the title "If You Talk in Your Sleep" is all on one line					
❑ APBO-0280	If You Talk in Your Sleep/Help Me	1974	—	3.00	6.00
—On label, the title "If You Talk" is on one line and "In Your Sleep" is on another line					
❑ APBO-0280 [PS]	If You Talk in Your Sleep/Help Me	1974	3.75	7.50	15.00
❑ HO7W-0808 [DJ]	Blue Christmas (same on both sides)	1957	375.00	750.00	1500.
❑ PB-10074	Promised Land/It's Midnight	1974	—	2.50	5.00
—Orange label (available at the same time as gray label)					
❑ PB-10074	Promised Land/It's Midnight	1974	—	2.50	5.00
—Gray label (available at the same time as orange label)					
❑ PB-10074	Promised Land/It's Midnight	1975	6.25	12.50	25.00
—Tan label (reissue)					
❑ PB-10074 [PS]	Promised Land/It's Midnight	1975	2.50	5.00	10.00
❑ GB-10156	Burning Love/Steamroller Blues	1975	2.00	4.00	8.00
—Gold Standard Series; red label					
❑ GB-10156	Burning Love/Steamroller Blues	1977	—	2.00	4.00
—Gold Standard Series; black label					
❑ GB-10157	Raised on Rock/If You Talk in Your Sleep	1975	2.00	4.00	8.00
—Gold Standard Series; red label					
❑ GB-10157	Raised on Rock/If You Talk in Your Sleep	1977	—	2.00	4.00
—Gold Standard Series; black label					
❑ PB-10191	My Boy/Thinking About You	1975	—	2.50	5.00
—Orange label					
❑ PB-10191	My Boy/Thinking About You	1975	—	2.50	5.00
—Tan label					
❑ PB-10191 [PS]	My Boy/Thinking About You	1975	2.50	5.00	10.00
❑ PB-10278	T-R-O-U-B-L-E/Mr. Songman	1975	—	2.50	5.00
—Orange label					
❑ PB-10278	T-R-O-U-B-L-E/Mr. Songman	1975	25.00	50.00	100.00
—Gray label					
❑ PB-10278	T-R-O-U-B-L-E/Mr. Songman	1975	2.50	5.00	10.00
—Tan label					
❑ PB-10278 [PS]	T-R-O-U-B-L-E/Mr. Songman	1975	2.50	5.00	10.00
❑ PB-10401	Bringing It Back/Pieces of My Life	1975	50.00	100.00	200.00
—Orange label					
❑ PB-10401	Bringing It Back/Pieces of My Life	1975	—	2.50	5.00
—Tan label					
❑ PB-10401 [PS]	Bringing It Back/Pieces of My Life	1975	2.50	5.00	10.00
❑ GB-10485	Take Good Care of Her/I've Got a Thing About You, Baby	1975	2.00	4.00	8.00
—Gold Standard Series; red label					
❑ GB-10486	Separate Ways/Always on My Mind	1975	2.00	4.00	8.00
—Gold Standard Series; red label					
❑ GB-10487	T-R-O-U-B-L-E/Mr. Songman	1975	2.00	4.00	8.00
—Gold Standard Series; red label					
❑ GB-10488	Promised Land/It's Midnight	1975	2.00	4.00	8.00
—Gold Standard Series; red label					
❑ GB-10489	My Boy/Thinking About You	1975	2.00	4.00	8.00
—Gold Standard Series; red label					
❑ PB-10601	Hurt/For the Heart	1976	—	2.50	5.00
—Originals on tan labels					
❑ PB-10601 [PS]	Hurt/For the Heart	1976	2.50	5.00	10.00
❑ 37-7850	Surrender/Lonely Man	1961	150.00	300.00	600.00
—"Compact Single 33" (small hole, plays at LP speed)					
❑ 37-7850 [PS]	Surrender/Lonely Man	1961	250.00	500.00	1000.
—Special picture sleeve for above record					
❑ 37-7880	I Feel So Bad/Wild in the Country	1961	250.00	500.00	1000.
—"Compact Single 33" (small hole, plays at LP speed)					
❑ 37-7880 [PS]	I Feel So Bad/Wild in the Country	1961	300.00	600.00	1200.
—Special picture sleeve for above record					
❑ 37-7908	(Marie's the Name) His Latest Flame/Little Sister	1961	375.00	750.00	1500.
—"Compact Single 33" (small hole, plays at LP speed)					
❑ 37-7908 [PS]	(Marie's the Name) His Latest Flame/Little Sister	1961	1000.	1500.	2000.
—Special picture sleeve for above record					
❑ 37-7908 [PS]	(Marie's the Name) His Latest Flame/Little Sister	1961	1125.	1688.	2250.
—Special picture sleeve for above record; says "Stereo-Orthophonic" on sleeve in error					
❑ 37-7968	Can't Help Falling in Love/Rock-a-Hula Baby	1961	1000.	1500.	2000.
—"Compact Single 33" (small hole, plays at LP speed)					
❑ 37-7968 [PS]	Can't Help Falling in Love/Rock-a-Hula Baby	1961	2000.	3000.	4000.
—Special picture sleeve for above record					
❑ 37-7992	Good Luck Charm/Anything That's Part of You	1962	1250.	1875.	2500.
—"Compact Single 33" (small hole, plays at LP speed)					
❑ 37-7992 [PS]	Good Luck Charm/Anything That's Part of You	1962	2500.	3750.	5000.
—Special picture sleeve for above record					
❑ 47-6357	I Forgot to Remember to Forget/Mystery Train	1955	15.00	30.00	60.00
—No horizontal line on label					
❑ 47-6357	I Forgot to Remember to Forget/Mystery Train	1955	15.00	30.00	60.00
—With horizontal line on label					
❑ 47-6357 [PS]	This Is His Life: Elvis Presley	1955	375.00	750.00	1500.
—Promo-only sleeve issued with above single; no stock picture sleeve was issued. This was formerly listed under "I Want You, I Need You, I Love You," as the sleeve does not have a number. Consensus opinion now places it with "Mystery Train."					
❑ 47-6380	That's All Right/Blue Moon of Kentucky	1955	15.00	30.00	60.00
—No horizontal line on label					
❑ 47-6380	That's All Right/Blue Moon of Kentucky	1955	15.00	30.00	60.00
—With horizontal line on label					
❑ 47-6381	Good Rockin' Tonight/I Don't Care If the Sun Don't Shine	1955	15.00	30.00	60.00
—With horizontal line on label					
❑ 47-6381	Good Rockin' Tonight/I Don't Care If the Sun Don't Shine	1955	15.00	30.00	60.00
—No horizontal line on label					
❑ 47-6382	Milkcow Blues Boogie/You're a Heartbreaker	1955	15.00	30.00	60.00
—No horizontal line on label					
❑ 47-6382	Milkcow Blues Boogie/You're a Heartbreaker	1955	15.00	30.00	60.00
—With horizontal line on label					

Number	Title (A Side/B Side)	Yr	VG	VG+	NM
❑ 47-6383	Baby Let's Play House/I'm Left, You're Right, She's Gone	1955	15.00	30.00	60.00
—With horizontal line on label					
❑ 47-6383	Baby Let's Play House/I'm Left, You're Right, She's Gone	1955	15.00	30.00	60.00
—No horizontal line on label					
❑ 47-6420	Heartbreak Hotel/I Was the One	1956	10.00	20.00	40.00
—No horizontal line on label					
❑ 47-6420	Heartbreak Hotel/I Was the One	1956	10.00	20.00	40.00
—With horizontal line on label					
❑ 47-6540	I Want You, I Need You, I Love You/My Baby Left Me	1956	10.00	20.00	40.00
—No horizontal line on label					
❑ 47-6540	I Want You, I Need You, I Love You/My Baby Left Me	1956	10.00	20.00	40.00
—With horizontal line on label					
❑ 47-6604	Don't Be Cruel/Hound Dog	1956	7.50	15.00	30.00
—No horizontal line on label					
❑ 47-6604	Don't Be Cruel/Hound Dog	1956	7.50	15.00	30.00
—With horizontal line on label					
❑ 47-6604 [PS]	Don't Be Cruel/Hound Dog	1956	50.00	100.00	200.00
—"Don't Be Cruel" listed on top of "Hound Dog!"					
❑ 47-6604 [PS]	Don't Be Cruel/Hound Dog	1956	30.00	60.00	120.00
—"Hound Dog!" listed on top of "Don't Be Cruel"					
❑ 47-6636	Blue Suede Shoes/Tutti Frutti	1956	20.00	40.00	80.00
—No horizontal line on label					
❑ 47-6636	Blue Suede Shoes/Tutti Frutti	1956	20.00	40.00	80.00
—With horizontal line on label					
❑ 47-6637	I Got a Woman/I'm Countin' On You	1956	20.00	40.00	80.00
—With horizontal line on label					
❑ 47-6637	I Got a Woman/I'm Countin' On You	1956	20.00	40.00	80.00
—No horizontal line on label					
❑ 47-6638	I'm Gonna Sit Right Down and Cry (Over You)/I'll Never Let You Go (Little Darlin')	1956	17.50	35.00	70.00
—No horizontal line on label					
❑ 47-6638	I'm Gonna Sit Right Down and Cry (Over You)/I'll Never Let You Go (Little Darlin')	1956	17.50	35.00	70.00
—With horizontal line on label					
❑ 47-6639	Tryin' to Get to You/I Love You Because	1956	17.50	35.00	70.00
—With horizontal line on label					
❑ 47-6639	Tryin' to Get to You/I Love You Because	1956	17.50	35.00	70.00
—No horizontal line on label					
❑ 47-6640	Blue Moon/Just Because	1956	15.00	30.00	60.00
—No horizontal line on label					
❑ 47-6640	Blue Moon/Just Because	1956	15.00	30.00	60.00
—With horizontal line on label					
❑ 47-6641	Money Honey/One-Sided Love Affair	1956	12.50	25.00	50.00
—With horizontal line on label					
❑ 47-6641	Money Honey/One-Sided Love Affair	1956	12.50	25.00	50.00
—No horizontal line on label					
❑ 47-6642	Lawdy Miss Clawdy/Shake, Rattle, and Roll	1956	10.00	20.00	40.00
—No horizontal line on label					
❑ 47-6642	Lawdy Miss Clawdy/Shake, Rattle, and Roll	1956	50.00	100.00	200.00
—With horizontal line on label, but with no dog					
❑ 47-6642	Lawdy Miss Clawdy/Shake, Rattle, and Roll	1956	10.00	20.00	40.00
—With horizontal line on label, dog on label as usual					
❑ 47-6643	Love Me Tender/Anyway You Want Me (That's How I Will Be)	1956	7.50	15.00	30.00
—No horizontal line on label					
❑ 47-6643	Love Me Tender/Anyway You Want Me (That's How I Will Be)	1956	7.50	15.00	30.00
—With horizontal line on label					
❑ 47-6643	Love Me Tender/Anyway You Want Me (That's How I Will Be)	1956	10.00	20.00	40.00
—No reference to the movie "Love Me Tender" on label					
❑ 47-6643 [PS]	Love Me Tender/Anyway You Want Me (That's How I Will Be)	1956	45.00	90.00	180.00
—Black and white sleeve					
❑ 47-6643 [PS]	Love Me Tender/Anyway You Want Me (That's How I Will Be)	1956	18.75	37.50	75.00
—Black and green sleeve					
❑ 47-6643 [PS]	Love Me Tender/Anyway You Want Me (That's How I Will Be)	1956	10.00	20.00	40.00
—Black and dark pink sleeve					
❑ 47-6643 [PS]	Love Me Tender/Anyway You Want Me (That's How I Will Be)	1956	7.50	15.00	30.00
—Black and light pink sleeve					
❑ 47-6800	Too Much/Playing for Keeps	1957	7.50	15.00	30.00
—No horizontal line on label					
❑ 47-6800	Too Much/Playing for Keeps	1957	50.00	100.00	200.00
—With horizontal line on label, but with no dog					
❑ 47-6800	Too Much/Playing for Keeps	1957	7.50	15.00	30.00
—With horizontal line on label, dog on label as normal					
❑ 47-6800 [PS]	Too Much/Playing for Keeps	1957	22.50	45.00	90.00
❑ 47-6870	All Shook Up/That's When Your Heartaches Begin	1957	7.50	15.00	30.00
—No horizontal line on label					
❑ 47-6870	All Shook Up/That's When Your Heartaches Begin	1957	7.50	15.00	30.00
—With horizontal line on label					
❑ 47-6870 [PS]	All Shook Up/That's When Your Heartaches Begin	1957	22.50	45.00	90.00
❑ 47-7000	(Let Me Be Your) Teddy Bear/Loving You	1957	10.00	20.00	40.00
—Label says "Let Me Be Your TEDDY BEAR" (no parentheses)					
❑ 47-7000	(Let Me Be Your) Teddy Bear/Loving You	1957	7.50	15.00	30.00
—Parentheses around "Let Me Be Your", no horizontal line on label					
❑ 47-7000	(Let Me Be Your) Teddy Bear/Loving You	1957	7.50	15.00	30.00
—Parentheses around "Let Me Be Your", with horizontal line on label					
❑ 47-7000 [PS]	(Let Me Be Your) Teddy Bear/Loving You	1957	30.00	60.00	120.00
❑ 47-7035	Jailhouse Rock/Treat Me Nice	1957	7.50	15.00	30.00
—No horizontal line on label					
❑ 47-7035	Jailhouse Rock/Treat Me Nice	1957	7.50	15.00	30.00
—With horizontal line on label					
❑ 47-7035 [PS]	Jailhouse Rock/Treat Me Nice	1957	25.00	50.00	100.00
❑ 47-7150	Don't/I Beg of You	1958	6.25	12.50	25.00
—No horizontal line on label					
❑ 47-7150	Don't/I Beg of You	1958	6.25	12.50	25.00
—With horizontal line on label					
❑ 47-7150 [PS]	Don't/I Beg of You	1958	22.50	45.00	90.00
❑ 47-7240	Wear My Ring Around Your Neck/Don'tcha Think It's Time	1958	6.25	12.50	25.00
❑ 47-7240 [PS]	Wear My Ring Around Your Neck/Don'tcha Think It's Time	1958	22.50	45.00	90.00
❑ 47-7280	Hard Headed Woman/Don't Ask Me Why	1958	6.25	12.50	25.00
❑ 47-7280 [PS]	Hard Headed Woman/Don't Ask Me Why	1958	17.50	35.00	70.00
❑ 47-7410	One Night/I Got Stung	1958	6.25	12.50	25.00
❑ 47-7410 [PS]	One Night/I Got Stung	1958	17.50	35.00	70.00
❑ 47-7506	(Now and Then There's) A Fool Such As I/I Need Your Love Tonight	1959	6.25	12.50	25.00
❑ 47-7506 [PS]	(Now and Then There's) A Fool Such As I/I Need Your Love Tonight	1959	250.00	500.00	1000.
—Sleeve promotes the "Elvis Sails" EP					
❑ 47-7506 [PS]	(Now and Then There's) A Fool Such As I/I Need Your Love Tonight	1959	15.00	30.00	60.00
—Sleeve lists Elvis' EPs and Gold Standard singles					
❑ 47-7600	A Big Hunk o'Love/My Wish Came True	1959	6.25	12.50	25.00
❑ 47-7600 [PS]	A Big Hunk o'Love/My Wish Came True	1959	17.50	35.00	70.00
❑ 47-7740	Stuck on You/Fame and Fortune	1960	5.00	10.00	20.00
❑ 47-7740 [PS]	Stuck on You/Fame and Fortune	1960	15.00	30.00	60.00
❑ 47-7777	It's Now or Never/A Mess of Blues	1960	250.00	500.00	1000.
—An early mispress is missing the piano part on the A-side. Has the number "L2WW-0100-3S" or "L2WW-0100-4S" in trail-off wax.					
❑ 47-7777	It's Now or Never/A Mess of Blues	1960	5.00	10.00	20.00
—All other pressings with overdubbed piano					
❑ 47-7777 [PS]	It's Now or Never/A Mess of Blues	1960	15.00	30.00	60.00
❑ 47-7810	Are You Lonesome To-Night?/I Gotta Know	1960	5.00	10.00	20.00
❑ 47-7810 [PS]	Are You Lonesome To-Night?/I Gotta Know	1960	15.00	30.00	60.00
❑ 47-7850	Surrender/Lonely Man	1961	5.00	10.00	20.00
❑ 47-7850 [PS]	Surrender/Lonely Man	1961	15.00	30.00	60.00
❑ 47-7880	I Feel So Bad/Wild in the Country	1961	5.00	10.00	20.00
❑ 47-7880 [PS]	I Feel So Bad/Wild in the Country	1961	12.50	25.00	50.00
❑ 47-7908	(Marie's the Name) His Latest Flame/Little Sister	1961	5.00	10.00	20.00
—All copies of this record actually read "Marie's the Name HIS LATEST FLAME" (no parentheses)					
❑ 47-7908 [PS]	(Marie's the Name) His Latest Flame/Little Sister	1961	12.50	25.00	50.00
❑ 47-7968	Can't Help Falling in Love/Rock-a-Hula Baby	1961	5.00	10.00	20.00
❑ 47-7968 [PS]	Can't Help Falling in Love/Rock-a-Hula Baby	1961	10.00	20.00	40.00
❑ 47-7992	Good Luck Charm/Anything That's Part of You	1962	5.00	10.00	20.00
❑ 47-7992 [PS]	Good Luck Charm/Anything That's Part of You	1962	10.00	20.00	40.00
—Titles in blue and pink letters					
❑ 47-7992 [PS]	Good Luck Charm/Anything That's Part of You	1962	10.00	20.00	40.00
—Titles in rust and lavender letters					
❑ 47-8041	She's Not You/Just Tell Her Jim Said Hello	1962	5.00	10.00	20.00
❑ 47-8041 [PS]	She's Not You/Just Tell Her Jim Said Hello	1962	10.00	20.00	40.00
❑ 47-8100	Return to Sender/Where Do You Come From	1962	5.00	10.00	20.00
❑ 47-8100 [PS]	Return to Sender/Where Do You Come From	1962	10.00	20.00	40.00
❑ 47-8134	One Broken Heart for Sale/They Remind Me Too Much of You	1963	3.00	6.00	12.00
❑ 47-8134 [PS]	One Broken Heart for Sale/They Remind Me Too Much of You	1963	7.50	15.00	30.00
❑ 47-8188	(You're the) Devil in Disguise/Please Don't Drag That String Along	1963	50.00	100.00	200.00
—First pressing with incorrect B-side title					
❑ 47-8188	(You're the) Devil in Disguise/Please Don't Drag That String Around	1963	3.00	6.00	12.00
—Second pressing with correct B-side title					
❑ 47-8188 [PS]	(You're the) Devil in Disguise/Please Don't Drag That String Around	1963	7.50	15.00	30.00
—All sleeves have correct B-side title					
❑ 47-8243	Bossa Nova Baby/Witchcraft	1963	3.00	6.00	12.00
❑ 47-8243 [PS]	Bossa Nova Baby/Witchcraft	1963	7.50	15.00	30.00
—"Coming Soon" on sleeve					
❑ 47-8243 [PS]	Bossa Nova Baby/Witchcraft	1963	7.50	15.00	30.00
—"Ask For" on sleeve					
❑ 47-8243 [PS]	Bossa Nova Baby/Witchcraft	1963	7.50	15.00	30.00
—No reference to another album on sleeve					
❑ 47-8307	Kissin' Cousins/It Hurts Me	1964	3.00	6.00	12.00
❑ 47-8307 [PS]	Kissin' Cousins/It Hurts Me	1964	6.25	12.50	25.00
❑ 47-8360	Viva Las Vegas/What'd I Say	1964	3.00	6.00	12.00
❑ 47-8360 [PS]	Viva Las Vegas/What'd I Say	1964	6.25	12.50	25.00
—"Coming Soon" on sleeve					
❑ 47-8360 [PS]	Viva Las Vegas/What'd I Say	1964	12.50	25.00	50.00
—"Ask For" on sleeve					
❑ 47-8400	Such a Night/Never Ending	1964	3.00	6.00	12.00
❑ 47-8400 [DJ]	Such a Night/Never Ending	1964	2500.	3750.	5000.
—An inexplicably rare regular white label promo					
❑ 47-8400 [PS]	Such a Night/Never Ending	1964	6.25	12.50	25.00
❑ 47-8440	Ain't That Loving You Baby/Ask Me	1964	2.50	5.00	10.00
❑ 47-8440 [PS]	Ain't That Loving You Baby/Ask Me	1964	6.25	12.50	25.00
—"Coming Soon" on sleeve					
❑ 47-8440 [PS]	Ain't That Loving You Baby/Ask Me	1964	6.25	12.50	25.00
—"Ask For" on sleeve					
❑ 47-8500	Do the Clam/You'll Be Gone	1965	2.50	5.00	10.00

Number	Title (A Side/B Side)	Yr	VG	VG+	NM
❑ 47-8500 [PS]	Do the Clam/You'll Be Gone	1965	6.25	12.50	25.00
❑ 47-8585	(Such An) Easy Question/It Feels So Right	1965	2.50	5.00	10.00
❑ 47-8585 [PS]	(Such An) Easy Question/It Feels So Right	1965	6.25	12.50	25.00
—"Coming Soon" on sleeve					
❑ 47-8585 [PS]	(Such An) Easy Question/It Feels So Right	1965	6.25	12.50	25.00
—"Ask For" on sleeve					
❑ 47-8657	I'm Yours/(It's a) Long, Lonely Highway	1965	2.50	5.00	10.00
❑ 47-8657 [PS]	I'm Yours/(It's a) Long, Lonely Highway	1965	6.25	12.50	25.00
❑ 47-8740	Tell Me Why/Blue River	1965	2.50	5.00	10.00
❑ 47-8740 [PS]	Tell Me Why/Blue River	1965	6.25	12.50	25.00
❑ 47-8780	Frankie and Johnny/Please Don't Stop Loving Me	1966	2.50	5.00	10.00
❑ 47-8780 [PS]	Frankie and Johnny/Please Don't Stop Loving Me	1966	6.25	12.50	25.00
❑ 47-8870	Love Letters/Come What May	1966	2.50	5.00	10.00
❑ 47-8870 [PS]	Love Letters/Come What May	1966	6.25	12.50	25.00
—"Coming Soon" on sleeve					
❑ 47-8870 [PS]	Love Letters/Come What May	1966	6.25	12.50	25.00
—"Ask For" on sleeve					
❑ 47-8941	Spinout/All That I Do	1966	2.50	5.00	10.00
❑ 47-8941 [PS]	Spinout/All That I Do	1966	6.25	12.50	25.00
—"Watch For" on sleeve					
❑ 47-8941 [PS]	Spinout/All That I Do	1966	6.25	12.50	25.00
—"Ask For" on sleeve					
❑ 47-8950	If Every Day Was Like Christmas/How Would You Like to Be	1966	5.00	10.00	20.00
❑ 47-8950 [PS]	If Every Day Was Like Christmas/How Would You Like to Be	1966	10.00	20.00	40.00
❑ 47-9056	Indescribably Blue/Fools Fall in Love	1966	2.50	5.00	10.00
❑ 47-9056 [PS]	Indescribably Blue/Fools Fall in Love	1966	6.25	12.50	25.00
❑ 47-9115	Long Legged Girl (With the Short Dress On)/That's Someone You Never Forget	1967	2.50	5.00	10.00
❑ 47-9115 [PS]	Long Legged Girl (With the Short Dress On)/That's Someone You Never Forget	1967	6.25	12.50	25.00
—"Coming Soon" on sleeve					
❑ 47-9115 [PS]	Long Legged Girl (With the Short Dress On)/That's Someone You Never Forget	1967	6.25	12.50	25.00
—"Ask For" on sleeve					
❑ 47-9287	There's Always Me/Judy	1967	2.50	5.00	10.00
❑ 47-9287 [PS]	There's Always Me/Judy	1967	6.25	12.50	25.00
❑ 47-9341	Big Boss Man/You Don't Know Me	1967	2.50	5.00	10.00
❑ 47-9341 [PS]	Big Boss Man/You Don't Know Me	1967	6.25	12.50	25.00
❑ 47-9425	Guitar Man/High Heel Sneakers	1968	2.50	5.00	10.00
❑ 47-9425 [PS]	Guitar Man/High Heel Sneakers	1968	6.25	12.50	25.00
—"Coming Soon" on sleeve					
❑ 47-9425 [PS]	Guitar Man/High Heel Sneakers	1968	6.25	12.50	25.00
—"Ask For" on sleeve					
❑ 47-9465	U.S. Male/Stay Away	1968	2.50	5.00	10.00
❑ 47-9465 [PS]	U.S. Male/Stay Away	1968	6.25	12.50	25.00
❑ 47-9547	Let Yourself Go/Your Time Hasn't Come Yet, Baby	1968	2.50	5.00	10.00
❑ 47-9547 [PS]	Let Yourself Go/Your Time Hasn't Come Yet, Baby	1968	6.25	12.50	25.00
—"Coming Soon" on sleeve					
❑ 47-9547 [PS]	Let Yourself Go/Your Time Hasn't Come Yet, Baby	1968	6.25	12.50	25.00
—"Ask For" on sleeve					
❑ 47-9600	You'll Never Walk Alone/We Call on Him	1968	3.00	6.00	12.00
❑ 47-9600 [PS]	You'll Never Walk Alone/We Call on Him	1968	25.00	50.00	100.00
❑ 47-9610	A Little Less Conversation/Almost in Love	1968	2.50	5.00	10.00
❑ 47-9610 [PS]	A Little Less Conversation/Almost in Love	1968	6.25	12.50	25.00
❑ 47-9670	If I Can Dream/Edge of Reality	1968	2.00	4.00	8.00
—First Elvis single on orange label					
❑ 47-9670 [PS]	If I Can Dream/Edge of Reality	1968	5.00	10.00	20.00
—Mentions his NBC-TV special on sleeve					
❑ 47-9670 [PS]	If I Can Dream/Edge of Reality	1968	5.00	10.00	20.00
—Does not mention his NBC-TV special on sleeve					
❑ 47-9731	Memories/Charro	1969	2.00	4.00	8.00
❑ 47-9731 [PS]	Memories/Charro	1969	5.00	10.00	20.00
❑ 47-9741	In the Ghetto/Any Day Now	1969	2.00	4.00	8.00
❑ 47-9741 [PS]	In the Ghetto/Any Day Now	1969	5.00	10.00	20.00
—"Coming Soon" on sleeve					
❑ 47-9741 [PS]	In the Ghetto/Any Day Now	1969	5.00	10.00	20.00
—"Ask For" on sleeve					
❑ 47-9747	Clean Up Your Own Back Yard/The Fair Is Moving On	1969	2.00	4.00	8.00
❑ 47-9747 [PS]	Clean Up Your Own Back Yard/The Fair Is Moving On	1969	5.00	10.00	20.00
❑ 47-9764	Suspicious Minds/You'll Think of Me	1969	2.00	4.00	8.00
❑ 47-9764 [PS]	Suspicious Minds/You'll Think of Me	1969	5.00	10.00	20.00
❑ 47-9768	Don't Cry Daddy/Rubberneckin'	1969	2.00	4.00	8.00
❑ 47-9768 [PS]	Don't Cry Daddy/Rubberneckin'	1969	3.75	7.50	15.00
❑ 47-9791	Kentucky Rain/My Little Friend	1969	2.00	4.00	8.00
❑ 47-9791 [PS]	Kentucky Rain/My Little Friend	1969	3.75	7.50	15.00
❑ 47-9835	The Wonder of You/Mama Liked the Roses	1970	2.00	4.00	8.00
❑ 47-9835 [PS]	The Wonder of You/Mama Liked the Roses	1970	3.75	7.50	15.00
❑ 47-9873	I've Lost You/The Next Step Is Love	1970	—	3.00	6.00
❑ 47-9873 [PS]	I've Lost You/The Next Step Is Love	1970	3.75	7.50	15.00
❑ 47-9916	You Don't Have to Say You Love Me/Patch It Up	1970	—	3.00	6.00
❑ 47-9916 [PS]	You Don't Have to Say You Love Me/Patch It Up	1970	3.75	7.50	15.00
❑ 47-9960	I Really Don't Want to Know/There Goes My Everything	1971	—	3.00	6.00
❑ 47-9960 [PS]	I Really Don't Want to Know/There Goes My Everything	1971	3.75	7.50	15.00
—"Coming Soon" on sleeve					
❑ 47-9960 [PS]	I Really Don't Want to Know/There Goes My Everything	1971	3.75	7.50	15.00
—"Ask For" on sleeve					
❑ 47-9980	Where Did They Go, Lord/Rags to Riches	1971	—	3.00	6.00
❑ 47-9980 [PS]	Where Did They Go, Lord/Rags to Riches	1971	5.00	10.00	20.00
❑ 47-9985	Life/Only Believe	1971	—	3.00	6.00
❑ 47-9985 [PS]	Life/Only Believe	1971	7.50	15.00	30.00
❑ 47-9998	I'm Leavin'/Heart of Rome	1971	—	3.00	6.00
❑ 47-9998 [PS]	I'm Leavin'/Heart of Rome	1971	5.00	10.00	20.00
❑ 48-1017	It's Only Love/The Sound of Your Cry	1971	—	3.00	6.00
❑ 48-1017 [PS]	It's Only Love/The Sound of Your Cry	1971	3.75	7.50	15.00
❑ 61-7740 [S]	Stuck on You/Fame and Fortune	1960	100.00	200.00	400.00
—"Living Stereo" (large hole, plays at 45 rpm)					
❑ 61-7777 [S]	It's Now or Never/A Mess of Blues	1960	100.00	200.00	400.00
—"Living Stereo" (large hole, plays at 45 rpm)					
❑ 61-7810 [S]	Are You Lonesome To-Night?/I Gotta Know	1960	150.00	300.00	600.00
—"Living Stereo" (large hole, plays at 45 rpm)					
❑ 61-7850 [S]	Surrender/Lonely Man	1961	200.00	400.00	800.00
—"Living Stereo" (large hole, plays at 45 rpm)					
❑ 68-7850 [S]	Surrender/Lonely Man	1961	1000.	1500.	2000.
—"Compact Stereo 33" in "Living Stereo"					
❑ 74-0130	How Great Thou Art/His Hand in Mine	1969	6.25	12.50	25.00
❑ 74-0130 [PS]	How Great Thou Art/His Hand in Mine	1969	37.50	75.00	150.00
❑ 74-0572	Merry Christmas Baby/O Come All Ye Faithful	1971	3.75	7.50	15.00
❑ 74-0572 [PS]	Merry Christmas Baby/O Come All Ye Faithful	1971	10.00	20.00	40.00
❑ 74-0619	Until It's Time for You to Go/We Can Make the Morning	1971	—	3.00	6.00
❑ 74-0619 [PS]	Until It's Time for You to Go/We Can Make the Morning	1971	3.75	7.50	15.00
❑ 74-0651	He Touched Me/The Bosom of Abraham	1972	37.50	75.00	150.00
—"He Touched Me" actually plays at about 35 rpm in error. A-side has "AWKS-1277" stamped in trail-off wax.					
❑ 74-0651	He Touched Me/The Bosom of Abraham	1972	2.00	4.00	8.00
—"He Touched Me" plays correctly. A-side has "APKS-1277" stamped in trail-off wax.					
❑ 74-0651 [PS]	He Touched Me/The Bosom of Abraham	1972	30.00	60.00	120.00
❑ 74-0672	An American Trilogy/The First Time Ever I Saw Your Face	1972	5.00	10.00	20.00
❑ 74-0672 [PS]	An American Trilogy/The First Time Ever I Saw Your Face	1972	10.00	20.00	40.00
❑ 74-0769	Burning Love/It's a Matter of Time	1972	—	3.00	6.00
—Originals have orange labels					
❑ 74-0769	Burning Love/It's a Matter of Time	1974	37.50	75.00	150.00
—Very rare reissues have gray labels					
❑ 74-0769 [PS]	Burning Love/It's a Matter of Time	1972	3.75	7.50	15.00
❑ 74-0815	Separate Ways/Always on My Mind	1972	—	3.00	6.00
❑ 74-0815 [PS]	Separate Ways/Always on My Mind	1972	3.75	7.50	15.00
❑ 74-0910	Steamroller Blues/Fool	1973	—	3.00	6.00
❑ 74-0910 [PS]	Steamroller Blues/Fool	1973	3.75	7.50	15.00
❑ 447-0600	I Forgot to Remember to Forget/Mystery Train	1959	3.75	7.50	15.00
—Note: All RCA Victor releases with a "447" prefix are from the Gold Standard Series. Black label, dog on top					
❑ 447-0600	I Forgot to Remember to Forget/Mystery Train	1965	2.50	5.00	10.00
—Black label, dog on left					
❑ 447-0600	I Forgot to Remember to Forget/Mystery Train	1969	6.25	12.50	25.00
—Orange label					
❑ 447-0600	I Forgot to Remember to Forget/Mystery Train	1970	2.00	4.00	8.00
—Red label					
❑ 447-0601	That's All Right/Blue Moon of Kentucky	1959	3.75	7.50	15.00
—Black label, dog on top					
❑ 447-0601	That's All Right/Blue Moon of Kentucky	1965	2.50	5.00	10.00
—Black label, dog on left					
❑ 447-0601	That's All Right/Blue Moon of Kentucky	1969	2.00	4.00	8.00
—Red label; B-side artist credit is misspelled "Elvis Presely"					
❑ 447-0601 [DJ]	That's All Right/Blue Moon of Kentucky	1964	25.00	50.00	100.00
❑ 447-0601 [PS]	That's All Right/Blue Moon of Kentucky	1964	50.00	100.00	200.00
❑ 447-0602	Good Rockin' Tonight/I Don't Care If the Sun Don't Shine	1959	3.75	7.50	15.00
—Black label, dog on top					
❑ 447-0602	Good Rockin' Tonight/I Don't Care If the Sun Don't Shine	1965	2.50	5.00	10.00
—Black label, dog on left					
❑ 447-0602	Good Rockin' Tonight/I Don't Care If the Sun Don't Shine	1970	2.00	4.00	8.00
—Red label					
❑ 447-0602 [DJ]	Good Rockin' Tonight/I Don't Care If the Sun Don't Shine	1964	25.00	50.00	100.00
❑ 447-0602 [PS]	Good Rockin' Tonight/I Don't Care If the Sun Don't Shine	1964	50.00	100.00	200.00
❑ 447-0603	Milkcow Blues Boogie/You're a Heartbreaker	1959	3.75	7.50	15.00
—Black label, dog on top					
❑ 447-0603	Milkcow Blues Boogie/You're a Heartbreaker	1965	2.50	5.00	10.00
—Black label, dog on left					
❑ 447-0603	Milkcow Blues Boogie/You're a Heartbreaker	1969	6.25	12.50	25.00
—Orange label					
❑ 447-0603	Milkcow Blues Boogie/You're a Heartbreaker	1970	2.00	4.00	8.00
—Red label					
❑ 447-0604	Baby Let's Play House/I'm Left, You're Right, She's Gone	1959	3.75	7.50	15.00
—Black label, dog on top					
❑ 447-0604	Baby Let's Play House/I'm Left, You're Right, She's Gone	1965	2.50	5.00	10.00
—Black label, dog on left					
❑ 447-0604	Baby Let's Play House/I'm Left, You're Right, She's Gone	1970	2.00	4.00	8.00
—Red label					
❑ 447-0605	Heartbreak Hotel/I Was the One	1959	3.75	7.50	15.00
—Black label, dog on top					
❑ 447-0605	Heartbreak Hotel/I Was the One	1965	2.50	5.00	10.00
—Black label, dog on left					

Number	Title (A Side/B Side)	Yr	VG	VG+	NM
❑ 447-0605 —Orange label	Heartbreak Hotel/I Was the One	1969	6.25	12.50	25.00
❑ 447-0605 —Red label	Heartbreak Hotel/I Was the One	1970	2.00	4.00	8.00
❑ 447-0605 [DJ]	Heartbreak Hotel/I Was the One	1964	25.00	50.00	100.00
❑ 447-0605 [PS]	Heartbreak Hotel/I Was the One	1964	50.00	100.00	200.00
❑ 447-0607 —Black label, dog on top	I Want You, I Need You, I Love You/My Baby Left Me	1959	3.75	7.50	15.00
❑ 447-0607 —Black label, dog on left	I Want You, I Need You, I Love You/My Baby Left Me	1965	2.50	5.00	10.00
❑ 447-0607 —Orange label	I Want You, I Need You, I Love You/My Baby Left Me	1969	6.25	12.50	25.00
❑ 447-0607 —Red label	I Want You, I Need You, I Love You/My Baby Left Me	1970	2.00	4.00	8.00
❑ 447-0608 —Black label, dog on top	Hound Dog/Don't Be Cruel	1959	3.75	7.50	15.00
❑ 447-0608 —Black label, dog on left	Hound Dog/Don't Be Cruel	1965	2.50	5.00	10.00
❑ 447-0608 —Orange label	Hound Dog/Don't Be Cruel	1969	6.25	12.50	25.00
❑ 447-0608 —Red label	Hound Dog/Don't Be Cruel	1970	2.00	4.00	8.00
❑ 447-0608 [DJ]	Hound Dog/Don't Be Cruel	1964	25.00	50.00	100.00
❑ 447-0608 [PS]	Hound Dog/Don't Be Cruel	1964	50.00	100.00	200.00
❑ 447-0609 —Black label, dog on top	Blue Suede Shoes/Tutti Frutti	1959	3.75	7.50	15.00
❑ 447-0609 —Black label, dog on left	Blue Suede Shoes/Tutti Frutti	1965	2.50	5.00	10.00
❑ 447-0609 —Orange label	Blue Suede Shoes/Tutti Frutti	1969	6.25	12.50	25.00
❑ 447-0609 —Red label	Blue Suede Shoes/Tutti Frutti	1970	2.00	4.00	8.00
❑ 447-0610 —Black label, dog on top	I Got a Woman/I'm Countin' On You	1959	3.75	7.50	15.00
❑ 447-0611 —Black label, dog on top	I'm Gonna Sit Right Down and Cry (Over You)/I'll Never Let You Go (Little Darlin')	1959	3.75	7.50	15.00
❑ 447-0612 —Black label, dog on top	Tryin' to Get to You/I Love You Because	1959	3.75	7.50	15.00
❑ 447-0613 —Black label, dog on top	Blue Moon/Just Because	1959	3.75	7.50	15.00
❑ 447-0613 —Black label, dog on left	Blue Moon/Just Because	1965	2.50	5.00	10.00
❑ 447-0613 —Orange label	Blue Moon/Just Because	1969	6.25	12.50	25.00
❑ 447-0613 —Red label	Blue Moon/Just Because	1970	2.00	4.00	8.00
❑ 447-0614 —Black label, dog on top	Money Honey/One-Sided Love Affair	1959	3.75	7.50	15.00
❑ 447-0614 —Black label, dog on left	Money Honey/One-Sided Love Affair	1965	2.50	5.00	10.00
❑ 447-0614 —Orange label	Money Honey/One-Sided Love Affair	1969	6.25	12.50	25.00
❑ 447-0614 —Red label	Money Honey/One-Sided Love Affair	1970	2.00	4.00	8.00
❑ 447-0615 —Black label, dog on top	Lawdy Miss Clawdy/Shake, Rattle, and Roll	1959	3.75	7.50	15.00
❑ 447-0615 —Black label, dog on left	Lawdy Miss Clawdy/Shake, Rattle, and Roll	1965	2.50	5.00	10.00
❑ 447-0615 —Orange label	Lawdy Miss Clawdy/Shake, Rattle, and Roll	1969	6.25	12.50	25.00
❑ 447-0615 —Red label	Lawdy Miss Clawdy/Shake, Rattle, and Roll	1970	2.00	4.00	8.00
❑ 447-0616 —Black label, dog on top	Love Me Tender/Anyway You Want Me (That's How I Will Be)	1959	3.75	7.50	15.00
❑ 447-0616 —Black label, dog on left	Love Me Tender/Anyway You Want Me (That's How I Will Be)	1965	2.50	5.00	10.00
❑ 447-0616 —Orange label	Love Me Tender/Anyway You Want Me (That's How I Will Be)	1969	6.25	12.50	25.00
❑ 447-0616 —Red label	Love Me Tender/Anyway You Want Me (That's How I Will Be)	1970	2.00	4.00	8.00
❑ 447-0617 —Black label, dog on top	Too Much/Playing for Keeps	1959	3.75	7.50	15.00
❑ 447-0617 —Black label, dog on left	Too Much/Playing for Keeps	1965	2.50	5.00	10.00
❑ 447-0617 —Orange label	Too Much/Playing for Keeps	1969	6.25	12.50	25.00
❑ 447-0617 —Red label	Too Much/Playing for Keeps	1970	2.00	4.00	8.00
❑ 447-0618 —Black label, dog on top	All Shook Up/That's When Your Heartaches Begin	1959	3.75	7.50	15.00
❑ 447-0618 —Black label, dog on left	All Shook Up/That's When Your Heartaches Begin	1965	2.50	5.00	10.00
❑ 447-0618 —Orange label	All Shook Up/That's When Your Heartaches Begin	1969	6.25	12.50	25.00
❑ 447-0618 —Red label	All Shook Up/That's When Your Heartaches Begin	1970	2.00	4.00	8.00
❑ 447-0618 [DJ]	All Shook Up/That's When Your Heartaches Begin	1964	25.00	50.00	100.00
❑ 447-0618 [PS]	All Shook Up/That's When Your Heartaches Begin	1964	50.00	100.00	200.00
❑ 447-0619 —Black label, dog on top	Jailhouse Rock/Treat Me Nice	1959	3.75	7.50	15.00
❑ 447-0619 —Black label, dog on left	Jailhouse Rock/Treat Me Nice	1965	2.50	5.00	10.00
❑ 447-0619 —Orange label	Jailhouse Rock/Treat Me Nice	1969	6.25	12.50	25.00
❑ 447-0619 —Red label	Jailhouse Rock/Treat Me Nice	1970	2.00	4.00	8.00
❑ 447-0620 —Black label, dog on top	(Let Me Be Your) Teddy Bear/Loving You	1959	3.75	7.50	15.00
❑ 447-0620 —Black label, dog on left	(Let Me Be Your) Teddy Bear/Loving You	1965	2.50	5.00	10.00
❑ 447-0620 —Orange label	(Let Me Be Your) Teddy Bear/Loving You	1969	6.25	12.50	25.00
❑ 447-0620 —Red label	(Let Me Be Your) Teddy Bear/Loving You	1970	2.00	4.00	8.00
❑ 447-0621 —Black label, dog on top	Don't/I Beg of You	1961	3.00	6.00	12.00
❑ 447-0621 —Black label, dog on left	Don't/I Beg of You	1965	2.50	5.00	10.00
❑ 447-0621 —Orange label	Don't/I Beg of You	1969	6.25	12.50	25.00
❑ 447-0621 —Red label	Don't/I Beg of You	1970	2.00	4.00	8.00
❑ 447-0622 —Black label, dog on top	Wear My Ring Around Your Neck/Don'tcha Think It's Time	1961	3.00	6.00	12.00
❑ 447-0622 —Black label, dog on left	Wear My Ring Around Your Neck/Don'tcha Think It's Time	1965	2.50	5.00	10.00
❑ 447-0622 —Orange label	Wear My Ring Around Your Neck/Don'tcha Think It's Time	1969	6.25	12.50	25.00
❑ 447-0622 —Red label	Wear My Ring Around Your Neck/Don'tcha Think It's Time	1970	2.00	4.00	8.00
❑ 447-0623 —Black label, dog on top	Hard Headed Woman/Don't Ask Me Why	1961	3.75	7.50	15.00
❑ 447-0623 —Black label, dog on left	Hard Headed Woman/Don't Ask Me Why	1965	2.50	5.00	10.00
❑ 447-0623 —Orange label	Hard Headed Woman/Don't Ask Me Why	1969	6.25	12.50	25.00
❑ 447-0623 —Red label	Hard Headed Woman/Don't Ask Me Why	1970	2.00	4.00	8.00
❑ 447-0624 —Black label, dog on top	One Night/I Got Stung	1961	3.00	6.00	12.00
❑ 447-0624 —Black label, dog on left	One Night/I Got Stung	1965	2.50	5.00	10.00
❑ 447-0624 —Orange label	One Night/I Got Stung	1969	6.25	12.50	25.00
❑ 447-0624 —Red label	One Night/I Got Stung	1970	2.00	4.00	8.00
❑ 447-0625 —Black label, dog on top	(Now and Then There's) A Fool Such As I/I Need Your Love Tonight	1961	3.75	7.50	15.00
❑ 447-0625 —Black label, dog on left	(Now and Then There's) A Fool Such As I/I Need Your Love Tonight	1965	2.50	5.00	10.00
❑ 447-0625 —Orange label	(Now and Then There's) A Fool Such As I/I Need Your Love Tonight	1969	6.25	12.50	25.00
❑ 447-0625 —Red label	(Now and Then There's) A Fool Such As I/I Need Your Love Tonight	1970	2.00	4.00	8.00
❑ 447-0626 —Black label, dog on top	A Big Hunk o'Love/My Wish Came True	1962	3.75	7.50	15.00
❑ 447-0626 —Black label, dog on left	A Big Hunk o'Love/My Wish Came True	1965	2.50	5.00	10.00
❑ 447-0626 —Orange label	A Big Hunk o'Love/My Wish Came True	1969	6.25	12.50	25.00
❑ 447-0626 —Red label	A Big Hunk o'Love/My Wish Came True	1970	2.00	4.00	8.00
❑ 447-0627 —Black label, dog on top	Stuck on You/Fame and Fortune	1962	3.00	6.00	12.00
❑ 447-0627 —Black label, dog on left	Stuck on You/Fame and Fortune	1965	2.50	5.00	10.00
❑ 447-0627 —Orange label	Stuck on You/Fame and Fortune	1969	6.25	12.50	25.00
❑ 447-0627 —Red label	Stuck on You/Fame and Fortune	1970	2.00	4.00	8.00
❑ 447-0628 —Black label, dog on top	It's Now or Never/A Mess of Blues	1962	3.00	6.00	12.00
❑ 447-0628 —Black label, dog on left	It's Now or Never/A Mess of Blues	1965	2.50	5.00	10.00
❑ 447-0628 —Orange label	It's Now or Never/A Mess of Blues	1969	6.25	12.50	25.00
❑ 447-0628 —Red label	It's Now or Never/A Mess of Blues	1970	2.00	4.00	8.00
❑ 447-0629 —Black label, dog on top	Are You Lonesome To-Night?/I Gotta Know	1962	3.75	7.50	15.00

Number	Title (A Side/B Side)	Yr	VG	VG+	NM
❑ 447-0629	Are You Lonesome To-Night?/I Gotta Know	1965	2.50	5.00	10.00
—Black label, dog on left					
❑ 447-0629	Are You Lonesome To-Night?/I Gotta Know	1969	6.25	12.50	25.00
—Orange label					
❑ 447-0629	Are You Lonesome To-Night?/I Gotta Know	1970	2.00	4.00	8.00
—Red label					
❑ 447-0630	Surrender/Lonely Man	1962	6.25	12.50	25.00
—Black label, dog on top					
❑ 447-0630	Surrender/Lonely Man	1965	2.50	5.00	10.00
—Black label, dog on left					
❑ 447-0630	Surrender/Lonely Man	1969	6.25	12.50	25.00
—Orange label					
❑ 447-0630	Surrender/Lonely Man	1970	2.00	4.00	8.00
—Red label					
❑ 447-0631	I Feel So Bad/Wild in the Country	1962	3.00	6.00	12.00
—Black label, dog on top					
❑ 447-0631	I Feel So Bad/Wild in the Country	1965	2.50	5.00	10.00
—Black label, dog on left					
❑ 447-0631	I Feel So Bad/Wild in the Country	1970	2.00	4.00	8.00
—Red label					
❑ 447-0634	(Marie's the Name) His Latest Flame/Little Sister	1962	3.00	6.00	12.00
—Black label, dog on top					
❑ 447-0634	(Marie's the Name) His Latest Flame/Little Sister	1965	2.50	5.00	10.00
—Black label, dog on left					
❑ 447-0634	(Marie's the Name) His Latest Flame/Little Sister	1969	6.25	12.50	25.00
—Orange label					
❑ 447-0634	(Marie's the Name) His Latest Flame/Little Sister	1970	2.00	4.00	8.00
—Red label					
❑ 447-0635	Can't Help Falling in Love/Rock-a-Hula Baby	1962	3.00	6.00	12.00
—Black label, dog on top					
❑ 447-0635	Can't Help Falling in Love/Rock-a-Hula Baby	1965	2.50	5.00	10.00
—Black label, dog on left					
❑ 447-0635	Can't Help Falling in Love/Rock-a-Hula Baby	1969	6.25	12.50	25.00
—Orange label					
❑ 447-0635	Can't Help Falling in Love/Rock-a-Hula Baby	1970	2.00	4.00	8.00
—Red label					
❑ 447-0636	Good Luck Charm/Anything That's Part of You	1962	3.00	6.00	12.00
—Black label, dog on top					
❑ 447-0636	Good Luck Charm/Anything That's Part of You	1965	2.50	5.00	10.00
—Black label, dog on left					
❑ 447-0636	Good Luck Charm/Anything That's Part of You	1969	6.25	12.50	25.00
—Orange label					
❑ 447-0636	Good Luck Charm/Anything That's Part of You	1970	2.00	4.00	8.00
—Red label					
❑ 447-0637	She's Not You/Just Tell Her Jim Said Hello	1963	3.00	6.00	12.00
—Black label, dog on top					
❑ 447-0637	She's Not You/Just Tell Her Jim Said Hello	1965	2.50	5.00	10.00
—Black label, dog on left					
❑ 447-0637	She's Not You/Just Tell Her Jim Said Hello	1969	6.25	12.50	25.00
—Orange label					
❑ 447-0637	She's Not You/Just Tell Her Jim Said Hello	1970	2.00	4.00	8.00
—Red label					
❑ 447-0638	Return to Sender/Where Do You Come From	1963	3.00	6.00	12.00
—Black label, dog on top					
❑ 447-0638	Return to Sender/Where Do You Come From	1965	2.50	5.00	10.00
—Black label, dog on left					
❑ 447-0638	Return to Sender/Where Do You Come From	1969	6.25	12.50	25.00
—Orange label					
❑ 447-0638	Return to Sender/Where Do You Come From	1970	2.00	4.00	8.00
—Red label					
❑ 447-0639	Kiss Me Quick/Suspicion	1964	2.50	5.00	10.00
—Black label, dog on top					
❑ 447-0639	Kiss Me Quick/Suspicion	1969	6.25	12.50	25.00
—Orange label					
❑ 447-0639	Kiss Me Quick/Suspicion	1970	2.00	4.00	8.00
—Red label					
❑ 447-0639 [PS]	Kiss Me Quick/Suspicion	1964	10.00	20.00	40.00
❑ 447-0640	One Broken Heart for Sale/They Remind Me Too Much of You	1964	6.25	12.50	25.00
—Black label, dog on top					
❑ 447-0640	One Broken Heart for Sale/They Remind Me Too Much of You	1965	2.50	5.00	10.00
—Black label, dog on left					
❑ 447-0640	One Broken Heart for Sale/They Remind Me Too Much of You	1969	6.25	12.50	25.00
—Orange label					
❑ 447-0640	One Broken Heart for Sale/They Remind Me Too Much of You	1970	2.00	4.00	8.00
—Red label					
❑ 447-0641	(You're the) Devil in Disguise/Please Don't Drag That String Around	1964	6.25	12.50	25.00
—Black label, dog on top					
❑ 447-0641	(You're the) Devil in Disguise/Please Don't Drag That String Around	1965	2.50	5.00	10.00
—Black label, dog on left					
❑ 447-0641	(You're the) Devil in Disguise/Please Don't Drag That String Around	1970	2.00	4.00	8.00
—Red label					
❑ 447-0642	Bossa Nova Baby/Witchcraft	1964	6.25	12.50	25.00
—Black label, dog on top					
❑ 447-0642	Bossa Nova Baby/Witchcraft	1965	2.50	5.00	10.00
—Black label, dog on left					
❑ 447-0642	Bossa Nova Baby/Witchcraft	1969	6.25	12.50	25.00
—Orange label					
❑ 447-0642	Bossa Nova Baby/Witchcraft	1970	2.00	4.00	8.00
—Red label					
❑ 447-0643	Crying in the Chapel/I Believe in the Man in the Sky	1965	2.50	5.00	10.00
—Black label, dog on left					
❑ 447-0643	Crying in the Chapel/I Believe in the Man in the Sky	1970	2.00	4.00	8.00
—Red label					
❑ 447-0643 [PS]	Crying in the Chapel/I Believe in the Man in the Sky	1965	7.50	15.00	30.00
❑ 447-0644	Kissin' Cousins/It Hurts Me	1965	2.50	5.00	10.00
—Black label, dog on left					
❑ 447-0644	Kissin' Cousins/It Hurts Me	1969	6.25	12.50	25.00
—Orange label					
❑ 447-0644	Kissin' Cousins/It Hurts Me	1970	2.00	4.00	8.00
—Red label					
❑ 447-0645	Such a Night/Never Ending	1965	10.00	20.00	40.00
—Black label, dog on top					
❑ 447-0645	Such a Night/Never Ending	1965	2.50	5.00	10.00
—Black label, dog on left					
❑ 447-0645	Such a Night/Never Ending	1969	6.25	12.50	25.00
—Orange label					
❑ 447-0645	Such a Night/Never Ending	1970	2.00	4.00	8.00
—Red label					
❑ 447-0646	Viva Las Vegas/What'd I Say	1965	6.25	12.50	25.00
—Black label, dog on top					
❑ 447-0646	Viva Las Vegas/What'd I Say	1965	2.50	5.00	10.00
—Black label, dog on left					
❑ 447-0646	Viva Las Vegas/What'd I Say	1969	6.25	12.50	25.00
—Orange label					
❑ 447-0646	Viva Las Vegas/What'd I Say	1970	2.00	4.00	8.00
—Red label					
❑ 447-0647	Blue Christmas/Santa Claus Is Back in Town	1965	3.00	6.00	12.00
—Black label, dog on side					
❑ 447-0647	Blue Christmas/Santa Claus Is Back in Town	1969	6.25	12.50	25.00
—Orange label					
❑ 447-0647	Blue Christmas/Santa Claus Is Back in Town	1970	2.00	4.00	8.00
—Red label					
❑ 447-0647 [PS]	Blue Christmas/Santa Claus Is Back in Town	1965	7.50	15.00	30.00
—Has "Gold Standard Series" on sleeve					
❑ 447-0648	Do the Clam/You'll Be Gone	1965	2.50	5.00	10.00
—Black label, dog on left					
❑ 447-0648	Do the Clam/You'll Be Gone	1970	2.50	5.00	10.00
—Red label					
❑ 447-0649	Ain't That Loving You Baby/Ask Me	1965	2.50	5.00	10.00
—Black label, dog on left					
❑ 447-0649	Ain't That Loving You Baby/Ask Me	1970	2.00	4.00	8.00
—Red label					
❑ 447-0650	Puppet on a String/Wooden Heart	1965	2.50	5.00	10.00
—Black label, dog on left					
❑ 447-0650	Puppet on a String/Wooden Heart	1970	2.00	4.00	8.00
—Red label					
❑ 447-0650 [PS]	Puppet on a String/Wooden Heart	1965	7.50	15.00	30.00
❑ 447-0651	Joshua Fit the Battle/Known Only to Him	1966	3.75	7.50	15.00
—Black label, dog on left					
❑ 447-0651	Joshua Fit the Battle/Known Only to Him	1970	2.00	4.00	8.00
—Red label					
❑ 447-0651 [PS]	Joshua Fit the Battle/Known Only to Him	1966	50.00	100.00	200.00
❑ 447-0652	Milky White Way/Swing Down Sweet Chariot	1966	3.75	7.50	15.00
—Black label, dog on left					
❑ 447-0652	Milky White Way/Swing Down Sweet Chariot	1970	2.00	4.00	8.00
—Red label					
❑ 447-0652 [PS]	Milky White Way/Swing Down Sweet Chariot	1966	50.00	100.00	200.00
❑ 447-0653	(Such An) Easy Question/It Feels So Right	1966	2.50	5.00	10.00
—Black label, dog on left					
❑ 447-0653	(Such An) Easy Question/It Feels So Right	1970	2.00	4.00	8.00
—Red label					
❑ 447-0654	I'm Yours/(It's a) Long, Lonely Highway	1966	2.50	5.00	10.00
—Black label, dog on left					
❑ 447-0654	I'm Yours/(It's a) Long, Lonely Highway	1970	2.00	4.00	8.00
—Red label					
❑ 447-0655	Tell Me Why/Blue River	1968	2.50	5.00	10.00
—Black label, dog on left					
❑ 447-0655	Tell Me Why/Blue River	1970	2.00	4.00	8.00
—Red label					
❑ 447-0656	Frankie and Johnny/Please Don't Stop Loving Me	1968	2.50	5.00	10.00
—Black label, dog on left					
❑ 447-0656	Frankie and Johnny/Please Don't Stop Loving Me	1969	6.25	12.50	25.00
—Orange label					
❑ 447-0656	Frankie and Johnny/Please Don't Stop Loving Me	1970	2.00	4.00	8.00
—Red label					
❑ 447-0657	Love Letters/Come What May	1968	2.50	5.00	10.00
—Black label, dog on left					
❑ 447-0657	Love Letters/Come What May	1970	2.00	4.00	8.00
—Red label					
❑ 447-0658	Spinout/All That I Do	1968	2.50	5.00	10.00
—Black label, dog on left					
❑ 447-0658	Spinout/All That I Do	1970	2.00	4.00	8.00
—Red label					
❑ 447-0659	Indescribably Blue/Fools Fall in Love	1969	6.25	12.50	25.00
—Orange label					
❑ 447-0659	Indescribably Blue/Fools Fall in Love	1970	2.00	4.00	8.00
—Red label					
❑ 447-0660	Long Legged Girl (With the Short Dress On)/That's Someone You Never Forget	1970	10.00	20.00	40.00
❑ 447-0661	There's Always Me/Judy	1970	3.75	7.50	15.00
❑ 447-0662	Big Boss Man/You Don't Know Me	1970	2.50	5.00	10.00
❑ 447-0663	Guitar Man/High Heel Sneakers	1970	2.00	4.00	8.00
❑ 447-0664	U.S. Male/Stay Away	1970	2.00	4.00	8.00

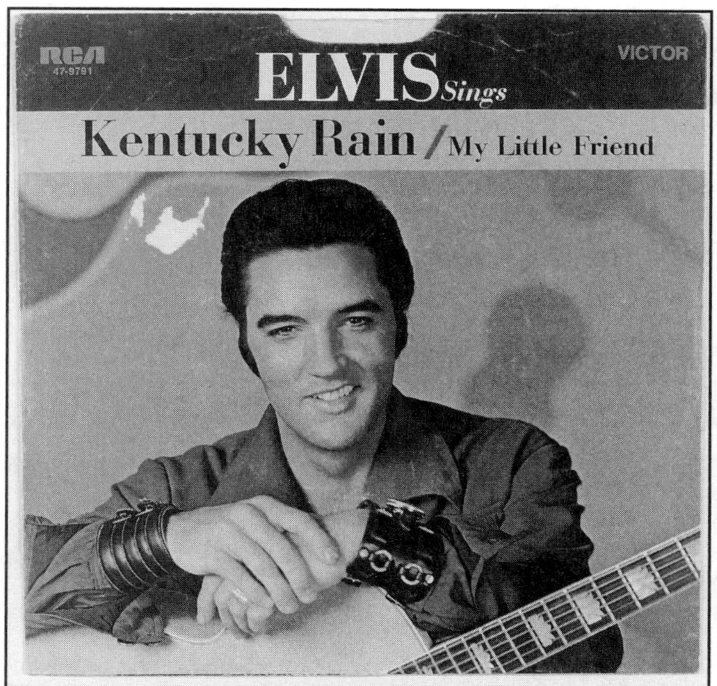

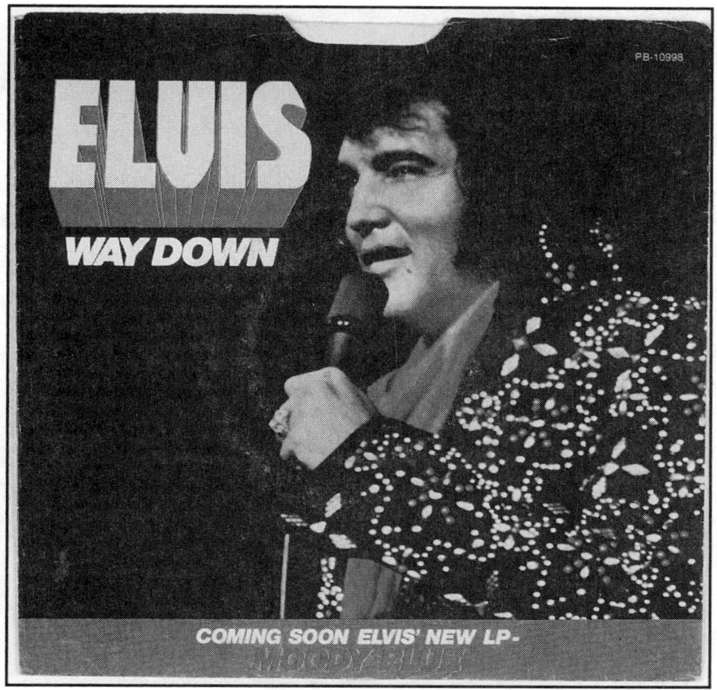

Elvis Presley was embraced by country audiences before he became a phenomenon, then was re-embraced after he became a parody of himself. Both his first and last No. 1 hits came on the country charts. (Top left) The first Elvis record to make any national chart was his fourth release on Sun, "Baby Let's Play House," which made the top five in the summer of 1955. (Top right) Four different Elvis singles pulled off the extremely rare feat of topping the pop, rhythm & blues *and* country & western charts. One of these was "All Shook Up." (Bottom left) After an eight-year hiatus, Elvis began to re-appear on the country charts in 1968. Though it only got to No. 31, "Kentucky Rain" was significant in that it gave a struggling young songwriter and singer named Eddie Rabbitt a big break. (Bottom right) In 1977, Elvis had two No. 1 singles on the country charts – and that was *before* he died! Atop the charts that were released the week of his death was "Way Down."

Number	Title (A Side/B Side)	Yr	VG	VG+	NM
❑ 447-0665	You'll Never Walk Alone/We Call on Him	1970	2.50	5.00	10.00
❑ 447-0666	Let Yourself Go/Your Time Hasn't Come Yet, Baby	1970	2.00	4.00	8.00
❑ 447-0667	A Little Less Conversation/Almost in Love	1970	2.00	4.00	8.00
❑ 447-0668	If I Can Dream/Edge of Reality	1970	2.00	4.00	8.00
❑ 447-0669	Memories/Charro	1970	2.00	4.00	8.00
❑ 447-0670	How Great Thou Art/His Hand in Mine	1970	2.50	5.00	10.00
❑ 447-0671	In the Ghetto/Any Day Now	1970	2.00	4.00	8.00
❑ 447-0672	Clean Up Your Own Back Yard/The Fair Is Moving On	1970	2.00	4.00	8.00
❑ 447-0673	Suspicious Minds/You'll Think of Me	1970	2.00	4.00	8.00
❑ 447-0674	Don't Cry Daddy/Rubberneckin'	1970	2.00	4.00	8.00
❑ 447-0675	Kentucky Rain/My Little Friend	1971	2.00	4.00	8.00
❑ 447-0676	The Wonder of You/Mama Liked the Roses	1971	2.00	4.00	8.00
❑ 447-0677	I've Lost You/The Next Step Is Love	1971	2.00	4.00	8.00
❑ 447-0678	You Don't Have to Say You Love Me/Patch It Up	1972	2.00	4.00	8.00
❑ 447-0679	I Really Don't Want to Know/There Goes My Everything	1972	2.00	4.00	8.00
❑ 447-0680	Where Did They Go, Lord/Rags to Riches	1972	2.00	4.00	8.00
❑ 447-0681	If Every Day Was Like Christmas/How Would You Like to Be	1972	2.00	4.00	8.00
❑ 447-0682	Life/Only Believe	1972	2.50	5.00	8.00
❑ 447-0683	I'm Leavin'/Heart of Rome	1972	2.00	4.00	8.00
❑ 447-0684	It's Only Love/The Sound of Your Cry	1972	2.00	4.00	8.00
❑ 447-0685	An American Trilogy/Until It's Time for You to Go	1973	2.00	4.00	8.00
❑ 447-0720	Blue Christmas/Wooden Heart	1964	3.75	7.50	15.00
❑ 447-0720 [PS]	Blue Christmas/Wooden Heart	1964	15.00	30.00	60.00

SUN

Number	Title (A Side/B Side)	Yr	VG	VG+	NM
❑ 209	That's All Right/Blue Moon of Kentucky	1954	2000.	4000.	6000.
—A mint copy of this has sold for over $17,000, but so far that is an aberration					
❑ 210	Good Rockin' Tonight/I Don't Care If the Sun Don't Shine	1954	1500.	2500.	3500.
❑ 215	Milkcow Blues Boogie/You're a Heartbreaker	1955	2000.	3500.	5000.
❑ 217	Baby Let's Play House/I'm Left, You're Right, She's Gone	1955	1000.	2000.	3000.
❑ 223	I Forgot to Remember to Forget/Mystery Train	1955	625.00	1250.	2500.

Selected 78s

RCA VICTOR

Number	Title (A Side/B Side)	Yr	VG	VG+	NM
❑ 20-6357	I Forgot to Remember to Forget/Mystery Train	1955	37.50	75.00	150.00
❑ 20-6380	That's All Right/Blue Moon of Kentucky	1955	37.50	75.00	150.00
❑ 20-6381	Good Rockin' Tonight/I Don't Care If the Sun Don't Shine	1955	37.50	75.00	150.00
❑ 20-6382	Milkcow Blues Boogie/You're a Heartbreaker	1955	37.50	75.00	150.00
❑ 20-6383	Baby Let's Play House/I'm Left, You're Right, She's Gone	1955	37.50	75.00	150.00
❑ 20-6420	Heartbreak Hotel/I Was the One	1956	25.00	50.00	100.00
❑ 20-6540	I Want You, I Need You, I Love You/My Baby Left Me	1956	25.00	50.00	100.00
❑ 20-6604	Don't Be Cruel/Hound Dog	1956	25.00	50.00	100.00
❑ 20-6636	Blue Suede Shoes/Tutti Frutti	1956	25.00	50.00	100.00
❑ 20-6637	I Got a Woman/I'm Countin' On You	1956	25.00	50.00	100.00
❑ 20-6638	I'm Gonna Sit Right Down and Cry (Over You)/I'll Never Let You Go (Little Darlin')	1956	25.00	50.00	100.00
❑ 20-6639	Tryin' to Get to You/I Love You Because	1956	25.00	50.00	100.00
❑ 20-6640	Blue Moon/Just Because	1956	25.00	50.00	100.00
❑ 20-6641	Money Honey/One-Sided Love Affair	1956	25.00	50.00	100.00
❑ 20-6642	Lawdy Miss Clawdy/Shake, Rattle, and Roll	1956	25.00	50.00	100.00
❑ 20-6643	Love Me Tender/Anyway You Want Me (That's How I Will Be)	1956	25.00	50.00	100.00
❑ 20-6800	Too Much/Playing for Keeps	1957	25.00	50.00	100.00
❑ 20-6870	All Shook Up/That's When Your Heartaches Begin	1957	25.00	50.00	100.00
❑ 20-7000	(Let Me Be Your) Teddy Bear/Loving You	1957	25.00	50.00	100.00
❑ 20-7035	Jailhouse Rock/Treat Me Nice	1957	25.00	50.00	100.00
❑ 20-7150	Don't/I Beg of You	1958	30.00	60.00	120.00
❑ 20-7240	Wear My Ring Around Your Neck/Don'tcha Think It's Time	1958	30.00	60.00	120.00
❑ 20-7280	Hard Headed Woman/Don't Ask Me Why	1958	30.00	60.00	120.00
❑ 20-7410	One Night/I Got Stung	1958	125.00	250.00	500.00

SUN

Number	Title (A Side/B Side)	Yr	VG	VG+	NM
❑ 209	That's All Right/Blue Moon of Kentucky	1954	750.00	1500.	3000.
❑ 210	Good Rockin' Tonight/I Don't Care If the Sun Don't Shine	1954	450.00	900.00	1800.
❑ 215	Milkcow Blues Boogie/You're a Heartbreaker	1955	625.00	1250.	2500.
❑ 217	Baby Let's Play House/I'm Left, You're Right, She's Gone	1955	375.00	750.00	1500.
❑ 223	I Forgot to Remember to Forget/Mystery Train	1955	250.00	500.00	1000.

7-Inch Extended Plays

RCA VICTOR

Number	Title (A Side/B Side)	Yr	VG	VG+	NM
❑ SPD-22 [PS]	Elvis Presley	1956	100.00	200.00	400.00
—Bonus given to buyers of a Victrola					
❑ SPD-22 [(2)]	Elvis Presley	1956	100.00	200.00	400.00
—Value is for both discs together					
❑ SPD-23 [PS]	Elvis Presley	1956	1000.	2000.	3000.
—Bonus given to buyers of a more expensive Victrola					
❑ SPD-23 [(3)]	Elvis Presley	1956	1000.	2000.	3000.
—Value is for all three discs together					
❑ SPA-7-37 [DJ]	Perfect for Parties	1956	15.00	30.00	60.00
—Without horizontal line on label					
❑ SPA-7-37 [DJ]	Perfect for Parties	1956	15.00	30.00	60.00
—With horizontal line on label					
❑ SPA-7-37 [PS]	Perfect for Parties	1956	15.00	30.00	60.00
❑ LPC-126	Flaming Star/Summer Kisses, Winter Tears//Are You Lonesome To-Night?/It's Now or Never	1961	10.00	20.00	40.00
—"Compact 33 Double" with small hole					
❑ LPC-126 [PS]	Elvis By Request	1961	10.00	20.00	40.00
❑ EPA-747	Blue Suede Shoes/Tutti Frutti//I Got a Woman/Just Because	1956	12.50	25.00	50.00
—Without horizontal line on label					
❑ EPA-747	Blue Suede Shoes/Tutti Frutti//I Got a Woman/Just Because	1956	12.50	25.00	50.00
—With horizontal line on label					
❑ EPA-747	Blue Suede Shoes/Tutti Frutti//I Got a Woman/Just Because	1956	50.00	100.00	200.00
—With horizontal line on label, but with no dog					
❑ EPA-747	Blue Suede Shoes/Tutti Frutti//I Got a Woman/Just Because	1956	50.00	100.00	200.00
—With incorrect label on Side 1 that lists, as song 3, "I'm Gonna Sit Right Down and Cry (Over You)," which does not appear on this record. Known copies of this version do not have horizontal line on label.					
❑ EPA-747	Blue Suede Shoes/Tutti Frutti//I Got a Woman/Just Because	1965	7.50	15.00	30.00
—Black label, dog on left					
❑ EPA-747	Blue Suede Shoes/Tutti Frutti//I Got a Woman/Just Because	1969	20.00	40.00	80.00
—Orange label					
❑ EPA-747 [PS]	Elvis Presley	1956	250.00	500.00	1000.
—Temporary envelope sleeve with dark blue print, "Blue Suede Shoes by Elvis Presley" in big letters					
❑ EPA-747 [PS]	Elvis Presley	1956	150.00	300.00	600.00
—Temporary envelope sleeve with black print, "Blue Suede Shoes by Elvis Presley" in big letters					
❑ EPA-747 [PS]	Elvis Presley	1956	12.50	25.00	50.00
—Five different back covers exist, all with titles on front cover; any are of equal value					
❑ EPA-747 [PS]	Elvis Presley	1965	7.50	15.00	30.00
—No titles at top of front cover					
❑ EPA-821	Heartbreak Hotel/I Was the One//Money Honey/I Forgot to Remember to Forget	1956	12.50	25.00	50.00
—Without horizontal line on label					
❑ EPA-821	Heartbreak Hotel/I Was the One//Money Honey/I Forgot to Remember to Forget	1956	12.50	25.00	50.00
—With horizontal line on label					
❑ EPA-821	Heartbreak Hotel/I Was the One//Money Honey/I Forgot to Remember to Forget	1956	50.00	100.00	200.00
—With horizontal line on label, but with no dog					
❑ EPA-821	Heartbreak Hotel/I Was the One//Money Honey/I Forgot to Remember to Forget	1965	7.50	15.00	30.00
—Black label, dog on left					
❑ EPA-821	Heartbreak Hotel/I Was the One//Money Honey/I Forgot to Remember to Forget	1969	20.00	40.00	80.00
—Orange label					
❑ EPA-821 [PS]	Heartbreak Hotel	1956	12.50	25.00	50.00
❑ EPA-830	Shake, Rattle and Roll/I Love You Because//Blue Moon/Lawdy, Miss Clawdy	1956	12.50	25.00	50.00
—Without horizontal line on label					
❑ EPA-830	Shake, Rattle and Roll/I Love You Because//Blue Moon/Lawdy, Miss Clawdy	1956	12.50	25.00	50.00
—With horizontal line on label					
❑ EPA-830	Shake, Rattle and Roll/I Love You Because//Blue Moon/Lawdy, Miss Clawdy	1956	50.00	100.00	200.00
—With horizontal line on label, but with no dog					
❑ EPA-830	Shake, Rattle and Roll/I Love You Because//Blue Moon/Lawdy, Miss Clawdy	1965	7.50	15.00	30.00
—Black label, dog on left					
❑ EPA-830	Shake, Rattle and Roll/I Love You Because//Blue Moon/Lawdy, Miss Clawdy	1969	20.00	40.00	80.00
—Orange label					
❑ EPA-830 [PS]	Elvis Presley	1956	12.50	25.00	50.00
❑ EPA-940	Don't Be Cruel/I Want You, I Need You, I Love You//Hound Dog/My Baby Left Me	1956	12.50	25.00	50.00
—Without horizontal line on label					
❑ EPA-940	Don't Be Cruel/I Want You, I Need You, I Love You//Hound Dog/My Baby Left Me	1956	12.50	25.00	50.00
—With horizontal line on label					
❑ EPA-940	Don't Be Cruel/I Want You, I Need You, I Love You//Hound Dog/My Baby Left Me	1956	50.00	100.00	200.00
—With horizontal line on label, but with no dog					
❑ EPA-940 [PS]	The Real Elvis	1956	12.50	25.00	50.00
❑ EPA-965	Anyway You Want Me (That's How I Will Be)/I'm Left, You're Right, She's Gone//I Don't Care If the Sun Don't Shine/Mystery Train	1956	10.00	20.00	40.00
—Without horizontal line on label					
❑ EPA-965	Anyway You Want Me (That's How I Will Be)/I'm Left, You're Right, She's Gone//I Don't Care If the Sun Don't Shine/Mystery Train	1956	10.00	20.00	40.00
—With horizontal line on label					
❑ EPA-965	Anyway You Want Me (That's How I Will Be)/I'm Left, You're Right, She's Gone//I Don't Care If the Sun Don't Shine/Mystery Train	1956	50.00	100.00	200.00
—With horizontal line on label, but with no dog					
❑ EPA-965	Anyway You Want Me (That's How I Will Be)/I'm Left, You're Right, She's Gone//I Don't Care If the Sun Don't Shine/Mystery Train	1965	7.50	15.00	30.00
—Black label, dog on left					
❑ EPA-965	Anyway You Want Me (That's How I Will Be)/I'm Left, You're Right, She's Gone//I Don't Care If the Sun Don't Shine/Mystery Train	1969	20.00	40.00	80.00
—Orange label					
❑ EPA-965 [PS]	Anyway You Want Me	1956	12.50	25.00	50.00
—With song titles and catalog number on front					

Number	Title (A Side/B Side)	Yr	VG	VG+	NM
❑ EPA-965 [PS]	Anyway You Want Me	196?	10.00	20.00	40.00
—Without song titles and catalog number on front					
❑ EPA-992	Rip It Up/Love Me//When My Blue Moon Turns to Gold Again/Paralyzed	1956	10.00	20.00	40.00
—Without horizontal line on label					
❑ EPA-992	Rip It Up/Love Me//When My Blue Moon Turns to Gold Again/Paralyzed	1956	10.00	20.00	40.00
—With horizontal line on label					
❑ EPA-992	Rip It Up/Love Me//When My Blue Moon Turns to Gold Again/Paralyzed	1956	50.00	100.00	200.00
—With horizontal line on label; bot with no dog					
❑ EPA-992	Rip It Up/Love Me//When My Blue Moon Turns to Gold Again/Paralyzed	1965	7.50	15.00	30.00
—Black label, dog on left					
❑ EPA-992	Rip It Up/Love Me//When My Blue Moon Turns to Gold Again/Paralyzed	1969	20.00	40.00	80.00
—Orange label					
❑ EPA-992 [PS]	Elvis (Volume 1)	1956	12.50	25.00	50.00
❑ EPA-993	So Glad You're Mine/Old Shep//Ready Teddy/Anyplace Is Paradise	1956	10.00	20.00	40.00
—Without horizontal line on label					
❑ EPA-993	So Glad You're Mine/Old Shep//Ready Teddy/Anyplace Is Paradise	1956	10.00	20.00	40.00
—With horizontal line on label					
❑ EPA-993	So Glad You're Mine/Old Shep//Ready Teddy/Anyplace Is Paradise	1956	50.00	100.00	200.00
—With horizontal line on label, but with no dog					
❑ EPA-993	So Glad You're Mine/Old Shep//Ready Teddy/Anyplace Is Paradise	1965	7.50	15.00	30.00
—Black label, dog on left					
❑ EPA-993	So Glad You're Mine/Old Shep//Ready Teddy/Anyplace Is Paradise	1969	20.00	40.00	80.00
—Orange label					
❑ EPA-993 [PS]	Elvis (Volume 2)	1956	12.50	25.00	50.00
—Titles at top of front cover					
❑ EPA-993 [PS]	Elvis (Volume 2)	1965	7.50	15.00	30.00
—No titles at top of front cover					
❑ EPA-994	Long Tall Sally/First in Line//How Do You Think I Feel/How's the World Treating You	1956	12.50	25.00	50.00
—Without horizontal line on label					
❑ EPA-994	Long Tall Sally/First in Line//How Do You Think I Feel/How's the World Treating You	1956	12.50	25.00	50.00
—With horizontal line on label					
❑ EPA-994	Long Tall Sally/First in Line//How Do You Think I Feel/How's the World Treating You	1956	50.00	100.00	200.00
—With horizontal line on label, but with no dog					
❑ EPA-994	Long Tall Sally/First in Line//How Do You Think I Feel/How's the World Treating You	1965	7.50	15.00	30.00
—Black label, dog on left					
❑ EPA-994	Long Tall Sally/First in Line//How Do You Think I Feel/How's the World Treating You	1969	20.00	40.00	80.00
—Orange label					
❑ EPA-994 [PS]	Strictly Elvis (Elvis, Vol. 3)	1956	12.50	25.00	50.00
—With titles listed on front cover					
❑ EPA-994 [PS]	Strictly Elvis (Elvis, Vol. 3)	1965	7.50	15.00	30.00
—No titles listed on front cover					
❑ EPB-1254 [PS]	Elvis Presley	1956	50.00	100.00	200.00
—Three different back covers exist hyping other non-Elvis RCA Victor releases; any are of equal value					
❑ EPB-1254 [PS]	Elvis Presley	1956	37.50	75.00	150.00
—With no hype of other non-Elvis releases on back					
❑ EPB-1254 [PS]	Elvis Presley... the most talked-about new personality in the last ten years of recorded music	1956	375.00	750.00	1500.
❑ EPB-1254 [(2)]	Elvis Presley	1956	50.00	100.00	200.00
—Without horizontal line on label; eight songs on two discs; value is for both discs together					
❑ EPB-1254 [(2)]	Elvis Presley	1956	50.00	100.00	200.00
—With horizontal line on label; eight songs on two discs; value is for both discs together					
❑ EPB-1254 [(2)]	Elvis Presley	1956	375.00	750.00	1500.
—Two records have three songs on each side (12 total), as opposed to the two of the standard release					
❑ EPA-1-1515	Loving You/Party//(Let Me Be Your) Teddy Bear/True Love	1957	10.00	20.00	40.00
—Without horizontal line on label					
❑ EPA-1-1515	Loving You/Party//(Let Me Be Your) Teddy Bear/True Love	1957	10.00	20.00	40.00
—With horizontal line on label					
❑ EPA-1-1515	Loving You/Party//(Let Me Be Your) Teddy Bear/True Love	1965	7.50	15.00	30.00
—Black label, dog on left					
❑ EPA-1-1515	Loving You/Party//(Let Me Be Your) Teddy Bear/True Love	1969	20.00	40.00	80.00
—Orange label					
❑ EPA-1-1515 [PS]	Loving You, Vol. I	1957	10.00	20.00	40.00
❑ EPA-2-1515	Lonesome Cowboy/Hot Dog//Mean Woman Blues/Got a Lot of Livin' to Do	1957	10.00	20.00	40.00
—Without horizontal line on label					
❑ EPA-2-1515	Lonesome Cowboy/Hot Dog//Mean Woman Blues/Got a Lot of Livin' to Do	1957	10.00	20.00	40.00
—With horizontal line on label					
❑ EPA-2-1515	Lonesome Cowboy/Hot Dog//Mean Woman Blues/Got a Lot of Livin' to Do	1965	7.50	15.00	30.00
—Black label, dog on left					
❑ EPA-2-1515	Lonesome Cowboy/Hot Dog//Mean Woman Blues/Got a Lot of Livin' to Do	1969	20.00	40.00	80.00
—Orange label					

Number	Title (A Side/B Side)	Yr	VG	VG+	NM
❑ EPA-2-1515 [PS]	Loving You, Vol. II	1957	10.00	20.00	40.00
—With song titles on top of front cover					
❑ EPA-2-1515 [PS]	Loving You, Vol. II	1965	7.50	15.00	30.00
—No song titles on top of front cover					
❑ EPA-4006	Love Me Tender/Let Me//Poor Boy/We're Gonna Move	1956	12.50	25.00	50.00
—Without horizontal line on label					
❑ EPA-4006	Love Me Tender/Let Me//Poor Boy/We're Gonna Move	1956	12.50	25.00	50.00
—With horizontal line on label					
❑ EPA-4006	Love Me Tender/Let Me//Poor Boy/We're Gonna Move	1956	50.00	100.00	200.00
—With horizontal line on label, but with no dog					
❑ EPA-4006	Love Me Tender/Let Me//Poor Boy/We're Gonna Move	1965	7.50	15.00	30.00
—Black label, dog on left					
❑ EPA-4006	Love Me Tender/Let Me//Poor Boy/We're Gonna Move	1969	20.00	40.00	80.00
—Orange label					
❑ EPA-4006 [PS]	Love Me Tender	1956	12.50	25.00	50.00
—With song titles on top of front cover					
❑ EPA-4006 [PS]	Love Me Tender	1965	7.50	15.00	30.00
—No song titles on top of front cover					
❑ EPA-4041	I Need You So/Have I Told You Lately//Blueberry Hill/Is It So Strange	1957	12.50	25.00	50.00
—Without horizontal line on label					
❑ EPA-4041	I Need You So/Have I Told You Lately//Blueberry Hill/Is It So Strange	1957	12.50	25.00	50.00
—With horizontal line on label					
❑ EPA-4041	I Need You So/Have I Told You Lately//Blueberry Hill/Is It So Strange	1957	50.00	100.00	200.00
—With horizontal line on label, but with no dog					
❑ EPA-4041	I Need You So/Have I Told You Lately//Blueberry Hill/Is It So Strange	1965	7.50	15.00	30.00
—Black label, dog on left					
❑ EPA-4041	I Need You So/Have I Told You Lately//Blueberry Hill/Is It So Strange	1969	20.00	40.00	80.00
—Orange label					
❑ EPA-4041 [PS]	Just for You (Elvis Presley)	1957	12.50	25.00	50.00
❑ EPA-4054	(There'll Be) Peace in the Valley (For Me)/It Is No Secret (What God Can Do)//I Believe/Take My Hand, Precious Lord	1957	10.00	20.00	40.00
—Without horizontal line on label					
❑ EPA-4054	(There'll Be) Peace in the Valley (For Me)/It Is No Secret (What God Can Do)//I Believe/Take My Hand, Precious Lord	1957	10.00	20.00	40.00
—With horizontal line on label					
❑ EPA-4054 [PS]	Peace in the Valley	1957	10.00	20.00	40.00
❑ EPA-4108	Santa Bring My Baby Back (To Me)/Blue Christmas//Santa Claus Is Back in Town/I'll Be Home for Christmas	1957	10.00	20.00	40.00
—Black label, dog on top					
❑ EPA-4108	Santa Bring My Baby Back (To Me)/Blue Christmas//Santa Claus Is Back in Town/I'll Be Home for Christmas	1965	7.50	15.00	30.00
—Black label, dog on left					
❑ EPA-4108	Santa Bring My Baby Back (To Me)/Blue Christmas//Santa Claus Is Back in Town/I'll Be Home for Christmas	1969	20.00	40.00	80.00
—Orange label					
❑ EPA-4108 [PS]	Elvis Sings Christmas Songs	1957	10.00	20.00	40.00
❑ EPA-4114	Jailhouse Rock/Young and Beautiful//I Want to Be Free/Don't Leave Me Now//(You're So Square) Baby I Don't Care	1957	10.00	20.00	40.00
—Black label, dog on top					
❑ EPA-4114	Jailhouse Rock/Young and Beautiful//I Want to Be Free/Don't Leave Me Now/(You're So Square) Baby I Don't Care	1965	7.50	15.00	30.00
—Black label, dog on left					
❑ EPA-4114	Jailhouse Rock/Young and Beautiful//I Want to Be Free/Don't Leave Me Now/(You're So Square) Baby I Don't Care	1969	20.00	40.00	80.00
—Orange label					
❑ EPA-4114 [PS]	Jailhouse Rock	1957	10.00	20.00	40.00
❑ EPA-4319	King Creole/New Orleans//As Long As I Have You/Lover Doll	1958	10.00	20.00	40.00
❑ EPA-4319 [PS]	King Creole	1958	12.50	25.00	50.00
—With copyright notice on front cover					
❑ EPA-4319 [PS]	King Creole	1958	10.00	20.00	40.00
—Without copyright notice on front cover					
❑ EPA-4321	Trouble/Young Dreams//Crawfish/Dixieland Rock	1958	10.00	20.00	40.00
—Black label, dog on top					
❑ EPA-4321	Trouble/Young Dreams//Crawfish/Dixieland Rock	1965	7.50	15.00	30.00
—Black label, dog on left					
❑ EPA-4321	Trouble/Young Dreams//Crawfish/Dixieland Rock	1969	20.00	40.00	80.00
—Orange label					
❑ EPA-4321 [PS]	King Creole, Vol. 2	1958	10.00	20.00	40.00
❑ EPA-4325	Press Interview with Elvis Presley//Elvis Presley's Newsreel Interview/Pat Hernon Interviews Elvis...	1958	20.00	40.00	80.00
❑ EPA-4325 [PS]	Elvis Sails	1958	20.00	40.00	80.00
—With 1959 calendar and a hole to make it suitable for hanging					

Number	Title (A Side/B Side)	Yr	VG	VG+	NM
❑ EPA-4340	White Christmas/Here Comes Santa Claus//Oh Little Town of Bethlehem/Silent Night	1958	17.50	35.00	70.00
—Black label, dog on top					
❑ EPA-4340	White Christmas/Here Comes Santa Claus//Oh Little Town of Bethlehem/Silent Night	1965	10.00	20.00	40.00
—Black label, dog on left					
❑ EPA-4340	White Christmas/Here Comes Santa Claus//Oh Little Town of Bethlehem/Silent Night	1969	10.00	40.00	80.00
—Orange label					
❑ EPA-4340 [PS]	Christmas with Elvis	1958	20.00	40.00	80.00
—With copyright notice and "Printed in U.S.A." at lower right					
❑ EPA-4340 [PS]	Christmas with Elvis	1965	10.00	20.00	40.00
—Without copyright notice and "Printed in U.S.A." at lower right					
❑ EPA-4368	Follow That Dream/Angel//What a Wonderful Life/I'm Not the Marrying Kind	1962	7.50	15.00	30.00
—Black label, dog on top, no playing times on label					
❑ EPA-4368	Follow That Dream/Angel//What a Wonderful Life/I'm Not the Marrying Kind	1962	10.00	20.00	40.00
—Black label, dog on top, with playing times on label					
❑ EPA-4368	Follow That Dream/Angel//What a Wonderful Life/I'm Not the Marrying Kind	1965	6.25	12.50	25.00
—Black label, dog on left					
❑ EPA-4368	Follow That Dream/Angel//What a Wonderful Life/I'm Not the Marrying Kind	1969	20.00	40.00	80.00
—Orange label					
❑ EPA-4368 [PS]	Follow That Dream	1962	37.50	75.00	150.00
—Paper sleeve with "Coin Operator -- DJ Prevue" at top; print is in red					
❑ EPA-4368 [PS]	Follow That Dream	1962	10.00	20.00	40.00
—Incorrect playing times on back cover; "Follow That Dream" is listed as 1:35 but is actually 1:38, and two others are wrong also					
❑ EPA-4368 [PS]	Follow That Dream	1965	6.25	12.50	25.00
—Correct playing times on back cover					
❑ EPA-4371	King of the Whole Wide World/This Is Living/ Riding the Rainbow//Home Is Where the Heart Is/I Got Lucky/A Whistling Tune	1962	10.00	20.00	40.00
—Black label, dog on top					
❑ EPA-4371	King of the Whole Wide World/This Is Living/ Riding the Rainbow//Home Is Where the Heart Is/I Got Lucky/A Whistling Tune	1965	7.50	15.00	30.00
—Black label, dog on left					
❑ EPA-4371	King of the Whole Wide World/This Is Living/ Riding the Rainbow//Home Is Where the Heart Is/I Got Lucky/A Whistling Tune	1969	20.00	40.00	80.00
—Orange label					
❑ EPA-4371 [PS]	Kid Galahad	1962	10.00	20.00	40.00
❑ EPA-4382	If You Think I Don't Need You/I Need Somebody to Lean On//C'mon Everybody/Today, Tomorrow and Forever	1964	10.00	20.00	40.00
—Black label, dog on top					
❑ EPA-4382	If You Think I Don't Need You/I Need Somebody to Lean On//C'mon Everybody/Today, Tomorrow and Forever	1965	7.50	15.00	30.00
—Black label, dog on left					
❑ EPA-4382	If You Think I Don't Need You/I Need Somebody to Lean On//C'mon Everybody/Today, Tomorrow and Forever	1969	20.00	40.00	80.00
—Orange label					
❑ EPA-4382 [PS]	Viva Las Vegas	1964	10.00	20.00	40.00
❑ EPA-4383	I Feel That I've Known You Forever/Slowly But Surely//Night Rider/Dirty Feeling	1965	7.50	15.00	30.00
—Black label, dog on left					
❑ EPA-4383	I Feel That I've Known You Forever/Slowly But Surely//Night Rider/Dirty Feeling	1969	20.00	40.00	80.00
—Orange label					
❑ EPA-4383 [PS]	Tickle Me	1965	7.50	15.00	30.00
—"Coming Soon" on front cover					
❑ EPA-4383 [PS]	Tickle Me	1965	7.50	15.00	30.00
—"Ask For" on front cover					
❑ EPA-4383 [PS]	Tickle Me	1969	8.75	17.50	35.00
—No blurb for new album on front cover					
❑ EPA-4387	Easy Come, Easy Go/The Love Machine/Yoga Is As Yoga Does//You Gotta Shop/Sing You Children/I'll Take Love	1967	7.50	15.00	30.00
—All copies appear to be black label, dog on left					
❑ EPA-4387 [PS]	Easy Come, Easy Go	1967	7.50	15.00	30.00
❑ EPA-5088	Hard Headed Woman/Good Rockin' Tonight// Don't/I Beg of You	1959	15.00	30.00	60.00
—Black label, dog on top					
❑ EPA-5088	Hard Headed Woman/Good Rockin' Tonight// Don't/I Beg of You	1959	100.00	200.00	400.00
—Maroon label					
❑ EPA-5088	Hard Headed Woman/Good Rockin' Tonight// Don't/I Beg of You	1965	7.50	15.00	30.00
—Black label, dog on left					
❑ EPA-5088	Hard Headed Woman/Good Rockin' Tonight// Don't/I Beg of You	1969	20.00	40.00	80.00
—Orange label					
❑ EPA-5088 [PS]	A Touch of Gold	1959	15.00	30.00	60.00
❑ EPA-5101	Wear My Ring Around Your Neck/Treat Me Nice/ /One Night/That's All Right	1959	15.00	30.00	60.00
—Black label, dog on top					
❑ EPA-5101	Wear My Ring Around Your Neck/Treat Me Nice/ /One Night/That's All Right	1959	100.00	200.00	400.00
—Maroon label					
❑ EPA-5101	Wear My Ring Around Your Neck/Treat Me Nice/ /One Night/That's All Right	1965	7.50	15.00	30.00
—Black label, dog on left					
❑ EPA-5101	Wear My Ring Around Your Neck/Treat Me Nice/ /One Night/That's All Right	1969	20.00	40.00	80.00
—Orange label					
❑ EPA-5101 [PS]	A Touch of Gold, Volume II	1959	15.00	30.00	60.00
❑ EPA-5120	Don't Be Cruel/I Want You, I Need You, I Love You//Hound Dog/My Baby Left Me	1959	15.00	30.00	60.00
—Black label, dog on top					
❑ EPA-5120	Don't Be Cruel/I Want You, I Need You, I Love You//Hound Dog/My Baby Left Me	1959	150.00	300.00	600.00
—Maroon label					
❑ EPA-5120	Don't Be Cruel/I Want You, I Need You, I Love You//Hound Dog/My Baby Left Me	1965	6.25	12.50	25.00
—Black label, dog on left					
❑ EPA-5120	Don't Be Cruel/I Want You, I Need You, I Love You//Hound Dog/My Baby Left Me	1969	20.00	40.00	80.00
—Orange label					
❑ EPA-5120 [PS]	The Real Elvis	1959	15.00	30.00	60.00
❑ EPA-5121	(There'll Be) Peace in the Valley (For Me)/It Is No Secret (What God Can Do)//I Believe/Take My Hand, Precious Lord	1959	7.50	15.00	30.00
—Black label, dog on top					
❑ EPA-5121	(There'll Be) Peace in the Valley (For Me)/It Is No Secret (What God Can Do)//I Believe/Take My Hand, Precious Lord	1959	100.00	200.00	400.00
—Maroon label					
❑ EPA-5121	(There'll Be) Peace in the Valley (For Me)/It Is No Secret (What God Can Do)//I Believe/Take My Hand, Precious Lord	1965	6.25	12.50	25.00
—Black label, dog on left					
❑ EPA-5121	(There'll Be) Peace in the Valley (For Me)/It Is No Secret (What God Can Do)//I Believe/Take My Hand, Precious Lord	1969	20.00	40.00	80.00
—Orange label					
❑ EPA-5121 [PS]	Peace in the Valley	1959	10.00	20.00	40.00
—Three slightly different cover variations with no difference in value					
❑ EPA-5122	King Creole/New Orleans//As Long As I Have You/Lover Doll	1959	7.50	15.00	30.00
—Black label, dog on top					
❑ EPA-5122	King Creole/New Orleans//As Long As I Have You/Lover Doll	1959	1000.	1500.	2000.
—Maroon label					
❑ EPA-5122	King Creole/New Orleans//As Long As I Have You/Lover Doll	1965	6.25	12.50	25.00
—Black label, dog on left					
❑ EPA-5122	King Creole/New Orleans//As Long As I Have You/Lover Doll	1969	20.00	40.00	80.00
—Orange label					
❑ EPA-5122 [PS]	King Creole	1959	10.00	20.00	40.00
—With "Gold Standard Series" on front cover					
❑ EPA-5122 [PS]	King Creole	1965	7.50	15.00	30.00
—Without "Gold Standard Series" on front cover					
❑ EPA-5141	All Shook Up/Don't Ask Me Why//Too Much/Blue Moon of Kentucky	1959	17.50	35.00	70.00
—Black label, dog on top					
❑ EPA-5141	All Shook Up/Don't Ask Me Why//Too Much/Blue Moon of Kentucky	1959	100.00	200.00	400.00
—Maroon label					
❑ EPA-5141	All Shook Up/Don't Ask Me Why//Too Much/Blue Moon of Kentucky	1959	7.50	15.00	30.00
—Black label, dog on left					
❑ EPA-5141	All Shook Up/Don't Ask Me Why//Too Much/Blue Moon of Kentucky	1959	20.00	40.00	80.00
—Orange label					
❑ EPA-5141 [PS]	A Touch of Gold, Volume 3	1959	17.50	35.00	70.00
❑ EPA-5157	Press Interview with Elvis Presley//Elvis Presley's Newsreel Interview/Pat Hernon Interviews Elvis...	1965	7.50	15.00	30.00
—Black label, dog on top					
❑ EPA-5157	Press Interview with Elvis Presley//Elvis Presley's Newsreel Interview/Pat Hernon Interviews Elvis...	1969	20.00	40.00	80.00
—Orange label					
❑ EPA-5157 [PS]	Elvis Sails	1965	7.50	15.00	30.00
❑ G8-MW-8705 [DJ]	TV Guide Presents Elvis Presley	1956	300.00	600.00	1200.
—Blue label, locked grooves (needle has to be lifted to play each of the four excerpts)					

Albums

BOXCAR

Number	Title	Yr	VG	VG+	NM
❑ (no #)	Having Fun with Elvis on Stage	1974	37.50	75.00	150.00
—All-talking record sold at Elvis concerts in 1974					

DCC COMPACT CLASSICS

Number	Title	Yr	VG	VG+	NM
❑ LPZ-2037 [S]	Elvis Is Back!	1997	6.25	12.50	25.00
—Audiophile vinyl					
❑ LPZ-2040 [(2)]	24 Karat Hits!	1997	7.50	15.00	30.00
—Audiophile vinyl					

FOTOPLAY

Number	Title	Yr	VG	VG+	NM
❑ FSP-1001 [PD]	To Elvis: Love Still Burning	1978	6.25	12.50	25.00
—Tribute-song picture disc of Elvis; in plastic bag with 11x11 insert					
❑ FSP-1001 [PD]	To Elvis: Love Still Burning	1978	7.50	15.00	30.00
—In white cardboard cover with black printing					
❑ FSP-1001 [PD]	To Elvis: Love Still Burning	1978	3.75	7.50	15.00
—In black cardboard cover with white printing					

GOLDEN EDITIONS

Number	Title	Yr	VG	VG+	NM
❑ KING-1	The First Year (Elvis, Scotty and Bill)	1979	3.75	7.50	15.00
❑ GEL-101	The First Year (Elvis, Scotty and Bill)	1979	5.00	10.00	20.00

Number	Title (A Side/B Side)	Yr	VG	VG+	NM
GREAT NORTHWEST					
❑ GV-2004	The King Speaks (February 1961, Memphis, Tennessee)	1977	2.50	5.00	10.00
—Label says this is on "Green Valley" while sleeve says "Great Northwest"					
❑ GNW-4005	The Elvis Tapes	1977	3.00	6.00	12.00
❑ GNW-4006	The King Speaks (February 1961, Memphis, Tennessee)	1977	2.00	4.00	8.00
—Both label and sleeve say this is on "Great Northwest"					
GREEN VALLEY					
❑ GV-2001/3 [(2)]	Elvis (Speaks to You)	1978	7.50	15.00	30.00
—Elvis interviews plus tracks by the Jordanaires					
❑ GV-2001	Elvis Exclusive Live Press Conference (Memphis, Tennessee, February 1961)	1977	10.00	20.00	40.00
—Issued with two slightly different covers					
GUSTO					
❑ SD-995	Interviews with Elvis (Canada 1957)	1978	10.00	20.00	40.00
—Reissue of Great Northwest album					
HALW					
❑ HALW-0001	The First Years	1978	7.50	15.00	30.00
—With stamped, limited edition number					
❑ HALW-0001	The First Years	1978	5.00	10.00	20.00
—Without limited edition number					
K-TEL					
❑ NU 9900	Love Songs	1981	5.00	10.00	20.00
LOUISIANA HAYRIDE					
❑ LH-3061	Beginning Years	1984	5.00	10.00	20.00
—With booklet and facsimile contract					
MARVENCO					
❑ 101	Beginning (1954-1955)	1988	3.75	7.50	15.00
—Pink vinyl with booklet and facsimile contract					
MOBILE FIDELITY					
❑ 1-059	From Elvis in Memphis	1982	12.50	25.00	50.00
—Audiophile vinyl					
MUSIC WORKS					
❑ PB-3601	The First Live Recordings	1984	3.75	7.50	15.00
❑ PB-3602	The Hillbilly Cat	1984	3.75	7.50	15.00
OAK					
❑ 1003	Vintage 1955 Elvis	1990	15.00	30.00	60.00
PAIR					
❑ PDL2-1010 [(2)]	Double Dynamite	1982	5.00	10.00	20.00
❑ PDL2-1037 [(2)]	Remembering	1983	7.50	15.00	30.00
❑ PDL2-1185 [(2)]	Elvis Aron Presley Forever	1988	5.00	10.00	20.00
PICKWICK					
❑ (no #) [(7)]	The Pickwick Pack (unofficial title)	1978	15.00	30.00	60.00
—Seven Pickwick albums in special package and cardboard wrapper; one of the LPs is Elvis' Christmas Album					
❑ (no #) [(7)]	The Pickwick Pack (unofficial title)	1979	15.00	30.00	60.00
—Seven Pickwick albums in special package and cardboard wrapper; one of the LPs is Frankie and Johnny					
❑ CAS-2304	Elvis Sings Flaming Star	1976	2.50	5.00	10.00
❑ CAS-2408	Let's Be Friends	1975	2.50	5.00	10.00
❑ CAL-2428 [M]	Elvis' Christmas Album	1975	3.00	6.00	12.00
—Same contents as RCA Camden LP; no Christmas trim on border					
❑ CAL-2428 [M]	Elvis' Christmas Album	1976	2.50	5.00	10.00
—Same as above, but with Christmas trim on cover border					
❑ CAS-2440	Almost in Love	1975	2.50	5.00	10.00
❑ CAL-2472	You'll Never Walk Alone	1975	2.50	5.00	10.00
❑ CAL-2518	C'mon Everybody	1975	2.50	5.00	10.00
❑ CAS-2533	I Got Lucky	1975	2.50	5.00	10.00
❑ CAS-2567	Elvis Sings Hits from His Movies, Volume 1	1975	2.50	5.00	10.00
❑ CAS-2595	Burning Love And Hits from His Movies, Vol. 2	1975	3.00	6.00	12.00
—First cover contains a notice about the upcoming "Aloha from Hawaii" show					
❑ CAS-2595	Burning Love And Hits from His Movies, Vol. 2	1976	2.00	4.00	8.00
—Reissue deletes the "Aloha from Hawaii" notice					
❑ CAS-2611	Separate Ways	1975	2.50	5.00	10.00
❑ DL2-5001 [(2)]	Double Dynamite	1975	6.25	12.50	25.00
❑ ACL-7007	Frankie and Johnny	1976	2.50	5.00	10.00
❑ ACL-7064	Mahalo from Elvis	1978	5.00	10.00	20.00
PREMORE					
❑ PL-589	Early Elvis (1954-1956 Live at the Louisiana Hayride)	1989	7.50	15.00	30.00
RCA					
❑ 2023-1-R	The Million Dollar Quartet	1990	3.00	6.00	12.00
—With Jerry Lee Lewis, Carl Perkins, and perhaps Johnny Cash					
❑ 2227-1-R	The Great Performances	1990	10.00	20.00	40.00
❑ 3114-1-R [(3)]	Collectors Gold	1991	—	—	—
—Rumored to exist on US vinyl, but unconfirmed					
❑ 5600-1-R	Return of the Rocker	1986	5.00	10.00	20.00
❑ 6221-1-R [(2)]	The Memphis Record	1987	7.50	15.00	30.00
❑ 6313-1-R	Elvis Talks!	1987	7.50	15.00	30.00
❑ 6382-1-R	The Number One Hits	1987	7.50	15.00	30.00
❑ 6383-1-R [(2)]	The Top Ten Hits	1987	7.50	15.00	30.00
❑ 6414-1-R [(2)]	The Complete Sun Sessions	1987	7.50	15.00	30.00
❑ 6738-1-R	Essential Elvis: The First Movies	1988	6.25	12.50	25.00
❑ 6985-1-R	The Alternate Aloha	1988	5.00	10.00	20.00
❑ 8468-1-R	Elvis in Nashville (1956-1971)	1988	10.00	20.00	40.00
❑ 9586-1-R	Elvis Gospel 1957-1971 (Known Only to Him)	1989	10.00	20.00	40.00
❑ 9589-1-R	Essential Elvis, Vol. 2 (Stereo '57)	1989	6.25	12.50	25.00
❑ 07863-67642-1	Elvis' Golden Records	1997	7.50	15.00	30.00
—Reissue for the Tower Records chain with 6 bonus tracks					
❑ 07863-67643-1	Elvis' Gold Records Volume 2 — 50,000,000 Elvis Fans Can't Be Wrong	1997	7.50	15.00	30.00
—Reissue for the Tower Records chain with 10 bonus tracks					

Number	Title (A Side/B Side)	Yr	VG	VG+	NM
RCA CAMDEN					
❑ CAS-2304	Elvis Sings Flaming Star	1969	7.50	15.00	30.00
❑ CAS-2408	Let's Be Friends	1970	7.50	15.00	30.00
❑ CAL-2428 [M]	Elvis' Christmas Album	1970	7.50	15.00	30.00
—Blue label, non-flexible vinyl					
❑ CAL-2428 [M]	Elvis' Christmas Album	1971	3.00	6.00	12.00
—Blue label, flexible vinyl					
❑ CAS-2440	Almost in Love	1970	10.00	20.00	40.00
—Last song on Side 2 is "Stay Away, Joe"					
❑ CAS-2440	Almost in Love	1973	6.25	12.50	25.00
—Last song on Side 2 is "Stay Away"					
❑ CAL-2472	You'll Never Walk Alone	1974	7.50	15.00	30.00
❑ CALX-2472	You'll Never Walk Alone	1971	3.75	7.50	15.00
❑ CAL-2518	C'mon Everybody	1971	5.00	10.00	20.00
❑ CAL-2533	I Got Lucky	1971	6.25	12.50	25.00
❑ CAS-2567	Elvis Sings Hits from His Movies, Volume 1	1972	5.00	10.00	20.00
❑ CAS-2595	Burning Love And Hits from His Movies, Vol. 2	1972	6.25	12.50	25.00
—With star on front cover advertising a bonus photo, the presence of which doubles the value of this LP					
❑ CAS-2595	Burning Love And Hits from His Movies, Vol. 2	1972	2.50	5.00	10.00
—No star on cover, no bonus photo					
❑ CAS-2611	Separate Ways	1973	7.50	15.00	30.00
RCA SPECIAL PRODUCTS					
❑ DPL2-0056(e) [(2)]	Elvis	1973	12.50	25.00	50.00
—Mustard labels					
❑ DPL2-0056(e) [(2)]	Elvis	1973	6.25	12.50	25.00
—Blue labels					
❑ DPL2-0056(e) [(2)]	Elvis Commemorative Album	1978	20.00	40.00	80.00
—Reissue of "Elvis" (same number) with new title and gold vinyl					
❑ DPL2-0168 [(2)]	Elvis in Hollywood	1976	15.00	30.00	60.00
—Blue labels; with 20-page booklet					
❑ DML5-0263 [(5)]	The Elvis Story	1977	15.00	30.00	60.00
—Available through Candelite Music via mail order					
❑ DML1-0264	His Songs of Inspiration	1977	3.75	7.50	15.00
❑ DPL5-0347 [(5)]	Memories of Elvis (A Lasting Tribute to the King of Rock 'N' Roll)	1978	20.00	40.00	80.00
❑ DML1-0348	The Greatest Show on Earth	1978	3.75	7.50	15.00
❑ DML6-0412 [(6)]	The Legendary Recordings of Elvis Presley	1979	25.00	50.00	100.00
❑ DML1-0413	The Greatest Moments in Music	1980	3.75	7.50	15.00
❑ DML1-0437	Rock 'N Roll Forever	1981	3.75	7.50	15.00
❑ DVL1-0461	The Legendary Magic of Elvis Presley	1980	3.75	7.50	15.00
❑ DML3-0632 [(3)]	The Elvis Presley Collection	1984	20.00	40.00	80.00
—Available through Candelite Music via mail order					
❑ DPL1-0647	Elvis Country	1984	7.50	15.00	30.00
❑ DVM1-0704	Elvis (One Night with You)	1984	15.00	30.00	60.00
—With poster (deduct 25% if missing)					
❑ SVL3-0710 [(3)]	50 Years — 50 Hits	1985	7.50	15.00	30.00
❑ DVL2-0728 [(2)]	His Songs of Faith and Inspiration	1986	12.50	25.00	50.00
❑ SVL2-0824 [(2)]	Good Rockin' Tonight	1988	5.00	10.00	20.00
❑ CAL-2428 [M]	Elvis' Christmas Album	1986	7.50	15.00	30.00
—Reissue for The Special Music Company					
RCA VICTOR					
❑ (no #)	International Hotel, Las Vegas Nevada, Presents Elvis, 1969	1969	1250.	1875.	2500.
—Gift box to guests at Elvis' July 31-Aug, 1, 1969 shows. Includes LPM-4088 and LSP-4155; press release; 1969 catalog; three photos; and thank-you note from Elvis and the Colonel. Most of the value is for the box.					
❑ (no #)	International Hotel, Las Vegas Nevada, Presents Elvis, 1970	1970	1250.	1875.	2500.
—Gift box to guests at Elvis' Jan. 28, 1970 show. Includes LSP-6020 and 47-9791; press release; 1970 catalog; photo; booklet; and dinner menu. Most of the value is for the box.					
❑ PRS-279	Singer Presents Elvis Singing Flaming Star and Others	1968	25.00	50.00	100.00
—Sold only at Singer sewing machine dealers; reissued on RCA Camden 2304					
❑ APL1-0283	Elvis	1973	12.50	25.00	50.00
❑ CPL1-0341	A Legendary Performer, Volume 1	1974	6.25	12.50	25.00
—Includes booklet (deduct 40% if missing); with die-cut hole in front cover					
❑ CPL1-0341	A Legendary Performer, Volume 1	1986	3.75	7.50	15.00
—No die-cut hole in cover and no booklet					
❑ APL1-0388	Raised on Rock/For Ol' Times Sake	1973	7.50	15.00	30.00
—Orange label					
❑ APL1-0388	Raised on Rock/For Ol' Times Sake	1975	7.50	15.00	30.00
—Tan label					
❑ APL1-0388	Raised on Rock/For Ol' Times Sake	1977	3.00	6.00	12.00
—Black label, dog near top					
❑ SP-33-461 [DJ]	Special Palm Sunday Programming	1967	175.00	350.00	700.00
—White label promo. Add 25% for cue sheet.					
❑ AFL1-0475	Good Times	1977	3.00	6.00	12.00
—Black label, dog near top; includes copies with sticker wrapped around spine with new number					
❑ CPL1-0475	Good Times	1974	12.50	25.00	50.00
—Orange label					
❑ CPL1-0475	Good Times	1976	3.00	6.00	12.00
—Black label, dog near top					
❑ SPS-33-571 [DJ]	Elvis As Recorded at Madison Square Garden	1972	75.00	150.00	300.00
—"Radio Station Banded Special Version"; came in plain white cover with stickers					
❑ AFL1-0606	Elvis Recorded Live on Stage in Memphis	1977	3.00	6.00	12.00
—Black label, dog near top; includes copies with sticker wrapped around spine with new number					
❑ APD1-0606 [Q]	Elvis Recorded Live on Stage in Memphis	1974	50.00	100.00	200.00
—"RCA QuadraDisc" labels					
❑ CPL1-0606	Elvis Recorded Live on Stage in Memphis	1974	6.25	12.50	25.00
—Orange label					
❑ CPL1-0606	Elvis Recorded Live on Stage in Memphis	1975	6.25	12.50	25.00
—Tan label					
❑ DJL1-0606 [DJ]	Elvis Recorded Live on Stage in Memphis	1974	75.00	150.00	300.00
—Special banded version for radio airplay					

Number	Title (A Side/B Side)	Yr	VG	VG+	NM
❑ AFM1-0818	Having Fun with Elvis on Stage	1977	6.25	12.50	25.00
—Black label, dog near top					
❑ CPM1-0818	Having Fun with Elvis on Stage	1974	7.50	15.00	30.00
—Commercial issue of Boxcar LP; orange label					
❑ CPM1-0818	Having Fun with Elvis on Stage	1975	5.00	10.00	20.00
—Tan label					
❑ DJM1-0835 [DJ]	Elvis Presley Interview Record: An Audio Self-Portrait	1984	20.00	40.00	80.00
—Promotional item for "50th Anniversary" series; later issued as RCA 6313-1-R					
❑ AFL1-0873	Promised Land	1977	3.75	7.50	15.00
—Black label, dog near top					
❑ APD1-0873 [Q]	Promised Land	1975	50.00	100.00	200.00
—"RCA QuadraDisc" label					
❑ APD1-0873 [Q]	Promised Land	1977	30.00	60.00	120.00
—Black label, dog near top; quadraphonic reissue					
❑ APL1-0873	Promised Land	1975	15.00	30.00	60.00
—Orange label					
❑ APL1-0873	Promised Land	1975	5.00	10.00	20.00
—Tan label					
❑ ANL1-0971(e)	Pure Gold	1975	3.75	7.50	15.00
—Orange label					
❑ ANL1-0971(e)	Pure Gold	1976	3.00	6.00	12.00
—Yellow label					
❑ LOC-1035 [M]	Elvis' Christmas Album	1957	125.00	250.00	500.00
—Gatefold cover; title printed in gold on LP spine; includes bound-in booklet but not sticker					
❑ LOC-1035 [M]	Elvis' Christmas Album	1957	125.00	250.00	500.00
—Gatefold cover; title printed in silver on LP spine; includes bound-in booklet but not sticker					
❑ LOC-1035 [M]	Elvis' Christmas Album	1957	7500.	11250.	15000.
—Red vinyl; unique					
❑ LOC-1035 [M]	Elvis' Christmas Album Sticker	1957	37.50	75.00	150.00
—Gold sticker with "To________" and "From_________" blanks					
❑ AFL1-1039	Elvis Today	1977	3.00	6.00	12.00
—Black label, dog near top; includes copies with sticker wrapped around spine with new number					
❑ APD1-1039 [Q]	Elvis Today	1975	50.00	100.00	200.00
—"RCA QuadraDisc" labels					
❑ APD1-1039 [Q]	Elvis Today	1977	37.50	75.00	150.00
—Black label, dog near top; quadraphonic reissue					
❑ APL1-1039	Elvis Today	1975	15.00	30.00	60.00
—Orange label					
❑ APL1-1039	Elvis Today	1975	7.50	15.00	30.00
—Tan label					
❑ AFL1-1254(e) [R]	Elvis Presley	1977	3.00	6.00	12.00
—Black label, dog near top; includes copies with sticker wrapped around spine with new number					
❑ LPM-1254 [M]	Elvis Presley	1956	125.00	250.00	500.00
—Version 1: "Long Play" on label; "Elvis" in pale pink, "Presley" in pale green on cover; pale green logo box in upper right front cover					
❑ LPM-1254 [M]	Elvis Presley	1956	100.00	200.00	400.00
—Version 2: "Long Play" on label; "Elvis" in pale pink, "Presley" in neon green on cover; neon green logo box in upper right front cover					
❑ LPM-1254 [M]	Elvis Presley	1956	62.50	125.00	250.00
—Version 3: "Long Play" on label; "Elvis" in pale pink, "Presley" in neon green on cover; black logo box in upper right front cover					
❑ LPM-1254 [M]	Elvis Presley	1958	50.00	100.00	200.00
—Version 4: "Long Play" on label; "Elvis" in neon pink, almost red, "Presley" in neon green on cover; black logo box in upper right front cover					
❑ LPM-1254 [M]	Elvis Presley	1963	30.00	60.00	120.00
—"Mono" on label; cover photo is slightly left of center, otherwise same as Version 4 above					
❑ LPM-1254 [M]	Elvis Presley	1964	15.00	30.00	60.00
—"Monaural" on label					
❑ LSP-1254(e) [R]	Elvis Presley	1962	50.00	100.00	200.00
—"Stereo Electronically Reprocessed" and silver "RCA Victor" on label					
❑ LSP-1254(e) [R]	Elvis Presley	1965	10.00	20.00	40.00
—"Stereo Electronically Reprocessed" and white "RCA Victor" on label					
❑ LSP-1254(e) [R]	Elvis Presley	1968	7.50	15.00	30.00
—Orange label, non-flexible vinyl					
❑ LSP-1254(e) [R]	Elvis Presley	1975	3.75	7.50	15.00
—Tan label					
❑ LSP-1254(e) [R]	Elvis Presley	1976	3.00	6.00	12.00
—Black label, dog near top					
❑ ANL1-1319 [S]	His Hand in Mine	1976	3.75	7.50	15.00
—Reissue with more tightly cropped photo of Elvis on front cover					
❑ CPL1-1349	A Legendary Performer, Volume 2	1976	7.50	15.00	30.00
—Includes booklet (deduct 40% if missing); with die-cut hole in front cover					
❑ CPL1-1349	A Legendary Performer, Volume 2	1976	15.00	30.00	60.00
—Without false starts and outtakes of "Such a Night" and "Cane and a High Starched Collar," which are supposed to be there. End of matrix number may be "31."					
❑ CPL1-1349	A Legendary Performer, Volume 2	1986	3.75	7.50	15.00
—No die-cut hole in cover and no booklet					
❑ AFL1-1382(e) [R]	Elvis	1977	3.00	6.00	12.00
—Black label, dog near top; includes copies with sticker wrapped around spine with new number					
❑ LPM-1382 [M]	Elvis	1956	75.00	150.00	300.00
—Back cover has ads for other albums. At least 11 different variations of this are known, all of equal value.					
❑ LPM-1382 [M]	Elvis	1956	75.00	150.00	300.00
—Back cover has no ads for other albums. "Long Play" on label.					
❑ LPM-1382 [M]	Elvis	1956	200.00	400.00	800.00
—With alternate take of "Old Shep" on side 2. Matrix number ends in "15S," "17S" or "19S," but should be played for positive ID. On alternate take, Elvis sings "he grew old AND his eyes were growing dim" (no AND on standard press)					
❑ LPM-1382 [M]	Elvis	1956	100.00	200.00	400.00
—With tracks listed on labels as "Band 1" through "Band 6"					
❑ LPM-1382 [M]	Elvis	1963	20.00	40.00	80.00
—"Mono" on label					
❑ LPM-1382 [M]	Elvis	1965	15.00	30.00	60.00
—"Monaural" on label					
❑ LSP-1382(e) [R]	Elvis	1962	50.00	100.00	200.00
—"Stereo Electronically Reprocessed" and silver "RCA Victor" on label					
❑ LSP-1382(e) [R]	Elvis	1964	12.50	25.00	50.00
—"Stereo Electronically Reprocessed" and white "RCA Victor" on label					
❑ LSP-1382(e) [R]	Elvis	1968	7.50	15.00	30.00
—Orange label, non-flexible vinyl					
❑ LSP-1382(e) [R]	Elvis	1971	5.00	10.00	20.00
—Orange label, flexible vinyl					
❑ LSP-1382(e) [R]	Elvis	1975	3.75	7.50	15.00
—Tan label					
❑ LSP-1382(e) [R]	Elvis	1976	3.00	6.00	12.00
—Black label, dog near top					
❑ AFL1-1506	From Elvis Presley Boulevard, Memphis, Tennessee	1977	3.00	6.00	12.00
—Black label, dog near top; with sticker wrapped around spine with new number (old number still on label)					
❑ AFL1-1506	From Elvis Presley Boulevard, Memphis, Tennessee	1977	2.50	5.00	10.00
—Black label, dog near top; new number is on cover and label					
❑ APL1-1506	From Elvis Presley Boulevard, Memphis, Tennessee	1976	7.50	15.00	30.00
—Tan label					
❑ AFL1-1515(e) [R]	Loving You	1977	3.00	6.00	12.00
—Black label, dog near top; includes copies with sticker wrapped around spine with new number					
❑ LPM-1515 [M]	Loving You	1957	75.00	150.00	300.00
—"Long Play" on label					
❑ LPM-1515 [M]	Loving You	1963	25.00	50.00	100.00
—"Mono" on label					
❑ LPM-1515 [M]	Loving You	1964	12.50	25.00	50.00
—"Monaural" on label					
❑ LSP-1515(e) [R]	Loving You	1962	37.50	75.00	150.00
—"Stereo Electronically Reprocessed" and silver "RCA Victor" on label					
❑ LSP-1515(e) [R]	Loving You	1964	12.50	25.00	50.00
—"Stereo Electronically Reprocessed" and white "RCA Victor" on label					
❑ LSP-1515(e) [R]	Loving You	1968	10.00	20.00	40.00
—Orange label, non-flexible vinyl					
❑ LSP-1515(e) [R]	Loving You	1971	5.00	10.00	20.00
—Orange label, flexible vinyl					
❑ LSP-1515(e) [R]	Loving You	1975	5.00	10.00	20.00
—Tan label					
❑ LSP-1515(e) [R]	Loving You	1976	3.00	6.00	12.00
—Black label, dog near top					
❑ AFM1-1675	The Sun Sessions	1977	3.75	7.50	15.00
—Black label, dog near top; includes copies with sticker wrapped around spine with new number					
❑ APM1-1675	The Sun Sessions	1976	5.00	10.00	20.00
—Tan label					
❑ APM1-1675	The Sun Sessions	1976	3.00	6.00	12.00
—Black label, dog near top					
❑ AFL1-1707(e) [R]	Elvis' Golden Records	1977	3.00	6.00	12.00
—Black label, dog near top; includes copies with sticker wrapped around spine with new number					
❑ AQL1-1707(e) [R]	Elvis' Golden Records	1979	2.50	5.00	10.00
—Another reissue with new prefix					
❑ LPM-1707 [M]	Elvis' Golden Records	1958	62.50	125.00	250.00
—Title on cover in light blue letters; no song titles listed on front cover					
❑ LPM-1707 [M]	Elvis' Golden Records	1958	37.50	75.00	150.00
—Title on cover in light blue letters; no song titles listed on front cover; "RE" on back cover					
❑ LPM-1707 [M]	Elvis' Golden Records	1963	15.00	30.00	60.00
—"Mono" on label; title on cover in white letters; song titles added to front cover					
❑ LPM-1707 [M]	Elvis' Golden Records	1964	10.00	20.00	40.00
—"Monaural" on label; "RE2" on back cover					
❑ LSP-1707(e) [R]	Elvis' Golden Records	1962	50.00	100.00	200.00
—"Stereo Electronically Reprocessed" and silver "RCA Victor" on label					
❑ LSP-1707(e) [R]	Elvis' Golden Records	1964	12.50	25.00	50.00
—"Stereo Electronically Reprocessed" and white "RCA Victor" on label					
❑ LSP-1707(e) [R]	Elvis' Golden Records	1968	7.50	15.00	30.00
—Orange label, non-flexible vinyl					
❑ LSP-1707(e) [R]	Elvis' Golden Records	1971	5.00	10.00	20.00
—Orange label, flexible vinyl					
❑ LSP-1707(e) [R]	Elvis' Golden Records	1975	5.00	10.00	20.00
—Tan label					
❑ LSP-1707(e) [R]	Elvis' Golden Records	1976	3.00	6.00	12.00
—Black label, dog near top					
❑ AFL1-1884(e) [R]	King Creole	1977	3.00	6.00	12.00
—Black label, dog near top; includes copies with sticker wrapped around spine with new number					
❑ LPM-1884 [M]	King Creole	1958	50.00	100.00	200.00
—"Long Play" on label; contrary to some other sources, this was NOT issued with a bonus photo					
❑ LPM-1884 [M]	King Creole	1963	20.00	40.00	80.00
—"Mono" on label					
❑ LPM-1884 [M]	King Creole	1964	15.00	30.00	60.00
—"Monaural" on label					
❑ LSP-1884(e) [R]	King Creole	1962	37.50	75.00	150.00
—"Stereo Electronically Reprocessed" and silver "RCA Victor" on label					
❑ LSP-1884(e) [R]	King Creole	1964	15.00	30.00	60.00
—"Stereo Electronically Reprocessed" and white "RCA Victor" on label					
❑ LSP-1884(e) [R]	King Creole	1968	10.00	20.00	40.00
—Orange label, non-flexible vinyl					
❑ LSP-1884(e) [R]	King Creole	1971	5.00	10.00	20.00
—Orange label, flexible vinyl					
❑ LSP-1884(e) [R]	King Creole	1975	5.00	10.00	20.00
—Tan label					
❑ LSP-1884(e) [R]	King Creole	1976	3.00	6.00	12.00
—Black label, dog near top					
❑ ANL1-1936	Elvis Sings the Wonderful World of Christmas	1975	3.75	7.50	15.00
—New number; same contents as LSP-4579. Orange label.					
❑ ANL1-1936	Elvis Sings the Wonderful World of Christmas	1976	3.00	6.00	12.00
—Tan label					
❑ ANL1-1936	Elvis Sings the Wonderful World of Christmas	1977	2.50	5.00	10.00
—Black label, dog near top					

Number	Title (A Side/B Side)	Yr	VG	VG+	NM
❑ LPM-1951 [M]	Elvis' Christmas Album	1958	37.50	75.00	150.00
—Same contents as LOC-1035, but with non-gatefold blue cover; "Long Play" at bottom of label					
❑ LPM-1951 [M]	Elvis' Christmas Album	1963	17.50	35.00	70.00
—"Mono" at bottom of label: "RE" on lower left front cover (photos on back were altered)					
❑ LPM-1951 [M]	Elvis' Christmas Album	1964	10.00	20.00	40.00
—"Monaural" at bottom of label; "RE" on lower left front cover					
❑ LSP-1951(e) [R]	Elvis' Christmas Album	1964	12.50	25.00	50.00
—Black label, dog on top; "Stereo Electronically Reprocessed" at bottom of label					
❑ LSP-1951(e) [R]	Elvis' Christmas Album	1968	15.00	30.00	60.00
—Orange label, non-flexible vinyl					
❑ AFL1-1990(e) [R]	For LP Fans Only	1977	3.00	6.00	12.00
—Black label, dog near top; includes copies with sticker wrapped around spine with new number					
❑ LPM-1990 [M]	For LP Fans Only	1959	62.50	125.00	250.00
—"Long Play" on label					
❑ LPM-1990 [M]	For LP Fans Only	1963	20.00	40.00	80.00
—"Mono" on label					
❑ LPM-1990 [M]	For LP Fans Only	1964	12.50	25.00	50.00
—"Monaural" on label					
❑ LSP-1990(e) [R]	For LP Fans Only	1965	75.00	150.00	300.00
—"Stereo Electronically Reprocessed" on label; error cover with same photo on both front and back					
❑ LSP-1990(e) [R]	For LP Fans Only	1965	12.50	25.00	50.00
—"Stereo Electronically Reprocessed" on label; normal cover with different front and back cover photos					
❑ LSP-1990(e) [R]	For LP Fans Only	1968	7.50	15.00	30.00
—Orange label, non-flexible vinyl					
❑ LSP-1990(e) [R]	For LP Fans Only	1975	5.00	10.00	20.00
—Tan label					
❑ LSP-1990(e) [R]	For LP Fans Only	1976	3.00	6.00	12.00
—Black label, dog near top					
❑ AFL1-2011(e) [R]	A Date with Elvis	1977	3.00	6.00	12.00
—Black label, dog near top; includes copies with sticker wrapped around spine with new number					
❑ LPM-2011 [M]	A Date with Elvis	1959	100.00	200.00	400.00
—"Long Play" on label; gatefold cover, no sticker on cover					
❑ LPM-2011 [M]	A Date with Elvis	1959	125.00	250.00	500.00
—"Long Play" on label; gatefold cover, with sticker on cover					
❑ LPM-2011 [M]	A Date with Elvis	1963	25.00	50.00	100.00
—"Mono" on label; no gatefold cover					
❑ LPM-2011 [M]	A Date with Elvis	1965	12.50	25.00	50.00
—"Monaural" on label					
❑ LSP-2011(e) [R]	A Date with Elvis	1965	12.50	25.00	50.00
—Black label, "Stereo Electronically Reprocessed" on label					
❑ LSP-2011(e) [R]	A Date with Elvis	1968	7.50	15.00	30.00
—Orange label, non-flexible vinyl					
❑ LSP-2011(e) [R]	A Date with Elvis	1971	5.00	10.00	20.00
—Orange label, flexible vinyl					
❑ LSP-2011(e) [R]	A Date with Elvis	1975	5.00	10.00	20.00
—Tan label					
❑ LSP-2011(e) [R]	A Date with Elvis	1977	3.00	6.00	12.00
—Black label, dog near top					
❑ AFL1-2075(e) [R]	Elvis' Gold Records Volume 2 — 50,000,000 Elvis Fans Can't Be Wrong	1977	3.00	6.00	12.00
—Black label, dog near top; includes copies with sticker wrapped around spine with new number					
❑ LPM-2075 [M]	Elvis' Gold Records Volume 2 — 50,000,000 Elvis Fans Can't Be Wrong	1960	50.00	100.00	200.00
—"Long Play" on label; "Magic Millions" on upper right front cover with RCA Victor logo					
❑ LPM-2075 [M]	Elvis' Gold Records Volume 2 — 50,000,000 Elvis Fans Can't Be Wrong	1963	20.00	40.00	80.00
—"Mono" on label; "RE" on lower right front cover					
❑ LPM-2075 [M]	Elvis' Gold Records Volume 2 — 50,000,000 Elvis Fans Can't Be Wrong	1964	12.50	25.00	50.00
—"Monaural" on label; label has words "50,000,000 Elvis Presley Fans Can't Be Wrong"					
❑ LPM-2075 [M]	Elvis' Gold Records Volume 2 — 50,000,000 Elvis Fans Can't Be Wrong	1964	12.50	25.00	50.00
—"Monaural" on label; label only has "Elvis' Gold Records - Vol. 2"					
❑ LSP-2075(e) [R]	Elvis' Gold Records Volume 2 — 50,000,000 Elvis Fans Can't Be Wrong	1962	37.50	75.00	150.00
—"Stereo Electronically Reprocessed" on label; label has words "50,000,000 Elvis Presley Fans Can't Be Wrong"					
❑ LSP-2075(e) [R]	Elvis' Gold Records Volume 2 — 50,000,000 Elvis Fans Can't Be Wrong	1964	12.50	25.00	50.00
—"Stereo Electronically Reprocessed" and white "RCA Victor" on label					
❑ LSP-2075(e) [R]	Elvis' Gold Records Volume 2 — 50,000,000 Elvis Fans Can't Be Wrong	1968	7.50	15.00	30.00
—Orange label, non-flexible vinyl					
❑ LSP-2075(e) [R]	Elvis' Gold Records Volume 2 — 50,000,000 Elvis Fans Can't Be Wrong	1971	5.00	10.00	20.00
—Orange label, flexible vinyl					
❑ LSP-2075(e) [R]	Elvis' Gold Records Volume 2 — 50,000,000 Elvis Fans Can't Be Wrong	1975	5.00	10.00	20.00
—Tan label					
❑ LSP-2075(e) [R]	Elvis' Gold Records Volume 2 — 50,000,000 Elvis Fans Can't Be Wrong	1976	3.00	6.00	12.00
—Black label, dog near top					
❑ AFL1-2231 [S]	Elvis Is Back!	1977	3.00	6.00	12.00
—Black label, dog near top; includes copies with sticker wrapped around spine with new number					
❑ LPM-2231 [M]	Elvis Is Back!	1960	37.50	75.00	150.00
—With sticker attached to front cover. Side 2, Song 4 is listed as "The Girl Next Door."					
❑ LPM-2231 [M]	Elvis Is Back!	1960	37.50	75.00	150.00
—With sticker attached to front cover. Side 2, Song 4 is listed as "The Girl Next Door Went a-Walking."					
❑ LPM-2231 [M]	Elvis Is Back!	1960	50.00	100.00	200.00
—With no sticker attached to front cover. Side 2, Song 4 is listed as "The Girl Next Door."					
❑ LPM-2231 [M]	Elvis Is Back!	1960	50.00	100.00	200.00
—With no sticker attached to front cover. Side 2, Song 4 is listed as "The Girl Next Door Went a-Walking."					
❑ LPM-2231 [M]	Elvis Is Back!	1963	15.00	30.00	60.00
—"Mono" on label; song titles printed on front cover					

Number	Title (A Side/B Side)	Yr	VG	VG+	NM
❑ LPM-2231 [M]	Elvis Is Back!	1964	15.00	30.00	60.00
—"Monaural" on label					
❑ LSP-2231 [S]	Elvis Is Back!	1960	75.00	150.00	300.00
—"Living Stereo" on label; with sticker attached to front cover. Side 2, Song 4 is listed as "The Girl Next Door."					
❑ LSP-2231 [S]	Elvis Is Back!	1960	75.00	150.00	300.00
—"Living Stereo" on label; with sticker attached to front cover. Side 2, Song 4 is listed as "The Girl Next Door Went a-Walking."					
❑ LSP-2231 [S]	Elvis Is Back!	1960	75.00	150.00	300.00
—"Living Stereo" on label; with no sticker attached to front cover. Side 2, Song 4 is listed as "The Girl Next Door."					
❑ LSP-2231 [S]	Elvis Is Back!	1960	75.00	150.00	300.00
—"Living Stereo" on label; with no sticker attached to front cover. Side 2, Song 4 is listed as "The Girl Next Door Went a-Walking."					
❑ LSP-2231 [S]	Elvis Is Back!	1964	15.00	30.00	60.00
—"Stereo" on label; song titles printed on front cover					
❑ LSP-2231 [S]	Elvis Is Back!	1968	10.00	20.00	40.00
—Orange label, non-flexible vinyl					
❑ LSP-2231 [S]	Elvis Is Back!	1975	5.00	10.00	20.00
—Tan label					
❑ LSP-2231 [S]	Elvis Is Back!	1976	3.75	7.50	15.00
—Black label, dog on top					
❑ AFL1-2256 [S]	G.I. Blues	1977	3.00	6.00	12.00
—Black label, dog near top; includes copies with sticker wrapped around spine with new number					
❑ LPM-2256 [M]	G.I. Blues	1960	125.00	250.00	500.00
—"Long Play" on label; with sticker on front cover advertising the presence of "Wooden Heart"					
❑ LPM-2256 [M]	G.I. Blues	1960	30.00	60.00	120.00
—"Long Play" on label; with no sticker on front cover					
❑ LPM-2256 [M]	G.I. Blues	1963	25.00	50.00	100.00
—"Mono" on label					
❑ LPM-2256 [M]	G.I. Blues	1964	12.50	25.00	50.00
—"Monaural" on label					
❑ LSP-2256 [S]	G.I. Blues	1960	150.00	300.00	600.00
—"Living Stereo" on label; with sticker on front cover advertising the presence of "Wooden Heart"					
❑ LSP-2256 [S]	G.I. Blues	1960	25.00	50.00	100.00
—"Living Stereo" on label; with no sticker on front cover					
❑ LSP-2256 [S]	G.I. Blues	1964	12.50	25.00	50.00
—"Stereo" on black label					
❑ LSP-2256 [S]	G.I. Blues	1968	10.00	20.00	40.00
—Orange label, non-flexible vinyl					
❑ LSP-2256 [S]	G.I. Blues	1971	5.00	10.00	20.00
—Orange label, flexible vinyl					
❑ LSP-2256 [S]	G.I. Blues	1975	6.25	12.50	25.00
—Tan label					
❑ LSP-2256 [S]	G.I. Blues	1976	3.00	6.00	12.00
—Black label, dog near top					
❑ AFL1-2274	Welcome to My World	1977	3.00	6.00	12.00
—Black label, dog near top; includes copies with sticker wrapped around spine with new number					
❑ APL1-2274	Welcome to My World	1977	5.00	10.00	20.00
—Black label, dog near top					
❑ AQL1-2274	Welcome to My World	1979	2.50	5.00	10.00
—Black label, dog near top; includes copies with sticker wrapped around spine with new number					
❑ LPM-2328 [M]	His Hand in Mine	1960	30.00	60.00	120.00
—"Long Play" on label					
❑ LPM-2328 [M]	His Hand in Mine	1963	15.00	30.00	60.00
—"Mono" on label					
❑ LPM-2328 [M]	His Hand in Mine	1964	12.50	25.00	50.00
—"Monaural" on label					
❑ LSP-2328 [S]	His Hand in Mine	1960	50.00	100.00	200.00
—"Living Stereo" on label					
❑ LSP-2328 [S]	His Hand in Mine	1964	150.00	300.00	600.00
—"Stereo" and silver "RCA Victor" on black label					
❑ LSP-2328 [S]	His Hand in Mine	1964	25.00	50.00	100.00
—"Stereo" and white "RCA Victor" on black label					
❑ LSP-2328 [S]	His Hand in Mine	1968	12.50	25.00	50.00
—Orange label, non-flexible vinyl					
❑ LSP-2328 [S]	His Hand in Mine	1975	5.00	10.00	20.00
—Tan label					
❑ LSP-2328 [S]	His Hand in Mine	197?	5.00	10.00	20.00
—Orange label, flexible vinyl					
❑ AHL1-2347	Greatest Hits, Volume One	1981	6.25	12.50	25.00
—With embossed cover					
❑ AHL1-2347	Greatest Hits, Volume One	1983	3.75	7.50	15.00
—Without embossed cover					
❑ AFL1-2370 [S]	Something for Everybody	1977	3.00	6.00	12.00
—Black label, dog near top; includes copies with sticker wrapped around spine with new number					
❑ LPM-2370 [M]	Something for Everybody	1961	30.00	60.00	120.00
—"Long Play" on label; back cover advertises RCA Compact 33 singles and doubles					
❑ LPM-2370 [M]	Something for Everybody	1963	20.00	40.00	80.00
—"Mono" on label; back cover advertises "Viva Las Vegas" EP					
❑ LPM-2370 [M]	Something for Everybody	1964	12.50	25.00	50.00
—"Monaural" on label; back cover advertises "Viva Las Vegas" EP					
❑ LSP-2370 [S]	Something for Everybody	1961	50.00	100.00	200.00
—"Living Stereo" on label; back cover advertises RCA Compact 33 singles and doubles					
❑ LSP-2370 [S]	Something for Everybody	1963	25.00	50.00	100.00
—"Stereo" and silver "RCA Victor" on black label; back cover advertises Elvis' Christmas Album and His Hand in Mine LPs and "Viva Las Vegas" EP					
❑ LSP-2370 [S]	Something for Everybody	1964	12.50	25.00	50.00
—"Stereo" and white "RCA Victor" on black label; back cover advertises "Viva Las Vegas" EP					
❑ LSP-2370 [S]	Something for Everybody	1968	10.00	20.00	40.00
—Orange label, non-flexible vinyl; final back cover change advertises Elvis (NBC-TV Special), Elvis' Christmas Album and His Hand in Mine LPs					
❑ LSP-2370 [S]	Something for Everybody	1971	5.00	10.00	20.00
—Orange label, flexible vinyl					
❑ LSP-2370 [S]	Something for Everybody	1975	5.00	10.00	20.00
—Tan label					

Number	Title (A Side/B Side)	Yr	VG	VG+	NM
❑ LSP-2370 [S]	Something for Everybody	1976	3.00	6.00	12.00
—Black label, dog near top					
❑ AFL1-2426 [S]	Blue Hawaii	1977	3.00	6.00	12.00
—Black label, dog near top; with sticker wrapped around spine with new number					
❑ LPM-2426 [M]	Blue Hawaii	1961	25.00	50.00	100.00
—"Long Play" on label; with sticker on cover advertising the presence of "Can't Help Falling in Love" and "Rock-a-Hula Baby"					
❑ LPM-2426 [M]	Blue Hawaii	1962	15.00	30.00	60.00
—"Long Play" on label; no sticker on front cover					
❑ LPM-2426 [M]	Blue Hawaii	1963	12.50	25.00	50.00
—"Mono" on label					
❑ LPM-2426 [M]	Blue Hawaii	1964	10.00	20.00	40.00
—"Monaural" on label					
❑ LSP-2426 [S]	Blue Hawaii	1961	37.50	75.00	150.00
—"Living Stereo" on label and upper right front cover; with sticker on cover advertising the presence of "Can't Help Falling in Love" and "Rock-a-Hula Baby"					
❑ LSP-2426 [S]	Blue Hawaii	1962	20.00	40.00	80.00
—"Living Stereo" on label and upper right front cover; no sticker on front cover					
❑ LSP-2426 [S]	Blue Hawaii	1964	12.50	25.00	50.00
—"Stereo" on label; "Victor Stereo" on upper right front cover					
❑ LSP-2426 [S]	Blue Hawaii	1968	10.00	20.00	40.00
—Orange label, non-flexible vinyl					
❑ LSP-2426 [S]	Blue Hawaii	1971	50.00	10.00	20.00
—Orange label, flexible vinyl					
❑ LSP-2426 [S]	Blue Hawaii	1975	50.00	10.00	20.00
—Tan label					
❑ LSP-2426 [S]	Blue Hawaii	1977	3.00	6.00	12.00
—Black label, dog near top					
❑ LSP-2426 [S]	Blue Hawaii	197?	250.00	500.00	1000.
—One-of-a-kind blue vinyl pressing with black label, dog near top					
❑ AFK1-2428	Moody Blue	1977	1500.	2250.	3000.
—Alternate cover slick (never put on an actual cover), with the words "Moody Blue" inside the large word "Elvis." See any late-1970s Elvis inner sleeve for a black and white photo of the scrapped cover.					
❑ AFL1-2428	Moody Blue	1977	2.50	5.00	10.00
—Blue vinyl					
❑ AFL1-2428	Moody Blue	1977	50.00	100.00	200.00
—Black vinyl					
❑ AFL1-2428 [DJ]	Moody Blue	1977	500.00	1000.	2000.
—Experimental colored vinyl pressings (with no cover), any color or combination except blue or black					
❑ AQL1-2428	Moody Blue	1979	6.25	12.50	25.00
—Reissue with new prefix					
❑ AFL1-2523 [S]	Pot Luck with Elvis	1977	3.00	6.00	12.00
—Black label, dog near top; includes copies with sticker wrapped around spine with new number					
❑ LPM-2523 [M]	Pot Luck with Elvis	1962	25.00	50.00	100.00
—"Long Play" on label					
❑ LPM-2523 [M]	Pot Luck with Elvis	1964	30.00	60.00	120.00
—"Monaural" on label					
❑ LSP-2523 [S]	Pot Luck with Elvis	1962	37.50	75.00	150.00
—"Living Stereo" on label					
❑ LSP-2523 [S]	Pot Luck with Elvis	1964	15.00	30.00	60.00
—"Stereo" on black label					
❑ LSP-2523 [S]	Pot Luck with Elvis	1968	10.00	20.00	40.00
—Orange label, non-flexible vinyl					
❑ LSP-2523 [S]	Pot Luck with Elvis	1975	5.00	10.00	20.00
—Tan label					
❑ LSP-2523 [S]	Pot Luck with Elvis	1976	3.00	6.00	12.00
—Black label, dog near top					
❑ CPD2-2542 [(2) Q]	Aloha from Hawaii Via Satellite	1975	6.25	12.50	25.00
—Reissue with new number; orange labels					
❑ CPD2-2542 [(2) Q]	Aloha from Hawaii Via Satellite	1975	5.00	10.00	20.00
—Reissue with new number; tan labels					
❑ CPD2-2542 [(2) Q]	Aloha from Hawaii Via Satellite	1977	5.00	10.00	20.00
—Black labels, dog near top					
❑ CPL2-2542 [(2) Q]	Aloha from Hawaii Via Satellite	1984	3.00	6.00	12.00
—New prefix; single-pocket instead of gatefold jacket					
❑ APL1-2558 [S]	Harum Scarum	1977	3.00	6.00	12.00
—Black label, dog near top					
❑ APL1-2560 [S]	Spinout	1977	3.00	6.00	12.00
—Black label, dog near top					
❑ APL1-2564 [S]	Double Trouble	1977	3.00	6.00	12.00
—Black label, dog near top; includes copies with sticker wrapped around spine with new number					
❑ APL1-2565	Clambake	1977	3.00	6.00	12.00
❑ APL1-2568 [S]	It Happened at the World's Fair	1977	3.00	6.00	12.00
❑ APL2-2587 [(2)]	Elvis in Concert	1977	6.25	12.50	25.00
❑ CPL2-2587 [(2)]	Elvis in Concert	1982	10.00	20.00	40.00
❑ AFL1-2621 [S]	Girls! Girls! Girls!	1977	3.00	6.00	12.00
—Black label, dog near top; includes copies with sticker wrapped around spine with new number					
❑ LPM-2621 [M]	Girls! Girls! Girls!	1962	20.00	40.00	80.00
—"Long Play" on label					
❑ LPM-2621 [M]	Girls! Girls! Girls!	1963	15.00	30.00	60.00
—"Mono" on label					
❑ LPM-2621 [M]	Girls! Girls! Girls!	1964	10.00	20.00	40.00
—"Monaural" on label					
❑ LPM/LSP-2621	Girls! Girls! Girls! Bonus 1963 Calendar	1962	37.50	75.00	150.00
—With listing of other Elvis records on back					
❑ LSP-2621 [S]	Girls! Girls! Girls!	1962	37.50	75.00	150.00
—"Living Stereo" on label					
❑ LSP-2621 [S]	Girls! Girls! Girls!	1964	15.00	30.00	60.00
—"Stereo" on black label					
❑ LSP-2621 [S]	Girls! Girls! Girls!	1968	10.00	20.00	40.00
—Orange label, non-flexible vinyl					
❑ LSP-2621 [S]	Girls! Girls! Girls!	1971	5.00	10.00	20.00
—Orange label, flexible vinyl					
❑ LSP-2621 [S]	Girls! Girls! Girls!	1975	6.25	12.50	25.00
—Tan label					
❑ LSP-2621 [S]	Girls! Girls! Girls!	1976	3.00	6.00	12.00
—Black label, dog near top					
❑ CPD2-2642 [(2) Q]	Aloha from Hawaii Via Satellite	1975	7.50	15.00	30.00
—Orange labels					
❑ CPD2-2642 [(2) Q]	Aloha from Hawaii Via Satellite	1977	20.00	40.00	80.00
—Black labels, dog near top					
❑ LPM-2697 [M]	It Happened at the World's Fair	1963	30.00	60.00	120.00
❑ LPM/LSP-2697	It Happened at the World's Fair Photo	1963	62.50	125.00	250.00
❑ LSP-2697 [S]	It Happened at the World's Fair	1963	50.00	100.00	200.00
—"Stereo" and silver "RCA Victor" on black label					
❑ LSP-2697 [S]	It Happened at the World's Fair	1964	20.00	40.00	80.00
—"Stereo" and white "RCA Victor" on black label					
❑ AFL1-2756 [S]	Fun in Acapulco	1977	3.00	6.00	12.00
—Black label, dog near top; includes copies with sticker wrapped around spine with new number					
❑ LPM-2756 [M]	Fun in Acapulco	1963	20.00	40.00	80.00
—"Mono" on label					
❑ LPM-2756 [M]	Fun in Acapulco	1964	12.50	25.00	50.00
—"Monaural" on label					
❑ LSP-2756 [S]	Fun in Acapulco	1963	25.00	50.00	100.00
—"Stereo" and silver "RCA Victor" on black label					
❑ LSP-2756 [S]	Fun in Acapulco	1964	15.00	30.00	60.00
—"Stereo" and white "RCA Victor" on black label					
❑ LSP-2756 [S]	Fun in Acapulco	1968	10.00	20.00	40.00
—Orange label, non-flexible vinyl					
❑ LSP-2756 [S]	Fun in Acapulco	1975	6.25	12.50	25.00
—Tan label					
❑ LSP-2756 [S]	Fun in Acapulco	1976	3.00	6.00	12.00
—Black label, dog near top					
❑ AFL1-2765 [S]	Elvis' Golden Records, Volume 3	1977	3.00	6.00	12.00
—Black label, dog near top; includes copies with sticker wrapped around spine with new number					
❑ LPM-2765 [M]	Elvis' Golden Records, Volume 3	1963	25.00	50.00	100.00
—"Mono" on label					
❑ LPM-2765 [M]	Elvis' Golden Records, Volume 3	1964	15.00	30.00	60.00
—"Monaural" on label					
❑ LSP-2765 [S]	Elvis' Golden Records, Volume 3	1963	37.50	75.00	150.00
—"Stereo" and silver "RCA Victor" on black label					
❑ LSP-2765 [S]	Elvis' Golden Records, Volume 3	1964	12.50	25.00	50.00
—"Stereo" and white "RCA Victor" on black label					
❑ LSP-2765 [S]	Elvis' Golden Records, Volume 3	1968	10.00	20.00	40.00
—Orange label, non-flexible vinyl					
❑ LSP-2765 [S]	Elvis' Golden Records, Volume 3	1975	5.00	10.00	20.00
—Tan label					
❑ LSP-2765 [S]	Elvis' Golden Records, Volume 3	1976	3.00	6.00	12.00
—Black label, dog near top					
❑ AFL1-2772	He Walks Beside Me	1978	6.25	12.50	25.00
—Includes 20-page photo booklet					
❑ AFL1-2894 [S]	Kissin' Cousins	1977	3.00	6.00	12.00
—Black label, dog near top; includes copies with sticker wrapped around spine with new number					
❑ LPM-2894 [M]	Kissin' Cousins	1964	20.00	40.00	80.00
—"Mono" on label; front cover has a small black and white photo of six cast members in lower right					
❑ LPM-2894 [M]	Kissin' Cousins	1964	50.00	100.00	200.00
—"Mono" on label; front cover does NOT have black and white photo in lower right					
❑ LPM-2894 [M]	Kissin' Cousins	1964	25.00	50.00	100.00
—"Monaural" on label; front cover has a small black and white photo of six cast members in lower right					
❑ LPM-2894 [M]	Kissin' Cousins	1964	50.00	100.00	200.00
—"Monaural" on label; front cover does NOT have black and white photo in lower right					
❑ LSP-2894 [S]	Kissin' Cousins	1964	30.00	60.00	120.00
—"Stereo" and silver "RCA Victor" on black label; front cover has a small black and white photo of six cast members in lower right					
❑ LSP-2894 [S]	Kissin' Cousins	1964	50.00	100.00	200.00
—"Stereo" and silver "RCA Victor" on black label; front cover does NOT have black and white photo in lower right					
❑ LSP-2894 [S]	Kissin' Cousins	1964	15.00	30.00	60.00
—"Stereo" and white "RCA Victor" on black label; all front covers have the cast photo in lower right					
❑ LSP-2894 [S]	Kissin' Cousins	1968	10.00	20.00	40.00
—Orange label, non-flexible vinyl					
❑ LSP-2894 [S]	Kissin' Cousins	1971	5.00	10.00	20.00
—Orange label, flexible vinyl					
❑ LSP-2894 [S]	Kissin' Cousins	1975	6.25	12.50	25.00
—Tan label					
❑ LSP-2894 [S]	Kissin' Cousins	1976	3.00	6.00	12.00
—Black label, dog near top					
❑ LSP-2894 [S]	Kissin' Cousins	1976	375.00	750.00	1500.
—Black label, dog near top; blue vinyl					
❑ CPL1-2901	Elvis Sings for Children and Grownups Too!	1978	5.00	10.00	20.00
—With two slits for removable greeting card on back cover (card should be with package)					
❑ CPL1-2901	Elvis Sings for Children and Grownups Too!	1978	2.50	5.00	10.00
—With greeting card graphic printed on back cover, and no slits on back cover					
❑ AFL1-2999 [S]	Roustabout	1977	3.00	6.00	12.00
—Black label, dog near top; includes copies with sticker wrapped around spine with new number					
❑ LPM-2999 [M]	Roustabout	1964	25.00	50.00	100.00
—"Mono" on label					
❑ LPM-2999 [M]	Roustabout	1965	15.00	30.00	60.00
—"Monaural" on label					
❑ LSP-2999 [S]	Roustabout	1964	150.00	300.00	600.00
—"Stereo" and silver "RCA Victor" on black label					
❑ LSP-2999 [S]	Roustabout	1964	15.00	30.00	60.00
—"Stereo" and white "RCA Victor" on black label					
❑ LSP-2999 [S]	Roustabout	1968	10.00	20.00	40.00
—Orange label, non-flexible vinyl					
❑ LSP-2999 [S]	Roustabout	1971	5.00	10.00	20.00
—Orange label, flexible vinyl					
❑ LSP-2999 [S]	Roustabout	1975	5.00	10.00	20.00
—Tan label					
❑ LSP-2999 [S]	Roustabout	1976	3.00	6.00	12.00
—Black label, dog near top					
❑ CPL1-3078 [PD]	A Legendary Performer, Volume 3	1978	6.25	12.50	25.00
—Picture disc applied to blue vinyl LP; with booklet (deduct 40% if missing)					

Number	Title (A Side/B Side)	Yr	VG	VG+	NM
❑ CPL1-3082	A Legendary Performer, Volume 3	1978	6.25	12.50	25.00
—Includes booklet (deduct 40% if missing); with die-cut hole in front cover					
❑ CPL1-3082	A Legendary Performer, Volume 3	1986	2.00	4.00	8.00
—No die-cut hole in cover and no booklet					
❑ AQL1-3279	Our Memories of Elvis	1979	5.00	10.00	20.00
❑ AFL1-3338 [S]	Girl Happy	1977	3.00	6.00	12.00
—Black label, dog near top; includes copies with sticker wrapped around spine with new number					
❑ LPM-3338 [M]	Girl Happy	1965	15.00	30.00	60.00
❑ LSP-3338 [S]	Girl Happy	1965	15.00	30.00	60.00
—"Stereo" on black label					
❑ LSP-3338 [S]	Girl Happy	1968	10.00	20.00	40.00
—Orange label, non-flexible vinyl					
❑ LSP-3338 [S]	Girl Happy	1971	5.00	10.00	20.00
—Orange label, flexible vinyl					
❑ LSP-3338 [S]	Girl Happy	1975	6.25	12.50	25.00
—Tan label					
❑ LSP-3338 [S]	Girl Happy	1976	3.00	6.00	12.00
—Black label, dog near top					
❑ AQL1-3448	Our Memories of Elvis, Volume 2	1979	5.00	10.00	20.00
❑ AFL1-3450 [P]	Elvis for Everyone	1977	3.00	6.00	12.00
—Black label, dog near top; includes copies with sticker wrapped around spine with new number					
❑ LPM-3450 [M]	Elvis for Everyone	1965	15.00	30.00	60.00
❑ LSP-3450 [P]	Elvis for Everyone	1965	15.00	30.00	60.00
—Black label, "Stereo" on label					
❑ LSP-3450 [P]	Elvis for Everyone	1968	10.00	20.00	40.00
—Orange label, non-flexible vinyl					
❑ LSP-3450 [P]	Elvis for Everyone	1971	5.00	10.00	20.00
—Orange label, flexible vinyl					
❑ LSP-3450 [P]	Elvis for Everyone	1975	5.00	10.00	20.00
—Tan label					
❑ LSP-3450 [P]	Elvis for Everyone	1976	3.00	6.00	12.00
—Black label, dog near top					
❑ DJL1-3455 [DJ]	Pure Elvis	1979	150.00	300.00	600.00
—Promo-only item for Our Memories of Elvis, Volume 2; contains original version of five songs on one side, "unsweetened" versions of same songs on the other					
❑ LPM-3468 [M]	Harum Scarum	1965	15.00	30.00	60.00
❑ LPM/LSP-3468	Harum Scarum Bonus Photo	1965	15.00	30.00	60.00
❑ LSP-3468 [S]	Harum Scarum	1965	15.00	30.00	60.00
—"Stereo" on black label					
❑ LPM-3553 [M]	Frankie and Johnny	1966	15.00	30.00	60.00
❑ LPM/LSP-3553	Frankie and Johnny Bonus Print	1966	15.00	30.00	60.00
❑ LSP-3553 [S]	Frankie and Johnny	1966	15.00	30.00	60.00
—"Stereo" on black label					
❑ AFL1-3643 [S]	Paradise, Hawaiian Style	1977	3.00	6.00	12.00
—Black label, dog near top; includes copies with sticker wrapped around spine with new number					
❑ LPM-3643 [M]	Paradise, Hawaiian Style	1966	15.00	30.00	60.00
❑ LSP-3643 [S]	Paradise, Hawaiian Style	1966	15.00	30.00	60.00
—"Stereo" on black label					
❑ LSP-3643 [S]	Paradise, Hawaiian Style	1968	10.00	20.00	40.00
—Orange label, non-flexible vinyl					
❑ LSP-3643 [S]	Paradise, Hawaiian Style	1971	5.00	10.00	20.00
—Orange label, flexible vinyl					
❑ LSP-3643 [S]	Paradise, Hawaiian Style	1975	3.75	7.50	15.00
—Tan label					
❑ LSP-3643 [S]	Paradise, Hawaiian Style	1976	3.00	6.00	12.00
—Black label, dog near top					
❑ AYL1-3683 [S]	Blue Hawaii	1980	2.50	5.00	10.00
—"Best Buy Series" reissue					
❑ AYL1-3684 [S]	Spinout	1980	2.00	4.00	8.00
—"Best Buy Series" reissue					
❑ CPL8-3699 [(8)]	Elvis Aron Presley	1980	25.00	50.00	100.00
—Box set; regular issue with booklet					
❑ CPL8-3699 [(8)]	Elvis Aron Presley	1980	62.50	125.00	250.00
—Box set; "Reviewer Series" edition (will be identified as such on the cover)					
❑ LPM-3702 [M]	Spinout	1966	15.00	30.00	60.00
❑ LPM/LSP-3702	Spinout Bonus Photo	1966	15.00	30.00	60.00
❑ LSP-3702 [S]	Spinout	1966	15.00	30.00	60.00
—"Stereo" on black label					
❑ DJL1-3729 [DJ]	Elvis Aron Presley (Excerpts)	1980	30.00	60.00	120.00
—Promo-only excerpts of songs from box set					
❑ AYL1-3732	Pure Gold	1980	2.00	4.00	8.00
—"Best Buy Series" reissue					
❑ AYL1-3733 [R]	King Creole	1980	2.00	4.00	8.00
—"Best Buy Series" reissue; includes copies with sticker wrapped around spine with new number					
❑ AYL1-3734 [S]	Harum Scarum	1980	2.00	4.00	8.00
—"Best Buy Series" reissue					
❑ AYL1-3735 [S]	G.I. Blues	1980	2.00	4.00	8.00
—"Best Buy Series" reissue					
❑ AFL1-3758 [S]	How Great Thou Art	1977	3.00	6.00	12.00
—Black label, dog near top; includes copies with sticker wrapped around spine with new number					
❑ AQL1-3758 [S]	How Great Thou Art	1979	2.50	5.00	10.00
—Reissue with new prefix					
❑ LPM-3758 [M]	How Great Thou Art	1967	15.00	30.00	60.00
—"Mono Dynagroove" on label					
❑ LSP-3758 [S]	How Great Thou Art	1967	15.00	30.00	60.00
—"Stereo Dynagroove" on black label					
❑ LSP-3758 [S]	How Great Thou Art	1968	10.00	20.00	40.00
—Orange label, non-flexible vinyl					
❑ LSP-3758 [S]	How Great Thou Art	1971	6.25	12.50	25.00
—Orange label, flexible vinyl					
❑ LSP-3758 [S]	How Great Thou Art	1975	5.00	10.00	20.00
—Tan label					
❑ LSP-3758 [S]	How Great Thou Art	1976	3.00	6.00	12.00
—Black label, dog near top					
❑ DJL1-3781 [DJ]	Elvis Aron Presley (Selections)	1980	30.00	60.00	120.00
—Promo-only complete versions of songs from box set					
❑ LPM-3787 [M]	Double Trouble	1967	15.00	30.00	60.00
—With bonus photo announcement on cover					
❑ LPM-3787 [M]	Double Trouble	1967	20.00	40.00	80.00
—With no bonus photo announcement on cover					
❑ LPM/LSP-3787	Double Trouble Bonus Photo	1967	12.50	25.00	50.00
❑ LSP-3787 [S]	Double Trouble	1967	15.00	30.00	60.00
—With bonus photo announcement on cover					
❑ LSP-3787 [S]	Double Trouble	1967	17.50	35.00	70.00
—With no bonus photo announcement on cover; black label "Stereo"					
❑ LSP-3787 [S]	Double Trouble	1968	10.00	20.00	40.00
—Orange label, non-flexible vinyl					
❑ LSP-3787 [S]	Double Trouble	1975	5.00	10.00	20.00
—Tan label					
❑ LSP-3787 [S]	Double Trouble	1977	3.00	6.00	12.00
—Black label, dog near top					
❑ AYL1-3892	Elvis in Person at the International Hotel, Las Vegas, Nevada	1981	2.00	4.00	8.00
—"Best Buy Series" reissue					
❑ AYM1-3893	The Sun Sessions	1981	2.00	4.00	8.00
—"Best Buy Series" reissue; includes copies with sticker wrapped around spine with new number					
❑ LPM-3893 [M]	Clambake	1967	62.50	125.00	250.00
❑ LPM/LSP-3893	Clambake Bonus Photo	1967	12.50	25.00	50.00
❑ LSP-3893 [S]	Clambake	1967	15.00	30.00	60.00
❑ AYM1-3894	Elvis (NBC-TV Special)	1981	2.00	4.00	8.00
—"Best Buy Series" reissue					
❑ AAL1-3917	Guitar Man	1981	7.50	15.00	30.00
❑ AFL1-3921 [P]	Elvis' Gold Records, Volume 4	1976	3.75	7.50	15.00
—Tan label with new prefix					
❑ AFL1-3921 [P]	Elvis' Gold Records, Volume 4	1977	3.00	6.00	12.00
—Black label, dog near top; includes copies with sticker wrapped around spine with new number					
❑ LPM-3921 [M]	Elvis' Gold Records, Volume 4	1968	500.00	1000.	2000.
—"Monaural" on label					
❑ LSP-3921 [P]	Elvis' Gold Records, Volume 4	1968	12.50	25.00	50.00
—"Stereo" and white "RCA Victor" on black label					
❑ LSP-3921 [P]	Elvis' Gold Records, Volume 4	1968	10.00	20.00	40.00
—Orange label, non-flexible vinyl					
❑ LSP-3921 [P]	Elvis' Gold Records, Volume 4	1975	6.25	12.50	25.00
—Tan label					
❑ LSP-3921 [P]	Elvis' Gold Records, Volume 4	1976	3.00	6.00	12.00
—Black label, dog near top					
❑ LSP-3921 [P]	Elvis' Gold Records, Volume 4	197?	5.00	10.00	20.00
—Orange label, flexible vinyl					
❑ AYL1-3935 [S]	His Hand in Mine	1981	2.00	4.00	8.00
—"Best Buy Series" reissue; includes copies with sticker wrapped around spine with new number					
❑ AYL1-3956	Elvis Country ("I'm 10,000 Years Old")	1981	2.00	4.00	8.00
—"Best Buy Series" reissue					
❑ AFL1-3989 [S]	Speedway	1977	3.00	6.00	12.00
—Black label, dog near top; includes copies with sticker wrapped around spine with new number					
❑ LPM-3989 [M]	Speedway	1968	500.00	1000.	2000.
❑ LPM/LSP-3989	Speedway Bonus Photo	1968	12.50	25.00	50.00
❑ LSP-3989 [S]	Speedway	1968	15.00	30.00	60.00
—"Stereo" on black label					
❑ LSP-3989 [S]	Speedway	1968	10.00	20.00	40.00
—Orange label, non-flexible vinyl					
❑ LSP-3989 [S]	Speedway	1971	5.00	10.00	20.00
—Orange label, flexible vinyl					
❑ LSP-3989 [S]	Speedway	1975	5.00	10.00	20.00
—Tan label					
❑ LSP-3989 [S]	Speedway	1976	3.00	6.00	12.00
—Black label, dog near top					
❑ CPL2-4031 [(2)]	This Is Elvis	1980	3.75	7.50	15.00
❑ AFM1-4088	Elvis (NBC-TV Special)	1977	3.00	6.00	12.00
—Black label, dog near top; includes copies with sticker wrapped around spine with new number					
❑ LPM-4088	Elvis (NBC-TV Special)	1968	10.00	20.00	40.00
—Orange label, non-flexible vinyl					
❑ LPM-4088	Elvis (NBC-TV Special)	1971	7.50	15.00	30.00
—Orange label, flexible vinyl					
❑ LPM-4088	Elvis (NBC-TV Special)	1975	5.00	10.00	20.00
—Tan label					
❑ LPM-4088	Elvis (NBC-TV Special)	1976	3.75	7.50	15.00
—Black label, dog near top					
❑ AYL1-4114	That's the Way It Is	1981	2.00	4.00	8.00
—"Best Buy Series" reissue; includes copies with sticker wrapped around spine with new number					
❑ AYL1-4115 [S]	Kissin' Cousins	1981	2.00	4.00	8.00
—"Best Buy Series" reissue; includes copies with sticker wrapped around spine with new number					
❑ AYL1-4116 [S]	Something for Everybody	1981	2.00	4.00	8.00
—"Best Buy Series" reissue; includes copies with sticker wrapped around spine with new number					
❑ AFL1-4155	From Elvis in Memphis	1977	3.00	6.00	12.00
—Black label, dog near top; includes copies with sticker wrapped around spine with new number					
❑ LSP-4155	From Elvis in Memphis	1969	10.00	20.00	40.00
—Orange label, non-flexible vinyl					
❑ LSP-4155	From Elvis in Memphis Bonus Photo	1969	10.00	20.00	40.00
❑ LSP-4155	From Elvis in Memphis	1971	7.50	15.00	30.00
—Orange label, flexible vinyl					
❑ LSP-4155	From Elvis in Memphis	1975	6.25	12.50	25.00
—Tan label					
❑ LSP-4155	From Elvis in Memphis	1976	3.75	7.50	15.00
—Black label, dog near top					
❑ AYL1-4232 [P]	Elvis for Everyone	1982	2.00	4.00	8.00
—"Best Buy Series" reissue					
❑ AFL1-4362	On Stage February, 1970	1977	3.00	6.00	12.00
—Black label, dog near top; includes copies with sticker wrapped around spine with new number					
❑ AQL1-4362	On Stage February, 1970	1983	2.00	4.00	8.00
—Reissue with some cover changes					
❑ LSP-4362	On Stage February, 1970	1970	10.00	20.00	40.00
—Orange label, non-flexible vinyl					

Number Title (A Side/B Side) Yr VG VG+ NM

❑ LSP-4362 On Stage February, 1970 1971 6.25 12.50 25.00
—Orange label, flexible vinyl
❑ LSP-4362 On Stage February, 1970 1975 6.25 12.50 25.00
—Tan label
❑ LSP-4362 On Stage February, 1970 1976 7.50 15.00 30.00
—Black label, dog near top
❑ CPL1-4395 Memories of Christmas 1982 3.75 7.50 15.00
—With greeting card (deduct 1/3 if missing)
❑ AFL1-4428 Elvis in Person at the International Hotel, Las Vegas, Nevada 1977 3.00 6.00 12.00
—Black label, dog near top; includes copies with sticker wrapped around spine with new number
❑ LSP-4428 Elvis in Person at the International Hotel, Las Vegas, Nevada 1970 12.50 25.00 50.00
—Orange label, non-flexible vinyl
❑ LSP-4428 Elvis in Person at the International Hotel, Las Vegas, Nevada 1971 10.00 20.00 40.00
—Orange label, flexible vinyl
❑ LSP-4428 Elvis in Person at the International Hotel, Las Vegas, Nevada 1975 6.25 12.50 25.00
—Tan label
❑ LSP-4428 Elvis in Person at the International Hotel, Las Vegas, Nevada 1976 3.75 7.50 15.00
—Black label, dog near top
❑ AFL1-4429 Back in Memphis 1977 3.00 6.00 12.00
—Black label, dog near top; with sticker wrapped around spine with new number
❑ LSP-4429 Back in Memphis 1970 10.00 20.00 40.00
—Orange label, non-flexible vinyl
❑ LSP-4429 Back in Memphis 1971 7.50 15.00 30.00
—Orange label, flexible vinyl
❑ LSP-4429 Back in Memphis 1975 6.25 12.50 25.00
—Tan label
❑ LSP-4429 Back in Memphis 1977 3.75 7.50 15.00
—Black label, dog near top
❑ AFL1-4445 That's the Way It Is 1977 3.00 6.00 12.00
—Black label, dog near top; includes copies with sticker wrapped around spine with new number
❑ LSP-4445 That's the Way It Is 1970 20.00 40.00 80.00
—Orange label, non-flexible vinyl
❑ LSP-4445 That's the Way It Is 1971 6.25 12.50 25.00
—Orange label, flexible vinyl
❑ LSP-4445 That's the Way It Is 1975 5.00 10.00 20.00
—Tan label
❑ LSP-4445 That's the Way It Is 1976 3.75 7.50 15.00
—Black label, dog near top
❑ AFL1-4460 Elvis Country ("I'm 10,000 Years Old") 1977 3.00 6.00 12.00
—Black label, dog near top; includes copies with sticker wrapped around spine with new number
❑ LSP-4460 Elvis Country ("I'm 10,000 Years Old") 1971 10.00 20.00 40.00
—Orange label, non-flexible vinyl
❑ LSP-4460 Elvis Country ("I'm 10,000 Years Old") 1971 6.25 12.50 25.00
—Orange label, flexible vinyl
❑ LSP-4460 Elvis Country ("I'm 10,000 Years Old") Bonus Photo 1971 3.75 7.50 15.00
—Available in either orange-label pressing
❑ LSP-4460 Elvis Country ("I'm 10,000 Years Old") 1975 6.25 12.50 25.00
—Tan label
❑ LSP-4460 Elvis Country ("I'm 10,000 Years Old") 1976 3.75 7.50 15.00
—Black label, dog near top
❑ LSP-4460 Elvis Country ("I'm 10,000 Years Old") 197? 500.00 1000. 2000.
—Green vinyl; black label, dog near top
❑ AFL1-4530 Love Letters from Elvis 1977 3.00 6.00 12.00
—Black label, dog near top; includes copies with sticker wrapped around spine with new number
❑ AHL1-4530 The Elvis Medley 1982 3.00 6.00 12.00
❑ LSP-4530 Love Letters from Elvis 1971 10.00 20.00 40.00
—Orange label; "Love Letters from" on one line of cover, "Elvis" on a second line
❑ LSP-4530 Love Letters from Elvis 1971 7.50 15.00 30.00
—Orange label; "Love Letters" on one line of cover; "from" on a second line, "Elvis" on a third line
❑ LSP-4530 Love Letters from Elvis 1975 7.50 15.00 30.00
—Tan label; "Love Letters from" on one line of cover, "Elvis" on a second line
❑ LSP-4530 Love Letters from Elvis 1975 6.25 12.50 25.00
—Tan label; "Love Letters" on one line of cover; "from" on a second line, "Elvis" on a third line
❑ LSP-4530 Love Letters from Elvis 1976 5.00 10.00 20.00
—Black label, dog near top
❑ LSP-4579 Elvis Sings the Wonderful World of Christmas 1971 7.50 15.00 30.00
—Orange label. Bonus postcard is priced separately
❑ LSP-4579 Elvis Sings the Wonderful World of Christmas Postcard 1971 5.00 10.00 20.00
❑ AFL1-4671 Elvis Now 1977 3.00 6.00 12.00
—Black label, dog near top; includes copies with sticker wrapped around spine with new number
❑ LSP-4671 Elvis Now 1972 7.50 15.00 30.00
—Orange label
❑ LSP-4671 Elvis Now 1975 6.25 12.50 25.00
—Tan label
❑ LSP-4671 Elvis Now 1976 3.75 7.50 15.00
—Black label, dog near top
❑ LSP-4671 [DJ] Elvis Now 1972 25.00 50.00 100.00
—Orange label; with white timing sticker on front cover
❑ AHL1-4678 I Was the One 1983 2.50 5.00 10.00
❑ AFL1-4690 He Touched Me 1977 3.00 6.00 12.00
—Black label, dog near top; includes copies with sticker wrapped around spine with new number
❑ LSP-4690 He Touched Me 1972 10.00 20.00 40.00
—Orange label
❑ LSP-4690 He Touched Me 1975 5.00 10.00 20.00
—Tan label
❑ LSP-4690 He Touched Me 1976 3.75 7.50 15.00
—Black label, dog near top
❑ LSP-4690 [DJ] He Touched Me 1972 25.00 50.00 100.00
—Orange label; with white timing sticker on front cover

Number Title (A Side/B Side) Yr VG VG+ NM

❑ AFL1-4776 Elvis As Recorded at Madison Square Garden 1977 3.00 6.00 12.00
—Black label, dog near top; includes copies with sticker wrapped around spine with new number
❑ AQL1-4776 Elvis As Recorded at Madison Square Garden 1980 2.00 4.00 8.00
—Another reissue with new prefix
❑ LSP-4776 Elvis As Recorded at Madison Square Garden 1972 7.50 15.00 30.00
—Orange label
❑ LSP-4776 Elvis As Recorded at Madison Square Garden 1975 5.00 10.00 20.00
—Tan label
❑ LSP-4776 Elvis As Recorded at Madison Square Garden 1976 3.75 7.50 15.00
—Black label, dog near top
❑ LSP-4776 [DJ] Elvis As Recorded at Madison Square Garden 1972 25.00 50.00 100.00
—Orange label; with white timing sticker on front cover
❑ CPL1-4848 A Legendary Performer, Volume 4 1983 7.50 15.00 30.00
—Includes booklet (deduct 40% if missing); with die-cut hole in front cover
❑ CPL1-4848 A Legendary Performer, Volume 4 1986 5.00 10.00 20.00
—No die-cut hole in cover
❑ AFL1-4941 Elvis' Gold Records, Volume 5 1984 2.50 5.00 10.00
❑ CPM6-5172 [(6)] A Golden Celebration 1984 25.00 50.00 100.00
❑ AFM1-5182 Rocker 1984 5.00 10.00 20.00
❑ AFM1-5196 [M] Elvis' Golden Records 1984 5.00 10.00 20.00
—50th Anniversary reissue in mono with banner
❑ AFM1-5197 [M] Elvis' Gold Records Volume 2 — 50,000,000 Elvis Fans Can't Be Wrong 1984 5.00 10.00 20.00
—50th Anniversary reissue in mono with banner
❑ AFM1-5198 [M] Elvis Presley 1984 5.00 10.00 20.00
—50th Anniversary reissue in mono with banner
❑ AFM1-5199 [M] Elvis 1984 5.00 10.00 20.00
—50th Anniversary reissue in mono with banner
❑ AFL1-5353 A Valentine Gift for You 1985 5.00 10.00 20.00
—Red vinyl
❑ AFL1-5353 A Valentine Gift for You 1985 2.50 5.00 10.00
—Black vinyl
❑ AFL1-5418 Reconsider Baby 1985 5.00 10.00 20.00
—All copies on blue vinyl
❑ AFL1-5430 Always on My Mind 1985 5.00 10.00 20.00
—All copies on purple vinyl
❑ AFM1-5486 [M] Elvis' Christmas Album 1985 5.00 10.00 20.00
—Same as LOC-1035; green vinyl with booklet
❑ AFM1-5486 [M] Elvis' Christmas Album 1985 3.75 7.50 15.00
—Same as LOC-1035; black vinyl with booklet
❑ UNRM-5697/8 [DJ] Special Christmas Programming 1967 300.00 600.00 1200.
—White label promo. Add 25% for script.
❑ LSP-6020 From Memphis to Vegas/From Vegas to Memphis Bonus Photos 1969 12.50 25.00 50.00
—Four different photos came with LP, but no more than two per set. Value is for any two different of the four photos.
❑ LSP-6020 [(2)] From Memphis to Vegas/From Vegas to Memphis 1969 25.00 50.00 100.00
—Orange labels, non-flexible vinyl; with composers of "Words" correctly listed as Barry, Robin and Maurice Gibb
❑ LSP-6020 [(2)] From Memphis to Vegas/From Vegas to Memphis 1969 37.50 75.00 150.00
—Orange labels, non-flexible vinyl; with composers of "Words" incorrectly listed as Tommy Boyce and Bobby Hart
❑ LSP-6020 [(2)] From Memphis to Vegas/From Vegas to Memphis 1971 10.00 20.00 40.00
—Orange labels, flexible vinyl
❑ LSP-6020 [(2)] From Memphis to Vegas/From Vegas to Memphis Bonus Photos 1975 7.50 15.00 30.00
—Tan labels
❑ LSP-6020 [(2)] From Memphis to Vegas/From Vegas to Memphis Bonus Photos 1976 5.00 10.00 20.00
—Black label, dog near top
❑ VPSX-6089 [(2) DJ] Aloha from Hawaii Via Satellite 1973 500.00 1000. 2000.
—Orange or dark orange label; with white timing sticker on front cover
❑ VPSX-6089 [(2) Q] Aloha from Hawaii Via Satellite 1973 25.00 50.00 100.00
—Dark orange labels, "QuadraDisc" on top, "RCA" on bottom
❑ VPSX-6089 [(2) Q] Aloha from Hawaii Via Satellite 1973 2500. 3750. 5000.
—Stokely-Van Camp employee version with Saturn-shaped sticker on front cover with "Chicken of the Sea" and mermaid
❑ VPSX-6089 [(2) Q] Aloha from Hawaii Via Satellite 1973 10.00 20.00 40.00
—Lighter orange labels, "RCA" on side
❑ LPM-6401 Worldwide 50 Gold Award Hits, Vol. 1 Photo Book 1970 10.00 20.00 40.00
—Two different books have been found in this LP box; price is for either
❑ LPM-6401 [(4)] Worldwide 50 Gold Award Hits, Vol. 1 1970 20.00 40.00 80.00
—Orange labels, non-flexible vinyl; with blurb for photo book on cover
❑ LPM-6401 [(4)] Worldwide 50 Gold Award Hits, Vol. 1 1970 20.00 40.00 80.00
—Orange labels, flexible vinyl; with blurb for photo book on cover
❑ LPM-6401 [(4)] Worldwide 50 Gold Award Hits, Vol. 1 1975 10.00 20.00 40.00
—Tan labels
❑ LPM-6401 [(4)] Worldwide 50 Gold Award Hits, Vol. 1 1977 7.50 15.00 30.00
—Black labels, dog near top
❑ LPM-6402 The Other Sides: Worldwide 50 Gold Award Hits, Vol. 2 Poster 1971 6.25 12.50 25.00
❑ LPM-6402 The Other Sides: Worldwide 50 Gold Award Hits, Vol. 2 Swatch and Envelope 1971 6.25 12.50 25.00
❑ LPM-6402 [(4)] The Other Sides: Worldwide 50 Gold Award Hits, Vol. 2 1971 17.50 35.00 70.00
—Orange labels, flexible vinyl; with blurb for inserts on cover
❑ LPM-6402 [(4)] The Other Sides: Worldwide 50 Gold Award Hits, Vol. 2 1975 7.50 15.00 30.00
—Tan labels
❑ LPM-6402 [(4)] The Other Sides: Worldwide 50 Gold Award Hits, Vol. 2 1977 5.00 10.00 20.00
—Black labels, dog near top
❑ KKL1-7065 A Canadian Tribute 1978 5.00 10.00 20.00
—Gold vinyl, embossed cover

Number	Title (A Side/B Side)	Yr	VG	VG+	NM
❑ R 213690 [(2)]	Worldwide Gold Award Hits, Parts 1 & 2	1974	30.00	60.00	120.00
	—RCA Record Club version; one label is orange, the other is tan (orange label on both records is unknown)				
❑ R 213690 [(2)]	Worldwide Gold Award Hits, Parts 1 & 2	1974	10.00	20.00	40.00
	—RCA Record Club version; tan labels				
❑ R 213690 [(2)]	Worldwide Gold Award Hits, Parts 1 & 2	1977	6.25	12.50	25.00
	—RCA Record Club version; black labels, dog near top				
❑ R 213736 [(2) S]	Aloha from Hawaii Via Satellite	1973	17.50	35.00	70.00
	—RCA Record Club edition in stereo instead of quadraphonic; orange labels				
❑ R 213736 [(2) S]	Aloha from Hawaii Via Satellite	1975	15.00	30.00	60.00
	—RCA Record Club edition in stereo instead of quadraphonic; tan labels				
❑ R 213736 [(2) S]	Aloha from Hawaii Via Satellite	1977	7.50	5.00	30.00
	—RCA Record Club edition in stereo instead of quadraphonic; black labels, dog near top				
❑ R 214657 [(2)]	Worldwide Gold Award Hits, Parts 3 & 4	1978	5.00	10.00	20.00
	—RCA Record Club version; black labels, dog near top				
❑ R 233299(e) [(2)]	Country Classics	1980	10.00	20.00	40.00
	—RCA Music Service exclusive				
❑ R 234340 [(2)]	From Elvis with Love	1978	10.00	20.00	40.00
	—RCA Music Service exclusive				
❑ R 244047 [(2)]	The Legendary Concert Performances	1978	10.00	20.00	40.00
	—RCA Music Service exclusive				
❑ R 244069 [(2)]	Country Memories	1978	10.00	20.00	40.00
	—RCA Music Service exclusive				
READER'S DIGEST					
❑ 010/A [(7)]	His Greatest Hits	1983	15.00	30.00	60.00
	—Yellow box				
❑ 010/A [(7)]	His Greatest Hits	1990	10.00	20.00	40.00
	—White box				
❑ RD-10/A [(8)]	His Greatest Hits	1979	100.00	200.00	400.00
	—White box				
❑ RBA-072/D	Great Hits of 1956-57	1987	5.00	10.00	20.00
❑ RD4A-181/D	Elvis Sings Inspirational Favorites	1983	5.00	10.00	20.00
❑ RB4-191/A [(7)]	The Legend Lives On	1986	15.00	30.00	60.00
❑ RDA-242/D	Elvis Sings Country Favorites	1984	15.00	30.00	60.00
SHOW-LAND					
❑ LP-2001	The First of Elvis	1979	25.00	50.00	100.00
SILHOUETTE					
❑ 10001/2 [(2)]	Personally Elvis	1979	7.50	15.00	30.00
	—Interview records; no music				
SUN					
❑ 1001	The Sun Years — Interviews and Memories	1977	6.25	12.50	25.00
	—With "Memphis, Tennessee" on label				
❑ 1001	The Sun Years — Interviews and Memories	1977	2.00	4.00	8.00
	—With "Nashville, U.S.A." on label; white cover with brown print				
❑ 1001	The Sun Years — Interviews and Memories	1977	3.75	7.50	15.00
	—With "Nashville, U.S.A." on label; dark yellow cover with brown print				
TIME-LIFE					
❑ STL-106 [(2)]	Elvis Presley: 1954-1961	1986	7.50	15.00	30.00
❑ STW-106	Country Music	1981	5.00	10.00	20.00
❑ STL-126 [(2)]	Elvis the King: 1954-1965	1989	20.00	40.00	80.00

PRESLEY, ELVIS (2)

45s

Number	Title (A Side/B Side)	Yr	VG	VG+	NM
CIN KAY					
❑ 064	Tell Me Pretty Baby (same on both sides)	1978	—	—	2.50
❑ 064 [PS]	Tell Me Pretty Baby (same on both sides)	1978	—	—	2.50
ELVIS CLASSIC					
❑ EC-5478	Tell Me Pretty Baby (same on both sides)	1978	—	—	2.50
❑ EC-5478 [PS]	Tell Me Pretty Baby (same on both sides)	1978	—	—	2.50

—The above are two different issues of a record that purported to be the "real" Elvis' first studio recording, but turned out to be an utter fake

PRESTON, EDDIE

45s

Number	Title (A Side/B Side)	Yr	VG	VG+	NM
PLATINUM					
❑ 101	When Did You Stop/Dance My Song	1989	—	2.50	5.00
❑ 102	Long Time Comin'/(B-side unknown)	1989	—	2.50	5.00
❑ 102 [PS]	Long Time Comin'/(B-side unknown)	1989	—	3.00	6.00

PRESTON, TERRY

See FERLIN HUSKY.

PRESTWOOD, HUGH

45s

Number	Title (A Side/B Side)	Yr	VG	VG+	NM
MTM					
❑ B-72097	Roller Coaster Run/By Heart	1988	—	2.00	4.00

PRICE, CHUCK

45s

Number	Title (A Side/B Side)	Yr	VG	VG+	NM
PLAYBOY					
❑ 5811	Cowboy Lemonade/What Is It	1977	—	2.50	5.00
❑ 6010	Slow Down/West Virginia Woman	1974	—	2.50	5.00
❑ 6030	Cheatin' Again/What Is It	1975	—	2.50	5.00
❑ 6052	Last of the Outlaws/Angels Have Days They Can't Fly	1975	—	2.50	5.00
❑ 6067	Cadillac Johnson/Trouble in Mind	1976	—	2.50	5.00
❑ 6072	I Don't Want It/Trouble in Mind	1976	—	2.50	5.00
❑ 6087	Rye Whiskey/Lucy Ain't Your Loser Lookin' Good	1976	—	2.50	5.00
❑ 6099	Is Anybody Goin' to San Antone/My Memories	1977	—	2.50	5.00

PRICE, DAVID

45s

Number	Title (A Side/B Side)	Yr	VG	VG+	NM
EPIC					
❑ 5-9494	Please Dim the Lights/Save a Little Room	1962	3.00	6.00	12.00
GAYLORD					
❑ 6430	Good Morning Self/You Make It Easy	1963	3.75	7.50	15.00
RICE					
❑ 1001	The World Lost a Man/I Need a Friend	1964	3.75	7.50	15.00
❑ 5013	National Everybody Hate Me Week/Invite Only Close Friends	196?	2.50	5.00	10.00
❑ 5016	Game of Chance/Lonely Corner	196?	2.50	5.00	10.00
❑ 5075	Love Him Tender, Sweet Jesus/I Need a Friend	1977	2.00	4.00	8.00
ROULETTE					
❑ 4639	If It's the Last Thing I Do/You Gotta Go Where It Is	1965	2.50	5.00	10.00
❑ 4676	Run From Lonely/Without a Tear	1966	2.50	5.00	10.00

PRICE, DENISE

45s

Number	Title (A Side/B Side)	Yr	VG	VG+	NM
DIMENSION					
❑ 1037	Two Hearts Can't Be Wrong/Somebody Everybody's Had	1982	—	2.50	5.00
❑ 1037 [PS]	Two Hearts Can't Be Wrong/Somebody Everybody's Had	1982	—	3.00	6.00

PRICE, KENNY

45s

Number	Title (A Side/B Side)	Yr	VG	VG+	NM
BOONE					
❑ 1024	The Secret of Losing the Blues/Low and Lonely	196?	3.00	6.00	12.00
❑ 1026	Somebody Told Mary/White Silver Sands	196?	3.00	6.00	12.00
❑ 1029	That's All That Matters/Tossin' Pennies	196?	3.00	6.00	12.00
❑ 1035	Goin' Out of Style/Hunky Dory	1966	2.50	5.00	10.00
❑ 1042	Walking on New Grass/Wasting My Time	1966	2.50	5.00	10.00
❑ 1051	Happy Tracks/The Clock	1966	2.50	5.00	10.00
❑ 1056	Pretty Girl, Pretty Clothes, Pretty Sad/You Made Me Lie to You	1967	2.50	5.00	10.00
❑ 1063	Grass Won't Grow on a Busy Street/Somebody Told Mary	1967	2.50	5.00	10.00
❑ 1067	My Goal for Today/Say Something Nice to Me	1967	2.50	5.00	10.00
❑ 1070	Going Home for the Last Time/Blame It on Me	1968	2.00	4.00	8.00
❑ 1075	Southern Bound/After All	1968	2.00	4.00	8.00
❑ 1081	It Don't Mean a Thing to Me/Big Operator	1968	2.00	4.00	8.00
❑ 1085	Who Do I Know in Dallas/I'm a Long Way from Home	1969	2.00	4.00	8.00
DIMENSION					
❑ 1003	Well Rounded Traveling Man/Everybody Needs Something	1980	—	2.50	5.00
❑ 1010	She's Leavin' (And I'm Almost Gone)/In Vain	1980	—	2.50	5.00
MRC					
❑ 1001	I'd Buy You Chattanooga/Mortar Mixing Mama	1977	—	2.50	5.00
❑ 1004	Leavin'/Boone County Weight Watchers of America	1977	—	2.50	5.00
❑ 1007	Afraid You'd Come Back/Walkin' in That California Sunshine	1977	—	2.50	5.00
❑ 1012	Sunshine Man/Sidewalk Satin Salesman	1978	—	2.50	5.00
❑ 1025	Hey There/Pickin' Up the Pieces	1979	—	2.50	5.00
RCA VICTOR					
❑ APBO-0083	You're Wearin' Me Down/The Closest Thing to Me (Is My Shadow)	1973	—	3.00	6.00
❑ AMAO-0127	Charlotte Fever/The Sheriff of Boone County	1973	—	2.50	5.00
	—"Gold Standard Series" reissue				
❑ APBO-0198	Turn On Your Light (And Let It Shine)/The First Song That Wasn't the Blues	1973	—	3.00	6.00
❑ APBO-0256	Que Pasa/Greener Grass to Walk On	1974	—	3.00	6.00
❑ PB-10039	Let's Truck Together/Super Hillbilly	1974	—	2.50	5.00
❑ PB-10141	Easy Look/Country Blues	1974	—	2.50	5.00
❑ PB-10260	Birds and Children Fly Away/Born in Country Music (Raised on Dixieland)	1975	—	2.50	5.00
❑ PB-10376	I've Changed Since I've Been Unchained/She Even Loves Me	1975	—	2.50	5.00
❑ PB-10460	Too Big a Price to Pay/Don't Boogie Woogie When You Say Your Prayers Tonight	1975	—	2.50	5.00
❑ 47-9787	Northeast Arkansas Mississippi County Bootlegger/Green, Green Grass of Home	1969	—	3.50	7.00
❑ 47-9869	Biloxi/The Shortest Song in the World	1970	—	3.50	7.00
❑ 47-9932	The Sheriff of Boone County/Six String Guitar	1970	—	3.50	7.00
❑ 47-9973	Tell Her You Love Her/Just Plain Me	1971	—	3.50	7.00
❑ 48-1015	Charlotte Fever/There's a Song in Everything	1971	—	3.50	7.00
❑ 74-0183	I'm a Long Way from Home/Who Do I Know in Dallas	1969	—	3.50	7.00
❑ 74-0260	Atlanta Georgia Stray/The Clock	1969	—	3.50	7.00
❑ 74-0617	Super Sideman/From Here to There	1971	—	3.00	6.00
❑ 74-0686	You Almost Slipped My Mind/Destination Anywhere	1972	—	3.00	6.00
❑ 74-0781	Sea of Heartbreak/Smiley	1972	—	3.00	6.00
❑ 74-0872	Don't Tell Me Your Troubles/Front of the Bus, Back of the Church	1973	—	3.00	6.00
❑ 74-0936	30 California Women/Love's Not Hard to Take	1973	—	3.00	6.00

Albums

Number	Title (A Side/B Side)	Yr	VG	VG+	NM
BOONE					
❑ 1211	One Hit Follows Another	1967	6.25	12.50	25.00
❑ 1214	Southern Bound	1968	6.25	12.50	25.00
DIMENSION					
❑ DLP-5000	The Best of Both	1980	3.00	6.00	12.00
RCA VICTOR					
❑ APL1-0208	30 California Women	1973	3.75	7.50	15.00
❑ LSP-4224	Happy Tracks	1969	5.00	10.00	20.00
❑ LSP-4225	Walking on New Grass	1969	5.00	10.00	20.00
❑ LSP-4292	The Heavyweight	1970	5.00	10.00	20.00

Number	Title (A Side/B Side)	Yr	VG	VG+	NM
❑ LSP-4373	Northeast Arkansas Mississippi County Bootlegger	1970	5.00	10.00	20.00
❑ LSP-4469	The Red Foley Songbook	1971	5.00	10.00	20.00
❑ LSP-4527	The Sheriff of Boone County	1971	5.00	10.00	20.00
❑ LSP-4605	Charlotte Fever	1971	5.00	10.00	20.00
❑ LSP-4681	Supersideman	1972	5.00	10.00	20.00
❑ LSP-4763	You Almost Slipped My Mind	1972	5.00	10.00	20.00
❑ LSP-4839	Sea of Heartbreak	1973	5.00	10.00	20.00

PRICE, RAY

Also see WILLIE NELSON.

45s

ABC

Number	Title (A Side/B Side)	Yr	VG	VG+	NM
❑ 12084	Roses and Love Songs/The Closest Thing to Love	1975	—	2.00	4.00
❑ 12095	Farthest Thing from My Mind/All That Keeps Me Going	1975	—	2.00	4.00

ABC DOT

Number	Title (A Side/B Side)	Yr	VG	VG+	NM
❑ 17588	Say I Do/I'll Still Love You	1975	—	2.00	4.00
❑ 17616	That's All She Wrote/I Didn't Feel Nothing	1976	—	2.00	4.00
❑ 17637	To Make a Long Story Short/We're Getting There	1976	—	2.00	4.00
❑ 17666	A Mansion on the Hill/Hey, Good Lookin'	1976	—	2.00	4.00
❑ 17690	Different Kind of Flower/Don't Let the Stars Get in Your Eyes	1977	—	2.00	4.00
❑ 17718	Born to Love Me/The Only Way to Say Good Morning	1977	—	2.00	4.00

COLUMBIA

Number	Title (A Side/B Side)	Yr	VG	VG+	NM
❑ 10006	Like a First Time Thing/You Are the Song	1974	—	2.50	5.00
❑ 10150	If You Ever Change Your Mind/Just Enough to Make Me Stay	1975	—	2.00	4.00
❑ 10503	Help Me/Nobody Wins	1977	—	2.00	4.00
❑ 10631	Born to Love Me/I'm Sorry for the Hateful Things I Did	1977	—	2.00	4.00
❑ 20810	You've Got My Troubles Now/If You're Ever Lonely Darling	1951	7.50	15.00	30.00
❑ 20833	I Saw My Castles Fall Today/Hey Lala	1951	7.50	15.00	30.00
❑ 20863	Heart Aching Blues/Till Death Do Us Part	1951	7.50	15.00	30.00
❑ 20883	I Made a Mistake and I'm Sorry/Weary Blues	1952	6.25	12.50	25.00
❑ 20913	Talk to Your Heart/I've Got to Hurry, Hurry, Hurry	1952	6.25	12.50	25.00
❑ 20943	Hot Diggity Dog/I've Got to Hurry, Hurry, Hurry	1952	5.00	10.00	20.00
—With Jimmy Dickens					
❑ 20963	Road of No Return/I Know I'll Never Win Your Love Again	1952	5.00	10.00	20.00
❑ 21015	I Can't Escape from You/Won't You Please Be Mine	1952	5.00	10.00	20.00
❑ 21025	Don't Let the Stars Get In Your Eyes/I Lost the Only Love I Know	1952	5.00	10.00	20.00
❑ 21053	You're Under Arrest/My Old Scrapbook	1953	5.00	10.00	20.00
❑ 21089	Price for Loving You/That's What I Got for Loving You	1953	5.00	10.00	20.00
❑ 21117	Cold Shoulder/You Weren't Ashamed to Kiss Me	1953	5.00	10.00	20.00
❑ 21149	Wrong Side of Town/Who Stole That Train	1953	5.00	10.00	20.00
❑ 21173	Leave Her Alone/You Always Get By	1953	5.00	10.00	20.00
❑ 21214	I'll Be There (If You Ever Want Me)/Release Me	1954	5.00	10.00	20.00
❑ 21249	Much Too Young to Die/I Love You So Much	1954	5.00	10.00	20.00
❑ 21299	I Could Love You More/What If He Don't Love You	1954	5.00	10.00	20.00
❑ 21315	If You Don't, Somebody Else Will/Oh Yes Darling	1954	5.00	10.00	20.00
❑ 21354	One Broken Heart/I'm Alone Because I Love You	1955	3.75	7.50	15.00
❑ 21402	Sweet Little Miss Blue Eyes/Let Me Talk to You	1955	3.75	7.50	15.00
❑ 21404	A Man Called Peter/Call the Lord and He'll Be There	1955	5.00	10.00	20.00
❑ 21442	I Can't Go On Like This/I Don't Want It on My Conscience	1955	3.75	7.50	15.00
❑ 21474	Run Boy/You Never Will Be True	1955	3.75	7.50	15.00
❑ 21510	Crazy Arms/You Done Me Wrong	1956	3.75	7.50	15.00
❑ 21562	I've Got a New Heartache/Wasted Words	1956	3.75	7.50	15.00
❑ 31428 [S]	(titles unknown)	1962	3.75	7.50	15.00
❑ 31429 [S]	(titles unknown)	1962	3.75	7.50	15.00
❑ 31430 [S]	(titles unknown)	1962	3.75	7.50	15.00
❑ 31431 [S]	(titles unknown)	1962	3.75	7.50	15.00
❑ 31432 [S]	(titles unknown)	1962	3.75	7.50	15.00
—Anyone who can fill in these gaps -- the above 5 all are Columbia "Stereo 7" singles -- please let us know.					
❑ 40889	I'll Be There (When You Get Lonely)/Please Don't Leave Me	1957	3.75	7.50	15.00
❑ 40951	My Shoes Keep Walking Back to You/Don't Do This to Me	1957	3.75	7.50	15.00
❑ 41105	Curtain in the Window/It's All Your Fault	1958	3.00	6.00	12.00
❑ 41191	City Lights/Invitation to the Blues	1958	3.00	6.00	12.00
❑ 41309	That's What It's Like to Be Lonesome/Kissing Your Picture	1958	3.00	6.00	12.00
❑ 41374	Heartaches By the Number/Wall of Tears	1959	3.00	6.00	12.00
❑ 41477	The Same Old Me/Under Your Spell Again	1959	3.00	6.00	12.00
❑ 41590	One More Time/Who'll Be the First	1960	3.00	6.00	12.00
❑ 41767	I Wish I Could Fall in Love Today/I Can't Run Away from Myself	1960	3.00	6.00	12.00
❑ 41947	Heart Over Mind/The Twenty-Fourth Hour	1961	2.50	5.00	10.00
❑ 42132	Soft Rain/Here We Are Again	1961	2.50	5.00	10.00
❑ 42310	I've Just Destroyed the World (I'm Living In)/Big Shoes	1962	2.50	5.00	10.00
❑ 42518	Pride/I'm Walking Slow	1962	2.50	5.00	10.00
❑ 42658	Walk Me to the Door/You Took Her Off My Hands (Now Please Take Her Off My Mind)	1963	2.50	5.00	10.00
❑ 42827	Make the World Go Away/Night Life	1963	2.50	5.00	10.00
❑ 42971	Burning Memories/That's All That Matters	1964	2.50	5.00	10.00
❑ 43086	Please Talk to My Heart/I Don't Know Why	1964	2.50	5.00	10.00
❑ 43162	A Thing Called Sadness/Here Comes My Baby Back Again	1964	2.50	5.00	10.00
❑ 43264	The Other Woman/Tearful Earful	1965	2.00	4.00	8.00
❑ 43427	Don't You Ever Get Tired of Hurting Me/Unloved, Unwanted	1965	2.00	4.00	8.00
❑ 43560	A Way to Survive/I'm Not Crazy Yet	1966	2.00	4.00	8.00
❑ 43795	Touch My Heart/It Should Be Easier Now	1966	2.00	4.00	8.00
❑ 44042	Danny Boy/I'll Let My Mind Wander	1967	2.00	4.00	8.00
❑ 44042 [PS]	Danny Boy/I'll Let My Mind Wander	1967	3.00	6.00	12.00
❑ 44195	I'm Still Not Over You/Crazy	1967	2.00	4.00	8.00
❑ 44374	Take Me As I Am (Or Let Me Go)/In the Summer of My Life	1967	2.00	4.00	8.00
❑ 44505	I've Been There Before/Night Life	1968	2.00	4.00	8.00
❑ 44628	She Wears My Ring/Goin' Away	1968	2.00	4.00	8.00
❑ 44747	Set Me Free/Trouble	1969	—	3.00	6.00
❑ 44761	Sweetheart of the Year/How Can I Write on Paper (What I Feel in My Heart)	1969	—	3.00	6.00
❑ 44931	Raining in My Heart/I Know Love	1969	—	3.00	6.00
❑ 45005	April's Fool/Make It Rain	1969	—	3.00	6.00
❑ 45046	Jingle Bells/Happy Birthday to You, Our Lord	1969	—	3.00	6.00
❑ 45095	You Wouldn't Know Love/Everybody Wants to Get to Heaven	1970	—	3.00	6.00
❑ 45178	For the Good Times/Grazin' in Greener Pastures	1970	—	3.00	6.00
❑ 45329	I Won't Mention It Again/Kiss the World Goodbye	1971	—	2.50	5.00
❑ 45425	I'd Rather Be Sorry/When I Loved Her	1971	—	2.50	5.00
❑ 45583	The Lonesomest Lonesome/That's What Leaving's About	1972	—	2.50	5.00
❑ 45724	She's Got to Be a Saint/Oh Lonesome Me	1972	—	2.50	5.00
❑ 45889	You're the Best Thing That Ever Happened to Me/What Kind of Love Is This	1973	—	2.50	5.00
❑ 46015	Storms of Troubled Times/Some Things Never Change	1974	—	2.50	5.00

DIMENSION

Number	Title (A Side/B Side)	Yr	VG	VG+	NM
❑ 1018	Getting Over You Again/Circle Driveway	1981	—	2.00	4.00
❑ 1021	It Don't Hurt Me Half As Bad/She's the Right Kind of Woman (Loving the Wrong Kind of Man)	1981	—	2.00	4.00
❑ 1024	Diamonds in the Stars/Grazing in Greener Pastures	1981	—	2.00	4.00
❑ 1031	Forty and Fadin'/Something to Forget You By	1982	—	2.00	4.00
❑ 1035	Will Till Those Bridges Are Gone/Angel in My Heart (Devil in My Mind)	1982	—	2.00	4.00
❑ 1038	Somewhere in Texas/Getting Down and Getting High	1982	—	2.00	4.00

MONUMENT

Number	Title (A Side/B Side)	Yr	VG	VG+	NM
❑ 45267	Feet/Let's Make a Nice Memory (Today)	1978	—	2.00	4.00
❑ 45277	There's Always Me/If It All the Same to You (I'll Be Leaving in the Morning)	1979	—	2.00	4.00
❑ 45283	That's the Only Way to Say Good Morning/All the Good Things Are Gone	1979	—	2.00	4.00
❑ 45290	Misty Morning Rain/We Can't Build a Fire in the Rain	1979	—	2.00	4.00

MYRRH

Number	Title (A Side/B Side)	Yr	VG	VG+	NM
❑ 146	Like Old Times Again/My First Day Without Her	1974	—	2.50	5.00
❑ 150	Roses and Love Songs/The Closest Thing to Love	1975	—	2.50	5.00

STEP ONE

Number	Title (A Side/B Side)	Yr	VG	VG+	NM
❑ 341	(She Got a Hold of Me Where It Hurts) She Won't Let Go/Memories to Burn	1985	—	2.00	4.00
❑ 344	I'm Not Leaving (I'm Just Getting Out of Your Way)/Why Don't Love Just Go Away	1985	—	2.00	4.00
❑ 350	Five Fingers/Lonely Like a Rose	1985	—	2.00	4.00
❑ 352	You're Nobody Till Somebody Loves You/I'm In the Mood for Love	1986	—	2.00	4.00
❑ 355	All the Way/Bummin' Around	1986	—	2.00	4.00
❑ 361	Please Don't Talk About Me When I'm Gone/For the Good Times	1986	—	2.00	4.00
❑ 366	When You Gave Your Love to Me/Forty and Fadin'	1986	—	2.00	4.00
❑ 370	Sentimental Journey/Better Class of Loser	1987	—	2.00	4.00
❑ 378	Just Enough Love/Why Don't Love Just Go Away	1987	—	2.00	4.00
❑ 381	For Christmas/With Christmas Near	1987	—	2.00	4.00
❑ 383	Big Ole Teardrops/The Season for Missing You	1988	—	2.00	4.00
❑ 388	Don't the Morning Always Come Too Soon/All You Have to Do Is Come Back	1988	—	2.00	4.00
❑ 393	I'd Do It All Over Again/Wind Beneath My Wings	1988	—	2.00	4.00
❑ 410	Love Me Down to Size/(B-side unknown)	1989	—	2.00	4.00
❑ 436	Memories That Last/A Whole Lot of You	1991	—	2.00	4.00
—With Faron Young					

VIVA

Number	Title (A Side/B Side)	Yr	VG	VG+	NM
❑ 29147	What Am I Gonna Do Without You/You've Been Leaving Me for Years	1984	—	—	3.00
❑ 29217	Better Class of Loser/Everytime I Sing a Love Song	1984	—	—	3.00
❑ 29277	A New Place to Begin/Everyone Gets Crazy Now and Then	1984	—	—	3.00
❑ 29458	Coors in Colorado/Living Her Life in a Song	1983	—	2.00	4.00
❑ 29543	Scotch and Soda/I Love You Eyes	1983	—	—	3.00

WARNER BROS.

Number	Title (A Side/B Side)	Yr	VG	VG+	NM
❑ 29691	Willie, Write Me a Song/I Love You Eyes	1983	—	—	3.00
❑ 29830	One Fiddle, Two Fiddle/San Antonio Rose	1982	—	2.00	4.00

Selected 78s

BULLET

Number	Title (A Side/B Side)	Yr	VG	VG+	NM
❑ 701	Jealous Lies/Your Wedding Corsage	1949	30.00	60.00	120.00

Number	Title (A Side/B Side)	Yr	VG	VG+	NM
7-Inch Extended Plays					
COLUMBIA					
❑ B-1786	(contents unknown)	195?	7.50	15.00	30.00
❑ B-1786 [PS]	Ray Price	195?	7.50	15.00	30.00
❑ B-2809	*I'll Be There/Release Me/Don't Let the Stars Get In Your Eyes/I Lost the Only Love I Knew	195?	3.75	7.50	15.00
❑ B-2809 [PS]	Ray Price (Hall of Fame Series)	195?	3.75	7.50	15.00
❑ B-2812	The Last Letter/My Shoes Keep Walking Back to You//Crazy Arms/I'm Alone Because I Love You	195?	3.75	7.50	15.00
❑ B-2812 [PS]	Ray Price (Hall of Fame Series)	195?	3.75	7.50	15.00
Albums					
ABC DOT					
❑ DO-2037	Say I Do	1975	3.00	6.00	12.00
❑ DO-2053	Rainbows and Tears	1976	3.00	6.00	12.00
❑ DO-2073	Reunited	1977	3.00	6.00	12.00
COLUMBIA					
❑ GP 28 [(2)]	The World of Ray Price	1970	3.75	7.50	15.00
❑ CL 1015 [M]	Ray Price Sings Heart Songs	1957	12.50	25.00	50.00
❑ CL 1148 [M]	Talk to Your Heart	1958	10.00	20.00	40.00
❑ CL 1494 [M]	Faith	1960	7.50	15.00	30.00
❑ CL 1566 [M]	Ray Price's Greatest Hits	1961	7.50	15.00	30.00
❑ CL 1756 [M]	San Antonio Rose	1962	5.00	10.00	20.00
❑ CL 1971 [M]	Night Life	1963	3.75	7.50	15.00
❑ CL 2189 [M]	Love Life	1964	3.75	7.50	15.00
❑ CL 2289 [M]	Burning Memories	1965	3.75	7.50	15.00
❑ CL 2339 [M]	Western Strings	1965	5.00	10.00	20.00
❑ CL 2382 [M]	The Other Woman	1965	3.75	7.50	15.00
❑ CL 2528 [M]	Another Bridge to Burn	1966	3.75	7.50	15.00
❑ CL 2606 [M]	Touch My Heart	1967	5.00	10.00	20.00
❑ CL 2670 [M]	Ray Price's Greatest Hits, Volume 2	1967	5.00	10.00	20.00
❑ CL 2677 [M]	Danny Boy	1967	5.00	10.00	20.00
❑ CL 2806 [M]	Take Me As I Am	1968	7.50	15.00	30.00
❑ CS 8285 [S]	Faith	1960	10.00	20.00	40.00
❑ CS 8556 [S]	San Antonio Rose	1962	7.50	15.00	30.00
❑ CS 8771 [S]	Night Life	1963	5.00	10.00	20.00
❑ CS 8866 [R]	Ray Price's Greatest Hits	1964	3.00	6.00	12.00
❑ PC 8866	Ray Price's Greatest Hits	198?	2.00	4.00	8.00
—Reissue with new prefix					
❑ CS 8989 [S]	Love Life	1964	5.00	10.00	20.00
❑ CS 9089 [S]	Burning Memories	1965	5.00	10.00	20.00
❑ CS 9139 [S]	Western Strings	1965	6.25	12.50	25.00
❑ CS 9182 [S]	The Other Woman	1965	5.00	10.00	20.00
❑ CS 9328 [S]	Another Bridge to Burn	1966	5.00	10.00	20.00
❑ CS 9406 [S]	Touch My Heart	1967	3.75	7.50	15.00
❑ CS 9470 [S]	Ray Price's Greatest Hits, Volume 2	1967	3.75	7.50	15.00
❑ CS 9477 [S]	Danny Boy	1967	3.75	7.50	15.00
❑ CS 9606 [S]	Take Me As I Am	1968	3.75	7.50	15.00
❑ CS 9733	She Wears My Ring	1968	3.75	7.50	15.00
❑ CS 9822	Sweetheart of the Year	1969	3.75	7.50	15.00
❑ CS 9861	Ray Price's Christmas Album	1969	3.75	7.50	15.00
❑ CS 9918	You Wouldn't Know Love	1970	3.75	7.50	15.00
❑ C 30106	For the Good Times	1970	3.00	6.00	12.00
❑ CQ 30106 [Q]	For the Good Times	1972	5.00	10.00	20.00
❑ C 30510	I Won't Mention It Again	1971	3.00	6.00	12.00
❑ CG 30878 [(2)]	Welcome to My World	1971	3.75	7.50	15.00
❑ KG 31364 [(2)]	Ray Price's All-Time Greatest Hits	1972	3.75	7.50	15.00
❑ KC 31546	The Lonesomest Lonesome	1972	3.00	6.00	12.00
❑ KC 32033	She's Got to Be a Saint	1973	3.00	6.00	12.00
❑ PC 32033	She's Got to Be a Saint	197?	2.00	4.00	8.00
—Reissue with new prefix					
❑ KC 32777	You're the Best Thing That Ever Happened to Me	1973	3.00	6.00	12.00
❑ PC 32777	You're the Best Thing That Ever Happened to Me	197?	2.00	4.00	8.00
—Reissue with new prefix					
❑ PC 33560	If You Change Your Mind	1975	3.00	6.00	12.00
❑ CG 33633 [(2)]	For the Good Times/I Won't Mention It Again	1975	3.75	7.50	15.00
—Reissue of two LPs in one package					
❑ PC 34160	The Best of Ray Price	1976	3.00	6.00	12.00
❑ PC 34710	Help Me	1977	3.00	6.00	12.00
❑ JC 37061	A Tribute to Willie and Kris	1982	2.50	5.00	10.00
HARMONY					
❑ HL 7372 [M]	Collectors' Choice	196?	3.00	6.00	12.00
❑ HL 7440 [M]	Born to Lose	1967	3.00	6.00	12.00
❑ HS 11172 [R]	Collectors' Choice	196?	3.00	6.00	12.00
❑ HS 11240 [S]	Born to Lose	1967	3.00	6.00	12.00
❑ HS 11373	I Fall to Pieces	1969	2.50	5.00	10.00
❑ KH 30272	Make the World Go Away	1970	2.50	5.00	10.00
MONUMENT					
❑ 7633	Always Me	1979	2.50	5.00	10.00
MYRRH					
❑ 6532	This Time, Lord	1975	3.00	6.00	12.00
PAIR					
❑ PDL2-1044 [(2)]	Happens to Be the Best	1986	3.00	6.00	12.00
❑ PDL2-1044 [(2)]	Ray Price Happens to Be the Best!	1986	3.00	6.00	12.00
❑ PDL2-1096 [(2)]	Priceless	1986	3.00	6.00	12.00
ROUNDER					
❑ SS-22	The Honky Tonk Years	1986	2.50	5.00	10.00
WORD					
❑ 8723	Precious Memories	197?	3.00	6.00	12.00
❑ 8780	How Great Thou Art	1978	3.00	6.00	12.00

PRICE, TONI

45s

Number	Title (A Side/B Side)	Yr	VG	VG+	NM
LUV					
❑ 114	Mississippi Breakdown/(B-side unknown)	1985	—	3.00	6.00

Number	Title (A Side/B Side)	Yr	VG	VG+	NM
MASTER					
❑ 01	How Much Do I Owe You/(B-side unknown)	1986	—	3.00	6.00
PRAIRIE DUST					
❑ 8744	I Want to Be Wanted/(B-side unknown)	1987	—	3.00	6.00

PRIDE, CHARLEY

Includes releases as "Country Charley Pride."

45s

Number	Title (A Side/B Side)	Yr	VG	VG+	NM
16TH AVENUE					
❑ 70400	Have I Got Some Blues for You/Ever Knowin'	1987	—	2.00	4.00
❑ 70402	If You Still Want a Fool Around/You Took Me There	1987	—	2.00	4.00
❑ 70408	Shouldn't It Be Easier Than This/Look in Your Mirror	1987	—	2.00	4.00
❑ 70414	I'm Gonna Love Her on the Radio/Shouldn't It Be Easier Than This	1988	—	2.00	4.00
❑ 70420	Where Was I/A Whole Lotta Lovin' (Goes a Long, Long Way)	1988	—	2.00	4.00
❑ 70425	White Houses/Shouldn't It Be Easier Than This	1989	—	2.00	4.00
❑ 70429	The More I Do/Heaven Help Us All	1989	—	2.00	4.00
❑ 70435	Amy's Eyes/I Made Love to You in My Mind	1989	—	2.00	4.00
❑ 70440	Woody Woman/Shouldn't It Be Easier Than This	1990	—	2.50	5.00
❑ 70446	Whole Lotta Love on the Line/Plenty Good Lovin'	1990	—	2.50	5.00
RCA					
❑ 2723-7-R	The Easy Part's Over/The Right to Do Wrong	1990	—	—	3.00
—"Gold Standard Series" reissue					
❑ PB-10757	A Whole Lotta Things to Sing About/The Hardest Part of Livin's Lovin' Me	1976	—	2.00	4.00
❑ PB-10875	She's Just An Old Love Turned Memory/Country Music	1977	—	2.00	4.00
❑ PB-10975	I'll Be Leaving Alone/We Need Lovin'	1977	—	2.00	4.00
❑ PB-11086	More to Me/Heaven Watches Over Fools Like Me	1977	—	2.00	4.00
❑ PB-11201	Someone Loves You Honey/Days of Our Lives	1978	—	2.00	4.00
❑ PB-11287	When I Stop Leaving (I'll Be Gone)/I Can See the Lovin' in Your Eyes	1978	—	2.00	4.00
❑ GB-11331	My Eyes Can Only See As Far As You/A Whole Lotta Things to Sing About	1978	—	—	3.00
—"Gold Standard Series" reissue					
❑ PB-11391	Burgers and Fries/Nothing's Prettier Than Rose Is	1978	—	2.00	4.00
❑ PB-11477	Where Do I Put Her Memory/The Best in the World	1979	—	2.00	4.00
❑ GB-11498	Someone Loves You Honey/When I Stop Leaving (I'll Be Gone)	1979	—	—	3.00
—"Gold Standard Series" reissue					
❑ PB-11655	You're My Jamaica/Let Me Have a Chance to Love You	1979	—	2.00	4.00
❑ PB-11736	Dallas Cowboys/When I Stop Leaving	1979	3.00	6.00	12.00
—Special blue and silver label edition					
❑ PB-11736	Dallas Cowboys/When I Stop Leaving	1979	—	3.00	6.00
—Regular black-label edition					
❑ PB-11751	Missin' You/Heartbreak Mountain	1979	—	2.00	4.00
❑ PB-11912	Honky Tonk Blues/I'm So Lonesome I Could Cry	1980	—	—	3.00
❑ GB-11992	Burgers and Fries/Where Do I Put Her Memory	1980	—	—	3.00
—"Gold Standard Series" reissue					
❑ PB-12002	You Win Again/There's a Little Bit of Hank in Me	1980	—	—	3.00
❑ PB-12100	You Almost Slipped My Mind/Ghost Written Love Letters	1980	—	—	3.00
❑ PB-12178	Roll On Mississippi/Fall Back on Me	1981	—	—	3.00
❑ PB-12294	Never Been So Loved (In All My Life)/I Call Her My Girl	1981	—	—	3.00
❑ GB-12371	Honky Tonk Blues/You Win Again	1981	—	—	3.00
—"Gold Standard Series" reissue					
❑ PB-13014	Mountain of Love/Love Is a Shadow	1981	—	—	3.00
❑ PB-13096	I Don't Think She's in Love Anymore/Oh What a Beautiful Love Song	1982	—	—	3.00
❑ PB-13293	You're So Good When You're Bad/I Haven't Loved This Way in Years	1982	—	—	3.00
❑ PB-13359	Let It Snow, Let It Snow, Let It Snow/Peace on Earth	1982	—	2.50	5.00
—B-side by Razzy Bailey					
❑ PB-13397	Why Baby Why/It's So Good to Be Together	1982	—	—	3.00
❑ PB-13451	More and More/Radio Heroes	1983	—	—	3.00
❑ PB-13542	Night Games/I Could Let Her Get Close to Me	1983	—	—	3.00
❑ PB-13648	Ev'ry Heart Should Have One/Lovin' It Up (Livin' It Down)	1983	—	—	3.00
❑ PB-13667	Let It Snow, Let It Snow, Let It Snow/O Holy Night	1983	—	2.00	4.00
❑ PB-13732	The Late Show/Love on a Blue Rainy Day	1984	—	2.00	4.00
❑ JK-13754	Stagger Lee (same on both sides)	1984	2.50	5.00	10.00
—Promo on red vinyl					
❑ PB-13821	The Power of Love/Ellie	1984	—	—	3.00
❑ PB-13936	Missin' Mississippi/Falling in Love Again	1984	—	—	3.00
❑ PB-14045	Down on the Farm/Now and Then	1985	—	—	3.00
❑ PB-14134	Let a Little Love Come In/Night Games	1985	—	—	3.00
❑ PB-14265	The Best There Is/The Tumbleweed and the Rose	1986	—	—	3.00
❑ PB-14296	Love on a Blue Rainy Day/I Used It All on You	1986	—	—	3.00
RCA VICTOR					
❑ APBO-0073	Amazing Love/Blue Ridge Mountains Turnin' Green	1973	—	2.50	5.00
❑ AMBO-0128	A Shoulder to Cry On/Don't Fight the Feelings of Love	1973	—	2.00	4.00
—"Gold Standard Series" reissue					
❑ APBO-0257	We Could/Love Put a Song in My Heart	1974	—	2.50	5.00
❑ PB-10030	Mississippi Cotton Picking Delta Town/Merry-Go-Round	1974	—	2.00	4.00
❑ PB-10126	Then Who Am I/Completely Helpless	1974	—	2.00	4.00

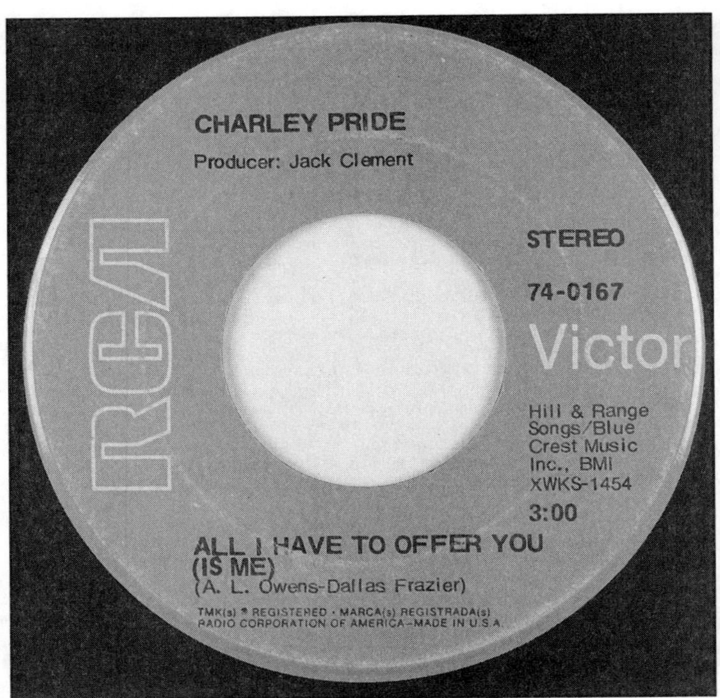

By far the most successful black country artist is Charley Pride. Once country audiences realized he was the real deal, he had a nearly unbroken string of hits from 1966 through 1984, and he ended up in the Country Music Hall of Fame. (Top left) After seven consecutive top 10 hits didn't hit the top, Pride finally got to the pinnacle with "All I Have to Offer You (Is Me)" in 1969. (Top right) Charley's third chart-topper, "Is Anybody Goin' to San Antone," is considered one of the classic country songs and has been remade frequently over the years. (Bottom left) His biggest hit, which spent over a month at the top, crossed over to the top 40 of the pop charts, and sold a million copies in its single form, was the late 1971-early 1972 hit "Kiss an Angel Good Mornin'." (Bottom right) Pride's last No. 1 single came in 1983 with "Night Games."

Number	Title (A Side/B Side)	Yr	VG	VG+	NM
PB-10236	I Ain't All Bad/Hard Times Will Be the Best Times	1975	—	2.00	4.00
PB-10344	Hope You're Feelin' Me (Like I'm Feelin' You)/ Searching for the Morning Sun	1975	—	2.00	4.00
PB-10455	The Happiness of Having You/Right Back Missing You Again	1975	—	2.00	4.00
GB-10507	Then Who Am I/Completely Helpless	1975	—	—	3.00
—"Gold Standard Series" reissue					
GB-10508	Mississippi Cotton Picking Delta Town/Merry-Go-Round	1975	—	—	3.00
—"Gold Standard Series" reissue					
GB-10509	Amazing Love/Blue Ridge Mountains Turning Green	1975	—	—	3.00
—"Gold Standard Series" reissue					
PB-10592	My Eyes Can Only See As Far As You/Oklahoma Morning	1976	—	2.00	4.00
PB-10643	In Jesus' Name I Pray/I Don't Deserve a Mansion	1976	—	3.00	6.00
GB-10674	I Ain't All Bad/Hope You're Feelin' Me (Like I'm Feelin' You)	1976	—	2.00	4.00
—"Gold Standard Series" reissue					
47-8738	Atlantic Coastal Line/Snakes Crawl at Night	1966	3.75	7.50	15.00
47-8862	Miller's Cave/Before I Met You	1966	3.75	7.50	15.00
47-9000	Just Between You and Me/Detroit City	1966	3.00	6.00	12.00
47-9162	I Know One/The Best Banjo Picker	1967	3.00	6.00	12.00
47-9281	Does My Ring Hurt Your Finger/The Spell of the Freight Train	1967	3.00	6.00	12.00
—Above three labeled as "Country Charley Pride"					
47-9403	The Day the World Stood Still/Gone, On the Other Hand	1967	2.00	4.00	8.00
47-9514	The Easy Part's Over/Right to Do Wrong	1968	2.00	4.00	8.00
47-9622	Let the Chips Fall/She Made Me Go	1968	2.00	4.00	8.00
47-9716	Kaw-Liga/Little Folks	1969	2.00	4.00	8.00
47-9777	Wings of a Dove/They Stood in Silent Prayer	1969	3.00	6.00	12.00
47-9806	Is Anybody Goin' to San Antone/Things Are Looking Up	1970	—	3.00	6.00
47-9855	Wonder Could I Live There Anymore/Piroque Joe	1970	—	3.00	6.00
47-9902	I Can't Believe That You've Stopped Loving Me/ Time	1970	—	3.00	6.00
47-9933	Christmas in My Home Town/Santa and the Kids	1970	2.00	4.00	8.00
47-9952	I'd Rather Love You/You Don't Belong	1971	—	3.00	6.00
47-9974	Let Me Live/Did You Think to Pray	1971	2.00	4.00	8.00
47-9996	I'm Just Me/A Place for the Lonesome	1971	—	3.00	6.00
74-0167	All I Have to Offer You (Is Me)/Brand New Bed of Roses	1969	2.00	4.00	8.00
74-0265	(I'm So) Afraid of Losing You Again/Good Chance of Tear-Fall Tonight	1969	2.00	4.00	8.00
74-0550	Kiss an Angel Good Mornin'/No One Could Ever Take Me from You	1971	—	3.00	6.00
74-0624	All His Children/You'll Still Be the One	1972	—	2.50	5.00
74-0707	It's Gonna Take a Little Bit Longer/You're Wanting Me to Stop Loving You	1972	—	2.50	5.00
74-0707 [PS]	It's Gonna Take a Little Bit Longer/You're Wanting Me to Stop Loving You	1972	2.00	4.00	8.00
74-0802	She's Too Good to Be True/She's That Kind	1972	—	2.50	5.00
74-0884	A Shoulder to Cry On/I'm Learning to Love Her	1973	—	2.50	5.00
74-0942	Don't Fight the Feelings of Love/Tennessee Girl	1973	—	2.50	5.00
447-0935	Christmas In My Home Town/Santa and the Kids	1972	—	2.00	4.00
—Gold Standard Series					

Albums

16TH AVENUE

Number	Title (A Side/B Side)	Yr	VG	VG+	NM
ST-70550	After All This Time	1987	3.00	6.00	12.00
D1-70551	I'm Gonna Love Her on the Radio	1988	3.00	6.00	12.00
D1-70554	Moody Woman	1989	3.00	6.00	12.00

PAIR

Number	Title (A Side/B Side)	Yr	VG	VG+	NM
PDL2-1023 [(2)]	Country in My Soul	1986	3.00	6.00	12.00

RCA CAMDEN

Number	Title (A Side/B Side)	Yr	VG	VG+	NM
CAS-2584	The Incomparable Charley Pride	1972	3.75	7.50	15.00

RCA VICTOR

Number	Title (A Side/B Side)	Yr	VG	VG+	NM
APD1-0217 [Q]	Sweet Country	1973	6.25	12.50	25.00
APL1-0217	Sweet Country	1973	3.75	7.50	15.00
APL1-0315	Charley Pride Presents the Pridesmen	1973	3.75	7.50	15.00
APD1-0397 [Q]	Amazing Love	1974	6.25	12.50	25.00
APL1-0397	Amazing Love	1974	3.75	7.50	15.00
APL1-0534	Country Feelin'	1974	3.75	7.50	15.00
APD1-0757 [Q]	Pride of America	1974	6.25	12.50	25.00
APL1-0757	Pride of America	1974	3.75	7.50	15.00
ANL1-0996	Charley Pride — In Person	1975	2.50	5.00	10.00
—Reissue of LSP-4094					
APD1-1038 [Q]	Charley	1975	6.25	12.50	25.00
APL1-1038	Charley	1975	3.75	7.50	15.00
ANL1-1214	I'm Just Me	1975	2.50	5.00	10.00
—Reissue of LSP-4560					
APD1-1241 [Q]	The Happiness of Having You	1975	6.25	12.50	25.00
APL1-1241	The Happiness of Having You	1975	3.75	7.50	15.00
APD1-1359 [Q]	Sunday Morning with Charley Pride	1976	6.25	12.50	25.00
APL1-1359	Sunday Morning with Charley Pride	1976	3.75	7.50	15.00
ANL1-1934	Christmas in My Home Town	1976	2.00	4.00	8.00
—Reissue of LSP-4406					
APL1-2023	The Best of Charley Pride, Vol. III	1976	3.00	6.00	12.00
APL1-2261	She's Just an Old Love Turned Memory	1977	3.00	6.00	12.00
AHL1-2478	Someone Loves You Honey	1978	3.00	6.00	12.00
AHL1-2963	Burgers and Fries	1978	3.00	6.00	12.00
AHL1-3441	You're My Jamaica	1979	3.00	6.00	12.00
AHL1-3548	There's a Little Bit of Hank in Me	1980	3.00	6.00	12.00
LPM-3645 [M]	Country Charley Pride	1966	6.25	12.50	25.00
LSP-3645 [S]	Country Charley Pride	1966	7.50	15.00	30.00
AYL1-3676	Someone Loves You Honey	1980	2.00	4.00	8.00
—"Best Buy Series" reissue					
AYL1-3740	Sunday Morning with Charley Pride	1980	2.00	4.00	8.00
—"Best Buy Series" reissue					
LPM-3775 [M]	The Pride of Country Music	1967	6.25	12.50	25.00
LSP-3775 [S]	The Pride of Country Music	1967	5.00	10.00	20.00
AYL1-3874	I'm Just Me	1981	2.00	4.00	8.00
—"Best Buy Series" reissue					
LPM-3895 [M]	The Country Way	1967	6.25	12.50	25.00
LSP-3895 [S]	The Country Way	1967	5.00	10.00	20.00
AHL1-3905	Roll On Mississippi	1981	2.50	5.00	10.00
AYL1-3943	The Happiness of Having You	1981	2.00	4.00	8.00
—"Best Buy Series" reissue					
LPM-3952 [M]	Make Mine Country	1968	15.00	30.00	60.00
LSP-3952 [S]	Make Mine Country	1968	5.00	10.00	20.00
LSP-4041	Songs of Pride — Charley, That Is	1968	5.00	10.00	20.00
AYL1-4074	Amazing Love	1981	2.00	4.00	8.00
—"Best Buy Series" reissue					
LSP-4094	Charley Pride — In Person	1969	5.00	10.00	20.00
AHL1-4151	Greatest Hits	1981	2.50	5.00	10.00
LSP-4153	The Sensational Charley Pride	1969	5.00	10.00	20.00
AYL1-4166	She's Just an Old Love Turned Memory	1981	2.00	4.00	8.00
—"Best Buy Series" reissue					
AHL1-4223	The Best of Charley Pride	198?	2.50	5.00	10.00
—Reissue of LSP-4223					
LSP-4223	The Best of Charley Pride	1969	5.00	10.00	20.00
AYL1-4252	Burgers and Fries	1982	2.00	4.00	8.00
—"Best Buy Series" reissue					
AHL1-4287	Charley Pride Sings Everybody's Choice	1982	2.50	5.00	10.00
LSP-4290	Just Plain Charley	1970	5.00	10.00	20.00
LSP-4367	Charley Pride's 10th Album	1970	5.00	10.00	20.00
LSP-4406	Christmas in My Home Town	1970	5.00	10.00	20.00
LSP-4468	From Me to You	1971	5.00	10.00	20.00
LSP-4513	Did You Think to Pray	1971	5.00	10.00	20.00
AHL1-4524	Charley Pride Live	1983	2.50	5.00	10.00
LSP-4560	I'm Just Me	1971	5.00	10.00	20.00
LSP-4617	Charley Pride Sings Heart Songs	1971	5.00	10.00	20.00
AHL1-4662	Country Classics	1983	2.50	5.00	10.00
AHL1-4682	The Best of Charley Pride, Volume 2	198?	2.50	5.00	10.00
—Reissue of LSP-4682					
LSP-4682	The Best of Charley Pride, Volume 2	1972	5.00	10.00	20.00
LSP-4742	A Sunshiny Day with Charley Pride	1972	5.00	10.00	20.00
AHL1-4822	Night Games	1983	2.50	5.00	10.00
AYL1-4831	There's a Little Bit of Hank in Me	1983	2.00	4.00	8.00
—"Best Buy Series" reissue					
LSP-4837	Songs of Love by Charley Pride	1973	3.75	7.50	15.00
AHL1-5031	The Power of Love	1984	2.50	5.00	10.00
AYL1-5147	Greatest Hits	1984	2.00	4.00	8.00
—"Best Buy Series" reissue					
AYL1-5148	The Best of Charley Pride	1984	2.00	4.00	8.00
—"Best Buy Series" reissue					
AHL1-5426	Greatest Hits, Volume 2	1985	2.50	5.00	10.00
AHL1-5851	Back to the Country	1986	2.50	5.00	10.00
CPL1-7049	Collector's Series	1985	2.50	5.00	10.00
AHL1-7174	The Best There Is	1986	2.50	5.00	10.00

READER'S DIGEST

Number	Title (A Side/B Side)	Yr	VG	VG+	NM
(# unknown) [(6)]	Charley Pride's Country	1979	10.00	20.00	40.00

TIME-LIFE

Number	Title (A Side/B Side)	Yr	VG	VG+	NM
STW-101	Country Music	1981	3.00	6.00	12.00

PROCTOR, PAUL

45s

19TH AVENUE

Number	Title (A Side/B Side)	Yr	VG	VG+	NM
1009	Ain't We Got Love/(B-side unknown)	1987	—	3.00	6.00
1012	Tied to the Wheel of a Runaway Heart/Feelin' My Way Through the Dark	1988	—	3.00	6.00

AURORA

Number	Title (A Side/B Side)	Yr	VG	VG+	NM
1003	Not Tonight/(B-side unknown)	1986	—	3.00	6.00
1005	He's Not Good Enough/(B-side unknown)	1987	—	3.00	6.00

PROPHET, ORVAL

45s

DECCA

Number	Title (A Side/B Side)	Yr	VG	VG+	NM
9-28206	The Judgment Day Express/A Crown of Thorns	1952	6.25	12.50	25.00
9-28338	Molly Darling/Tears on My Bridal Bouquet	1952	6.25	12.50	25.00
9-28870	With God's Hand in Mine/Beautiful Bells	1953	6.25	12.50	25.00
9-29302	Tired Little Mother/My Heart's on the Borderline	1954	6.25	12.50	25.00
9-46404	Don't Trade Your Love for Gold/I'm Going Back to Birmingham	1952	6.25	12.50	25.00

STARDAY

Number	Title (A Side/B Side)	Yr	VG	VG+	NM
771	Big River Joe/Traveling Snowman	1966	2.50	5.00	10.00

PROPHET, RONNIE

45s

CACHET

Number	Title (A Side/B Side)	Yr	VG	VG+	NM
4502	Everybody Needs a Love Song/Sundown	1979	—	3.00	6.00
4504	Phantom of the Opry/Livin' 'n' Lovin'	1979	—	3.00	6.00

RCA

Number	Title (A Side/B Side)	Yr	VG	VG+	NM
PB-50273	Big Big World/(B-side unknown)	1976	—	2.50	5.00
PB-50391	It Ain't Easy Lovin' Me/(B-side unknown)	1977	—	2.50	5.00

RCA VICTOR

Number	Title (A Side/B Side)	Yr	VG	VG+	NM
PB-50027	Sanctuary/Wild Outlaw	1975	—	2.50	5.00
PB-50136	Shine On/Last Night I Felt the Whole World Changing	1975	—	2.50	5.00
PB-50205	It's Enough/I Want to Be Touched by You	1976	—	2.50	5.00

PROPHET, RONNIE, AND GLORY-ANNE

45s

PROPHET

Number	Title (A Side/B Side)	Yr	VG	VG+	NM
❑ 1002	Seriously Love (same on both sides)	198?	—	3.00	6.00
❑ 1003	If This Is Love (same on both sides)	198?	—	3.00	6.00
❑ 1005	I'm Glad We're Bad at Something (same on both sides)	198?	—	3.00	6.00
❑ 1007	I'll Be There (same on both sides)	198?	—	3.00	6.00

PROSSER, JAMES

45s

WARNER BROS.

Number	Title (A Side/B Side)	Yr	VG	VG+	NM
❑ 7-16951	Angels Don't Fly/The Girl Next Door	1999	—	—	3.00
❑ 7-17111	Life Goes On/Sea of Heartbreak	1999	—	—	3.00

PRUETT, JEANNE

45s

AUDIOGRAPH

Number	Title (A Side/B Side)	Yr	VG	VG+	NM
❑ 454	Love Me/Safely in the Arms of Jesus	1983	—	2.50	5.00

—A-side with Marty Robbins

Number	Title (A Side/B Side)	Yr	VG	VG+	NM
❑ 467	Lady of the Eighties/(B-side unknown)	1983	—	2.00	4.00
❑ 477	We Came So Close/(B-side unknown)	1983	—	2.00	4.00
❑ 483	Star-Studded Nights/Wild Side of Life	1984	—	2.00	4.00

DECCA

Number	Title (A Side/B Side)	Yr	VG	VG+	NM
❑ 32383	One Woman Man/One Day Ahead of My Tears	1968	2.00	4.00	8.00
❑ 32435	Make Me Feel Like a Woman Again/Don't Hold Your Breath	1969	2.00	4.00	8.00
❑ 32614	It Ain't Fair That It Ain't Right/At the Sight of You	1970	—	3.00	6.00
❑ 32703	King Size Bed/One Day Ahead of My Tears	1970	—	3.00	6.00
❑ 32857	Hold On to My Unchanging Love/He's Calling Me Baby Again	1971	—	3.00	6.00
❑ 32929	Love Me/I'm Out Looking for You	1972	—	3.00	6.00
❑ 32977	Call On Me/Stay on His Mind	1972	—	3.00	6.00
❑ 33013	I Forgot More Than You'll Ever Know (About Him)/ Don't Hold Your Breath	1972	—	3.00	6.00

IBC

Number	Title (A Side/B Side)	Yr	VG	VG+	NM
❑ 0002	Please Sing Satin Sheets for Me/(B-side unknown)	1979	—	2.00	4.00
❑ 0005	Back to Back/(B-side unknown)	1979	—	2.00	4.00
❑ 0008	Temporarily Yours/(B-side unknown)	1980	—	2.00	4.00
❑ 00010	It's Too Late/(B-side unknown)	1980	—	2.00	4.00

MCA

Number	Title (A Side/B Side)	Yr	VG	VG+	NM
❑ 40015	Satin Sheets/Sweet Sweetheart	1973	—	3.00	6.00
❑ 40116	I'm Your Woman/Your Memory's Comin' On	1973	—	2.00	4.00
❑ 40207	You Don't Need to Move a Mountain/Hopefully	1974	—	2.00	4.00
❑ 40284	Welcome to the Sunshine (Sweet Baby Jane)/ What My Thoughts Do All the Time	1974	—	2.00	4.00
❑ 40340	Just Like Your Daddy/One More Time	1974	—	2.00	4.00
❑ 40395	Honey on His Hands/One of These Days	1975	—	2.00	4.00
❑ 40440	A Poor Man's Woman/Momma Let Me Find Shelter (In Your Sweet Woman's Arms)	1975	—	2.00	4.00
❑ 40490	My Baby's Gone/But Not Today	1975	—	2.00	4.00
❑ 40527	Driftin' Too Far Away/Sweet Sorrow	1976	—	2.00	4.00
❑ 40569	It Doesn't Hurt to Ask/If I'm Not Girl Enough to Hold You	1976	—	2.00	4.00
❑ 40605	I've Taken/Sweet and Warm and Right	1976	—	2.00	4.00
❑ 40678	I'm Living a Lie/My First Pay Day	1977	—	2.00	4.00
❑ 40723	She's Still All Over You/Fancy Place to Cry	1977	—	2.00	4.00

MERCURY

Number	Title (A Side/B Side)	Yr	VG	VG+	NM
❑ 55017	I'm a Woman/Midnight Exchange	1978	—	2.00	4.00
❑ 55034	I Guess I'm Not That Good at Being Bad/Where Do You Draw the Line	1978	—	2.00	4.00

MSR

Number	Title (A Side/B Side)	Yr	VG	VG+	NM
❑ 1956	Rented Room/(B-side unknown)	1987	—	2.00	4.00

PAID

Number	Title (A Side/B Side)	Yr	VG	VG+	NM
❑ 118	Sad Ole Shade of Gray/When I Stop Dreaming	1981	—	2.00	4.00
❑ 136	I Ought to Feel Guilty/Who'll Turn Out the Lights (In Your World)	1981	—	2.00	4.00

RCA VICTOR

Number	Title (A Side/B Side)	Yr	VG	VG+	NM
❑ 47-8157	Another Heart to Break/Just a Little After Heartaches	1963	3.75	7.50	15.00
❑ 47-8232	Little Black Book/The Things I Don't Know	1963	3.75	7.50	15.00
❑ 47-8297	As a Matter of Fact/Sing Me a Song I Can Cry By	1963	3.75	7.50	15.00

Albums

ALLEGIANCE

Number	Title (A Side/B Side)	Yr	VG	VG+	NM
❑ AV-5028	Stand By Your Man	1984	2.50	5.00	10.00

DECCA

Number	Title (A Side/B Side)	Yr	VG	VG+	NM
❑ DL 75320	Love Me	1972	3.75	7.50	15.00

DOT/MCA

Number	Title (A Side/B Side)	Yr	VG	VG+	NM
❑ 39031	Jeanne Pruett	1985	2.50	5.00	10.00

MCA

Number	Title (A Side/B Side)	Yr	VG	VG+	NM
❑ 338	Satin Sheets	1973	3.00	6.00	12.00
❑ 388	Jeanne Pruett	1974	3.00	6.00	12.00
❑ 479	Honey on His Hands	1975	3.00	6.00	12.00
❑ 503	Love Me	1975	3.00	6.00	12.00

—Reissue of Decca LP

PRUETT, LEWIS

45s

DECCA

Number	Title (A Side/B Side)	Yr	VG	VG+	NM
❑ 31038	Timbrook/(You'll Make) A Fool of Me	1959	3.75	7.50	15.00

—National reissue of Peach 725

Number	Title (A Side/B Side)	Yr	VG	VG+	NM
❑ 31095	Softly and Tenderly (I'll Hold You in My Arms)/ Riches and Gold	1960	3.75	7.50	15.00
❑ 31201	Crazy Bullfrog/The Hand That Held the Hand	1961	15.00	30.00	60.00
❑ 31295	This Little Girl (Has a Magic Touch)/I'll Never Forget You	1961	3.75	7.50	15.00

GREAT

Number	Title (A Side/B Side)	Yr	VG	VG+	NM
❑ 1135	Big Wheel from Boston/I'll Never Take Another Drink Again	1968	2.50	5.00	10.00

MUSIC TOWN

Number	Title (A Side/B Side)	Yr	VG	VG+	NM
❑ 020	If You've Been Better Than I've Been (You're Bored)/We're Going Down Together	1969	2.00	4.00	8.00

PEACH

Number	Title (A Side/B Side)	Yr	VG	VG+	NM
❑ 703	Pretty Baby/I'm in a Daze	1959	50.00	100.00	200.00
❑ 710	This Little Girl/I'll Never Forget	1959	50.00	100.00	200.00
❑ 725	Timbrook/(You'll Make) A Fool of Me	1959	6.25	12.50	25.00

VEE JAY

Number	Title (A Side/B Side)	Yr	VG	VG+	NM
❑ 502	Point of No Return/Thanks a Lot	1963	3.00	6.00	12.00
❑ 601	The Worst Is Yet to Come/I'd Rather Say Goodbye	1964	3.00	6.00	12.00

PRYOR, CACTUS

45s

4 STAR

Number	Title (A Side/B Side)	Yr	VG	VG+	NM
❑ 1558	My Heart Bawls for You/Hog Calling Champ of Arkansas	1951	10.00	20.00	40.00
❑ 1580	On Top of Old Baldy/Too Young #75	1951	7.50	15.00	30.00
❑ 1631	Don't Let the Stars Get In Your Eyes #2/I'll Ride Alone	1953	6.25	12.50	25.00
❑ 1661	Point of Order with the Senator and the Private (Parts 1 and 2)	1954	6.25	12.50	25.00
❑ 1676	Tweedlee Dee/What's the Score, Podner	1955	7.50	15.00	30.00
❑ 1689	16 Hours/Merrimac (Radio Service of NBZ)	1956	6.25	12.50	25.00

Selected 78s

4 STAR

Number	Title (A Side/B Side)	Yr	VG	VG+	NM
❑ 1404	Jackass Caravan/Red River Valley	1950	6.25	12.50	25.00
❑ 1442	Texas Tapper/Cool Water	1950	6.25	12.50	25.00
❑ 1459	Cry of the Dying Duck in a Thunder-Storm/Double Trouble	1950	6.25	12.50	25.00
❑ 1498	If I Know'd Youse a-Comin' I'd'a Cut My Throat/ Can't Yodel Blues	1950	6.25	12.50	25.00
❑ 1550	I Married the Thing/Burping the Baby	1951	5.00	10.00	20.00

PRYSOCK, ARTHUR

Best known as an R&B and soul singer, this was his only country chart hit.

45s

GUSTO

Number	Title (A Side/B Side)	Yr	VG	VG+	NM
❑ 9023	Today I Started Loving You Again/It Ain't No Big Thing	1979	—	3.00	6.00

PUCKETT, JERRY

45s

ATLANTIC AMERICA

Number	Title (A Side/B Side)	Yr	VG	VG+	NM
❑ 99860	Heart on the Run/Dance Alone	1983	—	2.00	4.00

PULLEN, DWIGHT

45s

CARLTON

Number	Title (A Side/B Side)	Yr	VG	VG+	NM
❑ 455	Sunglasses After Dark/Teenage Bug	1958	75.00	150.00	300.00

SAGE AND SAND

Number	Title (A Side/B Side)	Yr	VG	VG+	NM
❑ 279	By You, By the Bayou/It's Over With	1959	7.50	15.00	30.00
❑ 283	I Live a Lifetime Last Night/You'll Get Yours Some Day	1959	7.50	15.00	30.00

PULLEN, WHITEY

45s

SAGE AND SAND

Number	Title (A Side/B Side)	Yr	VG	VG+	NM
❑ 274	Walk My Way Back Home/Don't Make Me Cry	1958	62.50	125.00	250.00
❑ 294	Let's All Go Wild Tonight/Gently	1959	37.50	75.00	150.00
❑ 303	I'm Beggin' Your Pardon/Let Your Left Hand Know	1960	25.00	50.00	100.00
❑ 313	Tuscaloosa Lucy/Waltz of the Steel Guitar	1960	30.00	60.00	120.00
❑ 372	Crazy in Love/I Won the Day I Lost You	1962	10.00	20.00	40.00

Albums

CROWN

Number	Title (A Side/B Side)	Yr	VG	VG+	NM
❑ CST-332 [R]	Whitey Pullen	1963	3.00	6.00	12.00
❑ CLP-5332 [M]	Whitey Pullen	1963	10.00	20.00	40.00

PULLINS, LEROY

45s

KAPP

Number	Title (A Side/B Side)	Yr	VG	VG+	NM
❑ 758	I'm a Nut/Knee Deep	1966	2.00	4.00	8.00
❑ 775	Taterville Women's Auxiliary Sewing Circle/ Tickled Pink	1966	2.00	4.00	8.00
❑ 816	Meter Maid/Wall Around Your Heart	1967	2.00	4.00	8.00
❑ 863	Gypsy Rose (I Don't Give a Curse)/Oriental Girl	1967	2.00	4.00	8.00
❑ 889	The Interstate Is Coming Through My Outhouse/ Swimming at the Bottom	1968	2.00	4.00	8.00

Albums

KAPP

Number	Title (A Side/B Side)	Yr	VG	VG+	NM
❑ KL-1488 [M]	I'm a Nut	1966	6.25	12.50	25.00
❑ KS-3488 [S]	I'm a Nut	1966	7.50	15.00	30.00
❑ KS-3557	Funny Bones and Hearts	1968	6.25	12.50	25.00

PUMP BOYS AND DINETTES

From the original cast recording of the play of the same name (no other credit is given). The album is listed in the ORIGINAL CAST RECORDINGS section in back.

45s

CBS

Number	Title (A Side/B Side)	Yr	VG	VG+	NM
❑ 38-03549	The Night Dolly Parton Was Almost Mine/The Best Man	1983	—	2.50	5.00

PURE PRAIRIE LEAGUE

Also see VINCE GILL (lead singer on the Casablanca releases).

45s

CASABLANCA

Number	Title (A Side/B Side)	Yr	VG	VG+	NM
❑ 2266	Let Me Love You Tonight/Janny Lou	1980	—	2.00	4.00
❑ 2294	I'm Almost Ready/You're My True Love	1980	—	2.00	4.00
❑ 2319	I Can't Stop the Feelin'/A Lifetime of Nightime	1980	—	2.00	4.00
❑ 2332	Still Right Here in My Heart/Don't Keep Me Hangin'	1981	—	2.00	4.00
❑ 2337	You're Mine Tonight.Do You Love Me Truly, Julie	1981	—	2.00	4.00

RCA

Number	Title (A Side/B Side)	Yr	VG	VG+	NM
❑ PB-10829	Dance/Help Yourself	1976	—	2.00	4.00
❑ PB-10880	All the Way/Fade Away	1977	—	2.00	4.00
❑ PB-11148	The Sun Shone Lightly/Lucille Crawfield	1977	—	2.00	4.00
❑ PB-11260	Working in the Coal Mine/Bad Cream	1978	—	2.00	4.00
❑ PB-11282	Love Will Grow/Slim Pickin's	1978	—	2.00	4.00
❑ PB-11678	Can't Hold Back/Restless Woman	1979	—	2.00	4.00

RCA VICTOR

Number	Title (A Side/B Side)	Yr	VG	VG+	NM
❑ PB-10184	Amie/Memories	1975	—	2.50	5.00
❑ PB-10302	Two-Lane Highway/Sister's Keeper	1975	—	2.00	4.00
❑ PB-10382	Just Can't Believe It/Kentucky Moonshine	1975	—	2.00	4.00
❑ GB-10490	Amie/Memories	1975	—	—	3.00
—Gold Standard Series					
❑ PB-10580	Long Cold Winter/The Sun Shone Brightly	1976	—	2.00	4.00
❑ PB-10679	That'll Be the Day/I Can Only Dream of You	1976	—	2.00	4.00
❑ 48-1028	Tears/You're Between Me	1972	—	3.00	6.00
❑ 74-0742	Woman/She Darked the Sun	1972	—	3.00	6.00
❑ 74-0794	Early Morning Riser/Angel #9	1972	—	3.00	6.00

Albums

CASABLANCA

Number	Title (A Side/B Side)	Yr	VG	VG+	NM
❑ NBLP-7212	Firin' Up	1980	2.50	5.00	10.00
❑ NBLP-7255	Something in the Night	1981	2.50	5.00	10.00

PAIR

Number	Title (A Side/B Side)	Yr	VG	VG+	NM
❑ PDL2-1034 [(2)]	Home on the Range	1986	3.00	6.00	12.00

RCA VICTOR

Number	Title (A Side/B Side)	Yr	VG	VG+	NM
❑ APD1-0933 [Q]	Two Lane Highway	1975	5.00	10.00	20.00
❑ APL1-0933	Two Lane Highway	1975	3.00	6.00	12.00
❑ APD1-1247 [Q]	If The Shoe Fits	1976	5.00	10.00	20.00
❑ APL1-1247	If The Shoe Fits	1976	3.00	6.00	12.00
❑ APL1-1924	Dance	1976	3.00	6.00	12.00
❑ CPL2-2404 [(2)]	Live!! Takin' the Stage	1977	3.75	7.50	15.00
❑ AFL1-2590	Just Fly	1978	3.00	6.00	12.00
❑ AFL1-3335	Can't Hold Back	1979	3.00	6.00	12.00
❑ AYL1-3669	Two Lane Highway	1980	2.00	4.00	8.00
—"Best Buy Series" reissue					
❑ AYL1-3717	If the Shoe Fits	1981	2.00	4.00	8.00
—"Best Buy Series" reissue					
❑ AYL1-3718	Just Fly	1981	2.00	4.00	8.00
—"Best Buy Series" reissue					
❑ AYL1-3719	Pure Prairie League	1981	2.00	4.00	8.00
—"Best Buy Series" reissue					
❑ AYL1-3723	Dance	1981	2.00	4.00	8.00
—"Best Buy Series" reissue					
❑ AFL1-4650	Pure Prairie League	1977	2.50	5.00	10.00
—Reissue of LSP-4650					
❑ LSP-4650	Pure Prairie League	1972	3.00	6.00	12.00
❑ AYL1-4656	Bustin' Out	1984	2.00	4.00	8.00
—"Best Buy Series" reissue					
❑ AFL1-4769	Bustin' Out	1977	2.50	5.00	10.00
—Reissue of LSP-4769					
❑ LSP-4769	Bustin' Out	1972	3.00	6.00	12.00

PUTMAN, CURLY

45s

ABC

Number	Title (A Side/B Side)	Yr	VG	VG+	NM
❑ 10934	My Elusive Dreams/Hurtin' Like a Heartache	1967	2.00	4.00	8.00
❑ 10984	Set Me Free/Hummin' a Heartache	1967	2.00	4.00	8.00
❑ 11050	Little Bitty Soldier Boys/Untouchable You	1968	—	3.50	7.00
❑ 11095	Happy Shoes/Take It All Off	1968	—	3.50	7.00
❑ 11179	San Francisco Sun/If I Ever Get That Close Again	1969	—	3.50	7.00
❑ 11238	Wild Streak/You Can Always Come Home	1969	—	3.50	7.00

CHEROKEE

Number	Title (A Side/B Side)	Yr	VG	VG+	NM
❑ 504	The Prison Song/Forsaken	1960	5.00	10.00	20.00

RCA VICTOR

Number	Title (A Side/B Side)	Yr	VG	VG+	NM
❑ 47-9850	Army of Heartaches/Waiting for the Next Rainbow	1970	—	3.00	6.00
❑ 47-9910	Country Dreams/Woke Up with a Stranger	1970	—	3.00	6.00
❑ 47-9959	Danny the D.J./Goin' Home Blues	1971	—	3.00	6.00
❑ 48-1004	Divorce Sale/One Time	1971	—	3.00	6.00
❑ 74-0577	Old Ramblin' Alabama Me/You Love Me Into Staying	1971	—	3.00	6.00

Albums

ABC

Number	Title (A Side/B Side)	Yr	VG	VG+	NM
❑ ABC-618 [M]	Lonesome	1967	6.25	12.50	25.00
❑ ABCS-618 [S]	Lonesome	1967	3.75	7.50	15.00
❑ ABCS-686	World of Country Music	1969	3.75	7.50	15.00

PYLE, CHUCK

45s

URBAN SOUND

Number	Title (A Side/B Side)	Yr	VG	VG+	NM
❑ 782	Breathless in the Night/(B-side unknown)	1985	—	2.50	5.00
❑ 786	Drifter's Wind/Drifter's Wind (Long Version)	1985	—	2.50	5.00

Q

QUIST, JACK

45s

GRUDGE

Number	Title (A Side/B Side)	Yr	VG	VG+	NM
❑ 4756	Where Does Love Go (When It Dies)/South for the Winter	1989	—	3.00	6.00
❑ 4756 [PS]	Where Does Love Go (When It Dies)/South for the Winter	1989	2.00	4.00	8.00

MEMORY MACHINE

Number	Title (A Side/B Side)	Yr	VG	VG+	NM
❑ 1015	Memory Machine/I'm Comin' Home	1982	—	3.00	6.00

Albums

GRUDGE

Number	Title (A Side/B Side)	Yr	VG	VG+	NM
❑ 451	Where Does Love Go	1989	3.75	7.50	15.00

R

RABBITT, EDDIE

45s

20TH FOX

Number	Title (A Side/B Side)	Yr	VG	VG+	NM
❑ 474	Six Nights and Seven Days/Next to the Note	1964	5.00	10.00	20.00

CAPITOL

Number	Title (A Side/B Side)	Yr	VG	VG+	NM
❑ NR-44527	On Second Thought/Only One Love in My Life	1990	—	—	—
—Reissue of Universal 66025; unreleased on vinyl?					
❑ NR-44538	Runnin' with the Wind/Feel Like a Stranger	1990	—	2.00	4.00
❑ 7PRO-79999	Runnin' with the Wind (same on both sides)	1990	—	3.00	6.00
—White label promo number					

CAPITOL NASHVILLE

Number	Title (A Side/B Side)	Yr	VG	VG+	NM
❑ S7-19347	Rockin' Around the Christmas Tree/Have Yourself a Merry Little Christmas	1996	—	—	3.00

DATE

Number	Title (A Side/B Side)	Yr	VG	VG+	NM
❑ 1599	The Bed/Holding On	1968	3.00	6.00	12.00

ELEKTRA

Number	Title (A Side/B Side)	Yr	VG	VG+	NM
❑ 378 [DJ]	Song of Ireland (same on both sides)	1978	3.75	7.50	15.00
—Promo only on green vinyl; small center hole					
❑ 45237	Forgive and Forget/Pure Love	1975	—	2.50	5.00
❑ 45269	I Should Have Married You/Sweet Janine	1975	—	2.50	5.00
❑ 45301	Drinkin' My Baby (Off My Mind)/When I Was Young	1976	—	2.50	5.00
❑ 45315	Rocky Mountian Music/Do You Right Tonight	1976	—	2.50	5.00
—Butterfly label; most, if not all, copies misspell "Mountain" as above					
❑ 45315	Rocky Mountian Music/Do You Right Tonight	1976	—	3.00	6.00
—Red label; most, if not all, copies misspell "Mountain" as above					
❑ 45357	Two Dollars in the Jukebox/Don't Wanna Make Love	1976	—	2.50	5.00
—Butterfly label					
❑ 45357	Two Dollars in the Jukebox/Don't Wanna Make Love	1976	—	3.00	6.00
—Red label					
❑ 45381	Could You Love a Poor Boy, Dolly/There's Someone She Lies To (To Lie Here with Me)	1977	—	3.00	6.00
❑ 45390	I Can't Help Myself/She Loves Me Like She Means It	1977	—	2.00	4.00
❑ 45418	We Can't Go On Living Like This/We Made Love Beautiful	1977	—	2.00	4.00
❑ 45461	Hearts on Fire/Girl on My Mind	1978	—	2.00	4.00
❑ 45488	You Don't Love Me Anymore/Caroline	1978	—	2.00	4.00
❑ 45531	I Just Want to Love You/Crossin' the Mississippi	1978	—	2.00	4.00
❑ 45554	Every Which Way But Loose/Under the Double Eagle	1978	—	2.00	4.00
❑ 45895	You Get to Me/Que Pasa	1974	—	2.50	5.00
❑ 46053	Suspicions/I Don't Want to Make Love (With Anyone But You)	1979	—	2.00	4.00
❑ 46558	Pour Me Another Tequila/I Will Never Let You Go	1979	—	2.00	4.00
❑ 46613	Gone Too Far/Loveline	1980	—	2.00	4.00
❑ 46656	Drivin' My Life Away/Pretty Lady	1980	—	2.00	4.00
❑ 47066	I Love a Rainy Night/Short Road to Love	1980	—	2.00	4.00
❑ 47174	Step By Step/My Only Wish	1981	—	2.00	4.00
❑ 47174 [PS]	Step By Step/My Only Wish	1981	—	3.00	6.00

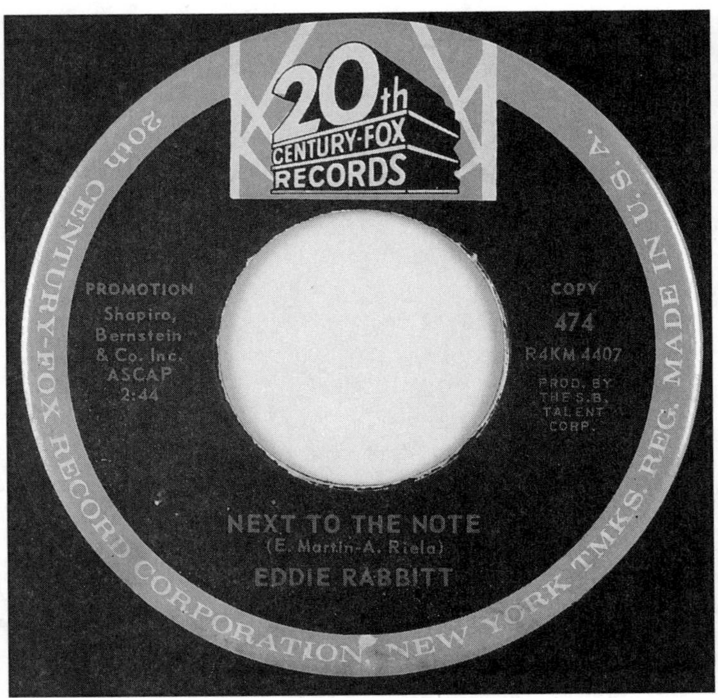

Before he finally became a recording star in the mid-1970s, Eddie Rabbitt had had several misfires, including from a record company that dropped him after he allowed Elvis Presley to record his "Kentucky Rain." In the end, he had hits from 1974 to the early 1990s. (Top left) His first single, on the 20th Century Fox label, was issued in 1964. (Top right) Rabbitt hit No. 1 on the country charts for the first time in 1976 with "Drinkin' My Baby (Off My Mind)." It was also his first top 10 record. (Bottom left) In the early 1980s, he had significant crossover success. One of the records that made the top 5 both on the pop and country charts was "Step By Step," his only solo 45 with a picture sleeve. (Bottom right) In 1989, Rabbitt signed with the short-lived Universal Records. His only single for the label before it was moved from MCA and folded into Capitol was "On Second Thought." Despite the changes in label – the song was reissued on Capitol, though probably only as a cassette single, in early 1990 – it became his last No. 1 single.

Number	Title (A Side/B Side)	Yr	VG	VG+	NM
❑ 47239	Someone Could Lose a Heart Tonight/Nobody Loves Me Like My Baby	1981	—	2.00	4.00
❑ 47435	I Don't Know Where to Start/Skip-A-Beat	1982	—	2.00	4.00
❑ 69936	You and I/All My Life, All My Love	1982	—	2.00	4.00
—A-side: With Crystal Gayle					
RCA					
❑ 5012-7-R	Gotta Have You/Singing in the Subway	1986	—	—	3.00
❑ 5093-7-R	When We Make Love/(B-side unknown)	1987	—	—	3.00
❑ 5238-7-R	Wanna Dance with You/Gotta Have You	1987	—	—	3.00
❑ 8306-7-R	The Wanderer/Workin' Out	1988	—	—	3.00
❑ 8716-7-R	We Must Be Doing Something Right/He's a Cheater	1988	—	—	3.00
❑ 8819-7-R	That's Why I Fell in Love with You/She's An Old Cadillac	1988	—	—	3.00
❑ PB-14192	A World Without Love/1-2-3, You Really Got a Hold on Me (The Wrestling Song)	1985	—	—	3.00
❑ PB-14317	Repetitive Love/Letter from Home	1986	—	—	3.00
❑ PB-14377	Both to Each Other (Friends and Lovers)/A World Without Love	1986	—	—	3.00
—With Juice Newton					
❑ PB-14377 [PS]	Both to Each Other (Friends and Lovers)/A World Without Love	1986	—	2.50	5.00
UNIVERSAL					
❑ UVL-66025	On Second Thought/Only One Love in My Life	1989	—	2.00	4.00
WARNER BROS.					
❑ 28976	She's Comin' Back to Say Goodbye/Dial That Telephone	1985	—	2.00	4.00
❑ 29089	Warning Sign/Go to Sleep, Big Bertha	1985	—	2.00	4.00
❑ 29186	The Best Year of My Life/Over There	1984	—	2.00	4.00
❑ 29279	B-B-B-Burnin' Up with Love/747	1984	—	2.00	4.00
❑ 29431	Nothing Like Falling in Love/Gone Too Far	1983	—	2.00	4.00
❑ 29512	Our Love Will Survive/You Put the Beat in My Heart	1983	—	2.00	4.00
❑ 29712	You Can't Run from Love/You Got Me Now	1983	—	2.00	4.00
Albums					
ELEKTRA					
❑ CM-3	Eddie Rabbitt	1975	3.75	7.50	15.00
❑ 6E-127	Variations	1978	3.00	6.00	12.00
❑ 6E-181	Loveline	1979	2.50	5.00	10.00
❑ 6E-235	The Best of Eddie Rabbitt	1979	2.50	5.00	10.00
❑ 6E-276	Horizon	1980	2.50	5.00	10.00
❑ 5E-532	Step By Step	1981	2.50	5.00	10.00
❑ 7E-1065	Rocky Mountain Music	1976	3.75	7.50	15.00
—Butterfly label					
❑ 7E-1065	Rocky Mountain Music	198?	2.00	4.00	8.00
—Red label					
❑ 7E-1105	Rabbitt	1977	3.75	7.50	15.00
—Butterfly label					
❑ 7E-1105	Rabbitt	198?	2.00	4.00	8.00
—Red label					
❑ 60160	Radio Romance	1982	2.50	5.00	10.00
RCA					
❑ 6373-1-R	I Wanna Dance with You	1988	2.00	4.00	8.00
RCA VICTOR					
❑ AHL1-7041	Rabbitt Trax	1986	2.00	4.00	8.00
WARNER BROS.					
❑ 6E-127	Variations	1983	2.00	4.00	8.00
—Reissue of Elektra LP					
❑ 6E-181	Loveline	1983	2.00	4.00	8.00
—Reissue of Elektra LP					
❑ 6E-235	The Best of Eddie Rabbitt	1983	2.00	4.00	8.00
—Reissue of Elektra LP					
❑ 6E-276	Horizon	1983	2.00	4.00	8.00
—Reissue of Elektra LP					
❑ 5E-532	Step by Step	1983	2.00	4.00	8.00
—Reissue of Elektra LP					
❑ 7E-1065	Rocky Mountain Music	1983	2.00	4.00	8.00
—Reissue of Elektra LP					
❑ 23925	Greatest Hits, Volume II	1983	2.50	5.00	10.00
❑ 25251	The Best Year of My Life	1984	2.50	5.00	10.00
❑ 25278	#1's	1985	2.50	5.00	10.00
❑ 60160	Radio Romance	1983	2.00	4.00	8.00
—Reissue of Elektra LP					

RABBITT, JIMMY

Number	Title (A Side/B Side)	Yr	VG	VG+	NM
45s					
ATCO					
❑ 6950	Everybody Needs Somebody That They Can Talk To/Wheels Rollin'	1973	—	3.00	6.00
CAPITOL					
❑ 4257	Ladies Love Outlaws/I Wish I Had Someone to Kiss	1976	—	2.50	5.00
Albums					
CAPITOL					
❑ ST-11491	Jimmy Rabbitt and Renegade	1976	3.00	6.00	12.00

RAE, LANA

Number	Title (A Side/B Side)	Yr	VG	VG+	NM
45s					
DECCA					
❑ 32927	You're My Shoulder to Lean On/Talking to the Wall	1972	—	3.00	6.00
❑ 33007	Will You Love Me Tomorrow/Get My Life Rollin' Again	1973	—	3.00	6.00

RAGSDALE, JOHNNY

Number	Title (A Side/B Side)	Yr	VG	VG+	NM
45s					
COLUMBIA					
❑ 4-21123	The Engineer's Song/Calamity Jane	1953	6.25	12.50	25.00
❑ 4-21163	Wrong Side of the Fence/Come Right In and Set	1953	5.00	10.00	20.00
❑ 4-21232	Ten Thousand Cows/Blue Memory	1954	5.00	10.00	20.00
❑ 4-21346	Words I Didn't Say/I'm Taking My Marbles Home	1955	5.00	10.00	20.00
❑ 4-21422	Stand-In Sweetheart/Someone Parted Our Love	1955	5.00	10.00	20.00

RAINES, LEON

Number	Title (A Side/B Side)	Yr	VG	VG+	NM
45s					
AMERICAN SPOTLITE					
❑ 103	I'll Be Seeing You/(B-side unknown)	1983	—	3.00	6.00
❑ 107	Don't Give Up on Her Now/Take Me Back	1984	—	3.00	6.00
ATLANTIC AMERICA					
❑ 99670	It Happens Every Time/Drunk on Love	1985	—	2.50	5.00
❑ 99700	Biloxi Lady/Listen to the Words	1984	—	2.50	5.00
SOUTHERN TRACKS					
❑ 1089	Most of All/No Losing You	1987	—	2.50	5.00
❑ 1094	I Keep Thinking to Myself/Tonight I Took Your...	1988	—	2.50	5.00
Albums					
ATLANTIC AMERICA					
❑ 90237	Leon Raines	1984	2.50	5.00	10.00

RAINFORD, TINA

Number	Title (A Side/B Side)	Yr	VG	VG+	NM
45s					
EPIC					
❑ 8-50340	Silver Bird/I'm Daddy's Girlfriend	1977	—	2.50	5.00
❑ 8-50455	Big Silver Angel/Guitar Man	1977	—	2.50	5.00
Albums					
EPIC					
❑ KE 35034	Silver Angel	1977	3.00	6.00	12.00

RAINSFORD, WILLIE

Number	Title (A Side/B Side)	Yr	VG	VG+	NM
45s					
CANDY					
❑ 1035 [DJ]	Christmas Shoes/There'll Be Rain, Dear This Christmas	197?	2.00	4.00	8.00
LOUISIANA HAYRIDE					
❑ 7615	No Relief in Sight/Piano Man Blues	1977	—	3.50	7.00
❑ 7629	Cheater's Kit/She's My Woman	1977	—	3.50	7.00

RAINWATER, JACK

Number	Title (A Side/B Side)	Yr	VG	VG+	NM
45s					
LAURIE					
❑ 3658	All I Want Is to Love You/A Place in the Sun	1977	—	3.50	7.00

RAINWATER, MARVIN

Also see CONNIE FRANCIS AND MARVIN RAINWATER.

Number	Title (A Side/B Side)	Yr	VG	VG+	NM
45s					
BRAVE					
❑ 1001	Part Time Lover/That Aching Heart	1963	2.50	5.00	10.00
—With Bill Guess					
❑ 1003	Love's Prison/These Thoughts of You	196?	2.50	5.00	10.00
—With Bill Guess					
❑ 1004	Bad Girl/I Saw Your New Love Today	196?	2.50	5.00	10.00
—With Bill Guess					
❑ 1017	The Old Gang's Gone/Run for Your Life Boy	196?	2.00	4.00	8.00
❑ 1028	Oklahoma Hills/Wedding Rings	196?	2.00	4.00	8.00
CORAL					
❑ 9-61342	I Gotta Go Get My Baby/Daddy's Glad You Came Home	1955	5.00	10.00	20.00
MGM					
❑ 12071	Sticks and Stones/Albino Stallion	1955	5.00	10.00	20.00
❑ 12090	Tennessee Houn' Dog Yodel/Tea Bag Romeo	1955	5.00	10.00	20.00
❑ 12152	Where Do We Go from Here/Dem Low Down Blues	1955	5.00	10.00	20.00
❑ 12240	Hot and Cold/Mr. Blues	1956	10.00	20.00	40.00
❑ 12313	Why Did You Have to Go and Leave Me/What Am I Supposed to Do	1956	5.00	10.00	20.00
❑ 12370	Get Off the Stool/(Sometimes) I Feel Like Leaving Town	1956	7.50	15.00	30.00
❑ 12412	Gonna Find Me a Bluebird/So You Think You've Got Troubles	1957	5.00	10.00	20.00
❑ 12511	My Brand of Blues/My Love Is Real	1957	5.00	10.00	20.00
❑ 12586	Lucky Star/Look for Me	1957	5.00	10.00	20.00
❑ 12609	Whole Lotta Woman/Baby Don't Go	1958	5.00	10.00	20.00
❑ 12653	Moanin' the Blues/Gamblin' Man	1958	6.25	12.50	25.00
❑ 12665	I Dig You Baby/Moanin' the Blues	1958	5.00	10.00	20.00
❑ 12701	Nothin' Needs Nothin' (Like I Need You)/(There's Always) A Need for Love	1958	5.00	10.00	20.00
❑ 12739	Lonely Island/Born to Be Lonesome	1958	5.00	10.00	20.00
❑ 12773	Love Me Baby (Like There's No Tomorrow)/That's When I'll Stop Loving You	1959	5.00	10.00	20.00
❑ 12803	Half-Breed/A Song of Love	1959	5.00	10.00	20.00
❑ 12829	Young Girls/Valley of the Moon	1959	5.00	10.00	20.00
❑ 12865	Pale Faced Indian/Wayward Angel	1960	3.75	7.50	15.00
❑ 12891	Hard Luck Blues/She's Gone	1960	3.75	7.50	15.00
❑ 12938	You're Not Happy ('Til I'm Cryin')/Yesterday's Kisses	1960	3.75	7.50	15.00
NU TRAYL					
❑ 902	Haircut/Looking Good	1976	—	3.00	6.00

Number	Title (A Side/B Side)	Yr	VG	VG+	NM
RALPH HIMSELF					
❑ 17094	Little Ralph the Robot (Poem)/Little Ralph the Robot (Song)	197?	—	2.50	5.00
UNITED ARTISTS					
❑ 837	It Wasn't Enough/My Old Home Town	1965	2.50	5.00	10.00
❑ 917	Black Sheet/Indian Burial Ground	1965	2.50	5.00	10.00
❑ 50023	Sorrow Brings a Good Man Down/The Troubles My Little Boy Had	1966	2.50	5.00	10.00
WARNER BROS.					
❑ 7373	Let Me Live Again/I Love My Country	1970	—	3.50	7.00
WARWICK					
❑ 666	Boo Hoo/I Can't Forget	1961	10.00	20.00	40.00
❑ 674	Tough Top Cat/(There's a) Honky Tonk in Your Heart	1962	6.25	12.50	25.00
(NO LABEL)					
❑ MR 1 [DJ]	Hearts Hall of Fame//Gotta Go Get My Baby/Albino Stallion	195?	25.00	50.00	100.00
—Called "Especially for Friends by Marvin Rainwater"; white label					
7-Inch Extended Plays					
MGM					
❑ X1464	(contents unknown)	1957	6.25	12.50	25.00
❑ X1464 [PS]	Songs by Marvin Rainwater, Vol. 1	1957	6.25	12.50	25.00
❑ X1465	Tennessee Houn' Dog Yodel/What Am I Supposed to Do//Why Did You Have to Go and Leave Me/Mr. Blues	1957	6.25	12.50	25.00
❑ X1465 [PS]	Songs by Marvin Rainwater Vol. 2	1957	6.25	12.50	25.00
❑ X1466	(contents unknown)	1957	6.25	12.50	25.00
❑ X1466 [PS]	Songs by Marvin Rainwater, Vol. 3	1957	6.25	12.50	25.00
Albums					
CROWN					
❑ CST-307 [R]	Marvin Rainwater	196?	3.00	6.00	12.00
❑ CLP-5307 [M]	Marvin Rainwater	196?	3.00	6.00	12.00
GUEST STAR					
❑ GS-1435 [M]	Country and Western Star	196?	3.00	6.00	12.00
MGM					
❑ E-3534 [M]	Songs by Marvin Rainwater	1957	37.50	75.00	150.00
❑ E-3721 [M]	Marvin Rainwater Sings with a Beat	1958	30.00	60.00	120.00
❑ E-4046 [M]	Gonna Find Me a Bluebird	1962	20.00	40.00	80.00
❑ SE-4046 [R]	Gonna Find Me a Bluebird	1962	12.50	25.00	50.00
SPIN-O-RAMA					
❑ SPM-109 [M]	Golden Country Hits	196?	3.00	6.00	12.00

RAITT, BONNIE

Not a country singer, but the below record, which appeared on the "Urban Cowboy" soundtrack, made the country charts.

Number	Title (A Side/B Side)	Yr	VG	VG+	NM
45s					
FULL MOON/ASYLUM					
❑ 47033	Don't It Make You Wanna Dance/Orange Blossom Special	1980	—	2.50	5.00
—B-side by Gilley's Urban Cowboy Band					
❑ 47033 [PS]	Don't It Make You Wanna Dance/Orange Blossom Special	1980	—	3.00	6.00

RAKES, PAL

Number	Title (A Side/B Side)	Yr	VG	VG+	NM
45s					
ATLANTIC					
❑ 88800	We Did It Once (We Can Do It Again)/Poor Boy	1989	—	—	3.00
ATLANTIC AMERICA					
❑ 99214	All You're Takin' Is My Love/I Feel a Change Comin' On	1989	—	—	3.00
❑ 99214 [PS]	All You're Takin' Is My Love/I Feel a Change Comin' On	1989	—	2.00	4.00
❑ 99276	I'm Only Lonely for You/One More Time	1988	—	—	3.00
COLUMBIA					
❑ 4-45168	Veronica/That Was Then	1970	2.00	4.00	8.00
—As "Palmer C. Rakes"					
❑ 4-45345	Turn the Corner/Some Hearts Never Learn	1971	2.00	4.00	8.00
—As "Palmer C. Rakes"					
VERVE					
❑ 10576	Old Shep/Can't Deny the Hurt	1967	2.50	5.00	10.00
WARNER BROS.					
❑ 8340	That's When the Lyin' Stops (And the Lovin' Starts)/Dirty Old Women	1977	—	2.50	5.00
❑ 8416	'Til I Can't Take It Anymore/Blue Summer	1977	—	2.50	5.00
❑ 8506	If I Ever Come Back/Lay It on the Line	1977	—	2.50	5.00
❑ 8656	Till Then/It's Sweet Business Doing Pleasure with You	1978	—	2.00	4.00
❑ 8765	You and Me and the Green Grass/Bad Deal	1979	—	2.00	4.00
Albums					
ATLANTIC AMERICA					
❑ 90964	Midnight Rain	1988	2.50	5.00	10.00

RAMBLING ROGUE, THE

See FRED ROSE.

RANCH, THE

Number	Title (A Side/B Side)	Yr	VG	VG+	NM
45s					
CAPITOL NASHVILLE					
❑ S7-19699	Walkin' the Country/Clutterbilly	1997	—	2.00	4.00

RANDALL, JON

Also see LORRIE MORGAN.

Number	Title (A Side/B Side)	Yr	VG	VG+	NM
45s					
RCA					
❑ 62833	This Heart/Only Game in Town	1994	—	—	3.00
❑ 64307	I Came Straight to You/This Heart	1995	—	—	3.00

RANDOLPH, BOOTS

Number	Title (A Side/B Side)	Yr	VG	VG+	NM
45s					
MONUMENT					
❑ 443	Fancy Dan/Hey, Daddy Daddy	1961	2.50	5.00	10.00
❑ 460	Bluebird of Happiness/Keep a Light in Your Window Tonight	1962	2.50	5.00	10.00
❑ 804	Yakety Sax/I Really Don't Want to Know	1963	2.50	5.00	10.00
❑ 821	Lonely Street/Windy and Warm	1963	2.00	4.00	8.00
❑ 835	Hey, Mr. Sax Man/Baby, Go to Sleep	1964	2.00	4.00	8.00
❑ 852	Mickey's Tune/I'll Take You Home Again, Kathleen	1964	2.00	4.00	8.00
❑ 884	King of the Road/Theme from a Dream	1965	2.00	4.00	8.00
❑ 928	These Boots Are Made for Walking/Honey in Your Heart	1966	2.00	4.00	8.00
❑ 950	Yodeling Sax/Miss You	1966	2.00	4.00	8.00
❑ 976	The Shadow of Your Smile/I'll Just Walk Away	1966	2.00	4.00	8.00
❑ 1009	Temptation/You've Lost That Lovin' Feelin'	1967	—	3.00	6.00
❑ 1038	Love Letters/Big Daddy	1967	—	3.00	6.00
❑ 1056	Wonderland by Night/Fred	1968	—	3.00	6.00
❑ 1081	Gentle on My Mind/Jackson	1968	—	3.00	6.00
❑ 1125	Games People Play/By the Time I Get to Phoenix	1969	—	3.00	6.00
❑ 1165	Hey Jude/Down Yonder	1969	—	3.00	6.00
❑ 1176	Sleigh Ride/White Christmas	1969	2.00	4.00	8.00
❑ 1199	Spanish Harlem/Anna	1970	—	2.50	5.00
❑ 1219	Sunday Morning Coming Down/Those Were the Days	1970	—	2.50	5.00
❑ 1226	Proud Mary/Without Love (There Is Nothing)	1970	—	2.50	5.00
❑ 1233	Take a Letter Maria/See See Rider	1970	—	2.50	5.00
❑ 1937	Sleigh Ride/White Christmas	1976	—	2.00	4.00
—Golden Series					
❑ 8500	My Sweet Lord/(B-side unknown)	1971	—	2.50	5.00
❑ 8534	Lookin'/Alligator Annie	1972	—	2.00	4.00
❑ 8541	Lonesome Ladies/Mountain Minuet	1972	—	2.00	4.00
❑ 8552	Love Theme from "The Godfather"/Rocky Top	1972	—	2.00	4.00
❑ 8588	Marie/Sentimental Journey	1973	—	2.00	4.00
❑ 8616	Behind Closed Doors/Old Joe Clarke	1974	—	2.00	4.00
❑ 8632	Sleigh Ride/White Christmas	1974	—	2.50	5.00
❑ 8634	Sanford & Son Theme/Ebb Tide	1974	—	2.50	5.00
❑ 45209	Honky Tonk/Memphis	1977	—	2.00	4.00
❑ 45227	Jive Talkin'/Blueberry Hill	1977	—	2.00	4.00
❑ 45263	You Light Up My Life/Movin' On Up	1978	—	2.00	4.00
❑ 45294	I Write the Songs/Motherland-Oluwa	1980	—	2.00	4.00
RCA VICTOR					
❑ 47-7278	Difficult/I'm Getting Your Message Baby	1958	3.75	7.50	15.00
—As "Randy Randolph"					
❑ 47-7395	Yakety Sax/Percolator	1958	5.00	10.00	20.00
—As "Randy Randolph"					
❑ 47-7515	Blue Guitar/Greenback Dollar	1959	3.00	6.00	12.00
—As "Randy Randolph"					
❑ 47-7611	Temptation/Sweet Talk	1959	3.00	6.00	12.00
❑ 47-7721	Red Light/La Golondrina	1960	3.00	6.00	12.00
❑ 47-7835	Bog Daddy/Bongo Band	1961	3.00	6.00	12.00
7-Inch Extended Plays					
MONUMENT					
❑ SMN-361 [DJ]	Sleigh Ride/Rudolph the Red-Nosed Reindeer//White Christmas/I'll Be Home for Christmas	1969	5.00	10.00	20.00
Albums					
MONUMENT					
❑ 6600	Boots Randolph's Yakety Sax	197?	2.50	5.00	10.00
—Reissue of 18002					
❑ 6601	Hip Boots	197?	2.50	5.00	10.00
—Reissue of 18015					
❑ 6602	Boots Randolph Plays More Yakety Sax	197?	2.50	5.00	10.00
—Reissue of 18037					
❑ 6603	The Fantastic Boots Randolph	197?	2.50	5.00	10.00
—Reissue of 18042					
❑ 6604	Boots with Strings	197?	2.50	5.00	10.00
—Reissue of 18066					
❑ 6605	Sax-Sational	197?	2.50	5.00	10.00
—Reissue of 18079					
❑ 6606	Boots Randolph with the Knightsbridge Strings & Voices	197?	2.50	5.00	10.00
—Reissue of 18082					
❑ 6607	Sunday Sax	197?	2.50	5.00	10.00
—Reissue of 18092					
❑ 6608	The Sound of Boots	197?	2.50	5.00	10.00
—Reissue of 18099					
❑ 6609	...With Love/The Seductive Sax of Boots Randolph	197?	2.50	5.00	10.00
—Reissue of 18111					
❑ 6610	Boots and Stockings	197?	2.50	5.00	10.00
—Reissue of 18127					
❑ 6611	Yakety Revisited	197?	2.50	5.00	10.00
—Reissue of 18128					
❑ 6612	Hit Boots 1970	197?	2.50	5.00	10.00
—Reissue of 18144					
❑ 6613	Boots with Brass	197?	2.50	5.00	10.00
—Reissue of 18147					

Number	Title (A Side/B Side)	Yr	VG	VG+	NM
❑ 6614	Homer Louis Randolph, III	197?	2.50	5.00	10.00
—Reissue of 30678					
❑ 6615	Boots Randolph Plays the Great Hits of Today	197?	2.50	5.00	10.00
—Reissue of 31908					
❑ 6616	Sentimental Journey	197?	2.50	5.00	10.00
—Reissue of 32292					
❑ 6617	Country Boots	197?	2.50	5.00	10.00
—Reissue of 32912					
❑ 6618	Cool Boots	197?	2.50	5.00	10.00
—Reissue of 33803					
❑ 7602	Greatest Hits	1977	2.50	5.00	10.00
❑ 7611	Sax Appeal	1977	2.50	5.00	10.00
❑ 7627	Put a Little Sax	1978	2.50	5.00	10.00
❑ MLP-8002 [M]	Boots Randolph's Yakety Sax	1963	5.00	10.00	20.00
❑ MLP-8015 [M]	Hip Boots	1964	3.75	7.50	15.00
❑ MLP-8029 [M]	12 Monstrous Sax Hits	1965	3.75	7.50	15.00
❑ MLP-8037 [M]	Boots Randolph Plays More Yakety Sax	1965	3.75	7.50	15.00
❑ MLP-8042 [M]	The Fantastic Boots Randolph	1966	3.75	7.50	15.00
❑ MLP-8066 [M]	Boots with Strings	1966	3.75	7.50	15.00
❑ MLP-8079 [M]	Sax-Sational	1967	5.00	10.00	20.00
❑ MLP-8082 [M]	Boots Randolph with the Knightsbridge Strings & Voices	1967	5.00	10.00	20.00
❑ 8604 [(2)]	Party Boots	197?	3.00	6.00	12.00
—Reissue of 34082					
❑ SLP-18002 [S]	Boots Randolph's Yakety Sax	1963	6.25	12.50	25.00
❑ SLP-18015 [S]	Hip Boots	1964	5.00	10.00	20.00
❑ SLP-18029 [S]	12 Monstrous Sax Hits	1965	5.00	10.00	20.00
❑ SLP-18037 [S]	Boots Randolph Plays More Yakety Sax	1965	5.00	10.00	20.00
❑ SLP-18042 [S]	The Fantastic Boots Randolph	1966	5.00	10.00	20.00
❑ SLP-18066 [S]	Boots with Strings	1966	5.00	10.00	20.00
❑ SLP-18079 [S]	Sax-Sational	1967	3.75	7.50	15.00
❑ SLP-18082 [S]	Boots Randolph with the Knightsbridge Strings & Voices	1967	3.75	7.50	15.00
❑ SLP-18092	Sunday Sax	1968	5.00	10.00	20.00
❑ SLP-18099	The Sound of Boots	1968	5.00	10.00	20.00
❑ SLP-18111	...With Love/The Seductive Sax of Boots Randolph	1969	3.75	7.50	15.00
❑ SLP 18127	Boots and Stockings	1969	3.75	7.50	15.00
❑ SLP-18128	Yakety Revisited	1969	3.75	7.50	15.00
❑ SLP-18144	Hit Boots 1970	1970	3.75	7.50	15.00
❑ SLP-18147	Boots with Brass	1970	3.75	7.50	15.00
❑ Z 30678	Homer Louis Randolph, III	1971	3.00	6.00	12.00
❑ Z2 30964 [(2)]	The World of Boots Randolph	1971	3.75	7.50	15.00
❑ KZ 31908	Boots Randolph Plays the Great Hits of Today	1972	3.00	6.00	12.00
❑ KZ 32292	Sentimental Journey	1973	3.00	6.00	12.00
❑ KZ 32912	Country Boots	1974	3.00	6.00	12.00
❑ KZ 33803	Cool Boots	1975	3.00	6.00	12.00
❑ Z2 34082 [(2)]	Party Boots	1976	3.75	7.50	15.00
❑ PW 38388	Greatest Hits	1983	2.50	5.00	10.00
❑ JW 38396	Dedication	1983	2.50	5.00	10.00
RCA CAMDEN					
❑ CAL-825 [M]	Yakin' Sax Man	1964	3.75	7.50	15.00
❑ CAS-825 [S]	Yakin' Sax Man	1964	3.75	7.50	15.00
❑ CAL-865 [M]	Sweet Talk	1965	3.75	7.50	15.00
❑ CAS-865 [R]	Sweet Talk	1965	3.00	6.00	12.00
❑ ACL-9003 [(2)]	Yakety Sax	1972	3.00	6.00	12.00
RCA VICTOR					
❑ LPM-2165 [M]	Yakety Sax	1960	10.00	20.00	40.00
❑ LSP-2165 [S]	Yakety Sax	1960	12.50	25.00	50.00

RANEY, WAYNE

45s

Number	Title (A Side/B Side)	Yr	VG	VG+	NM
BLAKE					
❑ 204	I'm in Love/My Beautiful Bouquet	196?	3.75	7.50	15.00
DECCA					
❑ 30212	Shake Baby Shake/Fortieth and Plum	1957	15.00	30.00	60.00
❑ 31004	Four Aces and a Queen/I Ain't Got Time	1959	3.75	7.50	15.00
KING					
❑ 956	Lost John Boogie/I'm On My Way	1951	10.00	20.00	40.00
❑ 974	I Want a Home in Dixie/I Had My Fingers Crossed	1951	10.00	20.00	40.00
❑ 989	Blues at My Door/You Better Treat Your Man Right	1951	10.00	20.00	40.00
❑ 1036	I'd Feel Just Like a Millionaire/Real Good Feelin'	1952	7.50	15.00	30.00
❑ 1058	Catfish Baby/Heads or Tails I Win	1952	7.50	15.00	30.00
❑ 1087	I'm Really Needin' You/Beatin' Round the Bush	1952	7.50	15.00	30.00
❑ 1116	When They Let the Hammer Down/Undertakin' Daddy	1952	7.50	15.00	30.00
❑ 1149	Child's Side of Life/If You Never Slip Around	1952	7.50	15.00	30.00
❑ 1160	No One's Crying But Me/Powerful Love	1953	7.50	15.00	30.00
❑ 1187	Betrayed Waltz/Falling	1953	7.50	15.00	30.00
❑ 1229	Gonna Row My Boat/Burning Your Love Letters	1953	7.50	15.00	30.00
❑ 1259	Adam/Roosters Are Crowing	1953	7.50	15.00	30.00
❑ 1331	Trying to Live Without You/Mama	1954	7.50	15.00	30.00
❑ 1469	I Was There/We Love to Live	1955	6.25	12.50	25.00
❑ 1480	Gone with the Wind This Morning/Tear Down the Mountains	1955	6.25	12.50	25.00
❑ 5327	Gathering in the Sky/Book of Revelations	1960	3.75	7.50	15.00
RIMROCK					
❑ 258	Grandma's Mini-Skirt/My Pot of Love	196?	2.00	4.00	8.00
STARDAY					
❑ 663	Mail Order Heart/Don't Try to Be What You Ain't	1964	3.00	6.00	12.00
❑ 677	Strictly Nothing/Love Thief	1964	3.00	6.00	12.00
❑ 689	Young Widow Brown/I Stumble, I Fumble, I Fall	1964	3.00	6.00	12.00

Selected 78s

Number	Title (A Side/B Side)	Yr	VG	VG+	NM
KING					
❑ 676	Fox Chase/Green Valley Waltz	1948	7.50	15.00	30.00
❑ 719	Lost John Boogie/Jole Blon's Ghost	1948	7.50	15.00	30.00
❑ 732	Jack and Jill Boogie/Lonesome Wind Blues	1948	7.50	15.00	30.00
❑ 759	The Book of Revelations/Gathering in the Sky	1949	7.50	15.00	30.00
❑ 791	Why Don't You Haul Off and Love Me/Don't Know Why	1949	7.50	15.00	30.00
❑ 824	I'm Square Dab from the Country/Red Ball to Natchez	1949	6.25	12.50	25.00
❑ 840	Del Rio Boogie/I Feel a Streak of Love Coming On	1950	6.25	12.50	25.00
❑ 856	Under the Double Eagle/Fast Train Through Arkansas	1950	6.25	12.50	25.00
❑ 887	I Want to Live with Mommy There/The Story of the Orphan	1950	6.25	12.50	25.00
❑ 910	Old Fashioned Matrimony in Mind/Pardon My Whiskers	1950	6.25	12.50	25.00
❑ 914	Real Hot Boogie/If You've Got the Money Honey (I've Got the Time)	1950	6.25	12.50	25.00
❑ 925	My Annabelle Lee/The Family Tree Musta Fell on Me	1951	5.00	10.00	20.00
❑ 939	I've Gone and Sold My Soul/I Love My Little Yo-Yo	1951	5.00	10.00	20.00

Albums

Number	Title (A Side/B Side)	Yr	VG	VG+	NM
KING					
❑ 588 [M]	Songs from the Hills	1958	25.00	50.00	100.00
NASHVILLE					
❑ NLP-2002	Radio Gospel and Sacred Favorites	196?	3.75	7.50	15.00
STARDAY					
❑ SLP-124 [M]	Wayne Raney and the Raney Family	1960	10.00	20.00	40.00
❑ SLP-279 [M]	Don't Try to Be What You Ain't	1964	10.00	20.00	40.00

RANGERS QUARTET, THE

45s

Number	Title (A Side/B Side)	Yr	VG	VG+	NM
DECCA					
❑ 9-46331	He Bore It All/I Shall Go Home in the Morning	1951	6.25	12.50	25.00

RATTLESNAKE ANNIE

45s

Number	Title (A Side/B Side)	Yr	VG	VG+	NM
COLUMBIA					
❑ 38-07024	Callin' Your Bluff/Goodbye to a River	1987	—	—	3.00
❑ 38-07250	Funky Country Livin'/Been Waiting That Long	1987	—	—	3.00
❑ 38-07634	Somewhere South of Macon/Outskirts of Town	1987	—	—	3.00

Albums

Number	Title (A Side/B Side)	Yr	VG	VG+	NM
COLUMBIA					
❑ B6C 40678	Rattlesnake Annie	1987	2.50	5.00	10.00

RAUSCH, LEON

Also see THE TEXAS PLAYBOYS.

45s

Number	Title (A Side/B Side)	Yr	VG	VG+	NM
DERRICK					
❑ 105	Through the Bottom of the Glass/Louisiana, My Home	1975	—	3.00	6.00
❑ 107	She's the Trip That I've Been On/I'll Say Your Goodbyes	1976	—	2.50	5.00
❑ 119	I'm Satisfied with You/(B-side unknown)	1978	—	2.50	5.00
❑ 122	Let's Have a Heart to Heart Talk/Did We Have to Come This Far to Say Goodbye	1978	—	2.50	5.00
❑ 124	You Can Be Replaced/Put Me to the Test	1979	—	2.50	5.00
❑ 128	Palimony/Love, Love, Love	1979	—	2.50	5.00

RAVEN, EDDY

45s

Number	Title (A Side/B Side)	Yr	VG	VG+	NM
ABC					
❑ 11370	Arkansas Sun/Killer of the Class of '53	1973	—	3.00	6.00
❑ 11392	Sam/Southern Queen	1973	—	3.00	6.00
❑ 11421	The Last of the Sunshine Cowboys/Sugah Kane	1974	—	2.50	5.00
❑ 11449	Carolina Country Morning/Killer of the Class of '53	1974	—	2.50	5.00
❑ 12037	Ain't She Somethin' Else/If Is a Bird on a Chain	1974	—	2.50	5.00
❑ 12083	Good News, Bad News/Sam	1975	—	2.50	5.00
❑ 12111	You're My Rainy Day Woman/Wild Man from Borneo	1975	—	2.50	5.00
ABC DOT					
❑ 17595	Free to Be/Country Green	1975	—	2.50	5.00
❑ 17618	I Wanna Live/I Don't Want to Talk It Over	1976	—	2.50	5.00
❑ 17646	The Curse of a Woman/Thank God for Kids	1976	—	3.00	6.00
❑ 17663	I'm Losing It All/Touch This Morning	1976	—	2.50	5.00
CAPITOL					
❑ NR-44528	Sooner or Later/Little Sheba	1990	—	2.00	4.00
—Reissue of Universal 66029					
❑ NR-44537	Island/A Woman's Place	1990	—	2.00	4.00
❑ 7PRO-79997	Island (same on both sides)	1990	—	2.50	5.00
—Originally issued only as a promo					
COSMOS					
❑ (# unknown)	Once a Fool/(B-side unknown)	1962	7.50	15.00	30.00
DIMENSION					
❑ 1001	Sweet Mother Texas/I Should've Called	1979	—	2.50	5.00
❑ 1005	Dealin' with the Devil/She Don't Cry	1980	—	2.50	5.00
❑ 1007	You've Got Those Eyes/Fais Do Do	1980	—	2.50	5.00
❑ 1012	Another Texas Song/Day After Day	1980	—	2.50	5.00
❑ 1017	Peace of Mind/Just Leave Me Alone	1980	—	2.50	5.00
ELEKTRA					
❑ 47136	I Should've Called/Young Girl	1981	—	2.00	4.00
❑ 47216	Who Do You Know in California/Thinking It Over	1981	—	2.00	4.00

Number	Title (A Side/B Side)	Yr	VG	VG+	NM
❑ 47233 [DJ]	Blue Christmas/White Christmas	1981	—	3.00	6.00
—B-side by Mel Tillis					
❑ 47413	A Little Bit Crazy/Loving Arms and Lying Eyes	1982	—	2.00	4.00
❑ 47469	She's Playing Hard to Forget/Desperate Dreams	1982	—	2.00	4.00
❑ 69929	San Antonio Nights/Free to Be	1982	—	2.00	4.00

LA LOUISIANNE

Number	Title (A Side/B Side)	Yr	VG	VG+	NM
❑ 8040	Christina/Maria	196?	6.25	12.50	25.00
❑ 8049	Your Picture/Lied to Judy	196?	5.00	10.00	20.00
❑ 8061	Misery/My Heart's Been Broken	196?	5.00	10.00	20.00
❑ 8073	Throw It Away/The Same Old Places	196?	5.00	10.00	20.00
❑ 8077	I Knew Better/Pictures	196?	5.00	10.00	20.00
❑ 8082	Cold, Cold Heart/Once Is Enough	196?	3.75	7.50	15.00
❑ 8095	Time Will Tell/I Did	196?	3.75	7.50	15.00
❑ 8100	One Way Love/Sincerely, Your Friend	196?	3.75	7.50	15.00
❑ 8126	Alligator Bayou/The Very Last Time	197?	2.50	5.00	10.00
❑ 8129	Home/I'm to Blame	197?	2.50	5.00	10.00
❑ 8130	Colinda/Red Was a Friend of Mine	197?	2.50	5.00	10.00

MONUMENT

Number	Title (A Side/B Side)	Yr	VG	VG+	NM
❑ 45-245	Colinda (Dancer Petite)/Touch and Go	1978	—	2.50	5.00
❑ 45-260	You're a Dancer/She Don't Cry	1978	—	2.50	5.00

RCA

Number	Title (A Side/B Side)	Yr	VG	VG+	NM
❑ 5032-7-R	Right Hand Man/I Got Mexico	1986	—	—	3.00
❑ 5128-7-R	You're Never Too Old for Young Love/Other Than Montreal	1987	—	—	3.00
❑ 5221-7-R	Shine, Shine, Shine/Stay with Me	1987	—	—	3.00
❑ 6831-7-R	I'm Gonna Get You/Other Than Montreal	1988	—	—	3.00
❑ 8303-7-R	Joe Knows How to Live/Looking for Ways	1988	—	—	3.00
❑ 8798-7-R	'Til You Cry/Just for the Sake of the Thrill	1988	—	—	3.00
❑ PB-13746	I Got Mexico/Love Burning Down	1984	—	—	3.00
❑ PB-13839	I Could Use Another You/Folks Out on the Road	1984	—	—	3.00
❑ PB-13939	She's Gonna Win Your Heart/Looking for Ways	1984	—	—	3.00
❑ PB-14044	Operator, Operator/Just for the Sake of the Thrill	1985	—	—	3.00
❑ PB-14164	I Wanna Hear It from You/Room to Run	1985	—	—	3.00
❑ PB-14258	You Should Have Been Gone by Now/We Robbed Trains	1985	—	—	3.00
❑ PB-14319	Sometimes a Lady/Just for the Sake of a Thrill	1986	—	—	3.00

UNIVERSAL

Number	Title (A Side/B Side)	Yr	VG	VG+	NM
❑ UVL-66003	In a Letter to You/Risky Business	1989	—	—	3.00
❑ UVL-66016	Bayou Boys/Angel Fire	1989	—	—	3.00
❑ UVL-66029	Sooner or Later/Little Sheba	1989	—	2.50	5.00

Albums

ABC DOT

Number	Title (A Side/B Side)	Yr	VG	VG+	NM
❑ DOSD-2031	This Is Eddy Raven	1975	3.75	7.50	15.00

DIMENSION

Number	Title (A Side/B Side)	Yr	VG	VG+	NM
❑ DLP-5001	Eyes	1980	3.75	7.50	15.00

ELEKTRA

Number	Title (A Side/B Side)	Yr	VG	VG+	NM
❑ 5E-545	Desperate Dreams	1981	3.00	6.00	12.00

LA LOUISIANNE

Number	Title (A Side/B Side)	Yr	VG	VG+	NM
❑ 127	That Cajun Country Sound	197?	5.00	10.00	20.00

MCA

Number	Title (A Side/B Side)	Yr	VG	VG+	NM
❑ 910	Thank God for Kids	198?	2.00	4.00	8.00

RCA

Number	Title (A Side/B Side)	Yr	VG	VG+	NM
❑ 5728-1-R	Right Hand Man	1987	2.00	4.00	8.00
❑ 6815-1-R	The Best of Eddy Raven	1988	2.00	4.00	8.00

RCA VICTOR

Number	Title (A Side/B Side)	Yr	VG	VG+	NM
❑ AHL1-5040	I Could Use Another You	1984	2.00	4.00	8.00
❑ AHL1-5456	Love and Other Hard Times	1985	2.00	4.00	8.00

UNIVERSAL

Number	Title (A Side/B Side)	Yr	VG	VG+	NM
❑ UVL-76003	Temporary Sanity	1989	2.50	5.00	10.00

WARNER BROS.

Number	Title (A Side/B Side)	Yr	VG	VG+	NM
❑ 5E-545	Desperate Dreams	1983	2.00	4.00	8.00
—Reissue of Elektra 5E-545					

RAY, MUNDO

See MUNDO EARWOOD.

RAY, WADE

45s

ANTENNA

Number	Title (A Side/B Side)	Yr	VG	VG+	NM
❑ 6433	Even at My Best/Two of the Usual	196?	2.50	5.00	10.00
❑ 6435	Tears Don't Stain/Meanwhile Back at My House	196?	2.50	5.00	10.00

CAPITOL

Number	Title (A Side/B Side)	Yr	VG	VG+	NM
❑ 54-40204	Flop-Eared Mule/Hell Amongst the Yearlin's	1949	12.50	25.00	50.00
❑ 54-40205	Forty Years Ago/Hilo Schottische	1949	12.50	25.00	50.00
❑ 54-40232	Cuddle Bug/I Want My Dime Back	1949	12.50	25.00	50.00

DOT

Number	Title (A Side/B Side)	Yr	VG	VG+	NM
❑ 15600	Two Red Red Lips/Burning Desire	1957	3.75	7.50	15.00

RCA VICTOR

Number	Title (A Side/B Side)	Yr	VG	VG+	NM
❑ 47-4429	Heart of a Clown/Just Like Taking Candy from a Baby	1951	7.50	15.00	30.00
❑ 47-4580	I Was Just Walkin' Out the Door/Fiddlin' Rag	1952	6.25	12.50	25.00
❑ 47-4751	June Bug Jitters/One Woman Man	1952	6.25	12.50	25.00
❑ 47-4930	The Echo of Your Voice/Bill Bailey Won't You Please Come Home	1952	6.25	12.50	25.00
❑ 47-5091	It's All Your Fault/The Things I Might Have Been	1952	6.25	12.50	25.00
❑ 47-5199	Call Me Up/If They Should Ask	1953	6.25	12.50	25.00
❑ 47-5302	Burned Fingers/Don't Wait to Baby Your Baby	1953	6.25	12.50	25.00
❑ 47-5377	That Love Makin' Melody/Did I Do Wrong	1953	6.25	12.50	25.00
❑ 47-5440	Let Me Go, Devil/Too Late Too	1953	7.50	15.00	30.00
❑ 47-5518	Saturday Night/First, Last and Always	1953	6.25	12.50	25.00
❑ 47-5624	Idaho Red/A Penny for Your Thoughts	1954	6.25	12.50	25.00
❑ 47-5696	The Best Man Must Smile/Easy Pickins	1954	5.00	10.00	20.00
❑ 47-5845	Rosetta/Letters Have No Arms	1954	5.00	10.00	20.00
❑ 47-5957	There's No Fool Like a Young Fool/No Mama, No Papa	1954	5.00	10.00	20.00
❑ 47-6061	Excuse Me/I Couldn't Be So Happy	1955	5.00	10.00	20.00
❑ 47-6110	Dipsey Doodle/A Sentimental Journey	1955	5.00	10.00	20.00
❑ 47-6219	Albino Stallion/I'll Keep On Being a Fool	1955	5.00	10.00	20.00
❑ 47-6313	Keep My Heart/Because of a Lie	1955	5.00	10.00	20.00
❑ 47-6457	Going Home All Alone/Any Old Time	1956	5.00	10.00	20.00
❑ 47-6818	When I Lost You/All or Nothin' Man	1957	5.00	10.00	20.00
❑ 47-6931	Wild Heart/Little Green Valley	1957	5.00	10.00	20.00

Albums

ABC-PARAMOUNT

Number	Title (A Side/B Side)	Yr	VG	VG+	NM
❑ ABC-539 [M]	A Ray of Country Sun	1966	3.75	7.50	15.00
❑ ABCS-539 [S]	A Ray of Country Sun	1966	5.00	10.00	20.00

RCA CAMDEN

Number	Title (A Side/B Side)	Yr	VG	VG+	NM
❑ CAS-2107	Walk Softly	1969	3.75	7.50	15.00

RAYBON BROS.

45s

MCA

Number	Title (A Side/B Side)	Yr	VG	VG+	NM
❑ 72016	Butterfly Kisses/(Instrumental)	1997	—	2.00	4.00
❑ 72017	The Way She's Lookin'/Tangled Up in Love	1997	—	—	3.00
❑ 72029	Falling/Your Love	1997	—	—	3.00
—A-side with Olivia Newton-John					

RAYE, COLLIN

Also see THE WRAYS.

45s

EPIC

Number	Title (A Side/B Side)	Yr	VG	VG+	NM
❑ 34-73831	All I Can Be (Is a Sweet Memory)/Good for You	1991	—	2.00	4.00
❑ 34-74051	Love, Me/Blue Magic	1991	—	2.00	4.00
❑ 34-74242	Every Second/Any Old Stretch of Blacktop	1992	—	—	3.00
❑ 34-74421	In This Life/Blue Magic	1992	—	2.00	4.00
❑ 34-74786	I Want You Bad (And That Ain't Good)/Let It Be Me	1992	—	—	3.00
❑ 34-74912	Somebody Else's Moon/You Can't Take It With You	1993	—	—	3.00
❑ 34-77118	That Was a River/Big River	1993	—	—	3.00
❑ 34-77308	That's My Story/Border and Beyond	1993	—	—	3.00
❑ 34-77436	Little Rock/Dreaming My Dreams with You	1994	—	2.00	4.00
❑ 34-77632	Man of My Word/Nothin' a Little Love Won't Cure	1994	—	—	3.00
❑ 34-77773	My Kind of Girl/Angel of No Mercy	1994	—	—	3.00
❑ 34-77859	If I Were You/A Bible and a Bus Ticket Home	1995	—	—	3.00
❑ 34-77973	One Boy, One Girl/I Love Being Wrong	1995	—	2.00	4.00
❑ 34-78189	Not That Different/Sweet Miss Behavin'	1995	—	2.00	4.00
❑ 34-78238	I Think About You/I Volunteer	1996	—	—	3.00
❑ 34-78348	Love Remains/I Love Being Different	1996	—	—	3.00
❑ 34-78452	What If Jesus Comes Back Like That/The Time Machine	1996	—	2.00	4.00
❑ 34-79353	Couldn't Last a Moment/You Still Take Me There	2000	—	—	3.00

RAYE, SUSAN

Also see BUCK OWENS AND SUSAN RAYE.

45s

CAPITOL

Number	Title (A Side/B Side)	Yr	VG	VG+	NM
❑ 2620	I Ain't Gonna Be Treated That-a-Way/Maybe If I Close My Eyes (It'll Go Away)	1969	—	3.00	6.00
❑ 2701	Put a Little Love in Your Heart/I've Carried This Torch Much Too Long	1969	—	3.00	6.00
❑ 2833	One Night Stand/She Don't Deserve You Anymore	1970	—	3.00	6.00
❑ 2950	Willy Jones/I'll Love You Forever (If You're Sure You'll Want Me Then)	1970	—	3.00	6.00
❑ 3035	L.A. International Airport/Merry-Go-Round of Love	1971	—	3.00	6.00
❑ 3129	Pitty, Pitty, Patter/I'll Be Gone	1971	—	3.00	6.00
❑ 3209	(I've Got a) Happy Heart/How Long Will My Baby Be Gone	1971	—	3.00	6.00
❑ 3289	A Song to Sing/Adios, Farewell, Goodbye, Good Luck, So Long	1972	—	2.50	5.00
❑ 3327	My Heart Has a Mind of Its Own/You'll Never Miss the Water	1972	—	2.50	5.00
❑ 3438	Wheel of Fortune/My Heart Skips a Beat	1972	—	2.50	5.00
❑ 3499	Love Sure Feels Good in My Heart/I've Got You on My Mind Again	1972	—	2.50	5.00
❑ 3569	Cheating Game/I'll Love You Forever and Ever	1973	—	2.50	5.00
❑ 3699	Plastic Trains, Paper Planes/I Won't Be Needing You	1973	—	2.50	5.00
❑ 3782	When You Get Back from Nashville/Nobody's Fool But Yours	1973	—	2.50	5.00
❑ 3850	Stop the World (And Let Me Off)/Love's Ups and Downs	1974	—	2.00	4.00
❑ 3927	You Can Sure See It from Here/I Wish I Was a Butterfly	1974	—	2.00	4.00
❑ 3980	Whatcha Gonna Do with a Dog Like That/That Loving Feeling	1974	—	2.00	4.00
❑ 4063	Ghost Story/Beginner's Luck	1975	—	2.00	4.00
❑ 4140	He Gives Me Something (To Forgive Him For)/You're the Piece That's Always Gone	1975	—	2.00	4.00
❑ 4197	Honey Toast and Sunshine/Only a Good Love Lasts Forever	1975	—	2.00	4.00

UNITED ARTISTS

Number	Title (A Side/B Side)	Yr	VG	VG+	NM
❑ XW870	Ozark Mountain Lullaby/Johnny Sunshine	1976	—	2.00	4.00
❑ XW934	Mr. Heartache/Turn Away	1977	—	2.00	4.00
❑ XW976	Saturday Night to Sunday Quiet/My Hiding Place	1977	—	2.00	4.00
❑ XW1026	It Didn't Have to Be a Diamond/My Hiding Place	1977	—	2.00	4.00

WESTEXAS AMERICA

Number	Title (A Side/B Side)	Yr	VG	VG+	NM
❑ 1	Put Another Notch in Your Belt/I Just Can't Take the Leaving Anymore	1984	—	2.00	4.00

Number	Title (A Side/B Side)	Yr	VG	VG+	NM
Albums					
CAPITOL					
❑ ST-543	One Night Stand	1970	3.75	7.50	15.00
❑ ST-736	Willy Jones	1971	3.75	7.50	15.00
❑ ST-807	Pitty, Pitty, Patter	1971	3.75	7.50	15.00
❑ ST-875	(I've Got a) Happy Heart	1972	3.75	7.50	15.00
❑ ST-11055	My Heart Has a Mind of Its Own	1972	3.00	6.00	12.00
❑ ST-11106	Wheel of Fortune	1972	3.00	6.00	12.00
❑ ST-11135	Love Sure Feels Good in My Heart	1973	3.00	6.00	12.00
❑ ST-11179	Cheating Game	1973	3.00	6.00	12.00
❑ ST-11223	Plastic Trains, Paper Planes	1973	3.00	6.00	12.00
❑ ST-11255	Hymns by Susan Raye	1974	3.00	6.00	12.00
❑ ST-11282	The Best of Susan Raye	1974	3.00	6.00	12.00
❑ ST-11333	Singing	1974	3.00	6.00	12.00
❑ ST-11393	Whatch Gonna Do with a Dog Like That	1975	3.00	6.00	12.00
UNITED ARTISTS					
❑ UA-LA764-G	Susan Raye	1977	3.00	6.00	12.00

RAZORBACK

See GRAYGHOST.

RECORD, DONNIE

Number	Title (A Side/B Side)	Yr	VG	VG+	NM
45s					
BRIARROSE					
❑ 1001	One More Goodbye, One More Hello/(B-side unknown)	1983	—	3.00	6.00

RED, WHITE AND BLUE (GRASS)

Number	Title (A Side/B Side)	Yr	VG	VG+	NM
45s					
GRC					
❑ 1009	July You're a Woman/High Ground	1973	2.00	4.00	8.00
❑ 2015	Linda Ann/(B-side unknown)	1974	2.00	4.00	8.00
Albums					
GRC					
❑ 5002	Red, White and Blue (Grass)	1973	3.75	7.50	15.00
❑ 10003	Red, White and Blue (Grass) Pickin' Up!	1974	3.75	7.50	15.00
MERCURY					
❑ SRM-1-1165	Red, White and Blue (Grass) and Company	1977	3.00	6.00	12.00

RED WILLOW BAND

Number	Title (A Side/B Side)	Yr	VG	VG+	NM
45s					
LOST					
❑ 1288	I Wish I Had Your Arms Around Me/Tying the Knot	1979	2.00	4.00	8.00

REDAY, EDDIE

Number	Title (A Side/B Side)	Yr	VG	VG+	NM
45s					
LITTLE DARLIN'					
❑ 8030	I've Got a Great American Dream/Mr. President	1980	—	3.50	7.00

REDDY, HELEN

The B-side of the below single by the pop singer spent a week in the country charts in 1977.

Number	Title (A Side/B Side)	Yr	VG	VG+	NM
45s					
CAPITOL					
❑ 4487	The Happy Girls/Laissez Les Bontemps Rouler	1977	—	2.00	4.00

REDMOND, ROBB

Number	Title (A Side/B Side)	Yr	VG	VG+	NM
45s					
NBC					
❑ 001	Lunch Time Lovers/Monday Morning Memory	1977	—	3.50	7.00

REECE, BEN

Number	Title (A Side/B Side)	Yr	VG	VG+	NM
45s					
20TH CENTURY					
❑ 2227	Mirror, Mirror/She's Winning	1975	—	2.50	5.00
❑ 2262	It Don't Bother Me/The Things to Do Today	1975	—	2.50	5.00
POLYDOR					
❑ 14329	Even If It's Wrong/Why'd the Last Time Have to Be the Best	1976	—	2.50	5.00
❑ 14356	Honky Tonk Fool/She Came to Me	1976	—	2.50	5.00
❑ 14376	I've Seen That Look on Me (A Thousand Times)/No One Will Ever Know	1977	—	2.50	5.00
❑ 14430	I Love My Neighbor/The Hand That Rocks the Cradle	1977	—	2.50	5.00

REED, BOBBY

Number	Title (A Side/B Side)	Yr	VG	VG+	NM
45s					
CBO					
❑ 132	If I Just Had My Woman/There's Love in the Air	1983	2.00	4.00	8.00

REED, JERRY

Number	Title (A Side/B Side)	Yr	VG	VG+	NM
45s					
CAPITOL					
❑ F3294	If the Good Lord's Willing and the Creeks Don't Rise/Here I Am	1955	5.00	10.00	20.00
❑ F3381	I'm a Lover, Not a Fighter/Honey Chile	1956	5.00	10.00	20.00
❑ F3429	When I Found You/Mister Whiz	1956	5.00	10.00	20.00
❑ F3504	Just a Romeo/This Great Big Empty Room	1956	5.00	10.00	20.00
❑ F3592	Too Busy Cryin' the Blues/You're Braggin', Boy	1956	5.00	10.00	20.00
❑ F3657	It's High Time/Forever	1957	3.75	7.50	15.00
❑ F3731	Rockin' in Bagdad/Oh Lonely Heart	1957	3.75	7.50	15.00
❑ F3823	In My Own Back Yard/Ba-Bee	1957	3.75	7.50	15.00
❑ F3882	Too Young to Be Blue/Bessie Baby	1958	3.75	7.50	15.00
❑ F3992	How Can I Go On This Way/Your Money Makes You Purty	1958	3.75	7.50	15.00
❑ B-5531	Big Time Fool/What Comes Around	1985	—	—	3.00
❑ B-5556	Country's Alive and Doing Well/Let It Go	1986	—	—	3.00
❑ B-5612	This Missin' You's a Whole Lotta Fun/There Was You	1986	—	—	3.00
❑ B-5660	You Can't Get the Hell Out of Texas/Old Fashioned Heart	1986	—	—	3.00
COLUMBIA					
❑ 42047	Love and War (Ain't Much Difference in the Two)/Love Is the Cause of It All	1961	2.50	5.00	10.00
❑ 42183	Hit and Run/Sure Is Blue Out Tonight	1961	2.50	5.00	10.00
❑ 42311	Pity the Fool/I've Got Everybody Fooled But Me	1962	2.50	5.00	10.00
❑ 42417	I'm Movin' On/Goodnight Irene	1962	2.50	5.00	10.00
❑ 42533	Twist-a-Roo/Hully Gully Guitars	1962	2.50	5.00	10.00
❑ 42639	Too Old to Cut the Mustard/Overlooked and Underloved	1962	2.50	5.00	10.00
❑ 42704	I Want to Be Loved/I'll See You in My Dreams	1963	2.50	5.00	10.00
❑ 42808	The Shock/Let's Get Ready for Summer	1963	2.50	5.00	10.00
❑ 42863	The Mountain Man/Love Don't Grow on Trees	1963	2.50	5.00	10.00
❑ 43052	June Night/Spilled Milk	1964	2.50	5.00	10.00
NRC					
❑ 014	Have Blues Will Travel/This Can't Be Happening to Me	1958	3.75	7.50	15.00
❑ 032	Just Right/Stone Eternal	1959	3.00	6.00	12.00
❑ 5008	Little Lovin' Liza/Soldier's Joy	1959	3.00	6.00	12.00
RCA					
❑ PB-10784	Remembering/Babe	1976	—	2.00	4.00
❑ PB-10893	Semolita/Phantom of the Opry	1977	—	2.00	4.00
❑ PB-11008	With His Pants in His Hand/We Called It Everything Else	1977	—	2.00	4.00
❑ PB-11056	East Bound and Down/(I'm Just A) Redneck in a Rock and Roll Bar	1977	—	2.00	4.00
❑ PB-11164	You Know What/Louisiana Lady	1977	—	2.00	4.00
—With Seidina					
❑ PB-11232	Sweet Love Feelings/You're Gonna Need Someone	1978	—	2.00	4.00
❑ PB-11281	(I Love You) What Can I Say/I Feel for You	1978	—	2.00	4.00
❑ PB-11281	(I Love You) What Can I Say/High Rollin'	1978	—	2.00	4.00
❑ PB-11370	Stars and Stripes Forever/Reedology	1978	—	2.00	4.00
❑ PB-11407	Gimme Back My Blues/Honkin'	1978	—	2.00	4.00
❑ PB-11472	Second-Hand Satin Lady (And a Bargain Basement Boy)/Jiffy Jam	1979	—	2.00	4.00
❑ PB-11638	(Who Was the Man Who Put) The Line in Gasoline/Piece of Cake	1979	—	2.00	4.00
❑ PB-11698	Hot Stuff/Nervous Breakdown	1979	—	2.00	4.00
❑ PB-11764	Sugar Foot Rag/I Wanna Go Back Home to Georgia	1979	—	2.00	4.00
❑ PB-11944	Age/Workin' at the Car Wash Blues	1980	—	2.00	4.00
❑ GB-11986	East Bound and Down/(I'm Just a) Redneck in a Rock and Roll Bar	1980	—	—	3.00
—Gold Standard Series					
❑ PB-12034	The Friendly Family Inn/Bandit	1980	—	2.00	4.00
❑ PB-12083	Texas Bound and Flyin'/Concrete Sailor	1980	—	2.00	4.00
❑ PB-12157	Caffein, Nicotine, Benzedrine (And Wish Me Luck)/If Love's Not Around the House	1981	—	2.00	4.00
❑ PB-12210	The Testimony of Soddy Hoe/Dreaming Fairy Tales	1981	—	2.00	4.00
❑ PB-12253	Good Friends Make Good Lovers/The Devil Went Down to Georgia	1981	—	2.00	4.00
❑ PB-12318	Patches/Stray Dogs and Stray Women	1981	—	2.00	4.00
❑ PB-13081	The Man with the Golden Thumb/East Bound and Down	1982	—	2.00	4.00
❑ PB-13268	She Got the Goldmine (I Got the Shaft)/44	1982	—	2.50	5.00
❑ PB-13355	The Bird/The Hobo	1982	—	2.50	5.00
—As "Jerry Reed and Friends"					
❑ PB-13422	Down on the Corner/Good Times	1983	—	2.00	4.00
❑ PB-13527	Good Ole Boys/She's Ready for Someone to Love Her	1983	—	2.00	4.00
❑ PB-13663	I'm a Slave/Nobody Ever Loved Me	1983	—	2.00	4.00
❑ JK-13666 [DJ]	Christmas Time's a-Coming (same on both sides)	1983	—	2.50	5.00
❑ PB-13666	Christmas Time's a-Coming/The Best I Ever Had	1983	—	2.50	5.00
❑ GB-14069	She Got the Goldmine (I Got the Shaft)/The Bird	1985	—	—	3.00
—Gold Standard Series					
RCA VICTOR					
❑ APBO-0194	The Uptown Poker Club/Honkin'	1973	—	2.50	5.00
❑ APBO-0224	The Crude Oil Blues/Pickie, Pickie, Pickie	1974	—	2.50	5.00
❑ APBO-0273	A Good Woman's Love/Everybody Needs Someone	1974	—	2.50	5.00
❑ PB-10013	You've Got It/Lightning Rod	1974	—	2.50	5.00
❑ PB-10063	Boogie Woogie Rock and Roll/In Between	1974	—	2.50	5.00
❑ PB-10132	Let's Sing Our Song/Grab Bag	1974	—	2.50	5.00
❑ PB-10247	Mind Your Love/Struttin'	1975	—	2.50	5.00
❑ PB-10325	The Telephone/City of New Orleans	1975	—	2.50	5.00
❑ PB-10389	You Got a Lock on Me/Reedology	1975	—	2.50	5.00
❑ GB-10510	Lord, Mr. Ford/Two-Timin'	1975	—	—	3.00
—Gold Standard Series					
❑ PB-10717	Gator/Good for Him	1976	—	2.50	5.00
❑ 47-8565	If I Don't Live Up to It/I Feel a Sin Coming On	1965	2.00	4.00	8.00
❑ 47-8667	Ain't That Just Like a Fool/Love's Battleground	1965	2.00	4.00	8.00
❑ 47-8730	Fighting for the U.S.A./Navy Blues	1965	2.00	4.00	8.00
❑ 47-8957	Woman Shy/I Feel for You	1966	2.00	4.00	8.00
❑ 47-9152	Guitar Man/It Don't Work That Way	1967	2.50	5.00	10.00
❑ 47-9334	Tupelo Mississippi Flash/Wabash Cannonball	1967	2.00	4.00	8.00
❑ 47-9493	Remembering/Fine on My Mind	1968	2.00	4.00	8.00

Number	Title (A Side/B Side)	Yr	VG	VG+	NM
❑ 47-9623	Alabama Wild Man/Twelve Bar Midnight	1968	2.00	4.00	8.00
❑ 47-9701	Oh, What a Woman/Losing Your Love	1968	2.00	4.00	8.00
❑ 47-9794	Turn It Around in Your Mind/Long Gone	1969	—	—	—
—Unreleased					
❑ 47-9804	Talk About the Good Times/Alabama Jubilee	1969	—	3.00	6.00
❑ 47-9870	Georgia Sunshine/Swinging '69	1970	—	3.00	6.00
❑ 47-9890	Tennessee Stud/Cannonball Rag	1970	—	3.00	6.00
—With Chet Atkins					
❑ 47-9904	Amos Moses/The Preacher and the Bear	1970	—	3.00	6.00
❑ 47-9976	When You're Hot, You're Hot/You've Been Crying Again	1971	—	3.00	6.00
❑ 48-1011	Ko Ko Joe/I Feel for You	1971	—	3.00	6.00
❑ 74-0124	Blues Land/There's Better Things in Life	1969	—	3.00	6.00
❑ 74-0211	Are You From Dixie/A Worried Man	1969	—	3.00	6.00
❑ 74-0242	A Thing Called Love/Hallelujah I Love Her So	1969	—	—	—
—Unreleased					
❑ 74-0613	Another Puff/Love Man	1971	—	2.50	5.00
❑ 74-0667	Smell the Flowers/If It Comes to That	1972	—	2.50	5.00
❑ 74-0738	Alabama Wildman/Take It Easy	1972	—	2.50	5.00
❑ 74-0775	Nashtownville/Jerry's Breakdown	1972	—	2.50	5.00
—With Chet Atkins					
❑ 74-0857	You Took All the Ramblin' Out of Me/I'm Not Playing Games	1972	—	2.50	5.00
❑ 74-0960	Lord, Mr. Ford/2-Timin'	1973	—	2.50	5.00
Albums					
CAPITOL					
❑ ST-12492	Lookin' at You	1986	2.00	4.00	8.00
HARMONY					
❑ H 30574	I'm Movin' On	1971	2.50	5.00	10.00
RCA CAMDEN					
❑ ACL1-0331	Tupelo Mississippi Flash	1973	2.50	5.00	10.00
❑ CAS-2585	Oh What a Woman!	1972	2.50	5.00	10.00
RCA VICTOR					
❑ APD1-0238 [Q]	Lord, Mr. Ford	1973	6.25	12.50	25.00
❑ APL1-0238	Lord, Mr. Ford	1973	3.00	6.00	12.00
❑ APL1-0356	The Uptown Poker Club	1973	3.00	6.00	12.00
❑ APL1-0544	A Good Woman's Love	1974	3.00	6.00	12.00
❑ APL1-1226	Red Hot Picker	1975	3.00	6.00	12.00
❑ ANL1-1345	When You're Hot, You're Hot	1975	2.50	5.00	10.00
—Reissue of 4506					
❑ APL1-1861	Both Barrels	1976	3.00	6.00	12.00
❑ ANL1-2167	Me and Chet	1976	2.50	5.00	10.00
—Reissue of 4707					
❑ AHL1-2346	Jerry Reed Rides Again	1977	3.00	6.00	12.00
❑ AHL1-2516	East Bound and Down	1977	3.00	6.00	12.00
❑ AHL1-2764	Sweet Love Feelings	1978	3.00	6.00	12.00
❑ AHL1-3359	Half Singin' & Half Pickin'	1979	3.00	6.00	12.00
❑ AHL1-3453	Jerry Reed Live!	1979	3.00	6.00	12.00
❑ AHl1-3604	Jerry Reed Sings Jim Croce	1980	3.00	6.00	12.00
❑ AYL1-3677	East Bound and Down	1980	2.00	4.00	8.00
—"Best Buy Series" reissue					
❑ LPM-3756 [M]	The Unbelievable Guitar and Voice of Jerry Reed	1967	6.25	12.50	25.00
❑ LSP-3756 [S]	The Unbelievable Guitar and Voice of Jerry Reed	1967	5.00	10.00	20.00
❑ AHL1-3771	Texas Bound and Flyin'	1980	3.00	6.00	12.00
❑ LPM-3978 [M]	Nashville Underground	1968	12.50	25.00	50.00
❑ LSP-3978 [S]	Nashville Underground	1968	5.00	10.00	20.00
❑ AHL1-4021	Dixie Dreams	1981	3.00	6.00	12.00
❑ LSP-4069	Alabama Wild Man	1968	5.00	10.00	20.00
❑ LSP-4147	Better Things in Life	1969	5.00	10.00	20.00
❑ AYL1-4167	Jerry Reed Live!	1982	2.00	4.00	8.00
—"Best Buy Series" reissue					
❑ LSP-4204	Jerry Reed Explores Guitar Country	1969	5.00	10.00	20.00
❑ LSP-4293	Cookin'	1970	5.00	10.00	20.00
❑ AHL1-4315	The Man with the Golden Thumb	1982	2.50	5.00	10.00
❑ LSP-4391	Georgia Sunshine	1970	5.00	10.00	20.00
❑ AYL1-4394	Texas Bound and Flyin'	1982	2.00	4.00	8.00
—"Best Buy Series" reissue					
❑ LSP-4506	When You're Hot, You're Hot	1971	3.75	7.50	15.00
❑ AHL1-4529	The Bird	1982	2.50	5.00	10.00
❑ LSP-4596	Ko-Ko Joe	1971	3.75	7.50	15.00
❑ LSP-4660	Smell the Flowers	1972	3.75	7.50	15.00
❑ AHL1-4692	Ready	1983	2.50	5.00	10.00
❑ LSP-4707	Me and Chet	1972	3.75	7.50	15.00
—With Chet Atkins					
❑ LSP-4729	The Best of Jerry Reed	1972	3.75	7.50	15.00
❑ LSP-4750	Jerry Reed	1972	3.75	7.50	15.00
❑ LSP-4838	Hot A' Mighty!	1973	3.75	7.50	15.00
❑ AYL1-5151	The Bird	1984	2.00	4.00	8.00
—"Best Buy Series" reissue					
❑ AHL1-5176	Greatest Hits	1984	2.50	5.00	10.00
❑ AHL1-5472	Collector's Series	1985	2.50	5.00	10.00

REEVES, DEL

Also see PENNY DeHAVEN.

Number	Title (A Side/B Side)	Yr	VG	VG+	NM
45s					
CAPITOL					
❑ F3819	Love, Love, Love/You're Not the Changing Kind	1957	7.50	15.00	30.00
—With Chester Smith					
❑ F3979	The Trot/Cool Drool	1958	7.50	15.00	30.00
❑ F4045	Two Teen Hearts/Baby I Love You	1958	7.50	15.00	30.00
CHART					
❑ 5082	Stand In/Bad, Bad Tuesday	1970	2.00	4.00	8.00
COLUMBIA					
❑ 4-43044	Talking to the Night Lights/Not Since Adam	1964	2.50	5.00	10.00
DECCA					
❑ 31307	Be Quiet Mind/As Far As I Can See	1961	3.00	6.00	12.00
❑ 31417	He Stands Real Tall/Empty House	1962	3.00	6.00	12.00
KOALA					
❑ 324	Good Ole Girls/Doin' Soft Time	1980	—	2.50	5.00
❑ 329	White Christmas/White Christmas (Second Version)	1980	—	2.50	5.00
❑ 333	Swinging Doors/Who Left the Door to Heaven Open	1981	—	2.50	5.00
❑ 336	Slow Hand/Take Off Time	1981	—	2.50	5.00
❑ 339	Ain't Nobody Gonna Get My Body But You/Let's Think About Livin'	1981	—	2.50	5.00
❑ 347	That's What I Like About the South/(B-side unknown)	1982	—	2.50	5.00
❑ 584	Take Me to Your Heart/What the Love of a Lady Can Do	1980	—	2.50	5.00
❑ 594	What Am I Gonna Do?/Night Out	1980	—	2.50	5.00
PEACH					
❑ 739	You Must Be an Angel/I Watched You Walk Away	1960	6.25	12.50	25.00
❑ 746	Time After Time/I Don't Wonder	1961	5.00	10.00	20.00
❑ 748	You Must Be an Angel/I Watched You Walk Away	1961	5.00	10.00	20.00
PLAYBACK					
❑ 1103	The Second Time Around/(B-side unknown)	1986	—	2.50	5.00
❑ 1301	Dear Dr. Ruth/Anywhere U.S.A.	1988	—	3.00	6.00
❑ 1302	Louisiana Legs/(B-side unknown)	1988	—	3.00	6.00
❑ 1303	I Used My Doodle-De-Doos/I Wish I Had Loved	1988	—	3.00	6.00
REPRISE					
❑ 20158	The Only Girl I Can't Forget/The Love She Offered Me	1963	2.50	5.00	10.00
❑ 20228	I Closed My Eyes and Saw the Light/Once a Fool	1963	2.50	5.00	10.00
UNITED ARTISTS					
❑ 0141	Girl on the Billboard/Bar Room Talk	1973	—	2.00	4.00
—"Silver Spotlight Series" reissue					
❑ XW249	Mm-Mm Good/Bridge That Wouldn't Burn	1973	—	2.50	5.00
❑ XW308	Lay a Little Lovin' on Me/Lay Me to Sleep	1973	—	2.50	5.00
❑ XW378	What a Way to Go/Sometimes Woman	1974	—	2.50	5.00
❑ XW427	Prayer from a Mobile Home/Three Years Late	1974	—	2.50	5.00
❑ XW532	She Likes Country Bands/A Rose Is Hard to Beat	1974	—	2.50	5.00
❑ XW564	Pour It All on Me/Belles of Broadway	1974	—	2.50	5.00
❑ XW593	But I Do/One More Round of Gin	1975	—	2.50	5.00
❑ XW639	Puttin' In Overtime at Home/Homemade Love	1975	—	2.50	5.00
❑ XW702	You Comb Her Hair Every Morning/Hell and Half of Georgia	1975	—	2.50	5.00
❑ XW760	I Ain't Got Nobody/I Would Like to See You Again	1976	—	2.50	5.00
❑ 824	Girl on the Billboard/Eyes Don't Come Crying to Me	1965	2.00	4.00	8.00
❑ XW829	Nobody Touches My Baby/She's the Best Thing I Ever Almost Had	1976	—	2.50	5.00
❑ XW885	My Better Half/Dig a Little Deeper in the Well	1976	—	2.50	5.00
❑ 890	The Belles of Southern Bell/Nothing to Write Home About	1965	2.00	4.00	8.00
❑ 940	Women Do Funny Things to Me/My Half of Our Part	1965	2.00	4.00	8.00
❑ XW989	Ladies Night/Cryin' in Arkansas Tonight	1977	—	2.50	5.00
❑ XW1047	Am I in Heaven/Rita Ballow	1977	—	2.50	5.00
❑ XW1191	When My Angel Turns Into a Devil/How Can Anything That Feels So Good (Hurt So Bad)	1978	—	2.50	5.00
❑ XW1230	Dig Down Deep/Darlin' I Love You	1978	—	2.50	5.00
❑ 50001	One Bum Town/Dead and Gone	1966	2.00	4.00	8.00
❑ 50035	Gettin' Any Feed for Your Chickens/Plain as the Tears on My Face	1966	2.00	4.00	8.00
❑ 50081	This Must Be the Bottom/Laughter Keeps Running Down My Cheeks	1966	2.00	4.00	8.00
❑ 50115	Christmas Is Lonely/Sajo	1966	2.50	5.00	10.00
❑ 50128	Blame It On My Do Wrong/I Don't Have Sense Enough	1967	2.00	4.00	8.00
❑ 50157	The Private/Things Her Memory Makes	1967	2.00	4.00	8.00
❑ 50157 [PS]	The Private/Things Her Memory Makes	1967	5.00	10.00	20.00
❑ 50210	A Dime at a Time/So Much Got Lost	1967	2.00	4.00	8.00
❑ 50270	Wild Blood/Lest We Forget	1968	—	3.50	7.00
❑ 50332	Looking at the World Through a Windshield/If I Lived Here (I'd Be Home Now)	1968	—	3.50	7.00
❑ 50487	Good Time Charlie's/These Feet	1968	—	3.50	7.00
❑ 50531	Be Glad/Moccasin Branch	1969	—	3.50	7.00
❑ 50564	There Wouldn't Be a Lonely Heart in Town/Little Bit of Somethin' Else	1969	—	3.50	7.00
❑ 50622	A Lover's Question/Spare Me	1970	—	3.50	7.00
❑ 50667	Son of a Coal Man/The Chair That Rocked Us All	1970	—	3.50	7.00
❑ 50714	Right Back Loving You Again/Gardenia Brown	1970	—	3.50	7.00
❑ 50743	Bar Room Talk/I'm Not Through Loving You	1971	—	3.00	6.00
❑ 50763	Working Like the Devil (For the Lord)/Sidewalks of Chicago	1971	—	3.00	6.00
❑ 50802	The Philadelphia Fillies/Belles of Broadway	1971	—	3.00	6.00
❑ 50840	A Dozen Pairs of Boots/A Rose Is Hard to Beat	1971	—	3.00	6.00
❑ 50877	The Best Is Yet to Come/Truth Can Hurt a Woman	1972	—	3.00	6.00
❑ 50906	No Rings — No Strings/Hey, Anybody Here Seen Cupid	1972	—	3.00	6.00
❑ 50964	Before Goodbye/Buck Jones Guitar	1972	—	3.00	6.00
❑ 51106	Trucker's Paradise/Gathering of My Memories	1973	—	3.00	6.00
Albums					
KOALA					
❑ KO 14188	Del Reeves	1980	3.00	6.00	12.00
PLAYBACK					
❑ 12002	Here's Del Reeves	1988	3.75	7.50	15.00

STARDAY

Number	Title (A Side/B Side)	Yr	VG	VG+	NM
❑ 998	Greatest Hits	197?	2.50	5.00	10.00

SUNSET

Number	Title (A Side/B Side)	Yr	VG	VG+	NM
❑ SUS-5230	Wonderful World of Country Music	1968	3.00	6.00	12.00
❑ SUS-5279	Country Concert Live!	1969	3.00	6.00	12.00
❑ SUS-5321	Out in the Country	1970	3.00	6.00	12.00

UNITED ARTISTS

Number	Title (A Side/B Side)	Yr	VG	VG+	NM
❑ UA-LA044-F	Trucker's Paradise	1973	3.75	7.50	15.00
❑ UA-LA204-G	Live at the Palomino Club	1974	3.75	7.50	15.00
❑ UA-LA235	The Very Best of Del Reeves	1974	3.75	7.50	15.00
❑ UA-LA364-G	Del Reeves with Strings and Things	1975	3.75	7.50	15.00
❑ UA-LA687-G	10th Anniversary	1977	3.00	6.00	12.00
❑ UAL-3441 [M]	Del Reeves Sings Girl on the Billboard	1965	6.25	12.50	25.00
❑ UAL-3458 [M]	Doodle-Oo-Doo-Doo	1965	5.00	10.00	20.00
❑ UAL-3468 [M]	Del Reeves Sings Jim Reeves	1966	5.00	10.00	20.00
❑ UAL-3488 [M]	Special Delivery	1966	5.00	10.00	20.00
❑ UAL-3528 [M]	Santa's Boy	1966	5.00	10.00	20.00
❑ UAL-3530 [M]	Gettin' Any Feed for Your Chickens?	1966	5.00	10.00	20.00
❑ UAL-3571 [M]	Struttin' My Stuff	1967	6.25	12.50	25.00
❑ UAL-3595 [M]	Six of One, Half a Dozen of the Other	1967	6.25	12.50	25.00
❑ UAL-3612 [M]	The Little Church in the Dell	1967	7.50	15.00	30.00
❑ UAS-6441 [S]	Del Reeves Sings Girl on the Billboard	1965	7.50	15.00	30.00
❑ UAS-6458 [S]	Doodle-Oo-Doo-Doo	1965	6.25	12.50	25.00
❑ UAS-6468 [S]	Del Reeves Sings Jim Reeves	1966	6.25	12.50	25.00
❑ UAS-6488 [S]	Special Delivery	1966	6.25	12.50	25.00
❑ UAS-6528 [S]	Santa's Boy	1966	6.25	12.50	25.00
❑ UAS-6530 [S]	Gettin' Any Feed for Your Chickens?	1966	6.25	12.50	25.00
❑ UAS-6571 [S]	Struttin' My Stuff	1967	5.00	10.00	20.00
❑ UAS-6595 [S]	Six of One, Half a Dozen of the Other	1967	5.00	10.00	20.00
❑ UAS-6612 [S]	The Little Church in the Dell	1967	6.25	12.50	25.00
❑ UAS-6635	The Best of Del Reeves	1968	5.00	10.00	20.00
❑ UAS-6643	Running Wild	1968	5.00	10.00	20.00
❑ UAS-6674	Looking at the World Through a Windshield	1968	5.00	10.00	20.00
❑ UAS-6705	Down at Good Time Charlie's	1969	5.00	10.00	20.00
❑ UAS-6733	Big Daddy Del	1970	5.00	10.00	20.00
❑ UAS-6758	The Best of Del Reeves, Vol. 2	1970	5.00	10.00	20.00
❑ UAS-6789	Friends and Neighbors	1971	5.00	10.00	20.00
❑ UAS-6820	The Del Reeves Album	1971	5.00	10.00	20.00
❑ UAS-6830	Before Goodbye	1972	5.00	10.00	20.00

REEVES, DEL, AND BOBBY GOLDSBORO

Also see each artist's individual listings.

45s

UNITED ARTISTS

Number	Title (A Side/B Side)	Yr	VG	VG+	NM
❑ 50243	I Just Wasted the Rest/Our Way of Life	1968	2.00	4.00	8.00
❑ 50591	She Thinks I Still Care/Take a Little Good Will Home	1969	—	3.50	7.00

Albums

UNITED ARTISTS

Number	Title (A Side/B Side)	Yr	VG	VG+	NM
❑ UAL 3615 [M]	Our Way of Life	1967	5.00	10.00	20.00
❑ UAS 6615 [S]	Our Way of Life	1967	5.00	10.00	20.00

REEVES, DEL, AND LIZ LYNDELL

Also see each artist's individual listings.

45s

KOALA

Number	Title (A Side/B Side)	Yr	VG	VG+	NM
❑ 321	We Must Have Been Out of Our Minds/We've Been Strong Long Enough	1980	—	2.50	5.00
❑ 323	Let's Go to Heaven Tonight/We've Been Strong Long Enough	1980	—	2.50	5.00

REEVES, DEL, AND BILLIE JO SPEARS

Also see each artist's individual listings.

45s

UNITED ARTISTS

Number	Title (A Side/B Side)	Yr	VG	VG+	NM
❑ XW797	On the Rebound/What's Our Love Coming To	1976	—	2.50	5.00
❑ XW832	Teardrops Will Kiss the Morning Dew/Nothing Seems to Work Anymore	1976	—	2.50	5.00

Albums

UNITED ARTISTS

Number	Title (A Side/B Side)	Yr	VG	VG+	NM
❑ UA-LA649-G	By Request: Del and Billie Jo	1976	3.75	7.50	15.00

REEVES, JIM

Also see GINNY WRIGHT.

45s

ABBOTT

Number	Title (A Side/B Side)	Yr	VG	VG+	NM
❑ 115	Wagon Load of Love/What Were You Doing Last Nite	1953	6.25	12.50	25.00
❑ 115	Wagon Load of Love/What Were You Doing Last Nite	1953	15.00	30.00	60.00
—Red vinyl					
❑ 116	Mexican Joe/I Could Cry	1953	15.00	30.00	60.00
—Red vinyl					
❑ 116	Mexican Joe/I Could Cry	1953	6.25	12.50	25.00
❑ 137	Let Me Love You Just a Little/Butterfly Love	1953	6.25	12.50	25.00
❑ 137	Let Me Love You Just a Little/Butterfly Love	1953	15.00	30.00	60.00
—Red vinyl					
❑ 143	El Rancho Del Rio/It's Hard to Love Just One	1953	6.25	12.50	25.00
❑ 143	El Rancho Del Rio/It's Hard to Love Just One	1953	15.00	30.00	60.00
—Red vinyl					
❑ 148	Bimbo/Gypsy Heart	1953	6.25	12.50	25.00
❑ 148	Bimbo/Gypsy Heart	1953	15.00	30.00	60.00
—Red vinyl					
❑ 160	Echo Bonita/Then I'll Stop Loving You	1954	5.00	10.00	20.00
❑ 164	Ramblin' Heart/Beatin' on the Ding Dong	1954	5.00	10.00	20.00
❑ 168	Padre of Old San Antone/Mother Went A-Walkin'	1954	5.00	10.00	20.00
❑ 170	Penny Candy/I'll Follow You	1954	5.00	10.00	20.00
❑ 174	Where Does a Broken Heart Go/The Wilder Your Heart Beats, The Sweeter You Love	1954	5.00	10.00	20.00
❑ 180	Drinking Tequila/Red Eyed and Rowdy	1955	5.00	10.00	20.00
❑ 182	Give Me One More Kiss/Tahiti	1955	5.00	10.00	20.00
❑ 184	Are You the One/How Many	1955	5.00	10.00	20.00
—With Alvadean Coker					
❑ 186	Let Me Remember/Hillbilly Waltz	1956	5.00	10.00	20.00

RCA

Number	Title (A Side/B Side)	Yr	VG	VG+	NM
❑ PB-10956	It's Nothin' to Me/I Won't Forget You	1977	—	2.00	4.00
❑ PB-11060	Little Ole Dime/A Letter to My Heart	1977	—	2.00	4.00
❑ PB-11187	You're the Only Good Thing (That's Happened to Me)/When You Are Gone	1978	—	2.00	4.00
❑ PB-11564	Don't Let Me Cross Over/I've Enjoyed As Much of This As I Can Stand	1979	—	2.00	4.00
❑ PB-11737	Oh, How I Miss You Tonight/The Talking Walls	1979	—	2.00	4.00
❑ PB-11946	Take Me in Your Arms and Hold Me/Missing Angel	1980	—	2.00	4.00
—With Deborah Allen (overdubbed)					
❑ PB-12118	There's Always Me/Somewhere Along the Line	1980	—	2.00	4.00
❑ PB-13410	The Jim Reeves Medley/He'll Have to Go	1982	—	2.00	4.00
❑ PB-13693	The Image of Me/Won't Come In While He's There	1983	—	2.00	4.00

RCA VICTOR

Number	Title (A Side/B Side)	Yr	VG	VG+	NM
❑ APBO-0255	I'd Fight the World/What's In It for Me	1974	—	2.00	4.00
❑ EP-10133	He Will/We Thank Thee	1974	—	2.00	4.00
❑ PB-10299	You Belong to Me/Maureen	1975	—	2.00	4.00
❑ PB-10418	You'll Never Know/There's That Smile Again	1975	—	2.00	4.00
❑ GB-10511	Missing You/I'd Fight the World	1975	—	2.00	4.00
—Gold Standard Series					
❑ 47-6200	Yonder Comes a Sucker/I'm Hurtin' Inside	1955	5.00	10.00	20.00
❑ 47-6274	I've Lived a Lot in My Time/Jimbo Jenkins	1955	5.00	10.00	20.00
❑ 47-6401	If You Were Mine/That's a Sad Affair	1956	5.00	10.00	20.00
❑ 47-6517	My Lips Are Sealed/Pickin' a Chicken	1956	5.00	10.00	20.00
❑ 47-6620	According to My Heart/The Mother of a Honky Tonk Girl	1956	5.00	10.00	20.00
—With Carol Johnson					
❑ 47-6625	Bimbo/Penny Candy	1956	5.00	10.00	20.00
❑ 47-6626	Mexican Joe/How Many	1956	5.00	10.00	20.00
❑ 47-6627	Then I'll Stop Loving You/Drinking Tequila	1956	5.00	10.00	20.00
❑ 47-6749	Am I Losing You/Waitin' for a Train	1956	5.00	10.00	20.00
❑ 47-6874	Four Walls/I Know and You Know	1957	3.75	7.50	15.00
❑ 47-6973	Young Hearts/Two Shadows on Your Window	1957	3.75	7.50	15.00
❑ 47-7070	Anna Marie/Everywhere You Go	1957	3.75	7.50	15.00
❑ 47-7171	I Love You More/Overnight	1958	3.75	7.50	15.00
❑ 47-7266	Blue Boy/Theme of Love (I Love to Say I Love You)	1958	3.75	7.50	15.00
❑ 47-7380	Billy Bayou/I'd Like to Be	1958	3.75	7.50	15.00
❑ 47-7479	Home/If Heartache Is the Fashion	1959	3.75	7.50	15.00
❑ 47-7557	Partners/I'm Beginning to Forget You	1959	3.75	7.50	15.00
❑ 47-7643	He'll Have to Go/In a Mansion Stands My Love	1959	3.00	6.00	12.00
❑ 47-7756	I'm Gettin' Better/I Know One	1960	3.00	6.00	12.00
❑ 47-7756 [PS]	I'm Gettin' Better/I Know One	1960	5.00	10.00	20.00
❑ 47-7800	Am I Losing You/I Missed Me	1960	3.00	6.00	12.00
❑ 47-7800 [PS]	Am I Losing You/I Missed Me	1960	5.00	10.00	20.00
❑ 47-7855	The Blizzard/Danny Boy	1961	3.00	6.00	12.00
❑ 47-7905	What Would You Do?/Stand At Your Window	1961	3.00	6.00	12.00
❑ 47-7950	Losing Your Love/(How Can I Write on Paper) What I Feel in My Heart	1961	3.00	6.00	12.00
❑ 47-8019	Adios Amigos/A Letter to My Heart	1962	2.50	5.00	10.00
❑ 47-8080	I'm Gonna Change Everything/Pride Goes Before a Fall	1962	2.50	5.00	10.00
❑ 47-8127	Is This Me?/Missing Angel	1963	2.50	5.00	10.00
❑ 47-8193	Guilty/Little Ole You	1963	2.50	5.00	10.00
❑ 47-8193 [PS]	Guilty/Little Ole You	1963	3.75	7.50	15.00
❑ 47-8252	An Old Christmas Card/Senor Santa Claus	1963	3.75	7.50	15.00
❑ 47-8252 [PS]	An Old Christmas Card/Senor Santa Claus	1963	10.00	20.00	40.00
❑ 47-8289	Welcome to My World/Good Morning Self	1963	2.50	5.00	10.00
❑ 47-8324	Love Is No Excuse/Look Who's Talking	1964	2.50	5.00	10.00
—With Dottie West					
❑ 47-8383	I Guess I'm Crazy/Not Until the Next Time	1964	2.50	5.00	10.00
❑ 47-8461	I Won't Forget You/Highway to Nowhere	1964	2.50	5.00	10.00
❑ 47-8508	This Is It/There's That Smile Again	1965	2.00	4.00	8.00
❑ 47-8625	Is It Really Over?/Rosa Rio	1965	2.00	4.00	8.00
❑ 47-8625 [PS]	Is It Really Over?/Rosa Rio	1965	3.00	6.00	12.00
❑ 47-8719	Snowflake/Take My Hand, Precious Lord	1965	2.00	4.00	8.00
❑ 47-8789	Distant Drums/Old Tige	1966	2.00	4.00	8.00
❑ 47-8902	Blue Side of Lonesome/It Hurts So Much (To See You Go)	1966	2.00	4.00	8.00
❑ 47-9057	I Won't Come In While He's There/Maureen	1966	2.00	4.00	8.00
❑ 47-9238	The Storm/Trying to Forget	1967	2.00	4.00	8.00
❑ 47-9343	I Heard a Heart Break Last Night/Golden Memories and Silver Tears	1967	2.00	4.00	8.00
❑ 47-9455	That's When I See the Blues (In Your Pretty Brown Eyes)/I've Lived a Lot in My Time	1968	2.00	4.00	8.00
❑ 47-9614	When You Are Gone/How Can I Write on Paper	1968	2.00	4.00	8.00
❑ 47-9880	Angels Don't Lie/You Kept Me Awake Last Night	1970	—	3.00	6.00
❑ 47-9969	Gypsy Feet/He Will	1971	—	3.00	6.00
❑ 74-0135	When Two Worlds Collide/Could I Be Falling in Love	1969	—	3.00	6.00
❑ 74-0286	Why Do I Love You (Melody of Love)/Nobody's Fool	1969	—	3.00	6.00
❑ 74-0626	The Writing on the Wall/You're Free to Go	1971	—	3.00	6.00
❑ 74-0744	Missing You/The Tie That Binds	1972	—	2.50	5.00

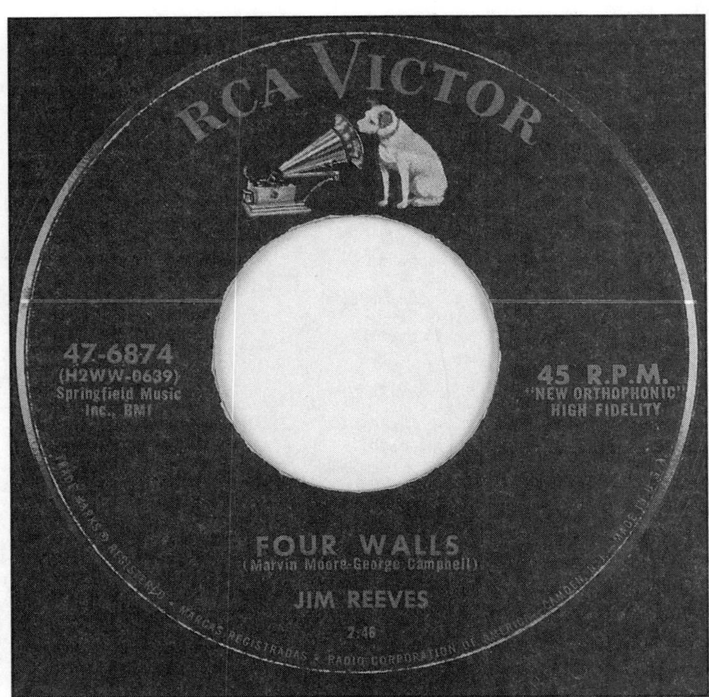

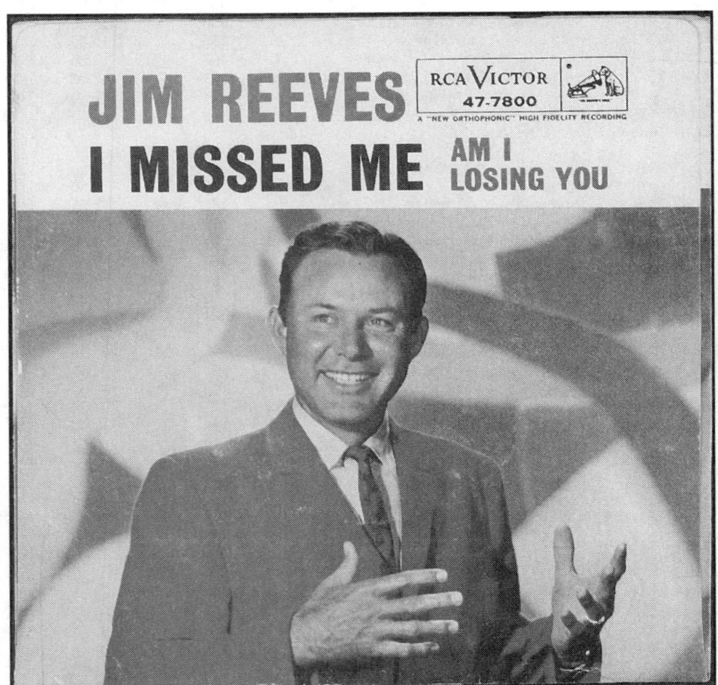

Jim Reeves recorded so prolifically that, for at least a decade after his death in a 1964 plane crash, "new" material emerged from the vaults and made the charts. The flow was so steady that some of his overseas fans thought he was still alive! (Top left) Country albums don't get more sought-after than this. Not including Elvis Presley rarities, *Jim Reeves Sings*, his only album for the Abbott label, is the msot valuable country record. Near-mint copies fetch in four figures. (Top right) Before RCA bought Elvis' contract from Sun, it bought Reeves' contract from the small Abbott label. It took longer for their purchase of Reeves to pay off, but he finally had his first RCA No. 1 country single with "Four Walls" in 1957. (Bottom left) In the early 1960s, Reeves routinely put both sides of his singles separately on the charts. Such was the case with "I Missed Me" and a new version of "Am I Losing You," each of which made the top 10 in 1960-61. (Bottom right) In the three years after his death, six of Reeves' eight singles hit No. 1 on the country charts. The biggest of these, "Distant Drums" in 1966, also hit No. 1 in England – on the pop charts.

Number	Title (A Side/B Side)	Yr	VG	VG+	NM
❑ 74-0859	Blue Christmas/Snowflake	1972	—	2.50	5.00
❑ 74-0963	Am I That Easy to Forget/Rosa Rio	1973	—	2.00	4.00
❑ 447-0884	An Old Christmas Card/Senor Santa Claus	1972	—	2.00	4.00
—Gold Standard Series					
❑ 447-0885	Snowflake/Take My Hand, Precious Lord	1972	—	2.00	4.00
—Gold Standard Series					

7-Inch Extended Plays

RCA VICTOR

Number	Title (A Side/B Side)	Yr	VG	VG+	NM
❑ EPA-4357	*He'll Have to Go/Wishful Thinking/Please Come Home/After Awhile	1960	5.00	10.00	20.00
❑ EPA-4357 [PS]	He'll Have to Go	1960	5.00	10.00	20.00

Albums

ABBOTT

Number	Title (A Side/B Side)	Yr	VG	VG+	NM
❑ LP-5001 [M]	Jim Reeves Sings	1956	1000.	1500.	2000.

COUNTRY MUSIC FOUNDATION

Number	Title (A Side/B Side)	Yr	VG	VG+	NM
❑ CMF-008	Live at the Opry	198?	2.50	5.00	10.00

PAIR

Number	Title (A Side/B Side)	Yr	VG	VG+	NM
❑ PDL2-1002 [(2)]	The Country Side of Jim Reeves	1986	3.00	6.00	12.00

RCA CAMDEN

Number	Title (A Side/B Side)	Yr	VG	VG+	NM
❑ ACL1-0123	Kimberley Jim	1973	3.75	7.50	15.00
❑ CAL-583 [M]	According to My Heart	1960	5.00	10.00	20.00
❑ CAS-583 [R]	According to My Heart	1960	5.00	10.00	20.00
❑ CAL-686 [M]	The Country Side of Jim Reeves	1962	5.00	10.00	20.00
❑ CAS-686 [S]	The Country Side of Jim Reeves	1962	5.00	10.00	20.00
❑ CAL-784 [M]	Good 'N' Country	1963	5.00	10.00	20.00
❑ CAS-784 [S]	Good 'N' Country	1963	5.00	10.00	20.00
❑ CAL-842 [M]	Have I Told You Lately That I Love You?	1964	5.00	10.00	20.00
❑ CAS-842 [S]	Have I Told You Lately That I Love You?	1964	5.00	10.00	20.00
❑ CAS-2532	Young and Country	1971	3.75	7.50	15.00
❑ CAX-9001 [(2)]	Jim Reeves	1972	5.00	10.00	20.00

RCA VICTOR

Number	Title (A Side/B Side)	Yr	VG	VG+	NM
❑ APL1-0039	Am I That Easy to Forget	1973	5.00	10.00	20.00
❑ APL1-0330	Great Moments with Jim Reeves	1973	5.00	10.00	20.00
❑ APL1-0537	I'd Fight the World	1974	5.00	10.00	20.00
❑ APL1-0793	The Best of Jim Reeves Sacred Songs	1974	5.00	10.00	20.00
❑ APL1-1037	Songs of Love	1975	5.00	10.00	20.00
❑ APL1-1224	I Love You Because	1976	5.00	10.00	20.00
❑ LPM-1256 [M]	Singing Down the Lane	1956	50.00	100.00	200.00
❑ LPM-1410 [M]	Bimbo	1957	50.00	100.00	200.00
—Reissue of Abbott LP					
❑ LPM-1576 [M]	Jim Reeves	1957	20.00	40.00	80.00
❑ LPM-1685 [M]	Girls I Have Known	1958	15.00	30.00	60.00
❑ CPL1-1891	A Legendary Performer	1976	5.00	10.00	20.00
❑ ANL1-1927	Twelve Songs of Christmas	1976	2.00	4.00	8.00
—Reissue of LSP-2758					
❑ LPM-1950 [M]	God Be With You	1958	10.00	20.00	40.00
❑ LSP-1950 [S]	God Be With You	1958	12.50	25.00	50.00
❑ LPM-2001 [M]	Songs to Warm the Heart	1959	10.00	20.00	40.00
❑ LSP-2001 [S]	Songs to Warm the Heart	1959	12.50	25.00	50.00
❑ LPM-2216 [M]	The Intimate Jim Reeves	1960	7.50	15.00	30.00
❑ LSP-2216 [S]	The Intimate Jim Reeves	1960	10.00	20.00	40.00
❑ LPM-2223 [M]	He'll Have to Go	1960	7.50	15.00	30.00
❑ LSP-2223 [S]	He'll Have to Go	1960	10.00	20.00	40.00
❑ LPM-2284 [M]	Tall Tales and Short Tempers	1961	6.25	12.50	25.00
❑ LSP-2284 [S]	Tall Tales and Short Tempers	1961	7.50	15.00	30.00
❑ APL1-2309	It's Nothin' to Me	1977	3.75	7.50	15.00
❑ LPM-2339 [M]	Talkin' to Your Heart	1961	6.25	12.50	25.00
❑ LSP-2339 [S]	Talkin' to Your Heart	1961	7.50	15.00	30.00
❑ LPM-2487 [M]	A Touch of Velvet	1962	6.25	12.50	25.00
❑ LSP-2487 [S]	A Touch of Velvet	1962	7.50	15.00	30.00
❑ LPM-2552 [M]	We Thank Thee	1962	6.25	12.50	25.00
❑ LSP-2552 [S]	We Thank Thee	1962	7.50	15.00	30.00
❑ LPM-2605 [M]	Gentleman Jim	1963	6.25	12.50	25.00
❑ LSP-2605 [S]	Gentleman Jim	1963	7.50	15.00	30.00
❑ LPM-2704 [M]	The International Jim Reeves	1963	6.25	12.50	25.00
❑ LSP-2704 [S]	The International Jim Reeves	1963	7.50	15.00	30.00
❑ AHL1-2720	Jim Reeves	1978	3.75	7.50	15.00
❑ LPM-2758 [M]	Twelve Songs of Christmas	1963	6.25	12.50	25.00
❑ LSP-2758 [S]	Twelve Songs of Christmas	1963	7.50	15.00	30.00
❑ LPM-2780 [M]	Kimberley Jim	1964	6.25	12.50	25.00
❑ LSP-2780 [S]	Kimberley Jim	1964	7.50	15.00	30.00
❑ LPM-2854 [M]	Moonlight and Roses	1964	6.25	12.50	25.00
❑ LSP-2854 [S]	Moonlight and Roses	1964	7.50	15.00	30.00
❑ LPM-2890 [M]	The Best of Jim Reeves	1964	5.00	10.00	20.00
❑ LSP-2890 [S]	The Best of Jim Reeves	1964	6.25	12.50	25.00
❑ LPM-2968 [M]	The Jim Reeves Way	1965	5.00	10.00	20.00
❑ LSP-2968 [S]	The Jim Reeves Way	1965	6.25	12.50	25.00
❑ ANL1-3014	Pure Gold, Volume 1	1978	3.00	6.00	12.00
❑ AHL1-3271	The Best of Jim Reeves, Volume IV	1979	3.75	7.50	15.00
❑ LPM-3427 [M]	Up Through the Years	1965	5.00	10.00	20.00
❑ LSP-3427 [S]	Up Through the Years	1965	6.25	12.50	25.00
❑ AHL1-3454	Don't Let Me Cross Over	1979	3.75	7.50	15.00
❑ LPM-3482 [M]	The Best of Jim Reeves, Vol. II	1966	5.00	10.00	20.00
❑ LSP-3482 [S]	The Best of Jim Reeves, Vol. II	1966	6.25	12.50	25.00
❑ LPM-3542 [M]	Distant Drums	1966	5.00	10.00	20.00
❑ LSP-3542 [S]	Distant Drums	1966	6.25	12.50	25.00
❑ AYL1-3678	The Best of Jim Reeves	1980	3.00	6.00	12.00
—"Best Buy Series" reissue					
❑ LPM-3709 [M]	Yours Sincerely, Jim Reeves	1966	5.00	10.00	20.00
❑ LSP-3709 [S]	Yours Sincerely, Jim Reeves	1966	6.25	12.50	25.00
❑ AYL1-3765	The Best of Jim Reeves Sacred Songs	1980	2.50	5.00	10.00
—"Best Buy Series" reissue					
❑ LPM-3793 [M]	Blue Side of Lonesome	1967	6.25	12.50	25.00
❑ LSP-3793 [S]	Blue Side of Lonesome	1967	5.00	10.00	20.00
❑ AHL1-3827	There's Always Me	1980	3.00	6.00	12.00
❑ LPM-3903 [M]	My Cathedral	1967	7.50	15.00	30.00
❑ LSP-3903 [S]	My Cathedral	1967	6.25	12.50	25.00
❑ AYL1-3936	Pure Gold, Volume 1	1980	2.50	5.00	10.00
—"Best Buy Series" reissue					
❑ LPM-3987 [M]	A Touch of Sadness	1968	15.00	30.00	60.00
❑ LSP-3987 [S]	A Touch of Sadness	1968	5.00	10.00	20.00
❑ LSP-4062	Jim Reeves On Stage	1968	5.00	10.00	20.00
❑ AYL1-4075	The Best of Jim Reeves, Volume IV	1981	2.50	5.00	10.00
—"Best Buy Series" reissue					
❑ LSP-4112	Jim Reeves and Some Friends	1969	5.00	10.00	20.00
❑ AYL1-4168	The Best of Jim Reeves, Vol. II	1981	2.50	5.00	10.00
—"Best Buy Series" reissue					
❑ LSP-4187	The Best of Jim Reeves Volume III	1969	5.00	10.00	20.00
❑ LSP-4475	Jim Reeves Writes You a Record	1971	5.00	10.00	20.00
❑ LSP-4528	Something Special	1971	5.00	10.00	20.00
❑ AHL1-4531	The Jim Reeves Medley	1983	2.50	5.00	10.00
❑ LSP-4646	My Friend	1972	5.00	10.00	20.00
❑ LSP-4749	Missing You	1972	5.00	10.00	20.00
❑ AYL1-4833	Don't Let Me Cross Over	1983	2.50	5.00	10.00
—"Best Buy Series" reissue					
❑ AYL1-4835	I Love You Because	1983	2.50	5.00	10.00
—"Best Buy Series" reissue					
❑ AYL1-4836	Songs of Love	1983	2.50	5.00	10.00
—"Best Buy Series" reissue					
❑ AYL1-4838	The Best of Jim Reeves Vol. III	1983	2.50	5.00	10.00
—"Best Buy Series" reissue					
❑ AYL1-4839	There's Always Me	1983	2.50	5.00	10.00
—"Best Buy Series" reissue					
❑ AYL1-4840	We Thank Thee	1983	2.50	5.00	10.00
—"Best Buy Series" reissue					
❑ AHL1-4865	A Special Collection	1983	3.00	6.00	12.00
❑ CPL2-5044 [(2)]	Just for You	1984	3.75	7.50	15.00
❑ AHL1-5424	Collector's Series	1985	3.00	6.00	12.00

REEVES, JIM, AND PATSY CLINE

Also see each artist's individual listings. Their duets were created electronically; they never actually recorded together.

45s

MCA

Number	Title (A Side/B Side)	Yr	VG	VG+	NM
❑ 52052	So Wrong/I Fall to Pieces	1982	—	2.00	4.00

RCA

Number	Title (A Side/B Side)	Yr	VG	VG+	NM
❑ PB-12346	Have You Ever Been Lonely (Have You Ever Been Blue)/Welcome to My World	1981	—	2.00	4.00

Albums

MCA

Number	Title (A Side/B Side)	Yr	VG	VG+	NM
❑ 5319	Remembering Jim Reeves and Patsy Cline	1982	3.75	7.50	15.00

RCA VICTOR

Number	Title (A Side/B Side)	Yr	VG	VG+	NM
❑ AHL1-4127	Greatest Hits	1981	3.75	7.50	15.00
❑ AYL1-5152	Greatest Hits	1984	2.50	5.00	10.00
—"Best Buy Series" reissue					

REEVES, JOHN REX

45s

SOC-A-GEE

Number	Title (A Side/B Side)	Yr	VG	VG+	NM
❑ 101	When We're Together/Something Has to Die	1979	—	3.00	6.00
❑ 102	This Time It's Over/(B-side unknown)	1979	—	3.00	6.00
❑ 103	Second Letter to Santa Claus/(B-side unknown)	1979	2.00	4.00	8.00
❑ 106	I'm Free from Your Love/Valley of Tears	1980	—	3.00	6.00
❑ 107	Love Is On the Move/I'm Living in Two Worlds	1980	—	3.00	6.00
❑ 109	What Would You Do/Jamaica Farewell	1981	—	3.00	6.00
❑ 110	You're the Reason/The Next One's on Me	1981	—	3.00	6.00
❑ 113	Till You Can Make It on Your Own/Old Used Daddy	1982	—	3.00	6.00
❑ 114	Safe in the Harbor/When You See It for Yourself	1982	—	3.00	6.00
❑ 115	After All These Years/You're the Best Thing	198?	—	3.00	6.00
❑ 116	A Million to One/You Can't Keep Me from Loving You	198?	—	3.00	6.00

REEVES, JULIE

45s

VIRGIN

Number	Title (A Side/B Side)	Yr	VG	VG+	NM
❑ 38671	Trouble Is a Woman/He Keeps Me in One Piece	1999	—	—	3.00

REEVES, RONNA

45s

MERCURY

Number	Title (A Side/B Side)	Yr	VG	VG+	NM
❑ 862260-7	Never Let Him See Me Cry/He's My Weakness	1993	—	—	3.00
❑ 864614-7	We Can Hold Our Own/Honky Tonk Hearts	1992	—	—	3.00
❑ 866380-7	The More I Learn (The Less I Understand About Love)/If I Were You	1992	—	2.00	4.00
❑ 866914-7	What If You're Wrong/Frontier Justice	1992	—	—	3.00
❑ 868230-7	Ain't No Future in the Past/Talk Back Trembling Lips	1991	—	—	3.00
❑ 878058-7	The Letter/Sadly Mistaken	1990	—	—	3.00
❑ 878554-7	Men/That's More About Love	1991	—	—	3.00

REGAN, BOB, AND LUCILLE STARR

See BOB AND LUCILLE; THE CANADIAN SWEETHEARTS.

REGINA REGINA

45s

Number	Title (A Side/B Side)	Yr	VG	VG+	NM
GIANT					
❑ 7-17360	Right Plan, Wrong Man/Border Town Road	1997	—	—	3.00
❑ 7-17426	More Than I Wanted to Know/She'll Let That Telephone Ring	1997	—	—	3.00

REID, BILL & MARY

45s

Number	Title (A Side/B Side)	Yr	VG	VG+	NM
COLUMBIA					
❑ 4-21497	Blue Ridge Waltz/In My Heart I Love You Yet	1956	5.00	10.00	20.00
❑ 4-21529	I'll Never Be Lonesome/Get Down on Your Knees and Pray	1956	5.00	10.00	20.00
❑ 4-21557	Your Sweet Loving Man/I Love Him Too	1956	5.00	10.00	20.00
❑ 4-40837	You're Stepping Out on Me/Who Knows Right from Wrong	1957	5.00	10.00	20.00

REID, MIKE

45s

Number	Title (A Side/B Side)	Yr	VG	VG+	NM
COLUMBIA					
❑ 38-73623	Walk on Faith/Turning for Home	1990	—	2.00	4.00
❑ 38-73736	Till You Were Gone/Everything to Me	1991	—	—	3.00
❑ 38-73888	As Simple As That/This Road	1991	—	—	3.00
❑ 38-74102	I'll Stop Loving You/Even a Strong Man	1991	—	—	3.00
❑ 38-74286	I Got a Life/Your Love Stays with Me	1992	—	—	3.00
❑ 38-74443	Keep On Walkin'/Working with the Right Tools	1992	—	—	3.00
❑ 38-74771	Call Home/Working with the Right Tools	1992	—	—	3.00
FRATERNITY					
❑ 3429	I'm the Singer/Looks Like I'm Lonely Again	197?	3.00	6.00	12.00

REMINGTON, HERB

45s

Number	Title (A Side/B Side)	Yr	VG	VG+	NM
COLUMBIA					
❑ 4-21347	Julida Polka/Westphalia Waltz	1955	5.00	10.00	20.00
—As "Herby Remington"					
D					
❑ 1129	Coo Coo Creek Hop/Chime Out for Love	1960	5.00	10.00	20.00
—As "Herby Remington"					
❑ 1186	Soft Shoe Slide/Fiddle Steel	1961	3.75	7.50	15.00
—As "Herby Remington"					
STARDAY					
❑ 332	Slush Pump/Station Break	1957	5.00	10.00	20.00
—As "Herby Remington"					
STONEWAY					
❑ 1102	Java/The Pookie	197?	—	3.00	6.00
❑ 1113	Sleep Walk/Elmer's Tune	197?	—	3.00	6.00
❑ 1139	The Texas Bump/Lovesick Blues	197?	—	3.00	6.00
UNITED ARTISTS					
❑ 482	Swinging Cow Bells/Pedal Softly	1962	3.75	7.50	15.00
—As "Herby Remington"					

Albums

Number	Title	Yr	VG	VG+	NM
D					
❑ 1376	Herby Remington Plays the Steel	197?	3.00	6.00	12.00
HILLTOP					
❑ JM-6020 [M]	Herby Remington Rides Again	196?	3.75	7.50	15.00
❑ JS-6020 [S]	Herby Remington Rides Again	196?	3.00	6.00	12.00
STONEWAY					
❑ 138	Pure Remington Steel	197?	3.00	6.00	12.00
UNITED ARTISTS					
❑ UAL-3167 [M]	Steel Guitar Holiday	1961	6.25	12.50	25.00
❑ UAS-6167 [S]	Steel Guitar Holiday	1961	7.50	15.00	30.00

REMINGTON, RITA

45s

Number	Title (A Side/B Side)	Yr	VG	VG+	NM
PLANTATION					
❑ 103	I've Never Been This Far Before/Wedding Cake	1973	—	2.50	5.00
❑ 111	Welcome Home/San Francisco Is a Lonely Town	1973	—	2.50	5.00
❑ 113	Days of Autumn Gold/Til the Morning Comes	1974	—	2.50	5.00
❑ 117	How Can I See/Til the Morning Comes	1974	—	2.50	5.00
❑ 124	We Tried/How Can I See	1975	—	2.50	5.00
❑ 137	Midnight Man (same on both sides)	1976	—	3.00	6.00
❑ 147	Rings on the Bar/Honky Tonk Angels and Wives	1976	—	2.50	5.00
—With James O'Gwynn					
❑ 150	Don't Love Me Half to Death/Feel My Love	1976	—	2.50	5.00
❑ 157	Every Song I Sing/My Melody of Love	1977	—	2.50	5.00
❑ 167	Don't Let the Flame Burn Out/Midnight Man	1977	—	2.50	5.00
❑ 171	To Each His Own/Rhythm of the Rain	1978	—	2.50	5.00
❑ 179	This Magic Moment/The Day Before the Night	1978	—	2.50	5.00
❑ 184	Chattanooga Choo Choo/(B-side unknown)	1979	—	2.50	5.00
❑ 190	We Were Meant to Be Lovers/This Bitter Earth	1979	—	2.50	5.00
❑ 190 [DJ]	We Were Meant to Be Lovers (same on both sides)	1979	2.00	4.00	8.00
—Promo only on green vinyl					
❑ 195	Baby Grand/Midnight Blue	1980	—	2.50	5.00
❑ 198	Lullaby Tissue Paper Company (same on both sides)	1981	—	3.00	6.00
❑ 202	Don't We Belong in Love/Easier Said Than Done	1981	—	2.50	5.00
❑ 207	The Flame/Blue Eyes Don't Make an Angel	1982	—	2.50	5.00

Albums

Number	Title	Yr	VG	VG+	NM
HILLTOP					
❑ JS-6050	The Loretta Lynn Songbook	197?	3.00	6.00	12.00
PLANTATION					
❑ 511	Country Girl Gold	197?	3.00	6.00	12.00

REMINGTONS, THE

45s

Number	Title (A Side/B Side)	Yr	VG	VG+	NM
BNA					
❑ 62063	A Long Time Ago/Takin' the Easy Way Out	1991	—	2.00	4.00
❑ 62201	I Could Love You (With My Eyes Closed)/Take a Little Love	1992	—	—	3.00
❑ 62276	Two Timin' Me/That's Easy for Me to Say	1992	—	—	3.00
❑ 62431	Nobody Loves You When You're Free/She's All I Got Going Now	1993	—	—	3.00
❑ 62527	Wall Around Her Heart/Lucky Boy	1993	—	—	3.00

RENO, DON

Also see RENO AND SMILEY; ARTHUR "GUITAR BOOGIE" SMITH.

45s

Number	Title (A Side/B Side)	Yr	VG	VG+	NM
DOT					
❑ 16693	Military Five String/Now I'm Willing to Give You My Heart	1965	2.50	5.00	10.00
EMH					
❑ 0020	Dueling Banjos/Tennessee Pride	1983	—	3.00	6.00
MONUMENT					
❑ 966	I'm Worried About Me/My Daddy's Uncle Sam (My Mommy's Miss America)	1966	3.00	6.00	12.00

RENO, DON, AND BILL HARRELL

45s

Number	Title (A Side/B Side)	Yr	VG	VG+	NM
DERBYTOWN					
❑ 101	Yellow Pages/Ex Misses Jones	197?	2.50	5.00	10.00
KING					
❑ 6143	Big Train/You Gave Me Your Love	1967	2.00	4.00	8.00
❑ 6150	I'm Just a Little Old Fashioned/Stepping Stones to Glory	1968	2.00	4.00	8.00
❑ 6180	Where Is Jones/Mister Bottle	1968	2.00	4.00	8.00
❑ 6233	Just a Phone Call Will Do/The Path That Leads Me Home	1969	2.00	4.00	8.00
❑ 6281	Welcome Home/Twelve String Time	1969	2.00	4.00	8.00
STARDAY					
❑ 952	Sweet Miss Sarah Jane/Truck Stop Boogie	1972	—	3.50	7.00

Albums

Number	Title	Yr	VG	VG+	NM
JALYN					
❑ JLP-108 [M]	Bluegrass Favorites	1964	6.25	12.50	25.00
❑ JLP-119 [M]	The Most Requested Songs	1966	6.25	12.50	25.00
KING					
❑ KSD-1029	A Variety of New Sacred Gospel Songs	1968	5.00	10.00	20.00
❑ KSD-1033	All the Way to Reno	1968	5.00	10.00	20.00
❑ KSD-1068	I'm Using My Bible for a Roadmap	1969	5.00	10.00	20.00

RENO, DON, AND BENNY MARTIN

Also see each artist's individual listings.

45s

Number	Title (A Side/B Side)	Yr	VG	VG+	NM
MONUMENT					
❑ 912	Soldier's Prayer in Viet Nam/Five by Eight	1965	3.00	6.00	12.00
❑ 931	Too Bad That You're No Good for Me/You Can't Make a Heel Toe the Line	1966	3.00	6.00	12.00

RENO, JACK

45s

Number	Title (A Side/B Side)	Yr	VG	VG+	NM
DERBYTOWN					
❑ 306	I Need You/Blue Roses	197?	—	3.00	6.00
❑ 309	Vevay Indiana/There's Nothing About You	197?	—	3.00	6.00
DOT					
❑ 17169	I Want One/Bigger Than Love	1968	—	3.00	6.00
❑ 17233	I'm a Good Man (In a Bad Frame of Mind)/Darling, Say It Again	1969	—	3.00	6.00
❑ 17293	We All Go Crazy/Albuquerque	1969	—	3.00	6.00
❑ 17340	That's the Way I See It/I've Heard That Song Before	1970	—	3.00	6.00
❑ 17412	Somebody Who Cares/Mrs. Miller Was a Pretty Woman	1972	—	3.00	6.00
JAB					
❑ 9009	Repeat After Me/You're Gonna Have to Come and Get It	1967	2.00	4.00	8.00
❑ 9015	How Sweet It Is (To Be in Love with You)/Juke Box	1968	2.00	4.00	8.00
TARGET					
❑ 113	Take My Hand/When Strangers Say Goodbye	1971	—	3.00	6.00
❑ 0133	Something Happened/Airline Girl	1971	—	3.00	6.00
❑ 0137	Hitchin' a Ride/You Are My Destiny	1971	—	3.00	6.00
❑ 0141	Heartaches by the Numbers/Airline Girl	1972	—	3.00	6.00
❑ 0150	Do You Want to Dance/I Get Too Lonely	1972	—	3.00	6.00
❑ 0154	Love Grows (Where My Rosemary Goes)/You Have Him	1972	—	3.00	6.00
UNITED ARTISTS					
❑ XW299	Beautiful Sunday/Sometimes Woman	1973	—	2.50	5.00
❑ XW374	Let the Four Winds Blow/Shackles and Chains	1973	—	2.50	5.00
❑ XW502	Jukebox/Goin' Through the Motions	1974	—	2.50	5.00

Albums

Number	Title	Yr	VG	VG+	NM
ATCO					
❑ SD 33-251	Meet Jack Reno	1968	6.25	12.50	25.00
DERBYTOWN					
❑ 101	Yellow Pages	197?	5.00	10.00	20.00
DOT					
❑ DLP 25921	I Want One	1968	6.25	12.50	25.00
❑ DLP 25946	I'm a Good Man in a Bad Frame of Mind	1969	6.25	12.50	25.00
TARGET					
❑ 1313	Hitchin' a Ride	1972	5.00	10.00	20.00

RENO, RONNIE

Also see RENO BROTHERS.

45s

EMH

Number	Title (A Side/B Side)	Yr	VG	VG+	NM
❑ 0010	Homemade Love/Hello Jesus	1982	—	3.00	6.00
❑ 0018	I Need That Shoulder After All/I Love the Way Your Loving Wakes Me Up	1983	—	3.00	6.00
❑ 0024	The Letter/Serious Love	1983	—	3.00	6.00
MCA					
❑ 40322	The Wintering Kind/September in Miami	1974	—	2.50	5.00
❑ 40494	Freedom Song/There's Been a Lot of Tears Today	1975	—	2.50	5.00
STEP ONE					
❑ 363	Midnight Perfume/Stand Up for the Music	1986	—	2.00	4.00
❑ 364	Limehouse Blues/Emotions	1986	—	2.00	4.00

Albums

MCA

Number	Title (A Side/B Side)	Yr	VG	VG+	NM
❑ 472	For the First Time	1974	3.00	6.00	12.00

RENO AND SMILEY

DON RENO and Red Smiley. Some of their records, especially the early ones, used their full names.

45s

DOT

Number	Title (A Side/B Side)	Yr	VG	VG+	NM
❑ 15588	Sawing on the Strings/Sweethearts in Heaven	1957	5.00	10.00	20.00
❑ 15649	Where Did Our Young Years Go/Cotton-Eyed Joe	1957	5.00	10.00	20.00
❑ 15700	Your Love Is Dying/Howdy Neighbor Howdy	1958	5.00	10.00	20.00
❑ 15760	One More Hill/Banjo Medley	1958	5.00	10.00	20.00
❑ 15835	One Teardrop and One Step Away/Unforgiveable You	1958	5.00	10.00	20.00
KING					
❑ 1045	Hear Jerusalem Mount/I'm Using My Bible for a Roadmap	1952	10.00	20.00	40.00
❑ 1063	There's Another Baby Waitin'/Drifting with the Tide	1952	7.50	15.00	30.00
❑ 1079	I Want to Live Like Christ/Let In the Guiding Light	1952	7.50	15.00	30.00
❑ 1104	Crazy Finger Blues/Maybe You Will Change Your Mind	1952	7.50	15.00	30.00
❑ 1128	The Lord's Last Supper/There's a Highway to Heaven	1952	7.50	15.00	30.00
❑ 1150	Tennessee Cutup Breakdown/I'm Gone Long Gone	1952	7.50	15.00	30.00
❑ 1162	Some Beautiful Day/Jesus Is Standing at My Right	1953	7.50	15.00	30.00
❑ 1199	A Pretty Wreath for Mother's Grave/A Rose on God's Shore	1953	7.50	15.00	30.00
❑ 1235	Choking the Strings/I'm the Talk of the Town	1953	7.50	15.00	30.00
❑ 1263	He's Coming Back to Earth Again/My Mother's Bible	1953	7.50	15.00	30.00
❑ 1283	Tennessee Breakdown/I Could Cry	1953	7.50	15.00	30.00
❑ 1303	I Can Hear the Angels Sing/The Mountain Church	1954	6.25	12.50	25.00
❑ 1332	Please Don't Feel Sorry for Me/Love Call Waltz	1954	6.25	12.50	25.00
❑ 1352	Tree of Life/Someone Will Love Me in Heaven	1954	6.25	12.50	25.00
❑ 1360	Emotions/Tally Ho	1954	6.25	12.50	25.00
❑ 1377	My Shepherd Is God/Since I've Used My Bible for a Roadmap	1954	6.25	12.50	25.00
❑ 1390	Dixie Breakdown/Your Tears Are Just Interest on the Loan	1954	6.25	12.50	25.00
❑ 1409	I'm Building a Mansion in Heaven/Springtime in Heaven	1954	6.25	12.50	25.00
❑ 1433	Mack's Hoedown/I'm the Biggest Liar in Town	1955	6.25	12.50	25.00
❑ 1458	Charlotte Breakdown/It's Grand to Have Someone	1955	6.25	12.50	25.00
❑ 1473	Jesus Is Waiting/How I Miss My Darling Mother	1955	6.25	12.50	25.00
❑ 1474	Green Mountain Hop/Home Sweet Home	1955	6.25	12.50	25.00
❑ 1490	Barefoot Nellie/Reno Ride	1955	6.25	12.50	25.00
❑ 1509	Double Banjo Blues/Trail of Sorrow	1955	6.25	12.50	25.00
❑ 1510	Cumberland Gap/Country Boy Rock and Roll	1955	7.50	15.00	30.00
❑ 4875	I'm So Happy/Family Altar	1956	6.25	12.50	25.00
❑ 4921	Old Home Place/Banjo Riff	1956	6.25	12.50	25.00
❑ 4944	Get Behind Me Satan/Jesus Answers My Prayers	1956	6.25	12.50	25.00
❑ 4962	Hen Scratchin' Stomp/Cruel Love	1956	6.25	12.50	25.00
❑ 4981	Remington Ride/If It Takes Me a Lifetime	1956	6.25	12.50	25.00
❑ 5002	Cumberland Rock/Country Boy Rock and Roll	1956	6.25	12.50	25.00
❑ 5024	Forgotten Men/Kneel Down	1957	5.00	10.00	20.00
❑ 5046	I Know You're Married/Beer Barrel Polka	1957	5.00	10.00	20.00
❑ 5065	I Never Get to Hold You in My Arms/When You and I...	1957	5.00	10.00	20.00
❑ 5079	No Longer a Sweetheart/Richmond Ruckus	1957	5.00	10.00	20.00
❑ 5126	Springtime in Dixie/Always Be Kind to Your Mother	1958	5.00	10.00	20.00
❑ 5169	Country Latin Special/Wall Around Your Heart	1959	5.00	10.00	20.00
❑ 5184	A Brighter Mansion Over There/Keep Me Humble	1959	5.00	10.00	20.00
❑ 5200	I Wouldn't Change You/Little Rock Getaway	1959	5.00	10.00	20.00
❑ 5221	The New Jerusalem/God's Record Book of Life	1959	5.00	10.00	20.00
❑ 5260	Pretending/Sockeye	1959	5.00	10.00	20.00
❑ 5277	Under Your Spell Again/Banjo Special	1959	5.00	10.00	20.00
❑ 5286	Jesus Will Save Your Soul/Whispering Hope	1959	5.00	10.00	20.00
❑ 5296	Lonesome Wind Blues/She Has Forgotten	1959	5.00	10.00	20.00
❑ 5320	Freight Train Boogie/Money, Marbles and Chalk	1960	3.75	7.50	15.00
❑ 5346	Mountain Rosa Lee/Eight More Miles to Louisville	1960	3.75	7.50	15.00
❑ 5369	Dark as a Dungeon/East Bound Freight Train	1960	3.75	7.50	15.00
❑ 5401	I'm Blue and I'm Lonesome/The Lord's Last Supper	1960	3.75	7.50	15.00
❑ 5432	Bringin' In the Georgia Trail/Please Remember That I Love You	1960	3.75	7.50	15.00
❑ 5469	Don't Let Your Sweet Love Die/Born to Lose	1961	3.75	7.50	15.00
❑ 5520	Love Oh Love, Please Come Home/Double Eagle	1961	3.75	7.50	15.00
❑ 5537	Jimmy Caught the Dickens (Pushing Ernest in the Tub)/Just Doing Rock and Roll	1961	3.00	6.00	12.00
—As "Chick and His Hot Rods Backed Up With Reno and Smiley"					
❑ 5554	That Moon Is No Stopping Place/Holiday Religion	1961	3.75	7.50	15.00
❑ 5583	Jesus Answers My Prayer/Higher	1961	3.75	7.50	15.00
❑ 5650	When It's Time for the Whip-Poor-Will to Sing/Washington and Lee Swing	1962	3.00	6.00	12.00
❑ 5673	The Everglades/Ten Faces	1962	3.00	6.00	12.00
❑ 5697	I'll See It Happen to You/Don't Let Temptation Turn You 'Round	1962	3.00	6.00	12.00
❑ 5728	It's a Sin/Grandfather's Clock	1963	3.00	6.00	12.00
❑ 5772	Just About Then/Lady of Spain	1963	3.00	6.00	12.00
❑ 5808	I'm Jealous of You/Only in a Dream World	1963	3.00	6.00	12.00
❑ 5814	Christmas Reunion/The True Meaning of Christmas	1963	3.00	6.00	12.00
❑ 5875	Things Are Gonna Be Different/Too Many Teardrops	1964	2.50	5.00	10.00
❑ 5905	Black and White Rag/Dill Pickles	1964	2.50	5.00	10.00
❑ 5915	There Ain't Nobody Gonna Kiss Me/I Don't Blame You	1964	2.50	5.00	10.00
❑ 5921	Mansion in the Sky/Amazing Grace	1964	2.50	5.00	10.00
❑ 5924	The Road of Broken Hearts/You're Living a Lie	1964	2.50	5.00	10.00
❑ 5935	Forever/Tragic Romance	1964	2.50	5.00	10.00
❑ 5936	A Lonely Road When You're All Alone/I Know Your Burdens	1964	2.50	5.00	10.00
❑ 5937	Chinese Breakdown/Just a Country Banjo	1964	2.50	5.00	10.00
❑ 5938	The River of Jordan/Echoes from the Burning Bush	1964	2.50	5.00	10.00
❑ 6010	Open Road/Little Mountain Road	1965	2.50	5.00	10.00
❑ 6054	Unwanted Love/Better Luck Next Time	1966	2.50	5.00	10.00
❑ 6060	I Want to Know/He's Not Ashamed of You	1966	2.50	5.00	10.00
❑ 6082	Sundown and Sorrow/The Last Mile	1967	2.00	4.00	8.00
STARDAY					
❑ 8009	I Know You're Married/Emotions	197?	—	3.00	6.00

Albums

DOT

Number	Title (A Side/B Side)	Yr	VG	VG+	NM
❑ DLP-3490 [M]	Bluegrass Hits	1963	6.25	12.50	25.00
❑ DLP-25490 [S]	Bluegrass Hits	1963	7.50	15.00	30.00
KING					
❑ 550 [M]	Sacred Songs	1958	30.00	60.00	120.00
❑ 552 [M]	Reno and Smiley Instrumentals	1958	25.00	50.00	100.00
❑ 579 [M]	Folk Ballads and Instrumentals	1958	25.00	50.00	100.00
❑ 617 [M]	Someone Will Love Me in Heaven	1959	25.00	50.00	100.00
❑ 621 [M]	Good Old Country Ballads	1959	25.00	50.00	100.00
❑ 646 [M]	A Variety of Country Songs	1959	25.00	50.00	100.00
❑ 693 [M]	Hymns Sacred and Gospel	1959	25.00	50.00	100.00
❑ 701 [M]	Country Songs	1959	25.00	50.00	100.00
❑ 718 [M]	Wanted	1961	25.00	50.00	100.00
❑ 756 [M]	Folk Songs of the Civil War	1961	25.00	50.00	100.00
❑ 776 [M]	Country Singing and Instrumentals	1962	20.00	40.00	80.00
❑ 787 [M]	Banjo Special	1962	20.00	40.00	80.00
❑ 816 [M]	Another Day with Reno and Smiley	1962	20.00	40.00	80.00
❑ 853 [M]	The 15 Greatest Hymns of All Time	1963	20.00	40.00	80.00
❑ 861 [M]	The World's Best Five String Banjo	1963	20.00	40.00	80.00
❑ 874 [M]	The True Meaning of Christmas	1963	25.00	50.00	100.00
❑ 874 [M]	The True Meaning of Christmas	1963	20.00	40.00	80.00
❑ 911 [M]	On the Road with Reno and Smiley	1964	20.00	40.00	80.00
❑ 914 [M]	A Bluegrass Tribute to Cowboy Copas	1964	20.00	40.00	80.00
❑ KSD-1044	I Know You're Married	1969	6.25	12.50	25.00
❑ KSD-1091	The Best of Reno and Smiley	1970	6.25	12.50	25.00

RENO BROTHERS

Also see RONNIE RENO.

45s

STEP ONE

Number	Title (A Side/B Side)	Yr	VG	VG+	NM
❑ 386	Midnight Lovers Express/Top of the Mountain	1988	—	2.00	4.00
❑ 387	Yonder Comes a Freight Train/Lay Your Heartache Down	1988	—	2.00	4.00
❑ 398	Love Will Never Be the Same/Southern Bound	1989	—	2.00	4.00

RESTLESS HEART

45s

RCA

Number	Title (A Side/B Side)	Yr	VG	VG+	NM
❑ 2503-7-R	Dancy's Dream/Lady Luck	1990	—	—	3.00
❑ 2663-7-R	When Somebody Loves You/A Little More Coal on the Fire	1990	—	—	3.00
❑ 2709-7-R	Long Lost Friend/I've Never Been So Sure	1990	—	—	3.00
❑ 5065-7-R	I'll Still Be Loving You/Victim of the Game	1986	—	2.00	4.00
❑ 5132-7-R	Why Does It Have to Be (Wrong or Right)/Hummingbird	1987	—	—	3.00
❑ 5280-7-R	Wheels/New York (Hold Her Tight)	1987	—	—	3.00
❑ 5280-7-R [PS]	Wheels/New York (Hold Her Tight)	1987	—	2.00	4.00
❑ 8382-7-R	Wheels/Why Does It Have to Be (Wrong or Right)	1988	—	—	3.00
—Gold Standard Series					
❑ 8386-7-R	Bluest Eyes in Texas/Eldorado	1988	—	—	3.00
❑ 8714-7-R	A Tender Lie/This Time	1988	—	—	3.00
❑ 8816-7-R	Big Dreams in a Small Town/The Ride of Your Life	1989	—	—	3.00
❑ 9034-7-R	Say What's in Your Heart/Jenny Come Back	1989	—	—	3.00
❑ 9115-7-R	Fast Movin' Train/The Truth Hurts	1989	—	—	3.00
❑ PB-13969	Let the Heartache Ride/Few and Far Between	1984	—	—	3.00
❑ PB-14086	I Want Everyone to Cry/She's Coming Home	1985	—	—	3.00

Number	Title (A Side/B Side)	Yr	VG	VG+	NM
❑ PB-14086 [PS]	I Want Everyone to Cry/She's Coming Home	1985	—	2.00	4.00
❑ PB-14190	(Back to the) Heartbreak Kid/She Danced Her Way (Into My Heart)	1985	—	—	3.00
❑ PB-14190 [PS]	(Back to the) Heartbreak Kid/She Danced Her Way (Into My Heart)	1985	—	2.00	4.00
❑ PB-14292	Til I Loved You/Shakin' the Night Away	1986	—	—	3.00
❑ PB-14376	That Rock Won't Roll/You Can't Outrun the Night	1986	—	—	3.00
❑ 62054	Familiar Pain/The Bluest Eyes in Texas	1991	—	—	3.00
❑ 62129	You Can Depend on Me/'Til I Loved You	1991	—	—	3.00
❑ 62334	When She Cries/Just in Time	1992	—	—	3.00
❑ 62419	Mending Fences/We're Gonna Be OK	1992	—	—	3.00
❑ 62468	Tell Me What You Dream/Mending Fences	1993	—	—	3.00
❑ 62510	We Got the Love/Meet Me on the Other Side	1993	—	—	3.00
❑ 62656	Big Iron Horses/Born in a High Wind	1993	—	—	3.00
❑ 62827	Baby Needs New Shoes/I'd Cross the Line	1994	—	—	3.00
❑ 62937	In This Little Town/Sweet Whiskey Lies	1994	—	—	3.00
❑ 65562	No End to This Road/For Lack of Better Words	1998	—	—	3.00
Albums					
RCA					
❑ 5648-1-R	Wheels	1986	2.00	4.00	8.00
❑ 8317-1-R	Big Dreams in a Small Town	1988	2.00	4.00	8.00
❑ 9961-1-R	Fast Movin' Train	1990	3.00	6.00	12.00
RCA VICTOR					
❑ CPL1-5369	Restless Heart	1985	2.00	4.00	8.00

REX, TIM, AND OKLAHOMA

Number	Title (A Side/B Side)	Yr	VG	VG+	NM
45s					
DEE JAY					
❑ 103	Arizona Highway/(B-side unknown)	1980	—	3.00	6.00
❑ 107	Gettin' Over You/Red Headed Lady	1980	—	3.00	6.00
❑ 111	Spread My Wings/Take Me Back to Oklahoma	1981	—	3.00	6.00

REY, ERNEST

Number	Title (A Side/B Side)	Yr	VG	VG+	NM
45s					
MCA					
❑ 40744	Don't Come to Texas/Trixie Delaney	1977	—	2.50	5.00
❑ 40895	Ain't This a Shame Sweet Marie/True Love Needs to Keep in Touch	1978	—	2.00	4.00
❑ 40991	Mama's Sugar/Don't Feel Like the Lone Ranger	1979	—	2.00	4.00

REYNOLDS, ALLEN

Number	Title (A Side/B Side)	Yr	VG	VG+	NM
45s					
CAMEO					
❑ 306	Julie Never Meant a Thing/You Beautiful Child	1964	2.50	5.00	10.00
CERTRON					
❑ 10016	Didn't He Shine/Ring Around the World	1970	—	3.50	7.00
HALLWAY					
❑ 1904	Just a Friend/She Really Lied	1962	3.00	6.00	12.00
JMI					
❑ 13	Back to the Country/If She Just Helps Me (Get Over You)	1973	—	3.00	6.00
❑ 44	Mississippi Memory/Gone Girl	1974	—	3.00	6.00
RCA VICTOR					
❑ 47-7885	Through the Eyes of Love/What a Pretty Little Girl	1961	3.00	6.00	12.00
❑ 47-8190	Here Comes Raggedy Ann/She Really Lied	1963	2.50	5.00	10.00
TRIPLE I					
❑ 496	Wrong Road Again/Ready for the Times to Get Better	1978	2.00	4.00	8.00

REYNOLDS, BURT

Number	Title (A Side/B Side)	Yr	VG	VG+	NM
45s					
MCA					
❑ 51004	Let's Do Something Cheap and Superficial/Rockin' Lone Star Style	1980	—	2.50	5.00
—B-side by the Bandit Band					
❑ 51004 [PS]	Let's Do Something Cheap and Superficial/Rockin' Lone Star Style	1980	—	3.00	6.00
MERCURY					
❑ 73441	Till I Get It Right/Room for a Boy Never Used	1973	—	3.00	6.00
❑ 73454	I Like Having You Around/She's Taken a Gentle Lover	1974	—	3.00	6.00
Albums					
MERCURY					
❑ MK-4 [DJ]	A Burt Reynolds Radio Special	1973	6.25	12.50	25.00
❑ SRM-1-693	Ask Me What I Am	1973	3.75	7.50	15.00

REYNOLDS, LAWRENCE

Number	Title (A Side/B Side)	Yr	VG	VG+	NM
45s					
COLUMBIA					
❑ 4-45722	Love Can Be a Drag (Sometimes)/Mr. Magician	1972	—	3.50	7.00
WARNER BROS.					
❑ 7322	Jesus Is a Soul Man/I Know a Good Girl (When I Hold One)	1969	2.00	4.00	8.00
❑ 7374	It Was Love/Messing with My Mind	1970	2.00	4.00	8.00
❑ 7384	Hey Mr. Preacher/Life Turned Her That Way	1970	2.00	4.00	8.00
❑ 7421	Does It Show/Doing His Thing	1970	2.00	4.00	8.00
Albums					
WARNER BROS.					
❑ WS 1825	Jesus Is a Soul Man	1969	5.00	10.00	20.00

RHOADS, RANDY

Number	Title (A Side/B Side)	Yr	VG	VG+	NM
45s					
BLUE RIDGE					
❑ 001	Honey Do Weekend/(B-side unknown)	1989	—	3.00	6.00

RICE, BILL

Also see LOIS JOHNSON.

Number	Title (A Side/B Side)	Yr	VG	VG+	NM
45s					
CAPITOL					
❑ 2724	For Life Goes On/Just Plain Lonely	1970	—	3.50	7.00
❑ 2904	Please Remember Me/What a Difference Your Love Makes	1970	—	3.50	7.00
❑ 3049	Travelin' Minstrel Man/Special	1971	—	3.50	7.00
❑ 3156	Honky-Tonk Stardust Cowboy/T.G.I.F. (Thank Goodness It's Forever)	1971	—	3.50	7.00
EPIC					
❑ 5-10833	A Girl Like Her Is Hard to Find/Here's to You, Darlin'	1972	—	3.00	6.00
❑ 5-10877	Something to Call Mine/She's Everything to Me	1972	—	3.00	6.00
❑ 5-10918	Man of Means/When I Want to Love a Lady	1972	—	3.00	6.00
POLYDOR					
❑ 14453	Beggars and Choosers/That's the Way It Is (With You and Me)	1978	—	2.50	5.00
❑ 14479	I Couldn't Help Myself/I'm Just Gettin' By	1978	—	2.50	5.00

RICE, BOBBY G.

Also see WAYNE KEMP AND BOBBY G. RICE.

Number	Title (A Side/B Side)	Yr	VG	VG+	NM
45s					
CHARTA					
❑ 161	I'm Movin' Up to You/Temperature's Risin'	1981	—	2.50	5.00
❑ 166	Pardon My French/Some Lovin' Time with You	1981	—	2.50	5.00
❑ 171	I Ain't Been Runnin' with Other Women/Pullin' Together	1982	—	2.50	5.00
DOOR KNOB					
❑ 213	I Can't Stop/Back to Love	1984	—	2.50	5.00
❑ 218	I Broke Down and Cried/I Can't Stop	1984	—	2.50	5.00
❑ 223	Easy Lady/You're Still a Part of Me	1984	—	2.50	5.00
❑ 228	State of the Union/Back to Love	1985	—	2.50	5.00
❑ 230	New Tradition/Those Words I Never Heard	1985	—	2.50	5.00
❑ 234	I'm Lookin' for Someone Who's Lookin' for Love/(B-side unknown)	1985	—	2.50	5.00
❑ 251	You've Taken Over My Heart/I'm Lookin' for Someone Lookin' for Love	1986	—	2.50	5.00
❑ 263	Makin' Love in Macon/You've Taken Over My Heart	1987	—	2.50	5.00
❑ 274	Rachel's Room/(B-side unknown)	1987	—	2.50	5.00
❑ 285	You Lay So Easy on My Mind/(B-side unknown)	1987	—	2.50	5.00
❑ 295	A Night of Love Forgotten/(B-side unknown)	1988	—	2.50	5.00
❑ 307	Clean Livin' Folk/(B-side unknown)	1988	—	2.50	5.00
—With Perry LaPointe					
❑ 312	Fire in the Hole/(B-side unknown)	1988	—	2.50	5.00
❑ 344	Until We Get It Right/(B-side unknown)	1990	—	2.50	5.00
❑ 355	For Cryin' Out Loud/(B-side unknown)	1990	—	2.50	5.00
GRT					
❑ 001	She Sure Laid the Lovelies on Me/Crystal Chandeliers	1974	—	3.00	6.00
❑ 009	Make It Feel Like Love Again/Darlin' Forever	1974	—	3.00	6.00
❑ 014	Write Me a Letter/Sweet Satisfying Feeling	1974	—	3.00	6.00
❑ 021	Freda Comes, Freda Goes/Love Me Tonight	1975	—	3.00	6.00
❑ 028	I May Never Be Your Lover (But I'll Always Be Your Friend)/It Was So Good While It Lasted	1975	—	3.00	6.00
❑ 036	Pick Me Up on Your Way Down/Right or Wrong	1975	—	3.00	6.00
❑ 038	Happy Anniversary/Old Rock and Roller (Will It Happen Again)	1976	—	3.00	6.00
❑ 061	You Are My Special Angel/I Want to Feel It	1976	—	3.00	6.00
❑ 084	Woman Stealer/Burning Bridges	1976	—	3.00	6.00
❑ 112	Somewhere Over the Rainbow/You Make It So Easy	1977	—	3.00	6.00
❑ 120	Just One Kiss Magdalena/The Love She Offered You	1977	—	3.00	6.00
METROMEDIA					
❑ BMBO-0075	The Whole World's Making Love Again Tonight/Baby, Lovin' You	1973	—	3.50	7.00
❑ BMBO-0168	My Christmas Wish for You/Holidays Are Happy Days	1973	2.00	4.00	8.00
❑ 68-0107	You Give Me You/Bring Your Love to Me Softly	1973	—	3.50	7.00
METROMEDIA COUNTRY					
❑ 902	You Lay So Easy on My Mind/There Ain't No Way Babe	1972	—	3.50	7.00
REPUBLIC					
❑ 023	Whisper It to Me/Sweet Cherry Lips	1978	—	2.50	5.00
❑ 031	The Softest Touch in Town/Passion	1978	—	2.50	5.00
❑ 041	Oh Baby Mine (I Get So Lonely)/Rainbows Are Back in Style	1979	—	2.50	5.00
ROYAL AMERICAN					
❑ 6	Sugar Shack/Sweet Lil' Ol' You	1970	2.00	4.00	8.00
❑ 18	Hey Baby/Hey, Hey, Santa Fe	1970	2.00	4.00	8.00
❑ 27	Lover Please/You're So Easy to Love	1970	2.00	4.00	8.00
❑ 32	Mountain of Love/Five O'Clock World	1971	2.00	4.00	8.00
❑ 48	Suspicion/The Birds and the Bees	1971	2.00	4.00	8.00
❑ 62	Just a Dream/A Hundred Pounds of Clay	1972	2.00	4.00	8.00
❑ 80	Guess Who/You're So Easy to Love	1972	2.00	4.00	8.00
❑ 120	The Love She Offered/Just One Kiss	1973	2.00	4.00	8.00

Number	Title (A Side/B Side)	Yr	VG	VG+	NM
SUNBIRD					
❑ 108	The Man Who Takes You Home/Sweet Molly Brown	1980	—	2.50	5.00
❑ 7558	Livin' Together (Lovin' Apart)/It Was So Good While It Lasted	1981	—	2.50	5.00
SUNSET					
❑ 102	You Make It So Easy/You Lay So Easy on My Mind	1979	—	2.50	5.00
Albums					
AUDIOGRAPH					
❑ 6000	Bobby G. Rice	1982	2.50	5.00	10.00
❑ 7772	Bobby's Back	1982	2.50	5.00	10.00
DOOR KNOB					
❑ 1008	New Beginning	198?	3.00	6.00	12.00
GRT					
❑ 8001	She Sure Laid the Lonelies on Me	1974	3.00	6.00	12.00
❑ 8003	Write Me a Letter	1975	3.00	6.00	12.00
❑ 8011	Instant Rice — The Best of Bobby G.	1976	3.00	6.00	12.00
❑ 8016	With Love from Bobby G. Rice	1977	3.00	6.00	12.00
METROMEDIA					
❑ BML1-0186	You Lay So Easy on My Mind	1973	5.00	10.00	20.00
ROYAL AMERICAN					
❑ 1003	Hit After Hit	1972	5.00	10.00	20.00
SUNBIRD					
❑ SN-50106	Greatest Hits	1980	3.00	6.00	12.00

RICH, CHARLIE

Number	Title (A Side/B Side)	Yr	VG	VG+	NM
45s					
ELEKTRA					
❑ 45553	I'll Wake You Up When I Get Home/Salty Dog Blues	1978	—	2.00	4.00
❑ 47047	A Man Just Doesn't Know What a Woman Goes Through/Marie	1980	—	2.00	4.00
❑ 47104	Are We Dreamin' the Same Dream/Angelina	1981	—	2.00	4.00
EPIC					
❑ 02058	You Made It Beautiful/How Good It Used to Be	1981	—	2.00	4.00
❑ 03165	Try a Little Tenderness/As Time Goes By	1982	—	2.00	4.00
❑ 10287	Set Me Free/I'll Just Go Away	1968	—	3.00	6.00
❑ 10358	Raggedy Ann/Nothing in the World	1968	—	3.00	6.00
❑ 10492	Life's Little Ups and Downs/It Takes Time	1969	—	3.00	6.00
❑ 10585	July 12, 1939/I'm Flying to Nashville Tonight	1970	—	3.00	6.00
❑ 10662	Nice 'N' Easy/I Can't Even Drink It Away	1970	—	3.00	6.00
❑ 10745	A Woman Left Lonely/Have a Heart	1971	—	2.50	5.00
❑ 10809	A Part of Your Life/A Sunday Kind of Woman	1971	—	2.50	5.00
❑ 10867	I Take It On Home/Peace on You	1972	—	2.50	5.00
❑ 10950	Behind Closed Doors/A Sunday Kind of Woman	1973	—	2.50	5.00
—Originals have yellow labels					
❑ 10950	Behind Closed Doors/A Sunday Kind of Woman	1973	—	2.00	4.00
—Repressings have orange labels					
❑ 11040	The Most Beautiful Girl/I Feel Like Going Home	1973	—	2.00	4.00
❑ 11091	A Very Special Love Song/I Can't Even Drink It Away	1974	—	2.00	4.00
❑ 20006	I Love My Friend/Why Oh Why	1974	—	2.00	4.00
❑ 50064	My Elusive Dreams/Whatever Happened	1975	—	2.00	4.00
❑ 50103	Every Time You Touch Me (I Get High)/Pass On By	1975	—	2.00	4.00
❑ 50142	All Over Me/You & I	1975	—	2.00	4.00
❑ 50182	Since I Fell for You/She	1975	—	2.00	4.00
❑ 50222	America the Beautiful (1976)/Down By the Riverside	1976	—	2.00	4.00
❑ 50268	Road Song/The Grass Is Always Greener	1976	—	2.00	4.00
❑ 50328	Easy Look/My Lady	1976	—	2.00	4.00
❑ 50392	Rollin' with the Flow/To Sing a Love Song	1977	—	2.00	4.00
❑ 50562	Beautiful Woman/Everybody Wrote That Song for Me	1978	—	2.00	4.00
❑ 50616	On My Knees/Mellow Melody	1978	—	2.00	4.00
❑ 50701	Spanish Eyes/I Do My Swingin' at Home	1979	—	2.00	4.00
❑ 50869	Even a Fool Would Let Go/Pretty People	1980	—	2.00	4.00
GROOVE					
❑ 58-0020	The Grass Is Always Greener/She Loved Everybody But Me	1963	3.75	7.50	15.00
❑ 58-0020 [PS]	The Grass Is Always Greener/She Loved Everybody But Me	1963	7.50	15.00	30.00
❑ 58-0025	Big Boss Man/Let Me Go My Merry Way	1963	3.75	7.50	15.00
❑ 58-0032	Lady Love/Why, Oh Why	1964	3.75	7.50	15.00
❑ 58-0035	The Ways of a Woman in Love/My Mountain Dew	1964	3.75	7.50	15.00
❑ 58-0041	Nice 'N' Easy/Turn Around and Face Me	1964	3.75	7.50	15.00
HI					
❑ 2116	Love Is After Me/Pass On By	1966	2.50	5.00	10.00
❑ 2123	My Heart Would Know/Nobody's Lonesome for Me	1967	2.50	5.00	10.00
❑ 2134	Hurry Up Freight Train/Only Me	1967	2.50	5.00	10.00
MERCURY					
❑ 73466	I Washed My Hands in Muddy Water/No Home	1974	—	2.50	5.00
❑ 73498	A Field of Yellow Daisies/Party Girl	1974	—	2.50	5.00
❑ 73646	Something Just Came Over Me/Best Years	1974	—	2.50	5.00
PHILLIPS INT'L.					
❑ 3532	Whirlwind/Philadelphia Baby	1959	6.25	12.50	25.00
❑ 3542	Rebound/Big Man	1959	6.25	12.50	25.00
❑ 3552	Lonely Weekends/Everything I Do Is Wrong	1960	6.25	12.50	25.00
❑ 3560	School Days/Gonna Be Waiting	1960	6.25	12.50	25.00
❑ 3562	On My Knees/Stay	1960	6.25	12.50	25.00
❑ 3566	Who Will the Next Fool Be/Caught in the Middle	1961	6.25	12.50	25.00
❑ 3572	Just a Little Sweet/It's Too Late	1962	5.00	10.00	20.00
❑ 3576	Easy Money/Midnight Blues	1962	5.00	10.00	20.00
❑ 3582	Sittin' and Thinkin'/Finally Found Out	1962	5.00	10.00	20.00
❑ 3584	There's Another Place I Can't Go/I Need Your Love	1963	5.00	10.00	20.00
RCA					
❑ PB-10859	My Mountain Dew/Nice 'N Easy	1976	—	2.00	4.00
❑ PB-10966	Nice 'N Easy/It's All Over Now	1977	—	2.00	4.00
RCA VICTOR					
❑ APBO-0195	There Won't Be Anymore/It's All Over Now	1973	—	2.50	5.00
❑ APBO-0260	I Don't See Me in Your Eyes Anymore/No Room to Dance	1974	—	2.00	4.00
❑ PB-10062	She Called Me Baby/$10 and a Clean White Shirt	1974	—	2.00	4.00
❑ GB-10159	There Won't Be Anymore/Tomorrow Night	1975	—	—	3.00
—Gold Standard Series					
❑ PB-10256	It's All Over Now/Big Jack	1975	—	2.00	4.00
❑ PB-10458	Not Everybody Knows/I've Got You Under My Skin	1975	—	2.00	4.00
❑ GB-10512	She Called Me Baby/$10 And a Clean White Shirt	1975	—	—	3.00
—Gold Standard Series					
❑ 47-8468	It's All Over Now/Too Many Teardrops	1964	3.75	7.50	15.00
❑ 47-8536	There Won't Be Anymore/Gentleman Jim	1965	5.00	10.00	20.00
❑ 47-8817	Nice 'N' Easy/Ol' Man River	1966	3.00	6.00	12.00
❑ 74-0983	Tomorrow Night/The Ways of a Woman in Love	1973	—	2.00	4.00
SMASH					
❑ 1993	Mohair Sam/I Washed My Hands in Muddy Water	1965	5.00	10.00	20.00
❑ 2012	Dance of Love/I Can't Go On	1965	3.75	7.50	15.00
❑ 2022	Hawg Jaw/Something Just Came Over Me	1966	3.75	7.50	15.00
❑ 2038	No Home/Tears a-Go-Go	1966	3.75	7.50	15.00
❑ 2060	That's the Way/When My Baby Comes Home	1966	3.75	7.50	15.00
SUN					
❑ 1110	Who Will the Next Fool Be/Stay	1970	—	2.50	5.00
❑ 1151	The Breakup/Be-Bop-a-Lula	1980	—	2.00	4.00
—B-side by Jerry Lee Lewis; both sides are duets with Orion					
UNITED ARTISTS					
❑ XW1193	Puttin' In Overtime at Home/Ghost of Another Man	1978	—	2.00	4.00
❑ XW1223	I Still Believe in Love/Wishful Thinking	1978	—	2.00	4.00
❑ XW1269	The Fool Strikes Again/I Loved You All the Way	1978	—	2.00	4.00
❑ XW1280	I Lost My Head/She Knows Just How to Touch Me	1979	—	2.00	4.00
❑ XW1307	Life Goes On/Standing Tall	1979	—	2.00	4.00
❑ 1325	You're Gonna Love Yourself in the Morning/Top of the Stairs	1979	—	2.00	4.00
❑ 1340	I'd Build a Bridge/All You Ever Have to Do Is Touch Me	1980	—	2.00	4.00
Albums					
BUCKBOARD					
❑ 1019	The Entertainer	197?	2.50	5.00	10.00
ELEKTRA					
❑ 6E-301	Once a Drifter	1981	2.50	5.00	10.00
EPIC					
❑ AS 50 [DJ]	Charlie Rich	1973	7.50	15.00	30.00
—Promo-only compilation					
❑ AS 139 [DJ]	Everything You Always Wanted to Hear by Charlie Rich But Were Afraid to Ask For	1976	6.25	12.50	25.00
—Promo-only sampler					
❑ BN 26376	Set Me Free	1968	5.00	10.00	20.00
❑ BN 26516	The Fabulous Charlie Rich	1970	5.00	10.00	20.00
❑ E 30214	Boss Man	1970	5.00	10.00	20.00
❑ CQ 31933 [Q]	The Best of Charlie Rich	1972	5.00	10.00	20.00
❑ KE 31933	The Best of Charlie Rich	1972	3.75	7.50	15.00
—Yellow label					
❑ KE 31933	The Best of Charlie Rich	1973	3.00	6.00	12.00
—Orange label					
❑ CQ 32247 [Q]	Behind Closed Doors	1973	5.00	10.00	20.00
❑ KE 32247	Behind Closed Doors	1973	3.00	6.00	12.00
❑ PE 32247	Behind Closed Doors	197?	2.00	4.00	8.00
—Reissue					
❑ PE 32531	Very Special Love Songs	1974	3.00	6.00	12.00
❑ PEQ 32531 [Q]	Very Special Love Songs	1974	5.00	10.00	20.00
❑ PE 33250	The Silver Fox	1974	3.00	6.00	12.00
❑ PEQ 33250 [Q]	The Silver Fox	1974	5.00	10.00	20.00
❑ PE 33455	Every Time You Touch Me (I Get High)	1975	3.00	6.00	12.00
❑ PEQ 33455 [Q]	Every Time You Touch Me (I Get High)	1975	5.00	10.00	20.00
❑ PE 33545	Silver Linings	1976	2.50	5.00	10.00
❑ PE 34240	Greatest Hits	1976	2.50	5.00	10.00
—Without bar code on cover					
❑ PE 34240	Greatest Hits	1979	2.00	4.00	8.00
—With bar code on cover					
❑ PE 34444	Take Me	1977	2.50	5.00	10.00
❑ PE 34444	Take Me	1977	2.50	5.00	10.00
❑ PE 34891	Rollin' with the Flow	1977	2.50	5.00	10.00
❑ JE 35394	Classic Rich, Vol. 1	1978	2.50	5.00	10.00
❑ JE 35624	Classic Rich, Vol. 2	1978	2.50	5.00	10.00
GROOVE					
❑ GM-1000 [M]	Charlie Rich	1964	37.50	75.00	150.00
❑ GS-1000 [S]	Charlie Rich	1964	75.00	150.00	300.00
HARMONY					
❑ KH 32166	I Do My Swingin' at Home	1973	3.00	6.00	12.00
HI					
❑ 8006	I'm So Lonesome I Could Cry	197?	3.00	6.00	12.00
❑ 8006	I'm So Lonesome I Could Cry	198?	2.00	4.00	8.00
—Reissue of Hi 32084					
❑ HL 12037 [M]	Charlie Rich Sings Country and Western	1967	7.50	15.00	30.00
❑ SHL 32037 [S]	Charlie Rich Sings Country and Western	1967	5.00	10.00	20.00

Number	Title (A Side/B Side)	Yr	VG	VG+	NM
❑ SHL 32084	Charlie Rich Sings the Songs of Hank Williams & Others	1974	3.00	6.00	12.00
—Reissue of 32037					
HILLTOP					
❑ 6139	Lonely Weekends	197?	2.50	5.00	10.00
❑ 6149	Songs for Beautiful Girls	1974	2.50	5.00	10.00
❑ 6160	Entertainer of the Year	197?	2.50	5.00	10.00
MERCURY					
❑ SRM-2-7505 [(2)]	Fully Realized	1974	3.75	7.50	15.00
PHILLIPS INTERNATIONAL					
❑ PLP-1970 [M]	Lonely Weekends	1960	150.00	300.00	600.00
PICKWICK					
❑ ACL-7001	Too Many Teardrops	1975	2.50	5.00	10.00
POWER PAK					
❑ PO-241	There Won't Be Anymore	197?	2.50	5.00	10.00
❑ PO-245	Arkansas Traveler	197?	2.50	5.00	10.00
❑ PO-252	The Silver Fox	197?	2.50	5.00	10.00
QUICKSILVER					
❑ QS-1005	Midnight Blue	198?	3.00	6.00	12.00
RCA CAMDEN					
❑ CAS-2417	The Versatile and Talented Charlie Rich	1970	2.50	5.00	10.00
RCA VICTOR					
❑ APL1-0258	Tomorrow Night	1973	3.00	6.00	12.00
❑ APL1-0433	There Won't Be Anymore	1974	3.00	6.00	12.00
❑ APL1-0686	She Called Me Baby	1974	3.00	6.00	12.00
❑ APL1-0857	Greatest Hits	1975	3.00	6.00	12.00
❑ APL1-1242	Now Everybody Knows	1975	3.00	6.00	12.00
❑ ANL1-1542	Tomorrow Night	1976	2.50	5.00	10.00
—Reissue					
❑ APL1-2260	Big Boss Man/My Mountain Dew	1977	3.00	6.00	12.00
❑ ANL1-2424	She Called Me Baby	1977	2.50	5.00	10.00
—Reissue of APL1-0686					
❑ LPM-3352 [M]	That's Rich	1965	10.00	20.00	40.00
❑ LSP-3352 [S]	That's Rich	1965	12.50	25.00	50.00
❑ LPM-3537 [M]	Big Boss Man	1966	10.00	20.00	40.00
❑ LSP-3557 [S]	Big Boss Man	1966	12.50	25.00	50.00
❑ AHL1-5496	Collector's Series	1985	2.00	4.00	8.00
SMASH					
❑ MGS-27070 [M]	The Many New Sides of Charlie Rich	1965	7.50	15.00	30.00
❑ MGS-27078 [M]	The Best Years	1966	7.50	15.00	30.00
❑ SRS-67070 [S]	The Many New Sides of Charlie Rich	1965	10.00	20.00	40.00
❑ SRS-67070 [S]	The Best Years	1966	10.00	20.00	40.00
SUN					
❑ LP 110	Lonely Weekend	1970	3.00	6.00	12.00
❑ LP 123	A Time for Tears	1971	3.00	6.00	12.00
❑ LP 132	The Early Years	1974	3.00	6.00	12.00
❑ LP 133	The Memphis Sound of Charlie Rich	1974	3.00	6.00	12.00
❑ LP 134	Golden Treasures	1974	3.00	6.00	12.00
❑ LP 135	Sun's Best of Charlie Rich	1974	3.00	6.00	12.00
❑ 1003	20 Golden Hits	1979	2.50	5.00	10.00
—Gold vinyl					
❑ 1007	The Original Charlie Rich	1979	2.50	5.00	10.00
SUNNYVALE					
❑ 9330	The Sun Story Vol. 2	1977	2.50	5.00	10.00
TIME-LIFE					
❑ STW 115	Country Music	1981	3.00	6.00	12.00
TRIP					
❑ TLP-8502 [(2)]	The Best of Charlie Rich	1974	3.00	6.00	12.00
UNITED ARTISTS					
❑ UA-LA876-H	I Still Believe in Love	1978	3.00	6.00	12.00
❑ UA-H	The Fool Strikes Again	1978	2.50	5.00	10.00
WING					
❑ SRW-16375	A Lonely Weekend	1969	3.00	6.00	12.00

RICH, DAVE

45s

Number	Title (A Side/B Side)	Yr	VG	VG+	NM
RCA VICTOR					
❑ 47-6327	I Forgot/I Think I'm Gonna Die	1955	7.50	15.00	30.00
❑ 47-6435	I'm Glad/Darling, I'm Lonesome	1956	7.50	15.00	30.00
❑ 47-6595	Your Pretty Blue Eyes/Ain't It Fine	1956	10.00	20.00	40.00
❑ 47-6687	I'm Sorry, Goodbye/I Love 'Em All	1956	7.50	15.00	30.00
❑ 47-6753	Lonely Street/Didn't Work Out, Did It	1956	7.50	15.00	30.00
❑ 47-6824	Tuggin' on My Heart Strings/Our Last Night Together	1957	7.50	15.00	30.00
❑ 47-6926	The Key to My Heart/Red Sweater	1957	7.50	15.00	30.00
❑ 47-7045	Chicken House/I've Learned	1957	7.50	15.00	30.00
❑ 47-7141	School Blues/I've Thought It Over	1958	7.50	15.00	30.00
❑ 47-7247	City Lights/Burn On Love Fire	1958	7.50	15.00	30.00
❑ 47-7334	Rosie Let's Get Cozy/Sunshine in My Heart	1958	7.50	15.00	30.00
REPUBLIC					
❑ 390	Because You're Gone/(B-side unknown)	1977	—	2.50	5.00
STOP					
❑ 122	When I've Learned/I Don't Need Nobody Else	196?	2.00	4.00	8.00
❑ 132	I Never Gave Up/On the Battlefield	196?	2.00	4.00	8.00
❑ 171	I Believe/Peace On Earth Begins Today	196?	2.00	4.00	8.00

Albums

Number	Title (A Side/B Side)	Yr	VG	VG+	NM
STOP					
❑ 10007	Soul Brother	196?	7.50	15.00	30.00

RICH, DEBBIE

45s

Number	Title (A Side/B Side)	Yr	VG	VG+	NM
DOOR KNOB					
❑ 311	I Ain't Gonna Take This Layin' Down/(B-side unknown)	1988	—	2.50	5.00
❑ 318	Don't Be Surprised If You Get It/(B-side unknown)	1989	—	2.50	5.00
❑ 321	I've Had Enough of You/(B-side unknown)	1989	—	2.50	5.00
❑ 327	Do It Again (I Think I Saw Diamonds)/(B-side unknown)	1989	—	2.50	5.00

RICH, DON

Also see THE BUCKAROOS. (Singles credited to "Don Rich and the Buckaroos" are listed there.)

Albums

Number	Title (A Side/B Side)	Yr	VG	VG+	NM
CAPITOL					
❑ ST-643	That Fiddlin' Man	1970	6.25	12.50	25.00

RICHARDS, DICK

45s

Number	Title (A Side/B Side)	Yr	VG	VG+	NM
COLUMBIA					
❑ 4-21532	Just Walkin' in the Rain/Born to Lose	1956	5.00	10.00	20.00
❑ 4-40957	Blue Jean Baby/We've Got a Right to Love	1957	10.00	20.00	40.00
❑ 4-41035	I Love You So Much It Hurts/Not Until I Pray for You	1957	6.25	12.50	25.00

RICHARDS, EARL

45s

Number	Title (A Side/B Side)	Yr	VG	VG+	NM
ACE OF HEARTS					
❑ 0461	Margie, Who's Watching the Baby/My Land	1972	—	3.00	6.00
❑ 0465	Things Are Kinda Slow at the House/Do My Playing at Home	1973	—	3.00	6.00
❑ 0470	The Sun Is Shining (On Everybody But Me)/Mother Nature's Daughter	1973	—	3.00	6.00
❑ 0477	Walkin' in Teardrops/How Can I Tell Her	1973	—	3.00	6.00
❑ 0501	Lay Around/(B-side unknown)	1974	—	3.00	6.00
❑ 7502	My Babe/Mother Nature's Daughter	1975	—	3.00	6.00
UNITED ARTISTS					
❑ 50462	Maggie/Shake 'Em Up and Let 'Em Roll	1968	2.00	4.00	8.00
❑ 50561	The House of Blue Lights/Hard Times a Comin'	1969	—	3.50	7.00
❑ 50619	Corrine, Corrina/Climbing a Mountain	1969	—	3.50	7.00
❑ 50704	Sunshine/San Francisco's Mabel Joy	1970	—	3.50	7.00
❑ 50752	Baby, I Need Your Lovin'/Our House on Paper	1971	—	3.50	7.00
❑ 50803	You Drove Her Right Into My Arms/You Were Crying	1971	—	3.50	7.00
❑ 50873	Let It Be/Down Along the Cove	1972	—	3.50	7.00

RICHARDS, SUE

Also see STAN HITCHCOCK.

45s

Number	Title (A Side/B Side)	Yr	VG	VG+	NM
ABC DOT					
❑ 17529	You Don't Have to Change the World/Make Me Believe It	1974	—	3.00	6.00
❑ 17547	Homemade Love/The Painter's Brush	1975	—	2.50	5.00
❑ 17572	Tower of Strength/Let Me Be Your Baby Tonight	1975	—	2.50	5.00
❑ 17600	Sweet Sensuous Feelings/He Plays for Me	1975	—	2.50	5.00
❑ 17622	Please Tell Him That I Said Hello/Love Is a Rose	1976	—	2.50	5.00
❑ 17645	I'll Never See Him Again/I've Got a Lot on My Mind	1976	—	2.50	5.00
❑ 17665	Love's Healing Touch/My Heart Won't Cry Anymore	1976	—	2.50	5.00
DOT					
❑ 17481	I Just Had You on My Mind/Wake Up Morning	1973	—	3.00	6.00
❑ 17508	Ease Me to the Ground/Make Me Believe It	1974	—	3.00	6.00
EPIC					
❑ 5-10411	That's Loneliness/Too Many Daddies	1968	2.00	4.00	8.00
❑ 5-10487	Don't Let a Little Thing Like That Stand in Your Way/First Lady	1969	2.00	4.00	8.00
❑ 5-10589	Givin' Out of Givin' In/I Let Him Know	1970	2.00	4.00	8.00
❑ 5-10657	Everything But a Dad/Hands Off	1970	2.00	4.00	8.00
❑ 5-10709	Feel Free to Go/No Special Occasion	1971	—	3.50	7.00
❑ 5-10764	I'll Leave Your Bags (At the Honky Tonk)/Simple Words	1971	—	3.50	7.00
❑ 8-50465	Someone Loves Him/Livin' in a House Full of Love	1977	—	2.50	5.00
❑ 8-50546	Hey, What Do You Say (We Fall in Love)/I'll Be Wearing Blue	1978	—	2.50	5.00

Albums

Number	Title (A Side/B Side)	Yr	VG	VG+	NM
ABC DOT					
❑ DOSD-2012	A Girl Named Sue	1974	3.00	6.00	12.00
❑ DOSD-2052	Sweet Sensuous Feelings	1976	3.00	6.00	12.00

RICHEY, KIM

45s

Number	Title (A Side/B Side)	Yr	VG	VG+	NM
MERCURY					
❑ 574184-7	I Know/It's Alright	1997	—	—	3.00
❑ 852300-7	Those Words We Said/Let the Sun Fall Down	1995	—	—	3.00
❑ 856832-7	Just My Luck/Just Like the Moon	1995	—	—	3.00

RICHEY, PAUL

45s

Number	Title (A Side/B Side)	Yr	VG	VG+	NM
CON BRIO					
❑ 138	Happy Birthday Honey/Thanks for Taking Me Along	1978	—	3.00	6.00

RICHIE, LIONEL

The R&B-pop singer, formerly of the Commodores, not only produced some of the biggest hits for KENNY ROGERS, but he also had two country hits of his own. The B-side of the second one, which features ALABAMA, made the top 10. Also, one of his albums made the country LP chart.

45s

MOTOWN

Number	Title (A Side/B Side)	Yr	VG	VG+	NM
❑ 1746	Stuck on You/Round and Round	1984	—	2.00	4.00
❑ 1746 [PS]	Stuck on You/Round and Round	1984	—	2.00	4.00
❑ 1873	Ballerina Girl/Deep River Woman	1986	—	—	3.00
—B-side with Alabama					
❑ 1873 [PS]	Ballerina Girl/Deep River Woman	1986	—	2.00	4.00

Albums

MOTOWN

Number	Title (A Side/B Side)	Yr	VG	VG+	NM
❑ 6059ML	Can't Slow Down	1983	2.00	4.00	8.00

RICKS, STEVE

45s

SOUTHWIND

Number	Title (A Side/B Side)	Yr	VG	VG+	NM
❑ 8205	Private Clown/(B-side unknown)	1986	—	3.50	7.00

RICOCHET

45s

COLUMBIA

Number	Title (A Side/B Side)	Yr	VG	VG+	NM
❑ 38-78088	What Do I Know/A Little Bit of Money (Is a Dangerous Thing)	1996	—	2.00	4.00
❑ 38-78097	Daddy's Money/I Wasn't Ready for You	1996	—	2.00	4.00
❑ 38-78098	Love Is Stronger Than Pride/I Wasn't Ready for You	1996	—	2.00	4.00
❑ 38-78688	Blink of an Eye/Don't Forget to Feed the Jukebox (While I'm Gone)	1997	—	2.00	4.00

RIDDLE, ALLAN

45s

PLAID

Number	Title (A Side/B Side)	Yr	VG	VG+	NM
❑ 1001	The Moon Is Crying/(B-side unknown)	1960	6.25	12.50	25.00

RIDE THE RIVER

45s

ADVANTAGE

Number	Title (A Side/B Side)	Yr	VG	VG+	NM
❑ 165	You Left Her Lovin' You/Soul of a Woman	1987	—	2.50	5.00
❑ 169	The First Cut Is the Deepest/(B-side unknown)	1987	—	2.50	5.00
❑ 182	It's Such a Heartache/(B-side unknown)	1987	—	2.50	5.00
❑ 189	After Last Night's Storm/(B-side unknown)	1988	—	2.50	5.00

RIDERS IN THE SKY

45s

ROUNDER

Number	Title (A Side/B Side)	Yr	VG	VG+	NM
❑ 4530	Cowboy Song/Here Comes the Santa Fe	1980	2.00	4.00	8.00
❑ 4537	Blue Bonnet Lady/Blue Montana Skies	1980	2.00	4.00	8.00
❑ 4543	Soon As the Roundup's Through/Back in the Saddle Again	1981	2.00	4.00	8.00
❑ 4548	Riding Along/Cowboy Jubilee	1981	2.00	4.00	8.00
❑ 4551	Prairie Serenade/Old El Paso	1982	2.00	4.00	8.00
❑ 4552	Christmas at the Triple X Ranch/Riding Home for Christmas	198?	2.00	4.00	8.00

Albums

MCA

Number	Title (A Side/B Side)	Yr	VG	VG+	NM
❑ 42040	The Cowboy Way	1987	2.00	4.00	8.00
❑ 42180	Riders Radio Theater	1988	2.00	4.00	8.00
❑ 42305	The Riders Go Commercial	1989	2.50	5.00	10.00

ROUNDER

Number	Title (A Side/B Side)	Yr	VG	VG+	NM
❑ 0102	Three on the Trail	1980	2.50	5.00	10.00
❑ 0147	Cowboy Jubilee	1981	2.50	5.00	10.00
❑ 0170	Prairie Serenade	1982	2.50	5.00	10.00
❑ 0186	Live	1984	2.50	5.00	10.00
❑ 0220	New Trails	1986	2.50	5.00	10.00
❑ 1038	Weeds and Water	1983	2.50	5.00	10.00
❑ 8011	Saddle Pals	1985	2.50	5.00	10.00

RIDERS OF THE PURPLE SAGE, THE

See FOY WILLING.

RILEY, DAN

45s

ARMADA

Number	Title (A Side/B Side)	Yr	VG	VG+	NM
❑ 103	Lily/If My Tears Could Fill a Lake I'd Throw You In	1979	—	3.00	6.00

RILEY, JEANNIE C.

45s

CAPITOL

Number	Title (A Side/B Side)	Yr	VG	VG+	NM
❑ 2378	The Price I Pay to Stay/How Can Anything So Right Be So Wrong	1969	—	2.50	5.00
❑ 2449	I Don't Know What I'm Doing Here/You've Got Me Singing Nursery Rhymes	1969	—	2.50	5.00

LITTLE DARLIN'

Number	Title (A Side/B Side)	Yr	VG	VG+	NM
❑ 0031	What About Them/You Write the Music	1967	3.75	7.50	15.00
—As "Jean Riley"					
❑ 0048	I Don't Know What I'm Doing Here/I'll Be a Woman of the World	1968	—	3.00	6.00

MCA

Number	Title (A Side/B Side)	Yr	VG	VG+	NM
❑ 52018	From Harper Valley to the Mountain/I Don't Have to Die to Get Into Heaven	1982	—	—	3.00

MERCURY

Number	Title (A Side/B Side)	Yr	VG	VG+	NM
❑ 73616	Plain Vanilla/Country Girl	1974	—	2.00	4.00

MGM

Number	Title (A Side/B Side)	Yr	VG	VG+	NM
❑ 14310	Houston Blues/How Hard I'm Trying	1971	—	2.00	4.00
❑ 14341	Give Myself a Party/Why You Been Gone So Long	1972	—	2.00	4.00
❑ 14382	Good Morning Country Rain/This Is for You	1972	—	2.00	4.00
❑ 14427	One Night/Without You	1972	—	2.00	4.00
❑ 14495	When Love Has Gone Away/Thou Shalt Not Kill	1973	—	2.00	4.00
❑ 14554	Hush/Not Looking Back	1973	—	2.00	4.00
❑ 14666	Another Football Year/Mother America	1973	—	2.00	4.00
❑ 14696	Missouri/Sing Jeannie Sing	1974	—	2.00	4.00

PLANTATION

Number	Title (A Side/B Side)	Yr	VG	VG+	NM
❑ 3	Harper Valley P.T.A./Yesterday All Day Long Today	1968	2.00	4.00	8.00
—Yellow label					
❑ 3	Harper Valley P.T.A./Yesterday All Day Long Today	1968	—	3.00	6.00
—Green and white label					
❑ 7	The Girl Most Likely/My Scrapbook	1968	—	2.50	5.00
❑ 16	There Never Was a Time/Back to School	1969	—	2.50	5.00
❑ 22	The Rib/I'm the Woman	1969	—	2.50	5.00
❑ 29	The Back Side of Dallas/Things Go Better with Love	1969	—	2.50	5.00
❑ 44	Country Girl/We Were Raised on Love	1970	—	2.50	5.00
❑ 59	Duty Not Desire/Holdin' On	1970	—	2.50	5.00
❑ 65	My Man/The Generation Gap	1970	—	2.50	5.00
❑ 72	Oh, Singer/I'll Take What's Left of You	1971	—	2.50	5.00
❑ 75	Good Enough to Be Your Wife/Light Your Light	1971	—	2.50	5.00
❑ 79	Roses and Thorns/Shed Me No Tears	1971	—	2.50	5.00
❑ 85	The Lion's Club/Tell the Truth and Shame the Devil	1972	—	2.50	5.00
❑ 93	If You Could Read My Mind/Will the Real Jesus Please Stand Up	1972	—	2.50	5.00
❑ 173	Harper Valley P.T.A. (Soundtrack Version)/I've Done a Lot of Living Since Then	1979	—	3.00	6.00

PLAYBACK

Number	Title (A Side/B Side)	Yr	VG	VG+	NM
❑ 1350	Here's to the Cowboys/Free	1989	—	3.00	6.00

WARNER BROS.

Number	Title (A Side/B Side)	Yr	VG	VG+	NM
❑ 8226	The Best I've Ever Had/Thank You for Forgiving	1976	—	2.00	4.00
❑ 8290	Pure Gold/Take Time	1976	—	2.00	4.00

Albums

ALLEGIANCE

Number	Title (A Side/B Side)	Yr	VG	VG+	NM
❑ AV-5026	Tears, Joys and Memories	198?	2.50	5.00	10.00

CAPITOL

Number	Title (A Side/B Side)	Yr	VG	VG+	NM
❑ ST-177	The Songs of Jeannie C. Riley	1969	3.75	7.50	15.00

LITTLE DARLIN'

Number	Title (A Side/B Side)	Yr	VG	VG+	NM
❑ SLD 8011	Sock Soul	1968	5.00	10.00	20.00

MGM

Number	Title (A Side/B Side)	Yr	VG	VG+	NM
❑ SE-4805	Give Myself a Party	1972	3.00	6.00	12.00
❑ SE-4849	Down to Earth	1973	3.00	6.00	12.00
❑ SE-4891	When Love Has Gone Away	1973	3.00	6.00	12.00
❑ SE-4909	Just Jeannie C. Riley	1973	3.00	6.00	12.00

PICKWICK

Number	Title (A Side/B Side)	Yr	VG	VG+	NM
❑ 6098	The Girl Most Likely	197?	2.50	5.00	10.00
❑ 6119	The World of Country	197?	2.50	5.00	10.00

PLANTATION

Number	Title (A Side/B Side)	Yr	VG	VG+	NM
❑ PLP 1	Harper Valley P.T.A.	1968	5.00	10.00	20.00
❑ PLP 2	Yearbooks and Yesterdays	1969	3.75	7.50	15.00
❑ PLP 3	Things Go Better with Love	1969	3.75	7.50	15.00
❑ PLP 8	Country Girl	1970	3.75	7.50	15.00
❑ PLP 11	The Generation Gap	1970	3.75	7.50	15.00
❑ PLP 13	Jeannie C. Riley's Greatest Hits	1971	3.75	7.50	15.00
❑ PLP 16	Jeannie	1971	3.75	7.50	15.00
❑ 508	Country Queens	197?	3.00	6.00	12.00

POWER PAK

Number	Title (A Side/B Side)	Yr	VG	VG+	NM
❑ 250	Country Gold	197?	2.50	5.00	10.00

RILEY, LARRY

45s

F&L

Number	Title (A Side/B Side)	Yr	VG	VG+	NM
❑ 507	Cheater's Last Chance/How Could I Ever Stop Loving You	1980	2.00	4.00	8.00
❑ 509	Code-a-Phone/(B-side unknown)	1981	2.00	4.00	8.00

RIMES, LEANN

Also see EDDY ARNOLD.

45s

CAPITOL

Number	Title (A Side/B Side)	Yr	VG	VG+	NM
❑ 88644	I Need You/Jesus, Theme from the Original Soundtrack	2000	—	2.00	4.00
—B-side by Patrick Williams					

CURB

Number	Title (A Side/B Side)	Yr	VG	VG+	NM
❑ D7-73022	How Do I Live/How Do I Live (Extended Mix)	1997	—	2.00	4.00
❑ D7-73027	You Light Up My Life/I Believe	1997	—	2.00	4.00
❑ D7-73055	Looking Through Your Eyes/Commitment	1998	—	2.00	4.00
❑ D7-73086	Big Deal/Leaving's Not Leaving	1999	—	2.00	4.00
❑ D7-76959	Blue/The Light in Your Eyes	1996	—	2.00	4.00

RISHARD, ROD

45s

SOUNDWAVES

Number	Title (A Side/B Side)	Yr	VG	VG+	NM
❑ 4715	You'd Better Believe It/You're the Closest I've Come	1983	—	2.50	5.00

Number	Title (A Side/B Side)	Yr	VG	VG+	NM
❑ 4717	How Do You Tell Someone You Love/Friday Night Love Affair	1983	—	2.50	5.00
❑ 4724	The More I Go Blind/The Next Exit Out of Love	1984	—	2.50	5.00
❑ 4734	Midnight Angel of Mercy/You're the Closest I've Come	1984	—	2.50	5.00

RITTER, TEX

45s

CAPITOL

Number	Title (A Side/B Side)	Yr	VG	VG+	NM
❑ F885	Deck of Cards/Rye Whiskey	1950	7.50	15.00	30.00
❑ F928	Boogie Woogie Cowboy/He's a Cowboy Auctioneer	1950	10.00	20.00	40.00
❑ F1058	Bad Brahma Bull/Blood on the Saddle	1950	7.50	15.00	30.00
❑ F1071	I've Got $5 and It's Saturday Night/Boiled Crawfish	1950	7.50	15.00	30.00
❑ F1098	Thief on the Cross/Beautiful Life	1950	7.50	15.00	30.00
❑ F1141	The Pledge of Allegiance/Fiery Bear	1950	7.50	15.00	30.00
❑ F1188	Coal Smoke, Valve Oil and Steam/Nobody's Fool	1950	7.50	15.00	30.00
❑ F1264	Merry Christmas Polka/Christmas Carols by the Old Corral	1950	7.50	15.00	30.00
❑ F1267	Daddy's Last Letter/Onward Christian Soldiers	1950	7.50	15.00	30.00
❑ F1334	Stay Away from My Heart/Big Blue Diamonds	1950	7.50	15.00	30.00
❑ F1388	You're Always Brand New/My Bucket's Been Fixed	1951	6.25	12.50	25.00
❑ F1453	If I Could Steal You/There's No One to Cry Over Me	1951	6.25	12.50	25.00
❑ F1581	Wearin' Out Your Walkin' Shoes/Coffee Pot	1951	6.25	12.50	25.00
❑ F1629	Jealous Heart/Green Grow the Lilacs	1951	6.25	12.50	25.00
—Reissue of 1940s material first issued on 78					
❑ F1631	Rye Whiskey/Blood on the Saddle	1951	6.25	12.50	25.00
—Reissue of 1940s material first issued on 78					
❑ F1665	Deck of Cards/Ol' Shorty	195?	6.25	12.50	25.00
—Reissue of 1940s material first issued on 78					
❑ F1698	High Noon (Do Not Forsake Me)/Let Me Go Devil	195?	3.75	7.50	15.00
—Reissue					
❑ F1783	Tennessee Blues/Rock All Babies	1951	6.25	12.50	25.00
❑ F1977	As Long As the River Flows On/When My Blue Moon Turns to Gold	1952	6.25	12.50	25.00
❑ F2034	The Letter Edged in Black/There Shall Be Showers	1952	6.25	12.50	25.00
❑ 2097	Bump Tiddle Dee Bum Bum/I Just Can't Get Away	1968	2.00	4.00	8.00
❑ F2120	High Noon (Do Not Forsake Me)/Go On! Get Out!	1952	7.50	15.00	30.00
❑ F2174	Boll Weevil Song/Have I Told You Lately That I Love You	1952	6.25	12.50	25.00
❑ 2232	Texas/Stranger on Boot Hill	1968	2.00	4.00	8.00
❑ F2368	My Woman Ain't Pretty/Buffalo Dream	1953	6.25	12.50	25.00
❑ 2388	A Funny Thing Happened (On the Way to Miami)/ The Governor and the Kid	1969	2.00	4.00	8.00
❑ F2475	The Marshall's Daughter/The San Antone Story	1953	6.25	12.50	25.00
❑ 2541	Growin' Up/A Letter to My Sons	1969	2.00	4.00	8.00
❑ F2594	Let Me Go, Devil!/Long Black Rifle	1953	6.25	12.50	25.00
❑ 2677	Wand'rin' Star/Chuckwagon Son of a Gun	1969	2.00	4.00	8.00
❑ F2686	Red Deck of Cards/Lord Send Me an Angel	1953	6.25	12.50	25.00
❑ F2756	Brave Man/Turn Around Boy	1954	5.00	10.00	20.00
❑ 2815	Green Green Valley/God Bless America Again	1970	—	3.50	7.00
❑ F2836	Lovely Veil of White/The Best Time of All	1954	5.00	10.00	20.00
❑ F2916	Prairie Home (Theme from The Vanishing Prairie)/The Bandit	1954	5.00	10.00	20.00
❑ F2957	Is There a Santa Claus/Ole Tex Kringle	1954	5.00	10.00	20.00
❑ F3003	A Whale of a Tale/High on a Mountain Top	1954	6.25	12.50	25.00
❑ 3154	Fall Away/Looking Back	1971	—	3.50	7.00
❑ F3179	Wichita/September Song	1955	5.00	10.00	20.00
❑ F3230	Gunsmoke/Remember the Alamo	1955	6.25	12.50	25.00
❑ 3286	Bourbon Man/Little Peanut Shell (Gotta Make It Grow)	1972	—	3.50	7.00
❑ F3324	These Hands/The Last Frontier	1956	5.00	10.00	20.00
❑ 3357	Lorena/The Keeper of the Key	1972	—	3.50	7.00
❑ F3363	If Jesus Came to Your House/Touch of the Master's Hand	1956	5.00	10.00	20.00
❑ F3430	The Wayward Wind/The Searchers (Ride Away)	1956	5.00	10.00	20.00
❑ 3457	Comin' After Jinny/You Will Have to Pay for Your Yesterday	1972	—	3.50	7.00
❑ F3538	The Last Wagon/Paul Bunyan Love	1956	5.00	10.00	20.00
❑ 3570	One Night for Willie/Sweet Bird of Youth	1973	—	3.00	6.00
❑ F3589	Green Grow the Lilacs/He Is There	1956	5.00	10.00	20.00
❑ F3640	Children and Fools/I Leaned on a Man	1957	5.00	10.00	20.00
❑ 3705	Willie, the Wandering Gypsy, and Me/Wind of Oklahoma	1973	—	3.00	6.00
❑ F3754	Trooper Hook (Chapter 1)/Trooper Hook (Chapter 2)	1957	5.00	10.00	20.00
❑ 3814	The Americans (A Canadian's Opinion)/He Who Is Without Sin	1974	—	3.00	6.00
❑ F3903	Here Was a Man/It Came Upon the Midnight Clear	1959	3.75	7.50	15.00
❑ F4006	Jealous Heart/Burning Sand	1958	3.75	7.50	15.00
❑ F4043	The History Song/I Look for a Love	1958	3.75	7.50	15.00
❑ F4217	Conversation with a Gun/Rye Whiskey	1959	3.75	7.50	15.00
❑ 4239	God Bless America Again/Lucy Let Your Lovelight Shine	1976	—	2.50	5.00
❑ F4285	Deck of Cards/Conversation with a Gun	1959	3.75	7.50	15.00
❑ 4364	The Vanishing American/The Gun, The Gold, and the Girl	1960	3.75	7.50	15.00
❑ 4567	I Dreamed of a Hill-Billy Heaven/The Wind and the Tree	1961	3.00	6.00	12.00
❑ 4644	Lonely Soldier Boy/Strange Little Melody	1961	3.00	6.00	12.00
❑ 4753	The Pledge of Allegiance/Ol' Shorty	1962	3.00	6.00	12.00
❑ 4849	Coo Se Coo/The Cookson Hills	1962	3.00	6.00	12.00
❑ 5004	The Gods Were Angry with Me/Will	1963	2.50	5.00	10.00
❑ 5159	That Son of a Saginaw Fisherman/Gallows Pole	1964	2.50	5.00	10.00
❑ 5224	Fool's Paradise/Gimme Some	1964	2.50	5.00	10.00
❑ 5347	She Loved This House/I Dreamed of a Hill-Billy Heaven	1965	2.50	5.00	10.00
❑ 5474	Bummin' Around/Take Him Fishin'	1965	2.50	5.00	10.00
❑ 5574	The Men in My Little Girl's Life/Custody	1966	2.00	4.00	8.00
❑ 5697	Mommy, Daddy, Tell Us/Remember Us	1966	2.00	4.00	8.00
❑ 5839	Just Beyond the Moon/Greedy Old Dog	1967	2.00	4.00	8.00
❑ 5966	A Working Man's Prayer/William Barrett Travis: A Message from the Alamo	1967	2.00	4.00	8.00
❑ 54-40179	The Chisholm Trail/San Antonio Rose	1949	7.50	15.00	30.00
❑ 54-40180	Try Me One More Time/Boll Weevil Song	1949	7.50	15.00	30.00
❑ 54-40181	Blood on the Saddle/Rounded Up in Glory	1949	7.50	15.00	30.00
❑ 54-40182	Rye Whiskey/Bad Brahma Bull	1949	7.50	15.00	30.00
—The above four comprise a box set					
❑ F40248	Never Mind My Tears/Some Sweet Day	1949	10.00	20.00	40.00

Selected 78s

CAPITOL

Number	Title (A Side/B Side)	Yr	VG	VG+	NM
❑ 110	Goodbye My Little Cherokee/Jingle, Jangle, Jingle	1942	3.75	7.50	15.00
❑ 132	Someone/I've Done the Best I Could	1943	3.75	7.50	15.00
❑ 147	Have I Stayed Away Too Long/There's a Gold Star in Her Window	1944	3.75	7.50	15.00
❑ 174	I'm Wasting My Tears on You/There's a New Moon Over My Shoulder	1944	3.75	7.50	15.00
❑ 179	Jealous Heart/We Live in Two Different Worlds	1944	3.75	7.50	15.00
❑ 206	You Two-Timed Once Too Often/Green Grow the Lilacs	1945	3.75	7.50	15.00
❑ 223	You Will Have to Pay/Christmas Carols by the Old Corral	1945	3.75	7.50	15.00
❑ 253	Long Time Gone/I'm Gonna Leave You Like I Found You	1946	3.75	7.50	15.00
❑ 296	When You Leave Don't Slam the Door/Have I Told You Lately That I Love You	1946	3.75	7.50	15.00
❑ 327	From Now On/Love Me Now	1947	3.75	7.50	15.00
❑ 366	One Little Teardrop Too Late/99 Years Is a Long Time	1947	3.75	7.50	15.00
❑ 15119	Rock and Rye/My Heart's As Cold As an Empty Jug	1948	5.00	10.00	20.00
❑ 15204	Merry Christmas Polka/Christmas Carols by the Old Corral	1948	6.25	12.50	25.00
❑ 15215	Jingle, Jangle, Jingle/There's a New Moon Over My Shoulder	1948	5.00	10.00	20.00
❑ 15256	Jealous Heart/I'm Gonna Leave You Like I Found You	1948	3.00	6.00	12.00
❑ 15257	Someone/You Two-Timed Me One Time Too Often	1948	3.00	6.00	12.00
❑ 15258	Have I Stayed Away Too Long/I'm Wasting My Tears on You	1948	3.00	6.00	12.00
—The above three were issued as a 78 rpm album (a 45 rpm box set may exist but is unconfirmed)					
❑ 15259	Green Grow the Lilacs/We Live in Two Different Worlds	1948	3.00	6.00	12.00
❑ 15260	Have I Told You Lately That I Love You/Love Me Now	1948	3.00	6.00	12.00
❑ 15261	Long Time Gone/When You Leave, Don't Slam the Door	1948	3.00	6.00	12.00
—The above three were issued as a 78 rpm album (a 45 rpm box set may exist but is unconfirmed)					
❑ 15309	Double Dealin' Darlin'/It's Never Too Late	1948	3.75	7.50	15.00
❑ 15375	Tenena, Timpson, Bobo and Blair/I Don't Want You Anymore	1949	3.75	7.50	15.00
❑ 40000	The Last Mile/Bats in Your Belfry	1947	5.00	10.00	20.00
❑ 40020	Toodle-Loo My Darlin'/Teach Me to Forget	1947	3.75	7.50	15.00
❑ 40036	I Can't Get My Foot Off the Rail/Don't Make Me Sorry	1947	3.75	7.50	15.00
❑ 40084	Rye Whiskey/Boll Weevil	1948	3.75	7.50	15.00
❑ 40090	Dallas Darlin'/I've Had Enough of Your Two-Timin'	1948	3.75	7.50	15.00
❑ 40106	Pecos Bill/Egg-a-Bread	1948	3.75	7.50	15.00
❑ 40114	Deck of Cards/Rounded Up in Glory	1948	5.00	10.00	20.00
❑ 40155	Careless Hands/Ol' Shorty	1949	3.75	7.50	15.00

CHAMPION

Number	Title (A Side/B Side)	Yr	VG	VG+	NM
❑ 45153	Nobody's Darling But Mine/(B-side unknown)	193?	7.50	15.00	30.00
❑ 45154	The Oregon Trail/(B-side unknown)	193?	7.50	15.00	30.00
❑ 45191	Bill the Bar Fly/(B-side unknown)	193?	7.50	15.00	30.00
❑ 45197	Answer to Nobody's Darling But Mine/(B-side unknown)	193?	6.25	12.50	25.00
❑ 45198	The Hills of Old Wyomin'/(B-side unknown)	193?	6.25	12.50	25.00

COLUMBIA

Number	Title (A Side/B Side)	Yr	VG	VG+	NM
❑ 20239	Rye Whiskey/Goodbye Old Paint	1948	3.00	6.00	12.00
—Reissue of 37640					
❑ 37640	Rye Whiskey/Goodbye Old Paint	1946	3.75	7.50	15.00
—Reissue of older material					

DECCA

Number	Title (A Side/B Side)	Yr	VG	VG+	NM
❑ 5076	Lady Killin' Cowboy/(B-side unknown)	1935	10.00	20.00	40.00
❑ 5112	Thirty-Three Years in Prison/(B-side unknown)	1935	10.00	20.00	40.00
❑ 5305	Bill the Bar Fly/(B-side unknown)	1936	7.50	15.00	30.00
❑ 5306	Jailhouse Lament/(B-side unknown)	1936	7.50	15.00	30.00
❑ 5315	High, Wide and Handsome/(B-side unknown)	1936	7.50	15.00	30.00
❑ 5389	Down the Colorado Trail/(B-side unknown)	1937	7.50	15.00	30.00
❑ 5405	I'm Hittin' the Trail (For Home)/(B-side unknown)	1937	7.50	15.00	30.00
❑ 5639	Singing in the Saddle/(B-side unknown)	1939	6.25	12.50	25.00
❑ 5648	titles unknown	1939	6.25	12.50	25.00
❑ 5922	titles unknown	1941	6.25	12.50	25.00

Number	Title (A Side/B Side)	Yr	VG	VG+	NM
Albums					
BUCKBOARD					
❑ BBS 1030	Tex Ritter	198?	2.50	5.00	10.00
CAPITOL					
❑ ST-213	Chuck Wagon Days	1969	5.00	10.00	20.00
❑ ST-467	Green Green Valley	1970	5.00	10.00	20.00
❑ T 971 [M]	Songs from the Western Screen	1958	20.00	40.00	80.00
—Turquoise or gray label					
❑ T 971 [M]	Songs from the Western Screen	1959	10.00	20.00	40.00
—Black colorband label, logo at left					
❑ T 971 [M]	Songs from the Western Screen	1962	6.25	12.50	25.00
—Black colorband label, logo at top					
❑ T 1100 [M]	Psalms	1959	12.50	25.00	50.00
—Black colorband label, logo at left					
❑ T 1100 [M]	Psalms	1962	6.25	12.50	25.00
—Black colorband label, logo at top					
❑ ST 1292 [S]	Blood on the Saddle	1960	10.00	20.00	40.00
—Black colorband label, logo at left					
❑ ST 1292 [S]	Blood on the Saddle	1962	6.25	12.50	25.00
—Black colorband label, logo at top					
❑ T 1292 [M]	Blood on the Saddle	1960	7.50	15.00	30.00
—Black colorband label, logo at left					
❑ T 1292 [M]	Blood on the Saddle	1962	5.00	10.00	20.00
—Black colorband label, logo at top					
❑ SW 1562 [S]	The Lincoln Hymns	1961	10.00	20.00	40.00
❑ W 1562 [M]	The Lincoln Hymns	1961	7.50	15.00	30.00
❑ ST 1623 [S]	Hillbilly Heaven	1961	10.00	20.00	40.00
—Black colorband label, logo at left					
❑ ST 1623 [S]	Hillbilly Heaven	1962	6.25	12.50	25.00
—Black colorband label, logo at top					
❑ T 1623 [M]	Hillbilly Heaven	1961	7.50	15.00	30.00
—Black colorband label, logo at left					
❑ T 1623 [M]	Hillbilly Heaven	1962	5.00	10.00	20.00
—Black colorband label, logo at top					
❑ ST 1910 [S]	Border Affair	1963	6.25	12.50	25.00
❑ T 1910 [M]	Border Affair	1963	5.00	10.00	20.00
❑ ST 2402 [S]	The Friendly Voice of Tex Ritter	1965	6.25	12.50	25.00
❑ T 2402 [M]	The Friendly Voice of Tex Ritter	1965	5.00	10.00	20.00
❑ DT 2595 [R]	The Best of Tex Ritter	1966	3.75	7.50	15.00
❑ T 2595 [M]	The Best of Tex Ritter	1966	6.25	12.50	25.00
❑ ST 2743 [S]	Sweet Land of Liberty	1967	6.25	12.50	25.00
❑ T 2743 [M]	Sweet Land of Liberty	1967	7.50	15.00	30.00
❑ ST 2786 [S]	Just Beyond the Moon	1967	6.25	12.50	25.00
❑ T 2786 [M]	Just Beyond the Moon	1967	7.50	15.00	30.00
❑ ST 2890 [S]	Bum Tiddil Dee Bum Bum!	1968	6.25	12.50	25.00
❑ T 2890 [M]	Bum Tiddil Dee Bum Bum!	1968	12.50	25.00	50.00
❑ ST 2974	Tex Ritter's Wild West	1968	6.25	12.50	25.00
❑ H 4004 [10]	Cowboy Favorites	195?	45.00	90.00	180.00
❑ ST-11037	Supercountrylegendary	1972	3.75	7.50	15.00
❑ SKC?-11241 [(3)]	An American Legend	1973	7.50	15.00	30.00
❑ ST-11351	Fall Away	1974	3.75	7.50	15.00
❑ ST-11503	Comin' After Jinny	1976	3.75	7.50	15.00
HILLTOP					
❑ PTP-2020 [(2)]	My Kinda Songs	197?	3.75	7.50	15.00
❑ JS-6043	Tex Ritter Sings His Hits	196?	3.00	6.00	12.00
❑ JS-6075	Love You As Big As Texas	196?	3.00	6.00	12.00
❑ JS-6138	High Noon	196?	3.00	6.00	12.00
❑ JS-6155	Tex	197?	3.00	6.00	12.00
LABREA					
❑ L-8036 [M]	Jamboree, Nashville Style	196?	5.00	10.00	20.00
❑ LS-8036 [S]	Jamboree, Nashville Style	196?	6.25	12.50	25.00
PREMIER					
❑ 9023	Tex Ritter and the Rio Grande River Boys	196?	3.00	6.00	12.00

RIVER ROAD

Number	Title (A Side/B Side)	Yr	VG	VG+	NM
45s					
CAPITOL NASHVILLE					
❑ S7-19580	I Broke It, I'll Fix It/A Day in the Life	1997	—	—	3.00
❑ S7-19647	Nickajack/Tears to the Tide	1997	—	—	3.00
❑ S7-19852	Somebody Will/As If You Didn't Know	1998	—	—	3.00
VIRGIN					
❑ 38699	Breathless/Somethin' in the Water	2000	—	—	3.00

RIVERS, EDDIE

Number	Title (A Side/B Side)	Yr	VG	VG+	NM
45s					
CHARTA					
❑ 102	Open Up Your Door/He's Still a Father in His Daughter's Eyes	1977	—	3.00	6.00
❑ 105	I Don't Care If the Sun Don't Shine/Soft Hearted Lady	1977	—	3.00	6.00
❑ 149	Christian Woman/If You Can't Bring It Home (You Leave It Alone)	1980	—	3.00	6.00
❑ 155	She Ain't the Best But She's Better Than Sleeping Alone/If You Can't Bring It Home You Better Leave It Alone	1980	—	—	—
—Canceled					
❑ 218	You Won the Battle/There's No Memories of Me (Ever Lovin' You)	1989	—	2.50	5.00
❑ 220	I Ain't Been Runnin' with Other Women/Walk On	1989	—	2.50	5.00

RIVERS, JACK

Number	Title (A Side/B Side)	Yr	VG	VG+	NM
45s					
CORAL					
❑ 9-64072	Haunted House Boogie/Bugle Call Baby	1951	7.50	15.00	30.00
❑ 9-64084	Shame, Shame on Jolie/Summer or Winter	1951	7.50	15.00	30.00
LISTEN					
❑ 1441	Navy Hot Rod/(B-side unknown)	1952	12.50	25.00	50.00
❑ 1445	titles unknown	1952	7.50	15.00	30.00
Selected 78s					
CAPITOL					
❑ 15169	Dear Oakie/A Million Memories	1948	5.00	10.00	20.00
CORAL					
❑ 64004	Draggin' the Steel/Watch Your Heart	1949	5.00	10.00	20.00
❑ 64005	I'm Just Living with My Sorrow/A Letter Asking for My Broken Heart	1949	5.00	10.00	20.00
❑ 64043	Me and My Teddy Bear/That Lucky Old Red-Nosed Mule	1950	3.75	7.50	15.00
❑ 64049	The Wild Guitar/Jelly Bean Rag	1950	3.75	7.50	15.00

RIVERS, JERRY

Number	Title (A Side/B Side)	Yr	VG	VG+	NM
Albums					
STARDAY					
❑ SLP-281 [M]	Fantastic Fiddlin' and Tall Tales	1964	7.50	15.00	30.00

RIVERS, JOHNNY

He had pop hits from 1964 through 1977, but his only country hit was the below single.

Number	Title (A Side/B Side)	Yr	VG	VG+	NM
45s					
ATLANTIC					
❑ 3028	Six Days on the Road/Artists and Poets	1974	—	2.50	5.00

ROBBINS, DENNIS

Also see BILLY HILL.

Number	Title (A Side/B Side)	Yr	VG	VG+	NM
45s					
GIANT					
❑ 7-18190	Walkin' on the Edge/Travelin' Music	1994	—	—	3.00
❑ 7-18294	Mona Lisa on Cruise Control/Walkin' on the Edge	1994	—	—	3.00
❑ 7-18786	My Side of Town/Hi O Silver	1992	—	—	3.00
❑ 7-18982	Home Sweet Home/The Only Slide I Ever Played On	1992	—	—	3.00
MCA					
❑ 52516	We Belong Together/Work for Love	1984	—	2.00	4.00
—As "Rockie Robbins"					
❑ 52584	I've Got Your Number/Work for Love	1985	—	2.00	4.00
—As "Rockie Robbins"					
❑ 52809	Hard Lovin' Man/Baby It's You	1986	—	2.00	4.00
❑ 52809 [DJ]	Hard Lovin' Man (same on both sides)	1986	2.50	5.00	10.00
—Promo only on blue vinyl					
❑ 52913	The First of Me/Sweet Sweet Lovin'	1986	—	2.00	4.00
❑ 52987	Long Gone Lonesome Blues/The Mountain Man and Me	1986	—	—	3.00
❑ 53143	Two of a Kind (Workin' on a Full House)/The Church on Cumberland Road	1987	—	2.50	5.00
NSD					
❑ 169	If I Could Get Over You/A Fire in Me	1983	—	3.00	6.00
Albums					
MCA					
❑ 5720	The First of Me	1986	2.00	4.00	8.00

ROBBINS, HARGUS "PIG"

Number	Title (A Side/B Side)	Yr	VG	VG+	NM
45s					
CHART					
❑ 1060	The Bridge Washed Out/Love's Apparition	1968	2.00	4.00	8.00
❑ 5022	Penguin Walk (Cool Theme)/Unknown Love	1969	2.00	4.00	8.00
❑ 5039	Tequila Float/Funk Chunkin'	1969	2.00	4.00	8.00
ELEKTRA					
❑ 45440	Diggin' In/Near You	1977	—	2.50	5.00
❑ 45469	Canadian Sunset/Roamin' 'Round	1978	—	2.50	5.00
❑ 45514	Little Bitty Pretty One/Forever	1978	—	2.50	5.00
❑ 46037	Chunky People/Whatever Happened to the Girls I Knew	1979	—	2.50	5.00
❑ 46512	Unbreakable Hearts/Love, Love, Love	1979	—	2.50	5.00
TIME					
❑ 1070	Forever/Happy Boy	1963	3.00	6.00	12.00
Albums					
CHART					
❑ CHS-1011	One More Time	196?	3.75	7.50	15.00
ELEKTRA					
❑ 6E-129	Pig in a Poke	1978	3.00	6.00	12.00
❑ 6E-185	Unbreakable Hearts	1979	3.00	6.00	12.00
❑ 7E-1110	Country Instrumentalist of the Year	1977	3.00	6.00	12.00
TIME					
❑ S-2107 [S]	A Bit of Country Piano	1963	6.25	12.50	25.00
❑ 52107 [M]	A Bit of Country Piano	1963	5.00	10.00	20.00

ROBBINS, JENNY

Number	Title (A Side/B Side)	Yr	VG	VG+	NM
45s					
EL DORADO					
❑ 152	You've Just Found Yourself Another Woman/All I've Got Left	1978	—	3.00	6.00

ROBBINS, MARTY

Also see JEANNIE PRUETT.

Number	Title (A Side/B Side)	Yr	VG	VG+	NM
45s					
COLUMBIA					
❑ 02444	Jumper Cable Man/Good Hearted Woman	1981	—	2.00	4.00
❑ 02575	Teardrops on My Heart/Honeycomb	1981	—	2.00	4.00
❑ 02854	Lover, Lover/Some Memories Just Won't Die	1982	—	2.00	4.00
❑ 03236	Tie Your Dream to Mine/That's All She Wrote	1982	—	2.00	4.00

Number	Title (A Side/B Side)	Yr	VG	VG+	NM
❑ 03789	Change of Heart/Devil in a Cowboy Hat	1983	—	2.00	4.00
❑ 03927	Baby That's Love/What If I Said I Love You	1983	—	2.00	4.00
❑ 10305	El Paso City/When I'm Gone	1976	—	2.50	5.00
❑ 10396	Among My Souvenirs/She's Just a Drifter	1976	—	2.50	5.00
❑ 10472	Adios Amigo/Helen	1977	—	2.50	5.00
❑ 10536	I Don't Know Why (I Just Do)/Inspiration for a Song	1977	—	2.50	5.00
❑ 10629	Don't Let Me Touch You/Tomorrow, Tomorrow, Tomorrow	1977	—	2.50	5.00
❑ 10673	Return to Me/More Than Anything, I Miss You	1978	—	2.50	5.00
❑ 10821	Please Don't Play a Love Song/Jenny	1978	—	2.50	5.00
❑ 10905	Touch Me with Magic/Confused and Lonely	1979	—	2.50	5.00
❑ 11016	All Around Cowboy/The Dreamer	1979	—	2.50	5.00
❑ 11102	Buenos Dias Argentina/Ballad of a Small Man	1979	—	2.50	5.00
❑ 11240	She's Made of Faith/Misery in My Soul	1980	—	2.00	4.00
❑ 11291	One Man's Trash (Is Another Man's Treasure)/I Can't Wait Until Tomorrow	1980	—	2.00	4.00
❑ 11372	An Occasional Rose/Holding On to You	1980	—	2.00	4.00
❑ 11425	Completely Out of Love/Another Cup of Coffee	1981	—	2.00	4.00
❑ 20925	Tomorrow You'll Be Gone/Love Me or Leave Me Alone	1952	7.50	15.00	30.00
❑ 20965	Crying 'Cause I Love You/I Wish Somebody Loved Me	1952	7.50	15.00	30.00
❑ 21022	I'll Go On Alone/You're Breaking My Heart	1952	7.50	15.00	30.00
❑ 21032	My Isle of Golden Dreams/Sweet Hawaiian Dream	1952	—	—	—
—Unreleased					
❑ 21075	I Couldn't Keep from Crying/After You Leave	1953	7.50	15.00	30.00
❑ 21111	A Castle in the Sky/A Half-Way Chance with You	1953	7.50	15.00	30.00
❑ 21145	Sing Me Something Sentimental/At the End of Long, Lonely Days	1953	7.50	15.00	30.00
❑ 21172	Blesserd Jesus Should I Fall Don't Let Me Lay/Kneel and Let the Lord Take Your Load	1953	7.50	15.00	30.00
❑ 21176	Don't Make Me Ashamed/It's a Long, Long Ride	1953	7.50	15.00	30.00
❑ 21213	My Isle of Golden Dreams/Aloha Oe	1954	7.50	15.00	30.00
❑ 21246	Pretty Words/Your Heart's Turn to Break	1954	7.50	15.00	30.00
❑ 21291	Call Me Up (And I'll Come Calling on You)/I'm Too Big to Cry	1954	7.50	15.00	30.00
❑ 21324	Time Goes By/It's a Pity What Money Can Do	1954	7.50	15.00	30.00
❑ 21351	That's All Right/Gossip	1955	12.50	25.00	50.00
❑ 21352	God Understands/Have Thine Own Way, Lord	1955	6.25	12.50	25.00
❑ 21388	Daddy Loves You/Pray for Me, Mother of Mine	1955	6.25	12.50	25.00
❑ 21414	It Looks Like I'm Just in the Way/I'll Love You Till the Day I Die	1955	6.25	12.50	25.00
❑ 21446	Maybellene/This Broken Heart of Mine	1955	12.50	25.00	50.00
❑ 21461	Pretty Mama/Don't Let Me Hang Around	1955	12.50	25.00	50.00
❑ 21477	Tennessee Toddy/Mean Mama Blues	1955	12.50	25.00	50.00
❑ 21508	Singing the Blues/I Can't Quit (I've Gone Too Far)	1956	10.00	20.00	40.00
❑ 21525	I'll Know You're Gone/How Long Will It Be	1956	6.25	12.50	25.00
—With Lee Emerson					
❑ 21545	Singing the Blues/I Can't Quit (I've Gone Too Far)	1956	7.50	15.00	30.00
❑ 30511 [S]	El Paso/Running Gun	1959	7.50	15.00	30.00
—"Stereo Seven" (small hole, plays at 33 1/3 rpm)					
❑ 30589 [S]	Big Iron/Saddle Tramp	1960	7.50	15.00	30.00
—"Stereo Seven" single (small hole, plays at 33 1/3 rpm)					
❑ 30771 [S]	Five Brothers/Ride, Cowboy, Ride	1960	7.50	15.00	30.00
—"Stereo Seven" single (small hole, plays at 33 1/3 rpm)					
❑ 30809 [S]	Ballad of the Alamo/A Time and a Place for Everything	1960	7.50	15.00	30.00
—"Stereo Seven" single (small hole, plays at 33 1/3 rpm)					
❑ 31124 [S]	To Each His Own/I Can't Help It	1961	5.00	10.00	20.00
—"Stereo Seven" single, small hole, plays at 33 1/3 rpm					
❑ 31125 [S]	Answer Me My Love/Clara	1961	5.00	10.00	20.00
—"Stereo Seven" single, small hole, plays at 33 1/3 rpm					
❑ 31126 [S]	Half As Much/Unchained Melody	1961	5.00	10.00	20.00
—"Stereo Seven" single, small hole, plays at 33 1/3 rpm					
❑ 31127 [S]	Are You Sincere?/Guess I'll Be Going	1961	5.00	10.00	20.00
—"Stereo Seven" single, small hole, plays at 33 1/3 rpm					
❑ 31128 [S]	To Think You've Chosen Me/Too Young	1961	5.00	10.00	20.00
—"Stereo Seven" single, small hole, plays at 33 1/3 rpm; the above five comprise set JS7-32, "Just a Little Sentimental"					
❑ 31190 [S]	Just a Little Sentimental/Hurt	1961	5.00	10.00	20.00
—"Stereo Seven" single, small hole, plays at 33 1/3 rpm					
❑ 31191 [S]	To Each His Own/I Can't Help It	1961	5.00	10.00	20.00
—"Stereo Seven" single, small hole, plays at 33 1/3 rpm					
❑ 31192 [S]	Answer Me My Love/Half As Much	1961	5.00	10.00	20.00
—"Stereo Seven" single, small hole, plays at 33 1/3 rpm					
❑ 31193 [S]	Unchained Melody/Are You Sincere?	1961	5.00	10.00	20.00
—"Stereo Seven" single, small hole, plays at 33 1/3 rpm					
❑ 31194 [S]	To Think You've Chosen Me/Too Young	1961	5.00	10.00	20.00
—"Stereo Seven" single, small hole, plays at 33 1/3 rpm; the above five comprise set JS7-37, an alternate compilation of "Just a Little Sentimental"					
❑ 31747 [S]	Devil Woman/Time Can't Make Me Forget	1963	5.00	10.00	20.00
—"Stereo Seven" single, small hole, plays at 33 1/3 rpm					
❑ 31748 [S]	In the Ashes of an Old Love Affair/The Hands You're Holding Now	1963	5.00	10.00	20.00
—"Stereo Seven" single, small hole, plays at 33 1/3 rpm					
❑ 31749 [S]	Worried/Little Rich Girl	1963	5.00	10.00	20.00
—"Stereo Seven" single, small hole, plays at 33 1/3 rpm					
❑ 31750 [S]	Progressive Love/Love Is a Hurting Thing	1963	5.00	10.00	20.00
—"Stereo Seven" single, small hole, plays at 33 1/3 rpm					
❑ 31751 [S]	Kinda Halfway Feel/The Wine Flowed Freely	1963	5.00	10.00	20.00
—"Stereo Seven" single, small hole, plays at 33 1/3 rpm; the above five comprise set JS7-78, "Devil Woman"					
❑ 40679	Long Tall Sally/Mr. Teardrop	1956	12.50	25.00	50.00
❑ 40706	Respectfully Miss Brooks/You Don't Owe Me a Thing	1956	12.50	25.00	50.00
❑ 40815	Knee Deep in the Blues/The Same Two Lips	1957	6.25	12.50	25.00
❑ 40864	A White Sport Coat (And a Pink Carnation)/Grown Up Tears	1957	6.25	12.50	25.00
❑ 40864 [PS]	A White Sport Coat (And a Pink Carnation)/Grown Up Tears	1957	10.00	20.00	40.00
❑ 40868	I Cried Like a Baby/Where D'Ja Go	1957	6.25	12.50	25.00
—With Lee Emerson					
❑ 40969	Please Don't Blame Me/Teen-Age Dream	1957	6.25	12.50	25.00
❑ 41013	The Story of My Life/Once-a-Week Date	1957	6.25	12.50	25.00
❑ 41013 [PS]	The Story of My Life/Once-a-Week Date	1957	10.00	20.00	40.00
❑ 41143	Just Married/Stairway of Love	1958	5.00	10.00	20.00
❑ 41208	She Was Only Seventeen (He Was One Year More)/Sittin' in a Tree House	1958	5.00	10.00	20.00
❑ 41208 [PS]	She Was Only Seventeen (He Was One Year More)/Sittin' in a Tree House	1958	10.00	20.00	40.00
❑ 41282	Ain't I the Lucky One/The Last Time I Saw My Heart	1958	5.00	10.00	20.00
❑ 41325	The Hanging Tree/The Blues, Country Style	1959	5.00	10.00	20.00
❑ 41325 [PS]	The Hanging Tree/The Blues, Country Style	1959	10.00	20.00	40.00
❑ 41408	Cap and Gown/Last Night About This Time	1959	5.00	10.00	20.00
❑ 41511 [M]	El Paso/Running Gun	1959	5.00	10.00	20.00
❑ 41511 [PS]	El Paso/Running Gun	1959	7.50	15.00	30.00
❑ 41589 [M]	Big Iron/Saddle Tramp	1960	3.75	7.50	15.00
❑ 41686	Is There Any Chance/I Told My Heart	1960	3.75	7.50	15.00
❑ 41766	Don't Worry/A Time and a Place for Everything	1960	—	—	—
—Unreleased					
❑ 41771 [M]	Five Brothers/Ride, Cowboy, Ride	1960	3.75	7.50	15.00
❑ 41809 [M]	Ballad of the Alamo/A Time and a Place for Everything	1960	3.75	7.50	15.00
❑ 41809 [PS]	Ballad of the Alamo/A Time and a Place for Everything	1960	7.50	15.00	30.00
❑ 41922	Don't Worry/Like All the Other Times	1961	3.75	7.50	15.00
❑ 41922 [PS]	Don't Worry/Like All the Other Times	1961	6.25	12.50	25.00
❑ 42008	Jimmy Martinez/Ghost Train	1961	3.75	7.50	15.00
❑ 42008 [PS]	Jimmy Martinez/Ghost Train	1961	6.25	12.50	25.00
❑ 42065	It's Your World/You Told Me So	1961	3.75	7.50	15.00
❑ 42065 [PS]	It's Your World/You Told Me So	1961	6.25	12.50	25.00
❑ 42246	I Told the Brook/Sometimes I'm Tempted	1961	3.75	7.50	15.00
❑ 42246 [PS]	I Told the Brook/Sometimes I'm Tempted	1961	6.25	12.50	25.00
❑ 42375	Love Can't Wait/Too Far Gone	1962	3.75	7.50	15.00
❑ 42375 [PS]	Love Can't Wait/Too Far Gone	1962	6.25	12.50	25.00
❑ 42486	Devil Woman/April Fool's Day	1962	3.75	7.50	15.00
❑ 42486 [PS]	Devil Woman/April Fool's Day	1962	6.25	12.50	25.00
❑ 42614	Ruby Ann/Won't You Forgive	1962	3.75	7.50	15.00
❑ 42614 [PS]	Ruby Ann/Won't You Forgive	1962	6.25	12.50	25.00
❑ 42672	Hawaii's Calling Me/Ka-Lu-A	1963	3.00	6.00	12.00
❑ 42701	Cigarettes and Coffee Blues/Teenager's Dad	1963	3.00	6.00	12.00
❑ 42701 [PS]	Cigarettes and Coffee Blues/Teenager's Dad	1963	6.25	12.50	25.00
❑ 42781	No Sign of Loneliness Here/I'm Not Ready Yet	1963	3.00	6.00	12.00
❑ 42781 [PS]	No Sign of Loneliness Here/I'm Not Ready Yet	1963	6.25	12.50	25.00
❑ 42831	Not So Long Ago/I Hope You Learn a Lot	1963	3.00	6.00	12.00
❑ 42890	Begging to You/Over High Mountain	1963	3.00	6.00	12.00
❑ 42968	Girl from Spanish Town/Kingston Girl	1964	2.50	5.00	10.00
❑ 43049	The Cowboy in the Continental Suit/Man Walks Among Us	1964	2.50	5.00	10.00
❑ 43134	One of These Days/Up in the Air	1964	2.50	5.00	10.00
❑ 43196	I Eish-Tay-Mah-Su (I Love You)/A Whole Lot Easier	1964	2.50	5.00	10.00
❑ 43258	Ribbon of Darkness/Little Robin	1965	2.50	5.00	10.00
❑ 43377	Old Red/Matilda	1965	2.00	4.00	8.00
❑ 43428	While You're Dancing/Lonely Too Long	1965	2.00	4.00	8.00
❑ 43500	Count Me Out/Private Wilson White	1965	2.00	4.00	8.00
❑ 43651	Ain't I Right/My Own Native Land	1966	—	—	—
—Unreleased					
❑ 43680	The Shoe Goes On the Other Foot Tonight/It Kind of Reminds Me of You	1966	2.00	4.00	8.00
❑ 43845	No Tears Milady/Fly Butterfly Fly	1966	2.00	4.00	8.00
❑ 43870	Mr. Shorty/Tall Handsome Strangers	1966	2.00	4.00	8.00
❑ 44128	Tonight Carmen/Waiting in Reno	1967	—	3.00	6.00
❑ 44271	Gardenias in Her Hair/In the Valley of the Rio Grande	1967	—	3.00	6.00
❑ 44509	Love Is In the Air/I've Been Leaving Everyday	1968	—	3.00	6.00
❑ 44633	I Walk Alone/Lily of the Valley	1968	—	3.00	6.00
❑ 44641	It Finally Happened/Big Mouthin' Around	1968	—	3.00	6.00
—By "Marty Robbins Jr. and Sr."					
❑ 44739	It's a Sin/I Feel Another Heartache Coming On	1969	—	2.50	5.00
❑ 44895	I Can't Say Goodbye/Hello Daily News	1969	—	2.50	5.00
❑ 44968	Girl from Spanish Town/Kingston Girl	1969	2.00	4.00	8.00
❑ 45024	Camelia/Virginia	1969	—	2.50	5.00
❑ 45091	My Woman, My Woman, My Wife/Martha Ellen Jenkins	1970	—	2.50	5.00
❑ 45215	Jolie Girl/The City	1970	—	2.50	5.00
❑ 45273	Padre/At Times	1970	—	3.00	6.00
❑ 45346	Little Spot in Heaven/Wait a Little Longer Please, Jesus	1971	—	3.00	6.00
❑ 45377	The Chair/Seventeen Years	1971	—	2.50	5.00
❑ 45442	Early Morning Sunshine/Another Day Has Gone By	1971	—	2.50	5.00
❑ 45520	The Best Part of Living/Gone with the Wind	1971	—	2.50	5.00
❑ 45668	I've Got a Woman's Love/A Little Spot in Heaven	1972	—	2.50	5.00
❑ 45775	Laura (What's He Got That I Ain't Got)/It Kind of Reminds Me of You	1973	—	2.50	5.00
❑ JZSP 49158/48863 [DJ]	El Paso (2:58)/El Paso (4:37)	1959	10.00	20.00	40.00

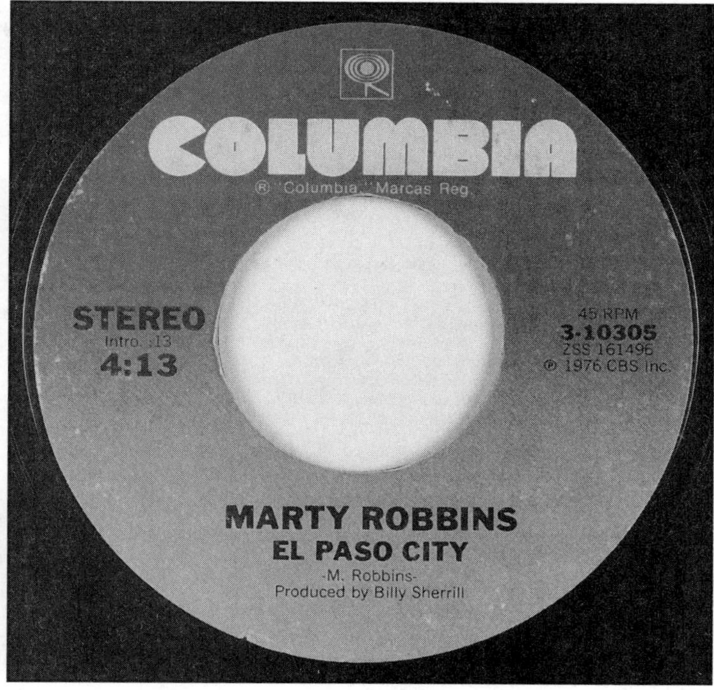

In his long career, which was cut short by a heart attack that killed him at age 57, Marty Robbins had 16 No. 1 hits on the *Billboard* country charts. (Top left) His biggest hit, which spent 13 weeks on top, was his version of "Singing the Blues." Even though Guy Mitchell's cover was the big hit on the pop side, Robbins' own version still made the Top 20 on the pop charts. (Top right) Columbia at first was reluctant to release Robbins' 1961 hit "Don't Worry" because of its distorted guitar sound, the result of a defective amplifier. But once the song came out, it spent two and a half months at No. 1 and was his second-biggest pop hit as well. (Bottom left) "Ruby Ann," another country chart-topper in 1962, was Marty's last Top 20 pop hit. (Bottom right) Robbins had not had a major country hit in two years when he came up with his "sequel" to his classic "El Paso." The new song, "El Paso City," was his first single upon his return to Columbia in 1976 after a short stay with Decca/MCA, and he was rewarded with his biggest hit in over a decade.

DECCA

Number	Title (A Side/B Side)	Yr	VG	VG+	NM
❑ 33006	This Much a Man/Guess I'll Stand Here Looking Dumb	1972	—	3.50	7.00

MCA

Number	Title (A Side/B Side)	Yr	VG	VG+	NM
❑ 40012	Franklin, Tennessee/Walking Piece of Heaven	1973	—	2.50	5.00
❑ 40067	A Man and a Train/Las Vegas, Nevada	1973	—	2.50	5.00
❑ 40134	Love Me/Crawling on My Knees	1973	—	2.50	5.00
❑ 40172	I'm Wanting To/Twentieth Century Drifter	1973	—	2.50	5.00
❑ 40236	Don't You Think/I Couldn't Believe It Was True	1974	—	2.50	5.00
❑ 40296	Two-Gun Daddy/Queen of the Big Rodeo	1974	—	2.50	5.00
❑ 40342	Life/It Takes Faith	1974	—	2.50	5.00
❑ 40425	These Are My Souvenirs/Shotgun Rider	1975	—	2.50	5.00
❑ 52197	Two Gun Daddy/Life	1983	—	2.50	5.00

WARNER BROS.

Number	Title (A Side/B Side)	Yr	VG	VG+	NM
❑ 29847	Honkytonk Man/Shotgun Rag	1982	—	2.00	4.00
—B-side by Johnny Gimble and the Texas Swing Band					

7-Inch Extended Plays

COLUMBIA

Number	Title (A Side/B Side)	Yr	VG	VG+	NM
❑ H-1785	I'll Go On Alone/Crying 'Cause I Love You//I Couldn't Keep from Crying/A Half-Way Chance with You	1953	15.00	30.00	60.00
❑ H-1785 [PS]	Marty Robbins	1953	15.00	30.00	60.00
❑ B-2116	*Singing the Blues/I Can't Quit/Long Gone Lonesome Blues/Lorelei	1956	12.50	25.00	50.00
❑ B-2116 [PS]	Singing the Blues	1956	12.50	25.00	50.00
❑ B-2134	*A White Sport Coat/Mean Mama Blues/Grown-Up Tears/Long Tall Sally	1957	10.00	20.00	40.00
❑ B-2134 [PS]	A White Sport Coat	1957	10.00	20.00	40.00
❑ B-2153	The Letter Edged in Black/The Little Rosewood Casket//The Dream of the Miner's Child/The Convict and the Rose	1957	7.50	15.00	30.00
❑ B-2153 [PS]	Marty Robbins	1957	7.50	15.00	30.00
❑ B-2808	I Couldn't Keep from Crying/Sing Me Something Sentimental//Tennessee Toddy/You Don't Owe Me a Thing	1957	12.50	25.00	50.00
❑ B-2808 [PS]	Marty Robbins	1957	12.50	25.00	50.00
❑ B-2814	*A White Sport Coat/The Story of My Life/Singing the Blues/I'm So Lonesome I Could Cry	1958	3.00	6.00	12.00
❑ B-2814 [PS]	Marty Robbins	1958	3.00	6.00	12.00
❑ B-9761	Lovesick Blues/I'm So Lonesome I Could Cry//It's Too Late Now/Rose of Ol' Pawnee	1957	3.75	7.50	15.00
❑ B-9761 [PS]	The Song of Robbins Vol. I	1957	3.75	7.50	15.00
❑ B-9762	I Never Let You Cross My Mind/I Hang My Head and Cry//You Only Want Me When You're Lonely/Moanin' the Blues	1957	3.75	7.50	15.00
❑ B-9762 [PS]	The Song of Robbins Vol. II	1957	3.75	7.50	15.00
❑ B-9763	I'll Step Aside/All the World Is Lonely Now//Bouquet of Roses/Have I Told You Lately That I Love You?	1957	3.75	7.50	15.00
❑ B-9763 [PS]	The Song of Robbins, Vol. III	1957	3.75	7.50	15.00
❑ B-10871	*Song of the Islands/Now Is the Hour/Sweet Leilani/Aloha Oe	1957	3.75	7.50	15.00
❑ B-10871 [PS]	Song of the Islands	1957	3.75	7.50	15.00
❑ B-11891	Kaw-Liga/Waltz of the Wind//Then I Turned and Walked Slowly Away/A House with Everything But Love	1958	3.75	7.50	15.00
❑ B-11891 [PS]	Marty Robbins	1958	3.75	7.50	15.00
❑ B-13491	El Paso/A Hundred and Sixty Acres//They're Hanging Me Tonight/The Strawberry Roan	1959	3.00	6.00	12.00
❑ B-13491 [PS]	Gunfighter Ballads and Trail Songs, Vol. I	1959	3.00	6.00	12.00
❑ B-13492	Big Iron/In the Valley//Running Gun/Utah Carol	1959	3.00	6.00	12.00
❑ B-13492 [PS]	Gunfighter Ballads and Trail Songs, Vol. II	1959	3.00	6.00	12.00
❑ B-13493	Cool Water/The Master's Call//Billy the Kid/The Little Green Valley	1959	3.75	7.50	15.00
❑ B-13493 [PS]	Gunfighter Ballads and Trail Songs, Vol. III	1959	3.75	7.50	15.00
❑ B-14811	*San Angelo/Prairie Fire/Streets of Laredo	1960	3.00	6.00	12.00
❑ B-14811 [PS]	More Gunfighter Ballads and Trail Songs, Vol. I	1960	3.00	6.00	12.00
❑ B-14812	*Five Brothers/Little Joe the Wrangler/Song of the Bandit/I've Got No Use for the Woman	1960	3.00	6.00	12.00
❑ B-14812 [PS]	More Gunfighter Ballads and Trail Songs, Vol. II	1960	3.00	6.00	12.00
❑ B-14813	*She Was Young and She Was Pretty/My Love/Ride Cowboy Ride/This Peaceful Sod	1960	3.00	6.00	12.00
❑ B-14813 [PS]	More Gunfighter Ballads and Trail Songs, Vol. III	1960	3.00	6.00	12.00

Albums

ARTCO

Number	Title (A Side/B Side)	Yr	VG	VG+	NM
❑ 110	The Best of Marty Robbins	1973	10.00	20.00	40.00

COLUMBIA

Number	Title (A Side/B Side)	Yr	VG	VG+	NM
❑ GP 15 [(2)]	Marty's Country	1969	6.25	12.50	25.00
❑ CL 976 [M]	The Song of Robbins	1957	25.00	50.00	100.00
—Red and black label with six "eye" logos					
❑ CL 976 [M]	The Song of Robbins	1963	5.00	10.00	20.00
—Red label with "Guaranteed High Fidelity" or "360 Sound Mono"					
❑ CL 1087 [M]	Song of the Islands	1957	30.00	60.00	120.00
—Red and black label with six "eye" logos					
❑ CL 1087 [M]	Song of the Islands	1963	5.00	10.00	20.00
—Red label with "Guaranteed High Fidelity" or "360 Sound Mono"					
❑ CL 1189 [M]	Marty Robbins	1958	20.00	40.00	80.00
—Red and black label with six "eye" logos					
❑ CL 1189 [M]	Marty Robbins	1963	5.00	10.00	20.00
—Red label with "Guaranteed High Fidelity" or "360 Sound Mono"					
❑ CL 1325 [M]	Marty's Greatest Hits	1959	20.00	40.00	80.00
—Red and black label with six "eye" logos					
❑ CL 1325 [M]	Marty's Greatest Hits	1963	5.00	10.00	20.00
—Red label with "Guaranteed High Fidelity" or "360 Sound Mono"					
❑ CL 1349 [M]	Gunfighter Ballads and Trail Songs	1959	7.50	15.00	30.00
—Red and black label with six "eye" logos					
❑ CL 1349 [M]	Gunfighter Ballads and Trail Songs	1963	3.75	7.50	15.00
—Red label with "Guaranteed High Fidelity" or "360 Sound Mono"					
❑ CL 1481 [M]	More Gunfighter Ballads and Trail Songs	1960	7.50	15.00	30.00
—Red and black label with six "eye" logos					
❑ CL 1481 [M]	More Gunfighter Ballads and Trail Songs	1963	3.75	7.50	15.00
—Red label with "Guaranteed High Fidelity" or "360 Sound Mono"					
❑ CL 1635 [M]	More Greatest Hits	1961	6.25	12.50	25.00
—Red and black label with six "eye" logos					
❑ CL 1635 [M]	More Greatest Hits	1963	3.75	7.50	15.00
—Red label with "Guaranteed High Fidelity" or "360 Sound Mono"					
❑ CL 1666 [M]	Just a Little Sentimental	1961	6.25	12.50	25.00
—Red and black label with six "eye" logos					
❑ CL 1666 [M]	Just a Little Sentimental	1963	3.75	7.50	15.00
—Red label with "Guaranteed High Fidelity" or "360 Sound Mono"					
❑ CL 1801 [M]	Marty After Midnight	1962	12.50	25.00	50.00
—Red and black label with six "eye" logos					
❑ CL 1801 [M]	Marty After Midnight	1962	5.00	10.00	20.00
—Red label with "Guaranteed High Fidelity"					
❑ CL 1801 [M]	Marty After Midnight	1965	3.75	7.50	15.00
—Red label with "360 Sound Mono"					
❑ CL 1855 [M]	Portrait of Marty	1962	10.00	20.00	40.00
❑ CL 1855/CS 8655	Portrait of Marty Bonus Photo	1962	7.50	15.00	30.00
❑ CL 1918 [M]	Devil Woman	1962	6.25	12.50	25.00
—Red label with "Guaranteed High Fidelity"					
❑ CL 1918 [M]	Devil Woman	1965	3.75	7.50	15.00
—Red label with "360 Sound Mono"					
❑ CL 2040 [M]	Hawaii's Calling Me	1963	6.25	12.50	25.00
—Red label with "Guaranteed High Fidelity"					
❑ CL 2040 [M]	Hawaii's Calling Me	1965	3.75	7.50	15.00
—Red label with "360 Sound Mono"					
❑ CL 2072 [M]	Return of the Gunfighter	1963	5.00	10.00	20.00
—Red label with "Guaranteed High Fidelity"					
❑ CL 2072 [M]	Return of the Gunfighter	1965	3.75	7.50	15.00
—Red label with "360 Sound Mono"					
❑ CL 2176 [M]	Island Woman	1964	7.50	15.00	30.00
—Red label with "Guaranteed High Fidelity"					
❑ CL 2176 [M]	Island Woman	1965	5.00	10.00	20.00
—Red label with "360 Sound Mono"					
❑ CL 2220 [M]	R.F.D.	1964	5.00	10.00	20.00
—Red label with "Guaranteed High Fidelity"					
❑ CL 2220 [M]	R.F.D.	1965	3.75	7.50	15.00
—Red label with "360 Sound Mono"					
❑ CL 2304 [M]	Turn the Lights Down Low	1965	6.25	12.50	25.00
—Red label with "Guaranteed High Fidelity"					
❑ CL 2304 [M]	Turn the Lights Down Low	1965	3.75	7.50	15.00
—Red label with "360 Sound Mono"					
❑ CL 2448 [M]	What God Has Done	1966	3.75	7.50	15.00
❑ CL 2527 [M]	The Drifter	1966	3.75	7.50	15.00
❑ CL 2601 [10]	Rock 'N Roll 'N Robbins	1956	250.00	500.00	1000.
❑ CL 2645 [M]	My Kind of Country	1967	6.25	12.50	25.00
❑ CL 2725 [M]	Tonight Carmen	1967	7.50	15.00	30.00
❑ CL 2735 [M]	Christmas with Marty Robbins	1967	12.50	25.00	50.00
❑ CL 2817 [M]	By the Time I Get to Phoenix	1968	15.00	30.00	60.00
❑ CS 8158 [S]	Gunfighter Ballads and Trail Songs	1959	10.00	20.00	40.00
—Red and black label with six "eye" logos					
❑ CS 8158 [S]	Gunfighter Ballads and Trail Songs	1963	5.00	10.00	20.00
—Red label with "360 Sound Stereo"					
❑ CS 8158 [S]	Gunfighter Ballads and Trail Songs	1971	2.50	5.00	10.00
—Orange label					
❑ PC 8158	Gunfighter Ballads and Trail Songs	198?	2.00	4.00	8.00
—Reissue with new prefix					
❑ CS 8272 [S]	More Gunfighter Ballads and Trail Songs	1960	10.00	20.00	40.00
—Red and black label with six "eye" logos					
❑ CS 8272 [S]	More Gunfighter Ballads and Trail Songs	1963	5.00	10.00	20.00
—Red label with "360 Sound Stereo"					
❑ CS 8272 [S]	More Gunfighter Ballads and Trail Songs	1971	2.50	5.00	10.00
—Orange label					
❑ PC 8272	More Gunfighter Ballads and Trail Songs				
❑ More		198?	2.00	4.00	8.00
—Reissue with new prefix					
❑ CS 8435 [S]	More Greatest Hits	1961	7.50	15.00	30.00
—Red and black label with six "eye" logos					
❑ CS 8435 [S]	More Greatest Hits	1963	5.00	10.00	20.00
—Red label with "360 Sound Stereo"					
❑ CS 8435 [S]	More Greatest Hits	1971	2.50	5.00	10.00
—Orange label					
❑ PC 8435	More Greatest Hits	198?	2.00	4.00	8.00
—Reissue with new prefix					
❑ CS 8466 [S]	Just a Little Sentimental	1961	7.50	15.00	30.00
—Red and black label with six "eye" logos					
❑ CS 8466 [S]	Just a Little Sentimental	1963	5.00	10.00	20.00
—Red label with "360 Sound Stereo"					
❑ CS 8601 [S]	Marty After Midnight	1962	20.00	40.00	80.00
—Red and black label with six "eye" logos					
❑ CS 8601 [S]	Marty After Midnight	1962	7.50	15.00	30.00
—Red label with "360 Sound Stereo" in black					
❑ CS 8601 [S]	Marty After Midnight	1965	5.00	10.00	20.00
—Red label with "360 Sound Stereo" in white					
❑ CS 8639 [P]	Marty's Greatest Hits	1962	7.50	15.00	30.00
—Red label with "360 Sound Stereo" in black					
❑ CS 8639 [P]	Marty's Greatest Hits	1965	5.00	10.00	20.00
—Red label with "360 Sound Stereo" in white					
❑ CS 8639 [P]	Marty's Greatest Hits	1970	2.50	5.00	10.00
—Orange label					

Number	Title (A Side/B Side)	Yr	VG	VG+	NM
❑ PC 8639	Marty's Greatest Hits	198?	2.00	4.00	8.00
—Reissue with new prefix					
❑ CS 8655 [S]	Portrait of Marty	1962	12.50	25.00	50.00
❑ CS 8718 [S]	Devil Woman	1962	7.50	15.00	30.00
—Red label with "360 Sound Stereo" in black					
❑ CS 8718 [S]	Devil Woman	1965	5.00	10.00	20.00
—Red label with "360 Sound Stereo" in white					
❑ CS 8718 [S]	Devil Woman	1970	2.50	5.00	10.00
—Orange label					
❑ CS 8840 [S]	Hawaii's Calling Me	1963	7.50	15.00	30.00
—Red label with "360 Sound Stereo" in black					
❑ CS 8840 [S]	Hawaii's Calling Me	1965	5.00	10.00	20.00
—Red label with "360 Sound Stereo" in white					
❑ CS 8872 [S]	Return of the Gunfighter	1963	6.25	12.50	25.00
—Red label with "360 Sound Stereo" in black					
❑ CS 8872 [S]	Return of the Gunfighter	1965	5.00	10.00	20.00
—Red label with "360 Sound Stereo" in white					
❑ CS 8872 [S]	Return of the Gunfighter	1970	2.50	5.00	10.00
—Orange label					
❑ CS 8976 [S]	Island Woman	1964	10.00	20.00	40.00
—Red label with "360 Sound Stereo" in black					
❑ CS 8976 [S]	Island Woman	1965	7.50	15.00	30.00
—Red label with "360 Sound Stereo" in white					
❑ CS 9020 [S]	R.F.D.	1964	6.25	12.50	25.00
—Red label with "360 Sound Stereo" in black					
❑ CS 9020 [S]	R.F.D.	1965	5.00	10.00	20.00
—Red label with "360 Sound Stereo" in white					
❑ CS 9104 [S]	Turn the Lights Down Low	1965	7.50	15.00	30.00
—Red label with "360 Sound Stereo" in black					
❑ CS 9104 [S]	Turn the Lights Down Low	1965	5.00	10.00	20.00
—Red label with "360 Sound Stereo" in white					
❑ CS 9248 [S]	What God Has Done	1966	5.00	10.00	20.00
—Red "360 Sound" label					
❑ CS 9248 [S]	What God Has Done	1970	2.50	5.00	10.00
—Orange label					
❑ CS 9327 [S]	The Drifter	1966	5.00	10.00	20.00
—Red "360 Sound" label					
❑ CS 9327 [S]	The Drifter	1970	2.50	5.00	10.00
—Orange label					
❑ CS 9421 [R]	The Song of Robbins	1967	3.75	7.50	15.00
—Red "360 Sound" label					
❑ CS 9421 [R]	The Song of Robbins	1970	2.50	5.00	10.00
—Orange label					
❑ CS 9425 [R]	Song of the Islands	1967	3.75	7.50	15.00
❑ CS 9445 [S]	My Kind of Country	1967	5.00	10.00	20.00
❑ CS 9525 [S]	Tonight Carmen	1967	5.00	10.00	20.00
—Red "360 Sound" label					
❑ CS 9525 [S]	Tonight Carmen	1970	2.50	5.00	10.00
—Orange label					
❑ 3C 9535	Christmas with Marty Robbins	198?	2.50	5.00	10.00
—Budget-line reissue					
❑ CS 9535 [S]	Christmas with Marty Robbins	1967	7.50	15.00	30.00
❑ CS 9617 [S]	By the Time I Get to Phoenix	1968	5.00	10.00	20.00
❑ CS 9725	I Walk Alone	1968	5.00	10.00	20.00
—Red "360 Sound" label					
❑ CS 9725	I Walk Alone	1970	2.50	5.00	10.00
—Orange label					
❑ CS 9811	It's a Sin	1969	5.00	10.00	20.00
—Red "360 Sound" label					
❑ CS 9811	It's a Sin	1970	2.50	5.00	10.00
—Orange label					
❑ CS 9978	My Woman, My Woman, My Wife	1970	5.00	10.00	20.00
—Red "360 Sound" label					
❑ CS 9978	My Woman, My Woman, My Wife	1970	3.75	7.50	15.00
—Orange label					
❑ PC 30316	El Paso	198?	2.00	4.00	8.00
—Reissue of Harmony 30316					
❑ C 30571	Marty Robbins' Greatest Hits Vol. III	1971	3.75	7.50	15.00
❑ PC 30571	Marty Robbins' Greatest Hits Vol. III	198?	2.00	4.00	8.00
—Budget-line reissue					
❑ CG 30811 [(2)]	The World of Marty Robbins	1971	4.50	9.00	18.00
❑ C 30816	Today	1971	3.75	7.50	15.00
❑ G 30881 [(2)]	The World of Marty Robbins	1971	5.00	10.00	20.00
❑ KC 31341	Bound for Old Mexico (Great Hits from South of the Border)	1973	3.75	7.50	15.00
❑ CG 31361 [(2)]	All Time Greatest Hits	1972	4.50	9.00	18.00
❑ KG 31361 [(2)]	Marty Robbins' All-Time Greatest Hits	1972	5.00	10.00	20.00
❑ KC 31628	I've Got a Woman's Love	1972	3.75	7.50	15.00
❑ KC 32586	Have I Told You Lately That I Love You	1974	3.75	7.50	15.00
❑ KC 33476	No Sign of Loneliness Here	1976	3.00	6.00	12.00
❑ CG 33630 [(2)]	Gunfighter Ballads and Trail Songs/My Woman, My Woman, My Wife	1976	3.75	7.50	15.00
❑ PC 34303	El Paso City	1976	3.00	6.00	12.00
—No bar code on cover					
❑ PC 34306	El Paso City	198?	2.00	4.00	8.00
—With bar code on cover					
❑ PC 34408	Adios Amigo	1977	3.00	6.00	12.00
—No bar code on cover					
❑ PC 34448	Adios Amigo	198?	2.00	4.00	8.00
—With bar code on cover					
❑ KC 35040	Don't Let Me Touch You	1977	3.00	6.00	12.00
❑ JC 35446	The Performer	1979	3.00	6.00	12.00
❑ KC 35629	Greatest Hits Vol. IV	1978	3.00	6.00	12.00
❑ JC 36085	All Around Cowboy	1979	3.00	6.00	12.00
❑ PC 36085	All Around Cowboy	198?	2.00	4.00	8.00
—Budget-line reissue					
❑ JC 36507	With Love	1980	3.00	6.00	12.00
❑ JC 36860	Everything I've Always Wanted	1981	3.00	6.00	12.00
❑ FC 37353	Encore	1981	3.00	6.00	12.00
❑ PC 37353	Encore	198?	2.00	4.00	8.00
—Budget-line reissue					
❑ FC 37541	The Legend	1982	3.00	6.00	12.00
❑ PC 37541	The Legend	1985	2.00	4.00	8.00
—Budget-line reissue					
❑ FC 37995	Come Back to Me	1982	3.00	6.00	12.00
❑ PC 37995	Come Back to Me	198?	2.00	4.00	8.00
—Budget-line reissue					
❑ FC 38309	Biggest Hits	1982	3.00	6.00	12.00
❑ FC 38603	Some Memories Just Won't Die	1983	3.00	6.00	12.00
❑ C2 38870 [(2)]	A Lifetime of Song 1951-1982	1983	3.75	7.50	15.00
❑ KC2 39575 [(2)]	Long, Long Ago	1984	3.75	7.50	15.00
COLUMBIA MUSICAL TREASURY					
❑ P5S 5812 [(5)]	Marty	1972	10.00	20.00	40.00
COLUMBIA RECORD CLUB					
❑ DS 445	Bend in the River	1968	10.00	20.00	40.00
COLUMBIA SPECIAL PRODUCTS					
❑ C 10980 [S]	Christmas with Marty Robbins	1972	3.75	7.50	15.00
—Stereo reissue; "Distributed by Apex Rendezvous, Inc." on back cover					
❑ C 11122	Marty's Greatest Hits	1972	3.00	6.00	12.00
❑ C 11311	By the Time I Get to Phoenix	1972	3.75	7.50	15.00
❑ C 11513	By the Time I Get to Phoenix	1973	3.75	7.50	15.00
❑ P 12416	Marty Robbins' Own Favorites	1974	3.75	7.50	15.00
❑ P 13358	Christmas with Marty Robbins	1976	3.00	6.00	12.00
❑ P 14035	Legendary Music Man	1977	3.00	6.00	12.00
❑ P 14613	The Best of Marty Robbins	1978	2.50	5.00	10.00
❑ P 15594	The Number One Cowboy	1981	2.50	5.00	10.00
❑ P 15812	Marty Robbins' Best	1982	2.50	5.00	10.00
❑ P 16561	Reflections	1982	2.50	5.00	10.00
❑ 3P 16578 [(3)]	Classics	1983	5.00	10.00	20.00
❑ P 16914	Country Classics	1983	2.50	5.00	10.00
❑ P 17120	Sincerely	1983	2.50	5.00	10.00
❑ P 17136	Forever Yours	1983	2.50	5.00	10.00
❑ P 17137	That Country Feeling	1983	2.50	5.00	10.00
❑ P 17138	Banquet of Songs	1983	2.50	5.00	10.00
❑ P 17159	The Great Marty Robbins	1983	2.50	5.00	10.00
❑ P 17206	The Legendary Marty Robbins	1983	2.50	5.00	10.00
❑ P 17209	Country Cowboy	1983	2.50	5.00	10.00
❑ P 17367	Song of the Islands	1983	2.50	5.00	10.00
DECCA					
❑ DL 75389	This Much a Man	1972	3.75	7.50	15.00
HARMONY					
❑ HS 11338	Singing the Blues	1969	3.75	7.50	15.00
❑ HS 11409	The Story of My Life	1970	3.75	7.50	15.00
❑ KH 30316	El Paso	1971	3.00	6.00	12.00
❑ KH 31257	Marty Robbins Favorites	1972	3.00	6.00	12.00
❑ H 31258	Songs of the Islands	1972	5.00	10.00	20.00
❑ KH 32286	Streets of Laredo	1973	3.00	6.00	12.00
MCA					
❑ 61	This Much a Man	1973	3.00	6.00	12.00
—Reissue of Decca LP					
❑ 342	Marty Robbins	1973	3.75	7.50	15.00
❑ 421	Good'n Country	1974	3.75	7.50	15.00

ROBBINS, RONNY

45s

Number	Title (A Side/B Side)	Yr	VG	VG+	NM
ARTIC					
❑ 878	The Last Lie I Told Her/Taste the Wine	1978	—	3.00	6.00
❑ 8782	Why'd the Last Time Have to Be the Best/Where Do I Put Her Memory	1979	—	3.00	6.00
COLUMBIA					
❑ 38-04506	Those You Lose/We've Been Lying Here Too Long	1984	—	2.00	4.00
❑ 38-05690	It's the Lovers That Give Love a Bad Name/Dynamite Nights	1985	—	2.00	4.00
❑ 38-05871	Black Check (On My Love)/Dynamite Nights	1986	—	2.00	4.00
MCA					
❑ 40055	Get Along Little Heartache/True Love's Forgiving	1973	—	3.50	7.00
❑ 40142	Too Much Love Between Us/Song for Ginny	1973	—	3.50	7.00
❑ 40197	Brand New You, Same Old Me/Broke Down and Alone	1974	—	3.50	7.00
❑ 40261	Let the Music Play/If This Is Love	1974	—	3.50	7.00
❑ 40393	What a Good Night's Love Will Do/Walk Your Kisses	1975	—	3.00	6.00
TRC					
❑ 081	I Know I'm Not Your Hero Anymore/The I Love You's Get Further Apart	1979	—	3.00	6.00

Albums

Number	Title (A Side/B Side)	Yr	VG	VG+	NM
COLUMBIA					
❑ CS 9944	Columbia Records Presents Marty Robbins Jr.	1970	6.25	12.50	25.00
—As "Marty Robbins, Jr."					

ROBERTS, HOUSTON

45s

Number	Title (A Side/B Side)	Yr	VG	VG+	NM
LITTLE DARLIN'					
❑ 0012	The All American Boy/Sorry, Wrong Number	1966	2.50	5.00	10.00
❑ 0024	If the Price Is Right/The Tie That Binds	1967	2.50	5.00	10.00

ROBERTS, KENNY
Also see THE DOWN HOMERS.

45s
BETHLEHEM

Number	Title (A Side/B Side)	Yr	VG	VG+	NM
❑ 3052	Cheer Up/Sing Me a Hurtin' Song	1962	3.00	6.00	12.00

CORAL

Number	Title (A Side/B Side)	Yr	VG	VG+	NM
❑ 9-60540	Beautiful Ohio/I Miss My Swiss	1951	6.25	12.50	25.00
❑ 9-60660	Kiwi Bird/Benny, Bunny	1952	5.00	10.00	20.00
❑ 9-60696	Ding Dong Bells (Are Ringing Again)/I'd Like to Kiss Susie Again	1952	5.00	10.00	20.00
❑ 9-60818	Honky Tonk Sweetheart/Mighty Pretty Waltz	1952	5.00	10.00	20.00
❑ 9-60884	Sleighbell Polka/Elfie the Elf	1952	5.00	10.00	20.00
❑ 9-60932	Sweet Little Cherokee/Hush Puppies	1953	5.00	10.00	20.00
❑ 9-61035	A Dear John Letter/She Taught Me How to Yodel	1953	5.00	10.00	20.00
❑ 9-61133	Wicked Little Cricket/Buzzy the Bumble Bee	1954	5.00	10.00	20.00
❑ 9-64059	I Finally Got Maggie Alone/Choo Choo Ch' Boogie	1950	7.50	15.00	30.00
❑ 9-64064	If You've Got the Money, I've Got the Time/ Molasses, Molasses	1950	7.50	15.00	30.00
❑ 9-64070	Cry Baby Blues/One Way Ticket	1950	7.50	15.00	30.00
❑ 9-64073	May the Good Lord Bless and Keep You/Wide Is the Gate	1951	6.25	12.50	25.00
❑ 9-64079	Mickey the Chickey/Casper, the Candy Cowboy	1951	6.25	12.50	25.00
❑ 9-64089	I Believe I'm Entitled to You/Just a Yodel for Me	1951	6.25	12.50	25.00
❑ 9-64105	He'll Be Coming Down the Chimney/Grandfather Kringle	1951	6.25	12.50	25.00
❑ 9-64115	F.O.B. Tennessee/Good Old Mountain Dew	1952	6.25	12.50	25.00
❑ 9-64142	Hillbilly Style/The Yodel Polka	1952	6.25	12.50	25.00
❑ 9-64151	Call of the Wild/Love Makes a New Fool Every Day	1952	6.25	12.50	25.00

DECCA

Number	Title (A Side/B Side)	Yr	VG	VG+	NM
❑ 9-30073	Broken Teen-Age Heart/I'm Looking for the Bully of the Town	1956	3.75	7.50	15.00
❑ 9-30472	Arizona Yodeler/Dream Little Cowboy	1957	5.00	10.00	20.00

DOT

Number	Title (A Side/B Side)	Yr	VG	VG+	NM
❑ 15140	Smoke Gets in Your Eyes/Wagon Wheels	1954	5.00	10.00	20.00

KING

Number	Title (A Side/B Side)	Yr	VG	VG+	NM
❑ 5543	Goodbye for Him (Hello for Me)/Two Steps Forward (Three Steps Back)	1961	3.75	7.50	15.00
❑ 5773	Choc'late Ice Cream Cone/24 Hours with the Blues	1963	3.00	6.00	12.00
❑ 5911	I Never See Maggie Alone/I'm Crying on the Inside	1964	3.00	6.00	12.00

STARDAY

Number	Title (A Side/B Side)	Yr	VG	VG+	NM
❑ 716	Tavern Town/Guitar Ringing	1965	2.50	5.00	10.00
❑ 736	Fly Away Mockingbird/If I'm a Man	1965	2.50	5.00	10.00
❑ 769	Anytime/Tying the Leaves	1966	2.50	5.00	10.00
❑ 788	Blue/Sioux City Sue	1966	3.00	6.00	12.00
❑ 805	Just Look, Don't Touch/Singing River	1967	2.00	4.00	8.00
❑ 851	Country Music Singing Sensation/Fugitive of Love	1968	2.00	4.00	8.00
❑ 869	Artificial Flowers/Gonna Whistle Me a Tune	1969	2.00	4.00	8.00
❑ 890	The Bottle Holds the Man/You Left Too Much	1970	—	3.50	7.00
❑ 908	Best Part of My Years/Green River	1970	—	3.50	7.00
❑ 924	Pistol Packin' Mama/Pretty Flowers	1971	—	3.50	7.00
❑ 947	Ding Dong Bell/Mule Skinner Blues	1972	—	3.50	7.00
❑ 7028	Chime Bells/She Taught Me How to Yodel	197?	—	3.00	6.00

Selected 78s
CORAL

Number	Title (A Side/B Side)	Yr	VG	VG+	NM
❑ 64012	I Never See Maggie Alone/Wedding Bells	1949	3.75	7.50	15.00
❑ 64015	River of Tears/I've Got the Blues	1949	3.75	7.50	15.00
❑ 64021	Jealous Heart/(There's a) Bluebird on Your Windowsill	1949	3.75	7.50	15.00
❑ 64025	The Christmas Cannonball/Christmas Roses	1949	3.75	7.50	15.00
❑ 64027	Slide Them Jugs Down the Mountain/When I'd Yoo-Hoo in the Valley	1950	3.75	7.50	15.00
❑ 64032	Choc'late Ice Cream Cone/Hillbilly Fever	1950	3.75	7.50	15.00
❑ 64045	Billy and Nanny Goat/Boogie Woogie Yodel Song	1950	3.00	6.00	12.00
—Unknown on 45; if one exists, it would be in the $40 NM range					
❑ 64053	Our Lady of Fatima/Mother Dear, O Pray for Me	1950	3.00	6.00	12.00
—Unknown on 45; if one exists, it would be in the $40 NM range					

Albums
STARDAY

Number	Title (A Side/B Side)	Yr	VG	VG+	NM
❑ SLP-336 [M]	Indian Love Call	1965	10.00	20.00	40.00
❑ SLP-406 [M]	The Incredible Kenny Roberts	1967	7.50	15.00	30.00
❑ SLP-434	Country Music Singing Sensation	1969	5.00	10.00	20.00

VOCALION

Number	Title (A Side/B Side)	Yr	VG	VG+	NM
❑ VL 73770	Kenny Roberts Sings Country Songs	196?	3.00	6.00	12.00

ROBERTS, KENNY, AND TOMMY SOSEBEE
Also see each artist's individual listings.

45s
CORAL

Number	Title (A Side/B Side)	Yr	VG	VG+	NM
❑ 9-64108	The Sissy Song/She Said	1951	6.25	12.50	25.00
❑ 9-64112	It's Great to Be a Christian/Let Jesus Come Into Your Heart	1951	6.25	12.50	25.00

ROBERTS, PAT

45s
ABC DOT

Number	Title (A Side/B Side)	Yr	VG	VG+	NM
❑ 17539	Airports and Planes/I Will Always Be Here	1974	—	2.50	5.00
❑ 17559	She's Out There Dancin' Alone/She Came Here for the Change	1975	—	2.50	5.00

DOT

Number	Title (A Side/B Side)	Yr	VG	VG+	NM
❑ 17434	Rhythm of the Rain/Without You	1972	—	3.00	6.00
❑ 17451	Thanks for Lovin' Me/A Whole Lotta Lovin'	1973	—	3.00	6.00
❑ 17465	Here Comes My Little Baby/Love Lives Again	1973	—	3.00	6.00
❑ 17478	I'm Gonna Keep Searching/Your Love's Been a Long Time Comin'	1973	—	3.00	6.00
❑ 17495	You Got Everything That You Want/Love Me, Love Me	1974	—	3.00	6.00

Albums
DOT

Number	Title (A Side/B Side)	Yr	VG	VG+	NM
❑ DLP-26011	This Is Pat Roberts	1973	3.75	7.50	15.00

ROBERTSON, JACK

45s
SOUNDWAVES

Number	Title (A Side/B Side)	Yr	VG	VG+	NM
❑ 4808	It's Not Easy/Cow Town Mama	1988	—	2.50	5.00

ROBERTSON, TEXAS JIM

45s
MGM

Number	Title (A Side/B Side)	Yr	VG	VG+	NM
❑ 11787	Hide-a-Way Love/Automatic Woman	1954	5.00	10.00	20.00
❑ 11860	Pride of My Heart/Walkin' and Talkin' with the Lord	1954	5.00	10.00	20.00

RCA VICTOR

Number	Title (A Side/B Side)	Yr	VG	VG+	NM
❑ 47-4326	Lonesome Whistle/Gotta Git a Glitter	1951	6.25	12.50	25.00
❑ 47-4548	Taffy/I'm Gonna Be Long Gone	1952	5.00	10.00	20.00
❑ 47-4710	Put Your Arms Around Me/Low in the Lehigh Valley	1952	5.00	10.00	20.00
❑ 47-4906	Blue Eyed Ellen/Life Passed Me By	1952	5.00	10.00	20.00
❑ 48-0071	Slipping Around/Wedding Bells	1949	10.00	20.00	40.00
—Originals on green vinyl					
❑ 48-0071	Slipping Around/Wedding Bells	1950	6.25	12.50	25.00
—Reissues on black vinyl					
❑ 48-0097	I Heard the Angels Weep/I'm So Low	1949	7.50	15.00	30.00
—Originals on green vinyl					
❑ 48-0133	I'll Never Slip Around Again/Revenge	1949	7.50	15.00	30.00
—Originals on green vinyl					
❑ 48-0178	I'll Walk This Weary Road Alone/I'm Back to Where I Started	1950	7.50	15.00	30.00
—Originals on green vinyl					
❑ 48-0304	Rubber Knuckle Sam/Wedding Bells Will Never Ring	1950	7.50	15.00	30.00
—Originals on green vinyl					
❑ 48-0334	One Kind Word/Yesterday's Kisses	1950	7.50	15.00	30.00
—Originals on green vinyl					
❑ 48-0365	Jaw, Jaw, Yap, Yap/It Hurts Me to See You with Somebody Else	1950	7.50	15.00	30.00
—Originals on green vinyl					
❑ 48-0398	I Don't Want No More of the Army Life/If You've Got the Money, I've Got the Time	1950	7.50	15.00	30.00
—Originals on green vinyl					
❑ 48-0427	Don't You Angel Me/You Can't Do Nothin' with a Woman	1951	6.25	12.50	25.00
❑ 48-0463	Wildcat Baby/Why Don't You Marry the Girl	1951	6.25	12.50	25.00
❑ 48-0492	Deadly Weapon/Bite Your Tongue and Say You're Sorry	1951	6.25	12.50	25.00

Selected 78s
BLUEBIRD

Number	Title (A Side/B Side)	Yr	VG	VG+	NM
❑ B-8186	Bouncin' Along/Things That Might Have Been	1940	5.00	10.00	20.00
❑ B-8207	I'm Gonna Throw My Lasso/What Good Is the Sunshine?	1940	5.00	10.00	20.00
❑ B-8435	Windy Ben/My Pony's Hair Turned Grey	1941	5.00	10.00	20.00
❑ B-8466	'Way Down in Texas/Purple Night on the Prairie	1941	5.00	10.00	20.00
❑ B-8606	The Cowboy Isn't Speaking to His Horse/I'll Be Back in a Year, Little Darling	1941	5.00	10.00	20.00
❑ B-8631	My Ma, She Told Me So/I'm Gonna Be Long Gone	1941	5.00	10.00	20.00
❑ B-8686	Brother Henry/Birmingham Woman	1941	5.00	10.00	20.00
❑ B- 8706	There's a Heart in the Heart of the Rockies/Too Blue to Cry	1941	5.00	10.00	20.00
❑ 33-0503	Sweet Baby/Miz O'Reilly's Daughter	1945	5.00	10.00	20.00

RCA VICTOR

Number	Title (A Side/B Side)	Yr	VG	VG+	NM
❑ 20-1975	Filipino Baby/Rainbow at Midnight	1946	3.75	7.50	15.00
❑ 20-2090	Land, Sky and Water/Seven Women in One	1947	3.75	7.50	15.00
❑ 20-2308	Don't Look Now/It Takes a Long Train	1947	3.75	7.50	15.00
❑ 20-2408	Don't Make Me Sorry/A Pal in Palo Alto	1947	3.75	7.50	15.00
❑ 20-2455	I Sure Got It from You/Answer to Rainbow at Midnight	1947	3.75	7.50	15.00
❑ 20-2651	Signed, Sealed and Delivered/Lost Deep in the Bottom of the Sea	1948	3.75	7.50	15.00
❑ 20-2764	The Letter I'm Mailing to You/Mountain Rosalie	1948	3.75	7.50	15.00
❑ 20-2907	In the Pines/Tears Today and Blues Tomorrow	1948	3.75	7.50	15.00

VICTOR

Number	Title (A Side/B Side)	Yr	VG	VG+	NM
❑ P-84 [PS]	Round the Campfire — Famous American Cowboy Songs	1941	5.00	10.00	20.00
—Folder for 78 rpm records 27550, 27551, 27552, 27553 (records priced separately)					
❑ 27550	Home on the Range/The Cowboy's Dream	1941	5.00	10.00	20.00
❑ 27551	O Bury Me Not on the Lone Prairie/In Texas for the Round-Up in the Spring	1941	5.00	10.00	20.00
❑ 27552	Red River Valley/The Border Affair	1941	5.00	10.00	20.00
❑ 27553	Ridin' Old Paint (And Leadin' Old Dan)/The Texas Song (A Cowboy Lament)	1941	5.00	10.00	20.00
—The above four 78s comprise album P-84, "Round the Campfire -- Famous American Cowboy Songs"					

Albums

Number	Title (A Side/B Side)	Yr	VG	VG+	NM
DESIGN					
❑ DLP-115 [M]	Golden Hits of Country and Western Music	196?	3.00	6.00	12.00
❑ DLP-132 [M]	Sacred Country & Western Songs	196?	3.00	6.00	12.00
GRAND PRIX					
❑ 185 [M]	Texas Jim Robertson Sings the Great Hits of Country & Western	196?	3.75	7.50	15.00
MASTERSEAL					
❑ (# unknown) [10]	Eight Top Western Hits	195?	15.00	30.00	60.00
STRAND					
❑ 1016 [M]	Texas Jim Robertson	1961	10.00	20.00	40.00

ROBEY, LORETTA

45s

Number	Title (A Side/B Side)	Yr	VG	VG+	NM
SOUNDWAVES					
❑ 4545	Sophisticated Country Lady/Lovin' Cup	1977	—	2.50	5.00
❑ 4551	Hey There/Lovin' Me All the Time	1977	—	2.50	5.00
❑ 4559	I've Done It Again/King of the Mountain	1977	—	2.50	5.00
❑ 4571	Mama/Hey There	1978	—	2.50	5.00
❑ 4576	So Busy Making a Living/When My Blue Moon Turns to Gold Again	1978	—	2.50	5.00
❑ 4590	I've Got It All This Time (same on both sides)	1979	—	3.00	6.00

ROBIN AND CRUISER

45s

Number	Title (A Side/B Side)	Yr	VG	VG+	NM
16TH AVENUE					
❑ 70404	Rings of Gold/Tie Me to Your Heart Again	1987	—	—	3.00
❑ 70409	No Heart Left to Break/Rings of Gold	1988	—	—	3.00

ROBINSON, BETTY JEAN

Also see CARL BELEW AND BETTY JEAN ROBINSON.

45s

Number	Title (A Side/B Side)	Yr	VG	VG+	NM
4 STAR					
❑ 1004	God Is Good/All I Need Is You	1975	—	2.50	5.00
❑ 1008	On Silver Wings/Boy, You're Getting Closer	1975	—	2.50	5.00
DECCA					
❑ 32912	Boy You're Getting Closer to Home/Daddy Can I Make It on My Own	1972	—	3.50	7.00
❑ 33017	Johnny's Secret/Another Football Year	1972	—	3.50	7.00
MCA					
❑ 40022	Love Is All Over Me/Baby Make the Sun Go Down	1973	—	2.50	5.00
❑ 40088	Lovin' You/Woman in Your Life	1973	—	2.50	5.00
❑ 40166	All I Need Is You/Jersey 33	1973	—	2.50	5.00
❑ 40300	On the Way Home/I've Got You	1974	—	2.50	5.00

ROBINSON, SHARON

45s

Number	Title (A Side/B Side)	Yr	VG	VG+	NM
NIGHTFALL					
❑ 001	Have You Hurt Any Good Ones Lately/Potential Strangers	1987	2.00	4.00	8.00

ROBISON, CARSON

Like VERNON DALHART, with whom he made some recordings, Robison made hundreds of records for many labels. Unlike Dalhart, Robison was still active into the 45 rpm era, so we've made an attempt to include all his 45s plus as many 78s as we could dig up. Additions are always welcome.

45s

Number	Title (A Side/B Side)	Yr	VG	VG+	NM
MGM					
❑ K10051	Head Couples Separate/Hook and Whirl	1949	5.00	10.00	20.00
—Reissue of 78 from 1947					
❑ K10052	Lady Round the Lady/Devil's Britches	1949	5.00	10.00	20.00
—Reissue of 78 from 1947					
❑ K10053	Bob's Favorite/Maverick	1949	5.00	10.00	20.00
—Reissue of 78 from 1947					
❑ K10054	Pokeberry Promenade/When Work's All Done This Fall	1949	5.00	10.00	20.00
—Reissue of 78 from 1947; the above four comprise 45 rpm box set K-5, "Square Dances"					
❑ K10435	Yodelling Tex/Too Big for His Britches	1950	7.50	15.00	30.00
❑ K10541	Remember This Song/Settin' by the Fire	1949	10.00	20.00	40.00
❑ K10732	Trail Drive/That Horse Named Pete	1950	7.50	15.00	30.00
❑ K10837	Texas Dan/The Devil Calls a Meeting	1950	7.50	15.00	30.00
❑ K10949	6 P.M./Our Silver Anniversary	1951	6.25	12.50	25.00
❑ K11044	Plumb Aggrevatin' Ain't It/Sunday Drivers	1951	6.25	12.50	25.00
❑ K11091	Old Tom the Turkey/Barnyard Square Dance	1951	6.25	12.50	25.00
❑ K11159	Square Dance Polka/Promenade Indian	1952	6.25	12.50	25.00
❑ K11293	I'm No Communist/Will Someone Please Tell Me	1952	7.50	15.00	30.00
❑ K11432	Ike's Letter to Harry/Harry's Reply	1953	7.50	15.00	30.00
❑ K11475	Spring! Spring! (Part 1)/Spring! Spring! (Part 2)	1953	6.25	12.50	25.00
❑ K11688	Denver, Dragon (Part 1)/Denver, Dragon (Part 2)	1954	5.00	10.00	20.00
❑ K11837	Just Lazy/Awkward Situation	1954	5.00	10.00	20.00
❑ K12266	Rockin' and Rollin' with Grandmaw/Hand Me Down My Walkin' Cane	1956	25.00	50.00	100.00
❑ K12355	I'm Going Back to Where I Come From/Will Someone Please Tell Me Who	1956	3.75	7.50	15.00
RCA VICTOR					
❑ 47-2868	Irish Washerwoman/Spanish Caballero	1949	5.00	10.00	20.00
❑ 47-2869	Solomon Levi/Comin' Round the Mountain	1949	5.00	10.00	20.00
❑ 47-2870	Jingle Bells/Paddy Dear	1949	5.00	10.00	20.00
❑ 47-2871	Golden Slippers/Turkey in the Straw	1949	5.00	10.00	20.00
—The above four comprise box set WP 155					

Selected 78s

Number	Title (A Side/B Side)	Yr	VG	VG+	NM
BANNER					
❑ 0615-B	Red River Valley/Down on the Old Plantation	193?	6.25	12.50	25.00
BLUEBIRD					
❑ B-11414	We're Gonna Have to Slap the Dirty Little Jap/Remember Pearl Harbor	1942	7.50	15.00	30.00
❑ B-11415	Get Your Gun and Come Along/I'm in the Army Now	1942	7.50	15.00	30.00
❑ B-11459	Mussolini's Letter to Hitler/Hitler's Reply to Mussolini	1942	7.50	15.00	30.00
❑ B-11460	1942 Turkey in the Straw/Here I Go to Tokio, Said Barnacle Bill, The Sailor	1942	7.50	15.00	30.00
❑ B-11527	The Story of Jitterbug Joe/It's Just a Matter of Time	1942	5.00	10.00	20.00
❑ 33-0509	Just Wait and See/Ramblin' Cowboy	1945	5.00	10.00	20.00
CLARION					
❑ 5109-C	Oklahoma Charley/Red River Valley	1931	7.50	15.00	30.00
❑ 5110-C	Leave the Purty Girls Alone/Darling Nellie Gray	1931	7.50	15.00	30.00
❑ 5243-C	Red River Valley/(B-side unknown)	193?	7.50	15.00	30.00
COLUMBIA					
❑ 2134-D	His Old Cornet/Smoky Mountain Bill	1930	6.25	12.50	25.00
❑ 2458-D	When It's Night Time in Nevada/Rocky Mountain Lullaby	1931	7.50	15.00	30.00
❑ 2550-D	Silvery Arizona Moon/When You're Alone (Try to Remember Me)	1931	7.50	15.00	30.00
❑ 2619-D	In the Cumberland Mountains/(B-side unknown)	1932	7.50	15.00	30.00
❑ 2642-D	Home on the Range/The Tree That Stands by the Road	1932	7.50	15.00	30.00
❑ 15548-D	Ohio Prison Fire/Why Are the Young Folks So Thoughtless?	1930	6.25	12.50	25.00
❑ 15588-D	Carry Me Back to the Mountains/Oklahoma Charley	1930	7.50	15.00	30.00
❑ 15627-D	I'm Gittin' Ready to Go/Abraham	1931	6.25	12.50	25.00
❑ 15644-D	My Heart Is Where the Mohawk Flows Tonight/Sleepy Hollow	1931	6.25	12.50	25.00
❑ 15768-D	titles unknown	1932	6.25	12.50	25.00
❑ 15773-D	Old Familiar Tunes/(B-side unknown)	1932	7.50	15.00	30.00
❑ 15779-D	Missouri Valley/When It's Springtime in the Blue Ridge Mountains	1932	7.50	15.00	30.00
❑ 36018	First Two Ladies Cross Over/Darling Nellie Gray	1941	5.00	10.00	20.00
❑ 36019	Buffalo Boy/Oh Susanna	1941	5.00	10.00	20.00
❑ 36020	Dive for the Oyster (Part 1)/Dive for the Oyster (Part 2)	1941	5.00	10.00	20.00
❑ 36021	Little Brown Jug/Possum in the Simmon Tree	1941	5.00	10.00	20.00
DIVA					
❑ 6066-G	Oklahoma Charley/Leave the Purty Girls Alone	1931	7.50	15.00	30.00
MGM					
❑ 10012	Predictions for 100 Years from Now/Ain't No Name Purdy As Arkansas	1947	5.00	10.00	20.00
❑ 10051	Head Couples Separate/Hook and Whirl	1947	3.75	7.50	15.00
❑ 10052	Lady Round the Lady/Devil's Britches	1947	3.75	7.50	15.00
❑ 10053	Bob's Favorite/Maverick	1947	3.75	7.50	15.00
❑ 10054	Pokeberry Promenade/When Work's All Done This Fall	1947	3.75	7.50	15.00
—The above four comprise 78 rpm album MGM-5, "Square Dances"					
❑ 10110	Shady Valley Waltz/Someday You Gotta Make Up Your Mind	1947	5.00	10.00	20.00
❑ 10173	Hold Your Hat/Midnight Express	1948	5.00	10.00	20.00
❑ 10224	Life Gits Tee-Jus Don't It/Wind in the Mountains	1948	5.00	10.00	20.00
❑ 10327	Little Darlin' Waltz/Seein' Red	1949	5.00	10.00	20.00
❑ 10389	More and More Tee-Jus Ain't It/Don't Make Sense Does It	1949	5.00	10.00	20.00
MONTGOMERY WARD					
❑ 3001	At the Close of a Long Day/(B-side unknown)	193?	5.00	10.00	20.00
OKEH					
❑ 45537	So I Joined the Navy/(B-side unknown)	193?	5.00	10.00	20.00
ORIOLE					
❑ 2021	I'm Drifting Back to Dreamland/(B-side unknown)	193?	5.00	10.00	20.00
❑ 8100	Twenty One Years/(B-side unknown)	193?	6.25	12.50	25.00
PERFECT					
❑ 12759	Twenty One Years/(B-side unknown)	193?	5.00	10.00	20.00
SUPERIOR					
❑ 2546	When the Sun Goes Down Again/(B-side unknown)	193?	12.50	25.00	50.00
❑ 2580	Cross-Eyed Sue/(B-side unknown)	193?	12.50	25.00	50.00
VELVET TONE					
❑ 7092-V	Oklahoma Charley/Leave the Purty Girls Alone	1931	7.50	15.00	30.00
VICTOR					
❑ 20382	Nola/Whistle-Itis	1927	5.00	10.00	20.00
❑ 20-1665	Hitler's Last Letter to Hirohito/Hirohito's Letter to Hitler	1945	5.00	10.00	20.00

Albums

Number	Title (A Side/B Side)	Yr	VG	VG+	NM
COLUMBIA					
❑ CL 2551 [10]	Square Dance	1955	20.00	40.00	80.00
❑ CL 6029 [10]	Square Dance	1949	20.00	40.00	80.00
MGM					
❑ E-13 [M]	Call Your Own Square Dances	195?	15.00	30.00	60.00
❑ E-557 [10]	Square Dances with Calls	1952	15.00	30.00	60.00
❑ E-3258 [M]	Square Dances	1955	7.50	15.00	30.00
❑ E-3594 [M]	Life Gets Tee-Jus, Don't It	1958	12.50	25.00	50.00
RCA VICTOR					
❑ LPM-1238 [M]	Square Dances	1956	7.50	15.00	30.00
❑ LPM-3030 [10]	Square Dances	1952	15.00	30.00	60.00

ROBISON, CHARLIE

45s

COLUMBIA

Number	Title (A Side/B Side)	Yr	VG	VG+	NM
❑ 79167	Barlight/You're Not the Best	1999	—	—	3.00

ROCK CITY BAND, THE

45s

HICKORY

Number	Title (A Side/B Side)	Yr	VG	VG+	NM
❑ 1617	Bad News/Grow	1971	2.00	4.00	8.00
❑ 1639	The Girl Who Loved Jack Daniels/Thoughtless Woman	1972	2.00	4.00	8.00
❑ 1663	A Country Song Is a Country Song/She's the Funny Turned Kind	1973	2.00	4.00	8.00

ROCKIN' SIDNEY

45s

EPIC

Number	Title (A Side/B Side)	Yr	VG	VG+	NM
❑ 34-05430	My Toot Toot/Jalapeno Lena	1985	—	2.00	4.00

GOLDBAND

Number	Title (A Side/B Side)	Yr	VG	VG+	NM
❑ 1158	Actions Speak Louder Than Words/Lais Per La Patate	196?	3.00	6.00	12.00
❑ 1159	My Poor Heart/Something Working Baby	196?	3.00	6.00	12.00
❑ 1163	Deedle Didie Da/Life Without Love	196?	2.50	5.00	10.00
❑ 1170	Gonna Be Looking/Shed So Many Tears	196?	2.50	5.00	10.00
❑ 1177	Corpus Christi/(B-side unknown)	196?	3.00	6.00	12.00
❑ 1178	Trust/Put On It	196?	2.50	5.00	10.00
❑ 1183	Soul Christmas (Part 1)/Soul Christmas (Part 2)	1966	3.00	6.00	12.00
❑ 1186	The Grandpa/Feel Delicious	1967	2.50	5.00	10.00

JIN

Number	Title (A Side/B Side)	Yr	VG	VG+	NM
❑ 110	My Little Girl/Don't Say Goodbye	1959	12.50	25.00	50.00
❑ 141	Walking Out on You/Rocky	1960	7.50	15.00	30.00
❑ 156	No Good Woman/You Ain't Nothin' But Fine	1960	7.50	15.00	30.00
❑ 164	Send Me Some Lovin'/Past Bedtime	196?	7.50	15.00	30.00
❑ 168	No Good Man/If I Could, I Win	196?	7.50	15.00	30.00
❑ 170	Don't Let Me Cross Over/You Don't Have to Go	196?	7.50	15.00	30.00
❑ 174	Something's Wrong/It Really Is a Hurtin' Thing	196?	7.50	15.00	30.00
❑ 177	Ya Ya/Wasted Days and Wasted Nights	196?	7.50	15.00	30.00

MAISON DE SOUL

Number	Title (A Side/B Side)	Yr	VG	VG+	NM
❑ 1017	Good Time Woman/You Ain't Nothin' But Fine	198?	—	3.00	6.00
❑ 1020	Dance and Show Off/Relax and Go Slow	198?	—	3.00	6.00
❑ 1021	Boogie for Me/Sweet Li'l Woman	198?	—	3.00	6.00
❑ 1024	My Toot Toot/Zydeco Shoes	1984	2.00	4.00	8.00
❑ 1025	Party This Christmas/Christmas Without You	1984	—	3.00	6.00

Albums

EPIC

Number	Title (A Side/B Side)	Yr	VG	VG+	NM
❑ 5E 40153 [EP]	My Toot Toot	1985	2.00	4.00	8.00

ZBC

Number	Title (A Side/B Side)	Yr	VG	VG+	NM
❑ LP-100	A Holiday Celebration with Rockin' Sidney	1983	3.75	7.50	15.00

ROCKINHORSE

45s

LONG SHOT

Number	Title (A Side/B Side)	Yr	VG	VG+	NM
❑ 1002	Have I Got a Heart for You/(B-side unknown)	1986	—	3.00	6.00
❑ 1003	Let a Little Love In (Tennessee Saturday Night)/(B-side unknown)	1986	—	3.00	6.00

RODGERS, JIMMIE (1)

Legendary country & western singer known as "The Singing Brakeman."

45s

RCA VICTOR

Number	Title (A Side/B Side)	Yr	VG	VG+	NM
❑ WPT 21 [PS]	Yodelingly Yours, Jimmie Rodgers, Volume 1	1950	5.00	10.00	20.00

—Box for 27-0098, 27-0099 and 27-0100

Number	Title (A Side/B Side)	Yr	VG	VG+	NM
❑ AMAO-0130	Mule Skinner Blues/Waiting for a Train	1973	2.00	4.00	8.00

—Gold Standard Series reissue

Number	Title (A Side/B Side)	Yr	VG	VG+	NM
❑ 27-0098	Blue Yodel (T for Texas)/Away Out on the Mountain	1950	5.00	10.00	20.00
❑ 27-0099	Never No Mo' Blues/Daddy and Home	1950	5.00	10.00	20.00
❑ 27-0100	Frankie and Johnny/The Brakeman's Blues	1950	5.00	10.00	20.00

—The above three comprise box set WPT 21

Number	Title (A Side/B Side)	Yr	VG	VG+	NM
❑ 47-6092	In the Jailhouse Now No. 2/Peach Pickin' Time Down in Georgia	1955	5.00	10.00	20.00
❑ 47-6205	Mule Skinner Blues/Mother, the Queen of My Heart	1955	5.00	10.00	20.00
❑ 47-6408	Never No Mo' Blues/Daddy and Home	1955	5.00	10.00	20.00

Selected 78s

BLUEBIRD

Number	Title (A Side/B Side)	Yr	VG	VG+	NM
❑ B-5000	Moonlight and Skies/Rock All Our Babies to Sleep	193?	5.00	10.00	20.00
❑ B-5037	Gambling Bar Room Blues/Looking for a New Mama	193?	7.50	15.00	30.00
❑ B-5057	Happy Till She Met You/(B-side unknown)	193?	7.50	15.00	30.00
❑ B-5061	You've Got Me Crying Again/(B-side unknown)	193?	7.50	15.00	30.00
❑ B-5076	Prairie Lullaby/Whippin' That Old T.B.	193?	7.50	15.00	30.00
❑ B-5080	Mother the Queen of My Heart/Peach Pickin' Time Down in Georgia	193?	7.50	15.00	30.00
❑ B-5081	Miss the Mississippi and You/Down the Old Road to Home	193?	7.50	15.00	30.00
❑ B-5082	Roll Along, Kentucky Moon/Why Should I Be Lonely?	193?	7.50	15.00	30.00
❑ B-5083	My Time Ain't Long/You and My Old Guitar	193?	7.50	15.00	30.00
❑ B-5084	What's It/Let Me Be Your Sidetrack	193?	7.50	15.00	30.00
❑ B-5085	Blue Yodel/Away Out on the Mountain	193?	7.50	15.00	30.00
❑ B-5136	Old Pal of My Heart/Mississippi Moon	193?	5.00	10.00	20.00
❑ B-5163	Waiting for a Train/When the Cactus Is in Bloom	193?	5.00	10.00	20.00
❑ B-5199	When It's Harvest Time/(B-side unknown)	193?	5.00	10.00	20.00
❑ B-5223	In the Jailhouse Now/Frankie and Johnny	193?	3.75	7.50	15.00
❑ B-5281	Jimmie Rodgers' Last Blue Yodel/Years Ago	193?	12.50	25.00	50.00
❑ B-5337	Lullaby Yodel/The Land of My Boyhood Dreams	193?	6.25	12.50	25.00
❑ B-5393	Mississippi River Blues/My Blue-Eyed Jane	193?	5.00	10.00	20.00
❑ B-5482	Mother Was a Lady/Ben Dewberry's Final Run	193?	5.00	10.00	20.00
❑ B-5556	The Yodeling Ranger/My Carolina Sunshine Girl	193?	5.00	10.00	20.00
❑ B-5609	My Old Pal/(B-side unknown)	193?	6.25	12.50	25.00
❑ B-5664	Tuck Away My Lonesome Blues/Any Old Time	193?	5.00	10.00	20.00
❑ B-5739	I'm Lonesome Too/The Mystery of Number Five	193?	6.25	12.50	25.00
❑ B-5784	In the Hills of Tennessee/(B-side unknown)	193?	5.00	10.00	20.00
❑ B-5838	My Little Lady/Treasures Untold	193?	5.00	10.00	20.00
❑ B-5892	I've Ranged, I've Roamed and I've Traveled/Why Did You Give Me Your Love	193?	6.25	12.50	25.00
❑ B-5942	My Good Gal's Gone Blues/(B-side unknown)	193?	15.00	30.00	60.00
❑ B-5991	Daddy and Home/Yodeling Cowboy	193?	5.00	10.00	20.00
❑ B-6198	Old Love Letters/(B-side unknown)	193?	10.00	20.00	40.00
❑ B-6225	Sleep, Baby, Sleep/Never No Mo' Blues	193?	5.00	10.00	20.00
❑ B-6275	Mule Skinner Blues/T.B. Blues	193?	7.50	15.00	30.00
❑ B-6698	Why There's a Tear in My Eye/We Miss Him When the Evening Shadows Fall	193?	12.50	25.00	50.00

—A-side with Sara Carter; B-side by "Mrs. Jimmie Rodgers"

Number	Title (A Side/B Side)	Yr	VG	VG+	NM
❑ B-6762	The Carter Family and Jimmie Rodgers in Texas/Where Is My Sailor Boy?	193?	6.25	12.50	25.00

—A-side with the Carter Family; B-side by Monroe Brothers

Number	Title (A Side/B Side)	Yr	VG	VG+	NM
❑ B-6810	I've Only Loved Three Women/The Wonderful City	193?	6.25	12.50	25.00

—B-side with Sara Carter

Number	Title (A Side/B Side)	Yr	VG	VG+	NM
❑ B-7280	Yodeling My Way Back Home/The One Rose	193?	6.25	12.50	25.00

—This is the first of Rodgers' Bluebird 78s to be issued originally on the familiar blue label. Earlier numbers came out originally on a cream label with blue print; blue label versions of those go for no more than 75 percent of the listed prices.

Number	Title (A Side/B Side)	Yr	VG	VG+	NM
❑ B-7600	Take Me Back Again/Dreaming with Tears in My Eyes	193?	7.50	15.00	30.00
❑ 33-0513	The Soldier's Sweetheart/The Sailor's Plea	1945	10.00	20.00	40.00

ELECTRADISC

Number	Title (A Side/B Side)	Yr	VG	VG+	NM
❑ E-1830	Moonlight and Skies/Rock All Our Babies to Sleep	193?	100.00	200.00	400.00
❑ E-1966	Gambling Bar Room Blues/Looking for a New Mama	193?	75.00	150.00	300.00
❑ E-1983	Whisper Your Mother's Name/(B-side unknown)	193?	75.00	150.00	300.00
❑ E-1999	Prairie Lullaby/Whippin' That Old T.B.	193?	75.00	150.00	300.00
❑ E-2008	Mother the Queen of My Heart/Peach Pickin' Time Down in Georgia	193?	75.00	150.00	300.00
❑ E-2009	My Time Ain't Long/You and My Old Guitar	193?	75.00	150.00	300.00
❑ E-2042	Old Pal of My Heart/Mississippi Moon	193?	75.00	150.00	300.00
❑ E-2060	Waiting for a Train/When the Cactus Is in Bloom	193?	75.00	150.00	300.00
❑ E-2109	In the Jailhouse Now/Frankie and Johnny	193?	75.00	150.00	300.00
❑ E-2155	Jimmie Rodgers' Last Blue Yodel/Years Ago	193?	100.00	200.00	400.00

MONTGOMERY WARD

Number	Title (A Side/B Side)	Yr	VG	VG+	NM
❑ M-3272	Blue Yodel/Away Out on the Mountain	193?	7.50	15.00	30.00
❑ M-4201	Prairie Lullaby/Whippin' That Old T.B.	193?	7.50	15.00	30.00
❑ M-4203	Gambling Barroom Blues/Looking for a New Mama	193?	7.50	15.00	30.00
❑ M-4209	Blue Yodel No. 9/(B-side unknown)	193?	15.00	30.00	60.00
❑ M-5014	My Good Gal's Gone Blues/(B-side unknown)	193?	15.00	30.00	60.00

SUNRISE

Number	Title (A Side/B Side)	Yr	VG	VG+	NM
❑ S-3104	Moonlight and Skies/Rock All Our Babies to Sleep	193?	62.50	125.00	250.00
❑ S-3131	Gambling Bar Room Blues/Looking for a New Mama	193?	62.50	125.00	250.00
❑ S-3142	Whisper Your Mother's Name/(B-side unknown)	193?	62.50	125.00	250.00
❑ S-3157	Prairie Lullaby/Whippin' That Old T.B.	193?	75.00	150.00	300.00
❑ S-3167	Mother the Queen of My Heart/Peach Pickin' Time Down in Georgia	193?	75.00	150.00	300.00
❑ S-3168	Miss the Mississippi and You/Down the Old Road to Home	193?	62.50	125.00	250.00
❑ S-3169	Roll Along, Kentucky Moon/Why Should I Be Lonely?	193?	62.50	125.00	250.00
❑ S-3170	My Time Ain't Long/You and My Old Guitar	193?	62.50	125.00	250.00
❑ S-3171	What's It/Let Me Be Your Sidetrack	193?	62.50	125.00	250.00
❑ S-3172	Blue Yodel/Away Out on the Mountain	193?	62.50	125.00	250.00
❑ S-3217	Old Pal of My Heart/Mississippi Moon	193?	62.50	125.00	250.00
❑ S-3244	Waiting for a Train/When the Cactus Is in Bloom	193?	62.50	125.00	250.00
❑ S-3306	In the Jailhouse Now/Frankie and Johnny	193?	62.50	125.00	250.00
❑ S-3362	Jimmie Rodgers' Last Blue Yodel/Years Ago	193?	75.00	150.00	300.00
❑ S-3418	Lullaby Yodel/The Land of My Boyhood Dreams	193?	62.50	125.00	250.00

VICTOR

Number	Title (A Side/B Side)	Yr	VG	VG+	NM
❑ 20864	The Soldier's Sweetheart/Sleep Baby Sleep	1927	10.00	20.00	40.00
❑ 21142	Blue Yodel/Away Out on the Mountain	1928	10.00	20.00	40.00
❑ 21245	In the Jail House Now/Ben Dewberry's Final Run	1928	10.00	20.00	40.00
❑ 21291	The Brakeman's Blues/Blue Yodel No. 2	1928	10.00	20.00	40.00
❑ 21433	Treasures Untold/Mother Was a Lady	1928	10.00	20.00	40.00
❑ 21531	Blue Yodel No. 3/Never No' Mo' Blues	1928	10.00	20.00	40.00
❑ 21574	Dear Old Sunny South by the Sea/My Little Old Home Town in New Orleans	1928	10.00	20.00	40.00
❑ 21636	Memphis Yodel/Lullaby Yodel	1928	10.00	20.00	40.00
❑ 21757	Daddy and Home/My Old Pal	1928	10.00	20.00	40.00
❑ 22072	Blue Yodel No. 5/I'm Sorry We Met	1929	10.00	20.00	40.00
❑ 22143	Frankie and Johnny/Everybody Does It in Hawaii	1929	10.00	20.00	40.00
❑ 22220	My Rough and Rowdy Ways/Tuck Away My Lonesome Blues	1930	12.50	25.00	50.00
❑ 22271	Blue Yodel No. 6/Yodeling Cowboy	1930	12.50	25.00	50.00
❑ 22319	The Drunkard's Child/Whisper Your Mother's Name	1930	12.50	25.00	50.00
❑ 22379	Train Whistle Blues/Jimmie's Texas Blues	1930	12.50	25.00	50.00
❑ 22421	Hobo Bill's Last Ride/That's Why I'm Blue	1930	12.50	25.00	50.00

Number	Title (A Side/B Side)	Yr	VG	VG+	NM
❑ 22488	Anniversary Yodel (Blue Yodel No. 7)/Any Old Time	1930	12.50	25.00	50.00
❑ 22523	In the Jailhouse Now No. 2/High Powered Mama	1930	12.50	25.00	50.00
❑ 22554	Pistol Packin' Papa/Those Gambler's Blues	1930	12.50	25.00	50.00
❑ 23503	Blue Yodel No. 8/Jimmie's Mean Mama Blues	1931	15.00	30.00	60.00
❑ 23518	Nobody Knows But Me/The Mystery of Number Five	1931	15.00	30.00	60.00
❑ 23535	T.B. Blues/Mississippi River Blues	1931	15.00	30.00	60.00
❑ 23549	Jimmie, The Kid/My Blue-Eyed Jane	1931	17.50	35.00	70.00
❑ 23564	I'm Lonesome, Too/Travellin' Blues	1931	17.50	35.00	70.00
❑ 23574	Moonlight and Skies/Jimmie Rodgers Visits the Carter Family	1931	17.50	35.00	70.00
❑ 23580	Blue Yodel No. 9 (Standin' on the Corner)/ Looking for a New Momma	1931	25.00	50.00	100.00

—Louis Armstrong plays trumpet on this recording!

Number	Title (A Side/B Side)	Yr	VG	VG+	NM
❑ 23609	What's It/Why Should I Be Lonely	1931	25.00	50.00	100.00
❑ 23621	Rodgers' Puzzle Record/Let Me Be Your Sidetrack	1931	25.00	50.00	100.00
❑ 23636	Gambling Polka Dot Blues/When the Cactus Is in Bloom	1932	25.00	50.00	100.00
❑ 23651	Roll Along, Kentucky Moon/For the Sake of Days Gone By	1932	25.00	50.00	100.00
❑ 23669	My Time Ain't Long/Ninety-Nine Years Blues	1932	25.00	50.00	100.00
❑ 23681	Home Call/She Was Happy Till She Met You	1932	25.00	50.00	100.00
❑ 23696	Blue Yodel No. 10/Mississippi Moon	1932	25.00	50.00	100.00
❑ 23711	Hobo's Meditation/Down the Old Road to Home	1932	25.00	50.00	100.00
❑ 23721	Mother, the Queen of My Heart/Rock All Our Babies to Sleep	1932	25.00	50.00	100.00
❑ 23736	Miss the Mississippi and You/In the Hills of Tennessee	1933	30.00	60.00	120.00
❑ 23751	Whippin' That Old T.B./No Hard Times	1933	30.00	60.00	120.00
❑ 23766	Gambling Bar Room Blues/Long Tall Mama Blues	1933	30.00	60.00	120.00
❑ 23781	Peach Pickin' Time in Georgia/Prairie Lullaby	1933	30.00	60.00	120.00
❑ 23796	Blue Yodel No. 11/Sweet Mama Hurry Home	1933	37.50	75.00	150.00
❑ 23811	The Southern Cannon Ball/The Land of My Boyhood Dreams	1933	50.00	100.00	200.00
❑ 23816	Mississippi Delta Blues/Old Pal of My Heart	1933	50.00	100.00	200.00
❑ 23830	The Yodeling Ranger/I'm Free	1934	50.00	100.00	200.00
❑ 23840	Old Love Letters/Somewhere Down Below the Mason-Dixie Line	1934	62.50	125.00	250.00
❑ 24456	Blue Yodel No. 12/The Cowhand's Last Ride	1933	62.50	125.00	250.00
❑ V40014	Waiting for a Train/California Blues (Blue Yodel No. 4)	1929	10.00	20.00	40.00
❑ V40054	The Sailor's Plea/I'm Lonely and Blue	1929	7.50	15.00	30.00
❑ V40072	My Little Lady/You and My Old Guitar	1929	10.00	20.00	40.00
❑ V40096	My Carolina Sunshine Girl/Desert Blues	1929	7.50	15.00	30.00
❑ 18-6000	Blue Yodel No. 12/The Cowhand's Last Ride	1935	375.00	750.00	1500.

—78 rpm picture disc

7-Inch Extended Plays

RCA VICTOR

Number	Title (A Side/B Side)	Yr	VG	VG+	NM
❑ EPAT 23	*My Carolina Sunshine Girl/Sleep, Baby, Sleep/ Blue Yodel No. 2/Tuck Away My Lonesome Blues	1952	5.00	10.00	20.00
❑ EPAT 23 [PS]	Yodelingly Yours, Jimmie Rodgers, Volume 3	1952	5.00	10.00	20.00
❑ EPAT 409	(contents unknown)	195?	5.00	10.00	20.00
❑ EPAT 409 [PS]	Yodelingly Yours, Jimmie Rodgers, Volume 4	195?	5.00	10.00	20.00
❑ EPAT 410	(contents unknown)	195?	5.00	10.00	20.00
❑ EPAT 410 [PS]	Yodelingly Yours, Jimmie Rodgers, Volume 5	195?	5.00	10.00	20.00
❑ EPAT 411	*You and My Old Guitar/Prairie Lullaby/Old Pal of My Heart/My Little Lady	195?	5.00	10.00	20.00
❑ EPAT 411 [PS]	Yodelingly Yours, Jimmie Rodgers, Volume 6	195?	5.00	10.00	20.00

Albums

RCA VICTOR

Number	Title (A Side/B Side)	Yr	VG	VG+	NM
❑ DPL2-0075 [(2)]	The Legendary Jimmie Rodgers, Vol. 1	1974	10.00	20.00	40.00

—Special-products issue for Country Music Magazine

Number	Title (A Side/B Side)	Yr	VG	VG+	NM
❑ ANL1-1209	My Rough and Rowdy Ways	1976	2.50	5.00	10.00
❑ LPM-1232 [M]	Never No Mo' Blues — A Memorial Album	1955	37.50	75.00	150.00
❑ LPM-1640 [M]	Train Whistle Blues	1957	37.50	75.00	150.00
❑ LPM-2112 [M]	My Rough and Rowdy Ways	1960	20.00	40.00	80.00
❑ LPM-2213 [M]	Jimmie the Kid	1961	20.00	40.00	80.00
❑ CPL1-2504	A Legendary Performer	1977	2.50	5.00	10.00
❑ LPM-2531 [M]	Country Music Hall of Fame	1962	20.00	40.00	80.00
❑ LPM-2634 [M]	The Short But Brilliant Life of Jimmie Rodgers	1963	20.00	40.00	80.00
❑ LPM-2865 [M]	My Time Ain't Long	1964	12.50	25.00	50.00
❑ LPM-3037 [10]	Jimmie Rodgers Memorial Album, Volume 1	1952	100.00	200.00	400.00
❑ LPM-3038 [10]	Jimmie Rodgers Memorial Album, Volume 2	1952	100.00	200.00	400.00
❑ LPM-3039 [10]	Jimmie Rodgers Memorial Album, Volume 3	1952	100.00	200.00	400.00
❑ LPM-3073 [10]	Travelin' Blues	1952	100.00	200.00	400.00
❑ AHL1-3315	The Best of the Legendary Jimmie Rodgers	197?	2.00	4.00	8.00

—Reissue with new prefix

Number	Title (A Side/B Side)	Yr	VG	VG+	NM
❑ LPM-3315 [M]	The Best of the Legendary Jimmie Rodgers	1965	10.00	20.00	40.00
❑ LSP-3315 [R]	The Best of the Legendary Jimmie Rodgers	1965	5.00	10.00	20.00
❑ VPS-6091(e) [(2)]	This Is Jimmie Rodgers	1971	5.00	10.00	20.00

ROUNDER

Number	Title (A Side/B Side)	Yr	VG	VG+	NM
❑ 1056	First Sessions 1927-1928	1990	3.00	6.00	12.00
❑ 1057	The Early Years 1928-1929	1990	3.00	6.00	12.00

RODGERS, JIMMIE (2)

Pop-country vocalist, no relation to the above.

45s

A&M

Number	Title (A Side/B Side)	Yr	VG	VG+	NM
❑ 842	I'll Say Goodbye/Shadows	1967	—	3.00	6.00
❑ 871	Child of Clay/Turnaround	1967	—	3.00	6.00
❑ 898	If I Were the Man/What a Strange Town	1967	—	3.00	6.00
❑ 902	I Believe It All/You Pass Me By	1968	—	3.00	6.00
❑ 930	How Do You Say Goodbye/I Wanna Be Free	1968	—	3.00	6.00
❑ 976	Today/The Lovers	1968	—	3.00	6.00
❑ 1055	The Windmills of Your Mind/L.A. Break Down (And Take Me Back In)	1969	—	3.00	6.00
❑ 1120	Father Paul/Me About You	1969	—	3.00	6.00
❑ 1152	Cycles/Tomorrow My Friends	1969	—	3.00	6.00
❑ 1213	Troubled Times/The Dum Dum Song	1970	—	2.50	5.00

DOT

Number	Title (A Side/B Side)	Yr	VG	VG+	NM
❑ 16378	No One Will Ever Know/Because	1962	2.50	5.00	10.00
❑ 16378 [PS]	No One Will Ever Know/Because	1962	3.75	7.50	15.00
❑ 16407	Rainbow at Midnight/Rhumba Boogie	1962	2.50	5.00	10.00
❑ 16428	I'll Never Stand in Your Way/Afraid	1963	2.50	5.00	10.00
❑ 16450	Lonely Tears/A Face in the Crowd	1963	2.50	5.00	10.00
❑ 16467	(I Don't Know Why) I Just Do/Load 'Em Up (And Keep a Steppin')	1963	2.50	5.00	10.00
❑ 16490	Poor Little Raggedy Ann/I'm Gonna Be the Winner	1963	2.50	5.00	10.00
❑ 16527	Two-Ten Six-Eighteen (Doesn't Anybody Know My Name)/The Banana Boat Song	1963	2.50	5.00	10.00
❑ 16561	Together/Mama Was a Cotton Picker	1963	2.50	5.00	10.00
❑ 16595	The World I Used to Know/I Forgot More Than You'll Ever Know	1964	2.50	5.00	10.00
❑ 16653	Water Boy/Someplace Green	1964	2.50	5.00	10.00
❑ 16673	Two Tickets/I Forgot More Than You'll Ever Know	1964	2.50	5.00	10.00
❑ 16694	(All My Friends Are Gonna Be) Strangers/Bon Soir Mademoiselle	1965	2.00	4.00	8.00
❑ 16720	Careless Love/When I'm Right You Don't Remember	1965	2.00	4.00	8.00
❑ 16749	Are You Going My Way (Little Beachcomber)/ Little Schoolgirl	1965	2.00	4.00	8.00
❑ 16781	Bye Bye Love/Hollow Words	1965	2.00	4.00	8.00
❑ 16795	The Chipmunk Song (Christmas Don't Be Late)/ In the Snow	1965	2.00	4.00	8.00
❑ 16826	A Falen Star/Brother, Where Are You	1966	2.00	4.00	8.00
❑ 16861	It's Over/Anita, You're Dreaming	1966	2.50	5.00	10.00
❑ 16916	Morning Means Tomorrow/New Ideas	1966	2.00	4.00	8.00
❑ 16973	Love Me, Please Love Me/Wonderful You	1966	2.00	4.00	8.00
❑ 17040	Time/Yours and Mine	1967	2.00	4.00	8.00

EPIC

Number	Title (A Side/B Side)	Yr	VG	VG+	NM
❑ 10828	Froggy's Fable/Daylight Lights the Dawning	1972	—	2.50	5.00
❑ 10857	Kick the Can/Go On By	1972	—	2.50	5.00

MGM

Number	Title (A Side/B Side)	Yr	VG	VG+	NM
❑ 11732	Mama, Don't Cry at My Wedding/You Don't Live Here No More	1954	6.25	12.50	25.00

ROULETTE

Number	Title (A Side/B Side)	Yr	VG	VG+	NM
❑ 4015	Honeycomb/Their Hearts Were Full of Spring	1957	5.00	10.00	20.00
❑ 4031	Kisses Sweeter Than Wine/Better Loved You'll Never Be	1957	5.00	10.00	20.00
❑ 4045	Oh-Oh, I'm Falling in Love Again/The Long Hot Summer	1958	5.00	10.00	20.00

—Red label

Number	Title (A Side/B Side)	Yr	VG	VG+	NM
❑ 4045	Oh-Oh, I'm Falling in Love Again/The Long Hot Summer	1958	3.75	7.50	15.00

—White label with colored spokes

Number	Title (A Side/B Side)	Yr	VG	VG+	NM
❑ 4070	Secretly/Make Me a Miracle	1958	5.00	10.00	20.00
❑ 4070 [PS]	Secretly/Make Me a Miracle	1958	10.00	20.00	40.00
❑ 4090	Are You Really Mine/The Wizard	1958	3.75	7.50	15.00
❑ 4090 [PS]	Are You Really Mine/The Wizard	1958	10.00	20.00	40.00
❑ 4116	Bimbombey/You Understand Me	1958	3.75	7.50	15.00
❑ 4129	I'm Never Gonna Tell/Because You're Young	1959	3.75	7.50	15.00
❑ 4158 [M]	Ring-a-Ling-a-Lario/Wonderful You	1959	3.75	7.50	15.00
❑ 4158 [PS]	Ring-a-Ling-a-Lario/Wonderful You	1959	6.25	12.50	25.00
❑ SSR-4158 [S]	Ring-a-Ling-a-Lario/Wonderful You	1959	7.50	15.00	30.00
❑ 4191	Tucumcari/That Night You Became Seventeen	1959	3.75	7.50	15.00
❑ 4205	It's Christmas Once Again/Wistful Willie	1959	5.00	10.00	20.00
❑ 4218 [M]	T.L.C. Tender Love and Care/Waltzing Matilda	1960	3.00	6.00	12.00
❑ SSR-4218 [S]	T.L.C. Tender Love and Care/Waltzing Matilda	1960	7.50	15.00	30.00
❑ 4234	Just a Closer Walk with Thee/Joshua Fit the Battle of Jericho	1960	3.00	6.00	12.00
❑ 4260	The Wreck of the John B/Four Little Girls in Boston	1960	3.00	6.00	12.00
❑ 4293	Woman from Liberia/Come Along Julie	1960	3.00	6.00	12.00
❑ 4293 [PS]	Woman from Liberia/Come Along Julie	1960	5.00	10.00	20.00
❑ 4318	When Love Is Young/The Little Shepherd of Kingdom Come	1960	3.00	6.00	12.00
❑ 4349	Everytime My Heart Sings/I'm On My Way	1961	3.00	6.00	12.00
❑ 4371	John Brown's Baby/I'm Going Home	1961	3.00	6.00	12.00
❑ 4384	A Little Dog Cried/Englidh Country Garden	1961	3.00	6.00	12.00
❑ 4439	You Are Everything to Me/Wanderin' Eyes	1962	3.00	6.00	12.00
❑ SSR-8001 [S]	Bo Diddley/Soldier Won't You Marry Me	1959	7.50	15.00	30.00
❑ SSR-8007 [S]	Froggy Went a-Courtin'/Lisa	1959	7.50	15.00	30.00
❑ SSR-8010 [S]	St. James Infirmary/Just a Wearyin' for You	1959	7.50	15.00	30.00

SCRIMSHAW

Number	Title (A Side/B Side)	Yr	VG	VG+	NM
❑ 1313	A Good Woman Likes to Drink with the Boys/ Dancing on the Moon	1977	—	2.00	4.00
❑ 1314	Everytime I Sing a Love Song/Just a Little Time	1978	—	2.00	4.00
❑ 1316	When Our Love Began (Cowboys and Indians)/ (B-side unknown)	1978	—	2.00	4.00
❑ 1318	Secretly/Shovelin' Coal	1978	—	2.00	4.00
❑ 1319/20	Easy to Love/Easy	1979	—	2.00	4.00

—With Michele

Number	Title (A Side/B Side)	Yr	VG	VG+	NM
7-Inch Extended Plays					
ROULETTE					
❑ EPR-1-303	Woman from Liberia/The Mating Call//Hey Little Baby/Water Boy	1957	12.50	25.00	50.00
❑ EPR-1-303 [PS]	Jimmie Rodgers	1957	12.50	25.00	50.00
❑ EPR-1-312	*Honeycomb/Oh-Oh, I'm Falling in Love Again/ The Preacher/Better Loved You'll Never Be	195?	12.50	25.00	50.00
❑ EPR-1-312 [PS]	Jimmie Rodgers Sings	195?	12.50	25.00	50.00
❑ EPR-1-313	*Tammy/The Song from Moulin Rouge/Love Letters in the Sand/Hey There	195?	12.50	25.00	50.00
❑ EPR-1-313 [PS]	The Number One Ballads, Part 1	195?	12.50	25.00	50.00
❑ EPR-1-315	Bo Diddley/Riddle Song//The Fox and the Goose/ Black Is the Color	1960	12.50	25.00	50.00
❑ EPR-1-315 [PS]	Jimmie Rodgers Sings Folk Songs, Part I	1960	12.50	25.00	50.00
❑ EPR-1-316	Waltzing Matilda/The Crocodile//Lord Randal/ Gotta Lotta Tunes in My Guitar	195?	12.50	25.00	50.00
❑ EPR-1-316 [PS]	Jimmie Rodgers Sings Folk Songs, Part II	195?	12.50	25.00	50.00
❑ EPR-1-317	Soldier, Won't You Marry Me?/Lassie O'Mine// Liza/Froggy Went a-Courtin'	1960	12.50	25.00	50.00
❑ EPR-1-317 [PS]	Jimmie Rodgers Sings Folk Songs, Part III	1960	12.50	25.00	50.00
Albums					
ACCORD					
❑ SN-7198	Honeycomb & Other Hits	198?	2.50	5.00	10.00
A&M					
❑ SP-130 [M]	Child of Clay	1967	6.25	12.50	25.00
❑ SP-4130 [S]	Child of Clay	1967	3.75	7.50	15.00
❑ SP-4187	Windmills of Your Mind	1969	3.75	7.50	15.00
❑ SP-4242	Troubled Times	1970	3.75	7.50	15.00
DOT					
❑ DLP-3453 [M]	No One Will Ever Know	1962	3.75	7.50	15.00
❑ DLP-3496 [M]	Jimmie Rodgers Folk Concert	1963	3.75	7.50	15.00
❑ DLP-3502 [M]	My Favorite Hymns	1963	3.75	7.50	15.00
❑ DLP-3525 [M]	Honeycomb & Kisses Sweeter Than Wine	1963	3.75	7.50	15.00
❑ DLP-3556 [M]	Town and Country	1964	5.00	10.00	20.00
❑ DLP-3556 [M]	The World I Used to Know	1964	3.75	7.50	15.00
—Retitled version of above					
❑ DLP-3579 [M]	12 Great Hits	1964	3.75	7.50	15.00
❑ DLP-3614 [M]	Deep Purple	1965	3.75	7.50	15.00
❑ DLP 3657 [M]	Christmas with Jimmie	1965	3.00	6.00	12.00
❑ DLP-3687 [M]	The Nashville Sound	1966	3.75	7.50	15.00
❑ DLP-3710 [M]	Country Music 1966	1966	3.75	7.50	15.00
❑ DLP-3717 [M]	It's Over	1966	3.75	7.50	15.00
❑ DLP-3780 [M]	Love Me, Please Love Me	1967	3.75	7.50	15.00
❑ DLP-3815 [M]	Golden Hits/15 Hits of Jimmie Rodgers	1967	5.00	10.00	20.00
❑ DLP-25453 [S]	No One Will Ever Know	1962	5.00	10.00	20.00
❑ DLP-25496 [S]	Jimmie Rodgers Folk Concert	1963	5.00	10.00	20.00
❑ DLP-25502 [S]	My Favorite Hymns	1963	5.00	10.00	20.00
❑ DLP-25525 [S]	Honeycomb & Kisses Sweeter Than Wine	1963	5.00	10.00	20.00
❑ DLP-25556 [S]	Town and Country	1964	6.25	12.50	25.00
❑ DLP-25556 [S]	The World I Used to Know	1964	5.00	10.00	20.00
—Retitled version of above					
❑ DLP-25579 [S]	12 Great Hits	1964	5.00	10.00	20.00
❑ DLP-25614 [S]	Deep Purple	1965	5.00	10.00	20.00
❑ DLP 25657 [S]	Christmas with Jimmie	1965	3.75	7.50	15.00
❑ DLP-25687 [S]	The Nashville Sound	1966	5.00	10.00	20.00
❑ DLP-25710 [S]	Country Music 1966	1966	5.00	10.00	20.00
❑ DLP-25717 [S]	It's Over	1966	5.00	10.00	20.00
❑ DLP-25780 [S]	Love Me, Please Love Me	1967	5.00	10.00	20.00
❑ DLP-25815 [S]	Golden Hits/15 Hits of Jimmie Rodgers	1967	3.75	7.50	15.00
FORUM					
❑ F-9025 [M]	At Home with Jimmie Rodgers: An Evening of Folk Songs	196?	3.00	6.00	12.00
❑ SF-9025 [S]	At Home with Jimmie Rodgers: An Evening of Folk Songs	196?	3.00	6.00	12.00
❑ F-9049 [M]	Just for You	196?	3.00	6.00	12.00
❑ SF-9049 [S]	Just for You	196?	3.00	6.00	12.00
❑ F-9059 [M]	Jimmie Rodgers Sings Folk Songs	196?	3.00	6.00	12.00
❑ SF-9059 [S]	Jimmie Rodgers Sings Folk Songs	196?	3.00	6.00	12.00
HAMILTON					
❑ HL-114 [M]	6 Favorite Hymns and 6 Favorite Folk Ballads	1964	3.00	6.00	12.00
❑ HL-148 [M]	12 Immortal Songs	196?	3.00	6.00	12.00
❑ HS-12114 [S]	6 Favorite Hymns and 6 Favorite Folk Ballads	1964	3.00	6.00	12.00
❑ HS-12148 [S]	12 Immortal Songs	196?	3.00	6.00	12.00
PARAMOUNT					
❑ PAS-2-1042 [(2)]	Honeycomb	1974	3.75	7.50	15.00
PICKWICK					
❑ PC-3040 [M]	Jimmie Rodgers	196?	3.00	6.00	12.00
❑ SPC-3040 [S]	Jimmie Rodgers	196?	3.00	6.00	12.00
❑ SPC-3599	Big Hits	197?	2.50	5.00	10.00
ROULETTE					
❑ R-25020 [M]	Jimmie Rodgers	1957	12.50	25.00	50.00
—Black label					
❑ R-25020 [M]	Jimmie Rodgers	1959	6.25	12.50	25.00
—White label with colored spokes					
❑ R-25033 [M]	Number One Ballads	1958	12.50	25.00	50.00
—Black label					
❑ R-25033 [M]	Number One Ballads	1959	6.25	12.50	25.00
—White label with colored spokes					
❑ R-25042 [M]	Jimmie Rodgers Sings Folk Songs	1958	12.50	25.00	50.00
—Black label					
❑ R-25042 [M]	Jimmie Rodgers Sings Folk Songs	1959	6.25	12.50	25.00
—White label with colored spokes					
❑ R-25057 [M]	His Golden Year	1959	6.25	12.50	25.00
❑ R-25071 [M]	TV Favorites	1959	7.50	15.00	30.00

Number	Title (A Side/B Side)	Yr	VG	VG+	NM
❑ SR-25071 [S]	TV Favorites	1959	12.50	25.00	50.00
❑ R-25081 [M]	Twilight on the Trail	1959	7.50	15.00	30.00
❑ SR-25081 [S]	Twilight on the Trail	1959	12.50	25.00	50.00
❑ R 25095 [M]	It's Christmas Once Again	1959	7.50	15.00	30.00
❑ SR 25095 [S]	It's Christmas Once Again	1959	12.50	25.00	50.00
❑ R-25103 [M]	When the Spirit Moves You	1960	7.50	15.00	30.00
❑ SR-25103 [S]	When the Spirit Moves You	1960	10.00	20.00	40.00
❑ R-25128 [M]	At Home with Jimmie Rodgers: An Evening of Folk Songs	1960	7.50	15.00	30.00
❑ SR-25128 [S]	At Home with Jimmie Rodgers: An Evening of Folk Songs	1960	10.00	20.00	40.00
❑ R-25150 [M]	The Folk Song World of Jimmie Rodgers	1961	7.50	15.00	30.00
❑ SR-25150 [S]	The Folk Song World of Jimmie Rodgers	1961	10.00	20.00	40.00
❑ R-25160 [M]	The Best of Jimmie Rodgers' Folk Tunes	1961	7.50	15.00	30.00
❑ SR-25160 [S]	The Best of Jimmie Rodgers' Folk Tunes	1961	10.00	20.00	40.00
—Black vinyl					
❑ SR-25160 [S]	The Best of Jimmie Rodgers' Folk Tunes	1961	62.50	125.00	250.00
—Red vinyl					
❑ R-25179 [M]	15 Million Sellers	1962	6.25	12.50	25.00
❑ SR-25179 [P]	15 Million Sellers	1962	7.50	15.00	30.00
❑ R-25199 [M]	Folk Songs	1963	5.00	10.00	20.00
❑ SR-25199 [S]	Folk Songs	1963	6.25	12.50	25.00
❑ SR-42006	Yours Truly	1968	3.75	7.50	15.00

RODMAN, JUDY

Number	Title (A Side/B Side)	Yr	VG	VG+	NM
45s					
MTM					
❑ B-72050	I've Been Had by Love Before/Do You Make Love As Well As You Make Music	1985	—	2.00	4.00
❑ B-72054	You're Gonna Miss Me When I'm Gone/She Thinks That She'll Marry	1985	—	2.00	4.00
❑ B-72061	I Sure Need Your Lovin'/Come Next Monday	1985	—	2.00	4.00
❑ B-72065	Until I Met You/Do You Make Love As Well As You Make Music	1986	—	2.50	5.00
❑ B-72076	She Thinks That She'll Marry/Our Love Is Fine	1986	—	2.00	4.00
❑ B-72083	Girls Ride Horses Too/Heart of a Gentleman	1987	—	2.00	4.00
❑ B-72089	I'll Be Your Baby Tonight/Love Comes from Inside of You	1987	—	2.00	4.00
❑ B-72092	I Want a Love Like That/Please Don't Take My Heart	1987	—	2.00	4.00
❑ B-72105	Goin' to Work/Please Don't Take My Heart	1988	—	2.00	4.00
❑ B-72112	I Can Love You/Come to Me	1988	—	2.00	4.00
Albums					
MTM					
❑ ST-71050	Judy	1986	2.50	5.00	10.00
❑ ST-71060	A Place Called Love	1987	2.50	5.00	10.00

RODRIGUEZ, JOHNNY

Number	Title (A Side/B Side)	Yr	VG	VG+	NM
45s					
CAPITOL					
❑ B-44071	I Didn't (Every Chance I Had)/I'm Not That Good at Goodbye	1987	—	2.00	4.00
❑ B-44204	I Wanta Wake Up with You/Someday I'm Gonna Finish Leaving You	1988	—	2.00	4.00
❑ B-44245	You Might Want to Use Me Again/She Loves Austin	1988	—	2.00	4.00
❑ B-44325	No Chance to Dance/Back to Stay	1989	—	2.00	4.00
❑ B-44403	Back to Stay/Someday I'm Gonna Finish Leaving You	1989	—	2.00	4.00
COLUMBIA					
❑ 02987	The Most Beautiful Girl/Too Far Gone	1982	—	2.00	4.00
—With Ray Conniff; B-side by Zella Lehr with Ray Conniff					
EPIC					
❑ 01033	I Want You Tonight/Your Love Isn't Mine Anymore	1981	—	—	3.00
❑ 02411	Trying Not to Love You/Mexico Rain	1981	—	—	3.00
❑ 02638	It's Not the Same Old You/Born with the Blues	1981	—	—	3.00
❑ 03275	He's Not Entitled to Your Love/Starting All Over Again	1982	—	—	3.00
❑ 03598	Foolin'/Because of You	1983	—	—	3.00
❑ 03972	How Could I Love Her So Much/Somethin' About a Jukebox	1983	—	—	3.00
❑ 04206	Back on Her Mind Again/Eleven Roses	1983	—	—	3.00
❑ 04336	Too Late to Go Home/No Memories Hangin' 'Round	1984	—	—	3.00
❑ 04460	Let's Leave the Lights On Tonight/What a Movie You'd Make	1984	—	—	3.00
❑ 04562	First Time Burned/Hand Me Another of Those	1984	—	—	3.00
❑ 04628	Rose of My Heart/Down in the Boondocks	1984	—	—	3.00
❑ 04838	Here I Am Again/Full Circle	1985	—	—	3.00
❑ 05732	She Don't Cry Like She Used To/Back on Her Mind Again	1985	—	—	3.00
❑ 05863	Maxine/Full Circle	1986	—	—	3.00
❑ 50671	Down on the Rio Grande/Mexico Holiday	1979	—	2.00	4.00
❑ 50735	Fools for Each Other/Street Walker	1979	—	2.00	4.00
❑ 50791	I Hate the Way I Love It/Almost Persuaded	1979	—	2.00	4.00
—With Charly McClain					
❑ 50808	What'll I Tell Virginia/Whatever Gets Me Through the Night	1979	—	2.00	4.00
❑ 50859	Love, Look At Us Now/Where Did It Go	1980	—	2.00	4.00
❑ 50932	North of the Border/When She Gets Around to Me	1980	—	2.00	4.00
MERCURY					
❑ 55004	Eres Tu/You Put a Hold on Me	1977	—	2.00	4.00
❑ 55012	Savin' This Love Song for You/Que Te Quiero	1977	—	2.00	4.00
❑ 55020	We Believe in Happy Endings/The Immigrant	1978	—	2.00	4.00

Number	Title (A Side/B Side)	Yr	VG	VG+	NM
❑ 55029	Love Me with All Your Heart (Cuando Caliente El Sol)	1978	—	2.00	4.00
❑ 55050	Alibis/Rest Your Love on Me	1978	—	2.00	4.00
❑ 73334	Pass Me By (If You're Only Passing Through)/ Jealous Heart	1972	—	2.50	5.00
❑ 73368	You Always Come Back (To Hurting Me)/I Wonder Where You Are Tonight	1973	—	2.50	5.00
❑ 73416	Ridin' My Thumb to Mexico/Release Me	1973	—	2.50	5.00
❑ 73446	That's the Way Love Goes/I Really Don't Want to Know	1973	—	2.50	5.00
❑ 73471	Something/Born to Lose	1974	—	2.50	5.00
❑ 73493	Dance with Me (Just One More Time)/Faded Love	1974	—	2.50	5.00
—Red label					
❑ 73493	Dance with Me (Just One More Time)/Faded Love	1974	—	2.00	4.00
—Chicago skyline label					
❑ 73621	We're Over/Oh I Miss You	1974	—	2.00	4.00
❑ 73659	I Just Can't Get Her Out of My Mind/Have I Told You Lately	1975	—	2.00	4.00
❑ 73682	Just Get Up and Close the Door/Am I That Easy to Forget	1975	—	2.00	4.00
❑ 73715	Love Put a Song in My Heart/Steppin' Out on You	1975	—	2.00	4.00
❑ 73769	I Couldn't Be Me Without You/Sometimes I Wish I Were You	1976	—	2.00	4.00
❑ 73815	I Wonder If I Ever Said Goodbye/Louisiana	1976	—	2.00	4.00
❑ 73855	Hillbilly Heart/Commonly Known As the Blues	1976	—	2.00	4.00
❑ 73878	Desperado/There'll Always Be Honky-Tonks in Texas	1976	—	2.00	4.00
❑ 73914	If Practice Makes Perfect/Hard Times	1977	—	2.00	4.00

Albums

Number	Title (A Side/B Side)	Yr	VG	VG+	NM
CAPITOL					
❑ C1-90040	Gracias	1988	2.50	5.00	10.00
EPIC					
❑ JE 36014	Rodriguez	1979	2.50	5.00	10.00
❑ JE 36274	Through My Eyes	1980	2.50	5.00	10.00
❑ JE 36587	Gypsy	1980	2.50	5.00	10.00
❑ FE 37103	After the Rain	1981	2.50	5.00	10.00
❑ FE 38321	Biggest Hits	1982	2.50	5.00	10.00
❑ FE 38806	For Every Rose	1983	2.50	5.00	10.00
❑ FE 39172	Foolin' with Fire	1984	2.50	5.00	10.00
❑ FE 39583	Full Circle	1985	2.50	5.00	10.00
MERCURY					
❑ SRM-1-686	All I Ever Meant to Do Was Sing	1973	3.75	7.50	15.00
❑ SRM-1-699	My Third Album	1974	3.75	7.50	15.00
❑ SRM-1-1012	Songs About Ladies and Love	1974	3.75	7.50	15.00
❑ SRM-1-1032	Just Get Up and Close the Door	1975	3.75	7.50	15.00
❑ SRM-1-1057	Love Put a Song in My Heart	1975	3.75	7.50	15.00
❑ SRM-1-1078	The Greatest Hits of Johnny Rodriguez	1976	3.75	7.50	15.00
❑ SRM-1-1110	Reflecting	1976	3.00	6.00	12.00
❑ SRM-1-1144	Practice Makes Perfect	1977	3.00	6.00	12.00
❑ SRM-1-5003	Just for You	1977	3.00	6.00	12.00
❑ SRM-1-5011	Love Me with All You Heart	1978	3.00	6.00	12.00
❑ SRM-1-5015	Johnny Rodriguez Was Here	1979	3.00	6.00	12.00
❑ SRM-1-5022	Sketches	1980	3.00	6.00	12.00
❑ SR-61378	Introducing Johnny Rodriguez	1973	3.75	7.50	15.00
❑ 826271-1	The Greatest Hits of Johnny Rodriguez	1985	2.00	4.00	8.00
—Reissue					

ROE, MARLYS

45s

Number	Title (A Side/B Side)	Yr	VG	VG+	NM
GRC					
❑ 1002	Carry Me Back/Somebody in Your Eyes	1973	—	3.00	6.00

ROE, TOMMY

Pop-rock-bubblegum singer who started making the country charts in 1973. Only his post-ABC material is included below.

45s

Number	Title (A Side/B Side)	Yr	VG	VG+	NM
AWESOME					
❑ 104	First Things First/(B-side unknown)	1984	—	3.00	6.00
❑ 108	Sittin' on a Mood/(B-side unknown)	1984	—	3.00	6.00
BGO					
❑ 1003	She Do Run Run/(B-side unknown)	1982	2.50	5.00	10.00
MCA CURB					
❑ 52711	Some Such Foolishness/Barbara Lou	1985	—	2.00	4.00
❑ 52778	Radio Romance/Barbara Lou	1986	—	2.00	4.00
MERCURY					
❑ 888206-7	Let's Be Fools Like That Again/Barbara Lou	1986	—	—	3.00
❑ 888497-7	Back When It Really Mattered/Radio Romance	1987	—	—	3.00
MGM SOUTH					
❑ 7001	Mean Little Woman, Rosalie/Skyline	1972	—	2.50	5.00
❑ 7008	Sarah My Love/Chewing on Sugar Cane	1972	—	2.50	5.00
❑ 7013	Working Class Hero/Sun in My Eyes	1973	—	2.50	5.00
❑ 7025	Silver Eyes/Memphis Me	1973	—	3.00	6.00
MONUMENT					
❑ 8644	Glitter and Gleam/Bad News	1975	—	2.50	5.00
❑ 8662	Snowing Me Under/Rita and Her Band	1975	—	2.50	5.00
❑ 8684	Slow Dancing/Burn On Love Light	1976	—	2.50	5.00
❑ 8705	Everybody/Energy	1976	—	2.50	5.00
❑ 45205	Early in the Morning/Bad News	1976	—	2.50	5.00
❑ 45228	Your Love Will See Me Through/Working Class Hero	1977	—	2.50	5.00
WARNER BROS.					
❑ 8660	Dreamin' Again/Love the Way You Love Me Up	1978	—	2.00	4.00
❑ 8720	Just Look at Me/Love the Way You Love Me Up	1978	—	2.50	5.00
❑ 8800	Massachusetts/Just Look at Me	1979	—	2.50	5.00
❑ 49085	You Better Move On/Just Look at Me	1979	—	2.00	4.00
❑ 49235	Charlie, I Love Your Wife/There Is No Sun on Sunset Boulevard	1980	—	2.00	4.00

Albums

Number	Title (A Side/B Side)	Yr	VG	VG+	NM
MONUMENT					
❑ 7604	Energy	1977	2.50	5.00	10.00
—Reissue of 34182					
❑ 7614	Full Bloom	1977	2.50	5.00	10.00
❑ PZ 34182	Energy	1976	3.00	6.00	12.00

ROGERS, CHUCK

45s

Number	Title (A Side/B Side)	Yr	VG	VG+	NM
DECCA					
❑ 9-46394	Five Little Girls/Ragtime Annie	1952	5.00	10.00	20.00

ROGERS, DANN

45s

Number	Title (A Side/B Side)	Yr	VG	VG+	NM
IA					
❑ 500	Looks Like Love Again/(B-side unknown)	1979	—	3.00	6.00
MCA					
❑ 53133	Just a Kid from Texas/We've Got to Stop Meeting This Way	1987	—	—	3.00
❑ 53202	Only One Girl/We Gotta Stop Meeting This Way	1987	—	—	3.00

Albums

Number	Title (A Side/B Side)	Yr	VG	VG+	NM
IA					
❑ 5000	Hearts Under Fire	1979	3.00	6.00	12.00
MCA					
❑ 42025	Still Runnin'	1987	2.00	4.00	8.00

ROGERS, DAVID

45s

Number	Title (A Side/B Side)	Yr	VG	VG+	NM
ATLANTIC					
❑ 4005	It'll Be Her/Singin' Star	1973	—	3.00	6.00
❑ 4012	Loving You Has Changed My Life/You Be You and I'll Be Gone	1973	—	3.00	6.00
❑ 4022	Hey There Girl/Someone That I Can Forget	1974	—	3.00	6.00
❑ 4204	I Just Can't Help Believin'/Now That You're a Woman	1974	—	3.00	6.00
COLUMBIA					
❑ 4-44430	I'd Be Your Fool Again/Loser's Shoes	1968	—	3.50	7.00
❑ 4-44561	I'm in Love with My Wife/Tessie's Bar Mystery	1968	—	3.50	7.00
❑ 4-44561 [PS]	I'm in Love with My Wife/Tessie's Bar Mystery	1968	3.00	6.00	12.00
❑ 4-44668	You Touched My Heart/Today and Tomorrow	1968	—	3.50	7.00
❑ 4-44796	Dearly Beloved/The Little White Cloud That Cried	1969	—	3.50	7.00
❑ 4-45007	A World Called You/A Picture of You	1969	—	3.50	7.00
❑ 4-45111	So Much in Love with You/The Edge of Your Memory	1970	—	3.50	7.00
❑ 4-45226	I Wake Up in Heaven/Baby Don't Cry	1970	—	3.50	7.00
❑ 4-45351	Bottle Do Your Thing/A Stranger in My Place	1971	2.00	4.00	8.00
❑ 4-45383	She Don't Make Me Cry/Bottle, Do Your Thing	1971	—	3.50	7.00
❑ 4-45478	Ruby, You're Warm/Is That All San Francisco Did for You	1971	—	3.50	7.00
❑ 4-45551	Need You/Sweet Vibrations (Some Folks Call It Love)	1972	—	3.50	7.00
❑ 4-45642	Goodbye/I'd Be Your Fool Again	1972	—	3.50	7.00
❑ 4-45714	All Heaven Breaks Loose/Completely Satisfied	1972	—	3.50	7.00
HAL KAT					
❑ 2083	I'm a Country Song/(B-side unknown)	1984	—	3.00	6.00
KARI					
❑ 108	The Only Way to Go/(B-side unknown)	1980	—	3.00	6.00
❑ 120	Houston Blue/Here's to You Darling	1981	—	3.00	6.00
MR. MUSIC					
❑ 016	You've Still Got Me/(B-side unknown)	1983	—	3.00	6.00
❑ 018	The Devil Is a Woman/Time for Lovin'	1983	—	3.00	6.00
MUSIC MASTER					
❑ 012	Crown Prince of the Barroom/Me and Ms. Chablis	1982	—	3.00	6.00
❑ 1004	Hold Me/Chuck Berry Music	1983	—	3.00	6.00
REPUBLIC					
❑ 001	I Love What My Woman Does to Me/(B-side unknown)	1977	—	3.00	6.00
❑ 006	Do You Hear My Heart Beat/They Went Together	1977	—	2.50	5.00
❑ 011	You and Me Alone/Time for Lovin'	1977	—	2.50	5.00
❑ 015	I'll Be There (When You Get Lonely)/Just for the Love of It	1978	—	2.50	5.00
❑ 020	Let's Try to Remember/That Woman Keeps This Cowboy Comin' Home	1978	—	2.50	5.00
❑ 029	When a Woman Cries/The Power of Positive Drinking	1978	—	2.50	5.00
❑ 038	Darlin'/How Long Has It Been	1979	—	2.50	5.00
❑ 042	You Are My Rainbow/If You Should Ask	1979	—	2.50	5.00
❑ 048	You're Amazing/Farewell Two Arms	1979	—	2.50	5.00
❑ 256	Whispers and Grins/Use Me Up	1976	—	3.00	6.00
❑ 311	Mahogany Bridge/It's a Crying Shame (That People Change)	1976	—	3.00	6.00
❑ 343	I'm Gonna Love You Right Out of This World/ Burning Bridges	1976	—	3.00	6.00
❑ 382	The Lady and the Baby/That Woman Keeps This Cowboy Coming Home	1977	—	3.00	6.00
UNITED ARTISTS					
❑ XW617	It Takes a Whole Lotta Livin' in a House/Since Never	1975	—	2.50	5.00
❑ XW720	Got You on My Mind Again/The Part of Me You Left Behind	1975	—	2.50	5.00

Albums

ATLANTIC

Number	Title (A Side/B Side)	Yr	VG	VG+	NM
❑ SD 7266	Just Thank Me	1973	3.75	7.50	15.00
❑ SD 7283	Farewell to the Ryman	1973	5.00	10.00	20.00
❑ SD 7306	Hey There Girl	1974	3.75	7.50	15.00

COLUMBIA

Number	Title (A Side/B Side)	Yr	VG	VG+	NM
❑ CS 1023	A World Called You	1970	3.75	7.50	15.00
❑ C 30972	She Don't Make Me Cry	1971	3.75	7.50	15.00
❑ KC 31506	Need You	1972	3.75	7.50	15.00

REPUBLIC

Number	Title (A Side/B Side)	Yr	VG	VG+	NM
❑ 5003	Lovingly	197?	3.00	6.00	12.00
❑ 5907	I'm Gonna Love You Right Out of This World	1976	3.00	6.00	12.00

UNITED ARTISTS

Number	Title (A Side/B Side)	Yr	VG	VG+	NM
❑ UA-LA422-G	A Whole Lotta Livin' in a House	1975	3.00	6.00	12.00

ROGERS, JAMES

45s

SOUNDWAVES

Number	Title (A Side/B Side)	Yr	VG	VG+	NM
❑ 4820	Something's Got a Hold on Me/This Is America	1989	—	2.50	5.00

ROGERS, JESSE

45s

ARCADE

Number	Title (A Side/B Side)	Yr	VG	VG+	NM
❑ 143	Jukebox Cannonball/You Can't Hang That Monkey on My Back	1957	10.00	20.00	40.00
❑ 162	Say It Again/Nightwind	1961	5.00	10.00	20.00
❑ 169	Jump Cats Jump/You've Changed My Whole Life Into a Dream	1962	25.00	50.00	100.00

MGM

Number	Title (A Side/B Side)	Yr	VG	VG+	NM
❑ K11369	An Old-Fashioned Christmas/Red, White and Blue	1952	6.25	12.50	25.00
❑ K11422	Howlin' and a Prowlin'/The Devil's Pitchfork	1953	6.25	12.50	25.00
❑ K11742	Foldin' Money/You're Sorry for Yourself	1954	6.25	12.50	25.00
❑ K11884	I Gotta Love Just Like I Like/I Never Knew I Needed You	1954	6.25	12.50	25.00
❑ K11983	The Waltz You Saved for Me/Impatient Heart	1955	6.25	12.50	25.00

RCA VICTOR

Number	Title (A Side/B Side)	Yr	VG	VG+	NM
❑ 48-0100	Blue Christmas/Here Comes Santa Claus	1949	12.50	25.00	50.00
—Originals on green vinyl					
❑ 48-0350	A Great Big Needle/I've Got Five Dollars	1950	7.50	15.00	30.00
—Originals on green vinyl					
❑ 48-0359	Slippin' Around with Jole Blon/Finder's Keepers	1950	7.50	15.00	30.00
—Originals on green vinyl					
❑ 48-0389	I Can Fool the World/Plain Old Lovin'	1950	7.50	15.00	30.00
—Originals on green vinyl					
❑ 48-0454	Beautiful Brown Eyes/Tellin' My Baby Bye	1951	6.25	12.50	25.00

Selected 78s

BLUEBIRD

Number	Title (A Side/B Side)	Yr	VG	VG+	NM
❑ 32-0001	Hadacol Blues/Country Boy	1949	5.00	10.00	20.00
❑ 32-0002	Wedding Bells/Tennessee Polka	1949	5.00	10.00	20.00

ROGERS, KENNY

Also see THE FIRST EDITION.

45s

CARLTON

Number	Title (A Side/B Side)	Yr	VG	VG+	NM
❑ 454	That Crazy Feeling/We'll Always Have Each Other	1958	25.00	50.00	100.00
—As "Kenneth Rogers"					
❑ 454	That Crazy Feeling/We'll Always Have Each Other	1958	25.00	50.00	100.00
—As "Kenny Rogers"					
❑ 468	For You Alone/I've Got a Lot to Learn	1958	15.00	30.00	60.00

KEN-LEE

Number	Title (A Side/B Side)	Yr	VG	VG+	NM
❑ 102	Jole Blon/Lonely	195?	25.00	50.00	100.00

LIBERTY

Number	Title (A Side/B Side)	Yr	VG	VG+	NM
❑ 1380	Lady/Sweet Music Man	1980	—	2.00	4.00
❑ 1380 [PS]	Lady/Sweet Music Man	1980	—	2.50	5.00
❑ 1391	Long Arm of the Law/You Were a Good Friend	1980	—	2.00	4.00
❑ 1415	I Don't Need You/Without You in My Life	1981	—	—	3.00
❑ 1415 [PS]	I Don't Need You/Without You in My Life	1981	—	2.00	4.00
❑ 1430	Share Your Love with Me/Greybeard	1981	—	—	3.00
❑ 1430 [PS]	Share Your Love with Me/Greybeard	1981	—	2.00	4.00
❑ 1438	Kentucky Homemade Christmas/Carol of the Bells	1981	—	2.50	5.00
❑ 1438 [PS]	Kentucky Homemade Christmas/Carol of the Bells	1981	—	3.00	6.00
❑ 1441	Blaze of Glory/The Good Life	1981	—	—	3.00
❑ 1444	Through the Years/So In Love with You	1981	—	—	3.00
❑ 1471	Love Will Turn You Around/I Want a Son	1982	—	—	3.00
❑ 1471 [PS]	Love Will Turn You Around/I Want a Son	1982	—	2.50	5.00
❑ 1485	A Love Song/Fool in Me	1982	—	—	3.00
❑ 1492	We've Got Tonight/You Are So Beautiful	1983	—	2.00	4.00
—A-side with Sheena Easton					
❑ 1492 [PS]	We've Got Tonight/You Are So Beautiful	1983	—	2.50	5.00
❑ 1495	All My Life/The Farther I Go	1983	—	—	3.00
❑ 1495 [PS]	All My Life/The Farther I Go	1983	—	2.00	4.00
❑ 1503	Scarlet Fever/What I Learned from Loving You	1983	—	—	3.00
❑ 1511	Sweet Music Man/You Were a Good Friend	1983	—	—	3.00
❑ 1524	A Stranger in My Place/Love Is What We Make It	1985	—	—	3.00
❑ 1525	Twentieth Century Fool/It Turns Me Inside Out	1985	—	—	3.00
❑ 1526	Abraham, Martin and John/Goodbye Marie	1985	—	—	3.00
❑ 4065 [DJ]	Christmas Everyday//Kentucky Homemade Christmas/Carol Of The Bells	198?	—	3.00	6.00

MERCURY

Number	Title (A Side/B Side)	Yr	VG	VG+	NM
❑ 72545	Here's That Rainy Day/Take Life in Stride	1966	6.25	12.50	25.00

RCA

Number	Title (A Side/B Side)	Yr	VG	VG+	NM
❑ 5016-7-R	They Don't Make Them Like They Used To/Just the Thought of Losing You	1986	—	—	3.00
❑ 5016-7-R [PS]	They Don't Make Them Like They Used To/Just the Thought of Losing You	1986	—	—	3.00
❑ 5078-7-R	Twenty Years Ago/The Heart of the Matter	1986	—	—	3.00
❑ 5209-7-R	Make No Mistake, She's Mine/You're My Love	1987	—	—	3.00
—With Ronnie Milsap					
❑ 5258-7-R	I Prefer the Moonlight/We're Doin' Alright	1987	—	—	3.00
❑ 6832-7-R	The Factory/One More Day	1987	—	—	3.00
❑ 8381-7-R	I Prefer the Moonlight/Make No Mistake, She's Mine	1988	—	—	3.00
—Gold Standard Series; B-side with Ronnie Milsap					
❑ 8390-7-R	I Don't Call Him Daddy/We're Doin' Alright	1988	—	—	3.00
❑ PB-13710	This Woman/Buried Treasure	1984	—	—	3.00
❑ PB-13710 [PS]	This Woman/Buried Treasure	1984	—	2.00	4.00
❑ JK-13713 [DJ]	Buried Treasure (same on both sides)	1984	—	2.50	5.00
❑ PB-13774	Eyes That See in the Dark/Hold Me	1984	—	—	3.00
❑ PB-13832	Evening Star/Midsummer Nights	1984	—	—	3.00
❑ PB-13899	What About Me/The Rest of Last Night	1984	—	—	3.00
—With Kim Carnes and James Ingram					
❑ PB-13899 [PS]	What About Me/The Rest of Last Night	1984	—	2.00	4.00
❑ PB-13944	The Christmas Song/Medley: Winter Wonderland-Sleigh Ride	1984	—	2.00	4.00
—B-side by Dolly Parton					
❑ PB-13975	Crazy/The Stranger	1984	—	—	3.00
❑ PB-13975 [PS]	Crazy/The Stranger	1984	—	2.00	4.00
❑ GB-14074	This Woman/What About Me	1985	—	—	3.00
—Gold Standard Series; B-side by Kenny Rogers, Kim Carnes and James Ingram					
❑ PB-14194	Morning Desire/People in Love	1985	—	—	3.00
❑ PB-14194 [PS]	Morning Desire/People in Love	1985	—	2.00	4.00
—Fold-out poster sleeve					
❑ PB-14298	Tomb of the Unknown Love/Our Perfect Song	1986	—	—	3.00
❑ PB-14298 [PS]	Tomb of the Unknown Love/Our Perfect Song	1986	—	2.00	4.00
❑ GB-14353	Crazy/Morning Desire	1986	—	—	3.00
—Gold Standard Series					
❑ PB-14384	The Pride Is Back/Didn't We?	1986	—	2.00	4.00
—A-side: With Nickie Ryder					
❑ PB-14384 [PS]	The Pride Is Back/Didn't We?	1986	—	2.00	4.00

REPRISE

Number	Title (A Side/B Side)	Yr	VG	VG+	NM
❑ PRO-S-3904 [DJ]	Maybe (same on both sides)	1990	—	3.00	6.00
—With Holly Dunn					
❑ 18835	Bed of Roses/I'll Be There for You	1992	—	—	3.00
❑ 18967	Someone Must Feel Like a Fool Tonight/ Sunshine	1992	—	—	3.00
❑ 19080	If You Want to Find Love/Sunshine	1991	—	—	3.00
❑ 19324	Walk Away/What I Did for Love	1991	—	—	3.00
❑ 19504	Lay My Body Down/Crazy in Love	1991	—	—	3.00
❑ 19972	Maybe/If I Knew Then What I Know Now	1990	—	—	3.00
—A-side with Holly Dunn; B-side with Gladys Knight					
❑ 22750	Christmas in America/Joy to the World	1989	—	—	3.00
❑ 22750 [PS]	Christmas in America/Joy to the World	1989	—	—	3.00
❑ 22828	The Vows Go Unbroken (Always True to You)/ One Night	1989	—	—	3.00
❑ 22853	(Something Inside) So Strong/When You Put Your Heart In It	1989	—	—	3.00
❑ 27690	Planet Texas/When You Put Your Heart in It	1988	—	—	3.00
❑ 27690 [PS]	Planet Texas/When You Put Your Heart in It	1988	—	—	3.00
❑ 27812	When You Put Your Heart In It/(Instrumental)	1988	—	—	3.00
❑ 27812 [PS]	When You Put Your Heart In It/(Instrumental)	1988	—	—	3.00

UNITED ARTISTS

Number	Title (A Side/B Side)	Yr	VG	VG+	NM
❑ XW746	Love Lifted Me/Home-Made Love	1975	—	2.00	4.00
❑ XW798	There's an Old Man in Our Town/Home-Made Love	1976	—	2.00	4.00
❑ XW812	I Would Like to See You Again/While the Feeling's Good	1976	—	2.00	4.00
❑ XW868	Laura (What's He Got That I Ain't Got)/I Wasn't Mad Enough	1976	—	2.00	4.00
❑ XW929	Lucille/Till I Get It Right	1976	—	2.00	4.00
❑ XW1027	Daytime Friends/We Don't Make Love Anymore	1977	—	2.00	4.00
❑ XW1095	Sweet Music Man/Lying Again	1977	—	2.00	4.00
❑ XW1151	Love Lifted Me/Reuben James	1978	—	2.00	4.00
❑ XW1152	Today I Started Loving You Again/Just Dropped In (To See What Condition My Condition Was In)	1978	—	2.00	4.00
❑ XW1153	Daytime Friends/But You Know I Love You	1978	—	2.00	4.00
❑ XW1154	Lucille/Something's Burning	1978	—	2.00	4.00
❑ XW1155	Sweet Music Man/Ruby, Don't Take Your Love to Town	1978	—	2.00	4.00
—B-sides of the above five singles are re-recordings of First Edition hits paired with early United Artists country hits					
❑ XW1210	Love Or Something Like It/Starting Again	1978	—	2.00	4.00
❑ XW1250	The Gambler/Momma's Waiting	1978	—	2.00	4.00
❑ XW1273	She Believes in Me/Morgana Jones	1979	—	2.00	4.00
❑ XW1273 [PS]	She Believes in Me/Morgana Jones	1979	—	2.50	5.00
❑ 1315	You Decorated My Life/One Man's Woman	1979	—	2.00	4.00
❑ 1315 [PS]	You Decorated My Life/One Man's Woman	1979	—	2.50	5.00
❑ 1327	Coward of the County/I Wanna Make You Smile	1979	—	2.00	4.00
❑ 1345	Don't Fall in Love with a Dreamer/Intro: Goin' Home to the Rock-Gideon Tanner	1980	—	2.00	4.00
—A-side: With Kim Carnes					
❑ 1345 [PS]	Don't Fall in Love with a Dreamer/Intro: Goin' Home to the Rock-Gideon Tanner	1980	—	2.50	5.00
❑ 1359	Love the World Away/Sayin' Goodbye-Requiem	1980	—	2.00	4.00

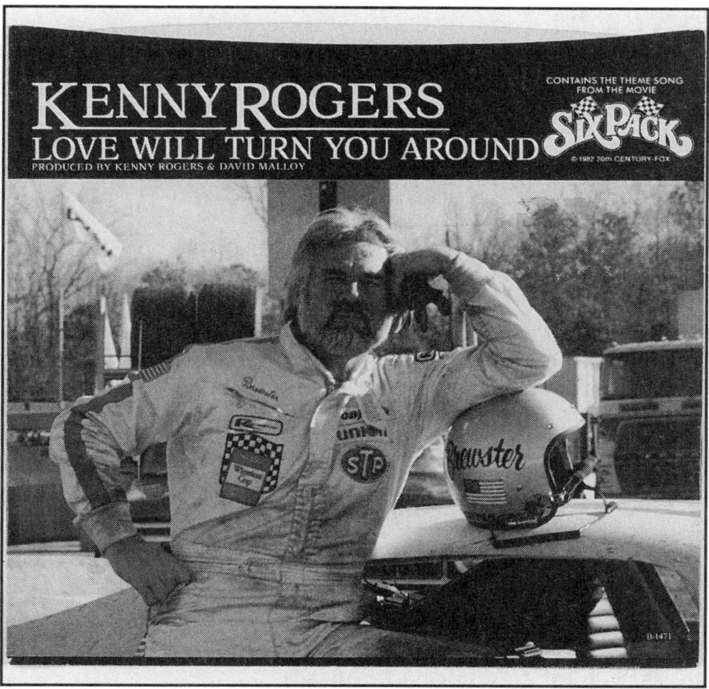

Amazingly, in 2000, Kenny Rogers defied the youth movement in country music and saw his song "Buy Me a Rose" hit No. 1 on the airplay charts (alas, no single was released to the public). It's the most recent highlight of a long career. (Top left) Early on, there were questions about how his first name would appear on the label. Here's a Carlton 45 from 1958 that spells his first name "Kenneth." Other copies of this same record have the name as "Kenny." (Top right) The first time Rogers appeared on the country charts was in 1969, when he was still with the First Edition. "Ruby, Don't Take Your Love to Town" was written by Mel Tillis and originally a hit by Johnny Darrell. (Bottom left) By 1980, Kenny was getting more adventurous in his choice of producer. Lionel Richie of the Commodores both wrote and produced "Lady," which got to the top of both the pop and country charts. (Bottom right) Rogers also branched out into acting. From the forgettable movie *Six Pack* came the unforgettable chart-topper "Love Will Turn You Around."

Albums

LIBERTY

Number	Title (A Side/B Side)	Yr	VG	VG+	NM
❑ LO-607	Love Lifted Me	1981	2.00	4.00	8.00
—Reissue of United Artists 607					
❑ LO-689	Kenny Rogers	1981	2.00	4.00	8.00
—Reissue of United Artists 689					
❑ LO-754	Daytime Friends	1981	2.00	4.00	8.00
—Reissue of United Artists 754					
❑ LO-835	Ten Years of Gold	1981	2.00	4.00	8.00
—Reissue of United Artists 835					
❑ LO-903	Love Or Something Like It	1981	2.00	4.00	8.00
—Reissue of United Artists 903					
❑ LO-934	The Gambler	1981	2.00	4.00	8.00
—Reissue of United Artists 934					
❑ LOO-979	Kenny	1981	2.00	4.00	8.00
—Reissue of United Artists 979					
❑ LOO-1035	Gideon	1981	2.00	4.00	8.00
—Reissue of United Artists 1035					
❑ LOO-1072	Kenny Rogers' Greatest Hits	1980	2.00	4.00	8.00
❑ LOO-1108	Share Your Love	1981	2.00	4.00	8.00
❑ LN-10207	Love Lifted Me	1984	—	3.00	6.00
—Budget-line reissue					
❑ LN-10208	Kenny Rogers	1983	—	3.00	6.00
—Budget-line reissue					
❑ LN-10240	Christmas	198?	2.00	4.00	8.00
—Reissue of LOO 51115					
❑ LN-10243	Gideon	1984	—	3.00	6.00
—Budget-line reissue					
❑ LN-10245	We've Got Tonight	1984	—	3.00	6.00
—Budget-line reissue					
❑ LN-10246	Love Will Turn You Around	1984	—	3.00	6.00
—Budget-line reissue					
❑ LN-10247	The Gambler	1984	—	3.00	6.00
—Budget-line reissue					
❑ LN-10248	Kenny	1984	—	3.00	6.00
—Budget-line reissue					
❑ LN-10249	Daytime Friends	1984	—	3.00	6.00
—Budget-line reissue					
❑ LN-10250	Love Or Something Like It	1984	—	3.00	6.00
—Budget-line reissue					
❑ LN-10254	Ten Years of Gold	1984	—	3.00	6.00
—Budget-line reissue					
❑ LOO-51115	Christmas	1981	2.50	5.00	10.00
❑ LO-51124	Love Will Turn You Around	1982	2.00	4.00	8.00
❑ LO-51143	We've Got Tonight	1983	2.00	4.00	8.00
❑ LV-51152	Twenty Greatest Hits	1983	2.00	4.00	8.00
❑ LO-51154	Duets	1984	2.00	4.00	8.00
❑ LO-51157	Love Is What We Make It	1985	2.00	4.00	8.00

MOBILE FIDELITY

Number	Title (A Side/B Side)	Yr	VG	VG+	NM
❑ 1-044	The Gambler	1981	5.00	10.00	20.00
—Audiophile vinyl					
❑ 1-049	Kenny Rogers' Greatest Hits	1981	5.00	10.00	20.00
—Audiophile vinyl					

RCA

Number	Title (A Side/B Side)	Yr	VG	VG+	NM
❑ 5833-1-R	They Don't Make Them Like They Used To	1986	2.00	4.00	8.00
❑ 6484-1-R	I Prefer the Moonlight	1987	2.00	4.00	8.00
❑ 8371-1-R	Greatest Hits	1988	2.00	4.00	8.00

RCA VICTOR

Number	Title (A Side/B Side)	Yr	VG	VG+	NM
❑ AFL1-4697	Eyes That See in the Dark	1983	2.00	4.00	8.00
❑ AJL1-5335	What About Me	1984	2.00	4.00	8.00
❑ AJL1-7023	The Heart of the Matter	1985	2.00	4.00	8.00

REPRISE

Number	Title (A Side/B Side)	Yr	VG	VG+	NM
❑ 25792	Something Inside So Strong	1989	2.50	5.00	10.00
❑ 25973	Christmas in America	1989	3.00	6.00	12.00
❑ R 144593	Love Is Strange	1990	5.00	10.00	20.00
—Only available on vinyl from BMG Direct Marketing					

UNITED ARTISTS

Number	Title (A Side/B Side)	Yr	VG	VG+	NM
❑ UA-LA607-G	Love Lifted Me	1976	3.75	7.50	15.00
❑ UA-LA689-G	Kenny Rogers	1976	2.50	5.00	10.00
❑ UA-LA754-G	Daytime Friends	1977	2.50	5.00	10.00
❑ UA-LA835-H	Ten Years of Gold	1978	2.50	5.00	10.00
❑ UA-LA903-H	Love Or Something Like It	1978	2.50	5.00	10.00
❑ UA-LA934-H	The Gambler	1978	2.50	5.00	10.00
❑ LWAK-979	Kenny	1979	2.50	5.00	10.00
❑ LOO-1035	Gideon	1980	2.50	5.00	10.00

ROGERS, KENNY, AND DOLLY PARTON

Also see each artist's individual listings.

12-Inch Singles

RCA

Number	Title (A Side/B Side)	Yr	VG	VG+	NM
❑ JR-13662 [DJ]	Islands in the Stream (same on both sides)	1983	2.00	4.00	8.00

45s

RCA

Number	Title (A Side/B Side)	Yr	VG	VG+	NM
❑ 5352-7-R	Christmas Without You/I Believe in Santa Claus	1987	—	—	3.00
—B-side by Dolly Parton					
❑ 9070-7-R	Christmas Without You/Medley: Winter Wonderland-Sleigh Ride	1989	—	—	3.00
—B-side by Dolly Parton					
❑ PB-13615	Islands in the Stream/I Will Always Love You	1983	—	—	3.00
❑ PB-13615 [PS]	Islands in the Stream/I Will Always Love You	1983	—	2.50	5.00
—Version 1: With "(Duet with Dolly Parton)" in small letters					
❑ PB-13615 [PS]	Islands in the Stream/I Will Always Love You	1983	—	2.00	4.00
—Version 2: With Dolly Parton's name the same size as Kenny Rogers'					
❑ PB-13945	The Greatest Gift of All/White Christmas	1984	—	2.00	4.00
❑ PB-14058	Real Love/I Can't Be True	1985	—	—	3.00
❑ GB-14073	Islands in the Stream/Eyes That See in the Dark	1985	—	—	3.00
—Gold Standard Series; B-side by Kenny Rogers					
❑ PB-14261	Christmas Without You/A Christmas to Remember	1985	—	—	3.00
❑ PB-14261 [PS]	Christmas Without You/A Christmas to Remember	1985	—	2.00	4.00

REPRISE

Number	Title (A Side/B Side)	Yr	VG	VG+	NM
❑ 19760	Love Is Strange/Walk Away	1990	—	—	3.00

Albums

RCA VICTOR

Number	Title (A Side/B Side)	Yr	VG	VG+	NM
❑ ASL1-5307	Once Upon a Christmas	1984	2.50	5.00	10.00

ROGERS, KENNY, AND THE FIRST EDITION

See THE FIRST EDITION.

ROGERS, KENNY, AND DOTTIE WEST

Also see each artist's individual listings.

45s

LIBERTY

Number	Title (A Side/B Side)	Yr	VG	VG+	NM
❑ 1516	Baby I'm-a Want You/Together Again	1984	—	—	3.00

UNITED ARTISTS

Number	Title (A Side/B Side)	Yr	VG	VG+	NM
❑ XW1137	Every Time Two Fools Collide/We Love Each Other	1978	—	2.00	4.00
❑ XW1234	Anyone Who Isn't Me Tonight/You and Me	1978	—	2.00	4.00
❑ XW1276	All I Ever Need Is You/Another Somebody Done Somebody Wrong Song	1979	—	2.00	4.00
❑ XW1299	Till I Can Make It on My Own/Midnight Flyer	1979	—	2.00	4.00

Albums

UNITED ARTISTS

Number	Title (A Side/B Side)	Yr	VG	VG+	NM
❑ UA-LA864-G	Every Time Two Fools Collide	1978	2.50	5.00	10.00
❑ UA-LA946-H	Classics	1979	2.50	5.00	10.00

ROGERS, RONNIE

45s

EPIC

Number	Title (A Side/B Side)	Yr	VG	VG+	NM
❑ 34-03953	Inside Story/Dixieland Delight	1983	—	2.00	4.00
❑ 34-04205	Modern Day Outlaws/Ten Toes Up, Ten Toes Down	1983	—	2.00	4.00

LIFESONG

Number	Title (A Side/B Side)	Yr	VG	VG+	NM
❑ 45094	Gonna Take My Angel Out Tonight/Neon Fool	1981	—	2.50	5.00
❑ 45095	My Love Belongs to You/Ramblers Never Change	1982	—	2.50	5.00
❑ 45116	First Time Around/Stoned Little Rat	1982	—	2.50	5.00
❑ 45118	Happy Country Birthday/Takin' It Back to the Hills	1982	—	2.50	5.00
❑ 45122	Peace/(B-side unknown)	1982	—	3.00	6.00
—With Tommy West					

MTM

Number	Title (A Side/B Side)	Yr	VG	VG+	NM
❑ B-72094	Good Timin' Shoes/Eyes of the Young	1987	—	2.00	4.00
❑ B-72098	Tough Times Don't Last/Fall in Tennessee	1988	—	2.00	4.00
❑ B-72110	Let's Be Bad Tonight/Honeymoon Mornin'	1988	—	2.00	4.00

Albums

MTM

Number	Title (A Side/B Side)	Yr	VG	VG+	NM
❑ ST-71065	Tough Times Don't Last	1988	2.50	5.00	10.00

ROGERS, ROY

Also see SONS OF THE PIONEERS.

45s

20TH CENTURY

Number	Title (A Side/B Side)	Yr	VG	VG+	NM
❑ 2154	Hoppy, Gene & Me/Good News, Bad News	1974	—	3.00	6.00
❑ 2173	Happy Trails/Don't Cry, Baby	1975	—	3.00	6.00
❑ 2209	Cowboy Heaven/Don't Ever Wear It for Him	1975	—	3.00	6.00

CAPITOL

Number	Title (A Side/B Side)	Yr	VG	VG+	NM
❑ 2895	Money Can't Buy Love/You and Me Against the World	1970	2.00	4.00	8.00
❑ 3016	Lovenworth/Vision at the Peace Table	1971	2.00	4.00	8.00
❑ 3117	Happy Anniversary/If I Ever Get That Close Again	1971	2.00	4.00	8.00
❑ 3263	These Are the Good Old Days/Pass It On	1972	2.00	4.00	8.00
❑ 3338	Homemade Love/Love Rides a Big White Horse	1972	2.00	4.00	8.00
❑ 3490	Talkin' About Love/In Another Lifetime	1972	2.00	4.00	8.00

MCA

Number	Title (A Side/B Side)	Yr	VG	VG+	NM
❑ 41294	Ride Concrete Cowboy Ride/Deliverance of the Wildwood Flower	1980	—	2.50	5.00
—With the Sons of the Pioneers; B-side by the Bandit Band					

RCA VICTOR

Number	Title (A Side/B Side)	Yr	VG	VG+	NM
❑ 47-0200	Pecos Bill — Part 1/Pecos Bill — Part 4	1949	10.00	20.00	40.00
—Blue label, yellow vinyl					
❑ 47-0201	Pecos Bill — Part 2/Pecos Bill — Part 3	1949	10.00	20.00	40.00
—Blue label, yellow vinyl; the above two records comprise set "WY 389"					
❑ 47-0228	Roy Rogers' Rodeo — Part 1/Roy Rogers' Rodeo — Part 4	1950	10.00	20.00	40.00
—Blue label, yellow vinyl					
❑ 47-0229	Roy Rogers' Rodeo — Part 2/Roy Rogers' Rodeo — Part 3	1950	10.00	20.00	40.00
—Blue label, yellow vinyl; the above two comprise album "WY 413"					
❑ 47-0255	Frosty the Snowman/Gabby the Gobbler	1950	10.00	20.00	40.00
—Blue label, yellow vinyl					
❑ 47-0306	Egbert the Easter Egg/Peter Cottontail	1951	10.00	20.00	40.00
—Blue label, yellow vinyl					
❑ 47-0306 [PS]	Egbert the Easter Egg/Peter Cottontail	1951	20.00	40.00	80.00
—Blue label, yellow vinyl					
❑ 47-2806	Don't Fence Me In/Roll On Texas Moon	1949	10.00	20.00	40.00
❑ 47-2807	The Yellow Rose of Texas/On the Old Spanish Trail	1949	10.00	20.00	40.00
❑ 47-2808	San Fernando Valley/Along the Navajo Trail	1949	10.00	20.00	40.00

Number	Title (A Side/B Side)	Yr	VG	VG+	NM
❑ 47-2809	Home in Oklahoma/A Gay Ranchero	1949	10.00	20.00	40.00
❑ 47-4237	Punky Punkin/The Kiwi Bird	1951	7.50	15.00	30.00
❑ 47-4242	I'm Gonna Lock You Out/Put All Your Kisses in an Envelope	1951	7.50	15.00	30.00
❑ 47-4301	Daddy's Cowboy/The Three Little Dwarfs	1951	7.50	15.00	30.00
❑ 47-4424	Horseshoe Moon/Home Sweet Oklahoma	1951	7.50	15.00	30.00
❑ 47-4526	Egbert the Easter Egg/Peter Cottontail	1952	7.50	15.00	30.00
❑ 47-4634	Four Legged Friend/There's a Cloud in My Valley of Sunshine	1952	7.50	15.00	30.00
❑ 47-4664	The Little White Duck/The Kiwi Bird	1952	7.50	15.00	30.00
❑ 47-4709	Happy Trails/California Rose	1952	10.00	20.00	40.00
❑ 47-4732	Peace in the Valley/Precious Memories	1952	7.50	15.00	30.00
❑ 47-4950	Hazy Mountains/You've Got a Rope Around My Heart	1952	7.50	15.00	30.00
❑ 48-0008	Don't Fence Me In/Roll On Texas Moon	1949	10.00	20.00	40.00
—Originals on green vinyl					
❑ 48-0009	The Yellow Rose of Texas/On the Old Spanish Trail	1949	10.00	20.00	40.00
—Originals on green vinyl					
❑ 48-0010	San Fernando Valley/Along the Navajo Trail	1949	10.00	20.00	40.00
—Originals on green vinyl					
❑ 48-0011	Home in Oklahoma/A Gay Ranchero	1949	10.00	20.00	40.00
—Originals on green vinyl					
❑ 48-0028	My Heart Went That-a-Way/No Children Allowed	1949	12.50	25.00	50.00
—Originals on green vinyl					
❑ 48-0034	The Kid with the Rip in His Pants/Dusty	1949	12.50	25.00	50.00
—Originals on green vinyl					
❑ 48-0035	Blue Shadows on the Trail/(There'll Never Be Another) Pecos Bill	1949	12.50	25.00	50.00
—Originals on green vinyl					
❑ 48-0074	Home on the Range/That Palomino Pal of Mine	1949	12.50	25.00	50.00
—Originals on green vinyl					
❑ 48-0115	My Chickashay Gal/A Little White Cross on the Hill	1949	10.00	20.00	40.00
—Originals on green vinyl					
❑ 48-0116	No Children Allowed/I Wish I Had Never Met Sunshine	1949	10.00	20.00	40.00
—Originals on green vinyl					
❑ 48-0117	My Heart Went That-a-Way/Dusty	1949	10.00	20.00	40.00
—Originals on green vinyl					
❑ 48-0152	Little Hula Honey/Mommy Can I Take My Doll to Heaven	1950	10.00	20.00	40.00
—Originals on green vinyl					
❑ 48-0161	Stampede/Church Music	1950	10.00	20.00	40.00
—Originals on green vinyl					
❑ 48-0207	Next to the X in Texas/Peter Cottontail	1950	10.00	20.00	40.00
—Originals on green vinyl					
❑ 48-0331	Buffalo Billy/Me and My Teddy Bear	1950	10.00	20.00	40.00
—Originals on green vinyl					
❑ 48-0374	Frosty the Snowman/Gabby the Gobbler	1950	10.00	20.00	40.00
—Originals on green vinyl					
❑ 48-0414	The Story of Bucky 'n' Dan/Ride, Son, Ride	1951	7.50	15.00	30.00
❑ 48-0423	Easter Parade/Peter Cottontail	1951	7.50	15.00	30.00
❑ 48-0438	Katy/Yogy the Doggie	1951	7.50	15.00	30.00
❑ 48-0458	Pliney Jane/Cowboy's Heaven	1951	7.50	15.00	30.00
❑ 48-0479	Buckeye Cowboy/I Wish I Wuz	1951	7.50	15.00	30.00
❑ 48-0496	The Lamp of Faith/Good Luck, Good Health	1951	7.50	15.00	30.00
Selected 78s					
DECCA					
❑ 6092	Think of Me/(B-side unknown)	1941	6.25	12.50	25.00
RCA VICTOR					
❑ 20-1782	You Can't Break My Heart/You Should Know	1946	6.25	12.50	25.00
❑ 20-1872	A Little White Cross on the Hill/I Can't Go On This Way	1946	6.25	12.50	25.00
❑ 20-2124	My Chickashay Gal/I Never Had a Chance	1947	6.25	12.50	25.00
❑ 20-2437	Do Ya or Don'tcha/Saddle Serenade	1948	6.25	12.50	25.00
❑ 20-2780	Blue Shadows on the Trail/(There'll Never Be Another) Pecos Bill	1948	6.25	12.50	25.00
—As "Roy Rogers and the Sons of the Pioneers"					
VOCALION					
❑ 04050	When a Cowboy Sings a Song/(B-side unknown)	1938	7.50	15.00	30.00
❑ 04051	Listen to the Rhythm of the Range/(B-side unknown)	1938	7.50	15.00	30.00
❑ 04091	Hi-Yo Silver/(B-side unknown)	1938	7.50	15.00	30.00
❑ 04263	I'm a Lonely Ranger/(B-side unknown)	1938	7.50	15.00	30.00
❑ 04389	When the Sun Is Setting on the Prairie/(B-side unknown)	1938	7.50	15.00	30.00
❑ 04453	Colorado Sunset/(B-side unknown)	1938	7.50	15.00	30.00
❑ 04544	Born to the Saddle/(B-side unknown)	1938	7.50	15.00	30.00
❑ 04840	Somebody's Smile/(B-side unknown)	1939	7.50	15.00	30.00
❑ 04923	Headin' for Texas and Home/(B-side unknown)	1939	7.50	15.00	30.00
❑ 04961	Let Me Build a Cabin/(B-side unknown)	1939	7.50	15.00	30.00
Albums					
20TH CENTURY					
❑ T-487	Happy Trails to You	1975	3.75	7.50	15.00
CAPITOL					
❑ ST-594	The Country Side of Roy Rogers	1970	5.00	10.00	20.00
❑ ST-785	A Man from Duck Run	1971	5.00	10.00	20.00
RCA					
❑ 3024-1-RRE [PD]	Roy Rogers Tribute	1991	10.00	20.00	40.00
—Picture disc; only vinyl edition of this release					
RCA CAMDEN					
❑ CAL-1054 [M]	Pecos Bill	1964	6.25	12.50	25.00
❑ CAS-1054(e) [R]	Pecos Bill	1964	3.75	7.50	15.00
❑ CAL-1074 [M]	Lore of the West	1966	6.25	12.50	25.00
❑ CAS-1074(e) [R]	Lore of the West	1966	3.75	7.50	15.00
❑ CAL-1097 [M]	Peter Cottontail and His Friends	1968	6.25	12.50	25.00
❑ CAS-1097 [R]	Peter Cottontail and His Friends	1968	3.75	7.50	15.00
RCA VICTOR					
❑ LBY-1022 [M]	Jesus Loves Me	1959	12.50	25.00	50.00
—On the "Children's Bluebird Series"					
❑ LPM-3041 [M]	Roy Rogers Souvenir Album	1952	75.00	150.00	300.00
❑ LPM-3168 [M]	Hymns of Faith	1954	50.00	100.00	200.00

ROGERS, ROY, AND CLINT BLACK

Also see each artist's individual listings.

Number	Title (A Side/B Side)	Yr	VG	VG+	NM
45s					
RCA					
❑ 62061	Hold On Partner/Alive and Kickin'	1991	—	2.50	5.00

ROGERS, ROY, AND SPADE COOLEY

Also see each artist's individual listings.

Number	Title (A Side/B Side)	Yr	VG	VG+	NM
45s					
RCA VICTOR					
❑ 48-0130	Skip to My Lou/Rickett's Reel	1949	10.00	20.00	40.00
—Originals on green vinyl					
❑ 48-0131	Old Joe Clark/Sycamore Reel	1949	10.00	20.00	40.00
—Originals on green vinyl					
❑ 48-0132	Oh Dem Golden Slippers/Lucky Leather Breeches	1949	10.00	20.00	40.00
—Originals on green vinyl					

ROGERS, ROY, AND DALE EVANS

Also see each artist's individual listings.

Number	Title (A Side/B Side)	Yr	VG	VG+	NM
45s					
CAPITOL					
❑ 2022	Merry Christmas My Darling/Sleigh Ride-Jingle Bells	1967	2.50	5.00	10.00
RCA VICTOR					
❑ WBY-43	Happy Trails/The Yellow Rose of Texas	195?	10.00	20.00	40.00
❑ WBY-43 [PS]	Happy Trails/The Yellow Rose of Texas	195?	20.00	40.00	80.00
❑ 47-0373	May the Good Lord Bless and Keep You/Smiles Are Made Out of Sunshine	1950	10.00	20.00	40.00
—Originals on green vinyl					
❑ 48-0128	Christmas on the Plains/Wonderful Christmas Night	1949	12.50	25.00	50.00
—Originals on green vinyl					
❑ 48-0336	What a Friend We Have in Jesus/I Love to Tell the Story	1950	10.00	20.00	40.00
—Originals on green vinyl					
❑ 48-0337	He Is So Precious to Me/When Jesus Came Into My Heart	1950	10.00	20.00	40.00
—Originals on green vinyl					
❑ 48-0338	Where He Leads Me/Love Lifted Me	1950	10.00	20.00	40.00
—Originals on green vinyl					
❑ 48-0344	The Old Rugged Cross/In the Garden	1950	10.00	20.00	40.00
—Originals on green vinyl					
❑ 48-0399	Yellow Bonnets and Polka Dot Shoes/No Bed of Roses	1950	10.00	20.00	40.00
—Originals on green vinyl					
❑ 48-0490	Snow on the Mountain/Strawberry Tears	1951	7.50	15.00	30.00
Albums					
CAPITOL					
❑ ST 1745 [S]	The Bible Tells Me So	1962	12.50	25.00	50.00
❑ T 1745 [M]	The Bible Tells Me So	1962	10.00	20.00	40.00
❑ ST 2818 [S]	Christmas Is Always	1967	7.50	15.00	30.00
❑ T 2818 [M]	Christmas Is Always	1967	7.50	15.00	30.00
GOLDEN					
❑ A198-6 [M]	Roy Rogers' and Dale Evans' Song Wagon	1958	20.00	40.00	80.00
—Originals have black labels and "198" prefix					
❑ A198-7 [M]	16 Great Songs of the Old West	1958	20.00	40.00	80.00
—Originals have black labels and "198" prefix					
❑ LP 7 [M]	A Child's Introduction to the West (16 Great Songs of the Old West)	196?	10.00	20.00	40.00
—Yellow label, "LP" prefix					
❑ A298-81 [M]	Peter Cottontail	1962	15.00	30.00	60.00
—Originals have black labels and "298" prefix					
RCA VICTOR					
❑ LPM-1439 [M]	Sweet Hour of Prayer	1957	20.00	40.00	80.00

ROGERS, SMOKEY

Number	Title (A Side/B Side)	Yr	VG	VG+	NM
45s					
CAPITOL					
❑ F40284	(Without Your) Wedding Ring/Dimples or Dumplin's	1950	10.00	20.00	40.00
Selected 78s					
CAPITOL					
❑ 15326	A Little Bird Told Me/Baby Me, Baby	1948	3.75	7.50	15.00
❑ 15406	Sui Sin Fa/Ten More Miles	1949	3.75	7.50	15.00
❑ 40080	Spanish Fandango/Drinkin' and a-Thinkin'	1948	5.00	10.00	20.00
❑ 40098	My Chickashay Gal/Slap 'Em Down Agin' Paw	1948	5.00	10.00	20.00
❑ 40123	Blue Bonnet Polka/Don't Come Cryin' to Me	1948	5.00	10.00	20.00
❑ 40199	The Spelling Song (I L-O-V-E You)/A Kiss to Remember	1949	3.75	7.50	15.00
❑ 40201	Queen for a Day Square Dance/Lady 'Round the Lady	1949	3.75	7.50	15.00
❑ 40230	Make Believe Heart/Rich Man, Poor Man	1949	3.75	7.50	15.00

ROHRS, DONNIE

45s

AD-KORP

Number	Title (A Side/B Side)	Yr	VG	VG+	NM
❑ 1223/24	Blues, Booze and Baby on My Mind/Mojo Small	197?	2.00	4.00	8.00
❑ 1233/34	Money/Woman in Your Eyes	197?	2.00	4.00	8.00
❑ 1243/44	Ugly Woman/Dang You Whiskey	1978	2.00	4.00	8.00
❑ 1245/46	Thank God for Music/Buster and the Boy	1978	2.00	4.00	8.00
❑ 1258	Hey Baby/(B-side unknown)	1978	2.00	4.00	8.00

PACIFIC CHALLENGER

Number	Title (A Side/B Side)	Yr	VG	VG+	NM
❑ 4504	Waltzes and Western Swing/Love Me Baby Tonight	1981	—	3.50	7.00

Albums

AD-KORP

Number	Title (A Side/B Side)	Yr	VG	VG+	NM
❑ 0112	Daddy and Daughter Time	197?	3.00	6.00	12.00

ROLAND, ADRIAN

45s

ALLSTAR

Number	Title (A Side/B Side)	Yr	VG	VG+	NM
❑ 7189	Mr. Bass Fiddle/Now I Know	1959	5.00	10.00	20.00
❑ 7196	The Night/When I'm in Your Arms	1960	5.00	10.00	20.00
❑ 7207	Imitation of Love/It Takes More Than a While	1960	5.00	10.00	20.00

ROLLING STONES, THE

"Far Away Eyes," the B-side of the No. 1 pop hit "Miss You," was actually distributed to country radio with the hope of gaining some airplay. Thus it is included in this book.

45s

ROLLING STONES

Number	Title (A Side/B Side)	Yr	VG	VG+	NM
❑ 19307	Miss You/Far Away Eyes	1978	—	2.00	4.00
❑ 19307 [DJ]	Far Away Eyes (same on both sides)	1978	50.00	100.00	250.00
❑ 19307 [PS]	Miss You/Far Away Eyes	1978	—	2.00	4.00

RONE, ROGER

45s

TRUE

Number	Title (A Side/B Side)	Yr	VG	VG+	NM
❑ 98	Holdin' On to Nothin'/Here I Stand	1989	—	3.00	6.00

RONICK, HOLLY

45s

HAPPY MAN

Number	Title (A Side/B Side)	Yr	VG	VG+	NM
❑ 822	Ain't No One Like Me in Tennessee/(B-side unknown)	1989	—	3.00	6.00
❑ 822 [PS]	Ain't No One Like Me in Tennessee/(B-side unknown)	1989	2.00	4.00	8.00

RONSTADT, LINDA

She has had 20 country hits. Many of the B-sides of her pop-rock hits charted country. Also see DOLLY PARTON/LINDA RONSTADT/EMMYLOU HARRIS.

12-Inch Singles

ASYLUM

Number	Title (A Side/B Side)	Yr	VG	VG+	NM
❑ 4935 [DJ]	What's New (same on both sides)	1983	2.00	4.00	8.00
❑ AS 11431 [DJ]	Blue Bayou/Lago Azul	1977	7.50	15.00	30.00
—Blue vinyl					

CAPITOL

Number	Title (A Side/B Side)	Yr	VG	VG+	NM
❑ ST-1003 [DJ]	Living Like a Fool (same on both sides)	1977	7.50	15.00	30.00
—Red vinyl; yellow label, "Capitol" in red at bottom					
❑ ST-1003 [DJ]	Living Like a Fool (same on both sides)	1977	10.00	20.00	40.00
—Red vinyl; yellow "SM" label with Capitol tower					

45s

ASYLUM

Number	Title (A Side/B Side)	Yr	VG	VG+	NM
❑ 11026	Love Has No Pride/I Can Almost See It	1973	—	2.50	5.00
❑ 11032	Silver Threads and Golden Needles/Don't Cry Now	1974	—	2.50	5.00
❑ 11039	Desperado/Colorado	1974	—	2.50	5.00
❑ 45271	Love Is a Rose/Silver Blue	1975	—	3.00	6.00
❑ 45282	Heat Wave/Love Is a Rose	1975	—	2.00	4.00
❑ 45295	Tracks of My Tears/The Sweetest Gift	1975	—	2.00	4.00
—B-side with Emmylou Harris					
❑ 45340	That'll Be the Day/Try Me Again	1976	—	2.00	4.00
—Clouds label					
❑ 45340	That'll Be the Day/Try Me Again	1976	—	2.50	5.00
—All-blue label					
❑ 45361	Someone to Lay Down Beside Me/Crazy	1976	—	2.00	4.00
❑ 45402	Lose Again/Lo Siento Mi Vida	1977	2.00	4.00	8.00
❑ 45431	Blue Bayou/Old Paint	1977	—	2.00	4.00
❑ 45438	It's So Easy/Lo Siento Mi Vida	1977	—	2.00	4.00
❑ 45462	Poor Poor Pitiful Me/Simple Man, Simple Dream	1978	—	2.00	4.00
❑ 45464	Lago Azul/Lo Siento Mi Vida	1978	2.00	4.00	8.00
❑ 45479	Tumbling Dice/I Never Will Marry	1978	—	2.00	4.00
❑ 45519	Back in the U.S.A./White Rhythm and Blues	1978	—	2.00	4.00
❑ 45519 [PS]	Back in the U.S.A./White Rhythm and Blues	1978	—	3.00	6.00
❑ 45546	Ooh Baby Baby/Blowing Away	1978	—	2.00	4.00
❑ 46011	Just One Look/Love Me Tender	1979	—	2.00	4.00
❑ 46034	Alison/Mohammed's Radio	1979	—	2.00	4.00
❑ 46602	How Do I Make You/Rambler Gambler	1980	—	2.00	4.00
❑ 46602 [PS]	How Do I Make You/Rambler Gambler	1980	—	2.50	5.00
❑ 46624	Hurt So Bad/Justine	1980	—	2.00	4.00
❑ 46654	I Can't Let Go/Look Out for My Love	1980	—	2.00	4.00
❑ 69476	(I Love You) For Sentimental Reasons/Straighten Up and Fly Right	1987	—	2.00	4.00
❑ 69507	When You Wish Upon a Star/Little Girl Blue	1986	—	2.00	4.00
❑ 69507 [PS]	When You Wish Upon a Star/Little Girl Blue	1986	—	2.00	4.00
❑ 69653	When I Fall in Love/It Never Entered My Mind	1985	—	2.00	4.00
❑ 69671	Lush Life/Skylark	1985	—	2.00	4.00
❑ 69725	Someone to Watch Over Me/What'll I Do	1984	—	2.00	4.00
❑ 69752	I've Got a Crush on You/Lover Man	1984	—	2.00	4.00
❑ 69780	What's New/Crazy He Calls Me	1983	—	2.00	4.00
❑ 69838	Easy for You to Say/Mr. Radio	1983	—	2.00	4.00
❑ 69853	I Knew You When/Talk to Me of Mendocino	1982	—	2.00	4.00
❑ 69853 [PS]	I Knew You When/Talk to Me of Mendocino	1982	—	2.50	5.00
❑ 69948	Get Closer/Sometimes You Just Can't Win	1982	—	2.00	4.00
❑ 69948 [PS]	Get Closer/Sometimes You Just Can't Win	1982	—	2.50	5.00

CAPITOL

Number	Title (A Side/B Side)	Yr	VG	VG+	NM
❑ 2438	Dolphins/The Long Way Around	1969	3.00	6.00	12.00
❑ 2767	Lovesick Blues/Will You Love Me Tomorrow	1970	2.00	4.00	8.00
❑ 2846	Long Long Time/Nobody's	1970	2.00	4.00	8.00
❑ 3021	The Long Way Around/(She's a) Very Lovely Woman	1971	—	3.00	6.00
❑ 3210	I Fall to Pieces/Can It Be True	1971	—	3.00	6.00
❑ 3273	Rock Me on the Water/Crazy Arms	1972	—	3.00	6.00
❑ 3990	You're No Good/I Can't Help It (If I'm Still in Love with You)	1974	—	2.00	4.00
❑ 4050	When Will I Be Loved/It Doesn't Matter Anymore	1975	—	2.00	4.00

ELEKTRA

Number	Title (A Side/B Side)	Yr	VG	VG+	NM
❑ 64427	The Waiting/Walk On	1995	—	—	3.00
❑ 64987	All My Life/Shattered	1990	—	—	3.00
—With Aaron Neville					
❑ 69261	Don't Know Much/Cry Like a Rainstorm	1989	—	—	3.00
—With Aaron Neville					

MCA

Number	Title (A Side/B Side)	Yr	VG	VG+	NM
❑ 52973	Somewhere Out There/(Instrumental)	1986	—	—	3.00
—With James Ingram					
❑ 52973 [PS]	Somewhere Out There/(Instrumental)	1986	—	2.00	4.00

Albums

ASYLUM

Number	Title (A Side/B Side)	Yr	VG	VG+	NM
❑ 6E-104	Simple Dreams	1977	2.50	5.00	10.00
❑ 6E-106	Greatest Hits	1977	2.50	5.00	10.00
❑ 6E-155	Living in the U.S.A.	1978	2.50	5.00	10.00
❑ DP-401 [PD]	Living in the U.S.A.	1978	4.50	9.00	18.00
❑ 5E-510	Mad Love	1980	2.50	5.00	10.00
❑ 5E-516	Greatest Hits, Volume 2	1980	2.50	5.00	10.00
❑ 5E-540	Keeping Out of Mischief	1981	—	—	—
—Canceled					
❑ 7E-1045	Prisoner in Disguise	1975	2.50	5.00	10.00
❑ 7E-1072	Hasten Down the Wind	1976	2.50	5.00	10.00
—"Clouds" label					
❑ 7E-1072	Hasten Down the Wind	1976	3.75	7.50	15.00
—Solid blue label with white stylized "a" at top					
❑ 7E-1092	Greatest Hits	1976	3.00	6.00	12.00
❑ SD 5064	Don't Cry Now	1973	2.50	5.00	10.00
❑ 60185	Get Closer	1982	2.50	5.00	10.00
❑ 60260	What's New	1983	2.50	5.00	10.00
❑ 60387	Lush Life	1984	2.50	5.00	10.00
❑ 60474	For Sentimental Reasons	1987	2.50	5.00	10.00
❑ 60489 [(3)]	'Round Midnight: The Nelson Riddle Sessions	1987	6.25	12.50	25.00
❑ 60765	Canciones De Mi Padre	1988	3.00	6.00	12.00

CAPITOL

Number	Title (A Side/B Side)	Yr	VG	VG+	NM
❑ ST-208	Hand Sown…Home Grown	1969	5.00	10.00	20.00
—Black label with colorband					
❑ ST-208	Hand Sown…Home Grown	1970	3.75	7.50	15.00
—Green label					
❑ ST-208	Hand Sown…Home Grown	1971	3.00	6.00	12.00
—Red label					
❑ ST-407	Silk Purse	1970	3.75	7.50	15.00
—Green label					
❑ ST-407	Silk Purse	1971	3.00	6.00	12.00
—Red label					
❑ ST-8-0407	Silk Purse	1970	5.00	10.00	20.00
—Capitol Record Club edition					
❑ SMAS-635	Linda Ronstadt	1972	3.00	6.00	12.00
❑ ST-11269	Different Drum	1974	3.00	6.00	12.00
—Also includes Stone Poneys tracks					
❑ ST-11358	Heart Like a Wheel	1974	3.00	6.00	12.00
❑ SW-11358	Heart Like a Wheel	1975	2.50	5.00	10.00
❑ SKBB-11629 [(2)]	A Retrospective	1977	3.75	7.50	15.00
—Also includes Stone Poneys tracks					
❑ SN-16130	Hand Sown…Home Grown	1980	2.00	4.00	8.00
❑ SN-16131	Silk Purse	1980	2.00	4.00	8.00
❑ SN-16132	Linda Ronstadt	1980	2.00	4.00	8.00
❑ SN-16133	Beginnings	1980	2.00	4.00	8.00
❑ SN-16299	Different Drum	198?	2.00	4.00	8.00
—Budget-line reissue					

ELEKTRA

Number	Title (A Side/B Side)	Yr	VG	VG+	NM
❑ 60872	Cry Like a Rainstorm, Howl Like the Wind	1989	3.00	6.00	12.00

MOBILE FIDELITY

Number	Title (A Side/B Side)	Yr	VG	VG+	NM
❑ 1-158	What's New	1984	12.50	25.00	50.00
—Audiophile vinyl					

NAUTILUS

Number	Title (A Side/B Side)	Yr	VG	VG+	NM
❑ NR-26	Simple Dreams	1982	12.50	25.00	50.00
—Audiophile vinyl					

PAIR

Number	Title (A Side/B Side)	Yr	VG	VG+	NM
❑ PDL2-1070 [(2)]	Prime of Life	1986	3.00	6.00	12.00
❑ PDL2-1125 [(2)]	Rockfile	1986	3.00	6.00	12.00

ROOFTOP SINGERS, THE

Folk group that saw the below #1 pop hit cross over to the country charts.

45s

VANGUARD

Number	Title (A Side/B Side)	Yr	VG	VG+	NM
❑ 35017	Walk Right In/Cool Water	1962	2.50	5.00	10.00

ROSE, FRED

Selected 78s

Number	Title (A Side/B Side)	Yr	VG	VG+	NM
COLUMBIA					
❑ 20018	Blues in My Mind/If It's Wrong to Love You	1948	3.00	6.00	12.00
—Reissue of 36951, evidently with credit revised to "Fred Rose"					
❑ 20436	No One Will Ever Know/Don't Feel Sorry for Me	1948	3.75	7.50	15.00
❑ 20507	Tender Hearted Sue/You're Only in My Arms (To Cry on My Shoulder)	1948	3.00	6.00	12.00
—Reissue of Okeh 6747					
❑ 36951	Blues in My Mind/If It's Wrong to Love You	1946	3.75	7.50	15.00
—As "The Rambling Rogue"					
OKEH					
❑ 6747	Tender Hearted Sue/You're Only in My Arms (To Cry on My Shoulder)	1945	5.00	10.00	20.00
—As "The Rambling Rogue"					

ROSE, JUANITA

45s

Number	Title (A Side/B Side)	Yr	VG	VG+	NM
HICKORY					
❑ 1667	Go On Back to the Honky Tonk/Tonight I'm Wantin' You Again	1973	2.00	4.00	8.00

ROSE, PAM

Also see CALAMITY JANE.

45s

Number	Title (A Side/B Side)	Yr	VG	VG+	NM
CAPITOL					
❑ 4440	Midnight Flight/Sing, Feelin', Sing	1977	—	2.50	5.00
❑ 4491	Runaway Heart/Break Down the Walls	1977	—	2.50	5.00
EPIC					
❑ 50819	It's Not Supposed to Be That Way/We're Gonna Try It Tonight	1979	—	2.00	4.00
❑ 50861	I'm Not Through Loving You Yet/When Love's in Your Heart, It's in Your Eyes	1980	—	2.00	4.00
❑ 50906	Memories for Sale/The Book of You and Me	1980	—	2.00	4.00

ROSE, RICHARD AND GARY

45s

Number	Title (A Side/B Side)	Yr	VG	VG+	NM
CAPITOL					
❑ B-44118	Younger Man, Older Woman/Until You're Mine	1987	—	—	3.00

ROSIE AND RETTA

45s

Number	Title (A Side/B Side)	Yr	VG	VG+	NM
COLUMBIA					
❑ 4-21385	Hoot Owl Melody/I'm Gonna Be Loved Tonight	1955	5.00	10.00	20.00
❑ 4-21447	Was There a Teardrop/Wild Wind	1955	5.00	10.00	20.00

ROSS, CHARLIE

45s

Number	Title (A Side/B Side)	Yr	VG	VG+	NM
BIG TREE					
❑ 16014	She's My Lady/(B-side unknown)	1974	—	3.00	6.00
❑ 16025	Can't Live With You, Can't Live Without You/Thanks for the Smiles	1974	—	3.00	6.00
❑ 16039	Your Side of the Bed/Can't Live With You, Can't Live Without You	1975	—	3.00	6.00
❑ 16056	Without Your Love (Mr. Jordan)/Sneaking Round Corners	1976	—	3.00	6.00
❑ 16068	Give Her What She Wants/(B-side unknown)	1976	—	3.00	6.00
TOWN HOUSE					
❑ 1057	The High Cost of Loving/She Sure Got Away with My Heart	1982	—	2.50	5.00
❑ 1060	Let's Start Over/(B-side unknown)	1982	—	3.00	6.00
❑ 1061	Are We in Love (Or Am I)/Shoot First, Ask Questions Later	1982	—	2.50	5.00
❑ 1063	The Name of the Game Is Cheating/Somebody Loves You	1982	—	2.50	5.00
ZODIAC					
❑ 1022	Lady Loretta/Without Your Love, Mr. Jordan, Part 2	1977	—	3.00	6.00

Albums

Number	Title (A Side/B Side)	Yr	VG	VG+	NM
ACCORD					
❑ SN-7007	High Cost of Loving	1982	2.50	5.00	10.00

ROSS, JERIS

45s

Number	Title (A Side/B Side)	Yr	VG	VG+	NM
ABC					
❑ 11397	Moontan/People Just Like You	1973	—	3.00	6.00
❑ 11436	I Know the Feeling/Everything You Always Wanted to Know	1974	—	3.00	6.00
❑ 12004	Come to Me/I Can Feel Love	1974	—	2.50	5.00
❑ 12038	Chapel of Love/Funny How the Bad Times Fade Away	1974	—	2.50	5.00
❑ 12064	Pictures on Paper/Won't You Meet Me at the Church	1975	—	2.50	5.00
ABC DOT					
❑ 17573	I'd Rather Be Picked Up Here (Than Be Put Down at Home)/Sing a Love Song to Your Baby	1975	—	2.50	5.00
❑ 17615	All the Cryin' in the World/Just Like Your Daddy	1976	—	2.50	5.00
❑ 17632	You Don't Need a Cadillac/Burning Love from Both Ends	1976	—	2.50	5.00
CARTWHEEL					
❑ 206	Brand New Key/Baby's Thinking of Leaving	1972	—	3.50	7.00
❑ 214	Old Fashioned Love Song/I Gotta Go to Memphis	1972	—	3.50	7.00
❑ 221	Midnight Cowboy/(B-side unknown)	1972	—	3.50	7.00
DOOR KNOB					
❑ 108	Little Bit More/Ease Me to the Ground	1979	—	2.50	5.00
❑ 117	You Win Again/Rock Me	1980	—	2.50	5.00
GAZELLE					
❑ 431	I Think I'll Say Goodbye/Rock Me	1977	—	2.50	5.00
SANTA'S LAND					
❑ 106	Hiding Behind the Christmas Tree/Joy, The Snow Flake	198?	—	2.50	5.00

Albums

Number	Title (A Side/B Side)	Yr	VG	VG+	NM
ABC DOT					
❑ DOSD-2046	Jeris Ross	1976	3.00	6.00	12.00

ROVERS, THE

45s

Number	Title (A Side/B Side)	Yr	VG	VG+	NM
CLEVELAND INT'L.					
❑ 02148	Mexican Girl/Pheasant Pluckers Son	1981	—	2.00	4.00
❑ 02728	Pain in My Past/Daddies (Bobby's Song)	1982	—	2.00	4.00
❑ 02911	People Who Read People Magazine/Roly Poly Ladies	1982	—	2.00	4.00
❑ 51007	Wasn't That a Party/Matchstalk Men and Matchstalk Cats & Dogs	1981	—	2.50	5.00
EPIC					
❑ 03089	Wasn't That a Party/Pain in My Past	1982	—	—	3.00
—Reissue					

Albums

Number	Title (A Side/B Side)	Yr	VG	VG+	NM
CLEVELAND INT'L.					
❑ JE 37107	Wasn't That a Party	1981	2.50	5.00	10.00
❑ FE 37706	Pain in My Past	1982	2.50	5.00	10.00

ROWE, JACK

45s

Number	Title (A Side/B Side)	Yr	VG	VG+	NM
DECCA					
❑ 9-46388	Bomb Bosh Boogie/Texas Stomp	1952	7.50	15.00	30.00

ROWE, STACEY

45s

Number	Title (A Side/B Side)	Yr	VG	VG+	NM
SABRE					
❑ 4510	I Couldn't Live Without Your Love/(B-side unknown)	1979	2.00	4.00	8.00

ROWELL, ERNIE

45s

Number	Title (A Side/B Side)	Yr	VG	VG+	NM
GRASS					
❑ 05	I'm Leavin' You Alone/He's the One	1979	—	3.00	6.00
❑ 07	Music in the Mountains/He's the One	1981	—	3.00	6.00
PRIZE					
❑ 02	Fire and Rain/Facing You	1971	2.00	4.00	8.00
❑ 08	Going Back to Louisiana/This Bottle Hides the Weakness in Me	1971	2.00	4.00	8.00
❑ 19	Four Roses/Those Two X's	1972	2.00	4.00	8.00
REVOLVER					
❑ 016	You Left My Heart for Broke/(B-side unknown)	1987	—	3.00	6.00

ROWLAND, DAVE

Also see DAVE AND SUGAR.

45s

Number	Title (A Side/B Side)	Yr	VG	VG+	NM
ELEKTRA					
❑ 47135	Fool By Your Side/Don't Let Our Dreams Die Young	1981	—	2.00	4.00
—As "Dave Rowland and Sugar"					
❑ 47177	The Pleasure's All Mine/One Step at a Time	1981	—	2.00	4.00
—As "Dave Rowland and Sugar"					
❑ 47234 [DJ]	Winter Wonderland/Rudolph the Red-Nosed Reindeer	1981	2.00	4.00	8.00
—As "Dave Rowland and Sugar"; B-side by Mel and Nancy (Tillis and Sinatra)					
❑ 47442	Natalie/Why Didn't I Think of That	1982	—	2.00	4.00
❑ 69998	Lovin' Our Lives Away/Women and Wine	1982	—	2.00	4.00

Albums

Number	Title (A Side/B Side)	Yr	VG	VG+	NM
ELEKTRA					
❑ 5E-525	Pleasure	1981	2.00	4.00	8.00
—As "Dave Rowland and Sugar"					
❑ 60011	Sugar Free	1982	2.00	4.00	8.00

ROY, BOBBIE

45s

Number	Title (A Side/B Side)	Yr	VG	VG+	NM
CAPITOL					
❑ 3301	One Woman's Trash (Another Woman's Treasure)/Due to a Heartache	1972	—	3.00	6.00
❑ 3428	Leavin' on Your Mind/Candle in the Wind	1972	—	3.00	6.00
❑ 3477	I Like Everything About Loving You/I Wanted So to Say It	1972	—	3.00	6.00
❑ 3513	I Am Woman/Till I Get It Right	1973	—	3.00	6.00
❑ 3587	Baby, I've Waited/Love Makes a Woman Feel Good	1973	—	3.00	6.00
❑ 3711	Things Are Looking Good/The World's Not Ready Yet	1973	—	3.00	6.00

Albums

Number	Title (A Side/B Side)	Yr	VG	VG+	NM
CAPITOL					
❑ ST-11086	I'm Your Woman	1972	3.00	6.00	12.00

ROYAL, BILLY JOE

By the 1970s, he was already recording in a country style, though he didn't start charting until 1985. We have opted to include his entire output, even his pop-oriented Columbia material, here. Also see DONNA FARGO.

45s

Number	Title (A Side/B Side)	Yr	VG	VG+	NM
ALL WOOD					
❑ 401	Wait for Me Baby/If It Wasn't for a Woman	1962	5.00	10.00	20.00
ATLANTIC					
❑ 2328	Never in a Hundred Years/We Haven't a Moment to Lose	1966	2.50	5.00	10.00
❑ 87770	If the Jukebox Took Teardrops/How Could You	1991	—	2.00	4.00
❑ 87867	Ring Where a Ring Used to Be/We Need to Walk	1990	—	2.00	4.00
❑ 87933	Searchin' for Some Kind of Clue/This Too Shall Pass	1990	—	2.00	4.00
❑ 88815	Till I Can't Take It Anymore/He Don't Know	1990	—	2.00	4.00
ATLANTIC AMERICA					
❑ 99217	Love Has No Right/Cross My Heart and Hope to Try	1989	—	—	3.00
❑ 99217 [PS]	Love Has No Right/Cross My Heart and Hope to Try	1989	—	2.00	4.00
❑ 99242	Tell It Like It Is/Losing You	1989	—	—	3.00
❑ 99242 [PS]	Tell It Like It Is/Losing You	1989	—	2.00	4.00
❑ 99295	It Keeps Right On Hurtin'/Let It Rain	1988	—	—	3.00
❑ 99295 [PS]	It Keeps Right On Hurtin'/Let It Rain	1988	—	—	3.00
❑ 99364	Out of Sight and On My Mind/She Don't Cry Like She Used To	1988	—	—	3.00
❑ 99364 [PS]	Out of Sight and On My Mind/She Don't Cry Like She Used To	1988	—	—	3.00
❑ 99404	I'll Pin a Note on Your Pillow/A Place for a Heartache	1987	—	—	3.00
❑ 99404 [PS]	I'll Pin a Note on Your Pillow/A Place for a Heartache	1987	—	—	3.00
❑ 99485	Old Bridges Burn Slow/We've Both Got a Lot to Learn	1987	—	—	3.00
❑ 99485 [PS]	Old Bridges Burn Slow/We've Both Got a Lot to Learn	1987	—	—	3.00
❑ 99519	I Miss You Already/Another Endless Night	1986	—	—	3.00
❑ 99555	Boardwalk Angel/Out of Sight and On My Mind	1986	—	—	3.00
❑ 99599	Burned Like a Rocket/Lonely Loving You	1985	—	—	3.00
COLUMBIA					
❑ 43305	Down in the Boondocks/Oh, What a Night	1965	2.50	5.00	10.00
❑ 43305 [DJ]	Down in the Boondocks (same on both sides)	1965	10.00	20.00	40.00
—Red vinyl promo					
❑ 43390	I Knew You When/Steal Away	1965	2.50	5.00	10.00
❑ 43390 [DJ]	I Knew You When (same on both sides)	1965	10.00	20.00	40.00
—Red vinyl promo					
❑ 43465	I've Got to Be Somebody/You Make Me Feel Like a Man	1965	2.00	4.00	8.00
❑ 43465 [DJ]	I've Got to Be Somebody (same on both sides)	1965	7.50	15.00	30.00
—Red vinyl promo					
❑ 43538	It's a Good Time/Don't Wait Up for Me Mama	1966	2.00	4.00	8.00
❑ 43622	Heart's Desire/Keep Inside Me	1966	2.00	4.00	8.00
❑ 43740	Campfire Girls/Should I Come Back	1966	2.00	4.00	8.00
❑ 43883	Yo-Yo/We Tried	1966	2.00	4.00	8.00
❑ 44003	Wisdom of a Fool/Everything Turned Blue	1967	2.00	4.00	8.00
❑ 44103	These Are Not My People/The Greatest Love	1967	2.00	4.00	8.00
❑ 44277	Hush/Watching from the Bandstand	1967	2.00	4.00	8.00
❑ 44468	Don't You Be Ashamed (To Call My Name)/Don't You Think It's Time	1968	2.00	4.00	8.00
❑ 44574	Storybook Children/Just Between You and Me	1968	2.00	4.00	8.00
❑ 44677	Movies in My Mind/Gabriel	1968	—	3.00	6.00
❑ 44743	Bed of Roses/The Greatest Love	1969	—	3.00	6.00
❑ 44814	Nobody Loves You But Me/Baby I'm Thinking of You	1969	—	2.50	5.00
❑ 44902	Cherry Hill Park/Helping Hand	1969	2.00	4.00	8.00
❑ 45085	Mama's Song/Me Without You	1970	—	2.50	5.00
❑ 45220	Burning a Hole/Every Night	1970	—	2.50	5.00
❑ 45289	Tulsa/Pick Up the Pieces	1970	—	2.50	5.00
❑ 45406	Poor Little Pearl/Lady Lives to Love	1971	—	2.50	5.00
❑ 45495	Colorado Rain/We Go Back	1971	—	2.50	5.00
❑ 45557	Later/The Family	1972	—	3.00	6.00
❑ 45620	Child of Mine/Natchez Trace	1972	—	3.00	6.00
FAIRLANE					
❑ 21009	Never in a Hundred Years/We Haven't a Moment to Lose	1961	7.50	15.00	30.00
❑ 21013	Dark Glasses/Perhaps	1962	7.50	15.00	30.00
KAT FAMILY					
❑ 01044	(Who is Like You) Sweet America/No Love Like a First Love	1981	—	2.00	4.00
❑ 02074	You Really Got a Hold on Me/No Love Like a First Love	1981	—	2.00	4.00
❑ 02297	Wasted Time/Outrun the Sun	1981	—	2.00	4.00
MERCURY					
❑ 76069	Mr. Kool/Let's Talk It Over	1980	—	2.00	4.00
MGM SOUTH					
❑ 7011	This Magic Moment/Mountain Woman	1973	—	2.50	5.00
❑ 7018	Summertime Skies/Look What I Found	1973	—	2.50	5.00
❑ 7022	If This Is the Last Time/Perfect Harmony	1973	—	2.50	5.00
❑ 7032	Star Again/Sugar Blue	1974	—	2.50	5.00
PLAYER'S					
❑ 1	I'm Specialized/Really You	1965	5.00	10.00	20.00
PRIVATE STOCK					
❑ 45192	Under the Boardwalk/Precious Time	1978	—	2.50	5.00
❑ 45212 [DJ]	Anchors Aweigh (mono/stereo)	1979	—	2.50	5.00
SCEPTER					
❑ 12419	All Night Rain/Time Don't Pass By Here	1976	—	2.00	4.00
TOLLIE					
❑ 9011	Mama Didn't Raise No Fools/Get Behind Me, Devil	1964	3.75	7.50	15.00

Albums

Number	Title	Yr	VG	VG+	NM
ATLANTIC AMERICA					
❑ 90508	Looking Ahead	1986	2.50	5.00	10.00
❑ 90658	The Royal Treatment	1987	2.50	5.00	10.00
❑ 91064	Tell It Like It Is	1989	2.50	5.00	10.00
COLUMBIA					
❑ CL 2403 [M]	Down in the Boondocks	1965	5.00	10.00	20.00
❑ CL 2781 [M]	Billy Joe Royal	1967	6.25	12.50	25.00
❑ CS 9203 [S]	Down in the Boondocks	1965	6.25	12.50	25.00
❑ CS 9581 [S]	Billy Joe Royal	1967	6.25	12.50	25.00
❑ CS 9974	Cherry Hill Park	1969	6.25	12.50	25.00
KAT FAMILY					
❑ JW 37342	Billy Joe Royal	1982	2.50	5.00	10.00
MERCURY					
❑ SRM-1-3837	Billy Joe Royal	1980	2.50	5.00	10.00

RUE, ARNIE

45s

Number	Title (A Side/B Side)	Yr	VG	VG+	NM
NSD					
❑ 19	Spare a Little Lovin' (On a Fool)/To Each His Own	1979	—	2.50	5.00
❑ 32	Rodle-Odeo-Home/Yesterday's Dreams	1979	—	2.50	5.00
❑ 42	Daddy Don't/Dreams	1980	—	2.50	5.00

RUN C & W

45s

Number	Title (A Side/B Side)	Yr	VG	VG+	NM
MCA					
❑ 54649	Itchy Twitchy Spot/Sweet Soul Music	1993	—	2.00	4.00

RUSHING, JIM

45s

Number	Title (A Side/B Side)	Yr	VG	VG+	NM
OVATION					
❑ 1153	Dixie Dirt/Two Hearts Don't Always Make a Pair	1980	—	2.50	5.00
❑ 1161	I've Loved Enough to Know/Two Hearts Don't Always Make a Pair	1980	—	2.50	5.00

RUSSELL, BOBBY

45s

Number	Title (A Side/B Side)	Yr	VG	VG+	NM
BUENA VISTA					
❑ 473	The Ballad of Smith & Gabriel Jimmy Boy/Summer Sweet	1969	2.50	5.00	10.00
❑ 474	The Ballad of Smith & Gabriel Billyboy/Summer Sweet	1969	2.50	5.00	10.00
COLUMBIA					
❑ 45901	Mid American Manufacturing Tycoon/Ships in the Night	1973	—	2.00	4.00
❑ 46045	The Night the Lights Went Out in Georgia/Go Chase Your Rainbow	1974	—	2.00	4.00
D					
❑ 1115	Not Even Friends/Shackled	1960	3.00	6.00	12.00
—With Sadie Russell					
ELF					
❑ 90014	Dusty/I Made You This Way	1968	—	3.00	6.00
❑ 90020	1432 Franklin Pike Circle Hero/Let's Talk About Them	1968	—	3.00	6.00
❑ 90023	Carlie/Ain't Society Great	1969	—	3.00	6.00
❑ 90027	Then She's a Lover/He Wrote a Song	1969	—	3.00	6.00
❑ 90031	Better Homes and Gardens/Summer Sweet	1969	—	3.00	6.00
FELSTED					
❑ 8520	The Raven/She's Gonna Be Sorry	1958	3.75	7.50	15.00
F&L					
❑ 518	Camp Getcha 'Losa Ya/Arm Chair Quarterback	1982	—	3.00	6.00
IMAGE					
❑ 1014	Goin' Steady Dream/To the Ones with Broken Hearts	1961	3.00	6.00	12.00
MONUMENT					
❑ 899	Once a Day/You Were Mine	1965	2.00	4.00	8.00
❑ 929	Friends and Memories/Wish I'd Say That	1966	2.00	4.00	8.00
NATIONAL GENERAL					
❑ 006	As Far As I'm Concerned/Traveling with a Star	1970	2.00	4.00	8.00
PRIVATE STOCK					
❑ 45046	Little Boxes/(B-side unknown)	1975	—	2.50	5.00
RISING SONS					
❑ 700	Bluebird/Tears Tell	1967	2.00	4.00	8.00
UNITED ARTISTS					
❑ 50788	Saturday Morning Confusion/Little Ole Song About Love	1971	—	2.50	5.00
❑ 50853	Goodbye/It Hurts	1971	—	2.50	5.00
❑ 50888	Easy Made for Lovin'/The Bell	1972	—	2.50	5.00
❑ 50904	You Babe/Back to Sausalito	1972	—	2.50	5.00
❑ 50959	Welcome to the U.S. Army/This Is the Life	1972	—	2.50	5.00

Albums

Number	Title	Yr	VG	VG+	NM
ELF					
❑ 5500	Words, Music, Laughter & Tears	1969	5.00	10.00	20.00
❑ 5501	Unlimited	1970	3.75	7.50	15.00
UNITED ARTISTS					
❑ UAS-5548	Saturday Morning Confusion	1971	3.00	6.00	12.00

RUSSELL, CLIFFORD

45s

SUGARTREE

Number	Title (A Side/B Side)	Yr	VG	VG+	NM
❑ 0509	She Feels Like a New Man Tonight/Sometimes When We Touch	1983	2.00	4.00	8.00
❑ 0509 [PS]	She Feels Like a New Man Tonight/Sometimes When We Touch	1983	2.50	5.00	10.00

RUSSELL, JIMMY

45s

CHARTA

Number	Title (A Side/B Side)	Yr	VG	VG+	NM
❑ 101	It's Been So Long Darling/Too Much of Her Rubbed Off	1976	—	3.00	6.00
❑ 103	You've Got to Move Two Mountains/It's Been So Long Darling	1976	—	3.00	6.00
❑ 113	Seventh Son/Yes, She Used to Be My Baby	1977	—	3.00	6.00

RUSSELL, JOHNNY

45s

Number	Title (A Side/B Side)	Yr	VG	VG+	NM
MERCURY					
❑ 55030	You'll Be Back (Every Night in My Dreams)/Is Anybody Leaving San Antone	1978	—	2.00	4.00
—Reissue of Polydor 14475					
❑ 55045	How Deep in Love Am I?/Shall We Gather at the Ridge	1978	—	2.00	4.00
❑ 55060	I Might Be Awhile in New Orleans/Make Up My Mind	1979	—	2.00	4.00
❑ 57008	Ain't No Way to Make a Bad Love Grow/Keep the Change	1979	—	2.00	4.00
❑ 57016	While the Choir Sang the Hymn (I Thought of Her)/Falsely Accused	1980	—	2.00	4.00
❑ 57026	We're Back in Love Again/Love Makes a Fool of Us All	1980	—	2.00	4.00
❑ 57038	Song of the South/I'm Gettin' Holes in My Boots (From Climbing the Walls)	1980	—	2.00	4.00
❑ 57050	Here's to the Horses/Take Me to Heart	1981	—	2.00	4.00
POLYDOR					
❑ 14475	You'll Be Back (Every Night in My Dreams)/Is Anybody Leavin' San Antone	1978	—	2.50	5.00
RCA					
❑ PB-10853	The Son of Hickory Holler's Tramp/I Wonder How She's Doing Now	1976	—	2.50	5.00
❑ PB-10984	Obscene Phone Call/If I Want to Get It Right	1977	—	2.50	5.00
❑ PB-11160	Leona/Your Fool	1977	—	2.50	5.00
RCA VICTOR					
❑ APBO-0021	Rednecks, White Socks and Blue Ribbon Beer/She's a Natural Woman	1973	—	3.00	6.00
❑ APBO-0165	The Baptism of Jesse Taylor/Making Plans	1973	—	3.00	6.00
❑ APBO-0248	She's in Love with a Rodeo Man/Someday I'll Sober Up	1974	—	3.00	6.00
❑ PB-10038	She Burn't the Little Roadside Tavern Down/It Sure Seemed Right	1974	—	2.50	5.00
❑ PB-10135	That's How My Baby Builds a Fire/Act Naturally	1974	—	2.50	5.00
❑ GB-10168	Rednecks, White Socks and Blue Ribbon Beer/The Baptism of Jesse Taylor	1975	—	2.00	4.00
—"Gold Standard Series" reissue					
❑ PB-10258	Hello I Love You/You Ain't Got No Class	1975	—	2.50	5.00
❑ PB-10403	Our Marriage Was a Failure/Catfish John	1975	—	2.50	5.00
❑ PB-10563	I'm a Trucker/Your Fool	1976	—	2.50	5.00
❑ PB-10667	This Man and Woman Thing/Over Georgia	1976	—	2.50	5.00
❑ 47-9990	Open Up the Door/Sure Gets Hard Being Me	1971	—	3.50	7.00
❑ 48-1000	Mr. and Mrs. Untrue/I'm Stayin'	1971	—	3.00	6.00
❑ 74-0570	What a Price/Listening to the Rain	1971	—	3.00	6.00
❑ 74-0665	Mr. Fiddle Man/Crying Takes More Practice Everyday	1972	—	3.00	6.00
❑ 74-0729	Rain Falling on Me/I'll Cry to That	1972	—	3.00	6.00
❑ 74-0810	Catfish John/Promise of Your Love	1972	—	3.00	6.00
❑ 74-0908	Chained/Drinkin' a Beer and Singin' a Country Song	1973	—	3.00	6.00

Albums

Number	Title	Yr	VG	VG+	NM
MERCURY					
❑ SRM-1-5019	Perspectives	1979	3.00	6.00	12.00
RCA VICTOR					
❑ APL1-0345	Rednecks, White Socks and Blue Ribbon Beer	1973	3.75	7.50	15.00
❑ APL1-0542	She's in Love with a Rodeo Man	1974	3.75	7.50	15.00
❑ APL1-1211	Here Comes Johnny Russell	1975	3.75	7.50	15.00
❑ ANL1-2165	Rednecks, White Socks and Blue Ribbon Beer	1977	2.50	5.00	10.00
—Reissue					
❑ LSP-4588	Mr. and Mrs. Untrue	1971	3.75	7.50	15.00
❑ LSP-4851	Catfish John/Chained	1973	3.75	7.50	15.00

RUSSELL, JOHNNY, AND LITTLE DAVID WILKINS

Also see each artist's individual listings.

45s

16TH AVENUE

Number	Title (A Side/B Side)	Yr	VG	VG+	NM
❑ B-70401	Butterbeans/Stone Country	1987	—	2.00	4.00
❑ B-70406	It's Quittin' Time (Hot Dama Lama)/I Owe, I Owe (It's Off to Work I Go)	1987	—	2.00	4.00

RUSSELL, LEON

At first, when he recorded country music, he did so under the pseudonym "Hank Wilson." Later, he dropped the alter ego and recorded country as well as rock under his real name. Also see WILLIE NELSON AND LEON RUSSELL.

45s

Number	Title (A Side/B Side)	Yr	VG	VG+	NM
ARK 21					
❑ S7-58714	Daddy Sang Bass/He Stopped Loving Her Today	1998	—	—	3.00
A&M					
❑ 734	Cindy/Misty	1964	5.00	10.00	20.00
DOT					
❑ 16771	Everybody's Talkin' 'Bout the Young/It's Alright with Me	1965	3.75	7.50	15.00
PARADISE					
❑ 628	Good Time Charlie's Got the Blues/Ain't No Love in the City	1984	—	2.00	4.00
❑ 629	Wabash Cannonball/Tennessee Waltz	1984	—	2.00	4.00
—As "Hank Wilson"; A-side with Willie Nelson					
❑ 631	Rescue My Heart/Lost Love	1985	—	2.00	4.00
❑ 631 [PS]	Rescue My Heart/Lost Love	1985	2.50	5.00	10.00
❑ 8208	Rainbow in Your Eyes/Love's Supposed to Be That Way	1976	—	2.00	4.00
—As "Leon and Mary Russell"					
❑ 8274	Satisfy You/Windsong	1976	—	2.00	4.00
—As "Leon and Mary Russell"					
❑ 8369	Love Crazy/Say You Will	1977	—	2.00	4.00
—As "Leon and Mary Russell"					
❑ 8438	Easy Love/Hold On to This Feeling	1977	—	2.00	4.00
—As "Leon and Mary Russell"					
❑ 8667	Elvis and Marilyn/Anita Bryant	1978	—	2.50	5.00
❑ 8667 [PS]	Elvis and Marilyn/Anita Bryant	1978	—	2.50	5.00
❑ 8719	Midnight Lover/From Maine to Mexico	1978	—	2.50	5.00
❑ 49662	Over the Rainbow/I've Just Seen a Face	1981	—	2.00	4.00
RCA VICTOR					
❑ 47-6884	(I Tasted) Tears on Your Lips/A Catchy Tune	1957	7.50	15.00	30.00
—As "Lee Russell"					
ROULETTE					
❑ 4049	Honky Tonk Woman/Rainbow at Midnight	1958	6.25	12.50	25.00
—As "Lee Russell"					
SHELTER					
❑ 301	Roll Away the Stone/Hummingbird	1970	—	3.00	6.00
❑ 7302	It Takes a Lot to Laugh, It Takes a Train to Cry/Home Sweet Oklahoma	1970	—	3.00	6.00
❑ 7305	A Hard Rain's A-Gonna Fall/Me and Baby Jane	1971	—	3.00	6.00
❑ 7316	A Song for You/A Hard Rain's A-Gonna Fall	1971	—	3.00	6.00
❑ 7325	Tight Rope/This Masquerade	1972	—	2.50	5.00
❑ 7328	Slipping Into Christmas/Christmas in Chicago	1972	—	2.50	5.00
❑ 7328 [PS]	Slipping Into Christmas/Christmas In Chicago	1972	6.25	12.50	25.00
❑ 7336	Roll in My Sweet Baby's Arms/I'm So Lonesome I Could Cry	1973	—	2.50	5.00
—As "Hank Wilson"					
❑ 7337	Queen of the Roller Derby/Roll Away the Stone	1973	—	2.50	5.00
❑ 7338	A Six Pack to Go/Uncle Pen	1973	—	2.50	5.00
—As "Hank Wilson"					
❑ 40210	If I Were a Carpenter/Wild Horses	1974	—	2.00	4.00
❑ 40210 [PS]	If I Were a Carpenter/Wild Horses	1974	2.00	4.00	8.00
❑ 40277	Time for Love/Leaving Whipporwhill	1974	—	2.00	4.00
❑ 40378	Lady Blue/Laying Right Here in Heaven	1975	—	2.00	4.00
❑ 40483	Back to the Island/Little Hideaway	1975	—	2.00	4.00
❑ 62004	Bluebird/Back to the Island	1976	—	2.00	4.00
❑ 65033	Slipping Into Christmas/Christmas in Chicago	1975	—	2.50	5.00
—Reissue of 7328					

Albums

Number	Title	Yr	VG	VG+	NM
MCA					
❑ 682	Leon Russell	1979	2.00	4.00	8.00
—Reissue of Shelter 52007					
❑ 683	Leon Russell and the Shelter People	1979	2.00	4.00	8.00
—Reissue of Shelter 52008					
❑ 685	Carney	1979	2.00	4.00	8.00
—Reissue of Shelter 52011					
❑ 686	Will O' the Wisp	1979	2.00	4.00	8.00
—Reissue of Shelter 52020					
❑ 37114	Best of Leon	1980	2.00	4.00	8.00
—Reissue of Shelter 52004					
PARADISE					
❑ 0002	Hank Wilson Vol. II	1984	3.00	6.00	12.00
❑ BS 2943	Wedding Album	1976	3.00	6.00	12.00
—As "Leon and Mary Russell"					
❑ BSK 3066	Make Love to the Music	1977	3.00	6.00	12.00
—As "Leon and Mary Russell"					
❑ BSK 3172	Americana	1978	3.00	6.00	12.00
❑ BSK 3341	Life and Love	1979	3.00	6.00	12.00
❑ BSK 3532	The Live Album	1981	2.50	5.00	10.00
SHELTER					
❑ SHE-1001	Leon Russell	1968	5.00	10.00	20.00
❑ SR 2108	Stop All That Jazz	1974	3.75	7.50	15.00
❑ SR 2118	Leon Russell	1974	3.00	6.00	12.00
—Reissue of 8901					
❑ SR 2119	Leon Russell and the Shelter People	1974	3.00	6.00	12.00
—Reissue of 8903					
❑ SR 2121	Carney	1974	3.00	6.00	12.00
—Reissue of 8911					
❑ SR 2138	Will O' the Wisp	1975	3.75	7.50	15.00
❑ SW-8901	Leon Russell	1970	3.75	7.50	15.00
—Early reissue of 1001					
❑ SW-8903	Leon Russell and the Shelter People	1971	3.75	7.50	15.00
❑ SW-8911	Carney	1972	3.75	7.50	15.00

Number	Title (A Side/B Side)	Yr	VG	VG+	NM
❑ STCO-8917 [(3)]	Leon Live	1973	5.00	10.00	20.00
❑ SW-8923	Hank Wilson's Back, Vol. 1	1973	3.75	7.50	15.00
—As "Hank Wilson"					
❑ 52004	Best of Leon	1976	2.50	5.00	10.00
❑ 52007	Leon Russell	1977	2.50	5.00	10.00
—Reissue of 2118					
❑ 52008	Leon Russell and the Shelter People	1977	2.50	5.00	10.00
—Reissue of 2119					
❑ 52011	Carney	1977	2.50	5.00	10.00
—Reissue of 2121					
❑ 52014	Hank Wilson's Back, Vol. 1	1977	2.50	5.00	10.00
—Reissue of 8923					
❑ 52016	Stop All That Jazz	1977	2.50	5.00	10.00
—Reissue of 2108					
❑ 52020	Will O' the Wisp	1977	2.50	5.00	10.00
—Reissue of 2138					

RUSTY AND DOUG

See RUSTY AND DOUG KERSHAW.

RUUD, NANCY

45s

Number	Title (A Side/B Side)	Yr	VG	VG+	NM
CALICO					
❑ 16425	A Good Love Is Like a Good Song/(B-side unknown)	1980	—	3.00	6.00
❑ 16493	Always, Sometimes, Never/Am I Too Late	1980	—	3.00	6.00
C&R					
❑ 101	I'm Gonna Hang Up This Heartache/(B-side unknown)	1981	—	3.00	6.00
❑ 102	Blue As the Blue in Your Eyes/(B-side unknown)	1981	—	3.00	6.00

RYAN, CHARLIE

45s

Number	Title (A Side/B Side)	Yr	VG	VG+	NM
4 STAR					
❑ 1733	Hot Rod Lincoln/Thru the Mill	1959	5.00	10.00	20.00
❑ 1745	Side Car Cycle/Steel Rock	1960	5.00	10.00	20.00
❑ 1749	Hot Rod Hades/Hot Rod Guitar	1961	5.00	10.00	20.00
❑ 1761	Hot Rod Race/Hot Rod Lincoln	1963	5.00	10.00	20.00
SOUVENIR					
❑ 101	Hot Rod Lincoln/(B-side unknown)	1955	15.00	30.00	60.00

Albums

Number	Title (A Side/B Side)	Yr	VG	VG+	NM
HILLTOP					
❑ JM-6006 [M]	Hot Rod Lincoln Drags Again	1964	12.50	25.00	50.00
❑ JS-6006 [R]	Hot Rod Lincoln Drags Again	1964	6.25	12.50	25.00
KING					
❑ 751 [M]	Hot Rod Lincoln	1961	100.00	200.00	400.00

RYAN, JAMEY

45s

Number	Title (A Side/B Side)	Yr	VG	VG+	NM
ATLANTIC					
❑ 4001	Keep On Loving Me/You Just Moved a Mountain	1973	—	3.00	6.00
COLUMBIA					
❑ 4-44045	21 Inches of Heaven/The Worst of the Hurt Is Over	1967	2.00	4.00	8.00
❑ 4-44169	You're Lookin' for a Plaything/Growin' Pains	1967	2.00	4.00	8.00
SHOW BIZ					
❑ 228	Willie and Laura Mae Jones/Sweet Wine and Bitter Tears	1969	2.00	4.00	8.00
❑ 232	Holy Cow/All a Woman Asks	1970	2.00	4.00	8.00
❑ 235	Baby, I Tried/Sunshine Blue	1970	2.00	4.00	8.00
❑ 239	Written on Your Heart/When I Want Some Hurt Again	1971	2.00	4.00	8.00
❑ 501	Wild Cat/Like Mother Like Daughter	1971	—	3.50	7.00
❑ 504	Memories to Spare/What Else Is There to Say	1972	—	3.50	7.00
❑ 505	A Taste of Money/(B-side unknown)	1972	—	3.50	7.00

RYAN, TIM

45s

Number	Title (A Side/B Side)	Yr	VG	VG+	NM
BNA					
❑ 62413	Idle Hands/One Life to Live	1992	—	—	3.00
❑ 62480	Love on the Rocks/Idle Hands	1993	—	—	3.00
EPIC					
❑ 34-73372	Dance in Circles/Honky Tonk Highway	1990	—	—	3.00
❑ 34-73578	Breakin' All the Way/A Little Love Won't Hurt a Thing	1990	—	—	3.00
❑ 34-73959	Seventh Direction/No More Sad Songs	1991	—	—	3.00
❑ 34-74124	I Will Love You Anyhow/Heartache Goin' Downtown Tonight	1991	—	—	3.00

RYAN, WESLEY

45s

Number	Title (A Side/B Side)	Yr	VG	VG+	NM
NSD					
❑ 93	Nothin' to Do But Just Lie/Take Good Care of My Baby	1981	—	2.50	5.00

RYLES, JOHN WESLEY

45s

Number	Title (A Side/B Side)	Yr	VG	VG+	NM
16TH AVENUE					
❑ 500	She Took It Too Well/(B-side unknown)	1984	—	3.00	6.00
ABC					
❑ 12348	Easy/Making Love Don't Make It Love	1978	—	2.50	5.00
❑ 12375	Kay/Next Time	1978	—	2.50	5.00
❑ 12410	Someday You Will/That All Over Feeling	1978	—	2.50	5.00
❑ 12432	Love Ain't Made for Fools/It's Raining Outside Your Door	1978	—	2.50	5.00
ABC DOT					
❑ 17679	Fool/I Fought the Law	1977	—	2.50	5.00
❑ 17698	Once in a Lifetime Thing/Wild Rose of Virginia	1977	—	2.50	5.00
❑ 17733	Shine on Me (The Sun Still Shines When It Rains)/Warming Love	1977	—	2.50	5.00
COLUMBIA					
❑ 4-44682	Kay/Come On Home	1968	—	3.50	7.00
❑ 4-44819	Heaven Below/A Mighty Fortress Is Our Love	1969	—	3.50	7.00
❑ 4-44966	The Most Beautiful Thing in the World Is a Woman/Eva Magdalena	1969	—	3.50	7.00
❑ 4-45018	The Weakest Kind of Man/We'll Try a Little Bit Harder	1969	—	3.50	7.00
❑ 4-45119	I've Just Been Wasting My Time/The House on the Hill	1970	—	3.50	7.00
GRT					
❑ 33	Your Kind of Man/Wash My Sins in the River	1970	—	3.50	7.00
MCA					
❑ 41033	Liberated Woman/She's On My Mind	1979	—	2.50	5.00
❑ 41124	You Are Always on My Mind/My Angel Got Her Wings Today	1979	—	2.00	4.00
❑ 41184	Perfect Strangers/Nothing But Love	1980	—	2.00	4.00
❑ 41278	May I Borrow Some Sugar from You/Let the Night Begin	1980	—	2.00	4.00
❑ 51013	Cheater's Trap/Two Beds	1980	—	2.00	4.00
❑ 51080	Somewhere to Come When It Rains/Your Old Love Letters	1981	—	2.00	4.00
❑ 51128	Mathilda/I'm Not That Crazy Anymore	1981	—	2.00	4.00
❑ 51174	Kiss and Say Goodbye/Slow Emotion	1981	—	2.00	4.00
MUSIC MILL					
❑ 214	Tell It Like It Is/Run Right Back	1976	—	3.50	7.00
❑ 240	When a Man Loves a Woman/I'm Gonna Make It Without You	1976	—	3.50	7.00
PLANTATION					
❑ 81	Reconsider Me/Mobile	1971	—	3.50	7.00
❑ 91	Two Shadows on the Wall/Louisiana	1972	—	3.50	7.00
❑ 95	I Almost Called Your Name/Love of This Woman	1973	—	3.50	7.00
❑ 158	Two Shadows on the Wall/(B-side unknown)	1977	—	3.00	6.00
PRIMERO					
❑ 1004	We've Got to Start Meeting Like This/(B-side unknown)	1982	—	2.50	5.00
❑ 1016	Just Once/Hideaway	1982	—	2.50	5.00
RCA VICTOR					
❑ APBO-0320	Satisfied Man/More Today Than Yesterday	1974	—	3.00	6.00
❑ PB-10146	When She Turns Off the Light/Leaning on Your Love	1974	—	3.00	6.00
WARNER BROS.					
❑ 7-27869	Nobody Knows/Freedom Feels Like Loneliness to Me	1988	—	2.00	4.00
❑ 7-28228	Louisiana Rain/Strong Heart	1987	—	2.00	4.00
❑ 7-28377	Midnight Blue/Starting Over Again	1987	—	2.00	4.00

Albums

Number	Title (A Side/B Side)	Yr	VG	VG+	NM
ABC					
❑ AB-1056	Shine on Me	1978	3.00	6.00	12.00
❑ AB-1112	Love's Sweet Pain	1979	3.00	6.00	12.00
ABC DOT					
❑ DO-2089	John Wesley Ryles	1977	3.00	6.00	12.00
COLUMBIA					
❑ CS 9768	Kay	1969	5.00	10.00	20.00
MCA					
❑ 643	Shine on Me	198?	2.00	4.00	8.00
—Budget-line reissue of ABC 1056					
❑ 644	John Wesley Ryles	198?	2.00	4.00	8.00
—Budget-line reissue of ABC Dot 2089					
❑ 750	Let the Night Begin	198?	2.00	4.00	8.00
—Budget-line reissue					
❑ 798	Love's Sweet Pain	198?	2.00	4.00	8.00
—Budget-line reissue of ABC 1112					
❑ 3183	Let the Night Begin	1979	3.00	6.00	12.00
PLANTATION					
❑ 517	Reconsider Me	197?	3.00	6.00	12.00

S

S-K-O
See SCHUYLER, KNOBLOCH & OVERSTREET.

SADLER, SAMMY
45s
EVERGREEN

Number	Title (A Side/B Side)	Yr	VG	VG+	NM
❑ 1088	Tell It Like It Is/(B-side unknown)	1988	—	2.50	5.00
❑ 1093	You Made It Easy/(B-side unknown)	1989	—	2.50	5.00
❑ 1106	Once in a Lifetime Thing/You Made It Easy	1989	—	2.50	5.00
❑ 1125	Mississippi Burning Tonight/(B-side unknown)	1990	—	3.00	6.00

SADLER, SSGT. BARRY
45s
RCA VICTOR

Number	Title (A Side/B Side)	Yr	VG	VG+	NM
❑ 47-8739	The Ballad of the Green Berets/Letter from Vietnam	1966	—	3.00	6.00
❑ 47-8739 [PS]	The Ballad of the Green Berets/Letter from Vietnam	1966	2.00	4.00	8.00
❑ 47-8804	The "A" Team/An Empty Glass	1966	—	3.00	6.00
❑ 47-8804 [PS]	The "A" Team/An Empty Glass	1966	2.00	4.00	8.00
❑ 47-8966	Not Just Lonely/One Day Nearer Home	1966	—	3.00	6.00
❑ 47-9008	I Won't Be Home This Christmas/A Woman Is a Weepin' Willow Tree	1966	2.00	4.00	8.00

Albums
RCA VICTOR

Number	Title (A Side/B Side)	Yr	VG	VG+	NM
❑ LPM-3547 [M]	Ballads of the Green Berets	1966	3.75	7.50	15.00
❑ LSP-3547 [S]	Ballads of the Green Berets	1966	5.00	10.00	20.00
❑ LPM-3605 [M]	The "A" Team	1966	3.75	7.50	15.00
❑ LSP-3605 [S]	The "A" Team	1966	5.00	10.00	20.00
❑ LPM-3691 [M]	Back Home	1967	5.00	10.00	20.00
❑ LSP-3691 [S]	Back Home	1967	3.75	7.50	15.00

SAHM, DOUG
Also see TEXAS TORNADOS.
45s

Number	Title (A Side/B Side)	Yr	VG	VG+	NM
ABC DOT					
❑ 17656	Cowboy Peyton Place/I Love the Way You Love (The Way I Love You)	1976	—	3.00	6.00
❑ 17674	Crying Inside Sometimes/I'm Missing You	1976	—	3.00	6.00
ATLANTIC					
❑ 2946	Is Anybody Going to San Antone/Don't Turn Around	1973	2.00	4.00	8.00
COBRA					
❑ 116	Just a Moment/Sapphire	1961	12.50	25.00	50.00
CRAZY CAJUN					
❑ 2004	If You Really Want/Not Tomato Man	1974	—	2.50	5.00
HARLEM					
❑ 108	Baby Tell Me/Sapphire	1960	12.50	25.00	50.00
❑ 108 [DJ]	Baby Tell Me/Sapphire	1960	25.00	50.00	100.00
—Gold vinyl promo					
❑ 113	More and More/Slow Down	1960	12.50	25.00	50.00
MERCURY					
❑ 73098	Be Real/I Don't Want to Go Home	1970	5.00	10.00	20.00
—As "Wayne Douglas"					
PERSONALITY					
❑ 260	Baby, What's On Your Mind/Crazy, Crazy Feeling	1962	12.50	25.00	50.00
RENNER					
❑ 212	Big Hat/Makes No Difference	1961	10.00	20.00	40.00
❑ 212 [DJ]	Big Hat/Makes No Difference	1961	25.00	50.00	100.00
—Red vinyl promo					
❑ 215	Baby, What's On Your Mind/Crazy, Crazy Feeling	1961	10.00	20.00	40.00
❑ 215 [DJ]	Baby, What's On Your Mind/Crazy, Crazy Feeling	1961	25.00	50.00	100.00
—Red vinyl promo					
❑ 226	Two Hearts in Love/Just Because	1962	10.00	20.00	40.00
❑ 232	Little Angel/Cry	1963	10.00	20.00	40.00
❑ 240	Lucky Me/A Year Ago Tonight	1963	10.00	20.00	40.00
❑ 247	Mr. Kool/Bill Beatty	1964	12.50	25.00	50.00
SARG					
❑ 113	A Real American Joe/Rolling Rolling	1958	25.00	50.00	100.00
—As "Little Doug"					
SATIN					
❑ 100	Crazy Daisy/I Can't Believe You Wanna Leave	1959	12.50	25.00	50.00
SOFT					
❑ 1031	Cry/Down the Pike	1965	7.50	15.00	30.00
SWINGIN'					
❑ 625	Why, Why, Why/If You Ever Need Me	1960	6.25	12.50	25.00
TEAR DROP					
❑ 3074	It's a Man Down There/4 A.M.	1966	6.25	12.50	25.00
—As "Him"					
TEARDROP					
❑ 3479	Who Were You Thinking Of/Velma	1982	—	2.00	4.00
—With Augie Myers					
❑ 3481	I'm Not a Fool Anymore/Don't Fight It	1982	—	2.00	4.00
—With Augie Myers					
WARNER BROS.					
❑ 7819	Girls Today/Groover's Paradise	1974	—	2.50	5.00
WARRIOR					
❑ 507	Crazy Daisy/If I Ever Need You	1958	20.00	40.00	80.00

Albums

Number	Title (A Side/B Side)	Yr	VG	VG+	NM
ABC DOT					
❑ DO-2057	Texas Rock for Country Rollers	1976	3.75	7.50	15.00
ANTONE'S					
❑ ANT-0008	Juke Box Music	1989	3.00	6.00	12.00
ATLANTIC					
❑ SD 7254	Doug Sahm and Band	1973	3.75	7.50	15.00
MERCURY					
❑ SRM-1-655	Rough Edges	1972	7.50	15.00	30.00
TAKOMA					
❑ TAK-7075	Hell of a Spell	1980	3.00	6.00	12.00
TEARDROP					
❑ TD-5000	The West Side Sound Rolls Again	1982	3.00	6.00	12.00
WARNER BROS.					
❑ BS 2810	Groovers Paradise	1974	5.00	10.00	20.00

ST. JOHN, TOMMY
45s
RCA

Number	Title (A Side/B Side)	Yr	VG	VG+	NM
❑ PB-13405	The Light of My Life (Has Gone Out Tonight)/Waitin' In Your Welfare Line	1982	—	2.00	4.00
❑ PB-13475	Where'd Ya Stay Last Night/She Can't Make Me What I Ain't	1983	—	2.00	4.00
❑ PB-13561	Stars on the Water/Wallflower	1983	—	2.00	4.00

ST. MARIE, SUSAN
45s

Number	Title (A Side/B Side)	Yr	VG	VG+	NM
CINNAMON					
❑ 768	All or Nothing with Me/Lonely After You	1973	2.00	4.00	8.00
❑ 784	Something's Wrong/Fever	1974	2.00	4.00	8.00
PINNACLE					
❑ 101	It's the Love in You/That's the Way Love Should Be	1977	—	3.00	6.00

SAMI JO
45s

Number	Title (A Side/B Side)	Yr	VG	VG+	NM
ELEKTRA					
❑ 47127	One Love Over Easy/You Got My Heart in Your Hands	1981	—	2.00	4.00
—As "Sami Jo Cole"					
❑ 47211	I Can't Help Myself (Here Comes the Feeling)/Carelessly	1981	—	2.00	4.00
—As "Sami Jo Cole"					
FAME					
❑ 1481	Get It On/Don't Hang No Halos on Me	1971	—	3.00	6.00
❑ 91003	Big Silver Angel/I Think I Love You Again	1972	—	3.00	6.00
MGM					
❑ 14773	I'll Do Anything You Say/Lovely Daughter	1974	—	2.50	5.00
❑ 14820	You're a Part of Me/I Can't See the Good in Your Goodbye	1975	—	2.50	5.00
MGM SOUTH					
❑ 7029	Tell Me a Lie/Stay Where You Are	1974	—	2.50	5.00
❑ 7034	It Could Have Been Me/Look at Us	1974	—	2.50	5.00
POLYDOR					
❑ 14315	God Loves Us (When We All Sing Together)/Partly Cloudy	1976	—	2.50	5.00
❑ 14341	Take Me to Heaven/Let Me Laugh (To Keep from Crying)	1976	—	2.50	5.00
SOUTHERN TRACKS					
❑ 1045	I'm Going Away (Before You Can Say Not to Go)/We Don't Live Here (We Just Love Here)	1985	—	3.00	6.00
WARNER BROS.					
❑ 29368	Emotions/I Can't Help the Way I Don't Feel	1984	—	2.00	4.00
—As "Sami Jo Cole"					

Albums

Number	Title (A Side/B Side)	Yr	VG	VG+	NM
MGM					
❑ M3G-4998	Sami Jo	1975	3.00	6.00	12.00
MGM SOUTH					
❑ 703	It Could Have Been Me	1974	3.00	6.00	12.00

SAMI JO AND SAMMY JOHNS
Also see each artist's individual listings.
45s
SOUTHERN TRACKS

Number	Title (A Side/B Side)	Yr	VG	VG+	NM
❑ 1054	Falling for You (same on both sides)	1986	—	3.00	6.00

SAMONE, STEPHANY
45s
MDJ

Number	Title (A Side/B Side)	Yr	VG	VG+	NM
❑ 1004	Do That to Me One More Time/Gotta Make You Mine	1980	—	2.50	5.00
❑ 1006	Somebody's Gotta Do the Losing/One Day at a Time	1980	—	2.50	5.00

SAMPLES, JUNIOR
45s
CHART

Number	Title (A Side/B Side)	Yr	VG	VG+	NM
❑ 1002	World's Biggest Whopper/It Happened to Junior	1967	2.00	4.00	8.00
—Reissue of 1460					
❑ 1009	Bird Mule/The Disorderly House	1967	2.00	4.00	8.00
❑ 1460	World's Biggest Whopper/It Happened to Junior	1967	2.50	5.00	10.00
❑ 5008	Birds, Bees, Girls and Stuff Like That/(B-side unknown)	1969	2.00	4.00	8.00

Number	Title (A Side/B Side)	Yr	VG	VG+	NM
❑ 5026	That's a Hee Haw/The Rabbit Song	1969	2.50	5.00	10.00
❑ 5050	Uncommonly Well/Doggone (My Dog Is Gone)	1969	2.00	4.00	8.00
❑ 5102	Dippin', Chewin' Acid and Pot/Sports Common Taters	1970	2.00	4.00	8.00
Albums					
CHART					
❑ CHM-1002 [M]	The World of Junior Samples	1967	5.00	10.00	20.00
❑ CHS-1002 [S]	The World of Junior Samples	1967	5.00	10.00	20.00
❑ CHS-1007	Bull Session at Bulls Gap	1968	3.75	7.50	15.00
❑ CHS-1021	That's a Hee Haw	1969	3.75	7.50	15.00
❑ CHS-1045	Best of Junior Samples	1970	3.75	7.50	15.00
HILLTOP					
❑ JS-6113	Moonshining	197?	2.50	5.00	10.00

SAMPLES, WILLIE

45s

Number	Title (A Side/B Side)	Yr	VG	VG+	NM
DOLLIE					
❑ 504	I Sure Was Happy Gettin' Sad/I'm Leaving My Heartaches to You	1966	2.50	5.00	10.00
❑ 507	Lock the Door Between Us/The Other You	1966	2.50	5.00	10.00
LITTLE DARLIN'					
❑ 0059	I'll Take You Home Kathleen/Your Little Boy	1969	2.50	5.00	10.00
❑ 0066	Ring the Bell/Down at Kelly's	1970	2.00	4.00	8.00

SAN FERNANDO VALLEY MUSIC BAND, THE

45s

Number	Title (A Side/B Side)	Yr	VG	VG+	NM
C&S					
❑ 017	Taken to the Line/Roll Your Own	1979	2.00	4.00	8.00

SANDERS, THE

45s

Number	Title (A Side/B Side)	Yr	VG	VG+	NM
AIRBORNE					
❑ 10001	You Fit Right Into My Heart/(B-side unknown)	1988	—	2.50	5.00
❑ 10009	Dancin' to the Radio/Starry Lullaby	1988	—	2.50	5.00
❑ 10013	Grandma's Old Wood Stove/Starry Lullaby	1989	—	2.50	5.00
❑ 10019	Who Needs You/Grandma's Old Wood Stove	1989	—	2.50	5.00
Albums					
AIRBORNE					
❑ 61003	Into Every Life	1988	3.00	6.00	12.00

SANDERS, BEN

45s

Number	Title (A Side/B Side)	Yr	VG	VG+	NM
LUV					
❑ 129	I'm Leavin' You/Good Advice	1988	—	3.00	6.00

SANDERS, CURLY

See RAY SANDERS.

SANDERS, DEBBIE

45s

Number	Title (A Side/B Side)	Yr	VG	VG+	NM
K-ARK					
❑ 1050	No Time at All/(B-side unknown)	1989	—	3.00	6.00

SANDERS, MACK

45s

Number	Title (A Side/B Side)	Yr	VG	VG+	NM
PILOT					
❑ 45101	Sweet Country Girl/Tonkin the Blues	1977	2.00	4.00	8.00

SANDERS, RAY

45s

Number	Title (A Side/B Side)	Yr	VG	VG+	NM
CONCEPT					
❑ 897	Dynamite/(B-side unknown)	1957	25.00	50.00	100.00
—As "Curly Sanders"					
❑ 898	This Time/(B-side unknown)	1957	15.00	30.00	60.00
—As "Curly Sanders"					
GNP CRESCENDO					
❑ 397	Soldier's Last Letter/Two People	1967	2.00	4.00	8.00
❑ 409	I Always Do the Best with What I've Got/Come Back to Me	1968	2.00	4.00	8.00
HILLSIDE					
❑ 7901	It Was Always Our Song/Mountain of Love	1979	—	3.00	6.00
❑ 7904	Loose Talk/Silver Wings	1979	—	3.00	6.00
❑ 8005	You're a Pretty Lady, Lady/My Special Angel	1980	—	3.00	6.00
❑ 8103	Don't You Believe Her/Walk On By	1981	—	3.00	6.00
❑ 8105	There's a Little Bit of Everything in Texas/Another Place, Another Time	1981	—	3.00	6.00
IMPERIAL					
❑ 66366	Beer Drinking Music/Gotta Find a Way	1969	—	3.50	7.00
❑ 66408	Three Tears (For the Sad, Hurt and Blue)/Lucille	1969	—	3.50	7.00
❑ 66433	Holly Would/So Softly and Tenderly	1970	—	3.50	7.00
JAMBOREE					
❑ 590	Brand New Rock and Roll/(B-side unknown)	1956	25.00	50.00	100.00
—As "Curly Sanders"					
LIBERTY					
❑ 55267	A World So Full of Love/A Little Bitty Tear	1960	2.50	5.00	10.00
❑ 55304	Lonelyville/I Haven't Gone Far Enough Yet	1961	2.50	5.00	10.00
❑ 55348	Walk Slow/Two Hearts Are Broken	1961	2.50	5.00	10.00
❑ 55373	Don't Tell Nell/When Love Forgets to Die	1961	2.50	5.00	10.00
❑ 55406	Punish Me Tomorrow/You're Welcome Anytime	1962	2.50	5.00	10.00
❑ 55486	If I Can Slip Away/See One Broken Heart	1962	2.50	5.00	10.00
❑ 55568	Rich Living Woman/It's Not Funny	1963	2.50	5.00	10.00
REPUBLIC					
❑ 003	I Don't Want to Be Alone Tonight/The Power of Positive Drinkin'	1977	—	2.50	5.00
❑ 008	She Was Alone/(B-side unknown)	1977	—	2.50	5.00
❑ 013	Tennessee/You Keep Right On Walking	1978	—	2.50	5.00
❑ 016	Here Comes That Feelin'/(B-side unknown)	1978	—	2.50	5.00
STADIUM					
❑ 1115	Christmas Letter/Missing Christmas Card	1964	2.50	5.00	10.00
TOWER					
❑ 232	My World Is Upside Down/Graveyard Dance	1966	2.00	4.00	8.00
❑ 270	The Only Way to Fly/Don't Let Our Love Grow Cold	1966	2.00	4.00	8.00
❑ 330	City of Sin/I'll Try to Work You In	1967	2.00	4.00	8.00
UNITED ARTISTS					
❑ XW201	Another Way to Say Goodbye/(B-side unknown)	1973	—	3.00	6.00
❑ 50689	Blame It on Rosey/Waikiki Sand	1970	—	3.00	6.00
❑ 50732	Judy/Wild Side of Life	1970	—	3.00	6.00
❑ 50774	Walk All Over Georgia/Tonight She'll Make You Happy	1971	—	3.00	6.00
❑ 50827	All I Ever Need Is You/Before I Met You	1971	—	3.00	6.00
❑ 50886	A Rose By Any Other Name (Is Still a Rose)/We've Gotta Learn to Help Each Other	1972	—	3.00	6.00
❑ 50933	Lucius Grinder/You Let My Love Live	1972	—	3.00	6.00
Albums					
IMPERIAL					
❑ LP-12447	Feelin' Good Is Easy	1969	3.75	7.50	15.00
REPUBLIC					
❑ 5004	I Don't Want to Be Alone Tonight	1977	3.00	6.00	12.00
UNITED ARTISTS					
❑ UAS-6822	Ray Sanders	1972	3.00	6.00	12.00

SARAH

45s

Number	Title (A Side/B Side)	Yr	VG	VG+	NM
HUB					
❑ 45	Lyin' Eyes/No Place to Run To	1987	—	3.00	6.00
❑ 46	Chains/You Can't Hurt Me	1988	—	3.00	6.00
❑ 48	Don't Send Me Roses/(B-side unknown)	1988	—	3.00	6.00

SARGEANTS, GARY

45s

Number	Title (A Side/B Side)	Yr	VG	VG+	NM
MERCURY					
❑ 73398	Everybody's Troubles But Mine/Red Hot Memories	1973	—	3.00	6.00
❑ 73440	Ode to Jolie Blon/Fair to Middlin', Lower Middle Class	1973	—	3.00	6.00
❑ 73474	I Just Started Hatin' Cheatin' Songs Today/Is This the Last Time We're Gonna Say Goodbye	1974	—	3.00	6.00
❑ 73608	Day Time Lover/Too Low to Get High	1974	—	3.00	6.00
❑ 73668	Don't Look Back/Love Me Wrong	1975	—	3.00	6.00
❑ 73733	Foolish Pleasure/Whiskey	1975	—	3.00	6.00

SASKIA AND SERGE

45s

Number	Title (A Side/B Side)	Yr	VG	VG+	NM
ABC HICKORY					
❑ 54020	Jambalaya (On the Bayou)/Don't Lay Your Head	1977	—	2.50	5.00
❑ 54028	When Will I Be Loved/You're a Dream	1978	—	2.50	5.00
❑ 54031	Oh Lonesome Me/Someone Broke Your Heart	1978	—	2.50	5.00
❑ 54035	Blue Eyes Crying in the Rain/Some Girls Grow Up	1978	—	2.50	5.00
❑ 54040	Crying/Emily	1978	—	2.50	5.00
Albums					
ABC HICKORY					
❑ HB-44008	Saskia and Serge	1978	2.50	5.00	10.00

SAULS, CORKEY

45s

Number	Title (A Side/B Side)	Yr	VG	VG+	NM
SAND MOUNTAIN					
❑ 822	There Goes That Smile Again/Home Is Where I Hang My Dungarees	1979	2.00	4.00	8.00

SAVANNAH

45s

Number	Title (A Side/B Side)	Yr	VG	VG+	NM
MERCURY					
❑ 814360-7	Backstreet Ballet/It Don't Get No Better Than This	1983	—	—	3.00
❑ 818439-7	Matinee Motel/St. Simon Sea	1984	—	—	3.00
❑ 880037-7	My Girl/Let's Get To It	1984	—	—	3.00

SAWMILL CREEK

See BRUCE HAUSER AND SAWMILL CREEK.

SAWYER, RAY

Also see DR. HOOK.

45s

Number	Title (A Side/B Side)	Yr	VG	VG+	NM
CAPITOL					
❑ 4344	(One More Year of) Daddy's Little Girl/I Need That High (But I Can't Stand the Taste)	1976	—	2.00	4.00
❑ 4386	Red-Winged Blackbird/The One I'm Holding Now	1977	—	2.00	4.00
❑ 4416	Walls and Doors/I Need That HIgh (But I Can't Stand the Taste)	1977	—	2.00	4.00
❑ 4592	Dancing Fool/Rhythm Guitar	1978	—	2.00	4.00
❑ 4747	What I'm Holding/I Want Johnny's Job	1979	—	2.00	4.00
❑ 4820	Drinking Wine Alone/I Don't Feel Like Smilin'	1980	—	2.00	4.00
SANDY					
❑ 1030	Rockin' Satellite/Bells in My Heart	1961	10.00	20.00	40.00
❑ 1037	I'm Gonna Leave/You Gave Me the Right	1961	6.25	12.50	25.00

Albums

CAPITOL

Number	Title (A Side/B Side)	Yr	VG	VG+	NM
❑ ST-11591	Ray Sawyer	1976	2.50	5.00	10.00

SAWYER BROWN

45s

CAPITOL

Number	Title (A Side/B Side)	Yr	VG	VG+	NM
❑ B-5403	Leona/Staying Afloat	1984	—	—	3.00
❑ B-5446	Step That Step/Feel Like Me	1985	—	—	3.00
❑ B-5446 [PS]	Step That Step/Feel Like Me	1985	—	2.00	4.00
❑ B-5477	Used to Blue/It's Hard to Keep a Good Love Down	1985	—	—	3.00
❑ B-5477 [PS]	Used to Blue/It's Hard to Keep a Good Love Down	1985	—	2.00	4.00
❑ B-5517	Betty's Bein' Bad/Lonely Girls	1985	—	—	3.00
❑ B-5517 [PS]	Betty's Bein' Bad/Lonely Girls	1985	—	2.00	4.00
❑ B-5548	Heart Don't Fall Now/That's a No No	1986	—	—	3.00
❑ B-5548 [PS]	Heart Don't Fall Now/That's a No No	1986	—	2.00	4.00
❑ B-5585	Shakin'/Betty Does Your Bulldog Bite	1986	—	—	3.00
❑ B-5629	Out Goin' Cattin'/The House Won't Rock	1986	—	—	3.00

—A-side with "Cat" Joe Bonsall

Number	Title (A Side/B Side)	Yr	VG	VG+	NM
❑ B-5629 [PS]	Out Goin' Cattin'/The House Won't Rock	1986	—	2.00	4.00
❑ B-5677	Gypsies on Parade/Not Ready to Let You Go	1987	—	—	3.00
❑ B-44007	Savin' the Honey for the Honeymoon/Lady of the Evening	1987	—	—	3.00
❑ B-44054	Somewhere in the Night/My Baby Drives a Buick	1987	—	—	3.00
❑ B-44054 [PS]	Somewhere in the Night/My Baby Drives a Buick	1987	—	2.00	4.00
❑ B-44108	This Missin' You Heart of Mine/A Mighty Big Broom	1987	—	—	3.00
❑ B-44108 [PS]	This Missin' You Heart of Mine/A Mighty Big Broom	1987	—	2.00	4.00
❑ B-44143	Old Photographs/In This Town	1988	—	—	3.00
❑ B-44218	My Baby's Gone/Blue Denim Soul	1988	—	—	3.00
❑ B-44282	It Wasn't His Child/Falling Apart at the Heart	1988	—	2.00	4.00
❑ B-44282 [PS]	It Wasn't His Child/Falling Apart at the Heart	1988	—	2.50	5.00
❑ B-44332	Old Pair of Shoes/What Am I Going to Tell My Heart	1989	—	2.00	4.00
❑ B-44431	The Race Is On/Passin' Train	1989	—	—	3.00
❑ B-44483	Did It for Love/The Heartland	1989	—	2.00	4.00

CAPITOL NASHVILLE

Number	Title (A Side/B Side)	Yr	VG	VG+	NM
❑ 7PRO-79040	Puttin' the Dark Back Into the Night (same on both sides)	1990	2.00	4.00	8.00

—Vinyl is promo only

Number	Title (A Side/B Side)	Yr	VG	VG+	NM
❑ 7PRO-79231	When Love Comes Callin' (same on both sides)	1990	2.00	4.00	8.00

—Vinyl is promo only

Number	Title (A Side/B Side)	Yr	VG	VG+	NM
❑ 7PRO-79432	One Less Pony (same on both sides)	1991	2.00	4.00	8.00

—Vinyl is promo only

Number	Title (A Side/B Side)	Yr	VG	VG+	NM
❑ 7PRO-79653	Mama's Little Baby Loves Me (same on both sides)	1991	2.00	4.00	8.00

—Vinyl is promo only

Number	Title (A Side/B Side)	Yr	VG	VG+	NM
❑ 7PRO-79750	The Walk (same on both sides)	1991	2.00	4.00	8.00

—Vinyl is promo only

CURB

Number	Title (A Side/B Side)	Yr	VG	VG+	NM
❑ D7-73016	Six Days on the Road/ This Night Won't Last Forever	1997	—	—	3.00
❑ D7-73075	Drive Me Wild/We're Everything to Me	1999	—	—	3.00
❑ D7-76930	This Time/Hard to Say	1995	—	—	3.00
❑ D7-76936	I Don't Believe in Goodbye/Outskirts of Town	1995	—	—	3.00
❑ D7-76955	(This Thing Called) Wantin' and Havin' It All/I Will Leave the Light On	1995	—	—	3.00
❑ D7-76975	'Round Here/I Will Leave the Light On	1995	—	—	3.00
❑ D7-76987	Treat Her Right/She's Gettin' There	1996	—	—	3.00

Albums

CAPITOL

Number	Title (A Side/B Side)	Yr	VG	VG+	NM
❑ ST-12391	Sawyer Brown	1985	2.00	4.00	8.00
❑ ST-12438	Shakin'	1985	2.00	4.00	8.00
❑ ST-12517	Out Goin' Cattin'	1986	2.00	4.00	8.00
❑ CLT-46923	Somewhere in the Night	1987	2.00	4.00	8.00
❑ C1-90417	Wide Open	1988	2.00	4.00	8.00
❑ C1-92358	The Boys Are Back	1989	2.50	5.00	10.00

SAYER, LEO

The British pop singer and songwriter had one charted country hit, listed below.

45s

WARNER BROS.

Number	Title (A Side/B Side)	Yr	VG	VG+	NM
❑ 8682	Raining in My Heart/No Looking Back	1978	—	2.00	4.00

SCARBURY, JOEY

Basically a pop singer with one major hit — "The Theme from The Greatest American Hero (Believe It Or Not)" — this was his only country hit.

45s

RCA

Number	Title (A Side/B Side)	Yr	VG	VG+	NM
❑ PB-13913	The Rover's Song/Billy's Home	1984	—	2.00	4.00

SCHAFFER, NORM

45s

DSP

Number	Title (A Side/B Side)	Yr	VG	VG+	NM
❑ 8712	Dallas Darlin'/(B-side unknown)	1987	—	3.00	6.00

SCHEREE

45s

COMPASS

Number	Title (A Side/B Side)	Yr	VG	VG+	NM
❑ 0027	I'm in Another World/(B-side unknown)	1979	—	3.00	6.00

SCHLITZ, DON

45s

CAPITOL

Number	Title (A Side/B Side)	Yr	VG	VG+	NM
❑ 4576	The Gambler/You Can't Take It With You	1978	—	2.50	5.00
❑ 4661	You're the One Who Rewrote My Life Story/I've Been Loved	1979	—	2.00	4.00
❑ 4860	Daily Bread/Senior Prom	1980	—	2.00	4.00
❑ 4917	I've Been Loved/Walkin' the Walk	1980	—	2.00	4.00

SCHMUCKER, PAUL

45s

STAR-FOX

Number	Title (A Side/B Side)	Yr	VG	VG+	NM
❑ 279	Steal Away/Lonely But Never Alone	1979	—	3.00	6.00
❑ 378	The Giver/You Never Gave Me You	1978	—	3.00	6.00
❑ 578	Makin' Love (Is a Beautiful Thing to Do)/Country Folks	1978	—	3.00	6.00
❑ 779	Rainy Days and Rainbows/It's Me Again	1979	—	3.00	6.00

SCHNEIDER, JOHN

45s

MCA

Number	Title (A Side/B Side)	Yr	VG	VG+	NM
❑ 52407	I've Been Around Enough to Know/Trouble	1984	—	—	3.00
❑ 52510	Country Girls/The Time of My Life	1984	—	—	3.00
❑ 52510 [PS]	Country Girls/The Time of My Life	1984	—	2.00	4.00
❑ 52567	It's a Short Walk from Heaven to Hell/Honeymoon Wine	1985	—	—	3.00
❑ 52648	I'm Going to Leave You Tomorrow/I Don't Feel Much Like a Cowboy Tonight	1985	—	—	3.00
❑ 52648 [PS]	I'm Going to Leave You Tomorrow/I Don't Feel Much Like a Cowboy Tonight	1985	—	2.00	4.00
❑ 52723	What's a Memory Like You (Doing in a Love Like This)/The One Who Got Away	1985	—	—	3.00
❑ 52723 [PS]	What's a Memory Like You (Doing in a Love Like This)/The One Who Got Away	1985	—	2.00	4.00
❑ 52827	You're the Last Thing I Needed Tonight/One More Night	1986	—	—	3.00
❑ 52901	At the Sound of the Tone/This Time	1986	—	—	3.00
❑ 52989	Take the Long Way Home/Better Class of Losers	1986	—	—	3.00
❑ 53069	Love, You Ain't Seen the Last of Me/Credit	1987	—	—	3.00
❑ 53144	When the Right One Comes Along/The Gunfighter	1987	—	—	3.00
❑ 53199	If It Was Anyone But You/So Good	1987	—	—	3.00

SCOTTI BROTHERS

Number	Title (A Side/B Side)	Yr	VG	VG+	NM
❑ ZS6-02105	It's Now or Never/Stay	1981	—	2.00	4.00
❑ ZS6-02105 [PS]	It's Now or Never/Stay	1981	—	3.00	6.00
❑ ZS5-02489	Them Good Old Boys Are Bad/Still	1981	—	2.00	4.00
❑ ZS5-02489 [PS]	Them Good Old Boys Are Bad/Still	1981	—	2.50	5.00
❑ ZS5-02606	Katey's Christmas Card/Silent Night, Holy Night	1981	—	3.00	6.00
❑ ZS5-02889	Dreamin'/Let Me Love You	1982	—	2.00	4.00
❑ ZS5-03062	In the Driver's Seat/They Got Nothin' on Him	1982	—	2.00	4.00
❑ ZS4-03369	Katey's Christmas Card/Silent Night, Holy Night	1982	—	2.00	4.00
❑ ZS4-03945	Are You Lonesome Tonight/Hurts Like the Devil	1983	—	2.00	4.00

—A-side with Jill Michaels

Number	Title (A Side/B Side)	Yr	VG	VG+	NM
❑ ZS4-04064	If You Believe/Every Night with You	1983	—	2.00	4.00

Albums

MCA

Number	Title (A Side/B Side)	Yr	VG	VG+	NM
❑ 5495	Too Good to Stop Now	1984	2.00	4.00	8.00
❑ 5583	Tryin' to Outrun the Wind	1985	2.00	4.00	8.00
❑ 5668	A Memory Like You	1986	2.00	4.00	8.00
❑ 5789	Take the Long Way Home	1986	2.00	4.00	8.00
❑ 5973	You Ain't Seen the Last of Me	1987	2.00	4.00	8.00
❑ 42033	Greatest Hits	1987	2.00	4.00	8.00

SCOTTI BROTHERS

Number	Title (A Side/B Side)	Yr	VG	VG+	NM
❑ FZ 37400	Now or Never	1981	2.50	5.00	10.00
❑ 3Z 37617	White Christmas	198?	2.00	4.00	8.00

—Budget-line reissue with new prefix

Number	Title (A Side/B Side)	Yr	VG	VG+	NM
❑ FZ 37617	White Christmas	1981	2.50	5.00	10.00
❑ FZ 37956	Quiet Man	1982	2.50	5.00	10.00
❑ FZ 38712	If You Believe	1983	2.50	5.00	10.00

SCHOONMAKER, LLOYD

45s

HITSVILLE

Number	Title (A Side/B Side)	Yr	VG	VG+	NM
❑ 6051	Little Sister/She Gives Me Love	1977	—	3.00	6.00

SCHUTT, DAWN

45s

MASTER

Number	Title (A Side/B Side)	Yr	VG	VG+	NM
❑ 10	Take Time/(B-side unknown)	1989	—	3.00	6.00

SCHUYLER, THOM

Also see SCHUYLER, KNOBLOCH & BICKHARDT; SCHUYLER, KNOBLOCK & OVERSTREET.

45s

CAPITOL

Number	Title (A Side/B Side)	Yr	VG	VG+	NM
❑ B-5239	A Little at a Time/The Softer I Try	1983	—	2.00	4.00
❑ B-5281	Brave Heart/Two Way Street	1983	—	2.00	4.00

Albums

CAPITOL

Number	Title (A Side/B Side)	Yr	VG	VG+	NM
❑ SQ-12298	Brave Heart	1983	2.50	5.00	10.00

SCHUYLER, KNOBLOCH & BICKHARDT

Also see CRAIG BICKHARDT; FRED KNOBLOCK; THOM SCHUYLER.

45s

MTM

Number	Title (A Side/B Side)	Yr	VG	VG+	NM
❑ B-72090	No Easy Horses/Too Good to Be Blue	1987	—	—	3.00
❑ B-72099	Givers and Takers/People Still Fall in Love	1988	—	—	3.00
❑ B-72100	This Old House/Living Without You	1987	—	—	3.00
❑ B-72115	Rigamarole/Major Repairs	1988	—	—	3.00

Albums

MTM

Number	Title (A Side/B Side)	Yr	VG	VG+	NM
❑ ST-71064	No Easy Horses	1987	2.50	5.00	10.00

SCHUYLER, KNOBLOCH & OVERSTREET

Also see FRED KNOBLOCK; PAUL OVERSTREET; THOM SCHUYLER.

45s

MTM

Number	Title (A Side/B Side)	Yr	VG	VG+	NM
❑ B-72071	You Can't Stop Love/Love Is the Hero	1986	—	2.00	4.00
❑ B-72081	Baby's Got a New Baby/Bitter Pill to Swallow	1986	—	2.00	4.00
—As "S-K-O"					
❑ B-72086	American Me/Country Heart	1987	—	2.00	4.00

Albums

MTM

Number	Title (A Side/B Side)	Yr	VG	VG+	NM
❑ ST-71058	S-K-O	1986	2.50	5.00	10.00

SCOTT, EARL

45s

DECCA

Number	Title (A Side/B Side)	Yr	VG	VG+	NM
❑ 31693	I'll Wander Back to You/Kiss My Lover Goodbye	1964	—	3.50	7.00
❑ 31804	Between My Heart and Home/I'm Comin' Home Mama	1965	—	3.50	7.00
❑ 31865	Don't Ask When I'll Be Back/Gotta Get Away	1965	—	3.50	7.00
❑ 31931	Wandering Boy/I Feel a Fool (Walkin' in My Shoes)	1966	—	3.50	7.00
❑ 32009	Conscience, Tell Me What to Do/Tearin' My Head Up Again	1966	—	3.50	7.00
❑ 32113	My Ex Mrs. Brown/Changing Arms	1967	—	3.50	7.00
❑ 32177	Daddy's Dead/G.I.	1967	—	3.50	7.00
❑ 32255	Mean Ole Man Made Things/That's the Hangup Baby	1968	—	3.50	7.00
❑ 32334	Cowboys Don't Care/Everytime I Fall In	1968	—	3.50	7.00
❑ 32397	Too Rough on Me/Bottle in My Hand	1968	—	3.50	7.00

KAPP

Number	Title (A Side/B Side)	Yr	VG	VG+	NM
❑ 854 (?)	Then a Tear Fell/Save a Minute (Lose a Wife)	1962	2.50	5.00	10.00

—Is this catalog number correct? This is the number we've found, but Kapp 854 -- a completely different record -- was issued in 1967!

MERCURY

Number	Title (A Side/B Side)	Yr	VG	VG+	NM
❑ 72110	Loose Lips/Guess I'll Never Learn	1963	2.00	4.00	8.00
❑ 72190	Restless River/The Best I Can Give Her	1963	2.00	4.00	8.00

SCOTT, JACK

45s

Number	Title (A Side/B Side)	Yr	VG	VG+	NM
ABC					
❑ 10843	Before the Bird Flies/Insane	1966	5.00	10.00	20.00
ABC-PARAMOUNT					
❑ 9818	Baby She's Gone/You Can Bet Your Bottom Dollar	1957	37.50	75.00	150.00
❑ 9860	Two Timin' Woman/I Need Your Love	1957	37.50	75.00	150.00
CAPITOL					
❑ 4554	A Little Feeling (Called Love)/Now That I	1961	6.25	12.50	25.00
❑ 4554 [PS]	A Little Feeling (Called Love)/Now That I	1961	12.50	25.00	50.00
❑ 4597	My Dream Came True/Strange Desire	1961	5.00	10.00	20.00
❑ 4597 [PS]	My Dream Came True/Strange Desire	1961	12.50	25.00	50.00
❑ 4637	Steps 1 and 2/One of These Days	1961	5.00	10.00	20.00
❑ 4637 [PS]	Steps 1 and 2/One of These Days	1961	12.50	25.00	50.00
❑ 4689	Cry, Cry, Cry/Grizzly Bear	1962	5.00	10.00	20.00
❑ 4689 [PS]	Cry, Cry, Cry/Grizzly Bear	1962	12.50	25.00	50.00
❑ 4738	The Part Where I Cry/You Only See What You Wanna See	1962	5.00	10.00	20.00
❑ 4796	Sad Story/I Can't Hold Your Letters	1962	5.00	10.00	20.00
❑ 4855	If Only/Green, Green Valley	1962	5.00	10.00	20.00
❑ 4903	Strangers/Laugh and the World Laughs With You	1963	5.00	10.00	20.00
❑ 4955	All I See Is Blue/Meo Myo	1963	5.00	10.00	20.00
CARLTON					
❑ 462	My True Love/Leroy	1958	7.50	15.00	30.00
❑ 483	With Your Love/Geraldine	1958	7.50	15.00	30.00
❑ 483 [PS]	With Your Love/Geraldine	1958	15.00	30.00	60.00
❑ 493	Goodbye Baby/Save My Soul	1959	7.50	15.00	30.00
❑ 493 [PS]	Goodbye Baby/Save My Soul	1959	15.00	30.00	60.00
❑ 504	I Never Felt Like This/Bella	1959	7.50	15.00	30.00
❑ 514	The Way I Walk/Midgie	1959	7.50	15.00	30.00
❑ 519 [M]	There Comes a Time/Baby Marie	1959	5.00	10.00	20.00
❑ ST-519 [S]	There Comes a Time/Baby Marie	1959	10.00	20.00	40.00
DOT					
❑ 17475	May You Never Be Alone/Face to the Wall	1973	—	2.50	5.00
❑ 17504	You're Just Getting Better/Walk Through My Mind	1974	—	2.50	5.00
GROOVE					
❑ 58-0027	There's Trouble Brewin'/Jingle Bell Slide	1963	5.00	10.00	20.00
❑ 58-0031	Blue Skies (Moving In on Me)/I Knew You First	1964	3.75	7.50	15.00
❑ 58-0037	Wiggle On Out/What a Wonderful Night Out	1964	5.00	10.00	20.00
❑ 58-0042	Thou Shalt Not Steal/I Prayed for an Angel	1964	3.75	7.50	15.00
❑ 58-0049	Flakey John/Tall Tales	1964	5.00	10.00	20.00
GRT					
❑ 35	Billy Jack/Mary, Marry Me	1971	—	2.50	5.00
GUARANTEED					
❑ 209	What Am I Living For/Indiana Waltz	1960	7.50	15.00	30.00
❑ 211	No One Will Ever Know/Go Wild Little Sadie	1960	7.50	15.00	30.00
JUBILEE					
❑ 5606	My Special Angel/I Keep Changin' My Mind	1967	5.00	10.00	20.00
PONIE					
❑ 7021-10	Geraldine/Midgie	197?	—	2.00	4.00
❑ 7021-11	There's Trouble Brewin'/Jingle Bell Slide	197?	—	2.00	4.00
❑ 7021-12	Flakey John/Wiggle On Out	197?	—	2.00	4.00
❑ 5121-15	Baby She's Gone/Two Timin' Woman	197?	—	2.00	4.00
❑ 6063-20	Leroy/Go Wild Little Sadie	197?	—	2.00	4.00
❑ 6083-20	Country Witch/Blues, Stay Away from Me-Stones	197?	—	2.00	4.00
❑ 4104-30	Spirit of '76/(Instrumental)	1976	—	2.00	4.00
RCA VICTOR					
❑ 47-8505	Separation's Now Granted/I Don't Believe in Tea Leaves	1965	3.75	7.50	15.00
❑ 47-8685	Looking for Linda/I Hope I Think I Wish	1965	3.75	7.50	15.00
❑ 47-8724	Don't Hush the Laughter/Let's Learn to Live and Love Again	1965	3.75	7.50	15.00
TOP RANK					
❑ 2028 [M]	What in the World's Come Over You/Baby Baby	1959	7.50	15.00	30.00
❑ 2028 [S]	What in the World's Come Over You/Baby Baby	1959	10.00	20.00	40.00
❑ 2041 [M]	Burning Bridges/Oh Little One	1960	6.25	12.50	25.00
❑ 2041 [PS]	Burning Bridges/Oh Little One	1960	15.00	30.00	60.00
❑ 2041 [S]	Burning Bridges/Oh Little One	1960	15.00	30.00	60.00
❑ 2055	It Only Happened Yesterday/Cool Water	1960	5.00	10.00	20.00
❑ 2075	Patsy/Old Time Religion	1960	5.00	10.00	20.00
❑ 2093	Is There Something on Your Mind/Found a Woman	1960	5.00	10.00	20.00
❑ 2093 [PS]	Is There Something on Your Mind/Found a Woman	1960	15.00	30.00	60.00

7-Inch Extended Plays

Number	Title (A Side/B Side)	Yr	VG	VG+	NM
CARLTON					
❑ EP 7/1070	Save My Soul/I Can't Help It//Geraldine/With Your Love	1959	50.00	100.00	200.00
❑ EP 7/1070 [PS]	Presenting Jack Scott (Volume 1)	1959	50.00	100.00	200.00
❑ EP 7/1071	Indiana Waltz,/Midgie//My True Love/Leroy	1959	50.00	100.00	200.00
❑ EP 7/1071 [PS]	Presenting Jack Scott (Volume 2)	1959	50.00	100.00	200.00
❑ EP 7/1072	No One Will Ever Know/Goodbye Baby//I'm Dreaming Of You/The Way I Walk	1959	50.00	100.00	200.00
❑ EP 7/1072 [PS]	Jack Scott Sings	1959	50.00	100.00	200.00
TOP RANK					
❑ 1001	(contents unknown)	1960	50.00	100.00	200.00
❑ 1001 [PS]	What in the World's Come Over You	1960	50.00	100.00	200.00

Albums

Number	Title (A Side/B Side)	Yr	VG	VG+	NM
CAPITOL					
❑ ST-8-2035	Burning Bridges	196?	50.00	100.00	200.00
—Capitol Record Club edition					
❑ ST 2035 [S]	Burning Bridges	1964	37.50	75.00	150.00
❑ T 2035 [M]	Burning Bridges	1964	20.00	40.00	80.00
CARLTON					
❑ LP-12-107 [M]	Jack Scott	1959	37.50	75.00	150.00
❑ STLP-12-107 [S]	Jack Scott	1959	100.00	200.00	400.00
—With "Stereo" in felt letters vertically along the left of cover					
❑ STLP-12-107 [S]	Jack Scott	1959	75.00	150.00	300.00
—With "Stereo" in felt letters horizontally along the top of cover					
❑ STLP-12-107 [S]	Jack Scott	1959	50.00	100.00	200.00
—With "Stereo" printed across the top					
❑ LP-12-122 [M]	What Am I Living For	1959	30.00	60.00	120.00
❑ STLP-12-122 [S]	What Am I Living For	1959	80.00	160.00	320.00
JADE					
❑ J33-113	Jack Is Back	198?	3.75	7.50	15.00
❑ J33-114	The Way I Rock	198?	3.75	7.50	15.00
PONIE					
❑ 563	Jack Scott	1974	3.75	7.50	15.00
❑ 7055	Jack Scott	1977	3.75	7.50	15.00
TOP RANK					
❑ RM-319 [M]	I Remember Hank Williams	1960	37.50	75.00	150.00
❑ RM-326 [M]	What in the World's Come Over You	1960	37.50	75.00	150.00
❑ RM-348 [M]	The Spirit Moves Me	1961	37.50	75.00	150.00
❑ SM-619 [S]	I Remember Hank Williams	1960	62.50	125.00	250.00
❑ SM-626 [S]	What in the World's Come Over You	1960	62.50	125.00	250.00
❑ SM-648 [S]	The Spirit Moves Me	1961	62.50	125.00	250.00

SCOTT, LANG

45s

MCA

Number	Title (A Side/B Side)	Yr	VG	VG+	NM
❑ 52359	Run Your Sweet Love By Me One More Time/It's Been One of Those Days	1984	—	2.00	4.00

SCRUGGS, EARL

Includes records as "The Earl Scruggs Revue." Also see FLATT AND SCRUGGS; TOM T. HALL AND EARL SCRUGGS.

45s

COLUMBIA

Number	Title (A Side/B Side)	Yr	VG	VG+	NM
❑ 38-03430	Sittin' on Top of the World/Lindsey	1983	—	2.00	4.00
—A-side vocals by Rodney Dillard					
❑ 38-03777	Could You Love Me One More/Roller Coaster	1983	—	2.00	4.00
—A-side vocals by Burrito Brothers					
❑ 38-04717	Pedal to the Metal/Leaving Louisiana in the Broad Daylight	1984	—	2.00	4.00
❑ 3-10433	Tall Texas Woman/Daydream	1976	—	3.00	6.00
❑ 3-10691	The Cabin/Our Love Is Home Grown	1978	—	2.50	5.00
❑ 10992	I Could Sure Use the Feeling/Drive to the Country	1979	—	2.50	5.00
❑ 11106	Play Me No Sad Songs/Morning After Kind of Man	1979	—	2.50	5.00
❑ 11176	Blue Moon of Kentucky/Give Me a Sign	1980	—	2.50	5.00
❑ 11306	It'll Be Alright/Country Comfort	1980	—	2.50	5.00
❑ 4-45218	Nashville Skyline Rag/Train Number Forty-Five	1970	2.00	4.00	8.00
❑ 4-45326	East Virginia Blues/Lonesome Ruben	1971	2.00	4.00	8.00
❑ 4-45413	Country Comfort/T for Texas	1971	—	3.50	7.00
❑ 4-45503	Foggy Mountain Breakdown/Brand New Tennessee Waltz	1971	—	3.50	7.00
❑ 4-45560	Lonesome and a Long Way from Home/Never Ending Song of Love	1972	—	3.50	7.00

Number	Title (A Side/B Side)	Yr	VG	VG+	NM
❑ 4-45919	If I'd Only Come and Gone/Station Break	1973	—	3.50	7.00
❑ 4-46014	Where the Lilies Bloom/All My Trials	1974	—	3.50	7.00
❑ 4-46051	Travelin' Prayer/Silver Eagle	1974	—	3.50	7.00
Albums					
COLUMBIA					
❑ CS 1007	Nashville's Rock	1970	3.75	7.50	15.00
❑ KC 31354	I Saw the Light	1972	3.75	7.50	15.00
❑ C 31758	Live at Kansas State	1972	3.00	6.00	12.00
❑ PC 31758	Live at Kansas State	198?	2.00	4.00	8.00
—Budget-line reissue with bar code					
❑ C 32268	Dueling Banjos	1973	3.00	6.00	12.00
❑ PC 32268	Dueling Banjos	198?	2.00	4.00	8.00
—Budget-line reissue with bar code					
❑ KC 32426	The Earl Scruggs Revue	1973	3.00	6.00	12.00
❑ KC 32943	Rockin' 'Cross the Country	1974	3.00	6.00	12.00
❑ PC 33416	Anniversary Special, Volume One	1975	2.50	5.00	10.00
❑ PC 34090	The Earl Scruggs Revue, Volume II	1976	2.50	5.00	10.00
❑ PC 34346	Family Portrait	1976	2.50	5.00	10.00
❑ PC 34464	Live from Austin City Limits	1977	2.50	5.00	10.00
—No bar code on back cover					
❑ PC 34464	Live from Austin City Limits	198?	2.00	4.00	8.00
—Budget-line reissue with bar code					
❑ PC 34878	Strike Anywhere	1977	2.50	5.00	10.00
❑ JC 35319	Bold & New	1978	2.50	5.00	10.00
❑ JC 36084	Today and Forever	1979	2.50	5.00	10.00
❑ PC 36084	Today and Forever	198?	2.00	4.00	8.00
—Budget-line reissue with bar code					
❑ JC 36509	Country Comfort	1980	2.50	5.00	10.00
❑ FC 38295	Top of the World	1983	2.50	5.00	10.00
❑ PC 38295	Top of the World	1985	2.00	4.00	8.00
—Budget-line reissue with new prefix					
❑ FC 39370	Super Jammin'	1984	2.50	5.00	10.00
❑ FC 39586	American Made, World Played	1984	2.50	5.00	10.00

SEA, JOHNNY

Number	Title (A Side/B Side)	Yr	VG	VG+	NM
45s					
CAPITOL					
❑ 4585	The Torch and the Flame/No Tears Tonight	1961	2.50	5.00	10.00
❑ 4646	Livin' Is Lovin'/The Wayward Wind	1961	2.50	5.00	10.00
COLUMBIA					
❑ 44423	Going Out to Tulsa/There's a Shadow Bar	1968	—	2.50	5.00
❑ 44542	Mama When I'm Gone Don't Cry for Me/Song Number 9 1/2 on the Album	1968	—	2.50	5.00
❑ 44634	Three Six-Packs, Two Arms and a Juke Box/ Loved Her Fine for a Time	1968	—	2.50	5.00
❑ 44717	I've Learned a Lot Today/A Poor Boy Just Trying to Get Along	1968	—	2.50	5.00
❑ 44805	Cryin' Gray Tombstone/Everybody's Friend	1969	—	2.50	5.00
NRC					
❑ 006	It Won't Be Easy to Forget/I Love You	1958	3.00	6.00	12.00
❑ 019	Frankie's Man, Johnny/Loneliness	1959	3.00	6.00	12.00
❑ 026	Stranger/Judy and Johnny	1959	3.00	6.00	12.00
❑ 049	Nobody's Darling But Mine/My Time to Cry	1959	3.00	6.00	12.00
❑ 060	Ghost Riders in the Sky/Mr. and Mrs. Sippi	1960	3.00	6.00	12.00
PHILIPS					
❑ 40164	My Baby Walks All Over Me/There's Another Man	1964	2.00	4.00	8.00
❑ 40214	All Mixed Up/Standing Room Only	1964	2.00	4.00	8.00
❑ 40267	My Old Faded Rose/It's a Shame	1965	2.00	4.00	8.00
❑ 40307	If It Wasn't for Hard Luck/Hitchin' and Hikin'	1965	2.00	4.00	8.00
VIKING					
❑ 1011	Fort Worth Girl/Willie's Drunk and Willie's Dying	1970	—	2.50	5.00
❑ 1017	Annie's Going to Sing Her Song/(B-side unknown)	1971	—	3.00	6.00
WARNER BROS.					
❑ 5820	Day for Decision/Mary Rocks Him to Sleep	1966	—	3.00	6.00
❑ 5861	Things You Gave Me/Wheels on the Highway	1966	—	3.00	6.00
❑ 5889	Nothin's Bad As Bein' Lonely/Ain't That Right	1967	—	3.00	6.00
Albums					
HILLTOP					
❑ 6018	Everybody's Favorite	196?	3.00	6.00	12.00
PHILIPS					
❑ PHM 200139 [M]	World of a Country Boy	1964	5.00	10.00	20.00
❑ PHM 200194 [M]	Live at the Bitter End	1965	5.00	10.00	20.00
❑ PHS 600139 [S]	World of a Country Boy	1964	6.25	12.50	25.00
❑ PHS 600194 [S]	Live at the Bitter End	1965	6.25	12.50	25.00
WARNER BROS.					
❑ W 1659 [M]	Day for Decision	1966	3.75	7.50	15.00
❑ WS 1659 [S]	Day for Decision	1966	5.00	10.00	20.00

SEAL, JIM

Number	Title (A Side/B Side)	Yr	VG	VG+	NM
45s					
NSD					
❑ 55	Empty Tables/She Loves My Troubles Away	1980	—	2.50	5.00
❑ 66	Bourbon Cowboy/From the Top to the Bottom	1980	—	2.50	5.00
❑ 82	No Body But Yours/My Love Keeps Reaching Out for You	1981	—	2.50	5.00

SEALS, BRADY

Also see LITTLE TEXAS.

Number	Title (A Side/B Side)	Yr	VG	VG+	NM
45s					
REPRISE					
❑ 7-17384	Still Standing Tall/Another You, Another Me	1997	—	—	3.00
❑ 7-17615	Another You, Another Me/You Can Have Your Way with Me	1996	—	—	3.00
WARNER BROS.					
❑ 7-17144	Whole Lotta Hurt/All My Devotion	1998	—	—	3.00
❑ 7-17198	I Fell/I Love You Too Much	1998	—	—	3.00

SEALS, DAN

Also see ENGLAND DAN AND JOHN FORD COLEY; MARIE OSMOND.

Number	Title (A Side/B Side)	Yr	VG	VG+	NM
45s					
ATLANTIC					
❑ 3674	Late at Night/(B-side unknown)	1980	2.00	4.00	8.00
—As "England Dan Seals"					
❑ 3769	Stones (Dig a Little Deeper)/Laugh or Cry	1980	2.00	4.00	8.00
—As "England Dan Seals"					
❑ 3786	Love Me Like the Last Time/(B-side unknown)	1980	2.00	4.00	8.00
—As "England Dan Seals"					
❑ 4015	Can't Get You Off My Mind/(B-side unknown)	1982	—	3.00	6.00
❑ 4042	I Could Be Lovin' You Right Now/(B-side unknown)	1982	—	3.00	6.00
CAPITOL					
❑ B-44077	One Friend/Bop	1987	—	2.00	4.00
❑ B-44077 [PS]	One Friend/Bop	1987	—	2.00	4.00
❑ B-44130	Addicted/Maybe I'm Missing You Now	1988	—	—	3.00
❑ B-44267	Big Wheels in the Moonlight/Factory Town	1988	—	—	3.00
❑ B-44345	They Rage On/Factory Town	1989	—	—	3.00
❑ B-44435	Love on Arrival/Those	1989	—	2.50	5.00
CAPITOL NASHVILLE					
❑ 7PRO-79120	Good Times (same on both sides)	1990	2.00	4.00	8.00
—Vinyl is promo only					
❑ 7PRO-79320	Bordertown (same on both sides)	1990	—	3.00	6.00
—Vinyl is promo only					
EMI AMERICA					
❑ B-8220	(You Bring Out) The Wild Side of Me/One Friend	1984	—	—	3.00
❑ B-8245	My Baby's Got Good Timing/She Thinks I Still Care	1984	—	—	3.00
❑ B-8261	My Old Yellow Car/On These Nights	1985	—	—	3.00
❑ B-8289	Bop/In San Antone	1985	—	2.00	4.00
❑ B-8311	Everything That Glitters (Is Not Gold)/So Easy to Need	1986	—	—	3.00
❑ B-8311 [PS]	Everything That Glitters (Is Not Gold)/So Easy to Need	1986	—	2.00	4.00
❑ B-8343	You Still Move Me/I'm Still Strung Out on You	1986	—	—	3.00
❑ B-8377	I Will Be There/Gonna Be Easy Now	1987	—	—	3.00
❑ B-8377 [PS]	I Will Be There/Gonna Be Easy Now	1987	—	2.00	4.00
❑ B-43023	Three Time Loser/On the Front Line	1987	—	—	3.00
LIBERTY					
❑ B-1496	Everybody's Dream Girl/The Banker	1983	—	2.00	4.00
❑ B-1504	After You/Candle in the Rain	1983	—	2.00	4.00
❑ B-1512	You Really Go for the Heart/On a Night Like This	1983	—	2.00	4.00
❑ B-1515	God Must Be a Cowboy/Nothin' Else Left to Do But Cry	1984	—	2.00	4.00
WARNER BROS.					
❑ 7-18058	Love Thing/A Good Place to Be	1994	—	—	3.00
❑ 7-18192	All Fired Up/Hillbilly Fever	1994	—	—	3.00
❑ 7-18710	We Are One/Sweet Little Shoe	1992	—	—	3.00
❑ 7-18813	When Love Comes Around the Bend/Sweet Little Shoe	1992	—	—	3.00
❑ 7-18968	Mason Dixon Line/Be My Angel	1992	—	—	3.00
❑ 7-19176	Sweet Little Shoe/Your Blue Heart	1991	—	—	3.00
Albums					
CAPITOL					
❑ 1P 7999	On Arrival	1990	5.00	10.00	20.00
—Only available on vinyl from Columbia House					
❑ C1-46976	Rage On	1988	2.00	4.00	8.00
❑ CLT-48308	The Best	1988	2.00	4.00	8.00
EMI AMERICA					
❑ ST-17131	San Antone	1984	2.00	4.00	8.00
❑ ST-17166	Won't Be Blue Anymore	1985	2.00	4.00	8.00
❑ PW-17231	On the Front Line	1986	2.00	4.00	8.00
LIBERTY					
❑ LT-51149	Rebel Heart	1983	2.50	5.00	10.00

SEALS, TROY

Also see JO ANN AND TROY.

Number	Title (A Side/B Side)	Yr	VG	VG+	NM
45s					
ATLANTIC					
❑ 4004	I Got a Thing About You Baby/Coal Town Blues	1973	—	3.00	6.00
❑ 4013	Star of the Bar/You Can't Judge a Book by the Cover	1973	—	3.00	6.00
❑ 4020	Honky Tonkin'/Let Me Make the Bright Lights Shine	1974	—	3.00	6.00
CALLA					
❑ 139	The Wedding of Society's Child/Sweet Love	1967	2.50	5.00	10.00
COLUMBIA					
❑ 3-10173	Easy/I'll Take You Down to San Antonio	1975	—	2.50	5.00
❑ 3-10227	Honky Tonk Dreams/San Antone-Ee-O	1975	—	2.50	5.00
❑ 3-10303	Sweet Dreams/In Our Rooms	1976	—	2.50	5.00
❑ 3-10354	Tall Texas Woman/We're Much Too Close (To Be So Far Apart)	1976	—	2.50	5.00
❑ 3-10435	Let's Go for a Ride/Me and Mama Used to Rock and Roll	1976	—	2.50	5.00
❑ 3-10511	Grand Ole Blues/One More Thrill	1977	—	2.50	5.00
ELEKTRA					
❑ 46573	One Night Honeymoon/Wanderin' Friends of Mine	1980	—	2.00	4.00

Number	Title (A Side/B Side)	Yr	VG	VG+	NM
POLYDOR					
❑ 14028	Where Did My Baby Go/Circles 'Round the Sun	1970	2.00	4.00	8.00
❑ 14053	Don't Blame Me/20 Miles from Home	1970	2.00	4.00	8.00
RCA					
❑ PB-13652	Good (Real Good)/We Had It All	1983	—	2.00	4.00
RISING SONS					
❑ 715	Mama, Hold My Hand/Ebony and Ivory	1969	7.50	15.00	30.00
Albums					
ATLANTIC					
❑ SD 7281	Now Prresenting Troy Seals	1973	3.00	6.00	12.00
COLUMBIA					
❑ KC 34271	Troy Seals	1976	3.00	6.00	12.00

SEARS, DAWN

Number	Title (A Side/B Side)	Yr	VG	VG+	NM
45s					
DECCA					
❑ 54834	Runaway Train/A Little at a Time	1994	—	2.50	5.00
❑ 54908	Nothin' But Good/No Relief in Sight	1994	—	2.00	4.00
WARNER BROS.					
❑ 7-19157	Good Goodbye/Till You Come Back to Me	1991	—	2.50	5.00

SEBASTIAN, JOHN

The former lead singer of the Lovin' Spoonful had one country hit, variations of which are listed below.

Number	Title (A Side/B Side)	Yr	VG	VG+	NM
45s					
REPRISE					
❑ 1349	Welcome Back Kotter/Warm Baby	1976	2.00	4.00	8.00
—Original A-side title					
❑ 1349	Welcome Back/Warm Baby	1976	—	2.00	4.00
—Revised A-side title					

SEELY, JEANNIE

Also see JACK GREENE AND JEANNIE SEELY.

Number	Title (A Side/B Side)	Yr	VG	VG+	NM
45s					
CHALLENGE					
❑ 59274	If I Can't Have You/Old Memories Never Die	1965	2.50	5.00	10.00
❑ 59298	Bring It On Back/World Without You	1965	2.50	5.00	10.00
❑ 59308	Today Is Not the Day/Please Release Me	1965	2.50	5.00	10.00
COLUMBIA					
❑ 3-10550	We're Still Hangin' In There Ain't We Jessi/I Don't Need Love Anymore	1977	—	2.50	5.00
❑ 3-10664	Take Me to Bed/Until You Have To	1978	—	2.50	5.00
DECCA					
❑ 32452	Just Enough to Start Me Dreamin'/How Big a Fire	1969	—	3.50	7.00
❑ 32524	Jeannie's Song/Out Loud	1969	—	3.50	7.00
❑ 32628	Please Be My New Love/Have You Found It Yet	1970	—	3.50	7.00
❑ 32757	Tell Me Again/What Kind of Bird Is That	1970	—	3.50	7.00
❑ 32838	You Don't Understand Him Like I Do/Another Heart for You to Break	1971	—	3.50	7.00
❑ 32882	Alright I'll Sign the Papers/All I Want Is You	1971	—	3.50	7.00
❑ 32964	Pride/I'm Afraid I Lied	1972	—	3.50	7.00
❑ 33042	Farm in Pennsyltucky/Between the King and I	1973	—	3.00	6.00
MCA					
❑ 40074	Can I Sleep in Your Arms/He'll Love the One He's With	1973	—	2.50	5.00
❑ 40162	Lucky Ladies/Hold Me	1973	—	2.50	5.00
❑ 40225	I Miss You/I'd Do As Much for You	1974	—	2.50	5.00
❑ 40287	He Can Be Mine/So Was He	1974	—	2.50	5.00
❑ 40372	If I Had the Chance/First Time	1975	—	2.50	5.00
❑ 40428	How Big a Fire/Take My Hand	1975	—	2.50	5.00
❑ 40528	Since I Met You Boy/Home to Him	1976	—	2.50	5.00
MONUMENT					
❑ 933	Don't Touch Me/You Tied Tin Cans to My Heart	1966	2.00	4.00	8.00
❑ 965	It's Only Love/Then Go Home to Her	1966	2.00	4.00	8.00
❑ 987	A Wanderin' Man/Darling Are You Ever Coming Home	1966	2.00	4.00	8.00
❑ 999	When It's Over/I'd Be Just As Lonely There	1967	2.00	4.00	8.00
❑ 1011	These Memories/Funny Way of Laughin'	1967	2.00	4.00	8.00
❑ 1029	I'll Love You More (Than You Need)/Enough to Lie	1967	2.00	4.00	8.00
❑ 1054	Welcome Home to Nothing/Maybe I Should Leave	1968	2.00	4.00	8.00
❑ 1075	How Is He?/A Little Unfair	1968	2.00	4.00	8.00
❑ 1100	Little Things/My Love Dies Hard	1968	2.00	4.00	8.00
Albums					
DECCA					
❑ DL 75093	Jeannie Seely	1969	3.75	7.50	15.00
❑ DL 75228	Please Be My New Love	1970	3.75	7.50	15.00
HARMONY					
❑ KH 31029	Make the World Go Away	1972	3.00	6.00	12.00
MCA					
❑ 385	Can I Sleep in Your Arms/Lucky Ladies	1973	3.00	6.00	12.00
MONUMENT					
❑ 6640	Greatest Hits	1977	3.00	6.00	12.00
—Reissue of 31911					
❑ MLP-8057 [M]	The Seely Style	1966	3.75	7.50	15.00
❑ MLP-8073 [M]	Thanks, Hank!	1967	6.25	12.50	25.00
❑ SLP-18057 [S]	The Seely Style	1966	5.00	10.00	20.00
❑ SLP-18073 [S]	Thanks, Hank!	1967	5.00	10.00	20.00
❑ SLP-18091	I'll Love You More	1968	5.00	10.00	20.00
❑ SLP-18104	Little Things	1968	5.00	10.00	20.00
❑ KZ 31911	Greatest Hits	1973	3.75	7.50	15.00

SEEVERS, LES

Number	Title (A Side/B Side)	Yr	VG	VG+	NM
45s					
CHESTNUT					
❑ 212	Stop, Look, Surrender/The Loser Who Can't Lose	196?	2.50	5.00	10.00
❑ 218	My Conscience/Lily	196?	2.50	5.00	10.00
❑ 219	Love Is Stronger Than Dirt/Loneliness	196?	2.50	5.00	10.00
❑ 221	There Goes My Life/Two Wrongs	196?	2.50	5.00	10.00
DECCA					
❑ 32363	My Conscience/Lily	1968	2.00	4.00	8.00
❑ 32434	What Kind of Magic/Stop, Look, Surrender	1969	2.00	4.00	8.00
EVENT					
❑ 4291	Wooden Angel/Something Old, Something New	1959	5.00	10.00	20.00

SEGER, BOB

The Detroit-area rocker made the top 20 of the Billboard country charts with the below A-side, which was written by RODNEY CROWELL.

Number	Title (A Side/B Side)	Yr	VG	VG+	NM
45s					
CAPITOL					
❑ B-5187	Shame on the Moon/House Behind a House	1982	—	—	3.00
❑ B-5187 [PS]	Shame on the Moon/House Behind a House	1982	—	2.00	4.00

SEGO BROTHERS AND NAOMI, THE

Number	Title (A Side/B Side)	Yr	VG	VG+	NM
45s					
SONGS OF FAITH					
❑ 8032	Sorry I Never Knew You/Since I Got This Feeling	1963	3.75	7.50	15.00
Albums					
GOSPEL TIME					
❑ 5007	From the Soul	196?	6.25	12.50	25.00
❑ 5018	Gospel Concert Special	196?	5.00	10.00	20.00
HARVEST					
❑ 1001	Keeping It Gospel	196?	6.25	12.50	25.00
HEART WARMING					
❑ 1952	With the Help of God	196?	7.50	15.00	30.00
❑ 1955	This World Has Turned Me Down	196?	7.50	15.00	30.00
❑ 3056	Happy Day	196?	6.25	12.50	25.00
❑ 3144	Meetin' Time	1972	6.25	12.50	25.00
❑ 3154	Featuring Naomi	1972	6.25	12.50	25.00
❑ 3186	Sorry I Never Knew You	1972	6.25	12.50	25.00
❑ 3206	The Dearest Friend I Ever Had	1973	6.25	12.50	25.00
❑ 3279	What a Happy Time	1974	6.25	12.50	25.00
❑ 3433	It Will Be Different the Next Time	1976	6.25	12.50	25.00
RUNA					
❑ 1941	Gospel Singing	196?	7.50	15.00	30.00
❑ 1942	Completely Gospel	196?	6.25	12.50	25.00
SCRIPTURE					
❑ 121	The Best of the Sego Brothers and Naomi	196?	7.50	15.00	30.00
❑ 122	Far Above the Starry Skies	196?	7.50	15.00	30.00
SILVER STAFF					
❑ 15003	I Pray My Way Out of Trouble	196?	6.25	12.50	25.00
SIMS					
❑ 134	With the Help of God	196?	10.00	20.00	40.00
SING					
❑ 9091M [M]	Sego Brothers and Naomi	196?	7.50	15.00	30.00
❑ 9091S [S]	Sego Brothers and Naomi	196?	10.00	20.00	40.00
❑ 9092M [M]	One Day Late	196?	7.50	15.00	30.00
❑ 9092S [S]	One Day Late	196?	10.00	20.00	40.00
SONGS OF FAITH					
❑ 103	Satisfied with Me	196?	7.50	15.00	30.00
❑ 110	The Sego Brothers and Naomi Sing the Gospel	1963	7.50	15.00	30.00
❑ 117	From the Soul	196?	7.50	15.00	30.00
❑ 121	The Award Winning Sego Brothers and Naomi	196?	7.50	15.00	30.00
❑ 126	Hem of His Garment	196?	7.50	15.00	30.00
❑ 133	He'll Walk By Your Side	196?	7.50	15.00	30.00
❑ 137	Will the Circle Be Unbroken	196?	7.50	15.00	30.00
❑ 141	Gospel Music On Stage with the Sego Brothers and Naomi	196?	7.50	15.00	30.00
❑ 143	I'm Longing for Home	196?	7.50	15.00	30.00
❑ 145	The Sego Brothers and Naomi Sing Weapon of Prayer	196?	5.00	10.00	20.00
❑ 147	Somebody Touched Me	196?	7.50	15.00	30.00
❑ 150	Daddy Sang Bass	1969	6.25	12.50	25.00
❑ 156	The Sego Brothers and Naomi Featuring W.R. Sego	1969	6.25	12.50	25.00
❑ 158	Golden Hits of the Sego Brothers and Naomi	1970	6.25	12.50	25.00
❑ 168	The Sego Brothers and Naomi at Grandfather Mountain	197?	6.25	12.50	25.00
SUPREME					
❑ 33003	I Pray My Way Out of Trouble	196?	7.50	15.00	30.00
VISTA					
❑ 1224	Old Time Singing	196?	7.50	15.00	30.00

SEINER, BARBARA

Number	Title (A Side/B Side)	Yr	VG	VG+	NM
45s					
STARSHIP					
❑ 109	Jealous Heart/Everybody Loves Somebody	1979	2.00	4.00	8.00

SELF, RONNIE

Number	Title (A Side/B Side)	Yr	VG	VG+	NM
45s					
ABC-PARAMOUNT					
❑ 9714	Pret[illegible] Bad Blues/Three Hearts Later	1956	25.00	50.00	100.00
❑ 9768	Alone/Sweet Love	1956	25.00	50.00	100.00
AMY					
❑ 11009	High on Life/The Road Keeps Winding	1968	2.50	5.00	10.00

COLUMBIA

Number	Title (A Side/B Side)	Yr	VG	VG+	NM
❑ 40875	Big Fool/Flame of Love	1957	10.00	20.00	40.00
❑ 40989	Ain't I'm a Dog/Rocky Road Blues	1957	10.00	20.00	40.00
❑ 41101	Bop-A-Lena/I Ain't Going Nowhere	1958	7.50	15.00	30.00
❑ 41166	Big Blon' Baby/Date Bait	1958	7.50	15.00	30.00
❑ 41241	Petrified/You're So Right for Me	1958	20.00	40.00	80.00

DECCA

Number	Title (A Side/B Side)	Yr	VG	VG+	NM
❑ 30958	Big Town/This Must Be the Place	1959	6.25	12.50	25.00
❑ 31131	I've Been There/So High	1960	6.25	12.50	25.00
❑ 31351	Instant Man/Some Things You Can't Change	1962	6.25	12.50	25.00
❑ 31431	Oh Me, Oh My/Past, Present and Future	1962	6.25	12.50	25.00

KAPP

Number	Title (A Side/B Side)	Yr	VG	VG+	NM
❑ 546	Houdini/Bless My Broken Heart	1963	5.00	10.00	20.00

7-Inch Extended Plays

COLUMBIA

Number	Title (A Side/B Side)	Yr	VG	VG+	NM
❑ B-2149	(contents unknown)	1957	50.00	100.00	200.00
❑ B-2149 [PS]	Ain't I'm a Dog	1957	50.00	100.00	200.00

SELF, TED

45s

PLAID

Number	Title (A Side/B Side)	Yr	VG	VG+	NM
❑ 1000	Little Angel (Come Rock Me to Sleep)/Walk Her Down the Aisle	1960	5.00	10.00	20.00

—Number also listed as "115"; we're not sure which is correct, or if perhaps both are correct!

SELLARS, MARILYN

45s

MEGA

Number	Title (A Side/B Side)	Yr	VG	VG+	NM
❑ 200	Sing Me a Song/How Is She	1973	—	3.00	6.00
❑ 1205	One Day at a Time/California	1974	—	2.50	5.00
❑ 1221	He's Everywhere/Good Love (I Knew I'd Find You)	1974	—	2.50	5.00
❑ 1230	Gather Me/Red Skies Over Georgia	1975	—	2.50	5.00
❑ 1237	Sometimes Sunshine/Red Skies Over Georgia	1975	—	2.50	5.00
❑ 1242	The Door I Used to Close/California	1975	—	2.50	5.00

WEST WIND

Number	Title (A Side/B Side)	Yr	VG	VG+	NM
❑ 7911	One Day at a Time/Storms of Troubled Times	1979	—	3.00	6.00

ZODIAC

Number	Title (A Side/B Side)	Yr	VG	VG+	NM
❑ 1001	He's Everywhere/One Day at a Time	1976	—	2.50	5.00
❑ 1008	When He Loved Me/California	1977	—	2.50	5.00

Albums

KOALA

Number	Title (A Side/B Side)	Yr	VG	VG+	NM
❑ 14154	Raised on Country Sunshine	198?	2.50	5.00	10.00

MEGA

Number	Title (A Side/B Side)	Yr	VG	VG+	NM
❑ MLPS-602	One Day at a Time	1974	3.00	6.00	12.00
❑ MLPS-609	Gather Me	1974	3.00	6.00	12.00

ZODIAC

Number	Title (A Side/B Side)	Yr	VG	VG+	NM
❑ ZLP-5001	One Day at a Time	1976	3.00	6.00	12.00
❑ ZLP-5005	Marilyn	1977	3.00	6.00	12.00

SELLERS, JASON

45s

BNA

Number	Title (A Side/B Side)	Yr	VG	VG+	NM
❑ 60209	Can't Help Calling Your Name/A Matter of Time	2000	—	—	3.00
❑ 64915	I'm Your Man/Divorce My Heart	1997	—	—	3.00
❑ 65322	That Does It/Walking in My Sleep	1997	—	—	3.00

SEMINOLE

45s

CURB/UNIVERSAL

Number	Title (A Side/B Side)	Yr	VG	VG+	NM
❑ 56094	She Knows Me by Heart/Honestly	1997	—	2.00	4.00

SERATT, KENNY

Includes records with his last name spelled "Serratt."

45s

HILLSIDE

Number	Title (A Side/B Side)	Yr	VG	VG+	NM
❑ 8106	I Never Go Around Mirrors/You're Free	1981	—	3.00	6.00

HITSVILLE

Number	Title (A Side/B Side)	Yr	VG	VG+	NM
❑ 6039	I've Been There Too/She Made Me Love You More	1976	—	2.50	5.00
❑ 6049	Daddy, They're Playing a Song About You/I Threw Away the Rose	1977	—	2.50	5.00

MC

Number	Title (A Side/B Side)	Yr	VG	VG+	NM
❑ 5007	She's the Trip I've Been On (Since You've Been Gone)/She Only Made Me Love You More	1978	—	2.50	5.00

MDJ

Number	Title (A Side/B Side)	Yr	VG	VG+	NM
❑ 1001	Never Gonna Be a Country Star/A Damn Good Drinking Song	1979	—	2.50	5.00
❑ 1003	Saturday Night in Dallas/We Made Memories	1980	—	2.50	5.00
❑ 1005	Until the Bitter End/Truckin' My Way to Glory	1980	—	2.50	5.00
❑ 1008	Sidewalks Are Grey/(B-side unknown)	1981	—	2.50	5.00

MELODYLAND

Number	Title (A Side/B Side)	Yr	VG	VG+	NM
❑ 6014	If I Could Have It Any Other Way/Not Too Old to Cry	1975	—	2.50	5.00
❑ 6024	Let's Hold On to What We've Got/Truly Great American Blues	1975	—	2.50	5.00

MGM

Number	Title (A Side/B Side)	Yr	VG	VG+	NM
❑ 14435	Goodbyes Come Hard for Me/The Man Who Picked the Wildwood Flower	1972	—	3.00	6.00
❑ 14517	This Just Ain't No Good Day for Leaving/The Way I Lose My Mind	1973	—	3.00	6.00
❑ 14636	Love and Honor/Running Kind	1973	—	3.00	6.00
❑ 14707	Just Like the Wind/Too Many Barrooms	1974	—	3.00	6.00

SESSIONS, RONNIE

45s

COMPLEAT

Number	Title (A Side/B Side)	Yr	VG	VG+	NM
❑ 161	I Bought the Shoes That Just Walked Out on Me/You're a Real Live Wire	1986	—	2.50	5.00
❑ 167	If I Owned a Honky Tonk/You Can't Keep a Good Love Down	1987	—	2.50	5.00

MCA

Number	Title (A Side/B Side)	Yr	VG	VG+	NM
❑ 40326	Cry/Poor Little Rich Girl	1974	—	2.50	5.00
❑ 40411	Lonesome Almost Always Feels the Same/Love Hangover	1975	—	2.50	5.00
❑ 40462	Makin' Love/Messin' Around	1975	—	2.50	5.00
❑ 40581	Support Your Local Honky Tonks/Showdown	1976	—	2.50	5.00
❑ 40624	Wiggle Wiggle/Baby Please Don't Stone Me Anymore	1976	—	2.50	5.00
❑ 40705	Me and Millie (Stompin' Grapes and Gettin' Silly)/The Losing End	1977	—	2.50	5.00
❑ 40758	Ambush/Victim of Life's Circumstances	1977	—	2.50	5.00
❑ 40831	I Like to Be with You/Sweet Annette	1977	—	2.50	5.00
❑ 40875	Cash on the Barrelhead/Lucy, Ain't Your Loser Lookin' Good	1978	—	2.50	5.00
❑ 40917	I Never Go Around Mirrors/Whole Lotta Hound	1978	—	2.50	5.00
❑ 40952	Juliet and Romeo/Poison Love	1978	—	2.50	5.00
❑ 41038	Do You Want to Fly/Hold On to Your Hiney	1979	—	2.50	5.00
❑ 41142	Honky Tonkin'/Come By Here	1979	—	2.50	5.00

MGM

Number	Title (A Side/B Side)	Yr	VG	VG+	NM
❑ 14394	Never Been to Spain/While I Play the Fiddle	1972	—	3.00	6.00
❑ 14445	Tossin' and Turnin'/Knock and Ring and Tap	1972	—	3.00	6.00
❑ 14482	Wrap Your Tender Love All Around Me/Christine Loves a Loser	1973	—	3.00	6.00
❑ 14528	She Feels So Good I Hate to Put Her Down/We May Never Get This Close Again	1973	—	3.00	6.00
❑ 14619	If That Back Door Could Talk/My Love Is Deep, My Love Is Wide	1973	—	3.00	6.00
❑ 14712	My Rockin' Days/You Say the Sweetest Things	1974	—	3.00	6.00

—With Patti Tierney

MOSRITE

Number	Title (A Side/B Side)	Yr	VG	VG+	NM
❑ 130/140	Last Night in Town/Queen of Snob Hill	196?	3.00	6.00	12.00
❑ 230	The Big O/Really	196?	3.00	6.00	12.00
❑ 320	I'm the Daddy/(B-side unknown)	196?	3.00	6.00	12.00

PIKE

Number	Title (A Side/B Side)	Yr	VG	VG+	NM
❑ 5904	Bunny Rabbit (Without Any Tail)/Mommy's Japanese	1961	5.00	10.00	20.00

—As "Little Ronnie Sessions"

Number	Title (A Side/B Side)	Yr	VG	VG+	NM
❑ 5908	Keep a-Knockin'/A Lot on My Mind Today	1961	5.00	10.00	20.00

REPUBLIC

Number	Title (A Side/B Side)	Yr	VG	VG+	NM
❑ 1401	My Daddy Was a Guitar Man/Walkin' Down the Road	1969	2.00	4.00	8.00
❑ 1412	More Than Satisfied/Sad But It's True	1970	2.00	4.00	8.00

STARVIEW

Number	Title (A Side/B Side)	Yr	VG	VG+	NM
❑ 1003	Life of Riley/Restless Old River	198?	—	3.00	6.00
❑ 1003 [PS]	Life of Riley/Restless Old River	198?	2.50	5.00	10.00

Albums

MCA

Number	Title (A Side/B Side)	Yr	VG	VG+	NM
❑ 2285	Ronnie Sessions	1977	2.50	5.00	10.00

SEXTON, MARK

45s

SUN-DE-MAR

Number	Title (A Side/B Side)	Yr	VG	VG+	NM
❑ 79101	Don't Say No to Me Tonight/Younger Than Tomorrow	1979	2.00	4.00	8.00

SHAFER, WHITEY

45s

ELEKTRA

Number	Title (A Side/B Side)	Yr	VG	VG+	NM
❑ 47063	You Are a Liar/Like I Want To	1980	—	2.00	4.00
❑ 47117	If I Say I Love You (Consider Me Drunk)/I'll Break Out Again Tonight	1981	—	2.00	4.00

HICKORY/MGM

Number	Title (A Side/B Side)	Yr	VG	VG+	NM
❑ 328	I'm Tired of Puttin' Up with Puttin' On/My House Is Your Honky Tonk	1974	—	3.00	6.00
❑ 335	I Need Someone Like Me/Warm Red Wine	1974	—	3.00	6.00
❑ 349	What Did You Expect Me to Do/Please Don't Do That Anymore	1975	—	3.00	6.00
❑ 359	Let's Love It Over Again/It's Much Too Late to Start Quitting Now	1975	—	3.00	6.00
❑ 366	Love Inflation/Love Always Makes Me Cry	1976	—	3.00	6.00

KING

Number	Title (A Side/B Side)	Yr	VG	VG+	NM
❑ 6335	Violet Mae/I Gave Up Getting Over You Today	1970	2.50	5.00	10.00

MUSICOR

Number	Title (A Side/B Side)	Yr	VG	VG+	NM
❑ 1287	You Better Not Come Along with Me/Your Tears Are Telling on You	1968	2.50	5.00	10.00
❑ 1294	Your Old Ex/Life of a Loser	1968	2.50	5.00	10.00

RCA VICTOR

Number	Title (A Side/B Side)	Yr	VG	VG+	NM
❑ 47-9597	Touching Home/By the Railroad Track	1968	2.00	4.00	8.00
❑ 47-9669	Honey Bees and Tulips/The Outskirts of Somewhere	1968	2.00	4.00	8.00
❑ 47-9845	Big, Big Show on Wheels/Between Winston-Salem and Nashville, Tennessee	1970	2.00	4.00	8.00
❑ 74-0180	The Bottle, Your Memory, and Me/Love Don't Live Here Anymore	1969	2.00	4.00	8.00
❑ 74-0273	I'm Lonesome When I'm Busted/I'll Break Out Again Tonight	1969	2.00	4.00	8.00

SHAMBLIN, MICHAEL

45s

F&L

Number	Title (A Side/B Side)	Yr	VG	VG+	NM
❑ 548	Foreign Affairs/(B-side unknown)	1986	—	2.50	5.00
❑ 549	Wishful Dreamin'/Livin' on Love	1986	—	2.50	5.00

HEART OF DIXIE

Number	Title (A Side/B Side)	Yr	VG	VG+	NM
❑ 0117	Thank God for Christmas/(B-side unknown)	198?	—	3.00	6.00

SHANE, MICHAEL

45s

REGAL

Number	Title (A Side/B Side)	Yr	VG	VG+	NM
❑ 1988	What's the Matter Baby/(B-side unknown)	1989	—	2.50	5.00
❑ 9891	Broken Dreams and Memories/(B-side unknown)	1989	—	2.50	5.00

SHANNON, BONNIE

45s

DOOR KNOB

Number	Title (A Side/B Side)	Yr	VG	VG+	NM
❑ 139	Lovin' You Lightly/(B-side unknown)	1980	—	2.50	5.00
❑ 147	The Thread of Life/(B-side unknown)	1981	—	2.50	5.00
❑ 154	His Daddy Was a Ladies' Man/The Thread of Life	1981	—	2.50	5.00
❑ 161	Love Is a Lifetime Thing/His Daddy Was a Ladies' Man	1981	—	2.50	5.00

SHANNON, DEL

Very late in his career, the rocker whose biggest hits were in the early 1960s recorded some country music for Warner Bros., as listed below.

45s

WARNER BROS.

Number	Title (A Side/B Side)	Yr	VG	VG+	NM
❑ 28853	Stranger on the Run/What You Gonna Do with That	1985	—	2.50	5.00
❑ 29098	In My Arms Again/You Can't Forgive Me	1985	—	2.50	5.00

SHANNON, GUY

45s

CINNAMON

Number	Title (A Side/B Side)	Yr	VG	VG+	NM
❑ 758	Naughty Girl/Lady Please Forgive	1973	—	3.00	6.00
❑ 769	Soul Deep/A Train That Never Runs	1973	—	3.00	6.00
❑ 778	Lover, Fighter, Wild Horse Rider/Personality	1974	—	3.00	6.00
❑ 803	Jenny/Pride Is a Foolish Thing	1974	—	3.00	6.00

SHARP, ROSEMARY

45s

CANYON CREEK

Number	Title (A Side/B Side)	Yr	VG	VG+	NM
❑ 0210	The Stairs/Until I Fall in Love Again	1988	—	2.50	5.00
❑ 0401	Real Good Heartache/(B-side unknown)	1987	—	3.00	6.00
❑ 0908	If You're Gonna Tell Me Lies (Tell Me Good Ones)/(B-side unknown)	1987	—	3.00	6.00
❑ 1226	Didn't You Go and Leave Me/(B-side unknown)	1986	—	3.00	6.00

SHARPE, SUNDAY

45s

PLAYBOY

Number	Title (A Side/B Side)	Yr	VG	VG+	NM
❑ 5806	I'm Not the One You Love (I'm the One You Make Love To)/Last Night's Lovin'	1977	—	2.50	5.00
❑ 5813	Hold On Tight/Welcome Stranger	1977	—	2.50	5.00
❑ 6090	A Little at a Time/Pour It in a Swinging Jug	1977	—	2.50	5.00

UNITED ARTISTS

Number	Title (A Side/B Side)	Yr	VG	VG+	NM
❑ XW507	I'm Having Your Baby/It's a Beautiful Life	1974	—	2.50	5.00
❑ XW571	Mr. Songwriter/I Gave All I Had to Him	1974	—	2.50	5.00
❑ XW602	Put Your Head on My Shoulder/Another Lonely Night	1975	—	2.50	5.00
❑ XW666	I Gave All I Had to Him/It's a Beautiful Night to Love	1975	—	2.50	5.00
❑ XW709	Fancy Satin Pillows/I've Never Loved Anyone More	1975	—	2.50	5.00
❑ XW758	Find a New Love, Girl/It's a Beautiful Night for Love	1976	—	2.50	5.00

Albums

UNITED ARTISTS

Number	Title (A Side/B Side)	Yr	VG	VG+	NM
❑ UA-LA362-G	I'm Having Your Baby	1975	3.00	6.00	12.00

SHATSWELL, DANNY

45s

MERCURY

Number	Title (A Side/B Side)	Yr	VG	VG+	NM
❑ 55027	I'm a Mender/She's My Shelter	1978	—	2.50	5.00
❑ 55044	Happy Birthday Honey/Sometimes You Don't Know It's Love (Until It's Gone)	1978	—	2.50	5.00

SHAVER, BILLY JOE

45s

CAPRICORN

Number	Title (A Side/B Side)	Yr	VG	VG+	NM
❑ 0263	America, You Are My Woman/Ride Me Down Easy	1976	—	2.50	5.00
❑ 0286	You Asked Me To/Silver Wings of Time	1978	—	2.50	5.00
❑ 0290	The Believe/Billy B. Damned	1978	—	2.50	5.00

COLUMBIA

Number	Title (A Side/B Side)	Yr	VG	VG+	NM
❑ 18-02460	When the Word Was Thunderbird/Mexico	1981	—	2.00	4.00
❑ 18-02853	Ride Me Down Easy/Love You Till the Cows Come Home	1982	—	2.00	4.00
❑ 18-02976	Amtrak/Cowboys	1982	—	2.00	4.00

MERCURY

Number	Title (A Side/B Side)	Yr	VG	VG+	NM
❑ 73133	Chicken on the Ground/Laying Here Lying in Bed	1970	2.00	4.00	8.00

MGM

Number	Title (A Side/B Side)	Yr	VG	VG+	NM
❑ 14774	I've Been Leaning Towards the Blues/(B-side unknown)	1974	—	3.00	6.00

MONUMENT

Number	Title (A Side/B Side)	Yr	VG	VG+	NM
❑ 8580	I Been to Georgia on a Fast Train/Old Five and Dimers Like Me	1973	—	3.00	6.00
❑ 8593	Black Rose/Bottom Dollar	1973	—	3.00	6.00

Albums

CAPRICORN

Number	Title (A Side/B Side)	Yr	VG	VG+	NM
❑ CPN 0171	Wings	1976	3.00	6.00	12.00
❑ CPN 0192	Gypsy Boy	1977	3.00	6.00	12.00

COLUMBIA

Number	Title (A Side/B Side)	Yr	VG	VG+	NM
❑ FC 37078	I'm Just an Old Chunk of Coal	1981	2.50	5.00	10.00
❑ FC 37959	Billy Joe Shaver	1982	2.50	5.00	10.00

MONUMENT

Number	Title (A Side/B Side)	Yr	VG	VG+	NM
❑ 7621	Old Five and Dimers Like Me	1978	2.50	5.00	10.00
—Reissue of 32293					
❑ KZ 32293	Old Five and Dimers Like Me	1973	3.75	7.50	15.00

ZOO

Number	Title (A Side/B Side)	Yr	VG	VG+	NM
❑ 1104	Unshaven: Live at Smith's Olde Bar	1995	3.75	7.50	15.00

SHAW, BRIAN

45s

RCA VICTOR

Number	Title (A Side/B Side)	Yr	VG	VG+	NM
❑ APBO-0058	The Devil Is a Woman/Just at Dawn	1973	—	3.00	6.00
❑ APBO-0186	Good Enough to Be Your Man/What Loving You Means to Me	1973	—	3.00	6.00
❑ APBO-0230	Friend Named Red/I'm Not Through Loving You	1974	—	3.00	6.00
❑ APBO-0300	Ohio — Why Did I Go/Place My Star in Her Crown	1974	—	3.00	6.00
❑ PB-10071	Here We Go Again/I'll Carry You	1974	—	3.00	6.00
❑ PB-10189	The One She's Cheating With/I'm There	1975	—	3.00	6.00
❑ PB-10292	You Burned the Love (Out of Me)/Don't Build a Wall	1975	—	3.00	6.00
❑ PB-10397	If You Want to Pick Me Up (I'm Where You Put Me Down)/What Have You Got Planned Tonight, Diana	1975	—	2.50	5.00

REPUBLIC

Number	Title (A Side/B Side)	Yr	VG	VG+	NM
❑ 306	Showdown/(B-side unknown)	1976	—	2.50	5.00
❑ 360	What Kind of Fool (Does That Make Me)/You Sure Were Good Last Night	1977	—	2.50	5.00

SCORPION

Number	Title (A Side/B Side)	Yr	VG	VG+	NM
❑ 0551	You Sure Were Good Last Night/You're Easy to Love	1978	—	2.50	5.00
❑ 0574	All the Time/Take the Gamble, Play the Game	1979	—	2.50	5.00

SHAW, RON

45s

PACIFIC CHALLENGER

Number	Title (A Side/B Side)	Yr	VG	VG+	NM
❑ 1503	Fairweather Woman/(B-side unknown)	1977	—	3.00	6.00
❑ 1511	Hurtin' Kind of Love/Like So Much Broken Glass	1977	—	3.00	6.00
❑ 1521	Free Born Man/The Blizzard	1978	—	2.50	5.00
❑ 1522	Goin' Home/Boogie Woogie Country Girl	1978	—	2.50	5.00
❑ 1631	Save the Last Dance for Me/If Walls Could Talk	1978	—	2.50	5.00
❑ 1633	I Cry Instead/Kansas City	1978	—	2.50	5.00
❑ 1635	One and One Make Three/I Can't Dance	1979	—	2.50	5.00
❑ 1636	What the World Needs Now (Is Love Sweet Love)/Fairweather Woman	1979	—	2.50	5.00
❑ 1637	Hurtin' Kind of Love/Like So Much Broken Glass	1980	—	2.50	5.00
❑ 1638	The Legend of Harry and the Mountain/With My Lady on My Mind	1980	—	2.50	5.00
❑ 1639	Reachin' for Freedom/(B-side unknown)	1981	—	2.50	5.00
❑ 2015	Tomorrow's Another Day/(B-side unknown)	198?	—	2.50	5.00

Albums

PACIFIC CHALLENGER

Number	Title (A Side/B Side)	Yr	VG	VG+	NM
❑ 152	Goin' Home	1978	3.00	6.00	12.00

SHAW, VICTORIA

45s

MPB

Number	Title (A Side/B Side)	Yr	VG	VG+	NM
❑ 5008	Break My Heart/Forever on My Mind	1984	—	3.00	6.00

REPRISE

Number	Title (A Side/B Side)	Yr	VG	VG+	NM
❑ 7-17380	Different Drum/In Spite of It All	1997	—	—	3.00
❑ 7-17773	(A Day in the Life of a) Single Mother/It's Not My Place to Say	1995	—	2.00	4.00
❑ 7-17886	Forgiveness/Bring My Baby Home	1995	—	2.00	4.00
❑ 7-18111	Tears Dry/Half Hearted	1994	—	2.00	4.00
❑ 7-18235	Cry Wolf/Love's Not Gonna Pass Me By	1994	—	2.00	4.00

SHAY, DOROTHY

She was known as "The Park Avenue Hillbilly," though she was more a comedienne (she sang with Spike Jones and His City Slickers for a time) than a country singer.

45s

COLUMBIA

Number	Title (A Side/B Side)	Yr	VG	VG+	NM
❑ 1-145 (?)	You Broke Your Promise/Mr. Sears and Mr. Roebuck	1949	10.00	20.00	40.00
—Microgroove 33 1/3 rpm 7-inch single, small hole					
❑ 1-252 (?)	Pappy's Predicament/Another Notch on Father's Shotgun	1949	10.00	20.00	40.00
—Microgroove 33 1/3 rpm 7-inch single, small hole					
❑ 1-450 (?)	Diamonds Are a Girl's Best Friend/Little Girl from Little Rock	1949	10.00	20.00	40.00
—Microgroove 33 1/3 rpm 7-inch single, small hole					
❑ 1-680 (?)	Jenny/Home Cookin'	1950	10.00	20.00	40.00
—Microgroove 33 1/3 rpm 7-inch single, small hole					

Number	Title (A Side/B Side)	Yr	VG	VG+	NM
❑ 1-750	Oh Them Dudes/Mr. Berlitz	1950	10.00	20.00	40.00

—Microgroove 33 1/3 rpm 7-inch single, small hole

Selected 78s

COLUMBIA

Number	Title (A Side/B Side)	Yr	VG	VG+	NM
❑ 37189	Feudin' and Fightin'/Say That We're Sweethearts Again	1947	3.75	7.50	15.00
❑ 37190	Efficiency/Mountain Gal	1947	3.75	7.50	15.00
❑ 37191	Flat River, Missouri/I've Been to Hollywood	1947	3.75	7.50	15.00
❑ 37192	Uncle Fud/I'm in Love with a Married Man	1947	3.75	7.50	15.00
❑ 37890	Just a Friendly Feeling/Mountain Lullaby	1948	3.75	7.50	15.00
❑ 37891	He's the One/The State to Which I've Become Accustomed	1948	3.75	7.50	15.00
❑ 37892	The Little Things That Count/A Little Indiscretion	1948	3.75	7.50	15.00
❑ 37893	The Drainpipe Song/Agnes Clung	1948	3.75	7.50	15.00
❑ 38140	Two Gun Harry from Tucumcari/Sample Song	1948	3.75	7.50	15.00
❑ 38238	Makin' Love Mountain Style/Finishing School	1948	3.75	7.50	15.00
❑ 38306	Pure as the Driven Snow/Joan of Arkansaw	1948	3.75	7.50	15.00
❑ 38307	No Ring on Her Finger/Why Don't Someone Marry Mary Anne	1948	3.75	7.50	15.00
❑ 38308	Since Mother Was a Girl/Love Isn't Born	1948	3.75	7.50	15.00
❑ 38309	The Old Apple Tree/Grandpa's Gettin' Younger	1948	3.75	7.50	15.00

SHELTON, RICKY VAN

45s

COLUMBIA

Number	Title (A Side/B Side)	Yr	VG	VG+	NM
❑ 38-06542	Wild-Eyed Dream/Think It Over	1986	—	2.00	4.00
❑ 38-07025	Crime of Passion/Don't We All Have the Right	1987	—	—	3.00
❑ 38-07311	Somebody Lied/Working Man's Blues	1987	—	—	3.00
❑ 38-07672	Life Turned Her That Way/I Don't Care	1987	—	—	3.00
❑ 38-07798	Don't We All Have the Right/Baby, I'm Ready	1988	—	—	3.00
❑ 38-08022	I'll Leave This World Loving You/Sometimes I Cry in My Sleep	1988	—	2.00	4.00
❑ 13-08391	Wild-Eyed Dream/Crime of Passion	1988	—	—	3.00

—"Hall of Fame" series; gray label

Number	Title (A Side/B Side)	Yr	VG	VG+	NM
❑ 38-08529	From a Jack to a King/The Picture	1988	—	—	3.00
❑ 38-68694	Hole in My Pocket/Let Me Live with Love (And Die with You)	1989	—	—	3.00
❑ 38-68994	Living Proof/Somebody's Back in Town	1989	—	—	3.00
❑ 38-73077	Statue of a Fool/He's Got You	1989	—	—	3.00
❑ 38-73263	I've Cried My Last Tear for You/I Still Love You	1990	—	—	3.00
❑ 38-73413	I Meant Every Word He Said/Sometimes I Cry in My Sleep	1990	—	—	3.00
❑ 38-73587	Life's Little Ups and Downs/Love Is Burnin'	1990	—	—	3.00
❑ 38-73780	I Am a Simple Man/Backroads	1991	—	2.00	4.00
❑ 38-73956	Keep It Between the Lines/Weekend World	1991	—	2.00	4.00
❑ 38-74104	After the Lights Go Out/Oh Heart of Mine	1991	—	—	3.00
❑ 38-74258	Backroads/Call Me Up	1992	—	—	3.00
❑ 38-74418	Wear My Ring Around Your Neck/Who'll Turn Out the Lights	1992	—	2.00	4.00
❑ 38-74748	Wild Man/If You're Ever in My Arms	1992	—	2.00	4.00
❑ 38-74896	Just As I Am/Slam That Door	1993	—	—	3.00
❑ 38-77130	A Couple of Good Years Left/My First Reaction	1993	—	—	3.00
❑ 38-77334	Where Was I/If It Weren't for Me	1993	—	—	3.00
❑ 38-77653	Wherever She Is/Thanks a Lot	1994	—	—	3.00
❑ 38-77792	Lola's Love/Been There, Done That	1995	—	—	3.00

Albums

COLUMBIA

Number	Title (A Side/B Side)	Yr	VG	VG+	NM
❑ B6C 40602	Wild-Eyed Dream	1987	2.00	4.00	8.00
❑ FC 44221	Loving Proof	1988	2.00	4.00	8.00
❑ C 45250	RVS III	1990	3.75	7.50	15.00
❑ FC 45269	Ricky Van Shelton Sings Christmas	1989	3.00	6.00	12.00
❑ C 46855	Backroads	1990	5.00	10.00	20.00

—Vinyl available only through Columbia House

SHENANDOAH

45s

CAPITOL NASHVILLE

Number	Title (A Side/B Side)	Yr	VG	VG+	NM
❑ S7-18730	Heaven Bound (I'm Ready)/Cabin Fever	1995	—	2.00	4.00
❑ S7-18903	Always Have, Always Will/Every Fire	1995	—	2.00	4.00
❑ S7-19116	All Over But the Shoutin'/Sunday in the South	1996	—	2.00	4.00
❑ S7-19344	There's a Way in the Manger/The Christmas Song (Chestnuts Roasting on an Open Fire)	1996	—	2.00	4.00

COLUMBIA

Number	Title (A Side/B Side)	Yr	VG	VG+	NM
❑ 38-07128	We Don't Make Love Like We Used To/Lily of the Alley	1987	—	2.00	4.00
❑ 38-07128 [PS]	We Don't Make Love Like We Used To/Lily of the Alley	1987	—	2.00	4.00
❑ 38-07654	Stop the Rain/What She Wants	1987	—	2.00	4.00
❑ 38-07779	She Doesn't Cry Anymore/What She Wants	1988	—	—	3.00
❑ 38-08042	Mama Knows/The Show Must Go On	1988	—	—	3.00
❑ 38-68550	The Church on Cumberland Road/She Doesn't Cry Anymore	1989	—	2.00	4.00
❑ 38-68892	Sunday in the South/Changes	1989	—	—	3.00
❑ 38-69061	Two Dozen Roses/Hard Country	1989	—	—	3.00
❑ 38-73237	See If I Care/Lily of the Valley	1990	—	—	3.00
❑ 38-73373	Next to You, Next to Me/Daddy's Little Man	1990	—	2.00	4.00
❑ 38-73520	Ghost in This House/She's Still Here	1990	—	—	3.00
❑ 38-73672	I Got You/The Road Not Taken	1991	—	—	3.00
❑ 38-73777	The Moon Over Georgia/Can't Stop Now	1991	—	—	3.00
❑ 38-73957	When You Were Mine/It Ain't Love Until It Hurts	1991	—	—	3.00

LIBERTY

Number	Title (A Side/B Side)	Yr	VG	VG+	NM
❑ S7-18484	Darned If I Do (Danged If I Don't)/Somewhere in the Vicinity of the Heart	1995	—	2.00	4.00

—B-side with Alison Krauss

Number	Title (A Side/B Side)	Yr	VG	VG+	NM
❑ S7-18556	Can't Buy Me Love/Get Back	1995	—	2.50	5.00

—B-side by Steve Wariner

RCA

Number	Title (A Side/B Side)	Yr	VG	VG+	NM
❑ 62199	Rock My Baby/Wednesday Night Prayer Meeting	1992	—	2.50	5.00
❑ 62290	Hey Mister (I Need This Job)/There Ain't No Beverly Hills in Tennessee	1992	—	—	3.00
❑ 62397	Leavin's Been a Long Time Comin'/I Was Young Once Too	1992	—	—	3.00
❑ 62504	Janie Baker's Love Slave/Right Where I Belong	1993	—	2.00	4.00
❑ 62642	I Want to Be Loved Like That/Just Say the Word	1993	—	2.00	4.00
❑ 62761	If Bubba Can Dance (I Can Too)/If It Takes Every Rib I've Got	1994	—	2.50	5.00
❑ 62867	I'll Go Down Loving You/The Blues Are Coming Over to Your House	1994	—	—	3.00

Albums

COLUMBIA

Number	Title (A Side/B Side)	Yr	VG	VG+	NM
❑ BFC 40788	Shenandoah	1987	2.50	5.00	10.00
❑ FC 44468	The Road Not Taken	1989	3.00	6.00	12.00
❑ C 48885	Greatest Hits	1992	5.00	10.00	20.00

—Vinyl available only through Columbia House

SHEPARD, JEAN

45s

CAPITOL

Number	Title (A Side/B Side)	Yr	VG	VG+	NM
❑ 2073	An Old Bridge/My New Darlin'	1968	2.00	4.00	8.00
❑ 2180	A Real Good Woman/The Trouble with Girls	1968	2.00	4.00	8.00
❑ 2273	Everyday's a Happy Day for Fools/My World Is New	1968	2.00	4.00	8.00
❑ F2358	Twice the Lovin'/Crying Steel Guitar Waltz	1953	7.50	15.00	30.00
❑ 2425	I'm Tied Around You Finger/You're Calling Me Sweetheart Again	1969	—	3.50	7.00
❑ F2502	A Dear John Letter/I'd Rather Die Young	1953	6.25	12.50	25.00

—A-side with "Ferlin Huskey"

Number	Title (A Side/B Side)	Yr	VG	VG+	NM
❑ 2585	Seven Lonely Days/Invisible Tears	1969	—	3.50	7.00
❑ F2586	Forgive Me, John/My Wedding Ring	1953	6.25	12.50	25.00

—A-side with "Ferlin Huskey"

Number	Title (A Side/B Side)	Yr	VG	VG+	NM
❑ 2694	Then He Touched Me/Only Mama That'll Walk the Line	1969	—	3.50	7.00
❑ F2706	The Glass That Stands Beside You/Let's Kiss and Try Again	1954	6.25	12.50	25.00

—With Ferlin Husky

Number	Title (A Side/B Side)	Yr	VG	VG+	NM
❑ 2779	A Woman's Hand/What Went Wrong	1970	—	3.50	7.00
❑ F2791	Two Whoops and a Holler/Why Did You Wait	1954	7.50	15.00	30.00
❑ 2847	I Want You Free/Be Nice to Everybody	1970	—	3.50	7.00
❑ F2905	Don't Fall in Love with Married Men/You'll Come Crawlin'	1954	6.25	12.50	25.00
❑ 2941	Another Lonely Night/Your Name's Become a Household Word	1970	—	3.50	7.00
❑ F2994	Don't Rush Me/Please Don't Divorce Me	1954	6.25	12.50	25.00
❑ 3033	With His Hand in Mine/Just Plain Lonely	1971	—	3.00	6.00
❑ F3051	Did You Tell Her About Me/You Sent Her an Orchid	1955	6.25	12.50	25.00
❑ F3118	A Satisfied Mind/Take Possession	1955	6.25	12.50	25.00
❑ 3153	Just As Soon As I Get Over Loving You/My Name Is Woman	1971	—	3.00	6.00
❑ F3222	Beautiful Lies/I Thought of You	1955	6.25	12.50	25.00
❑ 3238	Safe in These Lovin' Arms of Mine/The Closest Thing to Perfect	1971	—	3.00	6.00
❑ 3315	Virginia/We Go Good Together	1972	—	3.00	6.00
❑ F3340	I Learned It All from You/This Has Been Your Life	1956	6.25	12.50	25.00
❑ 3395	Just Like Walkin' in the Sunshine/Candlelighted World	1972	—	3.00	6.00
❑ F3401	You're Calling Me Sweetheart Again/He Loved Me Once and He'll Love Me Again	1956	6.25	12.50	25.00
❑ F3514	Just Give Me Love/Thank You Just the Same	1956	6.25	12.50	25.00
❑ F3618	If You Can Walk Away/Tomorrow I'll Be Gone	1957	6.25	12.50	25.00
❑ F3727	The Other Woman/Under Suspicion	1957	6.25	12.50	25.00
❑ F3796	Act Like a Married Man/It Scares Me Half to Death	1957	6.25	12.50	25.00
❑ F3881	You're Just the Kind of Guy/I Used to Love You	1958	5.00	10.00	20.00
❑ F4013	The Secret of Life/He's My Baby	1958	5.00	10.00	20.00
❑ F4068	I Want to Go Where No One Knows Me/Just Another Girl	1958	5.00	10.00	20.00
❑ F4129	Have Heart, Will Love/I'll Take the Blame	1959	5.00	10.00	20.00
❑ F4191	Jeopardy/Better Love Next Time	1959	5.00	10.00	20.00
❑ F4279	Heartaches, Teardrops and Sorrow/Sweetheart Don't Come Back	1959	5.00	10.00	20.00
❑ 4321	The One You Slip Around With/Mysteries of Life	1959	3.75	7.50	15.00
❑ 4365	Did I Turn Down a Better Deal/How Do I Tell It to the Child	1960	3.75	7.50	15.00
❑ 4423	Lonely Little World/For the Children's Sake	1960	3.75	7.50	15.00
❑ 4538	The Root of All Evil/No One Knows	1961	3.75	7.50	15.00
❑ 4584	How Long Does It Hurt/If You Were Losing Him to Me	1961	3.75	7.50	15.00
❑ 4640	The Biggest Cry/I've Got to Talk to Mary	1961	3.75	7.50	15.00
❑ 4719	Two Voices, Two Shadows, Two Faces/Your Conscience or Your Heart	1962	3.00	6.00	12.00
❑ 4858	One Less Heartache/It's Never Too Late	1962	3.00	6.00	12.00
❑ 4915	I've Learned to Live with You/It's Torture	1963	3.00	6.00	12.00
❑ 5062	That's What Lonesome Is/When Your House Is Not a Home	1963	3.00	6.00	12.00
❑ 5169	Second Fiddle (To an Old Guitar)/Two Little Boys	1964	2.50	5.00	10.00
❑ 5304	A Tear Dropped By/He Plays the Bongos (I Play the Banjo)	1964	2.50	5.00	10.00
❑ 5392	Someone's Gotta Cry/Don't Take Advantage of Me	1965	2.50	5.00	10.00
❑ 5508	Ain't You Ashamed/It's a Man	1965	2.50	5.00	10.00

Number	Title (A Side/B Side)	Yr	VG	VG+	NM
❑ 5585	Many Happy Hangovers to You/Our Past Is In My Way	1966	2.50	5.00	10.00
❑ 5681	If Teardrops Were Silver/Outstanding in Your Field	1966	2.00	4.00	8.00
❑ 5822	Heart, We Did All That We Could/My Momma Didn't Raise No Fools	1967	2.00	4.00	8.00
❑ 5899	Your Forevers (Don't Last Very Long)/Coming or Going	1967	2.00	4.00	8.00
❑ 5983	I Don't See How I Can Make It/Enough Heart to Hurt	1967	2.00	4.00	8.00

SCORPION

Number	Title (A Side/B Side)	Yr	VG	VG+	NM
❑ 157	The Real Thing/Break My Mind	1978	—	3.00	6.00
❑ 0557	Saturday Night Sin/(B-side unknown)	1978	—	3.00	6.00

UNITED ARTISTS

Number	Title (A Side/B Side)	Yr	VG	VG+	NM
❑ XW248	Slippin' Away/Think I'll Go Somewhere and Cry Myself to Sleep	1973	—	2.50	5.00
❑ XW317	Come On Phone/Are You Sincere?	1973	—	2.50	5.00
❑ XW384	At the Time/Love Came Pouring Down	1974	—	2.50	5.00
❑ XW442	I'll Do Anything It Takes (To Stay with You)/Safe in the Love of My Man	1974	—	2.50	5.00
❑ XW552	Poor Sweet Baby/I'm Not That Good at Goodbye	1974	—	2.50	5.00
❑ XW591	The Tip of My Fingers/Bright Lights and Country Music	1975	—	2.50	5.00
❑ XW701	I'm a Believer (In a Whole Lot of Lovin')/I Think I'll Wait Until Tomorrow	1975	—	2.50	5.00
❑ XW745	Another Neon Night/(Hey, Won't You Play) Another Somebody Done Somebody Wrong Song	1975	—	2.50	5.00
❑ XW776	Mercy/Wife of a Hard Working Man	1976	—	2.50	5.00
❑ XW818	Ain't Love Good/I Can Imagine	1976	—	2.50	5.00
❑ XW899	I'm Giving You Denver/He Loves Everything He Gets His Hands On	1976	—	2.50	5.00
❑ XW956	Hardly a Day Goes By/Lovin' You Comes So Easy	1977	—	2.50	5.00

Albums

CAPITOL

Number	Title (A Side/B Side)	Yr	VG	VG+	NM
❑ ST-321	Seven Lonely Days	1969	3.75	7.50	15.00
❑ ST-441	Best By Request	1970	3.75	7.50	15.00
❑ ST-559	A Woman's Hand	1970	3.75	7.50	15.00
❑ T 728 [M]	Songs of a Love Affair	1956	15.00	30.00	60.00
❑ ST-738	Here and Now	1971	3.75	7.50	15.00
❑ ST-815	Just As Soon As I Get Over Loving You	1971	3.75	7.50	15.00
❑ T 1126 [M]	Lonesome Love	1959	10.00	20.00	40.00
❑ T 1253 [M]	This Is Jean Shepard	1959	10.00	20.00	40.00
❑ ST 1525 [S]	Got You on My Mind	1961	7.50	15.00	30.00
❑ T 1525 [M]	Got You on My Mind	1961	6.25	12.50	25.00
❑ ST 1663 [S]	Heartaches and Tears	1962	7.50	15.00	30.00
❑ T 1663 [M]	Heartaches and Tears	1962	6.25	12.50	25.00
❑ DT 1922 [R]	The Best of Jean Shepherd	1963	3.75	7.50	15.00
❑ T 1922 [M]	The Best of Jean Shepherd	1963	6.25	12.50	25.00
❑ ST 2187 [S]	Lighthearted and Blue	1964	5.00	10.00	20.00
❑ T 2187 [M]	Lighthearted and Blue	1964	3.75	7.50	15.00
❑ ST 2416 [S]	It's a Man Every Time	1965	3.75	7.50	15.00
❑ T 2416 [M]	It's a Man Every Time	1965	3.00	6.00	12.00
❑ ST 2547 [S]	Many Happy Hangovers	1966	3.75	7.50	15.00
❑ T 2547 [M]	Many Happy Hangovers	1966	3.00	6.00	12.00
❑ ST 2690 [S]	Heart, We Did All That We Could	1967	3.75	7.50	15.00
❑ T 2690 [M]	Heart, We Did All That We Could	1967	3.75	7.50	15.00
❑ ST 2765 [S]	Your Forevers Don't Last Very Long	1967	3.75	7.50	15.00
❑ T 2765 [M]	Your Forevers Don't Last Very Long	1967	5.00	10.00	20.00
❑ ST 2871 [S]	Heart to Heart	1968	3.75	7.50	15.00
❑ T 2871 [M]	Heart to Heart	1968	10.00	20.00	40.00
❑ ST 2966	A Real Good Woman	1968	3.75	7.50	15.00
❑ ST-11049	Just Like Walkin' in the Sunshine	1972	3.00	6.00	12.00
❑ SM-11409	For the Good Times	1975	2.50	5.00	10.00

HILLTOP

Number	Title (A Side/B Side)	Yr	VG	VG+	NM
❑ JS-6068	Under Your Spell Again	197?	2.50	5.00	10.00

UNITED ARTISTS

Number	Title (A Side/B Side)	Yr	VG	VG+	NM
❑ UA-LA144-F	Slippin' Away	1973	3.00	6.00	12.00
❑ UA-LA307-R	I'll Do Anything It Takes	1974	3.00	6.00	12.00
❑ UA-LA363-G	Poor Sweet Baby and Ten More Bill Anderson Songs	1975	3.00	6.00	12.00
❑ UA-LA525-G	I'm a Believer	1975	3.00	6.00	12.00
❑ UA-LA609	Mercy, Ain't Love Good	1976	3.00	6.00	12.00
❑ UA-LA685-G	Greatest Hits	1976	2.50	5.00	10.00

SHEPARD, JEAN, AND RAY PILLOW

Also see each artist's individual listings.

45s

CAPITOL

Number	Title (A Side/B Side)	Yr	VG	VG+	NM
❑ 5633	I'll Take the Dog/I'd Fight the World	1966	2.00	4.00	8.00
❑ 5769	Mr. Do-It-Yourself/Strangers Nine to Five	1966	2.00	4.00	8.00

Albums

CAPITOL

Number	Title (A Side/B Side)	Yr	VG	VG+	NM
❑ ST 2537 [S]	I'll Take the Dog	1966	5.00	10.00	20.00
❑ T 2537 [M]	I'll Take the Dog	1966	3.75	7.50	15.00

SHEPPARD, T.G.

45s

CAPITOL NASHVILLE

Number	Title (A Side/B Side)	Yr	VG	VG+	NM
❑ 7PRO-79565	Born in a High Wind (same on both sides)	1991	—	3.00	6.00

—Vinyl is promo only

COLUMBIA

Number	Title (A Side/B Side)	Yr	VG	VG+	NM
❑ 38-04890	Fooled Around and Fell in Love/Livin' on the Edge	1985	—	—	3.00
❑ 38-04890 [PS]	Fooled Around and Fell in Love/Livin' on the Edge	1985	—	2.50	5.00
❑ 38-05591	Doncha?/Hunger for You	1985	—	—	3.00
❑ 38-05747	In Over My Heart/A Great Work of Art	1985	—	—	3.00
❑ 38-05905	Strong Heart/What You Gonna Do About Her	1986	—	—	3.00
❑ 38-06347	Half Past Forever (Till I'm Blue in the Heart)/The Bad Thing About Good Love	1986	—	—	3.00
❑ 38-06999	You're My First Lady/Paintin' the Town Blue	1987	—	—	3.00
❑ 38-07312	One for the Money/Come to Me	1987	—	—	3.00
❑ 38-08029	Don't Say It with Diamonds (Say It with Love)/There's a Lot of Heart	1988	—	—	3.00
❑ 38-08119	You Still Do/Something Worth Waiting For	1988	—	—	3.00
❑ 13-08392	One for the Money/You're My First Lady	1988	—	—	3.00
—Gray label reissue					
❑ 13-08404	Strong Heart/Half Past Forever (Till I'm Blue in the Heart)	1988	—	—	3.00
—Gray label reissue					
❑ 13-08405	Doncha?/In Over My Heart	1988	—	—	3.00
—Gray label reissue					
❑ 38-68685	She Didn't Break My Heart/Don't Say It with Diamonds (Say It with Love)	1989	—	—	3.00

CURB

Number	Title (A Side/B Side)	Yr	VG	VG+	NM
❑ D7-76993	I Can Help/Roots of Country	1996	—	2.00	4.00

—B-side by Jeffrey Steele

HITSVILLE

Number	Title (A Side/B Side)	Yr	VG	VG+	NM
❑ 6032	Solitary Man/Shame	1976	—	2.50	5.00
—Originally on Melodyland label					
❑ 6040	Show Me a Man/We Just Live Here (We Don't Love Here Anymore)	1976	—	2.50	5.00
❑ 6048	May I Spend Every New Years with You/I'll Always Remember That Song	1976	—	2.50	5.00
❑ 6053	Lovin' On/I'll Always Remember That Song	1977	—	2.50	5.00

MELODYLAND

Number	Title (A Side/B Side)	Yr	VG	VG+	NM
❑ 6002	Devil in the Bottle/Rollin' with the Flow	1974	—	2.50	5.00
❑ 6006	Tryin' to Beat the Morning Home/I'll Be Satisfied	1975	—	2.50	5.00
❑ 6016	Another Woman/I Can't Help Myself	1975	—	2.50	5.00
❑ 6028	Motels and Memories/Pigskin Charade	1975	—	2.50	5.00
❑ 6032	Solitary Man/Shame	1976	2.50	5.00	10.00

—Quickly reissued on Hitsville label

WARNER BROS.

Number	Title (A Side/B Side)	Yr	VG	VG+	NM
❑ 8490	Mister D.J./Easy to Love	1977	—	2.00	4.00
❑ 8525	Don't Ever Say Good-Bye/She Pretended We Were Married (While I Pretended She Was You)	1978	—	2.00	4.00
❑ 8593	When Can We Do This Again/Jenny, Don't Worry 'Bout the Kid	1978	—	2.00	4.00
❑ 8678	Daylight/Never Ending Crowded Circle	1978	—	2.00	4.00
❑ 8721	Happy Together/That's All She Wrote	1978	—	2.00	4.00
❑ 8808	You Feel Good All Over/I Wish That I Could Hurt That Way Again	1979	—	2.00	4.00
❑ 29071	You're Going Out of My Mind/Heat Lightning	1985	—	2.00	4.00
❑ 29167	One Owner Heart/I Could Get Used to This	1984	—	2.00	4.00
❑ 29343	Make My Day/Lucky We Are	1984	—	2.50	5.00
—A-side with Clint Eastwood					
❑ 29369	Somewhere Down the Line/It's a Bad Night for Good Girls	1984	—	2.00	4.00
❑ 29469	Slow Burn/First Things First	1983	—	2.00	4.00
❑ 29695	Without You/Where Did We Go Right?	1983	—	2.00	4.00
❑ 29934	War Is Hell (On the Homefront Too)/In Another Minute	1982	—	2.00	4.00
❑ 49024	Last Cheater's Waltz/You Do It to Me Every Time	1979	—	2.00	4.00
❑ 49110	I'll Be Coming Back for More/Faster Than I Could Dream	1979	—	2.00	4.00
❑ 49214	Smooth Sailin'/I Came Home to Make Love to You	1980	—	2.00	4.00
❑ 49515	Do You Wanna Go to Heaven/How Far Our Love Goes	1980	—	2.00	4.00
❑ 49615	I Feel Like Loving You Again/Let the Little Bird Fly	1980	—	2.00	4.00
❑ 49690	I Loved 'Em Every One/I Could Never Dream the Way You Feel	1981	—	2.00	4.00
❑ 49761	Party Time/You Waltzed Yourself Right Into My Life	1981	—	2.00	4.00
❑ 49858	Only One You/We Belong in Love Tonight	1981	—	2.00	4.00
❑ 50041	Finally/All My Cloudy Days Are Gone	1982	—	2.00	4.00

Albums

COLUMBIA

Number	Title (A Side/B Side)	Yr	VG	VG+	NM
❑ FC 40007	Livin' on the Edge	1985	2.00	4.00	8.00
❑ FC 40310	It Still Rains in Memphis	1986	2.00	4.00	8.00
❑ FC 40796	1ne 4 the $	1987	2.00	4.00	8.00
❑ FC 44307	Biggest Hits (1985-1987)	1988	2.00	4.00	8.00
❑ FC 44421	Crossroads	1989	2.50	5.00	10.00

HITSVILLE

Number	Title (A Side/B Side)	Yr	VG	VG+	NM
❑ H6-404S1	Solitary Man	1976	3.00	6.00	12.00

MELODYLAND

Number	Title (A Side/B Side)	Yr	VG	VG+	NM
❑ ME6-401S1	T.G. Sheppard	1975	3.00	6.00	12.00
❑ ME6-403S1	Motels and Memories	1976	3.00	6.00	12.00

WARNER BROS.

Number	Title (A Side/B Side)	Yr	VG	VG+	NM
❑ BSK 3133	T.G.	1978	2.50	5.00	10.00
—"Burbank" palm trees label					
❑ BSK 3133	T.G.	1979	2.00	4.00	8.00
—White label					
❑ BSK 3259	Daylight	1978	2.00	4.00	8.00
❑ BSK 3353	3/4 Lonely	1979	2.00	4.00	8.00
❑ BSK 3423	Smooth Sailin'	1980	2.00	4.00	8.00
❑ BSK 3528	I Love 'Em All	1981	2.00	4.00	8.00
❑ BSK 3600	Finally!	1982	2.00	4.00	8.00
❑ 23726	Perfect Stranger	1982	2.00	4.00	8.00

Number	Title (A Side/B Side)	Yr	VG	VG+	NM
❑ 23841	T.G. Sheppard's Greatest Hits	1983	2.00	4.00	8.00
❑ 23911	Slow Burn	1983	2.00	4.00	8.00
❑ 25149	One Owner Heart	1984	2.00	4.00	8.00
❑ 25282	T.G.	1985	2.00	4.00	8.00
❑ 25329	Greatest Hits, Volume 2	1985	2.00	4.00	8.00

SHEPPARD, T.G., AND KAREN BROOKS

Also see each artist's individual listings.

45s

WARNER BROS.

Number	Title (A Side/B Side)	Yr	VG	VG+	NM
❑ 29854	Faking Love/Reno and Me	1982	—	2.00	4.00

SHERLEY, GLEN

45s

MEGA

Number	Title (A Side/B Side)	Yr	VG	VG+	NM
❑ 0027	Greystone Chapel//Dialogue/Looking Back in Anger	1971	—	3.00	6.00
❑ 0041	Pud 'n' Tane/Look for Me	1971	—	3.00	6.00
❑ 0061	Robin/Just to Be That Close to You	1972	—	3.00	6.00

Albums

MEGA

Number	Title (A Side/B Side)	Yr	VG	VG+	NM
❑ 1006	Glen Sherley	1971	3.00	6.00	12.00

SHIBLEY, ARKIE

45s

4 STAR

Number	Title (A Side/B Side)	Yr	VG	VG+	NM
❑ 1737	Pick Pick Pickin' (My Guitar)/I'm a Poor Oakie	1959	7.50	15.00	30.00
❑ 1746	The House Next Door/In My Travels	1960	—	—	—
—Canceled					

GILT EDGE

Number	Title (A Side/B Side)	Yr	VG	VG+	NM
❑ 5021	Hot Rod Race/I'm Living Alone with an Old Love	1950	25.00	50.00	100.00
❑ 5030	Hot Rod Race No. 2/I Wish I Was Somebody's Rose	1951	25.00	50.00	100.00
❑ 5036	Arkie Meets the Judge (Hot Rod Race No. 3)/ Uncle Sam Has Called My Number	1951	25.00	50.00	100.00
❑ 5047	Hot Rod Race No. 4 (The Guy in the Mercury)/ This Feeling You Brought Over Me	1951	25.00	50.00	100.00
❑ 5054	Hot Rod Race No. 5 (The Kid in the Model-A)/My Beautiful Washington Rose	1951	25.00	50.00	100.00
❑ 5059	Shore Leave/Guitar Hoedown	1952	15.00	30.00	60.00
❑ 5065	Arkie's Letter from Home/Five String Banjo March	1952	15.00	30.00	60.00
❑ 5072	Three Day Pass/Hot Woodpecker Rag	1953	12.50	25.00	50.00
❑ 5078	Arkie's Talking Blues/Blue Guitar Ramble	1953	12.50	25.00	50.00
❑ 5089	Hard Times in Arkansas/Dusty Blossom Boogie	1954	12.50	25.00	50.00

Selected 78s

MOUNTAIN DEW

Number	Title (A Side/B Side)	Yr	VG	VG+	NM
❑ 101	Hot Rod Race/(B-side unknown)	1950	37.50	75.00	150.00
—Original issue of this song; unknown on 45 rpm					

SHINER, MERVIN

Also recorded as "Merv Shiner" and "Murv Shiner" (included below)

45s

CERTRON

Number	Title (A Side/B Side)	Yr	VG	VG+	NM
❑ 10012	Teach Your Children/Protest	1970	—	3.50	7.00

CORAL

Number	Title (A Side/B Side)	Yr	VG	VG+	NM
❑ 9-61080	I Dreamt That I Was Santa Claus/Don't Wait Until the Night Before Christmas	1953	5.00	10.00	20.00
❑ 9-64163	I'm Just Here to Get My Baby Out of Jail/ Castaway	1953	6.25	12.50	25.00
❑ 9-64170	Our Heart Breaking Waltz/River of Silver	1954	6.25	12.50	25.00
❑ 9-64178	Hide-Away/Bells of Memory	1954	6.25	12.50	25.00
—With Rusty Keefer					

DECCA

Number	Title (A Side/B Side)	Yr	VG	VG+	NM
❑ 9-28121	Almost/Let's Take a Trip to the Moon	1952	5.00	10.00	20.00
—With Grady Martin					
❑ 9-28220	Your Heart Is Too Crowded/The Man in the Moon Cried Last Night	1952	5.00	10.00	20.00
❑ 9-28424	Our Love Isn't Legal/Settin' the Woods on Fire	1952	5.00	10.00	20.00
—With Grady Martin					
❑ 9-28466	Landslide of Love/Me Without You	1952	5.00	10.00	20.00
❑ 9-28504	I Saw Mommy Kissing Santa Claus/Snowy White Snow-Jingle Bells	1952	6.25	12.50	25.00
❑ 9-28808	Candy Man/Candy Round-Up	1953	5.00	10.00	20.00
❑ 9-29363	Lord I'm Coming Home/Pass Me Not	1954	5.00	10.00	20.00
❑ 9-46221	Peter Cottontail/Floppy	1950	7.50	15.00	30.00
❑ 9-46231	Francis the Talking Mule/Me and My Teddy Bear	1950	7.50	15.00	30.00
❑ 9-46244	Little Liza Lou/Gra Mamou	1950	7.50	15.00	30.00
❑ 9-46253	Slippin' Around with Jole Blon/Steppin' Out	1950	7.50	15.00	30.00
❑ 9-46260	I Think I'm Gonna Cry Again/Ace in the Hole	1950	6.25	12.50	25.00
❑ 9-46272	The Lightning Express/Sweet Mama Blues	1950	6.25	12.50	25.00
❑ 9-46273	Walking with the Blues/Beloved, Be Faithful	1950	6.25	12.50	25.00
—With Eddie Crosby					
❑ 9-46274	I Overlooked an Orchid/If You've Got the Money (I've Got the Time)	1950	7.50	15.00	30.00
❑ 9-46280	Santa, Santa Don't Be Mad At Me/Fee Fi Fiddle	1950	6.25	12.50	25.00
❑ 9-46337	If Teardrops Were Pennies/Let's Live a Little	1951	6.25	12.50	25.00
❑ 9-46345	Ball and Chain Boogie/Memories of Mockingbird Hill	1951	7.50	15.00	30.00

LITTLE DARLIN'

Number	Title (A Side/B Side)	Yr	VG	VG+	NM
❑ 0065	In the Ghetto/El Bandito	1970	2.00	4.00	8.00
❑ 0068	Ain't That Sad/You Can Tell the World	1970	2.00	4.00	8.00

MGM

Number	Title (A Side/B Side)	Yr	VG	VG+	NM
❑ 13704	Big Brother/Big Shot, the Pool Shark	1967	2.00	4.00	8.00
❑ 13900	I'd Rather Be a Fool/How Are You, Brown Eyes	1968	2.00	4.00	8.00
❑ 14007	Too Hard to Say I'm Sorry/Tecumseh Valley	1968	—	3.50	7.00

RCA VICTOR

Number	Title (A Side/B Side)	Yr	VG	VG+	NM
❑ 47-5938	Mister Sandman/Penny Candy	1954	5.00	10.00	20.00
❑ 47-5983	Love with No Tomorrow/It's Nothin'	1955	5.00	10.00	20.00
❑ 47-6171	I Ain't Much of a Hand at Lovin'/Don't Believe	1955	5.00	10.00	20.00
❑ 47-6328	We're Off on a Race/You're Free to Go	1955	5.00	10.00	20.00

Selected 78s

DECCA

Number	Title (A Side/B Side)	Yr	VG	VG+	NM
❑ 46178	Why Don't You Haul Off and Love Me/Soft Lips	1949	5.00	10.00	20.00
❑ 46192	That's Christmas/An Old Christmas Card	1949	5.00	10.00	20.00
—With Nelson King					
❑ 46195	My Bucket's Got a Hole in It/Take a Little Silver	1949	5.00	10.00	20.00
❑ 46203	(I Won't Go Huntin' With You Jake) But I'll Go Chasin' Women/Anticipation Blues	1950	3.75	7.50	15.00
❑ 46210	Old Kentucky Waltz/I'm Gonna Tie a String	1950	3.75	7.50	15.00
❑ 46220	The Cry of the Wild Goose/Dust	1950	3.75	7.50	15.00

Albums

LITTLE DARLIN'

Number	Title (A Side/B Side)	Yr	VG	VG+	NM
❑ 8018	In the Ghetto	1970	3.75	7.50	15.00

SHIRLEY, DANNY

Also see CONFEDERATE RAILROAD.

45s

AMOR

Number	Title (A Side/B Side)	Yr	VG	VG+	NM
❑ 1002	Love and Let Love/(B-side unknown)	1984	—	3.50	7.00
❑ 1005	Christmas Needs Love to Be Christmas/(B-side unknown)	1984	—	3.50	7.00
❑ 1006	Yo Yo (The Right String But the Wrong Yo Yo)/ (B-side unknown)	1985	2.50	5.00	10.00
—With Piano Red					
❑ 2001	Deep Down (Everybody Wants to Be from Dixie)/ (B-side unknown)	1987	—	3.00	6.00
❑ 2002	Going to California/(B-side unknown)	1987	—	3.00	6.00
❑ 2004	I Make the Living (She Makes the Living Worthwhile)/(B-side unknown)	1988	—	3.00	6.00

SHIRLEY AND SQUIRRELY

45s

GRT

Number	Title (A Side/B Side)	Yr	VG	VG+	NM
❑ 054	Hey Shirley (This Is Squirrely)/(Instrumental)	1976	—	3.00	6.00
❑ 105	A Squirrely Christmas/Deck The Halls	1976	2.00	4.00	8.00

SHONDELL, TROY

45s

AVM

Number	Title (A Side/B Side)	Yr	VG	VG+	NM
❑ 14	(I'm Looking for Some) New Blue Jeans/(B-side unknown)	1988	—	3.50	7.00

BEAR

Number	Title (A Side/B Side)	Yr	VG	VG+	NM
❑ 2002	No One Knows/Sweet Enough	1989	—	3.00	6.00

BRITE STAR

Number	Title (A Side/B Side)	Yr	VG	VG+	NM
❑ 2453	This Time/You're Nobody's Child	1973	2.00	4.00	8.00
❑ 2459	Still Loving You/Rip It Up	1973	2.00	4.00	8.00
❑ 4691	Deeper and Deeper in Love/Love Stuff	1974	2.00	4.00	8.00

DECCA

Number	Title (A Side/B Side)	Yr	VG	VG+	NM
❑ 31712	You Can't Catch Me/Walkin' in a Memory	1964	2.50	5.00	10.00

EVEREST

Number	Title (A Side/B Side)	Yr	VG	VG+	NM
❑ 2015	Gone/Some People Never Learn	1963	2.50	5.00	10.00
❑ 2018	I've Got a Woman/No Fool Like an Old Fool	1963	2.50	5.00	10.00
❑ 2041	Trouble/Little Miss Tease	1964	2.50	5.00	10.00

GAYE

Number	Title (A Side/B Side)	Yr	VG	VG+	NM
❑ 2010	This Time/I Catch Myself Crying	1961	20.00	40.00	80.00

GOLDCREST

Number	Title (A Side/B Side)	Yr	VG	VG+	NM
❑ 161-A	This Time/Girl After Girl	1961	7.50	15.00	30.00
—With no "Distributed by Liberty" on label					
❑ 161-A	This Time/Girl After Girl	1961	6.25	12.50	25.00
—With "Distributed by Liberty Record Sales" on label					

ITCO

Number	Title (A Side/B Side)	Yr	VG	VG+	NM
❑ 105	And We Made Love/Imitation Woman	198?	—	2.50	5.00

LIBERTY

Number	Title (A Side/B Side)	Yr	VG	VG+	NM
❑ 55353	This Time/Girl After Girl	1961	5.00	10.00	20.00
❑ 55392	Tears from an Angel/Island in the Sky	1961	4.00	8.00	16.00
❑ 55445	Just Because/Na-No-No	1962	4.00	8.00	16.00

RIC

Number	Title (A Side/B Side)	Yr	VG	VG+	NM
❑ 174	Just a Dream/Just Like Me	1965	2.50	5.00	10.00
❑ 184	Big Windy City/I Thought That You Were Mine	1966	2.50	5.00	10.00

STAR-FOX

Number	Title (A Side/B Side)	Yr	VG	VG+	NM
❑ 77	Still Loving You/Doctor Love	1979	2.00	4.00	8.00

TELESONIC

Number	Title (A Side/B Side)	Yr	VG	VG+	NM
❑ 804	(Sittin' Here) Lovin' You/(Here I Am) Single Again	1980	2.00	4.00	8.00

TRX

Number	Title (A Side/B Side)	Yr	VG	VG+	NM
❑ 5001	A Rose and a Baby Ruth/Here It Comes Again	1967	2.00	4.00	8.00
❑ 5003	Head Man/She's Got Everything She Needs	1967	2.00	4.00	8.00
❑ 5015	Let's Go All the Way/Let Me Love You	1968	2.00	4.00	8.00
❑ 5019	Something's Wrong in Indiana/A Rose and a Baby Ruth	1969	2.00	4.00	8.00

Albums

EVEREST

Number	Title (A Side/B Side)	Yr	VG	VG+	NM
❑ SDBR-1206 [S]	The Many Sides of Troy Shondell	1963	20.00	40.00	80.00
❑ LPBR-5206 [M]	The Many Sides of Troy Shondell	1963	12.50	25.00	50.00

SUNSET

Number	Title (A Side/B Side)	Yr	VG	VG+	NM
❑ SUM-1174 [M]	This Time	1967	3.75	7.50	15.00
❑ SUS-5174 [S]	This Time	1967	3.75	7.50	15.00

SHOOTERS, THE
45s
EPIC

Number	Title (A Side/B Side)	Yr	VG	VG+	NM
❑ 34-06623	They Only Come Out at Night/Remote Control	1987	—	—	3.00
❑ 34-07131	'Til the Old Wears Off/Some Fools Were Made to Be Broken	1987	—	—	3.00
❑ 34-07367	Tell It to Your Teddy Bear/Dancing Alone	1987	—	—	3.00
❑ 34-07684	I Taught Her Everything She Knows About Love/I'll Cry Instead	1988	—	—	3.00
❑ 34-08082	Borderline/She's Steppin' Out	1988	—	—	3.00
❑ 34-68587	If I Ever Go Crazy/Leave and Learn	1989	—	—	3.00
❑ 34-68955	You Just Can't Lose 'Em All/If I Were You	1989	—	—	3.00

Albums
EPIC

Number	Title (A Side/B Side)	Yr	VG	VG+	NM
❑ FE 40885	The Shooters	1987	2.00	4.00	8.00
❑ FE 44326	Solid as a Rock	1989	2.50	5.00	10.00

SHOPPE, THE
45s
AMERICAN COUNTRY

Number	Title (A Side/B Side)	Yr	VG	VG+	NM
❑ 2	If You Think I Love You Now/(B-side unknown)	1984	—	3.00	6.00
❑ 3	Hurts All Over/(B-side unknown)	1985	—	3.00	6.00
MTM					
❑ B-72056	Holdin' the Family Together/The Sky Is Falling	1985	—	2.00	4.00
❑ B-72063	While the Moon's in Town/There's a Fire Inside	1985	—	2.00	4.00
❑ B-72069	Ain't Gonna Do You No Good/We'd Never Make It on the Outside	1986	—	2.00	4.00
NSD					
❑ 80	Doesn't Anybody Get High on Love Anymore/Paralyzed	1981	—	2.50	5.00
❑ 90	Dream Maker/Up to My Heart in Love	1981	—	2.50	5.00
❑ 122	Odds Are I'll Get Even/She Loves My Troubles Away	1982	—	2.50	5.00
RAINBOW SOUND					
❑ 8019	Three Way Love/Livin' in Your Lovin'	1980	—	3.00	6.00
❑ 8022	Star Studded Nights/The South's Gonna Rise Again	1980	—	3.00	6.00

Albums
MTM

Number	Title (A Side/B Side)	Yr	VG	VG+	NM
❑ ST-71051	The Shoppe	1986	2.50	5.00	10.00

SHRUM, WALTER, AND HIS COLORADO HILLBILLIES
Selected 78s
COAST

Number	Title (A Side/B Side)	Yr	VG	VG+	NM
❑ 2010	Triflin' Gal/You Two-Timed Me Once Too Often	1945	10.00	20.00	40.00

SHURFIRE
45s
AIR

Number	Title (A Side/B Side)	Yr	VG	VG+	NM
❑ 173	Bringin' the House Down/My Heart's in Louisiana	1987	—	2.50	5.00
❑ 180	Roll the Dice/I Want Some	1987	—	2.50	5.00
❑ 181	First in Line/(B-side unknown)	1988	—	2.50	5.00

SHYLO
45s
COLUMBIA

Number	Title (A Side/B Side)	Yr	VG	VG+	NM
❑ 3-10102	Fine Lovin' Woman/Sugar Love	1975	—	3.00	6.00
❑ 3-10267	Dog Tired of Cattin' Around/Heartbeat	1976	—	2.50	5.00
❑ 3-10343	Livin' on Love Street/Beyond the Sun	1976	—	2.50	5.00
❑ 3-10398	Ol' Man River (I've Come to Talk Again)/Showdown	1976	—	2.50	5.00
❑ 3-10456	Drinkin' My Way Back Home/Didn't Get No Lovin'	1976	—	2.50	5.00
❑ 3-10534	(I'm Coming Home to You) Dixie/Whiskey Fever	1977	—	2.50	5.00
❑ 3-10647	Gotta Travel On/The Drifter	1977	—	2.50	5.00
❑ 3-10918	Freckles/Wait Until Dark	1979	—	2.50	5.00
❑ 3-11048	I'm Puttin' My Love Inside You/What Kind of Dance Is That	1979	—	2.50	5.00
MERCURY					
❑ 76151	Crime in the Sheets/(I Wish You'd) Love Me Alone	1982	—	2.00	4.00
❑ 76171	Ain't That Fine/(B-side unknown)	1982	—	2.00	4.00

Albums
COLUMBIA

Number	Title (A Side/B Side)	Yr	VG	VG+	NM
❑ PC 34161	Flower of the South	1976	3.00	6.00	12.00

SIDE OF THE ROAD GANG, THE
45s
CAPITOL

Number	Title (A Side/B Side)	Yr	VG	VG+	NM
❑ 4298	Suitcase Life/Sittin' by the Side of the Road	1976	—	2.50	5.00
❑ 4338	What Am I Doin' Hangin' 'Round/People in Dallas Got Hair	1976	—	2.50	5.00

Albums
CAPITOL

Number	Title (A Side/B Side)	Yr	VG	VG+	NM
❑ ST-11526	The Side of the Road Gang	1976	3.00	6.00	12.00

SIERRA
45s
AWESOME

Number	Title (A Side/B Side)	Yr	VG	VG+	NM
❑ 101	Branded Man/Northern Lights	1984	—	3.00	6.00
❑ 106	Love Is the Reason/I'd Do It in a Heartbeat	1984	—	3.00	6.00
❑ 110	The Almighty Lover/How Many Angels	1985	—	3.00	6.00
❑ 111	What Two Hearts Can Do/(B-side unknown)	1985	—	3.00	6.00
CARDINAL					
❑ 052	Old Fashioned Lovin'/(B-side unknown)	1983	—	3.50	7.00
MUSICOM					
❑ 52701	Keep On Playin' That Country Music/(B-side unknown)	1983	—	3.50	7.00
❑ 52702	I'd Do It in a Heart Beat/(B-side unknown)	1983	—	3.50	7.00

SILVER CITY BAND
45s
COLUMBIA

Number	Title (A Side/B Side)	Yr	VG	VG+	NM
❑ 3-10601	If You Really Want Me To I'll Go/Georgia Girl	1977	—	2.50	5.00
❑ 3-10759	I'm Still Missing You/Valentine Partner	1978	—	2.50	5.00

SILVER CREEK
45s
CARDINAL

Number	Title (A Side/B Side)	Yr	VG	VG+	NM
❑ 8102	You and Me and Tennessee/(B-side unknown)	1981	—	3.00	6.00
—As "Roger Ivie and Silvercreek"					
❑ 8103	Lonely Women/(B-side unknown)	1981	—	3.00	6.00

SIMMONS, "JUMPIN'" GENE
Some were released as "Gene Simmons." He is no relation to the Gene Simmons of the rock band Kiss.

45s
AGP

Number	Title (A Side/B Side)	Yr	VG	VG+	NM
❑ 119	Back Home Again/Don't Worry About Me	1969	2.00	4.00	8.00
CHECKER					
❑ 948	Bad Boy Willie/Goin' Back to Memphis	1960	3.00	6.00	12.00
DELTUNE					
❑ 1201	Why Didn't I Think of That/Tennessee Party Time	1977	2.00	4.00	8.00
—As "Gene Simmons"					
EPIC					
❑ 10601	She's There When I Come Home/Magnolia Street	1970	—	3.00	6.00
HI					
❑ 2034	Teddy Bear/Your True Love	1961	2.50	5.00	10.00
❑ 2050	Caldonia/Be Her Number One	1962	2.50	5.00	10.00
❑ 2076	Haunted House/Hey, Hey Little Girl	1964	3.75	7.50	15.00
—As "Gene Simmons"					
❑ 2076	Haunted House/Hey, Hey Little Girl	1964	3.75	7.50	15.00
—As "Jumpin' Gene Simmons"					
❑ 2080	The Dodo/The Jump	1964	2.50	5.00	10.00
❑ 2086	Skinnie Minnie/I'm a Ramblin' Man	1965	2.50	5.00	10.00
❑ 2092	Mattie Rae/Folsom Prison Blues	1965	2.50	5.00	10.00
❑ 2102	The Batman/Bossy Boss	1966	3.75	7.50	15.00
❑ 2113	Go On Shoes/Keep That Meat in the Pan	1966	2.50	5.00	10.00
MALA					
❑ 12012	I'm Just a Loser/Lila	1968	2.50	5.00	10.00
SANDY					
❑ 1027	The Waiting Game/Shenandoah Waltz	1959	5.00	10.00	20.00
—As "Morris Gene Simmons"					
SUN					
❑ 299	Drinkin' Wine/I Done Told You	1958	37.50	75.00	150.00
—As "Gene Simmons"					

Albums
HI

Number	Title (A Side/B Side)	Yr	VG	VG+	NM
❑ HL 2018 [M]	Jumpin' Gene Simmons	1964	12.50	25.00	50.00
❑ SHL 32018 [S]	Jumpin' Gene Simmons	1964	17.50	35.00	70.00

SIMON, CARLY
The pop singer-songwriter had the below country hit.

45s
ELEKTRA

Number	Title (A Side/B Side)	Yr	VG	VG+	NM
❑ 45506	Devoted to You/Boys in the Trees	1978	—	2.00	4.00
—A-side with James Taylor					

SIMON AND VERITY
45s
EMI AMERICA

Number	Title (A Side/B Side)	Yr	VG	VG+	NM
❑ B-8257	We've Still Got Love/In Love and Out of Danger	1985	—	2.00	4.00
❑ B-8264	Your Eyes/In Love and Out of Danger	1985	—	2.00	4.00

SIMPSON, JENNY
45s
MERCURY

Number	Title (A Side/B Side)	Yr	VG	VG+	NM
❑ 566476-7	Ticket Out of Kansas/Til Then	1998	—	—	3.00

SIMPSON, RED
45s
CAPITOL

Number	Title (A Side/B Side)	Yr	VG	VG+	NM
❑ 2035	He Reminds Me a Whole Lot of Me/Honky Tonk Women	1967	2.00	4.00	8.00
❑ 3236	I'm a Truck/Where Love Used to Be	1971	—	3.50	7.00
❑ 3298	Country Western Truck Drivin' Singer/You're the First	1972	—	3.50	7.00
❑ 3364	Truckin' On Down the Road/Hold On Ma'am	1972	—	3.50	7.00
❑ 3495	Milesaver Man/Those Forgotten Trains	1972	—	3.50	7.00
❑ 3616	Awful Lot to Learn About Truck Drivin'/You Still Got a Hold on Me	1973	—	3.50	7.00
❑ 3745	I'm a Pretty Good Man/Bill Woods from Bakersfield	1973	—	3.50	7.00
❑ 3778	Truckin' Trees for Christmas/Blue Blue Christmas	1973	2.00	4.00	8.00
❑ 3807	If the World Ran Out of Diesel/Certainly	1973	—	3.50	7.00
❑ 3872	Honky Tonk Lady's Lovin' Man/Yip Yip	1974	—	3.00	6.00
❑ 5577	Roll Truck Roll/Runaway Truck	1966	2.50	5.00	10.00
❑ 5637	The Highway Patrol/Big Mack	1966	2.50	5.00	10.00

Number	Title (A Side/B Side)	Yr	VG	VG+	NM
❑ 5717	Sidewalk Patrol/I'm Turning In My Star	1966	2.00	4.00	8.00
❑ 5783	Diesel Smoke, Dangerous Curves/I'm Gonna Write Momma for Money	1966	2.50	5.00	10.00
❑ 5881	Jeannie with the Light Brown Cadillac/I've Just Lost You	1967	2.00	4.00	8.00
❑ 5956	Party Girl/Mini-Skirt Minnie	1967	2.00	4.00	8.00
K.E.Y.					
❑ 108	The Flying Saucer and the Truck Driver/I Miss You a Little	1979	2.50	5.00	10.00
WARNER BROS.					
❑ 8259	Truck Driver's Heaven/It Ain't Even Halloween	1976	—	3.00	6.00
Albums					
CAPITOL					
❑ ST-881	I'm a Truck	1972	3.75	7.50	15.00
❑ ST 2468 [S]	Roll, Truck, Roll	1966	5.00	10.00	20.00
❑ T 2468 [M]	Roll, Truck, Roll	1966	3.75	7.50	15.00
❑ ST 2569 [S]	The Man Behind the Badge	1966	5.00	10.00	20.00
❑ T 2569 [M]	The Man Behind the Badge	1966	3.75	7.50	15.00
❑ ST 2691 [S]	Truck Drivin' Fool	1967	5.00	10.00	20.00
❑ T 2691 [M]	Truck Drivin' Fool	1967	5.00	10.00	20.00
❑ ST 2829 [S]	A Bakersfield Dozen	1967	5.00	10.00	20.00
❑ T 2829 [M]	A Bakersfield Dozen	1967	6.25	12.50	25.00
❑ ST-11093	The Very Real Red Simpson	1973	3.75	7.50	15.00
❑ ST-11231	A Trucker's Christmas	1973	3.75	7.50	15.00
PORTLAND					
❑ 1005 [M]	Hello, I'm a Truck	1965	20.00	40.00	80.00
SEA SHELL					
❑ 16253	Ramblin' Road	198?	3.00	6.00	12.00

SINGING MCENTIRES, THE (PAKE, REBA AND SUSIE)

45s

Number	Title (A Side/B Side)	Yr	VG	VG+	NM
BOSS					
❑ SPS-194	The Ballad of John McEntire/Interview by the Grandchildren	1969	125.00	250.00	500.00

—Supposedly only 25 copies were pressed

SINGLETARY, DARYLE

45s

Number	Title (A Side/B Side)	Yr	VG	VG+	NM
GIANT					
❑ 7-17172	My Baby's Lovin'/Miracle in the Making	1998	—	—	3.00
❑ 7-17268	The Note/I Let Her Lie	1997	—	—	3.00
❑ 7-17399	The Used to Be's/That's What I Get for Thinkin'	1997	—	—	3.00
❑ 7-17650	Workin' It Out/What Am I Doing There	1996	—	—	3.00
❑ 7-17818	I Let Her Lie/Ordinary Heroes	1995	—	2.00	4.00
❑ 7-17902	I'm Living Up to Her Low Expectations/My Heart's Too Broke (To Pay Attention)	1995	—	—	3.00

SINGLETON, MARGIE

Also see LEON ASHLEY; GEORGE JONES.

45s

Number	Title (A Side/B Side)	Yr	VG	VG+	NM
ASHLEY					
❑ 200	The Little Girl I Didn't Have the Courage to Keep/Seemed You'd Never Been Good	197?	2.00	4.00	8.00
❑ 2000	Sooner or Later/Angel Hands	1967	2.50	5.00	10.00
❑ 2011	Ode to Billie Joe/Big Boys Don't Need Mamas	1967	2.50	5.00	10.00
❑ 2050	Wandering Mind/Your Conscience Sends Me Flowers	1968	2.50	5.00	10.00
❑ 2090	Chill Winds/Little Darlin'	1968	2.50	5.00	10.00
❑ 5000	Harper Valley P.T.A./(B-side unknown)	1968	2.50	5.00	10.00
❑ 7500	Jesus Is My Pusher/Lord Take Me Right Now	1969	2.50	5.00	10.00
❑ 35002	All That Love Is Gone/Blindness of the Wife	197?	—	3.00	6.00
❑ 35006	Enough of a Woman/Dreaming Bigger Than You	197?	—	3.00	6.00
❑ 35012	I Guess I've Just Loved You Too Long/The Well's Not Dry	197?	—	3.00	6.00
D					
❑ 1007	I Want to Be Where You're Gonna Be/Shattered Kingdom	1958	7.50	15.00	30.00
MERCURY					
❑ 71359	Oo-Wee, You're the One for Me/Teddy	1958	5.00	10.00	20.00
❑ 71672	Destination Love/Toss a Pebble	1960	3.75	7.50	15.00
❑ 71733	She Will Break Your Heart/Voices of Love	1960	3.75	7.50	15.00
❑ 71814	Your Old Love Letters/Are You Ever Too Young	1961	3.00	6.00	12.00
❑ 71928	I'll Just Walk On By/Her Image Keeps Getting in the Way	1962	3.00	6.00	12.00
❑ 72002	Chained to a Promise/Living in the Danger Zone	1962	3.00	6.00	12.00
❑ 72079	Magic Star (Telstar)/Only Your Shadow Knows	1963	3.00	6.00	12.00
❑ 72124	I Don't Have to Look Pretty/Walkin' Back to Happiness	1963	3.00	6.00	12.00
❑ 72213	Old Records/How Do You Say Goodbye	1963	3.00	6.00	12.00
❑ 72268	Forget Me Not/I Don't Want You This Way	1964	3.00	6.00	12.00
❑ 72363	Don't Be Good to Me/It's Too Much	1964	3.00	6.00	12.00
STARDAY					
❑ 287	One Step Nearer to You/Not What He's Got	1957	6.25	12.50	25.00
❑ 309	My Picture of You/Love Is a Treasure	1957	6.25	12.50	25.00
❑ 323	Beautiful Dawn/Take Time Out for Love	1957	6.25	12.50	25.00
❑ 443	Nothin' But True Love/It's Better to Know	1959	5.00	10.00	20.00
❑ 472	The Eyes of Love/Angel Hands	1959	5.00	10.00	20.00
❑ 502	For the Love of Jim/My Special Dream	1960	5.00	10.00	20.00
UNITED ARTISTS					
❑ 896	What Could I Do/You Shake My Hand and Kiss Me on the Cheek	1965	2.50	5.00	10.00
❑ 939	I'm Guilty This Time/You Took the Easy Way Out	1965	2.50	5.00	10.00
Albums					
ASHLEY					
❑ 3003	Margie Singleton Sings Country Music with Soul	1968	3.75	7.50	15.00
PICKWICK					
❑ SPC-3133	Harper Valley P.T.A.	197?	2.50	5.00	10.00
UNITED ARTISTS					
❑ UAL-3459 [M]	Crying Time	1965	3.75	7.50	15.00
❑ UAS-6459 [S]	Crying Time	1965	5.00	10.00	20.00

SINGLETON, MARGIE, AND FARON YOUNG

Also see each artist's individual listings.

45s

Number	Title (A Side/B Side)	Yr	VG	VG+	NM
MERCURY					
❑ 72237	Keeping Up with the Joneses/No Thanks, I Just Had One	1964	3.00	6.00	12.00
❑ 72237 [PS]	Keeping Up with the Joneses/No Thanks, I Just Had One	1964	5.00	10.00	20.00
❑ 72312	Another Woman's Man — Another Man's Woman/Honky Tonk Happy	1964	3.00	6.00	12.00

SKAGGS, RICKY

45s

Number	Title (A Side/B Side)	Yr	VG	VG+	NM
EPIC					
❑ 19-02034	Don't Get Above Your Raising/Low and Lonely	1981	—	2.00	4.00
❑ 14-02499	You May See Me Walkin'/So Round, So Firm, So Fully Packed	1981	—	2.00	4.00
❑ 14-02692	Crying My Heart Out Over You/Lost to a Stranger	1982	—	2.00	4.00
❑ 14-02931	I Don't Care/If That's the Way You Feel	1982	—	2.00	4.00
❑ 15-03096	Don't Get Above Your Raising/You May See Me Walkin'	1982	—	—	3.00
—Gray label reissue					
❑ 34-03212	Heartbroke/Don't Think I'll Cry	1982	—	2.00	4.00
❑ ENR-03265	Heartbroke	1982	—	3.50	7.00
—One-sided budget release					
❑ 34-03482	I Wouldn't Change You If I Could/One Way Rider	1982	—	2.00	4.00
❑ ENR-03491	I Wouldn't Change You If I Could	1982	—	3.50	7.00
—One-sided budget release					
❑ 34-03812	Highway 40 Blues/Don't Let Your Sweet Love Die	1983	—	2.00	4.00
❑ 34-04044	You've Got a Lover/Let's Love the Bad Times Away	1983	—	2.00	4.00
❑ 34-04668	Something in My Heart/Baby, I'm in Love with You	1984	—	2.00	4.00
❑ 34-04831	Country Boy/Wheel Hoss	1985	—	2.00	4.00
❑ 34-05585	You Make Me Feel Like a Man/Rendezvous	1985	—	2.00	4.00
❑ 34-05748	Cajun Moon/Rockin' the Boat	1985	—	2.00	4.00
❑ 34-05898	I've Got a New Heartache/She Didn't Say Why	1986	—	2.00	4.00
❑ 34-06327	Love's Gonna Get You Someday/Walkin' in Jerusalem	1986	—	2.00	4.00
❑ 34-06650	I Wonder If I Care As Much/Raisin' the Dickens	1987	—	2.00	4.00
❑ 34-07060	Love Can't Ever Get Better Than This/Daddy Was a Hardworking, Honest Man	1987	—	2.00	4.00
—With Sharon White					
❑ 34-07416	I'm Tired/San Antonio Rose	1987	—	2.00	4.00
❑ 34-07721	(Angel on My Mind) That's Why I'm Walkin'/Lord, She Sure Is Good at Lovin' Me	1988	—	2.00	4.00
❑ 34-07924	Thanks Again/If You Don't Believe the Bible	1988	—	2.00	4.00
❑ 34-08063	Old Kind of Love/Woman You Won't Break Mine	1988	—	2.00	4.00
❑ 15-08454	Cajun Moon/Love's Gonna Get You Someday	1988	—	—	3.00
—Gray label reissue					
❑ 15-08459	I've Got a New Heartache/Love Can't Ever Get Better Than This	1988	—	—	3.00
—Gray label reissue					
❑ 15-08464	Country Boy/You Make Me Feel Like a Man	1988	—	—	3.00
—Gray label reissue					
❑ 34-68693	Lovin' Only Me/Home Is Wherever You Are	1989	—	2.00	4.00
—B-side with Sharon White					
❑ 34-68995	Let It Be You/The Fields of Home	1989	—	2.00	4.00
❑ 34-73078	Heartbreak Hurricane/Casting My Shadows in the Road	1989	—	2.00	4.00
❑ 34-73312	Hummingbird/Kentucky Thunder	1990	—	2.00	4.00
❑ 34-73496	He Was On to Somethin' (So He Made You)/When I Love	1990	—	2.00	4.00
❑ 34-73947	Life's Too Long (To Live Like This)/Lonesome for You	1991	—	2.00	4.00
❑ 34-74147	Same Ol' Love/My Father's Son	1991	—	2.00	4.00
❑ 34-74311	From the Word Love/You Can't Take It With You When You Go	1992	—	2.00	4.00
SUGAR HILL					
❑ 3706	I'll Take the Blame/Could You Love Me One More Time	1980	2.50	5.00	10.00
SUGAR HILL/EPIC					
❑ 34-04245	Don't Cheat in Our Hometown/Children Go	1983	—	2.00	4.00
❑ 34-04394	Honey (Open That Door)/She's More to Be Pitied	1984	—	2.00	4.00
❑ 34-04527	Uncle Pen/I'm Head Over Heels in Love	1984	—	2.00	4.00
Albums					
ATLANTIC					
❑ 82834	Solid Ground	1995	3.75	7.50	15.00
EPIC					
❑ EAS 2022 [DJ]	The Ricky Skaggs Story	1990	7.50	15.00	30.00
—Promo-only interview record					
❑ FE 37193	Waitin' for the Sun to Shine	1981	2.50	5.00	10.00
❑ FE 37996	Highways and Heartaches	1982	2.50	5.00	10.00
❑ FE 39409	Favorite Country Songs	1985	2.50	5.00	10.00
❑ FE 39410	Country Boy	1984	2.50	5.00	10.00
❑ FE 40103	Live in London	1985	2.50	5.00	10.00
❑ FE 40309	Love's Gonna Get Ya!	1986	2.00	4.00	8.00

Number	Title (A Side/B Side)	Yr	VG	VG+	NM
❑ FE 40623	Comin' Home to Stay	1988	2.00	4.00	8.00
❑ FE 45027	Kentucky Thunder	1989	2.50	5.00	10.00
ROUNDER					
❑ 0151	Family and Friends	1982	3.00	6.00	12.00
SUGAR HILL					
❑ SH-3706	Sweet Temptation	1979	3.00	6.00	12.00
❑ SH-3711	Skaggs and Rice	1980	3.00	6.00	12.00
SUGAR HILL/EPIC					
❑ FE 38954	Don't Cheat in Our Hometown	1983	2.50	5.00	10.00

SKAGGS, RICKY, AND JAMES TAYLOR
Also see each artist's individual listings.

45s

EPIC

Number	Title (A Side/B Side)	Yr	VG	VG+	NM
❑ AE7 2569 [DJ]	New Star Shining (same on both sides)	1986	—	2.00	4.00
❑ AE7 2569 [PS]	New Star Shining	1986	—	2.00	4.00

SKAGGS, RICKY, AND KEITH WHITLEY
Also see each artist's individual listings.

Albums

REBEL

Number	Title (A Side/B Side)	Yr	VG	VG+	NM
❑ 1504	Second Generation Bluegrass	197?	5.00	10.00	20.00

SKINNER, JIMMIE
45s

CAPITOL

Number	Title (A Side/B Side)	Yr	VG	VG+	NM
❑ F1209	There Won't Be Much More Time/Will You Be Satisfied	1950	7.50	15.00	30.00
❑ F1339	It's My World/There's Nothing	1950	7.50	15.00	30.00
❑ F1413	Running Out of Time/Station Door Blues	1951	6.25	12.50	25.00
❑ F1476	Falling Rain Blues/It's All the Same	1951	6.25	12.50	25.00
❑ F1563	It's Bargain Day/I Can't Tell My Heart That	1951	6.25	12.50	25.00
❑ F1764	The Journey's End/Kentucky and You	1951	6.25	12.50	25.00
❑ F1889	Penny Post Card/'Tis Sweet	1951	6.25	12.50	25.00
❑ F1935	Holy Life Insurance/When the Book	1952	6.25	12.50	25.00
❑ F2007	It's Our Goodbye/Women Beware	1952	6.25	12.50	25.00
❑ F2108	Dreaming My Weary Life Away/Till Then	1952	6.25	12.50	25.00
❑ F2231	I Ain't Got Time/I Saw Your Face in the Crowd	1952	6.25	12.50	25.00
❑ F2351	Help Me Find My Broken Heart/Your Flyin' Days Are Through	1953	6.25	12.50	25.00
❑ F2401	Ready to Go Home/Singing Teacher in Heaven	1953	6.25	12.50	25.00
❑ F2513	I've Got a Lot of Love Baby/By Degrees	1953	6.25	12.50	25.00
DECCA					
❑ 9-28910	I'm Allergic to Your Kisses/Baby I Could Change My Ways	1953	6.25	12.50	25.00
❑ 9-29006	Don't Give Your Heart to a Rambler/What a Pleasure	1954	6.25	12.50	25.00
❑ 9-29053	Too Hot to Handle/My Broken Heart Is Startin' to Show	1954	6.25	12.50	25.00
❑ 9-29179	Don't Get Around Much Anymore/John Henry and the Water Boy	1954	6.25	12.50	25.00
❑ 9-29454	I Don't Need a Doctor/Blame the Right One	1955	6.25	12.50	25.00
❑ 9-30665	Beautiful/Jesus Loves Us All	1958	5.00	10.00	20.00
MERCURY					
❑ 70792	Steppin' Out on You/Want You for My Baby	1956	5.00	10.00	20.00
❑ 70854	Dime a Dozen/My Heart's on a Budget	1956	5.00	10.00	20.00
❑ 70894	Muddy Water Blues/Will You Be Satisfied That Way	1956	5.00	10.00	20.00
❑ 70956	Another Saturday Night/Just Ramblin' On	1956	5.00	10.00	20.00
❑ 71090	Born to Be Wild/No Fault of Mine	1957	5.00	10.00	20.00
❑ 71163	Hafta Do Something/No Maybe in My Baby's Eyes	1957	5.00	10.00	20.00
❑ 71192	I Found My Girl in the USA/Carroll County Blues	1957	5.00	10.00	20.00
❑ 71256	What Makes a Man Wander/We've Got Things in Common	1958	3.75	7.50	15.00
❑ 71341	Where My Sweet Baby Goes/Where Do We Go from Here	1958	3.75	7.50	15.00
❑ 71387	Dark Hollow/Walkin' My Blues Away	1958	3.75	7.50	15.00
❑ 71470	John Wesley Hardin/Misery Loves Company	1959	3.75	7.50	15.00
❑ 71539	Riverboat Gambler/Married to a Friend	1959	3.75	7.50	15.00
❑ 71606	Lonesome Road Blues/Two Squares Away	1960	3.75	7.50	15.00
❑ 71704	Careless Love/I'll Weaken and Call	1960	3.75	7.50	15.00
❑ 71719	The Hem of His Garment/God's Mansion in the Sky	1960	3.75	7.50	15.00
❑ 71785	Don't Let Love Get You Down/Please Don't Send Cecil Away	1961	3.00	6.00	12.00
❑ 71873	Four Walls, a Floor and a Ceiling/Big City	1961	3.00	6.00	12.00
❑ 71952	Hundred Proof Heartaches/I Know You're Married (But I Love You Still)	1962	3.00	6.00	12.00
❑ 72020	One Dead Man Ago/Wooden Angels	1962	3.00	6.00	12.00
STARDAY					
❑ 627	Trouble Walked In/Old Bill Dollar	1963	3.00	6.00	12.00
❑ 647	Try to Be Good/Yesterday's Wrong	1963	3.00	6.00	12.00
❑ 669	The Cork and the Bottle/Let's Say Goodbye Like We Said Hello	1964	3.00	6.00	12.00
❑ 687	This Old Road/Things That Might Have Been	1964	3.00	6.00	12.00
❑ 711	Hard Working Man/How It's Been (Since the Last Heartbreak)	1965	2.50	5.00	10.00
❑ 738	Twenty Beers/To Tell the World	1966	2.50	5.00	10.00
❑ 821	I'd Rather Take the Blame/The Kind of Love She Gave to Me	1967	2.50	5.00	10.00
❑ 836	The Story of Bonnie and Clyde/Bonnie and Clyde's Getaway	1968	2.50	5.00	10.00

—B-side by the Stanley Brothers

Selected 78s

RADIO ARTIST

Number	Title (A Side/B Side)	Yr	VG	VG+	NM
❑ 244	Tennessee Border/Candy Kisses	1949	7.50	15.00	30.00
❑ 246	On the Wrong Side of the Track/A Little Careless	1949	6.25	12.50	25.00
❑ 247	There Won't Be Much More/Will You Be Satisfied	1954	6.25	12.50	25.00
❑ 250	Capitol Letter/Going to Be	1949	6.25	12.50	25.00
❑ 253	The Rambler's Call/Here's My Goodbye to You	1950	5.00	10.00	20.00
❑ 254	You're My Big Baby Now/Yesterday's Winner	1950	5.00	10.00	20.00
❑ 255	I Believe in You/Jimmie's Blues	1950	5.00	10.00	20.00
❑ 256	You Don't Know My Mind/Lula Lee	1950	5.00	10.00	20.00

Albums

DECCA

Number	Title (A Side/B Side)	Yr	VG	VG+	NM
❑ DL 4132 [M]	Country Singer	1961	10.00	20.00	40.00
MERCURY					
❑ MG-20352 [M]	Songs That Make the Jukebox Play	1957	20.00	40.00	80.00
❑ MG-20700 [M]	Jimmie Skinner Sings Jimmie Rodgers	1962	6.25	12.50	25.00
❑ SR-60700 [S]	Jimmie Skinner Sings Jimmie Rodgers	1962	7.50	15.00	30.00
STARDAY					
❑ SLP-240 [M]	Jimmie Skinner	1963	10.00	20.00	40.00
VETCO					
❑ 3001	Jimmie Skinner Sings Bluegrass	1976	3.75	7.50	15.00
WING					
❑ MGW-12277 [M]	Country Blues	1964	6.25	12.50	25.00
❑ SRW-16277 [R]	Country Blues	1964	3.75	7.50	15.00

SKIP AND LINDA
45s

MDJ

Number	Title (A Side/B Side)	Yr	VG	VG+	NM
❑ 68178	If You Could See You Through My Eyes/The Clown	1982	—	2.50	5.00
❑ 68179	I Just Can't Turn Temptation Down/Don't Surrender Your Love	1982	—	2.50	5.00
❑ 68180	This Time/(B-side unknown)	1982	—	2.50	5.00

SKY KINGS, THE
45s

WARNER BROS.

Number	Title (A Side/B Side)	Yr	VG	VG+	NM
❑ 7-17610	That Just About Says It All/I Must Be Doin' Something Right	1996	—	2.50	5.00
❑ 7-17663	Picture Perfect/That's How You Learn About Love	1996	—	2.50	5.00

SLATER, DAVID
45s

CAPITOL

Number	Title (A Side/B Side)	Yr	VG	VG+	NM
❑ B-44129	I'm Still Your Fool/I've Met My Match	1988	—	—	3.00
❑ B-44184	The Other Guy/Rest Assured	1988	—	—	3.00
❑ B-44257	We Were Meant to Be Lovers/Losin' My Louisiana Blues	1988	—	—	3.00
❑ B-44351	She Will/The Story of Us	1989	—	2.00	4.00
❑ B-44443	Whatcha Gonna Do About Her/Be with Me	1989	—	2.00	4.00

Albums

CAPITOL

Number	Title (A Side/B Side)	Yr	VG	VG+	NM
❑ C1-48307	Exchange of Hearts	1988	2.00	4.00	8.00
❑ C1-91181	Be with Me	1989	2.50	5.00	10.00

SLEDD, PATSY
45s

EPIC

Number	Title (A Side/B Side)	Yr	VG	VG+	NM
❑ 5-10801	I Just Want to Hold On to You/Feeling Like a Woman	1971	2.00	4.00	8.00
MEGA					
❑ 0085	Nothing Can Stop My Loving You/Don't Fight the Feeling	1972	—	3.00	6.00
❑ 0098	I Hate You/What Will I Do	1973	—	2.50	5.00
❑ 0110	Thunderclouds of Love/We Gotta Lotta Love	1973	—	2.50	5.00
❑ 1203	Chip Chip/Don't Fight the Feeling	1973	—	2.50	5.00
❑ 1208	Lay Down/Stayin' Home Woman	1974	—	2.50	5.00
❑ 1217	See Saw/We Gotta Lotta Love	1974	—	2.50	5.00
❑ 1244	The Cowboy and the Lady/This Is It	1976	—	2.50	5.00
SHOWTIME					
❑ 1007	Don't Stay If You Don't Love Me/My Diamond Is Only a Stone	1987	—	2.50	5.00
❑ 1007 [PS]	Don't Stay If You Don't Love Me/My Diamond Is Only a Stone	1987	—	3.00	6.00
UNITED ARTISTS					
❑ 50574	You Mean to Say/Bouquets in My Mind	1969	—	3.50	7.00
❑ 50633	Ring Around Texas/If You Were Me	1970	—	3.50	7.00

Albums

MEGA

Number	Title (A Side/B Side)	Yr	VG	VG+	NM
❑ 1020	Yours Sincerely	1973	3.00	6.00	12.00

SLEWFOOT
45s

STEP ONE

Number	Title (A Side/B Side)	Yr	VG	VG+	NM
❑ 360	Nice to Be with You/Better Than This	1986	—	2.50	5.00

SLIGO STUDIO BAND
45s

GBS

Number	Title (A Side/B Side)	Yr	VG	VG+	NM
❑ 708	You're the Reason/She Offered Her Honor	1981	2.00	4.00	8.00

SLOAN, BONNIE

45s

COLUMBIA

Number	Title (A Side/B Side)	Yr	VG	VG+	NM
❑ 4-21311	Don't Call Me a Tramp/Alone I Cry	1954	6.25	12.50	25.00
❑ 4-21391	Nobody But You/Hog Tied and Branded	1955	6.25	12.50	25.00
❑ 4-21425	Poor Paper Kite/After the Wedding	1955	6.25	12.50	25.00
❑ 4-21463	Silly Boy/Idle Hours	1956	6.25	12.50	25.00
❑ 4-21502	The Next Waltz with You/Honky Tonk World	1956	6.25	12.50	25.00

SLYE, CARRIE

45s

FRIDAY

Number	Title (A Side/B Side)	Yr	VG	VG+	NM
❑ 42683	Ease the Fever/(B-side unknown)	1983	2.00	4.00	8.00

SMALLWOOD, LANEY

Also see CHARLIE McCOY.

45s

MONUMENT

Number	Title (A Side/B Side)	Yr	VG	VG+	NM
❑ 45-237	Undercover Man/He'll Sing the Blues	1978	—	2.50	5.00
❑ 45-255	That "I Love You, You Love Me Too" Love Song/I'm Sure to Cry	1978	—	2.50	5.00
❑ 45-271	Let's Fall in Love Again/We Got a Love Thing	1978	—	2.50	5.00

SMART, JIMMY

45s

Number	Title (A Side/B Side)	Yr	VG	VG+	NM
ALLSTAR					
❑ 7211	Broken Dream/It's Too Late for Me	1960	6.25	12.50	25.00
PLAID					
❑ 1004	Shorty/In My Dreams	1961	5.00	10.00	20.00

SMITH, ANDY LEE

45s

615

Number	Title (A Side/B Side)	Yr	VG	VG+	NM
❑ 1024	Invitation to the Blues/(B-side unknown)	1989	—	2.50	5.00
❑ 1024 [PS]	Invitation to the Blues/(B-side unknown)	1989	—	3.00	6.00

SMITH, ARTHUR "GUITAR BOOGIE"

Not to be confused with the Arthur Smith who recorded for Bluebird in the 1930s.

45s

Number	Title (A Side/B Side)	Yr	VG	VG+	NM
CHOICE					
❑ 6101	Shhh (With Dialogue)/Shhh (Without Dialogue)	1960	3.75	7.50	15.00
❑ 6102	I'm Afraid of Wimmin/Fishin' Fever	1961	3.75	7.50	15.00
DOT					
❑ 16695	The Billy Malone Story/I Look Up	1965	2.50	5.00	10.00
❑ 16852	Jet Set/New River Train	1966	2.50	5.00	10.00
❑ 17013	Today/Whitepoint	1967	2.50	5.00	10.00
MGM					
❑ K10516	Mountain Be-Bop/Don't Look for Trouble	1949	10.00	20.00	40.00
❑ K10551	Be-Bop Rag/I Never See Maggie Alone	1949	10.00	20.00	40.00
❑ K10577	Mule Train/Banjo Rag	1949	10.00	20.00	40.00
❑ K10608	Guitar and Piano Boogie/I'm Only Tellin' You	1950	7.50	15.00	30.00
❑ K10714	I.H. Boogie/I'm Afraid of Women	1950	7.50	15.00	30.00
❑ K10791	Mandolin Boogie/Conversation with a Mule	1950	7.50	15.00	30.00
❑ K10807	Memphis Blues/Beer Barrel Polka	1950	7.50	15.00	30.00
❑ K10829	Mr. Stalin, You're Eatin' Too High/Banjo Buster	1950	7.50	15.00	30.00
❑ K10847	Merry Christmas, Everyone/Guitar Jingle Bells	1950	7.50	15.00	30.00
❑ K10881	Hot Rod Race/Rhumba Boogie	1951	10.00	20.00	40.00
❑ K10914	Beautiful Brown Eyes (Vocal)/(Instrumental)	1951	7.50	15.00	30.00
❑ K10945	Chew Tobacco Rag/Big Mountain Shuffle	1951	7.50	15.00	30.00
❑ K10991	Who Shot Willie/Express Train Boogie	1951	7.50	15.00	30.00
❑ K11040	Fence Jumper/Tears Don't Always Mean a Broken Heart	1951	7.50	15.00	30.00
❑ K11096	Listen to the Mockingbird/BLue Moon Waltz	1951	7.50	15.00	30.00
❑ K11137	R.S.V.P. Uncle Sam/Shortnin' Bread	1952	6.25	12.50	25.00
❑ K11191	Just Lookin'/Fiddle Faddle	1952	6.25	12.50	25.00
❑ K11262	River Rag/Someone Left Another Young'un at Our House	1952	6.25	12.50	25.00
❑ K11317	Somebody's Knocking/I Know There's a Crown for Me	1952	6.25	12.50	25.00
❑ K11324	Make Me Know It/Five Foot Two, Eyes of Blue	1952	6.25	12.50	25.00
❑ K11361	Five String Banjo Boogie/Guitar Jamboree	1952	6.25	12.50	25.00
❑ K11379	The South/Lady of Spain	1952	6.25	12.50	25.00
❑ K11413	Indian Boogie/Cherokee Strut	1953	6.25	12.50	25.00
❑ K11433	In Memory of Hank Williams/I'm Richer Than You	1953	10.00	20.00	40.00
❑ K11503	Because You Love Me/Rainbow Waltz	1953	6.25	12.50	25.00
❑ K11558	He Went That-a-Way/Three "D" Boogie	1953	6.25	12.50	25.00
❑ K11605	Oklahoma Polka/You're Off Limits	1953	6.25	12.50	25.00
❑ K11657	The Honeymoon Is Over/Cotton Patch Rag	1954	6.25	12.50	25.00
❑ K11704	I Get So Lonely/Outboard	1954	6.25	12.50	25.00
❑ K11784	Red Headed Stranger/Sobbin' Women	1954	6.25	12.50	25.00
❑ K11817	Lonesome/Half-Moon	1954	6.25	12.50	25.00
❑ K11879	Hi-Lo Boogie/Truck Stop Grill	1954	6.25	12.50	25.00
❑ K11945	Midnight Rag/You're Hooked	1955	5.00	10.00	20.00
❑ K12006	Feudin' Banjos/'Bye 'Bye Back Smoke Choo Choo	1955	7.50	15.00	30.00
—With Don Reno					
❑ K12064	Your Way/Yes Sir, That's My Baby	1955	5.00	10.00	20.00
❑ K12135	Number One Street (Part 1)/Number One Street (Part 2)	1955	5.00	10.00	20.00
❑ K12176	Nobody, Somebody, Nobody/All Night Blues	1956	5.00	10.00	20.00
❑ K12224	The Gal with the Yaller Shoes/Buzz Saw	1956	5.00	10.00	20.00
❑ K12330	Blue Rock/More Foolish Questions	1956	5.00	10.00	20.00
❑ K12436	Freeze It Boogie/I Thought It Couldn't Happen to Me	1957	5.00	10.00	20.00
❑ K12458	Two Theme Calypso/Stamps	1957	5.00	10.00	20.00
❑ K12544	Teen-Age Rebel/Easy Rock	1957	6.25	12.50	25.00
❑ K12618	Rockin' the News/Guitar Bustin'	1958	5.00	10.00	20.00
❑ K12791	Banjo Boogie/Hard Boiled Boogie	1959	5.00	10.00	20.00
MONUMENT					
❑ 8572	Ringing Banjos/Battling Banjos Polka	1973	—	3.00	6.00
❑ 8583	Just Joshin'/Banjo Bustin'	1973	—	3.00	6.00
❑ 8604	Guitar Boogie/Right On	1974	—	3.00	6.00
❑ 8676	Theme from "Death Driver"/Moods from "Death Driver"	1975	—	3.00	6.00
STARDAY					
❑ 576	Guitar Boogie Twist/Napoleon's Retreat	1962	3.75	7.50	15.00
❑ 590	Heartaches/Foolish Questions — Silly Answers	1962	3.75	7.50	15.00
❑ 615	Philadelphia Guitar/Hospitality Blues	1962	3.75	7.50	15.00
❑ 634	Master of the Game/Travelin' Blues	1963	3.75	7.50	15.00
❑ 642	Tie My Hunting Dogs Down. Jed/Guitar Hop	1963	3.75	7.50	15.00
❑ 656	The Stuttering Song/Back to His Hole He Went	1963	3.75	7.50	15.00
❑ 701	I Like Lasses/Flat Top Hari Kari	1964	3.75	7.50	15.00
❑ 824	British Backbeat/Lynn's Gone	1968	2.00	4.00	8.00
❑ 861	What Is an American?/Psychoanalysis	1969	2.00	4.00	8.00
❑ 868	Guitar Unlimited/Summer Theme	1969	2.00	4.00	8.00
❑ 7007	Guitar Boogie Twist/Under the Double Eagle	197?	—	3.00	6.00
❑ 7018	The South/Memphis South	197?	—	3.00	6.00
❑ 8013	Guitar Boogie/Under the Double Eagle	197?	—	3.00	6.00

Selected 78s

MGM

Number	Title (A Side/B Side)	Yr	VG	VG+	NM
❑ 10229	Banjo Boogie/Have a Little Fun	1948	5.00	10.00	20.00
❑ 10268	Roundup Polka/Cabanola Glide	1948	5.00	10.00	20.00
❑ 10293	Guitar Boogie/Boomerang	1948	6.25	12.50	25.00
❑ 10294	12th Street Rag/Once Upon a Time	1948	5.00	10.00	20.00
❑ 10333	Raindrops and Teardrops/Foolish Questions	1949	5.00	10.00	20.00
❑ 10380	Careless Hands/Lady of Spain	1949	5.00	10.00	20.00
❑ 10441	Cracker Boogie/One Little, Two Little, Three Little Times	1949	5.00	10.00	20.00

Albums

Number	Title (A Side/B Side)	Yr	VG	VG+	NM
ABC-PARAMOUNT					
❑ ABC-441 [M]	Arthur "Guitar" Smith and Voices	1963	5.00	10.00	20.00
❑ ABCS-441 [S]	Arthur "Guitar" Smith and Voices	1963	6.25	12.50	25.00
DOT					
❑ DLP-3600 [M]	Original Guitar Boogie	1964	5.00	10.00	20.00
❑ DLP-3636 [M]	Great Country and Western Hits	1965	3.75	7.50	15.00
❑ DLP-3642 [M]	Singing on the Mountain with the Crossroads Quartet	1965	5.00	10.00	20.00
❑ DLP-3769 [M]	A Tribute to Jim Reeves	1966	3.75	7.50	15.00
❑ DLP-25600 [S]	Original Guitar Boogie	1964	6.25	12.50	25.00
❑ DLP-25636 [S]	Great Country and Western Hits	1965	5.00	10.00	20.00
❑ DLP-25642 [S]	Singing on the Mountain with the Crossroads Quartet	1965	6.25	12.50	25.00
❑ DLP-25769 [S]	A Tribute to Jim Reeves	1966	5.00	10.00	20.00
MGM					
❑ E-236 [10]	Foolish Questions	1954	30.00	60.00	120.00
❑ E-533 [10]	Fingers on Fire	1955	25.00	50.00	100.00
❑ E-3301 [M]	Specials	1955	20.00	40.00	80.00
❑ E-3525 [M]	Fingers on Fire	1957	20.00	40.00	80.00
MONUMENT					
❑ Z 32259	Battling Banjos	1973	3.00	6.00	12.00
STARDAY					
❑ SLP-173 [M]	Mister Guitar	1962	7.50	15.00	30.00
❑ SLP-186 [M]	Arthur Smith and the Crossroads Quartet	1962	10.00	20.00	40.00
❑ SLP-216 [M]	Arthur "Guitar Boogie" Smith Goes to Town	1963	7.50	15.00	30.00
❑ SLP-241 [M]	In Person	1963	7.50	15.00	30.00
❑ SLP-266 [M]	Down Home	1964	7.50	15.00	30.00

SMITH, BOBBY

45s

Number	Title (A Side/B Side)	Yr	VG	VG+	NM
AUTUMN					
❑ 398	Do You Wanna Make Love/Too Turned On	1977	—	3.00	6.00
LIBERTY					
❑ 1417	Just Enough Love (For One Woman)/Goin' in Circles	1981	—	2.00	4.00
❑ 1439	Too Many Hearts in the Fire/You Hit Me Right Where I Love	1981	—	2.00	4.00
❑ 1452	And Then Some/Everytime I Do	1982	—	2.00	4.00
❑ 1480	It's Been One of Those Days/Loving You Could Never Be Better	1982	—	2.00	4.00

Albums

CMH

Number	Title (A Side/B Side)	Yr	VG	VG+	NM
❑ 6225	Smokin' Bluegrass	198?	2.50	5.00	10.00

SMITH, CAL

Also see BILLY PARKER.

45s

DECCA

Number	Title (A Side/B Side)	Yr	VG	VG+	NM
❑ 32768	That's What It's Like to Be Lonesome/The Only Girl in the Game	1971	—	3.00	6.00
❑ 32815	Free Streets/Goin' Home to Do My Time	1971	—	3.00	6.00
❑ 32878	Woman on the Inside/To Save, My Wife	1971	—	3.00	6.00
❑ 32959	I've Found Someone of My Own/Lights of the Living	1972	—	3.00	6.00
❑ 33003	For My Baby/Handful of Stars	1972	—	3.00	6.00
❑ 33040	The Lord Knows I'm Drinking/Sweet Things I Remember About You	1972	—	3.00	6.00

Number	Title (A Side/B Side)	Yr	VG	VG+	NM
KAPP					
❑ 748	I'll Just Go On Home/Silver Dew on the Blue Grass Tonight	1966	2.50	5.00	10.00
❑ 788	The Only Thing I Want/Stranger in the House	1966	2.00	4.00	8.00
❑ 834	I'll Never Be Lonesome with You/If I Had My Life to Live Over	1967	2.00	4.00	8.00
❑ 851	I'll Sail My Ship Alone/You're Not Drowning Your Heartache	1967	2.00	4.00	8.00
❑ 884	Destination Atlanta G.A./Did She Ask About Me	1968	2.00	4.00	8.00
❑ 913	Jacksonville/I Love You a Thousand Ways	1968	2.00	4.00	8.00
❑ 938	Drinking Champagne/Honky Tonk Blues	1968	2.00	4.00	8.00
❑ 960	Empty Arms/So Much to Do	1969	2.00	4.00	8.00
❑ 994	It Takes All Night Long/Daddy's Arms	1969	2.00	4.00	8.00
❑ 2037	You Can't Housebreak a Tomcat/At the Sight of You	1969	—	3.00	6.00
❑ 2059	Heaven Is Just a Touch Away/I Overlooked an Orchid	1969	—	3.00	6.00
❑ 2076	The Difference Between Going and Really Gone/My Happiness Goes Off	1970	—	3.00	6.00
MCA					
❑ 40061	I Can Feel the Leavin' Comin' On/I've Loved You All Over the World	1973	—	2.50	5.00
❑ 40136	Bleep You/An Hour and a Six-Pack	1973	—	2.50	5.00
❑ 40191	Country Bumpkin/It's Not the Miles You Traveled	1974	—	2.50	5.00
❑ 40265	Between Lust and Watching TV/Some Kind of a Woman	1974	—	2.50	5.00
❑ 40335	It's Time to Pay the Fiddler/Love Is the Foundation	1974	—	2.50	5.00
❑ 40394	She Talked a Lot About Texas/Baby's Gone	1975	—	2.50	5.00
❑ 40467	Jason's Farm/You Slip Into My Mind	1975	—	2.50	5.00
❑ 40517	Thunderstorms/19 Years and 1800 Miles	1976	—	2.00	4.00
❑ 40563	MacArthur's Hand/Sunday Morning Christian	1976	—	2.00	4.00
❑ 40618	Woman Don't Try to Sing My Song/I Play a Man	1976	—	2.00	4.00
❑ 40671	I Just Came Home to Count the Memories/Feelin' the Weight of My Chains	1976	—	2.00	4.00
❑ 40714	Come See About Me/The In Crowd	1977	—	2.00	4.00
❑ 40789	Helen/I'm Forty Now	1977	—	2.00	4.00
❑ 40839	Throwin' Memories on the Fire/Tabernacle Tom	1977	—	2.00	4.00
❑ 40864	I'm Just a Farmer/The Ghost of Jim Bob Wilson	1978	—	2.00	4.00
❑ 40911	Bits and Pieces of Life/Leona	1978	—	2.00	4.00
❑ 40982	The Rise and Fall of the Roman Empire/Oklahoma Sunshine	1978	—	2.00	4.00
❑ 41001	One Little Skinny Rib/I Fed Her Love	1979	—	2.00	4.00
❑ 41128	The Room at the Top of the Stairs/Happy Anniversary	1979	—	2.00	4.00
PLAID					
❑ 1003	Eleven Long Years/Tear Stained Pillow	1961	5.00	10.00	20.00
STEP ONE					
❑ 353	Bein' Gone/I Know It's Not Over	1986	—	2.00	4.00
❑ 358	King Lear/Country Bumpkin	1986	—	2.00	4.00
SUN RIZE					
❑ 130	Take the Time to Love Somebody/Baby Can You Love Me Like She Used To	198?	—	3.00	6.00
Albums					
DECCA					
❑ DL 75369	I've Found Someone of My Own	1972	3.75	7.50	15.00
KAPP					
❑ KL-1504 [M]	All the World Is Lonely Now	1966	6.25	12.50	25.00
❑ KL-1537 [M]	Goin' to Cal's Place	1967	6.25	12.50	25.00
❑ KS-3504 [S]	All the World Is Lonely Now	1966	5.00	10.00	20.00
❑ KS-3537 [S]	Goin' to Cal's Place	1967	5.00	10.00	20.00
❑ KS-3544	Travelin' Man	1968	5.00	10.00	20.00
❑ KS-3608	Drinking Champagne	1968	5.00	10.00	20.00
❑ KS-3642	The Best of Cal Smith	1969	3.75	7.50	15.00
MCA					
❑ 70	The Best of Cal Smith	1973	2.50	5.00	10.00
—Reissue of Kapp 3642					
❑ 344	Cal Smith	1973	2.50	5.00	10.00
—Reissue of Decca LP					
❑ 424	Country Bumpkin	1974	2.50	5.00	10.00
❑ 467	It's Time to Pay the Fiddler	1975	2.50	5.00	10.00
❑ 485	My Kind of Country	1975	2.50	5.00	10.00
❑ 2172	Jason's Farm	1976	2.50	5.00	10.00
❑ 2266	I Just Came Home to Count the Memories	1977	2.50	5.00	10.00

SMITH, CARL

45s

Number	Title (A Side/B Side)	Yr	VG	VG+	NM
ABC HICKORY					
❑ 54004	A Way with Words/Till I Stop Meeting You	1976	—	2.50	5.00
❑ 54009	Show Me a Brick Wall/It's Teardrop Time	1977	—	2.50	5.00
❑ 54016	This Kinda Love Ain't Meant for Sunday School/There Stands the Glass	1977	—	2.50	5.00
❑ 54022	This Lady Loving Me/Loose Talk	1978	—	2.50	5.00
❑ 54030	Remembered by Someone (Remembered by Me)/It Takes Four Feet to Make a Yard	1978	—	2.50	5.00
❑ 54037	I Can't Get the Last Memory Down/Silver Tongued Cowboy	1978	—	2.50	5.00
COLUMBIA					
❑ 4-20712	Guilty Conscience/Washing My Dreams in Tears	1950	7.50	15.00	30.00
❑ 4-20741	I Overlooked an Orchid/I Betcha My Heart I Love You	1950	7.50	15.00	30.00
❑ 4-20765	This Side of Heaven/I Won't Be at Home	1950	7.50	15.00	30.00
❑ 4-20796	Let's Live a Little/There's Nothing As Sweet As My Baby	1951	6.25	12.50	25.00
❑ 4-20825	Mr. Moon/If Teardrops Were Pennies	1951	6.25	12.50	25.00
❑ 4-20862	Let Old Mother Nature Have Her Way/Me and My Broken Heart	1951	6.25	12.50	25.00
❑ 4-20893	(When You Feel Like You're in Love) Don't Just Stand There/The Little Girl in My Home Town	1952	6.25	12.50	25.00
❑ 4-20922	Are You Teasing Me/It's a Lovely, Lovely World	1952	6.25	12.50	25.00
❑ 4-20942	It's a Lovely, Lovely World/(When You Feel Like You're in Love) Don't Just Stand There	1952	6.25	12.50	25.00
❑ 4-21008	Our Honeymoon/Sing Her a Love Song	1952	6.25	12.50	25.00
❑ 4-21040	The Blood That Stained the Old Rugged Cross/Gethsemane	1951	7.50	15.00	30.00
—With the Carters					
❑ 4-21051	That's the Kind of Love I'm Looking For/My Lonely Heart's Runnin' Wild	1952	5.00	10.00	20.00
❑ 4-21087	Orchids Mean Goodbye/Just Wait 'Til I Get You Alone	1953	5.00	10.00	20.00
❑ 4-21110	Nail Scarred Hand/We Shall Meet Someday	1953	6.25	12.50	25.00
❑ 4-21119	Trademark/Do I Like It?	1953	5.00	10.00	20.00
❑ 4-21129	Hey Joe!/Darling Am I the One	1953	5.00	10.00	20.00
❑ 4-21166	Satisfaction Guaranteed/Who'll Buy My Heartaches	1953	5.00	10.00	20.00
❑ 4-21192	How About You/I'll Be Listening	1953	5.00	10.00	20.00
❑ 4-21197	Dog-Gone It, Baby, I'm in Love/What Am I Going to Do	1954	5.00	10.00	20.00
❑ 4-21226	Back Up Buddy/If You Tried As Hard to Love Me	1954	5.00	10.00	20.00
❑ 4-21266	Go, Boy, Go/If You Saw Her Through My Eyes	1954	5.00	10.00	20.00
❑ 4-21317	Loose Talk/More Than Anything Else in the World	1954	5.00	10.00	20.00
❑ 4-21340	Kisses Don't Lie/No, I Don't Believe I Will	1955	5.00	10.00	20.00
❑ 4-21368	Wait a Little Longer Please, Jesus/Works of the Lord	1955	6.25	12.50	25.00
❑ 4-21382	There She Goes/Old Lonesome Times	1955	5.00	10.00	20.00
❑ 4-21411	Baby I'm Ready/I Just Don't Care Anymore	1955	5.00	10.00	20.00
❑ 4-21429	Don't Tease Me/I Just Dropped In to Say Goodbye	1955	5.00	10.00	20.00
❑ 4-21462	You're Free to Go/I Feel Like Cryin'	1955	5.00	10.00	20.00
❑ 4-21493	I've Changed/If You Do Dear	1956	5.00	10.00	20.00
❑ 4-21507	Answers/My Dream of the Old Rugged Cross	1956	6.25	12.50	25.00
❑ 4-21522	You Are the One/Doorstep to Heaven	1956	5.00	10.00	20.00
❑ 4-21552	Before I Met You/Wicked Lies	1956	5.00	10.00	20.00
❑ 30848 [S]	(titles unknown)	1960	3.75	7.50	15.00
❑ 30849 [S]	(titles unknown)	1960	3.75	7.50	15.00
❑ 30850 [S]	(titles unknown)	1960	3.75	7.50	15.00
❑ 30851 [S]	(titles unknown)	1960	3.75	7.50	15.00
❑ 30852 [S]	(titles unknown)	1960	3.75	7.50	15.00
❑ 31473 [S]	(titles unknown)	1962	3.75	7.50	15.00
❑ 31474 [S]	(titles unknown)	1962	3.75	7.50	15.00
❑ 31475 [S]	(titles unknown)	1962	3.75	7.50	15.00
❑ 31476 [S]	(titles unknown)	1962	3.75	7.50	15.00
❑ 31477 [S]	(titles unknown)	1962	3.75	7.50	15.00
—The above 10 are "Stereo Seven" 7-inch 33 1/3 rpm singles with small holes					
❑ 4-40823	You Can't Hurt Me Anymore/That's the Way I Like You the Best	1957	3.75	7.50	15.00
❑ 4-40918	Mr. Lost/Try to Take It Like a Man	1957	3.75	7.50	15.00
❑ 4-40970	No Trespassing/Happy Street	1957	—	—	—
—Canceled					
❑ 4-40984	Why, Why/Emotions	1957	3.75	7.50	15.00
❑ 4-41092	Your Name Is Beautiful/You're So Easy to Love	1958	3.75	7.50	15.00
❑ 4-41170	Guess I've Been Around Too Long/Goodnight Mr. Sun	1958	3.75	7.50	15.00
❑ 4-41243	Walking the Slow Walk/A Love Was Born	1958	3.75	7.50	15.00
❑ 4-41290	The Best Years of Your Life/Mr. Moon	1958	3.75	7.50	15.00
❑ 4-41344	It's All My Heartache/I'll Kiss the Past Goodbye	1959	3.00	6.00	12.00
❑ 4-41417	Ten Thousand Drums/The Tall, Tall Gentleman	1959	3.00	6.00	12.00
❑ 4-41417 [PS]	Ten Thousand Drums/The Tall, Tall Gentleman	1959	6.25	12.50	25.00
❑ 4-41489	Tomorrow Night/I'll Walk with You	1959	3.00	6.00	12.00
❑ 4-41557	Make the Waterwheel Roll/Past	1960	3.00	6.00	12.00
❑ 4-41610	A Pain a Pill Can't Locate/If I Had You (I'd Live for You Only)	1962	3.00	6.00	12.00
❑ 4-41642	Cut Across Shorty/Why Did You Come My Way	1960	3.00	6.00	12.00
❑ 4-41729	If the World Don't End Tomorrow/Lonely Old Room	1960	3.00	6.00	12.00
❑ 4-41819	You Make Me Live Again/I Don't Know How	1960	3.00	6.00	12.00
❑ 4-41948	Are You True to Me/More Habit Than Desire	1961	3.00	6.00	12.00
❑ 4-42042	Kisses Never Lie/Why Can't You Be Satisfied with Me	1961	3.00	6.00	12.00
❑ 4-42222	Air Mail to Heaven/Things That Mean the Most	1961	3.00	6.00	12.00
❑ 4-42349	The Best Dressed Beggar (In Town)/I Used to Be	1962	3.00	6.00	12.00
❑ 4-42490	Gettin' Even/I Volunteer	1962	3.00	6.00	12.00
❑ 4-42610	A Pain a Pill Can't Locate/If I Had You (I'd Live for You Only)	1962	3.00	6.00	12.00
❑ 4-42686	Live for Tomorrow/Let's Talk This Thing Over	1963	3.00	6.00	12.00
❑ 4-42768	In the Back Room Tonight/Take My Love with You	1963	3.00	6.00	12.00
❑ 4-42858	Triangle/I Almost Forgot Her Today	1963	3.00	6.00	12.00
❑ 4-42949	The Pillow That Whispers/Sweet Little Country Girl	1964	3.00	6.00	12.00
❑ 4-43033	Take My Ring Off Your Finger/The Ballad of Hershel Lawson	1964	3.00	6.00	12.00
❑ 4-43124	Lonely Girl/When It's Over	1964	3.00	6.00	12.00
❑ 4-43200	She Called Me Baby/My Friends Are Gonna Be Strangers	1965	2.50	5.00	10.00
❑ 4-43266	Be Good to Her/Keep Me Fooled	1965	2.50	5.00	10.00
❑ 4-43361	Let's Walk Away Strangers/Ain't Love a Hurting Thing	1965	2.50	5.00	10.00
❑ 4-43485	Why Do I Keep Doing This to Us/Why Can't You Feel Sorry for Me	1966	2.50	5.00	10.00
❑ 4-43599	Sweet Temptation/(Is My) Ring on Your Finger	1966	2.50	5.00	10.00
❑ 4-43753	Man with a Plan/You Mean Ol' Moon	1966	2.50	5.00	10.00

Number	Title (A Side/B Side)	Yr	VG	VG+	NM
❑ 4-43866	You Better Be Better to Me/It's Only a Matter of Time	1966	2.50	5.00	10.00
❑ 4-44034	I Should Get Away for Awhile (From You)/Mighty Day	1967	2.00	4.00	8.00
❑ 4-44233	Deep Water/I Really Don't Want to Know	1967	2.00	4.00	8.00
❑ 4-44396	Foggy River/When Will the Rainbow Follow the Rain	1967	2.00	4.00	8.00
❑ 4-44486	You Ought to Hear Me Cry/I Used Up My Last Chance Last Night	1968	2.00	4.00	8.00
❑ 4-44620	There's No More Love/Remember Me (I'm the One Who Loves You)	1968	2.00	4.00	8.00
❑ 4-44702	Faded Love and Winter Roses/Until I Looked at You	1968	2.00	4.00	8.00
❑ 4-44816	Good Deal, Lucille/Never Gonna Cry No More	1969	2.00	4.00	8.00
❑ 4-44939	I Love You Because/Mister, Come and Get Your Wife	1969	2.00	4.00	8.00
❑ 4-45031	Heartbreak Avenue/It's Nice to See You Once Again	1969	2.00	4.00	8.00
❑ 4-45086	Pull My String and Wind Me Up/It's All Right	1970	2.00	4.00	8.00
❑ 4-45177	Pick Me Up on Your Way Down/Bonaparte's Retreat	1970	2.00	4.00	8.00
❑ 4-45225	How I Love Them Old Songs/Little Crop of Cotton Tops	1970	2.00	4.00	8.00
❑ 4-45262	Big Murph/My Mother's Eyes	1970	2.00	4.00	8.00
❑ 4-45293	Don't Worry 'Bout the Mule (Just Load the Wagon)/Darling Days	1970	2.00	4.00	8.00
❑ 4-45382	Lost It on the Road/I'm Wound Up Tight	1971	2.00	4.00	8.00
❑ 4-45436	Red Door/You Walked in My Sleep Last Night	1971	2.00	4.00	8.00
❑ 4-45497	Don't Say You're Mine/Country Soul Man	1971	2.00	4.00	8.00
❑ 4-45558	Mama Bear/Before My Time	1972	2.00	4.00	8.00
❑ 4-45648	If This Is Goodbye/If You Saw Her	1972	2.00	4.00	8.00
❑ 4-45832	What a Difference Your Love Would Make/When You're Gone (There Will Be Nothing Left)	1973	2.00	4.00	8.00
❑ 4-45923	I Need Help/Yesterday Is Gone	1973	2.00	4.00	8.00

HICKORY/MGM

Number	Title (A Side/B Side)	Yr	VG	VG+	NM
❑ 329	Dreaming Again/I Ain't Getting Nowhere with You	1974	—	3.00	6.00
❑ 337	The Way I Lose My Mind/Happy Birthday My Darlin'	1975	—	2.50	5.00
❑ 347	Everything I Touch Turns to Sugar/Lost Highway	1975	—	2.50	5.00
❑ 352	The Girl I Love/Me and My Broken Heart	1975	—	2.50	5.00
❑ 357	Roly Poly/Remembered by Someone (Remembered by Me)	1975	—	2.50	5.00
❑ 363	She Is/I Can't Go On Like This	1976	—	2.50	5.00
❑ 371	If You Don't, Somebody Else Will/It's Gonna Be One of Those Days	1976	—	2.50	5.00

7-Inch Extended Plays

COLUMBIA

Number	Title (A Side/B Side)	Yr	VG	VG+	NM
❑ B-10221	San Antonio Rose/Time Changes Everything//Lovin' Is Livin'/Oh, No!	1957	5.00	10.00	20.00
❑ B-10221 [PS]	Smith's the Name, Vol. I	1957	5.00	10.00	20.00
❑ B-10222	If I Could Hold Back the Dawn/That's What You Think//Live and Let Live/If You Want It, I've Got It	1957	5.00	10.00	20.00
❑ B-10222 [PS]	Smith's the Name, Vol. II	1957	5.00	10.00	20.00
❑ B-10223	Please Come Back Home/Look What Thoughts Done to Me//The House That Love Built/Come Back to Me	1957	5.00	10.00	20.00
❑ B-10223 [PS]	Smith's the Name, Vol. III	1957	5.00	10.00	20.00

Albums

ABC HICKORY

Number	Title (A Side/B Side)	Yr	VG	VG+	NM
❑ HB-44005	This Lady Loves Me	1977	3.00	6.00	12.00
❑ HB-44015	The Silver-Tongued Cowboy	1978	3.00	6.00	12.00

COLUMBIA

Number	Title (A Side/B Side)	Yr	VG	VG+	NM
❑ GP 31 [(2)]	The Carl Smith Anniversary Album/20 Years of Hits	1970	6.25	12.50	25.00
❑ CL 959 [M]	Sunday Down South	1957	12.50	25.00	50.00
❑ CL 1022 [M]	Smith's the Name	1957	12.50	25.00	50.00
❑ CL 1172 [M]	Let's Live a Little	1958	12.50	25.00	50.00
❑ CL 1532 [M]	The Carl Smith Touch	1960	6.25	12.50	25.00
❑ CL 1740 [M]	Easy to Please	1961	6.25	12.50	25.00
❑ CL 1937 [M]	Carl Smith's Greatest Hits	1962	5.00	10.00	20.00
❑ CL 2091 [M]	The Tall, Tall Gentleman	1963	5.00	10.00	20.00
❑ CL 2173 [M]	There Stands the Glass	1964	5.00	10.00	20.00
❑ CL 2293 [M]	I Want to Live and Love	1965	5.00	10.00	20.00
❑ CL 2358 [M]	Kisses Don't Lie	1965	5.00	10.00	20.00
❑ CL 2501 [M]	Man with a Plan	1966	5.00	10.00	20.00
❑ CL 2579 [10]	Carl Smith	1955	25.00	50.00	100.00
❑ CL 2610 [M]	The Country Gentleman	1967	5.00	10.00	20.00
❑ CL 2687 [M]	The Country Gentleman Sings His Favorites	1967	6.25	12.50	25.00
❑ CL 2822 [M]	Deep Water	1968	7.50	15.00	30.00
❑ CS 8352 [S]	The Carl Smith Touch	1960	7.50	15.00	30.00
❑ CS 8540 [S]	Easy to Please	1961	7.50	15.00	30.00
❑ CS 8737 [S]	Carl Smith's Greatest Hits	1962	6.25	12.50	25.00
❑ CS 8891 [S]	The Tall, Tall Gentleman	1963	6.25	12.50	25.00
❑ CS 8973 [S]	There Stands the Glass	1964	6.25	12.50	25.00
❑ CL 9023 [10]	Sentimental Songs	195?	25.00	50.00	100.00
❑ CL 9026 [10]	Softly and Tenderly	195?	20.00	40.00	80.00
❑ CS 9093 [S]	I Want to Live and Love	1965	6.25	12.50	25.00
❑ CS 9158 [S]	Kisses Don't Lie	1965	6.25	12.50	25.00
❑ CS 9301 [S]	Man with a Plan	1966	6.25	12.50	25.00
❑ CS 9410 [S]	The Country Gentleman	1967	6.25	12.50	25.00
❑ CS 9487 [S]	The Country Gentleman Sings His Favorites	1967	5.00	10.00	20.00
❑ CS 9622 [S]	Deep Water	1968	5.00	10.00	20.00
❑ CS 9688	Country on My Mind	1968	5.00	10.00	20.00
❑ CS 9786	Faded Love and Winter Roses	1969	5.00	10.00	20.00
❑ CS 9807	Carl Smith's Greatest Hits, Vol. 2	1969	5.00	10.00	20.00
❑ CS 9870	Carl Smith Sings a Tribute to Roy Acuff	1969	5.00	10.00	20.00
❑ CS 9898	I Love You Because	1970	5.00	10.00	20.00
❑ C 30215	Carl Smith with the Tunesmiths	1970	5.00	10.00	20.00
❑ C 30548	Bluegrass	1971	5.00	10.00	20.00
❑ C 31277	Don't Say You're Mine	1972	5.00	10.00	20.00
❑ KC 31606	If This Is Goodbye	1972	5.00	10.00	20.00
❑ FC 38906	Carl Smith	198?	2.50	5.00	10.00

HICKORY/MGM

Number	Title (A Side/B Side)	Yr	VG	VG+	NM
❑ H3G 4518	The Way I Lose My Mind	1975	3.00	6.00	12.00
❑ H3G 4522	The Girl I Love	1975	3.00	6.00	12.00

ROUNDER

Number	Title (A Side/B Side)	Yr	VG	VG+	NM
❑ SS-25	Old Lonesome Times	1988	2.50	5.00	10.00

SMITH, CARL; LEFTY FRIZZELL; MARTY ROBBINS

Albums

COLUMBIA

Number	Title (A Side/B Side)	Yr	VG	VG+	NM
❑ CL 2544 [10]	Carl, Lefty and Marty	1955	100.00	200.00	400.00

SMITH, CONNIE

45s

COLUMBIA

Number	Title (A Side/B Side)	Yr	VG	VG+	NM
❑ 10051	I've Got My Baby on My Mind/Why Don't You Love Me	1974	—	2.00	4.00
❑ 10086	I Got a Lot of Hurtin' Done Today/Back in the Country	1975	—	2.00	4.00
❑ 10135	Why Don't You Love Me/Loving You (Has Changed My Whole Life)	1975	—	2.00	4.00
❑ 10210	The Song We Fell in Love To/One Little Reason	1975	—	2.00	4.00
❑ 10277	('Til) I Kissed You/Ridin' on a Rainbow	1975	—	2.00	4.00
❑ 10345	So Sad (To Watch Good Love Go Bad)/Constantly	1976	—	2.00	4.00
❑ 10393	I Don't Wanna Talk It Over Anymore/You Crossed My Mind a Thousand Times	1976	—	2.00	4.00
❑ 10501	The Latest Shade of Blue/I'm All Wrapped Up in You	1977	—	2.00	4.00
❑ 45816	You've Got Me (Right Where You Want Me)/A Picture of Me	1973	—	2.50	5.00
❑ 45954	Ain't Love a Good Thing/I Still Feel the Same About You	1973	—	2.50	5.00
❑ 46008	Dallas/That's the Way Love Goes	1974	—	2.50	5.00
❑ 46058	I Never Knew (What That Song Meant Before)/Did We Have to Come This Far	1974	—	2.50	5.00

EPIC

Number	Title (A Side/B Side)	Yr	VG	VG+	NM
❑ 05414	A Far Cry from You/Don't Touch (The Pain's Not Dry)	1986	—	—	3.00
❑ 06250	Hold Me Back/Walk Me to the Door	1986	—	—	3.00

MONUMENT

Number	Title (A Side/B Side)	Yr	VG	VG+	NM
❑ 03857	Rough at the Edges/Don't Make Me Dream	1983	—	2.00	4.00
❑ 45219	Coming Around/You and Love and I	1977	—	2.00	4.00
❑ 45231	I Just Want to Be Your Everything/Scrapbook	1977	—	2.00	4.00
❑ 45241	Lovin' You Baby/All of a Sudden	1978	—	2.00	4.00
❑ 45252	There'll Never Be Another for Me/The Wayward Wind	1978	—	2.00	4.00
❑ 45266	Smooth Sailin'/Loving You Has Sure Been Good to Me	1978	—	2.00	4.00
❑ 45281	Lovin' You, Lovin' Me/Ten Thousand and One	1979	—	2.00	4.00
❑ 45284	Don't Say Love/I Don't Want to Be Free	1979	—	2.00	4.00

RCA VICTOR

Number	Title (A Side/B Side)	Yr	VG	VG+	NM
❑ APBO-0156	Everybody Loves Somebody/I Don't Want Your Memories	1973	—	2.50	5.00
❑ PB-10051	Someone to Give My Love To/I'm Sorry If My Love Got In Your Way	1974	—	2.50	5.00
❑ 47-8416	Once a Day/The Threshold	1964	2.50	5.00	10.00
❑ 47-8489	Then and Only Then/Tiny Blue Transistor Radio	1964	2.00	4.00	8.00
❑ 47-8551	I Can't Remember/Senses	1965	2.00	4.00	8.00
❑ 47-8663	If I Talk to Him/I Don't Have Anyplace to Go	1965	2.00	4.00	8.00
❑ 47-8746	Nobody But a Fool (Would Love Him)/I'll Never Get Over Loving You	1965	2.00	4.00	8.00
❑ 47-8842	Ain't Had No Lovin'/Five Fingers to Spare	1966	2.00	4.00	8.00
❑ 47-8964	The Hurtin's All Over/Invisible Tears	1966	2.00	4.00	8.00
❑ 47-9108	I'll Come Runnin'/It's Now or Never	1967	2.00	4.00	8.00
❑ 47-9214	Cincinnati, Ohio/Don't Feel Sorry for Me	1967	2.00	4.00	8.00
❑ 47-9335	Burning a Hole in My Mind/Only for Me	1967	2.00	4.00	8.00
❑ 47-9413	Baby's Back Again/It Only Hurts for a Little While	1967	2.00	4.00	8.00
❑ 47-9513	Run Away Little Tears/Let Me Halp You Work It Out	1968	2.00	4.00	8.00
❑ 47-9624	Cry, Cry, Cry/The Hurt Goes On	1968	2.00	4.00	8.00
❑ 47-9832	I Never Once Stopped Loving You/The Sun Shines Down on Me	1970	—	3.00	6.00
❑ 47-9887	Louisiana Man/Alone with You	1970	—	3.00	6.00
❑ 47-9938	Where Is My Castle/Clinging to a Saving Hand	1970	—	3.00	6.00
❑ 47-9981	Just One Time/Don't Walk Away	1971	—	3.00	6.00
❑ 74-0101	Ribbon of Darkness/A Lonely Woman	1969	2.00	4.00	8.00
❑ 74-0258	You and Your Sweet Love/I Can't Get Used to Being Lonely	1969	2.00	4.00	8.00
❑ 74-0535	I'm Sorry If My Love Got In Your Way/Plenty of Time	1971	—	3.00	6.00
❑ 74-0655	Just for What I Am/I'd Still Want to Serve Him Today	1972	—	3.00	6.00
❑ 74-0752	If It Ain't Love (Let's Leave It Alone)/Living Without You	1972	—	3.00	6.00
❑ 74-0860	Love Is the Look You're Looking For/My Ecstasy	1972	—	3.00	6.00
❑ 74-0971	Dream Painter/Once a Day	1973	—	3.00	6.00

Number	Title (A Side/B Side)	Yr	VG	VG+	NM
Albums					
COLUMBIA					
❑ KC 32185	A Lady Named Smith	1973	3.00	6.00	12.00
❑ KC 32492	God Is Abundant	1973	3.00	6.00	12.00
❑ KC 32581	That's the Way Love Goes	1974	3.00	6.00	12.00
❑ KC 33055	I Never Knew (What That Song Meant Before)	1974	3.00	6.00	12.00
❑ KC 33375	Got My Baby on My Mind	1975	3.00	6.00	12.00
❑ KC 33414	Connie Smith Sings Hank Williams Gospel	1975	3.00	6.00	12.00
❑ KC 33918	The Song We Fell in Love To	1976	3.00	6.00	12.00
❑ KC 34270	I Don't Want to Talk It Over Anymore	1976	3.00	6.00	12.00
❑ KC 34877	The Best of Connie Smith	1977	3.00	6.00	12.00
MONUMENT					
❑ 7609	Pure Connie Smith	1977	3.00	6.00	12.00
❑ 7624	New Horizons	1978	3.00	6.00	12.00
RCA CAMDEN					
❑ ACL1-0250	Even the Bad Times Are Good	1973	2.50	5.00	10.00
—With Nat Stuckey					
❑ CAL-2120 [M]	Connie in the Country	1967	3.75	7.50	15.00
❑ CAS-2120 [S]	Connie in the Country	1967	3.00	6.00	12.00
❑ CAS-2495	My Heart Has a Mind of Its Own	1971	2.50	5.00	10.00
❑ CAS-2550	City Lights — Country Favorites	1972	2.50	5.00	10.00
RCA VICTOR					
❑ APL1-0188	Dream Painter	1973	3.00	6.00	12.00
❑ APL1-0275	Connie Smith's Greatest Hits, Volume 1	1973	3.00	6.00	12.00
❑ APL1-0607	Now	1974	3.00	6.00	12.00
❑ LPM-3341 [M]	Connie Smith	1965	5.00	10.00	20.00
❑ LSP-3341 [S]	Connie Smith	1965	6.25	12.50	25.00
❑ LPM-3444 [M]	Cute 'n' Country	1965	5.00	10.00	20.00
❑ LSP-3444 [S]	Cute 'n' Country	1965	6.25	12.50	25.00
❑ LPM-3520 [M]	Miss Smith Goes to Nashville	1966	5.00	10.00	20.00
❑ LSP-3520 [S]	Miss Smith Goes to Nashville	1966	6.25	12.50	25.00
❑ LPM-3589 [M]	Connie Smith Sings Great Sacred Songs	1966	5.00	10.00	20.00
❑ LSP-3589 [S]	Connie Smith Sings Great Sacred Songs	1966	6.25	12.50	25.00
❑ LPM-3628 [M]	Born to Sing	1966	5.00	10.00	20.00
❑ LSP-3628 [S]	Born to Sing	1966	6.25	12.50	25.00
❑ LPM-3725 [M]	Downtown Country	1967	6.25	12.50	25.00
❑ LSP-3725 [S]	Downtown Country	1967	5.00	10.00	20.00
❑ LPM-3768 [M]	Connie Smith Sings Bill Anderson	1967	6.25	12.50	25.00
❑ LSP-3768 [S]	Connie Smith Sings Bill Anderson	1967	5.00	10.00	20.00
❑ LPM-3848 [M]	The Best of Connie Smith	1967	6.25	12.50	25.00
❑ LSP-3848 [S]	The Best of Connie Smith	1967	5.00	10.00	20.00
❑ LPM-3889 [M]	Soul of Country Music	1968	12.50	25.00	50.00
❑ LSP-3889 [S]	Soul of Country Music	1968	5.00	10.00	20.00
❑ LSP-4002	I Love Charley Brown	1968	5.00	10.00	20.00
❑ LSP-4077	Sunshine and Rain	1968	5.00	10.00	20.00
❑ LSP-4132	Connie's Country	1969	5.00	10.00	20.00
❑ LSP-4229	Back in Baby's Arms	1969	5.00	10.00	20.00
❑ LSP-4324	The Best of Connie Smith Volume II	1970	5.00	10.00	20.00
❑ LSP-4394	I Never Once Stopped Loving You	1970	5.00	10.00	20.00
❑ LSP-4474	Where's My Castle	1971	3.75	7.50	15.00
❑ LSP-4537	Just One Time	1971	3.75	7.50	15.00
❑ LSP-4598	Come Along and Walk with Me	1971	5.00	10.00	20.00
❑ LSP-4694	Ain't We Having a Good Time	1972	3.75	7.50	15.00
❑ LSP-4748	"If It Ain't Love" And Other Great Dallas Frazier Songs	1972	3.75	7.50	15.00
❑ LSP-4840	Love Is the Look You're Looking For	1973	3.75	7.50	15.00

SMITH, CONNIE, AND NAT STUCKEY

Number	Title (A Side/B Side)	Yr	VG	VG+	NM
45s					
RCA VICTOR					
❑ 47-9805	If God Is Dead (Who's That Living in My Soul)/His Love Takes Care of Me	1970	2.00	4.00	8.00
❑ 74-0181	Young Love/Something Pretty	1969	2.00	4.00	8.00
Albums					
RCA VICTOR					
❑ LSP-4190	Young Love	1969	5.00	10.00	20.00
❑ LSP-4300	Sunday Morning	1970	3.75	7.50	15.00

SMITH, DARDEN

Number	Title (A Side/B Side)	Yr	VG	VG+	NM
45s					
EPIC					
❑ 34-07709	Little Maggie/Place in Time	1988	—	—	3.00
❑ 34-07906	Day After Tomorrow/God's Will	1988	—	—	3.00
❑ 34-07997	Want You By My Side/Heart Don't Do This to Me	1988	—	—	3.00
Albums					
COLUMBIA					
❑ CAS 3034 [DJ]	Interchords	1988	3.75	7.50	15.00
—Promo-only interview record					
EPIC					
❑ EAS 1282 [EP]	Live Tracks: Darden Smith	1988	3.75	7.50	15.00
—Promo-only three-song live EP					
❑ E 40938	Darden Smith	1988	2.50	5.00	10.00
REDI MIX					
❑ RM 001	Native Soil	1986	5.00	10.00	20.00

SMITH, DAVID

Number	Title (A Side/B Side)	Yr	VG	VG+	NM
45s					
MDJ					
❑ 1002	Heroes and Idols (Don't Come Easy)/Loraine Phillips	1979	—	2.50	5.00

SMITH, DENNIS

Number	Title (A Side/B Side)	Yr	VG	VG+	NM
45s					
ADONDA					
❑ 79021	California Calling/Get It Together	1979	2.00	4.00	8.00

SMITH, EDDIE

Number	Title (A Side/B Side)	Yr	VG	VG+	NM
45s					
KING					
❑ 986	Down Yonder/A Sweet Bunch of Daisies	1951	7.50	15.00	30.00
❑ 1002	San Antonio Rose/Bow Wow Boogie	1951	7.50	15.00	30.00
❑ 1018	Ragtime Melody/Rag Rag Raggedy Moon	1951	6.25	12.50	25.00
❑ 1019	Red Wing/Annie's Rag	1951	6.25	12.50	25.00
❑ 1041	Beer Barrel Polka/Mourning Dove	1952	6.25	12.50	25.00
❑ 1095	The Preacher and the Bear/The Snow Deer	1952	6.25	12.50	25.00
❑ 1171	Back in Your Own Back Yard/Exhibition Special	1953	5.00	10.00	20.00
❑ 1204	When You and I Were Young Maggie/Hot Shot Rag	1953	5.00	10.00	20.00
❑ 1238	Red Suspender Blues/Eddie's Blues	1953	5.00	10.00	20.00

SMITH, GOLDIE HILL

See GOLDIE HILL.

SMITH, JERRY

Number	Title (A Side/B Side)	Yr	VG	VG+	NM
45s					
ABC					
❑ 11162	Truck Stop/My Happiness	1969	—	3.50	7.00
❑ 11230	Sweet 'n' Sassy/Sunrise Serenade	1969	—	3.50	7.00
❑ 11244	Speakeasy/Tokyo Butterfly	1969	—	3.50	7.00
❑ 11246	Papa Joe's Thing/Jean	1969	—	3.50	7.00
—As "Papa Joe's Music Box"					
AD					
❑ 5337	As Long As I Live/I Can't Tell You Why	19??	2.50	5.00	10.00
❑ 8823	Careless Love/Pins and Needles	19??	2.50	5.00	10.00
CHART					
❑ 1440	Annette/Lil' Ol' Me	1967	2.00	4.00	8.00
DECCA					
❑ 32679	Drivin' Home/Louisiana Blues	1970	—	3.00	6.00
❑ 32730	Steppin' Out/Closing Time	1970	—	3.00	6.00
❑ 32769	Papa Joe's Polka/The Toy Piano	1971	—	3.00	6.00
❑ 32814	By Special Request/Open All Night	1971	—	3.00	6.00
❑ 32869	Gear Jammer/Touch of Love	1971	—	3.00	6.00
❑ 32938	Cream and Sugar/Down in the Dumps	1972	—	3.00	6.00
❑ 32992	Jerry's Piano Boogie/When in Rome	1972	—	3.00	6.00
RANWOOD					
❑ 945	Faded Love/Moonlight and Roses	1973	—	2.50	5.00
❑ 953	Back Street/Scottish Waltz	197?	—	2.50	5.00
—As "Papa Joe's Music Box"					
❑ 954	Red Garter Saloon/Sioux City Sue	197?	—	2.50	5.00
❑ 964	One More North/(B-side unknown)	197?	—	2.50	5.00
—As "Papa Joe's Music Box"					
❑ 970	Johnson Rag/Rattle Trap	197?	—	2.50	5.00
❑ 975	White Silver Sands/Lover's Waltz	1974	—	2.50	5.00
—As "Papa Joe's Music Box"					
❑ 1002	Laura's Living Room/Give the World a Smile	1974	—	2.50	5.00
❑ 1024	Last Night/One Mile North of Town	1975	—	2.50	5.00
—As "Papa Joe's Music Box"					
❑ 1060	Heart and Soul/Louisiana Blues	1976	—	2.50	5.00
❑ 1065	The Inn Crowd/Sail Along Silvery Moon	1976	—	2.50	5.00
❑ 1067	Starlite Waltz/Truck Stop	1976	—	2.50	5.00
❑ 1077	Road Hog/Woodchopper's Ball	1977	—	2.50	5.00
❑ 1082	Cajun Gumbo/A Joyful Noise	197?	—	2.50	5.00
❑ 1086	Delicado/La Golondrina	197?	—	2.50	5.00
RICE					
❑ 5029	Shaky's Theme/Closing Time	1968	2.00	4.00	8.00
SOUND STAGE 7					
❑ 2542	Lil' Ol' Me/Wishy Washy	1965	2.50	5.00	10.00
Albums					
ABC					
❑ ABCS-692	Truck Stop	1969	3.75	7.50	15.00
DECCA					
❑ DL 75241	Drivin' Home, Steppin' Out	1970	3.75	7.50	15.00
❑ DL 75311	The Touch of Love	1972	3.75	7.50	15.00
RANWOOD					
❑ R-8111	The New Sound of Jerry Smith and His Pianos	197?	2.50	5.00	10.00
❑ R-8126	Ragtime	197?	2.50	5.00	10.00

SMITH, KATE

The famous radio and TV singer who popularized "God Bless America" had one country hit, listed below.

Number	Title (A Side/B Side)	Yr	VG	VG+	NM
Selected 78s					
MGM					
❑ 30059	Foggy River/Cool Water	1948	3.00	6.00	12.00

SMITH, LOGAN

Number	Title (A Side/B Side)	Yr	VG	VG+	NM
45s					
BRAND X					
❑ 6	Little Man/Down on the Farm	1973	2.00	4.00	8.00

SMITH, LOU

Number	Title (A Side/B Side)	Yr	VG	VG+	NM
45s					
KRCO					
❑ 103	If the World Was Mine/You're Always a Winner	1960	5.00	10.00	20.00
❑ 105	Cruel Love/Close to My Heart	1960	5.00	10.00	20.00

Number	Title (A Side/B Side)	Yr	VG	VG+	NM
SALVO					
❑ 2862	I'm Wondering/Aching Breaking Heart	1961	5.00	10.00	20.00
TOP RANK					
❑ 2069	Cruel Love/Close to My Heart	1960	3.75	7.50	15.00

SMITH, MARGO

Also see REX ALLEN JR.

45s

Number	Title (A Side/B Side)	Yr	VG	VG+	NM
20TH CENTURY					
❑ 2172	There I Said It/Hurt Me Twice	1975	—	3.00	6.00
❑ 2222	Paper Lovin'/We Don't Love Here	1975	—	3.00	6.00
❑ 2255	Meet Me Later/Baby's Hurtin'	1975	—	3.00	6.00
AMI					
❑ 1304	Either You're Married Or You're Single/Where the Heart Leads	1982	—	2.50	5.00
❑ 1309	Could It Be I Don't Belong Here Anymore/Ridin' High	1982	—	2.50	5.00
BERMUDA DUNES					
❑ 103	A Thin Ragged Edge/(B-side unknown)	1984	—	3.50	7.00
❑ 104	Sittin' on Santa's Knee/Tell Someone You Love Them on Christmas	1984	2.00	4.00	8.00
❑ 105	Take Your Memory When You Go/(B-side unknown)	1985	—	3.50	7.00
❑ 106	All I Do Is Dream of You/(B-side unknown)	1985	—	3.50	7.00
❑ 110	Everyday People/(B-side unknown)	1985	—	3.50	7.00
—With Tom Grant					
MOON SHINE					
❑ 3019	Wedding Bells/Ridin' High	1983	—	2.50	5.00
❑ 3021	Please Tell Him That I Said Hello/Waitin' Needin' Drives Me Crazy	1984	—	2.50	5.00
PLAYBACK					
❑ 1300	Echo Me/Love Letters in the Sand	1988	—	3.50	7.00
❑ 1313	Wheel of Fortune/I'm Only Fillin' In	1988	—	3.50	7.00
❑ 1325	Magic Man/(B-side unknown)	1989	—	3.50	7.00
WARNER BROS.					
❑ 8213	Save Your Kisses for Me/I'm About to Do It Again	1976	—	2.50	5.00
❑ 8261	Take My Breath Away/Where, When and Why	1976	—	2.50	5.00
❑ 8339	Love's Explosion/So Close Again	1977	—	2.50	5.00
❑ 8399	My Weakness/I'd Rather Have a Heart Abused	1977	—	2.50	5.00
❑ 8427	So Close Again/Saturday Night at the General Store	1977	—	2.50	5.00
—A-side with Norro Wilson					
❑ 8508	Don't Break the Heart That Loves You/Apt. #4, Sixth Street in Cincinnati	1977	—	2.50	5.00
❑ 8555	It Only Hurts for a Little While/Lookout Mountain	1978	—	2.50	5.00
❑ 8653	Little Things Mean a Lot/Make Love the Way We Used To	1978	—	2.50	5.00
❑ 8726	Still a Woman/Tennessee Sandman	1978	—	2.50	5.00
❑ 8806	If I Give My Heart to You/We'd Better Love It Over	1979	—	2.50	5.00
❑ 49038	Baby My Baby/The Bells of Buttercup Lane	1979	—	2.00	4.00
❑ 49109	The Shuffle Song/Move Over Juanita	1979	—	2.00	4.00
❑ 49250	My Guy/If You Remember Me	1980	—	2.00	4.00
❑ 49569	He Gives Me Diamonds, You Give Me Chills/Every Little Bit Hurts	1980	—	2.00	4.00
❑ 49701	My Heart Cries for You/Borrowed Angel	1981	—	2.00	4.00

Albums

Number	Title (A Side/B Side)	Yr	VG	VG+	NM
20TH CENTURY					
❑ T-490	Margo Smith	1975	3.00	6.00	12.00
WARNER BROS.					
❑ BS 2955	Song Bird	1976	2.50	5.00	10.00
❑ BS 3049	Happiness	1977	2.50	5.00	10.00
❑ BSK 3173	Don't Break the Heart That Loves You	1978	2.50	5.00	10.00
❑ BSK 3286	A Woman	1979	2.50	5.00	10.00
❑ BSK 3388	Just Margo	1979	2.50	5.00	10.00
❑ BSK 3464	Diamonds and Chills	1980	2.50	5.00	10.00

SMITH, RAY

45s

Number	Title (A Side/B Side)	Yr	VG	VG+	NM
CELEBRITY CIRCLE					
❑ 6901	I Walk the Line/Fool #1	1964	3.75	7.50	15.00
CINNAMON					
❑ 755	Tiilted Cup of Love/I'd Traded Better for Worse	1973	—	2.50	5.00
❑ 760	It Wasn't Easy/It's Just Not the Same	1973	—	2.50	5.00
❑ 773	The First Lonely Weekend/A Handful of Friends	1973	—	2.50	5.00
❑ 795	Ten Steps Out in Front/Because of Losing You	1974	—	2.50	5.00
COLUMBIA					
❑ 2-225 (?)	Rainbow/Waltz of the Alamo	1949	10.00	20.00	40.00
—Microgroove 33 1/3 rpm single, small hole					
❑ 2-290 (?)	Snowdeer/Roll Along Kentucky Moon	1949	10.00	20.00	40.00
—Microgroove 33 1/3 rpm single, small hole					
❑ 2-300 (?)	An Old Christmas Card/Jolly Old St. Nicholas	1949	10.00	20.00	40.00
—Microgroove 33 1/3 rpm single, small hole					
❑ 2-305 (?)	Wedding Bells/I'm Throwing Rice (At the Girl I Love)	1949	10.00	20.00	40.00
—Microgroove 33 1/3 rpm single, small hole					
❑ 2-310 (?)	Pretty Little Eyes of Blue/Tennessee Polka	1949	10.00	20.00	40.00
—Microgroove 33 1/3 rpm single, small hole					
❑ 2-530 (?)	Unfaithful One/Daddy's Little Girl	1950	10.00	20.00	40.00
—Microgroove 33 1/3 rpm single, small hole					
❑ 2-535 (?)	I'm Saving Mother's Wedding Ring for You/Mommy Can I Take My Doll	1950	10.00	20.00	40.00
—Microgroove 33 1/3 rpm single, small hole					
❑ 2-590 (?)	No Trespassing/The Sun Has Gone Down	1950	10.00	20.00	40.00
—Microgroove 33 1/3 rpm single, small hole					
DIAMOND					
❑ 193	Everybody's Goin' Somewhere/Au-Go-Go-Go	1965	3.75	7.50	15.00
ERA BACK TO BACK HITS					
❑ 048	Rockin' Little Angel/Robbin' the Cradle	197?	—	2.50	5.00
—B-side by Tony Bellus					
HEART					
❑ 250	Gone, Baby, Gone/(B-side unknown)	195?	1000.	1500.	2000.
INFINITY					
❑ 003	After This Night Is Through/Turn On the Moonlight	1961	3.75	7.50	15.00
❑ 007	Let Yourself Go/Johnny the Hummer	1961	3.75	7.50	15.00
JUDD					
❑ 1016	Rockin' Little Angel/That's All Right	1959	7.50	15.00	30.00
❑ 1017	Maria Elena/Put Your Arms Around Me Honey	1960	7.50	15.00	30.00
❑ 1019	One Wonderful Love/Makes Me Feel Good	1960	7.50	15.00	30.00
❑ 1021	Blonde Hair, Blue Eyes/You Don't Want Me	1960	7.50	15.00	30.00
NU-TONE					
❑ 1182	Deep in My Heart/She's Mine	1964	3.75	7.50	15.00
SHI-RAY					
❑ 101	Sleepy Eyed Woman/Pretty Juke Box	197?	—	3.00	6.00
SMASH					
❑ 1787	Room 503/These Four Precious Years	1962	3.75	7.50	15.00
SUN					
❑ 298	So Right/Right Behind You Baby	1958	7.50	15.00	30.00
❑ 308	Why, Why, Why/You Made a Hit	1958	7.50	15.00	30.00
❑ 319	Rockin' Bandit/Sail Away	1959	7.50	15.00	30.00
❑ 372	Travelin' Salesman/I Won't Miss You ('Til You're Gone)	1961	7.50	15.00	30.00
❑ 375	Hey Boss Man/Candy Doll	1962	7.50	15.00	30.00
TOLLIE					
❑ 9029	There Comes My Baby Back Again/Did We Have a Party	1964	5.00	10.00	20.00
TOPPA					
❑ 1071	Almost Alone/A Place Within My Heart	1962	5.00	10.00	20.00
VEE JAY					
❑ 579	Rockin' Robin/Robbin' the Cradle	1964	3.75	7.50	15.00
WARNER BROS.					
❑ 5371	I'm Snowed/Turn Over a New Leaf	1963	3.75	7.50	15.00
ZIRKON					
❑ 1055	After This Night Is Through/Turn On the Moonlight	1961	5.00	10.00	20.00

SMITH, RICK

45s

Number	Title (A Side/B Side)	Yr	VG	VG+	NM
CIN KAY					
❑ 110	The Way I Loved Her/Catchin' the 9:45	1976	—	2.50	5.00
❑ 114	Daddy How'm I Doin'/The Blues Was Here to Stay	1976	—	2.50	5.00

SMITH, RUSSELL

45s

Number	Title (A Side/B Side)	Yr	VG	VG+	NM
CAPITOL					
❑ B-5101	Your Eyes/Night Flight	1982	—	2.00	4.00
❑ B-5293	Where Did We Go Right/Hesitation	1983	—	2.00	4.00
EPIC					
❑ 34-07789	Three Piece Suit/Not Made of Stone	1988	—	—	3.00
❑ 34-07972	Betty Jean/Not Made of Stone	1988	—	—	3.00
❑ 34-68615	I Wonder What She's Doing Tonight/This Little Town	1989	—	—	3.00
❑ 34-68964	Anger and Tears/The Colorado Side	1989	—	—	3.00

Albums

Number	Title (A Side/B Side)	Yr	VG	VG+	NM
CAPITOL					
❑ ST-12197	Russell Smith	1982	2.00	4.00	8.00
EPIC					
❑ FE 40918	This Little Town	1988	2.00	4.00	8.00

SMITH, SAMMI

45s

Number	Title (A Side/B Side)	Yr	VG	VG+	NM
COLUMBIA					
❑ 44212	He Went a Little Bit Farther/Foxy Dan	1967	2.50	5.00	10.00
❑ 44370	So Long, Charlie Brown, Don't Look for Me Around/Turn Around	1967	2.00	4.00	8.00
❑ 44523	Why Do You Do Me Like You Do/22 Road Markers to a Mile	1968	2.00	4.00	8.00
❑ 44663	It's Not Time Now/Sand Covered Angels	1968	2.00	4.00	8.00
❑ 44905	Brownsville Lumberyard/Shadows of Your Mind	1969	2.00	4.00	8.00
CYCLONE					
❑ 100	What a Lie/It's Not My Way	1979	—	2.00	4.00
❑ 104	The Letter/It's a Day for Sad Songs	1979	—	2.00	4.00
ELEKTRA					
❑ 45292	Huckleberry Pie/I Won't Sing No Love Songs Anymore	1975	—	2.50	5.00
—With Even Stevens					
❑ 45300	As Long As There's a Sunday/Children	1976	—	2.00	4.00
❑ 45320	Rabbit Tracks/I'll Get Better	1976	—	2.00	4.00
❑ 45334	Sunday School to Broadway/Goodmornin', Sunshine, Goodbye	1976	—	2.00	4.00
❑ 45374	Loving Arms/I Just Wanted to Sing	1977	—	2.00	4.00
❑ 45398	I Can't Stop Loving You/De Grazia's Song	1977	—	2.00	4.00
❑ 45429	Days That End in "Y"/Hallelujah for Beer	1977	—	2.00	4.00
❑ 45476	It Just Won't Feel Like Cheating (With You)/I Ain't Got Time to Rock No Babies	1978	—	2.00	4.00
❑ 45504	Norma Jean/Lookin' for Lovin'	1978	—	2.00	4.00
MEGA					
❑ 0001	He's Everywhere/This Room for Rent	1970	—	2.50	5.00

Number	Title (A Side/B Side)	Yr	VG	VG+	NM
❑ 0015	Help Me Make It Through the Night/When Michael Calls	1970	—	3.00	6.00
❑ 0026	Then You Walk In/Willie	1971	—	2.50	5.00
❑ 0039	For the Ride/Saunder's Ferry Lane	1971	—	2.50	5.00
❑ 0056	Kentucky/The Marionette	1971	—	2.50	5.00
❑ 0068	Girl in New Orleans/Isn't It Sad	1972	—	2.50	5.00
❑ 0079	I've Got to Have You/Jimmy's in Georgia	1972	—	2.50	5.00
❑ 0097	The Toast of '45/Tony	1972	—	2.50	5.00
❑ 0109	I Miss You Most When You're Here/Billy Jacks	1973	—	2.50	5.00
❑ 0118	City of New Orleans/Don't Blow No Smoke on Me	1973	—	2.50	5.00
❑ 204	The Rainbow in Daddy's Eyes/Birmingham Mistake	1974	—	2.50	5.00
❑ 210	Never Been to Spain/It's Not Easy	1974	—	2.50	5.00
❑ 212	Help Me Make It Through the Night/When Michael Calls	1974	—	2.00	4.00
—Reissue of 0015					
❑ 1214	Long Black Veil/Paste Me On Some Feathers`	1974	—	2.50	5.00
❑ 1222	Cover Me/He Makes It Hard to Say Goodbye	1975	—	2.50	5.00
❑ 1233	She's in Love with a Rodeo Man/Fool for Something Years	1975	—	2.50	5.00
❑ 1236	Today I Started Loving You Again/Fine As Wine	1975	—	2.50	5.00
❑ 1246	My Window Faces the South/Before the Next Teardrop Falls	1976	—	2.50	5.00

PLAYBACK

Number	Title (A Side/B Side)	Yr	VG	VG+	NM
❑ 1340	Gonna Lay Me Down Beside My Memories/I'd Do It All Over Again	1989	—	2.50	5.00
❑ 1354	Cloudy Days/(B-side unknown)	1989	—	2.50	5.00

SOUND FACTORY

Number	Title (A Side/B Side)	Yr	VG	VG+	NM
❑ 425	I Just Want to Be with You/(B-side unknown)	1980	—	2.00	4.00
❑ 427	Cheatin's a Two-Way Street/(B-side unknown)	1981	—	2.00	4.00
❑ 446	Sometimes I Cry When I'm Alone/(B-side unknown)	1981	—	2.00	4.00
❑ 453	Gypsy and Joe/(B-side unknown)	1982	—	2.00	4.00

STEP ONE

Number	Title (A Side/B Side)	Yr	VG	VG+	NM
❑ 342	You Just Hurt My Last Feeling/Lying in My Arms	1985	—	2.00	4.00
❑ 347	An Offer I Couldn't Refuse/One Away from One Too Many	1985	—	2.00	4.00
❑ 351	Love Me All Over/Don't Let It Happen Again	1986	—	2.00	4.00

ZODIAC

Number	Title (A Side/B Side)	Yr	VG	VG+	NM
❑ 1000	Help Me Make It Through the Night/Saunder's Ferry Drive	1976	—	2.00	4.00
❑ 1005	Just You 'n' Me/Walking in the Sunshine	1976	—	2.00	4.00
❑ 1013	Rings for Sale/You Don't Want My Love	1976	—	2.00	4.00

Albums

ELEKTRA

Number	Title (A Side/B Side)	Yr	VG	VG+	NM
❑ 7E-1058	As Long As There's a Sunday	1976	2.50	5.00	10.00
❑ 7E-1108	Mixed Emotions	1977	2.50	5.00	10.00

HARMONY

Number	Title (A Side/B Side)	Yr	VG	VG+	NM
❑ H 30616	The World of Sammi Smith	1971	2.50	5.00	10.00

MEGA

Number	Title (A Side/B Side)	Yr	VG	VG+	NM
❑ 601	Rainbow in Daddy's Eyes	1974	3.00	6.00	12.00
❑ 612	Today I Started Loving You Again	1975	3.00	6.00	12.00
❑ 31-1000	Help Me Make It Through the Night	1971	3.00	6.00	12.00
❑ 31-1007	Lonesome	1971	3.00	6.00	12.00
❑ 31-1011	Something Old, Something New, Something Blue	1972	3.00	6.00	12.00
❑ 31-1019	The Best of Sammi Smith	1973	3.00	6.00	12.00
❑ 31-1021	The Toast of '45	1973	3.00	6.00	12.00

PICKWICK

Number	Title (A Side/B Side)	Yr	VG	VG+	NM
❑ 6167	Help Me Make It Through the Night	197?	2.50	5.00	10.00

ZODIAC

Number	Title (A Side/B Side)	Yr	VG	VG+	NM
❑ 5004	Her Way	1976	2.50	5.00	10.00

SMITH, WARREN

45s

LIBERTY

Number	Title (A Side/B Side)	Yr	VG	VG+	NM
❑ 55248	I Don't Believe I'll Fall in Love Today/Cave-In	1960	5.00	10.00	20.00
❑ 55302	Odds and Ends (Bits and Pieces)/A Whole Lot of Nothin'	1961	5.00	10.00	20.00
❑ 55336	Call of the Wild/Old Lonesome Feeling	1961	5.00	10.00	20.00
❑ 55361	Why Baby Why/Why I'm Walking	1961	5.00	10.00	20.00
—With Shirley Collie					
❑ 55409	Bad News Gets Around/Five Minutes of the Latest Blues	1962	5.00	10.00	20.00
❑ 55475	Book of Broken Hearts/160 Pounds of Hurt	1962	5.00	10.00	20.00
❑ 55615	Big City Ways/That's Why I Sing in a Honky Tonk	1963	3.75	7.50	15.00
❑ 55699	Blue Smoke/Judge and Jury	1964	3.75	7.50	15.00

MERCURY

Number	Title (A Side/B Side)	Yr	VG	VG+	NM
❑ 72825	Lie to Me/When the Heartaches Get to Me	1968	2.50	5.00	10.00

SUN

Number	Title (A Side/B Side)	Yr	VG	VG+	NM
❑ 239	Rock and Roll Ruby/I'd Rather Be Safe Than Sorry	1956	20.00	40.00	80.00
❑ 250	Ubangi Stomp/Black Jack David	1956	15.00	30.00	60.00
❑ 268	Miss Froggie/So Long, I'm Gone	1957	10.00	20.00	40.00
❑ 286	I Fell in Love/I've Got Love If You Want It	1958	7.50	15.00	30.00
❑ 314	Goodbye Mr. Love/Sweet Sweet Girl	1959	10.00	20.00	40.00

WARNER BROS.

Number	Title (A Side/B Side)	Yr	VG	VG+	NM
❑ 5125	Dear Santa/The Meaning of Christmas	1959	6.25	12.50	25.00

Albums

LIBERTY

Number	Title (A Side/B Side)	Yr	VG	VG+	NM
❑ LRP-3199 [M]	The First Country Collection of Warren Smith	1961	12.50	25.00	50.00
❑ LST-7199 [S]	The First Country Collection of Warren Smith	1961	17.50	35.00	70.00

SMOKIN' ARMADILLOS

45s

CURB

Number	Title (A Side/B Side)	Yr	VG	VG+	NM
❑ D7-76976	Let Your Heart Lead Your Mind/Miracle Man	1996	—	—	3.00
❑ D7-76989	Thump Factor/Miracle Man	1996	—	—	3.00

SNODGRASS, ELMER

45s

DECCA

Number	Title (A Side/B Side)	Yr	VG	VG+	NM
❑ 31048	Until Today/Sidelines	1960	3.75	7.50	15.00
❑ 31145	What a Terrible Feeling/Heartaches Over You	1960	3.75	7.50	15.00

SNOW, HANK

Also see CHET ATKINS.

45s

RCA

Number	Title (A Side/B Side)	Yr	VG	VG+	NM
❑ 2721-7-R	I've Been Everywhere/Ancient History	1990	—	—	3.00
—"Gold Standard Series" reissue					
❑ PB-10804	You're Wondering Why/Somewhere Someone Is Waiting for You	1976	—	2.50	5.00
❑ PB-11021	Trouble in Mind/Trying to Get My Baby Off My Mind	1977	—	2.50	5.00
❑ PB-11080	I'm Still Movin' On/I'm Gonna Bid My Blues Goodbye	1977	—	2.50	5.00
❑ PB-11153	Breakfast with the Blues/I've Done At Least One Thing	1977	—	2.50	5.00
❑ PB-11192	That Heart Belongs to Me/Love Is So Elusive	1978	—	2.50	5.00
❑ PB-11276	Nevertheless/Don't Rock the Boat	1978	—	2.50	5.00
❑ PB-11377	Ramblin' Rose/Red Roses	1978	—	2.50	5.00
❑ PB-11487	The Mysterious Lady from St. Martinique/Get On My Love Train	1979	—	2.50	5.00
❑ PB-11622	A Good Gal Is Hard to Find/I Wish My Heart Could Talk	1979	—	2.50	5.00
❑ PB-11734	It Takes Too Long/6 String Tennessee Flattop	1979	—	2.50	5.00

RCA VICTOR

Number	Title (A Side/B Side)	Yr	VG	VG+	NM
❑ APBO-0215	Hello Love/Until the End of Time	1974	—	3.50	7.00
❑ APBO-0307	That's You and Me/Brand on My Heart	1974	—	3.50	7.00
❑ PB-10108	Easy to Love/Just a Faded Petal from a Beautiful Bouquet	1974	—	3.00	6.00
❑ PB-10136	A Letter to Santa Claus/Christmas Roses	1974	—	3.50	7.00
❑ PB-10225	Merry-Go-Round of Love/My Filipino Love	1975	—	3.00	6.00
❑ PB-10338	Hijack/The Last Ride	1975	—	3.00	6.00
❑ PB-10439	Colorado Country Morning/I Keep Dreaming of You All the Time	1975	—	3.00	6.00
❑ PB-10459	Blue Christmas/Nestor, The Long Eared Christmas Donkey	1975	—	3.50	7.00
❑ GB-10513	Hello Love/Until the End of Time	1976	—	2.00	4.00
—"Gold Standard Series" reissue					
❑ PB-10681	Who's Been Here Since I've Been Gone/That's When He Dropped the World in My Hands	1976	—	3.00	6.00
❑ 37-7869	Beggar to a King/Poor Little Jimmie	1961	6.25	12.50	25.00
—"Compact Single 33" with small hole					
❑ 47-4095	Hobo Bill's Last Ride/Wreck of the Old 97	1951	5.00	10.00	20.00
❑ 47-4096	Ben Dewberry's Final Run/Engineer's Child	1951	5.00	10.00	20.00
❑ 47-4097	The Mystery of Number Five/One More Ride	1951	5.00	10.00	20.00
—The above three comprise a box set					
❑ 47-4346	Music Makin' Mama from Memphis/The Highest Bidder	1951	6.25	12.50	25.00
❑ 47-4398	Pray/These Things Shall Pass	1951	6.25	12.50	25.00
❑ 47-4522	The Gold Rush Is Over/Why Do You Promise Me	1952	6.25	12.50	25.00
❑ 47-4593	I'm Movin' On/Marriage Vow	1952	5.00	10.00	20.00
❑ 47-4594	Music Makin' Mama from Memphis/Down the Trail of Aching Hearts	1952	5.00	10.00	20.00
❑ 47-4595	Unwanted Sign Upon Your Heart/The Rhumba Boogie	1952	5.00	10.00	20.00
❑ 47-4596	The Golden Rocket/Bluebird Island	1952	5.00	10.00	20.00
—The above four comprise a box set					
❑ 47-4632	My Mother/I Just Telephone Upstairs	1952	6.25	12.50	25.00
❑ 47-4733	Lady's Man/Married by the Bible, Divorced by the Law	1952	6.25	12.50	25.00
❑ 47-4856	Jesus Wept/I'm in the Mood for Love	1952	6.25	12.50	25.00
❑ 47-4909	I Went to Your Wedding/Boogie Woogie Flying Cloud	1952	6.25	12.50	25.00
❑ 47-4973	Zeb Turney's Gal/Golden River	1952	5.00	10.00	20.00
❑ 47-4974	Moanin'/I Knew That We'd Meet Again	1952	5.00	10.00	20.00
❑ 47-4975	My Little Golden Horseshoe/The Yodeling Cowboy	1952	5.00	10.00	20.00
❑ 47-4976	Confused with the Blues/On That Old Hawaiian Shore	1952	5.00	10.00	20.00
—The above four comprise a box set					
❑ 47-5006	Broken Hearted/I Wonder Where You Are Tonight	1952	5.00	10.00	20.00
❑ 47-5026	Love Entered the Iron Door/I Cried But My Tears Were Too Late	1952	5.00	10.00	20.00
❑ 47-5034	(Now and Then, There's) A Fool Such As I/The Gal Who Invented Kissin'	1952	5.00	10.00	20.00
❑ 47-5155	Honeymoon on a Rocket Ship/There Wasn't an Organ at Our Wedding	1953	5.00	10.00	20.00
❑ 47-5220	Jimmie the Kid/My Blue Eyed Jane	1953	3.75	7.50	15.00
❑ 47-5221	When Jimmie Rodgers Said Goodbye/Treasure Untold	1953	3.75	7.50	15.00
❑ 47-5222	Southern Cannonball/Anniversary Blue Yodel	1953	3.75	7.50	15.00
❑ 47-5223	Why Did You Give Me Your Love/Mississippi River Blues	1953	3.75	7.50	15.00
—The above four comprise a box set					

Number	Title (A Side/B Side)	Yr	VG	VG+	NM
❑ 47-5249	Glory Land March/In Daddy's Footsteps	1953	5.00	10.00	20.00
❑ 47-5296	Spanish Fire Ball/Between Fire and Water	1953	5.00	10.00	20.00
❑ 47-5340	Christmas Roses/Reindeer Boogie	1953	6.25	12.50	25.00
❑ 47-5380	For Now and Always/A Message from the Tradewinds	1953	5.00	10.00	20.00
❑ 47-5490	When Mexican Joe Met Jole Blon/No Longer a Prisoner	1953	5.00	10.00	20.00
❑ 47-5548	I'm Glad I'm On the Inside/Invisible Hands	1953	5.00	10.00	20.00
❑ 47-5592	Panamama/Act 1, Act 2, Act 3	1954	5.00	10.00	20.00
❑ 47-5648	My Religion's Not Old Fashioned/Old Rattler	1954	6.25	12.50	25.00
—With Grandpa Jones					
❑ 47-5698	I Don't Hurt Anymore/My Arabian Baby	1954	5.00	10.00	20.00
❑ 47-5794	The Alphabet/My Religion's Not Old Fashioned	1954	5.00	10.00	20.00
❑ 47-5912	That Crazy Mambo Thing/The Next Voice You Hear	1954	5.00	10.00	20.00
❑ 47-5960	Let Me Go, Lover!/I've Forgotten You	1954	5.00	10.00	20.00
❑ 47-6057	Yellow Roses/Would You Mind	1955	3.75	7.50	15.00
❑ 47-6154	Cryin', Prayin', Waitin', Hopin'/I'm Glad I Got to See You Once Again	1955	3.75	7.50	15.00
❑ 47-6269	Born to Be Happy/Mainliner (The Hawk with Silver Wings)	1955	3.75	7.50	15.00
❑ 47-6326	In an Eighteenth Century Drawing Room/La Cucaracha	1955	3.75	7.50	15.00
❑ 47-6379	These Hands/I'm Moving In	1956	3.75	7.50	15.00
❑ 47-6578	Conscience I'm Guilty/Hula Rock	1956	6.25	12.50	25.00
❑ 47-6715	Stolen Moments/Two Won't Care	1956	3.75	7.50	15.00
❑ 47-6772	Oh, Wonderful World/Carnival of Venice	1957	3.75	7.50	15.00
❑ 47-6831	Calypso Sweethearts/Marriage and Divorce	1957	3.75	7.50	15.00
❑ 47-6955	Tangled Mind/My Arms Are a House	1957	3.75	7.50	15.00
❑ 47-7060	Unfaithful/Intro to Listeners-Squid Giggin' Ground	1957	3.75	7.50	15.00
❑ 47-7121	The Blue Danube Waltz/Under the Double Eagle	1957	3.75	7.50	15.00
❑ 47-7154	Whispering Rain/I Wish I Was the Moon	1958	3.75	7.50	15.00
❑ 47-7233	Big Wheels/I'm Hurting All Over	1958	3.75	7.50	15.00
❑ 47-7325	A Woman Captured Me/My Lucky Friend	1958	3.75	7.50	15.00
❑ 47-7448	Doggone That Train/Father Time and Mother Love	1959	3.75	7.50	15.00
❑ 47-7524	Chasin' a Rainbow/I Heard My Heart Break Last Night	1959	3.75	7.50	15.00
❑ 47-7586	The Last Ride/The Party of the Second Part	1959	3.75	7.50	15.00
❑ 47-7702	Rockin', Rollin' Ocean/Walkin' and Talkin'	1960	3.75	7.50	15.00
❑ 47-7748	Miller's Cave/The Change of the Tide	1960	3.75	7.50	15.00
❑ 47-7803	The Man Behind the Gun/I'm Asking for a Friend	1960	3.75	7.50	15.00
❑ 47-7869	Beggar to a King/Poor Little Jimmie	1961	3.00	6.00	12.00
❑ 47-7933	The Restless One/I Know	1961	3.00	6.00	12.00
❑ 47-8009	You Take the Future (And I'll Take the Past)/Dog Bone	1962	3.00	6.00	12.00
❑ 47-8072	I've Been Everywhere/Ancient History	1962	3.00	6.00	12.00
❑ 47-8151	The Man Who Robbed the Bank at Santa Fe/You're Losing Your Baby	1963	3.00	6.00	12.00
❑ 47-8151 [PS]	The Man Who Robbed the Bank at Santa Fe/You're Losing Your Baby	1963	6.25	12.50	25.00
❑ 47-8239	Ninety Miles an Hour (Down a Dead End Street)/Blue Roses	1963	3.00	6.00	12.00
❑ 47-8334	Breakfast with the Blues/I Stepped Over the Line	1964	3.00	6.00	12.00
❑ 47-8437	My Memory of You/Ninety Days	1964	3.00	6.00	12.00
❑ 47-8488	The Wishing Well (Down in the Well)/Human	1964	3.00	6.00	12.00
❑ 47-8548	Trouble in Mind/In the Misty Moonlight	1965	2.50	5.00	10.00
❑ 47-8655	The Queen of Draw Poker Town/Tears in the Trade Winds	1965	2.50	5.00	10.00
❑ 47-8713	I've Cried a Mile/Crazy Little Train (Of Love)	1965	2.50	5.00	10.00
❑ 47-8808	The Count Down/Isle of Sicily	1966	2.50	5.00	10.00
❑ 47-9012	Hula Love/Letter from Vietnam	1966	2.50	5.00	10.00
❑ 47-9030	Christmas Cannonball/God Is My Santa Claus	1966	3.00	6.00	12.00
❑ 47-9188	Down at the Pawn Shop/Listen	1967	2.50	5.00	10.00
❑ 47-9300	Learnin' a New Way of Life/Wild Flower	1967	2.50	5.00	10.00
❑ 47-9433	Who Will Answer? (Aleluya No. 1)/I Just Wanted to Know (How the Wind Was Blowing)	1968	2.50	5.00	10.00
❑ 47-9523	The Late and Great Love (Of My Life)/Born for You	1968	2.50	5.00	10.00
❑ 47-9685	The Name of the Game Was Love/The Gypsy and Me	1968	2.00	4.00	8.00
❑ 47-9856	Vanishing Breed/What More Can I Say	1970	2.00	4.00	8.00
❑ 47-9907	Come the Morning/Francesca	1970	2.00	4.00	8.00
❑ 47-9964	Duquesne, Pennsylvania/So Goes My Heart	1971	2.00	4.00	8.00
❑ 48-0056	Marriage Vow/The Star Spangled Waltz	1949	10.00	20.00	40.00
—Originals on green vinyl					
❑ 48-0056	Marriage Vow/The Star Spangled Waltz	195?	6.25	12.50	25.00
—Reissues on black vinyl					
❑ 48-0088	The Blind Boy's Dog/Anniversary of My Broken Heart	1949	10.00	20.00	40.00
—Originals on green vinyl					
❑ 48-0104	My Filipino Rose/The Law of Love	1949	10.00	20.00	40.00
—Originals on green vinyl					
❑ 48-0147	Nobody's Child/The Only Rose	1950	10.00	20.00	40.00
—Originals on green vinyl					
❑ 48-0214	Blue Ranger/Only a Rose from My Mother's Grave	1950	7.50	15.00	30.00
—Originals on green vinyl					
❑ 48-0224	Brand on My Heart/I'll Not Forget My Mother's Prayers	1950	7.50	15.00	30.00
—Originals on green vinyl					
❑ 48-0303	The Drunkard's Son/I Wonder Where You Are Tonight	1950	7.50	15.00	30.00
—Originals on green vinyl					
❑ 48-0328	I'm Movin' On/With This Ring I Thee Wed	1950	10.00	20.00	40.00
—Originals on green vinyl					
❑ 48-0328	I'm Movin' On/With This Ring I Thee Wed	1950	5.00	10.00	20.00
—Reissues on black vinyl					
❑ 48-0356	The Night I Stole Sammy Morgan's Gin/I Cried But My Tears Were Too Late	1950	7.50	15.00	30.00
—Originals on green vinyl					
❑ 48-0362	No Golden Tomorrow Ahead/You Broke the Chain That Held Our Hearts	1950	6.25	12.50	25.00
—Originals on green vinyl					
❑ 48-0363	Wasted Love/My Two Timin' Woman	1950	6.25	12.50	25.00
—Originals on green vinyl					
❑ 48-0364	Somewhere Along Life's Highway/Within This Broken Heart of Mine	1950	6.25	12.50	25.00
—Originals on green vinyl					
❑ 48-0400	The Golden Rocket/Paving the Highway with Tears	1950	7.50	15.00	30.00
—Originals on green vinyl					
❑ 48-0431	The Rhumba Boogie/You Pass Me By	1951	6.25	12.50	25.00
❑ 48-0498	Unwanted Sign Upon Your Heart/Your Locket Is My Broken Heart	1951	6.25	12.50	25.00
❑ 74-0151	Rome Wasn't Built in a Day/Like a Bird	1969	2.00	4.00	8.00
❑ 74-0251	That's When the Hurtin' Sets In/I'm Movin'	1969	2.00	4.00	8.00
❑ 74-0459	Blue Christmas/Nestor, The Long Eared Christmas Donkey	1971	—	—	—
—Unreleased					
❑ 74-0544	No One Will Ever Know/Seashores of Old Mexico	1971	2.00	4.00	8.00
❑ 74-0676	Canadian Pacific/My Way	1972	—	3.50	7.00
❑ 74-0818	The Governor's Hand/Rolling Thunder in My Mind	1972	—	3.50	7.00
❑ 74-0915	North to Chicago/Friend	1973	—	3.50	7.00

Albums

PAIR

Number	Title	Yr	VG	VG+	NM
❑ PDL2-1004 [(2)]	I'm Movin' On	1986	3.00	6.00	12.00

RCA CAMDEN

Number	Title	Yr	VG	VG+	NM
❑ ACL1-0124	Snowbird	1973	2.50	5.00	10.00
❑ ACL2-0337 [(2)]	When My Blue Moon Turns to Gold Again	197?	3.75	7.50	15.00
❑ CAL-514 [M]	The Singing Ranger	1959	5.00	10.00	20.00
❑ CAS-514 [R]	The Singing Ranger	196?	3.00	6.00	12.00
❑ ACL1-0540	I'm Movin' On	1974	2.50	5.00	10.00
❑ CAL-680 [M]	The Southern Cannonball	1961	5.00	10.00	20.00
❑ CAS-680 [R]	The Southern Cannonball	196?	3.00	6.00	12.00
❑ CAL-722 [M]	The One and Only Hank Snow	1962	5.00	10.00	20.00
❑ CAS-722 [R]	The One and Only Hank Snow	1962	3.00	6.00	12.00
❑ CAL-782 [M]	The Last Ride	1963	5.00	10.00	20.00
❑ CAS-782 [R]	The Last Ride	1963	3.00	6.00	12.00
❑ CAL-836 [M]	Old and Great Songs	1964	3.75	7.50	15.00
❑ CAS-836 [S]	Old and Great Songs	1964	3.00	6.00	12.00
❑ CAL-910 [M]	The Highest Bidder	1965	3.00	6.00	12.00
❑ CAS-910 [S]	The Highest Bidder	1965	3.75	7.50	15.00
❑ CAL-964 [M]	Travelin' Blues	1966	3.00	6.00	12.00
❑ CAS-964 [S]	Travelin' Blues	1966	3.75	7.50	15.00
❑ CAL-2160 [M]	My Early Favorites	1967	3.75	7.50	15.00
❑ CAS-2160 [S]	My Early Favorites	1967	3.00	6.00	12.00
❑ CAS-2257	My Nova Scotia Home	1968	3.00	6.00	12.00
❑ CAS-2348	I Went to Your Wedding	1969	3.00	6.00	12.00
❑ CAS-2443	Memories Are Made of This	1970	3.00	6.00	12.00
❑ CAS-2513	Lonesome Whistle	1972	3.00	6.00	12.00
❑ CAS-2560	The Legend of Old Doc Brown	1972	3.00	6.00	12.00
❑ CXS-9009 [(2)]	The Wreck of the 97	197?	3.75	7.50	15.00

RCA VICTOR

Number	Title	Yr	VG	VG+	NM
❑ DPL2-0134 [(2)]	The Living Legend	197?	25.00	50.00	100.00
—RCA Special Products release					
❑ APL1-0162	Grand Ole Opry Favorites	1973	3.75	7.50	15.00
❑ APL1-0441	Hello Love	1974	3.75	7.50	15.00
❑ APL1-0608	That's You and Me	1974	3.75	7.50	15.00
❑ APL1-0908	You're Easy to Love	1975	3.75	7.50	15.00
❑ LPM-1113 [M]	Just Keep a-Movin'	1955	25.00	50.00	100.00
❑ LPM-1156 [M]	Old Doc Brown and Other Narrations	1955	25.00	50.00	100.00
❑ ANL1-1207	Grand Ole Opry Favorites	1975	2.50	5.00	10.00
—Reissue of APL1-0162					
❑ LPM-1233 [M]	Country Classics	1956	20.00	40.00	80.00
❑ APL1-1361	Live from Evangel Temple	1976	3.00	6.00	12.00
—With Jimmy Snow					
❑ LPM-1419 [M]	Country and Western Jamboree	1957	20.00	40.00	80.00
❑ LPM-1435 [M]	Hank Snow's Country Guitar	1957	20.00	40.00	80.00
❑ LPM-1638 [M]	Hank Snow Sings Sacred Songs	1958	15.00	30.00	60.00
❑ LPM-2043 [M]	Hank Snow Sings Jimmie Rodgers Songs	1959	12.50	25.00	50.00
❑ LSP-2043 [S]	Hank Snow Sings Jimmie Rodgers Songs	1959	20.00	40.00	80.00
❑ ANL1-2194	The Jimmie Rodgers Story	1977	2.50	5.00	10.00
—Reissue of 4708					
❑ LPM-2285 [M]	Hank Snow Souvenirs	1961	7.50	15.00	30.00
❑ LSP-2285 [S]	Hank Snow Souvenirs	1961	10.00	20.00	40.00
❑ APL1-2400	#104 — Still Movin' On	1977	3.00	6.00	12.00
❑ LPM-2458 [M]	Big Country Hits	1961	7.50	15.00	30.00
❑ LSP-2458 [S]	Big Country Hits	1961	10.00	20.00	40.00
❑ LPM-2675 [M]	I've Been Everywhere	1963	7.50	15.00	30.00
❑ LSP-2675 [S]	I've Been Everywhere	1963	10.00	20.00	40.00
❑ LPM-2705 [M]	Railroad Man	1963	7.50	15.00	30.00
❑ LSP-2705 [S]	Railroad Man	1963	10.00	20.00	40.00
❑ LPM-2812 [M]	More Hank Snow Souvenirs	1964	6.25	12.50	25.00
❑ LSP-2812 [S]	More Hank Snow Souvenirs	1964	7.50	15.00	30.00
❑ LPM-2901 [M]	Songs of Tragedy	1964	6.25	12.50	25.00
❑ LSP-2901 [S]	Songs of Tragedy	1964	7.50	15.00	30.00
❑ LPM-3026 [10]	Country Classics	1952	50.00	100.00	200.00
❑ LPM-3070 [10]	Hank Snow Sings	1952	45.00	90.00	180.00

Number	Title (A Side/B Side)	Yr	VG	VG+	NM
❑ LPM-3131 [10]	Hank Snow Salutes Jimmie Rodgers	1953	45.00	90.00	180.00
❑ AHL1-3208	Mysterious Lady	1979	3.00	6.00	12.00
❑ LPM-3267 [10]	Hank Snow's Country Guitar	1954	45.00	90.00	180.00
❑ LPM-3317 [M]	Your Favorite Country Hits	1965	6.25	12.50	25.00
❑ LSP-3317 [S]	Your Favorite Country Hits	1965	7.50	15.00	30.00
❑ LPM-3378 [M]	Gloryland March	1965	6.25	12.50	25.00
❑ LSP-3378 [S]	Gloryland March	1965	7.50	15.00	30.00
❑ ANL1-3470	The Best of Hank Snow	1980	2.00	4.00	8.00
❑ LPM-3471 [M]	Heartbreak Trail - A Tribute to the Sons of the Pioneers	1966	6.25	12.50	25.00
❑ LSP-3471 [S]	Heartbreak Trail - A Tribute to the Sons of the Pioneers	1966	7.50	15.00	30.00
❑ LPM-3478 [M]	The Best of Hank Snow	1966	5.00	10.00	20.00
❑ LSP-3478 [S]	The Best of Hank Snow	1966	6.25	12.50	25.00
❑ AHL1-3511	Instrumentally Yours	1980	3.00	6.00	12.00
❑ LPM-3548 [M]	Guitar Stylings of Hank Snow	1966	6.25	12.50	25.00
❑ LSP-3548 [S]	Guitar Stylings of Hank Snow	1966	7.50	15.00	30.00
❑ LPM-3595 [M]	Gospel Train	1966	7.50	15.00	30.00
❑ LSP-3595 [S]	Gospel Train	1966	10.00	20.00	40.00
❑ LPM-3737 [M]	Snow in Hawaii	1967	7.50	15.00	30.00
❑ LSP-3737 [S]	Snow in Hawaii	1967	6.25	12.50	25.00
❑ LPM-3826 [M]	Christmas with Hank Snow	1967	7.50	15.00	30.00
❑ LSP-3826 [S]	Christmas with Hank Snow	1967	6.25	12.50	25.00
❑ LPM-3857 [M]	Spanish Fire Ball and Other Great Hank Snow Stylings	1967	7.50	15.00	30.00
❑ LSP-3857 [S]	Spanish Fire Ball and Other Great Hank Snow Stylings	1967	6.25	12.50	25.00
❑ LPM-3965 [M]	Hits, Hits and More Hits	1968	25.00	50.00	100.00
❑ LSP-3965 [S]	Hits, Hits and More Hits	1968	6.25	12.50	25.00
❑ LSP-4032	Tales of the Yukon	1968	6.25	12.50	25.00
❑ LSP-4122	Snow in All Seasons	1969	6.25	12.50	25.00
❑ LSP-4306	Hank Snow Sings in Memory of Jimmie Rodgers	1970	5.00	10.00	20.00
❑ LSP-4379	Cure for the Blues	1970	5.00	10.00	20.00
❑ LSP-4501	Tracks and Trains	1971	5.00	10.00	20.00
❑ LSP-4601	Award Winners	1971	5.00	10.00	20.00
❑ LSP-4708	The Jimmie Rodgers Story	1972	3.75	7.50	15.00
❑ LSP-4798	The Best of Hank Snow, Vol. 2	1972	3.75	7.50	15.00
❑ AHL1-5497	Collector's Series	1986	2.50	5.00	10.00
❑ LPM-6014 [(2) M]	This Is My Story	1966	10.00	20.00	40.00
❑ LSP-6014 [(2) S]	This Is My Story	1966	12.50	25.00	50.00
READER'S DIGEST					
❑ RDA-216 [(6)]	I'm Movin' On	197?	30.00	60.00	120.00
SCHOOL OF MUSIC					
❑ 1149 [M]	The Guitar	1958	62.50	125.00	250.00

—Deduct 20 percent if instruction book is missing

SNOW, HANK, AND CHET ATKINS

Albums

RCA VICTOR

Number	Title (A Side/B Side)	Yr	VG	VG+	NM
❑ LPM-2952 [M]	Reminiscing	1964	6.25	12.50	25.00
❑ LSP-2952 [S]	Reminiscing	1964	7.50	15.00	30.00
❑ LSP-4254	By Special Request - C.B. Atkins and C.E. Snow	1970	5.00	10.00	20.00

SNOW, HANK, AND ANITA CARTER

Also see each artist's individual listings.

45s

RCA VICTOR

Number	Title (A Side/B Side)	Yr	VG	VG+	NM
❑ 47-6500	Keep Your Promise, Willie Thomas/It's You, Only You, That I Love	1956	3.75	7.50	15.00
❑ 48-0441	Down the Trail of Achin' Hearts/Bluebird Island	1951	6.25	12.50	25.00

Albums

RCA VICTOR

Number	Title (A Side/B Side)	Yr	VG	VG+	NM
❑ LPM-2580 [M]	Together Again	1962	7.50	15.00	30.00
❑ LSP-2580 [S]	Together Again	1962	10.00	20.00	40.00

SNOW, HANK, AND KELLY FOXTON

Also see each artist's individual listings.

45s

RCA

Number	Title (A Side/B Side)	Yr	VG	VG+	NM
❑ PB-11891	Hasn't It Been Good Together/It Was Love	1980	—	2.50	5.00
❑ PB-11967	There's Something About You/All I Want to Do Is Touch You	1980	—	2.50	5.00
❑ PB-12102	Pain Didn't Shout/Check	1980	—	2.50	5.00
❑ PB-12235	Things/Forbidden Lovers	1981	—	2.50	5.00

Albums

RCA VICTOR

Number	Title (A Side/B Side)	Yr	VG	VG+	NM
❑ AHL1-3496	Lovingly Yours	1980	2.50	5.00	10.00
❑ AYL1-3987	Win Some, Lose Some, Lonesome	1981	2.50	5.00	10.00

SNOW, HANK; PORTER WAGONER; HANK LOCKLIN

Albums

RCA VICTOR

Number	Title (A Side/B Side)	Yr	VG	VG+	NM
❑ LPM-2723 [M]	Three Country Gentlemen	1963	7.50	15.00	30.00
❑ LSP-2723 [S]	Three Country Gentlemen	1963	10.00	20.00	40.00

SNOW, JIMMIE RODGERS

45s

RCA VICTOR

Number	Title (A Side/B Side)	Yr	VG	VG+	NM
❑ 47-5693	My Fallen Star/Well Whaddaya Know	1954	5.00	10.00	20.00
❑ 47-5900	How Do You Think I Feel/Why Don't You Let Me Go	1954	5.00	10.00	20.00
❑ 47-5986	Love Me/I Can't Spell	1955	5.00	10.00	20.00
❑ 47-6130	The Flame of Love/Someone Else's Heartaches	1955	5.00	10.00	20.00
❑ 47-6189	Go Back You Fool/I Care No More	1955	5.00	10.00	20.00
❑ 47-6303	Bee Line/The Meanest Thing in the World Is the Blues	1955	5.00	10.00	20.00
❑ 47-6430	The Milk Cow Blues/It Won't Do No Good	1956	5.00	10.00	20.00
❑ 47-6623	La Strada (The Road)/The One Note Polka	1956	3.75	7.50	15.00
❑ 47-7234	You Fool You/Rules of Love	1958	3.75	7.50	15.00

—As "Jimmie Snow"

SNUFF

45s

ELEKTRA

Number	Title (A Side/B Side)	Yr	VG	VG+	NM
❑ 69897	When Jokers Are Wild/Heaven in Your Eyes	1982	—	2.00	4.00
❑ 69996	(So This Is) Happy Hour/It Must Be Love	1982	—	2.00	4.00
WARNER BROS.					
❑ 29615	Bad, Bad Billy/Defiance	1983	—	2.00	4.00

Albums

ELEKTRA

Number	Title (A Side/B Side)	Yr	VG	VG+	NM
❑ 60149	Snuff	1982	2.50	5.00	10.00

SNYDER, JIMMY

45s

E.I.O.

Number	Title (A Side/B Side)	Yr	VG	VG+	NM
❑ 1126	Just to Prove My Love to You/Kiss Your Love Goodbye	1980	—	3.00	6.00
WAYSIDE					
❑ 001	Candy All Over My Face/Here Comes My Sunshine	1969	—	3.50	7.00
—Reissue of 1029					
❑ 006	Out of My Mind/Pretty One	1969	—	3.50	7.00
❑ 009	The Chicago Story/Take Her Flowers	1970	—	3.50	7.00
❑ 012	Husbands and Wives/Ain't That Something	1970	—	3.50	7.00
❑ 017	My Place in the Sun/Till I'm Out of My Mind	1970	—	3.50	7.00
❑ 1029	Candy All Over My Face/Here Comes My Sunshine	1969	2.00	4.00	8.00

SNYDER, RICK

45s

CAPITOL

Number	Title (A Side/B Side)	Yr	VG	VG+	NM
❑ B-44185	Losing Somebody You Love/I Know the Feeling	1988	—	—	3.00

SOLID GOLD BAND

45s

NSD

Number	Title (A Side/B Side)	Yr	VG	VG+	NM
❑ 92	Blackjack and Water/Lonesome Wind	1981	—	2.50	5.00
❑ 110	Cherokee Country/It's Just Your Memory	1981	—	2.50	5.00
❑ 121	I Never Had the One That I Wanted/Bandera, Texas	1982	—	2.50	5.00
❑ 127	Good Friends Are Hard to Find/Me, My Ol' Guitar and Merle	1982	—	2.50	5.00
❑ 138	Country Fiddles/The Sun Shines Bright in Oklahoma	1982	—	2.50	5.00
❑ 153	Another Night of Pickin' Country Music/Blackjack and Water	1983	—	2.50	5.00
❑ 208	The Swingin' Side of Them Swingin' Doors/If We Could Grow Young Not Old	198?	—	2.50	5.00
❑ 219	Alcohol of Fame/Big John Law	198?	—	2.50	5.00

SOME OF CHET'S FRIENDS

Also see CHET ATKINS.

45s

RCA VICTOR

Number	Title (A Side/B Side)	Yr	VG	VG+	NM
❑ 47-9229	Chet's Tune/Country Gentleman	1967	2.50	5.00	10.00
❑ 47-9229 [PS]	Chet's Tune/Country Gentleman	1967	3.75	7.50	15.00
❑ 74-0799	Chet's Tune (Part 1)/Chet's Tune (Part 2)	1972	—	3.00	6.00

SON VOLT

Albums

WARNER BROS.

Number	Title (A Side/B Side)	Yr	VG	VG+	NM
❑ 46518	Straightaways	1997	3.00	6.00	12.00
❑ 47059	Wide Swing Tremolo	1998	3.00	6.00	12.00

SONNIER, JO-EL

45s

CAPITOL NASHVILLE

Number	Title (A Side/B Side)	Yr	VG	VG+	NM
❑ 7PRO-79563	You May Change Your Mind (same on both sides)	1991	—	3.00	6.00
—Vinyl is promo only					
GOLDBAND					
❑ 1175	Turn Back/Eleven Years Innocent	196?	3.75	7.50	15.00
❑ 1189	Hurricane Audrey/Jump Little Frog	1969	2.50	5.00	10.00
❑ 1192	Take Me in Your Arms/Top Rocking Joe	1969	2.50	5.00	10.00
❑ 1193	My Girl of the Village/The Monkey Played Fiddle	1969	2.50	5.00	10.00
❑ 1195	I Won't Be Lonesome/Secret of Love	1970	2.00	4.00	8.00
❑ 1202	Where Can I Go/His Own Troubles	1970	2.00	4.00	8.00
❑ 1204	Curse of the Loser/The White Dove Has Died	197?	2.00	4.00	8.00
❑ 1216	Rat Race of Time/Together We're One	197?	2.00	4.00	8.00
❑ 1242	Merry Christmas Tonight/Coming for Christmas	197?	—	3.00	6.00
—B-side by Charles Page					
MERCURY					
❑ 55002	Cajun Born/It Don't Hurt Me Half As Bad	1977	—	2.50	5.00
❑ 73655	Cajun Woman/Blue Is Not a Word	1975	—	2.50	5.00
❑ 73702	I've Been Around Enough to Know/Brighter Shade of Blue	1975	—	2.50	5.00
❑ 73784	Always Late (With Your Kisses)/Knock, Knock, Knock	1976	—	2.50	5.00
❑ 73796	He's Still All Over You/Am I Just Your Friend	1976	—	2.50	5.00
❑ 73824	Showboat Gambler/Cheatin' Turns Her On	1976	—	2.50	5.00

Number	Title (A Side/B Side)	Yr	VG	VG+	NM
RCA					
❑ 5282-7-R	Come On Joe/Say You Love Me	1987	—	—	3.00
❑ 6895-7-R	No More One More Time/Louisiana 1927	1988	—	—	3.00
❑ 8304-7-R	Tear-Stained Letter/Say You Love Me	1988	—	—	3.00
❑ 8726-7-R	Rainin' in My Heart/Baby Hold On	1988	—	—	3.00
❑ 8918-7-R	(Blue, Blue, Blue) Blue, Blue/I've Got Dreams to Remember	1989	—	—	3.00
❑ 9014-7-R	If You Heart Should Ever Roll This Way Again/ You Done Me Wrong	1989	—	—	3.00
❑ 9123-7-R	The Scene of the Crime/Evangeline Special	1990	—	—	3.00
Albums					
RCA					
❑ 6374-1-R	Come On Joe	1988	2.00	4.00	8.00
❑ 8396-RDJ [DJ]	Jo-El	1989	3.75	7.50	15.00
—Promo-only sampler					
❑ 9718-1-R	Have a Little Faith	1990	3.00	6.00	12.00
ROUNDER					
❑ 3049	Cajun Life	1988	2.50	5.00	10.00

SONS OF THE DESERT

Number	Title (A Side/B Side)	Yr	VG	VG+	NM
45s					
EPIC					
❑ 34-78663	Hand of Fate/Burned in My Mind	1997	—	2.00	4.00
MCA NASHVILLE					
❑ 088 172156-7	Change/Albuquerque	2000	—	—	3.00
❑ 088 172179-7	Everybody's Gotta Grow Up Sometime/Ride	2000	—	—	3.00

SONS OF THE PIONEERS

Also see BOB NOLAN; ROY ROGERS.

Number	Title (A Side/B Side)	Yr	VG	VG+	NM
45s					
CORAL					
❑ 9-61186	River of No Return/The Lilies Grow High	1954	5.00	10.00	20.00
❑ 9-61316	Montana/Lonely Little Room	1954	5.00	10.00	20.00
❑ 9-64172	Sierra Nevada/If You Would Only Be Mine	1954	5.00	10.00	20.00
DECCA					
❑ 9-29814	Cool Water/Tumbling Tumbleweeds	1956	3.75	7.50	15.00
GRANITE					
❑ 550	Cool Water/Pretty Painted Ladies	1976	—	3.00	6.00
❑ 551	Indian Woman/(B-side unknown)	1977	—	3.00	6.00
RCA VICTOR					
❑ WBY-25	The Ballad of Davy Crockett/The Graveyard Filler of the West	1955	7.50	15.00	30.00
❑ WBY-27	A Whale of a Tale/Old Betsy	1955	6.25	12.50	25.00
❑ WBY-46	Home on the Range/Cheyenne	1957	5.00	10.00	20.00
❑ WBY-46 [PS]	Home on the Range/Cheyenne	1957	7.50	15.00	30.00
❑ 47-2836	Cool Water/Chant of the Wanderer	1949	7.50	15.00	30.00
❑ 47-2837	Tumbling Tumbleweeds/The Everlasting Hills of Oklahoma	1949	7.50	15.00	30.00
❑ 47-2838	Trees/The Timber Trail	1949	7.50	15.00	30.00
—The above three comprise a box set; quickly reissued as 48-0004, 0005 and 0006					
❑ 47-3983	America Forever/Little White Cross	1950	6.25	12.50	25.00
❑ 47-4071	Roses/Mexicali Rose	1951	5.00	10.00	20.00
❑ 47-4072	Moonlight and Roses/Bring Your Roses to Her Now	1951	5.00	10.00	20.00
❑ 47-4073	San Antonio Rose/Room Full of Roses	1951	5.00	10.00	20.00
—The above three comprise a box set					
❑ 47-4131	Daddy's Little Cowboy/Baby I Ain't Gonna Cry No More	1951	5.00	10.00	20.00
❑ 47-4264	Heart Break Hill/The Wind	1951	5.00	10.00	20.00
❑ 47-4347	The Lord's Prayer/Resurectus	1951	5.00	10.00	20.00
❑ 47-4431	Outlaws/I Still Do	1951	5.00	10.00	20.00
❑ 47-4459	I Told Them All About You/Ho-Le-O	1952	5.00	10.00	20.00
❑ 47-4571	Land Beyond the Sun/Waltz of the Roses	1952	5.00	10.00	20.00
❑ 47-4639	Diesel Smoke/Almost	1952	5.00	10.00	20.00
❑ 47-4937	Let's Pretend/The Everlasting Hills of Oklahoma	1952	5.00	10.00	20.00
❑ 47-6055	The Ballad of Davy Crockett/Graveyard Filler of the West	1955	6.25	12.50	25.00
❑ 47-6109	I Wonder When We'll Ever Know/The King's Highway	1955	3.75	7.50	15.00
❑ 47-6123	The Tennessee Rock 'n' Roll/The Three of Us	1955	6.25	12.50	25.00
❑ 47-6184	Be What You Want to Be/Epidemic	1955	3.75	7.50	15.00
❑ 47-6276	Yaller Yaller Gold/King of the River	1955	5.00	10.00	20.00
❑ 47-6376	How Great Thou Art/The Last Frontier	1956	3.75	7.50	15.00
❑ 47-6507	The Searchers/Song of the Prodigal Son	1956	3.75	7.50	15.00
❑ 47-6655	For the Love of You/Timmy's Tune	1956	3.75	7.50	15.00
❑ 47-6890	One More Time/Hasta La Vista	1957	3.75	7.50	15.00
❑ 47-7024	Ballad of the Cowboy Sailor/The Piney Woods	1957	3.75	7.50	15.00
❑ 47-7079	High Ridin' Woman/God Has His Arms Around Me	1957	3.75	7.50	15.00
❑ 47-7392	A Fiddle, a Rifle, an Ax and a Bible/My Last Goodbye	1958	3.00	6.00	12.00
❑ 47-8310	Crazy Arms/Cattle Call Rondolet	1963	2.50	5.00	10.00
❑ 47-8575	Destiny/Green Ice and Mountain Men	1965	2.50	5.00	10.00
❑ 47-9509	Gringo's Guitar/Margretta	1968	2.00	4.00	8.00
❑ 48-0004	Cool Water/Chant of the Wanderer	1949	7.50	15.00	30.00
—Green vinyl original					
❑ 48-0004	Cool Water/Chant of the Wanderer	1951	5.00	10.00	20.00
—Black vinyl reissue					
❑ 48-0005	Tumbling Tumbleweeds/Everlasting Hills of Oklahoma	1949	7.50	15.00	30.00
—Green vinyl original					
❑ 48-0005	Tumbling Tumbleweeds/Everlasting Hills of Oklahoma	1949	5.00	10.00	20.00
—Black vinyl reissue					
❑ 48-0006	Trees/The Timber Trail	1949	7.50	15.00	30.00
—Green vinyl original					
❑ 48-0006	Trees/The Timber Trail	1949	5.00	10.00	20.00
—Black vinyl reissue					
❑ 48-0007	Blue Prairie/Cowboy Camp Meetin'	1949	7.50	15.00	30.00
—Green vinyl original					
❑ 48-0007	Blue Prairie/Cowboy Camp Meetin'	1949	5.00	10.00	20.00
—Black vinyl reissue					
❑ 48-0060	Room Full of Roses/Riders in the Sky	1949	7.50	15.00	30.00
—Green vinyl original					
❑ 48-0094	Rounded Up in Glory/Too High, Too Wide, Too Low	1949	7.50	15.00	30.00
—Green vinyl original					
❑ 48-0095	Lead Me Gently Home Father/Power in the Blood	1949	7.50	15.00	30.00
—Green vinyl original					
❑ 48-0096	The Old Rugged Cross/Read the Bible Every Day	1949	7.50	15.00	30.00
—Green vinyl original					
❑ 48-0101	Lie Low Little Doggies/Bar None Ranch	1949	7.50	15.00	30.00
—Green vinyl original					
❑ 48-0141	Red River Valley/Santa Fe, New Mexico	1950	7.50	15.00	30.00
—Green vinyl original					
❑ 48-0171	Wedding Bells/Love at the County Fair	1950	7.50	15.00	30.00
—With Dale Evans; green vinyl original					
❑ 48-0183	Cigareets, Whusky and Wild, Wild Women/My Best to You	1950	7.50	15.00	30.00
—Green vinyl; reissue of hit 78 rpm from 1947					
❑ 48-0184	Let's Go West Again/Let Me Share Your Name	1950	7.50	15.00	30.00
—Green vinyl original					
❑ 48-0220	Teardrops in My Heart/You Don't Know What Lonesome Is	1950	7.50	15.00	30.00
—Green vinyl; reissue of hit 78 from 1947					
❑ 48-0221	The Sea Walker/The Touch of God's Hand	1950	7.50	15.00	30.00
—Green vinyl original					
❑ 48-0306	Roses/The Eagle's Heart	1950	6.25	12.50	25.00
—Green vinyl original					
❑ 48-0315	Rollin' Dust/Wagons West	1950	6.25	12.50	25.00
—Green vinyl original					
❑ 48-0345	Song of the Wagonmaster/Chuckawalla Swing	1950	6.25	12.50	25.00
—Green vinyl original					
❑ 48-0366	Land Beyond the Sun/I Told Them All About You	1950	6.25	12.50	25.00
—Green vinyl original					
❑ 48-0368	Old Man Atom/What This Country Needs	1950	6.25	12.50	25.00
—Green vinyl original					
❑ 48-0388	Where Are You/What This Country Needs	1950	6.25	12.50	25.00
—Green vinyl original					
❑ 48-0486	Lonesome/The Wondrous Word	1951	5.00	10.00	20.00
❑ 74-0199	Talli Wind/Hawaiian Lullaby	1969	2.00	4.00	8.00
Selected 78s					
COLUMBIA					
❑ 20226	I Love You, Nelly/When the Roses Bloom Again	1948	3.00	6.00	12.00
—Reissue of 37627					
❑ 20499	Hold That Critter Down/The Devil's Great Grandson	1948	3.75	7.50	15.00
❑ 20500	One More River to Cross/Open Road Ahead	1948	3.75	7.50	15.00
❑ 37627	I Love You, Nelly/When the Roses Bloom Again	1947	3.75	7.50	15.00
—Reissue of older material					
DECCA					
❑ 5013	Ridin' Home/(B-side unknown)	1934	6.25	12.50	25.00
❑ 5047	Tumbling Tumbleweeds/Moonlight on the Prairie	1934	7.50	15.00	30.00
—Original version of this classic					
❑ 5939	Cool Water/(B-side unknown)	1941	6.25	12.50	25.00
—Original version of this classic					
❑ 46027	Cool Water/Tumbling Tumbleweeds	1947	5.00	10.00	20.00
❑ 46059	There's a New Moon Over My Shoulder/Kelly Waltz	1947	5.00	10.00	20.00
❑ 46160	So Long to the Red River Valley/Empty Saddles	1949	5.00	10.00	20.00
RCA VICTOR					
❑ 20-1724	Stars and Stripes on Iwo Jima/Cool Water	1945	5.00	10.00	20.00
❑ 20-1764	Forgive and Forget/The Timber Trail	1945	5.00	10.00	20.00
❑ 20-1868	No One to Cry To/Grievin' My Heart Out for You	1946	5.00	10.00	20.00
❑ 20-1904	Tumbling Tumbleweeds/Cowboy Camp Meetin'	1947	5.00	10.00	20.00
❑ 20-1952	Out California Way/(B-side unknown)	1946	5.00	10.00	20.00
❑ 20-2078	Blue Prairie/Cowboy Camp Meetin'	1947	5.00	10.00	20.00
❑ 20-2086	Baby Doll/The Letter Marked Unclaimed	1947	5.00	10.00	20.00
❑ 20-2199	Cigareets, Whusky, and Wild, Wild Women/My Best to You	1947	5.00	10.00	20.00
❑ 20-2276	Teardrops in My Heart/You Don't Know What Lonesome Is	1947	5.00	10.00	20.00
❑ 20-2484	Out in Pioneertown/You'll Be Sorry	1947	5.00	10.00	20.00
❑ 20-2725	Happy Birthday Polka/Calico Apron	1948	5.00	10.00	20.00
❑ 20-3082	My Feet Takes Me Away/Missouri	1949	5.00	10.00	20.00
VOCALION					
❑ 03399	Power in the Blood/(B-side unknown)	193?	5.00	10.00	20.00
❑ 03880	Open Range Ahead/(B-side unknown)	193?	5.00	10.00	20.00
❑ 03881	Smilin' Through/(B-side unknown)	193?	5.00	10.00	20.00
❑ 03916	I Love You, Nelly/(B-side unknown)	193?	5.00	10.00	20.00
❑ 04136	Billy the Kid/(B-side unknown)	193?	5.00	10.00	20.00
❑ 04187	Hear Dem Bells/(B-side unknown)	193?	5.00	10.00	20.00
❑ 04264	Cajun Stomp/(B-side unknown)	193?	5.00	10.00	20.00
❑ 04328	Send Him Home to Me/(B-side unknown)	193?	5.00	10.00	20.00
Albums					
COLUMBIA					
❑ FC 37439	The Sons of the Pioneers: Columbia Historical Edition	1981	2.50	5.00	10.00

Number	Title (A Side/B Side)	Yr	VG	VG+	NM
MCA					
❑ 730	Tumbleweed Trails	198?	2.50	5.00	10.00
RCA CAMDEN					
❑ CAL-413 [M]	Wagons West	1958	5.00	10.00	20.00
❑ CAS-413 [R]	Wagons West	1963	3.00	6.00	12.00
❑ CAL-587 [M]	Room Full of Roses	1960	5.00	10.00	20.00
RCA VICTOR					
❑ PRM-104 [M]	Westward Ho!	1961	6.25	12.50	25.00
—Special-products issue					
❑ LPM-1130 [M]	Favorite Cowboy Songs	1955	12.50	25.00	50.00
❑ LPM-1431 [M]	How Great Thou Art	1957	12.50	25.00	50.00
❑ LPM-1483 [M]	One Man's Songs	1957	12.50	25.00	50.00
❑ LPM-2118 [M]	Cool Water	1960	6.25	12.50	25.00
❑ LSP-2118 [S]	Cool Water	1960	7.50	15.00	30.00
❑ ANL1-2332	A Country-Western Songbook	1977	3.75	7.50	15.00
❑ LPM-2356 [M]	Lure of the West	1961	6.25	12.50	25.00
❑ LSP-2356 [S]	Lure of the West	1961	7.50	15.00	30.00
❑ LPM-2456 [M]	Tumbleweed Trails	1962	6.25	12.50	25.00
❑ LSP-2456 [S]	Tumbleweed Trails	1962	7.50	15.00	30.00
❑ LPM-2603 [M]	Our Men Out West	1963	5.00	10.00	20.00
❑ LSP-2603 [S]	Our Men Out West	1963	6.25	12.50	25.00
❑ LPM-2652 [M]	Hymns of the Cowboy	1963	5.00	10.00	20.00
❑ LSP-2652 [S]	Hymns of the Cowboy	1963	6.25	12.50	25.00
❑ LPM-2737 [M]	Trail Dust	1963	5.00	10.00	20.00
❑ LSP-2737 [S]	Trail Dust	1963	6.25	12.50	25.00
❑ LPM-2855 [M]	Country Fare	1964	5.00	10.00	20.00
❑ LSP-2855 [S]	Country Fare	1964	6.25	12.50	25.00
❑ LPM-2957 [M]	Down Memory Trail	1964	5.00	10.00	20.00
❑ LSP-2957 [S]	Down Memory Trail	1964	6.25	12.50	25.00
❑ LPM-3032 [10]	Cowboy Classics	1952	25.00	50.00	100.00
❑ LPM-3095 [10]	Cowboy Hymns and Spirituals	1952	25.00	50.00	100.00
❑ LPM-3162 [10]	Western Classics	1953	25.00	50.00	100.00
❑ LPM-3351 [M]	Legends of the West	1965	3.75	7.50	15.00
❑ LSP-3351 [S]	Legends of the West	1965	5.00	10.00	20.00
❑ ANL1-3468	The Best of the Sons of the Pioneers	1980	2.50	5.00	10.00
❑ LPM-3476 [M]	The Best of Sons of the Pioneers	1966	3.75	7.50	15.00
❑ LSP-3476 [S]	The Best of Sons of the Pioneers	1966	5.00	10.00	20.00
❑ LPM-3554 [M]	The Songs of Bob Nolan	1966	3.75	7.50	15.00
❑ LSP-3554 [S]	The Songs of Bob Nolan	1966	5.00	10.00	20.00
❑ AYL1-3679	Cool Water	1980	2.50	5.00	10.00
❑ LPM-3714 [M]	Campfire Favorites	1967	6.25	12.50	25.00
❑ LSP-3714 [S]	Campfire Favorites	1967	5.00	10.00	20.00
❑ LPM-3964 [M]	South of the Border	1968	20.00	40.00	80.00
❑ LSP-3964 [S]	South of the Border	1968	5.00	10.00	20.00
❑ AYM1-4092	Let's Go West Again	1981	2.50	5.00	10.00

SONS OF THE PURPLE SAGE

Albums

Number	Title (A Side/B Side)	Yr	VG	VG+	NM
TOPS					
❑ L-1588 [M]	Western Favorites	1959	5.00	10.00	20.00
WALDORF					
❑ 143 [10]	Songs of the Golden West	1955	12.50	25.00	50.00

SOSEBEE, TOMMY

45s

Number	Title (A Side/B Side)	Yr	VG	VG+	NM
CORAL					
❑ 9-60916	Till I Waltz Again with You/All Night Boogie	1953	6.25	12.50	25.00
❑ 9-61406	Time/That's What I Call Love	1955	5.00	10.00	20.00
❑ 9-64071	I'm So Lonesome/You Can't Erase My Memory	1951	6.25	12.50	25.00
❑ 9-64080	She's My Easter Lily/Easter Parade	1951	6.25	12.50	25.00
❑ 9-64087	Mail Order Kisses/You're Always Brand New	1951	6.25	12.50	25.00
❑ 9-64094	The Singing Hills/You're Fixin' to Break My Heart	1951	6.25	12.50	25.00
❑ 9-64097	Wedding Blossoms/Honesick, Lonesome and Sorry	1951	6.25	12.50	25.00
❑ 9-64102	No Good Without You/Year After Year	1951	6.25	12.50	25.00
❑ 9-64107	Winter Wonderland/New Year Bells	1951	7.50	15.00	30.00
❑ 9-64110	Don't Trade Your Love for Gold/If You Don't Believe I'm Leaving	1951	6.25	12.50	25.00
❑ 9-64120	How Can You Smile/Don't Waste Your Tears	1952	6.25	12.50	25.00
❑ 9-64134	Many Miles/Pretty Little Girl	1952	6.25	12.50	25.00
❑ 9-64144	Saviour of the Rugged Cross/The Lord Lives at Your House	1952	6.25	12.50	25.00
❑ 9-64154	Love Is Deeper Than Pride/Nervous Feeling	1953	6.25	12.50	25.00
❑ 9-64158	Honky Tonk Waltz/Love Me	1953	6.25	12.50	25.00
❑ 9-64164	The Barber Shop Boogie/Anywhere, Anyplace, Anytime	1953	6.25	12.50	25.00
❑ 9-64183	If I Give My Heart to You/Don't Count Me Out	1954	6.25	12.50	25.00

SOUTH, JOE

45s

Number	Title (A Side/B Side)	Yr	VG	VG+	NM
ALLWOOD					
❑ 402	Just Remember You're Mine/Silly Me	1962	3.00	6.00	12.00
APT					
❑ 25084	Deep Inside Me/I Want to Be Somebody	1965	2.50	5.00	10.00
CAPITOL					
❑ 2060	Birds of a Feather/It Got Away	1967	2.00	4.00	8.00
❑ 2169	How Can I Unlove You/She's Almost You	1968	2.00	4.00	8.00
❑ 2248	Games People Play/Mirror of Your Mind	1968	2.00	4.00	8.00
❑ 2284	Redneck/Don't Throw Your Love to the Wind	1968	2.00	4.00	8.00
❑ 2491	Leanin' On You/Don't You Be Ashamed	1969	—	3.00	6.00
❑ 2532	Birds of a Feather/These Are Not My People	1969	—	3.00	6.00
❑ 2592	Don't It Make You Want to Go Home/Heart's Desire	1969	—	3.00	6.00
❑ 2704	Walk a Mile in My Shoes/Sheltered	1969	—	3.00	6.00
❑ 2755	Children/The Clock Up On the Wall	1970	—	2.50	5.00
❑ 2916	Why Does a Man Do What He Has to Do/Be a Believer	1970	—	2.50	5.00
❑ 3008	Rose Garden/Mirror of Your Mind	1971	—	3.00	6.00
❑ 3053	United We Stand/So the Seeds Are Growing	1971	—	2.50	5.00
❑ 3204	Fool Me/Devil May Care	1971	—	2.50	5.00
❑ 3450	One Man Band/Coming Down All Alone	1972	—	2.50	5.00
❑ 3487	I'm a Star/Misunderstanding	1972	—	2.50	5.00
❑ 3554	Real Thing/Save Your Best	1973	—	2.50	5.00
❑ 3717	Riverdog/It Hurts Me Too	1973	—	2.50	5.00
COLUMBIA					
❑ 43983	Backfield in Motion/I'll Come Back to You	1967	3.00	6.00	12.00
❑ 44218	A Fool in Love/Great Day	1967	3.00	6.00	12.00
FAIRLANE					
❑ 21006	You're the Reason/Jukebox	1961	5.00	10.00	20.00
❑ 21010	Masquerade/I'm Sorry for You	1961	3.75	7.50	15.00
❑ 21015	Slippin' Around/Just to Be with You Again	1962	3.75	7.50	15.00
ISLAND					
❑ 034	To Have, to Hold and Let Go/Midnight Rainbows	1975	—	2.00	4.00
MGM					
❑ 13145	Same Old Song/Standing Invitation	1963	2.50	5.00	10.00
❑ 13196	Concrete Jungle/The Last One to Know	1963	2.50	5.00	10.00
❑ 13276	Naughty Claudie/Little Queenie	1964	2.50	5.00	10.00
NRC					
❑ 002	I'm Snowed/It's Only You	1958	10.00	20.00	40.00
❑ 022	Chills/What a Night	1959	3.75	7.50	15.00
❑ 041	Little Bluebird/Play It Cool	1959	3.75	7.50	15.00
❑ 053	Tell the Truth/If You Only Knew Her	1960	3.75	7.50	15.00
❑ 065	Let's Talk It Over/Formality	1961	3.75	7.50	15.00
❑ 5000	The Purple People Eater Meets the Witch Doctor/My Fondest Memories	1958	3.75	7.50	15.00
❑ 5001	One Fool to Another/Texas Ain't the Biggest Anymore	1958	3.75	7.50	15.00

Albums

Number	Title (A Side/B Side)	Yr	VG	VG+	NM
ACCORD					
❑ SN-7119	Party People	1981	2.50	5.00	10.00
CAPITOL					
❑ ST-108	Introspect	1968	5.00	10.00	20.00
❑ ST-235	Games People Play	1969	3.75	7.50	15.00
❑ ST-392	Don't It Make You Want to Go Home	1969	3.75	7.50	15.00
❑ SM-450	Joe South's Greatest Hits	1977	2.00	4.00	8.00
—Reissue with new prefix					
❑ ST-450	Joe South's Greatest Hits	1970	3.75	7.50	15.00
❑ ST-637	So the Seeds Are Growing	1971	3.00	6.00	12.00
❑ ST-845	Joe South	1972	3.00	6.00	12.00
❑ ST-11074	A Look Inside	1972	3.00	6.00	12.00
ISLAND					
❑ ILPS-9328	Midnight Rainbows	1975	2.50	5.00	10.00
MINE					
❑ 1100	Walkin' South	1971	3.00	6.00	12.00
NASHVILLE					
❑ 2092	You're the Reason	1970	3.00	6.00	12.00
PICKWICK					
❑ SPC-3314	Games People Play	197?	2.50	5.00	10.00

SOUTH SIXTY FIVE

45s

Number	Title (A Side/B Side)	Yr	VG	VG+	NM
ATLANTIC					
❑ 84194	A Random Act of Senseless Kindness/Climbing Up Mt. Everest	1998	—	—	3.00
❑ 84457	No Easy Goodbye/All of This and More	1999	—	—	3.00
❑ 84531	Baby's Got My Number (Single Version)/(Dance Mix)	1999	—	—	3.00

SOUTHER, J.D.

Best known as a frequent collaborator with the EAGLES, he did make the country charts on a couple occasions. Also see LINDA RONSTADT.

12-Inch Singles

Number	Title (A Side/B Side)	Yr	VG	VG+	NM
WARNER BROS.					
❑ PRO-A-2140 [DJ]	Bad News/Homeby Down/Go Ahead	1984	—	3.00	6.00

45s

Number	Title (A Side/B Side)	Yr	VG	VG+	NM
ASYLUM					
❑ 11009	How Long/The Fast One	1972	—	2.50	5.00
❑ 45332	Silver Blue/Black Rose	1976	—	2.00	4.00
—As "John David Souther"					
❑ 45364	Faithless Love/Midnight Prowl	1976	—	2.00	4.00
—As "John David Souther"					
COLUMBIA					
❑ 02422	You're Only Lonely/If You Don't Want My Love	1981	—	—	3.00
—Reissue					
❑ 11079	You're Only Lonely/Songs of Love	1979	—	2.00	4.00
❑ 11196	White Rhythm and Blues/The Last in Love	1980	—	2.00	4.00
❑ 11302	'Til the Bar Burns Down/If You Don't Want My Love	1980	—	2.00	4.00
—With Johnny Duncan					
FULL MOON					
❑ 49612	You're Only Lonely/Once in a Lifetime	1980	—	2.00	4.00
—B-side by Bonnie Raitt					
WARNER BROS.					
❑ 29289	Go Ahead and Rain/All I Want	1984	—	—	3.00

Albums

Number	Title (A Side/B Side)	Yr	VG	VG+	NM
ASYLUM					
❑ 7E-1059	Black Rose	1976	2.50	5.00	10.00
❑ SD 5055	John David Souther	1972	3.00	6.00	12.00

COLUMBIA

Number	Title (A Side/B Side)	Yr	VG	VG+	NM
❑ JC 36093	You're Only Lonely	1979	2.50	5.00	10.00
❑ PC 36093	You're Only Lonely	198?	2.00	4.00	8.00

—Budget-line reissue

WARNER BROS.

Number	Title (A Side/B Side)	Yr	VG	VG+	NM
❑ 25081	Home By Dawn	1985	2.50	5.00	10.00

SOUTHERN ASHE

45s

SOUNDWAVES

Number	Title (A Side/B Side)	Yr	VG	VG+	NM
❑ 4641	Paradise/Loving on a Three-Way Street	1981	—	2.50	5.00

SOUTHERN PACIFIC

45s

WARNER BROS.

Number	Title (A Side/B Side)	Yr	VG	VG+	NM
❑ 19518	I Can't Complain/Memphis Queen	1991	—	2.00	4.00
❑ 19860	I Go to Pieces/Beyond Love	1990	—	2.00	4.00
❑ 19871	Reckless Heart/Side Saddle	1990	—	2.00	4.00
❑ 22714	Time's Up/Memphis Queen	1989	—	—	3.00

—A-side with Carlene Carter

Number	Title (A Side/B Side)	Yr	VG	VG+	NM
❑ 22965	Any Way the Wind Blows/Reno Bound	1989	—	—	3.00
❑ 22965 [PS]	Any Way the Wind Blows/Reno Bound	1989	—	2.00	4.00
❑ 27530	Dream On/All Is Lost	1989	—	—	3.00
❑ 27691	Honey I Dare You/Trail of Tears	1988	—	—	3.00
❑ 27691 [PS]	Honey I Dare You/Trail of Tears	1988	—	2.00	4.00
❑ 27790	New Shade of Blue/Just Hang On	1988	—	—	3.00
❑ 27952	Midnight Highway/What's It Gonna Take	1988	—	—	3.00
❑ 27952 [PS]	Midnight Highway/What's It Gonna Take	1988	—	2.00	4.00
❑ 28408	Don't Let Go of My Heart/What's It Gonna Take	1987	—	—	3.00
❑ 28554	Killbilly Hill/Bluegrass Blues	1986	—	—	3.00
❑ 28647	A Girl Like Emmylou/Hearts on the Borderline	1986	—	—	3.00
❑ 28722	Reno Bound/Someone's Gonna Love Me Tonight	1986	—	—	3.00
❑ 28870	Perfect Stranger/Bluebird Wine	1985	—	—	3.00
❑ 28943	Thing About You/Reno Bound	1985	—	—	3.00
❑ 29020	Someone's Gonna Love Me Tonight/The Blaster	1985	—	—	3.00

Albums

WARNER BROS.

Number	Title (A Side/B Side)	Yr	VG	VG+	NM
❑ 25206	Southern Pacific	1985	2.00	4.00	8.00
❑ 25409	Killbilly Hill	1986	2.00	4.00	8.00
❑ 25609	Zuma	1988	2.00	4.00	8.00

SOUTHERN REIGN

45s

REGAL

Number	Title (A Side/B Side)	Yr	VG	VG+	NM
❑ 1	The Auction/(B-side unknown)	1986	—	2.50	5.00
❑ 2	15 to 33/Sugary Sam	1986	—	2.50	5.00
❑ 3	Summer on the Mississippi/(B-side unknown)	1987	—	2.50	5.00

STEP ONE

Number	Title (A Side/B Side)	Yr	VG	VG+	NM
❑ 377	Cheap Motels (And One Night Stands)/Summer on the Mississippi	1987	—	2.00	4.00
❑ 385	Please Don't Leave Me Now/I Don't Think I Want to Love You Anymore	1988	—	2.00	4.00
❑ 391	There's a Telephone Ringing (In an Empty House)/Excuse Me for Loving You	1988	—	2.00	4.00

SOVINE, RED

45s

CHART

Number	Title (A Side/B Side)	Yr	VG	VG+	NM
❑ 5142	Old Pine Tree/Two Hearts on a Post Card	1971	—	2.50	5.00
❑ 5152	Six Broken Hearts/The Greatest Grand Ol' Opry	1972	—	2.50	5.00
❑ 5161	Down Through the Years/Petunia	1972	—	2.50	5.00
❑ 5176	The Guilty One/The Day the Preacher Came	1973	—	2.50	5.00
❑ 5207	Midnight Rider/Why the Grass Is Green	1974	—	2.50	5.00
❑ 5216	From Champagne to Beer/Mama's Birthday	1974	—	2.50	5.00
❑ 5220	It'll Come Back/Down Through the Years	1974	—	2.50	5.00
❑ 5230	Can I Keep Him Daddy/Red's So Fine	1974	—	2.50	5.00
❑ 5231	Santa Claus Is a Texas Cowboy/The Legend of the Christmas Rose	1974	—	2.50	5.00
❑ 7507	Daddy's Girl/(B-side unknown)	1975	—	2.50	5.00

DECCA

Number	Title (A Side/B Side)	Yr	VG	VG+	NM
❑ 29068	My New Love Affair/How Do You Think I Feel	1954	3.75	7.50	15.00
❑ 29211	Don't Drop It/Don't Be the One	1954	3.75	7.50	15.00
❑ 29335	Outlaw/Which One Should I Choose	1954	3.75	7.50	15.00
❑ 29411	Are You Mine/Ko Ko Mo	1955	3.75	7.50	15.00

—With Goldie Hill

Number	Title (A Side/B Side)	Yr	VG	VG+	NM
❑ 29529	I Hope You Don't Care/I'm Glad You Found a Place for Me	1955	3.75	7.50	15.00
❑ 29739	Why Baby Why/Sixteen Tons	1955	5.00	10.00	20.00

—A-side with Webb Pierce

Number	Title (A Side/B Side)	Yr	VG	VG+	NM
❑ 29755	Why Baby Why/Missing You	1955	3.75	7.50	15.00

—A-side with Webb Pierce

Number	Title (A Side/B Side)	Yr	VG	VG+	NM
❑ 29825	If Jesus Came to Your House/I Got Religion	1956	3.75	7.50	15.00
❑ 29876	Little Rosa/Hold Everything (Till I Get Home)	1956	3.75	7.50	15.00

—A-side with Webb Pierce

Number	Title (A Side/B Side)	Yr	VG	VG+	NM
❑ 30018	The Best Years of Your Life/My Little Rat	1956	3.00	6.00	12.00
❑ 30162	A Poor Man's Riches/Down on the Corner of Love	1956	3.00	6.00	12.00
❑ 30239	Juke Joint Johnny/No Thanks, Bartender	1957	7.50	15.00	30.00
❑ 30458	Wrong/Who Knows Better Than You and I	1957	3.00	6.00	12.00
❑ 30595	Once More/For Arms	1958	3.00	6.00	12.00
❑ 30715	Courtin' Time in Tennessee/Where Will Mommie Go	1958	3.00	6.00	12.00
❑ 30814	You Used to Be My Baby/Leave Me Alone	1959	2.50	5.00	10.00
❑ 30920	Cold Hands of Fate/One Sided Love Affair	1959	2.50	5.00	10.00
❑ 31028	A Lot Like You/Ooooh How I Love You	1959	2.50	5.00	10.00
❑ 31903	You Used to Be My Baby/Leave Me Alone	1966	2.00	4.00	8.00

GUSTO

Number	Title (A Side/B Side)	Yr	VG	VG+	NM
❑ 169	Woman Behind the Man Behind the Wheel/Jealous Heart	1977	—	2.00	4.00
❑ 175	Lay Down Sally/The Farmers and the Miners	1978	—	2.00	4.00
❑ 180	Lay Down Sally/The King's Last Concert	1978	—	3.00	6.00
❑ 188	The Days of Me and You/I'd Love to Make Love	1978	—	2.00	4.00
❑ 9005	A Place for Mama's Roses/Does Steppin' Out Mean Daddy Took a Walk	1978	—	2.00	4.00
❑ 9015	Christmas Is For Kids/What Does Christmas Look Like	1978	—	2.00	4.00
❑ 9016	The Waylon and Willie Machine/Colorado Cool-Aid	1979	—	2.50	5.00
❑ 9017	Mr. F.C.C./Flesh and Blood	1979	—	2.00	4.00
❑ 9019	The Prettiest Dress/Flesh and Blood	1979	—	2.00	4.00
❑ 9021	The Hero/Flesh and Blood	1979	—	2.00	4.00
❑ 9026	The First Time I Saw Her/18 Wheels a-Hummin' Home Sweet Home	1980	—	2.00	4.00
❑ 9028	The Little Family Soldier/She Was Loving Me Goodbye	1980	—	2.00	4.00
❑ 9030	It'll Come Back/Love Is	1980	—	2.00	4.00

MGM

Number	Title (A Side/B Side)	Yr	VG	VG+	NM
❑ 10717	When I Get Rich/You're Barking Up the Wrong Tree	1950	6.25	12.50	25.00
❑ 10782	Christmas Alone/Dear Mister Santa Claus	1950	6.25	12.50	25.00
❑ 10887	Billy Goat Boogie/Big Dipper	1951	5.00	10.00	20.00
❑ 10981	Four Flusher/Farewell, So Long	1951	5.00	10.00	20.00
❑ 11090	Don't Worry/Sundown Sue	1951	5.00	10.00	20.00
❑ 11214	It'd Surprise You/Loveless Marriage	1952	5.00	10.00	20.00
❑ 11323	Okey Dokey/Till Today	1952	5.00	10.00	20.00
❑ 11402	A Quarter's Worth of Heartaches/I'm Gonna Lock My Heart	1953	5.00	10.00	20.00
❑ 11567	You Taught Me How/If You'll Be a Baby	1953	5.00	10.00	20.00

RCA VICTOR

Number	Title (A Side/B Side)	Yr	VG	VG+	NM
❑ 47-7981	The Cajun Queen/Big Dreams	1962	3.00	6.00	12.00

RIC

Number	Title (A Side/B Side)	Yr	VG	VG+	NM
❑ 131	Big Ol' Ugly Fool/Hiding Out	1964	2.00	4.00	8.00
❑ 154	Losing My Grip/Star of the Show	1965	2.00	4.00	8.00
❑ 168	I Wish I Had Seen Sunshine/Salt on My Eggs	1965	2.00	4.00	8.00

STARDAY

Number	Title (A Side/B Side)	Yr	VG	VG+	NM
❑ 101	Phantom 309/(B-side unknown)	1975	—	2.00	4.00
❑ 137	Giddyup Go/Tonight My Lady Learns to Love	1976	—	2.00	4.00
❑ 142	Teddy Bear/Daddy	1976	—	2.50	5.00
❑ 144	Little Joe/Cold Love to Go	1976	—	2.00	4.00
❑ 147	Last Goodbye/Lonely Arms of Mine	1976	—	2.00	4.00
❑ 148	Just Gettin' By/I'm Gonna Move	1977	—	2.00	4.00
❑ 152	I'm Only Seventeen/No One's Too Big to Cry	1977	—	2.00	4.00
❑ 158	Daddy's Girl/Love Is All She Ever Wants from Me	1977	—	2.00	4.00
❑ 510	Burn the School/One Is a Lonely Number	1960	2.50	5.00	10.00
❑ 521	No Money in This Deal/If I Could Come Back	1960	2.50	5.00	10.00
❑ 540	Why Baby Why/Little Rosa	1961	2.50	5.00	10.00
❑ 553	Heart of a Man/Brand New Low	1961	2.50	5.00	10.00
❑ 567	Color of the Blues/Hold Everything	1961	2.50	5.00	10.00
❑ 579	East of West Berlin/Thanks for Nothing	1962	2.50	5.00	10.00
❑ 598	Rose of Love/She Can't Read My Writing	1962	2.50	5.00	10.00
❑ 616	Sittin' and Thinkin'/A Million to One	1962	2.50	5.00	10.00
❑ 632	Waltzing with Sin/I Forgot to Keep Her with Me	1963	2.50	5.00	10.00
❑ 650	Dream House for Sale/King of the Open Road	1963	2.50	5.00	10.00
❑ 672	Old Pipeliner/Peace of Mind	1964	2.50	5.00	10.00
❑ 737	Giddyup Go/A Kiss and the Keys	1965	2.00	4.00	8.00
❑ 757	Long Night/Too Much	1966	2.00	4.00	8.00
❑ 766	I'm the Man/I Think I Can Sleep Tonight	1966	2.00	4.00	8.00
❑ 774	Alabam/Nobody's Business	1966	2.00	4.00	8.00

—With Minnie Pearl

Number	Title (A Side/B Side)	Yr	VG	VG+	NM
❑ 779	Class of '49/I Hope My Wife Don't Find Out	1966	2.00	4.00	8.00
❑ 794	I Didn't Jump the Fence/Don't Let My Glass Run Dry	1967	2.00	4.00	8.00
❑ 811	Phantom 309/In Your Heart	1967	2.50	5.00	10.00
❑ 823	Tell Maude I Slipped/Not Like It Was with You	1967	2.00	4.00	8.00
❑ 831	Twenty-One/Sparkling Wine	1968	2.00	4.00	8.00
❑ 842	Loser Making Good/Good Enough for Nothing	1968	2.00	4.00	8.00
❑ 852	Normally, Norma Loves Me/Live and Let Live and Be Happy	1968	2.00	4.00	8.00
❑ 857	Between Closing Time and Dawn/The Father of Judy Ann	1968	2.00	4.00	8.00
❑ 864	Blues Stay Away from Me/Whiskey Flavored Kisses	1969	—	3.00	6.00
❑ 872	Who Am I/Three Hearts in a Tangle	1969	—	3.00	6.00
❑ 882	Truck Drivers Prayer/Chairman of the Board	1969	2.00	4.00	8.00
❑ 885	Castle of Shame/Why Don't You Haul Off and Love Me	1969	—	3.00	6.00

—With Lois Williams

Number	Title (A Side/B Side)	Yr	VG	VG+	NM
❑ 889	I Know You're Married But I Love You Still/Money, Marbles and Chalk	1970	—	3.00	6.00
❑ 896	Freightliner Fever/Mr. Sunday Sun	1970	—	3.00	6.00
❑ 915	Enough to Take the Me Out of Men/I'm Waiting Just for You	1970	—	3.00	6.00
❑ 918	Unfinished Letter/The Thought of Losing You	1970	—	3.00	6.00
❑ 926	Get in Touch/Violets Blue	1971	—	3.00	6.00
❑ 933	Happy Birthday, My Darlin'/I'll Sail My Ship Alone	1971	—	3.00	6.00
❑ 934	I Am a Pilgrim/Beautiful Life	1971	—	3.00	6.00
❑ 960	Go Hide John/Tear Stained Guitar	1973	—	2.50	5.00
❑ 977	Take Time to Remember/(B-side unknown)	1973	—	2.50	5.00
❑ 7004	Why Baby Why/Little Rosa	197?	—	2.00	4.00

—Reissue of 540

Number	Title (A Side/B Side)	Yr	VG	VG+	NM
❑ 7022	Six Days on the Road/Truck Drivin' Man	197?	—	2.00	4.00

Number	Title (A Side/B Side)	Yr	VG	VG+	NM
❑ 7037	He'll Have to Go/I'll Step Aside	197?	—	2.00	4.00
❑ 8000	Giddyup Go/Phantom 309	197?	—	2.00	4.00
❑ 8023	Little Rosa/Ruby, Don't Take Your Love to Town	197?	—	2.00	4.00
❑ 8033	Truck Driving Son-of-a-Gun/Radar Blues	197?	—	2.00	4.00
—B-side by Coleman Wilson					
Albums					
CHART					
❑ 1052	The Greatest Grand Ol' Opry	1972	3.75	7.50	15.00
❑ 2056	It'll Come Back	1974	3.75	7.50	15.00
DECCA					
❑ DL 4445 [M]	Red Sovine	1963	7.50	15.00	30.00
❑ DL 4736 [M]	Country Music Time	1966	7.50	15.00	30.00
❑ DL 74445 [R]	Red Sovine	1963	5.00	10.00	20.00
❑ DL 74736 [R]	Country Music Time	1966	5.00	10.00	20.00
GUSTO					
❑ 3010	16 All-Time Favorites	1978	3.00	6.00	12.00
MGM					
❑ E-3465 [M]	Red Sovine	1957	15.00	30.00	60.00
NASHVILLE					
❑ 2033	Giddy-Up Go	196?	3.00	6.00	12.00
❑ 2044	A Dear John Letter	196?	3.00	6.00	12.00
❑ 2056	Anytime	196?	3.00	6.00	12.00
❑ 2083	Don't Take Your Love to Town	1969	3.00	6.00	12.00
POWER PAK					
❑ 270	Phantom 309	197?	2.50	5.00	10.00
STARDAY					
❑ SLP-132 [M]	The One and Only Red Sovine	1961	10.00	20.00	40.00
❑ SLP-197 [M]	Golden Country Ballads of the 1960s	1962	10.00	20.00	40.00
❑ SLP-341 [M]	Little Rosa	1965	6.25	12.50	25.00
❑ SLP-357	That's Truckdrivin'	196?	5.00	10.00	20.00
❑ SLP-363 [M]	Giddy-Up Go	1966	5.00	10.00	20.00
❑ SLP-383 [M]	Town and Country Action	1966	5.00	10.00	20.00
❑ SLP-396 [M]	The Nashville Sound of Red Sovine	1967	5.00	10.00	20.00
❑ SLP-405 [M]	I Didn't Jump the Fence	1967	5.00	10.00	20.00
❑ SLP-414 [M]	Phantom 309	1967	5.00	10.00	20.00
❑ SLP-420	Tell Maude I Slipped	1968	5.00	10.00	20.00
❑ SLP-427	Sunday with Sovine	1968	5.00	10.00	20.00
❑ SLP-436	Classic Narrations	1968	5.00	10.00	20.00
❑ SLP-441	Closing Time 'Til Dawn	1969	5.00	10.00	20.00
❑ SLP-445	Who Am I	1969	5.00	10.00	20.00
❑ SLP-459	I Know You're Married But I Love You Still	1970	5.00	10.00	20.00
❑ 952	The Best of Red Sovine	197?	3.75	7.50	15.00
❑ 968	Teddy Bear	1976	3.75	7.50	15.00
❑ 970	Woodrow Wilson Sovine	1977	3.75	7.50	15.00
❑ 991	Red Sovine's 16 Greatest Hits	1977	3.75	7.50	15.00
VOCALION					
❑ VL 3829 [M]	The Country Way	196?	3.75	7.50	15.00
❑ VL 73829 [R]	The Country Way	196?	3.00	6.00	12.00

SOVINE, ROGER

Number	Title (A Side/B Side)	Yr	VG	VG+	NM
45s					
IMPERIAL					
❑ 66291	Culman, Alabam/Savannah Georgia Vagrant	1968	2.00	4.00	8.00
❑ 66322	Home Town Blues/River Girl	1968	2.00	4.00	8.00
❑ 66344	Love Took My Heart/A Railroad Trestle in California	1969	—	3.50	7.00
❑ 66398	Little Bitty Nitty Gritty Dirt Town/Son	1969	—	3.50	7.00
❑ 66449	Star/That Was Once Upon a Time	1970	—	3.50	7.00
STARDAY					
❑ 867	The Pledge of Allegiance/I Know You're Not an Angel	1969	2.00	4.00	8.00

SPACEK, SISSY

Number	Title (A Side/B Side)	Yr	VG	VG+	NM
45s					
ATLANTIC AMERICA					
❑ 99773	If You Could Only See Me Now/Have I Told You Lately That I Love You	1984	—	2.00	4.00
❑ 99801	If I Can Just Get Through the Night/Honky Tonkin'	1984	—	2.00	4.00
❑ 99847	Lonely But Only for You/Old Home Town	1983	—	2.00	4.00
❑ 99847 [PS]	Lonely But Only for You/Old Home Town	1983	—	2.50	5.00
MCA					
❑ 41221	Coal Miner's Daughter/I'm a Honky Tonk Girl	1980	—	2.00	4.00
❑ 41221 [PS]	Coal Miner's Daughter/I'm a Honky Tonk Girl	1980	2.00	4.00	8.00
❑ 41311	There He Goes/Back in Baby's Arms	1980	—	2.00	4.00
Albums					
ATLANTIC AMERICA					
❑ 90100	Hangin' Up My Heart	1983	2.50	5.00	10.00

SPEARS, BILLIE JO

Also see DEL REEVES.

Number	Title (A Side/B Side)	Yr	VG	VG+	NM
45s					
CAPITOL					
❑ 2331	He's Got More Love in His Little Finger/A Woman of the World	1968	—	3.50	7.00
❑ 2436	Mr. Walker, It's All Over/Tips and Tables	1969	—	3.50	7.00
❑ 2593	Stepchild/Softly and Tenderly	1969	—	3.50	7.00
❑ 2690	Daddy, I Love You/Look Out Your Window	1969	—	3.50	7.00
❑ 2769	Midnight Train/Meanwhile Back in My Heart	1970	—	3.50	7.00
❑ 2844	Marty Gray/True Love	1970	—	3.00	6.00
❑ 2964	I Stayed Long Enough/Come On Home	1970	—	3.00	6.00
❑ 3055	It Could 'A Been Me/Break Away	1971	—	3.00	6.00
❑ 3258	Souvenirs and California Mem'rys/What a Love I Have in You	1972	—	3.00	6.00
❑ 4272	Faded Love/Heart Over Mind	1976	—	2.50	5.00
CUTLASS					
❑ 133	Look What They've Done to My Song, Ma/(B-side unknown)	197?	2.00	4.00	8.00
LIBERTY					
❑ 1395	Your Good Girl's Gonna Go Bad/(I Never Promised You a) Rose Garden	1980	—	2.00	4.00
❑ 1409	What the World Needs Now Is Love/Snowbird	1981	—	2.00	4.00
PARLIAMENT					
❑ 1801	Midnight Blue/Midnight Love	1983	—	2.50	5.00
UNITED ARTISTS					
❑ XW549	See the Funny Little Clown/All I Want Is You	1974	—	2.50	5.00
❑ XW584	Blanket on the Ground/Come On Home	1975	—	2.50	5.00
❑ XW653	Stay Away from the Apple Tree/Before Your Time	1975	—	2.50	5.00
❑ XW712	Silver Wings and Golden Rings/Then Give Him Back to Me	1975	—	2.50	5.00
❑ XW764	What I've Got in Mind/Everytime Two Fools Collide	1976	—	2.50	5.00
❑ XW813	Misty Blue/Let's Try to Wake It Up Again	1976	—	2.50	5.00
❑ XW880	Never Did Like Whiskey/No Other Man	1976	—	2.50	5.00
❑ XW935	I'm Not Easy/Too Far Gone	1977	—	2.50	5.00
❑ XW985	If You Want Me/Don't Ever Let Go of Me	1977	—	2.50	5.00
❑ XW1041	Too Much Is Not Enough/The End of Me	1977	—	2.50	5.00
❑ XW1127	Lonely Hearts Club/His Little Something on the Side	1977	—	2.50	5.00
❑ XW1190	I've Got to Go/There's More to a Tear (Than Meets the Eye)	1978	—	2.00	4.00
❑ XW1229	'57 Chevrolet/The Lovin' Kind	1978	—	2.00	4.00
❑ XW1251	Love Ain't Gonna Wait for Us/Say It Again	1978	—	2.00	4.00
❑ XW1274	Yesterday/Miracle of Love	1979	—	2.00	4.00
❑ XW1292	I Will Survive/Rainy Days and Stormy Nights	1979	—	2.00	4.00
❑ X1309	Livin' Our Love Together/You	1979	—	2.00	4.00
❑ X1326	Rainy Days and Stormy Nights/Everyday I Have to Cry	1980	—	2.00	4.00
❑ X1336	Standing Tall/Freedom Song	1980	—	2.00	4.00
❑ X1358	Natural Attraction/You Could Know As Much About a Stranger	1980	—	2.00	4.00
❑ 50092	Not Enough of You to Go Around/You're Too Much Like Me	1966	2.50	5.00	10.00
❑ 50184	Easy to Be Evil/Much Too Busy to Cry	1967	2.00	4.00	8.00
Albums					
CAPITOL					
❑ ST-114	The Voice of Billie Jo Spears	1969	5.00	10.00	20.00
❑ ST-224	Mr. Walker, It's All Over!	1969	3.75	7.50	15.00
❑ ST-397	Miss Sincerity	1969	3.75	7.50	15.00
❑ ST-454	With Love	1970	3.75	7.50	15.00
❑ ST-560	Country Girl	1970	3.75	7.50	15.00
❑ ST-688	Just Singin'	1971	3.75	7.50	15.00
❑ SM-11887	The Best of Billie Jo Spears	1979	2.50	5.00	10.00
LIBERTY					
❑ LT-1074	Only the Hits	1981	2.00	4.00	8.00
❑ LN-10018	Blanket on the Ground	1980	2.00	4.00	8.00
❑ LN-10019	Love Ain't Gonna Wait for Us	1980	2.00	4.00	8.00
❑ LN-10020	I Will Survive	1980	2.00	4.00	8.00
❑ LN-10021	If You Want Me	1980	2.00	4.00	8.00
UNITED ARTISTS					
❑ UA-LA390-G	Blanket on the Ground	1975	2.50	5.00	10.00
❑ UA-LA508-G	Billie Jo	1975	2.50	5.00	10.00
❑ UA-LA608-G	What I've Got in Mind	1976	2.50	5.00	10.00
❑ UA-LA684-G	I'm Not Easy	1976	2.50	5.00	10.00
❑ UA-LA748-G	If You Want Me	1977	2.50	5.00	10.00
❑ UA-LA859-G	Lonely Hearts Club	1977	2.50	5.00	10.00
❑ UA-LA921-H	Love Ain't Gonna Wait for Us	1978	2.50	5.00	10.00
❑ LT-983	The Singles Album	1979	2.50	5.00	10.00
❑ LT-1018	Standing Tall	1980	2.50	5.00	10.00

SPEEGLE, DAVID

Number	Title (A Side/B Side)	Yr	VG	VG+	NM
45s					
BITTER CREEK					
❑ 07789	Tie Me Up (Hold Me Down)/Dim Lights and Candles	1989	—	3.00	6.00

SPEEKS, RONNIE

Number	Title (A Side/B Side)	Yr	VG	VG+	NM
45s					
DIMENSION					
❑ 1014	Baby Loved Me/You Almost Slipped My Mind	1980	—	2.50	5.00
FRATERNITY					
❑ 968	Oh Lonesome Me/I Who Have Nothing	1966	3.00	6.00	12.00
KING					
❑ 5548	Please Wait for Me/What Is Your Technique	1961	25.00	50.00	100.00
PALETTE					
❑ 5094	Mister Glenn/My Darling (I Love You So)	1962	2.50	5.00	10.00

SPELLING ON THE STONE

No artist name was given for this record, which saw some sort of message in the fact that Elvis Presley's middle name is misspelled on his gravestone.

Number	Title (A Side/B Side)	Yr	VG	VG+	NM
45s					
CURB					
❑ 10522	Spelling on the Stone (same on both sides)	1988	—	2.50	5.00
LS					
❑ 53	Spelling on the Stone (same on both sides)	1988	2.50	5.00	10.00

SPENCER, TEDDY

45s

OAK

Number	Title (A Side/B Side)	Yr	VG	VG+	NM
❑ 1052	Grass Is Greener/(B-side unknown)	1988	—	2.50	5.00

SPITZ, MICHELLE

45s

50 STATES

Number	Title (A Side/B Side)	Yr	VG	VG+	NM
❑ 72	Something I Never Got Over/Tear Time	1979	—	2.50	5.00
❑ 73	Waiting on You Still/Where Do You Go	1980	—	2.50	5.00
❑ 78	My Guns Are Loaded/(B-side unknown)	1980	—	2.50	5.00
❑ 83	Old Fashioned Lover (In a Brand New Love Affair)/If You Ever Need Me Again	1981	—	2.50	5.00

SPRINGER, ROGER

45s

GIANT

Number	Title (A Side/B Side)	Yr	VG	VG+	NM
❑ 16972	Ain't Nothin' But a Cloud/I Don't Understand (All I Know About Love)	1999	—	—	3.00
❑ 17137	Don't Try to Find Me/Love Lives On	1998	—	—	3.00

—As "Springer!"

MCA

Number	Title (A Side/B Side)	Yr	VG	VG+	NM
❑ 54250	The Right One Left/Honky Tonk Ways	1992	—	—	3.00

SPRINGER BROTHERS

45s

ELEKTRA

Number	Title (A Side/B Side)	Yr	VG	VG+	NM
❑ 45475	Twice As Strong/You and I	1978	—	2.50	5.00
❑ 45548	One More Broken Heart/You and I	1978	—	2.00	4.00
❑ 46062	Put Your Heart In It/You and I	1979	—	2.00	4.00
❑ 46575	What's a Nice Girl Like You (Doin' in a Love Like This)/Twice As Strong	1980	—	2.00	4.00
❑ 46622	Cathy's Clown/No Fair Fallin' in Love	1980	—	2.00	4.00

SPRINGFIELD, BOBBY LEE

Includes records as "Bobby Springfield."

45s

EPIC

Number	Title (A Side/B Side)	Yr	VG	VG+	NM
❑ 34-07110	Hank Drank/Wild Cat	1987	—	2.00	4.00
❑ 34-07310	Chain Gang/Wild Cat	1987	—	2.00	4.00
❑ 34-07628	All Fired Up/Opry Time	1987	—	2.00	4.00

KAT FAMILY

Number	Title (A Side/B Side)	Yr	VG	VG+	NM
❑ ZS5-02997	That's What You're Doing to Me/I Know Every Heartache by Name	1982	—	2.50	5.00
❑ ZS4-03211	You'll Never Have to Fall in Love Again/You're My Main Attraction	1982	—	2.50	5.00
❑ ZS4-03562	A Different Woman Every Night/Young and Hungry	1983	—	2.50	5.00

Albums

EPIC

Number	Title (A Side/B Side)	Yr	VG	VG+	NM
❑ B6E 40816	All Fired Up!	1987	2.00	4.00	8.00

SPRINGFIELDS, THE

The British folk group from which Dusty Springfield came, their version of "Silver Threads and Golden Needles" peaked higher on the country charts than it did on the pop charts.

45s

PHILIPS

Number	Title (A Side/B Side)	Yr	VG	VG+	NM
❑ 40038	Silver Threads and Golden Needles/Aunt Rhody	1962	3.75	7.50	15.00
❑ 40072	Dear Hearts and Gentle People/Gotta Travel On	1962	3.00	6.00	12.00
❑ 40092	Little By Little/Waf-Woof	1963	3.00	6.00	12.00
❑ 40099	Foggy Mountain Top/Island of Dreams	1963	3.00	6.00	12.00
❑ 40121	Say I Won't Be There/Little Boat	1963	3.00	6.00	12.00

Albums

PHILIPS

Number	Title (A Side/B Side)	Yr	VG	VG+	NM
❑ PHM 200052 [M]	Silver Threads and Golden Needles	1962	7.50	15.00	30.00
❑ PHM 200076 [M]	Folksongs from the Hills	1963	7.50	15.00	30.00
❑ PHS 600052 [S]	Silver Threads and Golden Needles	1962	10.00	20.00	40.00
❑ PHS 600076 [S]	Folksongs from the Hills	1963	10.00	20.00	40.00

SPURZZ

45s

EPIC

Number	Title (A Side/B Side)	Yr	VG	VG+	NM
❑ 50911	Cowboy Stomp!/Night Club	1980	—	2.00	4.00

STACK, BILLY

45s

CAPRICE

Number	Title (A Side/B Side)	Yr	VG	VG+	NM
❑ 2045	Love Can Make the Children Sing/The Big Time	1978	—	2.50	5.00
❑ 2048	Boogiewoogieitis/Rainbow Rider	1978	—	2.50	5.00
❑ 2050	Near Me/That Stranger Once Belonged to Me	1978	—	2.50	5.00
❑ 2058	No Greater Love/She Wanted So Bad to Be Good	1979	—	2.50	5.00

STAFF, BOBBI

45s

RCA VICTOR

Number	Title (A Side/B Side)	Yr	VG	VG+	NM
❑ 47-8689	I'm Available (Just for You)/Where Did the Summer Go	1965	2.50	5.00	10.00
❑ 47-8833	Chicken Feed/I Didn't Cry Today	1966	2.50	5.00	10.00
❑ 47-9093	Red Light Is Green/Straight to Helen	1967	2.50	5.00	10.00
❑ 47-9251	I Can't Find My Walking Shoes/Sun Tan and Wind Blown Time	1967	2.50	5.00	10.00
❑ 47-9363	Bobby Blows a Blue Note/He Chickened Out on Me	1967	2.50	5.00	10.00
❑ 47-9504	Back Away/A Ring Beats a Promise	1968	2.50	5.00	10.00

STAFFORD, JIM

45s

COLUMBIA

Number	Title (A Side/B Side)	Yr	VG	VG+	NM
❑ 04339	Little Bits and Pieces/Banjo Billy	1984	—	—	3.00

ELEKTRA

Number	Title (A Side/B Side)	Yr	VG	VG+	NM
❑ 47013	Don't Fool Around (When There's a Fool Around)/I Took Your Love Lightly	1980	—	2.00	4.00
❑ 47226	Isabel and Samantha/Yeller Dog Blues	1981	—	2.00	4.00

MGM

Number	Title (A Side/B Side)	Yr	VG	VG+	NM
❑ 14496	Swamp Witch/Nifty Fifties Blues	1973	—	2.00	4.00
❑ 14648	Spiders and Snakes/Undecided	1973	—	2.00	4.00
❑ 14718	My Girl Bill/L.A. Mama	1974	—	2.00	4.00
❑ 14737	Wildwood Weed/The Last Chant	1974	—	2.00	4.00
❑ 14775	Your Bulldog Drinks Champagne/Real Good Time	1974	—	2.00	4.00
❑ 14819	I Got Stoned and I Missed It/I Ain't Workin'	1975	—	2.00	4.00

POLYDOR

Number	Title (A Side/B Side)	Yr	VG	VG+	NM
❑ 14309	Jasper/I Can't Find Nobody Home	1976	—	2.00	4.00

TOWN HOUSE

Number	Title (A Side/B Side)	Yr	VG	VG+	NM
❑ 1062	What Mama Don't Know/That's What Little Kids Do	1982	—	2.00	4.00

WARNER BROS.

Number	Title (A Side/B Side)	Yr	VG	VG+	NM
❑ 8299	Turn Loose of My Leg/The Fight	1976	—	2.00	4.00
❑ 8538	You Can Call Me Clyde/One Step Ahead of the Law	1978	—	2.00	4.00
❑ 49611	Cow Patti/Texas Guitar Song	1980	—	2.00	4.00

Albums

MGM

Number	Title (A Side/B Side)	Yr	VG	VG+	NM
❑ M3G-4947	Jim Stafford	1974	2.50	5.00	10.00
❑ M3G-4984	Not Just Another Pretty Foot	1975	2.50	5.00	10.00

POLYDOR

Number	Title (A Side/B Side)	Yr	VG	VG+	NM
❑ PD-1-6072	Jim Stafford	1976	2.00	4.00	8.00

—Reissue of MGM 4947

STAFFORD, JO

The popular big band and solo singer had one country hit, listed below.

Selected 78s

CAPITOL

Number	Title (A Side/B Side)	Yr	VG	VG+	NM
❑ 443	Feudin' and Fightin'/Love and the Weather	1947	3.00	6.00	12.00

STAFFORD, TERRY

45s

ATLANTIC

Number	Title (A Side/B Side)	Yr	VG	VG+	NM
❑ 4006	Amarillo by Morning/Say, Has Anybody Seen My Sweet Gypsy Rose	1973	2.00	4.00	8.00
❑ 4015	Captured/It Sure Is Bad to Love Her	1974	—	3.00	6.00
❑ 4026	Stop If You Love Me/We've Grown Close	1974	—	3.00	6.00

A&M

Number	Title (A Side/B Side)	Yr	VG	VG+	NM
❑ 707	Heartaches on the Way/You Left Me Here to Cry	1963	3.00	6.00	12.00

CASINO

Number	Title (A Side/B Side)	Yr	VG	VG+	NM
❑ 113	It Sure Is Bad to Love Her/(B-side unknown)	1977	—	3.00	6.00

CRUSADER

Number	Title (A Side/B Side)	Yr	VG	VG+	NM
❑ 101	Suspicion/Judy	1964	3.75	7.50	15.00
❑ 105	I'll Touch a Star/Playing with Fire	1964	3.00	6.00	12.00
❑ 109	Follow the Rainbow/Are You a Fool Like Me	1964	3.00	6.00	12.00
❑ 110	A Little Bit Better/Hoping	1964	3.00	6.00	12.00

EASTLAND

Number	Title (A Side/B Side)	Yr	VG	VG+	NM
❑ 101	Back Together/Life's Railway to Heaven	198?	—	2.50	5.00

MELODYLAND

Number	Title (A Side/B Side)	Yr	VG	VG+	NM
❑ 6009	Darling, Think It Over/I Can't Find It	1975	—	2.50	5.00

MERCURY

Number	Title (A Side/B Side)	Yr	VG	VG+	NM
❑ 72538	Out of the Picture/Forbidden	1966	2.50	5.00	10.00

MGM

Number	Title (A Side/B Side)	Yr	VG	VG+	NM
❑ 14232	Mean Woman Blues-Candy Man/Chilly Chicago	1971	—	3.00	6.00
❑ 14271	California Dancer/The Walk	1971	—	3.00	6.00

PLAYER

Number	Title (A Side/B Side)	Yr	VG	VG+	NM
❑ 134	Lonestar Lonesome/(B-side unknown)	1989	—	3.00	6.00

SIDEWALK

Number	Title (A Side/B Side)	Yr	VG	VG+	NM
❑ 902	Soldier Boy/When Sin Stops, Love Begins	1966	2.50	5.00	10.00
❑ 914	A Step or Two Behind You/The Joke's on Me	1967	2.50	5.00	10.00

WARNER BROS.

Number	Title (A Side/B Side)	Yr	VG	VG+	NM
❑ 7286	Big in Dallas/Will a Man Ever Learn	1969	—	3.00	6.00

Albums

ATLANTIC

Number	Title (A Side/B Side)	Yr	VG	VG+	NM
❑ SD 7282	Say, Has Anybody Seen My Sweet Gypsy Rose	1974	3.00	6.00	12.00

CRUSADER

Number	Title (A Side/B Side)	Yr	VG	VG+	NM
❑ CLP-1001 [M]	Suspicion!	1964	10.00	20.00	40.00
❑ CLP-1001S [S]	Suspicion!	1964	15.00	30.00	60.00

STALEY, KAREN

45s

MCA

Number	Title (A Side/B Side)	Yr	VG	VG+	NM
❑ 53247	Oh Lonesome Me/Take Me Back to the Country	1988	—	—	3.00
❑ 53470	So Good to Be in Love/Keep Walkin' On	1988	—	—	3.00
❑ 53632	Now and Then/Looks Like Rain	1989	—	—	3.00

WARNER BROS.

Number	Title (A Side/B Side)	Yr	VG	VG+	NM
❑ 7-17142	Somebody's Child/Breakin' All the Rules	1998	—	2.00	4.00

Albums

MCA

Number	Title (A Side/B Side)	Yr	VG	VG+	NM
❑ 42112	Wildest Dreams	1988	2.50	5.00	10.00

STAMPLEY, JOE

Also see MOE BANDY AND JOE STAMPLEY; THE UNIQUES (1).

45s

ABC DOT

Number	Title (A Side/B Side)	Yr	VG	VG+	NM
❑ 17537	Penny/Backtrackin'	1974	—	2.50	5.00
❑ 17551	Unchained Melody/Dallas Alice	1975	—	2.50	5.00
❑ 17575	Cry Like a Baby/Try a Little Tenderness	1975	—	2.50	5.00
❑ 17599	You Make Life Easy/Clinging Vine	1975	—	2.50	5.00
❑ 17624	All These Things/My Louisiana Woman	1976	—	2.50	5.00
❑ 17642	The Night Time and My Baby/The Most Beautiful Girl	1976	—	2.50	5.00
❑ 17654	Everything I Own/Dallas Alice	1976	—	2.50	5.00

CHESS

Number	Title (A Side/B Side)	Yr	VG	VG+	NM
❑ 1798	Creation of Love/Teenage Picnic	1961	6.25	12.50	25.00

DOT

Number	Title (A Side/B Side)	Yr	VG	VG+	NM
❑ 17363	Take Time to Know Her/I Live to Love You	1970	—	3.00	6.00
❑ 17383	Two Weeks and a Day/Can You Imagine How I Feel	1971	—	3.00	6.00
❑ 17400	Hello Operator/Hello Charlie	1971	—	3.00	6.00
❑ 17421	If You Touch Me (You've Got to Love Me)/All the Praises	1972	—	3.00	6.00
❑ 17442	Soul Song/Not Too Long Ago	1972	—	3.00	6.00
❑ 17442 [PS]	Soul Song/Not Too Long Ago	1972	3.75	7.50	15.00

—Sleeve is promo only

Number	Title (A Side/B Side)	Yr	VG	VG+	NM
❑ 17452	Bring It On Home (To Your Woman)/You Make Life Easy	1973	—	3.00	6.00
❑ 17469	Too Far Gone/Night Time and My Baby	1973	—	3.00	6.00
❑ 17485	I'm Still Loving You/The Weatherman	1973	—	3.00	6.00
❑ 17502	How Lucky Can One Man Be/Can You Imagine How I Feel	1974	—	3.00	6.00
❑ 17522	Take Me Home to Somewhere/Hall of Famous Losers	1974	—	3.00	6.00

EPIC

Number	Title (A Side/B Side)	Yr	VG	VG+	NM
❑ 19-02097	Whiskey Chasin'/The Jukebox Never Plays Home Sweet Home	1981	—	2.00	4.00
❑ 14-02533	All These Things/Let's Get Together and Cry	1981	—	2.00	4.00
❑ 14-02791	I'm Goin' Hurtin'/The Fool	1982	—	2.00	4.00
❑ 14-03016	I Didn't Know You Could Break a Broken Heart/I Just Can't Get Over You	1982	—	2.00	4.00
❑ 15-03095	I'm Gonna Love You Back to Loving Me Again/Whiskey Chasin'	1982	—	—	3.00

—Gray label reissue

Number	Title (A Side/B Side)	Yr	VG	VG+	NM
❑ 34-03290	Backslidin'/I'm Willing to Try	1982	—	2.00	4.00
❑ 34-03558	Finding You/I'm Just Crazy Enough	1983	—	2.00	4.00
❑ 34-03966	Poor Side of Town/It's Over	1983	—	2.00	4.00
❑ 34-04173	Double Shot (Of My Baby's Love)/Penny	1983	—	2.00	4.00
❑ 34-04366	Brown Eyed Girl/A Winner Never Quits	1984	—	2.00	4.00
❑ 34-04446	Memory Lane/Could It Wait Until Forever	1984	—	2.00	4.00

—With Jessica Boucher

Number	Title (A Side/B Side)	Yr	VG	VG+	NM
❑ 34-05405	When Something Is Wrong with My Baby/Say It Like You Mean It	1985	—	2.00	4.00
❑ 34-05592	I'll Still Be Loving You/Heart Troubles	1985	—	2.00	4.00
❑ 34-05758	When You Were Blue and I Was Green/There's No You Left in Us Anymore	1986	—	2.00	4.00
❑ 8-50075	Roll On Big Mama/Love's Running Through My Veins	1975	—	2.50	5.00
❑ 8-50114	Dear Woman/Get On My Love Train	1975	—	2.50	5.00
❑ 8-50147	Billy, Get Me a Woman/She Has Love	1975	—	2.50	5.00
❑ 8-50179	She's Helping Me Get Over Loving You/Ray of Sunshine	1975	—	2.50	5.00
❑ 8-50199	Sheik of Chicago/Whiskey Talkin'	1976	—	2.50	5.00
❑ 8-50224	Was It Worth It/Live It Up	1976	—	2.50	5.00
❑ 8-50259	Whiskey Talkin'/Darlin' Raise the Shade	1976	—	2.50	5.00
❑ 8-50316	There She Goes Again/You Lift Me Up	1976	—	2.50	5.00
❑ 8-50361	She's Long Legged/Better Part of Me	1977	—	2.50	5.00
❑ 8-50410	Baby, I Love You So/Pour the Wine	1977	—	2.50	5.00
❑ 8-50453	Everyday I Have to Cry Some/What Would I Do Then	1977	—	2.50	5.00
❑ 8-50517	Red Wine and Blue Memories/Houston Treat My Lady Good	1978	—	2.50	5.00
❑ 8-50575	If You've Got Ten Minutes (Let's Fall in Love)/If This Is Freedom	1978	—	2.50	5.00
❑ 8-50626	Do You Ever Fool Around/Please Don't Throw Our Love Away	1978	—	2.50	5.00
❑ 8-50694	I Don't Lie/Draggin' Main	1979	—	2.00	4.00
❑ 50754	Put Your Clothes Back On/I Could Be Persuaded	1979	—	2.00	4.00
❑ 50854	After Hours/I'm Afraid to Know You That Well	1980	—	2.00	4.00
❑ 50893	Haven't I Loved You Somewhere Before/Whiskey Fever	1980	—	2.00	4.00
❑ 50934	There's Another Woman/No Love at All	1980	—	2.50	5.00
❑ 50972	I'm Gonna Love You Back to Loving Me Again/Back on the Road Again	1981	—	2.00	4.00

EVERGREEN

Number	Title (A Side/B Side)	Yr	VG	VG+	NM
❑ 1075	Cry Baby/(B-side unknown)	1988	—	2.50	5.00
❑ 1081	You Sure Got This Ol' Redneck Feelin' Blue/(B-side unknown)	1989	—	2.50	5.00
❑ 1100	If You Don't Know Me by Now/(B-side unknown)	1989	—	2.50	5.00

IMPERIAL

Number	Title (A Side/B Side)	Yr	VG	VG+	NM
❑ 5617	Glenda/We're Through	1959	5.00	10.00	20.00
❑ 5637	Heaven Dreams/Come a-Runnin'	1960	5.00	10.00	20.00

PARAMOUNT

Number	Title (A Side/B Side)	Yr	VG	VG+	NM
❑ 0025	All the Good Is GOne/Quonette McGraw	1970	2.00	4.00	8.00

PAULA

Number	Title (A Side/B Side)	Yr	VG	VG+	NM
❑ 403	Sometimes/Groovin' Out	1974	—	3.00	6.00

Albums

ABC

Number	Title (A Side/B Side)	Yr	VG	VG+	NM
❑ AC-30031	The ABC Collection	1976	3.00	6.00	12.00

ABC DOT

Number	Title (A Side/B Side)	Yr	VG	VG+	NM
❑ DOSD-2006	Take Me Home to Somewhere	1974	3.00	6.00	12.00
❑ DOSD-2023	Joe Stampley's Greatest Hits Volume 1	1975	3.00	6.00	12.00
❑ DOSD-2059	All These Things	1976	3.00	6.00	12.00

ACCORD

Number	Title (A Side/B Side)	Yr	VG	VG+	NM
❑ SN-7156	Early Years	1982	2.50	5.00	10.00

DOT

Number	Title (A Side/B Side)	Yr	VG	VG+	NM
❑ DLP-26002	If You Touch Me (You've Got to Love Me)	1972	3.75	7.50	15.00
❑ DLP-26007	Soul Song	1973	3.75	7.50	15.00
❑ DLP-26020	I'm Still Loving You	1974	3.75	7.50	15.00

EPIC

Number	Title (A Side/B Side)	Yr	VG	VG+	NM
❑ KE 33356	Joe Stampley	1975	3.00	6.00	12.00
❑ PE 33546	Billy, Get Me a Woman	1975	3.00	6.00	12.00
❑ KE 34036	The Sheik of Chicago	1976	3.00	6.00	12.00
❑ PE 34356	Ten Songs About Her	1976	3.00	6.00	12.00
❑ PE 34732	Saturday Nite Dance	1977	3.00	6.00	12.00
❑ KE 35543	Red Wine and Blue Memories	1978	3.00	6.00	12.00
❑ KE 35622	Greatest Hits	1978	2.50	5.00	10.00
❑ PE 35622	Greatest Hits	198?	2.00	4.00	8.00

—Budget-line reissue with new prefix

Number	Title (A Side/B Side)	Yr	VG	VG+	NM
❑ KE 36016	I Don't Lie	1979	2.50	5.00	10.00
❑ JE 36484	After Hours	1980	2.50	5.00	10.00
❑ FE 37055	I'm Gonna Love You Back to Loving Me Again	1981	2.50	5.00	10.00
❑ FE 37343	Encore	1981	2.50	5.00	10.00
❑ FE 37927	I'm Goin' Hurtin'	1982	2.50	5.00	10.00
❑ FE 38319	Biggest Hits	1982	2.50	5.00	10.00
❑ FE 38364	Backslidin'	1982	2.50	5.00	10.00
❑ FE 38964	Memory Lane	1983	2.50	5.00	10.00
❑ FE 39960	Still Be Lovin' You	1985	2.00	4.00	8.00

MCA

Number	Title (A Side/B Side)	Yr	VG	VG+	NM
❑ 27022	The Very Best of Joe Stampley	198?	2.00	4.00	8.00

STAMPS QUARTET, THE

45s

COLUMBIA

Number	Title (A Side/B Side)	Yr	VG	VG+	NM
❑ 2-600 (?)	Just a Closer Walk with Thee/Good News	1950	10.00	20.00	40.00

—Microgroove 33 1/3 rpm 7-inch single, small hole

Number	Title (A Side/B Side)	Yr	VG	VG+	NM
❑ 2-700 (?)	I'm a Little Bit Closer/What a Saviour	1950	10.00	20.00	40.00

—Microgroove 33 1/3 rpm 7-inch single, small hole

Number	Title (A Side/B Side)	Yr	VG	VG+	NM
❑ 4-20711	Lead My Children/Whispering Hope	1950	7.50	15.00	30.00
❑ 4-20751	Hallelujah Day/That Lonely Mile	1950	7.50	15.00	30.00
❑ 4-20773	Paradise Island/The Lord Is Coming By and By	1951	6.25	12.50	25.00
❑ 4-20802	Jesus Gave This One to Me/When the Lord Calls	1951	6.25	12.50	25.00
❑ 4-20824	What Could I Do/The Love of God	1951	6.25	12.50	25.00
❑ 4-20836	I Want to Know More About My Lord/Peace in the Valley	1951	6.25	12.50	25.00
❑ 4-20875	I'll Tell the World/Somewhere, Someday	1952	6.25	12.50	25.00
❑ 4-20889	I Heard the Saviour Call My Name/A Little Old Church	1952	6.25	12.50	25.00
❑ 4-20921	I Know My Saviour Is There/I've Put My All in His Care	1952	6.25	12.50	25.00
❑ 4-20971	You'll Find It in Paradise/You Need His Hand	1952	6.25	12.50	25.00
❑ 4-20993	He's the Lily of the Valley/He Made a Way for Me	1952	6.25	12.50	25.00
❑ 4-21005	Save Thy People, Lord/I've Found a City	1952	6.25	12.50	25.00
❑ 4-21055	Sing, Brother, Sing/One of His Own	1952	6.25	12.50	25.00
❑ 4-21067	Please Mention My Name/Sing	1953	6.25	12.50	25.00
❑ 4-21102	Somewhere/Headed for the Gloryland	1953	6.25	12.50	25.00
❑ 4-21121	A Roundup in the Sky/I Know That God Is Real	1953	6.25	12.50	25.00
❑ 4-21168	Joshua Led God's Children/Somebody Knows	1953	6.25	12.50	25.00
❑ 4-21201	Hide Me Rock of Ages/This I Know	1954	5.00	10.00	20.00
❑ 4-21245	Paradise Is Waiting/Oh When I Meet You	1954	5.00	10.00	20.00
❑ 4-21263	At the End of the Trail/Heaven Will Surely Be Worth It All	1954	5.00	10.00	20.00
❑ 4-21278	Jesus/Joy in My Soul	1954	5.00	10.00	20.00
❑ 4-21323	This Ole House/Promise You'll Meet Me	1954	6.25	12.50	25.00
❑ 4-21349	My Lord Is Caring for Me/God Is Right	1955	5.00	10.00	20.00
❑ 4-21363	My Thanks to Him/Way Up in Glory Land	1955	5.00	10.00	20.00
❑ 4-21377	There's a Ranch House in Heaven/I'll Have a Mansion of My Own	1955	5.00	10.00	20.00
❑ 4-21416	Heaven's Avenue/Sentimental Valley	1955	5.00	10.00	20.00
❑ 4-21445	Judgment Day/Treasure at the End of the Trail	1955	5.00	10.00	20.00
❑ 4-21476	It Won't Be Very Long Now/The Road That Leads to Tomorrow	1955	5.00	10.00	20.00
❑ 4-21492	I Cannot Bring Them Back/Meet Me Up in Heaven	1956	5.00	10.00	20.00
❑ 4-21520	Will the Lord Be With Me/His Name Is Jesus	1956	5.00	10.00	20.00
❑ 4-21553	Hide Me Rock of Ages/Oh When I Meet You	1956	5.00	10.00	20.00
❑ 4-40806	Father, Watch Over Thy Child/I Will Not Be a Stranger	1956	3.75	7.50	15.00
❑ 4-40891	Who?/When God's Chariot Comes	1957	3.75	7.50	15.00

STANLEY BROTHERS, THE

45s

COLUMBIA

Number	Title (A Side/B Side)	Yr	VG	VG+	NM
❑ 2-250 (?)	Let Me Be Your Friend/Little Glass of Wine	1949	10.00	20.00	40.00

—Microgroove 33 1/3 rpm single, small hole

Number	Title (A Side/B Side)	Yr	VG	VG+	NM
❑ 2-340 (?)	Angels Are Singing/It's Never Too Late	1949	10.00	20.00	40.00

—Microgroove 33 1/3 rpm single, small hole

Number	Title (A Side/B Side)	Yr	VG	VG+	NM
❑ 2-420 (?)	Have You Someone/Visions of Mother	1949	10.00	20.00	40.00

—Microgroove 33 1/3 rpm single, small hole

Number	Title (A Side/B Side)	Yr	VG	VG+	NM
❑ 2-490 (?)	The Fields Have Turned Brown/The Old Home	1950	10.00	20.00	40.00

—Microgroove 33 1/3 rpm single, small hole

Number	Title (A Side/B Side)	Yr	VG	VG+	NM
❑ 2-600 (?)	I Love No One But You/Too Late to Cry	1950	10.00	20.00	40.00

—Microgroove 33 1/3 rpm single, small hole

Number	Title (A Side/B Side)	Yr	VG	VG+	NM
❑ 4-20735	Drunkards Hell/We'll Be Sweethearts in Heaven	1950	7.50	15.00	30.00
❑ 4-20770	Hey, Hey, Hey/Pretty Polly	1950	7.50	15.00	30.00
❑ 4-20816	I'm a Man of Constant Sorrow/Lonesome River	1951	6.25	12.50	25.00
❑ 4-20953	Sweetest Love/Wandering Boy	1952	6.25	12.50	25.00

KING

Number	Title (A Side/B Side)	Yr	VG	VG+	NM
❑ 5155	She's More to Be Pitied/The Train	1958	5.00	10.00	20.00
❑ 5197	How Can We Thank Him/That Home Far Away	1959	3.75	7.50	15.00
❑ 5233	White Dove/Mother's Footsteps Guide Me	1959	3.75	7.50	15.00
❑ 5269	Mountain Girls Can Love/A Man of Constant Sorrow	1959	3.75	7.50	15.00
❑ 5291	Sunny Side of the Mountain/Shenandoah Waltz	1959	3.75	7.50	15.00
❑ 5306	How Far to Little Rock/Heaven Seems So Near	1960	3.75	7.50	15.00
❑ 5313	Pass Me Not/When Jesus Beckons Me Home	1960	3.75	7.50	15.00
❑ 5347	Mountain Dew/Old Rattler	1960	3.75	7.50	15.00
❑ 5355	Sweeter Than the Flowers/Next Sunday, Darling, Is My Birthday	1960	3.75	7.50	15.00
❑ 5367	Mother Left Me Her Bible/Over in Glory Land	1960	3.75	7.50	15.00
❑ 5384	Daybreak in Dixie/Finger Poppin' Time	1960	3.75	7.50	15.00
❑ 5415	An Old Love Letter/Little Benny	1960	3.75	7.50	15.00
❑ 5441	The Angel of Death/Jordan	1961	3.75	7.50	15.00
❑ 5460	The Window Up Above/The Wild Side of Life	1961	3.75	7.50	15.00
❑ 5494	Little Bessie/The Village Church Yard	1961	3.75	7.50	15.00
❑ 5518	I'll Take the Blame/I'd Worship You	1961	3.75	7.50	15.00
❑ 5557	There Is a Trap/Fast Express	1961	3.75	7.50	15.00
❑ 5582	Jacob's Vision/Thy Burdens Are Greater Than Mine	1961	3.75	7.50	15.00
❑ 5629	Still Trying to Get to Little Rock/String, Eraser and Blotter	1962	3.00	6.00	12.00
❑ 5637	I'm Only Human/Keep Them Cold Icy Fingers Off of Me	1962	3.00	6.00	12.00
❑ 5674	My Deceitful Heart/The Drunkard's Dream	1962	3.00	6.00	12.00
❑ 5688	I Just Came from Your Wedding/Mama Don't Allow	1962	3.00	6.00	12.00
❑ 5708	Who Will Sing for Me/Drinking from the Fountain	1963	3.00	6.00	12.00
❑ 5732	Old and In the Way/Six Months Ain't Long	1963	3.00	6.00	12.00
❑ 5754	Memories of Mother/Paul and Silas	1963	3.00	6.00	12.00
❑ 5763	Lips That Lie/He Went to Sleep — The Hogs Ate Him	1963	3.00	6.00	12.00
❑ 5809	Stone Walls and Steel Bars/Lonesome Night	1963	3.00	6.00	12.00
❑ 5869	Don't Cheat in Our Home Town/I See Through You	1964	2.50	5.00	10.00
❑ 5902	A Crown He Wore/John 3:16	1964	2.50	5.00	10.00
❑ 5916	Train 45/I Just Stood There	1964	2.50	5.00	10.00
❑ 5920	How Bad I Do Feel/Bully of the Town	1964	2.50	5.00	10.00
❑ 5932	He's Passing This Way/Shoutin' on the Hills of Glory	1964	2.50	5.00	10.00
❑ 5934	Five String Drag/Shout Little Lucie	1964	2.50	5.00	10.00
❑ 6005	Rollin' on Rubber Wheels/How You've Tortured My Mind	1965	2.50	5.00	10.00
❑ 6023	The End of the Road/Pray for the Boys	1966	2.50	5.00	10.00
❑ 6046	Never Again/Prayer of a Truck Driver's Son	1966	2.50	5.00	10.00
❑ 6053	A Soldier's Grave/Take Me Home	1966	2.50	5.00	10.00
❑ 6059	God's Highway/I Feel Like Going Home	1966	2.50	5.00	10.00
❑ 6079	Whiskey/A Little Birdie	1967	2.50	5.00	10.00
❑ 6089	The Hills of Roan County/I Don't Want Your Rambling Letters	1967	2.50	5.00	10.00

MERCURY

Number	Title (A Side/B Side)	Yr	VG	VG+	NM
❑ 70217	I'm Lonesome/That Weary Heart You Stole	1953	5.00	10.00	20.00
❑ 70270	Our Last Goodbye/Won't You Be Mine	1953	5.00	10.00	20.00
❑ 70340	A Voice from On High/I Long to See the Old Folks	1954	5.00	10.00	20.00
❑ 70400	Memories of Mother/Could You Love Me	1954	5.00	10.00	20.00
❑ 70453	Blue Moon of Kentucky/I Just Got Wise	1954	6.25	12.50	25.00
❑ 70483	Harbor of Love/Calling from Heaven	1954	5.00	10.00	20.00
❑ 70546	Hard Times/I Worship You	1955	5.00	10.00	20.00
❑ 70612	So Blue/You'd Better Get Right	1955	5.00	10.00	20.00
❑ 70663	Lonesome and Blue/Orange Blossom Special	1955	5.00	10.00	20.00
❑ 70718	I Hear My Savior Calling/Just a Little Talk with Jesus	1955	5.00	10.00	20.00
❑ 70789	Nobody's Love Like Mine/Big Tilda	1956	5.00	10.00	20.00
❑ 70886	Baby Girl/Say You'll Take Me Back	1956	5.00	10.00	20.00
❑ 71064	The Flood/I'm Lost, I'll Never Find the Way	1957	5.00	10.00	20.00
❑ 71135	The Cry from the Cross/Let Me Walk, Lord, By Your Side	1957	5.00	10.00	20.00
❑ 71207	Loving You Too Well/Fling Ding	1957	5.00	10.00	20.00
❑ 71258	If That's the Way You Feel/I'd Rather Be Forgotten	1957	5.00	10.00	20.00
❑ 71302	It's a Long Story/No Foolish Fling	1958	5.00	10.00	20.00

STARDAY

Number	Title (A Side/B Side)	Yr	VG	VG+	NM
❑ 406	Gonna Paint the Town/That Happy Night	1958	5.00	10.00	20.00
❑ 413	Christmas Is Near/Holiday Pickin'	1958	5.00	10.00	20.00
❑ 438	Trust Each Other/Beneath the Maple	1959	5.00	10.00	20.00
❑ 466	Highway of Regret/Another Night	1959	5.00	10.00	20.00
❑ 494	Ridin' the Midnight Train/A Little at a Time	1960	3.75	7.50	15.00
❑ 506	Rank Stranger/The Master's Bouquet	1960	3.75	7.50	15.00
❑ 522	Little Maggie/God Gave You to Me	1960	3.75	7.50	15.00
❑ 546	Don't Go Out Tonight/If I Lose	1961	3.75	7.50	15.00
❑ 565	Carolina Mountain Home/A Few More Sessions	1961	3.75	7.50	15.00
❑ 587	Come All Ye Tenderhearted/Choo Choo Comin'	1962	3.00	6.00	12.00
❑ 836	Bonnie and Clyde's Getaway/The Story of Bonnie and Clyde	1968	2.50	5.00	10.00

—B-side by Jimmie Skinner

Albums

CABIN CREEK

Number	Title (A Side/B Side)	Yr	VG	VG+	NM
❑ LP-203 [M]	Bluegrass Gospel Favorites	1966	15.00	30.00	60.00

HARMONY

Number	Title (A Side/B Side)	Yr	VG	VG+	NM
❑ HL 7291 [M]	The Stanley Brothers	1961	6.25	12.50	25.00

KING

Number	Title (A Side/B Side)	Yr	VG	VG+	NM
❑ 615 [M]	The Stanley Brothers	1959	25.00	50.00	100.00
❑ 645 [M]	Hymns and Sacred Songs	1960	20.00	40.00	80.00
❑ 690 [M]	Everybody's Country Favorites	1961	20.00	40.00	80.00
❑ KS-690 [S]	Everybody's Country Favorites	1961	25.00	50.00	100.00
❑ 698 [M]	For the Good People	1961	20.00	40.00	80.00
❑ 719 [M]	The Stanleys In Person	1961	20.00	40.00	80.00
❑ KS-719 [S]	The Stanleys In Person	1961	25.00	50.00	100.00
❑ 750 [M]	Old Time Camp Meeting	1962	20.00	40.00	80.00
❑ 772 [M]	The Stanley Brothers and the Clinch Mountain Boys Sing the Songs They Like Best	1962	20.00	40.00	80.00
❑ 791 [M]	Award Winners	1962	20.00	40.00	80.00
❑ KS-791 [S]	Award Winners	1962	25.00	50.00	100.00
❑ 805 [M]	Good Old Camp Meeting Songs	1963	20.00	40.00	80.00
❑ KS-805 [S]	Good Old Camp Meeting Songs	1963	25.00	50.00	100.00
❑ 834 [M]	Just Because	1964	12.50	25.00	50.00
❑ 864 [M]	Country Folk Music Spotlight	1964	12.50	25.00	50.00
❑ 872 [M]	Five String Banjo Hootenanny	1964	12.50	25.00	50.00
❑ 918 [M]	Hymns of the Cross	1964	12.50	25.00	50.00
❑ 924 [M]	The Remarkable Stanley Brothers Play and Sing Bluegrass Songs for You	1965	12.50	25.00	50.00
❑ 953 [M]	The Best of the Stanley Brothers	1966	6.25	12.50	25.00
❑ 963 [M]	A Collection of Gospel and Sacred Songs	1966	6.25	12.50	25.00
❑ 1013 [M]	The Stanley Brothers Sing the Best-Loved Sacred Songs of the Carter Family	1967	6.25	12.50	25.00
❑ KS-1013 [S]	The Stanley Brothers Sing the Best-Loved Sacred Songs of the Carter Family	1967	7.50	15.00	30.00

MERCURY

Number	Title (A Side/B Side)	Yr	VG	VG+	NM
❑ MG-20349 [M]	Country Pickin' and Singin'	1958	20.00	40.00	80.00
❑ MG-20884 [M]	Hard Times	1963	6.25	12.50	25.00
❑ SR-60884 [S]	Hard Times	1963	7.50	15.00	30.00

STARDAY

Number	Title (A Side/B Side)	Yr	VG	VG+	NM
❑ SLP-106 [M]	Mountain Song Favorites	1959	12.50	25.00	50.00
❑ SLP-122 [M]	Sacred Songs from the Hills	1960	12.50	25.00	50.00
❑ SLP-201 [M]	The Mountain Music Sound of the Stanley Brothers	1962	10.00	20.00	40.00
❑ SLP-384 [M]	Jacob's Vision	1966	7.50	15.00	30.00

VINTAGE

Number	Title (A Side/B Side)	Yr	VG	VG+	NM
❑ ZK-002 [M]	The Stanley Brothers Live at Antioch College	1961	17.50	35.00	70.00

STARCHER, BUDDY

45s

BOONE

Number	Title (A Side/B Side)	Yr	VG	VG+	NM
❑ 1038	History Repeats Itself/Sniper's Hill	1966	2.50	5.00	10.00

COLUMBIA

Number	Title (A Side/B Side)	Yr	VG	VG+	NM
❑ 2-380 (?)	I Planted a Rose/Isn't He Wonderful	1949	10.00	20.00	40.00

—Microgroove 33 1/3 rpm 7-inch single, small hole

Number	Title (A Side/B Side)	Yr	VG	VG+	NM
❑ 2-400 (?)	New Wildwood Flower/Walk Lightly, You're Stepping on My Heart	1949	10.00	20.00	40.00

—Microgroove 33 1/3 rpm 7-inch single, small hole

Number	Title (A Side/B Side)	Yr	VG	VG+	NM
❑ 2-490 (?)	Beyond the Sunset/Are You Facing the World All Alone	1949	10.00	20.00	40.00

—Microgroove 33 1/3 rpm 7-inch single, small hole

Number	Title (A Side/B Side)	Yr	VG	VG+	NM
❑ 2-580 (?)	Colored Child's Funeral/Oh Leave One Token of Your Love	1950	12.50	25.00	50.00

—Microgroove 33 1/3 rpm 7-inch single, small hole

Number	Title (A Side/B Side)	Yr	VG	VG+	NM
❑ 4-20723	I'll Forgive Dear But Never Forget/My Old Pal of Yesterday	1950	7.50	15.00	30.00

DECCA

Number	Title (A Side/B Side)	Yr	VG	VG+	NM
❑ 31975	Tax Payer's Lament/Day of Decision	1966	2.00	4.00	8.00
❑ 32012	Fall of a Nation/The Last Supper	1966	2.00	4.00	8.00

HEART WARMING

Number	Title (A Side/B Side)	Yr	VG	VG+	NM
❑ 5069	When Payday Comes/What Then?	1967	2.00	4.00	8.00

STARDAY

Number	Title (A Side/B Side)	Yr	VG	VG+	NM
❑ 439	The Battle of New Orleans/Pale Wildwood Flower	1959	3.75	7.50	15.00
❑ 460	Billy the Kid/Running Away from the Blues	1959	3.75	7.50	15.00
❑ 471	Ace of Hearts/Cryin'	1959	3.75	7.50	15.00
❑ 763	Little Red Riding Hood/Ace of Hearts	1966	2.00	4.00	8.00

Selected 78s

4 STAR

Number	Title (A Side/B Side)	Yr	VG	VG+	NM
❑ 1111	A Faded Rose, a Broken Heart/Bless Your Little Heart	1948	5.00	10.00	20.00
❑ 1112	It's Risky to Be Gone So Long/Song of the Waterwheel	1948	5.00	10.00	20.00
❑ 1113	I Won't Worry, I Won't Care/The Fire in My Heart	1948	5.00	10.00	20.00
❑ 1143	Wildwood Flower/Bless Your Little Heart	1948	5.00	10.00	20.00
❑ 1144	I Will Miss You Tonight/In Memory of Halloween	1948	5.00	10.00	20.00
❑ 1145	I'll Still Write Your Name in the Sand/Darling What More Can I Do	1948	5.00	10.00	20.00
❑ 1263	Darling What More Can I Do/You Can't Break the Chains of Love	1949	5.00	10.00	20.00

Albums

DECCA

Number	Title (A Side/B Side)	Yr	VG	VG+	NM
❑ DL 4796 [M]	History Repeats Itself	1966	5.00	10.00	20.00
❑ DL 74796 [S]	History Repeats Itself	1966	6.25	12.50	25.00

STARDAY

Number	Title (A Side/B Side)	Yr	VG	VG+	NM
❑ SLP-211 [M]	Buddy Starcher and His Mountain Guitar	1962	7.50	15.00	30.00
❑ SLP-382 [M]	History Repeats Itself	1966	7.50	15.00	30.00

STARK, DONNA

45s

RCI

Number	Title (A Side/B Side)	Yr	VG	VG+	NM
❑ 2341	I Wanna Be with You/If Pictures Could Talk	1980	—	3.00	6.00
❑ 2344	Why Don't You Believe Me/I'm So Lonesome and So Blue	1980	—	3.00	6.00
❑ 2345	Walking Away/Fascinating Stranger	1980	—	3.00	6.00
❑ 2347	Echoes of the Past/So the Rain Is Falling	1980	—	3.00	6.00
❑ 2348	Christmas Day Is Near/Set Me Free	1980	—	3.00	6.00
❑ 2351	Tomorrow I'll Remember/The Next Hundred Years	1981	—	3.00	6.00
❑ 2355	I've Gone Through Hell Just to Get to Heaven/ Time Alone	1981	—	3.00	6.00

STARLAND VOCAL BAND

45s

WINDSONG

Number	Title (A Side/B Side)	Yr	VG	VG+	NM
❑ CB-10588	Afternoon Delight/Starland	1976	—	2.00	4.00
❑ CB-10785	California Day/War Surplus Baby	1976	—	2.00	4.00
❑ CB-10855	Hail, Hail, Rock and Roll/Ain't It the Fall	1976	—	2.00	4.00
❑ GB-10943	Afternoon Delight/California Day	1977	—	—	3.00
—"Gold Standard Series" reissue					
❑ CB-11067	Light of My Life/Prism	1977	—	2.00	4.00
❑ CB-11168	Mr. Wrong/Too Long a Journey	1977	—	2.00	4.00
❑ CB-11261	Late Nite Radio/Please Mrs. Newslady	1978	—	2.00	4.00
❑ CB-11899	Loving You with My Eyes/Apartment for Rent	1980	—	2.00	4.00
❑ CB-12011	Thought I Would Never Find Love/Love Stuff	1980	—	2.00	4.00

Albums

WINDSONG

Number	Title (A Side/B Side)	Yr	VG	VG+	NM
❑ BHL1-1351	Starland Vocal Band	1976	2.50	5.00	10.00
❑ BHL1-2239	Rear View Mirror	1977	2.50	5.00	10.00
❑ BXL1-2598	Late Nite Radio	1978	2.50	5.00	10.00
❑ BXL1-3536	4 x 4	1980	2.50	5.00	10.00

STARR, KAY

Pop singer whose only country hits were two sides of the same record, listed below.

45s

CAPITOL

Number	Title (A Side/B Side)	Yr	VG	VG+	NM
❑ F1124	I'll Never Be Free/Ain't Nobody's Business But My Own	1950	6.25	12.50	25.00
—With Tennessee Ernie Ford					

STARR, KENNY

45s

MCA

Number	Title (A Side/B Side)	Yr	VG	VG+	NM
❑ 40023	That's a Whole Lotta Lovin' (You Give Me)/Carol	1973	—	2.50	5.00
❑ 40124	Ev'ryday Woman/My Lovin' Time with You	1973	—	2.50	5.00
❑ 40213	Highway of Love/You Make It Easy	1974	—	2.50	5.00
❑ 40350	Put Another Notch in Your Belt/Where Love Begins	1975	—	2.50	5.00
❑ 40474	The Blind Man in the Bleachers/Texas Proud	1975	—	2.50	5.00
❑ 40524	Tonight I'll Face the Man (Who Made It Happen)/ I Can't See in the Dark	1976	—	2.50	5.00
❑ 40580	The Calico Cat/Victims	1976	—	2.50	5.00
❑ 40637	I Just Can't (Turn My Habit Into Love)/The Upper Hand	1976	—	2.50	5.00
❑ 40672	Me and the Elephant/Smooth Talkin' Guy	1976	—	2.50	5.00
❑ 40769	Old Time Lovin'/Hobo on the Freight Train to Heaven	1977	—	2.50	5.00
❑ 40817	Hold Tight/Rockin' Robin	1977	—	2.50	5.00
❑ 40880	The Rest of My Life/Tuffy	1978	—	2.50	5.00
❑ 40922	Slow Drivin'/Watchin' the River Run	1978	—	2.50	5.00

SAGE

Number	Title (A Side/B Side)	Yr	VG	VG+	NM
❑ 281	Long, Long Time/My Tender Love	195?	5.00	10.00	20.00

Albums

MCA

Number	Title (A Side/B Side)	Yr	VG	VG+	NM
❑ 2177	The Blind Man in the Bleachers	1975	2.50	5.00	10.00

STARR, PENNY

See PENNY DeHAVEN.

STARR, RINGO

The former member of the Beatles recorded some country-oriented music, listed below. Also see BUCK OWENS.

45s

APPLE

Number	Title (A Side/B Side)	Yr	VG	VG+	NM
❑ 1826 [PS]	Beaucoups of Blues/Coochy-Coochy	1970	10.00	20.00	40.00
—Sleeve with wrong catalog number (actually 2969)					
❑ 2969	Beaucoups of Blues/Coochy-Coochy	1970	6.25	12.50	25.00
—With small Capitol logo on bottom of B-side label and star on A-side label					
❑ 2969	Beaucoups of Blues/Coochy-Coochy	1970	10.00	20.00	40.00
—With "Mfd. by Apple" on label and star on A-side label					
❑ 2969	Beaucoups of Blues/Coochy-Coochy	1970	2.00	4.00	8.00
—With "Mfd. by Apple" on label and no star on A-side label					
❑ 2969 [PS]	Beaucoups of Blues/Coochy-Coochy	1970	12.50	25.00	50.00
—Sleeve with correct catalog number					

CAPITOL

Number	Title (A Side/B Side)	Yr	VG	VG+	NM
❑ 2969	Beaucoups of Blues/Coochy-Coochy	1976	10.00	20.00	40.00
—Orange label					

Albums

APPLE

Number	Title (A Side/B Side)	Yr	VG	VG+	NM
❑ SMAS-3368	Beaucoups of Blues	1970	5.00	10.00	20.00

CAPITOL

Number	Title (A Side/B Side)	Yr	VG	VG+	NM
❑ SN-16235	Beaucoups of Blues	198?	5.00	10.00	20.00
—Green label budget-line reissue					

STARR, SALLY

45s

ARCADE

Number	Title (A Side/B Side)	Yr	VG	VG+	NM
❑ 157	Rocky the Rockin' Rabbit/Sing a Song of Happiness	1960	7.50	15.00	30.00

CLYMAX

Number	Title (A Side/B Side)	Yr	VG	VG+	NM
❑ 301	Rockin' in the Nursery/Little Pedro	1959	10.00	20.00	40.00

7-Inch Extended Plays

CLYMAX

Number	Title (A Side/B Side)	Yr	VG	VG+	NM
❑ EP-1001/2/3 [PS]	Our Gal Sal	1959	10.00	20.00	40.00
—Triple gatefold cover for all three EP-1001 records (despite what the cover says, the records are each numbered 1001)					
❑ EP-1001	Rockin' in the Nursery/Little Pedro//Rockin' Horse Cowgirl/Good Night Dear Lord	1959	7.50	15.00	30.00
—Third record of 3-EP set; master numbers are JB-144/JB-145					
❑ EP-1001	Toy Shop in the Town/Happy Birthday//Candy Red/Blue Ranger	1959	7.50	15.00	30.00
—First record of 3-EP set; master numbers are JB-140/JB-141					
❑ EP-1001	Cuckoo in the Clock/Sing a Song of Happiness// TV Pal/A.B.C. Rock	1959	7.50	15.00	30.00
—Second record of 3-EP set; master numbers are JB 142/JB 143					

Albums

ARCADE

Number	Title (A Side/B Side)	Yr	VG	VG+	NM
❑ 1001 [M]	Our Gal Sal	1960	20.00	40.00	80.00

CLYMAX

Number	Title (A Side/B Side)	Yr	VG	VG+	NM
❑ 1001 [M]	Our Gal Sal	1959	50.00	100.00	200.00

STATLER, DARRELL

45s

DOT

Number	Title (A Side/B Side)	Yr	VG	VG+	NM
❑ 17146	Tragedy's Girl/Been to Bakersfield	1968	2.00	4.00	8.00
❑ 17205	Hung Up on Your Love/It's Another World	1969	2.00	4.00	8.00
❑ 17275	Blue Collar Job/I'm Barely Gettin' By	1969	2.00	4.00	8.00
❑ 17333	Pasadena Penthouse/Handle to the Silver Spoon (Of Life)	1969	2.00	4.00	8.00
❑ 17359	The Good Guys and Bad Men/Those Country Folks	1970	2.00	4.00	8.00
❑ 17397	The Arms of Mary Lee/Where Are We Goin' This Time Mama	1971	2.00	4.00	8.00

STATLER BROTHERS, THE

45s

COLUMBIA

Number	Title (A Side/B Side)	Yr	VG	VG+	NM
❑ 43069	The Wreck of the Old 97/Hammer and Nails	1964	3.00	6.00	12.00
❑ 43146	I Still Miss Someone/You're a Foolish Game	1964	3.00	6.00	12.00
❑ 43315	Flowers on the Wall/Billy Christian	1965	2.50	5.00	10.00
❑ 43315 [DJ]	Flowers on the Wall (same on both sides)	1965	5.00	10.00	20.00
—Promo only on red vinyl					
❑ 43526	The Doodlin' Song/My Darling Hildegarde	1966	2.00	4.00	8.00
❑ 43624	The Right One/Is That What You'd Have Me Do	1966	2.00	4.00	8.00
❑ 43868	That'll Be the Day/Makin' Rounds	1966	2.00	4.00	8.00
❑ 44070	Ruthless/Do You Love Me Tonight	1967	2.00	4.00	8.00
❑ 44245	You Can't Have Your Kate and Edith, Too/ Walking in the Sunshine	1967	2.00	4.00	8.00
❑ 44480	Jump for Joy/Take a Bow, Rufus Humfry	1968	2.00	4.00	8.00
❑ 44608	Sissy/I Am the Boy	1968	2.00	4.00	8.00
❑ 44899	Oh Happy Day/How Great Thou Art	1969	2.00	4.00	8.00

MERCURY

Number	Title (A Side/B Side)	Yr	VG	VG+	NM
❑ DJ 557 [DJ]	Star Spangled Banner (With Spoken Intro)/Star Spangled Banner (Without Spoken Intro)	197?	2.00	4.00	8.00
❑ PRO 790-7 [DJ]	Don't Wait on Me (Live Edited Version/Live with Intro)	1989	2.00	4.00	8.00
—"US 99 10-In-a-Row Country Commemorative Edition" at top (other similar pressings may exist)					
❑ 55000	Silver Medals and Sweet Memories/The Regular Saturday Night Setback Card Game	1977	—	2.00	4.00
❑ 55013	Some I Wrote/Carried Away	1977	—	2.00	4.00
❑ 55022	Do You Know You Are My Sunshine/You're the First	1978	—	2.00	4.00
❑ 55037	Who Am I to Say/I Dreamed About You	1978	—	2.00	4.00
❑ 55046	I Believe in Santa's Cause/Who Do You Think	1978	—	2.00	4.00
❑ 55048	The Official Historian on Shirley Jean Berrell/The Best That I Can Do	1978	—	2.00	4.00
❑ 55057	How to Be a Country Star/A Little Farther Down the Road	1979	—	2.00	4.00
❑ 55066	Here We Are Again/Mr. Autry	1979	—	2.00	4.00
❑ 57007	Nothing As Original As You/Counting My Memories	1979	—	2.00	4.00
❑ 57012	(I'll Even Love You) Better Than I Did Then/ Almost in Love	1980	—	2.00	4.00
❑ 57031	Charlotte's Web/One Less Day to Go	1980	—	2.00	4.00
❑ 57037	Don't Forget Yourself/We Got Paid by Cash	1980	—	2.00	4.00
❑ 57048	In the Garden/How Are Things in Clay, Kentucky	1981	—	2.00	4.00
❑ 57051	Don't Wait on Me/Chet Atkins' Band	1981	—	2.00	4.00
❑ 57059	Years Ago/Dad	1981	—	2.00	4.00
❑ 73141	Bed of Rose's/The Last Goodbye	1970	—	2.50	5.00
❑ 73194	New York City/This Part of the World	1971	—	2.50	5.00
❑ 73229	Pictures/Making Memories	1971	—	2.50	5.00
❑ 73253	You Can't Go Home/Second Thoughts	1971	—	2.50	5.00
❑ 73275	Do You Remember These/Since Then	1972	—	2.50	5.00
❑ 73315	The Class of '57/Every Time I Trust a Gal	1972	—	2.50	5.00

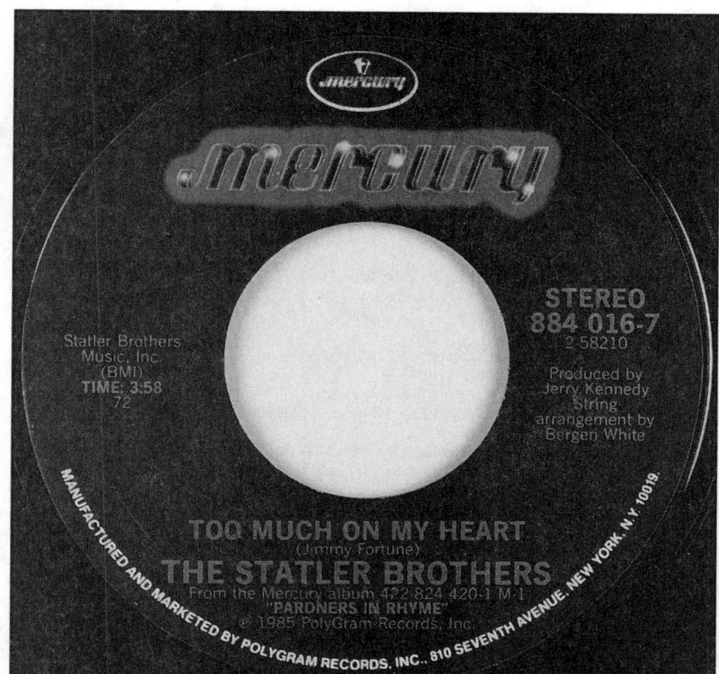

The Statler Brothers were not brothers (two of them were, but not all four), nor was anyone in the group named "Statler." But their harmonies were a prominent part of the country charts for two and a half decades. (Top left) After some early flops, their first hit single was "Flowers on the Wall." It got to No. 2 on the country charts and No. 4 on the pop charts. For the next 12-plus years, the Statlers would not have a bigger country hit. (Top right) They finally eclipsed their early classic when "Do You Know You Are My Sunshine" made it to No. 1 in 1978. (Bottom left) From 1983-86, the Statlers had their most consistent run of hits, three of which got all the way to the top. The third of them was 1985's "Too Much on My Heart." (Bottom right) Here's an interesting promotional 45 from 1989, given out by a radio station to push the live version of "Don't Wait on Me."

Number	Title (A Side/B Side)	Yr	VG	VG+	NM
❑ 73360	Monday Morning Secretary/Special Song for Wanda	1973	—	2.50	5.00
❑ 73392	Woman Without a Home/I'll Be Your Baby Tonight	1973	—	2.50	5.00
❑ 73415	Carry Me Back/I Wish I Could Be	1973	—	2.50	5.00
❑ 73448	Whatever Happened to Randolph Scott/The Strand	1974	—	2.50	5.00
❑ 73485	Thank You World/The Blackwood Brothers by the Statler Brothers	1974	—	2.50	5.00
❑ 73625	Susan When She Tried/She's Too Good	1974	—	2.50	5.00
❑ 73665	All American Girl/A Few Old Memories	1975	—	2.50	5.00
❑ 73687	I'll Go to My Grave Loving You/You've Been Like a Mother to Me	1975	—	2.50	5.00
❑ 73732	How Great Thou Art/Noah Found Grace in the Eyes of the Lord	1975	—	2.50	5.00
❑ 73785	Your Picture in the Paper/All the Times	1976	—	2.50	5.00
❑ 73846	Thank God I've Got You/Hat and Boots	1976	—	2.50	5.00
❑ 73877	The Movies/You Could Be Coming to Me	1976	—	2.50	5.00
❑ 73906	I Was There/Somebody New Will Be Coming Along	1977	—	2.50	5.00
❑ 76130	I Never Spend A Christmas That I Don't Think Of You/Who Do You Think?	1981	—	2.00	4.00
❑ 76142	You'll Be Back (Every Night in My Dreams)/We Ain't Even Started Yet	1982	—	—	3.00
❑ 76162	Whatever/Do You Know You Are My Sunshine	1982	—	—	3.00
❑ 76184	A Child of the Fifties/I'll Love You All Over Again	1982	—	—	3.00
❑ 811488-7	Oh Baby Mine (I Get So Lonely)/I'm Dyin' a Little Each Day	1983	—	—	3.00
❑ 812988-7	Guilty/I Never Want to Kiss You Goodbye	1983	—	—	3.00
❑ 814881-7	Elizabeth/Class of '57	1983	—	—	3.00
❑ 818700-7	Atlanta Blue/If It Makes Any Difference	1984	—	—	3.00
❑ 818700-7 [PS]	Atlanta Blue/If It Makes Any Difference	1984	—	2.00	4.00
❑ 866302-7	Atlanta Blue/Put It on the Card	1991	—	2.00	4.00
❑ 868140-7	Remember Me/My Music, My Memories and You	1991	—	—	3.00
❑ 868484-7	You've Been Like a Mother to Me/Jesus Is the Answer	1991	—	2.00	4.00
❑ 868892-7	There's Still Times/Elizabeth	1991	—	—	3.00
❑ 870164-7	The Best I Know How/I Lost My Heart to You	1988	—	—	3.00
❑ 870442-7	Am I Crazy?/Beyond Romance	1988	—	—	3.00
❑ 870681-7	Let's Get Started If We're Gonna Break My Heart/ Guilty	1988	—	—	3.00
❑ 872604-7	Moon Pretty Moon/I'll Be the One	1989	—	—	3.00
❑ 874196-7	More Than a Name on the Wall/Atlanta Blue	1989	—	—	3.00
❑ 875498-7	Small Small World/My Music, My Memories and You	1990	—	—	3.00
❑ 876112-7	Don't Wait on Me/A Hurt I Can't Handle	1989	—	—	3.00
❑ 876876-7	Walkin' Heartache in Disguise/The Official Historian on Shirley Jean Berrell	1990	—	—	3.00
❑ 878386-7	He Is There/Nobody Else	1991	—	2.00	4.00
❑ 880130-7	One Takes the Blame/Give It Your Best	1984	—	—	3.00
❑ 880411-7	My Only Love/Let's Just Take One Night at a Time	1984	—	—	3.00
❑ 880685-7	Hello Mary Lou/Remembering You	1985	—	—	3.00
❑ 884016-7	Too Much on My Heart/Her Heart or Mine	1985	—	—	3.00
❑ 884317-7	Sweeter and Sweeter/Amazing Grace	1985	—	—	3.00
❑ 884320-7	Christmas Eve (Kodia's Theme)/Mary's Sweet Smile	1985	—	—	3.00
❑ 884721-7	Count On Me/Will You Be There?	1986	—	—	3.00
❑ 888042-7	Only You/We Got the Mem'ries	1986	—	—	3.00
❑ 888219-7	Forever/More Like Daddy Than Me	1986	—	—	3.00
❑ 888650-7	I'll Be the One/Deja Vu	1987	—	—	3.00
❑ 888920-7	Maple Street Mem'ries/Jesus Showed Me So	1987	—	—	3.00
7-Inch Extended Plays					
MERCURY					
❑ DJ 577 [DJ]	I Never Spend a Christmas That I Don't Think of You/Jingle Bells//Away in a Manger/The Carols Those Kids Used to Sing	1978	—	3.00	6.00
❑ DJ 577 [PS]	A Very Merry Christmas from the Statler Brothers	1978	2.00	4.00	8.00
Albums					
COLUMBIA					
❑ CL 2449 [M]	Flowers on the Wall	1966	6.25	12.50	25.00
❑ CL 2719 [M]	The Big Hits	1967	7.50	15.00	30.00
❑ CS 9249 [S]	Flowers on the Wall	1966	7.50	15.00	30.00
❑ PC 9249	Flowers on the Wall	198?	2.00	4.00	8.00
—Reissue with new prefix					
❑ CS 9519 [S]	The Big Hits	1967	6.25	12.50	25.00
❑ PC 9519	The Big Hits	198?	2.00	4.00	8.00
—Reissue with new prefix					
❑ CS 9878	Oh Happy Day	1969	6.25	12.50	25.00
❑ PC 9878	Oh Happy Day	198?	2.00	4.00	8.00
—Reissue with new prefix					
❑ CG 31557 [(2)]	The World of the Statler Brothers	198?	3.00	6.00	12.00
—Reissue with new prefix					
❑ KG 31557 [(2)]	The World of the Statler Brothers	1972	5.00	10.00	20.00
❑ C 31560	How Great Thou Art	197?	2.50	5.00	10.00
—Reissue of Harmony 31560					
HARMONY					
❑ H 30610	Big Country Hits	1971	3.00	6.00	12.00
❑ KH 31560	How Great Thou Art	1972	3.00	6.00	12.00
❑ KH 32256	Do You Love Me Tonight	1973	3.00	6.00	12.00
MERCURY					
❑ SRM-2-101 [(2)]	Holy Bible/The Old and New Testaments	1978	5.00	10.00	20.00
—Reissue of 1051 and 1052 in one package					
❑ SRM-1-676	Carry Me Back	1973	3.75	7.50	15.00
❑ SRM-1-707	Thank You World	1974	3.75	7.50	15.00
❑ SRM-1-1019	Sons of the Motherland	1975	3.75	7.50	15.00
❑ SRM-1-1037	The Best of the Statler Brothers	1975	3.00	6.00	12.00
❑ SRM-1-1051	Holy Bible: Old Testament	1975	3.75	7.50	15.00
❑ SRM-1-1052	Holy Bible: New Testament	1975	3.75	7.50	15.00
❑ SRM-1-1077	Harold, Lew, Phil & Don	1976	3.75	7.50	15.00
❑ SRM-1-1125	The Country America Loves	1977	3.75	7.50	15.00
❑ SRM-1-4048	The Legend Goes On	1982	3.00	6.00	12.00
❑ SRM-1-5001	Short Stories	1977	3.00	6.00	12.00
❑ SRM-1-5007	Entertainers...On and Off the Record	1978	3.00	6.00	12.00
❑ SRM-1-5012	Christmas Card	1978	2.50	5.00	10.00
❑ SRM-1-5016	The Originals	1979	3.00	6.00	12.00
❑ SRM-1-5024	The Best of the Statler Brothers Rides Again, Volume II	1980	3.00	6.00	12.00
❑ SRM-1-5027	10th Anniversary	1980	3.00	6.00	12.00
❑ SRM-1-6002	Years Ago	1981	3.00	6.00	12.00
❑ SR-61317	Bed of Rose's	1970	3.75	7.50	15.00
❑ SR-61349	Pictures of Moments to Remember	1971	3.75	7.50	15.00
❑ SR-61358	Innerview	1972	3.75	7.50	15.00
❑ SR-61367	Country Music "Then and Now"	1972	3.75	7.50	15.00
❑ SR-61374	The Statler Brothers Sing Country Symphonies in E Major	1973	3.75	7.50	15.00
❑ 812184-1	Today	1983	2.50	5.00	10.00
❑ 812282-1	10th Anniversary	1983	2.00	4.00	8.00
❑ 812283-1	Entertainers...On and Off the Record	1983	2.00	4.00	8.00
❑ 812284-1	Carry Me Back	1983	2.00	4.00	8.00
❑ 818652-1	Atlanta Blue	1984	2.50	5.00	10.00
❑ 822524-1	The Best of the Statler Brothers	1984	2.00	4.00	8.00
❑ 822525-1	The Best of the Statler Brothers Rides Again, Volume II	1984	2.00	4.00	8.00
❑ 822743-1	Christmas Card	1985	2.00	4.00	8.00
❑ 824420-1	Pardners in Rhyme	1985	2.50	5.00	10.00
❑ 824785-1	Christmas Present	1985	2.50	5.00	10.00
❑ 826247-1	Bed of Rose's	1986	2.00	4.00	8.00
❑ 826259-1	Innerview	1986	2.00	4.00	8.00
❑ 826260-1	Country Music "Then and Now"	1986	2.00	4.00	8.00
❑ 826264-1 [(2)]	Holy Bible/The Old and New Testaments	1986	2.50	5.00	10.00
❑ 826267-1	Holy Bible: Old Testament	1986	2.00	4.00	8.00
❑ 826268-1	Holy Bible: New Testament	1986	2.00	4.00	8.00
❑ 826269-1	Harold, Lew, Phil & Don	1986	2.00	4.00	8.00
❑ 826275-1	The Country America Loves	1986	2.00	4.00	8.00
❑ 826278-1	The Legend Goes On	1986	2.00	4.00	8.00
❑ 826280-1	Short Stories	1986	2.00	4.00	8.00
❑ 826281-1	The Originals	1986	2.00	4.00	8.00
❑ 826710-1	Radio Gospel Favorites	1986	2.50	5.00	10.00
❑ 826782-1	Four for the Show	1986	2.50	5.00	10.00
❑ 832404-1	Maple Street Memories	1987	2.50	5.00	10.00
❑ 834626-1	The Statlers Greatest Hits	1988	2.50	5.00	10.00
❑ 838231-1	Statler Brothers Live — Sold Out	1989	3.75	7.50	15.00
PRIORITY					
❑ PU 37709	Country Gospel	1982	2.50	5.00	10.00

STEAGALL, RED

Includes records with his last name spelled "Stegall."

Number	Title (A Side/B Side)	Yr	VG	VG+	NM
45s					
ABC					
❑ 12337	Hang On Feelin'/Bob's Got a Swing Band in Heaven	1978	—	2.50	5.00
❑ 12381	Hot Roasted Peanuts/About Horses and Wars	1978	—	2.50	5.00
ABC DOT					
❑ 17610	Lone Star Beer and Bob Wills Music/I've Never Been This Loved Before	1976	—	2.50	5.00
❑ 17634	Truck Drivin' Man/Neons and Nylons	1976	—	2.50	5.00
❑ 17653	Rosie (Do You Wanna Talk It Over)/The Walls of This Old Honky Tonk	1976	—	2.50	5.00
❑ 17670	Her L-O-V-E's Gone/Take Me Back to Texas	1977	—	2.50	5.00
❑ 17684	I Left My Heart in San Francisco/Texas Red	1977	—	2.50	5.00
❑ 17709	Freckles Brown/My Adobe Hacienda	1977	—	2.50	5.00
❑ 17726	The Devil Ain't a Lonely Woman's Friend/The Rain Don't Stop in Oklahoma	1977	—	2.50	5.00
CAPITOL					
❑ 3119	Good Christian Soldier/Tell the Man I'm Coming Home	1971	—	3.50	7.00
❑ 3170	In a Jetway in Dallas/I've Been Here Ever Since	1971	—	3.50	7.00
❑ 3244	Party Dolls and Wine/Middle Tennessee Country Boy's Blues	1971	—	3.00	6.00
❑ 3318	Oklahoma Promise/Texas Silver Zephyr	1972	—	3.00	6.00
❑ 3375	Beer Drinkin' Music/You Came Awful Close to Lovin' Me	1972	—	3.00	6.00
❑ 3461	Somewhere, My Love/Give Me One More Chance	1972	—	3.00	6.00
❑ 3562	True Love/Something Nice and Easy	1973	—	3.00	6.00
❑ 3651	If You've Got the Time/Ol' Helen	1973	—	3.00	6.00
❑ 3724	The Fiddle Man/Neon Playboy	1973	—	3.00	6.00
❑ 3797	This Just Ain't My Day (For Lettin' Darlin' Down)/ Little Old Heartbreaker You	1973	—	3.00	6.00
❑ 3825	I Gave Up Good Mornin' Darling/Ballad of Billy's Lady	1974	—	3.00	6.00
❑ 3913	Finer Things in Life/Tight Levis and Yellow Ribbons	1974	—	3.00	6.00
❑ 3965	Someone Cares for You/Throw Away Heart	1974	—	3.00	6.00
❑ 4042	She Worshipped Me/April's Paintings	1975	—	3.00	6.00
❑ 4107	God Only Knows (Who'll Take Her Home)/Party Dolls and Wine	1975	—	3.00	6.00
❑ 4162	Lone Star Beer and Bob Wills Music/Cold Beer Signs and Country Songs	1975	2.00	4.00	8.00

Number	Title (A Side/B Side)	Yr	VG	VG+	NM
DOT					
❑ 17360	Alabama Woman/That Time Has Come and Gone	1970	2.50	5.00	10.00
ELEKTRA					
❑ 46527	Goodtime Charlie's Got the Blues/Songs About People in Love	1979	—	2.00	4.00
❑ 46590	3 Chord Country Song/Jackson Hole, Wyoming	1980	—	2.00	4.00
❑ 46633	Dim the Lights and Pour the Wine/He Ain't Got Nothin' on Me	1980	—	2.00	4.00
❑ 47014	Hard Hat Days and Honky Tonk Nights/Last Call for Alcohol	1980	—	2.00	4.00
U.S.					
❑ WS4-03361	You Can't Hold a Working Man Down/Born to Be a Cowboy	1982	—	2.00	4.00
Albums					
ABC					
❑ AB-1051	Hang On Feelin'	1978	3.00	6.00	12.00
ABC DOT					
❑ DOSD-2055	Lone Star Beer and Bob Wills Music	1976	3.75	7.50	15.00
❑ DOSD-2068	Texas Red	1976	3.00	6.00	12.00
❑ DO-2078	For All Our Cowboy Friends	1977	3.00	6.00	12.00
CAPITOL					
❑ ST-11056	Party Dolls and Wine	1972	5.00	10.00	20.00
❑ ST-11162	Somewhere My Love	1973	3.00	6.00	12.00
❑ ST-11228	If You've Got the Time, I've Got the Song	1973	3.00	6.00	12.00
❑ ST-11321	Finer Things in Life	1974	3.00	6.00	12.00
MCA					
❑ 680	For All Our Cowboy Friends	198?	2.00	4.00	8.00
—Reissue of ABC Dot 2078					
❑ 681	Hang On Feelin'	198?	2.00	4.00	8.00
—Reissue of ABC 1051					
❑ 985	Lone Star Beer and Bob Wills Music	1986	2.50	5.00	10.00
—Reissue of ABC Dot 2055					

STEARNS, JUNE

Also see JOHNNY DUNCAN.

Number	Title (A Side/B Side)	Yr	VG	VG+	NM
45s					
COLUMBIA					
❑ 4-44321	River of Regret/Where Did the Good Times Go	1967	2.00	4.00	8.00
❑ 4-44483	Empty House/I'm the Queen	1968	—	3.50	7.00
❑ 4-44575	Where He Stops Nobody Knows/I Cry Myself Awake	1968	—	3.50	7.00
❑ 4-44695	Walking Midnight Road/Plastic Saddle	1968	—	3.50	7.00
❑ 4-44795	No Good Man/Some of These Days	1969	—	3.50	7.00
❑ 4-44852	What Makes You So Different/Trouble in Mind	1969	—	3.50	7.00
❑ 4-44946	Some of These Days/A Piece at a Time	1969	—	3.50	7.00
❑ 4-45042	Drifting Too Far (From Your Arms)/He Was a Carpenter	1969	—	3.50	7.00
DECCA					
❑ 32726	Tyin' Strings/Don't Trouble Trouble	1970	—	3.00	6.00
❑ 32828	Sweet Baby on My Mind/How's My Ex Treating You	1971	—	3.00	6.00
❑ 32876	Your Kind of Lovin'/Another	1971	—	3.00	6.00
❑ 32986	Man/In Case of a Storm	1972	—	3.00	6.00
STARDAY					
❑ 639	Just Another Song/Three Sides to the Story	1963	3.00	6.00	12.00
—With Gene Martin					
❑ 660	Family Man/We've Got Things in Common	1963	3.00	6.00	12.00
—With Gene Martin					
Albums					
COLUMBIA					
❑ CS 9783	River of Regret	1969	5.00	10.00	20.00

STEEL, RIC

Number	Title (A Side/B Side)	Yr	VG	VG+	NM
45s					
PANACHE					
❑ 1001	The Radio Song/Third Time's the Charm	1987	—	3.00	6.00
❑ 1002	Whose Baby Are You/(B-side unknown)	1988	—	3.00	6.00

STEELE, JEFFREY

Number	Title (A Side/B Side)	Yr	VG	VG+	NM
45s					
CURB					
❑ D7-73012	A Girl Like You/My Greatest Love	1997	—	—	3.00
❑ D7-76993	Roots of Country/I Can Help	1996	—	2.00	4.00
—B-side by T.G. Sheppard					

STEELE, LARRY

Number	Title (A Side/B Side)	Yr	VG	VG+	NM
45s					
AIR STREAM					
❑ 001	Things Money Won't Do/Goody Goody People	1973	2.00	4.00	8.00
❑ 002	Heart Pepper Upper/A Little at a Time	1974	2.00	4.00	8.00
❑ 003	Hold On/Little Wine, Little Gin	1974	2.00	4.00	8.00
❑ 004	Daylight Losing Time/Watermelon Man	1974	2.00	4.00	8.00
❑ 006	Funny How Time Slips Away/Somethin' Ain't Home	1975	2.00	4.00	8.00
ASSAULT					
❑ 1847/8	My Own True Love/I Can't Help It	1963	3.00	6.00	12.00
K-ARK					
❑ 648	Baby Workout/My Lucky Day	1965	2.50	5.00	10.00
❑ 659	I Ain't Crying Mister/Ramblin Man	1965	2.50	5.00	10.00
❑ 802	Hard Times/The Apple or the Pair	1968	2.00	4.00	8.00
❑ 837	Hello Satan/Tall, Down on My Knees	196?	2.00	4.00	8.00
❑ 875	Three Men on a Mountain/How About It Young Lady	197?	2.00	4.00	8.00
❑ 893	Yesteryear's Man/Plain Simple Life	197?	2.00	4.00	8.00

STEFFIN SISTERS

Number	Title (A Side/B Side)	Yr	VG	VG+	NM
45s					
WINDWARD					
❑ 7	I Still Need You/Guitar Fiddlin' Joe	1989	—	3.00	6.00
❑ 7 [PS]	I Still Need You/Guitar Fiddlin' Joe	1989	2.50	5.00	10.00

STEGALL, KEITH

Number	Title (A Side/B Side)	Yr	VG	VG+	NM
45s					
CAPITOL					
❑ 4835	The Fool Who Fooled Around/Keep On Playing That Country Music	1980	—	2.00	4.00
❑ 4874	Goodbyes Don't Come Easy/Anything That Hurts You (Hurts Me)	1980	—	2.50	5.00
❑ 4967	Anything That Hurts You (Hurts Me)/She's Nobody's Babe But Mine	1981	—	2.00	4.00
❑ 5034	Won't You Be My Baby/Keep On Playing That Country Music	1981	—	2.00	4.00
EMI AMERICA					
❑ B-8107	In Love with Loving You/Hurry On Home	1982	—	2.00	4.00
EPIC					
❑ 34-04442	I Want to Go Somewhere/The Cowboy Thing to Do	1984	—	—	3.00
❑ 34-04590	Whatever Turns You On/Daylight Lovin' Time	1984	—	—	3.00
❑ 34-04590 [PS]	Whatever Turns You On/Daylight Lovin' Time	1984	—	2.00	4.00
❑ 34-04771	California/Straight Shooter	1985	—	—	3.00
❑ 34-04934	Pretty Lady/These Tears	1985	—	—	3.00
❑ 34-04934 [PS]	Pretty Lady/These Tears	1985	—	2.00	4.00
❑ 34-05643	Feed the Fire/Marylee	1985	—	—	3.00
❑ 34-05815	I Think I'm in Love/Sweet Love Bandit	1986	—	—	3.00
❑ 34-06418	Ole Rock and Roller (With a Country Heart)/On a Good Night	1986	—	—	3.00
MERCURY					
❑ 852618-7	1969/Fifty-Fifty	1996	—	2.00	4.00
Albums					
EPIC					
❑ B6E 39892	Keith Stegall	1985	2.00	4.00	8.00

STENMARK-MUELLER BAND

Number	Title (A Side/B Side)	Yr	VG	VG+	NM
45s					
ENVELOPE					
❑ 7004	Lover to Lover/(B-side unknown)	1987	2.00	4.00	8.00

STEPHENS, OTT

Number	Title (A Side/B Side)	Yr	VG	VG+	NM
45s					
CHANCELLOR					
❑ 107	Robert E. Lee/Never Tired of Loving You	1962	3.75	7.50	15.00
❑ 1120	Robert E. Lee/Never Tired of Loving You	1962	3.75	7.50	15.00
—We're not sure which is the original issue					
CHART					
❑ 1032	Hard Times (Are My Kind of Times)/Snow White Cloud	1968	2.00	4.00	8.00
❑ 1145	I Still Love Y-O-U/Little Bit of Blue	1964	2.50	5.00	10.00
❑ 1205	Enough Man for You/Never Tired of Loving You	1965	2.50	5.00	10.00
❑ 1260	You Go Your Way (I'll Go Mine)/Over There with You	1965	2.50	5.00	10.00
PEACH					
❑ 742	Victim of a Holiday Weekend/Why Does Everything Go Wrong	1961	5.00	10.00	20.00
❑ 749	Only a Friend/Oh Broken Hearted Me	1961	5.00	10.00	20.00
REPRISE					
❑ 0272	Be Quiet Mind/Hard Luck Story	1964	3.00	6.00	12.00

STEVENS, EVEN

Also see SAMMI SMITH.

Number	Title (A Side/B Side)	Yr	VG	VG+	NM
45s					
ELEKTRA					
❑ 45231	That's All She Wrote/I Wouldn't Do That to You	1975	—	2.50	5.00
❑ 45254	Let the Little Boy Dream/Josie's Comin' Home	1975	—	2.50	5.00
❑ 45325	Neon Rainbow/Farm Boy	1976	—	2.50	5.00
❑ 45430	The King of Country Music Meets the Queen of Rock & Roll/I'm from Outer Space	1977	—	2.50	5.00
—With Sherry Grooms					
❑ 45448	Thank You Lord//Piece of the Rock/Joshua/ Someone's Being Born	1977	—	2.50	5.00
Albums					
DAKAR					
❑ DK-76905	Even Stevens	1973	6.25	12.50	25.00
ELEKTRA					
❑ 7E-1113	Thorn on a Rose	1977	3.00	6.00	12.00

STEVENS, GERALDINE

In an earlier era, she recorded as "Dodie Stevens," under which she had a big pop hit in 1959 with "Pink Shoe Laces."

Number	Title (A Side/B Side)	Yr	VG	VG+	NM
45s					
WORLD PACIFIC					
❑ 77927	Billy, I've Got to Go to Town/It's Not Their Heartache, It's Mine	1969	2.00	4.00	8.00
❑ 77930	Play Me a Song/I've Got to Have More	1969	2.00	4.00	8.00
❑ 77934	Love Is Gonna Get You/You Ain't Goin' Nowhere	1970	2.00	4.00	8.00

STEVENS, JEFF, AND THE BULLETS

45s

ATLANTIC AMERICA

Number	Title (A Side/B Side)	Yr	VG	VG+	NM
❑ 99259	Johnny Lucky and Suzi 66/Change of Heart	1989	—	—	3.00
❑ 99259 [PS]	Johnny Lucky and Suzi 66/Change of Heart	1989	—	2.00	4.00
❑ 99433	Geronimo's Cadillac/Tamed by Love	1987	—	—	3.00
❑ 99475	You're in Love Alone/Tamed by Love	1987	—	—	3.00
❑ 99494	Darlington County/Tamed by Love	1986	—	—	3.00

Albums

ATLANTIC AMERICA

Number	Title (A Side/B Side)	Yr	VG	VG+	NM
❑ 90556	Bolt Out of the Blue	1987	2.50	5.00	10.00

STEVENS, LEE J.

45s

REGAL

Number	Title (A Side/B Side)	Yr	VG	VG+	NM
❑ 01	You'll Be the First to Know/(B-side unknown)	1988	—	3.00	6.00

STEVENS, RAY

45s

BARNABY

Number	Title (A Side/B Side)	Yr	VG	VG+	NM
❑ 514	Gitarzan/Unwind	197?	—	2.00	4.00
❑ 515	Everything Is Beautiful/Turn Your Radio On	197?	—	2.00	4.00
❑ 516	Mr. Businessman/Sunday Morning Comin' Down	197?	—	2.00	4.00
❑ 517	Ahab the Arab/Along Came Jones	197?	—	2.00	4.00
❑ 518	Freddie Feelgood (And His Funky Little Five Piece Band)/Isn't It Lonely Together	197?	—	2.00	4.00
❑ 519	Have a Little Talk with Myself/Bridget the Midget (The Queen of the Blues)	197?	—	2.00	4.00
—Barnaby releases in the 500 series are reissues; some may be re-recordings					
❑ 600	The Streak/You've Got the Music Inside	1974	—	2.50	5.00
—White label (not a promo)					
❑ 600	The Streak/You've Got the Music Inside	1974	—	2.00	4.00
—Multicolor label					
❑ 605	Moonlight Special/Just So Proud to Be Here	1974	—	2.00	4.00
❑ 610	Everybody Needs a Rainbow/Inside	1974	—	2.00	4.00
❑ 614	Misty/Sunshine	1975	—	2.00	4.00
❑ 616	Indian Love Call/Piece of Paradise	1975	—	2.00	4.00
❑ 618	Young Love/Deep Purple	1975	—	2.00	4.00
❑ 619	Lady of Spain/Mockingbird Hill	1976	—	2.00	4.00
❑ 2011	Everything Is Beautiful/A Brighter Day	1970	—	3.00	6.00
❑ 2016	America, Communicate with Me/Monkey See, Monkey Do	1970	—	2.50	5.00
❑ 2021	Sunset Strip/Islands	1970	—	2.50	5.00
❑ 2024	Bridget the Midget (The Queen of the Blues)/ Night People	1970	—	2.50	5.00
❑ 2024 [PS]	Bridget the Midget (The Queen of the Blues)/ Night People	1970	2.50	5.00	10.00
❑ 2029	A Mama and a Papa/Melt	1971	—	2.50	5.00
❑ 2039	All My Trials/Have a Little Talk with Myself	1971	—	2.50	5.00
❑ 2048	Turn Your Radio On/Loving You on Paper	1971	—	2.50	5.00
❑ 2058	Love Lifted Me/Glory Special	1972	—	2.50	5.00
❑ 2058	Love Lifted Me/Monkey See, Monkey Do	1972	—	2.50	5.00
❑ 2065	Losing Streak/Inside	1972	—	2.50	5.00
❑ 5020	Golden Age/Nashville	1973	—	2.00	4.00
❑ 5028	Love Me Longer/Float	1973	—	2.00	4.00

CAPITOL

Number	Title (A Side/B Side)	Yr	VG	VG+	NM
❑ F3967	Chickie Chickie Wah Wah/Crying Goodbye	1958	6.25	12.50	25.00
❑ F4030	Cat Pants/Love Goes On Forever	1958	7.50	15.00	30.00
❑ F4101	The School/The Clown	1958	6.25	12.50	25.00
❑ 7PRO-79430 [DJ]	Help Me Make It Through the Night (same on both sides)	1991	—	2.50	5.00
—Vinyl is promo only					

MCA

Number	Title (A Side/B Side)	Yr	VG	VG+	NM
❑ 52451	Joggin'/I'm Kissin' You Goodbye	1984	—	2.00	4.00
❑ 52492	Mississippi Squirrel Revival/Ned Nostril	1984	—	2.00	4.00
❑ 52548	It's Me Again, Margaret/Joggin'	1985	—	—	3.00
❑ 52657	The Haircut Song/Punk Country Love	1985	—	—	3.00
❑ 52738	Santa Claus Is Watching You/Armchair Quarterback	1985	—	2.00	4.00
❑ 52738 [PS]	Santa Claus Is Watching You/Armchair Quarterback	1985	—	2.00	4.00
❑ 52771	Vacation Bible School/The Ballad of the Blue Cyclone	1986	—	—	3.00
❑ 52906	The Camping Trip/Southern Air	1986	—	—	3.00
❑ 52924	People's Court/Dudley Doright (Of the Highway Patrol)	1986	—	—	3.00
❑ 53007	Can He Love You Half As Much As I Do/Dudley Doright (Of the Highway Patrol)	1987	—	—	3.00
❑ 53007 [DJ]	Can He Love You Half As Much As I Do (same on both sides)	1987	2.50	5.00	10.00
—Blue vinyl promo					
❑ 53101	Would Jesus Wear a Rolex?/Cool Down Willard	1987	—	2.00	4.00
❑ 53178	Three-Legged Man/Doctor, Doctor (Have Mercy on Me)	1987	—	—	3.00
❑ 53232	Sex Symbols/The Ballad of Cactus Pete and Lefty	1987	—	—	3.00
❑ 53372	Surfin' U.S.S.R./Language, Nudity, Violence & Sex	1988	—	—	3.00
❑ 53423	The Day I Tried to Teach Charlene MacKenzie How to Drive/I Don't Need None of That	1988	—	—	3.00
❑ 53661	I Saw Elvis in a U.F.O./I Used to Be Crazy	1989	2.50	5.00	10.00

MERCURY

Number	Title (A Side/B Side)	Yr	VG	VG+	NM
❑ 71843	Jeremiah Peabody's Poly Unsaturated Quick Dissolving Fast Acting Pleasant Tasting Green and Purple Pills/Teen Years	1961	3.75	7.50	15.00
❑ 71843 [PS]	Jeremiah Peabody's Poly Unsaturated Quick Dissolving Fast Acting Pleasant Tasting Green and Purple Pills/Teen Years	1961	6.25	12.50	25.00
❑ 71888	Scratch My Back/When You Wish Upon a Star	1961	3.75	7.50	15.00
❑ 71966	Ahab, the Arab/It's Been So Long	1962	3.75	7.50	15.00
❑ 71966 [PS]	Ahab, the Arab/It's Been So Long	1962	7.50	15.00	30.00
❑ 72039	Further More/Saturday Night at the Movies	1962	3.75	7.50	15.00
❑ 72058	Santa Claus Is Watching You/Loved and Lost	1962	3.75	7.50	15.00
❑ 72058 [PS]	Santa Claus Is Watching You/Loved and Lost	1962	6.25	12.50	25.00
❑ 72098	Funny Man/Just One of Life's Little Tragedies	1963	3.75	7.50	15.00
❑ 72125	Harry the Hairy Ape/Little Stone Statue	1963	3.75	7.50	15.00
❑ 72125 [PS]	Harry the Hairy Ape/Little Stone Statue	1963	6.25	12.50	25.00
❑ 72189	Speed Ball/It's Party Time	1963	3.75	7.50	15.00
❑ 72255	Butch Barbarian (Sure Footed Mountain Climber World Famous Yodeling Champion)/Don't Say Anything	1963	3.75	7.50	15.00
❑ 72307	Bubble Gum the Bubble Dancer/Laughing Over My Grave	1964	3.75	7.50	15.00
❑ 72382	Rockin' Teenage Mummies/It Only Hurts When I Love	1965	5.00	10.00	20.00
❑ 72430	Mr. Baker the Undertaker/Old English Surfer	1965	5.00	10.00	20.00
❑ 72816	Funny Man/Just One of Life's Little Tragedies	1968	3.00	6.00	12.00
❑ 812496-7	Pice of Paradise Called Tennessee/Mary Lou Nights	1983	—	2.00	4.00
❑ 812906-7	My Dad/Game Show Love	1983	—	2.50	5.00
❑ 814196-7	Love Will Beat Your Brains Out/Game Show Love	1983	—	2.00	4.00
❑ 818057-7	My Dad/Me	1984	—	2.00	4.00

MONUMENT

Number	Title (A Side/B Side)	Yr	VG	VG+	NM
❑ 911	A-B-C/Party People	1966	2.50	5.00	10.00
❑ 927	Devil-May-Care/Make a Few Memories	1966	2.50	5.00	10.00
❑ 946	Freddy Feelgood (And His Funky Little Five Piece Band)/There's One in Every Crowd	1966	2.50	5.00	10.00
❑ 1001	Mary, My Secretary/Answer Me, My Love	1967	2.00	4.00	8.00
❑ 1048	Unwind/For He's a Jolly Good Fellow	1968	2.00	4.00	8.00
❑ 1083	Mr. Businessman/Face the Music	1968	2.00	4.00	8.00
❑ 1099	Isn't It Lonely Together/The Great Escape	1968	2.00	4.00	8.00
❑ 1131	Gitarzan/Bagpipes-That's My Bag	1969	2.00	4.00	8.00
❑ 1150	Along Came Jones/Yakety Yak	1969	2.00	4.00	8.00
❑ 1163	Sunday Mornin' Comin' Down/The Minority	1969	—	3.00	6.00
❑ 1171	Have a Little Talk with Myself/Little Woman	1969	—	3.00	6.00
❑ 1187	I'll Be Your Baby Tonight/Fool on the Hill	1970	—	3.00	6.00

NRC

Number	Title (A Side/B Side)	Yr	VG	VG+	NM
❑ 031	High School Yearbook (Deck of Cards)/Truly True	1959	6.25	12.50	25.00
❑ 042	What Would I Do Without You/My Heart Cries for You	1959	6.25	12.50	25.00
❑ 057	Sergeant Preston of the Yukon/Who Do You Love	1960	6.25	12.50	25.00
❑ 063	Happy Blue Year/White Christmas	1960	6.25	12.50	25.00

PREP

Number	Title (A Side/B Side)	Yr	VG	VG+	NM
❑ 108	Rang Tang Ding Dong (I'm the Japanese Sandman)/Silver Bracelet	1957	6.25	12.50	25.00
❑ 122	Five More Steps/Tingle	1957	6.25	12.50	25.00

RCA

Number	Title (A Side/B Side)	Yr	VG	VG+	NM
❑ PB-11911	Shriner's Convention/You're Never Goin' to Tampa With Me	1980	—	2.00	4.00
❑ PB-12069	Night Games/Let's Do It Right This Time	1980	—	2.00	4.00
❑ PB-12170	One More Last Chance/I Believe You Love Me	1981	—	2.00	4.00
❑ PB-12185	The Streak/Misty	1981	—	2.00	4.00
❑ GB-12368	Everything Is Beautiful/Gitarzan	1981	—	—	3.00
—Gold Standard Series					
❑ GB-12370	Shriner's Convention/You're Never Goin' to Tampa with Me	1981	—	—	3.00
—Gold Standard Series					
❑ PB-13038	Written Down in My Heart/Country Boy, Country Club Girl	1981	—	2.00	4.00
❑ PB-13207	Where the Sun Don't Shine/Why Don't We Go Somewhere and Love	1982	—	2.00	4.00

WARNER BROS.

Number	Title (A Side/B Side)	Yr	VG	VG+	NM
❑ 8198	You Are So Beautiful/One Man Band	1976	—	2.00	4.00
❑ 8237	Honky Tonk Waltz/Om	1976	—	2.00	4.00
❑ 8301	In the Mood/Classical Cluck	1976	—	3.00	6.00
—As "Henhouse Five Plus Too"					
❑ 8318	Get Crazy with Me/Dixie Hummingbird	1977	—	2.00	4.00
❑ 8393	Dixie Hummingbird/Feel the Music	1977	—	2.00	4.00
❑ 8603	Be Your Own Best Friend/With a Smile	1978	—	2.00	4.00
❑ 8785	I Need Your Help Barry Manilow/Daydream Romance	1979	—	2.00	4.00
❑ 8785 [PS]	I Need Your Help Barry Manilow/Daydream Romance	1979	—	3.00	6.00
❑ 8849	The Feeling's Not Right Again/Get Crazy with Me	1979	—	2.00	4.00

Albums

BARNABY

Number	Title (A Side/B Side)	Yr	VG	VG+	NM
❑ 5004	Ray Stevens' Greatest Hits	1974	2.50	5.00	10.00
—Reissue of 30770					
❑ 5005	Nashville	1974	2.50	5.00	10.00
—Reissue of 15007					
❑ 6003	Boogity Boogity	1974	3.00	6.00	12.00
❑ 6012	Misty	1975	3.00	6.00	12.00
❑ 6018	The Very Best of Ray Stevens	1975	3.00	6.00	12.00
❑ 15007	Nashville	1973	3.00	6.00	12.00
❑ Z 30092	Ray Stevens...Unreal!!!	1970	3.00	6.00	12.00
❑ Z 30770	Ray Stevens' Greatest Hits	1971	3.00	6.00	12.00
❑ Z 30809	Turn Your Radio On	1972	3.00	6.00	12.00
❑ KZ 32139	Losin' Streak	1972	3.00	6.00	12.00
❑ Z12 35005	Everything Is Beautiful	1970	3.75	7.50	15.00

MCA

Number	Title (A Side/B Side)	Yr	VG	VG+	NM
5517	He Thinks He's Ray Stevens	1984	2.50	5.00	10.00
5635	I Have Returned	1985	2.50	5.00	10.00
5795	Surely You Joust	1986	2.50	5.00	10.00
5918	Greatest Hits	1987	2.50	5.00	10.00
42020	Crackin' Up!	1987	2.50	5.00	10.00
42062	Greatest Hits, Volume 2	1987	2.50	5.00	10.00
42172	I Never Made a Record I Didn't Like	1988	2.50	5.00	10.00
42303	Beside Myself	1989	2.50	5.00	10.00

MERCURY

Number	Title (A Side/B Side)	Yr	VG	VG+	NM
MG-20732 [M]	1,837 Seconds of Humor	1962	10.00	20.00	40.00
MG-20828 [M]	This Is Ray Stevens	1963	6.25	12.50	25.00
SR-60732 [S]	1,837 Seconds of Humor	1962	12.50	25.00	50.00
SR-60828 [S]	This Is Ray Stevens	1963	7.50	15.00	30.00
SR-61272	The Best of Ray Stevens	1968	3.75	7.50	15.00
812780-1	Me	1984	2.50	5.00	10.00

MONUMENT

Number	Title (A Side/B Side)	Yr	VG	VG+	NM
SLP-18102	Even Stevens	1968	3.75	7.50	15.00
SLP-18115	Gitarzan	1969	3.75	7.50	15.00
SLP-18134	Have a Little Talk with Myself	1970	3.75	7.50	15.00

PICKWICK

Number	Title (A Side/B Side)	Yr	VG	VG+	NM
SPC-3266	Rock and Roll Show	1971	2.50	5.00	10.00

PRIORITY

Number	Title (A Side/B Side)	Yr	VG	VG+	NM
PU 38075	Turn Your Radio On	1982	2.50	5.00	10.00
—Reissue of Barnaby 30809					

RCA VICTOR

Number	Title (A Side/B Side)	Yr	VG	VG+	NM
AHL1-3574	Shriner's Convention	1980	2.50	5.00	10.00
AHL1-3841	One More Last Chance	1981	2.50	5.00	10.00
AYL1-4253	Shriner's Convention	1982	2.00	4.00	8.00
—"Best Buy Series" reissue					
AHL1-4288	Don't Laugh Now	1982	2.50	5.00	10.00
AHL1-4727	Greatest Hits	1983	2.50	5.00	10.00
AYL1-5153	Greatest Hits	1985	2.00	4.00	8.00
—"Best Buy Series" reissue					
CPL1-7161	Collector's Series	1986	2.50	5.00	10.00

WARNER BROS.

Number	Title (A Side/B Side)	Yr	VG	VG+	NM
BS 2914	Just for the Record	1976	2.50	5.00	10.00
BS 2997	Feel the Music	1977	2.50	5.00	10.00
BS 3098	There Is Something...	1977	2.50	5.00	10.00
BS 3195	Be Your Own Best Friend	1978	2.50	5.00	10.00
BSK 3332	The Feeling's Not Right Again	1979	2.50	5.00	10.00

STEWART, GARY

45s

CORY

Number	Title (A Side/B Side)	Yr	VG	VG+	NM
101	Walk On By/(B-side unknown)	1964	6.25	12.50	25.00

DECCA

Number	Title (A Side/B Side)	Yr	VG	VG+	NM
32880	She's the Next Best Thing/Something to Believe In	1971	2.00	4.00	8.00

HIGHTONE

Number	Title (A Side/B Side)	Yr	VG	VG+	NM
506	Brand New Whiskey/Son of a Honky Tonk Woman	1988	—	2.50	5.00
507	An Empty Glass/Lucretia	1988	—	2.50	5.00
509	Rainin', Rainin', Rainin'/(B-side unknown)	1989	—	2.50	5.00
602	Nothin' But a Woman/(B-side unknown)	1989	—	3.00	6.00

KAPP

Number	Title (A Side/B Side)	Yr	VG	VG+	NM
934	Here Comes That Feeling Again/Merry-Go-Round	1968	2.00	4.00	8.00
2008	Sweet Tater and Cisco/Little Old Love	1969	2.00	4.00	8.00
2089	You're Not the Woman You Used to Be/Snuff Queen	1970	2.00	4.00	8.00

MCA

Number	Title (A Side/B Side)	Yr	VG	VG+	NM
40414	You're Not the Woman You Used to Be/I Owe It All to Mama	1975	—	2.50	5.00

RCA

Number	Title (A Side/B Side)	Yr	VG	VG+	NM
PB-10833	Your Place or Mine/Lord, What a Woman	1976	—	2.00	4.00
PB-10957	Ten Years of This/I Ain't Living Long Like This	1977	—	2.00	4.00
PB-11131	Quits/Dancing Eyes	1977	—	2.00	4.00
PB-11224	Whiskey Trip/Williamson County	1978	—	2.00	4.00
PB-11297	Single Again/Little Junior	1978	—	2.00	4.00
PB-11416	Stone Wall (Around Your Heart)/I Got Mine	1978	—	2.00	4.00
PB-11534	Shady Streets/Everything a Good Little Girl Needs	1979	—	2.00	4.00
PB-11623	Mazelle/One More	1979	—	2.00	4.00
PB-11960	Cactus and a Rose/Staring Each Other Down	1980	—	2.00	4.00
PB-12081	Are We Dreamin' the Same Dream/Roarin'	1980	—	2.00	4.00
PB-12203	Let's Forget That We're Married/Honky Tonk Man	1981	—	2.00	4.00
PB-12343	She's Got a Drinking Problem/Memories Swim in Whiskey	1981	—	2.00	4.00
PB-13261	She Sings Amazing Grace/Cold Turkey	1982	—	2.00	4.00

RCA VICTOR

Number	Title (A Side/B Side)	Yr	VG	VG+	NM
APBO-0035	Drinkin' Thing/I See the Want To in Your Eyes	1973	—	3.50	7.00
APBO-0144	Ramblin' Man/Williamson County	1973	—	3.00	6.00
APBO-0281	Drinkin' Thing/I See the Want To in Your Eyes	1974	—	2.50	5.00
PB-10061	Out of Hand/Draggin' Shackles	1974	—	2.50	5.00
PB-10222	She's Acting Single (I'm Drinking Doubles)/Williamson County	1975	—	2.50	5.00
PB-10351	Flat Natural Born Good-Timin' Man/This Old Heart Won't Let Go	1975	—	2.50	5.00
PB-10351 [PS]	Flat Natural Born Good-Timin' Man/This Old Heart Won't Let Go	1975	2.00	4.00	8.00
GB-10514	She's Acting Single (I'm Drinking Doubles)/Williamson County	1976	—	2.00	4.00
—"Gold Standard Series" reissue					
GB-10515	Out of Hand/Draggin' Shackles	1976	—	2.00	4.00
—"Gold Standard Series" reissue					
GB-10516	Drinkin' Thing/I See the Want To in Your Eyes	1976	—	2.00	4.00
—"Gold Standard Series" reissue					
PB-10550	Oh, Sweet Temptation/Hank Western	1976	—	2.50	5.00
PB-10680	In Some Room Above the Street/Easy People	1976	—	2.50	5.00

RED ASH

Number	Title (A Side/B Side)	Yr	VG	VG+	NM
8403	Hey, Bottle of Whiskey/Roadhouse Romances	1984	—	2.50	5.00
8406	I Got a Bad Attitude/Life's a Game	1984	—	2.50	5.00

Albums

HIGHTONE

Number	Title (A Side/B Side)	Yr	VG	VG+	NM
HT-8014	Brand New	1988	3.00	6.00	12.00

MCA

Number	Title (A Side/B Side)	Yr	VG	VG+	NM
488	You're Not the Woman You Used to Be	1975	3.00	6.00	12.00

RCA VICTOR

Number	Title (A Side/B Side)	Yr	VG	VG+	NM
APL1-0900	Out of Hand	1975	2.50	5.00	10.00
APL1-1225	Steppin' Out	1976	2.50	5.00	10.00
APL1-2199	Your Place or Mine	1977	2.50	5.00	10.00
AHL1-2779	Little Junior	1978	2.50	5.00	10.00
AHL1-3288	Gary	1979	2.50	5.00	10.00
AHL1-3627	Cactus and a Rose	1980	2.50	5.00	10.00
AYL1-3769	Steppin' Out	1981	2.00	4.00	8.00
—"Best Buy Series" reissue					
AYL1-3944	Out of Hand	1981	2.00	4.00	8.00
—"Best Buy Series" reissue					
AYL1-4254	Greatest Hits	1982	2.00	4.00	8.00
AHL1-5498	Collector's Series	1985	2.00	4.00	8.00

STEWART, GARY, AND DEAN DILLON

Also see each artist's individual listings.

45s

RCA

Number	Title (A Side/B Side)	Yr	VG	VG+	NM
PB-13049	Brotherly Love/Firewater Friends	1982	—	2.00	4.00
PB-13049 [PS]	Brotherly Love/Firewater Friends	1982	—	2.50	5.00
PB-13401	Those Were the Days/Drinkin' Thing	1982	—	2.00	4.00
PB-13472	Smokin' in the Rockies/Hard Time for Lovers	1983	—	2.00	4.00

Albums

RCA VICTOR

Number	Title (A Side/B Side)	Yr	VG	VG+	NM
AHL1-4310	Brotherly Love	1982	2.50	5.00	10.00
MHL1-8602 [EP]	Those Were the Days	1983	2.00	4.00	8.00

STEWART, LARRY

45s

COLUMBIA

Number	Title (A Side/B Side)	Yr	VG	VG+	NM
38-77638	Heart Like a Hurricane (2 mixes)	1994	—	2.00	4.00
38-77753	Losing Your Love/One Track Mind	1994	—	—	3.00
38-77857	Rockin' the Rock/I'm Not Through Lovin' You	1995	—	—	3.00
38-78307	Why Can't You/I'm Not Through Lovin' You	1996	—	—	3.00

RCA

Number	Title (A Side/B Side)	Yr	VG	VG+	NM
62474	Alright Already/The Boy Down the Road	1993	—	2.00	4.00
62546	I'll Cry Tomorrow/Brittany	1993	—	—	3.00
62696	We Can Love/When You Come Back to Me	1993	—	—	3.00

STEWART, LISA

45s

BNA

Number	Title (A Side/B Side)	Yr	VG	VG+	NM
62311	Somebody's in Love/Is It Love	1992	—	2.00	4.00
62441	Drive Time/Don't Touch Me	1993	—	—	3.00
62528	Under the Light of the Texaco/Forgive and Forget	1993	—	—	3.00

STEWART, REDD

Also see PEE WEE KING.

45s

BRIAR

Number	Title (A Side/B Side)	Yr	VG	VG+	NM
119	I'm Praying for the Day (That Peace Will Come)/Um-Pah-No-Lah	196?	3.75	7.50	15.00

DO-RA-ME

Number	Title (A Side/B Side)	Yr	VG	VG+	NM
1422	Levi Lady/River Road Rock Twist	1962	5.00	10.00	20.00

HICKORY

Number	Title (A Side/B Side)	Yr	VG	VG+	NM
1543	Bimbo/Big, Big Show	1969	2.00	4.00	8.00
1554	Cold, Cold Heart/Dreaming Again	1969	2.00	4.00	8.00
1572	Better Man/My Home Is the Dust of the Road	1970	2.00	4.00	8.00
1584	And the Rain Comes Down/Ballad of the Country Song Writer	1970	2.00	4.00	8.00
1603	My Friend/Sunshine Over the Hill	1971	2.00	4.00	8.00
1640	Plain Ole Country Me/Tennessee Waltz	1972	2.00	4.00	8.00
1658	Bonaparte's Retreat/Where Love Doesn't Live Anymore	1973	2.00	4.00	8.00

HICKORY/MGM

Number	Title (A Side/B Side)	Yr	VG	VG+	NM
325	Banjo/Talk to the Angels	1974	—	3.00	6.00
334	Cold, Cold Heart/I Remember	1974	—	3.00	6.00
343	Having Second Thoughts/Sunshine Over the Hill	1975	—	3.00	6.00
356	Bimbo/Cold, Cold Heart	1975	—	3.00	6.00

RCA VICTOR

Number	Title (A Side/B Side)	Yr	VG	VG+	NM
47-5928	I Did/Down Stream	1954	5.00	10.00	20.00
47-6036	Which One of Us Is to Blame/Don't Make Me Fall in Love with You	1955	5.00	10.00	20.00

Selected 78s

KING

Number	Title (A Side/B Side)	Yr	VG	VG+	NM
778	When I'm In My Indiana Home/Blow Out All the Candles	1949	5.00	10.00	20.00
781	Alone/Perhaps It Is Better That Way	1949	5.00	10.00	20.00

Number	Title (A Side/B Side)	Yr	VG	VG+	NM
❑ 797	Thy Burdens Are Greater Than Mine/When You Are Waltzing	1949	5.00	10.00	20.00
❑ 827	You Can't Divorce a Loving Heart/Baby Darling	1949	5.00	10.00	20.00
❑ 843	Brother Drop Dead/If You'll Come Back to Me	1950	5.00	10.00	20.00
❑ 860	It's All Over/My Little Wild Rose of the Hills	1950	5.00	10.00	20.00
❑ 877	Tomorrow You'll Be Married/Gotta Get Back to Dixie	1950	5.00	10.00	20.00
❑ 907	Take Back Your Paper Heart/Worried Cause I'm Losing You	1950	5.00	10.00	20.00
❑ 921	I've Decided/Peek-a-Boo Waltz	1951	5.00	10.00	20.00
❑ 940	I'm On My Last Go Round/I'll Never Love No One But You	1951	5.00	10.00	20.00

Albums

AUDIO LAB

Number	Title (A Side/B Side)	Yr	VG	VG+	NM
❑ AL-1528 [M]	Redd Stewart Sings Favorite Old Time Tunes	1959	50.00	100.00	200.00

HICKORY/MGM

Number	Title (A Side/B Side)	Yr	VG	VG+	NM
❑ H3G-4512	I Remember	1974	3.75	7.50	15.00

STEWART, VERNON

45s

BLU-J

Number	Title (A Side/B Side)	Yr	VG	VG+	NM
❑ 304	Christmas Tree in Heaven/Down to the Blues	196?	2.50	5.00	10.00

CHART

Number	Title (A Side/B Side)	Yr	VG	VG+	NM
❑ 501	The Way It Feels to Die/You're Not All Here	1962	3.75	7.50	15.00

PEACH

Number	Title (A Side/B Side)	Yr	VG	VG+	NM
❑ 740	I'm Tired of Make Believe/I'll Still Love You	1961	6.25	12.50	25.00
❑ 751	Mean, Mean Baby/Heal This Old Heart	1961	15.00	30.00	60.00

STEWART, WYNN

45s

ATLANTIC

Number	Title (A Side/B Side)	Yr	VG	VG+	NM
❑ 4025	When/Why Don't You Come to Me	1974	—	2.50	5.00

CAPITOL

Number	Title (A Side/B Side)	Yr	VG	VG+	NM
❑ 2012	Love's Gonna Happen to Me/Waltz of the Angels	1967	2.00	4.00	8.00
❑ 2012 [PS]	Love's Gonna Happen to Me/Waltz of the Angels	1967	3.00	6.00	12.00
❑ 2137	Something Pretty/Built in Love	1968	—	3.50	7.00
❑ 2137 [PS]	Something Pretty/Built in Love	1968	3.00	6.00	12.00
❑ 2240	In Love/My Own Little World	1968	—	3.50	7.00
❑ 2240 [PS]	In Love/My Own Little World	1968	3.00	6.00	12.00
❑ 2341	Strings/Happy Blues	1968	—	3.50	7.00
❑ 2421	Let the Whole World Sing It with Me/Who Are You	1969	—	3.50	7.00
❑ 2549	World-Wide Travelin' Man/Cry Baby	1969	—	3.50	7.00
❑ 2657	Yours Forever/Goin' Steady	1969	—	3.50	7.00
❑ 2751	You Don't Care What Happens to Me/Young As Spring	1970	—	3.00	6.00
❑ 2888	It's a Beautiful Day/Prisoner on the Run	1970	—	3.00	6.00
❑ 3000	Heavenly/You're No Secret of Mine	1970	—	3.00	6.00
❑ 3080	Baby, It's Yours/I Was the First One to Know	1971	—	3.00	6.00
❑ 3157	Hello Little Rock/You Can't Take It With You	1971	—	3.00	6.00
❑ F3408	The Waltz of the Angels/Why Do I Love You So	1956	5.00	10.00	20.00
❑ F3515	The Keeper of the Keys/Slowly But Surely	1956	5.00	10.00	20.00
❑ F3594	That Just Kills Me/You Took Her Off My Hands	1956	5.00	10.00	20.00
❑ F3651	Hold Back Tomorrow/New Love	1957	5.00	10.00	20.00
❑ F3803	A Night to Remember/I Wish I Could Say the Same	1957	5.00	10.00	20.00
❑ 5271	Half of This, Half of That	1964	2.00	4.00	8.00
❑ 5271 [PS]	Half of This, Half of That	1964	3.75	7.50	15.00
❑ 5397	Sha Marie/Does He Love You Like I Do	1965	2.00	4.00	8.00
❑ 5485	I Keep Forgettin' That I Forgot About You/My Rosalie	1965	2.00	4.00	8.00
❑ 5593	Angels Don't Lie/The Tourist	1966	2.00	4.00	8.00
❑ 5831	It's Such a Pretty World Today/Ol' What's Her Name	1967	2.00	4.00	8.00
❑ 5937	'Cause I Love You/That's the Only Way to Cry	1967	2.00	4.00	8.00
❑ 5937 [PS]	'Cause I Love You/That's the Only Way to Cry	1967	3.00	6.00	12.00

CHALLENGE

Number	Title (A Side/B Side)	Yr	VG	VG+	NM
❑ 9121	Big Big Love/One More Memory	1961	3.75	7.50	15.00
❑ 9142	I Done Done It/I Don't Feel at Home	1962	—	—	—
❑ 9155	Don't Look Back/Loversville	1962	3.75	7.50	15.00
❑ 9164	Another Day, Another Dollar/Donna on My Mind	1962	3.75	7.50	15.00
❑ 9192	Slightly Used/I'm Not the Man I Used to Be	1963	3.75	7.50	15.00
❑ 59061	Wishful Thinking/Uncle Tom Got Caught	1958	15.00	30.00	60.00
—The B-side is sought after by rockabilly collectors					
❑ 59084	Heartaches for a Dime/Playboy	1960	3.75	7.50	15.00
❑ 59095	If You See My Baby/I'd Rather Have America	1960	3.75	7.50	15.00
❑ 59216	Big City/One Way to Go	1963	3.75	7.50	15.00
❑ 59379	Girl in White/Fallin' for You	1967	2.00	4.00	8.00

FOUR STAR

Number	Title (A Side/B Side)	Yr	VG	VG+	NM
❑ 8001	Inflation Blues/Heartbreak Mountain	1980	—	3.00	6.00

JACKPOT

Number	Title (A Side/B Side)	Yr	VG	VG+	NM
❑ 48005	Come On/School Bus Love Affair	1959	75.00	150.00	300.00
❑ 48019	Open Up My Heart/Above and Beyond	1960	5.00	10.00	20.00

PLAYBOY

Number	Title (A Side/B Side)	Yr	VG	VG+	NM
❑ 6035	Lonely Rain/Just Now Thought of You	1975	—	2.50	5.00
❑ 6060	I'm Gonna Kill You/Seasons of My Heart	1976	—	3.00	6.00
❑ 6080	After the Storm/Don't Monkey with My Widow	1976	—	2.50	5.00
❑ 6091	Sing a Sad Song/It's Such a Pretty World Today	1976	—	2.50	5.00

PRETTY WORLD

Number	Title (A Side/B Side)	Yr	VG	VG+	NM
❑ 001	Wait Till I Get My Hands on You/Would You Want the World to End	1985	2.00	4.00	8.00

RCA VICTOR

Number	Title (A Side/B Side)	Yr	VG	VG+	NM
❑ APBO-0004	Love Ain't Worth a Dime Unless It's Free/Me and My Jesus Would Know	1973	—	2.50	5.00
❑ APBO-0114	It's Raining in Seattle/If I Were You	1973	—	2.50	5.00
❑ 74-0819	Paint Me a Rainbow/I Know They'll Make Room for You	1972	—	2.50	5.00
❑ 74-0891	Everything Needs a Little Woman's Touch/Search Through the Ashes	1973	—	2.50	5.00

WIN

Number	Title (A Side/B Side)	Yr	VG	VG+	NM
❑ 126	Eyes Big as Dallas/Such a Perfect Day for Making Love	1978	—	3.00	6.00
❑ 127	Could I Talk You Into Loving Me Again/I Was Raised Down on the Farm	1979	—	3.00	6.00

Albums

CAPITOL

Number	Title (A Side/B Side)	Yr	VG	VG+	NM
❑ ST-113	In Love	1969	5.00	10.00	20.00
❑ ST-214	Let the Whole World Sing It with Me	1969	5.00	10.00	20.00
❑ ST-324	Yours Forever	1969	5.00	10.00	20.00
❑ ST 2332 [S]	The Songs of Wynn Stewart	1965	6.25	12.50	25.00
❑ T 2332 [M]	The Songs of Wynn Stewart	1965	5.00	10.00	20.00
❑ ST 2737 [S]	It's Such a Pretty World Today	1967	6.25	12.50	25.00
❑ T 2737 [M]	It's Such a Pretty World Today	1967	5.00	10.00	20.00
❑ ST 2849 [S]	Love's Gonna Happen to Me	1968	5.00	10.00	20.00
❑ T 2849 [M]	Love's Gonna Happen to Me	1968	7.50	15.00	30.00
❑ ST 2921	Something Pretty	1968	5.00	10.00	20.00

HILLTOP

Number	Title (A Side/B Side)	Yr	VG	VG+	NM
❑ JM-6050 [M]	Above and Beyond the Call of Love	1967	3.75	7.50	15.00
❑ JS-6050 [S]	Above and Beyond the Call of Love	1967	3.00	6.00	12.00

PLAYBOY

Number	Title (A Side/B Side)	Yr	VG	VG+	NM
❑ PB 416	After the Storm	1976	2.50	5.00	10.00

WRANGLER

Number	Title (A Side/B Side)	Yr	VG	VG+	NM
❑ W-1006 [M]	Wynn Stewart	1962	7.50	15.00	30.00
❑ W-31006 [S]	Wynn Stewart	1962	10.00	20.00	40.00

STEWART, WYNN, AND JAN HOWARD

Also see each artist's individual listings.

45s

CHALLENGE

Number	Title (A Side/B Side)	Yr	VG	VG+	NM
❑ 59071	Wrong Company/We'll Never Love Again	1960	3.75	7.50	15.00
❑ 59264	How the Other Half Lives/We'll Never Love Again	1964	3.00	6.00	12.00

JACKPOT

Number	Title (A Side/B Side)	Yr	VG	VG+	NM
❑ 48014	How the Other Half Lives/Yankee Go Home	1960	5.00	10.00	20.00

Albums

CHALLENGE

Number	Title (A Side/B Side)	Yr	VG	VG+	NM
❑ CHL-611 [M]	Sweethearts of Country Music	1961	12.50	25.00	50.00

STARDAY

Number	Title (A Side/B Side)	Yr	VG	VG+	NM
❑ SLP-421	Wynn Stewart and Jan Howard Sing Their Hits	1968	6.25	12.50	25.00

STEWART, WYNN, AND WEBB PIERCE

Albums

DESIGN

Number	Title (A Side/B Side)	Yr	VG	VG+	NM
❑ DLP-604 [M]	Country and Western Stars	196?	3.00	6.00	12.00

STEREO-SPECTRUM

Number	Title (A Side/B Side)	Yr	VG	VG+	NM
❑ SLP-604 [R]	Country and Western Stars	196?	3.00	6.00	12.00

STOCKTON, SHANE

45s

DECCA

Number	Title (A Side/B Side)	Yr	VG	VG+	NM
❑ 72043	What If I'm Right/My Life's an Open Book	1998	—	—	3.00
❑ 72060	Gonna Have to Fall/Billy Saw the Light	1998	—	—	3.00

STONE, CLIFFIE

Also see SPEEDY WEST.

45s

CAPITOL

Number	Title (A Side/B Side)	Yr	VG	VG+	NM
❑ F966	Twilight Time in Texas/Steel Strike	1950	6.25	12.50	25.00
❑ F986	The Dipsey Doodle/Rubber Knuckle Sam	1950	6.25	12.50	25.00
❑ F1109	Westphalia Waltz/Put Your Little Foot	1950	6.25	12.50	25.00
❑ F1167	Fireball Mail/Blue Canadian Rockies	1950	6.25	12.50	25.00
❑ F1265	Christmas Waltz/Here Comes Santa Claus	1950	6.25	12.50	25.00
❑ F1354	Tater Pie/With a Kiss	1951	6.25	12.50	25.00
❑ F1406	Amen, Brother Ben/Red Head Polka	1951	6.25	12.50	25.00
❑ F1496	Jump Rope Boogie/The Hokey Pokey	1951	6.25	12.50	25.00
❑ F1606	Missouri Waltz/The Waltz You Saved for Me	1951	5.00	10.00	20.00
—Reissue					
❑ F1834	Bored of Education/The Grunt Song	1951	6.25	12.50	25.00
❑ F1960	Carolina Waltz/Dead End Street	1952	5.00	10.00	20.00
❑ 2270	Little Girl (With Calls)/Little Girl (Without Calls)	1968	2.00	4.00	8.00
❑ 2270 [PS]	Little Girl (With Calls)/Little Girl (Without Calls)	1968	3.00	6.00	12.00
❑ F2291	Dirty Dishes/Everyone's Sweetheart	1952	5.00	10.00	20.00
❑ F2362	Listen to the Mockingbird/When the Bloom Is On the Sage	1953	5.00	10.00	20.00
❑ F2407	The Last Roundup/Pretend	1953	5.00	10.00	20.00
❑ F2497	The Bunny Hop/In a Shanty in Old Shanty Town	1953	5.00	10.00	20.00
❑ F2571	Rocky Mountain Express/Cattle Call	1953	5.00	10.00	20.00
❑ F2910	Blue Moon of Kentucky/Please, Please	1954	7.50	15.00	30.00
❑ F3039	Melody of Love/Darling Je Vous Aime Beaucoup	1955	3.75	7.50	15.00
❑ F3323	Copenhagen/Milenberg Joys	1956	3.75	7.50	15.00
❑ F3585	Rudolph the Red-Nosed Reindeer/Jingle Bells	1956	3.75	7.50	15.00
❑ F4044	Near You/Nobody's Darling But Mine	1958	3.00	6.00	12.00
❑ F4079	Maybe/I Don't Want to Walk Without You	1958	3.00	6.00	12.00
❑ F4141	Blood on the Saddle/Cool Water	1959	3.00	6.00	12.00
❑ 5292	Jambalaya/Why Don't You Love Me	1964	2.50	5.00	10.00
❑ F40161	Devil's Dream/Old Joe Clark/Down Yonder/Buffalo Gals	1950	7.50	15.00	30.00
—78 first issued in 1949; other 45s in the 40000 series, in addition to those listed, may exist					
❑ F40190	Special Instructions for Square Dancing/The Arizona Double Star	1950	6.25	12.50	25.00

Number	Title (A Side/B Side)	Yr	VG	VG+	NM
❑ F40191	Catch All Eight/The Inside Out, The Outside In	1950	6.25	12.50	25.00
❑ F40192	Swing in the Center, Swing on the Side/Forward Six, Don't You Blunder	1950	6.25	12.50	25.00
❑ F40193	Right and Left Hand Star/Double Bow Knot	1950	6.25	12.50	25.00
❑ F40196	The Three Ladies Chain/Four-Gent Star	1949	6.25	12.50	25.00
❑ F40197	Right Hand Over, Left Hand Under/The Inside Arch, The Outside Under	1949	6.25	12.50	25.00
❑ F40198	Bird in the Cage, Seven Hands Around/The Lady Goes Half Way Round	1949	6.25	12.50	25.00
❑ F40265	Can I Canoe You Up the River/Just One Little Lie	1950	7.50	15.00	30.00
TOWER					
❑ 361	There Goes My Everything/Del Rio	1967	2.00	4.00	8.00
Selected 78s					
CAPITOL					
❑ 354	Silver Stars, Purple Sage, Eyes of Blue/If You Knew Susie	1947	3.75	7.50	15.00
❑ 378	Tiger Rag/My Pretty Girl	1947	3.75	7.50	15.00
❑ 15108	When My Blue Moon Turns to Gold Again/Take It Any Way You Can Get It	1948	3.75	7.50	15.00
❑ 15157	He's a Real Gone Oakie/So Long to the Red River Valley	1948	3.75	7.50	15.00
❑ 15205	Here Comes Santa Claus/The Christmas Waltz	1948	3.75	7.50	15.00
❑ 15303	Cream of Kentucky/There's a Gold Moon Shinin'	1949	3.75	7.50	15.00
❑ 15316	After You've Gone/Pretty Baby	1949	3.75	7.50	15.00
❑ 15362	Domino/I Don't Believe Them at All	1949	3.75	7.50	15.00
❑ 40013	Sugar Hill/T-N-Teasing Me	1947	5.00	10.00	20.00
❑ 40041	B-One Baby/Don't Do It Darlin'	1947	5.00	10.00	20.00
❑ 40064	Red, White and Blue/Watch It Neighbor	1948	5.00	10.00	20.00
❑ 40083	Peepin' Through the Keyhole (Watching Jole Blon)/Wabash Blues	1948	5.00	10.00	20.00
❑ 40096	Westphalia Waltz/Spanish Bells	1948	3.75	7.50	15.00
❑ 40113	Sugar Pie/Put Your Little Foot	1948	3.75	7.50	15.00
❑ 40147	The Waltz You Saved for Me/Moonlight on the Colorado	1949	3.75	7.50	15.00
❑ 40148	I'm Forever Blowing Bubbles/Missouri Waltz	1949	3.75	7.50	15.00
❑ 40149	Let Me Call You Sweetheart/There's a Silver Moon on the Ohio	1949	3.75	7.50	15.00
❑ 40150	When It's Springtime in the Rockies/The Beautiful Golden Gate	1949	3.75	7.50	15.00
❑ 40160	Tennessee Wagoner/Back Up and Push//Leather Breeches/Turkey in the Straw	1949	3.75	7.50	15.00
❑ 40165	Special Instructions for Square Dancing/Soldier's Joy	1949	3.75	7.50	15.00
❑ 40166	Sally Good'in/Cripple Creek	1949	3.75	7.50	15.00
❑ 40167	Bake Them Hoecakes Down/The Gal I Left Behind Me	1949	3.75	7.50	15.00
❑ 40168	O Dem Golden Slippers/Ragtime Annie	1949	3.75	7.50	15.00
❑ 40170	My Little Girl/Strummin' on the Old Banjo	1949	3.75	7.50	15.00
❑ 40207	The Blackhawk Waltz/Put Your Little Foot	1949	3.75	7.50	15.00
Albums					
CAPITOL					
❑ T 1080 [M]	The Party's on Me	1958	10.00	20.00	40.00
❑ ST 1230 [S]	Cool Cowboy	1959	10.00	20.00	40.00
❑ T 1230 [M]	Cool Cowboy	1959	7.50	15.00	30.00
❑ ST 1286 [S]	Square Dance Promenade	1960	10.00	20.00	40.00
❑ T 1286 [M]	Square Dance Promenade	1960	7.50	15.00	30.00
❑ KAO 1555 [M]	Original Cowboy Sing-A-Long	1961	7.50	15.00	30.00
❑ SKAO 1555 [S]	Original Cowboy Sing-A-Long	1961	10.00	20.00	40.00
❑ ST 1685 [S]	It's Fun to Square Dance	1962	6.25	12.50	25.00
❑ T 1685 [M]	It's Fun to Square Dance	1962	5.00	10.00	20.00
❑ H 4009 [10]	Square Dances	195?	15.00	30.00	60.00
TOWER					
❑ ST 5073 [S]	Together Again	1967	7.50	15.00	30.00
❑ T 5073 [M]	Together Again	1967	6.25	12.50	25.00

STONE, DOUG

Number	Title (A Side/B Side)	Yr	VG	VG+	NM
45s					
COLUMBIA					
❑ 38-77837	Faith in Me, Faith in You/Enough About Me (Let's Talk About You)	1995	—	—	3.00
❑ 38-77945	Sometimes I Forget/You Won't Outlive Me	1995	—	—	3.00
❑ 38-78039	Born in the Dark/Down on My Knees	1995	—	—	3.00
EPIC					
❑ 34-73246	I'd Be Better Off (In a Pine Box)/It's a Good Thing I Don't Love You Anymore	1990	—	2.00	4.00
❑ 34-73425	Fourteen Minutes Old/High Weeds and Rust	1990	—	2.00	4.00
❑ 34-73570	These Lips Don't Know How to Say Goodbye/We Always Agree on Love	1990	—	2.00	4.00
❑ 34-73741	In a Different Light/Turn This Thing Around	1991	—	2.00	4.00
❑ 34-73895	I Thought It Was You/(For Every Inch I've Laughed) I've Cried a Mile	1991	—	2.00	4.00
❑ 34-74089	A Jukebox with a Country Song/Remember the Ride	1991	—	2.00	4.00
❑ 34-74259	Come In Out of the Pain/The Feeling Never Goes Away	1992	—	2.00	4.00
❑ 34-74399	Warning Labels/Left, Leavin', Goin' or Gone	1992	—	2.00	4.00
❑ 34-74761	Too Busy Being in Love/The Working End of a Hoe	1992	—	2.00	4.00
❑ 34-74885	Made for Lovin' You/She's Got a Future in the Movies	1993	—	2.00	4.00
❑ 34-77025	Why Didn't I Think of That/This Empty House	1993	—	2.00	4.00
❑ 34-77228	I Never Knew Love/This Empty House	1993	—	—	3.00
❑ 34-77375	Addicted to a Dollar/That's a Lie	1994	—	—	3.00
❑ 34-77549	More Love/She Used to Love Me a Lot	1994	—	—	3.00
❑ 34-77716	Little Houses/I'd Be Better Off (In a Pine Box)	1994	—	—	3.00

STONEMANS, THE

Number	Title (A Side/B Side)	Yr	VG	VG+	NM
45s					
MGM					
❑ 13466	Tupelo County Jail/Spell of the Freight Train	1966	2.00	4.00	8.00
❑ 13557	The Five Little Johnson Girls/Goin' Back to Bowling Green	1966	2.00	4.00	8.00
❑ 13667	Back to Nashville, Tennessee/Bottle of Wine	1967	2.00	4.00	8.00
❑ 13755	West Canterbury Subdivision Blues/The Three Cent Opera	1967	2.00	4.00	8.00
❑ 13896	Cimarron/Tell It to My Heart Sometime	1968	2.00	4.00	8.00
❑ 13945	Christopher Robin/The Love I Left Behind	1968	2.00	4.00	8.00
❑ 14018	Travelin' Man/God Is Alive and Well	1968	—	3.50	7.00
RCA VICTOR					
❑ 47-9793	Get Together/Doesn't Anybody Know My Name	1969	—	3.50	7.00
❑ 47-9842	Who'll Stop the Rain/Proud to Be Together	1970	—	3.50	7.00
❑ 47-9882	California Blues/Looks Like Baby's Gone	1970	—	3.50	7.00
❑ 74-0266	Tecumseh Valley/Two Kids from Duluth, Minnesota	1969	—	3.50	7.00
STARDAY					
❑ 599	That Pal of Mine/Talking Fiddle Blues	1962	3.75	7.50	15.00
—As "The Stoneman Family"					
WORLD PACIFIC					
❑ 413	Groundhog/Take Me Home	1964	3.00	6.00	12.00
—As "The Stoneman Family"					
Albums					
MGM					
❑ GAS-124	The Stonemans (Golden Archive Series)	1970	3.75	7.50	15.00
❑ E-4363 [M]	Those Singin' Swingin' Stompin' Sensational Stonemans	1966	5.00	10.00	20.00
❑ SE-4363 [S]	Those Singin' Swingin' Stompin' Sensational Stonemans	1966	6.25	12.50	25.00
❑ E-4453 [M]	Stoneman's Country	1967	5.00	10.00	20.00
❑ SE-4453 [S]	Stoneman's Country	1967	6.25	12.50	25.00
❑ E-4511 [M]	All in the Family	1968	6.25	12.50	25.00
❑ SE-4511 [S]	All in the Family	1968	5.00	10.00	20.00
❑ SE-4578	The Great Stonemans	1968	5.00	10.00	20.00
❑ SE-4613	A Stoneman Christmas	1968	5.00	10.00	20.00
RCA VICTOR					
❑ LSP-4343	In All Honesty	1970	3.75	7.50	15.00
STARDAY					
❑ SLP-393 [M]	White Lightning	1965	10.00	20.00	40.00
WORLD PACIFIC					
❑ ST-1828 [S]	Big Ball in Monterey	1964	10.00	20.00	40.00
❑ WP-1828 [M]	Big Ball in Monterey	1964	7.50	15.00	30.00

STOREY, LEWIS

Number	Title (A Side/B Side)	Yr	VG	VG+	NM
45s					
EPIC					
❑ 34-05786	Ain't No Tellin'/Flo's Inn	1986	—	—	3.00
❑ 34-05786 [PS]	Ain't No Tellin'/Flo's Inn	1986	—	2.00	4.00
❑ 34-05890	Katie, Take Me Dancin'/Friday Fool's Parade	1986	—	—	3.00

STORIE, JAMES

Number	Title (A Side/B Side)	Yr	VG	VG+	NM
45s					
GMC					
❑ 1001	Lost Highway/Whispering Pines	1988	—	3.50	7.00
LS					
❑ 190	The Man I Used to Be/Dig a Little Deeper	198?	—	3.00	6.00
—As "Jim Storie"					

STORY, CARL

Number	Title (A Side/B Side)	Yr	VG	VG+	NM
45s					
COLUMBIA					
❑ 4-21137	Lonesome Hearted Blues/Love and Wealth	1953	6.25	12.50	25.00
❑ 4-21205	My Lord Keeps a Record/Someone to Lean On	1954	5.00	10.00	20.00
❑ 4-21250	Step It Up and Go/Have You Come to Say Goodbye	1954	6.25	12.50	25.00
❑ 4-21282	A Million Years in Glory/On the Other Shore	1954	5.00	10.00	20.00
❑ 4-21327	Love Me Like You Used to Do/It's a Lonesome Road	1954	6.25	12.50	25.00
❑ 4-21399	Reunion in Heaven/I Love the Hymns They Sing	1955	5.00	10.00	20.00
❑ 4-21444	What a Line/You've Been Tom-Cattin' Around	1955	5.00	10.00	20.00
MERCURY					
❑ 70785	Get On Board, Little Children/God Put the Rainbow in the Clouds	1956	3.75	7.50	15.00
❑ 70856	The Road of Prayer/Mother Is Old	1956	3.75	7.50	15.00
❑ 70932	Waiting for Me/Everybody Will Be Happy Over There	1956	3.75	7.50	15.00
❑ 71088	The Light at the River/Mocking Banjo	1957	3.75	7.50	15.00
❑ 71143	Got a Lot to Tell Jesus/Banjo on the Mountain	1957	3.75	7.50	15.00
❑ 71218	Family Reunion/Banjolina	1957	3.75	7.50	15.00
❑ 71268	The Saviour's Love/Fire on the Banjo	1958	3.75	7.50	15.00
STARDAY					
❑ 411	Old Country Baptizing/Angel Band	1958	3.75	7.50	15.00
❑ 427	Shout and Shine/A Beautiful City	1959	3.75	7.50	15.00
❑ 449	Set Your House in Order/The Old Gospel Ship	1959	3.75	7.50	15.00
❑ 465	I Heard My Mother Weeping/I'll Be a Friend	1959	3.75	7.50	15.00
❑ 492	(I Heard My Name) On the Radio/Sweeter Than the Flowers	1960	3.75	7.50	15.00
❑ 514	Someone's Last Day/The Ship That's Sailing Down	1960	3.75	7.50	15.00
❑ 531	Get Religion/Jerusalem Moan	1960	3.75	7.50	15.00
❑ 619	A Picture from Life's Other Side/Rank Stranger	1963	3.00	6.00	12.00
❑ 688	The Old Country Preacher/Listen to Your Radio	1964	2.50	5.00	10.00

Number	Title (A Side/B Side)	Yr	VG	VG+	NM
Albums					
MERCURY					
❑ MG-20323 [M]	Gospel Quartet Favorites	1958	10.00	20.00	40.00
❑ MG-20584 [M]	More Gospel Quartet Favorites	1961	7.50	15.00	30.00
❑ SR-60584 [S]	More Gospel Quartet Favorites	1961	10.00	20.00	40.00
STARDAY					
❑ SLP-107 [M]	America's Favorite Country Gospel Artist	1959	12.50	25.00	50.00
❑ SLP-127 [M]	Gospel Revival	1961	10.00	20.00	40.00
❑ SLP-137 [M]	All Day Singing with Dinner on the Ground	1961	10.00	20.00	40.00
❑ SLP-152 [M]	Get Religion	1962	10.00	20.00	40.00
❑ SLP-219 [M]	Mighty Close to Heaven	1963	10.00	20.00	40.00
❑ SLP-278 [M]	All Day Sacred Singing	1964	10.00	20.00	40.00
❑ SLP-315 [M]	Sacred Songs of Life and the Hereafter	1965	10.00	20.00	40.00
❑ SLP-348 [M]	There's Nothing on Earth (That Heaven Can't Cure)	1965	10.00	20.00	40.00
❑ SLP-411 [M]	My Lord Keeps a Record	1968	7.50	15.00	30.00

STOVALL, VERN

Number	Title (A Side/B Side)	Yr	VG	VG+	NM
45s					
CREST					
❑ 1080	Long Black Limousine/Loving on Borrowed Time	1961	5.00	10.00	20.00
❑ 1090	My Best Wasn't Good Enough/That's All It Takes	1961	3.75	7.50	15.00
❑ 1111	The World Had Too Much to See/Just Another Way to Get the Blues	1962	3.75	7.50	15.00
LONGHORN					
❑ 567	Wreck of the Olds 88/Break Time	196?	3.00	6.00	12.00
❑ 571	I'm Wild Bill Tonight/Not Worth the Paper	196?	3.00	6.00	12.00
—With Janet McBride					
❑ 575	Tell Me Again/Where Did the Other Dollar Go	196?	3.00	6.00	12.00
—With Janet McBride					
❑ 579	(I Didn't Know) Angels Flew This Close to the Ground/Funny Sense of Humor	1967	2.50	5.00	10.00
❑ 581	Dallas/Movin' Round	1967	2.50	5.00	10.00
❑ 584	Elbow Bender/Everybody Has a Price	1968	2.50	5.00	10.00
❑ 588	Sittin' Pretty/You Can't Roll a Seven Every Time	1968	2.50	5.00	10.00
MONUMENT					
❑ 1097	Cloud Burner/Honky Tonkers	1968	2.00	4.00	8.00
❑ 1126	Love Is/Brought On by the Wine	1969	2.00	4.00	8.00
❑ 1149	Pay Day/Code Alarm 7	1969	2.00	4.00	8.00

STRAIT, GEORGE

Number	Title (A Side/B Side)	Yr	VG	VG+	NM
45s					
MCA					
❑ S45-17234 [DJ]	Merry Christmas Strait to You/White Christmas	1986	5.00	10.00	20.00
—Promo only on red vinyl					
❑ S45-17451 [DJ]	For Christ's Sake, It's Christmas/When It's Christmas Time in Texas	1987	3.75	7.50	15.00
—Promo only on white vinyl					
❑ 51104	Unwound/She's Playing Hell Trying to Get Me to Heaven	1981	—	2.00	4.00
❑ 51170	Down and Out/Blame It on Mexico	1981	—	2.00	4.00
❑ 51228	If You're Thinking You Want a Stranger (There's One Coming Home)/Her Goodbye Hit Me in the Heart	1982	—	2.00	4.00
❑ 52066	Fool Hearted Memory/Steal of the Night	1982	—	2.00	4.00
❑ 52120	Marina Del Rey/I Can't See Texas from Here	1982	—	2.00	4.00
❑ 52162	Amarillo by Morning/Lover in Disguise	1983	—	2.00	4.00
❑ 52225	A Fire I Can't Put Out/Honky Tonk Crazy	1983	—	2.00	4.00
❑ 52279	You Look So Good in Love/A Little Heaven's Rubbing Off on Me	1983	—	2.00	4.00
❑ 52337	Right or Wrong/Fifteen Years Going Up (And One Night Going Down)	1984	—	—	3.00
❑ 52392	Let's Fall to Pieces Together/You're the Cloud I'm On (When I'm High)	1984	—	—	3.00
❑ 52458	Does Fort Worth Ever Cross Your Mind/Love Comes from the Other Side of Town	1984	—	—	3.00
❑ 52526	The Cowboy Rides Away/Any Old Time	1985	—	—	3.00
❑ 52586	The Fireman/What Did You Expect Me to Do	1985	—	—	3.00
❑ 52667	The Chair/In Too Deep	1985	—	—	3.00
❑ 52667 [DJ]	The Chair (same on both sides)	1985	3.75	7.50	15.00
—Promo only on blue vinyl					
❑ 52667 [PS]	The Chair/In Too Deep	1985	—	2.50	5.00
❑ 52764	You're Something Special to Me/Dance Time in Texas	1986	—	—	3.00
❑ 52817	Nobody in His Right Mind Would've Left Her/You Still Get to Me	1986	—	—	3.00
❑ 52914	It Ain't Cool to Be Crazy About You/Rhythm of the Road	1986	—	—	3.00
❑ 53021	Ocean Front Property/My Heart Won't Wander Very Far from You	1987	—	2.00	4.00
❑ 53021 [DJ]	Ocean Front Property (same on both sides)	1987	3.75	7.50	15.00
—Promo only on yellow vinyl					
❑ 53087	All My Ex's Live in Texas/I'm All Behind You Now	1987	—	2.00	4.00
❑ 53087 [DJ]	All My Ex's Live in Texas (same on both sides)	1987	3.75	7.50	15.00
—Promo only on yellow vinyl					
❑ 53165	Am I Blue/Someone's Walkin' Around Upstairs	1987	—	—	3.00
❑ 53165 [DJ]	Am I Blue (same on both sides)	1987	3.75	7.50	15.00
—Promo only on blue vinyl					
❑ 53248	Famous Last Words of a Fool/It's Too Late Now	1988	—	—	3.00
❑ 53340	Baby Blue/Back to Bein' Me	1988	—	—	3.00
❑ 53400	If You Ain't Lovin' (You Ain't Livin')/Is It That Time Again	1988	—	—	3.00
❑ 53486	Baby's Gotten Good at Goodbye/Bigger Man Than Me	1988	—	—	3.00
❑ 53648	What's Going On in Your World/Let's Get Down to It	1989	—	—	3.00
❑ 53693	Ace in the Hole/Oh Me, Oh My Sweet Baby	1989	—	2.50	5.00
❑ 53755	Overnight Success/Hollywood Squares	1989	—	2.00	4.00
❑ 53969	I've Come to Expect It from You/Stranger in My Arms	1990	—	2.00	4.00
❑ 54052	If I Know Me/Home in San Antone	1991	—	2.00	4.00
❑ 54127	You Know Me Better Than That/Baby Blue	1991	—	2.00	4.00
❑ 54180	The Chill of an Early Fall/Her Only Bad Habit Is Me	1991	—	2.00	4.00
❑ 54277	Drinking Champagne (A Toast to the Battlin' Bucs)/(B-side unknown)	1991	—	—	3.00
—Reissue of 79070 with new subtitle					
❑ 54318	Lovesick Blues/Is It Already Time	1992	—	—	3.00
❑ 54379	Gone as a Girl Can Get/Faults and All	1992	—	2.00	4.00
❑ 54439	So Much Like My Dad/Wonderland of Love	1992	—	2.00	4.00
❑ 54478	I Cross My Heart/You're Right I'm Wrong	1992	—	2.50	5.00
❑ 54563	Heartland/Baby Your Baby	1993	—	2.00	4.00
❑ 54642	When Did You Stop Loving Me/Where the Sidewalk Ends	1993	—	2.00	4.00
❑ 54717	Easy Come, Easy Go/She Lays It All on the Line	1993	—	2.00	4.00
❑ 54767	I'd Like to Have That One Back/That's Where My Baby Feels at Home	1993	—	2.00	4.00
❑ 54819	Love Bug/Just Look at Me	1994	—	2.00	4.00
❑ 54854	The Man in Love with You/We Must Be Loving Right	1994	—	2.00	4.00
❑ 54938	The Big One/No One But You	1994	—	2.00	4.00
❑ 54964	You Can't Make a Heart Love Somebody/What Am I Waiting For	1994	—	2.00	4.00
❑ 55019	Adalida/Down Louisiana Way	1995	—	2.00	4.00
❑ 55064	Lead On/I Met a Friend of Yours Today	1995	—	2.00	4.00
❑ 55127	Check Yes or No/Fly Me to the Moon	1995	—	2.00	4.00
—B-side with Frank Sinatra					
❑ 55163	I Know She Still Loves Me/Unwound	1995	—	2.00	4.00
—B-side with Frank Sinatra					
❑ 55187	Blue Clear Sky/I Ain't Never Seen No One Like You	1996	—	2.00	4.00
❑ 55204	Carried Away/Do the Right Thing	1996	—	2.00	4.00
❑ 55248	I Can Still Make Cheyenne/Need I Say More	1996	—	—	3.00
❑ 55288	King of the Mountain/I'd Just As Soon Go	1996	—	—	3.00
❑ 55321	One Night at a Time/Won't You Come Home (And Talk to a Stranger)	1997	—	—	3.00
❑ 72007	Carrying Your Love with Me/I've Got a Funny Feeling	1997	—	—	3.00
❑ 72019	Today My World Slipped Away/Round About Way	1997	—	—	3.00
❑ 72028	Round About Way/She'll Leave You with a Smile	1997	—	—	3.00
❑ 72046	I Just Want to Dance with You/Neon Row	1998	—	—	3.00
❑ 79015	Love Without End, Amen/Too Much of Too Little	1990	—	2.50	5.00
❑ 79070	Drinking Champagne/We're Supposed to Do That Now and Then	1990	—	2.50	5.00
MCA NASHVILLE					
❑ 72063	True/Remember the Alamo	1998	—	—	3.00
❑ 72071	We Really Shouldn't Be Doing This/Maria	1998	—	—	3.00
❑ 72084	Meanwhile/You Haven't Left Me Yet	1999	—	—	3.00
❑ 72095	Write This Down/4 Minus 3 Equals Zero	1999	—	—	3.00
❑ 72108	What Do You Say to That/4 Minus 3 Equals Zero	1999	—	—	3.00
❑ 088 172147 7	The Best Day/I Can Still Make Cheyenne	2000	—	—	3.00
❑ 088 172169 7	Go On/Murder on Music Row (a Duet with Alan Jackson)	2000	—	—	3.00
❑ 088 172194 7	Don't Make Me Come Over There and Love You/You're Stronger Than Me	2000	—	—	3.00
Albums					
HEARTLAND					
❑ HL 1172/3 [(2)]	The Very Best of George Strait	1991	3.75	7.50	15.00
MCA					
❑ 5248	Strait Country	1981	2.50	5.00	10.00
❑ 5320	Strait from the Heart	1982	2.50	5.00	10.00
❑ 5450	Right or Wrong	1983	2.50	5.00	10.00
❑ 5518	Does Fort Worth Ever Cross Your Mind	1984	2.50	5.00	10.00
❑ 5567	Greatest Hits	1985	2.50	5.00	10.00
❑ 5605	Something Special	1985	2.50	5.00	10.00
❑ 5750	#7	1986	2.50	5.00	10.00
❑ 5800	Merry Christmas Strait to You	1986	2.50	5.00	10.00
❑ 5913	Ocean Front Property	1987	2.50	5.00	10.00
❑ 6415	Livin' It Up	1990	3.00	6.00	12.00
❑ 10450	Ten Strait Hits	1992	5.00	10.00	20.00
—Only available on vinyl through Columbia House					
❑ 10532	Holding My Own	1992	5.00	10.00	20.00
—Only available on vinyl through Columbia House					
❑ 27092	Strait Country	1984	2.00	4.00	8.00
—Reissue of 5248					
❑ 42035	Greatest Hits, Volume Two	1987	2.00	4.00	8.00
❑ 42114	If You Ain't Lovin' You Ain't Livin'	1988	2.00	4.00	8.00
❑ 42266	Beyond the Blue Neon	1989	2.00	4.00	8.00
❑ R 134172	Merry Christmas Strait to You	1986	3.00	6.00	12.00
—Same as above, but BMG Direct Marketing version					
❑ R 153641	Chill of an Early Fall	1991	5.00	10.00	20.00
—Only released on vinyl through BMG Direct Marketing					

STRANGERS, THE

Backing group for MERLE HAGGARD.

Number	Title (A Side/B Side)	Yr	VG	VG+	NM
Albums					
CAPITOL					
❑ ST-169	Instrumental Sounds of Merle Haggard's Strangers	1969	5.00	10.00	20.00
❑ ST-445	Introducing My Friends the Strangers	1970	5.00	10.00	20.00
❑ ST-590	Getting to Know Merle Haggard's Strangers	1970	5.00	10.00	20.00

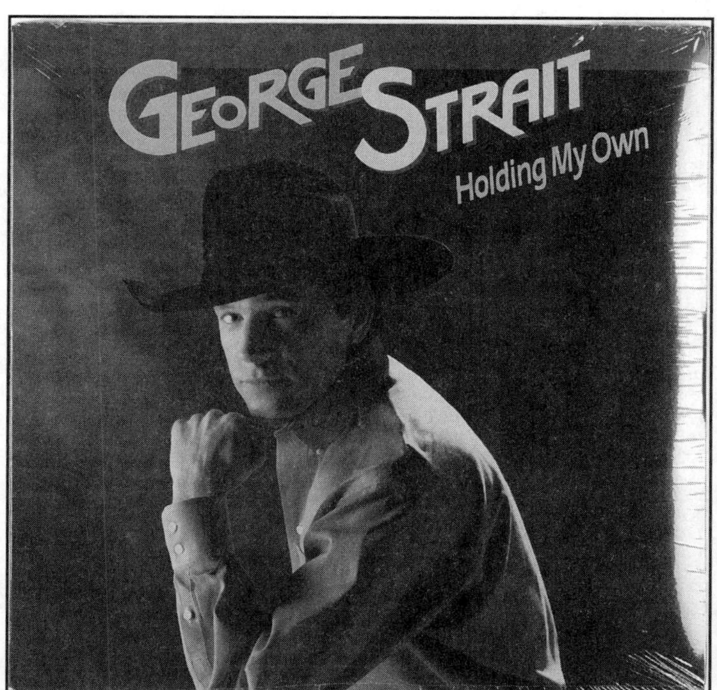

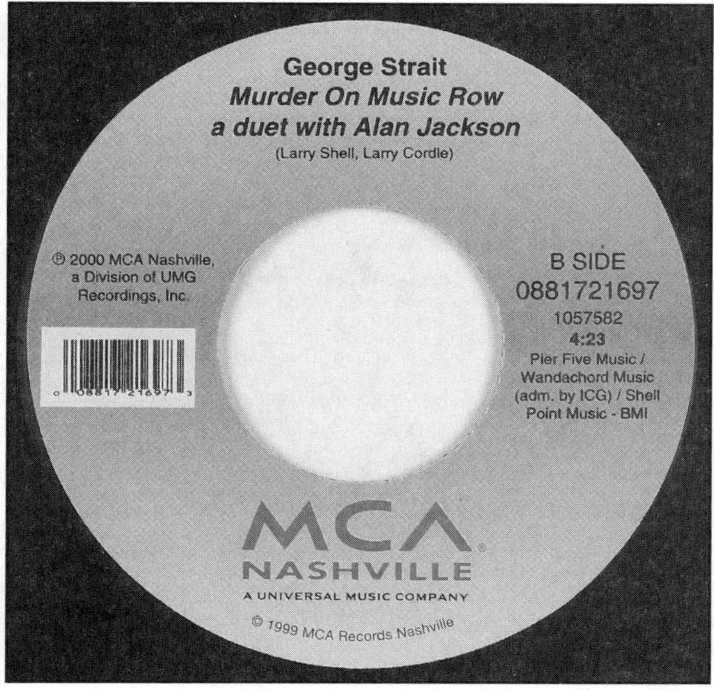

In today's country music environment, where longevity is much more rare than it used to be, it's amazing that George Strait has not only survived, but thrived. He has had at least one chart-topping single a year for 19 straight years! (Top left) The first of his No. 1 hits was "Fool Hearted Memory," which came from an obscure film called *The Soldier.* It was Strait's fourth single for MCA. (Top right) The only George Strait single issued with a picture sleeve was "The Chair," a song that broke almost every Nashville songwriting "rule," yet still topped the charts. (Bottom left) Strait's albums continued coming out on vinyl through record clubs two years after they stopped being issued otherwise. The last of these was *Holding My Own,* which Columbia House made available in 1992. (Bottom right) "Murder on Music Row," a duet with Alan Jackson that reflects the attitude of a portion of country music fans, made the top 40 on the country charts in 2000 despite not being promoted to radio. Its only single release was on 7-inch vinyl.

Number	Title (A Side/B Side)	Yr	VG	VG+	NM
❑ ST-796	Honky Tonkin'	1971	5.00	10.00	20.00
❑ ST-11141	Totally Instrumental with One Exception...	1973	3.75	7.50	15.00

STREET, MEL

45s

GRT

Number	Title (A Side/B Side)	Yr	VG	VG+	NM
❑ 002	You Make Me Feel More Like a Man/Green River	1974	—	3.00	6.00
❑ 012	Forbidden Angel/Don't Lead Me On	1974	—	3.00	6.00
❑ 017	Smokey Mountain Memories/Let's Put Out the Fire	1975	—	3.00	6.00
❑ 025	Even If I Have to Steal/Country Pride	1975	—	3.00	6.00
❑ 030	(This Ain't Just Another) Lust Affair/Strange Empty World	1975	—	3.00	6.00
❑ 043	The Devil in Your Kisses (And the Angel in Your Eyes)/Baby Don't Save Your Love for a Rainy Day	1976	—	3.00	6.00
❑ 057	I Met a Friend of Yours Today/She Boogies While He's Gone	1976	—	3.00	6.00
❑ 083	Looking Out My Window Through the Pain/ Virginia's Song	1976	—	3.00	6.00
❑ 109	An Old Christmas Card/You Cared Enough To Send Me The Very Best	1976	—	3.00	6.00
❑ 116	Rodeo Bum/Guilty As Sin	1977	—	3.00	6.00

MERCURY

Number	Title (A Side/B Side)	Yr	VG	VG+	NM
❑ 55043	Just Hangin' On/Easy Lovin' Kind	1978	—	2.50	5.00

METROMEDIA

Number	Title (A Side/B Side)	Yr	VG	VG+	NM
❑ BMBO-0018	The Town Where You Live/Body Man	1973	—	3.00	6.00
❑ BMBO-0143	Lovin' on Borrowed Time/Moonshine Man	1973	—	3.00	6.00

METROMEDIA COUNTRY

Number	Title (A Side/B Side)	Yr	VG	VG+	NM
❑ 901	Lovin' on Back Streets/Who'll Turn Out the Lights	1972	—	3.00	6.00
❑ 906	Walk Softly on the Bridges/Spoiled Lonely Man	1973	—	3.00	6.00

POLYDOR

Number	Title (A Side/B Side)	Yr	VG	VG+	NM
❑ 14399	Barbara Don't Let Me Be the Last to Know/My Friend the Jukebox	1977	—	2.50	5.00
❑ 14421	Close Enough for Lonesome/If This Is Having a Good Time	1977	—	2.50	5.00
❑ 14448	If I Had a Cheating Heart/Memory Eraser	1977	—	2.50	5.00
❑ 14468	Shady Rest/She's No Honky Tonk Angel	1978	—	2.50	5.00

ROYAL AMERICAN

Number	Title (A Side/B Side)	Yr	VG	VG+	NM
❑ 64	Borrowed Angel/House of Pride	1972	2.00	4.00	8.00

SUNBIRD

Number	Title (A Side/B Side)	Yr	VG	VG+	NM
❑ 103	Tonight Let's Sleep on It Baby/Muddy Mississippi	1980	—	2.50	5.00
❑ 7555	Who'll Turn Out the Lights/Lust Affair	1980	—	2.50	5.00
❑ 7568	Slip Away/Let's Put Out the Fire	1981	—	2.50	5.00

—With Sandy Powell

SUNSET

Number	Title (A Side/B Side)	Yr	VG	VG+	NM
❑ 100	The One Thing My Lady Never Puts Into Words/ Borrowed Angel	1979	—	2.50	5.00

Albums

GRT

Number	Title (A Side/B Side)	Yr	VG	VG+	NM
❑ 8002	Two Way Street	1974	3.00	6.00	12.00
❑ 8004	Smokey Mountain Memories	1975	3.00	6.00	12.00
❑ 8010	Mel Street's Greatest Hits	1976	3.00	6.00	12.00

METROMEDIA

Number	Title (A Side/B Side)	Yr	VG	VG+	NM
❑ BML1-0281	The Town Where You Live/Walk Softly on the Bridges	1973	3.00	6.00	12.00

METROMEDIA COUNTRY

Number	Title (A Side/B Side)	Yr	VG	VG+	NM
❑ 5001	Borrowed Angel	1972	3.75	7.50	15.00

POLYDOR

Number	Title (A Side/B Side)	Yr	VG	VG+	NM
❑ PD-1-6114	Mel Street	1977	2.50	5.00	10.00
❑ PD-1-6144	Country Soul	1978	2.50	5.00	10.00

SUNBIRD

Number	Title (A Side/B Side)	Yr	VG	VG+	NM
❑ 1000	Many Moods of Mel	1980	3.00	6.00	12.00
❑ ST-50101	The Very Best of Mel Street	1980	2.50	5.00	10.00
❑ ST-50102	Some Special Moments	1980	3.00	6.00	12.00

STREETFEET

45s

TRIPLE T

Number	Title (A Side/B Side)	Yr	VG	VG+	NM
❑ 2001	Where Do You Go/(B-side unknown)	1983	—	3.00	6.00

STREETS

See NIGHSTREETS.

STREISAND, BARBRA

See BARBRA AND NEIL.

STRENGTH, "TEXAS" BILL

45s

BRITE STAR

Number	Title (A Side/B Side)	Yr	VG	VG+	NM
❑ 2448	Nothing Is Sweeter Than You/Somehow, Someday, Someway	197?	3.00	6.00	12.00

CAPITOL

Number	Title (A Side/B Side)	Yr	VG	VG+	NM
❑ F3217	Yellow Rose of Texas/Cry, Cry, Cry	1955	5.00	10.00	20.00
❑ F3282	When Love Comes Knockin'/Turn Around	1955	5.00	10.00	20.00
❑ F3394	It Ain't Much, But It's Home/When the Bright Lights Grow Dim	1956	3.75	7.50	15.00
❑ F3477	Where Did My Heart Go/Gotta Lotta Love	1956	3.75	7.50	15.00
❑ F3568	North Wind/But Do You Think I'm Happy	1956	3.75	7.50	15.00
❑ F3701	Six Fools/I Wanna Ride On Your Merry-Go-Round	1957	3.75	7.50	15.00

CORAL

Number	Title (A Side/B Side)	Yr	VG	VG+	NM
❑ 9-61284	Nice to Be Living/Nobody Knows This More	1954	5.00	10.00	20.00
❑ 9-64117	Cherry Pie/Is Someone Else the Lucky One Tonight	1952	6.25	12.50	25.00
❑ 9-64133	Paper Boy Boogie/I Was Only Teasin' You	1952	6.25	12.50	25.00
❑ 9-64139	I Found My Love/It's a Shame	1952	6.25	12.50	25.00
❑ 9-64152	Rain or Shine/Heart, Don't Complain	1953	6.25	12.50	25.00
❑ 9-64171	Alone/Country Love	1954	5.00	10.00	20.00
❑ 9-64177	Let's Make Love or Go Home/You Can't Have My Love	1954	5.00	10.00	20.00

—With Tabby West

SUN

Number	Title (A Side/B Side)	Yr	VG	VG+	NM
❑ 346	Guess I'd Better Go/Senorita	1960	6.25	12.50	25.00

—As "Bill Strength"

Selected 78s

4 STAR

Number	Title (A Side/B Side)	Yr	VG	VG+	NM
❑ 1334	If I Could Buy Your Love/Please Don't Ever Forget Me	1949	5.00	10.00	20.00
❑ 1402	Action Speaks Louder Than Words/Mr. Moon Sailing High	1950	5.00	10.00	20.00
❑ 1465	Black Coffee Blues/Who's the Lucky One	1950	5.00	10.00	20.00
❑ 1532	It Could Be a Wonderful World/I'm Doing a Peach of a Job	1950	5.00	10.00	20.00
❑ 1554	I'm Walking in Heaven/Frown on the Moon	1951	5.00	10.00	20.00

Albums

RE-CAR

Number	Title (A Side/B Side)	Yr	VG	VG+	NM
❑ 2022	Greatest Hits	1967	6.25	12.50	25.00

STRODE, LANCE

45s

BOOTSTRAP

Number	Title (A Side/B Side)	Yr	VG	VG+	NM
❑ 0416	Dangerous Ground/(B-side unknown)	1989	2.00	4.00	8.00

STROMAN, GENE

45s

CAPITOL

Number	Title (A Side/B Side)	Yr	VG	VG+	NM
❑ B-5662	Goodbye Song/I'm Not That Crazy	1986	—	—	3.00
❑ B-44015	I Don't Feel Much Like a Cowboy Tonight/Too Many Rivers	1987	—	—	3.00

STRUNK, JUD

45s

AD-MEDIA

Number	Title (A Side/B Side)	Yr	VG	VG+	NM
❑ 6416	The Santa Song/A Special Christmas Tree	1969	2.50	5.00	10.00
❑ 6416 [PS]	The Santa Song/A Special Christmas Tree	1969	3.75	7.50	15.00

CAPITOL

Number	Title (A Side/B Side)	Yr	VG	VG+	NM
❑ 3960	My Country/The Will	1974	—	3.00	6.00

COLUMBIA

Number	Title (A Side/B Side)	Yr	VG	VG+	NM
❑ 4-45121	David's Place/Lion in the Park	1970	2.00	4.00	8.00
❑ 4-45189	Self-Eating Watermelon/Children at Play	1970	2.00	4.00	8.00

MCA

Number	Title (A Side/B Side)	Yr	VG	VG+	NM
❑ 40872	Tell Me Where I Am Tonight/Fool on My Shoulder	1978	—	2.00	4.00

MELODYLAND

Number	Title (A Side/B Side)	Yr	VG	VG+	NM
❑ 6015	The Biggest Parakeets in Town/I Wasn't Wrong About You	1975	—	2.50	5.00
❑ 6027	Pamela Brown/They're Tearing Down a Town	1975	—	2.50	5.00

MGM

Number	Title (A Side/B Side)	Yr	VG	VG+	NM
❑ 14388	Jacob Brown/Long Ride Home	1972	—	3.00	6.00
❑ 14463	Daisy a Day/The Searchers	1972	—	3.50	7.00
❑ 14572	Next Door Neighbor's Kid/I'd Prefer to Do It All Again	1973	—	3.00	6.00

Albums

COLUMBIA

Number	Title (A Side/B Side)	Yr	VG	VG+	NM
❑ CS 9990	Downeast Viewpoint	1970	3.75	7.50	15.00

HARMONY

Number	Title (A Side/B Side)	Yr	VG	VG+	NM
❑ KH 32344	Mr. Bojangles and Other Favorites	1973	2.50	5.00	10.00

MCA

Number	Title (A Side/B Side)	Yr	VG	VG+	NM
❑ 2309	A Semi-Reformed Tequila Crazed Gypsy	1977	2.50	5.00	10.00

MGM

Number	Title (A Side/B Side)	Yr	VG	VG+	NM
❑ SE-4790	Jones General Store	1972	3.00	6.00	12.00
❑ SE-4898	Daisy a Day	1973	3.00	6.00	12.00

STUART, MARTY

45s

COLUMBIA

Number	Title (A Side/B Side)	Yr	VG	VG+	NM
❑ 38-05724	Arlene/Midnight Moonlight	1985	—	2.00	4.00
❑ 38-05724 [PS]	Arlene/Midnight Moonlight	1985	2.00	4.00	8.00
❑ 38-05897	Honky Tonker/Anyhow I Love You	1986	—	2.00	4.00
❑ 38-06230	All Because of You/Maria (Love to See You Again)	1986	—	2.00	4.00
❑ 38-06425	Do You Really Want My Lovin'/Heart of Stone	1986	—	2.00	4.00
❑ 38-07729	Mirrors Don't Lie/Freight Train Boogie	1988	—	2.00	4.00
❑ 38-07914	Matches/Old Hat	1988	—	2.00	4.00

MCA

Number	Title (A Side/B Side)	Yr	VG	VG+	NM
❑ 53687	Cry Cry Cry/The Wild One	1989	—	—	3.00
❑ 53751	Don't Leave Her Lonely Too Long/The Coal Mine Blues	1989	—	—	3.00
❑ 53975	Little Things/Paint the Town Tonight	1990	—	2.00	4.00
❑ 54065	Till I Found You/Half a Heart	1991	—	2.00	4.00
❑ 54145	Tempted/I'm Blue, I'm Lonesome	1991	—	2.50	5.00
❑ 54253	Burn Me Down/Blue Train	1992	—	2.00	4.00
❑ 54477	Now That's Country/Me & Hank & Jumpin' Jack Flash	1992	—	2.00	4.00
❑ 54538	High on a Mountain Top/Just Between You and Me	1992	—	2.00	4.00
❑ 54607	Hey Baby/Down Home	1993	—	—	3.00

Number	Title (A Side/B Side)	Yr	VG	VG+	NM
54777	Kiss Me, I'm Gone/Marty Stuart Visits the Moon	1994	—	2.00	4.00
54840	Love and Luck/Oh What a Silent Night	1994	—	2.00	4.00
54915	That's What Love's About/Shake Your Hips	1994	—	—	3.00
55010	The Likes of Me/You Can Walk All Over Me	1995	—	—	3.00
55069	If I Ain't Got You/Wheels	1995	—	—	3.00
55226	Thanks to You/Country Girls	1996	—	—	3.00
55270	You Can't Stop Love/The Mississippi Mudcat and Sister Cheryl Crow	1996	—	—	3.00
79001	Hillbilly Rock/Western Girls	1990	—	3.00	6.00
79068	Western Girls/Me and Billy the Kid	1990	—	2.00	4.00

MCA NASHVILLE

Number	Title (A Side/B Side)	Yr	VG	VG+	NM
72096	Red, Red Wine and Cheatin' Songs/Goin' Nowhere Fast	1999	—	—	3.00

Albums

COLUMBIA

Number	Title (A Side/B Side)	Yr	VG	VG+	NM
B6C 40302	Marty Stuart	1986	7.50	15.00	30.00

MCA

Number	Title (A Side/B Side)	Yr	VG	VG+	NM
42312	Hillbilly Rock	1989	3.75	7.50	15.00
R 170076	Tempted	1990	6.25	12.50	25.00

—Vinyl version available only through BMG Direct Marketing

RIDGE RUNNER

Number	Title (A Side/B Side)	Yr	VG	VG+	NM
RRR 0013	Marty	1978	7.50	15.00	30.00

SUGAR HILL

Number	Title (A Side/B Side)	Yr	VG	VG+	NM
3726	Busy Bee Café	1981	7.50	15.00	30.00

STUART, MARTY, AND STEVE EARLE

Also see each artist's individual listings.

45s

DECCA

Number	Title (A Side/B Side)	Yr	VG	VG+	NM
55206	Crying, Waiting, Hoping/Maybe Baby	1996	—	—	3.00

—B-side by Nitty Gritty Dirt Band

STUART, MARTY, AND TRAVIS TRITT

Also see each artist's individual listings.

45s

MCA

Number	Title (A Side/B Side)	Yr	VG	VG+	NM
54405	This One's Gonna Hurt You (For a Long, Long Time)/The King of Dixie	1992	—	2.50	5.00
55197	Honky Tonkin's What I Do Best/Me & Hank & Jumpin' Jack Flash	1996	—	2.00	4.00

STUCKEY, NAT

Also see CONNIE SMITH AND NAT STUCKEY.

45s

MCA

Number	Title (A Side/B Side)	Yr	VG	VG+	NM
40519	Sun Comin' Up/Honky Tonk Dreams	1976	—	2.50	5.00
40568	The Way He's Treated You/At Least One Time	1976	—	2.50	5.00
40608	That's All She Ever Said Except Goodbye/After the Lovin' Has Passed	1976	—	2.50	5.00
40658	The Shady Side of Charlotte/They'd Love to Be Children Again	1976	—	2.50	5.00
40693	Fallin' Down/Please James	1977	—	2.50	5.00
40752	Buddy, I Lied/Don't You Believe Her	1977	—	2.50	5.00
40808	I'm Coming Home to Face the Music/Linda on My Mind	1977	—	2.50	5.00
40855	That Lucky Old Sun (Just Rolls Around Heaven All Day)/I'm Coming Home	1978	—	2.50	5.00
40923	The Days of Sand and Shovels/Mexican Divorce	1978	—	2.50	5.00

PAULA

Number	Title (A Side/B Side)	Yr	VG	VG+	NM
228	Hurtin' Again/Two Together	1965	3.00	6.00	12.00
233	Don't You Believe Her/Round and Round	1966	2.50	5.00	10.00
243	Sweet Thang/Paralyze My Mind	1966	2.50	5.00	10.00
243 [PS]	Sweet Thang/Paralyze My Mind	1966	6.25	12.50	25.00
257	Oh! Woman/On the Other Hand	1966	2.50	5.00	10.00
267	All My Tomorrows/You're Puttin' Me On	1967	2.50	5.00	10.00
276	Adorable Woman/I Knew Her When	1967	2.50	5.00	10.00
287	My Can Do Can't Keep Up With My Want To/If There's No Other Way	1967	2.50	5.00	10.00
288	Blue Christmas/How Can Christmas Be Merry	1967	2.50	5.00	10.00
300	Leave This One Alone/I Never Knew	1968	2.50	5.00	10.00
1204	She Thinks I Still Care/Two Together	1968	2.00	4.00	8.00
1217	Pop a Top/Love of the Common People	1970	2.00	4.00	8.00
1230	Mental Revenge/Waitin' in Your Welfare Line	1970	2.00	4.00	8.00
1295	Blue Christmas/How Can Christmas Be Merry	198?	—	3.00	6.00

RCA VICTOR

Number	Title (A Side/B Side)	Yr	VG	VG+	NM
APBO-0115	Got Leaving on Her Mind/Now Lonely Is Only a Word	1973	—	3.00	6.00
APBO-0222	You Never Say You Love Me Anymore/The Man That I Am	1974	—	3.00	6.00
APBO-0288	It Hurts to Know the Feeling's Gone/Plans for the Future	1974	—	3.00	6.00
PB-10090	You Don't Have to Go Home/I Sure Do Enjoy Loving You	1974	—	3.00	6.00
PB-10307	Boom Boom Barroom Man/Ain't Nothing Bad About Feeling Good	1975	—	3.00	6.00
47-9631	Plastic Saddle/Woman of Hurt	1968	2.00	4.00	8.00
47-9720	Joe and Mabel's 12th Street Bar and Grill/Loving You	1968	2.00	4.00	8.00
47-9786	Sittin' in Atlanta Station/Don't Wait for Me	1969	2.00	4.00	8.00
47-9833	Old Man Willis/Beauty of a Bar	1970	—	3.50	7.00
47-9884	Whiskey, Whiskey/What Am I Doing in L.A.	1970	2.00	4.00	8.00
47-9929	She Wakes Me With a Kiss Every Morning (And She Loves Me to Sleep Every Night)/The Devil Made Me Do That	1970	—	3.50	7.00
47-9977	Only a Woman Like You/Half the Love	1971	—	3.50	7.00
48-1010	I'm Gonna Act Right/Chained	1971	—	3.50	7.00
74-0163	Cut Across Shorty/Understand Little Man	1969	2.00	4.00	8.00
74-0238	Sweet Thang and Cisco/Son of a Bum	1969	2.00	4.00	8.00
74-0590	Forgive Me for Calling You Darling/He's Got the Whole World in His Hands	1971	—	3.50	7.00
74-0687	Is It Any Wonder That I Love You/Got It Comin' Day	1972	—	3.50	7.00
74-0761	Don't Pay the Ransom/There's Still You	1972	—	3.50	7.00
74-0879	Take Time to Love Her/Carry Me Back	1973	—	3.50	7.00
74-0973	I Used It All on You/I Know the Feelin'	1973	—	3.50	7.00

SIMS

Number	Title (A Side/B Side)	Yr	VG	VG+	NM
206	Leave the Door Open/Wills Crossing	1964	5.00	10.00	20.00

Albums

MCA

Number	Title (A Side/B Side)	Yr	VG	VG+	NM
2184	Independence	1976	3.00	6.00	12.00

PAULA

Number	Title (A Side/B Side)	Yr	VG	VG+	NM
LP-2192 [M]	Nat Stuckey Sings	1966	5.00	10.00	20.00
LPS-2192 [S]	Nat Stuckey Sings	1966	6.25	12.50	25.00
LP-2196 [M]	All My Tomorrows	1967	5.00	10.00	20.00
LPS-2196 [S]	All My Tomorrows	1967	6.25	12.50	25.00
LPS-2203	Country Favorites	1968	6.25	12.50	25.00

RCA CAMDEN

Number	Title (A Side/B Side)	Yr	VG	VG+	NM
ACL1-0780	In the Ghetto	1974	2.50	5.00	10.00

RCA VICTOR

Number	Title (A Side/B Side)	Yr	VG	VG+	NM
APD1-0080 [Q]	Take Time to Love Her/Used It All on You	1973	6.25	12.50	25.00

—"QuadraDisc"; may not exist in regular stereo

Number	Title (A Side/B Side)	Yr	VG	VG+	NM
APL1-0541	The Best of Nat Stuckey	1974	3.75	7.50	15.00
LSP-4090	Nat Stuckey Sings	1968	5.00	10.00	20.00
LSP-4123	Keep 'Em Country	1969	5.00	10.00	20.00
LSP-4226	New Country Roads	1969	5.00	10.00	20.00
LSP-4330	Old Man Willie	1970	3.75	7.50	15.00
LSP-4389	Country Fever	1970	3.75	7.50	15.00
LSP-4477	She Wakes Me with a Kiss Every Morning	1971	3.75	7.50	15.00
LSP-4559	Only a Woman Like You	1971	3.75	7.50	15.00
LSP-4635	Forgive Me for Calling You Darling	1972	3.75	7.50	15.00
LSP-4743	Is It Any Wonder That I Love You	1972	3.75	7.50	15.00

SUDDERTH, ANNA

45s

VERITE

Number	Title (A Side/B Side)	Yr	VG	VG+	NM
801	Not a Day Goes By/(B-side unknown)	1980	2.00	4.00	8.00

SULLIVAN, GENE

Also see WILEY AND GENE.

45s

COLUMBIA

Number	Title (A Side/B Side)	Yr	VG	VG+	NM
4-20902	Good Gosh Almighty/Walkin' and Talkin'	1952	6.25	12.50	25.00
4-20977	Would You Forgive Me/Inflated Love	1952	6.25	12.50	25.00
4-40971	Please Pass the Biscuits/Wash Your Feet Before Going to Bed	1957	3.75	7.50	15.00

SULLIVAN, PHIL

45s

STARDAY

Number	Title (A Side/B Side)	Yr	VG	VG+	NM
410	Love Never Dies/The Luckiest Man in Town	1958	5.00	10.00	20.00
437	Hearts Are Lonely/Rich Man — Po' Boy	1959	5.00	10.00	20.00
462	I Could Never Be Alone/You Get a Thrill	1959	5.00	10.00	20.00

SUMMER, SCOTT

45s

CON BRIO

Number	Title (A Side/B Side)	Yr	VG	VG+	NM
146	Flip Side of Today/I'm in Love	1979	—	2.50	5.00
152	I Don't Wanna Want You/Old Fashioned Lady	1979	—	2.50	5.00

SUN, JOE

45s

AMI

Number	Title (A Side/B Side)	Yr	VG	VG+	NM
1319	Bad for Me/(B-side unknown)	1984	—	2.50	5.00
1321	Why Would I Want to Forget/(B-side unknown)	1984	—	2.50	5.00
1324	West Texas Wind/(B-side unknown)	1985	—	2.50	5.00

ELEKTRA

Number	Title (A Side/B Side)	Yr	VG	VG+	NM
47229	Silent Night/Wings of My Victory	1981	—	2.50	5.00
47232 [DJ]	Silent Night/Oh Holy Night	1981	—	3.00	6.00

—B-side by Helen Cornelius

Number	Title (A Side/B Side)	Yr	VG	VG+	NM
47417	Holed Up in Some Honky Tonk/Boys in the Back of the Bus	1982	—	2.00	4.00
47467	Fraulein/I Ain't Honky Tonkin' No More	1982	—	2.00	4.00
69954	You Make Me Want to Sing/Midnight Train of Memories	1982	—	2.00	4.00

OVATION

Number	Title (A Side/B Side)	Yr	VG	VG+	NM
1107	Old Flames (Can't Hold a Candle to You)/I'll Find It Where I Can	1978	—	2.50	5.00
1117	High and Dry/Midnight Train of Memories	1978	—	2.50	5.00
1122	On Business for the King/Blue Ribbon Blues	1979	—	2.50	5.00
1127	I'd Rather Go On Hurtin'/I'm Still Crazy About You	1979	—	2.50	5.00
1137	Out of Your Mind/Mysteries of Life (My First Truckin' Song)	1979	—	2.50	5.00
1141	Shotgun Rider/Little Bit of Push	1980	—	2.50	5.00
1152	Bombed, Boozed and Busted/I'll Find It Where I Can	1980	—	2.50	5.00
1162	Ready for the Times to Get Better/Bottom Line	1980	—	2.50	5.00

Number	Title (A Side/B Side)	Yr	VG	VG+	NM
Albums					
ELEKTRA					
❑ 60010	I Ain't Honky Tonkin' No More	1982	2.00	4.00	8.00
OVATION					
❑ 1734	Old Flames	1978	2.50	5.00	10.00
❑ 1743	Out of Your Mind	1979	2.50	5.00	10.00
❑ 1755	Livin' on Honky Tonk Time	1980	2.50	5.00	10.00

SUNDOWN PLAYBOYS, THE

Number	Title (A Side/B Side)	Yr	VG	VG+	NM
45s					
APPLE					
❑ 1852	Saturday Night Special/Valse De Soleil Coucher	1972	3.75	7.50	15.00
GOLDBAND					
❑ 1073	Sundown Waltz/River Two Step	195?	7.50	15.00	30.00

SUNSHINE RUBY

Number	Title (A Side/B Side)	Yr	VG	VG+	NM
45s					
RCA VICTOR					
❑ 47-5250	Too Young to Tango/Hearts Weren't Meant to Be Broken	1953	5.00	10.00	20.00
❑ 47-5374	Datin'/Nobody Asked Me to Dance	1953	5.00	10.00	20.00
❑ 47-5467	Too Old for Toys/Little Girl Love	1953	5.00	10.00	20.00
❑ 47-5474	I Wanna Do Something for Santa Claus/Too Fat for the Chimney	1953	5.00	10.00	20.00
❑ 47-5582	I Got My First Kiss Last Night/That Ain't in Any Catalogue	1954	5.00	10.00	20.00
❑ 47-5806	I'm So Bashful/I Think He Winked at Me	1954	5.00	10.00	20.00
❑ 47-5931	My Daddy Has Two Sweethearts/I Don't Care What the General Said	1954	5.00	10.00	20.00

SUPER GRIT COWBOY BAND

Number	Title (A Side/B Side)	Yr	VG	VG+	NM
45s					
HOODSWAMP					
❑ 8002	If You Don't Know Me By Now/This Ol' Highway Song	1981	—	3.00	6.00
❑ 8003	Carolina by the Sea/Can't Play for Real	1981	—	3.00	6.00
❑ 8004	Semi Diesel Blues/Sweet Lady	1982	—	3.00	6.00
❑ 8005	She Is the Woman/Roar of the Crowd	1982	—	3.00	6.00
❑ 8006	I Bought the Shoes (That Just Walked Out on Me)/(B-side unknown)	1983	—	3.00	6.00

SUPERNAW, DOUG

Number	Title (A Side/B Side)	Yr	VG	VG+	NM
45s					
BNA					
❑ 62432	Honky Tonkin' Fool/You're Gonna Bring Back Cheatin' Songs	1993	—	—	3.00
❑ 62537	Reno/Daddy's Girl	1993	—	2.00	4.00
❑ 62638	I Don't Call Him Daddy/Honky Tonkin' Fool	1993	—	2.00	4.00
❑ 62757	Red and Rio Grande/Five Generations of Rock County Wilsons	1994	—	—	3.00
❑ 62851	State Fair/He Went to Paris	1994	—	—	3.00
❑ 62938	You Never Even Call Me By My Name/State Fair	1994	—	—	3.00
❑ 64214	What'll You Do About Me/Wishin' Her Well	1994	—	—	3.00
GIANT					
❑ 7-17687	She Never Looks Back/What in the World	1996	—	—	3.00
❑ 7-17764	Not Enough Hours in the Night/We're All Here	1995	—	—	3.00

SUTTON, GLENN

Number	Title (A Side/B Side)	Yr	VG	VG+	NM
45s					
EPIC					
❑ 5-10163	I Ain't Built That Way/Too Many Honky Tonks (Behind Her)	1967	2.50	5.00	10.00
MERCURY					
❑ 55052	The Football Card/The Ballad of the Blue Cyclone	1978	—	2.50	5.00
❑ 55056	Should Old Acquaintance Be Forgot/The Spaceship	1979	—	2.50	5.00
❑ 55064	Super Drunk/Under Pressure Like That	1979	—	2.50	5.00
❑ 57001	Red Neck Disco/Hip! Hip! Hooray for the U.S.A.	1979	—	2.50	5.00
❑ 57009	The Football Card/(B-side unknown)	1979	—	2.00	4.00
❑ 76188	Football Blues/The Football Card	1982	—	2.00	4.00
❑ 884563-7	Super Bowl Trip/Wild	1986	—	—	3.00
❑ 884974-7	I'll Go Steppin' Too/Hulk-A-Mania	1986	—	—	3.00
❑ 888544-7	I'm Gone This Time/Wild	1987	—	—	3.00
❑ 888564-7	Super Bowl Trip/T.V. Preacher Man Blues	1987	—	—	3.00
—B-side by Blue Water Dave					
MGM					
❑ 13273	Karate Sam/Fabulous Playboy Bill	1964	3.00	6.00	12.00
❑ 13333	Clarence, the Cross-Eyed Lion/Maurice the Police	1965	3.00	6.00	12.00
❑ 13352	Gee-Whopper/I Don't Wanna Go	1965	3.00	6.00	12.00
Albums					
MERCURY					
❑ SRM-1-5018	Close Encounters of the Sutton Kind	1979	2.50	5.00	10.00

SWAMPWATER

Number	Title (A Side/B Side)	Yr	VG	VG+	NM
45s					
KING					
❑ 6345	Louisiana Woman/River People	1971	2.00	4.00	8.00
❑ 6376	Take a City Bride/It's Your Game, Mary Jane	1971	2.00	4.00	8.00
RCA VICTOR					
❑ 74-0585	Ooh-Wee California/A Song I Heard	1971	—	3.50	7.00
Albums					
KING					
❑ KSD-1122	Swampwater	1971	3.75	7.50	15.00
RCA VICTOR					
❑ LSP-4572	Swampwater	1971	3.75	7.50	15.00

SWAN, BILLY

Number	Title (A Side/B Side)	Yr	VG	VG+	NM
45s					
A&M					
❑ 2046	Hello! Remember Me/Never Go Lookin' Again	1978	—	2.00	4.00
❑ 2103	No Way Around It (It's Love)/Forever in Your Love	1978	—	2.00	4.00
COLUMBIA					
❑ 10443	Shake, Rattle and Roll/I Got It for You	1976	—	2.00	4.00
❑ 10486	Swept Away/California Song (For Malibu)	1977	—	2.00	4.00
EPIC					
❑ 02196	I'm Into Lovin' You/Not Far from Forty	1981	—	—	3.00
❑ 02601	Stuck Right in the Middle of Your Love/Soft Touch	1981	—	—	3.00
❑ 02841	With Their Kind of Money and Our Kind of Love/Lay Down and Love Me Tonight	1982	—	—	3.00
❑ 03226	Your Picture Still Loves Me (And I Still Love You)/Give Your Lovin' to Me	1982	—	—	3.00
❑ 03505	Rainbows and Butterflies/Only Be You	1982	—	—	3.00
❑ 03917	Yes/I Can't Stop Writing Love Songs	1983	—	—	3.00
❑ 51000	Do I Have to Draw a Picture/I Want to Change Your Life	1981	—	—	3.00
MERCURY					
❑ 884668-7	You Must Be Lookin' for Me/Three Chord Rock & Roll	1986	—	—	3.00
❑ 888320-7	I'm Gonna Get You/Three Chord Rock & Roll	1987	—	—	3.00
MGM					
❑ 14008	El Paso/The Sweet Sound of Your Name	1968	2.50	5.00	10.00
MONUMENT					
❑ 940	Breakin' Up/Out of Her System	1966	3.00	6.00	12.00
❑ 988	I've Got to Have You/Below Average Everyday Girl	1966	3.00	6.00	12.00
❑ 8597	Wedding Bells/P.M.S.	1974	—	2.50	5.00
❑ 8621	I Can Help/The Ways of a Woman in Love	1974	—	2.50	5.00
❑ 8641	I'm Her Fool/I'd Like to Work for You	1975	—	2.00	4.00
❑ 8651	Come By/Woman Handled My Mind	1975	—	2.00	4.00
❑ 8661	Everything's the Same (Ain't Nothing Changed)/Overnite Thing (Usually)	1975	—	2.00	4.00
❑ 8682	Just Want to Taste Your Wine/Love You Baby to the Bone	1976	—	2.00	4.00
❑ 8697	Vanessa/Number 1	1976	—	2.00	4.00
❑ 8706	You're the One/Mr. Misery	1976	—	2.00	4.00
❑ 45275	Don't Be Cruel/Vanessa	1979	—	2.00	4.00
RISING SONS					
❑ 702	Friendship/You Got Me Laughing	1967	2.50	5.00	10.00
Albums					
A&M					
❑ SP-4686	You're OK, I'm OK	1978	2.50	5.00	10.00
COLUMBIA					
❑ PZ 33279	I Can Help	1977	2.00	4.00	8.00
—Reissue of Monument 33279					
❑ PZ 33805	Rock 'n' Roll Moon	1977	2.00	4.00	8.00
—Reissue of Monument 33805					
❑ PZ 34183	Billy Swan	1977	2.00	4.00	8.00
—Reissue of Monument 34183					
❑ PC 34473	Four	1977	2.50	5.00	10.00
EPIC					
❑ FE 37079	I'm Into Lovin' You	1981	2.50	5.00	10.00
MONUMENT					
❑ 7629	Billy Swan At His Best	1978	2.50	5.00	10.00
❑ KZ 33279	I Can Help	1974	2.50	5.00	10.00
❑ PZ 33805	Rock 'n' Roll Moon	1975	2.50	5.00	10.00
❑ PZ 34183	Billy Swan	1976	2.50	5.00	10.00

SWEAT, ISAAC PAYTON

Number	Title (A Side/B Side)	Yr	VG	VG+	NM
45s					
BELLAIRE					
❑ 5047	Goodbye Motor City/National Chili Anthem	1979	—	3.00	6.00
❑ 5081	Cotton Eyed Joe (Modest Version)/Cotton Eyed Joe (B.S. Version)	1980	—	3.00	6.00
❑ 5082	Home Is Anywhere You Hang Your Hat/Schottische	1980	—	3.00	6.00
❑ 5086	Jole Blon/I Could Never Pass a Honky Tonk	1980	—	3.00	6.00
❑ 5122	Shed So Many Tears/All This Ol' Wailin'	198?	—	2.00	4.00
GUSTO					
❑ 9010	Shed So Many Tears/All This Ol' Wailin'	1978	—	2.50	5.00
PAID					
❑ 137	Cotton Eyed Joe (The Modest Version)/Cotton Eyed Joe (B.S. Version)	1981	—	2.50	5.00
❑ 138	Walkin' Slowly/Little Foot and Hokey Pokey and Bunny Hop	1981	—	2.50	5.00
❑ 152	A Hangover Sure Hangs On/Say It's Not You	1982	—	2.50	5.00
Albums					
BELLAIRE					
❑ LP 1100	Cotton Eyed Joe/Shottish	1980	3.00	6.00	12.00
PAID					
❑ 2005	Cotton-Eyed Joe	1981	3.00	6.00	12.00

SWEET, RACHEL

Best known as a new wave/pop singer, she actually began her recording career as a preteen country singer.

12-Inch Singles

MCA

Number	Title (A Side/B Side)	Yr	VG	VG+	NM
❑ 17513 [DJ]	(Theme from) Hairspray (same on both sides)	1988	2.00	4.00	8.00

45s

COLUMBIA

Number	Title (A Side/B Side)	Yr	VG	VG+	NM
❑ 38-03411	Voo Doo/American Girl	1982	—	2.00	4.00
❑ 38-68580	Life Ain't Worth Living (When You're Dead)/ Romance (Love Theme from "Sing")	1989	—	2.00	4.00

—B-side by Paul Carrack and Terri Nunn

DERRICK

Number	Title (A Side/B Side)	Yr	VG	VG+	NM
❑ 0117	Any Port in a Storm/(B-side unknown)	197?	—	3.00	6.00
❑ 1000	We Live in Two Different Worlds/Paper Airplane	1976	—	3.00	6.00

MCA

Number	Title (A Side/B Side)	Yr	VG	VG+	NM
❑ 53303	(Theme from) Hairspray/Hairspray (Instrumental)	1988	—	2.00	4.00

STIFF/COLUMBIA

Number	Title (A Side/B Side)	Yr	VG	VG+	NM
❑ 02537	Then He Kissed Me/Be My Baby//Streetheart	1981	—	2.00	4.00
❑ 11052	I Go to Pieces/Suspended Animation	1979	—	2.50	5.00
❑ 11100	B-A-B-Y/Stranger in the House	1979	—	2.50	5.00
❑ 11245	Lover's Lane/Take Good Care of Me	1980	—	2.50	5.00
❑ 11272	Spellbound/Tonight	1980	—	2.50	5.00
❑ 11314	Lover's Lane/Tonight Ricky	1980	—	2.50	5.00

Albums

COLUMBIA

Number	Title (A Side/B Side)	Yr	VG	VG+	NM
❑ FC 38342	Blame It on Love	1982	2.50	5.00	10.00

STIFF/COLUMBIA

Number	Title (A Side/B Side)	Yr	VG	VG+	NM
❑ JC 36101	Fool Around	1979	3.00	6.00	12.00
❑ NJC 36337	Protect the Innocent	1980	2.50	5.00	10.00
❑ ARC 37077	...And Then He Kissed Me	1981	2.50	5.00	10.00

SWEET, RACHEL, AND REX ALLEN

45s

STIFF/COLUMBIA

Number	Title (A Side/B Side)	Yr	VG	VG+	NM
❑ 02169	Everlasting Love//Still Thinking of You/Billy and the Gun	1981	—	2.00	4.00

—B-side features one song each by Rex Allen and Rachel Sweet

Number	Title (A Side/B Side)	Yr	VG	VG+	NM
❑ 02169 [PS]	Everlasting Love//Still Thinking of You/Billy and the Gun	1981	—	2.50	5.00
❑ 02169 [PS]	Everlasting Love	1981	2.00	4.00	8.00

—"Demonstration -- Not for Sale" on rear

SWEETHEARTS OF THE RODEO

45s

COLUMBIA

Number	Title (A Side/B Side)	Yr	VG	VG+	NM
❑ 38-05824	Hey Doll Baby/Everywhere I Turn	1986	—	—	3.00
❑ 38-05824 [PS]	Hey Doll Baby/Everywhere I Turn	1986	—	2.50	5.00
❑ 38-06166	Since I Found You/Chosen Few	1986	—	—	3.00
❑ 38-06525	Midnight Girl/Sunset Town//I Can't Resist	1986	—	—	3.00
❑ 38-07023	Chains of Gold/Gotta Get Away	1987	—	—	3.00
❑ 38-07314	Gotta Get Away/Since I Found You	1987	—	—	3.00
❑ 38-07757	Satisfy You/One Time, One Night	1988	—	—	3.00
❑ 38-07985	Blue to the Bone/You Never Talk Sweet	1988	—	—	3.00
❑ 38-08504	I Feel Fine/Until I Stop Dancing	1988	—	—	3.00
❑ 38-68684	If I Never See Midnight Again/Gone Again	1989	—	—	3.00
❑ 38-73213	This Heart/So Sad (To Watch Good Love Go Bad)	1989	—	—	3.00
❑ 38-73360	Como Se Dice (I Love You)/I Don't Want You to Know	1990	—	2.00	4.00
❑ 38-73475	Hard Road to Go/What It Does to Me	1990	—	2.00	4.00
❑ 38-73907	Heard-Headed Man/Sisters	1991	—	2.00	4.00
❑ 38-74064	Devil and Your Deep Blue Eyes/Be Good to Me	1991	—	2.00	4.00

Albums

COLUMBIA

Number	Title (A Side/B Side)	Yr	VG	VG+	NM
❑ B6C 40406	Sweethearts of the Rodeo	1986	2.00	4.00	8.00
❑ FC 40614	One Time, One Night	1988	2.00	4.00	8.00

SWEETWATER

No relation to the late 1960s band of the same name that played at Woodstock. Also see DARRELL HOLT.

45s

FAUCET

Number	Title (A Side/B Side)	Yr	VG	VG+	NM
❑ 1592	I'd Throw It All Away/Antioch Church House Choir	1981	—	3.00	6.00

SWING SHIFT BAND, THE

Also see RAY PENNINGTON.

45s

STEP ONE

Number	Title (A Side/B Side)	Yr	VG	VG+	NM
❑ 392	(Turn Me Loose and) Let Me Swing/Loose Tights	1988	—	2.00	4.00

SYLVIA

Not to be confused with the Sylvia who had a hit pop and R&B single with "Pillow Talk" in 1973.

12-Inch Singles

RCA

Number	Title (A Side/B Side)	Yr	VG	VG+	NM
❑ PD-12303	Heart on the Mend/Rainbow Rider	1981	2.00	4.00	8.00

45s

RCA

Number	Title (A Side/B Side)	Yr	VG	VG+	NM
❑ 5127-7-R	Straight from My Heart/Makes You Wanna Slow Down	1987	—	—	3.00
❑ PB-11735	You Don't Miss a Thing/Cry Baby Cry	1979	—	2.00	4.00
❑ PB-11958	It Don't Hurt to Dream/No News Is Good News	1980	—	2.00	4.00
❑ PB-12077	Tumbleweed/Anytime, Anyplace	1980	—	2.00	4.00
❑ PB-12164	Drifter/Missin' You	1981	—	2.00	4.00
❑ PB-12164 [PS]	Drifter/Missin' You	1981	—	2.50	5.00
❑ PB-12214	The Matador/Cry Baby Cry	1981	—	2.00	4.00
❑ PB-12214 [PS]	The Matador/Cry Baby Cry	1981	—	2.50	5.00
❑ PB-12302	Heart on the Mend/Rainbow Rider	1981	—	2.00	4.00
❑ GB-12312	Drifter/Tumbleweed	1981	—	—	3.00

—"Gold Standard Series" reissue

Number	Title (A Side/B Side)	Yr	VG	VG+	NM
❑ PB-13020	Sweet Yesterday/I Feel Cheated	1981	—	2.00	4.00
❑ PB-13223	Nobody/I'll Make It Right with You	1982	—	—	3.00
❑ PB-13330	Like Nothing Ever Happened/Drifter	1982	—	—	3.00
❑ GB-13490	Nobody/Like Nothing Ever Happened	1983	—	—	3.00

—"Gold Standard Series" reissue

Number	Title (A Side/B Side)	Yr	VG	VG+	NM
❑ PB-13501	Snapshot/Tonight I'm Gettin' Friendly with the Blues	1983	—	—	3.00
❑ PB-13589	The Boy Gets Around/Who's Kidding Who	1983	—	—	3.00
❑ PB-13689	I Never Quite Got Back (From Loving You)/So Complete	1983	—	—	3.00
❑ PB-13755	Victims of Goodbye/Unguarded Moments	1984	—	—	3.00
❑ PB-13755 [PS]	Victims of Goodbye/Unguarded Moments	1984	—	2.00	4.00
❑ PB-13838	Love Over Old Times/I Just Don't Have the Heart	1984	—	—	3.00
❑ PB-13997	Fallin' in Love/True Blue	1985	—	—	3.00
❑ PB-14107	Cry Just a Little Bit/Only the Shadow Knows	1985	—	—	3.00
❑ PB-14375	Nothin' Ventured Nothin' Gained/Come to Me	1986	—	—	3.00

Albums

RCA

Number	Title (A Side/B Side)	Yr	VG	VG+	NM
❑ 5618-1-R	Greatest Hits	1987	2.00	4.00	8.00

RCA VICTOR

Number	Title (A Side/B Side)	Yr	VG	VG+	NM
❑ AHL1-3986	Drifter	1981	2.00	4.00	8.00
❑ AHL1-4312	Just Sylvia	1982	2.00	4.00	8.00
❑ AHL1-4672	Snapshot	1983	2.00	4.00	8.00
❑ AHL1-4960	Surprise	1984	2.00	4.00	8.00
❑ AYL1-5154	Drifter	1984	—	3.00	6.00

—"Best Buy Series" reissue

Number	Title (A Side/B Side)	Yr	VG	VG+	NM
❑ AHL1-5413	One Step Closer	1985	2.00	4.00	8.00
❑ AYL1-5439	Snapshot	1985	—	3.00	6.00

—"Best Buy Series" reissue

Number	Title (A Side/B Side)	Yr	VG	VG+	NM
❑ AYL1-7045	Surprise	1985	—	3.00	6.00

—"Best Buy Series" reissue

SYLVIA AND MICHAEL JOHNSON

Also see each artist's individual listings.

45s

RCA

Number	Title (A Side/B Side)	Yr	VG	VG+	NM
❑ PB-14217	I Love You by Heart/Eyes Like Mine	1985	—	—	3.00

SYLVIE AND HER SILVER DOLLAR BAND

45s

PLAYBACK

Number	Title (A Side/B Side)	Yr	VG	VG+	NM
❑ 75711	Where You Gonna Hang Your Hat/Warm Like a Fire	1989	—	3.00	6.00

T

TACKETT, MARLOW

45s

KARI

Number	Title (A Side/B Side)	Yr	VG	VG+	NM
❑ 114	Ride That Bull (Big Bertha)/Would You Know Love	1980	—	3.00	6.00

PALACE

Number	Title (A Side/B Side)	Yr	VG	VG+	NM
❑ 1006	Would You Know Love/South Bound Train	1979	2.00	4.00	8.00
❑ 1008	Midnight Fire/(B-side unknown)	1980	2.00	4.00	8.00

RCA

Number	Title (A Side/B Side)	Yr	VG	VG+	NM
❑ PB-13255	Ever-Lovin' Woman/Hang In There Teardrop	1982	—	2.00	4.00
❑ PB-13347	634-5789/She Couldn't Take It Anymore	1982	—	2.00	4.00
❑ PB-13471	I Know My Way to You by Heart/Big Old Teardrops	1983	—	2.00	4.00
❑ PB-13579	I Spent the Night in the Heart of Texas/Way Back When	1983	—	2.00	4.00

TAFF, RUSS

45s

A&M

Number	Title (A Side/B Side)	Yr	VG	VG+	NM
❑ 3004	Walk Between Lines/Shake	1988	—	2.50	5.00

HORIZON

Number	Title (A Side/B Side)	Yr	VG	VG+	NM
❑ 2744	I'm Not Alone/Silent Love	1985	—	2.50	5.00
❑ 2910	I'm Not Alone/Come Too Far	1987	—	2.50	5.00

MYRRH

Number	Title (A Side/B Side)	Yr	VG	VG+	NM
❑ 29	Pure in Heart/(B-side unknown)	1983	—	3.00	6.00
❑ 9016	Here I Am/God Only Knows	1985	—	3.00	6.00
❑ 9062	I'm Not Alone/Not Gonna Bow	1986	—	3.00	6.00

REPRISE

Number	Title (A Side/B Side)	Yr	VG	VG+	NM
❑ 7-17801	Bein' Happy/Heart Like Yours	1995	—	—	3.00
❑ 7-17918	One and Only Love/Home to You	1995	—	—	3.00
❑ 7-18029	Love Is Not a Thing/Once in a Lifetime	1994	—	—	3.00

TAFF, RUSS

Albums

HORIZON

Number	Title (A Side/B Side)	Yr	VG	VG+	NM
❑ SP-671	Russ Taff	198?	3.00	6.00	12.00
❑ SP-751	Medals	198?	3.00	6.00	12.00

MYRRH

Number	Title (A Side/B Side)	Yr	VG	VG+	NM
❑ MSB-6706	Walls of Glass	1983	3.00	6.00	12.00
❑ 701-679206-4	Medals	1985	3.00	6.00	12.00

TALBERT, BUBBA

45s

RANGER

Number	Title (A Side/B Side)	Yr	VG	VG+	NM
❑ 702	Downright Broke My Heart/(B-side unknown)	1983	—	3.00	6.00
❑ 5734	Easy Catch/Where Do We Go from Here?	1983	—	3.00	6.00
❑ 5734 [PS]	Easy Catch/Where Do We Go from Here?	1983	2.00	4.00	8.00

TALL, TOM

Also see GINNY WRIGHT.

45s

CHART

Number	Title (A Side/B Side)	Yr	VG	VG+	NM
❑ 1085	Walk Tall/Eyes Look Away	1964	2.50	5.00	10.00
❑ 1170	I Want You/In the Shadows of the Night	1965	2.50	5.00	10.00
—With Ginny Wright					
❑ 1225	Gravy Train/I've Seen Enough	1965	2.50	5.00	10.00
❑ 1305	Hill Above the City/Eyes Look Away	1966	2.50	5.00	10.00
❑ 1370	Bad, Bad Tuesday/A Little Miracle	1966	2.50	5.00	10.00
❑ 5195	Sugar in the Flowers/Bluegrass Valley	1973	—	3.50	7.00
❑ 5205	The La La Song/Reassuring Love	1974	—	3.50	7.00

CREST

Number	Title (A Side/B Side)	Yr	VG	VG+	NM
❑ 1038	Stack-a-Records/Mary Jo	1957	25.00	50.00	100.00
❑ 1052	High School Love/To Be Alone	1958	7.50	15.00	30.00

DECCA

Number	Title (A Side/B Side)	Yr	VG	VG+	NM
❑ 31151	The Fool's Side of Me/Was It Easy	1960	3.75	7.50	15.00
❑ 31240	One Thing's Wrong/You Call Everybody Darlin'	1961	3.75	7.50	15.00

FABOR

Number	Title (A Side/B Side)	Yr	VG	VG+	NM
❑ 108	Please Be Careful/I Gave My Heart to Two People	1954	7.50	15.00	30.00
❑ 115	I Want to Walk with You/You Loved Another One Better	1954	7.50	15.00	30.00
❑ 123	Underway/Goldie Jo Malone	1955	7.50	15.00	30.00
❑ 125	Give Me a Chance/Remembering You	1955	7.50	15.00	30.00
❑ 132	Hot Rod Is Her Name/Why Must I Wonder	1956	10.00	20.00	40.00
❑ 139	Don't You Know/If You Know What	1956	6.25	12.50	25.00
—With Ruckus Tyler					

PETAL

Number	Title (A Side/B Side)	Yr	VG	VG+	NM
❑ 1210	Bad, Bad Tuesday/Oohin' and Aahin'	1963	3.75	7.50	15.00

SAGE

Number	Title (A Side/B Side)	Yr	VG	VG+	NM
❑ 305	Three Walls/This Ireland	1959	5.00	10.00	20.00

SCORPION

Number	Title (A Side/B Side)	Yr	VG	VG+	NM
❑ 0501	Do the Wrong Again with Me/Daddy Wasn't There	197?	—	3.00	6.00

TALLEY, JAMES

45s

ATLANTIC

Number	Title (A Side/B Side)	Yr	VG	VG+	NM
❑ 2835	One Last Child/Mississippi River Whistle	1971	2.00	4.00	8.00

CAPITOL

Number	Title (A Side/B Side)	Yr	VG	VG+	NM
❑ 4112	W. Lee O'Daniel and the Light Crust Dough Boys/To Get Back Home	1975	—	2.50	5.00
❑ 4170	Red River Memory/No Opener Needed	1975	—	2.50	5.00
❑ 4218	Tryin' Like the Devil/Nothin' But the Blues	1976	—	2.50	5.00
❑ 4297	Are They Gonna Make Us Outlaws Again/Forty Hours	1976	—	2.50	5.00
❑ 4341	Sometimes I Think About Suzanne/Daddy's Song	1976	—	2.50	5.00
❑ 4410	Alabama Summertime/When the Fiddler Packs His Case	1977	—	2.50	5.00

Albums

CAPITOL

Number	Title (A Side/B Side)	Yr	VG	VG+	NM
❑ ST-11416	Got No Bread, No Milk, No Money, But We Sure Got a Lot of Love	1975	3.00	6.00	12.00
❑ ST-11494	Tryin' Like the Devil	1976	2.50	5.00	10.00
❑ ST-11605	Blackjack Choir	1977	2.50	5.00	10.00
❑ ST-11695	Ain't It Somethin'	1977	2.50	5.00	10.00

TALMADGE, BILLY

45s

DECCA

Number	Title (A Side/B Side)	Yr	VG	VG+	NM
❑ 9-46397	'Tis Sweet to Be Remembered/I Made a Mistake	1952	6.25	12.50	25.00

TAMMY JO

45s

RIDGETOP

Number	Title (A Side/B Side)	Yr	VG	VG+	NM
❑ 00880	I Go to Pieces/Don't Be Angry	1980	—	2.50	5.00
❑ 00980	Love Talking/Wishing Well	1980	—	2.50	5.00
❑ 1180	It'll Be Love/If I Had a Heart	1980	—	2.50	5.00

TANGO, CHARLIE

45s

MCA

Number	Title (A Side/B Side)	Yr	VG	VG+	NM
❑ 40688	He Ain't Country/Honky Tonk Song	1977	—	3.00	6.00
❑ 40827	In the Heart of Dixie/Honky Tonkin' Nights	1977	—	2.50	5.00

TANNER, FARGO

45s

AVCO

Number	Title (A Side/B Side)	Yr	VG	VG+	NM
❑ 612	Don't Drop It/I Go Crazy (But I Can't Let You Go)	1975	—	3.00	6.00

TAPP, DEMETRISS

45s

ABC

Number	Title (A Side/B Side)	Yr	VG	VG+	NM
❑ 11115	How Could He Do This to Me/Love Will Come Your Way	1968	2.50	5.00	10.00
❑ 11160	Ordinary Man/What Did Sister Do	1968	2.50	5.00	10.00
❑ 11201	Strain on My Heart/I'm All Alone Again	1969	2.00	4.00	8.00
❑ 11362	Love Me/I'm Missing You	1973	—	3.00	6.00
❑ 11383	Skinny Dippin'/Just Let Me Make Believe	1973	—	3.00	6.00
❑ 11401	Ain't You Gettin' Tired of Us, God/Takin' His Love Away from Me	1973	—	3.00	6.00

AVI

Number	Title (A Side/B Side)	Yr	VG	VG+	NM
❑ 297	Power of Love/Let It Come In	198?	—	2.50	5.00

BRUNSWICK

Number	Title (A Side/B Side)	Yr	VG	VG+	NM
❑ 55251	If You Find Love/Lipstick Paint a Smile on Me	1963	3.75	7.50	15.00
❑ 55257	Let Go of My Heart/Is This the Beginning of the End	1964	3.75	7.50	15.00
❑ 55264	What Kind of Girl/I Turn Blue	1964	3.75	7.50	15.00
❑ 55274	Ring Dang Doo/Little Girl Lost	1964	5.00	10.00	20.00

COLUMBIA

Number	Title (A Side/B Side)	Yr	VG	VG+	NM
❑ 4-42362	Am I the Keeper/Another Victory	1962	3.75	7.50	15.00
❑ 4-42603	It Isn't the End of the World/Act Your Age	1962	3.75	7.50	15.00

MONUMENT

Number	Title (A Side/B Side)	Yr	VG	VG+	NM
❑ 908	The First Word/I'm in Love with You	1965	3.75	7.50	15.00

TATE, MICHAEL

45s

OAK

Number	Title (A Side/B Side)	Yr	VG	VG+	NM
❑ 47102	Mexican Girl/True Love	1981	—	3.00	6.00

TAYLOR, CARMOL

45s

ELEKTRA

Number	Title (A Side/B Side)	Yr	VG	VG+	NM
❑ 45255	Back in the U.S.A./I'd Like to Sleep Til I Get Over You	1975	—	2.50	5.00
❑ 45277	Who Will I Be Loving Now/So Fine	1975	—	2.50	5.00
❑ 45299	Play the Saddest Song on the Jukebox/I'd Like to Sleep Til I Get Over You	1976	—	2.50	5.00
❑ 45312	I Really Had a Ball Last Night/Good Cheatin' Songs	1976	—	2.50	5.00
❑ 45342	That Little Difference/Love What's Left of Me	1976	—	2.50	5.00
❑ 45366	What Would I Do Then?/You're Looking at a Happy Man	1976	—	2.50	5.00
❑ 45367	Neon Women/Crying Steel Guitar	1976	—	2.50	5.00
—With Stella Parton					
❑ 45409	Good Cheatin' Songs/I Don't Want My Country Funky	1977	—	2.50	5.00
❑ 45446	Roll Over Beethoven/You're Looking at a Happy Man	1977	—	2.50	5.00

EPIC

Number	Title (A Side/B Side)	Yr	VG	VG+	NM
❑ 5-10615	Mama, Take Me Home/Someday I'll Leave You	1970	2.00	4.00	8.00
❑ 5-10803	Kiss the Baby/Standing in the Need of Love	1971	—	3.50	7.00

Albums

ELEKTRA

Number	Title (A Side/B Side)	Yr	VG	VG+	NM
❑ 7E-1069	Song Writer	1976	3.00	6.00	12.00

TAYLOR, CHET

45s

VISTA

Number	Title (A Side/B Side)	Yr	VG	VG+	NM
❑ 108	Barefoot Angel/Bet My Soul	1979	—	3.00	6.00

Albums

BRYLEN

Number	Title (A Side/B Side)	Yr	VG	VG+	NM
❑ BN-4408	Pretty Words	1982	2.50	5.00	10.00

TAYLOR, CHIP

45s

BUDDAH

Number	Title (A Side/B Side)	Yr	VG	VG+	NM
❑ 325	Angel of the Morning/(B-side unknown)	1972	—	3.00	6.00
❑ 344	Londonderry Company/(B-side unknown)	1973	—	3.00	6.00

CAPITOL

Number	Title (A Side/B Side)	Yr	VG	VG+	NM
❑ 4692	Saint Sebastian/One Night Out with the Boys	1979	—	2.00	4.00
❑ 4840	Stealin' Each Other Blind/He Ain't Makin' Music Anymore	1980	—	2.00	4.00

COLUMBIA

Number	Title (A Side/B Side)	Yr	VG	VG+	NM
❑ 10446	Hello Atlanta/Farmer's Daughter	1976	—	2.00	4.00
❑ 10520	Three Younger Bandits/Nothing Like You Girl	1977	—	2.00	4.00
❑ 44736	It's Such a Lonely Time of the Year/(B-side unknown)	1968	3.00	6.00	12.00

EPIC

Number	Title (A Side/B Side)	Yr	VG	VG+	NM
❑ 10567	It's Such a Lonely Time of Year/(Instrumental)	1969	2.50	5.00	10.00

MALA

Number	Title (A Side/B Side)	Yr	VG	VG+	NM
❑ 476	On My World/Joanie's Blues	1964	3.00	6.00	12.00
❑ 489	Suzannah (Comin' Home to Louisiana)/(B-side unknown)	1964	3.00	6.00	12.00
❑ 507	Young Love/Betty Ann	1965	2.50	5.00	10.00

MGM

Number	Title (A Side/B Side)	Yr	VG	VG+	NM
❑ 12993	Foolin' Around/Innocent Eyes	1961	5.00	10.00	20.00
❑ 13040	If You Don't Want Me Now/Sad Songs	1961	5.00	10.00	20.00

WARNER BROS.

Number	Title (A Side/B Side)	Yr	VG	VG+	NM
❑ 5314	Here I Am/I Love You But I Know	1962	3.75	7.50	15.00
❑ 5333	Lucky Star/A Guy Don't Need a Lot of Time	1963	3.75	7.50	15.00
❑ 8050	Me As I Am/Comin' From Behind	1974	—	2.00	4.00
❑ 8090	Early Sunday Morning/Shickshinny	1975	—	2.00	4.00

Number	Title (A Side/B Side)	Yr	VG	VG+	NM
❑ 8128	Big River/John Tucker's On the Wagon Again	1975	—	2.00	4.00
❑ 8159	Circle of Tears/You're Alright, Charlie	1975	—	2.00	4.00

Albums

BUDDAH

Number	Title	Yr	VG	VG+	NM
❑ BDS-5118	Gasoline	1972	3.00	6.00	12.00

CAPITOL

Number	Title	Yr	VG	VG+	NM
❑ ST-11909	Saint Sebastian	1979	2.50	5.00	10.00

COLUMBIA

Number	Title	Yr	VG	VG+	NM
❑ KC 34345	Somebody Shoot	1977	2.50	5.00	10.00

WARNER BROS.

Number	Title	Yr	VG	VG+	NM
❑ BS 2718	Last Chance	1973	3.00	6.00	12.00
❑ BS 2824	Some of Us	1974	3.00	6.00	12.00

TAYLOR, FRANK

45s

CHART ACTION

Number	Title	Yr	VG	VG+	NM
❑ 113	If You Were on Trial for Loving Me/Nobody's Darlin' But Mine	196?	5.00	10.00	20.00
❑ 117	Countryfied/Most of All	196?	5.00	10.00	20.00
❑ 801	Diesel on My Tail/Live and Let Live	196?	3.75	7.50	15.00

PARKWAY

Number	Title	Yr	VG	VG+	NM
❑ 869	Snow White Cloud/Send Her Back to Me	1963	3.75	7.50	15.00

TAYLOR, JAMES

Not a country artist, but he did have three charted country hits as a solo artist (the B-side of 10557 and the A-side of the other two), listed below. Also see CARLY SIMON; RICKY SKAGGS.

45s

COLUMBIA

Number	Title	Yr	VG	VG+	NM
❑ 05681	Everyday/Limousine Driver	1985	—	—	3.00
❑ 05681 [PS]	Everyday/Limousine Driver	1985	—	2.00	4.00
❑ 05785	Only One/Mona	1986	—	—	3.00
❑ 05785 [PS]	Only One/Mona	1986	—	—	3.00
❑ 10557	Handy Man/Bartender's Blues	1977	—	2.00	4.00

TAYLOR, JIM

45s

CHECKMATE

Number	Title	Yr	VG	VG+	NM
❑ 3069	I'll Still Need You Mary Ann/I'm Still Waiting for You	1978	—	3.50	7.00
❑ 3106	Leave It to Love/Too Many Tears Have Fallen	1978	—	3.50	7.00

TAYLOR, JUDY

45s

WARNER BROS.

Number	Title	Yr	VG	VG+	NM
❑ 29913	The End of the World/He Picked Me Up When You Let Me Down	1982	—	2.00	4.00
❑ 49859	A Married Man/I Wish That I Could Hurt That Way Again	1981	—	2.00	4.00
❑ 50061	A Step in the Right Direction/He Picked Me Up When You Let Me Down	1982	—	2.00	4.00

TAYLOR, KAREN

See KAREN TAYLOR-GOOD.

TAYLOR, LES

Also see SHELBY LYNNE.

45s

EPIC

Number	Title	Yr	VG	VG+	NM
❑ 34-73063	Coulda, Shoulda, Woulda Loved You/A Southern Breeze	1989	—	—	3.00
❑ 34-73264	Knowin' You Were Leavin'/A Southern Breeze	1990	—	—	3.00
❑ 34-73449	Every Time I Think It's Over/Shoulda, Coulda, Woulda Loved You	1990	—	—	3.00
❑ 34-73712	I Gotta Mind to Go Crazy/For the Rest of Your Life	1991	—	—	3.00

TAYLOR, LIVINGSTON, WITH LEAH KUNKEL

Neither of these singers are country, but they teamed up to make the country charts with the below record.

45s

CRITIQUE

Number	Title	Yr	VG	VG+	NM
❑ 99275	Loving Arms (Country Version)/Loving Arms (Pop Version)	1988	—	2.00	4.00
❑ 99275 [PS]	Loving Arms (Country Version)/Loving Arms (Pop Version)	1988	—	2.00	4.00

TAYLOR, MARY

Also see ROY CLARK.

45s

CAPITOL

Number	Title	Yr	VG	VG+	NM
❑ 5210	Please Don't Tell Them About Me/Johnny's Not the Only Boy	1964	2.00	4.00	8.00
❑ 5484	Finders Keepers/Before He Was Yours, He Was Mine	1965	2.00	4.00	8.00
❑ 5582	I'm Gonna Slip Around on You/Today Is Not the Day	1966	2.00	4.00	8.00
❑ 5776	Don't Waste Your Time/We Fooled 'Em Again	1966	2.00	4.00	8.00

DOT

Number	Title	Yr	VG	VG+	NM
❑ 17104	If I Don't Like the Way You Love Me/It Takes So Many	1968	—	3.50	7.00
❑ 17168	Feed Me One More Lie/I'll Be Better Off	1968	—	3.50	7.00
❑ 17225	Alexander/The Bridge I Tried to Burn	1969	—	3.50	7.00
❑ 17356	I'm a Honky Tonk Girl/He Used Me	1970	—	3.50	7.00

Albums

DOT

Number	Title	Yr	VG	VG+	NM
❑ DLP-25987	Mary Taylor's Very First Album	1971	3.00	6.00	12.00

TAYLOR, R. DEAN

A staff writer and sometime performer at Motown in the late 1960s and early 1970s ("Indiana Wants Me" was his pop hit), he made the country charts with the below single.

45s

STRUMMER

Number	Title	Yr	VG	VG+	NM
❑ 3748	Let's Talk It Over/(B-side unknown)	1982	—	3.00	6.00

TAYLOR, SHEILA

45s

MELODYLAND

Number	Title	Yr	VG	VG+	NM
❑ 6013	How Important Can It Be/She Satisfies	1975	—	2.50	5.00

TAYLOR-GOOD, KAREN

45s

MESA

Number	Title	Yr	VG	VG+	NM
❑ 1111	Diamond in the Rough/Doesn't Daddy Love Me Anymore	1982	—	2.50	5.00
—As "Karen Taylor"					
❑ 1112	Country Boy's Song/One Man Woman	1982	—	2.50	5.00
—As "Karen Taylor"					
❑ 1113	I'd Rather Be Doing Nothing with You/Sinking Kind of Feeling	1982	—	2.50	5.00
❑ 1114	Tenderness Place/When the Churchbell Stops Ringing	1983	—	2.50	5.00
❑ 1115	Don't Call Me/Begging of You	1983	—	2.50	5.00
❑ 1116	Handsome Man/Welcome to My World	1983	—	2.50	5.00
❑ 1117	We Just Gotta Dance/I'd Rather Be Doing Nothing with You	1984	—	2.50	5.00
❑ 1118	Starlite/Words Are Cheap	1985	—	2.50	5.00
❑ 1119	Up on Your Love/Afraid to Go to Sleep	1985	—	2.50	5.00
❑ 2011	Come On Planet Earth (Are You Listenin')/(B-side unknown)	1986	—	2.50	5.00

Albums

MESA

Number	Title	Yr	VG	VG+	NM
❑ 1111	Karen	1984	3.00	6.00	12.00

TEEL, LEO

45s

DECCA

Number	Title	Yr	VG	VG+	NM
❑ 9-46336	Fertilizer/He's Gazing at Daisy Boots Now	1951	6.25	12.50	25.00

TENNESSEANS, THE

Members of this group later joined SWEETWATER and MATTHEWS, WRIGHT AND KING.

45s

CAPITOL

Number	Title	Yr	VG	VG+	NM
❑ 4645	Nineteen Sixty-Something Songwriter of the Year/I Can Heal You	1978	—	2.50	5.00

TENNESSEE ERNIE

See TENNESSEE ERNIE FORD.

TENNESSEE EXPRESS

45s

RCA

Number	Title	Yr	VG	VG+	NM
❑ PB-12277	Big Like a River/Now	1981	—	2.00	4.00
❑ PB-12362	Little Things/How Much I Love You	1981	—	2.00	4.00
❑ PB-13078	The Arms of a Stranger/Someone Just Like You	1982	—	2.00	4.00
❑ PB-13265	Operator/Let Me In and Let Me Love You	1982	—	2.00	4.00
❑ PB-13423	How Long Will It Take/Lead Me Into Love	1983	—	2.00	4.00
❑ PB-13526	Cotton Fields/Good for Nothing	1983	—	2.00	4.00

TENNESSEE PULLEYBONE

45s

JMI

Number	Title	Yr	VG	VG+	NM
❑ 15	Good Time Charlie's Got the Blues/I Ain't in a Long, Long Time	1973	—	3.00	6.00
❑ 25	The Door's Always Open/Swinging Doors	1973	—	3.00	6.00
❑ 39	Clean Your Own Tables/May First	1974	—	3.00	6.00

TENNESSEE VALLEY BOYS, THE

Also see WALLY FOWLER.

45s

NASHWOOD

Number	Title	Yr	VG	VG+	NM
❑ 12684	Lo and Behold/It's Gonna Take Time	1984	2.00	4.00	8.00

TERRY, AL

45s

FEATURE

Number	Title	Yr	VG	VG+	NM
❑ 1061	I Wonder If I Can Lose the Blues This Way/Walking and Crying with the Blues	1953	12.50	25.00	50.00
❑ 1075	Say a Prayer for Me/I Nearly Made a Fool of My Heart	1953	12.50	25.00	50.00
❑ 1079	Will Christmas Be a Happy Day for Me/Santa Claus Is On His Way	1953	12.50	25.00	50.00
❑ 2000	You're Worse Than a Tramp/Please Think of Me	1954	12.50	25.00	50.00

HICKORY

Number	Title	Yr	VG	VG+	NM
❑ 1003	Good Deal, Lucille/Say a Prayer for Me	1954	10.00	20.00	40.00
❑ 1012	House of Glass/Show Me That You Love Me	1954	7.50	15.00	30.00
❑ 1017	Hey Whatta Y'Say/Let's Postpone Our Wedding	1954	10.00	20.00	40.00
❑ 1022	The Wall Around My Heart/Hate Me Not	1955	7.50	15.00	30.00

Number	Title (A Side/B Side)	Yr	VG	VG+	NM
❑ 1029	Gone Again/No No John	1955	7.50	15.00	30.00
❑ 1037	Goodbye Mr. Sunshine/I Love Her So	1955	7.50	15.00	30.00
❑ 1041	Not Anymore/We Make a Lovely Couple	1956	7.50	15.00	30.00
—With Wilma Lee (Cooper)					
❑ 1045	Follow Me/Lesson of Love	1956	7.50	15.00	30.00
❑ 1049	No Shrimp Today/Without You	1956	7.50	15.00	30.00
❑ 1056	Am I Seeing Things/Roughneck Blues	1956	7.50	15.00	30.00
❑ 1061	Money/If I Win, I Win	1957	7.50	15.00	30.00
—B-side by Rusty & Doug (Kershaw)					
❑ 1066	It's What You Are to Me/Last Date	1957	7.50	15.00	30.00
❑ 1071	Coconut Girl/Bring Me Some Rain	1957	7.50	15.00	30.00
❑ 1075	Good Deal, Lucille/Because I'm Yours	1958	7.50	15.00	30.00
❑ 1082	I'm Not the Girl/It's Just As Well	1958	7.50	15.00	30.00
—With Wilma Lee (Cooper)					
❑ 1088	My Baby Knows/Your Sweet Lies	1958	7.50	15.00	30.00
❑ 1093	It's Better Late Than Never/Then You're Living Just Like Me	1958	7.50	15.00	30.00
❑ 1111	Watch Dog/Passing the Blues Around	1960	6.25	12.50	25.00
INDEX					
❑ 5025	I've Been Losing You/I Saw the Enemy Today	196?	2.50	5.00	10.00
❑ 5026	Today's Another Day (Like Tomorrow)/Bourbon Street Parade	196?	2.50	5.00	10.00
❑ 5027	Only the Hangman (Gold in the Mountain)/Not Anymore	196?	2.50	5.00	10.00
—A-side with Bob Terry					
❑ 5029	I'm Beginning to Forget You/Hurricane Party	196?	2.50	5.00	10.00
Selected 78s					
FEATURE					
❑ 1003	I've Grown Lonesome for You/I Guess I'll Have to Face It All Alone	1949	7.50	15.00	30.00
❑ 1017	H-A-D-A-C-O-L/My Heart Cries Out with Pain	1949	7.50	15.00	30.00
❑ 1029	Better Late Than Never/I Really Tried	1950	7.50	15.00	30.00
❑ 1052	God Was So Good (When He Let Me Keep You)/How Can It Be	195?	6.25	12.50	25.00
❑ 1055	What Can I Do/I'm a Honky Tonkin' Man	195?	6.25	12.50	25.00
Albums					
INDEX					
❑ 5001	This Is Al Terry	196?	3.75	7.50	15.00

TERRY, GORDON

Number	Title (A Side/B Side)	Yr	VG	VG+	NM
45s					
CADENCE					
❑ 1316	Service with a Smile/Johnson's Old Gray Mule	1957	5.00	10.00	20.00
❑ 1317	Orange Blossom Special/Black Mountain Rag	1957	5.00	10.00	20.00
❑ 1334	Wild Honey/Run Little Joey	1957	5.00	10.00	20.00
❑ 1343	If You Don't Know It/I Lost Her	1958	5.00	10.00	20.00
CAPITOL					
❑ 2792	The Ballad of J.C./Untanglin' My Mind	1970	—	3.50	7.00
❑ 3092	The Hole/He'll Have to Go	1971	—	3.50	7.00
CHART					
❑ 1014	Easy Way Out/Togetherness	1967	2.50	5.00	10.00
❑ 1030	Baby Gets All Her Lovin' from Me/That's What Tears Me Up	1968	2.50	5.00	10.00
❑ 1049	Holding Trouble/A Little Bit	1968	2.50	5.00	10.00
❑ 5005	Charlie's Pride/Vision of Blindness	1969	2.00	4.00	8.00
❑ 5028	The Ballad of Biggersville/Day of the Gun	1969	2.00	4.00	8.00
COLUMBIA					
❑ 4-21484	You'll Regret/Hook, Line and Sinker	1956	5.00	10.00	20.00
❑ 4-21544	Keep Right On Talking/Maybe	1956	5.00	10.00	20.00
LIBERTY					
❑ 55500	Wild Honey/For Old Times' Sake	1962	3.00	6.00	12.00
❑ 55533	I Wish I'd Said That/In a Moment	1963	3.00	6.00	12.00
❑ 55558	Most of All/We've Got a Lot in Common	1963	3.00	6.00	12.00
❑ 55630	Sitting Just One Car from You/Almost Gone	1963	3.00	6.00	12.00
PLANTATION					
❑ 146	Orange Blossom Special/Smoking Violin	1977	—	2.50	5.00
❑ 156	Disco Mule/Tennessee Waltz	1977	—	2.50	5.00
RCA VICTOR					
❑ 47-7428	It Ain't Right/The Saddest Day	1958	5.00	10.00	20.00
❑ 47-7632	A Lotta Lotta Woman/Lonely Road	1959	10.00	20.00	40.00
❑ 47-7741	Trouble on the Turnpike/Almost Alone	1960	3.75	7.50	15.00
❑ 47-7788	Gonna Go Down to the River/When They Ring Those Wedding Bells	1960	3.75	7.50	15.00
❑ 47-7875	And Then I Heard the Bad News/I Had a Talk with Me	1961	3.75	7.50	15.00
❑ 47-7944	You Remembered Me/How My Baby Can Love	1961	3.75	7.50	15.00
❑ 47-7989	Long Black Limousine/Wild Desire	1962	3.75	7.50	15.00
Albums					
LIBERTY					
❑ LRP-3218 [M]	Liberty Square Dance Club	1962	5.00	10.00	20.00
—With calls					
❑ LRP-3219 [M]	Liberty Square Dance Club	1962	5.00	10.00	20.00
—Without calls					
PLANTATION					
❑ 514	Disco Country	1977	3.00	6.00	12.00

TEXAS PLAYBOYS, THE

Also see BOB WILLS.

Number	Title (A Side/B Side)	Yr	VG	VG+	NM
45s					
CAPITOL					
❑ 4332	Ida Red/Don't Let the Deal Go Down	1976	—	2.50	5.00
❑ 4401	Gambling Polka Dot Blues/Osage Stomp	1977	—	2.50	5.00
❑ 4437	Bring It On Down to My House/Lily Dale	1977	—	2.50	5.00
RIC					
❑ 163	I'll See You to the Door/Someday I'll Sober Up	1965	3.00	6.00	12.00
❑ 182	Footsteps to Nowhere/Livin', Laughin', and Lovin'	1966	3.00	6.00	12.00
Albums					
CAPITOL					
❑ ST-11612	Today	1977	3.75	7.50	15.00
❑ ST-11725	Live and Kickin'	1978	3.75	7.50	15.00

TEXAS RANGERS, THE

Number	Title (A Side/B Side)	Yr	VG	VG+	NM
Albums					
CUMBERLAND					
❑ MGC-29507 [M]	The Best of Western Swing	1963	5.00	10.00	20.00
❑ SRC-69505 [S]	The Best of Western Swing	1963	6.25	12.50	25.00

TEXAS TORNADOS, THE

Also see FREDDY FENDER; DOUG SAHM.

Number	Title (A Side/B Side)	Yr	VG	VG+	NM
12-Inch Singles					
REPRISE					
❑ PRO-A-8580 [DJ]	Little Bit Is Better Than Nada (The Cibola Mixes) (3 versions)	1996	2.50	5.00	10.00
45s					
REPRISE					
❑ 7-17587	Little Bit Is Better Than Nada/Amor	1996	—	2.00	4.00
❑ 7-18571	Guacamole/Hangin' On by a Thread	1993	—	2.50	5.00
❑ 7-19155	Is Anybody Goin' to San Antone/La Mucura	1992	—	2.50	5.00
❑ 7-19244	Adios Mexico/Rosa de Amor	1992	—	2.50	5.00
❑ 7-19516	A Man Can Cry/(Hey Baby) Que Paso	1990	—	2.50	5.00
❑ 7-19787	Who Were You Thinkin' Of/Soy de San Luis	1990	—	2.50	5.00

TEXAS TROUBADOURS, THE

Backing group for ERNEST TUBB.

Number	Title (A Side/B Side)	Yr	VG	VG+	NM
45s					
DECCA					
❑ 31627	Honey Love/Last Letter	1964	2.50	5.00	10.00
❑ 31699	Pan Handle Rag/Rhodes-Bud Boogie	1964	2.50	5.00	10.00
❑ 31770	Cain's Corner/Honky Tonks and You	1965	2.50	5.00	10.00
❑ 31837	Highway Man/Leon's Guitar Boogie	1965	2.50	5.00	10.00
❑ 32065	E.T. Blues/Walking the Floor Over You	1966	2.50	5.00	10.00
❑ 32121	Gardenia Waltz/Honey Fingers	1967	2.50	5.00	10.00
❑ 32185	Almost to Tulsa/Oklahoma Hills	1967	2.50	5.00	10.00
❑ 32587	Ridgetop Stomp/Jamming with C & C	1969	2.50	5.00	10.00
Albums					
DECCA					
❑ DL 4459 [M]	The Texas Troubadours	1964	6.25	12.50	25.00
❑ DL 4644 [M]	Country Dance Time	1965	5.00	10.00	20.00
❑ DL 4745 [M]	Ernest Tubb's Fabulous Texas Troubadours	1966	5.00	10.00	20.00
❑ DL 74459 [S]	The Texas Troubadours	1964	7.50	15.00	30.00
❑ DL 74644 [S]	Country Dance Time	1965	6.25	12.50	25.00
❑ DL 74745 [S]	Ernest Tubb's Fabulous Texas Troubadours	1966	6.25	12.50	25.00
❑ DL 75017	The Terrific Texas Troubadours and Guests	1968	5.00	10.00	20.00

TEXAS VOCAL COMPANY

Number	Title (A Side/B Side)	Yr	VG	VG+	NM
45s					
RCA					
❑ PB-13338	Why Did You Have to Be So Good/Didn't We Love	1982	—	2.00	4.00
❑ JK-13504 [DJ]	Two Hearts (same on both sides)	1983	2.50	5.00	10.00
—Promo only on green vinyl					
❑ PB-13504	Two Hearts/You Did It Again	1983	—	2.00	4.00
❑ JK-13566 [DJ]	It Had to Be You (same on both sides)	1983	2.50	5.00	10.00
—Promo only on yellow vinyl					
❑ PB-13566	It Had to Be You/Backsliding	1983	—	2.00	4.00

THOMAS, B.J.

His first charted country hit wasn't until 1975, but his country roots run deep. For example, he had the first really big hit version (on the pop charts, in 1966) of Hank Williams' "I'm So Lonesome I Could Cry." So we've chosen not to be selective.

Number	Title (A Side/B Side)	Yr	VG	VG+	NM
45s					
ABC					
❑ 12054	(Hey, Won't You Play) Another Somebody Done Somebody Wrong Song/City Blues	1974	—	2.00	4.00
❑ 12121	We Are Happy Together/Help Me Make It (To My Rockin' Chair)	1975	—	2.00	4.00
BRAGG					
❑ 103	Billy and Sue/Never Tell	1964	5.00	10.00	20.00
CLEVELAND INT'L.					
❑ 03492	Whatever Happened to Old Fashioned Love/I Just Sing	1983	—	2.00	4.00
❑ 04608	From This Moment On/The Girl Most Likely To	1984	—	2.00	4.00
COLUMBIA					
❑ 03985	New Looks from an Old Lover/You Keep the Man in Me Happy	1983	—	2.00	4.00
❑ 04237	Two Car Garage/Beautiful World	1983	—	2.00	4.00
❑ 04431	The Whole World's in Love When You're Lonely/We're Here to Love	1984	—	—	3.00
❑ 04531	Rock and Roll Shoes/Then I'll Be Over You	1984	—	—	3.00
—Ray Charles and B.J. Thomas					
❑ 05647	A Part of Me That Needs You Most/Northern Lights	1985	—	—	3.00
❑ 05771	America Is/Broken Toys	1986	—	—	3.00
❑ 05771 [PS]	America Is/Broken Toys	1986	—	2.00	4.00
❑ 06314	Night Life/Make the World Go Away	1986	—	—	3.00
HICKORY					
❑ 1395	Billy and Sue/Never Tell	1966	2.50	5.00	10.00

Number	Title (A Side/B Side)	Yr	VG	VG+	NM
LORI					
❑ 9547	I've Got a Feeling/Hey Judy	1963	6.25	12.50	25.00
❑ 9561	For Your Precious Love/Here I Am Again	1964	6.25	12.50	25.00
MCA					
❑ 40735	Don't Worry Baby/My Love	1977	—	2.00	4.00
❑ 40812	Still the Lovin' Is Fun/Play Me a Little Traveling Music	1977	—	2.00	4.00
❑ 40854	Everybody Loves a Rain Song/Dusty Roads	1978	—	2.00	4.00
❑ 40914	Sweet Young America/Aloha	1978	—	2.00	4.00
❑ 40986	We Could Have Been the Closest of Friends/In My Heart	1979	—	2.00	4.00
❑ 41134	God Bless the Children/On This Christmas Night	1979	—	2.00	4.00
❑ 41134 [PS]	God Bless the Children/On This Christmas Night	1979	—	2.50	5.00
❑ 41207	Nothin' Could Be Better/Walkin' on a Cloud	1980	—	2.00	4.00
❑ 41281	Everything Always Works Out for the Best/No Limit	1980	—	2.00	4.00
❑ 51087	Some Love Songs Never Die/There Ain't No Love	1981	—	2.00	4.00
❑ 51151	The Lovin' Kind/I Recall a Gypsy Woman	1981	—	2.00	4.00
❑ 52053	I Really Got the Feeling/But Love Me	1982	—	2.00	4.00
MYRRH					
❑ 166	Home Where I Belong/Hallelujah	1977	—	2.50	5.00
❑ 176	Without a Doubt/(B-side unknown)	1977	—	2.50	5.00
❑ 234	Uncloudy Day/(B-side unknown)	1981	—	2.50	5.00
PACEMAKER					
❑ 227	I'm So Lonesome I Could Cry/Candy Baby	1964	5.00	10.00	20.00
❑ 231	Mama/Wendy	1965	3.75	7.50	15.00
❑ 234	Bring Back the Time/I Don't Have a Mind of My Own	1965	3.75	7.50	15.00
❑ 239	Tomorrow Never Comes/Your Tears Leave Me Cold	1965	3.75	7.50	15.00
❑ 247	Plain Jane/My Home Town	1965	3.75	7.50	15.00
❑ 253	I'm Not a Fool Anymore/Baby Cried	1965	3.75	7.50	15.00
❑ 256	I Can't Help It (If I'm Still in Love with You)/Baby Cried	1965	3.75	7.50	15.00
❑ 259	Pretty Country Girl/Houston Town	1965	3.75	7.50	15.00
PARAMOUNT					
❑ 0218	Songs/Goodbye's a Long, Long Time	1973	—	2.50	5.00
❑ 0218 [PS]	Songs/Goodbye's a Long, Long Time	1973	—	3.00	6.00
❑ 0239	Sunday Sunrise/Talkin' Confidentially	1973	—	2.50	5.00
❑ 0239	Sunday Sunrise/Early Morning Rush	1973	—	2.50	5.00
❑ 0277	Play Something Sweet (Brickyard Blues)/Talkin' Confidentially	1974	—	2.50	5.00
REPRISE					
❑ 22837	Don't Leave Love (Out There All Alone)/One Woman	1989	—	—	3.00
SCEPTER					
❑ 12129	I'm So Lonesome I Could Cry/Candy Baby	1966	2.50	5.00	10.00
❑ 12139	Mama/Wendy	1966	2.00	4.00	8.00
❑ 12154	Bring Back the Time/I Don't Have a Mind of My Own	1966	2.00	4.00	8.00
❑ 12165	Tomorrow Never Comes/Your Tears Leave Me Cold	1966	2.00	4.00	8.00
❑ 12179	Plain Jane/My Home Town	1966	2.00	4.00	8.00
❑ 12194	I Can't Help It (If I'm Still in Love with You)/Baby Cried	1967	2.00	4.00	8.00
❑ 12200	Just the Wisdom of a Fool/Treasure of Love	1967	2.00	4.00	8.00
❑ 12201	Wisdom of a Fool/Human	1967	2.00	4.00	8.00
❑ 12205	The Girl Can't Help It/Walkin' Back	1967	2.00	4.00	8.00
❑ 12219	The Eyes of a New York Woman/I May Never Get to Heaven	1968	2.00	4.00	8.00
❑ 12230	Hooked on a Feeling/I've Been Down This Road Before	1968	2.00	4.00	8.00
❑ 12244	It's Only Love/You Don't Love Me Anymore	1969	—	3.00	6.00
❑ 12255	Pass the Apple Eve/Fairy Tale of Time	1969	—	3.00	6.00
❑ 12259	You Don't Love Me Anymore/Skip a Rope	1969	—	3.00	6.00
❑ 12265	Raindrops Keep Fallin' on My Head/Never Had It So Good	1969	—	3.50	7.00
❑ 12277	Everybody's Out of Town/Living Again	1970	—	3.00	6.00
❑ 12283	I Just Can't Help Believing/Send My Picture to Scranton, Pa.	1970	—	3.00	6.00
❑ 12299	Most of All/The Mask	1970	—	2.50	5.00
❑ 12307	No Love at All/Have a Heart	1971	—	2.50	5.00
❑ 12320	Mighty Clouds of Joy/Life	1971	—	2.50	5.00
❑ 12335	Long Ago Tomorrow/Burnin' a Hole in My Mind	1971	—	2.50	5.00
❑ 12344	Rock and Roll Lullaby/Are We Losing Touch	1972	—	3.00	6.00
❑ 12354	That's What Friends Are For/I Get Enthused	1972	—	2.50	5.00
❑ 12364	Happier Than the Morning Sun/We Have Got to Get Out Ship Together	1972	—	2.50	5.00
❑ 12379	Sweet Cherry Wine/Roads	1973	—	2.50	5.00
VALERIE					
❑ 226	I've Got a Feeling/Hey Judy	1963	5.00	10.00	20.00
WARNER BROS.					
❑ 5491	Billy and Sue/Never Tell	1964	5.00	10.00	20.00
Albums					
ABC					
❑ ABCD-858	Reunion	1975	2.50	5.00	10.00
❑ ABCD-912	Help Me Make It to My Rockin' Chair	1976	2.50	5.00	10.00
ACCORD					
❑ SN-7106	Lovin' You	198?	2.50	5.00	10.00
BUCKBOARD					
❑ 1023	B.J. Thomas Sings Hank Williams and Other Favorites	198?	2.50	5.00	10.00
CLEVELAND INT'L.					
❑ FC 38561	New Looks	1983	2.50	5.00	10.00
❑ PC 38561	New Looks	1984	2.00	4.00	8.00
—Budget-line reissue					
❑ FC 39111	The Great American Dream	1983	2.50	5.00	10.00
❑ PC 39111	The Great American Dream	1984	2.00	4.00	8.00
—Budget-line reissue					
❑ FC 39337	Shining	1984	2.50	5.00	10.00
❑ FC 40157	Throwing Rocks at the Moon	1985	2.50	5.00	10.00
COLUMBIA					
❑ PC 38400	Love Shines	1984	2.00	4.00	8.00
—Reissue of Priority 38400					
❑ PC 40148	All Is Calm, All Is Bright...	1985	2.50	5.00	10.00
❑ FC 40496	Night Life	1986	2.50	5.00	10.00
DORAL					
❑ (# unknown)	Doral Presents B.J. Thomas	1971	5.00	10.00	20.00
—Mail-order promotion from Doral cigarettes					
EVEREST					
❑ 4104	Golden Greats	1981	2.50	5.00	10.00
HICKORY					
❑ LPM-133 [M]	The Very Best of B.J. Thomas	1966	5.00	10.00	20.00
❑ LPS-133 [S]	The Very Best of B.J. Thomas	1966	6.25	12.50	25.00
❑ ST 90956 [S]	The Very Best of B.J. Thomas	1966	7.50	15.00	30.00
—Capitol Record Club edition					
❑ T 90956 [M]	The Very Best of B.J. Thomas	1966	6.25	12.50	25.00
—Capitol Record Club edition					
MCA					
❑ 746	Everybody Loves a Rain Song	1980	2.00	4.00	8.00
—Budget-line reissue					
❑ 2286	B.J. Thomas	1977	2.50	5.00	10.00
❑ 3035	Everybody Loves a Rain Song	1978	2.50	5.00	10.00
❑ 3231	For the Best	1979	2.50	5.00	10.00
❑ 5155	In Concert	1980	2.50	5.00	10.00
❑ 5195	Some Love Songs Never Die	1980	2.50	5.00	10.00
❑ 5296	As We Know Him	1982	2.50	5.00	10.00
❑ 27032	In Concert	198?	2.00	4.00	8.00
—Reissue of MCA 5155					
MYRRH					
❑ MSB-6574	Home Where I Belong	1978	2.50	5.00	10.00
❑ MSB-6593	A Happy Man	1979	2.50	5.00	10.00
❑ MSB-6633	You Gave Me Love	1979	2.50	5.00	10.00
❑ MSB-6653	The Best of B.J. Thomas	1980	2.50	5.00	10.00
❑ MSB-6675	Amazing Grace	1981	2.50	5.00	10.00
❑ MSB-6705	Miracle	1983	2.50	5.00	10.00
❑ MSB-6710	Peace in the Valley	1983	2.50	5.00	10.00
❑ MSB-6725	The Best of B.J. Thomas, Volume 2	1984	2.50	5.00	10.00
❑ WR-8153	Peace in the Valley	1985	2.50	5.00	10.00
—Reissue of 6710					
❑ WR-8200	Amazing Grace	1985	2.00	4.00	8.00
—Reissue of 6675					
PACEMAKER					
❑ PLP-3001 [M]	B.J. Thomas and the Triumphs	1965	50.00	100.00	200.00
PAIR					
❑ PDL2-1099 [(2)]	Greatest Hits	1986	3.00	6.00	12.00
PARAMOUNT					
❑ PAS 1020	Longhorns & Londonbridges	1974	3.00	6.00	12.00
❑ PAS-6052	B.J. Thomas Songs	1973	3.00	6.00	12.00
PICKWICK					
❑ SPC-3623	The Best of B.J. Thomas	197?	2.50	5.00	10.00
PRIORITY					
❑ JU 38400	Love Shines	1982	2.50	5.00	10.00
REPRISE					
❑ 25898	Midnight Minute	1989	3.00	6.00	12.00
SCEPTER					
❑ SPS-535 [S]	I'm So Lonesome I Could Cry	1966	6.25	12.50	25.00
❑ SRM-535 [M]	I'm So Lonesome I Could Cry	1966	5.00	10.00	20.00
❑ SPS-556 [S]	Tomorrow Never Comes	1966	5.00	10.00	20.00
❑ SRM-556 [M]	Tomorrow Never Comes	1966	3.75	7.50	15.00
❑ SPS-561 [S]	For Lovers and Losers	1967	3.75	7.50	15.00
❑ SRM-561 [M]	For Lovers and Losers	1967	5.00	10.00	20.00
❑ SPS-570	On My Way	1968	3.75	7.50	15.00
❑ SPS-576	Young and In Love	1969	3.75	7.50	15.00
❑ SPS-578	Greatest Hits, Volume 1	1969	3.00	6.00	12.00
❑ SPS-580	Raindrops Keep Fallin' on My Head	1970	3.00	6.00	12.00
—Remixed version; trail-off wax number on Side 1 is "SPS-580-A-1C" and on Side 2 is "SPS-580-B-1C"					
❑ SPS-580	Raindrops Keep Fallin' on My Head	1970	3.75	7.50	15.00
—Original "muddy mix"; trail-off wax number on Side 1 is "SPS-580-A-1B" and on Side 2 is "SPS-580-B-1A"					
❑ SPS-582	Everybody's Out of Town	1970	3.00	6.00	12.00
❑ SPS-586	Most of All	1970	3.00	6.00	12.00
❑ SPS-597	Greatest Hits, Volume Two	1971	3.00	6.00	12.00
❑ 5101	Billy Joe Thomas	1972	3.00	6.00	12.00
❑ 5108	B.J. Thomas Country	1972	3.00	6.00	12.00
❑ 5112 [(2)]	Greatest All-Time Hits	1973	3.75	7.50	15.00
STARDAY					
❑ 992	The Best of B.J. Thomas	197?	2.50	5.00	10.00
UNITED ARTISTS					
❑ UA-LA389-E	The Very Best of B.J. Thomas	1974	3.00	6.00	12.00

THOMAS, DARRELL

45s

Number	Title (A Side/B Side)	Yr	VG	VG+	NM
OZARK OPRY					
❑ 101	Waylon, Sing to Mama/The Conquered King	1979	2.00	4.00	8.00

THOMAS, DICK

45s

DECCA

Number	Title (A Side/B Side)	Yr	VG	VG+	NM
❑ 9-46229	One Man's Loss Is Another Man's Gain/You Better Stop	1950	7.50	15.00	30.00
❑ 9-46301	I'm Trying/Esmereldy	1951	6.25	12.50	25.00

Selected 78s

DECCA

Number	Title (A Side/B Side)	Yr	VG	VG+	NM
❑ 46114	Rosalinda/Can't You Take It Back and Change It for a Boy	1948	3.75	7.50	15.00
❑ 46118	Roses Have Thorns/My Guitar Is My Sweetheart	1948	3.75	7.50	15.00
❑ 46127	Born to Lose/When My Blue Moon Turns to Gold Again	1948	3.75	7.50	15.00
❑ 46132	The Beaut from Butte/Two Car Garage	1948	3.75	7.50	15.00
❑ 46141	Memories of France/My Daddy Is Only a Picture	1948	3.75	7.50	15.00
❑ 46147	The Sister of Sioux City Sue/Charlotte Belle (Carolina Waltz)	1949	3.75	7.50	15.00
❑ 46156	Sleepy Old Town/Give Me Back My Heart	1949	3.75	7.50	15.00
❑ 46163	Swiss Lullaby/Queen of the Poconos	1949	3.75	7.50	15.00
❑ 46191	Tennessee Local/Foolish Tears	1949	3.75	7.50	15.00

NATIONAL

Number	Title (A Side/B Side)	Yr	VG	VG+	NM
❑ 5001	You Never Loved Me/Broken Heart	194?	6.25	12.50	25.00
❑ 5002	Cowboy in Shaki/San Antonio Serenade	194?	5.00	10.00	20.00
❑ 5003	Down in Old Wyoming/If Memories Were Money	194?	5.00	10.00	20.00
❑ 5004	Never Take Texas Out of Me/To My Sweetheart	194?	5.00	10.00	20.00
❑ 5005	I'll Love You/Don't Want a Million Sweethearts	194?	5.00	10.00	20.00
❑ 5006	The Buds Begin to Blossom/Make Me Happy	1945	5.00	10.00	20.00
❑ 5007	Sioux City Sue/Tumbling Tumbleweeds	1945	5.00	10.00	20.00
❑ 5008	Honestly/Halfway to Montana	1945	5.00	10.00	20.00
❑ 5009	Ridin' 'Neath the Arizona Moon/Weary Nights and Broken Dreams	1946	5.00	10.00	20.00
❑ 5010	Some Day, Darlin'/Sioux City Sue	1946	3.75	7.50	15.00
❑ 5011	Can;t Get Back Too Soon to Tucson/Moanin' in the Mornin'	1946	3.75	7.50	15.00
❑ 5012	Ragtime Cowboy from Santa Fe/Sleepy Head	1946	3.75	7.50	15.00
❑ 5013	I've Got a Gal in Laramee/Gonna Dry Up My Tears	1947	3.75	7.50	15.00
❑ 5014	Rose of the Alamo/Lonely Cowboy's Dream	1947	3.75	7.50	15.00

THOMAS, GENE

Also see GENE AND DEBBE.

45s

HICKORY

Number	Title (A Side/B Side)	Yr	VG	VG+	NM
❑ 1592	Babe, I Wish You Well/Listen Buddy	1971	—	3.50	7.00
❑ 1608	Lay It Down/Remembered by Someone	1971	—	3.50	7.00
❑ 1631	Touch Something Good/Watching It Go	1972	—	3.50	7.00

UNITED ARTISTS

Number	Title (A Side/B Side)	Yr	VG	VG+	NM
❑ 583	Peace of Mind/The Puppet	1963	3.00	6.00	12.00
❑ 584	Baby's Gone/Stand By Love	1963	—	—	—
—Canceled					
❑ 640	Baby's Gone/Stand By Love	1963	3.00	6.00	12.00
❑ 725	The Last Song/Bobby and the Boys	1964	2.50	5.00	10.00
❑ 771	Playing Those Old Records/Together Again	1964	2.50	5.00	10.00
❑ 799	Half the Time/I'd Rather Not Talk About It	1964	2.50	5.00	10.00
❑ 871	Down the Road/It's a Sad World	1965	2.50	5.00	10.00

VENUS

Number	Title (A Side/B Side)	Yr	VG	VG+	NM
❑ 1439	Sometime/Every Night	1961	7.50	15.00	30.00
❑ 1441	Lamp of Love/Two Lips	1961	5.00	10.00	20.00
❑ 1444	Down the Road/(B-side unknown)	1962	20.00	40.00	80.00

THOMAS, JEFF

45s

REVOLVER

Number	Title (A Side/B Side)	Yr	VG	VG+	NM
❑ 012	Footloose (And Not So Fancy Free)/(B-side unknown)	1986	—	2.50	5.00
❑ 014	Hollywood's Dream/(B-side unknown)	1986	—	2.50	5.00

THOMPSON, HANK

45s

ABC

Number	Title (A Side/B Side)	Yr	VG	VG+	NM
❑ 12409	I'm Just Gettin' By/I Hear the South Callin' Me	1978	—	2.50	5.00
❑ 12447	Dance with Me Molly/Point of No Return	1979	—	2.50	5.00

ABC DOT

Number	Title (A Side/B Side)	Yr	VG	VG+	NM
❑ 17535	Mama Don't 'Low/Wait a Little Longer Baby	1974	—	3.00	6.00
❑ 17556	That's Just My Truckin' Luck/After You Have Made Me Over	1975	—	3.00	6.00
❑ 17583	Mona Lisa/Too Young	1975	—	3.00	6.00
❑ 17612	Asphalt Cowboy/Fifteen Miles to Clarksville	1976	—	3.00	6.00
❑ 17649	Big Band Days/Forgive Me	1976	—	3.00	6.00
❑ 17673	Honky Tonk Girl/Another Shot of Today	1976	—	3.00	6.00
❑ 17695	Just an Old Flame/Don't Get Around Much Anymore	1977	—	3.00	6.00

CAPITOL

Number	Title (A Side/B Side)	Yr	VG	VG+	NM
❑ F876	All That Goes Up Must Come Down/Standing on the Outside	1950	7.50	15.00	30.00
❑ F1016	Take a Look at This Broken Heart/She's a Girl Without a Sweetheart	1950	7.50	15.00	30.00
❑ F1113	Humpty Dumpty Heart/California Women	1950	6.25	12.50	25.00
❑ F1114	Soft Lips/Give a Little, Take a Little	1950	6.25	12.50	25.00
❑ F1115	Whoa Sailor/Today	1950	6.25	12.50	25.00
❑ F1116	Swing Wide/Tomorrow Night	1950	6.25	12.50	25.00
❑ F1117	Second Hand Gal/Don't Flirt with Me	1950	6.25	12.50	25.00
❑ F1118	Green Light/Mary Had a Little Lamb	1950	6.25	12.50	25.00
❑ F1119	The Grass Looks Greener/Rock in the Ocean	1950	6.25	12.50	25.00
❑ F1120	My Front Door Is Open/A Cat Has Nine Lives	1950	6.25	12.50	25.00
❑ F1121	I Find You Cheatin' on Me/You Remembered Me	1950	6.25	12.50	25.00
❑ F1163	When God Calls His Children Home/I Can't Feel at Home	1950	7.50	15.00	30.00
❑ F1198	Humpty Dumpty Boogie/Daddy Blues	1950	7.50	15.00	30.00
❑ F1327	A Broken Heart and a Glass of Beer/If I Cry	1950	7.50	15.00	30.00
❑ F1379	New Roving Gambler/Playin' Possum	1951	6.25	12.50	25.00
❑ F1444	Where Is Your Heart Tonight/Those Things Money Can't Buy	1951	6.25	12.50	25.00
❑ F1528	I Ain't Crying Over You/Hangover Heart	1951	6.25	12.50	25.00
❑ F1632	Humpty Dumpty Heart/Green Light	1951	5.00	10.00	20.00
—Reissue of hit A-sides from 1948					
❑ F1745	Love Thief/How Do You Feel	1951	6.25	12.50	25.00
❑ F1870	Teardrops on the Tea Leaves/I'll Be Your Sweetheart	1951	6.25	12.50	25.00
❑ F1942	The Wild Side of Life/Cryin' in the Deep Blue Sea	1952	6.25	12.50	25.00
❑ F2063	Waiting in the Lobby of Your Heart/Don't Make Me Cry Again	1952	6.25	12.50	25.00
❑ F2169	How Cold Hearted Can You Get/It's Better to Have Loved a Little	1952	6.25	12.50	25.00
❑ F2178	Whoa Sailor/Mary Had a Little Lamb	1952	5.00	10.00	20.00
❑ F2269	The New Wears Off Too Fast/You're Walking on My Heart	1952	6.25	12.50	25.00
❑ F2377	No Help Wanted/I'd Have Never Found Somebody New	1953	6.25	12.50	25.00
❑ F2445	Rub-a-Dub-Dub/I'll Sign My Heart Away	1953	6.25	12.50	25.00
❑ F2553	Yesterday's Girl/John Henry	1953	6.25	12.50	25.00
❑ F2646	Wake Up, Irene/Go Cry Your Heart Out	1953	6.25	12.50	25.00
❑ F2758	A Fooler, a Faker/Breakin' the Rules	1954	5.00	10.00	20.00
❑ F2792	Jersey Bounce/Sunrise Serenade	1954	6.25	12.50	25.00
❑ F2823	Honky-Tonk Girl/We've Gone Too Far	1954	5.00	10.00	20.00
❑ F2998	Dardanelle/Johnson Rag	1954	5.00	10.00	20.00
❑ F3030	If Lovin' You Is Wrong/Annie Over	1955	5.00	10.00	20.00
❑ F3106	Wildwood Flower/Breakin' In Another Heart	1955	5.00	10.00	20.00
—A-side with Merle Travis					
❑ F3188	Most of All/Simple Simon	1955	5.00	10.00	20.00
❑ F3235	Westphalia Waltz/Red Skin Gal	1955	5.00	10.00	20.00
❑ F3275	Don't Take It Out on Me/Honey, Honey Bee Ball	1955	5.00	10.00	20.00
❑ F3347	The Blackboard of My Heart/I'm Not Mad, Just Hurt	1956	5.00	10.00	20.00
❑ F3440	Weeping Willow/You Can Give Me Back My Heart	1956	5.00	10.00	20.00
❑ F3536	It Makes No Difference Now/Taking My Chances	1956	5.00	10.00	20.00
❑ F3623	Rockin' in the Congo/I Was the First One	1957	10.00	20.00	40.00
❑ F3709	Girl in the Night/Quicksand	1957	5.00	10.00	20.00
❑ F3781	Tears Are Only Rain/Under the Double Eagle	1957	5.00	10.00	20.00
❑ F3850	Just an Old Flame/If I'm Not Too Late	1957	5.00	10.00	20.00
❑ F3950	How Do You Hold a Memory/Li'l Liza Jane	1958	5.00	10.00	20.00
❑ F4017	Squaws Along the Yukon/Gathering Flowers	1958	5.00	10.00	20.00
❑ F4085	I've Run Out of Tomorrows/You're Going Back to Your Old Ways Again	1958	5.00	10.00	20.00
❑ F4138	Tuxedo Junction/The Cocoanut Grove	1959	5.00	10.00	20.00
❑ F4182	Anybody's Girl/Total Strangers	1959	5.00	10.00	20.00
❑ F4269	I Didn't Mean to Fall in Love/I Guess I'm Gettin' Over You	1959	5.00	10.00	20.00
❑ 4334	A Six Pack to Go/What Made Her Change	1960	5.00	10.00	20.00
❑ 4386	She's Just a Whole Lot Like You/There My Future Goes	1960	5.00	10.00	20.00
❑ 4454	It's Got to Be a Habit/Will We Start It All Over Again	1960	5.00	10.00	20.00
❑ 4502	Just One Step Away/Two Hearts Deep in the Blues	1961	5.00	10.00	20.00
❑ 4556	Oklahoma Hills/Teach Me How to Lie	1961	5.00	10.00	20.00
❑ 4605	Hangover Tavern/Give the World a Smile	1961	5.00	10.00	20.00
❑ 4649	Lost John/I've Convinced Everyone But Myself	1961	5.00	10.00	20.00
❑ 4649 [PS]	Lost John/I've Convinced Everyone But Myself	1961	7.50	15.00	30.00
❑ 4694	That's the Recipe for a Heartache/Drop Me Gently	1962	3.75	7.50	15.00
❑ 4722	Blue Skirt Waltz/Westphalia Waltz	1962	3.75	7.50	15.00
❑ 4786	How Many Teardrops Will It Take/I Cast a Lonesome Shadow	1962	3.75	7.50	15.00
❑ 4871	Honky Tonk Town/I'd Look Forward to Tomorrow	1963	3.75	7.50	15.00
❑ 4912	Yesterday's Girl/The Wild Side of Life	1963	3.75	7.50	15.00
❑ 4968	I Wasn't Even in the Running/The More in Love Your Heart Is	1963	3.75	7.50	15.00
❑ 5008	Too in Love/Blackboard of My Heart	1963	3.75	7.50	15.00
❑ 5071	Twice As Much/Reaching for the Moon	1964	3.75	7.50	15.00
❑ 5123	Just to Ease the Pain/Stirring Up the Ashes	1964	3.75	7.50	15.00
❑ 5217	Whatever Happened to Mary/Luckiest Heartache in Town	1964	3.75	7.50	15.00
❑ 5310	Mr. and Mrs. Snowman/I'd Like to Have an Elephant for Christmas	1964	3.75	7.50	15.00
❑ 5344	I'm Gonna Practice Freedom/Life's Sweetest Moment	1965	3.75	7.50	15.00
❑ 5422	Then I'll Start Believing in You/In the Back of Your Mind	1965	3.75	7.50	15.00
❑ 5507	Paper Doll/You Only Hurt the One You Love	1965	3.75	7.50	15.00
❑ 5535	Little Christmas/Gonna Wrap My Heart in Angel Ribbons	1965	3.75	7.50	15.00
❑ 5599	Pick Me Up on Your Way Down/You Nearly Lose Your Mind	1966	3.00	6.00	12.00
❑ F40264	Give a Little, Take a Little/A Cat Has Nine Lives	1949	7.50	15.00	30.00

CHURCHILL

Number	Title (A Side/B Side)	Yr	VG	VG+	NM
❑ 7779	Rockin' in the Congo/The Convict and the Rose	1981	2.00	4.00	8.00
❑ 7779 [PS]	Rockin' in the Congo/The Convict and the Rose	1981	2.50	5.00	10.00
❑ 94003	Cocaine Blues/Drop Me Gently	1982	—	2.50	5.00

Number	Title (A Side/B Side)	Yr	VG	VG+	NM
❑ 94009	Driving Nails in My Coffin/What Ever Happened to Mary	1982	—	2.50	5.00
❑ 94026	Once in a Blue Moon/Let's Stop What We Started	1983	—	2.50	5.00
❑ 94026 [PS]	Once in a Blue Moon/Let's Stop What We Started	1983	—	3.00	6.00

CURB

Number	Title (A Side/B Side)	Yr	VG	VG+	NM
❑ D7-73035	Gotta Sell Them Chickens/Total Stranger	1997	—	2.00	4.00

—A-side with Junior Brown; B-side with Lyle Lovett

DOT

Number	Title (A Side/B Side)	Yr	VG	VG+	NM
❑ 17108	On Tap, In the Can, or In the Bottle	1968	2.00	4.00	8.00
❑ 17163	Smoky the Bar/Clubs, Spades, Diamonds and Hearts	1968	2.00	4.00	8.00
❑ 17207	I See Them Everywhere/Today	1969	2.00	4.00	8.00
❑ 17262	The Pathway of My Life/At Certain Times	1969	2.00	4.00	8.00
❑ 17307	Oklahoma Home Brew/Let's Get Drunk and Be Somebody	1969	2.00	4.00	8.00
❑ 17347	But That's All Right/Take It All Away	1970	2.00	4.00	8.00
❑ 17354	One of the Fortunate Few/I'm Afraid I Lied	1970	2.00	4.00	8.00
❑ 17365	Next Time I Fall in Love (I Won't)/Big Boat Across Oklahoma	1971	—	3.50	7.00
❑ 17385	The Mark of a Heel/Promise Her Anything	1971	—	3.50	7.00
❑ 17390	Oklahoma Stomp/Maiden's Prayer	1971	—	3.50	7.00
❑ 17399	I've Come Awful Close/Teardrops on the Rocks	1971	—	3.50	7.00
❑ 17410	Cab Driver/Gloria	1972	—	3.50	7.00
❑ 17430	Glow Worm/You're Nobody Till Somebody Loves You	1972	—	3.50	7.00
❑ 17447	Roses in the Wine/That's Why I Sing	1973	—	3.50	7.00
❑ 17470	Kindly Keep It Country/Jill's Jack in the Box	1973	—	3.50	7.00
❑ 17490	The Older the Violin, the Sweeter the Music/A Six Pack to Go	1974	—	3.50	7.00
❑ 17512	Who Left the Door to Heaven Open/When My Blue Moon Turns to Gold Again	1974	—	3.50	7.00

MCA

Number	Title (A Side/B Side)	Yr	VG	VG+	NM
❑ 41079	I Hear the South Callin' Me/Through the Bottom of the Glass	1979	—	2.00	4.00
❑ 41176	Tony's Tank-Up, Drive-In Cafe/Point of No Return	1980	—	2.00	4.00
❑ 41274	You're Poppin' Tops/Rollin' in Your Sweet Sunshine	1980	—	2.00	4.00
❑ 51030	King of Western Swing/Take Me Back to Tulsa	1980	—	2.00	4.00

STEP ONE

Number	Title (A Side/B Side)	Yr	VG	VG+	NM
❑ 382	Here's to Country Music/The Hand I'm Holding Now	1988	—	2.00	4.00
❑ 394	If I Were You I'd Fall in Love with Me/(B-side unknown)	1988	—	2.00	4.00

WARNER BROS.

Number	Title (A Side/B Side)	Yr	VG	VG+	NM
❑ 5858	Where Is the Circus/Love Walked Out Long Before She Did	1966	2.50	5.00	10.00
❑ 5886	He's Got a Way with Women/Let the Four Winds Choose	1967	2.50	5.00	10.00

Selected 78s

BLUE BONNET

Number	Title (A Side/B Side)	Yr	VG	VG+	NM
❑ 107	A Lonely Heart Knows/My Starry-Eyed Texas Gal	1947	12.50	25.00	50.00
❑ 123	California Women/What Are You Gonna Do	1947	12.50	25.00	50.00

CAPITOL

Number	Title (A Side/B Side)	Yr	VG	VG+	NM
❑ 15132	Yesterday's Mail/What Are We Gonna Do About the Moonlight	1948	5.00	10.00	20.00
❑ 15187	Green Light/You Remembered Me	1948	5.00	10.00	20.00
❑ 15345	I Find You Cheating on Me/You Broke My Heart (In Little Bitty Pieces)	1949	5.00	10.00	20.00
❑ 40065	Humpty Dumpty Heart/Today	1948	5.00	10.00	20.00
❑ 40085	Don't Flirt with Me/Rock in the Ocean	1948	5.00	10.00	20.00
❑ 40112	California Women/Mary Had a Little Lamb	1948	5.00	10.00	20.00
❑ 40169	Tomorrow Night/My Front Door Is Open	1949	5.00	10.00	20.00
❑ 40211	Soft Lips/The Grass Looks Greener Over Yonder	1949	3.75	7.50	15.00
❑ 40218	Whoa Sailor/Swing Wide Your Gates of Love	1949	3.75	7.50	15.00

GLOBE

Number	Title (A Side/B Side)	Yr	VG	VG+	NM
❑ 124	Whoa Sailor!/Swing Wide Your Gate of Love	1946	50.00	100.00	200.00

7-Inch Extended Plays

CAPITOL

Number	Title (A Side/B Side)	Yr	VG	VG+	NM
❑ EAP 1-418	(contents unknown)	195?	5.00	10.00	20.00
❑ EAP 1-418 [PS]	Songs of the Brazos Valley, Part 1	195?	5.00	10.00	20.00
❑ EAP 2-418	(contents unknown)	195?	5.00	10.00	20.00
❑ EAP 2-418 [PS]	Songs of the Brazos Valley, Part 2	195?	5.00	10.00	20.00
❑ EAP 3-418	(contents unknown)	195?	5.00	10.00	20.00
❑ EAP 3-418 [PS]	Songs of the Brazos Valley, Part 3	195?	5.00	10.00	20.00
❑ EAP 1-601	(contents unknown)	195?	6.25	12.50	25.00
❑ EAP 1-601 [PS]	Hank Thompson	195?	6.25	12.50	25.00
❑ EAP 1-618	(contents unknown)	195?	5.00	10.00	20.00
❑ EAP 1-618 [PS]	North of the Rio Grande, Part 1	195?	5.00	10.00	20.00
❑ EAP 2-618	(contents unknown)	195?	5.00	10.00	20.00
❑ EAP 2-618 [PS]	North of the Rio Grande, Part 2	195?	5.00	10.00	20.00
❑ EAP 3-618	(contents unknown)	195?	5.00	10.00	20.00
❑ EAP 3-618 [PS]	North of the Rio Grande, Part 3	195?	5.00	10.00	20.00
❑ EAP 1-705	(contents unknown)	195?	6.25	12.50	25.00
❑ EAP 1-705 [PS]	Dancing Western Style	195?	6.25	12.50	25.00
❑ EAP 1-729	Humpty Dumpty Heart/Today//You Remembered Me/I'll Be Your Sweetheart for a Day	1957	3.75	7.50	15.00
❑ EAP 1-729 [PS]	New Recordings of Hank Thompson's All-Time Hits, Part 1	1957	3.75	7.50	15.00
❑ EAP 2-729	Don't Flirt with Me/The Grass Looks Greener//Swing Wide Your Gate of Love/I Find You Cheatin' on Me	1957	3.75	7.50	15.00
❑ EAP 2-729 [PS]	New Recordings of Hank Thompson's All-Time Hits, Part 2	1957	3.75	7.50	15.00
❑ EAP 3-729	My Front Door Is Open/Standing on the Outside//Whoa Sailor/Tomorrow Night	1957	3.75	7.50	15.00
❑ EAP 3-729 [PS]	New Recordings of Hank Thompson's All-Time Hits, Part 3	1957	3.75	7.50	15.00
❑ EAP 1-826	(contents unknown)	1957	3.75	7.50	15.00
❑ EAP 1-826 [PS]	Hank! Part 1	1957	3.75	7.50	15.00
❑ EAP 2-826	(contents unknown)	1957	3.75	7.50	15.00
❑ EAP 2-826 [PS]	Hank! Part 2	1957	3.75	7.50	15.00
❑ EAP 3-826	(contents unknown)	1957	3.75	7.50	15.00
❑ EAP 3-826 [PS]	Hank! Part 3	1957	3.75	7.50	15.00
❑ EAP 1-975	(contents unknown)	1958	3.75	7.50	15.00
❑ EAP 1-975 [PS]	Dance Ranch, Part 1	1958	3.75	7.50	15.00
❑ EAP 2-975	(contents unknown)	1958	3.75	7.50	15.00
❑ EAP 2-975 [PS]	Dance Ranch, Part 2	1958	3.75	7.50	15.00
❑ EAP 3-975	(contents unknown)	1958	3.75	7.50	15.00
❑ EAP 3-975 [PS]	Dance Ranch, Part 3	1958	3.75	7.50	15.00
❑ EAP 1-1111	Shenandoah Waltz/Wednesday Night Waltz//(B-side unknown)	1959	3.75	7.50	15.00
❑ EAP 1-1111 [PS]	Favorite Waltzes by Hank Thompson, Part 1	1959	3.75	7.50	15.00
❑ EAP 2-1111	(contents unknown)	1959	3.75	7.50	15.00
❑ EAP 2-1111 [PS]	Favorite Waltzes by Hank Thompson, Part 2	1959	3.75	7.50	15.00
❑ EAP 3-1111	(contents unknown)	1959	3.75	7.50	15.00
❑ EAP 3-1111 [PS]	Favorite Waltzes by Hank Thompson, Part 3	1959	3.75	7.50	15.00
❑ EAP 1-1246	(contents unknown)	1960	3.75	7.50	15.00
❑ EAP 1-1246 [PS]	Songs for Rounders, Part 1	1960	3.75	7.50	15.00
❑ EAP 2-1246	(contents unknown)	1960	3.75	7.50	15.00
❑ EAP 2-1246 [PS]	Songs for Rounders, Part 2	1960	3.75	7.50	15.00
❑ EAP 3-1246	(contents unknown)	1960	3.75	7.50	15.00
❑ EAP 3-1246 [PS]	Songs for Rounders, Part 3	1960	3.75	7.50	15.00

Albums

ABC

Number	Title	Yr	VG	VG+	NM
❑ AB-1095	Brand New Hank	1978	3.00	6.00	12.00

ABC DOT

Number	Title	Yr	VG	VG+	NM
❑ DOSD-2003	Moving On	1974	3.00	6.00	12.00
❑ DOSD-2032	Hank Thompson Sings Nat King Cole	1975	3.00	6.00	12.00
❑ DOSD-2060	Back in the Swing of Things	1976	3.00	6.00	12.00
❑ DOSD-2069	The Thompson Touch	1977	3.00	6.00	12.00
❑ DO-2091	Doin' My Thing	1977	3.00	6.00	12.00

CAPITOL

Number	Title	Yr	VG	VG+	NM
❑ H 418 [10]	Songs of the Brazos Valley	1953	30.00	60.00	120.00
❑ T 418 [M]	Songs of the Brazos Valley *—Turquoise or gray label*	1956	20.00	40.00	80.00
❑ T 418 [M]	Songs of the Brazos Valley *—Black colorband label, logo at left*	1959	7.50	15.00	30.00
❑ T 418 [M]	Songs of the Brazos Valley *—Black colorband label, logo at top*	1962	5.00	10.00	20.00
❑ H 618 [10]	North of the Rio Grande	1953	30.00	60.00	120.00
❑ T 618 [M]	North of the Rio Grande *—Turquoise or gray label*	1956	20.00	40.00	80.00
❑ H 729 [10]	New Recordings of Hank's All-Time Hits	195?	30.00	60.00	120.00
❑ T 729 [M]	New Recordings of Hank's All-Time Hits *—Turquoise or gray label*	1956	20.00	40.00	80.00
❑ T 729 [M]	New Recordings of Hank's All-Time Hits *—Black colorband label, logo at left*	1959	7.50	15.00	30.00
❑ T 729 [M]	New Recordings of Hank's All-Time Hits *—Black colorband label, logo at top*	1962	5.00	10.00	20.00
❑ T 826 [M]	Hank! *—Turquoise or gray label*	1957	20.00	40.00	80.00
❑ T 826 [M]	Hank! *—Black colorband label, logo at left*	1959	7.50	15.00	30.00
❑ T 826 [M]	Hank! *—Black colorband label, logo at top*	1962	5.00	10.00	20.00
❑ T 911 [M]	Hank Thompson Favorites *—Turquoise or gray label*	1957	20.00	40.00	80.00
❑ T 975 [M]	Hank Thompson's Dance Ranch *—Turquoise or gray label*	1958	20.00	40.00	80.00
❑ T 975 [M]	Hank Thompson's Dance Ranch *—Black colorband label, logo at left*	1959	7.50	15.00	30.00
❑ T 975 [M]	Hank Thompson's Dance Ranch *—Black colorband label, logo at top*	1962	5.00	10.00	20.00
❑ T 1111 [M]	Favorite Waltzes *—Black colorband label, logo at left*	1959	20.00	40.00	80.00
❑ T 1111 [M]	Favorite Waltzes *—Black colorband label, logo at top*	1962	5.00	10.00	20.00
❑ ST 1246 [S]	Songs for Rounders	1959	10.00	20.00	40.00
❑ T 1246 [M]	Songs for Rounders	1959	7.50	15.00	30.00
❑ ST 1360 [S]	Most of All *—Black colorband label, logo at left*	1960	10.00	20.00	40.00
❑ ST 1360 [S]	Most of All *—Black colorband label, logo at top*	1962	6.25	12.50	25.00
❑ T 1360 [M]	Most of All *—Black colorband label, logo at left*	1960	7.50	15.00	30.00
❑ T 1360 [M]	Most of All *—Black colorband label, logo at top*	1962	5.00	10.00	20.00
❑ ST 1469 [S]	This Broken Heart of Mine *—Black colorband label, logo at left*	1960	10.00	20.00	40.00
❑ ST 1469 [S]	This Broken Heart of Mine *—Black colorband label, logo at top*	1962	6.25	12.50	25.00
❑ T 1469 [M]	This Broken Heart of Mine *—Black colorband label, logo at left*	1960	7.50	15.00	30.00
❑ T 1469 [M]	This Broken Heart of Mine *—Black colorband label, logo at top*	1962	5.00	10.00	20.00
❑ ST 1544 [S]	An Old Love Affair *—Black colorband label, logo at left*	1961	7.50	15.00	30.00
❑ ST 1544 [S]	An Old Love Affair *—Black colorband label, logo at top*	1962	5.00	10.00	20.00
❑ T 1544 [M]	An Old Love Affair *—Black colorband label, logo at left*	1961	6.25	12.50	25.00

Number	Title (A Side/B Side)	Yr	VG	VG+	NM
❑ T 1544 [M]	An Old Love Affair	1962	3.75	7.50	15.00
—Black colorband label, logo at top					
❑ ST 1632 [S]	Hank Thompson at the Golden Nugget	1961	7.50	15.00	30.00
—Black colorband label, logo at left					
❑ ST 1632 [S]	Hank Thompson at the Golden Nugget	1962	5.00	10.00	20.00
—Black colorband label, logo at top					
❑ T 1632 [M]	Hank Thompson at the Golden Nugget	1961	6.25	12.50	25.00
—Black colorband label, logo at left					
❑ T 1632 [M]	Hank Thompson at the Golden Nugget	1962	3.75	7.50	15.00
—Black colorband label, logo at top					
❑ DT 1741 [R]	The #1 Country and Western Band	1962	5.00	10.00	20.00
—Black colorband label, logo at left					
❑ DT 1741 [R]	The #1 Country and Western Band	1962	3.00	6.00	12.00
—Black colorband label, logo at top					
❑ T 1741 [M]	The #1 Country and Western Band	1962	7.50	15.00	30.00
—Black colorband label, logo at left					
❑ T 1741 [M]	The #1 Country and Western Band	1962	5.00	10.00	20.00
—Black colorband label, logo at top					
❑ ST 1775 [S]	Cheyenne Frontier Days	1962	6.25	12.50	25.00
❑ T 1775 [M]	Cheyenne Frontier Days	1962	5.00	10.00	20.00
❑ ST 1878 [S]	The Best of Hank Thompson	1963	6.25	12.50	25.00
❑ T 1878 [M]	The Best of Hank Thompson	1963	5.00	10.00	20.00
❑ ST 1955 [S]	Hank Thompson at the State Fair of Texas	1963	6.25	12.50	25.00
❑ T 1955 [M]	Hank Thompson at the State Fair of Texas	1963	5.00	10.00	20.00
❑ ST 2089 [S]	Golden Country Hits	1964	6.25	12.50	25.00
❑ T 2089 [M]	Golden Country Hits	1964	5.00	10.00	20.00
❑ ST 2154 [S]	It's Christmas Time	1963	6.25	12.50	25.00
❑ T 2154 [M]	It's Christmas Time	1963	5.00	10.00	20.00
❑ ST 2274 [S]	Breakin' In Another Heart	1965	6.25	12.50	25.00
❑ T 2274 [M]	Breakin' In Another Heart	1965	5.00	10.00	20.00
❑ ST 2342 [S]	Luckiest Heartache in Town	1965	6.25	12.50	25.00
❑ T 2342 [M]	Luckiest Heartache in Town	1965	5.00	10.00	20.00
❑ ST 2460 [S]	A Six Pack to Go	1966	6.25	12.50	25.00
❑ T 2460 [M]	A Six Pack to Go	1966	5.00	10.00	20.00
❑ ST 2575 [S]	Breakin' the Rules	1966	6.25	12.50	25.00
❑ T 2575 [M]	Breakin' the Rules	1966	5.00	10.00	20.00
❑ ST 2661 [S]	The Best of Hank Thompson Vol. 2	1967	5.00	10.00	20.00
❑ T 2661 [M]	The Best of Hank Thompson Vol. 2	1967	6.25	12.50	25.00
❑ ST 2826 [S]	Just an Old Flame	1967	5.00	10.00	20.00
❑ T 2826 [M]	Just an Old Flame	1967	6.25	12.50	25.00

DOT

Number	Title (A Side/B Side)	Yr	VG	VG+	NM
❑ DOS-2000 [(2)]	Hank Thompson's 25th Anniversary Album	1971	5.00	10.00	20.00
❑ DLP-25864	Hank Thompson Sings the Gold Standards	1968	3.75	7.50	15.00
❑ DLP-25894	On Tap, In the Can, Or In the Bottle	1968	3.75	7.50	15.00
❑ DLP-25932	Smoky the Bar	1969	3.75	7.50	15.00
❑ DLP-25971	Hank Thompson Salutes Oklahoma	1969	3.75	7.50	15.00
❑ DLP-25991	Next Time I Fall in Love (I Won't)	1971	3.75	7.50	15.00
❑ DOS-25996	Cab Driver (A Salute to the Mills Brothers)	1972	3.75	7.50	15.00
❑ DOS-26004	Hank Thompson's Greatest Hits Vol. 1	1972	3.75	7.50	15.00
❑ DOS-26015	Kindly Keep It Country	1973	3.75	7.50	15.00

MCA

Number	Title (A Side/B Side)	Yr	VG	VG+	NM
❑ 689	Brand New Hank	198?	2.00	4.00	8.00
❑ 3250	Take Me Back to Tulsa	1980	2.50	5.00	10.00

WARNER BROS.

Number	Title (A Side/B Side)	Yr	VG	VG+	NM
❑ W 1664 [M]	Where Is the Circus and Other Heart Breakin' Hits	1966	3.75	7.50	15.00
❑ WS 1664 [S]	Where Is the Circus and Other Heart Breakin' Hits	1966	5.00	10.00	20.00
❑ W 1679 [M]	The Countrypolitan Sound of Hank Thompson	1967	3.75	7.50	15.00
❑ WS 1679 [S]	The Countrypolitan Sound of Hank Thompson	1967	5.00	10.00	20.00
❑ W 1686 [M]	The Gold Standard Collection of Hank Thompson	1967	3.75	7.50	15.00
❑ WS 1686 [S]	The Gold Standard Collection of Hank Thompson	1967	5.00	10.00	20.00

THOMPSON, J.W.

45s

CENTURY 21

Number	Title (A Side/B Side)	Yr	VG	VG+	NM
❑ 109	Hello Josephine/(B-side unknown)	1984	—	3.00	6.00

NSD

Number	Title (A Side/B Side)	Yr	VG	VG+	NM
❑ 44	Jesus Loves Cowboys the Same/Runaway Blues	1980	—	2.50	5.00
❑ 51	Hard Times/Louisiana Liquid Gold	1980	—	2.50	5.00
❑ 62	Halftime/Jesus Loves Cowboys the Same	1980	—	2.50	5.00
❑ 75	Two Out of Three Ain't Bad/Bubbles in My Beer	1981	—	2.50	5.00
❑ 86	Take These Chains from My Heart/Forever Waltz	1981	—	2.50	5.00
❑ 111	Doctor Doctor/Let's Stop the Fight	1981	—	2.50	5.00
❑ 117	House of Fools/I'm a Stepper	1982	—	2.50	5.00
❑ 141	Let It Be a Buddy of Mine/House of Fools	1982	—	2.50	5.00
❑ 159	One White Rose/No. 1 Fool of the Year	1983	—	2.50	5.00

SOUTHERN STAR

Number	Title (A Side/B Side)	Yr	VG	VG+	NM
❑ 309	The Visitor/When You're Honky Tonkin'	1979	—	3.00	6.00

USA COUNTRY

Number	Title (A Side/B Side)	Yr	VG	VG+	NM
❑ 1001	We've Got a Good Thing Goin'/Makin' Love with a Married Man	1983	—	3.00	6.00

THOMPSON, SUE

Also see DON GIBSON AND SUE THOMPSON.

45s

DECCA

Number	Title (A Side/B Side)	Yr	VG	VG+	NM
❑ 29314	Walkin' in the Snow/Come a Little Bit Closer	1954	6.25	12.50	25.00
—With Hank Penny					
❑ 29545	Day Dreaming/Your Mommie and Your Daddy	1955	6.25	12.50	25.00
❑ 30435	Walkin' to Missouri/Red Hot Honey Brown	1957	6.25	12.50	25.00

HICKORY

Number	Title (A Side/B Side)	Yr	VG	VG+	NM
❑ 308	Just Plain Country/Oh Johnny, Oh Johnny, Oh	1973	—	2.50	5.00
❑ 313	Find Out/Stay Another Day	1974	—	2.50	5.00
❑ 320	Making Love to You Is Just Like Eating Peanuts/Sweet Memories	1974	—	2.50	5.00
❑ 330	Trains/And Love Me	1974	—	2.50	5.00
❑ 339	The Thought of Losing You/Tennessee Waltz	1975	—	2.00	4.00
❑ 346	I Can't Stop Loving You/Any Other Morning	1975	—	2.00	4.00
❑ 354	Big Mabel Murphy/Big Daddy	1975	—	2.00	4.00
❑ 364	Never Naughty Rosie/He Cheats on Me	1976	—	2.00	4.00
❑ 370	Baby's Not Home/I Want It All	1976	—	2.00	4.00
❑ 1144	Throwin' Kisses/Angel, Angel	1961	5.00	10.00	20.00
❑ 1153	Sad Movies (Make Me Cry)/Nine Little Teardrops	1961	5.00	10.00	20.00
❑ 1159	Norman/Never Love Again	1961	5.00	10.00	20.00
❑ 1166	Two of a Kind/It Has to Be	1962	3.75	7.50	15.00
❑ 1174	Have a Good Time/If the Boy Only Knew	1962	3.75	7.50	15.00
❑ 1183	James (Hold the Ladder Steady)/My Hero	1962	3.75	7.50	15.00
❑ 1196	Willie Can/Too Much in Love	1962	3.75	7.50	15.00
❑ 1204	What's Wrong Bill/I Need a Harbor	1963	3.75	7.50	15.00
❑ 1204 [PS]	What's Wrong Bill/I Need a Harbor	1963	5.00	10.00	20.00
❑ 1217	True Confession/Suzie	1963	3.75	7.50	15.00
❑ 1217 [PS]	True Confession/Suzie	1963	5.00	10.00	20.00
❑ 1221	Too Hot to Dance/I Like Your Kind of Love	1963	3.00	6.00	12.00
—With Bob Luman					
❑ 1234	'Cause I Ask You To/It's 12:35	1963	3.00	6.00	12.00
❑ 1240	Big Daddy/I'd Like to Know You Better	1964	3.00	6.00	12.00
❑ 1255	Bad Boy/Toys	1964	3.00	6.00	12.00
❑ 1270	Big Hearted Me/Looking for a Good Boy	1964	3.00	6.00	12.00
❑ 1284	Paper Tiger/Mama, Don't Cry at My Wedding	1964	3.75	7.50	15.00
❑ 1308	Stop Th' Music/What I'm Needin' Is You	1965	3.00	6.00	12.00
❑ 1328	Afraid/It's Break-Up Time	1965	3.00	6.00	12.00
❑ 1340	Just Kiss Me/Sweet Hunk of Misery	1965	3.00	6.00	12.00
❑ 1359	Walkin' My Baby/I'm Lookin' (For a World)	1965	3.00	6.00	12.00
❑ 1381	What Should I Do/After the Heartache	1966	2.50	5.00	10.00
❑ 1403	I Can't Help It/Put It Back	1966	2.50	5.00	10.00
❑ 1423	Someone/From My Balcony	1966	2.50	5.00	10.00
❑ 1431	Language of Love/Let Me Down Hard	1967	2.50	5.00	10.00
❑ 1457	Don't Forget to Cry/Ferris Wheel	1967	2.50	5.00	10.00
❑ 1469	That's Just Too Much/Straight to Helen	1967	2.50	5.00	10.00
❑ 1488	Dear Boy/Love Has Come My Way	1967	2.50	5.00	10.00
❑ 1493	How Do You Start Over/Why Not	1968	2.00	4.00	8.00
❑ 1512	You Deserve Each Other/Doin' Nothing	1968	2.00	4.00	8.00
❑ 1524	Don't Try to Change Me/The Real Me	1968	2.00	4.00	8.00
❑ 1534	Tennessee Waltz/Who's Gonna Mow Your Grass	1969	2.00	4.00	8.00
❑ 1547	Pair of Broken Hearts/You Two-Timed Me One Time Too Often	1969	2.00	4.00	8.00
❑ 1560	I Just Keep Hangin' On/Lost Highway	1970	—	3.00	6.00
❑ 1577	Whole Lot of Walkin'/Guess Who's Coming to Dinner Tonight	1970	—	3.00	6.00
❑ 1587	Because You Love Me/Take a Little Time	1971	—	3.00	6.00
❑ 1596	Here's To Forever/What You See Is What You Get	1971	—	3.00	6.00
❑ 1612	Swiss Cottage Place/Thanks to Rumors	1971	—	3.00	6.00
❑ 1622	Let Your Thoughts Be Sweet/What a Woman in Love Won't Do	1972	—	3.00	6.00
❑ 1641	Sweet Memories/Take Me As I Am	1972	—	3.00	6.00
❑ 1652	Candy and Roses/Full Time Job	1972	—	3.00	6.00
❑ 1669	How I Love Them Old Songs/Just Two Young People	1973	—	2.50	5.00

MERCURY

Number	Title (A Side/B Side)	Yr	VG	VG+	NM
❑ 6325	You're Getting a Good Girl (When You Get Me)/What've You Got (That Makes Me Love You So)	1951	10.00	20.00	40.00
❑ 6377	Just Walking Out the Door/I'll Hate Myself in the Morning	1952	7.50	15.00	30.00
❑ 6390	Junior's a Big Boy Now/Tadpole	1952	7.50	15.00	30.00
❑ 6407	You Belong to Me/You're an Angel on the Outside	1952	7.50	15.00	30.00
❑ 6416	Red Hot Henrietta Brown/Last Night I Heard Somebody Cry	1952	7.50	15.00	30.00
❑ 70066	How Many Tears/If You Should Change	1953	6.25	12.50	25.00
❑ 70084	Take Care My Love/Things I Might Have Been	1953	6.25	12.50	25.00
❑ 70089	You and Me/Say It with Your Heart	1953	6.25	12.50	25.00
❑ 70152	I'm Not That Kind of Girl/I Long to Tell You	1953	6.25	12.50	25.00
❑ 70309	Donna Wanna/Gee But I Hate to Go Home Alone	1954	6.25	12.50	25.00

Albums

HICKORY

Number	Title (A Side/B Side)	Yr	VG	VG+	NM
❑ LPM-104 [M]	Meet Sue Thompson	1962	12.50	25.00	50.00
❑ LPS-104 [S]	Meet Sue Thompson	1962	20.00	40.00	80.00
❑ LPM-107 [M]	Two of a Kind	1962	7.50	15.00	30.00
❑ LPS-107 [S]	Two of a Kind	1962	10.00	20.00	40.00
❑ LPM-111 [M]	Sue Thompson's Golden Hits	1963	7.50	15.00	30.00
❑ LPS-111 [S]	Sue Thompson's Golden Hits	1963	10.00	20.00	40.00
❑ LPM-121 [M]	Paper Tiger	1965	7.50	15.00	30.00
❑ LPS-121 [S]	Paper Tiger	1965	10.00	20.00	40.00
❑ LPM-130 [M]	Sue Thompson with Strings Attached	1966	7.50	15.00	30.00
❑ LPS-130 [S]	Sue Thompson with Strings Attached	1966	10.00	20.00	40.00
❑ LPS-148	This Is Sue Thompson Country	1969	5.00	10.00	20.00
❑ H3F-4511	Sweet Memories	1974	3.75	7.50	15.00
❑ H3G-4515	...And Love Me	1974	3.75	7.50	15.00

WING

Number	Title (A Side/B Side)	Yr	VG	VG+	NM
❑ MGW-12317 [M]	The Country Side of Sue Thompson	1965	5.00	10.00	20.00
❑ SRW-16317 [R]	The Country Side of Sue Thompson	1965	3.75	7.50	15.00

THOMPSON BROTHERS BAND

45s

RCA

Number	Title (A Side/B Side)	Yr	VG	VG+	NM
❑ 64998	Drive Me Crazy/Back on the Farm	1997	—	—	3.00

THORNBURT, BILL

45s

MTM

Number	Title (A Side/B Side)	Yr	VG	VG+	NM
❑ B-72058	Time and Time Alone/The Biggest Fool She Ever Laid Her Lies On	1985	—	2.50	5.00

THORNTON, MARSHA

45s

MCA

Number	Title (A Side/B Side)	Yr	VG	VG+	NM
❑ 53711	Deep Water/Don't Tell Me What to Do	1989	—	2.00	4.00
❑ 53762	A Bottle of Wine and Patsy Cline/Don't Tell Me What to Do	1989	—	2.00	4.00
❑ 53995	Maybe the Moon Will Shine/A Far Cry from You	1991	—	2.00	4.00
❑ 79037	The Grass Is Greener/Next Time Around	1990	—	2.00	4.00

THRASHER BROTHERS, THE

45s

MCA

Number	Title (A Side/B Side)	Yr	VG	VG+	NM
❑ 51032	To Make a Long Story Longer/Wouldn't It Make a Good Country Song	1980	—	2.00	4.00
❑ 51049	Lovers Love/Wouldn't It Make a Good Country Song	1980	—	2.00	4.00
❑ 51123	Waitin' on Love/Smooth Southern Highway	1981	—	2.00	4.00
❑ 51175	As Long As We Keep Believing/Waitin' on Love	1981	—	2.00	4.00
❑ 51227	Best of Friends/The Captain and the Delta Queen	1982	—	2.00	4.00
❑ 52047	Sweet Country Music/I Think I Feel a Love Comin' On	1982	—	2.00	4.00
❑ 52093	Still the One/Long Tall Texan	1982	—	2.00	4.00
❑ 52153	Wherever You Are/Heart to Heart	1983	—	2.00	4.00
❑ 52192	I've Got Country in My Soul/I Wanna Be with You Tonight	1983	—	2.00	4.00
❑ 52242	Some Other Time/So Good	1983	—	2.00	4.00
❑ 52297	Whatcha Got Cookin' in Your Oven Tonight/Southern Swing	1983	—	2.00	4.00
❑ 52357	A Good Love Died Tonight/Southern Swing	1984	—	2.00	4.00

VULCAN

Number	Title (A Side/B Side)	Yr	VG	VG+	NM
❑ 10004	A Message to Khomeini/Maharishi	1979	—	3.00	6.00

—As "Roger Hallmark and the Thrasher Brothers"

Albums

MCA

Number	Title (A Side/B Side)	Yr	VG	VG+	NM
❑ 5352	Country in My Soul	1983	2.50	5.00	10.00

THROCKMORTON, SONNY

45s

CAPITOL

Number	Title (A Side/B Side)	Yr	VG	VG+	NM
❑ 3617	Angels in Red/Wake Up, John	1973	—	3.00	6.00
❑ 3728	The Windmill/Do Nothin' Somethin'	1973	—	3.00	6.00

HILLSIDE

Number	Title (A Side/B Side)	Yr	VG	VG+	NM
❑ 3026	All I've Got Going/Flowers of Darkness	196?	2.00	4.00	8.00
❑ 3032	Baby Hang On/Daddy Stand By Mama	196?	2.00	4.00	8.00

MCA

Number	Title (A Side/B Side)	Yr	VG	VG+	NM
❑ 51214	A Girl Like You/I've Broken My Own Heart	1981	—	2.00	4.00
❑ 52011	I Ain't Gonna Lie No More/I've Broken My Own Heart	1982	—	2.00	4.00
❑ 52121	Ain't No Way/I've Broken My Own Heart	1982	—	2.00	4.00

MERCURY

Number	Title (A Side/B Side)	Yr	VG	VG+	NM
❑ 55039	I Wish You Could Have Turned My Head (And Left My Heart Alone)/She Sure Makes Leavin' Look Easy	1978	—	2.00	4.00
❑ 55051	Smooth Sailin'/Last Cheater's Waltz	1979	—	2.00	4.00
❑ 55061	Can't You Hear That Whistle Blow/I Feel Like Lovin' You	1979	—	2.00	4.00
❑ 57002	Safely in the Arms of Jesus/There Must Be Something About Me That She Loves	1979	—	2.00	4.00
❑ 57018	Friday Night Blues/It Always Rains on Me	1980	—	2.00	4.00

STARCREST

Number	Title (A Side/B Side)	Yr	VG	VG+	NM
❑ 073	Rosie/Troublesome Waters	1976	—	3.00	6.00
❑ 073 [PS]	Rosie/Troublesome Waters	1976	2.00	4.00	8.00
❑ 094	Lovin' You, Lovin' Me/Don't Know How to Tell Her	1976	—	3.00	6.00

UNITED ARTISTS

Number	Title (A Side/B Side)	Yr	VG	VG+	NM
❑ 50823	Michael/Look What I Missed	1971	—	3.50	7.00
❑ 50863	I Wanna Kiss the Kids Goodnight/Let It Show	1971	—	3.50	7.00

WARNER BROS.

Number	Title (A Side/B Side)	Yr	VG	VG+	NM
❑ 28771	Bye Bye Baby Blues/You've Got the Longest Leaving Act in Town	1986	—	—	3.00

Albums

MERCURY

Number	Title (A Side/B Side)	Yr	VG	VG+	NM
❑ SRM-1-3736	Last Cheater's Waltz	1979	2.50	5.00	10.00

WARNER BROS.

Number	Title (A Side/B Side)	Yr	VG	VG+	NM
❑ 25374	Southern Train	1986	2.00	4.00	8.00

THUNDERKLOUD, BILLY, AND THE CHIEFTONES

45s

20TH CENTURY

Number	Title (A Side/B Side)	Yr	VG	VG+	NM
❑ 2116	You Touched My Life/When Love Is Right	1974	—	3.00	6.00
❑ 2164	Kick the Can/I'm Havin' a Party	1975	—	2.50	5.00
❑ 2181	What Time of Day/When Love Is Right	1975	—	2.50	5.00
❑ 2239	Pledging My Love/I Will Love You Until I Die	1975	—	2.50	5.00

POLYDOR

Number	Title (A Side/B Side)	Yr	VG	VG+	NM
❑ 14321	Indian Nation (The Lament of the Cherokee Reservation Indian)/I'm Going Right to Where I Do Wrong	1976	—	2.50	5.00
❑ 14338	Try a Little Tenderness/A Natural Feelin' for You	1976	—	2.50	5.00
❑ 14362	It's Alright/The Wanderer	1976	—	2.50	5.00
❑ 14383	Let Me Be Your Man/A Hundred Years from Now	1977	—	2.50	5.00
❑ 14412	Oklahoma Wind/The Trouble with Angels	1977	—	2.50	5.00
❑ 14449	Let Me Love You/My Lady	1977	—	2.50	5.00

Albums

20TH CENTURY

Number	Title (A Side/B Side)	Yr	VG	VG+	NM
❑ T-452	Off the Reservation	1974	3.00	6.00	12.00
❑ T-471	What Time of Day	1975	3.00	6.00	12.00

SUPERIOR

Number	Title (A Side/B Side)	Yr	VG	VG+	NM
❑ SR-103	All Through the Night	197?	3.75	7.50	15.00
❑ S-2010	Where Do I Begin to Tell the Story	1975	3.75	7.50	15.00

TIBOR BROTHERS, THE

45s

ARIOLA AMERICA

Number	Title (A Side/B Side)	Yr	VG	VG+	NM
❑ 7615	It's So Easy Lovin' You/Movin' Along	1976	—	3.00	6.00

Albums

JOMAR

Number	Title (A Side/B Side)	Yr	VG	VG+	NM
❑ S80-744-3631	The Tibor Brothers	1979	3.75	7.50	15.00

TIERNY, PATTI

45s

MGM

Number	Title (A Side/B Side)	Yr	VG	VG+	NM
❑ 14561	Cryin' Eyes/Jody's Face	1973	—	3.00	6.00

TILLIS, MEL

Also see BOB WILLS.

45s

COLUMBIA

Number	Title (A Side/B Side)	Yr	VG	VG+	NM
❑ 4-40845	It Takes a Worried Man to Sing a Worried Song/Honky Tonk Song	1957	5.00	10.00	20.00
❑ 4-40904	Case of the Blues/It's My Life	1957	5.00	10.00	20.00
❑ 4-40944	Juke Box Man/If You'll Be My Love	1957	6.25	12.50	25.00
❑ 4-41038	This Heart/Take My Hand	1957	5.00	10.00	20.00
❑ 4-41115	Teen Age Wedding/Lonely Street	1958	7.50	15.00	30.00
❑ 4-41189	The Violet and a Rose/No Song to Sing	1958	3.75	7.50	15.00
❑ 4-41277	Finally/The Brooklyn Bridge	1958	3.75	7.50	15.00
❑ 4-41632	It's So Easy/Loco Weed	1960	3.75	7.50	15.00
❑ 4-41863	Say/Walk On, Boy	1960	3.75	7.50	15.00
❑ 4-41986	Hearts of Stone/That's Where the Hurt Comes In	1961	5.00	10.00	20.00
❑ 4-42262	Party Girl/If I Lost Your Love	1962	5.00	10.00	20.00

DECCA

Number	Title (A Side/B Side)	Yr	VG	VG+	NM
❑ 31474	Don't Tell Mama/Half Laughing, Half Crying	1963	2.50	5.00	10.00
❑ 31528	Couldn't See the Forest for the Trees/It's No Surprise	1963	2.50	5.00	10.00
❑ 31623	It'll Be Easy/I'm Gonna Act Right	1964	2.50	5.00	10.00

ELEKTRA

Number	Title (A Side/B Side)	Yr	VG	VG+	NM
❑ 46536	Blind in Love/Blackjack, Arizona	1979	—	2.00	4.00
❑ 46583	Lying Time Again/Fooled Around and Fell in Love	1980	—	2.00	4.00
❑ 46628	Your Body Is an Outlaw/Rain on My Parade	1980	—	2.00	4.00
❑ 47015	Steppin' Out/Whiskey Chasin'	1980	—	2.00	4.00
❑ 47082	Southern Rains/Forgive Me for Giving You the Blues	1980	—	2.00	4.00
❑ 47116	A Million Old Goodbyes/Louisiana Lonely	1981	—	2.00	4.00
❑ 47178	One-Night Fever/Time Has Treated You Well	1981	—	2.00	4.00
❑ 47233 [DJ]	White Christmas/Blue Christmas	1981	—	3.00	6.00

—B-side by Eddy Raven

Number	Title (A Side/B Side)	Yr	VG	VG+	NM
❑ 47412	It's a Long Way to Daytona/Always You, Always Me	1982	—	2.00	4.00
❑ 47453	The One That Got Away/Why Ain't Life the Way It's S'posed to Be	1982	—	2.00	4.00
❑ 69963	Stay a Little Longer/Dream of Me	1982	—	2.00	4.00

KAPP

Number	Title (A Side/B Side)	Yr	VG	VG+	NM
❑ 764	Mental Revenge/Guide Me Home My Georgia Moon	1966	2.50	5.00	10.00
❑ 772	Stateside/Home Is Where the Hurt Is	1966	2.00	4.00	8.00
❑ 804	Life Turned Her That Way/If I Could Only Start Over	1967	2.00	4.00	8.00
❑ 804 [PS]	Life Turned Her That Way/If I Could Only Start Over	1967	3.75	7.50	15.00
❑ 837	Goodbye Wheeling/At the Sight of You	1967	2.00	4.00	8.00
❑ 867	Survival of the Fittest/The Old Gang's Gone	1967	2.00	4.00	8.00
❑ 881	All Right (I'll Sign the Papers)/Helpless, Hopeless Fool	1968	2.00	4.00	8.00
❑ 905	Something Special/You Name It	1968	2.00	4.00	8.00
❑ 941	Destroyed by Man/I Haven't Seen Mary in Years	1968	2.00	4.00	8.00
❑ 959	Who's Julie/Give Me One More Day	1968	2.00	4.00	8.00
❑ 986	Old Faithful/Sorrow Overtakes the Wine	1969	2.00	4.00	8.00
❑ 2031	These Lonely Hands of Mine/Cover Mama's Flowers	1969	—	3.50	7.00
❑ 2072	She'll Be Hanging 'Round Somewhere/Where Love Has Died	1970	—	3.50	7.00
❑ 2086	Heart Over Mind/Lingering Memories	1970	—	3.50	7.00
❑ 2103	Too Lonely, Too Long/Memories Made This House	1970	—	3.50	7.00
❑ 2121	One More Drink/I Could Never Be Ashamed by You	1971	—	3.50	7.00

MCA

Number	Title (A Side/B Side)	Yr	VG	VG+	NM
❑ KFC-001 [DJ]	There's No Turning Back/(B-side unknown)	1977	3.00	6.00	12.00

—Promo only; "America's Country Good Music from Kentucky Fried Chicken" on label

Number	Title (A Side/B Side)	Yr	VG	VG+	NM
❑ 40559	Love Revival/Gator Bar	1976	—	2.50	5.00
❑ 40627	Good Woman Blues/You Can't Trust a Crazy Man	1976	—	2.50	5.00
❑ 40667	Heart Healer/It's Just Not That Easy to Say	1976	—	2.50	5.00

Number	Title (A Side/B Side)	Yr	VG	VG+	NM
❑ 40710	Burning Memories/Golden Nugget Gambling Casino	1977	—	2.50	5.00
❑ 40764	I Got the Hoss/It's Been a Long Time	1977	—	2.50	5.00
❑ 40836	What Did I Promise Her Last Night/Woman, You Should Be in the Movies	1977	—	2.50	5.00
❑ 40900	I Believe in You/She Don't Trust You Daddy	1978	—	2.50	5.00
❑ 40946	Ain't No California/What Comes Natural to a Fool	1978	—	2.50	5.00
❑ 40983	Send Me Down to Tucson/Charlie's Angel	1978	—	2.50	5.00
❑ 41041	Coca Cola Cowboy/Cottonmouth	1979	—	2.50	5.00
❑ 52182	In the Middle of the Night/Even at Her Worst (She's Still the Best)	1983	—	—	3.00
❑ 52247	A Cowboy's Dream/After All This Time	1983	—	—	3.00
❑ 52285	She Meant Forever When She Said Goodbye/Try It Again	1983	—	—	3.00
❑ 52373	New Patches/Almost Like You Never Went Away	1984	—	—	3.00
MERCURY					
❑ 870192-7	You'll Come Back (You Always Do)/Try It Again	1988	—	—	3.00
MGM					
❑ 14148	Heaven Everyday/How Do You Drink the Wine	1970	—	3.00	6.00
❑ 14176	Commercial Affection/I Thought About You	1970	—	3.00	6.00
❑ 14211	The Arms of a Fool/Veil of White Lace	1971	—	3.00	6.00
❑ 14275	Brand New Mister Me/Brand New Wrapper	1971	—	3.00	6.00
❑ 14329	Untouched/I Went a Ramblin'	1971	—	3.00	6.00
❑ 14372	Would You Want the World to End/Things Have Changed a Lot	1972	—	3.00	6.00
❑ 14418	I Ain't Never/Border of Love	1972	—	3.00	6.00
❑ 14454	Neon Rose/It's My Love	1972	—	3.00	6.00
❑ 14522	Thank You for Being You/Over the Hill	1973	—	3.00	6.00
❑ 14585	Sawmill/Mama's Gonna Pray	1973	—	3.00	6.00
❑ 14689	Midnight, Me and the Blues/Modern Home Magazine	1974	—	3.00	6.00
❑ 14720	Stomp Them Grapes/Hang My Pictures in Your Heart	1974	—	3.00	6.00
❑ 14744	Memory Maker/Second Best	1974	—	3.00	6.00
❑ 14782	Best Way I Know How/Honey Dew Melon	1975	—	3.00	6.00
❑ 14804	Woman in the Back of My Mind/Kissing Your Picture (Is So Cold)	1975	—	3.00	6.00
❑ 14835	Lookin' for Tomorrow (And Findin' Yesterdays)/ Tennessee Banjo Man	1975	—	3.00	6.00
❑ 14846	Mental Revenge/My Bad Girl	1976	—	3.00	6.00
❑ 14850	Always Just a Memory Away/Come On Home	1976	—	3.00	6.00
RADIO					
❑ 001	City Lights/Who's Julie	1989	—	3.00	6.00
RCA					
❑ PB-14061	You Done Me Wrong/Another Heart Down	1985	—	—	3.00
❑ PB-14175	California Road/One More Time	1985	—	—	3.00
RIC					
❑ 150	Ode to the Little Brown Shack Out Back/Not in Front of the Kids	1965	3.00	6.00	12.00
❑ 158	Wine/Buried Alive	1965	3.00	6.00	12.00
❑ 178	Bring On the Blues/Mr. Dropout	1965	3.00	6.00	12.00
STARDAY					
❑ 8036	Wine/Stateside	197?	—	2.50	5.00
Albums					
COLUMBIA					
❑ CL 1724 [M]	Heart Over Mind and Other Big Country Hits	1962	7.50	15.00	30.00
❑ CS 8524 [S]	Heart Over Mind and Other Big Country Hits	1962	10.00	20.00	40.00
❑ C 30253	Heart Over Mind	1970	3.00	6.00	12.00
ELEKTRA					
❑ 6E-236	Me and Pepper	1979	2.50	5.00	10.00
❑ 6E-271	Your Body Is an Outlaw	1980	2.50	5.00	10.00
❑ 6E-310	Southern Rain	1980	2.50	5.00	10.00
❑ 60016	It's a Long Way to Daytona	1982	2.50	5.00	10.00
❑ 60192	Mel Tillis' Greatest Hits	1982	2.50	5.00	10.00
HARMONY					
❑ HL 7370 [M]	The Great Mel Tillis Sings "Walk On Boy" and Other Country Hits	196?	3.75	7.50	15.00
❑ HS 11170 [S]	The Great Mel Tillis Sings "Walk On Boy" and Other Country Hits	196?	3.00	6.00	12.00
❑ KH 31952	Mel	1972	3.00	6.00	12.00
HILLTOP					
❑ JS-6153	Detroit City	197?	2.50	5.00	10.00
KAPP					
❑ KL-1492 [M]	Stateside	1966	3.75	7.50	15.00
❑ KL-1514 [M]	Life Turned Her That Way	1967	3.75	7.50	15.00
❑ KL-1535 [M]	Mr. Mel	1967	5.00	10.00	20.00
❑ KS-3492 [S]	Stateside	1966	5.00	10.00	20.00
❑ KS-3514 [S]	Life Turned Her That Way	1967	5.00	10.00	20.00
❑ KS-3535 [S]	Mr. Mel	1967	3.75	7.50	15.00
❑ KS-3543	Let Me Talk to You	1968	3.75	7.50	15.00
❑ KS-3570	Something Special	1968	3.75	7.50	15.00
❑ KS-3589	Mel Tillis' Greatest Hits	1969	3.75	7.50	15.00
❑ KS-3594	Who's Julie	1969	3.75	7.50	15.00
❑ KS-3609	Mel Tillis Sings Old Faithful	1969	3.75	7.50	15.00
❑ KS-3630	She'll Be Hanging 'Round Somewhere	1970	3.75	7.50	15.00
❑ KS-3639	Mel Tillis In Person	1970	3.75	7.50	15.00
MCA					
❑ 66	Mel Tillis' Greatest Hits	1973	3.00	6.00	12.00
—Reissue of Kapp 3589					
❑ 550	Mel Tillis In Person	197?	2.50	5.00	10.00
—Reissue of Kapp 3639					
❑ 649	Love Revival	198?	2.00	4.00	8.00
—Reissue of 2204					
❑ 650	Heart Healer	198?	2.00	4.00	8.00
—Reissue of 2252					
❑ 651	Love's Troubled Waters	198?	2.00	4.00	8.00
—Reissue of 2288					
❑ 652	I Believe in You	198?	2.00	4.00	8.00
—Reissue of 2364					
❑ 653	Are You Sincere	198?	2.00	4.00	8.00
—Reissue of 3077					
❑ 789	M-M-Mel Live	198?	2.00	4.00	8.00
—Reissue of 3208					
❑ 2204	Love Revival	1976	3.00	6.00	12.00
❑ 2252	Heart Healer	1977	3.00	6.00	12.00
❑ 2288	Love's Troubled Waters	1977	3.00	6.00	12.00
❑ 2364	I Believe in You	1978	3.00	6.00	12.00
❑ 3077	Are You Sincere	1979	3.00	6.00	12.00
❑ 3167	Mr. Entertainer	1979	3.00	6.00	12.00
❑ 3208	M-M-Mel Live	1980	3.00	6.00	12.00
❑ 3274	The Very Best of Mel Tillis	1980	2.50	5.00	10.00
❑ 4091 [(2)]	The Best of Mel Tillis	1975	3.75	7.50	15.00
❑ 5378	After All This Time	1983	2.00	4.00	8.00
❑ 5472	New Patches	1984	2.00	4.00	8.00
❑ 37121	Mr. Entertainer	198?	2.00	4.00	8.00
—Reissue of 3167					
MERCURY					
❑ 835310-1	Brand New Mister Me	1988	2.00	4.00	8.00
MGM					
❑ SE-4681	One More Time	1970	3.75	7.50	15.00
❑ SE-4757	The Arms of a Fool/Commercial Affection	1971	3.75	7.50	15.00
❑ SE-4788	Recorded Live at the Sam Houston Coliseum, Houston, Texas	1971	3.75	7.50	15.00
❑ SE-4806	The Very Best of Mel Tillis and the Statesiders	1972	3.75	7.50	15.00
❑ SE-4841	Would You Want Your World to End	1972	3.75	7.50	15.00
❑ SE-4870	I Ain't Never/Neon Rose	1972	3.75	7.50	15.00
❑ SE-4889	Mel Tillis and the Statesiders On Stage at the Birmingham Municipal Auditorium	1973	3.75	7.50	15.00
❑ SE-4907	Sawmill	1973	3.75	7.50	15.00
❑ M3F-4960	Stomp Them Grapes	1974	3.00	6.00	12.00
❑ M3G-4970	Mel Tillis' Greatest Hits	1974	3.00	6.00	12.00
❑ M3G-4981	Mel Tillis Time	1975	—	—	—
—Canceled					
❑ M3G-4987	Mel Tillis and the Statesiders	1975	3.00	6.00	12.00
❑ MG-1-5002	M-M-Mel	1975	3.00	6.00	12.00
❑ MG-1-5021	The Best of Mel Tillis and the Statesiders	1976	3.00	6.00	12.00
❑ MG-1-5022	Welcome to Mel Tillis Country	1976	3.00	6.00	12.00
❑ MG-2-5402 [(2)]	24 Great Hits	1977	3.75	7.50	15.00
❑ MG-2-5404 [(2)]	Live at the Sam Houston Coliseum & Birmingham Municipal Auditorium	1978	3.75	7.50	15.00
—Combines 4788 and 4889 in one package					
POWER PAK					
❑ PO-295	Mel Tillis & Friends	197?	2.50	5.00	10.00
RCA VICTOR					
❑ AHL1-5483	California Road	1985	2.00	4.00	8.00
STARDAY					
❑ SLP-471	Stateside	1972	3.00	6.00	12.00
VOCALION					
❑ VL 73914	Big 'n' Country	1970	3.00	6.00	12.00

TILLIS, MEL, AND SHERRY BRYCE

Also see each artist's individual listings.

Number	Title (A Side/B Side)	Yr	VG	VG+	NM
45s					
MGM					
❑ 14255	Take My Hand/Life's Little Surprises	1971	—	3.00	6.00
❑ 14303	Living and Learning/Tangled Vines	1971	—	3.00	6.00
❑ 14365	Anything's Better Than Nothing/Then It Will Be All Over	1972	—	3.00	6.00
❑ 14472	Back to Life/Happyville	1972	—	3.00	6.00
❑ 14660	Let's Go All the Way Tonight/In the Vine	1973	—	3.00	6.00
❑ 14714	Don't Let Go/Why Not Do the Things (They Think We've Done)	1974	—	3.00	6.00
❑ 14776	You Are the One/I Saw Heaven in You	1974	—	3.00	6.00
❑ 14803	Mr. Right and Mrs. Wrong/Just Two Strangers Passing in the Night	1975	—	3.00	6.00
Albums					
MGM					
❑ SE-4800	Living and Learning/Take My Hand	1971	3.75	7.50	15.00
❑ SE-4937	Let's Go All the Way Tonight	1974	3.75	7.50	15.00

TILLIS, MEL, WITH GLEN CAMPBELL

Also see each artist's individual listings.

Number	Title (A Side/B Side)	Yr	VG	VG+	NM
45s					
MCA					
❑ 52474	Slow Nights/Midnight Love	1984	—	—	3.00

TILLIS, MEL, AND BILL PHILLIPS

Also see each artist's individual listings.

Number	Title (A Side/B Side)	Yr	VG	VG+	NM
45s					
COLUMBIA					
❑ 4-41416	Sawmill/You Are the Reason	1959	3.75	7.50	15.00
❑ 4-41530	Georgia Town Blues/Till I Get Enough of These Blues	1959	3.75	7.50	15.00

TILLIS, MEL, AND WEBB PIERCE

Also see each artist's individual listings.

45s

DECCA

Number	Title (A Side/B Side)	Yr	VG	VG+	NM
❑ 31445	How Come Your Dog Don't Bite Nobody But Me/ So Soon	1962	2.50	5.00	10.00

TILLIS, MEL, AND NANCY SINATRA

Also see MEL TILLIS (Nancy Sinatra's solo work is outside the scope of this book).

45s

ELEKTRA

Number	Title (A Side/B Side)	Yr	VG	VG+	NM
❑ 47157	Texas Cowboy Night/After the Lovin'	1981	—	2.50	5.00
❑ 47247	Play Me or Trade Me/Where Would I Be	1981	—	2.50	5.00

Albums

ELEKTRA

Number	Title (A Side/B Side)	Yr	VG	VG+	NM
❑ 5E-549	Mel and Nancy	1981	3.00	6.00	12.00

TILLIS, PAM

45s

ARISTA

Number	Title (A Side/B Side)	Yr	VG	VG+	NM
❑ 2129	Don't Tell Me What to Do/Melancholy Child	1990	—	2.50	5.00
❑ 2203	One of Those Things/Already Fallen	1991	—	2.00	4.00
❑ 10505	It's Lonely Out There/You Can't Have a Good Time Without Me	1996	—	2.00	4.00
❑ 12268	Put Yourself in My Place/I've Seen Enough to Know	1991	—	2.00	4.00
❑ 12371	Maybe It Was Memphis/Draggin' My Chains	1991	—	2.50	5.00
❑ 12408	Blue Rose Is/Ancient History	1992	—	2.00	4.00
❑ 12454	Shake the Sugar Tree/Maybe It Was Memphis	1992	—	2.00	4.00
❑ 12506	Let That Pony Run/Fine, Fine, Very Fine Love	1992	—	2.00	4.00
❑ 12539	Maybe It Was Memphis/Don't Tell Me What to Do	1993	—	—	3.00
—Reissue; black label with "Collectables" logo					
❑ 12552	Cleopatra, Queen of Denial/Homeward Looking Angel	1993	—	2.00	4.00
❑ 12606	Do You Know Where Your Man Is/We've Tried Everything Else	1993	—	2.00	4.00
❑ 12676	Spilled Perfume/'Til All the Lonely's Gone	1994	—	2.00	4.00
❑ 12726	When You Walk in the Room/'Til All the Lonely's Gone	1994	—	2.00	4.00
❑ 12759	Mi Vida Loca (My Crazy Life)/Ancient History	1994	—	2.50	5.00
❑ 12802	I Was Blown Away/Calico Plains	1995	—	2.00	4.00
❑ 12833	In Between Dances/They Don't Break 'Em Like They Used To	1995	—	2.00	4.00
❑ 12878	Deep Down/Tequila Mockingbird	1995	—	2.00	4.00
❑ 12958	The River and the Highway/All of This Love	1996	—	2.50	5.00
❑ 13045	Betty's Got a Bass Boat/Mandolin Rain	1996	—	—	3.00

ARISTA NASHVILLE

Number	Title (A Side/B Side)	Yr	VG	VG+	NM
❑ 13084	All the Good Ones Are Gone/Land of the Living	1997	—	2.00	4.00
❑ 13125	I Said a Prayer/Lay the Heartache Down	1998	—	—	3.00
❑ 13129	Every Time/You Put the Lonely on Me	1998	—	—	3.00

ELEKTRA

Number	Title (A Side/B Side)	Yr	VG	VG+	NM
❑ 47171	Every Home Should Have One/Holding On to What Is Gone	1981	3.00	6.00	12.00

WARNER BROS.

Number	Title (A Side/B Side)	Yr	VG	VG+	NM
❑ 28444	I Wish She Wouldn't Treat You That Way/Drawn to the Fire	1987	—	2.50	5.00
❑ 28676	I Thought I'd About Had It with You/Drawn to the Fire	1986	—	2.50	5.00
❑ 28806	Those Memories of You/Drawn to the Fire	1986	—	2.50	5.00
❑ 28984	One of Those Things/(B-side unknown)	1985	—	3.00	6.00
❑ 29155	Goodbye Highway/Somebody Else's	1984	—	3.00	6.00
❑ 29443	Killer Comfort/Weird	1983	2.50	5.00	10.00
❑ 29517	Love Is Sneakin' Up on You/Wish I Was in Love Tonight	1983	2.50	5.00	10.00

Albums

WARNER BROS.

Number	Title (A Side/B Side)	Yr	VG	VG+	NM
❑ 23871	Above and Beyond the Doll of Cutey	1983	6.25	12.50	25.00

TILLMAN, FLOYD

45s

CIMARRON

Number	Title (A Side/B Side)	Yr	VG	VG+	NM
❑ 4056	Daisy Mae/Let's Make Memories Tonight	1962	3.00	6.00	12.00

COLUMBIA

Number	Title (A Side/B Side)	Yr	VG	VG+	NM
❑ 2-216	Slipping Around/You Made Me Live, Love and Die	1949	12.50	25.00	50.00
—Microgroove 33 1/3 rpm 7-inch single, small hole					
❑ 2-320 (?)	I'll Never Slip Around Again/This Cold War with You	1949	10.00	20.00	40.00
—Microgroove 33 1/3 rpm 7-inch single, small hole					
❑ 2-400 (?)	I Gotta Have My Baby Back/It Had to Be That Way	1949	10.00	20.00	40.00
—Microgroove 33 1/3 rpm 7-inch single, small hole					
❑ 2-535 (?)	I Almost Lost My Mind/Precious Memories	1950	10.00	20.00	40.00
—Microgroove 33 1/3 rpm 7-inch single, small hole					
❑ 2-600 (?)	Just As Long As I Have You/The Last Straw	1950	10.00	20.00	40.00
—Microgroove 33 1/3 rpm 7-inch single, small hole					
❑ 4-20746	The Grandest Prize/I've Got the Craziest Feeling	1950	7.50	15.00	30.00
❑ 4-20771	Each Night at Nine/I'm Falling for You	1951	7.50	15.00	30.00
❑ 4-20793	I Love You/I Don't Care Anymore	1951	6.25	12.50	25.00
❑ 4-20823	You're That to Me/Rose of Old Monterrey	1951	6.25	12.50	25.00
❑ 4-20860	I'll Be Playing the Field From Now On/Why Do I Drink	1951	6.25	12.50	25.00
❑ 4-20894	Don't Say You Love Me/I'll Still Be Loving	1952	6.25	12.50	25.00
❑ 4-20956	It's Over, All Over/Take My Love With You Too	1952	6.25	12.50	25.00
❑ 4-21004	Goodbye Tomorrow, Hello Yesterday/I Finally Saw the Light	1952	6.25	12.50	25.00
❑ 4-21076	Small Little Town/The Worm Has Turned	1953	5.00	10.00	20.00
❑ 4-21200	More Than Anything/Just One More Time	1954	5.00	10.00	20.00
❑ 4-21257	I'll Never Be the Same/Call on Me	1954	5.00	10.00	20.00
❑ 4-21303	One More Day Wasted/Sometime Somewhere	1954	5.00	10.00	20.00
❑ 4-21372	She's Long Gone/Let's Make Memories Tonight	1955	5.00	10.00	20.00
❑ 4-33058	Slipping Around/I Love You So Much It Hurts	1961	2.00	4.00	8.00
—"Columbia Hall of Fame" series; red label					

LIBERTY

Number	Title (A Side/B Side)	Yr	VG	VG+	NM
❑ 55280	It Just Tears Me Up/The Song of Music	1960	3.75	7.50	15.00
❑ 55323	Whatever You Do/The Record Goes 'Round	1961	3.00	6.00	12.00

MAJOR

Number	Title (A Side/B Side)	Yr	VG	VG+	NM
❑ 1004	On You My Life Depends/I'm Free from the Love I Had for You	197?	—	3.00	6.00

MUSICOR

Number	Title (A Side/B Side)	Yr	VG	VG+	NM
❑ 1196	Only Where I Stand/Green Hills of Earth	1966	2.50	5.00	10.00
❑ 1230	One for the Money/You Won't Even Know That I Am Gone	1967	2.50	5.00	10.00
❑ 1254	Fightin' and Kissin'/A Memory's a Handy Thing to Have	1967	2.50	5.00	10.00
❑ 1279	I Didn't Keep My Big Mouth Shut/I Reap What I Sow	1967	2.50	5.00	10.00
❑ 1292	At Four O'Clock Each Morning/I Gotta Get Outta This House	1968	2.00	4.00	8.00
❑ 1304	Each Night at Nine/Dream On	1968	2.00	4.00	8.00
❑ 1316	Pour Me a Heartache/Because You're Gone	1968	2.00	4.00	8.00
❑ 1342	Autumn Song (I'm Losing You)/It Hurts So Hard So Long	1968	2.00	4.00	8.00
❑ 1355	It Makes No Difference Now/A Rainbow Is the Color of Love	1969	2.00	4.00	8.00

RCA VICTOR

Number	Title (A Side/B Side)	Yr	VG	VG+	NM
❑ 47-7157	Slipping Around/I Love You So Much It Hurts	1958	3.75	7.50	15.00

SIMS

Number	Title (A Side/B Side)	Yr	VG	VG+	NM
❑ 150	Gotta Have My Baby Back/I'll Never Get Over You	1963	3.00	6.00	12.00

Selected 78s

COLUMBIA

Number	Title (A Side/B Side)	Yr	VG	VG+	NM
❑ 20026	Drivin' Nails in My Coffin/Some Other World	1948	3.00	6.00	12.00
—Reissue of 36998					
❑ 20097	Sign on the Dotted Line/Go Out and Find Somebody New	1948	3.00	6.00	12.00
—Reissue of 37221					
❑ 20126	Gotta Have Something/Sweetheart, Darlin'	1948	3.00	6.00	12.00
—Reissue of 37393					
❑ 20388	I'm Leaving This Old World Someday/It's Got Me Down	1948	3.00	6.00	12.00
—Reissue of 37976					
❑ 20404	Houston Waltz/Westphalia Waltz	1948	3.00	6.00	12.00
—Reissue of 38086					
❑ 20430	I Love You So Much, It Hurts/I'll Take What I Can Get	1948	3.75	7.50	15.00
❑ 20496	Please Don't Pass Me By/Cold Cold Woman	1948	3.75	7.50	15.00
❑ 20532	Drinkin' and Thinkin'/Hot Lick Fiddlin' Man	1949	3.75	7.50	15.00
❑ 36998	Drivin' Nails in My Coffin/Some Other World	1946	3.75	7.50	15.00
❑ 37221	Sign on the Dotted Line/Go Out and Find Somebody New	1946	3.75	7.50	15.00
❑ 37393	Gotta Have Something/Sweetheart, Darlin'	1947	3.75	7.50	15.00
❑ 37976	I'm Leaving This Old World Someday/It's Got Me Down	1947	3.75	7.50	15.00
—Reissue of 37976					
❑ 38086	Houston Waltz/Westphalia Waltz	1948	3.75	7.50	15.00

DECCA

Number	Title (A Side/B Side)	Yr	VG	VG+	NM
❑ 6090	They Took the Stars Out of Heaven/Why Do You Treat Me This Way	1943	3.75	7.50	15.00
❑ 6104	Each Night at Nine/G.I. Blues	1944	3.75	7.50	15.00
❑ 46102	Each Night at Nine/Why Do You Treat Me This Way	1948	3.00	6.00	12.00
❑ 46182	Don't Be Blue/It's Been a Long, Long Time	1949	3.00	6.00	12.00

Albums

CIMARRON

Number	Title (A Side/B Side)	Yr	VG	VG+	NM
❑ C-2003 [M]	Let's Make Memories	1962	12.50	25.00	50.00

HARMONY

Number	Title (A Side/B Side)	Yr	VG	VG+	NM
❑ HL 7316 [M]	Floyd Tillman's Best	1964	6.25	12.50	25.00
❑ HS 11297	I'll Still Be Lovin' You	1969	6.25	12.50	25.00

MUSICOR

Number	Title (A Side/B Side)	Yr	VG	VG+	NM
❑ MM-2136 [M]	Floyd Tillman's Country	1967	5.00	10.00	20.00
❑ MS-3136 [S]	Floyd Tillman's Country	1967	6.25	12.50	25.00
❑ MS-3157	Dream On	1968	5.00	10.00	20.00

RCA VICTOR

Number	Title (A Side/B Side)	Yr	VG	VG+	NM
❑ LPM-1686 [M]	Floyd Tillman's Greatest	1958	15.00	30.00	60.00

STARDAY

Number	Title (A Side/B Side)	Yr	VG	VG+	NM
❑ SLP-310 [M]	Let's Make Memories	1965	7.50	15.00	30.00

TILLOTSON, JOHNNY

45s

AMOS

Number	Title (A Side/B Side)	Yr	VG	VG+	NM
❑ 117	Tears on My Pillow/Remember When	1969	—	3.00	6.00
❑ 125	What Am I Living For/Joy to the World	1969	—	3.00	6.00
❑ 128	Raining in My Heart/Today I Started Loving You Again	1969	—	3.00	6.00
❑ 136	Susan/Love Waits for Me	1970	—	3.00	6.00
❑ 146	I Don't Believe In It Anymore/Kansas City, Kansas	1970	—	3.00	6.00

ATLANTIC

Number	Title (A Side/B Side)	Yr	VG	VG+	NM
❑ 87978	Bim Bam Boom/(B-side unknown)	1990	—	2.00	4.00

BUDDAH

Number	Title (A Side/B Side)	Yr	VG	VG+	NM
❑ 232	Star Spangled Bus/Apple Bend	1971	—	2.50	5.00

Number	Title (A Side/B Side)	Yr	VG	VG+	NM
❑ 256	Welfare Hero/The Flower Kissed the Shoes That Jesus Wore	1971	—	2.50	5.00
❑ 279	Make Me Believe/The Flower Kissed the Shoes That Jesus Wore	1972	—	2.50	5.00
❑ 311	Your Love's Been a Long Time Comin'/Apple Bend	1972	—	2.50	5.00
CADENCE					
❑ 1353	Dreamy Eyes/Well, I'm Your Man	1958	5.00	10.00	20.00
❑ 1354	I'm Never Gonna Kiss You/Cherie, Cherie	1958	6.25	12.50	25.00
—With Genevieve					
❑ 1365	True True Happiness/Love Is Blind	1959	5.00	10.00	20.00
❑ 1372	Why Do I Love You So/Never Let Me Go	1959	5.00	10.00	20.00
❑ 1377	Earth Angel/Pledging My Love	1960	5.00	10.00	20.00
❑ 1377 [PS]	Earth Angel/Pledging My Love	1960	7.50	15.00	30.00
❑ 1384	Poetry in Motion/Princess, Princess	1960	5.00	10.00	20.00
❑ 1391	Jimmy's Girl/His True Love Said Godbye	1960	3.75	7.50	15.00
❑ 1391 [PS]	Jimmy's Girl/His True Love Said Godbye	1960	7.50	15.00	30.00
❑ 1404	Without You/Cutie Pie	1961	3.75	7.50	15.00
❑ 1409	Dreamy Eyes/Well, I'm Your Man	1961	3.75	7.50	15.00
❑ 1418	It Keeps Right On a-Hurtin'/She Gave Sweet Love to Me	1962	3.75	7.50	15.00
❑ 1424	Send Me the Pillow You Dream On/What'll I Do	1962	3.75	7.50	15.00
❑ 1432	I Can't Help It (If I'm Still in Love with You)/I'm So Lonesome I Could Cry	1962	3.75	7.50	15.00
❑ 1434	Out of My Mind/Empty Feelin'	1963	3.75	7.50	15.00
❑ 1437	You Can Never Stop Me Loving You/Judy, Judy, Judy	1963	3.75	7.50	15.00
❑ 1441	Funny How Time Slips Away/A Very Good Year for Girls	1963	3.75	7.50	15.00
COLUMBIA					
❑ 10125	Big Ole Jean/Mississippi Lady	1975	—	2.50	5.00
❑ 10199	Right Here in Your Arms/Willow County Request Live	1975	—	2.50	5.00
❑ 45842	Sunshine of My Life/If You Wouldn't Be My Lady	1973	—	2.50	5.00
❑ 45984	So Much of My Life/I Love How She Needs Me	1973	—	2.50	5.00
❑ 46065	Till I Can't Take It Anymore/Sunday Kind of Woman	1974	—	2.50	5.00
MGM					
❑ 13181	Talk Back Trembling Lips/Another You	1963	3.00	6.00	12.00
❑ 13181 [PS]	Talk Back Trembling Lips/Another You	1963	5.00	10.00	20.00
❑ 13193	Worried Guy/Please Don't Go Away	1963	2.50	5.00	10.00
❑ 13193 [PS]	Worried Guy/Please Don't Go Away	1963	5.00	10.00	20.00
❑ 13232	I Rise, I Fall/I'm Watching My Watch	1964	2.50	5.00	10.00
❑ 13232 [PS]	I Rise, I Fall/I'm Watching My Watch	1964	5.00	10.00	20.00
❑ 13255	Worry/Sufferin' from a Heartache	1964	2.50	5.00	10.00
❑ 13255 [PS]	Worry/Sufferin' from a Heartache	1964	5.00	10.00	20.00
❑ 13284	She Understands Me/Tomorrow	1964	2.50	5.00	10.00
❑ 13284 [PS]	She Understands Me/Tomorrow	1964	5.00	10.00	20.00
❑ 13316	Angel/Little Boy	1965	2.50	5.00	10.00
❑ 13316 [PS]	Angel/Little Boy	1965	5.00	10.00	20.00
❑ 13344	Then I'll Count Again/One's Yours, One's Mine	1965	2.50	5.00	10.00
❑ 13344 [PS]	Then I'll Count Again/One's Yours, One's Mine	1965	5.00	10.00	20.00
❑ 13376	Heartaches by the Number/Your Mem'ry Comes Along	1965	2.50	5.00	10.00
❑ 13376 [PS]	Heartaches by the Number/Your Mem'ry Comes Along	1965	5.00	10.00	20.00
❑ 13408	Our World/(Wait 'Till You See) My Gidget	1965	2.50	5.00	10.00
❑ 13445	Hello Enemy/I Never Loved You Anyway	1966	2.50	5.00	10.00
❑ 13499	Me, Myself and I/Country Boy, Country Boy	1966	2.50	5.00	10.00
❑ 13519	No Love at All/What Am I Gonna Do	1966	2.50	5.00	10.00
❑ 13598	More Than Before/Baby's Gone	1966	2.50	5.00	10.00
❑ 13598	More Than Before/Open Up Your Heart	1966	2.50	5.00	10.00
❑ 13633	Christmas Country Style/Christmas Is the Best of All	1966	2.50	5.00	10.00
❑ 13684	Strange Things Happen/Tommy Jones	1967	2.50	5.00	10.00
❑ 13738	Don't Tell Me It's Raining/Takin' It Easy	1967	2.50	5.00	10.00
❑ 13829	You're the Reason/Countin' My Teardrops	1967	2.50	5.00	10.00
❑ 13888	I Can Spot a Cheater/It Keeps Right On a-Hurtin'	1968	2.00	4.00	8.00
❑ 13924	I Haven't Begun to Love You Yet/Why So Lonely	1968	2.00	4.00	8.00
❑ 13977	Letter to Emily/Your Mem'ry Comes Along	1968	2.00	4.00	8.00
REWARD					
❑ 03327	Baby You Do It for Me (And I'll Do It for You)/She's Not As Married As She Used to Be	1982	—	2.00	4.00
❑ 03901	Crying/You're a Beautiful Place to Be	1983	—	2.00	4.00
❑ 04123	Burnin'/What's Another Year	1983	—	2.00	4.00
❑ 04346	Lay Back (In the Arms of Somebody)/What's Another Year	1984	—	2.00	4.00
SCEPTER					
❑ 12389	Song for Hank Williams (mono/stereo)	1973	2.00	4.00	8.00
—With John Edward Beland; may be promo-only					
UNITED ARTISTS					
❑ XW860	It Could've Been Nashville/Summertime Lovin'	1976	—	2.50	5.00
❑ XW986	Toy Hearts/Just An Ordinary Man	1977	—	2.50	5.00
7-Inch Extended Plays					
CADENCE					
❑ CEP-114	True True Happiness/Love Is Blind//Dreamy Eyes/Well I'm Your Man	1960	6.25	12.50	25.00
❑ CEP-114 [PS]	Johnny Tillotson	1960	6.25	12.50	25.00
Albums					
ACCORD					
❑ SN-7194	Scrapbook	1982	2.50	5.00	10.00
AMOS					
❑ 7006	Tears on My Pillow	1969	5.00	10.00	20.00
BARNABY					
❑ BR-4007	Johnny Tillotson's Greatest	1977	3.00	6.00	12.00
BUDDAH					
❑ BDS-5112	Johnny Tillotson	1972	3.75	7.50	15.00
CADENCE					
❑ CLP-3052 [M]	Johnny Tillotson's Best	1961	10.00	20.00	40.00
—Maroon and silver label					
❑ CLP-3052 [M]	Johnny Tillotson's Best	1962	6.25	12.50	25.00
—Red and black label					
❑ CLP-3058 [M]	It Keeps Right On a-Hurtin'	1962	7.50	15.00	30.00
❑ CLP-3067 [M]	You Can Never Stop Me Loving You	1963	7.50	15.00	30.00
❑ CLP-25052 [P]	Johnny Tillotson's Best	1961	12.50	25.00	50.00
—Maroon and silver label					
❑ CLP-25052 [P]	Johnny Tillotson's Best	1962	7.50	15.00	30.00
—Red and black label					
❑ CLP-25058 [S]	It Keeps Right On a-Hurtin'	1962	10.00	20.00	40.00
❑ CLP-25067 [P]	You Can Never Stop Me Loving You	1963	10.00	20.00	40.00
EVEREST					
❑ 4113	Johnny Tillotson's Greatest Hits	1982	2.50	5.00	10.00
METRO					
❑ M-561 [M]	Johnny Tillotson Sings Tillotson	1967	3.75	7.50	15.00
❑ MS-561 [S]	Johnny Tillotson Sings Tillotson	1967	5.00	10.00	20.00
MGM					
❑ E-4188 [M]	Talk Back Trembling Lips	1964	5.00	10.00	20.00
❑ SE-4188 [S]	Talk Back Trembling Lips	1964	6.25	12.50	25.00
❑ E-4224 [M]	The Tillotson Touch	1964	5.00	10.00	20.00
❑ SE-4224 [S]	The Tillotson Touch	1964	6.25	12.50	25.00
❑ E-4270 [M]	She Understands Me	1965	5.00	10.00	20.00
❑ SE-4270 [S]	She Understands Me	1965	6.25	12.50	25.00
❑ E-4302 [M]	That's My Style	1965	5.00	10.00	20.00
❑ SE-4302 [S]	That's My Style	1965	6.25	12.50	25.00
❑ E-4328 [M]	Our World	1965	5.00	10.00	20.00
❑ SE-4328 [S]	Our World	1965	6.25	12.50	25.00
❑ E-4395 [M]	No Love at All	1966	5.00	10.00	20.00
❑ SE-4395 [S]	No Love at All	1966	6.25	12.50	25.00
❑ E-4402 [M]	The Christmas Touch	1966	5.00	10.00	20.00
❑ SE-4402 [S]	The Christmas Touch	1966	6.25	12.50	25.00
❑ E-4452 [M]	Here I Am	1967	5.00	10.00	20.00
❑ SE-4452 [S]	Here I Am	1967	6.25	12.50	25.00
❑ E-4532 [M]	The Best of Johnny Tillotson	1968	7.50	15.00	30.00
—May be promo only (yellow label)					
❑ SE-4532 [S]	The Best of Johnny Tillotson	1968	5.00	10.00	20.00
❑ SE-4814	The Very Best of Johnny Tillotson	1971	3.00	6.00	12.00
❑ ST 90410 [S]	The Tillotson Touch	1965	7.50	15.00	30.00
—Capitol Record Club edition					
❑ T 90410 [M]	The Tillotson Touch	1965	7.50	15.00	30.00
—Capitol Record Club edition					
UNITED ARTISTS					
❑ UA-LA759-G	Johnny Tillotson	1977	2.50	5.00	10.00

TILTON, SHEILA

45s

Number	Title (A Side/B Side)	Yr	VG	VG+	NM
CON BRIO					
❑ 101	Brass Buckles/Good Old Pete	1975	—	3.00	6.00
❑ 104	I'll Be Whatever You Say/Let Your Lovin' Do the Talkin'	1976	—	2.50	5.00
❑ 107	I'm Beginning to See the Light/He's Coming Home	1976	—	2.50	5.00
❑ 110	Half As Much/I'll Be Whatever You Say	1976	—	2.50	5.00
❑ 115	Little Man/(B-side unknown)	1977	—	2.50	5.00

TINY TIM

The famous falsetto novelty singer had one record make the country charts, years after his pop success.

45s

Number	Title (A Side/B Side)	Yr	VG	VG+	NM
NLT					
❑ 1993	Leave Me Satisfied/I Wanna' Get Crazy with You	1988	2.00	4.00	8.00

TIPPIN, AARON

45s

Number	Title (A Side/B Side)	Yr	VG	VG+	NM
BNA					
❑ 62707	I'm So Lonesome I Could Cry/Crying Time	1993	—	2.00	4.00
—B-side by Lorrie Morgan					
LYRIC STREET					
❑ ED-11282	Kiss This/People Like Us	2000	—	2.50	5.00
—1,000 copies were pressed for a jukebox distributor					
❑ 64023	For You I Will/Back When I Knew Everything	1998	—	2.00	4.00
RCA					
❑ 2711-7-R	You've Got to Stand for Something/Up Against You	1990	—	3.00	6.00
❑ 2747-7-R	I Wonder How Far It Is Over You/You Should See Me Missing You	1991	—	—	3.00
❑ 62015	She Made a Memory Out of Me/The Sky's Got the Blues	1991	—	2.00	4.00
❑ 62181	There Ain't Nothin' Wrong with the Radio/I Miss Misbehavin'	1992	—	2.50	5.00
❑ 62241	I Wouldn't Have It Any Other Way/What I Can't Live Without	1992	—	2.00	4.00
❑ 62338	I Was Born with a Broken Heart/Read Between the Lines	1992	—	—	3.00
❑ 62430	My Blue Angel/The Sound of Your Goodbye (Sticks and Stones)	1993	—	2.00	4.00
❑ 62520	Working Man's Ph.D./When Country Took the Throne	1993	—	2.00	4.00
❑ 62657	The Call of the Wild/Nothin' in the World	1993	—	—	3.00

Number	Title (A Side/B Side)	Yr	VG	VG+	NM
❑ 62755	Honky-Tonk Superman/Let's Talk About You	1994	—	—	3.00
❑ 62832	Whole Lotta Love on the Line/I Promised You the World	1994	—	—	3.00
❑ 62947	I Got It Honest/Lookin' Back at Myself	1994	—	2.00	4.00
❑ 64272	She Feels Like a Brand New Man Tonight/Lovin' Me Into an Early Grave	1995	—	—	3.00
❑ 64392	That's As Close As I'll Get to Loving You/She Feels Like a Brand New Man Tonight	1995	—	2.00	4.00
❑ 64471	Without Your Love/Country Boy's Toolbox	1996	—	—	3.00
❑ 64544	Everything I Own/She Made a Man Out of a Mountain of Stone	1996	—	—	3.00
❑ 64640	How's the Radio Know/I Can Help	1996	—	—	3.00
❑ 64770	That's What Happens When I Hold You/Whole Lotta Love on the Line`	1997	—	—	3.00

TODD, DICK

He's not a country singer; one of his CD reissues calls him "The Canadian Crosby" as in Bing. But the below records either feature country backing or were aimed at the country market.

45s

DECCA

Number	Title (A Side/B Side)	Yr	VG	VG+	NM
❑ 9-28314	Too Old to Cut the Mustard/Waiting in the Lobby of Your Heart	1952	5.00	10.00	20.00
—With Grady Martin					
❑ 9-29361	Columbus Stockade/Sweethearts or Strangers	1954	5.00	10.00	20.00
—With Grady Martin					
❑ 32168	Big Wheel Cannonball/Return of the Double Eagle	1967	2.00	4.00	8.00
❑ 32251	Pennsylvania Turnpike, I Love You/White House Waltz	1968	2.00	4.00	8.00

TOLIVER, TONY

45s

CAPITOL NASHVILLE

Number	Title (A Side/B Side)	Yr	VG	VG+	NM
❑ 7PRO-79545	Bar Stool Fool (same on both sides)	1991	—	3.00	6.00
—Vinyl is promo only					

RISING TIDE

Number	Title (A Side/B Side)	Yr	VG	VG+	NM
❑ 56040	Bettin' Forever on You/Louisiana Lonely	1996	—	2.00	4.00
❑ 56042	He's On the Way Home/Swinging Doors	1996	—	2.00	4.00

TOM AND JERRY

Guitar duo of Tommy Tomlinson and Jerry Kennedy. No relation to the "Tom and Jerry" who recorded for Big and later became known as Simon and Garfunkel.

45s

MERCURY

Number	Title (A Side/B Side)	Yr	VG	VG+	NM
❑ 71753	Golden Wildwood Flower/South	1961	5.00	10.00	20.00
❑ 71827	Swing Low/Sungarfoot Rag	1961	5.00	10.00	20.00
❑ 71930	I'll Drown in My Tears/French Twist	1961	5.00	10.00	20.00

Albums

MERCURY

Number	Title (A Side/B Side)	Yr	VG	VG+	NM
❑ MG-20626 [M]	Guitar's Greatest Hits	1961	7.50	15.00	30.00
❑ MG-20671 [M]	Guitars Play the Sound of Ray Charles	1962	7.50	15.00	30.00
❑ MG-20756 [M]	Guitar's Greatest Hits, Vol. 2	1962	7.50	15.00	30.00
❑ MG-20842 [M]	Surfin' Hootenanny	1963	10.00	20.00	40.00
❑ SR-60626 [S]	Guitar's Greatest Hits	1961	10.00	20.00	40.00
❑ SR-60671 [S]	Guitars Play the Sound of Ray Charles	1962	10.00	20.00	40.00
❑ SR-60756 [S]	Guitar's Greatest Hits, Vol. 2	1962	10.00	20.00	40.00
❑ SR-60842 [S]	Surfin' Hootenanny	1963	12.50	25.00	50.00

TOMMY AND DONNA

45s

OAK

Number	Title (A Side/B Side)	Yr	VG	VG+	NM
❑ 1067	Take It Slow with Me/(B-side unknown)	1988	—	3.00	6.00

TOMORROW'S WORLD

All-star group of country artists singing in honor of the 20th anniversary of Earth Day. We have no evidence that this single was ever issued except as a promo.

45s

WARNER BROS.

Number	Title (A Side/B Side)	Yr	VG	VG+	NM
❑ PRO-S-4069	Tomorrow's World (same on both sides)	1990	—	2.50	5.00
—Only exists as a promo					
❑ PRO-S-4069 [PS]	Tomorrow's World (same on both sides)	1990	—	3.00	6.00

TOMPALL

See TOMPALL GLASER; TOMPALL AND THE GLASER BROTHERS.

TOMPALL AND THE GLASER BROTHERS

Also see CHUCK GLASER; JIM GLASER; TOMPALL GLASER.

45s

DECCA

Number	Title (A Side/B Side)	Yr	VG	VG+	NM
❑ 9-30805	Oh Little Mary/Lay Down the Gun	1959	3.75	7.50	15.00
❑ 9-30900	Ooie-Gooie/She Loves the Love I Give Her	1959	3.00	6.00	12.00
❑ 31011	I'll Never Tell/21 Miles from Home	1959	3.00	6.00	12.00
❑ 31051	Careless Love, Goodbye/Alibi	1960	3.00	6.00	12.00
❑ 31180	Same Old Memories/Sweet Love, Goodbye	1960	3.00	6.00	12.00
❑ 31258	Judy's Growin' Up/Words Come Easy	1961	3.00	6.00	12.00
❑ 31322	Tired of Crying Over You/Let Me Down Easy	1961	3.00	6.00	12.00
❑ 31398	I Can't Remember/I'm Losing Again	1962	3.00	6.00	12.00
❑ 31447	False Hearted Lover/Odds and Ends (Bits and Pieces)	1962	3.00	6.00	12.00
❑ 31494	Stand Beside Me/Trackin' Me Down	1963	2.50	5.00	10.00
❑ 31551	Blow Out the Candles/Mr. Lonesome	1963	2.50	5.00	10.00
❑ 31632	A Girl Like You/I've Got Troubles	1964	2.50	5.00	10.00
❑ 31736	Baby, They're Playing Our Song/Winner Take All	1965	2.50	5.00	10.00
❑ 31809	Back in Each Other's Arms Again/Teardrops 'Til Dawn	1965	2.50	5.00	10.00

ELEKTRA

Number	Title (A Side/B Side)	Yr	VG	VG+	NM
❑ 46595	Weight of My Chains/The Ballad of Lucy Jordan	1980	—	2.00	4.00
❑ 47056	Sweet City Woman/Tryin' to Outrun the Wind	1980	—	2.00	4.00
❑ 47134	Lovin' Her Was Easier (Than Anything I'll Ever Do Again)/United We Fall	1981	—	2.00	4.00
❑ 47193	Just One Time/Feelin' the Weight of My Chains	1981	—	2.00	4.00
❑ 47230 [DJ]	Silver Bells/Please Come Home for Christmas	1981	—	3.00	6.00
—B-side by Johnny Lee					
❑ 47405	It'll Be Her/A Mansion on the Hill	1982	—	2.00	4.00
❑ 47461	I Still Love You (After All These Years)/Feelin' the Weight of My Chains	1982	—	2.00	4.00
❑ 69947	Maria Consuela/I Can Never Live Alone Again	1982	—	2.00	4.00

MGM

Number	Title (A Side/B Side)	Yr	VG	VG+	NM
❑ 13531	The Last Thing on My Mind/More or Less	1966	2.50	5.00	10.00
❑ 13611	Gone, On the Other Hand/Streets of Baltimore	1966	2.00	4.00	8.00
❑ 13754	Through the Eyes of Love/She Loved the Wrong Man	1967	2.00	4.00	8.00
❑ 13880	The Moods of Mary/No End of Love	1967	2.00	4.00	8.00
❑ 13954	One of These Days/Where Has All the Love Gone	1968	2.00	4.00	8.00
❑ 14036	California Girl (And the Tennessee Square)/All That Keeps Ya Goin'	1969	—	3.50	7.00
❑ 14064	Wicked California/This Eve of Parting	1969	—	3.50	7.00
❑ 14113	All That Keeps Ya Goin'/Theme from "...tick ...tick ...tick"	1970	—	3.50	7.00
❑ 14169	Gone Girl/I'll Say My Words	1970	—	3.50	7.00
❑ 14249	Faded Love/Pretty Eyes	1971	—	3.00	6.00
—With Leon McAuliffe and the Cimarron Boys					
❑ 14291	Rings/That's When I Love You the Most	1971	—	3.00	6.00
❑ 14349	Sweet, Love Me Good Woman/Stand Beside Me	1971	—	3.00	6.00
❑ 14390	Ain't It All Worth Living For/Blue Ridge Mountain	1972	—	3.00	6.00
❑ 14462	A Girl Like You/Delta Lost	1972	—	3.00	6.00
❑ 14516	Charlie/Lovin' You Again	1973	—	3.00	6.00

RICH

Number	Title (A Side/B Side)	Yr	VG	VG+	NM
❑ 1004	The Cry of the Wild Goose/Yakety Yak	196?	3.75	7.50	15.00

ROBBINS

Number	Title (A Side/B Side)	Yr	VG	VG+	NM
❑ 1006	Sweet Lies/Yakety Yak	1958	7.50	15.00	30.00

Albums

DECCA

Number	Title (A Side/B Side)	Yr	VG	VG+	NM
❑ DL 4041 [M]	This Land Folk Songs	1960	7.50	15.00	30.00
❑ DL 74041 [S]	This Land Folk Songs	1960	10.00	20.00	40.00

ELEKTRA

Number	Title (A Side/B Side)	Yr	VG	VG+	NM
❑ 5E-542	Lovin' Her Was Easier	1981	2.50	5.00	10.00
❑ 60148	After All These Years	1982	2.50	5.00	10.00

MGM

Number	Title (A Side/B Side)	Yr	VG	VG+	NM
❑ E-4465 [M]	Tompall & the Glaser Brothers	1967	6.25	12.50	25.00
❑ SE-4465 [S]	Tompall & the Glaser Brothers	1967	5.00	10.00	20.00
❑ SE-4510	Through the Eyes of Love	1968	3.75	7.50	15.00
❑ SE-4620	Now Country	1969	3.75	7.50	15.00
❑ SE-4775	Award Winners	1971	3.75	7.50	15.00
❑ SE-4812	Rings and Things	1972	3.75	7.50	15.00
❑ SE-4888	Great Hits from Two Decades	1973	3.75	7.50	15.00
❑ SE-4976	Vocal Group of the Decade	1974	3.75	7.50	15.00

TONI AND TERRY

Albums

CAPITOL

Number	Title (A Side/B Side)	Yr	VG	VG+	NM
❑ ST-11137	Cross-Country	1973	3.00	6.00	12.00

TOPEL AND WARE

45s

RCI

Number	Title (A Side/B Side)	Yr	VG	VG+	NM
❑ 2399	Children of America (Liberty Tribute)/(B-side unknown)	1986	—	3.00	6.00
❑ 2406	Change of Heart/(B-side unknown)	1987	—	3.00	6.00

TOROK, MITCHELL

45s

ABBOTT

Number	Title (A Side/B Side)	Yr	VG	VG+	NM
❑ 136	Little Hoo-Wee/Judalina	1953	6.25	12.50	25.00
❑ 140	Caribbean/Weep Away	1953	7.50	15.00	30.00
❑ 150	Hootchy Kootchy Henry (From Hawaii)/Gigolo	1953	6.25	12.50	25.00
❑ 156	Edgar the Eager Easter Bunny/Living on Love	1954	6.25	12.50	25.00
❑ 162	Dancerette/Haunting Waterfall	1954	6.25	12.50	25.00

CAPITOL

Number	Title (A Side/B Side)	Yr	VG	VG+	NM
❑ 4846	Rio Grande/Fools Disguise	1962	2.00	4.00	8.00
❑ 4946	Mighty Mighty Man/For Someone Who's Supposed to Be Hurtin'	1963	2.00	4.00	8.00

DECCA

Number	Title (A Side/B Side)	Yr	VG	VG+	NM
❑ 29326	Roulette/Havana Huddle	1954	5.00	10.00	20.00
❑ 29408	Peasant's Guitar/The World Keeps Turning Around	1955	3.75	7.50	15.00
❑ 29576	Too Late Now/Smooth Talk	1955	3.75	7.50	15.00
❑ 29661	Marching My Blues Away/Country and Western	1955	3.75	7.50	15.00
❑ 29863	No Money Down/Red Light, Green Light	1956	3.75	7.50	15.00
❑ 29986	I Wish I Was a Little Bit Younger/When Mexico Gave Up Rhumba	1956	3.75	7.50	15.00
❑ 30134	Take This Heart/Drink Up and Go Home	1956	3.75	7.50	15.00
❑ 30230	Pledge of Love/What's Behind That Strange Door	1957	3.75	7.50	15.00
❑ 30424	Two Words/You're Tempting Me	1957	3.75	7.50	15.00
❑ 30599	Be Kind to Me/How Much Do I Love You	1958	3.00	6.00	12.00
❑ 30661	Sweet Revenge/Love Me Like You Mean It	1958	3.00	6.00	12.00
❑ 30742	Date with a Teardrop/These Things I Hold Dear	1958	3.00	6.00	12.00
❑ 30859	Go Ahead and Be a Fool/Memories of You Haunting Me Night and Day	1959	3.00	6.00	12.00
❑ 30901	PTA Rock and Roll/Teenie Weenie Bikini	1959	5.00	10.00	20.00

Number	Title (A Side/B Side)	Yr	VG	VG+	NM
GUYDEN					
❑ 2018	Caribbean/Hootchy Kootchy Henry (From Hawaii)	1959	3.00	6.00	12.00
❑ 2028	You Are the One/Mexican Joe	1959	2.50	5.00	10.00
❑ 2032	Guardian Angel/I Want to Know Everything	1960	2.50	5.00	10.00
❑ 2034	Pink Chiffon/What You Don't Know	1960	2.50	5.00	10.00
❑ 2034 [PS]	Pink Chiffon/What You Don't Know	1960	5.00	10.00	20.00
❑ 2040	Happy Street/Little Boy in Love	1960	2.50	5.00	10.00
MERCURY					
❑ 71826	El Tigre/Eating My Heart Out	1961	2.50	5.00	10.00
RCA VICTOR					
❑ 47-8646	I Needed All the Help I Can Get/Man with a Golden Hand	1965	2.00	4.00	8.00
❑ 47-8703	Caribbean/Witch Woman	1965	2.00	4.00	8.00
REPRISE					
❑ 0541	Instant Love/Put Me in the Driver's Seat	1966	—	3.00	6.00
❑ 0568	Falling in Love Again/Baby, Baby, Baby	1967	—	3.00	6.00
Albums					
GUYDEN					
❑ GLP-502 [M]	Caribbean	1960	10.00	20.00	40.00
❑ ST-502 [S]	Caribbean	1960	12.50	25.00	50.00
REPRISE					
❑ R 6223 [M]	Guitar Course	1966	5.00	10.00	20.00
❑ RS 6223 [S]	Guitar Course	1966	6.25	12.50	25.00

TOUCH OF COUNTRY

Number	Title (A Side/B Side)	Yr	VG	VG+	NM
45s					
OL					
❑ 127	I Won't Be Seeing Her No More/Long Talk with Myself	1988	—	2.50	5.00
❑ 130	Did I Leave My Heart at Your House/(B-side unknown)	1989	—	2.50	5.00
❑ 130 [PS]	Did I Leave My Heart at Your House/(B-side unknown)	1989	2.00	4.00	8.00
❑ 134	When I Look Into Your Eyes/Somebody Told Her	1989	—	2.50	5.00
❑ 143	Let Me Be the One/(B-side unknown)	1990	—	3.00	6.00

TRACTORS, THE

Number	Title (A Side/B Side)	Yr	VG	VG+	NM
45s					
ARISTA					
❑ 12717	Baby Likes to Rock It/Tulsa Shuffle	1994	—	2.00	4.00
❑ 12771	The Santa Claus Boogie/Swingin' Home for Christmas	1994	—	2.00	4.00
❑ 12784	Tryin' to Get to New Orleans/Doreen	1994	—	—	3.00
❑ 12818	Badly Bent/Thirty Days	1995	—	—	3.00
❑ 12923	Santa Claus Is Comin' (In a Boogie Woogie Choo Choo Train)/Santa Looked a Lot Like Daddy	1995	—	—	3.00
ARISTA NASHVILLE					
❑ 13147	Shortenin' Bread/How Long Will It Take	1998	—	—	3.00
❑ 13163	I Wouldn't Tell You No Lie/Hale Bop Boogie	1999	—	—	3.00

TRADER-PRICE

Number	Title (A Side/B Side)	Yr	VG	VG+	NM
45s					
UNIVERSAL					
❑ UVL-66022	Sad Eyes/Who's Gonna Know	1989	—	—	3.00
❑ UVL-66031	Lately Rose/Hideaway	1989	—	2.00	4.00

TRAMMELL, BOBBY LEE

Number	Title (A Side/B Side)	Yr	VG	VG+	NM
45s					
ABC-PARAMOUNT					
❑ 9890	Shirley Lee/I Sure Do Love You Baby	1958	20.00	40.00	80.00
ALLEY					
❑ 1001	It's All Your Fault/Arkansas Twist	1962	6.25	12.50	25.00
❑ 1004	Come On Baby/I Tried Not to Cry	1963	6.25	12.50	25.00
ATLANTA					
❑ 1101	Just Let Me Love You One More Time/Tator	196?	6.25	12.50	25.00
❑ 1501	Carolyn/Sally Twist	196?	6.25	12.50	25.00
❑ 1502	Come On/I Love 'Em All	196?	6.25	12.50	25.00
❑ 1503	Give Me That Good Lovin'/New Dance in France	196?	6.25	12.50	25.00
❑ 3001	I'll Step Aside/Mary Ann	196?	6.25	12.50	25.00
ATLANTIC					
❑ 2332	Shimmy Loo/You Make Me Feel So Fine	1966	3.00	6.00	12.00
CAPITOL					
❑ 3718	Love Don't Let Me Down/I Couldn't Believe My Eyes	1973	2.00	4.00	8.00
❑ 3801	You Mostest Girl/You Stand a Chance of Losing What You've Got	1973	2.00	4.00	8.00
CINNAMON					
❑ 797	The Warmth of Your Love/Marion County Tradition	1974	—	3.00	6.00
CONFEDERATE					
❑ 125	Shake Me Baby/Run Fool Run	195?	250.00	500.00	1000.
FABOR					
❑ 127	You Mostest Girl/Uh Oh	1964	3.00	6.00	12.00
❑ 4038	Shirley Lee/I Sure Do Love You Baby	1957	37.50	75.00	150.00
HOT					
❑ 101	Shimmy Lou/(B-side unknown)	1959	10.00	20.00	40.00
❑ 102	Betty Jean/(B-side unknown)	1959	10.00	20.00	40.00
RADIO					
❑ 102	You Mostest Girl/Uh Oh	1958	12.50	25.00	50.00
❑ 114	My Susie Jane/Should I Make Amends	1958	10.00	20.00	40.00
SANTO					
❑ 9052	Hi-O Silver/Don't You Know I Love You	196?	5.00	10.00	20.00
SIMS					
❑ 183	Good Lovin'/New Dance in France	1964	3.00	6.00	12.00
❑ 195	Come On and Love Me/If You Don't Wanna, You Don't Have To	1964	3.00	6.00	12.00
❑ 225	Twenty-Four Hours/Just Let Me Move You One More Time	1965	3.00	6.00	12.00
❑ 241	I Tried/Am I Satisfying You	1965	3.00	6.00	12.00
❑ 254	Long Tall Sally/The Saints Go Marchin' In	1965	3.00	6.00	12.00
SKYLA					
❑ 1307	You Mostest Girl/Uh Oh	1961	3.75	7.50	15.00
SOUNCOT					
❑ 1100	I Dare America to Be Great/A Gift from God	1970	—	3.00	6.00
❑ 1104	24 Hours a Day/I Lost the Girl I Love Tonight	1970	—	3.00	6.00
❑ 1113	You Mostest Girl/Whole Lotta Shakin' Goin' On	1971	—	3.00	6.00
❑ 1119	My Shoes Keep Walkin' Back to You/Let's Wash the World and Make It Clean	1971	—	3.00	6.00
❑ 1128	Don't Let the Stars Get In Your Eyes/Sheila	1971	—	3.00	6.00
❑ 1130	You Were Worth the Wait/Wadin' in the Water	1972	—	3.00	6.00
❑ 1135	Love Isn't Love (Till You Give It Away)/Tell Me That You Want Me	1972	—	3.00	6.00
❑ 1143	I Believe in You/My Love Keeps Growing	1972	—	3.00	6.00
❑ 1145	You Put Love Back in My Heart/I Lost the Girl I Love Tonight	1972	—	3.00	6.00
SUN					
❑ 1135	Jenny Lee/It's All Your Fault	1977	—	3.00	6.00
WARRIOR					
❑ 1554	Woe Is Me/(B-side unknown)	1959	20.00	40.00	80.00
Albums					
ATLANTA					
❑ 1503 [M]	Arkansas Twist	1962	250.00	500.00	1000.
SOUNCOT					
❑ SC-1102	I Dare America to Be Great	1971	5.00	10.00	20.00
❑ SC-1141	Love Isn't Love Till You Give It Away	1972	3.75	7.50	15.00

TRASK, DIANA

Number	Title (A Side/B Side)	Yr	VG	VG+	NM
45s					
ABC DOT					
❑ 17536	Oh Boy/Alone Again	1974	—	2.50	5.00
❑ 17555	There Has to Be a Loser/Sunshine	1975	—	2.50	5.00
❑ 17587	Cry/I Can Take a Little Heartache	1975	—	2.50	5.00
COLUMBIA					
❑ 4-41623	A Guy Is a Guy/Theme from "Our Man in Havana"	1960	3.75	7.50	15.00
❑ 4-41711	Long Ago Last Summer/Turn to Me	1960	3.75	7.50	15.00
❑ 4-41821	I'm So Lonesome I Could Cry/Our Language of Love	1960	3.75	7.50	15.00
❑ 4-41943	Waltzing Matilda/I Loved You Once in Silence	1961	3.75	7.50	15.00
DIAL					
❑ 4077	Lock, Stock and Tear Drops/Precious Time	1968	2.00	4.00	8.00
DOT					
❑ 17160	Hold What You've Got/This Heart Was Made for Lovin'	1968	—	3.50	7.00
❑ 17211	You Got What It Takes/Build Your Love (On a Solid Foundation)	1969	—	3.50	7.00
❑ 17286	Children/The Staying Kind	1969	—	3.50	7.00
❑ 17316	I Fall to Pieces/Long Ago Is Gone	1969	—	3.50	7.00
❑ 17342	Beneath Still Waters/Heartbreak Hotel	1970	—	3.00	6.00
❑ 17369	The Last Person to See Me Alive/A Stronger Hand to Hold	1970	—	3.00	6.00
❑ 17384	The Chokin' Kind/Let's Keep Her Free (America)	1971	—	3.00	6.00
❑ 17404	We've Got to Work It Out Between Us/I Keep It Hid	1972	—	3.00	6.00
❑ 17424	It Meant Nothing to Me/How Much Have I Hurt Thee	1972	—	3.00	6.00
❑ 17448	Say When/Old Southern Cotton Town	1973	—	3.00	6.00
❑ 17467	It's a Man's World (If You Had a Man Like Mine)/World of the Missing	1973	—	3.00	6.00
❑ 17486	When I Get My Hands on You/Shadow of My Man	1973	—	3.00	6.00
❑ 17496	Lean It All on Me/The King	1974	—	3.00	6.00
❑ 17520	(If You Wanna Hold On) Hold On to Your Man	1974	—	3.00	6.00
KARI					
❑ 121	This Must Be My Ship/(B-side unknown)	1981	—	3.00	6.00
❑ 123	Stirrin' Up Feelings/Give My Heart a Break	1981	—	3.00	6.00
❑ 125	Never Gonna Be Alright/(B-side unknown)	1981	—	3.00	6.00
ROULETTE					
❑ 4184	Soldier Won't You Marry Me/Love Is Another Name for a Fool	1959	5.00	10.00	20.00
Albums					
ABC					
❑ ABDP-948	Believe Me Now or Believe Me Later	1976	3.00	6.00	12.00
❑ AC-30030	The ABC Collection	1976	3.00	6.00	12.00
ABC DOT					
❑ DOSD-2007	Diana Trask's Greatest Hits	1974	3.00	6.00	12.00
❑ DOSD-2024	The Mood I'm In	1975	3.00	6.00	12.00
COLUMBIA					
❑ CL 1601 [M]	Diana Trask	1961	6.25	12.50	25.00
❑ CL 1705 [M]	Diana Trask on TV	1961	6.25	12.50	25.00
❑ CS 8401 [S]	Diana Trask	1961	7.50	15.00	30.00
❑ CS 8505 [S]	Diana Trask on TV	1961	7.50	15.00	30.00
DOT					
❑ DLP-25920	Miss Country Soul	1969	3.75	7.50	15.00
❑ DLP-25957	From the Heart	1969	3.75	7.50	15.00
❑ DOS-25989	Diana's Country	1971	3.75	7.50	15.00
❑ DOS-25999	Diana Trask Sings About Loving	1972	3.75	7.50	15.00
❑ DLP-26016	It's a Man's World	1973	3.75	7.50	15.00
❑ DLP-26022	Lean It All on Me	1974	3.75	7.50	15.00

TRAVIS, MERLE

Also see HANK THOMPSON.

45s

CAPITOL

Number	Title (A Side/B Side)	Yr	VG	VG+	NM
❑ F965	I Got a Mean Old Woman/Start Even	1950	7.50	15.00	30.00
❑ F1029	Guitar Rag/Cane Bottom Chair	1950	7.50	15.00	30.00
❑ F1146	Spoonin' Moon/Too Much Sugar for a Dime	1950	7.50	15.00	30.00
❑ F1241	El Reno/Trouble, Trouble	1950	7.50	15.00	30.00
❑ F1337	Dry Bread/Woncha Be My Baby	1950	7.50	15.00	30.00
❑ F1519	The Deep South/Boogie in A Minor	1951	6.25	12.50	25.00
❑ F1737	Lost John Boogie/Let's Settle Down	1951	6.25	12.50	25.00
❑ F1800	Done Rovin'/Faithful Fools	1951	6.25	12.50	25.00
❑ F2014	Rainy Day Feelin'/Kinfolks in Carolina	1952	6.25	12.50	25.00
❑ F2136	Ain't That a Cryin' Shame/Too Fast Past	1952	6.25	12.50	25.00
❑ F2175	Steel Guitar Rag/Merle's Boogie Woogie	1952	6.25	12.50	25.00
❑ F2176	I Am a Pilgrim/Nine Pound Hammer	1952	6.25	12.50	25.00
❑ F2245	I'll See You in My Dreams/Cannonball Rag	1952	6.25	12.50	25.00
❑ F2336	Bayou Baby/Knee Deep in Trouble	1953	6.25	12.50	25.00
❑ F2453	I'll Have Myself a Ball/Green Cheese	1953	6.25	12.50	25.00
❑ F2544	Gambler's Guitar/Shut Up and Drink Your Beer	1953	6.25	12.50	25.00
❑ F2563	Re-Enlistment Blues/Dance of the Golden Rod	1953	6.25	12.50	25.00
❑ F2757	Jole Fille/I Can't Afford the Coffee	1954	6.25	12.50	25.00
❑ F2902	Louisiana Boogie/Love Must Be Ketchin'	1954	6.25	12.50	25.00
❑ F3194	Beer Barrel Polka/Cuddle Up a Little Closer	1955	5.00	10.00	20.00
❑ F3247	Hunky Dory/If You Want It I've Got It	1955	5.00	10.00	20.00
❑ F3362	Lazy River/Turn My Picture Upside Down	1956	5.00	10.00	20.00
❑ 5657	John Henry, Jr./That Same Ol' Natural Urge	1966	2.50	5.00	10.00
❑ 5764	Moon Over the Motel/That Tennessee Beat	1966	2.50	5.00	10.00
❑ 5876	Wildwood Flower/Farther On Down the Road	1967	2.50	5.00	10.00
❑ 5965	Country Joe/You're a Little Bit Cuter	1967	2.50	5.00	10.00
❑ F40272	Petticoat Fever/I'm Pickin' Up the Pieces of My Heart	1950	10.00	20.00	40.00

Selected 78s

CAPITOL

Number	Title (A Side/B Side)	Yr	VG	VG+	NM
❑ BD-50 [(4)]	Folk Songs of the Hills	1947	25.00	50.00	100.00
—This is for all four 78s and the accompanying binder. We don't know the numbers or the A and B sides of the enclosed records, so we can't list them individually. We do know that one of the songs is the original version of "Sixteen Tons," which helps explain its value.					
❑ 258	Cincinnati Lou/No Vacancy	1946	3.75	7.50	15.00
❑ 290	Divorce Me C.O.D./Missouri	1946	5.00	10.00	20.00
❑ 349	So Round, So Firm, So Fully Packed/Sweet Temptation	1947	5.00	10.00	20.00
❑ 384	Steel Guitar Rag/Three Times Seven`	1947	3.75	7.50	15.00
❑ 15124	I Am a Pilgrim/Nine Pound Hammer	1948	3.75	7.50	15.00
❑ 15143	Crazy Boogie/I'm a Natural Born Gamblin' Man	1948	5.00	10.00	20.00
❑ 15212	T for Texas (Blue Yodel No. 1)/Leave My Honey Bee Alone	1948	5.00	10.00	20.00
❑ 15263	Divorce Me C.O.D./Steel Guitar Rag	1948	3.75	7.50	15.00
❑ 15264	Cincinnati Lou/So Round, So Firm, So Fully Packed	1948	3.75	7.50	15.00
❑ 15265	Missouri/No Vacancy	1948	3.75	7.50	15.00
❑ 15317	What a Shame/Dapper Dan	1949	3.75	7.50	15.00
❑ 40006	Lawdy, What a Gal/I'm Sick and Tired of You, Little Darlin'	1947	3.75	7.50	15.00
❑ 40026	Fat Gal/Merle's Boogie Woogie	1947	3.75	7.50	15.00
❑ 40050	I Like My Chicken Fryin' Size/Follow Thru	1947	3.75	7.50	15.00
❑ 40100	When My Baby Double Talks to Me/Kentucky Means Paradise	1948	3.75	7.50	15.00
❑ 40115	Alimony Bound/A Fool at the Steering Wheel	1948	3.75	7.50	15.00
❑ 40171	That's All/Get Along Blues	1949	5.00	10.00	20.00
❑ 40214	Blue Smoke/Walkin' the Strings, Fuller Blues	1949	5.00	10.00	20.00
❑ 40254	Blues Stay Away from Me/Philosophy	1949	5.00	10.00	20.00

Albums

CAPITOL

Number	Title (A Side/B Side)	Yr	VG	VG+	NM
❑ T 650 [M]	The Merle Travis Guitar	1956	30.00	60.00	120.00
—Turquoise or gray label					
❑ T 650 [M]	The Merle Travis Guitar	1959	7.50	15.00	30.00
—Black colorband label, logo at left					
❑ T 650 [M]	The Merle Travis Guitar	1962	5.00	10.00	20.00
—Black colorband label, logo at top					
❑ T 891 [M]	Back Home	1957	25.00	50.00	100.00
—Turquoise or gray label					
❑ T 891 [M]	Back Home	1959	7.50	15.00	30.00
—Black colorband label, logo at left					
❑ T 891 [M]	Back Home	1962	5.00	10.00	20.00
—Black colorband label, logo at top					
❑ T 1391 [M]	Walkin' the Strings	1960	20.00	40.00	80.00
—Black colorband label, logo at left					
❑ T 1391 [M]	Walkin' the Strings	1962	5.00	10.00	20.00
—Black colorband label, logo at top					
❑ ST 1664 [S]	Travis	1962	12.50	25.00	50.00
—Black colorband label, logo at left					
❑ ST 1664 [S]	Travis	1962	6.25	12.50	25.00
—Black colorband label, logo at top					
❑ T 1664 [M]	Travis	1962	10.00	20.00	40.00
—Black colorband label, logo at left					
❑ T 1664 [M]	Travis	1962	5.00	10.00	20.00
—Black colorband label, logo at top					
❑ ST 1956 [S]	Songs of the Coal Mines	1963	12.50	25.00	50.00
❑ T 1956 [M]	Songs of the Coal Mines	1963	10.00	20.00	40.00
❑ DT 2662 [R]	The Best of Merle Travis	1967	5.00	10.00	20.00
❑ T 2662 [M]	The Best of Merle Travis	1967	7.50	15.00	30.00
❑ ST 2938	Strictly Guitar	1968	6.25	12.50	25.00

TRAVIS, MERLE, AND JOE MAPHIS

Also see each artist's individual listings.

Albums

CAPITOL

Number	Title (A Side/B Side)	Yr	VG	VG+	NM
❑ ST 2102 [S]	Merle Travis and Joe Maphis	1964	12.50	25.00	50.00
❑ T 2102 [M]	Merle Travis and Joe Maphis	1964	10.00	20.00	40.00

TRAVIS, RANDY

45s

DREAMWORKS

Number	Title (A Side/B Side)	Yr	VG	VG+	NM
❑ 59007	Out of My Bones/Brinks Truck	1998	—	2.00	4.00

PAULA

Number	Title (A Side/B Side)	Yr	VG	VG+	NM
❑ 429	Dreamin'/I'll Take Any Willing Woman	1978	6.25	12.50	25.00
—As "Randy Traywick"					
❑ 431	She's My Woman/(Instrumental)	1978	6.25	12.50	25.00
—As "Randy Traywick"					

WARNER BROS.

Number	Title (A Side/B Side)	Yr	VG	VG+	NM
❑ PRO-S-2842 [DJ]	White Christmas Makes Me Blue/Sleigh Ride	1987	—	3.00	6.00
—B-side by Mark O'Connor					
❑ 7-17382	Price to Pay/I Wish It Would Rain	1997	—	—	3.00
❑ 7-17494	Would I/Don't Take Your Love Away from Me	1996	—	—	3.00
❑ 7-17619	Are We in Trouble Now/Nobody's Home	1996	—	—	3.00
❑ 7-17970	The Box/Honky Tonk Side of Town	1995	—	2.00	4.00
❑ 7-18062	This Is Me/Gonna Walk That Line	1994	—	—	3.00
❑ 7-18153	Whisper My Name/Oscar the Angel	1994	—	2.00	4.00
❑ 7-18208	Before You Kill Us All/The Box	1994	—	—	3.00
❑ 7-18274	Wind in the Wire/Down in the Old Corral	1994	—	—	3.00
❑ 18616	An Old Pair of Shoes/Promises	1993	—	—	3.00
❑ 18709	Look Heart, No Hands/The Heart to Climb the Mountain	1992	—	2.00	4.00
❑ 18792	If I Didn't Have You/I Told You So	1992	—	2.00	4.00
❑ 18943	I'd Surrender All/Let Me Try	1992	—	—	3.00
❑ 19067	Better Class of Losers/I'm Gonna Have a Little Talk	1991	—	2.00	4.00
❑ 19158	Forever Together/This Day Was Made for Me and You	1991	—	2.00	4.00
❑ 19283	Point of Light/Waiting on the Light to Change	1991	—	—	3.00
—B-side with B.B. King					
❑ 19469	Heroes and Friends/Shopping for Dresses	1991	—	2.00	4.00
—B-side with Loretta Lynn					
❑ 19586	A Few Ole Country Boys/Smokin' the Hive	1990	—	2.00	4.00
—A-side with George Jones; B-side with Clint Eastwood					
❑ 19878	He Walked on Water/Card Carryin' Fool	1990	—	—	3.00
❑ 19935	Hard Rock Bottom of Your Heart/When Your World Was Turning for Me	1990	—	2.00	4.00
❑ 22766	Oh, What a Silent Night/Winter Wonderland	1989	—	2.00	4.00
❑ 22841	It's Just a Matter of Time/This Day Was Made for You and Me	1989	—	2.00	4.00
❑ 22841 [PS]	It's Just a Matter of Time/This Day Was Made for You and Me	1989	2.00	4.00	8.00
❑ 22917	Promises/Written in Stone	1989	—	—	3.00
❑ 27551	Is It Still Over?/Here in My Heart	1989	—	2.00	4.00
❑ 27689	Deeper Than the Holler/It's Out of My Hands	1988	—	2.00	4.00
❑ 27689 [PS]	Deeper Than the Holler/It's Out of My Hands	1988	—	2.50	5.00
❑ 27707	An Old Time Christmas/How Do I Wrap My Heart Up for Christmas	1988	—	2.50	5.00
❑ 27707 [PS]	An Old Time Christmas/How Do I Wrap My Heart Up for Christmas	1988	—	2.50	5.00
❑ 27833	Honky Tonk Moon/Young Guns	1988	—	—	3.00
❑ 27833 [PS]	Honky Tonk Moon/Young Guns	1988	—	2.50	5.00
❑ 27969	I Told You So/Good Intentions	1988	—	—	3.00
❑ 27969 [PS]	I Told You So/Good Intentions	1988	—	2.50	5.00
❑ 28246	I Won't Need You Anymore (Always and Forever)/Tonight I'm Walking Out on the Blues	1987	—	2.00	4.00
❑ 28286	Too Gone Too Long/My House	1987	—	2.00	4.00
❑ 28286 [PS]	Too Gone Too Long/My House	1987	—	2.50	5.00
❑ 28384	Forever and Ever, Amen/Promises	1987	—	2.50	5.00
❑ 28384 [PS]	Forever and Ever, Amen/Promises	1987	—	2.50	5.00
❑ 28525	No Place Like Home/Send My Body	1986	—	2.00	4.00
❑ 28556	White Christmas Makes Me Blue/Pretty Paper	1986	—	2.50	5.00
❑ 28649	Diggin' Up Bones/There'll Always Be a Honky Tonk Somewhere	1986	—	2.00	4.00
❑ 28828	1982/Reasons I Quit	1985	—	2.00	4.00
❑ 28962	On the Other Hand/Can't Stop Now	1985	—	2.00	4.00
—Reissued in 1986 with the same label and number					

Albums

MUSIC VALLEY

Number	Title (A Side/B Side)	Yr	VG	VG+	NM
❑ (# unknown)	Randy Ray Live at the Nashville Palace	1982	75.00	150.00	300.00
—With no "Randy Travis" sticker on front cover					
❑ (# unknown)	Randy Ray Live at the Nashville Palace	1986	50.00	100.00	200.00
—With "Randy Travis" sticker on front cover; the records are the same as the first edition					

WARNER BROS.

Number	Title (A Side/B Side)	Yr	VG	VG+	NM
❑ 25435	Storms of Life	1986	2.50	5.00	10.00
❑ 25568	Always & Forever	1987	2.50	5.00	10.00
❑ 25738	Old 8x10	1988	2.50	5.00	10.00
❑ 25972	An Old-Fashioned Christmas	1989	3.00	6.00	12.00
❑ 25988	No Holdin' Back	1989	3.00	6.00	12.00
❑ R 174597	Heroes and Friends	1990	5.00	10.00	20.00
—Only released on vinyl through BMG Direct Marketing					

TRAYWICK, RANDY

See RANDY TRAVIS.

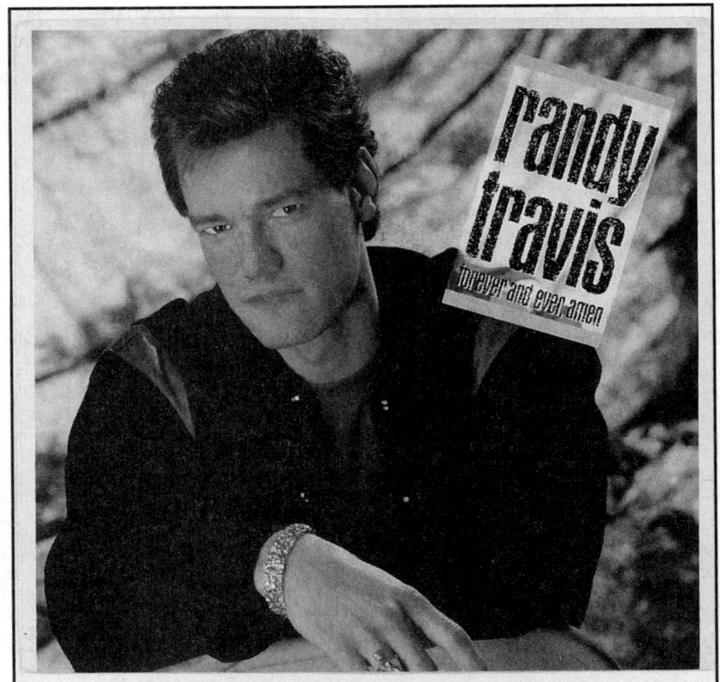

In the late 1980s, the revival of "older" country sounds led to a bunch of new stars. No one in that era was more popular than Randy Travis. (Top left) "Forever and Ever, Amen" became the biggest No. 1 hit in seven years when it spent three weeks atop the *Billboard* charts in 1987. (Top right) Another of Travis' chart-toppers from the late 1980s was "Deeper Than the Holler" from 1988. (Bottom left) His most recent No. 1 single was "Whisper My Name" in 1994. (Bottom right) After more than a decade with Warner Bros., Travis became one of the first country artists to sign with DreamWorks Records. His first single for the new label, "Out of My Bones," got to No. 2 before stalling.

TRENT, BUCK

45s

Number	Title (A Side/B Side)	Yr	VG	VG+	NM
ABC DOT					
❑ 17633	Bionic Banjo/Wrestling Matches	1976	—	2.50	5.00
❑ 17662	Donald Is a Duck/Buck's Hee-Haw Talkin' Blues	1976	—	2.50	5.00
❑ 17705	Why Don't You Haul Off and Love Me/You Are My Love Song	1977	—	2.50	5.00
BOONE					
❑ 1076	Five String General/The World Needs a Washin'	1968	2.50	5.00	10.00
RCA VICTOR					
❑ 74-0767	Goin' Home/Brand New Banjo	1972	—	3.50	7.00

Albums

Number	Title (A Side/B Side)	Yr	VG	VG+	NM
ABC DOT					
❑ DOSD-2058	Bionic Banjo	1976	2.50	5.00	10.00
❑ DO-2077	Oh Yeah!	1977	2.50	5.00	10.00
BOONE					
❑ 1212	Give Me Five	1967	5.00	10.00	20.00
RCA VICTOR					
❑ LSP-4705	Sounds of Now and Beyond	1972	3.00	6.00	12.00
SMASH					
❑ MGS-27002 [M]	The Sound of a Bluegrass Banjo	1962	5.00	10.00	20.00
—Smash LPs as "Charles Trent"					
❑ MGS-27017 [M]	The Sound of a Five String Banjo	1962	5.00	10.00	20.00
❑ SRS-67002 [S]	The Sound of a Bluegrass Banjo	1962	6.25	12.50	25.00
❑ SRS-67017 [S]	The Sound of a Five String Banjo	1962	6.25	12.50	25.00

TREVINO, RICK

45s

Number	Title (A Side/B Side)	Yr	VG	VG+	NM
COLUMBIA					
❑ 38-77159	Just Enough Rope/A Quarter at a Time	1993	—	2.00	4.00
❑ 38-77373	Honky Tonk Crowd/Un Momento Alla (For a Moment There)	1994	—	2.00	4.00
❑ 38-77535	She Can't Say I Didn't Cry/She Just Left Me Lounge	1994	—	2.00	4.00
❑ 38-77708	Doctor Time/What I'll Know Then	1994	—	2.00	4.00
❑ 38-77820	Looking for the Light/Life Can Turn on a Dime	1995	—	—	3.00
❑ 38-77903	Bobbie Ann Mason/San Antonio Rose to You	1995	—	—	3.00
❑ 38-77971	Cadillac Ranch/Fastest Horse in a One-Horse Town	1995	—	—	3.00
—B-side by Billy Ray Cyrus					
❑ 38-78329	Learning As You Go/I'm Here for You	1996	—	2.00	4.00
❑ 38-78331	Running Out of Reasons to Run/See Rock City	1996	—	2.00	4.00

TREVOR, VAN

45s

Number	Title (A Side/B Side)	Yr	VG	VG+	NM
ATLANTIC					
❑ 2175	Tuesday Girl/I Want to Cry	1963	2.50	5.00	10.00
BAND BOX					
❑ 367	Born to Be in Love with You/It's So Good to Be Loved	1966	2.00	4.00	8.00
❑ 371	Our Side/When You've Lost Your Baby	1966	2.00	4.00	8.00
❑ 373 [DJ]	Christmas In The Country/PSA Announcements	1966	2.50	5.00	10.00
❑ 374	He's Losing His Mind/A Fool Called Me	1967	2.00	4.00	8.00
CANADIAN AMERICAN					
❑ 181	Louisiana Hot Sauce/Satisfaction Is Guaranteed	1964	5.00	10.00	20.00
❑ 188	The Girl from the Main Street Diner/For This Girl	1965	3.75	7.50	15.00
CLARIDGE					
❑ 305	Christmas in Washington Square/Melting Snow	1965	3.75	7.50	15.00
DATE					
❑ 1565	You've Been So Good to Me/Sunday Morning	1967	2.00	4.00	8.00
❑ 1594	Take Me Along with You/Guitar	1968	2.00	4.00	8.00
ROYAL AMERICAN					
❑ 3	Mercy Hospital/Something Missing in Me	1970	—	2.50	5.00
❑ 9	Luziana River/Sweet Diana	1970	—	2.50	5.00
❑ 23	Wish I Was Home Instead/Did I Have a Good Time	1970	—	2.50	5.00
❑ 31	Lonely Looking Woman/Johnnie and Annie	1971	—	2.50	5.00
❑ 280	The Things That Matter/Band of Gold	1969	—	3.00	6.00
❑ 283	A Man Away from Home/I've Got Today to Live For	1969	—	3.00	6.00
❑ 289	Funny Familiar Forgotten Feelings/Daddy's Little Man	1969	—	3.00	6.00
VIVID					
❑ 1004	C'mon Now Baby/Fling of the Past	1963	7.50	15.00	30.00
—Backing group is The Four Seasons					

Albums

Number	Title (A Side/B Side)	Yr	VG	VG+	NM
BAND BOX					
❑ (# unknown)	Come On Over to Our Side	1967	5.00	10.00	20.00
DATE					
❑ DES-4008	You've Been So Good to Me	1967	3.75	7.50	15.00
ROYAL AMERICAN					
❑ 2800	Funny Familiar Forgotten Feelings	1969	3.75	7.50	15.00

TRIBBLE, MARK

45s

Number	Title (A Side/B Side)	Yr	VG	VG+	NM
PALOMA					
❑ 5	Lay Me Down Carolina/(B-side unknown)	1989	—	3.00	6.00
❑ 92787 [DJ]	The Year I Saw Santa Claus (same on both sides)	1987	—	3.00	6.00

TRICK PONY

45s

Number	Title (A Side/B Side)	Yr	VG	VG+	NM
WARNER BROS.					
❑ 7-16816	Pour Me/If You Think You've Got Trouble	2000	—	—	3.00

TRIGGS, TRINI

45s

Number	Title (A Side/B Side)	Yr	VG	VG+	NM
CURB					
❑ D7-73066	Straight Tequila/Horse to Mexico	1998	—	—	3.00

TRINITY, BOBBY

45s

Number	Title (A Side/B Side)	Yr	VG	VG+	NM
GRT					
❑ 127	I Love Everything I Get My Hands On/(B-side unknown)	1977	—	3.50	7.00

TRINITY LANE

45s

Number	Title (A Side/B Side)	Yr	VG	VG+	NM
CURB					
❑ 10507	For a Song/Don't Put It Past My Heart	1988	—	—	3.00
❑ 10511	Someday, Somenight/Suspicion	1988	—	—	3.00
❑ 10515	Ready to Take That Ride/How Can I Pull Myself Together	1988	—	—	3.00

TRIPP, ALLEN

45s

Number	Title (A Side/B Side)	Yr	VG	VG+	NM
NASHVILLE					
❑ 1001	Love Is/Lady Sorrow	1982	—	3.00	6.00

TRITT, TRAVIS

Also see BILL ENGVALL; MARTY STUART AND TRAVIS TRITT.

45s

Number	Title (A Side/B Side)	Yr	VG	VG+	NM
WARNER BROS.					
❑ 7-17108	No More Looking Over My Shoulder/Girls Like That	1999	—	—	3.00
❑ 7-17152	If I Lost You/Start the Car	1998	—	—	3.00
❑ 7-17451	Where Corn Don't Grow/She's Going Home with Me	1996	—	—	3.00
❑ 7-17606	More Than You'll Ever Know/Still in Love with You	1996	—	—	3.00
❑ 7-17792	Sometimes She Forgets/Only You (And You Alone)	1995	—	—	3.00
❑ 7-18003	Between an Old Memory and Me/Wishful Thinking	1994	—	—	3.00
❑ 7-18104	Ten Feet Tall and Bulletproof/Ten Feet Tall and Bulletproof (Acoustic Version)	1994	—	—	3.00
❑ 7-18180	Foolish Pride/No Vacation from the Blues	1994	—	2.00	4.00
❑ 7-18240	Take It Easy/I Wish I Could Go Back Home	1994	—	2.00	4.00
—No label name listed, but all indications are that it's Warner Bros.					
❑ 7-18463	Looking Out for Number One/Blue Collar Man	1993	—	2.00	4.00
❑ 7-18588	T-R-O-U-B-L-E/Leave My Girl Alone	1993	—	2.00	4.00
❑ 7-18669	Can I Trust You with My Heart/A Hundred Years from Now	1992	—	2.00	4.00
❑ 7-18703	Santa Looked a Lot Like Daddy/Winter Wonderland	1992	—	2.00	4.00
❑ 7-18779	Lord Have Mercy on the Working Man (Edit)/Lord Have Mercy on the Working Man (Album Version)	1992	—	2.00	4.00
—As "Travis Tritt & Friends"					
❑ 7-18984	Nothing Short of Dying/Bible Belt	1992	—	2.00	4.00
❑ 7-19097	The Whiskey Ain't Workin'/Bible Belt	1991	—	2.00	4.00
❑ 7-19190	Anymore/It's All About to Change	1991	—	2.50	5.00
❑ 7-19310	Here's a Quarter (Call Someone Who Cares)/If Hell Had a Jukebox	1991	—	2.50	5.00
❑ 7-19431	Drift Off to Dream/Son of the New South	1991	—	2.50	5.00
❑ 7-19715	Put Some Drive in Your Country/If I Were a Drinker	1990	—	2.00	4.00
❑ 7-19797	I'm Gonna Be Somebody/The Road Home	1990	—	2.00	4.00
❑ 7-19918	Help Me Hold On/All I'll Ever Be	1990	—	2.00	4.00
❑ 7-22882	Country Club/Sign of the Times	1989	—	2.00	4.00

Albums

Number	Title (A Side/B Side)	Yr	VG	VG+	NM
WARNER BROS.					
❑ W1-26589	It's All About to Change	1991	5.00	10.00	20.00
—Vinyl available only from Columbia House					

TRYTHALL, GIL

45s

Number	Title (A Side/B Side)	Yr	VG	VG+	NM
ATHENA					
❑ 5013	Yakety Moog/Foggy Mountain Breakdown	1970	—	3.00	6.00

Albums

Number	Title (A Side/B Side)	Yr	VG	VG+	NM
ATHENA					
❑ 6003	Switched On Nashville/Country Moog	1970	3.00	6.00	12.00
❑ 6004	Nashville Gold	1970	3.00	6.00	12.00

TUBB, ERNEST

Also see RED FOLEY AND ERNEST TUBB; THE TEXAS TROUBADOURS.

45s

Number	Title (A Side/B Side)	Yr	VG	VG+	NM
CACHET					
❑ 4501	Waltz Across Texas/Jealous Loving Heart	1979	—	3.00	6.00
❑ 4507	Walking the Floor Over You/Let's Say Goodbye	1979	—	3.00	6.00
DECCA					
❑ 9-28067	Somebody's Stolen My Honey/My Mother Must Have Been a Girl Like You	1952	5.00	10.00	20.00
❑ 9-28310	Fortunes in Memories/So Many Times	1952	5.00	10.00	20.00
❑ 9-28448	Somebody Loves You/Don't Trifle on Your Sweetheart	1952	5.00	10.00	20.00
❑ 9-28453	Merry Texas Christmas, You All/Blue Snowflakes	1952	6.25	12.50	25.00
❑ 9-28550	Dear Judge/I Will Miss You When You Go	1953	5.00	10.00	20.00
❑ 9-28630	Hank It Will Never Be the Same/Beyond the Sunset	1953	7.50	15.00	30.00

Number	Title (A Side/B Side)	Yr	VG	VG+	NM
❑ 9-28696	Jimmie Rodgers' Last Thoughts/When Jimmie Said Goodbye	1953	6.25	12.50	25.00
❑ 9-28777	Don't Brush Them on Me/My Wasted Past	1953	5.00	10.00	20.00
❑ 9-28837	A Dear John Letter/The Mean Age, In Between Age Blues	1953	5.00	10.00	20.00

—As "Bill and Ernest Tubb"

Number	Title (A Side/B Side)	Yr	VG	VG+	NM
❑ 9-28869	Divorce Granted/Counterfeit Kisses	1953	5.00	10.00	20.00
❑ 9-28946	I'm Trimming My Christmas Tree with Teardrops/We Need God for Christmas	1953	5.00	10.00	20.00
❑ 9-29011	Honky Tonk Heart/I'm Not Looking for an Angel	1954	5.00	10.00	20.00
❑ 9-29020	Jealous Loving Heart/Till We Two Are One	1954	5.00	10.00	20.00
❑ 9-29103	Baby Your Mother (Like She Babies You)/Your Mother, Your Darling, Your Friend	1954	6.25	12.50	25.00
❑ 9-29220	Two Glasses, Joe/Journey's End	1954	5.00	10.00	20.00
❑ 9-29350	I'll Be Walkin' the Floor This Christmas/Lonely Christmas Eve	1954	5.00	10.00	20.00
❑ 9-29415	Kansas City Blues/The Woman's Touch	1955	3.75	7.50	15.00
❑ 9-29520	It's a Lonely World/Have You Seen	1955	3.75	7.50	15.00
❑ 9-29624	I Met a Friend/When Jesus Calls	1955	3.75	7.50	15.00
❑ 9-29633	The Yellow Rose of Texas/A Million Miles from Here	1955	3.75	7.50	15.00
❑ 9-29731	Thirty Days (To Come Back Home)/Answer the Phone	1955	5.00	10.00	20.00
❑ 9-29836	So Doggone Lonesome/If I Never Have Anything Else	1956	3.75	7.50	15.00
❑ 9-29934	Jimmie Rodgers' Last Blue Yodel/Will You Be Satisfied That Way	1956	3.75	7.50	15.00
❑ 9-30098	Treat Her Right/Loving You Is My Weakness	1956	3.75	7.50	15.00
❑ 9-30219	Don't Forbid Me/God's Eye	1957	3.75	7.50	15.00
❑ 9-30305	Mister Love/Leave Me	1957	3.75	7.50	15.00
❑ 9-30422	My Treasure/Go Home	1957	3.75	7.50	15.00
❑ 9-30526	Geisha Girl/I Found My Girl in the U.S.A.	1957	3.75	7.50	15.00
❑ 9-30549	House of Glass/Heaven Help Me	1958	3.75	7.50	15.00
❑ 9-30610	Hey, Mr. Bluebird/How Do We Know	1958	3.75	7.50	15.00
❑ 9- 30685	Half a Mind/The Blues	1958	3.75	7.50	15.00
❑ 9-30759	What Am I Living For/Goodbye Sunshine, Hello Blues	1958	3.75	7.50	15.00
❑ 9-30872	I Cried a Tear/I'd Rather Be	1959	3.75	7.50	15.00
❑ 9-30952	Next Time/What I Know About Her	1959	3.75	7.50	15.00
❑ 9-31082	Live It Up/Accidentally on Purpose	1960	3.00	6.00	12.00
❑ 9-31119	Ev'rybody's Somebody's Fool/Let the Little Girl Dance	1960	3.00	6.00	12.00
❑ 31161	White Silver Sands/A Guy Named Joe	1960	3.00	6.00	12.00
❑ 31196	Girl from Abilene/Little Old Band of Gold	1961	3.00	6.00	12.00
❑ 31241	Thoughts of a Fool/Don't Just Stand There	1961	3.00	6.00	12.00
❑ 31300	Through That Door/What Will You Tell Them	1961	3.00	6.00	12.00
❑ 31334	Christmas Is Just Another Day for Me/Rudolph the Red-Nosed Reindeer	1961	3.00	6.00	12.00
❑ 31357	Go to Sleep Conscience (Don't Hurt Me This Time)/I Could Never Say No	1962	3.00	6.00	12.00
❑ 31399	I'm Looking High and Low for My Baby/Show Her Lots of Gold	1962	3.00	6.00	12.00
❑ 31428	House of Sorrow/No Letter Today	1962	3.00	6.00	12.00
❑ 31476	Mr. Juke Box/Walking the Floor Over You	1963	3.00	6.00	12.00
❑ 31526	Thanks a Lot/The Way That You're Living	1963	3.00	6.00	12.00
❑ 31614	Be Better to Your Baby/Think of Me, Thinking of You	1964	2.50	5.00	10.00
❑ 31706	Pass the Booze/(A Memory) That's All You'll Ever Be to Me	1964	2.50	5.00	10.00
❑ 31742	Do What You Do Well/Turn Around, Walk Away	1965	2.50	5.00	10.00
❑ 31824	Waltz Across Texas/Lots of Luck	1965	2.50	5.00	10.00
❑ 31861	It's for God, and Country, and You Mom (That's Why I'm Fighting in Viet Nam)/After the Boy Gets the Girl	1965	2.50	5.00	10.00
❑ 31866	Who's Gonna Be Your Santa Claus/Blue Christmas Tree	1965	2.50	5.00	10.00
❑ 31908	Till Me Getup Has Gotup and Gone/Just One More	1966	2.50	5.00	10.00
❑ 32022	Another Story/There's No Room in My Heart (For the Blues)	1966	2.50	5.00	10.00
❑ 32131	In the Jailhouse Now/Yesterday's Winner Is a Loser Today	1967	2.50	5.00	10.00
❑ 32237	Too Much of Not Enough/Nothing Is Better Than You	1968	2.00	4.00	8.00
❑ 32315	I'm Gonna Make Like a Snake/Mama, Who Was That Man	1968	2.00	4.00	8.00
❑ 32377	Just Pack and Go/It Sure Helps a Lot	1968	2.00	4.00	8.00
❑ 32448	Saturday Satan Sunday Saint/Tommy's Doll	1969	2.00	4.00	8.00
❑ 32532	Just a Drink Away/One More Memory	1969	2.00	4.00	8.00
❑ 32632	It's America/Somebody Better Than Me	1970	2.00	4.00	8.00
❑ 32690	Dear Judge/A Good Year for the Wine	1970	2.00	4.00	8.00
❑ 32800	One Sweet Hello/Once Ole Going Gets a-Goin'	1971	2.00	4.00	8.00
❑ 32849	Don't Back a Man in a Corner/Shenandoah Waltz	1971	2.00	4.00	8.00
❑ 32943	Say Something Nice to Sarah/Teach My Daddy How to Pray	1972	2.00	4.00	8.00
❑ 33014	Baby, It's So Hard to Be Good/In This Corner	1972	2.00	4.00	8.00
❑ 9-46018	Rainbow at Midnight/I Don't Blame You	1950	10.00	20.00	40.00

—78 first issued in 1946

Number	Title (A Side/B Side)	Yr	VG	VG+	NM
❑ 9-46186	White Christmas/Blue Christmas	1950	7.50	15.00	30.00

—78 first issued in 1949; black label, lines on either side of "Decca"

Number	Title (A Side/B Side)	Yr	VG	VG+	NM
❑ 9-46243	Throw Your Love My Way/Give Me a Little Old Fashioned Love	1950	10.00	20.00	40.00
❑ 9-46257	You Don't Have to Be a Baby to Cry/G-I-R-L Spells Trouble	1950	7.50	15.00	30.00
❑ 9-46268	Christmas Island/Christmas	1950	7.50	15.00	30.00

—Black label, lines on either side of "Decca"

Number	Title (A Side/B Side)	Yr	VG	VG+	NM
❑ 9-46269	(Remember Me) I'm the One Who Loves You/I Need Attention Bad	1950	7.50	15.00	30.00
❑ 9-46289	Tomorrow Never Comes/Are You Waiting Just for Me	1951	6.25	12.50	25.00
❑ 9-46295	When It's Prayer Meetin' Time in the Hollow/May the Good Lord Bless and Keep You	1951	6.25	12.50	25.00
❑ 9-46296	Don't Stay Too Long/If You Want Some Lovin'	1951	6.25	12.50	25.00
❑ 9-46306	Mother, Queen of My Heart/I'm Lonely and Blue	1951	5.00	10.00	20.00
❑ 9-46307	Why Did You Give Me Your Love/I'm Free from the Blues	1951	5.00	10.00	20.00
❑ 9-46308	Hobo's Meditation/Why Should I Be Lonely	1951	5.00	10.00	20.00
❑ 9-46309	Any Old Time/A Drunkard's Child	1951	5.00	10.00	20.00

—The above four comprise a box set

Number	Title (A Side/B Side)	Yr	VG	VG+	NM
❑ 9-46338	Hey La La/Precious Little Baby	1951	6.25	12.50	25.00
❑ 9-46343	Rose of the Mountain/I'm With the Crowd, But So Alone	1951	6.25	12.50	25.00
❑ 9-46377	Driftwood on the River/I'm Stepping Out of the Picture	1951	6.25	12.50	25.00
❑ 9-46389	Missing in Action/A Heartsick Soldier on Heartbreak Ridge	1952	6.25	12.50	25.00

FIRST GENERATION

Number	Title (A Side/B Side)	Yr	VG	VG+	NM
❑ 001	Sometimes I Do/Half My Heart's in Texas	1977	—	3.50	7.00

MCA

Number	Title (A Side/B Side)	Yr	VG	VG+	NM
❑ 40056	I've Got All the Heartaches I Can Handle/The Texas Troubadour	1973	—	3.00	6.00
❑ 40222	Anything But This/Don't Water Down the Bad News	1974	—	3.00	6.00
❑ 40436	If You Don't Quit Checkin' on Me (I'm Checkin' Out on You)/I'd Like to Live It Again	1975	—	3.00	6.00
❑ 65024	White Christmas/Blue Christmas	1973	—	2.00	4.00

—Black label with rainbow

Number	Title (A Side/B Side)	Yr	VG	VG+	NM
❑ 65024	White Christmas/Blue Christmas	1980	—	—	3.00

—Blue label with rainbow

RHINO

Number	Title (A Side/B Side)	Yr	VG	VG+	NM
❑ 74415	Walking the Floor Over You/(B-side unknown)	1991	3.00	6.00	12.00

—Black vinyl

Number	Title (A Side/B Side)	Yr	VG	VG+	NM
❑ 74415	Walking the Floor Over You/(B-side unknown)	1991	—	3.00	6.00

—Red vinyl

Number	Title (A Side/B Side)	Yr	VG	VG+	NM
❑ 74415	Walking the Floor Over You/(B-side unknown)	1991	—	3.50	7.00

—Blue vinyl

Number	Title (A Side/B Side)	Yr	VG	VG+	NM
❑ 74415 [PS]	Walking the Floor Over You/(B-side unknown)	1991	—	3.00	6.00

Selected 78s

BLUEBIRD

Number	Title (A Side/B Side)	Yr	VG	VG+	NM
❑ B-6693	The Passing of Jimmie Rodgers/(B-side unknown)	1936	125.00	250.00	500.00
❑ B-7000	Since That Black Cat Crossed My Path/T.B. Is Whipping Me	1938	62.50	125.00	250.00
❑ B-8899	Married Man Blues/Mean Old Bed Bug Blues	1942	37.50	75.00	150.00
❑ B-8966	My Mother Is Lonely/The Right Train to Heaven	1942	37.50	75.00	150.00

DECCA

Number	Title (A Side/B Side)	Yr	VG	VG+	NM
❑ 5825	titles unknown	1940	5.00	10.00	20.00
❑ 5846	titles unknown	1940	5.00	10.00	20.00
❑ 5900	titles unknown	1940	5.00	10.00	20.00
❑ 5910	titles unknown	1940	5.00	10.00	20.00
❑ 5920	titles unknown	1940	5.00	10.00	20.00
❑ 5938	titles unknown	1941	5.00	10.00	20.00
❑ 5958	Walking the Floor Over You/(B-side unknown)	1941	6.25	12.50	25.00
❑ 5976	titles unknown	1941	5.00	10.00	20.00
❑ 5993	titles unknown	1941	5.00	10.00	20.00
❑ 6007	titles unknown	1942	5.00	10.00	20.00
❑ 6023	Time After Time/When the World Has Turned You Down	1942	5.00	10.00	20.00
❑ 6040	titles unknown	1942	5.00	10.00	20.00
❑ 6093	Try Me One More Time/That's When It's Comin' Home to You	1943	5.00	10.00	20.00
❑ 6098	Soldier's Last Letter/Yesterday's Tears	1944	5.00	10.00	20.00
❑ 6106	Tomorrow Never Comes/Keep My Mem'ry in Your Heart	1945	5.00	10.00	20.00
❑ 6110	Careless Darlin'/Are You Waiting Just for Me	1945	5.00	10.00	20.00
❑ 6112	It's Been So Long Darling/Should I Come Back Home to You	1945	5.00	10.00	20.00
❑ 24592	I'm Bitin' My Fingernails and Thinking of You/Don't Rob Another Man's Castle	1949	5.00	10.00	20.00

—With the Andrews Sisters

Number	Title (A Side/B Side)	Yr	VG	VG+	NM
❑ 46006	Walking the Floor Over You/I'll Always Be Glad to Take You Back	1946	5.00	10.00	20.00

—A-side is a reissue of the original recording

Number	Title (A Side/B Side)	Yr	VG	VG+	NM
❑ 46007	I'll Never Cry Over You/I Wonder Why You Said Goodbye	1946	5.00	10.00	20.00
❑ 46013	You Were Only Teasing Me/I'm Beginning to Forget	1946	5.00	10.00	20.00
❑ 46018	Rainbow at Midnight/I Don't Blame You	1946	5.00	10.00	20.00
❑ 46019	Filipino Baby/Drivin' Nails in My Coffin	1946	5.00	10.00	20.00
❑ 46029	Answer to Walking the Floor Over You/You'll Want Me Back	1947	5.00	10.00	20.00
❑ 46030	I'm Free at Last/Those Simple Things Are Worth a Million	1947	5.00	10.00	20.00
❑ 46031	You Won't Ever Forget Me/Though the Days Were Only Seven	1947	5.00	10.00	20.00
❑ 46032	Those Tears in Your Eyes/How Can I Be Sure	1947	5.00	10.00	20.00
❑ 46040	Don't Look Now (But Your Broken Heart Is Showing)/So Round, So Firm, So Fully Packed	1947	5.00	10.00	20.00
❑ 46041	I'll Step Aside/There's Gonna Be Some Changes Made Around Here	1947	5.00	10.00	20.00
❑ 46047	Soldier's Last Letter/Try Me One More Time	1947	3.75	7.50	15.00
❑ 46048	It's Been So Long Darlin'/Careless Darlin'	1947	3.75	7.50	15.00

Number	Title (A Side/B Side)	Yr	VG	VG+	NM
❑ 46061	You Hit the Nail Right on the Head/Two Wrongs	1947	5.00	10.00	20.00
❑ 46078	Headin' Down the Wrong Highway/Answer to Rainbow at Midnight	1947	5.00	10.00	20.00
❑ 46091	I Hate to See You Go/Time After Time	1947	3.75	7.50	15.00
❑ 46092	I'll Get Along Somehow/When the World Has Turned	1947	3.75	7.50	15.00
❑ 46093	Blue Eyed Elaine/Our Baby's Back	1947	3.75	7.50	15.00
❑ 46113	A Lonely Heart Knows/A Woman Has Wrecked Many a Good Man	1948	5.00	10.00	20.00
❑ 46119	Seaman's Blues/Waiting for a Train	1948	5.00	10.00	20.00
❑ 46125	You Nearly Lose Your Mind/I Ain't Goin' Honky Tonkin' Anymore	1948	5.00	10.00	20.00
❑ 46134	Forever Is Ending Today/That Wild and Wicked Look in Your Eye	1948	5.00	10.00	20.00
❑ 46144	Have You Ever Been Lonely? (Have You Ever Been Blue)/Let's Say Goodbye Like We Said Hello	1948	5.00	10.00	20.00
❑ 46150	Till the End of the World/Daddy When Is Mommy Coming Home	1949	5.00	10.00	20.00
❑ 46162	Mama Mama Blues/Yesterday's Tears	1949	5.00	10.00	20.00
❑ 46173	Slipping Around/My Tennessee Baby	1949	5.00	10.00	20.00
❑ 46175	My Filipino Rose/Warm Red Wine	1949	5.00	10.00	20.00
❑ 46186	White Christmas/Blue Christmas	1949	5.00	10.00	20.00
❑ 46207	Letters Have No Arms/I'll Take a Back Seat to You	1950	5.00	10.00	20.00
❑ 46213	I Love You Because/Unfaithful One	1950	5.00	10.00	20.00

7-Inch Extended Plays

DECCA

Number	Title (A Side/B Side)	Yr	VG	VG+	NM
❑ ED 2026	(contents unknown)	195?	6.25	12.50	25.00
❑ ED 2026 [PS]	Ernest Tubb Sings	195?	6.25	12.50	25.00
❑ ED 2089	(contents unknown)	195?	6.25	12.50	25.00
❑ ED 2089 [PS]	White Christmas	195?	6.25	12.50	25.00
❑ ED 2356	(contents unknown)	1956	5.00	10.00	20.00
❑ ED 2356 [PS]	Ernest Tubb Favorites, Vol. 1	1956	5.00	10.00	20.00
❑ ED 2357	(contents unknown)	1956	5.00	10.00	20.00
❑ ED 2357 [PS]	Ernest Tubb Favorites, Vol. 2	1956	5.00	10.00	20.00
❑ ED 2521	*You're Breaking My Heart/I Know My Baby Loves Me in Her Own Peculiar Way/I've Got the Blues for Mammy/This Troubled Mind o' Mine	1957	5.00	10.00	20.00
❑ ED 2521 [PS]	The Daddy of 'Em All	1957	5.00	10.00	20.00
❑ ED 2522	*I Dreamed of an Old Love Affair/Mississippi Gal/When a Soldier Knocks and Finds Nobody Home/Daisy Mae	1957	5.00	10.00	20.00
❑ ED 2522 [PS]	Encores	1957	5.00	10.00	20.00
❑ ED 2523	*I Knew the Moment I Lost You/You're the Only Good Thing/My Hillbilly Baby/There's No Fool Like a Young Fool	1957	5.00	10.00	20.00
❑ ED 2523 [PS]	My Hillbilly Baby	1957	5.00	10.00	20.00
❑ ED 2563	*Geisha Girl/I Found My Girl in the U.S.A./Home of the Blues/Tangled Mind	1958	5.00	10.00	20.00
❑ ED 2563 [PS]	Ernest Tubb Sings the Hits	1958	5.00	10.00	20.00
❑ ED 2626	*House of Glass/My Treasure/Treat Her Right/Don't Forbid Me	1959	5.00	10.00	20.00
❑ ED 2626 [PS]	Ernest Tubb	1959	5.00	10.00	20.00
❑ ED 2627	*Mister Love/Leave Me/Hey Mr. Bluebird/How Do I Know	1959	5.00	10.00	20.00
❑ ED 2627 [PS]	Ernest Tubb and the Wilburn Brothers	1959	5.00	10.00	20.00
❑ ED 2643	*I'm a Long Gone Daddy/San Antonio Rose/Your Cheatin' Heart/It Makes No Difference Now	1959	5.00	10.00	20.00
❑ ED 2643	The Importance of Being Ernest	1959	5.00	10.00	20.00
❑ ED 2655 [M]	*Have You Ever Been Lonely/Rainbow at Midnight/Careless Darlin'/You Nearly Lost Your Mind	1959	5.00	10.00	20.00
❑ ED 2655 [PS]	The Ernest Tubb Story	1959	5.00	10.00	20.00
❑ ED 7-2655 [PS]	The Ernest Tubb Story	1959	7.50	15.00	30.00
❑ ED 7-2655 [S]	*Have You Ever Been Lonely/Rainbow at Midnight/Careless Darlin'/You Nearly Lost Your Mind	1959	7.50	15.00	30.00
❑ ED 2680	*He'll Have to Go/White Silver Sands/Am I That Easy to Forget/Guy Named Joe	1960	5.00	10.00	20.00
❑ ED 2680 [PS]	The Ernest Tubb Record Shop	1960	5.00	10.00	20.00
❑ ED 2691	*Ev'rybody's Somebody's Fool/Let the Little Girl Dance/Live It Up/Accidentally on Purpose	1960	5.00	10.00	20.00
❑ ED 2691 [PS]	Ernest Tubb	1960	5.00	10.00	20.00
❑ ED 2706	(contents unknown)	1962	5.00	10.00	20.00
❑ ED 2706 [PS]	Ernest Tubb	1962	5.00	10.00	20.00
❑ ED 2718	*What Will You Tell Them/Thoughts of a Fool/Go to Sleep Conscience/I Never Could Say No	1961	5.00	10.00	20.00
❑ ED 2718 [PS]	Ernest Tubb	1961	5.00	10.00	20.00
❑ ED 2728	*Show Her Lots of Gold/I'm Looking High and Low for My Baby/I Walk the Line/Crazy Arms	1962	6.25	12.50	25.00
❑ ED 2728 [PS]	Show Her Lots of Gold	1962	6.25	12.50	25.00
❑ ED 2739	*No Letter Today/Women Make a Fool Out of Me/House of Sorrow/Go On Home	1963	6.25	12.50	25.00
❑ ED 2739 [PS]	Ernest Tubb	1963	6.25	12.50	25.00
❑ ED 2769	(contents unknown)	1964	6.25	12.50	25.00
❑ ED 2769 [PS]	Ernest Tubb	1964	6.25	12.50	25.00
❑ ED 2774	*Thanks a Lot/Mr. Juke Box/Last Letter/Just Call Me Lonesome	1964	6.25	12.50	25.00
❑ ED 2774 [PS]	Thanks a Lot	1964	6.25	12.50	25.00
❑ ED 2787	(contents unknown)	1965	7.50	15.00	30.00
❑ ED 2787 [PS]	Be Better to Your Baby	1965	7.50	15.00	30.00
❑ ED 2797	(contents unknown)	1965	7.50	15.00	30.00
❑ ED 2797 [PS]	Pass the Booze	1965	7.50	15.00	30.00
❑ 7-4518 [PS]	Blue Christmas	1964	3.75	7.50	15.00
❑ 7-4518 [S]	(contents unknown)	1964	3.75	7.50	15.00

—33 1/3 rpm, small hole jukebox edition

Albums

CACHET

Number	Title (A Side/B Side)	Yr	VG	VG+	NM
❑ 33001	Ernest Tubb: The Legend and the Legacy, Volume One	1979	3.00	6.00	12.00

DECCA

Number	Title (A Side/B Side)	Yr	VG	VG+	NM
❑ DXA 159 [(2) M]	The Ernest Tubb Story *—Deduct 25 percent if book is missing*	1959	20.00	40.00	80.00
❑ DL 4042 [M]	The Ernest Tubb Record Shop	1960	10.00	20.00	40.00
❑ DL 4046 [M]	All Time Hits	1961	7.50	15.00	30.00
❑ DL 4118 [M]	Ernest Tubb's Golden Favorites	1961	7.50	15.00	30.00
❑ DL 4321 [M]	On Tour	1962	6.25	12.50	25.00
❑ DL 4385 [M]	Just Call Me Lonesome	1962	6.25	12.50	25.00
❑ DL 4397 [M]	The Family Bible	1963	6.25	12.50	25.00
❑ DL 4514 [M]	Thanks a Lot	1964	6.25	12.50	25.00
❑ DL 4518 [M]	Blue Christmas	1963	6.25	12.50	25.00
❑ DL 4640 [M]	My Pick of the Hits	1965	6.25	12.50	25.00
❑ DL 4681 [M]	Hittin' the Road	1965	6.25	12.50	25.00
❑ DL 4746 [M]	By Request	1966	6.25	12.50	25.00
❑ DL 4772 [M]	Ernest Tubb Sings Country Hits Old & New	1966	6.25	12.50	25.00
❑ DL 4867 [M]	Another Story	1967	7.50	15.00	30.00
❑ DL 4957 [M]	Ernest Tubb Sings Hank Williams	1968	12.50	25.00	50.00
❑ DL 5301 [10]	Ernest Tubb Favorites	1951	37.50	75.00	150.00
❑ DL 5334 [10]	The Old Rugged Cross	1951	37.50	75.00	150.00
❑ DL 5336 [10]	Jimmie Rodgers Songs Sung by Ernest Tubb	1951	37.50	75.00	150.00
❑ DL 5497 [10]	Sing a Song of Christmas	1954	37.50	75.00	150.00
❑ DXSA 7159 [(2) R]	The Ernest Tubb Story *—Deduct 25 percent if book is missing*	196?	7.50	15.00	30.00
❑ DL 8291 [M]	Ernest Tubb Favorites	1955	17.50	35.00	70.00
❑ DL 8553 [M]	The Daddy of 'Em All	1956	17.50	35.00	70.00
❑ DL 8834 [M]	The Importance of Being Ernest	1959	12.50	25.00	50.00
❑ DL 74042 [S]	The Ernest Tubb Record Shop	1960	12.50	25.00	50.00
❑ DL 74046 [S]	All Time Hits	1961	10.00	20.00	40.00
❑ DL 74118 [S]	Ernest Tubb's Golden Favorites	1961	10.00	2.00	40.00
❑ DL 74321 [S]	On Tour	1962	7.50	15.00	30.00
❑ DL 74385 [S]	Just Call Me Lonesome	1962	7.50	15.00	30.00
❑ DL 74397 [S]	The Family Bible	1963	7.50	15.00	30.00
❑ DL 74514 [S]	Thanks a Lot	1964	7.50	15.00	30.00
❑ DL 74518 [S]	Blue Christmas	1963	7.50	15.00	30.00
❑ DL 74640 [S]	My Pick of the Hits	1965	7.50	15.00	30.00
❑ DL 74681 [S]	Hittin' the Road	1965	7.50	15.00	30.00
❑ DL 74746 [S]	By Request	1966	7.50	15.00	30.00
❑ DL 74772 [S]	Ernest Tubb Sings Country Hits Old & New	1966	7.50	15.00	30.00
❑ DL 74867 [S]	Another Story	1967	6.25	12.50	25.00
❑ DL 74957 [S]	Ernest Tubb Sings Hank Williams	1968	6.25	12.50	25.00
❑ DL 75006	Ernest Tubb's Greatest Hits	1968	6.25	12.50	25.00
❑ DL 75072	Country Hit Time	1968	5.00	10.00	20.00
❑ DL 75122	Saturday Satan, Sunday Saint	1969	5.00	10.00	20.00
❑ DL 75222	A Great Year for the Wine	1970	5.00	10.00	20.00
❑ DL 75252	Ernest Tubb's Greatest Hits, Vol. 2	1970	5.00	10.00	20.00
❑ DL 75301	One Sweet Hello	1971	5.00	10.00	20.00
❑ DL 75345	Say Something Nice to Sarah	1972	5.00	10.00	20.00
❑ DL 75388	Baby, It's So Hard to Be Good	1972	5.00	10.00	20.00
❑ DL 78834 [S]	The Importance of Being Ernest	1959	15.00	30.00	60.00

FIRST GENERATION

Number	Title (A Side/B Side)	Yr	VG	VG+	NM
❑ LP-0002 [(2)]	The Legend and the Legacy *—No ads on back cover*	1979	12.50	25.00	50.00
❑ LP-0002 [(2)]	The Legend and the Legacy *—With ad for Ernest Tubb Record Shop on back cover*	1979	10.00	20.00	40.00
❑ TV-1033 [(2)]	The Legend and the Legacy *—Mail-order version*	1979	6.25	12.50	25.00

MCA

Number	Title (A Side/B Side)	Yr	VG	VG+	NM
❑ 16	Ernest Tubb's Greatest Hits *—Reissue of Decca 75006*	1973	3.00	6.00	12.00
❑ 24	Ernest Tubb's Greatest Hits, Vol. 2 *—Reissue of Decca 75252*	1973	3.00	6.00	12.00
❑ 84	Ernest Tubb's Golden Favorites *—Reissue of Decca 74118*	1973	3.00	6.00	12.00
❑ 341	I've Got All the Heartaches I Can Handle	1973	3.00	6.00	12.00
❑ 496	Ernest Tubb	1975	3.00	6.00	12.00
❑ 512	Baby, It's So Hard to Be Good *—Reissue of Decca 75388*	197?	3.00	6.00	12.00
❑ 4040 [(2)]	The Ernest Tubb Story *—Reissue of Decca DXSA 7159*	197?	3.75	7.50	15.00

TUBB, ERNEST, AND RED FOLEY

See RED FOLEY AND ERNEST TUBB.

TUBB, ERNEST, AND LORETTA LYNN

45s

DECCA

Number	Title (A Side/B Side)	Yr	VG	VG+	NM
❑ 31643	Mr. and Mrs. Used to Be/Love Was Right Here All the Time	1964	2.50	5.00	10.00
❑ 31793	Our Hearts Are Holding Hands/We're Not Kids Anymore	1965	2.50	5.00	10.00
❑ 32091	Sweet Thang/Beautiful, Unhappy Home	1967	2.50	5.00	10.00
❑ 32496	Who's Gonna Take the Garbage Out/Somewhere Between	1969	2.00	4.00	8.00
❑ 32570	I Chased You Till You Caught Me/If We Put Our Heads Together	1969	2.00	4.00	8.00

Albums

DECCA

Number	Title (A Side/B Side)	Yr	VG	VG+	NM
❑ DL 4639 [M]	Mr. and Mrs. Used to Be	1965	7.50	15.00	30.00
❑ DL 4872 [M]	Singin' Again	1967	7.50	15.00	30.00
❑ DL 74639 [S]	Mr. and Mrs. Used to Be	1965	10.00	20.00	40.00
❑ DL 74872 [S]	Singin' Again	1967	6.25	12.50	25.00
❑ DL 75115	If We Put Our Heads Together	1969	6.25	12.50	25.00

Number	Title (A Side/B Side)	Yr	VG	VG+	NM
MCA					
❑ 4000	The Ernest Tubb/Loretta Lynn Story	1973	3.75	7.50	15.00

TUBB, JUSTIN

45s

Number	Title (A Side/B Side)	Yr	VG	VG+	NM
CHALLENGE					
❑ 59081	Big Fool of the Year/Believing It Yourself	1960	3.75	7.50	15.00
DECCA					
❑ 9-28865	Ooh-La La/The Story of My Life	1953	5.00	10.00	20.00
❑ 9-29029	Somebody Ugghed On You/Something Called the Blues	1954	5.00	10.00	20.00
❑ 9-29169	I'm Lookin' for a Date Tonight/Sufferin' Heart	1954	5.00	10.00	20.00
❑ 9-29401	I Gotta Go Get My Baby/Chuga-Chuga, Chica-Mauga (Choo-Choo Train)	1955	5.00	10.00	20.00
❑ 9-29498	I'm Sorry I Stayed Away So Long/My Heart's Not for Little Girls to Play With	1955	5.00	10.00	20.00
❑ 9-29590	Within Your Arms/All Alone	1955	5.00	10.00	20.00
❑ 9-29720	Pepper Hot Baby/Who Will It Be	1955	5.00	10.00	20.00
❑ 9-29895	Lucky Lucky Someone Else/You Nearly Lost Your Mind	1956	3.75	7.50	15.00
❑ 9-30062	It Takes a Lot o' Heart/I'm Just Fool Enough	1956	3.75	7.50	15.00
❑ 9-30229	I'm a Big Boy Now/The Life I Have to Live	1957	3.75	7.50	15.00
❑ 9-30408	The Party Is Over/If You'll Be My Love	1957	3.75	7.50	15.00
❑ 9-30606	Sugar Lips/Rock It On Down to My House	1958	7.50	15.00	30.00
❑ 9-30792	Almost Lonely/Mine Is a Lonely Life	1958	3.75	7.50	15.00
❑ 9-30930	Buster's Gang/I Know You Do	1959	3.75	7.50	15.00
DOT					
❑ 17224	Blackjack County Change/The Great River Road Mystery	1969	2.00	4.00	8.00
GROOVE					
❑ 58-0017	Take a Letter, Miss Gray/Here I Sit a-Waiting	1963	2.50	5.00	10.00
❑ 58-0017 [PS]	Take a Letter, Miss Gray/Here I Sit a-Waiting	1963	10.00	20.00	40.00
❑ 58-0019	Little Miss Lonesome/Sorry About the World Out There	1963	2.50	5.00	10.00
❑ 58-0024	As Long As There's a Sunday/When Love Goes Wrong	1963	2.50	5.00	10.00
❑ 58-0034	If I Miss You (Half As Much As I Have Loved You)/John Mason Whitney III	1964	2.50	5.00	10.00
❑ 58-0047	Prematurely Blue/You'll Never Get a Better Chance	1964	2.50	5.00	10.00
RCA VICTOR					
❑ 47-8559	The Village Idiot/Where You're Concerned	1965	2.00	4.00	8.00
❑ 47-9082	But Wait There's More/The Second Thing I'm Gonna Do	1967	2.00	4.00	8.00
❑ 47-9428	A Funny Thing Happened/I'm Going Back to Louisiana	1968	2.00	4.00	8.00
STARDAY					
❑ 530	One Eyed Red/I'd Know You Anywhere	1960	3.75	7.50	15.00
❑ 549	My Heart Keeps Getting in the Way/One for You	1961	3.00	6.00	12.00
❑ 560	Your Side of the Story/How's It Feel	1961	3.00	6.00	12.00
❑ 582	Walking the Floor Over You/They Painted a Picture for Me	1962	3.00	6.00	12.00

Albums

Number	Title (A Side/B Side)	Yr	VG	VG+	NM
CUTLASS					
❑ 123	Travelin' Singin' Man	1972	7.50	15.00	30.00
DECCA					
❑ DL 8644 [M]	Country Boy in Love	1957	15.00	30.00	60.00
DOT					
❑ DLP-25922	Things I Still Remember Very Well	1969	3.75	7.50	15.00
FIRST GENERATION					
❑ 1	What's Wrong with the Way We're Doing It Now	1979	3.00	6.00	12.00
PHONORAMA					
❑ 5565	What's Wrong with the Way We're Doing It Now	1983	2.00	4.00	8.00
RCA VICTOR					
❑ LPM-3339 [M]	Where You're Concerned	1965	5.00	10.00	20.00
❑ LSP-3339 [S]	Where You're Concerned	1965	6.25	12.50	25.00
STARDAY					
❑ SLP-160 [M]	Star of the Grand Ole Opry	1962	10.00	20.00	40.00
❑ SLP-198 [M]	The Modern Country Sound of Justin Tubb	1962	10.00	20.00	40.00
❑ SLP-334 [M]	The Best of Justin Tubb	1965	6.25	12.50	25.00
VOCALION					
❑ VL 73802	That Country Style	196?	3.00	6.00	12.00

TUBB, JUSTIN, AND GOLDIE HILL

Also see each artist's individual listings.

45s

Number	Title (A Side/B Side)	Yr	VG	VG+	NM
DECCA					
❑ 9-29145	Looking Back to See/I Miss You So	1954	5.00	10.00	20.00
❑ 9-29349	Sure Fire Kisses/Fickle Heart	1954	5.00	10.00	20.00

TUBB, JUSTIN, AND LORENE MANN

Also see each artist's individual listings.

45s

Number	Title (A Side/B Side)	Yr	VG	VG+	NM
RCA VICTOR					
❑ 47-8659	Hurry, Mr. Peters/We've Got a Lot in Common	1965	2.00	4.00	8.00
❑ 47-8834	We've Gone Too Far Again/Together But Still Alone	1966	2.00	4.00	8.00

Albums

Number	Title (A Side/B Side)	Yr	VG	VG+	NM
RCA VICTOR					
❑ LPM-3591 [M]	Together and Alone	1966	7.50	15.00	30.00
❑ LSP-3591 [S]	Together and Alone	1966	10.00	20.00	40.00

TUCKER, JERRY LEE

45s

Number	Title (A Side/B Side)	Yr	VG	VG+	NM
OAK					
❑ 1057	Livin' in Shadows/(B-side unknown)	1988	—	3.00	6.00

TUCKER, JIMMY

45s

Number	Title (A Side/B Side)	Yr	VG	VG+	NM
GAR-PAX					
❑ 2715	I'm Gonna Move to the Country (And Get Away to It All)/(B-side unknown)	1979	—	3.00	6.00
NSD					
❑ 35	(You've Got That) Fire Goin' Again/Somebody Loves Me	1979	—	2.50	5.00
❑ 40	The Reading of the Will/It's Not Easy Loving You	1980	—	2.50	5.00

TUCKER, LA COSTA

See LA COSTA.

TUCKER, RICK

45s

Number	Title (A Side/B Side)	Yr	VG	VG+	NM
COLUMBIA					
❑ 4-41041	Patty Baby/Don't Do Me This Way	1957	25.00	50.00	100.00
HITSVILLE					
❑ 6035	I Heard a Song/Plans That We Made	1976	—	3.00	6.00
OAK					
❑ 1066	Honey I'm Just Walking Out the Door/(B-side unknown)	1989	—	2.50	5.00

TUCKER, TANYA

45s

Number	Title (A Side/B Side)	Yr	VG	VG+	NM
ARISTA					
❑ 0677	Feel Right/Cry	1982	—	2.00	4.00
❑ 1053	Changes/Too Long	1983	—	2.00	4.00
❑ 9006	Changes/Too Long	1983	—	—	3.00
❑ 9046	Baby I'm Yours/I Don't Want You to Go	1983	—	—	3.00
CAPITOL					
❑ 4986	Why Don't We Just Sleep on It Tonight/It's Your World	1981	—	2.00	4.00
—With Glen Campbell					
❑ B-5533	One Love at a Time/(B-side unknown)	1985	—	—	3.00
❑ B-5533 [PS]	One Love at a Time/(B-side unknown)	1985	—	—	3.00
❑ B-5604	Just Another Love/You Could Change My Mind	1986	—	—	3.00
❑ B-5604 [PS]	Just Another Love/You Could Change My Mind	1986	—	—	3.00
❑ B-5652	I'll Come Back As Another Woman/Somebody to Care	1986	—	—	3.00
❑ B-5694	It's Only for You/Girls Like Me	1987	—	2.50	5.00
—First pressing had erroneous A-side title					
❑ B-5694	It's Only Over for You/Girls Like Me	1987	—	—	3.00
❑ B-44036	Love Me Like You Used To/If I Didn't Love You	1987	—	—	3.00
❑ B-44036 [PS]	Love Me Like You Used To/If I Didn't Love You	1987	—	—	3.00
❑ B-44100	I Won't Take Less Than Your Love/Heartbreaker	1987	—	—	3.00
—With Paul Davis and Paul Overstreet					
❑ B-44142	If It Don't Come Easy/I'll Tennessee You in My Dreams	1988	—	—	3.00
❑ B-44188	Strong Enough to Bend/Back on My Feet	1988	—	—	3.00
❑ B-44271	Highway Robbery/Lonesome Town	1989	—	—	3.00
❑ B-44348	Call on Me/Daddy and Home	1989	—	—	3.00
❑ B-44401	Daddy and Home/Playing for Keeps	1989	—	—	3.00
❑ B-44469	My Arms Stay Open All Night/Love Me Like You Used To	1989	—	—	3.00
❑ NR-44520	Walking Shoes/This Heart of Mine	1990	—	2.00	4.00
❑ NR-44586	Don't Go Out/(B-side unknown)	1990	—	2.50	5.00
—With T. Graham Brown; may only have been released on cassette single					
❑ 7PRO-79810	My Arms Stay Open All Night (same on both sides)	1989	—	2.50	5.00
—Originally promo only; stock copy on 44469					
CAPITOL NASHVILLE					
❑ S7-19515	Little Things/You Don't Do It	1997	—	—	3.00
❑ S7-19628	Ridin' Out the Heartache/I Don't Believe That's How You Feel	1997	—	—	3.00
❑ NR-44774	(Without You) What Do I Do with Me/Oh What It Did to Me	1991	—	2.50	5.00
❑ 7PRO-79149	Don't Go Out (same on both sides)	1990	—	2.50	5.00
—With T. Graham Brown; vinyl may be promo only					
❑ 7PRO-79338	It Won't Be Me (same on both sides)	1990	—	3.00	6.00
—Vinyl is promo only					
❑ 7PRO-79535	Oh What It Did to Me (same on both sides)	1991	—	3.00	6.00
—Vinyl is promo only					
❑ 7PRO-79711	Down to My Last Teardrop (same on both sides)	1991	—	3.00	6.00
—Vinyl is promo only					
COLUMBIA					
❑ 10069	I Believe the South Is Gonna Rise Again/Old Dan Tucker's Daughter	1974	—	2.50	5.00
❑ 10127	Spring/Bed of Roses	1975	—	2.50	5.00
❑ 10236	Greener Than the Grass (We Laid On)/Guess I'll Have to Love Him More	1975	—	2.50	5.00
❑ 10577	You Are So Beautiful/Almost Persuaded	1977	—	2.00	4.00
❑ 45588	Delta Dawn/I Love the Way He Loves Me	1972	—	2.50	5.00
❑ 45588 [PS]	Delta Dawn/I Love the Way He Loves Me	1972	2.50	5.00	10.00
❑ 45721	Love's the Answer/The Jamestown Ferry	1972	—	2.50	5.00
❑ 45799	What's Your Mama's Name/Rainy Girl	1973	—	2.50	5.00
❑ 45892	Blood Red and Goin' Down/Missing Piece of Puzzle	1973	—	2.50	5.00
❑ 45991	Would You Lay with Me (In a Field of Stone)/No Man's Land	1974	—	2.50	5.00

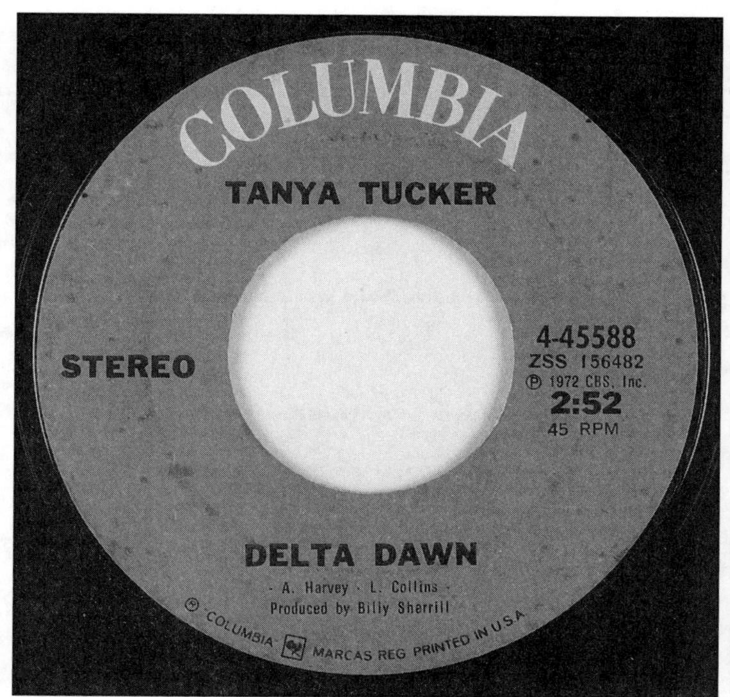

Tanya Tucker first recorded at age 13, went through a career slump in her early 20s, then became a factor on the country charts again after battling some personal demons. (Top left) Her first hit song was "Delta Dawn" in early 1972, which made the top 10 on the country charts. Helen Reddy would remake the song in 1973 and have a No. 1 pop hit with it. (Top right) Tucker began recording for MCA in 1975. Her time there got off to an auspicious start as her first single for the label, "Lizzie and the Rainman" hit No. 1. It also became her biggest pop hit by making the top 40. (Bottom left) After things turned sour at MCA, and after a very brief time with Arista, Tucker signed with Capitol in the mid-1980s and began having hits again. "Just Another Love," her second Capitol hit, was also her first No. 1 single in 10 years. (Bottom right) Tucker remained a chart fixture into the early 1990s, as five different songs hit No. 2 on the *Billboard* charts. The last of these was 1993's "Soon."

Number	Title (A Side/B Side)	Yr	VG	VG+	NM
❑ 46047	The Man That Turned My Mama On/Satisfied with Missing You	1974	—	2.50	5.00
LIBERTY					
❑ S7-17594	Soon/Sneaky Moon	1993	—	2.00	4.00
❑ S7-17803	We Don't Have to Do This/Silence Is King	1994	—	2.00	4.00
❑ S7-17908	Hangin' In/Let the Good Times Roll	1994	—	2.00	4.00
❑ S7-18135	You Just Watch Me/I Love You Anyway	1994	—	2.00	4.00
❑ S7-18485	Between the Two of Them/Love Will	1995	—	2.00	4.00
❑ S7-18583	Something/All My Loving	1995	—	2.00	4.00
—B-side by Suzy Bogguss and Chet Atkins					
❑ S7-56825	Two Sparrows in a Hurricane/Danger Ahead	1992	—	2.00	4.00
❑ S7-56953	It's a Little Too Late/Rainbow Rider	1993	—	2.00	4.00
❑ S7-56985	Tell Me About It/What Do They Know	1993	—	2.00	4.00
—A-side with Delbert McClinton					
❑ S7-57703	Some Kind of Trouble/Oh What It Did to Me	1992	—	2.50	5.00
❑ S7-57768	If Your Heart Ain't Busy Tonight/Down to My Last Teardrop	1992	—	2.50	5.00
❑ S7-57895	Winter Wonderland/What Child Is This	1992	—	2.00	4.00
MCA					
❑ 40402	Lizzie and the Rainman/Traveling Salesman	1975	—	2.00	4.00
❑ 40444	San Antonio Stroll/The Serenade That We Played	1975	—	2.00	4.00
❑ 40497	Don't Believe My Heart Can Stand Another You/ Depend on You	1975	—	2.00	4.00
❑ 40540	You've Got Me to Hold On To/Ain't That a Shame	1976	—	2.00	4.00
❑ 40598	Here's Some Love/The Pride of Franklin County	1976	—	2.00	4.00
❑ 40650	Ridin' Rainbows/Short Cut	1976	—	2.00	4.00
❑ 40708	It's a Cowboy Lovin' Night/Morning Comes	1977	—	2.00	4.00
❑ 40755	Dancing the Night Away/Let's Keep It That Way	1977	—	2.00	4.00
❑ 40902	Save Me/Slippin' Away	1978	—	2.00	4.00
❑ 40902 [PS]	Save Me/Slippin' Away	1978	—	3.00	6.00
❑ 40976	Texas (When I Die)/Not Fade Away	1978	—	2.00	4.00
❑ 40976 [PS]	Texas (When I Die)/Not Fade Away	1978	—	3.00	6.00
❑ 41005	I'm the Singer, You're the Song/Lover Goodbye	1979	—	2.00	4.00
❑ 41144	Lay Back in the Arms of Someone/By Day By Day	1979	—	2.00	4.00
❑ 41194	Tear Me Apart/Better Late Than Never	1980	—	2.00	4.00
❑ 41305	Pecos Promenade/King of Country Music	1980	—	2.00	4.00
❑ 41323	Dream Lover/Bronco	1980	—	2.00	4.00
—A-side with Glen Campbell					
❑ 51037	Can I See You Tonight/Let Me Count the Ways	1980	—	2.00	4.00
❑ 51096	Love Knows We Tried/Somebody (Trying to Tell You Something)	1981	—	2.00	4.00
❑ 51131	Should I Do It/Lucky Enough for Two	1981	—	2.00	4.00
❑ 51184	Rodeo Girls/Halfway to Heaven	1981	—	2.00	4.00
❑ 52017	Somebody Buy This Cowgirl a Beer/Delta Dawn	1982	—	2.00	4.00
Albums					
ARISTA					
❑ AL 8381	Changes	1984	2.00	4.00	8.00
—Reissue of 9596					
❑ AL 9596	Changes	1982	2.50	5.00	10.00
CAPITOL					
❑ ST-12474	Girls Like Me	1986	2.50	5.00	10.00
❑ CLT-46870	Love Me Like You Used To	1987	2.50	5.00	10.00
❑ C1-48865	Strong Enough to Bend	1988	2.50	5.00	10.00
❑ C1-91814	Greatest Hits	1989	3.00	6.00	12.00
CAPITOL NASHVILLE					
❑ 1P 8140	What Do I Do with Me	1991	5.00	10.00	20.00
—Only available on vinyl through Columbia House					
COLUMBIA					
❑ KC 31742	Delta Dawn	1972	3.75	7.50	15.00
❑ PC 31742	Delta Dawn	198?	2.00	4.00	8.00
❑ KC 32272	What's Your Mama's Name	1973	3.75	7.50	15.00
❑ KC 32744	Would You Lay with Me (In a Field of Stone)	1974	3.00	6.00	12.00
❑ PC 32744	Would You Lay with Me (In a Field of Stone)	197?	2.00	4.00	8.00
❑ PC 33355	Greatest Hits	1975	3.00	6.00	12.00
—No bar code on cover					
❑ PC 33355	Greatest Hits	197?	2.00	4.00	8.00
—With bar code on cover					
❑ PC 34733	You Are So Beautiful	1977	3.00	6.00	12.00
—No bar code on cover					
❑ PC 34733	You Are So Beautiful	197?	2.00	4.00	8.00
—With bar code on cover					
MCA					
❑ 654	Tanya Tucker	1980	2.00	4.00	8.00
—Reissue of 2141					
❑ 655	Lovin' and Learnin'	1980	2.00	4.00	8.00
—Reissue of 21??					
❑ 656	Here's Some Love	1980	2.00	4.00	8.00
—Reissue of 22??					
❑ 657	Ridin' Rainbows	1980	2.00	4.00	8.00
—Reissue of 2253					
❑ 2141	Tanya Tucker	1975	3.00	6.00	12.00
❑ 2167	Lovin' and Learnin'	1976	3.00	6.00	12.00
❑ 2213	Here's Some Love	1976	3.00	6.00	12.00
❑ 2253	Ridin' Rainbows	1977	3.00	6.00	12.00
❑ 3032	Tanya Tucker's Greatest Hits	1978	3.00	6.00	12.00
❑ 3066	TNT	1978	3.00	6.00	12.00
—Original gatefold cover					
❑ 5106	Tear Me Apart	1979	2.50	5.00	10.00
❑ 5140	Dreamlovers	1980	2.50	5.00	10.00
❑ 5228	Should I Do It	1981	2.50	5.00	10.00
❑ 5299	Tanya Tucker Live	1982	2.50	5.00	10.00
❑ 5357	The Best of Tanya Tucker	1983	2.50	5.00	10.00
❑ 27030	Dreamlovers	198?	2.00	4.00	8.00
—Reissue of 5140					
❑ 37075	TNT	1981	2.00	4.00	8.00
—Reissue of 3066; gatefold removed					
❑ 37158	Tear Me Apart	1981	2.00	4.00	8.00
—Reissue of 5106					
❑ 37225	Greatest Hits	1984	2.00	4.00	8.00
—Reissue of 3032					
❑ 37242	Tanya Tucker Live	1984	2.00	4.00	8.00
—Reissue of 5299					

TUNESMITHS, THE

Number	Title (A Side/B Side)	Yr	VG	VG+	NM
45s					
COLUMBIA					
❑ 4-21386	There's a Bottle Where She Used to Be/Oh Stop	1955	5.00	10.00	20.00
❑ 4-21485	Outlaw/Snowdeer	1956	5.00	10.00	20.00

TURNER, GRANT

Number	Title (A Side/B Side)	Yr	VG	VG+	NM
45s					
CHART					
❑ 1130	The Bible in Her Hand/Lord Don't Let Me Down	1964	3.75	7.50	15.00
❑ 1275	Old North Star/Maco Light	1965	3.00	6.00	12.00

TURNER, JACK

Number	Title (A Side/B Side)	Yr	VG	VG+	NM
45s					
HICKORY					
❑ 1050	Everybody's Rockin' But Me/I'm Gonna Get You If I Can	1956	6.25	12.50	25.00
❑ 1057	It's My Foolish Pride/Looking for Love	1956	5.00	10.00	20.00
RCA VICTOR					
❑ 47-5267	Hound Dog/(B-side unknown)	1953	7.50	15.00	30.00
❑ 47-5384	Gambler's Guitar/Butterfly Love	1953	7.50	15.00	30.00
❑ 47-5682	Walkin' a Chalk Line/Honey, I Reckon I Love You	1954	6.25	12.50	25.00
❑ 47-5815	If I Could Only Win Your Love/I'm Getting Married Tonight	1954	6.25	12.50	25.00
❑ 47-5901	I'm Not Jealous/Put It Down on Paper	1954	6.25	12.50	25.00
❑ 47-5997	Model T Baby/Hitchhikin' a Ride	1955	7.50	15.00	30.00
❑ 47-6163	Bama Bamboo Boy/The Story of the Smokey Mountain	1955	6.25	12.50	25.00
❑ 47-6305	Nightmare/Little Boy Why Do You Weep	1955	6.25	12.50	25.00

TURNER, MARY LOU

Also see BILL ANDERSON AND MARY LOU TURNER.

Number	Title (A Side/B Side)	Yr	VG	VG+	NM
45s					
CHURCHILL					
❑ 7741	Yours and Mine/You Can't Remember, And I Can't Forget	1979	—	2.50	5.00
❑ 7741 [PS]	Yours and Mine/You Can't Remember, And I Can't Forget	1979	2.00	4.00	8.00
❑ 7744	Caught with My Feelings Down/You Can't Remember, And I Can't Forget	1979	—	2.50	5.00
❑ 7751	I Wanna Love You Tonight/If You Cross That Bridge	1980	—	2.50	5.00
MCA					
❑ 40146	Poor Sweet Baby/Workin' on My Mind	1973	—	3.00	6.00
❑ 40244	All That Keeps Me Goin'/I'll Always Be Your Woman If You'll Always Be My Man	1974	—	2.50	5.00
❑ 40343	Come On Home/Tomorrow	1974	—	2.50	5.00
❑ 40448	I Wish It Was Love/The World Needs Country Music	1975	—	2.50	5.00
❑ 40566	It's Different with You/Old Habits Are Hard to Break	1976	—	2.50	5.00
❑ 40620	Love It Away/Must You Throw Dirt in My Face	1976	—	2.50	5.00
❑ 40674	Cheatin' Overtime/I Never Have the Time	1976	—	2.50	5.00
❑ 40727	The Man Still Turns Me On/Maybe It's Time to Start Calling It Love	1977	—	2.50	5.00
❑ 40828	He Picked Me Up When You Let Me Down/A Man Can't Live by Bed Alone	1977	—	2.50	5.00
❑ 40898	You Left Your Sunshine with Me/Oh, Boy	1978	—	2.50	5.00
NASHVILLE					
❑ 5239	The Frame of Mind You're In/I Lost My Biggest Race	196?	2.50	5.00	10.00
RCI					
❑ 2372	Have I Told You Lately That I Love You/You Can't Fall in Love When You're Cryin'	198?	—	3.00	6.00

TURNER, ZEB

Number	Title (A Side/B Side)	Yr	VG	VG+	NM
45s					
KING					
❑ 950	Chew Tobacco Rag/No More Nothin'	1951	10.00	20.00	40.00
❑ 960	I Got a Lot of Time for Lots of Things/Back, Back to Baltimore	1951	7.50	15.00	30.00
❑ 999	Sissy Song/Lonely Little Robin	1951	7.50	15.00	30.00
❑ 1001	Crazy Heart/I Got Loaded	1951	7.50	15.00	30.00
❑ 1009	Traveling Boogie/Oh She's Gone, Gone, Gone	1951	7.50	15.00	30.00
❑ 5492	It Just Tears Me All to Pieces/I Hung My Head and Cried	1961	3.75	7.50	15.00
Selected 78s					
BULLET					
❑ 629	Chattanooga Boogie/Ain't Had No Lovin'	194?	10.00	20.00	40.00
❑ 630	I'll Drift Along/When Love Is Gone	194?	10.00	20.00	40.00
❑ 636	Coal Miner's Blues/You Never Done Me Right	194?	7.50	15.00	30.00
❑ 651	I Guess That's Why I Love You/Don't That Moon Look Lonesome	194?	7.50	15.00	30.00
❑ 661	Things Just Happen That Way/Big Fat Papa	194?	7.50	15.00	30.00

Number	Title (A Side/B Side)	Yr	VG	VG+	NM
KING					
❑ 790	Tennessee Boogie/A Drunkard's Confession	1949	6.25	12.50	25.00
❑ 818	How Can I/You're Gonna Be Lonesome	1949	5.00	10.00	20.00
❑ 833	I Could Lose These Blues/Dolly Dimple Dance	1949	5.00	10.00	20.00
❑ 845	All Dressed Up/Why Don't You Haul Off and Get Religion	1950	5.00	10.00	20.00
❑ 861	Huckleberry Boogie/Never Been So Lonesome	1950	5.00	10.00	20.00
❑ 883	Hard Hearted You and Chicken Hearted Me/I'm Tying Up the Blues	1950	5.00	10.00	20.00
❑ 900	Boogie Woogie Lou/Outside Your Picture Frame	1950	5.00	10.00	20.00
Albums					
AUDIO LAB					
❑ AL-1537 [M]	Country Music in the Turner Style	1959	37.50	75.00	150.00

TURNER NICHOLS

45s

Number	Title (A Side/B Side)	Yr	VG	VG+	NM
BNA					
❑ 62577	Moonlight Drive-In/Anything	1993	—	—	3.00
❑ 62708	She Loves to Hear Me Rock/Harleys and Horses	1993	—	—	3.00
❑ 62819	Come Saturday Night/Rose Tattoo	1994	—	—	3.00

TUTTLE, WESLEY

45s

Number	Title (A Side/B Side)	Yr	VG	VG+	NM
CAPITOL					
❑ F1266	White Christmas/What I Want for Christmas	1950	6.25	12.50	25.00
❑ F1478	Too Bad About You/Before I'm Through	1951	6.25	12.50	25.00
❑ F1804	Detour/With Tears in My Eyes	1951	6.25	12.50	25.00
❑ F1916	Tennessee Rose/Heartbreak Ridge	1952	6.25	12.50	25.00
❑ F1992	Call of the Mountains/They Locked God Outside	1952	6.25	12.50	25.00
❑ F2091	Hillbilly Heaven/Devil's Heart	1952	6.25	12.50	25.00
❑ F2271	Known Only to Him/Gathering Home	1952	6.25	12.50	25.00
❑ F2408	Fill the Cup to Overflowing/I've Got a Round Trip Ticket	1953	6.25	12.50	25.00
❑ F2514	Vaya Con Dios/I Wonder Where You Are Tonight	1953	6.25	12.50	25.00
❑ F2545	Crying in the Chapel/For Me, For Me	1953	6.25	12.50	25.00
❑ F2577	Wonderful Waltz/Don't You Remember	1953	6.25	12.50	25.00
❑ F2768	I'll Have the Last Waltz with Mother/Sign Post	1954	5.00	10.00	20.00
❑ F3072	Penny Love Affair/That Little Boy of Mine	1955	5.00	10.00	20.00
❑ F3098	Jim, Johnny and Jonas/Say You Do	1955	5.00	10.00	20.00
❑ F3204	You, Nobody But You/I Promise You	1955	5.00	10.00	20.00
❑ F40271	Texas Yodel/A Picture in a Frame	1950	10.00	20.00	40.00
CORAL					
❑ 9-64068	The Lightning Express/That Silver Haired Daddy of Mine	1950	6.25	12.50	25.00
❑ 9-64076	One Diamond Ring/I'm Tired of Playing Second Fiddle to a Steel Guitar	1951	6.25	12.50	25.00
Selected 78s					
CAPITOL					
❑ 194	I Dreamed That My Daddy Came Home/Rainin' on the Mountain	1945	5.00	10.00	20.00
❑ 216	With Tears in My Eyes/Too Little Too Late	1945	3.75	7.50	15.00
❑ 233	Detour/I Wish I Had Never Met Sunshine	1946	3.75	7.50	15.00
❑ 267	Tho' I Tried (I Can't Forget You)/When You Cry (You Cry Alone)	1946	3.75	7.50	15.00
❑ 321	No Children Allowed/I've Loved You Too Long	1947	3.75	7.50	15.00
❑ 373	Little You Cared/A Broken Promise	1947	3.75	7.50	15.00
❑ 398	Excess Baggage/I'd Trade All of My Tomorrows	1947	3.75	7.50	15.00
❑ 15206	White Christmas/What I Want for Christmas	1948	3.75	7.50	15.00
❑ 15267	I Dreamed My Daddy Came Home/With Tears in My Eyes	1948	3.75	7.50	15.00
❑ 15268	Detour/I'd Trade All My Tomorrows	1948	3.75	7.50	15.00
❑ 15384	Don't Play Around with My Heart/The Time and the Place	1949	3.75	7.50	15.00
❑ 40007	Mail Order Mama/Until Dawn	1947	3.75	7.50	15.00
❑ 40021	If You Ever Need a Friend/Why Do I Love You, Oh Why	1947	3.75	7.50	15.00
❑ 40037	I Know It's Wrong/Please Be Like Your Daddy	1947	3.75	7.50	15.00
❑ 40073	There's a Star Spangled Rainbow/Go On and Cry Yourself to Sleep	1948	3.75	7.50	15.00
❑ 40104	Who Do You Spend Your Dreams With?/I'm Writing a Letter to Heaven	1948	3.75	7.50	15.00
❑ 40121	Mom Understands/You Can't Fool My Broken Heart	1948	3.75	7.50	15.00
❑ 40215	Hold Me, Hold Me/When You Lose	1949	3.75	7.50	15.00
❑ 40233	It May Be Too Late/God Put a Rainbow in the Clouds	1949	3.75	7.50	15.00
❑ 40241	This Cold War/Yodelin' Boogie	1949	3.75	7.50	15.00

TUTTLE, WESLEY AND MARILYN

45s

Number	Title (A Side/B Side)	Yr	VG	VG+	NM
CAPITOL					
❑ F2242	Our Love Isn't Legal/Don't Break the Sixth Commandment	1952	6.25	12.50	25.00
❑ F2850	Never/Friendly Love	1954	5.00	10.00	20.00
❑ F2983	Higher and Higher and Higher/Tennessee Mambo	1954	5.00	10.00	20.00
Selected 78s					
CAPITOL					
❑ 15423	Need You/I'm Bitin' My Fingernails	1949	3.75	7.50	15.00

TWAIN, SHANIA

45s

Number	Title (A Side/B Side)	Yr	VG	VG+	NM
MERCURY					
❑ 172123-7	Come On Over/Man! I Feel Like a Woman!	1999	—	2.00	4.00
❑ 562582-7	Rock This Country!/I'm Holdin' On to Love (To Save My Life)	2000	—	2.00	4.00
❑ 566220-7	Honey, I'm Home/That Don't Impress Me Much	1998	—	2.00	4.00
❑ 566450-7	From This Moment On (Pop Radio Mix)/From This Moment On (Single Remix)	1998	—	2.50	5.00
❑ 568062-7	Love Gets Me Every Time/Love Gets Me Every Time (Dance Mix)	1997	—	2.50	5.00
❑ 568242-7	Don't Be Stupid (You Know I Love You)/If It Don't Take Two	1997	—	2.50	5.00
❑ 568452-7	You're Still the One/Don't Be Stupid (You Know I Love You) (Remix)	1998	—	2.50	5.00
❑ 578384-7	Home Ain't Where His Heart Is (Anymore)/Whose Bed Have Your Boots Been Under?	1996	—	2.50	5.00
❑ 578748-7	God Bless the Child/(If You're Not In It for Love) I'm Outta Here! (Remix)	1996	—	3.00	6.00
❑ 852138-7	You Win My Love/Home Ain't Where His Heart Is (Anymore)	1996	—	2.50	5.00
❑ 852206-7	The Woman in Me (Needs the Man in You)/Any Man of Mine	1995	—	2.50	5.00
❑ 852498-7	(If You're Not In It for Love) I'm Outta Here!/The Woman in Me (Needs the Man in You)	1995	—	2.50	5.00
❑ 852986-7	No One Needs to Know/Leaving Is the Only Way Out	1996	—	2.50	5.00
❑ 856448-7	Whose Bed Have Your Boots Been Under?/Any Man of Mine	1995	2.50	5.00	10.00
❑ 862346-7	Dance with the One That Brought You/When He Leaves You	1993	—	3.00	6.00
❑ 862806-7	You Lay a Whole Lot of Love on Me/God Ain't Gonna Getcha for That	1993	—	3.00	6.00
❑ 864992-7	What Made You Say That/Crime of the Century	1993	—	3.00	6.00

TWISTER ALLEY

45s

Number	Title (A Side/B Side)	Yr	VG	VG+	NM
MERCURY					
❑ 862536-7	Dance/Billy Bill	1993	—	—	3.00
❑ 862846-7	Nothing In Common But Love/Redneck Ways	1993	—	—	3.00

TWITTY, CONWAY

45s

Number	Title (A Side/B Side)	Yr	VG	VG+	NM
ABC-PARAMOUNT					
❑ 10507	Go On and Cry/She Loves Me	1963	3.75	7.50	15.00
❑ 10550	Such a Night/My Baby Left Me	1964	6.25	12.50	25.00
DECCA					
❑ 31833	Together Forever/That Kind of Girl	1965	2.50	5.00	10.00
❑ 31897	Guess My Eyes Were Bigger Than Her Heart/Honky Tonk Man	1966	2.00	4.00	8.00
❑ 31983	Look Into My Teardrops/If You Were Mine to Lose	1966	2.00	4.00	8.00
❑ 32081	I Don't Want to Be with Me/Before I'll Set Her Free	1967	2.00	4.00	8.00
❑ 32147	Don't Put Your Hurt in My Heart/Walk Me to the Door	1967	2.00	4.00	8.00
❑ 32208	Funny (But I'm Not Laughing)/Working Girl	1967	2.00	4.00	8.00
❑ 32272	The Image of Me/Dim Lights, Truck Smoke (And Loud, Loud Music)	1968	2.00	4.00	8.00
❑ 32361	Next in Line/I'm Checking Out	1968	2.00	4.00	8.00
❑ 32424	Darling, You Know I Wouldn't Lie/Table in the Corner	1968	2.00	4.00	8.00
❑ 32481	I Love You More Today/Bad Girl	1969	2.00	4.00	8.00
❑ 32546	To See My Angel Cry/I Did the Best I Could	1969	2.00	4.00	8.00
❑ 32599	That's When She Started to Stop Loving You/I'll Get Over Losing You	1969	2.00	4.00	8.00
❑ 32661	Hello Darlin'/Girl at the Bar	1970	—	3.50	7.00
❑ 32742	Fifteen Years Ago/Up Comes the Bottle	1970	—	3.50	7.00
❑ 32801	How Much More Can She Stand/Just Like a Stranger	1971	—	3.50	7.00
❑ 32842	I Wonder What She'll Think About Me Leaving/A Heartache Just Walked In	1971	—	3.50	7.00
❑ 32895	I Can't See Me Without You/I Didn't Lose Her	1971	—	3.50	7.00
❑ 32945	(Lost Her Love) On Our Last Date/I'll Never Make It Home Tonight	1972	—	3.50	7.00
❑ 32988	I Can't Stop Loving You/She Needs Someone to Hold Her (When She Cries)	1972	—	3.50	7.00
❑ 32988	I Can't Stop Loving You/Since She's Not with the One She Loves	1972	—	3.50	7.00
❑ 33033	She Needs Someone to Hold Her (When She Cries)/This Road That I Walk	1972	—	3.50	7.00
ELEKTRA					
❑ 47302	The Clown/The Boy Next Door	1982	—	2.00	4.00
❑ 47302 [PS]	The Clown/The Boy Next Door	1982	—	2.50	5.00
❑ 47443	Slow Hand/When Love Was Something Else	1982	—	2.00	4.00
❑ 69854	The Rose/It's Only Make Believe	1982	—	2.00	4.00
❑ 69854 [PS]	The Rose/It's Only Make Believe	1982	—	2.50	5.00
❑ 69964	We Did But Now You Don't/(B-side unknown)	1982	—	2.00	4.00
MCA					
❑ 40027	Baby's Gone/Dim Lovely Places	1973	—	2.50	5.00
❑ 40094	You've Never Been This Far Before/You Make It Hard	1973	—	2.50	5.00
❑ 40173	There's a Honky Tonk Angel (Who'll Take Me Back In)/Don't Let It Go to Your Heart	1973	—	2.50	5.00
❑ 40224	I'm Not Through Loving You Yet/Before Your Time	1974	—	2.50	5.00
❑ 40282	I See the Want To in Your Eyes/Girl from Tupelo	1974	—	2.50	5.00
❑ 40339	Linda on My Mind/She's Just Not Over You Yet	1974	—	2.50	5.00
❑ 40407	Touch the Hand/Don't Cry Joni	1975	—	2.50	5.00
❑ 40492	This Time I've Hurt Her More Than She Loves Me/She Did, It Did, I Didn't	1975	—	2.50	5.00

Number	Title (A Side/B Side)	Yr	VG	VG+	NM
❑ 40534	After All the Good Is Gone/I Got a Good Thing Going	1976	—	2.50	5.00
❑ 40601	The Games That Daddies Play/There's More Love in the Arms You're Leaving	1976	—	2.50	5.00
❑ 40649	I Can't Believe She Gives It All to Me/I Can't Help It If She Can't Stop Loving Me	1976	—	2.50	5.00
❑ 40682	Play, Guitar, Play/One in a Million	1977	—	2.50	5.00
❑ 40754	I've Already Loved You in My Mind/I Changed My Mind	1977	—	2.50	5.00
❑ 40805	Talkin' 'Bout You/Georgia Keeps Pulling on My Ring	1977	—	2.50	5.00
❑ 40857	I'm Used to Losing You/The Grandest Lady of Them All	1978	—	2.50	5.00
❑ 40929	That's All She Wrote/Boogie Grass Band	1978	—	2.50	5.00
❑ 40963	Your Love Had Taken Me That High/My Woman Knows	1978	—	2.50	5.00
❑ 41002	Don't Take It Away/Draggin' Chains	1979	—	2.00	4.00
❑ 41059	I May Never Get to Heaven/Grand Ole Blues	1979	—	2.00	4.00
❑ 41135	Happy Birthday Darlin'/Heavy Tears	1979	—	2.00	4.00
❑ 41174	I'd Just Love to Lay You Down/She Thinks I Still Care	1980	—	2.00	4.00
❑ 41174	I'd Love to Lay You Down/She Thinks I Still Care	1980	—	2.50	5.00
—Note slightly different A-side title					
❑ 41271	I've Never Seen the Likes of You/Soulful Woman	1980	—	2.00	4.00
❑ 51011	A Bridge That Just Won't Burn/You'll Be Back	1980	—	2.00	4.00
❑ 51059	Rest Your Love on Me/I Am the Dreamer (You Are the Dream)	1981	—	2.00	4.00
❑ 51137	Tight Fittin' Jeans/I Made You a Woman	1981	—	2.00	4.00
❑ 51199	Red Neckin' Love Makin' Night/Hearts	1981	—	2.00	4.00
❑ 52032	Over Thirty (Not Over the Hill)/Love Salvation	1982	—	2.00	4.00
❑ 52154	We Had It All/Cheatin' Fire	1983	—	2.00	4.00
❑ 53034	Julia/Everybody Needs a Hero	1987	—	2.00	4.00
❑ 53134	I Want to Know You Before We Make Love/Snake Boots	1987	—	2.00	4.00
❑ 53200	That's My Job/Lonely Town	1987	—	2.00	4.00
❑ 53276	Goodbye Time/Your Loving Side	1988	—	2.00	4.00
❑ 53373	Saturday Night Special/If You Were Mine to Lose	1988	—	2.00	4.00
❑ 53456	I Wish I Was Still in Your Dreams/If You Were Mine to Lose	1988	—	2.00	4.00
❑ 53633	She's Got a Single Thing in Mind/Too White to Sing the Blues	1989	—	2.00	4.00
❑ 53688	The House on Old Lonesome Road/Nobody Can Fill Your Shoes	1989	—	2.00	4.00
❑ 53759	Who's Gonna Know/Private Part of My Heart	1989	—	2.00	4.00
❑ 53983	I Couldn't See You Leavin'/Just the Thought of Losing You	1991	—	2.00	4.00
❑ 54077	One Bridge I Didn't Burn/I'm Tired of Being Something	1991	—	2.00	4.00
❑ 54186	She's Got a Man on Her Mind/You Put It There	1991	—	2.00	4.00
❑ 54281	Who Did They Think He Was/Let the Pretty Lady Dance	1991	—	2.00	4.00
❑ 54717	I'm the Only Thing (I'll Hold Against You)/Final Touches	1993	—	2.00	4.00
❑ 54766	Don't It Make You Lonely/I Don't Love You	1993	—	2.00	4.00
❑ 79000	Fit to Be Tied Down/When You're Cool (The Sun Shines All the Time)	1990	—	2.00	4.00
❑ 79067	Crazy in Love/Hearts Breakin' All Over Town	1990	—	2.00	4.00

MERCURY

Number	Title (A Side/B Side)	Yr	VG	VG+	NM
❑ 71086	I Need Your Lovin'/Born to Sing the Blues	1957	10.00	20.00	40.00
❑ 71148	Maybe Baby/Shake It Up	1957	10.00	20.00	40.00
❑ 71384	Why Can't I Get Through to You/Double Talk Baby	1958	10.00	20.00	40.00

MGM

Number	Title (A Side/B Side)	Yr	VG	VG+	NM
❑ 12677 [M]	It's Only Make Believe/I'll Try	1958	6.25	12.50	25.00
❑ 12748	The Story of My Love/Make Me Know You're Mine	1959	6.25	12.50	25.00
❑ 12785	Hey Little Lucy! (Don'tcha Put No Lipstick On)/When I'm Not with You	1959	6.25	12.50	25.00
❑ 12804	Mona Lisa/Heavenly	1959	6.25	12.50	25.00
❑ 12826 [M]	Danny Boy/Halfway to Heaven	1959	6.25	12.50	25.00
—First pressings on yellow labels					
❑ 12826 [M]	Danny Boy/Halfway to Heaven	1959	5.00	10.00	20.00
—Second pressings on black labels					
❑ 12857	Lonely Blue Boy/Star Spangled Heaven	1959	5.00	10.00	20.00
❑ 12886	What Am I Living For/The Hurt in My Heart	1960	5.00	10.00	20.00
❑ 12886 [PS]	What Am I Living For/The Hurt in My Heart	1960	12.50	25.00	50.00
❑ 12911	Is a Blue Bird Blue/She's Mine	1960	5.00	10.00	20.00
❑ 12911 [PS]	Is a Blue Bird Blue/She's Mine	1960	12.50	25.00	50.00
❑ 12918	What a Dream/Tell Me One More Time	1960	3.75	7.50	15.00
❑ 12943	Teasin'/I Need You So	1960	3.75	7.50	15.00
❑ 12962	Whole Lot of Shakin' Going On/The Flame	1960	3.75	7.50	15.00
❑ 12969	C'est Si Bon (It's So Good)/Don't You Dare Let Me Down	1960	3.75	7.50	15.00
❑ 12969 [PS]	C'est Si Bon (It's So Good)/Don't You Dare Let Me Down	1960	12.50	25.00	50.00
❑ 12998	The Next Kiss (Is the Last Goodbye)/A Man Alone	1961	3.75	7.50	15.00
❑ 12998 [PS]	The Next Kiss (Is the Last Goodbye)/A Man Alone	1961	12.50	25.00	50.00
❑ 13011	I'm in a Blue, Blue Mood/A Million Teardrops	1961	3.75	7.50	15.00
❑ 13034	It's Drivin' Me Wild/Sweet Sorrow	1961	3.75	7.50	15.00
❑ 13034 [PS]	It's Drivin' Me Wild/Sweet Sorrow	1961	10.00	20.00	40.00
❑ 13050	Portrait of a Fool/Tower of Tears	1961	3.75	7.50	15.00
❑ 13072	Little Piece of My Heart/Comfy N' Cozy	1962	3.75	7.50	15.00
❑ 13089	There's Something on Your Mind/Unchained Melody	1962	3.75	7.50	15.00
❑ 13112	I Hope, I Think, I Wish/The Pickup	1962	3.75	7.50	15.00
❑ 13149	I Got My Mojo Working/She Ain't No Angel	1963	3.75	7.50	15.00
❑ 14172	It's Only Make Believe/Lonely Blue Boy	1970	—	2.50	5.00
❑ 14205	What Am I Living For/I'll Try	1970	—	2.50	5.00
❑ 14274	What a Dream/Long Black Train	1971	—	2.50	5.00
❑ 14355	It's Too Late/I Hope, I Think, I Wish	1972	—	2.50	5.00
❑ 14408	Walk On By/Hey Miss Ruby	1972	—	2.50	5.00
❑ 14447	Boss Man/Fever	1972	—	2.50	5.00
❑ 14582	Danny Boy/The Pickup	1973	—	2.50	5.00
❑ SK-50107 [S]	It's Only Make Believe/I'll Try	1958	25.00	50.00	100.00
❑ SK-50130 [S]	Danny Boy/Halfway to Heaven	1959	25.00	50.00	100.00

WARNER BROS.

Number	Title (A Side/B Side)	Yr	VG	VG+	NM
❑ 28577	Fallin' for You for Years/I'll Try	1986	—	2.00	4.00
❑ 28692	Desperado Love/I Can't See Me Without You	1986	—	2.00	4.00
❑ 28772	You'll Never Know How Much I Needed You Today/Fifteen Years Ago	1986	—	2.00	4.00
❑ 28866	The Legend and the Man/(I Can't Believe) She Gives It All to Me	1985	—	2.00	4.00
❑ 28966	Between Blue Eyes and Jeans/Baby's Gone	1985	—	2.00	4.00
❑ 29057	Don't Call Him a Cowboy/After All the Good Is Gone	1985	—	2.00	4.00
❑ 29129	White Christmas/Happy the Christmas Clown	1984	—	2.50	5.00
❑ 29129 [PS]	White Christmas/Happy The Christmas Clown	1984	—	2.50	5.00
❑ 29137	Ain't She Somethin' Else/The Games That Daddies Play	1984	—	2.00	4.00
❑ 29227	I Don't Know a Thing About Love (The Moon Song)/Don't Cry Joni	1984	—	2.00	4.00
❑ 29308	Somebody's Needin' Somebody/(Lying Here with) Linda on My Mind	1984	—	2.00	4.00
❑ 29395	Three Times a Lady/I Think I'm in Love	1983	—	2.00	4.00
❑ 29505	Heartache Tonight/Hello Darlin'	1983	—	2.00	4.00
❑ 29636	Lost in the Feeling/You've Never Been This Far Before	1983	—	2.00	4.00

7-Inch Extended Plays

MGM

Number	Title (A Side/B Side)	Yr	VG	VG+	NM
❑ X-1623	(contents unknown)	1958	37.50	75.00	150.00
❑ X-1623 [PS]	It's Only Make Believe	1958	37.50	75.00	150.00
❑ X-1640	It's Only Make Believe/Hallelujah, I Love Her So//First Romance/Make Me Know You're Mine	1959	25.00	50.00	100.00
❑ X-1640 [PS]	Conway Twitty Sings, Volume 1	1959	25.00	50.00	100.00
❑ X-1641	(contents unknown)	1959	25.00	50.00	100.00
❑ X-1641 [PS]	Conway Twitty Sings, Volume 2	1959	25.00	50.00	100.00
❑ X-1642	(contents unknown)	1959	25.00	50.00	100.00
❑ X-1642 [PS]	Conway Twitty Sings, Volume 3	1959	25.00	50.00	100.00
❑ X-1678	Danny Boy/Heavenly//She's Mine/Blueberry Hill	1959	25.00	50.00	100.00
❑ X-1678 [PS]	Saturday Night with Conway Twitty, Volume 1	1959	25.00	50.00	100.00
❑ X-1679	(contents unknown)	1959	25.00	50.00	100.00
❑ X-1679 [PS]	Saturday Night with Conway Twitty, Volume 2	1959	25.00	50.00	100.00
❑ X-1680	(contents unknown)	1959	25.00	50.00	100.00
❑ X-1680 [PS]	Saturday Night with Conway Twitty, Volume 3	1959	25.00	50.00	100.00
❑ X-1701	(contents unknown)	1960	25.00	50.00	100.00
❑ X-1701 [PS]	Lonely Blue Boy	1960	25.00	50.00	100.00

Albums

ACCORD

Number	Title (A Side/B Side)	Yr	VG	VG+	NM
❑ SN-7169	Early Favorites	1982	3.00	6.00	12.00

ALLEGIANCE

Number	Title (A Side/B Side)	Yr	VG	VG+	NM
❑ AV-5012	You Made Me What I Am	1983	3.75	7.50	15.00

DECCA

Number	Title (A Side/B Side)	Yr	VG	VG+	NM
❑ DL 4724 [M]	Conway Twitty Sings	1965	6.25	12.50	25.00
❑ DL 4828 [M]	Look Into My Teardrops	1966	6.25	12.50	25.00
❑ DL 4913 [M]	Conway Twitty Country	1967	7.50	15.00	30.00
❑ DL 4990 [M]	Here's Conway Twitty	1968	12.50	25.00	50.00
❑ DL 74724 [S]	Conway Twitty Sings	1965	7.50	15.00	30.00
❑ DL 74828 [S]	Look Into My Teardrops	1966	7.50	15.00	30.00
❑ DL 74913 [S]	Conway Twitty Country	1967	7.50	15.00	30.00
❑ DL 74990 [S]	Here's Conway Twitty	1968	7.50	15.00	30.00
❑ DL 75062	Next in Line	1968	6.25	12.50	25.00
❑ DL 75105	Darling, You Know I Wouldn't Lie	1968	5.00	10.00	20.00
❑ DL 75131	I Love You More Today	1969	5.00	10.00	20.00
❑ DL 75172	To See My Angel Cry	1970	5.00	10.00	20.00
❑ DL 75209	Hello Darlin'	1970	5.00	10.00	20.00
❑ DL 75248	Fifteen Years Ago	1970	5.00	10.00	20.00
❑ DL 75276	How Much More Can She Stand	1971	5.00	10.00	20.00
❑ DL 75292	I Wonder What She'll Think About Me Leaving	1971	5.00	10.00	20.00
❑ DL 75335	I Can't See Me Without You	1972	5.00	10.00	20.00
❑ DL 75352	Conway Twitty's Greatest Hits	1972	5.00	10.00	20.00
❑ DL 75361	I Can't Stop Loving You/Last Date	1972	5.00	10.00	20.00

ELEKTRA

Number	Title (A Side/B Side)	Yr	VG	VG+	NM
❑ 60005	Southern Confort	1982	2.50	5.00	10.00
❑ 60115	#1 Classics, Volume 1	1982	2.50	5.00	10.00
❑ 60182	Dream Maker	1982	2.50	5.00	10.00
❑ 60209	#1 Classics, Volume 2	1982	2.50	5.00	10.00

HEARTLAND

Number	Title (A Side/B Side)	Yr	VG	VG+	NM
❑ HL-1088/9 [(2)]	The Very Best of Conway Twitty	1989	5.00	10.00	20.00

MCA

Number	Title (A Side/B Side)	Yr	VG	VG+	NM
❑ 18	To See My Angel Cry	1973	3.00	6.00	12.00
—Reissue of Decca 75172					
❑ 19	Hello Darlin'	1973	3.00	6.00	12.00
—Reissue of Decca 75209					
❑ 52	Conway Twitty's Greatest Hits	1973	3.00	6.00	12.00
—Reissue of Decca 75352					
❑ 53	I Can't Stop Loving You/Last Date	1973	3.00	6.00	12.00
—Reissue of Decca 75361					
❑ 303	She Needs Someone to Hold Her (When She Cries)	1973	3.75	7.50	15.00
❑ 359	You've Never Been This Far Before/Baby's Gone	1973	3.75	7.50	15.00
❑ 376	Clinging to a Saving Hand	1973	15.00	30.00	60.00

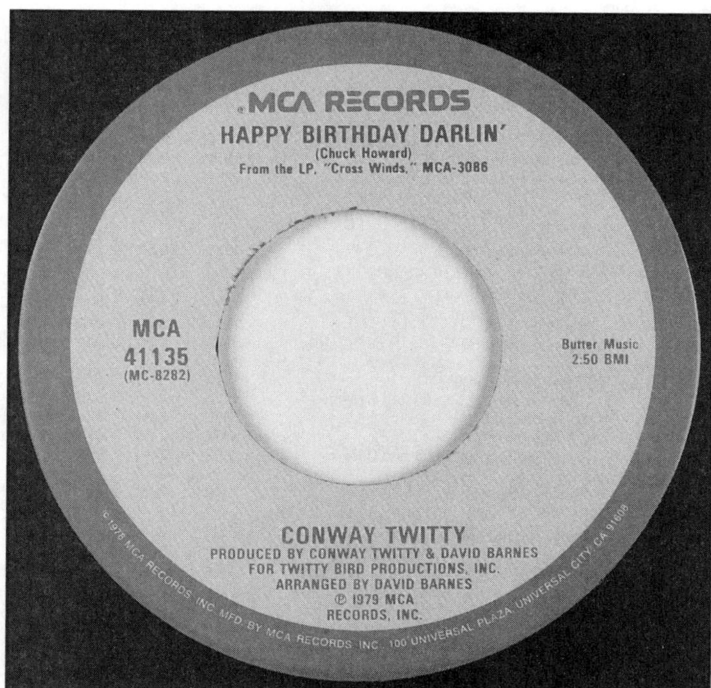

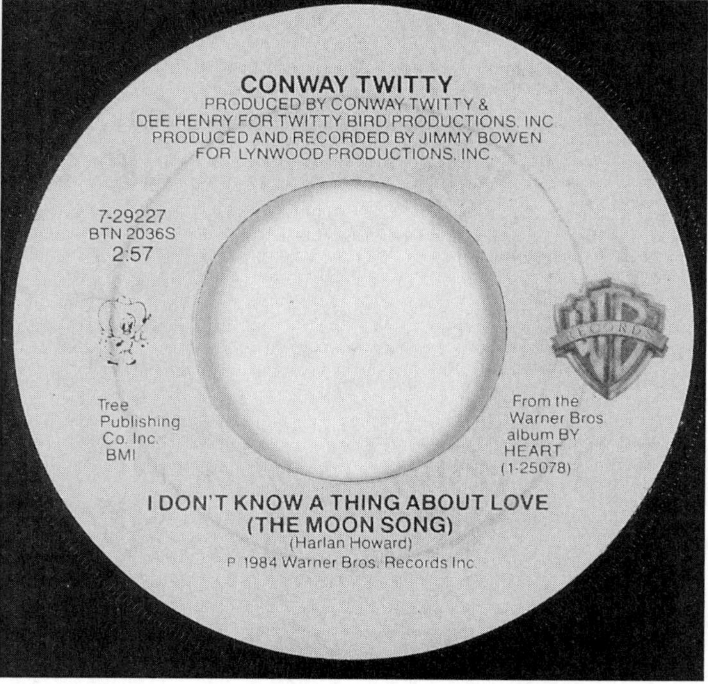

Taking his stage name from the towns of Conway, Arkansas and Twitty, Texas, the former Harold Jenkins first made the pop charts in 1958. After the hits faded away, he turned to his first love, country music, and had a long, successful chart career that lasted into the early 1990s. (Top left) The country song most closely associated with Twitty is "Hello Darlin'." It spent four weeks at No. 1 in 1970; later, Conway re-recorded it with Russian lyrics for use in one of the joint Apollo-Soyuz space missions in the 1970s. (Top right) During the mid-1970s, Twitty was accused of recording "country porn," as he had a string of hits with suggestive titles. The first of these, which also made the top 40 on the pop charts, was the 1973 hit "You've Never Been This Far Before." (Bottom left) In 1979, Twitty recorded a "sequel" to his biggest hit. Entitled "Happy Birthday Darlin'," this one, like its predecessor, also hit No. 1. (Bottom right) From 1982-86, Conway switched labels from MCA to Elektra/Warner Bros. While with WEA, he had eight No. 1 hits. One of the more significant was "I Don't Know a Thing About Love," because it was the first new hit for composer Harlan Howard in many years.

Number	Title (A Side/B Side)	Yr	VG	VG+	NM
❑ 406	Honky Tonk Angel	1974	3.75	7.50	15.00
❑ 441	I'm Not Through Loving You Yet/I See the Want To in Your Eyes	1974	3.75	7.50	15.00
❑ 469	Linda on My Mind	1975	3.75	7.50	15.00
❑ 625	High Priest of Country	197?	2.50	5.00	10.00
—Reissue of MCA 2144					
❑ 702	Conway	197?	2.50	5.00	10.00
—Reissue of MCA 3063					
❑ 2144	High Priest of Country Music	1975	3.75	7.50	15.00
❑ 2176	Twitty (This Time I've Hurt Her More Than She Loves Me)	1975	3.75	7.50	15.00
❑ 2206	Now and Then	1976	3.75	7.50	15.00
❑ 2235	Conway Twitty's Greatest Hits, Vol. 2	1976	3.75	7.50	15.00
❑ 2262	Play Guitar Play	1977	3.00	6.00	12.00
❑ 2293	I've Already Loved You in My Mind	1977	3.00	6.00	12.00
❑ 2328	Georgia Keeps Pullin' on My Ring	1978	3.00	6.00	12.00
❑ 2345	Conway Twitty's Greatest Hits, Vol. 1	1978	3.00	6.00	12.00
—Reissue of Decca 75352					
❑ 3042	The Very Best of Conway Twitty	1978	3.00	6.00	12.00
❑ 3063	Conway	1978	3.00	6.00	12.00
❑ 3086	Cross Winds	1979	3.00	6.00	12.00
❑ 3210	Heart and Soul	1980	3.00	6.00	12.00
❑ 5138	Rest Your Love on Me	1980	3.00	6.00	12.00
❑ 5204	Mr. T.	1981	3.00	6.00	12.00
❑ 5318	Number Ones	1982	3.00	6.00	12.00
❑ 5424	Classic Conway	1983	2.50	5.00	10.00
❑ 5700	Songwriter	1986	2.00	4.00	8.00
❑ 5817	A Night with Conway Twitty	1986	2.00	4.00	8.00
❑ 5969	Borderline	1987	2.00	4.00	8.00
❑ 37081	Georgia Keeps Pullin' on My Ring	198?	2.00	4.00	8.00
—Budget-line reissue					
❑ 37163	Cross Winds	198?	2.00	4.00	8.00
—Budget-line reissue					
❑ 37227	Heart and Soul	1983	2.00	4.00	8.00
—Budget-line reissue					
❑ 37228	Rest Your Love on Me	1983	2.00	4.00	8.00
—Budget-line reissue					
❑ 37229	Conway Twitty's Greatest Hits, Vol. 1	1983	2.00	4.00	8.00
—Budget-line reissue					
❑ 42115	Still in Your Dreams	1988	2.00	4.00	8.00
❑ 42297	House on Old Lonesome Road	1989	3.00	6.00	12.00
MCA CORAL					
❑ CB-20000	I'm So Used to Loving You	1973	3.00	6.00	12.00
METRO					
❑ M-512 [M]	It's Only Make Believe	1966	3.75	7.50	15.00
❑ MS-512 [S]	It's Only Make Believe	1966	5.00	10.00	20.00
MGM					
❑ GAS-110	Conway Twitty (Golden Archive Series)	1970	5.00	10.00	20.00
❑ E-3744 [M]	Conway Twitty Sings	1959	25.00	50.00	100.00
—Yellow label					
❑ E-3744 [M]	Conway Twitty Sings	1960	10.00	20.00	40.00
—Black label					
❑ E-3744 [M]	Conway Twitty Sings	196?	75.00	150.00	300.00
—Reissue with orange cover and a clean-cut photo of Conway					
❑ SE-3744 [S]	Conway Twitty Sings	1959	37.50	75.00	150.00
—Yellow label					
❑ SE-3744 [S]	Conway Twitty Sings	1960	12.50	25.00	50.00
—Black label					
❑ SE-3744 [S]	Conway Twitty Sings	196?	75.00	150.00	300.00
—Reissue with orange cover and a clean-cut photo of Conway					
❑ E-3786 [M]	Saturday Night with Conway Twitty	1960	17.50	35.00	70.00
❑ SE-3786 [S]	Saturday Night with Conway Twitty	1960	25.00	50.00	100.00
❑ E-3818 [M]	Lonely Blue Boy	1960	17.50	35.00	70.00
❑ SE-3818 [S]	Lonely Blue Boy	1960	25.00	50.00	100.00
❑ E-3849 [M]	Conway Twitty's Greatest Hits	1960	17.50	35.00	70.00
—With poster					
❑ E-3849 [M]	Conway Twitty's Greatest Hits	1960	10.00	20.00	40.00
—Without poster					
❑ SE-3849 [P]	Conway Twitty's Greatest Hits	1960	20.00	40.00	80.00
—With poster					
❑ SE-3849 [P]	Conway Twitty's Greatest Hits	1960	12.50	25.00	50.00
—Without poster					
❑ E-3907 [M]	The Rock and Roll Story	1961	12.50	25.00	50.00
❑ SE-3907 [S]	The Rock and Roll Story	1961	20.00	40.00	80.00
❑ E-3943 [M]	The Conway Twitty Touch	1961	12.50	25.00	50.00
❑ SE-3943 [S]	The Conway Twitty Touch	1961	20.00	40.00	80.00
❑ E-4019 [M]	Portrait of a Fool and Others	1962	10.00	20.00	40.00
❑ SE-4019 [S]	Portrait of a Fool and Others	1962	12.50	25.00	50.00
❑ E-4089 [M]	R & B '63	1963	10.00	20.00	40.00
❑ SE-4089 [S]	R & B '63	1963	12.50	25.00	50.00
❑ E-4217 [M]	Hit the Road	1964	6.25	12.50	25.00
❑ SE-4217 [S]	Hit the Road	1964	7.50	15.00	30.00
❑ SE-4650	You Can't Take the Country Out of Conway	1969	3.75	7.50	15.00
❑ SE-4799	Conway Twitty Hits	1971	3.75	7.50	15.00
❑ SE-4837	Conway Twitty Sings the Blues	1972	3.75	7.50	15.00
❑ SES-4844 [(2)]	20 Great Hits by Conway Twitty	1973	4.50	9.00	18.00
PICKWICK					
❑ SPC-3360	Shake It Up	1973	3.00	6.00	12.00
TEE VEE					
❑ 1009	20 Certified #1 Hits	1978	3.75	7.50	15.00
WARNER BROS.					
❑ 23869	Lost in the Feeling	1983	2.50	5.00	10.00
❑ 23971	Merry Twismas	1983	5.00	10.00	20.00
❑ 25078	By Heart	1984	2.50	5.00	10.00
❑ 25170	Conway's Latest Greatest Hits	1984	2.50	5.00	10.00
❑ 25207	Don't Call Him a Cowboy	1985	2.50	5.00	10.00
❑ 25294	Chasin' Rainbows	1985	2.50	5.00	10.00
❑ 25406	Fallin' for You for Years	1986	2.50	5.00	10.00
❑ 25777	#1's — The Warner Bros. Years	1988	2.00	4.00	8.00
❑ 60115	#1 Classics, Volume 1	1983	2.00	4.00	8.00
—Reissue of Elektra LP					
❑ 60182	Dream Maker	1983	2.00	4.00	8.00
—Reissue of Elektra LP					
❑ 60209	#1 Classics, Volume 2	1983	2.00	4.00	8.00
—Reissue of Elektra LP					

TWITTY, CONWAY, AND LORETTA LYNN

45s

Number	Title (A Side/B Side)	Yr	VG	VG+	NM
DECCA					
❑ 32776	After the Fire Is Gone/The One I Can't Live Without	1971	—	3.50	7.00
❑ 32873	Lead Me On/Four Glass Walls	1971	—	3.50	7.00
MCA					
❑ 40079	Louisiana Woman, Mississippi Man/Living Together Alone	1973	—	2.50	5.00
❑ 40251	As Soon As I Hang Up the Phone/A Lifetime Before	1974	—	2.50	5.00
❑ 40283	Trouble in Paradise/We've Already Tasted Love	1974	—	2.50	5.00
❑ 40420	Feelin's/You Done Lost Your Baby	1975	—	2.50	5.00
❑ 40572	The Letter/God Bless America Again	1976	—	2.50	5.00
❑ 40728	The Bed I'm Dreaming On/I Can't Love You Enough	1977	—	2.50	5.00
❑ 40920	You're the Reason Our Kids Are Ugly/From Seven Until Ten	1978	—	2.50	5.00
❑ 41141	The Sadness of It All/You Know Just What I'd Do	1979	—	2.50	5.00
❑ 41232	Hit the Road Jack/It's True Love	1980	—	2.00	4.00
❑ 51050	Lovin' What Your Lovin' Does to Me/Silent Partners	1981	—	2.00	4.00
❑ 51114	I Still Believe in Waltzes/Oh Honey	1981	—	2.00	4.00
❑ 53417	Making Believe/As Soon As I Hang Up the Phone (The Telephone Song)	1988	—	2.00	4.00

Albums

Number	Title (A Side/B Side)	Yr	VG	VG+	NM
DECCA					
❑ DL 75251	We Only Make Believe	1971	5.00	10.00	20.00
❑ DL 75326	Lead Me On	1972	5.00	10.00	20.00
HEARTLAND					
❑ HL-1059/60 [(2)]	The Best of Conway and Loretta	1987	5.00	10.00	20.00
MCA					
❑ 8	We Only Make Believe	1973	3.00	6.00	12.00
—Reissue of Decca 75251					
❑ 9	Lead Me On	1973	3.00	6.00	12.00
—Reissue of Decca 75326					
❑ 335	Louisiana Woman, Mississippi Man	1973	3.75	7.50	15.00
❑ 427	Country Partners	1974	3.75	7.50	15.00
❑ 629	United Talent	198?	2.50	5.00	10.00
—Reissue of MCA 2209					
❑ 722	Honky Tonk Heroes	198?	2.50	5.00	10.00
—Reissue of MCA 2372					
❑ 723	Diamond Duet	198?	2.50	5.00	10.00
—Reissue of MCA 3190					
❑ 2143	Feelins'	1975	3.75	7.50	15.00
❑ 2209	United Talent	1976	3.75	7.50	15.00
❑ 2278	Dynamic Duo	1977	3.00	6.00	12.00
❑ 2354	Country Partners	1978	2.50	5.00	10.00
—Reissue of MCA 427					
❑ 2372	Honky Tonk Heroes	1978	3.00	6.00	12.00
❑ 3164	The Very Best of Loretta and Conway	1979	3.00	6.00	12.00
❑ 3190	Diamond Duet	1979	3.00	6.00	12.00
❑ 5178	Two's a Party	1981	3.00	6.00	12.00
❑ 37237	The Very Best of Loretta and Conway	1983	2.00	4.00	8.00
—Budget-line reissue					
❑ 42216	Making Believe	1988	2.00	4.00	8.00
MCA CORAL					
❑ CDL-8006	Never Ending Song of Love	1973	3.00	6.00	12.00

TWITTY, KATHY

See JESSECA JAMES.

TWO HEARTS

45s

Number	Title (A Side/B Side)	Yr	VG	VG+	NM
MDJ					
❑ 5831	Two Hearts Can't Be Wrong/(B-side unknown)	1985	—	2.50	5.00
❑ 5831 [PS]	Two Hearts Can't Be Wrong/(B-side unknown)	1985	2.00	4.00	8.00
❑ 5832	Feel Like I'm Falling for You/All Wrapped Up in Your Love	1986	—	2.50	5.00
❑ 5832 [PS]	Feel Like I'm Falling for You/All Wrapped Up in Your Love	1986	2.00	4.00	8.00

TYLER, BONNIE

Her later material wasn't very country, but her RCA period was; "It's a Heartache" made the top 10 on both the pop and country charts.

45s

Number	Title (A Side/B Side)	Yr	VG	VG+	NM
CHRYSALIS					
❑ 2130	Lost in France/Baby I Remember You	1976	—	3.00	6.00
COLUMBIA					
❑ 03906	Total Eclipse of the Heart/Straight from the Heart	1983	—	2.00	4.00
❑ 04246	Take Me Back/Getttin' So Excited	1983	—	2.00	4.00
❑ 04246 [PS]	Take Me Back/Getttin' So Excited	1983	—	2.50	5.00
❑ 04370	Holding Out for a Hero/Faster Than the Speed of Night	1984	—	—	3.00

Number	Title (A Side/B Side)	Yr	VG	VG+	NM
❑ 04370 [PS]	Holding Out for a Hero/Faster Than the Speed of Night	1984	—	2.00	4.00
❑ 04548	Here She Comes/Obsession	1984	—	—	3.00
❑ 04548 [PS]	Here She Comes/Obsession	1984	—	2.00	4.00
❑ 05839	If You Were a Woman (And I Was a Man)/Under Suspicion	1986	—	—	3.00
❑ 05839 [PS]	If You Were a Woman (And I Was a Man)/Under Suspicion	1986	—	2.00	4.00
❑ 06151	Loving You's a Dirty Job (But Somebody's Gotta Do It)/Before This Night Is Through	1986	—	2.00	4.00
—With Todd Rundgren					
❑ 06527	Band of Gold/Tears	1986	—	—	3.00
❑ 07758	Hide Your Heart/Fire Below	1988	—	—	3.00
❑ 08497	Save Up All Your Tears/It's Not Enough	1988	—	—	3.00
RCA					
❑ PB-11249	It's a Heartache/It's About Time	1978	—	2.50	5.00
❑ PB-11349	If I Sing You a Love Song/Heaven	1978	—	2.00	4.00
❑ PB-11349 [PS]	If I Sing You a Love Song/Heaven	1978	—	2.50	5.00
❑ PB-11468	My Guns Are Loaded/Baby I Just Love You	1979	—	2.00	4.00
❑ PB-11630	Married Man/If You Ever Need Me Again	1979	—	2.00	4.00
❑ PB-11763	I Believe in Your Sweet Love/Come On, Give Me Loving	1979	—	2.00	4.00

Albums

Number	Title	Yr	VG	VG+	NM
CHRYSALIS					
❑ CHS-1140	The World Starts Tonight	1976	3.75	7.50	15.00
❑ PV 41140	The World Starts Tonight	198?	2.00	4.00	8.00
—Reissue of 1140					
COLUMBIA					
❑ BFC 38710	Faster Than the Speed of Night	1983	3.75	7.50	15.00
—Silver print on front cover					
❑ FC 38710	Faster Than the Speed of Night	1983	2.00	4.00	8.00
—Blue-green print on front cover					
❑ OC 40312	Secret Dreams and Forbidden Fire	1986	2.00	4.00	8.00
RCA VICTOR					
❑ AFL1-2821	It's a Heartache	1978	2.50	5.00	10.00
❑ AFL1-3072	Diamond Cut	1979	2.50	5.00	10.00
❑ AYL1-4110	It's a Heartache	1984	2.00	4.00	8.00
—"Best Buy Series" reissue					

TYLER, KRIS

45s

Number	Title (A Side/B Side)	Yr	VG	VG+	NM
RISING TIDE					
❑ 56045	Keeping Your Kisses/Rockin' Horse	1997	—	2.00	4.00
❑ 56051	What a Woman Knows/A Thousand Years Ago	1997	—	2.00	4.00

TYLER, T. TEXAS

45s

Number	Title (A Side/B Side)	Yr	VG	VG+	NM
4 STAR					
❑ 45-1228	Deck of Cards/Sweet Thing	195?	10.00	20.00	40.00
—Early 1950s reissue of the hit; first issued on 78 in 1948					
❑ 1555	If You Had a Heart/To Prove My Love Is True	1951	7.50	15.00	30.00
❑ 1565	Irma/Blue Kimono Blues	1951	7.50	15.00	30.00
❑ 1579	I Want to Learn to Do It/Curley Headed Baby	1951	7.50	15.00	30.00
❑ 1588	I Was the Last One to Know/When the White Azaleas Start Blooming	1952	6.25	12.50	25.00
❑ 1597	Get Out of My Life/Who's to Blame	1952	6.25	12.50	25.00
❑ 1612	It's My Heart, It's My Conscience/It's a Pity	1952	6.25	12.50	25.00
❑ 1621	Snow on the Mountain/Electric Guitar Polka	1952	6.25	12.50	25.00
❑ 1628	Wasted Tears/Let's Fly Away	1953	5.00	10.00	20.00
❑ 1649	Kiss Me Like Crazy/Tired of It All	1954	6.25	12.50	25.00
❑ 1658	Tattler's Wagon/The Soldier's Prayer Book	1954	6.25	12.50	25.00
❑ 1660	Courtin' in the Rain/Old Blue	1954	5.00	10.00	20.00
❑ 1669	A Million Teardrops/Little Miss Muffet	1955	5.00	10.00	20.00
❑ 1682	I Tickled Her Under the Chin/She Wouldn't Do for You	1955	5.00	10.00	20.00
❑ 1735	Deck of Cards/Dad Have My Dog Away	1959	3.75	7.50	15.00
❑ 1744	Remember Me/Oklahoma Hills	1960	3.75	7.50	15.00
DECCA					
❑ 9-28544	He Done Her Wrong/Much More Than the Past	1953	5.00	10.00	20.00
❑ 9-28579	Bumming Around/Jealous Love	1953	5.00	10.00	20.00
❑ 9-28760	Scratch and Itch/Let's Get Married	1953	5.00	10.00	20.00
❑ 9-28922	Pretender/Nothing at All	1953	5.00	10.00	20.00
❑ 9-29007	Hot Rod Rag/Lighthearted Guy	1954	6.25	12.50	25.00
❑ 9-29286	River Girl/Golden Wristwatch	1954	5.00	10.00	20.00
❑ 9-29598	That's What You Mean to Me/Ten-Ten-Tennessee Line	1955	3.75	7.50	15.00
KING					
❑ 5249	Deck of Cards/Dad Gave My Dog Away	1959	3.75	7.50	15.00
❑ 5380	Oklahoma Hills/Remember Me	1960	3.75	7.50	15.00
RCA VICTOR					
❑ 47-5679	Pie A La Mode/Here Goes	1954	5.00	10.00	20.00
❑ 47-5710	Deck of Cards/Ida Red	1954	5.00	10.00	20.00
STARDAY					
❑ 759	Texas Boogie Woogie/Just Like Dad	1966	2.50	5.00	10.00
❑ 783	It's a Long Road Back Home/I Still Love You (By the Way)	1966	2.50	5.00	10.00
❑ 806	Injun Joe/Crawdad Town	1967	2.50	5.00	10.00
❑ 8015	Deck of Cards/Remember Me	197?	—	3.00	6.00

Selected 78s

Number	Title (A Side/B Side)	Yr	VG	VG+	NM
4 STAR					
❑ 1008	Oklahoma Hills/Remember Me	1946	5.00	10.00	20.00
❑ 1009	Filipino Baby/You Were Only Teasin' Me	1946	5.00	10.00	20.00
❑ 1021	Home in San Antone/You'll Still Be in My Heart	1946	5.00	10.00	20.00
❑ 1022	Beautiful Morning Glory/Rough and Rocky	1946	5.00	10.00	20.00
❑ 1051	I Hung My Head and Cried/You Turned a Good Man Down	1947	5.00	10.00	20.00
❑ 1052	Gals Don't Mean a Thing/Black Jack David	1947	5.00	10.00	20.00
❑ 1062	You Nearly Lost Your Mind/Tex Tyler Ride	1947	5.00	10.00	20.00
❑ 1063	It's Been So Long Darlin'/T. Texas Blues	1947	5.00	10.00	20.00
❑ 1114	Guitar Boogie Woogie/Baby I Can't Sleep	1947	5.00	10.00	20.00
❑ 1115	I've Heard That Story Before/Smile When You Speak of Texas	1947	5.00	10.00	20.00
❑ 1140	Tell Your Lies to the Man in the Moon/Divorce Me C.O.D.	1947	5.00	10.00	20.00
❑ 1141	In My Little Red Book/I'm Gonna Get Mad (And Leave You)	1947	5.00	10.00	20.00
❑ 1149	You Doggone Son of a Gun/Pray for the Lights to Go Out	1947	5.00	10.00	20.00
❑ 1150	Frankie and Johnny/Much More Than the Rest	1947	5.00	10.00	20.00
❑ 1151	Fairweather Baby/So Round, So Firm, So Fully Packed	1947	5.00	10.00	20.00
❑ 1152	Red Light/Somebody's Rose	1947	5.00	10.00	20.00
❑ 1166	Old Fashioned Love/That's All	1947	5.00	10.00	20.00
❑ 1167	Ida Red/Follow Through	1947	5.00	10.00	20.00
❑ 1228	Deck of Cards/Sweet Thing	1948	5.00	10.00	20.00
❑ 1247	Deck of Cards/Remember Me	1948	5.00	10.00	20.00
❑ 1248	Dad Gave My Dog Away/Beautiful Life	1948	5.00	10.00	20.00
❑ 1249	Memories of France/Honky Tonk Gal	1948	5.00	10.00	20.00
❑ 1260	Fairweather Baby/I've Heard That Story Before	1948	5.00	10.00	20.00
❑ 1279	The Old Hymns/In the Sweet Bye and Bye	1948	5.00	10.00	20.00
❑ 1280	You've Got to Live Your Religion Every Day/That Beautiful Picture	1948	5.00	10.00	20.00
❑ 1281	God Put a Rainbow in the Sky/If I Could Hear My Mother Pray Again	1948	5.00	10.00	20.00
❑ 1285	New Baby Doll/Dead Ashes	1949	5.00	10.00	20.00
❑ 1290	There Ain't Gonna Be No Doggone After Awhile/Put My Little Shoes Away	1949	5.00	10.00	20.00
❑ 1321	Please Believe in Me/Soft Lips	1949	5.00	10.00	20.00
❑ 1346	Country Boy/Show Me the Way Back to Your Heart	1949	5.00	10.00	20.00
❑ 1383	My Bucket's Got a Hole in It/Cry-Baby Heart	1949	5.00	10.00	20.00
❑ 1403	Old Country Church/Colored Child's Funeral	1950	5.00	10.00	20.00
❑ 1411	Chattanoogie Shoe Shine Boy/I Love You Because	1950	5.00	10.00	20.00
❑ 1446	I'll Hate Myself Tomorrow/Goodnight Waltz	1950	5.00	10.00	20.00
❑ 1501	Wrong Side of Town/You'll Never Break My Trusting Heart Again	1950	5.00	10.00	20.00
❑ 1514	Mona Lisa/Trouble Then Satisfaction	1950	5.00	10.00	20.00
❑ 1539	Solitaire/Trouble Then Satisfaction	1950	5.00	10.00	20.00
❑ 1547	Cowboy's Prayer/Rag Monkey Song	1951	5.00	10.00	20.00

Albums

Number	Title	Yr	VG	VG+	NM
CAPITOL					
❑ ST 1662 [S]	Salvation	1962	7.50	15.00	30.00
❑ T 1662 [M]	Salvation	1962	6.25	12.50	25.00
❑ ST 2344 [S]	The Hits of T. Texas Tyler	1965	6.25	12.50	25.00
❑ T 2344 [M]	The Hits of T. Texas Tyler	1965	5.00	10.00	20.00
KING					
❑ 664 [M]	T. Texas Tyler	1959	30.00	60.00	120.00
❑ 689 [M]	The Great Texan	1960	30.00	60.00	120.00
❑ 721 [M]	T. Texas Tyler	1961	20.00	40.00	80.00
❑ 734 [M]	Songs Along the Way	1962	20.00	40.00	80.00
SOUND					
❑ 607 [M]	Deck of Cards	1958	20.00	40.00	80.00
STARDAY					
❑ SLP-379 [M]	The Man with a Million Friends	1966	6.25	12.50	25.00
WRANGLER					
❑ W-1002 [M]	T. Texas Tyler	1962	10.00	20.00	40.00
❑ W-31002 [S]	T. Texas Tyler	1962	12.50	25.00	50.00

TYNDALL, LYNNE

45s

Number	Title (A Side/B Side)	Yr	VG	VG+	NM
EVERGREEN					
❑ 1060	Lovin' the Blue/(B-side unknown)	1987	—	2.50	5.00
❑ 1071	This Is Me Leaving/(B-side unknown)	1988	—	2.50	5.00
❑ 1079	Love's Slippin' Up on Me/(B-side unknown)	1988	—	2.50	5.00
❑ 1091	I Promise/(B-side unknown)	1989	—	2.50	5.00

U

ULISSE, DONNA

45s

ATLANTIC

Number	Title (A Side/B Side)	Yr	VG	VG+	NM
❑ 7-87659	Out of Sight, Out of Mind/Trouble at the Door	1991	—	—	3.00
❑ 7-87739	When Was the Last Time/Legend in My Heart	1991	—	—	3.00
❑ 7-87862	Things Are Mostly Fine/Legend in My Heart	1991	—	—	3.00

UNCLE TUPELO

45s

ROCKVILLE

Number	Title (A Side/B Side)	Yr	VG	VG+	NM
❑ 6055	I Got Drunk/Sin City	1990	—	3.00	6.00
❑ 6055 [PS]	I Got Drunk/Sin City	1990	—	3.00	6.00
❑ 6069	Gun/I Wanna Destroy You	1991	—	2.50	5.00
❑ 6069 [PS]	Gun/I Wanna Destroy You	1991	—	2.50	5.00
❑ 6089	Sauget Wind/Looking for a Way Out	1992	2.00	4.00	8.00
—Clear vinyl					
❑ 6089 [PS]	Sauget Wind/Looking for a Way Out	1992	2.00	4.00	8.00
—Clear vinyl					

Albums

ROCKVILLE

Number	Title (A Side/B Side)	Yr	VG	VG+	NM
❑ 6050	No Depression	1990	3.00	6.00	12.00
❑ 6110 [(2)]	Still Feel Gone/March 16-20, 1992	1993	3.75	7.50	15.00

UNIQUES, THE

JOE STAMPLEY was a member of this group. Not to be confused with other groups on other labels with the same name.

45s

PARAMOUNT

Number	Title (A Side/B Side)	Yr	VG	VG+	NM
❑ 0017	Eunice/No One But You	1970	—	2.50	5.00
❑ 0058	Shadow of Love/Lazy Afternoon	1970	—	2.50	5.00
❑ 0116	Lucille/One Night with You	1971	—	2.50	5.00
❑ 0172	Will You Love Me Tomorrow/I Am a Gemini	1972	—	2.50	5.00

PAULA

Number	Title (A Side/B Side)	Yr	VG	VG+	NM
❑ 219	Not Too Long Ago/Fast Way of Living	1965	2.50	5.00	10.00
❑ 222	Too Good to Be True/Never Been in Love	1965	2.00	4.00	8.00
❑ 227	Lady's Man/Bolivar	1965	2.00	4.00	8.00
❑ 231	Strange/You Ain't Tuff	1966	2.00	4.00	8.00
❑ 238	All These Things/Tell Me What to Do	1966	2.00	4.00	8.00
❑ 245	Goodbye, So Long/Run and Hide	1966	2.00	4.00	8.00
❑ 255	Please Come Home for Christmas/(Instrumental)	1966	3.00	6.00	12.00
❑ 264	Groovin' Out/Areba	1967	2.00	4.00	8.00
❑ 275	Every Now and Then (I Cry)/Love Is a Precious Thing	1967	2.00	4.00	8.00
❑ 289	Go On and Leave/I'll Do Anything	1967	2.00	4.00	8.00
—B-side by University of Utah Chamber Choir					
❑ 299	It's All Over Now/All I Took Was Love	1968	—	3.00	6.00
❑ 307	It Hurts Me to Remember/I Sure Feel More (Like I Do Then I Did When I Got Here)	1968	—	3.00	6.00
❑ 313	How Lucky Can One Man Be/You Don't Miss Your Water	1968	—	3.00	6.00
❑ 320	Sha-La Love/You Know (That I Love You)	1970	—	2.50	5.00
❑ 324	My Babe/Toys Are Made for Children	1970	—	2.50	5.00
❑ 332	All These Things/You Know That I Love You	1970	—	2.50	5.00

Albums

PAULA

Number	Title (A Side/B Side)	Yr	VG	VG+	NM
❑ LP-2190 [M]	Uniquely Yours	1966	6.25	12.50	25.00
❑ LPS-2190 [S]	Uniquely Yours	1966	7.50	15.00	30.00
❑ LP-2194 [M]	Happening Now	1967	6.25	12.50	25.00
❑ LPS-2194 [S]	Happening Now	1967	7.50	15.00	30.00
❑ LP-2199 [M]	Playtime	1968	6.25	12.50	25.00
❑ LPS-2199 [S]	Playtime	1968	6.25	12.50	25.00
❑ LPS-2204	The Uniques	1969	6.25	12.50	25.00
❑ LPS-2208	Golden Hits	1970	6.25	12.50	25.00

URBAN, KEITH

45s

CAPITOL NASHVILLE

Number	Title (A Side/B Side)	Yr	VG	VG+	NM
❑ 58799	It's a Love Thing (same on both sides)	1999	—	—	3.00
❑ 58847	Your Everything/If You Wanna Stay	2000	—	—	3.00
❑ 58877	But for the Grace of God/I Thought You Knew	2000	—	2.00	4.00

USA FOR AFRICA

All-star group for charity. The most prominent country artists on this record are WILLIE NELSON and KENNY ROGERS. Three others who made the country charts at least once also appear on the song: KIM CARNES; RAY CHARLES; and LIONEL RICHIE.

12-Inch Singles

COLUMBIA

Number	Title (A Side/B Side)	Yr	VG	VG+	NM
❑ US2-05179	We Are the World/Grace	1985	2.50	5.00	10.00
—B-side by Quincy Jones					

45s

COLUMBIA

Number	Title (A Side/B Side)	Yr	VG	VG+	NM
❑ US7-04839	We Are the World/Grace	1985	—	—	3.00
—B-side by Quincy Jones					
❑ US7-04839 [PS]	We Are the World/Grace	1985	—	2.00	4.00

Albums

COLUMBIA

Number	Title (A Side/B Side)	Yr	VG	VG+	NM
❑ USA 40043	We Are the World	1985	3.75	7.50	15.00

V

VALENTINO

45s

RCA

Number	Title (A Side/B Side)	Yr	VG	VG+	NM
❑ PB-12269	She Took the Place of You/You Belong to My Heart	1981	—	2.00	4.00

VAN DYKE, BRUCE

45s

ARIA

Number	Title (A Side/B Side)	Yr	VG	VG+	NM
❑ 51688	It's All in the Touch/(B-side unknown)	1989	—	2.50	5.00
❑ 51689	Hard-Headed Heart/(B-side unknown)	1989	—	2.50	5.00
❑ 51689 [PS]	Hard-Headed Heart/(B-side unknown)	1989	—	3.00	6.00

VAN DYKE, LEROY

45s

ABC

Number	Title (A Side/B Side)	Yr	VG	VG+	NM
❑ 12070	Unfaithful Fools/What Will You Do Now, Mrs. Jones	1975	—	2.00	4.00

ABC/DOT

Number	Title (A Side/B Side)	Yr	VG	VG+	NM
❑ 17567	You Sure Look Good on My Pillow/Busted	1975	—	2.00	4.00
❑ 17597	Who's Gonna Run the Truck Stop in Tuba City When I'm Gone?/There Ain't No Roses in My Bed	1975	—	2.00	4.00
❑ 17691	Texas Tea/Las Vegas Girl	1977	—	2.00	4.00

DECCA

Number	Title (A Side/B Side)	Yr	VG	VG+	NM
❑ 32756	Mister Professor/People Gonna Turn You Off	1970	—	3.00	6.00
❑ 32825	Birmingham/What Am I Gonna Tell Them Now	1971	—	3.00	6.00
❑ 32866	I Get Lonely When It Rains/Party Girl	1971	—	3.00	6.00
❑ 32933	I'd Rather Be Wantin' Love/My Mind Is On You	1972	—	3.00	6.00
❑ 32999	I'll Be Around/Yesterday Will Come Again Tonight	1972	—	3.00	6.00
❑ 33055	Untie Me/Sittin' In for Me	1973	—	3.00	6.00

DOT

Number	Title (A Side/B Side)	Yr	VG	VG+	NM
❑ 15503	Auctioneer/I Fell in Love with a Pony Tail	1956	5.00	10.00	20.00
—Originals have maroon labels					
❑ 15503	Auctioneer/I Fell in Love with a Pony Tail	1956	3.75	7.50	15.00
—Second pressings have black labels					
❑ 15561	The Pocket Book Song/Honky Tonk Song	1957	3.75	7.50	15.00
❑ 15652	One Heart/Everytime I Ask My Heart	1957	3.75	7.50	15.00
❑ 15698	Leather Jacket/My Good Mind Went Bad	1958	25.00	50.00	100.00
❑ 16299	Auctioneer/I Fell in Love with a Pony	1961	2.50	5.00	10.00

KAPP

Number	Title (A Side/B Side)	Yr	VG	VG+	NM
❑ 908	Lonely Thing/One More Minute of Lonely	1968	—	3.00	6.00
❑ 931	You May Be Too Much for Memphis, Baby/Road of Love	1968	—	3.00	6.00
❑ 951	Lonesome Is/The Long Drive Home	1968	—	3.00	6.00
❑ 983	Goin' Back to Boston/The Straw	1969	—	3.00	6.00
❑ 2021	Steal Away/This Beginning of a Man	1969	—	3.00	6.00
❑ 2054	Crack in the World/Try a Little Bit Harder	1969	—	3.00	6.00
❑ 2091	Belle-O/An Old Love Affair Now Showing	1970	—	3.00	6.00

MCA

Number	Title (A Side/B Side)	Yr	VG	VG+	NM
❑ 40114	I'm O.K., You're O.K./Everytime Seems Like the First Time	1973	—	2.50	5.00

MERCURY

Number	Title (A Side/B Side)	Yr	VG	VG+	NM
❑ 71779	Faded Love/Big Man in a Big House	1961	3.00	6.00	12.00
❑ 71834	Walk On By/My World Is Caving In	1961	3.75	7.50	15.00
❑ 71926	If a Woman Answers (Hang Up the Phone)/A Broken Promise	1962	3.00	6.00	12.00
❑ 71988	The Life You Offered Me/Dim, Dark Corner	1962	3.00	6.00	12.00
❑ 72018	How Long Must You Keep Me a Secret/I Sat Back and Let It Happen	1962	3.00	6.00	12.00
❑ 72057	Black Cloud/Five Steps	1962	3.00	6.00	12.00
❑ 72097	Be a Good Girl/The Other Boys Are Talking	1963	3.00	6.00	12.00
❑ 72155	Wrong Side of the Tracks/What Are the Lips of Janet	1963	3.00	6.00	12.00
❑ 72198	Happy to Be Unhappy/Now I Lay Me Down	1963	3.00	6.00	12.00
❑ 72232	Night People/Baby (Where Can You Be)	1964	2.50	5.00	10.00
❑ 72277	Afraid of a Heartbreak/Your Money	1964	2.50	5.00	10.00
❑ 72360	Anne of a Thousand Days/Poor Guy	1964	2.50	5.00	10.00

PLANTATION

Number	Title (A Side/B Side)	Yr	VG	VG+	NM
❑ 170	Runaround Sue/House of the Rising Sun	1978	—	2.00	4.00
❑ 192	Don't Bite the Hand That Feeds You/A Gay Ranchero	1978	—	2.00	4.00

SUN

Number	Title (A Side/B Side)	Yr	VG	VG+	NM
❑ 1146	Save Me a Seat by the Fire/Rev. Edmond Giles	1979	—	2.00	4.00

WARNER BROS.

Number	Title (A Side/B Side)	Yr	VG	VG+	NM
❑ 5650	It's All Over Now, Baby Blue/Just a State of Mind	1965	2.50	5.00	10.00
❑ 5692	Big Wide Wonderful World of Country/Ol' Man Moses	1966	2.50	5.00	10.00
❑ 5807	(Now and Then There's) A Fool Such As I/You Couldn't Get My Love Back (If You Tried)	1966	2.50	5.00	10.00
❑ 5841	Roses from a Stranger/Before I Change My Mind	1966	2.00	4.00	8.00
❑ 7001	I've Never Been Loved/Less of Me	1967	2.00	4.00	8.00
❑ 7064	I'll Make It Up to You/What Am I Bid	1967	2.00	4.00	8.00
❑ 7155	Louisville/There's Always Tomorrow	1967	2.00	4.00	8.00

Albums

DOT

Number	Title (A Side/B Side)	Yr	VG	VG+	NM
❑ DLP 3693 [M]	Auctioneer	1966	5.00	10.00	20.00

HARMONY

Number	Title (A Side/B Side)	Yr	VG	VG+	NM
❑ HS 11308	I've Never Been Loved	196?	3.00	6.00	12.00

Number	Title (A Side/B Side)	Yr	VG	VG+	NM
KAPP					
❑ KS-3571	Lonesome Is	1968	3.75	7.50	15.00
❑ KS-3605	Greatest Hits	1969	3.75	7.50	15.00
❑ KS-3607	Just a Closer Walk with Thee	1969	3.75	7.50	15.00
MCA					
❑ 145	Greatest Hits	1973	3.00	6.00	12.00
MERCURY					
❑ MG-20682 [M]	Walk On By	1962	5.00	10.00	20.00
❑ MG-20716 [M]	Movin' Van Dyke	1963	5.00	10.00	20.00
❑ MG-20802 [M]	Leroy Van Dyke's Greatest Hits	1963	5.00	10.00	20.00
❑ MG-20922 [M]	Songs for Mom and Dad	1964	5.00	10.00	20.00
❑ MG-20950 [M]	Leroy Van Dyke at the Tradewinds	1964	5.00	10.00	10.00
❑ SR-60682 [S]	Walk On By	1962	6.25	12.50	25.00
❑ SR-60716 [S]	Movin' Van Dyke	1963	6.25	12.50	25.00
❑ SR-60802 [S]	Leroy Van Dyke's Greatest Hits	1963	6.25	12.50	25.00
❑ SR-60922 [S]	Songs for Mom and Dad	1964	6.25	12.50	25.00
❑ SR-60950 [S]	Leroy Van Dyke at the Tradewinds	1964	6.25	12.50	25.00
PLANTATION					
❑ 516	Gospel Greats	1977	3.00	6.00	12.00
SUN					
❑ 131	Golden Hits	1974	3.00	6.00	12.00
WARNER BROS.					
❑ W 1618 [M]	The Leroy Van Dyke Show	1965	3.75	7.50	15.00
❑ WS 1618 [S]	The Leroy Van Dyke Show	1965	5.00	10.00	20.00
❑ W 1652 [M]	Country Hits	1966	3.75	7.50	15.00
❑ WS 1652 [S]	Country Hits	1966	5.00	10.00	20.00
WING					
❑ MGW-12302 [M]	Out of Love	196?	3.00	6.00	12.00
❑ MGW-12322 [M]	Movin'	196?	3.00	6.00	12.00
❑ SRW-16302 [S]	Out of Love	196?	3.75	7.50	15.00
❑ SRW-16322 [S]	Movin'	196?	3.75	7.50	15.00

VAN SHELTON, RICKY

See listings under SHELTON, RICKY VAN. (Van is his given middle name, not part of his last name.)

VAN ZANDT, TOWNES

45s

Number	Title (A Side/B Side)	Yr	VG	VG+	NM
POPPY					
❑ XW170	Fraulein/Don't Let the Sunshine Fool You	1973	—	3.00	6.00
❑ XW238	Pancho and Lefty/(B-side unknown)	1973	2.50	5.00	10.00
❑ 506	Talking Karate Blues/Waiting Around to Die	1968	2.00	4.00	8.00
❑ 510	Second Lovers/(B-side unknown)	1968	2.00	4.00	8.00
❑ 90104	Come Tomorrow/Delta Momma Blues	1970	2.00	4.00	8.00
❑ 90108	Greensboro Woman/Stand-In	1971	2.00	4.00	8.00
❑ 90113	If I Needed You/Sunshine Boy	1971	2.00	4.00	8.00
❑ 90116	Honky Tonkin'/Snow Don't Fall	1972	2.00	4.00	8.00
TOMATO					
❑ 10003	Who Do You Love/(B-side unknown)	1977	—	2.50	5.00
❑ 10005	When She Don't Need Me/No Place to Fall	1978	—	2.50	5.00

Albums

Number	Title (A Side/B Side)	Yr	VG	VG+	NM
POPPY					
❑ PP-LA004-F	The Late Great Townes Van Zandt	1973	3.75	7.50	15.00
❑ PYS-5700	High, Low and In Between	1972	3.75	7.50	15.00
❑ PYS-40001	For the Sake of a Song	1968	6.25	12.50	25.00
❑ PYS-40004	Our Mother, The Mountain	1969	3.75	7.50	15.00
❑ PYS-40007	Townes Van Zandt	1969	3.75	7.50	15.00
❑ PYS-40012	Delta Momma Blues	1970	3.75	7.50	15.00
SUGAR HILL					
❑ SH-1020	At My Window	1987	2.50	5.00	10.00
❑ SH-1026	Live and Obscure	1989	2.50	5.00	10.00
TOMATO					
❑ 7001 [(2)]	Live at the Old Quarter, Houston, Texas	1977	3.75	7.50	15.00
❑ 7011	The Late Great Townes Van Zandt	1978	3.00	6.00	12.00
—Reissue of Poppy 004					
❑ 7012	High, Low and In Between	1978	3.00	6.00	12.00
—Reissue of Poppy 5700					
❑ 7013	Delta Momma Blues	1978	3.00	6.00	12.00
—Reissue of Poppy 40012					
❑ 7014	Townes Van Zandt	1978	3.00	6.00	12.00
—Reissue of Poppy 40007					
❑ 7015	Our Mother, The Mountain	1978	3.00	6.00	12.00
—Reissue of Poppy 40004					
❑ 7017	Flyin' Shoes	1978	3.00	6.00	12.00

VANCE, VINCE, AND THE VALIANTS

45s

Number	Title (A Side/B Side)	Yr	VG	VG+	NM
EMPIRE					
❑ (# unknown)	Bye Bye Baby/(B-side unknown)	1976	—	3.50	7.00
PAID					
❑ 109	Bomb Iran/Bye Bye Baby	1980	—	3.00	6.00
SCRATCHED					
❑ (# unknown)	Good-Bye Johnny/Sha-La-La-La, Goodbye	1982	—	3.00	6.00
SMC					
❑ (# unknown)	Fortune Teller/You'd Better Move On	1972	2.50	5.00	10.00
STONE MAVERICK					
❑ (# unknown)	The Silver and the Blue/(B-side unknown)	1981	—	3.00	6.00
VALIANT					
❑ 92689	All I Want For Christmas Is You/Exceptional Man	1989	—	3.00	6.00
❑ 92689 [PS]	All I Want For Christmas Is You/Exceptional Man	1989	2.00	4.00	8.00
❑ (# unknown)	Backseat Couch/Gloria	1975	2.00	4.00	8.00
❑ (# unknown)	Bomb Iran/Bye Bye Baby	1980	2.50	5.00	10.00
—Blue vinyl					
❑ (# unknown)	The Houston Love Song/Bye-Bye Steelers	1981	—	3.00	6.00
❑ (# unknown)	Amadago/You Don't Own Me	1986	—	2.50	5.00
❑ (# unknown)	Jackie and Jill/Bomb Iran	1987	—	2.50	5.00
❑ (# unknown)	All I Want for Christmas Is You/Christmas Time in Texas	1991	—	2.50	5.00

VANWARMER, RANDY

45s

Number	Title (A Side/B Side)	Yr	VG	VG+	NM
16TH AVENUE					
❑ 70407	I Will Hold You/I'll Be on the Next Dream Home	1987	—	2.00	4.00
❑ 70416	It's a Heartache/That's What Your Smile Does for Me	1988	—	2.00	4.00
❑ 70418	Where the Rocky Mountains Touch the Morning Sun/That's What Your Smile Does for Me	1988	—	2.00	4.00
❑ 70422	Love Will Wash It Away/I Am	1988	—	2.00	4.00
❑ 70434	I Never Got Over You/Stories, Trophies and Memories	1989	—	2.00	4.00
❑ 70442	Ain't Nothin' Comin' Down But the Rain/Stories, Trophies and Memories	1989	—	2.00	4.00
BEARSVILLE					
❑ 0334	Just When I Needed You Most/Your Light	1979	—	2.50	5.00
❑ 29431	Gonna Build Me a Rocket/I'm Still in Love	1983	—	2.00	4.00
❑ 29760	The Things That You Dream/Hester's Song	1983	—	2.00	4.00
❑ 49004	Convincing Lies/Gotta Get Out of Here	1979	—	2.00	4.00
❑ 49071	Call Me/Forever Loving You	1979	—	2.00	4.00
❑ 49258	Whatever You Decide/Doesn't Matter Anymore	1980	—	2.00	4.00
❑ 49567	All We Have Is Tonight/Farther Along	1980	—	2.00	4.00
❑ 49752	Suzi/Babel	1981	—	2.00	4.00

Albums

Number	Title (A Side/B Side)	Yr	VG	VG+	NM
16TH AVENUE					
❑ D1-70553	I Am/Randy Vanwarmer	1988	2.50	5.00	10.00
BEARSVILLE					
❑ BRK 3561	The Beat of Love	1981	2.50	5.00	10.00
❑ BRK 6988	Warmer	1979	2.50	5.00	10.00

VASSY, KIN

Also see THE FIRST EDITION.

45s

Number	Title (A Side/B Side)	Yr	VG	VG+	NM
EPIC					
❑ 5-10125	Gamblin' Man/Tracks Run Through the City	1967	2.50	5.00	10.00
IA					
❑ 501	Do I Ever Cross Your Mind/Sometimes Love Is Better When It's Gone	1979	—	3.00	6.00
❑ 502	Makes Me Wonder If I Ever Said Goodbye/Fort Worth Featherbed	1980	—	3.00	6.00
❑ 505	There's Nobody Like You/Nite Out	1980	—	3.00	6.00
LIBERTY					
❑ 1407	Likin' Him and Lovin' You/Hell and High Water	1981	—	2.00	4.00
❑ 1427	Sneakin' Around/Lonely Hearts	1981	—	2.00	4.00
❑ 1440	When You Were Blue and I Was Green/Honky Tonk Heart	1981	—	2.00	4.00
❑ 1458	Cast the First Stone/Lonely Hearts	1982	—	2.00	4.00
❑ 1469	Women in Love/Hell and High Water	1982	—	2.00	4.00
❑ 1488	Tryin' to Love Two/All for the Love of a Girl	1982	—	2.00	4.00
UNI					
❑ 55114	Farewell/Hello L.A., Bye Bye Birmingham	1969	2.00	4.00	8.00
❑ 55139	I Think I Just Found My Mind/That's the Bag I'm In	1969	2.00	4.00	8.00
❑ 55195	I Just Wanna Give My Love to You/Blue Bird	1970	2.00	4.00	8.00
❑ 55262	Revelation/After All (I Live My Life)	1971	2.00	4.00	8.00
UNITED ARTISTS					
❑ 1368	There's Nobody Like You/Nite Out	1980	—	2.00	4.00
—Reissue of IA 505					

VAUGHN, SAMMY

45s

Number	Title (A Side/B Side)	Yr	VG	VG+	NM
ALPINE					
❑ 100	Sunshine/(B-side unknown)	1979	—	2.50	5.00
OAK					
❑ 1007	This Time Around/(B-side unknown)	1978	—	3.00	6.00

VAUGHN, SHARON

Also see NARVEL FELTS AND SHARON VAUGHN.

45s

Number	Title (A Side/B Side)	Yr	VG	VG+	NM
ABC DOT					
❑ 17553	A Fire That Burns at Home/Go to Your Room and Play	1975	—	2.50	5.00
❑ 17590	You and Me, Me and You/The Time I've Had with You	1975	—	2.50	5.00
❑ 17639	I Always Will/Too Soon to Think of Love Again	1976	—	2.50	5.00
❑ 17677	Lay Down (And I'll Lay Down My Life for You)/One-of-a-Kind Kind of Me	1976	—	2.50	5.00
CINNAMON					
❑ 799	Never a Night Goes By/Take My Love Again	1974	—	3.00	6.00

VAUS, STEVE

45s

Number	Title (A Side/B Side)	Yr	VG	VG+	NM
RCA					
❑ 62308	We Must Take America Back/Never Had a Chance	1992	—	2.00	4.00

VEACH, GAIL

45s

Number	Title (A Side/B Side)	Yr	VG	VG+	NM
CHOICE					
❑ 101	Deepest Shade of Blue/(B-side unknown)	1988	—	3.00	6.00

Number	Title (A Side/B Side)	Yr	VG	VG+	NM
PRAIRIE DUST					
❑ 128	Would You Catch Me Baby (If I Fell for You)/(B-side unknown)	1987	—	3.00	6.00

VEGA, RAY

45s

Number	Title (A Side/B Side)	Yr	VG	VG+	NM
BNA					
❑ 64652	Remember When/Maria	1996	—	—	3.00

VEGA BROTHERS, THE

45s

Number	Title (A Side/B Side)	Yr	VG	VG+	NM
CURB					
❑ NR-76756	It's Out of My Hands/(B-side unknown)	1990	—	2.00	4.00
MCA					
❑ 52777	Heartache the Size of Texas/New Woman	1986	—	2.00	4.00
❑ 52874	There Goes My Heart/I Wanted to Fall in Love with You	1986	—	2.00	4.00

Albums

Number	Title (A Side/B Side)	Yr	VG	VG+	NM
MCA					
❑ 5686	The Vega Brothers	1986	2.00	4.00	8.00

VERA, BILLY

45s

Number	Title (A Side/B Side)	Yr	VG	VG+	NM
ALFA					
❑ 7002	I Can Take Care of Myself/Corner of the Night	1981	—	2.00	4.00
—As "Billy and the Beaters"					
❑ 7005	At This Moment/Someone Will School You, Someone Will Cool You	1981	—	2.50	5.00
❑ 7005 [PS]	At This Moment/Someone Will School You, Someone Will Cool You	1981	—	2.50	5.00
—As "Billy and the Beaters"					
❑ 7012	Millie, Make Me Some Chili/Someone Will School You, Someone Will Cool You	1981	—	2.00	4.00
—As "Billy and the Beaters"					
❑ 7020	We Got It All/You Own It	1982	—	2.00	4.00
ATLANTIC					
❑ 2526	With Pen in Hand/Good Morning Blues	1968	2.00	4.00	8.00
❑ 2555	I've Been Loving You Too Long/Are You Coming to My Party	1968	2.00	4.00	8.00
❑ 2586	Julie/Time Doesn't Matter Anymore	1968	2.00	4.00	8.00
❑ 2628	Bible Salesman/Are You Coming to My Party	1969	—	3.00	6.00
❑ 2700	I've Never Been Loved Like This Before/J.W.'s Dream	1970	—	3.00	6.00
CAPITOL					
❑ B-44149	Between Like and Love/Heart Be Still	1988	—	—	3.00
❑ B-44149 [PS]	Between Like and Love/Heart Be Still	1988	—	—	3.00
❑ B-44200	Ronnie's Song/Between Like and Love	1988	—	—	3.00
MACOLA					
❑ 8912	She Ain't Johnnie/My Girl Josephine	1987	—	2.00	4.00
MIDLAND INT'L.					
❑ MB-10639	Back Door Man/Run and Tell the People	1976	—	2.50	5.00
❑ MB-10909	Private Clown/Billy, Meet Your Son	1977	—	2.50	5.00
❑ MB-11042	I've Had Enough/Something Like Nothing Before	1977	—	2.50	5.00
❑ 72014	She Ain't Johnnie/I've Had Enough	1977	—	2.50	5.00
RHINO					
❑ 74403	At This Moment/I Can Take Care of Myself	1986	—	2.50	5.00
❑ 74403	At This Moment/Peanut Butter	1986	—	—	3.00
❑ 74404	I Can Take Care of Myself/(B-side unknown)	1987	—	—	3.00
❑ 74407	Hopeless Romantic/(B-side unknown)	1987	—	—	3.00
RUST					
❑ 5051	My Heart Cries/All My Love	1962	5.00	10.00	20.00

Albums

Number	Title (A Side/B Side)	Yr	VG	VG+	NM
ALFA					
❑ 10001	Billy and the Beaters	1981	3.75	7.50	15.00
❑ 10012	Billy Vera	1982	3.00	6.00	12.00
ATLANTIC					
❑ 8197 [M]	With Pen in Hand	1968	10.00	20.00	40.00
❑ SD 8197 [S]	With Pen in Hand	1968	6.25	12.50	25.00
CAPITOL					
❑ C1-46948	Retro Nuevo	1988	2.50	5.00	10.00
MACOLA					
❑ 961	The Billy Vera Album	1987	2.50	5.00	10.00
—Reissue of Midsong Int'l. LP					
MIDSONG INT'L.					
❑ BKL1-2219	Out of the Darkness	1977	3.00	6.00	12.00
RHINO					
❑ RNLP 70185	The Atlantic Years	1987	2.50	5.00	10.00
❑ RNLP 70858	By Request — The Best of Billy Vera and the Beaters	1986	3.00	6.00	12.00
THUNDER					
❑ TVLP 0018	The Hollywood Sessions	1987	2.50	5.00	10.00

VERNON, KENNY

45s

Number	Title (A Side/B Side)	Yr	VG	VG+	NM
CAPITOL					
❑ 3331	That'll Be the Day/I'd Go Right Back Again	1972	—	2.50	5.00
❑ 3430	Every Day with You/I Bought the Shoes	1972	—	2.50	5.00
❑ 3506	Feel So Fine/Would You Settle for Roses	1973	—	2.50	5.00
❑ 3590	Lady/What Kind of Mood (Will She Be In Tonight)	1973	—	2.50	5.00
❑ 3691	Loversville/Woman, I Just Want to Love You More	1973	—	2.50	5.00
❑ 3785	What Was Your Name Again?/Have I Ever Lied to You	1973	—	2.50	5.00
❑ 3925	Another Word for You/Your Steppin' Stone	1974	—	2.50	5.00
CARAVAN					
❑ 123	It Makes Me Happy (To Know You Make Me Blue)/Too Much Loving Turned Her Bad	1966	2.50	5.00	10.00
CHART					
❑ 1031	Oh Why Not Tonight/Woman, Won't You Make Up Your Mind	1968	2.00	4.00	8.00
❑ 1050	Free Born Man/I'll Tell You Where to Go	1968	2.00	4.00	8.00
❑ 5000	Yes Virginia/Seashores of My Mind	1969	—	3.00	6.00
❑ 5015	The Ba-Ba Song/Raining On a Sunny Day with You	1969	—	3.00	6.00
❑ 5038	Mississippi Woman/The Bridge Washed Out	1969	—	3.00	6.00
❑ 5075	Country Music Circus/The Part Inbetween	1970	—	3.00	6.00
❑ 5108	Up on Cripple Creek/Nashville Union Station Depot	1971	—	3.00	6.00
EPIC					
❑ 5-10192	Ain't That a Shame/Miles and Miles	1967	2.00	4.00	8.00

Albums

Number	Title (A Side/B Side)	Yr	VG	VG+	NM
CAPITOL					
❑ ST-11227	Loversville	1973	3.00	6.00	12.00
CHART					
❑ CHS-1018	Country Happening	1969	3.75	7.50	15.00
❑ CHS-1038	Nashville Union Station Depot	1971	3.75	7.50	15.00
MERCURY					
❑ SRM-1-606	Country Giants	1970	3.75	7.50	15.00

VICKERY, MACK

45s

Number	Title (A Side/B Side)	Yr	VG	VG+	NM
BOONE					
❑ 1073	Searching for a Baby/Jailbirds Can't Fly	1968	2.50	5.00	10.00
BRAGG					
❑ 203	Some Things Are Better Left Unsaid/She Calls Me Day, I Call Her Night	196?	3.00	6.00	12.00
MCA					
❑ 40233	That Kind of Fool/Starting All Over Again	1974	—	3.00	6.00
—As "Atlanta James"					
❑ 40291	Cardboard Pillow/Hold What You've Got	1974	—	3.00	6.00
—As "Atlanta James"					
❑ 40386	I'm the Only Hell My Mama Ever Raised/Down on the Levee	1975	—	3.00	6.00
—As "Atlanta James"					
❑ 40435	Honky Tonkin' Ladies/Meet Me at the Spring Annie	1975	—	3.00	6.00
—As "Atlanta James"					
MEGA					
❑ 0013	Meat Man/The Farther I Let Her Go	1970	2.00	4.00	8.00
—As "Atlanta James"					
PLAYBOY					
❑ 5800	Ishabilly/Think It Over	1977	—	2.50	5.00
❑ 5814	Here's to the Horses/When It Counted, You Could Never Count on Me	1977	—	2.50	5.00
PRINCETON					
❑ 101	High School Blues/(B-side unknown)	195?	25.00	50.00	100.00

Albums

Number	Title (A Side/B Side)	Yr	VG	VG+	NM
MEGA					
❑ 31-1002	Mack Vickery at the Alabama Women's Prison	1970	3.75	7.50	15.00

VINCENT, GENE

45s

Number	Title (A Side/B Side)	Yr	VG	VG+	NM
CAPITOL					
❑ F3450	Be-Bop-a-Lula/Woman Love	1956	17.50	35.00	70.00
—With large Capitol logo					
❑ F3450	Be-Bop-a-Lula/Woman Love	1956	12.50	25.00	50.00
—With small Capitol logo					
❑ F3530	Race with the Devil/Gonna Back Up, Baby	1956	10.00	20.00	40.00
❑ F3558	Bluejean Bop/Who Slapped John	1956	10.00	20.00	40.00
❑ F3617	Crazy Legs/Important Words	1956	12.50	25.00	50.00
❑ F3678	B-I-Bickey-Bi-Bo-Bo-Go/Five Days, Five Days	1957	12.50	25.00	50.00
❑ F3763	Lotta Lovin'/Wear My Ring	1957	12.50	25.00	50.00
❑ F3839	Dance to the Bop/I Got It	1957	7.50	15.00	30.00
❑ 3871	Be-Bop-a-Lula/Lotta Lovin'	1974	3.75	7.50	15.00
❑ F3874	Walkin' Home from School/I Gotta Baby	1958	10.00	20.00	40.00
❑ F3959	Baby Blue/True to You	1958	12.50	25.00	50.00
❑ F4010	Yes I Love You Baby/Rocky Road Blues	1958	10.00	20.00	40.00
❑ F4051	Little Lover/Git It	1958	10.00	20.00	40.00
❑ F4105	Say Mama/Be-Bop Boogie Boy	1958	12.50	25.00	50.00
❑ F4153	Over the Rainbow/Who's Pushin' Your Swing	1959	12.50	25.00	50.00
❑ F4237	The Night Is So Lonely/Right Now	1959	12.50	25.00	50.00
❑ F4237 [PS]	The Night Is So Lonely/Right Now	1959	500.00	1000.	2000.
❑ 4313	Wild Cat/Right Here on Earth	1959	12.50	25.00	50.00
❑ 4442	Pistol Packin' Mama/Anna Annabella	1960	10.00	20.00	40.00
❑ 4525	Mister Loneliness/If You Want My Lovin'	1961	6.25	12.50	25.00
❑ 4665	Lucy Star/Baby Don't Believe Him	1961	6.25	12.50	25.00
CHALLENGE					
❑ 59337	Bird Doggin'/Ain't That Too Much	1966	5.00	10.00	20.00
❑ 59347	Lonely Street/I've Got My Eyes on You	1966	5.00	10.00	20.00
❑ 59365	Born to Be a Rolling Stone/Pickin' Poppies	1967	5.00	10.00	20.00
FOREVER					
❑ 6001	Story of the Rockers/Pickin' Poppies	1969	12.50	25.00	50.00
KAMA SUTRA					
❑ 514	Sunshine/Geese	1970	3.00	6.00	12.00
❑ 518	High On Life/The Day the World Turned Blue	1971	3.00	6.00	12.00
PLAYGROUND					
❑ 100	Story of the Rockers/Pickin' Poppies	1968	50.00	100.00	200.00

7-Inch Extended Plays

CAPITOL

Number	Title (A Side/B Side)	Yr	VG	VG+	NM
EAP 1-764	Bluejean Bop/Jezebel//Jumps, Giggles and Shouts/Ain't She Sweet	1957	37.50	75.00	150.00
EAP 1-764 [PS]	Bluejean Bop! Part 1	1957	37.50	75.00	150.00
EAP 2-764	*Who Slapped John/Wedding Bells/Up a Lazy River/Bop Street	1957	37.50	75.00	150.00
EAP 2-764 [PS]	Bluejean Bop! Part 2	1957	37.50	75.00	150.00
EAP 3-764	*Jump Back, Honey, Jump Back/Waltz of the Wind/I Flipped/Peg o' My Heart	1957	37.50	75.00	150.00
EAP 3-764 [PS]	Bluejean Bop! Part 3	1957	37.50	75.00	150.00
EAP 1-811	*Red Bluejeans and a Ponytail/You Told a Fib/Hold Me, Hug Me, Rock Me/Unchained Melody	1957	37.50	75.00	150.00
EAP 1-811 [PS]	Gene Vincent and the Blue Caps, Part 1	1957	37.50	75.00	150.00
EAP 2-811	*Cruisin'/You Better Believe/Double Talkin' Baby/Blues Stay Away from Me	1957	37.50	75.00	150.00
EAP 2-811 [PS]	Gene Vincent and the Blue Caps, Part 2	1957	37.50	75.00	150.00
EAP 3-811	*Pink Thunderbird/Pretty, Pretty Baby/Cat Man/I Sure Miss You	1957	37.50	75.00	150.00
EAP 3-811 [PS]	Gene Vincent and the Blue Caps, Part 3	1957	37.50	75.00	150.00
EAP 1-970	*Frankie and Johnnie/In My Dreams/You'll Never Walk Alone/Brand New Beat	1958	37.50	75.00	150.00
EAP 1-970 [PS]	Gene Vincent Rocks! And the Blue Caps Roll, Part 1	1958	37.50	75.00	150.00
EAP 2-970	*By the Light of the Silvery Moon/Flea Brain/Rollin' Danny/Your Cheatin' Heart	1958	37.50	75.00	150.00
EAP 2-970 [PS]	Gene Vincent Rocks! And the Blue Caps Roll, Part 2	1958	37.50	75.00	150.00
EAP 3-970	*You Belong to Me/Time Will Bring You Everything/Should I Ever Love Again/It's No Lie	1958	37.50	75.00	150.00
EAP 3-970 [PS]	Gene Vincent Rocks! And the Blue Caps Roll, Part 3	1958	37.50	75.00	150.00
EAP 1-985	Lovely Loretta/Dance to the Bop//Dance in the Street/Baby Blue	1958	50.00	100.00	200.00
EAP 1-985 [PS]	Hot Rod Gang	1958	50.00	100.00	200.00
EAP 1-1059	*Five Feet of Lovin'/The Wayward Wind/Somebody Help Me/Keep It a Secret	1958	37.50	75.00	150.00
EAP 1-1059 [PS]	A Gene Vincent Record Date, Part 1	1958	37.50	75.00	150.00
EAP 2-1059	Git It/Teenage Partner//Hey, Good Lookin'/I Can't Help It	1958	37.50	75.00	150.00
EAP 2-1059 [PS]	A Gene Vincent Record Date, Part 2	1958	37.50	75.00	150.00
EAP 3-1059	*Look What You Gone and Done to Me/Peace of Mind/Summertime/I Love You	1958	37.50	75.00	150.00
EAP 3-1059 [PS]	A Gene Vincent Record Date, Part 3	1958	37.50	75.00	150.00

NORTON

Number	Title (A Side/B Side)	Yr	VG	VG+	NM
EP-076	My Love (In Love Again)/Lonesome Boy//The Night Is So Lonely/In My Dreams	1999	—	—	2.00
EP-076 [PS]	Blue Gene	1999	—	—	2.00

Albums

CAPITOL

Number	Title (A Side/B Side)	Yr	VG	VG+	NM
DKAO-380 [R]	Gene Vincent's Greatest	1969	12.50	25.00	50.00
SM-380 [R]	Gene Vincent's Greatest	197?	3.75	7.50	15.00
—Abridged reissue of DKAO-380					
T 764 [M]	Bluejean Bop!	1957	250.00	500.00	1000.
—Yellow label promo					
T 764 [M]	Bluejean Bop!	1957	250.00	500.00	1000.
—Black label promo					
T 764 [M]	Bluejean Bop!	1957	100.00	200.00	400.00
—Turquoise label stock copy					
T 811 [M]	Gene Vincent and the Blue Caps	1957	250.00	500.00	1000.
—Yellow label promo					
T 811 [M]	Gene Vincent and the Blue Caps	1957	250.00	500.00	1000.
—Black label promo					
T 811 [M]	Gene Vincent and the Blue Caps	1957	100.00	200.00	400.00
—Turquoise label stock copy					
T 970 [M]	Gene Vincent Rocks! And the Blue Caps Roll	1958	250.00	500.00	1000.
—Yellow label promo					
T 970 [M]	Gene Vincent Rocks! And the Blue Caps Roll	1958	250.00	500.00	1000.
—Black label promo					
T 970 [M]	Gene Vincent Rocks! And the Blue Caps Roll	1958	100.00	200.00	400.00
—Turquoise label stock copy					
T 1059 [M]	A Gene Vincent Record Date	1958	250.00	500.00	1000.
—Yellow label promo					
T 1059 [M]	A Gene Vincent Record Date	1958	250.00	500.00	1000.
—Black label promo					
T 1059 [M]	A Gene Vincent Record Date	1958	100.00	200.00	400.00
—Turquoise label stock copy					
T 1207 [M]	Sounds Like Gene Vincent	1959	75.00	150.00	300.00
—Black label with colorband, Capitol logo at left					
ST 1342 [S]	Crazy Times	1960	125.00	250.00	500.00
—Black label with colorband, Capitol logo at left					
T 1342 [M]	Crazy Times	1960	75.00	150.00	300.00
—Black label with colorband, Capitol logo at left					
SM-11287	The Bop That Just Won't Stop	1974	3.75	7.50	15.00
N-16208	Gene Vincent's Greatest	198?	3.00	6.00	12.00
—Budget-line reissue					
N-16209	The Bop That Just Won't Stop	198?	3.00	6.00	12.00
—Budget-line reissue					

DANDELION

Number	Title (A Side/B Side)	Yr	VG	VG+	NM
9-102	I'm Back and I'm Proud	1970	12.50	25.00	50.00

INTERMEDIA

Number	Title (A Side/B Side)	Yr	VG	VG+	NM
QS-5074	Rockabilly Fever	198?	3.00	6.00	12.00

KAMA SUTRA

Number	Title (A Side/B Side)	Yr	VG	VG+	NM
KSBS 2019	Gene Vincent	1970	12.50	25.00	50.00
KSBS 2027	The Day the World Turned Blue	1971	12.50	25.00	50.00

ROLLIN' ROCK

Number	Title (A Side/B Side)	Yr	VG	VG+	NM
022	Forever	1981	3.75	7.50	15.00

VINCENT, RHONDA

45s

GIANT

Number	Title (A Side/B Side)	Yr	VG	VG+	NM
7-17802	What More Do You Want from Me/The Best Is Yet to Come	1996	—	2.00	4.00
7-18243	What Else Could I Do/Mama Knows the Highway	1994	—	2.00	4.00
7-18517	I'm Not Over You/Passin' on the Train	1993	—	2.00	4.00

VINTON, BOBBY

He didn't make the country charts for the first time until 1970, but his basic sound was no different in the 1960s. So we've chosen to include his entire discography.

45s

ABC

Number	Title (A Side/B Side)	Yr	VG	VG+	NM
12022	My Melody of Love/I'll Be Loving You	1974	—	2.50	5.00
—Black label					
12022	My Melody of Love/I'll Be Loving You	1974	—	2.00	4.00
—Multi-colored label					
12056	Beer Barrel Polka/Dick and Jane	1974	—	2.00	4.00
12100	Wooden Heart/Polka Pose	1975	—	2.00	4.00
12131	My Gypsy Love/Midnight Show	1975	—	2.00	4.00
12178	Moonight Serenade/Why Can't I Get Over You	1976	—	2.00	4.00
12186	Save Your Kisses for Me/Love Shine	1976	—	2.00	4.00
12229	Love Is the Reason/Nobody But Me	1976	—	2.00	4.00
12265	Only Love Can Break a Heart/Once More with Feeling	1977	—	2.00	4.00
12293	Hold Me, Thrill Me, Kiss Me/Her Name Is Love	1977	—	2.00	4.00
12308	All My Todays/Strike Up the Band for Love	1977	—	2.00	4.00

ALPINE

Number	Title (A Side/B Side)	Yr	VG	VG+	NM
50	First Impression/You'll Never Forget	1959	7.50	15.00	30.00
59	The Sheik/A Freshman and a Sophomore	1960	6.25	12.50	25.00

BOBBY VINTON

Number	Title (A Side/B Side)	Yr	VG	VG+	NM
100	Santa Must Be Polish/Santa Claus Is Coming to Town	1987	—	—	3.00
100 [PS]	Santa Must Be Polish/Santa Claus Is Coming to Town	1987	—	—	3.00

CURB

Number	Title (A Side/B Side)	Yr	VG	VG+	NM
10512	The Last Rose/Sealed with a Kiss	1988	—	—	3.00
10541	Please Tell Her That I Said Hello/Getting Used to Being Loved Again	1989	—	—	3.00
10560	It's Been One of Those Days/(Now and Then There's) A Fool Such As I	1989	—	—	3.00
76751	The Only Fire That Burns/What Did You Do with Your Old 45's	1990	—	2.00	4.00

DIAMOND

Number	Title (A Side/B Side)	Yr	VG	VG+	NM
121	I Love You the Way You Are/You're My Girl	1962	5.00	10.00	20.00
—B-side by Chuck and Johnny					

ELEKTRA

Number	Title (A Side/B Side)	Yr	VG	VG+	NM
45503	My First, My Only Love/Summerlove Sensation	1978	—	2.00	4.00

EPIC

Number	Title (A Side/B Side)	Yr	VG	VG+	NM
06537	Blue Velvet/Blue on Blue	1986	—	2.50	5.00
9417	Posin'/Tornado	1960	3.75	7.50	15.00
9440	Corrina, Corrina/Little Lonely One	1961	3.75	7.50	15.00
9469	Hip-Swinging, High-Stepping, Drum Majorette/Will I Ask Ya	1961	3.75	7.50	15.00
9509	Roses Are Red (My Love)/You and I	1962	3.00	6.00	12.00
9509 [PS]	Roses Are Red (My Love)/You and I	1962	3.75	7.50	15.00
—Bobby Vinton looks straight ahead, chin in hand					
9509 [PS]	Roses Are Red (My Love)/You and I	1962	3.75	7.50	15.00
—Bobby Vinton looks toward the lower right corner					
9532	Rain, Rain Go Away/Over and Over	1962	3.00	6.00	12.00
9532 [PS]	Rain, Rain Go Away/Over and Over	1962	3.75	7.50	15.00
9550	Excerpts from "Roses Are Red"	1962	3.00	6.00	12.00
9551	Excerpts from "Roses Are Red"	1962	3.00	6.00	12.00
9552	Excerpts from "Roses Are Red"	1962	3.00	6.00	12.00
9553	Excerpts from "Roses Are Red"	1962	3.00	6.00	12.00
9554	Excerpts from "Roses Are Red"	1962	3.00	6.00	12.00
9561	Trouble Is My Middle Name/Let's Kiss and Make Up	1962	2.50	5.00	10.00
9561 [PS]	Trouble Is My Middle Name/Let's Kiss and Make Up	1962	3.75	7.50	15.00
9577	Over the Mountain (Across the Sea)/Faded Pictures	1963	2.50	5.00	10.00
9577 [PS]	Over the Mountain (Across the Sea)/Faded Pictures	1963	3.75	7.50	15.00
9593	Blue on Blue/Those Little Things	1963	3.00	6.00	12.00
9593 [PS]	Blue on Blue/Those Little Things	1963	3.75	7.50	15.00
9614	Blue Velvet/Is There a Place (Where I Can Go)	1963	3.00	6.00	12.00
9614 [PS]	Blue Velvet/Is There a Place (Where I Can Go)	1963	3.75	7.50	15.00
9638	There! I've Said It Again/The Girl with the Bow in Her Hair	1963	3.00	6.00	12.00
9638 [PS]	There! I've Said It Again/The Girl with the Bow in Her Hair	1963	3.75	7.50	15.00
9662	My Heart Belongs to Only You/Warm and Tender	1964	2.50	5.00	10.00
9662 [PS]	My Heart Belongs to Only You/Warm and Tender	1964	3.75	7.50	15.00
9687	Tell Me Why/Remembering	1964	2.00	4.00	8.00
9687 [PS]	Tell Me Why/Remembering	1964	3.75	7.50	15.00
9705	Clinging Vine/Imagination Is a Magic Dream	1964	2.00	4.00	8.00
9705 [PS]	Clinging Vine/Imagination Is a Magic Dream	1964	3.00	6.00	12.00
9730	Mr. Lonely/It's Better to Have Loved	1964	2.50	5.00	10.00
9730 [PS]	Mr. Lonely/It's Better to Have Loved	1964	3.00	6.00	12.00
9741	The Bell That Couldn't Jingle/Dearest Santa	1964	2.50	5.00	10.00
9768	Long Lonely Nights/Satin	1965	2.00	4.00	8.00

Number	Title (A Side/B Side)	Yr	VG	VG+	NM
❑ 9768 [PS]	Long Lonely Nights/Satin	1965	3.00	6.00	12.00
❑ 9791	L-O-N-E-L-Y/Graduation Tears	1965	2.00	4.00	8.00
❑ 9791 [PS]	L-O-N-E-L-Y/Graduation Tears	1965	3.00	6.00	12.00
❑ 9814	Theme from "Harlow" (Lonely Girl)/If I Should Lose Your Love	1965	2.00	4.00	8.00
❑ 9814 [PS]	Theme from "Harlow" (Lonely Girl)/If I Should Lose Your Love	1965	3.00	6.00	12.00
❑ 9846	What Color (Is a Man)/Love or Infatuation	1965	2.00	4.00	8.00
❑ 9869	Satin Pillows/Careless	1965	2.00	4.00	8.00
❑ 9869 [PS]	Satin Pillows/Careless	1965	3.00	6.00	12.00
❑ 9894	Tears/Go Away Pain	1966	—	3.00	6.00
❑ 10014	Dum-De-Da/Blue Clarinet	1966	—	3.00	6.00
❑ 10014 [PS]	Dum-De-Da/Blue Clarinet	1966	2.50	5.00	10.00
❑ 10048	Petticoat White (Summer Sky Blue)/All the King's Horses	1966	—	3.00	6.00
❑ 10048 [PS]	Petticoat White (Summer Sky Blue)/All the King's Horses	1966	2.50	5.00	10.00
❑ 10090	Coming Home Soldier/Don't Let My Mary Go Around	1966	—	3.00	6.00
❑ 10090 [PS]	Coming Home Soldier/Don't Let My Mary Go Around	1966	2.50	5.00	10.00
❑ 10136	For He's a Jolly Good Fellow/Sweet Maria	1967	—	3.00	6.00
❑ 10136 [PS]	For He's a Jolly Good Fellow/Sweet Maria	1967	2.50	5.00	10.00
❑ 10168	Red Roses for Mom/College Town	1967	—	3.00	6.00
❑ 10228	Please Love Me Forever/Miss America	1967	2.00	4.00	8.00
❑ 10228 [PS]	Please Love Me Forever/Miss America	1967	2.50	5.00	10.00
❑ 10266	Just As Much As Ever/Another Memory	1967	—	3.00	6.00
❑ 10266 [PS]	Just As Much As Ever/Another Memory	1967	2.50	5.00	10.00
❑ 10305	Take Good Care of My Baby/Strange Sensations	1968	—	3.00	6.00
❑ 10305 [PS]	Take Good Care of My Baby/Strange Sensations	1968	2.50	5.00	10.00
❑ 10350	Halfway to Paradise/(My Little) Christie	1968	—	3.00	6.00
❑ 10350	Halfway to Paradise/(My Little) Kristie	1968	2.50	5.00	10.00
—Note variation in B-side spelling					
❑ 10350 [PS]	Halfway to Paradise/(My Little) Christie	1968	2.50	5.00	10.00
❑ 10397	I Love How You Love Me/Little Barefoot Boy	1968	—	3.00	6.00
❑ 10397 [PS]	I Love How You Love Me/Little Barefoot Boy	1968	2.50	5.00	10.00
❑ 10461	To Know You Is to Love You/The Beat of My Heart	1969	—	2.50	5.00
❑ 10461 [PS]	To Know You Is to Love You/The Beat of My Heart	1969	2.50	5.00	10.00
❑ 10485	The Days of Sand and Shovels/So Many Lonely Girls	1969	—	2.50	5.00
❑ 10485 [PS]	The Days of Sand and Shovels/So Many Lonely Girls	1969	2.50	5.00	10.00
❑ 10554	Where Is Love/For All We Know	1969	—	2.50	5.00
❑ 10576	My Elusive Dreams/Over and Over	1970	—	2.50	5.00
❑ 10576 [PS]	My Elusive Dreams/Over and Over	1970	2.50	5.00	10.00
❑ 10629	No Arms Can Ever Hold You/I've Got That Lovin' Feelin'	1970	—	2.50	5.00
❑ 10629 [PS]	No Arms Can Ever Hold You/I've Got That Lovin' Feelin'	1970	2.00	4.00	8.00
❑ 10651	Why Don't They Understand/Where Is Love	1970	—	2.50	5.00
❑ 10651 [PS]	Why Don't They Understand/Where Is Love	1970	2.00	4.00	8.00
❑ 10689	Christmas Eve in My Home Town/The Christmas Angel	1970	—	3.00	6.00
❑ 10711	She Loves Me/I'll Make You My Baby	1971	—	2.50	5.00
❑ 10736	And I Love You So/She Loves Me	1971	—	2.50	5.00
❑ 10790	A Little Bit of You/God Bless America	1971	—	2.50	5.00
❑ 10822	Every Day of My Life/You Can Do It to Me Anytime	1972	—	2.50	5.00
❑ 10822 [PS]	Every Day of My Life/You Can Do It to Me Anytime	1972	2.00	4.00	8.00
❑ 10861	Sealed with a Kiss/All My Life	1972	—	2.50	5.00
❑ 10861 [PS]	Sealed with a Kiss/All My Life	1972	2.00	4.00	8.00
❑ 10936	But I Do/When You Love	1972	—	2.50	5.00
❑ 10936 [PS]	But I Do/When You Love	1972	2.00	4.00	8.00
❑ 10980	I Love You the Way You Are/Hurt	1973	—	2.50	5.00
❑ 11038	Where Are the Children/I Can't Believe That It's All Over	1973	—	2.50	5.00
❑ 50080	Clinging Vine/I Can't Believe That It's All Over	1975	—	2.50	5.00
❑ 50169	Christmas Eve in My Home Town/The Christmas Angel	1975	—	2.50	5.00
LARC					
❑ 81019	You Are Love/Ghost of Another Man	1983	—	2.50	5.00
MELODY					
❑ 5001/2	Always in My Heart/Harlem Nocturne	1960	6.25	12.50	25.00
TAPESTRY					
❑ 001	Disco Polka (Pennsylvania Polka)/I Could Have Danced All Night	1979	—	2.00	4.00
❑ 002	Make Believe It's Your First Time/I Remember Loving You	1979	—	2.00	4.00
❑ 003	He/My First and Only Love	1980	—	2.00	4.00
❑ 005	It Was Nice to Know You John/Ain't That Lovin' You	1981	—	2.50	5.00
❑ 006	Let Me Love You, Goodbye/You Are Love	1981	—	2.00	4.00
❑ 007	Forever and Ever/Ain't That Lovin' You	1982	—	2.00	4.00
❑ 008	She WIll Survive (Poland)/Love Is the Reason	1982	—	2.00	4.00
❑ 008 [PS]	She WIll Survive (Poland)/Love Is the Reason	1982	—	2.50	5.00
❑ 010	It Hurts to Be in Love/Love Makes Everything Better	1985	—	2.00	4.00
❑ 013	What Did You Do with Your Old 45s/(B-side unknown)	1986	—	2.00	4.00
❑ 1986	Sweet Lady of Liberty (same on both sides)	1986	—	2.00	4.00
❑ 4009	Bed of Roses/I Know a Goodbye	1984	—	2.00	4.00

Number	Title (A Side/B Side)	Yr	VG	VG+	NM
7-Inch Extended Plays					
ABC					
❑ LLP-271 [DJ]	The Most Beautiful Girl/My Melody of Love/Never Ending Song of Love//You'll Never Know/Am I Losing You/Here in My Heart	1974	2.50	5.00	10.00
—33 1/3 rpm, small hole jukebox issue					
❑ LLP-271 [PS]	Melodies of Love	1974	2.50	5.00	10.00
EPIC					
❑ EG 7215	Silver Bells/White Christmas//O Holy Night/The Christmas Song	1963	2.50	5.00	10.00
❑ EG 7215 [PS]	Songs of Christmas	1963	2.50	5.00	10.00
❑ 7-26437 [DJ]	Why Don't You Believe Me/Together/Save the Last Dance for Me//If I Didn't Care/Shangri-La/ It's No Sin	1968	2.50	5.00	10.00
—33 1/3 rpm, small hole jukebox issue					
❑ 7-26437 [PS]	I Love How You Love Me	1968	2.50	5.00	10.00
❑ 7-31642 [DJ]	Our Day Will Come/Song Sung Blue/Come Softly to Me//Some Kind of Wonderful/Somebody's Breaking My Heart/I'm Leaving It Up to You	1972	2.50	5.00	10.00
—33 1/3 rpm, small hole jukebox issue					
❑ 7-31642 [PS]	Sealed with a Kiss	1972	2.50	5.00	10.00
Albums					
ABC					
❑ X-851	Melodies of Love	1974	2.50	5.00	10.00
❑ D-891	Heart of Hearts	1975	2.50	5.00	10.00
❑ D-924	The Bobby Vinton Show	1975	2.50	5.00	10.00
❑ D-957	Serenades of Love	1976	2.50	5.00	10.00
❑ AB-981	The Name Is Love	1977	2.50	5.00	10.00
COLUMBIA LIMITED EDITION					
❑ LE 10140	Blue Velvet	197?	2.50	5.00	10.00
—Reissue of Epic 26068					
EPIC					
❑ BN 579 [S]	Dancing at the Hop	1961	12.50	25.00	50.00
❑ BN 597 [S]	Young Man with a Big Band	1961	12.50	25.00	50.00
❑ LN 3727 [M]	Dancing at the Hop	1961	7.50	15.00	30.00
❑ LN 3780 [M]	Young Man with a Big Band	1961	7.50	15.00	30.00
❑ LN 24020 [M]	Roses Are Red	1962	3.75	7.50	15.00
❑ LN 24035 [M]	Bobby Vinton Sings the Big Ones	1962	3.75	7.50	15.00
❑ LN 24049 [M]	The Greatest Hits of the Greatest Groups	1963	3.75	7.50	15.00
❑ LN 24068 [M]	Blue On Blue	1963	37.50	75.00	150.00
—Promo only on blue vinyl					
❑ LN 24068 [M]	Blue On Blue	1963	6.25	12.50	25.00
—Stock copy on black vinyl					
❑ LN 24068 [M]	Blue Velvet	1963	3.75	7.50	15.00
—Retitled version of "Blue On Blue"					
❑ LN 24081 [M]	There! I've Said It Again	1964	3.75	7.50	15.00
❑ LN 24098 [M]	Bobby Vinton's Greatest Hits	1964	3.00	6.00	12.00
—Despite lower number, this came out after "Tell Me Why"					
❑ LN 24113 [M]	Tell Me Why	1964	3.00	6.00	12.00
❑ LN 24122 [M]	A Very Merry Christmas	1964	3.00	6.00	12.00
❑ LN 24136 [M]	Mr. Lonely	1965	3.00	6.00	12.00
❑ LN 24154 [M]	Bobby Vinton Sings for Lonely Nights	1965	3.00	6.00	12.00
❑ LN 24170 [M]	Drive-In Movie Time	1965	3.00	6.00	12.00
❑ LN 24182 [M]	Satin Pillows and Careless	1966	3.00	6.00	12.00
❑ LN 24187 [M]	More of Bobby Vinton's Greatest Hits	1966	3.00	6.00	12.00
❑ LN 24188 [M]	Country Boy	1966	3.00	6.00	12.00
❑ LN 24203 [M]	Live at the Copa	1967	3.00	6.00	12.00
❑ LN 24245 [M]	Bobby Vinton's Newest Hits	1967	3.00	6.00	12.00
❑ LN 24341 [M]	Please Love Me Forever	1967	3.75	7.50	15.00
❑ BN 26020 [S]	Roses Are Red	1962	5.00	10.00	20.00
❑ BN 26035 [S]	Bobby Vinton Sings the Big Ones	1962	5.00	10.00	20.00
❑ BN 26049 [S]	The Greatest Hits of the Greatest Groups	1963	5.00	10.00	20.00
❑ BN 26068 [S]	Blue On Blue	1963	7.50	15.00	30.00
❑ BN 26068 [S]	Blue Velvet	1963	5.00	10.00	20.00
—Retitled version of "Blue On Blue"					
❑ BN 26081 [S]	There! I've Said It Again	1964	5.00	10.00	20.00
❑ BN 26098 [S]	Bobby Vinton's Greatest Hits	1964	3.75	7.50	15.00
—Despite lower number, this came out after "Tell Me Why"					
❑ PE 26098	Bobby Vinton's Greatest Hits	198?	2.00	4.00	8.00
—Budget-line reissue					
❑ BN 26113 [S]	Tell Me Why	1964	3.75	7.50	15.00
❑ BN 26122 [S]	A Very Merry Christmas	1964	3.75	7.50	15.00
—Same as above, but in stereo					
❑ BN 26136 [S]	Mr. Lonely	1965	3.75	7.50	15.00
❑ BN 26154 [S]	Bobby Vinton Sings for Lonely Nights	1965	3.75	7.50	15.00
❑ BN 26170 [S]	Drive-In Movie Time	1965	3.75	7.50	15.00
❑ BN 26182 [S]	Satin Pillows and Careless	1966	3.75	7.50	15.00
❑ BN 26187 [S]	More of Bobby Vinton's Greatest Hits	1966	3.75	7.50	15.00
❑ BN 26188 [S]	Country Boy	1966	3.75	7.50	15.00
❑ BN 26203 [S]	Live at the Copa	1967	3.75	7.50	15.00
❑ BN 26245 [S]	Bobby Vinton's Newest Hits	1967	3.75	7.50	15.00
❑ BN 26341 [S]	Please Love Me Forever	1967	3.75	7.50	15.00
❑ BN 26382	Take Good Care of My Baby	1968	3.75	7.50	15.00
❑ BN 26437	I Love How You Love Me	1968	3.75	7.50	15.00
❑ BN 26471	Vinton	1969	3.75	7.50	15.00
❑ BN 26510	Bobby Vinton's Greatest Hits of Love	1970	3.75	7.50	15.00
❑ BN 26540	My Elusive Dreams	1970	3.75	7.50	15.00
❑ KE 31286	Ev'ry Day of My Life	1972	3.00	6.00	12.00
❑ KEG 31487 [(2)]	Bobby Vinton's All-Time Greatest Hits	1972	3.75	7.50	15.00
❑ PEG 31487 [(2)]	Bobby Vinton's All-Time Greatest Hits	197?	3.00	6.00	12.00
—Reissue					
❑ KE 31642	Sealed with a Kiss	1972	3.00	6.00	12.00
❑ PE 32921	With Love	1974	2.50	5.00	10.00
❑ KEG 33468 [(2)]	Bobby Vinton Sings the Golden Decade of Love	1975	3.00	6.00	12.00

Number	Title (A Side/B Side)	Yr	VG	VG+	NM
❑ KEG 33767 [(2)]	Greatest Hits/Greatest Hits of Love	1976	3.00	6.00	12.00
❑ JE 35605	Autumn Memories	1979	2.50	5.00	10.00
❑ JE 35998	Spring Sensations	1979	2.50	5.00	10.00
❑ JE 35999	Summer Serenade	1979	2.50	5.00	10.00
HARMONY					
❑ KH 11402	Vinton Sings Vinton	197?	2.50	5.00	10.00
PICKWICK					
❑ SPC-3353	Melodies of Love	197?	2.00	4.00	8.00
TAPESTRY					
❑ TRS-1001 [EP]	Santa Must Be Polish	1987	2.50	5.00	10.00

VOLTAGE BROTHERS, THE
45s

MTM

Number	Title (A Side/B Side)	Yr	VG	VG+	NM
❑ B-72060	I Think I Miss You (After All)/Don't Jump the Gun	1985	—	2.50	5.00
❑ B-72067	Love's a Criminal/(B-side unknown)	1986	—	2.50	5.00
❑ B-72077	Insecure/(B-side unknown)	1986	—	2.50	5.00

VON, VICKI RAE
45s

ATLANTIC AMERICA

Number	Title (A Side/B Side)	Yr	VG	VG+	NM
❑ 99442	Torn-Up/Hold Me Like You've Never Had Me	1987	—	—	3.00
❑ 99471	Not Tonight I've Got a Heartache/It's All Over But the Lying	1987	—	—	3.00

Albums

ATLANTIC AMERICA

Number	Title (A Side/B Side)	Yr	VG	VG+	NM
❑ 90587	Not Tonight, I've Got a Heartache	1987	2.50	5.00	10.00

W

WADE, NORMAN
45s

NSD

Number	Title (A Side/B Side)	Yr	VG	VG+	NM
❑ 29	I'm a Long Gone Daddy/Arms of Someone Else	1979	—	3.00	6.00

WAGONEERS
45s

A&M

Number	Title (A Side/B Side)	Yr	VG	VG+	NM
❑ 1215	I Wanna Know Her Again/Stout and High	1988	—	2.00	4.00
❑ 1230	Every Step of the Way/It'll Take Some Time	1988	—	2.00	4.00
❑ 1260	Help Me Get Over You/Please Don't Think I'm Guilty	1988	—	2.00	4.00
❑ 1435	Sit a Little Closer/Spare Time	1989	—	2.00	4.00
❑ 1460	Test of Time/Atlanta	1989	—	2.50	5.00

Albums

A&M

Number	Title (A Side/B Side)	Yr	VG	VG+	NM
❑ SP-5200	Stout and High	1988	2.00	4.00	8.00

WAGONER, PORTER
45s

RCA

Number	Title (A Side/B Side)	Yr	VG	VG+	NM
❑ PB-10803	When Lea Jane Sang/Storm of Love	1976	—	2.00	4.00
❑ PB-10974	I Haven't Learned a Thing/Hand Me Down My Walking Cane	1977	—	2.00	4.00
❑ PB-11186	Mountain Music/Natural Wonder	1977	—	2.00	4.00
❑ PB-11411	Ole Slew Foot/I'm Gonna Feed 'Em Now	1978	—	2.00	4.00
❑ PB-11491	I Want to Walk You Home/Old Love Letter	1979	—	2.00	4.00
❑ PB-11671	Everything I've Always Wanted/No Bed of Roses	1979	—	2.00	4.00
❑ PB-11771	Hold On Tight/Someone Just Like You	1979	—	2.00	4.00
❑ PB-11998	Is It Only 'Cause You're Lonely/When She Was Mine	1980	—	2.00	4.00
RCA VICTOR					
❑ APBO-0013	Wake Up, Jacob/Stella, Dear Sweet Stella	1973	—	2.50	5.00
❑ APBO-0187	George Leory Chickashea/Cassie	1973	—	2.50	5.00
❑ APBO-0233	Tore Down/Nothing Between	1974	—	2.50	5.00
❑ APBO-0328	Highway Headin' South/Freda	1974	—	2.50	5.00
❑ PB-10124	Carolina Moonshiner/Not a Cloud in the Sky	1974	—	2.50	5.00
❑ PB-10281	It's My Time (To Say I Love You)/Just for the Lonely Ones	1975	—	3.00	6.00
❑ PB-10411	Indian Creek/Thank You for the Happiness	1975	—	2.50	5.00
❑ 47-4996	Settin' the Woods on Fire/Headin' for a Weddin'	1952	7.50	15.00	30.00
❑ 47-5086	Takin' Chances/I Can't Live with You	1952	7.50	15.00	30.00
❑ 47-5215	That's It/Don't Play That Song	1953	6.25	12.50	25.00
❑ 47-5330	Trademark/A Beggar for Your Love	1953	6.25	12.50	25.00
❑ 47-5430	Bringing Home the Bacon/An Angel Made for Love	1953	6.25	12.50	25.00
❑ 47-5527	Flame of Love/Dig That Crazy Moon	1953	6.25	12.50	25.00
❑ 47-5631	Trinidad/Bad News Travels Fast	1954	6.25	12.50	25.00
❑ 47-5754	Be Glad You Ain't Me/Love at First Sight	1954	6.25	12.50	25.00
❑ 47-5848	Company's Comin'/Tricks of the Trade	1954	6.25	12.50	25.00
❑ 47-6030	Hey, Maw/How Quick	1955	6.25	12.50	25.00
❑ 47-6105	A Satisfied Mind/Itchin' for My Baby	1955	5.00	10.00	20.00
❑ 47-6289	Eat, Drink and Be Merry (Tomorrow You'll Cry)/ Let's Squiggle	1955	5.00	10.00	20.00
❑ 47-6421	What Would You Do? (If Jesus Came to Your House)/How Can You Refuse Him Now	1956	5.00	10.00	20.00
❑ 47-6494	Uncle Pen/How I've Tried	1956	5.00	10.00	20.00
❑ 47-6598	Tryin' to Forget the Blues/I've Known You from Somewhere	1956	5.00	10.00	20.00
❑ 47-6803	I'm Day Dreamin' Tonight/I Should Be with You	1957	5.00	10.00	20.00
❑ 47-6844	Good Mornin', Neighbor/Who Will He Be	1957	5.00	10.00	20.00
❑ 47-6964	I Thought I Heard You Call My Name/Pay Day	1957	5.00	10.00	20.00
❑ 47-7073	Doll Face/Your Love	1957	5.00	10.00	20.00
❑ 47-7199	Tomorrow We'll Retire/Heaven's Just a Prayer Away	1958	3.75	7.50	15.00
❑ 47-7279	Haven't You Heard/Tell Her Lies and Feed Her Candy	1958	3.75	7.50	15.00
❑ 47-7374	Just Before Dawn/Dear Lonesome	1958	3.75	7.50	15.00
❑ 47-7457	Me and Fred and Joe and Bill/Out of Sight, Out of Mind	1959	3.75	7.50	15.00
❑ 47-7532	I'm Gonna Sing/I Thought of God	1959	3.75	7.50	15.00
❑ 47-7568	The Battle of Little Big Horn/Our Song of Love	1959	3.75	7.50	15.00
❑ 47-7638	The Girl Who Didn't Need Love/Your Kind of People	1959	3.75	7.50	15.00
❑ 47-7708	Legend of the Big Steeple/Wakin' Up the Crowd	1960	3.75	7.50	15.00
❑ 47-7770	Falling Again/An Old Log Cabin for Sale	1960	3.75	7.50	15.00
❑ 47-7837	Your Old Love Letters/Heartbreak Affair	1961	3.00	6.00	12.00
❑ 47-7901	Everything She Touches Gets the Blues/Sugar Foot Rag	1961	3.00	6.00	12.00
❑ 47-7967	Misery Loves Company/I Cried Again	1961	3.00	6.00	12.00
❑ 47-8026	Cold Dark Waters/Ain't It Awful	1962	3.00	6.00	12.00
❑ 47-8105	I've Enjoyed As Much of This As I Can Stand/One Way Ticket to the Blues	1962	3.00	6.00	12.00
❑ 47-8178	My Baby's Not Here (In Town Tonight)/In the Shadows of the Wine	1963	3.00	6.00	12.00
❑ 47-8257	Howdy Neighbor Howdy/Find Out	1963	3.00	6.00	12.00
❑ 47-8338	Sorrow on the Rocks/The Life of the Party	1964	3.00	6.00	12.00
❑ 47-8432	I'll Go Down Swinging/Country Music Has Gone to Town	1964	3.00	6.00	12.00
❑ 47-8524	I'm Gonna Feed You Now/The Bride's Bouquet	1965	2.50	5.00	10.00
❑ 47-8622	Green, Green Grass of Home/Dooley	1965	2.50	5.00	10.00
❑ 47-8723	Skid Row Joe/Love Your Neighbor	1965	2.50	5.00	10.00
❑ 47-8800	I Just Came to Smell the Flowers/I'm a Long Way from Home	1966	2.50	5.00	10.00
❑ 47-8882	I Dreamed I Saw America on Her Knees/When I Reach That City	1966	2.50	5.00	10.00
❑ 47-8977	Old Slew-Foot/Let Me In	1966	2.50	5.00	10.00
❑ 47-9067	The Cold Hard Facts of Life/You Can't Make a Heel Toe the Mark	1967	2.50	5.00	10.00
❑ 47-9243	Julie/Try Being Lonely	1967	2.50	5.00	10.00
❑ 47-9379	Woman Hungry/Out of the Silence (Came a Song)	1967	2.50	5.00	10.00
❑ 47-9530	Be Proud of Your Man/Wino	1968	2.00	4.00	8.00
❑ 47-9651	The Carroll County Accident/Sorrow Overtakes the Wine	1968	2.00	4.00	8.00
❑ 47-9802	You Got-Ta Have a License/Fairchild	1970	—	3.00	6.00
❑ 47-9811	Little Boy's Prayer/Roses Out of Season	1970	—	3.00	6.00
❑ 47-9895	Jim Johnson/One More Dime	1970	—	3.00	6.00
❑ 47-9939	The Last One to Touch Me/The Alley	1970	—	3.00	6.00
❑ 47-9979	Charley's Picture/As Simple As I Am	1971	—	3.00	6.00
❑ 48-1007	Be a Little Quieter/Watching	1971	—	3.00	6.00
❑ 74-0168	Big Wind/Tennessee Stud	1969	2.00	4.00	8.00
❑ 74-0267	When You're Hot You're Hot/The Answer Is Love	1969	2.00	4.00	8.00
❑ 74-0581	The Rubber Room/Late Love of Mine	1971	—	3.00	6.00
❑ 74-0648	What Ain't to Be, Just Might Happen/Little Bird	1972	—	3.00	6.00
❑ 74-0753	A World Without Music/Denise Mayree	1972	—	3.00	6.00
❑ 74-0820	Katy Did/Darlin' Debra Jean	1972	—	3.00	6.00
❑ 74-0923	Lightening the Load/Tomorrow Is Forever	1973	—	3.00	6.00
WARNER BROS.					
❑ 29596	That Was Then, This Is Now/Bottom of the Fifth	1983	—	2.00	4.00
❑ 29772	This Cowboy's Hat/She Don't Have a License to Drive Me Up the Wall	1983	—	—	3.00
❑ 29875	Turn the Pencil Over/Texas Moonbeam Waltz	1982	—	2.00	4.00

—B-side by Johnny Gimble/Texas Swing Band

7-Inch Extended Plays

RCA VICTOR

Number	Title (A Side/B Side)	Yr	VG	VG+	NM
❑ EPA-937	A Satisfied Mind/I Like Girls//Living in the Past/ Midnight	1956	6.25	12.50	25.00
❑ EPA-937 [PS]	Satisfied Mind	1956	6.25	12.50	25.00

Albums

Number	Title (A Side/B Side)	Yr	VG	VG+	NM
ACCORD					
❑ SN-7179	Down Home Country	1982	3.00	6.00	12.00
DOT/MCA					
❑ 39053	Porter Wagoner	1986	2.50	5.00	10.00
RCA CAMDEN					
❑ CAL-769 [M]	A Satisfied Mind	1963	3.00	6.00	12.00
❑ CAS-769(e) [R]	A Satisfied Mind	1963	2.50	5.00	10.00
❑ CAL-861 [M]	An Old Log Cabin for Sale	1965	3.00	6.00	12.00
❑ CAS-861 [S]	An Old Log Cabin for Sale	1965	3.00	6.00	12.00
❑ CAL-942 [M]	"Your Old Love Letters" And Other Country Hits	1966	3.00	6.00	12.00
❑ CAS-942 [S]	"Your Old Love Letters" And Other Country Hits	1966	3.00	6.00	12.00
❑ CAL-2116 [M]	I'm Day Dreamin' Tonight	1967	3.00	6.00	12.00
❑ CAS-2116 [S]	I'm Day Dreamin' Tonight	1967	3.00	6.00	12.00
❑ CAL-2191 [M]	Green, Green Grass of Home	1967	3.00	6.00	12.00
❑ CAS-2191 [S]	Green, Green Grass of Home	1967	3.00	6.00	12.00
❑ CAS-2321	Country Feeling	1968	3.00	6.00	12.00
❑ CAS-2409	Howdy Neighbor	1970	3.00	6.00	12.00
❑ CAS-2478	Porter Wagoner Country	1971	3.00	6.00	12.00
❑ CAS-2588	The Silent Kind	1972	3.00	6.00	12.00
❑ CXS-9010 [(2)]	Blue Moon of Kentucky	1971	3.75	7.50	15.00

RCA VICTOR

Number	Title (A Side/B Side)	Yr	VG	VG+	NM
❑ APL1-0142	I'll Keep on Lovin' You	1973	3.75	7.50	15.00
❑ APL1-0346	The Farmer	1974	3.75	7.50	15.00
❑ APL1-0496	Tore Down	1974	3.75	7.50	15.00
❑ APL1-0713	Highway Headin' South	1974	3.75	7.50	15.00
❑ APL1-1056	Sing Love	1975	3.75	7.50	15.00
❑ ANL1-1213	The Best of Porter Wagoner	1975	3.00	6.00	12.00
❑ LPM-1358 [M]	A Satisfied Mind	1956	50.00	100.00	200.00
❑ AHL1-2432	Porter	1977	3.00	6.00	12.00
❑ LPM-2447 [M]	A Slice of Life — Songs Happy 'N' Sad	1962	6.25	12.50	25.00
❑ LSP-2447 [S]	A Slice of Life — Songs Happy 'N' Sad	1962	7.50	15.00	30.00
❑ LPM-2650 [M]	The Porter Wagoner Show	1963	6.25	12.50	25.00
❑ LSP-2650 [S]	The Porter Wagoner Show	1963	7.50	15.00	30.00
❑ LPM-2706 [M]	Y'All Come	1963	6.25	12.50	25.00
❑ LSP-2706 [S]	Y'All Come	1963	7.50	15.00	30.00
❑ LPM-2840 [M]	In Person	1964	6.25	12.50	25.00
❑ LSP-2840 [S]	In Person	1964	7.50	15.00	30.00
❑ LPM-2960 [M]	The Bluegrass Story	1964	5.00	10.00	20.00
❑ LSP-2960 [S]	The Bluegrass Story	1964	6.25	12.50	25.00
❑ LPM-3389 [M]	The Thin Man from West Plains	1965	5.00	10.00	20.00
❑ LSP-3389 [S]	The Thin Man from West Plains	1965	6.25	12.50	25.00
❑ LPM-3488 [M]	Grand Old Gospel	1966	5.00	10.00	20.00
❑ LSP-3488 [S]	Grand Old Gospel	1966	6.25	12.50	25.00
❑ LPM-3509 [M]	On the Road	1966	5.00	10.00	20.00
❑ LSP-3509 [S]	On the Road	1966	6.25	12.50	25.00
❑ LPM-3560 [M]	The Best of Porter Wagoner	1966	5.00	10.00	20.00
❑ LSP-3560 [S]	The Best of Porter Wagoner	1966	6.25	12.50	25.00
❑ LPM-3593 [M]	Confessions of a Broken Man	1966	5.00	10.00	20.00
❑ LSP-3593 [S]	Confessions of a Broken Man	1966	6.25	12.50	25.00
❑ LPM-3683 [M]	Soul of a Convict	1967	6.25	12.50	25.00
❑ LSP-3683 [S]	Soul of a Convict	1967	5.00	10.00	20.00
❑ LPM-3797 [M]	The Cold Hard Facts of Life	1967	6.25	12.50	25.00
❑ LSP-3797 [S]	The Cold Hard Facts of Life	1967	5.00	10.00	20.00
❑ LPM-3855 [M]	More Grand Old Gospel	1967	6.25	12.50	25.00
❑ LSP-3855 [S]	More Grand Old Gospel	1967	5.00	10.00	20.00
❑ LPM-3968 [M]	The Bottom of the Bottle	1968	25.00	50.00	100.00
❑ LSP-3968 [S]	The Bottom of the Bottle	1968	5.00	10.00	20.00
❑ LSP-4034	Gospel Country	1968	5.00	10.00	20.00
❑ LSP-4116	The Carroll County Accident	1969	5.00	10.00	20.00
❑ LSP-4181	Me and My Boys	1969	5.00	10.00	20.00
❑ LSP-4286	You Got-ta Have a License	1970	5.00	10.00	20.00
❑ LSP-4321	The Best of Porter Wagoner, Volume 2	1970	5.00	10.00	20.00
❑ LSP-4386	Down in the Alley	1970	5.00	10.00	20.00
❑ LSP-4508	Simple As I Am	1971	5.00	10.00	20.00
❑ LSP-4586	Porter Wagoner Sings His Own	1971	3.75	7.50	15.00
❑ LSP-4661	What Ain't to Be	1972	3.75	7.50	15.00
❑ LSP-4734	Ballads of Love	1972	3.75	7.50	15.00
❑ LSP-4810	The Porter Wagoner Experience	1973	3.75	7.50	15.00
❑ AHL1-7000	Collector's Series	1985	2.50	5.00	10.00

WARNER BROS.

Number	Title (A Side/B Side)	Yr	VG	VG+	NM
❑ 23783	Viva Porter Wagoner!	1983	2.50	5.00	10.00

WAGONER, PORTER, AND SKEETER DAVIS

Albums

RCA VICTOR

Number	Title (A Side/B Side)	Yr	VG	VG+	NM
❑ LPM-2529 [M]	Porter Wagoner and Skeeter Davis Sing Duets	1962	6.25	12.50	25.00
❑ LSP-2529 [S]	Porter Wagoner and Skeeter Davis Sing Duets	1962	7.50	15.00	30.00

WAGONER, PORTER, AND DOLLY PARTON

45s

RCA

Number	Title (A Side/B Side)	Yr	VG	VG+	NM
❑ PB-11983	Making Plans/Beneath the Sweet Magnolia Trees	1980	—	2.00	4.00
❑ PB-12119	If You Go, I'll Follow You/Hide Me Away	1980	—	2.00	4.00

RCA VICTOR

Number	Title (A Side/B Side)	Yr	VG	VG+	NM
❑ PB-10010	Please Don't Stop Loving Me/Sounds of Nature	1974	—	2.00	4.00
❑ PB-10328	Say Forever You'll Be Mine/How Can I Help You Forgive Me	1975	—	2.00	4.00
❑ GB-10506	Please Don't Stop Loving Me/Sounds of Nature	1975	—	2.00	4.00
—Gold Standard Series					
❑ PB-10652	Is Forever Longer Than Always/If You Say I Can	1976	—	2.00	4.00
❑ GB-10675	Say Forever You'll Be Mine/How Can I Help You Forgive Me	1976	—	2.00	4.00
—Gold Standard Series					
❑ 47-9369	The Last Thing on My Mind/Love Is Worth Living	1967	2.00	4.00	8.00
❑ 47-9490	Holding On to Nothing/Just Between You and Me	1968	2.00	4.00	8.00
❑ 47-9577	We'll Get Ahead Someday/Jeannie's Afraid of the Dark	1968	2.00	4.00	8.00
❑ 47-9799	Tomorrow Is Forever/Mandy Never Sleeps	1969	—	3.00	6.00
❑ 47-9875	Daddy Was An Old Time Preacher Man/Good Understanding	1970	—	3.00	6.00
❑ 47-9958	Better Move It On Home/Two of a Kind	1971	—	3.00	6.00
❑ 47-9994	The Right Combination/The Part of Loving You	1971	—	3.00	6.00
❑ 74-0104	Malena/Yours, Love	1969	—	3.00	6.00
❑ 74-0172	Always, Always/No Need to Hurry Home	1969	—	3.00	6.00
❑ 74-0247	Just Someone I Used to Know/My Hands Are Tied	1969	—	3.00	6.00
❑ 74-0565	Burning the Midnight Oil/More Than Words Can Tell	1971	—	3.00	6.00
❑ 74-0675	Lost Forever in Your Kiss/The Fog Has Lifted	1972	—	2.50	5.00
❑ 74-0773	Together Always/Love's All Over	1972	—	2.50	5.00
❑ 74-0893	We Found It/Lord Have Mercy on Us	1973	—	2.50	5.00
❑ 74-0981	If Teardrops Were Pennies/Come to Me	1973	—	2.50	5.00

Albums

PAIR

Number	Title (A Side/B Side)	Yr	VG	VG+	NM
❑ PDL1-1013 [(2)]	Sweet Harmony	1986	3.00	6.00	12.00

RCA VICTOR

Number	Title (A Side/B Side)	Yr	VG	VG+	NM
❑ APL1-0248	Love and Music	1973	3.75	7.50	15.00
❑ APL1-0646	Porter 'N' Dolly	1974	3.75	7.50	15.00
❑ APL1-1116	Say Forever	1975	3.75	7.50	15.00
❑ AHL1-3700	Porter Wagoner and Dolly Parton	1980	3.00	6.00	12.00
❑ LPM-3926 [M]	Just Between You and Me	1968	25.00	50.00	100.00
❑ LSP-3926 [S]	Just Between You and Me	1968	5.00	10.00	20.00
❑ LSP-4039	Just the Two of Us	1968	5.00	10.00	20.00
❑ LSP-4186	Always, Always	1969	5.00	10.00	20.00
❑ AYL1-4251	Porter Wagoner and Dolly Parton	1982	2.00	4.00	8.00
—"Best Buy Series" reissue					
❑ LSP-4305	Porter Wayne and Dolly Rebecca	1970	5.00	10.00	20.00
❑ LSP-4388	Once More	1970	5.00	10.00	20.00
❑ LSP-4490	Two of a Kind	1971	5.00	10.00	20.00
❑ AHL1-4556	The Best of Porter Wagoner and Dolly Parton	1983	2.50	5.00	10.00
❑ LSP-4556	The Best of Porter Wagoner and Dolly Parton	1971	5.00	10.00	20.00
❑ LSP-4628	The Right Combination/Burning the Midnight Oil	1972	3.75	7.50	15.00
❑ LSP-4761	Together Always	1972	3.75	7.50	15.00
❑ LSP-4841	We Found It	1973	3.75	7.50	15.00

WAKELY, JIMMY

45s

ARTCO

Number	Title (A Side/B Side)	Yr	VG	VG+	NM
❑ 5012	If I Could Read Your Mind/Deep in the Heart of Texas	197?	—	3.00	6.00

CAPITOL

Number	Title (A Side/B Side)	Yr	VG	VG+	NM
❑ F929	Peter Cottontail/Mr. Easter Bunny	1950	5.00	10.00	20.00
❑ F1024	Under the Anheuser Bush/Home Town Rag	1950	5.00	10.00	20.00
❑ F1066	Sugar Plum Kisses/I Don't Have to Go to Heaven	1950	5.00	10.00	20.00
❑ F1151	Mona Lisa/Steppin' Out	1950	5.00	10.00	20.00
❑ F1240	Pot of Gold/Bandera Waltz	1950	5.00	10.00	20.00
❑ F1328	My Heart Cries for You/Music by the Angels	1950	5.00	10.00	20.00
❑ F1393	Beautiful Brown Eyes/At the Close of a Long Day	1951	5.00	10.00	20.00
❑ F1472	Did You Write a Letter to Your Sweetheart/Cryin' Just for Youq	1951	5.00	10.00	20.00
❑ F1534	Old Soldiers Never Die/I Like Wide Open Spaces	1951	5.00	10.00	20.00
❑ F1554	Don't Be Lonely/I'll Never Do a Thing	1951	5.00	10.00	20.00
❑ F1630	One Has My Name (The Other Has My Heart)/I Love You So Much It Hurts	1951	5.00	10.00	20.00
—Reissue of material first released on 78s					
❑ F1762	The Solid South/Another Fool Steps In	1951	5.00	10.00	20.00
❑ F1838	Each Step of the Way/Walk with the Lord	1951	5.00	10.00	20.00
❑ F1880	Keep a Light in Your Window/Won't You Ride in My Little Red Wagon	1951	5.00	10.00	20.00
❑ F1936	Missing in Action/Just a Little Waiting	1952	5.00	10.00	20.00
❑ F2028	Goodbye Little Girl/Love Song of the Waterfall	1952	5.00	10.00	20.00
❑ F2078	Forgive Me/Just Because	1952	5.00	10.00	20.00
❑ F2126	If You Would Only Be Mine/My Heart Has Room for You	1952	5.00	10.00	20.00
❑ F2161	Four Legged Friend/There's a Cloud in My Valley of Sunshine	1952	5.00	10.00	20.00
❑ F2172	When I Say Goodnight/There's the Same Old Lovelight in Your Eyes	1952	5.00	10.00	20.00
❑ F2221	I Went to Your Wedding/Pale Moon	1952	5.00	10.00	20.00
❑ F2272	Rainbow at Midnight/When It's Harvest Time Sweet Angeline	1952	5.00	10.00	20.00
❑ F2380	Lorelei/If You Knew What It Meant to Be Lonesome	1953	5.00	10.00	20.00
❑ F2484	The Orchid Means Goodbye/Out of Sight, Out of Mind	1953	5.00	10.00	20.00
❑ F2626	You Took My Name/Pride	1953	5.00	10.00	20.00
❑ F2644	It's Christmas/Thanks	1953	5.00	10.00	20.00
❑ F90040	Christmas Polka/If Santa Claus Could Bring You Back To Me	1949	6.25	12.50	25.00

CORAL

Number	Title (A Side/B Side)	Yr	VG	VG+	NM
❑ 9-61112	Red Deck of Cards/I've Had My Share of Tears	1953	5.00	10.00	20.00
❑ 9-61134	I Love You/I Stopped Livin'	1954	5.00	10.00	20.00
❑ 9-61143	Bimbo/Ain't She Sweet	1954	5.00	10.00	20.00
❑ 9-61175	Bright Eyed and Bushy Tailed/Twilight Time in Tennessee	1954	5.00	10.00	20.00
—With Eileen Barton					
❑ 9-61220	Here Lies My Heart/It's Lonely on the Trail	1954	5.00	10.00	20.00
❑ 9-61276	You Took My Name/When I Stop Loving You	1954	5.00	10.00	20.00
❑ 9-61320	Let Me Go Lover/Let the Rest of the World Go By	1954	5.00	10.00	20.00
❑ 9-61324	Punch/This-a-Way, That-a-Way	1954	5.00	10.00	20.00
—With Eileen Barton					
❑ 9-61341	Let's Walk into the Future/When He Grows Tired of You	1955	3.75	7.50	15.00
❑ 9-61389	Show Me the Way/What God Hath Joined Together	1955	3.75	7.50	15.00
❑ 9-61392	Jim, Johnny and Jonas/Please Have Mercy (On a Fool Like Me)	1955	3.75	7.50	15.00
❑ 9-61428	Are You Mine?/Yellow Roses	1955	3.75	7.50	15.00
❑ 9-61460	Tattle Tale Blues/I'd Love to Live in Loveland	1955	3.75	7.50	15.00
❑ 9-61509	Steal a Penny from a Beggar/Keep No Secrets	1955	3.75	7.50	15.00
❑ 9-61706	His Name Was Dean/Giant	1956	6.25	12.50	25.00
❑ 9-61722	Jimmy, Jimmy/James Dean	1956	6.25	12.50	25.00

DECCA

Number	Title (A Side/B Side)	Yr	VG	VG+	NM
❑ 9-29756	Are You Satisfied/Mississippi Dreamboat	1955	3.75	7.50	15.00
❑ 9-29875	Folsom Prison Blues/That's What the Lord Can Do	1956	3.75	7.50	15.00
❑ 9-29925	Goo Goo Da/Slow Down	1956	3.75	7.50	15.00
❑ 9-30019	The Lord's On My Side/Roundup for the Lord	1956	3.75	7.50	15.00
❑ 9-30270	Blue Nosed Mule/The Hand That Swept the Stars	1957	3.75	7.50	15.00
❑ 9-30372	Tweedle-O-Twill/The Image of Me	1957	3.75	7.50	15.00

Number	Title (A Side/B Side)	Yr	VG	VG+	NM
❑ 9-30524	Just a Boy and a Girl in Love/My Oh My	1957	3.75	7.50	15.00
—With Betsy Jones					
❑ 9-30632	Foreign Love Affair/The Blue Canadian Rockies	1958	3.75	7.50	15.00
❑ 31267	Blue Nosed Mule/Midnight Mule	1961	3.00	6.00	12.00
❑ 32271	Faded Love/Losing My Mind	1968	2.00	4.00	8.00
❑ 32324	Walking the Wet Streets/I Know How It Feels	1968	2.00	4.00	8.00
❑ 32381	Heartaches/I Gotta Have My Baby Back	1968	2.00	4.00	8.00
❑ 32459	I'll Steal Away in the Crowd/My Life Was Filled with Love	1969	2.00	4.00	8.00
❑ 32539	Brotherly Love/I Haven't Lived Enough	1969	2.00	4.00	8.00
❑ 32595	I Wanta Go Home/My Sweet Lovin' Wife	1969	2.00	4.00	8.00
❑ 32649	Any Way That You Want Me/That Silver-Haired Daddy of Mine	1970	2.00	4.00	8.00
❑ 32727	I'm Walkin' By/Peace in the World	1970	2.00	4.00	8.00
DOT					
❑ 16873	The Shelter of Your Arms/Look Back	1966	2.00	4.00	8.00
❑ 16986	Midnight Wind/Cowboy	1966	2.00	4.00	8.00
SHASTA					
❑ 104	Lonesome Lover/By the Waters of the Minnetonka	1958	3.00	6.00	12.00
❑ 105	I've Got a Secret/Tomorrow	1958	3.00	6.00	12.00
❑ 106	That's Santa Claus/Lonely Is the Hunter	1958	3.75	7.50	15.00
❑ 107	Slippin' Around/I Love You So Much It Hurts	1959	3.00	6.00	12.00
❑ 107 [PS]	Slippin' Around/I Love You So Much It Hurts	1959	6.25	12.50	25.00
❑ 110	When It's Springtime in Alaska/Keeper of the Key	1959	3.00	6.00	12.00
❑ 113	I Know How It Feels/Out in the Cold	1959	3.00	6.00	12.00
❑ 119	Sugar Candy/You Came Along	1959	3.00	6.00	12.00
❑ 124	Swinging Jingle Bells/Silver Bells	1959	3.00	6.00	12.00
❑ 127	Hoot and Holler/I Heard an Angel	1960	2.50	5.00	10.00
❑ 128	My Heart Cries for You/Beautiful Brown Eyes	1960	2.50	5.00	10.00
❑ 137	Please Help Me, I'm Falling/One Has My Name (The Other Has My Heart)	1960	2.50	5.00	10.00
—With Jeanne McManus					
❑ 140	High School Romance/Quail Hunt	1960	2.50	5.00	10.00
❑ 143	Come to Me/Cowboy	1960	2.50	5.00	10.00
❑ 145	Snow Flakes/Wang Wang Blues	1960	2.50	5.00	10.00
❑ 150	Goodnight Irene/Please Don't Hurt Me Anymore	1961	2.50	5.00	10.00
❑ 155	Oklahoma Hills/Your Cheatin' Heart	196?	2.50	5.00	10.00
❑ 160	Tennessee Waltz/(B-side unknown)	196?	3.00	6.00	12.00
❑ 162	Cry Fool Cry/Keeper of the Key	196?	2.50	5.00	10.00
❑ 165	Signifying Signs of the Lord/An Unfinished Prayer	196?	2.50	5.00	10.00
❑ 170	King's Airport/Magic Isle	196?	2.50	5.00	10.00
❑ 171	Cold, Cold Heart/Midnight Wind	196?	2.50	5.00	10.00
❑ 173	I Stopped Livin'/On and On	196?	2.50	5.00	10.00
❑ 176	Magic Isle/My Heart Cries for You	196?	2.50	5.00	10.00
❑ 177	Tomorrow/Lonely Is the Hunter	196?	2.50	5.00	10.00
❑ 178	Lonesome Guitar Man/You're Nobody 'Til Somebody Loves You	196?	2.50	5.00	10.00
❑ 179	Faded Love/Losin' My Mind	196?	2.50	5.00	10.00
❑ 201	Free from the Ghetto/Just a Closer Walk with Thee	197?	—	3.00	6.00
❑ 206	Jesus Is Alive/Peace in the World	197?	—	3.00	6.00
❑ 207	How Can You Mend a Broken Heart/Blue Moon of Kentucky	197?	—	3.00	6.00
❑ 209	Cimarron/Too Late	197?	—	3.00	6.00
❑ 210	Last Hour on Death Row/(B-side unknown)	197?	—	3.00	6.00
❑ 211	Goodbye Baby Goodbye/(B-side unknown)	197?	—	3.00	6.00
❑ 215	Ghost Riders in the Sky/In a Shanty in Old Shanty Town	197?	—	3.00	6.00
❑ 216	A Tribute to Bob Wills/Good Time Charlie's Got the Blues	197?	—	3.00	6.00
❑ 218	Corinna, Corinna/Stay a Little Longer	197?	—	3.50	7.00
❑ 219	Saturday's Heroes/I Could Be Beautiful	197?	—	3.00	6.00
SHASTONE					
❑ 103	High School Love/Puppy Love	1958	3.75	7.50	15.00
Selected 78s					
CAPITOL					
❑ 360	Somebody's Rose/Everyone Knew It But Me	1947	3.75	7.50	15.00
❑ 414	I'm Gonna Marry Mary/Too Many Sweethearts	1947	3.75	7.50	15.00
❑ 15162	One Has My Name (The Other Has My Heart)/You're the Sweetest Rose in Texas	1948	3.75	7.50	15.00
❑ 15236	Mine All Mine/Walking the Sidewalks of Shame	1948	3.75	7.50	15.00
❑ 15243	I Love You So Much It Hurts/I Don't Want Your Sympathy	1948	3.75	7.50	15.00
❑ 15333	Forever More/Think of Me Thinking of You	1949	3.75	7.50	15.00
❑ 15368	Till the End of the World/Moon Over Montana	1949	3.75	7.50	15.00
❑ 40016	I Hear You Talkin'/Song of the Sierras	1947	3.75	7.50	15.00
❑ 40040	I Can't Keep the Tears Out of My Eyes/Here Today and Gone Tomorrow	1947	3.75	7.50	15.00
❑ 40059	Sweethearts on Parade/When the Moon Plays Peek-a-Boo	1948	3.75	7.50	15.00
❑ 40078	Oklahoma Blues/Night After Night	1948	3.75	7.50	15.00
❑ 40088	Signed, Sealed and Delivered/Easy to Please	1948	3.75	7.50	15.00
❑ 40107	Bouquet of Roses/Milk Cow Blues	1948	3.75	7.50	15.00
❑ 40125	For the Sake of Days Gone By/Are You Ashamed	1948	3.75	7.50	15.00
❑ 40153	I Wish I Had a Nickel/Someday You'll Call My Name	1949	3.75	7.50	15.00
❑ 40187	Tellin' My Troubles to My Old Guitar/Try to Understand	1949	3.75	7.50	15.00
❑ F40252	You're Only in My Arms/I Don't Know Why I Love You	1949	7.50	15.00	30.00
❑ F40283	Dust/The Touch of God's Hand	1950	7.50	15.00	30.00
CORAL					
❑ 64002	You Can't Break the Chains of Love/I'm Sending You Red Roses	194?	3.75	7.50	15.00
❑ 64006	Blue Bonnet Blues/I Don't Care	1949	3.75	7.50	15.00
❑ 64011	A Broken Heart/Go Your Way and I'll Go Mine	1949	3.75	7.50	15.00
❑ 64014	Standing Outside of Heaven/When I Take My Vacation in Heaven	1949	3.75	7.50	15.00
❑ 64022	On the Strings of My Lonesome Guitar/When a Speck in the Sky Is a Bluebird	1949	3.75	7.50	15.00
❑ 64037	Be Honest with Me/Gone and Left Me Blues	1950	3.75	7.50	15.00
DECCA					
❑ 6059	Standing Outside of Heaven/(B-side unknown)	1943	5.00	10.00	20.00
❑ 6077	Maria Elena/Cimarron	1943	5.00	10.00	20.00
❑ 6091	Gone and Left Me Blues/After Tomorrow	1944	5.00	10.00	20.00
❑ 6095	I'm Sending You Red Roses/A Tiny Little Voice in a Tiny Little Prayer	1944	5.00	10.00	20.00
❑ 6109	Give Me Wings Like an Angel/(B-side unknown)	1945	5.00	10.00	20.00
❑ 46017	Texas Tornado/Blue Blue Eyes	1946	5.00	10.00	20.00
STERLING					
❑ 213	Cool Water/Saddle Pals	1947	5.00	10.00	20.00
❑ 214	I've Got Nuggets in My Pockets/If You Can't Go Right	1947	5.00	10.00	20.00
Albums					
CAPITOL					
❑ H 4008 [10]	Songs of the West	195?	30.00	60.00	120.00
❑ H-9004 [10]	Christmas on the Range	1950	37.50	75.00	150.00
DECCA					
❑ DL 8409 [M]	Santa Fe Trail	1956	20.00	40.00	80.00
❑ DL 8680 [M]	Enter and Rest and Pray	1957	15.00	30.00	60.00
❑ DL 75077	Heartaches	1969	3.75	7.50	15.00
❑ DL 75192	Now and Then	1970	3.75	7.50	15.00
DOT					
❑ DLP-3711 [M]	Slippin' Around	1966	5.00	10.00	20.00
❑ DLP-3754 [M]	Christmas with Jimmy Wakely	1966	5.00	10.00	20.00
❑ DLP-25711 [S]	Slippin' Around	1966	6.25	12.50	25.00
❑ DLP-25734 [S]	Christmas with Jimmy Wakely	1966	6.25	12.50	25.00
MCA CORAL					
❑ 20033	Blue Shadows	1973	2.50	5.00	10.00
MCR					
❑ 1250	Jimmy Wakely Sings a Tribute to Bob Wills	1974	3.75	7.50	15.00
❑ 1254	Jimmy Wakely Revisits Country Western Swing with the Big Band Sound	1974	3.75	7.50	15.00
SHASTA					
❑ 501	Country Million Sellers	195?	3.75	7.50	15.00
❑ 502	Merry Christmas	1959	3.75	7.50	15.00
❑ 505	Jimmy Wakely Sings	196?	3.75	7.50	15.00
❑ 512	The Jimmy Wakely Family Show	196?	3.75	7.50	15.00
❑ 528	J.W. Country	196?	3.75	7.50	15.00
TOPS					
❑ L-1601 [M]	A Cowboy Serenade	195?	6.25	12.50	25.00
VOCALION					
❑ VL 73857	Here's Jimmy Wakely	1968	3.00	6.00	12.00
❑ VL 73904	Big Country Songs	1970	3.00	6.00	12.00

WALKER, BILLY

45s

Number	Title (A Side/B Side)	Yr	VG	VG+	NM
CAPITOL					
❑ F941	Dirt 'Neath Your Feet/Too Many Times	1950	7.50	15.00	30.00
❑ F1097	Alcohol Love/The Last Kiss Is the Sweetest	1950	7.50	15.00	30.00
❑ 54-40244	Don't Be Afraid to Call Me Darlin'/Headed for Heartaches	1949	12.50	25.00	50.00
❑ F40277	I'm Gonna Take My Heart Away from You/You Didn't Try and Didn't Care	1950	10.00	20.00	40.00
CAPRICE					
❑ 2056	Lawyers/Why (Don't Ask Me Why)	1979	—	2.50	5.00
❑ 2057	Sweet Lovin' Things/Rainbow and Roses	1979	—	2.50	5.00
❑ 2059	A Little Bit Short on Love (A Little Bit Long on Tears)/I'm Gonna Leave You Tomorrow	1979	—	2.50	5.00
❑ 2060	You Turn My Love Light On/Love Is Free	1980	—	2.50	5.00
CASINO					
❑ 124	(If You Can) Why Can't I/The Magic Touch	1977	—	2.50	5.00
COLUMBIA					
❑ 4-20798	Beautiful Brown Eyes/I Ain't Got No Roses	1951	6.25	12.50	25.00
❑ 4-20847	Ting-a-Ling/Fifteen Hugs Past Midnight	1951	6.25	12.50	25.00
❑ 4-20874	Don't Tell a Soul/Millie My Darling	1952	6.25	12.50	25.00
❑ 4-20914	Anything Your Heart Desires/What Made Me Love You	1952	6.25	12.50	25.00
❑ 4-20994	If I Should Live That Long/One Heart's Beatin', One Heart's Cheatin'	1952	6.25	12.50	25.00
❑ 4-21003	Back Street Affair/You Can Talk Me Out of Anything	1952	6.25	12.50	25.00
❑ 4-21037	I Had a Dream/The One You Hurt	1952	6.25	12.50	25.00
❑ 4-21085	Mexican Joe/You Have My Heart Now	1953	5.00	10.00	20.00
❑ 4-21122	Time Will Tell/I Didn't Have the Nerve	1953	5.00	10.00	20.00
❑ 4-21154	I'm Looking for Love/Don't Let Your Pride Break Your Heart	1953	5.00	10.00	20.00
❑ 4-21191	I Got Lost Along the Way/I Can't Keep Girls Away	1953	5.00	10.00	20.00
❑ 4-21256	Thank You for Calling/Pretend You Don't Know Me	1954	5.00	10.00	20.00
❑ 4-21290	Going, Going, Gone/I'm a Fool to Care	1954	5.00	10.00	20.00
❑ 4-21326	Kissing You/You're the Only Good Thing	1954	5.00	10.00	20.00
❑ 4-21348	Let Me Hear from You/Hey!	1955	5.00	10.00	20.00
❑ 4-21392	Which One of Us Is to Blame/Let's Make Memories Tonight	1955	5.00	10.00	20.00
❑ 4-21439	Fool That I Am/The Record	1955	5.00	10.00	20.00
❑ 4-21471	Blue Mountain Waltz/Why Does It Have to Be	1955	5.00	10.00	20.00
❑ 4-21499	Whirlpool/Go Ahead and Make Me Cry	1956	5.00	10.00	20.00

Number	Title (A Side/B Side)	Yr	VG	VG+	NM
❑ 4-21531	I've Got Leavin' on My Mind/I'll Never Stand in Your Way	1956	5.00	10.00	20.00
❑ 4-21566	Little Baggy Britches/So Far	1956	5.00	10.00	20.00
❑ S7-31185 [S]	titles unknown	1961	3.75	7.50	15.00
❑ S7-31186 [S]	titles unknown	1961	3.75	7.50	15.00
❑ S7-31187 [S]	titles unknown	1961	3.75	7.50	15.00
❑ S7-31188 [S]	titles unknown	1961	3.75	7.50	15.00
❑ S7-31189 [S]	titles unknown	1961	3.75	7.50	15.00

—The above five are "Stereo Seven" 33 1/3 rpm jukebox issues with small holes

Number	Title (A Side/B Side)	Yr	VG	VG+	NM
❑ 4-40846	Especially for Fools/If You're Happy	1957	3.75	7.50	15.00
❑ 4-40920	On My Mind Again/Viva La Matador!	1957	3.75	7.50	15.00
❑ 4-41008	Anything Your Heart Desires/The Image of Me	1957	3.75	7.50	15.00
❑ 4-41099	Put Your Hand in Mine/I Need It	1958	3.75	7.50	15.00
❑ 4-41154	It'll Take Awhile/Where My Baby Goes	1958	3.75	7.50	15.00
❑ 4-41226	Ghost of a Promise/It's Doggone Tough on Me	1958	3.75	7.50	15.00
❑ 4-41319	Mr. Heartache/I Thought About You	1959	3.75	7.50	15.00
❑ 4-41433	A Woman Like You/The Storm Within My Heart	1959	3.75	7.50	15.00
❑ 4-41519	I Call It Heaven/One Way Give and Take	1959	3.75	7.50	15.00
❑ 4-41548	Forever/Changed My Mind	1960	3.00	6.00	12.00
❑ 4-41658	I'll Be True to You/Little Lover	1960	3.00	6.00	12.00
❑ 4-41763	I Wish You Love/Gotta Find a Way	1960	3.00	6.00	12.00
❑ 4-41872	Faded Lights and Lonesome People/Yes, I've Made It	1961	3.00	6.00	12.00
❑ 4-42050	Funny How Time Slips Away/Joey's Back in Town	1961	3.00	6.00	12.00
❑ 4-42287	Charlie's Shoes/Wild Colonial Boy	1962	3.00	6.00	12.00
❑ 4-42492	Willie the Weeper/Beggin' for Trouble	1962	3.00	6.00	12.00
❑ 4-42664	I've Got a New Heartache/Thank You for Calling	1963	2.50	5.00	10.00
❑ 4-42794	Heart, Be Careful/Storm of Love	1963	2.50	5.00	10.00
❑ 4-42794 [PS]	Heart, Be Careful/Storm of Love	1963	6.25	12.50	25.00
❑ 4-42891	The Morning Paper/Coming Back for More	1963	2.50	5.00	10.00
❑ 4-43010	Circumstances/It's Lonesome	1964	2.50	5.00	10.00
❑ 4-43120	Cross the Brazos at Waco/Down to My Last Cigarette	1964	2.50	5.00	10.00
❑ 4-43120 [PS]	Cross the Brazos at Waco/Down to My Last Cigarette	1964	10.00	20.00	40.00

—Sleeve is promo only

Number	Title (A Side/B Side)	Yr	VG	VG+	NM
❑ 4-43223	Matamoros/I'm Nothing to You	1965	2.00	4.00	8.00
❑ 4-43327	If It Pleases You/I'm So Miserable Without You	1965	2.00	4.00	8.00
❑ 4-43434	Come a Little Bit Closer/Nobody But a Fool	1965	2.00	4.00	8.00

DIMENSION

Number	Title (A Side/B Side)	Yr	VG	VG+	NM
❑ 1042	One Away from One Too Many/Looking Through the Eyes of Love (Will Make You Blind)	1983	—	2.50	5.00

MGM

Number	Title (A Side/B Side)	Yr	VG	VG+	NM
❑ 14134	When a Man Loves a Woman (The Way That I Love You)/She's As Close As I Can Get (To Loving You)	1970	—	3.00	6.00
❑ 14173	She Goes Walking Through My Mind/It's Your Fault I'm Cheating	1970	—	3.00	6.00
❑ 14210	I'm Gonna Keep On Lovin' You/It's a Long Way Down from Riches to Rags	1970	—	3.00	6.00
❑ 14239	It's Time to Love Her/She's Feeling Like a New Man Tonight	1971	—	3.00	6.00
❑ 14268	Don't Let Him Make a Memory Out of Me/A Fool and His Love	1971	—	3.00	6.00
❑ 14305	Traces of a Woman/You Gave Me a Mountain	1971	—	3.00	6.00
❑ 14377	Gone (Our Endless Love)/All I Have to Offer You Is Me	1972	—	3.00	6.00
❑ 14422	Sing Me a Love Song to Baby/The Day I Was Out and He Was In	1972	—	3.00	6.00
❑ 14488	My Mind Hangs On to You/Charlie's Shoes	1973	—	3.00	6.00
❑ 14565	The Hand of Love/Ranada	1973	—	3.00	6.00
❑ 14655	Margarita/I'll Still Be There	1973	2.00	4.00	8.00
❑ 14669	Too Many Memories/Margarita	1973	—	3.00	6.00
❑ 14693	I Changed My Mind/Heart Be Careful	1974	—	3.00	6.00
❑ 14717	How Far Our Love Goes/Love Me Back to Heaven (One More Time)	1974	—	3.00	6.00
❑ 14742	Fine As Wine/The Honky Tonks Are Calling Me Again	1974	—	3.00	6.00

MONUMENT

Number	Title (A Side/B Side)	Yr	VG	VG+	NM
❑ 932	The Old French Quarter (In New Orleans)/How Do You Ask?	1966	2.00	4.00	8.00
❑ 932 [PS]	The Old French Quarter (In New Orleans)/How Do You Ask?	1966	5.00	10.00	20.00
❑ 943	A Million and One/Close to Linda	1966	2.00	4.00	8.00
❑ 980	Bear With Me a Little Longer/It's Beginning to Hurt	1966	2.00	4.00	8.00
❑ 997	Anything Your Heart Desires/I Gotta Get Me Feelin' Better	1967	2.00	4.00	8.00
❑ 1013	In Del Rio/Wish I Could Love That Much Again	1967	2.00	4.00	8.00
❑ 1024	I Taught Her Everything She Knows/I Treat Her Like a Baby	1967	2.00	4.00	8.00
❑ 1055	Sundown Mary/Oh, Matilda	1968	—	3.50	7.00
❑ 1079	Ramona/One Inch Off the Ground	1968	—	3.50	7.00
❑ 1098	Age of Worry/Is This Desire	1968	—	3.50	7.00
❑ 1123	From the Bottle to the Bottom/She	1969	—	3.50	7.00
❑ 1140	Smoky Places/Elusive Butterfly	1969	—	3.50	7.00
❑ 1154	Better Homes and Gardens/If You See My Baby	1969	—	3.50	7.00
❑ 1174	Thinking 'Bout You, Babe/Invisible Tears	1969	—	3.50	7.00
❑ 1189	Darling Days/Pretend You Don't See Me	1970	—	3.50	7.00
❑ 1204	What Eva Doesn't Have/Curtains on the Windows	1970	—	3.50	7.00

MRC

Number	Title (A Side/B Side)	Yr	VG	VG+	NM
❑ 1003	It Always Brings Me Back Around to You/(B-side unknown)	1977	—	2.50	5.00
❑ 1005	Ringgold Georgia/Have I Told You Lately That I Love You	1977	—	2.50	5.00

—With Brenda Kaye Perry

Number	Title (A Side/B Side)	Yr	VG	VG+	NM
❑ 1009	Carlena and Jose Gomez/Every Cheatin' Thing She Knows	1977	—	2.50	5.00
❑ 1014	It's Not Over Till It's Over/Don't Let the Morning Sun Shine Shame on You	1978	—	2.50	5.00

RCA

Number	Title (A Side/B Side)	Yr	VG	VG+	NM
❑ PB-10821	Instead of Givin' Up (I'm Givin' In)/Curtains on the Windows	1976	—	2.50	5.00

RCA VICTOR

Number	Title (A Side/B Side)	Yr	VG	VG+	NM
❑ PB-10205	Word Games/I Can't Say No If She Keeps Saying Yes	1975	—	2.50	5.00
❑ PB-10345	If I'm Losing You/I'd Love to Feel You Loving Me Again	1975	—	2.50	5.00
❑ PB-10466	Don't Stop in My World (If You Don't Mean to Stay)/Honky Tonkitis	1975	—	2.50	5.00
❑ PB-10613	(Here I Am) Alone Again/When the Song Is Gone (The Music Dies)	1976	—	2.50	5.00
❑ PB-10729	Love You All to Pieces/Sierra Nevada	1976	—	2.50	5.00

SCORPION

Number	Title (A Side/B Side)	Yr	VG	VG+	NM
❑ 0552	You're a Violin That Never Has Been Played/Broken Pieces of Love	1978	—	2.50	5.00

TALL TEXAN

Number	Title (A Side/B Side)	Yr	VG	VG+	NM
❑ 52	Beautiful Texas/Your Ever Leavin' Lovin'	1984	—	3.00	6.00
❑ 55	Soap and Water/Someone Loves You	1985	—	3.00	6.00
❑ 56	He Sang the Song About El Paso/Welcome Back to My Heart	1985	—	3.00	6.00
❑ 57	Coffee Brown Eyes/Jesse	1985	—	3.00	6.00
❑ 58	Welcome Back to My Heart/(B-side unknown)	1986	—	3.00	6.00
❑ 59	One Day at a Time/And Now Mama	198?	—	3.00	6.00
❑ 60	Wild Texas Rose/Sweet Spanish Melodies	1988	—	3.00	6.00
❑ 62	Heartache in High Heel Shoes/I Can't Smile Without You	198?	—	3.00	6.00

Albums

COLUMBIA

Number	Title	Yr	VG	VG+	NM
❑ CL 1624 [M]	Everybody's Hits But Mine	1961	5.00	10.00	20.00
❑ CL 1935 [M]	Billy Walker's Greatest Hits	1963	3.75	7.50	15.00
❑ CL 2206 [M]	Thank You for Calling	1964	3.75	7.50	15.00
❑ CL 2331 [M]	The Gun, the Gold and the Girl/Cross the Brazos at Waco	1965	3.75	7.50	15.00
❑ CS 8424 [S]	Everybody's Hits But Mine	1961	7.50	15.00	30.00
❑ CS 8735 [S]	Billy Walker's Greatest Hits	1963	5.00	10.00	20.00
❑ CS 9006 [S]	Thank You for Calling	1964	5.00	10.00	20.00
❑ CS 9131 [S]	The Gun, the Gold and the Girl/Cross the Brazos at Waco	1965	5.00	10.00	20.00
❑ CS 9798	Billy Walker's Greatest Hits, Volume 2	1969	3.75	7.50	15.00
❑ C 30226	Goodnight	1971	3.00	6.00	12.00

HARMONY

Number	Title	Yr	VG	VG+	NM
❑ HL 7306 [M]	Anything Your Heart Desires	1964	3.75	7.50	15.00
❑ HL 7410 [M]	Big Country Hits	1967	3.75	7.50	15.00
❑ HS 11210 [S]	Big Country Hits	1967	3.00	6.00	12.00
❑ HS 11414	Charlie's Shoes	1970	3.00	6.00	12.00
❑ H 31177	There May Be No Tomorrow	1972	2.50	5.00	10.00

MGM

Number	Title	Yr	VG	VG+	NM
❑ SE-4682	When a Man Loves a Woman (The Way That I Love You)	1970	3.75	7.50	15.00
❑ SE-4756	I'm Gonna Keep On Lovin' You/She Goes Walking Through My Mind	1971	3.75	7.50	15.00
❑ SE-4789	Live!	1972	3.75	7.50	15.00
❑ SE-4863	The Billy Walker Show	1973	3.00	6.00	12.00
❑ SE-4887	All-Time Greatest Hits	1972	3.00	6.00	12.00
❑ SE-4938	Too Many Memories	1974	3.00	6.00	12.00

MONUMENT

Number	Title	Yr	VG	VG+	NM
❑ 6641	Greatest Hits	1976	2.50	5.00	10.00
❑ MLP-8047 [M]	A Million and One	1966	3.00	6.00	12.00
❑ MLP-8072 [M]	The Walker Way	1967	5.00	10.00	20.00
❑ SLP-18047 [S]	A Million and One	1966	3.75	7.50	15.00
❑ SLP-18072 [S]	The Walker Way	1967	3.75	7.50	15.00
❑ SLP-18090	I Taught Her Everything She Knows	1968	3.75	7.50	15.00
❑ SLP-18101	Billy Walker Salutes the Country Music Hall of Fame	1969	3.75	7.50	15.00
❑ SLP-18116	Portrait of Billy	1969	3.75	7.50	15.00
❑ SLP-18143	Darling Days	1970	3.75	7.50	15.00
❑ KZ 31912	Greatest Hits	1972	3.00	6.00	12.00

RCA VICTOR

Number	Title	Yr	VG	VG+	NM
❑ APL1-1160	Lovin' and Losin'	1975	3.00	6.00	12.00
❑ APL1-1489	Alone Again	1976	3.00	6.00	12.00

WALKER, BILLY, AND BARBARA FAIRCHILD

Also see each artist's individual listings.

45s

PAID

Number	Title (A Side/B Side)	Yr	VG	VG+	NM
❑ 102	Let Me Be the One/If We Take Our Time	1980	—	2.50	5.00
❑ 107	Bye Bye Love/Love's Slipping Through Our Fingers (Leaving Time on Our Hands)	1980	—	2.50	5.00
❑ 143	The Answer Game/Deep Purple	1981	—	2.50	5.00

WALKER, CHARLIE

45s

CAPITOL

Number	Title (A Side/B Side)	Yr	VG	VG+	NM
❑ 3922	Odds and Ends (Bits and Pieces)/Society's Got Us	1974	—	2.50	5.00
❑ 4040	Say You're Gone/The Last Supper	1975	—	2.50	5.00

COLUMBIA

Number	Title (A Side/B Side)	Yr	VG	VG+	NM
❑ 4-41211	Pick Me Up on Your Way Down/Two Empty Arms	1958	3.75	7.50	15.00
❑ 4-41388	I'll Catch You When You Fall/I Don't Mind Saying	1959	3.00	6.00	12.00

Number	Title (A Side/B Side)	Yr	VG	VG+	NM
❑ 4-41467	When My Conscience Hurts the Most/Bow Down Your Head and Cry	1959	3.00	6.00	12.00
❑ 4-41633	Who Will Buy the Wine/I Go Anywhere	1960	3.00	6.00	12.00
❑ 4-41820	Facing the Wall/I Walked Out on Heaven (When I Walked Out on You)	1961	3.00	6.00	12.00
❑ 4-42000	Right Back at Your Door/A Way to Free Myself	1961	3.00	6.00	12.00
❑ 4-42176	Good Deal, Lucille/Louisiana Bell	1961	3.00	6.00	12.00
❑ 4-42454	Life Goes On/Only Meant to Borrow	1962	3.00	6.00	12.00
❑ 4-42669	What's Wrong with Me/One in Every Crowd	1963	3.00	6.00	12.00
❑ 4-42860	Running Back to You/That's Where Katy Waits	1963	3.00	6.00	12.00
DECCA					
❑ 9-29715	Only You, Only You/Can't Get There from Here	1955	5.00	10.00	20.00
❑ 9-29908	Remembering/Stand Still	1956	5.00	10.00	20.00
EPIC					
❑ 5-9727	Close All the Honky Tonks/Truck Driving Man	1964	2.50	5.00	10.00
❑ 5-9759	Honky Tonk Song/Pick Me Up on Your Way Down	1965	2.50	5.00	10.00
❑ 5-9799	Wild as a Wildcat/Out of a Honky Tonk	1965	2.50	5.00	10.00
❑ 5-9852	He's a Jolly Good Fellow/Memory Killer	1965	2.50	5.00	10.00
❑ 5-9875	The Man in the Little White Suit/Fraulein	1966	2.50	5.00	10.00
❑ 5-10021	I'm Gonna Live (As Long As I Can)/Little Old Wine Drinker, Me	1966	2.00	4.00	8.00
❑ 5-10063	Daddy's Coming Home (Next Week)/I'm Gonna Hang Up My Gloves	1966	2.00	4.00	8.00
❑ 5-10118	The Town That Never Sleeps/The Way to Say Goodbye	1967	2.00	4.00	8.00
❑ 5-10174	Don't Squeeze My Sharmon/You Lied to Me	1967	—	3.50	7.00
❑ 5-10237	I Wouldn't Take Her to a Dogfight/Tonight, We're Calling It a Day	1967	—	3.50	7.00
❑ 5-10295	Truck Drivin' Cat with Nine Wives/Sweetheart of the Year	1968	—	3.50	7.00
❑ 5-10349	San Diego/When My Conscience Hurts the Most	1968	—	3.50	7.00
❑ 5-10426	Honky-Tonk Season/Too Many Nights in Too Many Arms	1969	—	3.50	7.00
❑ 5-10499	Moffett, Oklahoma/You're from Texas	1969	—	3.50	7.00
❑ 5-10565	Honky Tonk Women/Rosie Bokay	1970	—	3.50	7.00
❑ 5-10610	Let's Go Fishin' Boys (The Girls Are Bitin')/You're All Dressed Up	1970	—	3.50	7.00
❑ 5-10665	Becky Who/God Save the Queen (Of the Honky Tonks)	1970	—	3.50	7.00
❑ 5-10722	My Baby Used to Be That Way/Before I Found the Wine	1971	—	3.50	7.00
❑ 5-10799	Got My Mind on the Border of Mexico/Wild Women	1971	—	3.50	7.00
MERCURY					
❑ 71081	Gentle Love/Dancing Mexican Boy	1957	5.00	10.00	20.00
❑ 71111	I'll Never Let It Show/Take My Hand	1957	5.00	10.00	20.00
PLANTATION					
❑ 165	I've Had a Beautiful Time/Truck Driving Man	1977	—	2.50	5.00
❑ 168	T for Texas/Pick Me Up on Your Way Down	1978	—	2.50	5.00
❑ 172	Red Skies Over Georgia/My Shoes Keep Walking Back to You	1978	—	2.50	5.00
❑ 181	Tonight My Solitaire Turns Into Gin/My Shoes Keep Walking Back to You	1979	—	2.50	5.00
❑ 185	Don't Sing a Song About Texas/Please Mr. Please	1979	—	2.50	5.00
RCA VICTOR					
❑ 74-0730	I Don't Mind Goin' Under (If It'll Get Me Over You)/Honky Tonk Heart	1972	—	3.00	6.00
❑ 74-0870	Soft Lips and Hard Liquor/It's Better Than Going Home Alone	1973	—	3.00	6.00
❑ 74-0929	Gonna Drink Milwaukee Dry/Time Changes Everything	1973	—	3.00	6.00
Albums					
COLUMBIA					
❑ CL 1691 [M]	Charlie Walker's Greatest Hits	1961	5.00	10.00	20.00
❑ CS 8491 [S]	Charlie Walker's Greatest Hits	1961	7.50	15.00	30.00
EPIC					
❑ LN 24137 [M]	Close All the Honky Tonks	1965	3.75	7.50	15.00
❑ LN 24153 [M]	Born to Lose	1965	3.75	7.50	15.00
❑ LN 24209 [M]	Wine, Women and Walker	1966	3.75	7.50	15.00
❑ LN 24328 [M]	Don't Squeeze My Sharmon	1967	6.25	12.50	25.00
❑ BN 26137 [S]	Close All the Honky Tonks	1965	5.00	10.00	20.00
❑ BN 26153 [S]	Born to Lose	1965	5.00	10.00	20.00
❑ BN 26209 [S]	Wine, Women and Walker	1966	5.00	10.00	20.00
❑ BN 26328 [S]	Don't Squeeze My Sharmon	1967	5.00	10.00	20.00
❑ BN 26343	Greatest Hits	1968	3.75	7.50	15.00
❑ BN 26483	Recorded Live in Dallas	1969	3.75	7.50	15.00
❑ E 30660	Honky Tonkin'	1971	3.75	7.50	15.00
HARMONY					
❑ HL 7415 [M]	Golden Hits	1967	3.75	7.50	15.00
❑ HS 11215 [S]	Golden Hits	1967	3.00	6.00	12.00
PLANTATION					
❑ 535	Golden Hits	1978	2.50	5.00	10.00
RCA VICTOR					
❑ APL1-0181	Break Out the Bottle	1973	3.00	6.00	12.00
❑ LSP-4737	Charlie Walker	1972	3.75	7.50	15.00
VOCALION					
❑ VL 73814	The Style of Charlie Walker	1968	3.00	6.00	12.00

WALKER, CINDY

Selected 78s

Number	Title (A Side/B Side)	Yr	VG	VG+	NM
DECCA					
❑ 5992	Waltz Me Around Again/Don't Talk to ...	1942	3.75	7.50	15.00
❑ 6081	It Never Can Be/It's All Your Fault	1943	3.75	7.50	15.00
❑ 6103	When My Blue Moon Turns to Gold Again/Pins and Needles (In My Heart)	1944	3.75	7.50	15.00
❑ 46089	Blue Kimono Blues/Oh Darlin'	1948	3.75	7.50	15.00
Albums					
MONUMENT					
❑ MLP-8020 [M]	Words and Music by Cindy Walker	1964	5.00	10.00	20.00
❑ SLP-18020 [S]	Words and Music by Cindy Walker	1964	6.25	12.50	25.00

WALKER, CLAY

45s

Number	Title (A Side/B Side)	Yr	VG	VG+	NM
GIANT					
❑ 7-17158	You're Beginning to Get to Me/Lose Your Memory	1998	—	—	3.00
❑ 7-17210	Ordinary People/Next Step in Love	1998	—	—	3.00
❑ 7-17262	Then What?/Country Boy and City Girl	1998	—	—	3.00
❑ 7-17351	One, Two, I Love You/Country Boy and City Girl	1997	—	—	3.00
❑ 7-17704	Hypnotize the Moon/A Cowboy's Toughest Ride	1996	—	2.00	4.00
❑ 7-17771	Who Needs You Baby/Where Were You	1995	—	2.00	4.00
❑ 7-17887	My Heart Will Never Know/Money Ain't Everything	1995	—	—	3.00
❑ 7-17995	This Woman and This Man/Lose Your Memory	1995	—	2.00	4.00
❑ 7-18068	If I Could Make a Living/Down by the Riverside	1994	—	2.00	4.00
❑ 7-18139	Dreaming with My Eyes Open/Money Can't Buy (The Love We Had)	1994	—	2.00	4.00
❑ 7-18210	Where Do I Fit in the Picture/Money Can't Buy (The Love We Had)	1994	—	—	3.00
❑ 7-18332	Live Until I Die/The Silence Speaks for Itself	1993	—	2.00	4.00
❑ 7-18450	What's It To You/Where Do I Fit in the Picture	1993	—	2.00	4.00

WALKER, JERRY JEFF

45s

Number	Title (A Side/B Side)	Yr	VG	VG+	NM
ATCO					
❑ 6594	Mr. Bojangles/Round and Round	1968	2.50	5.00	10.00
❑ 6767	I'm Gonna Tell on You/But For the Time	1970	—	3.00	6.00
ELEKTRA					
❑ 46016	Comfort and Crazy/Eastern Ave. River Railway Blues	1979	—	2.00	4.00
MCA					
❑ 40054	L.A. Freeway/Charlie Dunn	1973	—	2.00	4.00
❑ 40167	Desperadoes Waitin' for a Train/Gettin' By	1973	—	2.00	4.00
❑ 40250	Sangria Wine/Hill Country Rain	1974	—	2.00	4.00
❑ 40389	Goodbye Easy Street/Salvation Army Band	1975	—	2.00	4.00
❑ 40487	Jaded Lover/I Love You	1975	—	2.00	4.00
❑ 40570	Dear John Letter Lounge/It's a Good Night for Singing	1976	—	2.00	4.00
❑ 40622	(Looking for the) Heart of Saturday Night/Stoney	1976	—	2.00	4.00
❑ 40760	Mr. Bojangles/Don't It Make You Wanna Dance	1977	—	2.00	4.00
❑ 40822	Ro-Deo-Deo Cowboy/Leavin' Texas	1977	—	2.00	4.00
SOUTH COAST					
❑ 51146	Got Lucky Last Night/Maybe Mexico	1981	—	2.00	4.00
❑ 51215	Take It As It Comes/She Knows Her Daddy Sings	1981	—	2.00	4.00
❑ 52122	Don't Think Twice, It's Alright/Laying My Life on the Line	1982	—	2.00	4.00
TRIED & TRUE					
❑ 1690	I Feel Like Hank Williams Tonight/Mr. Bojangles	1989	—	2.50	5.00
❑ 1695	The Pickup Truck Song/The Pickup Truck Song (Long Version)	1989	—	2.50	5.00
❑ 1698	Trashy Women/I Feel Like Hank Williams Tonight	1989	—	2.50	5.00
Albums					
ATCO					
❑ SD 33-259	Mr. Bojangles	1968	6.25	12.50	25.00
❑ SD 33-297	Five Years Gone	1969	7.50	15.00	30.00
❑ SD 33-336	Bein' Free	1970	5.00	10.00	20.00
BAINBRIDGE					
❑ 6222	Mr. Bojangles	198?	2.50	5.00	10.00
DECCA					
❑ DL 75384	Jerry Jeff Walker	1972	3.75	7.50	15.00
ELEKTRA					
❑ 6E-163	Jerry Jeff	1978	2.50	5.00	10.00
❑ 6E-239	Too Old to Change	1980	2.50	5.00	10.00
MCA					
❑ 382	Viva Terlingua!	1973	2.50	5.00	10.00
❑ 450	Walker's Collectibles	1974	2.50	5.00	10.00
❑ 510	Jerry Jeff Walker	1975	2.50	5.00	10.00
—Reissue of Decca LP					
❑ 2156	Ridin' High	1975	2.50	5.00	10.00
❑ 2202	It's a Good Night for Singin'	1976	2.50	5.00	10.00
❑ 2350	Viva Terlingua!	1977	2.00	4.00	8.00
—Reissue of MCA 382					
❑ 2355	Walker's Collectibles	1977	2.00	4.00	8.00
—Reissue of MCA 450					
❑ 2358	Jerry Jeff Walker	1977	2.00	4.00	8.00
—Reissue of MCA 510					
❑ 3041	Contrary to Ordinary	1978	2.50	5.00	10.00
❑ 5128	The Best of Jerry Jeff Walker	1980	2.50	5.00	10.00
❑ 5355	Cowjazz	1983	2.50	5.00	10.00
❑ 6003 [(2)]	A Man Must Carry On	198?	2.50	5.00	10.00
—Budget-line reissue					
❑ 8013 [(2)]	A Man Must Carry On	1977	3.00	6.00	12.00
❑ 27026	It's a Good Night for Singin'	198?	2.00	4.00	8.00
—Budget-line reissue					
❑ 27027	Walker's Collectibles	198?	—	3.00	6.00
—Budget-line reissue					
❑ 37004	Jerry Jeff Walker	198?	—	3.00	6.00
—Budget-line reissue					

Number	Title (A Side/B Side)	Yr	VG	VG+	NM
❑ 37005	Viva Terlingua!	198?	—	3.00	6.00
—Budget-line reissue					
❑ 37006	Ridin' High	198?	2.00	4.00	8.00
—Budget-line reissue					
❑ 37162	Contrary to Ordinary	198?	2.00	4.00	8.00
—Budget-line reissue					
SOUTHCOAST					
❑ 5199	Reunion	1981	2.50	5.00	10.00
VANGUARD					
❑ VSD-6521	Driftin' Way of Life	1969	5.00	10.00	20.00
❑ VMS-73124	Driftin' Way of Life	1985	2.00	4.00	8.00
—Reissue of 6521					

WALKER, KATHY

See TIM BLIXSETH; T.L. LEE.

WALKER, WILEY

Also see WILEY AND GENE.

Selected 78s

Number	Title (A Side/B Side)	Yr	VG	VG+	NM
COLUMBIA					
❑ 20130	I Might Have Known/I Want to Live and Love	1948	3.00	6.00	12.00
—Reissue of 37403					
❑ 20146	So Lonely/I Just Don't Want to Be Happy	1948	3.00	6.00	12.00
—Reissue of 37419					
❑ 37403	I Might Have Known/I Want to Live and Love	1947	3.75	7.50	15.00
❑ 37419	So Lonely/I Just Don't Want to Be Happy	1946	3.75	7.50	15.00
—Reissue					
OKEH					
❑ (# unknown)	So Lonely/I Just Don't Want to Be Happy	194?	5.00	10.00	20.00
❑ (# unknown)	I Might Have Known/I Want to Live and Love	194?	5.00	10.00	20.00

WALLACE, JERRY

45s

Number	Title (A Side/B Side)	Yr	VG	VG+	NM
4 STAR					
❑ 1035	I Wanna Go to Heaven/After You	1978	—	2.50	5.00
❑ 1036	Yours Love/There She Goes	1979	—	2.50	5.00
ALLIED					
❑ 5015	Little Miss One/Petrillo	1954	12.50	25.00	50.00
—B-side by Eddie Oliver and the Oliver Twisters					
❑ 5019	That's What a Woman Can Do/I Hate to Go Home Alone	1954	10.00	20.00	40.00
❑ 5023	Runnin' After Love/Dixie Anna	1954	10.00	20.00	40.00
BMA					
❑ 7-002	I Miss You Already/At the End of a Rainbow	1977	—	2.50	5.00
❑ 7-005	I'll Promise You Tomorrow/You're on the Run	1977	—	2.50	5.00
❑ 8-006	At the End of a Rainbow/Looking for a Memory	1978	—	2.50	5.00
❑ 8-008	My Last Sad Song/Wickenburg Way	1978	—	2.50	5.00
CHALLENGE					
❑ 1003	Blue Jean Baby/Fool's Hall of Fame	1957	5.00	10.00	20.00
❑ 9107	Life's a Holiday/I Can See an Angel Walking	1961	3.00	6.00	12.00
❑ 9117	Eyes (Don't Give My Secrets Away)/Lonesome	1961	3.00	6.00	12.00
❑ 9130	Rollin' River/I Hang My Head and Cry	1961	3.00	6.00	12.00
❑ 9139	Little Miss Tease/Mr. Lonely	1962	3.00	6.00	12.00
❑ 9152	Here I Go/You'll Never Know	1962	3.00	6.00	12.00
❑ 9171	Shutters and Boards/Am I That Easy to Forget	1962	3.00	6.00	12.00
❑ 9185	Move Over/On a Merry-Go-Round	1963	3.00	6.00	12.00
❑ 9195	Just Walking in the Rain/San Francisco Mama	1963	3.00	6.00	12.00
❑ 9205	Empty Arms Again/Bambola (My Darling One)	1963	3.00	6.00	12.00
❑ 59000	The Other Me/Good and Bad	1958	5.00	10.00	20.00
❑ 59013	How the Time Flies/With This Ring	1958	5.00	10.00	20.00
❑ 59027	Diamond Ring/All My Love Belongs to You	1958	5.00	10.00	20.00
❑ 59040	A Touch of Pink/Off Stage	1959	3.75	7.50	15.00
❑ 59047	Primrose Lane/By Your Side	1959	4.50	9.00	18.00
❑ 59060	Little Coco Palm/Mission Bell Blues	1959	3.75	7.50	15.00
❑ 59060 [PS]	Little Coco Palm/Mission Bell Blues	1959	10.00	20.00	40.00
❑ 59072	King of the Mountain/You're Singing Our Love Song to Somebody Else	1960	3.75	7.50	15.00
❑ 59082	Swingin' Down the Lane/Teardrops in the Rain	1960	3.75	7.50	15.00
❑ 59098	There She Goes/Angel on My Shoulder	1960	3.75	7.50	15.00
❑ 59223	Auf Wiedesehn/If I Make It Through Today	1963	2.50	5.00	10.00
❑ 59246	In the Misty Moonlight/Even the Bad Times Are Good	1964	2.50	5.00	10.00
❑ 59249	In the Misty Moonlight/Cannon Ball	1964	3.75	7.50	15.00
—B-side by the Soul Surfers					
❑ 59265	Even the Bad Times Are Good/Spanish Guitars	1964	2.50	5.00	10.00
❑ 59278	You're Driving You Out of My Mind/Helpless	1965	2.50	5.00	10.00
CLASS					
❑ 502	Taj Mahal/Autumn Has Come and Gone	1955	6.25	12.50	25.00
DECCA					
❑ 32777	After You/She'll Remember	1971	—	3.50	7.00
❑ 32859	The Morning After/I Can't Take It Anymore	1971	—	3.50	7.00
❑ 32914	To Get to You/Time	1972	—	3.50	7.00
❑ 32989	If You Leave Me Tonight I'll Cry/What's He Doin' in My World	1972	—	3.50	7.00
❑ 33036	Do You Know What It's Like to Be Lonesome/Where Did He Come From	1972	—	3.50	7.00
DOOR KNOB					
❑ 116	You've Still Got Me/Now That Sandy's Gone	1979	—	2.50	5.00
❑ 127	Cling to Me/Paper Madonna	1980	—	2.50	5.00
❑ 134	If I Could Set My Love to Music/Cling to Me	1980	—	2.50	5.00
GLENOLDEN					
❑ 159	Are You Ready/That's the Fool in Me	1968	—	3.00	6.00
LIBERTY					
❑ 55957	Runaway Bay/Dispossessed	1967	2.00	4.00	8.00
❑ 56001	This One's on the House/A New Sun Risin'	1967	2.00	4.00	8.00
❑ 56027	The Closest I Ever Came/That's What Fools Are For	1968	—	—	—
—Unreleased					
❑ 56028	Another Time, Another Place, Another World/That's What Fools Are For	1968	—	3.00	6.00
❑ 56059	Sweet Child of Sunshine/Our House on Paper	1968	—	3.00	6.00
❑ 56095	Temptation/Son	1969	—	3.00	6.00
❑ 56105	Venus/Soon We'll Be There	1969	—	3.00	6.00
❑ 56130	Swiss Cottage Place/With Aging	1969	—	3.00	6.00
❑ 56147	Honey Eyed Girl/Glory of My Girl	1969	—	3.00	6.00
❑ 56155	Even the Bad Times Are Good/For All We Know	1970	—	3.00	6.00
MCA					
❑ 40037	A Song Nobody Sings/Sound of Goodbye	1973	—	2.50	5.00
❑ 40111	Don't Give Up on Me/You Look Like Forever	1973	—	2.50	5.00
❑ 40183	Guess Who/All I Ever Want from You	1974	—	2.50	5.00
❑ 40248	My Wife's House/A Better Way to Say I Love You	1974	—	2.50	5.00
❑ 40321	Make Hay While the Sun Shines/I Wonder Whose Baby	1974	—	2.50	5.00
MERCURY					
❑ 70684	Taj Mahal/Autumn Has Come and Gone	1955	5.00	10.00	20.00
❑ 70758	The Greatest Magic of All/Walking in the Rain	1955	5.00	10.00	20.00
❑ 70812	One Night When Flowers Were Dancing/Gloria	1956	5.00	10.00	20.00
❑ 72246	In the Misty Moonlight/Even the Bad Times Are Good	1964	3.00	6.00	12.00
❑ 72258	Butterfly/Let the Tears Begin	1964	2.50	5.00	10.00
❑ 72292	It's a Cotton Candy World/Keep a Lamp Burning	1964	2.50	5.00	10.00
❑ 72356	Careless Hands/San Francisco d'Assisi	1964	2.50	5.00	10.00
❑ 72406	Rainbow/Time	1965	2.50	5.00	10.00
❑ 72461	Life's Gone and Slipped Away/Twelve Little Roses	1965	2.50	5.00	10.00
❑ 72529	Diamonds and Horseshoes/Will the Pain Fade Away	1966	2.50	5.00	10.00
❑ 72589	Wallpaper Roses/Son of a Green Beret	1966	2.50	5.00	10.00
❑ 72619	Not That I Care/Release Me	1966	2.50	5.00	10.00
MGM					
❑ 14788	Comin' Home to You/The River St. Marie	1975	—	2.50	5.00
❑ 14809	Wanted Man/Your Love	1975	—	2.50	5.00
❑ 14832	Georgia Rain/In the Garden	1975	—	2.50	5.00
POLYDOR					
❑ 14322	The Fool I've Been Today/Jenny Angel	1976	—	2.00	4.00
TOPS					
❑ 369	P.S. I Love You/Vaya Con Dios (May God Be With You)	1953	10.00	20.00	40.00
—B-side by Betty Ford					
UNITED ARTISTS					
❑ XW239	Take Me As I Am/Touch Me	1973	—	2.50	5.00
❑ XW618	With Pen in Hand/All I Want Is You	1975	—	2.50	5.00
❑ 50971	Funny How Time Slips Away/Thanks to You for Loving Me	1972	—	2.50	5.00
WING					
❑ 90065	Eyes of Fire, Lips of Wine/Monkey See, Monkey Do	1956	5.00	10.00	20.00

Albums

Number	Title	Yr	VG	VG+	NM
CHALLENGE					
❑ CHL 606 [M]	Just Jerry	1959	15.00	30.00	60.00
❑ CHL 612 [M]	There She Goes	1961	7.50	15.00	30.00
❑ CHS 612 [S]	There She Goes	1961	10.00	20.00	40.00
❑ CHL 616 [M]	Shutters and Boards	1962	7.50	15.00	30.00
❑ CHS 616 [S]	Shutters and Boards	1962	10.00	20.00	40.00
❑ CHL 619 [M]	In the Misty Moonlight	1964	5.00	10.00	20.00
❑ CHS 619 [S]	In the Misty Moonlight	1964	6.25	12.50	25.00
❑ 2002	Greatest Hits	1969	3.75	7.50	15.00
DECCA					
❑ DL 75294	This Is Jerry Wallace	1971	3.75	7.50	15.00
❑ DL 75349	To Get to You	1972	3.75	7.50	15.00
LIBERTY					
❑ LST-7545	This One's on the House	1967	5.00	10.00	20.00
❑ LST-7564	Another Time, Another World	1968	5.00	10.00	20.00
❑ LST-7597	Sweet Child of Sunshine	1968	5.00	10.00	20.00
MCA					
❑ 301	Do You Know What It's Like to Be Lonesome?	1973	3.00	6.00	12.00
❑ 366	Primrose Lane/Don't Give Up on Me	1973	3.00	6.00	12.00
❑ 408	For Wives and Lovers	1974	3.00	6.00	12.00
❑ 462	I Wonder Whose Baby (You Are Now)/Make Hay While the Sun Shines	1975	3.00	6.00	12.00
MERCURY					
❑ MG-21072 [M]	The Best of Jerry Wallace	1966	3.75	7.50	15.00
❑ SR-61072 [S]	The Best of Jerry Wallace	1966	5.00	10.00	20.00
MGM					
❑ M3G-4990	Greatest Hits	1975	2.50	5.00	10.00
❑ M3G-4995	Comin' Home to You	1976	3.00	6.00	12.00
❑ M3G-5007	Jerry Wallace	1976	2.50	5.00	10.00
SUNSET					
❑ SUS-5294	Primrose Lane	1969	3.00	6.00	12.00
UNITED ARTISTS					
❑ UXS-95 [(2)]	Jerry Wallace Superpak	1972	5.00	10.00	20.00

WALLACE, RON

45s

Number	Title (A Side/B Side)	Yr	VG	VG+	NM
COLUMBIA					
❑ 38-78021	I'm Listening Now/Don't Get Mad	1995	—	2.00	4.00
❑ 38-78091	Left Hand of God/Heartbreak	1995	—	2.00	4.00

WALSH, DAVID
45s
CHARTA

Number	Title (A Side/B Side)	Yr	VG	VG+	NM
❑ 180	Music Man/Ontario Nice	1983	—	3.00	6.00
❑ 182	Lady Alabama/I'll Drown Overnight in My Tears	1984	—	3.00	6.00
❑ 183	Slip It Off/Country Music Heroes	1984	—	3.00	6.00
❑ 185	Ain't No Way to Say Goodnight/Everybody Relax	1984	—	3.00	6.00
❑ 193	My Special Lady/Did She Tell You Daddy Loves You	1985	—	2.50	5.00
❑ 195	Manatee/Play to Win	1985	—	2.50	5.00
❑ 196	Alice, Rita and Donna/Music Man	1985	—	2.50	5.00
❑ 198	Tired of the Same Old Thing/Sweet Lydia's Biscuits	1985	—	2.50	5.00
❑ 200	Seven Little Stars/Rock 'n' Roll Country Music	1986	—	2.50	5.00
❑ 212	All the Things We Are Not/Two Sides to Lonesome	1988	—	2.50	5.00
❑ 215	Somewhere in Canada/She's the Newest Broken Heart	1989	—	2.50	5.00
❑ 219	We're Standing on the Edge/She Never Knew About You	1989	—	2.50	5.00

WARD, CHRIS
45s
GIANT

Number	Title (A Side/B Side)	Yr	VG	VG+	NM
❑ 7-17601	Fall Reaching/Somewhere Between Goodbye and Gone	1996	—	2.00	4.00

WARD, DALE
45s

Number	Title (A Side/B Side)	Yr	VG	VG+	NM
BOYD					
❑ 118	Here's Your Hat/Big Dale Trust	1962	5.00	10.00	20.00
❑ 150	Shake, Rattle and Roll/You Gotta Let Me Know	1965	2.50	5.00	10.00
❑ 152	I Tried/Living on Coal	1965	2.50	5.00	10.00
❑ 153	I Didn't Know/Pennies and Guitar Picks	1965	2.50	5.00	10.00
DOT					
❑ 16520	A Letter from Sherry/Oh Julie	1963	3.75	7.50	15.00
❑ 16590	Crying for Laura/I've Got a Girl Friend	1964	3.00	6.00	12.00
❑ 16632	I'll Never Love Again (After Loving You)/Young Lovers After Midnight	1964	3.00	6.00	12.00
❑ 16672	Fortune Teller/One Last Kiss Cherie	1964	3.00	6.00	12.00
❑ 16704	Dirty Old Town/River Goodbye	1965	3.00	6.00	12.00
❑ 16759	Lonely Mary Ann/You Little Flirt	1965	3.00	6.00	12.00
❑ 17389	Brand New Me/Woman Made Man	1971	—	3.50	7.00
❑ 17406	Sunrise Over Charlotte/Sweet, Sweet Jesus	1972	—	3.50	7.00
MONUMENT					
❑ 920	Hey You (I'm the One)/Kiss Him Goodbye	1966	2.50	5.00	10.00
❑ 945	Back in That World Again/Just Because I'm Lonely	1966	2.50	5.00	10.00
❑ 1014	Operator/Your Seventeenth Year	1967	2.00	4.00	8.00
❑ 1052	Don't Be Giving Away Your Love/Mama Don't Cry for Me	1968	2.00	4.00	8.00
❑ 1094	If Loving You Means Anything/River of Regret	1968	2.00	4.00	8.00
❑ 1101	How Much Can I Give/Saturday's Fool	1968	2.00	4.00	8.00
❑ 1136	Ruby, Don't Take Your Love to Town/Straight Down to Heaven	1969	2.00	4.00	8.00
PARAMOUNT					
❑ 0014	River Boat Annie/I Want the Best for You	1970	—	3.50	7.00
❑ 0020	I Try to Satisfy/Say I Love You (One More Time)	1970	—	3.50	7.00

WARD, JACKY
45s

Number	Title (A Side/B Side)	Yr	VG	VG+	NM
ASYLUM					
❑ 47424	Travelin' Man/Save a Little Love	1982	—	2.00	4.00
❑ 47468	Take the Mem'ry When You Go/Get Rhythm	1982	—	2.00	4.00
❑ 69844	The Night's Almost Over/Black and White Rainbows	1983	—	3.00	6.00
—Quickly reissued on Warner Bros.					
CINNAMON					
❑ 776	The One I Sing My Love Songs To/I've Got to Burn	1973	—	3.00	6.00
❑ 783	Smoky Places/Living Again	1974	—	3.00	6.00
❑ 800	Good Wine/Reachin' for You	1974	—	3.00	6.00
❑ 811	Baby Let's Do Something/(B-side unknown)	1974	2.00	4.00	8.00
—Quickly reissued on Mercury					
ELECTRIC					
❑ 105	Can't Get to You from Here/(B-side unknown)	1987	—	2.50	5.00
MEGA					
❑ 0099	Words/Pretty Girl, Pretty Clothes, Pretty Sad	1973	—	3.00	6.00
❑ 0112	Dream Weaver/Biggest Piece of Me	1973	—	3.00	6.00
MERCURY					
❑ 55003	Fools Fall in Love/Big Blue Diamond	1977	—	2.50	5.00
❑ 55018	A Lover's Question/She Belongs to Me	1978	—	2.50	5.00
❑ 55038	I Want to Be in Love/Hey Friend	1978	—	2.50	5.00
❑ 55047	Rhythm of the Rain/From Me to You	1978	—	2.50	5.00
❑ 55055	Wisdom of a Fool/One Day and a Night	1979	—	2.50	5.00
❑ 57004	You're My Kind of Woman/Rainbow	1979	—	2.50	5.00
❑ 57013	I'd Do Anything for You/Ain't It Just Like Me	1979	—	2.50	5.00
❑ 57022	Save Your Heart for Me/It Doesn't Matter Anymore	1980	—	2.50	5.00
❑ 57032	That's the Way a Cowboy Rocks and Rolls/I Learned All About Cheatin' from You	1980	—	2.50	5.00
❑ 57044	Somethin' on the Radio/Let Me Be Your Man	1981	—	2.50	5.00
❑ 73640	Baby Let's Do Something/No Guarantee	1974	—	2.50	5.00
❑ 73667	Stealin'/I Can't Stand the Pain	1975	—	2.50	5.00
❑ 73716	Dance Her By Me (One More Time)/Just Because	1975	—	2.50	5.00
❑ 73783	She'll Throw Stones at You/One Pillow Between Us	1976	—	2.50	5.00
❑ 73826	I Never Said It Would Be Easy/Nobody's Perfect	1976	—	2.50	5.00
❑ 73880	Texas Angel/Just Out of Reach	1976	—	2.50	5.00
❑ 73918	Why Not Tonight/The Feelin's Right	1977	—	2.50	5.00
TARGET					
❑ 0146	Big Blue Diamond/Just Hanging On	1972	—	3.50	7.00
❑ 0155	We're in Love/Two Right People in the Wrong Frame of Mind	1972	—	3.50	7.00
—With Lea Seagrave					
WARNER BROS.					
❑ 69844	The Night's Almost Over/Black and White Rainbows	1983	—	2.00	4.00

Albums

Number	Title	Yr	VG	VG+	NM
ASYLUM					
❑ 60013	Night After Night	1982	2.00	4.00	8.00
MERCURY					
❑ SRM-1-1170	Jacky Ward	1977	3.00	6.00	12.00
❑ SRM-1-5009	A Lover's Question	1978	2.50	5.00	10.00
❑ SRM-1-5013	Rainbow	1978	2.50	5.00	10.00
❑ SRM-1-5021	The Best of Jacky Ward ... Up 'Til Now	1979	2.50	5.00	10.00
❑ SRM-1-5030	More!	1980	2.50	5.00	10.00
TARGET					
❑ 1315	Big Blue Diamond	1972	3.00	6.00	12.00

WARD, JACKY, AND REBA MCENTIRE
45s
MERCURY

Number	Title (A Side/B Side)	Yr	VG	VG+	NM
❑ 55026	Three Sheets in the Wind/I'd Really Love to See You Tonight	1978	2.00	4.00	8.00
❑ 55054	That Makes Two of Us/Good Friends	1979	2.00	4.00	8.00

WARINER, STEVE
Also see GLEN CAMPBELL; ANITA COCHRAN.
45s

Number	Title (A Side/B Side)	Yr	VG	VG+	NM
ARISTA					
❑ 12349	Leave Him Out of This/Like the River to the Sea	1991	—	2.00	4.00
❑ 12392	The Tips of My Fingers/When Will I Let Go	1992	—	2.50	5.00
❑ 12426	A Woman Loves/Everything's Gonna Be Alright	1992	—	2.50	5.00
❑ 12461	Crash Course in the Blues/My How the Time Don't Fly	1992	—	2.00	4.00
❑ 12510	Like a River to the Sea/On My Heart Again	1993	—	2.00	4.00
❑ 12578	If I Didn't Love You/The Same Mistake Again	1993	—	2.00	4.00
❑ 12609	Drivin' and Cryin'/Drive	1993	—	2.00	4.00
❑ 12672	It Won't Be Over You/Missing You	1994	—	2.00	4.00
❑ 12744	Drive/The Same Mistake Again	1994	—	2.00	4.00
CAPITOL NASHVILLE					
❑ S7-19974	Holes in the Floor of Heaven/The Closer I Get to You	1998	—	2.00	4.00
❑ S7-58716	Burnin' the Roadhouse Down/Road Trippin'	1998	—	2.00	4.00
—A-side with Garth Brooks					
❑ 58753	Every Little Whisper/Love Me Like You Love Me	1999	—	—	3.00
❑ 58767	Two Teardrops/Cry No More	1999	—	—	3.00
❑ 58786	I'm Already Taken/Tattoos of Life	1999	—	—	3.00
❑ 58848	Faith in You/Blinded	2000	—	—	3.00
❑ 58878	Katie Wants a Fast One/I Just Do	2000	—	2.00	4.00
—A-side with Garth Brooks; B-side with the Nashville Super Pickers					
❑ 58900	Christmas in Your Arms/It Wouldn't Be Love	2000	—	2.00	4.00
LIBERTY					
❑ S7-18556	Get Back/Can't Buy Me Love	1995	—	2.50	5.00
—B-side by Shenandoah					
MCA					
❑ 52506	What I Didn't Do/Your Love Has Got a Hold on Me	1984	—	—	3.00
❑ 52506 [PS]	What I Didn't Do/Your Love Has Got a Hold on Me	1984	—	2.00	4.00
❑ 52562	Heart Trouble/As Long As Love's Been Around	1985	—	—	3.00
❑ 52644	Some Fools Never Learn/You Can't Cut Me Any Deeper	1985	—	—	3.00
❑ 52721	You Can Dream of Me/I Let a Keeper Get Away	1985	—	—	3.00
❑ 52721 [DJ]	You Can Dream of Me (same on both sides)	1985	2.50	5.00	10.00
—Promo only on yellow vinyl					
❑ 52721 [PS]	You Can Dream of Me/I Let a Keeper Get Away	1985	—	2.00	4.00
❑ 52786	Life's Highway/She's Crazy for Leaving	1986	—	—	3.00
❑ 52837	Starting Over Again/She's Leaving Me All Over Again	1986	—	—	3.00
❑ 52837 [DJ]	Starting Over Again (same on both sides)	1986	2.50	5.00	10.00
—Promo only on red vinyl					
❑ 53006	Small Town Girl/When It Rains	1987	—	—	3.00
❑ 53006 [DJ]	Small Town Girl (same on both sides)	1987	2.50	5.00	10.00
—Promo only on blue vinyl					
❑ 53068	The Weekend/Fastbreak	1987	—	—	3.00
❑ 53160	Lynda/There's Always a First Time	1987	—	—	3.00
❑ 53287	Baby I'm Yours/All That Matters	1988	—	—	3.00
❑ 53347	I Should Be with You/Caught Between Your Duty and Your Dream	1988	—	—	3.00
❑ 53419	Hold On (A Little Longer)/Runnin'	1988	—	—	3.00
❑ 53504	Where Did I Go Wrong/Plano Texas Girl	1989	—	—	3.00
❑ 53665	I Got Dreams/The Loser Wins	1989	—	—	3.00
❑ 53733	The Domino Theory/I Wanna Go Back	1990	—	2.00	4.00
❑ 53738	When I Could Come Home to You/Do You Want to Make Something Of It	1989	—	—	3.00
❑ 53936	There for Awhile/Why Do the Heroes Die So Young	1990	—	—	3.00
❑ 79051	Precious Thing/She's in Love	1990	—	2.00	4.00

RCA

Number	Title (A Side/B Side)	Yr	VG	VG+	NM
❑ PB-11173	I'm Already Taken/Daytime Dreamer	1978	—	2.50	5.00
❑ PB-11173 [PS]	I'm Already Taken/Daytime Dreamer	1978	2.00	4.00	8.00
❑ PB-11336	So Sad (To Watch Good Love Go Bad)//Atlanta/ My Greatest Loss	1978	—	2.50	5.00
❑ PB-11447	Marie/One Song in Everybody	1979	—	2.50	5.00
❑ PB-11658	Forget Me Not/Beside Me	1979	—	2.50	5.00
❑ JH-12029 [DJ]	The Easy Part's Over (stereo/mono)	1980	3.00	6.00	12.00
—Promo only on green vinyl					
❑ PB-12029	The Easy Part's Over/It's Your Move	1980	—	2.50	5.00
❑ PB-12139	Your Memory/Vince	1981	—	2.00	4.00
❑ PB-12204	By Now/Beverly (Take Care of Your Baby)	1981	—	2.00	4.00
❑ PB-12307	All Roads Lead to You/Here We Are	1981	—	2.00	4.00
❑ JK-13072 [DJ]	Kansas City Lights (same on both sides)	1982	2.50	5.00	10.00
—Promo only on yellow vinyl					
❑ PB-13072	Kansas City Lights/The Easy Part's Over	1982	—	2.00	4.00
❑ JK-13308 [DJ]	Don't It Break Your Heart (same on both sides)	1982	2.50	5.00	10.00
—Promo only on green vinyl					
❑ PB-13308	Don't It Break Your Heart/We'll Never Know	1982	—	2.00	4.00
❑ PB-13395	Don't Plan on Sleepin' Tonight/Your Memory	1982	—	2.00	4.00
❑ JK-13515 [DJ]	Don't Your Mem'ry Ever Sleep at Night (same on both sides)	1983	2.50	5.00	10.00
—Promo only on blue vinyl					
❑ PB-13515	Don't Your Mem'ry Ever Sleep at Night/Well, Hello Again	1983	—	2.00	4.00
❑ PB-13588	Midnight Fire/You Turn It All Around	1983	—	2.00	4.00
❑ PB-13691	Lonely Women Make Good Lovers/I Can Hear Kentucky Calling Me	1983	—	2.00	4.00
❑ PB-13768	Why Goodbye/Don't You Give Up on Love	1984	—	2.00	4.00
❑ PB-13862	Don't You Give Up on Love/When Is It All Gonna End	1984	—	2.00	4.00
❑ PB-13968	When We're Together/You Make Me Feel So Right	1984	—	2.00	4.00
❑ PB-14289	Drawn to the Fire/Those Memories of You	1986	—	2.00	4.00

Albums

ARISTA

Number	Title (A Side/B Side)	Yr	VG	VG+	NM
❑ AL 8691	I Am Ready	1992	5.00	10.00	20.00
—Vinyl version available only from Columbia House					

MCA

Number	Title (A Side/B Side)	Yr	VG	VG+	NM
❑ 5545	One Good Night Deserves Another	1985	2.00	4.00	8.00
❑ 5672	Life's Highway	1985	2.00	4.00	8.00
❑ 5926	It's a Crazy World	1987	2.00	4.00	8.00
❑ 42032	Greatest Hits	1987	2.00	4.00	8.00
❑ 42130	I Should Be with You	1988	2.00	4.00	8.00
❑ 42272	I Got Dreams	1989	2.50	5.00	10.00

RCA VICTOR

Number	Title (A Side/B Side)	Yr	VG	VG+	NM
❑ AHL1-4154	Steve Wariner	1982	2.50	5.00	10.00
❑ AHL1-4859	Midnight Fire	1983	2.50	5.00	10.00
❑ AHL1-5326	Greatest Hits	1985	2.00	4.00	8.00
❑ AYL1-5440	Steve Wariner	1985	2.00	4.00	8.00
—"Best Buy Series" reissue					
❑ AHL1-7164	Down in Tennessee	1986	2.00	4.00	8.00

WARNER, VIRGIL

45s

LHI

Number	Title (A Side/B Side)	Yr	VG	VG+	NM
❑ 1207	I'm Running Out/Next to You	1968	—	3.50	7.00
❑ 17009	Her Way, My Way/Telling You Goodbye	1967	2.00	4.00	8.00
❑ 17013	We're So Much Alike (In Different Ways)/ Suppose	1967	2.00	4.00	8.00

WARNER, VIRGIL, AND SUZI JANE HOKUM

Also see each artist's individual listings.

45s

LHI

Number	Title (A Side/B Side)	Yr	VG	VG+	NM
❑ 8	Angel of the Morning/Love County Fair	1969	—	3.50	7.00
❑ 1204	Storybook Children/Lady Bird	1968	—	3.50	7.00
❑ 1214	The House Song/Let It Be Me	1968	—	3.50	7.00
❑ 17001	Out of My Hands/Crying Shade	1967	2.00	4.00	8.00
❑ 17018	Here We Go Again/Hangin' On	1967	—	3.50	7.00

WARNES, JENNIFER

Includes records as "Jennifer." Also see STEVE GILLETTE; BILL MEDLEY; GARY MORRIS.

45s

ARISTA

Number	Title (A Side/B Side)	Yr	VG	VG+	NM
❑ 0223	Right Time of the Night/Daddy Don't Go	1976	—	2.50	5.00
❑ 0252	I'm Dreaming/Don't Lead Me On	1977	—	2.50	5.00
❑ 0430	I Know a Heartache When I See One/Frankie in the Rain	1979	—	2.00	4.00
❑ 0455	Don't Make Me Over/I'm Restless	1979	—	2.00	4.00
❑ 0497	When the Feeling Comes Around/Shot Through the Heart	1980	—	2.00	4.00
❑ 0611	Could It Be Love/I'm Restless	1982	—	2.00	4.00
❑ 0670	Come to Me/I'm Restless	1982	—	2.00	4.00

CASABLANCA

Number	Title (A Side/B Side)	Yr	VG	VG+	NM
❑ 814603-7	All the Right Moves/Theme — All the Right Moves	1983	—	2.00	4.00
—A-side with Chris Thompson; B-side by David Campbell					

CYPRESS

Number	Title (A Side/B Side)	Yr	VG	VG+	NM
❑ 661111-7	Ain't No Cure for Love/Famous Blue Raincoat	1986	—	2.00	4.00
❑ 661111-7 [PS]	Ain't No Cure for Love/Famous Blue Raincoat	1986	—	2.50	5.00
❑ 661115-7	First We Take Manhattan/Famous Blue Raincoat	1987	—	2.00	4.00

PARROT

Number	Title (A Side/B Side)	Yr	VG	VG+	NM
❑ 324	Here, There and Everywhere/Sunny Day Blue	1968	3.00	6.00	12.00
❑ 328	Chelsea Morning/The Park	1969	2.50	5.00	10.00
❑ 333	I Am Waiting/The Leaves	1969	2.50	5.00	10.00
❑ 336	Easy to Be Hard/Let the Sunshine In	1969	2.50	5.00	10.00
❑ 343	We're Not Gonna Take It/The Weather's Better	1970	2.00	4.00	8.00
❑ 346	Old Folks/Cajun Train	1970	2.00	4.00	8.00
—All of the above as "Jennifer"					

REPRISE

Number	Title (A Side/B Side)	Yr	VG	VG+	NM
❑ 1070	Last Song/These Days	1972	2.00	4.00	8.00
—As "Jennifer"					

WARNER BROS.

Number	Title (A Side/B Side)	Yr	VG	VG+	NM
❑ 29593	Nights Are Forever/Kick the Can	1983	—	2.00	4.00

Albums

ARISTA

Number	Title (A Side/B Side)	Yr	VG	VG+	NM
❑ AL 4062	Jennifer Warnes	1977	2.50	5.00	10.00
❑ AL 4217	Shot Through the Heart	1979	2.50	5.00	10.00
❑ AL 9560	The Best of Jennifer Warnes	1982	2.00	4.00	8.00

CYPRESS

Number	Title (A Side/B Side)	Yr	VG	VG+	NM
❑ 661111-1	Famous Blue Raincoat	1987	7.50	15.00	30.00

PARROT

Number	Title (A Side/B Side)	Yr	VG	VG+	NM
❑ PAS-71020	I Can Remember Anything	1968	5.00	10.00	20.00
—As "Jennifer"					
❑ PAS-71034	See Me	1970	5.00	10.00	20.00
—As "Jennifer"					

ROCK THE HOUSE

Number	Title (A Side/B Side)	Yr	VG	VG+	NM
❑ RTH 5052	Famous Blue Raincoat	1996	12.50	25.00	50.00
—Classic Records reissue					

WARREN, KELLI

Some of these spell her first name "Kelly."

45s

JEREMIAH

Number	Title (A Side/B Side)	Yr	VG	VG+	NM
❑ 1002	Don't Touch Me/Never Been to Spain	1979	—	3.00	6.00
—A-side with Jerry Naylor					
❑ 1004	Statue of a Fool/I'm Aimin' on Livin' Some	1980	—	3.00	6.00
❑ 1013	Good Hearted Woman/Just a Simple Phone Call	198?	—	3.00	6.00

RCA

Number	Title (A Side/B Side)	Yr	VG	VG+	NM
❑ PB-11428	One Man's Woman/If I Could Just Find My Way (Back to You)	1978	—	2.50	5.00
❑ PB-11521	I'll Love Your Leavin' Away/The Right Feeling at the Wrong Time	1979	—	2.50	5.00

WARREN BROTHERS, THE

45s

BNA

Number	Title (A Side/B Side)	Yr	VG	VG+	NM
❑ 65552	Guilty (same on both sides)	1998	—	—	3.00
❑ 65670	Better Man/Guilty	1999	—	—	3.00

BNA/RCA

Number	Title (A Side/B Side)	Yr	VG	VG+	NM
❑ 60213	That's the Beat of a Heart/Grow Young with You	2000	—	—	3.00
—A-side with Sara Evans; B-side by Coley McCabe with Special Guest Andy Griggs; odd record with BNA label on A-side and RCA label on B-side (not a misprint)					

WASHINGTON, JON

45s

DOOR KNOB

Number	Title (A Side/B Side)	Yr	VG	VG+	NM
❑ 310	One Dance Love Affair/(B-side unknown)	1988	—	2.50	5.00
❑ 315	Two Hearts/Lady of the Evening	1988	—	2.50	5.00

WATERS, CHRIS

45s

RIO

Number	Title (A Side/B Side)	Yr	VG	VG+	NM
❑ 1001	My Lady Loves Me (Just As I Am)/Nobody's Fool	1980	—	2.50	5.00
❑ 1002	It's Like Falling in Love (Over and Over Again)/ Long As I Can See the Light	1981	—	2.50	5.00

WATERS, JOE

45s

NEW COLONY

Number	Title (A Side/B Side)	Yr	VG	VG+	NM
❑ 6811	Livin' in the Light of Her Love/Wild Honey Mountain Girl	1981	—	3.50	7.00
❑ 6812	Some Day My Ship's Comin' In/Jubilee	1981	—	3.50	7.00
❑ 6812 [PS]	Some Day My Ship's Comin' In/Jubilee	1981	2.50	5.00	10.00
❑ 6813	The Queen of Hearts Loves You/Love Can Be Fatal	1982	—	3.50	7.00
❑ 6814	Harvest Moon/Sweet Georgia Clay (I'll Be Home Someday)	1983	—	3.50	7.00
❑ 6814 [PS]	Harvest Moon/Sweet Georgia Clay (I'll Be Home Someday)	1983	2.50	5.00	10.00
❑ 6815	Rise Above It All/Pay the Price for Love	1984	—	3.50	7.00

Albums

NEW COLONY

Number	Title (A Side/B Side)	Yr	VG	VG+	NM
❑ 831	Harvest Moon	1983	2.50	5.00	10.00

WATSON, B.B.

45s

BNA

Number	Title (A Side/B Side)	Yr	VG	VG+	NM
❑ 62039	Light at the End of the Tunnel/Honkytonk the Town Tonight	1991	—	2.00	4.00
❑ 62133	An Eye for an Eye/Hank Drank	1991	—	2.00	4.00
❑ 62195	Lover Not a Fighter/Bottle of Whiskey	1992	—	—	3.00
❑ 62260	Say Goodbye/Drop Dead Smile	1992	—	—	3.00

WATSON, CLYDE

45s

GROOVY

Number	Title (A Side/B Side)	Yr	VG	VG+	NM
❑ 100	The Touch of Her Fingers/Trouble	1977	—	3.00	6.00

Number	Title (A Side/B Side)	Yr	VG	VG+	NM
WATSON, DOC					
Includes records by the father-son duo of "Doc and Merle Watson."					
45s					
POPPY					
❑ XW169	If I Needed You/Bonaparte's Retreat	1973	—	2.00	4.00
—With Merle Watson					
❑ XW276	Bottle of Wine/Corinna, Corinna	1973	—	2.00	4.00
—With Merle Watson					
❑ XW370	New Born King/Peace in the Valley	1973	—	2.00	4.00
❑ XW414	Poor Boy Blues/Doc's Rag	1974	—	2.00	4.00
—With Merle Watson					
❑ 90110	Freight Train Boogie/Going Down the Road Feeling Bad	1971	—	2.50	5.00
❑ 90114	Summertime/I Couldn't Believe It Was True	1972	—	2.50	5.00
—With Merle Watson					
❑ 90119	New Born King/Peace in the Valley	1972	—	2.50	5.00
UNITED ARTISTS					
❑ XW713	Make Me a Pallet/Shady Grove	1975	—	2.00	4.00
❑ XW824	I Can't Help But Wonder (Where I'm Bound)/Southbound Passenger Train	1976	—	2.00	4.00
❑ XW894	Little Maggie/Cypress Grove Blues	1976	—	2.00	4.00
❑ XW1020	My Creole Belle/Minglewood Blues	1977	—	2.00	4.00
—With Merle Watson					
❑ 1231	Don't Think Twice, It's All Right/Under the Double Eagle	1978	—	2.00	4.00
—With Merle Watson					
❑ 1275	All I Have to Do Is Dream/'Rangement Blues	1979	—	2.00	4.00
—With Merle Watson					
VANGUARD					
❑ 35079	Peach Picking Time in Georgia/Memphis Blues	1968	—	3.00	6.00
Albums					
FLYING FISH					
❑ FF-252	Red Rocking Chair	1981	3.00	6.00	12.00
❑ FF-301	Guitar Album	1983	3.00	6.00	12.00
❑ FF-352	Pickin' the Blues	1985	2.50	5.00	10.00
FOLKWAYS					
❑ FA-2366 [M]	Doc Watson and Family	1963	6.25	12.50	25.00
❑ FA-31021 [S]	Doc Watson and Family	196?	3.75	7.50	15.00
INTERMEDIA					
❑ QS-5031	Out in the Country	198?	2.50	5.00	10.00
LIBERTY					
❑ LWB-423	Memories	1981	3.00	6.00	12.00
—Reissue of United Artists 423					
❑ LW-601	Doc and the Boys	1981	2.50	5.00	10.00
—Reissue of United Artists 601					
❑ LT-887	Look Away!	1981	2.50	5.00	10.00
—Reissue of United Artists 887					
❑ LT-943	Live and Pickin'	1981	2.50	5.00	10.00
—Reissue of United Artists 943					
❑ LN-10027	Lonesome Road	1981	2.00	4.00	8.00
—Budget-line reissue					
POPPY					
❑ PP-LA022-F	Then and Now	1973	3.75	7.50	15.00
❑ PP-LA210-G	Two Days in November	1974	3.75	7.50	15.00
❑ PYS-5703	The Elementary Doc Watson	1972	3.75	7.50	15.00
SMITHSONIAN/FOLKWAYS					
❑ SF-40012	The Doc Watson Family	1990	3.00	6.00	12.00
—Reissue of Folkways LP					
SUGAR HILL					
❑ SH-3742	Down South	1985	2.50	5.00	10.00
❑ SH-3752	Riding the Midnight Train	1986	2.50	5.00	10.00
❑ SH-3759	Portrait	1987	2.50	5.00	10.00
UNITED ARTISTS					
❑ UA-LA423-G [(2)]	Memories	1975	3.75	7.50	15.00
❑ UA-LA601-G	Doc and the Boys	1976	3.00	6.00	12.00
❑ UA-LA725-G	Lonesome Road	1977	3.00	6.00	12.00
❑ UA-LA887-H	Look Away!	1978	3.00	6.00	12.00
❑ UA-LA943-H	Live and Pickin'	1979	3.00	6.00	12.00
VANGUARD					
❑ VSD-9/10 [(2)]	Doc Watson on Stage	1970	5.00	10.00	20.00
❑ VSD 45/46 [(2)]	The Essential Doc Watson	1973	5.00	10.00	20.00
❑ VSD 107/8 [(2)]	Old Timey Concert	1977	5.00	10.00	20.00
❑ VSD-6576	Ballads from Deep Gap	1971	3.75	7.50	15.00
❑ VRS-9152 [M]	Doc Watson	1964	5.00	10.00	20.00
❑ VRS-9170 [M]	Doc Watson and Son	1965	5.00	10.00	20.00
❑ VRS-9213 [M]	Southbound	1966	3.75	7.50	15.00
❑ VRS-9239 [M]	Home Again	1967	3.75	7.50	15.00
❑ VMS-73108	The Essential Doc Watson, Vol. 1	1985	2.50	5.00	10.00
❑ VMS-73121	The Essential Doc Watson, Vol. 2	1985	2.50	5.00	10.00
❑ VSD-79152 [S]	Doc Watson	1964	6.25	12.50	25.00
❑ VSD-79170 [S]	Doc Watson and Son	1965	6.25	12.50	25.00
❑ VSD-79213 [S]	Southbound	1966	5.00	10.00	20.00
❑ VSD-79239 [S]	Home Again	1967	5.00	10.00	20.00
❑ VSD-79276	Good Deal	1968	3.75	7.50	15.00
WATSON, GENE					
45s					
BROADLAND					
❑ 192	One and One and One/She's No Lady	1992	—	2.50	5.00
CAPITOL					
❑ 4076	Love in the Hot Afternoon/Through the Eyes of Love	1975	—	2.50	5.00
❑ 4143	Where Love Begins/Long Enough to Care	1975	—	2.50	5.00
❑ 4214	You Could Know As Much About a Stranger/Harvest Time	1976	—	2.50	5.00
❑ 4279	Because You Believed in Me/When My World Left Town	1976	—	2.50	5.00
❑ 4331	Her Body Couldn't Keep You (Off My Mind)/If I'm a Fool for Leaving	1976	—	2.50	5.00
❑ 4378	Paper Rosie/Don't Look at Me (In That Tone of Voice)	1976	—	2.50	5.00
❑ 4458	The Old Man and His Horn/Just at Dawn	1977	—	2.50	5.00
❑ 4513	I Don't Need a Thing at All/Hey Barnum and Bailey	1977	—	2.50	5.00
❑ 4556	Cowboys Don't Get Lucky All the Time/I'd Love to Live with You Again	1978	—	2.00	4.00
❑ 4616	One Sided Conversation/I Know What It's Like in Her Arms	1978	—	2.00	4.00
❑ 4680	Farewell Party/I Don't Know How to Tell Her (She Don't Love Me Anymore)	1979	—	2.00	4.00
❑ 4723	Pick the Wildwood Flower/Mama Sold Roses	1979	—	2.00	4.00
❑ 4772	Should I Come Home (Or Should I Go Crazy)/Beautiful You	1979	—	2.00	4.00
❑ 4814	Nothing Sure Looked Good on You/The Beer at Dorsey's Bar	1979	—	2.00	4.00
❑ 4854	Bedroom Ballad/After the Party	1980	—	2.00	4.00
❑ 4898	Raisin' Cane in Texas/A Cold Day in July	1980	—	2.00	4.00
❑ 4940	No One Will Ever Know/Down and Out This Way Again	1980	—	2.00	4.00
EPIC					
❑ 34-05407	Cold Summer Day in Georgia/The Note	1985	—	—	3.00
❑ 34-05633	Memories to Burn/Get Along Little Doggie	1985	—	—	3.00
❑ 34-05817	Carmen/The New York Times	1986	—	—	3.00
❑ 34-06057	Bottle of Tears/Stranger in Our House Tonight	1986	—	—	3.00
❑ 34-06290	Everything I Used to Do/I Saved Your Place	1986	—	—	3.00
❑ 34-06987	Honky Tonk Crazy/Starting New Memories Today	1987	—	—	3.00
❑ 34-07308	Everybody Needs a Hero/When She Touched Me	1987	—	—	3.00
MCA					
❑ 51039	Between This Time and the Next Time/I'mTellin' Me a Lie	1981	—	—	3.00
❑ 51127	Maybe I Should Have Been Listening/I'm Gonna Kill You	1981	—	—	3.00
❑ 51183	Fourteen Carat Mind/Lonely Me	1981	—	2.00	4.00
❑ 52009	Speak Softly (You're Talking to My Heart)/'Til Melinda Comes Around	1982	—	—	3.00
❑ 52074	This Dream's On Me/This Torch That I Carry for You	1982	—	—	3.00
❑ 52131	What She Don't Know Won't Hurt Her/Fightin' Fire with Fire	1982	—	—	3.00
❑ 52191	You're Out Doing What I'm Here Doing Without/You're Just Another Beer Drinking Song	1983	—	—	3.00
❑ 52243	Sometimes I Get Lucky and Forget/You Put Out an Old Flame Last Night	1983	—	—	3.00
❑ 52309	Drinkin' My Way Back Home/My Memories of You	1983	—	—	3.00
❑ 52356	Forever Again/Growing Apart	1984	—	—	3.00
❑ 52410	Little by Little/The Ballad of Richard Lindsey	1984	—	—	3.00
MCA CURB					
❑ 52457	Got No Reason Now for Goin' Home/A Memory Away	1984	—	—	3.00
❑ 52533	One Hell of a Heartache/Sailing Home to Me	1985	—	—	3.00
RESCO					
❑ 616	To Have Conquered/Through the Eyes of Love	1974	2.00	4.00	8.00
❑ 619	Burning Memories/Do You Have Any Plans for Me	1974	2.00	4.00	8.00
❑ 627	Shadows on the Wall/I Told a Lie	1974	2.00	4.00	8.00
❑ 630	Bad Water/I'll Run Right Back	1974	2.00	4.00	8.00
❑ 634	Love in the Hot Afternoon/Through the Eyes of Love	1975	2.00	4.00	8.00
STEP ONE					
❑ 468	Snake in the House/You Can't Believe a Thing I Say	1993	—	2.00	4.00
❑ 472	Glass Hearts/Hold That Thought	1994	—	2.00	4.00
STONEWAY					
❑ 1120	If I'm a Fool for Leaving/Two Right People	197?	2.50	5.00	10.00
❑ 1130	It's Just a Matter of Time/Walking Back to Birmingham	197?	2.50	5.00	10.00
❑ 1142	I Feel a Sin Coming On/I'm Not Strong Enough	197?	2.50	5.00	10.00
❑ 1165	Listen They're Playing Our Song/I'm Not Strong Enough	197?	2.50	5.00	10.00
TRI-DEC					
❑ 8357	My Rockin' Baby/(B-side unknown)	1958	200.00	400.00	800.00
WARNER BROS.					
❑ 7-19540	This Country's Bigger Than Texas/You Can't Get Arrested in Nashville	1990	—	2.00	4.00
❑ 7-22751	The Great Divide/Ain't No Fun to Be Alone in San Antone	1989	—	—	3.00
❑ 7-22912	The Jukebox Played Along/Somewhere Over You	1989	—	—	3.00
❑ 7-27532	Back in the Fire/Just How Little I Know	1989	—	—	3.00
❑ 7-27692	Don't Waste It on the Blues/I Picked a San Antonio Rose	1988	—	—	3.00
❑ 49648	Any Way You Want Me/Those Eyes That Lie to Me	1981	—	2.00	4.00
WIDE WORLD					
❑ 1001	Autumn in June/I'll Run Right Back to You	1970	3.00	6.00	12.00
❑ 1002	Before the Next Teardrop Falls/I Told a Lie	1970	3.00	6.00	12.00
❑ 1003	Florence Jean/John's Back in Town	1970	3.00	6.00	12.00
❑ 1007	I Went All to Pieces/Two Right People (In the Wrong Frame of Mind)	1970	3.00	6.00	12.00

Number	Title (A Side/B Side)	Yr	VG	VG+	NM
❑ 1010	I Feel a Sin Coming On/Lie to Me	1970	3.00	6.00	12.00
❑ 1014	If I'm a Fool for Leaving/The Only Difference	1971	3.00	6.00	12.00
❑ 1016	Eli Funkelby/When My Daddy Danced	1971	3.00	6.00	12.00
❑ 1019	I Feel Fine/I'm Not Strong Enough	1971	3.00	6.00	12.00
❑ 1021	The Birds and the Bees/My Eyes Are Jealous	197?	3.00	6.00	12.00
Albums					
CAPITOL					
❑ ST-11443	Love in the Hot Afternoon	1975	3.00	6.00	12.00
❑ ST-11529	Because You Believe in Me	1976	3.00	6.00	12.00
❑ ST-11597	Paper Rosie	1977	3.00	6.00	12.00
❑ ST-11715	Beautiful Country	1977	3.00	6.00	12.00
❑ ST-11782	The Best of Gene Watson	1978	3.00	6.00	12.00
❑ SW-11805	Reflections	1978	3.00	6.00	12.00
❑ ST-11947	Should I Come Home	1979	3.00	6.00	12.00
❑ ST-12102	No One Will Ever Know	1980	3.00	6.00	12.00
❑ SN-16124	Paper Rosie	198?	2.00	4.00	8.00
—Budget-line reissue					
❑ SN-16241	The Best of Gene Watson, Vol. 2	198?	2.00	4.00	8.00
❑ SN-16304	Reflections	198?	2.00	4.00	8.00
—Budget-line reissue					
❑ C1-91641	The Best of Gene Watson	1989	3.00	6.00	12.00
EPIC					
❑ BFE 40076	Memories to Burn	1985	2.00	4.00	8.00
❑ FE 40306	Starting New Memories	1986	2.00	4.00	8.00
❑ FE 40644	Honky Tonk Crazy	1987	2.00	4.00	8.00
MCA					
❑ 950	Sometimes I Get Lucky	1985	2.00	4.00	8.00
—Reissue of 5384					
❑ 951	Little by Little	1985	2.00	4.00	8.00
—Reissue of 5440					
❑ 5170	Between This Time and the Next Time	1981	2.50	5.00	10.00
❑ 5241	Old Loves Never Die	1981	2.50	5.00	10.00
❑ 5302	This Dream's on Me	1982	2.50	5.00	10.00
❑ 5384	Sometimes I Get Lucky	1983	2.50	5.00	10.00
❑ 5440	Little by Little	1984	2.50	5.00	10.00
❑ 5572	Greatest Hits	1985	2.00	4.00	8.00
MCA CURB					
❑ 5520	Heartaches, Love and Stuff	1984	2.00	4.00	8.00
❑ 5670	Texas Saturday Night	1985	2.00	4.00	8.00
WARNER BROS.					
❑ 25832	Back in the Fire	1989	2.50	5.00	10.00

WAYLON AND JESSI

Also see JESSI COLTER; WAYLON JENNINGS.

Number	Title (A Side/B Side)	Yr	VG	VG+	NM
45s					
RCA					
❑ PB-12176	Storms Never Last/I Ain't the One	1982	—	2.00	4.00
❑ PB-12245	Wild Side of Life/It Wasn't God Who Made Honky Tonk Angels	1982	—	2.00	4.00
RCA VICTOR					
❑ PB-10653	Suspicious Minds/I Ain't the One	1976	—	2.50	5.00
❑ 47-9920	Suspicious Minds/I Ain't the One	1970	—	3.00	6.00
❑ 47-9992	Under Your Spell Again/Bridge Over Troubled Water	1971	—	3.00	6.00
Albums					
RCA VICTOR					
❑ AHL1-3931	Leather and Lace	1981	2.50	5.00	10.00

WAYLON AND WILLIE

For convenience's sake, we've listed all the variations of their credits here, including "Willie Nelson and Waylon Jennings." Also see WAYLON JENNINGS; WILLIE NELSON.

Number	Title (A Side/B Side)	Yr	VG	VG+	NM
45s					
COLUMBIA					
❑ 04131	Take It to the Limit/Till I Gain Control Again	1983	—	2.00	4.00
❑ 04131 [PS]	Take It to the Limit/Till I Gain Control Again	1983	—	2.50	5.00
EPIC					
❑ 73832	If I Can Find a Clean Shirt/Put Me on a Train Back to Texas	1991	—	—	3.00
❑ 74024	Tryin' to Outrun the Wind/The Makin's of a Song	1991	—	—	3.00
RCA					
❑ PB-11198	Mammas Don't Let Your Babies Grow Up to Be Cowboys/I Can Get Off on You	1978	—	2.00	4.00
❑ GB-11499	Mammas Don't Let Your Babies Grow Up to Be Cowboys/Luckenbach, Texas (Back to the Basics of Love)	1979	—	2.00	4.00
—Gold Standard Series					
❑ GB-11996	Mammas Don't Let Your Babies Grow Up to Be Cowboys/I Can Get Off on You	1980	—	—	3.00
—Gold Standard Series					
❑ PB-13073	Just to Satisfy You/Get Naked With You	1982	—	2.00	4.00
❑ PB-13319	(Sittin' On) The Dock of the Bay/Luckenbach, Texas	1982	—	2.00	4.00
RCA VICTOR					
❑ PB-10529	Good Hearted Woman/Heaven or Hell	1975	—	2.50	5.00
Albums					
COLUMBIA					
❑ FC 38562	Take It to the Limit	1983	2.50	5.00	10.00
RCA VICTOR					
❑ AAL1-2686	Waylon and Willie	198?	2.00	4.00	8.00
—Reissue with new prefix					
❑ AFL1-2686	Waylon and Willie	1978	2.50	5.00	10.00
❑ AFL1-2686 [DJ]	Waylon and Willie	1978	6.25	12.50	25.00
—Promo only on gold vinyl					
❑ AHL1-4455	WW II	1982	2.50	5.00	10.00
❑ AYL1-5134	Waylon and Willie	198?	2.00	4.00	8.00
—"Best Buy Series" reissue					
❑ AYL1-5138	WW II	198?	2.00	4.00	8.00
—"Best Buy Series" reissue					

WAYLON AND WILLIE/WAYLON AND JESSI

Number	Title (A Side/B Side)	Yr	VG	VG+	NM
45s					
RCA					
❑ GB-10928	Good Hearted Woman/Suspicious Minds	1977	—	—	3.00
—Gold Standard Series					

WAYLORS, THE

Backing group for WAYLON JENNINGS.

Number	Title (A Side/B Side)	Yr	VG	VG+	NM
45s					
RCA VICTOR					
❑ PB-10738	Crazy Arms/Shopping	1976	—	2.50	5.00

WAYNE, BOBBY

Also see THE STRANGERS. Not to be confused with the Bobby Wayne who had several pop hits in the early 1950s.

Number	Title (A Side/B Side)	Yr	VG	VG+	NM
45s					
CAPITOL					
❑ 2826	Let's Pretend We're Kids Again/The Way His Woman Does	1970	—	3.50	7.00
❑ 2931	Repeat Performance/What's So Bad About Feelin' Good	1970	—	3.50	7.00
❑ 3025	Harold's Super Service/I Can't Stand Me	1971	—	3.50	7.00
❑ 3106	The Ties That Bind/Sixty-Four Dollar Delta Night Flight to Dallas	1971	—	3.50	7.00
❑ 3158	If I Live Again/Jukebox Charlie	1971	—	3.50	7.00
❑ 3237	Fill It Up/How Can We Make It Alone	1971	—	3.50	7.00
❑ 3290	Baby's Home/Just Sit Down and Cry	1972	—	3.50	7.00

WAYNE, JOHN

Number	Title (A Side/B Side)	Yr	VG	VG+	NM
45s					
CASABLANCA					
❑ 1002	I Have Faith/The Prayer	1979	—	3.00	6.00
Albums					
RCA VICTOR					
❑ AFL1-3484	America, Why I Love Her	1979	2.50	5.00	10.00
—Reissue of 4828					
❑ AYL1-3959	America, Why I Love Her	1981	2.00	4.00	8.00
—"Best Buy Series" reissue					
❑ LSP-4828	America, Why I Love Her	1973	6.25	12.50	25.00

WAYNE, NANCY

Number	Title (A Side/B Side)	Yr	VG	VG+	NM
45s					
20TH CENTURY					
❑ 2086	The Back Door of Heaven/The Greatest Show on Earth	1974	—	2.50	5.00
❑ 2124	Gone/'Til I Can't Take It Anymore	1974	—	2.50	5.00
❑ 2165	Arkansas First Time/Cheatin' Was the Last Thing on My Mind	1975	—	2.50	5.00
❑ 2184	I Wanna Kiss You/Cold Carolina Morning	1975	—	2.50	5.00
Albums					
20TH CENTURY					
❑ T-442	Cheatin' Was the Last Thing on My Mind	1974	3.00	6.00	12.00
❑ T-472	I Wanna Kiss You	1975	3.00	6.00	12.00

WEATHERLY, JIM

Number	Title (A Side/B Side)	Yr	VG	VG+	NM
45s					
20TH CENTURY FOX					
❑ 565	I'm Gonna Make It/Wise Men Never Speak	1965	3.75	7.50	15.00
ABC					
❑ 12193	(Apples Won't Grow In) Colorado Snow/To a Gentler Time	1976	—	2.50	5.00
❑ 12213	Gonna Shine It On Again/People Some People Choose to Love	1976	—	2.50	5.00
❑ 12252	Storms of Troubled Times/(B-side unknown)	1977	—	2.50	5.00
❑ 12288	All That Keeps Me Going/I Hope It Never Rains Like That Again	1977	—	2.50	5.00
BUDDAH					
❑ 420	The Need to Be/Like Old Times Again	1974	—	2.50	5.00
❑ 420 [PS]	The Need to Be/Like Old Times Again	1974	—	3.00	6.00
❑ 444	I'll Still Love You/My First Day Without Her	1974	—	2.50	5.00
❑ 467	It Must Have Been the Rain/Mississippi	1975	—	2.50	5.00
❑ 505	What's One More Time/How'd We Ever Get This Way	1975	—	2.50	5.00
ELEKTRA					
❑ 46547	Smooth Sailin'/Let Me Love It Away	1979	—	2.00	4.00
❑ 46592	Gift from Missouri/All I Need to Know	1980	—	2.00	4.00
❑ 47027	Safe in the Arms of Your Love (Cold in the Streets)/All I Need to Know	1980	—	2.00	4.00
❑ 47096	Love That Went Away/(B-side unknown)	1980	—	2.00	4.00
RCA VICTOR					
❑ APBO-0020	Leavin' Dallas/It Must Be Love This Time	1973	—	2.50	5.00
❑ APBO-0153	Rebel Keeps On Rollin'/Same Old Song and Dance	1973	—	2.50	5.00
❑ PB-10134	High on Love/Like a First Time Thing	1974	—	2.50	5.00
❑ 74-0828	Loving You Is Just an Old Habit/Between His Goodbye and My Hello	1972	—	3.00	6.00
❑ 74-0897	Old Kentucky Moon/Until Your Ship Comes In	1973	—	3.00	6.00
❑ 74-0949	Where Peaceful Waters Flow/Like a First Time Thing	1973	—	3.00	6.00

Number	Title (A Side/B Side)	Yr	VG	VG+	NM
Albums					
ABC					
❑ D-937	People Choose to Love	1976	2.50	5.00	10.00
❑ D-982	Pictures and Rhymes	1977	2.50	5.00	10.00
BUDDAH					
❑ BDS-5608	The Songs of Jim Weatherly	1974	2.50	5.00	10.00
RCA VICTOR					
❑ APL1-0090	A Simpler Time	1973	3.00	6.00	12.00
❑ APL1-0267	Jim Weatherly	1974	3.00	6.00	12.00
❑ LSP-4747	Weatherly	1972	3.00	6.00	12.00

WEAVERS, THE

The famous and influential folk group had this one charted country hit.

Number	Title (A Side/B Side)	Yr	VG	VG+	NM
45s					
DECCA					
❑ 9-27515	On Top of Old Smoky/Across the Wide Missouri	1951	5.00	10.00	20.00
—With Terry Gilkyson					

WEBB, JAY LEE

Number	Title (A Side/B Side)	Yr	VG	VG+	NM
45s					
DECCA					
❑ 32087	I Come Home a-Drinking (To a Worn-Out Wife Like You)/Since You Made a Wreck Out of Me	1967	2.50	5.00	10.00
—As "Jack Webb"					
❑ 32145	Bottle Turn Her Off/You Never Were Mine	1967	2.00	4.00	8.00
❑ 32286	I'll Build Her Up/Tootsie's Wall	1968	—	3.50	7.00
❑ 32430	She's Lookin' Better by the Minute/The House Where Losers Go	1969	—	3.50	7.00
❑ 32512	Broad Minded Man/Get a Lot While You're Young	1969	—	3.50	7.00
❑ 32591	Your Cow's Gonna Get Out/Finance Company Waltz	1969	—	3.50	7.00
❑ 32710	Bloomin' Fools/If I Go On a-Livin'	1970	—	3.00	6.00
❑ 32798	I Was Ready for the World/Whole Lot of Nothin'	1971	—	3.00	6.00
❑ 32887	The Happiness of Having You/Don't Blow Your Horn, Gabe	1971	—	3.50	7.00
❑ 32960	You're Not Here/Love Me Back to Life	1972	—	3.50	7.00
O'BRIEN					
❑ 329	Country Queens/More Than I Love You	197?	—	3.00	6.00
❑ 332	Let's Make Memories Together/You Are the One	197?	—	3.00	6.00
❑ 333	Together We'll Make It/More Than I Love You	197?	—	3.00	6.00
—Possibly as "Jay Lee and Luanne"					
Albums					
DECCA					
❑ DL 4933 [M]	I Come Home a-Drinkin'	1967	6.25	12.50	25.00
❑ DL 74933 [S]	I Come Home a-Drinkin'	1967	5.00	10.00	20.00
❑ DL 75121	She's Looking Better by the Minute	1969	5.00	10.00	20.00

WEBB, JUNE

Number	Title (A Side/B Side)	Yr	VG	VG+	NM
45s					
HICKORY					
❑ 1079	I'm So Lonesome I Could Cry/Love	1958	5.00	10.00	20.00
❑ 1086	A Mansion on the Hill/Friendly Enemy	1958	5.00	10.00	20.00
❑ 1096	Conscience/You Take the Table	1959	5.00	10.00	20.00
❑ 1105	I Wonder If You Know/What a Price to Pay	1959	5.00	10.00	20.00
❑ 1120	Love Has Come My Way/Sweeter Than Flowers	1960	3.75	7.50	15.00
❑ 1129	Take Me Home (To My Lover)/I Was Just Meant to Be Lonely	1960	3.75	7.50	15.00

WEBSTER, CHASE

Number	Title (A Side/B Side)	Yr	VG	VG+	NM
45s					
CAMEO					
❑ 288	Uptown/Where Are You	1963	3.00	6.00	12.00
❑ 312	Cry Cry Darling/Suit Cash	1964	3.00	6.00	12.00
DOT					
❑ 16270	Could This Be Magic/Sweethearts in Heaven	1961	3.75	7.50	15.00
❑ 16318	For Sale/Patty Cake	1961	3.75	7.50	15.00
❑ 16367	Handful of Friends/I Can't Walk Away	1962	3.75	7.50	15.00
❑ 16384	I'll Light a Candle/Like I've Never Been Gone	1962	3.75	7.50	15.00
❑ 16466	Your Old Love Letters/The Town Sleeps Through It	1963	3.75	7.50	15.00
HICKORY					
❑ 1283	Life Can Have Meaning/Where Is Your Heart Tonight	1964	2.50	5.00	10.00
❑ 1303	Cry Cry Darling/Find Out	1965	2.50	5.00	10.00
SHOW BIZ					
❑ 226	Reuben James/Strange Day	1969	2.50	5.00	10.00
❑ 230	You're So Easy to Love/Livin' Laughin' Love-In	1970	2.50	5.00	10.00
❑ 233	Moody River/Turn Out the Lights	1970	2.50	5.00	10.00
❑ 237	Happy in the Morning/Love or the Wine	1970	2.50	5.00	10.00
❑ 241	Honky Tonkin'/I'll Just Have to Pay	1970	2.50	5.00	10.00
SOUTHERN SOUND					
❑ 101	Moody River/The Dreamer	196?	5.00	10.00	20.00

WEBSTER BROTHERS, THE

Number	Title (A Side/B Side)	Yr	VG	VG+	NM
45s					
COLUMBIA					
❑ 4-21421	Seven Year Blues/Road of Broken Hearts	1955	5.00	10.00	20.00
❑ 4-21473	Looking Through the Windows of Heaven/Walking in God's Sunshine	1955	5.00	10.00	20.00
❑ 4-21503	Only One Heart/Watching the Clock	1956	5.00	10.00	20.00
❑ 4-21563	Where We Never Grow Old/Somebody Touched Me	1956	5.00	10.00	20.00

WEISS, LARRY

Number	Title (A Side/B Side)	Yr	VG	VG+	NM
45s					
20TH CENTURY					
❑ 2084	Rhinestone Cowboy/Sweet Ophelia	1974	2.00	4.00	8.00
—This recording of the A-side, by its composer, predates the hit by Glen Campbell					
❑ 2122	The World Was Filled with Love/She's Everything She Doesn't Want to Be	1974	—	2.50	5.00
Albums					
20TH CENTURY					
❑ T-428	Black and Blue Suite	1974	3.75	7.50	15.00

WEISSBERG, ERIC, AND MARSHALL BRICKMAN

Number	Title (A Side/B Side)	Yr	VG	VG+	NM
Albums					
ELEKTRA					
❑ EKL-238 [M]	New Dimensions in Banjo and Bluegrass	1963	5.00	10.00	20.00
❑ EKS-7238 [S]	New Dimensions in Banjo and Bluegrass	1963	6.25	12.50	25.00
—Mandolin-player label					
❑ EKS-7238 [S]	New Dimensions in Banjo and Bluegrass	1967	5.00	10.00	20.00
—Tan label with large stylized "E" at top					
❑ EKS-7238 [S]	New Dimensions in Banjo and Bluegrass	1969	3.75	7.50	15.00
—Red label with large stylized "E" at top					
❑ EKS-7238 [S]	New Dimensions in Banjo and Bluegrass	1971	3.00	6.00	12.00
—Butterfly label					
❑ EKS-7238 [S]	New Dimensions in Banjo and Bluegrass	1980	2.50	5.00	10.00
—Red label with Warner Communications logo in lower right					

WEISSBERG, ERIC, AND DELIVERANCE

Number	Title (A Side/B Side)	Yr	VG	VG+	NM
45s					
EPIC					
❑ 50072	Yakety Yak/Meadow Muffins	1975	—	2.00	4.00
WARNER BROS.					
❑ 7718	Reuben's Train/Scalded Cat	1973	—	2.00	4.00
❑ 7756	Opening Day/Concrete Canyon Boogie	1973	—	2.00	4.00
Albums					
WARNER BROS.					
❑ BS 2720	Rural Free Delivery	1973	2.50	5.00	10.00

WEISSBERG, ERIC, AND STEVE MANDELL

Number	Title (A Side/B Side)	Yr	VG	VG+	NM
45s					
WARNER BROS.					
❑ 7659	Dueling Banjos/End of a Dream	1972	—	3.00	6.00
—First pressings mark the A-side as "from the Warner Bros. motion picture Deliverance" with no artist mentioned on the B-side					
❑ 7659	Dueling Banjos/End of a Dream	1973	—	2.00	4.00
—Later pressings credit the musicians					
Albums					
WARNER BROS.					
❑ BS 2683	Dueling Banjos from Deliverance	1973	2.50	5.00	10.00
—Except for the title song and "End of a Dream," this is actually a reissue of Elektra 7238; green label					
❑ BS 2683	Dueling Banjos from Deliverance	1973	2.00	4.00	8.00
—"Burbank" palm trees label					
❑ BS 2683	Dueling Banjos from Deliverance	1979	—	3.00	6.00
—Tan or white label					

WELCH, ERNIE

Number	Title (A Side/B Side)	Yr	VG	VG+	NM
45s					
DUCK TAPE					
❑ 021	Who Have You Got to Lose/(B-side unknown)	1989	—	3.00	6.00

WELCH, KEVIN

Number	Title (A Side/B Side)	Yr	VG	VG+	NM
45s					
REPRISE					
❑ 7-18844	Something 'Bout You/I Look for You	1992	—	2.00	4.00
❑ 7-19440	True Love Never Dies/Some Kind of Paradise	1991	—	—	3.00
❑ 7-19585	Praying for Rain/The Mother Road	1990	—	—	3.00
❑ 7-19873	Till I See You Again/A Letter to Dustin	1990	—	—	3.00
WARNER BROS.					
❑ 7-22972	I Came Straight to You/Hello, I'm Gone	1989	—	—	3.00
❑ 7-27647	Stay November/I Am No Drifter	1989	—	—	3.00

WELLER, FREDDY

Number	Title (A Side/B Side)	Yr	VG	VG+	NM
45s					
ABC DOT					
❑ 17554	Love You Back to Georgia/Show Me the Way to Your Love	1975	—	2.50	5.00
❑ 17577	Stone Crazy/Still Making Love to You	1975	—	2.50	5.00
APT					
❑ 25096	Walk Away Slowly/You Better Go Join the Campfire	1966	2.50	5.00	10.00
COLUMBIA					
❑ 10016	You're Not Getting Older (You're Getting Better)/Are We Makin' Love	1974	—	2.00	4.00
❑ 10300	Ask Any Old Cheater Who Knows/A Legend in My Home	1976	—	2.00	4.00
❑ 10352	Liquor, Love and Life/Celia Brown	1976	—	2.00	4.00
❑ 10411	Room 269/I Drank Myself Sober	1976	—	2.00	4.00
❑ 10482	Strawberry Curls/When You Were Mine	1977	—	2.00	4.00
❑ 10539	Merry-Go-Round/One Man Show	1977	—	2.00	4.00
❑ 10598	Nobody Cares But You/Love Doctor	1977	—	2.00	4.00
❑ 10682	Let Me Fall Back in Your Arms/Snuff Queens	1978	—	2.00	4.00
❑ 10769	Bar Wars/One of the Mysteries of Love	1978	—	2.00	4.00
❑ 10837	Love Got in the Way/You Win Again	1978	—	2.00	4.00
❑ 10890	Fantasy Island/Take a Little Bit	1979	—	2.00	4.00

Number	Title (A Side/B Side)	Yr	VG	VG+	NM
❑ 10973	Nadine/Too Many Memories	1979	—	2.00	4.00
❑ 11044	That Run-Away Woman of Mine/Atlanta	1979	—	2.00	4.00
❑ 11149	Go for the Night/Two Makes One Wonderful	1979	—	2.00	4.00
❑ 11221	A Million Old Goodbyes/Sleep with Me	1980	—	2.00	4.00
❑ 11266	Lost in Austin/Explosion!	1980	—	2.00	4.00
❑ 11394	Still Your Fool/Tonight I'm Drinkin'	1980	—	2.00	4.00
❑ 44800	Games People Play/Home	1969	—	2.50	5.00
❑ 44916	These Are Not My People/Never Knew Julie	1969	—	2.50	5.00
❑ 45026	Down in the Boondocks/Amarillo, Texas	1969	—	2.50	5.00
❑ 45087	I Shook the Hand/We Gotta All Get Together	1970	—	2.50	5.00
❑ 45138	Listen to the Young Folks/That Little Boy	1970	—	3.00	6.00
❑ 45276	The Promised Land/Goodnight Sandy	1970	—	2.50	5.00
❑ 45388	Indian Lake/Over You	1971	—	2.50	5.00
❑ 45451	Another Night of Love/Always Something Special	1971	—	2.50	5.00
❑ 45542	Ballad of a Hillbilly Singer/Good Old-Fashioned Music	1972	—	2.50	5.00
❑ 45624	The Roadmaster/Who Do You Love	1972	—	2.50	5.00
❑ 45723	She Loves Me (Right Out of My Mind)/Angel on My Shoulder	1972	—	2.50	5.00
❑ 45827	Too Much Monkey Business/It Sure Feels Good	1973	—	2.50	5.00
❑ 45902	The Perfect Stranger/Betty Ann and Shirley Cole	1973	—	2.50	5.00
❑ 45968	I've Just Got to Know (How Loving You Would Be)/Georgia Girl	1973	—	2.50	5.00
❑ 46040	Sexy Lady/Bobby Crabtree's Grave	1974	—	2.50	5.00
DORE					
❑ 595	No One to Love/Mary, I'm Glad to See You	1961	3.75	7.50	15.00

Albums

Number	Title	Yr	VG	VG+	NM
ABC DOT					
❑ DOSD-2026	Love You Back to Georgia	1975	3.00	6.00	12.00
COLUMBIA					
❑ CS 1036	Listen to the Young Folks	1970	3.75	7.50	15.00
❑ CS 9904	Games People Play/These Are Not My People	1969	3.75	7.50	15.00
❑ C 30638	Promised Land	1971	3.00	6.00	12.00
❑ KC 31769	Roadmaster	1972	3.00	6.00	12.00
❑ KC 32218	Too Much Monkey Business	1973	3.00	6.00	12.00
❑ KC 32958	Sexy Lady	1974	3.00	6.00	12.00
❑ KC 33883	Greatest Hits	1975	3.00	6.00	12.00
❑ KC 34244	Liquor, Love and Life	1976	2.50	5.00	10.00
❑ PC 34709	One Man Show	1977	2.50	5.00	10.00
❑ KC 35658	Love Got in the Way	1979	2.50	5.00	10.00
HARMONY					
❑ KH 31784	Country Collection	1972	2.50	5.00	10.00

WELLMAN, TINY

45s

Number	Title	Yr	VG	VG+	NM
LEE ANN					
❑ 7342	Nothing Left to Lose/(B-side unknown)	1988	—	3.00	6.00

WELLS, CHUCK

45s

Number	Title	Yr	VG	VG+	NM
COLUMBIA					
❑ 4-21134	I'm Not Ashamed/I'm Setting You Free	1953	5.00	10.00	20.00
❑ 4-21183	Just a-Lookin'/If You Could Just Be Mine	1953	5.00	10.00	20.00
❑ 4-21224	Barroom Girl/Three Memories	1954	5.00	10.00	20.00
❑ 4-21275	I Saw the Lord/Heavenly Road	1954	5.00	10.00	20.00
❑ 4-21312	Foot Loose and Fancy Free/Marryin' Preacher Man	1954	5.00	10.00	20.00
❑ 4-21360	Is This the Day/Someone Cares	1955	5.00	10.00	20.00

WELLS, KITTY

Also see ROY ACUFF; RAYBURN ANTHONY.

45s

Number	Title	Yr	VG	VG+	NM
CAPRICORN					
❑ 0208	Too Much Love Between Us/What About You	1974	—	3.00	6.00
❑ 0226	I've Been Loving You Too Long/Too Stubborn	1975	—	3.00	6.00
❑ 0240	Anybody Out There Wanna Be a Daddy/Somewhere Down the Road (There's a Country Girl)	1975	—	3.00	6.00
❑ 0264	Mary Hartman, Mary Hartman/Nickel Candy Bar	1976	—	3.00	6.00
DECCA					
❑ 9-28232	It Wasn't God Who Made Honky Tonk Angels/I Don't Want Your Money, I Want Your Time	1952	7.50	15.00	30.00
❑ 9-28432	I Heard the Juke Box Playing/A Wedding Ring Ago	1952	6.25	12.50	25.00
❑ 9-28525	Divided by Two/The Things I Might Have Been	1953	6.25	12.50	25.00
❑ 9-28578	Paying for That Back Street Affair/Crying Steel Guitar Waltz	1953	6.25	12.50	25.00
❑ 9-28666	You Said You Could Do Without Me/Honky Tonk Waltz	1953	6.25	12.50	25.00
❑ 9-28753	I Don't Claim to Be an Angel/The Life They Live in Songs	1953	6.25	12.50	25.00
❑ 9-28797	Hey Joe/My Cold Cold Heart Is Melted Now	1953	6.25	12.50	25.00
❑ 9-28931	Cheatin's a Sin/I Gave My Wedding Dress Away	1953	6.25	12.50	25.00
❑ 9-29023	Release Me/After Dark	1954	6.25	12.50	25.00
❑ 9-29134	You're Not Easy to Forget/He's Married to Me	1954	6.25	12.50	25.00
❑ 9-29313	Thou Shalt Not Steal/I Hope My Divorce Is Never Granted	1954	6.25	12.50	25.00
❑ 9-29419	Makin' Believe/Whose Shoulder Will You Cry On	1955	5.00	10.00	20.00
❑ 9-29577	There's Poison in Your Heart/I'm in Love with You	1955	5.00	10.00	20.00
❑ 9-29728	Lonely Side of Town/I've Kissed You My Last Time	1955	5.00	10.00	20.00
❑ 9-29823	How Far Is Heaven/Dust on the Bible	1956	5.00	10.00	20.00
—A-side with Carol Sue					
❑ 9-29956	Searching (For Someone Like You)/I'd Rather Stay Home	1956	5.00	10.00	20.00
❑ 9-30094	Repenting/I'm Counting on You	1956	5.00	10.00	20.00
❑ 9-30288	Three Ways (To Love You)/A Change of Heart	1957	3.75	7.50	15.00
❑ 9-30415	(I'll Always Be Your) Fraulein/What I Believe	1957	3.75	7.50	15.00
❑ 9-30551	I Can't Stop Loving You/She's No Angel	1958	3.75	7.50	15.00
❑ 9-30662	Jealousy/I Can't Help Wondering	1958	3.75	7.50	15.00
❑ 9-30736	Touch and Go Heart/He's Lost His Love for Me	1958	3.75	7.50	15.00
❑ 9-30804	Mommy for a Day/All the Time	1959	3.75	7.50	15.00
❑ 9-30890	Your Wild Life's Gonna Get You Down/You'll Never Be Mine Again	1959	3.75	7.50	15.00
❑ 9-30987	Amigo's Guitar/Lonely Is a Word	1959	3.75	7.50	15.00
❑ 31065	Left to Right/Memory of Love	1960	3.75	7.50	15.00
❑ 31123	Carmel by the Sea/The Man I Used to Know	1960	3.00	6.00	12.00
❑ 31192	The Other Cheek/Fickle Fun	1961	3.00	6.00	12.00
❑ 31246	Heartbreak U.S.A./There Must Be Another Way to Live	1961	3.00	6.00	12.00
❑ 31313	Day Into Night/Our Mansion Is a Prison Now	1961	3.00	6.00	12.00
❑ 31349	Unloved Unwanted/Au Revoir (Goodbye)	1962	3.00	6.00	12.00
❑ 31392	Will Your Lawyer Talk to God/The Big Let Down	1962	3.00	6.00	12.00
❑ 31422	We Missed You/Wicked World	1962	3.00	6.00	12.00
❑ 31441	Christmas Ain't Like Christmas Anymore/Dancer (With the Light Upon His Tail)	1962	3.75	7.50	15.00
❑ 31457	Cold and Lonely (Is the Forecast for Tonight)/Is It Asking Too Much	1963	2.50	5.00	10.00
❑ 31501	I Gave My Wedding Dress Away/A Heartache for a Keepsake	1963	2.50	5.00	10.00
❑ 31580	This White Circle on My Finger/(I Didn't Have to) Break Up Someone's Home	1964	2.50	5.00	10.00
❑ 31622	Password/I've Thought of Leaving You	1964	2.50	5.00	10.00
❑ 31705	I'll Repossess My Heart/Kill Him with Kindness	1964	2.50	5.00	10.00
❑ 31749	You Don't Hear/Six Lonely Hours	1965	2.50	5.00	10.00
❑ 31817	Meanwhile, Down at Joe's/Leavin' Town Tonight	1965	2.50	5.00	10.00
❑ 31881	A Woman Half My Age/When Your Little High Horse Runs Down	1966	2.50	5.00	10.00
❑ 31957	It's All Over (But the Crying)/You Left Your Mark on Me	1966	2.50	5.00	10.00
❑ 32024	Only Me and My Hairdresser Know/A Woman Never Forgets	1966	2.50	5.00	10.00
❑ 32088	Love Makes the World Go Around/I'm Just Not Smart	1967	2.00	4.00	8.00
❑ 32163	Queen of Honky Tonk Street/Wasting My Time	1967	2.00	4.00	8.00
❑ 32247	My Big Truck Drivin' Man/You Want Her Not Me	1967	2.00	4.00	8.00
❑ 32343	Gypsy King/When Hearts Grow Hard and Cold	1968	2.00	4.00	8.00
❑ 32389	Happiness Hill/You're No Angel Yourself	1968	2.00	4.00	8.00
❑ 32455	Guilty Street/Shape Up or Get Out	1969	2.00	4.00	8.00
❑ 32455 [PS]	Guilty Street/Shape Up or Get Out	1969	5.00	10.00	20.00
—Her only known Decca picture sleeve					
❑ 32535	Just a Cheap Affair/Don't Call Me Your Darling	1969	2.00	4.00	8.00
❑ 32629	I Don't See What I Say/Gonna Find Me a Bluebird	1970	2.00	4.00	8.00
❑ 32700	Your Love Is the Way/It's Written All Over Your Face	1970	2.00	4.00	8.00
❑ 32795	They're Stepping All Over My Heart/Your Old Love Letters	1971	2.00	4.00	8.00
❑ 32840	Pledging My Love/Thank You for Loving Me	1971	2.00	4.00	8.00
❑ 32889	I'm the Wreck of Number Two/Reno Airport Nashville Plane	1971	2.00	4.00	8.00
❑ 32931	Sincerely/J.J. Sneed	1972	2.00	4.00	8.00
❑ 32976	A Bridge I Just Can't Burn/Love Is the Answer	1972	2.00	4.00	8.00
❑ 33016	I've Got Yesterday/Less Than a Lady	1972	2.00	4.00	8.00
❑ 33047	Full Grown Man/Every Step of the Way	1973	2.00	4.00	8.00
❑ 7-34185 [S]	Dasher (With the Light Upon His Tail)/C-H-R-I-S-T-M-A-S	1962	5.00	10.00	20.00
—Small hole, plays at 33 1/3 rpm					
❑ 7-34186 [S]	Santa's On His Way/(B-side unknown)	1962	5.00	10.00	20.00
—Small hole, plays at 33 1/3 rpm					
❑ 7-34187 [S]	titles unknown	1962	5.00	10.00	20.00
—Small hole, plays at 33 1/3 rpm					
❑ 7-34188 [S]	Rudolph the Red-Nosed Reindeer/Blue Christmas	1962	5.00	10.00	20.00
—Small hole, plays at 33 1/3 rpm					
❑ 7-34189 [S]	Ole Kris Kringle/(B-side unknown)	1962	5.00	10.00	20.00
—Small hole, plays at 33 1/3 rpm					
❑ 9-46409	Precious Memories/Gloryland March	1952	10.00	20.00	40.00
MCA					
❑ 40057	Easily Persuaded/It Doesn't Say	1973	—	3.00	6.00
❑ 40123	If I Was a Bottle/Mississippi Missus	1973	—	3.00	6.00
RCA VICTOR					
❑ 47-5686	Kiss Me/Why Fall So Slowly	1954	6.25	12.50	25.00
❑ 48-0084	Love or Hate/Don't Wait for the Last Minute to Pray	1949	15.00	30.00	60.00
—Originals on green vinyl					
❑ 48-0333	Make Up Your Mind/All Smiles Tonight	1950	12.50	25.00	50.00
—Originals on green vinyl					
❑ 48-0384	How Far Is Heaven/My Mother	1950	12.50	25.00	50.00
—Originals on green vinyl					
RUBOCA					
❑ 122	Thank You for the Roses/Loving You Was All I Ever Needed	1979	2.00	4.00	8.00
❑ 123	Old Milwaukee Talking/I Never Told Him I Loved Him	1979	2.00	4.00	8.00
❑ 124	I Can't Help It/I'll Hold You in My Heart	1980	2.00	4.00	8.00

7-Inch Extended Plays

Number	Title	Yr	VG	VG+	NM
DECCA					
❑ ED 2163	(contents unknown)	1955	6.25	12.50	25.00
❑ ED 2163 [PS]	Kitty Wells Sings	1955	6.25	12.50	25.00
❑ ED 2361	(contents unknown)	1956	5.00	10.00	20.00

Number	Title (A Side/B Side)	Yr	VG	VG+	NM
❑ ED 2361 [PS]	Kitty Wells, Vol. 1	1956	5.00	10.00	20.00
❑ ED 2362	(contents unknown)	1956	5.00	10.00	20.00
❑ ED 2362 [PS]	Kitty Wells, Vol. 2	1956	5.00	10.00	20.00
❑ ED 2363	(contents unknown)	1956	5.00	10.00	20.00
❑ ED 2363 [PS]	Kitty Wells, Vol. 3	1956	5.00	10.00	20.00
❑ ED 2518	*Winner of Your Heart/Right or Wrong/Pace That Kills/Dancing with a Stranger	1957	5.00	10.00	20.00
❑ ED 2518 [PS]	Winner of Your Heart, Vol. 1	1957	5.00	10.00	20.00
❑ ED 2519	*Each Day/She's No Angel/Broken Marriage Vows/Change of Heart	1957	5.00	10.00	20.00
❑ ED 2519 [PS]	Winner of Your Heart, Vol. 2 (Change of Heart)	1957	5.00	10.00	20.00
❑ ED 2520	*Mansion on the Hill/Standing Room Only/I Guess I'll Go On Dreaming/Stubborn Heart	1957	5.00	10.00	20.00
❑ ED 2520 [PS]	Winner of Your Heart, Vol. 3 (Stubborn Heart)	1957	5.00	10.00	20.00
❑ ED 2584	That's Me Without You/Waltz of the Angels//Lonely Street/Love Me to Pieces	1958	5.00	10.00	20.00
❑ ED 2584 [PS]	Lonely Street	1958	5.00	10.00	20.00
❑ ED 2646 [M]	*Dust on the Bible/I Dreamed I Searched Heaven for You/Lonesome Valley/My Loved Ones Are Waiting for Me	1959	5.00	10.00	20.00
❑ ED 2646 [PS]	Dust on the Bible	1959	5.00	10.00	20.00
❑ ED 7-2646 [PS]	Dust on the Bible	1959	7.50	15.00	30.00
❑ ED 7-2646 [S]	*Dust on the Bible/I Dreamed I Searched Heaven for You/Lonesome Valley/My Loved Ones Are Waiting for Me	1959	7.50	15.00	30.00
❑ ED 2677	*Sugartime/Dark Moon/Bonaparte's Retreat/When the Moon Comes Over the Mountain	1960	5.00	10.00	20.00
❑ ED 2677 [PS]	Kitty's Choice	1960	5.00	10.00	20.00
❑ ED 2684	*Seasons of My Heart/Lonely Is a Word/Send Me the Pillow You Dream On/Amigo's Guitar	1960	5.00	10.00	20.00
❑ ED 2684 [PS]	Seasons of My Heart	1960	5.00	10.00	20.00
❑ ED 2692	(contents unknown)	1961	5.00	10.00	20.00
❑ ED 2692 [PS]	Kitty Wells	1961	5.00	10.00	20.00
❑ ED 2699	*Heartbreak U.S.A./Heart to Heart Talk/This Old Heart/Cold, Cold Heart	1961	5.00	10.00	20.00
❑ ED 2699 [PS]	Heartbreak U.S.A.	1961	5.00	10.00	20.00
❑ ED 2710	(contents unknown)	1962	5.00	10.00	20.00
❑ ED 2710 [PS]	Kitty Wells	1962	5.00	10.00	20.00
❑ ED 2717	(contents unknown)	1962	5.00	10.00	20.00
❑ ED 2717 [PS]	Kitty Wells	1962	5.00	10.00	20.00
❑ ED 2732	*Will Your Lawyer Talk to God/The Big Let Down/I'm Couting on You/I've Got a New Heartache	1962	5.00	10.00	20.00
❑ ED 2732 [PS]	Kitty Wells	1962	5.00	10.00	20.00
❑ ED 2737	*Wicked World/We Missed You/Your Old Love Letters/Slowly	1963	5.00	10.00	20.00
❑ ED 2737 [PS]	Wicked World	1963	5.00	10.00	20.00
❑ ED 2749	*I Can't Stop Loving You/All the Time/Your Wild Life's Gonna Get You Down/Hey Joe	1963	5.00	10.00	20.00
❑ ED 2749 [PS]	All the Time	1963	5.00	10.00	20.00
❑ ED 2763	*I Gave My Wedding Dress Away/A Heartache for a Keepsake/Cold and Lonely/Is It Asking Too Much	1963	5.00	10.00	20.00
❑ ED 2763 [PS]	Kitty Wells	1963	5.00	10.00	20.00
❑ ED 2777	*Talk Back Trembling Lips/Busted/Ring of Fire/Guilty	1964	6.25	12.50	25.00
❑ ED 2777 [PS]	Talk Back Trembling Lips	1964	6.25	12.50	25.00
❑ ED 2780	*Password/B.J. the D.J./Old Records/As Usual	1964	6.25	12.50	25.00
❑ ED 2780 [PS]	Password	1964	7.50	15.00	30.00
❑ ED 2781	(contents unknown)	1965	7.50	15.00	30.00
❑ ED 2781 [PS]	This White Circle	1965	7.50	15.00	30.00
❑ ED 2804	(contents unknown)	1965	7.50	15.00	30.00
❑ ED 2804 [PS]	Burning Memories	1965	7.50	15.00	30.00

Albums

DECCA

Number	Title (A Side/B Side)	Yr	VG	VG+	NM
❑ DXB 174 [(2) M]	The Kitty Wells Story	1963	7.50	15.00	30.00
❑ DL 4075 [M]	Seasons of My Heart	1961	7.50	15.00	30.00
❑ DL 4108 [M]	Kitty Wells' Golden Favorites	1961	7.50	15.00	30.00
❑ DL 4141 [M]	Heartbreak U.S.A.	1961	7.50	15.00	30.00
❑ DL 4197 [M]	Queen of Country Music	1962	7.50	15.00	30.00
❑ DL 4270 [M]	Singing on Sunday	1962	7.50	15.00	30.00
❑ DL 4349 [M]	Christmas Day with Kitty Wells	1962	6.25	12.50	25.00
❑ DL 4493 [M]	Especially for You	1964	6.25	12.50	25.00
❑ DL 4554 [M]	Country Music Time	1964	6.25	12.50	25.00
❑ DL 4612 [M]	Burning Memories	1965	6.25	12.50	25.00
❑ DL 4658 [M]	Lonesome Sad and Blue	1965	6.25	12.50	25.00
❑ DL 4679 [M]	Family Gospel Sing	1965	6.25	12.50	25.00
❑ DL 4741 [M]	Kitty Wells Sings Songs Made Famous by Jim Reeves	1966	6.25	12.50	25.00
❑ DL 4776 [M]	Country All the Way	1966	6.25	12.50	25.00
❑ DL 4831 [M]	The Kitty Wells Show	1966	6.25	12.50	25.00
❑ DL 4857 [M]	Love Makes the World Go Around	1967	7.50	15.00	30.00
❑ DL 4929 [M]	Queen of Honky Tonk Street	1967	10.00	20.00	40.00
❑ DXSB 7174 [(2) P]	The Kitty Wells Story	1963	10.00	20.00	40.00
❑ DL 8293 [M]	Kitty Wells' Country Hit Parade	1956	15.00	30.00	60.00
—Black label, silver print					
❑ DL 8293 [M]	Kitty Wells' Country Hit Parade	1961	7.50	15.00	30.00
—Black label with color bars					
❑ DL 8552 [M]	Winner of Your Heart	1957	15.00	30.00	60.00
—Black label, silver print					
❑ DL 8552 [M]	Winner of Your Heart	1961	7.50	15.00	30.00
—Black label with color bars					
❑ DL 8732 [M]	Lonely Street	1958	15.00	30.00	60.00
—Black label, silver print					
❑ DL 8732 [M]	Lonely Street	1961	7.50	15.00	30.00
—Black label with color bars					
❑ DL 8858 [M]	Dust on the Bible	1959	15.00	30.00	60.00
—Black label, silver print					
❑ DL 8858 [M]	Dust on the Bible	1961	7.50	15.00	30.00
—Black label with color bars					
❑ DL 8888 [M]	After Dark	1959	15.00	30.00	60.00
—Black label, silver print					
❑ DL 8888 [M]	After Dark	1961	7.50	15.00	30.00
—Black label with color bars					
❑ DL 8979 [M]	Kitty's Choice	1960	12.50	25.00	50.00
—Black label, silver print					
❑ DL 8979 [M]	Kitty's Choice	1961	6.25	12.50	25.00
—Black label with color bars					
❑ DL 74075 [S]	Seasons of My Heart	1961	10.00	20.00	40.00
❑ DL 74108 [R]	Kitty Wells' Golden Favorites	196?	5.00	10.00	20.00
❑ DL 74141 [S]	Heartbreak U.S.A.	1961	10.00	20.00	40.00
❑ DL 74197 [S]	Queen of Country Music	1962	10.00	20.00	40.00
❑ DL 74270 [S]	Singing on Sunday	1962	10.00	20.00	40.00
❑ DL 74349 [S]	Christmas Day with Kitty Wells	1962	7.50	15.00	30.00
❑ DL 74493 [S]	Especially for You	1964	7.50	15.00	30.00
❑ DL 74554 [S]	Country Music Time	1964	7.50	15.00	30.00
❑ DL 74612 [S]	Burning Memories	1965	7.50	15.00	30.00
❑ DL 74658 [S]	Lonesome Sad and Blue	1965	7.50	15.00	30.00
❑ DL 74679 [S]	Family Gospel Sing	1965	7.50	15.00	30.00
❑ DL 74741 [S]	Kitty Wells Sings Songs Made Famous by Jim Reeves	1966	7.50	15.00	30.00
❑ DL 74776 [S]	Country All the Way	1966	7.50	15.00	30.00
❑ DL 74831 [S]	The Kitty Wells Show	1966	7.50	15.00	30.00
❑ DL 74857 [S]	Love Makes the World Go Around	1967	7.50	15.00	30.00
❑ DL 74929 [S]	Queen of Honky Tonk Street	1967	6.25	12.50	25.00
❑ DL 74961	Kitty Wells Showcase	1968	6.25	12.50	25.00
❑ DL 75001	Kitty Wells' Greatest Hits	1968	6.25	12.50	25.00
❑ DL 75067	Cream of Country Hits	1968	6.25	12.50	25.00
❑ DL 75098	Guilty Street	1969	6.25	12.50	25.00
❑ DL 75164	Bouquet of Country Hits	1969	5.00	10.00	20.00
❑ DL 75221	Singin' 'Em Country	1970	5.00	10.00	20.00
❑ DL 75245	Your Love Is the Way	1970	5.00	10.00	20.00
❑ DL 75277	They're Stepping All Over My Heart	1971	5.00	10.00	20.00
❑ DL 75313	Pledging My Love	1971	5.00	10.00	20.00
❑ DL 75325	Heartwarming Gospel Songs	1972	5.00	10.00	20.00
❑ DL 75350	Sincerely	1972	5.00	10.00	20.00
❑ DL 75382	I've Got Yesterday	1972	5.00	10.00	20.00
❑ DL 78293 [R]	Kitty Wells' Country Hit Parade	196?	5.00	10.00	20.00
❑ DL 78552 [R]	Winner of Your Heart	196?	5.00	10.00	20.00
❑ DL 78732 [R]	Lonely Street	196?	5.00	10.00	20.00
❑ DL 78858 [R]	Dust on the Bible	196?	5.00	10.00	20.00
❑ DL 78979 [S]	Kitty's Choice	1960	15.00	30.00	60.00
—Maroon label, silver print					
❑ DL 78979 [S]	Kitty's Choice	1961	7.50	15.00	30.00
—Black label with color bars					

WELLS, KITTY, AND ROY DRUSKY

Also see each artist's individual listings.

45s

DECCA

Number	Title (A Side/B Side)	Yr	VG	VG+	NM
❑ 31164	I Can't Tell My Heart That/When Do You Love Me	1960	3.00	6.00	12.00
❑ 31523	Another Chance to Fall in Love/My World's Losing You	1963	2.50	5.00	10.00

WELLS, KITTY, AND RED FOLEY

Also see each artist's individual listings.

45s

Number	Title (A Side/B Side)	Yr	VG	VG+	NM
❑ 9-29065	One by One/I'm a Stranger in My Home	1954	6.25	12.50	25.00
❑ 9-29228	Skinnie Minnie (Fishtart)/Thank You for Calling	1954	6.25	12.50	25.00
❑ 9-29390	As Long As I Live/Make Believe ('Til We Can Make It Come True)	1955	5.00	10.00	20.00
❑ 9-29740	You and Me/No One But You	1955	5.00	10.00	20.00
❑ 32126	Happiness Means You/Hello Number One	1967	2.00	4.00	8.00
❑ 32223	Living as Strangers/Loved and Wanted	1967	2.00	4.00	8.00
❑ 32427	Have I Told You Lately That I Love You?/We Need One More Chance	1968	2.00	4.00	8.00

7-Inch Extended Plays

DECCA

Number	Title (A Side/B Side)	Yr	VG	VG+	NM
❑ ED 2667	(contents unknown)	1959	6.25	12.50	25.00
❑ ED 2667 [PS]	Kitty Wells and Red Foley	1959	6.25	12.50	25.00

Albums

DECCA

Number	Title (A Side/B Side)	Yr	VG	VG+	NM
❑ DL 4109 [M]	Golden Favorites	1961	7.50	15.00	30.00
❑ DL 4906 [M]	Together Again	1967	7.50	15.00	30.00
❑ DL 74109 [S]	Golden Favorites	1961	10.00	20.00	40.00
❑ DL 74906 [S]	Together Again	1967	6.25	12.50	25.00

WELLS, KITTY, AND WEBB PIERCE

Also see each artist's individual listings.

45s

Number	Title (A Side/B Side)	Yr	VG	VG+	NM
❑ 9-30183	Oh So Many Years/Can You Find It in Your Heart	1957	3.75	7.50	15.00
❑ 9-30489	One Week Later/When I'm with You	1957	3.75	7.50	15.00
❑ 31663	Finally/He Made You for Me	1964	2.50	5.00	10.00

7-Inch Extended Plays

DECCA

Number	Title (A Side/B Side)	Yr	VG	VG+	NM
❑ ED 2666	*Oh So Many Years/One Week Later/When I'm With You/Can You FInd It in Your Heart	1959	6.25	12.50	25.00
❑ ED 2666 [PS]	Kitty Wells and Webb Pierce	1959	6.25	12.50	25.00

WELLS, KITTY, AND JOHNNY WRIGHT

Also see each artist's individual listings.

45s

DECCA

Number	Title (A Side/B Side)	Yr	VG	VG+	NM
❑ 32294	We'll Stick Together/Heartbreak Waltz	1968	2.00	4.00	8.00
❑ 32604	There Won't Be Any Tree This Christmas/White Christmas	1969	2.00	4.00	8.00

Albums

DECCA

Number	Title (A Side/B Side)	Yr	VG	VG+	NM
❑ DL 75028	We'll Stick Together	1968	6.25	12.50	25.00

WELLS, MIKE

45s

PLAYBOY

Number	Title (A Side/B Side)	Yr	VG	VG+	NM
❑ 6029	Sing a Love Song, Porter Wagoner/Detour	1975	—	2.50	5.00
❑ 6042	Shoe-Top Clover/Have You Ever Had an Angel (Love the Devil Out of You)	1975	—	2.50	5.00
❑ 6061	Wild World/The Lady and the Tramp	1976	—	2.50	5.00

WENCE, BILL

45s

LAMON

Number	Title (A Side/B Side)	Yr	VG	VG+	NM
❑ 10129	Christmas in Dixie/(B-side unknown)	198?	—	3.00	6.00

—Possibly as "Bill Wentz"

RUSTIC

Number	Title (A Side/B Side)	Yr	VG	VG+	NM
❑ 1003	Quicksand/(B-side unknown)	1979	—	3.00	6.00
❑ 1005	Break Away/(B-side unknown)	1980	—	3.00	6.00
❑ 1009	I Wanna Do It Again/Quicksand	1980	—	3.00	6.00
❑ 1012	Night Lies/(B-side unknown)	1980	—	3.00	6.00

WEST, DOTTIE

Also see JIM REEVES; KENNY ROGERS AND DOTTIE WEST.

45s

ATLANTIC

Number	Title (A Side/B Side)	Yr	VG	VG+	NM
❑ 2155	You Said I'd Never Love Again/I'll Pick Up My Heart (And Go Home)	1962	3.75	7.50	15.00

LIBERTY

Number	Title (A Side/B Side)	Yr	VG	VG+	NM
❑ 1392	Are You Happy Baby/Right or Wrong	1980	—	—	3.00
❑ 1404	What Are We Doin' in Love/Choosin' Means Losin'	1981	—	—	3.00

—Duet with Kenny Rogers, who is not credited on the label

Number	Title (A Side/B Side)	Yr	VG	VG+	NM
❑ 1419	(I'm Gonna) Put You Back on the Rack/Sorry Seems to Be the Hardest Word	1981	—	—	3.00
❑ 1436	It's High Time/Don't Be Kind	1981	—	—	3.00
❑ 1451	You're Not Easy to Forget/Something's Missing	1982	—	—	3.00
❑ 1479	She Can't Get My Love Off the Bed/Hurt	1982	—	—	3.00
❑ 1490	If It Takes All Night/Try to Win a Friend	1982	—	—	3.00
❑ 1500	Tulsa Ballroom/A Woman in Love with You	1983	—	—	3.00
❑ 1506	The Night Love Let You Down/He's All I Need	1983	—	—	3.00

PERMIAN

Number	Title (A Side/B Side)	Yr	VG	VG+	NM
❑ 82006	What's Good for the Goose (Is Good for the Gander)/Tell Me Again	1984	—	2.00	4.00
❑ 82007	Let Love Come Lookin' for You/Blue Fiddle Waltz	1984	—	2.00	4.00
❑ 82010	We Know Better Now/Let Love Come Lookin' for You	1985	—	2.00	4.00

RCA

Number	Title (A Side/B Side)	Yr	VG	VG+	NM
❑ PB-12284	Once You Were Mine/Dream Baby (How Long Must I Dream)	1981	—	2.00	4.00

RCA VICTOR

Number	Title (A Side/B Side)	Yr	VG	VG+	NM
❑ APBO-0072	Country Sunshine/Wish I Didn't Love You Any More	1973	2.00	4.00	8.00
❑ APBO-0231	Last Time I Saw Him/Everybody Bring a Song	1974	—	2.50	5.00
❑ APBO-0321	House of Love/Love As Long As We Can	1974	—	2.50	5.00
❑ PB-10125	Lay Back Lover/Good Lovin' You	1974	—	2.50	5.00
❑ PB-10269	Rollin' in Your Sweet Sunshine/Carolina Cousins	1975	—	2.50	5.00
❑ PB-10553	Here Come the Flowers/He's Not for You	1976	—	2.50	5.00
❑ PB-10699	If I'm a Fool for Loving You/Home Made Love	1976	—	2.50	5.00
❑ 47-8166	Touch Me/More Than I Meant To	1963	3.00	6.00	12.00
❑ 47-8225	Let Me Off at the Corner/I Wish You Wouldn't Do That	1963	2.50	5.00	10.00
❑ 47-8324	Love Is No Excuse/Look Who's Talking	1964	2.50	5.00	10.00

—With Jim Reeves

Number	Title (A Side/B Side)	Yr	VG	VG+	NM
❑ 47-8374	Here Comes My Baby/(How Can I Face) These Heartaches Alone	1964	2.50	5.00	10.00
❑ 47-8467	Didn't I/In Its Own Little Way	1964	2.50	5.00	10.00
❑ 47-8525	Gettin' Married Has Made Us Strangers/It Just Takes Practice	1965	2.50	5.00	10.00
❑ 47-8615	No Sign of Living/Night Life	1965	2.50	5.00	10.00
❑ 47-8702	Before the Ring on Your Finger Turns Green/Wear Away	1965	2.50	5.00	10.00
❑ 47-8770	Would You Hold It Against Me/You're Just the Only World I Know	1965	2.00	4.00	8.00
❑ 47-8900	Mommy, Can I Still Call Him Daddy/Suffertime	1966	2.00	4.00	8.00
❑ 47-9011	What's Come Over My Baby/How Many Lifetimes Will It Take	1966	2.00	4.00	8.00
❑ 47-9118	Paper Mansions/Someone's Gotta Cry	1967	2.00	4.00	8.00
❑ 47-9267	Like a Fool/Everything's a Wreck	1967	2.00	4.00	8.00
❑ 47-9377	Childhood Places/No One	1967	2.00	4.00	8.00
❑ 47-9497	Country Girl/That's Where Our Love Must Be	1968	2.00	4.00	8.00
❑ 47-9604	Reno/My Heart Has Changed Its Mind	1968	2.00	4.00	8.00
❑ 47-9792	I Heard Our Song/Makin' Memories	1969	—	3.00	6.00
❑ 47-9834	Jack Daniels, Old Grand-Dad, Johnnie Walker and You/Long Black Limousine	1970	—	3.00	6.00
❑ 47-9872	It's Dawned on Me You're Gone/Love's Farewell	1970	—	3.00	6.00
❑ 47-9911	Forever Yours/Cold Hand of Fate	1970	—	3.00	6.00
❑ 47-9947	Slowly/Sweet Thang	1971	—	3.00	6.00

—With Jimmy Dean

Number	Title (A Side/B Side)	Yr	VG	VG+	NM
❑ 47-9957	Careless Hands/Only One Thing Left to Do	1971	—	3.00	6.00
❑ 47-9982	Lonely Is/Cancel Tomorrow	1971	—	3.00	6.00
❑ 48-1012	Six Weeks Every Summer (Christmas Every Day)/Wish I Didn't Love You Anymore	1971	—	2.50	5.00
❑ 74-0239	Clinging to My Baby's Hand/Don't Say a Word	1969	—	3.00	6.00
❑ 74-0601	Cold Hand of Fate/You're the Other Half of Me	1971	—	3.00	6.00
❑ 74-0711	I'm Only a Woman/Baby, I Tried	1972	—	2.50	5.00
❑ 74-0828	If It's All Right with You/Special Memory	1972	—	2.50	5.00
❑ 74-0930	Just What I've Been Looking For/Everything's a Wreck	1973	—	2.50	5.00

STARDAY

Number	Title (A Side/B Side)	Yr	VG	VG+	NM
❑ 517	Angel on Paper/No Time Will I Ever	1960	5.00	10.00	20.00
❑ 547	I Lost, You Win, I'm Leavin'/I Should Start Runnin'	1961	5.00	10.00	20.00
❑ 574	My Big John/Men with Evil Hearts	1961	5.00	10.00	20.00
❑ 724	I'd Be Lying/Walking in the Dark	1965	2.50	5.00	10.00

UNITED ARTISTS

Number	Title (A Side/B Side)	Yr	VG	VG+	NM
❑ XW898	When It's Just You and Me/We Love Each Other	1976	—	2.00	4.00
❑ XW946	Every Word I Write/We Love Each Other	1977	—	2.00	4.00
❑ XW1010	Tonight You Belong to Me/Tiny Fingers	1977	—	2.00	4.00
❑ XW1084	That's All I Wanted to Know/Who's Gonna Love Me Now	1977	—	2.00	4.00
❑ XW1209	Come See Me and Come Lonely/Decorate Your Conscience	1978	—	2.00	4.00
❑ XW1257	Reaching Out to Hold You/My Two Empty Arms	1978	—	2.00	4.00
❑ 1324	You Pick Me Up (And Put Me Down)/We Got Tonight	1979	—	2.00	4.00
❑ 1339	A Lesson in Leavin'/Love's So Easy for Two	1980	—	2.00	4.00
❑ 1352	Leavin's for Unbelievers/Blue As I Want To	1980	—	2.00	4.00

Albums

LIBERTY

Number	Title (A Side/B Side)	Yr	VG	VG+	NM
❑ LT-740	When It's Just You and Me	1981	2.00	4.00	8.00

—Reissue of United Artists 740

Number	Title (A Side/B Side)	Yr	VG	VG+	NM
❑ LT-860	Dottie	1981	2.00	4.00	8.00

—Reissue of United Artists 860

Number	Title (A Side/B Side)	Yr	VG	VG+	NM
❑ LT-1000	Special Delivery	1981	2.00	4.00	8.00

—Reissue of United Artists 1000

Number	Title (A Side/B Side)	Yr	VG	VG+	NM
❑ LT-1062	Wild West	1981	2.50	5.00	10.00
❑ LT-51114	High Times	1982	2.50	5.00	10.00
❑ LT-51129	Full Circle	1982	2.50	5.00	10.00
❑ LT-51145	New Horizons	1983	2.50	5.00	10.00
❑ LT-51155	Greatest Hits	1984	2.50	5.00	10.00

POWER PAK

Number	Title (A Side/B Side)	Yr	VG	VG+	NM
❑ 274	Country Girl Singing Sensation	197?	2.50	5.00	10.00

RCA CAMDEN

Number	Title (A Side/B Side)	Yr	VG	VG+	NM
❑ ACL1-0125	Would You Hold It Against Me	1973	2.50	5.00	10.00
❑ ACL1-0482	Loving You	1974	2.50	5.00	10.00
❑ CAL-2155 [M]	The Sound of Country Music	1967	3.75	7.50	15.00
❑ CAS-2155 [S]	The Sound of Country Music	1967	3.00	6.00	12.00
❑ CAS-2454	A Legend in My Time	1971	3.00	6.00	12.00

RCA VICTOR

Number	Title (A Side/B Side)	Yr	VG	VG+	NM
❑ APD1-0151 [Q]	If It's All Right with You	1973	5.00	10.00	20.00
❑ APL1-0151	If It's All Right with You	1973	3.00	6.00	12.00
❑ APL1-0344	Country Sunshine	1973	3.00	6.00	12.00
❑ APL1-0543	House of Love	1974	3.00	6.00	12.00
❑ APL1-1041	Carolina Cousins	1975	3.00	6.00	12.00
❑ ANL1-2327	Country Sunshine	1977	2.50	5.00	10.00

—Reissue of APL1-0344

Number	Title (A Side/B Side)	Yr	VG	VG+	NM
❑ LPM-3368 [M]	Here Comes My Baby	1965	6.25	12.50	25.00
❑ LSP-3368 [S]	Here Comes My Baby	1965	7.50	15.00	30.00
❑ LPM-3490 [M]	Dottie West Sings	1966	6.25	12.50	25.00
❑ LSP-3490 [S]	Dottie West Sings	1966	7.50	15.00	30.00
❑ LPM-3587 [M]	Suffer Time	1966	6.25	12.50	25.00
❑ LSP-3587 [S]	Suffer Time	1966	7.50	15.00	30.00
❑ LPM-3693 [M]	With All My Heart and Soul	1967	7.50	15.00	30.00
❑ LSP-3693 [S]	With All My Heart and Soul	1967	6.25	12.50	25.00
❑ LPM-3784 [M]	Dottie West Sings Sacred Ballads	1967	7.50	15.00	30.00
❑ LSP-3784 [S]	Dottie West Sings Sacred Ballads	1967	6.25	12.50	25.00
❑ LPM-3830 [M]	I'll Help You Forget Her	1967	7.50	15.00	30.00
❑ LSP-3830 [S]	I'll Help You Forget Her	1967	6.25	12.50	25.00
❑ LPM-3932 [M]	What I'm Cut Out to Be	1968	12.50	25.00	50.00
❑ LSP-3932 [S]	What I'm Cut Out to Be	1968	6.25	12.50	25.00
❑ LSP-4004	Country Girl	1968	6.25	12.50	25.00
❑ LSP-4095	Feminine Fancy	1969	5.00	10.00	20.00
❑ AHL1-4117	Once You Were Mine	1981	2.50	5.00	10.00
❑ LSP-4154	Dottie Sings Eddy	1969	5.00	10.00	20.00
❑ LSP-4276	Makin' Memories	1970	5.00	10.00	20.00
❑ AYL1-4302	Once You Were Mine	1982	2.00	4.00	8.00
❑ LSP-4332	Country and West	1970	5.00	10.00	20.00
❑ LSP-4433	Forever Yours	1970	5.00	10.00	20.00
❑ LSP-4482	Careless Hands	1971	3.75	7.50	15.00
❑ LSP-4606	Have You Heard	1971	3.75	7.50	15.00
❑ LSP-4704	I'm Only a Woman	1972	3.75	7.50	15.00
❑ LSP-4811	The Best of Dottie West	1973	3.75	7.50	15.00
❑ CPL1-7047	Collector's Series	1985	2.50	5.00	10.00

STARDAY

Number	Title (A Side/B Side)	Yr	VG	VG+	NM
❑ SLP-302 [M]	Country Girl Singing Sensation	1964	10.00	20.00	40.00

UNITED ARTISTS

Number	Title (A Side/B Side)	Yr	VG	VG+	NM
❑ UA-LA740-G	When It's Just You and Me	1977	2.50	5.00	10.00
❑ UA-LA860-G	Dottie	1978	2.50	5.00	10.00
❑ LT-1000	Special Delivery	1980	2.50	5.00	10.00

WEST, DOTTIE, AND DON GIBSON

Also see each artist's individual listings.

45s

RCA VICTOR

Number	Title (A Side/B Side)	Yr	VG	VG+	NM
❑ 47-9715	Rings of Gold/Final Examination	1969	—	3.00	6.00
❑ 47-9867	Till I Can't Take It Anymore/I Love You Because	1970	—	3.00	6.00
❑ 74-0178	Sweet Memories/How's the World Treating You	1969	—	3.00	6.00
❑ 74-0291	There's a Story (Goin' 'Round)/Lock, Stock and Teardrops	1969	—	3.00	6.00

Albums

RCA VICTOR

Number	Title (A Side/B Side)	Yr	VG	VG+	NM
❑ LSP-4131	Dottie and Don	1969	5.00	10.00	20.00

WEST, JIM

45s

MACHO

Number	Title (A Side/B Side)	Yr	VG	VG+	NM
❑ 002	Honky Tonk Disco/(B-side unknown)	1979	—	3.00	6.00
❑ 003	Can't Love on Lies/(B-side unknown)	1979	—	3.00	6.00
—With Carol Chase					
❑ 008	Slip Away/(B-side unknown)	1980	—	3.00	6.00
❑ 009	Lovin' Night/Dancin' Round and Round	1981	—	3.00	6.00

Albums

HOME COMFORT

Number	Title (A Side/B Side)	Yr	VG	VG+	NM
❑ 1011	Good Things Goin' Down	1977	3.00	6.00	12.00

WEST, SHELLY

Also see DAVID FRIZZELL AND SHELLY WEST.

45s

VIVA

Number	Title (A Side/B Side)	Yr	VG	VG+	NM
❑ 29106	Now There's You/I'll Still Be Loving You	1985	—	—	3.00
❑ 29265	Somebody Buy This Cowgirl a Beer/Small Talk	1984	—	—	3.00
❑ 29353	Now I Lay Me Down to Cheat/Let's Make a Little Love Tonight	1984	—	—	3.00
❑ 29461	Another Motel Memory/Suite Sixteen	1983	—	—	3.00
❑ 29597	Flight 309 to Tennessee/Sexy Song	1983	—	—	3.00

WARNER BROS.

Number	Title (A Side/B Side)	Yr	VG	VG+	NM
❑ 28648	Love Don't Come Any Better Than This/My Heart Feels Like Dancing Again	1986	—	—	3.00
❑ 28769	What Would You Do/Why Must the Ending Be So Sad	1986	—	—	3.00
❑ 28857	Hold Tight/If I Could Sing Something in Spanish	1985	—	—	3.00
❑ 28909	I'll Dance the Two Step/Why Must the Ending Be So Sad	1985	—	—	3.00
❑ 28997	Don't Make Me Wait on the Moon/Let's Stay the Way We Are Tonight	1985	—	—	3.00
❑ 29778	Jose Cuervo/Country Lullabye	1983	—	2.50	5.00

Albums

VIVA

Number	Title (A Side/B Side)	Yr	VG	VG+	NM
❑ 23983	Red Hot	1983	2.00	4.00	8.00
❑ 25189	Don't Make Me Wait on the Moon	1985	2.00	4.00	8.00

WARNER BROS.

Number	Title (A Side/B Side)	Yr	VG	VG+	NM
❑ 23775	West by West	1983	2.00	4.00	8.00

WEST, SPEEDY

45s

CAPITOL

Number	Title (A Side/B Side)	Yr	VG	VG+	NM
❑ F1805	Hub Cap Roll/Truck Drivers Ride	1951	6.25	12.50	25.00
❑ F1991	Crackerjack/Roadside Rag	1952	6.25	12.50	25.00
❑ F2448	Lover Man/Pennies from Heaven	1953	6.25	12.50	25.00
❑ F3669	On the Alamo/Shawnee Trot	1957	3.75	7.50	15.00

Albums

CAPITOL

Number	Title (A Side/B Side)	Yr	VG	VG+	NM
❑ T 956 [M]	West of Hawaii	1958	20.00	40.00	80.00
❑ ST 1341 [S]	Steel Guitar	1960	15.00	30.00	60.00
❑ T 1341 [M]	Steel Guitar	1960	10.00	20.00	40.00
❑ ST 1835 [S]	Guitar Spectacular	1962	10.00	20.00	40.00
❑ T 1835 [M]	Guitar Spectacular	1962	7.50	15.00	30.00

WEST, SPEEDY, AND JIMMY BRYANT

45s

CAPITOL

Number	Title (A Side/B Side)	Yr	VG	VG+	NM
❑ F2444	Serenade to a Frog/Bryant's Bounce	1953	6.25	12.50	25.00
❑ F2519	Speedin' West/Skiddle Dee Boo	1953	6.25	12.50	25.00
❑ F2892	Bustin' Thru/Our Paradise	1954	6.25	12.50	25.00
❑ F2964	Deep Water/Stratosphere Boogie	1954	6.25	12.50	25.00
❑ F3026	West of Samoa/Flippin' the Lid	1955	5.00	10.00	20.00
❑ F3150	Cotton Pickin'/Sleepwalkers' Lullaby	1955	5.00	10.00	20.00
❑ F3208	Steelin' Moonlight/Caffeine Patrol	1955	5.00	10.00	20.00
❑ F3276	Frettin' Fingers/Chatterbox	1955	5.00	10.00	20.00
❑ F3348	Shuffleboard Rag/Yankee Clover	1956	5.00	10.00	20.00
❑ F3454	Pickin' Peppers/Pushin' the Blues	1956	5.00	10.00	20.00
❑ F3537	Water Baby Blues/Sand Canyon Swing	1956	5.00	10.00	20.00
❑ F3635	Night Rider/Rolling Sky	1957	5.00	10.00	20.00

IMPERIAL

Number	Title (A Side/B Side)	Yr	VG	VG+	NM
❑ 66219	Shinbone/Tabasco Road	1966	2.00	4.00	8.00
—As "Orville and Ivy"					
❑ 66249	Slow Poke/Please Pass the Biscuits	1967	2.00	4.00	8.00
—As "Orville and Ivy"					

7-Inch Extended Plays

CAPITOL

Number	Title (A Side/B Side)	Yr	VG	VG+	NM
❑ EAP 1-520	Hop, Skip and Jump/Old Joe Clark//(B-side unknown)	195?	7.50	15.00	30.00
❑ EAP 1-520 [PS]	2 Guitars Country Style	195?	7.50	15.00	30.00

Albums

CAPITOL

Number	Title (A Side/B Side)	Yr	VG	VG+	NM
❑ H 520 [10]	Two Guitars Country Style	1954	50.00	100.00	200.00
❑ T 520 [M]	Two Guitars Country Style	1954	30.00	60.00	120.00

WEST, SPEEDY, AND CLIFFIE STONE

45s

CAPITOL

Number	Title (A Side/B Side)	Yr	VG	VG+	NM
❑ F1464	Railroadin'/Stainless Steel	1951	6.25	12.50	25.00
❑ F2620	Steel Guitar Rag/One Rose	1953	6.25	12.50	25.00

WESTERN FLYER

45s

STEP ONE

Number	Title (A Side/B Side)	Yr	VG	VG+	NM
❑ 479	Western Flyer/I Would Give Anything	1994	—	2.00	4.00
❑ 485	She Should've Been Mine/I Would Give Anything	1994	—	2.00	4.00

WESTERN UNION BAND, THE

45s

SHAWN-DEL

Number	Title (A Side/B Side)	Yr	VG	VG+	NM
❑ 2201	Bed of Roses/L.A. Freeway	1988	—	3.00	6.00
❑ 2202	Rising Cost of Loving You/So Much Love	1988	—	3.00	6.00

Albums

SHAWN-DEL

Number	Title (A Side/B Side)	Yr	VG	VG+	NM
❑ (# unknown)	The Western Union Band	1987	2.50	5.00	10.00

WHEELER, BILLY EDD

45s

CAPITOL

Number	Title (A Side/B Side)	Yr	VG	VG+	NM
❑ 4149	Humperdink (The Coon Huntin' Monkey)/Baby Martin	1975	—	2.50	5.00
❑ 4231	The Hole (In Uncle Vincent's Wooden Leg)/Dust Marks	1976	—	2.50	5.00

KAPP

Number	Title (A Side/B Side)	Yr	VG	VG+	NM
❑ 595	On the Outside (Lookin' In)/The Right Foot in His World	1964	2.50	5.00	10.00
❑ 606	The Bachelor/Anne	1964	2.50	5.00	10.00
❑ 617	Ode to the Little Shack Out Back/Goin' Down to Town	1964	2.50	5.00	10.00
❑ 655	Burning Bridges/Tonight I'm Singing Just for You	1965	2.00	4.00	8.00
❑ 670	Jackson/The Politician's Dog	1965	2.00	4.00	8.00
❑ 687	Hillbilly Bossa Nova/The Waltz of Miss Sarah Green	1965	2.00	4.00	8.00
❑ 739	The Coming of the Roads/The Doves of San Morey	1966	2.00	4.00	8.00
❑ 845	Half a Man/She	1967	2.00	4.00	8.00
❑ 873	High Flying Bird/They Can't Put It Back	1967	2.00	4.00	8.00
❑ 928	I Ain't the Worryin' Kind/It's More Than Home	1968	2.00	4.00	8.00

NSD

Number	Title (A Side/B Side)	Yr	VG	VG+	NM
❑ 47	Mama's Going Down in the Mine/Time to Make Love	1980	—	2.50	5.00
❑ 84	Bald Headed Men/The Spinster and the Cowboy	1981	—	2.50	5.00
❑ 94	Daddy/Long Arm of the Law	1981	—	2.50	5.00
—With Rashell Richmond					
❑ 108	In Your Spanish Eyes/The Memory	1981	—	2.50	5.00
❑ 124	Pepsi/Chain Gang of Love	1982	—	2.50	5.00

RADIO CINEMA

Number	Title (A Side/B Side)	Yr	VG	VG+	NM
❑ 001	Duel Under the Snow/Ode to the Little Brown Shack Out Back	1979	2.00	4.00	8.00

RCA VICTOR

Number	Title (A Side/B Side)	Yr	VG	VG+	NM
❑ 47-9898	The Day After Tomorrow/Soon As Buddy Gets Home	1970	—	3.00	6.00
❑ 47-9943	Woman's Talkin' Liberation Blues/Little Lucy	1971	—	3.00	6.00
❑ 48-1001	Ode to a Critter/Sally	1971	—	3.00	6.00
❑ 74-0610	Plutebobelle/Gifts	1971	—	3.00	6.00
❑ 74-0656	Betty Bow Legs/Does Mel Tillis Really Stutter	1972	—	3.00	6.00
❑ 74-0739	200 Lbs. o' Slingin' Hound/The Hoedown	1972	—	3.00	6.00
❑ 74-0832	The Girl Who Loved the Man Who Robbed the Bank at Santa Fe/Gabriel's Horn	1972	—	3.00	6.00
❑ 74-0881	Gentle Big Man/Peter Gonzales	1973	—	3.00	6.00

UNITED ARTISTS

Number	Title (A Side/B Side)	Yr	VG	VG+	NM
❑ 50507	West Virginia Woman/One Stop	1969	—	3.50	7.00
❑ 50579	Fried Chicken and a Country Tune/One Excuse	1969	—	3.50	7.00
❑ 50583	Bow of Love/Young Billy Young	1969	—	3.50	7.00
❑ 50597	Coon Hunters/Fried Chicken and a Country Tune	1969	—	3.50	7.00

Albums

FLYING FISH

Number	Title (A Side/B Side)	Yr	VG	VG+	NM
❑ FF-085	Wild Mountain Flowers	1979	3.00	6.00	12.00

FOLKWAYS

Number	Title (A Side/B Side)	Yr	VG	VG+	NM
❑ 31014	When Kentucky Had No Union Men	196?	5.00	10.00	20.00

KAPP

Number	Title (A Side/B Side)	Yr	VG	VG+	NM
❑ KL-1351 [M]	A New Bag of Songs Written and Sung by Billy Edd Wheeler	1964	3.75	7.50	15.00
❑ KL-1425 [M]	Memories of America/Ode to the Little Brown Shack Out Back	1965	3.75	7.50	15.00
❑ KL-1443 [M]	Wheeler Man	1965	3.75	7.50	15.00
❑ KL-1479 [M]	Goin' Town and Country	1966	3.75	7.50	15.00
❑ KL-1533 [M]	Paper Birds	1967	5.00	10.00	20.00
❑ KS-3351 [S]	A New Bag of Songs Written and Sung by Billy Edd Wheeler	1964	5.00	10.00	20.00
❑ KS-3425 [S]	Memories of America/Ode to the Little Brown Shack Out Back	1965	5.00	10.00	20.00
❑ KS-3443 [S]	Wheeler Man	1965	5.00	10.00	20.00
❑ KS-3479 [S]	Goin' Town and Country	1966	5.00	10.00	20.00

Number	Title (A Side/B Side)	Yr	VG	VG+	NM
❑ KS-3533 [S]	Paper Birds	1967	3.75	7.50	15.00
❑ KS-3567	I Ain't the Worryin' Kind	1968	3.75	7.50	15.00
MONITOR					
❑ MF-354 [M]	Billy Edd U.S.A.	1961	7.50	15.00	30.00
❑ MF-367 [M]	Billy Edd and Bluegrass	1962	7.50	15.00	30.00
RCA VICTOR					
❑ LSP-4491	Love	1971	3.75	7.50	15.00
UNITED ARTISTS					
❑ UAS-6711	Nashville Zodiac	1969	3.75	7.50	15.00

WHEELER, KAREN

Also see BOBBY HARDEN.

45s

Number	Title (A Side/B Side)	Yr	VG	VG+	NM
BOONE					
❑ 1074	Best of Two Worlds/I've Heard a Big Wind Blow Before	1968	2.00	4.00	8.00
CAPITOL					
❑ 4697	Ain't No Mountain High Enough/How Will I Get Over You	1979	—	2.50	5.00
CHART					
❑ 5166	The First Time for Us/A Special Day	1972	—	3.00	6.00
❑ 5179	Life Is Life and Life's Like That/Keeper of the Keys	1973	—	3.00	6.00
❑ 5185	I Miss You Already/One Hurt at a Time	1973	—	3.00	6.00
HILLTOP					
❑ 3027	Listen Spot/Deception	1969	2.00	4.00	8.00
❑ 3031	Mama's Kitchen/Stand By Your Man	1969	2.00	4.00	8.00
K-ARK					
❑ 616	Wait Till I'm Sixteen/Going to Hold My Baby	196?	3.00	6.00	12.00
❑ 641	The Bad with the Good/I've Been There	1965	2.50	5.00	10.00
❑ 654	More of Mr. Peters/I've Been There	196?	2.50	5.00	10.00
—With Curtis Keen					
RCA VICTOR					
❑ APBO-0223	Born to Love and Satisfy/A Woman in Love	1974	—	2.50	5.00
❑ APBO-0223 [PS]	Born to Love and Satisfy/A Woman in Love	1974	2.00	4.00	8.00
❑ PB-10034	What Can I Do (To Make You Happy)/You're Smothering Me	1974	—	2.50	5.00
❑ PB-10196	I'm Getting Tired of Holding Hands/A Woman in Love	1975	—	2.50	5.00
❑ PB-10611	In the Middle of the Night/Love Made	1976	—	2.50	5.00

WHEELER, ONIE

45s

Number	Title (A Side/B Side)	Yr	VG	VG+	NM
CHARTA					
❑ 122	I Don't Believe We're Through/Pick Up the Pieces	1978	—	3.00	6.00
❑ 129	Lucie Ann's Song/I Don't Believe We're Through	1978	—	3.00	6.00
❑ 148	Onie's Bop/I'd Rather Scratch with the Chickens	1979	—	3.00	6.00
COLUMBIA					
❑ 4-21371	Little Mama/She Wiggled and Giggled	1955	5.00	10.00	20.00
❑ 4-21418	My Home Is Not a Home at All/That's What I Like	1955	5.00	10.00	20.00
❑ 4-21454	Cut It Out/I'm Satisfied with My Dreams	1955	5.00	10.00	20.00
❑ 4-21500	No I Don't Guess I Will/I Tried and I Tried	1956	5.00	10.00	20.00
❑ 4-21523	Onie's Bop/I Wanna Hold My Baby	1956	15.00	30.00	60.00
❑ 4-40787	A Beggar for Your Love/A Booger Gonna Getcha	1956	12.50	25.00	50.00
❑ 4-40911	Steppin' Out/Going Back to the City	1957	3.75	7.50	15.00
EPIC					
❑ 9540	What About Tomorrow/Sunnyland Farmer	1962	2.50	5.00	10.00
JAB					
❑ 9003	Just Leave Her to Me/Water Your Flower	1967	2.00	4.00	8.00
❑ 9013	Dirt Behind My Years/Burn Another Honky Tonk Down	1968	2.00	4.00	8.00
K-ARK					
❑ 606	Too Hot to Handle/I Need to Go Home	196?	3.75	7.50	15.00
❑ 617	You're Getting All Over Me/All Day, All Night, Always	196?	3.75	7.50	15.00
❑ 620	Go Home/I Saw Mother with God Last Night	196?	3.75	7.50	15.00
❑ 626	White Lightning Cherokee/Stubborn Heart	196?	3.75	7.50	15.00
❑ 671	Too Hot to Handle/I Need to Go Home	1966	2.50	5.00	10.00
❑ 856	Please Don't Plant Pretty Flowers/Which-A-Way, That-A-Way	197?	2.00	4.00	8.00
MUSICOR					
❑ 1096	I'm Gonna Hang My Britches Up/You're Too Good for Me	1965	2.50	5.00	10.00
❑ 1121	Her Porch Came Up to My Knees/Pretty Little Tomboy	1965	2.50	5.00	10.00
OKEH					
❑ 18022	When We All Get There/Run 'Em Off	1952	7.50	15.00	30.00
❑ 18026	Mother Prayed Loud in Her Sleep/A Million Years in Glory	195?	6.25	12.50	25.00
❑ 18037	Closing Time/I'll Swear You Don't Love Me	195?	6.25	12.50	25.00
❑ 18058	Would You Like to Wear a Crown/I Saw Mother with God Last Night	1954	6.25	12.50	25.00
RANWOOD					
❑ 1025	EIO (The Sawmill Man)/Train to Louisville	1975	—	3.00	6.00
ROYAL AMERICAN					
❑ 76	John's Been Shucking My Corn/Make 'Em All Go Home	1973	—	2.50	5.00
❑ 85	Shuckin' My Way to the Hall of Fame/I Can't Pass an Orchard	1973	—	2.50	5.00
STARDAY					
❑ 767	Mr. Free/Dancing	1966	2.50	5.00	10.00
❑ 785	Playing Tricks/I Closed My Book Last Night	1966	2.50	5.00	10.00
SUN					
❑ 315	Jump Right Out of This Jukebox/Tell 'Em Off	1959	7.50	15.00	30.00

Albums

Number	Title (A Side/B Side)	Yr	VG	VG+	NM
BRYLEN					
❑ BN 4448	Something New and Something Old	1982	2.50	5.00	10.00

WHIPPLE, STERLING

45s

Number	Title (A Side/B Side)	Yr	VG	VG+	NM
ELEKTRA					
❑ 46594	The Lady and the Tramp/Really Get to You	1980	—	2.00	4.00
EPIC					
❑ 50282	Hungry/Silence on the Line	1976	—	2.50	5.00
❑ 50366	Believe in Them/Exit 59	1977	—	2.50	5.00
RCA VICTOR					
❑ PB-10349	Maybe Tomorrow Baby Blue/In Some Room Above the Street	1975	—	2.50	5.00
WARNER BROS.					
❑ 8552	Dirty Work/Don't Give Up on Me	1978	—	2.00	4.00
❑ 8632	Then You'll Remember/Nice Guys Always Finish Last	1978	—	2.00	4.00
❑ 8747	Love Is Hours in the Making/What Do You Do with Your Hands	1979	—	2.00	4.00

WHISPERING WILL

45s

Number	Title (A Side/B Side)	Yr	VG	VG+	NM
VISTA					
❑ 104	Double W/(B-side unknown)	1979	—	3.50	7.00

WHITE, BILL

45s

Number	Title (A Side/B Side)	Yr	VG	VG+	NM
PRAIRIE DUST					
❑ 7625	Unbreakable Hearts/Lovely One	1978	—	3.00	6.00

WHITE, BRIAN

45s

Number	Title (A Side/B Side)	Yr	VG	VG+	NM
OAK					
❑ 1050	It's Too Late to Love You Now/(B-side unknown)	1988	—	3.00	6.00

WHITE, BRYAN

45s

Number	Title (A Side/B Side)	Yr	VG	VG+	NM
ASYLUM					
❑ 64267	So Much for Pretending/On Any Given Night	1996	—	2.50	5.00
❑ 64313	I'm Not Supposed to Love You Anymore/Blindhearted	1996	—	2.00	4.00
❑ 64360	Rebecca Lynn/Nothing Less Than Love	1995	—	2.50	5.00
❑ 64435	Someone Else's Star/This Town	1995	—	2.50	5.00
❑ 64489	Look at Me Now/Restless Heart	1994	—	2.00	4.00
❑ 64510	Eugene You Genius/Going, Going, Gone	1994	—	2.00	4.00

WHITE, CHARLEY

45s

Number	Title (A Side/B Side)	Yr	VG	VG+	NM
NSD					
❑ 22	Rocket 'Til the Cows Come Home/My Babe	1979	—	3.50	7.00

WHITE, DANNY

45s

Number	Title (A Side/B Side)	Yr	VG	VG+	NM
GRAND PRIX					
❑ 2	You're a Part of Me/Let It Be Me	1983	3.00	6.00	12.00
—With Linda Nail					
❑ 4	Then You Can Tell Me Goodbye/(B-side unknown)	1983	3.00	6.00	12.00

Albums

Number	Title (A Side/B Side)	Yr	VG	VG+	NM
GRAND PRIX					
❑ 101	Danny White Sings Country	1983	6.25	12.50	25.00

WHITE, JOY LYNN

Her first three Columbia singles were as "Joy White."

45s

Number	Title (A Side/B Side)	Yr	VG	VG+	NM
COLUMBIA					
❑ 38-74412	Little Tears/Maybe in Mayberry	1992	—	—	3.00
❑ 38-74845	True Confessions/Let's Talk About Love Again	1993	—	—	3.00
❑ 38-74952	Cold Day in July/Bittersweet End	1993	—	—	3.00
❑ 38-77565	Wild Love/You Were Right from Your Side	1994	—	—	3.00
❑ 38-77699	Bad Loser/Why Can't I Stop Loving You	1994	—	—	3.00

WHITE, LARI

45s

Number	Title (A Side/B Side)	Yr	VG	VG+	NM
CAPITOL					
❑ B-44251	Flying Above the Rain/Good in Blue	1988	—	2.50	5.00
LYRIC STREET					
❑ 64019	Stepping Stone/Tired	1998	—	2.00	4.00
RCA					
❑ 62420	What a Woman Wants/Good, Good Love	1993	—	2.00	4.00
❑ 62511	Lead Me Not/Anything Goes	1993	—	2.00	4.00
❑ 62622	Lay Around and Love on You/Don't Leave Me Lonely	1993	—	2.00	4.00
❑ 62764	That's My Baby/Where the Lights Are Low	1994	—	2.50	5.00
❑ 62896	Now I Know/It's Love	1994	—	2.50	5.00
❑ 64233	That's How You Know (When You're in Love)/If I'm Not Already Crazy	1995	—	2.00	4.00
❑ 64455	Ready, Willing and Able/Don't Fence Me In	1995	—	—	3.00
❑ 64520	Wild at Heart/Do It Again	1996	—	—	3.00

Number	Title (A Side/B Side)	Yr	VG	VG+	NM
WHITE, L.E.					
45s					
DECCA					
❑ 32968	Face to Face/I Just Wanted You to Know	1972	—	3.00	6.00
❑ 33029	City of New Orleans/Short on Love Too Long	1972	—	3.00	6.00
WHITE, L.E., AND LOLA JEAN DILLON					
45s					
EPIC					
❑ 50389	Hone Sweet Home/It's Almost as Cold Outside	1977	—	3.00	6.00
❑ 50474	You're the Reason Our Kids Are Ugly/The Vacation	1977	—	3.00	6.00
❑ 50504	As Far As I Can Go/If We Only Looked (Closer to Home)	1978	—	3.00	6.00
HO-HO					
❑ 20445	The Big One/What a Day I've Had	19??	—	3.50	7.00
WHITE, MACK					
45s					
COMMERCIAL					
❑ 00033	Just Out of Reach/You Can Have Her	1978	—	3.00	6.00
❑ 00040	Goodbyes Don't Come Easy/(B-side unknown)	1978	—	3.00	6.00
❑ 121	Kiss the Hurt Away/(B-side unknown)	1982	—	3.00	6.00
❑ 1313	Blue Eyes Crying in the Rain/Wild Wild Man	1973	—	3.00	6.00
❑ 1314	Too Much Pride/By the Circle on Your Finger	1973	—	3.00	6.00
❑ 1315	Sweet and Tender Feeling/Thou Shalt Not Steal	1974	—	3.00	6.00
❑ 1316	Ain't It All Worth Living For/Thou Shalt Not Steal	1974	2.00	4.00	8.00
❑ 1317	Let Me Be Your Friend/That Woman of Mine	1976	—	3.00	6.00
❑ 1319	Take Me As I Am (Or Let Me Go)/By the Circle on Your Finger	1976	—	3.00	6.00
❑ 1320	A Stranger to Me/That Woman of Mine	1976	—	3.00	6.00
PLAYBOY					
❑ 6016	Ain't It All Worth Living For/Thou Shalt Not Steal	1974	—	2.50	5.00
❑ 6033	My Heart Would Know/Walking on a Cloud	1975	—	2.50	5.00
Albums					
COMMERCIAL					
❑ 782	Lonely in the Crowd	197?	3.75	7.50	15.00
WHITE, MICHAEL					
45s					
REPRISE					
❑ 7-18499	Country Conscience/The Best Thing I've Ever Done Wrong	1993	—	—	3.00
❑ 7-18694	She Likes to Dance/She Likes to Dance (Dance Mix)	1992	—	—	3.00
❑ 7-18881	Familiar Ground/Me or the Whiskey	1992	—	—	3.00
❑ 7-19128	Professional Fool/Hard Hearted Broken Hearted	1991	—	—	3.00
WHITE, PAUL					
45s					
COUNTRY JUBILEE					
❑ 0101	Elvis, Christmas Won't Be Christmas Without You/(B-side unknown)	1977	3.00	6.00	12.00
SPIN CHECK					
❑ (no #)	Merry Christmas Elvis/I'm So Lonesome I Could Cry	1978	3.00	6.00	12.00
WHITE, ROGER					
45s					
BIG A					
❑ 103	Mystery of Tallahatchie Bridge/Wild Roses	1967	3.00	6.00	12.00
WHITE, TONY JOE					
12-Inch Singles					
CASABLANCA					
❑ NBD 20218	I Get Off On It	1980	3.00	6.00	12.00
—B-side is blank					
45s					
20TH CENTURY					
❑ 2276	It Must Be Love/Susie-Q	1976	—	2.00	4.00
❑ 2322	Texas Woman/Hold On to Your Hiney	1976	—	2.00	4.00
ARISTA					
❑ 0376	We'll Live on Love/You and Me Baby	1978	—	2.00	4.00
❑ 0395	It Must Be Love/We'll Live on Love	1979	—	2.00	4.00
CASABLANCA					
❑ 2279	I Get Off on It/Feelin' Loose	1980	—	2.50	5.00
❑ 2304	Mamas Don't Let Your Cowboys Grow Up to Be Babies/Disco Blues	1980	—	2.50	5.00
COLUMBIA					
❑ 38-03967	Swamp Rap/Living in the River City	1983	—	2.00	4.00
❑ 38-04134	The Lady in My Life/We Belong Together	1983	—	2.00	4.00
❑ 38-04356	We Belong Together/Naughty Lady	1984	—	2.00	4.00
❑ 38-04476	You Just Get Better All the Time/Do You Have a Garter Belt	1984	—	2.00	4.00
❑ 38-04683	Nobody's Baby Tonight/Down by the Border	1984	—	2.00	4.00
MONUMENT					
❑ 1003	Georgia Pines/Ten More Miles to Louisiana	1967	2.00	4.00	8.00
❑ 1053	Watching the Trains Go By/Old Man Willie	1968	2.00	4.00	8.00
❑ 1070	I Protest/Man Can Only Stand So Much Pain	1968	2.00	4.00	8.00
❑ 1086	Soul Francisco/Whompt Out on You	1968	2.00	4.00	8.00
❑ 1104	Polk Salad Annie/Aspen Colorado	1968	2.50	5.00	10.00
❑ 1169	Roosevelt and Ira Lee (Night of the Moccasin)/The Migrant	1969	—	3.00	6.00
❑ 1193	High Sheriff/Groupy Girl	1970	—	3.00	6.00
❑ 1206	Save Your Sugar for Me/My Friend	1970	—	3.00	6.00
❑ 1227	Old Man Willie/Scratch My Back	1970	—	3.00	6.00
WARNER BROS.					
❑ 7468	The Daddy/Voodoo Village	1971	—	2.50	5.00
❑ 7477	My Kind of Woman/I Just Walked Away	1971	—	2.50	5.00
❑ 7505	Lustful Earl and the Married Woman/I Just Walked Away	1971	—	2.50	5.00
❑ 7523	Delta Love/That On the Road Look	1971	—	2.50	5.00
❑ 7591	Even Trolls Love Rock and Roll/If I Ever Saw a Good Thing	1972	—	2.50	5.00
❑ 7607	I've Got a Thing About You, Baby/Gospel Singer	1972	—	2.50	5.00
❑ 7712	Backwoods Preacher Man/Saturday Night in Oak Grove, La.	1973	—	2.50	5.00
❑ 7780	Love 'Tween You and Me/Sign of the Lion	1974	—	2.50	5.00
❑ 8042	Wishful Thinking/Don't Let the Door	1974	—	2.50	5.00
Albums					
20TH CENTURY					
❑ T-523	Eyes	1977	3.00	6.00	12.00
CASABLANCA					
❑ NBLP 7233	Real Thang	1980	2.50	5.00	10.00
COLUMBIA					
❑ FC 38817	Dangerous	1983	2.50	5.00	10.00
MONUMENT					
❑ SLP-18114	Black and White	1969	3.75	7.50	15.00
❑ SLP-18133	...Continued	1969	3.75	7.50	15.00
❑ SLP-18142	Tony Joe	1970	3.75	7.50	15.00
WARNER BROS.					
❑ WS 1900	Tony Joe White	1971	3.00	6.00	12.00
❑ BS 2580	The Train I'm On	1972	3.00	6.00	12.00
❑ BS 2708	Homemade Ice Cream	1973	3.00	6.00	12.00
WHITE WATER JUNCTION					
45s					
JUNGLE ROGUE					
❑ 1004	Sleeping Back to Back/(B-side unknown)	1984	—	3.00	6.00
WHITEHAWK, JOHN					
45s					
LITTLE DARLIN'					
❑ 0064	It Shows on Your Face/I Need Love, Love, Love	1970	2.50	5.00	10.00
❑ 0071	Is It Love/You Live Your Life, I'll Live Mine	1970	2.50	5.00	10.00
WHITEHEAD, BENNY					
45s					
REPRISE					
❑ 1081	Queen of My Heart/Looms of Love	1972	—	3.00	6.00
❑ 1121	Baby My Heart/Looms of Love	1972	—	3.00	6.00
❑ 1131	Blue Eyed Jane/So Long Gone	1972	—	3.00	6.00
WHITES, THE					
45s					
CANAAN					
❑ 689357	Doing It by the Book/(B-side unknown)	1989	—	2.50	5.00
❑ (# unknown)	It's Not What You Know (It's Who You Know)/(B-side unknown)	1988	—	2.50	5.00
CAPITOL					
❑ 5004	Send Me the Pillow You Dream On/West Virginia Memories	1980	—	2.00	4.00
ELEKTRA					
❑ 69855	Hangin' Around/West Virginia Mem'ries	1982	—	2.00	4.00
❑ 69980	You Put the Blue in Me/Old River	1982	—	2.00	4.00
MCA CURB					
❑ 52381	Forever You/(Our Own) Jole Blon	1984	—	—	3.00
❑ 52432	Pins and Needles/Move It On Over	1984	—	—	3.00
❑ 52535	If It Ain't Love (Let's Leave It Alone)/I Don't Care	1985	—	—	3.00
❑ 52615	Hometown Gossip/No One Has to Tell Me (What Love Is)	1985	—	—	3.00
❑ 52697	I Don't Want to Get Over You/Down in Louisiana	1985	—	—	3.00
❑ 52825	Love Won't Wait/Daddy's Hands	1986	—	—	3.00
❑ 52953	It Should Have Been Easy/Love Won't Wait	1986	—	—	3.00
❑ 53038	There Ain't No Binds/Mama's Rockin' Chair	1987	—	—	3.00
WARNER BROS.					
❑ 29411	Give Me Back That Old Familiar Feeling/Pipeline Blues	1983	—	2.00	4.00
❑ 29513	When the New Wears Off of Our Love/Blue Letters	1983	—	2.00	4.00
❑ 29659	I Wonder Who's Holding My Baby Tonight/Follow the Leader	1983	—	2.00	4.00
Albums					
MCA CURB					
❑ 5490	Forever You	1984	2.00	4.00	8.00
❑ 5562	Whole New World	1985	2.00	4.00	8.00
❑ 5717	Greatest Hits	1986	2.00	4.00	8.00
❑ 5820	Ain't No Binds	1987	2.00	4.00	8.00
WARNER BROS.					
❑ 23872	Old Familiar Feeling	1983	2.00	4.00	8.00

WHITING, MARGARET, AND JIMMY WAKELY

Whiting never made the country charts as a solo act, so those records are not listed in this book. Also see JIMMY WAKELY.

45s

CAPITOL

Number	Title (A Side/B Side)	Yr	VG	VG+	NM
❑ F800	Broken Down Merry-Go-Round/The Gods Were Angry with Me	1950	5.00	10.00	20.00
❑ F960	Let's Go to Church (Next Sunday Morning)/Why Do You Say Those Things	1950	5.00	10.00	20.00
❑ F1065	Close Your Pretty Eyes/Fools' Paradise	1950	5.00	10.00	20.00
❑ F1234	A Bushel and a Peck/Beyond the Reef	1950	3.75	7.50	15.00
❑ F1255	Silver Bells/Christmas Candy	1950	5.00	10.00	20.00
❑ F1500	When You and I Were Young Maggie Blues/Till We Meet Again	1951	3.75	7.50	15.00
❑ F1555	Star of Hope/Why Am I Losing You	1951	3.75	7.50	15.00
❑ F1634	Slipping Around/Wedding Bells	1951	3.75	7.50	15.00
—Reissue of 78 rpm hits from 1948					
❑ F1816	Let's Live a Little/I Don't Want to Be Free	1951	3.75	7.50	15.00
❑ F1965	Give Me More, More, More/Let Old Mother Nature Have Her	1952	3.75	7.50	15.00
❑ F2402	Gomen Nasai/I Learned to Love You Too Late	1953	3.75	7.50	15.00
❑ F2528	My Heart Knows/When Love Goes Wrong	1953	3.75	7.50	15.00
❑ F2689	Tennessee Church Bells/There's a Silver Moon on Golden Gate	1953	3.75	7.50	15.00
❑ F3905	Silver Bells/Christmas Candy	1958	3.00	6.00	12.00
❑ 54-40224	Slipping Around/Wedding Bells	1949	10.00	20.00	40.00
❑ 54-40246	I'll Never Slip Around Again/Six Times a Week and Twice on Sunday	1949	7.50	15.00	30.00

7-Inch Extended Plays

CAPITOL

Number	Title (A Side/B Side)	Yr	VG	VG+	NM
❑ EAP 1-403	Slipping Around/Wedding Bells//I'll Never Slip Around Again/Six Times a Week and Twice on Sundays	195?	5.00	10.00	20.00
❑ EAP 1-403 [PS]	Margaret Whiting and Jimmy Wakely Sing	195?	5.00	10.00	20.00

WHITLEY, KEITH

Also see RICKY SKAGGS.

45s

BNA

Number	Title (A Side/B Side)	Yr	VG	VG+	NM
❑ 62934	Charlotte's in North Carolina/A Voice Still Rings True	1994	—	2.00	4.00
—B-side credited to "Various Artists"					
❑ 64277	Charlotte's in North Carolina/When You Say Nothing at All	1995	—	2.00	4.00
—B-side by Alison Krass and Union Station					
❑ 64424	Wherever You Are Tonight/Tell Me Something I Don't Know	1995	—	—	3.00

RCA

Number	Title (A Side/B Side)	Yr	VG	VG+	NM
❑ 3711-7-R	There's a New Kid in Town/A Christmas Letter	1990	—	2.50	5.00
❑ 5013-7-R	Homecoming '63/On the Other Hand	1986	—	2.00	4.00
❑ 5050-7-R	A Christmas Letter/Santa Are You Coming to Atlanta	1986	—	2.50	5.00
—B-side by Pake McEntire					
❑ 5116-7-R	Hard Livin'/Quittin' Time	1987	—	2.00	4.00
❑ 5226-7-R	Some Old Side Road/Light at the End of the Tunnel	1987	—	2.00	4.00
❑ 5237-7-R	Would These Arms Be in Your Way/Someone New	1987	—	2.00	4.00
❑ 5237-7-R [PS]	Would These Arms Be in Your Way/Someone New	1987	—	2.50	5.00
❑ 6901-7-R	Don't Close Your Eyes/Lucky Dog	1988	—	2.00	4.00
❑ 8637-7-R	When You Say Nothing at All/Lucky Dog	1988	—	2.00	4.00
❑ 8797-7-R	I'm No Stranger to the Rain/A Day in the Life	1989	—	2.00	4.00
❑ 8940-7-R	I Wonder Do You Think of Me/Brother Jukebox	1989	—	2.00	4.00
❑ 9024-7-R	Miami, My Amy/Homecoming '63	1989	—	—	3.00
—"Gold Standard Series" reissue					
❑ 9025-7-R	Don't Close Your Eyes/I'm No Stranger to the Rain	1989	—	—	3.00
—"Gold Standard Series" reissue					
❑ 9059-7-R	It Ain't Nothin'/Heartbreak Highway	1989	—	2.00	4.00
❑ 9122-7-R	I'm Over You/Tennessee Courage	1990	—	2.00	4.00
❑ PB-13810	Turn Me to Love/Pick Me Up on Your Way Down	1984	—	2.00	4.00
❑ PB-13967	Living Like Tomorrow (Finally Got to Me Tonight)/Don't Our Love Look Natural	1984	—	2.50	5.00
❑ PB-13996	A Hard Act to Follow/Don't Our Love Look Natural	1985	—	2.00	4.00
❑ PB-14173	I've Got the Heart for You/I Gotta Get Drunk	1985	—	2.00	4.00
❑ PB-14238	A Christmas Letter/If You Think I'm Crazy Now	1985	—	2.50	5.00
❑ PB-14285	Miami, My Amy/I've Got the Heart for You	1985	—	2.00	4.00
❑ PB-14363	Ten Feet Away/Nobody Is His Right Mind Would've Left Her	1986	—	2.00	4.00
❑ 62166	Somebody's Doin' Me Right/Would These Arms Be in Your Way	1991	—	2.00	4.00

Albums

RCA

Number	Title (A Side/B Side)	Yr	VG	VG+	NM
❑ 6494-1-R	Don't Close Your Eyes	1988	2.50	5.00	10.00
❑ 9809-1-R	I Wonder Do You Think of Me	1989	3.00	6.00	12.00

RCA VICTOR

Number	Title (A Side/B Side)	Yr	VG	VG+	NM
❑ AEL1-5870	L.A. to Miami	1986	2.50	5.00	10.00
—Reissue of 7043, has 10 tracks					
❑ AHL1-7043	L.A. to Miami	1986	3.75	7.50	15.00
—Original issue, has 7 tracks					
❑ MHL1-8525 [EP]	A Hard Act to Follow	1984	3.00	6.00	12.00

WHITLEY, KEITH, AND EARL THOMAS CONLEY

Also see each artist's individual listings.

45s

RCA

Number	Title (A Side/B Side)	Yr	VG	VG+	NM
❑ 62037	Brotherly Love/Backbone Job	1991	—	2.00	4.00

WHITLEY, KEITH, AND LORRIE MORGAN

Also see each artist's individual listings.

45s

RCA

Number	Title (A Side/B Side)	Yr	VG	VG+	NM
❑ 2619-7-R	'Til a Tear Becomes a Rose/Lady's Choice	1990	—	2.00	4.00

WHITMAN, SLIM

45s

CLEVELAND INT'L.

Number	Title (A Side/B Side)	Yr	VG	VG+	NM
❑ 02402	Can't Help Falling in Love with You/Oh My Darlin' (I Love You)	1981	—	2.00	4.00
❑ 02544	If I Had My Life to Live Over/Flowers	1981	—	2.00	4.00
❑ 02779	My Melody of Love/Open Up Your Heart	1982	—	2.00	4.00
❑ 03370	Where Is the Christ in Christmas/Sleep My Child (All Through the Night)	1982	—	2.00	4.00
❑ 50912	When/Since You Went Away	1980	—	2.00	4.00
❑ 50946	That Silver-Haired Daddy of Mine/If I Could Only Dream	1980	—	2.00	4.00
❑ 50957	Where Is the Christ in Christmas/Sleep My Child (All Through the Night)	1980	—	2.00	4.00
❑ 50971	I Remember You/Where Do I Go from Here	1981	—	2.00	4.00

EPIC

Number	Title (A Side/B Side)	Yr	VG	VG+	NM
❑ 04358	Blue Memories/Cry Baby Heart	1983	—	2.00	4.00
❑ 04549	Four Walls/Tryin' to Outrun the Wind	1984	—	2.00	4.00

IMPERIAL

Number	Title (A Side/B Side)	Yr	VG	VG+	NM
❑ 5731	Remember Me/Just Call Me Lonesome	1961	2.50	5.00	10.00
❑ 5746	The Bells That Broke My Heart/I'd Climb the Highest Mountain	1961	2.50	5.00	10.00
❑ 5766	Once in a Lifetime/When I Call on You	1961	2.50	5.00	10.00
❑ 5778	The Old Spinning Wheel/In a Hundred Years	1961	2.50	5.00	10.00
❑ 5791	Yesterday's Love/It Sure Looks Lonesome Outside	1961	2.50	5.00	10.00
❑ 5821	Valley of Tears/Annie Laurie	1962	2.50	5.00	10.00
❑ 5859	I Forgot More Than You'll Ever Know (About Her)/Backward, Turn Backward	1962	2.50	5.00	10.00
❑ 5871	Blues Stay Away from Me/You Have My Heart	1962	2.50	5.00	10.00
❑ 5900	The Wayward Wind/Straight from Heaven	1962	2.50	5.00	10.00
❑ 5919	Love Letters in the Sand/You're the Only One	1963	2.50	5.00	10.00
❑ 5938	What'll I Do/So Long Mary	1963	2.50	5.00	10.00
❑ 5966	Broken Down Merry-Go-Round/Never	1963	2.50	5.00	10.00
❑ 5990	My Wild Irish Rose/Chime Bells	1963	2.50	5.00	10.00
❑ 8134	Love Song of the Waterfall/My Love's Growing Stale	1951	6.25	12.50	25.00
❑ 8144	Bandera Waltz/(B-side unknown)	1952	6.25	12.50	25.00
❑ 8147	Cold Empty Arms/In a Hundred Years or More	1952	6.25	12.50	25.00
❑ 8156	Indian Love Call/China Doll	1952	6.25	12.50	25.00
—Black vinyl					
❑ 8156	Indian Love Call/China Doll	1952	12.50	25.00	50.00
—Opaque red vinyl					
❑ 8163	By the Waters of the Winnetonka/An Amateur in Love	1952	6.25	12.50	25.00
❑ 8169	Keep It a Secret/My Heart Is Broken in Threes	1952	6.25	12.50	25.00
❑ 8180	How Can I Tell/All That I'm Asking Is Sympathy	1953	6.25	12.50	25.00
❑ 8189	Restless Heart/Song of the Old Water Wheel	1953	6.25	12.50	25.00
❑ 8194	Once Before/Have Mercy on Me	1953	6.25	12.50	25.00
❑ 8201	Danny Boy/There's a Rainbow in Every Teardrop	1953	6.25	12.50	25.00
❑ 8208	North Wind/Darlin' Don't Cry	1953	6.25	12.50	25.00
❑ 8223	Secret Love/Why	1954	5.00	10.00	20.00
❑ 8236	Rose-Marie/We Stood at the Altar	1954	5.00	10.00	20.00
❑ 8257	Beautiful Dreamer/Ride Away	1954	5.00	10.00	20.00
❑ 8267	Singing Hills/I Hate to See You Cry	1954	5.00	10.00	20.00
❑ 8281	Cattle Call/When I Grow Too Old to Dream	1954	5.00	10.00	20.00
❑ 8290	Roll On Silvery Moon/Haunted Hungry Heart	1955	5.00	10.00	20.00
❑ 8298	I'll Never Stop Loving You/I'll Never Take You Back Again	1955	5.00	10.00	20.00
❑ 8299	Song of the Wild/You Have My Heart	1955	5.00	10.00	20.00
❑ 8304	Tumbling Tumbleweeds/Tell Me	1955	5.00	10.00	20.00
❑ 8305	I'm a Fool/Serenade	1956	5.00	10.00	20.00
❑ 8307	The Whiffenpoof Song/Dear Mary	1956	5.00	10.00	20.00
❑ 8308	Smoke Signals/Curtain of Tears	1956	5.00	10.00	20.00
❑ 8309	Careless Love/I Must Have Been Blind	1957	3.75	7.50	15.00
❑ 8310	I'll Take You Home Again Kathleen/Lovesick Blues	1957	3.75	7.50	15.00
❑ 8312	Unchain My Heart/Hush-a-Bye	1957	3.75	7.50	15.00
❑ 8316	A Very Precious Love/Careless	1958	3.75	7.50	15.00
❑ 8317	Candy Kisses/Tormented	1958	3.75	7.50	15.00
❑ 8318	When It's Springtime in the Rockies/Put Your Trust in Me	1958	3.75	7.50	15.00
❑ 8319	At the End of Nowhere/Wherever You Are	1958	3.75	7.50	15.00
❑ 8320	The Letter Edged in Black/I Never See Maggie	1959	3.75	7.50	15.00
❑ 8321	A Tree in the Meadow/What Kind of God	1959	3.75	7.50	15.00
❑ 8322	A Fool Such As I/The Prisoner's Song	1959	3.75	7.50	15.00
❑ 8323	Indian Love Call/Haunted Hungry Heart	1960	3.00	6.00	12.00
❑ 8326	Roll, River, Roll/Twilla Lee	1960	3.00	6.00	12.00
❑ 8327	Sunrise/I'll Walk with God	1960	3.00	6.00	12.00
❑ 8328	A Lonesome Heart/The Wind	1960	3.00	6.00	12.00
❑ 8329	Vaya Con Dios/Ramona	1960	3.00	6.00	12.00
❑ 66002	Maria Elena/Gortamona	1963	2.50	5.00	10.00
❑ 66012	Tell Me Pretty Words/Only You And You Alone	1964	2.00	4.00	8.00

Number	Title (A Side/B Side)	Yr	VG	VG+	NM
❑ 66040	I'll Hold You in My Heart (Till I Can Hold You in My Arms)/No Other Arms, No Other Lips	1964	2.00	4.00	8.00
❑ 66077	Love Song of the Waterfall/Virginia	1964	2.00	4.00	8.00
❑ 66103	Mansion on the Hill/Reminiscing	1965	2.00	4.00	8.00
❑ 66130	More Than Yesterday/La Golondrina	1965	2.00	4.00	8.00
❑ 66153	The Twelfth of Never/Straight from Heaven	1966	2.00	4.00	8.00
❑ 66181	I Remember You/Travelin' Man	1966	2.50	5.00	10.00
❑ 66212	One Dream/Jerry	1966	2.00	4.00	8.00
❑ 66226	What's This World a-Comin' To/You Bring Out the Best in Me	1967	2.00	4.00	8.00
❑ 66248	I'm a Fool/North Wind	1967	2.00	4.00	8.00
❑ 66262	The Keeper of the Key/Broken Wings	1967	2.00	4.00	8.00
❑ 66283	Rainbows Are Back in Style/How Could I Not Love You	1968	—	3.00	6.00
❑ 66311	Happy Street/My Heart Is In the Roses	1968	—	3.00	6.00
❑ 66337	Livin' On Lovin' (And Lovin' Livin' with You)/ Heaven Says Hello	1968	—	3.00	6.00
❑ 66358	My Happiness/Promises	1969	—	3.00	6.00
❑ 66384	Irresistible/Flower of Love	1969	—	3.00	6.00
❑ 66411	When You Were 16/Love Song of the Waterfall	1969	—	3.00	6.00
❑ 66441	Tomorrow Never Comes/Come Take My Hand	1970	—	3.00	6.00

RCA VICTOR

Number	Title (A Side/B Side)	Yr	VG	VG+	NM
❑ 47-5431	There's a Rainbow in Every Teardrop/I'm Casting My Lasso	1953	6.25	12.50	25.00
❑ 47-5557	Birmingham Jail/Wabash Waltz	1953	6.25	12.50	25.00
❑ 47-5724	I'll Never Pass This Way Again/Please Paint a Rose on the Garden Wall	1954	6.25	12.50	25.00
❑ 48-0069	Please Paint a Rose on the Garden Wall/Tears Can Never Drown the Flame	1949	15.00	30.00	60.00
—Green vinyl					
❑ 48-0145	I'll Never Pass This Way Again/Birmingham Jail	1949	15.00	30.00	60.00
—Green vinyl					
❑ 48-0358	I'm Crying for You/Wabash Waltz	1950	15.00	30.00	60.00
—Green vinyl					

UNITED ARTISTS

Number	Title (A Side/B Side)	Yr	VG	VG+	NM
❑ 0138	Indian Love Call/China Doll	1973	—	2.00	4.00
—"Silver Spotlight Series" reissue					
❑ 0139	Rose Marie/Secret Love	1973	—	2.00	4.00
—"Silver Spotlight Series" reissue					
❑ XW178	Hold Me/So Close to Home	1973	—	2.50	5.00
❑ XW269	Where the Lilacs Grow/Something Beautiful	1973	—	2.50	5.00
❑ XW402	It's All in the Game/Make Believe	1974	—	2.50	5.00
❑ XW530	Happy Anniversary/What I Had with You	1974	—	2.00	4.00
❑ XW619	The Most Beautiful Girl/Foolish Question	1975	—	2.00	4.00
❑ XW690	Everything Leads Back to You/I'm Beginning to Love You	1975	—	2.00	4.00
❑ XW731	Mexicali Rose/As You Take a Walk Through My Mind	1975	—	2.00	4.00
❑ XW1022	Red River Valley/Somewhere My Love	1977	—	2.00	4.00
❑ 50697	Shutters and Boards/I Pretend	1970	—	2.50	5.00
❑ 50731	Guess Who/From Heaven to Heartache	1970	—	2.50	5.00
❑ 50775	Something Beautiful (To Remember)/Jerry	1971	—	2.50	5.00
❑ 50806	It's a Sin to Tell a Lie/That's Enough for Me	1971	—	2.50	5.00
❑ 50852	Loveliest Night of the Year/Near You	1971	—	2.50	5.00
❑ 50899	Little Drops of Silver/Tammy	1972	—	2.50	5.00
❑ 50952	(It's No) Sin/(B-side unknown)	1972	—	2.50	5.00

7-Inch Extended Plays

IMPERIAL

Number	Title (A Side/B Side)	Yr	VG	VG+	NM
❑ IMP 104	(contents unknown)	1954	12.50	25.00	50.00
❑ IMP 104 [PS]	America's Favorite Folk Artist	1954	12.50	25.00	50.00
❑ IMP-130	(contents unknown)	1956	10.00	20.00	40.00
❑ IMP-130 [PS]	Slim Whitman Singing…	1956	10.00	20.00	40.00
❑ IMP-131	(contents unknown)	1956	10.00	20.00	40.00
❑ IMP-131 [PS]	Songs by Slim Whitman	1956	10.00	20.00	40.00
❑ IMP-132	(contents unknown)	1956	10.00	20.00	40.00
❑ IMP-132 [PS]	Songs by Slim Whitman	1956	10.00	20.00	40.00
❑ IMP-133	(contents unknown)	1956	10.00	20.00	40.00
❑ IMP-133 [PS]	Songs by Slim Whitman	1956	10.00	20.00	40.00
❑ IMP-134	(contents unknown)	1956	10.00	20.00	40.00
❑ IMP-134 [PS]	Songs by Slim Whitman	1956	10.00	20.00	40.00
❑ IMP-135	(contents unknown)	1956	10.00	20.00	40.00
❑ IMP-135 [PS]	Slim Whitman	1956	10.00	20.00	40.00
❑ IMP-136	(contents unknown)	1956	10.00	20.00	40.00
❑ IMP-136 [PS]	Songs by Slim Whitman	1956	10.00	20.00	40.00
❑ IMP-137	(contents unknown)	1956	10.00	20.00	40.00
❑ IMP-137 [PS]	Slim Whitman	1956	10.00	20.00	40.00

Albums

CLEVELAND INT'L.

Number	Title (A Side/B Side)	Yr	VG	VG+	NM
❑ AS99-875 [DJ]	Songs I Love to Sing	1980	7.50	15.00	30.00
—Promo-only picture disc					
❑ JE 36768	Songs I Love to Sing	1980	2.50	5.00	10.00
❑ JE 36847	Christmas with Slim Whitman	1980	3.00	6.00	12.00
❑ FE 37403	Mr. Songman	1982	2.50	5.00	10.00

COLUMBIA SPECIAL PRODUCTS

Number	Title (A Side/B Side)	Yr	VG	VG+	NM
❑ P 16323	Christmas with Slim Whitman	1981	2.50	5.00	10.00

EPIC

Number	Title (A Side/B Side)	Yr	VG	VG+	NM
❑ PE 36768	Songs I Love to Sing	198?	2.00	4.00	8.00
—Reissue of Cleveland Int'l. JE 36768					
❑ PE 36847	Christmas with Slim Whitman	1981	2.00	4.00	8.00
—Reissue of Cleveland Int'l. JE 36847					

IMPERIAL

Number	Title (A Side/B Side)	Yr	VG	VG+	NM
❑ LP-3004 [10]	America's Favorite Folk Artist	1954	150.00	300.00	600.00
❑ LP-9003 [M]	Favorites	1956	12.50	25.00	50.00
—Maroon label					
❑ LP-9003 [M]	Favorites	1958	7.50	15.00	30.00
—Black label with stars on top					
❑ LP-9003 [M]	Favorites	1964	5.00	10.00	20.00
—Black and pink label					
❑ LP-9003 [M]	Favorites	1966	3.75	7.50	15.00
—Black and green label					
❑ LP-9026 [M]	Slim Whitman Sings	1957	12.50	25.00	50.00
—Maroon label					
❑ LP-9026 [M]	Slim Whitman Sings	1958	7.50	15.00	30.00
—Black label with stars on top					
❑ LP-9026 [M]	Slim Whitman Sings	1964	5.00	10.00	20.00
—Black and pink label					
❑ LP-9026 [M]	Slim Whitman Sings	1966	3.75	7.50	15.00
—Black and green label					
❑ LP-9056 [M]	Slim Whitman Sings	1958	12.50	25.00	50.00
—Maroon label					
❑ LP-9056 [M]	Slim Whitman Sings	1958	7.50	15.00	30.00
—Black label with stars on top					
❑ LP-9056 [M]	Slim Whitman Sings	1964	5.00	10.00	20.00
—Black and pink label					
❑ LP-9056 [M]	Slim Whitman Sings	1966	3.75	7.50	15.00
—Black and green label					
❑ LP-9064 [M]	Slim Whitman Sings	1959	7.50	15.00	30.00
—Black label with stars on top					
❑ LP-9064 [M]	Slim Whitman Sings	1964	5.00	10.00	20.00
—Black and pink label					
❑ LP-9064 [M]	Slim Whitman Sings	1966	3.75	7.50	15.00
—Black and green label					
❑ LP-9088 [M]	I'll Walk with God	1960	7.50	15.00	30.00
—Black label with stars on top					
❑ LP-9088 [M]	I'll Walk with God	1964	5.00	10.00	20.00
—Black and pink label					
❑ LP-9088 [M]	I'll Walk with God	1966	3.75	7.50	15.00
—Black and green label					
❑ LP-9102 [M]	Million Record Hits	1960	7.50	15.00	30.00
—Black label with stars on top					
❑ LP-9102 [M]	Million Record Hits	1964	5.00	10.00	20.00
—Black and pink label					
❑ LP-9102 [M]	Million Record Hits	1966	3.75	7.50	15.00
—Black and green label					
❑ LP-9135 [M]	Slim Whitman's First Visit to Britain	1960	6.25	12.50	25.00
—Black label with stars on top					
❑ LP-9135 [M]	Slim Whitman's First Visit to Britain	1964	3.75	7.50	15.00
—Black and pink label					
❑ LP-9135 [M]	Slim Whitman's First Visit to Britain	1966	3.00	6.00	12.00
—Black and green label					
❑ LP-9137 [M]	Just Call Me Lonesome	1961	6.25	12.50	25.00
—Black label with stars on top					
❑ LP-9137 [M]	Just Call Me Lonesome	1964	3.75	7.50	15.00
—Black and pink label					
❑ LP-9137 [M]	Just Call Me Lonesome	1966	3.00	6.00	12.00
—Black and green label					
❑ LP-9156 [M]	Once in a Lifetime	1961	6.25	12.50	25.00
—Black label with stars on top					
❑ LP-9156 [M]	Once in a Lifetime	1964	3.75	7.50	15.00
—Black and pink label					
❑ LP-9156 [M]	Once in a Lifetime	1966	3.00	6.00	12.00
—Black and green label					
❑ LP-9163 [M]	Slim Whitman Sings Annie Laurie	1961	6.25	12.50	25.00
—Black label with stars on top					
❑ LP-9163 [M]	Slim Whitman Sings Annie Laurie	1964	3.75	7.50	15.00
—Black and pink label					
❑ LP-9163 [M]	Slim Whitman Sings Annie Laurie	1966	3.00	6.00	12.00
—Black and green label					
❑ LP-9171 [M]	Forever	1961	6.25	12.50	25.00
—Black label with stars on top					
❑ LP-9171 [M]	Forever	1964	3.75	7.50	15.00
—Black and pink label					
❑ LP-9171 [M]	Forever	1966	3.00	6.00	12.00
—Black and green label					
❑ LP-9194 [M]	Slim Whitman Sings	1962	6.25	12.50	25.00
—Black label with stars on top					
❑ LP-9194 [M]	Slim Whitman Sings	1964	3.75	7.50	15.00
—Black and pink label					
❑ LP-9194 [M]	Slim Whitman Sings	1966	3.00	6.00	12.00
—Black and green label					
❑ LP-9209 [M]	Heart Songs and Love Songs	1962	6.25	12.50	25.00
—Black label with stars on top					
❑ LP-9209 [M]	Heart Songs and Love Songs	1964	3.75	7.50	15.00
—Black and pink label					
❑ LP-9209 [M]	Heart Songs and Love Songs	1966	3.00	6.00	12.00
—Black and green label					
❑ LP-9226 [M]	I'm a Lonely Wanderer	1963	6.25	12.50	25.00
—Black label with stars on top					
❑ LP-9226 [M]	I'm a Lonely Wanderer	1964	3.75	7.50	15.00
—Black and pink label					
❑ LP-9226 [M]	I'm a Lonely Wanderer	1966	3.00	6.00	12.00
—Black and green label					
❑ LP-9235 [M]	Yodeling	1963	6.25	12.50	25.00
—Black label with stars on top					
❑ LP-9235 [M]	Yodeling	1964	3.75	7.50	15.00
—Black and pink label					
❑ LP-9235 [M]	Yodeling	1966	3.00	6.00	12.00
—Black and green label					
❑ LP-9245 [M]	Irish Songs The Whitman Way	1963	6.25	12.50	25.00
—Black label with stars on top					

Number	Title (A Side/B Side)	Yr	VG	VG+	NM
❑ LP-9245 [M]	Irish Songs The Whitman Way	1964	3.75	7.50	15.00
—Black and pink label					
❑ LP-9245 [M]	Irish Songs The Whitman Way	1966	3.00	6.00	12.00
—Black and green label					
❑ LP-9252 [M]	All-Time Favorites	1964	7.50	15.00	30.00
—Black label with stars on top					
❑ LP-9252 [M]	All-Time Favorites	1964	3.75	7.50	15.00
—Black and pink label					
❑ LP-9252 [M]	All-Time Favorites	1966	3.00	6.00	12.00
—Black and green label					
❑ LP-9268 [M]	Country Songs/City Hits	1964	3.75	7.50	15.00
—Black and pink label					
❑ LP-9268 [M]	Country Songs/City Hits	1966	3.00	6.00	12.00
—Black and green label					
❑ LP-9277 [M]	Love Song of the Waterfall	1964	3.75	7.50	15.00
—Black and pink label					
❑ LP-9277 [M]	Love Song of the Waterfall	1966	3.00	6.00	12.00
—Black and green label					
❑ LP-9288 [M]	Reminiscing	1965	3.75	7.50	15.00
—Black and pink label					
❑ LP-9288 [M]	Reminiscing	1966	3.00	6.00	12.00
—Black and green label					
❑ LP-9303 [M]	More Than Yesterday	1965	3.75	7.50	15.00
—Black and pink label					
❑ LP-9303 [M]	More Than Yesterday	1966	3.00	6.00	12.00
—Black and green label					
❑ LP-9308 [M]	God's Hand in Mine	1966	3.00	6.00	12.00
❑ LP-9313 [M]	A Travelin' Man	1966	3.00	6.00	12.00
❑ LP-9333 [M]	A Time for Love	1966	3.00	6.00	12.00
❑ LP-9342 [M]	15th Anniversary	1967	3.75	7.50	15.00
❑ LP-9356 [M]	Country Memories	1967	3.75	7.50	15.00
❑ LP-12032 [S]	I'll Walk with God	1959	10.00	20.00	40.00
—Black label with silver top					
❑ LP-12032 [S]	I'll Walk with God	1964	6.25	12.50	25.00
—Black and pink label					
❑ LP-12032 [S]	I'll Walk with God	1966	5.00	10.00	20.00
—Black and green label					
❑ LP-12077 [S]	Slim Whitman Sings Annie Laurie	1961	7.50	15.00	30.00
—Black label with silver top					
❑ LP-12077 [S]	Slim Whitman Sings Annie Laurie	1964	5.00	10.00	20.00
—Black and pink label					
❑ LP-12077 [S]	Slim Whitman Sings Annie Laurie	1966	3.75	7.50	15.00
—Black and green label					
❑ LP-12100 [R]	Slim Whitman	1964	3.75	7.50	15.00
—Black and pink label					
❑ LP-12100 [R]	Slim Whitman	1966	3.00	6.00	12.00
—Black and green label					
❑ LP-12102 [R]	Song of the Old Waterwheel	1964	3.75	7.50	15.00
—Black and pink label					
❑ LP-12102 [R]	Song of the Old Waterwheel	1966	3.00	6.00	12.00
—Black and green label					
❑ LP-12194 [S]	Slim Whitman Sings	1962	7.50	15.00	30.00
—Black label with silver top					
❑ LP-12194 [S]	Slim Whitman Sings	1964	5.00	10.00	20.00
—Black and pink label					
❑ LP-12194 [S]	Slim Whitman Sings	1966	3.75	7.50	15.00
—Black and green label					
❑ LP-12268 [S]	Country Songs/City Hits	1964	5.00	10.00	20.00
—Black and pink label					
❑ LP-12268 [S]	Country Songs/City Hits	1966	3.75	7.50	15.00
—Black and green label					
❑ LP-12277 [S]	Love Song of the Waterfall	1964	5.00	10.00	20.00
—Black and pink label					
❑ LP-12277 [S]	Love Song of the Waterfall	1966	3.75	7.50	15.00
—Black and green label					
❑ LP-12288 [S]	Reminiscing	1965	5.00	10.00	20.00
—Black and pink label					
❑ LP-12288 [S]	Reminiscing	1966	3.75	7.50	15.00
—Black and green label					
❑ LP-12303 [S]	More Than Yesterday	1965	5.00	10.00	20.00
—Black and pink label					
❑ LP-12303 [S]	More Than Yesterday	1966	3.75	7.50	15.00
—Black and green label					
❑ LP-12313 [S]	A Travelin' Man	1966	3.75	7.50	15.00
❑ LP-12333 [S]	A Time for Love	1966	3.75	7.50	15.00
❑ LP-12342 [S]	15th Anniversary	1967	3.00	6.00	12.00
❑ LP-12356 [S]	Country Memories	1967	3.00	6.00	12.00
❑ LP-12375	In Love, The Whitman Way	1968	3.00	6.00	12.00
❑ LP-12411	Happy Street	1969	3.00	6.00	12.00
❑ LP-12436	Slim	1969	3.00	6.00	12.00
❑ LP-12448	The Slim Whitman Christmas Album	1969	3.75	7.50	15.00
LIBERTY					
❑ LM-1005	The Very Best of Slim Whitman	1981	2.00	4.00	8.00
—Reissue of United Artists 1005					
❑ LM-1067	The Slim Whitman Christmas Album	1980	2.00	4.00	8.00
—Abridged reissue of Imperial 12448					
❑ SL-8128	All My Best	1981	3.00	6.00	12.00
—Mail-order album					
❑ LN-10033	Red River Valley	1981	2.00	4.00	8.00
—Budget-line reissue					
❑ LN-10123	Till We Meet Again	1981	2.00	4.00	8.00
—Budget-line reissue					
❑ LN-10124	Ghost Riders in the Sky	1981	2.00	4.00	8.00
—Budget-line reissue					
❑ LN-10125	The Best of Slim Whitman, Vol. 2	1981	2.00	4.00	8.00
—Budget-line reissue					
❑ LN-10152	God's Hand in Mine	1981	2.00	4.00	8.00
—Budget-line reissue					
❑ LN-10153	Country Songs/City Hits	1981	2.00	4.00	8.00
—Budget-line reissue					
PAIR					
❑ PDL2-1085 [(2)]	One of a Kind	1986	3.00	6.00	12.00
PICKWICK					
❑ SPC-3590	Happy Anniversary	1978	2.50	5.00	10.00
RCA CAMDEN					
❑ CAL-954 [M]	Birmingham Jail	1966	5.00	10.00	20.00
❑ CAS-954(e) [R]	Birmingham Jail	1966	3.00	6.00	12.00
RCA VICTOR					
❑ LPM-3217 [10]	Slim Whitman Sings and Yodels	1954	75.00	150.00	300.00
❑ AYL1-3774	Birmingham Jail	1980	2.00	4.00	8.00
—"Best Buy Series" reissue					
SUNSET					
❑ SUM-1112 [M]	Unchain Your Heart	1966	3.00	6.00	12.00
❑ SUM-1167 [M]	Lonesome Heart	1967	3.00	6.00	12.00
❑ SUS-5112 [R]	Unchain Your Heart	1966	3.00	6.00	12.00
❑ SUS-5167 [R]	Lonesome Heart	1967	3.00	6.00	12.00
❑ SUS-5267	Slim Whitman	1969	3.00	6.00	12.00
❑ SUS-5320	Ramblin' Rose	1970	2.50	5.00	10.00
UNITED ARTISTS					
❑ UA-LA046-F	I'll See You When I Get There	1973	2.50	5.00	10.00
❑ UA-LA245-G	The Very Best of Slim Whitman	1974	2.50	5.00	10.00
❑ UA-LA319-G	Happy Anniversary	1974	2.50	5.00	10.00
❑ UA-LA386-E	The Very Best of Slim Whitman	1974	2.50	5.00	10.00
❑ UA-LA513-G	Everything Leads Back to You	1975	2.50	5.00	10.00
❑ UA-LA752-G	Red River Valley	1977	2.50	5.00	10.00
❑ UA-LA787-G	Home on the Range	1978	2.50	5.00	10.00
❑ LM-1005	The Very Best of Slim Whitman	1980	2.50	5.00	10.00
❑ UAS-6763	Tomorrow Never Comes	1970	3.00	6.00	12.00
❑ UAS-6783	Guess Who	1970	3.00	6.00	12.00
❑ UAS-6819	It's a Sin to Tell a Lie	1971	3.00	6.00	12.00
❑ UAS-6832	The Best of Slim Whitman	1972	3.00	6.00	12.00

WHITTAKER, ROGER

British singer generally regarded as "easy listening." He did make the country charts once, and late in his career he was recording for country labels in the U.S.

Number	Title (A Side/B Side)	Yr	VG	VG+	NM
45s					
CAPITOL NASHVILLE					
❑ 7PRO-79035	I'd Fall in Love Tonight (same on both sides)	1990	—	3.00	6.00
—Vinyl is promo only					
❑ 7PRO-79036	But She Loves Me (same on both sides)	1990	—	3.00	6.00
—Vinyl is promo only					
❑ 7PRO-79397	Take Away My Pain (same on both sides)	1990	—	3.00	6.00
—Vinyl is promo only					
MAIN STREET					
❑ 93016	I Love You Because/Eternally	1983	—	2.50	5.00
❑ 93018	There Goes My Everything/(B-side unknown)	1984	—	2.50	5.00
RCA					
❑ PB-10874	Here We Stand/Before She Breaks My Heart	1976	—	2.00	4.00
❑ PB-11218	Last Song/Sea Gull	1978	—	2.00	4.00
❑ PB-11300	Love Last Forever/If I Knew Just What to Say	1978	—	2.00	4.00
❑ PB-11760	You Are My Miracle/Blow Gentle Breeze	1979	—	2.00	4.00
❑ PB-11941	You Are My Miracle/Blow Gentle Breeze	1980	—	—	3.00
❑ PB-11966	Wishes/I Was Born	1980	—	—	3.00
❑ PB-12096	River Lady/Lighthouse	1980	—	—	—
—Unreleased					
❑ PB-12110	A Man Without Love/I Am But a Small Voice	1980	—	—	3.00
❑ PB-12165	Tall Dark Stranger/Goodbye	1981	—	—	3.00
❑ PB-12330	How Does It Feel/Moonshine	1981	—	—	3.00
❑ PB-13030	River Lady/Smooth Sailing	1981	—	—	3.00
❑ JB-13379 [DJ]	Too Beautiful to Cry/Together	1982	—	2.50	5.00
❑ PB-14043	Take a Little-Give a Little/Dover to Calais	1985	—	—	3.00
❑ PB-14147	My Silver Eagle/Chicago Girl	1985	—	—	3.00
❑ PB-14333	The Genius of Love/Everybody's Got a Lonely Heart	1986	—	—	3.00
RCA VICTOR					
❑ PB-10356	I Don't Believe In It Anymore/New World in the Morning	1975	—	2.00	4.00
❑ PB-10447	Durham Town (The Leaving)/Mexican Whistler	1975	—	2.00	4.00
❑ GB-10494	The Last Farewell/Paradise	1975	—	—	3.00
—Gold Standard Series					
❑ PB-10732	Summer Days/The First Hello, The Last Goodbye	1976	—	2.00	4.00
❑ PB-50030	The Last Farewell/Paradise	1975	—	2.00	4.00
—Canadian number, but pressed and released in the U.S. as well					
❑ 74-0320	New World in the Morning/Durham Town	1970	2.00	4.00	8.00
❑ 74-0355	I Don't Believe in It Anymore/I Should Have Taken My Time	1970	—	3.00	6.00
❑ 74-0442	Why/Moonshine	1971	—	3.00	6.00
❑ 74-0501	The Mexican Whistler/What Love Is	1971	—	3.00	6.00
UNIVERSAL					
❑ UVL-66010	Have I Told You Lately That I Love You/Just Across the Rio Grande	1989	—	2.00	4.00
❑ UVL-66030	There Goes My Everything/Love Still Means You to Me	1989	—	2.00	4.00
Albums					
CAPITOL NASHVILLE					
❑ C1 594058	World's Most Beautiful Christmas Songs	1990	3.75	7.50	15.00
—Available on vinyl through Columbia House only					
PAIR					
❑ PDL2-1039 [(2)]	Golden Tones	1986	3.00	6.00	12.00
❑ PDL2-1111 [(2)]	Fire and Rain	1986	3.00	6.00	12.00

Number	Title (A Side/B Side)	Yr	VG	VG+	NM
RCA VICTOR					
❑ AFL1-0078	Traveling with Roger Whittaker	1978	2.50	5.00	10.00
—Reissue of APL1-0078					
❑ APL1-0078	Traveling with Roger Whittaker	1973	3.75	7.50	15.00
❑ AFL1-0855	"The Last Farewell" and Other Hits	1978	2.50	5.00	10.00
—Reissue of APL1-0855					
❑ APL1-0855	"The Last Farewell" and Other Hits	1975	3.00	6.00	12.00
❑ AQL1-0855	"The Last Farewell" and Other Hits	198?	2.00	4.00	8.00
—Reissue of AFL1-0855					
❑ AFL1-1313	The Magical World of Roger Whittaker	1978	2.50	5.00	10.00
—Reissue of APL1-1313					
❑ APL1-1313	The Magical World of Roger Whittaker	1976	3.00	6.00	12.00
❑ ANL1-1405	Roger Whittaker	1976	3.00	6.00	12.00
❑ AFL1-1853	Reflections of Love	1978	2.50	5.00	10.00
—Reissue of APL1-1853					
❑ APL1-1853	Reflections of Love	1976	3.00	6.00	12.00
❑ AFL1-2255	The Best of Roger Whittaker	1978	2.50	5.00	10.00
—Reissue of APL1-2255					
❑ APL1-2255	The Best of Roger Whittaker	1977	3.00	6.00	12.00
❑ AQL1-2255	The Best of Roger Whittaker	198?	2.00	4.00	8.00
—Reissue of AFL1-2255					
❑ AFL1-2525	Folk Songs	1978	3.00	6.00	12.00
❑ AQL1-2525	Folk Songs	198?	2.50	5.00	10.00
—Reissue of AFL1-2525					
❑ ANL1-2933	The Roger Whittaker Christmas Album	1978	3.00	6.00	12.00
❑ AFL1-3077	Imagine	1978	3.00	6.00	12.00
❑ AQL1-3077	Imagine	198?	2.00	4.00	8.00
—Reissue of AFL1-3077					
❑ AFL1-3355	When I Need You	1979	2.50	5.00	10.00
❑ AFL1-3501	Mirrors of My Mind	1979	2.50	5.00	10.00
❑ AQL1-3501	Mirrors of My Mind	198?	2.00	4.00	8.00
—Reissue of AFL1-3501					
❑ AFL1-3518	Voyager	1980	2.50	5.00	10.00
❑ AQL1-3518	Voyager	198?	2.00	4.00	8.00
—Reissue of AFL1-3518					
❑ AYL1-3670	The Magical World of Roger Whittaker	1980	2.00	4.00	8.00
—"Best Buy Series" reissue					
❑ AFL1-3778	With Love	1980	2.50	5.00	10.00
❑ AYL1-3911	When I Need You	1981	2.00	4.00	8.00
—"Best Buy Series" reissue					
❑ AYL1-3946	A Special Kind of Man	1981	2.00	4.00	8.00
—"Best Buy Series" reissue					
❑ CPL2-4057 [(2)]	Live in Concert	1981	3.00	6.00	12.00
❑ AFL1-4129	Changes	1982	2.50	5.00	10.00
❑ AYL1-4177	I Don't Believe in It Any More	1982	2.00	4.00	8.00
—"Best Buy Series" reissue					
❑ AYL1-4178	New World in the Morning	1982	2.00	4.00	8.00
—"Best Buy Series" reissue					
❑ AFL1-4321	The Wind Beneath My Wings	1983	2.50	5.00	10.00
❑ AFL1-4340	New World in the Morning	1978	2.50	5.00	10.00
—Reissue of LSP-4340					
❑ LPM-4340	New World in the Morning	1970	3.75	7.50	15.00
❑ AFL1-4405	I Don't Believe in It Any More	1978	2.50	5.00	10.00
—Reissue of LSP-4405					
❑ LPM-4405	I Don't Believe in It Any More	1970	3.75	7.50	15.00
❑ AFL1-4505	A Special Kind of Man	1978	2.50	5.00	10.00
—Reissue of LSP-4505					
❑ LPM-4505	A Special Kind of Man	1971	3.75	7.50	15.00
❑ LPM-4652	Loose and Fiery	1972	3.75	7.50	15.00
❑ AYL1-5166	The Best of Roger Whittaker	1985	—	3.00	6.00
—"Best Buy Series" reissue					
❑ AFL1-5803	The Genius of Love	1986	2.50	5.00	10.00
❑ NFL1-8047	Take a Little — Give a Little	1985	2.50	5.00	10.00

WICHITA LINEMEN, THE

Number	Title (A Side/B Side)	Yr	VG	VG+	NM
45s					
LINEMEN					
❑ 773	Everyday of My Life/(B-side unknown)	1977	—	3.00	6.00
❑ 10838	You're a Pretty Lady, Lady/Magic Herds	1979	—	3.00	6.00

WICKHAM, LEWIE

Number	Title (A Side/B Side)	Yr	VG	VG+	NM
45s					
MCA					
❑ 40928	$60 Duck/Trucker's Lament	1978	—	2.00	4.00
STARDAY					
❑ 888	Little Bit Late/Endless Love Affair	1970	2.00	4.00	8.00
❑ 902	Hippy Love Song/How Come My Dog Don't Bark	1970	2.00	4.00	8.00

WICKLINE

Number	Title (A Side/B Side)	Yr	VG	VG+	NM
45s					
CASCADE MOUNTAIN					
❑ 2325	Do Fish Swim?/(B-side unknown)	1981	—	3.00	6.00
❑ 2424	Banjo Fantasy/Do Fish Swim?	1982	—	3.00	6.00
❑ 2425	Take Time/(B-side unknown)	1982	—	3.00	6.00
❑ 3030	True Love's Getting Pretty Hard to Find/(B-side unknown)	1983	—	3.00	6.00
❑ 4045	Ski Bumpus/Banjo Fantasy II//Powder Winter	1984	—	3.00	6.00
—As "Wickline Band Featuring Scott Gavin"					
Albums					
CASCADE MOUNTAIN					
❑ 2	Wickline	198?	3.00	6.00	12.00

WIDE LOAD

Number	Title (A Side/B Side)	Yr	VG	VG+	NM
45s					
16TH AVENUE					
❑ 70412	Bread and Butter/Jamestown Ferry	1988	—	2.50	5.00

WIER, RUSTY

Number	Title (A Side/B Side)	Yr	VG	VG+	NM
45s					
20TH CENTURY					
❑ 2188	I Heard You Been Layin' My Old Lady (Apologies to Susie)/Aqua Dulce	1975	—	2.50	5.00
❑ 2219	Don't It Make You Wanna Dance/I Believe in the Way That You Love Me	1975	—	2.50	5.00
❑ 2273	I Don't Want to Lay This Guitar Down/Long and Lonesome Highway Blues	1976	—	2.50	5.00
ABC					
❑ 12019	Stoned, Slow and Rugged/Jeremiah Black	1974	—	3.00	6.00
BLACK HAT					
❑ 102	Close Your Eyes/Kum-Back Bar and Grill	1987	—	3.00	6.00
❑ 103	(Lover of the) Other Side of the Hill/I Kept Thinkin' About You	1987	—	3.00	6.00
COLUMBIA					
❑ 3-10445	I Think It's Time (I Learned How to Let Her Go)/Me and Daisy on the Run	1976	—	2.00	4.00
COMPLEAT					
❑ 107	Don't It Make You Wanna Dance/You Gave Me a Reason	1983	—	2.50	5.00
❑ 121	Lone Star Lady/I Still Believe in You	1984	—	2.50	5.00
LONGHORN					
❑ 101	(Lover of the) Other Side of the Hill/(B-side unknown)	1965	3.75	7.50	15.00
Albums					
20TH CENTURY					
❑ T-469	Don't It Make You Wanna Dance?	1975	2.50	5.00	10.00
❑ T-495	Rusty Wier	1975	2.50	5.00	10.00
ABC					
❑ D-820	Stoned, Slow and Rugged	1974	3.00	6.00	12.00
COLUMBIA					
❑ KC 34319	Black Hat Saloon	1976	2.50	5.00	10.00
❑ PC 34775	Stacked Deck	1977	2.50	5.00	10.00
MCA					
❑ 820	Stoned, Slow and Rugged	1980	2.00	4.00	8.00
—Reissue of ABC 820					

WIGGINS, JOHN AND AUDREY

Number	Title (A Side/B Side)	Yr	VG	VG+	NM
45s					
MERCURY					
❑ 574300-7	Somewhere in Love/I Can Sleep When I'm Dead	1997	—	—	3.00
❑ 856296-7	She's in the Bedroom Crying/New Mexico	1994	—	—	3.00
❑ 858476-7	Falling Out of Love/Memory Making Night	1994	—	—	3.00
❑ 858920-7	Has Anybody Seen Amy/Memory Making Night	1994	—	—	3.00

WIGGINS, ROY

Includes records as "Little Roy Wiggins."

Number	Title (A Side/B Side)	Yr	VG	VG+	NM
45s					
DOT					
❑ 15053	It's a Sin/Cimarron	1953	5.00	10.00	20.00
O'BRIEN					
❑ 321	What Makes My Steel Guitar Cry/Just Plain Country	197?	—	3.00	6.00
❑ 324	Fair and Warm/Jimmy and Me	197?	—	3.00	6.00
❑ 326	Ting-a-Ling Waltz/Hoy Hoy Little Boy	197?	—	3.00	6.00
❑ 328	Fraulein/Candy Kisses	197?	—	3.00	6.00
❑ 330	Cold, Cold Heart/Fair and Warm	197?	—	3.00	6.00
❑ 331	Filipino Baby/Ting-a-Ling Waltz	197?	—	3.00	6.00
❑ 334	No Way Mama/Born to Lose	197?	—	3.00	6.00
PALMER					
❑ 39567	Millie/Steel Guitar Rag	197?	—	3.50	7.00
STARDAY					
❑ 584	Through the Night/Love Theme	1962	3.00	6.00	12.00
❑ 787	You're the One/Annette	1966	2.00	4.00	8.00
Albums					
DIPLOMAT					
❑ DPL 2615 [M]	Songs I Played for Eddy Arnold	196?	3.75	7.50	15.00
STARDAY					
❑ SLP-188 [M]	Mister Steel Guitar	1962	7.50	15.00	30.00
❑ SLP-259 [M]	The Fabulous Steel Guitar Artistry of Roy Wiggins	1963	7.50	15.00	30.00
❑ SLP-392 [M]	Nashville Steel Guitar	1965	6.25	12.50	25.00

WILBOURN, BILL, AND KATHY MORRISON

Number	Title (A Side/B Side)	Yr	VG	VG+	NM
45s					
UNITED ARTISTS					
❑ 50310	The Lovers/Your Gentle Way of Loving Me	1968	—	3.50	7.00
❑ 50474	Him and Her/You're Driving Me Out of My Mind	1969	—	3.50	7.00
❑ 50537	Lovin' Season/Model Couple	1969	—	3.50	7.00
❑ 50603	Mr. Work and Mrs. Play/Don't Try to Change Me	1969	—	3.50	7.00
❑ 50660	A Good Thing/That's the Way I Want It to Be	1970	—	3.50	7.00
❑ 50718	Look How Far We've Come/The Hand That Feeds You	1970	—	3.50	7.00
Albums					
UNITED ARTISTS					
❑ UAS-6685	The Lovers	1969	3.75	7.50	15.00

WILBURN BROTHERS, THE

45s

DECCA

Number	Title (A Side/B Side)	Yr	VG	VG+	NM
❑ 29190	If You Love Me/A Little Time Out for Love	1954	5.00	10.00	20.00
❑ 29277	Carefree Moments/Let Me Be the First to Know	1954	5.00	10.00	20.00
❑ 29459	I Wanna Wanna Wanna/My Heart or My Mind	1955	5.00	10.00	20.00
❑ 29614	Temptation Go Away/Mixed-Up Medley	1955	5.00	10.00	20.00
❑ 29747	You're Not Play Love/Look Around, Take a Look at Me	1955	5.00	10.00	20.00
❑ 29887	I'm So in Love with You/Deep Elem Blues	1956	5.00	10.00	20.00
❑ 30087	Go Away with Me/Great Big Love	1956	5.00	10.00	20.00
❑ 30228	Nothing at All/I'm Setting You Free	1957	3.75	7.50	15.00
❑ 30428	I Close My Eyes/I Got Over the Blues	1957	3.75	7.50	15.00
❑ 30591	Oo Bop Sha Boom/My Baby Ain't My Baby No More	1958	7.50	15.00	30.00
❑ 30686	Cry Baby Cry/Till I'm the Only One	1958	3.75	7.50	15.00
❑ 30787	Which One Is to Blame/The Knoxville Girl	1958	3.75	7.50	15.00
❑ 30871	Somebody's Back in Town/I Love Everybody	1959	3.75	7.50	15.00
❑ 30968	A Woman's Intuition/A Town That Never Sleeps	1959	3.75	7.50	15.00
❑ 31062	Sentenced to Die/You Can't Take It With You	1960	3.00	6.00	12.00
❑ 31114	When Will You Know It/Big Heartbreak	1960	3.00	6.00	12.00
❑ 31152	The Best of All My Heartaches/Someone Else's Love	1960	3.00	6.00	12.00
❑ 31214	The Flame's Still Burning/The Legend of the Big River Train	1961	3.00	6.00	12.00
❑ 31276	Blue Blue Day/No Legal Right	1961	3.00	6.00	12.00
❑ 31333	Tag Along/Gift of the Blues	1961	3.00	6.00	12.00
❑ 31363	Trouble's Back in Town/Young But True Love	1962	3.00	6.00	12.00
❑ 31425	The Sound of Your Footsteps/Day After Day	1962	3.00	6.00	12.00
❑ 31464	Roll Muddy River/Not That I Care	1963	3.00	6.00	12.00
❑ 31520	Tell Her So/Here Comes a Million Memories	1963	3.00	6.00	12.00
❑ 31578	Hangin' Around/Never Alone	1964	2.50	5.00	10.00
❑ 31625	Impossible/I'll Take What's Left of Me	1964	2.50	5.00	10.00
❑ 31674	I'm Gonna Tie One On Tonight/Making Plans	1964	2.50	5.00	10.00
❑ 31764	I Had One Too Many/Left Out	1965	2.50	5.00	10.00
❑ 31819	It's Another World/My Day Won't Be Complete	1965	2.50	5.00	10.00
❑ 31894	Someone Before Me/Something About You	1966	2.50	5.00	10.00
❑ 31974	I Can't Keep Away from You/I'm Gonna Dress Up	1966	2.50	5.00	10.00
❑ 32038	Hurt Her Once for Me/Just to Be Where You Are	1966	2.50	5.00	10.00
❑ 32117	Roarin' Again/Go Mena Si (I'm Sorry)	1967	2.00	4.00	8.00
❑ 32169	Goody, Goody Gumdrop/You're Standing in the Way	1967	2.00	4.00	8.00
❑ 32225	I'm Leavin'/Wastin' My Time	1967	2.00	4.00	8.00
❑ 32292	Shakiest Gun in the West/She'll Walk All Over You	1968	2.00	4.00	8.00
❑ 32386	We Need a Lot More Happiness/If You're with Me	1968	2.00	4.00	8.00
❑ 32449	It Looks Like the Sun's Gonna Shine/Make My Heart Die Away	1969	2.00	4.00	8.00
❑ 32531	Signs Are Everywhere/Who Could Ask for More	1969	2.00	4.00	8.00
❑ 32597	Gift of the Blues/Tag Along	1969	2.00	4.00	8.00
❑ 32608	Little Johnny from Down the Street/Which Side's the Wrong Side	1970	2.00	4.00	8.00
❑ 32683	Lilacs in Winter/Country Boy (Sing Your Heart Out)	1970	2.00	4.00	8.00
❑ 32771	Little Eyes That Look at Me/I've Gotta Hang My Hat Up on the Wind	1971	2.00	4.00	8.00
❑ 32835	That She's Leaving Feeling/Everything I Am	1971	2.00	4.00	8.00
❑ 32909	The War Keeps Draggin' On/Bloomin' Fools	1971	2.00	4.00	8.00
❑ 32921	Arkansas/Santa Fe Rolls Royce	1972	2.00	4.00	8.00
❑ 32978	Opryland/Hard Times Have Been There	1972	2.00	4.00	8.00
❑ 33027	The City's Goin' Country/Minds of Lonely Men	1972	2.00	4.00	8.00

MCA

Number	Title (A Side/B Side)	Yr	VG	VG+	NM
❑ 40042	Simon Crutchfield's Grave/Treat the Dog Like a Dog	1973	—	2.50	5.00
❑ 40264	There Must Be More to Love Than This/You've Still Got a Place in My Heart	1974	—	2.50	5.00
❑ 40473	Country Honey/Milwaukee, You're in Trouble	1975	—	2.50	5.00
❑ 40577	Country Kind of Feeling/Goin' and Comin'	1975	—	2.50	5.00

SCORPION

Number	Title (A Side/B Side)	Yr	VG	VG+	NM
❑ 0558	Mama's Shoe Box/What a Way to Go	1978	—	2.00	4.00

7-Inch Extended Plays

DECCA

Number	Title (A Side/B Side)	Yr	VG	VG+	NM
❑ ED 2537	*That's When I Miss You/Cry, Cry Darling/I Know You Don't Love Me Anymore/Always Alone	1957	6.25	12.50	25.00
❑ ED 2537 [PS]	The Wilburn Brothers	1957	6.25	12.50	25.00
❑ ED 2551	*You Win Again/I'll Sail My Ship Alone/Don't Sweetheart Me/Time Changes Everything	1957	6.25	12.50	25.00
❑ ED 2551 [PS]	The Wilburn Brothers	1957	6.25	12.50	25.00
❑ ED 2588	*If It's Wrong to Love You/One Has My Name, The Other Has My Heart/You Can't Break the Chains of Love/Much Too Often	1958	5.00	10.00	20.00
❑ ED 2588 [PS]	The Wilburn Brothers	1958	5.00	10.00	20.00
❑ ED 2617	*Need Someone/A Boy's Faithful Friend/Faded Love/Great Speckled Bird	1959	5.00	10.00	20.00
❑ ED 2617 [PS]	Side by Side	1959	5.00	10.00	20.00
❑ ED 2681	*Never Be Anyone Else But You/Big Heartbreak/ Empty Arms/I Almost Lost My Mind	1960	5.00	10.00	20.00
❑ ED 2681 [PS]	Big Heartbreak	1960	5.00	10.00	20.00
❑ ED 2689	*When Will You Know It/A Town That Never Sleeps/Sentenced to Die/You Can't Take It With You	1961	5.00	10.00	20.00
❑ ED 2689 [PS]	The Wilburn Brothers	1961	5.00	10.00	20.00
❑ ED 2727	*Trouble's Back in Town/Young But True Love/ Roll On Buddy, Roll On/Michael	1962	5.00	10.00	20.00
❑ ED 2727 [PS]	Trouble's Back in Town	1962	5.00	10.00	20.00
❑ ED 2756	Which One Is to Blame/No Legal Right//Blue Blue Day/Day After Day	1963	5.00	10.00	20.00
❑ ED 2756 [PS]	The Wilburn Brothers	1963	5.00	10.00	20.00
❑ ED 2782	*Roll Muddy River/Talk Back Trembling Lips/ Hangin' Around/A Fool Never Learns	1964	6.25	12.50	25.00
❑ ED 2782 [PS]	Roll Muddy River	1964	6.25	12.50	25.00
❑ ED 2783	(contents unknown)	1964	6.25	12.50	25.00
❑ ED 2783 [PS]	Take Up Thy Cross	1964	6.25	12.50	25.00
❑ ED 2803	(contents unknown)	1965	6.25	12.50	25.00
❑ ED 2803 [PS]	I'm Gonna Tie One On Tonight	1965	6.25	12.50	25.00

Albums

DECCA

Number	Title	Yr	VG	VG+	NM
❑ DL 4058 [M]	The Big Heartbreak	1960	7.50	15.00	30.00
❑ DL 4142 [M]	The Wilburn Brothers Sing	1961	7.50	15.00	30.00
❑ DL 4211 [M]	City Limits	1961	7.50	15.00	30.00
❑ DL 4225 [M]	Folk Songs	1962	5.00	10.00	20.00
❑ DL 4391 [M]	Trouble's Back in Town	1963	5.00	10.00	20.00
❑ DL 4464 [M]	Take Up Thy Cross	1964	5.00	10.00	20.00
❑ DL 4544 [M]	Never Alone	1964	5.00	10.00	20.00
❑ DL 4615 [M]	Country Gold	1965	5.00	10.00	20.00
❑ DL 4645 [M]	I'm Gonna Tie One on Tonight	1965	5.00	10.00	20.00
❑ DL 4721 [M]	The Wilburn Brothers Show	1966	15.00	30.00	60.00
—With guests Loretta Lynn, Ernest Tubb, Harold Morrison					
❑ DL 4764 [M]	Let's Go Country	1966	5.00	10.00	20.00
❑ DL 4824 [M]	Two for the Show	1967	6.25	12.50	25.00
❑ DL 4871 [M]	Cool	1967	7.50	15.00	30.00
❑ DL 4954 [M]	It's Another World	1968	10.00	20.00	40.00
❑ DL 8576 [M]	The Wilburn Brothers	1957	10.00	20.00	40.00
❑ DL 8774 [M]	Side by Side	1958	10.00	20.00	40.00
❑ DL 8959 [M]	Livin' in God's Country	1959	10.00	20.00	40.00
❑ DL 74058 [S]	The Big Heartbreak	1960	10.00	20.00	40.00
❑ DL 74142 [S]	The Wilburn Brothers Sing	1961	10.00	20.00	40.00
❑ DL 74211 [S]	City Limits	1961	10.00	20.00	40.00
❑ DL 74225 [S]	Folk Songs	1962	7.50	15.00	30.00
❑ DL 74391 [S]	Trouble's Back in Town	1963	7.50	15.00	30.00
❑ DL 74464 [S]	Take Up Thy Cross	1964	6.25	12.50	25.00
❑ DL 74544 [S]	Never Alone	1964	6.25	12.50	25.00
❑ DL 74615 [S]	Country Gold	1965	6.25	12.50	25.00
❑ DL 74645 [S]	I'm Gonna Tie One on Tonight	1965	6.25	12.50	25.00
❑ DL 74721 [S]	The Wilburn Brothers Show	1966	20.00	40.00	80.00
—With guests Loretta Lynn, Ernest Tubb, Harold Morrison					
❑ DL 74764 [S]	Let's Go Country	1966	6.25	12.50	25.00
❑ DL 74824 [S]	Two for the Show	1967	5.00	10.00	20.00
❑ DL 74871 [S]	Cool	1967	5.00	10.00	20.00
❑ DL 74954 [S]	It's Another World	1968	5.00	10.00	20.00
❑ DL 75173	Little Johnny from Down the Street	1970	5.00	10.00	20.00
❑ DL 75214	Sing Your Heart Out Country Boy	1971	5.00	10.00	20.00
❑ DL 75291	That She's Leaving Feeling	1972	5.00	10.00	20.00
❑ DL 88774 [S]	Side by Side	1959	15.00	30.00	60.00
❑ DL 88959 [S]	Livin' in God's Country	1959	15.00	30.00	60.00

KING

Number	Title	Yr	VG	VG+	NM
❑ 746 [M]	The Wonderful Wilburn Brothers	1961	25.00	50.00	100.00

MCA

Number	Title	Yr	VG	VG+	NM
❑ 4011 [(2)]	Portrait	197?	3.75	7.50	15.00

MCA CORAL

Number	Title	Yr	VG	VG+	NM
❑ 20058	That Country Feeling	1973	2.50	5.00	10.00

VOCALION

Number	Title	Yr	VG	VG+	NM
❑ VL 3691 [M]	Carefree Moments	1962	3.75	7.50	15.00
❑ VL 73691 [S]	Carefree Moments	1962	3.75	7.50	15.00
❑ VL 73876	That Country Feeling	197?	3.00	6.00	12.00
❑ VL 73889	I Walk the Line	197?	3.00	6.00	12.00

WILCO

Albums

SIRE

Number	Title	Yr	VG	VG+	NM
❑ 45857	A.M.	1995	3.00	6.00	12.00
—Red vinyl in generic plastic sleeve with sticker in upper left corner					

WARNER BROS.

Number	Title	Yr	VG	VG+	NM
❑ 46236 [(2)]	Being There	1996	3.75	7.50	15.00

WILCOX, HARLOW

45s

IMPEL

Number	Title (A Side/B Side)	Yr	VG	VG+	NM
❑ 002	Groovy Grubworm/(B-side unknown)	1969	6.25	12.50	25.00

PLANTATION

Number	Title (A Side/B Side)	Yr	VG	VG+	NM
❑ 28	Groovy Grubworm/Moose Trot	1969	2.00	4.00	8.00
❑ 28 [PS]	Groovy Grubworm/Moose Trot	1969	2.50	5.00	10.00
❑ 45	Golden Guitar Flower/The Gold Eagle	1970	—	3.50	7.00
❑ 60	Cripple Cricket/The Last Time	1970	—	3.50	7.00

Albums

PLANTATION

Number	Title	Yr	VG	VG+	NM
❑ PLP-7	Groovy Grubworm and Other Golden Guitar Greats	1970	3.75	7.50	15.00
❑ PLP-12	Cripple Cricket and Other Country Critters	1971	3.75	7.50	15.00

WILD CHOIR

Also see GAIL DAVIES.

45s

RCA

Number	Title (A Side/B Side)	Yr	VG	VG+	NM
❑ PB-14337	Next Time/Love Back	1986	—	—	3.00

WILD COUNTRY

See ALABAMA.

WILD ROSE

45s

CAPITOL

Number	Title (A Side/B Side)	Yr	VG	VG+	NM
❑ NR-44529	Go Down Swingin'/Wild Rose	1990	—	—	—
—Reissue of Universal 66033; unreleased on vinyl?					

CAPITOL NASHVILLE

Number	Title (A Side/B Side)	Yr	VG	VG+	NM
❑ 7PRO-79042	Where Did We Go Wrong (same on both sides)	1990	—	2.50	5.00
—Vinyl is promo only					
❑ 7PRO-79192	Everything He Touches (same on both sides)	1990	—	2.50	5.00
—Vinyl is promo only					

UNIVERSAL

Number	Title (A Side/B Side)	Yr	VG	VG+	NM
❑ UVL-66018	Breaking New Ground/Home Sweet Highway	1989	—	2.00	4.00
❑ UVL-66033	Go Down Swingin'/Wild Rose	1989	—	2.00	4.00

WILEY AND GENE

Duo of WILEY WALKER and GENE SULLIVAN.

45s

COLUMBIA

Number	Title (A Side/B Side)	Yr	VG	VG+	NM
❑ 4-20729	Stolen Kisses/Tear Drop Waltz	1950	7.50	15.00	30.00
❑ 4-20750	I'm Sorry for the One Who's Losing You/My Prison	1950	7.50	15.00	30.00

Selected 78s

COLUMBIA

Number	Title (A Side/B Side)	Yr	VG	VG+	NM
❑ 20004	Make Room in Your Heart for a Friend/Forgive Me	1948	3.00	6.00	12.00
—Reissue of 36869					
❑ 20070	After I'm Gone/Bothered by the Blues	1948	3.00	6.00	12.00
—Reissue of 37056					
❑ 20095	Take Away Those Blues Around My Heart/Kansas City Blues	1948	3.00	6.00	12.00
—Reissue of 37216					
❑ 20116	Don't That Moon Look Lonesome/Love Ain't Worrying Me	1948	3.00	6.00	12.00
—Reissue of 37331					
❑ 20191	Bring Back the Sunshine/Losing My Sleep Over You	1948	3.00	6.00	12.00
—Reissue of 37572					
❑ 20264	When My Blue Moon Turns to Gold Again/Live and Let Live	1948	3.00	6.00	12.00
—Reissue of 37665					
❑ 20368	Don't You Dare/Empty Future	1948	3.00	6.00	12.00
—Reissue of 37886					
❑ 20401	My Memory Picture of You/No Parting Word, No Parting Kiss	1948	3.00	6.00	12.00
—Reissue of 38077					
❑ 20434	Please Change Your Mind/Slow Marching and Sad Music	1948	3.75	7.50	15.00
❑ 20465	Give Me Your Heart/Tiny Baby Bonnet	1948	3.75	7.50	15.00
❑ 20520	No Hope for Love/You Little Sweet Little You	1949	3.75	7.50	15.00
❑ 20554	How Does One Forget/I've Stopped Dreaming About You	1949	3.75	7.50	15.00
❑ 36869	Make Room in Your Heart for a Friend/Forgive Me	1945	3.75	7.50	15.00
❑ 37056	After I'm Gone/Bothered by the Blues	1946	3.75	7.50	15.00
❑ 37216	Take Away Those Blues Around My Heart/Kansas City Blues	1946	3.75	7.50	15.00
❑ 37331	Don't That Moon Look Lonesome/Love Ain't Worrying Me	1946	3.75	7.50	15.00
❑ 37572	Bring Back the Sunshine/Losing My Sleep Over You	1947	3.75	7.50	15.00
❑ 37665	When My Blue Moon Turns to Gold Again/Live and Let Live	1947	3.75	7.50	15.00
—Reissue					
❑ 37886	Don't You Dare/Empty Future	1947	3.75	7.50	15.00
❑ 38077	My Memory Picture of You/No Parting Word, No Parting Kiss	1948	3.75	7.50	15.00

OKEH

Number	Title (A Side/B Side)	Yr	VG	VG+	NM
❑ 6700 (?)	When My Blue Moon Turns to Gold Again/Live and Let Live	1944	5.00	10.00	20.00

WILKINS, LITTLE DAVID

45s

EPIC

Number	Title (A Side/B Side)	Yr	VG	VG+	NM
❑ 8-50571	Motel Rooms/If There's an Easy Way for Love to Die	1978	—	2.00	4.00

JERE

Number	Title (A Side/B Side)	Yr	VG	VG+	NM
❑ 1003	Lady in Distress/(B-side unknown)	1986	—	2.50	5.00

MCA

Number	Title (A Side/B Side)	Yr	VG	VG+	NM
❑ 40034	Love in the Back Seat/To My One and Only	1973	—	2.50	5.00
❑ 40115	Too Much Hold Back/You Can't Stop Me from Loving You	1973	—	2.50	5.00
❑ 40200	Georgia Keeps Pulling on My Ring/Run It By Me One More Time	1974	—	2.50	5.00
❑ 40299	Not Tonight/My Love for You	1974	—	2.50	5.00
❑ 40345	Whoever Turned You On Forgot to Turn You Off/Butterbeans	1974	—	2.50	5.00
❑ 40427	One Monkey Don't Stop No Show/Make Me Stop Loving Her	1975	—	2.50	5.00
❑ 40510	The Good-Night Special/Let's Do Something (Even If It's Wrong)	1976	—	2.50	5.00
❑ 40579	Disco-Tex/Half the Way In, Half the Way Out	1976	—	2.50	5.00
❑ 40646	The Greatest Show on Earth/King of All the Taverns	1976	—	2.50	5.00
❑ 40668	He'll Play the Music (But You Can't Make Him Dance)/He Cries Like a Baby	1976	—	2.50	5.00
❑ 40734	Is Everybody Ready/Makin' Love in Waltz Time	1977	—	2.50	5.00

PLANTATION

Number	Title (A Side/B Side)	Yr	VG	VG+	NM
❑ 11	Just Blow in His Ear/Government Inspected	1969	—	3.50	7.00
❑ 23	A Little Dab Will Do Me/Maggie	1969	—	3.50	7.00
❑ 30	You Get Burned/Irving	1969	—	3.50	7.00
❑ 53	Put a Little Lovin' on Me/Yesterday, Today and Tomorrow	1970	—	3.50	7.00
❑ 70	She Hates to Be Alone/Yesterday, Tomorrow and Today	1970	—	3.50	7.00

PLAYBOY

Number	Title (A Side/B Side)	Yr	VG	VG+	NM
❑ 5822	Agree to Disagree/Her Old Stomping Ground	1977	—	2.00	4.00
❑ 5825	Don't Stop the Music (You're Playing My Song)/The Only Good Part of Leaving	1978	—	2.00	4.00

Albums

MCA

Number	Title (A Side/B Side)	Yr	VG	VG+	NM
❑ 445	Little David Wilkins	1974	3.00	6.00	12.00
❑ 2215	King of All the Taverns	1976	3.00	6.00	12.00

PLAYBOY

Number	Title (A Side/B Side)	Yr	VG	VG+	NM
❑ KZ 35028	New Horizons	1977	3.00	6.00	12.00

WILKINSONS, THE

45s

GIANT

Number	Title (A Side/B Side)	Yr	VG	VG+	NM
❑ 16887	Jimmy's Got a Girlfriend/Williamstown	2000	—	—	3.00
❑ 16986	Boy Oh Boy/The Word	1999	—	—	3.00
❑ 17131	Fly (The Angel Song)/26 Cents (Special Acoustic Version)	1998	—	—	3.00
❑ 17197	26c//Boy Oh Boy/Williamstown/Nothing But Love (Standing in the Way) (excerpts)	1998	—	—	3.00

WILLCOX, PETE

45s

M&M

Number	Title (A Side/B Side)	Yr	VG	VG+	NM
❑ 105	The King/(B-side unknown)	1982	2.50	5.00	10.00

WILLET, SLIM

45s

4 STAR

Number	Title (A Side/B Side)	Yr	VG	VG+	NM
❑ 1614	Don't Let the Stars (Get In Your Eyes)/Hadacol Corners	1952	7.50	15.00	30.00
❑ 1625	Let Me Know/My Love Song for You	1953	6.25	12.50	25.00
❑ 1637	Red Rose/Live While You're Young	1953	6.25	12.50	25.00
❑ 1642	Hungry Slim/Villa Cuna	1953	6.25	12.50	25.00
❑ 1643	Hard to Love Just One/Little Bluebird Keeps Singin'	1953	6.25	12.50	25.00
❑ 1645	Don't Waste Your Heart/Shibuya	1953	6.25	12.50	25.00
❑ 1653	Will There Be Stars in My Crown/Life Today As You Know	1954	6.25	12.50	25.00
❑ 1663	Lonely Tide/Don't Laugh at Me Now	1954	6.25	12.50	25.00
❑ 1672	Love Me Baby/When Lovers Go By	1955	5.00	10.00	20.00
❑ 1677	Mata Hari/Tell Me Now	1955	5.00	10.00	20.00
❑ 1679	When Nobody Cares/Tall Men	1955	5.00	10.00	20.00
❑ 1698	It Ain't Gonna Rain/(B-side unknown)	1956	5.00	10.00	20.00

DECCA

Number	Title (A Side/B Side)	Yr	VG	VG+	NM
❑ 9-29066	Leave Me Alone Now/Starlight Waltz	1954	5.00	10.00	20.00

EDMORAL

Number	Title (A Side/B Side)	Yr	VG	VG+	NM
❑ 1010	I've Been a-Wonderin'/Don't Be Afraid of the Moonlight	1956	6.25	12.50	25.00

WINSTON

Number	Title (A Side/B Side)	Yr	VG	VG+	NM
❑ 1019	Pandemonium/Crazy Crazy	1957	5.00	10.00	20.00
❑ 1036	Boom Town Man/Tool Pusher (On a Rotary Rig)	1959	5.00	10.00	20.00
❑ 1038	Billy Tremain/Marching Down	1959	5.00	10.00	20.00
❑ 1043	Abilene Waltz/Blue Eagle	1959	5.00	10.00	20.00
❑ 1044	Sweet Sally/Smell That Sweet Perfume	1959	5.00	10.00	20.00
❑ 1056	If the Stars Get In Your Eyes/Memories When I Grow Old	196?	3.75	7.50	15.00
❑ 1061	Everything Is Shakin' Fine/Big Money	196?	3.75	7.50	15.00
❑ 1067	I Don't Cry/Moonlight and Stardust	196?	3.75	7.50	15.00
❑ 1068	Hold Me Close/I Love You	196?	3.75	7.50	15.00
❑ 1077	The World Has Ended/Hangin' Day	196?	3.00	6.00	12.00
❑ 1078	You're the Only Woman/The Lights Don't Shine	196?	3.00	6.00	12.00

Albums

AUDIO LAB

Number	Title (A Side/B Side)	Yr	VG	VG+	NM
❑ AL-1542 [M]	Slim Willet	1959	25.00	50.00	100.00

WILLIAMS, BECKY

45s

COUNTRY PRIDE

Number	Title (A Side/B Side)	Yr	VG	VG+	NM
❑ 0011	Tie Me Up (Hold Me Down)/(B-side unknown)	1988	—	2.50	5.00
❑ 0011 [PS]	Tie Me Up (Hold Me Down)/(B-side unknown)	1988	2.00	4.00	8.00

WILLIAMS, BETH

45s

BGM

Number	Title (A Side/B Side)	Yr	VG	VG+	NM
❑ 13087	Man at the Backdoor/The Way I Do	1967	—	2.50	5.00
❑ 71086	Wrong Train/Blue Tonight	1986	—	2.50	5.00
❑ 92486	These Eyes/(B-side unknown)	1986	—	2.50	5.00

WILLIAMS, COOTIE

The jazz trumpeter had one record make the country charts, listed below.

Selected 78s

HIT

Number	Title (A Side/B Side)	Yr	VG	VG+	NM
❑ 7084	Red Blues/Things Ain't What They Used to Be	1944	7.50	15.00	30.00

WILLIAMS, DIANA

45s

Number	Title (A Side/B Side)	Yr	VG	VG+	NM
CAPITOL					
❑ 4317	Teddy Bear's Last Ride/If You Cared Enough to Cry	1976	—	2.50	5.00
❑ 4351	Everybody Sing/Storm in Tupelo	1976	—	2.00	4.00
❑ 4400	Little One/An Old Fashioned Love Song	1977	—	2.00	4.00
LITTLE GEM					
❑ 1022	One More Christmas/Goodbye Bing, Elvis and Guy	1977	2.00	4.00	8.00

Albums

Number	Title (A Side/B Side)	Yr	VG	VG+	NM
CAPITOL					
❑ ST-11587	Diana Williams	1976	3.00	6.00	12.00

WILLIAMS, DON

Also see EMMYLOU HARRIS; THE POZO-SECO SINGERS.

45s

Number	Title (A Side/B Side)	Yr	VG	VG+	NM
ABC					
❑ 12332	I've Got a Winner in You/Overlookin' and Underthinkin'	1978	—	2.00	4.00
❑ 12373	Rake and Ramblin' Man/Too Many Tears	1978	—	2.00	4.00
❑ 12425	Tulsa Time/When I'm With You	1978	—	2.50	5.00
❑ 12458	Lay Down Beside Me/I Would Like to See You Again	1979	—	2.50	5.00
ABC DOT					
❑ 17531	The Ties That Bind/Goodbye Isn't Really Good at All	1974	—	2.00	4.00
❑ 17550	You're My Best Friend/Where Are You	1975	—	2.00	4.00
❑ 17568	(Turn Out the Light And) Love Me Tonight/ Reason to Be	1975	—	2.00	4.00
❑ 17604	Till the Rivers All Run Dry/Don't You Think It's Time	1976	—	2.00	4.00
❑ 17631	Say It Again/I Don't Want the Money	1976	—	2.00	4.00
❑ 17658	She Never Knew Me/Ramblin'	1976	—	2.00	4.00
❑ 17683	Some Broken Hearts Never Mend/I'll Forgive But I'll Never Forget	1977	—	2.00	4.00
❑ 17717	I'm Just a Country Boy/It's Gotta Be Magic	1977	—	2.00	4.00
CAPITOL					
❑ B-5526	We've Got a Good Fire Goin'/Shot Full of Love	1985	—	—	3.00
❑ B-5588	Heartbeat in the Darkness/Light in Your Eyes	1986	—	—	3.00
❑ B-5638	Then It's Love/It's About Time	1986	—	—	3.00
❑ B-5683	Senorita/Send Her Roses	1987	—	—	3.00
❑ B-44019	I'll Never Be in Love Again/Send Her Roses	1987	—	—	3.00
❑ B-44066	I Wouldn't Be a Man/Light in Your Eyes	1987	—	—	3.00
❑ B-44131	Another Place, Another Time/Running Out of Reasons to Run	1988	—	—	3.00
❑ B-44216	Desperately/You Loved Me Through It All	1988	—	—	3.00
❑ B-44274	Old Coyote Town/You Loved Me Through It All	1988	—	—	3.00
DOT					
❑ 17516	I Wouldn't Want to Live If You Didn't Love Me/Fly Away	1974	—	2.50	5.00
GIANT					
❑ 17126	Pretty Little Baby Child/'Twas the Night Before Christmas	1998	—	—	3.00
JMI					
❑ 7	Don't You Believe/You Have a Star	1972	—	3.00	6.00
❑ 12	The Shelter of Your Eyes/Playin' Around	1972	—	3.00	6.00
❑ 24	Come Early Morning/Amanda	1973	—	3.00	6.00
❑ 32	Atta Way to Go/I Recall a Gypsy Woman	1973	—	3.00	6.00
❑ 36	We Should Be Together/Miller's Cave	1974	—	3.00	6.00
❑ 42	Down the Road I Go/She's in Love with a Rodeo Man	1974	—	3.00	6.00
MCA					
❑ S45-1763 [DJ]	A Special Message from Don Williams For Your Radio Station and Audience	1982	3.00	6.00	12.00
❑ 12458	Lay Down Beside Me/I Would Like to See You Again	1979	—	—	3.00
—Reissue of ABC 12458					
❑ 41069	It Must Be Love/Not a Chance	1979	—	—	3.00
❑ 41155	Love Me Over Again/Circle Driveway	1979	—	—	3.00
❑ 41205	Good Ole Boys Like Me/We're All the Way	1980	—	—	3.00
❑ 41304	I Believe in You/It Only Rains on Me	1980	—	2.00	4.00
❑ 51065	Falling Again/I Keep Putting Off Getting Over You	1981	—	—	3.00
❑ 51134	Miracles/I Don't Want to Love You	1981	—	—	3.00
❑ 51207	Lord, I Hope This Day Is Good/Smooth Talking Baby	1981	—	—	3.00
❑ 52037	Listen to the Radio/Only Love	1982	—	—	3.00
❑ 52097	Mistakes/Fool, Fool Heart	1982	—	—	3.00
❑ 52152	If Hollywood Don't Need You/Help Yourselves to Each Other	1982	—	—	3.00
❑ 52205	Love Is on a Roll/I'll Take Your Love Anytime	1983	—	—	3.00
❑ 52245	Nobody But You/If Love Gets There Before I Do	1983	—	—	3.00
❑ 52310	Stay Young/Pressure Makes Diamonds	1983	—	—	3.00
❑ 52389	That's the Thing About Love/I'm Still Looking for You	1984	—	—	3.00
❑ 52448	Maggie's Dream/Leavin'	1984	—	—	3.00
❑ 52514	Walkin' a Broken Heart/True Blue Hearts	1984	—	—	3.00
❑ 52692	It's Time for Love/I'll Never Need Another You	1985	—	—	3.00
RCA					
❑ 2507-7-R	Maybe That's All It Takes/We're All the Way	1990	—	2.00	4.00
❑ 2677-7-R	Back in My Younger Days/Diamonds to Dust	1990	—	2.00	4.00
❑ 2745-7-R	True Love/Learn to Let It Go	1990	—	2.00	4.00
❑ 2820-7-R	Lord Have Mercy on a Country Boy/Jamaica Farewell	1991	—	2.00	4.00
❑ 8867-7-R	One Good Well/Flowers Won't Grow (In a Field of Stone)	1989	—	2.00	4.00
❑ 9017-7-R	I've Been Loved by the Best/If You Love, Won't You Love Me	1989	—	2.00	4.00
❑ 9119-7-R	Just As Long As I Have You/Why Get Up	1989	—	2.00	4.00
❑ 62055	Donald and June/Come a Little Closer	1991	—	2.00	4.00
❑ 62180	Too Much Love/Back on the Street Again	1992	—	2.00	4.00
❑ 62240	It's Who You Love/The Old Trail	1992	—	2.00	4.00
❑ 62317	Catfish Bates/That Song About the River	1992	—	2.00	4.00

Albums

Number	Title (A Side/B Side)	Yr	VG	VG+	NM
ABC					
❑ AA-1069	Expressions	1978	3.00	6.00	12.00
ABC/DOT					
❑ DO-2004	Don Williams, Vol. III	1974	3.00	6.00	12.00
❑ DO-2014	Don Williams, Vol. 1	1974	3.00	6.00	12.00
—Reissue of JMI 4004					
❑ DO-2018	Don Williams, Vol. 2	1974	3.00	6.00	12.00
—Reissue of JMI 4006					
❑ DO-2021	You're My Best Friend	1975	3.00	6.00	12.00
❑ DO-2035	Greatest Hits	1975	3.00	6.00	12.00
❑ DO-2049	Harmony	1976	3.00	6.00	12.00
❑ DO-2064	Visions	1976	3.00	6.00	12.00
❑ DO-2088	I'm Just a Country Boy	1977	3.00	6.00	12.00
CAPITOL					
❑ ST-12440	New Moves	1987	2.00	4.00	8.00
❑ CLT-48034	Traces	1988	2.00	4.00	8.00
❑ C1-91444	Prime Cuts	1989	2.00	4.00	8.00
JMI					
❑ 4004	Don Williams	1973	6.25	12.50	25.00
❑ 4006	Don Williams, Vol. 2	1974	5.00	10.00	20.00
MCA					
❑ 1442	The Best of Don Williams, Vol. 3	1985	2.00	4.00	8.00
—Budget-line reissue					
❑ 3096	The Best of Don Williams, Vol. 2	1979	2.50	5.00	10.00
❑ 3192	Portrait	1980	2.50	5.00	10.00
❑ 3279	Expressions	1980	2.00	4.00	8.00
—Reissue of ABC 1069					
❑ 5133	I Believe in You	1980	2.50	5.00	10.00
❑ 5210	Especially for You	1981	2.50	5.00	10.00
❑ 5306	Listen to the Radio	1982	2.50	5.00	10.00
❑ 5407	Yellow Moon	1983	2.50	5.00	10.00
❑ 5465	The Best of Don Williams, Vol. 3	1984	2.50	5.00	10.00
❑ 5493	Café Carolina	1984	2.50	5.00	10.00
❑ 5671	The Best of Don Williams, Vol. 4	1985	2.50	5.00	10.00
❑ 5697	Don Williams Sings Bob McDill	1986	2.50	5.00	10.00
❑ 5803	Lovers and Best Friends	1986	2.50	5.00	10.00
❑ 37135	Greatest Hits	198?	2.00	4.00	8.00
—Budget-line reissue					
❑ 37155	The Best of Don Williams, Vol. 2	198?	2.00	4.00	8.00
—Budget-line reissue					
❑ 37230	Visions	198?	2.00	4.00	8.00
—Budget-line reissue					
❑ 37231	Portrait	198?	2.00	4.00	8.00
—Budget-line reissue					
❑ 37232	I'm Just a Country Boy	198?	2.00	4.00	8.00
—Budget-line reissue					
❑ 37233	Especially for You	198?	2.00	4.00	8.00
—Budget-line reissue					
❑ 37234	I Believe in You	198?	2.00	4.00	8.00
—Budget-line reissue					
RCA					
❑ 9656-1-R	One Good Well	1989	2.50	5.00	10.00
❑ R 124814	True Love	1990	3.75	7.50	15.00
—BMG Music Service pressing; only US vinyl edition					

WILLIAMS, HANK

45s

Number	Title (A Side/B Side)	Yr	VG	VG+	NM
MGM					
❑ 8010	Lovesick Blues/Never Again	1949	17.50	35.00	70.00
❑ 10352	Lovesick Blues/Never Again	1950	12.50	25.00	50.00
—Reissue has original 45 rpm number in parentheses under this number					
❑ 10401	Wedding Bells/I've Just Told Mama Goodbye	1949	15.00	30.00	60.00
❑ 10434	Dear Brother/Lost on the River	1949	15.00	30.00	60.00
❑ 10461	Mind Your Own Business/There'll Be No Teardrops Tonight	1949	15.00	30.00	60.00
❑ 10506	You're Gonna Change (Or I'm Gonna Leave)/Lost Highway	1949	15.00	30.00	60.00
❑ 10560	My Bucket's Got a Hole In It/I'm So Lonesome I Could Cry	1949	15.00	30.00	60.00
❑ 10609	I Just Don't Like This Kind of Lovin'/May You Never Be Alone	1950	10.00	20.00	40.00
❑ 10630	Beyond the Sunset/The Funeral	1950	15.00	30.00	60.00
—As "Luke the Drifter"					
❑ 10645	Long Gone Lonesome Blues/My Son Calls Another Man Daddy	1950	10.00	20.00	40.00
❑ 10696	Why Don't You Love Me/A House Without Love	1950	10.00	20.00	40.00
❑ 10718	Everything's OK/Too Many Parties	1950	15.00	30.00	60.00
—As "Luke the Drifter"					
❑ 10760	They'll Never Take Her Love from Me/Why Should We Try Anymore	1950	10.00	20.00	40.00
❑ 10806	No, No, Joe/Help Me Understand	1950	15.00	30.00	60.00
—As "Luke the Drifter"					
❑ 10813	I Heard My Mother Praying for Me/Jesus Remembered Me	1950	12.50	25.00	50.00
❑ 10832	Moanin' the Blues/Nobody's Lonesome for Me	1950	10.00	20.00	40.00

Number	Title (A Side/B Side)	Yr	VG	VG+	NM
❑ 10904	Cold, Cold Heart/Dear John	1951	7.50	15.00	30.00
❑ 10932	Just Waitin'/Men with Broken Hearts	1951	12.50	25.00	50.00
—As "Luke the Drifter"					
❑ 10961	I Can't Help It (If I'm Still in Love with You)/Howlin' at the Moon	1951	7.50	15.00	30.00
❑ 11000	Hey, Good Lookin'/My Heart Would Know	1951	7.50	15.00	30.00
❑ 11017	I Dreamed About Mama Last Night/I've Been Down That Road Before	1951	12.50	25.00	50.00
—As "Luke the Drifter"					
❑ 11054	Crazy Heart/Lonesome Whistle	1951	7.50	15.00	30.00
❑ 11083	Leave Us Women Alone/If You See My Baby	1951	10.00	20.00	40.00
❑ 11100	Baby, We're Really in Love/I'd Still Want You	1951	7.50	15.00	30.00
❑ 11120	Ramblin' Man/A Picture from Life's Other Side	1952	10.00	20.00	40.00
—As "Luke the Drifter"					
❑ 11160	Honky Tonk Blues/I'm Sorry for You My Friend	1952	7.50	15.00	30.00
❑ 11202	Half As Much/Let's Turn Back the Years	1952	7.50	15.00	30.00
❑ 11283	Jambalaya (On the Bayou)/Window Shopping	1952	7.50	15.00	30.00
❑ 11309	Be Careful of Stones That You Throw/Why Don't You Make Up Your Mind	1952	10.00	20.00	40.00
—As "Luke the Drifter"					
❑ 11318	Settin' the Woods On Fire/You Win Again	1952	7.50	15.00	30.00
❑ 11366	I'll Never Get Out of This World Alive/I Could Never Be Ashamed	1952	7.50	15.00	30.00
❑ 11416	Kaw-Liga/Your Cheatin' Heart	1953	7.50	15.00	30.00
❑ 11479	Take These Chains from My Heart/Ramblin' Man	1953	6.25	12.50	25.00
❑ 11533	I Won't Be Home No More/My Love for You	1953	6.25	12.50	25.00
❑ 11574	Weary Blues from Waitin'/I Can't Escape from You	1953	6.25	12.50	25.00
❑ 11628	Calling You/When God Comes and Gathers His Jewels	1953	6.25	12.50	25.00
❑ 11675	You Better Keep It on Your Mind/Low Down Blues	1954	6.25	12.50	25.00
❑ 11707	How Can You Refuse Him Now/A House of Gold	1954	6.25	12.50	25.00
❑ 11768	I Ain't Got Nothin' But Time/I'm Satisfied with You	1954	6.25	12.50	25.00
❑ 11861	Angel of Death/(I'm Gonna) Sing, Sing, Sing	1954	6.25	12.50	25.00
❑ 11928	Please Don't Let Me Love You/Faded Love and Winter's Roses	1955	6.25	12.50	25.00
❑ 11975	Message to My Mother/Mother Is Gone	1955	6.25	12.50	25.00
❑ 12029	A Teardrop on a Rose/Alone and Forsaken	1955	6.25	12.50	25.00
❑ 12077	Someday You'll Call My Name/The First Fall of Snow	1955	6.25	12.50	25.00
❑ 12127	The Battle of Armageddon/Thank God	1955	6.25	12.50	25.00
❑ 12185	California Zephyr/Thy Burdens Are Greater Than Mine	1956	6.25	12.50	25.00
❑ 12244	I Wish I Had a Nickel/There's No Room in My Heart	1956	6.25	12.50	25.00
❑ 12332	Blue Love (In My Heart)/Singing Waterfall	1956	6.25	12.50	25.00
❑ 12394	The Pale Horse and His Rider/A Home in Heaven	1956	5.00	10.00	20.00
—As "Hank and Audrey Williams"					
❑ 12431	Alimony Blues/Because You've Been Away	1957	5.00	10.00	20.00
❑ 12438	Ready to Go Home/We're Getting Closer	1957	5.00	10.00	20.00
❑ 12484	Leave Me Alone with the Blues/With Tears in My Eyes	1957	5.00	10.00	20.00
❑ 12535	No One Will Ever Know/The Waltz of the Wind	1957	5.00	10.00	20.00
❑ 12611	Why Don't You Love Me/I Can't Help It (If I'm Still in Love with You)	1958	5.00	10.00	20.00
❑ 12635	We Live in Two Different Worlds/My Bucket's Got a Hole In It	1958	5.00	10.00	20.00
❑ 12727	Just Waitin'/Roly-Poly	1958	5.00	10.00	20.00
❑ 13305	Your Cheatin' Heart/Lovesick Blues	1964	3.00	6.00	12.00
❑ 13305 [PS]	Your Cheatin' Heart/Lovesick Blues	1964	5.00	10.00	20.00
❑ 13489	I'm So Lonesome I Could Cry/You Win Again	1966	3.00	6.00	12.00
❑ 13542	Kaw-Liga/Let's Turn Back the Years	1966	3.00	6.00	12.00
❑ 13630	There'll Be No Teardrops Tonight/They'll Never Take Her Love from Me	1966	3.00	6.00	12.00
❑ 13717	Long Gone Lonesome Blues/Hang On the Bell, Nellie	1967	3.00	6.00	12.00
❑ 14849	Why Don't You Love Me/Ramblin' Man	1976	—	3.00	6.00

Selected 78s

MGM

Number	Title (A Side/B Side)	Yr	VG	VG+	NM
❑ 10033	Move It On Over/(Last Night) I Heard You Cryin' in Your Sleep	1947	20.00	40.00	80.00
❑ 10073	Fly Trouble/On the Banks of the Old Pontchartrain	1947	15.00	30.00	60.00
❑ 10124	Rootie Tootie/My Sweet Love Ain't Around	1948	15.00	30.00	60.00
❑ 10171	Honky Tonkin'/I'll Be a Bachelor 'Til I Die	1948	12.50	25.00	50.00
❑ 10212	I'm a Long Gone Daddy/Please Come Around	1948	12.50	25.00	50.00
❑ 10226	Pan American/I Don't Care	1948	12.50	25.00	50.00
❑ 10271	I Saw the Light/Six More Miles	1948	12.50	25.00	50.00
❑ 10328	Mansion on the Hill/I Can't Get You Off My Mind	1949	10.00	20.00	40.00
❑ 10352	Lovesick Blues/Never Again	1949	7.50	15.00	30.00
❑ 10401	Wedding Bells/I've Just Told Mama Goodbye	1949	7.50	15.00	30.00
❑ 10434	Dear Brother/Lost on the River	1949	7.50	15.00	30.00
❑ 10461	Mind Your Own Business/There'll Be No Teardrops Tonight	1949	7.50	15.00	30.00
❑ 10506	You're Gonna Change (Or I'm Gonna Leave)/Lost Highway	1949	7.50	15.00	30.00
❑ 10560	My Bucket's Got a Hole In It/I'm So Lonesome I Could Cry	1949	7.50	15.00	30.00

STERLING

Number	Title (A Side/B Side)	Yr	VG	VG+	NM
❑ 201	Calling You/Never Again (Will I Knock on Your Door)	1946	200.00	400.00	800.00
❑ 204	Wealth Won't Save Your Soul/When God Comes and Gathers His Jewels	1946	125.00	250.00	500.00
—With correct B-side title as above					
❑ 204	Wealth Won't Save Your Soul/When God Comes and Fathers His Jewels	1946	125.00	250.00	500.00
—With incorrect B-side title as above					
❑ 207	I Don't Care (If Tomorrow Never Comes)/My Love for You (Has Turned to Hate)	1947	125.00	250.00	500.00
❑ 210	Honky Tonkin'/Pan American	1947	100.00	200.00	400.00

7-Inch Extended Plays

MGM

Number	Title (A Side/B Side)	Yr	VG	VG+	NM
❑ X-168 [PS]	Moanin' the Blues	1953	10.00	20.00	40.00
—Cover with X-4041 and X-4042					
❑ X-202 [PS]	The Hank Williams Memorial Album	1953	10.00	20.00	40.00
—Cover with X-4102 and X-4103					
❑ X-1014	Crazy Heart/Baby We're Really in Love//My Heart Would Know/I Can't Help It (If I'm Still in Love with You)	1953	20.00	40.00	80.00
—Yellow label					
❑ X-1014	Crazy Heart/Baby We're Really in Love//My Heart Would Know/I Can't Help It (If I'm Still in Love with You)	1960	5.00	10.00	20.00
—Black label					
❑ X-1014 [PS]	Crazy Heart	1953	5.00	10.00	20.00
❑ X-1047	Pictures from Life's Other Side/Men with Broken Hearts//Help Me Understand/Too Many Parties (And Too Many Pals)	1955	15.00	30.00	60.00
—Yellow label					
❑ X-1047	Pictures from Life's Other Side/Men with Broken Hearts//Help Me Understand/Too Many Parties (And Too Many Pals)	1960	5.00	10.00	20.00
—Black label					
❑ X-1047 [PS]	Hank Williams As Luke the Drifter	1955	5.00	10.00	20.00
❑ X-1076	Move It On Over/Fly Trouble//Window Shopping/Pan American	1955	15.00	30.00	60.00
—Yellow label					
❑ X-1076	Move It On Over/Fly Trouble//Window Shopping/Pan American	1960	5.00	10.00	20.00
—Black label					
❑ X-1076 [PS]	Move It On Over	1955	5.00	10.00	20.00
❑ X-1082	(contents unknown)	1955	15.00	30.00	60.00
—Yellow label					
❑ X-1082	(contents unknown)	1960	5.00	10.00	20.00
—Black label					
❑ X-1082 [PS]	There'll Be No Teardrops Tonight	1955	5.00	10.00	20.00
❑ X-1101	I Saw the Light/Mansion on the Hill//Six More Miles/Wedding Bells	1955	15.00	30.00	60.00
—Yellow label					
❑ X-1101	I Saw the Light/Mansion on the Hill//Six More Miles/Wedding Bells	1960	5.00	10.00	20.00
—Black label					
❑ X-1101 [PS]	Hank Williams Sings	1955	5.00	10.00	20.00
❑ X-1102	Lost Highway/I've Just Told Mama Goodbye//Wealth Won't Save Your Soul/A House Without Love	1955	15.00	30.00	60.00
—Yellow label					
❑ X-1102	Lost Highway/I've Just Told Mama Goodbye//Wealth Won't Save Your Soul/A House Without Love	1960	5.00	10.00	20.00
—Black label					
❑ X-1102 [PS]	Hank Williams Sings Vol. 2	1955	5.00	10.00	20.00
❑ X-1135	Ramblin' Man/My Son Calls Another Man Daddy//I Can't Escape from You/Nobody's Lonesome for Me	1955	10.00	20.00	40.00
—Yellow label					
❑ X-1135	Ramblin' Man/My Son Calls Another Man Daddy//I Can't Escape from You/Nobody's Lonesome for Me	1960	3.75	7.50	15.00
—Black label					
❑ X-1135 [PS]	Ramblin' Man Vol. 1	1955	3.75	7.50	15.00
❑ X-1136	Lonesome Whistle/I Jus' Don't Like This Kind of Livin'//Take These Chains from My Heart/Why Don't You Love Me?	1955	10.00	20.00	40.00
—Yellow label					
❑ X-1136	Lonesome Whistle/I Jus' Don't Like This Kind of Livin'//Take These Chains from My Heart/Why Don't You Love Me?	1960	3.75	7.50	15.00
—Black label					
❑ X-1136 [PS]	Ramblin' Man Vol. 2	1955	3.75	7.50	15.00
❑ X-1165	Why Don't You Make Up Your Mind/I've Been Down That Road Before//Just Waitin'/Everything's Okay	1955	10.00	20.00	40.00
—Yellow label					
❑ X-1165	Why Don't You Make Up Your Mind/I've Been Down That Road Before//Just Waitin'/Everything's Okay	1960	3.75	7.50	15.00
—Black label					
❑ X-1165 [PS]	Luke the Drifter	1955	3.75	7.50	15.00
❑ X-1215	(contents unknown)	1956	10.00	20.00	40.00
—Yellow label					
❑ X-1215	(contents unknown)	1960	3.75	7.50	15.00
—Black label					
❑ X-1215 [PS]	Moanin' the Blues Vol. 1	1956	3.75	7.50	15.00
❑ X-1216	Moanin' the Blues/I'm So Lonesome I Could Cry//My Sweet Love Ain't Around/Honky Tonk Blues	1956	10.00	20.00	40.00
—Yellow label					
❑ X-1216	Moanin' the Blues/I'm So Lonesome I Could Cry//My Sweet Love Ain't Around/Honky Tonk Blues	1960	3.75	7.50	15.00
—Black label					
❑ X-1216 [PS]	Moanin' the Blues Vol. 2	1956	3.75	7.50	15.00
❑ X-1217	Lovesick Blues/The Blues Come Around//I'm a Long Gone Daddy/Long Gone Lonesome Blues	1956	10.00	20.00	40.00
—Yellow label					

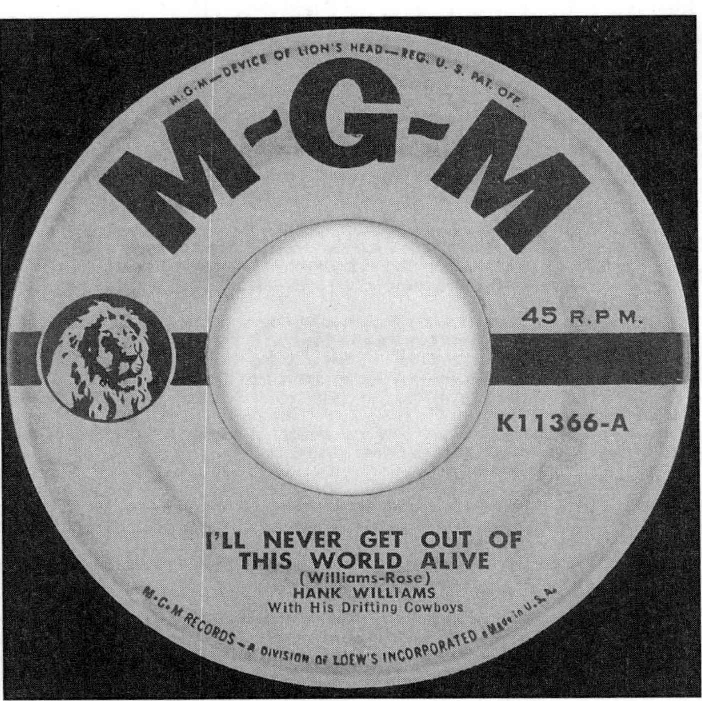

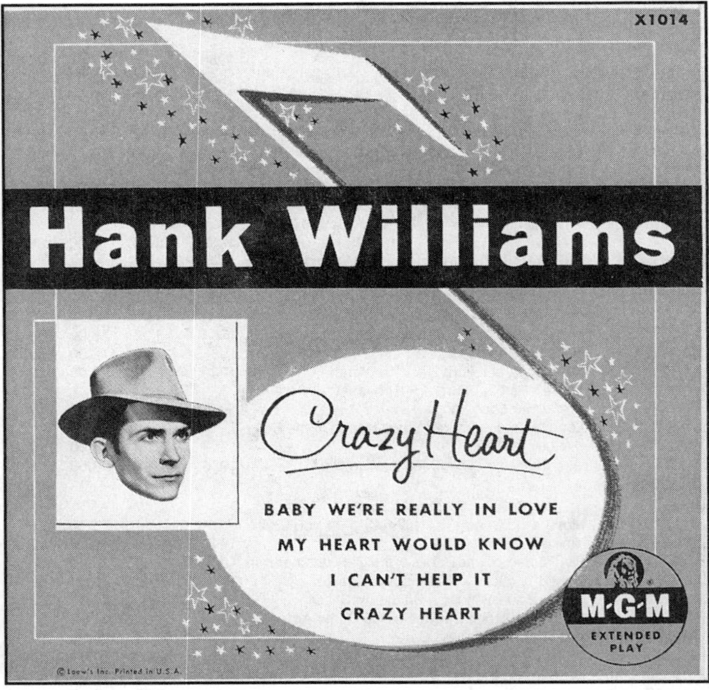

Though he didn't live to see his 30th birthday, Hank Williams' music and legacy have lived long beyond. In addition to his place as one of country music's most important figures, he was one of America's greatest songwriters of any era and genre. (Top left) Oddly, his first monster hit, and the one that was the biggest in his lifetime, was a song he didn't write, "Lovesick Blues." But he made it so much his own that many people think it's his. (Top right) The last record to be released while he was still living was, ironically, "I'll Never Get Out of This World Alive." It was on the charts when he died on January 1, 1953. (Bottom left) Right after Williams' death, two of the last songs he was working on came out as a double A-side; both sides, "Kaw-Liga" and "Your Cheatin' Heart," hit the top individually. (Bottom right) It didn't take long for MGM, his record label, to realize the gold mine it had. Repackagings started quickly, including this early extended-play single, "Crazy Heart."

Number	Title (A Side/B Side)	Yr	VG	VG+	NM
❑ X-1217	Lovesick Blues/The Blues Come Around//I'm a Long Gone Daddy/Long Gone Lonesome Blues	1960	3.75	7.50	15.00
—Black label					
❑ X-1217 [PS]	Moanin' the Blues Vol. 3	1956	3.75	7.50	15.00
❑ X-1218	I'm Gonna Sing/Message to My Mother//Thank God/The Angel of Death	1956	10.00	20.00	40.00
—Yellow label					
❑ X-1218	I'm Gonna Sing/Message to My Mother//Thank God/The Angel of Death	1960	3.75	7.50	15.00
—Black label					
❑ X-1218 [PS]	I Saw the Light	1956	3.75	7.50	15.00
❑ X-1235	*Honky Tonkin'/Mind Your Own Business/Rootie Tootie/I Ain't Got Nothing But Time	1956	10.00	20.00	40.00
—Yellow label					
❑ X-1235	*Honky Tonkin'/Mind Your Own Business/Rootie Tootie/I Ain't Got Nothing But Time	1960	3.75	7.50	15.00
—Black label					
❑ X-1235 [PS]	Honky Tonkin'	1956	3.75	7.50	15.00
❑ X-1317	Jambalaya (On the Bayou)/I Won't Be Home No More//Honky Tonk Blues/I'll Never Get Out of This World Alive	1957	10.00	20.00	40.00
—Yellow label					
❑ X-1317	Jambalaya (On the Bayou)/I Won't Be Home No More//Honky Tonk Blues/I'll Never Get Out of This World Alive	1960	3.75	7.50	15.00
—Black label					
❑ X-1317 [PS]	Honky Tonkin' Vol. 1	1957	3.75	7.50	15.00
❑ X-1318	Honky Tonkin'/Howlin' at the Moon//My Bucket's Got a Hole in It/Baby, We're Really in Love	1957	10.00	20.00	40.00
—Yellow label					
❑ X-1318	Honky Tonkin'/Howlin' at the Moon//My Bucket's Got a Hole in It/Baby, We're Really in Love	1960	3.75	7.50	15.00
—Black label					
❑ X-1318 [PS]	Honky Tonkin' Vol. 2	1957	3.75	7.50	15.00
❑ X-1319	Mind Your Own Business/Rootie Tootie//I Ain't Got Nothin' But Time/You Better Keep It on Your Mind	1957	10.00	20.00	40.00
—Yellow label					
❑ X-1319	Mind Your Own Business/Rootie Tootie//I Ain't Got Nothin' But Time/You Better Keep It on Your Mind	1960	3.75	7.50	15.00
—Black label					
❑ X-1319 [PS]	Honky Tonkin' Vol. 3	1957	3.75	7.50	15.00
❑ X-1491	Wedding Bells/May You Never Be Alone//Lost Highway/Why Should We Try Anymore	1958	7.50	5.00	30.00
—Yellow label					
❑ X-1491	Wedding Bells/May You Never Be Alone//Lost Highway/Why Should We Try Anymore	1960	3.75	7.50	15.00
—Black label					
❑ X-1491 [PS]	Sing Me a Blue Song Vol. 1	1958	3.75	7.50	15.00
❑ X-1492	I Heard You Crying in Your Sleep/Blue Love//Mansion on the Hill/They'll Never Take Her Love from Me	1958	7.50	15.00	30.00
—Yellow label					
❑ X-1492	I Heard You Crying in Your Sleep/Blue Love//Mansion on the Hill/They'll Never Take Her Love from Me	1960	3.75	7.50	15.00
—Black label					
❑ X-1492 [PS]	Sing Me a Blue Song Vol. 2	1958	3.75	7.50	15.00
❑ X-1493	I've Just Told Mama Goodbye/House Without Love//Six More Miles/Singing Waterfall	1958	7.50	15.00	30.00
—Yellow label					
❑ X-1493	I've Just Told Mama Goodbye/House Without Love//Six More Miles/Singing Waterfall	1960	3.75	7.50	15.00
—Black label					
❑ X-1493 [PS]	Sing Me a Blue Song Vol. 3	1958	3.75	7.50	15.00
❑ X-1554	There's No Room in My Heart/Waltz of the Wind//Pan American/With Tears in My Eyes	1958	7.50	15.00	30.00
—Yellow label					
❑ X-1554	There's No Room in My Heart/Waltz of the Wind//Pan American/With Tears in My Eyes	1960	3.75	7.50	15.00
—Black label					
❑ X-1554 [PS]	The Immortal Hank Williams Vol. 1	1958	3.75	7.50	15.00
❑ X-1555	I Wish I Had a Nickel/Fly Trouble//Please Don't Let Me Love You/I'm Satisfied with You	1958	7.50	15.00	30.00
—Yellow label					
❑ X-1555	I Wish I Had a Nickel/Fly Trouble//Please Don't Let Me Love You/I'm Satisfied with You	1960	3.75	7.50	15.00
—Black label					
❑ X-1555 [PS]	The Immortal Hank Williams Vol. 2	1958	3.75	7.50	15.00
❑ X-1556	No One Will Ever Know/Faded Love and Winter Roses//First Fall of Snow/California Zephyr	1958	7.50	15.00	30.00
—Yellow label					
❑ X-1556	No One Will Ever Know/Faded Love and Winter Roses//First Fall of Snow/California Zephyr	1960	3.75	7.50	15.00
—Black label					
❑ X-1556 [PS]	The Immortal Hank Williams Vol. 3	1958	3.75	7.50	15.00
❑ X-1612	Your Cheatin' Heart/Settin' the Woods on Fire//You Win Again/Hey, Good Lookin'	1959	7.50	15.00	30.00
—Yellow label					
❑ X-1612	Your Cheatin' Heart/Settin' the Woods on Fire//You Win Again/Hey, Good Lookin'	1960	3.75	7.50	15.00
—Black label					
❑ X-1612 [PS]	Hank Williams Memorial Album Vol. 1	1959	3.75	7.50	15.00
❑ X-1613	Cold, Cold Heart/Kaw-Liga//I Could Never Be Ashamed of You/Half As Much	1959	7.50	15.00	30.00
—Yellow label					
❑ X-1613	Cold, Cold Heart/Kaw-Liga//I Could Never Be Ashamed of You/Half As Much	1960	3.75	7.50	15.00
—Black label					
❑ X-1613 [PS]	Hank Williams Memorial Album Vol. 2	1959	3.75	7.50	15.00
❑ X-1614	Crazy Heart/Move It On Over//My Heart Would Know/I'm Sorry for You My Friend	1959	7.50	15.00	30.00
—Yellow label					
❑ X-1614	Crazy Heart/Move It On Over//My Heart Would Know/I'm Sorry for You My Friend	1960	3.75	7.50	15.00
—Black label					
❑ X-1614 [PS]	Hank Williams Memorial Album Vol. 3	1959	3.75	7.50	15.00
❑ X-1637	*I Can't Get You Off My Mind/I Don't Care (If Tomorrow Never Comes)/Dear John/My Love for You (Has Turned to Hate)	1959	7.50	15.00	30.00
—Yellow label					
❑ X-1637	*I Can't Get You Off My Mind/I Don't Care (If Tomorrow Never Comes)/Dear John/My Love for You (Has Turned to Hate)	1959	3.75	7.50	15.00
—Black label					
❑ X-1637 [PS]	The Unforgettable Hank Williams, Vol. 1	1959	3.75	7.50	15.00
❑ X-1643	Pictures from Life's Other Side/Men with Broken Hearts//Help Me Understand/Too Many Parties and Too Many Pals	1959	7.50	15.00	30.00
—Yellow label					
❑ X-1643	Pictures from Life's Other Side/Men with Broken Hearts//Help Me Understand/Too Many Parties and Too Many Pals	1960	3.75	7.50	15.00
—Black label					
❑ X-1643 [PS]	Hank Williams As Luke The Drifter	1959	3.75	7.50	15.00
❑ X-1644	Be Careful of Stones That You Throw/I Dreamed About Mama Last Night//Funeral/Beyond the Sunset	1959	7.50	15.00	30.00
—Yellow label					
❑ X-1644	Be Careful of Stones That You Throw/I Dreamed About Mama Last Night//Funeral/Beyond the Sunset	1960	3.75	7.50	15.00
—Black label					
❑ X-1644 [PS]	Hank Williams As Luke The Drifter	1959	3.75	7.50	15.00
❑ X-1698	(contents unknown)	1960	3.75	7.50	15.00
❑ X-1698 [PS]	The Lonesome Sound of Hank Williams Vol. 1	1960	3.75	7.50	15.00
❑ X-1699	(contents unknown)	1960	3.75	7.50	15.00
❑ X-1699 [PS]	The Lonesome Sound of Hank Williams Vol. 2	1960	3.75	7.50	15.00
❑ X-1700	(contents unknown)	1960	3.75	7.50	15.00
❑ X-1700 [PS]	The Lonesome Sound of Hank Williams Vol. 3	1960	3.75	7.50	15.00
❑ X-4041	Moanin' the Blues/I'm So Lonesome I Could Cry//My Sweet Love Ain't Around/Honky Tonk Blues	1953	10.00	20.00	40.00
—One record of "X168"					
❑ X-4042	Lovesick Blues/The Blues Come Around//I'm a Long Gone Daddy/Long Gone Lonesome Blues	1953	10.00	20.00	40.00
—One record of "X168"					
❑ X-4102	Your Cheatin' Heart/Settin' the Woods on Fire//You Win Again/Hey, Good Lookin'	1953	10.00	20.00	40.00
—One record of "X202"					
❑ X-4103	Cold, Cold Heart/Kaw-Liga//I Could Never Be Ashamed of You/Half as Much	1953	10.00	20.00	40.00
—One record of "X202"					

Albums

COUNTRY MUSIC FOUNDATION

Number	Title	Yr	VG	VG+	NM
❑ CMF-006	Just Me and My Guitar	198?	2.50	5.00	10.00
❑ CMF-007	The First Recordings	198?	2.50	5.00	10.00

METRO

Number	Title	Yr	VG	VG+	NM
❑ M-509 [M]	Hank Williams	1966	5.00	10.00	20.00
❑ MS-509 [R]	Hank Williams	1966	3.00	6.00	12.00
❑ M-547 [M]	Mr. and Mrs. Hank Williams	1966	5.00	10.00	20.00
❑ MS-547 [R]	Mr. and Mrs. Hank Williams	1966	3.00	6.00	12.00
❑ M-602 [M]	The Immortal Hank Williams	1967	5.00	10.00	20.00
❑ MS-602 [R]	The Immortal Hank Williams	1967	3.00	6.00	12.00

MGM

Number	Title	Yr	VG	VG+	NM
❑ 3E-2 [(3) M]	36 of Hank Williams' Greatest Hits	1957	50.00	100.00	200.00
—Yellow labels					
❑ 3E-2 [(3) M]	36 of Hank Williams' Greatest Hits	1960	25.00	50.00	100.00
—Black labels					
❑ 3E-4 [(3) M]	36 More of Hank Williams' Greatest Hits	1958	50.00	100.00	200.00
—Yellow labels					
❑ 3E-4 [(3) M]	36 More of Hank Williams' Greatest Hits	1960	25.00	50.00	100.00
—Black labels					
❑ E-107 [10]	Hank Williams Sings	1952	100.00	200.00	400.00
❑ E-168 [10]	Moanin' the Blues	1952	100.00	200.00	400.00
❑ E-202 [10]	Memorial Album	1953	100.00	200.00	400.00
❑ E-203 [10]	Hank Williams as Luke the Drifter	1953	100.00	200.00	400.00
❑ E-242 [10]	Honky Tonkin'	1954	100.00	200.00	400.00
❑ E-243 [10]	I Saw the Light	1954	100.00	200.00	400.00
❑ E-291 [10]	Ramblin' Man	1954	100.00	200.00	400.00
❑ PRO-912 [(3) DJ]	Reflections of Those Who Loved Him	1975	62.50	125.00	250.00
—Promo-only box set					
❑ E-3219 [M]	Ramblin' Man	1955	25.00	50.00	100.00
—Yellow label					
❑ E-3219 [M]	Ramblin' Man	1960	10.00	20.00	40.00
—Black label					
❑ E-3267 [M]	Hank Williams as Luke the Drifter	1955	25.00	50.00	100.00
—Yellow label					
❑ E-3267 [M]	Hank Williams as Luke the Drifter	1960	10.00	20.00	40.00
—Black label					
❑ E-3272 [M]	Memorial Album	1955	25.00	50.00	100.00
—Yellow label					

Number	Title (A Side/B Side)	Yr	VG	VG+	NM
❑ E-3272 [M]	Memorial Album	1960	10.00	20.00	40.00
—Black label					
❑ E-3330 [M]	Moanin' the Blues	1956	25.00	50.00	100.00
—Yellow label					
❑ E-3330 [M]	Moanin' the Blues	1960	10.00	20.00	40.00
—Black label					
❑ E-3331 [M]	I Saw the Light	1956	50.00	100.00	200.00
—Yellow label; green cover					
❑ E-3331 [M]	I Saw the Light	1959	25.00	50.00	100.00
—Yellow label; church on cover					
❑ E-3331 [M]	I Saw the Light	1960	10.00	20.00	40.00
—Black label					
❑ SE-3331 [R]	I Saw the Light	1968	3.00	6.00	12.00
—Blue and gold label					
❑ E-3412 [M]	Honky Tonkin'	1957	25.00	50.00	100.00
—Yellow label					
❑ E-3412 [M]	Honky Tonkin'	1960	10.00	20.00	40.00
—Black label					
❑ E-3560 [M]	Sing Me a Blue Song	1957	25.00	50.00	100.00
—Yellow label					
❑ E-3560 [M]	Sing Me a Blue Song	1960	10.00	20.00	40.00
—Black label					
❑ E-3605 [M]	The Immortal Hank Williams	1958	25.00	50.00	100.00
—Yellow label					
❑ E-3605 [M]	The Immortal Hank Williams	1960	10.00	20.00	40.00
—Black label					
❑ E-3733 [M]	The Unforgettable Hank Williams	1959	25.00	50.00	100.00
—Yellow label					
❑ E-3733 [M]	The Unforgettable Hank Williams	1960	10.00	20.00	40.00
—Black label					
❑ SE-3733 [R]	The Unforgettable Hank Williams	1968	3.00	6.00	12.00
—Blue and gold label					
❑ E-3803 [M]	The Lonesome Sound of Hank Williams	1960	10.00	20.00	40.00
❑ E-3850 [M]	Wait for the Light to Shine	1960	10.00	20.00	40.00
❑ SE-3850 [R]	Wait for the Light to Shine	1968	3.00	6.00	12.00
—Blue and gold label					
❑ E-3918 [M]	Hank Williams' Greatest Hits	1961	10.00	20.00	40.00
❑ SE-3918 [R]	Hank Williams' Greatest Hits	1963	5.00	10.00	20.00
—Black label					
❑ SE-3918 [R]	Hank Williams' Greatest Hits	1968	3.00	6.00	12.00
—Blue and gold label					
❑ E-3923 [M]	Hank Williams Lives Again	1961	10.00	20.00	40.00
❑ E-3924 [M]	Sing Me a Blue Song	1961	10.00	20.00	40.00
❑ E-3925 [M]	Wanderin' Around	1961	10.00	20.00	40.00
❑ E-3926 [M]	I'm Blue Inside	1961	10.00	20.00	40.00
❑ E-3927 [M]	Luke the Drifter	1961	10.00	20.00	40.00
❑ E-3928 [M]	First, Last and Always	1961	10.00	20.00	40.00
❑ SE-3928 [R]	First, Last and Always	1968	3.00	6.00	12.00
—Blue and gold label					
❑ E-3955 [M]	The Spirit of Hank Williams	1961	10.00	20.00	40.00
❑ SE-3955 [R]	The Spirit of Hank Williams	1968	3.00	6.00	12.00
—Blue and gold label					
❑ E-3999 [M]	On Stage! Hank Williams Recorded Live	1962	15.00	30.00	60.00
❑ E-3999 [M]	Hank Williams on Stage Recorded Live	1962	10.00	20.00	40.00
—Note revised title					
❑ SE-3999 [R]	Hank Williams on Stage Recorded Live	1968	3.00	6.00	12.00
—Blue and gold label					
❑ E-4040 [M]	Hank Williams' Greatest Hits, Volume 2	1962	10.00	20.00	40.00
❑ SE-4040 [R]	Hank Williams' Greatest Hits, Volume 2	1963	3.75	7.50	15.00
—Black label					
❑ SE-4040 [R]	Hank Williams' Greatest Hits, Volume 2	1968	3.00	6.00	12.00
—Blue and gold label					
❑ E-4109 [M]	Hank Williams on Stage, Volume 2	1963	10.00	20.00	40.00
❑ SE-4109 [R]	Hank Williams on Stage, Volume 2	1963	5.00	10.00	20.00
—Black label					
❑ SE-4109 [R]	Hank Williams on Stage, Volume 2	1968	3.00	6.00	12.00
—Blue and gold label					
❑ E-4138 [M]	Beyond the Sunset	1963	7.50	15.00	30.00
❑ SE-4138 [R]	Beyond the Sunset	1963	3.75	7.50	15.00
—Black label					
❑ E-4140 [M]	14 More of Hank Williams' Greatest Hits (Volume 3)	1963	7.50	15.00	30.00
❑ SE-4140 [R]	14 More of Hank Williams' Greatest Hits (Volume 3)	1963	3.75	7.50	15.00
—Black label					
❑ SE-4140 [R]	14 More of Hank Williams' Greatest Hits (Volume 3)	1968	3.00	6.00	12.00
—Blue and gold label					
❑ E-4168 [M]	The Very Best of Hank Williams	1963	7.50	15.00	30.00
❑ SE-4168 [R]	The Very Best of Hank Williams	1963	3.75	7.50	15.00
—Black label					
❑ SE-4168 [R]	The Very Best of Hank Williams	1968	3.00	6.00	12.00
—Blue and gold label					
❑ E-4227 [M]	The Very Best of Hank Williams, Volume 2	1964	7.50	15.00	30.00
❑ SE-4227 [R]	The Very Best of Hank Williams, Volume 2	1964	3.75	7.50	15.00
—Black label					
❑ SE-4227 [R]	The Very Best of Hank Williams, Volume 2	1968	3.00	6.00	12.00
—Blue and gold label					
❑ E-4254 [M]	Lost Highway (and Other Folk Ballads)	1964	10.00	20.00	40.00
❑ SE-4254 [R]	Lost Highway (and Other Folk Ballads)	1964	5.00	10.00	20.00
—Black label					
❑ SE-4254 [R]	Lost Highway (and Other Folk Ballads)	1968	3.00	6.00	12.00
—Blue and gold label					
❑ E-4267-4 [(4) M]	The Hank Williams Story	1965	15.00	30.00	60.00
❑ E-4300 [M]	Kaw-Liga and Other Humorous Songs	1965	7.50	15.00	30.00
❑ SE-4300 [R]	Kaw-Liga and Other Humorous Songs	1965	3.75	7.50	15.00
—Black label					
❑ SE-4300 [R]	Kaw-Liga and Other Humorous Songs	1968	3.00	6.00	12.00
—Blue and gold label					
❑ E-4377 [M]	The Legend Lives Anew — Hank Williams with Strings	1966	5.00	10.00	20.00
❑ SE-4377 [S]	The Legend Lives Anew — Hank Williams with Strings	1966	6.25	12.50	25.00
—Black label					
❑ SE-4377 [S]	The Legend Lives Anew — Hank Williams with Strings	1968	3.75	7.50	15.00
—Blue and gold label					
❑ E-4380 [M]	Movin' on — Luke the Drifter	1966	7.50	15.00	30.00
❑ SE-4380 [R]	Movin' on — Luke the Drifter	1968	3.00	6.00	12.00
—Blue and gold label					
❑ E-4429 [M]	More Hank Williams and Strings	1966	5.00	10.00	20.00
❑ SE-4429 [S]	More Hank Williams and Strings	1966	6.25	12.50	25.00
—Black label					
❑ SE-4429 [S]	More Hank Williams and Strings	1968	3.75	7.50	15.00
—Blue and gold label					
❑ E-4481 [M]	I Won't Be Home No More	1967	7.50	15.00	30.00
❑ SE-4481 [S]	I Won't Be Home No More	1967	5.00	10.00	20.00
—Black label					
❑ SE-4481 [S]	I Won't Be Home No More	1968	3.75	7.50	15.00
—Blue and gold label					
❑ E-4529 [M]	Hank Williams and Strings, Volume 3	1968	10.00	20.00	40.00
❑ SE-4529 [S]	Hank Williams and Strings, Volume 3	1968	5.00	10.00	20.00
❑ E-4576 [M]	Hank Williams in the Beginning	1968	10.00	20.00	40.00
❑ SE-4576 [R]	Hank Williams in the Beginning	1968	3.75	7.50	15.00
❑ SE-4651	Essential Hank Williams	1969	3.00	6.00	12.00
❑ SE-4680	Life to Legend	1970	3.00	6.00	12.00
❑ SE-4755-2 [(2)]	24 Greatest Hits	1971	3.75	7.50	15.00
❑ M3G-4954	Archetypes	1974	3.00	6.00	12.00
❑ MG-1-5019	Hank Williams, Sr., Live at the Grand Old Opry	1976	3.00	6.00	12.00
❑ MG-2-5401 [(2)]	24 Greatest Hits, Volume 2	197?	3.75	7.50	15.00
❑ ST-90511 [R]	The Very Best of Hank Williams	1965	5.00	10.00	20.00
—Capitol Record Club edition					
❑ T-90511 [M]	The Very Best of Hank Williams	1965	10.00	20.00	40.00
—Capitol Record Club edition					
❑ ST-90884 [R]	Movin' on — Luke the Drifter	1968	3.75	7.50	15.00
—Capitol Record Club edition; blue and gold label					
❑ ST-91115 [S]	The Legend Lives Anew — Hank Williams with Strings	1968	5.00	10.00	20.00
—Capitol Record Club edition; blue and gold label					
POLYDOR					
❑ 821233-1 [(2)]	40 Greatest Hits	1984	3.75	7.50	15.00
❑ 823291-1	Hank Williams' Greatest Hits	1984	2.00	4.00	8.00
❑ 823292-1	The Very Best of Hank Williams	1984	2.00	4.00	8.00
❑ 823293-1 [(2)]	24 Greatest Hits	1984	3.00	6.00	12.00
❑ 823294-1 [(2)]	24 Greatest Hits, Volume 2	1984	3.00	6.00	12.00
❑ 823695-1	Rare Takes and Radio Cuts	1984	2.50	5.00	10.00
❑ 825531-1	On the Air	1985	2.50	5.00	10.00
❑ 825548-1	I Ain't Got Nothin' But Time	1985	2.50	5.00	10.00
❑ 825551-1	Lovesick Blues	1985	2.50	5.00	10.00
❑ 825554-1	Lost Highway	1986	2.50	5.00	10.00
❑ 825557-1	I'm So Lonesome I Could Cry	1986	2.50	5.00	10.00
❑ 831574-1	Beyond the Sunset	1987	2.50	5.00	10.00
❑ 831633-1	Long Gone Lonesome Blues	1987	2.50	5.00	10.00
❑ 831634-1	Hey, Good Lookin'	1987	2.50	5.00	10.00
❑ 833749-1	Let's Turn Back the Years	1988	2.50	5.00	10.00
❑ 833752-1	I Won't Be Home No More	1988	2.50	5.00	10.00
TIME-LIFE					
❑ 3003 [(3)]	Country and Western Classics	1981	7.50	15.00	30.00

WILLIAMS, HANK /ROY ACUFF

Albums

Number	Title (A Side/B Side)	Yr	VG	VG+	NM
LAMB AND LION					
❑ LL-706 [(3)]	Hank Williams, Sr./Roy Acuff "Collector's Item!"	197?	10.00	20.00	40.00
—Sides 1-4 are reissues of Hank Williams; side 5-6 are Roy Acuff					

WILLIAMS, HANK, AND HANK WILLIAMS, JR.

Also see each artist's individual listings.

Albums

Number	Title (A Side/B Side)	Yr	VG	VG+	NM
MGM					
❑ E-4276 [M]	Father and Son	1965	5.00	10.00	20.00
❑ SE-4276 [S]	Father and Son	1965	6.25	12.50	25.00
❑ E-4378 [M]	Again	1966	5.00	10.00	20.00
❑ SE-4378 [S]	Again	1966	6.25	12.50	25.00
❑ 2SES-4865 [(2)]	Hank Williams: The Legend in Story and Song	1973	3.75	7.50	15.00
❑ M3HB 4975 [(2)]	Insights Into Hank Williams in Song and Story	1974	3.75	7.50	15.00

WILLIAMS, HANK, JR.

12-Inch Singles

Number	Title (A Side/B Side)	Yr	VG	VG+	NM
WARNER BROS.					
❑ PRO-A-2088 [DJ]	Woman on the Run (same on both sides)	1983	2.00	4.00	8.00
❑ PRO-A-2662 [DJ]	My Name Is Bocephus (same on both sides)	1987	2.00	4.00	8.00

45s

Number	Title (A Side/B Side)	Yr	VG	VG+	NM
CAPRICORN					
❑ 18486	Diamond Mine/Dirty Mind	1993	—	—	3.00
❑ 18614	Everything Comes Down to Money and Love/S.O.B. I'm Tired	1993	—	—	3.00
❑ 18800	Lyin' Jukebox/Fax Me a Beer	1992	—	—	3.00
❑ 18923	Come On Over to the Country/Wild Weekend	1992	—	—	3.00
❑ 19023	Hotel Whiskey/The Count Song	1992	—	—	3.00

Number	Title (A Side/B Side)	Yr	VG	VG+	NM
ELEKTRA					
❑ 46018	To Love Somebody/We Can Work It All Out	1979	—	2.50	5.00
❑ 46046	Family Tradition/Paying On Time	1979	—	2.50	5.00
❑ 46535	Whiskey Bent and Hell Bound/O.D.'d in Denver	1979	—	2.50	5.00
❑ 46593	Women I've Never Had/Tired of Being Johnny B. Goode	1980	—	2.50	5.00
❑ 46636	Kaw-Liga/The American Way	1980	—	2.50	5.00
❑ 47012	If You Don't Like Hank Williams/Outlaw Women	1980	—	3.00	6.00
❑ 47016	Old Habits/Won't It Be Nice	1980	—	2.50	5.00
❑ 47102	Texas Women/You Can't Find Many Kisses	1981	—	2.50	5.00
❑ 47137	Dixie on My Mind/Ramblin' Man	1981	—	2.50	5.00
❑ 47191	All My Rowdy Friends (Have Settled Down)/ Everytime I Hear That Song	1981	—	2.50	5.00
❑ 47231 [DJ]	Little Drummer Boy/The Christmas Song	1981	2.00	4.00	8.00
—B-side by Sonny Curtis					
❑ 47257	A Country Boy Can Survive/Weatherman	1982	—	2.50	5.00
❑ 47462	Honky Tonkin'/High and Pressurized	1982	—	2.50	5.00
❑ 69846	Gonna Go Huntin' Tonight/Twodot, Montana	1983	—	2.00	4.00
❑ 69960	The American Dream/If Heaven Ain't a Lot Like Dixie	1982	—	2.00	4.00
MCG CURB					
❑ 76932	I Ain't Goin' Peacefully/Greeted in Enid	1995	—	2.00	4.00
❑ 76948	Hog Wild/Wild Thing	1995	—	2.00	4.00
MGM					
❑ 13208	Long Gone Lonesome Blues/Doesn't Anybody Know My Name	1964	3.00	6.00	12.00
❑ 13253	Guess What, That's Right, She's Gone/Goin' Steady with the Blues	1964	3.00	6.00	12.00
❑ 13278	Endless Sleep/My Bucket's Got a Hole In It	1964	3.00	6.00	12.00
❑ 13318	I'm So Lonesome I Could Cry/Is It That Much Fun to Hurt Someone	1965	3.00	6.00	12.00
❑ 13353	I Went to All That Trouble for Nothin'/Mule Skinner Blues	1965	3.00	6.00	12.00
❑ 13392	Pecos Jail/You're Ruinin' My Life	1965	3.00	6.00	12.00
❑ 13443	Rainmaker/The River	1966	3.00	6.00	12.00
❑ 13504	Standing in the Shadows/It's Written All Over Your Face	1966	3.00	6.00	12.00
❑ 13640	I Can't Take It No Longer/You Can Hear a Tear Drop	1966	3.00	6.00	12.00
❑ 13730	I'm In No Condition/I'm Gonna Break Your Heart	1967	3.00	6.00	12.00
❑ 13782	Nobody's Child/The Next Best Thing to Nothing	1967	3.00	6.00	12.00
❑ 13857	I Wouldn't Change a Thing About You (But Your Name)/No Meaning and No End	1967	3.00	6.00	12.00
❑ 13922	The Old Ryman/I Wonder Where You Are Tonight	1968	2.50	5.00	10.00
❑ 13968	It's All Over But the Crying/Rock in My Shoes	1968	2.50	5.00	10.00
❑ 14002	I Was With Red Foley (The Night He Passed Away)/On Trial	1968	3.00	6.00	12.00
—As "Luke the Drifter, Jr."					
❑ 14020	Custody/My Home Town Circle "R"	1968	3.00	6.00	12.00
—As "Luke the Drifter, Jr."					
❑ 14024	A Baby Again/Swim Across a Tear	1969	2.50	5.00	10.00
❑ 14047	Cajun Baby/My Heart Won't Let Me Go	1969	2.50	5.00	10.00
❑ 14062	Be Careful of Stones That You Throw/Book of Memories	1969	2.50	5.00	10.00
—As "Luke the Drifter, Jr."					
❑ 14077	I'd Rather Be Gone/Try, Try Again	1969	2.50	5.00	10.00
❑ 14095	Something to Think About/(There Must Be) A Better Way to Love	1969	2.50	5.00	10.00
—As "Luke the Drifter, Jr."					
❑ 14107	I Walked Out on Heaven/Your Love's One Thing	1970	2.00	4.00	8.00
❑ 14120	It Don't Take But One Mistake/Goin' Home	1970	2.00	4.00	8.00
—As "Luke the Drifter, Jr."					
❑ 14152	All for the Love of Sunshine/Ballad of the Moonshine	1970	2.00	4.00	8.00
❑ 14194	Rainin' in My Heart/A-Eee	1970	2.00	4.00	8.00
❑ 14240	I've Got a Right to Cry/Jesus Loved the Devil Out of Me	1971	2.00	4.00	8.00
❑ 14277	After All They All Used to Belong to Me/Happy Kind of Sadness	1971	2.00	4.00	8.00
❑ 14317	Ain't That a Shame/End of a Bad Day	1971	2.00	4.00	8.00
❑ 14371	Eleven Roses/Richmond Valley Breeze	1972	2.00	4.00	8.00
❑ 14421	Pride's Not Hard to Swallow/Hamburger Steak, Holiday Inn	1972	2.00	4.00	8.00
❑ 14486	After You/Knoxville Courthouse Blues	1973	—	3.00	6.00
❑ 14550	Hank/Hank (Part 2)	1973	—	3.00	6.00
❑ 14656	The Last Love Song/Those Tear Jerking Songs	1973	—	3.00	6.00
❑ 14700	Rainy Night in Georgia/Country Music in My Soul	1974	—	3.00	6.00
❑ 14731	I'll Think of Something/Country Music Lover	1974	—	3.00	6.00
❑ 14755	Angels Are Hard to Find/Getting Over You	1974	—	3.00	6.00
❑ 14794	Where He's Going, I've Already Gone/The Kind of Woman I've Got	1975	—	3.00	6.00
❑ 14813	The Same Old Story/Country Love	1975	—	3.00	6.00
❑ 14833	Stoned at the Jukebox/The Devil in the Bottle	1975	—	3.00	6.00
❑ 14845	Living Proof/Brothers of the Road	1976	—	3.00	6.00
VERVE					
❑ 10540	Meter Reader Maid/Just a Dream	1967	12.50	25.00	50.00
—As "Bocephus"					
❑ 10572	Mental Revenge/Splish Splash	1967	10.00	20.00	40.00
—As "Bocephus"					
WARNER BROS.					
❑ PRO-S-3838 [DJ]	All My Rowdy Friends (Are Here on Monday Night) (same on both sides)	1989	3.75	7.50	15.00
❑ PRO-S-4492 [DJ]	Don't Give Us a Reason (same on both sides)	1990	2.00	4.00	8.00
❑ 8345	She's the Star (On the Stage of My Mind)/Call Me, Honey, Won't You	1977	—	2.50	5.00

Number	Title (A Side/B Side)	Yr	VG	VG+	NM
❑ 8361	Mobile Boogie/She's the Star (On the Stage of My Mind)	1977	—	2.50	5.00
❑ 8410	I'm Not Responsible/(Honey, Won't You) Call Me	1977	—	2.50	5.00
❑ 8451	One Night Stands/I'm Not Responsible	1977	—	2.50	5.00
❑ 8507	Feelin' Better/Once and For All	1977	—	2.50	5.00
❑ 8549	The New South/Storms Never Last	1978	—	3.00	6.00
❑ 8564	You Love the Thunder/I Just Ain't Been Able	1978	—	2.50	5.00
❑ 8641	I Fought the Law/It's Different with You	1978	—	2.50	5.00
❑ 8715	Old Flame, New Fire/Payin' On Time	1978	—	2.50	5.00
❑ 19193	Angels Are Hard to Find/Hollywood Honeys	1991	—	—	3.00
❑ 19352	If It Will It Will/Won't It Be Nice	1991	—	—	3.00
❑ 19463	I Mean I Love You/Stoned at the Jukebox	1990	—	—	3.00
❑ 19542	Don't Give Us a Reason/U.S.A. Today	1990	—	—	3.00
❑ 19818	Man to Man/Whiskey Bent and Hell Bound	1990	—	—	3.00
❑ 19872	Good Friends, Good Whiskey, Good Lovin'/ Family Tradition	1990	—	—	3.00
❑ 19957	Ain't Nobody's Business/Big Mamou	1990	—	—	3.00
❑ 22945	Finders Are Keepers/What You Don't Know (Won't Hurt You)	1989	—	—	3.00
❑ 27584	There's a Tear in My Beer/You Brought Me Down to Earth	1989	—	2.00	4.00
—A-side with Hank Williams Sr.					
❑ 27722	Early in the Morning and Late at Night/I'm Just a Man	1988	—	—	3.00
❑ 27862	If the South Woulda Won/Wild Steak	1988	—	—	3.00
❑ 28120	Young Country/Buck Naked	1988	—	—	3.00
❑ 28227	Heaven Can't Be Found/Doctor's Song	1987	—	—	3.00
❑ 28369	Born to Boogie/What It Boils Down To	1987	—	—	3.00
❑ 28452	When Something Is Good (Why Does It Change)/ Loving Instructor	1987	—	—	3.00
❑ 28581	Mind Your Own Business/My Name Is Bocephus	1986	—	2.00	4.00
❑ 28691	Country State of Mind/Fat Friends	1986	—	2.00	4.00
❑ 28794	Ain't Misbehavin'/I've Been Around	1986	—	2.00	4.00
❑ 28912	This Ain't Dallas/I Really Like Girls	1985	—	2.00	4.00
❑ 29022	I'm for Love/Lawyers, Guns and Money	1985	—	2.00	4.00
❑ 29095	Major Moves/Mr. Lincoln	1985	—	2.00	4.00
❑ 29184	All My Rowdy Friends Are Coming Over Tonight/ Video Blues	1984	—	2.00	4.00
❑ 29253	Attitude Adjustment/Knoxville Courthouse Blues	1984	—	2.00	4.00
❑ 29382	Man of Steel/Now I Know How George Feels	1984	—	2.00	4.00
❑ 29500	Queen of My Heart/She Had Me	1983	—	2.00	4.00
❑ 29633	Leave Them Boys Alone/The Girl in the Front Row at Fort Worth	1983	—	2.00	4.00
Albums					
CAPRICORN					
❑ W1-26806	Maverick	1992	5.00	10.00	20.00
—Columbia House edition (only U.S. vinyl release)					
ELEKTRA					
❑ 6E-194	Family Tradition	1979	3.00	6.00	12.00
❑ 6E-237	Whiskey Bent and Hell Bound	1979	2.50	5.00	10.00
❑ 6E-278	Habits Old and New	1980	2.50	5.00	10.00
❑ 6E-330	Rowdy	1981	2.50	5.00	10.00
❑ 5E-535	The Pressure Is On	1981	2.50	5.00	10.00
❑ 5E-538	One Night Stands	1982	2.50	5.00	10.00
—Reissue					
❑ 5E-539	The New South	1982	2.50	5.00	10.00
—Reissue					
❑ 60100	High Notes	1982	2.50	5.00	10.00
❑ 60193	Hank Williams, Jr.'s, Greatest Hits	1982	2.50	5.00	10.00
❑ 60223	Strong Stuff	1983	3.75	7.50	15.00
MGM					
❑ GAS-119	Hank Williams, Jr. (Golden Archive Series)	1970	3.75	7.50	15.00
❑ E-4213 [M]	Sings the Songs of Hank Williams	1964	5.00	10.00	20.00
❑ SE-4213 [S]	Sings the Songs of Hank Williams	1964	6.25	12.50	25.00
❑ E-4260 [M]	Your Cheatin' Heart	1964	5.00	10.00	20.00
❑ SE-4260 [S]	Your Cheatin' Heart	1964	6.25	12.50	25.00
❑ E-4316 [M]	Ballads of the Hills and Plains	1965	5.00	10.00	20.00
❑ SE-4316 [S]	Ballads of the Hills and Plains	1965	6.25	12.50	25.00
❑ E-4344 [M]	Blues My Name	1966	5.00	10.00	20.00
❑ SE-4344 [S]	Blues My Name	1966	6.25	12.50	25.00
❑ E-4391 [M]	Country Shadows	1966	5.00	10.00	20.00
❑ SE-4391 [S]	Country Shadows	1966	6.25	12.50	25.00
❑ E-4428 [M]	In My Own Way	1967	5.00	10.00	20.00
❑ SE-4428 [S]	In My Own Way	1967	6.25	12.50	25.00
❑ E-4513 [M]	The Best of Hank Williams, Jr.	1967	5.00	10.00	20.00
❑ SE-4513 [S]	The Best of Hank Williams, Jr.	1967	6.25	12.50	25.00
❑ E-4527 [M]	My Songs	1968	—	—	—
—Unreleased?					
❑ SE-4527 [S]	My Songs	1968	6.25	12.50	25.00
❑ SE-4540	A Time to Sing	1968	6.25	12.50	25.00
❑ SE-4559	Luke the Drifter, Jr.	1969	5.00	10.00	20.00
❑ SE-4621	Songs My Father Left Me	1969	5.00	10.00	20.00
❑ SE-4632	Luke the Drifter, Jr. (Vol. 2)	1969	5.00	10.00	20.00
❑ SE-4644	Live at Cobo Hall, Detroit	1969	5.00	10.00	20.00
❑ SE-4656	Hank Williams, Jr.'s Greatest Hits	1970	3.75	7.50	15.00
❑ SE-4657	Sunday Morning	1970	3.75	7.50	15.00
❑ SE-4673	Luke the Drifter, Jr. (Vol. 3)	1970	3.75	7.50	15.00
❑ SE-4675	Hank Williams, Jr., Singing My Songs (Johnny Cash)	1970	3.75	7.50	15.00
❑ SE-4721	Removing the Shadows	1971	3.75	7.50	15.00
❑ SE-4774	I've Got a Right to Cry/They All Used to Belong to Me	1971	3.75	7.50	15.00
❑ SE-4798	Sweet Dreams	1972	3.00	6.00	12.00
—With the Mike Curb Congregation					
❑ SE-4822	Hank Williams, Jr.'s Greatest Hits, Volume 2	1972	3.00	6.00	12.00

Number	Title (A Side/B Side)	Yr	VG	VG+	NM
❑ SE-4843	Eleven Roses	1972	3.00	6.00	12.00
❑ SE-4862	After You/Pride's Not Hard to Swallow	1973	3.00	6.00	12.00
❑ M3G-4906	Just Pickin' — No Singin'	1973	3.00	6.00	12.00
❑ M3G-4936	The Last Love Song	1973	3.00	6.00	12.00
❑ M3G-4971	Living Proof	1974	3.00	6.00	12.00
❑ M3G-4988	Bocephus	1974	3.00	6.00	12.00
❑ MG-1-5009	Hank Williams, Jr., and Friends	1975	10.00	20.00	40.00
❑ MG-1-5020	14 Greatest Hits	1976	3.00	6.00	12.00
❑ ST-90695 [S]	Blues My Name	1966	7.50	15.00	30.00
—Capitol Record Club edition					
❑ T-90695 [M]	Blues My Name	1966	6.25	12.50	25.00
—Capitol Record Club edition					
PAIR					
❑ PDL2-1164 [(2)]	I'm Walkin'	1987	3.00	6.00	12.00
POLYDOR					
❑ 811902-1	Live at Cobo Hall, Detroit	1983	2.00	4.00	8.00
—Reissue					
❑ 811903-1	Hank Williams, Jr.'s Greatest Hits	1983	2.00	4.00	8.00
❑ 811906-1	Hank Williams, Jr.'s Greatest Hits, Volume 2	1983	2.00	4.00	8.00
❑ 825091-1	14 Greatest Hits	1985	2.00	4.00	8.00
❑ 831575-1	Hank Williams, Jr., and Friends	1987	3.00	6.00	12.00
❑ 833069-1	Blues My Name	1987	2.00	4.00	8.00
❑ 833070-1	Eleven Roses	1987	2.00	4.00	8.00
❑ 835132-1	Standing in the Shadows	1988	2.00	4.00	8.00
WARNER BROS.					
❑ 6E-194	Family Tradition	1983	2.00	4.00	8.00
❑ 6E-237	Whiskey Bent and Hell Bound	1983	2.00	4.00	8.00
❑ 6E-278	Habits Old and New	1983	2.00	4.00	8.00
❑ 6E-330	Rowdy	1983	2.00	4.00	8.00
❑ 5E-535	The Pressure Is On	1983	2.00	4.00	8.00
❑ 5E-538	One Night Stands	1983	2.00	4.00	8.00
❑ 5E-539	The New South	1983	2.00	4.00	8.00
❑ PRO-A-2092 [DJ]	The Hank Williams, Jr., Interview	1983	6.25	12.50	25.00
❑ BS 2988	One Night Stands	1977	3.00	6.00	12.00
❑ BS 3127	The New South	1977	3.00	6.00	12.00
❑ 23924	Man of Steel	1983	2.50	5.00	10.00
❑ 25088	Major Moves	1984	2.50	5.00	10.00
❑ 25267	Five-O	1985	2.50	5.00	10.00
❑ 25328	Greatest Hits — Volume 2	1985	2.00	4.00	8.00
❑ 25412	Montana Café	1986	2.00	4.00	8.00
❑ 25538	Hank "Live"	1987	2.00	4.00	8.00
❑ 25593	Born to Boogie	1987	2.00	4.00	8.00
❑ 25725	Wild Streak	1988	2.00	4.00	8.00
❑ 25834	Greatest Hits III	1989	2.00	4.00	8.00
❑ 26090	Lone Wolf	1990	3.00	6.00	12.00
❑ 60100	High Notes	1983	2.00	4.00	8.00
❑ 60193	Hank Williams, Jr.'s, Greatest Hits	1983	2.00	4.00	8.00
❑ 60223	Strong Stuff	1983	2.50	5.00	10.00
❑ R 120612	America (The Way I See It)	1990	5.00	10.00	20.00
—BMG Music Service edition (no regular vinyl release)					
❑ R 160351	Pure Hank	1991	5.00	10.00	20.00
—BMG Music Service edition (no regular vinyl release)					

WILLIAMS, HANK, JR., AND LOIS JOHNSON

Also see each artist's individual listings.

45s

Number	Title (A Side/B Side)	Yr	VG	VG+	NM
MGM					
❑ 14136	Removing the Shadow/Party People	1970	2.00	4.00	8.00
❑ 14164	So Sad (To Watch Good Love Go Bad)/Let's Talk It Over Again	1970	2.00	4.00	8.00
❑ 14356	Send Me Some Lovin'/What We Used to Hang On To	1972	2.00	4.00	8.00
❑ 14443	Whole Lotta Loving/Why Should We Try Anymore	1972	2.00	4.00	8.00

Albums

Number	Title (A Side/B Side)	Yr	VG	VG+	NM
MGM					
❑ SE-4750	All for the Love of Sunshine	1971	5.00	10.00	20.00
❑ SE-4857	Send Me Some Lovin'/Whole Lotta Lovin'	1972	5.00	10.00	20.00

WILLIAMS, JASON D.

45s

Number	Title (A Side/B Side)	Yr	VG	VG+	NM
RCA					
❑ 8869-7-R	Where There's Smoke/Tore Up Over You	1989	—	—	3.00
❑ 9026-7-R	Waitin' on Ice/Get Out You Big Roll Daddy	1989	—	—	3.00

Albums

Number	Title (A Side/B Side)	Yr	VG	VG+	NM
RCA					
❑ 9782-1-R	Tore Up	1989	3.00	6.00	12.00

WILLIAMS, JOHNNY

45s

Number	Title (A Side/B Side)	Yr	VG	VG+	NM
CINNAMON					
❑ 812	Love Me for a While/That's All That Matters	1974	—	3.00	6.00
COLUMBIA					
❑ 4-42777	Black Knight/Augie's Great Piano	1963	2.50	5.00	10.00
EPIC					
❑ 5-10797	The Other Man/Lifed Go	1971	—	3.50	7.00
❑ 5-10845	He Will Break Your Heart/If Loving You Means Anything	1972	—	3.50	7.00
❑ 5-10921	I Still Belong to You/Sweet Memories	1972	—	3.50	7.00

WILLIAMS, LAWTON

45s

Number	Title (A Side/B Side)	Yr	VG	VG+	NM
D					
❑ 1120	I Don't Care Who Knows/Satan's Bell	1960	3.75	7.50	15.00
DECCA					
❑ 9-30709	Texas vs. Alaska/Don't Let Anybody Tell You	1958	3.75	7.50	15.00
❑ 9-30839	Iron Curtain/House Full of Love	1959	3.75	7.50	15.00
DISCUS					
❑ 912	The Nairy County Sheriff/Don't Play Angel with Me	197?	—	3.00	6.00
GROOVE					
❑ 58-0011	The Carpetbaggers/Mama Pinch a Penny	1963	3.00	6.00	12.00
MEGA					
❑ 0035	Asphalt Cowboy/Cold, Cold Hands	1971	—	3.50	7.00
MERCURY					
❑ 71780	The Big Fire/John and Mary Doe	1961	3.00	6.00	12.00
❑ 71867	Anywhere There's People/Ploughed Ground	1961	3.00	6.00	12.00
PLANTATION					
❑ 56	The Preacher and the Movie/Ain't That Bad About Mrs. Jones	1970	—	3.50	7.00
❑ 64	The Ballad of Morgan/Ain't That Bad About Mrs. Jones	1970	—	3.50	7.00
RCA VICTOR					
❑ 47-7105	Foreign Love/Don't Burn the Bridge Behind You	1957	5.00	10.00	20.00
❑ 47-7188	Casino on the Hill/If You're Waitin' on Me	1958	5.00	10.00	20.00
❑ 47-8142	Don't Destroy Me/Rock of Gibraltar	1963	2.50	5.00	10.00
❑ 47-8203	Mountain of a Man/In Love with You	1963	2.50	5.00	10.00
❑ 47-8300	Squawlein/It Looks Like You Love Me	1963	2.50	5.00	10.00
❑ 47-8359	I'm Not All Here/Stay on the Ball	1964	2.50	5.00	10.00
❑ 47-8407	Everything's OK on the LBJ/Don't Look Down	1964	2.50	5.00	10.00
❑ 47-8514	War on Poverty/Power of Love	1965	2.50	5.00	10.00
❑ 74-0109	Everything's OK on the LBJ/I'm Not All Here	1969	—	3.50	7.00

WILLIAMS, LEONA

Also see MERLE HAGGARD AND LEONA WILLIAMS.

45s

Number	Title (A Side/B Side)	Yr	VG	VG+	NM
ELEKTRA					
❑ 47114	I'm Almost Ready/The End of the World	1981	—	2.00	4.00
❑ 47162	You Can't Find Many Kisses/Guitar Pickin' Man	1981	—	2.00	4.00
❑ 47217	Always Late with Your Kisses/Startin' Today	1981	—	2.00	4.00
HICKORY					
❑ 1501	A Woman's Man/Ten Minutes Till Heartaches	1968	2.00	4.00	8.00
❑ 1511	Broadminded/Papa's Medicine Show	1968	2.00	4.00	8.00
❑ 1523	I Want Some More of This/They'll Never Take His Love from Me	1968	2.00	4.00	8.00
❑ 1532	Once More/I Narrowed This Triangle (Down to Two)	1969	2.00	4.00	8.00
❑ 1544	Baby, We're Really in Love/Circle of Love	1969	2.00	4.00	8.00
❑ 1555	Just Because of You/When I Stop Dreaming	1969	2.00	4.00	8.00
❑ 1565	This Ain't a Home No More/Yes Ma'am (He Found Me in a Honky Tonk)	1970	2.00	4.00	8.00
❑ 1578	If I'd Only Listened to Mama and Dad/Watch Her Go	1970	2.00	4.00	8.00
❑ 1590	Somewhere Inside/He's Just You Made Over	1971	2.00	4.00	8.00
❑ 1606	Country Girl with Hot Pants On/Babe, Just for You	1971	2.00	4.00	8.00
❑ 1619	Country Music in My Soul/The Boys and Lucy Brown	1972	—	3.50	7.00
❑ 1635	Happy Anniversary, Baby/The Old Place Is Gone	1972	—	3.50	7.00
❑ 1650	Out of Hand/Gentleman on My Mind	1972	—	3.50	7.00
❑ 1662	A Woman's Life Is More Than Just a Man/I'd Rather Die	1973	—	3.50	7.00
❑ 1670	Papa's Medicine Show/I Can't Tell My Heart That	1973	—	3.50	7.00
HICKORY/MGM					
❑ 304	Your Shoeshine Girl/Since I'm Not with the One I Love (I'll Love the One I'm With)	1973	—	3.00	6.00
❑ 310	Anything Goes/I Spent a Week There Last Night	1973	—	3.00	6.00
❑ 315	I'm Not Supposed to Love You Anymore/Once More	1974	—	3.00	6.00
MCA					
❑ 40515	If Anyone Ought to Know/I Wonder Where I'll Find You At Tonight	1976	—	2.50	5.00
❑ 40557	Cotton-Eyed Joe/San Quentin	1976	—	2.50	5.00
❑ 40856	Mama I've Got to Go to Memphis/That Lonely Unloved Wife Look	1978	—	2.50	5.00
❑ 40926	Rockin' Rollin' Stoned/Bright Morning Light	1978	—	2.50	5.00
❑ 40988	The Baby Song/Call Me Crazy Lady	1979	—	2.50	5.00
❑ 41006	Yes Ma'am (He Found Me in a Honky Tonk)/Good Nights Make Good Mornings	1979	—	2.50	5.00
❑ 41196	Catchin' Crawfish/Any Port in a Storm	1980	—	2.50	5.00
MERCURY					
❑ 818946-7	Midnight Love/My First Night Away from Home	1984	—	2.00	4.00
RCA VICTOR					
❑ PB-10097	Just Like a Prayer/A Lifetime to Forget	1974	—	3.00	6.00
❑ PB-10300	Shape Up or Ship Out/You Don't Love Me Like You Mean It	1975	—	3.00	6.00

Albums

Number	Title (A Side/B Side)	Yr	VG	VG+	NM
HICKORY					
❑ LPS-151	That Williams Girl	1971	3.75	7.50	15.00
❑ LPS-165	The Best of Leona Williams	1972	3.75	7.50	15.00
MCA					
❑ 2212	San Quentin's First Lady	1976	3.00	6.00	12.00
MERCURY					
❑ 822424-1	Someday When Things Are Good	1984	2.00	4.00	8.00

WILLIAMS, LOIS

Also see RED SOVINE.

45s

STARDAY

Number	Title (A Side/B Side)	Yr	VG	VG+	NM
❑ 873	Corner of Your World/He's the Man	1969	—	3.50	7.00
❑ 877	A Girl Named Sam/We've Got Another Chance	1969	2.00	4.00	8.00
❑ 886	From Miss to Mistake/You Low-Down Son of a Gun	1969	—	3.50	7.00
❑ 899	I Fell in Love with a Feller on the Hee Haw Show/What It Takes	1970	—	3.50	7.00
❑ 913	Don't Take My Child Away/I'm Looking for a Man, Boy	1970	—	3.50	7.00

Albums

STARDAY

Number	Title (A Side/B Side)	Yr	VG	VG+	NM
❑ SLP-448	A Girl Named Sam	1970	5.00	10.00	20.00

WILLIAMS, OTIS, AND HIS CHARMS

Otis Williams' group, after it became The Midnight Cowboys, recorded some country music from 1968-73.

45s

SCEPTER

Number	Title (A Side/B Side)	Yr	VG	VG+	NM
❑ 12376	Here Lie the Bones of Nellie Jones/When You Turn On the Love	1973	2.00	4.00	8.00

STOP

Number	Title (A Side/B Side)	Yr	VG	VG+	NM
❑ 301	Begging to You/(B-side unknown)	1968	2.50	5.00	10.00
❑ 306	Begging to You/Everybody's Got a Song But Me	1968	2.50	5.00	10.00
❑ 346	Jesus Is a Soul Man/Make a Woman Feel Like a Woman	1969	2.50	5.00	10.00
❑ 360	Ling, Ting, Tong/For the Love	1970	2.50	5.00	10.00
❑ 388	I Wanna Go Country/Rocky Top	1971	2.00	4.00	8.00

—As "Otis Williams and the Midnight Cowboys"

Albums

STOP

Number	Title (A Side/B Side)	Yr	VG	VG+	NM
❑ STLP-1022	Otis Williams and the Midnight Cowboys	1971	6.25	12.50	25.00

WILLIAMS, PAUL

45s

A&M

Number	Title (A Side/B Side)	Yr	VG	VG+	NM
❑ 1325	We've Only Just Begun/Waking Up Alone	1972	—	2.00	4.00
❑ 1356	My Love and I/I Never Had It So Good	1972	—	2.00	4.00
❑ 1409	I Won't Last a Day Without You/Little Girl	1973	—	2.00	4.00
❑ 1429	Lady in Waiting/Look What I Found	1973	—	2.00	4.00
❑ 1479	What Would They Say/Inspiration	1973	—	2.00	4.00
❑ 1525	That's What Friends Are For/Dream Away	1974	—	2.00	4.00
❑ 1659	A Little Bit of Love/Nice to Be Around	1975	—	2.00	4.00
❑ 1686	One More Angel/This Is Supposed to Be a Party	1975	—	2.00	4.00
❑ 1797	Don't Call It Love/Time and Tide	1976	—	2.00	4.00
❑ 1853	Even Better Than I Know Myself/Time and Tide	1976	—	2.00	4.00
❑ 1868	Bugsy Malone/Ordinary Fool	1976	—	2.00	4.00
❑ 1961	Love Theme from "A Star Is Born"/Waking Up Alone	1977	—	2.00	4.00

PAID

Number	Title (A Side/B Side)	Yr	VG	VG+	NM
❑ 146	Making Believe/Oh, How I Miss You Tonight	1981	—	2.00	4.00

PORTRAIT

Number	Title (A Side/B Side)	Yr	VG	VG+	NM
❑ 70029	The Gift/A Little on the Windy Side	1979	—	2.00	4.00

REPRISE

Number	Title (A Side/B Side)	Yr	VG	VG+	NM
❑ 0903	Someday/Mornin' I'll Be Movin' On	1970	—	3.00	6.00

Albums

A&M

Number	Title (A Side/B Side)	Yr	VG	VG+	NM
❑ SP-3131	Just an Old Fashioned Love Song	198?	2.00	4.00	8.00
—Budget-line reissue					
❑ SP-3606	Here Comes Inspiration	1974	2.50	5.00	10.00
❑ SP-3655	A Little Bit of Love	1974	2.50	5.00	10.00
❑ SP-4327	Just an Old Fashioned Love Song	1971	2.50	5.00	10.00
❑ SP-4367	Life Goes On	1972	2.50	5.00	10.00
❑ SP-4550	Ordinary Fool	1975	2.50	5.00	10.00
❑ SP-4701	Classics	1977	2.50	5.00	10.00

PORTRAIT

Number	Title (A Side/B Side)	Yr	VG	VG+	NM
❑ JR 35610	Windy Side	1979	2.50	5.00	10.00

REPRISE

Number	Title (A Side/B Side)	Yr	VG	VG+	NM
❑ RS 6401	Someday Man	1970	3.00	6.00	12.00

WILLIAMS, TEX

Also see REX ALLEN.

45s

BOONE

Number	Title (A Side/B Side)	Yr	VG	VG+	NM
❑ 1028	Too Many Tigers/Winter Snow	1965	2.00	4.00	8.00
❑ 1032	Big Tennessee/My Last Two Tens	1965	2.00	4.00	8.00
❑ 1036	Bottom of a Mountain/Tears Are Only Rain	1965	2.00	4.00	8.00
❑ 1040	Bottom Land/First Step Down	1966	2.00	4.00	8.00
❑ 1044	Another Day, Another Dollar in the Hole/The Big Man	1966	2.00	4.00	8.00
❑ 1052	Crazy Life/The Toy Piano	1966	2.00	4.00	8.00
❑ 1059	Black Jack County/Ain't Gonna Walk Your Dog	1967	2.00	4.00	8.00
❑ 1065	Mother's Flower Garden/She's Somebody Else's Heartache Now	1967	2.00	4.00	8.00
❑ 1069	Smoke, Smoke, Smoke — '68/Lonely One	1968	2.00	4.00	8.00
❑ 1072	Here's to You and Me/If Not for You There Could Go Me	1968	2.00	4.00	8.00
❑ 1080	The Tail's Been Wagging/Look Beyond Your Dreams	1969	2.00	4.00	8.00

CAPITOL

Number	Title (A Side/B Side)	Yr	VG	VG+	NM
❑ F940	My San Fernando Rose/Was Yesterday a Dream	1950	6.25	12.50	25.00
❑ F1006	Birmingham Bounce/Great Big Needle	1950	6.25	12.50	25.00
❑ F1087	Happy Feet/You Two Time Me, I'll Two Time You	1950	6.25	12.50	25.00
❑ F1166	Wild Card/Tamburitza Boogie	1950	6.25	12.50	25.00
❑ F1286	Alimony/I Want Gold	1950	6.25	12.50	25.00
❑ F1345	Cheaters Never Prosper/Don't Make Love	1950	6.25	12.50	25.00
❑ F1390	She Didn't Even Kiss Me Goodbye/Tulsa Trot	1951	5.00	10.00	20.00
❑ F1437	That's Where I Live/Smoke! Smoke! Smoke! (That Cigarette)	1951	5.00	10.00	20.00
❑ F1475	I Lost My Gal from Memphis/One Way Ticket	1951	5.00	10.00	20.00
❑ F1540	Sugar Coated Love/Goodnight Cincinnati, Good Morning Tennessee	1951	5.00	10.00	20.00
❑ F1700	Love and Devotion/Black Strap Molasses	1951	5.00	10.00	20.00
❑ F1799	Cocker Spaniel Polka/I Want to Be Near You	1951	5.00	10.00	20.00
❑ 4413	Smoke! Smoke! Smoke! (That Cigarette)/That's What I Like About the West	1960	3.00	6.00	12.00
❑ 4479	Are You Sure/Think It Over Boys	1960	3.00	6.00	12.00
❑ 4690	A Hundred Years from Now/How Do You Lie to a Heart	1962	2.50	5.00	10.00
❑ 4776	You Gotta Have a License/Ghost of a Honky Tonk Slave	1962	2.50	5.00	10.00
❑ F40001	Smoke! Smoke! Smoke! (That Cigarette)/Roundup Polka	1949	10.00	20.00	40.00
❑ F40183	Cowboy Polka/Big Bass Polka	1950	6.25	12.50	25.00
❑ F40184	Beer Barrel Polka/Banjo Polka	1950	6.25	12.50	25.00
❑ F40185	Capitol Polka/Milkman Polka	1950	6.25	12.50	25.00
❑ F40186	Cow Bell Polka/Yodeling Polka	1950	6.25	12.50	25.00
—The above four, which comprise a box set entitled "Polkas!", were issued on 78 in 1948					
❑ F40276	With Men Who Know Tobacco Best (It's Women Two to One)/Three Little Girls Dressed in Blue	1950	7.50	15.00	30.00

DECCA

Number	Title (A Side/B Side)	Yr	VG	VG+	NM
❑ 9-28660	Big Big Lie/Changeable	1953	5.00	10.00	20.00
❑ 9-28721	Hey Mister Cotton-Picker/Don't Call My Name	1953	5.00	10.00	20.00
—With Roberta Lee					
❑ 9-28809	The Deck of Cards/Seven Days in Heaven	1953	5.00	10.00	20.00
❑ 9-29077	If You'd Believe in Me/Honey	1954	5.00	10.00	20.00
❑ 9-29133	River of No Return/Down in the Meadow	1954	5.00	10.00	20.00
❑ 9-29202	They Were Doing the Mambo/That's the Good Lord Saying "Good Morning"	1954	5.00	10.00	20.00
❑ 9-29308	Sidetracked/Can I Say the Same About You	1954	5.00	10.00	20.00
❑ 9-29385	Air Mail Special/Williams Rag	1954	5.00	10.00	20.00
❑ 9-29469	Roses and Revolvers/Rancho Boogie	1955	3.75	7.50	15.00
❑ 9-29578	Old Betsy/Be Sure You're Right (Then Go Ahead)	1955	6.25	12.50	25.00
❑ 9-29764	New Nine Pound Hammer/Pauline	1956	3.75	7.50	15.00
❑ 9-29900	Shake the Hand of a Stranger/Revival Is On Its Way	1956	3.75	7.50	15.00
❑ 9-30037	Artichokes/Reno, Town of Broken Hearts	1956	3.75	7.50	15.00
❑ 9-30161	When I Call the Roll/You're Cold, So Cold	1956	3.75	7.50	15.00
❑ 9-30328	Every Night/Talkin' to the Blues	1957	3.75	7.50	15.00
❑ 9-30459	Let's Go Rockabilly/Long Lost Love	1957	5.00	10.00	20.00
❑ 9-30553	False Face/Danny Boy of San Angelo	1958	3.75	7.50	15.00
❑ 9-30672	The Ballad of Thunder Road/Bad Man's Country	1958	3.75	7.50	15.00
❑ 9-30774	You Rocked When You Should-a Rolled/The Killer	1958	6.25	12.50	25.00

DOT

Number	Title (A Side/B Side)	Yr	VG	VG+	NM
❑ 16850	Bummin' Around/Keeper of Boot Hill	1966	2.00	4.00	8.00

GRANITE

Number	Title (A Side/B Side)	Yr	VG	VG+	NM
❑ 505	Is This All You Hear/Roll, Muddy River	1974	—	3.00	6.00
❑ 507	Those Lazy, Hazy, Crazy Days of Summer/Nowhere, West Virginia	1974	—	3.00	6.00
❑ 512	Bum, Bum, Bum/Mother Was a Sideman	1974	—	3.00	6.00

LIBERTY

Number	Title (A Side/B Side)	Yr	VG	VG+	NM
❑ 55537	Where the Sad People Are/Five Foot Deep in Teardrops	1963	2.50	5.00	10.00
❑ 55583	Risin' High/Go Into the Mountains	1963	2.50	5.00	10.00
❑ 55652	Late Movies/Long John	1963	2.50	5.00	10.00
❑ 55698	Mr. All Alone/Pickin' White Gold	1964	2.50	5.00	10.00
❑ 55711	Empty Letter/Closer, Closer, Closer	1964	2.50	5.00	10.00
❑ 55760	Smokey Hollow/Between Today and Tomorrow	1965	2.50	5.00	10.00

MONUMENT

Number	Title (A Side/B Side)	Yr	VG	VG+	NM
❑ 1200	Big Oscar/Wasted Dreams	1970	—	3.50	7.00
❑ 1216	It Ain't No Big Thing/I Never Knew What Doing Was ('Til I Got Done by You)	1970	—	3.50	7.00
❑ 8503	The Night Miss Nancy Ann's Hotel for Single Girls Burned Down/If It's All the Same to You	1971	—	3.50	7.00
❑ 8533	Everywhere I Go (He's Already Been There)/Pretty in Blue	1972	—	3.50	7.00
❑ 8538	Glamour of the Night/The House	1972	—	3.50	7.00
❑ 8544	I Pledge Allegiance/Tennessee Travelin' Man	1972	—	3.50	7.00
❑ 8551	Cynthia Ann/Walkin' on the Wind	1972	—	3.50	7.00

RCA VICTOR

Number	Title (A Side/B Side)	Yr	VG	VG+	NM
❑ 47-4409	Shrimp Boats/Urn on the Mantel	1951	5.00	10.00	20.00
❑ 47-4506	Only Politickin'/Shame on You	1952	5.00	10.00	20.00
❑ 47-4561	Double Shuffle/Senator from Tennessee	1952	5.00	10.00	20.00
—With Dinah Shore					
❑ 47-4708	Sinful/Bronco Buster's Ball	1952	5.00	10.00	20.00
❑ 47-4897	Miracle Waltz/Sweet Little Boogalie	1952	5.00	10.00	20.00

SHASTA

Number	Title (A Side/B Side)	Yr	VG	VG+	NM
❑ 109	Yankee Go Home/I'll Hold You in My Heart	1959	3.00	6.00	12.00
—With Bonnie Sloan					
❑ 116	The Battle of New Orleans/Keeper of Boot Hill	1959	3.00	6.00	12.00
❑ 122	Bummin' Around/Keeper of Boot Hill	1959	3.00	6.00	12.00
❑ 129	River Stay 'Way from My Door/Thunder on the River	1960	3.00	6.00	12.00
❑ 130	Where Do We Go from Here/Blue Ribbons	1960	3.00	6.00	12.00
—With Bonnie Sloan					

Selected 78s

CAPITOL

Number	Title (A Side/B Side)	Yr	VG	VG+	NM
❑ 302	The California Polka/Rose of Alamo	1946	3.75	7.50	15.00
❑ 333	I Got Texas in My Soul/Leaf of Love	1947	3.75	7.50	15.00
❑ 15101	Banjo Polka/Pretty Red Lights	1948	3.00	6.00	12.00
❑ 15113	Who, Me?/Foolish Tears	1948	3.00	6.00	12.00
❑ 15175	Talking Boogie/Just a Pair of Blue Eyes	1948	3.00	6.00	12.00
❑ 15217	Hair of Gold, Eyes of Blue/Ball of Fire	1948	3.00	6.00	12.00
—With Smokey Rogers					
❑ 15262	California Polka/I've Got Texas in My Soul	1948	3.00	6.00	12.00
❑ 15271	Life Gits Tee-Jus, Don't It?/Big Hat Polka	1948	3.00	6.00	12.00
❑ 15321	Hurry Don't Delay/Old Paint's Complaint	1949	3.00	6.00	12.00
❑ 15398	You Broke Your Promise/I Cried Myself to Sleep	1949	3.00	6.00	12.00
❑ 40001	Smoke! Smoke! Smoke! (That Cigarette)/ Roundup Polka	1947	3.75	7.50	15.00
—Red label; 78 first issued in 1947					
❑ 40031	That's What I Like About the West/Downtown Poker Club	1947	3.75	7.50	15.00
❑ 40054	Never Trust a Woman/What It Means to Be Blue	1947	3.75	7.50	15.00
❑ 40081	Don't Telephone — Don't Telegraph (Tell a Woman)/Blue as a Heart Ache	1948	3.75	7.50	15.00
❑ 40095	Happy Birthday Polka/Artistry in Western Swing	1948	3.75	7.50	15.00
❑ 40109	Suspicion/Flo from St. Joe Mo.	1948	3.75	7.50	15.00
❑ 40159	Castle of My Dreams/Johnstown Polka	1949	3.00	6.00	12.00
❑ 40194	Cowpuncher's Waltz/Ham 'n' Eggs	1949	3.75	7.50	15.00
❑ 40200	Texas Star/Ocean Waves	1949	3.00	6.00	12.00
❑ 40202	Ocean Waves/Chinese Breakdown	1949	3.00	6.00	12.00
❑ 40203	Rakes of Mallow/A & E Rag	1949	3.00	6.00	12.00
❑ 40206	Hot Pretzels/Cotton-Eyed Joe	1949	3.00	6.00	12.00
❑ 40225	(There's a) Bluebird on Your Windowsill/A Letter Asking for My Heart	1949	3.00	6.00	12.00
❑ 40253	Crocodile Tears/The Winter Song	1949	3.00	6.00	12.00

7-Inch Extended Plays

DECCA

Number	Title (A Side/B Side)	Yr	VG	VG+	NM
❑ ED 2174	(contents unknown)	1955	6.25	12.50	25.00
❑ ED 2174 [PS]	All Time Greats	1955	6.25	12.50	25.00
❑ ED 2229	(contents unknown)	1955	6.25	12.50	25.00
❑ ED 2229 [PS]	Dance-O-Rama	1955	6.25	12.50	25.00

Albums

Number	Title (A Side/B Side)	Yr	VG	VG+	NM
BOONE					
❑ LP-1210 [M]	The Two Sides of Tex Williams	1966	5.00	10.00	20.00
❑ LSP-1210 [S]	The Two Sides of Tex Williams	1966	6.25	12.50	25.00
CAPITOL					
❑ ST 1463 [S]	Smoke! Smoke! Smoke!	1960	10.00	20.00	40.00
❑ T 1463 [M]	Smoke! Smoke! Smoke!	1960	7.50	15.00	30.00
DECCA					
❑ DL 4295 [M]	Country Music Time	1962	5.00	10.00	20.00
❑ DL 5565 [10]	Dance-O-Rama #5	1955	75.00	150.00	300.00
❑ DL 74295 [S]	Country Music Time	1962	7.50	15.00	30.00
IMPERIAL					
❑ LP-9309 [M]	The Voice of Authority	1966	5.00	10.00	20.00
❑ LP-12309 [S]	The Voice of Authority	1966	6.25	12.50	25.00
LIBERTY					
❑ LRP-3304 [M]	Tex Williams in Las Vegas	1963	5.00	10.00	20.00
❑ LST-7304 [S]	Tex Williams in Las Vegas	1963	7.50	15.00	30.00
MONUMENT					
❑ Z 30909	A Man Called Tex	1971	5.00	10.00	20.00
RCA CAMDEN					
❑ CAL-363 [M]	Tex Williams' Best	1958	6.25	12.50	25.00

WILLIAMS, TUCKER

45s

YATAHEY

Number	Title (A Side/B Side)	Yr	VG	VG+	NM
❑ 999	Donna-Earth Angel (Medley)/Honey Love	1980	—	3.50	7.00

WILLIAMS BROS.

These are not Andy Williams' nephews Andrew and David, who also recorded as The Williams Brothers; this is an unrelated duo, Jimmy and Bobby Williams.

45s

DEL-MAR

Number	Title (A Side/B Side)	Yr	VG	VG+	NM
❑ 1008	Bad Old Memories/The Last Time	1963	5.00	10.00	20.00

WILLING, FOY, AND THE RIDERS OF THE PURPLE SAGE

45s

Number	Title (A Side/B Side)	Yr	VG	VG+	NM
CHALLENGE					
❑ 1011	Cool Water/No One to Cry To	1958	5.00	10.00	20.00
DECCA					
❑ 9-46365	Detour/Address Unknown	1951	6.25	12.50	25.00
ROULETTE					
❑ 4055	Cowboy/Soft Winds	1958	3.75	7.50	15.00
ROYALE					
❑ 4520	Song of the Sierras/(B-side unknown)	195?	5.00	10.00	20.00
❑ 45212	Cool Water/(B-side unknown)	195?	5.00	10.00	20.00
❑ 45341	Divorce Me C.O.D./(B-side unknown)	195?	5.00	10.00	20.00
VARSITY					
❑ 4520	Song of the Sierras/(B-side unknown)	195?	5.00	10.00	20.00
❑ 45212	Cool Water/(B-side unknown)	195?	5.00	10.00	20.00
❑ 45341	Divorce Me C.O.D./(B-side unknown)	195?	5.00	10.00	20.00

Selected 78s

Number	Title (A Side/B Side)	Yr	VG	VG+	NM
CAPITOL					
❑ 162	Texas Blues/Hang Your Head in Shame	1944	3.00	6.00	12.00
❑ 15163	Sometime/I'll Have Somebody Else	1948	3.75	7.50	15.00
❑ 15221	Just a Little Lovin'/Lay Your Little Head on My Shoulder	1948	3.75	7.50	15.00
❑ 15290	Brush Those Tears from Your Eyes/Rose of Ol' Pawnee	1948	3.75	7.50	15.00
❑ 15355	I Care No More/Goodbye, Good Luck	1948	3.75	7.50	15.00
❑ 40108	Anytime/I'm Waltzing with a Broken Heart	1948	3.75	7.50	15.00
❑ 40151	You Told a Lie/I Had My Heart Set on You	1948	3.75	7.50	15.00
❑ 40164	Riders in the Sky/I Cried Myself to Sleep	1949	3.75	7.50	15.00
❑ 40228	Your Tears Came Too Late/You'll Never Have My Love Anymore	1949	3.75	7.50	15.00
DECCA					
❑ 9000	Detour/Someone Won Your Heart Little Darlin'	1946	3.75	7.50	15.00
❑ 46088	No One to Cry To/A Hundred and Sixty Acres	1948	3.75	7.50	15.00
MAJESTIC					
❑ 6000	Have I Told You Lately (That I Love You)/Cool Water	1946	3.75	7.50	15.00
❑ 6001	Chained to a Memory/Live and Learn	1946	3.75	7.50	15.00
❑ 6002	Divorce Me C.O.D./Darling What More Can I Do	1946	3.75	7.50	15.00
❑ 6003	So Round, So Firm (So Fully Packed)/No One to Cry To	1946	3.75	7.50	15.00
❑ 6013	I Wonder Who's Kissing Her Now/Wait'll I Get My Sunshine in the Moonlight	1947	3.75	7.50	15.00
❑ 6014	Tumbling Tumbleweeds/Twilight on the Trail	1947	3.75	7.50	15.00
❑ 6015	Holiday for the Blues/Where the Cool Clear Water Spills	1947	3.75	7.50	15.00
❑ 6016	When the Sun Goes Down/Be My Darlin'	1947	3.75	7.50	15.00
❑ 6021	That's What I Like About the West/Never Trust a Woman	1947	3.75	7.50	15.00
❑ 6030	Little White House/Blue Shadows on the Trail	1947	3.75	7.50	15.00
❑ 6031	Song of the Sierras/I Couldn't Believe It Was True	1947	3.75	7.50	15.00

Albums

Number	Title (A Side/B Side)	Yr	VG	VG+	NM
CROWN					
❑ CST-582	Country & Western Favorites	196?	2.50	5.00	10.00
❑ CLP-5306 [M]	Cool Water	196?	3.00	6.00	12.00
CUSTOM					
❑ CS 1017	Cool, Cool Water	197?	2.50	5.00	10.00
JUBILEE					
❑ JL-5028 [M]	The New Sound of American Folk	1962	5.00	10.00	20.00
❑ JLS-5028 [S]	The New Sound of American Folk	1962	6.25	12.50	25.00
ROULETTE					
❑ R-25035 [M]	Cowboy	1958	10.00	20.00	40.00
ROYALE					
❑ 6032 [10]	The Riders of the Purple Sage	1952	25.00	50.00	100.00
VARSITY					
❑ 6032 [10]	The Riders of the Purple Sage	1950	30.00	60.00	120.00

WILLIS, ANDRA

Also see TENNESSEE ERNIE FORD.

45s

Number	Title (A Side/B Side)	Yr	VG	VG+	NM
CAPITOL					
❑ 3525	Down Home Lovin' Woman/Cryin' Cause You're Gone	1973	—	3.00	6.00
❑ 3591	The Last Thing I Need/A Little Bit of Love in the Morning	1973	—	3.00	6.00
❑ 3666	Til I Can't Take It Anymore/After You	1973	—	3.00	6.00
❑ 3747	He Makes Me Feel Like a Woman/Little Old Heartbreaker You	1973	—	3.00	6.00
❑ 4114	After You/Only for My Man	1975	—	3.00	6.00
MCA					
❑ 40594	You in Me/Except I Love You	1976	—	2.50	5.00
❑ 40676	I'm Sorry/It's Me and You	1976	—	2.50	5.00

WILLIS, HAL

45s

Number	Title (A Side/B Side)	Yr	VG	VG+	NM
ATHENS					
❑ 704	Crazy Little Mama/Walkin' Dream	1958	37.50	75.00	150.00
ATLANTIC					
❑ 1114	Bop-A-Dee, Bop-A-Doo/My Pink Cadillac	1956	50.00	100.00	200.00
DECCA					
❑ 30949	Poor Little Jimmy/That's the Way It Goes	1959	3.00	6.00	12.00
MERCURY					
❑ 71933	Bayou Pierre/I Love You (Around the World)	1962	3.00	6.00	12.00
SIMS					
❑ 207	The Lumberjack/Dig Me a Hole	1964	3.00	6.00	12.00
❑ 224	The One I Love/What's Left of Me	1965	3.00	6.00	12.00
❑ 235	Klondike Mike/So Right But So Wrong	1965	3.00	6.00	12.00
❑ 243	Thumb and Shoes/Nopper the Topper	1965	3.00	6.00	12.00
❑ 250	Creole Rose/When It's Springtime in Alaska	1965	3.00	6.00	12.00
❑ 288	Doggin' in the U.S. Mail/The Battle of Viet Nam	1966	3.00	6.00	12.00
❑ 307	Parson from Paint Rock/Private Dick	1966	3.00	6.00	12.00

WILLIS, KELLY

45s

MCA

Number	Title (A Side/B Side)	Yr	VG	VG+	NM
❑ 53944	Looking for Someone Like You/I'm Just Lonely	1990	—	2.00	4.00
❑ 54050	Baby Take a Piece of My Heart/Standing by the River	1991	—	2.00	4.00
❑ 54198	The Heart That Love Forgot/Too Much to Ask	1991	—	2.00	4.00
❑ 54251	Settle for Love/Bang Bang	1991	—	2.00	4.00
❑ 54678	Whatever Way the Wind Blows/World Without You	1993	—	—	3.00
❑ 54733	Heaven's Just a Sin Away/Get Real	1993	—	—	3.00
❑ 79002	I Don't Want to Love You (But I Do)/Drive South	1990	—	2.00	4.00
❑ 79053	River of Love/Red Sunset	1990	—	2.00	4.00

WILLIS BROTHERS, THE

45s

STARDAY

Number	Title (A Side/B Side)	Yr	VG	VG+	NM
❑ 518	Pretty Diamonds/Billy the Kid	1960	3.75	7.50	15.00
❑ 532	Little Footprints in the Snow/Y'All Come	1960	3.75	7.50	15.00
❑ 555	Everlovin' Dixieland/Tattooed Lady	1961	3.75	7.50	15.00
❑ 570	Big Daddy/It's the Miles	1961	3.75	7.50	15.00
❑ 592	Sally's Bangs/Honey, Do You Love Your Man	1962	3.00	6.00	12.00
❑ 604	Yankee Dollar/Morning Glory	1962	3.00	6.00	12.00
❑ 625	Private Lee/Ax Cabin	1963	3.00	6.00	12.00
❑ 645	Truck Driver's Queen/Who's Next on Your List	1963	3.00	6.00	12.00
❑ 662	Linda Do the Bubble Up/Wash Up	1964	3.00	6.00	12.00
❑ 681	Give Me 40 Acres (To Turn This Rig Around)/ Gonna Buy Me a Juke Box	1964	2.50	5.00	10.00
❑ 703	Blazing Smokestack/Too Early to Get Up	1964	2.50	5.00	10.00
❑ 713	A Six Foot Two by Four/Strange Old Town	1965	2.50	5.00	10.00
❑ 730	Pinball Anonymous/When I Came Driving Through	1965	2.50	5.00	10.00
❑ 748	Swing 'Til My Rose Breaks/Love Thy Neighbor	1965	2.50	5.00	10.00
❑ 760	Three Sheets in the Wind/Waltzing with Sin	1966	2.50	5.00	10.00
❑ 782	Ain't It Funny/Goin' to Town	1966	2.50	5.00	10.00
❑ 796	Bob/Show Her Lots of Gold	1967	2.00	4.00	8.00
❑ 812	Somebody Knows My Dog/The End of the Road	1967	2.00	4.00	8.00
❑ 830	Ode to Big Joe/Drivin's in My Blood	1968	2.00	4.00	8.00
❑ 848	Diesel Driving Donut Dunkin' Dan/A Moonlight Ride in a Diesel	1968	2.00	4.00	8.00
❑ 863	Alcohol and No. 2 Diesel/My Ramblin' Boy	1969	2.00	4.00	8.00
❑ 874	Buyin' Popcorn/1,000 Acres	1969	2.00	4.00	8.00
❑ 884	Cold North Wind/Gypsy Rose and Me	1969	2.00	4.00	8.00
❑ 903	Nashville Ace in the Hole/There Goes the Farm	1970	2.00	4.00	8.00
❑ 923	For the Good Times/Women's Liberation	1971	—	3.50	7.00
❑ 938	She's Living in Sin/You Make My Heart Want a Sniff of Snuff	1971	—	3.50	7.00
❑ 962	John Told Jack/Why Don't You Haul Off and Love Me	1973	—	3.50	7.00
❑ 7006	Truck Driver's Queen/Diesel Smoke, Dangerous Curves	197?	—	3.00	6.00
❑ 8027	Give Me 40 Acres (To Turn This Rig Around)/ Truck Driver's Queen	197?	—	3.00	6.00

Albums

STARDAY

Number	Title	Yr	VG	VG+	NM
❑ SLP-163 [M]	The Willis Brothers in Action	1962	15.00	30.00	60.00
❑ SLP-229 [M]	Code of the West	1963	12.50	25.00	50.00
❑ SLP-306 [M]	Let's Hit the Road	1965	10.00	20.00	40.00
❑ SLP-323 [M]	Give Me 40 Acres	1965	10.00	20.00	40.00
❑ SLP-353 [M]	Road Stop Juke Box Hits	1966	7.50	15.00	30.00
❑ SLP-369 [M]	The Wild Side of Life	1966	7.50	15.00	30.00
❑ SLP-387 [M]	Goin' to Town	1966	7.50	15.00	30.00
❑ SLP-403 [M]	Bob	1967	6.25	12.50	25.00
❑ SLP-428	Hey, Mister Truck Driver	1968	6.25	12.50	25.00
❑ SLP-442	Bummin' Around	1969	6.25	12.50	25.00
❑ SLP-466	The Best of the Willis Brothers	1970	5.00	10.00	20.00
❑ SLP-472	For the Good Times	1971	5.00	10.00	20.00

WILLOUGHBY, LARRY

45s

ATLANTIC AMERICA

Number	Title (A Side/B Side)	Yr	VG	VG+	NM
❑ 99759	Angel Eyes/The Devil's on the Loose	1984	—	2.00	4.00
❑ 99797	Building Bridges/(B-side unknown)	1984	—	2.00	4.00
❑ 99826	Heart on the Line (Operator, Operator)/Stone Cold	1983	—	2.00	4.00

Albums

ATLANTIC AMERICA

Number	Title	Yr	VG	VG+	NM
❑ 90112	Building Bridges	1983	2.50	5.00	10.00

WILLS, BOB

Also see THE TEXAS PLAYBOYS.

45s

COLUMBIA

Number	Title (A Side/B Side)	Yr	VG	VG+	NM
❑ 2-220	Misery/You're There	1949	12.50	25.00	50.00
—Microgroove 7-inch 33 1/3 single, small hole					
❑ 4-52029	San Antonio Rose/New San Antonio Rose	195?	3.75	7.50	15.00
—Early "Hall of Fame Series" issue					

DECCA

Number	Title (A Side/B Side)	Yr	VG	VG+	NM
❑ 9-29432	Sincerely/Cornball Rag	1955	5.00	10.00	20.00
❑ 9-29453	The Boston Fancy/Don't Keep It a Secret	1955	5.00	10.00	20.00
❑ 9-29604	San Antonio Rose/I'll Follow Wherever You Go	1955	5.00	10.00	20.00
❑ 9-29682	New Osage Stomp/Blue Yodel	1955	5.00	10.00	20.00
❑ 9-30068	Texas Fiddler/My Shoes Keep Walking Back to You	1956	5.00	10.00	20.00

KAPP

Number	Title (A Side/B Side)	Yr	VG	VG+	NM
❑ 744	She's Killin' Me/She Won't Let Me Forget Her	1966	2.50	5.00	10.00
❑ 780	You're the Only Star in My Blue Heaven/My Adobe Hacienda	1966	2.50	5.00	10.00
❑ 842	I Wish I Felt This Way at Home/Looking Over My Shoulder	1967	2.50	5.00	10.00
—With Mel Tillis					
❑ 886	Born to Love You/Fiddle Bird	1968	2.50	5.00	10.00
❑ 918	Across the Alley from the Alamo/I'm Living in the Middle of Nowhere	1968	2.50	5.00	10.00
❑ 988	Milk Cow Blues/It's a Good World	1969	2.50	5.00	10.00
❑ 2019	What Kind of Girl Are You/Look What Trouble Left Behind	1969	2.50	5.00	10.00
❑ 2067	Southwestern Waltz/If I Just Had a Home to Go Home To	1969	2.50	5.00	10.00

LIBERTY

Number	Title (A Side/B Side)	Yr	VG	VG+	NM
❑ 55260	Heart to Heart Talk/What's the Matter with the Mill	1960	3.75	7.50	15.00
❑ 55264	The Image of Me/Goodbye Liza Jane	1960	3.75	7.50	15.00
❑ 55311	After All/It May Be Too Late	1961	3.75	7.50	15.00
❑ 55378	Siesta/I'm Crying My Heart Out	1961	3.75	7.50	15.00
❑ 55450	Oklahoma Gals/Tomorrow I'll Cry	1962	3.75	7.50	15.00
❑ 55594	Rosetta/Blues in "A"	1963	3.75	7.50	15.00

LONGHORN

Number	Title (A Side/B Side)	Yr	VG	VG+	NM
❑ 544	Buffalo Twist/Sooner or Later (You'll Fall)	1964	3.75	7.50	15.00
❑ 545	All Night Long/You Can't Break a Heart	1964	3.00	6.00	12.00
❑ 550	If He's Movin' In/Get It Over and Done With	1965	3.00	6.00	12.00
❑ 560	Faded Love/Wills Junction	1965	3.00	6.00	12.00

MGM

Number	Title (A Side/B Side)	Yr	VG	VG+	NM
❑ K10570	Ida Red Likes the Boogie/A King Without a Queen	1949	7.50	15.00	30.00
❑ K10620	She's Gone/Mean Woman with Green Eyes	1950	7.50	15.00	30.00
❑ K10681	Jole Blon Likes the Boogie/Pastime Blues	1950	7.50	15.00	30.00
❑ K10731	Rockabye Baby Blues/Nothin' But the Best for My Baby	1950	7.50	15.00	30.00
❑ K10786	Faded Love/Boot Heel Rag	1950	7.50	15.00	30.00
❑ K10836	Tater Pie/I Didn't Realize	1950	7.50	15.00	30.00
❑ K10898	End of the Line/Anything	1951	6.25	12.50	25.00
❑ K10934	I Betcha My Heart I Love You/I Laugh When I Think	1951	6.25	12.50	25.00
❑ K10980	Cross My Heart/I'm Dotting Every I	1951	6.25	12.50	25.00
❑ K11024	Plain Jane/I'm Tired of Living	1951	6.25	12.50	25.00
❑ K11082	Silver Bells/Last Goodbye	1951	6.25	12.50	25.00
❑ K11119	Brown Skin Gal/Send Me a Red Rose	1951	6.25	12.50	25.00
❑ K11163	Twinkle Star/Can't Stand Loneliness	1952	6.25	12.50	25.00
❑ K11213	Hubbin' It/I'll Be Lucky Someday	1952	6.25	12.50	25.00
❑ K11241	I Want to Be Wanted/Snatchin' Grabbin'	1952	6.25	12.50	25.00
❑ K11288	I'm All Alone/Three Miles South of Cash in Arkansas	1952	6.25	12.50	25.00
❑ K11322	Red Hot Needle/Trouble Blues	1952	6.25	12.50	25.00
❑ K11377	Awake But Dreaming/Steamboat Stomp	1952	6.25	12.50	25.00
❑ K11452	Little Girl, Little Girl/Sittin' on Top of the World	1953	6.25	12.50	25.00
❑ K11516	I Want to Go to Mexico/Broken Heart for a Souvenir	1953	6.25	12.50	25.00
❑ K11568	I Won't Be Back Tonight/B. Bowman Hop	1953	6.25	12.50	25.00
❑ K11635	As I Sit Broken-Hearted/Bottle Baby Boogie	1953	6.25	12.50	25.00
❑ K11709	She's the Quarter Horse Type (Of a Gal)/ (Everyone Is Callin' You) A Fallen Angel	1954	6.25	12.50	25.00
❑ K11767	Texas Blues/I Hit the Jackpot	1954	6.25	12.50	25.00
❑ K11832	St. Louis Blues/I've Got a New Road	1954	6.25	12.50	25.00
❑ K11883	Cadillac in Model "A"/Waltzing in Ole San Antone	1954	6.25	12.50	25.00
❑ K11985	So Long, I'll See You Later/I Live for You	1955	6.25	12.50	25.00

UNITED ARTISTS

Number	Title (A Side/B Side)	Yr	VG	VG+	NM
❑ XW556	San Antonio Rose/Faded Love	1974	—	3.00	6.00

Selected 78s

COLUMBIA

Number	Title (A Side/B Side)	Yr	VG	VG+	NM
❑ 20002	Silver Dew on the Blue Grass Tonight/Texas Playboy Rag	1948	3.75	7.50	15.00
—Reissue of 36841					
❑ 20008	White Cross on Okinawa/Empty Chair at the Christmas Table	1948	3.75	7.50	15.00
—Reissue of 36881					
❑ 20019	New Spanish Two Step/Roly-Poly	1948	3.75	7.50	15.00
—Reissue of 36966					
❑ 20035	San Antonio Rose/The Convict and the Rose	1948	3.75	7.50	15.00
—Reissue of 37009					
❑ 20040	New San Antonio Rose/Bob Wills' Special	1948	3.75	7.50	15.00
—Reissue of 37014					
❑ 20048	Oh You Pretty Woman/I Knew the Moment I Lost You	1948	3.75	7.50	15.00
—Reissue of 37022					
❑ 20051	My Life's Been a Pleasure/Please Don't Leave Me	1948	3.75	7.50	15.00
—Reissue of 37025					
❑ 20055	My Confession/Whose Heart Are You Breaking Now	1948	3.75	7.50	15.00
—Reissue of 37030					
❑ 20059	We Might As Well Forget It/You're from Texas	1948	3.75	7.50	15.00
—Reissue of 37034					
❑ 20078	Stay a Little Longer/I Can't Go On This Way	1948	3.75	7.50	15.00
—Reissue of 37097					
❑ 20093	I'm Gonna Be Boss from Now On/There's a Big Rock in the Road	1948	3.75	7.50	15.00
—Reissue of 37205					
❑ 20094	Cotton Eyed Joe/Staccato Waltz	1948	3.75	7.50	15.00
—Reissue of 37212					
❑ 20109	Trouble in Mind/New San Antonio Rose	1948	3.00	6.00	12.00
—Reissue of 37306					
❑ 20110	I Can't Go On This Way/Take Me Back to Tulsa	1948	3.00	6.00	12.00
—Reissue of 37307					
❑ 20111	Time Changes Everything/Big Beaver	1948	3.00	6.00	12.00
—Reissue of 37308					
❑ 20112	Miss Molly/Roly Poly	1948	3.00	6.00	12.00
—Reissue of 37309; the above four were issued in an album/binder					
❑ 20113	Sugar Moon/Brain Cloudy Blues	1948	3.75	7.50	15.00
—Reissue of 37313					
❑ 20122	Bob Wills Boogie/Rose of Old Pawnee	1948	3.75	7.50	15.00
—Reissue of 37357					
❑ 20132	Ten Years/Let's Ride with Bob	1948	3.75	7.50	15.00
—Reissue of 37405					
❑ 20147	It's All Your Fault/Dusty Skies	1948	3.75	7.50	15.00
—Reissue of 37420					
❑ 20149	Cherokee Maiden/Ride On	1948	3.75	7.50	15.00
—Reissue of 37422					

Number	Title (A Side/B Side)	Yr	VG	VG+	NM
❑ 20155	Corrine Corrina/Goodnight Little Sweetheart	1948	3.75	7.50	15.00
—Reissue of 37428					
❑ 20188	How Can It Be Wrong/Punkin Stomp	1948	3.75	7.50	15.00
—Reissue of 37564					
❑ 20204	St. Louis Blues/Four or Five Times	1948	3.75	7.50	15.00
—Reissue of 37605					
❑ 20206	Mexicali Rose/Good Old Oklahoma	1948	3.75	7.50	15.00
—Reissue of 37607					
❑ 20211	Black and Blue Rag/Sitting on Top of the World	1948	3.75	7.50	15.00
—Reissue of 37612					
❑ 20215	Old Fashioned Love/Oklahoma Rag	1948	3.75	7.50	15.00
—Reissue of 37616					
❑ 20217	Basin Street Blues/Red Hot Gal of Mine	1948	3.75	7.50	15.00
—Reissue of 37618					
❑ 20218	Sugar Blues/Fan It	1948	3.75	7.50	15.00
—Reissue of 37619					
❑ 20219	Steel Guitar Rag/Swing Blues #1	1948	3.75	7.50	15.00
—Reissue of 37620					
❑ 20221	She's Killing Me/What's the Matter with the Mill	1948	3.75	7.50	15.00
—Reissue of 37622					
❑ 20222	Right or Wrong/Get Along Home Cindy	1948	3.75	7.50	15.00
—Reissue of 37623					
❑ 20223	Mean Mama Blues/Bring It On Down to My House	1948	3.75	7.50	15.00
—Reissue of 37624					
❑ 20224	Too Busy/No Matter How She Done It	1948	3.75	7.50	15.00
—Reissue of 37625					
❑ 20227	Steel Guitar Stomp/Sunbonnet Sue	1948	3.75	7.50	15.00
—Reissue of 37628					
❑ 20228	Empty Bed Blues/Keep Knocking	1948	3.75	7.50	15.00
—Reissue of 37629					
❑ 20236	I Wonder If You Feel the Way I Do/That's What	1948	3.75	7.50	15.00
—Reissue of 37637					
❑ 20238	You're Okay/Liza Pull Down the Shade	1948	3.75	7.50	15.00
—Reissue of 37639					
❑ 20241	The Waltz You Saved for Me/Beaumont Rag	1948	3.75	7.50	15.00
—Reissue of 37642					
❑ 20246	Blue Bonnet Rag/Medley of Spanish Waltzes	1948	3.75	7.50	15.00
—Reissue of 37647					
❑ 20263	Bob Wills Stomp/Lil' Liza Jane	1948	3.75	7.50	15.00
—Reissue of 37664					
❑ 20280	Osage Stomp/Get With It	1948	3.75	7.50	15.00
—Reissue of 37701					
❑ 20282	Never No More Blues/I Can't Give You Anything But Love	1948	3.75	7.50	15.00
—Reissue of 37703					
❑ 20289	New St. Louis Blues/Oozin' Daddy Blues	1948	3.75	7.50	15.00
—Reissue of 37712					
❑ 20302	Little Red Head/Tulsa Stomp	1948	3.75	7.50	15.00
—Reissue of 37725					
❑ 20304	Moonlight and Roses/I Wish I Could Shimmy Like My Sister Kate	1948	3.75	7.50	15.00
—Reissue of 37727					
❑ 20305	Oh You Beautiful Doll/Oh Lady Be Good	1948	3.75	7.50	15.00
—Reissue of 37728					
❑ 20308	Whoa Babe/Little Girl Go and Ask Your Mama	1948	3.75	7.50	15.00
—Reissue of 37731					
❑ 20312	Ida Red/Carolina in the Morning	1948	3.75	7.50	15.00
—Reissue of 37735					
❑ 20316	Drunkard Blues/Don't Let the Deal Go Down	1948	3.75	7.50	15.00
—Reissue of 37739					
❑ 20326	I Don't Lov'a Nobody/Lone Star Rag	1948	3.75	7.50	15.00
—Reissue of 37749					
❑ 20359	Fat Boy Rag/You Should Have Thought of That Before	1948	3.75	7.50	15.00
—Reissue of 37824					
❑ 20391	Cowboy Stomp/A Sweet Kind of Love	1948	3.75	7.50	15.00
—Reissue of 37988					
❑ 20412	Deep Water/This Is Southland	1948	3.75	7.50	15.00
—Reissue of 38137					
❑ 20424	Texarkana Baby/New Texas Playboy Rag	1948	3.75	7.50	15.00
—Reissue of 38179					
❑ 20458	Bob Willis Schottische/The Devil Ain't Lazy	1948	5.00	10.00	20.00
❑ 20473	Maiden's Prayer/Never No More Hard Time Blues	1948	5.00	10.00	20.00
❑ 20487	Hometown Stomp/Honeymoon Trail	1948	5.00	10.00	20.00
❑ 20498	Silver Bells/Spanish Two Step	1948	5.00	10.00	20.00
❑ 20513	Can't Get Enough to Texas/Let Me Call YoU Sweetheart	1949	5.00	10.00	20.00
❑ 20531	Good Time Cake Walk/Hot Lick Fiddlin' Man	1949	5.00	10.00	20.00
❑ 20555	Goodbye Liza Jane/I'm Feelin' Bad	1949	5.00	10.00	20.00
❑ 36841	Silver Dew on the Blue Grass Tonight/Texas Playboy Rag	1945	5.00	10.00	20.00
❑ 36881	White Cross on Okinawa/Empty Chair at the Christmas Table	1945	5.00	10.00	20.00
❑ 36966	New Spanish Two Step/Roly-Poly	1946	5.00	10.00	20.00
❑ 37009	San Antonio Rose/The Convict and the Rose	1947	5.00	10.00	20.00
—Reissue of Vocalion 04755					
❑ 37014	New San Antonio Rose/Bob Wills' Special	1946	5.00	10.00	20.00
—Reissue of Okeh 5694					
❑ 37022	Oh You Pretty Woman/I Knew the Moment I Lost You	1946	5.00	10.00	20.00
—Reissue of Okeh 78					
❑ 37025	My Life's Been a Pleasure/Please Don't Leave Me	1946	5.00	10.00	20.00
—Reissue of Okeh 78					
❑ 37030	My Confession/Whose Heart Are You Breaking Now	1946	5.00	10.00	20.00
—Reissue of Okeh 78					

Number	Title (A Side/B Side)	Yr	VG	VG+	NM
❑ 37034	We Might As Well Forget It/You're from Texas	1946	5.00	10.00	20.00
—Reissue of Okeh 6722					
❑ 37097	Stay a Little Longer/I Can't Go On This Way	1946	5.00	10.00	20.00
❑ 37205	I'm Gonna Be Boss from Now On/There's a Big Rock in the Road	1947	5.00	10.00	20.00
❑ 37212	Cotton Eyed Joe/Staccato Waltz	1947	5.00	10.00	20.00
❑ 37306	Trouble in Mind/New San Antonio Rose	1947	3.75	7.50	15.00
❑ 37307	I Can't Go On This Way/Take Me Back to Tulsa	1947	3.75	7.50	15.00
❑ 37308	Time Changes Everything/Big Beaver	1947	3.75	7.50	15.00
❑ 37309	Miss Molly/Roly Poly	1947	3.75	7.50	15.00
—The above four were issued in an album/binder					
❑ 37313	Sugar Moon/Brain Cloudy Blues	1947	5.00	10.00	20.00
❑ 37357	Bob Wills Boogie/Rose of Old Pawnee	1947	5.00	10.00	20.00
❑ 37405	Ten Years/Let's Ride with Bob	1947	5.00	10.00	20.00
—Reissue of Okeh 78					
❑ 37420	It's All Your Fault/Dusty Skies	1947	5.00	10.00	20.00
—Reissue of Okeh 78					
❑ 37422	Cherokee Maiden/Ride On	1947	5.00	10.00	20.00
—Reissue of earlier 78					
❑ 37428	Corrine Corrina/Goodnight Little Sweetheart	1947	5.00	10.00	20.00
—Reissue of Okeh 06530					
❑ 37564	How Can It Be Wrong/Punkin Stomp	1947	5.00	10.00	20.00
❑ 37605	St. Louis Blues/Four or Five Times	1947	5.00	10.00	20.00
—Reissue					
❑ 37607	Mexicali Rose/Good Old Oklahoma	1947	5.00	10.00	20.00
—Reissue					
❑ 37612	Black and Blue Rag/Sitting on Top of the World	1947	5.00	10.00	20.00
—Reissue					
❑ 37616	Old Fashioned Love/Oklahoma Rag	1947	5.00	10.00	20.00
—Reissue					
❑ 37618	Basin Street Blues/Red Hot Gal of Mine	1947	5.00	10.00	20.00
—Reissue					
❑ 37619	Sugar Blues/Fan It	1947	5.00	10.00	20.00
—Reissue					
❑ 37620	Steel Guitar Rag/Swing Blues #1	1947	5.00	10.00	20.00
—Reissue					
❑ 37622	She's Killing Me/What's the Matter with the Mill	1947	5.00	10.00	20.00
—Reissue					
❑ 37623	Right or Wrong/Get Along Home Cindy	1947	5.00	10.00	20.00
—Reissue					
❑ 37624	Mean Mama Blues/Bring It On Down to My House	1947	5.00	10.00	20.00
—Reissue					
❑ 37625	Too Busy/No Matter How She Done It	1947	5.00	10.00	20.00
—Reissue					
❑ 37628	Steel Guitar Stomp/Sunbonnet Sue	1947	5.00	10.00	20.00
—Reissue					
❑ 37629	Empty Bed Blues/Keep Knocking	1947	5.00	10.00	20.00
—Reissue					
❑ 37637	I Wonder If You Feel the Way I Do/That's What	1947	5.00	10.00	20.00
—Reissue					
❑ 37639	You're Okay/Liza Pull Down the Shade	1947	5.00	10.00	20.00
—Reissue					
❑ 37642	The Waltz You Saved for Me/Beaumont Rag	1947	5.00	10.00	20.00
—Reissue					
❑ 37647	Blue Bonnet Rag/Medley of Spanish Waltzes	1947	5.00	10.00	20.00
—Reissue					
❑ 37664	Bob Wills Stomp/Lil' Liza Jane	1947	5.00	10.00	20.00
—Reissue					
❑ 37701	Osage Stomp/Get With It	1947	5.00	10.00	20.00
—Reissue					
❑ 37703	Never No More Blues/I Can't Give You Anything But Love	1947	5.00	10.00	20.00
—Reissue					
❑ 37712	New St. Louis Blues/Oozin' Daddy Blues	1947	5.00	10.00	20.00
—Reissue					
❑ 37725	Little Red Head/Tulsa Stomp	1947	5.00	10.00	20.00
—Reissue					
❑ 37727	Moonlight and Roses/I Wish I Could Shimmy Like My Sister Kate	1947	5.00	10.00	20.00
—Reissue					
❑ 37728	Oh You Beautiful Doll/Oh Lady Be Good	1947	5.00	10.00	20.00
—Reissue of Okeh 04515					
❑ 37731	Whoa Babe/Little Girl Go and Ask Your Mama	1947	5.00	10.00	20.00
—Reissue					
❑ 37735	Ida Red/Carolina in the Morning	1947	5.00	10.00	20.00
—Reissue					
❑ 37739	Drunkard Blues/Don't Let the Deal Go Down	1947	5.00	10.00	20.00
—Reissue					
❑ 37749	I Don't Lov'a Nobody/Lone Star Rag	1947	5.00	10.00	20.00
—Reissue					
❑ 37824	Fat Boy Rag/You Should Have Thought of That Before	1947	5.00	10.00	20.00
❑ 37988	Cowboy Stomp/A Sweet Kind of Love	1948	5.00	10.00	20.00
❑ 38137	Deep Water/This Is Southland	1948	5.00	10.00	20.00
❑ 38179	Texarkana Baby/New Texas Playboy Rag	1948	6.25	12.50	25.00
MGM					
❑ 10116	Bubbles in My Beer/Spanish Fandango	1948	5.00	10.00	20.00
❑ 10139	Closed for Repairs/Little Cowboy Lullaby	1948	5.00	10.00	20.00
❑ 10175	Keeper of My Heart/I'll Have Somebody Else	1948	5.00	10.00	20.00
❑ 10213	I Had a Little Mule/Blues for Dixie	1948	5.00	10.00	20.00
❑ 10236	Thorn in My Heart/'Neath Hawaiian Palms	1948	5.00	10.00	20.00
❑ 10276	Still Water Runs the Deepest/Go Home with the Girls	1948	5.00	10.00	20.00
❑ 10291	Cotton Patch Blues/Hop, Skip and Jump Over Texas	1948	5.00	10.00	20.00
❑ 10292	Sally Goodin/Blackout Blues	1948	5.00	10.00	20.00
❑ 10334	Texas Drummer Boy/I Want to Be Near You	1949	5.00	10.00	20.00

Number	Title (A Side/B Side)	Yr	VG	VG+	NM
❑ 10370	Playboy Chimes/Dog House Blues	1949	5.00	10.00	20.00
❑ 10415	Don't Be Ashamed of Your Age/Silver Lake Blues	1949	5.00	10.00	20.00
❑ 10459	I Ain't Got Nobody/Papa's Jumpin'	1949	5.00	10.00	20.00
❑ 10469	Bob Wills Square Dance No. 1/Bob Wills Square Dance No. 2	1949	5.00	10.00	20.00
❑ 10491	Warm Red Wine/Nothing But Trouble	1949	5.00	10.00	20.00
❑ 10512	Santa's on the Way/When It's Christmas	1949	5.00	10.00	20.00
OKEH					
❑ 03230	Blue River/Spanish Two Step	194?	6.25	12.50	25.00
—Reissue of Vocalion 03230					
❑ 04515	Oh You Beautiful Doll/Oh Lady Be Good	194?	6.25	12.50	25.00
—Reissue of Vocalion 04515					
❑ 05694	New San Antonio Rose/Bob Wills' Special	1940	6.25	12.50	25.00
❑ 05753	Time Changes Everything/(B-side unknown)	194?	6.25	12.50	25.00
❑ 05905	Big Beaver/(B-side unknown)	194?	6.25	12.50	25.00
❑ 06101	Worried Mind/Take Me Back to Tulsa	1941	6.25	12.50	25.00
❑ 06530	Corrine Corrina/Goodnight Little Sweetheart	1942	6.25	12.50	25.00
❑ 06568	Cherokee Maiden/Ride On	194?	6.25	12.50	25.00
❑ 6692	Ten Years/Let's Ride with Bob	1942	6.25	12.50	25.00
❑ 6703	My Confession/Whose Heart Are You Breaking Now	1943	6.25	12.50	25.00
❑ 6710	Home in San Antone/Miss Molly	1943	6.25	12.50	25.00
❑ 6722	We Might As Well Forget It/You're from Texas	1944	6.25	12.50	25.00
❑ 6736	Smoke on the Water/Hang Your Head in Shame	1945	6.25	12.50	25.00
❑ 6742	Stars and Stripes on Iwo Jima/You Don't Care What Happens to Me	1945	6.25	12.50	25.00
VOCALION					
❑ 03076	St. Louis Blues/Four or Five Times	193?	10.00	20.00	40.00
❑ 03086	Mexicali Rose/Good Old Oklahoma	193?	10.00	20.00	40.00
❑ 03096	Osage Stomp/Get With It	193?	10.00	20.00	40.00
❑ 03139	Black and Blue Rag/Sitting on Top of the World	193?	10.00	20.00	40.00
❑ 03173	Wang Wang Blues/(B-side unknown)	193?	10.00	20.00	40.00
❑ 03206	I Ain't Got Nobody/(B-side unknown)	193?	7.50	15.00	30.00
❑ 03230	Blue River/Spanish Two Step	193?	7.50	15.00	30.00
❑ 03264	Never No More Blues/I Can't Give You Anything But Love	193?	7.50	15.00	30.00
❑ 03295	Old Fashioned Love/Oklahoma Rag	193?	7.50	15.00	30.00
❑ 03343	Trouble in Mind/(B-side unknown)	193?	7.50	15.00	30.00
❑ 03344	Basin Street Blues/Red Hot Gal of Mine	193?	7.50	15.00	30.00
❑ 03361	Sugar Blues/Fan It	193?	7.50	15.00	30.00
❑ 03394	Steel Guitar Rag/Swing Blues #1	193?	7.50	15.00	30.00
❑ 03424	She's Killing Me/What's the Matter with the Mill	193?	7.50	15.00	30.00
❑ 03451	Right or Wrong/Get Along Home Cindy	193?	7.50	15.00	30.00
❑ 03492	Mean Mama Blues/Bring It On Down to My House	193?	7.50	15.00	30.00
❑ 03537	Too Busy/No Matter How She Done It	193?	7.50	15.00	30.00
❑ 03578	Swing Blues #2/(B-side unknown)	193?	7.50	15.00	30.00
❑ 03597	Bleeding Hearted Blues/(B-side unknown)	193?	7.50	15.00	30.00
❑ 03614	White Heat/(B-side unknown)	193?	7.50	15.00	30.00
❑ 03659	Rosetta/(B-side unknown)	193?	7.50	15.00	30.00
❑ 03693	New St. Louis Blues/Oozin' Daddy Blues	193?	7.50	15.00	30.00
❑ 03924	Maiden's Prayer/(B-side unknown)	193?	7.50	15.00	30.00
❑ 03977	Steel Guitar Stomp/Sunbonnet Sue	193?	7.50	15.00	30.00
❑ 04132	Black Rider/(B-side unknown)	193?	7.50	15.00	30.00
❑ 04184	Empty Bed Blues/Keep Knocking	193?	7.50	15.00	30.00
—Reissue					
❑ 04275	Gambling Polka Dot Blues/(B-side unknown)	193?	7.50	15.00	30.00
❑ 04325	Little Red Head/Tulsa Stomp	193?	7.50	15.00	30.00
—Reissue					
❑ 04387	Loveless Love/(B-side unknown)	193?	7.50	15.00	30.00
❑ 04439	Moonlight and Roses/I Wish I Could Shimmy Like My Sister Kate	193?	7.50	15.00	30.00
❑ 04515	Oh You Beautiful Doll/Oh Lady Be Good	193?	7.50	15.00	30.00
❑ 04566	That's What I Like 'Bout the South/(B-side unknown)	1939	7.50	15.00	30.00
❑ 04625	Whoa Babe/Little Girl Go and Ask Your Mama	1939	7.50	15.00	30.00
❑ 04755	San Antonio Rose/The Convict and the Rose	1939	7.50	15.00	30.00
❑ 04839	titles unknown	1939	7.50	15.00	30.00
❑ 04934	Silver Bells/Yearning	1939	7.50	15.00	30.00
❑ 04999	titles unknown	1939	7.50	15.00	30.00
❑ 05079	Ida Red/Carolina in the Morning	1939	7.50	15.00	30.00
❑ 05161	titles unknown	1939	7.50	15.00	30.00
❑ 05228	If I Could Bring Back My Buddy/Prosperity Special	1940	7.50	15.00	30.00
❑ 05282	Drunkard Blues/Don't Let the Deal Go Down	1940	7.50	15.00	30.00

7-Inch Extended Plays

Number	Title (A Side/B Side)	Yr	VG	VG+	NM
UNITED ARTISTS					
❑ SP-102 [DJ]	San Antonio Rose/Faded Love//Stay All Night (Stay a Little Longer)/Yearning (Just for You)	1974	2.50	5.00	10.00
❑ SP-102 [PS]	For the Last Time	1974	3.75	7.50	15.00

Albums

Number	Title (A Side/B Side)	Yr	VG	VG+	NM
ANTONES					
❑ 6000 [10]	Old Time Favorites	195?	125.00	250.00	500.00
—Fan club release					
❑ 6010 [10]	Old Time Favorites	195?	125.00	250.00	500.00
—Fan club release					
CAPITOL					
❑ SKBB-11550 [(2)]	Bob Wills and His Texas Playboys in Concert	1976	5.00	10.00	20.00
COLUMBIA					
❑ CL 9003 [10]	Bob Wills Round-Up	1949	75.00	150.00	300.00
❑ KG 32416 [(2)]	Anthology	1973	5.00	10.00	20.00
DECCA					
❑ DL 5562 [10]	Dance-O-Rama #2	1955	75.00	150.00	300.00
❑ DL 8727 [M]	Bob Wills and His Texas Playboys	1957	25.00	50.00	100.00
—Black label, silver print					
❑ DL 8727 [M]	Bob Wills and His Texas Playboys	1961	10.00	20.00	40.00
—Black label with color bars					
❑ DL 78727 [R]	Bob Wills and His Texas Playboys	196?	5.00	10.00	20.00
HARMONY					
❑ HL 7036 [M]	Bob Wills Special	1957	10.00	20.00	40.00
—Maroon label					
❑ HL 7036 [M]	Bob Wills Special	196?	5.00	10.00	20.00
—Black label					
❑ HL 7304 [M]	The Best of Bob Wills	1963	6.25	12.50	25.00
❑ HL 7345 [M]	The Great Bob Wills	1965	5.00	10.00	20.00
KAPP					
❑ KL-1506 [M]	From the Heart of Texas	1966	5.00	10.00	20.00
❑ KL-1523 [M]	King of Western Swing	1967	6.25	12.50	25.00
❑ KS-3506 [S]	From the Heart of Texas	1966	6.25	12.50	25.00
❑ KS-3523 [S]	King of Western Swing	1967	6.25	12.50	25.00
❑ KS-3542	Here's That Man Again	1968	6.25	12.50	25.00
❑ KS-3569	Time Changes Everything	1969	5.00	10.00	20.00
❑ KS-3587	The Living Legend	1969	5.00	10.00	20.00
❑ KS-3601	The Greatest String Band Hits	1969	5.00	10.00	20.00
❑ KS-3639	Bob Wills in Person	1970	5.00	10.00	20.00
❑ KS-3641	The Best of Bob Wills	1971	5.00	10.00	20.00
LIBERTY					
❑ LRP-3173 [M]	Together Again	1960	7.50	15.00	30.00
❑ LRP-3182 [M]	Living Legend	1961	7.50	15.00	30.00
❑ LRP-3194 [M]	Mr. Words and Mr. Music	1961	7.50	15.00	30.00
❑ LRP-3303 [M]	Bob Wills Sings and Plays	1963	7.50	15.00	30.00
❑ LST-7173 [S]	Together Again	1960	10.00	20.00	40.00
❑ LST-7182 [S]	Living Legend	1961	10.00	20.00	40.00
❑ LST-7194 [S]	Mr. Words and Mr. Music	1961	10.00	20.00	40.00
❑ LST-7303 [S]	Bob Wills Sings and Plays	1963	10.00	20.00	40.00
LONGHORN					
❑ LP-001 [M]	My Keepsake Album	1965	20.00	40.00	80.00
MGM					
❑ E-91 [10]	Ranch House Favorites	1951	75.00	150.00	300.00
❑ GAS-141	A Tribute (Golden Archive Series)	1971	6.25	12.50	25.00
❑ E-3352 [M]	Ranch House Favorites	1956	37.50	75.00	150.00
STARDAY					
❑ SLP-375 [M]	San Antonio Rose	1965	10.00	20.00	40.00
UNITED ARTISTS					
❑ UA-LA216-J [(2)]	For the Last Time	1974	10.00	20.00	40.00
—Box set with booklet					
❑ UAS-9962 [(2)]	Legendary Masters	1971	6.25	12.50	25.00
VOCALION					
❑ VL 3735 [M]	Western Swing Band	1965	5.00	10.00	20.00

WILLS, DAVID

45s

Number	Title (A Side/B Side)	Yr	VG	VG+	NM
EPIC					
❑ 34-08043	Paper Thin Walls/Honey Baby	1988	—	—	3.00
❑ 8-50036	There's a Song on the Jukebox/I Can't Even Drink It Away	1974	—	3.00	6.00
❑ 8-50090	From Barrooms to Bedrooms/I'll Be More Than Happy	1975	—	2.50	5.00
❑ 8-50118	The Barmaid/Make Me Hate You	1975	—	2.50	5.00
❑ 8-50154	She Deserves My Very Best/Lady of the Evening	1975	—	2.50	5.00
❑ 8-50188	Queen of the Starlight Ballroom/Long Tall Sally	1976	—	2.50	5.00
❑ 8-50228	Woman/Paint Me a Picture	1976	—	2.50	5.00
❑ 8-50260	(I'm Just Pouring Out) What She Bottled Up in Me/The Happy Hour	1976	—	2.50	5.00
RCA					
❑ JK-13460 [DJ]	Those Nights, These Days (same on both sides)	1983	2.50	5.00	10.00
—Promo only on red vinyl					
❑ PB-13460	Those Nights, These Days/Tennessee Moon	1983	—	—	3.00
❑ JK-13541 [DJ]	The Eyes of a Stranger (same on both sides)	1983	2.50	5.00	10.00
—Promo only on yellow vinyl					
❑ PB-13541	The Eyes of a Stranger/Give Her a Break	1983	—	—	3.00
❑ PB-13653	Miss Understanding/First to Make It Last	1983	—	—	3.00
❑ PB-13737	Lady in Waiting/First Time Feeling	1984	—	—	3.00
❑ JK-13833 [DJ]	Thank God for Friday (same on both sides)	1984	2.50	5.00	10.00
—Promo only on blue vinyl					
❑ PB-13833	Thank God for Friday/Racin' Down the Highway	1984	—	2.00	4.00
❑ PB-13940	Macon Love/Racin' Down the Highway	1984	—	2.00	4.00
UNITED ARTISTS					
❑ XW988	The Best Part of My Days (Are My Nights with You)/I'm Gonna Save It for My Baby	1977	—	2.00	4.00
❑ XW1042	Cheatin' Turns Her On/I'm Gonna Save It for My Baby	1977	—	2.00	4.00
❑ XW1097	Do You Wanna Make Love/The Fool Strikes Again	1977	—	2.00	4.00
❑ XW1196	You Snap Your Fingers (And I'm Back in Your Hands)/To Make a Long Story Short	1978	—	2.00	4.00
❑ XW1271	I'm Being Good/Women Have a Feeling ('Bout These Things)	1979	—	2.00	4.00
❑ XW1319	Endless/One, Two, Three, We Were Lovers	1979	—	2.00	4.00
❑ XW1350	She's Hangin' In There (I'm Hangin' Out)/Take It Back	1980	—	2.00	4.00
❑ X1375	The Light of My Life (Has Gone Out Again Tonight)/Marriage on the Rocks	1980	—	2.00	4.00

Albums

Number	Title (A Side/B Side)	Yr	VG	VG+	NM
EPIC					
❑ KE 33353	Barrooms to Bedrooms	1975	3.00	6.00	12.00
❑ KE 33548	Everybody's Country	1975	3.00	6.00	12.00
RCA VICTOR					
❑ MHL1-8516 [EP]	New Beginnings	1984	2.00	4.00	8.00

WILLS, JOHNNIE LEE

45s

DELTA

Number	Title (A Side/B Side)	Yr	VG	VG+	NM
❑ 11323	In the Mood/Big Beaver	198?	—	3.00	6.00

SIMS

Number	Title (A Side/B Side)	Yr	VG	VG+	NM
❑ 129	Blue Twist/Your Love for Me Is Losing Light	1962	3.75	7.50	15.00
❑ 133	Lazy John/Milk Cow Blues	1963	3.75	7.50	15.00

Selected 78s

BULLET

Number	Title (A Side/B Side)	Yr	VG	VG+	NM
❑ 696	Rag Mop/Near Me	1950	5.00	10.00	20.00
❑ 700	Peter Cottontail/Shattered Dreams	1950	5.00	10.00	20.00
❑ 710	Champagne Polka/I'm That Way About You	1950	5.00	10.00	20.00
❑ 711	Boogie Woogie Highball/Coyote Blues	1950	5.00	10.00	20.00
❑ 717	A Bad Deal All Around/Tom Cat Boogie	1950	5.00	10.00	20.00
❑ 721	This Room Is So Crowded/Si Te Amo (Yes I Love You)	1950	5.00	10.00	20.00
❑ 724	I Like You Best of All/I'm Leaving (Yes Indeedy)	1950	5.00	10.00	20.00
❑ 726	Oklahoma That's for Me/I Needed You	1951	5.00	10.00	20.00
❑ 737	That Band's a-Rockin'/I'm Not Sorry I Cried Over You	1951	5.00	10.00	20.00
❑ 741	Careless Me/Big Chief Wamp-Pa-Setti	1951	3.75	7.50	15.00
❑ 743	Levee Blues/I'll Make You Happy	1952	3.75	7.50	15.00

DECCA

Number	Title (A Side/B Side)	Yr	VG	VG+	NM
❑ 46012	Milk Cow Blues/I'm Sorry We Said Goodbye	1946	5.00	10.00	20.00
❑ 46053	Late Evening Blues/Square Dance Boogie	1947	5.00	10.00	20.00
❑ 46054	Lazy John/Texas Sundown	1947	5.00	10.00	20.00
❑ 46064	Green Grow the Lilacs/Queen of Joaquin	1947	5.00	10.00	20.00
❑ 46070	Who's Gonna Love Me/I Never Knew How Much	1947	5.00	10.00	20.00

Albums

FLYING FISH

Number	Title (A Side/B Side)	Yr	VG	VG+	NM
❑ FF-069	Reunion	1978	3.00	6.00	12.00

ROUNDER

Number	Title (A Side/B Side)	Yr	VG	VG+	NM
❑ 1027	Tulsa Swing	1978	3.00	6.00	12.00

SIMS

Number	Title (A Side/B Side)	Yr	VG	VG+	NM
❑ LP-101 [M]	Where There's a Wills, There's a Way	1962	10.00	20.00	40.00
❑ LPS-101 [S]	Where There's a Wills, There's a Way	1962	15.00	30.00	60.00
❑ LP-108 [M]	Johnny Lee Wills at the Tulsa Stampede	1963	7.50	15.00	30.00
❑ LPS-108 [S]	Johnny Lee Wills at the Tulsa Stampede	1963	12.50	25.00	50.00

WILLS, MARK

45s

MERCURY

Number	Title (A Side/B Side)	Yr	VG	VG+	NM
❑ 172153-7	Almost Doesn't Count/Permanently	2000	—	—	3.00
❑ 562530-7	Back at One/Because I Love You	1999	—	—	3.00
❑ 566054-7	Don't Laugh at Me/I Can't Live with Myself	1998	—	—	3.00
❑ 566746-7	She's in Love/Don't Think I Won't	1999	—	—	3.00
❑ 566764-7	Wish You Were Here/Emily Harper	1999	—	—	3.00
❑ 568602-7	I Do (Cherish You)/You Can't Go Wrong Loving Me	1998	—	—	3.00
❑ 574150-7	Places I've Never Been/Ace of Hearts	1997	—	—	3.00
❑ 578004-7	Jacob's Ladder/High Low and In Between	1996	—	—	3.00

WILLS, TOMMY

45s

AIRTOWN

Number	Title (A Side/B Side)	Yr	VG	VG+	NM
❑ 001	Night Train/Honky Tonk II	196?	2.00	4.00	8.00
❑ 004	Born to Lose-I Can't Stop Loving You/Funky Sax	196?	2.00	4.00	8.00
❑ 007	Four Corners/Since You've Been Gone	196?	2.00	4.00	8.00
❑ 013	Lost Dreams/Since I Fell for You	196?	2.00	4.00	8.00
❑ 2001	Funny How Time Slips Away/Crying Time	196?	2.50	5.00	10.00
❑ 2004	Born to Lose-I Can't Stop Loving You/Funky Sax	196?	2.50	5.00	10.00

CLUB MIAMI

Number	Title (A Side/B Side)	Yr	VG	VG+	NM
❑ 501	Let 'Em Roll/(B-side unknown)	195?	75.00	150.00	300.00

COUNTRY INT'L.

Number	Title (A Side/B Side)	Yr	VG	VG+	NM
❑ 103	Green, Green Grass of Home/Saxy Boogie	1975	—	3.00	6.00
❑ 108	Georgia on My Mind/Help Me Make It Through the Night	1975	—	3.00	6.00

GOLDEN MOON

Number	Title (A Side/B Side)	Yr	VG	VG+	NM
❑ 004	Wildwood Flower/Ram-Bunk-Shush	1978	2.00	4.00	8.00

JUKE

Number	Title (A Side/B Side)	Yr	VG	VG+	NM
❑ 2014	Moonglow/Soul Yakety Sax	196?	2.50	5.00	10.00
❑ 2018	Together Again/Sweet Soul	196?	2.50	5.00	10.00
❑ 2020	Blue Christmas/What Are You Doing New Year's Eve	196?	2.50	5.00	10.00
❑ 2021	Tuff Times/We'll Be Together Again	196?	2.50	5.00	10.00
❑ 2025	Kansas City/K.C. Drive	196?	2.50	5.00	10.00

TERRY

Number	Title (A Side/B Side)	Yr	VG	VG+	NM
❑ 106	Mr. Movin' Is Groovin'/Third Man Theme "Rock"	1962	3.75	7.50	15.00
❑ 110	Aw Shucks/Tuffer Than Tuff	1962	3.75	7.50	15.00

WILSON, BENNY

45s

COLUMBIA

Number	Title (A Side/B Side)	Yr	VG	VG+	NM
❑ 38-04197	Lay Down and Lie/Boy Was I Wrong	1983	—	2.00	4.00
❑ 38-04724	Acres of Diamonds/I Just Don't Love You, That's All	1984	—	—	3.00
❑ 38-05829	If You Wanna Talk Love/Where the Light Comes From	1986	—	—	3.00

WILSON, COLEMAN

45s

KING

Number	Title (A Side/B Side)	Yr	VG	VG+	NM
❑ 5388	Radar Blues/(B-side unknown)	1960	5.00	10.00	20.00
❑ 5512	Passing Zone Blues/Flat-Footed Mama	1961	5.00	10.00	20.00
❑ 5596	A Green Truck Driver's First Experience/Hot Rod Baby	1962	5.00	10.00	20.00

WILSON, HANK

See LEON RUSSELL.

WILSON, JIM

45s

MERCURY

Number	Title (A Side/B Side)	Yr	VG	VG+	NM
❑ 70635	Daddy, You Know What?/Plans for Divorce	1955	5.00	10.00	20.00
❑ 70702	I Wonder When We'll Ever Know/Don't Point Your Finger	1955	5.00	10.00	20.00
❑ 70755	Daddy, Who Is Santa Claus/Round, Round the Christmas Tree	1955	5.00	10.00	20.00
❑ 70859	Thank You, Lord, for Dinner/My Greatest Possession	1956	5.00	10.00	20.00

REED

Number	Title (A Side/B Side)	Yr	VG	VG+	NM
❑ 1032	Have a Tear on Me/Just for You	1959	3.75	7.50	15.00

WILSON, LARRY JON

45s

MONUMENT

Number	Title (A Side/B Side)	Yr	VG	VG+	NM
❑ 45-276	It's Just a Matter of Time/Stagger Lee	1978	—	2.50	5.00
❑ 45-287	The Bigger the Fool (The Harder They Fall)/Another Friend Song	1979	—	2.50	5.00
❑ 8647	Broomstraw Philosophers and Scupperoog Wine/Bertrand, My Son	1975	—	3.00	6.00
❑ 8663	Melt Not My Igloo/Choopee River Bottom Land	1975	—	3.00	6.00
❑ 8675	Through the Eyes of Little Children/The Truth Ain't in You	1975	—	3.00	6.00
❑ 8692	Think I Feel a Hitchhike Coming On/Drowning in the Mainstream	1976	—	3.00	6.00

Albums

MONUMENT

Number	Title (A Side/B Side)	Yr	VG	VG+	NM
❑ 7615	Loose Change	1978	2.50	5.00	10.00
❑ KZ 33382	New Beginnings	1975	2.50	5.00	10.00
❑ KZ 34041	Let Me Sing My Song to You	1976	2.50	5.00	10.00

WILSON, MERI

45s

BNA

Number	Title (A Side/B Side)	Yr	VG	VG+	NM
❑ 8248	Peter the Meter Reader/(B-side unknown)	1981	2.50	5.00	10.00

GRT

Number	Title (A Side/B Side)	Yr	VG	VG+	NM
❑ 127	Telephone Man/Itenerary	1977	—	2.50	5.00

WMOT

Number	Title (A Side/B Side)	Yr	VG	VG+	NM
❑ WS9 02405	Peter the Meter Reader/My Heat Walkin'	1981	—	2.50	5.00

Albums

GRT

Number	Title (A Side/B Side)	Yr	VG	VG+	NM
❑ 8023	First Take	1977	3.75	7.50	15.00

WILSON, NORRO

Also see MARGO SMITH.

45s

CAPITOL

Number	Title (A Side/B Side)	Yr	VG	VG+	NM
❑ 3886	Loneliness (Can Break a Good Man Down)/I Want to Hold You in My Arms	1974	—	3.00	6.00
❑ 4004	Thanks But No Thanks/Come On, Come On, Pour Your Lovin' on Me	1974	—	3.00	6.00

HICKORY

Number	Title (A Side/B Side)	Yr	VG	VG+	NM
❑ 1379	Let's Think About Living/Oh Lonesome Me	1966	3.00	6.00	12.00
—As "Norris Wilson"					

MERCURY

Number	Title (A Side/B Side)	Yr	VG	VG+	NM
❑ 73077	Do It to Someone You Love/No One Will Ever Know	1970	—	3.50	7.00
❑ 73125	Old Enough to Want To (Fool Enough to Try)/State Line Daddy	1970	—	3.50	7.00
❑ 73213	If You Get to Where the Heart Is/Show Me the Way to Her Arms	1970	—	3.50	7.00

MGM

Number	Title (A Side/B Side)	Yr	VG	VG+	NM
❑ 13323	Chantilly Lace/Where the Action Is	1965	3.00	6.00	12.00
—As "Norris Wilson"					
❑ 14038	Chantilly Lace/Love Hurts	1969	2.00	4.00	8.00
—As "Norris Wilson"					

MONUMENT

Number	Title (A Side/B Side)	Yr	VG	VG+	NM
❑ 453	Ma Baker's Island/(My Heart's in) Mexico	1962	3.75	7.50	15.00
—As "Norris Wilson"					
❑ 466	For a Little While/Honolulu	1962	3.75	7.50	15.00
—As "Norris Wilson"					

RCA VICTOR

Number	Title (A Side/B Side)	Yr	VG	VG+	NM
❑ APBO-0062	Ain't It Good (To Feel This Way)/It's All in the Game	1973	—	3.00	6.00
❑ 74-0677	A Gift of Love/Sweet Lips That Kiss Me Good Morning	1972	—	3.00	6.00
❑ 74-0762	Times Like These Make the Roses Sweet/Little Old Lady	1972	—	3.00	6.00
❑ 74-0824	Everybody Needs Lovin'/The Strange Little Girl	1972	—	3.00	6.00
❑ 74-0909	Darlin' Raise the Shade/Keep Me from Blowin' Away	1973	—	3.00	6.00

SMASH

Number	Title (A Side/B Side)	Yr	VG	VG+	NM
❑ 2151	Stranger to Me/Mama McCluskie	1968	2.00	4.00	8.00
❑ 2184	Sunset and Vine/I'd Rather Do It Than Eat	1968	2.00	4.00	8.00
❑ 2192	Only You/Hey Mister	1968	2.00	4.00	8.00
❑ 2210	Love Comes But Once in a Lifetime/All the Time	1969	2.00	4.00	8.00

Number	Title (A Side/B Side)	Yr	VG	VG+	NM
❑ 2236	Shame on Me/Let Me Go Back	1969	2.00	4.00	8.00
❑ 2262	In the Loneliness of the City/Roses in the Snow	1970	2.00	4.00	8.00

Albums

SMASH

Number	Title (A Side/B Side)	Yr	VG	VG+	NM
❑ SRS-67116	Dedicated to: Only You	1969	3.75	7.50	15.00

WILSON, TIM

45s

CAPITOL NASHVILLE

Number	Title (A Side/B Side)	Yr	VG	VG+	NM
❑ 58855	The Ballad of John Rocker/Michael McDonald Had a Farm	2000	—	2.00	4.00
❑ 58901	Darryl Stokes (That Dumb Sonofa) Almost Shot Santa Claus/The Family Reunion	2000	—	2.00	4.00

SOUTHERN TRACKS

Number	Title (A Side/B Side)	Yr	VG	VG+	NM
❑ 0035	Garth Brooks Has Ruined My Life/Help Me Find Jimmy Hoffa	1993	—	2.00	4.00

WINSLOW, STEPHANIE

45s

MCA

Number	Title (A Side/B Side)	Yr	VG	VG+	NM
❑ 52291	Kiss Me Darling/Another Night	1983	—	2.00	4.00
❑ 52327	Dancin' with the Devil/I Don't Want to Talk About It	1983	—	2.00	4.00
❑ 52372	Baby, Come to Me/Kisses Like Fire	1984	—	2.00	4.00

OAK

Number	Title (A Side/B Side)	Yr	VG	VG+	NM
❑ 1056	Nobody Else for Me/Another Night	1983	—	2.50	5.00
❑ 1060	Kiss Me Darling/Another Night	1983	—	3.00	6.00

PRIMERO

Number	Title (A Side/B Side)	Yr	VG	VG+	NM
❑ 1003	Slippin' and Slidin'/Another Night	1982	—	2.50	5.00
❑ 1007	Don't We Belong in Love/Another Night	1982	—	2.50	5.00
❑ 1012	In Between Lovers/Try	1982	—	2.50	5.00

WARNER BROS.

Number	Title (A Side/B Side)	Yr	VG	VG+	NM
❑ 49074	Say You Love Me/Oh, Mister	1979	—	2.50	5.00
❑ 49146	Crying/Try	1979	—	2.50	5.00
❑ 49201	I Can't Remember/Don't Go	1980	—	2.50	5.00
❑ 49257	Try It On/Me Without You	1980	—	2.50	5.00
❑ 49557	Baby, I'm-a Want You/Pretend	1980	—	2.00	4.00
❑ 49628	Anything But Yes Is Still a No/Cold, Cold Heart	1980	—	2.00	4.00
❑ 49693	Hideaway Healing/Will This Be the Last Time	1981	—	2.00	4.00
❑ 49753	I've Been a Fool/Sometimes When We Touch	1981	—	2.00	4.00
❑ 49831	When You Walk in the Room/Somebody to Love	1981	—	2.00	4.00

Albums

WARNER BROS.

Number	Title (A Side/B Side)	Yr	VG	VG+	NM
❑ BSK 3406	Crying	1980	2.50	5.00	10.00
❑ BSK 3529	Dakota	1981	2.50	5.00	10.00

WINTERMUTE, JOANN

45s

CANYON CREEK

Number	Title (A Side/B Side)	Yr	VG	VG+	NM
❑ 1225	Two Old Flames One Cheatin' Fire/My Heart Just Doesn't Know	1989	—	2.50	5.00

DOOR KNOB

Number	Title (A Side/B Side)	Yr	VG	VG+	NM
❑ 324	I Wouldn't Trade for Your Love/(B-side unknown)	1989	—	2.50	5.00
❑ 330	How I Love You in the Morning/(B-side unknown)	1989	—	2.50	5.00

WINTERS, DON

45s

COIN

Number	Title (A Side/B Side)	Yr	VG	VG+	NM
❑ 102	Be My Baby, Baby/Pretty Moon	195?	20.00	40.00	80.00

DECCA

Number	Title (A Side/B Side)	Yr	VG	VG+	NM
❑ 31067	Someday Baby/That's All I Need	1960	3.00	6.00	12.00
❑ 31253	Too Many Times/Shake Hands with a Loser	1961	3.00	6.00	12.00
❑ 31352	Disappointed/Blue Sun Down	1962	3.00	6.00	12.00

HAMILTON

Number	Title (A Side/B Side)	Yr	VG	VG+	NM
❑ 50039	Jamaica Joe/It's All My Fault	196?	3.75	7.50	15.00

WISEMAN, MAC

Also see LESTER FLATT AND MAC WISEMAN.

45s

CAPITOL

Number	Title (A Side/B Side)	Yr	VG	VG+	NM
❑ 4701	Footprints in the Snow/Just Outside	1962	2.50	5.00	10.00
❑ 4781	Bluegrass Fiesta/What's Gonna Happen to Me	1962	2.50	5.00	10.00
❑ 4854	Pistol Packin' Preacher/Sing Little Birdie	1962	2.50	5.00	10.00
❑ 4898	Wildfire/I Like Good Bluegrass Music	1963	2.50	5.00	10.00
❑ 5011	Your Best Friend and Me/When the Moon Comes Over the Mountain	1963	2.50	5.00	10.00
❑ 5116	Scene of the Crime/'Tis Sweet to Be Remembered	1964	2.50	5.00	10.00
❑ 5256	Heads You Win, Tails I Lose/Old Pair of Shoes	1964	2.50	5.00	10.00

CHURCHILL

Number	Title (A Side/B Side)	Yr	VG	VG+	NM
❑ 7706	Never Going Back Again/Goodbye Mexico Rose	1978	—	3.00	6.00
❑ 7735	My Blue Heaven/It Must Be True	1979	—	3.00	6.00
—With Woody Herman					
❑ 7738	Scotch and Soda/Dancing Bear	1979	—	3.00	6.00

DOT

Number	Title (A Side/B Side)	Yr	VG	VG+	NM
❑ 1062	Are You Coming Back to Me/'Tis Sweet to Be Remembered	1951	6.25	12.50	25.00
❑ 1075	Little White Church/I'm a Stranger	1951	6.25	12.50	25.00
❑ 1091	I Still Write Your Name in the Sand/Four Walls Around Me	1952	6.25	12.50	25.00
❑ 1092	Georgia Waltz/Dreaming of a Little Cabin	1952	6.25	12.50	25.00
❑ 1115	I Wonder How the Old Folks Are/You're the Girl of My Dreams	1952	6.25	12.50	25.00
❑ 1126	Fire in My Heart/Going to See My Baby	1952	6.25	12.50	25.00
❑ 1131	By the Side of the Road/Waiting for the Boys	1953	6.25	12.50	25.00
❑ 1146	Six More Miles/It's Goodbye and So Long to You	1953	6.25	12.50	25.00
❑ 1149	My Little Home in Tennessee/I Haven't Got the Right to Love You	1953	6.25	12.50	25.00
❑ 1150	Shackles and Chains/Going Like Wildfire	1953	6.25	12.50	25.00
❑ 1158	You're Sweeter Than the Honey/Don't Let Your Sweet Love Die	1953	6.25	12.50	25.00
❑ 1168	Crazy Blues/Rainbow in the Valley	1953	6.25	12.50	25.00
❑ 1173	You'd Better Wake Up/I'd Rather Die Young	1953	6.25	12.50	25.00
❑ 1182	Remembering/Let Me Borrow Your Heart for Just Tonight	1953	6.25	12.50	25.00
❑ 1191	The Waltz You Saved for Me/Love Letters in the Sand	1954	6.25	12.50	25.00
❑ 1192	Dreams of Mother and Home/Reveille in Heaven	1954	6.25	12.50	25.00
❑ 1194	My Little Home in Tennessee/I Haven't Got the Right	1954	6.25	12.50	25.00
❑ 1202	I Saw Your Face in the Moon/You Can't Judge a Book	1954	6.25	12.50	25.00
❑ 1224	Keep on the Sunny Side/I Love You Best of All	1954	6.25	12.50	25.00
❑ 1230	I Didn't Know/Don't Blame It All on Me	1954	6.25	12.50	25.00
❑ 1236	When I Get Money Made/The Little Old Church in the Valley	1955	5.00	10.00	20.00
❑ 1240	The Ballad of Davy Crockett/Danger Heartbreak Ahead	1955	6.25	12.50	25.00
❑ 1262	The Kentuckian Song/Wabash Cannonball	1955	5.00	10.00	20.00
❑ 1266	Fire Ball Mail/When the Roses Bloom Again	1955	5.00	10.00	20.00
❑ 1273	I Hear You Knockin'/Camptown Races	1955	5.00	10.00	20.00
❑ 1276	These Hands/I'm Eatin' High on the Hog	1956	5.00	10.00	20.00
❑ 1282	Meanest Blues in the World/Be Good Baby	1956	5.00	10.00	20.00
❑ 1285	Smilin' Through/I'm Drifting Back to Dreamland	1956	5.00	10.00	20.00
❑ 15497	One Mint Julep/I'm Waiting for the Ships That Never Come	1956	3.75	7.50	15.00
❑ 15544	Step It Up and Go/Sundown	1957	7.50	15.00	30.00
❑ 15578	Love Letters in the Sand/Because We Are Young	1957	3.75	7.50	15.00
❑ 15638	I'll Still Write Your Name in the Sand/'Tis Sweet to Be	1957	3.75	7.50	15.00
❑ 15731	Put Me in Your Pocket/When the Work's All Done	1958	3.75	7.50	15.00
❑ 15796	Thinkin' About You/Promise of Things	1958	3.75	7.50	15.00
❑ 15929	Each Ring of the Hammer/Did You Stop to Pray This Morning	1959	3.75	7.50	15.00
❑ 15946	Jimmy Brown the Newsboy/I've Got No Use for the Women	1959	3.75	7.50	15.00
❑ 16008	The Preacher and the Bear/When It's Lamp Lightin' Time in the Valley	1959	3.75	7.50	15.00
❑ 16045	Drifting on the River/One Mint Julep	1960	3.00	6.00	12.00
❑ 16107	Darling Nelly Gray/There's a Star Spangled Banner Waving Somewhere	1960	3.00	6.00	12.00
❑ 16148	Glad Rags/Now That You Have Me	1960	3.00	6.00	12.00
❑ 16194	Dark as a Dungeon/Darling, How Can You Forget So Soon	1961	3.00	6.00	12.00
❑ 16901	Just a Baby's Prayer at Twilight/White Silver Sands	1966	2.00	4.00	8.00
❑ 16980	Little Bird/This Is Where I Came In	1966	2.00	4.00	8.00

MGM

Number	Title (A Side/B Side)	Yr	VG	VG+	NM
❑ 13986	Got Leavin' on Her Mind/She Simply Left	1968	2.00	4.00	8.00

RCA VICTOR

Number	Title (A Side/B Side)	Yr	VG	VG+	NM
❑ APBO-0034	At the Crossroad/You Can't Go in the Red Playin' Bluegrass	1973	—	3.00	6.00
❑ APBO-0276	It Comes and Goes/I've Got to Catch That Train	1974	—	3.00	6.00
❑ 47-9814	Me and Bobby McGee/Ring of Fire	1969	—	3.50	7.00
❑ 47-9883	Things You Have Turned To/Wrinkled, Crinkled, Wadded Dollar Bill	1970	—	3.50	7.00
❑ 74-0283	Johnny's Cash and Charley's Pride/Mama, Put My Little Shoes Away	1969	—	3.50	7.00
❑ 74-0639	I'd Rather Live by the Side of the Road/Sing Little Birdie	1972	—	3.50	7.00
❑ 74-0758	On Susan's Floor/Song of the Wildwood	1972	—	3.50	7.00
❑ 74-0834	Eight More Miles to Louisville/Let Time Be Your Friend	1972	—	3.50	7.00

Albums

ABC

Number	Title (A Side/B Side)	Yr	VG	VG+	NM
❑ 4009	16 Great Performances	1974	3.00	6.00	12.00
❑ AC-30033	The ABC Collection	1976	3.00	6.00	12.00

CAPITOL

Number	Title (A Side/B Side)	Yr	VG	VG+	NM
❑ ST 1800 [S]	Bluegrass Favorites	1962	10.00	20.00	40.00
❑ T 1800 [M]	Bluegrass Favorites	1962	7.50	15.00	30.00

CMH

Number	Title (A Side/B Side)	Yr	VG	VG+	NM
❑ 4502	Greatest Bluegrass Hits	198?	2.50	5.00	10.00
❑ 6202	Country Memories	197?	3.00	6.00	12.00
❑ 6217	Mac Wiseman Sings Gordon Lightfoot	197?	3.00	6.00	12.00
❑ 9001 [(2)]	The Mac Wiseman Story	197?	3.75	7.50	15.00
❑ 9021 [(2)]	Songs That Made the Juke Box Play	197?	3.75	7.50	15.00

DOT

Number	Title (A Side/B Side)	Yr	VG	VG+	NM
❑ DLP-3084 [M]	Tis Sweet to Be Remembered	1958	12.50	25.00	50.00
❑ DLP-3135 [M]	Beside the Still Waters	1959	7.50	15.00	30.00
❑ DLP-3213 [M]	Great Folk Ballads	1959	7.50	15.00	30.00
❑ DLP-3313 [M]	12 Great Hits	1960	7.50	15.00	30.00
❑ DLP-3336 [M]	Keep on the Sunny Side	1960	10.00	20.00	40.00
❑ DLP-3373 [M]	Best Loved Gospel Hymns	1961	7.50	15.00	30.00
❑ DLP-3408 [M]	Fireball Mail	1961	10.00	20.00	40.00
❑ DLP-3697 [M]	This Is Mac Wiseman	1966	5.00	10.00	20.00
❑ DLP-3730 [M]	A Master at Work	1966	5.00	10.00	20.00
❑ DLP-3731 [M]	Bluegrass	1966	5.00	10.00	20.00
❑ DLP-25084 [R]	Tis Sweet to Be Remembered	196?	5.00	10.00	20.00
❑ DLP-25135 [S]	Beside the Still Waters	1959	10.00	20.00	40.00

Number	Title (A Side/B Side)	Yr	VG	VG+	NM
❑ DLP-25213 [S]	Great Folk Ballads	1959	10.00	20.00	40.00
❑ DLP-25313 [S]	12 Great Hits	1960	10.00	20.00	40.00
❑ DLP-25336 [R]	Keep on the Sunny Side	196?	5.00	10.00	20.00
❑ DLP-25373 [S]	Best Loved Gospel Hymns	1961	10.00	20.00	40.00
❑ DLP-25408 [R]	Fireball Mail	196?	5.00	10.00	20.00
❑ DLP-25697 [S]	This Is Mac Wiseman	1966	6.25	12.50	25.00
❑ DLP-25730 [S]	A Master at Work	1966	6.25	12.50	25.00
❑ DLP-25731 [S]	Bluegrass	1966	6.25	12.50	25.00
❑ DLP-25896	Golden Hits of Mac Wiseman	1968	5.00	10.00	20.00
HAMILTON					
❑ HLP-12130 [M]	Sincerely	1964	5.00	10.00	20.00
❑ HLP-12167 [M]	Songs of the Dear Old Days	1965	5.00	10.00	20.00
HILLTOP					
❑ JM-6047 [M]	Mac Wiseman	1967	3.75	7.50	15.00
❑ JS-6047 [R]	Mac Wiseman	1967	3.00	6.00	12.00
MCA					
❑ 4009	16 Great Performances	198?	2.00	4.00	8.00
—Reissue of ABC 4009					
RCA VICTOR					
❑ ANL1-1208	Concert Favorites	1975	2.50	5.00	10.00
—Reissue of 4845					
❑ LSP-4336	Johnny's Cash and Charley's Pride	1970	3.75	7.50	15.00
❑ LSP-4845	Concert Favorites	1972	3.75	7.50	15.00
VETCO					
❑ 508	New Traditions, Vol. 1	197?	3.75	7.50	15.00
❑ 509	New Traditions, Vol. 2	197?	3.75	7.50	15.00

WOFFORD, E.D.

45s

Number	Title (A Side/B Side)	Yr	VG	VG+	NM
MC					
❑ 5012	Baby I Need Your Lovin'/Why Not Try Lovin' Me	1978	—	2.50	5.00

WOLF, GARY

45s

Number	Title (A Side/B Side)	Yr	VG	VG+	NM
COLUMBIA					
❑ 18-02986	Love Never Dies/Ages and Pages Ago	1982	—	—	3.00
❑ 38-03272	The Perfect Picture (To Fit My Frame of Mind)/If I Could Only Go Back to Goodbye	1982	—	—	3.00
❑ 38-03493	Livin' on Memories/Lone Wolf	1983	—	—	3.00
MERCURY					
❑ 822244-7	You Bring the Heartache (I'll Bring the Wine)/Call on Me	1984	—	—	3.00
❑ 880246-7	Gettin' Into Tennessee Tonight/(B-side unknown)	1984	—	—	3.00
❑ 880564-7	It's My Life/First Things First	1985	—	—	3.00
❑ 880967-7	Soft Touch/Who Turns You On	1985	—	—	3.00

WOLFPACK, THE

Also see KENNY EARL; NARVEL FELTS; LOBO.

45s

Number	Title (A Side/B Side)	Yr	VG	VG+	NM
LOBO					
❑ VI	Bull Smith Can't Dance the Cotton-Eyed Joe/I Don't Want to Want You	1982	—	3.00	6.00

WOMACK, LEE ANN

45s

Number	Title (A Side/B Side)	Yr	VG	VG+	NM
DECCA					
❑ 55320	Never Again, Again (3:10)/Never Again, Again (3:22)	1997	—	2.00	4.00
❑ 72009	The Fool/Trouble's Here	1997	—	—	3.00
❑ 72023	You've Got to Talk to Me/A Man with 18 Wheels	1997	—	—	3.00
❑ 72041	Buckaroo/Make Memories with Me	1998	—	—	3.00
❑ 72049	A Man with 18 Wheels/Drivin' My Life Away	1998	—	—	3.00
—B-side by Rhett Akins					
❑ 72068	A Little Past Little Rock/If You're Ever Down in Dallas	1998	—	—	3.00
❑ 72076	I'll Think of a Reason Later/I'd Rather Have What We Had	1999	—	—	3.00
❑ 088-172132-7	Don't Tell Me/I Keep Forgetting	1999	—	—	3.00
MCA NASHVILLE					
❑ 72111	(Now You See Me) Now You Don't/The Preacher Won't Have to Lie	1999	—	—	3.00
❑ 088-172158-7	I Hope You Dance/Lonely Too	2000	—	—	3.00
❑ 088-172182-7	Ashes by Now/Lonely Too	2000	—	—	3.00
❑ 088-172185 7	I Hope You Dance (Pop Version)/I Hope You Dance (Album Version)	2000	—	—	3.00

WOOD, BOBBY

45s

Number	Title (A Side/B Side)	Yr	VG	VG+	NM
CHALLENGE					
❑ 9160	The Day After Forever/Everybody's Searchin'	1962	2.50	5.00	10.00
CINNAMON					
❑ 790	I'm a Fool for Loving You/Secret Love Affair	1974	—	2.00	4.00
JOY					
❑ 277	I Still Hurt/Just the Same	1963	2.50	5.00	10.00
❑ 279	Do Darlin' (Do Remember Me)/That's All I Need	1963	2.50	5.00	10.00
❑ 285	If I'm a Fool for Loving You/My Heart Went Boing! Boing! Boing!	1964	2.50	5.00	10.00
❑ 288	That's All I Need to Know/This Time	1964	2.50	5.00	10.00
❑ 291	So Cruel/I'd Do It Again	1964	2.50	5.00	10.00
❑ 295	Bed of Roses/Show Me	1965	2.00	4.00	8.00
❑ 298	Human Emotions/When a Lonely Boy Meets a Lonely Girl	1965	2.00	4.00	8.00
❑ 301	Fool's Paradise/What Am I Gonna Tell Myself	1965	2.00	4.00	8.00
LUCKY ELEVEN					
❑ 361	One Day Behind/Sound of Sadness	1973	—	2.50	5.00
MALA					
❑ 526	My Special Angel/I'd Rather Forgive You	1966	2.00	4.00	8.00
MGM					
❑ 13729	My Last Date (With You)/Everybody's Baby	1967	—	3.00	6.00
❑ 13797	Break My Mind/This Thing Called Love	1967	—	3.00	6.00
❑ 13912	Is That All There Is To It/Say It's Not You	1968	—	3.00	6.00
❑ 13952	Mary/Big Buildup	1968	—	3.00	6.00
❑ 14051	(Margie's at the) Lincoln Park Inn/I'm the Name of Her Game	1969	—	3.00	6.00
SUN					
❑ 369 [DJ]	Everybody's Searchin'/Human Emotions	1961	200.00	400.00	600.00
—No stock copies known; should one be discovered, it would be worth much more					

Albums

Number	Title (A Side/B Side)	Yr	VG	VG+	NM
JOY					
❑ 1001 [M]	Bobby Wood	1964	10.00	20.00	40.00

WOOD, DANNY

45s

Number	Title (A Side/B Side)	Yr	VG	VG+	NM
AVION					
❑ 102	Tribute to Hag/I Can't Hold Us Together Alone	1983	—	3.00	6.00
LONDON					
❑ 242	If This Is Freedom (I Want Out)/I Won't Be Sleeping Alone	1976	—	2.50	5.00
❑ 248	I Need Somethin' Easy Tonight/Permanent Thing	1977	—	2.50	5.00
❑ 258	Opposites Attract/Back to Your Old Ways Again	1977	—	2.50	5.00
RCA					
❑ PB-11968	A Heart's Been Broken/All the Kind Young Strangers	1980	—	2.00	4.00
❑ PB-12123	It Took Us All Night Long to Say Goodbye/Crazy Dreams	1980	—	2.00	4.00
❑ PB-12181	Fool's Gold/Where Were You (When I Came Home Last Night)	1981	—	2.00	4.00

WOOD, DEL

45s

Number	Title (A Side/B Side)	Yr	VG	VG+	NM
CHART					
❑ 5115	Are You from Dixie/Kentucky Turnpike	1971	—	3.50	7.00
❑ 5155	Gloryland March/Standing Room Only	1972	—	3.50	7.00
DECCA					
❑ 9-28611	The Eyes of Texas Are Upon You/Washington and Lee Swing	1953	5.00	10.00	20.00
❑ 9-28795	Listen to the Mockingbird/Margie	1953	5.00	10.00	20.00
MERCURY					
❑ 71899	Creole Fandango/My Adobe Hacienda	1961	3.00	6.00	12.00
❑ 71972	Down Yonder/Lady of Spain	1962	3.00	6.00	12.00
❑ 72158	Columbus Georgia Blues/Old Piano Roll Blues	1963	3.00	6.00	12.00
❑ 72351	I Walk the Line/Night Train to Memphis	1964	2.50	5.00	10.00
RCA VICTOR					
❑ 47-6080	Home Sweet Home/That Naughty Waltz	1955	5.00	10.00	20.00
❑ 47-6275	Rocky Mountain Express/Dream Train	1955	5.00	10.00	20.00
❑ 47-6397	Josephine/Ain't She Sweet	1956	5.00	10.00	20.00
❑ 47-6489	Down Yonder/Tie Me to Your Apron	1956	5.00	10.00	20.00
❑ 47-6613	Are You from Dixie/Intermission at the Opry	1956	5.00	10.00	20.00
❑ 47-6725	On the Sunny Side of the Street/Crazy	1956	5.00	10.00	20.00
❑ 47-6817	Rockin' 88/After Five	1957	7.50	15.00	30.00
❑ 47-6978	Piano Roll Waltz/Chicka-Boo	1957	5.00	10.00	20.00
❑ 47-7088	Maggie Blues/Whirl-A-Way	1957	5.00	10.00	20.00
❑ 47-7212	Raggin' the Keys/Echo Waltz	1958	3.75	7.50	15.00
❑ 47-7421	Shortcake/Sunday Down South	1958	3.75	7.50	15.00
❑ 47-7594	Swanee River Soft Shoe/Gismo Rag	1959	3.75	7.50	15.00
REPUBLIC					
❑ 7036	Pickin' and Grinnin'/12th Street Rag	1953	6.25	12.50	25.00
❑ 7043	Elmer's Tune/Jersey Bounce	1953	6.25	12.50	25.00
❑ 7051	Ricky-Tic Piano/Moonlight Cocktail	1953	6.25	12.50	25.00
—With Don Estes					
❑ 7057	Ragtime Annie/Back Room Polka	1953	6.25	12.50	25.00
❑ 7070	Columbus Stockade Blues/Bye Bye Blackbird	1954	6.25	12.50	25.00
❑ 7085	It's a Grand Old Flag/When I Lost You	1954	6.25	12.50	25.00
❑ 7087	It's a Sin/I Like Mountain Music	1954	6.25	12.50	25.00
❑ 7105	Are You from Dixie/There's a Tavern in the Town	1955	6.25	12.50	25.00
TENNESSEE					
❑ 775	Down Yonder/Mine, All Mine	1951	7.50	15.00	30.00

Albums

Number	Title (A Side/B Side)	Yr	VG	VG+	NM
COLUMBIA					
❑ CL 2539 [M]	Upright, Low Down and Honky Tonk	1966	3.00	6.00	12.00
❑ CS 9339 [S]	Upright, Low Down and Honky Tonk	1966	3.75	7.50	15.00
LAMB & LION					
❑ 1009	Rag Time Glory Special	197?	3.00	6.00	12.00
MERCURY					
❑ MG-20674 [M]	Ragtime Goes South of the Border	1962	3.00	6.00	12.00
❑ MG-20713 [M]	Ragtime Goes International	1962	3.00	6.00	12.00
❑ MG-20804 [M]	Piano Roll Blues	1963	3.00	6.00	12.00
❑ MG-20978 [M]	Roll Out the Piano	1964	3.00	6.00	12.00
❑ SR-60674 [S]	Ragtime Goes South of the Border	1962	3.75	7.50	15.00
❑ SR-60713 [S]	Ragtime Goes International	1962	3.75	7.50	15.00
❑ SR-60804 [S]	Piano Roll Blues	1963	3.75	7.50	15.00
❑ SR-60978 [S]	Roll Out the Piano	1964	3.75	7.50	15.00
RCA CAMDEN					
❑ CAL-684 [M]	Honky Tonk Piano	1962	3.00	6.00	12.00
❑ CAS-684 [R]	Honky Tonk Piano	1962	2.50	5.00	10.00
❑ CAL-796 [M]	It's Honky Tonk Time	1964	3.00	6.00	12.00
❑ CAS-796 [R]	It's Honky Tonk Time	1964	2.50	5.00	10.00

Number	Title (A Side/B Side)	Yr	VG	VG+	NM
RCA VICTOR					
❑ LPM-1129 [M]	Down Yonder	1955	5.00	10.00	20.00
❑ LPM-1437 [M]	Hot, Happy and Honky	1957	5.00	10.00	20.00
❑ LPM-1633 [M]	Rags to Riches	1958	3.75	7.50	15.00
❑ LSP-1633 [S]	Rags to Riches	1958	5.00	10.00	20.00
❑ LPM-2091 [M]	Mississippi Show Boat	1959	3.75	7.50	15.00
❑ LSP-2091 [S]	Mississippi Show Boat	1959	5.00	10.00	20.00
❑ LPM-2203 [M]	Flivvers, Flappers and Fox Trots	1960	3.75	7.50	15.00
❑ LSP-2203 [S]	Flivvers, Flappers and Fox Trots	1960	5.00	10.00	20.00
❑ LPM-2240 [M]	Buggies, Bustles and Barrelhouse	1960	3.75	7.50	15.00
❑ LSP-2240 [S]	Buggies, Bustles and Barrelhouse	1960	5.00	10.00	20.00
❑ LPM-3907 [M]	The Best of Del Wood	1968	6.25	12.50	25.00
❑ LSP-3907 [S]	The Best of Del Wood	1968	3.00	6.00	12.00
VOCALION					
❑ VL 3609 [M]	There's a Tavern in the Town	196?	3.00	6.00	12.00

WOOD, NANCY

45s

Number	Title (A Side/B Side)	Yr	VG	VG+	NM
MONTAGE					
❑ 1202	Imagine That/Turn Your Love Light On	1981	—	3.00	6.00

WOODRUFF, BOB

45s

Number	Title (A Side/B Side)	Yr	VG	VG+	NM
ASYLUM					
❑ 64523	Alright/Caroline	1994	—	2.00	4.00
❑ 64553	Bayou Girl/Poisoned at the Well	1994	—	2.00	4.00
❑ 64575	Hard Liquor, Cold Women, Warm Beer/The Year We Tried to Kill the Pain	1994	—	2.00	4.00

WOODS, GENE

45s

Number	Title (A Side/B Side)	Yr	VG	VG+	NM
HAP					
❑ 1004	The Ballad of Wild River/Afraid	1960	6.25	12.50	25.00

WOODY, BILL

45s

Number	Title (A Side/B Side)	Yr	VG	VG+	NM
ABC HICKORY					
❑ 54008	Morning Girl/Go Away Slow	1977	—	2.50	5.00
—As "Woody"					
❑ 54017	Never Meant to Be/Silly Boy	1977	—	2.50	5.00
—As "Woody"					
❑ 54023	Just for You Babe/Waltz of the Wind	1978	—	2.50	5.00
—As "Woody"					
❑ 54032	Makin' Changes/Ridin' Rainbows	1978	—	2.50	5.00
—As "Woody"					
❑ 54043	Just Between Us/I Love You	1979	2.50	5.00	10.00
—Quickly reissued on MCA					
MCA					
❑ 41070	Love Wouldn't Leave Us Alone/Organized Noise	1979	—	2.00	4.00
❑ 54043	Just Between Us/I Love You	1979	—	2.00	4.00
—Reissue of ABC Hickory 54043					

Albums

Number	Title (A Side/B Side)	Yr	VG	VG+	NM
ABC HICKORY					
❑ HB-44009	Just for You Babe	1977	3.00	6.00	12.00
—As "Woody"					
MCA					
❑ 3095	Organized Noise	1979	2.50	5.00	10.00

WOOLERY, CHUCK

45s

Number	Title (A Side/B Side)	Yr	VG	VG+	NM
COLUMBIA					
❑ 45017	I've Been Wrong/Soft Velvet Love	1969	—	3.00	6.00
❑ 45135	Heaven Here on Earth/Pleasure of Her Company	1970	—	3.00	6.00
❑ 45224	Your Name Is Woman/Soft Velvet Love	1970	—	3.00	6.00
❑ 45274	Hey, Baby/Soft Velvet Love	1970	—	3.00	6.00
EPIC					
❑ 50897	The Greatest Love Affair/Heroes and Lovers	1980	—	2.00	4.00
RCA VICTOR					
❑ 74-0554	Deja Vu/Forgive My Heart	1971	—	2.50	5.00
❑ 74-0703	Kiss Me Three Times/If Only	1972	—	2.50	5.00
❑ 74-0771	Time and Time Again/Pen of a Poet	1972	—	2.50	5.00
❑ 74-0865	Forgive My Heart/Love Me, Love Me	1973	—	2.50	5.00
WARNER BROS.					
❑ 8381	Painted Lady/Growing Up in a Country Way	1977	—	2.50	5.00

WOOLEY, AMY

45s

Number	Title (A Side/B Side)	Yr	VG	VG+	NM
MCA					
❑ 51168	Ain't No Reason to Be Teasin'/Have a Heart	1981	—	2.00	4.00
❑ 52084	If My Heart Had Windows/Burned by Love	1982	—	2.00	4.00
❑ 52143	My Turn/Back Door of Heaven	1982	—	2.00	4.00

Albums

Number	Title (A Side/B Side)	Yr	VG	VG+	NM
MCA					
❑ 5240	Amy Wooley	1981	2.50	5.00	10.00

WOOLEY, SHEB

45s

Number	Title (A Side/B Side)	Yr	VG	VG+	NM
BLUE BONNET					
❑ 124	Wooley's Polka/Lazy Mary	1954	17.50	35.00	70.00
❑ 125	Peeping Thru the Keyhole/Time Won't Heal an Achin' Heart	1954	17.50	35.00	70.00
❑ 130	Too Long with the Wrong Mama/Your Papa Ain't Steppin' Anymore	1954	15.00	30.00	60.00
MGM					
❑ 10697	Mule Boogie/Changing Your Name	1950	7.50	15.00	30.00
❑ 10960	Hoot Owl Boogie/Country Kisses	1951	7.50	15.00	30.00
❑ 11059	Over the Barrel/Air Castles	1951	7.50	15.00	30.00
❑ 11180	Backroom Boogie/Down in the Toolies	1952	7.50	15.00	30.00
❑ 11272	You're the Cat's Meow/Wha' Happened to Me Baby	1952	7.50	15.00	30.00
❑ 11308	A Cowboy Had Ought to Be Single/You Never Can Tell	1952	7.50	15.00	30.00
❑ 11403	Heart Bound in Chains/Freight Train Cinders	1953	6.25	12.50	25.00
❑ 11580	Love Is a Merry-Go-Round/Texas Tango	1953	6.25	12.50	25.00
❑ 11640	Goodbye Texas, Hello Tennessee/I'll Rerturn the Letters	1953	6.25	12.50	25.00
❑ 11665	Don't Stop Kissing Me Goodnight/Knew I Had Lost	1954	5.00	10.00	20.00
❑ 11717	Blue Guitar/Panama Pete	1954	5.00	10.00	20.00
❑ 11792	White Lightnin'/Fool About You	1954	5.00	10.00	20.00
❑ 11836	Hillbilly Mambo/I Go Outta My Mind	1954	5.00	10.00	20.00
❑ 11910	38-24-35/I Flipped	1955	3.75	7.50	15.00
❑ 11976	Speak of the Devil/Love at First Sight	1955	3.75	7.50	15.00
❑ 12048	Listening to Your Footsteps/Love Is a Prayer	1955	3.75	7.50	15.00
❑ 12060	It Takes a Heap of Livin'/Listen for Your Footsteps	1955	3.75	7.50	15.00
❑ 12114	Are You Satisfied/Humdinger	1955	3.75	7.50	15.00
❑ 12202	The Birth of the Rock 'N' Roll/A King or a Clown	1956	3.75	7.50	15.00
❑ 12260	You Can Do It/Do I Remember?	1956	3.75	7.50	15.00
❑ 12328	First Day of School/The Lonely Man	1956	3.75	7.50	15.00
❑ 12382	Honey I'm Lonesome/Let the Big Winds Blow	1956	3.75	7.50	15.00
❑ 12467	Plenty of Love/I Won't Come Back	1957	3.00	6.00	12.00
❑ 12541	Recipe for Love/I'm Too Young	1957	3.00	6.00	12.00
❑ 12584	So Close to Heaven/I Found Me An Angel	1957	3.00	6.00	12.00
❑ 12651	The Purple People Eater/I Can't Believe You're Mine	1958	4.50	9.00	18.00
❑ 12704	The Chase/Monkey Jive	1958	3.00	6.00	12.00
❑ 12733	Santa and the Purple People Eater/Star of Love	1958	5.00	10.00	20.00
❑ 12733 [PS]	Santa and the Purple People Eater/Star of Love	1958	10.00	20.00	40.00
❑ 12743	Cherry Street/Star of Love	1958	3.00	6.00	12.00
❑ 12778	More/Deep Goes the Love	1959	2.50	5.00	10.00
❑ 12781	Sweet Chile/More	1959	2.50	5.00	10.00
❑ 12817	Careless Hands/Pigmy Love	1959	2.50	5.00	10.00
❑ 12851	Love Like Mine/Josie	1959	2.50	5.00	10.00
❑ 12853	It's Almost Time/Roughneck	1959	2.50	5.00	10.00
❑ 12882	Luke the Spook/My Only Treasure	1960	2.50	5.00	10.00
❑ 12931	Taste of Ashes/Reach for the Moon	1960	2.50	5.00	10.00
❑ 13013	Skin Tight, Pin Striped, Pink Pedal Pushers/Till the End of the World	1961	2.50	5.00	10.00
❑ 13046	That's My Pa/Meet Mr. Lonely	1961	2.50	5.00	10.00
❑ 13065	Laughin' the Blues/Somebody Please	1962	2.50	5.00	10.00
❑ 13079	That's My Ma/Land of No Love	1962	2.50	5.00	10.00
❑ 13094	The Leged of Echo Mountain/Give That Ball to Willie B	1962	2.50	5.00	10.00
❑ 13104	Don't Go Near the Eskimos/Louisiana Trapper	1962	2.50	5.00	10.00
—As "Ben Colder"					
❑ 13122	Hello Wall No. 2/Shudders and Screams	1963	2.50	5.00	10.00
—As "Ben Colder"					
❑ 13125	Little Bitty Bilbo Abernathy Nathan Allen Quincy Jones/Daddy Kiss and Make It Well	1963	2.50	5.00	10.00
❑ 13147	Still No. 2/Goin' Surfin'	1963	3.75	7.50	15.00
—As "Ben Colder"					
❑ 13152	Buildin' a Railroad/Cowboy Hero	1963	2.50	5.00	10.00
❑ 13166	Hootenanny Hoot/Old Rag Doll	1963	2.50	5.00	10.00
❑ 13167	Detroit City No. 2/Ring of Smoke	1963	2.50	5.00	10.00
—As "Ben Colder"					
❑ 13195	Papa's Ole Fiddle/She Called Me Baby	1963	2.50	5.00	10.00
❑ 13197	I Walk the Line No. 2/Talk Back Blubberin' Lips	1963	2.50	5.00	10.00
—As "Ben Colder"					
❑ 13241	Blue Guitar/Natchez Landing	1964	2.00	4.00	8.00
❑ 13262	TV Westerns/Dobro's Catchin' On Again (And I'm Gonna Be a Star)	1964	2.00	4.00	8.00
—As "Ben Colder"					
❑ 13294	Wild and Wooley, Big Unruly Me/Sittin' and Thinkin'	1964	2.00	4.00	8.00
❑ 13351	Silver (The Wonder Horse)/Blistered	1965	2.00	4.00	8.00
❑ 13395	Big Land/Sally's Arms	1965	2.00	4.00	8.00
❑ 13444	Make the World Go Away No. 2/May the Bird of Paradise Fly Up Your Snoot	1966	2.00	4.00	8.00
—As "Ben Colder"					
❑ 13477	Buba Hoo Boba Dee/I'll Leave the Singin' to the Bluebirds	1966	2.00	4.00	8.00
❑ 13556	Tonight's the Night My Angel's Halo Fell/Anchors Aweigh	1966	2.00	4.00	8.00
❑ 13590	Almost Persuaded No. 2/A Packet of Pencils	1966	2.00	4.00	8.00
—As "Ben Colder"					
❑ 13668	There Goes My Everything No. 2/Great Men Repeat Themselves	1967	2.00	4.00	8.00
—As "Ben Colder"					
❑ 13705	Letter to Daddy/Draggin' the River	1967	2.00	4.00	8.00
❑ 13771	The Purple People Eater No. 2/Undertaker's Love Lament	1967	2.00	4.00	8.00
—As "Ben Colder"					
❑ 13806	Number One on the Survey/Big Ole, Good Ole Girl	1967	2.00	4.00	8.00
❑ 13827	The Love-In/Wildwood Flower on the Autoharp	1967	2.00	4.00	8.00
❑ 13897	Ain't It Funny How Wine Sips Away/The Doo-Hickey Song	1968	2.00	4.00	8.00
—As "Ben Colder"					

Number	Title (A Side/B Side)	Yr	VG	VG+	NM
❑ 13914	By the Time I Get to Phoenix No. 2/Skip a Rope No. 2	1968	2.00	4.00	8.00
—As "Ben Colder"					
❑ 13938	Make 'Em Laugh/Tie a Tiger Down	1968	—	3.00	6.00
❑ 13997	Harper Valley P.T.A. (Later That Same Day)/ Folsom Prison Blues No. 1 1/2	1968	2.50	5.00	10.00
—As "Ben Colder"					
❑ 14005	That Girl/I Remember Loving You	1968	—	3.00	6.00
❑ 14015	Little Green Apples No. 2/It's Such a Pretty World Tonight	1968	2.00	4.00	8.00
—As "Ben Colder"					
❑ 14044	Ode to the Little Shack Out Back/You're a Real Good Friend	1969	—	3.00	6.00
—As "Ben Colder"					
❑ 14065	The Carroll County Accident No. 2/His Lincoln's Parked at Margie's Again	1969	—	3.00	6.00
—As "Ben Colder"					
❑ 14070	The Recipient/Big Ole, Good Ole Girl	1969	—	3.00	6.00
❑ 14076	Ruby Please Bring Your Love to Town/Yet	1969	—	3.00	6.00
—As "Ben Colder"					
❑ 14085	One Man Band/You Still Turn Me On	1969	—	3.00	6.00
❑ 14111	Big Sweet John/Games People Play	1970	—	3.00	6.00
—As "Ben Colder"					
❑ 14123	Daddy's Home/The Will	1970	—	3.00	6.00
❑ 14133	Tennessee Bird Talk/What Is Youth	1970	—	3.00	6.00
—As "Ben Colder"					
❑ 14165	One of Them Roarin' Songs/I Don't Belong in Her Arms	1970	—	3.00	6.00
❑ 14209	Fifteen Beers Ago/Sunday Mornin' Fallin' Down	1970	—	3.00	6.00
—As "Ben Colder"					
❑ 14247	Help Me Fake It Through the Night/Rose Garden	1971	—	3.00	6.00
—As "Ben Colder"					
❑ 14287	Goodbye Wabash Cannonball/Joy	1971	—	3.00	6.00
❑ 14327	Easy Loving No. 2/Sing a Drinkin' Song	1971	—	3.00	6.00
—As "Ben Colder"					
❑ 14384	Life Is a Fountain/Somebody Gonna Come Along	1972	—	3.00	6.00
❑ 14420	The Unhappiest Squirrel in the Whole U.S.A./ Runnin' Bare	1972	—	2.50	5.00
—As "Ben Colder"					
❑ 14444	A Kick in the Head/Personality	1972	—	3.00	6.00
❑ 14471	Glossy 8 x 10/Moontan	1972	—	2.50	5.00
—As "Ben Colder"					
❑ 14610	Early in the Morning/Getting High on Love	1973	—	3.00	6.00
❑ 14639	Behind Cloe's Door/Satin Sheets	1973	—	2.50	5.00
—As "Ben Colder"					
❑ 14647	The Purple People Eater/I Can't Believe You're Mine	1973	2.50	5.00	10.00
SCORPION					
❑ 0556	Lucille No. 2/Senior Citizen's Lament	1978	—	2.00	4.00
—As "Ben Colder"					
SUNBIRD					
❑ 104	The Rambler/Amazania	1979	—	2.00	4.00
—As "Ben Colder"					
❑ 109	Flower of the County (Censored Version)/Flower of the County (Uncensored Version)	1980	—	2.00	4.00
—As "Ben Colder"					
❑ 7566	Jack Hammer Man/Belly Button	1981	—	2.00	4.00
Selected 78s					
BULLET					
❑ 603	Oklahoma Honky Tonk Gal/I Can't Live (On) Without You	1945	15.00	30.00	60.00
Albums					
MGM					
❑ GAS-139	Ben Colder (Golden Archive Series)	1970	3.75	7.50	15.00
—As "Ben Colder"					
❑ E-3299 [M]	Sheb Wooley	1956	37.50	75.00	150.00
❑ E-3904 [M]	Songs from the Days of Rawhide	1961	10.00	20.00	40.00
❑ SE-3904 [S]	Songs from the Days of Rawhide	1961	12.50	25.00	50.00
❑ E-4026 [M]	That's My Ma and That's My Pa	1962	7.50	15.00	30.00
❑ SE-4026 [S]	That's My Ma and That's My Pa	1962	10.00	20.00	40.00
❑ E-4117 [M]	Spoofing the Big Ones	1961	10.00	20.00	40.00
❑ SE-4117 [S]	Spoofing the Big Ones	1961	12.50	25.00	50.00
—MGM 4117 as "Ben Colder"					
❑ E-4136 [M]	Tales of How the West Was Won	1963	7.50	15.00	30.00
❑ SE-4136 [S]	Tales of How the West Was Won	1963	10.00	20.00	40.00
❑ E-4173 [M]	Ben Colder	1963	7.50	15.00	30.00
❑ SE-4173 [S]	Ben Colder	1963	10.00	20.00	40.00
—MGM 4173 as "Ben Colder"					
❑ E-4275 [M]	The Very Best of Sheb Wooley	1965	5.00	10.00	20.00
❑ SE-4275 [S]	The Very Best of Sheb Wooley	1965	6.25	12.50	25.00
❑ E-4325 [M]	It's a Big Land	1965	5.00	10.00	20.00
❑ SE-4325 [S]	It's a Big Land	1965	6.25	12.50	25.00
❑ E-4421 [M]	Big Ben Strikes Again	1967	5.00	10.00	20.00
❑ SE-4421 [S]	Big Ben Strikes Again	1967	5.00	10.00	20.00
—MGM 4421 as "Ben Colder"					
❑ E-4482 [M]	Wine, Women and Song	1967	5.00	10.00	20.00
❑ SE-4482 [S]	Wine, Women and Song	1967	5.00	10.00	20.00
—MGM 4482 as "Ben Colder"					
❑ SE-4530	The Best of Ben Colder	1968	5.00	10.00	20.00
—As "Ben Colder"					
❑ SE-4614	Harper Valley P.T.A.	1968	5.00	10.00	20.00
—As "Ben Colder"					
❑ SE-4615	Warm and Wooley	1969	5.00	10.00	20.00
❑ SE-4629	Have One On	1969	3.75	7.50	15.00
—As "Ben Colder"					
❑ SE-4674	Wild Again	1970	3.75	7.50	15.00
—As "Ben Colder"					
❑ SE-4758	Live and Loaded	1971	3.75	7.50	15.00
—As "Ben Colder"					
❑ SE-4807	Warming Up to Colder	1972	3.75	7.50	15.00
—As "Ben Colder"					
❑ SE-4876	The Wacky World of Ben Colder	1973	3.75	7.50	15.00
—As "Ben Colder"					

WOPAT, TOM

Number	Title (A Side/B Side)	Yr	VG	VG+	NM
45s					
CAPITOL					
❑ B-44144	Hey Little Sister/A Letter in the Fire	1988	—	—	3.00
❑ B-44243	Not Enough Love/A Letter in the Fire	1988	—	—	3.00
❑ B-44346	Red Hot and Blue/The Rain Don't Care	1989	—	—	3.00
COLUMBIA					
❑ 38-03486	Full Moon, Empty Pockets/Savannah	1983	—	2.00	4.00
❑ 38-03884	I Kissed You/Luckiest Man in the World	1983	—	2.00	4.00
❑ 38-03947	Sha-Marie/Savannah	1983	—	2.00	4.00
EMI AMERICA					
❑ B-8316	True Love (Never Did Run Smooth)/Some Day, Some Night	1986	—	—	3.00
❑ B-8334	I Won't Let You Down/Wheels	1986	—	—	3.00
❑ B-8364	The Rock and Roll of Love/A Good Woman's Love	1986	—	—	3.00
❑ B-43010	Put Me Out of My Misery/Daylight Loving Time	1987	—	—	3.00
❑ B-43034	Susannah/Cars	1987	—	—	3.00
EMI MANHATTAN					
❑ B-50112	A Little Bit Closer/Bad Thing About Good Love	1987	—	—	3.00
EPIC					
❑ 34-73862	Too Many Honky Tonks (On My Way Home)/I've Been There	1991	—	2.00	4.00
❑ 34-74063	Back to the Well/Always a Blue Moon	1991	—	2.00	4.00

WORK, JIMMY

Number	Title (A Side/B Side)	Yr	VG	VG+	NM
45s					
CAPITOL					
❑ F2372	If I Should Lose You/Don't Play with My Heart	1953	6.25	12.50	25.00
❑ F2565	Crazy Moon/Out of My Mind	1953	6.25	12.50	25.00
❑ F2682	How Can I Love You/I'm Lonesome for Someone	1953	6.25	12.50	25.00
DOT					
❑ 1221	Making Believe/Just Like Downtown	1954	5.00	10.00	20.00
❑ 1245	That's What Makes the Juke Box Play/Don't Give Me a Reason	1955	5.00	10.00	20.00
❑ 1267	Don't Knock, Just Come On In/Let 'Em Talk	1955	5.00	10.00	20.00
❑ 1272	There's Only One You/When She Said You All	1955	5.00	10.00	20.00
❑ 1277	My Old Stomping Ground/Hands Away from My Heart	1956	5.00	10.00	20.00
❑ 1279	Rock Island Line/That's the Way It's Gonna Be	1956	5.00	10.00	20.00
❑ 1284	Blind Heart/You've Got a Heart Like a Merry-Go-Round	1956	3.75	7.50	15.00
❑ 1287	Digging My Own Grave/That Cold, Cold Look in Your Eyes	1957	3.75	7.50	15.00
Selected 78s					
BULLET					
❑ 699	Mr. and Mrs. Cloud/Hospitality	1950	7.50	15.00	30.00
DECCA					
❑ 46166	Blue Grass Tickling My Feet/Please Don't Let Me	1949	5.00	10.00	20.00
❑ 46181	Smokey Mountain Moon/I Would Send Roses	1949	5.00	10.00	20.00
❑ 46223	Surrounded by Water and Bars/Who's Been Here	1950	5.00	10.00	20.00

WORTH, MARION

Number	Title (A Side/B Side)	Yr	VG	VG+	NM
45s					
CHEROKEE					
❑ 503	Are You Willing, Willie/This Heart of Mine	1959	7.50	15.00	30.00
COLUMBIA					
❑ 4-41799	I Think I Know/Tomorrow at a Quarter Till Nine	1960	3.75	7.50	15.00
❑ 4-41799 [PS]	I Think I Know/Tomorrow at a Quarter Till Nine	1960	7.50	15.00	30.00
❑ 4-41972	There'll Always Be Sadness/I'm Not at All Sorry for You	1961	3.75	7.50	15.00
❑ 4-42184	Go On Home/Imitation	1961	3.75	7.50	15.00
❑ 4-42453	It's So Funny I Could Cry/Lover's Hymn	1962	3.75	7.50	15.00
❑ 4-42640	Shake Me I Rattle (Squeeze Me I Cry)/Tennessee Teardrops	1962	3.75	7.50	15.00
❑ 4-42640 [PS]	Shake Me I Rattle (Squeeze Me I Cry)/Tennessee Teardrops	1962	6.25	12.50	25.00
❑ 4-42703	Crazy Arms/Lovers' Lane	1963	3.75	7.50	15.00
❑ 4-42904	Shake Me I Rattle (Squeeze Me I Cry)/My Dolly Has a Pain in Her Sawdust	1963	3.00	6.00	12.00
❑ 4-42992	You Took Him Off My Hands (Now Please Take Him Off My Mind)/He Loves Me, He Loves Me Not	1964	3.00	6.00	12.00
❑ 4-43119	The French Song/Kentucky Waltz	1964	3.00	6.00	12.00
❑ 4-43214	The Hands You're Holding Now/I'm Not Myself	1965	3.00	6.00	12.00
❑ 4-43308	Does the Sun Rise in the East/Seven Roses	1965	3.00	6.00	12.00
❑ 4-43405	I Will Not Blow Out the Light/Twenty-One Days of Darkness	1965	3.00	6.00	12.00
DECCA					
❑ 32150	Baby For You/Only You Can Make Me Cry	1967	2.00	4.00	8.00
❑ 32195	A Woman Needs Love/I've Got That Sad and Lonely Feeling	1967	2.00	4.00	8.00
❑ 32278	Mama Sez/Then I'll Be Over	1968	2.00	4.00	8.00
❑ 32398	Spreadin' My Wings/Are You Sleeping Well at Night	1968	2.00	4.00	8.00
❑ 32457	Love Is a Very Strange Thing/Wonder What to Do	1969	2.00	4.00	8.00

Number	Title (A Side/B Side)	Yr	VG	VG+	NM
❑ 32579	Sock It To 'Em Sister Nell/He's Mean to Me	1969	2.00	4.00	8.00
❑ 32717	If I Kiss You/Just Leave Me Alone	1970	—	3.50	7.00
GUYDEN					
❑ 2026	Are You Willing, Willie/This Heart of Mine	1959	5.00	10.00	20.00
—Reissue of Cherokee 503					
❑ 2033	That's My Kind of Love/I Lost Johnny	1960	5.00	10.00	20.00
Albums					
COLUMBIA					
❑ CL 2011 [M]	Marion Worth's Greatest Hits	1963	5.00	10.00	20.00
❑ CL 2287 [M]	Marion Worth Sings Marty Robbins	1964	5.00	10.00	20.00
❑ CS 8811 [S]	Marion Worth's Greatest Hits	1963	6.25	12.50	25.00
❑ CS 9087 [S]	Marion Worth Sings Marty Robbins	1964	6.25	12.50	25.00
DECCA					
❑ DL 4936 [M]	A Woman Needs Love	1967	6.25	12.50	25.00
❑ DL 74936 [S]	A Woman Needs Love	1967	5.00	10.00	20.00

WORTH, MARION, AND GEORGE MORGAN

Also see each artist's individual listings.

Number	Title (A Side/B Side)	Yr	VG	VG+	NM
45s					
COLUMBIA					
❑ 4-42848	In His Own Quiet Way/Play a Blue Guitar (For Me)	1963	3.75	7.50	15.00
❑ 4-43020	Slipping Around/I Love You So Much It Hurts	1964	3.75	7.50	15.00
❑ 4-43543	Too Busy Saying Goodbye/Saving All My Love (For You)	1966	3.75	7.50	15.00
❑ 4-43874	The Wheel of Hurt/Married	1966	3.75	7.50	15.00
Albums					
COLUMBIA					
❑ CL 2197 [M]	Slippin' Around	1964	5.00	10.00	20.00
❑ CS 8997 [S]	Slippin' Around	1964	6.25	12.50	25.00

WRAYS, THE

COLLIN RAYE was a member of this group while using the name "Bubba Wray."

Number	Title (A Side/B Side)	Yr	VG	VG+	NM
45s					
CIS					
❑ 3011	Reason to Believe/(B-side unknown)	1983	2.00	4.00	8.00
—As "The Wray Brothers Band"					
MERCURY					
❑ 884621-7	I Don't Want to Know Your Name/Here's to the Men Who Can Cry	1986	—	2.50	5.00
❑ 884900-7	Come On Joe/Here's to the Men Who Can Cry	1986	—	2.50	5.00
❑ 888542-7	You Lay a Lotta Love on Me/Until We Meet Again	1987	—	2.50	5.00
SASPARILLA					
❑ 0003	Until We Meet Again/(B-side unknown)	1985	2.00	4.00	8.00
—As "The Wray Brothers Band"					
WRAY					
❑ 002	Need Someone Bad Tonight/(B-side unknown)	198?	2.00	4.00	8.00
—As "The Wray Brothers Band"					

WREN, LARRY

Number	Title (A Side/B Side)	Yr	VG	VG+	NM
45s					
50 STATES					
❑ 51	Lie to Me/It's Saturday Night	1977	—	3.00	6.00
❑ 54	There's Something About You Girl/Talk It Over	1977	—	3.00	6.00

WRIGHT, B.J.

Number	Title (A Side/B Side)	Yr	VG	VG+	NM
45s					
SOUNDWAVES					
❑ 4577	Memory Bound/Don't Say Love	1978	—	2.50	5.00
❑ 4581	Leaning on Each Other/California Rose	1979	—	2.50	5.00
❑ 4589	I've Got a Right to Be Wrong/Free at Last	1979	—	2.50	5.00
❑ 4593	Nobody's Darlin' But Mine/(Somewhere There's a) Rainbow Over Texas	1979	—	2.50	5.00
❑ 4604	J.R./Memory Bound	1980	—	2.50	5.00
❑ 4610	Lost Love Affair/You're Drivin' Me Crazy	1980	—	2.50	5.00
❑ 4624	I Know an Ending (When It Comes)/Baby Blue	1980	—	2.50	5.00

WRIGHT, BOBBY

Number	Title (A Side/B Side)	Yr	VG	VG+	NM
45s					
ABC					
❑ 11390	Lovin' Someone on My Mind/This Time	1973	—	2.50	5.00
❑ 11418	Seasons in the Sun/Live and Let Live	1974	—	2.50	5.00
❑ 11443	Everybody Needs a Rainbow/I'll Surely Fall in Love with You	1974	—	2.50	5.00
❑ 12028	Baby's Gone/Love Look (At Us Now)	1974	—	2.50	5.00
❑ 12062	I Just Came Home to Count the Memories/No One Has Ever Loved Me Like You	1975	—	2.50	5.00
❑ 12093	It's for You Hon/You Won't Find Another Fool Like Me	1975	—	2.50	5.00
DECCA					
❑ 32107	Lay Some Happiness on Me/How Much Lonelier Can Lonely Be	1967	—	3.00	6.00
❑ 32193	That See Me Later Look/Nail My Shoes to the Floor	1967	—	3.00	6.00
❑ 32280	Something Called Happiness/It Happens in the Best of Families	1968	—	3.00	6.00
❑ 32367	Old Before My Time/Shutting Out the Light	1968	—	3.00	6.00
❑ 32464	Upstairs in the Bedroom/My Home Away from Home	1969	—	3.00	6.00
❑ 32564	Sing a Song About Love/If You Don't Swing — Don't Ring	1969	—	3.00	6.00
❑ 32633	Take Me Back to the Goodtimes, Sally/Something Called Happiness	1970	—	3.00	6.00
❑ 32705	Hurry Home to Me/My Home Away from Home	1970	—	3.00	6.00
❑ 32792	If You Want Me To I'll Go/Rain Falling on Me	1971	—	3.00	6.00
❑ 32839	Here I Go Again/If You Don't Swing...Don't Ring	1971	—	3.00	6.00
❑ 32903	Search Your Heart/I'll Walk on Water	1971	—	3.00	6.00
❑ 32954	There She Goes/Somebody's Breakin' My Heart	1972	—	3.00	6.00
❑ 32985	Just Because I'm Still in Love with You/Pledging My Love	1972	—	3.00	6.00
❑ 33034	If Not for You/Searching	1972	—	3.00	6.00
UNITED ARTISTS					
❑ XW913	Neon Lady/'57 Chevrolet	1976	—	2.00	4.00
❑ XW963	In Our Room/Lay Down Beside Me	1977	—	2.00	4.00
❑ XW1051	Playing with the Baby's Mama/Lay Down Beside Me	1977	—	2.00	4.00
❑ XW1197	Caroline's Footsteps/I'm Comin' Down Lonely	1978	—	2.00	4.00
❑ XW1238	Takin' a Chance/I Don't Know What to Tell Her	1978	—	2.00	4.00
❑ XW1281	Gettin' Down, Gettin' Together, Gettin' in Love/Same Old Song	1979	—	2.00	4.00
❑ X1300	I'm Turning You Loose/Going Home	1979	—	2.00	4.00
❑ X1337	I Wish You Could Have Turned My Head (And Left My Heart Alone)/I'm Comin' Down Lonely	1980	—	2.00	4.00
Albums					
ABC					
❑ ABCD-842	Seasons of Love	1974	3.00	6.00	12.00
DECCA					
❑ DL 75319	Here I Go Again	1971	3.75	7.50	15.00

WRIGHT, CHELY

Number	Title (A Side/B Side)	Yr	VG	VG+	NM
45s					
MCA					
❑ 72012	Shut Up and Drive/Emma Jean's Guitar	1997	—	2.00	4.00
❑ 72025	Just Another Heartache/Feelin' Single and Seein' Double	1997	—	—	3.00
❑ 72044	I Already Do/Is It Love Yet	1998	—	—	3.00
MCA NASHVILLE					
❑ 72092	Single White Female/Let Me In	1999	—	2.00	4.00
❑ 088-172113-7	It Was/Rubbin' It In	1999	—	—	3.00
❑ 088-172161-7	She Went Out for Cigarettes/Some Kind of Somethin'	2000	—	—	3.00
POLYDOR					
❑ 577282-7	Listenin' to the Radio/Till All Her Tears Are Dry	1995	—	2.00	4.00
❑ 577936-7	The Love That We Lost/Gotta Get Good at Givin' Again	1996	—	2.00	4.00
❑ 851430-7	Sea of Cowboy Hats/Nobody But a Fool	1995	—	2.00	4.00
❑ 853056-7	He's a Good Ole Boy/Go On and Go	1994	—	2.00	4.00
❑ 853810-7	Till I Was Loved by You/He Don't Do Bars Anymore	1994	—	2.00	4.00

WRIGHT, CURTIS

Also see ORRALL AND WRIGHT.

Number	Title (A Side/B Side)	Yr	VG	VG+	NM
45s					
AIRBORNE					
❑ 75746	She's Got a Man on Her Mind/(B-side unknown)	1989	—	2.50	5.00

WRIGHT, GINNY

Number	Title (A Side/B Side)	Yr	VG	VG+	NM
45s					
FABOR					
❑ 101	I Love You/I Want You Yes (You Want Me No)	1953	10.00	20.00	40.00
—With Jim Reeves					
❑ 102	Wait/Lonesome Seagull	1954	7.50	15.00	30.00
—With Jerry Rowley					
❑ 105	My Chihuahua Dog/I Saw Esau	1954	7.50	15.00	30.00
❑ 110	Indian Moon/Your Eyes Feasted Upon Her	1954	7.50	15.00	30.00
❑ 114	Turn Around My Darling/How to Get Married	1954	7.50	15.00	30.00
❑ 130	Please Leave My Darling Alone/I Could Still Tell You	1955	7.50	15.00	30.00
❑ 133	Where Were You/Whirlwind	1956	6.25	12.50	25.00

WRIGHT, GINNY, AND TOM TALL

Number	Title (A Side/B Side)	Yr	VG	VG+	NM
45s					
FABOR					
❑ 117	Are You Mine/Somebody New	1954	7.50	15.00	30.00
❑ 121	Out of Line/Boom Boom Boomerang	1955	7.50	15.00	30.00
❑ 127	Will This Dream of Mine Come True/Come with Me	1955	7.50	15.00	30.00
ZERO					
❑ 106	Are You Mine/I've Got Somebody New	1960	5.00	10.00	20.00

WRIGHT, JOHNNY

Also see JOHNNIE AND JACK; KITTY WELLS AND JOHNNY WRIGHT.

Number	Title (A Side/B Side)	Yr	VG	VG+	NM
45s					
DECCA					
❑ 31537	Sweet Snow Dear/What's Gonna Happen to Me	1963	2.50	5.00	10.00
❑ 31593	Walkin', Talkin', Cryin', Barely Beatin' Broken Heart/They're All Going Home But One	1964	2.00	4.00	8.00
❑ 31679	Don't Give Up the Ship/Guitar Lessons	1964	2.00	4.00	8.00
❑ 31740	Blame It on the Moonlight/Rest in Peace	1965	2.00	4.00	8.00
❑ 31821	Hello Vietnam/Mexico City	1965	2.00	4.00	8.00
❑ 31875	Keep the Flag Flying/You're Over There (And I'm Over Here)	1965	2.00	4.00	8.00
❑ 31927	Nickels, Quarters and Dimes/Is Love Worth All the Heartaches	1966	2.00	4.00	8.00
❑ 32002	I'm Doing This for Daddy/Racing Man	1966	2.00	4.00	8.00
❑ 32061	Mama's Little Jewel/Something for Nothing	1966	2.00	4.00	8.00
❑ 32133	Ole Honky Tonk/Why	1967	2.00	4.00	8.00
❑ 32162	American Power/Settle Back Down to Earth	1967	2.00	4.00	8.00
❑ 32216	Music to Cry By/Cheaters Can't Win	1967	2.00	4.00	8.00

Number	Title (A Side/B Side)	Yr	VG	VG+	NM
❑ 32267	Go Get It/Atlanta Georgia Baby	1968	2.00	4.00	8.00
❑ 32402	(They Always Come Out) Smellin' Like a Rose/ One Little Taco	1968	2.00	4.00	8.00
❑ 32466	Wabash Cannonball/Love Ain't Gonna Die	1969	2.00	4.00	8.00
❑ 32627	Rainbow in the Clouds/A Dear John Letter	1970	—	3.00	6.00
❑ 32704	Love Everybody/Mama Set the Table with Love	1970	—	3.00	6.00
❑ 32770	Something to Come Home To/Where the Heartaches Hang Around	1971	—	3.00	6.00
❑ 32799	She's Gone, Gone, Gone/Old Honky Tonk	1971	—	3.00	6.00
❑ 32832	High Cost of Livin'/Let Jesus Turn You On	1971	—	3.00	6.00
❑ 32883	Going to the Country/South in New Orleans	1971	—	3.00	6.00
❑ 33012	Doo-Hickey/Hoping That You're Hoping	1972	—	3.00	6.00
❑ 33053	Don't Let the Stars Get In Your Eyes/(B-side unknown)	1973	—	3.00	6.00
MCA					
❑ 40138	Ode to a Country Bar/They're Writing Her Name	1973	—	2.50	5.00
RUBOCA					
❑ 213	Pressure/Harry Truman	198?	—	3.50	7.00
Albums					
DECCA					
❑ DL 4698 [M]	Hello Vietnam	1965	6.25	12.50	25.00
❑ DL 4770 [M]	Country Music Special	1966	6.25	12.50	25.00
❑ DL 4846 [M]	Country the Wright Way	1967	6.25	12.50	25.00
❑ DL 74698 [S]	Hello Vietnam	1965	7.50	15.00	30.00
❑ DL 74770 [S]	Country Music Special	1966	7.50	15.00	30.00
❑ DL 74846 [S]	Country the Wright Way	1967	5.00	10.00	20.00
❑ DL 75019	Johnny Wright Sings Country Favorites	1968	5.00	10.00	20.00

WRIGHT, JUSTIN

45s

Number	Title (A Side/B Side)	Yr	VG	VG+	NM
BEAR					
❑ 195	Settin' at the Kitchen Table/(B-side unknown)	1989	—	3.00	6.00
❑ 2001	Hank and Lefty/(B-side unknown)	1989	—	3.00	6.00
❑ 2004	Redneck Blue Monday/(B-side unknown)	1989	—	3.00	6.00
❑ 2009	Girls Like Her/(B-side unknown)	1989	—	3.00	6.00

WRIGHT, LEE

45s

Number	Title (A Side/B Side)	Yr	VG	VG+	NM
PRAIRIE DUST					
❑ 5185	The Eyes Have It/(B-side unknown)	1985	—	3.00	6.00
❑ 7628	Capricorn Kings/Wait Till Morning	1978	—	3.00	6.00
❑ 7635	Good Night for Drinking/The Hand That Rocks the Cradle	1979	—	3.00	6.00
❑ 92784	Memory Machine/The Afternoon Soaps	1984	—	3.00	6.00

WRIGHT, MICHELLE

45s

Number	Title (A Side/B Side)	Yr	VG	VG+	NM
ARISTA					
❑ 2002	New Kind of Love/As Far As Lonely Goes	1990	—	2.00	4.00
❑ 2090	Woman's Intuition/As Far As Lonely Goes	1990	—	2.00	4.00
❑ 2152	A Heartbeat Away/The Longest Night	1991	—	2.00	4.00
❑ 2208	All You Really Wanna Do/The Longest Night	1991	—	2.00	4.00
❑ 12406	Take It Like a Man/Guitar Talk	1992	—	2.50	5.00
❑ 12444	One Time Around/A Little More Comfortable	1992	—	2.00	4.00
❑ 12480	He Would Be Sixteen/The Change	1992	—	2.00	4.00
❑ 12528	The Change/If I'm Over You	1993	—	2.00	4.00
❑ 12727	One Good Man/Where Do We Go from Here	1994	—	2.00	4.00
❑ 13023	Nobody's Girl/I'm Not Afraid	1996	—	2.00	4.00
ARISTA NASHVILLE					
❑ 13053	The Answer Is Yes/Cold Kisses	1996	—	2.00	4.00

WRIGHT, RANDY

45s

Number	Title (A Side/B Side)	Yr	VG	VG+	NM
MCA					
❑ 52273	There's Nobody Lovin' at Home/Times Like This (Make Me Want Times Like That)	1983	—	2.00	4.00
❑ 52358	If You're Serious About Cheating/Times Like This	1984	—	2.00	4.00

WRIGHT, RUBY

There are two different singers named Ruby Wright. One is a former band singer who was born in 1914 and isn't country. The other, born in 1938, is the daughter of KITTY WELLS and JOHNNY WRIGHT. The records listed below are the only ones we're sure are by the country "Ruby Wright."

45s

Number	Title (A Side/B Side)	Yr	VG	VG+	NM
CHART					
❑ 5171	He's a Night Owl/The Fire That Burns at Home	1973	—	3.00	6.00
EPIC					
❑ 5-10055	A New Place to Hang Your Hat/A Kick in the Conscience	1966	2.50	5.00	10.00
❑ 5-10150	(I Can Find) A Better Deal Than That/Everything, All the Time	1967	2.50	5.00	10.00
PLANTATION					
❑ 51	Yester-Me, Yester-You, Yesterday/Listen to the Words	1970	—	3.50	7.00
RIC					
❑ 126	Dern Ya/Such a Silly Notion	1964	3.75	7.50	15.00
❑ 145	Billy Broke My Heart at Walgrains/You're Not Really Leaving Me	1964	3.75	7.50	15.00
❑ 157	Webster, You Wrote the Book/Up the Path (and In My Door)	1965	3.75	7.50	15.00
❑ 166	Adios Aloha/Smile on My Lips	1965	3.75	7.50	15.00

WRIGHT, SONNY

Also see PEGGY SUE AND SONNY WRIGHT.

45s

Number	Title (A Side/B Side)	Yr	VG	VG+	NM
COLUMBIA					
❑ 4-44320	Leftover Love/Running Drunk	1967	2.00	4.00	8.00
❑ 4-44496	Pain Remover/Hung to Another Man	1968	2.00	4.00	8.00
DOOR KNOB					
❑ 040	Motel Mourning/When I Start Drinking	1977	—	2.50	5.00
❑ 057	Same Old Highway/Motel Mourning	1978	—	2.50	5.00
❑ 076	If This Isn't It/Same Old Highway	1978	—	2.50	5.00
❑ 100	You Make Me Feel Brand New/If This Isn't It	1979	—	2.50	5.00
❑ 128	Molly (And the Texas Rain)/It Wasn't Me Who Said I Owned a Gold Mine	1980	—	2.50	5.00
KAPP					
❑ 2009	I Love You, Loretta Lynn/Rose	1969	2.50	5.00	10.00
❑ 2040	Hung Over/The Trash You Threw Away	1969	2.00	4.00	8.00
❑ 2090	My Long Gone Reason/Mama Didn't Bend the Twig	1970	2.00	4.00	8.00
Albums					
KAPP					
❑ KS-3614	I Love You, Loretta Lynn	1968	5.00	10.00	20.00

WRIGHT BROTHERS, THE

45s

Number	Title (A Side/B Side)	Yr	VG	VG+	NM
AIRBORNE					
❑ 10006	Come On Rain/(B-side unknown)	1988	—	2.50	5.00
MERCURY					
❑ 818653-7	Southern Women/Love's Slippin' Up on Me	1984	—	—	3.00
❑ 880055-7	Radio Lover/So Close	1984	—	—	3.00
❑ 880316-7	Eight Days a Week/She's a Diamond	1984	—	—	3.00
❑ 880596-7	Fire in the Sky/Pride	1985	—	—	3.00
❑ 880868-7	Country Stroll/Dixie Road	1985	—	—	3.00
WARNER BROS.					
❑ 29839	So Easy to Love/We Don't Know Why	1982	—	2.00	4.00
❑ 29926	Made in the U.S.A./Words of Love	1982	—	2.00	4.00
❑ 49837	Family Man/Engine Engine Number Nine	1981	—	2.00	4.00
❑ 50033	When You Find Her, Keep Her/Let the Little Bird Fly	1982	—	2.00	4.00
Albums					
MERCURY					
❑ 818654-1	Easy Street	1984	2.00	4.00	8.00
WARNER BROS.					
❑ 23736	Made in the U.S.A.	1982	2.50	5.00	10.00

WYATT, GENE

45s

Number	Title (A Side/B Side)	Yr	VG	VG+	NM
DOLLIE					
❑ 502	Fightin' for the Free Land/Searching for a New Love Affair	1966	2.50	5.00	10.00
EBB					
❑ 123	Love Fever/Lover Boy	1957	25.00	50.00	100.00
LUCKY SEVEN					
❑ 101	Prettiest Girl at the Dance/(B-side unknown)	1959	15.00	30.00	60.00
MERCURY					
❑ 72752	I Stole the Flowers/I'm a One Woman Man	1967	2.50	5.00	10.00
PAULA					
❑ 308	I Just Ain't Got (As Much As He's Got Going for Me)/Chains Around My Heart	1968	2.50	5.00	10.00
❑ 1206	Little Liza Jane/Country Music Peyton Place	1968	2.50	5.00	10.00
❑ 1211	My Story of Love/Evangeline	1969	2.50	5.00	10.00
❑ 1216	Milk and Honey Memories/Failure of T Crop	1969	2.50	5.00	10.00
❑ 1223	Twelve Men/Back Door of My Mind	1970	2.00	4.00	8.00
❑ 1224	Go Together/As Long As I Live	1970	2.00	4.00	8.00

WYATT, NINA

45s

Number	Title (A Side/B Side)	Yr	VG	VG+	NM
CHARTA					
❑ 207	Richer Now with You/You're Not Playing Love by the Rules	1988	—	2.50	5.00
❑ 209	Raised on Radio/You Lay So Easy on My Mind	1988	—	2.50	5.00
❑ 210	After the Passion Leaves/Love Finally Got the Best of Me	1988	—	2.50	5.00
❑ 216	A Clean and Even Break/Willie	1989	—	2.50	5.00

WYATT BROTHERS

45s

Number	Title (A Side/B Side)	Yr	VG	VG+	NM
WYATT					
❑ 103	Wyatt Liquor/(B-side unknown)	1986	2.00	4.00	8.00

WYNETTE, TAMMY

45s

Number	Title (A Side/B Side)	Yr	VG	VG+	NM
COLUMBIA					
❑ 77294	Silver Threads and Golden Needles/Let Her Fly	1993	—	—	3.00
—With Dolly Parton and Loretta Lynn					
EPIC					
❑ TW 1 [DJ]	The Wonders You Perform (stereo/mono)	1969	5.00	10.00	20.00
—Red vinyl; included with some early copies of the LP "Inspiration"					
❑ AS 60 [DJ]	White Christmas/One Happy Christmas	1973	2.00	4.00	8.00
—1973 Christmas Seals promotional record					
❑ AS 60 [PS]	White Christmas/One Happy Christmas	1973	2.50	5.00	10.00
❑ 02439	Crying in the Rain/Bring Back My Baby to Me	1981	—	2.00	4.00
❑ 02770	Another Chance/What's It Like to Be a Woman	1982	—	2.00	4.00

Number	Title (A Side/B Side)	Yr	VG	VG+	NM
❑ 03064	You Still Get To Me in My Dreams/If I Didn't Have a Heart	1982	—	2.00	4.00
❑ 03384	A Good Night's Love/I'm Going On with Everything Gone	1982	—	2.00	4.00
❑ 03811	I Just Heard a Heart Break (And I'm So Afraid It's Mine)/Back to the Wall	1983	—	2.00	4.00
❑ 03971	Unwed Fathers/I'm So Afraid That I'd Live Through It	1983	—	2.00	4.00
❑ 04101	Still in the Ring/Midnight Love	1983	—	2.00	4.00
❑ 04467	Lonely Heart/(I'm Not) A Candle in the Wind	1984	—	—	3.00
❑ 05399	You Can Lead a Heart to Love (But You Can't Make It Fall)/He Talks to Me	1985	—	—	3.00
❑ 06263	Alive and Well/I'll Be Thinking of You	1986	—	—	3.00
❑ 07226	Your Love/I Wasn't Meant to Live My Life Alone	1987	—	—	3.00
❑ 07635	Talkin' to Myself Again/A Slow Burning Fire	1987	—	—	3.00
❑ 07788	Beneath a Painted Sky/Some Things Will Never Change	1988	—	—	3.00
❑ 10095	Apartment No. 9/I'm Not Mine to Give	1966	2.50	5.00	10.00
❑ 10134	Your Good Girl's Gonna Go Bad/Send Me No Roses	1967	2.00	4.00	8.00
❑ 10211	I Don't Wanna Play House/Soakin' Wet	1967	2.00	4.00	8.00
❑ 10269	Take Me to Your World/Good	1967	2.00	4.00	8.00
❑ 10315	D-I-V-O-R-C-E/Don't Make It Now	1968	2.00	4.00	8.00
❑ 10398	Stand By Your Man/I Stayed Long Enough	1968	2.50	5.00	10.00
❑ 10462	Singing My Song/Too Far Gone	1969	—	3.00	6.00
❑ 10462 [PS]	Singing My Song/Too Far Gone	1969	2.50	5.00	10.00
❑ 10512	The Ways to Love a Man/Still Around	1969	—	3.00	6.00
❑ 10571	I'll See Him Through/Enough of a Woman	1970	—	3.00	6.00
❑ 10612	He Loves Me All the Way/One Last Night Together	1970	—	3.00	6.00
❑ 10653	Run, Woman, Run/My Daddy Doll	1970	—	3.00	6.00
❑ 10687	The Wonders You Perform/Gentle Shepherd	1970	—	3.00	6.00
❑ 10690	One Happy Christmas/(Merry Christmas) We Must Be Having One	1970	2.00	4.00	8.00
❑ 10707	We Sure Can Love Each Other/Fun	1971	—	3.00	6.00
❑ 10759	Good Lovin' (Makes It Right)/I Love You, Mr. Jones	1971	—	3.00	6.00
❑ 10818	Bedtime Story/Reach Out Your Hand	1971	—	3.00	6.00
❑ 10856	Reach Out Your Hand/Love's the Answer	1972	—	3.00	6.00
❑ 10909	My Man/Things I Love to Do	1972	—	3.00	6.00
❑ 10969	Kids Say the Darnedest Things/I Wish I Had a Mommy Like You	1973	—	3.00	6.00
❑ 11044	One Final Stand/Crying Steel Guitar	1973	—	—	—
—Canceled?					
❑ 11079	Another Lonely Song/The Only Time I'm Really Me	1973	—	3.00	6.00
❑ 50008	Woman to Woman/Love Me Forever	1974	—	2.50	5.00
❑ 50071	(You Make Me Want to Be) A Mother/I'm Not a Has-Been	1975	—	2.50	5.00
❑ 50145	I Still Believe in Fairy Tales/Your Memory's Gone to Rest	1975	—	2.50	5.00
❑ 50196	'Til I Can Make It on My Own/Love Is Something Good for Everybody	1976	—	2.50	5.00
❑ 50264	You and Me/When Love Was All We Had	1976	—	2.50	5.00
❑ 50349	(Let's Get Together) One Last Time/Hardly a Day Goes By	1977	—	2.50	5.00
❑ 50450	One of a Kind/Loving You, I Do	1977	—	2.50	5.00
❑ 50538	I'd Like to See Jesus (On the Midnight Special)/Love Doesn't Always Come (On the Night It's Needed)	1978	—	2.50	5.00
❑ 50574	Womanhood/50 Words or Less	1978	—	2.50	5.00
❑ 50661	They Call It Making Love/Let Me Be Me	1979	—	2.50	5.00
❑ 50722	No One Else in the World/Mama, Your Little Girl Fell	1979	—	2.50	5.00
❑ 50868	He Was There (When I Needed You)/Only the Names Have Been Changed	1980	—	2.50	5.00
❑ 50915	Starting Over/I'll Be Thinking of You	1980	—	2.50	5.00
❑ 51011	Cowboys Don't Shoot Straight (Like They Used To)/You Brought Me Back	1981	—	2.00	4.00
❑ 68570	Next to You/When a Girl Becomes a Wife	1989	—	—	3.00
❑ 68894	Thank the Cowboy for the Ride/We Called It Everything But Quits	1989	—	—	3.00
❑ 73427	Let's Call It a Day Today/When a Girl Becomes a Wife	1990	—	2.00	4.00
❑ 73579	I'm Turning You Loose/Just a Minute There	1990	—	2.00	4.00
❑ 73656	What Goes with Blue/Let's Call It a Day Today	1991	—	2.00	4.00
❑ 73958	We're Strangers Again/If You Were the Friend	1991	—	2.00	4.00
—A-side with Randy Travis					

Albums

EPIC

Number	Title (A Side/B Side)	Yr	VG	VG+	NM
❑ EGP 503 [(2)]	The World of Tammy Wynette	1970	6.25	12.50	25.00
❑ LN 24305 [M]	Your Good Girl's Gonna Go Bad	1967	7.50	15.00	30.00
❑ BN 26305 [S]	Your Good Girl's Gonna Go Bad	1967	5.00	10.00	20.00
❑ BN 26353	Take Me to Your World	1968	5.00	10.00	20.00
❑ BN 26392	D-I-V-O-R-C-E	1968	5.00	10.00	20.00
❑ BN 26423	Inspiration	1969	5.00	10.00	20.00
❑ BN 26451	Stand By Your Man	1969	5.00	10.00	20.00
❑ BN 26486	Tammy's Greatest Hits	1969	5.00	10.00	20.00
❑ PE 26486	Tammy's Greatest Hits	198?	2.00	4.00	8.00
—Budget-line reissue					
❑ BN 26519	The Ways to Love a Man	1970	5.00	10.00	20.00
❑ BN 26549	Tammy's Touch	1970	5.00	10.00	20.00
❑ E 30212	The First Lady	1970	5.00	10.00	20.00
❑ E 30343	Christmas with Tammy	1970	5.00	10.00	20.00
❑ KEG 30358 [(2)]	The First Songs of the First Lady	1970	5.00	10.00	20.00
❑ E 30658	We Sure Can Love Each Other	1971	5.00	10.00	20.00
❑ EQ 30658 [Q]	We Sure Can Love Each Other	1972	7.50	15.00	30.00
❑ E 30733	Tammy's Greatest Hits, Volume II	1971	5.00	10.00	20.00
❑ PE 30733	Tammy's Greatest Hits, Volume II	198?	2.00	4.00	8.00
—Budget-line reissue					
❑ KE 31285	Bedtime Story	1972	3.75	7.50	15.00
❑ KE 31717	My Man	1972	3.75	7.50	15.00
❑ KE 31937	Kids Say the Darndest Things	1973	3.75	7.50	15.00
❑ KE 32745	Another Lonely Song	1974	3.00	6.00	12.00
❑ KE 33246	Woman to Woman	1975	3.00	6.00	12.00
❑ KE 33396	Tammy's Greatest Hits, Volume III	1975	3.00	6.00	12.00
❑ PE 33396	Tammy's Greatest Hits, Volume III	198?	2.00	4.00	8.00
—Budget-line reissue					
❑ KE 33582	I Still Believe in Fairy Tales	1975	3.00	6.00	12.00
❑ BG 33773 [(2)]	Stand By Your Man/Bedtime Story	1976	3.75	7.50	15.00
❑ PE 34075	'Til I Can Make It on My Own	1976	3.00	6.00	12.00
❑ PE 34289	You and Me	1976	3.00	6.00	12.00
❑ PE 34694	Let's Get Together One Last Time	1977	3.00	6.00	12.00
❑ KE 35044	One of a Kind	1977	3.00	6.00	12.00
❑ KE 35442	Womanhood	1978	3.00	6.00	12.00
❑ KE 35630	Tammy's Greatest Hits, Volume IV	1978	3.00	6.00	12.00
❑ KE 36013	Just Tammy	1979	3.00	6.00	12.00
❑ JE 36485	Only Lonely Sometimes	1980	2.50	5.00	10.00
❑ FE 37104	You Brought Me Back	1981	2.50	5.00	10.00
❑ FE 37344	Encore	1981	2.50	5.00	10.00
❑ PE 37344	Encore	198?	2.00	4.00	8.00
—Budget-line reissue					
❑ FE 37980	Soft Touch	1982	2.50	5.00	10.00
❑ FE 38312	Biggest Hits	1984	2.50	5.00	10.00
❑ FE 38372	Good Love and Heartbreak	1983	2.50	5.00	10.00
❑ FE 38744	Even the Strong Get Lonely	1983	2.50	5.00	10.00
❑ FE 39971	Sometimes When We Touch	1985	2.50	5.00	10.00
❑ EG 40625 [(2)]	Anniversary: 20 Years of Hits	1987	3.75	7.50	15.00
❑ FE 40832	Higher Ground	1987	2.50	5.00	10.00
❑ FE 44498	Next to You	1989	3.00	6.00	12.00

HARMONY

Number	Title (A Side/B Side)	Yr	VG	VG+	NM
❑ KH 30096	Send Me No Roses	1970	3.00	6.00	12.00
❑ KH 30914	Just a Matter of Time	1971	3.00	6.00	12.00

PAIR

Number	Title (A Side/B Side)	Yr	VG	VG+	NM
❑ PDL2-1073 [(2)]	From the Bottom of My Heart	1986	3.00	6.00	12.00

WYNONNA

See WYNONNA JUDD.

WYNTERS, GAIL

Today a jazz singer, she began her career in a failed attempt to become a country star.

45s

HICKORY

Number	Title (A Side/B Side)	Yr	VG	VG+	NM
❑ 1453	Snap Your Fingers/Find Myself a New Love	1967	2.50	5.00	10.00
❑ 1461	Have a Good Time/You've Got the Power	1967	2.50	5.00	10.00
❑ 1478	My Man/You Don't Have to Be in Love	1967	2.50	5.00	10.00
❑ 1520	When I Stop Dreaming/You Don't Even Know the Meaning of the Word	1968	2.00	4.00	8.00
❑ 1530	Crawling Back/It's Daytime	1968	2.00	4.00	8.00
❑ 1548	I Like Your Kind of Love/Who Am I	1969	2.00	4.00	8.00
❑ 1591	Help Me Make it Through the Night/Rainbow Sign	1971	2.00	4.00	8.00
❑ 1613	Snap Your Fingers/Going Out of My Head	1971	2.00	4.00	8.00
❑ 1625	I'll Sing for You/Young Tears Don't Fall Forever	1972	2.00	4.00	8.00
❑ 1644	Basic Blue/Bring the Boys Around	1972	2.00	4.00	8.00

RCA

Number	Title (A Side/B Side)	Yr	VG	VG+	NM
❑ PB-10973	Gonna Love You, Love You, and Love You Some More/Remember	1977	—	2.50	5.00

Albums

HICKORY

Number	Title (A Side/B Side)	Yr	VG	VG+	NM
❑ LPM-138 [M]	A Girl for All Seasons	1967	5.00	10.00	20.00
❑ LPS-138 [S]	A Girl for All Seasons	1967	3.75	7.50	15.00

RCA VICTOR

Number	Title (A Side/B Side)	Yr	VG	VG+	NM
❑ APL1-2285	Let the Lady Sing	1977	5.00	10.00	20.00

WYRICK, BARBARA

45s

MELODYLAND

Number	Title (A Side/B Side)	Yr	VG	VG+	NM
❑ 6010	Baby I Love You Too Much/You've Been Doing Wrong for So Long	1975	—	2.50	5.00
❑ 6023	Crazy Love/Pity Little Billy Jo	1975	—	2.50	5.00

WYRICK, JIM, AND UNION GOLD

45s

NSD

Number	Title (A Side/B Side)	Yr	VG	VG+	NM
❑ 157	The Memory/First to Be the Last	1983	—	2.50	5.00

Y

YANKOVIC, FRANKIE

The king of "Cleveland-style" polka had three singles make the country charts; the first and third of these made the top 10!

Selected 78s

COLUMBIA

Number	Title (A Side/B Side)	Yr	VG	VG+	NM
❑ 12359	Just Because/A Night in May	1948	3.00	6.00	12.00
❑ 12381	The Iron Range/Linda's Lullaby	1948	3.00	6.00	12.00
❑ 12394	Blue Skirt Waltz/Charlie Was a Boxer	1949	3.00	6.00	12.00

YARBROUGH, BOB

45s

CINNAMON

Number	Title (A Side/B Side)	Yr	VG	VG+	NM
❑ 788	Steady As She Goes/Country Music	1974	—	3.50	7.00

MUSIC MILL

Number	Title (A Side/B Side)	Yr	VG	VG+	NM
❑ 186	50 Ways to Leave Your Lover/You Only Look Me Up When You're Down	1976	—	3.00	6.00

SUGAR HILL

Number	Title (A Side/B Side)	Yr	VG	VG+	NM
❑ 013	You're Just More a Woman/In the Palm of My Hand	1971	2.00	4.00	8.00
❑ 016	Cause God Made You Mine/(B-side unknown)	1971	2.00	4.00	8.00
❑ 018	When's the Last Time/(B-side unknown)	1971	2.00	4.00	8.00
❑ 021	Rose, You've Left a Thorn in My Heart/My Woman Satisfies	1972	2.00	4.00	8.00
❑ 023	Eight O'Clock Saturday Night/You Make My Day	1972	2.00	4.00	8.00
❑ 024	Before I Knew Love Was Here/Eight O'Clock Saturday Night	1972	2.00	4.00	8.00

Albums

SUGAR HILL

Number	Title (A Side/B Side)	Yr	VG	VG+	NM
❑ 002	Because You're Just More a Woman	1971	3.75	7.50	15.00

YATES, BILLY

45s

ALMO SOUNDS

Number	Title (A Side/B Side)	Yr	VG	VG+	NM
❑ 89010	I Smell Smoke/Goodbye Makes the Saddest Sound	1997	—	2.00	4.00
❑ 89013	When the Walls Come Tumblin' Down/Broken Hearted Me	1997	—	2.00	4.00

YATES, JENNY

45s

MERCURY

Number	Title (A Side/B Side)	Yr	VG	VG+	NM
❑ 884973-7	Let It Be Love/Everybody Has Got Somebody	1986	—	2.00	4.00
❑ 888428-7	A Whole Month of Sundays/Holding Out for Love	1987	—	—	3.00

YATES, LORI

45s

COLUMBIA

Number	Title (A Side/B Side)	Yr	VG	VG+	NM
❑ 38-08055	Scene of the Crime/Cowboy	1988	—	—	3.00
❑ 38-68596	Promises, Promises/Heart in a Suitcase	1989	—	—	3.00

Albums

COLUMBIA

Number	Title (A Side/B Side)	Yr	VG	VG+	NM
❑ FC 44278	Can't Stop the Girl	1988	2.00	4.00	8.00

YEARWOOD, TRISHA

45s

COLLECTABLES

Number	Title (A Side/B Side)	Yr	VG	VG+	NM
❑ 90041	She's in Love with the Boy/Victim of the Game	1995	—	—	3.00

MCA

Number	Title (A Side/B Side)	Yr	VG	VG+	NM
❑ 54076	She's in Love with the Boy/Victim of the Game	1991	2.00	4.00	8.00
❑ 54172	Like We Never Had a Broken Heart/The Whisper of Your Heart	1991	—	—	3.00
❑ 54270	That's What I Like About You/When Goodbye Was a Word	1991	—	—	3.00
❑ 54362	The Woman Before Me/You Done Me Wrong (And That Ain't Right)	1992	—	—	3.00
❑ 54414	Wrong Side of Memphis/Lonesome Dove	1992	—	—	3.00
❑ 54495	Walkaway Joe/You Don't Have to Move That Mountain	1992	—	—	3.00
❑ 54600	You Say You Will/Hearts in Armor	1993	—	—	3.00
❑ 54670	Down on My Knees/For Reasons I've Forgotten	1993	—	—	3.00
❑ 54734	The Song Remembers When/Oh Lonesome You	1993	—	—	3.00
❑ 54786	Better Your Heart Than Mine/Promises to Keep	1994	—	—	3.00
❑ 54836	I Fall to Pieces/(Instrumental)	1994	—	—	3.00
—With Aaron Neville					
❑ 54898	XXX's and OOO's (An American Girl)/One in a Row	1994	—	—	3.00
❑ 54940	It Wasn't His Child/Reindeer Boogie	1994	—	2.00	4.00
❑ 54973	Thinkin' About You/Fairytale	1995	—	—	3.00
❑ 55025	You Can Sleep While I Drive/Two Days from Knowing	1995	—	—	3.00
❑ 55078	I Wanna Go Too Far/The Restless Kind	1995	—	—	3.00
❑ 55141	On a Bus to St. Cloud/O Mexico	1995	—	—	3.00
❑ 55211	Believe Me Baby (I Lied)/Little Hercules	1996	—	—	3.00
❑ 55250	Everybody Knows/A Love Is Forever	1996	—	—	3.00
❑ 55308	I Need You/Hello, I'm Gone	1997	—	—	3.00
❑ 72015	How Do I Live (4:25)/How Do I Live (4:02)	1997	—	2.50	5.00
❑ 72021	In Another's Eyes/I Want to Live Again	1997	—	—	3.00
—A-side with Garth Brooks					
❑ 72034	A Perfect Love/I Need You	1998	—	—	3.00
❑ 72048	There Goes My Baby/One More Chance	1998	—	—	3.00

MCA NASHVILLE

Number	Title (A Side/B Side)	Yr	VG	VG+	NM
❑ 72070	Where Your Road Leads/Bring Me All Your Lovin'	1998	—	2.50	5.00
—A-side with Garth Brooks					
❑ 72082	Powerful Thing/Never Let You Go Again	1998	—	—	3.00
❑ 72089	I'll Still Love You More/Wouldn't Any Woman	1999	—	—	3.00
❑ 088 172146 7	Real Live Woman/I'm Still Alive	2000	—	—	3.00
❑ 088 172170 7	Where Are You Now/Some Days	2000	—	—	3.00

Albums

MCA

Number	Title (A Side/B Side)	Yr	VG	VG+	NM
❑ 1P-8161	Trisha Yearwood	1991	6.25	12.50	25.00
—Vinyl edition available only from Columbia House					

YOAKAM, DWIGHT

12-Inch Singles

REPRISE

Number	Title (A Side/B Side)	Yr	VG	VG+	NM
❑ PRO-A-3799 [DJ]	Long White Cadillac (Edit)/Long White Cadillac (FM)	1989	2.00	4.00	8.00

45s

EPIC

Number	Title (A Side/B Side)	Yr	VG	VG+	NM
❑ 34-74753	Suspicious Minds/Burning Love	1992	—	2.00	4.00
—B-side by Travis Tritt					

REPRISE

Number	Title (A Side/B Side)	Yr	VG	VG+	NM
❑ 7-16938	Crazy Little Thing Called Love/Thinking About Leaving	1999	—	—	3.00
❑ 7-17143	These Arms/That's Okay	1998	—	—	3.00
❑ 7-17273	Silver Bells/Come On Christmas	1997	—	—	3.00
❑ 7-17275	Santa Can't Stay/The Christmas Song (Chestnuts Roasting on an Open Fire)	1997	—	—	3.00
❑ 7-17734	Nothing/Gone (That'll Be Me)	1995	—	—	3.00
❑ 7-18239	Try Not to Look So Pretty/Wild Ride	1994	—	2.00	4.00
❑ 7-18341	Fast As You/Home for Sale	1993	—	2.50	5.00
❑ 7-18528	A Thousand Miles from Nowhere/Ain't That Lonely Yet	1993	—	2.00	4.00
❑ 7-18590	Ain't That Lonely Yet/Lonesome Roads	1993	—	2.00	4.00
❑ 7-18846	Send a Message to My Heart/Takes a Lot to Rock You	1992	—	2.00	4.00
—A-side with Patti Loveless					
❑ 7-18966	The Heart That You Own/Dangerous Man	1992	—	2.00	4.00
❑ 7-19148	It Only Hurts When I Cry/Let's Work Together	1991	—	2.50	5.00
❑ 7-19256	Nothing's Changed Here/Sad, Sad Music	1991	—	2.00	4.00
❑ 7-19405	You're the One/If There Was a Way	1991	—	2.00	4.00
❑ 7-19543	Turn It On, Turn It Up, Turn Me Loose/Since I Started Drinkin' Again	1990	—	2.00	4.00
❑ 7-21868	I Sang Dixie/Long White Cadillac	1989	—	—	3.00
—"Back to Back Hits" reissue					
❑ 7-21898	Streets of Bakersfield/Please Please Baby	198?	—	—	3.00
—"Back to Back Hits" reissue; A-side with Buck Owens					
❑ 7-21947	Little Sister/Little Ways	198?	—	—	3.00
—"Back to Back Hits" reissue					
❑ 7-21957	Honky Tonk Man/Guitars, Cadillacs	198?	—	—	3.00
—"Back to Back Hits" reissue					
❑ 7-22799	Long White Cadillac/Little Ways	1989	—	—	3.00
❑ 7-22799 [PS]	Long White Cadillac/Little Ways	1989	—	2.00	4.00
❑ 7-22944	Buenas Noches from a Lonely Room (She Wore Red Dresses)/What I Don't Know	1989	—	—	3.00
❑ 7-27567	I Got You/South of Cincinnati	1989	—	—	3.00
❑ 7-27715	I Sang Dixie/Floyd County	1988	—	—	3.00
❑ 7-27715 [PS]	I Sang Dixie/Floyd County	1988	—	2.00	4.00
❑ 7-27964	Streets of Bakersfield/One More Name	1988	—	2.50	5.00
—A-side with Buck Owens					
❑ 7-27964 [PS]	Streets of Bakersfield/One More Name	1988	—	2.50	5.00
—With Buck Owens					
❑ 7-27994	Always Late with Your Kisses/1,000 Miles	1988	—	—	3.00
❑ 7-27994 [PS]	Always Late with Your Kisses/1,000 Miles	1988	—	2.00	4.00
❑ 7-28156	Santa Claus Is Back in Town/Christmas Eve With The Babylonian Cowboys: Jingle Bells	1987	—	2.50	5.00
❑ 7-28156 [PS]	Santa Claus Is Back in Town/Christmas Eve With The Babylonian Cowboys: Jingle Bells	1987	—	2.50	5.00
❑ 7-28174	Please, Please Baby/Throughout All Time	1987	—	—	3.00
❑ 7-28310	Little Ways/Readin', Rightin', Rt. 23	1987	—	—	3.00
❑ 7-28310 [PS]	Little Ways/Readin', Rightin', Rt. 23	1987	—	2.00	4.00
❑ 7-28432	Little Sister/This Drinkin' Will Kill Me	1987	—	—	3.00
❑ 7-28432 [PS]	Little Sister/This Drinkin' Will Kill Me	1987	—	2.00	4.00
❑ 7-28565	It Won't Hurt/Bury Me (Duet with Maria McKee)	1986	—	—	3.00
❑ 7-28688	Guitars, Cadillacs/I'll Be Gone	1986	—	—	3.00
❑ 7-28688 [PS]	Guitars, Cadillacs/I'll Be Gone	1986	2.00	4.00	8.00
❑ 7-28793	Honky Tonk Man/Miner's Prayer	1986	—	—	3.00

WARNER BROS.

Number	Title (A Side/B Side)	Yr	VG	VG+	NM
❑ PRO-S-2424 [DJ]	This Drinkin' Will Kill Me (Live)/Miner's Prayer (Live)	1985	3.00	6.00	12.00

Albums

OAK

Number	Title (A Side/B Side)	Yr	VG	VG+	NM
❑ OR 2356 [EP]	Guitars, Cadillacs, Etc., Etc.	1984	200.00	400.00	800.00
—Six-song EP; cover is in black and white; the song "Guitars, Cadillacs" does NOT appear on this release					

REPRISE

Number	Title (A Side/B Side)	Yr	VG	VG+	NM
❑ 25372	Guitars, Cadillacs, Etc., Etc.	1986	2.50	5.00	10.00
—LP has 10 songs rather than the six on the Oak EP; front cover has color on it					
❑ W1-25372	Guitars, Cadillacs, Etc., Etc.	1986	3.00	6.00	12.00
—Columbia House edition					
❑ 25567	Hillbilly Deluxe	1987	2.50	5.00	10.00
❑ W1-25567	Hillbilly Deluxe	1987	3.00	6.00	12.00
—Columbia House edition					
❑ 25749	Buenas Noches from a Lonely Room	1988	2.50	5.00	10.00

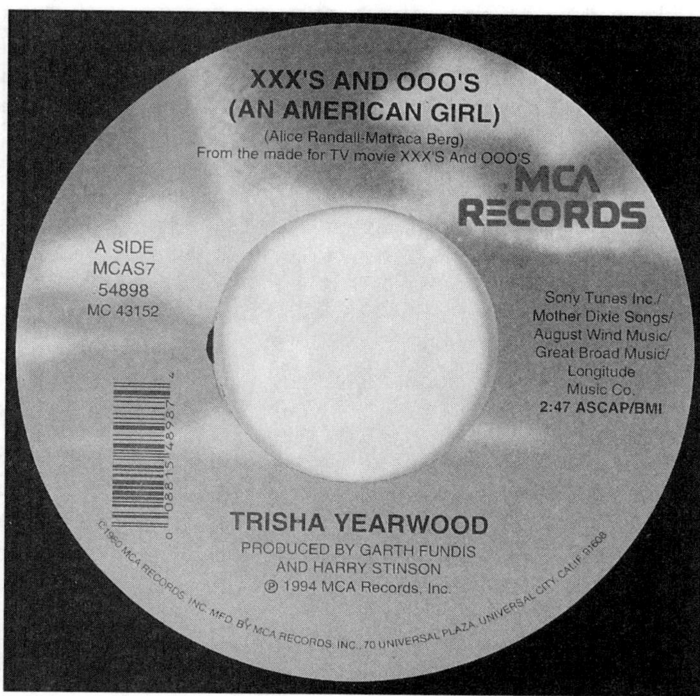

In 1991, Trisha Yearwood's "She's in Love with the Boy" became the first debut single by a female singer to hit No. 1 since Connie Smith's "Once a Day" did so in 1964, and she's never looked back since. (Top left) Her self-titled debut album made a brief appearance on vinyl through Columbia House; otherwise, all her albums have been on cassette and CD only. (Top right) After her first single topped the charts, she didn't return to the top until "XXX's and OOO's (An American Girl)" turned the trick in 1994. At the time it was a hit, it was only available as a single. (Bottom left) Yearwood's version of "How Do I Live," the version used in the movie *Con Air*, was more popular than LeAnn Rimes' version on country radio, as it got to No. 2 in 1997. (Bottom right) Here's the second of two released duets with Garth Brooks, "Where Your Road Leads." This one got to No. 18 in 1998.

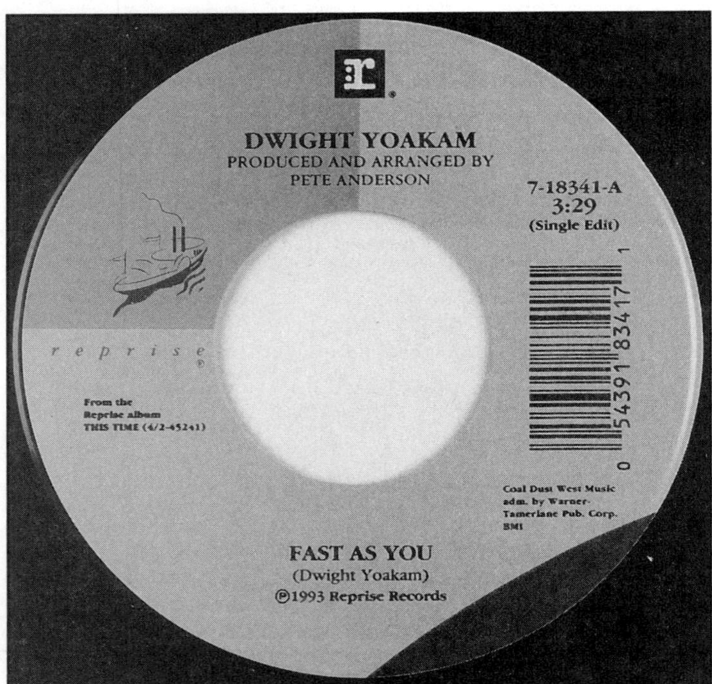

One of the foremost of the "New Traditionalist" acts of the late 1980s, Dwight Yoakam continues to carry that mantle. His mainstream airplay has largely disappeared, but his albums remain critical favorites. (Top left) Yoakam had two No. 1 singles back-to-back in 1988-89. The second of these, and the first by him alone, was "I Sang Dixie." (Top right) The vinyl version of *If There Was a Way*, issued by the BMG Music Service in 1991, had 12 songs on it, while the CD version had 14. That was still an improvement over the average country album of the time, most of which had 10 songs. (Bottom left) Channeling the spirit of Roy Orbison, Yoakam took "Fast as You" to No. 2 in 1993. It was the third consecutive runner-up single from his CD *This Time.* (Bottom right) In 1999, Yoakam recorded the old Queen track "Crazy Little Thing Called Love" for a TV commercial. The full-length version, issued on his second greatest-hits collection, made it to the top 20 of the country charts.

Number	Title (A Side/B Side)	Yr	VG	VG+	NM
❑ W1-25749	Buenas Noches from a Lonely Room	1988	3.00	6.00	12.00
—Columbia House edition					
❑ 25989	Just Lookin' for a Hit	1989	2.50	5.00	10.00
❑ W1-25989	Just Lookin' for a Hit	1989	3.00	6.00	12.00
—Columbia House edition					
❑ R 100009	Buenas Noches from a Lonely Room	1988	3.00	6.00	12.00
—BMG Direct Marketing edition					
❑ R 150223	Guitars, Cadillacs, Etc., Etc.	1986	3.00	6.00	12.00
—RCA Music Service edition					
❑ R 164146	Hillbilly Deluxe	1987	3.00	6.00	12.00
—BMG Direct Marketing edition					
❑ R 164310	If There Was a Way	1990	5.00	10.00	20.00
—BMG Direct Marketing edition; only U.S. vinyl version					
❑ R 174052	Just Lookin' for a Hit	1989	3.00	6.00	12.00
—BMG Direct Marketing edition					

YOUNG, COLE

45s

EVERGREEN

Number	Title (A Side/B Side)	Yr	VG	VG+	NM
❑ 1005	I'd Keep My Heart in Line/(B-side unknown)	1983	—	2.50	5.00
❑ 1008	Just Give Me One More Night/I'd Keep My Heart in Line	1983	—	2.50	5.00

YOUNG, DONNY

See JOHNNY PAYCHECK.

YOUNG, FARON

Also see MARGIE SINGLETON.

45s

CAPITOL

Number	Title (A Side/B Side)	Yr	VG	VG+	NM
❑ F2039	Tattle Tale Tears/Have I Waited Too Long	1952	10.00	20.00	40.00
❑ F2133	Foolish Pride/I Knew You When	1952	7.50	15.00	30.00
❑ F2171	Saving My Tears/What Can I Do with My Sorrow	1952	7.50	15.00	30.00
❑ F2299	Goin' Steady/Just Out of Reach (Of My Two Open Arms)	1952	6.25	12.50	25.00
❑ F2461	I Can't Wait (For the Sun to Go Down)/What's the Use to Love You	1953	6.25	12.50	25.00
❑ F2570	That's What I'd Do for You/Baby My Heart	1953	6.25	12.50	25.00
❑ F2629	You're an Angel on My Christmas Tree/I'm Gonna Tell Santa Claus on You	1953	7.50	15.00	30.00
❑ F2690	Just Married/I Hardly Knew It Was You	1953	6.25	12.50	25.00
❑ F2780	They Made Me Fall in Love with You/You're Right	1954	6.25	12.50	25.00
❑ F2859	A Place for Girls Like You/In the Chapel in the Moonlight	1954	6.25	12.50	25.00
❑ F2953	If You Ain't Lovin' (You Ain't Livin')/If That's the Fashion	1954	6.25	12.50	25.00
❑ F3056	Live Fast, Love Hard, Die Young/Forgive Me, Dear	1955	6.25	12.50	25.00
❑ F3107	Where Could I Go/God Bless God	1955	6.25	12.50	25.00
❑ F3169	All Right/Go Back You Fool	1955	6.25	12.50	25.00
❑ F3258	It's a Great Life (If You Don't Weaken)/For the Love of a Woman Like You	1955	6.25	12.50	25.00
❑ F3369	You're Still Mine/I've Got Five Dollars and It's Saturday Night	1956	5.00	10.00	20.00
❑ F3443	Sweet Dreams/Until I Met You	1956	5.00	10.00	20.00
❑ F3549	Turn Her Down/I'll Be Satisfied with Love	1956	5.00	10.00	20.00
❑ F3611	I Miss You Already (And You're Not Even Gone)/I'm Gonna Live Some Before I Die	1957	5.00	10.00	20.00
❑ F3696	The Shrine of St. Cecilia/He Was There	1957	5.00	10.00	20.00
❑ F3753	Love Has Finally Come My Way/Moonlight Mountain	1957	5.00	10.00	20.00
❑ F3805	Vacation's Over/Honey Stop	1957	5.00	10.00	20.00
❑ F3855	The Locket/Snowball	1957	5.00	10.00	20.00
❑ F3898	Rosalie/I Can't Dance	1958	5.00	10.00	20.00
❑ F3982	Alone with You/Every Time I'm Kissing You	1958	5.00	10.00	20.00
❑ F4050	That's the Way I Feel/I Hate Myself	1958	5.00	10.00	20.00
❑ F4113	A Long Time Ago/Last Night at a Party	1959	5.00	10.00	20.00
❑ F4164	That's the Way It's Gotta Be/We're Talking It Over	1959	5.00	10.00	20.00
❑ F4233	Country Girl/I Hear You Talkin'	1959	5.00	10.00	20.00
❑ F4291	Riverboat/Face to the Wall	1959	5.00	10.00	20.00
❑ 4351	Your Old Used to Be/I'll Be Alright (In the Morning)	1960	3.75	7.50	15.00
❑ 4410	There's Not Any Like You Left/is She All You Thought She'd Be	1960	3.75	7.50	15.00
❑ 4463	Forget the Past/A World So Full of Love	1960	3.75	7.50	15.00
❑ 4533	Hello Walls/Congratulations	1961	3.75	7.50	15.00
❑ 4616	Backtrack/I Can't Find the Time	1961	3.75	7.50	15.00
❑ 4616 [PS]	Backtrack/I Can't Find the Time	1961	7.50	15.00	30.00
❑ 4696	Three Days/I Let It Slip Away	1962	3.75	7.50	15.00
❑ 4696 [PS]	Three Days/I Let It Slip Away	1962	7.50	15.00	30.00
❑ 4754	The Comeback/Over Lonely and Under Kissed	1962	3.75	7.50	15.00
❑ 4868	Down by the River/Safely in Love Again	1962	3.75	7.50	15.00

MCA

Number	Title (A Side/B Side)	Yr	VG	VG+	NM
❑ 41004	The Great Chicago Fire/Old Songs	1979	—	2.50	5.00
❑ 41046	That Over Thirty Look/Second Hand Emotion	1979	—	2.00	4.00
❑ 41177	(If I'd Only Known) It Was the Last Time/Free and Easy	1980	—	2.00	4.00
❑ 41292	Tearjoint/I May Lose You Tomorrow	1980	—	2.00	4.00
❑ 51088	Until the Bitter End/Motel with No Phone	1981	—	2.00	4.00
❑ 51176	Pull Up a Pillow/Ain't Your Memory Got No Pride at All	1981	—	2.00	4.00

MERCURY

Number	Title (A Side/B Side)	Yr	VG	VG+	NM
❑ 55019	Loving Here and Living There and Lying In Between/City Lights	1978	—	3.00	6.00
❑ 72085	The Yellow Bandana/How Much I Must Have Loved You	1963	3.00	6.00	12.00
❑ 72114	Nightmare/I've Come to Say Goodbye	1963	3.00	6.00	12.00
❑ 72167	We've Got Something in Common/Think About the Old Days	1963	3.00	6.00	12.00
❑ 72201	You'll Drive Me Back (Into Her Arms Again)/What Will I Tell My Darling	1963	3.00	6.00	12.00
❑ 72271	Rhinestones/Old Courthouse	1964	3.00	6.00	12.00
❑ 72313	My Friend on the Right/The World's Greatest Love	1964	3.00	6.00	12.00
❑ 72375	Walk Tall/Heartbreak Valley	1965	2.50	5.00	10.00
❑ 72375	Walk Tall/The Weakness of a Man	1965	2.50	5.00	10.00
❑ 72440	Nothing Left to Lose/Dingaka (The Witch Doctor)	1965	2.50	5.00	10.00
❑ 72490	My Dreams/You Had a Call	1965	2.50	5.00	10.00
❑ 72576	Sweet Love and Happiness/You Don't Treat Me Right	1966	2.50	5.00	10.00
❑ 72617	Unmitigated Gall/Some of Your Memories (Hurt Me All of the Time)	1966	2.50	5.00	10.00
❑ 72656	I Guess I Had Too Much to Dream Last Night/I Just Don't Know How to Say No	1967	2.50	5.00	10.00
❑ 72728	Wonderful World of Women/All I Can Stand	1967	2.50	5.00	10.00
❑ 72774	She Went a Little Bit Farther/Stay, Love	1968	2.00	4.00	8.00
❑ 72774 [PS]	She Went a Little Bit Farther/Stay, Love	1968	3.75	7.50	15.00
❑ 72827	I Just Came to Get My Baby/Missing You Is All I Did Today	1968	2.00	4.00	8.00
❑ 72889	I've Got Precious Memories/You Stayed Just Long Enough	1969	2.00	4.00	8.00
❑ 72936	Wine Me Up/That's Where My Baby Feels at Home	1969	2.00	4.00	8.00
❑ 72983	Your Time's Comin'/Painted Girls and Wine	1969	2.00	4.00	8.00
❑ 73018	Occasional Wife/The Guns of Johnny Rondo	1970	—	3.50	7.00
❑ 73065	If I Ever Fall in Love (With a Honky Tonk Girl)/A Bunch of Young Ideas	1970	—	3.50	7.00
❑ 73112	Goin' Steady/That's My Way	1970	—	3.50	7.00
❑ 73191	Step Aside/Seems Like I'm Always Leaving	1971	—	3.50	7.00
❑ 73220	Leavin' and Sayin' Goodbye/She Was the Color of Love	1971	—	3.50	7.00
❑ 73250	It's Four in the Morning/It's Not the Miles	1971	—	3.50	7.00
❑ 73308	This Little Girl of Mine/It Hurts So Good	1972	—	3.50	7.00
❑ 73337	A Woman's Touch/It's Four in the Morning	1972	—	3.50	7.00
❑ 73359	She Fights That Lovin' Feeling/I'm in Love with Everything	1973	—	3.50	7.00
❑ 73403	Just What I Had in Mind/All at Once It's Forever	1973	—	3.50	7.00
❑ 73464	Some Kind of a Woman/Again Today	1974	—	3.50	7.00
❑ 73500	The Wrong in Loving You/Almost Dawn in Denver	1974	—	3.50	7.00
❑ 73633	Another You/God's Been Good to Me	1974	—	3.00	6.00
❑ 73692	Here I Am in Dallas/Too Much of Not Enough of You	1975	—	3.00	6.00
❑ 73731	Feel Again/Some Old Rainy Mornin'	1975	—	3.00	6.00
❑ 73782	I'd Just Be Fool Enough/What You See Is What You Get	1976	—	3.00	6.00
❑ 73847	(The Worst You Ever Gave Me Was) The Best I Ever Had/You Get the Feelin'	1976	—	3.00	6.00
❑ 73925	Crutches/The Last Goodbye	1977	—	3.00	6.00

STEP ONE

Number	Title (A Side/B Side)	Yr	VG	VG+	NM
❑ 390	Stop and Take the Time/Misty Morning Rain	1988	—	2.50	5.00
❑ 397	Here's to You/You're Just Another Beer Drinking Song	1989	—	2.50	5.00
❑ 408	After the Lovin'/Let Me Walk	1989	—	2.50	5.00
❑ 414	Baxter Hill/A Waste of Love	1990	—	2.50	5.00
❑ 429	Just an Ol' Heartache/(B-side unknown)	1991	—	2.50	5.00
❑ 436	Memories That Last/A Whole Lot of You	1991	—	2.50	5.00
—With Ray Price					
❑ 440	Too Big to Fight/Now She's in Paris	1992	—	2.50	5.00
❑ 455	White Christmas/The Christmas Song	1992	—	3.00	6.00
—Red vinyl					

7-Inch Extended Plays

CAPITOL

Number	Title (A Side/B Side)	Yr	VG	VG+	NM
❑ EAP 1-450	Goin' Steady/Tattle Tale Tears//Saving My Tears (For Tomorrow)/I Knew You When	1954	7.50	15.00	30.00
❑ EAP 1-450 [PS]	Goin' Steady with Faron Young	1954	7.50	15.00	30.00
❑ EAP 1-611	(contents unknown)	1956	7.50	15.00	30.00
❑ EAP 1-611 [PS]	Faron Young	1956	7.50	15.00	30.00
❑ EAP 1-778	Sweethearts or Strangers/Your Cheatin' Heart//Shame on You/I Can't Tell My Heart	1957	6.25	12.50	25.00
❑ EAP 1-778 [PS]	Sweethearts or Strangers, Part 1	1957	6.25	12.50	25.00
❑ EAP 2-778	You Call Everybody Darlin'/Better Things Than These//Worried Mind/I'll Be Yours	1957	6.25	12.50	25.00
❑ EAP 2-778 [PS]	Sweethearts or Strangers, Part 2	1957	6.25	12.50	25.00
❑ EAP 3-778	I'm a Poor Boy/I Can't Help It//You Are My Sunshine/That's What It's Like to Be Lonesome	1957	6.25	12.50	25.00
❑ EAP 3-778 [PS]	Sweethearts or Strangers, Part 3	1957	6.25	12.50	25.00
❑ EAP 1-869	(contents unknown)	1957	6.25	12.50	25.00
❑ EAP 1-869 [PS]	The Shrine of St. Cecilia	1957	6.25	12.50	25.00
❑ EAP 1-921	(contents unknown)	1958	5.00	10.00	20.00
❑ EAP 1-921 [PS]	Country Music Holiday, Part 1	1958	5.00	10.00	20.00
❑ EAP 2-921	(contents unknown)	1958	5.00	10.00	20.00
❑ EAP 2-921 [PS]	Country Music Holiday, Part 2	1958	5.00	10.00	20.00
❑ EAP 3-921	(contents unknown)	1958	5.00	10.00	20.00
❑ EAP 3-921 [PS]	Country Music Holiday, Part 3	1958	5.00	10.00	20.00
❑ EAP 1-1096	(contents unknown)	1959	5.00	10.00	20.00
❑ EAP 1-1096 [PS]	This Is Faron Young, Part 1	1959	5.00	10.00	20.00
❑ EAP 2-1096	(contents unknown)	1959	5.00	10.00	20.00
❑ EAP 2-1096 [PS]	This Is Faron Young, Part 2	1959	5.00	10.00	20.00
❑ EAP 3-1096	(contents unknown)	1959	5.00	10.00	20.00
❑ EAP 3-1096 [PS]	This Is Faron Young, Part 3	1959	5.00	10.00	20.00
❑ EAP 1-1185	(contents unknown)	1959	5.00	10.00	20.00
❑ EAP 1-1185 [PS]	My Garden of Prayer, Part 1	1959	5.00	10.00	20.00

Number	Title (A Side/B Side)	Yr	VG	VG+	NM
❑ EAP 2-1185	(contents unknown)	1959	5.00	10.00	20.00
❑ EAP 2-1185 [PS]	My Garden of Prayer, Part 2	1959	5.00	10.00	20.00
❑ EAP 3-1185	(contents unknown)	1959	5.00	10.00	20.00
❑ EAP 3-1185 [PS]	My Garden of Prayer, Part 3	1959	5.00	10.00	20.00
❑ EAP 1-1245	(contents unknown)	1959	5.00	10.00	20.00
❑ EAP 1-1245 [PS]	Talk About Hits, Part 1	1959	5.00	10.00	20.00
❑ EAP 2-1245	(contents unknown)	1959	5.00	10.00	20.00
❑ EAP 2-1245 [PS]	Talk About Hits, Part 2	1959	5.00	10.00	20.00
❑ EAP 3-1245	(contents unknown)	1959	5.00	10.00	20.00
❑ EAP 3-1245 [PS]	Talk About Hits, Part 3	1959	5.00	10.00	20.00
Albums					
ALLEGIANCE					
❑ AV-5008	The Sheriff	198?	2.50	5.00	10.00
CAPITOL					
❑ T 778 [M]	Sweethearts or Strangers	1957	15.00	30.00	60.00
—Turquoise or gray label					
❑ T 778 [M]	Sweethearts or Strangers	1959	6.25	12.50	25.00
—Black colorband label, logo at left					
❑ T 1004 [M]	The Object of My Affection	1958	12.50	25.00	50.00
❑ T 1096 [M]	This Is Faron Young	1959	12.50	25.00	50.00
❑ T 1185 [M]	My Garden of Prayer	1959	10.00	20.00	40.00
❑ ST 1245 [S]	Talk About Hits	1959	10.00	20.00	40.00
❑ T 1245 [M]	Talk About Hits	1959	7.50	15.00	30.00
❑ ST 1450 [S]	The Best of Faron Young	1960	10.00	20.00	40.00
❑ T 1450 [M]	The Best of Faron Young	1960	7.50	15.00	30.00
❑ ST 1528 [S]	Hello Walls	1961	10.00	20.00	40.00
❑ T 1528 [M]	Hello Walls	1961	7.50	15.00	30.00
❑ ST 1634 [S]	The Young Approach	1961	10.00	20.00	40.00
❑ T 1634 [M]	The Young Approach	1961	7.50	15.00	30.00
❑ DT 1876 [P]	The All-Time Great Hits of Faron Young	1963	5.00	10.00	20.00
❑ T 1876 [M]	The All-Time Great Hits of Faron Young	1963	6.25	12.50	25.00
❑ DT 2037 [R]	Faron Young's Memory Lane	1964	5.00	10.00	20.00
❑ T 2037 [M]	Faron Young's Memory Lane	1964	6.25	12.50	25.00
❑ ST 2307 [S]	Falling in Love	1965	6.25	12.50	25.00
❑ T 2307 [M]	Falling in Love	1965	5.00	10.00	20.00
❑ DT 2536 [R]	If You Ain't Lovin' You Ain't Livin'	1966	5.00	10.00	20.00
❑ T 2536 [M]	If You Ain't Lovin' You Ain't Livin'	1966	6.25	12.50	25.00
HILLTOP					
❑ JM-6037 [M]	Faron Young	1966	3.75	7.50	15.00
❑ JS-6037 [S]	Faron Young	1966	3.00	6.00	12.00
❑ JS-6073	I'll Be Yours	1968	3.00	6.00	12.00
MARY CARTER					
❑ MC 1000 [M]	Faron Young Sings on Stage for Mary Carter Paints	196?	15.00	30.00	60.00
—Promotional item for sponsor of The Faron Young Show					
MCA					
❑ 757	Chapter Two	198?	2.00	4.00	8.00
—Budget-line reissue of 3092					
❑ 3092	Chapter Two	1979	3.00	6.00	12.00
❑ 3212	Free and Easy	1980	3.00	6.00	12.00
MERCURY					
❑ SRM-1-674	Just What I Had in Mind	1973	3.75	7.50	15.00
❑ SRM-1-698	Faron Young Sings "Some Kind of a Woman"	1974	3.75	7.50	15.00
❑ SRM-1-1016	A Man and His Music	1974	3.00	6.00	12.00
❑ SRM-1-1075	I'd Just Be Fool Enough	1976	3.00	6.00	12.00
❑ SRM-1-1130	The Best of Faron Young, Vol. 2	1977	3.00	6.00	12.00
❑ SRM-1-5005	Young Feelin'	1978	3.00	6.00	12.00
❑ MG 20785 [M]	This Is Faron	1963	5.00	10.00	20.00
❑ MG 20840 [M]	Faron Young Aims at the West	1963	5.00	10.00	20.00
❑ MG 20896 [M]	Story Songs for Country Folks	1964	5.00	10.00	20.00
❑ MG 20931 [M]	Country Dance Favorites	1964	5.00	10.00	20.00
❑ MG 20971 [M]	Story Songs of Mountains and Valleys	1965	5.00	10.00	20.00
❑ MG 21007 [M]	Pen and Paper	1965	5.00	10.00	20.00
❑ MG 21047 [M]	Faron Young's Greatest Hits	1965	5.00	10.00	20.00
❑ MG 21058 [M]	Faron Young Sings the Best of Jim Reeves	1966	5.00	10.00	20.00
❑ MG 21110 [M]	Unmitigated Gall	1967	6.25	12.50	25.00
❑ SR 60785 [S]	This Is Faron	1963	6.25	12.50	25.00
❑ SR 60840 [S]	Faron Young Aims at the West	1963	6.25	12.50	25.00
❑ SR 60896 [S]	Story Songs for Country Folks	1964	6.25	12.50	25.00
❑ SR 60931 [S]	Country Dance Favorites	1964	6.25	12.50	25.00
❑ SR 60971 [S]	Story Songs of Mountains and Valleys	1965	6.25	12.50	25.00
❑ SR 61007 [S]	Pen and Paper	1965	6.25	12.50	25.00
❑ SR 61047 [S]	Faron Young's Greatest Hits	1965	6.25	12.50	25.00
❑ SR 61058 [S]	Faron Young Sings the Best of Jim Reeves	1966	6.25	12.50	25.00
❑ SR 61110 [S]	Unmitigated Gall	1967	5.00	10.00	20.00
❑ SR 61143	Greatest Hits Vol. 2	1968	5.00	10.00	20.00
❑ SR 61174	Here's Faron Young	1968	5.00	10.00	20.00
❑ SR 61212	I've Got Precious Memories	1969	5.00	10.00	20.00
❑ SR 61241	Wine Me Up	1969	5.00	10.00	20.00
❑ SR 61267	The Best of Faron Young	1970	5.00	10.00	20.00
❑ SR 61275	Faron Young Sings "Occasional Wife" and "If I Ever Fall in Love with a Honky Tonk Girl"	1970	5.00	10.00	20.00
❑ SR 61337	Step Aside	1971	5.00	10.00	20.00
❑ SR 61354	Faron Young Sings "Leavin' and Sayin' Goodbye"	1971	3.75	7.50	15.00
❑ SR 61359	Evening	1972	5.00	10.00	20.00
—Original title?					
❑ SR 61359	It's Four in the Morning	1972	3.75	7.50	15.00
—Revised title to reflect the hit?					
❑ SR 61364	Faron Young Sings This Little Girl of Mine	1972	3.75	7.50	15.00
❑ SR 61376	This Time the Hurtin's on Me	1973	3.75	7.50	15.00
PICCADILLY					
❑ 3547	Hello Walls	198?	2.50	5.00	10.00
SEARS					
❑ SPS-124	Candy Kisses	1969	6.25	12.50	25.00

Number	Title (A Side/B Side)	Yr	VG	VG+	NM
SESAC					
❑ (# unknown) [DJ]	Church Songs	196?	20.00	40.00	80.00
TOWER					
❑ DT 5022 [R]	It's a Great Life	1966	3.00	6.00	12.00
❑ T 5022 [M]	It's a Great Life	1966	5.00	10.00	20.00
❑ DT 5121	The World of Faron Young	1968	3.75	7.50	15.00

YOUNG, NEIL

The impossible-to-pigeonhole singer did a full-blown country album, complete with a Top 40 country single, in 1985. Only the material relating to that album, "Old Ways," is listed below. Also see CROSBY, STILLS, NASH AND YOUNG; WILLIE NELSON.

Number	Title (A Side/B Side)	Yr	VG	VG+	NM
12-Inch Singles					
GEFFEN					
❑ PRO-A-2373 [DJ]	Get Back to the Country (Long)/Get Back to the Country (Short)	1985	2.50	5.00	10.00
45s					
GEFFEN					
❑ 28753	Old Ways/Once an Angel	1986	—	—	3.00
❑ 28883	Get Back to the Country/Misfits	1985	—	—	3.00
Albums					
GEFFEN					
❑ GHS 24068	Old Ways	1985	3.00	6.00	12.00
❑ R 163233	Old Ways	1985	3.75	7.50	15.00
—RCA Music Service edition					
MOBILE FIDELITY					
❑ 1-252	Old Ways	1996	5.00	10.00	20.00
—Audiophile vinyl					

YOUNG, ROGER

Number	Title (A Side/B Side)	Yr	VG	VG+	NM
45s					
DESSA					
❑ 79-2	Skip a Rope/(B-side unknown)	1979	—	3.50	7.00

YOUNG, STEVE

Number	Title (A Side/B Side)	Yr	VG	VG+	NM
45s					
A&M					
❑ 1083	Seven Bridges Road/I'm a One Woman Man	1969	5.00	10.00	20.00
BLUE CANYON					
❑ 135	My Oklahoma/The White Trash Song	1973	2.00	4.00	8.00
❑ 135 [PS]	My Oklahoma/The White Trash Song	1973	3.00	6.00	12.00
RCA					
❑ PB-10769	Renegade Picker/Old Memories (Mean Nothing to Me)	1976	—	2.50	5.00
❑ PB-10823	Broken Hearted People (Take Me to a Barroom)/Light of My Life	1976	—	2.50	5.00
❑ PB-10868	It's Not Supposed to Be That Way/Lonesome, On'ry and Mean	1976	—	2.50	5.00
❑ PB-11233	Don't Think Twice, It's All Right/Montgomery in the Rain	1978	—	2.50	5.00
❑ PB-11361	Whiskey/Mid-Nite Fever	1978	—	2.50	5.00
REPRISE					
❑ 0946	Crash on the Levee/Sea Rock City	1969	2.00	4.00	8.00
❑ 1001	Call Me Up in Dreamland/I Can't Hold Myself in Line	1971	2.00	4.00	8.00
❑ 1013	Come Sit By My Side/Golden Rocket	1971	2.00	4.00	8.00
❑ 1100	Seven Bridges Road/Many Rivers	1972	3.00	6.00	12.00
Albums					
BLUE CANYON					
❑ 505	Seven Bridges Road	197?	3.75	7.50	15.00
MOUNTAIN RAILROAD					
❑ 52776	Honky-Tonk Man	197?	3.75	7.50	15.00
RCA VICTOR					
❑ APL1-1759	Renegade Picker	1976	3.75	7.50	15.00
❑ APL1-2510	No Place to Fall	1978	3.75	7.50	15.00
REPRISE					
❑ MS 2081	Seven Bridges Road	1972	3.75	7.50	15.00
ROUNDER					
❑ 3057	To Satisfy You	198?	2.50	5.00	10.00
❑ 3058	Seven Bridges Road	198?	2.50	5.00	10.00
❑ 3087	Honky-Tonk Man	198?	2.50	5.00	10.00

YOUNGBLOOD, JACK

Number	Title (A Side/B Side)	Yr	VG	VG+	NM
45s					
COLUMBIA					
❑ 4-21103	Bile Dem Cabbage Down/Wednesday Night Waltz	1953	5.00	10.00	20.00
❑ 4-21298	Hitch-Hiker's Blues/Twinkle, Twinkle, Little Star	1954	5.00	10.00	20.00

YOUNGER, JAMES AND MICHAEL

Number	Title (A Side/B Side)	Yr	VG	VG+	NM
45s					
AIR					
❑ 102	Back on the Radio Again/Women Like Her Are in Dreams	1986	—	2.50	5.00
❑ 106	She Wants to Marry a Cowboy/(B-side unknown)	1986	—	2.50	5.00
MCA					
❑ 52030	Lonely Hearts/A Taste of the Wind	1982	—	2.00	4.00
—As "Younger Brothers"					
❑ 52076	Nothing But the Radio On/A Taste of the Wind	1982	—	2.00	4.00
—As "Younger Brothers"					
❑ 52148	There's No Substitute for You/Here Comes the Tempter	1982	—	2.00	4.00
—As "Younger Brothers"					

Number	Title (A Side/B Side)	Yr	VG	VG+	NM
❑ 52183	Somewhere Down the Line/Blame It on Mexico	1983	—	2.00	4.00
—As "Younger Brothers"					
❑ 52222	A Taste of the Wind/Lost in the Feeling	1983	—	2.00	4.00
❑ 52263	Lovers on the Rebound/Here Comes the Tempter	1983	—	2.00	4.00
❑ 52317	Shoot First, Ask Questions Later/Thinking 'Bout Leaving	1983	—	2.00	4.00
PERMIAN					
❑ 82011	My Special Angel/In South Texas	1985	—	2.50	5.00
Albums					
MCA					
❑ 900	James and Michael Younger	198?	2.00	4.00	8.00
—Budget-line reissue of 5391					
❑ 5391	James and Michael Younger	1983	2.50	5.00	10.00

YOUNGER BROTHERS
See JAMES AND MICHAEL YOUNGER.

YOUNGER BROTHERS BAND, THE
45s

Number	Title (A Side/B Side)	Yr	VG	VG+	NM
ERP					
❑ 04094	Making Love to Dixie/I Don't Want to Be Your Friend	1984	—	3.00	6.00
Albums					
HME					
❑ FW 39978	The Younger Brothers Band	1985	2.00	4.00	8.00

Z

ZACA CREEK
45s

Number	Title (A Side/B Side)	Yr	VG	VG+	NM
COLUMBIA					
❑ 38-69062	Sometimes Love's Not a Pretty Thing/Rock Me Back	1989	—	—	3.00
❑ 38-73096	Ghost Town/Time's Up	1989	—	—	3.00
❑ 38-73351	War Paint/Mean Old Moon	1990	—	—	3.00
GIANT					
❑ 7-18495	Fly Me South/Maverick Saloon	1993	—	2.00	4.00

ZACK, EDDIE
45s

Number	Title (A Side/B Side)	Yr	VG	VG+	NM
COLUMBIA					
❑ 4-21148	Little Donkey/You Knew Men When You Were Lonely	1953	10.00	20.00	40.00
DECCA					
❑ 9-46302	Beautiful Brown Eyes/Shenandoah Waltz	1951	10.00	20.00	40.00
❑ 9-46330	The Clouds Will Soon Roll By/You Remind Me of So Much	1951	10.00	20.00	40.00

ZACK, EDDIE, AND COUSIN RICHIE
45s

Number	Title (A Side/B Side)	Yr	VG	VG+	NM
COLUMBIA					
❑ 4-21199	I've Lost Again/I Never Saw Her Again	1954	12.50	25.00	50.00
❑ 4-21261	Positively No Dancing/Dancing Country Style	1954	12.50	25.00	50.00
❑ 4-21307	You're Out of My Sight/Cryin' Tears	1954	37.50	75.00	150.00
❑ 4-21387	Rocky Road Blues/Lover, Lover	1955	37.50	75.00	150.00
❑ 4-21441	I'm Gonna Rock and Roll/Foolish Me	1955	37.50	75.00	150.00

ZADORA, PIA
Before attempting to become a dance diva, and before attempting to become an actress, she attempted to become a country star. The discography only includes those early attempts.
45s

Number	Title (A Side/B Side)	Yr	VG	VG+	NM
WARNER BROS.					
❑ 8612	Come Share My Love/Just Make Believe You Love Me	1978	—	2.00	4.00
❑ 8766	Bedtime Stories/Tell Him	1979	—	2.00	4.00
❑ 49065	I Know a Good Thing When I Feel It/Trouble	1979	—	2.00	4.00
❑ 49148	Baby It's You/Roses Ain't Red	1979	—	2.00	4.00

ZEILER, GAYLE
Also see ETHEL AND THE SHAMELESS HUSSIES.
45s

Number	Title (A Side/B Side)	Yr	VG	VG+	NM
EQUA					
❑ 670	No Place to Hide/(B-side unknown)	1982	—	3.50	7.00

ORIGINAL CAST RECORDINGS

Number / Title (A Side/B Side)	Yr	VG	VG+	NM
THE BEST LITTLE WHOREHOUSE IN TEXAS				
❑ MCA 3049	1978	3.00	6.00	12.00
BIG RIVER				
❑ MCA 6147	1985	2.50	5.00	10.00
—Music written by Roger Miller				
PUMP BOYS AND DINETTES				
❑ CBS FM 37790	1982	3.75	7.50	15.00

SOUNDTRACKS

Number / Title (A Side/B Side)	Yr	VG	VG+	NM
ANY WHICH WAY YOU CAN				
❑ Warner Bros. HS 3499	1980	2.50	5.00	10.00
THE BEST LITTLE WHOREHOUSE IN TEXAS				
❑ MCA 1499	198?	2.00	4.00	8.00
—Reissue of 6112				
❑ MCA 6112	1982	2.50	5.00	10.00
BRONCO BILLY				
❑ Elektra 5E-512	1980	2.50	5.00	10.00
COAL MINER'S DAUGHTER				
❑ MCA 5107	1980	3.75	7.50	15.00
CONVOY				
❑ United Artists UA-LA910-H	1978	3.00	6.00	12.00
EVERY WHICH WAY BUT LOOSE				
❑ Elektra 5E-503	1978	3.00	6.00	12.00
HARD COUNTRY				
❑ Epic SE 37367	1981	2.50	5.00	10.00
HONKYTONK MAN				
❑ Warner Bros. 23739	1982	2.50	5.00	10.00
THE NIGHT THE LIGHTS WENT OUT IN GEORGIA				
❑ Mirage SD 16051	1981	2.50	5.00	10.00
OUTLAW BLUES				
❑ Capitol ST-11691	1977	3.75	7.50	15.00
PINK CADILLAC				
❑ Warner Bros. 25922	1989	2.50	5.00	10.00
RUSTLERS' RHAPSODY				
❑ Warner Bros. 25284	1985	2.50	5.00	10.00
SMOKEY AND THE BANDIT				
❑ MCA 2099	1977	3.00	6.00	12.00
SMOKEY AND THE BANDIT 2				
❑ MCA 6101	1980	2.50	5.00	10.00
SMOKEY AND THE BANDIT 3				
❑ MCA 36006	1983	2.50	5.00	10.00
TAKE THIS JOB AND SHOVE IT!				
❑ Epic SE 37177	1981	3.00	6.00	12.00
TICK...TICK...TICK				
❑ MGM SE-4667	1970	6.25	12.50	25.00
URBAN COWBOY				
❑ Full Moon/Asylum DP-90002 [(2)]	1980	3.00	6.00	12.00
URBAN COWBOY II (MORE MUSIC FROM THE ORIGINAL SOUNDTRACK)				
❑ Full Moon/Epic SE 36291	1980	2.50	5.00	10.00

TELEVISION RECORDS

Number / Title (A Side/B Side)	Yr	VG	VG+	NM
THE BEVERLY HILLBILLIES				
❑ Columbia CL 2402 [M]	1965	10.00	20.00	40.00
❑ Columbia CS 9202 [S]	1965	15.00	30.00	60.00
DALLAS: THE MUSIC STORY				
❑ Warner Bros. 25325	1985	2.00	4.00	8.00
THE DUKES OF HAZZARD				
❑ Scotti Brothers FZ 37712	1982	3.00	6.00	12.00

VARIOUS ARTISTS COLLECTIONS

Number / Title (A Side/B Side)	Yr	VG	VG+	NM
10 GIANT COUNTRY HITS/10 SUPER COUNTRY STARS, VOL. 1				
❑ MGM SE-4920	1972	2.50	5.00	10.00
10 GIANT COUNTRY HITS/10 SUPER COUNTRY STARS, VOL. 2				
❑ MGM SE-4921	1972	2.50	5.00	10.00
10 GIANT COUNTRY HITS/10 SUPER COUNTRY STARS, VOL. 3				
❑ MGM SE-4922	1972	2.50	5.00	10.00
10 GIANT COUNTRY HITS/10 SUPER COUNTRY STARS, VOL. 4				
❑ MGM SE-4923	1972	2.50	5.00	10.00
14 GREAT ALL TIME C&W WALTZES				
❑ King 890 [M]	1964	17.50	35.00	70.00
14 #1 COUNTRY HITS				
❑ RCA Victor AHL1-7004	1985	3.00	6.00	12.00
16 TOP COUNTRY HITS (VOLUME 1)				
❑ MCA R 174207	1990	3.75	7.50	15.00
—Only available on vinyl from BMG Direct Marketing				
16 TOP COUNTRY HITS (VOLUME 2)				
❑ MCA R 134217	1990	3.75	7.50	15.00
—Only available on vinyl from BMG Direct Marketing				
18 ALL TIME COUNTRY AND WESTERN HITS				
❑ King 1027 [M]	1968	7.50	15.00	30.00
18 KING-SIZE COUNTRY HITS				
❑ Columbia CL 2668 [M]	1967	5.00	10.00	20.00
❑ Columbia CS 9468 [R]	1967	5.00	10.00	20.00
19 HOT COUNTRY REQUESTS				
❑ Epic FE 39597	1985	2.00	4.00	8.00
19 HOT COUNTRY REQUESTS, VOL. 2				
❑ Epic FE 40175	1985	2.00	4.00	8.00
19 HOT COUNTRY REQUESTS, VOL. 3				
❑ Epic FE 40479	1986	2.00	4.00	8.00
20 GREAT COUNTRY HITS				
❑ RCA Victor CPL2-1286 [(2)]	1975	5.00	10.00	20.00
22 HIGH-BALLIN' HITS!				
❑ GRT 2103-709 [(2)]	1976	3.00	6.00	12.00
25 YEARS OF COUNTRY AND WESTERN SACRED SONGS				
❑ King 807 [M]	1962	25.00	50.00	100.00
25 YEARS OF C&W HITS				
❑ King 1006 [M]	1966	7.50	15.00	30.00
30 GOLDEN COUNTRY HITS				
❑ RCA Special Products DVL2-0447 [(2)]	1980	3.00	6.00	12.00
—Mail-order offer from Sessions				
30 YEARS OF NO. 1 COUNTRY HITS				
❑ Reader's Digest RBA-215-A [(7)]	1986	12.50	25.00	50.00
30X30: 30 GREAT HITS BY 30 GREAT COUNTRY ARTISTS, VOL. 1				
❑ Columbia Musical Treasuries P2S 5218 [(2)]	1968	5.00	10.00	20.00
30X30: 30 GREAT HITS BY 30 GREAT COUNTRY ARTISTS, VOL. 2				
❑ Columbia Musical Treasuries P2S 5220 [(2)]	1968	5.00	10.00	20.00
5-STRING BANJO PICKIN' AND SINGIN'				
❑ King 994 [M]	1966	10.00	20.00	40.00
50 YEARS OF BLUEGRASS HITS, VOL. 1				
❑ CMH 9033 [(2)]	198?	3.75	7.50	15.00
50 YEARS OF BLUEGRASS HITS, VOL. 2				
❑ CMH 9034 [(2)]	198?	3.75	7.50	15.00
50 YEARS OF BLUEGRASS HITS, VOL. 3				
❑ CMH 9035 [(2)]	198?	3.75	7.50	15.00
50 YEARS OF BLUEGRASS HITS, VOL. 4				
❑ CMH 9036 [(2)]	198?	3.75	7.50	15.00
60 YEARS OF COUNTRY MUSIC				
❑ RCA Victor CPL2-4351	1982	5.00	10.00	20.00
60 YEARS OF THE GRAND OLE OPRY				
❑ RCA Victor CPL2-9507 [(2)]	1986	3.75	7.50	15.00
ALL-AMERICAN COWBOYS				
❑ Kat Family FZ 38126	1983	2.50	5.00	10.00
ALL-STAR COUNTRY AND WESTERN				
❑ Diplomat DS 2623	196?	3.00	6.00	12.00
ALL STAR COUNTRY				
❑ MGM SE-4690	1970	3.75	7.50	15.00
❑ RCA Victor PRS-387	1970	3.00	6.00	12.00
ALL STAR COUNTRY HITS				
❑ MGM SE-4787	1971	3.00	6.00	12.00
ALL TIME COUNTRY AND WESTERN				
❑ Decca DL 4010 [M]	1960	7.50	15.00	30.00
❑ Decca DL 74010 [R]	196?	5.00	10.00	20.00

Number Title (A Side/B Side)	Yr	VG	VG+	NM
ALL TIME COUNTRY AND WESTERN HITS				
❑ King 537 [M]	1956	37.50	75.00	150.00
❑ King 710 [M]	1961	25.00	50.00	100.00
—Not a reissue of King 537, but a different collection				
ALL TIME COUNTRY AND WESTERN, VOL. 2				
❑ Decca DL 4090 [M]	1961	6.25	12.50	25.00
❑ Decca DL 74090 [R]	196?	3.75	7.50	15.00
ALL TIME COUNTRY AND WESTERN, VOL. 3				
❑ Decca DL 4134 [M]	1961	6.25	12.50	25.00
❑ Decca DL 74134 [R]	196?	3.75	7.50	15.00
ALL TIME COUNTRY AND WESTERN, VOL. 4				
❑ Decca DL 4359 [M]	1963	6.25	12.50	25.00
❑ Decca DL 74359 [R]	196?	3.75	7.50	15.00
ALL TIME COUNTRY AND WESTERN, VOL. 5				
❑ Decca DL 4549 [M]	1964	6.25	12.50	25.00
❑ Decca DL 74549 [R]	1964	3.75	7.50	15.00
ALL TIME COUNTRY AND WESTERN, VOL. 6				
❑ Decca DL 4657 [M]	1965	5.00	10.00	20.00
❑ Decca DL 74657 [R]	1965	3.00	6.00	12.00
ALL TIME COUNTRY AND WESTERN, VOL. 7				
❑ Decca DL 4775 [M]	1966	5.00	10.00	20.00
❑ Decca DL 74775 [R]	1966	3.00	6.00	12.00
ALL TIME COUNTRY AND WESTERN, VOL. 8				
❑ Decca DL 4881 [M]	1967	5.00	10.00	20.00
❑ Decca DL 74881 [S]	1967	5.00	10.00	20.00
ALL TIME COUNTRY AND WESTERN, VOL. 9				
❑ Decca DL 75025	1968	5.00	10.00	20.00
AMERICA'S GREATEST COUNTRY STARS LIVE AND IN PERSON				
❑ Harmony HL 7414 [M]	1967	3.75	7.50	15.00
❑ Harmony HS 11214 [S]	1967	3.75	7.50	15.00
AWARD WINNERS				
❑ RCA Victor APL1-2262	1977	3.00	6.00	12.00
BACK IN THE SADDLE AGAIN: AMERICAN COWBOY SONGS				
❑ New World 314/5 [(2)]	198?	3.75	7.50	15.00
BANDED TOGETHER				
❑ Epic JE36177	1979	2.50	5.00	10.00
❑ Epic PE36177	198?	2.00	4.00	8.00
—Budget-line reissue				
BANJO COUNTRY STYLE				
❑ Audio Lab AL-1569 [M]	1962	20.00	40.00	80.00
BEST OF BAKERSFIELD				
❑ Capitol ST-11111	1972	3.75	7.50	15.00
BEST OF BLUEGRASS				
❑ Wing MGW-12267 [M]	1964	3.75	7.50	15.00
❑ Wing SRW-16267 [S]	1964	3.75	7.50	15.00
THE BEST OF CHRISTMAS				
❑ RCA Victor CPL1-7013	1985	2.50	5.00	10.00
THE BEST OF COUNTRY DUETS				
❑ RCA Victor LSP-4082	1968	3.75	7.50	15.00
BEST OF THE '50S				
❑ RCA Victor AEL1-5800	1986	3.75	7.50	15.00
BEST OF THE '50S, '60S AND '70S				
❑ RCA Victor AEL1-5838	1986	3.75	7.50	15.00
BEST OF THE '60S				
❑ RCA Victor AEL1-5802	1986	3.75	7.50	15.00
BEST OF THE '70S				
❑ RCA Victor AEL1-5837	1986	3.75	7.50	15.00
BEST OF THE 80'S... SO FAR!				
❑ RCA Victor AHL1-5058	198?	2.50	5.00	10.00
BIG COUNTRY HITS, VOL. 1				
❑ RCA Victor LPM-3606 [M]	1966	3.75	7.50	15.00
❑ RCA Victor LSP-3606 [S]	1966	5.00	10.00	20.00
BLUE RIBBON COUNTRY				
❑ Capitol STBB 2969 [(2)]	1968	6.25	12.50	25.00
BLUE RIBBON COUNTRY, VOL. 2				
❑ Capitol STBB-217 [(2)]	1969	6.25	12.50	25.00
THE BLUEGRASS ALBUM				
❑ Rounder 0140	198?	2.50	5.00	10.00
THE BLUEGRASS ALBUM, VOL. 2				
❑ Rounder 0164	198?	2.50	5.00	10.00
THE BLUEGRASS ALBUM, VOL. 3				
❑ Rounder 0180	198?	2.50	5.00	10.00
THE BLUEGRASS ALBUM, VOL. 4				
❑ Rounder 0210	198?	2.50	5.00	10.00
BLUEGRASS OLDIES BUT GOODIES				
❑ Cumberland MGC-29520 [M]	1965	3.75	7.50	15.00
❑ Cumberland SRC-69520 [S]	1965	3.75	7.50	15.00
❑ Smash MGS-27028 [M]	1963	5.00	10.00	20.00
❑ Smash SRS-67028 [S]	1963	5.00	10.00	20.00
BLUEGRASS SPECTACULAR				
❑ CMH 5902 [(2)]	198?	3.75	7.50	15.00
❑ Starday SLP-232 [M]	1963	6.25	12.50	25.00
BLUEGRASS: THE WORLD'S GREATEST SHOW				
❑ Sugar Hill SH-2201 [(2)]	198?	3.75	7.50	15.00
BRIGHT LIGHTS AND HONKY TONKS				
❑ Starday SLP-239 [M]	1963	6.25	12.50	25.00
THE BRISTOL SESSIONS				
❑ Country Music Foundation CMF-011 [(2)]	198?	3.75	7.50	15.00
CHRISTMAS COUNTRY				
❑ Elektra 5E-554	1981	3.00	6.00	12.00
CHRISTMAS DAY IN THE COUNTRY				
❑ Columbia Special Products P 11887	1973	2.50	5.00	10.00
CHRISTMAS FOR THE 90'S, VOLUME 1				
❑ Capitol Nashville 1P 8117	1990	3.75	7.50	15.00
—Available on vinyl through Columbia House only				
CHRISTMAS FOR THE 90'S, VOLUME 2				
❑ Capitol Nashville 1P 8118	1990	3.75	7.50	15.00
—Available on vinyl through Columbia House only				
CHRISTMAS GREETINGS FROM NASHVILLE				
❑ Columbia PC 39467	1984	2.50	5.00	10.00
A CHRISTMAS TRADITION				
❑ Warner Bros. 25630	1987	3.00	6.00	12.00
A CHRISTMAS TRADITION, VOLUME II				
❑ Warner Bros. 25762	1988	2.50	5.00	10.00
CHRISTMAS WITH GLEN CAMPBELL AND THE HOLLYWOOD POPS ORCHESTRA				
❑ Capitol Creative Products SL-6699	1971	3.00	6.00	12.00
CLASSIC COUNTRY				
❑ Epic FE 38630	1983	2.50	5.00	10.00
❑ Epic PE 38630	1985	2.00	4.00	8.00
—Budget-line reissue				
CLASSIC COUNTRY MUSIC				
❑ Columbia Special Products P8 15640 [(8)]	1981	12.50	25.00	50.00
—Boxed set; sold only by the Smithsonian; original version				
❑ RCA Special Products DML6-0914 [(6)]	1990	12.50	25.00	50.00
—Boxed set; sold only by the Smithsonian; revised version				
CLASSIC LOVE SONGS				
❑ RCA Victor AEL1-7195	1986	2.00	4.00	8.00
COLLECTOR'S SERIES: DUETS				
❑ RCA Victor CPL1-7059	1985	2.00	4.00	8.00
COLLECTOR'S SERIES: DUETS DUETS				
❑ RCA Victor CPL1-7130	1985	2.00	4.00	8.00
COME TOGETHER: AMERICA SALUTES THE BEATLES				
❑ Liberty 31712	1995	5.00	10.00	20.00
COUNTRY'S BEST				
❑ Capitol T 1179 [M]	1959	7.50	15.00	30.00
COUNTRY'S GREATEST HITS				
❑ Power Pak PO-227	197?	2.50	5.00	10.00
COUNTRY AFTER DARK				
❑ Intermedia QS-5073	198?	2.50	5.00	10.00
COUNTRY AND WESTERN AWARD WINNERS 1964				
❑ Decca DL 4622 [M]	1965	5.00	10.00	20.00
❑ Decca DL 74622 [S]	1965	6.25	12.50	25.00
COUNTRY AND WESTERN AWARD WINNERS 1966				
❑ Decca DL 4837 [M]	1967	5.00	10.00	20.00
❑ Decca DL 74837 [S]	1967	3.75	7.50	15.00
COUNTRY AND WESTERN FAVORITES				
❑ Metro M-530 [M]	1965	3.00	6.00	12.00
❑ Metro MS-530 [R]	1965	2.50	5.00	10.00
COUNTRY AND WESTERN FAVORITES, VOLUME 2				
❑ Metro M-572 [M]	1966	3.00	6.00	12.00
❑ Metro MS-572 [R]	1966	2.50	5.00	10.00
COUNTRY AND WESTERN JAMBOREE				
❑ King 697 [M]	1961	37.50	75.00	150.00
COUNTRY AND WESTERN, VOLUME 1				
❑ Dot DLP-3700 [M]	1966	3.75	7.50	15.00
COUNTRY AND WESTERN, VOLUME 2				
❑ Dot DLP-3701 [M]	1966	3.75	7.50	15.00
COUNTRY AND WESTERN, VOLUME 3				
❑ Dot DLP-3702 [M]	1966	3.75	7.50	15.00

Number Title (A Side/B Side)	Yr	VG	VG+	NM
COUNTRY AND WESTERN, VOLUME 4				
❑ Dot DLP-3703 [M]	1966	3.75	7.50	15.00
COUNTRY BONANZA				
❑ Columbia Musical Treasury P2S 5372 [(2)]	1969	3.75	7.50	15.00
COUNTRY BOY — COUNTRY GIRL				
❑ Decca DL 4201 [M]	1962	6.25	12.50	25.00
❑ Decca DL 74201 [S]	1962	7.50	15.00	30.00
COUNTRY CHRISTMAS				
❑ Columbia CS 9888	1968	3.75	7.50	15.00
❑ Columbia Special Products CSS 1434	1970	3.00	6.00	12.00
❑ Columbia Special Products/Sessions P 16365	1981	2.50	5.00	10.00
❑ Epic JE 36823	1980	2.50	5.00	10.00
❑ King 811 [M]	1962	25.00	50.00	100.00
❑ Monument SLP-18125	1969	5.00	10.00	20.00
❑ RCA Victor CPL1-4396	1982	2.50	5.00	10.00
❑ RCA Victor AYL1-4812	1983	2.00	4.00	8.00
—Reissue of CPL1-4396				
❑ Time-Life STL-109 [(3)]	1988	5.00	10.00	20.00
—Available from Time-Life by mail order only; boxed set				
A COUNTRY CHRISTMAS WITH LORETTA LYNN AND FRIENDS				
❑ MCA Special Markets 34979	197?	3.00	6.00	12.00
A COUNTRY CHRISTMAS, VOLUME 2				
❑ RCA Victor AYL1-4809	1983	3.00	6.00	12.00
A COUNTRY CHRISTMAS, VOLUME 3				
❑ RCA Victor CPL1-5178	1984	2.50	5.00	10.00
A COUNTRY CHRISTMAS, VOLUME 4				
❑ RCA Victor CPL1-7012	1985	2.50	5.00	10.00
COUNTRY CLASSICS				
❑ RCA Victor LPM-2313 [M]	1961	6.25	12.50	25.00
❑ RCA Victor LSP-2313 [S]	1961	7.50	15.00	30.00
COUNTRY EXPRESS				
❑ Starday SLP-109 [M]	1959	10.00	20.00	40.00
COUNTRY FAIR				
❑ Capitol SWBB-562 [(2)]	1970	6.25	12.50	25.00
COUNTRY GIRLS SING COUNTRY SONGS				
❑ RCA Camden CAL-959 [M]	1966	3.00	6.00	12.00
❑ RCA Camden CAS-959 [S]	1966	3.75	7.50	15.00
COUNTRY GOLD				
❑ RCA Special Products DPL1-0561	1980	5.00	10.00	20.00
COUNTRY GOLD, VOL. 1				
❑ Plantation PL-5	1969	3.00	6.00	12.00
COUNTRY HIT PARADE				
❑ Starday SLP-110 [M]	1959	10.00	20.00	40.00
COUNTRY HITS BY COUNTRY STARS				
❑ Capitol T 1912 [M]	1963	5.00	10.00	20.00
❑ Capitol ST 1912 [S]	1963	6.25	12.50	25.00
COUNTRY JUBILEE				
❑ Decca DL 4172 [M]	1961	7.50	15.00	30.00
COUNTRY MEMORIES				
❑ Reader's Digest RBA-066-A [(7)]	1989	12.50	25.00	50.00
COUNTRY MUSIC BY THE WAYSIDE				
❑ Wayside 1013	1968	5.00	10.00	20.00
COUNTRY MUSIC HALL OF FAME				
❑ Starday SLP-164 [(2) M]	1962	7.50	15.00	30.00
COUNTRY MUSIC HALL OF FAME, VOL. 2				
❑ Starday SLP-190 [(2) M]	1963	7.50	15.00	30.00
COUNTRY MUSIC HALL OF FAME, VOL. 3				
❑ Starday SLP-256 [(2) M]	1963	7.50	15.00	30.00
COUNTRY MUSIC HALL OF FAME, VOL. 4				
❑ Starday SLP-295 [(2) M]	1964	7.50	15.00	30.00
COUNTRY MUSIC HALL OF FAME, VOL. 5				
❑ Starday SLP-360 [M]	1966	6.25	12.50	25.00
COUNTRY MUSIC HALL OF FAME, VOL. 6				
❑ Starday SLP-390	1967	6.25	12.50	25.00
COUNTRY MUSIC HALL OF FAME, VOL. 7				
❑ Starday SLP-409	1969	5.00	10.00	20.00
COUNTRY MUSIC HALL OF FAME, VOL. 8				
❑ Starday SLP-430	1969	5.00	10.00	20.00
COUNTRY MUSIC HALL OF FAME, VOL. 9				
❑ Starday SLP-449	1970	5.00	10.00	20.00
COUNTRY MUSIC HITS BY COUNTRY MUSIC STARS				
❑ RCA Camden CAL-689 [M]	1962	5.00	10.00	20.00
❑ RCA Camden CAS-689 [R]	196?	3.75	7.50	15.00
COUNTRY MUSIC HOOTENANNY				
❑ Capitol ST 2009 [S]	1963	7.50	15.00	30.00
❑ Capitol T 2009 [M]	1963	6.25	12.50	25.00

Number Title (A Side/B Side)	Yr	VG	VG+	NM
COUNTRY MUSIC JAMBOREE				
❑ Mercury MG-20350 [M]	1958	10.00	20.00	40.00
COUNTRY MUSIC SPECTACULAR				
❑ Starday SLP-117 [M]	1961	10.00	20.00	40.00
COUNTRY MUSIC WHO'S WHO				
❑ Starday SLP-304 [M]	1964	7.50	15.00	30.00
—With 52-page booklet				
❑ Starday SLP-304 [M]	1964	5.00	10.00	20.00
—Without booklet				
COUNTRY OLDIES BUT GOODIES				
❑ Smash MGS-27016 [M]	1962	5.00	10.00	20.00
❑ Smash SRS-67016 [S]	1962	5.00	10.00	20.00
A COUNTRY SALUTE TO HANK WILLIAMS				
❑ Harmony HL 7265 [M]	1960	5.00	10.00	20.00
THE COUNTRY SIDE OF CHRISTMAS/ALL-TIME FAVORITES IN THE TRADITIONAL STYLE				
❑ Capitol Creative Products SL-6586	1968	3.00	6.00	12.00
COUNTRY SOFT AND MELLOW				
❑ Reader's Digest RB4-200 [(7)]	1989	12.50	25.00	50.00
COUNTRY SPECIAL				
❑ Capitol STBB-402 [(2)]	1969	6.25	12.50	25.00
COUNTRY SPECTACULAR				
❑ Columbia CL 894 [M]	1956	12.50	25.00	50.00
COUNTRY STAR PARADE VOL. 1				
❑ Vocalion VL 3768 [M]	1966	3.00	6.00	12.00
❑ Vocalion VL 73768 [R]	1966	3.00	6.00	12.00
COUNTRY STAR PARADE, VOL. 2				
❑ Vocalion VL 3804 [M].	1967	3.75	7.50	15.00
❑ Vocalion VL 73804 [R]	1967	3.00	6.00	12.00
COUNTRY STARS OF TODAY				
❑ Power Pak PO-287	197?	2.50	5.00	10.00
COUNTRY STARS SING SACRED SONGS				
❑ RCA Camden CAL-2136 [M]	1967	3.75	7.50	15.00
❑ RCA Camden CAS-2136 [S]	1967	3.00	6.00	12.00
COUNTRY STARS, COUNTRY HITS				
❑ RCA Camden CAL-793 [M]	1964	5.00	10.00	20.00
❑ RCA Camden CAS-793 [S]	1964	5.00	10.00	20.00
COUNTRY USA: 1950				
❑ Time-Life CTR-23 [(2)]	1991	5.00	10.00	20.00
COUNTRY USA: 1951				
❑ Time-Life CTR-22 [(2)]	1991	5.00	10.00	20.00
COUNTRY USA: 1952				
❑ Time-Life CTR-16 [(2)]	1990	3.75	7.50	15.00
COUNTRY USA: 1953				
❑ Time-Life CTR-20 [(2)]	1990	3.75	7.50	15.00
COUNTRY USA: 1954				
❑ Time-Life CTR-15 [(2)]	1990	5.00	10.00	20.00
COUNTRY USA: 1955				
❑ Time-Life CTR-19 [(2)]	1990	5.00	10.00	20.00
COUNTRY USA: 1956				
❑ Time-Life CTR-13 [(2)]	1990	5.00	10.00	20.00
COUNTRY USA: 1957				
❑ Time-Life CTR-02 [(2)]	1988	3.75	7.50	15.00
COUNTRY USA: 1958				
❑ Time-Life CTR-07 [(2)]	1989	5.00	10.00	20.00
COUNTRY USA: 1959				
❑ Time-Life CTR-09 [(2)]	1989	3.75	7.50	15.00
COUNTRY USA: 1960				
❑ Time-Life CTR-12 [(2)]	1989	3.75	7.50	15.00
COUNTRY USA: 1961				
❑ Time-Life CTR-01 [(2)]	1988	3.75	7.50	15.00
COUNTRY USA: 1962				
❑ Time-Life CTR-03 [(2)]	1988	3.75	7.50	15.00
COUNTRY USA: 1963				
❑ Time-Life CTR-11 [(2)]	1989	3.75	7.50	15.00
COUNTRY USA: 1964				
❑ Time-Life CTR-14 [(2)]	1990	3.75	7.50	15.00
COUNTRY USA: 1965				
❑ Time-Life CTR-10 [(2)]	1989	3.75	7.50	15.00
COUNTRY USA: 1966				
❑ Time-Life CTR-21 [(2)]	1991	5.00	10.00	20.00
COUNTRY USA: 1967				
❑ Time-Life CTR-17 [(2)]	1990	3.75	7.50	15.00

Number Title (A Side/B Side)	Yr	VG	VG+	NM
COUNTRY USA: 1968				
❑ Time-Life CTR-06 [(2)]	1989	3.75	7.50	15.00
COUNTRY USA: 1969				
❑ Time-Life CTR-08 [(2)]	1989	5.00	10.00	20.00
COUNTRY USA: 1970				
❑ Time-Life CTR-04 [(2)]	1988	3.75	7.50	15.00
COUNTRY USA: 1971				
❑ Time-Life CTR-05 [(2)]	1989	3.75	7.50	15.00
COUNTRY USA: 1972				
❑ Time-Life CTR-18 [(2)]	1990	3.75	7.50	15.00
A DAY IN THE COUNTRY				
❑ Audio Lab AL-1519 [M]	1959	20.00	40.00	80.00
DIESEL SMOKE, DANGEROUS CURVES AND OTHER TRUCK DRIVERS FAVORITES				
❑ Starday SLP-250 [M]	1963	7.50	15.00	30.00
A DOWN-HOME COUNTRY CHRISTMAS				
❑ Columbia Special Products P 14992	1979	2.00	4.00	8.00
THE EARLY DAYS OF BLUEGRASS VOL. 3: NEW SOUNDS RAMBLIN' FROM COAST TO COAST				
❑ Rounder 1015	198?	2.50	5.00	10.00
THE EARLY DAYS OF BLUEGRASS, VOL. 1				
❑ Rounder 1013	198?	2.50	5.00	10.00
THE EARLY DAYS OF BLUEGRASS, VOL. 2				
❑ Rounder 1014	198?	2.50	5.00	10.00
FANTASTIC COUNTRY				
❑ RCA Victor PRS-423	1972	3.00	6.00	12.00
FIDDLER'S HALL OF FAME				
❑ Starday SLP-209 [M]	1963	7.50	15.00	30.00
FIDDLIN' COUNTRY STYLE				
❑ Nashville NLP-2015 [M]	1965	5.00	10.00	20.00
❑ Power Pak PO-296	197?	2.50	5.00	10.00
❑ Starday SLP-114 [M]	1960	10.00	20.00	40.00
FIRE ON THE STRINGS				
❑ Starday SLP-221 [M]	1963	7.50	15.00	30.00
FIRST OF THE FAMOUS				
❑ Capitol T 2275 [M]	1965	6.25	12.50	25.00
GET HOT OR GO HOME: VINTAGE RCA ROCKABILLY '56-'59				
❑ Country Music Foundation CMF-014 [(2)]	1990	3.75	7.50	15.00
GOLDEN AGE OF COUNTRY MUSIC 1940-1970				
❑ Reader's Digest RBA-005-A [(7)]	1987	10.00	20.00	40.00
GOLDEN COUNTRY GROUPS				
❑ Reader's Digest RBA-201-A [(7)]	1988	10.00	20.00	40.00
GOLDEN COUNTRY HITS				
❑ Harmony HL 7362 [M]	1966	3.00	6.00	12.00
❑ Harmony HS 11162 [S]	1966	3.75	7.50	15.00
❑ United Artists UAL-3327 [M]	1964	3.75	7.50	15.00
❑ United Artists UAS-6327 [S]	1964	5.00	10.00	20.00
GOLDEN INSTRUMENTALS COUNTRY STYLE				
❑ Wing MGW-12261 [M]	1964	5.00	10.00	20.00
❑ Wing SRW-16261 [S]	1964	5.00	10.00	20.00
GRAND OLE OPRY HITS				
❑ RCA Camden CAL-737 [M]	1963	5.00	10.00	20.00
❑ RCA Camden CAS-737 [R]	1966	3.75	7.50	15.00
GRAND OLE OPRY SPECTACULAR				
❑ Starday SLP-242 [(2) M]	1963	7.50	15.00	30.00
GREAT COUNTRY AND WESTERN STARS				
❑ Wing MGW-12268 [M]	1964	5.00	10.00	20.00
❑ Wing SRW-16268 [S]	1964	5.00	10.00	20.00
GREAT COUNTRY FAVORITES				
❑ MGM E-4211 [M]	1964	5.00	10.00	20.00
❑ MGM SE-4211 [S]	1964	6.25	12.50	25.00
GREAT COUNTRY GOSPEL GROUPS				
❑ Wing MGW-12262 [M]	1964	3.75	7.50	15.00
❑ Wing SRW-16262 [S]	1964	3.75	7.50	15.00
GREAT COUNTRY HITS				
❑ United Artists UAL-3159 [M]	1961	6.25	12.50	25.00
GREAT COUNTRY MUSIC, VOLUME 1				
❑ Dot DLP-3732 [M]	1966	3.00	6.00	12.00
❑ Dot DLP-25732 [S]	1966	3.75	7.50	15.00
GREAT COUNTRY MUSIC, VOLUME 2				
❑ Dot DLP-3733 [M]	1966	3.00	6.00	12.00
❑ Dot DLP-25733 [S]	1966	3.75	7.50	15.00
GREAT MOMENTS AT THE GRAND OLE OPRY				
❑ RCA Victor CPL2-1904 [(2)]	1977	5.00	10.00	20.00

Number Title (A Side/B Side)	Yr	VG	VG+	NM
THE GREAT ONES				
❑ Capitol T 1718 [M]	1962	6.25	12.50	25.00
❑ Capitol ST 1718 [S]	1962	7.50	15.00	30.00
GREATEST COUNTRY AND WESTERN HITS NO. 3				
❑ Columbia CL 1816 [M]	1962	5.00	10.00	20.00
GREATEST COUNTRY AND WESTERN HITS NO. 4				
❑ Columbia CL 2081 [M]	1963	5.00	10.00	20.00
❑ Columbia CS 8881 [S]	1963	6.25	12.50	25.00
GREATEST COUNTRY HITS FROM THE MOVIES				
❑ Epic FE 39001	1984	2.50	5.00	10.00
GREATEST COUNTRY HITS OF THE '80S: 1980				
❑ Columbia FC 44281	1988	2.50	5.00	10.00
GREATEST COUNTRY HITS OF THE '80S: 1981				
❑ Columbia FC 44431	1988	2.50	5.00	10.00
GREATEST COUNTRY HITS OF THE '80S: 1982				
❑ Columbia FC 44430	1988	2.50	5.00	10.00
GREATEST COUNTRY HITS OF THE '80S: 1983				
❑ Columbia FC 44429	1988	2.50	5.00	10.00
GREATEST COUNTRY HITS OF THE 70'S				
❑ Columbia JC 36549	1980	2.50	5.00	10.00
❑ Columbia PC 36549	198?	2.00	4.00	8.00
—Budget-line reissue				
GREATEST COUNTRY HITS OF THE 70'S, VOL. 2				
❑ Columbia JC 36802	1980	2.50	5.00	10.00
❑ Columbia PC 36802	198?	2.00	4.00	8.00
—Budget-line reissue				
GREATEST COUNTRY HITS OF THE 70'S, VOL. 3				
❑ Columbia JC 36969	1981	2.50	5.00	10.00
❑ Columbia PC 36969	198?	2.00	4.00	8.00
—Budget-line reissue				
THE GREATEST GREATEST HITS				
❑ RCA Victor AHL1-7185	1986	2.00	4.00	8.00
THE GREATEST HITS, VOL. 1				
❑ Power Pak PO-248	197?	2.50	5.00	10.00
THE GREATEST HITS, VOL. 2				
❑ Power Pak PO-249	197?	2.50	5.00	10.00
GREATEST WESTERN HITS				
❑ Columbia CL 1257 [M]	1959	7.50	15.00	30.00
❑ Columbia CS 8776 [R]	1963	5.00	10.00	20.00
GREATEST WESTERN HITS NO. 2				
❑ Columbia CL 1408 [M]	1960	7.50	15.00	30.00
❑ Columbia CS 8777 [R]	1963	5.00	10.00	20.00
HEAVY HAULERS				
❑ Power Pak PO-290	197?	2.50	5.00	10.00
HILLBILLY HEAVEN				
❑ Capitol Special Markets SL-8118	1979	3.00	6.00	12.00
HILLBILLY HIT PARADE				
❑ Mercury MG-20282 [M]	1957	12.50	25.00	50.00
HILLBILLY HIT PARADE				
❑ Starday SLP-102 [M]	1956	25.00	50.00	100.00
HILLBILLY HOLIDAY				
❑ Rhino R1 70195	1988	3.00	6.00	12.00
HIT PARADE OF COUNTRY MUSIC				
❑ Starday SLP-184 [M]	1962	7.50	15.00	30.00
THE HITS OF '86				
❑ RCA Victor 5768-1-R	1987	2.00	4.00	8.00
THE HITS OF '87				
❑ RCA 6496-1-R	1987	2.00	4.00	8.00
HONEST TO GOODNESS COUNTRY MUSIC HITS				
❑ RCA Victor LPM-2564 [M]	1962	5.00	10.00	20.00
❑ RCA Victor LSP-2564 [S]	1962	6.25	12.50	25.00
HONEST TO GOODNESS COUNTRY MUSIC HITS, VOL. 2				
❑ RCA Victor LPM-2633 [M]	1963	5.00	10.00	20.00
❑ RCA Victor LSP-2633 [S]	1963	6.25	12.50	25.00
HOT NO. 1 COUNTRY HITS				
❑ Realm 1P 8196	1992	3.75	7.50	15.00
—Only available on vinyl through Columbia House				
HUM-N-STRUM: THE BEST OF FOLK AND COUNTRY				
❑ Columbia Special Products CSP 309 [M]	1966	3.75	7.50	15.00
—For General Electric				
IN CONCERT				
❑ RCA Victor CPL2-1014 [(2)]	1975	5.00	10.00	20.00
INSTRUMENTALLY YOURS				
❑ RCA 6492-1-R	1987	2.00	4.00	8.00

Number Title (A Side/B Side)	Yr	VG	VG+	NM
THE JOY OF CHRISTMAS, FEATURING MARTY ROBBINS AND HIS FRIENDS				
❑ Columbia Special Products C 11087	1972	3.75	7.50	15.00
LADIES GET THE BLUES				
❑ Mercury 834199-1	1988	2.00	4.00	8.00
LE GRAN MAMOU: A CAJUN MUSIC ANTHOLOGY, THE HISTORIC VICTOR AND BLUEBIRD SESSIONS 1928-1941				
❑ Country Music Foundation CMF-013 [(2)]	1990	3.75	7.50	15.00
THE LEGEND OF JESSE JAMES				
❑ A&M SP-3718	1980	3.00	6.00	12.00
MEMPHIS COUNTRY				
❑ Sun 120	1970	3.75	7.50	15.00
MGM MILLION SELLERS: COUNTRY & WESTERN HITS, VOLUME 1				
❑ MGM E-3825 [M]	1960	6.25	12.50	25.00
MIDNIGHT JAMBOREE				
❑ Decca DL 4041 [M]	1961	6.25	12.50	25.00
❑ Decca DL 74041 [S]	1961	7.50	15.00	30.00
MONUMENTAL COUNTRY HITS				
❑ Monument SLP-18095	1968	5.00	10.00	20.00
MORE COUNTRY CLASSICS				
❑ RCA Victor LPM-2467 [M]	1961	6.25	12.50	25.00
❑ RCA Victor LSP-2467 [S]	1961	7.50	15.00	30.00
MORE COUNTRY MUSIC SPECTACULAR				
❑ Starday SLP-140 [M]	1961	10.00	20.00	40.00
MORE HOT COUNTRY REQUESTS				
❑ Epic FE 44279	1988	2.00	4.00	8.00
MORE HOT COUNTRY REQUESTS, VOL. 2				
❑ Epic FE 44280	1988	2.00	4.00	8.00
NASCAR GOES COUNTRY				
❑ MCA 474	1975	7.50	15.00	30.00
NASHVILLE'S GREATEST CHRISTMAS HITS				
❑ Columbia PC 44412	1988	2.50	5.00	10.00
NASHVILLE'S GREATEST CHRISTMAS HITS, VOLUME II				
❑ Columbia PC 44413	1988	2.50	5.00	10.00
NASHVILLE BANDSTAND				
❑ King 813 [M]	1962	25.00	50.00	100.00
NASHVILLE BANDSTAND, VOLUME 2				
❑ King 847 [M]	1963	20.00	40.00	80.00
THE NASHVILLE CHRISTMAS ALBUM				
❑ Epic PE 40418	1986	2.50	5.00	10.00
NASHVILLE SATURDAY NIGHT				
❑ Columbia House 1P 6215	1975	2.50	5.00	10.00
❑ Nashville NLP-2009 [M]	1965	5.00	10.00	20.00
❑ Starday SLP-128 [M]	1961	10.00	20.00	40.00
NASHVILLE STEEL GUITAR				
❑ Nashville NLP-2017 [M]	1965	5.00	10.00	20.00
❑ Starday SLP-138 [M]	1961	7.50	15.00	30.00
THE NEW BREED				
❑ RCA Victor CPL1-5491	1986	2.00	4.00	8.00
THE NEW TRADITION SINGS THE OLD TRADITION				
❑ Warner Bros. R 124450	1989	3.75	7.50	15.00
—BMG Direct Marketing edition				
OLD TIME BANJO PROJECT				
❑ Elektra EKL-276 [M]	1964	5.00	10.00	20.00
❑ Elektra EKS-7276 [S]	1964	6.25	12.50	25.00
ON STAGE AT THE GRAND OLE OPRY				
❑ Decca DL 4393 [M]	1964	6.25	12.50	25.00
❑ Decca DL 74393 [S]	1964	7.50	15.00	30.00
OPRY OLD TIMERS				
❑ Starday SLP-182 [M]	1962	7.50	15.00	30.00
OPRY TIME IN TENNESSEE				
❑ Starday SLP-177 [M]	1962	7.50	15.00	30.00
THE ORIGINAL COUNTRY HITS #1				
❑ Liberty LRP-3305 [M]	1963	5.00	10.00	20.00
THE ORIGINAL COUNTRY HITS #2				
❑ Liberty LRP-3345 [M]	1964	5.00	10.00	20.00
THE ORIGINAL COUNTRY HITS #3				
❑ Liberty LRP-3382 [M]	1964	5.00	10.00	20.00
ORIGINAL GOLDEN COUNTRY GREATS, VOLUME 1				
❑ Liberty LST-7569 [R]	1968	3.00	6.00	12.00
—Reissue of "The Original Country Hits #1," Liberty 3305, in rechanneled stereo				
ORIGINAL GOLDEN COUNTRY GREATS, VOLUME 2				
❑ Liberty LST-7570 [R]	1968	3.00	6.00	12.00
—Reissue of "The Original Country Hits #2," Liberty 3345, in rechanneled stereo				
ORIGINAL GOLDEN COUNTRY GREATS, VOLUME 3				
❑ Liberty LST-7571 [R]	1968	3.00	6.00	12.00
—Reissue of "The Original Country Hits #3," Liberty 3382, in rechanneled stereo				
THE ORIGINAL GREATEST HITS OF THE GREAT COUNTRY AND WESTERN STARS				
❑ Mercury MG-20825 [M]	1963	5.00	10.00	20.00
❑ Mercury SR-60825 [S]	1963	6.25	12.50	25.00
PICK OF THE COUNTRY				
❑ RCA Victor LPM-2094 [M]	1960	6.25	12.50	25.00
❑ RCA Victor LSP-2094 [S]	1960	7.50	15.00	30.00
PICK OF THE COUNTRY, VOL. 2				
❑ RCA Victor LPM-2956 [M]	1964	5.00	10.00	20.00
❑ RCA Victor LSP-2956 [S]	1964	6.25	12.50	25.00
POP COUNTRY HITS				
❑ RCA Victor LPM-2949 [M]	1964	3.75	7.50	15.00
❑ RCA Victor LSP-2949 [S]	1964	5.00	10.00	20.00
QUEENS OF COUNTRY				
❑ Columbia KC 32719	1974	3.00	6.00	12.00
RAILROAD SONGS				
❑ King 869 [M]	1963	17.50	35.00	70.00
RAMBLIN' COUNTRY				
❑ Columbia Special Products P 12484	1974	3.00	6.00	12.00
RFD CHRISTMAS				
❑ Columbia Special Products P 15427	1981	2.50	5.00	10.00
SATURDAY NIGHT GRAND OLE OPRY				
❑ Decca DL 4303 [M]	1962	6.25	12.50	25.00
❑ Decca DL 74303 [S]	1962	7.50	15.00	30.00
SATURDAY NIGHT GRAND OLE OPRY, VOL. 2				
❑ Decca DL 4539 [M]	1964	5.00	10.00	20.00
❑ Decca DL 74539 [S]	1964	6.25	12.50	25.00
SATURDAY NIGHT GRAND OLE OPRY, VOL. 3				
❑ Decca DL 4671 [M]	1965	5.00	10.00	20.00
❑ Decca DL 74671 [S]	1965	6.25	12.50	25.00
SOLID COUNTRY GOLD				
❑ RCA Victor CPL1-4841	1983	2.50	5.00	10.00
SONGS OF THE HILLS				
❑ Audio Lab AL-1515 [M]	1959	20.00	40.00	80.00
STAR-SPANGLED COUNTRY				
❑ RCA Victor AEL1-5849	1986	2.00	4.00	8.00
STARS				
❑ Sun 148	1982	5.00	10.00	20.00
—Includes two early Alabama tracks				
THE STARS ARE OUT IN TEXAS				
❑ RCA Victor CPL1-7165	1986	2.00	4.00	8.00
STARS OF BLUEGRASS MUSIC				
❑ CMH 5903 [(2)]	198?	3.75	7.50	15.00
STARS OF THE GRAND OLE OPRY 1926-1974				
❑ RCA Victor CPL2-0466 [(2)]	1974	5.00	10.00	20.00
SWEET DREAMS OF COUNTRY				
❑ Reader's Digest RBA-049A [(7)]	1990	12.50	25.00	50.00
SWING BILLIES				
❑ Audio Lab AL-1546 [M]	1960	30.00	60.00	120.00
SWING BILLIES VOLUME 2				
❑ Audio Lab AL-1566 [M]	1960	30.00	60.00	120.00
TENNESSEE CHRISTMAS				
❑ MCA 5620	1985	3.00	6.00	12.00
❑ MCA R 134563	1985	3.00	6.00	12.00
—RCA Music Service edition				
TENNESSEE MOUNTAIN BLUEGRASS FESTIVAL				
❑ CMH 9014 [(2)]	198?	3.75	7.50	15.00
TEXAS HONKY TONK HITS				
❑ CMH 9038	198?	3.00	6.00	12.00
THIS IS YOUR COUNTRY				
❑ Realm 1P 8126	1991	3.75	7.50	15.00
—Only available on vinyl through Columbia House				
TRUCK DRIVER SONGS				
❑ King 866 [M]	1963	17.50	35.00	70.00
TRUCK STOP FAVORITES				
❑ Starday/Power Pak PO 298	1977	2.50	5.00	10.00
—Label says only "Power Pak" but the cover has both label names				
TV COUNTRY JAMBOREE				
❑ RCA Camden CAL-925 [M]	1965	3.00	6.00	12.00
❑ RCA Camden CAS-925 [S]	1965	3.75	7.50	15.00
VOLUNTEER JAM III AND IV				
❑ Epic E2 35368 [(2)]	1978	5.00	10.00	20.00

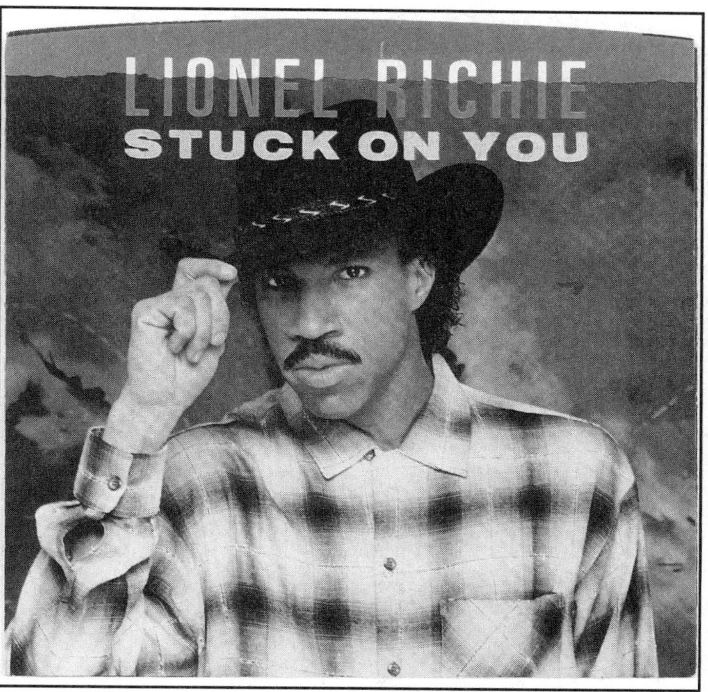

Not everybody who has made the country charts is a country artist. Here are a few "unlikely" country singers. (Top left) In 1974-75, Paul McCartney and Wings had a double-sided hit. "Junior's Farm" was the A-side; the B-side, recorded with some Nashville session pros, was "Sally G." That B-side spent over two months on the country charts. (Top right) The B-side of "Too Much Heaven," a late 1978 hit by the Bee Gees, was the wonderful "Rest Your Love on Me." The Gibb brothers' version made the top 40 on the country charts, and was later remade by Conway Twitty, whose version went all the way to the top. (Bottom left) Bob Seger made the top 20 of the country charts with his version of the Rodney Crowell-penned "Shame on the Moon." (Bottom right) Considering that Lionel Richie had produced more than an LP's worth of Kenny Rogers material without harming Rogers' country standing, maybe it's not so unlikely that one of Richie's solo hits would make the top 30 of the country charts. "Stuck on You" pulled off the feat in 1984. He later did a song with Alabama, "Deep River Woman," that made the top 10.

Number	Title (A Side/B Side)	Yr	VG	VG+	NM
WE WISH YOU A COUNTRY CHRISTMAS					
❑ Columbia Special Products P 14991		1979	2.00	4.00	8.00
WELCOME TO MUSIC CITY U.S.A.					
❑ Columbia CL 2590 [M]		1966	3.00	6.00	12.00
❑ Columbia CS 9390 [S]		1966	3.75	7.50	15.00
WESTERN STAR PARADE					
❑ Vocalion VL 3805 [M]		1967	3.75	7.50	15.00
❑ Vocalion VL 73805 [R]		1967	3.00	6.00	12.00
WESTERN SWING IN HI-FI					
❑ Decca DL 8730 [M]		1958	10.00	20.00	40.00
WHITE MANSIONS					
❑ A&M SP 6004 [(2)]		1978	5.00	10.00	20.00
THE WHO'S WHO OF COUNTRY AND WESTERN MUSIC					
❑ Capitol T 2538 [M]		1966	5.00	10.00	20.00
❑ Capitol ST 2538 [S]		1966	5.00	10.00	20.00
THE WONDERFUL WORLD OF GOSPEL AND SACRED MUSIC					
❑ Starday SLP-255 [M]		1963	7.50	15.00	30.00
THE WORLD'S GREATEST BLUEGRASS BAND					
❑ CMH 5900 [(2)]		197?	3.75	7.50	15.00
THE WORLD'S GREATEST BLUEGRASS BANDS, VOL. 2					
❑ CMH 5901 [(2)]		197?	3.75	7.50	15.00
THE WORLD OF COUNTRY MUSIC					
❑ Capitol NPB-5 [(3)]		1965	7.50	15.00	30.00
YOU AND I/CLASSIC COUNTRY DUETS					
❑ Warner Bros. 25171		1984	2.50	5.00	10.00